THE WORLD OF EROS

finest products · worldwide

Made in Germany

Neu / New

pjur group: www.pjurEROS.com

Luxembourg: Phone (++352) 748 989
Fax (++352) 748 990
USA (NYC): Phone (++1) 212-337-3767
Fax (++1) 212-367-9389

PEOPLE™

Nationwide Service

Whenever you are in Amsterdam or elsewhere in the Netherlands, our boys are just a phone call away

- we understand your personal desires
- we go to the utmost to get you the boy you are looking for
- home/ hotel visiting service
- reliable & absolutely discreet
- The leading gay escortservice

very & *affordable*

International Outcalls

Wherever you are, no matter which part of the world, we are only a flight away

Visit our website for more information, or just give us a call at any time

http://www.boysescort.com
extensive interactive website available

10 years of reliability

020- 662 999 0

from outside the Netherlands, please dial +31 20 662 999 0
24 hours a day, cards welcome

- The largest selection of boys in the country
- Carefully selected boys in any type, selected on a.o. looks and personality

Male Escorts, Company & Guides
AMSTERDAM

Beate Uhse

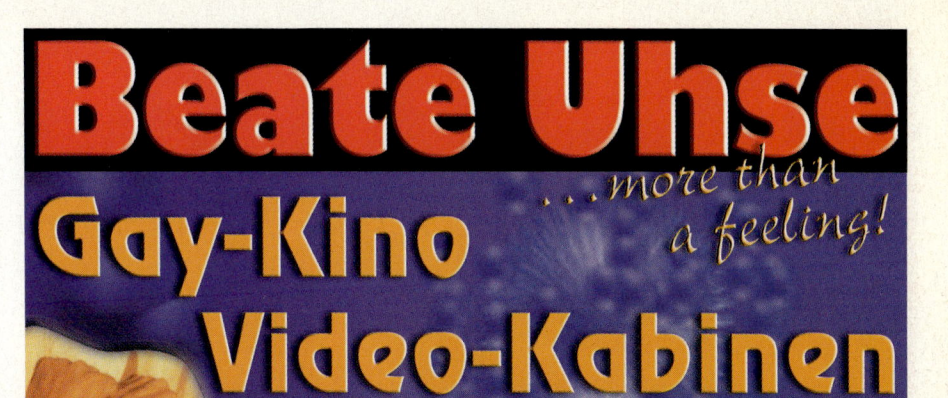

...more than a feeling!

Gay-Kino
Video-Kabinen

Täglich von **9h - 24h**

Internationale Spitzenfilme

Ständiger Programm-Wechsel

Kinotage
Sonntag und Dienstag
4 Kinos – 1 Preis
11,00 DM
inclusive Getränk!

Berlin · Joachimstaler Str. 4/Ecke Kantstr.

LONDON PARIS NEW YORK MUNICH PARIS BARCELONA ROME IBIZIA BERLIN AMSTERDAM MADRID

for the most comprehensive queer city guides and travel services, be in queercompany.

queercompany

WWW.QUEERCOMPANY.COM

Big RUBYS
GUESTHOUSE

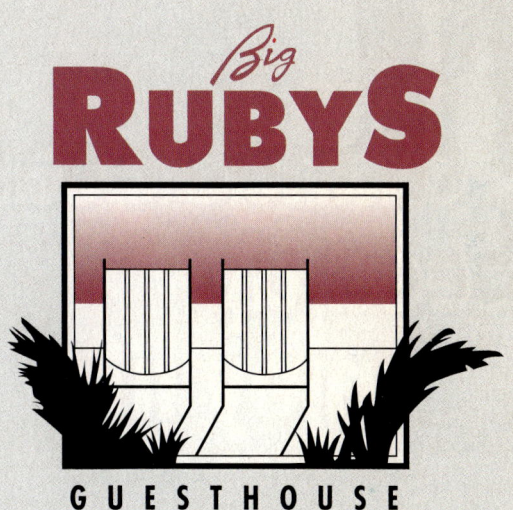

KEY WEST, USA
305-296-2323

LA PLANTACION
MANUEL ANTONIO, COSTA RICA
506-777-1332

L'ORANGERIE
AIGUES-MORTES, FRANCE
33-4-66-53-10-23

1-800-477-7829 USA/CANADA
www.BigRubys.com

change gear
speed up
enjoy life

leather, rubber, army, bdsm, toys.
fun accelerators available at:

H·M LEDER!

www.hm-leder.com

Online Shop

Neukirchstr. 18
D-28215 Bremen
Germany
Tel. +49 4 21 - 37 14 30
Fax - 37 49 53

kink shop

www.kink.ch

Online Shop

Engelstr. 62
CH-8004 Zurich
Switzerland
Tel. +41 1 - 241 32 15
Fax - 241 32 19

Tonight... Go DeLuxe
ForPlay
Lube de Luxe
Gel
Water Based
Liquid
Gel/Plus
Water Based
Cream
Lube de Luxe
"the pure pleasure of personal luxury"
Available in: Gel · Liquid · Cream · Gel/Plus
TRIMENSA PHARMACEUTICALS, NEWBURY PARK, CA 91320 800/ 554-1313 VISIT OUR WEB SITE @ forplay.com

revista-magazine
zero

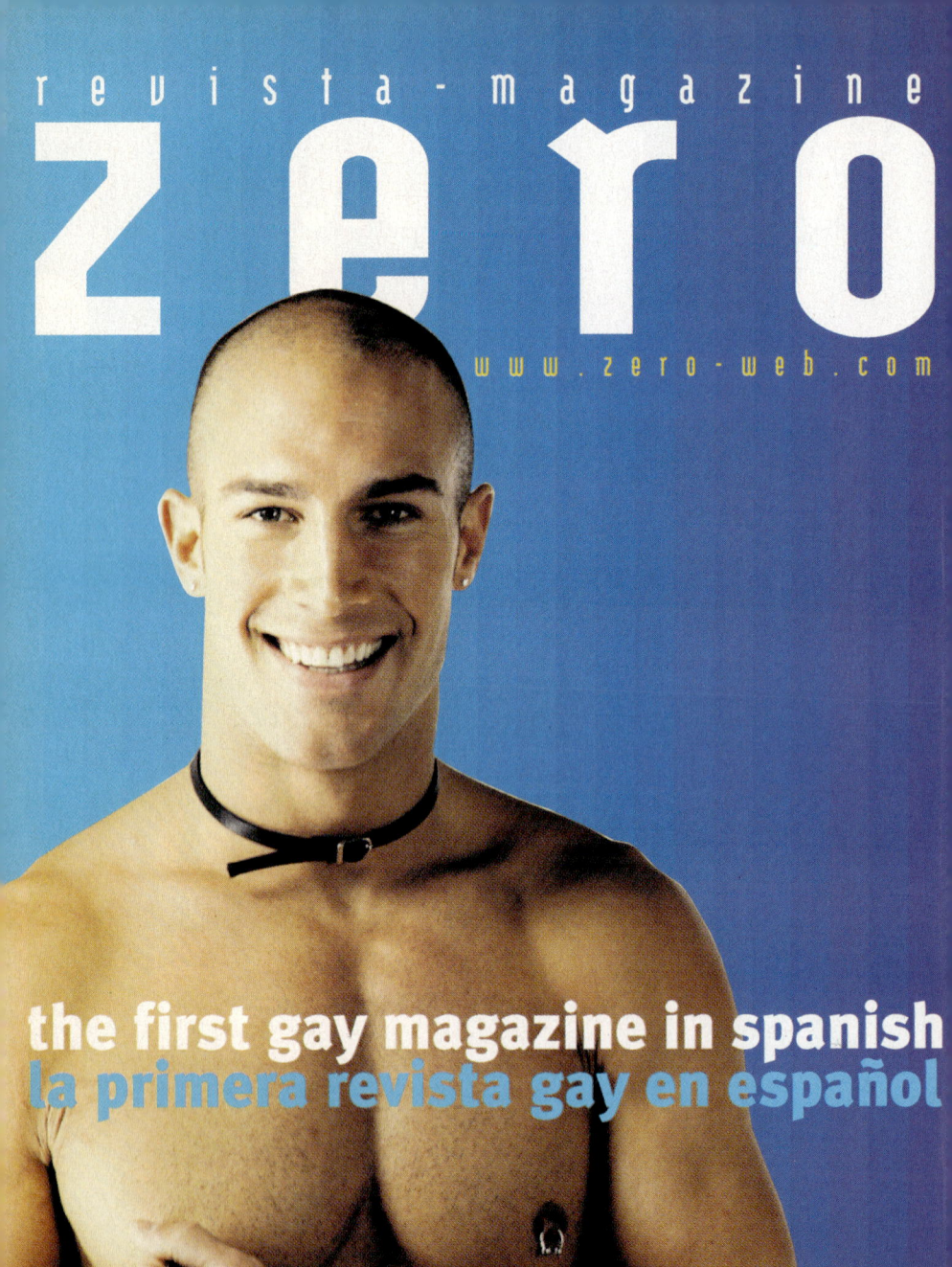

www.zero-web.com

the first gay magazine in spanish
la primera revista gay en español

have a taste for free!

get **3 free issues.** If you decide to subscribe for a year, pay only **23,5** € (spain) - **48,2** € (europe) - **60,3** € (rest of the world)

www.zero-web.com

#1 #2 #3 #4 #5 #6 #7 #8 #9 #10 #11
#12 #13 #14 #15 #16 #17 #18 #19 #20 #21 #22

¡pruébanos gratis!

recibe **3 números gratis** y si decides seguir todo el año paga sólo **3.900** ptas. (españa) **8.000** ptas. (europa) - **10.000** ptas. (resto del mundo)

e-mail: **suscripciones@zeropress.com** tel.: **+34 91 701 00 91**

name / nombre
last name / apellidos
occupation / ocupación
age / edad
city / población
zip / c.p.
address / dirección
tel./fax
e-mail
bill me / contra reembolso
visa
signature / firma
expire / caduca __ __ / __ __ n°. __ __ __ __ / __ __ __ __ / __ __ __ __ / __ __ __ __

EUROPE 8.000 ptas. / 48,2 €   RESTO DEL MUNDO REST OF THE WORLD 10.000 ptas. / 60,3 €
NÚMEROS ATRASADOS PAST ISSUES 500 ptas. c/u. / 3 €   GRATIS 3 MESES 3 MONTHS FREE
1 AÑO (ESPAÑA) 1 YEAR (SPAIN) 3.900 ptas. / 23,5 €

send cupon to / envía cupón a: apdo. de correos 18207- madrid 28080 (spain) / fax: 34 91 531 51 17

KEY WEST
SAUNA CLUB

Open everyday from 12h00 to 1h00 am
except on friday and saturday until 2h00 am
141, rue Lafayette 75010 Paris
+33 (0)1 45 26 31 74 - M° Gare du Nord

DOUBLE YOUR PLEASURE !
Buy one admission and get half price on your admission
at IDM Sauna Club
4, rue du Faubourg Montmartre 75009 Paris - M° Grands Boulevards - +33 (0)1.45.23.10.03

SPARTACUS
INTERNATIONAL GAY GUIDE
2001/2002

30th Edition

BRUNO GMÜNDER

Imprint

PUBLISHER	BRUNO GMÜNDER VERLAG GMBH Leuschnerdamm 31· D-10999 Berlin · GERMANY Tel +49 / (0)30 / 615 00 30 Fax +49 / (0)30 / 615 90 07 E-mail : info@spartacus.de
EDITOR IN CHIEF	Briand Bedford · Robin Rauch
EDITORIAL TEAM	Stefan Santoprete · Yvan Ladurner · Felix Rasche Oliver Ambach · Martin Bober · Tsafrir Cohen · Carsten Hinz · Peo Månestad Finn Jagow · Chris Nicolas · Renato de Mederios Filho Facharzt Dirk Lohr
TRANSLATION	Oliver Ambach · Briand Bedford · F. R. Bock · Yvan Ladurner Carsten Sinner · Susanne Purrmann
ADVERTISING SALES	BRUNO GMÜNDER VERLAG GMBH Leuschnerdamm 31· D-10999 Berlin · GERMANY Tel +49 / (0)30 / 615 00 3-42 Fax +49 / (0)30 / 615 91 34
COVER PHOTOGRAPH	© VistaVideo Int'l · Ron Williams
COVER DESIGN	Rudolph Haas
LAYOUT DESIGN	Rudolph Haas
LAYOUT & MAPS	Print Eisenherz, Berlin · Reinhold Fischer
PRINTING	GGP Media GmbH, Pößneck, GERMANY

© 2001 Bruno Gmünder Verlag

SPARTACUS® is a registered Trademark ™

No part of this work may be reproduced or utilized in any form or by any means, electronic or mechanical, including photocopying or by any information storage and retrieval system without permission in writing by the publisher.

Please note that **SPARTACUS**® published by BRUNO GMÜNDER VERLAG has no connection with any other business with the name of „SPARTACUS", even if advertised in this book.

Please note that the inclusion of any establishment, business or organisation in this book or the appearance on the cover or on advertisements in **SPARTACUS**® does not necessarily reflect the sexual orientation of owners, staff or models.

ISBN 3-86187-192-0

Member of **IGLTA** (International Gay & Lesbian Travel Association)

Distribution

Worldwide Distribution

■ BRUNO GMÜNDER Verlag GmbH
Abteilung Vertrieb
Wrangelstr. 100
10997 Berlin · Germany
Ph. +49 (30) 61 00 11 20
Fax. +49 (30) 615 90 08
Email: vertrieb@brunogmuender.com

USA/Canada

■ Bookazine Company, Inc.
75 Hook Road
Bayonne, NJ 07002
Toll-free (800) 548-3855
Fax. (201) 339-7778
www.bookazine.com

■ KOEN Book Distributor, Inc.
10 Twosome Drive, Box 600
Moorestown, NJ 08057
Toll-free (800) 257-8481
Fax. (856) 727-6914
E-Mail: kbd@koen.com

■ PDC Publishers Distributing Company
1045 Westgate Drive
St. Paul, MN 55114
Ph. (800) 464-4574
Fax. (323) 467-0152

UK/Ireland

■ Turnaround
Unit 3, Olympia Trading Estate
Coburg Road
London N22 6TZ
Ph. (020) 8829-3000 · Fax. (020) 8881-5088
Email: orders@turnaround.uk.com

France

■ I.E.M. (Travel Guides)
208 Rue Saint-Maur
75010 Paris
Ph. (01) 4018-5151 · Fax. (01) 4018-5150
E-Mail: iem.management@wanadoo.fr

BeNeLux

■ SCALA AGENTUREN B.V.
Contactweg 28
1014 AN Amsterdam
Ph. +31 (20) 687 06 87 · Fax. +31 (20) 687 06 00
Email: eddyd@scala-nl.com

Spain

■ M.G. Triangulo Distribuciones S.L.
Calle Gravina 11
28004 Madrid
Ph. + Fax. (91) 532 01 22

■ HARMONY LOVE S.A.
Calle Caballero 79
08014 Barcelona
Ph. +34 (93) 405 33 00
Fax. +34 (93) 405 11 48

Italy

■ Les Durham
Cascina Antonietta
27050 Bagnaria PV
Ph. 0383 542 104
Fax. 0383 542 105
E-Mail : durham@libero.it

Hong Kong/Taiwan

■ ASIA 2000
15 B, The Parkside
#263 Hollywood Road
Sheung Wan, Hong Kong
Ph. (00852) 2530-1409
Fax. (00852) 2526-1107

Japan

■ Taisei Trading
2-2-10 Nakakaigan
Chigasaki Kanagawa 253-0055
Toll-free (120) 33 33 65
Fax. (3) 5772-1789

Australia/New Zealand

■ Bulldog Books
P.O.Box 300, Beaconsfield
NSW 2014
Ph. (02) 9699-3507
Fax. (02) 9699-3527
Email: bulldog@rainbow.net.au

Single copies and our free mail order brochure
may be ordered by mail from:

BRUNO GMÜNDER · Mail Order
Zeughofstraße 1 · 10997 Berlin · GERMANY

A cooperative action of the BZgA Bundeszentrale für gesundheitliche Aufklärung
and BRUNO GMÜNDER VERLAG

GIB AIDS KEINE CHANCE

✱ Welcome to the new SPARTACUS ✱

Dear reader!

In front of you is the 30th edition of the SPARTACUS International Gay Guide.

A reason to celebrate!
You are holding the new, completely updated and annually revised edition of SPARTACUS. As a novelty the jubilee edition the entire guide has been printed in full color!
We have given the SPARTACUS International Gay Guide a face-lift for its birthday: A new millennium in a new design.
In order that you can find your way around, the information about each country as well as the country and city maps stand out in full color.

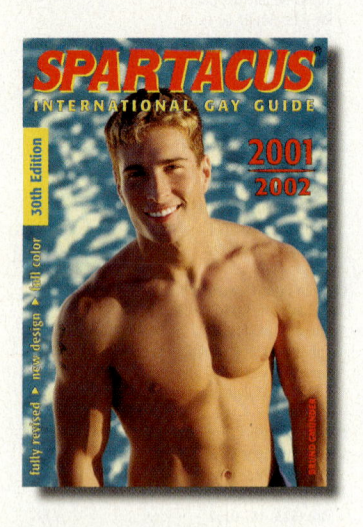

That is not the only change: SPARTACUS goes online!
The launch is on the 01st May 2001. Here is the long awaited address:
www.SpartacusWorld.com
All purchasers of this jubilee copy have the one-off chance to immediately register free of charge at www.SpartacusWorld.com. The registration card is to be found at the back of this guide, fill out and sign this original card, then send it off by post! All registered users can take advantage of the regularly updated SPARTACUS address data bank, free of charge until 31st December 2001.

Your doorway to the gay world!
30 years of SPARTACUS, 30 years of information and addresses from the international gay world. We are proud to present information from all corners of the globe from Albania to Zimbabwe, which, with help from our new internet presence, will be even more up-to-date!

We wish you lots of pleasure with your new
SPARTACUS International Gay Guide

Briand Bedford
CHIEF EDITOR

+++ register now +++ constantly updated +++ all current info

Lifestyle

Shopping

Personals

Gay Chat

Adult Entertainment

www.SpartacusWorld.com

Travel

Events

Spartacus Gay Guide

Free newsletter

Entertainment

Launch date: 1st May 2001!

As purchaser of the jubilee edition of SPARTACUS International Gay Guide 2001/2002, after I have registered myself, I have the possibility to use and research in the SPARTACUS address data bank free of charge until the 31st December 2001.

The registration card should be completed in full, signed and sent off by post to:
SpartacusWorld.com GmbH
P.O.Box 17 01 23 • 10203 Berlin • Germany

Your personal password will be sent to you promptly.

+++ all current information +++ register now +++ constantly

✳ How to use SPARTACUS ✳

Listing of countries

SPARTACUS is divided into countries which are listed alphabetically in English. An exception to this rule is the Caribbean where all islands and countries in the Caribbean are listed under "C". Each country is broken down into cities and towns which are in the local language and also alphabetically listed. For the countries Australia, Canada & USA the state, territory or province has been listed alphabetically and divided into cities or towns. Should you have problems, refer to our index on page 1362, where all states, countries, cities and towns are alphabetically listed in all five SPARTACUS languages: English, German, French, Spanish and Italian.

Each country listed has specific information on the legal and social situation for gay men, including the legal age of consent. Furthermore information on gay festivals and special events are included.

Before this introduction for each country, you will find the following information :

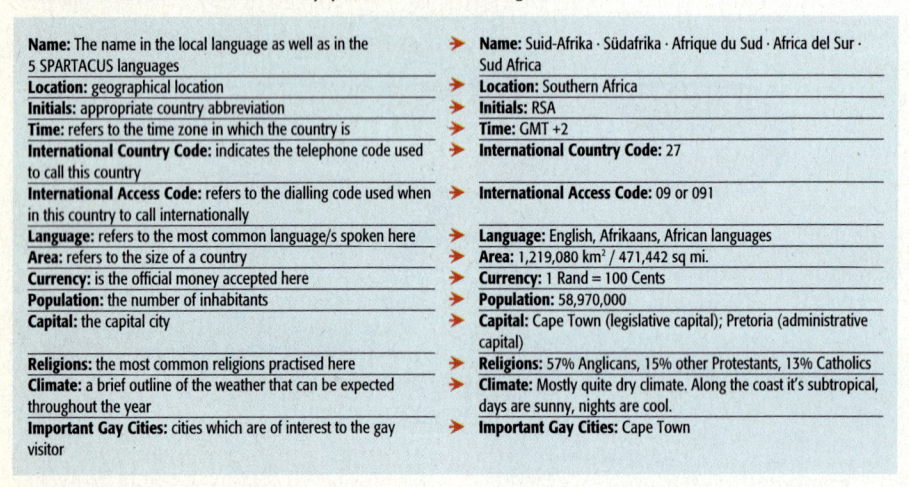

Name: The name in the local language as well as in the 5 SPARTACUS languages	**Name:** Suid-Afrika · Südafrika · Afrique du Sud · Africa del Sur · Sud Africa
Location: geographical location	**Location:** Southern Africa
Initials: appropriate country abbreviation	**Initials:** RSA
Time: refers to the time zone in which the country is	**Time:** GMT +2
International Country Code: indicates the telephone code used to call this country	**International Country Code:** 27
International Access Code: refers to the dialling code used when in this country to call internationally	**International Access Code:** 09 or 091
Language: refers to the most common language/s spoken here	**Language:** English, Afrikaans, African languages
Area: refers to the size of a country	**Area:** 1,219,080 km^2 / 471,442 sq mi.
Currency: is the official money accepted here	**Currency:** 1 Rand = 100 Cents
Population: the number of inhabitants	**Population:** 58,970,000
Capital: the capital city	**Capital:** Cape Town (legislative capital); Pretoria (administrative capital)
Religions: the most common religions practised here	**Religions:** 57% Anglicans, 15% other Protestants, 13% Catholics
Climate: a brief outline of the weather that can be expected throughout the year	**Climate:** Mostly quite dry climate. Along the coast it's subtropical, days are sunny, nights are cool.
Important Gay Cities: cities which are of interest to the gay visitor	**Important Gay Cities:** Cape Town

Information in an address entry

Each listing is made up of the name ❶, the corresponding SPARTACUS codes ❷, the opening hours ❸, the address with postal code ❹, the telephone number ❺, telefax number ❻, e-mail address ❼, & website address ❽.

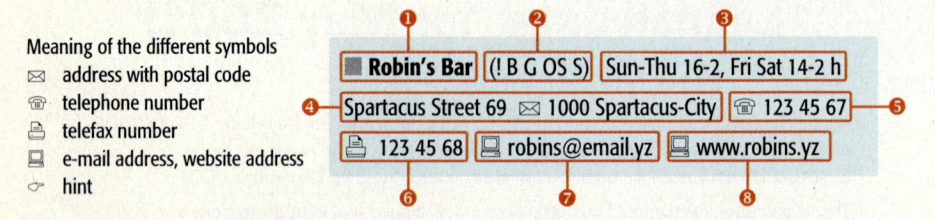

Meaning of the different symbols
- ✉ address with postal code
- ☏ telephone number
- 🖨 telefax number
- 💻 e-mail address, website address
- ☞ hint

■ **Robin's Bar** (! B G OS S) Sun-Thu 16-2, Fri Sat 14-2 h
Spartacus Street 69 ✉ 1000 Spartacus-City ☏ 123 45 67
🖨 123 45 68 💻 robins@email.yz 💻 www.robins.yz

■ A red square in front of the address shows further information is available in a corresponding advertisement.

✹ How to use SPARTACUS ✹

Listing of categories

Within the different countries and cities the individual addresses are sorted into categories as follows:

National Gay Info
National Help Lines
National Publishers
National Companies
National Groups
Health Groups
Going Out
▼
Bars
Cafés
Danceclubs
Restaurants
▼
Sex Shops/Blue Movies
Cinemas
▼
Saunas/Baths
Fitness Studios
Massage
▼
Book Shops
Fashion Shops
Leather & Fetish Shops
Travel & Transport
▼
Hotels
Guest Houses
Apartments
Private Accommodation
▼
Groups
▼
Swimming
Cruising

Please use our freepost information card to be found at the back of this guidebook to inform us of any changes you might have come across while travelling. Please try to give us as much information as possible. We would be delighted to receive any information you may have which does not appear in this edition of SPARTACUS:

Bruno Gmünder Verlag GmbH • SPARTACUS-Redaktion
P.O.Box 61 01 04 • 10921 Berlin • GERMANY
info@spartacus.de

Code description

SPARTACUS codes mean the following (codes in small letters mean in general a restriction):

!	A must
A	Art exhibitions
AC	Air conditioning
AYOR	At your own risk. Danger of personal attack or police activity
B	Bar with full range of alcoholic beverages
BF	Full breakfast
CC	All major credit cards accepted
D	Dancing / Discotheque
DR	Darkroom
E	Elegant. Appropriate dress necessary
F	Food. Extensive menu available
G	Gay. Exclusively or almost exclusively gay men
GLM	Gay and lesbian mixed crowd
H	Hotel or other accommodation welcoming gay men
LJ	Leather, fetish or uniform
MA	Mixed ages
MG	Middle-aged gay men
msg	Massage on offer
N	Local interest with local patrons
NG	Not gay but possibly of interest to gay men
NU	Nudist area
OG	Mostly older gay men
OS	Outdoor seating, terrace or garden
P	Private club or strict door control
PI	Swimming pool
R	Frequented by hustlers
S	Shows or other events
SA	Dry sauna
SB	Steam bath
SNU	Strip shows
SOL	Solarium
STV	Drag shows
TV	Transvestites and / or transsexual clientele
VS	Video shows
WE	More popular at the weekend
WH	Whirlpool / Jacuzzi / Hot tub
WO	Work-out equipment available
YG	Younger gay men (18–28)

The SPARTACUS codes are also available as practical bookmark at the back of this guide!

Health Information

1. Introduction

There is no other area of medical research in which the pursuit of knowledge changes at such as pace as it has done in the research of HIV infections and AIDS. 20 years after the first known case of AIDS there are still many new cases of HIV infection despite all public awareness campaigns and precautions. Nevertheless the number of new AIDS infections or deaths have remain unchanged. This is thanks to new and more effective therapies which aim to combat the virus infection and other possible related illnesses. Knowledge regarding the paths of infection reduce the chance of infection and break down the anxiety and prejudice which prevails within the general population. Knowledge regarding the infection, illness and the path it takes as well as the possible therapy alternatives improve the prognosis as well as the quality of life for those affected.

2. HIV Infection and AIDS

Both the above are a result of contact with a so-called HI virus, in which the H stands for Human and I for immune defect. AIDS is an infectious disease which is brought about by a virus, the so-called HIV. The HIV damages the human immune system and as a result weakens the resistance. In this way the body is susceptible to harmful organisms which would normally not be a problem for a healthy body. The virus can also cause other disruptions in the body and may induce skin and nervous disorders. Even the growth of tumours can be caused by the virus. Once the virus has landed in the body, it attacks the cells of the human immune system and adapts the metabolism to its own advantage. The virus can therefore multiply inside the cells leading to their destruction. Non-infected HIV cells of the immune system try to destroy the virus. It is however impossible for the immune system to destroy the virus completely. When infected with the virus one may notice after a couple of days non specific type of flu like side effects, such as high temperature, sweating, muscle pains and swollen glands. These symptoms disappear rapidly. A new possibility to confirm the infection is a so-called PCR-analysis which can deliver the results after the first few days of being infected and can trace micro-biological virus bodies. The building of anti-bodies, which are the basis of the HIV test, take place after a period of two, three or even more weeks. The virus then takes over in the body and especially the immune system as well as the brain and nerve cells. The human cells are attacked, partly destroyed and the metabolism changes. The immune system along with T-cells hold out as long and as best as they can, depending upon the physical condition of the infected person or supplementary stress as well as the psychological condition caused by other infections. Should it come to an overburdening on the part of the virus on the immune system it may lead to opportune infections, which would be no problem for a healthy person but which are a serious threat to those with a weakened immune system.

Apart from this the development of other, serious illnesses such as the development of malignant lymph tumours or inflammation of the brain, the lungs or many other organs is possible (full blown AIDS stage). A complete destruction of all viral bodies is no longer possible either by the bodies own immune system or the best therapy available. Nevertheless, in all stages of the disease excellent and partly very promising therapies have become available. The most important thing for all of us to remember is however, prevention and for those who are directly effected the saying "keep calm and think clearly" is applicable.

3. Transmission of HIV

As a rule, the virus is transmitted via body secretions such as blood and sperm from someone who is HIV-positive. If blood or sperm containing the virus lands on an open wound or on the mucous membrane this could result in a HIV-infection. This means one should avoid contact with the body fluids.

High risk practises include
- Anal intercourse without the use of a condom (principally risky for both involved, although the passive partner is probably more at risk)

An average risk practise would be
- Oral sex in which sperm is ejaculated into the partners mouth. The pre-ejaculation fluid contains very small traces of the virus and saliva may even be able to destroy the virus.
- Fisting (anal sex using the fist) without the use of rubber gloves

Transmission cannot be caused by kissing, by using the same drinking glass or cutlery, clothing, swimming pools saunas or toilets. Even so is touching door handles, telephones etc. or contact such as handshaking or hugging as well as transmission by air or insects without risk. In all the above the HIV cannot be transmitted.

4. Safer Sex

To protect oneself when having sex from HIV transmission, one should note a few safer-sex "rules":
- The correct use of condoms by anal and oral sex. This also protects against other sexually transmitted diseases such as Syphilis, Gonorrhoea and Hepatitis.
- Use of condoms even when both partners are HIV-positive! This prevents the re-infection from other strains of the virus causing additional complications in therapy
- No sperm in the mouth of your partner
- No fisting without rubber gloves
- Drug addicts should only use their own needles.

Care should be taken with newly shaved skin and open wounds. The sharing of dildos should only be practised in combination with new condoms for each partner.

Use only tested condoms which are "extra strong" and will not tear. Protect then from high and low temperatures and sunlight and only use water based lubricants in combination with condoms. Creams or lubricants which are oil based tend to weaken the condom and make it porous.

Most people do not display the effects of an HIV infection. For this reason one should automatically assume that with unknown sexual partners an HIV infection is possible and protect oneself when having sex.

✳ Health Information ✳

5. Treatment possibilities

A note to start with: there is at present no vaccination against a HIV-infection, there are however various medications (called anti-virus medications) which can be used to reduce the proliferation of the virus.

When a therapy is to be undertaken is a decision which is to be made by the patient and his doctor, who can recommend the various therapy possibilities. This is based on the T4 count (helper cells) and the concentration of the virus in the blood.

To reduce the concentration of the virus in the blood, a series of medications (at least 3) are combined in order to prevent the adaptable viruses from becoming immune.

After a while a resistance to the medications used may result, in which case other medications must be prescribed. For this reason, it is important to use a condom, to prevent the transfer of resistant virus types. Antibiotics are used to treat the side-effects.

The most important medications available at this stage are listed below. There are several new medications which will shortly appear on the market, some of which are combination medications, which will simplify the use of medications. The medications are listed with the international substance name along with the local trade name in brackets:

Zidovudin (Retrovir)
Lamivudin (Epivir), together also available as Combivir
Didanosin (Videx)
Zalcitabin (Hivid)
Stavudin (Zerit)
Abacavir (Ziagen)
Saquinavir (Invirase/Fortovase)
Indinavir (Crixivan)
Nelfinavir (Viracept)
Ritonavir (Norvir)
Amprenavir (Agenerase)
Delavirdin (Rescriptor)
Efavirenz (Sustiva)
Nevirapin (Viramune)

With the use of a combination of the above medications in a controlled and therapy it is possible to reduce the virus concentration. The risk of transferring the virus however remains – even when the level of the virus falls below the level at which it can be traced.

These anti-virus medications must however be taken on a regular basis. Although the number of tablets (sometimes as many as 20 per day) along with the restrictions imposed on the day to day lifestyle and the sometimes resulting strong side-effects from the medications make things difficult for the patient, a disciplined approach is important for an effective therapy.

When problems arise and you are currently "on the road" you are advised to consult a doctor or visit a hospital which specialises in HIV therapy practises.

6. Travelling with HIV and AIDS

As the virus which causes AIDS can be found on a global basis, one should adhere to the "safe-sex" rules in foreign countries too. For those who are infected a restriction in mobility is not necessarily applicable. One should however take a list with you of possible medical practises or hospitals which are specialists in the field of HIV and AIDS in the area which you will visit.

Due to the fact that in some countries the correct quality condoms and medications are difficult to obtain, one is advised to take these with you when travelling.

It is also recommended that you seek the advise of a doctor who will be able to inform you of the possible diseases which one can come into contact with.

By following simple rules such as protecting oneself against the sun, wearing the appropriate clothing and following simple rules of hygiene (taking care with drinking water and raw foods) one can avoid many of the common problems which arise while on holiday. A further series of sexually transferred diseases such as Hepatitis, Gonorrhoea, Syphilis as well as others can be avoided by inoculations (such as Hepatitis A and B). Even HIV patients may be inoculated after consultation with their doctor.

Last but not least, two final points : before taking a trip, check up on the health insurance cover abroad and enquire whether restrictions apply to tourist wishing to visit who have HIV. One should also enquire as to whether it is possible to take all the necessary medications into the country which you intend visiting or are they perhaps available on site ?

Dirk Lohr
General practitioner
Berlin-Charlottenburg

★ Willkommen beim neuen SPARTACUS ★

Lieber Leser,

vor Dir liegt die 30. Ausgabe vom
SPARTACUS International Gay Guide.

Ein Grund zu feiern!
Wie jedes Jahr hältst Du eine komplett überarbeitete und aktualisierte Version in den Händen. Als Novum zur Jubiläums-Ausgabe erscheint der gesamte Guide in Farbe!
Wir haben dem SPARTACUS International Gay Guide zu seinem Geburtstag ein Facelift verpasst: ein neues Jahrtausend im neuen Design. Damit Du dich noch schneller zurecht findest, sind die Länderinformationen, Landkarten und Stadtpläne farblich hervorgehoben.

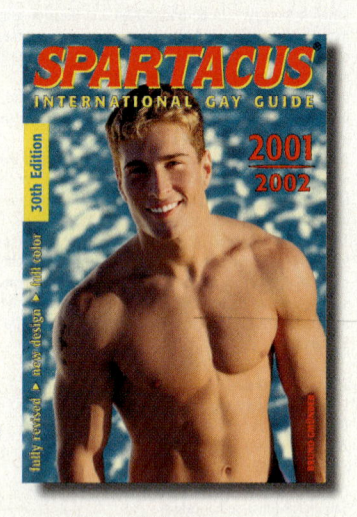

Das ist noch nicht alles: SPARTACUS goes online!
Die Premiere ist am 1. Mai 2001, und hier die heißersehnte Adresse:
www.SpartacusWorld.com
Das bedeutet für alle Käufer dieser Jubiläumsausgabe die einmalige Möglichkeit, sich ab sofort kostenlos bei www.SpartacusWorld.com registrieren zu lassen. Die Registrierungskarte findest Du im hinteren Teil des Buches. Die vollständig ausgefüllte und unterschriebene Registrierungskarte im Original per Post abschicken, fertig!
Alle registrierten Benutzer können dann kostenfrei bis zum 31. Dezember 2001 in der ständig aktualisierten SPARTACUS-Adressdatenbank recherchieren.

Dein Tor zur schwulen Welt!
30 Jahre SPARTACUS, 30 Jahre Informationen und Adressen aus der ganzen schwulen Welt. Wir freuen uns, Dir seit drei Dekaden von Albanien bis Zimbabwe Infos aus jeder Ecke des Globus zu bieten: durch den Internetauftritt noch aktueller und besser!

Wir wünschen allen viel Spaß mit dem neuen
SPARTACUS International Gay Guide

Briand Bedford
CHEFREDAKTEUR

+++ jetzt registrieren lassen +++ ständige Aktualisierung +++

Lifestyle

Shopping

Kleinanzeigen

Gay Chat

Adult Entertainment

www.SpartacusWorld.com

Travel

Events

Spartacus Gay Guide

kostenloser Newsletter

Entertainment

Premiere: 1. Mai 2001!

Als Käufer der Jubiläumsausgabe von SPARTACUS International Gay Guide 2001/2002 habe ich nach Registrierung die Möglichkeit, in der SPARTACUS-Adressdatenbank kostenfrei bis zum 31. Dezember 2001 zu recherchieren.

Die vollständig ausgefüllte und unterschriebene Registrierungskarte im Original und per Post einschicken an: **SpartacusWorld.com GmbH**
Postfach 17 01 23 • 10203 Berlin • Germany

Deinen persönlichen Zugangscode erhältst Du rechtzeitig von uns zugeschickt.

+++ alle aktuellen Infos +++ jetzt registrieren lassen +++

★ Wie man den SPARTACUS benutzt ★

Sortierung der Länder

Der SPARTACUS ist in alphabetischer Reihenfolge nach den englischen Bezeichnungen der jeweiligen Länder aufgeteilt. Eine Ausnahme bildet die Karibik mit den jeweiligen Inseln und Ländern, die man unter dem Buchstaben „C" findet. Innerhalb der Länder erfolgt die Sortierung ebenfalls alphabetisch, jedoch sind die Namen der Städte in der jeweiligen Landessprache aufgelistet. Australien, Kanada und die USA sind jeweils noch in Bundesstaaten/Territorien/Provinzen eingeteilt und erst innerhalb dieser Listung werden die jeweiligen Städte alphabetisch aufgeführt. Sollten Sie dennoch Probleme haben, schlagen Sie einfach in unserem Inhaltsverzeichnis auf Seite 1362 nach. Dort sind alle Staaten, Länder und Städte in allen fünf SPARTACUS-Sprachen, also Englisch, Deutsch, Französisch, Spanisch und Italienisch, aufgeführt.

Für jedes Land haben wir spezifische Informationen über die rechtliche und soziale Situation von Gays zusammengetragen, dazu gehört auch das Mündigkeitsalter sowie Informationen zu Gay-Festivals und besonderen Events.

Vor der Einführung über jedes Land, finden Sie nachstehende Informationen:

Name: Der Name in der Landessprache sowie in den fünf SPARTACUS-Sprachen	**Name:** Suid-Afrika · Südafrika · Afrique du Sud · Africa del Sur · Sud Africa
Location: geographische Lage	**Location:** Southern Africa
Initials: übliche Landesabkürzung	**Initials:** RSA
Time: bezieht sich auf die Zeitzone, in der ein Land liegt	**Time:** GMT +2
International Country Code: gibt die internationale Vorwahlnummer des Landes für Anrufe aus dem Ausland an	**International Country Code:** 27
International Access Code: ist die Vorwahlnummer des jeweiligen Landes, um von dort ins Ausland zu telefonieren	**International Access Code:** 09 or 091
Language: bezieht sich auf die meistgesprochene/n Sprache/n im Land	**Language:** English, Afrikaans, African languages
Area: Fläche des Landes	**Area:** 1,219,080 km^2 / 471,442 sq mi.
Currency: ist die offizielle Landeswährung	**Currency:** 1 Rand = 100 Cents
Population: Einwohnerzahl	**Population:** 58,970,000
Capital: Hauptstadt	**Capital:** Cape Town (legislative capital); Pretoria (administrative capital)
Religions: sind die im Land verbreiteten Religionen	**Religions:** 57% Anglicans, 15% other Protestants, 13% Catholics
Climate: Hier finden Sie eine kurze Übersicht über das Klima	**Climate:** Mostly quite dry climate. Along the coast it's subtropical, days are sunny, nights are cool.
Important Gay Cities: Städte, die für den schwulen Touristen von Interesse sind	**Important Gay Cities:** Cape Town

Gliederung der Adresseinträge

Der einzelne Eintrag enthält: den Namen ❶, die entsprechenden SPARTACUS Codes ❷, die Öffnungszeiten ❸, die Adresse mit Postleitzahl ❹, die Telefonnummer ❺, die Fax-Nummer ❻, die E-mail Adresse ❼ und schließlich die Website Adresse ❽.

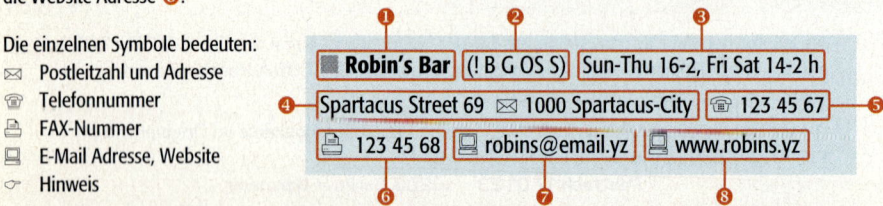

Die einzelnen Symbole bedeuten:
- ✉ Postleitzahl und Adresse
- ☎ Telefonnummer
- 🖨 FAX-Nummer
- 💻 E-Mail Adresse, Website
- ☞ Hinweis

Robin's Bar (! B G OS S) Sun-Thu 16-2, Fri Sat 14-2 h
Spartacus Street 69 ✉ 1000 Spartacus-City ☎ 123 45 67
🖨 123 45 68 💻 robins@email.yz 💻 www.robins.yz

■ Ein rotes Quadrat zu Beginn des Adresseintrags verweist auf weitergehende Informationen in der jeweiligen Kundenwerbung

SPARTACUS 2001/2002

★ Wie man den SPARTACUS benutzt ★

Sortierung der Rubriken

Innerhalb der Länder und Städte sind die einzelnen Adresseinträge folgendermaßen sortiert:

National Gay Info
National Help Lines
National Publishers
National Companies
National Groups
Health Groups
Going Out
▼
Bars
Cafés
Danceclubs
Restaurants
▼
Sex Shops/Blue Movies
Cinemas
▼
Saunas/Baths
Fitness Studios
Massage
▼
Book Shops
Fashion Shops
Leather & Fetish Shops
Travel & Transport
▼
Hotels
Guest Houses
Apartments
Private Accommodation
▼
Groups
▼
Swimming
Cruising

Beschreibung der Codes

Die SPARTACUS Codes bedeuten (Codes in Kleinbuchstaben bedeuten im allgemeinen eine Einschränkung):

!	Ein Muss
A	Kunstausstellungen
AC	Klimaanlage
AYOR	Auf eigenes Risiko, möglicherweise gefährlich oder häufige Polizeikontrollen
B	Bar mit breitem Angebot alkoholischer Getränke
BF	Umfangreiches Frühstück
CC	Alle gängigen Kreditkarten akzeptiert
D	Tanzmöglichkeit/Diskothek
DR	Darkroom
E	Elegant, entsprechende Kleidung notwendig
F	Restaurant mit umfangreicher Karte
G	Ausschließlich oder überwiegend schwules Publikum
GLM	Ausschließlich oder überwiegend schwul-lesbisches Publikum
H	Schwulenfreundliche Unterkunft
LJ	Leder, Fetisch oder Uniform
MA	Gemischte Altersklassen
MG	Schwule mittleren Alters
msg	Massage möglich
N	Nachbarschaftsbar
NG	Nicht schwul, aber interessant
NU	FKK/Nacktbademöglichkeit
OG	Eher ältere Schwule
OS	Außenplätze; Straßencafé, Terrasse, Garten
P	Privatclub oder strenge Einlasskontrolle
PI	Swimmingpool
R	Von Strichern frequentiert
S	Shows/Veranstaltungen
SA	Trockensauna/Finnische Sauna
SB	Dampfsauna
SNU	Stripshows
SOL	Solarium
STV	Travestieshows
TV	Transvestiten, transsexuelles Publikum
VS	Videoshows
WE	Betrieb vor allem am Wochenende
WH	Whirlpool/Jacuzzi
WO	Bodybuilding möglich
YG	Junge Schwule (18–28)

Möchten Sie uns über eventuelle Veränderungen aufmerksam machen, die Sie im Laufe Ihrer Reise bemerkt haben? Dann benutzen Sie bitte, für Ihre natürlich kostenlose Infopost an uns, die beiliegende Karte am Ende des SPARTACUS Reiseführers. Bitte stellen Sie uns so viele Informationen wie möglich zur Verfügung. Wir freuen uns über jede Art von Information, über die Sie vielleicht verfügen, die aber noch nicht im SPARTACUS steht. Ihre Infos senden Sie bitte an:

Bruno Gmünder Verlag GmbH • SPARTACUS-Redaktion
Postfach 61 01 04 • 10921 Berlin • GERMANY
info@spartacus.de

Die SPARTACUS Codes gibt es auch als praktisches heraustrennbares Lesezeichen am Ende des Buches!

★ Gesundheitsinformationen ★

1. Vorwort

Es gibt kaum ein Gebiet der Medizin, in dem das Wissen so rasch voranschreitet wie bei HIV-Infektionen und AIDS. 20 Jahre nach dem ersten Auftreten von AIDS-Erkrankungen gibt es immer noch eine große Zahl von neuen HIV-Infektionen pro Jahr – trotz Aufklärungsarbeit und Vorsorgemaßnahmen. Doch der Stand der neu hinzukommenden AIDS-Erkrankungen oder gar Todesfälle hat sich kaum verändert durch hochwirksame Therapien gegen die Virusinfektion und gegen die möglichen Folgeerkrankungen. Wissen über die Ansteckungswege mindert das Infektionsrisiko für alle und baut Vorurteile und Ängste in der Bevölkerung ab. Wissen über die Infektion, Erkrankung, deren Verlauf und Therapiemöglichkeiten verbessert die Prognose und oft auch die Lebensqualität von Betroffenen.

2. HIV-Infektion und AIDS

Beiden liegt eine Infektion mit sogenannten HI-Viren zugrunde, wobei H für human (menschlich) und I für Immunschwäche steht. Eine Akutinfektion mit den Viren löst nach einer Inkubationszeit von einigen Tagen bis wenigen Wochen oft eine Art Grippeerkrankung aus; bei vielen Betroffenen können jedoch Symptome wie Fieber, Schweißausbrüche, Muskel- und Gelenkschmerzen, Lymphknotenschwellungen oder Hauterscheinungen auch fehlen oder sehr schnell wieder verschwinden. Um in diesem Stadium bei entsprechenden Verdachtsmomenten eine Infektion nachzuweisen, gibt es inzwischen die Möglichkeit, eine sogenannte PCR-Analyse durchführen zu lassen, die oft schon nach wenigen Tagen positiv wird und molekularbiologisch Virusmaterial nachweist. Die Ausbildung spezifischer Antikörper, die man bei dem bekannteren HIV-Test nachweist, erfolgt dagegen frühestens nach zwei, drei oder noch mehr Wochen. Danach kommt es zur Ausbreitung der Viren im Körper, vor allem im Bereich des Immunsystems, aber auch in anderen Bereichen wie Gehirn und Nerven, Schleimhäuten etc. Menschliche Zellen werden befallen, teilweise zerstört oder ihr Stoffwechsel wird verändert. Das Immunsystem (und als Teil dessen auch die T-Helferzellen) hält dagegen so gut und so lange es kann, abhängig von der körperlichen Verfassung des Erkrankten (z.B. durch bestehende Krankheiten) oder zusätzliche Belastungen des Körpers oder der Seele durch andere Infektionen. Kommt es schließlich zu einem Übergewicht der Virusbelastung gegenüber dem Immunsystem, kann es zu sog. opportunistischen Infektionen kommen, also solchen, die für Gesunde kein Problem darstellen, für Immungeschwächte aber umso mehr. Außerdem sind weitere, schwere Erkrankungen wie die Entwicklung eines Kaposi-Sarkoms, bösartiger Lympherkrankungen oder Entzündungen des Gehirns, der Lungen oder vieler anderer Organe möglich (Stadium AIDS). Eine komplette Vernichtung aller Viren gelingt (bisher) weder dem Immunsystem, noch den besten Therapien, doch in allen Stadien der Erkrankung kommen inzwischen hervorgende und teilweise vielversprechende Therapien zum Einsatz. Den wichtigsten Beitrag jedoch leistet jeder einzelne von uns: vorbeugen, mitarbeiten und am wichtigsten für Betroffene: den berühmten „kühlen und klaren Kopf" bewahren.

3. Übertragungswege der HI-Viren

Im Prinzip werden die HI-Viren durch Körperflüssigkeiten eines HIV-positiven Menschen übertragen, wozu im wesentlichen Blut und Sperma gehören. Die Weitergabe erfolgt meist über den Kontakt dieser Körperflüssigkeiten mit der Schleimhaut oder Wunden eines Gesunden. Auch Kontakt mit Haut, gerade wenn sie verletzt ist, scheint zumindest ein Restrisiko zu bergen.
Ein hohes Ansteckungsrisiko haben Praktiken wie
- Analverkehr ohne Kondom (prinzipiell für beide Sexualpartner riskant, auch wenn der passive Partner das höhere Risiko trägt)
Mittleres Risiko haben folgende Praktiken:
- Oralverkehr beim Mann mit Samenerguss in den Mund. Die sog. Vorflüssigkeit beim Mann enthält meist nur geringe Virusmengen; Speichel kann eventuell sogar Viren abtöten.
- Fisting (Analsex mit der Faust, ohne Schutz z.B. durch Gummihandschuhe)
Geringes Risiko birgt Analverkehr bei Verwendung eines Kondoms in sich oder Oralverkehr ohne Samenerguss in den Mund. Tränensekret, Speichel und Schweiß enthalten Viren in nur geringer; Urin und Stuhl in mäßiger Konzentration. Vor allem durch Kot besteht jedoch die Möglichkeit, Parasiten zu übertragen.
Keinesfalls besteht jedoch eine Ansteckungsmöglichkeit über den herkömmlichen Alltagskontakt wie Händeschütteln, Benutzung von Gläsern anderer, Toiletten, Schwimmbädern und Saunas. Die Übertragung von HI-Viren über Atemluft, Niesen oder durch Insekten gehört in den Bereich der Mythologie und Fabeln.

4. Safer Sex

- Unbedingt Kondome benutzen! Sie bieten einen hohen Schutz vor virushaltiger Körperflüssigkeit und Schutz vor weiteren sexuell übertragbaren Krankheiten wie Syphillis (harter Schanker) und Tripper (Gonorrhoe), die inzwischen wieder an Häufigkeit zunehmen sowie Hepatitisinfektionen
- Kondome auch benutzen, wenn beide Partner HIV-positiv sind! Nur so kann ein Austausch verschiedener Virusstämme vermieden werden; andernfalls würden spätere Therapien erschwert
- kein Samenerguss in den Mund
- kein Fisting ohne Gummihandschuhe
- jeder Drogenabhängige muss eigene Spritzutensilien benutzen. Vorsicht bei frischen Wunden, verletzter oder frisch rasierter (!) Haut. Austausch von Dildos nur mit neuem Kondom für jeden Partner. Kondome sollten qualitativ hochwertig sein und nur mit wasserlöslichen Gleitgels verwendet werden, weil sie sonst undicht werden können. Bei allem ist zu beachten: Vorsichtsmaßnahmen können nur schützen, wenn man sie konsequent anwendet. Ein Restrisiko bleibt jedoch immer; Achtung daher ganz besonders bei fremden Sexpartnern, denn eine Infektion ist ihnen in der Regel nicht anzusehen.

★ *Gesundheitsinformationen* ★

5. Therapiestrategien

Gleich vorneweg: es gibt (noch) keine Impfung gegen eine HIV-Infektion, aber inzwischen eine Vielzahl von Medikamenten, die während der einzelnen Erkrankungsstadien eingesetzt werden können.

Wann eine Therapie notwendig ist, entscheidet der Patient zusammen mit seinem Arzt, der die Therapie nur vorschlagen kann. Man orientiert sich dabei zum einen an verschiedenen Symptomen, zum anderen auch an bestimmten Laborwerten, wie der Höhe der Viruskonzentration im Blut (Viruslast) und der Zahl der T4-Lymphozyten (Helferzellen).

Um die Viruslast zu senken, werden in der Regel mehrere Medikamente (meist drei) kombiniert, damit die Viren, die „intelligent" und damit lernfähig sind, möglichst lange gegen die Medikamente empfindlich bleiben.

Nach einer gewissen Zeit kann es zu Resistenzen kommen, so dass andere Medikamente genommen werden müssen. Auch aus diesem Grund ist es wichtig, Kondome zu verwenden, um nämlich die Übertragung resistenter Viren zu verhindern. Zusätzlich auftretende Infektionen, z.B. die bereits beschriebenen opportunistischen Erkrankungen, müssen natürlich ebenfalls z.B. durch Antibiotika bekämpft werden.

Die wichtigsten im Einsatz befindlichen Medikamente sind im folgenden gelistet; weitere Medikamente sind in Entwicklung und stehen teilweise kurz vor ihrer Zulassung – darunter auch Kombinationspräparate, die vor allem die Einnahme vereinfachen sollen. Genannt wird zuerst der internationale Substanzname, in Klammern der Handelsname:

Zidovudin (Retrovir)
Lamivudin (Epivir), beide zusammen auch als Combivir erhältlich
Didanosin (Videx)
Zalcitabin (Hivid)
Stavudin (Zerit)
Abacavir (Ziagen)
Saquinavir (Invirase/Fortovase)
Indinavir (Crixivan)
Nelfinavir (Viracept)
Ritonavir (Norvir)
Amprenavir (Agenerase)
Delavirdin (Rescriptor)
Efavirenz (Sustiva)
Nevirapin (Viramune)

Entsprechend der jeweiligen Therapie werden nun nach bestimmten Kriterien die oben genannten Medikamente miteinander kombiniert, wodurch die Viruskonzentration deutlich und nachhaltig gesenkt werden kann. Weiterhin besteht aber das Risiko einer Virenübertragung auf gesunde Personen, selbst wenn die Viruskonzentration unter die Nachweisgrenze sinkt.

Das Wichtigste an einer effektiven Therapie ist die Disziplin und Kooperation des Patienten, der oft viele Jahre hinweg bis zu zwanzig Tabletten pro Tag nach einem genau festgelegten Zeitplan nehmen und dabei manchmal auch noch mit recht starken Nebenwirkungen rechnen muss.

Bei auftretenden Beschwerden zu Hause und auf Reisen – dies betrifft sowohl Nebenwirkungen als auch weitere Infektionen – sollte immer eine Arzt oder ein Krankenhaus mit entsprechenden HIV-Therapieerfahrungen aufgesucht werden.

6. Reisen mit HIV-Infektion und AIDS

Es bestehen prinzipiell dieselben Regeln wie im Heimatland bezüglich Safer Sex bzw. der Einnahme von Medikamenten. HIV-Infektionen haben bisher kein Land der Welt verschont. Selbst bei einer Erkrankung besteht kaum eine Einschränkung der Reisefähigkeit. Es empfiehlt sich, vor der Abreise Adressen von Ärzten und Schwerpunktkliniken zu besorgen (in der Regel in größeren Ballungszentren bzw. Unikliniken).

Man sollte auch daran denken, sich mit einem ausreichenden Vorrat an Medikamenten, an Kondomen und anderen Dingen, die im Urlaubsland unter Umständen schwer zu bekommen sind, zu versorgen.

Auch bezüglich der meisten Reise- und Tropenkrankheiten empfiehlt sich die Rücksprache mit einem Arzt oder Tropeninstitut.

Durch Sonnenschutz, entsprechende Kleidung, das Einhalten von Hygienevorschriften (Vorsicht bei nicht abgekochtem Wasser und rohen Speisen!) können viele unangenehme Reiseerinnerungen vermieden werden. Gegen viele Krankheiten kann man sich vorbeugend impfen lassen (Hepatitis A und B, Typhus, Polio etc.), bei Reisen in ein Malariagebiet kann eine Prophylaxe erwogen werden. Auch HIV-Kranke sollen geimpft werden; dies muss im Einzelfall zusammen mit dem Arzt entschieden werden.

Zum Schluss sei noch auf zwei Dinge hingewiesen: Vor der Reise unbedingt den Krankenversicherungsschutz fürs Ausland überprüfen (lassen) und sich bei der zuständigen Botschaft des Urlaubslandes nach den neuesten Einreisebeschränkungen für HIV-Infizierte erkundigen. Abzuklären ist hierbei auch, ob Medikamente besser aus dem Heimatland mitgenommen werden (Zollbestimmungen?) oder ob sie auch am Zielort erhältlich sind.

Dirk Lohr
Facharzt
Berlin-Charlottenburg

✱ Bienvenue dans le nouveau SPARTACUS ✱

Cher Lecteur!

Vous tenez dans vos mains la 30ème édition de SPARTACUS International Gay Guide.

Un anniversaire à célébrer!
Comme chaque année, vous vous trouvez en possession d'une édition complètement révisée et actualisée. Pour marquer cette édition anniversaire, le guide est pour la première fois tout en couleur! Nous avons offert à SPARTACUS International Gay Guide un lifting pour son anniversaire: un nouveau visage pour un nouveau millénaire. Pour une consultation facilitée du guide, vous trouverez maintenant les informations sur les pays ainsi que les cartes des pays et plans de villes tout en couleur.

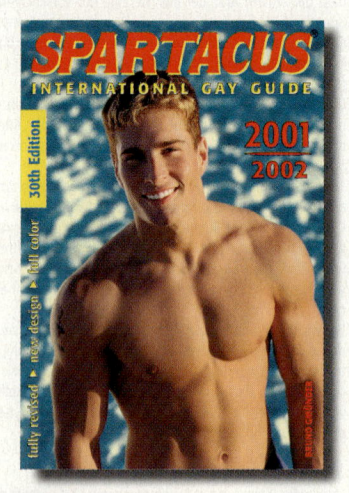

Et ce n'est pas tout: SPARTACUS se lance aussi dans l'Internet. Enfin!
A partir du 1er mai 2001, à l'adresse suivante:
www.SpartacusWorld.com
Cela signifie que tous les acquéreurs de cette édition anniversaire du livre peuvent exclusivement s'inscrire gratuitement sur le site www.SpartacusWorld.com. Il vous suffit de nous renvoyer par courrier le bulletin d'inscription original que vous trouverez en fin de livre dûment complété et signé. Tous les utilisateurs inscrits peuvent alors consulter la banque de données SPARTACUS continuellement mise à jour. Et cela gratuitement jusqu'au 31 décembre 2001.

La porte d'entrée vers un vibrant monde gai!
30 ans de SPARTACUS, 30 ans d'informations et d'adresses gaies du monde entier. Nous nous réjouissons depuis trois décennies de vous offrir depuis l'Albanie jusqu'au Zimbabwe des informations sur chaque recoin du monde: et ceci désormais avec une mise à jour encore plus rapide grâce à l'Internet!

Nous vous souhaitons beaucoup de plaisirs avec votre nouveau SPARTACUS International Gay Guide!

Briand Bedford
EDITEUR EN CHEF

+++ inscrivez-vous maintenant +++ mise à jour constante +++

- Lifestyle
- Achats
- Annonces
- Messagerie
- Erotisme

www.SpartacusWorld.com

- Voyages
- Loisirs

Spartacus Gay Guide

- Informations actuelles
- Manifestations

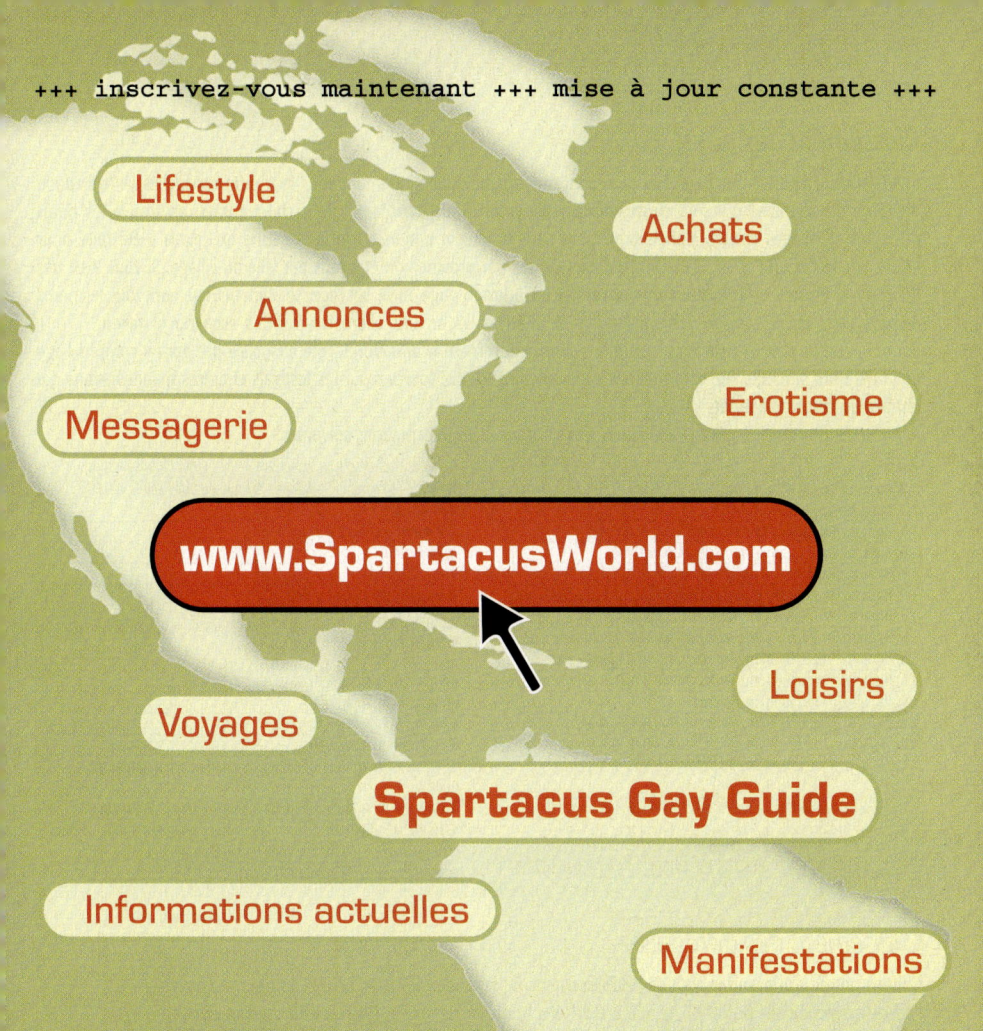

Lancement: 1er mai 2001!

En tant qu'acquéreur de l'édition anniversaire de SPARTACUS International Gay Guide 2001/2002, j'ai la possibilité après inscription de consulter gratuitement la banque de données SPARTACUS jusqu'au 31 décembre 2001.

Veuillez nous renvoyer par courrier la carte d'inscription originale dûment complétée et signée à l'adresse suivante: **SpartacusWorld.com GmbH**
P.O. Box 17 01 23 • 10203 Berlin • Allemagne

Vous recevrez votre mot de passe dans les plus brefs délais.

+++ informations actuelles +++ inscrivez-vous maintenant +++

✻ *Comment utiliser votre SPARTACUS* ✻

Classement des pays

SPARTACUS est classé par pays. Les pays sont ordonnés alphabétiquement sous leur nom en anglais, à l'exception des pays des caraïbes qui sont classés alphabétiquement sous Caribbean. Pour chaque pays, on trouve les noms des villes et villages classés alphabétiquement dans la langue nationale ou locale. Une exception a été faite pour l'Australie, le Canada et les Etats-Unis qui sont divisés par province ou état puis par ville ou village. Si vous avez des difficultés à trouver un lieu, veuillez vous référer à l'index en page 1362 qui recense alphabétiquement tous les noms de pays, villes et villages dans les cinq langues de SPARTACUS: anglais, allemand, français, espagnol et italien.

Pour chaque pays vous trouverez des informations concernant la situation légale et sociale des gais, y compris l'âge de la majorité sexuelle. Des informations supplémentaires sont fournies sur les festivals et autres manifestations qui ont lieu au cours de l'année.

Avant cette introduction pour chaque pays, vous trouverez les informations suivantes:

Name: indique le nom du lieu dans la langue régionale et dans les cinq langues de SPARTACUS	**Name:** Suid-Afrika · Südafrika · Afrique du Sud · Africa del Sur · Sud Africa
Location: indique la situation géographique du pays	**Location:** Southern Africa
Initials: indique à l'abréviation générale du pays	**Initials:** RSA
Time: indique le fuseau horaire du pays	**Time:** GMT +2
International Country Code: indique l'indicatif à composer pour joindre le pays depuis l'étranger	**International Country Code:** 27
International Access Code: indique l'indicatif à composer pour joindre le réseau téléphonique international depuis le pays	**International Access Code:** 09 or 091
Language: indique les principales langues parlées dans le pays	**Language:** English, Afrikaans, African languages
Area: indique la superficie du pays	**Area:** 1,219,080 km^2 / 471,442 sq mi.
Currency: indique la monnaie en cours dans le pays	**Currency:** 1 Rand = 100 Cents
Population: indique le nombre d'habitants du pays	**Population:** 58,970,000
Capital: indique la capitale du pays	**Capital:** Cape Town (legislative capital); Pretoria (administrative capital)
Religions: indique les religions pratiquées dans le pays	**Religions:** 57% Anglicans, 15% other Protestants, 13% Catholics
Climate: indique les caractéristiques climatiques du pays	**Climate:** Mostly quite dry climate. Along the coast it's subtropical, days are sunny, nights are cool.
Important Gay Cities: indique les principales villes gaies	**Important Gay Cities:** Cape Town

Classement des adresses

Chaque entrée comprend le nom de l'établissement ❶, les codes SPARTACUS ❷, les heures d'ouverture ❸, l'adresse avec le code postal ❹, le numéro de téléphone ❺, de fax ❻, l'adresse du courrier électronique ❼, et du site Internet ❽.

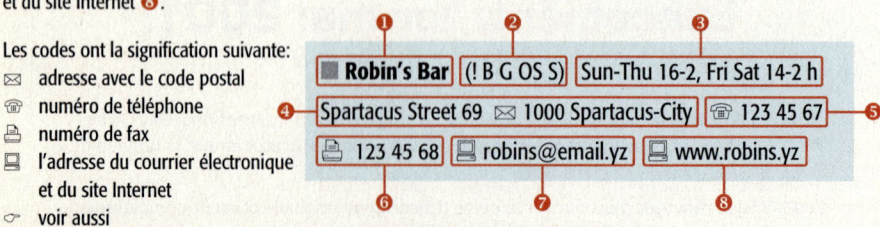

Les codes ont la signification suivante:
- ✉ adresse avec le code postal
- ☏ numéro de téléphone
- 🖨 numéro de fax
- 💻 l'adresse du courrier électronique et du site Internet
- ☞ voir aussi

■ Un carré rouge au début d'une adresse renvoie aux informations supplémentaires données par une annonce publicitaire.

✸ Comment utiliser votre SPARTACUS ✸

Classement des rubriques

Pour chaque pays et ville, vous trouverez les adresses classées sous les rubriques dans l'ordre suivant:

National Gay Info
National Help Lines
National Publishers
National Companies
National Groups
Health Groups
Going Out
▼
Bars
Cafés
Danceclubs
Restaurants
▼
Sex Shops/Blue Movies
Cinemas
▼
Saunas/Baths
Fitness Studios
Massage
▼
Book Shops
Fashion Shops
Leather & Fetish Shops
Travel & Transport
▼
Hotels
Guest Houses
Apartments
Private Accommodation
▼
Groups
▼
Swimming
Cruising

Veuillez utilisez les coupons-réponse (sans frais de port) disponibles en fin de guide pour nous indiquer tous les changements que vous noterez au cours de vos voyages. Essayez d'être le plus complet possible dans vos indications. Nous serons ravis de recevoir toute information qui n'apparaît pas dans cette édition de SPARTACUS:

Bruno Gmünder Verlag GmbH • SPARTACUS-Redaktion
B.P. 61 01 04 • 10785 Berlin • ALLEMAGNE
info@spartacus.de

Signification des codes

Les codes SPARTACUS signifient (Un code en minuscule implique une restriction):

!	un must
A	exposition d'art
AC	climatisation
AYOR	à vos risques et périls!
B	bar avec boissons alcoolisées
BF	petit déjeuner complet
CC	principales cartes de crédit acceptées
D	discothèque
DR	darkroom
E	élégant / tenue correcte exigée
F	restauration / repas servis
G	clientèle majoritairement gaie
GLM	clientèle majoritairement gaie et lesbienne
H	hôtel / lieu d'hébergement où les gais sont bienvenus
LJ	cuir, latex ou uniforme
MA	tous âges
MG	gais d'âge moyen
msg	massage possible
N	établissement de quartier, clientèle du coin
NG	pas forcément gai mais intéressant
NU	nudisme possible
OG	gais plutôt âgés
OS	plein air, terrasse ou jardin
P	club privé ou contrôle strict à l'entrée
PI	piscine
R	fréquenté aussi par des gigolos
S	spectacle ou autre manifestation
SA	sauna finlandais
SB	bain turc, hammam
SNU	strip-tease
SOL	solarium
STV	spectacle de transformisme
TV	fréquenté aussi par des travestis/transsexuels
VS	projection de vidéos
WE	fréquenté plutôt le week-end
WH	jacuzzi / bain à tourbillons
WO	musculation possible
YG	jeunes gais (18–28 ans)

Les codes de SPARTACUS sont aussi disponibles sous la forme d'un signet détachable en fin de livre.

SPARTACUS 2001/2002 | XIX

❋ Informations sur la santé ❋

1. Introduction

La recherche sur les infections du VIH et le SIDA est le domaine de la recherche médicale dont les progrès dans la connaissance s'effectuent le plus rapidement. 20 ans après le premier cas connu de SIDA, des infections par le VIH se produisent toujours malgré toutes les campagnes de prévention et d'information. Cependant le nombre de nouvelles infections et de décès reste inchangé, ceci grâce aux nouvelles thérapies plus efficace qui permettent de combattre le virus et les maladies qui y sont liées. Les connaissances sur les modes de transmission réduisent les chances d'infection et permettent d'amoindrir l'angoisse et le préjugés du grand public. Les connaissances sur la maladie, son évolution et son traitement thérapeutique permettent d'améliorer les pronostics médicaux et la qualité de vie des personnes infectées.

2. La transmission du VIH et du SIDA

Elle résulte du contact avec le VIH, ou Virus Immunodéficitaire Humain. Le SIDA est une maladie infectieuse causée par le virus dénommé VIH. Le VIH affaibli le système immunitaire du corps humain et diminue ainsi sa force de résistance. Le corps atteint devient vulnérable face à des organismes inoffensifs pour un corps sain. Le virus peut aussi provoquer certaines maladies, par exemple cutanées ou nerveuses, mais aussi l'apparition de tumeurs. Une fois que le virus se trouve dans le corps humain, il attaque les cellules du système immunitaire et programme leur métabolisme à son avantage. Le virus peut alors se développer dans ces cellules jusqu'à provoquer leur destruction. Les cellules du système immunitaire qui ne sont pas infectés par le VIH tentent de combattre le virus. Le système immunitaire ne peut cependant se débarrasser complètement du virus. Une personne infectée par le virus remarquera probablement après quelques jours les symptômes d'une grippe, tels que fièvre, transpiration, douleurs musculaires et inflammation des ganglions. Ces symptômes disparaissent rapidement. Une nouvelle possibilité de confirmer le diagnostic d'une infection est l'analyse PCR qui donne un résultat quelques jours après la date de l'infection en traçant les corps microbiologiques du virus. La production d'anticorps, qui sont à la base du test VIH, ne commence que plusieurs semaines (deux, trois, ou plus) après la date de l'infection. Le virus se répand alors dans le corps, particulièrement dans le système immunitaire et dans les cellules cérébrales et nerveuses. Les cellules sont attaquées, en partie détruites et leur métabolisme est modifié. Le système immunitaire existe mais les cellules T (T cells) résistent du mieux et aussi longtemps qu'elles le peuvent. Leur capacité de résistance dépend de la condition physique et psychologique de la personne infectée qui peuvent être déja amoindries par le stress supplémentaire causé par d'autres maladies.
Si le virus prend trop d'importance dans le système immunitaire, il peut provoquer des infections qui serait inoffensives pour une personne saine mais qui sont part contre un réel danger pour une personne dont le système immunitaire est affaibli. De plus, le développement d'autre maladies graves, comme une tumeur maligne, une encéphalite, une pneumonie ou l'inflammation d'autres organes peut se produire (stade du SIDA déclaré). Une destruction complète des corps viraux n'est plus possible, que ce soit par le corps lui-même ou par la meilleure des thérapies. Cependant, il existe maintenant des thérapies efficaces et en partie prometteuses qui peuvent être appliquées aux différents stades la maladie. Il est donc très important pour tous d'observer les règles strictes de prévention et, pour les personnes qui sont affectées, d'essayer de rester zen.

3. Transmission du VIH

Le virus se transmet à travers les fluides corporels (sang et sperme) d'une personne séropositive. Une transmission du HIV peut se produire si du sang ou du sperme contenant du virus se trouve en contact avec une plaie ouverte ou des muqueuses. Il est donc nécessaire d'éviter tout contact avec ces fluides corporels.
Une pratique sexuelle à haut risque est:
- la pénétration anale sans préservatif (dangereux pour les deux partenaires même si le partenaire passif courre probablement plus de risque).
Une pratique sexuelle à risque moyen est:
- la fellation lorsque du sperme est éjaculé dans la bouche du partenaire. Le liquide pré-éjaculatoire contient de petites quantités de virus mais la salive peut parvenir à les détruire,
- le fist-fucking (la pénétration anale par une main) sans gant.
Un baiser ou l'utilisation commune d'un verre, de services de table, l'échange d'habits, la fréquentation de saunas ou de toilettes publiques ne présentent aucun danger de contamination. Toucher une poignée de porte ou un appareil téléphonique, serrer une main ou étreindre une personne, être en contact avec l'air ou se faire piquer par un insecte ne présentent également aucun danger.

4. Safer Sex

- Afin de se protéger d'une transmission du VIH lors de rapports sexuels, il est impératif d'observer certaines règles de comportement (les règles du "safer sex"). Concrètement, cela signifie:
- Une utilisation appropriée de préservatifs lors de rapports sexuels anaux ou oraux. Cela permet de se protéger également d'autres maladies sexuellement transmissibles (MST) comme la syphilis, la blennorragie ou l'hépatite. L'utilisation de préservatifs est aussi indiquée pour deux partenaires séropositifs. Cela évite la recontamination par d'autres souches du virus qui peuvent créer des complications thérapeutiques.
- Pas de sperme dans la bouche du partenaire.
- Pas de pénétration anale avec la main sans gant en latex.
- Les toxicomanes ne doivent pas s'échanger leurs seringues.
Il faut faire attention avec la peau fraîchement rasée et avec les plaies ouvertes. L'échange de godemichés ne doit se faire qu'avec une préservatif neuf pour chaque nouvel utilisateur.
N'utilisez que des préservatifs extra résistants ("extra strong") qui ne se déchirent pas. Protégez-les des températures extrêmes (chaudes et froides) et des rayons directs du soleil, et n'utilisez que des lubrifiants soluble à l'eau. Les crèmes et lubrifiants à base de graisse ont tendance à rendre les préservatifs plus poreux.
La plupart des personnes infectées par le VIH n'ont pas de symptômes apparents. Pour cette raison, il faut considérer toute relation sexuelle avec un partenaire occasionnel comme à risque et se protéger en conséquence.

✱ *Informations sur la santé* ✱

5. Possibilités de traitement

Une remarque pour commencer: il n'existe à ce jour aucun vaccin contre le VIH. Il existe cependant plusieurs médicaments (appelés antiviraux) qui permettent de réduire la prolifération du virus.
La décision de commencer une thérapie doit être prise en commun accord entre le patient et son médecin traitant qui peut proposer différents types de thérapies. Il se base pour cela sur le nombre de T4 et sur la concentration de virus dans le sang.
Pour réduire la concentration de virus dans le sang, une combinaison de médicaments (au moins trois) est prescrite afin d'éviter que le virus ne s'adapte et devienne résistant.
Après un certain temps, le virus peut devenir résistant aux médicaments. Il faut alors prescrire d'autres médicaments. C'est une des raisons pour laquelle il est important d'utiliser des préservatifs afin d'éviter la transmission de virus résistants. Des antibiotiques sont aussi utilisés pour réduire les effets secondaires.
La plupart des médicaments disponibles à ce jour sont mentionnés ci-dessous. Il y a plusieurs nouveaux médicaments qui vont prochainement apparaître sur le marché, certains d'entre eux étant une combinaison de médicaments déjà disponibles destinés à alléger la médication. Les médicaments suivants sont ici cités avec le nom international de la substance qui les compose et avec leur nom sur le marché local entre parenthèses:

Zidovudin (Retrovir)
Lamivudin (Epivir),
aussi disponibles ensemble sous le nom de Combivir
Didanosin (Videx)
Zalcitabin (Hivid)
Stavudin (Zerit)
Abacavir (Ziagen)
Saquinavir (Invirase/Fortovase)
Indinavir (Crixivan)
Nelfinavir (Viracept)
Ritonavir (Norvir)
Amprenavir (Agenerase)
Delavirdin (Rescriptor)
Efavirenz (Sustiva)
Nevirapin (Viramune)

Une utilisation combinée de ces médicaments dans le cadre d'une thérapie contrôlée permet de réduire la concentration du virus. Le risque de transmission du virus persiste toutefois, même quand le virus diminue au point de n'être plus traçable.
Ces médicaments antiviraux doivent être pris de manière régulière. Même si le nombre de médicaments (parfois jusqu'à 20 par jour), leurs effets secondaires parfois importants, et les restrictions dans la vie quotidienne qu'ils impliquent sont contraignants pour les patients, une approche disciplinée de la médication est importante pour le succès de la thérapie.
Si vous rencontrez des problèmes lors d'un voyage, il est recommandable de consulter un médecin ou de se rendre dans un hôpital spécialisé dans le traitement du VIH.

6. Voyages et SIDA

Puisque le virus du SIDA est répandu dans le monde entier, il est important d'observer les règles du "safer sex" aussi à l'étranger. Il n'y a pas forcément de restrictions de la mobilité des personne infectées. Il leur est toutefois recommandé de se renseigner à l'avance sur les différents spécialistes dans le domaine du SIDA qui se trouvent dans la région de leur destination.
Il est aussi avisé d'emporter avec soi des préservatifs de qualité et ses médicaments, la fiabilité des produits sur le marché de certains pays étrangers n'étant pas assurée.
Il est également recommandé de demander l'avis de son médecin sur les risques de maladies qui sont encourus dans le pays de destination.
En observant des précautions de base (se protéger du soleil et porter des habits appropriés) et en suivant des règles d'hygiène de base (ne pas boire de l'eau du robinet ou ne pas manger de la nourriture crue) vous pouvez éviter bien des problèmes qui peuvent survenir lors d'un séjour à l'étranger. Plusieurs autres maladies sexuellement transmissibles comme l'hépatite, la blennorragie, la syphilis peuvent également être évitées avec des vaccins (par exemple l'hépatite A et B). Même les personnes séropositives peuvent se faire vacciner si elles consultent leur médecin traitant.

Deux points importants pour conclure: avant de partir en voyage, renseignez-vous pour savoir si votre assurance maladie vous couvre à l'étranger et s'il existe des restrictions quant à l'entrée de touristes séropositifs dans votre pays de destination. Il est également important de savoir si vous pouvez importer vos médicaments. Ces informations vous seront peut-être fournies sur le site ?

Dirk Lohr
Médecin spécialiste
Berlin-Charlottenburg

✖ ¡Bienvenidos al nuevo SPARTACUS! ✖

Querido lector:

En tus manos se encuentra la 30 edición de la SPARTACUS International Gay Guide.

¡Es un verdadero motivo para celebrar!
Como todos los años, te hemos enviado una versión completamente revisada y actualizada. La novedad de esta edición de jubileo es que itoda la guía es a colores!
Además como regalo de cumpleaños, a la SPARTACUS International Gay Guide la hemos embellecido con un nuevo diseño para iniciar el milenio. Para que te ubiques más rápidamente, la información sobre los países, así como los mapas y los planos de las ciudades están resaltados a colores.

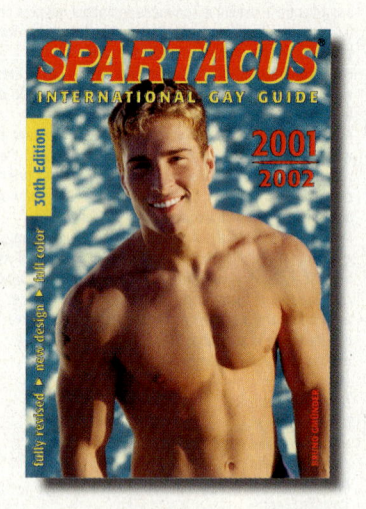

Pero esto no es todo: ¡SPARTACUS se va al internet!
El estreno es el 1 de mayo de 2001, y aquí la anhelada dirección:
www.SpartacusWord.com
Todos los que compren la edición conmemorativa tienen la posibilidad de registrarse gratuitamente en www.SpartacusWord.com. Para ello, encontrarás la tarjeta de registro en la parte trasera de esta guia, rellénala, envíala por correo, ¡y listo!
Todos los usuarios registrados podrán acceder gratuitamente al banco de datos de direcciones SPARTACUS continuamente actualizado (hasta el 31-12-2001 de forma gratuita).

¡Es tu puerta al universo gay!
30 años de SPARTACUS, 30 años de información y direcciones de todo el mundo gay. Nos complace muchísimo continuar ofreciéndote, como desde hace tres décadas, información sobre todos los rincones del mundo, desde Albania hasta Zimbabwe. Con la presentación en Internet, nuestra información será más actual y mejor.

A todos les deseamos mucha alegría y entretenimiento con la nueva SPARTACUS International Gay Guide

Briand Bedford
REDACTOR JEFE

-++ Registrarse ahora gratuitamente +++ Actualización continua +++

Acontecimientos

Ir de compras

Clasificados

Chat gay

Entretenimiento para adultos

www.SpartacusWorld.com

Events

Viaje

Spartacus Gay Guide

Buletín de novedades

Entretenimiento

¡Estreno: 1 de mayo del 2001!

Como comprador de la edición conmemorativa de SPARTACUS International Gay Guide 2001/2002, una vez registrado puedo acceder gratuitamente y hasta el 31 de diciembre del 2001 al banco de datos de direcciones de SPARTACUS.

Complementar la tarjeta de registro y enviar el original de la tarjeta, firmado, a:
SpartacusWorld.com GmbH
P.O. Box 17 01 23 • 10203 Berlin • Germany

Recibirás tu código personal de acceso por correo.

++ informaciones actuales +++ Registrarse ahora gratuitamente +++

✖ Cómo usar el SPARTACUS ✖

Orden de los países

SPARTACUS se ha dividido por países enlistados alfabéticamente (siguiendo los nombres en inglés). Las islas y países del caribe constituyen una excepción y se encuentran bajo la letra "C". Todos los países están subdivididos por ciudades, indicados en la lengua local e igualmente enlistados alfabéticamente. En los casos de Australia, Canadá y Estados Unidos de América, los diferentes Estados o provincias figuran por alfabeto y están, a su vez, subdivididos por ciudades. En caso de no encontrar algo, puede consultarse el índice en la página 1362, donde los países y las ciudades se indican por orden alfabético en las cinco lenguas empleadas en la guía SPARTACUS: alemán, español, francés, inglés e italiano.
Como información específica sobre todos los países incluidos en la guía se explica, por ejemplo, la situación legal y social de los hombres gays, así como la edad de consentimiento para las relaciones sexuales. Además, ofrecemos información sobre festivales gays, acontecimientos especiales, etc.
Antes de la introducción a cada país, el lector encontrará la siguiente información:

Name: El nombre en la lengua local así como en las cinco lenguas empleadas en la guía SPARTACUS	**Name:** Suid-Afrika · Südafrika · Afrique du Sud · Africa del Sur · Sud Africa
Location: ubicación geográfica	**Location:** Southern Africa
Initials: indican la abreviatura usual del país	**Initials:** RSA
Time: hace referencia al huso horario en que se encuentra el país	**Time:** GMT +2
International Country Code: indica el prefijo telefónico empleado para llamar al país	**International Country Code:** 27
International Access Code: indica el prefijo telefónico empleado para realizar llamadas internacionales desde el país	**International Access Code:** 09 or 091
Language: indica la(s) lengu(s) más comunes habladas en el país	**Language:** English, Afrikaans, African languages
Area: indica la superficie del país	**Area:** 1,219,080 km^2 / 471,442 sq mi.
Currency: indica la monena oficial aceptado en el país	**Currency:** 1 Rand = 100 Cents
Population: el número de habitantes	**Population:** 58,970,000
Capital: la ciudad capital del país	**Capital:** Cape Town (legislative capital); Pretoria (administrative capital)
Religions: las religiones más importantes practicadas en el país	**Religions:** 57% Anglicans, 15% other Protestants, 13% Catholics
Climate: breve descripción del clima que se puede esperar a lo largo del año	**Climate:** Mostly quite dry climate. Along the coast it's subtropical, days are sunny, nights are cool.
Important Gay Cities: ciudades de especial interés para visitantes gays	**Important Gay Cities:** Cape Town

Orden de la información en los encabezados

Cada lista está constituida por el nombre ❶, los códigos SPARTACUS correspondientes ❷, los horarios de apertura ❸, la dirección con código postal ❹, el número de teléfono ❺, el número de fax ❻, la dirección de correo electrónico ❼ y la dirección en internet ❽.

Los siguientes símbolos significan:
- ✉ dirección con código postal
- ☎ número de teléfono
- 🖨 número de fax
- 💻 dirección de correo electrónico, dirección en internet
- ☞ sugerencias

❶ Robin's Bar ❷ (! B G OS S) ❸ Sun-Thu 16-2, Fri Sat 14-2 h
❹ Spartacus Street 69 ✉ 1000 Spartacus-City ☎ 123 45 67 ❺
🖨 123 45 68 💻 robins@email.yz 💻 www.robins.yz
❻ ❼ ❽

■ Un cuadrado rojo al principio de una entrada con una dirección remite a información adicional publicada por el cliente en cuestión

XXIV *SPARTACUS* 2001/2002

✖ Cómo usar el SPARTACUS ✖

Orden de los apartados

Bajo los encabezados de los países y de las ciudades, los títulos de las diferentes direcciones están ordenados de la siguiente manera:

> National Gay Info
> National Help Lines
> National Publishers
> National Companies
> National Groups
> Health Groups
> Going Out
> ▼
> Bars
> Cafés
> Danceclubs
> Restaurants
> ▼
> Sex Shops/Blue Movies
> Cinemas
> ▼
> Saunas/Baths
> Fitness Studios
> Massage
> ▼
> Book Shops
> Fashion Shops
> Leather & Fetish Shops
> Travel & Transport
> ▼
> Hotels
> Guest Houses
> Apartments
> Private Accommodation
> ▼
> Groups
> ▼
> Swimming
> Cruising

Usa la tarjeta postal de información (de franqueo pagado) que encontrarás al final de esta guía para comunicarnos cualquier dato nuevo o cambio de los datos señalados que hayas notado durante tu viaje. Es importante indicar el máximo de información posible. Estamos especialmente interesados en recibir información todavía no incluida en la presente edición de la guía SPARTACUS.

Bruno Gmünder Verlag GmbH • SPARTACUS-Redaktion
P.O. Box 61 01 04 • 10921 Berlin • GERMANY
info@spartacus.de

Descripción de los códigos

Los códigos de SPARTACUS significan lo siguiente (estando en minúscula significan una limitación del significado del código en mayúscula):

!	Sin falta
A	Exposiciones de arte
AC	Aire acondicionado
AYOR	Bajo su propio riesgo. Peligro de ser atacado o de actividades de la policía
B	Bar con todo tipo de bebidas alcohólicas
BF	Desayuno completo
CC	Se aceptan las más importantes tarjetas de crédito
D	Para bailar / discoteca
DR	Cuarto oscuro / sala oscura
E	Elegante. Es necesario vestirse de manera adecuada
F	Comida. Disponibilidad de menús completos
G	Exclusivamente o casi exclusivamente público gay
GLM	Público gay y lésbico mezclado
H	Hotel o tipo parecido de alojamiento donde se recibe bien a los gays
LJ	Cuero, fetichismo o uniforme
MA	Edades mixtas
MG	Hombres gays de edades medias
msg	Se hacen masajes
N	Sobre todo de interés para el público local / los asistentes son del lugar
NG	No gay pero posiblemente de interés para gays
NU	Área de nudismo
OG	Sobre todo hombres gays mayores
OS	Posibilidad de sentarse al aire libre / terraza o jardín
P	Club privado o control estricto en la entrada
PI	Piscina
R	Frecuentado por personas que ejercen la prostitución
S	Espectáculos o otros acontecimientos
SA	Sauna finlandesa
SB	Baño de vapor
SNU	Espectáculos de striptease
SOL	Solarium / Rayos UV
STV	Espectáculo de travestis
TV	Travestis y / o clientela transsexual
VS	Video
WE	Más animado los fines de semana
WH	Whirlpool / jacuzzi / bañera
WO	Posibilidad de ejercer culturismo
YG	Gays más jóvenes (18 a 28 años)

Los códigos de SPARTACUS también se encuentran impresos en el práctico separador que se encuentra al final del libro.

✖ Informaciones de salud ✖

1. Introducción

No existe apenas ningún otro campo de la medicina en el que se avance tan deprisa como en el de la infección por el HIV y el sida. 20 años tras los primeros casos de sida y a pesar de las campañas informativas y las medidas preventivas se siguen produciendo un gran número de nuevas infecciones por HIV. Sin embargo, el número de nuevos casos de desarrollo de la enfermedad e incluso el de las muertes apenas si ha variado, lo que se debe al empleo de tratamientos muy eficaces contra la infección con el virus y las enfermedades subsiguientes. El conocimiento de las vías de contagio reduce el riesgo de infección para todos y reduce los prejuicios y temores de la población. Los conocimientos sobre la infección, la enfermedad, su desarrollo y las posibilidades de tratamiento mejoran las esperanzas y la calidad de vida de los afectados.

2. Infección por el HIV y sida

Ambos tienen su origen en los llamados virus HI, estando la H por humana y la I por inmunodeficiencia. Una infección aguda con el virus provoca que en un período de incubación de pocas semanas se produzca habitualmente una especie de enfermedad gripal; sin embargo, en muchos casos síntomas tales como fiebre, sudores, dolores musculares o articulares, inflamación de los ganglios linfáticos, o inflamaciones cutáneas, o bien no se presentan o desaparecen al poco tiempo. Para sobre la base de las correspondientes sospechas poder detectar la infección en este estadio hoy es posible recurrir al llamado análisis PCR, que incluso tras pocos días da resultados positivos y detecta la estructura biológico-molecular del virus. La formación de anticuerpos específicos, que es lo que los más conocidos análisis del HIV detectan, se produce como muy pronto tras dos, tres o más semanas. A continuación tiene lugar la difusión del virus por el cuerpo, sobre todo en el sistema inmunitario pero también en otros lugares como el cerebro, nervios, mucosas, etc. El virus ataca las células, las destruye parcialmente o bien modifica su metabolismo. Ni el sistema inmunitario (y como parte del mismo también las células T) resiste tan bien y tanto tiempo como puede, y según el estado físico del enfermo (p. ej. debido a enfermedades preexistentes) o de otros factores de estrés físico o mental originados por otras infecciones. Si finalmente se rompe el equilibrio a favor del virus y contra el sistema inmunitario, se producen las llamadas infecciones oportunistas, esto es aquellas que no suponen problema alguno para una persona sana, pero que para inmunodeficientes resultan tanto más graves.
También es posible que se desarrollen otras graves enfermedades tales como: el sarcoma de Kaposi, malignas enfermedades de los ganglios linfáticos, del cerebro, de los pulmones o de muchos otros órganos (fase sida). Ni el sistema inmunitario, ni el mejor de los tratamientos, han conseguido (hasta ahora) la destrucción completa de todos los virus, si bien ya se están aplicando excelentes y prometedores tratamientos en todas las fases de desarrollo de la enfermedad.Sin embargo, la ayuda principal la prestamos cada uno de nosotros: prevenir, ayudar y los más importante para los afectados: conservar la famosa "cabeza clara y fría".

3. Vías de transmisión del VIH

La transmisión del VIH se produce a través de los fluidos corporales de una persona infectada con el HIV, sobre todo a través de la sangre y el semen. La transmisión se produce mediante el contacto de estos con las mucosas o con las heridas de una persona sana. El contacto con la piel cuando esta registra pequeñas heridas también parece implicar cuando menos un riesgo residual de contagio.
Se consideran de alto riesgo las siguientes prácticas:
- Penetración anal sin preservativo (en principio con riesgo para ambas partes, aun cuando la parte pasiva soporta el mayor riesgo)
Las siguientes prácticas conllevan un riesgo medio:
- Sexo oral con eyaculación en la boca. La llamada secreción previa del hombre contiene en la mayoría de los casos solamente pequeñas cantidades del virus; la saliva puede llegar incluso a matar el virus.
- Fisting (sexo anal con el puño realizado sin protección alguna como por ej. guantes de goma)
La práctica del sexo anal con preservativo o del sexo oral sin eyaculación en la boca entrañan un pequeño riesgo. Lágrimas, saliva y sudor contienen muy pequeñas concentraciones del virus; orina y heces cantidades moderadas. Sin embargo, a través de los excrementos existe la posibilidad de transmitir parásitos.
En ningún caso existe la posibilidad de contagio mediante los contactos de la vida cotidiana como: estrecharse la mano, compartir el vaso de otra persona, el uso de servicios públicos, piscinas o saunas. La transmisión del HIV a través del aire, estornudos o insectos pertenece al ámbito de la mitología y los cuentos.

4. Sexo seguro

- Es imprescindible el uso de preservativos! ya que ofrecen una gran protección contra los fluidos corporales contaminados con el virus y otras enfermedades de transmisión sexual como la sífilis (chancro venéreo) y la gonorrea, que han ganado en frecuencia, así como la hepatitis vírica.
- También se deben usar preservativos aún cuando ambas partes sean seropositivas! ya que solamente de esta manera se puede evitar el intercambio de distintas cepas del virus; que de otro modo dificultarían futuros tratamientos.
- No eyacular en la boca.
- No realizar "fisting" desprovisto de guantes de goma.
- cada drogadicto debe utilizar sus propios instrumentos para inyectarse.
Cuidado con las heridas frescas y con la piel herida o recién afeitada (!). Intercambio de dildos solo con un nuevo preservativo por ambas partes. Los preservativos deben ser de buena calidad y usarse solo junto con gels solubles en água; pues de lo contrario pueden dañarse. Y esto vale en todos los casos: las medidas precautorias solamente son eficaces si se emplean de manera consecuente. Sin embargo, siempre queda un riesgo residual; por lo tanto se debe tener un especial cuidado con nuevos compañeros sexuales, ya que por lo general la infección no se reconoce a simple vista.

✖ Informaciones de salud ✖

5. Posibles tratamientos

Queremos dejarlo claro desde el principio: no existe (todavía) ninguna vacuna contra la infección con el HIV, pero sí una gran cantidad de medicamentos que se pueden emplear durante las distintas fases de la enfermedad.

El momento adecuado para iniciar un tratamiento es algo que deciden el paciente junto con su médico, que solamente puede proponer el tratamiento. Para lo que deben servir de orientación por un lado los distintos síntomas y por otro determinados valores como el grado de concentración del virus en la sangre (carga viral) y la cantidad de linfocitos-T4 (células T).

Para reducir la carga viral se combinan varios medicamentos (en la mayoría de los casos tres), de modo que los virus, que son "inteligentes" y, por tanto, capaces de aprender, permanezcan el mayor tiempo posible sensibles al tratamiento.

Tras un cierto tiempo se pueden presentar resistencias, de modo que sea preciso tomar otros medicamentos. Por lo que también por este motivo es importante el uso de preservativos, evitándose así la transmisión de virus resistentes. Dándose por supuesto que otras infecciones como las ya citadas enfermedades oportunistas se deberán combatir también, p. ej. mediante antibióticos.

A continuación se detallan los más importantes medicamentos actualmente en uso; otros medicamentos se encuentra en fase de desarrollo y en parte a punto de obtener su homologación, entre ellos algunas combinaciones que deberán facilitar sobre todo la ingestión. En primer lugar se cita la denominación internacional de la sustancia y entre paréntesis el nombre comercial:

Zidovudin (Retrovir)
Lamivudin (Epivir),
adquiribles también conjuntamente bajo el nombre Combivir
Didanosin (Videx)
Zalcitabin (Hivid)
Stavudin (Zerit)
Abacavir (Ziagen)
Saquinavir (Invirase/Fortovase)
Indinavir (Crixivan)
Nelfinavir (Viracept)
Ritonavir (Norvir)
Amprenavir (Agenerase)
Delavirdin (Rescriptor)
Efavirenz (Sustiva)
Nevirapin (Viramune)

Los medicamentos aquí citados y según el tratamiento respectivo se combinan de acuerdo con determinados criterios, pudiéndose reducir así la concentración del virus de manera clara y duradera. Sin embargo, y aún cuando la concentración del virus quede por debajo del valor constatable, se mantiene el riesgo de transmisión a personas sanas.

Los elementos más importantes para un tratamiento efectivo son la disciplina y la cooperación del paciente, que por lo común debe ingerir durante varios años hasta 20 comprimidos diarios de acuerdo con un horario prefijado y en algunos casos contar también con unos efectos secundarios bastante fuertes.

Siempre que se presenten molestias, sea en el domicilio habitual o en el transcurso de viajes y tanto si se trata de efectos secundarios como de otras infecciones, se debe acudir a un médico o hospital con la correspondiente experiencia en el tratamiento del HIV.

6. Viajes con la infección HIV y con el sida

En principio son de aplicación las mismas reglas que en el país de origen en lo que respecta al sexo seguro y la ingestión de medicamentos. Hasta hoy el sida no ha perdonado a ningún país. Incluso en caso de enfermedad no existen limitaciones en cuanto a los viajes. Siendo recomendable la recogida de direcciones de médicos o clínicas especializadas antes de iniciar el viaje (por lo habitual en grandes centros urbanos o en clínicas universitarias).

Es también aconsejable proveerse de una cantidad suficiente de medicamentos, preservativos y otros objetos que en determinadas circunstancias pueda ser difícil conseguir.

También es aconsejable mantener una entrevista en relación con enfermedades tropicales con un médico o una clínica especializados en el tema.

Mediante protección contra el sol, la ropa adecuada y el mantenimiento de reglas de higiene (cuidado con el água sin cocer y los alimentos crudos!) se pueden evitar muchos recuerdos desagradables de las vacaciones. Es posible vacunarse de manera profiláctica contra muchas enfermedades (hepatitis A y B, tifus, polio, etc.). En caso de viajes a regiones afectadas por el paludismo se puede valorar la utilización de medidas preventivas. Los enfermos con el HIV también deben vacunarse; lo que debe decidirse de acuerdo con el médico.

Y para terminar debemos hacer hincapié en dos cosas: (dejar) comprobar antes de salir de viaje el seguro de enfermedad e informarse en la correspondiente embajada del país de destino de las más recientes restricciones relacionadas con la entrada de infectados por el HIV. Al mismo tiempo se debe valorar si es mejor proveerse de medicamentos en el país de origen (¿normas aduaneras?) o si también es posible adquirirlos en el país de destino.

Dirk Lohr
Médico especialista
Berlin-Charlottenburg

Benvenuti all'nuovo SPARTACUS

Caro lettore,

ecco finalmente la 30ª edizione di
SPARTACUS International Gay Guide.

Un motivo per festeggiare!
Come ogni anno hai in mano una versione completamente
rielaborata ed attualizzata. E come novità per l'edizione
dell'anniversario la guida è stata realizzata tutta a colori!
Per l'occasione abbiamo dato più peso all'estetica di questa
guida: un nuovo millennio con un nuovo design.
Affinchè tu possa orientarti più rapidamente, le informazioni
sui diversi paesi, le carte geografiche e le piante delle città
sono a colori.

Ma non è tutto: SPARTACUS goes online!
A partire dal 1º maggio 2001 ci potete raggiungere su Internet:
www.SpartacusWorld.com
Tutti gli acquirenti di questa edizione del giubileo del 30º avranno il privilegio di
registrasi gratuitamente fin d'ora sul sito www.SpartacusWorld.com (il tagliando di
registrazione lo trovi alla fine del libro: basta compilarlo, firmarlo e spedirlo).
Tutti gli utenti registrati potranno usare la nostra banca dati (sempre attuale)
gratuitamente fino al 31 Dicembre 2001.

Il tuo portale per il mondo gay!
30 anni di SPARTACUS, 30 anni di informazioni e di indirizzi da tutto il mondo gay.
Siamo lieti di offrire da ben tre decenni tutte le informazioni da ogni angolo del globo,
dall'Albania allo Zimbabwe: ancora più attuali e migliori grazie alla nostra presenza
su Internet!

Auguriamo a tutti buon divertimento con la nuova guida
SPARTACUS International Gay Guide!

Briand Bedford
REDATTORE CAPO

+++ registrarsi adesso +++ aggiornamento continuo +++ tutte le

Lifestyle

Shopping

Piccoli annunci

Chat gay

Intrattenimento per adulti

www.SpartacusWorld.com

Viaggi

Eventi

Spartacus Gay Guide

Bollettino d'informazione

Intrattenimento

Première: 1° maggio 2001!

Avendo acquistato l'edizione speciale per il 30° anniversario della SPARTACUS International Gay Guide 2001/2002, avrò la possibilità, a registrazione avvenuta, di consultare gratuitamente l'indirizzario on line di SPARTACUS fino al 31. Dicembre 2001.

Compilare integralmente la scheda di registrazione ed inviare l'originale firmato a:
SpartacusWorld.com GmbH
P.O.Box 17 01 23 • 10203 Berlin • Germania

Il codice di accesso personale ti verrà inviato tempestivamente.

+++ tutte le informazioni attuali +++ registrarsi adesso +++

Come utilizzare lo SPARTACUS

Classificazione dei paesi

Lo SPARTACUS è diviso in paesi che sono elencati in inglese secondo l'ordine alfabetico. Fanno eccezione i Caraibi con i loro rispettivi stati e le isole che si trovano sotto la voce "C" come Carribian/Caraibi. I paesi stessi poi, sono elencati secondo l'ordine alfabetico, ma i nomi delle città sono nella lingua nazionale del rispettivo paese. Per quanto riguarda l'Australia, il Canada e gli USA le città o province sono elencate in ordine alfabetico e sono divise in metropoli e città. Per ulteriori chiarimenti si raccomanda di andare a vedere l'indice su pagina 1362, dove tutti i paesi, metropoli e città sono elencati in ordine alfabetico e nelle cinque lingue dello SPARTACUS e cioè in inglese, tedesco, francese e spagnolo.

Per ogni paese abbiamo collezionato informazioni specifiche sulla situazione sociale e legale dei gay, incluso l'eta legale per avere rapporti sessuali. Ne fanno naturalmente anche parte le informazioni su eventuali festival gay e su eventi particolari.

Prima dell'introduzione su ogni paese si trovano le seguenti informazioni:

Name: il nome nella lingua locale e in tutte le 5 lingue dello SPARTACUS	**Name:** Suid-Afrika · Südafrika · Afrique du Sud · Africa del Sur · Sud Africa
Location: posizione geografica	**Location:** Southern Africa
Initials: indica l'abbreviazione commune des nome del paese	**Initials:** RSA
Time: indica il fuso orario	**Time:** GMT +2
International Country Code: indica il prefisso internazionale del paese per telefonare dall'estero in questo paese	**International Country Code:** 27
International Access Code: indica il prefisso del respettivo paese che viene utilizzato per chiamare da questo paese all'estero	**International Access Code:** 09 or 091
Language: si riferisce alla/e lingua/e più parlata/e	**Language:** English, Afrikaans, African languages
Area: è l'estensione territoriale del paese	**Area:** 1,219,080 km_ / 471,442 sq mi.
Currency: è la moneta ufficiale del paese	**Currency:** 1 Rand = 100 Cents
Population: numero degli abitanti	**Population:** 58,970,000
Capital: capitale	**Capital:** Cape Town (legislative capital); Pretoria (administrative capital)
Religions: sono le religioni più diffuse nel paese	**Religions:** 57% Anglicans, 15% other Protestants, 13% Catholics
Climate: qui si trovano informazioni sul probabile clima	**Climate:** Mostly quite dry climate. Along the coast it's subtropical, days are sunny, nights are cool.
Important Gay Cities: città che sono interessanti per turisti gay	**Important Gay Cities:** Cape Town

Strutturazione degli indirizzi

Ogni singolo elenco contiene il nome ❶, i rispettivi codici SPARTACUS ❷, gli orari d'apertura ❸, l'indirizzo con il codice postale ❹, il numero di telefono ❺, il numero di fax ❻, l'indirizzo e-mail ❼ e l'indirizzo del website ❽.

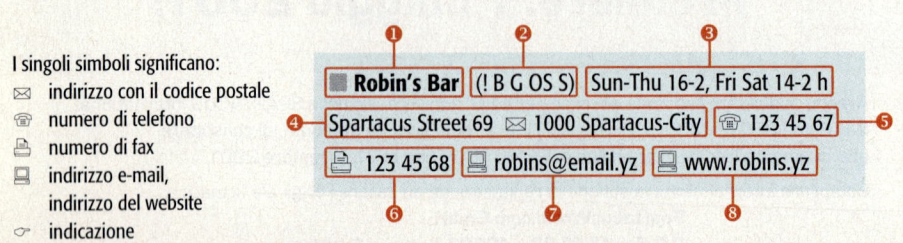

I singoli simboli significano:
- ✉ indirizzo con il codice postale
- ☎ numero di telefono
- 🖨 numero di fax
- 💻 indirizzo e-mail, indirizzo del website
- ☞ indicazione

❶ **Robin's Bar** ❷ (! B G OS S) ❸ Sun-Thu 16-2, Fri Sat 14-2 h
❹ Spartacus Street 69 ✉ 1000 Spartacus-City ☎ ❺ 123 45 67
❻ 🖨 123 45 68 ❼ 💻 robins@email.yz ❽ www.robins.yz

■ Un quadrato rosso all'inizio di un'indirizzo rimanda alle informazioni supplementarie date da un'annuncio pubblicitario

● Come utilizzare lo SPARTACUS ●

Classificazione delle rubriche

Per ogni paese e città troverete gli indirizzi classificati sotto le rubriche nell'ordine seguente:

National Gay Info
National Help Lines
National Publishers
National Companies
National Groups
Health Groups
Going Out
▼
Bars
Cafés
Danceclubs
Restaurants
▼
Sex Shops/Blue Movies
Cinemas
▼
Saunas/Baths
Fitness Studios
Massage
▼
Book Shops
Fashion Shops
Leather & Fetish Shops
Travel & Transport
▼
Hotels
Guest Houses
Apartments
Private Accommodation
▼
Groups
▼
Swimming
Cruising

Vuole informarci su eventuali cambiamenti che ha scoperto durante il Suo viaggio? In questo caso La preghiamo di utilizzare per la sua informazione la "Users information card" che si trova alla fine di questa edizione dello SPARTACUS. Naturalmente le spese di spedizione vanno a carico del destinatario. Quante informazioni ci dà meglio è. Le siamo grati di ogni tipo di informazione di cui Lei forse già dispone e che non si trova ancora in questa edizione dello SPARTACUS.

Bruno Gmünder Verlag GmbH • SPARTACUS-Redaktion
P.O. Box 61 01 04 • 10921 Berlin • GERMANY
info@spartacus.de

Significato dei codici

I codici dello SPARTACUS significano (Codici in lettere minuscule significano in generale una restrizione):

!	Di obbligo
A	Mostre d'arte
AC	Aria condizionata
AYOR	A Suo rischio. Forse luogo pericoloso.
B	Bar con bevande alcoliche
BF	Colazione abbondante
CC	Si accettano le più importanti carte di credito
D	Discoteca
DR	Darkroom
E	Pubblico elegante, si consiglia un abbigliamento adatto
F	Ristorante
G	Esclusivamente uomini omosessuali
GLM	Esclusivamente pubblico gay e lesbico
H	Gay benvenuti nell'alloggio
LJ	Feticisti
MA	Età mista
MG	Omossesuali di età media
msg	Massaggio possibile
N	Località con gente del quartiere
NG	Non omosessuale, ma interessante
NU	Nudismo / è possibile bagnarsi nudo
OG	Piùttosto omossesuali più vecchi
OS	Tavoli all'aperto; caffè, terazza, giardino
P	Club privato / controlli severi alla porta
PI	Piscina
R	Frequentato da Prostituti
S	Shows/evenementi
SA	Sauna finnica
SB	Sauna a vapore
SNU	Spettacoli di spogliarello
SOL	Solario
STV	Spettacoli di travesti
TV	Travestiti nel pubblico
VS	Videospettacoli
WE	Più frequentato il fine settimana
WH	Whirlpool / jacuzzi
WO	È possibile fare bodybuilding
YG	Omossesuali giovani (18–28 anni)

I codici SPARTACUS sono anche disponibili sotto la forma di un segnalibro strappabile alla fine della guida SPARTACUS.

● Informazioni sulla salute ●

1. Introduzione

Non c'è praticamente alcun settore della medicina in cui la scienza compia tali passi da gigante come nel caso delle infezioni da HIV e dell'AIDS. A 20 anni di distanza dal primo manifestarsi dell'AIDS, continua ad esserci ogni anno un grande numero di nuovi sieropositivi, nonostante il lavoro di informazione e le misure di prevenzione. Tuttavia il numero dei nuovi casi di AIDS o perfino dei decessi è rimasto praticamente invariato, grazie all'adozione di terapie molto efficaci contro l'infezione virale e le possibili malattie che ne possono derivare. L' informazione sulle modalità del contagio riduce per tutti il rischio d'infezione e combatte pregiudizi e timori nella popolazione. L'informazione sull'infezione, sul manifestarsi della malattia, sul suo sviluppo e sulle terapie possibili, migliora la prognosi e spesso anche la qualità della vita di coloro che ne sono affetti.

2. Infezione da HIV e AIDS

Entrambi hanno alla base un'infezione dai cosiddetti virus HI, dove H significa Human (umano) e I immunodeficienza. Un'infezione acuta con questi virus provoca, dopo un periodo di incubazione che va da alcuni giorni fino a qualche settimana, una specie di sindrome influenzale; tuttavia in molti casi i sintomi quali febbre, sudorazione improvvisa, dolori muscolari ed articolari o l'ingrossamento dei linfonodi, mancano del tutto o riscompaiono rapidamente. Per accertare un'infezione in questo stadio, nel caso ci sia motivo di sospetti in questo senso, c'è la possibilità di far eseguire una cosiddetta analisi mediante PCR che spesso già dopo pochi giorni diventa positiva e dimostra la presenza di materiale virale tramite le analisi microbiologiche. Lo sviluppo di anticorpi specifici, che si prova con il più noto test dell'HIV, non risulta invece prima di due, tre o più settimane. Ne segue la proliferazione dei virus nel corpo, soprattutto a livello del sistema immunitario, ma anche in altri organi quali il cervello ed i nervi, le mucose ecc. Le cellule umane vengono colpite, in parte distrutte o ne viene alterato il metabolismo. Il sistema immunitario (e con esso anche i linfociti T helper) cerca di difendersi il meglio possibile e quanto più a lungo possibile, in dipendenza dalla costituzione del malato (indebolita per esempio da altre affezioni preesistenti) o dall'insorgere di ulteriori patologie fisiche e psichiche. Se infine l'affezione virale riesce a sopraffare il sistema immunitario, si possono verificare le cosiddette infezioni opportunistiche, ossia quelle infezioni che per le persone sane non rappresentano alcun pericolo, ma che lo sono per quelle affette da immunodeficienza.
Inoltre è possibile che insorgano altre malattie gravi, come lo sviluppo di un sarcoma di Kaposi, di un tumore maligno nel sistema linfatico, di encefalopatite, polmonite o infiammazioni di molti altri organi (stadio dell'AIDS). Né il sistema immunitario né le migliori terapie sono riuscite (finora) a distruggere completamente tutti i virus, tuttavia in tutti gli stadi della malattia c'è ora la possibilità di ricorrere a terapie eccellenti e talvolta molto promettenti. Tuttavia il contributo più importante lo fornisce ognuno di noi: la prevenzione, la collaborazione e, cosa più importante per le persone contagiate, quella di "non lasciarsi prendere dal panico e mantenere il sangue freddo".

3. Modalità di trasmissione dei virus HI

Fondamentalmente i virus HI vengono trasmessi attraverso i liquidi corporei di una persona HIV positiva, ossia essenzialmente tramite il sangue e lo sperma. Il contagio avviene per lo più tramite il contatto di questi liquidi corporei con le mucose o con le ferite di una persona sana. Anche il contatto cutaneo, proprio quando l'epidermide presenta delle lesioni, sembra presentare per lo meno un rischio residuo.
Un grande rischio di contagio presentano le attività quali
- i rapporti sessuali anali senza profilattici (fondamentalmente per tutti e due i partner, anche se il rischio maggiore è per il partner passivo).

Un rischio medio presentano le seguenti attività:
- i rapporti sessuali orali nell'uomo con eiaculazione di sperma in bocca. Il liquido seminale dell'uomo prima dell'eiaculazione contiene per lo più una quantità limitata di virus e la saliva può addirittura uccidere i virus;
- fisting (penetrazione anale con il pugno senza protezione, per esempio con guanti di gomma).

Un rischio limitato viene rappresentato di per sé dai rapporti sessuali anali se si usa un preservativo oppure dai rapporti sessuali orali senza eiaculazione in bocca. Il liquido lacrimale, la saliva ed il sudore contengono virus solo in concentrazione limitata, le urine e le feci in concentrazione modesta. Ma soprattutto tramite gli escrementi sussiste la possibilità di trasmettere parassiti.
Non sussiste comunque nessuna possibilità di contagio tramite i comuni contatti quotidiani, quali la stretta di mano, l'uso di bicchieri già usati da altri, della toilette, della piscina e della sauna. La trasmissione di virus HI tramite l'aria espirata, lo starnuto o gli insetti deve essere relegata al campo della mitologia e delle favole.

4. Sesso sicuro

- Usare assolutamente i profilattici! Essi offrono un'alta protezione dai liquidi corporei che contengono virus e proteggono inoltre da altre malattie che vengono trasmesse con le pratiche sessuali come la sifilide o la gonorrea, la cui frequenza ricomincia ad aumentare come i casi di epatite.
- Usare i preservativi anche quando tutti e due i partner sono sieropositivi! Solo in questo modo si può evitare lo scambio di ceppi di virus diversi e rendere più difficili eventuali terapie successive.
- Evitare l'eiaculazione in bocca
- Non praticare il fisting senza guanti di gomma
- Ciascuno deve usare siringa ed utensili propri per le iniezioni di sostanze stupefacenti

Attenzione nel caso di ferite recenti e di zone cutanee che presentino lesioni o appena rasate (!). Lo scambio di vibratori deve avvenire solo con un nuovo profilattico per ciascun partner. I preservativi devono essere di buona qualità e venire usati solo con gelatine idrosolubili, perché altrimenti possono perdere la tenuta. In ogni caso si deve tenere presente che le misure precauzionali possono essere di protezione solo se vengono applicate con costanza. Un rischio residuo rimane comunque, fare perciò particolare attenzione in caso di rapporti sessuali con partner sconosciuti, perché di solito non si nota se siano infetti o meno.

● *Informazioni sulla salute* ●

5. *Strategie terapeutiche*

Per mettere subito le cose in chiaro: non esiste (ancora) nessun vaccino contro un'infezione da HIV, ma finalmente una molteplicità di farmaci che possono venire impiegati nei singoli stadi della malattia.
È il paziente stesso, insieme al medico che può solo proporre la terapia, a decidere quando questa si renda necessaria. Al riguardo ci si basa da un lato sui diversi sintomi, dall'altro anche su determinati risultati delle analisi, quali il valore della concentrazione del virus nel sangue (carica virale) ed il numero dei linfociti T4 (cellule helper).
Per diminuire la carica virale si combinano di solito diversi farmaci (per lo più tre) in modo che i virus che sono "intelligenti" e quindi capaci di apprendere, rimangano sensibili ai preparati il più a lungo possibile.
Dopo un certo tempo si possono verificare dei fenomeni di resistenza che rendono necessario l'impiego di altri farmaci. Anche per questo motivo è importante usare profilattici, per evitare cioè la trasmissione di virus resistenti. Anche altre infezioni che sopravvengono, come le infezioni opportunistiche menzionate in precedenza, devono venire naturalmente combattute, per esempio con l'impiego di antibiotici.
I farmaci più importanti in uso sono elencati qui di seguito; altri farmaci sono ancora in fase di sviluppo e in parte saranno disponibili fra breve, tra di essi anche farmaci combinati che dovrebbero facilitarne l'assunzione. Prima viene riportato il nome internazionale della sostanza e poi fra parentesi il nome commerciale:

Zidovudin (Retrovir),
Lamivudin (Epivir),
tutte e due insieme disponibili anche come Combivir
Didanosin (Videx)
Zalcitabin (Hivid)
Stavudin (Zerit)
Abacavir (Ziagen)
Saquinavir (Invirase/Fortvase)
Indinavir (Crixivan)
Nelfinavir (Viracept)
Ritonavir (Norvir)
Amprenavir (Agenerase)
Delavirdin (Rescriptor)
Efavirenz (Sustiva)
Nervirapin (Viramune)

In modo corrispondente alla relativa terapia i preparati sopra nominati vengono combinati gli uni con gli altri secondo determinati criteri, tramite i quali può venire ridotta notevolmente ed a lungo la concentrazione dei virus. Tuttavia continua a rimanere il rischio di una trasmissione dei virus ad una persona sana, anche se la concentrazione virale scende al di sotto del limite dell'accettabilità.
Gli elementi più importanti per una terapia efficace sono la disciplina e la cooperazione del paziente che spesso per anni deve prendere fino a venti pastiglie al giorno secondo degli orari prestabiliti e che talvolta si trova anche ad affrontare degli effetti collaterali molto seri.
In caso di disturbi a casa o in viaggio – ciò riguarda sia gli effetti collaterali che il sopraggiungere di nuove infezioni – ci deve sempre rivolgere ad un medico o ad un ospedale con la rispettiva esperienza HIV.

6. *Viaggi con l'infezione da HIV e AIDS*

Valgono principalmente le stesse regole come nel paese di provenienza relativamente al sesso sicuro o all'assunzione di farmaci. Le infezioni da HIV non hanno risparmiato finora nessun paese del mondo. Anche nel caso che la malattia si sia manifestata non esistono praticamente limiti alla possibilità di viaggiare. Si consiglia di procurarsi prima della partenza indirizzi di medici o di cliniche specializzate (di solito nelle zone più densamente popolate o nelle cliniche universitarie).
Non si deve nemmeno dimenticare di procurarsi una quantità sufficiente di medicinali, profilattici ed altre cose che eventualmente possono essere difficile da reperire nel paese di destinazione.
Anche per quanto riguarda la maggior parte delle malattie legate ai viaggi o di quelle tropicali si consiglia di consultarsi con un medico od un istituto per malattie tropicali.
Proteggendosi dal sole, adottando un abbigliamento adeguato, rispettando le norme igieniche (attenzione nel caso di acqua non bollita e cibi crudi!) si possono evitare molti spiacevoli episodi che rimarrebbero un ricordo spiacevole. Contro molte malattie ci si può far vaccinare in modo preventivo (epatite A e B, tifo, poliomielite ecc.), in caso di viaggi in zone di diffusione della malaria si può anche prendere in considerazione la relativa profilassi. Anche i malati di HIV dovrebbero venire vaccinati, ma ciò deve venire discusso nel singolo caso con il medico.

Infine si devono fare presente ancora due cose: prima del viaggio (fare) controllare assolutamente l'assicurazione contro le malattie per l'estero ed informarsi presso l'ambasciata competente del paese meta del viaggio in merito alle limitazioni più recenti per i sieropositivi. Al riguardo si deve anche chiarire se si devono portare con sé i farmaci dal paese di provenienza (disposizioni doganali) oppure se siano disponibili anche nel paese di destinazione.

Dirk Lohr
Medico specialista
Berlino-Charlottenburg

International

INTERNATIONAL ORGANISATIONS

■ **Amnesty International Members for G&L Concerns**
77 Maitland Place, Suite 820 ✉ M4Y 2V6 Toronto, Canada
🖥 www.amnesty.org
Support human and gay rights worldwide by writing letters to governments urging them to respect international standards.

■ **European Gay and Lesbian Sports Federation (EGLSF)**
Breedstraat 28 ✉ 2513 TT Den Haag, The Netherlands ☎ +31 70 364 24 42

■ **European Pride Organizers Association**
c/o Hartmut Schönknecht, Elberfelder Straße 23 ✉ 10555 Berlin, Germany ☎ +49 30 392 53 11 📠 +49 30 392 43 19
Voluntarily working European network of Lesbian & Gay Pride Organizations and licenser of the Europride title.

■ **Federation of Gay Games**
584 Castro Street, Suite 343 ✉ CA 94114 San Francisco
☎ +1 415 6950-222

■ **International Gay and Lesbian Archives**
PO Box 69679, West Hollywood ✉ CA 90069 Los Angeles, USA
☎ +1 310 845-0271

■ **International Gay and Lesbian Travel Association (IGLTA)**
52 West Oakland Park Boulevard 237 ✉ FL 33311 Wilton Manors, USA ☎ +1 954 776-2626 ☎ +1 800 448-8550
📠 +1 954 776-3303 📧 iglta@iglta.org 🖥 www.iglta.org
IGLTA is an international network of travel industry business and professionals dedicated to the support of its members who have joined together to encourage gay travel throughout the world. IGLTA is committed to the welfare of gay and lesbian travelers, and to "shrinking the gay globe". Spartacus is member of IGLTA.

■ **International Gay Penpals**
Ste. 320, PO Box 7304 ✉ CA 91603 Los Angeles, USA

■ **International Lesbian and Gay Association (ILGA)**
81 Rue du Marché au Charbon ✉ 1000 Bruxelles, Belgium
☎ +32 2 502 24 71 📠 +32 2 502 24 71
📧 ilga@ilga.org
🖥 www.ilga.org
ILGA's aim is to work for the equality of lesbians, gay men, bisexuals and transgendered people and their liberation from all forms of discrimination.

■ **Lesbian & Gay Hospitality Exchange International**
PO Box 612, Station C ✉ QC H2L 4K5 Montréal, Canada
☎ +1 514 593 03 00 📠 +1 514 593 03 00
📧 info@lghei.org 🖥 www.lghei.org
Non-profit home stay network, with 500 listings in 40 different countries.

■ **UNAIDS**
20 Avenue Appia ✉ 1211 Genève 27, Switzerland ☎ +41 22 791 36 66 ☎ +41 22 791 41 87
📧 unaids@unaids.org
🖥 www.unaids.org/contact/index.html
As the main advocate for global action on HIV/AIDS, UNAIDS leads, strengthens and supports an expanded response aimed at preventing the transmission of HIV, providing care and support, reducing the vulnerability of individuals and communities to HIV/AIDS, and alleviating the impact of the epidemic.

Albania

Name: Shqipëria • Albanien • Albanie • Albania
Location: Southeast Europe
Initials: AL
Time: GMT +1
International Country Code: ☏ 355 (leave the first 0 of area codes)
International Access Code: ☏ 00
Language: Albanian, Greek
Area: 28,750 km2 / 11,100 sq mi.
Currency: 1 Lek = 100 Qindarka
Population: 3,324,000
Capital: Tiranë
Religions: 70% Muslim, 30% Christians
Climate: Mild and moderate. Winters are cool, cloudy and wet, summers hot, clear and dry. The interior is cooler and wetter.

In Albania homosexual acts are no longer punishable. Thanks to the work of the "Society Gay Albania" group and also the ILGA which has its offices in Brussels. The discussion surrounding the legal changes also helped increase awareness of homosexuality among the general public. Nevertheless, homophobia and ignorance are widespread among Albanians in general.

In Albanien stehen homosexuelle Handlungen nicht mehr unter Strafe, was dem Einsatz der Gruppe "Society Gay Albania" und der ILGA mit Sitz in Brüssel zu verdanken ist. Durch die Änderung des Sexualstrafrechts wurde das Thema Homosexualität in die Öffentlichkeit gerückt, jedoch begegnet ein Großteil der Bevölkerung diesem Thema noch immer mit Ablehnung und Ignoranz.

En Albanie, l'homosexualité n'est plus considérée comme un délit, grâce à l'engagement du groupe "Society Gay Albania" et à celui de l'ILGA siégeant à Bruxelles. La modification du droit pénal relatif aux infractions contre les moeurs, a permis d'ouvrir un débat public sur le sujet de l'homosexualité. La majorité de la population reste toutefois homophobe.

Los actos homosexuales ya no están penados en Albania, gracias a los esfuerzos de la asociación "Society Gay Albania" y de la ILGA con sede en Bruselas. Aunque este cambio legislativo despertó el interés público, la mayoría de los albanos sigue teniendo una actitud homófoba e ignorante acerca de los homosexuales.

In Albania gli atti tra omosessuali non sono più considerati reato, grazie agli sforzi del gruppo "Society Gay Albania" e dell'ILGA di Bruxelles. Attraverso il cambiamento del diritto penale sessuale il tema dell'omosessualità è diventato di dominio pubblico, la popolazione in gran parte però si dimostra pur sempre sfavorevole ed ignorante verso questo tema.

NATIONAL GAY INFO

■ **Society Gay Albania (SGA)** (GLM) 14-20 h
Kutie Postare 104 Tirane ☏ (43) 739 73
✉ Albgaysoc@hotmail.com
AIDS information and anti-discrimination.

NATIONAL GROUPS

■ **Albania Lesbian and Gay Association** (GLM)
Kutie Postare 8299 Tirana

Tiranë ☏ 042

HEALTH GROUPS

■ **Action Plus**
Spitali ☏ 355 53   📠 336 44
AIDS information group affiliated with a Tirana hospital.

CRUISING

- Rruga „Deshmorët e 4 Shkurtit" (AYOR) (between Rruga „Myslym Shyri" and the River Lana)
- Park across from Hotel Dajiti (ayour) (evenings best)

Argentina

Name: Argentinien • Argentine
Location: South America
Initials: RA
Time: GMT -3
International Country Code: ☎ 54 (leave the first 0 of area codes)
International Access Code: ☎ 00
Language: Spanish
Area: 2,780,400 km2 / 1,068,298 sq mi.
Currency: 1 Peso (Arg$) = 100 Centavos
Population: 36,265,463
Capital: Buenos Aires
Religions: 91 % Roman Catholic
Climate: Mostly moderate climate. The southeast is very dry, the southwest subantarctic.
Important gay cities: Buenos Aires, Córdoba

✱ In Argentina homosexual acts are not forbidden. Homosexual acts in public deemed to be against public morality may lead to arrest.
Under most circumstances the Argentinians are liberally minded in the major cities with regard to gays. Buenos Aires has a multifaceted gay scene and is seen as the gay metropolis of South America. In other major cities, such as Rosario or Cordoba there continues to be a positive development of the gay movement. As in many other countries in rural districts the acceptance of homosexuality continues to be restrictive. Especially in rural areas of Argentina the Catholic Church still has a major influence on the non-acceptance of homosexuality.

✱ In Argentinien sind homosexuelle Handlungen grundsätzlich nicht verboten. Vor allzu freizügigem Verhalten in der Öffentlichkeit sei jedoch gewarnt, da dies unter Umständen eine Verhaftung wegen „Verstoßes gegen die öffentliche Moral" zur Folge haben kann.
Im allgemeinen verhalten sich die Argentinier in den Großstädten Schwulen gegenüber recht liberal. Buenos Aires hat eine vielfältige schwule Szene, aber auch andere Großstädte wie Rosario oder Cordoba entwickeln sich zunehmend positiv. Wie in vielen Ländern ist auch in Argentinien die Akzeptanz von Homosexualität auf dem Lande bei weitem geringer. Gerade in ländlichen Gebieten hat die katholische Kirche immer noch starken Einfluß.

✱ En Argentine, l'homosexualité n'est en principe pas interdite. Mais il est toujours possible de se faire arrêter pour „atteinte à la morale publique". Dans les grandes villes, les argentins se comportent généralement très libéralement envers les homosexuels. Buenos Aires a une scène gaie variée, et d'autres grandes villes comme Rosario ou Cordoba se développent de plus en plus. Comme dans de nombreux pays, l'homosexualité est moins bien acceptée dans les régions rurales. N'oublions pas que l'église catholique a encore une forte influence dans ces régions.

✱ En Argentina no existe ninguna ley que prohibe las relaciones homosexuales. Sin embargo, no se recomienda un comportamiento demasiado abierto en público, ya que este podría causar una detención por „ofensa a la moral pública" En general los argentinos de las ciudades grandes se muestran relativamente liberales con los homosexuales. Buenos Aires ofrece un variado ambiente gay, pero también ciudades como Rosario y Cordoba se desarrollan en este sentido muy positivamente. Como en la mayoría de los paises, la acceptación de los homosexuales entre la población rural es mucho más reducida. Argentina no es ninguna excepción, ya que en los pueblos la iglesia católica sigue teniendo una fuerte influencia.

✖ Generalmente gli atti tra omosessuali in Argentina non sono proibiti, è meglio però evitare un comportamento troppo libero in pubblico, perché ciò potrebbe portare all'arresto per „lesione della pubblica morale". Generalmente gli argentini nelle grande città si dimostrano abbastanza liberali verso i gay. Per i gay, Buenos Aires offre varie possibilità, ma anche altre città come Rosario o Cordoba stanno sviluppandosi in modo positivo. Come in altri paesi, in posti di campagna l'omossessualità è meno accettata. Soprattutto nelle zone rurali la chiesa cattolica esercita un forte influsso.

NATIONAL PUBLICATIONS

■ **NX** Mon-Fri 10-21, Sat 16-20 h
Av. Callao 339, 4° piso ✉ 1022 Buenos Aires
(next to Callao Station, Subway B, 4th floor) ☎ (011) 4375-0366
📠 (011) 4375-0366 ✉ nx@netline.com.ar
🖥 www.nexo.org
Argentinas gay monthly magazine with agenda map published by Grupo Nexo. AIDS information. Numerous erotic photos. Gay guide. A$ 6.-

■ **Otra Guia. La** (GLM)
Casilla de Correo 78, Suc. Olivos ✉ 1636 Buenos Aires
✉ loguia@satlink.com
Free gay monthly agenda.

NATIONAL GROUPS

■ **Comunidad Homosexual Argentina (CHA)** (GLM)
Tomás Liberti 1080 ✉ 1165 Buenos Aires ☎ (011) 4361-6382
✉ cha@ciudad.com.ar 🖥 mundogay.com/cha

Buenos Aires | Argentina

■ **Deportistas Argentinos Gays (D.A.G.)** (GLM) Mon, Wed, Thu Sat 18.30-21.30 h
Defensa 1120, San Telmo Buenos Aires ☏ (011) 4362-9052
✉ info@dag.com.ar ✉ www.dag.com.ar
■ **Gays y Lesbianas por los Derechos Civiles** (GLM)
Paraná 157, Dto. F ✉ 1017 Buenos Aires ☏ (011) 4373-8955
☏ (011) 4373-8955 ✉ gaylesdc@arnet.com.ar
Argentina's most important organisation for gay liberation and a member of the International Lesbian & Gay Association (ILGA). They deal with political activities, legal advice, and give general information.

Buenos Aires - Capital Federal ☏ 011

Buenos Aires is developing into the gay metropolis of South America. Compared with other cities in South America, Buenos Aires seems to be traditionally much more European and the people are open minded and tolerant. The gay tourist has a wide choice of bars and discos and something to suit every taste. Night life begins late; hardly anybody goes out before 2 am and the discos tend to close around 7 am. Buenos Aires will, however set you back a bit. A visit to a disco will cost around $ 15.

Buenos Aires ist im Begriff, sich zu der schwulen Metropole Südamerikas zu entwickeln. Im Vergleich zu anderen Städten des Kontinents gibt sich Buenos Aires traditionell sehr europäisch, die Menschen gelten als weltoffen und tolerant.
Der schwule Tourist hat hier die Qual der Wahl, unter einer Vielzahl von Bars und Discos auszuwählen. Die Szene wird kaum einen Wunsch unerfüllt lassen. Das Nachtleben beginnt spät: Vor 1 Uhr ist es in den meisten Bars noch ruhig, die Discotheken füllen sich nicht vor 2 Uhr und schließen in der Regel erst um 7 Uhr früh. Allerdings ist Buenos Aires auch ein teures Pflaster, der Eintritt in die Disco kann durchaus $ 15 kosten.

Buenos Aires est en train de devenir la métropole gaie d'Amérique du Sud. Comparée aux autres villes du continent, Buenos Aires ressemble beaucoup à une ville traditionelle européenne. Les gens passent pour être compréhensifs et tolérants. Le touriste homosexuel a ici l'embarras du choix : la scène est à même de satisfaire tous les désirs parmi la multiplicité des bars et discothèques. La vie nocturne commence tard: jusqu'à 1 heure du matin, tous et encore tranquille dans la plupart des bars, les discothèques ne se remplissent pas avant 2 heures et ferment en général seulement vers 7 heure du matin. A Buenos Aires, il est vrai, la vie est chère, l'entrée dans une discothèque peut facilement coûter $ 15.

Buenos Aires está a punto de convertirse en la indiscutible capital gay de Sudamérica. En comparación con otras ciudades del continente, Buenos Aires se mostró tradicionalmente muy europeo y sus habitantes tienen fama de ser abiertos y tolerantes. El turista gay tiene aqui la dificultad de elegir entre los innumerables bares y discotecas que ofrecen un ambiente que satisface cualquier tipo de deseo. La vida nocturna empieza muy tarde: la mayoría de los bares no se animan antes de la 1 de la madrugada, las discoteca no empiezan ha llenarse antes de las 2 y no suelen cerrar sus puertas antes de las 7 de la mañana. Pero Buenos Aires también es una ciudad bastante cara, donde nadie se extraña en pagar $15 por la entrada en una discoteca.

Buenos Aires sta sviluppandosi alla metropoli gay dell'America meridionale. Rispetto ad altre città di questo continente la tradizione di Buenos Aires assomiglia più a quella europea, la gente viene considerata cosmopolita e aperta. Il turista gay soffre dell'imbarazzo della scelta tra una grande varietà di bar e discoteche che soddisfanno quasi tutti i gusti. La vita notturna comincia tardi: Prima dell'una nei bar è ancora abbastanza tranquillo, e nelle discoteche, che chiudono alle sette, ci si va solo dopo le due. Buenos Aires è comunque molto cara, l'entrata in discoteca costa circa 15 dollari.

GAY INFO
■ **La Hora**
PO Box 12, suc 27 B ✉ 1427

CULTURE
■ **Área de Estudios Queer** (GLM)
Avenida Corrientes 2038, 2° p ✉ 1045 *(2nd floor)*
■ **Centro de Documentación Gay-lesbico**
Paraná 157, F ✉ 1017 ☏ 4373-8955 ☏ 4373-8955
✉ gaylesdc@aenet.com.ar

TOURIST INFO
■ **Oficina Central de Información Turística**
Avenida Santa Fe 883 ✉ 1059 ☏ 4312-2232 ☏ 3312-5550

BARS
■ **Bacco** Fri Sat 23-? h
Riobamba 189 ☏ 4374-2874
■ **Bach Bar** (B d GLM s WE YG) Tue-Sun 23-? h
José A. Cabrena 4390 ✉ 1414 *(Between Julián Alvarez & Lavallevja)* ☏ 4388-2875
Shows at Firday nights, Karaoke at Sunday nights.
■ **Bar Alvear** (B F Glm MA) 22-6 h
Avenida Marcelo T. de Alvear 1461 ☏ 4816-9227
Pub, restaurant and pre-danceclub place.
■ **Downtown Cafe** (AC B CC d F G MA snu) Thu & Fri 22-3, Sat -7, Sun 20-23 h
Alsina 975 *(Metro. Av. de Mayo)* ☏ 4334-6110
also restaurant
■ **Garbo** (B GLM MA S snu)
Gascón 992 ☏ 4867-4416
Tue-Sat shows, Wed strippers.
■ **Gasoil New Generation** (AC B Glm MA snu stv) Mon-Sun 23-? Wed closed. Shows 1.30 h
Bulnes 1250 *(at Avenida Córdoba)* ☏ 4864-4056
■ **Hall Bar-Café-Cine** (B g MA VS) Mon-Thu 10-4, Fri -6, Sat 12-6, Sun 12-4 h
Avenida Roque Saénz Peña 1150 ✉ 1035 *(between Cerrito and Libertad, next to „Obelisco")* ☏ 4382-7934
Café-bar in the hall of a xxx-cinema
■ **In Vitro** (B G MA S) Mon-Sun 23-? Shows at 0 and 1.30 h
Azcuénaga 1007 ✉ 1115 *(at Avenida M. T. de Alvear)* ☏ 4824-0932
■ **New Manhattan. The** (B G S MG) 22-? Shows at 1 h
Anchorena 1347 *(between Avenida Santa Fé and Charcas)* ☏ 4824-8550
■ **Puerto Tulum** (B G MA S)
Gascón 1172 ☏ 4862-9429
■ **Scream** (B G MA) Thu-Sun 22-? h
Cerrito 306 ☏ 4382-5253
Pre-dance bar & pub.
■ **Sitges** (B d GLM MA s) Wed-Sun 22.30-? h
Avenida Córdoba 4119 ☏ 4861-3763
Table telephones for quick contacts.

CAFES
■ **Elegant** (B f g OS)
Avenida Equador *(at Avenida Santa Fe)*
A typical café bar during the day, but in the evening the terrace is a well known gay meeting place.

SPARTACUS 2001/2002 | 3

Argentina | Buenos Aires

Contramano
DISCO-PUB

SINCE 1984

A tradition that lasts in time

Rodriguez Peña 1082
(1020) Buenos Aires
Argentina
www.contramano.com
info@contramano.com

DANCECLUBS

■ **Amerika** (GLM D YG) Wed, Fri Sat & Sun 0- 6 h
Gascón 1040 *(at Avenida Córdoba)* ☏ 4865-4416
Three dance floors (house, disco and latin music). Capacity 2500 people.
■ **Angel's** (B D G MA r snu) Thu-Sun 0-? h
Viamonte 2168 ✉ 1056
■ **Confusión** (B D GLM TV)
Scalabrini Ortiz 1721
■ **Contramano** (AC B D G lj MA r) Wed-Sat 0-5, Sun 19-5 h
Rodriguez Peña 1082 ✉ 1020 *(at Avenida Santa Fé)*
CONTRAMANO is the oldest gay bar in Buenos Aires, opened in 1984. Traditional place to meet men
■ **Glam** (B D GLM)
Cabrera 3046
Disco-pub.
■ **Milenio 5to** (B D GLM MA) Fri 1-? h
Avenida Rivadavia 1910
■ **OXEN** (B D Glm S YG) Fri-Sa 0-? h, Shows 3 h
Sarmiento 1662
Pop, latino, marcha, performances,...

RESTAURANTS

■ **Enriqueta** (F g) 20-? h
Bulnes 1730 ☏ 4823-6209
■ **Memorabilia** (AC B CC glm s) Mon-Fri 12-16, 20-?, Sat 20-? h
Maipú 761 ☏ 4322-7630
Many musicians or artists eat here.
■ **Tacla** (! A B CC DR F Glm OS S snu) 16-3, WE -6 h
Avenida de Mayo 1114 *(at Avenida 9 de Julio)* ☏ 4381-8764
Restaurant with downstairs bar and darkroom. Show Fri & Sat nights 1 h. Good for gay information.

SEX SHOPS/BLUE MOVIES

■ **Adult Video News** (g VS)
Maipú 484, 3° Piso ☏ 4393-8695
■ **Once Plus** (G VS) 10-6, Sun 14-2 h
Avenida Ecuador 54

CINEMAS

■ **ABC** (G VS) Mon-Fri 9-6, Sat 12-6, Sun 14-6 h
Esmeralda 506
4 cinemas. Mon gay leather night 24-6 h
■ **Box Cinema** (G VS) 14-6, Sun 16-4 h
Laprida 1423 *(at Avenida Santa Fé)*
■ **City** (G VS) 8-6 h
Libertad 429 *(at Avenida Corrientes)* ☏ 4384-9083
■ **Edén** (G VS) 0-24 h
Avenida Santa Fé 1833 *(Galeria Bozzini)*
■ **Equix** (G VS) Mon-Thu 8-2, Fri-Sat -6, Sun 12-2 h
Hipólito Yrigoyen 945
■ **Ideal** (G VS) 10-6, Sun and public holidays 14-6 h
Suipacha 378 *(at Avenidas Corrientes)*
■ **Multicine** (G VS) 0-24 h
Lavalle 750, Galeria *(between Maipú and Esmeralda, Sala Oscar Wilde)*
■ **Nuevo Victoria** (b G MA VS) 8-2, Sun 10-24 h
Hipólito Yrigoyen 965 *(Metro Av. de Mayo, Piedras)* ☏ 4331-4686

SAUNAS/BATHS

■ **A Full** (B BF DR f G MA msg SA SB SOL VS WH) Mon-Thu 12-3 h, Fri-Sun 0-24 h
Viamonte 1770 ✉ 1055 *(Subway D-Callao)* ☏ 4371-7263
Well designed sauna. One of the largest in Argentinia.
■ **Baño Salud** (B G og SA SB VS)
Bravard 1105
■ **Unikus** (B DR f G MA r SA SB VS) 13-24 h
Pueyrredón 1180 ✉ 1118

FITNESS STUDIOS

■ **American Hot Gym** (CC g WO) Mon-Fri 8-24, Sat 9-21 h, Sun closed
Ayacucho 449 ✉ 1026 *(Metro Callao, Linea B)* ☏ 4951-7679

TRAVEL AND TRANSPORT

■ **Arcadia** (GLM)
Florida 142, 6°N ✉ 1337 *(Metro Plaza de Mayo)* ☏ 4326-4910
🖷 4326-8449 💻 info@arcadiatur.com.ar

HOTELS

■ **O'tello** (AC b BF CC E g H)
Arregni 4241, Devoto ✉ 1417 ☏ 4568-2056 🖷 4568-8829
💻 info@otello.com.ar 💻 www.otello.com.ar
Rooms by the hour, luxurious thematic rooms. All night also possible.

GUEST HOUSES

■ **First. The** (BF CC G H SA SOL)
Defensa 1120 ✉ 1065 *(San Telmo)* ☏ 4300-4747
💻 thefirstgay@infovia.com.ar
Located in the historic San Telmo district, 6 double rooms, 2 single rooms, all with WC, partly with shared bathroom.

PRIVATE ACCOMMODATION

■ **Faraón** (AC b BF CC E g H) 0-24 h
Gallardo 340 ✉ 1408 ☏ 4642-3643 🖷 4642-4293
💻 info@faraon.com.ar 💻 www.faraon.com.ar
Rooms by the hour with high standards. Also all night possible.

Buenos Aires ▶ Corrientes | **Argentina**

GENERAL GROUPS
■ **Grupo Nexo** (GLM) Mon-Fri 10-21 h
Avenida Callao 339, Pisos 4 y 5 ✉ 1002 ☏ 4375-0366
☏ 4374-4484 (Hotline) 📠 4375-0366 📧 nexo@nexo.org
🖥 www.nexo.org
NEXO are the publishers of the monthly magazine NX. Many activities for different interest groups. Just call and ask. Friendly staff. Any information about AIDS.
■ **Lugar de Gay de Buenos Aires** (GLM)
Defensa 1120 ☏ 4300-4747 📧 thefirstgay@infovia.com.ar
Debates, brainstorming, films.
■ **SIGLA** (GLM) Mon-Sat 18-22
Paraná 122, 2° Piso ✉ 1017 *(2nd floor)* ☏ 4382-4540
☏ 4382-2584 📧 hs.sigla@sudnet.com.ar
Political and social G&L group.

FETISH GROUPS
■ **Fierro Leather Club** (G LJ)
☏ 4537-2639 📧 fierroleather@yahoo.com
🖥 www.geocities.com/fierroleather/club.html

HEALTH GROUPS
■ **Fundación HUESPED**
Pje. Avenida Peluffo 3932 ☏ 4981-1828 ☏ 4981-2071
■ **Hospital de Clinicas - P.E.T.S.**
Avenida Córdoba 2351 ☏ 4961-6001 ☏ 4961-7575
Specialised in STDs.

RELIGIOUS GROUPS
■ **Iglesia Communitaria Metropolitana** (I.C.M.)
Virrey Cevallos 463, 1°, 6 ✉ 1043 ☏ 4381-2327
📧 icmbas@infovia.com.ar

SWIMMING
-Outdoor pool „Balneario Norte"

CRUISING
-Avenida Santa Fé (at Avenida Pueyrredón, best 1 h)
-Avenida Santa Fé (at Avenida Callao)
-Avenida Cabildo (between Virrey del Pino and Av Monroe)
-Plaza Las Heras (Av. Las heras and Coronel Días)
-Ciudad Universitaria: Behind Universities in Nuñez by the river, in the bushes on the left hand side on the road. (Sat, Sun afternoon, Bus 37, 45, 160)
-Reserva Ecológica (Av. Belgrano and Av. Costanera)
-Reserva Ecológica (Viamonte and Av. Costanera)

Córdoba - Córdoba ☏ 0351

BARS
■ **Beep Pub** (B DR MA S SNU STV TV WE) Thu-Sun midnight-07h
Sucre 173 ✉ 5000 ☏ 425 6521

DANCECLUBS
■ **Hangar 18** (A AC B CC D DR glm MA snu STV VS WE)
Fri-Sun 0.30-6 h
Boulevard Las Heras 116/18 ☏ 424 3824
■ **La Piaf** (B D GLM MA STV tv WE)
Fri, Sat and before holidays 23.30-6 h
Obispo Ceballos 45 ✉ 5000 *(San Martín)* ☏ 471 7914
■ **Planta Baja** (B D G) Tue-Sun 0-? h
San Martín 666 ☏ 421 4704
■ **Universo Pub** (B D glm MA) Fri-Sun 0.30-6h
Boulevard Las Heras 118 ☏ 424 3824

BUENOS AIRES
♂ FULL
RELAX CENTER FOR MEN
SAUNA·GYM
JACUZZI·STEAM BATH
INDIVIDUAL RELAX BOXES
VIDEO ROOM·MASAGES·BAR·CAFE
RELAX ROOM
Students under 30 years old: 30% disccount
Viamonte 1770
One block away from Callao station, Subway D
Monday thru Thursday 12 to 3 am
Friday thru Sunday open 24 hs
INFORMATION: (54-11) 4371-7263
Cedex. Imágex (5411) 4187-8950

SAUNAS/BATHS
■ **Va.X** (B g SA WO) 15-3 h
Corro 467

GENERAL GROUPS
■ **Asociación contra la Discriminación Homosexual** (A.Co.D.Ho.)
San Martin 666 PB ✉ 5000 ☏ 421-4704 ☏ 422-5186
📧 acodho@hotmail.com

CRUISING
-Plaza San Martin
-Plaza Vélez-Sarsfield
-Avenida Argentina to Plaza Centenario on to Parque Sarmiento
-Rio Primero (along the bank)
-Calle Buenos Aires (between Boulevard Illia and 27 de Abril)
-Calle Rivadavia (between 27 de Abril and 25 de Mayo)
-25 de Mayo (between Alvear and San Martín)
-9 de Julio (between San Martín and La Cañada)
-Dean Funes (between General Paz and San Martín)
-Santa Rosa (between Maipú and General Paz)
-Rosario de Santa Fé (between San Martín and Alvear)
-Galería San Martín (San Martín 50)
-Paseo de las Artes (this is a handcrafts market on WE)
-Avenida Hipólito Yrigoyen (around the area of Teatro San Martín)

Corrientes - Corrientes ☏ 03783

DANCECLUBS
■ **Contramarcha** (B D G)
Piambre 2280 ✉ 3400 *(at Cazadores Correntinos)*

Argentina La Plata ▶ San Juan

La Plata - Buenos Aires ☎ 0221

DANCECLUBS
■ **Back Disco** (B D G S) Fri Sat 1.30-5.30 h
Calle 53 esq. 5 ✉ 1900
■ **Depper** (B D GLM) Sat 1-? h
Calle 13, #77 esq. 33 y 34 ✉ 1900 ☎ 15-428-6029
■ **Divina Pub. La** (B D GLM MA) Fri 0-8, Sat 5-8 h
Calle 51 #496 esq. 4 y 5 ✉ 1900

HEALTH GROUPS
■ **Campaña Stop Sida**
Calle 69 #683 ✉ 1900

Mar del Plata - Buenos Aires ☎ 0223

BARS
■ **Dicroika** (B G MA S) 22-8 h
Bolivar 2152 ✉ 7600
■ **Kromo Café** (B g MA)
Moreno 2884 ✉ 7600
Internet café busy in the early evening.

DANCECLUBS
■ **Milenium** (B D G MA) 0-? h
Arenales 2272 ✉ 7600

CINEMAS
■ **Cine A** (g VS) 12-6 h
San Martin ✉ 7600 *(at Corrientes, Galeria Florida)*
■ **Cine Sex** (g VS) 12-4 h
Belgrano 2331 ✉ 7600

HEALTH GROUPS
■ **Fundación Un Lugar**
Falucho 2576, 1° Piso, Of. 5 ✉ 7600 *(1st floor)* ☎ 492-0777
■ **Homo Sapiens**
Avenida Independencia 1101 4to A ✉ 7600 ☎ 494-7025
🖨 494-7025 📧 hsapiens@infovia.com.ar

CRUISING
-La Rambla (between Punta Iglesia and Playa Chica, at night)
-Peatonal San Martin (between Buenos Aires and San Luis, at night)
-Playa Chica (Dec-Mar, during the day)

Mendoza - Mendoza ☎ 0261

DANCECLUBS
■ **Queen Disco** (B D GLM STV)
Ejército de Los Andos 656 ✉ 5519 *(Dorrego, Guayamallén)*
☎ 431-6990
■ **Reserva. La** (B D GLM)
Rivadavia 43 ✉ 5500

SEX SHOPS/BLUE MOVIES
■ **Sex Shop** (g VS)
c/o Galería Tonsa, Avenida San Martín ✉ 5500
(Catamarca, 1° piso/1st floor)

SAUNAS/BATHS
■ **Hangar 21** (B D glm MA)
Avenida Costanera esq. Godoy Cruzy ✉ 5500 *(P. Taso)*

CRUISING
-Avenida San Martín (between Rivadavia and Las Heras)
-Avenida Las Heras (between Avenida San Martín and Avenida Mitre)
-Avenida Mitre (between Avenida Las Heras and Espejo)
-Calle Espejo (between Avenida San Martín and Chile)
-Calle Chile (beteen Calle Espejo and Avenida Las Heras)
-Calle Gutierrez (between Calle Chile and Avenida San Martín)
-Calle 25 de Mayo (between Las Heras and Calle Gutierrez)
-Plaza Chile and Plaza Italia
-Plaza Independencia
-Calle Necochea (between San Martín and 25 de Mayo)
-Plaza San Martín
-Plazoleta O'Higgins
-Plazoleta Barraquero

Rosario - Santa Fe ☎ 0341

BARS
■ **El Beso** (B G MA)
Güemes 2631 ✉ 2000
■ **Inizio** (B G) 22-? h
Mitre 1880

DANCECLUBS
■ **Oscar Wilde** (B D G) Thu-Sun 23-? h
Chacabuco esq. E. Zeballos ✉ 2000
■ **Station G** (B D G)
Avenida Rivadaria 2481

HOTELS
■ **Ava Miriva** (g H)
Avenida Circunv. y Rondeau ✉ 2000

GENERAL GROUPS
■ **Colectivo ARCO IRIS**
Pte Roca 663, Of. 5, PO Box 208 Correo Central ✉ 2000
☎ 447-0268 ☎ 449-9099 🖨 449-9098

HEALTH GROUPS
■ **Voluntario contra el SIDA**
Pasco 1840 ✉ 2000 ☎ 485-0308

CRUISING
-Peatonal Córdoba (at night)
-Peatonal San Martín (at night)

Salta - Salta ☎ 0387

BARS
■ **Estacion Tequila** (B G MA) 22-3, Fri Sat -8 h
San Luis 348
■ **Nosotros** (B D glm MA)
Juan M. Güemes 11 ✉ 4400 *(Don Emilio)*
■ **O'Clock Disco** (B D GLM MA P s WE) Fri-Sun & before public holidays 1-5 h
La Rioja 111 ✉ 4400 *(at Santa Fe)*

CRUISING
-Peatonal Alberti (G) (at night)
-Parque San Martin (tv) (at night)

San Juan - San Juan ☎ 0264

DANCECLUBS
■ **Uomo-Man** (B D G MA) Fri Sat 1-? h
Avenida de Circunvalación 489 ✉ 8500 *(Oeste)*

San Miguel de Tucumán ▶ Santa Fe **Argentina**

San Miguel de Tucumán - Tucumán ☎ 0381

BARS
■ **Margaritos** (B G MA TV)
Corrientes 1902

DANCECLUBS
■ **Madonna** (B D G MA)
Santiago casi Avenida Ejér. del Norte

CRUISING
-Plaza Independencia
-Plaza Belgrano
-Parque 9 de Julio
-Parque Avellaneda
-Around Government Palace

Santa Fe - Santa Fe ☎ 0342

BARS
■ **Paloma. La** (B glm MA)
Santa Rosa esq. Orrego ✉ 3000 *(Santo Tomé)* ☎ 460-3238

DANCECLUBS
■ **Tudor Taberna** (B D G YG) Sat (D)
Javier de la Rosa 325
✉ 3000 *(Barrio de Guadalupe)*

CRUISING
-Plaza Mayo
-Plaza San Martín

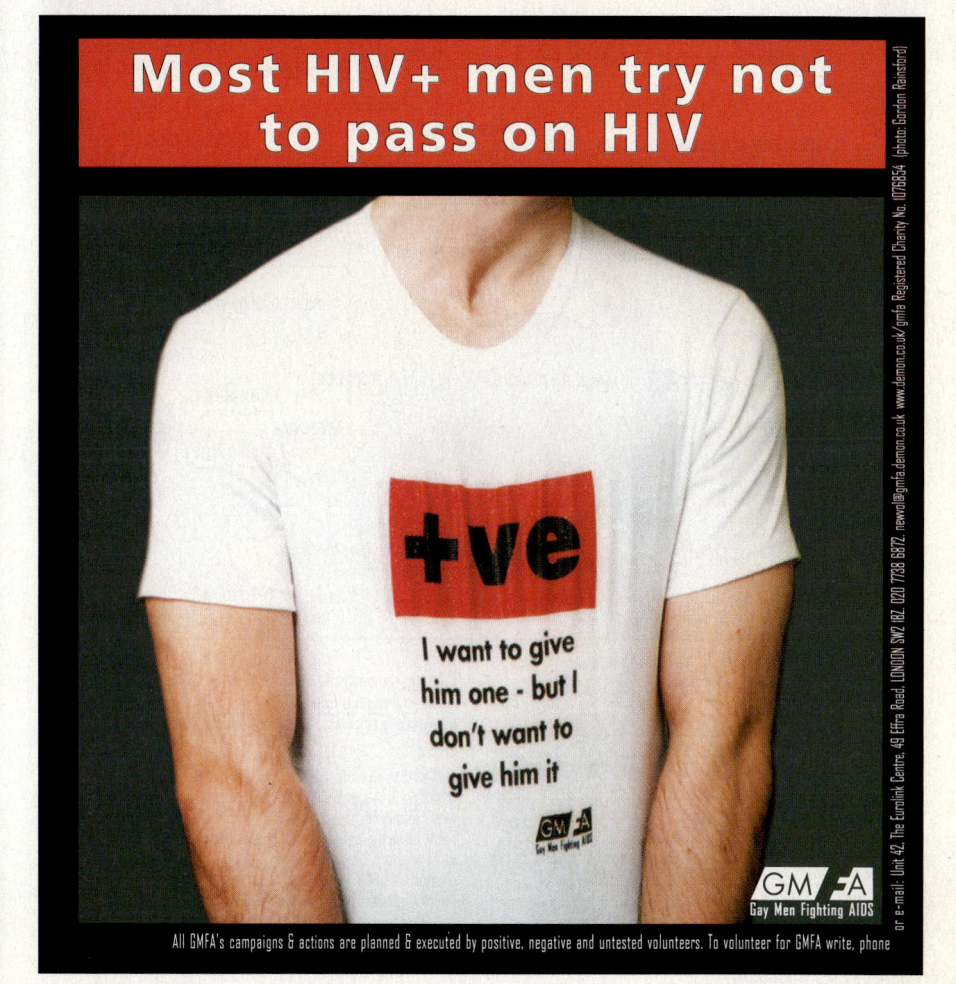

Australia

Australia

[Map of Australia showing states, territories, and major cities including Darwin, Alice Springs, Cairns, Rockhampton, Brisbane, Surfers Paradise, Sydney, Canberra, Melbourne, Hobart, Adelaide, Perth, Albany, and features like Ayors Rock, Great Australian Bight, Gulf of Carpentaria, Timor Sea, Coral Sea, Tasman Sea, Indian Ocean]

Name: Australien • Australie • Austrália
Location: Oceania
Initials: AUS
Time: GMT +8/+9.5/+10
International Country Code: ☏ 61 (leave away the first 0 of area codes)
International Access Code: ☏ 0011
Language: English
Area: 7,686,300 km2 / 2,967,897 sq mi.
Currency: 1 Australian Dollar (A$) = 100 Cents
Population: 18,710,000
Capital: Canberra
Religions: 71% Christians, 26% Catholics, 22% Anglicans

Climate: Generally the climate is dry. The south and east are moderate, the north is tropical.
Important gay cities: Sydney, Melbourne, Brisbane, Perth and Adelaide

✴ Australia consists of six federal states and two territories. Each Australian state and territory has different legislation with respect to homosexuality. For this reason there is no agreement as to the age of sexual consent or on anti-discrimination laws. For more exact details on a federal state refer to the corresponding capital.
There is a strong gay movement in Australia with the most recent success in Tasmania in which homosexuality was legalised. The gay scene of this continent is professionally organised. There are

Australia

many local newspapers and regional magazines, including „Campaign" and „Outrage", allowing the gay community to consciously express itself.
Cairns in the federal state of Queensland has developed into a much beloved holiday destination. Sydney in New South Wales is seen by many as the most important Gay Metropolis outside of course Europe and North America. Moreover, one of the most important gay events the Mardi Gras takes place in Sydney each February.

★ Australien besteht aus 6 Bundesstaaten und 2 Territorien. Die Verfassung Australiens gewährt den Bundesstaaten und Territorien weitgehende Selbständigkeit. Aus diesem Grunde gibt es in Australien kein einheitliches Schutzalter und keine einheitlichen Antidiskriminierungsgesetze. Die genauen Angaben für die einzelnen Bundesstaaten und Territorien finden Sie in den entsprechenden Kapiteln.
Die Schwulenbewegung Australiens ist stark. Als jüngster Erfolg ist die Legalisierung homosexueller Handlungen im Bundesstaat Tasmanien zu nennen. Die schwule Szene des Kontinents ist sehr professionell organisiert. Neben zahlreichen Lokalzeitungen geben die überregionalen Magazine „Campaign" und „Outrage" ein interessantes Bild des gestiegenen Selbstbewußtseins.
Im Bundesstaat Queensland entwickelt sich Cairns zu einem schwulen Urlaubsziel von internationaler Bedeutung. Außerhalb Europas und Nordamerikas gilt Sydney in Neusüdwales als die bedeutenste schwule Metropole. Entsprechend großartig fällt auch eines der weltweit wichtigsten schwulen Ereignisse aus, der Mardi Gras von Sydney (jeweils im Februar).

★ L'Australie se compose de 6 Etats fédéraux et de 2 territoires. La Constitution australienne accorde aux Etats fédéraux et territoires une large indépendance. Pour cette raison, un âge de protection et des lois antidiscriminatoires uniformes n'existent pas. Vous trouverez les données exactes des Etats fédéraux et territoires individuels aux chapitres correspondants.
Le mouvement homosexuel d'Australie est puissant. Notons le succès législatif récent en Tasmanie. La scène gaie est organisée de manière professionnelle. A part les nombreux journaux locaux, les magazines nationaux „Campaign" et „Outrage" donnent une image intéressante du sentiment accru de sa propre valeur.
Dans l'Etat fédéral du Queensland, Cairns est en train de devenir un lieu de villégiature gai d'une dimension internationale. Sydney est considérée comme la métropole homosexuelle la plus impor-

tante en dehors de l'Europe et de l'Amérique du Nord. Un événement gai international s'y tient chaque année: le Mardi gras au mois de février.

★ Australia se compone de 6 estados federales y 2 territorios. La constitución australiana garantiza en gran medida la autonomía de sus estados federales y territorios. Por esta razón no existe una sola edad de protección o leyes de antidiscriminación aplicables para toda Australia. Para informaciones más detalladas respecto a cada estado federal o territorio sírvanse tomar nota del capítulo correspondiente.
El movimiento gay en Australia es muy fuerte. Uno de los últimos éxitos alcanzados es sin duda la legalización de relaciones homosexuales en el estado federal de Tasmania. La comunidad gay en Australia está organizada muy profesionalmente. A parte de sus numerosos periodicos locales, las revistas „Campaign" y „Outrage", de publicación nacional, reflejan la creciente autoconfianza de los gays australianos.
Cairns, en el estado federal de Queensland, se está desarollando como un lugar vacacional gay con prestigio internacional. Sydney en New South Wales está considerada hoy en día la metrópoli gay más importante a nivel mundial fuera de Europa y Norteamérica. Así que uno de los eventos más espectaculares en el mundo gay tiene lugar aqui: La Mardi Gras que se celebra cada año en febrero.

✗ L'Australia comprende 6 Stati e 2 Territori. Secondo la costituzione dell'Australia gli Stati ed i Territori godono di un'ampia indipendenza. Per questo motivo non esistono su scala nazionale né un'età legale né una legge contro la discriminazione. Le indicazioni esatte per i singoli Stati e Territori si trovano nei rispettivi capitoli.
C'è un forte movimento gay, il cui successo più recente è stato, nello stato federale di Tasmania, la legalizzazione di atti omosessuali. In tutto il continente la vita gay è organizzata in modo molto professionale. A parte i numerosi giornali locali le riviste su livello nazionale „Campaign" e „Outrage" danno un'imagine interessante dell'aumentato orgoglio dei gay.
Nello stato di Queensland la città di Cairns sta sviluppandosi come luogo di vacanze su livello internazionale. Al di fuori dell'Europa e dell'America del Nord, Sydney in New South Wales viene considerata la metropoli gay più importante. In corrispondenza a questo fatto uno degli avvenimenti più famosi, il Mardi Gras di Sydney (sempre in febbraio) risulta essere una delle feste più grandi.

NATIONAL GAY INFO

■ Australian Gay and Lesbian Travel Association
PO Box 2174, ✉ VIC 3065 Fitzroy, Melbourne
☎ (1902) 9419-5230
📠 (03) 9419-5230   📧 peterkj@ozemail.com.au
🌐 www.galta.com.au

■ National Network
247-251 Flinders Lane, Melbourne ✉ WA 2000 Victoria
☎ (03) 9650-5103
A political activist and social support group for lesbian, gay and bisexual people under 26 years of age.

NATIONAL PUBLICATIONS

■ Campaign
1st floor, Suite 6, 66 Oxford Street ✉ NSW 2010 Darlinghurst, Sydney
☎ (02) 9332-3666 📠 (02) 9361-5962
Australia's longest running gay magazine. Published monthly and containing classifieds, news, arts, entertainment and community listings.

■ DNA
PO Box 400 ✉ NSW 1340 Kings Cross, Sydney ☎ (02) 9380-4211
☎ (02) 9380-4288   📧 andrew@dnamagazine.com.au
Monthly magazine featuring articles on gay trends, politics, culture and fashion. About 80 pages in colours. A$ 7.60

■ Gay Maps Australia
PO Box 1401 ✉ NSW 2022 Bondi Junction, Sydney ☎ (02) 9369 2738
📠 (02) 9389 5450
📧 gaymaps@tma.com.au

■ OutRage
85 King William Street ✉ VIC 3065 Fitzroy, Melbourne
☎ (03) 9926 1160
📠 (03) 9926-1199
outrage_subscriptions@satellitemedia.com.au
One of Australia premier gay mens magazines, packed with news, fashion, food gossip and much more.
Published monthly.

Australia/Australia Capital Territory — Canberra

gaydar.au.com
what you want, when you want it

NATIONAL COMPANIES
■ **Gaylink Tours** (CC GLM)
PO Box 11-462 ✉ 6001 Wellington ☎ 384 18 65 📠 384 18 35
💻 reznz@gaylink.co.nz 💻 www.gaylinktours.com
For online reservations and vacation planning on Internet for New Zealand, Australia and South Pacific.

NATIONAL GROUPS
■ **Acceptance Australia**
PO Box 277 ✉ QLD 4170 ☎ (07) 3399-2528
Cannon Hill ☎ (07) 12 12 12
📠 (07) 12 12 12
National office of the support and counselling group for gay Catholics.
■ **AIDS Trust of Australia**
PO Box 300, Australia Square ✉ NSW 2000
Sydney ☎ (02) 9221-2955 📠 (02) 9221-2939
National Fundraising Body for AIDS Education Research and Care.
■ **Australian Federation of AIDS Organizations (AFAO)**
Level 8, Kindersley House, 33 Bligh Street ✉ QLD 2000 Sydney
☎ (02) 9231-2111
📠 (02) 9231-2092.
Representing the eight states and territory community-based AIDS organizations at a national and international level. Also the National Association of people with AIDS/HIV.
■ **Australian Gay Medical Association (AGMA)**
PO Box 145 ✉ VIC 3214 Corio
Support/education for gay friendly doctors and medical students.
■ **Australian National Council on AIDS**
PO Box 9848 ✉ ACT 2601 Canberra ☎ (06) 2289-7767

AUS-Australian Capital Territory
Location: Southeast AUS
Initials: ACT
Time: GMT +10
Area: 2,330km2 / 926 sq mi.
Population: 309,000
Capital: Canberra

✱ In the A.C.T. the age of consent is fixed at 16 years.

✱ Im A.C.T. liegt das Schutzalter bei 16 Jahren.

✱ Dans l'A.C.T. la majorité sexuelle est fixée à 16 ans.

✱ En el A.C.T., la edad de consentimiento está estipulada en 16 años.

✖ Nell'A.C.T. l'età legale per rapporti sessuali è di 16 anni.

Canberra ☎ 02

BARS
■ **Heaven** (B F GLM) Sun, Tue-Thu 20-1 h, Fri-Sat 20-4 h.
Grema Place Civic Centre, City ✉ ACT 2600 *(off Bunda Street Civic Center)* ☎ 6257-6180
■ **Meridian Club** (AC B d GLM lj MA s) Tue Wed 18-1, Thu -2, Fri 17-3, Sat 20-3 h, closed Sun Mon
34 Mort Street, Braddon ✉ ACT 2614 ☎ 6248-9966
Admission A$ 5. Hellfire club on various nights.
■ **Republic. The** (B F g)
Allara Street ✉ ACT 2601 *Civic Center*
■ **Tilley's** (B F glm OS s) 9-24 h
13 Wattle Street/Brigalow Street, Lyneham ✉ ACT 2602 *4 kms from city centre on bus route. Close to youth hostel.* ☎ 6249-1543
Mixed bar and restaurant.

MEN'S CLUBS
■ **John's JO-Club** (g MA NU P VS) 2nd Thu / month
PO Box 44 33, Kingston ✉ ACT 2604 ☎ 6297 9967
Social relaxing evenings for like minded men. Safe sex only.

CAFES
■ **Da Cesare** (B F g)
Lonsdale Street/Eloura Street, Braddon ✉ ACT 2601
☎ 6247-2946

SEX SHOPS/BLUE MOVIES
■ **Adam & Eve** (A AC CC g S VS) 9-24 h
125 Gladstone Street, Fyshwick ✉ ACT 2609 ☎ 6239-1121
Sex shop with video arcade.
■ **Champions Headquarters** (AC CC DR G MA msg NU r s VS) 9-24 h
83 Woolongong Street, Fyshwick ✉ ACT 2609 ☎ 6280 6969
Sex shop, back room, cinema.
■ **Ram Lounges and Video**
Unit 6, 83 Wollongong Street, Fyshwick ✉ ACT 2601
(Next to Club X) ☎ 6280-4568

HOUSE OF BOYS
■ **Male Company** 10-4 h
161 Newcastle Street, Fyshwick ✉ ACT 2601 ☎ 6280-7642
Studio, outcalls, appointments.

Canberra ▶ Adelong — Australia Capital Territory - New South Wales/Australia

SAUNAS/BATHS
■ **Canberra City Steam** (AC CC DR G MA SA SB VS WH WO) Sun-Thu 12-1, Fri-Sat -3 h
161 Newcastle Street, Fishwick ✉ ACT 2609 *(on bus route 80)*
☎ 6280-6980
New premises sauna with retail shop. Busy on Fri.

GUEST HOUSES
■ **Northbourne Lodge** (AC BF CC glm MA OS) 24 hours
522 Northbourne Avenue, Downer ✉ ACT 2602 *(Next to Dickson Shopping Centre)* ☎ 6257-2599 📠 6257-2599
Rates from A$ 75.

GENERAL GROUPS
■ **Club 19** (G MA) 2nd Sat & 4th Wed
PO Box 4703 Kingston ✉ ACT 2604 ☎ 6297 9967
💻 googong@interact.au
Friendship club for male gays. Can arrange accomodation for overseas visitors.

FETISH GROUPS
■ **Griffin Motor Club, The**
GPO Box 10 48 ✉ ACT 2601 ☎ 6258-8716

HEALTH GROUPS
■ **AIDS Action Council of the A.C.T.** Mon-Fri 9-17 h
13 Lonsdale Street, PO Box 229, Braddon ✉ ACT 2601
☎ 6257-2855 📠 6257-4839
Office and Healthline.
■ **Peer Support Network (PSN)** Mo-Fr 10:00-16:00h
Westlund House, 16 Gordon Street ✉ ACT 2601 ☎ 6257 4985
📠 6257 4838 💻 plwhaact@hotmail.com
Support for positive people, friends and family

RELIGIOUS GROUPS
■ **Acceptance Canberra**
✉ ACT 2601 ☎ 6281-3977
Catholic group.

SWIMMING
-Kambah Pool (A "free beach" on the Murrumbidgee River. West of Canberra. Walk downstream from the last car park for about 1 km to a large sandy beach. Cruising very active downstream on both sides.)

CRUISING
-Museum site (off Lady Denman Drive on shores of Lake Burley Griffin)

Deakin ☎ 02

TRAVEL AND TRANSPORT
■ **Just Travel** Mon-Fri 8.30-18.30h, Sat 9-12.30h
Suite 2, 6 Napier Close ✉ ACT 2600 ☎ 6285 2644 📠 6282 2430
💻 www.justtravel.com
Gay and lesbian travel services.

AUS-New South Wales

Location: South East AUS
Initials: NSW
Time: GMT +10
Area: 801,600 km2 / 309,498 sq mi.
Population: 6,330,000
Capital: Sydney

CITYSTEAM
161 Newcastle St Fyshwick ACT
Sun to Thu - 12 noon to 1am
Fri to Sat - 12 noon to 3am
Telephone 02 6280 6980
www.citysteam.com.au

※ In New South Wales the age of consent is fixed at 16 years of age for heterosexuals and 18 for homosexuals. There is an anti-discrimination law protecting homosexuals concerning issues regarding housing and social / medical care.

★ In Neu-Südwales liegt das Schutzalter bei 16 Jahren für Heterosexuelle und bei 18 Jahren für Homosexuelle. Es gibt zudem ein Antidiskriminierungsgesetz, das Homosexuelle in den Bereichen Wohnen und Versorgung schützt.

※ En Nouvelle Galles du Sud, la majorité sexuelle est fixée à 16 ans pour les hétérosexuels et à 18 ans pour les homosexuels. Une loi anti-discriminatoire garantit aux homosexuels les mêmes droits que les autres citoyens dans les domaines du logement et de la sécurité sociale.

● En New South Wales la edad de consentimiento es de 16 años para heterosexuales y de 18 años para homosexuales. Existe además una ley de antidiscriminación que protege la igualdad de los gays en areas como vivienda y empleo.

✕ In New South Wales l'età legale per rapporti eterosessuali è di 16 anni, per quelli omosessuali di 18 anni. Esiste una legge contro la discriminazione per la tutela degli omosessuali negli ambiti del domicilio e dell'assistenza sociale.

Adelong ☎ 02

HOTELS
■ **Adelong's Beaufort House**
77 Tumut Street ✉ 2729 ☎ 6946 2273 📠 6946 2553
💻 Beaufort@dragnet.com.au 💻 Beaufort.dragnet.com.au
Rates A$ 45-75 .

Australia/New South Wales — Albury ▶ Penrith

Albury ☎ 02

HEALTH GROUPS
■ **AIDS Task Group**
PO Box 10 76 ✉ NSW 2640 ☎ 6023 0340 ☎ 6023 0370
Information, resources, seminars, community education, support and counselling on AIDS issues.

CRUISING
-Botanical gardens
-Billson Park (AYOR) (David Street; daytime)

Byron Bay ☎ 02

HEALTH GROUPS
■ **Aids Council of New South Wales (ACON) Northern Rivers Branch**
147 Laurel Avenue, Lismore ✉ NSW 2480 ☎ 6622 1555
🖷 6622 1520

SWIMMING
-Kingshead Beach (NU) (7 km south of Byron on Brokenhead Road. Make a left to Seven Miles Beach Road, drive to first [P] south of Broken Head Beach, walk down to Kingshead Beach through rainforest.)

Coffs Harbour ☎ 02

HOTELS
■ **Santa Fe Luxury Bed & Breakfast** (f g H PI)
Gaudrons Road, The Mountain Way, PO Box 17 63 ✉ NSW 2450
☎ 6653 7700 🖷 6653 7050
10 km north of Coffs Harbour. Located on 5 acres. En suite rooms with TV & VCR.

GENERAL GROUPS
■ **Four Seasons Social Group**
PO Box 16 54 ✉ NSW 2450 ☎ 6652-7643
Provides social activities, dances, barbecues, bush walks, etc..

HEALTH GROUPS
■ **AIDS Council of NSW**
c/o 93 High Street, ✉ NSW 2450 ☎ 6651-4056

SWIMMING
-Little Diggers (g NU) (5 km north of Coffs Harbour. Opposite the Big Banana. On the beach facing the sea to the left .

Corowa ☎ 02

HOTELS
■ **Motor Inn** (AC b BF f G H PI SA)
PO Box 122 ✉ NSW 2646 ☎ 6033-1255

Dargan ☎ 02

HOTELS
■ **Gays Lodge** (GLM)
57 Valley View Road ✉ NSW 2786 ☎ 957 3811 🖷 957 1385

Hunter Valley Wine Country ☎ 02

HOTELS
■ **Pokolbin Village**
☞ *Pokolbin*

Hurstville ☎ 02

TRAVEL AND TRANSPORT
■ **Breakout Tours**
PO Box 504 ✉ NSW 2220 ☎ 9570-5900 🖷 9570-9200
Gay and lesbian travel services.

Leura ☎ 02

GUEST HOUSES
■ **Leura House** (AC b BF CC E f g H)
7 Britain Street ✉ NSW 2780 ☎ 4784-2035 🖷 4784-3329
🖳 www.bluemts.com.au/leurahouse
Beautiful historic guest houses. 11 rooms with bath/WC and balcony/terrace. 2 cottages.

APARTMENTS
■ **Bygone Beauty's Cottages** (E g)
20-22 Grose Street ✉ NSW 2780 ☎ 4784 3117 🖷 4784 3078
🖳 bygonebeautys.com.au

Newcastle ☎ 02

BARS
■ **Islington Barracks** (B D GLM S STV YG) 18-? h, closed Mon
139 Maitland Road, Islington ✉ NSW 2300 ☎ 4969-1848
■ **Wickham Park Hotel** (b D f GLM STV WE) Mon-Sat 12-3, Sun 12-22 h
61 Maitland Road, Islington ✉ NSW 2296 ☎ 4969-2017

RESTAURANTS
■ **Barry & Paul's "Little Swallows Cafe"** (F GLM)
Cleary Street/Beaumont Street ✉ NSW 2300 ☎ 4969-2135
■ **Gina's on Beaumont** (AC b CC F glm MA OS WE)
Lunch: Wed-Fri 11.30-14.30, Diner: Tue-Sun 18-? h
47 Beaumont Street, Haminton ✉ NSW 2303 ☎ 4961-6844
Northern Italian style food.

GENERAL GROUPS
■ **Newcastle University Students Association (NUSA)**
Shortland Union Bdg., University of Newcastle ✉ NSW 2308
☎ 4968-1281 🖷 4968-3559 🖳 smusa@alinga.newcastle.edu.au

HEALTH GROUPS
■ **AIDS Council of NSW (ACON)**
Hunter Branch, PO Box 1081 ✉ NSW 2300 ☎ 4929-3464

CRUISING
-Dangar Park, Maitland Road, Mayfield
-Gregson Park, Hamilton
-Islington Park, Maitland Road (exit to Criterion Hotel)
-Rocks at Susan Gilmore Beach, Memorial Drive

Penrith ☎ 02

BOOK SHOPS
■ **Way Out West Bookshop** (g)
Shop 2, Carmina Arcade ✉ NSW 2750 ☎ 4731-3094
General bookstore with gay section.

Pokolbin ▶ Sydney **New South Wales/Australia**

Style & Convenience...

Set on 40 acres in the heart of Hunter Valley Wine Country. Pokolbin Village Resort offers a unique standard of affordable accommodation in a very enticing location. With the convenience of two fine restaurants, an alfresco café and quaint general store, the Resort provides the ideal setting for a relaxing holiday in the vineyards. Guests have a choice of two styles of accommodation. Our new art deco suites provide a contemporary ambience, while our traditional country style suites offer a cosy alternative.

188 Broke Road, Pokolbin N.S.W 2320
Telephone: (02) 4998 7670 · Facsimile: (02) 4998 7377
www.pokolbinvillage.com.au

Pokolbin ☏ 02

HOTELS

■ **Pokolbin Village Resort & Conference Center** (AC BF CC F glm H)
188 Broke Road ✉ NSW 2320 ☏ 4998-7670 🖷 4998-7377
⌨ www.pokolbinvillage.com.au
Gay owned resort in one of the main vineyard districts 2 hours north of Sydney. Horse riding. 12 doubles, 1 single, 3 studios and 4 apartments with bath or shower/WC, balcony, telephone, Fax, TV/video, radio, safe, kitchenette (studios) or kitchen (apartments).

Port Kembla ☏ 02

BOOK SHOPS

■ **Venus Adult Book Shop**
121 Wentworth Road ✉ NSW 2505 ☏ 4275-2121

HEALTH GROUPS

■ **AIDS Council of New South Wales**
✉ 2505 ☏ 4276-2399

Robertson ☏ 02

HOTELS

■ **Ranelagh House** (f g H PI SA WH)
Illawarra Highway ✉ 2577 ☏ 4885-1111
Historic guest house for a quiet romantic weekend located in the suburbs.

Rylestone ☏ 02

HOTELS

■ **High Tweeters** (BF glm H MA NU)
Nullo Mountain Road NSW 2849 ✉ 2849 ☏ 6379-6351
Farmstay accomodation in beautiful landscape, close to Wollemi National Park. Rates A$ 50,- double incl. continental bf (full bf $ 7,50 extra), minimum of 2 nights. Guided trekking tours. 270 km from Sydney.

Sydney ☏ 02

✱ The capital of New South Wales is Sydney. It is the oldest and largest city in Australia and probably the most well known.

The hustle and bustle of the metropolis with its sub-tropical climate and spectacular Sydney Harbour Bridge and the well known Opera House. Sydney has a large gay and lesbian community which celebrates at the end of February each year the world famous Gay Parade, the Sydney Gay and lesbian Mardi Gras. Hundreds of thousands gather on the streets to watch the spectacular costume parade and or to party to dawn. The „Sleeze Ball" at the end of September or another Mardi-Gras event attracts up to 20,000 gays, lesbians and their friends.
The gay scene has established itself around the Golden Mile of Oxford Street in the suburb of Darlinghurst. Another gay centre has emerged around King Street (New Town) the gay and lesbian presence is clearly seen. The city beaches of Manly and Bondi are also attractive meeting points for gays. The cafés and restaurants offer an interesting range of typical Pacific area cuisine in which Sydney's young chefs are leaders.
Sydney is ideally located for the tourist to get to the Blue Mountains (a couple of hours away from the city). Newcastle and Wollongong, the Southern Highlands, Canberra are only a short trip away from Sydney. Further North of New South Wales is the liberal district of the Northern Rivers located on Byron Bay which has a small but lively gay community. Sydney will also maintain its reputation as a gay metropolis in the future with the taking place of the Gay Games in the year 2002.

✱ Sydney, Hauptstadt von Neusüdwales, ist die älteste und größte Stadt Australiens. Die geschäftige Metropole mit ihrem subtropischen Klima erstreckt sich um den spektakulären Hafen mit der Harbour Bridge und dem berühmten Opera House. Sydney hat eine große schwul-lesbische Gemeinde, die sich jedes Jahr Ende Februar mit der weltweit größten Schwulenparade, der „Sydney Gay and Lesbian Mardi Gras" feiert. Hunderttausende drängen sich in den Straßen, um die kostümierte Parade an sich vorbeiziehen zu lassen oder um bis zum Morgengrauen mitzufeiern.
Der „Sleaze Ball" Ende September bzw. Anfang Oktober ist ein weiteres Mardi-Gras-Event, zu dem mehr als 20 000 Schwule, Lesben und ihre Freunde zusammenkommen. Die schwule Szene hat sich rings um die „Goldene Meile" Oxford Street in der Vorstadt Darlinghurst etabliert. Neben einem weiteren schwulen Zentrum um die King Street (Newtown) wird praktisch der ganze zentrale Stadtbereich von Schwulen und Lesben in Beschlag genommen, deren Präsenz auch dem ungeübten Auge kaum entgeht. Nicht weniger

Australia/New South Wales — Sydney

interessant für Schwule sind die Stadtstrände von Manly und natürlich der berühmte Bondi-Strand.
Die Cafés und Restaurants der Stadt bieten die interessante und abwechslungsreiche Küche des Pazifischen Raumes, in der Sydneys junge Chefs kräftig mitmischen.
Schwule Bars, schwule Hotels, schwule Saunas, schwule Fitneßstudios, schwule Strände, schwule Organisationen: selbst nüchtern betrachtet genügt es nicht, Sydney als schwules Dienstleistungszentrum zu beschreiben, es ist die schwule Hauptstadt des südpazifischen Raums.
Für den Touristen ist Sydney äußerst günstig gelegen. Die Blue Mountains sind nur einige Stunden entfernt, weitere interessante Tagesausflüge sind die benachbarten Städte Newcastle und Wollongong, die Southern Highlands bei Berri, das Weinanbaugebiet Hunter Valley oder die Hauptstadt Australiens, Canberra. Im äußersten Norden von Neusüdwales liegt der liberale Bezirk Northern Rivers um Byron Bay, das eine kleine aber lebhafte schwule Gemeinde hat.
Auch in Zukunft wird Sydney seinem Ruf als schwule Metropole gerecht, wenn sich im August 2002 schwule und lesbische SportlerInnen aus aller Welt hier zu den Gay Games 2002 treffen.

※ Sydney, capitale de la Nouvelle Galles du Sud, est la ville la plus ancienne et la plus grande d'Australie et probablement aussi la plus connue. La métropole commerciale au climat subtropical s'étend autour d'un port spectaculaire avec le Harbourg Bridge et le célèbre Opera House. Sydney a une grande communauté homosexuelle qui fête chaque année, à la fin de février la plus grande parade homosexuelle mondiale, la „Sydney Gay and Lesbian Mardi Gras". Des centaines de milliers de spectateurs se pressent dans la rue pour voir défiler devant eux la parade costumée ou pour faire la fête jusqu'à l'aube. Le „Sleaze Ball" vers la fin de septembre ou le début d'octobre est un autre événement de Mardi gras, où se rencontrent plus de 20.000 homosexuels, lesbiennes et amis.
La scène s'est établie tout autour de l'Oxford Street au faubourg de Darlinghurst. Une autre zone gaie se développe aux environs de la King Street (Newtown). Les plages de la ville, Manly et Bondi, sont aussi assidûment fréquentées par les homosexuels. Les cafés et restaurants de la ville offrent une cuisine variée et intéressante de la région du Pacifique avec de nombreux jeunes chefs à la pointe de l'innovation. Sydney est idéalement située pour des excusions touristiques. Les Blue Mountains ne se trouvent qu'à quelques heures de la capitale, les villes voisines Newcastle et Wollongong, les Southern Highlands près de Berri, la région viticole de Hunter Valley ou la capitale de l'Australie, Canberra valent également un détour. A l'extrême nord de la Nouvelle Galles du Sud se trouve le district libéral de Northern Rivers autour de Byron Bay qui possède une petite communauté gaie très active.
Sydney va encore renforcer sa réputation de métropole gaie au mois d'août 2002 quand se tiendront les Gay Games.

● Sydney, la capital de New South Wales, es la ciudad más antigua y más grande de Australia y con toda seguridad la más famosa. La vivaz metrópoli con su clima subtropical se caracteriza por su puerto espectacular con el *Harbour Bridge* y su famoso *Opera House*. Sydney cuenta con una extensa comunidad gay, que se reune cada año a finales de febrero para celebrar la fiesta más grande de homosexuales en el mundo, la *Sydney Gay and Lesbian Mardi Gras*. Miles de personas llenan las calles para ver el desfile con sus impresionantes disfraces o para participar en las fiestas que duran hasta la madrugada. El *Sleaze Ball* que se celebra a finales de septiembre o a principios de octubre es otro evento de Mardi Gras, donde se reunen más que 20.000 homosexuales, lesbianas y sus simpatizantes. El ambiente gay surgió en la „Golden Mile" de Oxford Street y sus alrededores, en los surburbios de Darlinghurst. A parte del otro centro gay que se encuentra en los alrededores de la King Street (Newton), los homosexuales y lesbianas se han apoderado casi de todo el centro de la ciudad, donde su fuerte presencia es notable hasta para los ojos nada experimentados. De especial interés para el turista gay son las playas de Manly y por supuesto la famosa Bondi playa. Los locales y restaurantes ofrecen una interesante y variada cocina de la región del Pacífico, preparados por los innovativos cocineros de la ciudad. Bares gay, hoteles gay, saunas gay, gimnasios gay, playas gay, organizaciones gay, hasta considerándolo friamente destaca el hecho que Sydney no se puede describir como centro de servicios gay, sino que es la metrópoli homosexual en la región del Pacífico. Para el turista, Sydney está situado perfectamente. Los Blue Mountains están a unas horas de distancias y otros excursiones interesantes se pueden hacer a las ciudades cercanas de Newcastle y Wollongong, a los Southern Highlands cerca de Berri, a la región vinícola Hunter Valley o a la capital australiana Canberra. En el extremo norte de New South Wales se encuentra el barrio liberal de Northern Rivers en los alrededores de Byron Bay, que cuenta con una pequeña, pero extremadamente vivaz comunidad gay. Sydney se consagrará también en el futuro como metrópoli gay, cuando en el mes de agosto en el año 2002 se reunerán aqui deportistas homosexuales y lesbianas de todo el mundo para los Gay Games 2002.

✕ Sydney, capitale del New South Wales, è la più vecchia e più grande città dell'Australia, e magari anche quella più conosciuta. La metropoli vivace con il suo clima subtropicale si estende attorno allo spettacolare porto con l'Harbour Bridge e la famosa Opera House. Sydney ha una grande comunità gay e lesbica che ha ottenuto fama internazionale grazie alla „Sydney Gay and Lesbian Mardi Gras", la più grande sfilata gay del mondo che si svolge sempre verso la fine di febbraio. Centinaia di migliaia di persone assistono alla manifestazione e festeggiano fino all'alba. A „Sleaze Ball", a fine settembre, all'inizio dell'ottobre, c'è un'altro avvenimento „Mardi Gras" che attira più di 20.000 gay e lesbiche e i loro amici. La vita gay è situata intorno alla „Golden Mile" nella Oxford Street nel distretto di Darlinghorst. Oltre a un'altro centro gay attorno alla King Street quasi tutta la città in quei giorni viene occupata dai gay e dalle lesbiche. La loro presenza dà nell'occhio anche a quelli meno „esperti". Altrettanto interessante per i gay sono le spiagge di Manly e di Bondi. I locali e ristoranti offrono le diverse cucine tipiche del pacifico, dove i giovani chef contribuiscono al loro successo. Bar gay, alberghi gay, saune gay, palestre gay, spiagge gay, organizzazioni gay: dal punto di vista obiettivo non basta descrivere Sydney come centro gay nel settore dei servizi, ma bensí come capitale gay del Pacifico Meridionale. Per il turista Sydney è una comoda base per escursioni. Alle Blue Mountains si arriva entro poche ore, altri posti interessanti sono le città vicine di Newcastle e Wollongong, le Southern Highlands presso Berri, le Vigne della Hunter Valley, o la capitale australiana Canberra. Nella parte più a nord del New South Wales si trova il distretto di Northern Rivers attorno alla Byron Bay con una piccola ma vivace comunità gay. Anche nel futuro Sydney soddisferà le aspettative che vengono poste ad una metropoli gay, perché nell'agosto del 2002 si incontreranno sportive/i lesbiche e gay in occasione delle Gay Games 2002.

GAY INFO

■ **Capital Q**
263 Liverpool Street, Darlinghurst ✉ NSW 2010 ☎ 9332-4988
🖨 9380-5104 📧 capq@ipacific.net.au 🌐 www.capitalq.com.au
Published weekly. Free at gay venues.

■ **Gaywaves** Thu 19.30-20.30h (2 SER FM 107.3 Mhz)
PO Box 473, Broadway ✉ NSW 2007 ☎ 9514 9514
🖨 9514 9599 📧 gaywaves@hotmail.com 🌐 www.2ser.com
Gay and lesbian radio program.

Sydney — New South Wales/Australia

Sydney

1. City Gym Fitness
2. Stellar Suites
3. Macquarie Boutique Hotel
4. DCM-Sydney Night Disco Club
5. Exchange Hotel Bar & Phoenix Bar
6. Kingsteam Sauna
7. Signal Men's Club
8. FOD Travel Service & Midnight Shift
9. Numbers Bar
10. Mephisto Leather Shop
11. The Den Men's Club
12. The Probe
13. Byblos Disco
14. Oxford Hotel Bar
15. Bookshop Darlinghurst
16. Green Park Diner
17. Beauchamp Hotel Bar
18. Albury Hotel Bar
19. Banana Bar
20. Manor House Boutique Hotel
21. Bodyline Sauna
22. Taxi Club Bar
23. Flinders Hotel Bar
24. Beresford Hotel Bar
25. Pelican Hotel
26. The Villa Private Hotel
27. 415 on Bourke Hotel
28. The Piercing Urge Shop
29. Headquarters Men's Club
30. City Crown Lodge Hotel
31. Governors on Fitzroy Guest House
32. Brickfield Inn B&B
33. Radical Leather Shop
34. Ken's at Kensington
35. Oasis on Flinders

Australia/New South Wales — Sydney

■ **Sydney Gay and Lesbian Mardi Gras Association**
PO Box 557 Newtown ✉ NSW 2042 ☎ 9557-4332 🖷 9516-4446
Association organizes the annual Sydney Gay and Lesbian Mardi Gras Party, Parade, Festival, and Sleaze Ball.
■ **Sydney Star Observer**
PO Box 939, Darlinghurst ✉ NSW 1300 ☎ 9380-5577
🖷 9331 2118 📧 mail@ssonet.com.au 💻 www.ssonet.com.au
Sydney's weekly published gay and lesbian community newspaper. One of Australia's leading gay newspapers. Very professional. Free at gay venues.

TOURIST INFO

■ **Sydney Visitors Information Kiosk** Mon-Fri 9-17 h
Martin Plaza, ✉ NSW 2000 ☎ 9235 2424

BARS

■ **Albury Hotel** (B F G MA STV YG) Sun-Thu 12-24, Fri-Sat 12-1 h
6 Oxford Street, Paddington ✉ NSW 2021 ☎ 9361-6555
Popular bar, with body-builder barmen, drag shows.
■ **Banana Bar** (A AC B CC d F GLM S YG) Mon-Sat 15-3, Sun 15-24 h
1-5 Flinders Street, Darlinghurst ✉ NSW 2010 (Taylor Square)
☎ 9360-6373
Cocktail bar and restaurant.
■ **Barracks Bar** (! LJ) Mon-Sun 17-03h
Cnr Flinders and Bourke Street, Taylor Square (Rear of Taylor Square Hotel)
An underground haven for leather fans, bears and others. The bar for men who know what they want.
■ **Beauchamp Hotel. The** (AC B cc d G LJ MA N VS) Mo- We & Su 12-24h Th -01am, Fr & Sa -02h
267 Oxford Street, Darlinghurst ✉ NSW 2010 Opposite St. Vincents Hospital. Courner of Oxford and South Downing Street. ☎ 9331-2575
■ **Caesar's Bar** (B G MA)
Petersham Inn Hotel, 388 Parramatta Road, Petersham ✉ NSW 2049 ☎ 9569-4448
■ **Cleveland** (AC B CC d F glm MA N OS) Mon-Sat 11-4, Sun 12-24 h
433 Cleveland Street, Redfern ☎ 9698 1908
■ **Exchange Hotel** (B D glm MA S) Mon-Fri 112-2, Sat 18-3, Sun 18-2 h
34 Oxford Street, Darlinghurst ✉ NSW 2010 ☎ 9331-1936
3 Bars and Dancefloor.
■ **Flinders Hotel** (AC B d G S SNU YG) Mon-Thu 20-3, Fri-Sat 22-7, Sun 20-24 h; shows Thu-Sun; strippers Sat 23 h
63 Flinders Street, Darlinghurst ✉ NSW 2010 ☎ 9360-4929
■ **Imperial Hotel** (B D GLM s) Sun-Thu 10-?, Fri Sat -8 h
35 Erskineville Road ✉ NSW 2000 ☎ 9519-9899
Thu-Sun drag shows. Fri Sat Theatre Restaurant.
■ **Newtown Hotel** (AC B D F G S VS YG) Mon-Sat 10-24, Sun 12-22 h
174 King Street, Newtown ✉ NSW 2042 ☎ 9557-1329
2 bars.
■ **Numbers** (B D G) 10-? h
95 Oxford Street, Darlinghurst ✉ NSW 2010 (1st floor)
☎ 9331-6099
■ **Oxford Hotel** (! B G lj YG) Mon-Thu 17-2, Fri sat -3, Sun -24 h
134 Oxford Street, Darlinghurst ✉ NSW 2010 ☎ 9331-3467
Cocktail bar „Gilligans" on the 1st floor. One of the most popular bars in Sydney.
■ **Phoenix Bar** (AC B CC D DR GLM lj MA r VS WE)
Wed & Thu 22-5, Fr, Sat & Sun 22-7 h
c/o Exchange Hotel, 34 Oxford Street, Darlinghurst ✉ NSW 2010
(200 m east from Hyde Park on Oxford St.) ☎ 9331 1936

■ **Stonewall Hotel** (A AC B BF CC D F GLM MA OS S WE)
Mon-Fri 12-3, Sat Sun -5 h
173-175 Oxford Street, Darlinghurst ✉ NSW 2010 ☎ 9360-1963
🖷 9331-4733 📧 stonewall@ozemail.com.au
■ **Taxi Club** (B D F glm STV) 0-24 h
40 Flinders Street, Darlinghurst ✉ NSW 2010 ☎ 9331-4256

MEN'S CLUBS

■ **Den. The** (CC DR G lj VS) Mon-Thu 20-5, Fri 20-Mon 5 h
97 Oxford Street, Darlinghurst ✉ NSW 2010 (1st floor)
☎ 9332-3402
Sexclub with coffee bar, TV & video lounge. Entry A$ 10.
■ **Headquarters on Crown** (AC BF CC DR f G LJ MA NU VS)
Mon-Thu 12-7, Fri 12-Mon 7 h
273 Crown Street, Darlinghurst ✉ NSW 2010 (100m from Oxford Street) ☎ 9331 6217
■ **Signal** (AC DR G LJ MA s VS WE) Sun-Thu 11-3, Fr-Sat 11-6
Riley Street/Arnold Square ✉ NSW 2010 (above 81, Oxford Street)
☎ 9331-8830
A range of toys, magazines, books, underwear, leather clothing, etc. Men's sex club.

CAFES

■ **Memento**
479 Bronte Road ☎ 9389 1613
Snacks and BYO. Breakfast on the beach.
■ **X-Core Cafe** (BF F glm OS)
191 King Street, Newtown ✉ NSW 2042
Unique atmosphere with pleasant cuisine.

DANCECLUBS

■ **Byblos** (B D G) Thu-Sat 22-? h
169 Oxford Street, Darlinghurst ✉ NSW 2010
■ **DCM-Sydney Night Club** (AC B D glm MA S STV) Thu-Sun 23-? h
33 Oxford Street, Darlinghurst ✉ NSW 2000 ☎ 9267-7036
Popular disco with mixed nights and gay nights. Check gay newspapers.
■ **Midnight Shift Hotel** (A AC B D GLM MA S STV VS) Bars downstairs: Mon-Sun 12-5, nightclub upstairs: Thu-Sun 23-6h
85 Oxford Street, Darlinghurst ✉ NSW 2010 (between Crown & Riley) ☎ 9360 4319
Upstairs: Midnight Shift Nightclub, downstairs: The Shift Video Bar and the Locker Room. Every Sat night „boys-only zone" upstairs.

RESTAURANTS

■ **Californian Cafe. The** (F GLM MA) 0-24 h
177 Oxford Street, Darlinghurst ✉ NSW 2010 ☎ 9331-5587
All meals under A$ 10.
■ **Green Park Diner** (A BF F GLM OS) 11-23, Fri Sat -24, Sun 11-22 h
219 Oxford Street, Darlinghurst ✉ NSW 2010 ☎ 9361 6171
Burgers and fresh simple food. Sydney's oldest gay restaurant. Very popular.
■ **Kink**
137 Oxford Street, Darkinghurst ☎ 9380 6494
■ **Nova** (A BF CC F GLM MA OS)
191-195 Oxford Street, Darlinghurst ✉ NSW 2010 (level 1&2, Taylor Square) ☎ 9380 6545
■ **Side door Restaurant** (B F G MA s)
283 Australia Street, Newtown ✉ NSW 2000 ☎ 9516-3691
■ **Thai Panic** (F GLM OS YG) Mon-Thu 11-23, Fri-Sun 11-3 h
80 Oxford Street, Darlinghurst ☎ 9361-6406
Fresh food and funky atmosphere.
■ **Yipiyiyo** (AC CC F GLM MA) Mon-Thu 18.30-22, Fri Sat -23 h, closed Sun
290 Crown Street, Darlinghurst ✉ NSW 2010 (100 m south of Oxford Street) ☎ 9332 3114

Sydney | New South Wales/Australia

Ken's at Kensington

SYDNEY'S LEGENDARY GAY MEN'S SAUNA

SWIMMING POOL • STEAM ROOM • SAUNA • SPA • GYMNASIUM
PRIVATE RETREATS • VIDEO LOUNGE • BIG SCREEN TV LOUNGE
COFFEE LOUNGE • OUTDOOR SMOKING AREA
FULLY AIR-CONDITIONED

★ GAY OWNED & OPERATED ★

83 ANZAC PARADE KENSINGTON • TELEPHONE: (02) 9662 1359

SEX SHOPS/BLUE MOVIES

■ **Adultworld** (CC g VS) 0-24 h
124 A Oxford Street, Darlinghurst ✉ NSW 2010 ☎ 9360-8527
■ **Body Play** (g)
159 Oxford Street, Darlinghurst ✉ NSW 2010 *(level 2)*
Only all male peep show in Australia.
■ **Club X** (G VS)
26 Bayswater Road, Kings Cross ✉ NSW 2011 ☎ 9357-1902
■ **Numbers** (G VS) 0-24 h
95 Oxford Street, Darlinghurst ✉ NSW 2010 *(1st floor)*
☎ 9331-6099
Gay magazines, novels etc. Action area. Entry A$ 5.
■ **Probe. The** (CC DR G MA SNU VS) 11-1, Fri-Sun 0-24 h
159 Oxford Street, Darlinghurst ✉ NSW 2010 *(level 1)*
☎ 9361-5924
■ **Ram Lounge and Video** (G VS) 9-1 h
380 Pitt Street ✉ NSW 2000 *(Club X entrance. 1st floor)*
☎ 9264-3249
All day membership pass A$ 10.
■ **Tool Shed. The** (G VS) 11-1.30, Fri Sat 11-?, Sun 13.30-23 h
198 King Street, Newtown ✉ NSW 2042 ☎ 9565-1599
Adult boutique.
■ **Toolshed** (B G)
81 Oxford Street, Darlinghurst ✉ NSW 2010

HOUSE OF BOYS

■ **Knightcall Male Escorts** (AC CC G R) 11:00-late, every day.
P.O. Box 812, Kingscross ✉ NSW 2011 ☎ 9368-0511
Sydney's premier male escort agency.

SAUNAS/BATHS

■ **Bodyline** (! AC CC DR f G MA OS P SA SB VS WH WO) Mon-Thu 12-7, Fri 12-Mon 7 h
10 Taylor Street, Darlinghurst ✉ NSW 2010 *(just off Oxford Street at Taylor Square)* ☎ 9360-1006
A steamy adventure on three floors with sun deck. Free condoms and lubricant in all sex areas. Popular with the club scene and orientals.
■ **Ken's at Kensington** (! AC dr f G MA msg PI SA SB VS WH WO) Mon-Thu 12-6, Fri 12-Mon 6 h
83 Anzac Parade, Kensington ✉ NSW 2033 *(Bus 391-398-Taylor Square)* ☎ 9662-1359
Sydney's well-known gay sauna with friendly staff. Popular and cruisy. Gay owned & operated.
■ **Kingsteam** (DR f G OG P SA SB VS WH WO) Mon 10-1, Tue-Fri -6, Sat-Sun 0-24 h
38-42 Oxford Street, Darlinghurst ✉ NSW 2010 *(next to Exchange Hotel, 1st floor)* ☎ 9360-3431
Friendly sauna with free condoms and lube available.
■ **Man Club** (G MA SA SB) 10-24, Fri-Sun -23 h
170 Parmatta Road, Granville ✉ NSW 2142 *(near Granville station)*
Clothes optional sauna.

FITNESS STUDIOS

■ **Bayswater Fitness** (g SOL WO) Mon-Fri 6.-22, Sat 7-22, Sun 7-9h
33 Bayswater Road, Kings Cross ✉ NSW 2011 ☎ 9356-2555
■ **City Gym** (AC CC SB msg SA) Mo-Fr 0-24 h, Su 08-22h
107- 113 Crown Street East ✉ NSW 2010 *(East Sydney)*
☎ 9360 6541
Sydney's premier gay gymnasium.

Australia/New South Wales | **Sydney**

MACQUARIE BOUTIQUE HOTEL
· 42 WENTWORTH AVE, SYDNEY 2000 ·

- 2 Bars & Restaurants
- All rooms with private facilities
- 50mtrs to Oxford St
- Television
- Tea & coffee facilities
- Air-conditioned

Tariffs

Single $185 p/night (tax included)

Double/Twin $235 p/night (tax included)

(All prices are subject to change)

Built earlier this century, the Macquarie Boutique Hotel has been extensively restored. The atmosphere is reminiscent of a bygone era. Centrally located and great value for money.

Ph 9264 8888   Fax 9267 5037   E-mail hotel@cafesydney.net.au

---

■ **Fitness Exchange. The** (G) 17-? h
33 Wellington Street, Chippendale ✉ NSW 2008 ☏ 9699-6514
Non-profit making gymnasium owned and run by gay members. Has weight-lifting and body-building, fitness classes, and tuition in karate.
■ **Newtown Gym** (AC CC G msg SA SOL WO) Mon-Fri 6-22,
Sat Sun 8-20 h
328-338 King Street, Newtown ✉ NSW 2042 *(Newtown Plaza level 2)*
☏ 9557-2219

BODY & BEAUTY SHOPS

■ **Piercing Urge. The** (AC CC) Mon- Fri 10-20h, Sat -18h, Sun 12-18h
Shop 3, 322 Bourke Street, Darlinghurst ✉ NSW 2010
☏ 9360 3179

BOOK SHOPS

■ **Bookshop Darlinghurst. The** (AC CC GLM) Mon-Wed 10-23,
Thu-Sat -24, Sun 11-24 h
207 Oxford Street, Darlinghurst ✉ NSW 2010 *Taylor Square*
☏ 9331-1103
Australia's oldest gay and lesbian bookshop, magazines and cards plus local info.
■ **Club X** (G) 09.30-01h
429 Pitt Street ✉ NSW 2000 ☏ 9211 5345
Adult book store.
■ **Gleebooks** 8-21 h
49 Glebe Point Road, Glebe ✉ NSW 2037 ☏ 9660-2333
General bookstore with gay section.

FASHION SHOPS

■ **Pile up**
238 Oxford Street, Paddington ✉ NSW 2321 ☏ 9360-1279
Wild Dance Party Gear for the Gay Community. Fashion Sunglasses.

LEATHER & FETISH SHOPS

■ **Mephisto Leather**
135 Oxford Street, Darlinghurst ✉ NSW 2010 *(Ground floor)*
☏ 9332 3218
Relocated and expanded.
■ **Radical Leather** (CC GLM) Tue-Fri 11-18, Sat -16 h
20 Hutchinson Street, Surry Hills ✉ NSW 2310 *(in the basement)*
☏ 9331-7544
S&M leathergoods and made to measure apparel.

TRAVEL AND TRANSPORT

■ **Beyond the Blue**
685 South Dowling Street, Surrey Hills ✉ NSW 2010 ☏ 8399 0070
🖷 8399 0073 🖳 www.beyondtheblue.net
Gay and lesbian travel service

■ **Creative Tours**
3/55 Grafton Street, Bondi Junction ✉ NSW 2022 ☏ 9386-2111
🖷 9386-2199
Gay and lesbian travel services and products.
■ **Destination Downunder** Mon-Fr 8.30-18h
130 Elizabeth St. Sydney ✉ NSW 2000 ☏ 9268-2111
🖷 9267-9733
Gay and lesbian travel agents.
■ **Friends of Dorothy • FOD Travel** 9-17.30, Sat 9-13 h
77 Oxford Street, Darlinghurst ✉ NSW 1300 *(2nd floor)*
☏ 9360-3616 🖷 9332-3326 🖳 fod@dot.net.au
■ **HHK Travel**
50 Oxford Street, Paddington ✉ NSW 2021 ☏ 9332-4299
🖷 9360-2164
Travel agency for gays.
■ **Jornada** (CC GLM)
263 Liverpool Street, Darlinghurst ✉ NSW 2010 *(Level 1)*
☏ 9360-9611 ☏ (1 800) 672 120 🖷 9326 0199
🖳 justask@jordana.com.au 🖳 www.jordana.com.au
■ **Rosemary Hopkins-In Any Event**
2 Isabella Street, Balmain ✉ NSW 2041 ☏ 9810-2439
🖷 9810-3420
Project management in tourism and hospitality for the gay and lesbian community.
■ **Silke's Travel**
263 Oxford Street ✉ NSW 2010 ☏ 9380-6244
Travel agent. Member of IGLTA and AGLTA, Mardi Gras Tour Operator.

VIDEO SHOPS

■ **Videodrama** Sun-Thu 10-22, Fri Sat 10-24 h
135 Oxford Street, Darlinghurst ✉ NSW 2010
Gay owned video hire. Not x-rated but gay relevant films.

HOTELS

■ **Beresford Hotel** (B CC D GLM LJ MA OS TV WE) Sun Mon 5-24,
Tue-Thu 12-24, Fri Sat 5-3 h
354 Bourke Street, Surry Hills ✉ NSW 2010 ☏ 9331-1045
🖷 9360-4857
Pub & hotel offering food and drink.
■ **Chelsea Guest House** (AC BF CC glm H OS WO) 0-24 h
49 Womerah Avenue, Darlinghurst ✉ NSW 2010 *(5 minutes to Oxford Street 7 Kings Cross)* ☏ 9380-5994 🖷 9332 2491
🖳 xchelsea@ozemail.com.au
Single A$ 70, double 110 incl. breakfast

Sydney | **New South Wales/Australia**

SYDNEY's Premier Gay Boutique Hotel

Incorporating Lush restaurant and bar   *300m from Oxford St*

Featuring 20 elegantly appointed rooms and 5 serviced apartments

- Continental breakfast included
- King size beds
- Air conditioning
- Mini bar
- Electronic safe
- TV video

Telephone: 612 9380 6633
Facsimile: 612 9380 5016
Email: info@manorhouse.com.au
Website: www.manorhouse.com.au

MANOR HOUSE
Boutique Hotel

86 Flinders St Darlinghurst SYDNEY NSW 2010 Australia

Australia/New South Wales — Sydney

Sydney's Friendliest
Gay Owned & Operated

US$ 50
US$119

SYDNEY PARK LODGE HOTEL
747 South Dowling St, Moore Park 2016

Centrally located - walk to Oxford St, restaurants, clubs, bars & dance party venues (incl. Mardi Gras & Sleeze ball). Only 10-15 minutes from Sydney Harbour, Opera House, Bondi Beach. 15 minutes to Airport, close to public transport.

- Features -
★ Fantastic & enthusiastic staff ★ Ensuite Rooms ★ Air conditioning ★ Colour TV ★ Tea & Coffee facilitie ★ Iron & board ★ wall safe ★ Direct dial phone ★ Refridgerator ★ E-mail/Internet facility ★ Continental Breakfast ★ Guest laundry ★ Tours organised ★ credit cards accepted ★ 24 hr Reception ★VCR

Tel: +61 2 9318 2393   Fax :+61 2 9318 2513
glodge@parklodgehotel.com
www.parklodgesydney.com

■ **City Crown Lodge International** (BF CC E GLM H MA OS P VS) 8-23 h
289 Crown Street, Surry Hills ✉ NSW 2010 *(One minute walk to Oxford Street/Gay scene)* ☎ 9331-2433 ☎ (1800) 358 666
📠 9360-7760 💻 citycrown@bigpond.com
💻 wheretostay.com.au/citycrownlodge
19 double rooms with shower/WC, balcony or terrace, telephone. Own key. Rates A$ 100 + tax. Elegant atmosphere. Breakfast extra.

■ **Furama Hotel Central** (AC B CC glm H OS PI SA WH WO)
28 Albion Street, Surry Hills ✉ NSW 2010 *(Near Central station)*
☎ 9213 3820   📠 9281 0222   💻 fhctr@furama-hotels.com
💻 www.furama-hotels.com
Located minutes walk from Oxford Street. It's a four-star gay-friendly hotel.

■ **Macquarie Boutique** (AC B BF G H)
42 Wentworth Avenue ✉ 2000 *(50m from Oxford Street)*
☎ 9264 8888   📠 9267 5037   💻 hotel@cafesydney.net.au
Near gay scene. Singles from A$ 185, doubles from A$ 235, per night, incl. tax.

■ **Manor House Boutique Hotel** (AC B BF CC F GLM H MA OS PI S WH)
86 Flinders Street, Darlinghurst ✉ NSW 2010 *(300m from Oxford Street)* ☎ 9380 6633   📠 9380 5016   💻 info@manorhouse.com.au
💻 www.manorhouse.com.au
All rooms with private facilities, TV/Video, radio, safe, own key. Rates A$ 130-200 + tax (low season), 165-275 + tax (high season) includes continental breakfast. 24 elegant rooms and 6 service apartments.

■ **Park Lodge Hotel** (AC BF CC glm H OS VS) All year.
747 South Dowling Street/Thurlow Street ✉ NSW 2016 *(St. Moore Park)* ☎ 9318-2393   📠 9318-2513
💻 glodge@parklodgehotel.com   💻 www.parklodgesydney.com
Ten minutes to the airport. Five minutes to gay venues. Restored Victorian Hotel. Rates A$ 50-119.

■ **Pelican, The** (BF G H OS)
411 Bourke Street, Darlinghurst ✉ NSW 2010 *(near Taylor Square)*
☎ 9331-5344   📠 9331-3150
In the heart of the gay scene.

■ **Rooftop Motel** (AC BF CC glm PI)
146-148 Glebe Point Road ✉ NSW 2037   ☎ 9660-7777
📠 9660 7155   💻 rooftop@ral.net.au
Located 2 km from central Sydney. 39 Rooms with shower/WC, phone, TV, radio, AC, own key.

Victoria Court HOTEL–SYDNEY

122 Victoria Street
Sydney-Potts Point 2011
Tel: +61-2-9357 3200
Fax: +61-2-9357 7606
www.VictoriaCourt.com.au
E-mail: info@VictoriaCourt.com.au

Small Historic Boutique Hotel in an elegant 1880's Victorian terrace house. Centrally located on quiet, leafy Victoria Street in lively Potts Point - the heart of Sydney's gastronomic precinct - and within minutes of the Opera House, Central Business District, Oxford Street and Beaches. All rooms have private en-suite bathrooms, TV, telephones and air-conditioning. An airport bus and parking are available. Reasonable rates.

Sydney — New South Wales/Australia

Brickfield Hill Bed & Breakfast Inn
Sydney's warmest and most inviting guesthouse
'gay owned & operated'
visit us on the web at http:www.zip.com.au/~fields
403 Riley Street, Surry Hills, Sydney, N.S.W. 2010 Australia
Ph: (+61-2) 9211 4886 Fax:: (+61-2) 9212 2556 Email: fields@zip.com.au

■ **Stellar Suites** (CC NG) All year 7-23h
4 Wentworth Ave, Wentworth ✉ NSW 2000 ☎ 9264 9754
☎ (1800) 025 575 (free call) 🖨 9261 8006
💻 reservations@stellarsuites.com.au 💻 www.stellarsuites.com.au
Newly refurbished, Stellar Suites on Wentworth are close to the heart of the City and provide guests with quality accommodation at affordable rates. Public transport at your door.

■ **Sullivans Hotel** (AC BF CC glm H MA OS PI)
21 Oxford Street, Paddington ✉ NSW 2021 ☎ 9361-0211
☎ 936 3735 💻 sydney@sullivans.com.au
💻 www.sullivans.com.au
Located in fashionable Paddington near nightlife, art galleries, shopping. 11 km to airports, 6 km to beach. 62 rooms with shower/WC, TV and phone. Rates A$ 125-140. Bicycle hire.Free inhouse movies.

■ **Victoria Court Sydney** (AC BF CC g H)
122 Victoria Street, Potts Point ✉ NSW 2011 ☎ 9357 3200
☎ (1800) 63 05 05 🖨 9357 7606 💻 info@VictoriaCourt.com.au
💻 www.VictoriaCourt.com.au
Historic boutique Hotel. Close to Opera House, Oxford Street and beaches. All rooms with bath/WC, TV and phone. Rates A$ 125-250. 10% discount for SPARTACUS readers.

■ **415 on Bourke** (G H)
415 Bourke Street, Darlinghurst ✉ NSW 2010 ☎ 9360-9443
🖨 9331-3150
Close to gay venues. 4 rooms with antique furniture.

GUEST HOUSES

■ **Barracks. The** (CC G H lj)
19 Palmer Lane, Darlinghurst ✉ NSW 2010 (5 minutes walk to Oxford Street/Gay scene) ☎ 9360-5823 🖨 9358-4996
💻 barracks@chilli.net.au 💻 www.chilli.net.au/~barracks.

■ **Brickfield Hill-Bed and Breakfast Inn** (AC BF cc f GLM H MA)
403 Riley Street, Surry Hills ✉ NSW 2010 ☎ 9211 4886
🖨 9212 2556 💻 fields@zip.com.au 💻 www.zip.com.au/~fields
A warm and friendly guest house in the gay district, close to public transport, the city and beaches.5 rooms, some with private baths. Rates from A$95 to A$ 150.

■ **Governors on Fitzroy** (BF CC G H) All year
64 Fitzroy Street, Surry Hills ✉ NSW 2010 ☎ 9331-4652
🖨 9361-5094 💻 Info@governors.com.au
💻 www.governors.com.au
In the heart of gay Sydney, 3 blocks from Oxford Street. 6 rooms. Rates single A$ 85, double A$ 110 including breakfast.

■ **Oasis on Flinders** (CC G H OS NU WH) 0-24 h
106 Flinders Street ✉ NSW 1300 (2 min walk from Taylor Square)
☎ 9331 8791 🖨 9332 2247 💻 admin@oasisonflinders.com.au
💻 www.oasisonflinders.com.au

Exclusively for gay male naturalists, in the heart of Sydney. A large Victorian terrace with jacuzzi and sundecks.
Three bedrooms have TV, VCR, celing fans. One with en-suite.
Rates from A$ 110, per room
including continental breakfast.

OASIS on FLINDERS
SYDNEY AUSTRALIA
"Like staying with friends!"

A private retreat for
GAY MALE NATURISTS

Bed & Breakfast · In the heart of the city
Your hosts Colin and Gary
PO Box 532 Darlinghurst 1300 NSW
AUSTRALIA
Phone: +61.2.9331 8791
Fax: +61.2.9332 2247
Website www.oasisonflinders.com.au
Email admin@oasisonflinders.com.au

Australia/New South Wales — Sydney

SYDNEY'S Stellar Suites Boutique Hotel

Our location and friendly staff put us ahead of the rest.
All our Suites offer our guests spacious comfortable living. All rooms have Queen or King beds, ensuites, in-house movies, kitchenettes, air conditioning, mini bar, TV & Video.
Nothing is too much trouble for our staff from organizing a day tour to party tickets. If there is a way we will find it.
The Bus from the airport stops at our door.

4 Wentworth Avenue Sydney NSW 2000
Near the corner of Oxford St
Ph 61 2 9264 9754
Fax 61 2 9261 8006
www.stellarsuites.com.au
reservation@stellarsuites.com.au

■ **Villa Private Hotel. The** (GLM H)
413 Bourke Street, Darlinghurst ✉ NSW 2010 ☎ 9331-3602
🖷 9331-2101
Centrally located. 6 rooms with shared bath, TV, radio, kitchenette.

APARTMENTS

■ **Addison's on Anzac** (AC B CC E F g H)
147 Anzac Parade, Kensington ✉ NSW 2033 ☎ 9663 0600
☎ 1800 336 336 (free in AUS) 🖷 9313 6216
42 apartments. Fully furnished and serviced apartments, conveniently located.
■ **Apartment 902** (GLM H)
28 Macleay Street, Pott Point ✉ NSW 2011 ☎ 9358-1036
🖷 9358-1036 💻 apart902@khsnet.com.au
💻 www.khsnet.com/apart902
Central, self-catering studio with harbour views. Non-smoking. AU$ 130.-
■ **Seventeen Elizabeth Bay Road**
17 Elizabeth Bay Road ✉ NSW 2011 ☎ 9358 8999 🖷 9356 2491

PRIVATE ACCOMMODATION

■ **Ross & Hunter's B&B** (AC BF glm) All year
361 Empire Road, Enmore ✉ NSW 2340 (30 mins to city center, Bus 355,423,426 & 428) ☎ 9516 1193 🖷 rosshunter@ar.com.au
💻 www.ar.com.au/~rosshunter/guest/house.htm
■ **Share Accommodation for Travellers** (GLM) Mo-Fr 09:30-19h, Sa 10-16h
Level 1, 263 Oxford Street, Darlinghurst ✉ NSW 2010
☎ 9360 7744 🖷 9361 3729 ✉ service@asharespace.com.au
💻 www.sharespace.com.au
Share accommodation from 1 week to 1 year at prices to meet all budgets.

GENERAL GROUPS

■ **Cronulla Gay Group** every 2nd Wed 20 h
PO Box 195, Cronulla ✉ NSW 2230 ☎ 9521-7914
(Brian) Exists to provide both friendship and support for gay women and men.
■ **Gay & Lesbian Rights Lobby**
74-78 Oxford Street, Darlinghurst ✉ NSW 2010 ☎ 9360-6650
Postal Address: PO Box 9, Darlinghurst 2010 Anti-violence project, advice on legal, custody and educational problems.
■ **Gay Fathers**
103/412 Oxford Street, Paddington ✉ NSW 2021 ☎ 9360-3063
■ **Icebreakers** Tue 20-22 h
197 Albion Street, Surry Hills ✉ NSW 2010 ☎ 9360-2211
Gay social group for people of any age looking for new friends. Counselling Service.
■ **Lesbian & Gay Anti-Violence Project** (GLM)
PO Box 1178, Darlinghurst ✉ NSW 1300 ☎ 9360-6687
☎ (008) 637360 (toll free) 🖷 9380-5844 ✉ avp@kbdnet.net.au
💻 www.kbdnet.net.au
■ **Parents-FLAG**
PO Box 1152, Castle Hill ✉ NSW 2154 ☎ 9899-1101
(Heather) or ☎ 9630-5681 (Mollie) Parents and friends of gays and lesbians.

FETISH GROUPS

■ **Dolphin Motor Club** (LJ) Meets 2nd Fri at „The Keep"
PO Box E362, St. James ✉ NSW 2000 ☎ 9699-6588
■ **Sydney Roadrunners Motorcycle Club** Meeting 1st Mon at „Newtown Hotel"
PO Box 405 ✉ NSW 2015 ☎ 9699-9386
Meet every 3rd Sun. Phone Ian for information.

HEALTH GROUPS

■ **AIDS Council of NSW (ACON)** Mon-Fri 10-18 h
9 Commonwealth Street, Surry Hill ✉ NSW 2010 ☎ 9206-2000
■ **Kendall Centre. The**
26 Kendall Centre, Harris Park ✉ NSW 2150 ☎ 9893-9522
AIDS information and support, condoms, needle exchange and counselling.
■ **Order of Perpetual Indulgence**
PO Box 426, Grosvenor Place, ✉ NSW 2000
Part of the international Order.

HELP WITH PROBLEMS

■ **Twenty Ten Youth Service** (GLM p YG) Mo-Fr 10:00-18:30h
PO Box 213, Glebe ✉ NSW 2037 ☎ 9660-0539 🖷 9552 6324
✉ twenty@rainbow.net.au
Youth housing and support services for young gays and lesbians.

RELIGIOUS GROUPS

■ **Acceptance Sydney** Church service 20h Fri
28 Roslyn Gardens, Elizabeth Bay ✉ NSW 2011 ☎ 9361-5290
💻 sites.netscape.net/acceptsyd
Full name : Acceptance Sydney for gay and lesbian Catholics Incorporated.
■ **Aleph**
PO Box 120, 60 Blair Street, Bondi North ✉ NSW 2026
☎ 9300-9700
(Michael) Social group for gay & lesbian Jews.

Sydney ▶ Wollongong New South Wales/Australia

Ross and Hunter's Bed and Breakfast

All rooms have
- ensuites
- queen size bed
- air-conditioning
- breakfast included
- 5 minutes walk to Newtown

To make a reservation contact Ross or Hunter on
Sydney (02) 9516 1193 or visit
www.ar.com.au/~rosshunter/guest/house.htm

■ **Metropolitan Community Church of the Good Shepherd** Sun 19 h
15 Francis Street, Darlinghurst ✉ NSW 2011 ☎ 9638-3885
📠 9387-8371

SPECIAL INTEREST GROUPS

■ **Asian & Friends** Fri 19.30-22 h
PO Box 238, Darlinghurst ✉ NSW 2010 ☎ 9558-0061
(Gus or Jim) Social group.
■ **Choir Sydney Gay and Lesbian**
PO Box 649, Darlinghurst ✉ NSW 2010 ☎ 9698-2151
(Stephen) or ☎ 9361-6980 (Rob)
■ **Queer Screen Limited** (CC GLM MA)
PO Box 1081, Darlinghurst ✉ NSW 2010 ☎ 9332 4938
📠 9331 2988 💻 info@queerscreen.com.au
🖥 www.queerscreen.com.au
Group which organises the Sydney International Mardi Gras Film Festival
■ **Silk Road**
c/o Acon, 9 Commonwealth Street ✉ NSW 2010 ☎ 9206 2080
📠 9206 2069 💻 asia@acon.org.au
Asian gay and bisexual men. Free membership.
■ **Sydney Bisexual Support Network** 2nd/4th Mon
66 Albion Street, Surry Hills ✉ NSW 2010 ☎ 9698-1207
■ **Sydney Gay and Lesbian Business Association** (GLM MA)
PO Box 394, Darlinghurst ✉ NSW 1300 ☎ 9552 2000
📠 9225 9096 💻 sglba@iname.com 🖥 www.gaybusiness.com.au
Social networking for gays and lesbian business people. Monthly dinners & cocktail nights.

SPORT GROUPS

■ **Southern Cross Outdoor Group**
PO Box 411, Dee Why ✉ NSW 2099 ☎ 9907-9144
💻 scog@pinkboard.com.au 🖥 /www.pinkboard.com.au/~scog
Walking & social group for gay men in Greater Sydney.
■ **Team Sydney**
PO Box 1037, Darlinghurst ✉ NSW 2010 ☎ 9427-7729
Call Brian or Wayne ☎ 9311-3062 Sports group, regular newsletter.

SWIMMING

-Lady Jane Beach (g NU) (near South Head. Official nude beach. Lady Jane is very small and picturesque and is reached by taking the bush walk from Camp Cove.)
-Tamarama and nearby Bondi Beach (The rock area between the two beaches is the site of much heavy cruising)
-Obelisk Beach (g NU) (at Mosman, opposite side of the Harbour (from Lady Jane Bay) and next to Naval base)

CRUISING

All AYOR
-Centennial Park (Beecroft Road/Pennant Hill Road)
-Wentworth Hotel lobby (Bligh Street entrance)
-Opposite Clifford Park (Market Street, Parramatta)
-South side of Cooks River Bridge at Tempe
(Princes Highway, busy)
-Circular Quay
-Town Hall Station
-Belmore Park (Isabella Street, Parramatta)
-Chiswick Gardens (Ocean Street, Woolahra)
-Rocks at Balmoral (daytime)
-Centennial Park (AYOR)
-Lady Jane Beach (amongst the rocks, but be discreet)
-Grant's Park (south side of Coogee Beach from Surf Club to Sunstrip Pool; 11-2 h)
-Cremorne Wharf (north side of harbor; 10-1 h)
-Obelisk Beach, Mosman
-Reef Beach (NU) (Seaforth)
-Rifle Range at Maroubra
-Red Leaf Pool (Woollahra on harbor)
-Rushcutters Bay Park (AYOR at night) (all day long)
-Green Park (AYOR) (Darlinghurst)
-Rocks between Bondi Beach and Tamarama
-Alamein Fountain (AYOR R)(Fitzroy Park, Kings Cross)

Tweed Heads ☎ 02

BOOK SHOPS

■ **Borderline Books** (g)
28 Bay Street ✉ 2485 ☎ 5536-4271
■ **Keyhole Bookshop** (g)
9 Bay Street ✉ 2485 ☎ 7536-3197

Wollongong ☎ 02

DANCECLUBS

■ **Castaways** (AC b D f GLM MA OS S STV WE) 2nd & 4th Sat 20-2 h
17 Chopin Street ✉ NSW 2147 *(at Parramatta Golf Club, 10 min walk from Westmead & Parramatta stations)* ☎ 9674 5903
Entry A$ 5.00 - supporting people with HIV/AIDS
■ **Chequers** (A AC B CC D f GLM MA S STV) Wed-Sat 20-3 h
341 Crown Street ✉ 2500 *(on the rooftop of Piccadilly Shopping Centre)* ☎ 4226-3788
Bar and dance club with pool tables and pin ball machines. No entrance-fee on Thu and before 22 h on Wed Fri Sat.

SPARTACUS 2001/2002 | 23

Australia/New South Wales - Queensland | Wollongong ▶ Darwin

GENERAL GROUPS
■ **Men's Gay & Bisexual Coming Out Group**
PO Box 1144 ✉ 2500 ☎ 4221-4012
Advice and help.
■ **Wollongong Out Now**
☎ 4226-1163
Social group for gays & bis under 26.

HEALTH GROUPS
■ **AIDS Council of NSW**
129 Kembla Street, PO Box 1073 ✉ 2500 ☎ 4226-1163
📠 4226-9838.

SWIMMING
-Windang Beach (NU)

CRUISING
-Fairy Meadow Surf Club (at night)
-McCabe Park (AYOR-Police) (Fri and Sat night)

AUS-Northern Territory

Location: Northern AUS
Initials: NT
Time: GMT +9.5
Area: 1,346,200 km2 / 519,768 sq mi.
Population: 191,000
Capital: Darwin

✱ In the Northern Territory the age of consent is fixed at 18 years of age.

✱ In Northern Territory liegt das Schutzalter bei 18 Jahren.

✱ En Northern Territory, la majorité sexuelle est fixée à 18 ans.

⬢ En Northern Territory, la edad de consentimiento está estipulado en 18 años.

✖ In Northern Territory l'età legale per rapporti sessuali è di 18 anni.

Alice Springs ☎ 08

BARS
■ **Oasis Motel** (B F g h MA) gayish Fri 17-19 h
Gap Road ✉ NT 0870 ☎ 8952 1444
■ **Simpsons Gap Bar in Alice Springs** (B g) 18-2 h
Sheraton, Barrett Drive ✉ NT 0870 ☎ 8952 8000

RESTAURANTS
■ **Casa Nostra** (B F g)
Undoolya Road ✉ NT 0870 ☎ 8952 6749
■ **Swingers Café** (A F glm OS S) Mon-Tue 7.30-18, Wed-Sat -23 h, closed Sun
off Todd Mall ✉ NT 0870 ☎ 8952 9291
Mainly vegetarian.

GUEST HOUSES
■ **Rainbow Connection** (AC BF GLM MA msg Pl S)
Fri 08 - Mon 18h
22-24 Raggatt Street ✉ 0870 *(1.2 km from town center)*
☎ 889 526 411 📠 889 526 441 💻 rainbow@dove.net.au
Airport transfer and tours by arrangement. Social events available.

HEALTH GROUPS
■ **AIDS Council of Central Australia** Mon-Fri 9-17 h
19 Todd Street, PO Box 910 ✉ NT 0871 ☎ 8953 1118
📠 8953 4584.
■ **Alice Springs Hospital STD Unit** Mon-Fri 8-16 h
Gap Road/Steward Terrace ✉ NT 0870 ☎ 8950 2638

Darwin ☎ 08

BARS
■ **Mississippi Queen Restaurant-Rail Car Bar** (AC B CC F g MA N OS r s) 19-2 h
6 Gardiner Street ✉ NT 0800 ☎ 8981-3358
Bar restaurant.

RESTAURANTS
■ **Genghis Khan** (F g)
44 East Point Road ✉ NT 0800 ☎ 8981 3883

SEX SHOPS/BLUE MOVIES
■ **Fantasy Lane/Champions Two** (AC DR g MA P VS) 9-24 h
4 Charles Street, Stuart Park ✉ NT 0820 ☎ 8941-2441
Sex shop with gay back room.

TRAVEL AND TRANSPORT
■ **Gray Link Tour Operators**
PO Box 3826 ✉ NT 0801 ☎ 8948-1777 📠 8948-1777

HOTELS
■ **Mirambeena Resort Darwin** (AC b CC F H MA PI WO) 24 hours
64 Cavenagh Street ✉ NT 0800 *(city center)* ☎ 8946-0111
☎ (01800) 89-1100 📠 8981-5116 💻 info@mirambeena.com.au
💻 www.mirambeena.com.au
Single from A$ 140, double 140. Rates per room per night including 10% general sales tax.

HEALTH GROUPS
■ **Communicable Diseases Centre**
Block 4, Royal Darwin Hospital, Rocklands Drive ☎ 8920 8007
Antibody testing, inpatient and outpatient services.
■ **Northern Territory AIDS Council Inc.** (B GLM MA)
Mon-Fri 8.30-17h
6 Manton Street ✉ NT 0800 ☎ 8941 1711 ☎ 8981 6690
📠 8941 2590 💻 info@ntac.org.au 💻 www.ntac.org.au

CRUISING
-Vesty's Beach (between Sailing Club and Ski Club showers, good at night; fairly safe, take insect repellent)
-Mindil Beach (either side of the casino)
-Lameroo Beach (NU) (below the Darwin Hotel)
-Casarina Free Beach (NU) (turn right towards the gun turret)

AUS-Queensland

Location: North East AUS
Initials: QLD
Time: GMT +10
Area: 1,727,200 km2 / 666,872 sq mi.
Population: 3,451,000
Capital: Brisbane

✱ In Queensland the age of consent is fixed at 16 years of age and 18 years when anal sex is involved.

Brisbane Queensland/Australia

★ In Queensland liegt das Schutzalter bei 16 Jahren und bei 18, wenn Analverkehr praktiziert wird.

❋ En Queensland, la majorité sexuelle est fixée à 16 ans et à 18 pour la sodomie.

● En Queensland, la edad de consentimiento estipulada es de 16 años y de 18 años para el sexo anal.

✖ In Queensland l'età legale per rapporti sessuali è di 16 anni ed di 18 per i rapporti anali.

Brisbane ☎ 07

❋ This is the capital of Queensland, also known as the Sunshine State. After much needed legal reform the somewhat conservative city has become a popular holiday destination for gays. Although Brisbane is an important economic centre it has not developed as rapidly as Melbourne or Sydney. Brisbane is close to the beaches and to the Gold Coast (forty minutes to the South) and the Sunshine State is only an hour and a half to the North. There have emerged in the past few years a vast number of gay bars; restaurants and guest houses. Even the far North of Queensland is interesting for the gay tourist.
The people from Queensland are friendly and proud of their state with its sub-tropical climate. A major attraction is the Mr. Gay Queensland competition held in July. This competition invites contestants from throughout the state and has been a major contribution to the development of the gay movement in Queensland.

★ Brisbane ist die Hauptstadt des Bundesstaates Queensland, der auch den Namen „Sunshine-State" trägt. Nach einigen Gesetzesreformen ist die traditionell eher konservative Stadt heute ein sehr angenehmes Reiseziel für Schwule. Obwohl Brisbane ein wichtiges wirtschaftliches Zentrum ist, entwickelt es sich nicht so rasant wie etwa Melbourne oder Sydney. Von hier aus ist es nicht weit zu den Stränden und der Gold Coast (vierzig Minuten nach Süden) oder den Sunshine Coast (eineinhalb Stunden nach Norden). Dort und natürlich in Brisbane selbst haben in den letzten Jahren eine ganze Reihe von schwulen Bars, Restaurants und Pensionen eröffnet. Selbst der äußerste Norden von Queensland ist heute für den schwulen Touristen interessant.
Den Menschen hier wird nachgesagt, sie seien natürlich, freundlich und sehr stolz auf ihren Bundesstaat mit seinem subtropischen Klima. Eine große Attraktion ist der Mr.-Gay-Queensland-Wettbewerb im Juli. Er zieht Schwule aus dem ganzen Land an und stellt einen wesentlichen Beitrag zur Entwicklung des schwulen Selbstbewußtseins in Queensland dar.

❋ Brisbane, la capitale du Queensland („l'état du soleil") a 1,350 millions d'habitants. Brisbane s'est débarrassée de son esprit rétrograde depuis que le Queensland a commencé à attirer les touristes. La législation concernant l'homosexualité en fait aujourd'hui un des hauts lieux du tourisme gay. Brisbane est une ville très active et un centre économique important, sans avoir toutefois le côté tentaculaire de Melbourne ou Sydney.
De Brisbane, il faut 40 minutes pour atteindre les plages et les sites touristiques de Gold Coast (au sud) et une heure et demie pour aller à Sunshine Coast (au nord). Comme à Brisbane, vous y trouverez toute une série d'établissements gays (bars, restaurants, pensions et, dans le nord du Queensland, centres de vacances gays) tous assez récents. Les habitants du Queensland ont la réputation d'être simples, décontractés, sympathiques, très fiers de leur état et de son climat tropical. Depuis quelques années, on procède en juillet à l'élection de M. Gay-Queensland. Les candidats affluent des quatre coins de l'état. C'est un évènement important qui renforce la „gay pride".

● Brisbane es la capital del estado federal Queensland, que se conoce también como „Sunshine- State". En esta ciudad, tradicionalmente muy conservadora, se han llevado a cabo algunas reformas legislativas en los últimos año y como consecuencia Brisbane se ha convertido en un destino vacacional muy agradable para homosexuales. Aunque la ciudad es un importante centro económico, no se está desarrollando con la misma velocidad como por ejemplo Melbourne or Sydney. Brisbane está situada cerca de la las playas como la de Gold Coast (a 40 minutos dirección sur) o de Sunshine Coast (a hora y media hacia el norte). En estos lugares, así como en la misma ciudad de Brisbane se establecieron en el transcurso de los últimos años bares, restaurantes y hoteles gay. Incluso el extremo norte de Queensland es hoy en día interesante para el turista homosexual. La gente de Queensland tienen fama de ser sencillos y amables, así como muy orgullosos de su estado federal con su clima subtropical. Una de las mayores atracciones es la elección de „Mr.-Gay-Queensland" que tiene lugar cada año en el mes de julio. Este evento atrae homosexuales de todo el mundo y es una de las mayores contribuciones al desarrollo de la autoconfianza gay en Queensland.

✖ Brisbane è la capitale dello stato federale di Queensland che viene chiamato anche „Sunshine State". Dopo alcune riforme di legge la città tradizionalmente più conservatrice si presenta oggi come piacevole posto per i turisti gay. Sebbene Brisbane sia un'importante centro economico, non sta sviluppandosi altrettanto veloce come Melbourne e Sydney. Da qui non è lontano arrivare alle spiagge ed alla Gold Coast (a 40 minuti verso sud) o alla Sunshine Coast (a un'ora e mezzo verso nord). In questi posti ed anche a Brisbane stessa hanno aperto vari bar, ristoranti e pensioni gay. Perfino l'estremo nord di Queensland risulta interessante per il turista gay. Si dice, che gli abitanti di Queensland siano cordiali, rilassati e molto orgogliosi del loro clima tropicale. Una grande attrazione nel luglio è il concorso del Mr.-Gay- Queensland, che attira i gay di tutto il paese e rappresenta un'importante contributo allo sviluppo dell'orgoglio gay.

GAY INFO

■ **Gayline** 19-22 h
✉ 4000 ☎ 3839-3277 ☎ 3891-7377
Information and counselling.

■ **Gaywaves** Wed 18-21 h (FM 102.1 MHz)
✉ 4000 ☎ 3252-1555

■ **Queensland Pride**
PO Box 591, Mount Gravatt ✉ 4000 ☎ 3392-2922 📠 3392-2923
Free monthly publication.

■ **Queer Radio** every 2nd Wed 19-21 h on 4ZZZ fm, 102.1
☎ 3252-1555 📧 john@4zzz.org.au

TOURIST INFO

■ **Brisbane Visitors & Convention Bureau**
PO Box 12260, Elizabeth Street ✉ 4002 ☎ 3221-8411
📠 322 95 126

BARS

■ **Beat Nightclub** (AC B D f glm MA s SNU STV) 20-5 h
677 Ann Street, Fortitude Valley ✉ 4006 Brunswick train station, in Mall. ☎ 3252-2543
Also Cockatoo Club

■ **Options Niteclub & Cafe** (B D F GLM S STV) Café 17-?, Club 20-? h, shows Fri-Sat
18 Little Edward Street, Spring Hill ✉ 4000 ☎ 3831-4214

Australia/Queensland — Brisbane

■ **Raptors** (B G MA) Tue-Sat 17-?, Sun 16-? h
c/o The Brunswick Hotel, Brunswick Street, New Farm
☎ (015) 72-5004
■ **Russel's Longbar** (B G MA)
Shamrock Hotel, 186 Brunswick Street, Fortitude Valley
☎ 3252 2421
■ **Wickham** (B CC D F glm H MA S VS) Mon 9-24h, Tue-Thu -03h, Fri -05h, Sat 10-05h Sun -03h
308 Wickham Street, Fortitude Valley ✉ QLD 4006 ☎ 3852 1301
3 bars - a DJ party bar, a lounge for relaxing with cocktails and the Gayming Room for those who like to gamble.

MEN'S CLUBS
■ **Den. The** (B CC G) Mon-Thu 20-?, Fri 20-Mon ? h
187 Brunswick Street, Fortitude Valley ✉ 4006 *courner of Brunswick St.& Barry Drive* ☎ 3854-1981
Gay men's club and bookshop. Large range of toys, books, leather.

CAFES
■ **Moray Café** (B F g OS) 9-22, Sun 10-15.30 h, closed Mon
Moray Street/Merthyr Road, New Farm ✉ 4000 ☎ 3254-1342
■ **Ric's Café**
Brunswick Street Mall, Fortitude Valley ✉ 4006 ☎ 3854-1772
■ **Three Monkees Coffee & Tea House**
58 Mollison Street, South Brisbane ✉ 4101 ☎ 3844-6045

RESTAURANTS
■ **Boticelli's** (B F glm)
The Broadwalk, Breakfast Creek Wharf, Newstead ☎ 3257 1501
■ **Francesca's Restaurant**
195 Wickham Terrace, Spring Hill ✉ 4000 ☎ 3831-4125

ESCORTS & STUDIOS
■ **Male Order**
☎ (0500) 55 66 40

SAUNAS/BATHS
■ **Bodyline Spa & Sauna** (AC b BF G MA msg P SA SB VS WH) Sun-Thu 12-3, Fri Sat 12-7 h
43 Ipswich Road, Woollongabba ✉ QLD 4102 ☎ 3391 4285
Free breakfast at the week ends.
■ **Wet Spa & Sauna** (AC CC f G MA P SA SB VS WH) Mon-Thu 11-1, Fri Sat -3 h
22 Jeays Street, Bowen Hills ✉ QLD 4005 *(5 min walk from Bowen Hills railways station)* ☎ 3854-1383
Modern sauna with many facilities. Busy on Sun for Wet Day.

BOOK SHOPS
■ **Signal Bookshop** (g) Mon-Thu 10-24, Fri-Sun 0-24 h
191 Brunswick Street, Fortitude Valley ✉ 4006 ☎ 3252-7191

HOTELS
■ **Sportsman Hotel** (AC B CC f GLM H MA STV) 13-? h
130 Leichardt Street, Spring Hill ✉ QLD 4000 ☎ 3831-2892
🖷 3839-2106
Rates from A$ 25-40 (bf incl.) Gay hotel and 3 bars.

GENERAL GROUPS
■ **Foothold**
☎ 3349-0897 ☎ 3348-8387 (Richard)
Social and contact group for gay and bisexual men over 26.
■ **GLADS**
☎ 3844-9599
Gay and lesbian alcohol and drug support group. Meets Wed 20 h, Gladstone Road Medical.

■ **Jumbucks**
PO Box 205, Red Hill ✉ 4000
Club for men over 21.
■ **QUT Campus Queers**
PO Box 511, Bulimba ✉ 4171 ☎ 3844-4565
or ☎ 3255 0215 (Damien) or ☎ 3399 5471 (Lorelle). Gay & Lesbian student group.

FETISH GROUPS
■ **Brisbane Boot Co**
PO Box 187, Red Hill ✉ 4059
Meeting 1st Sat 21 h at Russels Longbar, Shamrock Hotel, Brunswick Street, Fortitude Valley.
■ **Brisbears** 3rd Sat 21 h
PO Box 6, Nundah ✉ 4012 ☎ 3266 8847
📧 brisbears@geocities.com
Social Club for men who like hairy men. Meets at Sportsman Hotel, downstairs bar.

HEALTH GROUPS
■ **Brisbane Gay & Lesbian Health Service**
38 Gladstone Road, Highgate Hill ✉ 4101 ☎ 3844-6806
Gay male doctor, comprehensive medical service.
■ **Gay & Lesbian Welfare Association** Helpline 19-22 h
PO Box 1078, Fortitude Valley ✉ QLD 4006 ☎ 3891 7377 (gay line) ☎ (1800) 249 377 (toll free)
Information & counselling.
■ **Queensland AIDS Council** Mon-Fri 9-17 h
32 Peel Street, /PO Box 3142, South Brisbane QLD 4101 ✉ 4000
☎ 3444-1990 ☎ (800) 177-434. 🖷 844-4206
HIV/AIDS information and support.
■ **Queensland Positive People**
PO Box 3142, South Brisbane ✉ 4000 ☎ 3846-3939
HIV+ support group, Tue social day, Fri night open social support, counselling, workshops and more.
■ **QUIVAA** Mon-Fri 9-17 h
191 Brunswick Street, Fortitude Valley ✉ QLD 4006 *(city center)*
☎ 3252-5390 🖷 3252-5392 📧 quivaa@quivaa.org.au
Advice and help for injecting drug users. Needle exchange. HIV education & support.

HELP WITH PROBLEMS
■ **Brisbane AA-Gay & Lesbian Alcoholics Anonymous** Sat at RBH
☎ 3844-7840
(Matt) or ☎ 3359-0035 (Janice).

SPECIAL INTEREST GROUPS
■ **Australian Bisexual Network**
PO Box 490, Lutwyche ✉ 4030 ☎ 3857-2500
■ **Rangers**
☎ 3349-0897
Camping, adventure and social club for gay men.
■ **Sunboys**
☎ 3848-5268
Nudist club for men. Swim nights 3rd Sun each month.

SPORT GROUPS
■ **AFAA-Australian Free Athletic Association**
PO Box 428, Spring Hill ✉ 4000
Queensland gay sports group.

Bundaberg ☎ 07

GENERAL GROUPS
■ **Bundaberg Gay & Lesbian Support**
PO Box 2695 ✉ 4670 ☎ 4152-9999
Social/support group.

SWIMMING
-Mon Repos (G NU) (All year round. Go north, past first set of rocks only)

CRUISING
-Corner of Quay and Targo Streets (in toilets or in park during the day and early evening - be discreet)

Cairns ☎ 07

TOURIST INFO
■ **Far North Queensland Promotion Bureau Ltd.**
Grafton Street/Hartley Street ✉ 4870 ☎ 4051-3588

BARS
■ **Chapel Café** (AC B CC F NG s) 12-2 h
91 Esplanade, Level 1 ✉ 4870 ☎ 4041-4222
Great ocean views and the best bar in Cairns. Best after 22 h.
■ **John Henrys Bar and Café** (A AC B F MA NG OS WE) Thu-Tue 17-1 h, closed Wed
92 Abbott Street ✉ 4870 *(upstairs)* ☎ 4031-4849
■ **Nu Trix** (B D GLM TV) Wed-Sun 21-05 h
53 Spence Street ✉ QLD 4870 *(upstairs)* ☎ 4051-8223

RESTAURANTS
■ **Red Ochre Grill** (AC B CC F g) Mon-Sat lunch & dinner, Sat Sun dinner
43 Shields Street ✉ QLD 4870 ☎ 4051-0100
Seafood and Australian specialities. Sun outside dining and men's strip show.

TRAVEL AND TRANSPORT
■ **Boyz Brick Road** (CC G) 8.30-17.30
256 Sheridan Street ✉ 4870 ☎ 4041 0661 📠 4041 0662
✉ sales@boyz-brick-road.com.au 💻 www.boyz-brick-road.com.au
Gay mens tour company offering information on touring around Australia.
■ **Ocean Spirit Cruises** (B CC glm)
143 Lake Street ☎ 4031-2920 📠 4031-4344
Cruises, also gay-lesbian only.
■ **Out Touring Australia** (CC GLM) 0-24 h
PO Box 12 14 ☎ 4051-1485 📠 4052-1478
Tour and accomodation booking service.

HOTELS
■ **Lugger Bay Beach Resort** (A AC B BF CC F GLM H lj MA msg NU P PI WH WO)
PO Box 18, Mission Beach ✉ QLD 4852 ☎ 4068-8400
📠 4068-8586
Beachfront luxury private resort. Room rates from A$ 45 pp/pn to 650 pn (penthouse).
■ **Marlin Cove Quest Resort** (AC CC H MA msg OS PI WH)
2 Keem Street, PO Box 365, Trinity Beach ✉ QLD 4079
☎ 4057-8299 📠 4057-8909 ✉ regency@cairns.net.au
Located 15 minutes drive north of Cairns. 100 apartments with bath/shower/WC, balcony/patio, radio, kitchenette, phone. Hotel provides own key, car park, bicycle hire and tennis lawn. Rates A$ 120-190, add. bed 15.

THE ONLY GAY HOTEL
Cairns • Australia

New Hotel — *Pool/Spa*
26 Rooms — *Sauna/Gym*
Restaurant — *Tour desk*
Bar — *Car Rental*

P.O. Box 7544 Cairns 4870.
Phone: +61 7 40514644 Fax: +61 7 40510103
E-Mail: 18_24 James@internetnorth.com.au
Web Site: http://www.18-24James.com.au

■ **Tentative Nests** (BF F CC g H)
26 Barron Falls Road, Kuranda ✉ QLD 4872 ☎ 4093-9555
📠 4093-9053
Open all year. 8 cabine style tents on platforms. Located deep in the rainforest. Rates from A$ 55 per person, half-board A$ 88. Car park.
■ **Turtle Cove Resort** (! AC B BF CC F GLM H MA msg NU OS PI VS WH WO) All year, 24h
PO Box 158 Smithfield ✉ QLD 4878 *(Captain Cook Highway between Cairns and Port Douglas)* ☎ 4059-1800 📠 4059-1969
✉ gay@turtlecove.com.au 💻 www.turtlecove.com.au
Turtle cove with 31 first class rooms, all with private facilities and ocean views as well as a private beach. Rates A$ 110-265 per room. Airport pick-up. Australias leading resort with many facilities and great fun.
■ **18-24 James** (AC b BF CC F G H MA N OS PI SA WH WO)
Bar/restaurant 10-24, reception 7-21 h
18-24 James Street ✉ QLD 4870 *(in city centre)* ☎ 4051 4644
📠 4051 0103 ✉ 18_24james@internetnorth.com.au
💻 www.18-24James.com.au
Free airport pickup. All rooms with TV, radio, phone, tea & coffee makers, refrigerator, shower/WC, king-size beds. Rates include free tropical breakfast. Single from A$ 95, double or twin A$ 120 per room. Additional person A$ 25 and shared rooms (max. 4) A$ 55 per person. Car hire and tours can be arranged by hotel.

Australia/Queensland — Cairns ▶ Surfer's Paradise

HELP WITH PROBLEMS
■ **Gayline** Wed-Sun 19-23 h
☏ 4051-0279

SWIMMING
-Bucchans Point/Ellis Beach (25 km north of Cairns. Take bus 2xx or 1A from city. Unofficial nude beach)
-Yorkey's Knob (20 km north of Cairns)

CRUISING
-Cairns Esplanada (from city north to hospital).

Noosa ☏ 07

RESTAURANTS
■ **Berardo's Restaurant and Bar** (B F glm) 7 days a week for dinner.
50 Hastings Street ✉ QLD 4567 ☏ 5447 5666
Friendly with quality service and fine contemporary Australian cuisine.

TRAVEL AND TRANSPORT
■ **Australian Gay Travel Service**
PO Box 302 ✉ QLD 4567 ☏ 5448 3444 📠 5448 3711
✉ rods@ozemail.com.au 🖥 Gaytravelaustralia.com
Australian and South Pacific gay travel consultants. Over 20 years experience in the gay travel industry.

GUEST HOUSES
■ **Falcons At Peregian** (BF CC G msg lj MA msg NU OS PI WO) All year
PO Box 254 ✉ QLD 4573 ☏ 5448 3710 📠 5448 3712
✉ falconsap@hotmail.com 🖥 www.linstar.com.au/falcons
Located in the „sunshine coast" region of Queensland, 100 km north of Brisbane. 6 rooms with bath/WC, own key. Rates single from A$ 60, double from 70. Free continental bf.

APARTMENTS
■ **Hideaway. The** (AC CC glm H NU OS PI) Open all year 24h
386 David Low Way ✉ 4573 (10km south of Noosa & 100km north of Brisbane) ☏ 5448 1006 📠 5448 3891
Fully self-contained holiday apartments near Noosa. Rates per double from A$ 55, – to A$ 110 per night. Weekly rates available.
■ **Noosa Cove Holiday Apartments** (CC GLM H MA NU OS PI)
82 Upper Hastings Street ✉ QLDS 4567 5 mins walk from Noosa bus transit terminal ☏ 5449 2668 📠 5447 5373
✉ noosacove@bigpond.com
🖥 www.users.bigpond.com/noosacove
Luxury studio, 1 and 2 bedroom holiday apartments- self contained- in tropical garden setting. Only 3 mins walk to beach.

SWIMMING
-Alexandria Beach (45 minutes through National Park from Noosa Heads. Nude beach. Popular with gays.)
-The Spit (end of Hastings street)
-Noosa wods (mouth of Noosa river)
-Bay Beach (second beach back-river beach)

Peregian Beach ☏ 07

APARTMENTS
■ **Horizons at Peregian** (AC CC GLM H MA NU OS PI WH) 07-22h
45 Lorikeet Drive ✉ QLD 4573 (80 mins north of Brisbane.300m to gay beach) ☏ 5448 3444 📠 5448 3711

✉ admin@horizons-peregian.com
🖥 www.horizons-peregian.com/gay
Apartments from A$ 98 per night. Suites with private roof garden and spa. Situated on the beachfront.

Rockhampton ☏ 07

GENERAL GROUPS
■ **Mackay M.A.G.S.**
PO Box 1145, Mackay ✉ QLD 4740 ☏ 4953 0888
Support and social group.

CRUISING
-Central Park (AYOR) (between St. Joseph Cathedral and fountain)

Surfer's Paradise ☏ 07

BARS
■ **Meeting Place Bar & Club** Tu-Sa 20:00-05:00h, Su 17:00-?
26 Orchard Avenue ✉ 4217 ☏ 5526 2337
■ **R.U.1.2.** (B G MA) 16-? h
Paradise Center ✉ 4217 (1st floor, enter from beach and upstairs)
☏ (015) 59-0867

SEX SHOPS/BLUE MOVIES
■ **Club R 18+** (AC b CC DR G LJ MA msg P SNU VS) 16-24 h
1/3 Allsion Street ✉ QLD 4217 (in basement car park at Parkrise building. Look for big number ONE on front door) ☏ 5539 9955

TRAVEL AND TRANSPORT
■ **Surfers Paradise Gay Vacations** (CC G)
PO Box 7260, G.C.M.C. ✉ 4217 ☏ 5592-2223 📠 5592-2209
This gay-run agency specializes in finding gay friendly accommodation at discount rates from budget (from A$55 per night) to 5 star. Also multi-share at A$30 per night. Call or write for free brochure. It has its own all male gay guesthouse at A$ 50 per night.

HOTELS
■ **Islander Resort Hotel** (g H) 24 hours
6 Beach Road ✉ QLD 4217 (Central Surfer's Paradise)
☏ 5538 8000 📠 5592 2762 ✉ info@parkregis.com.au
🖥 www.parkregis.com
■ **Sleeping Inn Surfers** (BF CC GLM H PI) 8-22 h
26 Whelan Street ✉ QLD 4217 (5 minutes to gay beach & venues)
☏ 5592-4455 📠 5592-5266 ✉ sleepinginn@hotmail.com
🖥 www.sleepinginn.com.au
8 double, 8 single rooms, 5 apartments, also shared rooms and dorms backpacker style. Rates - double from A$ 40, single A$ 30, additional bed A$ 15. Apartment A$ 60. Shared room or dormatory A$15 per person.

GUEST HOUSES
■ **Paradise Retreat** (AC BF G MA msg NU OS PI VS WH) 24 hours a day, 7 days a week
102 Admiralty Drive ✉ 4217 ☏ 5571 1414 ☏ (1800) 060 069
📠 5531 0614 ✉ staygay@ion.com.au
The only exclusively Gay accomodation in Surfers Paradise. Central Dress Circle Location, Stunning Water Views. All Amenities including Pool, Sundeck, and Video Lounge Relaxed and friendly gay environment. Comprehensive knowledge of Gay venues and activiteies on the Gold Coast.

Queensland/Australia

Turtle Cove is the hottest spot in the South Pacific. On its own gay, private beach between Cairns & Port Douglas in Australia's Tropical North, it has all the facilities for a vacation...

...with the emphasis on gay fun, sun and service.

TURTLE COVE
CAIRNS
AUSTRALIA

Opposite the Great Barrier Reef

TURTLE COVE RESORT

Between Cairns & Port Douglas in the Tropical North

Phone: +61 7 40 591 800
Fax: +61 7 40 591 969
gay@turtlecove.com.au
www.turtlecove.com.au

SPARTACUS 2001/2002 | 29

Australia/Queensland - South Australia | Surfer's Paradise ▶ Adelaide

APARTMENTS
■ **Stay Gay Apartments** (CC G H msg)
PO Box 7260, Gold Coast Mail Centre ✉ QLD 4217 ☎ 5592-2223
📠 5592-2209

GENERAL GROUPS
■ **Gold Coast Gay Info-Line**
☎ 5592-2377

HEALTH GROUPS
■ **Gold Coast Branch, Queensland AIDS Commitee** Wed 19-22 h
PO Box 13 30 ✉ 4217 ☎ 5538-4611
■ **Queensland AIDS Council**
105 Frank Street, Labrador ✉ 4295 *Runaway Bay* ☎ 5538-8922

SWIMMING
-Broadbeach (AYOR) (Opposite Broadbeach International Hotel & Oasis Shopping Complex. Be a little bit more discreet, as it is usually mixed and touristy)
-Southport Spit (AYOR) (Opposite Seaworld Dolphin and Whale Arena, very popular on Sat and Sun)

CRUISING
-The spit (dunes oposite Seaworld)
-Southport swimming pool (opposite Southport's Australia Fair Complex, best at night)
-Broadbeach Surf Life Saving Club (on the beach, best at night)

Toowoomba ☎ 07

HEALTH GROUPS
■ **Queensland AIDS Council** 0-24 h
8 Anzac Avenue ✉ QLD 4352 ☎ 4639-1820

CRUISING
-Margaret Street, near Queens Park
-Queens Park

Townsville ☎ 07

BARS
■ **Sovereign Hotel** (B GLM MA) Wed-Sun
807 Flinders Street ✉ QLD 4810 ☎ 4771 2909

SEX SHOPS/BLUE MOVIES
■ **Sweethearts Adult Bookshop**
206a Charters Towers Road, Hermit Park ✉ QLD 4810
☎ 4725-1431

GUEST HOUSES
■ **Sandy´s on the Strand** (AC BF E G msg OS PI)
PO Box 193 ✉ QLD 4810 ☎ 4772 1193 📠 4772 1193
Situated on the beach front. Facilities of the room includes shower/WC, telephone and balcony. Rates from A$ 55-75 (breakfast inc.).

SWIMMING
-Balding Bay/Rocky Bay (AYOR) (on Magnetic Island. Popular with gays who tend to congregate at the far end.)
-Beyond Pallaranda (g NU)

CRUISING
-Flinders Mall (in centre of city; daytime on week days)
-Beach and park (after dark)
-[P] between Rower's Bay and Pallaranda
-Strand Park
-Queen Park

AUS-South Australia

Location: South AUS
Initials: SA
Time: GMT +9.5
Area: 984,000 km2 / 379,922 sq mi.
Population: 1,485,000
Capital: Adelaide

※ In South Australia the age of consent is fixed at 17 years of age.

★ In South Australia liegt das Schutzalter bei 17 Jahren.

※ En South Australia, la majorité sexuelle est fixée à 17 ans.

● En South Australia, la edad de consentimiento está estipulado en 17 años.

✖ In South Australia l'età legale per rapporti sessuali è di 17 anni.

Adelaide ☎ 08

※ The elegant capital of South Australia with a population of 1,000,000 is a beautiful city, with hills to one side, beaches on the other, and parks and gardens throughout the central city area. The journey to the picturesque wine-growing areas of the Barossa Valley or McClaren Vale is a must. From Adelaide the tourist can strike out to the opal mines of Coober Pedy (a full day's journey by car) or the wildlife of Kangaroo Island (six hours). South Australia is a State with a history of social reform. It was the first State in Australia to give women the vote. In 1976 it was the first state to legalise homosexual activity.
Gay life in Adelaide is like the city itself, quiet, friendly, polite, even a little repressed for most of the year, but erupting into periods of considerable activity and fun at certain times. The International Arts Festival every two years in April (next one in 2002) has a Fringe Festival with significant gay and lesbian activities. The Gay Community celebrates Stonewall in June „Sleaze Ball" as well as a gay/lesbian arts festival in November („Feast").

★ Eingebettet zwischen Hügeln auf der einen Seite und Stränden auf der anderen liegt Adelaide, die schöne und elegante 1-Mio.-Einwohner-Hauptstadt South Australias. Parks und Gärten durchziehen das Stadtzentrum. Die Fahrt zu den malerischen Weinanbaugebieten von Barossa Valley oder McClaren Vale ist ein Muß. Von Adelaide aus kann der Tourist den Weg zu den Opalminen von Coober Pedy (eine Tagesreise mit dem Auto) oder zu den wildlebenden Tieren von Kangaroo Island (sechs Stunden) einschlagen. South Australia ist ein Staat mit einer von sozialen Reformen geprägten Geschichte: Es war der erste Staat Australiens, der Frauen das Wahlrecht einräumte. 1976 war es der erste Staat, der homosexuelle Aktivitäten legalisierte.
Schwules Leben in Adelaide ist wie die Stadt: still, freundlich und höflich. Während es den größten Teil des Jahres sehr ruhig zugeht, gibt es doch zu bestimmten Zeiten reges Treiben: das „International Arts Festival" findet alle zwei Jahre im April statt (das nächste 2002); es wird begleitet vom „Fringe Festival" mit bedeutender schwuler und lesbischer Anteilnahme. Die Schwule Gemeinde feiert im Juni ihr Stonewall- Fest und einen "Sleaze Ball" (abgehalten in einem alten Gefängnis) im August.

※ Adélaïde, élégante métropole du sud de l'Australie (plus d'un million d'habitants) est située sur plusieurs collines bordées

Adelaide — South Australia/Australia

de plages. Au centre de la ville, il y a de nombreux parcs et jardins. A voir absolument: les vignobles pittoresques de Barossa Valley ou de Mc Claren Vale. D'Adélaïde, on atteint sans problème les mines d'opale de Coober Pedy (une journée de voiture) ou le parc d'animaux sauvages de Kangoroo Island (six heures de voiture). South Australia est un état dont l'histoire est marquée par les réformes sociales: c'est le premier Etat d'Australie qui a accordé le droit de vote aux femmes et qui, en 1976, a légalisé l'homosexualité.

A Adélaïde, la vie gay est à l'image de la ville: calme, sympathique et polie. Diverses manifestations culturelles apportent un peu d'animation dans cette ville plutôt calme toute l'année. En avril, la biennale International Arts Festival (la prochaine en 2002) est suivie du Fringe Festival où les gays et les lesbiennes sont largement représentés.

Situada entre lomas y playas paradisiacas se encuentra Adelaide, la elegante capital de South Australia con 1 millon de habitantes. El centro de la ciudad esta lleno de parques y jardines. Se recomienda la visita de sus pintorescas regiones vinícolas, Barossa Valley y McClaren. Desde Adelaide se puede hacer una excursión en coche a las minas de ópalo de Coober Pedy o bien visitar los animales de Kangoroo Island que viven alli en su entorno natural sin jaulas (a 6 horas de distancia). South Australia es un estado que se caracteriza por su história de reformas sociales: Fue el primer estado australiano, que concedió a las mujeres el derecho al voto, así como en 1976 fue el primer estado que legalizó las actividades homosexuales. La vida gay en Adelaide es como la ciudad misma: tranquila, amable y respetuosa. Aunque la mayoria del año transcurre con relativa tranquilidad, hay algunas fechas cuando realmente se anima: Uno de los eventos más importantes es el Internacional Arts Festival, que se celebra cada dos años (el próximo en 2002) en el mes de abril, que junto con el Fringe Festival cuenta con una gran participación de homosexuales y lesbianas. La comunidad gay celebra en junio su festival de Stonewall y un "Sleaze Ball" (fiesta y baile) que tiene lugar en una antigua cárcel en el mes de agosto.

La capitale dell'Australia del sud conta un milione di abitanti, è una bella città situata tra spiagge e colline, ricca di parchi e di giardini. Un'escursione ai pittoreschi vigneti di Barossa Valley o di Mc Claren Valley è obbligatoria. Da Adelaide si possono raggiungere le miniere di opale di Coober Pedy (un giorno di viaggio in auto) o il parco faunistico di Kangoroo Island (sei ore di viaggio). Importanti riforme sociali caratterizzano la storia dell'Australia del sud. Questo stato concesse per primo il diritto di voto alle donne, e nel 1976 legalizzo per primo alcune attività omosessuali. La vita gay in Adelaide è come la città: tranquilla, socievole ed educata. Durante l'anno piuttosto appartata, ma in certi periodi ricca di considerevoli attività. L'International Arts Festival (biennale in aprile, il prossimo nel 2002) accompagna il Fringe Festival con molti partecipanti omosessuali. Le comunità gay festeggiano in giugno la Stonewallfest e in agosto la Sleaze Ball (tenuta in una ex prigione).

GAY INFO

■ "GT" Adelaide Gay Times
18 Freemasons Lane ✉ SA 5000 ☎ 8232-1544 📠 8232 1560
💻 AdelaideGT_reception@satellitemedium.comau
Fortnightly publication. Free at gay venues throughout Adelaide.
■ Gay Radio Sun 12-14 h (3 D Radio 93.7 FM)
☎ 8410-0937

CULTURE

■ Gay and Lesbian Community Library (GLM) Mon-Fr 9-17, Sat 14-17h
Darling House, 64 Fullarton Road, Norwood ✉ SA 5061 ☎ 8362 3106 📠 8363 1046 💻 glcssa@glcssa.org.au
💻 www.glcssa.org.au

TOURIST INFO

■ South Australian Travel Centre
1 King William Street ☎ 8212-1505 📠 8303-2231

BARS

■ Edinburgh Castle Hotel (B D F GLM MA OS STV) Mon-Thu-24, Fri& Sat -03, Sun -02h
Gray Street/Currie Street ✉ SA 5000 ☎ 8410 1211

CAFES

■ Universal Wine Bar (B g)
258 Rundle Street ✉ 5000 ☎ 8232-5000

DANCECLUBS

■ Mars Bar (B D g MA S) 21-? h
122 Gouger Street ✉ 5000 ☎ 8231-9639
Popular Fri. Fri-Sun entry A$ 5.

RESTAURANTS

■ Magic Flute (B F g)
109 Melbourne Street ✉ 5000 ☎ 8267-3172

SEX SHOPS/BLUE MOVIES

■ Pink Pussy (g)
135 b Goodwood Road, Goodwood ✉ 5034 ☎ 8271-5975
Full range of adult books, toys and novelties.
■ Ram Lounge and Video (G VS) 11-2 h
71 Hindley Street ✉ 5000 (*Nightlife Centre. Via Club X*)
☎ 8410-0444
■ Windsor Adult Bookshop (g)
364 North East Road ✉ 5000 (*Shop 1*) ☎ 8369-0088

SAUNAS/BATHS

■ Phoenix (AC b DR F G lj MA p SA SB sol VS WH WO) Mon-Thu 12-3, Fri-Sat 12-7 h
147 Waymouth Street, Light Square ✉ SA 5000 (*near main train station and main bus terminal, 1st floor*) ☎ 8221 7002
Sling rooms, maze area, internet cafe.
■ Pulteney 431 (AC b DR f G MA PI SA SB WH) 12-1, Fri Sat -3 h
431 Pulteney Street ✉ SA 5000 (*next to Astor Hotel*) ☎ 8223 7506

BOOK SHOPS

■ Imprints Booksellers (CC glm) Mon-Thu, Sat 9-18, Fri -21, Sun 12-18 h
80 Hindley Street ✉ 5000 ☎ 8231-4454

TRAVEL AND TRANSPORT

■ Parkside Travel Mo-Fri 8.30-17.30, Sat 9-12 h
70 Glen Osmond Road ✉ 5063 (*Parkside*) Bus stop 2
☎ 8274 1222 📠 8272 7371 💻 parkside@harveyworld.com.au

HOTELS

■ Rochdale Bed & Breakfast (AC BF CC F glm H OS p PI) 24h
349 Glen Osmond Road, Glen Osmond ✉ 5064 ☎ 8379-7498
📠 8379-2483 💻 rochdale@camtech.net.au
All ensuite traditional B&B with fully enclosed solar heated pool. Close to city center. Easy access to beach

APARTMENTS

■ Greenways Apartments (AC CC g H MA N) All year
45 King William Road ✉ SA 5006 ☎ 8267 5903 📠 8267 1790

Australia/South Australia — Adelaide ▶ Clare Valley

PRIVATE ACCOMMODATION
■ **City Apartments** (g H) Reservations: 8.30-17.30 h, Sat 8.30-12 h
70 Glen Osmond Road, Parkside ✉ 5063 ☎ 8274-1222 🖷 8272-7371
Centrally located 1-3 bedroom apartments. Economy, Executive, and Superior in different locations in the city. Rates from A$ 50-105.

GENERAL GROUPS
■ **Gay and Lesbian Immigration Task Force**
PO Box 110, Woodville ✉ 5011
Immigration Advice.
■ **Inside Out/Work It Out**
c/o The Second Story Youth Health Service, 57 Hyde St.
☎ 8232-0233
Workshops and educational programms for gays and bis under 26.
■ **Thursday Night Drop-in Centre** (b f G MA) Thu 19.30-22.30 h
Box Factory Community Centre, 59 Regent Street South ✉ 5000
(between Carrington and Halifax Street, side entrance)
Social group.

HEALTH GROUPS
■ **AIDS Council of South Australia**
PO Box 907, Kent Town ✉ 5000 ☎ 8362-1611 ☎ (008) 88-8559 (toll free)
Services for people living with HIV/AIDS and their lovers, families and carers, including counselling advocacy, treatments info, referrals, housing and financial assistance.
■ **Clinic 275** Mon Thu Fri 10-16.30, Tue Wed 12-19h
275 North Terrace ✉ 5000 *(1st floor)* ☎ 8226-6375
📧 stdservices@dhs.sa.gov.au 🖥 www.stdservices.on.net
HIV-testing.
■ **Flinders Medical Centre**
Flinders Drive, Bedford Park ✉ 5042 ☎ 8204-5192
HIV testing. HIV clinic. Wed mornings by appointment only.
■ **South Australian Bobby Goldsmith Foundation**
PO Box 247, Kent Town ✉ 5000 ☎ 8362-1611 ☎ 1800 888 559 (toll free) or ☎ 8212-2382 (Chris).
Organization which provides living expenses for PWA in financial difficulty.

HELP WITH PROBLEMS
■ **Gay & Lesbian Counselling Service of South Australia** 19-22, Sat Sun 14-17 h
PO Box 2011 ✉ SA 5063 ☎ 8362-3223 ☎ (1 800) 182 233 (toll-free)
■ **People living with HIV/AIDS** (MA s)
PO Box 2603 Kenttown ✉ 5031 ☎ 8231-0300 🖷 8231-9989
Antibody positive support group.

RELIGIOUS GROUPS
■ **Acceptance**
☎ 8337-8720 *(Robert)*
Catholic group.
■ **Metropolitan Community Church** Sun service 19-? h at Quaker Meeting Hall
40 A Pennington Terrace, GPO Box 10 06, ✉ 5000 ☎ 8298-4374
■ **Mitrasasana**
PO Box 39, Woodville ✉ 5011
Gay group inspired by the teachings of Buddha.

SPECIAL INTEREST GROUPS
■ **Rainbow Connection**
☎ 8268-9266 (Bob)
Gay & lesbian business group.

■ **Young Asians**
c/o The Second Story Youth Health Centre, 57 Hyde St.
☎ 8232-0233
Social/support group for gay and bisexual Asians. Asians and their friends meet 4th Sun and Asians only 2nd Sun.

SPORT GROUPS
■ **Adelaide Happy Wanderers** Meeting 9am outside Al Fresco Gelateria
260 Rundle Street ✉ SA 5006 ☎ 8267 5112 (Bart) ☎ 8333 0667 (Jeff) 🖷 8267 5112
Day walks every first Sun of each month. Also bicycling, canoeing and camping.
■ **Team Adelaide Incorporated**
GPO Box 271 ✉ 5001 ☎ 8232 4231 ☎ 8411 1003 (voice mail)
📧 mang01@senet.com.au
🖥 www.freeyellow.com/members4/mang01/index.html
formerly known as SAGSAA Inc a.k.a. South Australian Gay Sports & Arts Association. Umbrella body for Gay & Lesbian Sports and Arts in South Australia; organises tennis, ten pin bowling, squash, racquetball, movie nights, annual cabaret and coordinates Team Adelaide teams for Gay Games and Australian Gaymes. Contacts available for other gay sporting groups. Please contact Bryan Thalbourne, President.

SWIMMING
- The Broadway (South from Glenelg near kiosk and toilet block)
- Maslin's Beach (about 50 minutes drive from Adelaide. Or take train from North Terrace, Adelaide to Noarlunga Centre and transfer to bus 741 or 742. Best on south end .
- Tennyson Beach (tram from North Terrace to Port Adelaide then bus 340 or 115 to West Lakes, some police surveillance)

CRUISING
- Unley Road Park (between Greenhill Road and South Terrace, days only)
- Glen Osmond Road (AYOR) (night and day)
  All Cruising Areas are AYOR!
- Cresserell Gardens (near Adelaide oval)
- Rundle Road, Parklands

Barossa Valley ☎ 08

HOTELS
■ **Lodge. The** (AC B BF CC F g H MA Pl) 0-24 h
RSD 120, Seppeltsfield ✉ 5355 ☎ 8562-8277 🖷 8562-8344
📧 thelodge@dove.net.au 🖥 thelodge.mtx.net
Private Georgian style homestead with en suites. Rates single A$ 230, double 285 (bf incl.).
■ **Top of the Valley** (g H Pl)
49 Murray Street, Nuiootpa ✉ 5355 ☎ 8562-2111
Tourist Motel.

Burra ☎ 08

HOTELS
■ **Wildildie Homestead** (AC BF CC F g MA)
PO Box 135, Burra ✉ 5417 ☎ 8892-2394
Located in typical Australian setting with kangaroos and emus. Close to Barossa Valley and Clare wine regions. Rates on request.

Clare Valley ☎ 08

HOTELS
■ **Oldfields** (glm F)
Young Street, Mintaro, PO Box 544, ✉ 5453 ☎ 8843-9038

Clare Valley ▶ Ulverstone — South Australia - Tasmania/Australia

■ **Thorn Park Country House** (AC B BF CC F glm H MA OS) Open all year.24 hours
College Road, Sevenhill ✉ SA 5453 ☎ 8843-4304 📠 8843-4296
📧 thornpk@capri.net.au 🌐 www.thornpark.com.au
Country house suites with en suites. Rates single A$ 195, double 295 (bf incl.). Apartment A$295.

Elizabeth ☎ 08

CRUISING
- Town Centre
- The Park
- Grove Shopping Centre

AUS-Tasmania

Location:	South AUS
Initials:	TAS
Time:	GMT +10
Area:	67,800 km2 / 26,177 sq mi.
Population:	471,000
Capital:	Hobart

✳ In Tasmania the age of consent is fixed at 17 years of age.

★ In Tasmanien liegt das Schutzalter bei 17 Jahren.

✱ En Tasmanie, la majorité sexuelle est fixée à 17 ans.

⬢ En Tasmania, la edad de consentimiento está estipulado en 17 años.

✖ In Tasmania l'età legale per rapporti sessuali è di 17 anni.

Hobart ☎ 03

GAY INFO
■ **Gay Information Line**
✉ 7000 ☎ 6234 8179
(24 hours recorded information)

BARS
■ **Bav Tav** (B glm)
Liverpool Street ✉ TAS 7000
Dance party held every 1st Sat in month.
■ **Good Woman Inn** (B F glm H) Mon-Thu 12-23, Fri-Sun 19-23. Sun 20.30 h Dance
186 Argyle Street/Worwick, North Hobart ✉ 7000 ☎ 6234 4796
Front bar every evening, also budget accommodation.
■ **ICQ Club** (F GLM) Wed-Sat 17-?, Sat 19-?h
7 Despard Street ✉ TAS 7000 ☎ 6224 4411

RESTAURANTS
■ **Indiscretions Restaurant** (F glm) open every day for dinner, lunch Mon-Fri
186 Argyle Street ✉ 7000 *(upstairs at the Good Woman Inn)*
☎ 6234 4796
■ **Kaos Cafe** (AC F glm) Mon-Fri 12-24 , Sat 10-24, Sun -22 h
237 Elizabeth Street ✉ 7000 ☎ 6231-5699
Bring your own.

■ **Rockerfellas Restaurant and Cocktail Bar** (B F G)
11 Morrison Street ✉ TAS 7000 *(on Water Front)*
■ **Syrup** (D F GLM) Dinners Wed-Sat 18-23h, Closed Tue & Sun.
39 Salamanca Place ✉ TAS 7000 ☎ 6224 8249

SEX SHOPS/BLUE MOVIES
■ **Black Rose, The** (g)
108 Harrington Street ✉ TAS 7000

BOOK SHOPS
■ **Akashic Bookshop** (g)
Cat and Fiddle Arcade ✉ 7000

HOTELS
■ **Lodge on Elizabeth, The** (BF CC g H)
249 Elizabeth Street ✉ TAS 7000 ☎ 6231 3830 📠 6234 2566
📧 lodgeoneliz@tassie.net.au

GUEST HOUSES
■ **Corinda's Cottages** (BF CC GLM H MA) All year, 24h
17 Glebe Street, Glebe ✉ TAS 7000 ☎ 6234 1590 📠 6234 2744
📧 info@corindascottages.com.au
🌐 www.corindascottages.com.au
Gay owned, fully self-contained, 2 bedrooms with antique furnishings, coulour TV. Beautiful setting, 1 km to city centre, 15 km to airport. Prices from A$ 170-190.

GENERAL GROUPS
■ **Tasmanian Gay and Lesbian Rights Group**
G.P.O Box 1773 ✉ 7000 ☎ 6224 3556
📠 6223 6136.

SWIMMING
- Seven Mile Beach (Situated about 7 km out of Hobart, the southern end of the beach attracts a large gay attendance. No nudity, but cruisy)

Launceston ☎ 03

GAY INFO
■ **Gay Information Line**
✉ TAS 7250 ☎ 6234 3254

BARS
■ **Tramshed Bar in Great Northern Hotel** (B g h) 10-1 h
3 Earl Street ✉ TAS 7250 ☎ 6231-9999

HOTELS
■ **1A Accommodation** (BF G)
1A Canning Street ✉ TAS 7250 ☎ 6234 1170 📠 6331 3454
Single studio available for gay travelers.

GENERAL GROUPS
■ **Free Sexual Health Service**
☎ 6236 22116
HIV testing, support and counselling.

Ulverstone ☎ 03

BARS
■ **Furners Hotel** (B g H) Mon-Sat 11-23 h
42 Reiby Street ✉ TAS 7315 ☎ 6225 1488
Gay group meets 2nd and 4th Fri.

Australia/Victoria — Ballarat ▶ Melbourne

AUS-Victoria
Location: South East AUS
Initials: VIC
Time: GMT +10
Area: 227,600 km2 / 87,876 sq mi.
Population: 4,648,000
Capital: Melbourne

✻ In Victoria the age of consent is fixed at 16 years of age.

✻ In Victoria liegt das Schutzalter bei 16 Jahren.

✻ Dans l'Etat de Victoria, la majorité sexuelle est fixée à 16 ans.

✻ En Victoria, la edad de consentimiento es de 16 años.

✻ In Victoria l'età legale per rapporti sessuali è di 16 anni.

Ballarat ☎ 03
GENERAL GROUPS
■ **Ballarat Gays (BGS)**
PO Box 369 ✉ VIC 3350

CRUISING
-Lake Wendouree Drive

Bendigo ☎ 03
GENERAL GROUPS
■ **Bendigo Gay Society**
PO Box 1123 ✉ VIC 3550 ☎ 5427-0312
Social and supporting group.

Cape Schanck ☎ 03
HOTELS
■ **Cape Lodge** (BF CC glm msg OS P PI SA)
134 Cape Schanck Road ✉ VIC 3939 ☎ 5988-6395 📠 5988-6395
Rates double A$ 110 per night. Dinner by arrangement 30.

Clunes ☎ 03
GUEST HOUSES
■ **Keebles of Clunes** (BF CC F GLM)
114 Bailey Street ✉ VIC 3370 (90 minutes drive from Melbourne)
☎ 5345 3200 📠 5345 3200 💻 keeblesofclunes@bigpond.com
💻 www.ballarat.com/keebles.htm

Daylesford ☎ 03
CAFES
■ **Boathouse** (AC BF CC F glm MA OS) 9-24 h
Lake Daylesford Foreshore, Leggat Street ✉ VIC 3460
☎ 5348-1387

RESTAURANTS
■ **Double Nut Of Switzerland** (B BF CC E F glm OS WH)
Fri-Mon 10-23 h
5 Howe Street ✉ VIC 3460 ☎ 5348-3981

GUEST HOUSES
■ **Balconies of Daylesford** (BF CC f GLM lj MA msg N NU OS PI WH)
35 Perrins Street ✉ VIC 3460 (10 min from center of town)
☎ 5348-1322 💻 balconys@netconnect.com.au
💻 www.spacountry.net.au/balconys
Gay owned on 3 acres of garden and overlooks Lake Daylesford. 2 rooms with shower/WC. Cooked breakfast inc.
■ **Holly Lodge** (BF CC glm H MA msg OS p VS)
15 Grenville Street ✉ VIC 3460 ☎ 5348-3670
Victorian home in large garden. 4 rooms. Gay owned.
■ **Holyrood House** (BFCC F GLM MA msg OS) Thu-Sun (Malasian restaurant)
Crn Stanbridge & Duke Street ✉ VIC 3460 ☎ 5348-4818
📠 5348 4818 💻 brownell@netconnect.com.au
Set in the heart of Daylesford. Hosted accommodation.
■ **Illoura Cottage** (BF cc G OS)
Main Road, Hepburn Springs ☎ 5348-3151
Gay owned.
■ **Turner's Farm House** (g H)
Caslemaine-Daylesford Road, Guilford ☎ 5476-4288
☎ (018) 506 087
Also horse-riding school.
■ **Villa Vita** (BF CC F GLM H)
Main Road, Kingston ☎ 5345-6448 ☎ (019) 358 839

Echuca ☎ 03
GUEST HOUSES
■ **Echuca Gardens** (BF CC GLM)
103 Mitchell Street ✉ VIC 3564 ☎ 5480-6522
💻 echucagardens@origin.net.au

Geelong ☎ 03
SWIMMING
-Point Impossible (take beach road out of Torquay to Breamlea)
-Point Addis (Situated off the Geelong road to Angleseo. Turn off 2 km past Bell's Beach. Popular.)

CRUISING
-King's Park, King's Wharf
-behind Newton Library

Marysville ☎ 03
GUEST HOUSES
■ **Fruit Salad Farm** (g H)
30-32 Aubrey Couzens Drive ✉ VIC 3711 ☎ 5963 3232
📠 5965 3681 💻 reservations@fruitsaladfarm.com.au
Fully self-contained cottages, with open fires. Gay owned and staffed.
■ **Mathildes of Marysville** (BF CC GLM)
19 Red Hill Road ✉ VIC 3779 ☎ 5963-3797
💻 www.discover-australia.com

Melbourne ☎ 03
✻ The capital of Victoria has a large multicultural population of 3,200,000. Ever since it was founded in 1835, the city has exercised a big political and cultural influence on the history of Australia. Melbourne has a very European feel, and is famous for its restaurants, wine bars, cafés, as well as its parks and gardens. In the central city suburbs of Carlton, South Yarra and South Melbourne beautiful examples of Victorian terrace house archtecture can be seen. The bohemian quarters of Fitzroy and St. Kilda, the clothes shops of Prahran and Toorak are of interest to the gay visitor and

Melbourne Victoria/Australia

here most of the gay venues are located. Melbourne has a relatively cold climate, which results in a more „indoors" and sophisticated lifestyle. In Sidney, the only fashion accessory you need is a worked-out body, whereas in Melbourne clothing and grooming are highly estimated. The gay calendar starts with the Mid-Summa Festival in late January with the popular Red Raw Gay Dance Party taking place on the weekend nearest Australia Day (January 26th). Other dance parties are held on major public holidays. Also of interest to gays is the Melbourne International Arts Festival, which is held annually in September. Melbourne is a good base if you want to visit the local vineyards of the Yarra Valley, the penguins on Phillip Island or the scenic beauty of the Grampians or Wilson's Promontory. An especially worthwhile destination is Daylesford, a country town and former spa (around 1900), which today is a popular resort for country-loving lesbians and gays.

★ Seit der Gründung 1835 hat die Hauptstadt des Bundesstaates Victoria einen enormen politischen und kulturellen Einfluß auf die Geschichte Australiens ausgeübt. Melbourne wirkt sehr europäisch und ist berühmt für seine Restaurants, Weinlokale, Kaffeehäuser und ebenso für seine Parks und Gärten. In den Vorstädten Carlton, South Yarra und South Melbourne finden sich schöne Beispiele viktorianischer Terrassenhaus-Architektur. Die Bohème-Viertel Fitzroy und St. Kilda, die Bekleidungsgeschäfte von Prahran und Toorak sind für den schwulen Besucher von Interesse. In diesen Vierteln findet man auch die meisten schwulen Einrichtungen. Melbourne liegt klimatisch in gemäßigten Breiten und so spielt sich die Kultur eher „innen" und damit „gepflegt" ab. Während in Sydney der Körper das einzige Modezubehör ist, sind in Melbourne Bekleidung und Pflege hoch geschätzt. Der schwule Kalender beginnt mit dem „Mid-Summa-Festival" im späten Januar und der populären „Red Raw Gay Dance Party", die an dem Wochenende stattfindet, das dem „Australia Day" (26. Januar) am nächsten ist. Andere Parties werden an wichtigen Feiertagen abgehalten. Das „Melbourne International Arts Festival" im September jeden Jahres ist für Schwule von Interesse.

Melbourne ist ein guter Ausgangspunkt, um die Weingärten des Yarra Valley, die Pinguine auf Phillip Island oder die malerische Schönheit der Grampians sowie des Wilson's Promontory zu besuchen. Ein besonders lohnenswertes Ziel ist Daylesford, ein ländlicher Ort, der um 1900 Kurort war und heute ein beliebter Erholungsort für landliebende Lesben und Schwule ist.

✱ Avec ses 3.200.000 habitants, Melbourne est le modèle même d'une ville multiculturelle. Depuis sa fondation en 1835, Melbourne joue un rôle décisif tant sur le plan politique que culturel. L'atmosphère de Melbourne est très européenne. On y trouve d'excellents restaurants, tavernes et cafés et de splendides parcs et jardins. A Carlton, South Yarra et South Melbourne, vous admirerez les joyaux de l'architecture victorienne que sont les maisons à terrasses. Vous vous promènerez dans les quartiers artistes de Fitzroy et St Kilda et pourrez aussi faire du lèche-vitrines à Prahan et Toorak (boutiques de mode) qui sont les quartiers gais de la ville.
Le climat de Melbourne est relativement rude. La vie culturelle a lieu surtout en intérieur et est assez guindée. Alors qu'à Sydney, le corps est au centre des préoccupations de la mode, on préfère de loin à Melbourne le style et les vêtements de marque. Le calendrier des manifestations gaies: le Mid-Summa Festival fin janvier, puis la "Red Raw Gay Dance Party" qui a lieu le week-end le plus proche du Australia Day (26 janvier). On organise d'autres soirées à l'occasion des jours fériés importants. Le Melbourne International Arts Festival (tous les ans en septembre) attire de nombreux gais. Melbourne est le point de départ idéal pour visiter les vignobles de Yarra Valley, aller admirer les sites des Grampians et de Wilsons Promontory ou bien encore aller dire bonjour aux pingouins de Phillip Island. Daylesford, autrefois petite ville, est depuis 1990 une station balnéaire aujourd'hui très prisée par les gais et les lesbiennes recherchant le calme et la détente.

◆ Desde su fundación en 1835, no se convirtió solamente en la capital de Victoria, sino también en eje político y cultural del

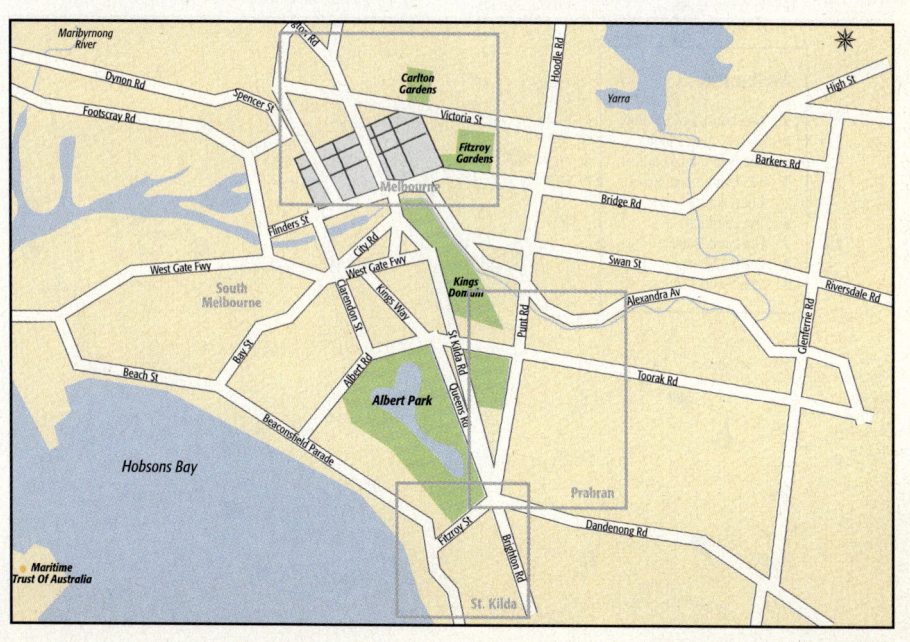

SPARTACUS 2001/2002 | 35

Australia/Victoria — Melbourne

continente australiano. Melbourne es una ciudad conocida por su ambiente europeo, que no es famosa solamente por sus restaurantes, tabernas y cafeterías, sino también por sus parques y jardines. En las afueras de la ciudad, en Carlton, South Yarra y South Melbourne, se encuentran ejemplos de la arquitectura victoriana, unas impresionantes casas con terrazas. Los barrios de Fitzroy y St. Kild, así como las tiendas de ropa de Prahran y Toorak son de especial interés para el turista gay. En estas zonas están situados también la mayoría de los locales con clientela homosexual. Melbourne tiene un clima moderado. Por esta razón la vida no se concentra en las calles, como por ejemplo en Sydney, donde la gente lleva debido al clima poca ropa y el culto al cuerpo está siempre presente. En Melbourne se cuida mucho más la manera de vestir. El calendario gay comienza a finales de enero con el Mid-Summa-Festival y la pópular „Red Raw Gay Dance Party" que tiene lugar el fin de semana que más se acerque al Australia Day (26. de enero). Otras fiestas se llevan también a cabo durante festivos importantes. De gran atracción para gays es también el Melbourne Internacional Arts Festival, que se celebra cada año en septiembre. Melbourne es un punto de partida ideal para visitar las regiones vinícolas de Yarra Valley, los pingüinos en la Phillip Island o la pintoresca belleza de Grampians o de Wilson's Promotory. Si se quiere disfrutar de la tranquilidad rural, es digno de mención el balneario Daylesford, fundado alrededor de 1900, que se ha convertido hoy en día en un atractivo lugar para homosexuales y lesbianas.

✖ I 3.200.000 di abitanti della capitale dello stato di Victoria sono un esempio di una particolare multiculturalità. Dalla sua fondazione, nel 1835, a oggi la città ha avuto una grande influenza politico-culturale sulla storia dell'Australia. Melbourne è molto europea ed è famosa per i suoi ristoranti, le sue enoteche, i suoi bar e altrettanto per i suoi parchi e giardini. Nei distretti periferici di Carlton, South Yarra e South Melbourne si trovano esempi molto belli di case a schiera. Per i visitatori gay i quartieri boemi di Fitzroy e St.Kilda e i negozi di abbigliamento di Prahran e Toorak sono di particolare interesse. In questi quartieri si trova la maggior parte dei locali d'ambiente. Il clima piuttosto freddo di Melbourne fa sí che la vita sociale e culturale urbana sia più raffinata che in altre città. Se a Sidney si sfoggiano bellezza e muscoli, a Melbourne contano invece abbigliamento e maniere. Il calendario gay inizia con il „Mid-Summa Festival" alla fine di gennaio durante il quale ha luogo il „Red Raw Gay Dance Party" durante il fine settimana più prossimo all'Australia Day (26 gennaio). Altri party hanno luogo in importanti giorni festivi. Il Melbourne International Arts Festival, che si svolge annualmente in settembre, è di interesse per i gay. Melbourne è un buon punto di partenza per visitare i vigneti di Yarra Valley, la stazione balneare di Daylesford, i pinguini di Phillip Island, le pittoresche bellezze di Grampians o il promontorio di Wilson. Una meta particolarmente interessante è Daylesford, stazione termale in campagna intorno al 1900, divenuta ora un luogo di villeggiatura per gay e lesbiche amanti della vita bucolica.

PUBLICATIONS

■ **Brother Sister** 9.30-17.30 h
Suite 33a, 1st fl, 261 Bridge Road, Richmond ✉ VIC 3121
☎ 9429 8844 📠 9429 8966 📧 brosisv@webtime.com.au
🖥 www.brothersister.com.au
Biweekly gay and lesbian paper. Free of charge.

■ **Melbourne Star Observer** Mon-Fri 08.30-17h
PO Box 205, Fitzroy ✉ 3065 *(Inner city)* ☎ 9926 1111
📠 9926 1199 📧 mso_reception@satellitemedia.com.au
Popular publication containing news, information about Melbourne's gay and lesbian scene. Published every Fri.

TOURIST INFO

■ **Melbourne Tourist Information**
City Square, Swanstan Walk/Collins Street ☎ 9790-3333

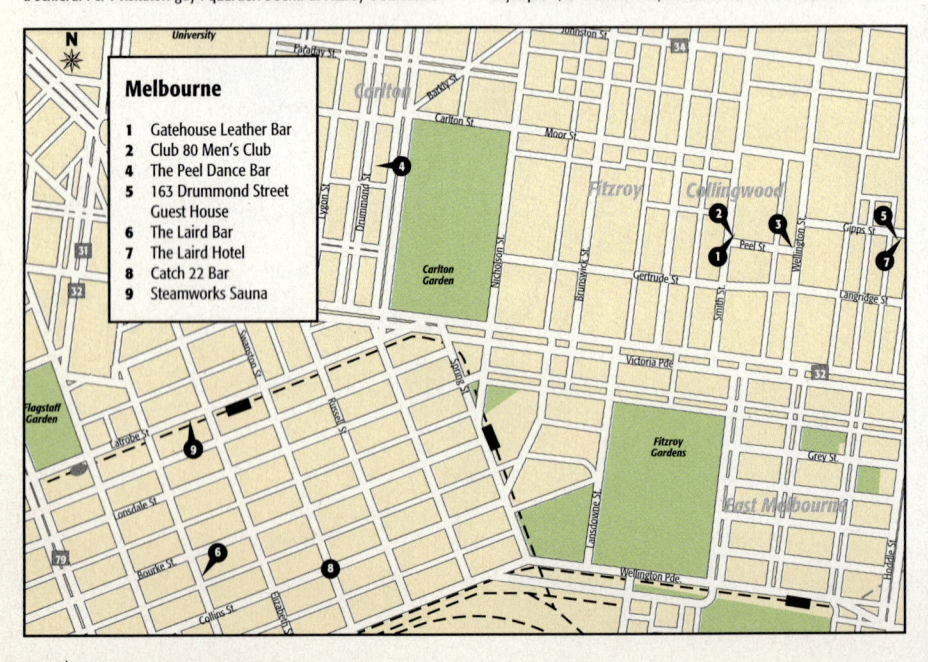

Melbourne

1 Gatehouse Leather Bar
2 Club 80 Men's Club
4 The Peel Dance Bar
5 163 Drummond Street Guest House
6 The Laird Bar
7 The Laird Hotel
8 Catch 22 Bar
9 Steamworks Sauna

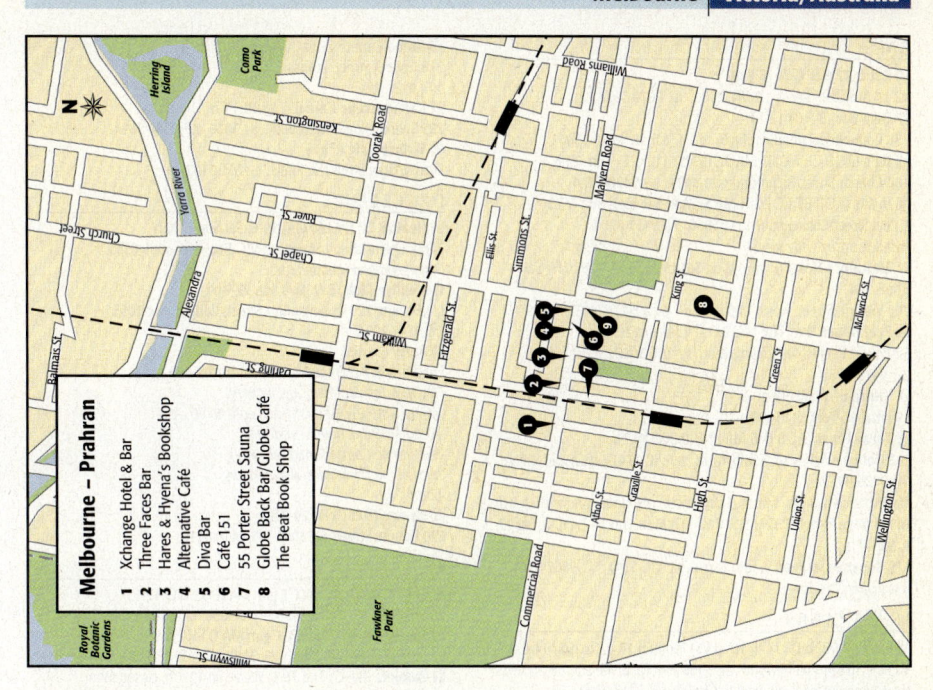

Melbourne — Victoria/Australia

Melbourne – Prahran

1. Xchange Hotel & Bar
2. Three Faces Bar
3. Hares & Hyena's Bookshop
4. Alternative Café
5. Diva Bar
6. Café 151
7. 55 Porter Street Sauna
8. Globe Back Bar/Globe Café
9. The Beat Book Shop

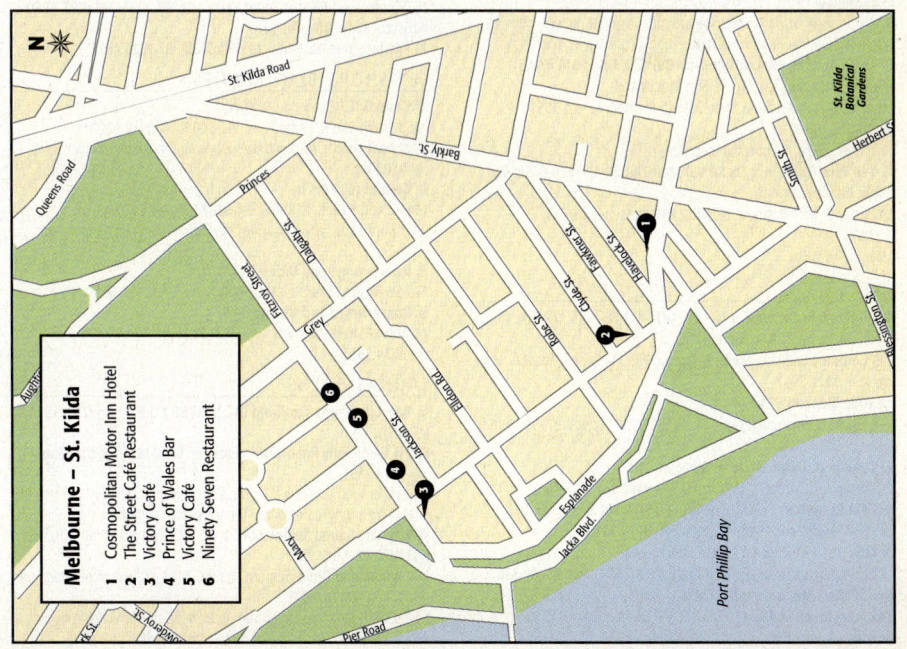

Melbourne – St. Kilda

1. Cosmopolitan Motor Inn Hotel
2. The Street Café Restaurant
3. Victory Café
4. Prince of Wales Bar
5. Victory Café
6. Ninety Seven Restaurant

Australia/Victoria | Melbourne

BARS

■ **Catch 22 Bar Café** (B F g)
12-14 McKillop Street ✉ VIC 3000 ☎ 9670 3638
■ **Diva Bar** (B F G) 12-1 h
153 Commercial Road, Prahran ✉ 3181 ☎ 9826 5500
■ **DT's** (AC B CC F GLM MA S STV VS) 11.30-1 , Sun -23 h
164 Church Strret, Richmond ✉ 3121 ☎ 9428-5724
■ **Jock's** (AC B BF CC f G H MA S) Mon-Sat 16-1, Sun -23.30 h
9 Peel Street Collingwood ✉ 3066 ☎ 9417 6700
Popular, close to gay scene.
■ **Mulcahy's Hotel** (B glm) Wed-Sat 18-1, Sun 14-23 h, Fri-Sat Bootscout
700 Victoria Street, North Melbourne ✉ 3051 ☎ 9329 0699
■ **Peel Dance Bar. The** (AC B C D G lj MA s) 22-3 h
Sir Robert Peel Hotel, Collingwood ✉ VIC 3066 *(at Peel Street)* ☎ 9419-4762
■ **Prince of Wales** (B g)
29 Fitzroy Street ✉ 3000
■ **Three Faces** (AC B C D G MA S) Thu-Sun 19-? h
143 Commercial Road, South Yarra ✉ VIC 3141 *(at Chapel Street)* ☎ 9826-0933
Modern exclusivly gay venue. 3 bars, disco, pool table. Show at 22.30 h.
■ **Xchange Hotel** (B G N S STV VS YG) Mon-Thu 14-?, Fri -3, Sat 12-3, Sun -? h
119 Commercial Road, South Yarra ✉ VIC 3141 ☎ 9867 5144
Bistro open Tue-Sat

MEN'S CLUBS

■ **Club 80** (AC b DR f G lj MA p VS) Mon-Fri 17-8, Sat-Sun 14-8 h
10 Peel Street, Collingwood ✉ 3066 *2km NE of Melbourne city center. 300m from tram stopSmithSt/Peel St* ☎ 9417 2182
Three floors of cruising, video lounge with the latest movies, cyber lounge with internet access and coffee bar. Private rooms, pool table.
■ **Eagle Melbourne Leather Club Bar** (B DR G LJ MA P s VS) (G) Fri 21-1, (glm) Sat 21-1 h, Sun-Thu closed
Munster Terrace/Victoria Street, North Melbourne ✉ 3051 ☎ 9417-2100
Strict dress code, membership necessary.
■ **Ten Plus** (DR G msg OS SA VS) Mon-Thu 20-4, Fri 20-6, Sat Sun public holidays 14-6 h
59 Porter Street, Prahran ✉ VIC 3181 *(Near gay venues)* ☎ 9525 0469
Male cruise club.

CAFES

■ **Alternative Cafe & Bar** (B CC F GLM MA N OS TV YG) Tue 18-?, Wed-Sun 12-? h, closed Mon
149 Commercial Road, South Yarra ✉ VIC 3141 *(near Prahran Market)* ☎ 9827 5997
■ **Blue Elephant. The** (B F G)
194 Commercial Road, Prahran ✉ VIC 3181 *(opposite Prahran market)* ☎ 9510 3654
■ **Café de los Santos** (B F g) Tue-Sun 11-1
175 Brunswick Street ✉ VIC 3000 ☎ 9417 1567
■ **Café Rumours** (F GLM) Tue-Fri 11-23.30, Sat Sun 10-23.30 h
199 Brunswick Street ✉ VIC 3000 ☎ 9419 5219
■ **Café 151** (AC b BF CC F GLM OS) 12-24 h
151 Commercial Road, South Yarra ✉ VIC 3141 ☎ 9826 5336
■ **Galleon Café** (b F glm) 10-24 h
9 Carlisle Street, St. Kilda ✉ 3182 ☎ 9534 8934
Bohemian café with good food, not expensive.

■ **Globe Café** (b f GLM) Mon-Sun 10-23 h
218 Chapel Street, Prahran ✉ 3181 ☎ 9510 8693
50's style café.
■ **Kaleidoscope Café** (B F g) 10-17 h
295 Sydney Road, Brunswick ✉ 3056 ☎ 9380 9894
■ **Victory Café** (F g)
Fitzroy/Grey Street, St. Kilda ✉ VIC 3182

DANCECLUBS

■ **Heat** (B CC D GLM MA) 19-6, Sat Sun 14-6 h
2/111 Quensbridge Street ✉ VIC 3205 ☎ 3699-6555
Discotheque and cocktail bar.
■ **Hellfire Club** (B D glm) Sun 22-? h
c/o Dream, 229 Queensberry Street, Carlton ✉ 3053 ☎ 9349 1924
■ **Party events:**
Enquiries to ALSO foundation ☎ 9510 5569
-Red Raw (on Australia Day, January)
-Winter Daze (Queens Birthday, early June)
-World AIDS day (late November)
-Midsumma Carnival (mid February)
-Midsumma Street Party (late January)
-Easter Party
■ **Savage** (B D G) Fri 24-9 h
629 Bourke Street ✉ 3000 ☎ 9419 4110

RESTAURANTS

■ **Col's Café** (A AC B CC F glm MA N OS WE) 12-1 h
20 Smith Street, Collingwood ✉ 3066 ☎ 9486 9433
■ **Ninety Seven** (B BF CC F glm MA OS WE)
97 Fitzroy Street, St. Kilda ✉ 3182 ☎ 9525 5922
■ **Ramjets** (B F G) Tue 18-1, Wed-Sun 12-1 h, closed Mon
147 Ccommercial Road, South Yarra ✉ VIC 3141 ☎ 9827 6260
■ **Street Café. The** (B F g)
23 Fitzroy Street, St. Kilda ✉ VIC 3182 ☎ 9525 4655

SEX SHOPS/BLUE MOVIES

■ **Gemini** (G) Every day 10-02h.
235a Smith Street, Fitzroy ✉ VIC 3065 ☎ 9419 6270
Adult book shop: Gay magazines, sex aids, underwear, leather gear, cards, videos...
■ **Gemini** (G) 10-3 h
164 Acland Street, St. Kilda ✉ 3182 ☎ 9534 6074
Adult book shop: gay magazines, sex aids, underwear, leather gear, cards,...
■ **Ram Lounge and Video** (G VS)
216 Swanston Street ✉ VIC 3000 *(Via Club X)* ☎ 9663 8094
■ **Ram Lounge and Video** (G VS)
74 Acland Street, St. Kilda ✉ VIC 3182 *(Via Club X. 1st floor)* ☎ 9534 5835

SAUNAS/BATHS

■ **Bay City Sauna Caulfield** (AC b CC DR f G MA msg N SA SB SOL VS WH) 12-3 h
482 D Glenhuntly Road, Elsternwick ✉ VIC 3185 *(Tram 67, Stop 47)* ☎ 9528 2381
Neighbourhood sauna with maze, free condoms and lube. 2nd and 4th Mon of the month „Melbourne Wankers" jack off parties.
■ **Bay City Sauna Seaford** (AC b CC DR f msg NU SA SB SOL VS WH WO) 12-3 h
16 Cumberland Drive, Seaford ✉ VIC 3198 *(10 min from Kananook station)* ☎ 9776 9279
Sauna with clothing optional sun deck, maze, free lube and condoms. 2nd Sun of every 2nd month 9-12 h nudist breakfast.

Melbourne | Victoria/Australia

BEAT BOOKSHOP AND Video Lounge / CRUISE AREA

COME VISIT THE NEW LOOK STORE...
MORE VIDEOS...
MORE BOOKS...
MORE TOYS...
MORE MAGS...
MORE ACTION...

OPEN 7 DAYS

157 COMMERCIAL ROAD ☎ 03 9827 8748
SOUTH YARRA VIC. 3141 AUSTRALIA

■ **Spa Guy** (f G OG P SA WH VS) Mon-Thu 17-1, Fri-Sat -3, Sun 16-3 h
553 Victoria Street, Abbotsford ✉ VIC 3067 ☎ 9428 5494
Frequented by an older crowd.
■ **Steamworks** (AC b CC DR F G lj MA msg P Pl SA SB SOL VS WH WO) Mon-Thu 12-5, Fri 11-Mon 5 h
279 Latrobe Street ✉ VIC 3000 *(at Elizabeth Street)* ☎ 9602 4493
Sauna on five floors with free condoms, glory holes, and dark maze. Leather & fetish night 1st Fri of the month.
■ **Subway** (AC CC DR G MA msg SA SB VS WH) 24 hours - 7 days a week
Vault 13, Banana Alley Vaults ✉ 3184 *(on courner of Flinders & Queensbridge Streets)* ☎ 9620 77 66
■ **55 Porter Street** (AC b CC DR f G MA msg P SA SB SOL VS WH WO) Mon-Fri 14-7, Sat 14-Mon 7 h
55 Porter Street, Prahran ✉ VIC 3181 ☎ 9529 5166
Bath house on two levels with large cruising maze and four glory holes cubicles.

BODY & BEAUTY SHOPS

■ **Piercing Urge. The** (AC CC) Mon-Wed 11-19, Thu & Fri 11-20, Sat 10-18 h, Sun 12-17h.
206 Commercial Road, Prahran ✉ VIC 3181 ☎ 9530 2244
Body Jewellery shop.

BOOK SHOPS

■ **Beat Bookshop** (AC CC G DR MA VS) Mon-Thu 10-20, Fri 10-2, Sat 9-2, Sun 12-20h
157 Commercial Road, South Yarra, ✉ VIC 3141 *(Commercial Road precinct)* ☎ 9827 8748
The best adult bookshop in Melbourne. A wide selection of gay magazines, books, toys etc.
■ **Hares & Hyenas** (CC GLM) 10-20h
135 Commercial Road, South Yarra ✉ VIC 3141 ☎ 9824 0110

LEATHER & FETISH SHOPS

■ **Eagle Leather** (CC glm LJ MA) Su-Th 12-18h, Fr & Sa 12-21h - other times by appointment
58 Hoddle Street, Abbotsford ✉ VIC 3067 ☎ 9417 2100
Locally made leather and latex clothing, toys & accessories. Imports from UK, USA and Canada. Co-ordinates Melbournes Leather Festival each year (1-20 September).

TRAVEL AND TRANSPORT

■ **Pride Travel and Tours** Mon-Fri 9-17.30, Sat 10-13h
254 Bay Street, Brighton ✉ VIC 3186 ☎ 9596 7100 ☎ 1800 061 427 (toll free) 🖷 9596 7761 ✉ jetbay@ergo.com.au
Gay Travel agency service.

HOTELS

■ **California Motor Inn** (AC B CC BF F H MA msg N NG OS PI) 0-24 h
138 Barkers Road, Hawthorn ✉ VIC 3122 ☎ 9818 0281
🖷 9819 6585. ✉ california_motel@bigpond.com
✉ www.californiamotel.com.au
Situated in pleasant suburb 1/2 h from city center. Close to gay venues. Restaurant, bar, free parking, guest laundry. Rates single A$ 110, double 150, studio 145. Open all year. Long-term rates available.
■ **Cosmopolitan Motor Inn St. Kilda** (F g N)
6 Carlisle Street, St. Kilda ✉ 3182 *(near Melbourne bayside cosmopolitan suburb)* ☎ 9534 0781 🖷 9534 8262
All rooms with facilities. Rates A$ 70-110.
■ **Laird Hotel. The** (AC B BF CC G H LJ MA OS S) Mon-Thu 17-2, Fri-Sat 17-3, Sun 17-24 h
149 Gipps Street, Abbotsford ✉ VIC 3067 ☎ 9417 2832
🖷 9417 2109 ✉ hotel@airdhotel.com ✉ www.lairdhotel.com
Home of Melbournes leather scene. TV lounge area, beer garden, 2 bars, pooltable, games area. 9 double rooms, share bathrooms. Room rate A$ 55.

Australia/Victoria | Melbourne

■ **Saville. Hotel** (BF CC H F g)
5 Commercial Road, South Yarra ✉ 3141 ☏ 9867 2755
🖷 9020-9726

GUEST HOUSES

■ **Eagle Lodge SM Playhouse** (DR G LJ MA P)
647 Nicholson Street, North Carlton, ✉ 3054 ☏ 9417-2100
☏ 9419-4509 🖷 9416-4235
SM-Playhouse, for hire, parties, education.
■ **Gatehouse. The** (AC BF CC G H LJ MA)
97 Cambridge Street, Collingwood ✉ 3066 Checkin at the Club80
☏ 9471 2182 🖷 9416 0474 📧 gatehouse@club80.net
Men only accommodation for leathermen / players. Every room has its own play area with sling, bondage bed & wall. Guests receive complimentary entry to Club80 and the Peel Dance Bar.
■ **Heathville House** (BF CC GLM H)
171 Aitken Street, Williamstown ✉ VIC 3016 ☏ 9397-5959
🖷 9397-5959
■ **Palm Court** (BF CC e GLM H)
22 Grattan Place, Richmond ✉ VIC 3121 ☏ 9427 7365
🖷 9427 7365 📧 palmc@ozemail.com.au
💻 www.ozemail.com.au/~palmc
Open all year. 8 double rooms with shower/WC, telephone/fax, TV/radio, own key. Rates A$ 40-90 off season, 50-100 on season (bf incl.).
■ **The Gatehouse** (AC BF CC G H)
97 Cambridge Street, Collingwood ✉ VIC 3066 ☏ 9417 2182
🖷 9416 0474 💻 www.club80.net.au
Guest house catering to the male SM scene. 4 double guest rooms. Each has its own play room complete with sling, mezanine sleeping area, communal TV lounge room, bathrooms. Room rate A$ 70. Comp. entry to Club 80 for guests.
■ **163 Drummond Street** (AC BF CC f GLM) All year, 24 h
163 Drummond Street ✉ VIC 3053 ☏ 9663 3081 🖷 9663 6500
📧 enquiries@163drummond.com.au
💻 www.163drummond.com.au

PRIVATE ACCOMMODATION

■ **Gayshare Accomodation** Mon-Fri 9-17 h
501 Latrobe Street, Level 4 ✉ 3000 ☏ . 🖷 9602-4484
📧 mckenzie@wire.net.au
Long and short term accomodation for Gays, Lesbians and gay friendly people.
■ **Holly Lodge Bed & Breakfast** (BF CC glm MA msg OS)
19 Grenville Street, Daylesford ✉ VIC 3460 ☏ 5348 3670
🖷 5348 3670 📧 hollylodgings@hotmail.com

GENERAL GROUPS

■ **ALSO Foundation**
35 Cato Street, Pahran ✉ VIC 3182 ☏ 9510 5569
Supports all manner of Lesbian and Gay community initiatives.
■ **Gay and Lesbian Immigration Task Force**
PO Box 2387, Richmond South ✉ 3121 ☏ 9822-0794
or ☏ 9523-7864. Help and support for immigration equality as well as gays and lesbians with overseas partners.
■ **Gay and Lesbian Organisation of Business and Enterprise (GLOBE)** (CC E f GLM MA S)
PO Box 20 63, Albert Park ✉ 3206 ☏ 9686 2499
📧 GLOBE@hotmail.com
Dinner -1st Mo in month, „fruits in suits" -3rd Th in month
■ **G.L.A.D.** 2nd/4th Mon 18.30 h at 3CR, 21 Smith Street, Fitzroy
PO Box 4215, Melbourne University Post Office, ✉ VIC 3052 Parkville ☏ 9576 1994
Gay men & lesbians against discrimination (and homophobia).

■ **Motafrenz** (GLM)
PO Box 351, Blackburn ✉ 3130 ☏ 9557 9635
Phone Ross. Gay and Lesbian motor social group.
■ **Multicultural** Meets at St. Kilda Community Health Centre, 18 Milford Street
PO Box 1052, Elsternwick ✉ 3185 ☏ 9525 6233
Call for information and dates.

FETISH GROUPS

■ **Jackaroos** (LJ) Tue 21.30-24 h at The Laird Bar
PO Box 50 64 ✉ 3000 ☏ 9663 8168
A group for gays into leather, denim and the great outdoors.

HEALTH GROUPS

■ **AIDSLINE** Mon-Fri 11-22, Sat Sun 11-14, 19-22 h
✉ VIC 3000 ☏ 9347 6099 ☏ 008-13 339
Telephone counselling, support and education. Staffed by trained volunteers.
■ **Carlton Clinic** (CC GLM) Mon-Fri 8.30-19, Sat Sun 9.30-12.30h
88 Rathdowne Street, Carlton ✉ VIC 3053 (Courner Elgin Str. Bus 200, 203, 205) ☏ 9347 9422 🖷 9349 2991
📧 carclin@corplink.com.au 💻 www.thecarltonclinic.com.au
Gay and lesbian clinic.
■ **Melbourne Sexual Health Centre**
580 Swanston Street, Carlton ✉ VIC 3053 Trams 1,3,5,6,8, Melbourne Central station 10 min walk. ☏ 9347 0244 ☏ (008) 032 017
■ **Middle Park Clinic**
41 Armstrong Street, Middle Park ✉ VIC 3206 (near St. Kilda)
☏ 9699 3758 ☏ 9699 4626
Gay medical practice.

SPECIAL INTEREST GROUPS

■ **Alsounds • Choir for lesbians and gay men** (GLM) Meetings Wed 19.30 h at 325 Dorcas Street
PO Box 142, Coburg ✉ VIC 3058 ☏ 9380 5538

SWIMMING

Most city and inner suburb swimming pools are cruisy.
-Beaconsfield Parade/Victoria Avenue.
-Middle Park/South Melbourne Beach (known as „Screech Beach") Situated at the end towards the Port Melbourne Lifesaving Club. Most popular gay beach in Melbourne)
-Somers Beach (NU) (Two-hour drive from Melbourne on the Merrington Peninsula)
-St. Kilda Beach (on the lawn outside Jean Jacques restaurant)
-Prahran swimming pool. 41 Essex Street, Prahran, ☏ 522-3248. (Open Oct-May. Outdoors heated public swimming. Popular with gays.)

CRUISING

Victorian police have regular plain clothes surveillance, so all areas are AYOR.
-Princes Park
-Beaconsfield Parade (from Fitzroy Street, St. Kilda along beach front to Port Melbourne)
-Footscray Park
-Ashburton shopping centre
-Canterbury Park, Canterbury
-Albert Park (AYOR) (along Aughtie Drive and bushy areas at night)
-Point Ormond Beach (AYOR) (end of Glenhuntly Road. Occasional bashers)
-Eildon Park, off Ackland Street next to the church.
Most beats around the city are busy (be guided by the graffiti) as are those on Bayside beaches and the Yarra river bank for 4-5 km out of the city up the river. In the suburbs most shopping complexes are

Melbourne ▶ Perth   Victoria - Western Australia/Australia

busy but patrolled by in house security.)
-Flinders Street Station (AYOR) (several facilities including entrance from Elizabeth Street and at nearby Princes Bridge.)
-Spencer Street station (AYOR) (on platforms 11 and 12, very busy)
-Footscray Park
-Queens Park Sunshine
-Near boatsheds on Yarra River (AYOR) (regular police raids)

Mornington ☎ 03
SWIMMING
-Sunnyside Beach (between Mornington and Mount Eliza on the Peninsula. Although this is a family beach gays tend to congregate at the far end of this scenic beach. 50 minutes drive from central city.)

Olinda ☎ 03
HOTELS
■ **Delvin Country House** (BF cc F GLM msg)
25 Monash Avenue ✉ VIC 3788 ☎ 9751-1800 📠 9751-1829
Rates from A$85 (single) to A$110 (double). Special theme dinners (e.g. murder mysteries).

Portarlington ☎ 03
GUEST HOUSES
■ **Roses by the Sea** (BF GLM)
16 Evandale Avenue ✉ VIC 3223 ☎ 5293-8097

Stanley ☎ 03
GUEST HOUSES
■ **Stanley Croft** (AC BF CC GLM H MA NU OS P WE)
Masons Road, Beechworth ✉ VIC 3747 *(Located between Sydney & Melbourne. Bushland setting)* ☎ 5728-6626 📠 5728-6626
💻 scroft@netc.net.au 🌐 home.netc.net.au/~scroft/
One double room with shower/WC, radio, kitchenette, own key. Rates from A$ 100 (single usage 65). Additional bed 50.

Warburton ☎ 03
GUEST HOUSES
■ **St. Lawrence** (BF CC GLM)
13 Richards Road ✉ VIC 3799 *(close to Yarra Valley wineries)*
☎ 5966-6493

Werribee ☎ 03
SWIMMING
-Campbell's Cove (NU) (at Werribee)

AUS-Western Australia

Location: West AUS
Initials: WA
Time: GMT +8
Area: 2,525,500 km2 / 975,096 sq mi.
Population: 1,822,000
Capital: Perth

✱ In Western Australia the age of consent is fixed at 16 years for lesbians and heterosexuals and 21 for gay men.

★ In Westaustralien liegt das Schutzalter bei 16 Jahren für Lesben und Heterosexuelle und bei 21 Jahren für Schwule.

✱ En Australie occidentale, la majorité sexuelle est fixée à 16 ans pour les lesbiennes et les hétérosexuels et à 21 ans pour les gais.

▌ La edad de consentimiento en Australia Occidental es de 16 años para lesbianas y heterosexuales, para homosexuales está estipulada en los 21 años.

✖ In Western Australia l'età legale per rapporti sessuali tra eterosessuali e tra donne è di 16 anni, quello tra uomini di 21 anni.

Perth ☎ 08

✱ The capital of Western Australia was founded in 1829 and has a population of 1,200,000. Perth is beautifully located on the Swan River and is not too far away from the harbour city of Fremantle. Perth looks out on the Indian Ocean and has many airlince connections with Africa and Asia. It has become the first Australian city that many Europeans have contact with.
It has developed into an interesting and lively gay scene with many different things on offer for the gay tourist. Perth has many wonderful shops and diverse architecture (e.g. London Court in the Tudor look). There is plenty of attractive natural beauty. In the centrally situated Kings Park are prime examples of Australian bush flora and the wild flowers that that bloom in November are beautiful. A beloved holiday destination is Rottnest Island with a huge beach and home to the perculiar animal the Quokka. Further afield is the Darling Ranges and the wine district of the Margaret River.
Every year in October takes place for five weeks the Gay Pride Festival.

★ Die Hauptstadt des Bundesstaates Western Australia wurde 1829 gegründet und zählt heute 1 200 000 Einwohner. Perth ist malerisch am Swan River gelegen und nicht weit von der Hafenstadt Fremantle entfernt. Im Westen Australiens gelegen blickt Perth auf den Indischen Ozean. Die Stadt hat viele direkte Flugverbindungen mit Afrika und Asien und ist oft für viele Besucher die erste australische Stadt, mit der sie Kontakt haben.
In der Stadt hat sich eine interessante und lebhafte Szene entwickelt, aber auch Perth selbst hat sehr viel Abwechslungsreiches zu bieten. Central Perth ist eine tolle Einkaufsgegend, die Architektur ist vielfältig (z.B. London Court im Tudor-Look).
Die Natur hat ihren besonderen Reiz: Im zentral gelegenen Kings Park ist die australische Buschflora vertreten und die Blüte der Wildblumen im November ist fantastisch. Ein beliebtes Reiseziel ist Rottnest Island mit seinem großen Strand, wo ein eigentümliches Tier, der Quokka beheimatet ist. Etwas weiter entfernt liegen die Darling Ranges und das Weinanbaugebiet Margaret River.
Jährlich im Oktober findet für fünf Wochen das Gay Pride Festival statt.

✱ Capitale de l'état Western Australia, fondée en 1829, Perth compte aujourd'hui 1.200.000 habitants. La ville est située sur la Swan River, près de Fremantle (ville portuaire). Géographiquement et psychologiquement coupée du reste du pays, Perth tourne ses regards vers l'Océan indien et entretient d'excellentes relations aériennes avec l'Asie et l'Afrique. Beaucoup de touristes européens découvre l'Australie ici pour la première fois.
La scène gaie à Perth est diversifiée et animée. La ville propose une foule de magasins à l'architecture intéressante (London Court dans le style Tudor, par exemple). Mais la ville regorge aussi de

Australia/Western Australia — Perth

splendeurs naturelles. En novembre, pendant la floraison, la végétation est d'une rare beauté. Kings Park, au centre ville, présente les merveilles de la flore australienne. Sur Rottnest Island, (haut lieu touristique près de Perth), on trouve de magnifiques plages et ce curieux animal que l'on appelle „Quokka". Les Darling Ranges et les vignobles de Margaret River, bien qu'un peu loin, valent également le détour.
Chaque année en octobre, on célèbre pendant 5 semaines la Gay Pride.

La capital del estado federal de Australia Occidental se fundó en 1829 y cuenta hoy en día con 1.200.000 habitantes. Perth está situado a orillas del río Swan y muy cerca de la ciudad portuária de Freemantle. Situado en la parte occidental de Australia, Perth tiene vistas al Océano ndico. La ciudad dispone de muchas conexiones aereas directas con Africa y Asia, así que para muchos visitantes europeos es la primera ciudad que conocen de Australia. En Perth no solo se ha desarrollado un ambiente gay interesante y vivaz, sino también la ciudad misma tiene mucho que ofrecer. Central Perth es una zona de compras estupenda y los diferentes estilos de arquitectura son dignos de ver (como por ejemplo London Court). La naturaleza tiene un encanto especial. Es incréible el poder contemplar en el mismo centro de la ciudad (Kings Park) ejemplos de la flora salvaje australiana, que en el mes de noviembre, cuando todas las plantas están en plena floración, alcanza su mayor esplendor. De los destinos de especial interés se podrían citar Rottnest Island, no solamente por sus extensas playas, sino por el curiosísimo animal, que exclusivamente en esta región habita, el Quokka. Alejándonos un poco, encontramos Darling Ranges y la región vinícola Margaret River. Anualmente, en el mes de octubre se celebra durante cinco semanas el Gay Pride Festival.

La capitale dello stato federale fu fondata nel 1829. Oggi ha 1.200.000 abitanti. Situato pittorescamente sulle rive dello Swan River, all'ovest del continente sull'oceano indiano, non dista molto dal porto di Fremantle. La città possiede collegamenti aerei diretti con l'Africa e l'Asia, e spesso è la prima città australiana con cui molti turisti europei vengono in contatto. A parte la vita gay interessante e vivace, la città offre varie attrazioni. Central Perth è pieno di bellissimi negozi, l'architettura è svariata (p.es. London Court nel Tudor-Look). La natura ha il suo fascino: il Kings Park ospita molte specie della flora australiana, ed i fiori selvaggi in novembre sono spettacolari. Rottnest Island vicino a Perth è una meta turistica interessante per la sua grande spiaggia ed una sua caratteristica specie animale: il Quokka. Un po' più lontano si trovano I Darling Ranges ed i vigneti di Margaret River. Ogni anno in ottobre ha luogo per cinque settimane il Gay Pride Festival.

GAY INFO

■ **Beats per Minute** Thu/Fri night RTR 92.1 FM
PO Box 298, Belmont ✉ WA 6984 ☎ 9277 4268 🖷 9277 4268
🖳 www.iinet.net.au/~6pm/
■ **Gay and Lesbian Community Services** (GLM MA P) Mon-Fri 19.30-22.30, Tue 13-16 h
City West Lotteries House, 2 Delhi Street ✉ WA 6005
☎ 9420 7201 ☎ 9420 7201 (counselling) 🖷 9486 9855
Information on the gay and lesbian scene. Telephone counselling. Groups such as Breakaway, 26up, galen, groovygirls and wow.
■ **Westside Observer**
79 Lindsay Street ✉ WA 6906 ☎ 9228 1044 🖷 9228 1055
🖳 editorial@wso.com.au 🖳 www.wso.com.au
Fortnightly publication, free at gay venues.

TOURIST INFO

■ **Western Australian Tourism Commission**
6th Floor, 16 St. Georges Terrace, ✉ WA 6000 ☎ 9220-1700
🖷 220 17 02.

BARS

■ **Connections Night Club** (AC B D GLM MA S SNU STV YG) Tue (G) 22-4, Wed Fri 22-6, Sat 21-6, Sun 20-1 h, Mon Thu closed
81 James Street, Northbridge ✉ WA 6003 *(above Plaka Café)*
☎ 9328-1870
First hour every night - free entry and „nice price" drinks. Gay owned and managed.
■ **Court Hotel. The** (B F glm H S) Mon-Sat 11-23, Sun 15-21 h
50 Beaufort Street/James Street, Northbridge ✉ WA 6003
☎ 9328-5292

DANCECLUBS

■ **Dive Bar** (B D G MA) Thu-Sun 18-? h
232 William Street, Northbridge ✉ WA 6003 ☎ 9328-1822

SEX SHOPS/BLUE MOVIES

■ **Ram Lounge and Video** (G VS) Mon-Wed 9-23, Thu-Sat 9-24, Sun 11-24 h
114 Barrack Street ✉ WA 6000 *(via Club X)* ☎ 9325-3815
■ **Vibrations Adult Shop** (AC CC G MA SNU VS)
354 A Charles Street, North Perth ✉ WA 6006 *(opposite McDonald's)* ☎ 9242-4501

SAUNAS/BATHS

■ **Beaufort 565** (AC CC DR f G lj MA msg SA SB SOL VS WH) Daily 12-01 h
565 Beaufort Street, Mount Lawley ✉ WA 6050 *(at Vincent St.)*
☎ 9328-7703
Friendly and private atmosphere bath house used by many groups as their home base: West Oz Leather, Perth Bears,...
■ **Perth Steam Works** (AC CC DR f G MSG SA SB WH)
Sun-Thu 12-1, Fri-Sat 12-3 h
369 William Street, Northbridge ✉ WA 6003 *(15 min walk from railway station, entry Forbes Road)* ☎ 9328-2930
Sauna with mirror room, bondage and maze frequented by a mixed age group, younger in the evenings.

BOOK SHOPS

■ **Arcane Bookshop. The** (CC GLM) Mon-Thu 10-17.30, Fri 10-20, Sat 10-17, Sun 12-17 h
212 William Street, Northbridge ✉ WA 6000 ☎ 9328-5073
Largest range of gay/lesbian books in Perth and ticket seller for gay lesbian events.

HOTELS

■ **Court Hotel** (B BF CC D F GLM H MA N OS S)
50 Beaufort Street ✉ WA 6000 ☎ 9328-5292 ☎ 9328-5282
🖷 9227-1570
Central location. Rates from A$ 35. Also Bar.
■ **Criterion Hotel** (B BF CC D E F glm H MA OS)
560 Hay Street ✉ WA 6000 ☎ 9325-5155 🖷 9325-4176
Comfortable hotel directly in the heart of the city. Rooms with bath or shower/WC, telephone, TV, radio, minibar, room service, own key. Rates (excl. tax) for single AUS$ 95, double AUS$ 112 and triple AUS$ 130 incl. full bf. Car park.
■ **Metro Inn Apartment Hotel** (AC B BF CC F H PI) 7-23 h
22 Nile Street, East Perth ✉ WA 6004 ☎ 9325-1866
🖷 1800 022 523 🖷 9325-5374
Rates from A$ 86 (one bedroom apartment) to 144 (interconnecting apartments).

Perth ▸ Scarborough — Western Australia/Australia

■ **Sullivans Hotel** (AC B BF CC F MA NG OS PI)
166 Mounts Bay Road ✉ WA 6000 ☎ 9321-8022 📠 9481-6762
📧 perth@sullivans.com.au 🖥 www.sullivans.com.au
Near Kings Park, free bus to city centre. 70 rooms AND 2 apartments with TV, shower/WC, phone, radio. Partly with balcony and safe. Rates from A$ 98,–

GUEST HOUSES

■ **Abaca Palms** (AC BF CC F G Ij MA NU OS SA WH WO)
34 Whatley Crescent, Mount Lawley ✉ WA 6050 ☎ 9271-2117
📠 9371-5370 📧 abacpalm@multiline.com.au
Guest house close to city and venues. 8 rooms and one apartment with bath/WC, telephone, TV/video, radio, own key. Rates single A$ 50, double 65, apartment 130.

■ **Lawley on Guildford, The** (AC BF CC GLM H OS WH)
72 Guildford Road, Mount Lawley ✉ WA 6065 ☎ 9272 5501
📠 9272 5501
Large double rooms, private and shared bath, guest lounge, Spa, gym, grass tennis court, close to all amenities. Rates from A$ 55.

■ **Swanbourne Guest House** (AC b BF CC f g H lj MA msg N NU p Pl OS VS WO) All year
5 Myera Street, Swanbourne ✉ WA 6010 (Bus 36-Beach/Perth City)
☎ 9383-1981 📠 9383-1981 📧 ralphk@wantree.com.au
🖥 www.wantree.com.au/~ralphh
5 min outside of Perth, 2 km to gay nude beach. All rooms with cable television. Guest House provides room service. Rates A$ 55-95 per night.

GENERAL GROUPS

■ **Breakaway Gay Youth Group** (G YG) Every 2nd Sa 12-17h
c/o GLCS, 2 Delhi Street ✉ WA 6005 ☎ 9420 7201 📠 9486 9855
Support group via the GLCS.

■ **Breakaway-Gay Youth Group**
PO Box 406 ✉ WA 6001
A social and support group for people under 26. For details Gayline ☎ 9328 9044.

■ **Club West Social Group**
PO Box 283 ✉ WA 6006 ☎ 9307-5740
📧 clubwest@merriweb.com.au
🖥 www.merriweb.com.au/clubwest

■ **Country Network**
GPO Box 1031 ✉ WA 6001
For details Gayline ☎ 9328-9044.

■ **GAGS-Gays Activities Group Services**
PO Box 8234, Stirling Street ✉ WA 6000

■ **GALE-Coalition for Gay and Lesbian Equality**
PO Box 912, West Perth ✉ WA 6005

■ **Gay Outdoors Group**
PO Box 263, Cottesloe ✉ WA 6011

■ **MUGALS-Murdoch Uni Gay and Lesbian Society**
Student Guild, Murdoch Uni, South St., Murdoch ✉ WA 6150 ☎ 9332-6335

■ **Pride Collective**
PO Box 156, Northbridge ✉ WA 6003 ☎ 9227 1767
🖥 www.pridewa.asn.au
Organizers of gay pride.

■ **Stonewall Union of Students**
c/o The Secretary, PO Box 156, Northbridge ✉ WA 6003
Social and support group for gay, lesbian and bisexual students.

HEALTH GROUPS

■ **Act Up Perth**
PO Box 231, Northbridge ✉ WA 6003 ☎ 9227-6706

■ **AIDS Youthline**
☎ 9227-9644

■ **Mount Lawley Medical Centre** 9-18 h
689 Beaufort Street, Mount Lawley ✉ WA 6050 ☎ 9227-2455

■ **Murray St STD Clinic**
70 Murray Street ✉ WA 6000 ☎ 9270-1122

■ **People Living with AIDS**
U10/105 Lord Street ✉ WA 6000 ☎ 9221-3002
FAX 9221-3035

■ **Sida Centre** Mo 12-20, Tue-Fr 9-7
Unit 10, 105 Lord Street, East Perth ✉ WA 6004 ☎ 9221-3002
📠 9221-9035
Centre for people with HIV and Aids

■ **WA AIDS Council** Mon-Fri 08.30-17h, closed Sat & Sun.
664 Murray Street, West Perth ✉ WA 6005 ☎ 9429 9900
📠 9429 9901 📧 waa@waaids.asn.au 🖥 www.waaids.asn.au
Support, information, education.

RELIGIOUS GROUPS

■ **Acceptance West**
PO Box 83 30, Stirling Street Private Boxes ✉ WA 6849
☎ 9383-3188
Catholic group.

■ **Aleph c/o Gay and Lesbian Counselling Service**
c/o Gay and Lesbian Counselling Service, PO Box 405, *Mt. Lawley WA 6050* ☎ 9328-9044
Social group for gay & lesbian Jews.

■ **Resurrection Community Church** Worship Sun 19.30 h
317 Bagot Road, Subiaco ✉ WA 6008 ☎ 9478-3657

SPECIAL INTEREST GROUPS

■ **Parents, Families & Friends of Lesbians & Gays** Mondays 9-12h
PO Box 354, Northbridge ✉ WA 6865 ☎ 9228 1005
☎ 9228 1006 📧 plagperth@telstra.easymail.com.au
🖥 www.p-flag.org.au

SPORT GROUPS

■ **Loton Park Tennis Club** (GLM) Oct-May: Sat Sun 13-17 h
PO Box 8330, Bulwer Street/Lord Street ✉ WA 6849 ☎ 9328-5065
🖥 www.geocities.com/lotonpark
Gay and lesbian tennis club.

SWIMMING

-Floriat Beach (AYOR) (Not a nude beach but attract quite a few gay people, particularly at the northern end.)
-South City Beach/Swanbourne (AYOR). (Nude beaches. Gays congregate at the southern end of South City Beach and North Swanbourne.)
-Warnbro Beach (Rockingham)
-Whitford's Beach

CRUISING

All AYOR
-Fremantle (under bridges)
-Swanbourne Beach (at night, but helicopter surveillance).
-Fawkner Park (South Perth)
-Mosman Park (south end of Mosman Bay)
-Kings Park (near barbeque area; entrance from Thomas Street)

Scarborough ☎ 08

HOTELS

■ **Scarborough's By The Sea** (g H)
96a Stanley Street ✉ WA 6019 ☎ 9341 1411

Austria

Name: Österreich • Autriche
Location: Central Europe
Initials: A
Time: GMT +1
International Country Code: 43 (leave the first 0 of area codes)
International Access Code: 00
Language: German
Area: 83,857 km2 / 34,307 sq mi.
Currency: 1 Austrian Schilling (öS) = 100 Rappen.
1 EURO = 13,764 Schilling
Population: 8,030,000
Capital: Wien
Religions: 78% Catholic
Climate: Alpine climate with hot summers and cold, snowy winters.

Austria is one of the more backward countries in Europe when it comes to the updating of its laws. There is still a difference in the age of consent for homosexuals (18) and heterosexuals (14), and strangely lesbians. Violation of this law can be punished with up to five years imprisonment. The §209 which can be implemented by the courts can result in a minimum of six months imprisonment.. The conservative party (ÖVP) and the (FPÖ), a extreme right wing party declined all amendments of §209 in July 1998. Whether these two political parties will change their standpoint now that they are the government parties is doubtful. The international pressure on Austria is growing. The European parliament and the UNO commission for human rights have repeatedly demanded the abolishment of §209.
The Austrians are said to be very conservative and conventional. This is most probably not exaggerated. In the last few years much has changed however. The general attitude of the press and public opinion has undergone a positive change. The most noticeable change has taken place in Vienna. The (gay) capital and the only really large city in Austria. With a colourful and lively scene, Vienna has become a popular gay city in the German-speaking countries of Europe.
A small but interesting „scene" can also be found in Linz, Graz, Salzburg and Innsbruck.
The remaining parts of Austria are uninteresting in terms of the gay scene, but are certainly well worth a visit due to the breathtaking landscapes, historical buildings as well as cultural history and leisure activities in the mountain and lake landscapes.

Österreich ist in Sachen Gesetzgebung einer der rückständigsten Staaten Europas. Noch immer gibt es im Strafrecht eine Bestimmung, die ein unterschiedliches Mindestalter für Homosexuelle Männer (18) als für Heterosexuelle bzw. Lesben (14) vorsieht. Ein Verstoß wird mit Haftstrafe bis zu fünf Jahren bedroht. Die Bestimmung (§ 209) muß von den Gerichten auch angewendet werden, die zu verhängende Mindeststrafe beträgt 6 Monate Gefängnis. Eine Aufhebung des § 209 wurde zuletzt im Juli 1998 von der konservativen Volkspartei (ÖVP) und der rechtsextremen Freiheitlichen Partei (FPÖ) abgelehnt. Ob die beiden Parteien nach ihrem Regierungsantritt im Februar 2000 ihre Haltung ändern werden, ist eher zu bezweifeln. Allerdings wird der internationale Druck auf Österreich immer größer: Europarat, Europaparlament und der UNO-Ausschuß für Menschenrechte haben Österreich namentlich und mehrfach zur Streichung des § 209 aufgefordert.
Den Österreichern wird nachgesagt, eher sehr konservativ und in Konventionen verhaftet zu sein. Was sicherlich nicht übertrieben ist. In den letzten Jahren jedoch hat sich viel getan. Die Einstellung der Bevölkerung und der meisten Medien hat sich zum Positiven verändert. Das gesellschaftliche Klima hat sich gewandelt und ist wohl im europäischen Durchschnitt anzusiedeln. Besonders deutlich zeigt sich diese Klimaveränderung in Wien, der (schwulen) Hauptstadt und einzigen wirklichen Großstadt Österreichs. Mit ihrer bunten und lebendigen Szene nimmt sie heute einen Spitzenplatz im deutschsprachigen Raum ein.
Eine kleine, zum Teil auch feine Szene findet sich in Linz, Graz, Salzburg und Innsbruck. Der Rest Österreichs wird von schwulen Touristen wohl kaum wegen der aufregenden Szene besucht, sondern vielmehr wegen seiner landschaftlichen Schönheiten, historischen Bauten, seiner Festspiele und vielfältigen anderen kulturellen Veranstaltungen sowie der Sport- und Freizeitmöglichkeiten an den Seen und in den Bergen.

L'Autriche est un des pays les plus rétrogrades en Europe au niveau de la législation homosexuelle. Le Code pénal fait une différence entre la majorité sexuelle des hétérosexuels et lesbiennes (14 ans) et celle des homosexuels (18 ans). Les contrevenants s'exposent à des peines allant jusqu'à 5 ans d'emprisonnement. Le Paragraphe 209 précise encore que les contrevenants seront jugés avec une peine minimale de 6 mois. Une tentative d'abolition de ce paragraphe a échoué en juillet 1998 devant le refus des partis conservateur (ÖVP) et d'extrême droite (FPÖ). Un changement de position de ces deux partis depuis leur entrée au gouvernement en février 2000 est peu probable. La pression internationale sur le pays est pourtant toujours plus grande: Le Conseil Européen, le Parlement Européen et la Commission des Droits de l'Homme des Nations Unies ont sommé plusieurs fois l'Autriche de supprimer le Paragraphe 209.
Les Autrichiens sont réputés pour être plutôt conservateurs et attachés aux conventions. Cela est certainement vrai, même si l'opinion publique et les médias on évolués dans un sens positif ces

Austria

dernières années. La société s'est transformée pour se trouver plus en accord avec ses voisins européens. Ce changement de mentalité est particulièrement visible à Vienne, la seule métropole et capitale (gaie) du pays. Grâce à une scène diversifiée et active, Vienne s'est faite une place de choix parmi les villes germanophones.
On trouve également un milieu gai restreint mais intéressant dans les villes de Linz, Graz, Salzburg et Innsbruck. Le reste du pays n'attire certainement pas les touristes pour son milieu gai, mais plutôt pour la beauté de ses paysages, ses sites historiques, ses festivals et ses nombreuses manifestations culturelles, ainsi que pour ses offres en matière de sport et de loisirs sur les nombreux lacs et montagnes.

En cuanto a la legislación, Austria sigue siendo uno de los países más retrasados de Europa. Todavía hay una ley en el código penal austríaco según la cual la edad de consentimiento es diferente para hombres homosexuales (18) que para heterosexuales y mujeres homosexuales (14). La infracción de esta ley puede ser penalizada con hasta cinco años de prisión. Los tribunales han de aplicarlLa disposición legal (artículo 209) obligatoriamente, y la pena mínima es de seis meses de prisión. En julio de 1998, la abolición del artículo 209 fue rechazada por el Partido Conservador Popular (ÖVP) y el partido de extrema derecha Patrido Liberal (FPÖ). Es poco probable que estos dos partidos, que desde febrero del 2000 forman el gobierno austríaco, cambien de postura. Sin embargo, la presión internacional contra la política austríaca es cada vez más grande. El Consejo Europeo, el Parlamento Europeo y la Comisión de Derechos Humanos de la ONU exigieron repetidas veces que Austria ratifique la abolición del artículo 209.
Se dice de los austríacos que son bastante conservadores y muy profundamente arraigados en tradiciones y convenciones anticuadas, lo que sin duda no es una exageración, si bien en los últimos años mucho ha cambiado. La postura de la población y de la mayoría de los medios de comunicación ha mejorado. El clima general ha mejorado, de manera que en Europa, la sociedad austríaca ahora ocupa una posición media. Este cambio de la situación se nota especialmente en Viena, la capital (y capital gay) del país y única verdadera gran ciudad de Austria. Con su ambiente gay animado y variado es una de las ciudades más importantes en el área de habla alemana.

En las ciudades de Linz, Graz, Salzburgo e Innsbruck hay un ambiente gay pequeño, pero nada malo. El resto del país no es visitado por los turistas gays por tener un ambiente gay particularmente espectacular, sino por su belleza de paisajes, construcciones históricas, festivales y demás actividades culturales así como por las muy variadas oportunidades de ocio, deporte, etc. en los lagos y en las montañas.

L'Austria è in materia di legislazione uno degli stati più arretrati d'Europa. Nel codice penale esiste ancora una normativa che stabilisce per gli omosessuali (18) un'età minima differente da quella di eterosessuali e lesbiche (14) e punisce i trasgressori con un massimo di cinque anni di pena carceraria. La normativa (§ 209), deve essere applicata dai tribunali; la pena minima prevede 6 mesi di carcere. L'ultima proposta di abolizione del § 209 è stata respinta nel luglio 1998 dal partito popolare conservatore (ÖVP; Partito popolare austriaco; n.d.t.) e dal partito liberale di estrema destra (FPÖ; Partito liberale austriaco). È improbabile che ambo i partiti cambino la loro posizione dopo essere andati al governo a febbraio del 2000. Tuttavia la pressione internazionale che si esercita sull'Austria diventa sempre più forte: Il Consiglio d'Europa, il Parlamento Europeo e la Commissione per i diritti umani dell'UNO hanno invitato più volte e specificatamente l'Austria a cancellare il § 209.
Degli Austriaci si dice che siano piuttosto conservatori e legati alle convenzioni, e ciò non rappresenta senza dubbio un'esagerazione. Tuttavia molte cose sono state fatte negli ultimi anni. L'opinione pubblica e la posizione della maggior parte dei media è mutata positivamente. Il clima sociale è cambiato e può essere annoverato entro la media europea.
Il mutamento di clima si manifesta con particolare chiarezza a Vienna, capitale (gay) e unica vera metropoli austriaca, che con la sua vivace e variopinta scena gay occupa una posizione di punta nell'ambiente di lingua tedesca.
A Linz, Graz, Salisburgo e Innsbruck troviamo una scena gay in parte raffinata ma piuttosto ridotta. Il resto dell'Austria è meta turistica gay non tanto per l'attraente scena locale, quanto per le bellezze del paesaggio, il retaggio storico dell'architettura, i festival e le altre svariate manifestazioni culturali, così come per la possibilità di praticare attività sportive e di tempo libero ai laghi e in montagna.

NATIONAL PUBLICATIONS

■ **Bussi**
Graf-Starhemberg-Gasse 9/4 ✉ 1040 Wien ☎ (01) 505 07 42

📠 (01) 505 49 41-5
Magazine with lots of stories, gossip, events, listings-mostly about the scene in Vienna.

Austria | Bregenz ▶ Fügen-Zillertal

☎ **0676 / 77 30 149 oder 0049-177/6826436**
eMail: **MasterIngo@gmx.net**

Dominanter Er, 34, Deutscher, kräftig, **männlich,** gut bestückt, aktiv, tabulos, in diversen Outfits (Leder, Uniform, Skin, Handwerker, Jeans, Sportswear...) **absolut diskret,** gibt Dir was Du brauchst. Soft bis extrem! Wien-Salzburg-Linz-bundesweit (eigenes Appartement in Wien). Auch Reisebegleitung (weltweit) sowie Wäsche- und Fotoversand möglich!   **www.smcallboy.at.gs**

■ **LAMBDA-Nachrichten**
c/o HOSI Wien, Novaragasse 40 ✉ 1020 Wien ☎ (01) 216 66 04
📠 (01) 216 66 04 📧 lambda@hosiwien.at 💻 www.hosiwien.at
Published four times a year. öS 60 per issue. Approximately 88 pages. Austria's oldest and leading news magazine for gays and lesbians, published by HOSI/Wien. Features national and international reports. Feuilleton. Some commercial and classified advertisements.

■ **XTRA!**
Postfach 77 ✉ 1043 Wien 📧 xtra@nextra.at
Monthly magazine with calendar of events, listing of Vienna's bars and organisations and other information about Vienna's gay scene. Free at gay venues. Official magazine of Safe Way.

NATIONAL COMPANIES

■ **American Discount**
☎ (02236) 22 596 📠 (02236) 47 127
Comics, magazines and books / Comics, Magazine und Bücher.

NATIONAL GROUPS

■ **AG.PRO - Austrian Gay Professionals**
Postfach 95 ✉ 1050 Wien ☎ (01) 548 61 38
📠 (01) 548 61 86-66 📧 info@agpro.at 💻 www.agpro.at

■ **AIDS-Informationszentrale Austria** Mon-Thu 9-15, Fri 9-12.30 h
Eggerthgasse 10/1 ✉ 1060 Wien (near/nahe Naschmarkt)
☎ (01) 585 76 21-3 📠 (01) 585 76 21-6
📧 aidsinfo@aidshilfe.or.at 💻 www.aidshilfe.at

■ **CSD Wien** Office hours Mon Wed 10-20 h
Wasagasse 12/3/5 ✉ 1090 Wien ☎ (01) 319 44 72 33
📠 (01) 319 44 72 99 📧 info@pride.at 💻 www.pride.at
Meetings every 1st Mon/month 19 h. Organisation for a better acceptance of gays,lesbians and transgender persons in society.Regular events „Regenbogenball" in February, "Regenbogenparade" in June, EUROPRIDE 1-30.6.2001.

■ **HOSI Wien-1. Lesben- und Schwulenverband Österreichs/HOSI-Zentrum** Tue Wed (L) 19-?, Thu 17-20 newcomer (coming out-group) Thu 20-? h youth group „Hungrige Herzen"
Novaragasse 40 ✉ 1020 Wien (U-Praterstern/Nestroyplatz)
☎ (01) 216 66 04 (helpline) 📠 (01) 216 66 04
📧 office@hosiwien.at
💻 www.hosiwien.at
Helpline „Rosa Telefon" during office hours.

■ **Rechtskomitee Lambda**
Linke Wienzeile 102 ✉ 1060 Wien ☎ (01) 876 30 61
📠 (01) 876 30 61 📧 rk.lambda@magnet.at
💻 www.ourworld.compuserve.com/homepages/RKlambda/
Legal counselling & help. Newsletter IUS AMANDI.

COUNTRY CRUISING
A2 (Südautobahn) P "P14", last P ➤ Wien, behind km 13,5, from sunset/ ab Dämmerung
A7 P Franzosenhausweg 22-? h
A14 (E60) Lindau ➤ Feldkirch P "Hohenems" 12-3 h

Bregenz ☎ 05574

BARS
■ **Wunderbar** (! B BF glm MA) 9-1 h
Bahnhofstraße 4 ✉ 6900 (near pedestrian zone/nahe Fußgängerzone) ☎ 477 58

HEALTH GROUPS
■ **AIDS-Hilfe Vorarlberg** Counselling: Tue Thu 17-19, Wed Fri 10-13. Test: 17-19 h
Neugasse 5 ✉ 6900 ☎ 465 26 📠 469 04 14

Dornbirn ☎ 05572

SEX SHOPS/BLUE MOVIES
■ **Blue Box Erotik Discount Videothek** (CC GLM LJ VS) Mon-Sat 11-22 h
Bahnhofstraße 26-28 ✉ 6850 (near/nahe Hauptbahnhof)
☎ 555 30
Video rental and purchase, toys and tools, magazines, CD-roms, books.

GENERAL GROUPS
■ **Homosexuelle Initiative (HOSI) Vorarlberg** Counselling Thu 18-20 h
PO Box 841 ✉ 6854 ☎ 469 04 14

Feldkirch ☎ 05522

RELIGIOUS GROUPS
■ **Homosexualität und Glaube (HuG)**
Postfach 522 ✉ 6803

Fügen-Zillertal ☎ 05288

HOTELS
■ **Hotel-Garni Alpenhof** (B BF g H lj MA msg OS SA SB SOL WO) mid Dec-mid Apr, mid May-mid Oct
Sängerweg 490 ✉ 6263 ☎ 620 50 📠 620 50 50
📧 info@alpenhof.cc 💻 www.alpenhof.cc
Gay owned hotel in a romantic setting, ideal for summer and winter holidays. Special gay weeks in winter. 50 km to Innsbruck airport. 20 rooms with bath/shower, balcony, phone, TV, safe, heating, own key. Rates from single room 460-670 ÖS, double 360-470 p.p.

46 SPARTACUS 2001/2002

Gmunden ▶ Graz | Austria

Phil & Jür
Natural Spa™
GAY-BADEHAUS
Wellness - Cruising - Fun 8042 Graz, St. Peter Hauptstrasse 119a
So.......14 - 24 Uhr Mo, Di, Do.......15 - 24 Uhr Mi.......closed Fr.......15 - 01 Uhr Sa.......14 - 02 Uhr

Gmunden ☎ 07612

CRUISING
-Traunbrücke (YG) (below the bridge/unter der Brücke -18 h)

Graz ☎ 0316

GAY INFO
■ **Schwulen- und Lesbenzentrum „feel free"**
Rapoldgasse 24 ✉ 8010 ☎ 32 80 80 📠 31 85 40
💻 rlp@homo.at 💻 www.rlp.homo.at
„Rosa-Lila PantherInnen, Schwulen- und Lesbenzentrum 'feel free'" gives information, counselling also with bibliotheque, café and events.

BARS
■ **Bang** (D DR GLM OS s VS YG) Bar:Thu Sun 21-2, Disco: Fri Sat -4 h
Dreihackengasse 4-10 ✉ 8020 ☎ 71 95 49
■ **BARcelona** (B f GLM MA r P) Mon-Sat 20-4 h
Reitschulgasse 20 ✉ 8010 ☎ 84 52 48
■ **Pepi's** (B glm MA) 18-? h
Griesplatz 36 ✉ 8020 ☎ 71 92 77

CAFES
■ **Na Und?** (B f glm) 16-2 h
Babenbergerstraße 28 ✉ 8020 ☎ 72 38 32

SEX SHOPS/BLUE MOVIES
■ **Erotic Bazar** (CC g) Mo-Sat 10-19
Bindergasse 8 ✉ 8010 ☎ 83 17 65

■ **Sexworld Gayshop Austria** (DR G r VS) Mon-Fri 10-13 h 14-19 h, Sat 10-17 h
Quergasse 1 ✉ 8020 *(near main station/nahe Hauptbahnhof)*
Videos, magazines, PP, toys.

ESCORTS & STUDIOS
■ **Amsterdam-Club** (B CC DR G p R VS) 22-2 h, closed Sun
Quergasse 1/Annenstraße 53 ✉ 8020 ☎ 76 54 59
Gay Swinger Club

SAUNAS/BATHS
■ **Phil & Jür „Natural Spa"** (Ac B d DR f G MA msg p S SA SB VS)
Mon Tue Thu 15-24, Fri-1 Sat 14-2 Sun -24 h Wed closed
St. Peter Hauptstr. 119 a ✉ 8042 *(tram 6, bus 36)* ☎ 42 74 218
Wellness,cruising and fun on 2 floors.

BOOK SHOPS
■ **American Discount** Mon-Fri 9-13 14-18, Sat 9-12 h
Jakoministraße 12 ✉ 8020 ☎ 83 23 24
International magazines, comics, books-including a gay section/ Zeitungs- und Buchladen mit schwuler Abteilung.

GENERAL GROUPS
■ **Hochschülerschaft an der TU Graz, Referat für gleichgeschlechtl. Lebensweisen** (YG) Tue 18-19 h
Lessingstraße 27 ✉ 8010 ☎ 873 51 22 ☎ (0676) 30 54 896
💻 tu@gaystudent.at 💻 www.gaystudent.at
Information office for homosexual students.
■ **Rosalila PantherInnen-Schwul-Lesbische Arbeitsgemeinschaft Steiermark** Mon Thu 19 -22.30 h (Fri women only)
c/o feel free, Rapoldgasse 24 ✉ 8010 ☎ 32 80 80 📠 31 85 40
💻 rlp@homo.at 💻 www.rlp.homo.at

SPARTACUS 2001/2002 | 47

Austria | Graz ▸ Innsbruck

RELAXEN ...
Sauna
Dampfbad
Solarium
Fitneßraum ...

GAY-Wochen im Winter

Fordert doch tel. oder schriftlich unsere GAY-INFO an!

Hotel Alpenhof
Josef R. Kofler
A-6263 Fügen/Zillertal/Tirol-Austria
Sängerweg 490
Phone 0043/(0)5288/62050 · Fax 0043/(0)5288/6205050
Mobiltel. 00 43/(0) 664 337 56 39
www.alpenhof.cc · email: info@alpenhof.cc

HEALTH GROUPS

■ **Steirische AIDS-Hilfe** Mon Wed 11-13, Fri 17-19 consellung, Tue Thu 16.30-19.30 h HIV-test
Schmiedgasse 38/I ✉ 8010 ☎ 81 50 50 📠 81 50 50-6
📧 steirische@aids-hilfe.at ⌨ www.aids-hilfe.at
■ **Stop AIDS Verein zur Förderung von sicherem Sex** Office: Tue 10-12, hotline: Tue 19-20 h
Rapoldgasse 24 ✉ 8010 ☎ 36 66 00 📠 31 85 40
📧 stopaids@homo.at ⌨ www.geilundsafe.at

RELIGIOUS GROUPS

■ **Homosexuelle und Glaube (HuG)** 1st and 3rd Fri/month 19.30 h
c/o feel free, Rapoldgasse 24 ✉ 8010 ☎ 32 80 80 📠 31 85 40
📧 hug-steiermark@gmx.at

CRUISING

-municipal park (fountain)
-Schlammteich -Hauptplatz -Jakominiplatz -Hauptbahnhof -Annenpassage -University: Vorklinisches Institutsgebäude, Parterre
-Hauptplatz
-Jakominiplatz

Innsbruck ☎ 0512

GAY INFO

■ **Homosexuelle Initiative (HOSI) Tirol** (b G MA s) Thu 20.30-23.30 h
Innrain 100 / 1. Stock ✉ 6020 ☎ 56 24 03 📠 57 45 06
📧 hosi.tirol@tirol.com
Different events. Call for details.

BARS

■ **Bacchus** (CC D GLM MA S) Sun-Thu 21-4, Fri Sat -6 h
Salurnerstraße 18 ✉ 6020 (opposite to/gegenüber Spielcasino)
☎ 57 08 94
Bar / Disco with a DJ every day. New chatroom
■ **Piccolo Bar** (b G MA p) 21-4 h
Seilergasse 2 ✉ 6020 (near/nahe „Goldenes Dachl") ☎ 58 21 63

CAFES

■ **Café im Hotel Central** (B glm) 11-23 h
Erlerstraße 11 ✉ 6020 ☎ 59 20
Piano music.

DANCECLUBS

■ **Utopia Kulturverein** (B C glm lj MA S WE) Café Utopia: Mon-Fri 18-3, Basement: Wed-Sat 21-2/3 h
Tschamlerstraße 3 ✉ 6020 ☎ 58 85 87

RESTAURANTS

■ **Emil & Christian's Bistro Café** (BF F g OS) Mon-Fri 7.30-21 h
Anichstraße 29 ✉ 6020 ☎ 58 27 80

Laufend Veranstaltungen

BACCHUS
DAS SCHRILLE SZENELOKAL
BEI DER TRIUMPHPFORTE

jetzt auch im internet:
www.bacchus-bar.com

Auf euren Besuch freut sich das Bacchus Team

FOR GAYS
LESBIANS
TRANSVESTITES
AND FRIENDS

6020 Innsbruck
Salurnerstraße 18
Tel. 0043-512/570894

Täglich ab 21.00 Uhr geöffnet

Innsbruck ▶ Linz Austria

AUCH FÜR DICH GIBT'S BEI UNS BERATUNG + BLUTTESTS GRATIS UND ANONYM

aidsHilfe KÄRNTEN

8.- Mai-Straße 19, 4. Stock, A-9020 Klagenfurt - Tel. 0463/55128, Fax 0463/516492
Öffnungszeiten: Mo, Di, Do von 17 bis 19 Uhr - Blutabnahme: Di von 17 bis 19 Uhr
http://www.aidshilfe.or.at/aidshilfe   e-mail:kaernten@aidshilfe.or.at
ENGLISH COUNSELLING + BLOOD TESTS CONFIDENCIAL AND FREE OF CHARGE

HOTELS
■ **Hotel-Garni Alpenhof**
⇒ Fügen-Zillertal.

HEALTH GROUPS
■ **AIDS-Hilfe Tirol** Mon-Fri 10-15 h
Bruneckerstraße 8 ✉ 6020 ☎ 56 36 21 📠 563 62 19 💻
tirol@aidshilfen.at 💻 www.aidshilfe-tirol.at
HIV and hepatitis testing Tue 13.30-15, Wed 16.30-18 h

SPECIAL INTEREST GROUPS
■ **Libertine**
PO Box 5 ✉ 6027
S/M Initiative.

SWIMMING
-Kranebitter Au (G MA NU) (Leave motorway A 12 Innsbruck to Bregenz at Innsbruck-Kranebitten, take road 171 to Zirl. ℗ at „St. Schüt. Kasern" and get to the left bank of the river Inn. Summer only)

CRUISING
-Hofgarten (Rennweg)
-Boznerplatz
-Hofgarten (Rennweg)

Klagenfurt ☎ 0463

BARS
■ **Absolut** (B d f GLM lj MA OS s TV WE) Mon-Fri 10-4, Sat, Sun & holidays 19-4 h
St. Veiter Straße 3 ✉ 9020 *(near/nahe Stadtpfarrkirche)*
☎ 59 99 99

GENERAL GROUPS
■ **Queer Klagenfurt** (GLM)
PO Box 146 ✉ 9010
Hotline ☎ 50 46 90 Wed 19-21 h

HEALTH GROUPS
■ **AIDS-Hilfe Kärnten** Mon Tue Thu 17-19 counselling, Tue 17-19 h HIV-test
8.-Mai-Straße 19. 4. Etage ✉ 9020 *(4th Floor/4. Etage)* ☎ 551 28
☎ (0676) 718 53 00 (infoline YG) 📠 51 64 92
💻 kaernten@aidshilfe.or.at 💻 www.aidshilfe.or.at/aidshilfe
Also meeting point for gay youth group "Die Welpen" (Fri 19h).
Contact: welpen@gay.or.at; www.welpen.gay.or.at

SWIMMING
-Keutschacher See (NU) (camping)
-Forstsee

CRUISING
-Schubert Park (hinter dem Theater, abends/behind theatre, evenings)
-Heiliger Geist Platz (vor Quelle, spät nachmittags/in front of Quelle Store, late evenings)
-Zwischen/between Bahnhofstraße & Bushaltestelle/bus station (abends/ evenings)
-Bahnhof/railway station

Kolbnitz ☎ 04783

GUEST HOUSES
■ **Gasthof Herkuleshof** (F H OS) 8-24 h, closed mid-January to mid-February.
Am Danielsberg 9815 ✉ 9815 ☎ 22 88 📠 30 02
💻 herkuleshof@utanet.at 💻 www.herkuleshof.com
Rates double from 340 öS per person (bf incl.), 480 half-board.

Krems ☎ 02734

GENERAL GROUPS
■ **Schwuler Stammtisch Krems-Waldviertel** (G MA) biweekly Fri from 20 h
PO Box 2 ✉ 3507 *(pls call for furher information)*
☎ (0664) 325 83 78 📠 2734 36 36 💻 stammtisch-krems@aon.at
💻 members.aon.at/stammtisch-krems

Leoben ☎ 03842

CRUISING
-Bahnhof/station

Linz ☎ 0732

PUBLICATIONS
■ **PRIDE - das schwul/lesbische Bundesländermagazin**
Postfach 43 ✉ 4013 ☎ 60 98 98 📠 60 98 98 1
💻 pride@hosilinz.at 💻 www.pride.or.at
Regional gay paper.

BARS
■ **Blue Heaven** (AC B D DR f G MA s WE) Sun-Thu 20-2, Fri Sat -4 h. Mon closed
Starhembergstrasse 11 ✉ 4020 *(Neustadtviertel, Bus 21)*
☎ 77 43 67
■ **My Way** (B CC GLM MA) Daily 19-? h
Goethestrasse 51 ✉ 4020 ☎ 65 27 60

SPARTACUS 2001/2002 | 49

Austria Linz ▶ Salzburg

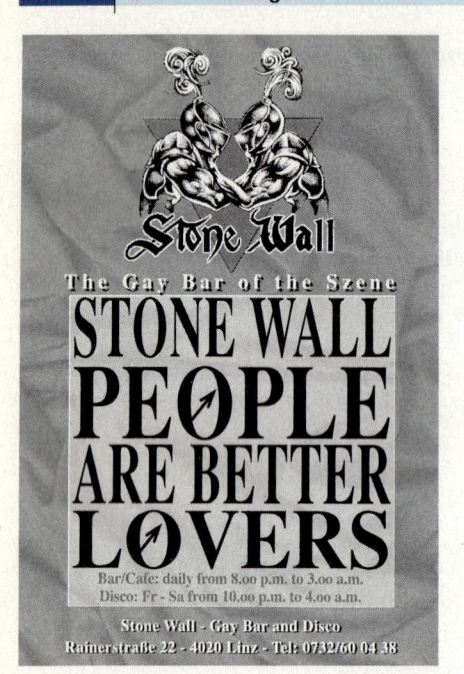

■ **Stone Wall** (AC B CC D f G MA r S WE) Bar/Café: daily from 20-3, Disco: Fri-Sat 22-4 h
Rainerstraße 22 ✉ 4020 ☎ 60 04 38

CAFES
■ **Coffee Corner** (B f GLM MA YG) 18-2 h, closed Sun
Betlehemstraße 30 ✉ 4020 ☎ 77 08 62
■ **Gösser Stub'n** (B F glm MA) 11-1, Sat Sun 17-1 h
Starhembergstraße 11 ✉ 4020 *(Neustadtviertel, Bus 21)*
☎ 79 70 95

SEX SHOPS/BLUE MOVIES
■ **Erotic Center Linz** (CC g) Mo-Sat 9-23 h
Goethe Straße 41 ✉ 4020

GENERAL GROUPS
■ **Homosexuelle Initiative Linz (HOSI)** (GLM MA) Counselling Mon 20-22; Thu 18:30-22 h
Schubertstraße 36 ✉ 4020 ☎ 60 98 98-1/-4 🖷 ooe@hosilinz.at
💻 www.hosilinz.at
Publisher of PRIDE-magazine.

HEALTH GROUPS
■ **AIDS-Hilfe Oberösterreich** Mon 14-18, Wed 16-20, Fri 10-14 h counselling
Langgasse 12 ✉ 4020 ☎ 21 70 🖷 21 70-20
💻 office@aidshilfe-ooe.at 💻 www.aidshilfe-ooe.at

HELP WITH PROBLEMS
■ **Rosa Telefon** Mon 20-22, Thu 18.30-22 h
☎ 60 98 98

SWIMMING
-Weikerlsee (NU YG) (south of Linz in Pichling)
-Pleschingersee (G NU YG) (Linz-Urfahr, southeastern corner of lake)

CRUISING
-Hinsenkampplatz (AYOR) (subway)
-Sonnensteinstraße
-Wiener Straße (OG) (near tram-stop "Unionkreuzung")
-Hauptbahnhof/Main rail station (r)
-Lokalbahnhof (YG)
-Hessenplatz (WE YG)
-Volksgarten (ayor R) (am Bahnhof/near railway station)

Pörtschach am Wörther See ☎ 04272

GUEST HOUSES
■ **Pension Schweiger** (BF CC glm OS) April-October
Annastraße 22 ✉ 9210 ☎ 35 35
Rates from ATS 300-500/person incl. bf.

Salzburg ☎ 0662

GAY INFO
■ **Homosexuelle Initiative Salzburg (HOSI)** (B GLM lj MA) Wed from 19, Fri Sat from 20 h
Müllner Hauptstraße 11 ✉ 5020 ☎ 43 59 27 🖷 43 59 27-27
💻 office@hosi.or.at 💻 www.hosi.or.at

BARS
■ **Kupferpfandl** (B glm lj MA p) 17-4 h
Paracelsusstraße 14 ✉ 5020 *(near main station/nahe Hauptbahnhof)* ☎ 87 57 60

Stone Wall
The Gay Bar of the Szene
STONE WALL PEOPLE ARE BETTER LOVERS
Bar/Cafe: daily from 8.oo p.m. to 3.oo a.m.
Disco: Fr - Sa from 10.oo p.m. to 4.oo a.m.
Stone Wall - Gay Bar and Disco
Rainerstraße 22 - 4020 Linz - Tel: 0732/60 04 38

Die etwas *andere* Pension am Wörthersee

Pension Schweiger
Annastraße 22
9210 Pörtschach
☎ 04272 / 3535

Salzburg ▶ St. Pölten | **Austria**

■ **Oscar's Gay Bistro-Bar** (B GLM MA) Tue-Sat 20-4 h
Gstättengasse 25 ✉ 5020 ☎ 84 38 08
■ **Vis a Vis** (B CC d glm MA s WE) Sun-Wed 20-4, Thu-Sat -5 h
Rudolfskai 27 ✉ 5020 ☎ 84 12 90
■ **2-Stein** (A AC B CC D f GLM MA OS p SNU STV) Sun-Thu 18-4,
Fri Sat -5 h
Giselakai 9 ✉ 5020 (near/nahe Staatsbrücke) ☎ 88 02 01
Disco from 22 h.

RESTAURANTS
■ **Daimler's** (AC CC F glm lj MA N) Bar 18-4, Thu, Sat -5, Restaurant
18-2 h, Mon & holidays closed
Giselakai 17 ✉ 5020 ☎ 87 39 67

SEX SHOPS/BLUE MOVIES
■ **Erotic Center Salzburg** (CC g) Mo-Sat 9-23 h
Ferd. Porsche-Str. 7 ✉ 5020

BOOK SHOPS
■ **American Discount** (g) Mon-Fri 9-13 14-18, Sat 9-12 h
Waggplatz ✉ 5020 ☎ 84 56 40

HEALTH GROUPS
■ **Aidshilfe Salzburg** Counselling: Mon Wed Thu 17-19, HIV- and
Hepatitis-test: Mon Thu 17-19 h
Gabelsbergerstraße 20 ✉ 5020 ☎ 88 14 88 📠 881 94 43
💻 salzburg@aidshilfen.at 💻 www.aidshilfen.at

HELP WITH PROBLEMS
■ **Rosa Telefon** Fri 19-21 h
☎ 43 59 27 📠 43 59 27-27 💻 office@hosi.or.at
💻 www.hosi.or.at

RELIGIOUS GROUPS
■ **Homosexuelle und Glaube (HuG) Salzburg** Meetings 1st and
3rd Wed 20 h
c/o KHG, Philharmonikergasse 2 ✉ 5020 ☎ 84 13 27

CRUISING
-Staatsbrücke (daytime only/nur tagsüber between/zwischen "Café
Bazar" & "Staatsbrücke")
-Philharmonikergasse (under church/unter der Kirche)
-Mirabellgarten (AYOR R) (Rosenhügel. Condom vending machine at
the WC)

Sölden ☎ 05254

GUEST HOUSES
■ **Frühstückspension Herrmann Fiegl** (BF glm H MA OS)
Schmiedhof 35 ✉ 6450 ☎ 26 36 📠 26 36
💻 www.members.aon.at/schmiedhof35
Nice rooms with a view. All rooms with shower/WC, balcony and bf incl.
Rates/person single ÖS 350, double 320. Apartment 90 sqm with kitchen, tiled stove and sat-TV ÖS 300/person up to 6/8 persons. Pool and sauna within 10 minutes walk. Newly renovated.

St. Pölten ☎ 02742

CRUISING
-hinter der Sparkasse am Domplatz/behind the bank at Domplatz
-Ende der/End of Julius-Raab-Promenade (YG)

Daimler's
Restaurant · Bar

Wir freuen uns

auf Ihren Besuch

in unseren

vollklimatisierten

Räumlichkeiten.

Giselakai 17 · 5020 Salzburg
Tel. +43-(0)662-87 39 67
email: daimlersalzburg@aol.com

Öffnungszeiten: tägl. von
18.00 - 2.00 Uhr
Montag und Feiertag Ruhetag

!AidshilfeSalzburg

Gabelsbergerstraße 20
A- 5020 Salzburg
Tel.: 0043-662-88 14 88
Fax: 0043-662-88 19 443
E-Mail: Salzburg@aidshilfen.at
www.aidshilfen.at

Telefonische Beratung & allgemeine Auskünfte:
Montag bis Freitag 10-12 Uhr
Montag, Mittwoch, und Donnerstag 17-19 Uhr

Persönliche Beratung:
Montag, Mittwoch und Donnerstag 17-19 Uhr

Blutabnahme für HIV- bzw. Hepatitis-Test:
Montag und Donnerstag 17-19 Uhr

Psychosoziale Beratung & Betreuung für Betroffene:
Montag bis Freitag 10-12 Uhr

Austria Steyr ▶ Wien

Steyr ☏ 07252

SEX SHOPS/BLUE MOVIES
■ **Sex-Shop Steyr** (CC g) Mon-Sat 9-19 h
Damberggasse 19 ✉ 4400

CRUISING
-Main station/Hauptbahnhof (YG) (15-22 h)

Velden am Wörther See ☏ 04274

SWIMMING
-Forstsee (NU) (between Velden and Pörtschach)

CRUISING
-Park gegenüber/opposite Hotel Corinthia

Villach ☏ 04242

SWIMMING
-Erlebnistherme Warmbad (g sa) (11-20 h)

Wels ☏ 07242

CRUISING
-Volksgarten (near/Nahe Messegelände, summer/Sommer)
-Busbahnhof (YG)
 (12-15 h, near the SAB-IN-Buffet, popular)
-Hauptbahnhof (16-22 h)

Wien ☏ 01

✱ The annual rainbow parade is probably the most obvious sign from Vienna's gay viewpoint, in which the city attempts to return to being one of the central European metropolis. Tens of thousands of gays and lesbians, with their friends have shown how change can be brought about by standing up and showing themselves for what and who they are in public.

The scene in Vienna has mirrored this concept for a long time now. It is nevertheless astonishing how many cafés, bars, discos, shops and saunas/bath houses there are in this so-called conservative city. The majority of theses gay places are to be found in the south west boundary of the city, around the attractive Naschmarkt.

Other places of interest and saunas are to be found in the near of the Ringstraße, where the City Hall of Vienna is to be found. Here the annual spectacular - the LifeBall takes place. From here it is not far to Stephens Dome or Hofburg, in which , as well as in Schönbrunn, the Empress Sisi lived.

✱ Die jährliche Regenbogenparade ist wohl das deutlichste Zeichen dafür, daß sich Wien anschickt, aus schwuler Sicht in die Reihe der aufstrebenden zentraleuropäischen Metropolen aufzurücken. Zehntausende von Schwulen, Lesben und ihre Freunde haben gezeigt, daß öffentliche Präsenz doch sehr viel ausmacht und in dieser Form auch einen Aufbruch markieren kann.

Die Wiener Szene hat dies schon lange deutlich gemacht. Es ist doch erstaunlich, wie viele Cafés, Bars, Discos, Läden, Saunen es gibt in dieser als konservativ verschrienen Stadt. Die meisten dieser Einrichtungen mit ihrem eigenen Charme finden sich südwestlich an den Stadtkern angrenzend um den sehenswerten Naschmarkt.

Weitere Lokale und Saunen finden sich innerhalb der Ringstraße, an

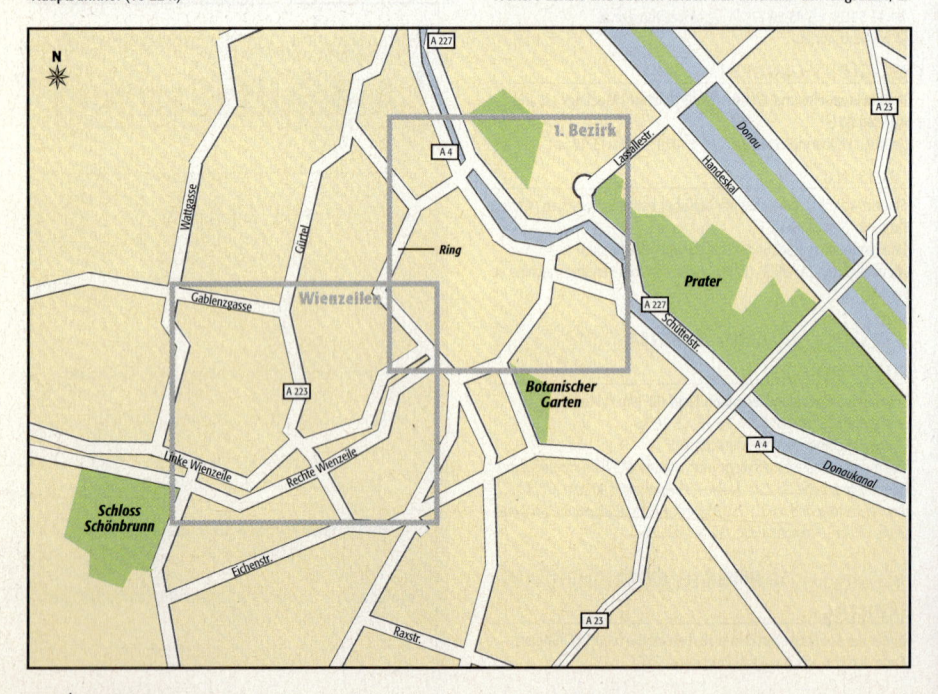

Wien | **Austria**

EURO PRIDE
VIENNA 2001

1st June - 30th June 2001
Vienna/Austria

CSD Wien – Christopher Street Day Vienna
Wasagasse 12/3/5
A-1090 Wien

tel ++43 - 1 - 319 44 72 - 33
e-mail info@pride.at
www.pride.at   and   www.europride.at

© Sebastian Menschhorn

Austria — Wien

denen übrigens auch das Wiener Rathaus liegt, das jährliche Wiener Megaspektakel LifeBall beherbergt. Von hier aus ist es nicht weit zum Stephansdom oder zur Hofburg, in der - wie in Schönbrunn - unser aller Sisi (die Kaiserin) wohnte.

2001 wird EUROPRIDE in Wien stattfinden. Den ganzen Juni über wird es zahlreiche Veranstaltungen geben: einen richtigen Wiener Eröffnungsball, Sportturniere, ein Fetisch-Wochenende, Straßenfest, politische Debatten, Film, Literatur, Medien. Gekrönt wird das Spektakel durch die Regenbogenparade am 30. Juni, zu der einige hunderttausend Menschen auf der Wiener Ringstraße erwartet werden, und anschließendem Riesenfest.

✻ La parade Arc-en-ciel est la démonstration que Vienne est en passe de devenir une des métropoles gaies d'Europe centrale. Des dizaines de milliers de gais et lesbiennes - et leurs amis - ont montré que manifester publiquement permet de faire progresser les choses dans le bon sens.

La capitale a déjà fait ses preuves dans ce domaine; il est étonnant de voir à quel point les cafés, bars, clubs, magasins et saunas gais sont nombreux dans cette ville si conservatrice. La plupart de ces établissements au charme certain se trouve dans le sud-ouest de la ville, tout près du remarquable marché, le Naschmarkt. D'autres établissements et saunas se situent à l'intérieur du Ring, près de l'Hôtel de Ville qui accueille aussi chaque année la grandiose fête qu'est le Life Ball. D'ici, il ne faut pas loin pour aller admirer la cathédrale Saint Etienne ou le château de la Hofburg qui, avec Schönbrunn, était la résidence de l'inoubliable impératrice Sissi.

La Europride de 2001 se tiendra à Vienne. Tout le mois de juin sera prétexte à de nombreuses manifestations: un vrai bal d'ouverture à la viennoise, des tournois de sport, un week-end fétiche, une fête de rue, des débats politiques, du cinéma et de la littérature sont au programme. Le summum des festivités sera atteint le 30 juin, lorsque des centaines de milliers de personnes descendront dans les rues de la ville pour célébrer une gigantesque fête.

● El "Desfile del Arcoiris" (desfile del orgullo gay) anual es la demostración más clara de que Viena se está convirtiendo en una de las metrópolis gays centroeuropeas. Decenas de miles de gays y lesbianas acompañados por sus amigos y amigas demostraron que la presencia pública puede cambiar mucho y puede marcar un verdadero punto de partida. El ambiente gay vienés lleva tiempo enseñándolo: es asombrosa la cantidad de cafeterías, bares, tiendas y saunas homosexuales que se pueden encontrar en esta ciudad supuestamente tan conservadora. La mayoría de los sitios con un encanto muy particular se encuentran en la zona situada al sudoeste del centro, alrededor del llamado Naschmarkt.

Otros locales y saunas se encuentran dentro de la zona delimitada por la Ringstraße, la gran Avenida de Circunvalación donde también se encuentra el Ayuntamiento, que una vez al año hospeda el gran espectáculo LifeBall. Desde el Ring no quedan lejos la catedral famosa Stephansdom o el palacio Hofburg donde, igual que en Schönbrunn, vivió Sisi emperatriz.

En 2001, Viena será anfitrión de EUROPRIDE. Durante el mes de junio habrá muchas actividades: un gran baile de inauguración, manifestaciones deportivas, un fin de semana para los fetichistas, fiestas callejeras, debates políticos, películas, literatura, medios de comunicación ... El momento culminante del espectáculo será el "Desfile del Arcoiris" el día 30 de junio. Se espera que varios cientos de miles de personas participen en el desfile en la Ringstraße, la gran Avenida de Circunvalación, y a continuación en la gran fiesta final.

✖ L'annuale "Regenbogenparade" [Parata dell'Arcobaleno; n.d.t.] è la testimonianza più lampante che Vienna dal punto di vista gay si accinge ad essere promossa tra le file delle più ambiziose metropoli del centroeuropa. Decine di migliaia di gay, lesbiche e i loro amici hanno dimostrato che la loro presenza pubblica conta veramente molto e che queste forme segnano un passo in avanti.

La scena gay viennese l'ha già messo in chiaro da molto tempo: è sorprendente quanti café, bar, discoteche, negozi e saune ci siano in questa città tacciata di conservatorismo.

La maggior parte di queste istituzioni dal fascino singolare si trovano a sud-ovest nel cuore della città ai margini del "Naschmarkt", un'attrazione locale.

Altri locali e saune si trovano sulla Ringstraße, dove tra l'altro c'è anche il palazzo del municipio, che ospita il megaspettacolo annuale "LifeBall". Da qui non distano molto il duomo di S. Stefano e la Hofburg, dove, così come il castello di Schönbrunn, visse la nostra cara Sisi (l'imperatrice).

Nel 2001 a Vienna avrà luogo EUROPRIDE. Per tutto il mese di giugno ci saranno numerose manifestazioni: un vero ballo viennese di apertura, gare sportive, un weekend feticista, feste di strada, dibattiti politici, cinema, letteratura e media. Lo spettacolo sarà incoronato il 30 giugno dalla Regenbogenparade, per cui si prevede l'arrivo a Vienna sulla Ringstraße di alcune centinaia di migliaia di persone, e dalla gigantesca festa che seguirà.

GAY INFO

■ **Schwulen- und Lesbenberatung Rosa Lila Tip** Mon-Fri 17-20 h
Linke Wienzeile 102/103 ✉ 1060 (U4-Pilgramgasse) ☏ 585 4343
(G) ☏ 586 8150 (L) 🖷 587 1778 📧 info@villa.at
🌐 www.villa.at
Betreuung, Infos, Schwulen-, Lesben und Elterngruppen. Bibliothek, Kondome, Gleitmittel/Gay-lesbian switchboard : Counselling, infos, glb-groups, library, condoms, lubricants.

Wien | Austria

Des vacances à Vienne? Placez votre ordre et nous vous ferons recevoir un exemplaire gratuit!

Vacanze a Vienna? Ordina subito il tuo esemplare gratuito!

Urlaub in Wien? Bestelle jetzt Dein Gratis-Exemplar!

Planning a vacation in Vienna? Order your free sample copy now!

Das Wiener Szene-Magazin
Vienna's Gay Mag • Periodico gay di Vienna

XTRA!

P.O.Box 77 • A–1043 Vienna
Austria • Europe   E-mail: xtra@nextra.at

Austria Wien

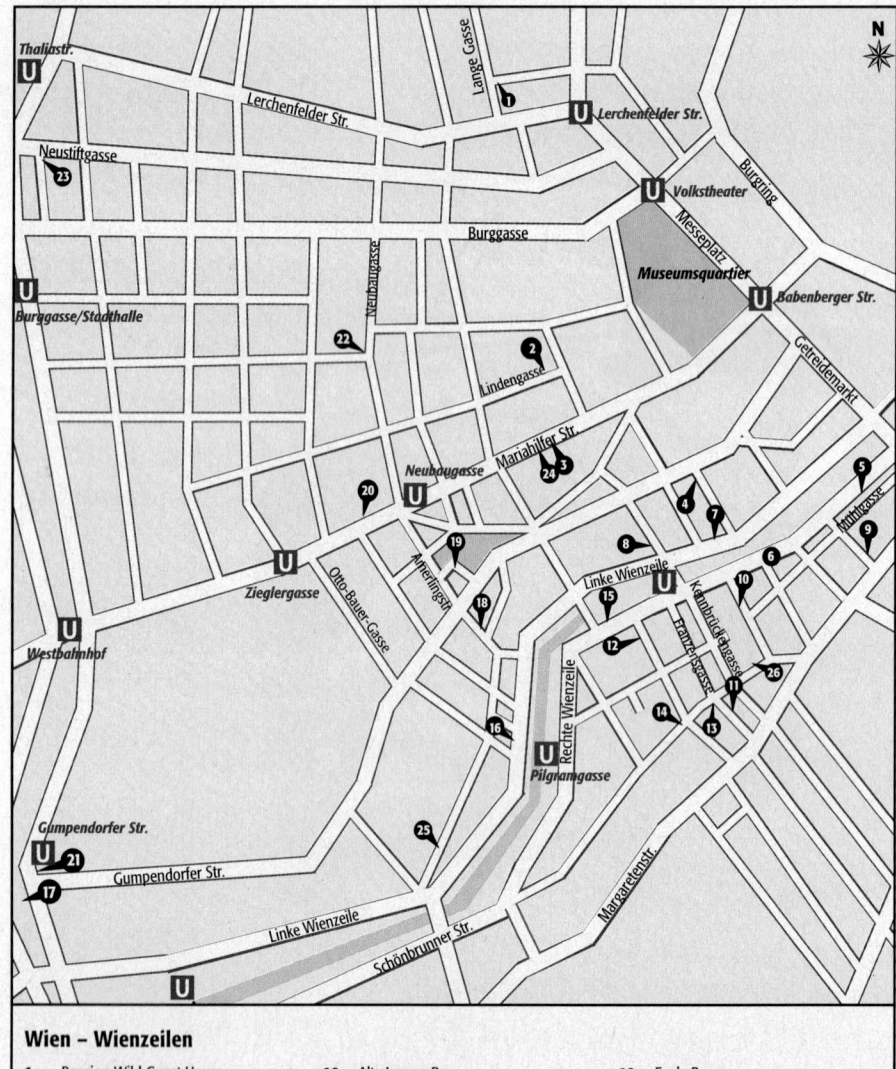

Wien – Wienzeilen

1. Pension Wild Guest House Sport-Sauna
2. Tiberius Fetish Shop
3. X-Bar
4. Mango Bar
5. American Discount Book Shop
6. Willi's Lounge Bar
7. Café Savoy
8. Alfi's Goldener Spiegel
9. Nanu Bar
10. Alte Lampe Bar
11. Café Reiner Bar
12. Living Room Bar
13. Café Joy Bar
14. Wiener Freiheit Bar
15. Man for Man Sex Shop/ Blue Movie
16. Café Willendorf Restaurant Rosa Lila Villa Gay Info
17. Love & Fun Sex Store
18. Nightshift Bar
19. Eagle Bar
20. Skyline Sex Shop
21. Arcotel Hotel Wimberger
22. American Discount Book Shop
23. Apollo Sauna
24. Stöger Restaurant
25. Sexworld International Sex Shop/Blue Movie
26. Orlando Restaurant

Wien | Austria

BOYS & MEN
Escortservice for Gentlemen

9820622

www.boys-men.com

Good
Times

All creditcards!

Escorts von 19-35 haben Zeit für Dich! Service in ganz Österreich und weltweit. Eines der exklusivsten Gay-Escortservices Europas seit 1993. Diskret und prompt.
Escorts aged 19-35 have time for you! Service in Austria and worldwide. One of Europe's most exclusive Gay Escort Services since 1993. Discrete and prompt.

Call 982 06 22
täglich 13-2 Uhr/daily 1 p.m. - 2 a.m.

Austria Wien

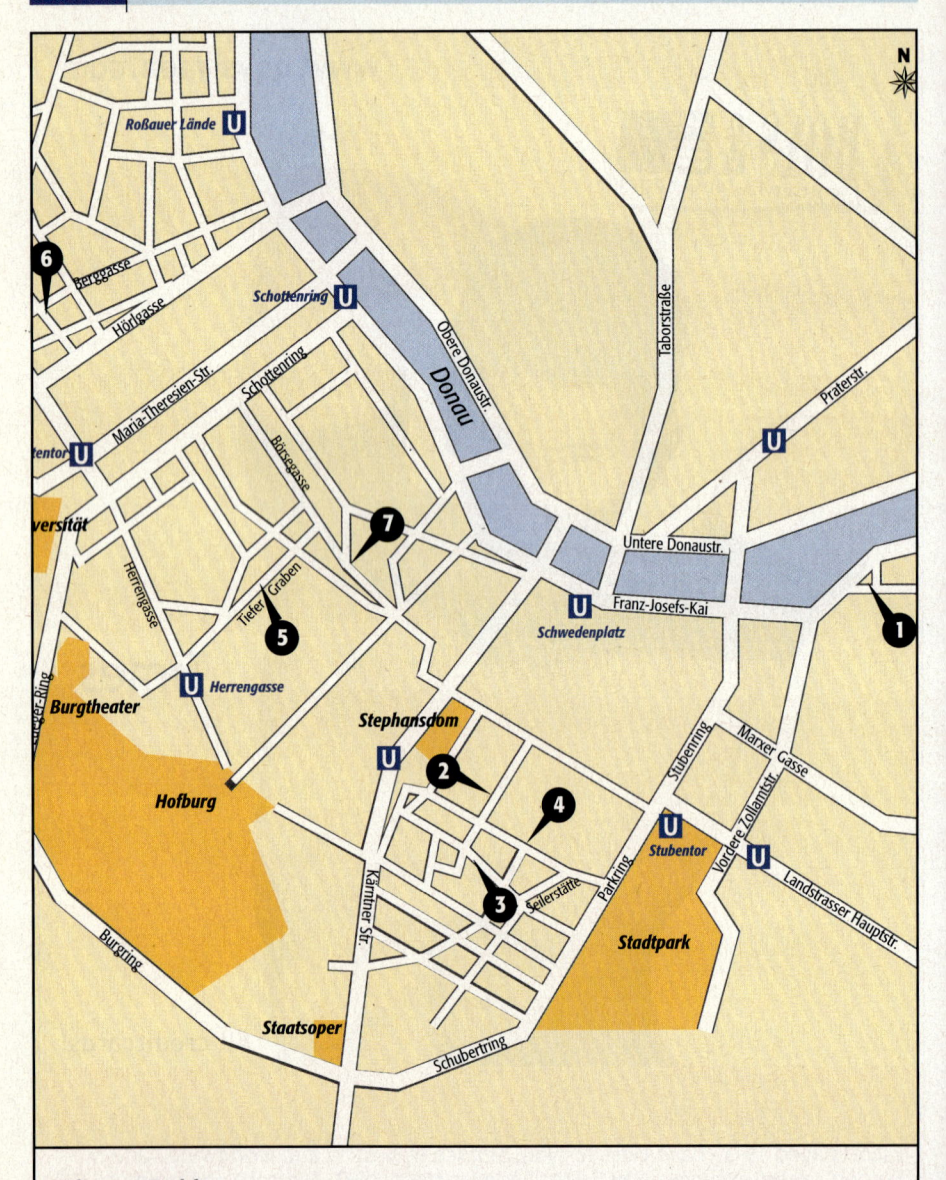

Wien – 1. Bezirk

1. Urania Hotel
2. Das Versteck Bar
3. Kaiserbründl Sauna
4. Santo Spirito Restaurant
5. Why Not Danceclub
6. Café Berg / Löwenherz Bookshop
7. Papageno Reisen Travel Agent

SPARTACUS 2001/2002

Wien | Austria

WHY NOT
CLUBDISKOTHEK

GAY BAR DISCOTHEK
ON 2 FLOORS

Friday + Saturday + night before public hollydays
10PM - 6AM

1010 Wien, Tiefer Graben 22
Tel: +43 1 925 30 24
www.why-not.at

ROSA LILA VILLA

LESBEN UND SCHWULEN HAUS

ROSA TIP
SCHWULE BERATEN & INFORMIEREN
01-585 4343

LILA TIP
LESBEN BERATEN & INFORMIEREN
01-586 8150

PERSÖNLICH UND TELEFONISCH

bar restaurant café
willendorf
01-587 17 89

LINKE WIENZEILE 102, A-1060 WIEN
U4/Pilgramgasse

Austria | Wien

PUBLICATIONS

■ **Vienna Gay Guide**
c/o Pink Advertising, Wurmsergasse 35/17 ✉ 1150 ☎ 789 97 37
🖨 789 97 37 office@gayguide.at
💻 www.gayguide.at

TOURIST INFO

■ **Wiener Tourismusverband** 9-19 h
Albertinaplatz ✉ 1025 *(at Maysedergasse)* ☎ 211 14-222
🖨 216 84 92 info@info.wien.at
💻 www.info.wien.at

BARS

■ **Alfi's Goldener Spiegel** (B F G MA p R) 19-2 h, Tue closed
Linke Wienzeile 46 ✉ 1060 *(U4-Kettenbrückengasse. Entrance/Eingang Stiegengasse)* ☎ 586 66 08
Bar and restaurant. Good Viennese cuisine.

■ **Alte Lampe** (! AC B f G MG S) Sun Wed Thu 18-1, Fri Sat 20-3 h
Heumühlgasse 13 ✉ 1040 *(U4-Kettenbrückengasse)*
☎ 587 34 54
Vienna's oldest gay bar. Happy hour 18-20 h. Relaxed atmosphere, sometimes piano bar.

■ **Café Joy** (AYOR B f G MA N R) 20-4 h, Sun closed
Franzengasse 2 ✉ 1050 *(U4-Kettenbrückengasse)* ☎ 586 59 38
Small and run-down bar frequented by a dubious crowd.

■ **Café Reiner** (B CC DR G MA p r VS) 21-4 h
Kettenbrückengasse 4 ✉ 1040 *(U4-Kettenbrückengasse)*
☎ 586 23 62
Darkroom with cubicals; late night meeting place.

■ **Mango Bar** (AC B G p s YG) 21-4 h
Laimgrubengasse 3 ✉ 1060 *(U4-Kettenbrückengasse)*
☎ 587 44 48
Best 23-1 h. Popular and trendy.

■ **Nanu Bar** (AC B f G MA N OS) 18-2 h
Schleifmühlgasse 11 ✉ 1040 *(U4-Kettenbrückengasse)*
☎ 587 29 87 *Internet-café.*

■ **Old Inn** (B d F g MA OS STV WE) Tue-Thu 18-2, Fri Sat 18-4 (kitchen until 3) Sun Mon closed
Schönbrunnerstrasse 4 ✉ 1040 *(U4-Kettenbrückengasse, near/Nähe Naschmarkt)* ☎ 586 1787

■ **Versteck. Das** (B glm N YG) Mon-Fri 18-24, Sat 19-24 h, closed Sun
Grünangergasse 10 ✉ 1010 *(U1-Stephansplatz - entrance downstairs)* ☎ 513 40 53 *Vienna's smallest bar.*

■ **Warm Up** (AC B CC F G MA N s) Sun-Thu 18-2, Fri Sat -4 h
Preßgasse 30 ✉ 1040 *(U4-Kettenbrückengasse)* ☎ 585 41 27

■ **Wiener Freiheit** (B D f g MA N OS p r s WE) Mon-Sat 20-4 h, Sun closed
Schönbrunner Straße 25 ✉ 1050 *(U4-Kettenbrückengasse)*
☎ 913 91 11

■ **X Bar. Café** (B CC f G MA) Mon-Sun 16-2 h
Mariahilfer Straße 45 ✉ 1060 *(Raimundhofpassage. U3-Neubaugasse)* ☎ 585 24 37

MEN'S CLUBS

■ **Eagle-Bar** (! AC B DR G lj MA p VS) 21-4 h
Blümelgasse 1/Amerlingstrasse ✉ 1060 *(U3-Neubaugasse/Amerlinggasse)* ☎ 587 26 61
Sex shop integrated: leather, rubber, videos and magazines.

---

vienna's number one
mango bar

täglich/daily 21-4h
a-1060 vienna, laimgrubengasse 3; t. +43.1.587 44 48

Wien | Austria

EAGLE VIENNA

Leather Jeans **BAR**

OPEN DAILY 21 - 04

1060 WIEN
BLÜMELGASSE 1
TEL. 587 26 61

www.eagle-vienna.com

LMC VIENNA

[lo:sch]
DIE LMC VIENNA LOCATION

A-1150 Wien, Fünfhausgasse 1
Telefon: + 43 1 895 99 79
http://www.tiberius.at

Grafik: SCHLEICHWERBUNG; © ART by SEPP of VIENNA

Austria — Wien

■ **[lo:sch]** (B DR G LJ MA P) Fri & Sat 22-2, sometimes Sun 18-22 h
Fünfhausgasse 1 ✉ 1150 *(Ecke/on the corner of Sechshauer Str)*
☎ 895 99 79
Home of the LMC Vienna. Ask for dates and parties. Dresscode. 2 floors with darkroom, sling, changing room & shower available. Fri-Sun parties see homepage www.tiberius.at/lmc.htm
■ **Nightshift** (AC B DR G lj MA VS) 22-4, Fri Sat-5 h
Corneliusgasse 8/Kopernikusgasse ✉ 1060 *(U4-Kettenbrückengasse)* ☎ 586 23 37
Billards. A late night bar.
■ **Stiefelknecht** (B DR f G LJ MA p s VS) 22-2, Fri Sat -4 h
Wimmergasse 20 ✉ 1050 *(Tram 62/65-Kliebergasse. Entrance/Eingang Stolberggasse)* ☎ 545 23 01

CAFES

■ **Berg, das Café** (! A AC B BF F G MA) 10-1 h
Berggasse 8/Wasagasse ✉ 1090 *(near/Nähe Universität, U2- Schottentor)* ☎ 319 57 20
Next to the Löwenherz bookshop.
■ **Savoy. Café** (! B f GLM MA OS) Mon-Fri 17-2, Sat 9-2 h, closed Sun
Linke Wienzeile 36 ✉ 1060 *(U4-Kettenbrückengasse)* ☎ 586 73 48
Popular. Century old traditional café. Enjoy the 6 m high ceiling and the possibly largest mirrors in Europe.

DANCECLUBS

■ **Liquid Gay Club Night** (D G) Fri 23- ? h
Rotgasse 9 ✉ 1010
■ **U4 Heaven Gay Night** (AC B D DR GLM lj s TV YG) Thu 23-5 h
Schönbrunnerstraße 222 ✉ 1120 *(U4-Meidlinger Hauptstraße)*
Tradition Thu night-out.

■ **Why Not** (AC B CC D f GLM p s YG) Fri-Sat and before public holidays 22- ? h
Tiefer Graben 22 ✉ 1010 ☎ 925 30 24

RESTAURANTS

■ **Café Willendorf** (! B F GLM MA OS) 18-2 (meals -24 h)
Linke Wienzeile 102 ✉ 1060 *(U4-Pilgramgasse)* ☎ 587 17 89
Many vegetarian dishes. Near to the city center.
■ **Living Room** (! A B CC F G MA OS) 18-4 h (kitchen-3.30)
Franzensgasse 18/Grüngasse ✉ 1050 *(U4-Kettenbrückengasse)* ☎ 585 37 07
Good Austrian wines&food as well as international cuisine. In winter piano music on Fridays.
■ **Motto Bar-Restaurant** (A AC B F g MA OS) Mon-Sun 18-4 h
Schönbrunnerstraße 30 ✉ 1050 *(Eingang / Entrance Rüdigergasse)* ☎ 587 06 72
Chic restaurant&bar. Reservation recommended.
■ **Orlando** (A CC F gLM MA OS S) 18-2 h (meals 18-24 h)
Mollardgasse 3 ✉ 1060 *(U4-Pilgramgasse)* ☎ 967 35 50
Lesbian run. Very fine daily menu.
■ **Santo Spirito** (B BF CC F glm OS) Mon-Thu 18-2, Fri Sat 11-3, Sun 10-2 h
Kumpfgasse 7 ✉ 1010 *(U1-Stephansplatz)* ☎ 512 99 98
Classical music and bohemian atmosphere. Best after 21 h. Trendy

SEX SHOPS/BLUE MOVIES

■ **Austria Gay Markt** (CC g p VS) Mon-Fri 10-19 Sat -17 h
Mariahilferstraße 72 ✉ 1070 *(1. Stock/upstairs, U3-Neubaugasse)* ☎ 523 75 07
Large selection of videos, toys, aphrodisiacs, cabins

Ein Traum in Nostalgie

CAFE SAVOY

A nostalgic Dream

A - 1060 Wien
Linke Wienzeile 36
Tel. 586-73-48

Wien | Austria

SANTO SPIRITO
the classical music
Café – Restaurant – Bar

Mon–Thu 18–02   Fri + Sat 11–03   Sun 10–02   Dinner until midnight

A-1010 Wien • Kumpfgasse 7 • ✆ +43/(0)1/512 99 98

Living Room
Bar · Restaurant

18 – 04 h (warme Küchekitchen open until – 03.30 a.m.)

Telefon 585 37 07
Franzensgasse 18/Grüngasse

CAFÉ REINER

...cool drinks - hot darkrooms - horny guys...

...nightly from 09.00 p.m. - 04.00 a.m. possible...

WIEN 4., KETTENBRÜCKENGASSE 4

Austria | Wien

■ **Erotic Center Naschmarkt** (CC g VS) Mon-Sat 9-23 h
Rechte Wienzeile 21 ✉ 1040
Big gay courner selection. Individual cubicals

■ **Man for Man. Gay Sex Shop** (AC CC DR G MA VS) Mon-Sat 11-23 h, closed Sun & public holidays
Hamburgerstraße 8 ✉ 1050 *(U4-Kettenbrückengasse)*
☎ 585 20 64
Only gay sex shop in town. Cabins, gay-cinema, toys, books, videos.

■ **Man's World** (CC G) Mon-Sat 10-20 Sun& on public holidays -18 h
Odoakergasse 21 ✉ 1160 ☎ 40 23 462

■ **Sexworld International** (AC b CC DR g MA VS) Mon-Sat 10-21 h, closed Sun & public holidays
Mariahilfer Straße 49 ✉ 1060 *(U-Neubaugasse)* ☎ 587 66 56
Large gay selection. Video cabins. Cruising area on 500 mts.

---

man for man
1. WIENER GAYSHOP
Tel.: 585 20 64

seit Nov. 2000 auch:
GAY-KINO
GAY-CINEMA
4 Programme gleichzeitig
jede Woche 8 neue Filme
DARKROOMS - KABINEN

★ BÜCHER UND MAGAZINE
★ VIDEOS (VERKAUF - VERLEIH)
★ TOYS

geöffnet: Mo.-Sa. 11-23 Uhr

man for man
1050 Wien, Hamburgerstr. 8
-50m von U4-Station-Kettenbrückengasse-

Cruising Area on 500 meters

Video Rooms   Darkroom   Rest Room
31 Cabins   Condoms   16 Films + Drink = 1 Price
Videos   Toys   Day Ticket

das führende Fachgeschäft in Wien:

SEXWORLD
international

Mariahilfer Straße 49 (U-Neubaugasse – exit Stiftgasse)
www.sexworld.at · Mo–Sa 10–21 Uhr

SPARTACUS 2001/2002

Wien | Austria

GAY MARKT

DEINE ERSTE WAHL IN WIEN !
DISKRET, FREUNDLICH, SAUBER – RIESENAUSWAHL

ca. 2000 GAY-VIDEOS ALLER RICHTUNGEN
GROSSE AUSWAHL AN CD-ROM + DVD
DONGS · BUTT PLUGS · REALISTICS
ADJUSTABLES · NATURALS · LOVE RINGS
CONDOMS · APHRODISIACS · LOTIONS · LUBRICANTS
VERSAND: EUROPAWEIT !

MONDAY–FRIDAY 10–19 UHR

1070 WIEN, MARIAHILFERSTR. 72

DISKRET IM GESAMTEN 1. STOCK

WWW.GAYMEGASHOP.COM

Austria Wien

Dynamisch Vertrauensvoll Dynamic Prompt Discreet Diskret

Nationwide exclusive escorts
Österreichweit niveauvolle Escorts
Daily/Tgl. 10:00-24:00

www.Model-Escort.com

Tel. +43 (0)699 176 176 17

Pictured - Lucas

CINEMAS

■ **Fortuna-Kino** (g VS) Wed 20-24 Sun 18-24 h
Favoritenstr. 147 *(10.Bezirk)* ☎ 603 90 45
entrance fee 90,- ÖS. Also sale of videos rubber, lubricants and other useful stuff.

■ **Tivoli-Kino, „Cinema Erotic"** (g VS) Sun(G) 18.30-22 h
Winckelmannstr. 128 *(15.Bezirk)*
☎ 893 69 58
Entrance fee S 70,-

■ **Währinger Gürtelkino** (g VS) Gay on Mon&Sat 20-24 h
Schulgasse 1 *(18.Bezirk)*
☎ 405 22 21
Entrance fee 90,- ÖS. Slightly shabby& rather uncomfortable squeeky benches.

ESCORTS & STUDIOS

■ **Boys & Men Escort Service Wien, Linz, Graz, Salzburg, Innsbruck, Klagenfurt** (CC G msg LJ) 13-2 h
PO Box 8 ✉ 1131 ☎ 982 06 22
Well known gay escort service, established 1993. Home and hotel visits, menstrip, international travelescorts.

■ **Model Escort Agency** (CC G) 17-24 h
Postfach 155 ✉ 3302 ☎ (0699) 17 61 76 17
House/hotel visits anywhere in Austria. Also international travel escorts.

SAUNAS/BATHS

■ **Apollo City** (B CC DR f G MA msg OS P SA SB SOL VS YG) 14-2 h
Wimbergergasse 34 ✉ 1070 *(U-Burggasse)*
☎ 523 08 14/13
Sauna on two floors with terrace. Own parking place.

1. Man´s World Gay Shop

Gay Videos, Toys und vieles mehr!

MAN´S WORLD

alle Versandangebote jetzt auch zum Abholen!

**Odoakerg. 32
1160 Wien**

Nähe Wilhelminenstr. Sandleiteng.

Mo-Sa.
10-20 Uhr

Tel: 01 402 34 62
mansworld@telering.at
www.mansworld.at

MODELS BY **CAZZO** FILM BERLIN

SPARTACUS 2001/2002

Wien | Austria

apollo
city - sauna - wien

sauna - dampfkammer
swimmingpool - solarium
ruhekabinen - video / tv
bar & snacks
eigener parkplatz

mo - partnertag
mi - jugendtag

ermäßigung f. studenten u. militär

1070 Wien, Wimbergergasse 34
Täglich 14 - 2h   Tel.: 523 08 14

U6 - 5 - 48A

E-Mail: apollo-city-sauna.gmbh@chello.at
www.geocities.com/apollo_city_sauna

Austria — Wien

SPORT SAUNA
die junge gay Sauna zum Verlieben

Lange Gasse 10
A-1080 Wien
Tel. +43 1 4067156
15 – 1 Uhr (3 pm – 1 am)
http://www.sportsauna.at

■ **Kaiserbründl** (! AC B CC DR F G MA msg Pl s SA SB SOL VS WO) Mon-Thu 14-24, Fri-Sat -2, Sun 12-24 h
Weihburggasse 18-20 ✉ 1010 *(U1-Stephansplatz, entrance green door)* ☏ 513 32 93
Beautiful interior: Built in 1887 in Moorish style. Newly renovated on 1200 m², 3 floors, 3 bars, darkroom-maze. Mon coffee & cake free. WE Viennese buffet, Fri Satyricon temple shows, 1/2 price for under 25.

■ **Sport-Sauna** (AC B CC f G p SA SB VS YG) 15-1 h
Lange Gasse 10 ✉ 1080 *(U2-Lerchenfelder Strasse/Bus 13A-Piaristengasse)* ☏ 406 71 56
Intimate sauna frequented by a young crowd along with gay hotel Pension Wild.

BOOK SHOPS

■ **American Discount** Mon-Fri 9-18, Sat 9-12 h
Neubaugasse 39 ✉ 1070 ☏ 523 37 07

■ **American Discount** Mon-Fri 9.30-18.30, Sat 9-13 h
Rechte Wienzeile 5 ✉ 1040 ☏ 587 57 72

■ **American Discount**
Donaustadtstrasse 1 (Donauzentrum) ✉ 1220
☏ 203 95 18

■ **Löwenherz** (CC G) Mon-Fri 10-19, Sat 10-17 h
Berggasse 8 ✉ 1090 *(Entrance Wasagasse. Near Universität. U2-Schottentor)* ☏ 317 29 82

LEATHER & FETISH SHOPS

■ **Tiberius Leather Latex & Tools** (A CC GLM LJ S) Mon-Fri 15-18.30, Sat 11-15 h and by appointment
Lindengasse 2a ✉ 1070 *(U3-Neubaugasse)* ☏ 522 04 74
Fetish store, leather, latex, toys etc.

BLUE BOX
EROTIK DISCOUNT
A-6850 Dornbirn, Bahnhofstrasse 26-28 Tel. 0043 (0)5572 55750 Fax. 372828
www.the-bluebox.com
Online Shop with more then 1.500 Articel for Him and Her.
Free Picture Announcment, Chatroom and a lot more!
STOP for a free Visit!
Any Question! Mail to: info@the-bluebox.com

10% OFF Each Order with Code: SP410

VIENNA'S GAY SAUNA Nº ONE
KAISERBRÜNDL
SAUNA.FITNESS.CRUISING.BAR
1010 WIEN, WEIHBURGGASSE 18-20 TEL: 01/5133293
MO - DO 14-24H, FR - SA 14-02H, SO 12-24H
WWW.GAYSAUNA.AT

Austria | Wien

HOTEL URANIA BETRIEBS GMBH

1030 WIEN, OBERE WEISSGERBERSTRASSE 7
TELEFON 713 17 11 · TELEFAX 713 56 94
E-mail Adresse: hotel.urania@chello.at

First Art Hotel Vienna
all rooms individually designed; gays welcome; centrally located;
gay information available at the reception; friendly and comfortable

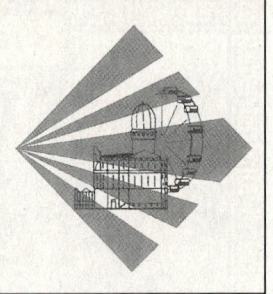

---

complete offer
see page Germany/Berlin

VIENNA – from ATS 280 –
overnight accomodation service
· about 750 beds · more than 28 cities ·

enjoy bed & breakfast

central booking office Berlin ☏ **+49-30-236 236 10** 4:30-9:00 pm local time
Fax +49-30-23623619 · info@ebab.com · www.ebab.com

**DER REISEPARTNER FÜR DEN
"SPEZIELLEN" URLAUB WELTWEIT ODER
IN ÖSTERREICH**

MANTOURS

Ein Produkt von Papageno Reisen
1010 Wien
Passauer Platz 6

Tel.: 0043 1 533 06 60
FAX: 0043 1 533 06 50

Wien | Austria

Hotel-Pension WILD

GAY-ONLY
GAY-SAUNA

Bitte zeitgerecht buchen
www.pension-wild.at
Phone: +43 1 406 51 74
Fax: +43 1 402 21 68
e-Mail: info@pension-wild.at
Lange Gasse 10   A-1080 WIEN

TRAVEL AND TRANSPORT

■ **Papageno** (CC) Mon-Fri 9-18 h
Passauer Platz 6 ⊠ 1010 *(U-Schwedenplatz)* ☎ 533 06 60
🖨 533 06 50
Gay travel service./Anbieter schwuler Reisen.

HOTELS

■ **Urania. Hotel** (B BF CC F G H)
Obere Weißgerberstraße 7 ⊠ 1030 *(U-Schwedenplatz, Tram N, O)*
☎ 713 17 11   🖨 713 56 94   💻 hotel.urania@chello.at
All rooms with shower, WC, telefone & cable TV. Rates from EZ 750 ÖS, DZ 950 ÖS. Rooms per hour 380-780 ÖS.

GUEST HOUSES

■ **Pension Wild** (BF CC G H msg SA SB)
Lange Gasse 10 ⊠ 1080 *(U2-Lerchenfelder Strasse)* ☎ 406 51 74
🖨 402 21 68   💻 info@pension-wild.at   💻 www.pension-wild.at
Centrally located. Gay sauna in the house, 3 single rooms, rates at ATS 690,- (shower, WC, cableTV, minibar, telephone), 3 double rooms, rates ATS 790,- (shower, telephone), 3 double rooms rates 590,- (standard) bf. incl., 3 appartments for 1-4 persons.

PRIVATE ACCOMMODATION

■ **Enjoy Bed & Breakfast** (BF G H MA YG) 16:30-21 h
☎ +49 (30) 236 236 10   🖨 +49 (30) 236 236 19
💻 Info@ebab.com   💻 www.ebab.com
Accommodation sharing agency. All with shower & bf. DM 40-45p.p.

American Discount
more books, more magazines, more sports...more dreams

more shops

EKZ Donauzentrum	Neubaugasse 39	Rechte Wienzeile 5
A 1220 Wien	A 1070 Wien	A 1040 Wien
T +43-1-203 95 18	T +43-1-523 37 07	T/F +43-1-587 57 72

Austria | Wien

GENERAL GROUPS
■ **Rechtskomitee Lambda**
Linke Wienzeile 102 ✉ 1020 ☎ 876 30 61 🖥 rk.lambda@magnet.at

FETISH GROUPS
■ **LMC Vienna** (G LJ MA) irregular events Fri-Sun
PO Box 34 ✉ 1011 📠 587 50 60 🖥 lmcvienna@tiberius.at
🖥 www.tiberius.at
Member of ECMC. Leather & Motorbike Community of Vienna. Weekly events in leather bar [Lo:sch]

HEALTH GROUPS
■ **Aids Hilfe Wien** (A BF glm F S) Mon 8.30-23,Tue -19, Wed Fri -20, Thu -22 h
Mariahilfer Gürtel 4 ✉ 1060 (U6-Gumpendorfer Straße) ☎ 599 37
📠 599 37 16 🖥 wien@aids.at 🖥 www.aids.at
Kostenlose HIV Antikörpertests / Free HIV testing. Counselling Mon Wed 16-20, Thu 9-13, Fri 14-18 h.
■ **Aids-Informationszentrale Austria**
Eggerthgasse 10/1 ✉ 1060 (near/nahe Naschmarkt)
☎ 585 76 21-3 📠 585 76 21-6 🖥 aidsinfo@aidshilfe.or.at
🖥 www.aidshilfe.at
No counselling.

HELP WITH PROBLEMS
■ **Anonyme-Alkoholiker-Gruppe für homosexuelle Männer und lesbische Frauen** Sat 19 h
c/o Zentrale Kontaktstelle, Geblergasse 45/III ✉ 1170
☎ 408 53 77

RELIGIOUS GROUPS
■ **Homosexuelle und Kirche (HuK)**
PO Box 513 ✉ 1011 ☎ 405 87 78 (Johannes) ☎ (02732) 85 403 (Wolfgang) 🖥 huk-wien@gmx.at
■ **Re'uth-Vereinigung Jüdischer Homosexueller in Österreich**
Scheugasse 12/18 ✉ 1100 ☎ 952 35 66 🖥 re_uth@hotmail.com (John)

SPECIAL INTEREST GROUPS
■ **Libertine. S/M-Initiative Wien** Meeting every 2nd &4th Fri 20 h at Stiftgasse 8, 1070 Wien (Amerlinghaus)
Postfach 63 ✉ 1011 ☎ (0664) 488 31 12 🖥 contact@libertine.at
🖥 www.libertine.at
S/M-initiative. Publishes newsletter „Unter Druck". Reunion every 3rd Tue/month Café SMart, Köstlerg. 6, 1060 Wien.

SPORT GROUPS
■ **Volleyballverein Aufschlag** Mon-Fri 10-18 h
c/o Rosa Lila Villa, Linke Wienzeile 102 ✉ 1060 ☎ 587 17 78
🖥 Aufschlag@gay.or.at

SWIMMING
-Dechantlacke in der Lobau (NU) (Bus 91 A vom Vienna International Center zum Restaurant Roter Hiasl, dann 10 Minuten Fußweg/take Bus 91 A from Vienna International Center to Restaurant Roter Hiasl, then 10 minutes walk)
-Donauinsel (NU) (vis-à-vis Leopoldsberg; Bus 33 B vom Franz-Jonas-Platz bis Überfuhrstrasse, dann über die "Jedleseer Fußgängerbrücke" 500 m rechts/take Bus 33 B from Franz-Jonas-Platz to Überfuhrstrasse, cross the "Jedleseer Bridge", then 500 m to the right)
-Donauinsel "Toter Grund" (! NU) (Bus 91 A bis Steinspornbrücke. Über die Brücke, dann ca 500 m nach links. Populär./take bus 91 A to Steinspornbrücke. After crossing the bridge 500 m to the left. Very popular)
-Wienerberg 1010 (Tram 65 ☞ "Raxstraße", go to Sickingengasse via Raxstraße. There's a small lake, gay in the nude area)

CRUISING
-U-Bahn-Stationen/subway stations:
Vorgartenstraße, Donauinsel, Keplerplatz, Lerchenfelderstraße (afternoons/nachmittags)
-Albertina Passage (left of opera, very popular afternoons and nights/links neben der Oper, nachmittags und nachts)
-Florianigasse/Langegasse (AYOR) (afternoons/nachmittags/)
-Beginning of/Anfang der Prater Hauptallee (ayor)
-Türkenschanzpark (Hasenauerstraße / Litrowgasse & Hasenauerstraße / Gregor-Mendel-Straße, nachts/at night)
-Babenberger Passage/Burgring (cruising in the toilets)
-Rathauspark (after sunset till dawn, very popular/von Sonnenuntergang bis Sonnenaufgang, populär)
-Schweizer Garten (AYOR r) (am/next to Südbahnhof; Turks, Arabs)
-Waldmüllerpark (AYOR) Landgutgasse/Neilreichgasse
-Nepomukberger Platz (cruising in the toilets)

Wiener Neustadt ☎ 02622

SEX SHOPS/BLUE MOVIES
■ **Art-X** (AC CC glm MA) Mon-Fri 10-20 h, Sat 10-17 h
Stadionstraße 38 ✉ 2700 (at FMZ) ☎ 895 55
One of Austria's biggest erotic shops.
■ **Erotic-Center Wr. Neustadt** (CC g) Mo-Sat 9-20 h
Grazer Straße 81 ✉ 2700

GENERAL GROUPS
■ **Mattersburger Gay-Clique**
PO Box 219 ✉ 2700

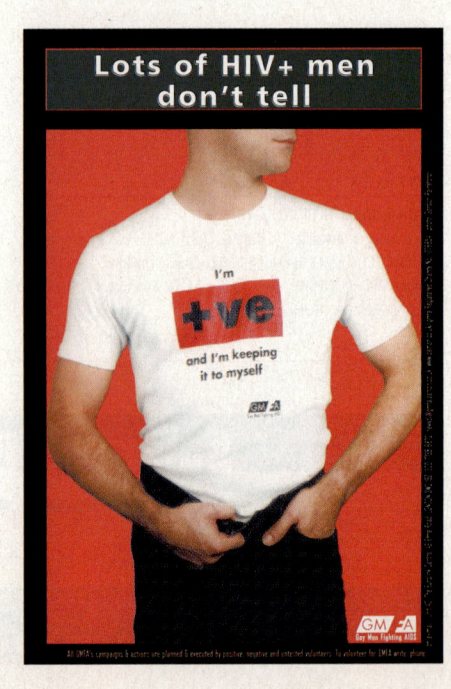

Belarus

Name: Weißrussland • Biélorussie • Bielorussia • Russa Bianca
Location: Eastern Europe
Initials: BY
Time: GMT +2
International Country Code: ☎ 375
International Access Code: ☎ 8 (wait for tone) 10
Language: Bielorussian, Russian
Area: 207,600 km² / 80,154 sq mi.
Currency: 1 Belarus-Ruble (BYR) = 100 Kopecks
Population: 10,410,000
Capital: Minsk
Religions: 60% Russian Orthodox, 8% Greek Catholic
Climate: Winters are generally cold, summers are cool and moist. Belarus is in between continental and maritime climates.

✳ Homosexuality between consenting adults is legal. The age of consent is set at 18 years for both gays and straights.

★ Einvernehmliche Homosexualität zwischen Erwachsenen ist legal. Das Schutzalter liegt für Hetero- wie Homosexuelle bei 18 Jahren.

✳ L'homosexualité entre adultes consentants n'est pas un délit. La majorité sexuelle est fixée à 18 ans pour tous.

⬢ La homosexualidad por acuerdo entre dultos es legal. La edad de consentimiento es de 18 años, independientemente de la orientación sexual.

✖ L'omosessualità tra adulti consenzienti è legale. La maturità sessuale è di 18 anni per tutti.

NATIONAL GAY INFO

▪ **Gay.ru**
PO Box 1 ✉ 109 457 Moscow 🖥 www.gay.ru
Russian National website of Gays, Lesbians, Bi- and Transsexuals. The most comprehensive website covering all aspects of gay life in all Republics of the former USSR, including Belarus. Reliable, exhaustive and up-to-date information. English version available.

NATIONAL PUBLICATIONS

▪ **Forum Lambda**
PO Box 23 ✉ 220 006 Minsk ☎ (017) 213 26 93
📧 gayforum@irex.minsk.by 🖥 www.irex.minsk.by/~gayforum
Monthly gay, lesbian and transsexual magazine. Published since June 1998.

NATIONAL GROUPS

▪ **Belarus Lambda League for Freedom of Sexual Minorities (BLL)**
PO Box 23 ✉ 220 006 Minsk 📧 gayforum@irex.minsk.by

🖥 www.irex.minsk.by/~gayforum
Founded in 1998. ILGA member. AIDS prevention.

Minsk ☎ 17

DANCECLUBS

▪ **Mayak (Lighthouse)** (B D f G R STV WE) Thu-Sat 24-6 h
43 Platonova vulitsa *(Metro Ploschad Yakuba Kolasa)*

SAUNAS/BATHS

▪ **Bathhouse** (g SA SB) 9-22 h
Moskovskaya vulitsa *(Metro-Institute of Culture)*

CRUISING

- „Panikovka" (YG, OG) (Metro Oktyabryaskaya, behind Yanka Kupala Theater)
- Park Gor'kogo (AYOR) (pathways near the central WC)
- Railway station (area behind the WC on bobruyskaya vulitsa)
- Park Cheluskintsev (AYOR) (WC with interesing graffiti)

Belgium

Name: Belgique/België • Belgien • Bélgica • Belgio
Location: Western Europe
Initials: B
Time: GMT +1
International Country Code: ☎ 32 (leave the first 0 of area codes)
International Access Code: ☎ 00
Language: French, Dutch, also German in one province
Area: 30,518 km2 / 11,787 sq mi.
Currency: 1 Belgian Franc (BFr) = 100 Centimes. 1 EURO = 100 EURO Cents (The Euro can only be used in the clearance system)
Population: 10,213,000
Capital: Bruxelles/Brussel
Religions: 88% Roman Catholic
Climate: Moderate climate with mild winters and cool summers. It's rainy, humid and cloudy.
Important gay cities: Bruxelles/Brussel, Antwerpen, Gent

✱ The most topical conflict in Belgium, which has been going on for many decades now, is the language. Flemish (a Dutch dialect) is spoken in the north of the country (Flanders), and French in the south (Wallony) and German in the east. The city of Brussels is bilingual. Even the street names are in both French and Dutch. This all has a certain influence on the Belgian gay life. There are no national homosexual organisations (with the exception of the BLGP - Belgian Lesbian & Gay Pride). There are, however, many regional organisations such as the FWH in Flanders and Tels Quels in Brussels and Wallony.
Homosexuality in Belgium was decriminalised in the 19th century. In 1998 the parliament voted in a law which permits non married couples the right to draw up a legal contract of co-habitation and includes homosexual couples under this law. This law has been adversely effected by the opposition on behalf of the Christian socialist political party in Flanders. Since the elections in June 1999 this party is an opposition party and there is a good chance that this law may finally come into force. At present the discussions are further to include the right for homosexual couples to marry and the right to adopt children.
The age of consent is set at 16 years of age. The general attitude towards homosexuals is open-minded. Rainbow flags can be seen in increasing numbers flying above bars and other gay establishments.
Over and above their sense for hospitality, the Belgians are renown for their cuisine, their chocolates and beers which are internationally renowned.
Tels Quels

★ Einer der größten Konflikte in Belgien ist das nunmehr schon seit Jahrzehnten andauernde Sprachproblem. Flämisch (ein niederländischer Dialekt) wird im Norden des Landes (Flandern) gesprochen, Französisch hingegen spricht man in Wallonien und Deutsch im Osten des Landes. Die Hauptstadt Brüssel selbst ist zweisprachig und sogar die Namen der Straßen sind sowohl in französischer als auch in flämischer Sprache vertreten. Diese Gegebenheiten haben einen gewissen Einfluß auf das Gay-Leben in Belgien. Es gibt zwar keine nationale Homosexuellen-Organisation (eine Ausnahme bildet das BLGP – Belgian Lesbian & Gay Pride), aber viele regionale Organisationen wie der die der "FWH" in Flandern und die Organisation "Tels Quels" in Brüssel und in Wallonien. Seit dem 19. Jahrhundert ist in Belgien Homosexualität nicht mehr strafbar. 1998 verabschiedete das belgische Parlament ein Gesetz, das es nicht verheirateten Paaren gestattet einen legalen Vertrag des Zusammenlebens zu entwerfen; dieses Gesetz gilt auch für homosexuelle Paare. Dieses Gesetz wurde durch die christlich soziale Partei Flanderns blockiert. Seit den Wahlen im Juni 1999 ist diese Partei eine oppositionelle Partei und die Chancen stehen gut, damit dieses Gesetz endlich in Kraft treten kann. Derzeit gehen die Diskussionen in Richtung einer Einbeziehung des Rechts für homosexuelle Paare zu heiraten und Kinder adoptieren zu dürfen.
Das Schutzalter liegt bei 16 Jahren. Die allgemeine Haltung gegenüber Homosexuellen ist offen. Regenbogenflaggen wehen immer öfter über Bars und anderen Gay-Treffpunkten. Für ihre Gastfreundschaft und darüber hinaus sind die Belgier für ihre Küche, ihre Schokolade und ihre vielen international bekannten Biersorten berühmt.
Tels Quels

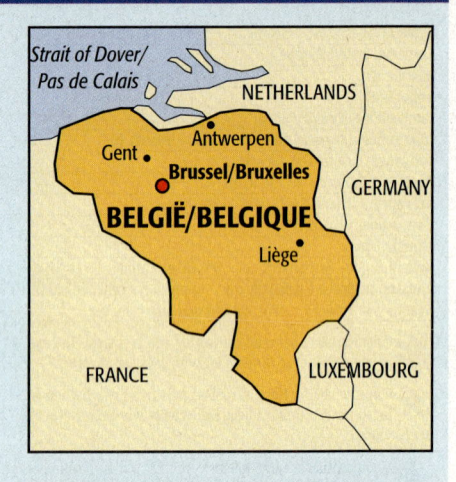

✱ La chose la plus frappante en Belgique est certainement le conflit linguistique qui date maintenant depuis plusieurs décennies. Le flamand (un dialecte néerlandais) est parlé dans la partie nord du pays (Flandre), le français dans la partie sud (Wallonie) et l'allemand dans les cantons de l'est. La ville de Bruxelles est bilingue. Même les noms de rues sont indiqués en français et en néerlandais. Cela influence bien sûr la vie homosexuelle belge : il n'existe - à l'exception de la BLGP (Belgian Lesbian & Gay Pride) - aucune association homosexuelle nationale. Il existe par contre plusieurs organisations régionales dont la FWH en Flandre et Tels Quels à Bruxelles et en Wallonie.
L'homosexualité en Belgique n'est plus incriminée depuis le 19e siècle. En 1998, le Parlement votait une loi permettant aux couples non mariés de conclure un contrat de cohabitation légale et reconnaissait de ce fait les couples homosexuels. Cette loi ne fut cependant mise en application qu'en 2000 en raison du blocage opéré par le parti social-chrétien flamand. Depuis les élections de juin 1999, celui-ci s'est retrouvé dans l'opposition et la nouvelle majorité a pu mettre la loi en application. Actuellement, des dis-

Belgium

cussions ont lieu afin de permettre aux couples homosexuels l'accès au mariage, le droit à l'adoption et à la coparentalité.
La majorité sexuelle est fixée à 16 ans. L'attitude générale envers les homosexuels est ouverte. On peut voir de plus en plus souvent des drapeaux arc-en-ciel orner les façades des bars et autres établissements gais.
En plus de leur sens de l'hospitalité, les Belges sont connus pour leur cuisine, leur chocolat et leurs bières qui ont acquis une renommée internationale.
Tels Quels

El conflicto más tópico de este país es la cuestión de la lengua.que lleva varias décadas debatiéndose. Flamenco, un dialecto del neerlandés, es hablado en el norte del país, en Flandres, el francés se habla en la zona del sur, en Valonia, y el alemán en la parte oriental de Bélgica. La ciudad de Bruselas es bilingüe, y hasta los nombres de las calles se indican en flamenco y en francés. Todo ello tiene cierta repercusión en la vida gay en Bélgica. No existen organizaciones homosexuales a nivel nacional (con excepción de la BLGP, "Orgullo Lésbico y Gay Belga"). Hay, sin embargo, muchas organizaciones regionales como la FWH en Flandres y Tels Quels en Bruselas y Valonia.
La homosexualidad fue legalizada en en siglo XIX. En 1998, el parlamento votó una ley que concede el derecho de firmar contratos de convivencia a parejas no casadas (parejas de hecho) e incluyó a las parejas homosexuales en esta ley. El partido socialista cristiano de Flandres se opuso a esta ley. Desde las elecciones en junio de 1999, este partido forma parte de la oposición, por lo que es probable que la ley finalmente pueda entrar en vigor. Actualmente, los debates se centran en la inclusión en esta ley del derecho de casarse y adoptar niños también para homosexuales.
La edad de consentimiento es de 16 años. La actitud general hacia los homosexuales es muy abierta. Cada vez hay más bares y otros establecimientos gays con banderas del arcoiris. Los belgas tienen fama de ser muy hospitalarios, pero también son famosos por su cocina, sus chocolates y cervezas con reputación internacional.
Tels Quels

In Belgio il conflitto più notevole che si manifesta già da molti anni, è il problema della lingua. Il fiammingo, un dialetto ollandese, è parlato al
nord del paese, in Fiandra, mentre invece si parla il francese al sud, in Vallonia, e il tedesco nella parte orientale del Belgio. La città di
Bruxelles è bilingue e pure i nomi delle strade sono sia in francese che in fiammingo. Tutto ciò ha una certa influenza sulla vita gay belga. A livello nazionale non vi sono organizzazioni gay; un1eccezione è il BLGP – il Belgian Lesbian & Gay Pride. Tuttavia esistono tante organizzazioni regionali come ad esempio la FWH in Fiandra e la Tels Quels a Bruxelles e in Vallonia.
In Belgio, l1omosessualità non viene più punita dal 19 secolo. Nel 1998 il parlamento ha approvato una legge che permette alle coppie non sposate, omosessuali inclusi, di stendere un contratto di coabitazione. Questa legge è stata bloccata dall1opposizione e cioè dal partito Cristiano sociale in Fiandra. Dal giugno 1999 questo partito è un partito d1opposizione e buone sono le possibilità che tale legge potrebbe finalmente entrare in vigore. In questo momento le discussioni vanno persino nella direzione di permettere alle coppie omosessuali di sposarsi e di conferirle il diritto di adottare dei figli.
L1età minima per contatti omosessuali è di 16 anni. L1attitudine generale nei confronti di omosessuali è aperta e il numero delle bandiere con i
colori dell1arcobaleno sventolando sopra i bar ed altri luoghi gay è in forte aumento. Oltre che per la loro ospitalità, i belgi sono conosciuti per
la cucina, il cioccolato e le birre di fama internazionale.
Tels Quels

NATIONAL GAY INFO
■ **Belgian Lesbian & Gay Pride (BLGP)**
Kammerstraat 22 ✉ 9000 Gent ☎ (09) 223 69 29
🖷 (09) 223 58 21
Organisers of the national pride in Brussels, each year in May.
■ **Gay Info Line** 9-17 h
☎ (09) 223 69 29 ☎ (09) 223 58 21 🖷 (09) 223 58 21

NATIONAL PUBLICATIONS
■ **Gay Kiss Kontaktmagazine**
Postbus 69 ✉ 2100 Deurne ☎ (03) 320 98 27 🖷 (03) 320 98 29
💻 info@gaykiss.net 💻 www.gaykiss.net
Monthly magazine in Dutch with classifieds and ads of gay venues.
■ **Gus**
Rue de Verrewinkel 5a ✉ 1180 Bruxelles ☎ (02) 375 93 96
🖷 (02) 375 36 59
Gay monthly magazine available for free at gay venues.
■ **Potins de Bruxelles. Les** (GLM)
43 Rue du Midi ✉ 1000 Bruxelles ☎ (02) 512 28 76
🖷 (02) 512 58 69 💻 lespotinsdebruxelles@busmail.net
Gay and lesbian monthly magazine available for free at Brussels gay venues.
■ **Regard** (GLM)
B.P. 215 ✉ 1040 Bruxelles 4 ☎ (02) 733 10 24 🖷 (02) 732 10 81
💻 regard@euronet.be
Bi-monthly magazine featuring cultural, international, local news for the French speaking gay community. About 50 pages. FB 90.-

■ **Secret Magazine**
P.B. 1400 ✉ 1000 Bruxelles ☎ (02) 223 10 09 🖷 (02) 223 10 09
SM-magazine with gay and non-gay ads.
■ **Tels Quels Magazine**
Rue du Marché au Charbon 81 ✉ 1000 Bruxelles
☎ (02) 512 45 87 🖷 (02) 511 31 48 💻 telsquels@skynet.be
Cultural and political reports and comments. Interviews. List of events. International and national ads. Photos. Monthly magazine for the French speaking gay community. More than 30 pages. For BF 100 at numerous points of sale.
■ **Uitkomst**
c/o Gespreks- en Onthaal Centrum, Dambruggestraat 204
✉ 2060 Antwerpen ☎ (03) 233 10 71 🖷 (03) 234 33 39
Articles of general interest, gay liberation, book and film reviews, political commentary. Free copy on request.
■ **Zizo** (GLM) 9-17 h
Kammerstraat 22 ✉ 9000 Gent ☎ (09) 223 69 29
🖷 (09) 223 58 21 💻 zizo@fwh.be 💻 www.fwh.be
News, politics, culture, interviews, short stories, list of events and classifieds in Dutch.

NATIONAL HELPLINES
■ **Aidstelefoon** Mon-Fri 14-22, Sat -17 h
Postbus 169 ✉ 2060 Antwerpen ☎ (078) 15 15 15
💻 info@aidstelefoon.be 💻 www.aidstelefoon.be
Helpline for people with HIV/AIDS in Dutch.

Belgium Aalst

NATIONAL COMPANIES

■ **G Mail** (G LJ MA VS)
Postbus 5 ✉ 9000 Gent 1 ☎ (077) 35 02 55 (Dutch) ☎ (077) 35 02 56 (French) 📠 g-mail@skynet.be 🖥 www.g-mail.com
Gay-erotic postmail.

NATIONAL GROUPS

■ **BGMC-Knalpijp**
Vlaanderenstraat 22 ✉ 9000 Gent ☎ (09) 221 60 56 ☎ (02) 270 01 05 📠 (02) 270 14 91
Belgian Gay Motor Club.

■ **Commission Homosexualité et Droits Humains (Amnesty International)**
9 Rue Berckmans ✉ 1060 Bruxelles ☎ (02) 538 81 77 (Brian May) 📠 bmay@aibf.be

■ **Federatie Werkgroepen Homoseksualiteit (FWH)** (GLM MA)
Mon-Tri 9-12.30, 13-17.15, Fri until 16.30 h
Kammerstraat 22 ✉ 9000 Gent ☎ (09) 223 69 29 📠 (09) 223 58 21 📠 info@fwh.be 🖥 www.fwh.be

■ **Fédération des Associations Gayes et Lesbiennes (FLAG)** (GLM)
44 Rue du Souvenir ✉ 1070 Bruxelles 📠 fagl_be@hotmail.com

■ **Girth & Mirth - Belgium** (CC G lj MA)
B.P. 1014 ✉ 6000 Charleroi 1 ☎ (071) 56 05 80 📠 (071) 51 84 01 📠 girth&mirth@must.be 🖥 www.biggerworld.com
Club for fat men, bears and their admirers. Publishes a magazine „Fat Angel Times". Organizes events and conventions mostly in Brussels. Regular meetings in Oasis Sauna. Call for information on activites.

■ **HIV-Vereniging Vlaanderen** Mon-Fri 11-16, Positive line: Mon 14-16 Wed 19-21 h
Kipdorpvest 50 ✉ 2000 Antwerpen *(Tram 2-VII Olympiadelaan)*
☎ (03) 238 68 68 📠 (03) 248 42 70 📠 info@hiv-vereniging.be 🖥 www.hiv-vereniging.be
Working group of and for people with HIV/AIDS and their relatives and friends in Flanders.

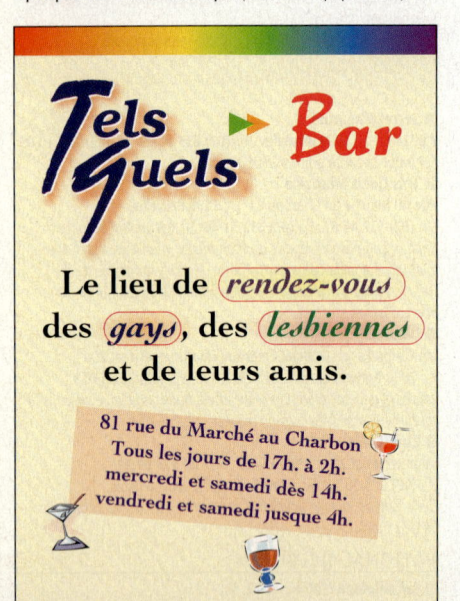

■ **Liga van Gespreks- en Onthaalcentra voor Homo's**
Mon-Fri 12-18 h
Dambruggestraat 204 ✉ 2060 Antwerpen ☎ (03) 233 10 71 📠 (03) 234 33 39

■ **MSC Belgium** (G LJ MA) Meeting: 1st. Fri 22-? h at the Duquesnoy, Bruxelles
P.B. 699 ✉ 1000 Bruxelles ☎ (02) 293 08 48
📠 mscbelgium@compuserve.com
National fetish group. Member of ECMC.

■ **Tels Quels** (A B GLM) Mon-Fri 10-16.30 h
Rue du Marché au Charbon 81 ✉ 1000 Bruxelles
☎ (02) 512 45 87 📠 (02) 511 31 48 📠 telsquels@skynet.be
Social service, bar, library, magazine, choir, young group, lesbian group, Brussel gay & lesbian film festival/Service social, bar, bibliothèque, magazine, chorale, groupe jeunes, groupe lesbien, festival du film gay et lesbien de Bruxelles.

■ **Tiberias** (GLM MA)
C. Meunierstraat 95/8 ✉ 3000 Leuven ☎ (016) 22 76 09
National Dutch religious organisation.

■ **Wel Jong, Niet Hetero** (GLM YG)
PO Box 323 ✉ 9000 Gent 📠 info@weljongniethetero.be
🖥 www.weljongniethetero.be
Gay youth groups of Flanders and Brussels. Organises a summer camp each year.

■ **Werkgroep Homoseksualiteit en Geloof**
C. Meunierstraat 95/8 ✉ 3000 Leuven ☎ (016) 22 76 09
Religious gay group.

■ **Werkgroep Ouders van Homofielen (WOH)** (GLM)
Ullenshofstraat 5 ✉ 2170 Merksem *(bus 11)* ☎ (03) 647 18 58

COUNTRY CRUISING

-A3 (E40) Bruxelles ⇌ Liège [P] past Exit "Sterrebeek" (both sides)
-A7 (E19) Bruxelles ⇌ Paris [P] km 22.5
-A7 (E19) Bruxelles ⇌ Paris [P] km 39
-A7 (E19) Bruxelles ⇌ Paris [P] Nivelles-Nord (both sides)
-A7 (E19) Bruxelles ⇌ Paris [P] Hall (both sides)
-A8 (E19) Tournai ⇌ Lille [P] Froynnes (both sides)
-A13 (E313) Liège ⇌ Antwerpen [P] km 42.8/ Exit 24 (Wooded picnic area at the right. Day and night)
-A13 (E313) Liège ⇌ Antwerpen [P] km 62.6 (Parking area and wooded area on both sides)
-A14 (E17) Antwerpen ⇌ Gent Exit km 79.0 (Leave motorway. [P] beside the forest. Cruising in forest and parked cars. Day and night) Exit Linkeroever, cruising in [P] and in wooded area
-A15 (E42) Charleroi ⇌ Namur [P] between Fleurus and Gosselies
-A16 (E42) Mons ⇌ Tournai [P] Antoing (afternoon and evening)

Aalst ✉ 9300 ☎ 053

GAY INFO

■ **Advies Kontakt Centrum 't Koerken (HAK)** 10.30-13.30, 15.30-24 h, closed Sat Sun
St. Martensplein 2 ✉ 9300 ☎ 70 38 88

BARS

■ **Poeskaffee** (AC B GLM MA TV WE) Wed-Fri 15-?, Sat 10-4 Sun 16-4 h, closed on Mon Tue
Gentsestraat 14 ✉ 9300 *(centre)* ☎ 77 46 79

CAFES

■ **Allegro ma non troppo** (B CC F glm MA) Tue-Thu Sun 12-24, Fri -1, Sat 10-1 h, closed on Mon
Gentsestraat 16 ✉ 9300 *(centre)* ☎ 78 44 46

Aalst ▸ Antwerpen Belgium

RESTAURANTS
■ **Da Galeria** (A B CC F glm MA s) 16-1 h, closed on Tue
Gentsestraat 6 ✉ 9300 *(5 min from centre)* ☎ 77 40 63
Café bar restaurant with Bazilian food, music, and exhibitions.

GENERAL GROUPS
■ **Homo- en Lesbiennegroep Vice Versa** (GLM)
PO Box 67 ✉ 9300

Antwerpen ✉ 2000 ☎ 03

✱ Antwerp is the national centre for the diamond market. Innumerable jewellers can be found along the street known as Lange Herentalsesstraat. Antwerp has however more to offer than just diamonds : in the centre of the old city one can find well preserved remains of ancient museums and markets. The flee market (Vlooienmarkt) is a must. The city has also one of the most beautiful botanical gardens, situated at the end of the magnificent central railway station.
The gay scene is to be found in three principal areas : the Vanschoonhovenstraat, the ideal place for one to flirt with the locals which who are enjoying a drink in one of the many bars and discos in this street. In the centre of the old city in the direction of l'Esaut (het Schelde) the bars and restaurants are in the historical buildings. For those interested in trying authentic Flemish specialities, one should try „Waterzooi", a creamy soup. Leather fans should visit the bars and leather clubs in the Van Aerdtstraat with their impressive darkrooms.
Tels Quels

✱ Antwerpen ist das nationale Zentrum für den Diamantenhandel. Unzählige Juweliergeschäfte befinden sich in der bekannten Lange Herentasesstraat. Antwerpen hat jedoch weitaus mehr als nur Diamanten zu bieten: Im Zentrum der alten Stadt findet man gut erhaltene Überbleibsel alter Museen und Märkte. Der Flohmarkt (Vlooienmarkt) ist ein absolutes Muss! Außerdem besitzt die Stadt einen der schönsten botanischen Gärten, der sich am Ende des wunderschönen Zentralbahnhofes befindet.
Die Gay-Szene ist vor allem in drei Hauptgegenden anzufinden: in der Vanschoonhovenstraat – ein idealer Ort um mit den Einheimischen zu flirten und dabei einen Drink in den vielen Bars oder Diskotheken der Straße zu genießen. Im Zentrum der alten Stadt in Richtung Esaut (het Schelde) befinden sich die Bars und Restaurants in historischen Gebäuden. Wer auf echte flämische Spezialitäten neugierig ist, probiert am besten "Waterzooi", eine cremige Suppe. Lederfans sollten die Bars und Clubs in der Van Aerdtstraat mit ihren eindrucksvollen Darkrooms besuchen.
Tels Quels

✱ Anvers est le siège principal du marché national du diamant. On trouve d'innombrables joailliers dans la Lange Herentalestraat. Mais Anvers offre davantage que des diamants : au centre de l'ancienne ville, se trouvent nombre d'édifices anciens bien conservés, des musées et marchés. Le marché aux puces (vlooienmarkt) est particulièrement renommé. La ville possède également l'un des plus beaux jardins zoologiques, situé juste à la sortie de la magnifique gare centrale.
La scène homosexuelle très animée se répartit entre trois aires principales : la Vanschoonhovenstraat est le véritable lieu pour flirter lors d'un drink avec des Belges sympathiques, dans les nombreux bars et discothèques de cette rue. Au centre de la vieille ville, en direction de l'Escaut (het Schelde), se trouvent des bars et restaurants dans des bâtiments historiques. Si l'on recherche des spécialités flamandes authentiques, on devrait essayer le Waterzooi, un potage velouté succulent. Les adeptes du cuir se tourneront plutôt vers la Van Aerdtstraat où se concentrent les bars et clubs " cuir " avec leurs darkrooms impressionnantes.
Tels Quels

✱ Amberes es el centro nacional del mercado del diamante. Innumerables joyeros tienen sus negocios a lo largo de la Lange Herentalsesstraat. Pero Amberes tiene mucho más que ofrecer que diamantes: en el centro de la ciudad vieja se pueden ver los restos muy bien conservados de antiguos museos y mercados. No hay que perder el rastro (Vlooienmarkt). La ciudad tienen uno de los jardines botánicos más bonitos, situado al final de la magnífica estación central.
El ambiente gay de la ciudad está repartido por tres áreas principales: la Vanschoonhovenstraat, el lugar ideal para encontrar un flirteo con los gays de Amberes tomando una copa en uno de los muchos bares y discotecas ubicados en esta calle. En el centro de la ciudad vieja en dirección de l'Esaut (en flamenco het Schelde), los bares y restaurantes se encuentran en los edificios históricos. Las personas que quieran probar una especialidad auténtica de Flandres deberían pedir una "Waterzooi", una sopa cremosa. Los amigos del cuero pueden visitar los bares y clubs leather con sus cuartos oscuros impresionantes en la Van Aerdtstraat.
Tels Quels

✱ Anversa è il centro nazionale del mercato dei diamanti. Lungo la Lange Herentalsesstraat si trovano i negozi di tantissimi gioiellieri. Ma Anversa
offre molto di più che solo diamanti. Nel centro storico troverete musei antichi e mercati in buono stato di preservazione. Andare al mercato delle pulci (Vlooienmarkt) è un dovere assoluto. Anversa ha anche uno dei giardini botanici più belli del mondo, trovandosi alla fine della magnifica stazione centrale.
La vita gay si svolge principalmente in tre settori: nella Vanschoonhovenstraat, il luogo ideale per un flirt con i belgi prendendo un drink in uno degli innumerevoli bar e discoteche trovandosi in questa strada. nel centro vecchio della città, nella direzione di l1Esaut (het Schelde) i bar e ristoranti si trovano in edifici storici. Coloro che sono interessati a provare delle specialità autentiche fiammingne, dovrebbero assaggiare la "Waterzooi", una zuppa cremosa. Gli amanti del cuoio dovrebbero andare nei bar e nei club nella Van Aerdtstraat con i loro impressionanti darkrooms.
Tels Quels

GAY INFO
■ **G.O.C. Antwerpen** (B D G) 20-24, Fri -2, Sat sun 22-4.30, closed Mon
Dambruggestraat 204 ✉ 2060 ☎ 233 10 71 🖷 234 33 39
Also Parties. Call for info.
■ **Uitkomst**
Dambruggestraat 204 ✉ 2060 ☎ 233 10 17 🖷 234 33 39
Local gay newspaper.

PUBLICATIONS
■ **Antwerpen Homo Gids 2000**
Kipdorvest 50 ✉ 2000 🖥 info@aidsteam.be
🌐 www.aidsteam.be
Gay map of the city published by the health group Aidsteam.

TOURIST INFO
■ **Dienst voor Toerisme** Mon-Fri 9-18, Sat Sun 9-17 h
Grote Markt 15 ✉ 2000 ☎ 232 01 03 🖷 231 19 37

BARS
■ **Bacchus** (B G LJ MA) Mon-Thu 17-?, Fri-Sun 16-? h
Van Schoonhovenstraat 28 ✉ 2060 ☎ 233 96 66

Belgium — Antwerpen

■ **Den Bazaar** (AC B D GLM MA) Mon-Thu 12-24, Fri-Sun -5 h
Van Schoonhovenstraat 22 ✉ 2060 ☎ 232 91 20
■ **Body Boys** (B GLM) 14-5 h
Van Schoonhovenstraat 30 ✉ 2060 ☎ 203 05 43
■ **Boots. The** (! AC B DR G LJ MA P VS WE) Fri Sat 22.30-5 h
Van Aerdtstraat 22 ✉ 2060 *(near St. Jansplein)* ☎ 233 21 36
Fetish sex club, skinhead hangout.
■ **Borsalino** (! AC B D f G MA) 21-? h, closed on Wed
Van Schoonhovenstraat 48 ✉ 2060 ☎ 226 91 62
■ **Cafe de Fiets** (A B f GLM MA) 17-?, Fri 8.30-?, closed on Wed
Vrijdagmarkt 5 ✉ 2000 *(near Vrijdagmarkt)* ☎ 231 45 99
■ **Cafe Hessenhuis** (B f GLM MA) 10-? h
Falconrui 53 ✉ 2000 ☎ 231 13 56
■ **Cafe Strange** (B D G OS) 21-5, Sun 16-5 h
Dambruggestraat 161 ✉ 2060 ☎ 226 00 72
Summertime barbecue parties.
■ **Den Beiaard** (B F g OS) 9-? h closed on Thu
Handschoenmarkt 21 ✉ 2000 ☎ 232 40 14
■ **Den Houten Kop** (B f GLM MA tv) 19-8 h closed Tue
St. Lambertusstraat 73 ✉ 2600 ☎ 218 91 79
■ **Envers d'Anvers. L'** (B d f G snu stv) 11.30-5, Fri Sat -7 h
Pacificatiestraat 97 ✉ 2000 ☎ 237 33 36
■ **Fifty-Fifty** (AC B D f GLM p) 21-?, Sun 16-? h
Van Schoonhovenstraat 40 ✉ 2060 ☎ 225 11 73
Very popular bar with upstairs quiet area for snacks and conversation.
■ **Hanky Code Bar** (B DR f G LJ MA NU OS) Sun-Thu 20-5 h
Van de Wervestraat 69 ✉ 2060 *(Bus 81-86-St. Jansplein)*
☎ 226 81 72
Terrace in summer from 15 h (WE).
■ **Hanky Code's Cellar** (B D DR G LJ MA P WE) Fri-Sat 20-9 h
Van de Wervestraat 69 ✉ 2060 *(Bus 81-86-St. Jansplein)*
☎ 226 81 72
Many special parties, nude, SM, FF, etc.
■ **In de Roskam** (B GLM MA) 17-?, WE 15-? h
Vrijdagmarkt 12 ✉ 2000 ☎ 226 24 10
■ **Katshuis. 'T** (B G MA H) 20-?, Fri-Sun 16-? h
Grote Pieter Potstraat 18 ✉ 2000 ☎ 234 03 69
✉ kats.an@skynet.be *Café and guest house with private entrance. Rooms with shower and TV. Single FB 950.- double 1500.-*
■ **Kinkies. The** (AC B g DR LJ P VS) 21-?h closed Wed.
Lange Beeldekenstraat 10 ✉ 2060 *(Near central station)*
☎ 295 06 40
■ **New Queens** (B CC G MA R) 12-5 h
Van Schoonhovenstraat 4 ✉ 2000 *(near central station)*
☎ 213 32 03
■ **Nutsville Café & Danceclub** (AC B D DR G MA S) Café: 16-2, Danceclub: Fri-Sun 23-7 h
Sudermanstraat 20/20a ✉ 2000 *(centre)* ☎ 232 33 19
■ **Playboy** (AC B D GLM h MA p s tv) 17-3, Sat Sun -8 h
Van Schoonhovenstraat 42 ✉ 2060 ☎ 231 60 06
Rooms available.
■ **Popi Café** (B F GLM) 15-? h
Riemstraat 22-24 ✉ 2000 ☎ 238 15 30
■ **Rimbaud** (B GLM MA) 20-?, Sun 17-? h, closed Mon Tue
Hessenbrug 5 ✉ 2000 ☎ 232 79 18
■ **Rubbzz** (B G LJ MA) 22-? h
Geulincxstraat 28 ✉ 2000 *(15 min from the railway station)*
☎ 0495/52 03 57
Clubhouse of the Fenix skinhead movement of Antwerpen with its own skingear shop.
■ **Twilight** (AC B CC G MA OS) 16-? h
Van Schoonhovenstraat 54 ✉ 2060 *(near central station)*
☎ 232 67 04
Cosy bar with garden terrace.

CAFES

■ **Het Gebaar** (BF glm) 10.30-18 h, closed on Mon
Schuttershofstraat 14 ✉ 2000 ☎ 232 37 10

DANCECLUBS

■ **Havanna Beach** (B D GLM) Fri-Sun 22-? h
Van Schoonhovenstraat 24 ✉ 2060 ☎ 232 01 43
■ **Red & Blue** (! AC B CC D DR E G SNU YG) Sat 23-? h
Lange Schipperskapelstraat 11-13 ✉ 2000 *(near the Red Light district)* ☎ 213 05 55
One of the biggest gay clubs in Benelux.

RESTAURANTS

■ **Grote Witte Arend** (B F glm) 11.30-22.30 h, closed Tue, Nov-Apr Tue & Wed
Reynderstraat 18 ✉ 2000 ☎ 226 31 90
■ **In de Schaduw v.d. Kathedraal** (B BF F GLM)
Wed-Sat 12-15 18-20, Sun 18-22 h.
Handschoenmarkt 17 ✉ 2000 *(near Kathedraal)* ☎ 232 40 14
■ **Kertosono Indonesian Restaurant** (B E F glm OS) 18.30-23 h
Provinciestraat 118 ✉ 2018 ☎ 225 02 74
■ **O' Kontreir Restaurant** (F glm) Tue-Fri 12-14.30, 18-22.30, Sat Sun 18-22.30 h, closed on Tue
Isabellalei 145 ✉ 2018 ☎ 281 39 76
Gay-friendly restaurant.
■ **Kule** (B F g) Tue-Sun 12-1 h
Cuylitsstraat 1 ✉ 2018 ☎ 237 17 95
Turkish cuisine.
■ **Nouveau Zirk** (B CC F glm)
Zirkstraat 29 ✉ 2000
■ **Ogenblick. 'T** (B G MA) Wed-Sat 11-24 h
Grote Markt 10-12 ✉ 2000 ☎ 233 62 62
■ **Oi!** (F glm)
Kleine Kraaiwijk 10 ✉ 2000 ☎ 231 06 71
Together with the SM - Fetish Roxy shop.
■ **Preud Homme** (b F g)
Suikerrui 28 ✉ 2000 ☎ 233 42 00
High quality Belgian cuisine.
■ **Quicherie Eiland** (A AC CC F glm MA OS) Tue-Sat 12-14, 17-21 h
Isabellalei 8 ✉ 2018 ☎ 230 16 60
Daily meal restaurant with vegetarian/fish dishes. Friendly staff.
■ **Quick** (B F g) 12-6, WE 17-6 h
De Coninckplein 29 ✉ 2060 ☎ 225 22 16
Sandwich bar.
■ **Tafeltje Rond** (AC B CC F g) 11.30-22 h, Mon Sun & holidays closed
Hoge Weg 14 ✉ 2600 ☎ 230 99 48
■ **Tafeltje Rond** (B F g)
Gildekamerstraat 10 ✉ 2000 ☎ 231 65 81
Tea room and restaurant.

SEX SHOPS/BLUE MOVIES

■ **Adonis** (G VS) 12-22, Sat 14-23, Sun 13-22 h
Dambruggestraat 174 ✉ 2060 ☎ 226 91 51
■ **Erotheek International** (g) 12-24, Sat 12-22 h
Van Schoonhovenstraat 34 ✉ 2060 ☎ 233 29 40
■ **Libidos Erotheek** (g) 12-22 h
Carnotstraat 35 ✉ 2060 *(near central station)* ☎ 226 02 45
■ **Roxy** (g lj) 12-24 h
Kleine Kraaiwijk 10 ✉ 2000 ☎ 227 45 57
Rubber, leather, films.
■ **Videotheek Gay-Ron** (DR G MA VS) Mon-Fri 12-23, Sat Sun 14-22 h
Van Wesenbekestraat 54 ✉ 2060 *(near centralstation)*
☎ 234 04 43

Antwerpen | Belgium

KOUROS SAUNA
Botermelkbaan 50
2900 Schoten
BELGIUM
Tel.: 0032(0)3/658.09.37
(15 km.from center Antwerp)

* INDOOR SWIMMINGPOOL 27 °C
  (with underwater music)
* BIG GARDEN WITH SWIMMINGPOOL
  (possibility of naturism & nude sunbathing)
* HAMMAM
  (turkish bath)
* WHIRLPOOL
  (jacuzzi)
* FINNISH SAUNA
* BAR / RESTAURANT
* T.V. ROOM
* RELAX ROOMS
* DARKROOM
* SOLARIUM
* PRIVATE PARKING
* HOTEL ACCOMODATIONS NEARBY
  (if full, many places 200m. further)
* SUNDAY: FREE BRUNCH
  (from 11.00h. till 14.00h)
* WEDNESDAY: 250 ENTRY FOR YEARS BOYS.

* Take bus 61: From Antwerp-Rooseveldplaats to Schoten Koningshof.
  Ask the driver to Botermelkbaan.
* Motorway: Antwerp-Breda exit nr.4 St.Job in 't Goor, at the end turn left. At 1st. traffic lights turn right. At the 2nd traffic lights turn left (direction Schilde). After 1km. on your right side, KOUROS SAUNA nr.50

Open every day from 13.00h till 01.00h
Sunday from 11.00 till 01.00h

SPARTACUS 2001/2002 | 79

Belgium — Antwerpen

**sauna·club
sanderusstraat 55
2018 antwerp
tel 03/2383137
open daily 14-24h**

■ **Walhalla** (G) 12-2 h
St.-Paulusplaats 21 ✉ 2000 ☎ 233 62 91
Videos, magazines, rubber/leather, piercing, removable tattoos.
■ **Warehouse. The** (G LJ) Fri-Sat 22.30-5 h
Van Aerdtstraat 22 ✉ 2060 ☎ 225 23 76
In „Boots" bar.

SAUNAS/BATHS

■ **City** (B F DR G MA SA SB VS WH) 14-24 h
Olijftakstraat 35 ✉ 2060 ☎ 234 19 25
■ **Dimitry's Sauna Bath** (B DR G MA SA SB VS) Mon-Fri 14-23, S at 20 h, Sun closed
Greinstraat 47 ✉ 2060 *(10 min walk from station, Subway 3-Elisabeth)* ☎ 235 00 87
Naked group sex parties on Sat.
■ **Herenhuis. 'T** (AC B C d DR F G MA msg DJ SA SB SOL VS WH) 12-24, Fri Sat -6 h
De Lescluzestraat 63 ✉ 2600 *(in Berchem)* ☎ 239 51 95
Entrance fee BEF 450 except Wed and Tue for those under 25 (BEF 300).
■ **Kouros** (AC B CC DR F G MA msg OS P PI SA SB SOL VS WH) Mon-Sat 13-1, Sun 11-1 h
Botermelkbaan 50 ✉ 2900 *(In Schoten, Bus 61)* ☎ 658 09 37
Friendly atmosphere sauna and garden on 1800 m². In and outdoor swimming pool.
■ **Metropolitan International** (B DR G MA SA SB VS WH) 14-23, Fri -2, Sat -20 h, closed Sun
Sint Elisabethstraat 47 ✉ 2060 ☎ 213 48 21
Free condoms available.
■ **Park** (B CC F DR G MA PI SA SB VS WH) 15-1, Fri Sat -6 h
Florisstraat 10 ✉ 2018 ☎ 226 03 93
Former Macho I.
■ **SPA 55** (B DR f G MA MSG OS p SA SB VS WH) 14-24 h
Sanderusstraat 55 ✉ 2018 *(Behind Justitie Paleis)* ☎ 238 31 37
5 floors, friendly atmosphere, professional massage, sun terrace.

BOOK SHOPS

■ **De Groene Waterman** (G)
Wolstraat 7 ✉ 2000 ☎ 232 93 94
■ **Pourquoi Pas**
Quellinstraat 51 ✉ 2000 ☎ (02) 227 23 27

■ **Verschil. 'T** (A b BF CC GLM MA OS) Fri 12-18, Sat 12-19, Sun 12-18 bf 12-14 h
Minderbroedersrui 42 ✉ 2000 *(Tram 4,11, next to shopping centre Antwerp & Groenplaats)* ☎ 226 08 04
Gay and Lesbian book and coffeeshop.

LEATHER & FETISH SHOPS

■ **Roxy Piercingstudio** (g) 14-23 h
Kleine Kraaiwijk 12 ✉ 12000 ☎ 232 82 89
Specialised in intimate piercings.

TRAVEL AND TRANSPORT

■ **Dimane Travel + Promotion** (CC GLM) Tue-Fri 10-20, Sat -14 h
Mechelse Steenweg 39 ✉ 2018 ☎ 213 17 85 📠 213 17 86
✉ dimane-pr@skynet.be 🖥 www.dimane-pr.com
Gay travel & events, direct marketing, promotion, concept design, etc.
■ **Fiesta Gay Planet (Fiesta Reizen N.V.)** (CC GLM) Mon-Fri 9.30-13, 14-18 h, closed Sat Sun
Leopoldstraat 3 ✉ 2000 *(next to Bourla theater)* ☎ 231 05 81
📠 231 05 82

HOTELS

■ **Astrid Park Plaza** (A B CC BF g H msg SA SOL PI WH WO)
Koningin Astridplein 7 ✉ 2018 *(opposite to Central station)*
☎ 203 12 34 📠 203 12 75 ✉ astrid.plaza@euronet.be
🖥 www.parkplazaastrid.com
229 double rooms with bath/WC phone, fax, TV, radio, minibar, safe, own key.
■ **Hanky Code Hotel** (B BF CC G H LJ NU OS)
Van de Wervestraat 67 ✉ 2060 *(Bus 81-86-St. Jansplein)* ☎ 226 81 72 📠 226 26 78 ✉ info@hankycode.com
🖥 www.hankycode.com
Own key. 36 rooms, 1 dormitory room. Rates single Bfr 1.300.-, double 1.600.-
■ **Ideal** (g H)
Waghemakerstraat 17 ✉ 2060 ☎ 234 00 70
■ **President** (g H)
Rotterdamstraat 62 ✉ 2060 ☎ 234 8172

PRIVATE ACCOMMODATION

■ **Sweet Ours** (BF G H OS)
Krugerpark, Mertenstraat 31 ✉ 2140 *(Tram 10/24, 10 min for train*

80 **SPARTACUS** 2001/2002

Antwerpen ▶ Blankenberge | **Belgium**

't HERENHUIS
de Lescluzestraat, 63
2600 Berchem – Antwerpen
Tel. (03) 239 51 95

Open every day 12–24
Fri & Sat 12–06
& cold buffet 20–22
Sat & Sun Brunch

station, located in a little quiet city park area) ☎ (0479) 91 09 34
✉ boa@tucrail.be
Bed & Breakfast within walking distance from the gay nightlife run by a gay couple. One room with kitchen, bathroom and room service.

GENERAL GROUPS
■ **ANTAR vzw** (GLM)
Helenalei 20 bus 15 ✉ 2018 ☎ 12 88 16 95 ✉ antar@pi.be
Social and cultural activities gays and lesbians.
■ **HAGAR - Homobisische Aktiegroep**
Kloosterstraat 5 ✉ 2000 ☎ 237 66 25
■ **Het Roze Huis**
P/a Breughelstraat 31-33 ✉ 2018 ☎ 440 51 40 ☎ 568 74 43
■ **Holebijongeren Kast en Co** (GLM)
PO Box 346 ✉ 2000
■ **Landelijke Belangenverdediging Homoseksualiteit**
Dambruggestraat 204 ✉ 2060 ☎ 223 10 71
Gay liberation organization.
■ **Roze Aktie Front (RAF)** (GLM)
Congresstraat 41 ✉ 2060 ☎ 236 50 76

HEALTH GROUPS
■ **Aidsteam** Mon-Fri 9-12.30, 13.30-17 h
Kipdorpvest 50 ✉ 2000 ☎ 238 68 68 🖨 248 42 90
✉ info@aidsteam.be ✉ www.aidsteam.be
Aids prevention for gay, lesbian and bisexual people. Also publishers of a gay map of the city.
■ **De Witte Raven** Mon-Fri 10-17, Tue -19 h
Schijfwepersstraat 145 ✉ 2020 ☎ 826 69 00 🖨 825 40 13
✉ hiv.de.witte.raven@skynet.be
■ **Instituut voor Tropische Geneeskunde** Mon-Fri 9-17 h (by appointment only)
Kronenburgstraat 43 ✉ 2000 ☎ 247 64 25
AIDS test & STDs consultation.

HELP WITH PROBLEMS
■ **D.O.K. (Konsultatieburo voor Relaties en Seksualiteit)** 9-12.30, 13.30-17, Tue Thu also 19-21.30 h, closed Sat Sun
Rotterdamstraat 127 ✉ 2000 ☎ 234 08 48

SPECIAL INTEREST GROUPS
■ **Classico Club**
Dambruggestraat 204 ✉ 2060 ☎ 233 10 71
Classical music lovers.
■ **GanymedeS Homojongeren** (GLM YG)
Dambruggestraat 204 ✉ 2060 ☎ 223 10 71
Gay youth group.

■ **Holebi-jongeren Enig Verschil** (GLM YG)
PO Box 22 ✉ 2060 ☎ 216 37 37
■ **Kring Homoseksuele Senioren** (GLM OG)
Dambruggestraat 204 ✉ 2060 ☎ 223 10 71
Group for older gays.

CRUISING
-Stadspark (AYOR)
-Wooded area (between Berchem station and Grote Steenweg)
-Het Rot (linker oever, drive through Waasland tunnel, ca 1 km sooded area on left-hand side)
-Conincplein (AYOR OG)
-Multi-story parking garage (on Van Schoonhovenstraat)

Arlon ✉ 6700 ☎ 063

GENERAL GROUPS
■ **Tels Quels Arlon** (GLM) 2nd Sat/month 10.30-12.30, 4th Sat/month 16-18 h
☎ 23 10 18

CRUISING
-Le Belvédère (across from the church St. Donant, in summer, evenings)

Assenede ✉ 9960 ☎ 09

DANCECLUBS
■ **Passé** (B D G MA) Thu Mon 17-?, Sat Sun 14-? h
Doornend 1 ✉ 9960

GUEST HOUSES
■ **Staaksken. T'** (AC BF Glm H lj MA NU OS WO)
Staakstraat 136/138 A ✉ 9960 (between Antwerp, Gent and Bruges)
☎ 344 09 54 🖨 344 09 54 ✉ staaksken@skynet.be
✉ www.come.to/staaksken
Non-smoking 4* B&B holiday cottage located in the nature. Call for rates.

Blankenberge ✉ 8370 ☎ 050

BARS
■ **Oosterstaketsel** (B BF F g MA N)
✉ 8370 (on end of east pier harbour entrance) ☎ 41 19 12
NU in dunes nearby.

HOTELS
■ **E.T.M. Bach** (GLM H MA msg SOL)
Vissersstraat 20 ✉ 8370 ☎ 41 97 71

Belgium | **Blankenberge** ▶ **Brussel/Bruxelles**

BAR - RESTO
Place de la Vieille Halle aux Blés 26
1000 BRUSSELS
Tel & Fax: +32 2 514 05 00
Open: Bar 19h - 03h
Resto 19h - 00h (01h W-E)

APARTMENTS
■ **Johan Dockx Apartments** (GLM H) 10-16.30 h (Call ahead)
Molenstraat 13 ✉ 8370 ☎ (0479) 33 12 11 📠 (058) 42 27 38

CRUISING
-Dunes direction Zeebrugge

Braffe ✉ 7600 ☎ 069

DANCECLUBS
■ **Starmania. Le** (B D G) Fri & Sat 21-? h
12 Rue de la Place ✉ 7204 ☎ 77 68 49

Brugge ✉ 8000 ☎ 050

BARS
■ **Passe-Partout** (AC B CC d DR f G lj MA p s VS) 16-?, Sun 14.30-? h, closed Wed
St. Jansstraat 3 ✉ 8000 (near the big market place) ☎ 33 47 42

RESTAURANTS
■ **Hollywood** (B CC F glm H) 11-23.30 h, closed Thu
'T Zand 24 ✉ 8000 ☎ 33 72 52
■ **Miramar** (b CC F g OS) 11-23 h, closed on Thu
Mariastraat 13 ✉ 8000 (near Church of our Lady) ☎ 34 72 62

HOTELS
■ **Memling** (b BF f g H)
Kuiperstraat 8 ✉ 8000 ☎ 33 20 96
Centrally located, all rooms with telephone, priv. bath.

GUEST HOUSES
■ **Het Wit Beertje** (BF glm H)
Witte Beerstraat 4 ✉ 8200 (Bus 5/15 2nd stop from the station, 10 min on foot) ☎ 45 08 88 ☎ 31 87 62 📠 45 08 80
📧 jp.defour@worldonline.be 🌐 home.worldonline.be/~jpdefour

GENERAL GROUPS
■ **Homocentrum Brugge Idem-Dito** Meeting Fri 20, Sun 15-18 h at Bar Passe-Partout
PO Box 131 ✉ 8000 ☎ 33 47 42

RELIGIOUS GROUPS
■ **Effeta Brugge**
PO Box 136 ✉ 8000 ☎ 33 77 14

SPECIAL INTEREST GROUPS
■ **Boomerang** (GLM WE YG)
Koningin Elisabethlaan 92 ✉ 8000 ☎ (075) 33 38 63
📧 postboomerang@hotmail.com
Group of young gays, lesbians and bisexuals. E-mail or call for information on activities (WE).
■ **Holebi-Jongeren** (GLM YG)
PO Box 131 ✉ 8000 ☎ 37 47 02

CRUISING
-Minnewaterpark

Brussel/Bruxelles ✉ 1000 ☎ 02

✱ Brussels is not only the headquarters of the EU, there are also some interesting sights which can be found here: the impressive Grand' Place with its imposing architecture. In the Palace des Beaux Arts the amateur modern artists can marvel at the interesting exhibitions of contemporary masters. Not to be missed is the statue Manneken Pis who urinates day and night. No tourist information guide is able to give a plausible explanation for this statue. It has become a national emblem, like the Atomium ever since the exposition from 1958.
The gay scene is centred around the two streets „Marché au Charbon" and „ rue des Pierres". Although Brussels is bilingual, you will make more use of your French. A recommendation : the large gay parties „à La Démence". They attract gay men from around the world and reflect the true cosmopolitan character of Brussels. To be seen in January : the gay film festival which takes place over roughly 10 days. Brussels is also the home to the head office of the International Lesbian and Gay Association (IGLA) as well as the city in which the gay pride takes to the streets in May.
Tels Quels

★ Brüssel ist nicht nur das Hauptquartier der EU – sondern auch eine Stadt mit vielen interessanten Sehenswürdigkeiten. Die eindrucksvolle Grande Place mit ihrer imposanten Architektur. Im Palais des Beaux Arts kann der Liebhaber moderner Kunst interes-

Brussel/Bruxelles | **Belgium**

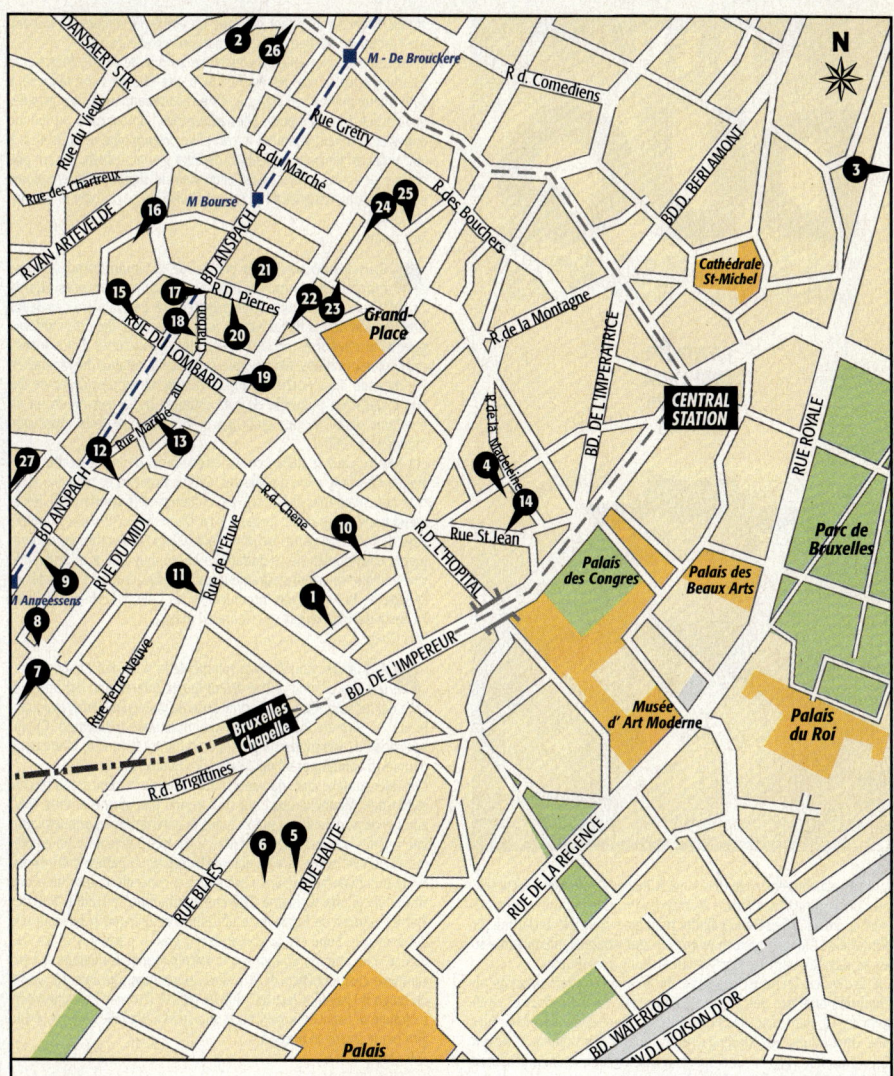

Brussel

1. La Griffe Sauna
2. Hôtel Noga
3. Oasis Sauna
4. Le Duquesnoy Bar
5. La Démence Danceclub
6. Le Lagon Sauna
7. Club 3000 Sauna
8. El Papagayo Café
9. Erot'X'Stars Adult Entertainment
10. Le Comptoir Bar
11. Strong Danceclub
12. Le Macho 2 Sauna
13. Tels Quels Bar
14. Le Kiosque du Gay Délire
15. Why Not Danceclub
16. La Potinière Hotel
17. Boulev'Art Bar
18. The Slave Bar
19. The Soum Bar
20. Incognito Bar
21. Chez Maman Bar
22. Can-Can Taverne Bar
23. La Dolce Bar
24. La Réserve Bar
25. Le Pretext Bar
26. Les Ecrins Hôtel
27. Spades 4our Sauna

Belgium | Brussel/Bruxelles

statue. Elle est cependant devenue un emblème national, tout comme l'Atomium, vestige de l'exposition universelle de 58.
La scène homosexuelle se concentre autour de la rue Marché au Charbon et de la rue des Pierres. Bien que Bruxelles soit bilingue, il vaut mieux utiliser son français. Une recommandation : les grandes gay-parties à La Démence. Elles attirent les homosexuels du monde entier et décrivent vraiment le caractère cosmopolite de Bruxelles. A voir aussi en janvier : le Festival du Film gay et lesbien, durant une dizaine de jours. Bruxelles est également le siège de l'International Lesbian & Gay Association (ILGA) et la ville où se déroule la gay pride, en mai.
Tels Quels

Bruselas no sólo es la central de la Unión Europea. Tiene muchos sitios muy interesantes como la impresionante Grand' Place con su imponente arquitectura. En el Palace des Beaux Arts (Palacio de las Bellas Artes), los aficionados del arte moderno pueden maravillarse con las interesantes exposiciones de los maestros contemporáneos. No hay que perderse la estatua del Manneken Pis, meando día y noche ... Ningún guía de turismo es capaz de dar una explicación plausible de esta estatua. Se ha convertido en un emblema de la nación, igual que el Atomium desde la exposición mundial en 1958.
Los locales gays se hallan en los alrededores de las dos calles Marché au Charbon y Rue des Pierres. Si bien Bruselas es bilingüe, el turista necesitará más el francés que el flamenco (o neerlandés). Recomendamos las grandes fiestas "à La Démence". Atraen a hombres gays de todas las partes del mundo y reflejan el carácter verdaderamente cosmopolita de la ciudad. En enero, hay que ir al festival de cine gay que se celebra durante unos diez días. Además, Bruselas es la sede de la Asociación Internacional de Gays y Lesbianas (IGLA). La fiesta del orgullo gay se celebra en mayo.
Tels Quels

A Bruxelles non si trova solamente la sede dell'Unione Europea ma ci sono anche alcuni luoghi interessanti dal punto di vista del turismo. Una delle prime cose da vedersi è l'impressionante piazza "Grande Place" con la sua imponente architettura. Gli appassionati d'arte moderna possono ammirare le mostre interessanti di maestri contemporanei nel Musée des Beaux Arts.
Nell'elenco delle cose da vedersi non deve però mancare la piccola statua del "Manneken-pis" chi sta facendo pipi giorno e notte. Fino ad oggi nessuna guida è stata capace di dare una spiegazione plausibile relativa a questa statua. Il Manneken-pis è diventato un emblema nazionale, come lo è diventato l'Atomium a partire dall'esposizione mondiale nel 1958. La scena gay è concentrata intorno a due strade di cui una si chiama "Marché au Charbon" e l'altra "Rue des Pierres". Anche se Bruxelles è ufficialmente bilingue si farà più uso del francese. Sono da raccomandare i grandi party gay a "La Démence" che attirano uomini gay di tutto il mondo e riflettono il vero carattere cosmopolitico di Bruxelles. In gennaio, durante 10 giorni, ha luogo il "gay film festival". Anche l'ILGA (l'organizzazione internationale di lesbiche e gay) ha la sua sede a Bruxelles e il gay pride gira per le strade in maggio.
Tels Quels

CULTURE

■ **Brussels Gay & Lesbian Film Festival** (GLM)
81 Rue Marché au Charbon ✉ 1000 ☏ 512 45 87
✉ info@fglb.org 🌐 www.fglb.org
Organised by Tels Quels asbl in January each year (lasts 10 days).
■ **Gaye Attitude** (GLM)
98 Avenue Dailly ✉ 1030 ☏ 245 94 84 📠 242 38 06
Group promoting gay culture.

TOURIST INFO

■ **T.I.B.** 9-18, winter: Mon-Sat 9-18 h
Grote Markt (Stadhuis) ✉ 1000 ☏ 513 89 40 📠 514 45 38

sante Ausstellungen zeitgenössischer Künstler bewundern. Nicht fehlen darf natürlich das kleine Manneken-Pis, das tag und nacht uriniert. In keinem Reiseführer findet man eine plausible Erklärung für diese kleine Statue, dennoch wurde sie zum nationalen Emblem – so wie es das Atomium seit der Weltausstellung von 1958 ist.
Die Schwulen-Szene ist rund um die beiden Straßen "Marché au Charbon" und Rue des Pierres" angesiedelt. Obwohl Brüssel zweisprachig ist, wird man das Französische öfter verwenden. Und hier eine Empfehlung: die Riesengay-Partys in der "La Démence" ziehen Gays aus aller Welt an und spiegeln den wahren cosmopolitischen Charakter Brüssels wider. Alljährlich im Januar findet in Brüssel das zehn Tage ndauernde Gay-Filmfestival statt. Brüssel beheimatet auch das Hauptquartier der internationalen Schwulen- und Lesbenorganisation (IGLA) und die Stadt, in der im Mai die Gay-Parade stattfindet.
Tels Quels

Bruxelles n'est pas seulement le siège principal de l'UE, elle offre également quelques curiosités intéressantes : notons l'imposante Grand' Place avec son architecture impressionnante. Les amateurs d'art moderne trouveront des expositions intéressantes d'artistes contemporains au Palais des Beaux Arts. A ne pas manquer : la statue de Manneken Pis, qui urine du matin au soir. Aucune information touristique n'a donné une explication plausible sur cette

Brussel/Bruxelles | Belgium

BARS

■ **Amour Fou. L'** (A AC B BF CC F g MA) 9-3 h
Chaussee d'Ixelles 185 ✉ 1050 ☎ 514 27 09
■ **Belgica. Le** (B GLM MA) Thu-Sun 22-3 h
32 Rue du Marché au Charbon ✉ 1000
■ **Boulev'Art. Le** (B f G MA N OS) 10-2 h
108 Boulevard Anspach ✉ 1000 *(Near the stock exchange and "Grand Place)* ☎ 512 53 62
■ **Can-Can. Le** (AC B G MA P p s) 16-? h
Rue des Pierres 55 ✉ 1000 *(near Grand Place)* ☎ 512 97 75
Karaoke nights on Fri, Shows last Sat/month.
■ **Carrousel. Le** (B F GLM MA r) 10-? h
12 Place Fontainas ✉ 1000 ☎ 512 15 03
■ **Chez Maman** (AC B E G MA p S) Thu-Sun 19-?
Rue des Grands Carmes 7 ✉ 1000 *(100 m from the Manneken Pis, Metro-Bourse)* ☎ 502 86 96
■ **Club. Le** (B Glm MA) 15-6 h
18 Rue des Pierres ✉ 1000 ☎ 502 71 00
■ **Club 73** (B G MA) 12-6 h
73 Rue des Bouchers ✉ 1000 ☎ 502 99 41
■ **Comptoir** (B F G MA s YG) 19-3, restaurant -24, WE -1 h
Place de la Vieille Halle aux Blés 26 ✉ 1000 *(près du/near Manneken Pis)* ☎ 514 05 00
Restaurant on 1st floor.
■ **Copa. Le** (B G YG) 19-? h
42 rue du Marché au Charbon ✉ 1000
■ **Coucou. Le** (B Glm STV) 21-? h, closed on Mon
8 Rue Jardin des Olives ✉ 1000 ☎ 511 33 36
■ **Dolce. La** (B G) 15-? h
Petit-Rue-au-Beurre 8 ✉ 1000 ☎ 502 78 66
■ **Duquesnoy** (AC B DR G LJ MA p VS) Mon-Thu 21-3, Fri Sat -5, Sun 18-3 h, 1st Fri MSC Belgium, 3rd Sun Spanklub
Rue Duquesnoy 12 ✉ 1000 *(M-Gare Centrale)* ☎ 502 38 83
■ **Gate. The** (B D GLm) Tue-Fri 12-?, Sat 15-?, Sun 18-? h
36 Rue Fossé aux Loups ✉ 1000 ☎ 223 04 34
■ **Gémeau. Le** (AC B D G MA P s) Thu-Sat 22-? Sun 16-? h
Rue de Laeken 12 ✉ 1000 *(centre, Metro-Bourse)* ☎ 219 23 36
Café dansant. Typical Brussel atmosphere.
■ **Homo Erectus. L'** (B Glm) 11-6 h
57 Rue des Pierres ✉ 1000 *(near Grand Place)* ☎ 514 74 93
■ **Horeca** (B d G MA p S) Mon 14-? Tue-Fri 11-?, Sat Sun 16-? h
Rue de la Fourche 21 ✉ 1000 *(close to Grand Place)* ☎ 502 50 84
Cosy bar with soft music.
■ **Incognito. L'** (AC B D G MA p STV) 11-? h
Rue des Pierres 36 ✉ 1000 *(near Grand Place)* ☎ 513 37 88
■ **Iris. L'** (AC B CC GLM MG N OS s) 15-? h
Rue de la Fourche 12 ✉ 1000 ☎ 219 88 83
■ **Jourdan. Le** (B G MA)
Avenue d'Audergem 140 ✉ 1040 ☎ 724 71 90
■ **Pretext. Le** (B GLM MA) 11-3, Sat Sun 16-3 h
21 Rue de la Fourche ✉ 1000 ☎ 502 50 84
■ **Réserve. La** (AC B d E G MG) Mon Thu Fri 11-24, Sat Sun 15-24, Wed 16-22 h, Tue closed
Petit Rue-au-Beurre 2A ✉ 1000 *(metro Bourse)* ☎ 511 66 06
■ **Rijk der Zinnen. Het** (B G MA r) 12-?, Fri-Sat 21-? h
14 Rue des Pierres ✉ 1000 ☎ 511 26 59
■ **Slave. The** (B DR G LJ MA p) 22-4, Fri Sat 22-6 h
Rue Plattesteen 7 ✉ 1000 *(Near Grand Place)* ☎ 513 47 46
■ **Soum. Le** (AC B D GLM SNU) 12-? h
44 Rue Marché-au-Charbon ✉ 1000 ☎ 514 07 11
■ **Tels Quels Lesbian & Gay Meeting Point** (A B f GLM MA) 17-2, Wed 14-2, Fri 17-4, Sat 14-4 h
81 Rue Marché au Charbon ✉ 1000 ☎ 512 32 34

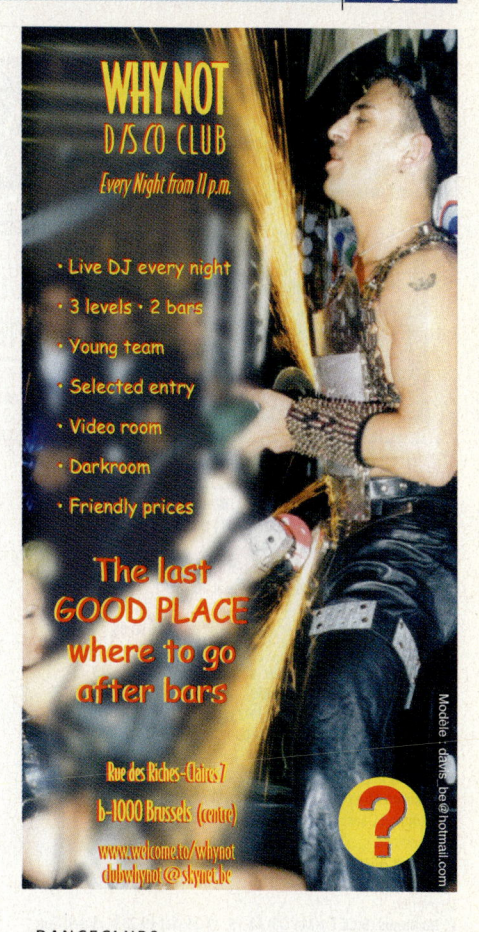

WHY NOT
DISCO CLUB
Every Night from 11 p.m.

• Live DJ every night
• 3 levels • 2 bars
• Young team
• Selected entry
• Video room
• Darkroom
• Friendly prices

The last **GOOD PLACE** where to go after bars

Rue des Riches-Claires 7
b-1000 Brussels (centre)
www.welcome.to/whynot
clubwhynot@skynet.be

Modèle : davis_be@hotmail.com

DANCECLUBS

■ **Cabaret. Le** (AC B D GLM WE YG) Sun 23-7 h
Rue de l'Ecuyer 41 ✉ 1000 *(near La Monnaie)* ☎ 503 58 40
■ **Démence. La** (! AC B CC D DR G MA s VS) 23-10 h,
Rue Blaes 208 ✉ 1000 *(Near Gare du Midi)* ☎ 511 97 89
Big parties 12 times/year. 3 floors, 4 bars, 2 dancefloors,... Call or check website for exact dates.
■ **Different** (B D GLM) 1st Sat 23-6 h
112 Rue du Marché au Charbon ✉ 1000 ☎ 514 30 64
■ **Strong** (AC B D DR G lj s VS WE YG) Sat 23-12 h
Rue Saint Christophe 1 ✉ 1000 *(Metro-Bourse)* ☎ 503 58 40
■ **Why Not** (AC B CC D DR G lj MA P s VS) 23-6, Fri Sat -7 h
Rue des Riches-Claires 7 ✉ 1000 *(Near stock exchange and Grande Place)* ☎ 512 63 63
The only disco open every night.
■ **Wing's. Le** (B D GLM MA WE) Fri (GLM) Sat (L) 23-? h
Rue du Cypre 3 ✉ 1000 *(near Place Sainte Catherine)*
☎ (075) 66 09 90

Belgium — Brussel/Bruxelles

SAUNA
ROOF-GARDEN · STEAM BATH
VIDEO SHOWS · SAUNA
WHIRLPOOL · LABYRINTH
DARK ROOMS · SM CATACOMB

SPADES 4OUR ★★★★★
The next generation

★ VERY CLEAN
★ YOUNG TRENDY PEOPLE
★ VERY BUSY
★ LUXURIOUS
★ FRIENDLY STAFF

Nr 1 in Belgium

Open every day

WWW.SAUNASPADES4.BE
+ 32 (0) 2 502 07 72

7 FLOORS
SWIMMINGPOOL
UV-SOLARIUM · BAR
RESTO · MASSAGE
FITNESS · FOOT-BATH

Rue Bodeghem 23-25
b-1000 Brussels

RESTAURANTS

■ **Au Boeuf que rit** (F glm) 12-15, 18-24 h
Rue des Bouchers 32 ✉ 1000 ☎ 511 96 02

■ **Comptoir. Le** (F GLM) 19-24 h
24-25 Place Vieille Halle aux Blés ✉ 1000 ☎ 514 05 00

■ **El Papagayo** (B F G OS YG) 12-2, Sat Sun 18-2, winter Mon-Sun 18-2 h
Place Rouppe 6 ✉ 1000 *(M-Anneessens)* ☎ 514 50 83

■ **Entre Deux. L'** (CC B F s)
Place de la Vieille Halle aux Blés 42 ✉ 1000 ☎ 511 68 73
Show-dinner every 3rd Sun/month.

■ **H2O** (A AC B E F glm MA p) 19-2 h, closed Dec 23-Jan 7.
Rue Marché-au-Charbon 27 ✉ 1000 ☎ 512 38 43

■ **Imperial. L'** (B F g) 8.30-0 h
Place Saint Josse 21 ✉ 1040 ☎ 230 35 04

■ **Mamma Mia** (CC F glm) closed on Wed and Sun noon
Rue Antoine Dansaert 158 ✉ 1000 ☎ 512 46 24
Italian cuisine.

■ **Monde Allant Vert. Le** (F glm) closed Sun/Mon
Chee de Vleurgatsesteenweg 316 ✉ 1050 ☎ 649 37 27
Vegetarian.

■ **Mykonos** (B CC F g MA OS) 12-15, 17-23, Sat 19-23 h, closed Sun
Rue Archimède 63 ✉ 1040 ☎ 735 17 59

■ **Padoum Center** (F msg)
Boulevard Jamar Laan 9b ✉ 1070 ☎ 522 10 50
Vegetarian Restaurant, Meditation hall, Californian Massage, Dietetics.

■ **Pom' Touline. La** (F g N MA s) Tue-Sat
Place du Béguinage 6 ✉ 1000 *(10 min from Grand Place, Metro-Sainte Catherine)* ☎ 223 33 40

■ **Salons de l'Atalaide. Les** (B F glm)
Chaussée de Charleroi 89 ✉ 1060 ☎ 537 21 54

■ **Vie Sauvage. La** (B F glm)
Rue de Naples 12 ✉ 1050

■ **Y'a pas de Miracle** (B F glm) Mon-Sat 19-1 h
Avenue Paul Dejaer 20 ✉ 1060 ☎ 538 48 93

SEX SHOPS/BLUE MOVIES

■ **Erot' X Stars** (G VS) 11-21 h
Rue de Malines 30 ✉ 1000 ☎ 217 77 27

■ **Europa X** (g VS) 10.30-2 h
Boulevard Adolphe Max 60 ✉ 1000 ☎ 219 71 40

■ **Orly Center** (G DR VS) 10-24, Fri-Sun 12-24 h
Boulevard Jamar 9 ✉ 1070 ☎ 522 10 50

SAUNAS/BATHS

■ **Club 3000** (B CC DR F G MA MSG OS SA SB SOL VS WH WO) Mon-Fri 11-24, Sat Sun and holidays 12-24 h
Boulevard Jamar 9 ✉ 1060 *(near the gare du Midi)* ☎ 522 10 50
No attitude sauna on 600 m² with 3 cinemas. Brunch on Sat & Sun.

■ **Griffe. La** (B DR G MG SA SB VS WH) Mon-Thu 11-22, Fri Sat -2, Sun 14-22 h
Rue de Dinat 41-43 ✉ 1000 ☎ 512 62 51
Renovated sauna with a big-screen video. Established since 1975.

■ **Lagon. Le** (B f DR G MA msg SA SB SOL WH WO) Wed Sat 14-2, Sun 14-24 h (mixed the other days)
86 Rue de Livourne ✉ 1050 *(near Palais de la Justice)*
☎ 534 20 74
Sauna on three floors in the centre of Brussels.

■ **Macho 2** (! AC B F g MA PI s SA SB SOL VS WH WO) 12-2, Sat -4, Sun 12-24 h
Rue du Marché au Charbon 106 ✉ 1000 *(Metro-Bourse, near Grand Place)* ☎ 513 56 67
Tropical sauna frequented by a young crowd.

■ **Oasis. L'** (B F DR G H MA SA SB SOL WH WO) 12-1, Fri Sat-2 h.
Rue van Orley 10 ✉ 1000 *(M° Botanic/Madou)* ☎ 218 08 00
Very big and luxurious bath house. Fri Sat 20-21.30 h cold buffet Bfr 100.

■ **Spades 4our** (AC b CC DR F G MSG OS p PI SA SB SOL WH WO YG) 12-24, Fri -2, Sat 14-2, Sun -24 h
Rue Bodeghem 23-25 ✉ 1000 *(M°-Anneessens, 5 min from Gare Midi)* ☎ 502 07 72
One of the biggest sauna in Belgium on 1200 m². Nude sunbathing on the terrace in summer.

MASSAGE

■ **Institut de Relaxtherapie**
Boulevard Emile Bockstaellaan 293 ✉ 1020 ☎ 420 21 86

BOOK SHOPS

■ **Darakan** (glm)
Rue du Midi 9 ✉ 1000 ☎ 512 20 76

Brussel/Bruxelles | **Belgium**

Sauna...simply the best

macho

Rue marché au charbon, 106 - 1000 Brussels ☎ : 02/513 56 67

Sauna
Whirlpool
Steam bath
Swimming pool
Relax rooms
Dark room
Fitness
Solarium
Air - co
Resto
Bar
Tv
Video
Shop

Open every day at 12:00
Admission: 450 Bef.
Under 25 years: 300 Bef.
Wednesday «School Day» student: 250 Bef
Thursday: 300 Bef

SPARTACUS 2001/2002 | 87

Belgium — Brussel/Bruxelles

■ **Kiosque du Gay Délire. Le** (GLM) 12-19.30 h
Rue Saint Jean 13 ✉ 1000 *(near station railway)* ☎ 511 22 87
Bookshop, gadgets, postcards, videos. Mailorder under www.kiosquegay.com

LEATHER & FETISH SHOPS

■ **Boutique Minuit** (g LJ TV) 10.30-18.30 h, closed Sun
Galerie du Centre 60 ✉ 1000 ☎ 213 09 14
Also Mail Order.

TRAVEL AND TRANSPORT

■ **Sfera Tours** (glm)
Rue Grétry 22 ✉ 1000 ☎ 223 49 48 ✉ sferatours@skynet.be

VIDEO SHOPS

■ **Vidéo Square at Woluwe Shopping Center** (g VS)
Woluwe Saint Lambert 1200 ✉ 1000 ☎ 762 97 80

HOTELS

■ **Bedford** (B E F g)
Rue du Midi 135 ✉ 1000 ☎ 512 78 40 📠 514 17 59
Downtown location/au centre, 20 km to the airport. All rooms with telephone, private bath, WC, and fridge.

■ **Ecrins. Les** (AC b BF CC G H MG)
Rue du Rouleau 15 ✉ 1000 *(Centrally located. 12 km to Zaventhem Airport, M-Sainte Catherine)* ☎ 219 36 57 📠 223 57 40
✉ les.ecrins@skynet.be 🖥 www.lesecrins.com
Comfortable, hospitable 100-year old hotel. Beautiful, spacious rooms. Rates bfr 1500-2800.-

■ **Noga** (B BF CC f glm H)
Rue du Beguinage 38 ✉ 1000 *(Metro-Sainte Catherine)*
☎ 218 67 63 📠 218 16 03 ✉ info@nogahotel.com

■ **Potinière. La** (B g H)
Place St. Géry 29-30 ✉ 1000 *(M-Bourse)* ☎ 511 01 25
📠 511 01 25
Centrally located. All rooms with shower/WC. Single bfr 950, double 1500 (bf incl).

GUEST HOUSES

■ **Bruxelles, Ma Belle** (AC BF GLM H MA p VS)
(quiet street in Quartier Louise) ☎ (0496) 93 92 52
✉ toniet@smart.belgacom.be
2 to 6 people, comfortable rooms with central heating, private bath. TV, VCR, library, videos.

GENERAL GROUPS

■ **Andere Krant. De** (GLM)
14 Fraikinstraat ✉ 1030 ☎ 245 00 41
Flemish-speaking gay group.

FETISH GROUPS

■ **Spanklub** Meeting: 3rd. Sun 15 h at the Duquesnoy
☎ 532 68 78

HEALTH GROUPS

■ **Act Together**
5 Rue d'Artois ✉ 1000 ☎ 512 05 05 (helpline) ☎ 511 33 33
📠 512 09 09
Helping group for English-speaking people with HIV/AIDS.

■ **Act up Bruxelles** Meetings Tue & Sat 14-17 h
Rue Van Artevelde 145 ✉ 1000 ☎ 512 02 02 📠 512 00 07
✉ info@actup.orp 🖥 www.actup.org

■ **Aide Info Sida** (GLM) Mon-Fri 9-20, helpline 18-21 h
45 Rue Duquesnoy ✉ 1000 ☎ 514 29 65 ☎ (0800) 20120 (Helpline)

■ **Elisa** Tue Thu 17-20, Wed Fri 11-14 h
46 Rue d'Artois ✉ 1000 ☎ 513 26 51
Free anonymous HIV tests.

■ **Ex Aequo** Mon-Fri 9.30-17 h
Rue de Tervaete 89 ✉ 1040 *(Metro-Thieffry)* ☎ 736 38 61
☎ 733 96 17 ✉ info@exaequo.be 🖥 www.exaequo.be
Gay association for Aids and other sexual diseases prevention . Also shop selling condoms & lubricants. Publisher of a gay map of Brussels.

■ **Foundation. The** Mon-Fri 10-13, 17-20 h
Diksmuidelaan 49-51 ✉ 1000 ☎ 219 33 51 📠 219 40 00
✉ info@foundation.be 🖥 www.foundation.be
Counselling, care and buddy system for PWAs.

HELP WITH PROBLEMS

■ **Infor Homo** (AC B GLM MA) Wed Fri 20-24, Helpline: Mon-Fri 20-22 h
Avenue de l'Opale 100 ✉ 1030 *(near R.T.B.F, Metro-Diamant)*
☎ 733 10 24 📠 732 10 81 ✉ regard@eurnet.be
Gay Switch Board Centre.

■ **Service Social de Tels Quels** Mon-Fri 10.30-16.30 h
Rue du Marché au Charbon 81 ✉ 1000 ☎ 512 45 87
📠 511 31 48 ✉ telsquels@skynet.be

■ **Télégal** 20-24 h
BP 1969 ✉ 1000 ☎ 502 79 38
French speaking anonymous gay & lesbian info-line/Ecoute-info gaye et lesbienne dans l'anonymat.

RELIGIOUS GROUPS

■ **Communauté. La** (b GLM MA P WE) 2nd 4th Sun 18.30-21 h
BP 104 ✉ 1000 ☎ 672 37 98 ✉ ccl_be@hotmail.com
🖥 www.geocities.com/WestHollywood/Village/4897
Gay christian group.

Le kiosque du gay déLIRE

livres
magazines
cartes-postales
gadgets

13 rue Saint-Jean
B-1000 Bruxelles
tel 32 2 511.22.87
www.kiosquegay.com

Brussel/Bruxelles ▸ De Panne Belgium

"Les Ecrins" Résidence

air conditioning
15, rue du Rouleau 1000 Bruxelles -
Tel. +32 (0) 2 219 36 57 - Fax: +32 (0) 2 223 57 40

e.mail: les.ecrins@skynet.be
www.lesecrins.com

A large century-old building situated in the heart of Brussels, near the major monuments, restaurants, shopping and night life. New spacious rooms equipped with full bathrooms, tel direct & TV

SPECIAL INTEREST GROUPS

■ **Basta Brussel** (GLM YG)
Postbus 1696 ✉ 1000 💻 basta@advalvas.be 💻 surf.to/basta
Young Flemish gay group.

■ **CHE (Cercle Homosexuel Etudiant)** (d GLM YG) meetings
c/o Aimer à l'ULB, 38 Avenue Jeanne ✉ 1050 ☎ 650 25 40
Gay students. Call for info on activities.

■ **English-speaking Gay Group (E.G.G.)** (GLM)
B.P. 198 ✉ 1060 💻 tomhoemig@skynet.be
💻 www.geocities.com/eggbrussels
Social group that organises parties on Sun from 15 h.

■ **Kelmabel** (GLM)
BP 1038 ✉ 1000 ☎ 280 46 60 💻 kelmabelgium@hotmail.com
💻 multimania.com/kelmabelgique
North-African and Middle East gay & lesbian group.

■ **Roze Atomium Rose** (GLM)
BP 696 ✉ 1000 ☎ 345 90 96
Gay deaf group.

SPORT GROUPS

■ **Brussels Gay Sports** (GLM)
32 Rue du Midi ✉ 1000 *(Metro-Bourse)* ☎ 514 50 88
🖨 514 51 09 💻 bgs@bgs.org 💻 www.bgs.org
Contact them for details on activities.

■ **Fédération Arc-en-Ciel** (g)
175/2 Avenue Winston Churchill ✉ 1180 ☎ 646 25 83

CRUISING

-Bois de la Cambre „drève de Lorraine" (near Chaussée de La Hulpe, from noon till sunset)
-Parc du Cinquantenaire (when you come from Shuman, enter the park and turn to the right) (AYOR)
-Place Fontainas (R)
-Parc Royal (until 22 h)
-Lobby of Line 3 underground station „De Brouckere" (especially exit opposite of the movie theater Eldorado)

Charleroi ✉ 6000 ☎ 071

BARS

■ **Bahamas. Le** (B GLM p TV) 21-6 h
Rue Vauban 13 ✉ 6000 *(Ville Haute)* ☎ 32 63 15

■ **Différence. La** (B GLM)
64 Rue du Grand Central ✉ 6000

■ **Entre Deux. L'** (B GLM)
61 Boulevard J. Bertrand ✉ 6000 ☎ 30 03 35

■ **Fifty-Fifty. Le** (B glm)
62 Boulevard J. Bertrand ✉ 6000 ☎ 30 88 60

■ **Petit Chariot. Le** (B D GLM P S) 22-? h
5 Rue de la Bienfaisance ✉ 6000 *(opposite Robert La Frite)*
☎ (0486) 57 00 44
Theme nights on WE.

■ **Provence. Le** (B GLM) 11-3 h
69 Rue de la Régence ✉ 6000 ☎ 30 17 21

SEX SHOPS/BLUE MOVIES

■ **Cine Turenne** (g VS) 12-21 h
Rue Turenne 35 ✉ 6000 ☎ 32 55 97

■ **Fantasme** (g VS)
Rue de la Turenne 45 ✉ 6000 ☎ 30 23 29

BOOK SHOPS

■ **Nouvelle** (g)
4-6 Passage de la Bourse ✉ 6000 ☎ 31 81 33

GENERAL GROUPS

■ **Tels Quels Charleroi** (GLM)
BP 1067 ✉ 6000 ☎ 70 33 63

HEALTH GROUPS

■ **Coordination Sida - Hainaut**
87 Grand-Rue ✉ 6000 ☎ 48 94 20

■ **Sida MST info** Mon-Fri 8-16 h
13 Boulevard Joseph II ✉ 6000 ☎ 23 31 11

CRUISING

-Park near Palais de Justice (AYOR) (near lion statues)

De Panne ✉ 8470 ☎ 058

BARS

■ **Oasis** (B G)
Duikerkelaan ✉ 8470
Cocktail Bar.

Belgium — De Panne ▶ Gent

CAFES
■ **Tearoom The Classics** (B F g YG) 10-24 h
Zeedijk 1 ✉ 8470 ☎ 41 20 19

CRUISING
-Monument Léopold Ier (Esplanade. Evenings)
-Leffrinckouke (+1 h walk near factory hall. Very popular.)

Dendermonde ✉ 9220 ☎ 052

RESTAURANTS
■ **Blaffertuurken. 'T** (CC B F g) 11.30-23 h
Hierbaan 27 ✉ 9220 ☎ 21 80 95
International specialities.

GENERAL GROUPS
■ **Homo- & lesbi-jongerengroep Liever Spruitjes** (GLM)
PO Box 130 ✉ 9200 ☎ 21 59 43

Dinant ✉ 5500 ☎ 082

GENERAL GROUPS
■ **Tels Quels Dinant** (GLM) Fri 20-22 h
7 Place Saint-Nicolas ✉ 5500 ☎ (02) 512 45 87

Genk ✉ 3600 ☎ 011

CAFES
■ **Cheers** (b glm OS) winter 11-21 summer 10-1 h
Rootenstraat 19, Shopping II ✉ 3600 ☎ 35 49 56

Gent ✉ 9000 ☎ 09

GAY INFO
■ **Boys Town** (GLM MA) Sun 20-21 on FM 107.7; Tue 20-21 on 103.3 (Aalst); Wed 20-21 h on 103.3 (Tremolo)
Vlaanderenstraat 22 ✉ 9000 ☎ 329 82 38 ✉ Boystown@usa.net
💻 listen.to/boystown
■ **Holebi-Foon** (GLM) Mon-Sat 18-22, Wed 14-22 h
Kammerstraat 22 ✉ 9000 ☎ 223.69.29 📠 223.58.21
✉ info@fwh.be 💻 www.fwh.be
Gay and lesbian information switchboard. Also home of the FWH (Federatie Werkgroepen Homoseksualiteit).

CULTURE
■ **Fonds Suzan Daniel** (GLM)
Postbus 569 ✉ 9000 ☎ 223 58 79 📠 223 63 74
✉ suzan.daniel@skynet.be
Gay-Lesbian archives and documentation centre.

BARS
■ **Dandy's Club** (B D E G h MA os p tv) Tue-Thu 20-?, Fri-Sun 18-? h, closed Mon
Princes Clementinalaan 195 ✉ 9000 *(next to St. Pieters train station)* ☎ 329 68 91
■ **King Street** (B G MA) 21-7 h
Kammerstraat 49 ✉ 9000
■ **Krypton** (B D g) Sat Sun 20-? h
Ter Kameren 2 ✉ 9620 ☎ 360 63 27
■ **Oase** (B g)
Botestraat 84 ✉ 9032 ☎ 091/53 08 08
■ **Pablo** (B CC D G MA OS p YG) 21-? h
Princes Clementinalaan 195 ✉ 9000 ☎ 245 02 99
New decoration every two months.

■ **Paradox** (A AC B d GLM MA) Café: Thu-Sun 20-?; Club: Wed 22-?; Café + Club Sat 21-? h
Vlaanderenstraat 22 ✉ 9000 ☎ 233 70 40
■ **Por que no** (B g) Thu-Mon 21-? h
St. Denijslaan 155 ✉ 9000 ☎ 222 53 70
■ **Zénon** (B G MA) 11-1, Fri Sat 14-2 h
St. Veerleplein 7 ✉ 9000

CAFES
■ **Cocteau** (F g) Tue-Sun 11-? h
Jan Palfijnstraat 19 ✉ 9000 ☎ 233 52 68
■ **Grote Avond. De** (F g) Wed-Sun 18-3 h
Huidevetterskaai 40 ✉ 9000 ☎ 224 31 21
■ **Ludwig** (glm) Tue-Sun 11-1 h
Hoogpoort 37 ✉ 9000 ☎ 223 71 65
■ **Sphinx** (glm) Mon-Fri 19-2, Sat Sun 14-2 h
Sint Michelshelling 3 ✉ 9000 ☎ 225 60 86

DANCECLUBS
■ **7th Heaven** (B D DR G NU STV VS YG) Thu Sat Sun (G), Fri (GLM), closed Mon-Wed
Grote Baan 218 ✉ 9920 *(take E40, E17, then R4 direction Eeklo)*
☎ 372 59 57

RESTAURANTS
■ **Avalon** (B F glm) 12-14 h, closed Sun
Geldmunt 37 ✉ 9000
■ **Cassis** (AC CC F g MA OS) 10-23 h
Vrijdagmarkt 5 ✉ 9000 *(centre)* ☎ 233 85 46
■ **Malcontenta. La** (B F glm) Tue-Sat 12-14, Thu-Sat 20-22 h
Haringsteeg 7 ✉ 9000 ☎ 224 18 01
■ **Olivier's** (AC B E F g OS) 12-23 h
Vrijdagmarkt 16 ✉ 9000 ☎ 224 20 40
Traditional cuisine.
■ **Oranjerie** (CC F glm) 12-14, 18-22 h, closed Tue Wed
Corduwaniersstraat 8 (Patershol) ✉ 9000 ☎ 224 10 08
■ **Vier Tafels. De** (b F g) Mon-Sun 11.30-14.30 h
Plotersgracht 6 ✉ 9000 ☎ 225 05 25
■ **Walry** (B F glm) 8-18 h, closed Sun
Zwijnaarsesteenweg 6 ✉ 9000

SEX SHOPS/BLUE MOVIES
■ **Libidos-Erotheek** (g MA VS) Mon-Sat 12-22 h
Kuiperskaai 4 ✉ 9000 ☎ 223 93 88

SAUNAS/BATHS
■ **Boys Avenue** (B F DR G MA SA SB VS) 12-24, Fri -1, Sun 15-24 h
Oude Schaapsmark 1A ✉ 9000 ☎ 225 40 78

BOOK SHOPS
■ **De Brug** (glm) 6.30-22, Sun 9-21 h
Phoenixstraat 1 ✉ 9000 ☎ 226 38 69
■ **Walry** (g)
Zwijnaardsesteenweg 6 ✉ 9000 ☎ 221 85 08

HOTELS
■ **Erasmus** (BF CC g H OS) closed from 15th Dec to 15th Jan
Poel 25 ✉ 9000 *(central)* ☎ 225 75 91 📠 224 21 95
📠 233 42 41 ✉ hotel.erasmus@proximedia.be
💻 www.proximedia.com/web/hotel-erasmus.html
Small friendly hotel in a 16th century house. All rooms with bath, TV. Own keys.

GUEST HOUSES
■ **Chambres d'Amis** (BF H glm OS)
Schoolstraat 14 ✉ 9040 *(2 km from the city centre, near Campo Santo and Sint-Amandsberg)* ☎ 238 43 47 ☎ (04) 77 89 71 57
💻 chambres@come.to 💻 come.to/chambres
Recently renovated and redecorated „gentleman's house".

GENERAL GROUPS
■ **Casa Rosa** (GLM)
Kammerstraat 22 ✉ 9000 ☎ 222 83 01 💻 surf.to/CasaRosa
Gay and lesbian association providing information, organising cultural events and parties.
■ **Het Gehoor** (GLM MA)
Sint-Niklaasstraat 7 ✉ 9000 ☎ 225 75 99
💻 hetgehoor@poboxes.com 💻 come.to/hetgehoor
Gent gay and lesbian group.
■ **Werkgroep Gehuwde Homo's, Lesbiennes en Partners Gent** (GLM)
Kalkoenlaan 37 ✉ 9032 ☎ 253 80 65
■ **Werkgroep Ouders van Homo's en Lesbiennes**
Coupure 604 ✉ 9000 ☎ 223 58 79

RELIGIOUS GROUPS
■ **Lieve Deugd. Gelovige Holebi's Gent** (GLM MA) Wed 20-22, Sat 10-12 h
Postbus 40 ✉ 9030 ☎ 226 13 30 💻 lieve.deugd@advalvas.be
💻 surf.to/lieve.deugd

SPECIAL INTEREST GROUPS
■ **Verkeerd Geparkeerd** (GLM YG)
PO Box 535 ✉ 9000 💻 vege@student.rug.ac.be
Young gay and lesbian group. Write for info.

SPORT GROUPS
■ **Sportclub Auricula** (GLM)
Korenveldstraat 17 ✉ 9032 ☎ 236 53 39

CRUISING
-Blaarmeersen (Watersportbaan, at foot of hill)
-Station (M. Hendrikaplein)
-Citadelpark (Leopold II laan)

Hasselt ✉ 3500 ☎ 011

BARS
■ **Renegade** (AC B d f glm MA s) 20-? h closed Sun
Fonteinstraat 2 ✉ 3500 ☎ 28 10 28

GENERAL GROUPS
■ **Limburgs Actie Centrum Homofilie (LACH)** (GLM MA)
Tue Fri 20-22
c/o C.G.S.O., Wijngaardstraat 1 ✉ 3500 ☎ 21 20 20
■ **Werkgroep Gehuwde Homo's, Lesbiennes & Partners Hasselt** (GLM)
Wijngaardstraat 1 ✉ 3500
■ **Werkgroep Ouders van Holebi's**
✉ 3500 ☎ 23 26 05

RELIGIOUS GROUPS
■ **Cristen Gewoon Anders (H & G Limburg)**
p/a Wijngaardstraat 1 ✉ 3500 ☎ 28 47 62

SPECIAL INTEREST GROUPS
■ **Holebi-Jongeren Nota Bene** (GLM YG)
PO Box 137 ✉ 3500 ☎ (089) 85 65 06

Herentals ✉ 2200 ☎ 014

LEATHER & FETISH SHOPS
■ **Philippe Moda Pelle** (CC GLM LJ) Mon-Fri 8-16.30, Sat 11-16.30 h
Bovenrij 25 ✉ 2200 *(20 min from Antwerpen, next to the Townhall)*
☎ 21 91 03
Hand made top quality leather clothing.

Huy ✉ 4500 ☎ 085

GENERAL GROUPS
■ **Tels Quels Huy** (GLM) Tue 10-12, 20-22, Sun 20-22 h
22 Rue Portelette ✉ 4500 ☎ 25 34 19

Knokke-Heist ✉ 8300 ☎ 050

BARS
■ **Apero. L'** (AC B CC f g OS s) 21-6 h
Zoutelaan 3 ✉ 8300 *(near Lippenslaan)* ☎ 62 75 40
■ **Night Flash Bistro** (B F g MA) 19-7 h, closed Tue
Lippenslaan 48 ✉ 8300 ☎ 61 23 50

RESTAURANTS
■ **De Bolle** (B BF CC F GLM H MA) 11.30-14.30, 18-24 h
Vlamingstraat 62 ✉ 8301 *(Heist)* ☎ 51 43 04
Restaurant bar with rooms to rent.

Koekelaere ✉ 8280 ☎ 051

CAFES
■ **'T Vosmotje** (B F GLM)
Marktplein 8280 ✉ 8280 ☎ 58 97 48

Kortrijk ✉ 8500 ☎ 056

GAY INFO
■ **G.O.C. Kortrijk** Wed, Thu, Sun 20-24, Fri -2, Sat -? h
Papenstraat 9 ✉ 8500 ☎ 21 75 42

BARS
■ **Bronx. The** (A AC B CC D E GLM MA P) Mon, Wed, Thu 22-?, Fri-Sun 21-? h, closed Tue
Kasteelkaai 5 ✉ 8500 ☎ 21 96 74
■ **Burning Love** (B G MA)
Doorniksewijk 113 ✉ 8500
■ **Café Del Mar** (B GLM MA) 20-5 h, Tue closed
Gentsestraat 1 ✉ 8500
■ **Pink Panther. The** (B G MA) Fri-Sun 20-2 h
Papenstraat 9 ✉ 8500
■ **Vagabond** (AC B CC D E f GLM lj MA p VS) 22-? h
Meensesteenweg 80 ✉ 8500 ☎ 35 41 13

DANCECLUBS
■ **Bamba. La** (B CC D GLM MA p SNU VS WE) Fri Sat 20-5 h
Kasteelkaai 5 ✉ 8500

RESTAURANTS
■ **Kopje. 'T** (b F g) 13-1 h
Grote Markt ✉ 8500

Belgium | Kortijk ▶ Liège

SAUNAS/BATHS

■ **Aquarius** (B cc DR f G MA NU OS p PI SA SB VS WH) 13-24 h
Moeskroensesteenweg 1 ✉ 8511 *(between Mouscron and Kortrijk, highway N43)* ☎ 20 25 33
Nice sauna in a white villa with a lovely garden with whirlpool and swimming pool for nude sun bathing.

GENERAL GROUPS

■ **Korthom / Kortrijkse Homowerking** (G)
Minister Tacklaan 99 ✉ 8500 ☎ 22 60 71
■ **Werkgroep gehuwde homo`s en partners** (GLM)
Papenstraat 9 ✉ 8500 ☎ 21 75 42

RELIGIOUS GROUPS

■ **Homo & Geloof Kortrijk** (GLM)
Beekstraat 38 ✉ 8500 ☎ 22 12 61

SPECIAL INTEREST GROUPS

■ **Detrain Homojongeren** (GLM YG)
Papenstraat 9 ✉ 8500 ☎ 21 75 42
Gay youth group.

CRUISING

-Kasteelkaai-Rooseveltplein

Kuurne ✉ 8520 ☎ 056

DANCECLUBS

■ **After Nine** (AC B D E GLM MA p s) 21-? h, closed Tue
Brugsesteenweg 102 ✉ 8520 ☎ 35 76 18

La Louvière ✉ 7100 ☎ 064

BARS

■ **Pub. The** (B d GLM MA) 11-?, Sat 15-?, Sun 18-? h
Rue Kerasmis 31 ✉ 7100 ☎ 28 00 80

Leuven ☎ 016

BARS

■ **Charly's Brasserie** (B CC F glm MA) 10.30-? h
Martelarenplein 11 ✉ 3000 ☎ 23 23 33
■ **Exkeet** (B glm) 21-? h, closed on Sun
Nerviersstraat ✉ 3000 ☎ 22 30 42
■ **Frenkies. The** (A AC B d G lj MA TV) 21-? h, closed Wed-Thu
Schapenstraat 105 ✉ 3000 *(near Begijnhof)* ☎ 22 77 66

CAFES

■ **Couperus en Cocteau** (B GLM MA OS) 20-1.30 h, closed on Tue & Sat
Diestsestraat 245 ✉ 3000 *(near station)*
On Thu host of the local gay organisation.

HEALTH GROUPS

■ **De Witte Raven HIV-café** Fri 20 h
St.-Michielscentrum, Naamsestraat 57a ✉ 3000 ☎ 20 09 06

SPECIAL INTEREST GROUPS

■ **Holebi-Jongeren Het Goede Spoor** (GLM YG)
PO Box 113 ✉ 3000 ☎ 20 06 06

Liège ✉ 4000 ☎ 04

BARS

■ **Blue Note** (B glm MA)
29 Place du Marché ✉ 4000 ☎ 221 38 64
■ **Chez Danny** (B GLM MA) 10-? h
15 Place Xavier Neujean ✉ 4000 ☎ 232 04 68
■ **Petit Paris. Le** (B BF glm MA OS) 11-? h, closed Mon
31 Place du Marché ✉ 4000 ☎ 223 54 96
■ **Relax Café. Le** (B d f GLM MA OS S TV) Mon-Sat 11-?, Sun 14-? h
22 Rue Pont d'Avroy ✉ 4000 *(in front of the cinema „Palace")*
☎ 223 16 46
Drag queen shows every 3rd week.
■ **Rio. Le** (B GLM) 11-23 h
Galerie Opéra ✉ 4000 *(1st floor)* ☎ 223 19 28
■ **Scène. La** (B glm) 11-?, Sun 15-? h
Rue de la Casquette 1 ✉ 4000 ☎ 223 11 43
■ **Spartacus** (AC B CC d DR G LJ MA P VS WE) 16-6, Fri-Sun -6 h
12 Rue Saint-Jean en Isle ✉ 4000 *(centre)* ☎ 223 12 59

DANCECLUBS

■ **Jungle. La** (B gL MA) 22-? h, closed Mon Tue Wed
20 Rue Léon Mignon ✉ 4000 ☎ 222 07 75
■ **Mama Roma** (AC B D GLM MA stv) 22-? h, closed Mon Tue
16 Rue des Célestines ✉ 4000 ☎ 223 47 69
Shows on Fri & Sun.
■ **Milord. Le** (B D GLM MA) 20-? h, closed Tue
32 Rue Souverain Pont ✉ 4000 ☎ 221 41 08

RESTAURANTS

■ **Bruit Qui Court. Le** (CC B F glm) 11-24, Fri Sat -2 h, closed Sun noon
142 Boulevard de la Sauvenière ✉ 4000 *(centre, near the „Carré" and other gay places)* ☎ 232 18 18
Brasserie-Restaurant.

SEX SHOPS/BLUE MOVIES

■ **Majestix** (g VS)
Rue de la Cathédrale 9 ✉ 4000 ☎ 232 10 51

SAUNAS/BATHS

■ **Espace Man** (B CC f G MA SA SB VS WS) 14-24, Fri-Sun -3 h
Rue des Célestines 9 ✉ 4000 ☎ 222 47 41
■ **Sauna 2000** (B cc F DR G SA SOL VS WH WO) Mon-Thu 15-24, Fri Sat 15-6, Sun 14-23 h
Rue des Français 139 ✉ 4430 *(in Ans)* ☎ 246 32 54
The bar area is accessible without visiting the sauna. Younger crowd during the WE.

BOOK SHOPS

■ **Entretemps. L'** (glm)
19-21 Rue Pierreuse ✉ 4000

HOTELS

■ **Must. Le** (g H) 9-24 h, Sun closed
9 Rue Henri de Dinant ✉ 4000 ☎ 243 35 63
Room with bath BFR 980.-, bf 75.-

GENERAL GROUPS

■ **Alliàge** (GLM) Meetings 2nd & 4th Fri 19-23 h
45 Rue des Bayards ✉ 4000 ☎ 228 04 77
✉ alliage@geocities.com 🖥 come.to/alliage

HEALTH GROUPS
■ **Coordination Sida - Liège**
7 rue Hors-Château ✉ 4000 ☎ 223 29 13

SPECIAL INTEREST GROUPS
■ **CHEL** (GLM YG) Thu 17-19 h
9 Rue Soeurs-de-Hasque ✉ 4000 *(next to „Le Pot au Lait")*
☎ 222 33 76 📠 223 24 69 💻 chel@sips.be 💻 www.sips.be/chel
Young (up to 30) gay and lesbian organisation.

CRUISING
-Canal Albert, Ile-de-Monsin (near Albert I Monument)
-Parc d'Avroy
-Place de la Cathédrale
-Place de la République Française (AYOR)

Lignières ✉ 6900 ☎ 0496

DANCECLUBS
■ **Queen 69** (B D GLM) Wed, Fri-Sun 22-? h
4 Bras de Lignières ✉ 6900 ☎ 47 74 22

Lommel ✉ 3920 ☎ 011

BARS
■ **Patho** (B glm)
Dorp 63 ✉ 3920

RESTAURANTS
■ **Lommelshuisje** (F glm H) 16-? h closed Thu
Adelberg 51 ✉ 3920 ☎ 55 13 04

Mechelen ✉ 2800 ☎ 015

BARS
■ **Bonaparte** (B glm) 12-? h
Veemarkt 17 ✉ 2800 ☎ 21 85 46
■ **Sebastiaan** (AC BF B d GLM H MA OS) 12-?, Sat 14-?, Sun 16-? h, closed Thu
Brusselsesteenweg 203-205 ✉ 2800 ☎ 43 00 10
Provides bed & breakfast.

GENERAL GROUPS
■ **HLWM (Homo- en Lesbiennewerking Mechelen)** (GLM MA N)
Fri 20-? h Gay Café
Hanswijkstraat 74 ✉ 2800 ☎ 43 21 20

SPECIAL INTEREST GROUPS
■ **Jong Geleerd** (GLM N YG)
Postbus 4 ✉ 2800 💻 jonggeleerd@hotmail.com
💻 www.geocities.com/jonggeleerd
Weekly activities for young (-26 years) gay and lesbian. Check website for details and dates.

CRUISING
-Railway station (especially near north entrance)
-In front of bus station (AYOR) (next to post office; 17-? h, and on Sat Sun afternoons)

Menen ✉ 8930 ☎ 056

BARS
■ **Lagoen** (B g MA)
Wervikstraat ✉ 8930

Mol ✉ 2400 ☎ 014

CAFES
■ **Cher** (B glm MA) 16-3, Tue 7-3, Sun 9-3 h
St.-Pieterstraat 5 ✉ 2400 ☎ 31 95 83

Mons ✉ 7000 ☎ 065

BARS
■ **Half and Half Bar** (B g) 20-? h
Rue de la Coupe 36 ✉ 7000

SEX SHOPS/BLUE MOVIES
■ **New Sexy World** (g) 10-23 h
Rue Léopold II 17 ✉ 7000 ☎ 35 16 61

GENERAL GROUPS
■ **Tels Quels Mons** (GLM)
☎ (0477) 92 01 34 ☎ (02) 512 45 87
Meetings, entertainment, information/Rencontres, animations, informations.

CRUISING
-Around church gardens
-[P] Heppignies near Fleurus (highway from Mons to Namur, 10 km from Charleroi; both sides, day and night)

Namur ✉ 5000 ☎ 081

DANCECLUBS
■ **Caves d'Apollon. Les** (B D G) Wed 19-? h, Fri Sat 22-? h
Rue des Tanneures 13 B ✉ 5000 ☎ (075) 68 00 77

HOTELS
■ **New Hôtel de Lives** (B BF CC F glm H MA OS)
Chaussée de Liege 1178 ✉ 5101 *(6 km from centre of Namur, Bus 12 / bus stop in front of the hotel)* ☎ 58 05 13 📠 58 15 77
💻 francis40@infonie.be 💻 perso.infonie.fr/francis35
Hotel, restaurant, pub completely renovated. Ancient style.

GENERAL GROUPS
■ **Tandem** (GLM)
BP 70 ✉ 5100 ☎ 74 60 49

HEALTH GROUPS
■ **Coordination Sida Assuétude**
Rue Château-des-Balances 3 boîte 13 ✉ 5000 ☎ 72 16 21
📠 72 16 20 💻 sida.toxicomanie@province.namur.be
HIV tests, condoms and lubricants.

CRUISING
-Parc Louise Marie (R MA WE) (evenings)

Nieuwpoort ✉ 8620 ☎ 058

BARS
■ **Boat. De** (B D F glm YG) 18-2 h closed Mon
Watersportlaan ✉ 8620 ☎ 23 80 56

Oostende ✉ 8400 ☎ 059

GAY INFO
■ **GOW Oostende**
PO Box 131 ✉ 8400 ☎ 50 25 58

Belgium — Oostende ▶ Tournai

BARS
- **Art Gallery Bistro Mercurius** (A B F g MA) 10-? h
  Van Iseghemlaan 28 ✉ 8400 ☏ 80 67 44
- **Azo** (B G MA)
  Ooststraat 57 ✉ 8400 ☏ 51 18 92
- **Calypso** (AC B f GLM MA OS) 16-?, Jul-Sep 10.30-? h
  Groentenmarkt 15 ✉ 8400 ☏ 80 15 69
- **Rapsody** (AC B D G MA YG) 21-? h, closed Tue
  St. Franciscusstraat 29 ✉ 8400 ☏ 80 84 73
- **Taverne Ushuaia** (B d Glm) 16-? h
  Kleine Weststraat 13 ✉ 8400 *(near Wapenplein/Casino)*
  ☏ 075/27 43 18
- **Valentino** (B D G MA) 22-? h
  Schipperstraat 50 ✉ 8400 ☏ 50 29 26

CAFES
- **Café de Flore. Le** (B F GLM M) 10-5 h, closed Tue
  Kursaal (Oosthelling) ✉ 8400
- **Caruso** (B BF f) bf from 6 h
  Nieuwstraat ✉ 8400
- **Croisette. La** (B F GLM) 11-? h, off-season closed Thu
  Promenade Albert I 50 a ✉ 8400 ☏ 70 91 65
- **Dewulf** (A B BF f glm) 7.30-19.30 h
  Kapellestraat 32-34 ✉ 8400 ☏ 70 05 69
  Gay bf place.
- **Mercurius** (! A B BF CC E f g h MA OS) 10-? h, closed Tue
  Van Iseghemlaan 28 ✉ 8400 ☏ 80 67 44
  Provides rooms & apartments.
- **Piaf's. Le** (B F GLM) closed Tue
  Langestraat 90 ✉ 8400 ☏ 70 57 65

DANCECLUBS
- **Men 4 Men** (AC B D DR G MA P S TV VS) 21.30-? h
  Sint- Franciscusstraat 22 ✉ 8400 ☏ 70 30 67

RESTAURANTS
- **Cormoran. Le** (B F GLM)
  Langestraat 63 ✉ 8400 ☏ 70 11 60
- **Komedie. De** (B F glm) 10-? h
  Louisastraat 5 ✉ 8400 ☏ 51 27 98
  Snacks and Indian specialties.
- **New Sint James** (AC B BF F g MA OS) 7.30-22 h, closed Mon
  Canadaplein 2 ✉ 8400 ☏ 51 18 36
- **Van Eyck** (B F glm) 19-?, closed Thu, meals -2 h
  Hertstraat 10 ✉ 8400 ☏ 70 35 81

SEX SHOPS/BLUE MOVIES
- **Adonis** (DR G MA VS) 12-22 h
  Dwarsstraat 1B ✉ 8400 *(Old Town)* ☏ 51 43 01
- **Paradise** (CC g VS) 11-23 h
  Madridstraat 15 ✉ 8400 *(80 m from the casino)* ☏ 51 36 72
  Books and magazines, rubber/leather and SM toys.

SAUNAS/BATHS
- **Aquarius II** (B f DR G MA MSG SA SB SOL VS WH WO) 15-24, Sat Sun 14-24 h
  Peter Benoitstraat 77 ✉ 8400 *(10 min from station)* ☏ 51 34 55
  Recent sauna frequented by a mixed age crowd.
- **Thermos** (B F G SA SB SOL VS WO) 14-24 h
  Kaaistraat 34 ✉ 8400 *(5 min from train station)* ☏ 51 59 23

HEALTH GROUPS
- **De Witte Raven HIV-café**
  Nieuwpoortsteenweg 85 ✉ 8400 ☏ 50 28 82

CRUISING
- Bredene (at the beginning of the dunes near the Military Hospital on the Blankenberghe side of Oostende in afternoons)
- Beach opposite Digue de Mer
- Lido Beach (afternoons)
- Maria-Hendrika Park

Pipaix ✉ 7904 ☏ 069

DANCECLUBS
- **Escargot. L'** (B D Glm MA) Fri Sat 21-? h
  13 Chaussée de Mons ✉ 7904 ☏ 66 36 50

Pittem ✉ 8740 ☏ 051

BARS
- **Retro** (B d f G MA p) Wed Thu 20-5, Fri-Sun 21.30-6 h
  Tieltstraat 38 ✉ 8740 *(between Brugge and Kortrijk)* ☏ 46 74 47

Rekkem ✉ 8930 ☏ 056

BARS
- **Blue Night** (AC B d E f GLM p s) Thu-Mon 20-? h, Sun gay, closed Tue Wed
  Vagevuurstraat 67 ✉ 8930 ☏ 40 16 55

Rillaar ✉ 3202 ☏ 016

DANCECLUBS
- **Viertap** (B D g OS TV YG) Fri-Sun & holidays 20-8 h
  Molenstraat 1 ✉ 3202 ☏ 50 08 63

Roeselare ✉ 8800 ☏ 051

BARS
- **Patrick's Pub** (AC B d G OS P YG) Fri-Tue 18-?, every 3rd Wed 19-? h (DR NU)
  St. Jorisstraat 25 ✉ 8800 *(5 min from station)* ☏ 075/46 42 34

GENERAL GROUPS
- **Werkgroep Ouders van Holebis**
  Spechtenwegel 8 ✉ 8800 ☏ 051/22 32 68

Sint-Niklaas ✉ 9100 ☏ 03

GENERAL GROUPS
- **Homo- en Lesbiennegroep Roze Waas** (GLM) Fri 20-24 h
  Truweelstraat 85 ✉ 9100 💻 rozewaas@email.com

Tielt ✉ 8700 ☏ 051

BARS
- **Barneyz** (AC B D DR G MA OS P S SNU VS) 21-? h
  Brugstokwegel 2-4 ✉ 8700

Tienen ✉ 3300 ☏ 016

RESTAURANTS
- **Verleiding. De** (F glm)
  Minderbroederstraat 16 ✉ 3300 ☏ 81 32 80

Tournai ✉ 7500 ☏ 069

BARS
- **Diva. La** (B glm)
  Rue Saint-Piat ✉ 7500

Tournai ▶ Wichelen — Belgium - Belize

DANCECLUBS
■ **Midnight. Le** (B D GLM)
14 Rue de Dorez ✉ 7500 ☎ 21 13 78

RESTAURANTS
■ **Roi de Rome** (b F g)
Rue des Maux ✉ 7500

SHOWS
■ **Merlin. Le** (B GLM MA STV) 10-? h closed Wed
13 Place de Lille ✉ 7500 ☎ 84 09 98

GENERAL GROUPS
■ **Tels Quels Tournai** (GLM)
29 Rue de la Construction ✉ 7500 ☎ (0496) 98 30 45

Turnhout ✉ 2300 ☎ 014

BARS
■ **Kasteeltje. 'T** (B d glm) Tue-Sat 11-?, Sun 14-? h
Kateelplein 8 ✉ 2300

GENERAL GROUPS
■ **Kempische Werkgroep Homofielie** (B GLM) Wed, Fri-Sun 21-3 h
Driezenstraat 25 ✉ 2300 ☎ 42 35 83
Contact Enter Plus (G MA), Exit (YG) and Werkgroep ouders van homo's at this address.

RELIGIOUS GROUPS
■ **Homoseksualiteit en Geloof** (GLM)
Polderstraat 33 ✉ 2360 (Oud-Turnhout) ☎ 41 24 25

CRUISING
P between Exit 24 and 25 (A 34)

Veurne ✉ 8630 ☎ 058

CAFES
■ **Fortuintje** (B f glm MA N) 11-?, closed on Thu
Appelmarkt 1 ✉ 8630 ☎ 31 14 21

RESTAURANTS
■ **Oude Vesten. D'** (AC B CC F glm MA) 10.30-1 h
Oude Vestingstraat 69 ✉ 8630 ☎ 31 40 74

Waasmunster ✉ 9250 ☎ 052

GENERAL GROUPS
■ **Werkgroep Ouders van Holebis**
Rhodendries 53 ✉ 9250 ☎ 47 90 37

Wichelen ✉ 9260 ☎ 09

BARS
■ **Cadillac** (B D GLM YG) Sat 22-6 h
Watermolenweg 100 ✉ 9260 ☎ 369 53 60

Belize

Name: Belice
Location: Central America
Initials: BH
Time: GMT -6
International Country Code: ☎ 501 (leave the first 0 of area codes)
International Access Code: ☎ 00
Language: English. Spanish, Creole, Carib, Mayan
Area: 22,965 km2 / 8,867 sq mi.
Currency: 1 Belize Dollar (Bz$) = 100 Cents.
Population: 230,000
Capital: Belmopan
Religions: 58% Roman Catholic, 28% Protestant
Climate: Tropical climate, very hot and humid. The rainy season lasts from May to February.

✳ Homosexuality is legal in Belize. However, it is worth keeping in mind that tolerance of gays among the general populace is limited.

★ Die Ausübung homosexueller Handlungen ist in Belize legal. Allerdings sollte man beachten, daß sich die Toleranz der Bevölkerung gegenüber Schwulen in Grenzen hält.

✳ L'homosexualité est légale au Belize. Notons cependant que la tolérance de la part de la population vis-à-vis des gais reste limitée.

En Belize la práctica del comportamiento homosexual es legal. De todas formas se debería tener en cuenta, que la tolerancia hacia los homosexuales es bastante limitada.

✖ In Belize l'omosessualità è legale, senonché conviene tener presente che la tolleranza della popolazione è limitata.

Map showing Belize with neighboring Mexico, Guatemala, Caribbean Sea, and capital Belmopan.

Belize - Bolivia — Belize City ▸ La Paz

Belize City ☎ 02

BARS
■ **Bellevue Hotel** (B CC D G WE YG) 22-? h
Southern Foreshore *(upstairs bar/main floor disco)*
■ **Red Roof Lounge** (B F g MA OS) Tue-Fri 17-24, Sat-3 h
3580 Sittee Street ☎ .

ESCORTS & STUDIOS
■ **C & C Services**
PO Box 22 31 ☎ 353 08

FITNESS STUDIOS
■ **Body 2000**
Carribbean Shores *(1 mile from Save U Supermarket towards Airport)*
$5 Daypass.

HOTELS
■ **Bakadeer Inn** (AC BF)
Gleghorn Street *(5 min. from downtown in quiet side street)*
☎ 314 00
8 rooms with bath. Single $45 Double 55.

SPECIAL INTEREST GROUPS
■ **For Us Club** (g)
PO Box 2270

SWIMMING
-San Pedro/Ambergris Caye (Beach/Strand near/bei Ramons Village g NG YG)
-Punta Gorda (G MA) (beach at the mouth of the Moho River, only reachable by boat, boat reservations at Tourism Centre in Punta Gorda, 11 Front Street. ☎ (07) 2 834)

CRUISING
-Lindsbergs Landing (from Ramad to Pub Amnesia, Thu-Sat ca.3-2 h)

Bolivia

Name: Bolivien • Bolivie
Location: South America
Initials: BOL
Time: GMT -4
International Country Code: ☎ 591 (leave the first 0 of area codes)
International Access Code: ☎ 00
Language: Spanish
Area: 1,098,581 km2 / 424,162 sq mi.
Currency: 1 Boliviano (Bs) = 100 Centavos
Population: 7,958,000
Capital: La Paz
Religions: 95% Roman Catholic
Climate: The climate varies with the altitude from humid and tropical to cold and dry.

✱ Homosexuality is not mentioned in the Bolivian law books. According to our information, the age of consent is 21. Violations may be punished with up to 5 years' imprisonment.

★ Das bolivianische Strafgesetzbuch erwähnt Homosexualität nicht. Die Schutzaltersgrenze liegt nach unseren Informationen bei 21 Jahren. Auf Zuwiderhandlung stehen ein bis fünf Jahre Gefängnis.

✱ Le Code Pénal bolivien ne fait pas mention de l'homosexualité. D'après ce que nous savons, la majorité sexuelle est fixée à 21 ans. Les contrevenants risquent jusqu'à 5 ans d'emprisonnement.

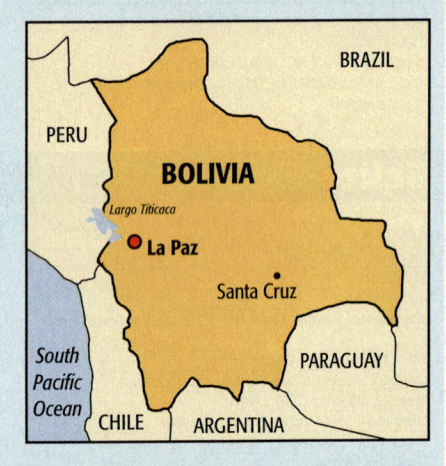

⬢ El Código Penal boliviano no menciona la homosexualidad. Según nuestras informaciones, la edad de consentimiento es de 21 años. La contravención de esta disposición supone una pena que va desde uno hasta cinco años de cárcel.

✖ Il Codice Penale boliviano non nomina l'omosessualità. Secondo le nostre informazioni l'età minima per i rapporti è di 21 anni. I trasgressori possono essere condannati alla reclusione per una durata da uno a cinque anni.

Cochabamba ☎ 042

CRUISING
-La Plaza (dia o noche/day or night)
-El Prado (AYOR) (by night)

La Paz ☎ 02

BARS
■ **Chichara. La** (G MA TV) Mon-Sat evenings 'til late
Pichincha 664/Indaburo
Difficult to find as there are no signs outside. Toilets rather grubby but interesting crowd.

La Paz ▶ Sucre | **Bolivia - Bosnia-Herzegovnia**

DANCECLUBS
■ **Extasis** (g MA) Thu, Fri, Sat nights
Calle Diego de Peralta/Calle Onduras *(No house number but a red light hangs outside)*
Entrance US$ 4,– includes one drink and cloak room)

CINEMAS
■ **Cine Papillon** (NG) Daily 22h
Calle Pichincha 524
In the last row you may find gay activities. Entrance fee US$ 2,–. Busy from 22h (3 or 4 films)

HOTELS
■ **Panamericano** (B F H NG)
Avenida Manco Kapac 454 ☎ 34 08 10
Downtown location. 7 km from the airport. All rooms with telephone, private bath. Single US$ 6.50, double 12.
■ **Residencial Rosario** (b F H M NG OS SA SB WH)
Calle Illampu 704
All rooms with shower, WC, heating. Rate double US$ 27. Booking essential.

CRUISING
-Plaza P. Velasco
-Plaza Mendoza
-Plaza San Francisco
-El Prado/Plaza de Estudieantes(mediodia y noche/midday and night)

Santa Cruz ☎ 03

BARS
■ **Las Brujas** (AYOR B glm R) -6 h
Avenida Cañoto/Avenida Landivar
■ **Line** (B D GLM r) 19-? h
Avenida 26 de Febrero, 1005

CRUISING
-Plaza 24 de septiembre
-Parque del Arenal (AYOR)
-Avenida Coñoto
-El Christo

Sucre ☎ 064

CAFES
■ **Biblio Café** (B NG)
Calle Nicolas Ortiz
En frente de la catedral/across from the cathedral.

CRUISING
-La Plaza(noche/night)

Bosnia-Herzegovnia

Name: Bosna i Hercegovina • Bosnien & Herzegowina • Bosnie-Herzégovine
Location: Southeast Europe
Initials: BIH
Time: GMT +1
International Country Code: ☎ 387 (leave the first 0 of area codes)
International Access Code: ☎ 00
Language: Serbocroatian
Area: 51,129 km2 / 19,741 sq mi.
Currency: Bosnian Dinar
Population: 3,365,000
Capital: Sarajevo
Religions: 44% Muslim 31% Serbian-Orthodox 17% Catholics
Climate: Summers are hot, winters cold. Areas of high elevation have short, cool summers and long, severe winters. Along the coast winters are mild and rainy.

✳ According to our information, homosexual acts between men in Bosnia-Hercegovina are not illegal.

✴ Nach unseren Informationen sind homosexuelle Handlungen zwischen Männern in Bosnien-Herzegowina nicht verboten.

✳ D'après ce que nous savons, l'homosexualité n'est pas un délit en Bosnie-Herzégovine.

⬢ Según nuestras informaciones la homosexualidad (entre hombres) en Bosnia-Herzegovina no está prohibida.

✖ Secondo le nostre informazioni l'omosessualità non è vietata in Bosnia-Erzegovina. Ciò vale però solo per l'omosessualità tra uomini.

Map: Bosnia-Herzegovina with Sarajevo, bordered by Croatia, Yugoslavia, Albania, Italy, Adriatic Sea

Bosnia-Herzegovnia - Brazil   Sarajevo

NATIONAL GAY INFO

■ **Gay Bosnia**
✉ editor@gaybih.com
🖥 www.gaybih.com
*Internet site supporting the development of a gay (lesbian, transsexual and bi) community in Bosnia and Hercegovina.
Cultural news, health information, going out info and chat pages.*

Sarajevo ☏ 071

BARS

■ **Bar. The** (B f glm)
Titiva 7 (Marsala Tita)
You'll find more gays on Fri and Sat 11-2 h

CRUISING

-Main Station
-Park close to the presidency building and The Bar
-Beside the Zeljeznica River in Ilidza

Brazil

Name: Brasil • Brasilien • Brésil • Brasile
Location: Central & northeastern South America
Initials: BR
Time: GMT -3/-4
International Country Code: ☏ 55 (leave the first 0 of area codes)
International Access Code: ☏ 00
Language: Portuguese
Area: 8,511,996 km2 / 3,285,632 sq mi.
Currency: 1 Real (R$) = 100 Centavos.
Population: 169,806,557
Capital: Brasilia
Religions: 70% Roman Catholic
Climate: Mostly tropical climate, but the south is moderate.
Important gay cities: Rio de Janeiro, São Paulo, Salvador, Belo Horizonte, Recife

✱ The legal age of consent in Brazil is 18. A law has even been passed here to prevent the discrimination of sexual minorities. However, we have no information as to whether the police is continuing to arrest gays under the precept of "safeguarding morality and public decency". However, there are large and colourful gay scenes in the big cities like Rio, Sao Paulo or Salvador.

★ Das Schutzalter liegt in Brasilien bei 18 Jahren. Es existiert ein Gesetz gegen die Diskriminierung sexueller Minderheiten. Allerdings wird von häufigen Übergriffen der Sicherheitskräfte vor allem auf Transvestiten und Transsexuelle berichtet. In den großen Städten aber, wie Rio, Sao Paulo oder Salvador, gibt es große und sehr bunte schwule Szenen.

✱ Au Brésil, la majorité sexuelle est fixée à 18 ans pour tous. La loi protège les gais de toute discrimination liée à leur sexualité. Nous ne pouvons pas dire avec exactitude si la police continue à vouloir „protéger la morale et les bonnes moeurs" à sa façon. Dans les grandes villes comme Rio, Sao Paolo ou Salvador, ça bouge beaucoup au niveau gai.

⬢ La edad de consentimiento es de 18 años. Existe una ley contra la discriminación de las minorías sexuales. No nos es conocido si las fuerzas de seguridad continuan "protejiendo las costumbres y la moral pública". Pero en las grandes ciudades como Río, Sao Paulo o Salvador hay un ambiente gay muy colorido.

✖ In Brasile l'età legale per avere rapporti omosessuali é di 18 anni. Esiste una legge contro la discriminazione di minoranze sessuali. Non sappiamo se le forze dell'ordine proteggono ancora la „morale pubblica". Tuttavia nelle grandi città come Rio, San Paolo e Salvador esiste un'effervescente e variopinta vita gay.

NATIONAL GAY INFO

■ **Grito De Alerta**
Avenida Amaral Peixoto, 36 sala 1209, Niterói Rio de Janeiro
☏ (021) 722 14 58   📠 (021) 625 45 90
■ **Nós por Exemplo**
Rua da Glória, 30-Glória, Rio de Janeiro   ☏ (021)2 52 47 57
■ **OK Magazine c/o Trama Editorial Ltda.**
PO Box 19113   ✉ 04.505-970 São Paulo - São Paulo

CULTURE

■ **Festival of Sexual Diversity**
Rua Joao Moura 2432 cj 01, Pinheiros   ☏ (011) 2127 3901
📠 (011) 3819 5360
Every year in November there is this very important international film festival for gays and lesbians, with directors from all over the world.

Aracaju-Sergipe ▶ Brasilia-Distrito Federal | **Brazil**

NATIONAL GAY INFO
■ **Grito De Alerta**
Avenida Amaral Peixoto, 36 sala 1209, Niterói Rio de Janeiro
☎ (021) 14 58 📠 (021) 625 45 90.
■ **Nós por Exemplo**
Rua da Glória, 30-Glória, Rio de Janeiro ☎ (021) 252 47 57
■ **OK Magazine c/o Trama Editorial Ltda.**
PO Box 19113 ✉ 04.505-970 São Paulo - São Paulo

NATIONAL GROUPS
■ **Festival of Sexual Diversity**
Rua Joao Moura 2432 cj 01, Pinheiros
São Paulo ☎ (011) 2127 3901
📠 (011) 3819 5360
Every year in November there is this very important international film festival for gays and lesbians, with directors from all over the world.

Aracaju - Sergipe ☎ 079

GAY INFO
■ **O Capital**
Avenida Ivo Prado, 948 *(Centro)* ☎ 222-4868

BARS
■ **Aldo's Drink Bar**
Rua Mal. Deodoro, 1185 *(Bairro Getúlio Vargas)*
■ **Bug House**
Rua Mariano Salmeron, 283 *(Bairro Siqueira Campos)*
■ **Caras e Caras**
Rua Napoleão Dórea, 355 *(Bairro Atalája)*
■ **Chico's Bar**
Rua do Rosário, 555 *(Bairro Santo Antônio)*
■ **Cine Ria Branco** *(g)*
Calçadão da Rua São João
■ **Tenda do Moisés**
Avenida Ivo Prado, 106 *(Centro)*

GENERAL GROUPS
■ **Dialogay**
PO Box 298 ✉ 49000 ☎ 235-8169
■ **Núcleo Homossexual**
Caixa Postal 24 ✉ 49001-970

CRUISING
-O Calçadão (Rua João Pessôa; 18-24 h)
-Rua 24 horas (praia de Atalaia)

Belem - Parà ☎ 091

BARS
■ **Bar do Parque** (AYOR b f G OS R) 0-24 h
Praça da República *(near Hilton)*

DANCECLUBS
■ **Boite Luau Sexta** (B D GLM OS) 22-4 h
Travessa Rui Barbosa, 729 ☎ 223-7629
■ **Guetto** (AC B D G STV SNU) Fri - Sat 23-?
Municipalidade 383 ☎ 223 6323
■ **Mix** (B D GLM) Fri - Sat 23-?
Rua Almirante Wanderlock 985 *(2nd floor)*

SAUNAS/BATHS
■ **Narcissus** (B G msg SA SB PI R S VS) 15-24h
Rua Arthur Bernardes / Rua Pratinha 332 ☎ 258 0289

GENERAL GROUPS
■ **Movimento Homossexual de Belém**
PO Box 15 59 ✉ PA 66017-9

CRUISING
-Bar do Parque
-Bosque de Rodrigues
-Praça da Republica (YG) (Rua St. Antonio and J. Alfredo)
-Pierside and Market (during the day and early evening)

Belo Horizonte - Minas Gerais ☎ 031

BARS
■ **Bar do Fernando** (B g) closed Mon
Rua Sergipe/Avenida Brasil ✉ 30130 *(Savassi-suburb)*
■ **Blue Way** (B g) closed Mon
Rua Sergipe/Avenida Brasil *(Savassi-suburb)*
■ **Caminho de Casa** (B g)
Rua Barão de Macaúbas, 212 A *(Santo Antonio)*
■ **Cantina Do Lucas** (B F GLM YG)
Avenida de Lima 223, Loja 18 ✉ 30660 ☎ 226-7153
■ **Point** (B d f glm) Tue-Sat 19-? h Sun 16-? h
Rua Rio de Janeiro 1562
■ **SO-HO** (B G)
Rua Santa Rita Durão, 432 ☎ 221-7743

DANCECLUBS
■ **Fashion** (B D G)
Rua Cláudio Manoel, 240 ☎ 223-7171
■ **Opera 60** (A AC B D E G VS YG)
Avenida Prudente de Morais, 921 ✉ 30380 *(Telemig Cid. Jadin)*
■ **The Biggof's** (B D G)
Rua São Paulo, 1245 Galpão Centro *(Gâlpao)*

CINEMAS
■ **Cine Brasil** (g)
Praça Sete de Setembro
■ **Cine Candelária** (g)
Praça Raul Soares s/n ✉ 30180

SAUNAS/BATHS
■ **Hot House** (b f G MA N SA SB)
Rua Guajajaras 1097, Centro ✉ 30180 ☎ 292-6778
■ **Off 2000** (AC B CC DR f G MA msg PI SA SB VS WH WO) 0-24 h
Av. Oiapoque 85, Centro ✉ 30111-070 ☎ 224-7904
■ **Vapore** (AC B CC DR f G MA msg PI SA SB VS WH WO) 0-24 h
Rua Timbiras, 2523, Centro ✉ 30140-061 ☎ 275-2001
Big sauna with relax rooms, scotch bar and many specials.

HOTELS
■ **Papillon** (H NG)
Rua Rio de Janeiro, 639 Praça Sete *(Centro)* ☎ 212-3811

CRUISING
-Avenida Alfonso Pena (from Rodoviaria to the town hall)
-Praca Raul Soares (R)
-Rua Goitacazes
-Parque Municipal (at sunset)

Brasilia - Distrito Federal ☎ 061

BARS
■ **Barulho** (B g) Sun
Parque da Cidade

Brazil Brasilia-Distrito Federal ▶ Fortaleza-Ceará

■ **Beirute** (B F GLM)
109 W 3 Sul ☎ 244 1717
■ **Karekas** (B f g)
C-08 lote 18, loja 02, Taguatinga
■ **Lobo Mau**
W 3 Norte

CAFES

■ **Café Savana** (B F glm MA OS) 11.30-1 h, closed Sun
SCLN 116 Bloco A Loja 4 ✉ 70.773-510 ☎ 347-9403
■ **Cassis** (B F g)
CLS 214 Bloco B, Lj. 22 - Asa Sul

DANCECLUBS

■ **Boate New Aquarius** (B D G WE) Fr-Sat - 23-?
SDS - Ed. Acropol, Bloco N Loja 12 ☎ 225 9328
■ **Garagem** (B D GLM WE) Fri-Sat 23-?
SOF/Sul-Qd. 16 - Cj.A - Lt. 5/6

RESTAURANTS

■ **Universal Diner** (B F g)
CLS 210 Sul ☎ 4432089

CINEMAS

■ **Cine Bristol** (g)
Ed. Konic Seto de Divers°es Sul
■ **Cine Karin** (g)
W 3 Sul

SAUNAS/BATHS

■ **Calígola** (G MA SA SB)
Setor de Diversão Sul, Ed. Venâncio Jr. ✉ 70300 *(Subsolo)*
☎ 321-423
■ **Soho** (B G SA SB)
Setor Comercial Sul ✉ 70300 *(Lojas Americanas)*

HOTELS

■ **Byblos** (H NG)
SHN 3, Lote E ✉ 70710 ☎ 223 2570
If travelling alone, there is no problem taking someone home with you for the night if you have reserved a room for two.
■ **Nacional Brasilia** (H NG)
SHS, Lote 1 ✉ 70300 ☎ 226-8181
Still one of the best hotels in town, but very expensive. If there is no official guest of the government while staying there, you can take a well dressed visitor to your room during the day. There is also a sauna where things can happen, but don't be too optimistic. 10 km to the airport. Single US$ 62, double 69 (bf incl.).

GENERAL GROUPS

■ **Estruturação**
PO Box 3636 ✉ 70084-970

CRUISING

-Avenida W-3 (after 24 h)
-Parque Nacional (swimming pools with warm mineral water; anywhere near the pool or the waterfall. Avoid toilets: military police!)
-Conjunto Nacional Shopping Mall, Commercial Sector South. Cruisy toilets: downstairs near middle of mall; upstairs on exterior terrace. „Constant action." Located across from the main bus terminal.

Curitiba - Paraná ☎ 041

BARS

■ **Blue Jeans Bar** (B g)
Alameda Dom Pedro II, 448
■ **Classic Bar** (B g)
Avenida Iguaçu, 550
■ **Memories Bar** (B g)
Avenida Visconte de Guarapuava, 3602

DANCECLUBS

■ **Insanus**
Rua Fernando Moreira, 185 ☎ 223-1838

SAUNAS/BATHS

■ **Caracala** (G MA SA VS) 16-23h
Rua Alferos Poli, 1039 ✉ 80000 ☎ 333-6766

CRUISING

-Rua XV de Novembre (park at the end of Rua das Flores)

Diamantina - Minas Gerais ☎ 038

BARS

■ **Bar** (B g)
Beco Alegrim, 39 ✉ 39100

Fortaleza - Ceará ☎ 088

BARS

■ **Barraca A Pin E A Tosa** (B d F glm MA N OS s WE) 0-24 h
Avenida Beira Mar 3101 23b-24a, Meireles ✉ 60.165-000
☎ 242-4962
■ **Barraca do Joca** (B BF F g N) 0-24 h
Avenida Presidente Kennedy, 3101, barraca 25-a ✉ 60165 *(on the Iracema Beach, across from Hotel Beira-Mar)* ☎ 261-4603
■ **Navy** (B G)
Avenida da Abolicao, 3303 c ☎ 263-3122

DANCECLUBS

■ **Kinze Trinta** (AC B D G MA S WE) 23-6 h
Rua General Sampaio, 1530 ✉ 60020 *(Faculdade de Direito)*
☎ 252-1549
■ **Periferia** (AC B D GLM S WE YG) 23-6 h
Rua Dragão do Mar, 260 ✉ 60060 *(near Cappitania dos Portos)*
☎ 252-3208

SAUNAS/BATHS

■ **Apollo** (AC B DR f G msg p Pl SA SB VS WO) 16.30-24h
Rua Rodrigues Junior 1425 ✉ 60060-001 *(Bus-Av. Dom Manuel, 15 min from the airport)* ☎ 221-6667
■ **Iracema** (B cc DR G MA SA SB VS WO) 15-23 h
Rua Vicente Leite 2020, Aldeota ✉ 60135-420 *(near Av. Antônio Sales)*
☎ 244-1999
Nice sauna with extended facilities.

HOTELS

■ **Hotel Passeio** (AC BF g H MA)
Rua Dr. João Moreira 221 ✉ 60.030-000 *Centro, nearby Mercado Central* ☎ 226-9640 ☎ 253-6165 253-6165

GENERAL GROUPS

■ **GRAB • Grupo de resistência asa branca**
PO Box 421, ✉ 60001-970 grabqbrhs.com.br

Grupo Canto Livre
Rua Erico Mota, 1029, Parquelândia, ✉ 60540-170

SWIMMING
- Praia de Iracema
- Praia Canoa Quebrada (NU) (several hours from the city)
- Praia do Cumbuco (nu) (in the dunes at the far western end, 1 hour from the city, near Icarai)
- Praia Jericoacoara (several hours to the west of the city)

CRUISING
- Stone jetty(at the west end of Praia de Iracema, opposite Iracema Hotel)
- Southwest corner of the Praça do Ferreira
- Praça do Carmo (behind the church)
- Along the downtown section of Duque de Caixas Avenue
- Downtown cinemas (by the entryways and in the restrooms)

Foz do Iguaçu - Paraná ☎ 045

HOTELS
Das Cataratas (AC B F H NG OS PI)
Rod. BR 469 km 28 ✉ 86750 ☎ 74-2666
Right on the waterfall. Nice but expensive.

Goiânia - Goiás ☎ 062

DANCECLUBS
Jump! (B D glm WE) Wed-Sun
Av. Republica do Libano 1752 - Setor Oeste

SAUNAS/BATHS
Musculo e Poder (B g DR SA SB VS WO) 9-19h
Av. Araguaia / Av. Contorno *(Next to Muritana park)*

HEALTH GROUPS
Grupo pela Vida
Rua 19, 35-Edificio Dom Abel (Centro) ✉ 74036-901
☎ 225-8639

Guarujá - São Paulo ☎ 013

BARS
Boate Aquarius (B g)
Avenida Floriano Peixoto, 913 ✉ 11410 *(Morro do Maluf)*
☎ 86-4148

RESTAURANTS
Faro. II (B F g)
Rua Tracema, 38 ✉ 11400 *(Praia da Enseada)* ☎ 53-3117

HOTELS
Casa Grande (H NG)
Avenida Miguel Stefano, 999 ✉ 11440 *(Enseada)* ☎ 86-2223
Single US$ 57, double US$ 129.
Guarujá Inn (H NG)
Ave da Inn Hotel ✉ 11440 ☎ 87-2332
Single US$ 81, double US$ 110.

CRUISING
- Seashore Promenade around the facilities in City center
- Beach 30 km west of the city

Ilhéus - Bahia ☎ 073

HOTELS
Motel Barravento (B H NG R)
Rua N. S. des Gracas ✉ 45660 *(situated on Malhado beach)*
Get a room in the annex with a refrigerator and priv. bath.

João Pessoa - Paraíba ☎ 083

RESTAURANTS
Peixada do João (F g)
Rua Coração de Jesus ✉ 58035 *(Tambaú)*
Simple atmosphere but very good food.

HOTELS
Sol-Mar (H NG PI)
Avenida Rui Carneiro, 500 ✉ 58043 *(Near airport)* ☎ 226-1350

GENERAL GROUPS
All-Ação Pela Liberdade Licás
Rua Abel Silva, 532, Cruz das Alomas ✉ 58000-000
Movimento do Espírito Lilás
PO Box 524 ✉ 58001-970

SWIMMING
- Praia da Tambaba (first "official" nude beach in the northeast; about 30miles south of the town)

Macapá - Amapá ☎ 096

CRUISING
- The Jetty (active promenade)
- Zoological Gardens and steps to the cathedral on a small hill, downtown
- Sea Front
- Avenida Ribeiros

Maceió - Alagoas ☎ 082

BARS
Bye Bar Brasil (B g)
Rua Olavo Machado ribeiro 320 - Jaiuca
LLe (B GLM YG)
Avenida Duque de Caxias ✉ 57000

DANCECLUBS
Number One Disco Bar (B D glm WE) Fri-Sat 23-?h
Rua do Uruguai 288 - Jaragua
Singles (B D G STV WE)
Rua Silverio Jorge 598 - Centro
Trup e Dance (B D glm WE)
Rua jangadeiros 115

CINEMAS
Ideal
Avenida Dezesseis de Septiembro ✉ 57015 *(Levada)*

SAUNAS/BATHS
Ele/Ela (B g SA SB MG) 15-23h
Rua Silverio Jorge 514
Eros (B G SA SB VS) 17-?h
Rua Sete de Setembro 74 - Centro ☎ 2214601

Brazil | Maceió-Alagoas ▸ Nova Iguaçu-Rio de Janeiro

HOTELS
■ **Pousada Cavalo Marinho** (BF F glm H) 24 h
Rua da Praia 55, Riacho Doce ✉ 57039.280 ☎ 355-1247
🖨 355-1265 📧 cavmar@dialnet.com.br

SWIMMING
-Praia de Ponta Verde (YG) (popular)
-Jatiúca (in front of Praia Verde Hotel)
-Ilha do Croa (NU) (across the river at Barra de Santo Antonio)

CRUISING
-Praça Sinimbú (Avenida Duque de Caxias, evenings)
-Praia de Jatiúca
-Praia do Francês
-Praia de Pajuçara
-Praia da Avenida
-Praia de Sacarecica
-Praia do Sabral

Manaus - Amazonia ☎ 092

DANCECLUBS
■ **Bancrevia Club** (B D g)
Av. Getulio Vargas, Centro
■ **Chiek Club** (B D G)
Av. Getulio Vargas, Centro
■ **Madame Butterfly** (BDG)
Av. Djalma Batista *(Near Shopping Amazonas)*
■ **Notivagos** (B D DR GLM) Thu - Sat
Rua Wilken de Matos s/n - Aparecida
■ **TS** (B D G WE) Fri - Sun 23-?h
Blvd. Dr. V. de Lima, 33 ☎ 081 228 6828

Maricá - Rio de Janeiro ☎ 021

HOTELS
■ **Hotel Solar Tabauna** (B BF glm M H MA OS PI SA)
Rua Caxambú - Alto do Farol ✉ 24900-000 *(nearby the beaches)*
☎ 648-1626 📧 solartabauna@aol.com
🖥 www.brasil-solartabauna.de

Natal - Rio Grande do Norte ☎ 084

BARS
■ **Rainbow** (B D G WE)
Rua João Alves Flor 3025 - Parque das Colinas ☎ 988 6626

DANCECLUBS
■ **Vice e Versa**
Rua Coronel Cascudo 127 - Centro ☎ 222 2349
■ **Vogue** (B D G S SNU WE) Thu-Sun
Rua Presidente Bandeira 385 - Alecrim

SAUNAS/BATHS
■ **Eunapius** (AC B G msg OS PI SA SB VS WO) 17-23 h
Rua dos Tororós, 2535, Lagoa Nova *(20 min from airport)*
☎ 234-8246
Large sauna with outdoor pool and garden, game room with a pool table.
■ **Eunapius Termas Club** (AC B g SA SB msg VS WO) 17-24h
Rua dos Tororos 2535 - Lagoa Nova ☎ 234 8246
■ **Medieval II** (B G DR S SA SB) Mon-Fri 17-23h, Sat-Sun 16-23h
Rua Ceara Mirim / Nizario Gurgel 2013 - Centro ☎ 991 3338

■ **Rio Branco** (B G MA SA VS) 16-22 h
Avenida Rio Branco, 821, Centro ☎ 201-2086

HOTELS
■ **Oasis Swiss Hotel** (g OS)
Rua Joaquim Fabricio 291 ✉ 59.012-340 *between centre and beach*
☎ 202-2766 🖨 202-2766 📧 rshswiss@digi.com.br
🖥 www.oasisswisshotel.com.br
Double room with shower 25-30 US$ incl. bf.

GENERAL GROUPS
■ **GOLH (Grupo Oxente de Libertação Homossexual)**
Rua Câmara Cascudo, 123 Sala 102 ✉ 59012-390
■ **Grupo Habeus Corpus Potiguá**
PO Box 576 ✉ 59022-970
■ **SINTA**
Rua Doctor José Neves, 25

RELIGIOUS GROUPS
■ **Comunidade Fratriarcal**
PO Box 346 ✉ RN 59001-970

Niterói - Rio de Janeiro ☎ 021

DANCECLUBS
■ **Disco Clube Imperial** (B D F G PI S SB VS) 21-4 h. Fri & Sat shows.
Rua 2, No.20 *Recanto de Itaipuaçu. Last bus stop on the route Niterói-Itaipuaçu.* ☎ 709-2242
■ **Vollupya** (B D G S VS)
Rua Coronel Tamarindo, 35 *(São Domingos)*

CINEMAS
■ **Cine Central** (g)
Avenida Visconde do Rio Branco

HOTELS
■ **Icarai Palace Hotel** (AC B F NG SA)
Belisário Augusto, 21 ✉ 24230 ☎ 714-1414
■ **Hotel Pousada & Club Imperale** (B D DR G H PI VS S)
Rua 2 n. 20 Recanto ✉ 24.900-000 *(Itaipuaçu)* ☎ 638-1581

SWIMMING
-Itaipu
-Recanto de Itaipuaçu

CRUISING
-São Francisco Beach and Ica Beach (from ferry take bus "Canto de Rio")

Nova Iguaçu - Rio de Janeiro ☎ 021

BARS
■ **Encantus**
Rua Coronel Francisco Soares, 268 *(Centro)*
■ **Nevada**
Santa Luzia, 180 *Centro*
■ **Rosa Choque**
Avenida Governador Portela, 775 *(Centro)*

GENERAL GROUPS
■ **28 de Junho**
Rua Ataíde Pimenta de Moraes, 37 ✉ 26.210-210

Olinda-Pernambuco ▶ Porto Alegre-Rio Grande Do Sul | **Brazil**

Olinda - Pernambuco ☏ 081

BARS
■ **Frutapão** (B F glm OS) 17-24, Sun 16-22 h (GLM YG)
Rua do Sol 349 *(Sea Front near Busstop Olinda Carmo)*
■ **Itapoã** (! B GLM OS) 16-24 h
Avenida Markus Freire 897 *(Sea Front)*
■ **Pool Bar at Hotel Pousada D'Olinda** (B glm OS PI)
Praça João Alfredo, 178 *(opposite San Pedro Church-Busstop Olina Carmo)* ☏ 439 11 63

RESTAURANTS
■ **Atelier. l'** (E F glm MA OS)
Rua San Bento 91 *(Quatro Cantos)*
■ **Mourisco** (A E F glm MA)
Praça João Alfredo 1st floor *(opposite Hotel Pousada D'Olinda-Busstop Olinda Carmo)*
■ **Oficina do Sabor** (E F glm MA OS)
Rua do Amparo 335 *(near Busstop Amparo)*

HOTELS
■ **Hotel Pousada D'Olinda** (AC B BF F glm H OS PI SOL)
Praça João Alfredo 178 ✉ 53110 *(Olindo Historico-opposite Igreja San Pedro)* ☏ 439 11 63 📠 439 11 63
■ **Pousada Peter** (A AC B BF CC F H NG PI)
Rua do Amparo 215 ✉ 53.020-170 *(in the historical centre of Olinda)* ☏ 439 2171 📠 439 2171 ✉ pousadapeter@uol.com.br
💻 www.pousadapeter.com.br
Hotel with art gallery, tropical garden with pool and nice view.

SWIMMING
-Olinda Casa Caiada
-Janga
-Pau Amarelo
-Maria Farinha (beach)
-Itamaraca Island (beach) (a few miles from Olind, easily accessible by bus, action possible at far end of the beach.)

CRUISING
-Beach at Praia da Enseada (from afternoon, opposite Rio Doce)
-Praça João Alfredo (Olina Carmo)

Ouro Preto - Minas Gerais ☏ 031

BARS
■ **Beco de Sata** (B G S)
93 Rua San Jose

Porto Alegre - Rio Grande Do Sul ☏ 051

BARS
■ **Bahamas** (B G MA S TV VS YG) 23-? h
Avenida Farrapos, 2025 ✉ 90220-006
■ **Fim de Seculo** (B D G) Thu Sun 23-?h
Avenida Plinio Brasil Milano, 427 ✉ 90210 *(Auxiliadora)*
☏ 312 2220

DANCECLUBS
■ **Enigma/Pandora Privé** (! B D E GLM OS WE YG) Fri-Sat 23-? h
Rua Pinto Bandeira, 485 - Centro ✉ 90030 *(Downtown)*
■ **Escandalo Lounge** (A B D G S STV)
Av. Venancio Aires 59 - Cidade Baixa ☏ 222 3856
■ **Planet Club** (B D G S SNU WE) Sun 23:30-?h
Av. Venancio Aires 59 ☏ 337 0544

CINEMAS
■ **Aurea**
Avenida Julio de Castilhos
■ **Capitólio**
Avenida Borges de Medeiros
■ **Carlos Gomes** (g LJ)
Rua Vig. José Inacio, 335
■ **Cine Apolo** (g)
Rua Voluntarios da Patria - Galeria Santa Catarina
■ **Cine Area** (g)
Av. Julio de Castillo 76 - Centro
■ **Eroticos Videos** (AC G) MoFri 11-20h, Sat 12-19h
Av. julio de Castilhos 648 ☏ 286 2479
■ **Lido** (G)
Avenida Borges de Medeiros ✉ 90020

SAUNAS/BATHS
■ **Arpoador** (B G MA SA SB VS) 15-24, Sat Sun & public holidays - 23 h
Rua Prof. Ivo Corseuil, 210, Petrópolis ☏ 338-4306
Condoms and lube for free.
■ **Convés Sauna Clube** (AC G MA SB VS) Mon-Fri 11-21, Sat -18 h
Avenida Mauá 1897
Condoms and lube for free.
■ **Coruja** (B G SA SB) 14-22:30h
Rua Comendador Coruja 189 - Floresta ☏ 291 3430
■ **Hero** (G B SA SB msg MA R VS) 15-23 h closed Sun
Rua Visconde do Rio Branco, 390 ✉ 90460 *(Floreste. Between Travessa Azevedo & Rua Santa Rita)* ☏ 395 5458
Young men in underwear are hustlers (michés).
■ **Plataforma** (G SA SB msg)
Avenida Pernambuco, 2765, Bairro São Geraldo ☏ 395-1633
■ **Sauna Alternativa** (B G SA SB R VS)
Rua Augusto Severo 291 - Sãio João ☏ 337 2252
■ **Thermas Point Sul Ltda** (AC B G MA SA SB PI VS) 15-23 h
Rua Cabral, 468, Moinho de Vento *(near Av. Mariante)* ☏ 331-6324

TRAVEL AND TRANSPORT
■ **Pink Side Travel Agency** 9-? h
St. Mostardeiro, 157/CJS. 907/908 ✉ 90430-001 ☏ 222 2144
☏ 222-2653 📠 346-2650

GENERAL GROUPS
■ **Nuances**
PO Box 1747 ✉ 90.001-970 ☏ 221 63 63

HEALTH GROUPS
■ **G.A.P.A. (HIV Positive Advice and AIDS)**
Rua Luiz Alfonso, 234 ✉ 90001 *(Disque:Soliedariedade)*
☏ 221 63 67

CRUISING
-Praça Da Alfandega (toilets)
-Rua dos Andradas
-Avenida Borges de Medeiros
-Rua Salgado Filho
-Avenida Independencia
-Ipanema Bathing Resort (close to town)
-Belem Novo Bathing Resort
-Avenida Jose Bonifácio (across from Parque Farroupilha-car necessary)
-Parque Marinha do Brasil-Avenida Beida Rio (car useful)
-Parque da Redenção
-Parque Farroupilha (Park-dangerous at night.)
-Rua da Praia Shopping

Brazil | Porto Seguro-Bahia ▶ Rio de Janeiro

Porto Seguro - Bahia ☏ 073

HOTELS
■ **Pousada Cheiro Verde** (b BF g H PI)
Estrada do Mucuge 448 ✉ 45820 *(near arrial d'Ajuda)*
☏ 575 12 05

Porto Vehlo - Roraima ☏ 069

DANCECLUBS
■ **Claudio's Club Prive** (B D G)
Rua Gonçalves Dias 784, Olaria

Recife - Pernambuco ☏ 081

BARS
■ **Bangue** (B g OS YG) 17-22 h
Pátio de São Pedro ✉ 50020 *(Santo Antonio)*
■ **Kibe** (g MA OS R) Fri- Sat 24-2 h
Avenida Herculano Bandeira (Pina)
Gay on Fri & Sat.
■ **Mustang** (B F g MA OS)
Avenida Conde da Boa Vista *(near Mesbla)*
The gayest hours are 20-1 h.
■ **Pit House** (g MA OS)
Rua do Progresso *(Boa Vista-near Mustang)*
■ **Porção Magica** (g MA OS)
Rua do Progresso (Boa Vista-near Mustang)
■ **Savoy** (B g MA OS R)
Avenida Guararapes, 147 ✉ 50010 *(Santo Antonio)* ☏ 224 2291
■ **Sete Cores** (B D GLM MA OS R S)
Rua do Progreso, (Boa Visto-near Mustang)

SAUNAS/BATHS
■ **Athenas** (AC B CC DR f G MA msg p SA SB VS) 10-23, Fri-Sat -9 h
Avenida Conselheiro Aguiar, 4790/207, Boa Viagem ✉ 51021 *(2nd floor)* ☏ 326-5010
■ **Center** (B G MA msg OS SA VS)
Rua do Sossego 62, Boa Vista ✉ 56380-000 ☏ 221-5498
■ **Clube Spartacus** (AC B CC F G MA msg OS p R s SA SB VS WO) 15-23, Fri-Sat -5 h
Rua João Ivo da Silva, 95, Madalena ✉ 50720-100 *(close to Bradesko Bank on Ave. Caxangá)* ☏ 228-6828
A discreet and friendly sauna. Parties once a month with free food and drinks as well as music on the patio.

TRAVEL AND TRANSPORT
■ **Personalité Tour-Impresarial João Roma**
Avenida Conselheiro Aguiar 2333 *(Boa Viagem)* ☏ 465 63 36
Travel Agent.

SWIMMING
-also see Olinda
-Calhetas (near Gaibu, Cabo)
-Porto das Galinhas (40 miles from Recife)
-Gaibu- Beach (by bus from airport to Cabo and transfer)

CRUISING
-Shopping Center Recife (near C&A, ground floor)
-Avenida Conde de Boa Vista (AYOR r) (day and night)
-Casa de Cultura (AYOR, TV) (shopping center on Avenida Beberibe)
-Praça do Carmo (AYOR) (on the steps of the law building)
-Promenade at Boa Viagem
-Beach at Avenida Boa Viagem (AYOR, R) (daytime)
-Praça de Casa Forte

Rio de Janeiro ☏ 021

✱ Rio is one of the largest and most cosmopolitan cities in the world. Including the suburbs, the city now numbers almost 16 million people. Rio has something to offer for everyone's taste. If you want to spend your days sunning on the beach and watching the masses of gorgeous gods of all races go by, and then in the evening throw yourself into the malestrom of bars and discos, then the Copacabana district is the place for you. If all this commotion is too much, try the Ipanema section of town, where the pace is slower and there are fewer crowds. If you're more of a daytime person and want to see what Rio's shops and markets have to offer, you will find what you are looking for in the Rio Branco district downtown. The bus service between Copacabana and the center of town is cheap and also runs regularly at night. The ride takes about ½ hour.
The Carnival, which has made Rio de Janeiro famous throughout the world, takes place every year, some time between the end of February and the beginning of March. You would be well advised to protect yourself against the high rate of criminal activity during this period.

★ Rio gehört zu den aufregendsten Mammutstädten der Erde. Die Außenbezirke eingerechnet, zählt sie mittlerweile fast 16 Millionen Einwohner. Unterschiedlichste Bedürfnisse kommen hier zu ihrem Recht. Falls Sie gern tagsüber am weißen Strand schmoren (wo es von Schönheiten aller Rassen nur so wimmelt), um sich anschließend abends und nachts in das wilde Getümmel der Bars und Discos zu stürzen, so finden Sie Ihr Paradies vermutlich in Copacabana. Ein wenig gesetzter geht es in Ipanema zu, hier sind auch nicht ganz so viele Menschen. Wenn Sie jedoch eher ein Tagmensch sind und erleben möchten, was Rios Märkte und Läden Ihnen so alles zu bieten haben, dann sind Sie am besten in der Zentrumsgegend des Rio Branco aufgehoben. Die Busverbindungen zwischen Copacabana und der Innenstadt sind billig und werden auch nachts aufrecht erhalten. Die Fahrzeit beträgt, je nach Uhrzeit, eine halbe bis eine Stunde. Der legendäre "Carneval", der die Stadt Rio de Janeiro auf der ganzen Welt berühmt gemacht hat, findet, je nach Jahr, zwischen Ende Februar und Anfang März statt. Hier muß man sich allerdings auch auf eine sehr hohe Kriminalitätsrate einstellen.

✱ Rio est une des plus excitantes mégapoles du monde. 16 millions de personnes vivent dans son agglomération. Ici, tous vos souhaits seront exaucés! A Copacabana, vous pouvez vous faire dorer sur la plage au milieu de beautés de toutes races pour, le soir venu, vous plonger dans l'animation des nombreux bars et night clubs. Le paradis! A Ipanema, c'est un peu plus calme et beaucoup moins agité. Si vous êtes plutôt diurne et que vous voulez faire du lèche-vitrines, vous traînerez sûrement du côté de Rio Branco, dans le centre. Les bus entre Copacabana et le centre de la ville sont bon marché et circulent aussi la nuit. La durée du trajet varie d'une demi-heure à une heure.
Rio est connue dans le monde entier pour son carnaval qui a lieu chaque année vers la fin février et le début mars. Soyez sur vos gardes: recrudescence de la délinquance à cette époque-là!

● Río es una de las mega-ciudades más excitantes de nuestro planeta, incluyendo los barrios circundantes, cuenta actualmente con un total de casi 16 millones de habitantes. Aqui realmente es posible encontrar satisfacción para los deseos más dispares. Así sea dejarse tostar por el sol sobre las blancas arenas de la playa, donde se pueden observar bellezas de todas razas o por las noches dejarse precipitar en el tumulto incesante de bares y discotecas, si esto es lo que se busca, el paraíso está en Copacabana. En Ipanema el ritmo no es tan acelerado, y además todo está un poco menos abarrotado. En caso que usted sea un pájaro del día y desee con-

104 *SPARTACUS* 2001/2002

Rio de Janeiro | Brazil

- THE BEST DANCING CLUB GAY IN RIO -

LE BOY BY GILLES

Raul Pompéia, 102 - Copacabana - Tel.: 513-4993

- SAUNA NUMBER ONE -

LE BOY BY GILLES - FITNESS -

www.leboy.com.br

Raul Pompéia, 102 - Copacabana - Tel.: 522-9175

- THE FASHION STYLE -

GILLES - RIO -

- OUTDOOR & UNDERWEAR -

SHOW ROOM - TEL.: 287-6995
R. Visconde de Pirajá - 365 B - Ipanema - RJ - Brasil

Brazil — Rio de Janeiro

templar todo lo que pueden llegar a ofrecer los comercios y mercados de Río, su lugar ideal de residencia encontraría en el centro, en los alrededores de Río Branco.
Las líneas de autobúses entre Copacabana y el centro urbano son baratas y funcionan también de noche. El trayecto suele durar de 30 minutos a una hora. El carnaval, que tan famoso ha hecho a Río de Janeiro en el mundo entero, tiene lugar entre finales de febrero y principios de marzo, dependiendo del año. Lamentablemente, estos días conllevan una alta criminalidad.

Rio è una della città più cosmopolite del mondo. La popolazione, periferie incluse, ha raggiunto approssivamente i 16 milioni. Questa città offre qualcosa per i gusti di ognuno. Se volete abbronzarvi sulla spiaggia e guardare splendide bellezze di ogni razza e durante la sera tuffarvi nel tumulto di discoteche e bar, allora Copacabana è il posto che fa per voi. Ipanema al contrario è una parte della città un po' più quieta e meno affollata. Se invece preferite vivere di „giorno", visitate i mercati e i negozi che Rio ha da offrirvi, il quartiere di Rio Branco saprà prendersi cura di voi. Il servizio di autobus che collega Copacabana al centro della città è conveniente e funziona anche la notte. La durata degli spostamenti varia da mezz'ora a un'ora. Il leggendario carnevale che ha reso Rio famosa in tutto il mondo ha luogo, secondo l'anno, tra la fine di febbraio e l'inizio di marzo. In questo periodo aumenta anche il tasso di criminalitá.

TOURIST INFO
■ **Companhia de Turismo da Cidade do Rio de Janeiro (Riotur)**
Rua da Assembléia, 10 / 7. e 8. andares ✉ 20011-000
☎ 531 15 75 🖷 531 25 06

BARS
■ **Casa Grande** (B D G R TV WE)
Rua Coronel Tamarindo, 2552 ✉ 20030 *(Bangu)* ☎ 331 21 71
■ **Guetto** (B D G MA) Tue-Sun 22-?h
Rua Muniz Barreto 448 *(Botafogo)* ☎ 961 8697
■ **Jumpin Jack** (AC B d E F G N YG)
Rua Visconde Silva N° 13 *(Botafogo)*

DANCECLUBS
■ **Boemio** (B D G S) Disco Fri-Sun 23-?, show 2 h
Rua Santa Luzia, 760 *(Centro)* ☎ 240 72 59
■ **Boite 1140** (AC B D G S YG) Fri Sat 22-?, Sun 20.30-? h
Rua Captião Menezes, 1140 ✉ 21320 *(Praça Seca)* ☎ 390 76 90
■ **Boy Club. Le** (! AC B D G S SNU YG) Tue-Sun 21-3 h, closed Mon
Rua Raul Pompeia 102, Copacabana ✉ 22080-000 ☎ 513 4993
Show at 1.30 h. Popular on Tue, Sat and Sun.
■ **Cabaré Casa Nova** (B D G MA S) 23-?, show 1.30 h
Avenida Mém de Sá, 25 ✉ 20230 *(Lapa)*
■ **Cueva. La** (B D G OG R) 23-? h, closed Mon
Rua Miguel Lemos, 51 ✉ 22071 *(Copacabana)* ☎ 23767 57
■ **Gaivota** (B D G) Tue-Sun 23-? h, closed Mon
Avenida Rodolfo de Amoedo, 347 *(Barra da Tijuca)*
Popular on Sun
■ **Incontru's Disco** (B D G S) 21-3 h, WE longer
Praça Serzedelo Correia, 15A, Copacabana ✉ 22040 *(between Avenues Copacabana and Atlantica)( )* ☎ 257 64 98

RESTAURANTS
■ **Amarelinho/Verdinho** (B F g)
Praça de Cinelandia/Rua Alvaro Alvim, 52 *(Centro)*

■ **Cantina Donanna** (B g F)
Rua Domingos Ferreira, 63 B ✉ 22050 ☎ 255 88 41
Italian cuisine.
■ **Tamino** (B F G OS) 19-4 h
Rua Arnaldo Quintela 26 *(Botafogo)* ☎ 295 18 49

SHOWS
■ **Teatro Brigitte Blair I** (B g S TV)
Senador Dantas ✉ 22071 ☎ 220 50 33
■ **Teatro Brigitte Blair II** (B g S TV)
Rua Miguel Lemos 51 H ✉ 22071 ☎ 220 50 33

CINEMAS
■ **Astor** (G)
Avenida Ministro Edgar Romeiro, 236 *(Madureira)*
■ **Botafogo** (g)
Rua Voluntários da Pátria, 35 *(Metro Botafogo)*
■ **Bruni-Meyer** (G)
Rua Amaro Cavalcante, 1 ☎ 591 27 46
■ **Bruni-Tijuca** (G)
Rua Conde de Bonfim, 370 *(Saens Pena)*
■ **Iris** (g)
Rua da Carioca, 49/51 ✉ 20050 *(Centro. Metro Carioca)*
■ **Odeon** (G)
Mahatma Gandi, 2 ✉ 22250 *(Cinelândia)*
■ **Orly** (G)
Rua Alcindo Guanabara, 17 *(Metro Cinelândia)*
■ **Scala/Coral** (G)
Praia de Botafogo, 316 C-B ✉ 22250 *(Botafogo)* ☎ 266 25 45
■ **Tijuca II** (G)
Rua Conde de Bonfim, 422 *(Saens Pena)* ☎ 264-5246

SAUNAS/BATHS
■ **Boy Fitness. Le** (! B CC G msg SA SB VS WO YG) Tue-Sun 15-? h
Rua Raul Pompéia, 102, Copacabana ✉ 22080-000 *(Left of the disco entrance 'til 23h)* ☎ 522-9175
Together with Le Boy Club (free entrance to the club with your sauna ticket). From 23h entrance via the Le Boy disco. Very large, clean.
■ **Catete** (B G MA SA SB) Mon-Thu 14-1, Fri-Sun -6 h
Rua Correia Dutra, 34, Catete ✉ 22210 *(Subway-Catete)*
☎ 265-5478
■ **Club 117** (AC B CC G MA R SNU SB VS WE) Tue-Sun 15-1 h
Rua Cândido Mendes 117, Glória *(Metro-Glória)* ☎ 252-0160
Also hotel. Regular strip shows.
■ **Club 29** (G MA SA SB VS)
Rua Prof. Alfredo Gomes 29, Botafogo ☎ 286-6380
Very small, no facilities, cruisy atmosphere.
■ **Ibiza** (AC B DR G MA msg SA SB VS WO) 15-3, Fri Sat 13-3, Sun 13-1 h
Rua Siqueira Campos 202 ✉ 22031 *(Copacabana)* ☎ 256 6693
Popular sauna with cyber café.
■ **Kabalk** (B f G SA VS WO) Tue-Sun 15-24 h
Rua Santa Luiza, Maracanã ☎ 572-6210
Reading room and snack bar.
■ **Meio Mundo** (B G R SA SNU) 15-24, Fri-Sun -2 h
Rua Teófilo Otoni, 18, Centro *(near Candelária)* ☎ 9167-2900
Sauna with young men awaiting the generosity of gentlemen.
■ **Nova Leblon** (B f G MA msg SA SB SOL R VS) 12-6, Sat Sun 9-6 h
Rua Barão da Torre, 522, Ipanema *(off Rua Garcia D'Avila)*
☎ 287-8899
Sauna with hairdresser and beauty salon.

Rio de Janeiro ▶ Rio Verde-Goiás **Brazil**

CLUB 117
SAUNA SECA E A VAPOR
PHONE: (21) 252-0160

OPEN TUES.
- SUNDAY FROM 03 p.m. TO 01 a.m.
3 FLOORS OF PURE PLASURE
TV AND VIDEO ROOMS
AMERICAN STYLE BAR
MASSAGE AVAILABLE
ESCORT BOY SERVICE
DRY AND STEAM ROOM SAUNAS
CREDIT CARDS ACCEPTED

■ **Roger's** (B f G msg R SA) 15-1, Thu-Sat -3 h
Rua Ministro Alfredo Valadão 36, Copacabana ✉ 22031 *(between Rua Figueiredo de Magalhaes and Rua Siqueira Campos)*
☎ 549-9096
■ **Studio 64** (b CC DR f G msg SA SB VS WO YG) 15-3 h
Rua Redentor, 64, Ipanema *(between Joana Angélica and Maria Quitéria)* ☎ 523-5670
Many special events (check website or call).

HOTELS
■ **Agres** (G H)
Rua Farme de Amoedo 135, Ipanema
■ **Caprice Hotel** (G H)
Avenida Nossa Sra. de Copacabana, 1079a ✉ 22060 ☎ 28758 41
☎ 521 76 29
■ **Gomes Freire** (G H)
Avenida Gomes Freire, 343 *(centro)*
■ **Lips** (AC B d glm H)
Rua Senador Dantas, 46 *(Centro)* ☎ 210 32 35
All rooms with TV and minibar.

FASHION SHOPS
■ **Gilles**
R. Vísconda de Pirajá 365 b ☎ 287 69 95

GENERAL GROUPS
■ **ARCO-IRIS**
Rua do Bispo, 316/805 *(Tijuca)* ☎ 254 65 46
■ **ASTRAL**
☎ 265 57 47
■ **Atoba**
Rua Professor Carvalho de Melo, 471, RJ 21735-110 *(Megalhães Bastos)* ☎ 331 1527 ☎ 332 07 87 (hot-Line) 📠 331 1527
✉ atobamehomos@ax.ibase.org.br
■ **Triangulo Rosa**
PO Box 14.601 ✉ 22412-970
■ **Turma OK**
Rua do Resende, 43 *(Centro)*

HEALTH GROUPS
■ **ABIA-Associação Brasileira Interdisciplinar de AIDS**
Rua sete de Septembro, 48/12 ☎ 224 16 54 📠 224 34 14.
■ **AIDS Hotline-AIDS Pela Vida**
☎ 518 22 21 ☎ 518 39 93.

■ **NOSS-Núcleo de Orientação em Saúde Social**
☎ 242 47 57
Publishes "Nós por Exemplo".

SWIMMING
-The beach at the end of the Rua Fame de Amvedo in Ipanema is popular with gays (on the left side, mainly on WE).
-Recreio Beach. Nude sun bathing and cruisy woods. „Great gay beach, discreet nudity, lots of action in the woods across the highway." Located several miles outside of the city. A car is best but the bus is possible (553); head past Barra de Tijuca but keep going to Recreio (before Grumari Beach) until the view of the beach is obstructed by tall grass. Park on the right side of the highway and hop over the wire fence to the beach.

CRUISING
-Ipanema Beach (in front of Rua Farme de Amoedo)
-Copacabana Beach (just above Copacabana Palace Hotel known as "Stock Market" / bolsa de Copacabana)
-Botafogo Beach (AYOR) (weekdays until midnight and on Saturdays until 2 h, very dangerous)
-Avenida Atlantica-Av. Copacabana
-Avenida Rio Branco in Cinelandia
-Praça Floriano (R) (there are small hotels in this area called "Somente Cavalheiros", which means "men only"; you will have no problem bringing someone home with you whenever you want)
-Quinta da Boa Vista (AYOR) (closes at night)
-Parque do Flamengo (AYOR) (between Hotel Gloria and Botafogo, day and night)
-Between Santos Dumont airport and Praça XV (AYOR) (at night)
-Praia do Arpoador
-Corner Ataulfo de Paiva/Aristides Espinola
-Praça da Bandeira (closes at night)
-Via Apia (AYOR R) (Rua 1° de Marçc/Pres. Antonio Carlos, Santa Luzia. Dangerous. Police.)
-Incontrus on the plaza between Siqueira Campos and Hilario de Gouvea. Cruisy toilet.

Rio Verde - Goiás ☎ **075**

RELIGIOUS GROUPS
■ **Comunidade Pacifista TUNKER**
PO Box 214 ✉ 75.901-970

Brazil: Salvador-Bahia

Salvador - Bahia ☏ 071

Salvador was formerly the capital of Brazil and is still the cultural centre of the nation. Its culture was strongly influenced by black people brought over from Africa as slaves in colonial times. Salvador is considered the most African city in Brazil. Brazil's gays hold their own Carnival here in February on the "Praça Castro Alves".

Salvador ist die ehemalige Hauptstadt Brasiliens und auch heute noch das kulturelle Zentrum. Die Stadt ist stark geprägt von den Nachfahren der früher von den Kolonialisten aus Afrika deportierten schwarzen Zwangsarbeitern. Man nennt Salvador die afrikanischste Stadt Brasiliens. In dieser Stadt feiern Brasiliens Schwule im Februar ihren Carnaval: sie treffen sich auf dem Platz "Praça Castro Alves".

Salvador est l'ancienne capitale du Brésil. Elle en est restée la capitale culturelle. Fortement marquée par les descendants des esclaves noirs africains d'autrefois, on dit que c'est la ville la plus africaine du pays. C'est ici que les gais, chaque année en février, organisent leur propre carnaval. On s'y rencontre sur la place Praça Castro Alves.

Salvador es la antigua capital del Brasil y sigue siendo el centro cultural del país. Se hace notar la fuerte influencia de los descendientes de los esclavos, traidos desde el continente africano. Salvador se considera la ciudad más africana del Brasil. En esta ciudad los gays celebran anualmente en el mes de febrero su carnaval en la plaza „Castro Alves".

Salvador era in origine la capitale del Brasile è ancora adesso il centro culturale della nazione. La sua cultura è stata fortemente influenzata dagli schiavi neri portati dall'Africa. Salvador è nominata la città più africana del Brasile. Qui festeggiano gli omosessuali brasiliani il loro carnevale; il luogo d'incontro è la piazza Castro Alves.

TOURIST INFO

■ **Empresa de Turismo da Bahia-Bahiatursa**
Ed. Sede do Centro de Convençes da Bahia, Praia da Armação
✉ 41750-270   ☏ 370 84 01
Tourist office.

BARS

■ **Adé Aló** (B g S)
Rua Pedro Autran, 71, 1st floor
■ **Aruba** (B F G WE)
Praia de A rmação *(Beach bar at Armacao beach)*
■ **Atelier Maria Adair** (B f glm OS)
Pelourinho   ☏ 321 3363
■ **Cantina da Lua** (B g)
Terreiro de Jesus
■ **Charles Chaplin** (B G R WE)
Rua Carlos Gomes/Rua Pedro Autran
■ **Connexão** (B f GLM OS) Tue - Sun
Rua Cecilia Lima, 11 *(At Beco dos Artistas near Teatro castro Alves)*
☏ 32 80199
■ **Empório** (B f G) 19-? h
Avenida Sete Setembro,3089/Farol da Barra
■ **Espaço Alternativo**
Rua Carlos Gomes, 141
■ **Holmes New Look Bar** (AC B D G MA WE) Fri-Sun 22-6 h
Rua Newton Prado, 24   ✉ 40120 *(Gamboa de Cirne)*   ☏ 336 49 49
■ **Minos Bar** (B g)
Rua Carlos Gomes 15

■ **Nos Dois** (B G WE)
Rua Odilon Santos 40 - Rio Vermelho *(Near Shopping Rio Vermelho)*
☏ 334 6707
■ **Stylus** (B g)
Rua Carlos Gomes, 102

CAFES

■ **Aquarela** (B Fglm S)
Rua dias Davila s/n - Farol da Barra *(Near Lighthouse of Barra)*
■ **Touche Creperia** (B f GLM)
Rua Belo Horizonte - Jardim Brasil - Barra   ☏ 9121 9084

DANCECLUBS

■ **Augustu's Space** (B D DR R WE) Fri-Sat 21-?h
Travessa Salvador Pires, 3 - Aflitos *(Near Aflitos Place)* ☏ 329 4274
■ **Banana República** (B D g)
Rua Braulio Xavier *(Vitoria)*
■ **Caverna** (B D G R TV WE)
Rua Carlos Gomes, 133
■ **Close up** (B D GLM) 22-6 h, Sat Gay
Avenida Oceânica *(Ondina)*
Sometimes gay parties.
■ **Club Mix Ozone** (B D G MA snu TV) Sat 23-? h
Rua Augusto Franca, 55   ☏ 321-5373
Entrance fee 10 Reals incl. one free drink.
■ **Off Club** (B D f GLM S SNU WE) Wed - Sun 23-?
Rua Dias D'avila 33 - Barra *(Near Farol da Barra)* ☏ 2676215
■ **Queens** (B D DR SNU STV) Wed-Sat 0.-5 h Sun 17-22h
Teodoro Sampaio Str.160, Barris ✉ 40 070150 ☏ 328 62 20
It's also a sex shop with cruising area and video cabins.
■ **Red Blue** (B f GLM S OS WE) Fri- Sun 15-23h
Rua Pinto Aguiar 24 - Patamares   ☏ 3635580
■ **Tropical** (AYOR B D G r stv)
Rua do Pau da Bandeira, Sé *(cross street from Rua de Chile)*

RESTAURANTS

■ **Felipe Camarão** (B F g)
Rio Vermelho
■ **Ibiza** (B F g) 11-24 h
Rua Alfredo Brito, 11 *(Pelourinho)*

CINEMAS

■ **Astor**
Rua da Ajuda, 5   ✉ 40020 *(Centro Histórico)*
■ **Cine Tamoio**
Rua Rui Barbosa *(Centro)*
■ **Liceu**
Rua do Saldanha, 16 *(Centro Histórico)*
■ **Tupi**
Rua J.J. Seabra, 347 *(Baixa do Sapateiro)*

SAUNAS/BATHS

■ **Campus** (G MA SA SB)
Rua Días Dávila, 25 *(Farol da Barra)* ☏ 235-2247
■ **Esgrima** (B G MA msg SA SB VS WO) 15-23, Fri-Sun -1 h
Ladeira de Santa Tereza, 2 - Centro *(near Museu de Arte Sacra, a side street from Rua C. Gomes)* ☏ 322-3783
Also with game room. Wed with women. 4 floors rather sterile atmosphere.
■ **Olympus** (B G MA msg SA SB VS) 14.30-22.30 h
Rua Tuiuti, 183, Aflitos ✉ 40060-020 *(off Carlos Gomes/Ladeira dos Aflitos, near post office)* ☏ 329-0060
English, French, Spanish & Italian spoken. Small but friendly atmosphere. Busy on Sat.

108 **SPARTACUS** 2001/2002

Salvador-Bahia ▸ São Paulo — Brazil

■ **Persona** (B G MA msg SNU SA SB VS) 15-23 h
Rua Junqueira Ayres, 230 (antigo 37) *(Barris)* ☎ 329-1273
Strip shows Sat & Sun 20 h
■ **Phoenix** (B G MA msg OS R SA SB VS)
Rua Prado Valadares, 16 ✉ 40000 *(Nazaré)* ☎ 243-5495
■ **Space New Relax** (B msg R SA SB VS) Sun-Thu 14-24, Fri-Sat 14-?h
Travessa Salvador Pires, 3 Aflitos *(Near Aflitos Place)* ☎ 329 4274

HOTELS

■ **Capri** (g H)
Largo Dois de Julho - Centro ☎ 322 4617
■ **Costa de Marfim Guesthouse** (AC BF GLM OS WH)
Rua Felipe Camarao, 442 *(Saude)* ☎ 242 40 62
All rooms with TV, bath, WC.
■ **Don Juan** (g H)
Rua Rui Barbosa - Centro ☎ 321 4793
■ **Enseada Porto da Barra** (g H)
Rua Barão de Itapuã *(Porto da Barra)*
■ **Hotel Angelo-Americano** (g H)
Avenida Sete de Septiembre *(Barra)*
■ **Santiago** (g H)
Rua Forte de São Pedro 52/54 - Campo Grande *(Near Campo Grande Place)* ☎ 245 9293

GENERAL GROUPS

■ **Grupo Gay da Bahia / Centro Baiano Anti-Aids** Meetings Wed-Fri 20 h.
Rua do Sodré, 45, PO Box 2552 ✉ 40.022-260 *(Bairro Dois de Julho-near Museu de Arte Sacra)* ☎ 243 49 02 📠 322 37 82
Publications: Boletim Do GGB „Candreno De Textos Do GGB" „AIDS E Candomble" „Guia Gay Do Cidade Do Salvador" „O Que Todo Munde Deve Saber Sobre A Homossexualidade".

HEALTH GROUPS

■ **Disk-AIDS**
PO Box 25 52 ✉ 40022-260 ☎ 245 85 00
■ **GAPA-Bahia**
Rua Dias D'Ávila 109 ✉ 40140-270 *(Farol da Barra)* ☎ 267 1727 📠 267 1587 💻 gapaba@svn.com.br 💻 www.gapabahia.org.bf

SWIMMING

-Porto da Barra (main gay beach, mostly at the weekend)
-Farol da Barra (especially at the rocks)
-Praia dos Artistas (Boca do Rio beach)
-Jardim de Ala
-Stella Maris

CRUISING

-Small park behind Governor's Palace
-Mercado Modelo (market Sat 8-18 h)
-Jardin da Piedade
-Campo Grande
-Praça Municipal (Sucupira graveyard)
-Shopping Barra
-Shopping Iguatemi
-Shopping Piedad
-Aero Clube Plaza Show.

Santa Maria - Rio Grande do Sul ☎ 055

BARS

■ **Bus Club**
Rua Andradas, 1900

■ **Over Busy** (B D G WE) Thu-Sun 22-?h
Rua Riachuelo 244 ☎ 2227541
■ **Panacéia**
Rua Angelo Uglione ✉ 1697
■ **Skato Bar** (B g)
Avenida Presidente Vargas, 1450 ✉ 11100 ☎ 221 4500
■ **Yellow House**
Rua Riachuelo

HOTELS

■ **Hotel Moratim**
Rua Angelo Uglione, 1629 ✉ 11100 ☎ 222 44 53
■ **Hotel Rio**
Avenida Rio Branco, 126 ☎ 221 17 01

Santos - São Paulo ☎ 013

RESTAURANTS

■ **Churrascaria Tertulia** (B F g)
Avenida Bartolomeu de Gusmao 187 ✉ 11030 *(Ponta da Praia)* ☎ 36 16 41
■ **Gug's** (B F g)
Avenida Bartolomeu de Gusmao 131 ✉ 11045 *(near Canal 6, Embaré)* ☎ 36 05 80

CINEMAS

■ **Fugitive** (g)
Rua Da. Adelina 31 ✉ 11013 *(Paquetá)* ☎ 32 36 79

CRUISING

-Bars and Cafés in Plaza St. Vincente and Avenida Ana Costa
-Near Oslo Bar and Rua General Camara
-Itararé Beach
-Beach to the side of St. Vicente
-Embaré Beach between Canal 2 and 3
-Promenade from Gonzoga to Avenida Conselheiro
-Praça Independencia (in the evening)
-Praça Maua (at bus stop)

São João Del Rei - Minas Gerais ☎ 032

RESTAURANTS

■ **Cantinho da Canja** (B F g)
Rua Balbino da Cunha 168

São Luiz - Maranhão ☎ 098

GENERAL GROUPS

■ **Grupo Gay e Lésbico do Maranhão-TIBRO**
Rua do Sol, 472 ✉ 65010-950 *(Altos São Luis)*

CRUISING

-Praia do Olho D'água (beach)
-Praia do Caolho
-Praia do Calhao
-Praça Central. (near Postoffice)

São Paulo - São Paulo ☎ 011

❋ One of the largest city in the world, São Paulo is the cultural and financial capital of Brazil. This busy and multi-cultural profile is a very welcoming city for gay people with a scene that caters for all tastes.

Brazil — São Paulo

★ Als eine der größten Städte der Welt, ist Sao Paulo die kulturelle und finanzielle Hauptstadt Brasiliens. Das geschäftige und multikulturelle Profil in dieser für Gays weltoffenen Stadt verfügt über eine Szene, die für jeden Geschmack etwas zu bieten hat.

★ Sao Paulo, une des plus grandes ville du monde, est la capitale culturelle et financière du Brésil. La ville, grâce à une intense activité et à sa diversité culturelle, propose un milieu gai très accueillant qui a de quoi satisfaire les goûts de tout un chacun.

★ São Paulo, una de las ciudades más grandes del mundo, es la capital cultural y financiera del Brasil. Esta ciudad animada y pluricultural, con su ambiente que complace a todos los gustos, es el lugar ideal para gente gay.

★ San Paolo, una delle città più grandi del mondo, è la capitale culturale ed economica del Brasile. Con il suo carattere vivace e multiculturale la città accoglie di buon grado e amichevolmente tutte le persone gay e offre opportunità per tutti i gusti.

TOURIST INFO
■ **Embratur**
Rua São Bento 380 7o andar, Centro ☏ 3104 3991

BARS
■ **A Revelia** (B G S)
Alameda Itu 1493 - Jardins ☏ 883 6258
■ **Allegro** (B f GLM YG) Tue-Sun 20-4h
Rua da Consolação, 3055 - Jardins *(Jardins)* ☏ 3064 4294
■ **Bocage** (B F g) Thu-Sun 20-3h
Al Itu x R da Consolaçao, Jardins
■ **Burger & Beer** (B f G) Sun-Thu -3h, Fri-Sat -6h
Av. Consolação 2376 - Centro ☏ 214 1079
■ **Caneca de Prata** (B G OG R) Daily open from 19-4h
Avenida Vieira de Carvalho, 55 *(near Rep)* ☏ 223-6420
■ **Carto** (B glm) Thu-Sun 20-03h
Al Itu 1536, Jardins
■ **Chope Escuro** (B F OG) Daily open from 17-04h
Rua Marques de Itu 252, Centro ☏ 221 0812
■ **DJ Clube Bar teatro** (A B d GLM YG VS) Wed-Sat 22-4 h
Alameda Franca 241 - Jardins ☏ 289 0090
■ **Farol Madalena** (A B F GLM S) Open daily from 18-04h
Rua Jericó 179, Vila Madalena ☏ 210 6470
■ **Feitiços** (B F GLM) Thu-Sat 21-3h, Sun-17-22h
Alameda Itú, 1542, Jardins
■ **Ferros** (B F glm) Open daily from 17h
Rua Martinho Prado 119, centro ☏ 258 0004
■ **Gourmet** (B GLM) Tue-Sun 21-3h
Al Franca 1552 , Jardins ☏ 3064 7958
■ **Habeas Copus** (B G OG F) Open daily from 17-5h
Av Vieira de Carvalho 94 , Centro ☏ 222 7080
■ **Lord Byron** (F G OG) Daily 18-3h
Rua Viera de Carvalho 60, Centro ☏ 220 0368
■ **Matrix** (B D glm) Tue-Sat 21-05h
Al Franca 1552, Jardins ☏ 814 6056
■ **Paparazzi** (AC B F GLM) Wed-Sat 21-4h
Rua da Consolação, 3050 *(next to Disco Galpao-Jardins)* ☏ 881 6665
■ **Pitombas** (B F glm) Daily open from 19-3h
Rua da Consolação 3161, Jardins ☏ 852 4058
■ **Pix** (B D glm) Tue-Sun 18-4h
Rua Alagoas 852, Higienopolis ☏ 3666 0723
■ **Pride** (B GLM S) Wed-Sun 21-03h
Al Itu 1576, Jardins ☏ 853 1213

■ **Rainha Victoria** (B F G MA) Tue-Sun 19-04h
Largo do Arouche 06, Centro ☏ 3362 0157
■ **Station** (DR G p) Tue- private club SM only for members 21h
Sun-Thu 21-3h, Fri & Sat 22-5h
Rua dos Pinheiros 352, Pinheiros
■ **Torre do Dr. Zero** (B D glm) Thu-Sun 23-04 hs
Rua Mourato Coelho 569, Pinheiros ☏ 212 1858

CAFES
■ **Moon Café** (B D F G) Mon-Sat 17-4h, Sun-14-18h
Rua Bela Cintra 1900, Jardins ☏ 34867890
■ **Vermont** (B F G MA) Daily open from 19-3hs
Rua Vieira de Carvalho 10 - Vila Buarque ☏ 222 5848

DANCECLUBS
■ **Avalon. The** Thu-Sat 22-?h
Al Itu 1564 Jardins ☏ 2590 859
■ **Blue Space** (D DR G STV SNU) Fri & Sat 23h Su-18h
Rua Brigadeiro Galvão, 723, Barra Funda ☏ 3666 1616
■ **Boite Blackout Cruising Bar** (AYOR B D DR GLM MA R STV SNU TV) 24-6 h, closed Mon-Wed
Rua Amaral Gurgel, 253 ✉ CEP 01221-001 *(Vila Buarque. M° República)* ☏ 3333-2840
■ **Club Stereo** (! B D glm) Wed-Sat 23-5h
Al Olga, 168, Barra Funda ☏ 3664 7925
■ **Diesel na Base** (! B G D DR)
Rua Brigadeiro Luis Antonio 1137, Centro ☏ 3106 3244
■ **Disco Fever** (B D G YG) Wed-Sun 23.30-?h
Rua da Consolação 3032 ✉ 01302 *(Jardim Paulista. M° Consolação)* ☏ 881 5496
■ **Discoteque** (B D G) Thu-Sat 23:30h
Rua Augusta 2203 Jardins ☏ 852 6345
■ **Galpao** (B D G ma s) Fri-Sat 24-5 h
Rua Concolaçao 3046 *(located in the quarter Jardins)* ☏ 881 66 65
■ **Gent's Theater House** (AC B D E f G MA OS S VS) 23-4, closed Mon Tue, shows 1.30 h
Avenida Ibirapuera, 1911, (Moema) ✉ 04029 *(Indianópolis)* ☏ 572 82 27
■ **Ipisis** (B D GLM) Thu-Sat 22-?h
Rua Garcia Velho 63 Pinheiros ☏ 813 2744
■ **Mad Queen** (B D G) Thu-Sun 23-?h
Al Arapanes 1364 Moema ☏ 240 0088
■ **Massivo** (B D G) Tue-Sat 23-?h
Al Itu 1548 Jardins ☏ 883 7505
■ **Nostromundo 2000** (B D G MA LJ SNU) 22-4, Sun 18-1 h, closed Mon & Tue.
Rua da Consolação, 2554 ✉ 01302 *(M° Consolação)* ☏ 259 2945
Oldest gay disco in town: For 26 years!
■ **Sky Pere** (B D GLM MA S WE) Fri-Sat 21-?h, Sun 18-24h.
Rua Santo Antonio, 570, Centro *(Bela Vista. M° Anhangabaú)* ☏ 3105 4345
■ **SoGo** (AC CC B D DR G VS) Thu-Sun 23-?h, Wed women only.
Al. Franca 1368 ☏ 306 155 13
■ **Tunnel** (AC B D f GLM MA S) Fri & Sat 23-? h, Sun 19-? h
Rua Dos Ingleses 355 *(nearby subway station Bribadeiro, Green Line)* ☏ 286-0246
■ **Volúpia** (AC B D F gLM MA OS P S) 22-4, Sun 21-3 h, closed Mon-Wed
Rua dos Pinheiros 688 ☏ 852 38 77

RESTAURANTS
■ **Allegro** (B F G) Tue-Sun 20-?h
Rua da Consolação 3055, Jardins ☏ 3064 4294

São Paulo | Brazil

■ **Consulado Mineiro** (B CC F glm) 12-1:00h
Rua Conego Eugenio Leite 504, Pinheiros ☎ 853 0281
Brazilian food.
■ **Gato Que Ri. O** (F g)
Largo do Arouche, 47-41 ✉ 01219 *(Vila Buarque)* ☎ 221 26 99
Italian food.
■ **Ritz** (! AC F B GLM) Mon-Frir 12-15h & 19:30-1:30h Sat & Sun 13-1:30h
Al Franca 1088, Jardins ☎ 280 6808

CINEMA

■ **Cine Cairo** (g)
Rua Formosa 401, Vale do Anhangabau, Centro ☎ 221 3080

SEX SHOPS/BLUE MOVIES

■ **L'amour** (G) Mon-Sat 9-2h, Sun 18-24h
Av. 9 de Julho 3287 ☎ 3884 7362
■ **Ponto G** (g) (G) Sun-Wed 10-3h, Thu-Sat 23-3h
Rua Amaral Gurgel 206 ☎ 223 30 11
■ **R&R Amigos** (g) Mon-Fri 10-22h, Sat- 12-20h
Rua Sena Madureira 755, Vila Mariana ☎ 5571 1614

CINEMAS

■ **América** (g)
Avenida Rio Branco, 49
■ **Art Palácio** (g)
Avenida São João, 419 ✉ 01035 *(Centro)*
■ **Cine Ipiranga** (g)
Avenida Ipiranga, 786 ✉ 01040 *(Centro)* ☎ 222 06 32
■ **Cine Saci** (g)
Avenida São João, 285 ✉ 01035 *(Centro)* ☎ 223 9191
■ **Cine Shopping Roma** (g)
Avenida São João, 577 ✉ 01035 *(Centro)* ☎ 222 7336
■ **Novo Cine Studio**
Rua Aurora, 710 ☎ 220 6236
Straight men and boys looking for sex. Stalls in the toilets very busy. Best action Mon-Thu.
■ **Republica** (g)
Avenida Ipiranga, 752 ☎ 222 7236
■ **Windsor** (g)
Avenida Ipiranga, 974 ✉ 01040 *(Centro)* ☎ 222 25 53

SAUNAS/BATHS

■ **Alterosas** (B G R SA SB WH) 13-22 h
Avenida das Alterosas, 40A ✉ 03544 *(Near M° Patriarca)* ☎ 958-1712
■ **Champion** (B G SA) Mon-Fri 14-24, Sat & Sun 14-?h
Largo do Arouche, 336 ✉ 01219 *(opposite flower market, Vila Buarque)* ☎ 222-4973
■ **Fragata** (B G R SA SB SNU VS WO) 14-24 h
Rua Francisco Leitão, 71, Jardim América ☎ 853-7061
Sauna with regular strip shows.
■ **Labirinttu's 1** (B DR G msg SA SB VS WH) 0-24 h
Alameda Nothmann, 1220, Santa Cecília ☎ 825-0932
Hydromassage available.
■ **Labirinttu's 2** (AC B DR G MA msg SA SB VS WH WO) 0-24 h
Rua frei Caneca, 135, Consolação ☎ 259-4938
Big sauna with strip shows, sex shop and many other extras.
■ **Lagoa** (AC b CC DR f G MA msg PI R SA SB SNU VS WH WO) 14-24, Fri -5 h
Rua Borges Lagoa 287, Vila Clementino ✉ 04038-030 *(3 blocks from M° Santa Cruz)* ☎ 577 396 89
Sauna frequented by young men (18-30 years) awaiting the generosity of older men. Cinema, heated swimming pool, suite with bath, Wed & Fri- Sun strip shows, Tue bingo night, Thu live music and Sat Arena lagoa.

Termas for Friends

open daily 14 – 24 hs

R Morgado de Mateus 365

Vila Mariana

Fone/fax:
011-5579-1887/5579-9768

São Paulo – Brazil

www.termasforfriends.com.br

e-mail ffriends@uol.com.br

all credit cards

Brazil | São Paulo ▶ Teresina-Piauí

THERMAS LAGOA
São Paulo, SP - Brasil

TURKISH BATH – FINNISH SAUNA – SNACKS – AMERICAN BAR
DRINKS – VIDEOS (GAY & HETERO) – BODY BUILDING – MASSAGE
DARK ROOM – RESTROOM – PRIVATE CABIN WITH VIDEO – TV
JACUZZI – SWIMMING POOL – SOLARIUM – CINE DOLBY DIGITAL

Open every day from 2:00pm to Midnight
Fridays from 2:00pm to 5:00am

www.netgay.com.br/lagoaIII.htm

Rua Borges Lagoa, 287, metrô Santa Cruz - São Paulo, SP - Brasil - Phone/fax (011) 5573-9689 e 5539-3008

■ **Rouge. Le** (B G MA PI SA SB VS) 14-1, Fri Sat -5 h
Rua Arruda Alvim, 175, Pinheiros ✉ 05410 *(Mº-Clinicas)*
☎ 852-3043
■ **Termas for Friends** (! B CC DR f G MA OSPI SA SB VS WH) 14-24 h
Rua Morgado de Matheus 365, Vila Mariana ✉ 04015-050 *(Mº Ana Rosa, near Ibirapuera's Park)* ☎ 5579-1887
Big clean sauna on 700 m² with a great atmosphere and a winter garden.

BOOK SHOPS
■ **Futuro Ininito** (A B CC GLM) Mon-Sat 10-22h Sun 10-18hs
Rua Oscar Freire 2303, Pinheiros ☎ 3064 5358

TRAVEL AND TRANSPORT
■ **Inter Rainbow**
Rua da Consolacao 359 cj 53 ☎ 214.0380
📧 geotrave@greco.com.br

HOTELS
■ **Caesar Park** (g H)
Rua Agusta 1508, Paulista ☎ 253 6622
■ **Grant's** (g H)
Avenida Amaral Gurgel, 392 ✉ 01221 *(Vila Buarque)*
☎ 259 60 06
■ **Luver II** (g H)
Rua Frei Caneca, 963 ✉ 01307 *(Consolação)* ☎ 287 70 40
■ **Pergamon** (g H)
Rua Frei Caneca 80, Bela Vista ☎ 3120 2021
■ **Renaissance** (g H)
Al Santos 2233, Jardins ☎ 3069 2223

HEALTH GROUPS
■ **Centro de Saude Santa Cecilia** Mon-Fri 7-17 h
Rua Vitorino Camilo, 599 *(Santa Cecilia. Mº Marechal Deodoro)*
☎ 826-7970
HIV-tests and treatment for free.
■ **C.O.A. Centro de Orientação e Aconselhamento em AIDS e Doeças Sexualmente Transmissíveis** Mon-Fri 8-14 h
Galeria Prestes Maia, Terreo *(Centro)* ☎ 239 22 24
Information on AIDS and free HIV-tests.
■ **GAPA • Grupo de Apoio a Pacientes de AIDS**
Rua Barão de Tatui, 375
■ **Hospital São Paulo**
Rua Napoleão de Barros 715 ✉ 01246 *(Vila Clementino)*
☎ 549 87 77
■ **SAMPA • Solidariedade, Apoio Moral e Psicologico Aplicados a AIDS**
Rua Manuel de Paiva 218 *(Vila Mariana)* ☎ 571 73 96
By appointment only. Psychological treatment charged according to patient capabilities.

CRUISING
- Avenida Ipiranga (AYOR R) (intersection of São João and São Luiz and São Luiz and Praça Roosevelt)(tv)
- Avenida República de Libano (TV) (area between Parque do Ibarapuera and the residential district of Avenida Sto. Amaro)
- Galeria Califórnia (R) (Rua Barão de Itapetininga 255, connecting the Barão de Itapetininga with Dom José Gaspar)
- Parque do Ibirpuera (WE) (Try the cycle paths or go by car at night)
- Praça Roosevelt (at night and at the weekend)
- Rua Rui Barbosa (from Zaccaro Theatre to Village Station Cabaret)
- Rua Santo Antonio (area leading from Major Quedinho á Treze de Maio)
- MASP-São Paulo Art Museum (Avenida Paulista 1578)(Sun afternoon)
- "Autorama"-area in Ibirapera park (between DETRAN & BIENAL. Where the cars park. At night)
- Most restrooms of subway stations (AYOR)
- Republica Square
- Mappin department store (Praça Ramos Azevedo)

São Vicente - São Paulo ☎ 013

BARS
■ **Terraco Chopp** (B g)
Alameda Ari Barroso 79 ✉ 11320 *(Ilha Porchat)* ☎ 681 159

RESTAURANTS
■ **Itapura** (B F g)
Avenida Newton Prado 179 ✉ 11320 *(Road to Ponte Pensil, Morro dos Barbosas)* ☎ 685 143
■ **Terraco** (B F g)
Al. Almirante Barroso 77 *(Ilha Porchat)* ☎ 687 527

SWIMMING
- Praia Itararé (near Ilha Porchat)

Teresina - Piauí ☎ 086

BARS
■ **Carinhoso Bar**
Rua Alvaro Mendes

CRUISING
- Praça Pedro II
- Praça Saraiva (at night, action in front of the church)

Tiradentes - Minas Gerais ☎ 032

BARS
■ **Aluarte** (A B g)
Largo do ó 1

Vitória - Espirito Santo ☎ 027

BARS
■ **Beleza's Sorveteria** (B f g)
Avenida Florentino Avidos 532 *(in Hotel Grand Estoril, Centro)*
■ **Bengalo Bar** (B f GLM P) 12-5 h
Rua Professor Baltazar 136 *(Centro)*

SAUNAS/BATHS
■ **Tempu's** (B G R msg SA SB VS) 16-22h
Rua Dr. Antônio Ataíde, 982, Vila Velha *(Centro)* ☎ 239 1413

CRUISING
- Jardin de Penha Gamburi
- Praia Compridor
- Praia de Camburi
- Praia de Guarapari (Castanheiras Beach)
- Parque Moscoso
- Promenade Embarcadouro
- In front of Sao Luis Theatre (Rua 23 de Maio)
- Plaza Costa Pereira (R)

Bulgaria

Name: Bâlgarija • Bulgarien • Bulgarie
Location: Southeastern Europe
Initials: BG
Time: GMT +2
International Country Code: ☎ 359 (leave the first 0 of area codes)
International Access Code: ☎ 00
Language: Bulgarian
Area: 111,993 km2 / 42,854 sq mi.
Currency: 1 Lew (Lw) = 100 Stótinki.
Population: 8,240,426
Capital: Sofija
Religions: 88% Orthodox Christian
Climate: For the most part continental, milder on the Black Sea coast.

✱ The age of consent for homosexual activity is 16, while for heterosexuals it is 14. There are some signs of an emerging gay movement, although this has yet to lead to any kind of a gay scene.

★ Das Schutzalter für Schwule und Lesben liegt bei 16, ansonsten bei 14 Jahren. Es gibt erste Zeichen einer sich entwickelnden schwulen Bewegung; eine schwule Szene aber muß sich noch entwickeln.

✱ La majorité sexuelle en Bulgarie est fixée à 16 ans pour les homosexuels et à 14 ans pour les hétérosexuels. Malgré tout, les choses sont en train de changer et les gais commencent à s'organiser, lentement mais sûrement.

⬣ La edad de consentimiento para la homosexualidad es de 16 años, para la heterosexualidad es de 14 años. A pesar de todo, ya se pueden notar los primeros indicios de una organización gay, aún cuando los gays apenas se han movilizado.

✖ L'età minima per avere dei rapporti omosessuali è di 16 anni, di 14 per rapporti eterosessuali. Tuttavia stanno apparendo i primi segni di un movimento gay.

NATIONAL GAY INFO
■ **BULGA**
PO Box 32 ✉ 1330 Sofija ☎ (02) 58 52 71 📠 (02) 44 38 04
■ **Gemini** (GLM)
PO Box 123 ✉ 1784 Sofija ☎ (088) 30 90 98
📧 geminibg@hotmail.com 🖥 people.bulgaria.com/gemini
Bulgarian gay organisation.

Burgas ☎ 056
CRUISING
- At the main railway station and in the city park

Sofija ☎ 02
BARS
■ **Adonis** (A AC B d GLM lj MA P p SNU) Mon-Sun 19-6 h
Kniaz Boris I 122 *(opposite Sheraton Hotel)*
■ **Gayzer** (B G p)
Rakovsky Str. 77 *(Tsar Simeon Str.)* ☎ (088) 80 84 67
■ **George** (AC B d GLM LJ MA N P p) 19.30-4 h
Lavale 17 *(Center, behind the National Museum of History)*
■ **Miami Club** (B G d dr MA p r VS)
Pirotska 49 ☎ (0799) 603 70
☎ 981 71 11

Bulgaria - Cambodia | Sofija ▸ Phnom Penh

■ **Private Club - Kayo's** (AC CC B G MA P p SNU) Mon-Sun 19-6 h
Yuri Venelin 27 *(opposite National Stadium)* ☎ 986 40 02
■ **Why Not...** (B G p) 20-4 h
Alexander Stamboliysky Boulevard 31 *(downstairs under Capri Pizzeria)* ☎ 986 66 30

DANCECLUBS

■ **Spartacus** (B D G P S TV WE) Tue-Sun 0-6 h
Vassil Levsky Boulevard *(at underground passage in front of Sofia University)*

RESTAURANTS

■ **Malkiyat Printz** (F g MA) Mon-Sun 11-2 h
24 Slavyansky Str. ☎ 980 81 51
Malkiyat Printz (The Little Prince) offers good food at affordable prices.

SEX SHOPS/BLUE MOVIES

■ **Flamingo** (B DR g VS) 14-2 h
Tsar Simeon St. 208 ✉ 1680 *(1st floor)* ☎ 97 46 47
Also video rental.

CRUISING

-Orlov Most
-Vazrazhdane Square (A. Stamboliysky Blvd./H. Botev Blvd.)
-Garden behind Main Library („Doctor's Garden", near University)

Varna ☎ 052

DANCECLUBS

■ **Spartacus** (B D GLM P S TV WE) Tue-Sun 23-5 h
(in the cellar of Varna Stae Theater)

GENERAL GROUPS

■ **Contact**
PO Box 707, Central Post Office ✉ 9000

SWIMMING

-The WC in front of the tennis court at Sea garden (day and night)
-The thermal source at the beach near the lift, know as „BADEN BADEN" (day and night, down in front of the zoological Garden)
-Adam Beach (men's nudist beach, just in the central beach of Varna)
-Golden Sands Resort (The nudist beach, after the yacht port in front of Hotel Glarus)
-Albena Resort (Nudist beach after Hotel Gergana)

Cambodia

Name: Kâmpuchéa • Kambodscha • Cambodge • Camboya • Cambogia
Location: Southeast Asia
Initials: K
Time: GMT +7
International Country Code: ☎ 855 (leave the first 0 of area codes)
International Access Code: ☎ 00
Language: Khmer. French
Area: 181,035 km2 / 69,898 sq mi.
Currency: 1 Riel = 10 Kak = 100 Sen
Population: 11,339,562
Capital: Phnom Penh
Religions: 95% Theravada Buddhism
Climate: Tropical climate. The rainy monsoon season lasts from May to November, the dry season from December to April. There's little seasonal temperature variation.

✱ We have no information concerning the legal status of homosexuals in Cambodia. However ILGA states, that the attitude of Cambodians should be seen as being rather hostile.

★ Uns liegen keinerlei Informationen zur gesetzlichen Lage Homosexueller in Kambodscha vor. Die ILGA stellt allerdings fest, daß die Haltung der Kambodschaner eher als feindselig betrachtet werden muß.

✱ Nous ne disposons d'aucune information sur la situation des gais au Cambodge. L'ILGA nous a fait savoir que les Cambodgiens ne semblent pas être particulièrement homophiles.

● No poseemos información alguna sobre la situación legal de los homosexuales en Camboya. La ILGA constata que el comportamiento de los camboyanos se puede calificar de agresivo.

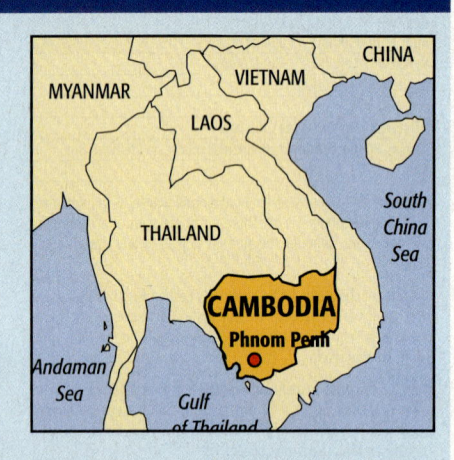

✖ Non abbiamo alcun tipo di informazione sulla situazione giuridica degli omosessuali in Cambogia. L'ILGA ha costatato un'attitudine ostile della popolazione nei confronti dei gay.

Phnom Penh ☎ 023

BARS

■ **Martini Pub** (B D glm MA OS) 20-? h
402 Keo Mony Bud *(Near Olympic Stadium)*

■ **Heart of Darkness** (B glm MA) 19-? h
No 26 Street 51 *(Pasteur)*
■ **Tamarind Bar** (B F GLM MA OS) 11-1 h
No. 31, Street 240 *(near Royal Place)* ☎ 015-914743

Phnom Penh | Cambodia

CAFES
■ **No Problem**
178th Street

RESTAURANTS
■ **Athena Restaurant & Bar** (AC B F glm MA OS) 11-24 h
140 Norodom Boulevard *(nearby Independence Mounument)*
☎ 802 330

FITNESS STUDIOS
■ **Parkway Gym**
Mao Tse Tung Street

GUEST HOUSES
■ **Bert's Books Guest House**
79, Sithowath Quay ☎ 360 806

HEALTH GROUPS
■ **Tropical & Travellers Medical Clinic**
No. 88, Street 108 *(Near Wat Phnom)* ☎ 023-366 802
Tropical medicine, sexual diseases, HIV test the Doctor is from the UK.

CRUISING
- Olympic stadium (inside)
- Park near Independence Monument (ayor)
- Along the corniche on the riverfront at night (AYOR).
- Le Cercle Sportif 96th St. (pi W)
- Phnom Penh pagoda (ayor r)

CAMBODIA Vietnam Laos Bali Thailand
local gay guides, private holidays, a world of new friends.
www.utopia-tours.com
Asia's gay & lesbian travel pioneers
Utopia Tours
info@utopia-tours.com

Most HIV+ men try not to pass on HIV

+ve
I want to give him one - but I don't want to give him it

GMFA's campaigns and actions are designed, planned and executed by positive, negative and untested volunteers.
To volunteer for GMFA write, phone or email:
Unit 43, Eurolink Centre, 49 Effra Road, LONDON, SW2 1BZ.
020 7738 6872. newvol@gmfa.demon.co.uk
www.demon.co.uk/gmfa
Registered Charity no. 1076854

GMFA
Gay Men Fighting AIDS

Canada

Name: Kanada
Location: North America
Initials: CDN
Time: GMT -4/ -5/ -6/ -7/ -8
International Country Code: ☎ 1
International Access Code: ☎ 011
Language: English, French
Area: 9,976,319 km2 / 3,844,910 sq mi.
Currency: 1 Canadian Dollar (Can$) = 100 Cents
Population: 30,675,398
Capital: Ottawa
Religions: 87,7% Christian (46,5% Catholic, 41,2% Protestant)
Climate: Varies from Moderate in the south to subarctic and arctic in the north.
Important gay cities: Montréal, Toronto, Vancouver

Canada is the second largest country in the world. For the convenience of the readers, listings are organised alphabetically according to province or territory. The country is made up of 10 provinces and 3 territories, with the creation of Nunavut in April 1999.

The legal age of consent for homosexual acts in Canada is 14. Exceptions include anal intercourse, prostitution, and sexual exploitation of a dependent relationships where the age of consent is 18 for both heterosexuals and homosexuals.

Federal legislation prohibits discrimination on the basis of sexual orientation. In British Colombia and Ontario it is possible for gay / lesbian couples to adopt children. Moreover, gays and lesbians can serve in the Canadian Army.

Canada's liberal attitudes are similar to those of the northern US. Language differences (i.e. French in Quebec) is part of every day li-

Canada

fe. Canada is culturally aware and accepts different religions of its people. The population of metropolitan Toronto is already as big as that of Boston in the US. The European roots of the Eastern part of Canada provide for its general tolerance of gays and lesbians.

Three very important gay cities are Montreal (Quebec), Toronto (Ontario) and Vancouver (British Columbia). The two Eastern cities differ noticeably in character from Vancouver. The pace of life in Vancouver is more relaxed and the gay scene is less diverse than in Montreal or Toronto. In 1998 Glen Murray was elected mayor of Winnipeg. He is the first open gay mayor in Canada.

★ Kanada ist das zweitgrößte Land der Erde. Damit Sie sich besser zurechtfinden, haben wir das Listing nach Provinzen bzw. Territorien neu sortiert. Darin folgen die Städte in alphabetischer Ordnung.

Das Schutzalter für homosexuelle Handlungen liegt bei 14 Jahren. Ausgenommen sind Analverkehr, Prostitution und Ausnützung eines Abhängigkeitsverhältnisses; in diesen Fällen liegt die Altersgrenze generell bei 18 Jahren, egal ob es sich um hetero- oder homosexuelle Handlungen handelt.

Es gibt seit einigen Jahren kanadaweit gesetzlichen Schutz vor Diskrimierung aufgrund der sexuellen Identität. In British Columbia und Ontario können Schwule und Lesben problemlos Kinder adoptieren. Die kanadische Armee sieht in der Beschäftigung Homosexueller kein Problem.

Dieser relative Liberalismus liegt vor allem in einem, im Vergleich zu den benachbarten USA, wesentlich moderateren Lebensstil. Sprachdifferenzen (z.B. im frankophonen Québéc) sind Alltag, die Kultur der Inuit gehört selbstverständlich zu Kanada. Religion spielt dagegen im Alltag keine herausragende Rolle. Der Regionalismus sorgt dafür, daß die Nation nicht überhöht wird. Das Land ist zwar verstädtert, doch der größte Ballungsraum (um Toronto) ist gerade so groß wie der des US-amerikanischen Boston. Und gerade die im Osten des Landes offensichtlichen europäischen Wurzeln sorgen für ein maßvolles Klima in Kanada.

Die drei wichtigsten schwulen Städte des Landes sind Montreal (Quebec), Toronto (Ontario) und Vancouver (British Columbia). Die Unterschiede zwischen den beiden östlichen Städten und Vancouver sind allerdings beträchtlich. Während die Szene in den Städten des Westens eher beschaulich wirkt und sich Gay-Pride-Veranstaltungen noch im Wachsen befinden, sind die Großstädte des Ostens wahre Szene-Hochburgen. Entsprechend vielfältig ist die Szene, entsprechend stark ist die schwul-lesbische Bewegung.

★ Le Canada est le deuxième plus grand pays du monde par sa superficie. Pour vous aider à mieux vous y retrouver, nous avons regroupé notre liste par provinces et territoires, puis par ordre alphabétique de ville. Le pays comprend 10 provinces et 3 territoires depuis la création du Nunavut en avril 1999.

La majorité sexuelle est fixée à 14 ans pour les gais, avec cependant une exception pour les rapports anaux, la prostitution et la mise à profit d'un rapport de dépendance. Dans ces cas, la limite d'âge se situe généralement à 18 ans, qu'il s'agisse de rapports hétérosexuels ou homosexuels.

Depuis quelques années, il existe dans tout le Canada une protection contre la discrimination liée à l'identité sexuelle. En Colombie-Britannique et en Ontario, les homosexuels et lesbiennes peuvent adopter des enfants sans difficulté. L'armée canadienne est également ouverte à l'engagement des gais.

Le Canada est de manière générale plus libéral que son voisin les Etats-Unis. Les différences linguistiques (par exemple du Québec francophone) font partie de la vie quotidienne. Le pays est culturellement riche et tolérant vis-à-vis des pratiques religieuses. La plus grande agglomération urbaine (celle de Toronto) est aujourd'hui aussi grande que la ville américaine de Boston. Les racines européennes évidentes à l'est du pays contribuent certainement à une plus grande tolérance à l'égard des gais.

Les trois villes homosexuelles les plus importantes du pays sont Montréal (Québec), Toronto (Ontario) et Vancouver (Colombie-Britannique). Des différences entre l'est et l'ouest sont cependant à noter. A Vancouver. le mode de vie est plus détendu et la scène gaie moins diversifiée qu'à Montréal ou Toronto. Glen Murray, élu en 1998 à Winnipeg, a été le premier maire ouvertement homosexuel du pays.

★ Canada es el segundo país más grande del mundo. Para su mejor orientación hemos ordenado el listado por provincias o territorios, indicando las ciudades correspondientes por orden alfabético. Al inicio damos una lista con todas las ciudades canadienses. La edad de consentimiento para homosexuales es de 14 años, haciendo excepción de las relaciones anales, la prostitución o el aprovechamiento de una relación de dependencia. Para estos casos la ley estipula una edad de 18 años, independientemente de la orientación sexual. Desde hace algunos años existe una ley en Canada que garantiza la igualdad de derechos para homosexuales. Por ejemplo, en British Columbia parejas gay o lesbianas pueden adoptar niños sin problema alguno y el ejército canadiense no considera problemático el reclutamiento de hombres homosexuales. Ese relativo liberalismo (en comparación con los vecinos Estados Unidos) se debe sobre todo a una postura más abierta hacia minorias. Las diferencias lingüisticas (por ejemplo en la provincia de habla francesa Québec) son rutina y la cultura de los Inuit (esquimales) forma parte de la vida canadiense. Por otro lado, la religión no juega ningún papel predominante. Debido al fuerte regionalismo, para los canadienses el concepto de la nación no tiene gran importancia. Aunque hay muchas ciudades, la mayor aglomeración urbana (Toronto y sus alrededores) es apenas tan grande como la ciudad estadounidense de Boston. En la parte oriental arraigó con más fuerza la tradición europea, garantizando de este modo un ambiente más abierto y liberal. Las tres ciudades de mayor importancia para gays son Montreal (Québec), Toronto (Ontario) y Vancouver (British Columbia), aunque las diferencias entre las dos ciudades orientales y Vancouver son enormes. Mientras el ambiente gay en las ciudades del Oeste es bastante tranquilo y fiestas como la Gay-Pride se organizan hace muy poco, las grandes ciudades del Este son verdaderas bastiones homosexuales. Estas ciudades ofrecen un ámplio ambiente y como es de esperar el movimiento gay posee gran impulso.

★ Canadà è il secondo paese più grande del mondo in superficie. Per un migliore orientamento abbiamo cambiato la lista a seconda delle province e dei territori nel cui capitolo vengono elencate le rispettive città. All'inizio di questa lista troverete un'elenco di tutte le città canadesi. L'età legale per avere rapporti omossesuali è di 14 anni. Sono esclusi i rapporti anali, la prostituzione e lo sfruttamento di una relazione di dipendenza. In questi casi, l'età del consenso è di 18 anni per gli atti sia eterosessuali sia omossessuali. Da alcuni anni esistono leggi che proteggono in tutto il paese i gay e le lesbiche contro la discriminazione del loro orientamento sessuale. Nella Colombia britannica ed in Ontario gay e lesbiche possono adottare bambini. L'esercito canadese non esclude gli omossessuali dalle proprie file. Il motivo per questo liberalismo è lo stile di vita abbastanza riservato, rispetto a quello degli USA. Le difficoltà con le

Canada/Alberta — Calgary

lingue (p.es. nel Quebec francofono) fanno parte della vita quotidiana, come anche la cultura degli Inuit è parte della Canada. Grazie al regionalismo, la religione non svolge un ruolo essenziale per tutta la nazione. Anche se il paese è urbanizzato, la zona con la più alta concentrazione di abitanti (attorno a Toronto) è grande come Boston negli USA. Sono le radici europee nella parte orientale del paese che contribuiscono a un buon clima sociale. Le tre città gay più importanti sono Montreal (Quebec), Toronto (Ontario) e Vancouver (Colombia britannica). Ci sono differenze notevoli tra le due città orientali e Vancouver. Mentre la vita gay nelle città dell'occidente è piuttosto tranquilla e gli avvenimenti di Gay Pride si stanno ancora sviluppando, e mentre le grandi città dell'oriente sono veri baluardi del movimento gay e lesbico con una grande varietà di locali e possibilità d'incontro.

NATIONAL GAY INFO

■ **Canadian Gay, Lesbian & Bisexual Resource Directory. The** (GLM)
386 Montrose Street ✉ MB R3M 3M8 Winnipeg
☎ (204) 488-1805 ☎ (1-800) 245-2734 (toll-free)
🖨 (204) 663-6001
📧 cglbrd@cglbrd.com 💻 www.cglbrd.com
Internet listing of gay and lesbian business organisation.

■ **Canadian Lesbian & Gay Archives. The** (GLM MA) Tue-Thu 19.30-22 h (and by appointment)
PO Box 639, Station A ✉ ON M5W 1G2 Toronto *(56 Temperance Street, Suite 201)* ☎ (416) 777-2755
Archives, library and research centre. Large collection of periodicals.

■ **GAYroute**
CP 1036, Stn. „C" ✉ QC H2L 4V3 Montréal
For more details about all types of gay businesses in Canada send a fee of US$ 5, – or 3x IRC and a self addressed envelope. Mail order only.

■ **INFO - all about gay Canada**
☎ (514) 899 4636
Information about all services offered to visitors to Canada. Free service.

NATIONAL PUBLICATIONS

■ **Fab Magazine** (GLM)
110 Spadina Avenue, Suite 201 ✉ ON M5V 2K4 Toronto
☎ (416) 306-0180 🖨 (416) 306-0182

■ **Go Big** (GLM)
c/o Pink Triangle Press, 2nd floor, 491 Church Street ✉ ON M4Y 2C6 Toronto ☎ (416) 925-6665 🖨 (416) 925-6674
📧 gobig@xtra.ca
Trends magazine published twice a year with portraits and fashion. About 30 pages, free at gay venues.

NATIONAL COMPANIES

■ **Cachet Accommodations Network (C.A.N.)** (GLM) 10-22 h
PO Box 60542 ✉ QC H1V 3L8 Montréal ☎ (514) 254 1250 ext. 2
☎ (1 877) 487-7448 (Toll-free) 📧 be-brief@sympatico.ca
Since 1984, the gay and lesbian room booking service for visitors to Canada.

■ **Footprints** (GLM)
506 Church Street, Ste 200 ✉ ON M4Y 2C8 Toronto
☎ (416) 962-8111 ☎ (1-888) 962-6211 (toll-free)
🖨 (416) 962-6621
📧 trips@footprintstravel.com 💻 www.footprintstravel.com
Tour operator specializing in the provision of worldwide adventure travel for the gay and lesbian community.

■ **Homelink International** (GLM)
PO Box 762, Station C ✉ QC H2L 4L6 Montréal ☎ (514) 523-4462
☎ (800) 429-4983 (Toll-free) 🖨 (514) 879-3299
Gay & Lesbian accomodation club. Hospitality and home exchange.

■ **Wega Video** (CC GLM VS)
930 Rue Sainte-Catherine Est ✉ QC H2S 3K6 Montréal *(M° Beaudry)* ☎ (514) 987-5993 ☎ (1-800) 361-9929 (toll-free)
🖨 (514) 987-5994 📧 wega@wegavideo.com
💻 www.wegavideo.com
One of Canada's largest online adult gay video store. Over 1300 titles in stock with new ones available every month!

NATIONAL GROUPS

■ **Canadian AIDS Society** 8.30-17 h
900-130 Albert Street, ✉ ON K1P 5G4 Ottawa ☎ 613-230-3580
🖨 613-563-4998 📧 casinfo@web.net

■ **Gay Mates-Men's national pen pal contact club**
PO Box 3043, ✉ SK S7K 3S9 Saskatoon

■ **MGL. Regroupement de militaires gais, lesbiennes, bisexuels et transsexuelles** (GLM) 0-24 h
C.P. 4111, Succ. Terminus ✉ QC G1K 2Z2 Québec *(in Montreal and Quebec City)* ☎ (418) 524-7949 (Québec) ☎ (514) 932-8258 (Montréal) 📧 mgl.qc@pfa-qc.com 💻 www.algi.qc.ca/asso/mgl
Military gays, lesbians, bisexuals and transsexuals group.

CDN-Alberta

Location: Southwest CDN
Initials: AB
Time: GMT -7
Area: 661,000 km2 / 255,212 sq mi.
Population: 2,847,000
Capital: Edmonton
Important gay cities: Calgary and Edmonton

Calgary ☎ 403

GAY INFO

■ **Gay & Lesbian Community Services Association** 19-22 h
206, 223 12th Avenue South West ✉ AB T2R 0G3 ☎ 234-8973
☎ 234-9752 (infoline) 💻 www.glcsa.org
Peer support, information, library and drop-in center.

PUBLICATIONS

■ **Outlooks** (GLM MA) Mon-Fri 9-17 h
Box 439, Suite 100, 1039 17th Avenue South West ✉ AB T2T 0B2
☎ 228-1157 🖨 228-7735 📧 outlooks@cadvision.com
💻 www.outlooks.ab.ca
Monthly newspaper distributed nationally in Canada.

TOURIST INFO

■ **Calgary Convention & Visitors Bureau** Mon-Fri 8-17 h
237-8 Avenue South East ✉ AB T2G 0K8 ☎ 263-8510
☎ (1-800) 661-1678 (toll-free) 🖨 262-3809
📧 destination@visitors.ab.ca

Calgary ▶ Edmonton | **Alberta/Canada**

BARS
■ **Loading Dock. The** (B G N) 15-3 h
c/o Detour, 318 17th Avenue South West ✉ AB T2S 0A8
☎ 244-8537
■ **Money Pennies** (B F GLM OS) 11-3 h
1742 10th Avenue South West ☎ 263-7411
■ **Rekroom** (B G lj MA N p) 16-3 h
213-A 10th Avenue South West ✉ AB T2R 0A4 (lower level)
☎ 265-4749

CAFES
■ **Grabbajabba** (AC b CC F GLM MA) Mon-Thu 7-23, Fri -24, S un 8-23 h
1610-10th Street South West ✉ AB T2R 1G1 (off 17th Ave)
☎ 244-7750
■ **Midnight Café** (B F glm MA) Mon-Fri 7-2, Sat 9-2, Sun 11-24 h
840 - 14th Avenue ☎ 229-9322

DANCECLUBS
■ **Arena** (B D G MA) Thu-Sat 21-3 h
310 17th Avenue South West ✉ AB T2S 0A8 ☎ 228-5730
■ **Backlot. The** (B D GLM OS) 16-? h
209 10th Avenue SW ✉ AB T2R 0A4 ☎ 265-5211
■ **Detour** (B D Glm MA) Wed-Sun 22-3 h. Fri men only
318 17th Avenue South West ✉ AB T2S 0A8 ☎ 244-8537
■ **Metro Boyztown** (B CC D G MA P snu) 21-3 h
213 10h Avenue South West ✉ AB T2R 0A4 ☎ 265-2028
Men only exept on Wed.

RESTAURANTS
■ **Entre Nous** (F glm) Mon-Sat 11-23, Sun 11-14 h
1800 4th Street South West ☎ 228-5525
French cuisine.
■ **Victoria's** (AC B CC F glm OS) 11-24, Fri-Sat -2 h
306 17th Avenue South West ✉ AB T2S 0A8 ☎ 244-9991

SEX SHOPS/BLUE MOVIES
■ **After Dark** (g VS)
1314 1st Street South West ✉ AB T2R 0V7 ☎ 264-7399
Videos, toys, lingerie, magazines, peep shows.

SAUNAS/BATHS
■ **Goliath's Saunatel** (b f G MA SB WH VS) 0-24 h
308 17th Avenue South West ✉ AB T2S 0A8 (rear entrance)
☎ 229-0911

BOOK SHOPS
■ **Rainbow Pride Resource Center** (A AC CC GLM MA S)
2-2, Sun -21 h
L100 - 822 11th Avenue South West ☎ 266-5685
Adult videos, gifts, cards, books & magazines

LEATHER & FETISH SHOPS
■ **B&B Emporium** (glm LJ TV) Mon-Sat 10.30-18 h. Party every 2nd/4th Fri Sat.
426 8th Avenue South East ✉ AB T2G 0L7 ☎ 203-0703

GUEST HOUSES
■ **Foxwood B&B** (BF CC GLM MA H OS WH)
1725 12th Street South West ✉ AB T3T 3N1 ☎ 244-6693
📠 244-4098 ✉ foxwoodband@home.com
💻 www.thefoxwood.com
3 rooms with shared bath and one suite with private bath. TV, video. Please call for rates.

■ **Westways Guest House** (AC BF CC GLM H msg WH)
216 25th Avenue South West ✉ AB T2S 0L1 (close to nightlife)
☎ 229-1758 📠 228-6265 ✉ calgary@westways.ab.ca
💻 www.westways.ab.ca
All rooms with private baths, cable TV, VCR and phone.
■ **11th Street Lodging** (BF GLM H) 10-21 h
1307 11th Street South West ✉ AB T2R 1G5 (downtown)
☎ 209-0111 📠 209-2571 ✉ dulj@cadvision.com
💻 www.11street.com
5 doubles, 4 singles with shared bath and 1 studio and 1 apartment with private bath. Rooms with balcony, radio and TV/VCR.

GENERAL GROUPS
■ **Camp 181** (GLM)
PO Box 702 Station M ✉ AB T2P 2J3 ☎ 234-8973
Social, recreational gay and lesbian group.

HEALTH GROUPS
■ **Southern Alberta Clinic** Mon-Fri 8-16 h
#213, 906 8 Avenue South West ✉ AB T2P 1H9 ☎ 234-2399
📠 262-4893 💻 www.health.ab.ca/clin/sac/sac.htm
For people living with HIV in Southern Alberta.

HELP WITH PROBLEMS
■ **Gay Lines Calgary** 19-22 h
206, 223 12th Avenue South West ✉ AB T2R 0G3 ☎ 234-8973
📠 261-9776

RELIGIOUS GROUPS
■ **MCC Calgary**
PO Box 82054, Scarboro Postal Outlet ✉ AB T3C 3M5
☎ 265-6222 ✉ mcccalgary@hotmail.com
Services at Bankview Community centre..

SPECIAL INTEREST GROUPS
■ **GLASS**
PO Box 47, MacEwan Hall, University of Calgary, 2500 University Drive, North West ✉ AB T2N 1N4 ☎ 220-2872
✉ glass@acs.ucalgary.ca 💻 www.ucalgary.ca/~glass
Gay & Lesbian Academics, Students & Staff.

SPORT GROUPS
■ **Alberta Rockies Gay Rodeo Association (ARGRA)**
#208, 223 12th Avenue South West ✉ AB T2R 0G9 ☎ 541-8140
■ **Alpine Frontrunners Club**
PO Box 22054, Bankers Hall ✉ AB T2P 4J1 ☎ 244-4644
■ **Apollo: Friends in Sports** (GLM)
PO Box 6481, Station D ✉ AB T2P 4J1 (Bankers Hall) ☎ 281 3572
Gay, lesbian sports club.

CRUISING
-East end of Prince Island
-Tennis Court on 2nd Street (between 13th & 14th Avenue South West)
-University of Calgary (Education Building, men's restroom, 2nd floor)
-13th Avenue South West (r) (between 6th & 7th Street South West)

Edmonton ☎ 780

GAY INFO
■ **Gay and Lesbian Community Centre of Edmonton (GLCCE)**
(GLM) Info Line: Mon-Fri 19-22, Wed 13-16 / Youth phone line: Sat 20-22 h
PO Box 1852 ✉ AB T5J 2P2 ☎ 488-3234 (Infoline) ☎ 488-1574 (Youthline) ✉ glcce@freenet.edmonton.ab.ca
💻 www.freenet.edmonton.ab.ca/glcce

SPARTACUS 2001/2002 | 119

Canada/Alberta - British Columbia — Edmonton ▶ Fernie

BARS
- **Boots'n Saddle** (B G LJ MA N P SNU STV WE) 15-2 h
10240 106th Street/103rd Avenue ✉ AB T5J 1H7 ☎ 423-5014
Private club. Sun buffet.
- **Buddy's Bar** (B Glm MA)
10116 124th Street ✉ AB T5N 1P6 *(above Jazzberry's)*
☎ 488-6636
- **Secrets Bar and Grill** (B F GLM) Mon-Sat 16-3 h
10249 107th Street ☎ 990-1818

DANCECLUBS
- **Roost. The** (AC B CC D f GLM MA OS s WE) Mon-Sun 20-3 h
10345-104 Street ✉ AB T5J 1B9 ☎ 426-3150

RESTAURANTS
- **Café de Ville** (F glm)
10137 124 Street ✉ AB T5N 1P5 ☎ 488-9188

SEX SHOPS/BLUE MOVIES
- **Executive Express** (CC G VS) 13-21 h, closed Tue
202-11745 Jasper Avenue ✉ AB T5K 0N5 ☎ 482-7480
Adult video sales, rentals and clothing.
- **Pride Video** (G VS)
10121 124 Street North West ✉ AB T5N 1P5 ☎ 452-7743

SAUNAS/BATHS
- **Down Under** (AC CC f DR G MA SA VS WH) 0-24 h
12224 Jasper Avenue ✉ AB T5N 3K3 *(at 122th Street, basement location)* ☎ 482-7960
Sauna with glory holes or sling rooms on offer.
- **Georgia Baths** (G SA SB WH)
9668 Jasper Avenue ✉ AB T5H 3V5 ☎ 422-2581

BOOK SHOPS
- **Front Page. The** (glm) Mon-Sat 9-20 h
10356 Jasper Avenue ✉ AB T5J 1Y7 *(central)* ☎ 426-1206

GUEST HOUSES
- **Northern Lights Bed & Breakfast** (G H NU PI)
8216, 151 Street ✉ AB T5R 1H6 ☎ 483-1572
💻 nlight69@hotmail.com

FETISH GROUPS
- **NLA Edmonton** Fetish nights, 2nd fri in Roost
PO Box 35015, 11229 Jasper Avenue ✉ AB T5K 2R8
💻 nlaedmonton@canada.com

HEALTH GROUPS
- **AIDS Network of Edmonton Society** Mon-Fri 9-16 h
#201 11456 Jasper Avenue ✉ AB T5K 0M1 ☎ 488-5816
- **HIV Network of Edmonton Society**
600 10242-105 Street ✉ AB T5J 3L5 ☎ 488-5742
💻 mail@hivedmonton.com
Health promotion, advocacy, support & education. Home of the Gay Men's Outreach Crew.

SPECIAL INTEREST GROUPS
- **Outreach** (GLM)
PO Box 75, Room 620, Students Union Building ✉ AB T6G 2J7
☎ 988-4166 💻 outreach@gpu.srv.ulaberta.ca
Students and staff GL group of the University of Alberta.

CRUISING
- Victoria Park (near the golf course)
- Hill (across from McDonald Hotel)

Lethbridge ☎ 403

GAY INFO
- **Gay & Lesbian Alliance of Lethbridge and Area** Mon 19-22 h
1129-41 Avenue North ✉ AB T1H 6A4 ☎ 329-4666
💻 gaylethbridge@hotmail.com

HEALTH GROUPS
- **Lethbridge HIV Connection Society** Mon-Thu 9-17 h
1206 6th Avenue South ✉ AB T1J 1A4 ☎ 328-8186 📠 328-8564

Red Deer ☎ 403

BARS
- **Other Place. The** (AC BC CC D F GLM MA N STV) Tue-Sun 16-3 h
Bay 3 & 4, 5579-47 Street ✉ AB T4N 1S1 ☎ 342-6440

GENERAL GROUPS
- **Gay & Lesbian Association of Central Alberta (GALACA)** (GLM) Wed 19-22 h
PO Box 1078 ✉ AB T4N 6S5 ☎ 340-2198

HEALTH GROUPS
- **Central Alberta AIDS Network Society**
400 5000-50 Street ✉ AB T4N 6C2 ☎ 346-8858

CRUISING
- Canyon Park

CDN-British-Columbia

Location: Southwest CDN
Initials: BC
Time: GMT -8
Area: 949,000 km2 / 366,409 sq mi
Population: 3,933,000
Capital: Victoria

Bowen Island ☎ 604

GUEST HOUSES
- **Espérance. L'** (A BF CC GLM msg NU WH)
567 Cowan Road RR#1 Q93 ✉ BC V0N 1G0 *(20 min from Vancouver with ferry)* ☎ 947-0672 📠 947-0672
💻 sergealex@hotmail.com
1 double room & 1 studio with kitchenette, fireplace, whirlpool in the forest.

Castlegar ☎ 250

HEALTH GROUPS
- **AIDS Network, Outreach & Support Society (ANKORS)**
903 4th Street ☎ 365-2437

Duncan ☎ 250

GENERAL GROUPS
- **Island Gay and Lesbian Association**
PO Box 129 ✉ BC V9L 3X1 ☎ 748-7689

Fernie ☎ 250

GUEST HOUSES
- **Fernie Westways Guest House** (BF CC e g H msg WH)
PO Box 658, 202 4 A Avenue ✉ BC V0B 1M0 ☎ 423-3058
📠 423-3059 💻 fernie@westways.ab.ca 🌐 www.westways.ab.ca
Small B&B in remote but beautiful setting. All rooms with private bath, radio and TV/VCR.

Kamloops ☎ 250

GENERAL GROUPS
■ **Gay and Lesbian Association** (GLM MA)
PO Box 2071, Station A ✉ BC V2B 7K6 ☎ 376-3111
✉ galakam@yahoo.com 🖥 www.gaycanada.com/kamloops-gala
Call or check website for details.

Kelowna ☎ 250

GAY INFO
■ **Okanagan Gay & Lesbian Organization** (OGLO) (GLM) Infoline Mon, Thu 19-21.30h, Wed & Fri 16.30-17.30h
1180 Houghton Road ✉ BC V1X 2C9 ☎ 860-8555
✉ okrainbow@hotmail.com
Support groups, social events, lending library. Dances usually held at Laurel Bldg, 1600 Ellis St.

CAFES
■ **Bean Scene** (glm) Gay coffee night Mon 20-22 h
274 Bernard Avenue ✉ BC V1Y 6N4 ☎ 763-1814

GUEST HOUSES
■ **Flags Bed and Breakfast, The** (AC BF G H NU PI SA SOL WH) All year
2295 McKinley Road ✉ BC V1V 2B6 ☎ 868-2416 📠 868-2416
Country setting. 3 double rooms and 1 single with bath/shower and WC on the floor. Clothing optional.

Nanaimo ☎ 250

BARS
■ **Neighbours Lounge** (B CC GLM MA stv) Mon-Wed 19-2, Thu-Sat 16-2, Sun 15-24 h
70 Church Street ✉ BC V9R 5H4 *(under the Dorchester Hotel)*
☎ 716-0505
Bar with karaoke shows on Wed.

GIFT & PRIDE SHOPS
■ **A Different Drummer** (CC GLM)
189 Commercial Street ✉ BC V9R 5G5 ☎ 753-0030

GUEST HOUSES
■ **Stonewall Guest House** (BF CC F GLM H MA msg nu OS WH)
4171 Stoneall Drive ✉ BC V9G 1G1 *(20 min south of Nanaimo)*
☎ 245-3346 📠 245-3316 ✉ relax@stonewallinn.bc.ca
🖥 www.stonewallinn.bc.ca

HEALTH GROUPS
■ **AIDS Vancouver Island** (GLM)
201-55 Victoria Street ☎ 1 800 665-2437 (helpline) ☎ 753-2437 (office)

Nelson ☎ 250

PRIVATE ACCOMMODATION
■ **Dragon Fly Inn** (glm)
1016 Hall Mines Road ☎ 354-1128 📠 354-1128
✉ dragonfly@netidea.com

GENERAL GROUPS
■ **West Kootenay Gays and Lesbians Society** (ANKORS)
101 Baker Street ✉ BC V1L 4H1 ☎ 354-4297
✉ ankors@wkpowerlink.com
Support and advocacy services, community care teams.

New Westminster ☎ 604

SAUNAS/BATHS
■ **Fahrenheit 212°** (b CC G MA P SB VS WO) 0-24 h
430 Columbia Street ✉ BC V3L 1B1 ☎ 540-2117
Photo ID required for membership.

Prince George ☎ 250

GUEST HOUSES
■ **Hawthorne Bed and Breakfast** (BF CC F glm H MG NU OS WO WH)
829 PG Pulp Mill Road ✉ BC V2K 5P4 ☎ 563-8299 📠 563-0899

GENERAL GROUPS
■ **Gay and Lesbian Association**
36-1306 7th Avenue ☎ 562-6253

Prince Rupert ☎ 250

GAY INFO
■ **Gay Info Line**
PO Box 881 ☎ 627-8900 ✉ box881@hotmail.com

Revelstoke ☎ 250

GENERAL GROUPS
■ **Lothlorien** (GLM)
PO Box 8557 ✉ BC V0E 3G0
Gay & lesbian support group.

Salt Spring Island ☎ 250

GUEST HOUSES
■ **Green Rose Bed & Breakfast** (CC GLM H OS)
388 Scott Point Drive ✉ BC V8K 2R2 ☎ 537-9927 📠 537-9927
Ocean-side suite with own entrance, gas fireplace, kitchenette and bath. All rooms face the sea.
■ **Summerhill Guest House** (glm H)
209 Chu-An Drive ✉ BC V8K 1H9 ☎ 537-2727 📠 531-4301
✉ summerhill@saltspring.com
🖥 www.bestinns.net/canada/bc/rdsummerhill.html
An island guest house overlooking magnificent Sansum Narrows. 3 rooms with shower/bath, balcony, own key.

PRIVATE ACCOMMODATION
■ **Blue Ewe, The** (BF CC H GLM msg NU SA WH)
1207 Beddis Road ✉ BC V8K 2C8 *(on the Gulf Islands)*
☎ 537-9344 ✉ blueewe@saltspring.com
🖥 www.saltspring.com/blueewe
3 double rooms with shower/bath & WC.

Tofino ☎ 250

GUEST HOUSES
■ **West Wind** (BF CC f GLM NU OS VS WH WO)
1321 Pacific Rim, Box 436BC ✉ V0R 2Z0 ☎ 725-2224
📠 725-2212 ✉ westwind@island.net
🖥 www.island.net/~westwind
Small B&B located in beautiful landscape. All rooms with private bath, balcony, Sat-TV/VCR, radio, kitchenette and hair-dryer. Free airport pick up.

Canada/British Columbia — Vancouver

Vancouver ☎ 604

Vancouver is often compared to Hong Kong because of over a quarter million Hong Kong-Chinese people who have established themselves in this city, giving Vancouver an international flair. Investments by new immigrants have led to an economic boom, a dramatic increase in the value of properties and the construction of many new high-rise apartment and office blocks. Vancouver has a beautiful and natural setting, with the Coastal Mountains on the one side and the Pacific Ocean on the other. First class ski resorts are within easy reach. The best known ski resort „Whistler" is about 90 minutes drive from Vancouver. Whistler's Gay Ski Week attracts gay and lesbian skiers from all over the world. Stanley Park is the largest urban park in North America, with over 9 kilometres of pathways.
Vancouver is well known for its rainy weather, but it also has the mildest winters in the country. In January the average temperature is zero while the rest of Canada lies under heavy blankets of snow. In the summer the average temperature from May to September is around 20°C. Popular attractions include the Capilano Suspension Bridge, Chinatown, the food market on Granville Island, the Museum of Anthropology and the shops and cafés along Robinson Street.
Many of the gay bars, cafés and guest houses are located in the West End. One would, however, expect more gay gay bars and danceclubs in a city with a population of over 2 million people. The strict regulations regarding opening and closing times effect the bar buisness. Vancouver offers the gay tourist a wide spectrum of activities from bars, clubs, saunas, gay beaches and many cruising areas. Vancouver Island is also well worth a visit.

Nicht umsonst wird Vancouver immer häufiger mit Hongkong verglichen. Über eine Viertel Million Hongkong-Chinesen haben sich in den letzten Jahren hier niedergelassen und geben der Stadt, trotz Ihrer abgeschiedenen Lage, ein internationales Flair.
Die Stadt erlebt einen regelrechten Boom. Überall entstehen neue Wolkenkratzer, die Grundstückspreise schnellen in die Höhe und neue Wirtschaftszweige lassen sich an der Stadt am Pazifik nieder.
Vancouver liegt von viel Wasser umgeben eindrucksvoll am Fuße der Pacific Ranges. Erstklassige Skigebiete sind in kürzester Zeit zu erreichen. Den bekannten Skiort *Whistler* erreicht man in knapp 90 Minuten. Mit dem Stanley Park verfügt Vancouver zudem über einen der weltgrößten Stadtparks, den man auf einem 9 Kilometer langen Klippenweg umrunden kann.
Zwar ist Vancouver bekannt für seine große Anzahl an Regentagen, doch während der Rest Kanadas im Winter im Schnee versinkt, läßt es sich hier bei Temperaturen über 0°C gut aushalten. Im warmen Sommer (Durschnittstemperatur am Tag von Mai-September über 20°C) tummeln sich Einheimische und Touristen an den zahlreichen Stränden und genießen ein Bad im kühlen aber glasklaren Wasser.
Das schwule Zentrum Vancouvers ist das West End in Downtown gelegen. Hier finden sich die meisten Bars und Cafés, einige sehr gute schwule Bed&Breakfast-Unterkünfte sowie der sehr gut sortierte schwulen Buchladen Little Sister's. Die schwule Szene ist sicherlich nicht so abwechslungsreich, wie man es von einer so großen (Ballungsraum mit mehr als 2 Mio. Einwohner) und lebendigen Stadt erwarten würde. Dies liegt wohl zum größten Teil an der sehr restriktiven Vergabe von Ausschanklizensen sowie der frühen Sperrstunde. Alle Bars und Clubs schließen spätestens um 2 Uhr morgens.
Doch wenn Einheimische sich vielleicht auch über mangelnde Ausgehmöglichkeiten beklagen, so bietet Vancouver dem schwulen Touristen mit seinen Bars, Saunen, schwulen Stränden und zahlreichen Cruising Areas doch genügend Unterhaltungsmöglichkeiten. Und wer etwas länger in der Pazifikmetropole verweilt, sollte auf jeden Fall einen Abstecher zur landschaftlich einmaligen Vancouver Island mit einplanen.

Ce n'est pas pour rien que Vancouver est de plus en plus comparé à Hongkong. Plus d'un quart de million de chinois de Hongkong se sont établis ici au cours de ces dernière années et confèrent à la ville, en dépit de sa situation isolée, une atmosphère internationale. La ville connaît un véritable boom. De nouveaux gratte-ciel naissent partout, les prix des terrains augmentent de façon vertigineuse et de nouveaux secteurs économiques s'établissent dans la ville du pacifique. Vancouver se trouve au pied du Pacific Ranges entourée de manière impressionnante de beaucoup d'eau. On accède à des régions de ski de premier ordre en peu de temps. Le lieu de ski *Whistler* est atteint en moins de 90 minutes. Vancouver dispose, en outre, du parc municipal le plus grand du monde que l'on peut parcourir le long d'un chemin d'écueil de 9 kilomètres de long. Certes, la région de Vancouver est connue pour son grand nombre de jours de pluie, tandis que le reste du Canada est englouti en hiver dans la neige, on se trouve bien ici grâce à des températures de plus de 0°C. En été, où la température moyenne pendant la journée est de 20°C, et ce du mois de mai à septembre, les natifs et les touristes s'ébattent sur les nombreuses plages et jouissent d'un bain dans l'eau froide mais limpide. Le centre d'homosexuels de Vancouver est le „West End" situé au centre de la ville. C'est ici que se trouvent ainsi que la librairie d'homosexuels Little Sister's bien assortie. La scène d'homosexuels n'est assurément pas aussi variée de ce qu'on pourrait attendre d'une ville aussi grande (zone de concentration urbaine de plus de 2 millions d'habitants) et aussi animée. Ceci est probablement dû en grande partie à l'attribution très restrictive des licences de débit de boissons et aux heures de fermeture avancées. Tous les bars et clubs ferment à 2 heures du matin au plus tard. Pourtant, si les natifs se plaignent peut-être du manque de possibilités de sortie, Vancouver offre cependant aux touristes homosexuels suffisamment de possibilités de divertissement grâce à ses bars, saunas, plages réservées aux homosexuels et nombreuses zones d'excursion (Cruising Areas). Et celui qui séjourne un peu plus longtemps dans la métropole du Pacifique devrait en tous cas faire un crochet sur l'île de Vancouver unique quant à son paysage.

Vancouver se compara mucho, y con razón, con Hongkong. En los últimos años más de 250.000 chinos han fijado su residencia aqui. A pesar que Vancouver se encuentre, geográficamente hablando, muy aislada, sus emigrantes le dan un carácter muy cosmopolita. La ciudad vive un auge vertiginoso, por todas partes se construyen rascacielos, los precios de vivienda suben sin parar y nuevas industrias se están estableciendo. Vancouver está situado a orillas del Pacífico al pie de las montañas Pacific Ranges. Por esta razón ofrece la zona verdaderos paraísos para la práctica del esqui, buen ejemplo es „II" a solamente 90 minutos de distancia. Vancouver se enorgullece de tener uno de los parques de mayor extensión en todo el mundo, el impresionante Stanley Park. Aunque la ciudad tiene fama por sus numerosos dias de lluvia, en invierno, cuando el resto de Canada se cubre de nieve, aqui se disfruta de temperaturas que sobrepasan los 0°C. Durante los veranos calurosos (Con temperaturas medias de 20°C de mayo a septiembre) los inumerables playas se llenan de gente, que disfrutan de un baño en aguas cristalinas. El centro gay de Vancouver se encuentra en West End, Downtown. Aqui se concentra el mayor número de bares y cafeterias, algunos excelentes hotels gays (Bed&Breakfast), y la libería Little Sister's con una amplia oferta de literatura homosexual. Sin embargo, el ambiente gay no ofrece tanta variedad, como es de esperar de una ciudad tan grande (aglomeración úrbana con más de 2 millones de habitantes) y vivaz. Esto se debe en gran parte a las restrictivas concesiones para la venta de bebidas alcohólicas, como a la hora temprana del cierre. Todos los bares y clubs cierran como muy tarde a las 2

Vancouver | British Columbia/Canada

Vancouver

1. Lola's at the Century House Restaurant
2. Ms T's Bar
3. Club Vancouver Sauna
4. Heritage House Hotel / Uncle Charlies Bar
5. Dufferin Hotel
6. Mack's Leather Shop
7. Royal Hotel & Bar
8. The Odyssey Danceclub
9. Number Danceclub
10. Xtra West Gay Info
11. Fahrenheit 212° Sauna
12. Doll & Penny's Restaurant
13. Colibri Bed & Breakfast
14. Little Sister's Bookshop
15. West End Guest House
16. Delilah's Restaurant
17. Denmans Station Bar

Canada/British Columbia — Vancouver

de la mañana. Aunque la gente de Vancouver se queje sobre las pocas posibilidades de diversión, el turista encuentra en los bares, saunas, playas gay y las numerosas areas de cruising abundantes sitios para pasárlo bien. Uno de los sitios dignos de visitar es Vancouver Island con su impresionante paisaje.

Non per caso si fa il confronto tra Vancouver e Hongkong. Negli ultimi anni più di 250.000 cinesi di Hongkong si sono stabiliti qui e, malgrado la sua posizione isolata, danno alla città un carattere internazionale. La città vede un vero e proprio boom economico. Dappertutto emergono nuovi grattacieli, i prezzi degli immobili salgono alle stelle e si sviluppano nuovi settori economici nella città sul pacifico. Vancouver, situato pittorescamente ai piedi delle Pacific Ranges, è circondato da molta acqua. Le zone di prima classe per sciare sono facili da raggiungere, p.es. al famoso *Whistler* si arriva entro un'ora e mezzo. Il Stanley Park, uno dei più grandi parchi comunali, si può percorrere per mezzo di una strada sopra uno scoglio lunga 9 kilometri. Anche se Vancouver viene nominata come la città con i massimi giorni di pioggia, mentre però nel resto del paese in inverno si sprofonda nella neve, Vancouver può vantarsi di temperature sopra lo zero. Nelle calde estati (temperatura media giornaliera da maggio a settembre sopra i 20 gradi) gli abitanti e i turisti si divertono sulle numerose spiagge e godono di fare il bagno nelle acque limpide e fresche. Il centro gay di Vancouver è il West End in Downtown. Qui si trova la maggior parte dei bar, alcuni buoni soggiorni Bed&Breakfast per gay e la libreria gay Little Sister's con un buon assortimento. L'ambiente gay non è tanto vasto come ci si potrebbe aspettare da una città così grande (città e hinterland con più di 2 milioni di abitanti); questo può dipendere da una restrittiva aggiudicazione delle licenze per lo spaccio e dall'orario d'apertura. Tutti i bar e i club chiudono infatti alle due di notte. Ma anche se gli abitanti si lamentano per le poche possibilità di uscire, Vancouver con i suoi numerosi bar, saune, spiagge gay e Cruising Areas offre al turista gay abbastanza occasioni per divertirsi. E per chi intende intrattenersi un po' più a lungo nella metropoli sul pacifico, dovrebbe in ogni caso fare un salto alla Vancouver Island che vanta di un'unico paesaggio.

GAY INFO

■ **Gay and Lesbian Center** (GLM) Business line: 10-19 / Switchboard: 19-22 h
1170 Bute Street, Suite 4 *(2nd floor)* ☎ 684-5307 (Business line) ☎ 684-6869 (Switchboard)
Houses gay/lesbian switchboard, counselling services, library, food bank and a legal clinic.

PUBLICATIONS

■ **XTRA West** Mon-Fri 9-17 h
501-1033 Davie Street ✉ BC V6E 1M7 ☎ 684-9696 📠 684-9697
📧 XWeditor@Xtra.ca 🌐 www.xtra.ca
Vancouver's gay and lesbian bi-weekly newspaper. Contains news, arts, and entertainment information.

CULTURE

■ **Out On The Shelves** Mon 19.30-21.30, Wed 15-18 h
1170 Bute Street ✉ BC V6E 1Z6 ☎ 684-5309
One of Canada's largest G&L Library.

BARS

■ **Denman Station** (B D G lj MA s) 19-2 h
860 Denman Street ✉ BC V6G 2L8 *(at Haro Street)* ☎ 669-3448
■ **Dufferin** (B Glm MA OS SNU STV)
900 Seymour Street ✉ BC V6B 3L9 ☎ 683-4251

■ **Fountainhead** (B GLM MA)
1025 Davie Street ✉ BC V6E 1M5 ☎ 687-2222
■ **Lava Lounge** (B GLM)
1180 Greanville Street ✉ BC V6Z 1L8 *(at Davie Street)* ☎ 605-6136
■ **Ms T's** (B G LJ) Mon-Sat 20- h
339 West Pender Street ✉ BC V6E 1T3 ☎ 682-8096
■ **Royal Hotel Pub** (B GLM S) 11-24 h
1025 Granville Street ✉ BC V6Z 1L4 ☎ 685-5335
Live entertainment and many special parties.
■ **Uncle Charlies** (B G MA)
c/o Heritage House Hotel, 455 Abbott Street ☎ 685-7777

CAFES

■ **Edge Coffee Bar. The** (b BF f glm) Mon-Sat 7-4, Sun -2 h
1148 Davie Street ✉ BC V6E 1N1 ☎ 688-3395

DANCECLUBS

■ **Numbers** (AC B D G MA VS) 20-2, Sun -24 h
1042 Davie Street, Burrard ✉ BC V6E 1M3 ☎ 685-4077
■ **Odyssey. The** (AC B D G OS s YG) 19-2 h
1251 Howe Street ☎ 689-5256

RESTAURANTS

■ **Delilah's** (B E F glm)
1739 Comox ☎ 687-3424
■ **Doll and Penny's** (B F glm TV) Mon-Thu 7-4, Fri Sat 0-24 h
1167 Davie Street ✉ BC V6E 1N2 ☎ 685-3417
■ **Harry's Off Commercial** (B F glm)
1716 Charles Street ☎ 253-1789
■ **Homer's Bar** (b BF F glm)
1249 Howe Street ☎ 689-2444
■ **Lola's at the Century House** (B F glm)
432 Richards Street ✉ BC V6B 2Z3 ☎ 684-5652
Award-winning cooking in elegant setting.
■ **Mongolie Grill. The** (F glm)
1108-4th Street , SW ☎ 262-7773
■ **Taki's Taverna** (B F glm)
1106 Davie Street ☎ 682-1336
■ **Water Street Café. The** (B F glm)
300 Water Street ☎ 689-2832

SHOWS

■ **Lotus Cabaret** (B GLM MA STV) 20-2 h
c/o Heritage House Hotel, 455 Abbott Street ✉ V6B 2L2 ☎ 685-7777
Cabaret and bar. Popular.

SEX SHOPS/BLUE MOVIES

■ **Willy's Books & Video** (glm) 10-23 h
1109 Granville Street ☎ 685-3226

SAUNAS/BATHS

■ **Club Vancouver** (AC CC DR f G MA P SB VS WO) 0-24 h
399 West Pender Street ✉ BC V6B 1T3 *(2 blocks north of stadium, corner Homer)* ☎ 681-5719
Sauna attracting gay/bi men of all ages.
■ **Fahrenheit 212°** (AC cc DR f G P SB VS WH WO YG) 0-24 h
1048 Davie Street ✉ BC V6E 1M3 *(between Burrard St. and Thurlow St.)* ☎ 689-9719
Very clean and well-equipped sauna on 6500 sq ft in the heart of the gay community. Tue Buddy night.
■ **Richards Street Service Club** (b DR f G SA SB VS) 0-24 h
1169 Richards Street ✉ BC V6B 3E7 *(at Davie Street)* ☎ 684-6010
Sauna established since 1970 frequented by a mixed age crowd. Free condoms and towels. Sling and glory holes.

Vancouver | **British Columbia/Canada**

BOOK SHOPS
■ **Little Sisters Book and Art Emporium** (AC GLM JSF) 10-23 h
1238 Davie Street ✉ BC V6E 1N4 ☎ 669-1753
Free maps of gay Vancouver available. Literary events.

LEATHER & FETISH SHOPS
■ **Mack's Leathers Incorporated** (glm LJ MA) Sun-Wed 11-19, Thu-Fri -20 h
1043 Granville Street ✉ BC L1V 3A5 ☎ 688-6225
Leather articles, accessories and toys. Also body piercing. Mail order under www.macks.bc.ca

TRAVEL AND TRANSPORT
■ **Gaytour Vancouver** (GLM)
208-2333 Triumph Street ✉ BC V5L 1L4 ☎ 377-3584
🖶 253-4512 ✉ audience@integrate.ca
Guided city tours, meet & greet services, adventure tours, cycling tours, walking tours & other related services.

VIDEO SHOPS
■ **Videomatica** (glm MA VS) 10-22 h
1855 West 4th Avenue ✉ BC V6J 1M4 ☎ 734-5452
Good selection of gay and lesbian films.

HOTELS
■ **Dufferin Hotel** (B CC F G H lj MA)
900 Seymour Street/Smithe ✉ BC V6B 3L9 (*Downtown Vancouver, close to the scene*) ☎ 683-4251 🖶 683-0611 ✉ indigo@direct.ca
✉ www.dufferinhotel.com
Hotel with restaurant and bar located in the heart of the city.
■ **Heritage House Hotel** (AC B CC d GLM H MA)
455 Abbott Street ✉ BC V6B 2L2 (*Convenient location, 10 km to the airport*) ☎ 685-7777 🖶 685-7067
110 double rooms. TV and phone (local calls free of charge) in all rooms.
■ **Royal Hotel** (AC B CC GLM H MA)
1025 Granville Street ✉ BC V6Z 1L4 ☎ 685-5335,
☎ (1-877) 685-5337 (toll-free) 🖶 685-5331
✉ frontdesk@attheroyal.com ✉ www.attheroyal.com
Newly renovated gay accommodation. 82 rooms with ensuite bath (Can$ 79-129.-) or semi-private bath (59-99.-) available in a variety of combinations of single, double and queen-sized beds on four different levels. Also gay pub „ The Royal".

GUEST HOUSES
■ **Albion Guest House** (BF CC GLM H)
592 West 19th Avenue ✉ BC V5Z 1W6 (*Centrally located*)
☎ 873-2287 🖶 879-5682
■ **Colibri Bed & Breakfast** (BF CC GLM H MA) All year
1101 Thurlow Street ✉ BC V6E 1W9 (*City centre, 2 blocks from bars, clubs and restaurants*) ☎ 689-5100 🖶 682-3925
✉ colibri@home.com
■ **Don's Home Away From Home Guest House** (g H)
6870 MacPherson Avenue, Burnaby B.C. ☎ 435-3037
■ **Nelson House** (BF CC GLM H) closed Christmas and New Year's week
977 Broughton Street ✉ BC V6G 2A4 ☎ 684-9793
✉ bestinvan@lightspeed.bc.ca
Walking distance to downtown. Suite with jacuzzi, 3 rooms with private bath, 2 rooms which share a bath.
■ **West End Guest House** (BF glm H) Reservations 8-21 h
1362 Haro Street ✉ BC V6E 1G2 (*in the West End*) ☎ 681-2889
🖶 688-8812 ✉ wegh@idmail.com
✉ www.westendguesthouse.com
Victorian style house. Rooms decorated with antiques.

VISIT VANCOUVER'S #1 GAY HOTEL/BAR COMPLEX

STAY GAY

Royal Hotel
Vancouver, Canada

1025 Granville St.
Vancouver, B.C.,
Canada V6Z 1L4

Tel: (604) 685-5335
Toll Free: 1-877-685-5337
   (within North America)
Fax: (604) 685-5351

www.attheroyal.com

GENERAL GROUPS
■ **Gays, Lesbians and Bisexuals of UBC**
SUB, PO Box 9, UBC ✉ BC V6T 1W5 ☎ 822-4638

FETISH GROUPS
■ **Vancouver Leather Alliance (VLA)**
c/o Northwind, PO Box 2253 ✉ BC V6B 3W2 ☎ 88-9378 ext. 2035

HEALTH GROUPS
■ **AIDS Vancouver** 24 hours
1107 Seymour Street (*at Helmcken*) ☎ 687-5220
Houses AIDS Research Centre (switchboard, library).
■ **Helpline**
☎ 687-2437

SPECIAL INTEREST GROUPS
■ **Lesbian and Gay Youth**
SUB, PO Box 9, UBC ✉ BC V6T 1W5 ☎ 684-6869
Support and activity group for teenagers.
■ **Over 40's Group** Meets last Sat
SUB, PO Box 9, UBC ✉ BC V6T 1W5 ☎ 689-9219

SPORT GROUPS
■ **Vancouver Tennis Association**
1170 Bute Street ✉ BC V6E 1Z6 ☎ 875-8646

SWIMMING
-**Wreck Beach** (G NU) (*Near the University of British Columbia campus, plenty of action in the wooded area. Access by several paths with about 200 steps down from* P *along roadside*)

Canada/British Columbia - Manitoba

Vancouver ▶ Winnipeg

CRUISING
-Stanley Park (day and night. East of [P] 2nd beach)
-Central Park
-English Bay Bath House
-Kitsilano Park (at the pool)
-Burnette River Park (New Westminster)

Vernon ☎ 250

GUEST HOUSES
■ **Rainbow's End B & B** (BF GLM H MA WH)
8282 Jackpine Road ✉ BC V1B 3M7 *(near Silver Star Park)*
☎ 542-4842 💻 rainbowsend@telus.net

Victoria ☎ 250

BARS
■ **BJ's Lounge** (AC B CC d f GLM MA STV VS) 12-2, Sun -24 h
642 Johnson Street ✉ BC V8W 1M6 *(Corner of Broad and Johnson Street)* ☎ 388-0505

RESTAURANTS
■ **Friends of Dorothy's Café** (F GLM) Mon-Wed 11.30-20, Thu-Sat -4, Sun 11-20 h
615 Johnson Street ☎ 381 2277
Will deliver to BJ's Lounge.

SAUNAS/BATHS
■ **Steamworks** (b DR f G MA p SA VS) 19-9 h
582 Johnson Street ✉ BC V9W 1M6 ☎ 383-6623
Sauna with juice bar frequented by a young-middle aged crowd.

HOTELS
■ **Camellia House** (BF GLM H)
1994 Leighton Road ✉ BC V8R 1N6 ☎ 370-2816

GUEST HOUSES
■ **Weekender Bed & Breakfast** (BF GLM H msg)
10 Eberts Street ✉ BC V8S 5L6 ☎ 389-1688
💻 www.bctravel.com/weekender.html
Located along Victoria's scenic drive. All rooms with shower/bath/WC, telephone, heating, own key.

HEALTH GROUPS
■ **AIDS Vancouver Island**
304-733 Johnson Street ✉ BC V8W 3C7 ☎ 384-4554

CRUISING
-Beacon Hill Park (along Dallas Road)
-The Causeway (in front of the Embassy Hotel)
-Government Street (in front of the Empress Hotel)

CDN-Manitoba

Location:	Central CDN
Initials:	MB
Time:	GMT -6
Area:	650,000 km2 / 250,965 sq mi.
Population:	1,145,000
Capital:	Winnipeg

Brandon ☎ 204

GENERAL GROUPS
■ **Gays and Lesbians of Brandon & Elsewehre (GLOBE)** Fri 19-21 h
PO Box 220 39 ✉ MB R7A 6Y2 ☎ 727-4297

HEALTH GROUPS
■ **AIDS Brandon**
PO Box 32 ✉ MB R7A 6Y2 ☎ 726-4020 📠 728-4344

Winnipeg ☎ 204

GAY INFO
■ **Rainbow Resource Centre** (GLM) Mon-Sat 19.30-22, Wed-Fri 13-16.30 h
222 Osborne Street South, #1 ✉ MB R3C 2Z6 ☎ 284-5208
📠 478-1160 💻 wglrc@escape.ca
💻 www.rainbowresourcecentre.homepage.com
Phone-line, Drop-in/groups, library archive, meeting place for gay/lesbian groups. Non-profit organisation.

PUBLICATIONS
■ **Swerve Newsmagazine** (GLM) Mon Wed Fri 10-15 h
200-63 Albert Street ✉ MB R3B 1G4 *(2nd floor)* ☎ 942-4599
📠 947-0554 💻 swerve@pangea.ca
Monthly newspaper.

BARS
■ **Gio's** (B D Glm MA P SNU) 21-2, Fri -3.30 h
272 Sherbrook Street ✉ MB R3C 2B9 ☎ 786-1236

DANCECLUBS
■ **Club 200** (AC B CC D F GLM MA STV WE) Mon-Sat 16-2, Sun -22 h
190 Garry Street ✉ MB R3C 1G6 ☎ 943-6045
Gay & lesbian bar, restaurant & danceclub.
■ **Happenings** (AC B D GLM snu stv VS WE YG)
Mon-Wed 21-2.30, Thu 20-3.45 (SNU), Fri -3 (STV), Sat -3.30 h
274 Sherbrook Street ✉ MB R3C 2B9 *(at Broadway Avenue, upstairs)* ☎ 774-3576
Very popular on Sat nights. Gay dance bar & lounge.

SAUNAS/BATHS
■ **Adonis Spa** (AC G MA SA SB VS) 0-24 h
1060 Main Street ✉ MB R2W 3R7 *(at Burrows Street, just north of downtown)* ☎ 589-6133
Newly renovated. Regular & Deluxe rooms on offer.

BOOK SHOPS
■ **McNally Robinson** (glm)
1120 Grant Avenue, Unit 4000 ☎ 475-0483

GUEST HOUSES
■ **Masson's Bed and Breakfast** (AC BF glm H MA)
181 Masson Street ✉ MB R2H 0H3 *(15 min walk to centre)*
☎ 237-9230 📠 237-9230 💻 massbnb@home.com
💻 www.members.home.net/massbnb
Victorian B&B. All rooms furnished in quaint turn-of-the-century decor. Single rooms Can$ 40.-, double 50-55.- incl. BF. Parking available.
■ **Winged Ox Guest House** (GLM H)
82 Spence Street ✉ MB R3C 1Y3 ☎ 783-7408 📠 783-7408
💻 winged-ox@gaycanada.com 💻 www.gaycanada.com/winged-ox

GENERAL GROUPS
■ **Federal Sexual Orientation Lobby** (GLM)
PO Box 1661 ✉ MB R3C 2Z6 ☎ 284-5208
Political group working for equality of gays and lesbians in federal legislation.
■ **Prime Timers** (G MG OG) 4th Wed. 19 h at Gio's
26072, 116 Sherbrook Street ✉ MB R3K 4K9 ☎ 889-2835
📠 888-0451
For men over 40.

Winnipeg ▸ Saint John — Manitoba - New Brunswick/Canada

FETISH GROUPS
■ **Club Winnipeg**
PO Box 1697 ✉ MB R3C 2Z6 ☎ 582-6331
Country, leather, uniforms, bears mixed social group.

HEALTH GROUPS
■ **Nine Circles**
705 Broadway ✉ MB R3G 0X2 ☎ 940-6000
■ **Provincial AIDS/STD Line** Mon-Fri 8.30-20.30 h
☎ 945-2437 ☎ 1-800-782-2437

SWIMMING
-Beaconia Beach (AYOR g nu) (located on Lake Winnipeg; drive on Hwy 59 about 70 km north of Winnipeg; turn west on PR 500. After you pass the gas station, continue due west on the gravel road until you reach parking lot. Walk to beach, turn left and walk about fifteen minutes to reach nudist area. Gay section is at far south end of beach)

CRUISING
-Bonnycastle Park (ayor) (at night)
-Assiniboine Park (AYOR) (washrooms & parking lot, 250 m west of Pavilion weekday afternoons)
-[P] Assiniboine Avenue (between Main and Fort Street)
-TD Centre concourse (AYOR) (washrooms near the food courts)

CDN-New Brunswick

Location: East CDN
Initials: NB
Time: GMT -4, -5
Area: 73,000 km2 / 28,185 sq mi.
Population: 762,000
Capital: Fredericton

Bathurst ☎ 506

GENERAL GROUPS
■ **Gales nor Gays (GNG)**
PO Box 983 ✉ NB E2A 4H8 ☎ 783-7440 📧 andre@nbnet.nb.ca

Fredericton ☎ 506

DANCECLUBS
■ **G Spot** (B CC D glm MA) 20-2 h, closed Mon
377 King Street ✉ NB E3B 1E4 *(3r floor)* ☎ 455-7768

BOOK SHOPS
■ **Beegie's Bookstore**
Fredericton Mall, Prospect Street ☎ 459-3936

GENERAL GROUPS
■ **Fredericton Lesbians & Gays (FLAG)** (GLM MA)
PO Box 1556, Station A ✉ NB E3B 5G2 ☎ 457-2156
📧 jwhitehe@unb.ca
📧 www.geocities.com/WestHollywood/3074/contente.htm
■ **New Brunswick Coalition for Human Rights Reform**
785 Aberdeen Street ✉ NB E3B 1S7 ☎ 457-2514
📧 righters@nbnet.nb.ca
National political advocacy group.
■ **Rainbow Pride (Fredericton lesbian, gay and bisxeual youth group)**
📧 www.gaycanada.com/rp_nb/low_rpf.htm

HEALTH GROUPS
■ **AIDS New Brunswick** Mon-Fri 8.30-16.30 h
c/o Victoria Health Centre, 65 Brunswick Street ✉ NB E3B 1G5
☎ 459-7518 ☎ (800) 561-4009 (toll-free) ☎ 459-5782
📧 sidaids@nbnet.nb.ca 📧 www.aidsnb.com
Information, referral and counselling.

RELIGIOUS GROUPS
■ **Living Waters Community Church** Sun 19 h
c/o E. Gibson, 98 Cityview Avenue ✉ NB E3A 1S8
☎ 472-3376 📧 living_waters@hotmail.com

SPECIAL INTEREST GROUPS
■ **East Coast Bears** (G)
PO Box 1492, Station A ✉ NB E3B 5G2 📧 lairbear@nbnet.nb.ca
📧 www.personal.nbnet.nb.ca/lairbear/
Group of Bears and their fans.
■ **Gay & Lesbian Alliance of University of New Brunswick (GA-LA)** (GLM) Meets Wed 19 h at room 19E1, Alumni Memorial Bldg. at UNB/STU
c/o Help Centre, UNB SUB, PO Box 4400 ✉ NB E3B 5A3
☎ 453-4955 📠 453-4958. 📧 gala@unb.ca
📧 www.unb.ca/web/gala/webpages/gala.html

CRUISING
-Riverside park (AYOR) (located between the Lord Beaverbrook Hotel and the railway bridge)
-Regent Mall
-YMCA swimming bath

Moncton ☎ 506

BARS
■ **Triangles** (B GLM MA)
234 St. George Street ✉ NB E1C 1V8 ☎ 857-8779

HEALTH GROUPS
■ **SIDA/AIDS Moncton**
165-A Gordon Street ✉ NB E1C 1N1 ☎ 859-9616 📠 855-4526

Saint John ☎ 506

DANCECLUBS
■ **Bogarts** (B D GLM) Wed-Sat 21-2 h
9 Sydney Street ✉ NB E2L 2L1 ☎ 652-2004

GUEST HOUSES
■ **Mahogany Manor** (CC e glm H)
220 Germain Street ✉ NB E2L 2G4 ☎ 636-8000 📠 636-8001
📧 leavittr@nbnet.nb.ca 📧 www.sjnow.com/mm
Victorian house with five elegant guest rooms located in the heart of uptown Saint John. Rooms with private bath/WC, telephone, radio and heating. TV room with video. No pets. Smoke-free environment. Special diets may be accomodated. Open all year.

HEALTH GROUPS
■ **AIDS Saint John**
115 Hazen Street ✉ NB E2L 3L3 ☎ 652-2437 📠 652-2438
📧 aidssj@fundy.net

CRUISING
-Carlton Street (r) (near Old Stone Church)
-City Market
-Princess Street (near Union)
-Rockwood Park (beach and trails)

Canada/Newfoundland - Nova Scotia | Saint John's ▶ Halifax

CDN-Newfoundland

Location: East CDN
Initials: NF
Time: GMT -4
Area: 405,000 km2 / 156,370 sq mi.
Population: 564,000
Capital: St. John's

Saint John's ☎ 709

GAY INFO

■ **Gay & Lesbian Support & Info Line** Thu 19-22 h
PO Box 6121 ✉ A1C 6J9 ☎ 753-4297 ⌨ glbt_cbt@yahoo.ca
🖥 ngalecb.tripod.com/
24-hour message service.

BARS

■ **Junctions** (B d glm MA)
208 Water Street ✉ NF A1C 6E7 ☎ 579-2557
■ **Zone 2-1-6** (B CC D GLM lj MA STV VS WE) Wed Sun 21-2, Fri-Sat -4.30 h
216 Water Street ✉ NF A1C 1A9 ☎ 754-2492
The only gay bar in St. John's.

RESTAURANTS

■ **Biarritz On The Square** (b F glm)
188 Duckworth Street ✉ NF A1C 1G5 ☎ 726-3885
Seafood, lunch and dinner specials.
■ **Stella's Restaurant** (b F glm)
106 Water Street ✉ NF A1C 1A7 ☎ 753 96 25
Vegetarian dishes, seafood and delicious desserts.

BOOK SHOPS

■ **Bennington Gate Bookstore** (glm)
8-10 Rowan Street (Lower Level, terrace on the Square, Churchill Square) ☎ 576-6600
Large selection of gay and lesbian books.
■ **Wordplay Bookstore** (glm)
221 Duckworth Street ✉ NF A1C 1G7 ☎ 726-9193

PRIVATE ACCOMMODATION

■ **Abba Inn** (AC BF CC f glm H WH)
36 Queen's Road ✉ NF A1C 2A5 (near City Hall) ☎ 754-0047
☎ (800) 563 3959 (toll-free) 📠 754-0047 ⌨
abba@roadrunner.nf.net 🖥 www.wordplay.com/abba_inn
Comfortable Bed and Breakfast in a refurbished Queen Anne townhouse. All rooms with en-suite bathroom, cable TV, alarm clock, radio, telephone and ceiling-fan. Non-smoking. Free BF.
■ **Banberry House Bed & Breakfast** (BF CC glm H) 9-22:30 h
116 Military Road ✉ NF A1C 2C9 ☎ 579-8006 📠 579 3443
⌨ banberry@bigfoot.com 🖥 www.bbcanada.com/1780.html
Small B&B in nice Victorian home. All rooms with private bath, radio, hair-dryer and own key.

GENERAL GROUPS

■ **NGALE (NF Gays & Lesbians for Equality)** Please call for details
PO Box 6121 ✉ NF A1C 6J9 (Conference Room C, at Corporate Office, St. John's Health Care Corporation, Waterford Bridge Road)
☎ 753-4297 ⌨ ngale@geocities.com
🖥 www.geocities.com/WestHollywood/4291
■ **PFLAG (Parents, Family & Friends of Lesbians & Gays)**
PO Box 6121 ✉ NF A1C 6J9 ☎ 753-4297
🖥 www.geocities.com/westhollywood/4291

HEALTH GROUPS

■ **Newfoundland and Labrador AIDS Committee**
198 Water Street (3rd floor) ☎ 579-8656 ☎ (1 800) 563-1575
⌨ nlac@avalon.nf.ca

CDN-Nova Scotia

Location: East CDN
Initials: NS
Time: GMT -4
Area: 56,000 km2 / 21,612 sq mi.
Population: 948,000
Capital: Halifax

Antigonish ☎ 902

GENERAL GROUPS

■ **GLBX (Gays, Lesbians and Bisexuals at X)**
PO Box 1842, Town Post Office ✉ NS B2G 1F4 ☎ 867-5007
⌨ glbx@stfx.ca 🖥 www.juliet.sfx.ca/~glbx/

Halifax ☎ 902

PUBLICATIONS

■ **Wayves**
PO Box 340 90 ✉ NS B3J 3S1 ☎ 826-7356
⌨ wayves@fox.nstn.ca
🖥 www.chebucto.ns.ca/CommunitySupport/Wayves
Gay and Lesbian monthly magazine for Atlantic Canadians. Free at many locations.

BARS

■ **Club NRB** (B CC D f GLM MA N OS STV YG)
2099 Gottingen Street ✉ NS B3K 3B3
■ **Eagle. The** (B CC f G MA N) Mon-Fri 11.30-2h, Sat & Sun 15-2h
2104 Gottingen Street ✉ B3K 3B3 (upstairs) ☎ 425-6976
Home of the Mr Gay Leatherman Atlantic competition.
■ **Reflections** (AC B CC f GLM LJ MA STV) 16-4 h
5184 Sackville Street ✉ NS B3S 2N1 ☎ 422-2957
Popular club. Various theme nights.

CAFES

■ **Grabbajabba** (b glm MA)
5475 Spring Garden Road ✉ NS B3J 3T2 ☎ 423-1651

RESTAURANTS

■ **Bistro. Le** (b F glm)
1333 South Park ☎ 423-8428

SAUNAS/BATHS

■ **Apollo Sauna Bath** (DR G MA p SA) 19-24 h, closed Sun
1547 Barrington Street ✉ NS B3J 1Z4 (at Blowers Street)
☎ 423-6549

BOOK SHOPS

■ **Atlantic News** (AC CC GLM) Mon-Sat 8-22, Sun 9-22 h
5560 Morris Street ✉ NS B3J 1C2 (at Queen St.)
☎ 429-5468
Gay and international magazines.

GUEST HOUSES

■ **Bob's B&B** (BF glm H WH)
2715 Windsor Street ✉ NS B3K 5EI (5 minutes drive to town center, 30 min to airport) ☎ 454-4374
Non-smoking bed and breakfast, 6 rooms with shared and private baths, balcony and radio.

Halifax ▶ Guelph — Nova Scotia - Ontario/Canada

PRIVATE ACCOMMODATION
■ **Centretown B&B** (AC BF CC GLM H)
2016 Oxford Street ✉ NS B3L 2T2 ☎ 422-2380
📧 stephenp@fox.nstn.ca
1920's style bungalow with veranda in central location. Own key. Non-smoking. Laundry facilities.
■ **Fresh Start B&B** (BF CC glm H)
2720 Gottingen Street ✉ NS B3K 3C7 ☎ 453-6316
🖨 453-6617

GENERAL GROUPS
■ **Humans against Homophobia (HAH)**
☎ 494-6662 📧 nspirg@is2.dal.ca
■ **PFLAG (Parents, Family & Friends of Lesbians & Gays)** 3rd Mon 14 h
☎ 443-3747 (Ron Gamett-Doucette) 📧 ab274@chebucto.na.ca

FETISH GROUPS
■ **Tightrope**
PO Box 33067 ✉ NS B3L 4T6 ☎ 423-6127
🌐 www.geocities.com/tightropeehfx/
Men's leather, denim, uniform group.

HEALTH GROUPS
■ **AIDS Coalition of Nova Scotia** Mon-Fri 10-16 h
5675 Spring Garden Road, Suite 600 ✉ NS B3J 1H1 ☎ 425-4882
☎ 425-7922 🖨 422-6200 📧 acns@kayhay.com
🌐 www.nsnet/org/acns/
■ **Anonymous HIV/AIDS Testing**
☎ 455-9656

RELIGIOUS GROUPS
■ **Affirm United**
PO Box 33067 ✉ NS B3H 4T6 📧 stewarar@gov.ns.ca

SPECIAL INTEREST GROUPS
■ **BGLAD (Bisexual, Gay and Lesbian Association of Dalhousie)**
c/o SUB, 6136 University Avenue ✉ NS B3H 4J2 ☎ 494-1256
📧 bglad@is2.dal.ca
Group for LGB students.
■ **Gay, Lesbian & Bisexual Youth Group at Q.E.H.**
☎ 421-6797 (Jeannie Buffet)
■ **JUKA (Black, Gay, Lesbian, Bisexuals & Friends)**
☎ 454-5884 (Les Gray)

SWIMMING
-Crystal Crescent (g NU) (25 km from Halifax. 15 min walk from [P]. Best on the rocks)

CRUISING
-Citadel Hill (at night)
-Public Gardens

New Glasgow ☎ 902

HEALTH GROUPS
■ **Pictou County AIDS Coalition**
PO Box 964 ✉ NS B2H 5K7 ☎ 752-6218

Sydney ☎ 902

HEALTH GROUPS
■ **AIDS Coalition of Cape Breton (ACCB)**
PO Box 177 ✉ NS B1P 6H1 ☎ 567-1766
📧 sharpadvice@hotmail.com 🌐 www.accb.ns.ca/sane.html

Wolfville ☎ 902

GENERAL GROUPS
■ **Valley Pride Group** Meets Tue 19 h at Coffee Merchant, 334 Main Street
🌐 www.geocities.com/WestHollywood/Heights/2377

CDN-Ontario
Location: Central-West CDN
Initials: ON
Time: GMT -5
Area: 1,067,000 km2 / 411,969 sq mi.
Population: 11,408,000
Capital: Toronto

Cambridge ☎ 519

BARS
■ **Robin's Nest** (B glm MA)
26 Hobson Street ☎ 621-2688

Fort Erie ☎ 905

SAUNAS/BATHS
■ **Fort Erie Sauna** (G SA SB) 0-24 h
216 Jarvis Street ✉ ON L2A 2S5 ☎ 871-0023

Grand Valley ☎ 519

HOTELS
■ **Manfred's Meadow Guest House** (F G H NU SA SOL WH WO)
R.R. N° 1 ✉ ON L0N 1G0 ☎ 925-5306 🖨 925 0447
📧 milton@frexnet.com 🌐 www.geocities.com/WestHollywood
With a man made lake. All rooms with private bath and balcony. Full board possible.

Guelph ☎ 519

GAY INFO
■ **Gay Lesbian Bi Transgendered Outline** 0-24 h
☎ 836-4550
Recorded information.

CAFES
■ **Bookshelf Café. The** (b f glm) 9-21 h
41 Quebec Street ☎ 821-3311

GENERAL GROUPS
■ **Guelph Queer Equality**
c/o CSA, UC, University of Guelph ✉ ON N1G 2W1 ☎ 824-4120
📧 gqe@uoguelph.ca
■ **Rainbow Chorus**
☎ 821-2539

HEALTH GROUPS
■ **AIDS Committee of Guelph & Wellington County** Mon-Fri 8-18 h
204-85 Norfolk Street ☎ 763-2255 ☎ 763-8265 (infoline)
🖨 763-8125

CRUISING
-Royal City Park (along Wellington Street)
-Exhibition Park (parking lots at night)

SPARTACUS 2001/2002 | 129

Hamilton ☎ 905

BARS
■ **Amigos Bar** (B glm)
121 Hughson Street ✉ ON L8R 1G7 ☎ 546-5258
■ **Bombay Club. The** (AC B D F GLM MA N TV) 12-2 h
121 Hughson Street North ✉ ON L8R 1G7 *(between Wilson & Cannon Street)* ☎ 540-8008
■ **Windsor Bar** (B g)
31 John Street ✉ ON L8R 1H2 *(at King William Street)* ☎ 522-5990

DANCECLUBS
■ **Embassy Club** (B D Glm)
54 King Street East ✉ ON L8N 1A6 ☎ 522-7783
Dance bar.

BOOK SHOPS
■ **Gomorrah's Books** (CC GLM) Mon-Thu 12-18, Fri -20, Sat 10-18, Sun 12-16 h
158 James Street South ✉ ON L8P 3A2 *(Near GO station)* ☎ 526-1074
Books, cards, gifts, magazines, adult-toys.

HEALTH GROUPS
■ **Hamilton AIDS Network (HANDS)** Mon-Fri 9-17, Tue Thu 18.30-21 h
PO Box 120, Station A ✉ ON L8N 3C8 *(143 James Street South, Suite 900)* ☎ 528-0854
Dialogue, support, information.

HELP WITH PROBLEMS
■ **Hamilton Gay, Lesbian and Bisexual Youth Line**
☎ (800) 268-9688 (toll-free)

Kingston ☎ 613

GAY INFO
■ **Kingston Lesbian, Gay, Bisexual Association**
Infoline: Mon-Fri 19-21 h
51 Queens Cres ✉ ON K7L 2S7 ☎ 545-2960
☎ 531-8981 (infoline)

BARS
■ **Club 477** (B glm) Mon-Thu 16-1, Fri Sat 16-3 h
477 Princess Street ✉ ON K7L 1C3 ☎ 547-2923

HEALTH GROUPS
■ **Kingston AIDS Project**
PO Box 120 ✉ ON K7L 4V6 ☎ 545-3698
☎ (1-800) 565-2209 (toll-free)

Kitchener ☎ 519

BARS
■ **Club Renaissance** (B D F Glm YG) Wed-Sun 21-3 h
24 Charles Street West ✉ ON N2G 1H2 *(opposite Transit Center)* ☎ 570-2406

CRUISING
-Victoria Park (AYOR) (parking lots at night)
-King Street (between Frederick and Victoria Streets late at night)
-Waterloo Park (summer time)

London ☎ 519

GAY INFO
■ **Gay Line** Mon Thu 19-22 h, or tape
☎ 433-3551

BARS
■ **Apartment. The** (B f D GLM)
186 Dundas Street ✉ ON N6A 1G7 ☎ 679-1255
■ **Club H2O** (B d GLM) Thu-Sun 17-3 h
194 Dundas Street West ✉ ON N6A 1G7 ☎ 850-9922
■ **Diversity** (B GLM MA) 19-23 h, Sun closed
355 Talbot Street ✉ ON N6A 2R5 ☎ 432-8181

DANCECLUBS
■ **Sinnz** (B D GLM) Thu-Sat 20-3 h
347 Clarence Street ✉ ON N6A 3M4 ☎ 423-0622

SAUNAS/BATHS
■ **Club London** (AC B BF CC DR f G lj MA P SA SB SOL VS WH WO) 0-24 h
722 York Street ✉ ON N5W 2S8 *(rear entrance from parking lot)* ☎ 438-2625
Big sauna on three floors and 15 000 sq ft with game room (video games, pool table), licensed lounge, TV lounge with fireplace, toys and leather store. Leather night last Sat of the month. Established since 1975.

CAMPING
■ **Enchanted Forest Resort** (G NU PI SA WH)
20237 Kennedy Road ☎ (800) 477-5858

GENERAL GROUPS
■ **Halo Club** (B GLM) Fri Sat -?, Mon 19-22 h
649 Colborne Street/Pall Mall ✉ ON N6A 3Z2 ☎ 433-3762

HEALTH GROUPS
■ **AIDS Committee of London**
200-343 Richmond Street ✉ ON N6A 3C2 ☎ 434-1601
📠 434-1843

HELP WITH PROBLEMS
■ **AA Gay/Lesbian**
☎ 473-4738
■ **AIDS Hotline**
☎ 434-8160

CRUISING
-Victoria Park (at Wellington Street and Dufferin Avenue)
-Harris Park (end of Dufferin Avenue along Thames, only in summer)

Maynooth ☎ 613

GUEST HOUSES
■ **Wildewood Guest House** (BF F GLM MA WH) Reservations 9-22 h
970 Madawaska Road, Box 121 ✉ ON K0L 2S0 *(30 minutes from Algonquin Park. 3 hours drive from Toronto or Ottawa)* ☎ 338-3134
📠 338-3134
All your meals lovingly prepared, two guest rooms with views, two washrooms, comfortable queen-size beds. Rates include full breakfast and 3 course dinner.

Oshawa ▶ Peterborough | **Ontario/Canada**

Oshawa ☎ 905

BARS
■ **Club 717** (B D GLM MA TV) Thu 21-3, Sun -1 h
717 Wilson Road South ✉ ON L1H 6E9 ☎ 434-4297

Ottawa ☎ 613

GAY INFO
■ **Pink Triangle Services** (GLM) Gayline: 19-22 h
71 Bank Street ✉ ON K1P 6H6 (2nd floor) ☎ 238-1717

PUBLICATIONS
■ **Capital XTRA!** (GLM) Mon-Fri 9-18 h
506-177 Nepean Street ✉ ON K2P 0B4 ☎ 237-7133 🖷 237-6651
📧 capxtra@capital.xtra.ca 🖳 www.capitalxtra.on.ca
Ottawa's gay and lesbian monthly paper.

TOURIST INFO
■ **Ottawa Tourism and Convention Authority**
130 Albert Street, Suite 1800 ✉ ON K1P 5G4 ☎ 237-5150
🖷 237-7339 📧 info@tourottawa.org 🖳 www.tourottawa.org

BARS
■ **Cellblock** (AC B d G LJ MA) Wed-Sat 21-2, Sun 18-2 h
340 Somerset Street West ✉ ON K2P 0J9 (upstairs) ☎ 594-0233
■ **Centretown Pub** (AC B CC D Glm lj MA N OS VS) Wed-Sat 21-2, Sun 18-2 h
340 Somerset Street West/Bank ✉ ON K2P 0J9 ☎ 594-0233
■ **Franky's** (B G MA SNU) Mon-Fri 16-2, Sat Sun 14-2 h
303 Frank Street ✉ ON K2P 0X7 ☎ 233-9195
■ **Lookout Bar and Bistro. The** (B F GLM MA)
41 York Street ✉ ON K1N 5S7 (2nd floor) ☎ 789-1624
■ **Silhouette Piano Bar** (AC B CC GLM MG S) Thu-Sat 21-1 h
340 Somerset Street West ✉ ON K2P 0J9 (downstairs) ☎ 594-0234
■ **Village Inn Pub** (B f GLM) 11-2 h
313 Bank Street ✉ ON K2P 1X9 ☎ 594-8287

CAFES
■ **Market Station** (b f GLM)
15 George Street ✉ ON K1N 8W5 ☎ 562-3540

DANCECLUBS
■ **Club Polo Pub** (B D f GLM) 11-2 h
65 Bank Street ✉ ON K1P 5N2 (near Sparks) ☎ 235-5995
■ **Icon** (B D G YG) Thu-Sat 20-3, Sun 23-2 h
366 Lisgar Street ✉ ON K2P 2J3 ☎ 235-4005

RESTAURANTS
■ **News. The** (! B F GLM)
284 Elgin Street ✉ ON K2P 1M3 ☎ 567-6397
■ **Rock Bottom Grill** (B F GLM MA)
307 Dalhousie Street ✉ ON K1N 7E8 ☎ 562-1414
■ **William Street Café** (AC B F GLM)
47 William Street ✉ ON K1N 6Z9 ☎ 241-4254

SEX SHOPS/BLUE MOVIES
■ **Wilde's** (G)
367 Bank Street ☎ 234-5512

SAUNAS/BATHS
■ **Club Ottawa** (AC B G MA SA SB SOL VS MX) 0-24 h
1069 Wellington Street ✉ ON K1Y 2Y2 (at Merton Street) ☎ 722-8978

■ **Steamworks** (AC b f G SA SB VS MX) 0-24 h
487 Lewis Street ✉ ON K2P 0T2 (between O'Connor St. and Bank St.) ☎ 230-8431
Sauna with snack and juice counter and a TV lounge.

BOOK SHOPS
■ **After Stonewall** (CC GLM MA) Mon-Tue Wed-Thu Sat 10-18, Fri -21, Sun 12-17 h
370 Bank Street ✉ ON K2P 1Y4 (2nd floor opp. Wilde's) ☎ 567-2221

GIFT & PRIDE SHOPS
■ **One in Ten** (GLM) Mon-Sat 11-23, Sun 11-20 h
216 Bank Street ☎ 563-0110
Pride accessories, videos, lingerie, t-shirts, etc.

GUEST HOUSES
■ **Inn on Somerset** (AC BF CC glm H)
282 Somerset Street West ✉ K2P 0J6 ☎ 236-9309 🖷 237-6842
📧 rideau@istar.ca 🖳 www.home.istar.ca/~rideau
Friendly staff and atmosphere. Eight rooms, two with private bath.
■ **Ottawa House** (GLM H)
264 Stewart Street ☎ 233-4433
■ **Rainbow Bed & Breakfast** (GLM)
203 York Street ☎ 789-3286

GENERAL GROUPS
■ **EGALE**
306-177 Nepean Street ✉ ON K2P 0B4 ☎ 230-1043 🖷 230-9395

HEALTH GROUPS
■ **AIDS Committee of Ottawa**
111 Lisgar Street (Council Hall) ☎ 238-5014 ☎ 233-4443
🖳 www.theaco.on.ca
Anonymous AIDS Testing at Centretown Community Health Centre.

RELIGIOUS GROUPS
■ **Dignity** Tue 19.30 h at 386 Bank Street
PO Box 21 02, Station D ✉ ON K1P 5W3 ☎ 231-2393

SWIMMING
-Meech Lake Rapids Widerness Federal Park (! G NU WE YG) (North of Hull in Gatineau Park near Old Chelsea Park in Meech Lake Beach parking lot, then take the hiking trail at the side of the lot for about 15 min. to a small bridge, take the first path on the right and follow the edge of the lake around to the falls. Lots of winding wilderness paths to cruise.)

CRUISING
-Rockcliff Park (daytime; close to parking lots)
-Major's Hill Park (very AYOR)
-Nepean Point (very AYOR)
-Remic Rapids Park (along walking paths very busy during summer days)
-Mackenzie Street (AYOR G R)
-Rideau Canal (between Somerset Street and Waverly Street and action in bushes around the German embassy during summer months)
-Rideau Shopping Centre (3rd floor near coffee & muffin shop mainly in winter)

Peterborough ☎ 705

GAY INFO
■ **Rainbow Community Centre & Service Organization**
☎ 876-1845

Canada/Ontario — Peterborough ▸ Toronto

■ **Trent Lesbian & Gay Collective**
☏ 734-5414

HEALTH GROUPS
■ **Peterborough AIDS Resource Network**
PO Box 15 82 ✉ ON K9J 7H7 ☏ 749-9110

Port Sydney ☏ 705

HOTELS
■ **Divine Lake Resort** (b BF E F glm H MA msg PI SA WH WO)
R.R. 1, Clearwater Lake Road 848 ✉ ON P0B 1L0 *(two hours from downtown Toronto)* ☏ 385-1212 🖶 385-1283
✉ divinelk@vianet.on.ca ⌂ www.divinelake.com
Chalets for 2 to 4 persons and cottages for 2 persons. All with facilities, balcony, TV, video, radio, kitchenette.

Stratford ☏ 519

BARS
■ **Down the Street** (B glm MA)
30 Ontario Street ✉ ON N5A 3G8 ☏ 273-5886
■ **Old English Parlour** (B g MA)
101 Wellington Street ✉ ON N5A 2L4 ☏ 271-2372

PRIVATE ACCOMMODATION
■ **Burnside Guest Home** (AC BF glm H msg NU WH) 8-2 h
139 William Street ✉ ON N5A 4X9 *(80 miles west of Toronto)*
☏ 271-7076 🖶 271-0265
2 rooms with shared bath/WC, phone, fax, TV, video, radio, own key.

Sudbury ☏ 705

DANCECLUBS
■ **Zig's** (AC B CC D f GLM lj MA N r STV) Sun-Tue 20-1, Wed-Sat -2 h
33 Elgin Street ✉ ON P3C 5B3 ☏ 677-0614

HEALTH GROUPS
■ **AIDS Commitee of Sudbury**
23 Durham Street, ✉ ON P3C 5E2 ☏ 688-0500

Thunder Bay ☏ 807

BARS
■ **Backstreet Dance Klub** (B GLM) Tue-Sat 16-3 h
24 S Cumberland Street/Red River Road *(no sign)* ☏ 344-5437

GENERAL GROUPS
■ **Lesbian Gay Bisexual Centre at Lakehead University**
c/o L.U. Student Union, 955 Oliver Road ✉ ON P7B 5E1
☏ 343-8813

HEALTH GROUPS
■ **AIDS Info Line** Mon-Fri 8.30-17 h
☏ 345-7233

Toronto ☏ 416

✱ Toronto is Canada's largest city. Since the 70's it has been growing in prominence and economic prosperity. Toronto is the financial and communications centre of the nation and home to many corporate headquaters. Toronto is home to Canada's most prestigious cultural insitutions, such as the Toronto Symphony, the National Ballet and the Canadian Opera Company. Toronto has shed its boring image and has become more cosmopolitan with the influx of immigrants from all over the world. Some popular tourist attractions include the CN Tower, Casa Loma, Eaton Centre, the Ontario Science Centre and the Royal Ontario Museum.
The heart of the gay village is Church Street, between Alexander and Wellesley Streets. There are also several gay bars on the parallel strech of Yonge Street. The popularity of the Gay Pride Parade has grown considerably in the past decade, attracting more than 100,000 spectators in recent years.

★ Toronto umgibt der größte Ballungsraum des Landes. Seit den 70ern ist die Stadt auf Kosten Montreals erheblich gewachsen. In Toronto haben sich die großen Banken, Medienkonzerne und Firmenzentralen niedergelassen. Entsprechend prestigeträchtig sind Symphonieorchester, Ballett und Oper der Stadt. Aus der langweiligen und angestaubt wirkenden Stadt ist ein lebendiges und buntes Zentrum Kanadas geworden. Dazu tragen vor allem die vielen Einwanderer, die nach der Einreise in Toronto hängen bleiben, aber auch die Angehörigen der First Nation (der kanadischen Ureinwohner) bei.
Die *gay community* konzentriert sich um die Ecke Church Street/ Wellesley Street bis hinein in die Yonge Street. Toronto ist eine durchaus sichere Stadt. Für das nächtliche Heimkommen von einer schwulen Kneipentour ist dennoch ein Taxi sehr empfehlenswert. Ob es bis dahin allerdings so spät wird, ist eher fraglich: die meisten Kneipen schließen um ein Uhr. Doch auch danach bleiben Discos, Clubs und die vielen special events, um die Nacht zum Tag zu machen.
Der Gay-Pride-Day Torontos hat sich zu einer beachtlichen Veranstaltung von enormen Ausmaßen (über 100.000 Teilnehmer) entwickelt.

✱ Toronto est la plus grande ville du Canada. Elle a considérablement grandi en importance et s'est beaucoup enrichie depuis les années 70. Elle est devenue le centre économique et financier du pays et le siège de nombreuses entreprises nationales. Elle abrite également diverses institutions culturelles prestigieuses, telles que l'Orchestre Symphonique de Toronto ou l'Opéra et le Ballet nationaux. Toronto a réussi à se débarrasser de son image de ville ennuyeuse pour devenir un centre cosmopolite grâce, entre autres, à l'arrivée d'immigrés venus du monde entier. Ses attractions touristiques les plus cotées sont la CN Tower, la Casa Loma, l'Eaton Centre, le Ontario Science Centre et le Royal Ontario Museum.
La scène gaie se concentre aux abords de la Church Street entre Alexander Street et Wellesley Street et sur la rue parallèle, la Yonge Street. La Gay Pride de Toronto s'est développé de manière exponentielle ces dernières années pour atteindre plus de 100.000 participants lors de sa dernière édition.

✱ Toronto está situado en la mayor zona de aglomeración del país. Desde los años 70 la ciudad creció enormemente a costa de Montreal. En Toronto se establecieron los grandes bancos, empresas de comunicación y las oficinas centrales de las multinacionales. Como consecuencia, la orquesta sinfónica, el ballet y la ópera de la ciudad gozan de gran prestigio. La ciudad, que antes daba una impresión de aburida y anticuada, se ha convertido actualmente en un vivaz y colorido centro canadiense. Esto se debe en gran parte a los numerosos emigrantes, que se establecieron en Toronto tanto como a los miembros de la First Nation (los indigenos de Canada). La comunidad gay se concentra en la zona que comprende la esquina que forman Church Street y Wellesley Street, extendiendose hasta la Yonge Street. Toronto es una ciudad muy segura, sin embargo se recomienda coger un taxi para regresar a casa despúes de una noche de marcha por los bares gay. Pero en general no se hará muy

Toronto   Ontario/Canada

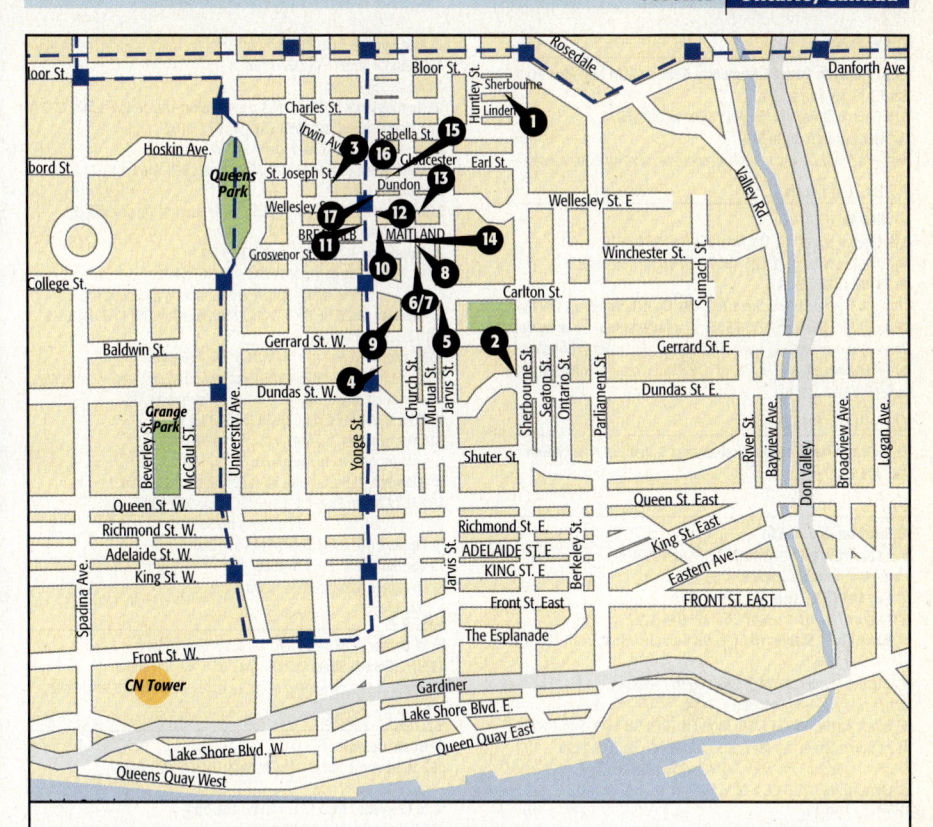

Toronto

1. Selby Hotel / Boots Complex Danceclub
2. Amazing Space B&B Guest House
3. Toolbox Bar
4. Remington's Bar
5. Club Toronto Sauna
6. Woody's Bar
7. Priape Sex Shop
8. Black Eagle Bar
9. The Barn / Stables Bar
10. Trax V Bar
11. Sneakers Bar
12. St. Marc Spa Sauna
13. Bar 501
14. Crews Bar
15. Dundonald B&B Guest House
16. Victoria's Mansion
17. El Convente Rico Danceclub

tarde, ya que la mayoría de los bares y pubs cierren a la una. Sin embargo, la ciudad ofrece discotecas, clubs y eventos especiales, donde se puede disfrutar de la noche hasta horas tempranas. El Gay-Pride-Day se ha convertido en un evento notable con una participación enorme (más que 100.000 participantes).

✖ Toronto è circondata dalla zona più abitata del Canada. Sin dagli anni '70 la città è cresciuta a scapito di Montreal. A Toronto si sono stabilite grandi banche, l'industria delle mass-media e le centrali delle imprese. Corrispondentemente l'orchestra sinfonica, il balletto e l'opera della città sono di un'alto livello. La città noiosa e antiquata di una volta è diventata un centro canadese vivace e svariato. A ciò contribuiscono soprattutto i molti immigranti che si fermano a Toronto, ma anche gli appartenenti alla *First Nation*, cioè la popolazione originaria. Il centro della *gay comunity* si trova all'angolo della Church Street/Wellesley Street e comprende anche la Yonge Street. Anche se Toronto è una città abbastanza sicura, conviene prendere un taxì dopo un giro dei bar. Dipende però se questo giro si allunga fino a tardi, perché i bar chiudono all'una di notte. Dopo si può andare in una delle discoteche, in un club o partecipare ad uno dei numerosi eventi che fanno della notte il giorno. Il Gay Pride Day di Toronto si è sviluppato ad un avvenimento di enormi misure con più di 100.000 partecipanti.

Canada/Ontario — Toronto

GAY INFO
■ **519 Church Street Community Centre** (GLM MA) Mon-Fri 9-22, Sat 12-17.30, Sun 9-17 h
519 Church Street ✉ ON M4Y 3C9 ☏ 392-6874
🖳 www.icomm.ca/the519/
Home of many GL groups and location for numerous gay events.

PUBLICATIONS
■ **Attitude** (GLM YG)
519 Church Street ✉ ON M4Y 2C9 ☏ 964-1916
The official Lesbian and Gay Youth of Toronto newsletter.
■ **XTRA!** (GLM) 8-24 h
c/o Pink Triangle Press, Suite 200, 491 Church Street ✉ ON M4Y 2C6 ☏ 925-6665 📠 925-6503 ✉ info@xttra.ca 🖳 www.xtra.ca
Biweekly magazine with calendar of events, and other information about Toronto gay scene. Free at gay venues, retail & entertainment outlets all over Toronto.

TOURIST INFO
■ **Metropolitan Toronto Convention & Visitors Association**
☏ 203-2600

BARS
■ **Babylon** (B GLM YG)
553 Church Street ✉ M4Y 2E2 ☏ 923-2626
Three floors of hip ambience.
■ **Bar 501** (B CC GLM MA STV) 11-2 h
501 Church Street ✉ M4Y 2C6 ☏ 944-3272
■ **Barn. The / Stables** (B CC D DR Glm LJ s VS) Mon-Thu 21-3, Fri-Sat -4, Sun 16-4 h
418 Church Street ✉ M5B 2A3 ☏ 977-4702
Dance club and leather shop.
■ **Black Eagle** (! B G LJ MA) Mon-Fri 16-2, Sat 14-2, Sun 12-2 h
459 Church Street ✉ M4Y 2C5 (2nd floor) ☏ 413-1219
Leather cruise bar. Thu Bear Night and Sun Naked Night.
■ **Byzantium** (AC B CC F GLM lj MA N OS TV) 17.30-1, Thu-Sat 17.30-2 h
499 Church Street ✉ M4Y 2C6 ☏ 922-3859
Hip bar and restaurant.
■ **Carringtons Sports Bar** (B Glm MA) 11-2 h
618 Yonge Street (2nd floor) ☏ 944-0559
Pool Bar.
■ **Cell Block** (B D G)
72 Carlton Street (rear entrance)
Popular in the after hours.
■ **Ciao Edie** (B GLm MA) 20-2 h, Women on Sat
489 College Street ✉ M6G 1A5 ☏ 927-7774
■ **Crews** (B CC GL STV) 11-2, shows Wed-Sun at 23 h
508 Church Street ✉ M4Y 2C8 ☏ 972-1662
Gay bar in old Victorian house.
■ **Hair of the Dog** (F G MA)
425 Church Street ✉ M5B 2A3
Cocktail bar & restaurant.
■ **Pegasus Billiard Lounge** (AC B CC GLM MA) Mon-Fri 11-2, Sat-Sun 12-2 h
489B Church Street ✉ M4Y 2C6 (2nd floor) ☏ 927-8832
If you prefer playing pool, video games or NTN satellite trivia game to dancing, then this is the place for you.
■ **Pimblett's Pub** (B CC f GLM MA N TV) 16-2 h
263 Gerrard Street East ✉ M5A 2G1 ☏ 929-5375
Friendly pub.

■ **Red Spot** (B F GLM)
459 Church Street ☏ 967-7768
Many special parties.
■ **Remington's** (AC B f G MA p SNU) Mon-Thu 15-2, Fri-Sun 13-2 h
379 Yonge Street ✉ M5B 1S1 ☏ 977-2160
Male Strip club with two stages and two bars.
■ **Slack Alice** (B F GLM MA) Mon-Wed 16-2, Thu Fri 12-2, Sat Sun 11-2 h
562 Church Street ✉ M4Y 2E3 (in the heart of the gay Village)
☏ 969-8742
■ **Sneakers** (AC B CC f G MA N R) 11-2 h
502A Yonge Street ✉ M4Y 1X9 ☏ 961-5808
Cruisy atmosphere with a mature crowd looking for young men.
■ **Toolbox** (AC B BF DR F G H LJ MA OS) Mon-Thu 17-3, Fri 14-3, Sat 12-3, Sun 11-3 h
508 Eastern Avenue ✉ M4M 1C5 ☏ 466-8616
Patio, leather shop, restaurant, guesthouse with priv. and shared baths. Non smoking rooms with air conditioner and cable TV.
■ **Trax V** (AC B CC d f G lj MA OS S) 11-2 h
529 Yonge Street ✉ M4Y 1Y5 ☏ 962-5196
Fun atmosphere in this piano bar.
■ **Woody's** (! B CC f Glm MA STV) Mon-Fri 12-2, Sat 11-3 h
465-467 Church Street ✉ M4Y 2C5 ☏ 972-0887
Popular 5 bars with live drag shows on Sun.
■ **Zipperz** (AC B CC D GLM MA S) 12-2h
72 Carlton Street ☏ 921-0066
Piano lounge, show and dance bar.

CAFES
■ **IX Below** (b BF f glm MA) 8-24, Sat Sun 10-24 h
473-1/2 Church Street ✉ ON M4Y 2C5 ☏ 944-3265
Popular coffee shop serving delicious cakes, desserts and sandwiches.

DANCECLUBS
■ **Boots Complex** (! B D G S YG) 21-3 h
592 Sherbourne Street ✉ ON M4X 1L4 ☏ 921-0665
Dance bar and lounge.
■ **El Convento Rico** (B D glm tv) Thu-Sun
750 College Street ☏ 588-7800
Latino dance club.
■ **Fly** (AC B CC D f glm LJ MA p s tv) Sat 21-8 h
6 Gloucester Street ✉ ON M4Y 1L5 ☏ 410-5426
■ **Industry Nightclub** (AC B CC D GLM lj STV WE YG) Fri-Sat 22-8 h
901 King Street West, Box 20 ✉ ON M5V 3H5 ☏ 260-2660
Club with international DJs busy very late.
■ **5ive** (! B D F Glm YG) Tue-Sun 17-2 h
5 St. Joseph Street ✉ ON M4Y 1J6 ☏ 964-8685

RESTAURANTS
■ **Auntie Emm's Diner** (b BF F Glm MA)
105 Carlton Street ☏ 260-6864
■ **Living Well Restaurant** (A AC B CC d F glm MA N OS) Restaurant: Sun-Thu 11,30-1, Fri Sat -1.30, Bar: 18-2 h
692 Yonge Street ✉ ON M4Y 2A6 (at Isabella Street) ☏ 922-6770
■ **Mango. The** (AC B CC F GLM MA N OS) 11-1, Thu-Sat 11-2 h
580 Church Street ✉ ON M4Y 2E5 (Subway Wellesly) ☏ 922-6925
International cuisine.
■ **Marshall's** (B CC F glm MA) 11.30-22, Sun 11-22 h
471 Church Street ✉ ON M4Y 2E5 ☏ 925-0341
High quality French cuisine.
■ **Village Rainbow. The** (AC B BF CC F G WE) 7-23 h
477 Church Street ✉ ON M4Y 2C6 ☏ 961-0616
Bar & Restaurant. Good breakfasts.

Toronto | Ontario/Canada

VICTORIA'S MANSION
In the Village

Beautiful Victorian Mansion in the heart of downtown Toronto and The Gay Village. Walking distance to shopping, dining, theatre, museums, University of Toronto, business district and public transit.

Clean, affordable rooms with private bathroom, refrigerator, microwave, coffee maker, cable T.V., A/C. Laundry and parking available. Rates start at $65.00.

Reservations (416) 921-4625
Fax: (416) 944-1092
Email: victorias.mansion@sympatico.ca
http://www3.sympatico.ca/victorias.mansion

INN & GUEST HOUSE

■ **Wilde Oscar's** (B CC F glm OS) 12-3 h
518 Church Street ✉ ON M4Y 2C8 ☎ 921-8142
In the heart of the gay village good and hearty meals are served e.g. pizzas, steak, pastas and sea food.
■ **Youki Asian Bar & Bistro** (B CC F glm OS) 17.30-22.30, Sun 17-21 h
4 Dundonald Street ✉ ON M4Y 1K2 ☎ 924-2925
Reasonably priced Asian cuisine.
■ **Zelda's Bar, Restaurant & Lounge** (B CC F GLM MA N OS s STV WE) 11-2 h
76 Wellesley Street East ✉ ON M4Y 1H2 *(M° Wellesley, at Church Street)* ☎ 922-2526

SHOWS
■ **Tallulah's Cabaret** (AC B CC D GLM S WE) Tue-Sat 10-18, Sun 12-15 h, closed Mon. Club: Fri-Sat 22.30-3 h
12 Alexander Street ✉ ON M4Y 1B4 *(M° College Street)* ☎ 975-8555

SEX SHOPS/BLUE MOVIES
■ **New Release Adult Video** (CC G MA VS) 9-2, Sun 10-1 h
489 Church Street ✉ ON M4Y 2C6 *(lower level)* ☎ 966-9815
Sales, rentals, magazines and toys.
■ **Priape** (CC GLM LJ) 10-19, Thu-Sat -21, Sun 12-18 h
465 Church Street ✉ ON M4X 1T8 ☎ 586-9914
Everything for leather fans.

SAUNAS/BATHS
■ **Barracks. The** (AC b CC G lj S SA SB) 0-24 h
56 Widmer Street/Richmond ✉ ON M5V 2E9 ☎ 593-0499
Popular with the leather crowd. Sling rooms and sex toy store available.

■ **Bijou. The** (B DR G MA VS) 21-4 h
370 Church Street *(near Gerrard)* ☎ 960-1272
■ **Cellar. The** (b G MA SA VS) 0-24 h
78 Wellesley Street East ✉ ON M4Y 1H2 *(basement-black door)* ☎ 944-3779
Very raunchy sauna.
■ **Central Spa** (f G msg SA SB WH VS WO) 12-3 h
1610 Dundas Street West ✉ ON M6K 1T8 *(at Brock Avenue)* ☎ 588-6191
■ **Club Toronto** (AC CC G OS P Pl r SA SB SOL VS WH) 0-24 h
231 Mutual Street ✉ ON M5B 2B4 *(one block East of Mapple Leaf Garden)* ☎ 977-4629
Popular sauna on four floors established since 1974 with swimming pool (in summer only). Sundays complimentary buffet 16-20 h.
■ **Spa Excess** (AC B DR F G MA OS SA SB VS) 0-24 h
105 Carlton Street ✉ ON M5B 1M1 *(near corner of Carlton and Jarvis Street)* ☎ 260-2363
One of the biggest sauna in Canada on 4 floors offering many special facilities: internet connection, billiard table, TV bar, and many private rooms. Coming soon: work-out room and massage.
■ **Spa on Maitland. The** (AC B CC f G MG r SA SB VS) 0-24 h
66 Maitland Street ✉ ON M4Y 1C5 *(west of Church Street, 2nd floor)* ☎ 925-1571
Big sauna on 11,800 sq ft with two dry saunas, two steam rooms and a licensed bar. Middle aged to older crowd.
■ **St. Marc Spa** (CC DR G f msg SA SB VS WH WO YG)
543 Yonge Street ✉ ON M4Y 1Y5 *(Between Wellesley and Maitland. Top floor. M°-Wellesley)* ☎ 927-0210
Sauna popular with a younger crowd. Dark room with glory holes, disco nights on Sat. Reservation on their website possible.

Canada/Ontario — Toronto

AMAZING SPACE B&B

Clean, economical,
accommodation in downtown Toronto!

Walking distance to shopping, the
Gay Village, theatres and restaurants!
Public Transit at the door!

Breakfast included, parking available.
Air conditioned, cable TV in each room,
shared and private baths,
clothing optional sun deck.

Reservations
416-968-2323
800-205-3694
FAX: 416-968-7194
Email: hughes99@home.com
http://www.immaculate-reception.com
Visa accepted

BOOK SHOPS

■ **Glad Day Books** (CC glm) Mon-Wed 11-18.30, Thu-Fri -21, Sat 10-18, Sun 12-18 h
598 A Yonge Street ✉ ON M4Y 1Z3 (2nd floor, at St.Joseph)
☎ 961-4161 FAX 961-1624

■ **Rosedale Library** (GLM) 10-22, Fri-Sat -24, Sun 13-21 h
483 Church Street ✉ ON M4Y 2C6 ☎ 929-9912

LEATHER & FETISH SHOPS

■ **Doc's Leather and Latex** (AC CC GLM LJ MA r WE) 11-19, Sun 12-17 h
726 Queen Street West ✉ ON M6J 1E8 ☎ 504-8888
New and second-hand leather/fetish wear.

■ **Northbound Leather Ltd.** (A AC CC glm LJ) Mon-Wed Sat 10-18, Thu Fri -21, Sun 12-17 h
586 Yonge Street ✉ ON M4Y 1Z3 (1 block from gay centre)
☎ 972-1037
300 m^2 showroom on Toronto's main street.

HOTELS

■ **Selby Hotel** (AC B BF CC D GLM H OS S)
592 Sherbourne Street ✉ ON M4X 1L4 (M° Sherbourne).
☎ 921-3142 ☎ (800) 387-4788 (toll-free) 📠 923-3177
📧 selby@inforamp.net
Minutes from gay area and city centre. Rooms with private baths, historic rooms with fireplaces.

■ **Victoria's Mansion** (CC glm H MA)
68 Gloucester Street ✉ ON M4Y 1L5 (close to the gay village)
☎ 921-4625 📠 944-1092 📧 victorias.mansion@sympatico.ca
🌐 www.3.sympatico.ca/victorias.mansion
13 double rooms, 8 single, 1 studio and 1 apartment. Rooms with facilities, TV, AC, own key.

GUEST HOUSES

■ **Aberdeen Guest House** (AC BF CC E GLM H)
52 Aberdeen Avenue ✉ ON M4X 1A2 ☎ 922-8697 📠 922-5011
📧 aberdeengh@aol.com 🌐 www.interlog.com/~aberinn
Small B&B in Historic town centre. All rooms with shared bath and TV. Non-smoking establishment.

■ **Acorn House B&B** (BF GLM H lj)
255 Donlands Avenue ✉ ON M4J 3R5 ☎ 463-8274 📠 463-9136
Small B&B. Rooms with shared bath.

■ **Amazing Space B&B** (AC BF CC GLM H NU OS)
246 Sherbourne Street ✉ ON M5A 2S1 (20 min to airport, downtown, close to gay scene) ☎ 968-2323 ☎ (800) 205-3694 (toll-free)
📠 968-7194 📧 hughes99@home.com
🌐 www.immaculate-reception.com
All rooms with AC, cable TV, shared or private baths. Clothing optional sun deck.

■ **Banting House** (AC BF CC e G H lj)
73 Homewood Avenue ✉ ON M4Y 2K1 ☎ 924-1458
📠 922-2718 📧 bantingghs@aol.com
🌐 www.bbcanada.com/1960.html
Rooms with shower/WC, SAT-TV, kitchen(ette), balcony.

■ **Catnaps Guesthouse** (CC GLM H)
246 Sherbourne Street ✉ ON M5A 2S1 ☎ 1-800-205-3694
📧 catnaps@onramp.ca

■ **Cawthra Square Inn & Ten Cawthra Square B&B** (AC CC E GLM H OS WH)
10 Cawthra Square ✉ ON M4Y 1K8 (in the gay village)
☎ 966-3074 ☎ (800) 259-5474 (toll-free) 📠 966-4494
📧 host@cawthra.com 🌐 www.cawthra.com
Two quality guesthouses in elegant historic homes. 1 single, 8 double, 3 Premium, and 3 x 2 bedrooms suites. All with phone, TV, VCR. Most with private bath, somme with terrace. Rates Can$ 79-349 (bf incl.).

■ **DunDonald Bed and Breakfast** (AC BF CC GLM H MA msg OS SA WH WO)
35 Dundonald Street ✉ ON M4Y 1K3 (M° Wellesley) ☎ 961-9888
☎ (1-800) 260 7227 (toll-free) 📠 961-2120
📧 dundonal@idirect.com 🌐 www.dundonaldhouse.com
Friendly B&B in the heart of the gay village. 5 double and 1 single room with TV/video and radio. Sauna, hot tub, work out room free of charge. Bicycles and parking available. Check website or call for rates.

■ **House on McGill, The** (AC BF CC glm H) 8-20 h
110 McGill Street ✉ ON M5B 1H6 (M° College Street) ☎ 351-1503
📧 mcgillbb@interlog.com 🌐 www.interlog.com/~mcgillbb/
Small B&B. All rooms with shared bath, baclony, radio, TV/VCR. Rates double Can$ 70-90, add. bed 15, Single 50-70 incl. bf buffet.

■ **Two Aberdeen** (AC BF CC GLM) 7-21 h
2 Aberdeen Avenue ✉ ON M4X 1A2 (close to gay village & downtown) ☎ 944-1426 📠 944-3523 📧 twoaberdeen@interlog.com
🌐 www.twoaberdeen.com
Rooms with private or shared bath, balcony, Sat-TV/VCR.

PRIVATE ACCOMMODATION

■ **Muther's Guesthouse at the Toolbox** (AC B CC F G LJ H MA NU)
508 Eastern Avenue ✉ ON M4M 1C5 ☎ 466-8316
🌐 www.torque.net/~toolbox
Clean and comfortable rooms. Can $ 60-80.-

GENERAL GROUPS

■ **Gay Lesbian and Bisexual International** (GLINT) (GLM MA)
42A St. George Street ✉ ON M5S 2E4 ☎ 591-7949
Support group for all those whose first language is not English. Call for info.

Toronto Ontario/Canada

■ **Primetimers Toronto** (G OG) 3rd Sat 14-16 h
c/o Community Centre, 519 Church Street ✉ ON M4Y 2C9
☎ 925-9872 (ext. 2970). 💻 cg520@torfree.net
Social group for gay and bisexual men over 40. Newsletter available.
■ **Toronto Bisexual Network** 1st Thu 18-20, 3rd Thu 20-22 h
c/o Community Centre, 519 Church Street ✉ ON M4Y 2C9
☎ 925-9872 (ext. 2015). 💻 steve@bi.org

HEALTH GROUPS

■ **AIDS Action Now** Mon-Fri 13-16.30, meets 2nd/4th Tue 20-22 h
519 Church Street ✉ ON M6G 4A2 ☎ 928-2206 📠 928-2185
Political group.
■ **AIDS Committee of Toronto (ACT)**
399 Church Street ✉ ON M5B 2J6 *(4th floor)* ☎ 340-2437
☎ 340-8844 (hotline) 📠 340-8224 💻 www.actoronto.org
Largest non-profit organisation in Canada. AIDS-related resource library, counselling, support groups and practical help for those affected by AIDS.
■ **Asian Community AIDS Services (ACAS)** Mon-Fri 11-19 h
107-33 Isabella Street ✉ ON M4Y 2P7 ☎ 963-4300 📠 963-4371
💻 info@acas.org 💻 www.acas.org
Counselling, education and support services for the East and Southeast Asian communities.
■ **Community AIDS Treatment Information Exchange (CATIE)**
Mon Fri Sat 10-18 h, Tue-Thu 10-22 h
517 College Street, Suite 420 ✉ ON M6G 4A2 ☎ 416-944-1916
☎ (800) 263-1638 (toll free) 📠 416-928-2185.
■ **Hassle Free Clinic** Mon Wed 16-21, Tue Thu 10-15, Fri 16-19,
Sat 10-14 h
556 Church Street ✉ ON M4Y 2E3 *(2nd floor)* ☎ 922-0603
💻 hfclinic@interlog.com
Sexual health clinic providing counselling, information and support for men.
■ **Toronto PWA Foundation**
399 Church Street ✉ ON M5B 2J6 *(2nd floor)* ☎ 506-1400
📠 506-1404

HELP WITH PROBLEMS

■ **New Start Lesbian and Gay Counselling Centre**
☎ 944-3858 ☎ (800) 363-4363 (toll-free)
Clinical, health, social, addiction and planning services with gay doctors, counsellors and staff.

RELIGIOUS GROUPS

■ **Integrity Toronto** (GLM) 1st Mon/month 19.30 h at Church of the Redeemer, Bloor St., W. at Avenue Rd.
PO Box 873, Station F ✉ ON M4Y 2N9 ☎ 323-0389
💻 www.whirlwind.ca/integrity
Group of Anglican gays, lesbians and friends.

SPECIAL INTEREST GROUPS

■ **Bear Buddies Toronto** (G MA)
PO Box 926, Station F ✉ ON M4Y 2N9 ☎ 925-9872
💻 bearbuddiestoronto.com
Group of hairy man and their fans.
■ **LGBT OUT** (GLM)
Room 133, 73 St. George Street ✉ ON M5S 2E5 ☎ 946-5542
💻 lgbtout@hotmail.com
💻 www.campuslife.utoronto.ca/groups/lgbout/
Lesbians, Gays, Bisexuals of the University of Toronto.
■ **TNT!MEN** (G MA NU)
PO Box 19, 552 Church Street ✉ ON M4Y 2E3 ☎ 925-9872 ext 3010 💻 tnt@gypsy.rose.utoronto.ca
💻 gypsy.rose.utoronto.ca/people/david_dir/tnt/
Not-for-profit recreational nudist club for men of all ages, races, shapes, and sizes.

Voted Best Bed & Breakfast

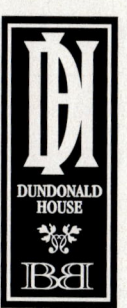

DUNDONALD HOUSE
BED & BREAKFAST

- Full Breakfast
- Parking Available
- Touring Bikes
- Hot tub
- Sauna
- Work Out Room
- Right In the gay village

Your Hosts **David & Warren**

35 Dundonald St.
Toronto, ON M4Y 1K3
email: dundonal@idirect.com
http://www.dundonaldhouse.com

(416) 961-9888 or 1 800 260-7227

■ **Transgendered, Bisexual, Lesbian and Alliance at York** (GLM YG)
C449 Student Centre York University, 4700 Keele, North York
✉ ON M3J 1P3 ☎ 736-2100 ext. 20494
Student organisation.

SPORT GROUPS

■ **Frontrunners Toronto** (GLM MA) Meets Thu afternoon, Sun mornings at Church Community Centre, 519 Church St.
PO Box 892, Station F ✉ ON M4Y 2N9 ☎ 925-9872
Running club for gay/lesbian/bisexual and transgender people.
■ **Out & Out Club**
PO Box 331, Station F ✉ ON M4Y 2L7 ☎ 925-9872
Sports and leisure activities for gays, lesbians and friends e.g. horseback riding, cycling, skiing, canoeing, tennis, volleyball, hiking, weekend excursions and BBQs. Newsletter available.

SWIMMING

- Hanlans Point Beach (g NU) (Toronto Island; take ferry from Harbour Castle Westin Hotel)
- Scarborough Beach (East of Warden Avenue; mostly gay, mostly nude, but occasional police hassle if nude)
- Cherry Beach (at the foot of Cherry Street)
- Kew Beach (at the foot of Woodbine Avenue)

CRUISING

- Balfour Park (AYOR) (St. Clair Avenue east of Yonge Street)
- Backyard (between Alexander and Maitland Streets, near Church Street)
- Church Street (between Carlton and Isabella Streets)
- Grosvenor/Bay and Yonge Streets (AYOR R)

Canada/Ontario – Québec   Toronto ▶ Magog

-High Park (AYOR at night) (south end near Colbourne Lodge, very busy summer days too)
-Cloverdale Shopping Mall (in Etobicoke)
-Cawthra Park (behind 519 Community Centre)

Whitby ☎ 905

BARS
■ **Bar. The** (B g MA)
110 Dundas Street West ✉ ON L1N 2L7 ☎ 666-3121

Windsor ☎ 519

GAY INFO
■ **Gay Hotline** Thu Fri 20-22 h or tape
☎ 973-4951

BARS
■ **Club Happy Tap** (AC B D GLM MA N SNU VS) Danceclub Sun 20-2, Mon 16-2, Tue-Sat 14-2, Stripclub Mon-Sat 17-2 h
1056 Wyandotte Street East ✉ ON N9A 3K2 ☎ 256-8998

SAUNAS/BATHS
■ **Vesuvio Steam Bath** (G OS SA SB VS) 0-24 h
563 Brant Street ✉ ON N9A 3E5 ☎ 977-8578

HEALTH GROUPS
■ **AIDS Committee of Windsor**
PO Box 2503 ✉ ON N9C 3Z1 ☎ 973-0222

SPECIAL INTEREST GROUPS
■ **Gay Youth Line** (GLM YG) Mon-Fri 9-17h, Tue & Thu 6.30-9.30h
1168 Drouillard ☎ 973-7671
🖥 www.geocities.com/windsor-youth
For youngsters under 30.

CDN-Prince-Edward-Island

Location: East CDN
Initials: PE
Time: GMT -4
Area: 6,000 km2 / 2,316 sq mi.
Population: 137,000
Capital: Charlottetown

Charlottetown ☎ 902

BOOK SHOPS
■ **Reading Well Bookstore** (CC glm) Summer: 10-20 h, closed Sun
84 Great George Street ✉ PE C1A 4K4 ☎ 566-2703
Gay and Lesbian section.

HEALTH GROUPS
■ **AIDS PEI**
PO Box 2762 ✉ PE C1A 8C4 ☎ 566-2437 ☎ (1-800) 344-2437 (toll-free) 📠 626 3400 🖥 aidspei@cdngateway.pe.ca

Vernon Bridge ☎ 902

GUEST HOUSES
■ **Rainbow Lodge** (BF CC GLM H MA) June-September
Station Main ✉ PE C0A 2E0 ☎ 651-2202 ☎ (1-800) 268-7005 (toll-free) 🖥 jimculbert@hotmail.com 🖥 www.gaypei.com
Rates Can$ 80.- incl. BF.

CDN-Québec

Location: West CDN
Initials: PQ
Time: GMT -5
Area: 1,541,000 km2 / 594,980 sq mi.
Population: 7,419,000
Capital:
Important gay cities: Montréal and Québec

Chicoutimi ☎ 418

BARS
■ **Bistro des Anges** (B GLM) 15-3 h
332 rue du Havre ✉ QC G7N 1N4 ☎ 698-4829

Drummondville ☎ 819

BARS
■ **Nuance. Le** (B D GLM MA s) Wed-Sun 30-3 h
336 Rue Lindsay ✉ QC J2B 1G5 (2nd floor) ☎ 471-4252

HOTELS
■ **Motel Alouette** (AC glm H MA WH)
1975 Boulevard Mercure ✉ QC J2B 3P3 ☎ 478-4166
📠 478-0090 🖥 info@motel-alouette.qc.ca
🖥 www.motel-alouette.qc.ca

CRUISING
-Parc Woodyat (evenings)

Granby ☎ 450

CAMPING
■ **Bain Gai de Nature** (BF F G NU OS PI SA VS WH) 9-21 h
127 Rue Lussier, St-Alphonse-de-Granby ✉ QC J0E 2A0 *(Ca. 10 min from Granby)* ☎ 375-4765 📠 375-4765 🖥 info@editpaix.qc.ca
🖥 www.editpaix.qc.ca
Luxurious house with private lake and forest. Overnight accommodation possible as well as day visits.

Joliette ☎ 450

BARS
■ **Flirt. Le** (B G MA)
343 rue Beaudry ✉ QC J6E 6B9 ☎ 753-7295

Jonquière ☎ 418

BARS
■ **Stool. Le** (B GLM) Thu-Sat 21-3, Sun 14-3 h
2732 Boulevard du Saguenay ✉ QC G7S 5C3 ☎ 548-0168

Magog ☎ 819

GUEST HOUSES
■ **Au Gîte du Cerf Argenté** (BF GLM MA H)
2984 Chemin Georgeville ✉ ON J1X 3W4 *(Highway 10, exit 18, right at km 13)* ☎ 4847-426 🖥 info@cerfargente.com
🖥 www.cerfangente.com
Rates CAN$ 38-72.-

Montréal Québec/Canada

Montréal ☎ 514

Montreal, a metropolis of over 3.4 million people, has a gay and lesbian community that makes up a significant segment of its population. Through the years, this has resulted in the forging of a special spirit of openness and tolerance between the general public and Montreal's gay community. Such open-mindedness has made the city, particularly the Village (one of the largest gay neighbourhoods in the world), a preferred destination for the gays and lesbians from around the world. Many gay visitors have fond memories of the city and keep coming back making Montreal a frequent gay-friendly destination, not only because of the gay life, but also because of the joie de vivre that permeates the city and give it a charm that visitors absolutely cannot resist!
Montreal has great gay events and activities: Divers/Cité, the Montreal Pride Celebration, fabulous circuit parties such as the Black & Blue Festival and the oldest gay & lesbian film festival of Canada: Image&Nation. Montreal has it all: bars, saunas, male strippers, places, people and the Quebec and Canadian Governments recognise same sex partners.

Montreal, eine Metropole in der mehr als 3,4 Millionen Menschen leben, hat eine Gay- und Lesbencommunity, die einen bedeutenden Teil der Einwohner ausmachen. Im Laufe der Jahre führte dies vor allem dazu, daß zwischen der allgemeinen Öffentlichkeit und Montreals Gay-Community ein großes Maß an Offenheit und Toleranz herrscht. Diese Offenheit führte dazu, daß die Stadt und besonders der Stadtteil Village, eine der größten Gay-Gegenden der Welt, eine der beliebtesten Reiseziele für Schwule und Lesben überhaupt ist. Viele schwule Besucher der Stadt verbinden mit Montreal liebevollen Erinnerungen und kommen hier immer wieder sehr gerne zurück. Die Stadt ist eine sehr schwulenfreundlich, nicht nur wegen des schwulen Lebens, sondern auch wegen der "joie de vivre", die sie Stadt durchdringt und ihr einen Charme verleiht, dem Besucher nicht widerstehen können!
In Montreal gibt es sehr viele Gay-Events und Aktivitäten: Divers/Cité, die Gay-Pride Celebration, wunderbare Großveranstaltungen wie das Black & Blue Festival und natürlich das älteste schwul-lesbische Filmfestival in ganz Kanada: "Image & Nation". Montreal hat einfach alles zu bieten: Bars, Saunen, Stripper, Plätze, Menschen. Hinzu kommt, daß die Regierung Quebecs und Kanadas gleichgeschlechtliche Partner anerkennen.

La communauté gaie de Montréal, une métropole de plus de 3,4 million d'habitants, représente un pourcentage significatif de la population. Au fil des ans, un esprit d'ouverture et de tolérance s'est développé entre le milieu gai et le public. Ceci explique pourquoi Montréal, et plus particulièrement le Village (un des plus grands quartiers gai au monde) est devenu une destination privilégiée pour les touristes gais et lesbiennes internationaux. Beaucoup de visiteurs gardent un souvenir impérissable de la ville et y reviennent régulièrement, non seulement pour son milieu, mais également pour sa joie de vivre qui lui confère un charme difficile à résister.
Montréal propose une palette riche d'événements et d'activités : Divers/Cité, les Célébrations de la Fierté (Gay Pride), des événements de danse et de culture comme le Festival Black & Blue, ou le plus vieux festival cinématographique gai et lesbien du pays: Image & Nation.
Montréal, avec ses bars, restos, saunas, boîtes de strip-tease et ses chaleureux habitants, a de quoi satisfaire les goûts de tout un chacun, d'autant plus que le partenariat entre homosexuels est reconnu par les gouvernements du Québec et du Canada.

Montreal, metrópoli con más de 3,4 millones de personas, tiene una comunidad gay y lesbiana que representa un segmento importante de la población. Esto, a lo largo de los años ha llevado al desarrollo de un espíritu de tolerancia en la sociedad en general y en la comunidad homosexual de Montreal. Esta falta de prejuicios ha convertido a la ciudad, especialmente a la Village (una de las mayores zonas gays del mundo) en uno de los destinos preferidos por los gays y lesbianas de todo el mundo. Muchos visitantes homosexuales tienen muy buenos recuerdos de la ciudad y vuelven una y otra vez. Es un destino especialmente ideal para el turista homosexual, no sólo por la vida gay que se lleva en la ciudad, sino también por las ganas de vivir que se notan en Montreal a cada paso, dando a la ciudad un encanto especial que difícilmente se puede resistir.

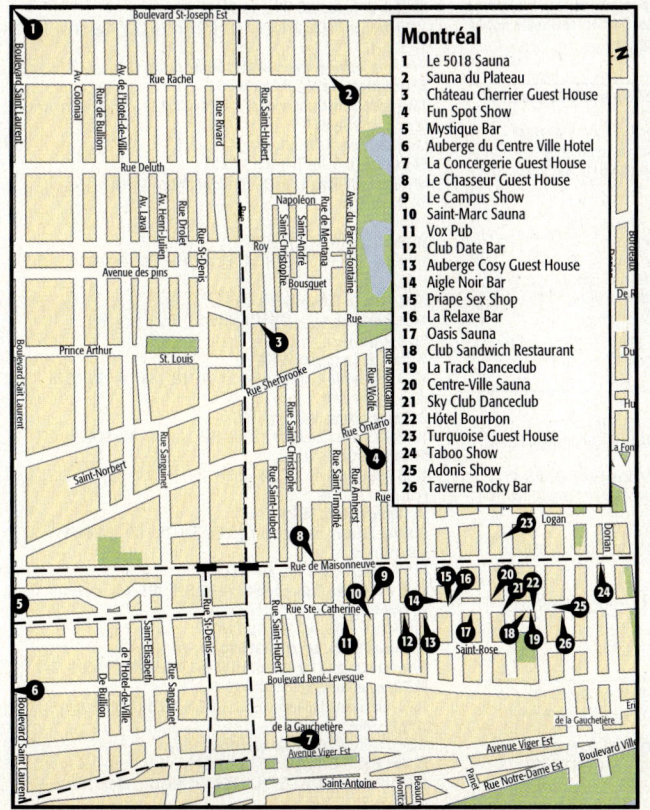

Montréal

1 Le 5018 Sauna
2 Sauna du Plateau
3 Château Cherrier Guest House
4 Fun Spot Show
5 Mystique Bar
6 Auberge du Centre Ville Hotel
7 La Concergerie Guest House
8 Le Chasseur Guest House
9 Le Campus Show
10 Saint-Marc Sauna
11 Vox Pub
12 Club Date Bar
13 Auberge Cosy Guest House
14 Aigle Noir Bar
15 Priape Sex Shop
16 La Relaxe Bar
17 Oasis Sauna
18 Club Sandwich Restaurant
19 La Track Danceclub
20 Centre-Ville Sauna
21 Sky Club Danceclub
22 Hôtel Bourbon
23 Turquoise Guest House
24 Taboo Show
25 Adonis Show
26 Taverne Rocky Bar

Canada/Québec — Montréal

Montreal cuenta con actividades y acontecimientos gays fantásticos: Divers/Cité, la fiesta del orgullo gay de Montreal Pride, fiestas fabulosas como el festival Black & Blue (negro y azul) así como el festival del cine gay y lesbiano más antiguo del Canadá, la Image&Nation (imagen y nación). Montreal lo tiene todo: bares, saunas, stiptease masculino, sitios, gente ... Los gobiernos de la provincia de Quebec así como del Canadá reconocen las relaciones de personas del mismo sexo.

✖ Montreal, una metropoli con più di 3,4 milioni d'abitanti, ospita una comunità di gay e lesbiche che costituisce una parte importante della popolazione.
Nel corso degli anni la popolazione di Montreal ha sviluppato una maggiore apertura e tolleranza nei confronti della comunità gay. Tale apertura ha fatto di tale città ed in particolar modo del "Village", una delle zone gay più grandi al mondo, una delle mete turistiche più ambite in assoluto per gay e lesbiche. Molti di questi visitatori associano alla città di Montreal ricordi meravigliosi e ci ritornano molto volentieri.
La città è molto favorevole ai gay, non solo per quanto riguarda la vita gay, ma anche per la "joie de vivre" che permea la città conferendole un fascino irresistibile!
A Montreal ci sono molte manifestazioni e attività per omosessuali: Divers/Cité, Gay-Pride Celebration, grandi spettacoli splendidi come il Festival Black & Blue e naturalmente il più antico festival per il cinema omosessuale in tutt'il Canada: Image & Nation. Montreal offre proprio di tutto: bar, saune, strip- tease, piazze, e la gente. Inoltre va menzionato che il governo del Quebec, così come quello del Canada riconoscono le coppie omosessuali.

GAY INFO
■ **Centre Communautaire des Gais et Lesbiennes de Montréal (CCGLM)** (GLM MA) Mon-Fri 9-12, 13-17 h
C.P. 476, Succ. „C" ✉ QC H2L 4K4 (2nd floor) ☎ 528-8424
🖨 528-9908 📧 info@ccglm.qc.ca 🖥 www.ccglm.qc.ca
Organisation with library aimed at improving the gay and lesbian condition through the creation of a dialogue.
■ **Fondation BBCM. La**
C.P. 1253, Station „B" ✉ QC H3B 3K9 ☎ 875-7070
📧 information@bbcm.org 🖥 www.bbcm.org
Organisers of the 5 annual party events in Montreal : „Black & Blue", „Wild & Wet", „Twist/Gay Pride", „Red" and „Bal de Boys" Please call, send an e-mail or visit the website for further information and exact dates.
■ **Gay Events & More** (GLM) 0-24 h
☎ 252-4429
Recorded message, changes weekly.

PUBLICATIONS
■ **Fugues**
1212 Rue Saint Hubert ✉ QC H2L 3Y7 ☎ 848-1854
☎ (888) 848-1854 (Toll-free) 🖨 845-7645 📧 info@fugues.com
🖥 www.fugues.com
Monthly magazine with calendar of events, advertising, classifieds, personal ads. Mainly French, some English. Subscription Can$ 30 per year. Free at gay venues.
■ **Homo Sapiens**
C.P. 8888, station centre-ville ✉ QC H3C 3P8 ☎ 987-3039
🖨 987-3615
■ **RG**
c/o Editions Homeureux, C.P. 915, succ. C ✉ QC H2L 4V2
☎ 523-9463 🖨 523-2214
Monthly magazine in French.

CULTURE
■ **Archives Gaies Du Québec. Les** (G) Wed 19.30-21.30 h
C.P. 395, Succ. Place-du-Parc ✉ QC H2W 2N9 (4067 Boulevard St.Laurent, #202) ☎ 287-9987
■ **Diffusions Gaies et Lesbiennes du Québec** (GLM MA)
4067 Boulevard Saint-Laurent, Bureau 300 ✉ QC H2W 1Y7
☎ 285-4467 🖨 285-1562
Organisers of the gay & lesbian film festival of Montreal.

TOURIST INFO
■ **Tourisme Montréal** 1st Jun-4th Sep: 7-20, 5th Sep-31st May: 9-18 h, colsed the 25th of Dec & 1st of Jan
1001 du Square-Dorchester ☎ 844-5400 🖨 844-5757
📧 perrier.jean-francois@tourisme-montreal.org
🖥 www.tourism-montreal.org

BARS
■ **Agora** (B G N) Tue-Sat 16-3, Sun & Mon 16-23 h
1160 rue Mackay ✉ QC H3G 2H4 (M°Guy-Concordia)
☎ 934-1428
■ **Aigle Noir** (B G LJ)
1315 rue Sainte Catherine Est ✉ QC H2L 2H4 (M° Beaudry)
☎ 529-0040
■ **Autre Bar. L'** (B GLM YG)
278 rue Laurier Ouest ✉ QC H2V 2K2 ☎ 278-1519
To see and be seen.
■ **Bar Cajun** (B GLM MA)
1574 Rue Sainte Catherine Est ✉ QC H2L 2J2 (M° Papineau/Beaudry) ☎ 523-4679
Intimate atmosphere bar.
■ **Club Bolo** (AC B GLM lj MA) Course: Mon Tue Thu 19-22.30, Dancing: Fri Sat 21-3, Sun 16-21 h
960 Rue Amherst ✉ QC H2L 3K5 (M° Beaudry) ☎ 849-4777
Country dance club and bar. Friendly atmosphere.
■ **Club Date** (ac B G OS s) 13-3 h
1218 rue Sainte-Catherine Est ✉ QC H2L 2G9 (M° Beaudry)
☎ 521-1242
Piano bar with live singers on WE. Karoke nights.
■ **Drugstore. Le** (AC B GLM MA OS)
1364 rue Sainte-Catherine Est ✉ QC H2L 2H6 (M°Beaudry/Papineau) ☎ 524-1960
Complex of eight bars, including Le Trou (LJ).
■ **Exotica** (B GLM) Thu-Sun 22-3 h
417 Rue Saint-Pierre ✉ QC H2Y 2M3 (Victoria Square)
☎ 218-1773
Latino bar.
■ **Mystique** (B G OG) 16-3 h
1424 Rue Stanley ✉ QC H3A 1P7 (M° Peel) ☎ 844-5711
English Pub.
■ **Q Zone** (B G MA) 12-3 h
1401 Rue Mackay ✉ ON H3G 2H6 (M° Guy-Concordia)
☎ 841-3131
■ **Relaxe. La** (B glm MA N)
1309 Rue Sainte-Catherine Est ✉ QC H2L 2H4 ☎ 523-0578
Friendly mixed bar.
■ **Resurrection** (B D Glm) 15-3 h
108 Rue Sainte-Catherine ✉ ON H2L 2G2 ☎ 845-5045
■ **Sona** (B Glm YG)
1439 Rue Bleury ✉ QC H3A 2H5
Popular in the after hours.
■ **Stéréo** (B D GLM) 23-11 h
858 Rue Sainte-Catherine Est ✉ QC H2L 2E3 ☎ 284-4475
New after hours bar.
■ **Stud** (AC CC B D G LJ MA N s) 10-3 h
1812 Rue Sainte Catherine Est ✉ QC H2K 2H3 (M°Papineau)
☎ 598-8243
Video-poker, free pool table 10-15 h
■ **Talons Noirs. Les** (B GLM MA) 15-3 h
3945 Rue Ontario Est ✉ ON H1W 1S8 (M° Pie-IX) ☎ 598-1342
■ **Taverne Rocky** (B G lj OG) 10-24 h
1673 Rue Sainte-Catherine Est ✉ QC H2L 2J5 (M° Papineau)
☎ 521-7865
Ballroom and line dancing for a mature crowd.
■ **Vox Pub** (AC B G MA OS VS) 10-24 h
1295 rue Amherst ✉ QC H2L 3K9 (M° Beaudry, at rue Sainte Catherine) ☎ 522-2766

Montréal Québec/Canada

CAFES

■ **Eden Café** (B f GLM OS)
1334 Rue Sainte-Catherine Est ✉ QC H3G 1P6 ☎ 524-2107
■ **Ôgâtô** (b BF CC F Glm)
1301 Rue Sainte-Catherine Est ✉ QC H2L 2H4 ☎ 528-6222
Good breakfast for a good looking men.
■ **Toasteur. Le** (b BF CC F GLM)
950 Rue Roy Est ✉ QC H2L 1E8 ☎ 527-8500
Crepes, waffles, eggs,...

DANCECLUBS

■ **Sky Club** (B D GLM MA STV)
1474 Rue Ste Catherine Est ✉ QC H2L 2J1 (M°Beaudry/Papineau) ☎ 529-6969
Pub and night club with different music and atmospheres on three levels.
■ **Track. La** (AC B G LJ MA WE) 21-3, Sat Sun 15-3 h
1584 Rue Sainte-Catherine Est ✉ QC H2L 2J2 (M° Papineau) ☎ 521-1419
Cruisy danceclub on three floors. Alternative rock and disco music.
■ **Unity** (! AC B D Glm OS snu YG)
1400 Rue Montcalm ✉ QC H2L 3G8 (M° Beaudry) ☎ 523-4429
Big danceclub on several floors. Sex nights on Thu, Women on Fri & Queen size on Sun.

RESTAURANTS

■ **Avenue. L'** (B CC F GLM)
922 Avenue Mont-Royal Est ✉ QC H2J 1X2 (M° Mont-Royal) ☎ 523-8780
North-American cuisine in a hip atmosphere.
■ **Bazou** (AC B CC F GLM MA OS)
2004 Hôtel de Ville ✉ QC H2X 1H5 ☎ 982-0853
Californian cuisine in a kitsch decor.
■ **Camembert. Le** (b CC F G H MA) 9-23 h
1641 Rue Amherst ✉ QC H2L 3L4 (M° Berri-UQAM) ☎ 597-0878
French and continental cuisine
■ **Chablis** (b CC F GLM MA OS) 11-23.20, Sat Sun 16-23.30 h
1639 Rue Saint-Hubert ✉ QC H2L 3Z1 (M°Berri) ☎ 523-0053
*French and Spanish cuisine. Brunch Sun 11 h.
Popular in the after hours.*
■ **Entretiens. Les** (B CC F GLM) 10-24 h
1577 Avenue Laurier Est ✉ QC H2J 1J1 (M° Laurier) ☎ 521-2934
*Vegetarian cuisine.
Hamburgers, fries, vegetarian dishes.*
■ **Piccolo Diavolo** (A AC b CC E F GLM LJ MA) Sat-Wed 17-23, Thu 11.30-14, 17-23, Fri 11.30-14, 14-24 h
1336 Rue Sainte-Catherine Est ✉ QC H2L 2H5 ☎ 526-1336
Italian cuisine.
■ **Planète. Le** (CC F GLM)
1451 Rue Sainte-Catherine Est ✉ QC H2L 2H9 ☎ 528-6953
Original cuisine.
■ **Saint-Charles. Le** (B CC E F G MA) 17-? h
1799 Rue Amherst ✉ QC H2L 3L7 (M° Beaudry) ☎ 526-1799
International cuisine.
■ **Stromboli** (B CC F Glm)
1019 Avenue Mont-Royal Est ✉ QC H2V 2H4 ☎ 528-5020
Italian cuisine in a theater decor.

SHOWS

■ **Adonis** (B G SNU YG) 15-3 h
1681 Rue Sainte Catherine Est ✉ QC H2L 2J5 (M°Papineau) ☎ 521-1355
■ **Cabaret l'Entre-Peau** (B Glm STV) 21-3, Sun 15-3 h
1115 Rue Sainte-Catherine Est ✉ QC H2L 2G6 (M° Beaudry) ☎ 525-7566
One of the most famous drag show of Montreal.
■ **Campus. Le** (AC B G SNU) 15-3 h, Ladies's night on Sun
1111 Rue Sainte Catherine Est ✉ QC H2L 2G6 (M° Beaudry) ☎ 526-3616
■ **Chez Cleopatra** (B G STV)
1230 Boulevard Saint-Laurent ✉ QC H2X 2S5 ☎ 871-8065
Drags shows in this recently renovated bar.

■ **Fun Spot** (B G MA STV) 10-24 h
1151 Ontario Est ✉ QC H2L 1R3 (M° Beaudry) ☎ 522-0416
■ **Stock Bar** (B G SNU) Wed-sun 20-3 h
1278 Saint-André ✉ QC H2L 3S9 (M° Berri-UQAM) ☎ 842-1366
Also pool bar.
■ **Taboo** (AC B G SNU YG) 15-3 h
1950 Boulevard de Maisonneuve Est ✉ QC H2K 2C8 (M° Papineau) ☎ 597-0010

SEX SHOPS/BLUE MOVIES

■ **Priape** (CC G LJ MA) Mon-Sat 10-21, Sun 12-21 h
1311 Rue Sainte Catherine Est ✉ QC H2L 2H4 ☎ 521-8451
Magazines, leather, jeans, rubber, toys etc.

ESCORTS & STUDIOS

■ **Agence Flèche** (G MSG) 0-24 h
☎ 254-5478

SAUNAS/BATHS

■ **Aux Berges** (B G MA SB OS WH) 0-24 h
1070 Rue Mackay ✉ QC H3G 2H1 (M°Lucien l'Allier ou Guy Concordia) ☎ 938-9393
■ **Bain Colonial** (CC G SA SB VS WH)
3963 Avenue Colonial ☎ 285-0132
■ **Bourbon** (B G MA SB VS) 0-24 h
1574 Rue Sainte-Catherine Est ✉ QC H2L 2J2 (Métro Beaudry & Papineau) ☎ 523-4679
Small sauna part of a resort complex.
■ **Centre-Ville** (AC CC F G MA SA SB VS WH) 0-24 h
1465 Rue Sainte Catherine Est ✉ QC H2L 2H9 (M°Berri/Papineau) ☎ 524-3486
Sauna frequented by a mixed age crowd.
■ **Oasis. L'** (AC B f G SA SB VS WH YG) 0-24 h
1390 Rue Sainte Catherine Est ✉ QC H2L 2H6 (M°Beaudry) ☎ 521-0785
Recently refurbished, this popular sauna in the heart of the gay village gets really busy with a young crowd after the bars close.
■ **Saint Hubert** (AC G SA VS) Mon-Thu 11-24, Fri-Sun 0-24 h
6527 Saint Hubert ✉ QC H2S 2M5 (near Plaza Saint-Hubert) ☎ 277-0176
Discreet sauna where it is not unusual to meet married men.
■ **Saint-Marc. Le** (AC B DR f G MA lj SA VS WH) 0-24 h
1168 Rue Sainte Catherine Est ✉ QC H2L 2G7 (M°Beaudry) ☎ 525-8404
Sauna on two floors frequented by a leather crowd.
■ **Sauna du Plateau** (f G MA OS SA SB VS WH) 0-24 h
961 Rue Rachel Est ✉ QC H2J 2J4 (near Parc Lafontaine) ☎ 528-1679
Recent sauna on four floors with summer terrace. Room to room telephone service.
■ **Verdun Sauna** (AC f G MG SA VS) 11-24, Fri-Sun 0-24 h
5785 Avenue Verdun, Verdun ✉ QC H4H 1L7 (M° Verdun) ☎ 769-6034
Intimate sauna frequented by middle aged professionals, often bi-men.
■ **1286** (AC b G SA MA VS WH) 0-24 h
1286 Chemin Chambly, Longueuil ✉ QC J4J 3W6 (M°Longueuil. Bus8/88) ☎ (450) 677-1286
Frequented by a mixed age crowd from Montreal-East.
■ **226** (G MG SA SB SOL VS WO) 0-24 h
243 Boulevard des Laurentides, Laval ✉ QC H7G 2T6 (M° Henry Bourassa) ☎ (450) 975-4556
Sauna busy from noon until evening with a professional middle aged crowd.
■ **3481. Le** (G SA SB VS WH) 0-24 h
3481 Montée Saint-Hubert (on Montreal's South shore) ☎ (450) 462-1511
■ **456. Le** (B CC DR F G MA PI SA SB VS WH WO) 0-24 h
456 de La Gauchetière Ouest ✉ QC H2Z 1E3 (M°Square Victoria/McGill) ☎ 871-8341
Big sauna with numerous special parties throughout the year. Check website for dates.

SPARTACUS 2001/2002 | 141

Canada/Québec Montréal

CANADA'S FINEST ALL MALE HOTEL

**42 ROOM HOTEL · AIR-CONDITIONED
PRIVATE BATHROOMS · TELEVISION
VIDEOS · TELEPHONES · BOUTIQUE
CONTINENTAL BREAKFAST**

aux Berges AUBERGE

**SAUNA · STEAM
JACUZZI · COMMUNAL SHOWERS
ROOFTOP TERRACE · BAR
GARDEN · PATIO**

LUCIEN-L'ALLIER

GUY-CONCORDIA

www.auxberges.ca

AUBERGE DU CENTRE VILLE INC.
1070, RUE MACKAY, MONTRÉAL H3G 2H1 (514) 938-9763 (800) 668-6253

---

la Conciergerie GUEST HOUSE

Your resort in the city!

EDITOR'S CHOICE AWARDS 1999 OUT & ABOUT

1019, rue Saint-Hubert, Montréal (Qc) H2L 3Y3 Canada
Tel:(514) 289-7553 Fax:(514) 289-0845
www.laconciergerie.ca info@laconciergerie.ca

■ **5018. Le** (AC cc f G MA msg OS SA SB VS WH) 0-24 h
5018 Boulevard St-Laurent ✉ QC H2T 1R7 *(M° Laurier, between Rue St-Joseph and Rue Laurier)* ☎ 277-3555
Big sauna on four floors with roof top. Mixed friendly crowd.

MASSAGE
■ **Tropicales Services** (G MA MSG) 0-24 h
☎ 253-2255
Excellent serious and safe male masseurs. 24 h answering service, student rates with ID card.

BOOK SHOPS
■ **Androgyne. L'** (CC GLM MA) Mon-Wed 9-18, Thu Fri 9-21, Sat 9-18, Sun 11-18 h
3636 Boulevard Saint-Laurent ✉ QC H2X 2V4 *(at Prince Arthur)* ☎ 842-4765
Gay, lesbian books in French, English.

FASHION SHOPS
■ **Body Body** (G)
1326 Rue Sainte-Catherine Est ✉ QC H2L 2H5 *(M° Beaudry or Papineau)* ☎ 523-0645
Men's clothing, clubwear.

LEATHER & FETISH SHOPS
■ **Il Bolero** (glm LJ) Mon-Wed 9.30-18, Thu Fri -21, Sat -17, Sun 12.30-17 h
6842 Rue Saint Hubert ✉ QC H2S 2M6 *(M° Jean Talon)* ☎ 270-6065
Fetish fashion & clubwear.
■ **U-Bahn** (CC G LJ)
1285 Rue Amherst ✉ QC H2L 3K9 ☎ 529-0808
Leather, rubber and PVC clothing for men.

Montréal Québec/Canada

AUBERGE COSY
BED & BREAKFAST

14 SPACIOUS ROOMS
COLOR TV & CABLE
FULL EUROPEAN BREAKFAST
WHIRLPOOL
AIR CONDITIONING
ROOFTOP TERRACE

www.aubergecosy.com

Your hosts Eric & Eric

1274 SAINTE-CATHERINE EAST, MONTREAL • 514-525-2151

HOTELS

■ **Auberge du Centre-Ville** (AC B BF CC f G H MA NU OS SA BF VS WH)
1070 Rue Mackay ✉ QC H3G 2H1 *Downtown, M°Guy-Concordia, at Rue René-Levesque)* ☎ 938-9393 ☎ (800) 668-9393 (free-call)
📠 938 -1616 📧 info@auxberges.ca 💻 www.auxberges.ca
42 rooms, most with bath/shower/WC, all with phone, radio, TV, AC and room service. For more details, please see website. Rates start at CAN$ 80.-

GUEST HOUSES

■ **Alacoque** (AC BF CC F Glm H OS)
2091 St Urbain ✉ QC H2X 2N1 *(South of Sherbrooke)* ☎ 842-0430
📠 842-7585 📧 christian.alacoque@sympatico.ca
💻 www.3.sympatico.ca/christian.alacoque
An authentic town house from 1830. Well furnished. Downtown. Rates Can$ 50-100.

■ **Auberge Cosy** (AC BF CC GLM H WH)
1274 Rue Sainte-Catherine Est ✉ QC H2l 2H2 *(M° Beaudry)*
☎ 525-2151 📠 525-2579 📧 info@aubergecosy.com
💻 www.aubergecosy.com
14 spacious rooms with AC, colour TV & cable. Check website or call for rates.

■ **Chambres au Village** (BF f G H MA)
850 Rue de la Gauchetière Est ✉ QC H2L 2N2 *(M° Berri/Bus 150)*
☎ 844-6901 📧 info@chambresauvillage.com
💻 www.chambresauvillage.com

■ **Chasseur. Le** (BF CC G H MA OS)
1567 Rue Saint-André ✉ QC H2L 3T5 *(M° Berri-Uqam, central)*
☎ 521-2238 📠 849-2051
5 rooms with bath/WC on the corridor, 1 en-suite. Rooms with balcony, radio, heating.

■ **Château Cherrier** (AC BF CC GLM H) Apr 15-Nov 15
550 Rue Cherrier ✉ QC H2L 1H3 *(M°Sherbrooke)* ☎ 844-0055
☎ (800) 816-0055 (toll-free) 📠 844-8438
📧 chateau.cherrier@sympatico.ca
Located in the „quartier latin", close to gay village. 8 rooms in an old Tudor building, with authentic period furniture. Gay owned and operated.

■ **Conciergerie Guest House. La** (AC BF CC G LJ msg QS WH WO)
1019 Rue Saint Hubert ✉ QC H2L 3Y3 *(central location. 20 km to airport. 4 min walk to the gay bars of the Village, M° Berri)*
☎ 289-9097 📠 289-0201 📧 info@laconciergerie.ca
💻 www.laconciergerie.ca
Nice guest house with sundeck surrounded by a cruisy area. Open year round. Rates from Can $ 97.- (bath/shower/WC), 82.- (without).

■ **Hôtel Bourbon** (B BF F GLM H SB)
1574 Rue Sainte-Catherine Est ✉ QC H2L 2J2 *(Métro Beaudry & Papineau)* ☎ 523-4679 ☎ (1 800) 268-4679 📠 523-4679
37 comfortable rooms in a gay shopping en entertainment complex.

■ **Houseboy Bed & Breakfast. Le** (AC BF GLM H MA)
1281 Rue Beaudry ✉ QC H2L 3E3 *(in the gay Village)*
☎ 525-1459 📠 525-1459 📧 lehouseboy@excite.com
Nice cozy rooms in a renovated Victorian House, Single rooms CAN $ 50-60.-, double 75-80.- incl. full BF.

Château Cherrier
Bed & Breakfast

Déjeuners hors-pair — Healty & Hearty Breakfast
550, Cherrier, Montréal, Québec
Canada H2L 1H3
Tél : (514) 844-0055—Fax: (514) 844-8438

SPARTACUS 2001/2002   143

Canada/Québec — Montréal

CLASSIFICATION GÎTES TOURISTIQUES
BED & BREAKFASTS RATING

Hébergement Québec

The colorful Bed & Breakfast
in the heart of the Gay Village

▼ Great location
▼ Quiet
▼ Shared bathrooms
▼ Private garden

1576, Alexandre-DeSève
Montréal (Québec)
Canada H2L 2V7
(514) 523.9913
1.877.707.1576
www.turquoisebb.com

■ **Maison Chablis** (AC BF CC F G H MA OS SOL) Reception: 11-23 h
1641 Rue St-Hubert ✉ QC H2L 3Z1 (M° Berri) ☎ 527-8346
🖥 596-1519 ✉ chablis@mlink.com 🖥 www.mlink.net/~chablis/
Downtown location near gay village. 8 double rooms, 5 single rooms.

■ **Roy d'Carreau Guest House. Le** (A AC BF CC GLM MSG NU OS) 8-23 h
1637 Amherst ✉ QC H2L 3L4 (M°Beaudry/Berry-UQAM)
☎ 524-2493 ☎ (888) 304-2443 (toll-free) ✉ info@leroydcarreau.com 🖥 www.leroydcarreau.com

■ **Saint-Christophe. Le** (BF CC G H NU OS SOL WH)
1597 Rue Saint-Christophe ✉ QC H2L 3W7 (M° Berri)
☎ 527-7836 🖥 526-6488 ✉ info@stchristophe.com
🖥 www.stchristophe.com

■ **Three Cats Guest House. The** (BF G H LJ MA p)
c/o POB/CP 1036, Station „C" ✉ QC H2L 4V3 ☎ 899-5582
For leather fetish guests. Close to East Village area. Call for further information and address.

■ **Turquoise** (BF G H NU OS)
1576 rue Alexandre de Sève ✉ QC H2L 2V7 (M°Beaudry)
☎ 523-9943 ☎ (1-877) 707 15 76 (call-free) 🖥 523-9943
🖥 www.turquoisebb.com
B&B in a Victorian mansion with a large and sunny garden. 4 rooms and one suite (2 queen size beds) with shared bath/WC, own key. Rates single Can$ 40-50, double 50-60 and suite 60-90, bf buffet included.

PRIVATE ACCOMMODATION

■ **Au Stade B+B** (ac BF G F MA p SOL WO) 10-22 h
C.P. 60542 ✉ QC H1V 3T8 (close to Olympic Village, 20 min. to airport & 7 min. to gay area) ☎ 254-1250, ext. 1
✉ be-brief@sympatico.ca
3 rooms with shared baths. Balcony, phone, fax, TV, video, and radio. Call for rates.

■ **Bed and Breakfast du Village** (BF GLM H OS WH)
1279 Rue Montcalm ✉ QC H2L 3G6 ☎ 522-4771 🖥 522-7118
✉ bbv@total.net 🖥 www.gaibec.com/bbv

■ **Un et l'Autre B&B. L'** (AC b BF CC G)
1641 Rue Amherst ✉ QC H2L 3L4 ☎ 597 0878
✉ info@aubergell.com 🖥 www.aubergell.com
Beautifully renovated house in the heart of Montréal's gay village with outdoor terrace/Jolie maison rénovée sise au coer du Village avec terrasse-soleil.

■ **Zip Centre-Ville** (AC BF G MA SA WH) 8-21 h
1210 Dalcourt ✉ QC H2L 2W6 (M° Beaudry) ☎ 524-4372
✉ rbarrette@cedep.com 🖥 www.pointzip.qc.ca
5 rooms with bath/WC, radio, kitchenette, own key.

CAMPING

■ **Camping Plein Bois** (B CC D F G LJ MG NU OS PI) 9-24 h, open May-Sep
550 Chemin St-Henri, Sainte-Marthe, Cté Vaudreuil ✉ QC J0P 1W0

(45 min. from Montreal, 1.30 h. from Ottawa) ☎ (450) 459-4646
☎ (1 888) 505-1010 (toll-free) 🖥 (450) 459-9417
✉ info.camping.pb@qc.aira.com 🖥 www.campingpb.qc.ca
Campground for men only. There are so many activities possible, that we suggest you contact André for further information.

GENERAL GROUPS

■ **Aux Prismes, Plein Air et Culture** (GLM)
C.P. 5461 Succ. B ✉ QC H3B 4P1 ☎ 963-9710
✉ aux_prismes@moncourrier.com 🖥 pages.infinit.net/benmarc
A non profit organisation offering gays, lesbians and their friends a large selction of social/outdoors/cultural events. See the calendar of events on the website. [3]

FETISH GROUPS

■ **Club de Cuir Les Prédateurs Montréal** (G LJ MA)
C.P. 171, Succ. „C" ✉ QC H2L 4K1
Social group for men interested in leather.

■ **M.C. Faucon Montréal** (G LJ)
C.P. 152, Succ. „C" ✉ QC H2L 4K1

HEALTH GROUPS

■ **ACCM** (G)
2075 Rue Plessis ✉ QC H2L 2Y4 ☎ 527-0918
Support groups, counselling, legal and financial services.

■ **Fonds de Recherche pour l'Etude sur le Sida**
1150 Boulevard Saint-Joseph, Bureau 020 ✉ QC H2J 1L5
☎ 521-1572

■ **Info-SIDA**
☎ 521-7432
Information about transmission, symptoms, treatment etc. in French.

■ **Séro-Zéro** (G)
C.P. 246, Succ. „C" ✉ QC H2L 4K1 (2075 Rue Plessis) ☎ 521-7778
🖥 521-7665 🖥 www.sero-zero.qc.ca
Prevention & information about HIV/AIDS.

HELP WITH PROBLEMS

■ **Gai Ecoute** 19-23 h
c/o Gay Line, C.P. 384, Stn. H ✉ QC H3G 2L1 ☎ 866-0103
French info-line.

■ **Gay Line** 19-23 h
C.P. 384, Stn. H ✉ QC H3G 2L1 ☎ 866-5090
Non-profit listening & referal service for the gay, lesbian and bisexual English-speaking community of Quebec.

SPECIAL INTEREST GROUPS

■ **Association des Lesbiennes et des Gais de l'Université de Québec à Montréal (ALGUQAM)** (GLM YG)
1259 Rue Berri ✉ QC H2L 4C7 *(9th floor)* ☎ 987-3000 # 3039
Student group publisher of the monthly information magazine "Homo sapiens".

■ **Association des Motocyclistes Gais du Québec (AMGQ)** (G MA)
C.P. 47618, Succ. Mont Royal ✉ QC H2H 2S8 ☎ 597-2246
📧 amgq_mtl@yahoo.com 🌐 www.algi.qc.ca/asso/amgq/
Social group promoting gay presence in motorcycling world; bi-monthly newsletter; garage and driving school.

■ **Jeunesse Lambda** (GLM YG)
C.P. 5514, Succ. „B" ✉ QC H3B 4P1 ☎ 528-5315 📠 528-5316
Youth group.

■ **Ours Montréal Bears** (G)
C.P. 613, Succ. „C" ✉ QC H2L 4L5 ☎ 855-8922
Club for bears and their admirers.

CRUISING

- Rue Sainte-Catherine Est (Saint-Hubert Street to Wolfe Street, after 21 h)
- In front, in the little park west of Church Marie-Reine-du-Monde
- Parc Baldwin (M°Papineau)
- Rue Champlain (R) (between Sainte-Catherine est and René-Lévesque Est boulevard)
- Parc Mont-Royal (daytime east side of the hill, both sides of the main branch of Camilien-Houde-street. Nighttime, 23-? h, only on the left side)

Mont-Tremblant ☎ 819

PRIVATE ACCOMMODATION

■ **Versant Ouest** (BF CC GLM) all year
110 Chemin Labelle ✉ QC J0T 1Z0 ☎ 425-5315
📧 verso@cil.qc.ca 🌐 www.versant-ouest.qc.ca
Open year round. 90 min. by car from Montreal and 5 min. from the skiing resort of Tremblant. Nice country B&B house. 4 rooms with bath/WC.

Québec ☎ 418

✱ Quebec City is the capital of the same named province and is seen as the heart of the French speaking culture in Canada. The outer suburbs are very American in style and the inner part of the city is predominantly French architecture with many of the old building under historical protection. Quebec is a strange mixture of North America and France.
The gay scene is rather small but lively. The city has many first class restaurants heavily frequented by gays and lesbians. In Quebec the winter is very long and lasts from November to April. February is one of the coldest months with temperatures sinking to under minus 20° Celsius. The cold winter does not prevent the Quebecoise from celebrating their Winter Carnival. The colourful Quebec Carnival is heavily visited by tourists and it is even worth making a trip from Montreal or Toronto.

✱ Quebec City ist die Hauptstadt der gleichnamigen Provinz und gilt als Wiege der französischsprachigen Kultur in Kanada. Während sich die Stadt in ihren Außenbezirken mit ihren Highways, Shoppingmalls und ausgedehnten Wohngebieten sehr amerikanisch gibt, strahlt die denkmalgeschützte und äußerst sehenswerte Altstadt ein geschichtsträchtiges Flair aus, das eher an Frankreich als an Nordamerika erinnert.
Die Szene ist klein aber lebendig. Die Stadt verfügt über zahlreiche erstklassige Restaurants, von denen einige fast ausschließlich von Schwulen und Lesben besucht werden.
Nicht vergessen sollten Besucher, daß Quebec auch die Kältekammer Kanadas genannt wird, und dies nicht ohne Grund. Der Winter ist lang und dauert von November bis April, wobei die Temperaturen im Februar zum Teil unter minus 20° C absinken. Dies hindert die Quebecoise aber nicht daran, jedes Jahr im Februar ausgiebig ihren Winterkarneval zu feiern. Dieses bunte Spektakel lockt auch viele Touristen an und lohnt auf jeden Fall einen Abstecher von Montreal oder Toronto aus.

✱ La métropole du Québec est la capitale de la province de même nom et est considérée comme le berceau de la culture francophone du Canada. Bien que la ville dans ses quartiers extérieurs avec ses highways, shoppingmalls et zones résidentielles soient très américains, la remarquable vieille ville classée monuments historiques reflète une atmosphère historique rappelant plutôt la France que l'Amérique du Nord. La scène est petite, mais animée. La ville dispose d'un grand nombre de restaurants de première catégorie dont certains sont fréquentés presque exclusivement par les homosexuels et les lesbiennes. Les visiteurs ne devraient pas oublier que le Québec est également désigné „chambre froide" du Canada, et cela non sans raison. L'hiver est long et dure du mois de novembre jusqu'au mois d'avril, encore qu'il faille souligner que les températures descendent au mois de février au-dessous de 20⁰ C. Cela n'empèche cependant pas les québécoises de fêter amplement leur carnaval d'hiver. Ce spectacle de variétés attire aussi de nombreux touristes et un crochet de Montréal ou de Toronto en vaut la peine.

✱ Québec City es la capital de la provincia del mismo nombre y es considerada como la cuna de la cultura francófona en Canada. Mientras las afueras de la ciudad se semeja mucho a los Estados Unidos, con sus grandes careteras, centros comerciales y extensas zonas de viviendas, el centro de la ciudad refleja un ambiente muy especial que recuerda más a Francia con sus antiguos edificios dignos de ver. El ambiente gay es pequeño, pero muy vivaz. La ciudad cuenta con excelentes restaurantes, algunos de ellos visitados exclusivamente por clientela gay. El apodo de Québec es, y con mucha razón, „cámara frigorífica de Canadá", debido a su largo invierno que dura desde noviembre hasta abril, con temperaturas que bajan frecuentemente a menos de 20°C. Pero este hecho no significa ningún obstáculo para que anualmente sus habitantes celebren apasionadamente la fiesta de carnavales en febrero. Este fantástico espectáculo atrae siempre muchos turistas, que vienen desde Montreal o Toronto para no perderse estas fiestas.

✱ Quebec City è la capitale della provincia omonima e viene considerata la culla della cultura francofona in Canada. Mentre i quartieri periferici con gli Highways, Shoppingmalls e le estese zone residenziali sono tipici per l'America, il bel centro storico pieno di monumenti nazionali rievoca il passato e le sue radici francesi. La vita gay è piccola ma vivace. Si trovano numerosi ristoranti di prima classe, di cui alcuni vengono frequentati esclusivamente dai gay e lesbiche. Non è da dimentacare che Quebec viene nominato il „frigorifero" di Canada. C'è un motivo. L'inverno è lungo e dura da novembre fino ad aprile, e le temperature calano fino ai 20 gradi sotto zero, un fatto che non inibisce i Quebecoise a festeggiare il carnavale. Questo allegro avvenimento attrae anche molti turisti, e vale la pena fare una scappata da Montreal o Toronto.

Canada/Québec — Québec ▶ Rouyn-Noranda

PUBLICATIONS
■ **Magaizine de Québec. Le**
707 Boulevard Charest Ouest ✉ QC G1N 4T1 ☎ 529-5892
Monthly newspaper published in French.

BARS
■ **Amour Sorcier** (A B d f GLM MA N OS s) 14-3 h
789 Côte Sainte-Geneviève ✉ QC G1R 3L6 ☎ 523-3395
■ **Bar de la Couronne** (B G S) 15-3 h
310 Rue de la Couronne ✉ QC G1K 6E5 ☎ 525-6593
■ **Drague. Le** (B G lj N OS STV VS) 9-24 h
815 rue St. Augustin ✉ QC G1R 3N4 *(at Rue St. Joachim)*
☎ 649-7212
Very popular.
■ **Eveil. L'** (B G MA)
670 rue Bouvier ✉ QC G2J 1A7 ☎ 628-0610
■ **Lazbyboy** (B GLM YG)
811 rue Saint Jean ✉ QC G1R 1R2 ☎ 647-9227
■ **Mâle.** Le (B G LJ MA)
770 Côte Sainte Geneviève ✉ QC G1R 3L3 ☎ 648-9497
■ **Paradisio** (B GLM MA)
161 rue St-Jean ✉ QC G1R 1N4 ☎ 522-6014
■ **Taverne Bar** (B G MA)
321 rue de la Couronne ✉ QC G1K 6E5 ☎ 525-5107

DANCECLUBS
■ **Ballon Rouge. Le** (B D G YG) 22-3 h
811 rue Saint Jean ✉ QC G1R 1R2 ☎ 647-9227

RESTAURANTS
■ **Chez Garbo** (B F glm)
157 Chemin Sainte Foy ✉ QC G1R 1T1 ☎ 529-9903
■ **Hobbit. Le** (B BF F glm)
700 rue Saint Jean ✉ QC G1R 1P9 ☎ 647-2677
■ **Restaurant Diana** (B F glm) 20-1 h
849 rue St. Jean ✉ QC G1R 1R2 ☎ 524-5794
Italian and Greek cuisine.

SEX SHOPS/BLUE MOVIES
■ **Empire Lyon** (G LJ)
873 rue Saint Jean ✉ QC G1R 1R2 ☎ 648 2301
Videos, magazines, clothing, leather & sex toys.
■ **Gai Serpentin** (G LJ VS)
101 boulevard du Pont, Saint Nicolas ✉ QC G7A 2T3
☎ 831-4055
■ **Importation Delta** (CC G LJ MA) Sun & Mon 12-18, Tue, Wed & Sat 10-18, Thu & Fri -21 h
875 rue Saint Jean ✉ QC G1R 1R2 ☎ 647-6808
Men's underwear, leather, toys, videos, pride & bears products & more.

SAUNAS/BATHS
■ **Backboys** (b CC DR f G MA SB WH) 0-24 h
264 Rue de la Couronne ✉ QC G1K 6C8 ☎ 521 6686
Sauna with mirrors rooms, glory holes, sling and TV lounge.
■ **Bloc 225** (B G MA SA SB) 0-24 h
225 rue Saint Jean ✉ QC G1R 1N8 ☎ 523-2562
Also sale of underwear and sale/rental of videos.
■ **Hippocampe** (b CC G H SA SB SOL WH) 0-24 h
31 rue McMahon ✉ QC G1R 3S5 ☎ 692-1521
Sauna with comfortable hotel rooms and free coffee in the morning.

■ **853** (AC f G SA SB SOL VS WO) 0-24 h
853 rue St-Jean ✉ QC G1R 1R2 ☎ 522 5525
Sauna with free gym facilities, tanning beds and parking place. Also hotel rooms, shop and glory holes.

GUEST HOUSES
■ **Coureur des Bois Guest House. Le** (BF GLM H MA OS)
15 rue Sainte Ursule ✉ QC G1R 4C7 ☎ 692-1117
☎ (800) 269-6414 (Toll-free) ≞ 692-4308
🖳 www.gayquebec.com
Located within the walls of old Quebec City. All rooms with shared baths. Rates Can$ 30-65 incl. cont. bf. No kids, pets on request.
■ **727 Guest House. Le** (AC BF GLM H msg OS SOL WH)
727 Rue d'Aiguillon ✉ QC G1R 1M8 ☎ 648-6766
☎ (800) 652-6766 (Toll-free) ≞ 648-1474
European-style guest house located in the old part. Rooms with private and shared bath, color TV. Rates Can$ 30-66 incl. cont. bf.

FETISH GROUPS
■ **Cuirassés du Québec. Les**
C.P. 52064, Succ. St. Fidèle ✉ QC G1L 5A4
🖳 cuir_qc@yahoo.com

HEALTH GROUPS
■ **MIELS Québec**
281 Chemin Sainte-Foy ✉ QC G1R 1T5 ☎ 649-1720
■ **Regroupement des personnes vivant avec le VIH/SIDA**
281 Chemin Sainte-Foy, bureau 100 ✉ QC G1R 1T5 ☎ 529-1942

SPECIAL INTEREST GROUPS
■ **Adam Et Compagnie** (G MA)
C.P. 55042 Succ. St. Vallier ✉ QC G1K 9A4 ☎ 525-8447
🖳 adam_et_cie@hotmail.com 🖳 www.geocities.com/adam
Gay & bi nudist club.
■ **Groupe Gai de l'Université Laval** (GLM YG)
C.P. 2500, Pav. Ernest-Lemieux, Cité universitaire ✉ QC G1K 7P4
(Université Laval, Pavillon Pollack, local 2223) ☎ 656-2131 ext. 8950
Information, support, gay library.

CRUISING
- Lac Vert
- Rue St.Denis
- Rue St. Jean (north of Place d'Youville)
- Plains of Abraham (path along the cliffs, evenings)
- Terrace Dufferin

Rimouski ☎ 418

GENERAL GROUPS
■ **Regroupement des lesbiennes et gais de l'est du Québec** (B D GLM)
C.P. 31 ✉ QC G5L 7B7 ☎ 721-0097

Rouyn-Noranda ☎ 819

BARS
■ **Station D** (B GLM MA) Wed 16-24, Thu-Sun -3 h
82 Perreault Ouest ✉ QC J9X 2T4 ☎ 797-8696

GENERAL GROUPS
■ **Action Gaie de l'Abitibi-Témiscamingue** (GLM)
C.P. 576 ✉ J9X 5C6
Gay & lesbian social and support group.

Saint François-Du-Lac ▶ Regina   Québec - Saskatchewan/Canada

Saint François-Du-Lac ☎ 450

CAMPING
■ **Domaine Gay Luron** (B CC D F G MA NU PI stv WE) May 1st-Sep 15th
261 Grande-Terre ✉ QC J0G 1M0 ☎ 568-3634 🖨 568-2055
🖳 www.freeyellow.com/members8/gayluron
Camp ground, appartments and cabins Can$ 7-60.-

Saint Georges ☎ 418

BARS
■ **Stare. Le** (B GLM MA) Thu-Sun 16-3, Sat 20-3 h
11270 1ère Avenue ✉ QC G5Y 2C3 *(5th floor)* ☎ 227-6131

Saint Hyacinthe ☎ 450

BARS
■ **Main Gauche. La** (AC B D E GLM MA OS S)
470 rue Mondor ✉ QC J2S 5A7 ☎ 774-5556

Saint Jérôme ☎ 450

BARS
■ **O Différent** (B GLM MA) Wed-Sun 21-3 h
257 St-Georges ✉ QC J7Z 5A1 ☎ 569-8769

Sept-Iles ☎ 418

GAY INFO
■ **Unigai(es)** (GLM)
☎ 962-7130

CAFES
■ **Café du Port** (b glm) 11-24 h
495 Avenue Brochu ✉ QC G4R 2X2 ☎ 962-9311

Sherbrooke ☎ 819

BARS
■ **Complexe 13-17** (B Glm D)
13-15-17 Bowen sud ✉ QC J1G 2C4 ☎ 569-5580

HELP WITH PROBLEMS
■ **Gai Ecoute** (GLM) 19-23 h
☎ (1-888) 505-1010 (Toll-free)

CRUISING
-Rue Wellington
-Carrefour de l'Estrie Centre

Trois Rivières ☎ 819

BARS
■ **Station MP. La** (B GLM MA)
1198 Rue Champflour ✉ QC G9A 1Z9 ☎ 376-0481

RESTAURANTS
■ **Embuscade. L'** (A AC B d F glm MA N OS s) 12-3 h GLM on Thu
1571 Place Badeaux ✉ QC G9A 4T4 ☎ 374 0652
Café-galerie with live music on Sat.

HELP WITH PROBLEMS
■ **Gai Ecoute** (GLM) 19-23 h
☎ (1-888) 505-1010 (Toll-free)

CDN-Saskatchewan

Location: Central CDN
Initials: SK
Time: GMT -6
Area: 652,000 km2 / 251,737 sq mi.
Population: 1,024,000
Capital: Regina

Lashburn ☎ 306

GENERAL GROUPS
■ **Support and Education for Gays, Lesbians, their Families & Friends** (GLM)
PO Box 9 ✉ SK S0M 1H0 ☎ 285-3823

Ravenscrag ☎ 306

GUEST HOUSES
■ **Spring Valley Guest Ranch** (BF F g H)
PO Box 10 ✉ SK S0N 2C0 ☎ 295-4124
Bed and breakfast with licensed tearoom.

Regina ☎ 306

GAY INFO
■ **Pink Triangle Community Services** Tue Fri 20.30-23 h
PO Box 24031, Broad Street PO ✉ SK S4P 4J8 ☎ 526-6046
📧 ptcsregina@canada.com 🖳 members.xoom.com/ptcs
Health, education and support group. Also library.

CAFES
■ **Just Bean Brewed** (f glm)
2201 Broad Street ✉ SK S4P 1Y7 ☎ 522-5535

DANCECLUBS
■ **Outside** (B D GLM)
2070 Broad Street ✉ SK S4P 3J8 ☎ 522-7343

GIFT & PRIDE SHOPS
■ **Homo Depot** (GLM) 16-? h
2070 Broad Street PO ✉ SK S4P 4J8
T-shirts, cards, jewellery, gifts, etc

GENERAL GROUPS
■ **EGALE Regina** (GLM)
PO Box 24031, Broad Street PO ✉ SK S4P 4J8
Gay/Lesbian rights lobbying group.
■ **Gay and Lesbian Community of Regina (GLCR)** (GLM) 16-? h
2070 Broad Street, PO Box 3414 ✉ SK B4P 3J8 ☎ 522-7343
📧 glcr@sk.sympatico.ca
Non-profit society operating the community centre, lounge, café and disco.
■ **Lesbian, Bisexual & Gay Pride Committee of Regina** (GLM)
PO Box 24031, Broad Street PO ✉ SK S4P 4J8 ☎ 545-9472
📧 regina-pride@gaycanada.com

Canada/Saskatchewan - Yukon Territory   Regina ▶ Whitehorse

HEALTH GROUPS
■ **AIDS Regina**
1504B Albert Street ✉ SK S4P 2S4 ☎ 525-0905 (info-tape)
☎ 924-8420 (hotline)

RELIGIOUS GROUPS
■ **Dignity Regina Dignité** (GLM)
PO Box 482 ✉ SK S4P 3A2 ☎ 569-3666 (Donald)
Gay roman catholics and friends. Potluck supper/service on 3rd Sun.

CRUISING
-Scarth Street (R) (2000 & 2100 blocks)
-Cornwall Centre Mall
-Wascana Park (College Avenue section)

Saskatoon ☎ 306

PUBLICATIONS
■ **Perceptions** (GLM)
PO Box 8581 ✉ SK S7K 6K7 ☎ 244-1930 📠 665-1280
📧 perceptions@home.com
Prairie gay/lesbian newsmagazine.

BARS
■ **Diva's** (B GLM MA P) Tue-Sat 20-2.30, Sun -0.30 h
110-220 3rd Avenue South ✉ SK S7K 1M1 *(side alley entrance)*
☎ 665-0100

GIFT & PRIDE SHOPS
■ **Out of the Closet** (GLM) Mon-Fri 12-22, Sat 12-18 h
203-220 3rd Avenue South ✉ SK S7K 6K7
Queer shop with shirts, magazines, cards, jewellery, gifts. Funraising venture of GLHS.

GENERAL GROUPS
■ **PFLAG (Parents & Friends of Lesbians and Gays)** 1st Sun meetings
☎ 664-4228 (Dennis Morrison) ☎ 477-1476 (Kay)
Support/education group for parents and families of gays.

HEALTH GROUPS
■ **AIDS Saskatoon** AIDS Hotline: Mon-Fri 9-17 h
130 Idylwyld North Street ✉ SK S7L OY7 ☎ 242-5005
☎ (1-800) 667-6876 (Toll-free) 📠 665-9976
📧 aids.saskatoon@home.com
Non-profit association, gay and non-gay people welcome.
■ **Gay and Lesbian Health Services (GLHS)** (GLM)
203-220 3rd Avenue South ✉ SK S7K 6K7 ☎ 665-1224
☎ (1-800) 358-1833 (Toll-free) 📧 glhs@home.com
Lesbian and gay health agency. Organises also many social activities.
■ **PLWA (Persons Living With AIDS). Network of Saskatchewan**
PO Box 7123 ✉ SK S4K 4J1 ☎ 373-7766
☎ (1-800) 226-0944 (Toll-free) 📠 374-7746
Support and services for PLWA, families, friends and partners.

SWIMMING
-Cranberry Flats

CRUISING
-Spadina Crescent (R) (between Medical Arts Building and Broadway Bridge, evening and night)
-Kiwanis Park (known as Bessborough Park; next to Spadina Crescent, evening and night, daytime occasionally)
-Midtown Plaza (main mall)
-Eatons (lower main floor)
-Kinsmen Park (closed in winter)

CDN-Yukon Territory

Location: Northwest CDN
Initials: YT
Time: GMT -8
Area: 536,000 km2 / 206,949 sq mi.
Population: 32,000
Capital: Whitehorse

Whitehorse ☎ 403

GENERAL GROUPS
■ **Gay and Lesbian Alliance of the Yukon Territory**
PO Box 56 04 ✉ YT Y1A 5H4 ☎ 667-7857

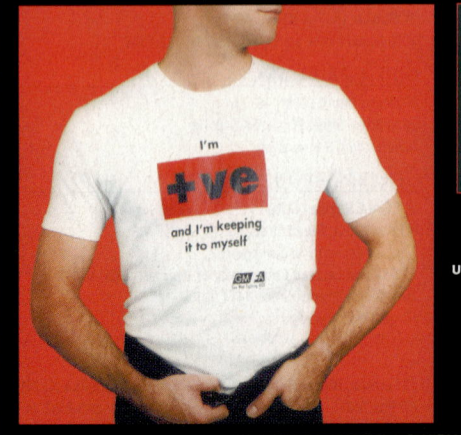

Lots of HIV+ men don't tell

GMFA's campaigns and actions are designed, planned and executed by positive, negative and untested volunteers.
To volunteer for GMFA write, phone or email:
Unit 43, Eurolink Centre, 49 Effra Road, LONDON, SW2 1BZ. 020 7738 6872. newvol@gmfa.demon.co.uk
www.demon.co.uk/gmfa
Registered Charity no. 1076854

GMFA
Gay Men Fighting AIDS

Caribbean

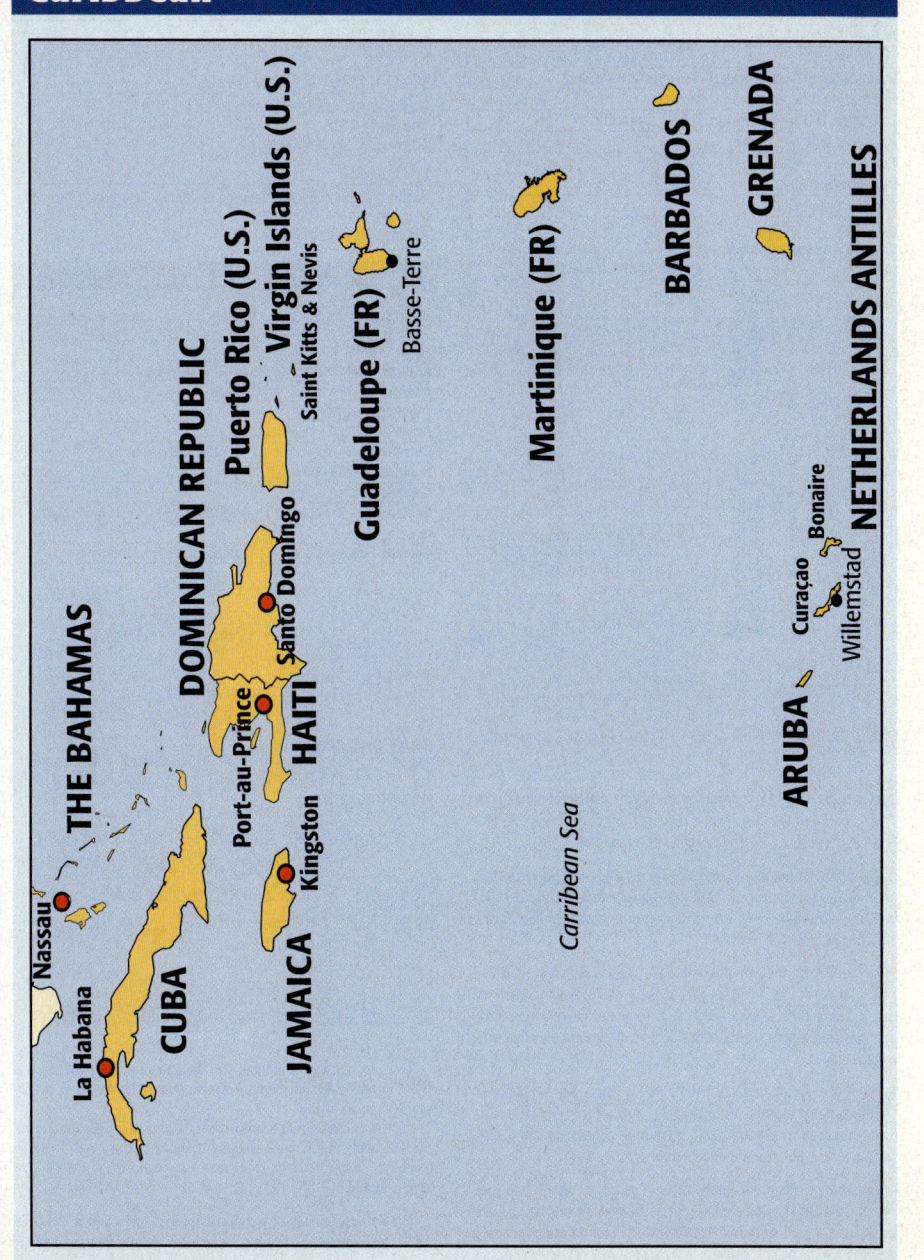

Caribbean/Aruba - Bahamas — Oranjestad

Caribbean - Aruba

Location: Caribbean
Initials: ARU (NL)
Time: GMT -4
International Country Code: ☎ 297 (no area Codes)
International Access Code: ☎ 00
Language: Dutch, Papiamento, English, Spanish
Area: 193 km2 / 75 sq mi.
Currency: 1 Aruba-Florin (Afl) = 100 Cents
Population: 69,000
Capital: Oranjestad
Religions: over 80% Catholic
Climate: Tropical marine climate with little seasonal temperature variation.

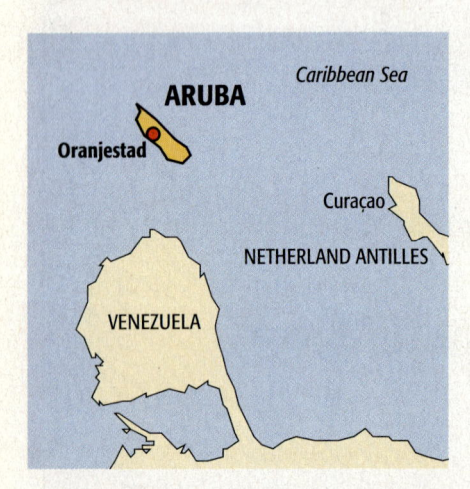

★ Aruba is an autonomous territory of the Netherlands with special status. Gays lead a relatively untroubled and safe life. The age of consent is 16 and sex between men is legal.

★ Aruba ist autonomer Teil der Niederlande mit Sonderstatus. Schwule können auf Aruba relativ unbehelligt und sicher leben. Das Schutzalter liegt bei 16 Jahren und einvernehmlicher Sex zwischen Männern ist legal.

★ Aruba est une île autonome des Pays-Bas jouissant d'un statut particulier. Pour les gais, la vie y est relativement sûre et calme. La majorité sexuelle est fixée à 16 ans et les relations entre hommes sont légales si elles sont placées sous le signe du consentement mutuel.

★ Aruba es una parte autónoma de los Países Bajos que posee un status especial. Homosexuales pueden vivir en la isla relativamente seguros y tranquilos. La edad de protección son los 16 años, y el sexo por acuerdo entre hombres es legal.

★ Aruba è una parte autonoma dei Paesi Bassi con statuto speciale. Qui i gay possono vivere senza essere importunati. L'età legale per rapporti sessuali è di 16 anni, ed i rapporti tra uomini sono legali purché biconsensuali.

Oranjestad

BARS
■ **Cellar** (B G MA) Wed Thu-Sat 22-4
Klipstraat 2

SEX SHOPS/BLUE MOVIES
■ **Hot Spot Adult Entertainment** (AC CC GLM MA)
Mon-Sat 14-22 h
Waterweg 1   ☎ 826 932

CRUISING
- Eagle Beach 16-sunset h (between La Quinta Resort and Dutch Village Hotel)
- Malmok 14-18 h (by the beach)

Caribbean - Bahamas

Location: Caribbean
Initials: BS
Time: GMT-4
International Country Code: ☎ 242 (no area codes)
International Access Code: ☎ 001
Language: English and Creole
Area: 13 939 km2 / 5,381 sq mi.
Currency: 1 Bahma Dollar (B$) =100 Cents
Population: 289 000
Capital: Nassau
Religions: 32 % Baptist, 20% Anglican, 19% Catholic & 6% Methodist
Climate: Subtropical climate Tropical storms in autumn.

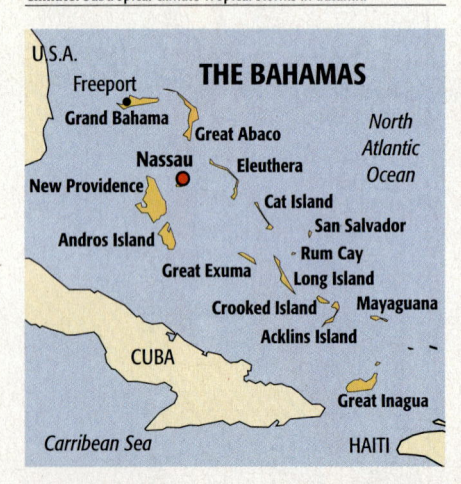

★ Homosexuality is not illegal in the Bahamas. Only gay sex acts in public are deemed an offense punishable by up to twenty years in prison.
The age of consent for heterosexuals is 16 and 18 for gays and lesbians. Residents and visitors alike are asked to comply with the laws relating to public decency. One cannot say that the general attitude here is hostile.

★ Homosexualität ist auf den Bahamas nicht illegal. Sexuelle Handlungen zwischen Gays werden jedoch als Vergehen erachtet, das mit bis zu zwanzig Jahren Gefängnis bestraft werden kann. Das Schutzalter für Heterosexuelle liegt bei 16 Jahren und für Gays und Lesben bei 18 Jahren. Ortsansässige und Besucher sind in gleichem Maße angehalten nicht gegen die Gesetze bezüglich des öffentlichen Anstands zu verstoßen. Man kann nicht sagen, daß die allgemeine Haltung gegenüber Homosexuellen feindlich wäre.

✴ L'homosexualité n'est pas illégale aux Bahamas. Seuls les rapports sexuels entre gais en public sont considérés comme une offense punissable par une peine d'emprisonnement allant jusqu'à 20 ans.
La majorité sexuelle est fixée à 16 ans pour les hétérosexuels et à 18 pour les homosexuels. Les habitants tout autant que les touristes sont tenus à respecter les lois de décence publique. On ne peut pour autant pas dire que l'attitude générale est homophobe.

✴ La homosexualidad no es ilegal en las Bahamas. Sin embargo, actos sexuales (homosexuales) en público se consideran un delito y son penalizados con hasta veinte años de prisión.
La edad de cconsentimiento es de 16 años para heterosexuales y de 18 años para gays y lesbianas. Se espera tanto de los residentes de las islas como de los turistas que cumplan con las leyes relacionadas con la "decencia en público" . No se puede decir que la actitud general hacia los gays sea hostil.

✖ L'omossessualità alle Bahamas non è illegale. Tuttavia le relazioni sessuali tra gay sono considerate reato, punibile con carcere fino a venti anni. L'età minima per eterosessuali è di 16 anni e 18 per gay e lesbiche. Residenti e visitatori sono tenuti in egual misura a rispettare le leggi che si riferiscono al pubblico decoro. Non si può dire che l'opinione generale sia ostica nei confronti degli omosessuali.

Nassau

GAY INFO
■ **Hope** Wed & Thu 20-22h MET
Nassau ☏ 328-1816 ✉ hopetea@yahoo.com
✉ members.nbci.com/hope_tea/HopeTea/Home.html
Support group for the gay, lesbian bisexual and transgender community of the Bahamas.

BARS
■ **Drop off Pub. The** (B f D NG MA) Best Sun - Thu from 22h
Bay Street (Opp. Planet Hollywood) ☏ 322 3444
■ **Pineapple Lounge** (B g MA) Best Fri & Sat from 22h
Rockcrusher Road

CAFES
■ **Paradiso** (B glm MA)
The Island Station, Downtown Bay Street ☏ 356 5282

DANCECLUBS
■ **Dangerous Beach** (B D MA) Fri & Sat 23-?h
Stip Mall (In shopping centre)
Information in Café Paradiso.

SWIMMING
-Westend Esplanade, near the El Greco hotel (cruising at night).

Caribbean - Barbados

Name: Barbade
Location: Caribbean
Initials: BDS
Time: GMT -4
International Country Code: ☏ 1-246 (no area codes)
International Access Code: ☏ 011
Language: English, Bajan
Area: 430 km2 / 166 sq. mi.
Currency: 1 Barbados Dollar (BDS$) = 100 Cents
Population: 263,000
Capital: Bridgetown
Religions: 70% Christian
Climate: Tropical climate. The rainy season lasts from June to October.

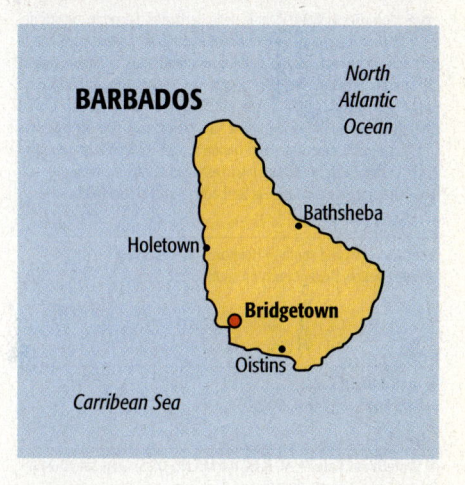

✴ Homosexuality is illegal in Barbados. According to reports, gays are however not bothered by the police, and Barbados is said to be one of the most liberal islands of the English-speaking South Caribbean. Nonetheless, the gay scene is rather hidden from the public eye. Gay life takes place mostly on the southern coast (St. Michael, Christ Church) as well as on the west coast (St. James). Cruising is done on the beach and from cars. Especially worth mentioning are the Thanksgiving Festival which takes place in July and the Arts Festival in November.

★ Homosexualität ist auf Barbados illegal. Allerdings werden Schwule nicht von der Polizei verfolgt: Barbados gilt als eine der liberalsten Inseln der anglophonen südlichen Karibik. Trotzdem ist die einheimische Schwulenszene von der Öffentlichkeit abgeschirmt. Das schwule Leben spielt sich vor allem an der Südküste (St. Michael, Christ Church) sowie an der Westküste (St. James) ab. Man cruist am Strand oder per Auto-Blickkontakt. Erwähnenswert sind vor allem das im Juli stattfindende „Erntedank-Festival" und das sogenannte „Künstlerfest" im November.

✴ A la Barbade, l'homosexualité est un délit. D'après ce que nous savons, la police laisse les gais en paix. La Barbade passe pour être l'une des îles les plus tolérantes des Caraïbes. Pourtant, les gais s'y font très discrets. Les principaux lieux gais se trouvent

Caribbean/Barbados — Bridgetown ▸ Worthing

surtout sur la côte sud (St. Michael, Christ Church) et sur la côte ouest (St. James). On drague à la plage et en voiture. A voir: la grande fête de la Grâce (pour la récolte, en juin) et la fête des Artistes (en novembre).

La homosexualidad es ilegal en Barbados. De acuerdo a los informes, los gays no son perseguidos por la policía. Barbados es considerada como una de las islas más liberales de los anglo-parlantes del Pacífico Sur. A pesar de todo, el ambiente gay de los nativos se mantiene en cubierto, la vida gay se da sobre todo en la costa sur (St. Michael, Christ Church) así como también en la costa Occidental (St. James). El „cruising" se practica en la playa o viajando en coche con contactos a primera vista. Digno de mención es el Festival de la Cosecha (en julio de cada año), así como la llamada Fiesta de los Artistas (noviembre).

L'omosessualità è illegale nelle Barbados. Secondo i nostri dati però i gay non vengono disturbati dalla polizia; pare che le Barbados siano tra le isole Caraibiche meridionali di lingua inglese più liberali. Stranamente però la vita gay è piuttosto nascosta e ha luogo soprattutto sulla costa meridionale (St. Michael, Christ Church) e su quella occidentale (St. James). Ci si incontra sulla spiaggia e nelle macchine. Qui hanno luogo in luglio il grande Cropover Festival e in novembre l'Art Festival due ragioni in più per evitare l'alta stagione e godersi le Barbados senza grandi folle.

SWIMMING
- Beaches north and south of Holetown on west coast
- Rockley beach, Dover beach on south coast

Bridgetown

BARS
■ **John's Night Cap**
Baxters Road ☎ 246-436 2207

CAFES
■ **Waterfront Cafe** (A AC B CC d F MA NG OS S) Mon-Sat 10-24 h
Cavans Lane ☎ 427 00 93

CRUISING
- Broad Street

Christ Church

BARS
■ **Buddies** (AC B CC d F GLM MA S STV YG) 18-? h
„Iriston" Worthing (opposite to Sandy Beach Hotel) ☎ 435 65 45

APARTMENTS
■ **Roman Beach Apartments** (glm H)
Enterprise Coast Road, Oistin Town ☎ 428 76 35
Modest, reasonably priced accomodation. Sharing possible. Self-catering rooms with electric fans. Informal and friendly.

CRUISING
- Long Bay Beach (near the airport, also called „Chancery Lane Beach", usually quiet, lots of bushes, discreet nude bathing, take no valuables!)
- Rockley Beach (also called „Accra Beach", crowded on weekends and evenings. Easy contacts)
- Saint Lawrence Gap (AYOR R) (after dark)

Lower Carlton

BARS
■ **John Moore's Bar** (B g MA)

Speightstown

BARS
■ **Derrick's Bar** (B g MA)
■ **Fisherman's Pub** (B g MA)

St. James

RESTAURANTS
■ **Coach House** (B F g) 12-15/18-2 h
Paynes Bay ☎ 432 11 63
Live music most nights.

GUEST HOUSES
■ **Hogarth House** (B BF CC E F MA NG)
Lot 5, Holders Hill ☎ 432 64 02   432 71 73
✉ Hogarthhouse@hotmail.com
Rooms with shower/WC and balcony.

St. Joseph

RESTAURANTS
■ **Restaurant at Atlantis Hotel** (B F g)
Tent Bay, Bathsheba ☎ 433 94 45

SWIMMING
- Cattlewash Beach (along East Coast Road, best part is between holiday houses and Barclays Park. Discreet NU possible.)
- Batts Rock Beach (popular with bushes, cliffs, etc. West Coast)

St. Michael

RESTAURANTS
■ **Waterfront Café** (B F g OS) 10-24 h, closed Sun
The Careenage, Bridgetown ☎ 427 00 93
Very popular. Live music.

CRUISING
- Baxter's Road (AYOR R RT WE) (off Broad Street, at night)

St. Peter

HOTELS
■ **The Palace** (B F g H)
Road View (located on the oceanfront, near Mullins Beach)
☎ +1-246-422 32 40

Worthing

DANCECLUBS
■ **Shells** 22-? h.
(off main road near Police Station)
Gay Party every two weeks on Sat. Very popular. Reasonable prices.

La Habana | Cuba/Caribbean

Caribbean - Cuba

Name: Kuba
Location: Caribbean
Initials: C
Time: GMT -5
International Country Code: ☏ 53 (leave the first 0 of area codes)
International Access Code: ☏ 119
Language: Spanish
Area: 110,860 km2 / 42,803 sq mi.
Currency: 1 Cuban Peso (Cub) = 100 Centavos
Population: 11,115,000
Capital: La Habana
Religions: 40% Roman Catholic
Climate: Tropical climate that is moderated by trade winds. The dry season lasts from November to April, the rainy season from May to October.

According to Article 303 of the Cuban penal code it is illegal to display homosexuality in public. It has been said that the police have been targeting gay meeting places and controlling young locals in the accompaniment of older men. Care should be taken when approaching young men. There has been a dramatic crack down on prostitution and crime against visitors. There are not many gay places or events in Havana. In Havana there are three meeting points where information about local events can be obtained. These are Coppelia - La Ramba (21-23h), El Malecon and La Fiat.
Cuba is economically poor but rich in culture and history. Its people are well educated and extremely friendly. Those looking for gay lifestyle bars in Cuba have come to the wrong place.

Nach Artikel 303 des kubanischen Strafgesetzbuches ist die Zurschaustellung von Homosexualität in der Öffentlichkeit gesetzwidrig. Es wird berichtet, daß die Polizei Schwulentreffpunkte beobachtet und junge Einheimische in Begleitung älterer Männer kontrolliert. Vorsicht also bei der Kontaktaufnahme zu jungen Männern. Prostitution und Straftaten gegenüber Besuchern sind in der letzten Zeit stark zurückgegangen. In Havanna findet man nicht viele Schwulentreffpunkte oder -veranstaltungen, es gibt jedoch drei Treffs, wo man sich über lokale Veranstaltungen informieren kann: im Coppelia - La Ramba (21-23 Uhr), im El Malecon und im El Fiat.
Kuba ist ein armes Land, dafür aber reich an Kultur und Geschichte. Die Bevölkerung ist gebildet und außerordentlich freundlich. Wer in Kuba nach typischen Gaybars sucht, ist ins falsche Land gereist.

Selon l'article 303 du Code pénal cubain, il est interdit d'afficher son homosexualité en public. Il paraît que la police cible les lieux de rencontres gais et contrôle les jeunes cubains accompagnés par des personnes plus âgées. La plus grande prudence est donc à observer si vous rencontrez des jeunes autochtones. Une forte diminution de la prostitution et des agressions contre les visiteurs a été observée ces derniers temps. Il n'y a pas beaucoup d'établissements ou de manifestations gais à la Havane. Pour se renseigner sur les événements locaux, nous vous recommandons trois lieux de rencontres: Coppelia - La Ramba (21-23 h), El Malecon et La Fiat. Cuba est économiquement pauvre mais historiquement et culturellement riche. Ses habitants ont beaucoup d'éducation et sont très amicaux. Ceux qui se rendent à Cuba pour trouver des bars typiquement gais seront certainement déçus.

Según el artículo 303 del código penal cubano, la manifestación de la orientación homosexual en público constituye un acto ilegal. Se dice que los puntos de encuentro de los homosexuales se han convertido en el blanco preferido de la policía que suele pedir la documentación a las personas cubanas jóvenes acompañadas por hombres mayores. Por ello, hay que tener cuidado al hacerles propuestas a los hombres jóvenes. Ha habido en los últimos tiempos una dramática disminución de la prostitución y de los crímenes contra visitantes de la isla.
No hay muchos locales gays o acontecimientos gays en La Habana. La ciudad cuenta con tres puntos de encuentro donde se puede obtener información acerca de los acontecimientos actuales. Son Coppelia - La Ramba (21-23h), El Malecón y La Fiat. Cuba es pobre económicamente hablando, pero muy rica en cultura e historia. Sus gentes son muy educados y extremadamente amables. Quien está en búsqueda de bares de diseño y estilo gay, en Cuba no los encontrará.

Secondo l'articolo 303 del codice penale cubano mostrare l'omosessualità in pubblico è illegale. Gira voce che la polizia tenga sotto sservazione i posti d'incontro degli omosessuali e che controlli giovani cubani accompagnati da uomini piu anziani. Fate allora attenzione quando tentate un'approccio con un uomo più giovane. Negli ultimi tempi la prostituzione e i delitti contro visitatori sono in forte ribasso. In Havanna non si trovano molti posti o avvenimenti gay, esistono però tre posti d'incontro dove si possono ottenere informasioni su eventi locali: Il Coppelia - La Ramba (ore 21-23), El Malecon e La Fiat. Cuba è un paese economicamente povero, ma ricco di cultura e storia. I cubani sono un popolo colto ed estremamente disponibile. Chi cerca dei tipici bar gay a Cuba ha scelto il posto sbagliato.

La Habana ☏ 07

BARS

■ **Casa de las Infusiones** (B glm) 11-22 h
Mercaderes/Obispo *(Old Town)*

SPARTACUS 2001/2002 | 153

Caribbean/Cuba - Dominican Republic | La Habana

■ **Karachy Club** (B D glm YG)
17 y K *(Vedado)*

CAFES
■ **D'Giovanni** (B F GLM)
Empedrado/Tacón *(Old Town)*
Gay especially in the afternoon. Italian cuisine, pastries.

DANCECLUBS
■ **Disco Jocker** (AC B D GLM YG) Tue-Sun 21-4 h, closed Mon
Linea y 10 *(Vedado)*
■ **Eco Disco** (B D GLM YG) Tue-Sun 21-4 h, closed Mon
Linea y F *(Vedado)*

SHOWS
■ **Castropole** (G) Shows around 23h
El Malécon, between Genios and Crespo

CINEMAS
■ **Yara Movie** (g YG)
(Vedado near Hotel Habana Libre)

PRIVATE ACCOMMODATION
■ **Casa Alberto** (H)
Calle Aguila 361 *(between San Miguel and Neptuno)* ☎ 634 834
✉ casalberto@w-i-t.com ● www.w-i-t.com
Contact Alberto for further details about private accommodation in Cuba.

SWIMMING
-Santa Maria Beach/Mi Cayito (G) *(east of Havana from Mar Azul Hotel to Itabo Hotel)*
-El Chivo (AYOR g) *(east of Havana)*

CRUISING
All cruising areas are AYOR.
-Fraternidad Park
-Central Park
-Monte street
-Feria de la Juventud
-Teatro Nacional (especially after opera performances)
-Heladeria Copelia (WE)
-Prado Street
-Santa Maria Beach

Caribbean - Dominican Republic

Name:	Dominikanische Republik • République Dominicaine • República Dominicana
Location:	Caribbean
Initials:	DOM
Time:	GMT -4
International Country Code:	☎ 1-809 (no area codes)
International Access Code:	☎ 011
Language:	Spanish, English
Area:	48,422 km2 / 18,696 sq mi.
Currency:	1 Dominican Peso (Dop) = 100 Centavos
Population:	8,232,000
Capital:	Santo Domingo
Religions:	94% Roman Catholic
Climate:	Tropical maritime climate with little seasonal temperature variation and variation in rainfall.

※ This country is a popular vacation spot for tourists from the U.S. and Western Europe. The laws of the Dominican Republic make no distinction between gay and straight relations between adults (over 18 years). However, Article 330 of the penal code punishes "every violation of decorum and good behavior on public streets" with a penalty of up to two years in prison, so it is advisable not to display too much affection in public. Although the law is rarely applied, the police can take a very hostile attitude. For getting around in Santo Domingo, we recommend the use of taxis, because although the bus system is cheap and communicative, it is not very effective. You should, however, agree on the cost with the taxi-driver before starting your journey.

★ Das Land ist ein beliebter Urlaubsort US-amerikanischer und westeuropäischer Touristen. Die Gesetze der Dominikanischen Republik machen zwischen schwulen und heterosexuellen Beziehungen Erwachsener (über 18 Jahre) keinen Unterschied. Allerdings kann nach Paragraph 330 des Strafgesetzes „...jedes Übertreten der Schicklichkeit und des guten Betragens auf öffentlichen Straßen mit einer Haftstrafe von bis zu zwei Jahren Gefängnis..." geahndet werden. Zu intensive Liebesbekundungen sind also in der Öffentlichkeit nicht empfehlenswert. Auch wenn dieser Paragraph nicht oft angewandt wird, kann die Polizei doch sehr feindselig werden. In Santo Domingo sollten Sie lieber ein Taxi nehmen als die nicht besonders effektiven aber kommunikativen und billigen Kleinbusse. Vorher aber unbedingt den Preis aushandeln!

※ La République Dominicaine est un lieu de villégiature très prisé par les Américains et les Européens. La législation dominicaine ne fait pas de distinction entre homosexuels et hétérosexuels, mais protège les mineurs (majorité: 18 ans). Signalons cependant que, selon l'article 330 du code pénal, on risque 2 ans de prison pour tout „débordement de décence ou de comportement dans les lieux publics". Il n'est donc pas conseillé d'afficher ses préférences au grand jour! Même si cet article n'est quasiment plus appliqué, vous risquez d'avoir des ennuis avec la police locale. A San Diego, circulez en taxi, mais veillez bien à fixer le prix de la course auparavant. Evitez les petits bus ni bon marché, ni efficaces, mais où on peut, en revanche, faire des rencontres!

◆ Este país es uno de los lugares vacacionales más preferidos por los turistas norteamericanos y europeos. Las leyes domi-

Las Terrenas ▶ Santo Domingo | Dominican Republic/Caribbean

nicanas no hacen ninguna comparación en lo referente a actividades heterosexuales u homosexuales entre adultos mayores de 18 años. Se puede sin embargo ser penado por "cualquier incumplimiento a la descencia o al buen comportamiento en las vías públicas" con una pena máxima de 2 años de prisión. No son recomendadas intensivas demostraciones amorosas en público. Aunque este artículo muy pocas veces es aplicado, se recomienda tener cuidado, ya que la policía puede comportarse bastante impertinente. En Santo Domingo es preferible viajar en taxi, ya que los pequeños autobuses no son nada de puntuales, aunque baratos y con un ambiente bastante comunicativo. Antes de montarse en el taxi se recomienda acordar el precio del viaje.

Questo paese è un luogo di vacanze fra i preferiti dai turisti americani. Le leggi della Repubblica Dominicana non fanno distinzioni tra i rapporti eterosessuali e omosessuali olte i 18 anni. Peraltro il paragrafo 330 del codice penale punisce le „offese alla morale pubblica" con una pena massima di 2 anni. Quindi in pubblico non sono consigliabili lunghe e appassionate prove d'amore. Anche se questo paragrafo viene raramente applicato, la polízia non essere molto intollerante. In Santo Domingo è meglio spostarsi in taxi che con i poco efficienti ma economici e comunicativi autobus. Cercate di trattare sempre il prezzo prima di salire!

Las Terrenas

APARTMENTS
■ **Paraiso Suizo** (BF glm H OS)
Playa Bonita ☏ 240-6118 📠 240-6118
Bungalows. On premises restaurant El Coco.

Puerto Plata

HOTELS
■ **Hotel Barlovento** (AC B BF CC D E F G H PI s WO)
Costambar ☏ 586 44 26 📠 320 86 10. 📧 t.vacacional@codetel.net.do

GUEST HOUSES
■ **Bugalows el Carite** (B BF D F H PI R S YG)
Cabarete ☏ 571 04 15 📠 571 04 16
■ **Laguna Bonito** (B glm H PI SA WH)
Escondido Bay (Casa 73) *(Sosua)* ☏ 471 16 94 📠 471 16 94
📧 www.DomRep-Reisen.de

Samaná

HOTELS
■ **El Paraiso** (AC B BF CC F G NU OS PI S VS WO YG)
☏ +49-171-890 66 94 📠 368 25 45

Santiago

RESTAURANTS
■ **Pez Dorado. El** (B F glm)
C. El Sol # 43 ☏ 582 25 18

HOTELS
■ **Mercedes Hotel** (b f glm H)
C. 30 de Marzo # 18 ☏ 583 11 71

CRUISING
-Parc at Calle El Sol (after 18 h)

Santo Domingo

BARS
■ **Café Capri** (B F glm MA OS s) Thu-Sun 21-3 h
Avenida Tiradentes # 20, Naco *(beside the Naco Hotel)*
■ **Drake's Bar** (B glm MA OS r)
C. La Atarazana, Colonial City *(in front of Alcazar de Colon)*
■ **O'Hara's Place** (B f GLM MA OS) Wed-Sun 19-2 h, closed Mon Tue
C. Danae # 3, Gascue. ☏ 682 84 08
■ **Phönix** (ayor B G OG R) Wed-Sun 18-23 h
Calle Polvorín 10 *(Zona Colonial)* ☏ 688 79 05
■ **St. Michael's Grand Café & Restaurant** (B e F glm ma OS s YG) Wed-Sun 18-3 h
Avenida Lope de Vega # 26, Naco. ☏ 541 66 55

CAFES
■ **Yuca Cafe** (B BF h F) 8.00-2.00 h
Calle Proyecto Paredes 3 *(Bocachica)*

DANCECLUBS
■ **Disco Free** (AC B D glm MA N S TV WE YG) Thu-Sun 10-5 h
Avenida Ortega y Gaset, 13 *(near Avenida John F. Kennedy)*
☏ 565 81 00
■ **Güácara Taína Disco. La** (AC B D e MA NG S) Wed-Sun 20-3 h
Avenida Mirador de Sur *(near Parque Paseo de los Indios)*
☏ 533 10 51
Located in a natural cave.
■ **Penthouse. El** (ayor B D GLM MA R S tv WE) 23-5 h
Calle El Seybo/20, altos.

RESTAURANTS
■ **Cafe Cogo** (b F g)
Calle Sánchez 153 ☏ 687 96 24
■ **Pitiri** (AC B E F glm MA) 12-15, 19-24, closed Sun 12-15 h
C. Nicolás de Bar # 6/Eduardo Gener, La Esperilla *(in front of the National Conservatory of Music)* ☏ 541 54 78

CINEMAS
■ **Lido** (AYOR glm r) 17-23.30 h
Avenida Mella

APARTMENTS
■ **Laurel Apartments** (AC BF F glm H)
Avenida Caonabo # 41 ☏ 530 47 24
Kitchenettes in all units. Good value but a few miles away from the centre.

GENERAL GROUPS
■ **Colectivo Ciguay**
PO Box 156-9

HEALTH GROUPS
■ **AIDS Hotline** Mon-Fri 8-18 h
☏ 541 44 00
■ **Amigos Siempre Amigos**
PO Box 22231, El Huacal ☏ 759 88 32

SWIMMING
-Boca Chica Beach (50 km from the city)
-Embassy Beach (About 65 km from the city. Take Avenida Las Americas, highway to San Pedro de Macoris. Beach on the right filled with cocconut palms.)

Caribbean/Dominican Republic - Guadeloupe | Santo Domingo ▶ St. George's

CRUISING
- Plaza Independencia (r)
- Parque Colón (r)
- Playa Guibia (r) (Avenida Washington, El Malecon)
- Parque Mirador Sur (evenings)

Caribbean - Grenada

Name: Grenade
Location: Caribbean
Initials: WG
Time: GMT -4
International Country Code: ☏ 1-473
International Access Code: ☏ 011
Language: English
Area: 344 km² / 133 sq mi.
Currency: 1 East Caribbean Dollar (EC$) = 100 Cents
Population: 95,000
Capital: Saint George's
Religions: 59% Catholic, 34% Protestant
Climate: Tropical climate that is temperated by northeast trade winds.

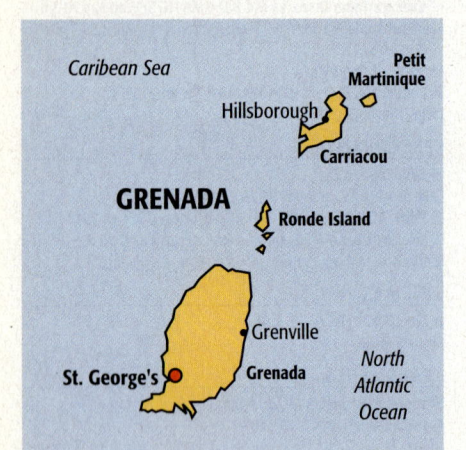

[Map of Grenada showing Caribean Sea, Petit Martinique, Hillsborough, Carriacou, Ronde Island, Grenville, St. George's, Grenada, North Atlantic Ocean]

✱ According to our knowledge, homosexuality is illegal in Grenada and the neighboring island of Carriacou to the north. The tourist industry is developing steadily, and is concentrated around St. George to the south. There is no gay scene as such; the following places should only be used as starting points.

★ Unseres Wissens nach ist Homosexualität auf Grenada illegal, wie auch auf der nördlich gelegenen Nachbarinsel Carriacou. Die Tourismusindustrie hat sich in den letzten Jahren stark weiterentwickelt, ist aber vor allem um die Stadt St. George's im Süden konzentriert. Es gibt keine Schwulenszene; die folgenden Adressen sollten nur als Ausgangspunkte dienen.

✱ D'après ce que nous savons, l'homosexualité est un délit à Grenade et sur l'île voisine de Carriacou (au nord). L'industrie touristique est en plein essor, tout particulièrement à St George, dans le sud. Pas de vie gaie à proprement parler. Les établissements mentionnés ci-dessous ne sont cités qu'à titre d'information.

⬢ Por lo que sabemos la homosexualidad es ilegal en Grenada y en Carriacou, la isla vecina que queda al norte. La industria de turismo se está desarrollando y estableciendo casi exclusivamente en St. George, en el sur del país. No existe un ambiente gay propiamente dicho; las siguientes direcciones sirven sólo como punto de partida.

✖ Per quanto ne sappiamo, l'omosessualitè è illegale a Grenada e su Carriacou, l'isola vicina situata al nord. L'industria del turismo si sta sviluppando quasi esclusivamente nel territorio di St. George al sud. Non c'è una vita gay vera e propria; i seguenti luoghi dovrebbero essere usati solo come punti di riferimento e di base.

St. George's

BARS
▪ **Fantasia 2001** (AC B D) 20.30-? h
Morne Rouge ☏ 444 42 24
▪ **Internatinal Cubby Hole** (B D F)
The Caranage ☏ 440 29 27
▪ **St. James Hotel Bar** (g)
Grand Etang Road *(downtown)* ☏ 440 20 41

RESTAURANTS
▪ **Coconuts** (B F g) 10-22 h
Grande Anse Beach ☏ 444 46 44
French and local cuisine; beachfront; live band most nights.
▪ **Nutmeg Restaurant & Bar** (B F g)
The Caranage Water Front ☏ 440 25 39
Open daily for breakfast, lunch and dinner.
▪ **Rudolf's** (B F g) 10-24 h, closed Sun
The Caranage ☏ 440 22 41

SWIMMING
- Grand Anse Beach (3.5 miles of white sand)

Caribbean - Guadeloupe

Name: Guadalupe
Location: Caribbean
Initials: GUA (F)
Time: GMT -4
International Country Code: ☏ 590 (no area codes)
International Access Code: ☏ 00
Language: French, Créole
Area: 1,780 km2 / 687 sq mi.
Currency: 1 French Franc (FF) = 100 Centimes
Population: 444,000
Capital: Basse-Terre
Religions: 95% Roman Catholic
Climate: Subtropical climate that is tempered by trade winds. The humidity is relatively high.

Basse-Terre ▶ Saint Martin Guadeloupe - Caribbean

Guadeloupe (FRANCE)

Carribean Sea
Port-Louis
Grande-Terre
La Désirade
Deshaies
Point-à-Pitre
Basse-Terre
Iles de la Petite Terre
Basse-Terre
Saint Louis
Marie-Galante
Les Saintes

Pointe-à-Pitre

HEALTH GROUPS

■ **Centre Hospitalier de Pointe-à-Pitre**
Route de Chauvel ✉ 97110 *(north tower, 1st floor)* ☎ 89 13 41

CRUISING

-Rue Duplessis (along La Darse, the old port)
-Rue de Nozieres
-Rue Frebault
-Rue René Boisneuf

Saint François

BARS

■ **Iguane Café** (b F g MA OS) Dinner every night except Tue Sun lunch & dinner
Route de la Pointe des Chateaux ✉ 97118 ☎ 88 61 37
A friendly smile and great food. A must on the way back from the gay beach at Pointe Tarare.

SWIMMING

-Pointe Tarare (legal nudist beach)

Saint Martin

❋ St. Martin's falls under the jurisdiction of faraway Guadeloupe and thus belongs to France's overseas territories. The northern part of the island is French, the south is Dutch. The island of St. Martin is the perfect place for a relaxing holiday and has wonderful beaches (also with nude sunbathing).

❋ St. Martin wird vom Regionalparlament des weit entfernten Guadeloupe regiert und ist damit Teil des französischen Überseedepartements. Der Nordteil der Insel ist französisch, der Süden niederländisch.
St. Martin ist eine herrliche Insel für Urlaub und Erholung mit wundervollen Stränden (FKK ist möglich).

❋ St Martin est administrée par la lointaine Guadeloupe et fait ainsi partie de l'Union Européenne. Le nord de l'île est français, le sud est hollandais. On passe d'agréables et reposantes vacances à St Martin. On y trouve de merveilleuses plages, accessibles également aux naturistes.

❋ A pesar de que St. Martin queda bastante lejos de Guadalupe, está bajo su jurisdicción y forma parte de la colonia francesa. No obstante la isla está dividida en la parte francesa del norte y la parte holandesa del sur.
St. Martin es una hermosa isla para las vacaciones y el descanso, con playas maravillosas (también para amantes del nudismo).

❋ San Martino viene governato dal parlamento regionale della lontana Guadalupa e insieme a quest'ultima fa parte dei territori d'oltre mare francesi. La parte settentrionale dell'isola è francese, quella meridionale olandese. Quest'isola meravigliosa con le sue splendide spiagge (anche per nudisti) è un posto ottimo per passare le vacanze e per rilassarsi.

RESTAURANTS

■ **Kontiki Plage** (B F g)
(Orient-Bay Beach) ☎ 87 43 27

SWIMMING

-Baie Rouge
-Baie Orientale (NU) (Cruising area is between Boo Boo Sam and Coco Beach restaurants and in the far south of the beach just after the Club Orient)

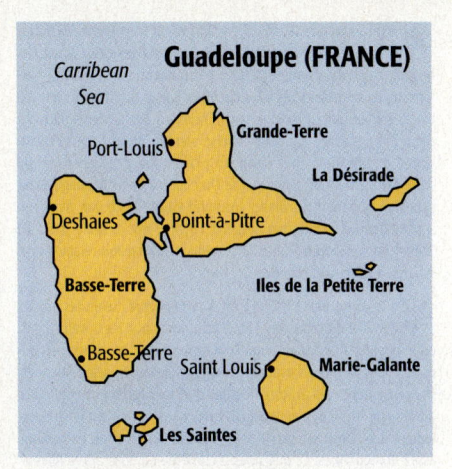

❋ The French penal code is in effect here (⇨ France). The island is sunny and, in every sense of the word, heavenly. Most of the people are of African descent. Compared with other Caribbean countries, the cost of living is somewhat higher.

★ Es gelten die Strafbestimmungen ⇨ Frankreichs. Die Insel ist sonnig und paradiesisch, die meisten Menschen sind afrikanischer Herkunft. Die Lebenshaltungskosten liegen hier, verglichen mit anderen karibischen Ländern, eher hoch.

❋ La législation française (⇨France) est en vigueur en Guadeloupe. Ile ensoleillée et paradisiaque. La population est d'origine africaine. Le coût de la vie est, comparé aux autres pays des Caraïbes, plutôt élevé.

❋ El Código Penal francés (⇨ Francia) es vigente en esta isla caribeña. Guadalupe disfruta de un clima soleado y es verdaderamente paradisíaca, la mayoría de los habitantes son de origen africano. El costo de la vida es aquí más bien alto si se compara con el de otros países caribeños.

❋ E'in vigore il codice penale francese (⇨Francia). L'isola è soleggiata e paradisiaca. La maggior parte degli abitanti è di origine africana, il costo della vita è, in confronto agli altri paesi dei Caraibi, piuttosto elevato.

Basse-Terre

RESTAURANTS

■ **Orangerie. L'** (b F glm)
Desmarais ✉ 97100 ☎ 81 01 01

Les Saintes

HOTELS

■ **Petits Saints aux Anacardiers. Les** (A AC B F MA g Pl SA)
La Savasse - Terre-de-Haut ✉ 97137 ☎ 99 50 99 ☎ 995455
📠 99 54 51 ✉ petitsaints@yahoo.fr 🌐 www.petitssaints.com
An ideal island get-away. Take boat or plane from Guadeloupe.

SWIMMING

-Beach/Plage Crawen

Caribbean/Guadeloupe - Jamaica | Sainte Anne ▸ Kingston

Sainte Anne

BARS
■ **Chez Elles** (B F glm) Wed-Sun 19-? h
Les Galbas ✉ 97180 *(opposite Village artisanal)* ☎ 88 92 36

SWIMMING
-Plage de la Caravelle (NU) (possible contacts with tourists and locals in the afternoon; best part of island Plage de Tarare, on road to Pointe des Châteaux)

Caribbean - Jamaica

Name:	Jamaika • Jamaique • Giamaica
Location:	Caribbean
Initials:	JA
Time:	GMT -5
International Country Code:	☎ 1-876 (no area codes)
International Access Code:	☎ 011
Language:	English
Area:	10,990 km² / 4,243 sq mi.
Currency:	1 Jamaican Dollar (J$) = 100 Cents
Population:	2,539,000
Capital:	Kingston
Religions:	48% Protestant, 5% Catholic, 26% other religions
Climate:	Tropical climate, hot and humid. The interior is more moderate.

Homosexual acts are unconditionally prohibited. Paragraphs 76-79 of the Jamaican penal code prescribe imprisonment with hard labour for up to ten years. Attempted gay seduction is likewise harshly punished with up to seven years imprisonment with or without labour, according to the judgement of the court. Fortunately, these laws are only rarely enforced, but they do have an influence on the lifestyle of gay men in Jamaica. The general population is quite homophobic, as was confirmed by the German embassy in Kingston. Not surprisingly, under these circumstances, Jamaica offers no gay scene in the western sense of the word, although Kingston is said to be relatively open-minded.

Homosexuelle Handlungen sind ohne Ausnahme verboten. Die Art. 76-79 des jamaikanischen Strafgesetzes sehen Gefängnisstrafen mit Zwangsarbeit bis zu 10 Jahren vor. Versuchte Verführung zu schwulem Sex wird ebenfalls hart bestraft, und zwar mit bis zu sieben Jahren Haft -je nach Ermessen des Gerichts mit oder ohne Zwangsarbeit. Glücklicherweise werden diese Gesetze relativ selten angewandt, aber dennoch prägen sie das Lebensgefühl schwuler Männer auf Jamaica. Die Durchschnittsbevölkerung ist entsprechend homophob. Dieser Umstand wurde auch von der deutschen Botschaft in Kingston bestätigt. Folglich gibt es keine „schwule Szene" im westlichen Sinne, auch wenn sich Kingston relativ aufgeschlossen gibt.

L'homosexualité est un délit à la Jamaïque. Selon les articles 76 à 79 du code pénal jamaïcain, on risque les travaux forcés ou la prison, 10 ans maximum. Tout rapport avec un mineur est puni de 7 ans de prison avec ou sans travaux forcés, selon les jurés. Heureusement, ces articles ne sont que très rarement appliqués, mais il n'en reste pas moins qu'ils influencent fortement le comportement des homosexuels du pays. Les Jamaïcains sont, en général, assez homophobes, ce que nous a confirmé l'ambassade d'Allemagne à Kingston. Ceci explique l'absence de vie gaie à l'occidentale, même si Kingston est une ville assez ouverte et tolérante.

Las actividades homosexuales están rotundamente prohibidas. Los párrafos 76-79 del Código Penal jamaica preveen penas de encarcelamiento con trabajos forzados de hasta 10 años. Los intentos de seducción homosexual son igualmente perseguidos con dureza, incluso hasta con 7 años de prisión -dependiendo de la decisión del tribunal el que sea o no con trabajos forzados. Afortunadamente estas leyes son aplicadas muy raramente, pero determinan en gran medida la vida y la situación de los gays jamaicanos. En general la sociedad jamaicana es muy homófoba, esta situación fue confirmada por la embajada alemana en Kingston. Debido a ello, no existe un ambiente gay como el que se conoce en Europa occidental, aunque la ciudad de Kingston se muestra relativamente liberal.

Gli atti omosessuali sono incondizionatamente proibiti. I paragrafi 76-79 del codice penale giamaicano prescrivono l'imprigionamento e i lavori forzati fino a 10 anni. Anche i tentativi di seduzione gay vengono puniti duramente, cioè con prigione fino a sette anni (secondo l'apprezzamento del giudice con o senza lavori forzati). Anche se queste leggi vengono per fortuna raramente applicate, influiscono lo stile di vita dei gay giamaicani. Dunque la popolazione è abbastanza omofoba. Questa situazione è stata confermata anche dall'ambasciata tedesca a Kingston. Quindi non esiste un ambiente gay nel senso occidentale del termine, anche se la popolazione si dimostra abbastanza aperta.

Kingston

HOTELS
■ **Lawrence Bed & Breakfast** (F g H MA) Easiest to reach 6-13 h
1 Denham Avenue, Meadow Brook Estate, Kingston 19 ☎ 933 13 72 📠 933 13 72
■ **Muscle and Art-Bed and Breakfast** (BF g H)
1 Denham Avenue ✉ 19 ☎ 933 13 72

SWIMMING
-Wyndham Rosehall Resort Beach (next to cruise ship terminal)

Negril ▶ Sainte Anne   Jamaica - Martinique/Caribbean

Negril
GUEST HOUSES
■ **Tingalaya's**
West End Road ☎ 957 01 26

Savanna la Mar
GUEST HOUSES
■ **Moun Tambrin Resort** (CC g H)
PO Box 210 ☎ 997 58 95 ✉ jamountambrin@toj.com
🖥 www.jamaicaescapes.com
Located in the south-west of the island. Rates from US$ 210 per person per night.

Caribbean - Martinique

Name:	Martinica
Location:	Caribbean
Initials:	MAR
Time:	GMT -4
International Country Code:	☎ 596 (no area code)
International Access Code:	☎ 00
Language:	French, Créole
Area:	1,102 km2 / 425 sq mi.
Currency:	1 French Franc (FF) = 100 Centimes
Population:	375,000
Capital:	Fort-de-France
Religions:	95% Roman Catholic
Climate:	Tropical climate with warm days and ocean breezes. Heat is seldom excessive.

✱ Martinique is a French "Departement d'Outre-Mer/D.O.M.", i.e., it belongs to France's overseas territories. The inhabitants (and visitors) are therefore subject to the same laws as in ⇒ France. Martinique has become a very popular vacation island for Europeans, combining exotic tropical beauty with European and French comforts. This makes a holiday here particularly uncomplicated and enjoyable.

✱ Martinique ist ein französisches "Département d'Outre-Mer/D.O.M." und gilt damit als Teil des französischen Mutterlandes. Es gelten für die Bewohner (und Besucher) dieselben gesetzlichen Rechte und Pflichten wie in ⇒ Frankreich. Martinique ist ein beliebtes Touristenziel für Europäer geworden, verbinden sich doch auf dieser Insel tropische Schönheit und Exotik mit europäischem Komfort. Das macht den Urlaub hier natürlich besonders einfach und angenehm.

✱ La Martinique est un département d'outre-mer français et fait donc partie intégrante de la France. Les habitants et les touristes ont les mêmes droits et les mêmes obligations qu'en ⇒ France métropolitaine. C'est un lieu de villégiature apprécié des Européens. La douceur tropicale, l'exotisme et le confort à la française rendront votre séjour particulièrement agréable.

✱ Martinica es un "Dèpartement d' Outre-Mer/D.O.M" francés, y como tal es también considerada parte de la Madre Patria: Francia. Tanto para visitantes como para sus habitantes son valederas ⇒ las leyes francesas. Martinica es hoy en día una atracción turística para europeos, donde se conjugan a la perfección las bellezas exóticas de una isla tropical con el confort europeo. Por esta razón el turista puede disfrutar aqui unas vacaciones agradables sin complicaciones.

✱ La Martinica è un „département d'outre mer/D.O.M." francese, quindi una parte della Francia. Legalmente i suoi abitanti ed i suoi visitatori sono soggetti agli stessi obblighi e doveri dei francesi. La Martinica è diventata un'amata meta turistica per gli europei che trovano su quest'isola una buona fusione di bellezza esotica e confort francese, un fatto che vi permette di passare delle vacanze piacevoli senza complicazioni.

Fort-de-France
HEALTH GROUPS
■ **Action Sida Martinique** Call Wed 15-18, Thu 19-21 h
B.P. 1075 ✉ 97200 ☎ 63 12 36 📠 63 91 91
🖥 actionsidamart@wanadoo.fr

CRUISING
-Parc de la Savanne (in front of Hotel Impératrice along the sea)

Les Trois Islets
GUEST HOUSES
■ **Carbet. Le** (AC BF G MA NU OS WH)
18 Rue des Alamandas, Anse Mitan ✉ 97229 *(20 min from the airport)* ☎ 66 03 31 📠 66 03 31 ✉ dominique.celma@wanadoo.fr
🖥 www.lecarbet-gaybandb.com
Near the beach. 3 rooms with loggia and kitchenette. Quiet and intimate location.

Sainte Anne
SWIMMING
-Les Petites Salines aka La Pointe Pie (when arriving in les Salines, take on the right and walk along the beach until the end. After the parking place, floow the pathway about 5 min. No nudism allowed but possible. Keeps your shorts handy)

Caribbean/Netherlands Antilles
Bonaire - Sorobon

Caribbean - Netherlands Antilles

Name: Nederlandse Antillen • Niederländische Antillen • Antilles Néerlandaises • Antillas Neerlandesas
Location: Caribbean
Initials: NA
Time: GMT -4
International Country Code: ☎ 599 (leave the first 0 of area codes)
International Access Code: ☎ 00
Language: Dutch, Papiamento, English, Spanish
Area: 800 km2 / 309 sq mi.
Currency: 1 Netherland Antilles Guilder (ANG) = 100 Cents
Population: 198,000
Capital: Willemstad (on Curaçao)
Religions: predominantly Roman Catholic
Climate: Tropical climate that is moderated by northeast trade winds.

Caribbean Dreams

Delfina Hotel

on St. Maarten

P.O. Box 5305
Netherlands Antilles
Fax/Fon: ++5995/453300

www.delfinahotel.com
delfina@sintmaarten.net

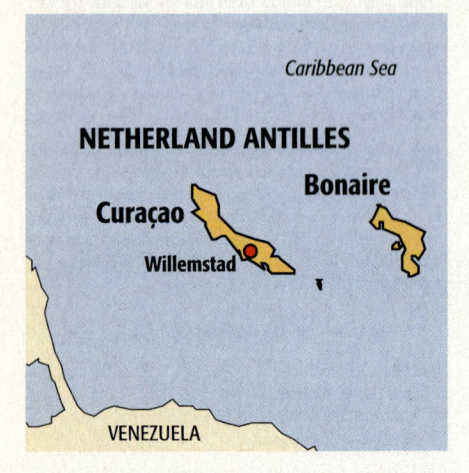

✱ Under Article 255 of the penal code, homosexual acts are legal between adult males, and the age of consent is set at 16. The attitude of the general public towards homosexuality, however, is somewhat less tolerant than that in the Netherlands.

✱ Homosexuelle Handlungen werden in Artikel 255 des Strafgesetzbuches abgehandelt. Zwischen erwachsenen Männern sind sie legal, und das Schutzalter liegt bei 16 Jahren. Allerdings ist die öffentliche Meinung Homosexuellen gegenüber hierzulande etwas weniger tolerant als im niederländischen "Mutterland".

✱ Selon l'article 255 du code pénal l'homosexualité n'est pas considérée comme un délit. La majorité sexuelle est fixée à 16 ans. Notons toutefois que l'attitude de la population vis-à-vis des gais n'est pas aussi tolérante que dans les Pays-Bas.

✱ El artículo 255 del Código Penal dictamina sobre las actividades homosexuales. Estas son declaradas legales entre hombres adultos y la edad mínima de consentimiento queda fijada en 16 años. La opinión pública de este país es menos tolerante con los gays que la de la madre patria; Holanda.

✖ Gli atti omosessuali vengono trattati nel paragrafo 255 del codice penale. Sono legali tra uomini adulti, l'età del consenso è di 16 anni. Comunque, l'opinione pubblica verso l'omosessualità è meno tollerante rispetto a quella della „madrepatria" olandese.

Bonaire - Sorobon ☎ 07

BARS
■ **Karels Beach Bar** (B NG YG) live music on Sat evening
Kaya Kachi Craane *(opposite Zeezicht Bar)*

APARTMENTS
■ **Ocean View Villas** (AC CC GLM H NU)
Kaya Statius van Eps 6 ☎ 61 05 📠 43 09
✉ info@oceanviewvillas.com
3 apartments with shower/WC, terrace, TV, kitchen, own key. Rates from US$ 80 / night.
■ **Sorobon Beach Resort** (H NG NU)
PO Box 14, Island Bonair ☎ 80 80
■ **Sunset Beach Hotel-Bonaire Sunset Villas** (B F H NG OS)
PO Box 333 ☎ 84 48
Double from US$ 80.

St. Maarten | **Netherlands Antilles - Puerto Rico/Caribbean**

St. Maarten ☎ 05

BARS
■ **Mary's Boon Hotel** (AC B BF F glm H MA OS)
Juliana, PO Box 2078 *(at the beach)* ☎ 442 35
Twin US$ 75-125. 3 minutes from the airport.

HOTELS
■ **Delfina** (AC B BF cc f GLM MA OS PI s WH WO) 07-22h
Tigris Road 14-16, Cote d' Azur ☎ 453 300 📠 453 300
✉ delfina@sintmaarten.net 🌐 www.delfinahotel.com
12 rooms. Within walking distance from nudist beach and the gay beach Cupecoy.

■ **White Sands Beach Club** (glm H) 7-17 h
PO Box 3043 ☎ 543 70 📠 522 45
17 chalets, suites and 2 bedrooms with/without kitchen. All beachfront. Call for rates.

SWIMMING
-Cupecoy Beach (g NU) (take bus from Philipsberg to Mullet Bay, then walk 20 min. following the road across the golf course and over the hill, then turn left onto the beach)

Caribbean - Puerto Rico

Name: Porto Rico
Location: Caribbean
Initials: PR
Time: GMT -5
International Country Code: ☎ 1-787 (no area codes)
International Access Code: ☎ 011
Language: Spanish, English
Area: 8,897 km2 / 3,435 sq mi.
Currency: 1 US Dollar (US$) = 100 Cents
Population: 3,806,000
Capital: San Juan
Religions: 80% Catholic
Climate: Tropical marine climate that is mild. There's little seasonal temperature variation.
Important gay cities: San Juan

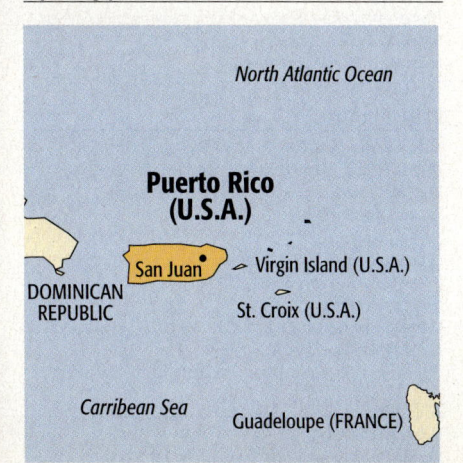

North Atlantic Ocean

Puerto Rico (U.S.A.)

San Juan
Virgin Island (U.S.A.)
DOMINICAN REPUBLIC
St. Croix (U.S.A.)

Carribean Sea
Guadeloupe (FRANCE)

※ Puerto Rico is neither a state of the US, nor independent, but 'freely associated' with the US. The Puertoricans are US-citizens but they are not entitled to vote in US-elections. This political position 'in between' and considerable customs privileges ensure economical prosperity for this Caribbean island. We do not have any information concerning the penal code, but we assume, that homosexuality is open to prosecution. Still Puerto Rico is the most liberal island in the whole of the Caribbean Sea. Gay activities take place wholly in the capital San Juan.

※ Puerto Rico ist weder ein US-Staat, noch selbständig, sondern mit den USA „frei assoziiert". Die Puertoricaner sind zwar Bürger der USA, besitzen aber kein Stimmrecht bei US-Wahlen. Diese politische Mittelstellung und erhebliche Zollvergünstigungen sichern dieser Karibikinsel wirtschaftliches Wohlergehen. Zwar liegen uns keine juristischen Informationen vor, aber wir gehen davon aus, daß Homosexualität strafbar ist. Trotzdem ist Puerto Rico die liberalste Insel in der gesamten Karibik. Schwule Aktivitäten konzentrieren sich ganz und gar auf die Hauptstadt San Juan.

※ Porto Rico ne fait pas partie de la Confédération américaine et n'est pas non plus indépendante. L'île est „associée" aux Etats-Unis. Les gens là-bas ont la citoyenneté américaine, mais ne disposent pas du droit de vote. Grâce à son statut mixte et à une liberté en matière de douanes, l'île jouit d'une certaine prospérité. Nous ne disposons d'aucune information concernant la situation des gais face à la loi. Il semblerait cependant que l'homosexualité soit condamnable. Il n'empêche que Porto Rico est une des îles les plus tolérantes des Caraïbes. La capitale gaie de l'île est San Juan.

※ Puerto Rico no es ni independiente ni un estado norteamericano, sino un estado libre asociado a los Estados Unidos. Los puertorriqueños son ciudadanos norteamericanos sin tener el derecho al voto en las elecciones norteamericanas. Esta situación política asi como las suntuosas ventajas aduaneras y migratorias, le brindan gran auge económico a esta isla caribeña. No poseemos informaciones judiciales respecto al trato de la homosexualidad en la isla, pero suponemos que ella es penada. A pesar de ello, Puerto Rico es una de las islas caribeñas más liberales. Las actividades homosexuales se concentran por completo en la capital San Juan.

※ Porto Rico non è nè indipendente nè uno stato degli USA, ma „liberamente associato"agli USA. I portoricani sono cittadini degli USA, però non hanno diritto di voto nelle elezioni parlamentari degli USA. Questo compromesso politico e le agevolazioni doganali assicurano il benessere economico di quest'isola caraibica. Non abbiamo informazioni concrete ma presumiamo che qui l'omosessualità sia illegale. Nonostante ciò Porto Rico è l'isola più liberale dei Caraibi. Le attività gay sono concentrati alla capitale di San Juan.

NATIONAL PUBLICATIONS
■ **Caribbean Heat**
1505 Loiza Street, Suite 78 ✉ PR 00911 Santurce ☎ 726 18 07
About 32 pages, US$ 4. The only gay magazine in the Caribbean. Articles about health, entertainment, arts and travel.

■ **Puerto Rico Breeze**
400 Calaf Suite 100 ✉ PR 00918-1323 San Juan ☎ 282 71 84

NATIONAL GROUPS
■ **Concra Puerto Rico**
112 Avenida Universidad Santa Rito, Rio Piedras, Puerto Rico
☎ 753-9449
■ **Sabana Litigation and AIDS Civil Rights Project**
1056 Muñoz Rivera, Suite 1004 ✉ PR 00927 Rio Piedras
☎ 759-8832

Caribbean/Puerto Rico Aguada ▸ San Juan

CAFE BERLIN
restaurant bakery delikatessen

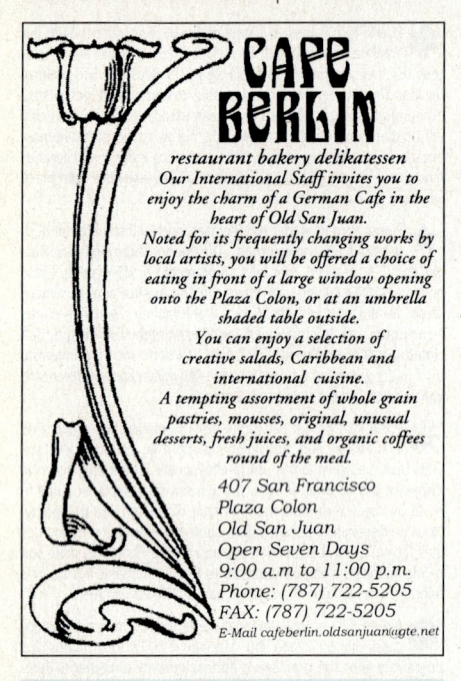

Our International Staff invites you to enjoy the charm of a German Cafe in the heart of Old San Juan.
Noted for its frequently changing works by local artists, you will be offered a choice of eating in front of a large window opening onto the Plaza Colon, or at an umbrella shaded table outside.
You can enjoy a selection of creative salads, Caribbean and international cuisine.
A tempting assortment of whole grain pastries, mousses, original, unusual desserts, fresh juices, and organic coffees round of the meal.

407 San Francisco
Plaza Colon
Old San Juan
Open Seven Days
9:00 a.m to 11:00 p.m.
Phone: (787) 722-5205
FAX: (787) 722-5205
E-Mail cafeberlin.oldsanjuan@qte.net

Aguada

HOTELS
■ **San Max** (H NG) closed May & Jun
PO Box 12 94 ✉ 00602 ☏ 868 29 31
Room with bath. Rates US$ 25. Two persons 30. Full kitchen. Minimum stay 3 days.

San Juan

For the Caribbean, San Juan, with its highways and highrise buildings in the tourist quarter *Condado*, seems to have a very American feel to it. In this quarter (with its most beautiful bathing beach) and in Ocean View right next to it are most of the gay accomodations, venue and clubs. Approximately one kilometre distant lies the old town of San Juan, *Viejo San Juan*, which is so remarkable that its inscribed in the World Heritage List of UNESCO. Here is the right place to go shopping and there are many nightclubs and bars.

Für karibische Verhältnisse wirkt das von Highways durchzogene San Juan mit den Hochhäusern im Urlauberviertel *Condado* sehr amerikanisch. In diesem Viertel (mit wunderschönem Badestrand) und nebenan in Ocean View liegen auch die meisten schwulen Unterkünfte und Ausgehmöglichkeiten. Etwa einen Kilometer entfernt liegt die Altstadt San Juans, *Viejo San Juan*, die so sehenswert ist, daß die UNESCO sie in ihrer Welterbeliste verzeichnet. Alt-San-Juan ist auch die richtige Gegend zum Shoppen und Bummeln.

Les autoroutes urbaines traversent San Juan, les tours se dressent dans le quartier résidentiel de Condado: on a l'impression d'être aux Etats-Unis. C'est à Condado (plages merveilleuses) et à Ocean View que vous trouverez la plupart des pensions gaies, des bars et des boîtes. A un kilomètre de là, vous avez le vieille ville de San Juan. Elle fait partie du patrimoine de l'UNESCO. Viejo San Juan est le lieu idéal pour faire du shopping et sortir le soir.

San Juan, con sus Highways y sus rascacielos en la región vacacional *Condado*, se caracteriza por su apariencia norteamericana. En Condado, con sus maravillosas playas, y en el sector Ocean View se encuentran la mayoría de locales, pensiones y lugares de diversión gay. A 1 km. de distancia se encuentra la ciudad vieja San Juan, que por su belleza e importancia histórica, fue incluída dentro de la lista Patrimonio Cultural Mundial de la UNESCO. San Juan Viejo es el lugar ideal para ir de compras y disfrutar de la vida nocturna.

San Juan ha un aspetto molto americano: è attraversata da autostrade, il suo orizzonte è disegnato dai grattacieli del quartiere turistico di *Condado*. In questo quartiere (con una spiaggia favolosa) ed nell'*Ocean View* si concentrano gli alberghi e i locali gay. Ad un chilometro di distanza si trova il centro di San Juan, *viejo San Juan*, che per la sua bellezza è stato messo sotto protezione artistica dall'Unesco. Questa zona è la migliore per fare un giro dei negozi e per uscire di sera.

BARS
■ **Barefoot Bar** (B F g H MA N R) 9.00-4.00 h
2 Calle Vendig ✉ PR 00907 (*Condado*) ☏ +1-809-725 20 55 or ☏ 725-2055. Meals 9-17, happy hour 17-19 h. Rooms & apartments available.
■ **Juniors Bar** (B D g N P SNU) 18-2, Sun 15-2 h
602 Calle Condado (*Condado*)

DANCECLUBS
■ **Abbey in the Lazer, The** (B D C) Sun
251 Calle Cruz
■ **Eros** (B D G MA SNU) Wed-Sun 21-4 h, Mon closed
1257 Avenida Ponce de Leon, Stop 18 Santurce (next to Metro Cinema) ☏ 722 11 31
Extiting hightech disco. Regular parties and theme night, AIDS benefit. Shows Thu and Sun, strippers, bands.
■ **Escape** (B D G MA S) Sat 20-? h
181 O'Neill Street, Hato Rey

RESTAURANTS
■ **Cafe Berlin** (A AC B BF CC F GLM MA OS) 9-23 h
407 San Francisco, Plaza Colon (*Old San Juan*) ☏ 722 52 05
Restaurant, bakery, delicatessen. Mostly vegetarian cuisine.
■ **Cafe Gambaro** (B F g)
320 Calle Fortaleza ☏ 724 45 92
■ **Condado Inn** (B GLM MA) 11-? h
6 Avenida Condado (*Condado*) ☏ 724 71 45
Dinner only. Home style food.
■ **Panaché Restaurant & Bar** (AC B F G MA N OS) 11.30-15, 18-23 h
1127 Calle Seaview *Condado* ☏ 725 82 84
Excellent southern French cuisine. Overlooking beach. Inexpensive.

SEX SHOPS/BLUE MOVIES
■ **Condom Mania** (g)
353 San Francisco Street (*Old San Juan*) ☏ 722 53 87

San Juan | **Puerto Rico/Caribbean**

ATLANTIC BEACH HOTEL
san juan

The jewel of the Caribean

Where you and the blue sea come together

On the beach • Deck bar • Sea View Restaurant

Tel. (787) 721-6900, Fax (787) 721-9617

WWW.atlanticbeachhotel.net

P.O. Box 16876 San Juan, Puerto Rico 00908-6876 / One calle Vendig, Condado, San Juan, Puerto Rico 00907

EMBASSY
Guest House Condado

Best location in San Juan

Pool & Jacuzzi on the beach, Kitchenette available

Only steps to Casinos & Night life

Phone (787) 725-8284 • Fax (787) 725-2400 • http//home.att.net/~embassyguesthouse/
1126 Calle Seaview, Condado, San Juan, Puerto Rico. 00907

Caribbean/Puerto Rico | San Juan

STEAMWORKS
saca la presión

BAÑOS TURCOS — BERKELEY CA CHICAGO IL SAN JUAN PR

205 Calle Luna / Old San Juan PR / 787.725.4993 / www.SteamworksOnLine.com

OCEAN PARK BEACH INN

Calle Elena #3
San Juan
Puerto Rico
00911
787 728 7418
Phone & Fax

Privacy
Breakfast
Gay Beach
Cafe & Bar
Redesigned
Weekly Rates

Tropical Gardens By The Ocean
1 800 292 9208
E-mail:opbi@coqui.net - Web http://home.coqui.net/opbi

San Juan — Puerto Rico - Saint Kitts & Nevis/Caribbean

SAUNAS/BATHS
■ **Steamworks** (AC b CC f G MA P SA SB VS WH WO) 0-24 h
205 Calle Luna ✉ PR 00902 *(Old San Juan)* ☎ 725 49 93
Popular sauna in historic old San Juan.

HOTELS
■ **Atlantic Beach Hotel** (AC B BF CC d F GLM H MA OS S SNU STV WH) All year
1 Calle Vendig ✉ PR 00907 *(Condado, Center of hotel area)*
☎ 721-6900 721-6917 ✉ reservations@atlanticbeachhotel.net
 www.atlanticbeachhotel.net
Central location on beach. Restaurant. Deckbar and Sundeck. Jacuzzi. 37 rooms with direct dial telephone, cable TV, priv. bath and WC. Single US$70, double $100 (off-season). Single $115, double $150 (high-season). Reservation essential in high-season Dec-Apr.
■ **Beach Buoy Inn Guest House** (glm H)
1853 Mc Leary *(Ocean Park)* ☎ 728 81 19
■ **Casa del Caribe** (AC BF CC H)
57 Calle Caribe ✉ 00907 ☎ (877) 722-7139 *(toll-free)*
■ **Condado Inn** (B F GLM H s)
6 Avenida Condado *Condado* ☎ 724 71 45
■ **Numero Uno On the Beach** (B F glm H Pl)
1 Calle Santa Ana, Ocean Park ✉ PR 00911 ☎ 726 50 10
 727 54 82

GUEST HOUSES
■ **Embassy Guest House** (AC B CC F GLM H MA OS)
1126 Calle Seaview ✉ PR 00907 *(Condado)* ☎ 725 82 84
☎ 724 74 40 725 24 00
 www.home.att.net/embassyguesthouse/
All rooms with private bath and TV. Rates US$ 45-85 (low season), 65-135 (high season). All rooms have private bath, air-condition, ceiling fans, refrigerator, coffee maker and color cable TV.
■ **LaCondessa Inn Guest House** (glm H)
2071 Calle Cacique ✉ PR 00912 *(Ocean Park)* ☎ 727 36 98
■ **L'Habitation Beach** (AC B BF CC F glm MA OS p r SOL)
1957 Calle Italia, Ocean Park ✉ PR 00911 *(Condado)*
☎ 727 24 99 727-2599 ✉ habitationbeach@msn.com
Central location directly on the beach. All rooms have private baths. Rates US$ 66-87 (Dec 15-Apr 15) and US$ 47-69 (Apr 16-Dec 14), bf incl.
■ **Ocean Park Beach Inn** (BF CC glm H OS) All year
3 Calle Elena ✉ 00911 *(Ocean Park)* ☎ 728-7418
☎ +1 800 292-9208 *(tollfree)* 728-7418 ✉ opbi@coqui.net
 home.coqui.net/opbi
Single rooms from US$ 55 (low season) to $ 100, (high season), double rooms from $80,(low season) to $ 130, (high season). Special rates available.

SWIMMING
-Beach between La Concha Hotel and Dupont Plaza Hotel (R) (especially next to Atlantic Beach Hotel, more tourists than locals)
-Ocean Park (more locals, busy on Sun)

CRUISING
-Plaza Rio Piedras (near University, Hato Rey)
-Calle San Francisco, Old San Juan (R)
-Plaza de Armas, Old San Juan
-Plaza de las Americas
-Plaza Colon (bus stop)

Caribbean - Saint Kitts & Nevis
Location: Caribbean
Initials: KN
Time: GMT -4
International Country Code: ☎ 1-869 (no area codes)
International Access Code: ☎ 011
Language: English
Area: 261 km2 / 101 sq mi.
Currency: 1 East Caribbean Dollar (EC$) = 100 Cents
Population: 42,000
Capital: Basseterre
Religions: 87% Christian
Climate: Subtropical climate, that is tempered by constant sea breezes. The rainy season lasts from May to November.

✳ We have no information about Saint Kitts and Nevis except that gay life is extremely hidden. Nevertheless it is a wonderful place to recover from the stress of everyday urban life.

★ Über Saint Kitts und Nevis stehen uns keine Informationen zur Verfügung; wir wissen nur, daß das Leben der Homosexuellen sehr diskret verläuft. Dennoch kann man sich auf dieser wunderschönen Insel vom städtischen Alltagsstress erholen.

✳ Nous ne possédons aucune information sur Saint Kitts and Nevis si ce n'est que les gais n'affichent pas leur homosexualité publiquement. L'archipel reste cependant un lieu idyllique pour se reposer du stress quotidien de la ville.

⬢ No tenemos informaciones sobre San Cristóbal y Nevis. Sólo sabemos que los gays llevan una vida extremadamente discreta. No obstante, estas islas maravillosas son ideales para olvidarse del estrés de la vida ajetreada en la ciudad.

✕ Non disponiamo di informazioni per quanto riguarda Saint Kitts e Nevis. Sappiamo soltanto che la vita gay è estremamente nascosta. Nonostante ciò questa meravigliosa isola è il posto ideale per riprendersi dallo stress quotidiano della vita urbana.

Caribbean/Saint Kitts & Nevis - Virgin Island of the USA | Charlestown ▶ Saint John

Nevis - Charlestown

HOTELS

■ **Four Season Resort** (AC B F H NG PI)
PO Box 565
Single/double US$ 220-385. Reservations: New York (212) 980-0101, London 834 44 22, Düsseldorf (0211) 35 41 98, Paris (01) 42088390

Saint Kitts - Basseterre

HOTELS

■ **Ocean Terrace Inn** (B F H NG PI)
PO Box 65, W1 ☎ 465 27 54

CRUISING
-Frigate Beach (WE)
-Along seafront (dock area and particularly where local buses depart)

Caribbean - Virgin Islands of the USA

Name: Jungferninseln • Iles Vierges • Islas Vírgenes
Location: Caribbean
Initials: VI
Time: GMT -4
International Country Code: ☎ 1-340 (no area codes)
International Access Code: ☎ 011
Language: English
Area: 344 km² / 133 sq mi.
Currency: 1 US Dollar (US$) = 100 Cents
Population: 105,000
Capital: Charlotte Amalie (on St. Thomas)
Religions: 42% Baptist, 34% Roman Catholic, 17% Episcopalian
Climate: Subtropical climate, that is tempered by constant sea breezes. The rainy season lasts from May to November.

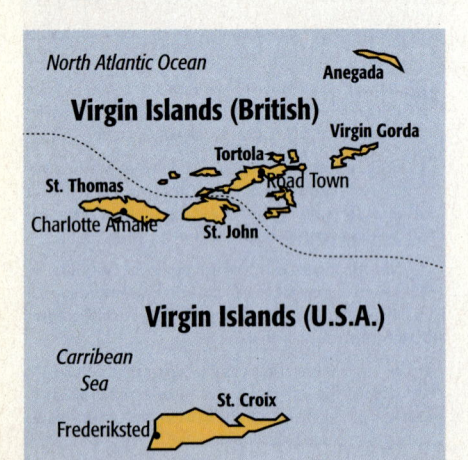

North Atlantic Ocean
Anegada
Virgin Islands (British)
Virgin Gorda
Tortola
St. Thomas — **Road Town**
Charlotte Amalie — **St. John**
Virgin Islands (U.S.A.)
Carribean Sea
St. Croix
Frederiksted

✱ The Virgin Islands are the nearest neighbours to Puerto Rico. For the average tourist these islands are mainly a station on their Caribbean cruise to buy duty free goods. Next to that there are gay hotels and the fundamental gay entertainment amenities in Frederiksted on *St. Croix*. And more is not needed. You don't take a gay holiday on a Caribbean island. You go here to lounge on a beautiful beach in a lovely tropical climate, to recreate and play in a sparkling ocean.

✱ Die Jungferninseln liegen in unmittelbarer Nachbarschaft zu Puerto Rico. Der Durchschnittstourist besucht diese Inseln vor allem als Station einer Karibik-Kreuzfahrt und um hier günstig zollfrei einzukaufen. Daneben gibt es auf *St. Croix* in Frederiksted und auf *St. Thomas* schwule Hotels und eine Grundausstattung an schwulen Unterhaltungsmöglichkeiten. Mehr ist auch nicht nötig, denn auf einer Karibikinsel macht man keinen schwulen Urlaub. Hierher fährt man, um sich im angenehmen tropischen Klima an einem wunderschönen Strand im herrlichen Meer zu tummeln und zu erholen.

✱ Les Iles Vierges sont voisines de Porto Rico. En général, on y vient pour faire des achats en duty free. A Frederiksted sur Sainte Croix et sur Saint Thomas, il y a plusieurs hôtels et établissements gais. Cela suffit largement, car on ne vient pas aux Caraïbes pour passer des vacances 100% gaies. On y vient pour la douceur du climat et pour les plages enchanteresses.

✱ Las Islas Vírgenes se localizan en las cercanías de Puerto Rico. La mayoria de los turistas que hacen un crucero por el Caribe bacen aquí una parada para aprochevar los interesantes precios de esta zona libre de impuestos. Pero en *St. Thomas* existen también unas cuantas pensiones y locales de diversión gay. Mucho más tampoco hace falta, ya que el objetivo de la mayoría de los turistas gay es disfrutar del excelente clima, las bella playas y el mar azul, y no se echa de menos una infrastructura homosexual.

✱ Le Isole Vergini sono situate nelle immediate vicinanze di Porto Rico. Normalmente i turisti si fermano solo per fare scalo durante una crociera e per fare acquisti senza pagare tasse doganali. A Frederiksted, in *St. Croix* e a St. Thomas vi sono alcuni hotel e locali per gay. Non ci vuole di più, dato che ai Caraibi non si viene per il sesso, ma per godersi il clima e le spiaggie.

Saint Croix

BARS

■ **St. Tropez** (B glm)
67 King Street

HOTELS

■ **On The Beach** (AC B BF F glm H MA OS PI WH)
PO Box 1908, Frederiksted, ✉ VI 00841 ☎ 772 12 05
☎ (800) 524-2018 (toll free)
Beautiful beachfront hotel welcoming gays and non-gays alike. Reservation necessary. All rooms with kitchenette, priv. bath, and balcony.

SWIMMING
-Frederiksted, Beach of Hotel On the Beach

CRUISING
-Old Fortress (at Christiansted)

Saint John

GUEST HOUSES

■ **Oscar's Guesthouse** (AC CC H NU YG)
Estate Pastory #27, P.O.Box 117, Cruz Bay ✉ VI 00831 ☎ 776 61 93

Saint Thomas

TRAVEL AND TRANSPORT
■ **Rafting Adventures** (NG)
Maritime Services Int'l., Inc., 82 Red Hook Center ☎ 779 20 32
Snorkel-Sightsee-Tours.

HOTELS
■ **Blackbeard's Castle** (AC B CC F glm MA N OS PI)
38 Dronningens Gade, ✉ VI 00804 ☎ 776 12 34 📠 976 432
■ blackbeards.stt@postoffice.worldnet.att.net.
Rates (single/double) US$ summer 60-95 / 75-110, winter 110-150 / 125-175 (all prices + tax, bf incl.)
■ **Danish Chalet Guest House** (AC B H NG OS PI)
Solberg Road, Charlotte Amalie ✉ VI 00803 (Gamble Norisideve's)
☎ 774 57 64
☎ (800) 635-1531 *Toll-free* Central location, 10 min to the airport.

All rooms with fridge, priv. bath. Single US$ 45-80 (bf incl.)
■ **Harbor Lites** (glm H)
Nisky Mail Box 442 ☎ 775 24 76
■ **Hotel 1829** (AC B CC F H NG PI)
Goverment Hill, Charlotte Amalie ✉ VI 00802, *(above the post office)* ☎ 776 18 29
Downtown location, 15 min to the airport. The gourmet restaurant offers French and American specialities (try the soufflés). All rooms have AC, telephone, priv. bath, frigidaire, cable TV.
Toll-free ☎ (800) 524-2002 *Toll-free*
■ **Secret Harbor Beach Resort** (g H)
6280 Estate Nazareth ☎ 775 65 50
☎ (800) 524-2250 *Toll free*

SWIMMING
-Little Magen's Bay (g NU) (right side of Magen's Bay Beach)

Chile

Name: Chili • Cile
Location: South America
Initials: RCH
Time: GMT -4
International Country Code: ☎ 56 (Leave away the first 0 of area codes)
International Access Code: ☎ 00
Language: Spanish
Area: 756,945 km2 / 292,256 sq mi.
Currency: 1 Chilean Peso (chil$) = 100 Centavos.
Population: 14,824,000
Capital: Santiago de Chile
Religions: 89% Roman Catholic
Climate: Moderate climate. Desert climate in the north, the south is cool and damp.

※ The new Chilean legislation has repealed earlier laws passed in 1998 that criminalised same-sex relations between consenting adults. The age of consent for same-sex partners is now set at 18 years.

Chile is a wonderful country well worth a visit. With a wide variation of climate and vegetation zones, from the Atacama desert (the driest desert in the world) and the geysers at over 5000m to the cool and wet tip of south Chile.

★ Die neue chilenische Gesetzgebung hat frühere Gesetze, die 1998 noch gültig waren und gleichgeschlechtliche Beziehungen zwischen mündigen Erwachsenen unter Strafe stellten, aufgehoben. Das Mündigkeitsalter für gleichgeschlechtliche Partner ist nunmehr auf 18 Jahre festgesetzt.

Chile ist ein wunderbares Land, das einen Besuch wert ist. Es verfügt über verschiedenen Klima- und Vegetationszonen, die von der Atacama-Wüste (die trockenste Wüste der Welt) über die Geysiere gehen, die sich auf einer Höhe von über 5000 m befinden, und bis hin zur kühlen und feuchten Südspitze des Landes reichen.

※ la nouvelle législation chilienne a aboli en 1998 les lois qui interdisaient les relations entre personnes de même sexe. La majorité sexuelle est fixée maintenant à 18 ans pour les homosexuels.
Le Chili est un pays magnifique qui mérite une visite. Il offre de grandes variations de climat et de végétation, entre le désert d'Atacama (le désert le plus sec du monde), des geysers à plus de 5000 mètres d'altitude ou les régions plus humides au sud.

● La nueva legislación chilena revocó leyes anteriores aprobadas en 1998 que criminalizaron las relaciones consentidas entre adultos del mismo sexo. La edad de consentimiento para relaciones sexuales con personas del mismo sexo ahora se está fijada en 18 años.

Chile es un país maravilloso que bien merece una visita. Tiene una gran variación de zonas climáticas con vegetaciones muy diversas, desde el desierto de Atacama (el desierto más seco del mundo) pasando por los géiseres a más de 5000 metros sobre el nivel del mar hasta la parte fría y húmeda del sur de Chile.

✖ La nuova leggislazione del Cile ha abrogato le leggi che erano ancora in vigore nel 1998 e che prevedevano una pena per rapporti tra adulti
maggiorenni dello stesso sesso. Ora, l'età maggiore per partner dello stesso sesso è fissato a 18 anni. Il Cile è un paese meraviglioso dove vale la pena andarci. Cile dispone di varie zone climatiche e vegetative che vanno dal deserto Atacama (il deserto più secco nel mondo), attraverso i geyseri, trovandosi in una altezza di oltre 5000 metri, fino alla fredda e umida punta meridionale del Cile.

Chile — Antofagasta ▶ Horcon

NATIONAL GAY INFO
■ **El Otro Lado**
PO Box 512 64 Correo Central Santiago-1 Santiago
☎ (0)2543 27 05
■ **Follies**
PO Box 34, Santiago-35 Santiago   ☎ (0)2-285 15 43
🖷 (0)2-233 63 24   ✉ Centrum@cernet.net

NATIONAL PUBLICATIONS
■ **Lambda News**
Augustinas 2095, PO Box 53575, Correo Central Santiago Santiago *(esquina Avenida Brasil, Santiago Centro)*   ☎ (02) 673 00 57
🖷 (02) 673 00 57   ✉ lambdanews@interactiva.cl
🖳 www.lambdanews.cl
Chiles monthly gay magazine.

NATIONAL GROUPS
■ **Comisión Nacional del SIDA**
Mac Iver 541 Santiago ☎ 630 06 73   ☎ 630 06 74   ✉ cilaids@cchps.mic.cl
Also Corporación Chilena de Prevención del Sida
■ **Corporación Chilena de Prevención del Sida** Mon-Fri 10-22 h
General Jofré 179 Santiago☎ (02) 222 52 55   🖷 (02) 222 8356
✉ chilaids@cchps.mic.cl
■ **Movimiento Unificado de Minorías Sexuales** 13-22h
Casilla Postal 52834, Correo Central, Santiago 1 Santiago
☎ (02) 7373 0892   🖷 (02) 732 0863   ✉ movim@minorias.in.cl
🖳 www.minorias.in.cl

Antofagasta ☎ 055
DANCECLUBS
■ **Boy´s** (ac B D G S MA) Fri & Sat 22-5 h
Calma frente a la Vega Central *(Calama opposite of Vega Central)*
■ **Máscaras** (ac B D G S MA) Fri & Sat 22-5 h
Taltal esq. Calbuco *(At the corner Taltal/Calbuco)*

RESTAURANTS
■ **Bavaria** (B F glm)
José Santos Ossa *(At the corner Baquedano)*
Typical cuisine

HOTELS
■ **Antofagasta** (AC BF glm F H OS PI WO)
Balmaceda s/n°   ☎ 26 8259
■ **Apart Hotel Diego de Almagro** (BF F glm H)
Condell 2624   ☎ 26 8331
■ **Plaza** (AC BF glm F H)
Baquedano 461   ☎ 26 9246

CRUISING
-Plaza Colòn (g MA r)

Arica ☎ 058
HOTELS
■ **Diego de Almagro** (BF F glm H)
Sotomayor 490   ☎ 22 4444
■ **Hostería Arica** (BF F glm H OS PI)
Avenida Commandante San Martín 599   ☎ 25 4540
■ **San Marcos Hotel** (BF glm F H)
Sotomayor 367   ☎ 23 2970
Centrally located hotel with garden. All rooms with telephone, TV, private bath, WC.

CRUISING
-Beach "El Laucho" (next to the Hotel Arica in the Avenida Costanera, in the early evening)
-Plaza Colón (Square in front of City Hall and the Vicuña Square next to it, in the early evening).
-Plaza Vicuña Mackenna, (in the early evening)

Calama ☎ 055
RESTAURANTS
■ **Maracuyá** (B F glm)
Avenida Commandante San Martin 0321   ☎ 22 7600

HOTELS
■ **Alfa** (BF F glm H)
Sotomayor 2016   ☎ 34 2496
■ **Hosteriá Calama** (BF F glm H)
Latorre 1521   ☎ 34 1511
■ **Park Hotel Calama** (BF f glm H)
Camino Aeropuerto 1392   ☎ 34 2208

Castro - Isla de Chiloe ☎ 065
RESTAURANTS
■ **Central** (B F MA NG)
Avenida Pedro Montt   ☎ 63 4749
■ **Sancho** (b F MA NG)
Thompson 213   ☎ 63 2079

HOTELS
■ **Unicornio Azul** (AC BF F glm H)
Avenida Pedro Montt 228   ☎ 63 2359

GUEST HOUSES
■ **Hospedaje Llapui** (ac BF glm) 24 h
O'Higgins 657   ☎ 63 3217   ☎ 63 7497

Chillan ☎ 042
BARS
■ **Kalhúa** (B D G MA)
Panamericana Sur km 412   ☎ 23 78 74

Concepción ☎ 041
RESTAURANTS
■ **Chateau. Le** (AC B F glm)
Colo-Colo/O'Higgins

HOTELS
■ **Alborada** (AC B BF F glm H)
Barros Arana 457   ☎ 24 2144
■ **Araucano. El** (AC B BF F glm H)
Caupolicán 521   ☎ 23 0606

SWIMMING
-Playa Blanca (G MA) (Located south of Concepción, approximately one hour by bus/car between the cities of Coronel and Lota).

CRUISING
-Plaza de la Independencia (g MA) (At the corner Barros Arana/Aníbal Pinto).
-Paseo Peatonal Barros Arana (g MA) (busy after 21 h).
-Paseo Peatonal Aníbal Pinto (g MA) (busy after 21 h).

Horcon ☎ 032
HOTELS
■ **Hosteriá Arancibia** (BF F glm H)
Avenida La Playa s/n.

Horcon ▶ Santiago — Chile

■ **Residencial Juan Esteban** (BF glm H)
Pasaje Miramar 2 ☎ 33 5153
Clean, comfortable rooms with private bathroom.

SWIMMING
-Cau-Cau (G MA NU)

Iquique ☎ 057

DANCECLUBS
■ **Escape** (B D G MA)
Bajo Molle, km 8

Isla de Pascua - Rapanui ☎ 032

DANCECLUBS
■ **Tavake** (D glm) 23-? h
Hanga Roa

HOTELS
■ **Hanga Roa** (BF F glm H)
Avenida Pont s/n., Hanga Roa ☎ 10 0299
■ **Hotu Matúa** (BF F glm H)
Avenida Pont s/n., Hanga Roa ☎ 10 0242
■ **Orongo Easter Island** (BF F glm H)
Avenida Policarpo Toro s/n., Hanga Roa ☎ 10 0294

La Serena ☎ 051

BARS
■ **Remaking** (ac B D GLM MA)
Avenida Francisco de Aguirre 062 ☎ 21 0632

DANCECLUBS
■ **Best** (ac B D GLM MA S)
Balmaceda 3390, Paradero 6 1/2, La Pampa ☎ 24 2607
■ **Diva** (B D G MA) Fri Sat
Colo-Colo 4456 *(Loteo Aeroparque)*

RESTAURANTS
■ **La Miá Pizza** (b F glm MA)
Avenida del Mar 2100 ☎ 21 2232

HOTELS
■ **Berlin** (BF F glm H)
Cordovez 535 ☎ 22 2927
■ **Casablanca** (AC BF F glm H)
Vicuña 414 ☎ 22 5573
■ **Francisco de Aguirre** (AC BF F glm H)
Cordovez 210 ☎ 22 2991

CRUISING
-Playa El Faro (g MA) (Dunes north of El Faro Monument.)

Punta Arenas ☎ 061

BARS
■ **Bossanova** (B G MA)
Avenida España 1198 ☎ 24 19 78

Rocas de Santo Domingo ☎ 035

HOTELS
■ **Intihuasi** (BF F glm H)
Avenida Litoral 54 ☎ 28 3104 📠 28 3104
■ **Rocas de Santo Domingo** (BF F glm H)
La Ronda 130 ☎ 44 4356

SWIMMING
-Dunas de Rocas de Santo Domingo (G MA NU) (Dunes south of the town).

San Antonio ☎ 035

RESTAURANTS
■ **D'Borques** (b F glm MA)
Avenida Chile del Balneario Llo-Lleo
■ **Juanita** (b F glm MA)
Antofagasta 159

HOTELS
■ **Hotel de Turismo del Jockey Club** (BF F glm H)
Avenida 21 de Mayo 202 ☎ 21 1777
■ **Imperial** (BF F glm H)
Avenida Centenario 330 ☎ 21 1676

SWIMMING
-Dunas de Llo-Lleo (G MA NU) (South towards the end of the dunes).

CRUISING
-Plaza Central de Llo-Lleo (g MA) (In the public pool/Balneario).

San Pedro de Atacama ☎ 055

RESTAURANTS
■ **Estaka. La** (B bf CC glm MA) 9-0.30h
Caracoles 259-b ✉ 6061 ☎ 851 201
Traditional food, meat and vegetarian dishes.
■ **Tambo Cañaveral** (b BF F glm)
Caracoles *(esquina Toconao)*
Traditional food

HOTELS
■ **San Pedro de Atacama. Hosteriá** (BF F glm H)
Solcor s/n.
■ **Takha Takha. Hosteriá** (BF F glm H)
Tocopilla s/n.

GUEST HOUSES
■ **Residencial Juanita** (BF F glm H)
La Plaza s/n.

CRUISING
-Plaza de San Pedro (g)

Santiago ☎ 02

GAY INFO
■ **Disque Amistad** (g MA) 0-24 h
☎ 700 1010
■ **Radio Nuevo Mundo 93 AM** (G) Sat 15.30 h
The program „Triángulo Abierto" is produced by the MOVILH.
■ **Radio Tierro 130 AM** Mon-Fri 19.20 h
Program „Crónicas Radiales"

Chile — Santiago

BARS

■ **Bar Willy / Bar Fox** (B glm MA S) 22-4, WE -5 h
Avenida 11 de Septiembre 2214 *(Comun Providencia, Passeo Las Palmas)* ☎ 381 1806
During the day mixed public, in the evening turns into Bar Willy - gay with stripshow on the 1st floor.
■ **Dionisio** (B F GLM MA S) Mon-Sat 21-? h
Bombero Nuñez 111 *(esquina Dardinac, Barrio Bellavista, Recoleta)*
☎ 737 6065
Shows Wed-Sat 0-3 h
■ **Tu club** (B GLM MA) Wed-Sat 22-5 h
Copiapó 685 ☎ 634 1963

CAFES

■ **Tavelli** (! AC BF f glm OS)
Avenida Providencia *(between Andrés de Fuenzalida and Las Urbinas, Providencia)* ☎ 231 9862
Very popular.

DANCECLUBS

■ **Bokhara** (B D G MA S) 20-5, WE-7 h
Pio Nono 430 *(Bellavista)* ☎ 732 1050
■ **Bunker Santiago** (! B D GLM MA S) Fri, Sat & before holidays 0-6 h. Shows 2 h
Bombero Nuñez 159/Andrés Bello *(Barrio Bellavista, Recoleta)*
☎ 777 3760
■ **Cero** (B D G MA) Fri & Sat 23-6 h
Euclides 1204, Par. 2 Gr. Avenida ☎ 551 7228
■ **Fausto** (! AC B D G MA S VS) Mon-Sat 22:30-? h, Show 2 h
Avenida Santa María 0826/Paso Hondo *(Providencia)* ☎ 777 1041
■ **Naxos** (ac B D G MA S) Tue-Sun 24-? h
Alameda Bernardo O'Higgins 776/San Francisco *(Centro)*
☎ 639 9629
■ **Quasar** (ac B D G MA S STV VS) Fri & Sat 0-6 h
Coquimbo 1458/Aldunate *(Santiago Sur)* ☎ 671 1367
Large, very popular disco.
■ **Queen** (B D Glm MA STV) 23-? h
Coronel Santiago Bueras 128/Irene Morales *(Centro)* ☎ 639 8703
Shows 1.30, WE 3 h

RESTAURANTS

■ **Capricho Español** (! A AC B CC F G MA OS s) 20-3 h
Purisima 65 *(M°-Baquedano)* ☎ 777 76 74
Spanish and international cuisine
■ **Eneldo** (B F glm)
Ernesto Pinto Lagarrigue 195 *(Bellavista)* ☎ 732 0428
International cuisine.
■ **Pizza Nostra. La** (A B F glm MA OS)
Avenida Providencia 1975/Pedro de Valdivia *(Providencia)*
☎ 231 9853
Italian food. Nice atmosphere.
■ **Prosit** (b f glm MA OS)
Avenida Providencia/Avenida Vicuña Mackenna *(Plaza Italia. Providencia)*
Fast food. Popular with gays later at night and on WE.

SEX SHOPS/BLUE MOVIES

■ **Freeshop Magazine** (g) Mon-Sat 12-24, Sun 18-24 h
Huérfanos 530/Santa Lucía, local 10 *(Centro)* ☎ 664 4240
■ **Novelty** (glm)
Merced 839, Local 96 ☎ 697 2547
■ **Sex Shop Chile** (g P VS)
Caracol Madrid, Av. Pedro de Valdivia 1783, local 186 *(esquina Avenida Francisco Bilbao, cuarto piso, Ñuñoa)* ☎ 251 67 29

CINEMAS

■ **Capri** (ayor g MA VS) 11-23 h
Santo Domingo 834 ☎ 639 2414
Please note that showing anal penetration in films is forbidden under Chilean law.

SAUNAS/BATHS

■ **Baños Chacabuco** (b g MA OG r SB) 10-21, Sun 10-14 h
Chacabuco 33 *(Centro)* ☎ 681 74 62
The cabins on the first floor are for the straights, gays can rent cabins on the second floor. Be discreet.
■ **Baños Turcos Miraflores** (b g OG r SB) 7-21, Sun 7-14 h
Miraflores 353 *(Segundo Subterráneo, Centro)* ☎ 639 55 04
Relaxed atmosphere. Be discreet.

FITNESS STUDIOS

■ **Gimnasio JR** (! b G MA p SB WO) 15-21 h
Ricardo Matte Pérez 0372/Condell *(Providencia)*
☎ 225 1970
Cabines available.
■ **Protec** (g WO)
Alonso Ovalle 1585 *(Santiago Sur)* ☎ 688 5412

NEWS STANDS

■ **Ediciones Yugoslavia** (g)
Pasaje Catedral, Catedral 1063/Bandera, local 512 *(Centro)*

VIDEO SHOPS

■ **Video Club** (g P VS)
Rosas 3017 *(esquina Maipú, Centro)* ☎ 681 3662
Magazines and videos may be bought by adults (18 years and older) for private use only.

HOTELS

■ **Sao Paulo** (BF F glm H)
San Antonio 356/Huérfanos *(Santiago Centro)* ☎ 39 80 31

GENERAL GROUPS

■ **PAFALH (Padres, Famialares y Amigos de Lesbianas y Homosexuales)**
Aduana 936, Dept.21 *(Nuñoa)* ☎ 272 2040

HEALTH GROUPS

■ **Comisión Nacional del SIDA (CONASIDA)**
Monjitas 689 *(6th floor, Santiago Centro)* ☎ 639 4001
Information and education.
■ **EDUK**
☎ 737 5267
Education and information about AIDS.
■ **FRENASIDA (Frente Nacional de prevención del SIDA)**
Dieciocho 120 *(Santiago Sur)* ☎ 698 1180 ☎ 697 3711
Library containing lots of information about HIV/AIDS.
■ **GEAM (Gente para un Amor Nuevo)**
☎ 635 1760
For people living with HIV/AIDS.
■ **R.E.O.S.S. (Redes de Orientación en Salud Social)**
Melipilla 3432, Avenida Independencia al 3400 *(Conchalí)*
☎ 736 5542
HIV information, counselling and testing.

HELP WITH PROBLEMS

■ **CAPVIH (Centro de Apoyo a personas viviendo con VIH)**
San Antonio 501, dpto. 702 *(Santiago Centro)* ☎ 633 6966
Legal help and advice for gays and lesbians and people living with HIV/AIDS.
■ **Corporación Chilena de Prevención del SIDA (CCPS)**
General Jofré 179 *(esq. San Camilo, Santiago-Sur)* ☎ 222 8356
☎ 222 5255

Santiago ▶ Viña del Mar Chile

■ **Teléfono SIDA** 0-24 h
☎ 800 2021
Helpline

CRUISING
-Plaza de Armas (g MA R) (Ahumada esquina. Compañia, after 21 h)
-Avenida Providencia (g MA) (from 22 h)
-Parque Metropolitano (AYOR g MA) (Cerro San Cristóbalo, daytime)
-Parque Uruguay (AYOR g MA) (from Avenida Los Leones and Avenida Manuel Montt, along Mapocho river in Providencia, after 15 h)
-Parque Gran Bretaña (AYOR g MA) (Between Avenida Providencia and the River Mapocho, from Avenida Elcondoro Yáñez hasta Avenia Vicuña Mackenna in Providencia, after 21 h)
-Cerro Santa Lucia (AYOR g MA R) (daytime only)
-Plaza Indira Gandhi (AYOR g R YG) (Avenida Santa Mariá, next to the clinic INDISA and the Sheraton Hotel in Providencia, along the river and next tp Plaza Indira Gandhi, after 15 h, busy at night)
-Parque Forestal (AYOR g MA) (from Plaza Italia to Miraflores, along the river Mapocho in Santiago Centro, be very careful at night)
-Paseo Ahumada (g MA) (from the Alameda Bernardo O'Higgins to the Plaza del Armas in Santiago Centro, after 21 h)
-Paseo Huérfanos (g MA) (from calle Santa Lucía to Calle Bandera, Santiago Centro, after 21 h)
-Plaza Italia (g MA) (Avenida Vicuña Mackenna esquina Avenida Providencia, next to entrance of Metro station Baquedano and the Restaurante Prosit, after 22 h, very busy on WE)

Talca ☎ 071

DANCECLUBS
■ **Halloween** (ac b D g MA TV)
Flor de llano, Parcela 1

HOTELS
■ **Marco Gómez** (AC BF glm)
1 Oriente 1070 ☎ 22 3388
■ **Plaza** (AC B BF glm H)
Poniente 1141 ☎ 22 6150

Talcahuano ☎ 041

DANCECLUBS
■ **Divine** (B D G MA STV) Fri-Sat 0-? h
Caupolicán 52

HOTELS
■ **De la Costa** (BF glm H)
Colón 648 ☎ 54 5930
■ **France** (BF glm H)
Aníbal Pinto 44 ☎ 54 21 30

Valparaiso ☎ 032

BARS
■ **Foxy** (AC B D GLM MA SNU STV VS) Tue-Sun 24-5 h
Independencia Nros. 2436-2440-2442-2446 *(entre/between San Ignacio y/and Simón Bolivar)* ☎ 23 3577
■ **Tacones** (B glm) 22-2 h
Huito 301/Brasil

DANCECLUBS
■ **Scándal** (B D G)
Yungay 2229 ☎ 55 6083

RESTAURANTS
■ **Bar Inglés** (B F glm)
Cochrane 851 ☎ 21 4625
Chilean cuisine

■ **Bote Salvavidas** (B F glm)
Muelle Prat s/n *(2nd floor)* ☎ 25 1477
Specialized in seafood
■ **Café Turri** (B F glm)
Templeman 147 *(Cerro Concepción)* ☎ 25 2091
International cuisine

HOTELS
■ **Lancaster** (BF F glm H)
Chacabuco 2362 ☎ 21 7391
■ **Reina Victoria** (BF glm H)
Plaza Sotomayor 190 *(next to the Plaza Sotomayor)* ☎ 21 2203

CRUISING
-Plaza Victoria (g MA r) (17-24 h)
-Avenida Pedro Montt (the two blocks leading to Plaza Victoria, late afternoon until late at night).

Viña del Mar ☎ 032

DANCECLUBS
■ **New Soviet** (ac b D GLM STV) 23-? h
Arlegui 346 *(at the end of the alley)* ☎ 68 5514

RESTAURANTS
■ **Cap Ducal** (B F glm MA)
Avenida Marina 51 ☎ 62 6655
International cuisine
■ **Chez Gerald** (AC B F glm MA)
Avenida Perú 496 ☎ 68 9243
International cuisine
■ **Club Alemán** (B F glm MA)
Salvador Donóso 1337 ☎ 23 33 50
German and Chilean food.
■ **El Castillo** (B F glm MA)
Washington 714 ☎ 28 1974
Chilean cuisine.

FASHION SHOPS
■ **Gaivota** (G MA)
Galería Cristal, Local 20

HOTELS
■ **Alcanzar** (BF F glm H)
Alvarez 646 ☎ 68 3214
Rooms with private bath, telephone and TV.
■ **Miramar** (AC BF F H NG OS WO)
Calceta Abarca s/n ☎ 62 6677
Very luxurious hotel in beachfront location. Very expensive.
■ **O'Higgins** (AC BF F H NG OS WO)
Plaza Vergara s/n ☎ 88 2016
■ **San Martin** (AC BF F glm H OS)
Avenida San Martín 667 ☎ 68 9191

SWIMMING
-Caleta Abarea (g MA) (next to Hotel Miramar)
-Los Marineros (g MA) (at the south end of Las Salinas, next to the Escuela Armamentos de la Marina Nacional)
-Las Salinas (g MA) (2 km north of the city, popular with marines)
-Dunas de Mantagua (G MA) (north of Viña, between the beaches playa Ritoque and playa Roca Negra. Very popular. Take the bus P to Punta Piedra and exit at the beach between Concón and Quintero).

CRUISING
-Calle Valparaíso (g MA) (main shopping area downtown, especially in the evening and late at night, near Samoiedo Cafe)
-Plaza Vergara (g MA) (busy at night)

China

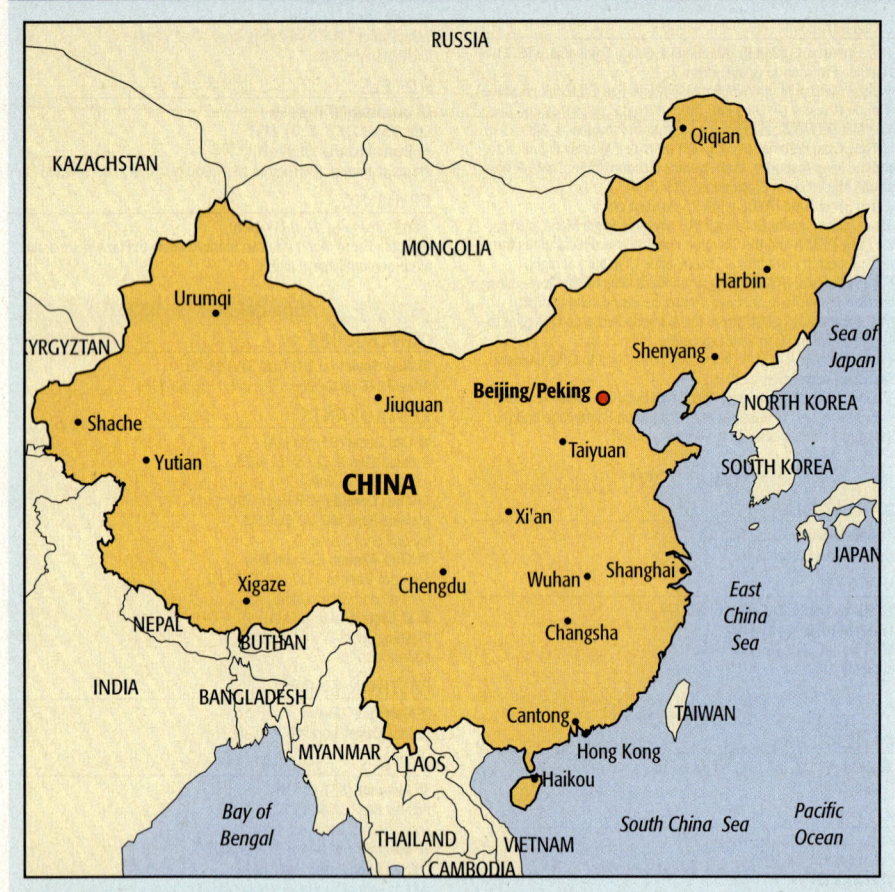

Name:	Ta Chung-hua Min-kuo • Chine • Cina
Location:	Eastern Asia
Initials:	RC
Time:	GMT +8
International Country Code:	☏ 86 (leave the first 0 of area codes)
International Access Code:	☏ 00
Language:	Chinese (Putonghua) or Mandarin
Area:	9,560,980 km^2 / 3,691,494 sq mi.
Currency:	1 Renminbi uan (RMB.) = 100 Fen
Population:	1,255,091,000
Capital:	Beijing
Religions:	Confucianism, northern Buddhism (Mahajana 100 Million), Taoism, Sunnite Moslem (14 Million)
Climate:	The climate is extremely diverse and ranges from tropical in the south to subarctic in the north.

✱ There is no paragraph explicitly against homosexuality in the Chinese penal code. It is, however, considered to disrupt the „principle of harmony". The gradual process of liberalisation in China is nevertheless making itself felt for homosexuals, too. Gay scenes are beginning to emerge in Peking and Shanghai, and tolerance is increasing.
Guests have to pay for any objects which are broken in their hotel rooms during their stay (even if it is only a toothmug), so it is a good idea to check the condition of your room(s) upon arrival.
People with HIV/AIDS are not allowed to enter China. Anyone trying to do so may be turned away.

✱ Immer wieder wird deutlich, daß die chinesische Gesellschaft nicht von Toleranz gegenüber Schwulen und Lesben geprägt wird. Doch die (wirtschaftliche) Öffnung des Landes und die Angliederung Hong Kongs üben auch einen liberalisierenden Einfluß auf die Menschen und den Staat aus.

Anshan ▸ Guangzhou China

Die chinesischen Gesetze gehen auf Homosexualität nicht ein. In Hong Kong sind einvernehmliche Kontakte zwischen Männern über 21 entkriminalisiert.
Die schwule Szene Hong Kongs gehört zu den sehenswertesten Asiens. Die Angliederung des Stadtstaates an das Mutterland hat nicht zu den befürchteten schweren Repressionen geführt. Die Volksrepublik hält sich an die Vereinbarung „Ein Land, zwei Systeme". In China selbst haben sich in Beijing, Guangzhou und Shanghai kleine schwule Szenen gebildet. Und man wird davon ausgehen können, daß zunehmende wirtschaftliche Prosperität diesen Trend verstärken wird.
Für HIV/AIDS infizierte Personen besteht in China ein Einreiseverbot.

En Chine, l'homosexualité n'est pas un délit. Elle est, toutefois, considérée comme une atteinte au principe d'harmonie. Les homosexuels chinois commencent à sentir les effets de l'ouverture du pays sur l'Occident. A Pékin et Shangaï on assiste premiers signes de la mise en place d'un milieu gai et d'une certaine tolérance vis-à-vis des gais.
Si vous cassez ou endommagez quoi que ce soit à l'hôtel (le verre à dents par exemple), vous devez le remplacer à vos frais. En entrant dans votre chambre, pensez bien à dresser un état des lieux et un inventaire. Les séropositifs et les sidéens n'ont pas le droit d'entrer et de séjourner en Chine. On les refoule à la frontière.

En el código penal chino no existe ninguna ley en contra de la homosexualidad: se considera como contravención al principio de la armonía. La lenta apertura del país se ha dejado también sentir por los gays. Muy cuidadosamente se han ido formando en ciudades como Peking y Shanghai lo que podría llamarse el principio de la tolerancia frente a la homosexualidad. Si se rompen objetos que están en la habitación del hotel (por ejemplo el vaso para cepillarse los dientes), deben ser pagados por el huésped. Es conveniente asegurarse del estado de la habitación al llegar al hotel. Turistas infectados con HIV se les niega la entrada al país. En caso contrario podrían ser deportados.

Nella legge cinese non c'è un paragrafo contro l'omosessualità, che però viene considerata contraria al principio d'armonia. Tuttavia anche i gay beneficiano della lenta riapertura del paese. A Pechino e a Shangai si stanno creando le basi per lo sviluppo della comunità gay; è consigliabile di accertarsi esattamente dello stato in cui si trovano le stanze d'albergo prima del pernottamento: ogni oggetto che viene rovinato deve essere rimborsato. Turisti infettati di HIV non possono entrare in Cina; possono essere rimandati indietro.

Anshan ☏ 0412
CRUISING
Square in front of Main station
-Xiaodongmen Park

Baoding ☏ 0312
CRUISING
-Opposite Hebei Yingjuyuan/Theatre

Beijing ☏ 010
BARS
■ **Butterfly Bar** (AC B CC D G MA)
Sanlitun Road 10 (At the bginning of Sanlitun Road) ☏ 64 15 14 13
■ **Half & Half Café** (B G N YG) 11.30-1 h
Sanlitun Nanlu 15 ☏ 641 669 19

DANCECLUBS
■ **Nightman Disco** (AC B D glm N VS WE YG)
2 Xibahenanli ☏ 64 66 25 62

CRUISING
-Quinghuachi at Zhushikou Street (after dark)
-Wangfujing Street and Bathhall (after dark)
-Tiantan Park (after dark)
-Worker's Cultural Palace (after dark)
-Dungtan Park (after dark)
-Grey brick WC in N°2 Taijizhang Lane (after dark)
-Toilet at the intersection of Sidan
-Roadside WC in front of the Peking Exhibition Centre
-Youyi Shangdian (Friendship Store, WC 2nd floor)

Cangzhou ☏ 0317
CRUISING
-Long Distance Bus Terminal
-Jiuhe Hotel (opposite the hotel)

Chengdu ☏ 028
CRUISING
-Sichuan newspaper building (in front of)
-Workers cultural palace

Chongqing ☏ 0811
HOTELS
■ **Renmin Hotel** (H NG)
175 Renmin Lu FAX ☏ 385 14 21 ✆ 385 20 76
■ **Shaping Grand Hotel** (H NG)
84 Xiaolonkan New Street, PO Box 6300030 ☏ 686 31 94
✆ 686 32 98

Dalian ☏ 0411
CRUISING
-Jianmin Bath Hall
-Railway station (square in front of it)
-Zhongshan Park

Guangzhou ☏ 020
BARS
■ **42nd Street** (B F glm MA)
399 Huanshi Dong Lu

China Guangzhou ▶ Shanghai

RESTAURANTS
■ **Milano's** (B F glm)
3-103 Xin Chen Bei Jie, Tianhe Dong Lu

HOTELS
■ **Nanhu Resort Hotel** (H NG)
Nanhu South Lake *(at the foot of White Cloud Mountain)*
☎ 87 77 63 67
■ **White Swan Hotel** (AC B CC F H NG PI SA SB WO)
Shaiman Island

CRUISING
-Cultural Park (after dark among the movie watching audience)
-Toilet facing Cultural Park entrance
-Beijing Road WC

Haicheng ☎ 0412

CRUISING
-Zhongjie Bath Hall

Harbin ☎ 041

BARS
■ **Bu Luo Bar** (B glm MA) 18-2 h
257 West Da Zhi Street *(Nangang)*
☎ 632 01 10
■ **Pop Bar** (B glm MA)
47 Gexin Street *(Nangang)*
☎ 262 09 29

CRUISING
-Jiuzhan Park
-Yiman Street
-Zoological Garden

Nanjing ☎ 025

HOTELS
■ **Shuang Men Lou Guest House** (H NG)
185 North Hu Ju Road ☎ 880 59 61
40 minutes to the airport. Single US$ 30, double 36.

CRUISING
-Intersection at downtown Sinjiekuo
-Worker's Cultural Palace
-Near the Wutaishan Gymnasium and on the hills nearby

Shanghai ☎ 021

✱ Nowadays, the only major Chinese city with a visible gay presence apart from Hong Kong is Shanghai. The harbour quarter, which dates back to colonial times, is called the „Bund" and is the most popular cruising area in Shanghai. Many gays meet there in the afternoon, and towards evening the paths are full of promenading couples. WARNING: Beware of invitations to any so-called „Gay Bar", and to avoid trouble, do not order anything until you have seen the price list.

★ Shanghai ist heute die einzige Stadt ausser Hong Kong mit einer sichtbaren schwulen Präsenz in ganz China. „Der Bund" heißt das alte Hafenviertel aus der Kolonialzeit und ist die beliebteste Cruising Area der Stadt. Schon in den frühen Nachmittagsstunden treffen sich täglich zahlreiche Schwule, abends füllen sich die Wege des Parks mit Pärchen. Eine Warnung: Vorsicht bei Einladungen in eine sogenannte „Gay Bar". Um Ärger zu vermeiden sollte man nichts bestellen, ohne vorher die Karte mit den Preisen gesehen zu haben.

✱ Shanghaï est aujourd'hui la seule ville de Chine à part Hong Kong qui peut se vanter d'avoir une infrastructure gay digne de ce nom. L'ancien quartier portuaire, „The Bund", (héritage de l'époque coloniale) est le lieu de drague le plus fréquenté de la ville. Dès les premières heures de l'après-midi, on se retrouve ici et, le soir venu, on se promène en couples dans le parc, ignorant apparemment les risques auxquels on s'expose en affichant ainsi son homosexualité.
Attention: Méfiez-vous des invitations dans un soi-disant „Gay Bar". Pour éviter les ennuis, ne commandez qu'après avoir jeté un coup d'oeil sur la carte des consommations.

◆ Shanghai es hoy en día la única ciudad en toda la China aparte de Hong Kong que tiene un ambiente gay. El viejo barrio portuario, que data del tiempo colonial y llamado „La alianza" es hoy en día la zona favorita para practicar el „cruising" (ligue). Ya a horas tempranas de la tarde se reunen aquí todos los días muchos gays. Por las noches, los caminos del parque se llenan con parejas.
Advertencia: ten cuidado con invitaciones en el llamado „Gay Bar". Para evitar malos entendidos no pidas nada antes de mirar la lista de precios.

✖ Shanghai è l'unica città cinese con una visibile presenza gay aparte Hong Kong. Il vecchio quartiere portuale *Der Bund*, il cui nome risale ai tempi coloniali, è la cruising area della città. Tutti i giorni già nel primo pomeriggio si incontrano numerosi gay, e di sera le coppiette affollano i sentieri del parco. Fate attenzione se venite invitati in un cosidetto „gay bar". Per evitare problemi controllare sempre la lista dei prezzi prima di ordinare.

BARS
■ **Anton's Bar** (B G YG)
500 Zhongshan East No. 1 Road *(Bund)*
■ **Asia Blue** (B d G)
181 Jin-xian Road ☎ 62 17 60 65
■ **Eddy´s Bar** (AC B D G MA STV S) 18-4 h
No. 1 Lane 860, Nanjing Xi Lu Road ☎ 62 71 90 57
■ **Eddy's Two** (AC B D G MA STV S) Tue-Sat 14-4h
Dixiashi no.207 Xiang Yang Nan Road ☎ 64-959466
■ **Feeling Bar** (B G MA)
Ruijin Road 207 ☎ 64 73 60 97
■ **Hawallan Bar** (B G MA N)
Wei Hai Road *(Near Nanjing Road 904)* ☎ 62 47 78 68
■ **Judy's Too** (B F glm)
176 Mao Ling Lu ☎ 64 73 14 17
■ **K.M. Bar** (AC B G MA N) 18-4 h
No. 513 Hai Fang Road ☎ 62 56 42 09

DANCECLUBS
■ **Xiang-yin (Eddy's)** (! AC B D G MA N S WE) 14-4 h
1, Lane 860 Nanjing West Road ☎ 62 71 90 57

RESTAURANTS
■ **Frankie's Place** (B F glm)
81 Tong Ren Road ☎ 62 47 08 86

HOTELS
■ **Jinjiang Hotel** (H NG)
59 Maoming Nanlu ☎ 62 53 42 42 ☎ 62 58 25 82-45 67
One of the largest and best equipped hotels in Shanghai; very conveni-

ent for exhibition hall, Jing Jiang Club and the Jin An Park. Rates RMB 136-195.

■ **Peace Hotel** (B D H NG)
20 Nanjingdonglu *(downtown)* ☎ 63 21 12 44
Bar, disco and hotel near the cruising area; has replaced the former disco of the Jing Jiang Hotel. The lobby and the café are also very cruisy. RMB 85-171.

SWIMMING

-Jin Jiang Club (the indoor swimming pool of the hotel is opened in winter)
-Guoji Julebu (International) Club (a favorite summertime watering spot for foreign residents)

CRUISING

-Waitan (near Huangpu Park on The Bund, downstream from the Peace Hotel and Nanjing Road; area below the sightseeing boat dock and the bus loop)
-Jin An Park (not far from the Exhibition Hall and Jin Jiang Hotel)
-WC and newspaper displays near the people's park
-Outside the railway station
-at the intersection near Qingan Temple

Shijiazhuang ☎ 0311

CRUISING

-WC to the right of the Norman Bethune Memorial entrance (very cruisy, even during daytime).
-2 WCs near entrances of Ping'An Park (after dark)
-WC in front of Teachers' University (Shi Da) on Yu Hua road (very cruisy after dark, especially in summer).

Tianjin ☎ 022

HOTELS

■ **Nendels Victory Hotel** (H NG)
11 Jin Tang Road *(Tanggu)* ☎ 938 58 33 998 44 70

Wuhan ☎ 027

HOTELS

■ **Xuangong Hotel** (H NG)
45 Jianghan Yi Road *(Wu Han)* ☎ 281 44 04
Rates RMB 24-45.

CRUISING

-Port
-Changjiang bridge

Xian ☎ 029

HOTELS

■ **New World Dynasty Hotel** (CC H NG PI SA SB WO)
48 Lian Hu Lu ☎ 721 68 68 721 97 54.
■ **Renmin (People's) Mansion** (H NG)
319 Dongxin Jie ☎ 222 51 11
Lots of young tourists. Twin RMB 83-140.

CRUISING

-In front of the Hotel „Dasha"
-Railway station

Shanghai ▶ Hong Kong Island | China

China - Hong Kong

Location: Eastern Asia
Initials: HK
Time: GMT +8
International Country Code: ☎ 852 (no area codes)
International Access Code: ☎ 001 or 0080 or 009
Language: English, Chinese
Area: 1,071 km2 / 414 sq mi.
Currency: 1 Hong Kong Dollar (HK$) = 100 Cents
Religions: Christian majority; Buddism; Confucianism
Climate: Tropical monsoon climate. Winters are cool and humid. Spring through summer is hot and rainy, fall warm and sunny.

NATIONAL HELPLINES

■ **AIDS Hotline**
c/o Red Ribbon Center, Department of Health Hong Kong
☎ 2780-2211 2870-9580 aids@health.gen.gov.hk
 www.info.gov.hk/aids

NATIONAL PUBLICATIONS

■ **HK Magazine c/o Asia City Publishing Ltd.**
Hollywood Center, 233 Hollywood Road Hong Kong Island
☎ 2850-5065 2543-1880 asiacity@asia-city.com.hk
Pick up your FREE copy in most bars , hotels, restaurants.

Hong Kong Island

BARS

■ **Babylon** (AC B f G YG) Mon-Sat 19-24h
5Fl. King Power Commercial Bldg. 409-413 Jaffe Rd - Causeway Bay
■ **CE Top** (AC B CC D DR G MA NU OS p SA VS WH)
Mon-Sun 21-4h
2nd Floor, 37-43 Cochraine Str. - Upper Central *(above Dublin Jack)*
☎ 2581-9951 *2nd floor sauna, 9th floor disco & rooftop.*
■ **General Eye's Café Bar** Mon-Thu 16.30-1h, Fri & Sat -3h Sun -24h
1/F Bloom House, 2 Tang Lung Street Causeway Bay
☎ 2295-6168
■ **Rice Bar** (AC B CC F GLM MA N s) Tue-Sat 13-2h
33 Jervois str. Grnd.Fl. - Central-Sheung Wan *(at Mercer, near Sheung Wan MTR Station, Exit A-2)* ☎ 2851-4800
Live DJs on WE, „malebox", college night on Tue. Lunch is also served.
■ **UFO** (AC B G YG) Tue-Sat 19-24h
3Fl Yeung lu Chi Commercial Bldg. 460-462 Jaffe Rd. - Causeway Bay ☎ 2893-2788
New.
■ **Why Not** (AC B G N YG) Sun-Thu 20-2h
12Fl Kyoto Plaza, 491-499 Lockhardt Rd. Causeway Bay
☎ 2572-7808
Karaoke lounge.
■ **Works** (AC B CC D G MA VS) Tue-Sat 19-1.30h Sun 3.30h
1 Fl 30-32 Wyndham Str. Central
(MTR Central, opposite Fridge Club)) ☎ 2868-6102
The largest GLM bar in Hong Kong
■ **ZIP** (AC B CC d F G OS s YG) Tue-Sun 19-4h
Ground Floor, 2 Glenealy Str. Upper Central *(ground floor)*
☎ 2533-3595

CAFES

■ **G2K Station** (AC GLM) Tue-Sat 16-22h
460-462 Jaffe Rd. Causeway Bay *(15th floor Yeung Lu Chi Commercial Bldg)* ☎ 2892-1391

SPARTACUS 2001/2002 | 175

IT IS NOT GOOD

FOR MAN TO BE ALONE.

I WILL MAKE A COMPANION FOR HIM

WHO CORRESPONDS TO HIM

Genesis 2:18 - 19

Photography by Almond Chu

PROPAGANDA

THE ALTERNATIVE CLUB FOR ALL CREATURES, GREAT AND SMALL.

Unless, of course, you'd rather stay home and lick your own balls.

WORKS
bar.club.breeding ground

China — Hong Kong Island

CENTRAL ESCALATOR
SAUNA
STEAM BATH
JACUZZI
RESTROOMS
REFRESHMENTS

1/2 PRICE ENTRY WITH THIS AD

Tel. 9198 2836, 2581 9951 Opening Hrs. 1400-0000

2/F. 37-43 Cochrane St., Central Hong Kong.

(Taxi ask for Lyndhurst Terrace, above Dublin Jack Pub)

中環閣麟街 37-43 號祥興商業大廈電梯 2 字樓
(近中環半山電動樓梯,的士由擺花街入,在 Dublin Jack Pub 樓上)

DANCECLUBS
- **Propaganda** (! AC B CC E GLM MA VS) Sun-Fri 19-3.30, Sat. 4.30h
Lower Ground Floor. 1 Hollywood Rd. - Upper Central *(MTR Central Station, opposite Central Police Station)* ☏ 2868-1316
Largest GLM-Bar/Disco in Hong Kong.

RESTAURANTS
- **Alternatives** (AC F GLM) Tue-Sun 16-1h
27 Floor. Wellington Centre, 97A Wellington Str. - Central
☏ 2850-4111
- **Blue** (AC B CC E F glm)
Ground Floor. 43-45 Lyndhurst Terrace - Upper Central
☏ 2815-4005
- **Wyndham Street Thai** (AC b F g) Mon-Sat 12-23h
Ground Floor, 38 Wyndham Str. - Upper Central *(next to WORKS)*
☏ 2869-6216

ESCORTS & STUDIOS
- **Guy** (G msg) Mon-Sun 12-4h
☏ 8101-6996

SAUNAS/BATHS
- **A Emale** (AC b G MG SB VS) Sun-Sat 14-23h
1st Floor, Kwon Ah Building, 114 Thomson Rd.- Wanchai *(1st floor)*
☏ 2591-0500
AE stands for American Eagle. Karaoke room and some mirror rooms.
- **Central Escalator** (B f G SB VS WE YG) 14-24 h
2/F Cheung Hing Comm. Building, 37-43 Cochrane Street *(Central Hillside Escalator, MTR)* ☏ 2581-9951
or ☏ 9198-2836. Entrance from Gage Street, opposite Park'n'Shops main entrance.
- **Chaps** (AC DR G MA NU p SA SB VS) Tue-Sun 14-1h
Ground Floor, 15 Ming Yuen Western Street - North Point
☏ 2570-9339
Tue+Thur = nude.
- **Dream Factory Member Club** (AC G p SA VS YG) Tue-Sun 15-1h
Ho Lee Commercial Building, 17-22 Lan Kwai Fong, Central *(Unit E, 2nd floor)* ☏ 2868-2786
Nice sauna with free condoms, drinks and food.
- **EM-motion@l** (AC B DR G MA NU p SA SB SOL VS WE) Mon-Thur 16-21, Fri-Sun + Pub Holiday 15-12h
26/F. Workingview Commercial Building, 21 Yiu Wa Str. - Causeway Bay ☏ 2572-1318
- **Game Boy Fitness Club** (AC b DR f G SA WO YG) Mon-Sun 12-2h
324-330A Lockhardt Rd, Fook Yee Building. - Wanchai *(2nd floor)*
☏ 2574-3215
Tue+Thur = nude, incl. Karaoke. Admission only with your ID.
- **WE Club** (AC b CC DR F G MG NU p SA SB SOL VS WE WO) Mon-Fri 15-24, Sat Sun & public holidays 14-24 h
Thai Kong Bldg, 482 Hennessy Road, Causeway Bay *(MTR Station, Exit B Entrance in Tang Lung St., 3rd floor)* ☏ 2833-6677
Over 1000 sq ft of gym area, 2 karaoke rooms and one reading room.

BOOK SHOPS
- **Angelo de Capri** (AC b GLM MA) Tue - Sun 12-21h
18 Wo On Lane, Lane Kwai Fong, Central ☏ 2857-7148
- **General Gay's Bookshop** (AC GLM) 13-22, Sun 14.30-22h
10F United Bldg, 449 Hennessey Road. Causeway Bay
☏ 2588-1792
- **Oasis** (AC GLM) Mon-Fri 11-20, Sat 11-13h
1Fl. 458 Lockhardt Rd- Causeway Bay
- **P.O.V. Bookstore** (AC GLM) Mon-Fri 11-22, Sat 11-12, Sun 13-22h
Shop A 1Fl. Hong Kong Mansion, 137-147 Lockhardt Rd. Wanchai
☏ 2865-5116

GENERAL Gay's BookShop
10/F., Unitd Building,
449 Hennessy Road,
Causeway Bay
Tel : (852) 2588 1792
Mon~Sat: 1:00~10:00p.m.
Sun   : 2:30~10:00p.m.

Hong Kong No.1
Book Shop
Eye's Cafe

GENERAL Eye's Cafe' Bar
1/F., Bloom House,
2 Tang Lung Street,
Causeway Bay
Tel : (852) 2295 6168
Mon~Thu: 4:30~ 1:00p.m.
Fri~Sat   : 4:30~ 3:00a.m.
Sun   : 4:30~12:00p.m.

www.gaybuilding.com / info@gaybuilding.com

Hong Kong Island — China

LEATHER & FETISH SHOPS

■ **Fetish Fashion** (AC CC GLM LJ S) Tue-Sun 11-19 h, closed Mon
M/Fl Merlin Bldg. , 32 Cochraine Street - Upper Central *(along Central escalator)* ☎ 2544-1155
Fetish shop with 2 SM playrooms.

TRAVEL AND TRANSPORT

■ **Concorde Travel** (GLM) Mon-Fri 10-19, Sat 10-13h
1Fl. 8-10 On Lan Street - Central ☎ 2526-3391 ☎ 2524-5121
🖨 2845-0485 ✉ concorde@netvigator.com

HOTELS

■ **Harbour View International House** (H NG)
4 Harbour Road, Wanchai *(next to Convention & Exhibition Center)*
☎ 2520-1111
Run by the YMCA. Not expensive but a good standard. Single HK$450, twin HK$550.

HEALTH GROUPS

■ **AIDS Concern** Thu-Sat 19-22h
GPO Box 33 50 ☎ 2898-4422
Counselling in Cantonese and English.
■ **HIV Information & Drop-In Centre**
St. John's Cathedral, Garden Road, Central ☎ 2525-7207
☎ 2525-7208 or ☎ 2525-7208.
■ **HK AIDS Foundation**
☎ 2560-8528 ☎ 2513-0513 (helpline), 2170-222-170 (infoline)
General Enquires ☎ 2560-8528
Helpline ☎ 2513-0513
Infoline ☎ 2170 222 170
■ **Horizons** Mon-Thu 19.30-22.30h
☎ 2815-9268
counselling in English and Cantonese.
■ **10% Club** Wed 19.30-21.30h
☎ 2314-8726

SWIMMING

-Middle Bay (G) (Take bus 320 or 6a from Central to Repulse Bay. Walk along the beach towards the South. Cruisy Sat afternoon and on Sunday. Action on the rocks between Middle Bay and South Bay. Wear good shoes because of the rocks)
-Morisson Hill Swimming Pool (g) (Wanchai)
-Victoria Park Swimming Pool
-South Bay, next to Middle Bay.

CRUISING

-Lan Kwai Fong (AYOR-police)
-Ice House Street (near Queen Road Central)

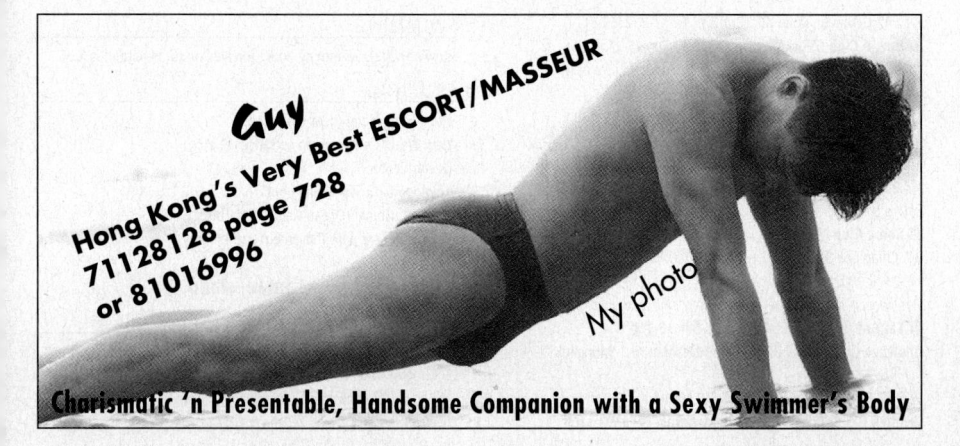

EM-motion@l

EM-MOTIONAL SAUNA, YOUR DREAM SAUNA.
A NEW, CLEAN, COMFORTABLE & INNOVATIVE SAUNA IN HONG KONG.

EM-MOTIONAL サウナ、香港で最も新しい、
清潔でおちつける君の夢のサウナです。

EM-MOTIONAL SAUNA, 你夢想中的SAUNA。
一所香港全新、整潔、舒適及革新的 S A U N A 。

香港銅鑼灣耀華街21號華耀商業大廈26樓
26/F WORKINGVIEW COMMERCIAL BUILDING,
21 YIU WA STREET, CAUSEWAY BAY, HONG KONG.
TEL: 852-25721318

OPEN: Monday ～ Thursday (4:00p.m. - 12:00 Midnight)
      Friday ～ Sunday   (3:00p.m. - 12:00 Midnight)
      Public Holiday   (3:00p.m. - 12:00 Midnight)

(*TO ENTER AFTER 8:00 p.m. EVERYDAY OR ON PUBLIC HOLIDAYS, PLEASE JUST UNCLICK THE GATE OF THE BUILDING & COME IN.)
(註：每晚8:00p.m. 後鐵閘鎖閉用手掣自行"CLICK"大鐵入口鎖(空上鎖)。)

Guy
Hong Kong's Very Best ESCORT/MASSEUR
71128128 page 728
or 81016996

My photo

Charismatic 'n Presentable, Handsome Companion with a Sexy Swimmer's Body

China | Hong Kong Island ▶ Lantau Island

-Shing Wong Street (stairs on Hollywood Road, between Aderdeen Street and Man Mo Temple)
-MTR-Wanchai
-Queens Road East/Queensway
-IFC Bldg. (on top of airport express-Central station) B/Fl. toilets /far end bldg
-on the Central Escalator , between New York Fitness and Staunton Café/ SOHO district.
-Middle Bay
-Morrison Hill Road Public Swimming Bath (Oi Kwan Road, Wanchai)
-Pacific Place Shopping Mall

Kowloon

BARS

■ **New Wally Matt** (AC B CC f G MA N) Mon-Sun 12-1h
Grnd/Fl. 5A Humphreys Avenue - Tsim Sha Tsui ☎ 2721-2568
■ **New Wally Matt Lounge** (AC B CC f G MA N) Mon-Sun 18-3h
3A Grnd/Fl Granville Circuit - Tsim Sha Tsui
(behind Ramada Hotel) ☎ 2721-2568
Internet bar.

CAFES

■ **MY Coffee** (AC F GLM) Mon-Sat 12-21h
Shop 6E Bo Yip Bldg. , 6 Ashley rd. - Tsim Sha Tsui

SAUNAS/BATHS

■ **Babylon** (AC B DR G VS YG) Mon-Sun 15-24h
2nd floor. Chun Lee Commercial Bldg. 494-496 Nathan Rd. - Mongkok ☎ 2388-5963
■ **Blue Blood** (AC b DR G VS) 14-24 h
3rd floor, Perfect Commercial Building, 20 Austin Avenue, Tsim Sha Tsui *(3rd floor)* ☎ 2302-0780
■ **Bobson's Fitness Club** (AC B DR G VS YG) Mon-Sun 15-24h
3rd floor, Flat D, Ma's Building, 35-37 Hankow Road *(M° Tsim Sha Tsu)* ☎ 2376-2208
■ **D.F. Concept** (B DR g SB VS) 15.30-23, Sat-Sun & public holiday 14-23 h
2/F., 42 Carnavon Road *(M° Tsim Sha Tsu)* ☎ 2369-8174
■ **Jungle Club** (DR G MA SB) 16-24, Sat Sun 15-24 h
Unit 301, Cheong Hing Building, 72 Nathan Road *(3rd floor)* ☎ 2367-5337
Karaoke room and reading room with local gay magazines.
■ **Rainbow** (AYOR G MA VS) Mon-Sun 15-24 h
K.K. Centre, No. 46-54 Temple Street, Yau Ma Tei *(14th floor)* ☎ 2385-6652
Sauna on 43000 sq ft with karaoke and specials for buddies.
■ **Rome Club** (AC b DR G SA SB YG) Mon-Sun 15-24 h
2/F Chiap Lee Building, 27 Ashley Road *(M° Tsim Sha Tsu)* ☎ 2376-0602
Two floors with dark maze, private rooms and a karaoke room.
■ **Tai Fan** (AC b DR G SA YG) Mon-Sun 15-24h
Chun Lee Commercial Bldg. 494-496 Nathan rd. - Mongkok *(1st floor)* ☎ 2770-7673
■ **Yuk Tak Chee** (AC G msg OG SB) Mon-Sun 12-24h
Grnd/Fl. 123 Prince Edward rd. - Mongkok ☎ 2393-1109

BOOK SHOPS

■ **Park Book Store Ltd** (AC CC GLM MA) 11-21.30h
Flat A, 1/Fl., Rex House, 648 Nathan Road, Mongkok ☎ 2787-7988
■ **Rainbow House** (AC GLM)
Rm 1109 Good Hope Bldg. 5 Sai Yeung Choi Str. - South Mongkok ☎ 2384-2387

TRAVEL AND TRANSPORT

■ **IGTC** (CC G) Mon-Fri 10-18, Sat 10-13
M/Fl. 305 Lai Chi Kok Rd. - Shamshuipo ☎ 8106-5810

HOTELS

■ **Y.M.C.A. Hotel** (AC F g H Pl r SA WH)
41 Salisbury Road -Tsim Sha Tsui *(next to Peninsula Hotel)*
☎ 2369-2211
Downtown location, 10-15 minutes to the airport. Hotel with garden. All rooms with telephone, partly kitchenette, bath/WC.
■ **Y.M.C.A. International House** (AC F H NG)
23 Waterloo Road ☎ 2771-9111
4 km from the airport. Downtown location. Single HK$ 300, double 330-400. Bf not included.

GENERAL GROUPS

■ **10% Club**
PO Box 722 07, Central post Office ☎ 2314-8726
Registered association that fights for political and social acceptance. Servicing, social and educational gatherings.

HELP WITH PROBLEMS

■ **AIDS Couselling & Health Education Service**
c/o Queen Elizabeth Hospital, Wylie Road
☎ 2710-2429

RELIGIOUS GROUPS

■ **Isavara**
PO Box 743 42, Kowloon Central Post Office
☎ 2782-0649 📠 2374-5948
Gay Buddhist group.

SWIMMING

-Kowloon Park Swimming Pool - (on Nathan rd. behind mosque).

CRUISING

-Hong Kong Hotel (near coffeeshop)
-New World Centre (main entrance, 12-20 h)
-Ocean Center
-Kowloon Park Swimming Pool
-Ocean Terminal (Ocean Center & Harbour City)
-Yau Ma Tei car park (basement and 1st floor)

Lantau Island

HOTELS

■ **Babylon Villa** (glm H)
29 Cheung Sha, Lower Village ☎ 2980-3145 📠 2980-3024
📧 babylon@wlink.net 🌐 www.babylon-villa-hotel.com
Located on the white sandy beach of Cheng Sha.

Armenia | Colombia

Colombia

Name: Kolumbien • Colombie
Location: Northwest coast of South America
Initials: CO
Time: GMT -5
International Country Code: ☎ 57 (leave away the first 9 of area codes)
International Access Code: ☎ 009
Language: Spanish; Indian languages
Area: 1,138,914 km² / 439,735 sq mi.
Currency: 1 Columbian Peso (col$) = 100 Centavos
Population: 38,580,949
Capital: Santafé de Bogotá
Religions: over 95% Roman Catholic
Climate: Tropical climate along the coast and eastern plains. Highlands are cooler.

✱ Although homosexuality is not mentioned in the law and the age of consent is 18 years, Columbian society in general has a negative attitude towards homosexuality. The police are known to harass gay men. Contact with male prostitutes can sometimes be dangerous. Also, we strongly recommend that you leave valuables in your hotel safe, as the crime rate is very high. Tourists generally do not need an HIV test. A test may be required, however, from citizens of the USA, Haiti and African nationals. For visas other than tourist visas, one must be free of infectious diseases.

✱ Obwohl Homosexualität im Gesetz nicht erwähnt wird, und das Schutzalter bei 18 Jahren liegt, hat die Gesellschaft eine überwiegend negative Einstellung zu Schwulen. Es ist bekannt, daß die Polizei schwule Männer verfolgt.
Das Land leidet unter einen hoher Kriminalitätsrate. Zudem haben die gewalttätigen Auseinandersetzungen zwischen der Drogenmafia und dem Staat, denen auch zahlreiche Zivilisten zum Opfer gefallen sind, zu einer Verrohung der Gesellschaft geführt. Für die Schwulen und Lesben Kolumbiens bedeutet dies, daß sie häufig nicht nur verbalen Angriffen ausgesetzt sind.
Trotz dieser ungünstigen Voraussetzungen finden sich in vielen Städten, vor allem aber natürlich in der Hauptstadt Santafé de Bogota, zahlreiche schwule Lokale, die relativ sichere Orte in diesem unsicheren Land darstellen.

✱ Bien que le code pénal ne fasse pas état de l'homosexualité et que la majorité sexuelle soit fixée à 18 ans, les Colombiens sont dans l'ensemble plutôt homophobes. La police ne cesse de harceler les gais. Evitez donc les ennuis! La délinquance est un problème sérieux en Colombie. Laissez donc votre argent et vos objets de valeur à l'hôtel!
Les touristes ne sont pas obligés de se soumettre à un test de dépistage pour entrer en Colombie, à l'exception des personnes venant des Etats-Unis, de Haïti et d'Afrique. Pour obtenir un visa (à l'exception d'un visa touristique), il faut prouver que l'on n'est pas atteint d'une maladie contagieuse.

✱ A pesar de que la homosexualidad no se menciona en la ley y la edad de consentimiento es de 18 años, la opinión pública es negativa ante los homosexuales. También se sabe que la policía molesta a los gays. El contacto con prostitutos es peligroso. Debido a que existe un alto porcentaje de criminalidad, es recomendable dejar los objetos de valor en el hotel. En general los turistas no necesitan someterse a una prueba de SIDA. Sin embargo, esta puede ser exigida a visitantes provenientes de los EEUU, Haiti y Africa. De igual forma todas las personas que solicitan un visado (excepto el visado de turista) tienen que demostrar que no non portadores de enfermedades contagiosas.

✖ Sebbene l'omosessualità non sia menzionata dalla legge e l'età del consenso sia di 18 anni, la società in generale ha un atteggiamento negativo verso il problema. La polizia è conosciuta per la sua durezza verso i gay. I contatti con i prostituti maschi possono essere piuttosto pericolosi a causa dei furti. Vi raccomandiamo di lasciare i vostri soldi e gli oggetti di valore in albergo. Turisti non devono presentare il risultato di un HIV-test. Però è possibile che venga richiesto dai turisti proveniente dagli USA, da Haiti o dall'Africa. Chi richiede un visto (se non si tratta di un visto per turismo) deve provare di non soffrire di una malattia contagiosa.

Armenia ☎ 967

BARS

■ **Amemonos Amor** (B D GLM MA) 20-3 h
Carrera 18

■ **Copa** (B GLM MA)
Pasaje Comercial, Carrera 14

HOTELS

■ **Maitamá** (B F glm H)
Carrera 17, N°21-29 ☎ 44 34 00
Central location, 20 min to the airport. All rooms have telephone, frigde, priv. bath, color TV.

■ **Zuldemayda** (B glm H)
Calle 20, N° 15-38 ☎ 44 42 00

Colombia — Barranquilla ▶ Medellin

Barranquilla ☎ 958

BARS
- **Baco Bar** (B d G)
  Carrera 44 B, N°70-46
- **Del Prado Bar** (AC B E g MA R)
  Carrera 54, N°70-10 *(in Hotel Del Prado)*

CINEMAS
- **Cine Rex** (r)
  Carrera 45, N° 37-20 Centro ☎ 370 43

CRUISING
-Plaza Colón
-Plaza Bolivar and Paseo Bolivar

Calí ☎ 92

BARS
- **Bonston** (B G MA)
  Avenida Colombia, 8-58
- **Chapien** (B G MA)
  Avenida Colombia, 6-28
- **Charles** (B G MA)
  Carrera 3, 10-55
- **Golden** (B G MA)
  Calle 9, 3-36
- **Mandonna** (B G MA)
  Avenida Colombia, 8-74
- **Manhattan** (B G S TV)
  Calle 16, N°4-25
- **Pine Manor** (B D g)
  Calle 17 N, N°6-23
- **Tropical Video Bar** (B G MA VS)
  Avenida 8a Norte, 10-118 ☎ 661 00 58
- **Unicornio Club Campestre** (B D G)
  Avenida 4 A Oeste, N°6-30

DANCECLUBS
- **Ulises Club Discotec** (B D g)
  Avenida Colombia 8-47 ☎ 881 64 69

SHOWS
- **Romanos Club Discotec** (B D g STV) Show Tue Thu-Sun
  Carrera 3, N° 9-47 ☎ 880 40 65

SAUNAS/BATHS
- **Romanos** (B G SA)
  Carrera 3a, 9-47 ☎ 880 40 65
- **Spartacus** (G SA)
  Carrera 23a, 8A-15

CRUISING
-Parque de Cayzedo / Calle 12 (R)
-Cali River
-Avenida Colombia
-Avenida 6a Norte

Cartagena ☎ 95

DANCECLUBS
- **Saffari's Club** (B D G)
  Calle del Quartel con Estanco del Aguardiente
- **Vía Libre** (B D G)
  Calle de la Soledad 9-52

HOTELS
- **Montecarlo** (B F H NG)
  La Matuna, Centro ☎ 664 50 13

CRUISING
-Beach "Playa Boca Granda" (AYOR) (all day long)
-Carrera 2 (AYOR) (known as "Avenida San Martin", Boca Grande)
-Beach close to Hotel Capilla del Mar, Boca Grande (AYOR)
-Beach in front of Hotel Don Blas, Boca Grande (AYOR)
-La boca Chica (AYOR) (1 hour boat ride from pier in centre of town)
-La Boquilla (AYOR) (beach near the airport with little restaurants)
-Under Clock Tower at the entrance to the Old City (AYOR) (19-23 h)

Cúcuta ☎ 975

BARS
- **Baru** (B g)
  Avenida la 6-95
- **Cervezeria** (B G)
  Avenida 4, N°6-72

HOTELS
- **Amaruc** (AC B F H NG)
  Avenida 5, N°9-73 ☎ 72 76 25
  Centrally located, 15min to the airport. All rooms with telephone, priv. bath and balcony.
- **Casablanca** (AC B F H NG PI)
  Avenida 6, N°14-55 ☎ 72 29 93
  Centrally located, all rooms with telephone, priv. bath and balcony.

CRUISING
-Avenida 0
-Avenida Simón Bolivar
-Calle 17 (between Avenida 6 and Avenida 1)
-Parque Santander(after 18 h)

Medellin ☎ 94

BARS
- **Baru Bar** (AC B D G R WE)
  Carrera 50, N° 55A-05 *(Downtown, 2nd floor)* ☎ 512 15 10
  Be careful. Surrounding area is unsafe at night.
- **Camerata, La** (B E glm N)
  Calle 51, N° 64C-27 ☎ 230 22 97
- **Centauros** (B G YG)
  Carrera 47 #54-27 *(2nd floor)*
- **Ceres** (B G OG)
  Calle 56, N° 49-69 *(Downtown)* ☎ 512 16 46 *Be careful, surrounding area is unsafe at night.*
- **Ebano & Marfil** (! AC B CC E F GLM YG)
  Calle 56, N°45-73 *(Downtown)* ☎ 254 50 74
  Big old house turned into big bar.
- **Luchos II** (B CC D G YG)
  Calle 58, N° 47-18 *(Downtown)* ☎ 284 52 20
- **Mision, La** (! B E G MA WE YG)
  Calle 44, N° 73-53 ☎ 270 57 22
- **Tebes** (AYOR B D G MA WE)
  Calle 58, N° 53-101 *(Downtown, second floor)* ☎ 251 48 57
  Be careful, surrounding are is unsafe at night, no sign at the door.

DANCECLUBS
- **Labias** (B D G YG)
  Cra. 52, N°57-55 ☎ 512 56 69

Medellin ▶ Santafé de Bogotá | **Colombia**

■ **Plataforma** (! AC D E G S YG) Thu-Sat
Calle 44, N°68-59 *(San Juan)*
Three floors. Popular.
■ **Skala** (B D glm MA VS WE)
Calle 44, N° 79-75 ☎ 250 48 88
■ **Teatro** (! AC B CC D E G WE)
Calle 44, N° 73-51
3 bars, 1 disco, videos, no sign at doors.
■ **Toque de Queda** (! AC B D E G MA VS WE YG) Tue-Sat
Calle 44, N° 73-51 ☎ 412 09 55

RESTAURANTS
■ **La Isla** (B g R)
Calle 56, N°49-101

SAUNAS/BATHS
■ **Barbacoas** (B G msg NU P SB SOL VS)
Calle 57A, N° 46-47
■ **Club Casa Loma** (B E G msg NU P PI SA SB SOL VS) Tue-Sun 13-22 h
Calle 50, N° 38-25 *(Downtown)* ☎ 217 24 51
■ **Tabomar** (b g SA SB SOL VS) Tue-Sun 10-20 h
Carrera 45, 46-27 ☎ 251 54 32

GENERAL GROUPS
■ **Movimiento de Liberación Sexual**
c/o León Zuleta, PO Box 65 25 ☎ 238 26 91
Publisher of "El Otro".

CRUISING
-Carrera Junin between Calles 56 and 47
-Parque de Bolívar (R) (corner of Sayonara only)
-Avenida San Juan (R) (between Carreras 70 and 80; students)
-Loraita (male prostitution in the area of Universidad de Antioquia, Highway 51-49 and Calles 67-71)

Neiva ☎ 988

BARS
■ **Marion** (B D g)
Calle 25, N°4-88

CRUISING
-Carrera 4 (between calles 8 and 9)

Pasto ☎ 927

DANCECLUBS
■ **Peko's** (B D G)
16-62, Carrera 27

San Andrés ☎ 9811

HOTELS
■ **Casablanca** (glm H PI)
Avenida Costa Rica, N°1-40 ☎ 233 30
■ **Isleño** (gLM H)
Avenida Colombia, N°5-11 ☎ 239 90

CRUISING
-Along Avenida Colombia (from Hotel Isleño to Hotel Aquarium; in the evening on the beach opposite Avenida Colombia)

Santa Marta ☎ 95

DANCECLUBS
■ **40 Disco Bar** (B D G)
Carrera 2a, 19-49

CRUISING
-Avenida Rodrigo Carrera 1C

Santafé de Bogotá ☎ 91

BARS
■ **Anónimos** (B G MA) Tue-Sun 18-1, Fri Sat -3 h
Avenida Caracas, 52-77
■ **Bar Frances** (B G MA)
Calle 86, 13 A 28 ☎ 217 52 89
■ **Blues Bar** (B G MA)
Calle 86, 13 A 30
■ **Cabo'e** (B G MA)
Carrera 7/Calle 49
■ **Calles de San Francisco** (B D g MA S) Mon-Sat 9-3 h
Carrera 10, 24-42
■ **C.D. Bar** (B G MA)
Avenida Caracas, 56-13
■ **Figaro** (B G MA)
Calle 23, 6-07, int. 6
■ **Muy Personal** (B G MA)
Calle 58, 10-07
■ **Paco's Club** (B G MA)
Calle 57, 8-69, Local 114
■ **Pantera Roja** (B D GLM MA S) 18-? h
Calle 32, N°14-14 ☎ 288 51 40
Dance club, local music, reservation necessary.
■ **Secretos y Compañia** (B G MA)
Avenida Caracas 51-85
■ **Te Odio Bar** (B G) Wed-Sat 22-3 h
Calle 80, N° 13A-28 ☎ 618 33 37

DANCECLUBS
■ **Babilonia Club** (B D G)
Carrera 15, 72-48
■ **Bianca** (B D G)
Carrera 22, 67-27 ☎ 255 47 94
■ **Boys Club** (B D G MA S) Wed-Sat 22-4 h
Avenida Caracas N°37-68 *(Barrio Teusaquillo)* ☎ 28724 42
■ **Champang Club** (B D G)
Carrera 13, 33-82
■ **Cruising Bar** (B D G)
Carrera 7, 48-93 ☎ 245 53 37
■ **Doble Via** (B D G)
Carrera 9, 61-84
■ **Enjalma y Loma** (B D G) Fri-Sat 19-1, Sun 12-1 h
Vía La Calera, km 4.5 ☎ 632 08 80
■ **Estudio Uno** (B D G)
Calle 100, 17-55, Sotano
■ **Extaxis** (B D G)
Calle 66, 13-41
■ **Flag** (B D G)
Carrera 18/Calle 82 ☎ 616 73 56
■ **Giros Club** (B D G)
Carrera 13, 35-31
■ **Lujuria** (B D G S VS) Thu-Sat 20.30-3 h
Transversal 18, N° 79-59 *(Centro Comercial "Los Heroes", 1st floor)*
☎ 257 32 70

Colombia — Santafé de Bogotá

■ **Playa Blanca** (B D G)
Calle 57, 9-27 ☏ 235 72 25
■ **Punto 59** (B D G MA) Tue-Sat 20-2, Sun 15-23 h
Carrera 13, N° 59-24, Interior 6 *(Centro Comercial "Acuario")*
■ **Saffari's Club** (! B D G MA S) Thu-Sat 22-3 h
Avenidas Caracas N° 73-26 ☏ 217 82 62
■ **Septima Estacion** (B D F G) Fri-Sun
Via La Calera, km 7 ☏ 860 89 18
■ **Seven** (B D G)
Calle 66, 13-50, int 101
■ **Tasca Santamaria** (B D G)
Calle 23, 6-7, int. 101
■ **Zona Franca** (! AC B CC D E G MA S WE) Fri Sat 20-0.30 h
Calle 74, 15-51 ☏ 235 31 48

RESTAURANTS
■ **San Antonio** (AC B CC F G MG OS s WE YG) Restaurant 12-18, Disco 19-0.30 h
Via La Calera, km 6 *(Near Peaje de Patios)*

SEX SHOPS/BLUE MOVIES
■ **Centro Eros Videos** (glm VS)
Carrera 9, N° 18-51, Local 113-114 ☏ 281 88 11
Mixed sex shop with gay/bi/hetero and tanssexual videos!
■ **Chapinero Eros Videos** (glm VS)
Carrera 13, N° 64-67, Local 204 ☏ 217 28 45
Mixed sex shop with gay/bi/hetero and transsexual videos!
■ **Ibiza Club** (G VS) 12-23 h
Calle 66, 15-50 ☏ 255 38 38
■ **Monte Carlo Club** (G VS)
Calle 66, 10-81
■ **Unicentro Sex Video** (glm VS)
Avenida 15, N° 119A-03, Local 230 ☏ 215 53 57
Mixed sex shop with gay/bi/hetero and transsexual videos!
■ **Vea Videos** (G VS)
Carrera 13, 64-67 ☏ 217 27 40

CINEMAS
■ **Dorado, El** 13-21 h
Calle 17, N°4-60
■ **Teatro Esmeralda** 11-21 h
Carrera 7, N°22-20

SAUNAS/BATHS
■ **Baltimore** (b CC f g msg SA SB SOL VS WH WO) 0-24 h
Calle 33/Carrera 15-17 *In Hotel Maria Isabel* ☏ 245 26 50
Reduced student rates. Recommended!
■ **Monroe's Club** (B DR G SA SB VS WH) Sun-Tue 14-22, Wed Thu - 24, Fri Sat -1 h
Carrera 16A No. 79-24, El Lago ☏ 218 07 31
Wed & Sun nudism parties, Thu beer festival
■ **Turcos 82** (G SA SB)
Carrera 13, 24-70
■ **Turcos 82** (B f G SA SB) 0-24 h
Calle 82, N°15-73 ☏ 256 6136
■ **Ulises** (B DR f G MA SA SB VS WO) 0-24 h
Carrera 15, N°32-26 ☏ 232 58 09

HOTELS
■ **Spartacus** (B G H)
Avenida Caracas 44-34 ☏ 232 27 95

GENERAL GROUPS
■ **Proyecto Lambda**
☏ 287 05 01 ☏ 287 79 14
Gay group

HEALTH GROUPS
■ **Fundacion Eudes**
Casa "El Tonel", Calle 85, N° 35-28 ☏ 256 56 29
Information about AIDS, and help for HIV+ and People With AIDS (PWA).
■ **Servicio de Salud de Bogotá** 7-12 h
Carrera 23, N° 22A-26 ☏ 268 10 64
V.D. treatment.

CRUISING
-Carrera 7 (AYOR) (between Calles 24 and 16)
-Calle 24 (AYOR) (between Carreras 7 and 13)
-Calle 19 (AYOR) (between Carreras 3 and 7)
-Avenida Lima (AYOR) (between Carreras 5 and 7)
-Centro Comercial El Lago, Carrera 15 and Calle 79 (AYOR)
-Centro Comercial, Hotel Tequendama (AYOR)
-Centro Comercio Unicentro at Carrera 15, Calle 133 (AYOR)
-Parque de la Independencia (AYOR) (Calle 16, between Carreras 5 and 7)
-Entrance of post office in Avianca Building between Carrera 7a and Calle 16 (AYOR)

Alajuela ▶ Playa Tortuga Costa Rica

Costa Rica

Location: Central America
Initials: CR
Time: GMT -6
International Country Code: ☎ 506 (no area codes)
International Access Code: ☎ 00
Language: Spanish
Area: 51,100 km2 / 19,730 sq mi.
Currency: 1 Costa Rica Colón = 100 Céntimos
Population: 3,604,642
Capital: San José
Religions: 89% Roman Catholic
Climate: The dry season lasts from December to April. In the Rainy season from May to November by mid-afternoon it is mostly cloudy and it'll rain often during the night.
Important gay cities: San José, Quepos/Manuel Antonio

✱ The age of legal protection in Costa Rica is 18. Since 1999 a law has been introduced which can legally punish discrimination of minorities and on the basis of sexual orientation. Especially in San José and Quepos/Manuel Antonio homosexuality is widely tolerated by the general public.

✱ Das Schutzalter liegt in Costa Rica bei 18 Jahren. Seit 1999 existiert ein Gesetz, welches die Diskriminierung von sexuellen und anderen Minderheiten unter Strafe stellt. Insbesondere in den homosexuellen Zentren San José und Quepos/Manuel Antonio toleriert die Gesellschaft Homosexualität weitestgehend.

✱ La majorité sexuelle est fixée à 18 ans au Costa Rica. Depuis 1999, une nouvelle loi qui permet sanctionner la discrimination de minorités sur la base de l'orientation sexuelle a été introduite. A San José et à Quepos/Manuel Antonio, l'homosexualité est bien tolérée par la population.

✱ La edad de protección es de 18 años en Costa Rica. Desde 1999 hay una ley de antidiscriminación de minorías, incluyendo las que lo son por su orientación sexual. Especialmente en San José y Quepos/Manuel Antonio, los centros gays, la población suele tolerar la homosexualidad.

✱ In Costa Rica la maggiore età è 18 anni. Dal 1999 esiste una legge che considera reato la discriminazione di minoranze (anche degli omosessuali). Soprattutto nei centri gay San José e Quepos/Manuel Antonio l'omosessualità viene largamente tollerata dalla società.

NATIONAL GAY INFO

■ **Asociación de Lucha por el Respecto a la Diversidad Sexual**
PO Box 1766-2050 San José ☎ 250-9481

■ **Fundación Vida**
Calle 1 y 3, Avenida 1 San José ☎ 221-5819

■ **Triangulo Rosa**
PO Box 366-2200 Coronado ☎ 223-1370 📠 223-3964

NATIONAL PUBLICATIONS

■ **Gayness**
PO Box 1581-1002 San José ☎ 280-4792 📠 253-7675
✉ gayness@sol.racsa.co.cr ✉ www.gaynesscr.com
Monthly newspaper.

■ **Gente 10**
PO Box 1910-2100 San José
Bimonthly magazine.

Alajuela

BARS

■ **Tsunami** (GLM MA N) 17-2-30, Sun 17-24 h
Frente a Agua Cristal (100 m east of the beer brewery, opposite „Agua Cristal")

Limon

BARS

■ **El Duende Feliz** (B BF F NG) 9-22 h
Punta Ura (Puerto Viejo) ☎ 750-0188
Bar and restaurant. Italian cuisine.

Nosara

GUEST HOUSES

■ **Roger Harrison** (G H)
PO Box 9-5233 (Nicoya, Guanacaste) ☎ 680-0749

Playa Jaco

HOTELS

■ **Poseidón** (AC glm)
(near the beach) ☎ 643-1642 📠 643-3558
✉ poseidon@sol.racsa.co.cr

Playa Tortuga

GUEST HOUSES

■ **Villas el Bosque** (H MA)
(between Costanera and Playa Tortuga on the Pacific) 📠 786-6358
✉ villaselbosque@yahoo.com

Costa Rica — Puerto Viejo ▶ Quepos / Manuel Antonio

HOTEL VILLA ROCA — Costa Rica

Es operado por sus propios dueños y es exclusivo para gays, lesbianas y sus amigos/as.
Localizado en la mejor área de Quepos, Manuel Antonio con espectacular vista al mar.

Gay-owned and operated and exclusive for gays, lesbians and their friends.
Located in the best area of Quepos, Manuel Antonio with a spectacular view to the Pacific Ocean.

100 mts. del Hotel "si como no"
Tel/Fax: 777-1349
Internet: www.villaroca.com
E-mail: mantonio@villaroca.com

Los precios son accesibles. The rates are reasonables

Big RUBYS GUESTHOUSE

KEY WEST, USA
305-296-2323

LA PLANTACION
MANUEL ANTONIO, COSTA RICA
506-777-1332

L'ORANGERIE
AIGUES-MORTES, FRANCE
33-4-66-53-10-23

1-800-477-7829 USA/CANADA
www.BigRubys.com

Puerto Viejo

HOTELS

■ **Cabinas Villa Paradiso** (BF glm F H)
(4 km south of Puerto Viejo) ☎ 750-0322 750-0322
✉ palmetto@sol.racsa.co.cr

Puntarenas

CRUISING

-Paseo de Los Turistas (next to the beach)

Quepos / Manuel Antonio

BARS

■ **Cockatoo** (! B GLM MA OS) Low season: 17-23, high season: 17-? h
Carretera al Parcque Nacional (on rooftop of a restaurant El Gato Negro, at Hotel Eclipse)
■ **Tio Fernando** (glm MA N) 17-24 h
(Quepos downtown, across from hotel Melissa)

DANCECLUBS

■ **Acro Iris** (glm MA WE) Fri-Sat until 2 h
(100m after the bridge to San José on the right hand side)

RESTAURANTS

■ **Barba Roja** (B F glm) 7-22, Mon 16-22 h
Carretera al Parcque Nacional (besides Hotel Casa Blanca, next to Karolas on the right)
American style, steaks and seafood.

■ **Café Milagro** (! B F glm) 6-22 h
Carretera al Parque Nacional (across from Hotel Casa Blanca)
☎ 777-1707
■ **El Gato Negro** (B F glm) Lunch and dinner
Carretera al Parcque Nacional (at Hotel Eclipse, under the cockatoo bar) ☎ 777-1728
Very good Pasta. Rather expensive.
■ **El Gran Escape** (B NG)
Quepos bayfront ☎ 777-0395
The best fish in town.
■ **Karolas** (B F NG) 11-23 h
Carretera al Parcque Nacional (next to Barba Roja on the left)
☎ 777-1557
Not cheap. Located in the rain forest with a tropical atmosphere.
■ **Mar y Sombra** (B d F glm) 11-23 h
(1km before the park, on the beach behind „Cabinas Ramirez")
Nice atmosphere, young people, directly on the beach, at the weekend disco.

HOTELS

■ **Casa Blanca** (BF CC GLM H OS PI)
Carretera Manuel Antonio, Apartado 194 ✉ 6350 (Manuel Antonio. Entrada „La Mariposa") ☎ 777-1316 ☎ 777-1790 777-0253
✉ cblanca@sol.racsa.co.cr www.hotelcasablanca.com
Guest house and „Miranon Center" overlooking the pacific ocean near Manuel Antonia National Park. 4 rooms with bath, 2 suites and 2 apartments (4-5 persons). 20 minutes walking distance to nude/gay beach. Rates upon request.
■ **Big Ruby's La Plantación** (BF CC F G H NU PI)
PO Box 94-6350 (3 miles from Quepos and near M. Antonio)
☎ 777-1332 777-0432 ✉ costarica@bigrubys.com

Quepos / Manuel Antonio ▶ San José | **Costa Rica**

📧 www.bigrubys.com
Please call or see the website for details on special prices. Restaurant on site. Nude sunbathing.

■ **California** (glm H)
Carretera al Parque Nacional *(entrance/entrada „El Salto")*
☎ 777-1234 📠 777-1062 📧 hotelcal@sol.racsa.co.cr
📧 www.icr.co.cr/hcalifornia
Children welcome !

■ **Makanda By The Sea** (B glm H Pl)
Carretera al Parque Nacional *(entrance/entrada „La Mariposa")*
☎ 777-0442 📠 777-1032 📧 makanda@sol.racsa.co.cr
📧 www.makanda.com
Rates: US$ 85 - 185, good atmosphere for the sunset-drink.

■ **Villa Roca** (AC BF CC GLM H OS)
Apdo 143. Carretera al Parque Nacional ✉ 6350 ☎ 777-1349
📠 777-1349 📧 mantonio@villaroca.com 📧 www.villaroca.com
Comment: 5 double rooms and 3 apartments with bath/WC, balcony, ocean view, telephone and minibar. Short walking distance to the beaches and all the gay places. Rates: US$ 39 - 95. Further information see website.

SWIMMING
-Playita (at Espadilla beach opposite of National Park) Nude swimming and sunbathing.

Samara

HOTELS
■ **Casa Naranja** (H F glm)
Samara centro ☎ 656 0220

San José

BARS
■ **Backroom** (DR G LJ MA) Sun.Thur 18- midnight, Fri & Sat -02h
Avenida 7-9 / Calle Central ☎ 258-0774
Used to be the Kashbah, behind MECCA, best on Saturdays.

■ **Buenas Vibraciones** (gLM)
Avenida 14 between Calle 7 and 9 ☎ 223-4573
Mostly lesbians.

■ **Cantábrico. El** (B f GLM MA N) From 15 till 3h
Avenida 6 between Calle Central and Calle 2 ☎ 233-5797
Best early evening.

■ **Casita, La** (G DR MA SNU) 20-02h, Fri. and Sat. openend
Calle 11 between Av. 8 / 6
Best on friday- and saturday nights after 1:30am in the backroom.

■ **El Pucho** (! B G DR MA SNU STV) daily: 20 till 02h
Corner Avenida 8 / Calle 11 ☎ 256-1147
Very popular, with darkroom (attention pick pockets!), funny stripper- and dragshows on friday- and saturdaynights.

■ **Highlander** (B g F SNU) 18-2.30h
Between Calle 2 & Calle 4

CAFES
■ **Uno @ Diez** (GLM MA) Mon-Sat 9-20h
Calle 1 / Avenida 9-11 ☎ 258-4561
Internetcafe, gay-tourist information-center, gallery, shop.

DANCECLUBS
■ **Avispa. La** (! AC B D GLM S YG) 20-2/?, Sun 17-02 h, Mon closed
Calle 1 between Avenida 8 and Avenida 10 ☎ 223-5343
No sign. Downhill from Cucharones on left side of the street.very popular for gays and lesbians, 2nd Wed men only, last Wed women only. Two dance floors, great lighting.Best on Sun from 18h and Tue after 21h.

■ **BoysBar** (B D G SNU) Fri Sat 22-? h
Complejo Convoy *(Antiguo Kilates, Tibás)*

■ **Chuca. Los** (B D GLM MA R snu STV TV) Wed-Sun 19-? (19-21 h entrance free)
Avenida 6 between Calle Central / Calle 1 *(black door across the street from the Chinese restaurant)* ☎ 223-4710
Was previously the „Los Chucarones". Some shows, mostly local people, good music, Fri SNU.

■ **Coliseo** (AC B D F GLM YG OS)
Calle 3, between Avenida 9 and 11
Young people, two floors, restaurant, big terrace.

■ **Deja-Vú** (! AC B D f GLM MA S YG) Wed-Sat 21-03h
Calle 2, between Avenida 14 and 16 ☎ 223-3758
Rave and techno , young people, very big, for your own security it is best to take a taxi. 2 dancefloors.

RESTAURANTS
■ **Bochinche. El** (B F GLM MA YG VS) Tue-Thur 19-02h, Fri & Sat - 5am. Closed Sun & Mon.
Avenida 10/Calle 11 *(between Avenida 10 and 12)* ☎ 221-0500
Very good bar, good music, young people, gigantic screen, best Fri & Sat around midnight.

■ **Café Mundo** (! A AC B CC F g MA OS YG) Mon-Fri 11.00 to 23.00 h, Sat 5.00-24.00 h, Sun closed
Avenida 9, Calle 15, Casa1372 *Locatet in the historic district of Amón-Otoya* ☎ 222 61 90

■ **Esquina. La** (F GLM MA OS) 18-23h
Boulevard Rohrmoser *(in the „Hotel Colours")* ☎ 296-1880
From 18-19.30h „two for one".

SEX SHOPS/BLUE MOVIES
■ **XXX Adult World** (glm MA)
Calle 2 between Avenida 3 and 5 ☎ 221-7165

SAUNAS/BATHS
■ **Bedevau Club** (g)
Avenida 10 *(between 1st & 3rd Street)*

■ **Dionisos** (b G MG MSG SA VS) Mon-Thu 11-23, Fri-Sat -?, Sun -21 h
Avenida 16, # 941, 2nd Floor *(between Calle 9 and 11)*
☎ 221-0534
Only the massage is good.

■ **Hispalis** (! AC b DR f G OS SA SB VS WH WO) Sun-Thu 12-2h, Fri & Sat-4h
Avenida Segunda, 1762 *(between Calles 17 and 19, difficult to find)*
Clean sauna for gays only. Large cruising area with many cubicals.

■ **Jano** (G MA N SA VS) 14-23 h
Calle 1 *(between Avenida 4 and 6)*
Small sauna frequented by a mixed local age crowd.

■ **Leblón** (b G MA N SA SB VS WO) 14-23, Sun 13-21 h
Calle 9 *(between Avenida 1 / Avenida 3)* ☎ 221-9485
Local men, not clean.

■ **Paris** (b DR G MSG SA SB WS WH WO) 12-2, Fri Sat -4 h
Calle 7, Avenida 7 *(100 north of the park Morazano, 100 from Holiday Inn)* ☎ 222-2737
Large area, condoms for free.

EDUCATION SERVICES
■ **ILISA Instituto de Idiomas** (CC f glm MA OS) Mon-Fri 7.30-16.30 h
☎ 225 24 95 📠 225 46 65
Spanish language school located in San Pedroin the suburb of San José. Call for exact location.

Costa Rica - Croatia | San José ▶ San Ramón

TRAVEL AND TRANSPORT
■ **Chase Travel Service** (glm)
☏ 221-6681 📠 221-9387 ✉ agchase@sol.racsa.co.cr
www.chasetravel.co.cr
■ **Costa Rican Trails** (GLM)
Avenida 15 / Calle 23 ☏ 221-3011 ☏ 1-800-803-3344 (USA)
📠 257-4655 ✉ crtrails@sol.racsa.co.cr
■ **Maguines Travel Service** (GLM)
PO Box 11366-1000 ☏ 283-4510 📠 283-4510
✉ manfredg@sol.racsa.co.cr

HOTELS
■ **Colours Costa Rica** (b BF CC d F GLM H N MA PI WH) 8-21 h
Boulevard Rohmoser (Northwest corner of the triangle) ☏ 232-3504
☏ 296-1880 📠 296-1597 ✉ colours@sol.racsa.co.cr
🖥 www.colours.net
10 minutes from downtown. English speaking staff. Rates US$ 59-109 (bf incl.) It's also a bar & restaurant (La Esquina) as well as a tour service for entire country.
■ **Kekoldi** (BF CC glm H)
Avenida 9, Calle 3 Bis, PO Box 12150-1000 ☏ 223-3244
📠 257-5476 ✉ kekoldi@sol.racsa.co.cr 🖥 www.kekoldi.com
14 rooms with shower/WC, telephone, safe. Rates in the low season: single: $32 , double:$45, triple: $60 plus 16,39% tax. Rates between Dec.15 and Jan. 30 are higher.

GUEST HOUSES
■ **Joluva Guest House** (BF CC GLM H MA)
Calle 3 bis, Avs 9 y 11, Barrio Amón (beetween Avenida 9 and 11)
☏ 223-7961 📠 257-7668 ✉ joluva@sol.racsa.co.cr
🖥 www.joluva.com
Close to gay scene. 3 double, 5 single rooms, with satellite TV and partly shower/WC.

PRIVATE ACCOMMODATION
■ **Taylor's Inn** (BF H)
PO Box 531-1000, Barrio Amón ☏ 257-4333 📠 221-1475
✉ taylor@catours.co.cr
7 blocks north of the National Theatre and within walking distance of the Pueblo Shopping Center.

CRUISING
AYOR! The police regularly carry out raids at the following cruising areas! All the crusing areas are dangerous at night!
-Parque Central, Calle Central and Avenida Segunda (especially at the Café Soda Palace and Perla Café)
-Parque Morazán (Avenidas 5a & 7a, Calles 5a and 7a) (r tv) (in the woods, day and night)
-Parque La Sabana (busy and dangerous at night) (popular) (between „Rohrmoser" and city; in the southwest, next to Municipal Stadium)
-Plaza de la Cultura (popular) (in front of the National Theater and at the Plaza and also in the basement; between Calle 3 and 5; busy in the late afternoon and evening)
-Parque Nacional (Avenidas 1 and 3, Calles 15 and 19; dangerous at night)
-Ojo de Agua (NG).

San Ramón ✉ 4250

GUEST HOUSES
■ **Hacienda Los Alpes** (AC BF G H MA NU OS) Nov-Aug
PO Box 231 ✉ 4250 (17 km from San Ramón, to reach by taxi or own 4-wheel) ☏ 284-6291 📠 445-5718 (post office)
Minimum stay 1 week, reservation needed. Please call for prices.

Croatia

Name:	Hrvatska • Kroatien • Croatie
Location:	Central Europe
Initials:	HR
Time:	GMT +1
International Country Code:	☏ 385 (leave the first 0 of area codes)
International Access Code:	☏ 00
Language:	Croatian
Area:	56,538 km2 / 21,829 sq mi.
Currency:	1 Kuna (HRK) = 100 Lipa
Population:	4,4671,584
Capital:	Zagreb
Religions:	76% Catholic, 11% Orthodox, 1% Slavic Muslim
Climate:	Mediterranean and continental climate. The continental climate is predominant with hot summers and cold winters. Along the coast, winters are mild and summers dry.

✴ Homosexuality is legal in Croatia (it was decriminalised in 1977), and the age of consent is 18 for homosexuals. However, the age of consent remains unequal, being only 14 for heterosexuals. Although there isn't any outspoken anti-gay legislation there have been a few cases of police harassments, such as id-checks etc, on places gathering homosexuals. The gay movement in Croatia is led by lesbian, feminist and Human Right's organisations. These groups can mainly be found in the capital city of Zagreb and tia is led by lesbian, feminist and Human Right's organisations. These groups can mainly be found in the capital city of Zagreb and their activities don't reach far beyond the city limits. Since changes on the political scene homosexuals has become more visible in the media and the society is going towards liberation in its view of homosexuality. In general homosexuality is tolerated as long as it's not obvious. People in larger cities have a largely open-

Croatia

minded attitude towards homosexuality while people in rural areas often view it negatively. The youth is in general more positive towards homosexuality. Some find homosexuality to be an illness and hand in hand walking threw the streets is not to recommend. Such „behaviour" could cause unpleasant reactions.
The gay life in Croatia is rather bleak and invisible. Homosexuals generally meet each other outdoors on public places that don't specifically count as being gay. Most of these unofficial meeting spots can be found in Zagreb and in the popular tourist-resorts on the Rivera. Croatia is a paradise for naturists and the foreign tourist who visits here will come upon a friendly and surprisingly laid-back people, as well as some of the most beautiful scenery to be found on the European continent.

★ Homosexualität ist in Kroatien legal und seit 1977 nicht mehr strafbar. Das Mündigkeitsalter für Homosexuelle liegt bei 18 Jahren und liegt damit wesentlich höher als das vorgeschriebene Mündigkeitsalter für Heterosexuelle, das auf 14 Jahre festgesetzt wurde. Obwohl es keine ausgesprochene Anti-Gay-Gesetzgebung gibt, gab es seitens der Polizei einige Fälle von Schikanen wie zum Beispiel Überprüfungen der Identität usw. an Gay-Treffpunkten. Die Gay-Bewegung in Kroatien wird von lesbischen, feministischen und Menschenrechtsorganisationen geleitet. Diese Gruppen findet man vor allem in der Hauptstadt Zagreb, wobei gesagt werden muß, daß die Aktivitäten nicht weit über die Stadtgrenze hinaus reichen. Seit den politischen Veränderungen im Land ist Homosexualität auch in den Medien sichtbar und die Gesellschaft bewegt sich in Richtung einer Befreiung, was die Haltung gegenüber der Homosexualität betrifft. Im allgemeinen wird Homosexualität toleriert wenn sie nicht eindeutig sichtbar ist, und, wie immer, haben die Menschen in den größeren Städten eine offenere Haltung gegenüber Homosexuellen als die Landbevölkerung. Bei den Jugendlichen hingegen findet man im allgemeinen eine positivere Einstellung zur Homosexualität. Einige halten Homosexualität jedoch für eine Krankheit, und aus diesem Grund ist es nicht ratsam Hand in Hand durch die Straßen zu laufen, da ein solches "Benehmen" unangenehme Reaktionen hervorrufen könnte.
Das Gay-Leben in Kroatien ist eher trostlos und kaum sichtbar. Im allgemeinen treffen sich Homosexuelle eher an öffentlichen Orten im Freien, die nicht unbedingt als Gay-Treffpunkte bekannt sind. Die meisten dieser inoffiziellen Treffpunkte findet man in Zagreb und in den bekannten Ferienorten entlang der Küste.
Kroatien ist ein Paradies für Naturliebhaber, und ausländische Touristen, die das Land besuchen, werden nicht nur auf erstaunlich entspannte Menschen treffen, sondern auch eine der schönsten europäischen Landschaften genießen können.

✱ L'homosexualité est légale en Croatie (elle a été dépénalisée en 1977). La majorité sexuelle est inégalement fixée à 18 ans pour les homosexuels et à 14 ans pour les lesbiennes et les hétérosexuels. Bien qu'il n'y ait pas législation homophobe, plusieurs cas de harcèlement policier, comme des contrôles d'identité, se sont tenus dans des lieux attirant une clientèle gaie. Le mouvement homosexuel croate est dirigé par des organisations lesbiennes, féministes et de droits de l'homme. Ces groupes sont tous basés dans la capitale Zagreb, et leur action ne dépasse généralement pas les confins de la ville. Depuis les changements intervenus dans la scène politique, les homosexuels sont plus présents dans les médias et l'image des gais est mieux perçue par la société. Les homosexuels sont aujourd'hui tolérés pour autant que leur attitude ne soit pas trop ostentatoire. L'ouverture d'esprit des citadins et des jeunes est plus grande que celles des habitants des régions rurales. Se promener dans la rue en se tenant la main n'est cependant pas recommandé car un tel comportement peut provoquer des réactions désagréables de la part de certaines personnes qui considèrent encore l'homosexualité comme une maladie.

Le milieu gai croate est presque inexistant. Les homosexuels se rencontrent généralement dans des lieux publics, pas spécifiquement gais. La plupart de ces lieux de rencontre officieux se trouvent à Zagreb ou dans les stations balnéaires touristiques. La Croatie est un paradis pour naturistes et ses visiteurs seront agréablement surpris de rencontrer des gens très sympathiques et parmi les plus beaux paysages du continent européen.

● La homosexualidad es legal in Croacia (se legalizó en 1977), y la edad de consentimiento es de dieciocho para personas homosexuales. De todas formas, la edad de consentimiento sigue siendo diferente para heterosexuales y homosexuales, puesto que para los primeros es sólo de catorce años. A pesar de que no existe una legislación expresadamente anti-gay, hubo algunos casos de coacción policial como control de carnets de identidad, etc. en lugares de encuentro de homosexuales. El movimiento gay de Croacia es liderado por organizaciones de lesbianas, organizaciones feministas y de derechos humanos. Estos grupos se encuentran sobre todo en la capital del país, Zagreb, y sus actividades no van mucho más allá de los limites de la ciudad. Desde los cambios políticos en Croacia, el ambiente homosexual se ha hecho más visible en los medios de comunicación y la sociedad se está haciendo más liberal en cuanto a la actitud hacia la homosexualidad. Generalmente, homosexualidad es tolerada siempre que no se haga demasiado obvia. Las personas en ciudades más grandes tienen una actitud abierta hacia los homosexuales, mientras que los habitantes de las áreas rurales a menudo la ven de forma negativa. La juventud generalmente tiene una postura más positiva hacia la homosexualidad. Algunos creen que la homosexualidad es una enfermedad, y para homosexuales no es recomendable andar por la calle cogidos de la mano, ya que este 'comportamiento' podría provocar reacciones desagradables. La vida gay de Croacia es más bien sombría e invisible. Los homosexuales suelen encontrarse en sitios públicos que no son considerados particularmente gays. La mayoría de estos lugares de encuentro 'inoficiales' se hallan en Zagreb y en los sitios de turismo de la Riviera. Croacia es un paraíso para naturistas y los turistas extranjeros que visitan el país encontrará personas amables y sorprendentemente relajadas, así como uno de los paisajes más bonitos que se pueden ver en el continente europeo.

✖ In Croazia l'omossessualità è legale e non viene più punita dal 1977. Per rapporti sessuali tra omosessuali bisogna aver compiuto i 18 anni mentre per eterosessuali l'età legale è di 14 anni. Bensì non vi esiste una legislazione anti gay sono noti alcuni casi di dispetto da parte della polizia in luoghi d'incontro per gay come per esempio controlli d'identità ecc. In Croazia il movimento gay viene diretto da organizzazioni lesbiche, femministiche e organizazzioni del diritto dell'uomo. Questi gruppi si trovano soprattutto nella capitale Zagabria ma spesso le loro attività non vanno oltre i limiti della città. Da quando la situazione politica è cambiata lOomosessualità viene tematizzata anche nei mass media e la popolazione sta facendo un passo verso la liberazione per quanto riguarda la sua vista dell'omosessualità. In generale l'omosessualità viene tollerata finché non diventa visibile. La gente nelle città grandi ha uno attitudine più aperta nei riguardi degli omosessuali che la popolazione rurale. Alcuni ritengono che l'omosessualità sia una malattia e per ciò non si raccomanda camminare per le strade tenendosi la mano perché un tale "comportamento" potrebbe causare delle reazioni poco piacevoli. In Croazia la vita gay è piuttosto triste e quasi invisibile. In generale gli omosessuali si incontrano in luoghi che non contano esplicitamente come luoghi dOincontro gay. La maggior parte di questi luoghi si trovano a Zagabria e nelle località turistiche lungo la Riviera. La Croazia è un paradiso per amatori della natura e il turista straniero vi troverà non solo gente gentilissima e molto rilassata ma anche uno dei più belli paesaggi sul continente europeo.

Croatia Cres ▶ Rijeka

NATIONAL GAY INFO
■ **Crogay : The Croatian Gay Portal**
info@crogay.com   www.crogay.com/eng/
Information in English about the gay scene and movement in Croatia and chat rooms.

Cres ✉ 51000 ☎ 051
SWIMMING
-Beach (g NU) (after the auto-camp in the beginning of the bay)
-Martincica (g NU) (take the road from the town of Cres towards the Island of Mali Loinj, near Lake Vransko (Vransko jezero). The beach is to be found near the camping-site)
-Miholacica (g NU) (The main beach near the tourist area)

Dubrovnik ✉ 20000 ☎ 020
SWIMMING
-Lokrum Island (MA NU) (Boat from the old harbour of Dubrovnik. At the end of nudist beach and the rocks on the south side. Action in woods behind)
-Camp Solitudo (take bus 6 and get off at the last station. Popular)

Hvar ✉ 21000 ☎ 021
SWIMMING
-Sveti Jerolim Island (g MA NU) (Boat from the harbour of Hvar (city). South side of the island. Action in the bushes. Popular in summer)

Kanegra ✉ 52000 ☎ 052
SWIMMING
-Beach near the Slovenian border on the southern coast of the Bay of Piran (MA NU WE) (Roads from Umag or Savudrija in Croatia or Portoro. Action in the woods behind the nudist beach)

Karlovac ✉ 47000 ☎ 047
CRUISING
-Park near Korana River, behind Hotel Korana and the wooden bridge (evenings)

Koprivnica ✉ 48000 ☎ 048
CRUISING
-Glavni Kolodvor/Main railway station (check out the toilets)

Krk ✉ 51000 ☎ 051
SWIMMING
-Njivice (MA NU) (trough village and auto-camp, enter forest by doors in fence, gay area 10-15 min walk along sea shore)
-Baka (near camping site Bunculuka)
-Krk (town) (near the camping-site Politin)

Makarska ✉ 21000 ☎ 021
SWIMMING
-Nugal (g NU YG) (On the Osejava Peninsula, towards Tucepi. If you're coming from Split with a car, turn right when you see the sign for the tennis centre and then go all the way down. Turn right on the gravelled road and drive until you reach the end of the road. Approximately 1km)

Nin ✉ 23000 ☎ 023
SWIMMING
-Zaton (g NU) (near the sea outside the camping-site)

Osijek ✉ 33000 ☎ 031
BARS
■ **Copacabana**
On the bank of the Drava River
Well-known and busy.
CRUISING
-Behind the Hotel Osijek
-City Park on the Drava

Poreč ✉ 52000 ☎ 052
SWIMMING
-Cervar Porata (G NU) (along the coast in the direction of Autocamp Ulika)
-White Bay/Bijela uvala (G NU) (4 km south of Poreč, between Autocamp Bijela Uvala and Funtana)

Primošten ✉ 22000 ☎ 022
SWIMMING
-Beach (g NU) (in front of Hotel Marina Lučic)

Rab ✉ 51000 ☎ 051
BARS
■ **Celestina** (B g MA) 9-2 h
Biskupa Draga 2 ✉ 51 280 *(old town, opposite post office)*
SWIMMING
-Beach of the city of Rab (G MA NU) (by boat from the harbour. At the end of the nudist beach. Action in the woods)
-Frankj (G NU) (take a boat from Rab or a car to Suha Punta. Walk to the beach right next to Hotel Eva, turn left and at the end of the beach you will find the nudist area. You have to pay an entrance to enter the nudist area. When you have entered, walk through the woods and then turn right and walk approximately 300 m to reach the gay area which is told to be one of the most popular on the Croatian Rivera)
CRUISING
-Park (between Hotel Istra and Hotel Imperijal)
-Park Dorka (small park in old town)

Rijeka ✉ 51000 ☎ 051
CAFES
■ **Python** (B g YG) 18-2 h
Fiorella la Guardia, Guvernerova palača
Many young bi and gay men.
DANCECLUBS
■ **Quorum** (B D g s YG) Thu-Sun 22-5 h, gayest on Thu Fri in summer
Preluk 1 *(Bus 32 to Preluka)*
Popular unofficial gay club of Rijeka. Very cool atmosphere but stay discreet.
CAMPING
■ **Autocamp Preluk** (g)
Preluk 1 ☎ (034) 255-051 📠 (034) 255-066
Very popular among gays who like camping. Just 50 m from the Quorum. 200m along the sea shore you will find one of the most popular GAY-beaches in Croatia - "Bunker". Please note that the camp is an unofficial gay camp and most campers are straight (heterosexual).
SWIMMING
-Bunker (G NU) (take bus 32 to Preluka, then walk back through the big curve, turn down to sea-shore)
-Medveja (g NU YG) (25 km west of Rijeka, on the Istrian peninsula, not far from Opatija and Moscenicka draga. The nude section is outside the village)

Rovinj ▶ Zagreb **Croatia**

Rovinj ✉ 52000 ☎ 052

SWIMMING
- Monsena (G NU) (at the end of autocamp, direction of Lim fjord)
- Crveni otok (NU) MA (In the center, near the temple)
- Polari Camping (g NU YG)

Slavonski Brod ✉ 35000 ☎ 035

CRUISING
- Park next to the main railway station (Glavni kolodvor)

Split ✉ 21000 ☎ 021

HEALTH GROUPS
■ **Teleapel Split** 19-7 h
☎ 365-666

SWIMMING
- Duilovo (G) (take bus 15 going there, then walk by the sea to the rocky end, between the Hotel Zagreb and the village of Stobrec)
- Io (g NU) (take the bus 12 from the Church of St. Francis, near Hotel Bellevue. The rocky beach and the hilly area just before IO, the Institute of Oceanography (Instituta za oceanografiju). The beach can be found on the tip of the Marjan peninsula)

CRUISING
- Bacvice (from intercity bus station and walk 200m to a little park with a few benches. If a guy crosses the street to enter the park (called „Schwarzwald" by the local gay people) on the opposite side and disappears into the bushes, this could be a „signal" to you. Popular from around 19.30 h or later in summertime.
- Hotel Park (The whole area surrounding the hotel, including two parks, is very popular and cruisy. Most likely to meet somebody here is after midnight and WE)
- Main bus station and the park and beach behind (very active and popular)

Šibenik ✉ 22000 ☎ 022

SWIMMING
- Zablace (g NU MA) (The beach near Solaris camping-site. Walk by the seashore from Solaris camping centre towards Zablace camping centre. The gay spot is somewhere in the middle. Action in the bushes.)

Trogir ✉ 21000 ☎ 021

SWIMMING
- Beach (G) (walk to Hotel Medena. At the end of the hotel pavement begins a rocky beach. Action at the hill on the right side)

Umag ✉ 52000 ☎ 052

SWIMMING
- Polynezia (after the Village of Katoro, but before Zambratia. The best way to get there is to go to Zambratia and then walk from the small harbour to the beach. The gay spot is to be found in front of and on the peninsula)

Varaždin ✉ 42000 ☎ 042

BARS
■ **Purgar** (b g MA)
(opposite side to the City Park and the theatre building)

SWIMMING
- Artificial Lakes (g NU) (to get there go by the road from Varaždin to Koprivnica. Popular)

CRUISING
City Park (behind the theatre building. 22-24 in summer and 19-21 h in winter)

Zadar ✉ 23000 ☎ 023

SWIMMING
Puntamika (afternoons)

CRUISING
Park near the Seamen College (evenings)

Zagreb ✉ 10000 ☎ 01

BARS
■ **Bad Boy** (AC B CC D DR G MA SNU tv VS) 17-1 h, Fri-Sun -4 h
Ksaver 210 ✉ 10 000 *(Tramcar 8/14-Zvijezda)* ☎ 46 77 501
Only existing gay club in Croatia opened in March 1999. Small but very popular.

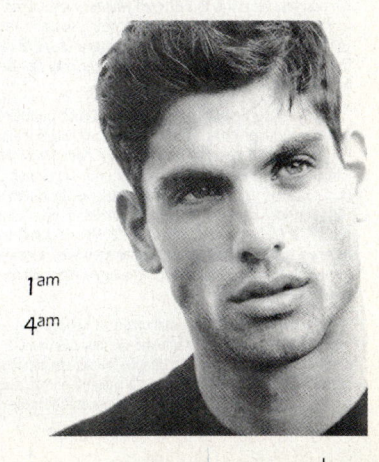

BADBOY
Ksaver 210, 10 000 Zagreb
Croatia

Opening hours:

every day: 5ᵖᵐ - 1ᵃᵐ
fri - sun: 5ᵖᵐ - 4ᵃᵐ

phone & fax
+385 (0)1 - 46 77 501

Croatia - Cyprus   Zagreb

CAFES
■ **Bacchus** (b BF glm MA)
Trg kralja Tomislava 11

DANCECLUBS
■ **Aquarius** (AC B D glm YG) Gayest on Sat 23-? h
Aleja mira, Jarun *(Tramcar 5/17-Recreational center Jarun)*
■ **Gjuro** (B D g YG)
Medveščak 58
Most popular unofficial gay club in Zagreb. Busy Fri and Sun with a young crowd.

SEX SHOPS/BLUE MOVIES
■ **Eros** (g VS)
Obrtnički prolaz 1a
■ **Pigalle** (g VS) Mon-Fri 10-20, Sat 10-14 h
Gajeva 17 ✉ 10 000 *(centre)*
☎ 48 72 671

SAUNAS/BATHS
■ **Kupalište Diana** (B g MA MSG NU PI SA SB) Gayest Tue Fri 12-19, Sat 10-15 h
Ilica 8 *(In the passage, last building)*
Very popular and active.

HEALTH GROUPS
■ **Referalni centar za AIDS** 12-15 h
Mirogojska 8   ☎ 42 56 31

SWIMMING
-Jarun lake (G MA NU) (Southern part of the eastern peninsula. Otok mladosti (Island of Youth). From noon on)

CRUISING
-Botanički vrt/Botanical garden (g MA R) (Mihanovičeva Street. Mostly in the afternoon -20 h)
-Maksimir Park (g MA) (entrance from Bukovacka/Petrova Street. Western edge of the woods, late afternoon & evening)
-Trg Bana Jelačica/Ban Jelačic Square (meeting point near the WC at Branimir's market place (Branimirova tržnica))

Cyprus

Name: Kypros/Kibris • Zypern • Chypre • Chipre • Cipro
Location: Eastern Mediterranean Sea
Initials: CY
Time: GMT +2
International Country Code: ☎ 357 (south) and 90 (north)
International Access Code: ☎ 00
Language: Greek, Turkish, English
Area: 9,251 km2 / 3,572 sq mi.
Currency: 1 Cypriot Pound (Z =100 Cents (south part). 1 Turkish Lira (TL) =100 Kurus
Population: 748,982
Capital: Nicosia (south part), Lefkosa (north part)
Religions: 78% Greek Orthodox, 18% Muslim
Climate: Moderate, mediterranean climate with hot, dry summers and cool, wet winters.

✱ From international pressure in May 1998 the notorious paragraph 171 has been abolished, which totally forbid homosexual acts. Although the old paragraph has been barely applied over the past few years it is to be feared with new regulations or agreements that there will be a worsening of the situation for homosexuals in Cyprus including the setting the age of sexual consent for homosexuals at 18 and the forbidding of personal classified ads for homosexuals.

★ Zwar wurde auf internationalen Druck im Mai 1998 der berüchtigte Paragraph 171 abgeschafft, welcher ein Totalverbot homosexueller Handlungen beinhaltet hatte. Während der alte Paragraph in den letzten Jahren kaum noch angewandt wurde, ist zu befürchten, daß neue Bestimmungen eine Verschlechterung der Lage der Homosexuellen auf Zypern mit sich bringen könnte. Dazu gehört die Erhöhung des Schutzalters für Homosexuelle auf 18 Jahre sowie die Einführung eines sogenannten Werbeverbots für Homosexualität, welches unter anderem auch die Schaltung von Kontaktanzeigen verbietet.

✱ Sous la pression internationale, la Chypre a aboli en mai 1998 son célèbre Paragraphe 171 qui interdisait les rapports homosexuels. Même si ce Paragraphe n'avait été appliqué que rarement ces dernières années, il est à craindre que de nouvelles législations (par exemple une loi fixant la majorité sexuelle des gais à 18 ans ou encore l'interdiction pour les homosexuels de faire paraître des petites annonces de rencontre) détériorent le statut des homosexuels dans l'île.

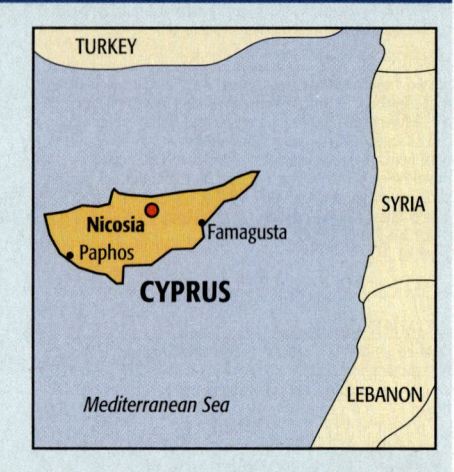

■ El artículo 171 que prohiba terminantemente las relaciones homosexuales, fue abolido en mayo de 1998 por presión internacional. Sin embargo, con las nuevas regulaciones legislativas no se espera ninguna mejora para los gays del país. Esto se hace notar por la edad de consentimiento que está estipulada ahora en 18 años y la llamada „prohibición de publicidad homosexual", que por ejemplo no permite poner anuncios de contacto.

✖ Dopo la pressione internazionale nel maggio 1998 è stato abilito il famigerato paragrafo 171 che vietava tutti gli atti omosessuali. Mentre negli ultimi anni questo vecchio paragrafo era stato applicato solo raramente, si può aspettare che nuovi regolamenti peggioreranno la situazione dei gay del Cipro. A ciò appartiene l'aumento dell'età legale per atti omosessualità, qui incluso tra l'altro il divieto di mettere inserzioni d'annunci d'incontro.

Famagusta ▶ Paphos Cyprus

Famagusta (north part)

SWIMMING
-Bedis Beach (between town and ruins; behind the bushes)

CRUISING
-City Walls (on top of main entrance to city. Climb up through the ramp way)
-Road from Port Gate toward Petek Pastanesi

Kyrenia (north part)

SWIMMING
-Kale arkasi (swimming behind the castle)

CRUISING
-Old Harbour Pier (Towards lighthouse. Pick up along the pier)

Larnaca (south part) ☏ 04

CRUISING
-Phinikoudes Beach (day and night)

Limassol (south part) ☏ 05

BARS
■ **Alaloum Disco Bar** (AC B D glm) 21-3 h
Loutron 1, Old Port *(in old town)* ☏ 36 97 26
■ **Irodion** (AC B D G MA) 21.30-3.30 h
St. Andrew Street 238 *(near Molos seafront)* ☏ 36 34 27
■ **J & A-Jacarè Bar** (B MA NG STV) 21-1 h
Popiland, 67, Georgiou A'Yermassoyia *(opposite Park Beach Hotel. Entrance at rear)* ☏ 32 06 35
Recommended.

SAUNAS/BATHS
■ **Spartacus** (G MA msg SA SB) 14-20 h
17 Voltaire Street *(in the Yermassoyias area)*
☏ 36 97 26

SWIMMING
-Dhassoudi Beach (through main entrance, then to the far end)
-Pissouri Beach (NU) (5 km west of Evdimou)
-White Rocks (between "Govenor's Beach" and "Ayios Georgios Alamanos"- monastery)

-Beach at Amathous hotel (500m from the hotel behind a stone wall, for 200 m)

CRUISING
-Anexartisias Street (at night)
-Hagios Andreas Street (only during hours when shops are open)
-Makarios Avenue (SWC g)
-Municipal gardens (all day until sunset)
-Sea front-Molos (next to the Old Port; at night)
-Dhassoudi Beach (at day)
-Behind the Central Bus Station (daytime)

Nicosia/Lefkosa ☏ 02

BARS
■ **Bastione** (B F NG s)
6 Athina Avenue *(near „green line" in old town)* ☏ 43 31 01
Busy late.
■ **Edvokia Bar** (B f MA NG)
30, Athena Avenue *(Old town near Famagusta gate)*
Best place to start.

GENERAL GROUPS
■ **Gay Liberation Movement of Cyprus**
☏ 44 33 46

CRUISING
South part:
-Eleftherias Square and Park below, also toilets
-Garden Café (opposite museum)
-Constantinos Palelogos Avenue (from Eleftheria Square to Ochi Square)
-Municipal parking place and toilets (close to the Central Post Office 16-19, 22-? h)
North part:
-Kugulu Park (next to Kyrenia Gate)
-Arasta (Shopping Centre towards the cathedral and market place, late at night)

Paphos (south part) ☏ 06

CRUISING
-Apostolus Pavlos Avenue(between „day and night newspaper shop" and castle.)

YOU CAN BE FRANK WITH ME

Ask our Virtual Nurse whatever you want to know about gay sex, safe sex or male bodies and he'll get right back to you by e-mail. Nothing surprises him and with New Zealand AIDS Foundation backing him, you know you can trust his answers. You'll find the Virtual Nurse on our website under 'queeries'.
Frank, anonymous answers to questions about sex.
WWW.NZAF.ORG.NZ/COMMED/QUEERIES.HTML

NEW ZEALAND AIDS FOUNDATION

Czech Republic

Name: Ceská Republika • Tschechische Republik • République Tchèque • República Checa • Repubblica Ceca
Location: Central Europe
Initials: CZ
Time: GMT +1
International Country Code: ☎ 420
International Access Code: ☎ 00
Language: Czech
Area: 78,864 km2 / 30,449 sq mi.
Currency: 1 Koruna (Kˇc) = 100 Haléˇru
Population: 10,286,470
Capital: Praha
Religions: 30% Catholic; 8% Protestant
Climate: Moderate climate. Summers are cool, winters cold, cloudy and humid.
Important gay cities: Praha

✳ Homosexuality was decriminalised in 1961. Laws against homosexual relations were repealed in 1990. The legal minimum age of consent (for heterosexual and homosexual relations alike) is 15 years (if no money is involved). Additionally, it is an offence to expose a minor (under 18) to the „danger of depravation" by enabling him an „idle or indecent life" or by seducing him into such a life. Prague is a liberal city where many gay Czechs choose to live. There are no laws concerning tourists with HIV/AIDS. Prostitution and the promotion of prostitution is legal, if the prostitute is at least 18 years old. Registered partnerships have been discussed twice in the Parliament, but no law has been agreed upon as yet
Czech society is liberal and open minded, perhaps because the church never had much influence within the society. This liberal stand also covers sexuality and different lifestyles. The number of gay bars, clubs, cafes and accommodations is permanently growing. The gay movement is well organised: 30 organisations and groups from all over the republic belong to the national SOHO association, that also organises several regular annual events like the Culture & Film Festival in Karlovy Vary; the Gay Men of Czech Republic event; the Candlelight March or the Rainbow Spring - a gay sport festival. Although these are semi-public events, SOHO's members don't like public events like Gay Pride Days - for this reason this has never taken place as yet.

✳ Homosexualität wurde 1961 außer Strafe gestellt. 1990 wurden die letzten Rechtsvorschriften gegen homosexuelle Beziehungen außer Kraft gesetzt. Das Mindestschutzalter liegt sowohl für heterosexuelle als auch für homosexuelle Beziehungen (und solange kein Geld im Spiel ist) bei 15 Jahren. Es gilt als Vergehen, einen Minderjährigen (unter 18) der „Gefahr der Lasterhaftigkeit" auszusetzen, indem man ihm einen „müßigen oder unzüchtigen Lebensstil" ermöglicht oder ihn zu einem solchen verführt. Prag ist eine sehr liberale Stadt, die viele tschechische Gays als Wohnort wählen. Rechtsvorschriften für Touristen mit HIV/Aids gibt es nicht. Prostitution und ihre Förderung ist legal, solange die sich prostituierenden Personen, das 18. Lebensjahr erreicht haben. Über eingetragene Partnerschaften wurde bereits zwei Mal im Parlament debattiert, doch konnte man sich bis heute nicht auf eine gesetzliche Grundlage einigen. Die tschechische Gesellschaft ist liberal und aufgeschlossen, vielleicht weil die Kirche niemals einen großen Einfluss innerhalb der Gesellschaft hatte. Diese liberale Einstellung zeigt sich auch bei Fragen der Sexualität und anderen Lebensstilen gegenüber. Die Zahl der Gaybars, -clubs, -cafés und -unterkünfte steigt stetig. Die Schwulen- und Lesbenbewegung ist gut organisiert: 30 Organisationen und Gruppen aus der ganzen Republik gehören dem nationalen SOHO-Dachverband an, der auch regelmäßig verschiedenste jährlich stattfindende Veranstaltungen organisiert, so das Kultur & Filmfestival in Karlovo Vary, das Treffen der Schwulen Männer der Tschechischen Republik, den Kerzenmarsch oder das Rainbow Spring - ein schwules Sportfest. Obwohl diese Veranstaltungen alle halböffentlich sind, mögen die Mitglieder der SOHO Massenveranstaltungen wie Gay-Prides nicht, weshalb eine solche Veranstaltung bis heute nicht organisiert worden ist.

✳ L'homosexualité a été dépénalisée en 1961 en République Tchèque. Une modification ultérieure des lois est entrée en vigueur en 1990. La majorité sexuelle est fixée à 15 ans pour tous (si de l'argent n'est pas impliqué). Il est en outre interdit d'exposer un mineur de moins de 18 ans à un „danger de dépravation" en le laissant ou en l'entraînant dans une „vie frivole ou indécente". Prague est une ville libérale et beaucoup de Tchèques choisissent d'y vivre. Il n'existe pas de loi restrictive concernant les touristes séropositifs. La prostitution et sa promotion sont légales si le prostitué est âgé d'au moins 18 ans. Une partenariat enregistré (PAC) a déjà été discuté deux fois au Parlement mais n'a pas encore abouti à une loi.
La société tchèque est libérale et ouverte d'esprit, peut-être parce que l'Eglise n'a jamais eu beaucoup d'emprise sur le pays. Cette ouverture d'esprit comprend également la sexualité et les modes de vie alternatifs. Le nombre de bars, clubs, restaurants et lieux d'hébergement gais ne cesse de croître. Le mouvement gai est très bien organisé: 30 organisations et groupes répartis dans tout le pays sont chapeautés par l'organisation nationale SOHO, qui propose plusieurs événements tout au long de l'année: le Festival culturel et cinématographique de Karlovy Vary, l'élection de Mister Gay, la Marche aux bougies, ou la manifestation sportive nommée „Printemps arc-en-ciel". Les membres de SOHO n'aiment pas les manifestations publiques, ces événements restent semi-privés. Ceci explique pourquoi aucune Gay Pride ne s'est encore tenue dans le pays.

Brno | Czech Republic

La homosexualidad fue legalizada en 1961. Las leyes contra relaciones homosexuales se abolieron en 1990. La edad mínima de consentimiento es de 15 años (siempre que no haya dinero por en medio) y es igual para heterosexuales y homosexuales. Además, es considerado un delito exponer a menores (es decir menores de 18 años) al peligro de la „depravación" posibilitándoles una „vida ociosa o indecente" o seduciéndoles para que lleven una vida así.

Praga es una ciudad liberal donde se mudan muchos gays del resto de la República Checa. No existen diposiciones legales especiales para turistas con HIV/AIDS. La prostitución y la promoción de la prostitución son legales, siempre que la persona que se prostituye haya cumplido ya los 18. Las relaciones registradas se debatieron ya dos veces en el parlamento, pero de momento no se ha aprobado ninguna ley al respecto.

La sociedad checa es liberal y muy abierta, posiblemente porque la iglesia nunca tuvo mucha influencia en el seno de la sociedad. Esta postura liberal también incluye la sexualidad y estilos de vida diferentes. El número de bares, clubs, cafeterías y alojamientos gays crece constantemente. El movimiento gay está muy bien organizado: 30 organizaciones y grupos de la entera República Checa están integrados en la asociación nacional SOHO. Esta asociación organiza varios acontecimientos y fiestas anuales como el Festival de Cine y Teatro en Karlovo Vary; la fiesta 'Hombres Gays de la República Checa Men'; el Desfile de Velas y la Fiesta Arcoiris en Primavera - un festival de deporte. A pesar de que estos acontecimientos son 'semipúblicos', los miembros de SOHO no quieren actos públicos como lo es el Día del Orgullo Gay, etc.; por esta razón hasta el momento no hubo un Desfile del Orgullo Gay en este país

L'omosessualità non è più reato nella Repubblica ceca dal 1961. Le ultime disposizioni di legge contro l'omosessualità sono state abolite nel 1990. L'età minima tanto per i rapporti eterosessuali quanto per quelli omosessuali è di 15 anni (finchè il fattore denaro non entra in gioco). È considerato reato esporre un minorenne (sotto i 18 anni) al "pericolo di corruzione2 permettendogli e inducendolo a uno stile di vita ozioso e lussurioso.

Praga è una città molto liberale che molti gay cechi eleggono a proprio domicilio. Non esistono disposizioni di legge riguardanti turisti portatori di HIV/Aids. L'offerta e la domanda di prostituzione è legale se le persone che si prostituiscono hanno superato il diciottesimo anno d'età. L'unione legale di persone dello stesso sesso è stata già due volte oggetto di dibattito in parlamento. Fino ad oggi tuttavia non si è raggiunto l'accordo per una piattaforma di legge unitaria. Probabilmente la società ceca è liberale ed aperta perchè la chiesa non vi ha mai avuto una grande influenza. Questa disposizione liberale si nota anche di fronte alle questioni di sessualità e di stili di vita diversi.

Il numero dei locali notturni, club, café e servizi alberghieri gay aumenta continuamente. Il movimento di gay e lesbiche, è ben organizzato: 30 organizzazioni e gruppi di tutta la repubblica fanno capo alla SOHO, la confederazione nazionale, che organizza regolarmente le più svariate rassegne annuali, come il Festival di cultura e cinema a Karlovy Vary, momento d'incontro dei gay della repubblica ceca, la Marcia delle candele o il Rainbow Spring, una festa sportiva gay.

Malgrado tutte queste manifestazioni siano ancora semipubbliche, i membri della SOHO non sembrano prediligere grandi appuntamenti di massa come il Gay-Prides, ragione per cui questo tipo di manifestazione non è mai stata organizzata fino ad oggi.

NATIONAL PUBLICATIONS

■ **Amigo** (G)
c/o Amigo International, PO Box 60 ✉ 100 21 Praha 8
☎ (02) 684 65 48 ☎ (0602) 64 12 74 🖷 (02) 684 65 48
📧 amigo@czn.cz 🖥 www.amigo.cz
Bimonthly gay contact magazine and guide to the Czech Republic scene. Includes a coloured map of gay Prague. Free private adds. Useful information also in English and German.

■ **Maxxx** (G)
c/o Amigo International, PO Box 60 ✉ 180 21 Praha 8
☎ (02) 684 65 48 ☎ (0602) 641 274 📧 amigo@czn.cz
🖥 www.maxxx.cz
Czech gay erotic magazine with many photos. Free privat adds with photos. Maxxx video also on sale.

■ **Princ Gay Sex Magazine, Princ Story, Gaycko**
PO Box 73, Komárkova 21 ✉ 14801 Praha 414
☎ (02) 679 107 70 🖷 (02) 679 118 04 📧 princ@iol.cz
Gaycko, magazine published in cooperation with the countrywide gay organisation Soho. Princ Gay Sex Magazine is a porn magazin. Four times a year Princ Story - a magazine featuring erotic stories in Czech language.

NATIONAL PUBLISHERS

■ **Fox Press** (G)
PO Box 3 ✉ 360 05 Karlovy Vary 5 ☎ (017) 390 11 11
🖷 (017) 390 11 11 📧 foxpress@cmail.cz
Publisher of the Czech gay videomagazine "Fox Boy". Video production.

NATIONAL COMPANIES

■ **Amigo International**
PO Box 60 ✉ 180 21 Praha 8 ☎ (02) 684 65 48
🖷 (02) 684 65 48 📧 amigo@czn.cz 🖥 www.amigo.cz
Mail order company: magazines, books, videos.

■ **Rainbow Travel** (CC GLM) 8-18 h
Lidická 569 ✉ 252 63 Roztoky u Prahy *(from Prague Metro A-Dejvi vkà, then Bus 340/350)* ☎ (02) 20 91 08 55 🖷 (0603) 551 757
🖷 (02) 20 91 08 55 📧 rainbowtravel@mbox.vol.cz
🖥 www.rainbowtravel.cz
Gay tour operator.

NATIONAL GROUPS

■ **Association of Organisations of Gay Citizens in the Czech Republic - Sdruzení Organizací Homosexuálních Obcanů v CR (SO-HO)**
Senovázné námésti 2 ✉ 110 00 Praha 1 ☎ (02) 24 22 38 11
☎ (0603) 21 38 40 📧 haq-foreign@post.cz 🖥 www.bosko.cz
30 organisations and groups from all over the Rebublic belong to SOHO. Organiser of several regular annual events. April 2001: „Aprilfest" (lesbian festival) in Prague; 22nd-24th of June 2001: „Rainbow Festival" in Karlovy Vary; 11th-17th of June 2001: „Gay Film Festival" in Brno; October 2001: „Gay Man" in Prague.

Brno ☎ 05

BARS

■ **Barclub „H46"** (B f GLM MA N p YG) 18-4 h daily
Hybešova 46 ✉ 602 00 *(Tram 1/2-Hybesova, 10 min form main railway station in direction fair area)* ☎ 43 23 49 45
Friendly, reasonable prices.

■ **Marcus Bar** (AC B CC glm MA p VS) 15-24 h
Uvoz 24 ✉ 602 00 *(in the city centre)* ☎ 43 24 54 04
Also sex shop with video shows.

■ **Philadelphia Club** (B GLM MA) 16-3 h
Milady Horákové 1a ☎ 57 77 30

Czech Republic — Brno ▶ Plzeň

DANCECLUBS
- **Gibon Club** (B DR G MA P VS) Mon-Sat 18-2/? h
Pekarska 38 ☎ 43 24 66 77
Also sexshop.
- **King's Club** (B D DR G SNU) Wed-Sat 21-? h
Pekarska 7 ☎ 43 23 71 06
- **U Richarda** (AC B D F GLM MA p VS) Fri, Sat 20-10 h
Lužova 29 ✉ 613 00 ☎ 57 29 37

SAUNAS/BATHS
- **Las Palmas** (AC B DR G SA SB) 14-3h
Galandauerova 17 ☎ 9222 94

GENERAL GROUPS
- **Lambda Brno** (GLM)
Lužova 29 ✉ 613 00 ☎ 57 29 37
- **Stud** (G)
Roubalova 5 ✉ 602 00 ☎ 43 21 58 45 ✉ stud-brno@seznam.cz
💻 www.stud.cz/

HEALTH GROUPS
- **AIDS Centrum Brno - Infekční Klinika Nemocnice** Mon 16-18 h
Jíhlavská 20 ✉ 639 01 ☎ 43 19 22 71 ☎ 43 19 22 65

CRUISING
-Ceská ulice
-Park in front of New Opera House

Česká Lipá ☎ 0425

HOTELS
- **Ranc U Dedka** (BF F glm H) 0-24 h
Kvitkov 4 ☎ (0601) 29 45 75

Cheb ☎ 0166

BARS
- **Bert** (B D G MA) Thu-Sun 18-2 h
Evropska 30 ☎ 336 88

Děčin ☎ 0412

DANCECLUBS
- **Diplomat Club** (B D DR glm)
U Dvora 1083/1 ☎ 51 02 60

Hoštka ☎ 0411

GUEST HOUSES
- **Penzion U Vikomta** (B d F glm H NU P PI SA stv)
Pod Nádražím 281 ✉ 41172 *(50 km north-west of Prague)*
☎ 81 41 71 📠 81 41 71
Drag shows on Sat. Busy on WE & summer.

Hradec Králové ☎ 049

DANCECLUBS
- **Millenium** (B D F glm S) Mon,Tue,Thu 13-23, Wed 15-23, Fri: 13-18, 21-3 (GLM), Sat 21-5 (GLM), Sun 17-21 h
Gocarova 218 ☎ 38 938

Karlovy Vary ☎ 017

BARS
- **E & T Bar** (B F glm) 10-24 h
Zeyerova 3

DANCECLUBS
- **Mandragora** (B D G H SA) 15-24-? h
Sopecna 37 ☎ 322 10 07

Liberec ☎ 048

BARS
- **Bar Marek** (B GLM) 16-24, Fri-Sat 18-? h
Delnicka 23/194 ☎ (0601) 24 23 26

Most ☎ 035

HOTELS
- **Hotel Sebastian** (B F glm H S SA)
Nova Ves v Horach 143 ☎ 6303 015 📠 6307 043

GENERAL GROUPS
- **Most k Nadeji** (GLM)
c/o Dum humanity, Jílemnického 1929 ✉ 434 01 ☎ 610 48 77
☎ (0602) 33 80 92 📠 610 48 77 ✉ slapota.lubomir@seznam.cz

Olomouc ☎ 068

BARS
- **Retrobar Diva** (B GLM MA) 18-2/? h
Pavelčákova 17 ✉ 77100

SEX SHOPS/BLUE MOVIES
- **Maxxx Shop** (b G MA VS) Tue-Sat 10-11.30, 12.30-20 h
Sokolská 44 ☎ 523 39 75

Ostrava ☎ 069

BARS
- **G-Centrum** (B D DR F G H SA) 16-? h (D on Wed, Fri & Sat)
Frdecká 62

GENERAL GROUPS
- **Klub Lambda**
PO Box 377 ✉ 730 77 ☎ (0603) 92 88 47 ☎ 682 00 78 (aidsline)
💻 mendrok@opr.ova.cdrail.cz

CRUISING
-In front of Hotel Ostrava Imperial (at New Church, námesti Národni)

Pardubice ☎ 040

DANCECLUBS
- **Cadinote Club** (B D glm LJ) 16-2, Fri: 20-4 (glm), Sat 20-? h (GLM)
Hronovicka 708 ☎ (0606) 45 37 74

Plzeň ☎ 019

DANCECLUBS
- **Misa** (B D GLM H snu stv) 18-?, Fri Sat 20-? h
c/o Hotel Morrison, Thámova Street 9 ✉ 320 02 *(Tram 4-Chodské námesti, in the basement of the hotel)* ☎ 27 09 52

Plzeň ▸ Praha Czech Republic

GENERAL GROUPS

■ **Patrick Klub** (G)
Politickch Veznu 31 ✉ 320 02 ☏ 27 42 54 ☏ 27 42 54
🖳 patrick.plzen@telecom.cz
🖳 www.mujweb.cz/www/pilsen_gay_pages

Praha 02

✱ Prague has become a major destination for gay tourists, but also for gay immigrants. The bar and club scene is highly differentiated, separating older from younger guys, Czechs from tourists, cruising from chatting, sex-workers and their clients from others. The main gay areas are Vinohrady & Zizkov (Prague 2/10 & 3). Prague castle „Hradcany", seen from Charles' Bridge at night, is an unforgettable sight. But with the Town Hall in the old part of the city, the National Gallery and Hotel Europa on Wenceslas Square (being a perfect example of Art Nouveau), Prague offers one breathtaking sight after another. Here you will find one of the most unspoilt historic city centres in Central Europe. The best way to get around Prague is by metro (fast, cheap and reliable). Trams and buses complete the public transport system. In light of the hordes of tourists who visit Prague, spring or autumn are probably better times to visit than in the busy summer period.

✱ Prag ist zu einem der beliebtesten Reiseziele von schwulen Touristen geworden und immer mehr Schwule ziehen hierher. Die Bar- und Clubszene ist ausgesprochen vielfältig, man unterscheidet hier zwischen alten und jungen Männern, zwischen Tschechen und Touristen, Cruising und Unterhaltung, kommerziellen Sexanbietern mit ihren Kunden und dem Rest. Die wichtigsten Schwulen-Bezirke sind die Stadtteile Vinohrady und Zizkov (Prag 2/10 und 3). Mit der Prager Burg Hradshin, von der Karlsbrücke aus betrachtet bei Nacht, der Stadthalle in der Altstadt, der Nationalgalerie und dem Hotel Europa (einem perfekten Beispiel des Jugendstils), bieten sich dem Besucher zahlreiche atemberaubende Anblicke. Die historische Stadtmitte Prags zählt zu den besterhaltenen in Mitteleuropa. In der Stadt bewegt man sich am besten mit der U-Bahn fort (schnell, preiswert und verlässlich), Straßenbahnen und Busse vervollständigen das Netz der öffentlichen Verkehrsmittel. Angesichts der Horden von Touristen, die Prag bereisen, ist es wahrscheinlich am günstigsten, die Stadt nicht im Sommer, wenn es am vollsten ist, sondern im Frühjahr oder im Herbst zu besuchen.

✱ Prague est devenue une destination privilégiée des touristes et immigrants gais. La scène est très diversifiée et spécialisée, offrant des lieux pour jeunes ou pour personnes plus âgées, pour les touristes ou pour les tchèques, pour draguer ou pour discuter, pour les gigolos et leurs clients ou pour les autres.
Les quartiers gais sont Vinohrady & Zizkov (Prague 2/10 & 3). Le Château de Prague „Hradcany" vu depuis le Pont Charles la nuit est d'une splendeur inoubliable. L'ancien Hôtel de Ville sur la place du Marché, la Galerie Nationale et l'hôtel Europa (joyau du style Art Nouveau) sur la place Wenceslas sont d'autres exemples des vues imprenables qu'offre la ville. Prague est une des villes d'Europe centrale qui a su le mieux conserver son centre historique. Le métro, rapide, bon marché et fiable, est le meilleur moyen pour se déplacer. Des trams et bus complètent le réseau de transports en commun. A cause des hordes de touristes qui envahissent la ville en été, il est préférable de visiter Prague au printemps ou en automne.

✱ Praga se ha convertido en uno de los destinos preferidos por los turistas gays, pero también por inmigrantes homosexuales. El ambiente gay con sus bares y clubs está extremadamente diferenciado, separando los gays jóvenes de los gays mayores, checos de turistas, ligar de charlar, prostitución y clientes del resto.
Los áreas gays principales son Vinohrady y Zizkov (Praga 2/10 y 3). El castillo de Praga „Hradcany", visto desde el puente de Carlos por la noche, es una imagen inolvidable. Pero con el Ayuntamiento en la parte vieja de la ciudad, la Galería Nacional y el hotel Europa en la Plaza de Venceslao, un perfecto ejemplo del Modernismo, Praga ofrece una vista expectacular tras otra. El centro de Praga es uno de los centros de ciudad más conservados de toda Europa Central. La mejor manera de moverse por la ciudad es en metro (rápido, barato y de fiar). El sistema de transporte público es completado por tranvías y autobuses. Por las masas de turistas que viajan a Praga, probablemente sea mejor visitar la ciudad en primavera u otoño y no durante el ajetreado período estival.

✱ Praga è diventata una delle mete predilette del turismo gay e sempre più omosessuali vengono a viverci. La scena dei locali notturni e dei club è particolarmente varia: c`è quella dei giovani e quella dei meno giovani, dei cechi e dei turisti, del cruising e dell'intrattenimento, dei prestatori di servizi sessuali con i loro clienti e del resto. Le zone gay più importanti sono i quartieri Vinohrady e Zizkov (Praga 2/10 e 3).
La vista notturna della castello praghese Hradschi dal ponte Carlo é già un'avvenimento indimenticabile. Ma Praga offre un panorama mozzafiato dopo l´altro, come la Stadthalle nella città vecchia, la Galleria Nazionale e l´hotel Europa (un magnifico esempio di stile liberty) in piazza Wenzel. Il centro storico è tra i meglio conservati in Europa.In città ci si sposta meglio con la metropolitana (veloce, conveniente e affidabile); tram e autobus completano la rete dei mezzi di trasporto pubblici. Considerando le orde di turisti che affollano Praga soprattutto d´estate, è probabilmente più opportuno visitare la cittá piuttosto in primavera.

Prosim

gayGUIDE.NET
PRAGUE

prague@gayguide.net
www.gayguide.net » link Prague

Czech Republic | Praha

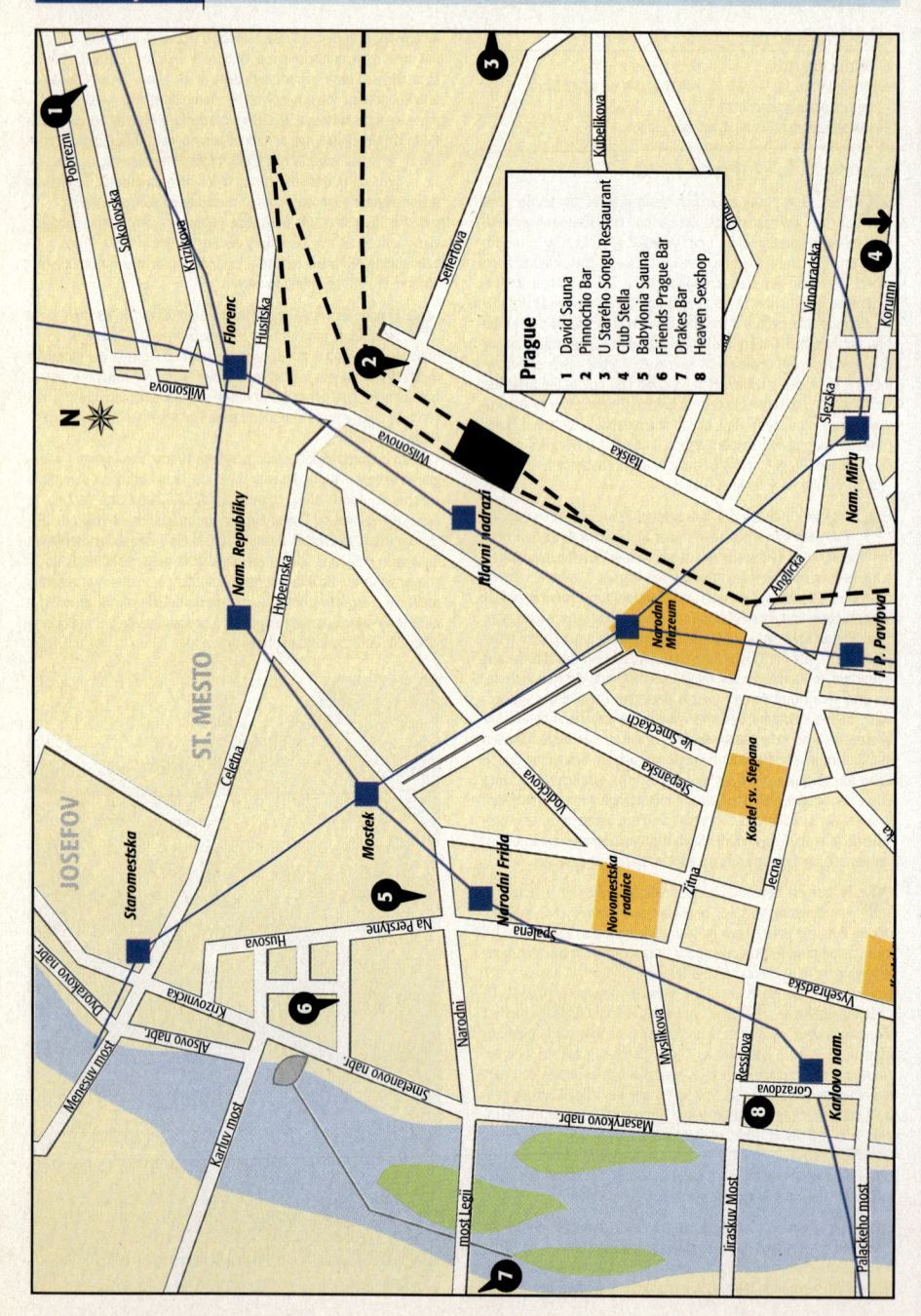

Prague
1. David Sauna
2. Pinnochio Bar
3. U Starého Songu Restaurant
4. Club Stella
5. Babylonia Sauna
6. Friends Prague Bar
7. Drakes Bar
8. Heaven Sexshop

Praha | Czech Republic

BARS

■ **A-Club** (B D gLm MA s) 19-6 h, Fri (L only) Sat disco
Milčova 25, Zizkov ✉ 130 00 (Tram 5/9/26/55/58-Lipanska, Bus 133/207-Tachovsé námestí) ☎ 22 78 16 23
Prague's only lesbian club ! On Sun sometimes transvestite & strip show. Entrance: Fri 25 Kc, Sat 50 Kc.

■ **Club Angel** (AC B CC D DR f G MA SNU STV VS) 19-3 h
Kmochova 8, Smichov ✉ 150 00 (M-Andél/Tram 4/7/9/10/58 Bertramka/Bus 176-Holeckova) ☎ 57 31 61 27

■ **Club Stella** (B F GLM OS p) 20-5 h
Lužická 10 ✉ 120 00 (Tram 4/22/23/34/57-Jana Masaryká then 3 min walk through Budecská, take the first on the right)
☎ 24 25 78 69
Nightbar, candlelight, several couches.

■ **Drake's** (B CC DR f G MA msg r SNU VS) 0-24 h
Zborovská 50 ✉ 150 00 (M-Andel, Tram 6/9/12, corner of Petrinska)
Free buffet Sun at 20 h, nightly shows at 21 & 23 h. Entrance Kc 500.- for tourists, 150.- for Czechs.

■ **Friends Prague** (AC B GLM) 16-3 h
Náprstkova 1 ✉ 110 00 ☎ 21 63 54 08
Cellar Music & Video Bar in the core of Prague. Wed to Sat DJ Parties.

■ **La Provence/ Banana Café/Tapas Bar** (A AC CC D E F g MA s snu) Restaurant 12-24, Tapas Bar 11-1, Banana Café 20-1 h
Štupartská 9 ✉ 110 00 (near Oldtown Place) ☎ 90 05 45 10
Happy Hour 12-17 h, Live piano 18.30-21.30 h, every WE - programm. French cuisine.

■ **Piano Bar** (B f g MA) 17-22/? h
Milesovská 10 ✉ 130 00 (M° A-Námestí Jiriho z Podebrad, appr. 100 meters in TV-Tower-direction)
Thu Soho and Logo members meet here for 'Charles Day'. Small pub in the cellar.

■ **Pinocchio** (B D f G H MA R SNU STV VS) 15-6 h
Seifertova 3 ✉ 130 00 (near train station, Metro C „Hlavni Nádrazí" or Tram 5/9/26/night Tram 55/58-Olzanova) ☎ 22 71 07 73
Disco, erotic centre, sex-shop and accomodation

■ **Tom's Bar** (B D DR F G MA p s VS WE) 21-2 h
Pernerova 4 ✉ 186 00 (Karlín. M-Krizíkova/Florenc, Tram 3/24, Nighttram 52-Karlinske Námestí) ☎ 24 81 38 02
Bar, small dancefloor surrounded wih tables. Room for chatting with videos. Entrance 50 Kc.

■ **U Strelce** (B G STV) Wed, Fri & Sat 21.30-?
Karoliny Svetlé 12 ✉ 110 00 (Tram 6/9/18/21/22/51/54/57/58-Národní opera, Metro B-Národní trida, Tram 17/18-Národní divadlo) ☎ 24 23 82 78
Focus on drag shows. 2nd Thu/month SOHO organises a culture evening with readings and performances with Czech actors. Entrance fee: minimum 100 Kc.

■ **Vinny Sklipek u sv.Prokopa** (B G MA) Mon-Fri 14-23, Sat 17-24
V. Nejedleho 20 ✉ 130 00 (Tram 5/9/26-Husinecka)
☎ 22 71 10 27
Cozy cellar wine and beer pub.

MEN'S CLUBS

■ **Alcatraz** (AC B DR f G LJ MA N p s VS) Tue-Sat 21.30- 4 h
Borivojova 58 ✉ 130 00 (Tram 5/9/26-Lipanska) ☎ 22 71 14 58
Modern sex club for uniforms, rubber & leather types. Naked and underwear parties every first & third Sat.

■ **SAM** (AC B DR G LJ p) 21-4/? h, Fri parties
Cajkovského 34, Žižkov ✉ 130 00 (Tram 5/9/26-Lipanska)
☎ 24 23 96 57
It is possible here to change clothes and rent leather gear. Hard to find. Red light by the door.

Friends PRAGUE

MUSIC VIDEO BAR

3 ROOMS
- PROFESSIONAL MUSIC / VIDEO SYSTEM
- SUPER VENTILATION
- GREAT LIGHTING

EACH ROOM INDIVIDUALLY CONTROLLED

ASSORTMENT OF COFFEES (SEGAFREDO)

TAP BEER (KRUŠOVICE) & BOTTLED

MORAVIAN WINES

EXCELLENT RANGE OF ALCOHOL AND SOFT DRINKS

TOP SHELF AND COCKTAIL MENU
AVAILABLE AT BAR

CHECK OUR BULLETIN BOARD FOR CALENDAR OF SPECIALS AND EVENTS

Open: Sun - Sat: 4 p.m. - 3 a.m. (?)

NÁPRSTKOVA 1, 110 00 PRAHA 1

tel./fax: +420 2 2163 5408   www.friends-prague.cz

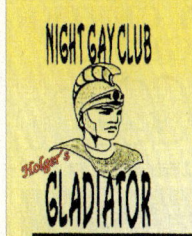

NIGHT GAY CLUB

Holger's GLADIATOR

Rokycanova 29
130 00 Praha 3 - Žižkov
Tel: 02/ 22 78 25 59

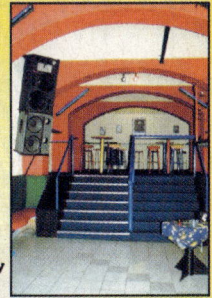

! ENTRY FREE !

Open daily: 8 pm - 4 am

2 Bars & Disco
Strip show
Go-go dancer
Friendly atmosphere
Good music

! EINTRITT FREI !
Täglich: 20.00 - 4.00 Uhr

Czech Republic — Praha

RESTAURANT - DISCOBAR - EROTIC CLUB

ESCAPE
GAY CLUB
TO PARADISE

THE BEST IN PRAGUE

RESTAURANT DISCOBAR CLUB
19 - 04/7pm-4am   22 - 05/10pm-5am

Relax in a pleasant
untraditional
EROTIC, EXOTIC
Surrounding

Open Daily 19-05/7pm-5am
V Jámě 8, Praha 1, 110 00
www.volny.cz/escapeclub   Tel: +420 602 403 744
escapeclub@volny.cz   Fax: +420 2 22 71 07 77

BIGGEST GAY CENTER IN PRAGUE

PINOCCHIO GAY CENTER

OPEN NONSTOP
DISCO - BAR, EROTIC CENTER,
POKER MACHINES, SIMULATORS
TRAVESTIES, LIVE - STRIP SHOW,
ACCOMMODATION-PARKING

Seifertova 3, Praha 3, 130 00
Tel.Reception:+420 2 22 71 07 73   e-mail: pinocchio@volny.cz
Fax: +420 2 22 71 07 77   http://www.volny.cz/pinocchio

■ **Tunel** (AC B DR G LJ p VS) Mon-Thu 22-4, Fri-Sat 22-5/? h
Plzeňská 41, Smichov ✉ 150 00 *(Metro B-Andel, Tram 4/7/9/10/58-Bertramka, Bus 176-Holeckova)*
Leather, uniform and rubber friends. You may store clothes in the cloak room. Minimum consumption 50 Kc, Fri & Sat 80 Kc.

CAFES

■ **Érra Café** (A AC B BF f GLM OS) 11-24 h
Konviktská 11 ✉ 110 00 *(M-Narodni Trida, Tram 6/9/17/18/22)*
☏ 22 22 05 68
Stylished by Roman Reznicek, a prominent Czech restaurateur.
■ **Fajn Bar** (B f GLM) 11-?, Sat-Sun 14-? h
Dittrichova 5 ✉ 120 00 *(Tram 3/7/10/14/16/17-Palackého námesti, M° Palackého námesti)* ☏ 24 91 74 09
■ **Kafírna U Českého Pána** (B G) Mon-Fri 11-22 h, Sat, Sun 14-22 h
Kozí 13 ✉ 110 00 *(Metro A-Staromestská, Tram 5/14/53-Dvorákovo nabrezi)* ☏ 232 82 83
Small cosy café-bar near the Jewish quarter.

DANCECLUBS

■ **Escape** (B D F G) Disco 22-5, Restaurant 19-4 h
V Jamě 8 ✉ 11000 ☏ 602 403 744
■ **Gejzee..r** (AC B D DR GLM snu stv VS YG) Tue-Thu 18- 4/?, Fri-Sat 18-5/? h
Vinohradská 40 ✉ 120 00 *(Metro-Námesti Miru)* ☏ 22 51 60 36
Biggest gay dance club in Prague.
■ **Holger's Gladiator** (B D G MA r S SNU) 20-4 h
Rokycanova 29 ✉ 130 00 *(Bus 136-Rokycanova, Bus 133/204-Husitska)* ☏ 22 78 25 59
2 bars, disco, shows & strip shows. Entry free.

RESTAURANTS

■ **U Kapra** (B F MA NG OS) 11-1 h
Eatecká 7 ✉ 110 00 *(M-Staroměstská)* ☏ 24 81 36 35
Czech and international cuisine.
■ **U Starého Songu** (B F glm) 16 -24/?, Fri Sat 18 -2/? h, Sun closed
Štítného 27 ✉ 130 00 *(Tram 5/9/26, Nighttram 56/58-Lipanská, and appr. 3 min walk through the street Chlumova)* ☏ 22 78 20 47

SEX SHOPS/BLUE MOVIES

■ **City Fox** (G MA VS) 11-22 h
Príbenická 12 ✉ 130 00 *(Žizkov)* ☏ 627 85 42
■ **Drake's** (B CC DR G MA msg r S VS) 0-24, SNU 21 h, Sun free buffet
Petřinska/Zborovská, 150 00 Praha 5 *(Smíchov. M-Andel, Tram 6, 9, 12)*
☏ 53 49 09
■ **Heaven** (b DR G VS) Mon-Fri 11-24, Sat & Sun 14-24 h
Gorazdova 11 ✉ 120 00 *(M-Karlovo nam.)* ☏ 24 92 12 82
■ **Lambda City Man** (G VS) Mon-Sat 14-20 h
Krakovská 2 ✉ 110 00 *(Nové Mesto, very close to Wenceslas Square)*
☏ 96 23 00 15

HOUSE OF BOYS

■ **Caligula** (B D G MA R) 18-6 h
Vita Nejedleho 7 ✉ 130 00 *(Tram 5/9/26-Husinecka)*
☏ (0602) 184 278
Small but very comfortable with sofas for sitting, bar, small dance floor, and a bedroom in the back with a double bed! Quite unique. No entrance fee. Minimum consumption 100 Kc.
■ **Pharao** (B D F G R SNU) Restaurant 11-4, Club 21-4 h
Prokopova 19 ✉ 130 00 *(Tram 5/9/26-Stop Lipanska)*
☏ 22 78 25 80
Casino with roulette table, restaurant, large stage, booths for sitting. Strip and erotic shows from 22 h. 3 bedrooms with double beds, available for rental. Entrance fee 100 Kc.

Praha | Czech Republic

William Higgins'

Drake's Prague

"Discover Prague, the New Amsterdam"

Central Europe's Most Important Gay Sex Club: Cruise & Pick-Up Bar, Gay Erotic Kino/Cinema, Private Video Cockpits, Maze, Erotic Shop, Video Relax Rooms, Leather Dungeon, Daily Total Nudity Boy & Male Strip+Erotic Shows, Massages, Escorts,
Europe's Gay Hyper-Mart!

Non-Stop - 0-24 Hours 365 Days *"We Never Close!!!"*

Visit Drake's/Find a Friend
Besuchen Sie Drake's und finden Sie sich einen Freund.

Corner of - *Ecke der* - **Zborovská & Petřinská** Streets, *Straße,* **Smíchov, Praha 5, CZ 150 00**
Tel. & Fax (+42 2) 534 909

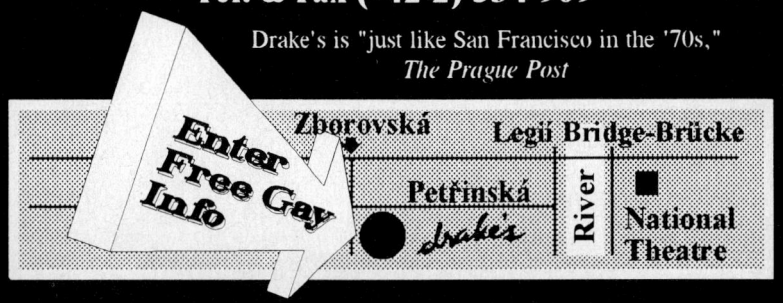

Drake's is "just like San Francisco in the '70s,"
The Prague Post

Enter Free Gay Info

Zborovská — Legií Bridge-Brücke
Petřinská — River — National Theatre
drake's

Czech Republic | Praha

HEAVEN
ALL MALE MOVIE & SHOP & VIDEOTHEK

Gorazdova 11
U-Station: Karlovo nám.
CZ - 120 00 PRAHA 2

Cinema - Video - Books - Drinks - Toys

Phone: +420 2 249 212 82

Mo. - Fr. 11:00 - 24:00
Sa. - Su. 14:00 - 24:00

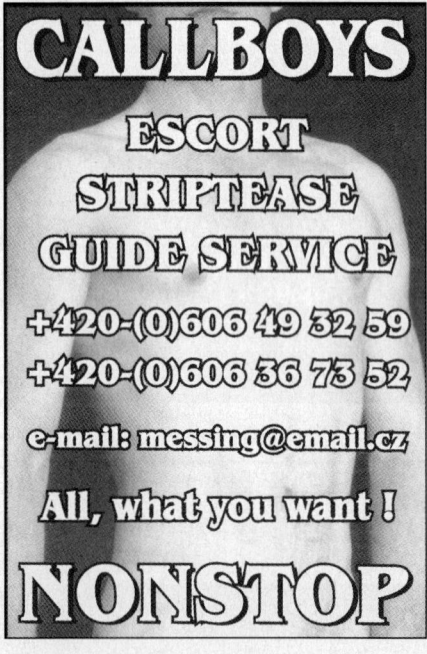

CALLBOYS
ESCORT
STRIPTEASE
GUIDE SERVICE

+420-(0)606 49 32 59
+420-(0)606 36 73 52

e-mail: messing@email.cz

All, what you want!

NONSTOP

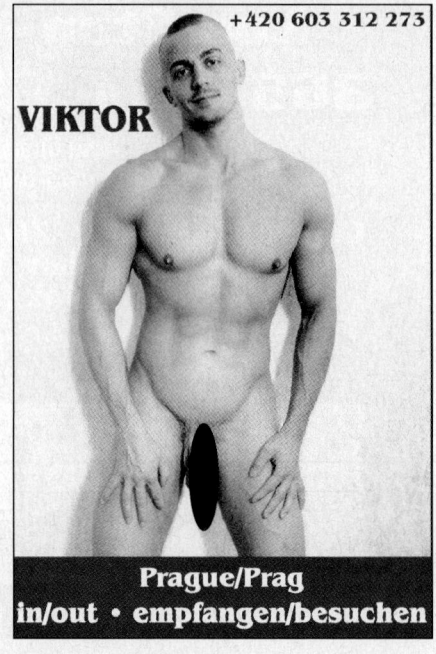

+420 603 312 273

VIKTOR

Prague/Prag
in/out • empfangen/besuchen

Praha | Czech Republic

BABYLONIA
Täglich - Daily: 14.00 - 03.00
Martinská 6, Praha 1
Tel: 00420 - 2 - 24 23 23 04

sauna, steam, whirlpool, video-room, bar, relax-room, massage, fitness
Internet: http://www.amigo.cz/babylonia

SAUNAS/BATHS
- **Babylonia** (AC B f G MA msg SA SB VS WH WO) 14-3 h
Martinská 6 ✉ 110 00 *(next to St. Martin church, Metro B/Tram 6/9/18/22/54/57/58-Národní trida)* ☎ 24 23 23 04
Very popular and friendly sauna on 500 m².
- **David** (AC b CC DR f G MA msg N P SA SB SOL VS WH) 12-24 h
Sokolouská 44 ✉ 186 00 *(M-Florenc, Tram 8/24)* ☎ 231 78 69
This was the first gay sauna of Prague. Small, cosy and intimate.
- **Marco** (B DR G MA SA SB VS WH) 14-3 h
Lublanská 17 ✉ 120 00 *(M° C.I.Pavlova, Tram 4/6/11/16/22/34/51/56/57-Pavlova)* ☎ 24 26 28 33
Small but popular.
- **Plavecky Stadion Podolí** (B g Pl SA SB) Mon-Fri 6-21.45, Sat-Sun 8.30-19.35; Men sauna daily 9-18.30 h
Podolská 74 ✉ 140 00 *(Tram 3/16/17/21/54-Kublov plus 100 meter walk)* ☎ 61 21 43 43
Public bath where you will find a lot of gay people all over the year.

HOTELS
- **Holger's Hotel** (B BF F G H MA OS p) bar 9-22, restaurant 12.30-21.30 h
Nad přívozem 52 ✉ 147 00 ☎ (0602) 31 15 17 ☎ (0602) 31 15 16
📠 444 606 43 📧 holger@atlas.cz 🖥 www.amigo.cz/holger
Also bar, restaurant and beer garden. All rooms with shower/WC, sat-TV, minibar und phone. Very busy, friendly, good BF.
- **U Cervené Sklenice** (B BF CC F glm H MA OS)
Na Kampě 513/10 ✉ 118 00 ☎ 57 53 29 18
☎ (0602) 357 700 📠 57 53 29 18 📧 recepce@hotel-kampa.cz
🖥 www.hotel-kampa.cz
Hotel with bar and international restaurant and a summer garden on the river. All rooms with WC, bath, cable TV, safe, minibar and phone. Rates: 2900 Kc during the winter; 4600 Kc during the summer, BF incl.
- **Villa Mansland** (B BF CC F G MA msg OS P R SA SNU SOL VS WH)
Štěpnicná ulice 9-11 ✉ 182 00 *(Tram 10/17/24, Nightline 54-Stepnicna)*
☎ (0603) 52 00 45 ☎ 86 88 44 11 (restaurant) 📠 86 88 44 05
📧 pragconnect@mbox.vol.cz 🖥 www.pragconnect.com
Gay hotel and holiday apartments, gay info and booking service, nightclub, restaurant and sauna. Also apartments in Prague Palmovka. Rates Kc 1600- 3000.-

GUEST HOUSES
- **Gayconnect House** (B BF G H MA) 0-24 h
Ke Krci 35/593 ✉ 147 00 *(Tram 3/17, 10 min fom centre by car)*
☎ 44 46 24 10 📠 44 46 50 41 📧 Gayconnect@atlas.cz

🖥 www.gayconnect.cz
5 single rooms, 2 double rooms & 1 apartment with shower/bath & WC, phone, radio, kitchenette, safe. Own keys. Parking places in courtyard. Rates Kc 1200-3000.-
- **Pension Haus Holger** (b BF G H MA OS)
Pod Sychrovem II/47 ✉ 101 00 *(Tram 11-Chodovská)*
☎ 72 76 40 42 ☎ (0602) 81 62 88 (Reservations) 📠 72 76 40 42
📧 pensionholger@gmx.net 🖥 www.gayprague.org
5 double rooms with private bath/WC, 2 apartments with living room. Rooms with balcony, Sat-TV, radioclock, phone. Room rates from 1500 Kc; Apartment rates from 1900 Kc. Breakfast and snacks in the Bistro.

Rainbow Travel
Gay incoming tour operator for the Czech Republic

Sightseeing trips in Prague and the entire country
Private tours with chauff/guides in deluxe cars
Arrangements for small group tours
Accommodation and restaurant reservations
Tickets for cultural performances
Airport transfers
Gay info service
Please, contact us at ph/fax:
+420-2-20 91 08 55
or
rainbowtravel@mbox.vol.cz
http://www.rainbowtravel.cz

SPARTACUS 2001/2002 | 203

Czech Republic — Praha

HOTEL U ČERVENÉ SKLENICE

NA KAMPĚ 513/10
PRAHA 1, 118 00

reception: tel/fax +4202 57532918
reservations: +42 0602 357700
http://www.hotel-kampa.cz
e-mail: recepce@hotel-kampa.cz

Accommodation in the old centre of Prague with a view to the Prague Castle and the Charles bridge.

HOTEL VILLA ANDY ★★★

U Šípků 10
Barrandov
Prague 5
CZ - 154 00

Reservation:
Tel.: +4202 5816681
Fax: + 4202 5816682
Internet:
www.amigo.cz/villa-andy

hotel
restaurant
bar
sauna
whirlpool

GAY HOLIDAY — HOLGER'S Hotel

Restaurant "U Myslivce"

Nad přívozem 52, 147 00 Praha 4 - Braník

The friendly gay hotel with restaurant and beergarden.

INFORMATION AND RESERVATION:
++420-602-311516
++420-602-311517
RESERVATION - FAX:
++420-2-44460643
INTERNET: http://www.amigo.cz/holger

GAYCONNECT HOUSE PRAG

Ke Krci 35/593·14700 Praha 4

Zimmer/Apartments mit Bad/WC & Kochgelegenheit zu vermieten für den Kurzaufenthalt oder für länger, wenige Minuten vom Stadtzentrum, vom Schwimmbad und Podoli-Gay-Treffpunkt entfernt. Eine gute Gastwirtschaft sowie eine freundliche Bar im Haus runden unser Angebot ab – damit Sie Ihren Prag-Aufenthalt nicht vergessen.

Rooms/Apartments with bathroom and kitchenette – for short or long visits; within walking distance to the city centre, the swimming pool and the Podoli gay meeting place. Our restaurant and bar at the premises and a pleasant atmosphere will ensure an enjoyable stay in Prag.

Gayconnect@atlas.cz
www.gayconnect.cz
Tel / Fax: +42 02 44462410 / -5041

Praha | **Czech Republic**

VILLA MANSLAND
A CLASS OF ITS OWN
Hotel & Apartments

Gay Hotel & Private Holiday Flats
Erotic Night Club "Boysworld"
Restaurant, Sauna & Shows
Escorts for In/Out Calls
Club daily 6:00 pm till 6:00 am
Stepnicna 9-11, Prague 8
Reservation: 00420 (0)603 520 045

e-mail: pragconnect@mbox.vol.cz
www.pragconnect.com

■ **Ron's Rainbow Guesthouse** (BF G H MA)
Bulharská 4 ✉ 101 00 *(near centre, Tram 4/22/23-Ruska)*
☎ 71 72 56 64 ☎ (0604) 87 6694 (mobile) 📠 71 72 28 86
💻 ronprague@hotmail.com 💻 www.gay-prague.com
2 luxury and 2 economy rooms with private baths/wc, Sat TV, fridge in all rooms plus kitchenette. Rates from $50-65 incl. breakfast. Excellent personal tourist information given by Ron. 10% discount for 4 days stays or more.

■ **Villa Andy** (B BF CC F GLM H MA msg OS PI r SA WH)
U Šipku 10 ✉ 154 00 *(non-central, Metro B-Smichovkd nadrazi then Bus 126 -Zahorskeho, no public transportaion at night)*
☎ 581 66 81 📠 581 66 82 💻 www.amigo.cz/villa-andy
16 rooms with shower/WC, SAT-TV, phone. Rates Single room 1600 Kc, Double room 2100 Kc.

GENERAL GROUPS
■ **Men-Klub Lambda Praha** (G)
PO Box 120 ✉ 110 01
Local organisation of SOHO.

HEALTH GROUPS
■ **CSAP - Ceská Spolecnost AIDS Pomoc & Lighthouse** 9-21 h
Malého 3 ✉ 186 21 ☎ 248 142 84 📠 248 103 45
💻 AIDS-pomoc@iol.cz 💻 web.telecom.cz/aids-pomoc
Czech organisation for Aids prevention and support for people with Aids/HIV. HIV testing and counselling Mon 16-19 h

■ **Institute of Sexuology** Mon-Fri 8-12 h
Karlovo námestí 32 ✉ 120 00 ☎ 249 043 79 ☎ 249 046 10
📠 249 046 09

■ **KHS - Kranská Hygienická Stanice** Mon-Thu 13-18 h
Dittrichova 57 ✉ 120 00 ☎ (0800) 1 444 444 (helpline)
Free and anonymous HIV tests Mon-Fri 8-12 h

RELIGIOUS GROUPS
■ **Logos** (GLM) Helpline: Wed 19-22 h
c/o Fara CCE, U Školské Zahrady 1 ✉ 182 00 *(Kobylisy)*
☎ 22 51 40 40 (helpline) 💻 logos_prg@post.cz
💻 www.ecn.cz/private/logos
Gay and lesbian ecumenical group. Meetings first Sun/month 14-17.30 h.

Pension Haus Holger Prague

The comfort of our guests is our prime concern

Tidy rooms and apartments with sat-tv and minibar in a pleasant atmosphere.
Enjoy our breakfast offerings all day
Our staff is eager to serve you at all times
Visit us on the Internet: www.gayprague.org

Pod Sychrovem II / 47 - 10100 Praha 10
Reservationphone: 00420-602-816288   Rezeption/Fax: 00420-2-72764042
E-mail: PensionHolger@gmx.net

Czech Republic   Praha ▸ Ustí nad Labem

RON'S RAINBOW GUEST HOUSE

Located in a 1910 Art Nouveau Building very close to the city center and within walking distance of some of Prague's most popular **GAY HOT SPOTS**.

Bulharska 4, Prague 10, Czech Republic

RON'S RAINBOW GUEST HOUSE

www.gay-prague.com
ronprague@hotmail.com
Tel: +420-2-717-25-664
Mobile: +420-604-876-694

SPECIAL INTEREST GROUPS

■ **Degales** (GLM)
Habova 1571   ✉ 155 00   📠 (0326) 78 62 67
📧 degales@deafnet.cz   🖥 www.deafnet.cz/degales
Deaf gay and lesbian group.

SWIMMING

-Seberak Lake (g NU) (take the metro to Kácerov, then a bus till Seberak (end station). From the bus stop walk to the opposite side of the lake)
-Sarka Lake (g NU) (take the metro to Dejvicka the Tram 26 to the end station)

CRUISING

All are very AYOR!
-Park Letna, Praha 7 (the area near the 'Metronom' on the top and next to the Belvedere Palace. In the bushes on both sides of the pavillion, near the Hanovsky Pavillion Restaurant)
-Hlavni nadrazi (Main Railway Station - gallery above the ticket counters)
-Petrin Hill & Petrin Park (paved walkways, bushes and toilets)
-Toilets at the University of Economy
-Namesti Rebubliki toilets
-Park close to Karlovo Namesti

Prostějov ☏ 0508

GENERAL GROUPS

■ **PV Klub Prostějov** (GLM MA VS) 13-21 h
Dolní 43   ✉ 796 01   ☏ 33 55 63   📧 pvklub@centrum.cz
🖥 www.hyperlink.cz/pvklub
Photos, organiser of a gay film festival.

Ustí nad Labem ☏ 047

BARS

■ **Eurobar** (B D G) 17-2, Fri-Sat 19-4/? h, closed on Sun
Hrncirska 8750 (Na Predmosti) ✉ 400 00 ☏ (0602) 40 97 57

GENERAL GROUPS

■ **Sokrates** (GLM)
Jilemnického 1929   ✉ 434 01   ☏ (0602) 81 29 39
☏ (0603) 935220   📧 sokrates.ul@post.cz

HEALTH GROUPS

■ **AIDS Centrum Ústí nad Labem**
Masarykova nemocnice   ✉ 401 13   ☏ 568 26 02   ☏ 568 26 03

CRUISING

-Západni nádrazi (West Railway Station)

SpartacusWorld.com

▶ click and ▶ win!

www.spartacusworld.com

# Denmark

Name: Danmark • Dänemark • Danemark • Dinamarca • Danimarca
Location: Northern Europe
Initials: DK
Time: GMT +1
International Country Code: ☏ 45 (no area codes)
International Access Code: ☏ 00
Language: Danish, Faeroes, Greenlandic
Area: 43,093 km² / 16,634 sq mi.
Currency: 1 Danish Krone (dkr) = 100 Öre
Population: 5,333,617
Capital: København
Religions: 91% Evangelical Lutheran
Climate: Considering its northern latitude, the climate in Denmark is fairly mild (similar to that of London/Amsterdam) February is usually the coldest month and July/August the warmest.
Important gay cities: København

✳ Denmark, along with Norway, Sweden and the Netherlands, is one of the most liberal and gay-friendly countries in the world. The age of consent is 15. Anti-discrimination laws have been in effect since 1987, homosexual couples enjoy the same inheritance rights as heterosexuals. The national Association for Gays and Lesbians (LBL) was founded in 1948 as the first of its kind. In 1989, Denmark was the first country in the world to recognise marriage between two persons of the same sex. In 1999, it became possible for married gays to adopt the children of their partners - a major step towards the recognition of a broader definition of the family. Gay visitors will find that Danes are exceptionally friendly and tolerant.
Copenhagen has long been a tolerant and relaxed capital for both gay Danes and tourists. The first gay bar, Centralhjørnet, opened over 75 years ago, and is still going strong - along with a wealth of other newer cafés & bars. It even boasts its own gay radio station, Copenhagen, Denmark and Malmö, Sweden welcome the new fixed link across the strait of Øresund as it marks the beginning of a new era for Northern Europe. The fixed link, Øresundsbron, opened on July 1, 2000 and offers new possibilities and opportunities as two Scandinavian countries are brought together in one region: The Øresund Region. Now it takes you only 35 minutes by train from central Copenhagen to explore the gay life of Swedens 3rd largest city: Malmö. Other cities in Denmark such as Århus also have much to offer the gay tourist. Visit Denmark and discover a beautiful country and the very friendly and helpful people.

✳ Neben Norwegen, Schweden und den Niederlanden gehört Dänemark zu den liberalsten und Homosexuellen gegenüber aufgeschlossensten Ländern der Welt. Das Mündigkeitsalter liegt bei 15 Jahren. Anti-Diskriminierungsgesetze sind bereits seit 1987 in Kraft, homosexuelle Paare sind heterosexuellen erbrechtlich gleichgestellt. Die nationale Vereinigung für Schwule und Lesben (LBL) wurde 1948 gegründet und war die erste Organisation dieser Art überhaupt. 1989 erkannte Dänemark als erstes Land der Welt die Heirat von gleichgeschlechtlichen Paaren an. Seit 1999 ist es Schwulen und Lesben erlaubt, die Kinder ihrer Partner zu adoptieren, was einen großen Schritt in Richtung einer weitergefassten Definition von Familie bedeutet. Homosexuelle Besucher werden die Dänen als außerordentlich freundliches und tolerantes Volk erleben.
Kopenhagen ist bei homosexuellen Dänen wie auch bei Touristen schon seit langem als tolerante und entspannte Hauptstadt bekannt. Die erste Gaybar, das Centralhjørnet, öffnete bereits vor über 75 Jahren ihre Pforten und erfreut sich neben einer Vielzahl von neueren Cafés und Bars immer noch großer Beliebtheit. Selbst einen eigenen Gay-Radiosender kann sie aufweisen.
Die dänische Hauptstadt Kopenhagen und das schwedische Malmö freuen sich indes über die erste feste Landverbindung zwischen den beiden Städten, den den Beginn einer neuen Ära für Nordeuropa kennzeichnet. Die Öresundbrücke, welche die Öresund-Meerenge überquert, wurde am 1. Juli 2000 für den Verkehr freigegeben und eröffnet völlig neue Möglichkeiten, da die beiden skandinavischen Länder nun in einer Region vereint sind: in der Öresund-Region. Vom Zentrum Kopenhagens braucht man mit dem Zug jetzt nur noch 35 Minuten um das Gay-Leben der drittgrößten Stadt Schwedens, Malmö, zu erkunden. Auch andere dänische Städte, wie z.B. Århus, haben Gay-Touristen viel zu bieten. Besuchen Sie Dänemark und entdecken Sie dieses wunderschöne Land und seine freundlichen und hilfsbereiten Bewohner.

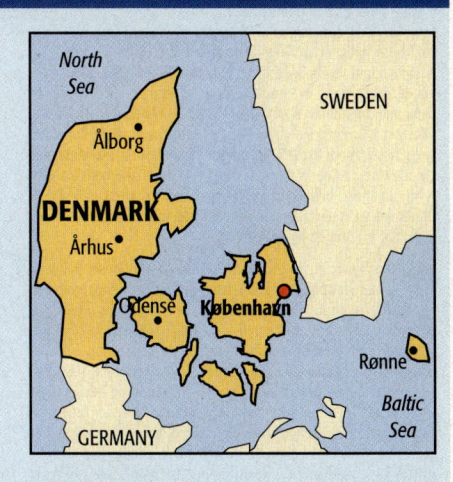

✳ Le Danemark, avec la Norvège, la Suède et les Pays-Bas, est un des pays les plus libéral et ouvert à l'homosexualité du monde. La majorité sexuelle est fixée à 15 ans. Dois lois anti-discriminatoires sont en vigueur depuis 1987 et les couples gais bénéficient des mêmes droits de succession que les hétérosexuels. L'association nationale des gais et lesbiennes (LBL) a été fondée en 1948 et était la première du genre au monde. Le Danemark a été aussi le premier pays à reconnaître, en 1989, le mariage entre personnes de même sexe. Un grand pas en avant pour une définition plus large de la famille a été fait en 1999 avec une nouvelle loi qui permet aux gais d'adopter les enfants de leur partenaire.
Les touristes trouveront les habitants du pays très sympathiques et tolérants. Copenhague est depuis longtemps une ville ouverte et accueillante autant pour les danois que pour ses visiteurs. Le premier bar gai de la ville, le Centralhjørnet, existe depuis 75 ans

Denmark

et bénéficie, avec les nombreux autres nouveaux bars et cafés de la ville, d'une grande popularité.
Les villes de Copenhague au Danemark et de Malmö en Suède sont aussi maintenant liées à travers le détroit de Øresund: un nouveau pont, le Øresundsbron, inauguré le 1er juillet 2000, marque le début d'une ère nouvelle pour le nord de l'Europe car les deux pays scandinaves sont maintenant réunis en une région : le Øresund. 35 minutes de train depuis la gare centrale de Copenhague suffisent pour explorer la vie gaie de Malmö, la troisième plus grande ville de Suède. Mais d'autres villes du Danemark, comme Arhus, ont aussi beaucoup à offrir aux touristes gais. Une visite au Danemark vous permettra de découvrir un magnifique pays et des gens très amicaux et serviables.

Dinamarca, junto con Noruega, Suecia y los Países Bajos, es uno de los países más liberales del mundo y muy amigo de los gays. La edad de consentimiento es de quince años. Leyes antidiscriminatorias entraron en vigor en 1987 y las parejas homosexuales disfrutan de los mismos derechos de herencia que las parejas heterosexuales. La Asociación de Gays y Lesbianas (LBL) danesa se fundó en 1948 como primera asociación de este tipo. En 1989, Dinamarca fue el primer país del mundo en reconocer el matrimonio entre dos personas del mismo sexo. Desde 1999, homosexuales casados tienen la posibilidad de adoptar los hijos de su pareja, lo que constituye un importante primer paso hacia el reconocimiento de una definición más amplia de la familia. Los visitantes gays de este país enseguida se darán cuenta de que los daneses son excepcionalmente amables y tolerantes.
Copenhague lleva muchísimo tiempo siendo una capital tolerante y relajada tanto para gays daneses como para los turistas gays. El primer bar gay, Centralhjørnet, abrió hace más de 75 años, y sigue funcionando muy bien, junto con una gran cantidad de otros cafés y bares más nuevos, y hasta puede presumir de tener su propia emisora de radio.
Copenhague en Dinamarca y Malmö en Suecia están encantadas con la nueva conexión a través del estrecho de Øresund, pues marca el principio de una nueva era para el norte de Europa. El puente, Øresundsbron, se inauguró el 1 de julio del 2000 y ofrece nuevas posibilidades y oportunidades, puesto que se ha unido en una región, la región de Øresund, a dos países escandinavos. Ahora, sólo se tarda 35 minutos en tren desde el centro de Copenhague a Malmö para poder explorar la vida gay de esta ciudad, la tercera ciudad más grande de Suecia. Otras ciudades danesas, como Århus, por ejemplo, también tienen mucho que ofrecer a los turistas gays. Visita Dinamarca y discubre un país maravilloso y a sus gentes tan amables y atentas.

Insieme alla Norvegia, alla Svezia e ai Paesi Bassi, la Danimarca è uno dei paesi più liberali e aperti nei confronti degli omosessuali al mondo. La maggiore età (per quel che concerne i rapporti sessuali) è 15 anni. Leggi contro la discriminazione sono in vigore già dal 1987, le coppie omosessuali godano degli stessi diritti ereditari di quelle eterosessuali. L'associazione nazionale di gay e lesbiche (LBL) è stata fondata nel 1948 come prima organizzazione di questo tipo. Nel 1989 la Danimarca è stata il primo paese del mondo a riconoscere il matrimonio tra due persone dello stesso sesso. Nel 1999 per i gay sposati è diventato possibile adottare i figli del partner, un ulteriore passo questo verso una definizione più ampia del concetto di famiglia. Visitatori gay scopriranno che i danesi sono un popolo straordinariamente cortese e tollerante.
Da tempo sia gli omosessuali danesi che i turisti hanno scoperto Copenaghen come una capitale tollerante e rilassata.
Il primo bar gay, il Centralhjørnet, apri più di 75 anni fa e gode ancora oggi, insieme a numerosi caffè e bar più recenti, di una grande popolarità. Il Centralhjørnet può perfino vantarsi di una propria stazione radio gay.
La capitale danese Copenaghen e la città svedese Malmö hanno accolto con gioia la realizzazione della prima via terrestre che, attraversando lo stretto di Oresund, unisce le due città e marca l'inizio di una nuova era per l'Europa settentrionale. Il ponte Oresund è stato aperto al traffico il primo luglio del 2000 e offre nuove possibilità e opportunità visto che ora i due paesi scandinavi hanno nella regione di Oresund una regione comune. Dal centro di Copenaghen ci vogliono oramai solo 35 minuti di treno per andare ad esplorare la vita gay di Malmö, la terza città svedese in ordine di grandezza. Anche altre città danesi, come per esempio Århus, hanno molto da offrire ai turisti gay. Visitate la Danimarca e scoprite questo bellissimo paese ed i suoi cortesi e disponibili abitanti.

NATIONAL GAY INFO

■ **Landsforeningen for Bøsser og Lesbiske, Århus-afd** Thu 18-19 h
Jægergårdsgade 42, ✉ 8100 Århus *(stair A, 1st floor, same building as PAN Disco/Club)* ☎ 86/ 13 19 48
Denmarks national organization for gay men and lesbian women, founded in 1948. Local groups in all areas.
■ **PAN-Info** Thu,Sun & Mon 20-22 h
☎ 33 36 00 86
Information on what's going on in gay and lesbian Denmark.

NATIONAL PUBLICATIONS

■ **PAN Bladet & X-Pansion**
Teglgårdstræde 13 København ☎ 33 11 19 61 33 39 00 83
✉ lbl-panblad@lbl.dk
Magazine for the members of LBL. National gay and lesbian list of events. Also lists, addresses etc. of non-LBL-groups. Founded in 1954. Approximately 28 pages. Monthly publication including personal ads, news, AIDS info, book, film and theater reviews. Free to members, institutions, libraries, etc. Dkr 150 per year.

NATIONAL COMPANIES

■ **Danske Bjørne Video ApS** (CC G) 08-17h
Risbrgvej 10 -Industri III, PO Box 162 ✉ 6330 Padborg
☎ 73/ 67 47 20 73 67 47 37 info@gayvideoshop.com
 www.gayshop.com
Videos, toys, magazines, CDs etc.
■ **Euro Shop APS**
Stationsvej, PO Box 57 ✉ 6360 Tinglev ☎ 73 /67 00 77
 73 67 00 80.

NATIONAL GROUPS

■ **Copenhagen Gay & Lesbian Film Festival**
c/o Det Danske Filminstitut, 55 Gothersgade
København ☎ 28 40 35 45
✉ www.gayfilm.com
■ **LBL - National Association for Gays and Lesbians**
Mon-Fri 10-16 h
Teglgårdstræde 13 ✉ 1452 København ☎ 3313 1948

Aabenraa ▸ Århus **Denmark**

PAN CAFE DISCO — Århus

Great mirrowball, Favorable prices, mainstream music og frendly exquisite service

Gay and Lesbian mixed crowd
Mixed ages

Pan Club, Jægergårdsgade 42, DK 8000 Århus
tel. 86 13 43 80, Website: panclub.dk e-mail: panclub@mail1.stofanet.dk

Aabenraa

GENERAL GROUPS
■ **LBL Sønderjyllandsafdelingen** Tue 19-21 h
PO Box 282, Nygade 55A ✉ 6200 ☎ 74 62 11 48
Discussions, social activities. Pan Café Fri-Sat 20-24 h

Aalborg

BARS
■ **PAN Aalborg** (B D GLM MA s WE) Wed 20-0h, Thu -02h, Fri & Sat 22-05h
Danmarksgade 27 A ✉ 9000 *(Main railway station)* ☎ 981 222 45
Bar and night club.

GENERAL GROUPS
■ **Landsforeningen for Bøsser og Lesbiske, Ålborg-afdeling** (b GLM S) Wed 17-19 h, Thu 19-23 h
PO Box 12 44, Tolbodgade 27 ✉ 9100 *(Near habour)*
☎ 98 16 45 07

CRUISING
-Kildeparken (entrance from Vesterbro near toilets and Gammel Kaervej)
-Area of bushes and trees near race course (entrance up the slope from Skydebanevej just after the race course entrance; daytime, summer only)

Århus

BARS
■ **Mens Club Århus** (B DR G LJ MA P VS) Fri-Sat 22-2 h,
Østbanetorvet 8 st.th., PO Box 5049 ✉ 8100 ☎ 86 19 10 89
Leather bar for gay men only.

CAFES
■ **Pan Club** (B D F GLM OS) Mon-Thu 18-1 h, Thu -3, Fri & Sat 20-6h
Jægergårdsgade 42 ✉ 8000 *(From train station 5 min walk. South on M.P. Bruunsg, right into Jægergårdsgade)* ☎ 86 13 43 80

SEX SHOPS/BLUE MOVIES
■ **A Center Video** (AC DR g MA VS) 12-24 h
Rosenkrantzgade 16 ✉ 8000 *(near railway station)* ☎ 86 13 01 73
■ **Gay Club Århus**
Paradisgade 11 ✉ 8000
Gay sex-cinema, videos, magazines etc.

FETISH GROUPS
■ **SMil S/M Club** Tue 20-22 h
PO Box 198 ✉ 8100 ☎ 86 13 70 23
Leather/SM group for heteros and gays.

HEALTH GROUPS
■ **Aids-Info Århus** 19-23 h
Vestergade 5B ✉ 8000 ☎ 86 13 65 13
■ **AktHIV-Huset** 9-16 h
Vestergade 5B ✉ 8000 ☎ 86 18 16 46 🖷 86 19 11 56
Information about HIV and AIDS. Help for HIV+ and PWA. Café for HIV+ Wed 12-18, Thu 19-22 h.
■ **STOP AIDS** Mon-Thu 11-16, Fri -15, Wed 20-22h
Frederiksgade 20, 3.sal, Postboks 477 ✉ 8100 ☎ 86 12 88 00
✉ Aarhus@stopaids.dk 🖳 www.stopaids.dk
Information regarding HIV and safe sex for gays only.

HELP WITH PROBLEMS
■ **HIV-Groups** Mon-Fri 09-15h
Vestergade 5, 2nd Floor ✉ 8000 ☎ 86 12 43 13
✉ akthivhuset@akthivhuset.dk 🖳 www.akthivhuset.dk
Tue 19-22 h, HIV positive only, Wed 12-16 h, for everyone, Wed 19-22 h for everyone.
■ **Rådgivning** Thu 18-20 h
Jægergårdsgade 42, opg. A, I. ✉ 8000 ☎ 86 13 19 48
Gay and lesbian consultation service.

SPECIAL INTEREST GROUPS
■ **Danish D-Lite** office hours 19.30 - 20.30
at LBL-Århus'office ✉ 8000 ☎ 86 13 19 48
🖳 www.gaysport.org/danish dlite/
Sport acitvities for gays and lesbians
■ **Halvstuderede Homoer** Thu in odd weeks 19.30 (except Jul and Aug)
Studenternes Hus, Nordre Ringgade ✉ 8000
Activities for gay and lesbian students in Århus

SWIMMING
-Den Permanente (NU) (at Risskov)
-Mariendal Havbakker (NU)
-Ballehage (nu) (near Højbjerg, afternoon)
-Fløjstrup Stand (NU)

CRUISING
-Central Station
Botanisk Have (main entrance to Den Gamle By at Eugen Warmings Vej)
-Mindeparken (Near Oddervej).
-Havnen Pier 3
-Tangkrogen (near Chr. Filtenborgs Plads, along the beach, summer after dark)

Års

HOTELS
■ **Haus Branabur** (BF G H)
Svoldruprej 101, Vognsild ✉ 9600 ☏ 98 65 86 75

Ballerup

GENERAL GROUPS
■ **Bisværmen** (G)
✉ 2750 ☏ 33 25 60 65
Gay and Lesbian Group

HELP WITH PROBLEMS
■ **Lokalforening for bøsser og lesbiske i Ballerup og omegn**
✉ 2750 ☏ 33 25 60 65

Esbjerg

CAFES
■ **Tulipan** (B GLM) Thu 19.30-22.30, Sat 20-24 (even weeks only), Sun 14-17 h (1 Oct-1 Apr only)
Nørrebrogade 102 ✉ 6700 ☏ 75 45 19 48
Café Thu 19.30-22.30 h. Parties 2nd Sat/month 21-?

SEX SHOPS/BLUE MOVIES
■ **Week-End Sex** (g)
Torvegade 11 ✉ 6700

GENERAL GROUPS
■ **LBL** Thu 19.30-22.30
Nørrebrogade 102, PO Box 10 33, 6701 ☏ 75 45 19 48

SWIMMING
-Houstrup Strand (G NU) (near Lønne. From the [P] walk 500m in direction of the nude beach. Very popular.)

CRUISING
-City park/byparken (cruising near the water tower and the art museum)
-Banegaarden/Central station
-Vestkraftvej (at toilet and phone booth, best late evening and night)
-Molevej (at toilet)

Fanø Sønderho

HOTELS
■ **Kromann's Hotel Fiskerestaurant** (B BF F glm H MA OS SOL)
Easter-October, Christmas/sylvester
Sønderland 7 ✉ 6720 ☏ 75 16 44 45 🖷 75 16 43 26

Faxe Ladeplads

SWIMMING
-Beach on the „Feddet" (by the inlet of Præsto Fjord; after the [P] there is a nudist beach, and further on the beach will become more and more gay)

Fredericia

BARS
■ **Club 77** (B D GLM h MA) Thu 22-2, Fri-Sat 23-5 h
Dalegade 77 ✉ 7000 *(ground floor)* ☏ 75 93 12 28

SWIMMING
-Trelde Næs

CRUISING
-Stationen/railway station
-The battlement "Volden"
-Norgesgade (toilet)

Frederikshavn

GENERAL GROUPS
■ **Get-Together Group**
☏ 98 42 81 74 ☏ 98 43 50 70 🖳 www.gaynord.dk/bliv.htm

Grenaa

SWIMMING
-The island of "Anholt" (g) (very long and wonderful beach)

Haderslev

GENERAL GROUPS
■ **Profil** (GLM) 2nd Fri
PO Box 112 ☏ 74 54 31 94

CRUISING
-Toilets on the "Jomfrustien"

Helsingør

GENERAL GROUPS
■ **B.I.H.** (G) Thu 18-20 h
✉ 3000 ☏ 49 20 23 03
Gay and Bisexual men in Helsingør. Café meetings 1st and 3rd Sat 20 h

CRUISING
-railway station

Herning

GENERAL GROUPS
■ **Club Fristedet** (GLM)
PO Box 48, Nørregade 7 7400 ✉ 7400 ☏ 97 12 12 42
Café in room 7-06, Kulturellen, Nørregade 7 on Thu 19.30-22 h. Parties 1st Sat in Feb, Apr, Jun, Aug, Oct and Dec.

CRUISING
-[P] in Danmarksgade
-Toilets at the [P] behind supermarket Føtex on Bredgade.

Hillerød

GENERAL GROUPS
■ **S.L.O.T.S.B.I.O.** (GLM) Last Sat in Butikken, Møllestrade 3
✉ 3400 ☏ 42 26 17 41

Hjørring

GENERAL GROUPS
■ **GayNordDK**
Postboks 243 ✉ 9800 🖳 Redaktion@gaynord.dk
🖳 www.gaynord.dk/
Infos on gay and lesbian activities in the north of Jutland.

Holbæk ▸ København   **Denmark**

Holbæk

BARS
■ **Café Oasen** (B GLM) Fri 19.30-24; lesbian night 2nd Fri 19-23 h Foreninghuset, Jernbanevej 16 ✉ 4300 *(entrance in courtyard, 1st floor)*

GENERAL GROUPS
■ **Landsforeningen for Bøsser of Lesbiske**
✉ 4300 ☏ 53 63 45 09
■ **LBL Sjæland**
✉ 4300 ☏ 59 43 19 95

Karrebæksminde

SWIMMING
Beach on the Vesterhave side (just before the bridge turn to the right, after the P walk about 500 m to the north-west)

København

Denmark's capital city is an economical, commercial and cultural center, in addition to being the undisputed fun-metropolis in Scandinavia with a relatively large gay scene. Copenhagen is a cheerful, colourful and open-minded city where the people are very friendly and the scene is very non-pretentious.
The city is not a huge sprawling metropolis, which makes finding your way around simple and convenient - everything is within walking distance. For visitors to Copenhagen, the year offers a varied selection of gay events: In April, The National Film House presents a cavalcade of classic gay movies. June sees the St. Hans Midsummer bonfire. August presents the popular biennial beauty contest for drag queens „Miss World Goes Gay" (2002/2004) as well as the annual gay pride parade „Mermaid Pride". In October there is the Copenhagen Gay and Lesbian film festival which goes on for nine days. On the 1st of December - International AIDS day - various events take place throughout the city. Art, design and fashion has become popular in recent years and the Copenhagen café, bar and restaurant scene has boomed.

Dänemarks Hauptstadt ist nicht nur Wirtschafts- und Handelszentrum, sondern auch Kulturmetropole des Landes. Hinzu kommt ihre Stellung als unbestrittene Fun-Metropole in Skandinavien mit einer relativ großen Gay-Szene. Kopenhagen ist eine heitere, abwechslungsreiche und offene Stadt in der die Menschen sehr freundlich sind und in der Szene keine hohen Ansprüche gestellt werden.
Die Stadt ist keine sehr ausgebreitete Metropole - alles ist einfach und bequem zu finden und zu Fuß erreichbar. Für die Besucher Kopenhagens bietet die Stadt das ganze Jahr über eine unterschiedliche Auswahl an Gay-Events: Im April präsentiert das Nationale Filmhaus eine Reihe klassischer Gay-Filme. Im Juni gibt es das St. Hans Mittsommer-Freudenfeuer und im August den alle zwei Jahre stattfindenden Schönheitswettbewerb für Drag-Queens „Miss World goes Gay" (2002/2004) sowie die jährlich stattfindende Gay-Parade „Mermaid-Pride". Im Oktober findet das neuntägige schwullesbische Filmfestival statt. Am ersten Dezember, dem internationalen Aids-Tag, finden in der ganzen Stadt verschiedene Events statt. Kunst, Design und Mode wurden in den letzten Jahren recht populär und die Kopenhagener Café- Bar- und Restaurantszene erfuhr einen regelrechten Boom.

La capitale du Danemark est non seulement le centre économique, commercial et culturel du pays mais aussi la métropole scandinave indiscutée de la fête avec sa scène gaie bien développée. Copenhague est une ville accueillante, bigarrée et ouverte. Ses habitants sont très sympathiques et sa scène sans trop de prétentions.
La ville n'est pas énorme, ce qui permet de trouver son chemin facilement et de tout faire à pied. Pour les touristes, Copenhague offre une multitude d'événements variés tout au long de l'année: En avril, la National Film House présente une myriade de films gais classiques. En juin a lieu le grand feu de joie de St. Hans. En août se tient tous les deux ans le concours de beauté pour drag queens „Miss World Goes Gay" (prochaines dates 2002 et 2004), bien sûr, la Gay Pride annuelle „Mermaid Pride". En octobre on peut assister pendant 9 jours au festival du film gai et lesbien „Copenhagen Gay and Lesbian Film Festival". Et le 1er décembre, pour la journée internationale du SIDA, diverses manifestations sont organisées dans toute la ville. L'art, le design et la mode bénéficient d'une popularité grandissante depuis quelques années et de nombreux cafés, bars et restaurants fleurissent dans les rues de la ville.

La capital de Dinamarca es un centro cultural, de la economía y del comercio. Con un ambiente gay relativamente grande, sin duda es la metrópoli de la diversión de Escandinavia.
Copenhague es una ciudad alegre, animada y sin prejuicios donde la gente es muy amable y el ambiente es muy poco pretencioso.
No es una metrópoli grande y desorganizada, por lo que es muy fácil orientarse y moverse en ella, pues todo está a dos pasos. Para los visitantes de Copenhague, hay una amplia gama de acontecimientos gays: En abril, la Casa Nacional del Cine presenta una larga serie de clásicos del cine gay, y en junio hay la 'hoguera de verano', el día de San Juan. Agosto es el mes del „Miss World Goes Gay", el gran concurso de belleza bienal para las drag queens (2002/2004) así como el „Mermaid Pride", la manifestación del orgullo gay anual. En octubre se celebra el festival de cine gay y lesbiano (Copenhagen Gay and Lesbian film festival) que dura nada menos que nueve días. El día 1 de diciembre (Día Internacional del SIDA) hay diferentes acontecimientos en toda la ciudad. Moda, arte y Arte se han puesto de moda durante los últimos años y las cafeterías, bares y restaurantes de la ciudad han experimentado un auténtico boom.

La capitale della Danimarca non è solo un importante centro economico, commerciale e culturale, ma anche l'incontrastata metropoli del divertimento in Scandinavia con una scena gay relativamente grande. Copenaghen è una città allegra, colorata e spregiudicata, i suoi abitanti sono molto cortesi e la scena gay non è tutt'altro che arrogante.
Non essendo Copenaghen una metropoli immensa ed estesa è facile ed economico andare in giro, tutto è raggiungibile a piedi. I visitatori trovano durante tutto l'anno una vasta scelta di eventi gay: in aprile, il National Film House presenta una maratona cinematografica imperniata sui classici del cinema gay, in giugno c'è il „St. Hans Midsummer bonfire" per il festeggiamento della mezza estate. Ad agosto si tengono il popolare concorso biennale di bellezza delle drag queen „Miss World Goes Gay" (2002/2004) e l'annuale sfilata gay „Mermaid Pride". In ottobre c'è il Copenaghen Gay and Lesbian Film Festival, una rassegna cinematografica che dura nove giorni. Il primo dicembre - giornata internazionale dell'AIDS - diversi avvenimenti hanno luogo in tutta la città. Negli ultimi anni l'arte, il design e la moda sono diventati sempre più popolari e la scena dei caffè, dei bar e dei ristoranti di Copenaghen ha vissuto un vero e proprio boom.

SPARTACUS 2001/2002 | 211

Denmark | København

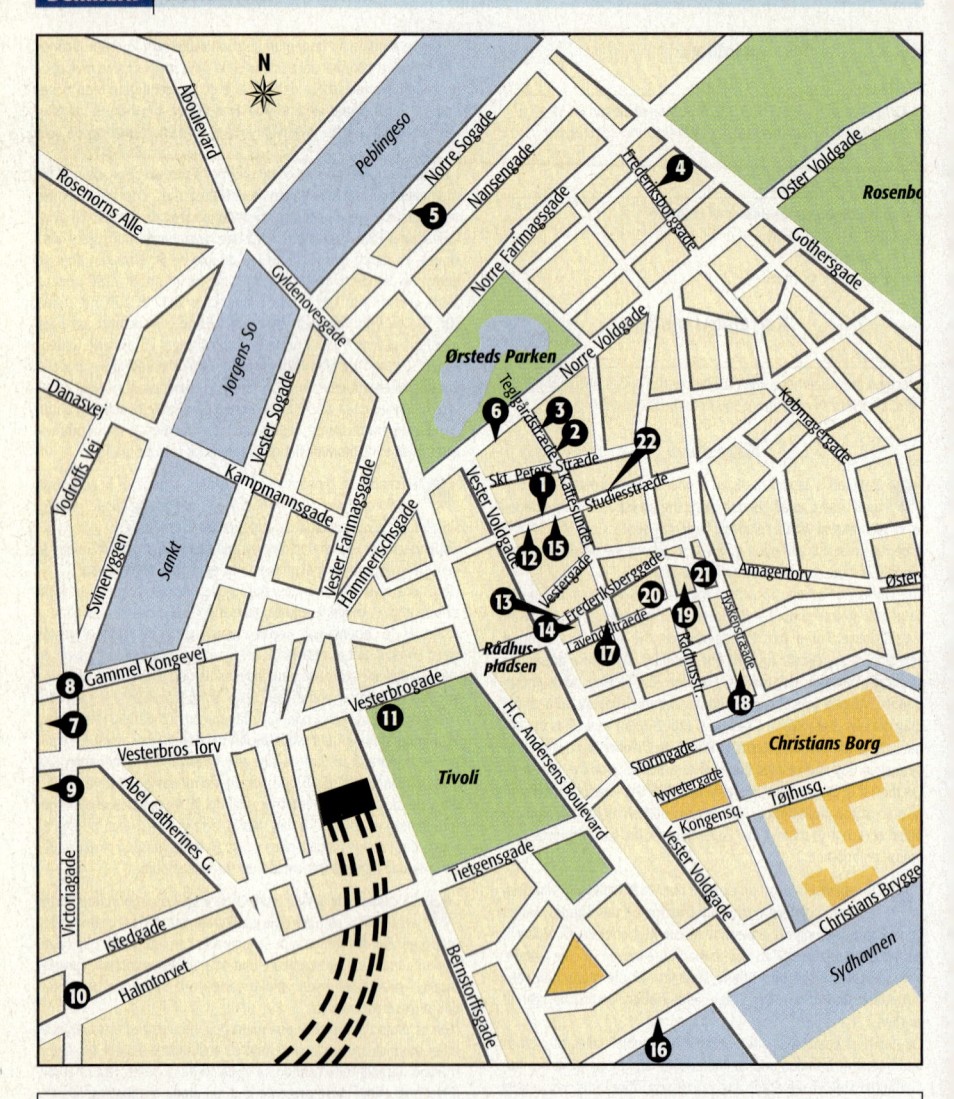

København

1. Cosy Bar
2. Men's Bar
3. LBL Gay Info
4. Windsor Hotel
5. Loke Cinema
6. Never Mind Bar
7. Amigo Bar
8. Café Intime
9. Body Bio Sauna
10. Men's Shop
11. Wonderful Copenhagen Tourist Information
12. Masken Bar
13. Rainbow Guest House
14. Can Can Bar
15. Amigo Sauna
16. At Carsten's Guesthouse
17. Cenralhjørnet Bar
18. Queen Victoria Restaurant
19. PAN Danceclub
20. Heaven Bar, Café/Restaurant
21. Sebastian Bar & Café
22. Kelleren Gay Café & Restaurant

København | Denmark

Contact Copenhagen

Copenhagen and the Øresund Region combines a high level of cultural events with a new era of modern design. Get in contact and see for yourself.

Contact Copenhagen at www.visitcopenhagen.dk or www.copenhagen-gay-life.dk
Call Copenhagen at tel: +45 7022 2442
fax: +45 7022 2452 for more information.

Wonderful Copenhagen®

EXPERIENCE ØRESUND

Denmark | **København**

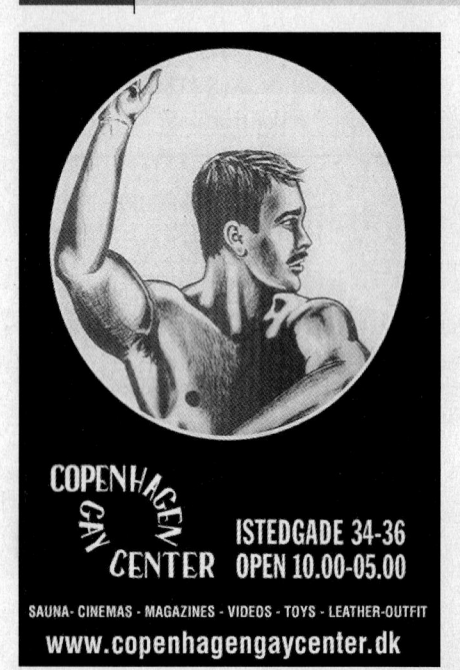

COPENHAGEN GAY CENTER
ISTEDGADE 34-36
OPEN 10.00-05.00
SAUNA- CINEMAS - MAGAZINES - VIDEOS - TOYS - LEATHER-OUTFIT
www.copenhagengaycenter.dk

GAY INFO
■ **Bøssehuset**
Fristaden Christiania *(Entrance Refshalevej 2)* ☎ 32 95 98 72
🖥 www.christiana.org/~bhuset
Call for info.
■ **Copenhagen Gay Life**
☎ 3314 7676 🖥 www.copenhagen-gay-life.dk
Copenhagen's own network for gay buisnesses and organisations.
■ **Landsforeningen for Bøsser og Lesbiske/LBL** Mon - Fri 11-15 h
Teglgårdstræde 13 ☎ 33 13 19 48 🖂 lbl@lbl.dk 🖥 www.lbl.dk
-Københavnsafdelingen *(=local section of the LBL)*
-Aftenskolen for bøsser og lesbiske / *night school for gays and lesbians with lectures of interest to students*
-LBL library (🖥 www.lbl.dk)
-Pan-Bladet & Zink Magazine (🖥 www.ezink.dk)
-Pan Idræt *(athletic association within LBL.* 🖥 www.panik.dk)
-Rådgivningen *(personal consultation* Thu 18-20 h, 1 33 13 19 48)
-Ungdomsgruppen *(group for young gays and lesbians)* Fri 20h in Café Intime.
-Youth hotline ☎ 33 36 00 80 Tue 19-21 h
■ **LBL Library** (GLM) Mon-Fri 17-19h.
Teglgårdstræde 13 🖂 1007 K ☎ 33 36 00 85 📠 33 36 00 83
🖥 www.lbl.dk
Library of the National Association for gays and lesbians.
■ **Radio Rosa**
Teglgårdstræde 13, baghuset 🖂 1452 ☎ 33 33 04 04
📠 33 36 00 83 🖂 lbl-radiorosa@lbl.dk
🖥 www.radiorosa.dk
FM 91.4 and cable FM 91.4.

MEN'S BAR
HAPPY HOURS 15 - 21
TEGLGÅRDSTRÆDE 3 - 1252 COPENHAGEN K
Open all day 15 - 02

København | **Denmark**

MLN'S SHOP

The largest selection of magazines and books, videos, leather- and rubber-gear

Cinemas NON STOP Video-Rental

Every Thursday S/M-video-show

Viktoriagade 24 - 1655 København V
Tel. 33 25 44 75

The Best Gay Place in Town

TOURIST INFO

■ **Wonderful Copenhagen Tourist Information**
Bernstorffsgad 1 ✆ 1610 ☏ 70 22 24 42 📠 70 22 24 52
✉ touristinfo@woco.dk ■ www.visitcopenhagen.dk
For a visitor to Copenhagen, the year offers a varied selection of gay events. Check our website for all further information on Copenhagen.

BARS

■ **Amigo Bar** (B g) 22-?
Schønbergsgade 4 ✉ 1906 Frederiksberg ☏ 31 21 49 15
Kareoke bar.
■ **Café Intime** (B d g) 17-02 h, Sat 20-02 h
Allegade 25, ✉ 2000 Frederiksberg ☏ 38 34 19 58
Old fashioned piano bar but very friendly. Piano music Wed-Sun.
■ **Can Can** (AC CC GLM MA TV) Mon-Sun 14-2 h
Mikkel Bryggers Gade 11/Lavendel Strade ✉ 1460 *(50 m to Town Hall)* ☏ 33 11 50 10
Friendly gay bar in the center of the city. Music is a mixture of Eurovision and Kylie Mynogue.
■ **Centralhjørnet** (! B G MA) Mo - Fri 11-01 h, Sat - Sun 05-10 h, 15-01 h
Kattesundet 18/Lavendelstræde ✉ 1458 ☏ 33 11 85 49
Oldest gay bar in Copenhagen.
■ **Cosy Bar** (B G MA) Sun-Wed 23-6, Thu-Sat 23-7 h
Studiestræde 24 ✉ 1455 ☏ 33 12 74 27
Popular and cruisy. One of the oldest bars in Copenhagen. Best in the early hours of the morning. Great music and interesting atmosphere.
■ **Måsken Bar** (B GLM MA) 16-2, Sat-Sun 15-02 h, Thur 20-2h
„Girls' night"
Studiestræde 33 ✉ 1455 ☏ 33 91 67 80

■ **Men's Bar** (AC B G LJ MA) 15-2 h, Happy Hour 15-21 h
Teglgardstræde 3 ✉ 1252 ☏ 33 12 73 03
A must if you are into jeans or leather, Friendly atmosphere, popular brunch on the first Sunday in the month.
■ **Never Mind** (B d G MA) 22-6 h
Nørre Voldgade 2 ✉ 1358 ☏ 33 11 33 08
Late night bar.
■ **PAN** (! B CC GLM OS YG) Wed-Sat 20-5, Sun-Tue only in summer
Knabrostræde 3 ✉ 1210 ☏ 33 11 37 8
Wed-Sat café from 20h, disco from 23h.
■ **Sebastian Bar & Café** (! AC B CC F GLM MA N YG) 12-02h
Hyskenstræde10 ✉ 1207
This is the first stop on a night out. Very popular and a young crowd. New kitchen. Try out the new menucard.

CAFES

■ **Heaven Bar, Café and Restaurant** (! A B CC F GLM MA) Mon-Sun 12-24h
Kompagnistraede 18 ☏ 33 15 19 00
2 floors, newly opened October 2000!
■ **Kafe Knud** (B G MA) Wed-Thu 14-22 h
Skindergade 26
HIV+ and PWA cafe.

DANCECLUBS

■ **PAN** (! B CC D GLM YG) Bar: Mon-Sun 20-05h, Disco: Thu 23-05, Fri & Sat -06h
Knabrostræde 3 ✉ 1210 ☏ 33 11 37 84
A vibrant and exciting place. Popular and crowded. Cruisy.
■ **Scandinavian Leather Men/SLM** (B DR G LJ MA P VS)
Fri 22- 04h Doors close at 02h
Studiestræde 14 A ✉ 1455 ☏ 33 32 06 01
Members only, but foreigners just show their ID and get a daily membership. Leather club in basement.

SPARTACUS 2001/2002

Denmark København

AMIGO SAUNA

Over 20 years and still the best cruising place in Copenhagen
Night & Day

Studiestræde 31 A
1455 Copenhagen

Everyday all year 12 am to 7 am   Fri + Sat 12 am to 8 am

ROOMS IN A PRIVATE GAY & LESBIAN HOME IN COPENHAGEN.

On Christians Brygge 28, 5th. floor
only 5 minutes walk from gay scene.
Sun terrace. Own key. Shared bath, kitchen and laundry facilities.
Double DKK 460, extra persons DKK 110.
Up to 4 persons/room.
Also shared dormitory for back packers DKK 130-.
Call Carsten Appel: 33149107
Mobile phone: 40509107

AT CARSTEN'S GUEST HOUSE

More information on:
http://www.circuitq.dk
EMAIL: CARSTENS@VIP.CYBERCITY.DK

RESTAURANTS

■ **Kelleren Café & Restaurant** (B F G)
12 Studiestræde ☏ 33 15 22 55
An exclusive and upmarket gay restaurant on two floors.

■ **Queen Victoria** (B BF CC e F glm) 17-24 h
Snaregade 4 ✉ 1205 ☏ 33 91 01 91
Popular restaurant owned by a well known drag queen. Good Danish cuisine. Rather expensive, but here you dine with the local celebrities. Reservations recommended for dinner.

SEX SHOPS/BLUE MOVIES

■ **Body Bio** (b DR G MA SA VS) 12-01 h
Kingosgade 7, ✉ 1623 *(Take Bus No. 6 to Kingosgade)*
Popular cruising place. Some straight guys looking for fun and don't be afraid, sometimes some straight couples.

■ **ep-production** (g) Mon-Sat 11-19:00h
Kattesundet 10 ✉ 1458 ☏ 3311 6406
Shop for gay and straight clientele. Publisher of the Danish gay magazine "Cock".

■ **Men's Shop** (CC G MA VS) 10-02h
Viktoriagade 24/Istedgade, ✉ 1655 V ☏ 33 25 44 75
Copenhagen's largest and best equipped pornoshop for gay men with magazines, books, toys, leather and rubber items. Two small video rooms.

CINEMAS

■ **Loke** (DR G MA p) 15-01 h. Closed on Saterdays.
Nørre Søgade 23 ✉ 1370 ☏ 33 32 19 73
Biggest gay cinema in town with cubicals and small dark zone area. Three video rooms. Shop with magazines, toys and videos. Cover charge 40DKr.

SAUNAS/BATHS

■ **Amigo** (B DR f G MA SA SB SOL VS) 12-7, Fri Sat -8 h
Studiestræde 31A ✉ 1455 ☏ 33 15 20 28
Copenhagen's only real gay sauna on 800 m². Recently renovated. Three floors with lots of cubicals, dark rooms, several video rooms as well as sling rooms and mazes. Busy on WE.

■ **Copenhagen Gay Center** (b cc DR f G SA VS) 10-05h
Istedgade 34-36 ✉ 1650 ☏ 33 22 23 00
Also rents porno videos. Free coffee. Slight shabby video rooms.

SPARTACUS 2001/2002

København | Denmark

Copenhagen's exclusively Gay Hotel

Hotel Windsor

Frederiksboggade 30, DK-1360 Copenhagen

Internet: http://www.hotelwindsor.dk

Email: hotelwindsor@inet.uni2.dk

Cable TV

Tel.: +45 33 11 08 30 – Fax: +45 33 11 63 87

Visa – Eurocard – Mastercard

BOOK SHOPS
■ **Bookshop Café** (b f GLM) Mon-Thu 17-19 h
Teglgårdstræde 13 ✉ 1452 ☏ 33 36 00 81
Non-commercial bookshop run by LBL with internet café.

FASHION SHOPS
■ **Underwear for Gentlemen** (g)
Gothersgade 27 ✉ 1123 ☏ 33 14 04 84
Special shop for sexy and trendy underwear.

LEATHER & FETISH SHOPS
■ **Cruz Leather Works** (G LJ MA) 11-17.30, Sat -14 h
Studiestræde 29, ✉ 1455 ☏ 33 14 90 17
Call for appointment outside store hours. Everything made to measure within a few days.

complete offer
see page Germany/Berlin

■ **SM-Bladet/SM-Shop** 11-18, Fri -19, Sat 10-14 h, closed Sun
Studiestræde 27, ✉ 1455 København K ☏ 33 32 33 03

TRAVEL AND TRANSPORT
■ **Inter-Travel ApS** 10-17.30 h
Frederiksholms Kanal 2 ✉ 1220 ☏ 33 15 00 77

HOTELS
● **Windsor** (BF CC G H MA) Check in 8-23 h
Frederiksborggade 30 ✉ 1360 (2nd floor. S-Tog Nørreport)
☏ 33 11 08 30 33 11 63 87 hotelwindsor@inet.uni2.dk
 www.hotelwindsor.dk
The only gay hotel in Copenhagen. Traditional and unpretentious hotel. Within walking distance to all gay locations. Single rooms from 400 DKK, Double rooms form 500 DKK, breakfast included.

KØBENHAVN - from DKK 150 -
overnight accomodation service
· about 750 beds · more than 28 cities ·

enjoy bed & breakfast

central booking office Berlin ☏ **+49-30-236 236 10** 4:30-9:00 pm local time
Fax +49-30-23623519 · info@ebab.de · www.ebab.de

SPARTACUS 2001/2002

Denmark København

Your new Guesthouse/B&B in Central Copenhagen

Cosy, comfortable, small, gays-only penthouse right on the main pedestrian street by Tivoli Gardens and City Hall. As close to bars, clubs etc. as you can be. 4 double rooms - overlooking the rooftops and towers of Central Copenhagen - w/wo private toilet/shower. Free Web-access. Own key.

Welcome !

copenhagen rainbow

Frederiksberggade 25 C,   DK-1459 Copenhagen K
Phone: +45 33 14 10 20   Fax: +45 33 14 10 25
www.copenhagen-rainbow.dk   info@copenhagen-rainbow.dk

GUEST HOUSES

■ **Copenhagen Rainbow Guesthouse** (AC BF CC G lj) All year Frederiksberggade 25c ✉ 1459 ☎ 33 14 10 20 📠 33 14 10 25 📧 info@copenhagen-rainbow.dk 🌐 www.copenhagen-rainbow.dk
The Rainbow is a very centrally situated privately gay-owned and -managed small, gays-only Guesthouse/ Bed & Breakfast. The Rainbow is on Frederiksberggade (the main pedestrian street), right next to the City Hall and Tivoli - the famous amusement park. There are 4 comfortable rooms.

PRIVATE ACCOMMODATION

■ **At Carsten's (B&B)** (! BF CC GLM H OS YG) Reservation 11-21 h Christians Brygge 28 ✉ 1559 V (5th floor) ☎ 33 14 91 07 📧 Carstens@vip.cybercity.dk 🌐 www.circuitq.dk
Centrally located, 5 min. walk to gay scene. Own key, shared bath, kitchen and laundry. Rates double Dkr. 470. Extra persons Dkr. 125. Also shared dormitory for back packers. Rates Dkr. 125. Also small studio apartments Dkr. 750. Wonderful location, good views. Now with even more rooms available. Rooftop parties in summer.

■ **Enjoy Bed & Breakfast** (BF G H MA YG)
☎ 32 960 206 📧 Info@ebab.dk 🌐 ebab.dk
Price 20 Euro. Accommodation sharing agency. All with shower & bf

GENERAL GROUPS

■ **HOVSA Club for Gay Hikers**
☎ 38 87 80 71 ☎ 48 17 47 70
■ **Mermaid Pride Copenhagen**
🌐 www.mermaidpride.dk
Annual Gay Pride Parade - known in Copenhagen as „Mermaid Pride", where thousands of spectators line the parade route, as around a thousand gays and lesbians strut their stuff through the capital, jamming the traffic with floats, rainbow flags „dykes on bikes, screaming queens and leather people". The year 2000 saw the innauguration of the homo -and homophobia awards - presented, provocatively enough, in front of the Danish parliament building.

HEALTH GROUPS

■ **Positivgruppen** Mon-Thu 10-16, Fri 12-14 h
PO Box 159 ✉ 2000 Frederiksberg ☎ 31 86 32 33
Group of gays or bisexual men who are HIV-positive and live in Copenhagen or Sjælland (Sealand). Organized in small groups.

■ **STOP AIDS** Mon-Fri 10-16:00h
Amagertorv 33 ✉ 1160 ☎ 33 11 29 11
A non profit organisation, supported by the government promoting AIDS awareness

HELP WITH PROBLEMS

■ **AIDS Hotline** 9-23:00h every day.
☎ 3391 1119
„Kafe Knud" - Skindergade 26 is the meeting place for PWA

RELIGIOUS GROUPS

■ **Markens Liljer/Metropolitan Community Church**
Teglgårdstræde 13 ☎ 31 83 32 86

SPECIAL INTEREST GROUPS

■ **SMil S&M Club** (g LJ) Mon 18-21 h.
Sorgenfrigade 8 A (2nd floor) ☎ 31 81 05 50
Association for S/M; gay and straight persons can become members. Publishes an own SM magazine. Gay-Together party last Sun 20h (Dress-code).

SWIMMING

- Bellevue Strand (Public beach 8 km north of Copenhagen city. Used by many gay men; especially the northern part of the beach against the wall)
- Charlottenlund (8 km from København)
- Frederiksberg Svømmehal (g MA pi sa sol) (8-20, Sat 7-13 h, closed Sun. Helgesvej 29, 2000 Frederiksberg; take bus N°2 or 11 from 2002 get off at Friederiksberg Metro Station
- Tisvilde Strand (Public beach in North Sjælland (Sealand). Go by train E to Hillerød, then change to private railroad for Tisvildeleje. The beach is about 2 km from the station; pass the P and go 1-2 km further west.

CRUISING

- Amor parken (Tagemsvej-Blegdamsvej)
- Charlottenlund Skov (Take the S-train to Charlottenlund Station and pass under the railway into the wood in direction of the castle; the action is usually between the castle and the Danmarks Akvarium in the evenings and at night.)
- Ørstedsparken Centrally located between Nørre Voldgade and Nørre Farimagsgade. Action during the day but mostly nights
- Utterslev Mose (Follow the motorway to Hillerød. About 8-9 km from the city you will find a P with a public convenience building on your right. Round this building and in the bushes 100 m away you will find the action. Take bus 63 from Rådhuspladsen. Daytime and evenings, summernights.)

Køge ▸ Slagelse **Denmark**

Køge

SWIMMING
-ølsemagle Revle (about 4 km north of Køge)

CRUISING
-At the harbor/ved havnen

Kolding

BARS
■ **Lobito** (B D G MA) Wed 19-23, Sat 21-2 h
Dyrehavegårdsvej 38 ✉ 6000 *(1st floor)* ☏ 75 54 10 23

Næstved

GENERAL GROUPS
■ **LBL Næstved** (GLM) Café Rosa at Agora, Glentevej 23 every 2nd/4th Fri 19-24 h
Glentevej 23 ✉ 4700

Nykøbing F

GAY INFO
■ **SABL** See website
Vendersgade 8 ✉ 4800 ☏ 55 85 55 19 ✉ sabl@forum.dk
🖥 sabl.homestead.com

GENERAL GROUPS
■ **Klubben for bøsser og lesbiske i Nykøbing F**
Ejegodskolen, Fjordvej 46 ✉ 4800 ☏ 53 88 00 70
or ☏ 53 87 34 78 or 54 94 33 26

SWIMMING
-Marielyst Strand (near the nude area)

Odense

BARS
■ **Lambda Bar and Café** (B D GLM MA s WE) Wed 10-24, Fri -2, Sat 22-2, 1st & 3rd Sat Homopowerparty 22-4 h
Vindegade 100 KLD ✉ 5000 ☏ 66 17 76 92

SEX SHOPS/BLUE MOVIES
■ **Antikvaren** (g)
Dronningegade 24, Odense C ✉ 5000 ☏ 66 12 86 08
■ **Pornocentrum** (g) 10-22 h
St. Gråbrødrestræde 7 B, Odense C ✉ 5000
Also sex shop. 4 film rooms, 1 with gay-porno films. Video rentals.

■ **Sexshop** (glm VS)
Vindegade 110 ✉ 5000 ☏ 66 19 05 33
3 film rooms, one with gay film. Video rental.

HEALTH GROUPS
■ **AIDS-Info (døgnvagt)** Mon-Fri 08-23 h, Sat, Sun 14-23 h
Sankt Anne Plads 2 ✉ 5000 ☏ 65 91 11 19
Information and help with questions about AIDS and HIV-antibodies.

SWIMMING
-Hverringe Strand (Nude bathing near Kerteminde. About 2 km on the road along the "Nordstranden" in direction of Hverringe Slot. The entrance to the beach is at the P in the "Hverringe-skoven")

CRUISING
-Park „Munke Mose" (along the brook, evening and night)

Roskilde

GENERAL GROUPS
■ **Trianglen** (GLM) Tue 19, 2n/4th Fri 19 h, party 1st Fri
Køgevej 44 ✉ 4000 ☏ 42 38 23 02

CRUISING
-Railway station

Skagen

HOTELS
■ **Finns Hotel Pension** (BF CC F glm H MA OS)
Østre Strandvej 63 ✉ 9990 ☏ 98 45 01 55
🖥 www.skaw.dk/finnshotelpension
Old woodhouse with a private atmosphere. Own key, car park. Rates single Dkr 275-325, double 525-725.

SWIMMING
-Beautiful long beach on the west coast (g NU)

Slagelse

GENERAL GROUPS
■ **Lesbiske og bøsser i Vestsjælland** 1 & 3 Fri. mixed cafe 19-23h, every 4th Fri gay cafe 19-h?
Nordre Stationsvej 3c ✉ 4200 ☏ 58 50 61 12

SWIMMING
-Egerup strand between Korsør and Skælskør
-P-plats at Egerup strand. Walk 600 meters north.

Art, Culture and Nature...

Finns Hotel Pension

Østre Strandvej 63 · DK-9990 Skagen · Denmark
Tlf. +45 98 45 01 55 · Fax +45 98 45 05 55
Gay friendly hotel in the most famous holiday place in Denmark.
Open all year on request, open daily in summerseason May to September.
E-Mail: info@finnshotelpension.dk · www.skaw.dk/Finnshotelpension

IGLTA

Denmark | Slagelse ▸ Viborg

CRUISING
-Picnic area on the motorway Slagelse, both sides.

Sønderborg
GENERAL GROUPS
■ Sønderbrog-gruppen (G p)
PO Box 102 6400 ✉ 6400 ☎ 74 42 24 49
■ 1'eren
✉ 6400 ☎ 74 43 05 14

CRUISING
-At [P] behind supermarket "Kvickly"
-Esplanade (Strandpromenaden) (between castle and yacht-harbor)

Sorø
GENERAL GROUPS
■ LBL Sjælland
Rylevænget 18 4180 ✉ 4180 ☎ 53 63 01 64

Svendborg
SWIMMING
-Beach on the south-eastern part of the small island of "Thurø".

CRUISING
-Railway station (in front of Hotel Svendborg)

Tisvilde
SWIMMING
-Tisvilde strand (NU)

Vanloese
FETISH GROUPS
■ ECMC Secretariat
Clausholmvej 3 A ✉ 2720 🖥 ecmc-slm@post3.tele.dk
ECMC's European Club's secretariat.

Vejle
CRUISING
-Railway station

Viborg
GENERAL GROUPS
■ Ny Manton (G)
☎ 20 95 95 14
Gay Group meetings every 1st and 3rd Wed 19-22 at Medborgerhuset (Blue Room), Vesterbrogade.

CRUISING
-[P] behind the supermarket "Schou-Epa"
-Around the cathedral
-[P] A13

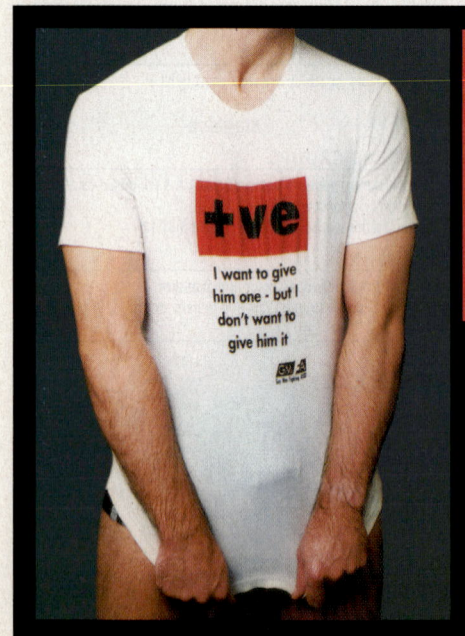

Most HIV+ men try not to pass on HIV

I want to give him one - but I don't want to give him it

GMFA's campaigns and actions are designed, planned and executed by positive, negative and untested volunteers.
To volunteer for GMFA write, phone or email:
Unit 43, Eurolink Centre, 49 Effra Road, LONDON, SW2 1BZ.
020 7738 6872. newvol@gmfa.demon.co.uk
www.demon.co.uk/gmfa
Registered Charity no. 1076854

GMFA Gay Men Fighting AIDS

Ecuador

Name: Equateur
Location: Northwestern South America
Initials: EC
Time: GMT -5
International Country Code: ☏ 593
International Access Code: ☏ 00
Language: Spanish, Quechua
Area: 283,561 km2 / 109,483 sq mi.
Currency: 1 Sucre (S/.) = 100 Centavos
Population: 12,336,572
Capital: Quito
Religions: 95% Roman Catholic
Climate: Tropical climate along the coast that becomes cooler towards the inland.

With the introduction of the new constitution which was amended during a revision which took place from November 1997 until July 1998, the legal discrimination against homosexuals disappeared. Same-sex relationships between people over the age of 18 are no longer punishable.
Despite the general prejudice against homosexuals, this new legal situation has lead to the creation of groups and associations focusing on gay issues. Along with this a few bars, restaurants and hotels have discovered the gay market and started advertising.
Especially noticeable is the emerging gay scene in the capital city Quito, which until recently was confined to a couple of cruising areas and one grubby disco. This city has several interesting bars, clubs and meeting places to offer the traveller from Europe and North America
E. Stakel

Mit der neuen Staatsverfassung, die von November 1997 bis Juli 1998 von einer freigewählten Verfassungsversammlung ausgearbeitet wurde, ist auch in Ecuador zumindest formell die gesetzliche Diskriminierung der Homosexualität verschwunden. Gleichgeschlechtliche Beziehungen zwischen Personen, die das 18. Lebensjahr vollendet haben, sind damit nicht mehr strafbar.
Diese neue Situation hat, trotz der weiterhin bestehenden Vorurteile in der Bevölkerung gegenüber Homosexuellen, zur Gründung einiger Initiativen und Verbände geführt, die sich der Interessen der Schwulen und Lesben Ecuadors annehmen. Außerdem haben Bars, Restaurants und Hotels für Homosexuelle inzwischen begonnen öffentlich Werbung zu betreiben, wodurch dieser Bereich der ecuadorianischen Gastronomie aus dem Schattendasein herausgetreten ist.
Vor allem die Schwule Szene in der Hauptstadt Quito, die noch bis vor kurzer Zeit auf zwei bis drei Cruisinggelände und eine schmuddelige Discobar beschränkt war, hat sich inzwischen erfreulich entwickelt und bietet auch dem verwöhnten Reisenden aus Europa und Nordamerika sichere und freundlich gestaltete Treffpunkte.
E. Stakel

Avec l'introduction d'une nouvelle Constitution, écrite par un comité librement élu entre novembre 1997 et juillet 1998, la discrimination juridique des gais en Equateur a disparue. Les relations homosexuelles entre partenaires de plus de 18 ans ne sont aujourd'hui plus punissables.
Cette nouvelle situation a permis la création de plusieurs groupes et associations qui défendent les droits des gais et lesbiennes dans le pays face à une population plutôt homophobe. Les bars, restaurants et hôtels sont ainsi sorti de placard et font aujourd'hui ouvertement de la publicité.
La scène de la capitale Quito, qui n'offrait il y a peu d'années que quelques lieux de drague et une discothèque douteuse, s'est développée et propose aujourd'hui aux touristes avertis d'Europe et d'Amérique du Nord des endroits de rencontres modernes et amicaux.
E. Stakel

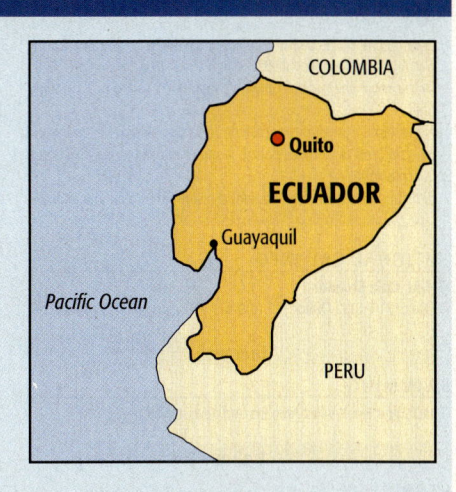

Entre noviembre de 1997 y julio de 1998, una asamblea constitucional elegida en elecciones libres elaboró una nueva constitución. Con ella, también en Ecuador desapareció, por lo menos formalmente, la discriminación legal de los homosexuales. Las relaciones entre personas del mismo sexo que han cumplido los dieciocho años han dejado de constituir un acto punible.
A pesar de que en la población siga habiendo prejuicios contra los homosexuales, esta situación nueva llevó a la fundación de algunas iniciativas y asociaciones que abogan por los intereses de los gays y lesbianas de Ecuador. Además, los bares, restaurantes y hoteles para homosexuales empezaron a hacer publicidad para sus establecimientos, lo que acabó con la vida oculta de esta rama de la gastronomía ecuatoriana.
Sobre todo el ambiente gay de la capital, Quito, hasta hace bien poco limitado a tres zonas de cruising y un descuidado discopub, está viviendo un desarrollo muy positivo, y también los viajantes exigentes de Europa y Norteamérica encontrarán lugares de encuentro seguros y de un agradable diseño.
E. Stakel

Ecuador | Atacames ▶ Quito

Grazie alla nuova costituzione dello Stato elaborata dal novembre 1997 fino a luglio 1998 da uno assemblea costituente, anche nell'Ecuador è sparita finalmente la discriminazione per legge dell'omosessualità. Rapporti sessuali tra persone dello stesso sesso che hanno compiuti i 18 anni non sono più condannabili.
Nonostante i pregiudizi persistenti della popolazione ecuadoriana nei confronti degli omosessuali, la nuova situazione ha portato alla ormazione
di alcune iniziative e associazioni che si prendono cura degli interessi dei gay e delle lesbiche nell'Ecuador. Tra l'altro i bar, ristoranti ed alberghi per Gay hanno cominciato a fare vera e propria pubblicità, permettendo così a questa parte della gastronomia ecuadoriana di uscire finalmente dalla sua esistenza oscura.
Soprattutto la scena gay della capitale Quito, che fino a poco tempo fà si è limitata a due o tre luoghi per il cruising e ad un bar in una discoteca piuttosto sporco, si è trasformata in una direzione piacevole ed offre anche al turista europeo o degli Stati Uniti dei luoghi d'incontro sicuri e gradevoli.
E. Stakel

NATIONAL GAY INFO
■ **G&L Guia Ecuador**
PO Box 1717-1002 Quito ☎ (0)9 477 776 ✉ giguia@hotmail.com

Atacames
SWIMMING
-Beach near Hotel Villas Arco Iris and newsstand Cheers.

Baños
BARS
■ **Bar Illusions** (B g)
Luis A. Martínez (16 de diciembre & 12 de noviembre)

Cuenca ☎ 07
BARS
■ **Santo y Seña** (B glm H)
Psje. 3 de Noviembre 471 ☎ 841 981
alternative bar, café and hostal

DANCECLUBS
■ **Manú** (B D glm) Wed-Sat 22-2 h
Honorato Vásquez y J. Arriaga Esq.

CRUISING
-Plaza in front of the hew cathedral (especially Sun afternoon)

Guayaquil ☎ 04
BARS
■ **Club. El** (B GLM s) Mon-Thu 19-24 h, Fri, Sat 19-2 h
Luis Urdaneta y Ximena 608 ☎ 302 113
■ **Marco´s** (B D GLM) Wed-Sat 22-3 h
V. E. Estrada 1310 A

DANCECLUBS
■ **JUDA** (B D GLM) Wed-Sat 22-3 h
10 de Agoste & Los Rios

HOTELS
■ **Hotel Velez** (H)
Velez 1021 y Quito *(1 1/2 blocks from Parque del Centenario)*
☎ 52 54 30 ☎ 52 62 92

CRUISING
-Promenade, Avenida 9 de Octubre
-Parque Centenario (ayor)

Quito ☎ 02
BARS
■ **Bar-ril (Ana Maria)** (B G) Wed-Sat 17-24 h
L. García & 6 de Diciembre
■ **Dionisios** (B GLM S SNU STV) Wed-Sat 18-2h
Manuel Larrea 550 y Riofrío *(Manuel Larrea between the streets Checa and Riofrío, near Parque Ejido)* ☎ 557 759
Friendly and popular, access through outside stairs. Thu-Sat cultural events.
■ **Habana Café** (B GLM) 17-2 h
Juan Leon Mera 134 ES y Calama *(Mariscal, located at the corner.)*
☎ (0)9-590 911
Alternative bar

CAFES
■ **Cafecito. EL** (B F glm) 17-24 h
Cordero 1124 *(Mariscal)*
Café Alternativo, with a mixture of guests. Very good meals - mainly vegetarian although rather too expensive.
■ **Pobre Diablo. El** (B f glm) Mon-Sat 17- ? h
Santa Maria y J. L. Mera
Gay owned mixed alternative café. Small snacks. Periodical exhibitions such as photographical expositions.
■ **Portón Azul. El** (B glm) Tue-Sat 17-24 h
Rábida y Colón *(in the North of Mariscal)*
In the lively northern part of the city (La Mariscal) where the Yuppie scene from Quito is to be found every Friday night.

DANCECLUBS
■ **Footloose (Victor´s)** (B D G TV P) Fri, Sat 22-5 h
General Bassano & Av. 6 de Diciembre *(Right on the corner of both streets, Mariscal)*
Has a bad reputation but is, as always, a good meeting place. Ring the door bell.
■ **Lunatika** (B D glm) Wed-Sat 21.30-2 h
Orellana 899 & Yánes Pinzón *(In the new city center)*
■ **Matrioshka** (B D G MA) Thu-Sat 20-2.30 h
Joaquin Pinto 376 & Juan Leon Mera *(In the new city center)*
☎ 552-669

Quito Ecuador - Egypt

■ **Seseribó** (B D glm YG) Fri Sat 21-4 h
Veintimilla 325 & Av. 12 de Octobre *(In the Basement)*
Mostly Salsa music. Gays and lesbians dance as mixed couples. The majority of the guests are heterosexual.

■ **Spartakus** (B D GLM TV p) Thu-Sun 22-2 h
UNP e Iñaquito *(In the north at the corner of UNP and Iñaquito)*
Very popular

SEX SHOPS/BLUE MOVIES
■ **Condomanía**
Paris 740 y Pasteur

CINEMAS
■ **Hollywood** (NG)
Av. Venezuela
No gay videos, but very cruisy.

GUEST HOUSES
■ **Ciprés. El** (H G)
Lérida 381 & Pontevedra *(In the La FIresta area)*

☏ 549 561   549 558
Not the most attractive guesthouse, but exclusively gay and inexpensive.

PRIVATE ACCOMMODATION
■ **Cumbre Andina** (BF f g H)
Av. 18 de Septiembre 368 & Av. Amazonas 2nd Floor
☏ +49-7851-480 345   ☏ 541 441   +49-7851-480 562
info@ecuatour.com   www.ecuatour.com
It's also a language school and a gay info center for Ecuador. Call for further information.

HELP WITH PROBLEMS
■ **Linea. La**
☏ 526 527   ☏ 55 99 99

CRUISING
- Parque El Ejido (by daytime, in the new city center, at night AYOR beware of the police!)
- Avenida Rio Amazonas (R) (after sunset, near Hotel Hilton-colón)
- La Moriscal (AYOR)

Egypt

Name: Misr • Ägypten • Egypte • Egipto • Egitto
Location: Northeastern Africa
Initials: ET
Time: GMT +2
International Country Code: ☏ 20 (leave the first 0 of area codes)
International Access Code: ☏ 00
Language: Arabic. French and English as languages of commerce.
Area: 997,739 km2 / 385,227 sq mi.
Currency: 1 Egyptian Pound (E) = 100 Piasters (PT)
Population: 66,050,004
Capital: Cairo (Al-Qáhirah)
Religions: 94% Moslem (almost all Sunni)
Climate: Desert climate. Summers are hot and dry, winters moderate.

✱ Homosexuality is not illegal in Egypt. Caution should however be taken, as Egypt also has regulations on „offences against public morals and sensitivities" which are vague enough that they could be used against you. Men are not openly gay in Egypt, so as not to be outcast by their families and society. The police cannot be considered gay-friendly. In light of recent attacks against tourists by militants Muslims, we strongly recommend you not to openly display homosexuality; this opinion was confirmed by the German embassy in Cairo. When entering the country, it is important to demand that your currency declaration be stamped and signed. It is also advisable to declare all valuables before entering, as they could otherwise be confiscated upon departure.

★ Homosexualität ist in Ägypten nicht verboten. Allerdings gilt auch für Ägypten, daß ein „Verstoß gegen die öffentliche Moral oder die allgemeinen Empfindungen" nicht näher definiert wird. Schwule treten in Ägypten nicht öffentlich in Erscheinung, um nicht von Familie und Gesellschaft geächtet zu werden. Die Polizei kann nicht als schwulenfreundlich bezeichnet werden. Angesichts der Angriffe auf Touristen von seiten radikaler Moslems kann nur empfohlen werden, sein Schwulsein nicht „zu demonstrieren", wie die deutsche Botschaft in Kairo meint. Bei der Einreise ist es nicht ganz unwichtig, darauf zu bestehen, daß die Währungsdeklaration abgestempelt und unterschrieben wird. Man sollte auch die mitgeführten Wertsachen deklarieren, da sie sonst bei der Ausreise konfisziert werden können.

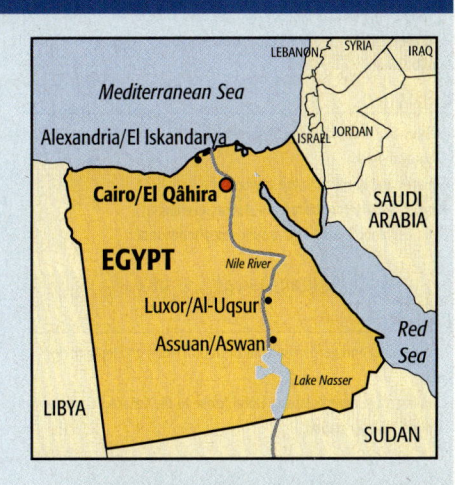

✱ L'homosexualité n'est pas interdite en Egypte. Signalons cependant que personne ne définit de façon précise ce qu'est une enfreinte à „la morale publique et au bon ordre". Les gais n'affichent pas leur homosexualité en public pour ne pas s'exposer au mépris des leurs ou de la société. La police est plutôt homophobe. Compte tenu des attentats perpétrés par les extrémistes contre des touristes, l'ambassade d'Allemagne au Caire recommande de ne pas trop faire état de son homosexualité.
A votre arrivée en Egypte, n'oubliez pas de bien faire tamponner et signer votre déclaration de devises. Déclarez aussi les objets de valeur que vous possédez. Ils pourraient vous être confisqués lors de votre sortie du pays.

SPARTACUS 2001/2002 | 223

Egypt Alexandria/El Iskandarya ▶ Luxor/Al-Uqsur

En Egipto la homosexualidad no está prohibida, no obstante aquí tampoco se define claramente la famosa cláusula "incumplimiento contra la moral pública o sentimientos generales". Para no ser discriminados por la familia y la sociedad, los gay no se muestran en público. La policía no es precisamente conocida por su amabilidad con los homosexuales. Debido a los ataques de musulmanes radicales contra turistas se recomienda no „demostrar abiertamente" la homosexualidad, como lo formula la embajada alemana en el Cairo. A la hora de entrar al país es importante insistir en que la declaración de divisas sea sellada y firmada. Se deberían también declarar los objetos de valor, ya que a la hora de salir del país podrían ser confiscados.

L'omosessualità non è illegale in Egitto, tuttavia vengono punite le "offese alla morale pubblica". I gay egiziani non manifestano la loro condizione per non sconvolgere la famiglia e la società. La polizia non può essere definita tollerante nei confronti dei gay. L'ambasciata tedesca in Cairo consiglia, dopo l'esperienza dei passati attacchi ai turisti da parte di estremisti musulmani, di non ostentare la propria omosessualità in pubblico. Entrando nel paese è importante farsi timbrare e firmare la dichiarazione della valuta. Vi consigliamo inoltre di dichiarare i vostri oggetti di valore all'arrivo nel paese, per evitare che alla partenza vi possano essere confiscati.

Alexandria/El Iskandarya ☎ 03

HOTELS
■ **Cecil** (AC B F H NG OS)
16 Saad Zaghoul Square ☎ 480 70 55
Downtown location, 10 min to the airport. All rooms have AC, telephone, fridge, private bath, balcony, TV and radio. US$ 26-30.
■ **Crillon** (g H)
5 Adib Street

CRUISING
- Stanley Bay and Sidi Bich (city beach)
- Montuzah Park
- Squares and gardens in the city center
- Ramleh Square (opposite tram station, evenings)
- Saad Zaghloul Square and around telephone kiosk

Assuan/Aswan ☎ 097

CRUISING
- Boat landing and garden in front of Oberoi Hotel on Elephantine Island
- Landing stage near Kalabsha Hotel (close to the Cataract Gardens)
- Around Railway station

Cairo/El Qâhira ☎ 02

BARS
■ **Al American** (B NG)
Tal'at Harb/Sitta W-'Asshrin Julyu
■ **Cafeteria Bodega** (AYOR g RT) 22-24h
Tawfik Street *(Pedestrian street)*
Local bars in Egypt are called "Cafeteria".
■ **Cafeteria Tawfik** (AYOR g RT) 11-02h
Tawfik Square
■ **Grapp D'Or** (g) 11-02h
Sarwat Street
Very crowded.
■ **Harry's Bar** (B NG)
Cairo Marriott Hotel ☎ 340 88 88

Uruba Street, Horreya ☎ 266 55 00
The Swan Bar & The Lobby Bar.

CAFES
■ **Amphitrion Café** (B F NG)
Al-Ahram Street, Nozha, Heliopolis
3 min. walk from Roxy Square. Open-air and indoor bar, café and restaurant.

DANCECLUBS
■ **Amonn Disco** (B D NG)
Sphinx Square
■ **Disco at Borg Hotel** (B D NG)

SAUNAS/BATHS
■ **Atfet el Manam** (AYOR R)
Sharia el Azhar
■ **Qualaqua** Best 9-19 h
Khan Al-Khalyly

CRUISING
- Talaat Harb-Street/Tahrir Square
- Tahrir Square (little garden in the middle, at night, best Wed and Thu)
- Café Fishaawi, Khan El Khalili, El Hussein quarter
- Café Umm Kulthuum (downtown near Tawfikia square, best Thu)

Luxor/Al-Uqsur ☎ 095

BARS
■ **Etap Hotel Bar** (B G H r)
Nile Corniche
Also try the Dakka Bar and the swimming pool (8-20 h).

CRUISING
- The Corniche (from the Museum to the winter Palace Hotel)
- Park between Temple of Amon and Luxor Hotel
- Landing place for Nile river-boats (near Winter Palace Hotel)
- Banana Island (at night)

El Salvador

Location: Pacific coast of Central America
Initials: ES
Time: GMT -6
International Country Code: ☎ 503 (no area codes)
International Access Code: ☎ 0
Language: Spanish; regional Nahuatl, Maya
Area: 21,041 km2 / 8,124 sq mi.
Currency: 1 El-Salvador-Colon (¢) = 100 Centavos
Population: 5,752,067
Capital: San Salvador
Religions: 92% Roman Catholic
Climate: Tropical climate. The rainy season lasts from May to October, the dry season from November to April.

✱ El Salvador's constitution does not mention homosexuality at all. The age of consent is set at 18 years, regardless of the sexual orientation. In general, the situation of gays in this country is nowadays much like that of gay men in western countries, not in a very sophisticated sense but discreetly acceptable. This improvement applies mainly to gay men and not to lesbians, who unfortunately do not have any organisations. Outside the larger cities being gay is however still a taboo and many people living in rural areas do not want to talk about it. For this reason most gay men move to the large cities.

El Salvador's main attraction is the diversity of people (Mestizo, Caucasian and Indigenous), places, landscapes and climates. There are impressive volcanoes, small lakes, black sand beaches (ideal for swimming, surfing and many other water sports) and archaeological sites with presence of the Mayan culture. The climate is very tropical. Parks and towns in higher altitudes have cool weather.

San Salvador is roughly 2,000 feet / 610m above sea level. It is a modern city. The picturesque „plazas" in the old part of the city are well worth visiting. There are several gay organisations as well as gay bars and discos. Most gay men, however, are to be found cruising in the main city malls (like Metrocentro) or in the Zona Rosa (exclusive part of the city). Since 1996 a Gay Pride parade takes place in the city in the month of June.
(Roberto Quintanilla - Interlengua)

✱ In der Verfassung El Salvadors wird auf Homosexualität mit keinem Wort eingegangen. Das Mündigkeitsalter liegt, unabhängig von der sexuellen Orientierung, bei 18 Jahren. Insgesamt gesehen ist die Situation von Gays in El Salvador heute annähernd mit der von Schwulen in westlichen Ländern vergleichbar, sie genießen zwar kein ausgeprägtes Verständnis, werden aber diskret geduldet. Dieser Fortschritt gilt hauptsächlich für Schwule, nicht für Lesben, die leider von keiner Organisation vertreten werden. Außerhalb der größeren Städte ist Schwulsein jedoch immer noch ein Tabu und viele Menschen, die in ländlichen Gebieten leben, möchten daher nicht darüber sprechen. Aus diesem Grund ziehen die meisten Schwulen in die größeren Städte.

Die unterschiedliche Herkunft der Menschen (Mestizen, Kaukasier und Einheimische) sowie die Vielfalt von Orten, Landschaften und Klimas machen die Attraktivität El Salvadors aus. Das Land besitzt eindrucksvolle Vulkane, kleine Seen, schwarze Sandstrände (das Meer ist ideal zum Schwimmen, Surfen und für viele andere Wassersportarten) sowie archäologische Stätten, an denen man die alte Mayakultur bewundern kann. Das Klima ist tropisch, in höher gelegenen Naturparks und Städten ist es dagegen kühl.

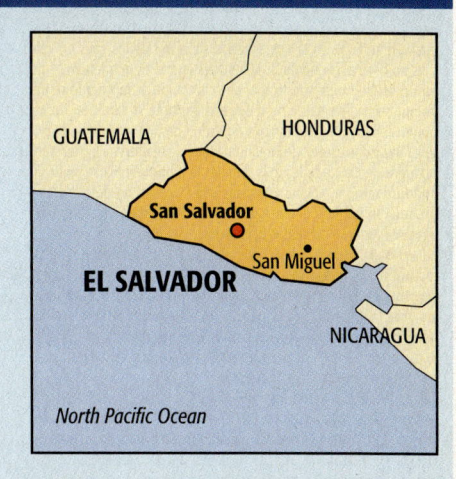

Die Hauptstadt San Salvador liegt ca. 2.000 Fuß/ 610 m über dem Meeresspiegel und ist eine moderne Stadt. Die pittoresken „Plazas" in der Altstadt sind einen Besuch wert. Hier gibt es mehrere Gay-Organisationen sowie Gaybars und -discos. Die meisten Schwulen halten sich edoch in den großen Einkaufszentren (wie dem Metrocentro) oder in der Zona Rosa, dem reichen und vornehmen Bezirk der Stadt, auf. Seit 1996 findet jedes Jahr im Juni eine Gay-Pride-Parade statt.
(Roberto Quintanilla - Interlengua)

✱ La constitution de El Salvador ne mentionne pas l'homosexualité. La majorité sexuelle est fixée à 18 ans pour tous. La condition des gais du pays est aujourd'hui semblable à celle des pays occidentaux, même si une plus grande discrétion est observée. Cette amélioration de la situation n'est cependant valable que pour les hommes, les lesbiennes n'ayant pas d'organisation de défense nationale. Dans les régions rurales, l'homosexualité reste un sujet tabou et beaucoup de gais se murent dans le silence ou immigrent dans les grandes villes.

L'attrait principal du pays réside dans la diversité de sa population (Mestizo, Caucasiens et indigènes), de ses régions et paysages, et de son climat. El Salvador possède des volcans impressionnants, des petits lacs, des plages de sable noir (idéales pour nager, surfer ou pratiquer d'autres sports nautiques) et des sites archéologiques empruntsde culture maya. Le climat est très tropical, les parcs nationaux et villes en haute altitude bénéficient d'un temps plus frais.

La capitale San Salvador, ville moderne, se situe à peine à plus de 610 m (2000 pieds) au dessus du niveau de la mer. Les magnifiques "plazas" de la partie historique de la ville valent un détour. Il existe plusieurs organisations, bars et clubs gais. Cependant, beaucoup de gais préfèrent draguer dans les centres commerciaux (par exemple Metrocentro) ou dans la Zona Rosa (quartier chic de la ville). Depuis 1996, une Gay Pride se tient chaque année au mois de juin.
(Roberto Quintanilla - Interlengua)

El Salvador — San Salvador

En la constitución de El Salvador ni siquiera se menciona la homosexualidad. La edad de consentimiento es de 18 años para todos, es decir que no guarda relación con la orientación sexual. En general, en la actualidad la situación de los gays en este país no difiere mucho de la de los gays en países occidentales - no en un sentido muy sofisticado, pero aceptada siempre que se lleve una vida discreta. Si ha mejorado bastante la situación de los hombres, las lesbianas todavía no gozan de una gran mejora, pues El Salvador carece de organizaciones de lesbianas. No obstante, fuera de las ciudades más grandes la homosexualidad sigue siendo un tabú, y muchas personas que viven en las áreas rurales no quieren hablar del tema. Por ello, la mayoría de los hombres gays se mudan a las ciudades grandes.

La atracción principal de El Salvador es la gran diversidad de gentes (mestizos, indígenas, europeos), paisajes y climas. Hay volcanes impresionantes, pequeños lagos, playas de arena negra (ideales para la natación, surf y muchos más deportes acuáticos) y lugares de interés arqueológico por los vestigios de la cultura Maya. El clima es tropical; los parques y las ciudades ubicados a más altura tienen un clima más moderado.

La capital San Salvador, una ciudad moderna, se encuentra a unos 610 metros (2.000 pies) sobre el nivel del mar. Las plazas pintorescas de la parte antigua de la ciudad merecen una visita. Hay varias organizaciones gays así como también bares y discotecas gays. Sin embargo, la mayoría de los gays pueden encontrarse en las zonas de cruising en los principales centros comerciales (como Metrocentro) o en la Zona Rosa (!), la parte exclusiva de la ciudad. Desde 1996, en el mes de junio se festeja una desfile de orgullo Gay en la ciudad.

(Roberto Quintanilla - Interlengua)

Nella costituzione di El Salvador non vi è alcun espresso riferimento alla parola omosessualità. Il raggiungimento della maggior età avviene al compimento del diciottesimo anno d1età, a prescindere dall1orientamento sessuale di ciascuno. Complessivamente la situazione dei gay a El Salvador è oggi tutto sommato paragonabile a quella degli omosessuali nei paesi occidentali, dove essi, sebbene non siano accettati senza riserve, sono perlomeno tollerati. Questo progresso verso l1emancipazione riguarda soprattutto gli omosessuali, non invece le lesbiche, che purtroppo non sono rappresentate da nessuna organizzazione. Al di fuori delle città più grandi l1essere gay rimane tuttavia ancora un tabù, e molte persone che vivono nelle zone rurali preferiscono perciò non parlare dell1argomento. Per questo motivo la maggior parte degli omosessuali si trasferisce nelle città più grandi.

La diversa provenienza etnica della popolazione (meticci, caucasici, e indigeni), così come la molteplicità dei luoghi, paesaggi e dei climi rendono El Salvador un paese attraente. Esso possiede vulcani impressionanti, piccoli laghi e spiagge di sabbia nera (il mare è ideale per nuotare, per praticare il surf, e per molti altri sport d1acqua), così come siti archeologici, nei quali si può ammirare la cultura dei Maya. Il clima è tropicale, ma nei parchi naturali e nelle città ad alta altitudine prevale invece il clima piuttosto rigido.

La capitale San Salvador è situata a circa 610 metri (2000 piedi) sopra il livello del mare ed è una città moderna. Assolutamente da non perdere le pittoresche "Plazas2 della città vecchia. Qui ci sono diverse organizzioni gay così come bar e discotebe per gay. La maggior parte degli omosessuali dimorano nei pressi del grandi centri commerciali (come il Metrocentro) oppure nella Zona Rosa, il ricco e signorile quartiere della città. Dal 1996 ogni anno in giugno ha luogo la Parata del Gay- Pride.

(Roberto Quintanilla - Interlengua)

San Salvador

BARS
■ **Kroll** (B D G)
Col. Flor Blanca
■ **Luna. La** (A NG)
2289 Calle Berlin, Urb Buenos Aires 3 (north of Boulevard Los Heroes) ☎ 260 292
Bar with live music.
■ **Silver Cup** (B G)
Condominio Juan Pablo II (Other end of the shopping center where Millenium is)
Not such good reviews about this place.

MEN'S CLUBS
■ **Opciones** (G msg P SNU S)
☎ 841 0929
Call Tony to become a member of this private club.

DANCECLUBS
■ **Kairos** (B D NG)
(in front of Bloom Hospital)
■ **Milenium** (B G D MA WE)
Alamenda Juan Pablo II (Opp. Sir Speedy copy shop)
More middle/lower class patronage.
■ **Olimpo** (B D G) Wed-Sat 22-?, Sun 17-24 h, closed Mon Tue
Alameda Juan Pablo II/Condominio Juan Pablo II No.315 (600m west of Boulevard de Los Héroes)
■ **Oráculos** (B D G YG TV) Wed-Sat 21-4 h
Condominio 2000/Boulevard de los Héroes (1st floor, near Las Tres Torres) ☎ 225 04 27
This is an anything goes disco with lots of transvestites.
■ **Scape** (AC B CC D G S)
1a Calle Pte. (Behingd Pizza Hut, in a shopping center with a sign for a big copyshop.)
Probably the most upscale gay disco in San Salvador.

RESTAURANTS
■ **Ventana. La** (A CC NG)
Calle San Antonio Abad ✉ 2335 (in front of San Luis Mall)
☎ 226 5129

CINEMAS
■ **Dario** (AYOR NG)
Calle Ruben Darío
■ **Majestic** (AYOR NG)
Avenida España

EDUCATION SERVICES
■ **Interlengua** (NG)
Col. Lourder 6G, Planes de Rend ☎ 280 52 85
✉ interlengua@yahoo.com ✉ www.geocities.com/interlengua

GENERAL GROUPS
■ **Entre Amigos**
Col. Y Pje. Sta Victoria # 50 ☎ 225 42 13
■ **Mano Amigo**
☎ 260 72 49
■ **Roca Blanda**
✉ vegeta42@latinmail.com
Upper class gay group.

San Salvador ▶ Tallinn | **El Salvador - Estonia**

HEALTH GROUPS
■ **Fundasida**
☎ 225 42 13

SWIMMING
-Majagual Beach
-La Libertad Beach

CRUISING
-Morazan Park/2nd Avenue (AYOR R)
-Metrocentro Mall(Centro Comercial, Boulevard de los Heroes)
-Boulevard Hypodromo
-Zona Rosa (Boulevard Hipodromo)
-Acajutla Port (R)

Estonia

Name: Eesti • Estland • Estonie
Location: Northeastern Europe
Initials: EST
Time: GMT +2
International Country Code: ☎ 372
International Access Code: ☎ 8 (wait for tone) 00
Language: Estonian, Russian, Ukrainian
Area: 45,100 km2 / 17,413 sq mi.
Currency: 1 Estonian Crown (ekr) = 100 Senti
Population: 1,421,335
Capital: Tallinn
Religions: Evangelical Lutheran, Russian Orthodox
Climate: Maritime climate. Winters are wet and moderate, summers cool.

Homosexuality between consenting adults is leagal. The age of consent is 14 for girls and 16 for boys, regardless of sexual orientation.

Einvernehmliche Homosexualität zwischen Erwachsenen ist legal. Das Schutzalter liegt, ungeachtet der sexuellen Orientierung, für Mädchen bei 14, für Jungen bei 16 Jahren.

L'homosexualité entre adultes consentants n'est pas un délit. En Estonie, la majorité sexuelle est fixée à 14 ans pour les filles et à 16 ans pour les garçons et ce, quelle que soit leur orientation sexuelle.

La homosexualidad por acuerdo entre dultos es legal. La edad de consentimiento, sin importar la orientación sexual, es de 16 años para varones; para mujeres es de 14 años.

L'omosessualità tra adulti consenzienti è legale. L'età legale per avere rapporti sessuali è, indipendentemente dall'orientamento, di 14 anni per le ragazze e di 16 per i ragazzi.

NATIONAL GROUPS
■ **Eesti Gayliit** (GLM)
PO Box 142 ✉ 10502 Tallinn 📧 gayliit@hotmail.com
Estonian Gay League.
■ **Estonian Leathermen's Club** (G LJ MA P)
PO Box 5705 ✉ 10302 Tallinn 📧 LMC_Estonia@lycus.com
For more information contact the club.

Pärnu ☎ 044

SWIMMING
-Beach of Pärnu

Tallinn ☎ 02

TOURIST INFO
■ **Estonian Tourist Board**
Mündi 2 ✉ 10146 ☎ 699 04 20 📠 699 04 32
📧 e-mail etb@tourism.ee 🌐 www.tourism.ee

BARS
■ **X Baar** (AC B DR F GLM) 15-1.30 h
Sauna 1 ☎ 620 92 66
Relaxed, discreet atmosphere.

DANCECLUBS
■ **Nightman** (AC B CC D F GLM MA S) Wed Thu 21-4, Fri Sat -6 h
Vineeri 4 *(Bus 5/18/36-Vineeri)* ☎ 26 18 47
One of the biggest gay club in the Baltics.

HOTELS
■ **Amarellius** (AC B CC GLM H)
Amarulluse 4, Viimsi, Viimsi vald ☎ 519 22 081
A small gay and lesbian hotel in Tallinn suburbs.

HEALTH GROUPS
■ **AIDS Support Centre** 15-18, Sat 12-14 h, Sun closed
Kopli 32 ☎ 641 31 65 📠 641 31 65
Support for people with HIV/AIDS.

Estonia - Fiji | Tallinn ▶ Suva

SWIMMING
- Pirita Rand. Beach on the right side from beach station to the end of the beach (area befor the stones and in forest)
- Klooga Rand. in the dunes (40 minutes by train from Tallinn)
- Stromi Rand. On the left side form beach station cruising in forest

CRUISING
- Harju Mägi-Park (entrance from Vabaduse Väljak, the best is Linda Monument)
- Toompea

Tartu ☏ 027

BARS
■ **Helleri Baar** (AC B DR F Glm) 21-4 h
Lossi street

CRUISING
- Banks of Emajögi River
- Laululava (the song festival field. Wed to Sat from April to October from 19-22 h)

Fiji

Name: Viti • Fidschi
Location: South Pacific Ocean
Initials: FJI
Time: GMT +12
International Country Code: ☏ 679 (no area codes)
International Access Code: ☏ 05
Language: English and Fijian, Hindi
Area: 18,274 km2 / 7,056 sq mi.
Currency: 1 Fiji-Dollar ($F) = 100 Cents
Population: 822,000
Capital: Suva
Religions: 53% various Christian denominations, 38% Hindu, 8% Moslem
Climate: Tropical marine climate. There's only slight seasonal temperature variation.

✳ Paragraphs 168-170 of the Fiji penal code make homosexuality completely illegal. Even an attempt is punishable. The maximum penalty for gay sex is 14 years imprisonment and for "attempted gay sex" seven years.

★ Gemäß den Artikeln 168-170 des Strafgesetzbuches der Fidschi-Inseln sind homosexuelle Handlungen verboten, selbst der "Versuch" ist strafbar. Die Höchststrafe für vollzogenen schwulen Sex ist 14 Jahre, die für "versuchten" schwulen Sex sieben Jahre Haft.

✳ Aux Iles Fidji, toute forme d'homosexualité est un délit (articles 168 à 170 du code pénal), même les „tentatives". On risque 14 ans de prison maximum. Pour une „tentative", on risque 7 ans.

✳ Según establecen los artículos 168-170 del Código Penal de estas islas, todo tipo de actividad homosexual queda terminantemente prohibida, incluso el intento está penalizado. La pena más alta por actos sexuales de tipo homosexual son 14 años de cárcel, por un "intento" de acto sexual pueden caer siete años de condena.

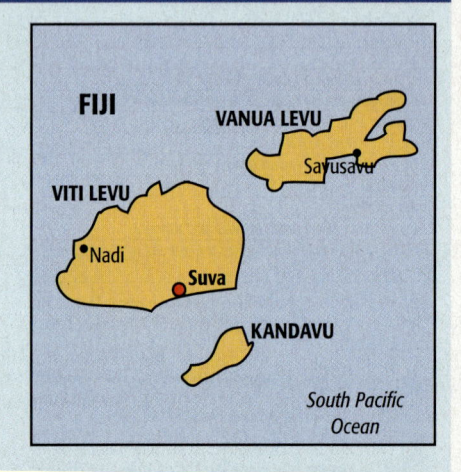

✖ I paragrafi 168-170 del codice penale delle isole Figi vietano ogni atto omosessuale e lo puniscono con la reclusione fino a 14 anni. Anche i tentativi di seduzione omosessuale sono punibili, la pena massima è di sette anni.

Korolevu

HOTELS
■ **Man Friday Resort** (B F GLM H)
PO Box 20 *(Coral Coast)* ☏ 500 185 📠 520 666

Nadi

HOTELS
■ **The West's Motor Inn** (AC B F CC NG PI)
Queens Road ☏ 72 00 44 📠 72 00 71
✉ westsmotelinn@is.com.fj
Located near international airport. 62 rooms with bath/shower/WC. All rooms with phone, balcony/terrace, radio. Hotel provides own key, car park and room service.

Suva

BARS
■ **Dragon. The** (B g)
Victoria Parade
■ **O'Reilly's** (B g)
5 McArthur Street ☏ 312 884

DANCECLUBS
■ **Lucky Eddie's / Urban Jungle** (B D g)
217 Victoria Parade *(Above O'Reilly's Bar)*
■ **Sugar Shack** (B D g)
54 Camavon Street ☏ 305 707
■ **Traps** (B D g) Mon-Sat
305 Victoria Parade ☏ 312 922

Suva Fiji - Finland

RESTAURANTS
■ **Bad Dog Café** (A F g)
McArthur Street/Victoria Parade *(Next to O'Reilly's)*
■ **Leonardo's** (B F g) Lunch & dinner, closed Sun
215 Victoria Parade ☏ 312 968

■ **Scott's** (B F g) Mon-Sat lunch & dinner, Sun dinner only
59 Gordon Street ☏ 305 620

APARTMENTS
■ **Town House Apartments** (AC B F g H)
3 Forster Street, Central Suva ☏ 300 055 📠 303 446
Rooms with private baths.

Finland

Name:	Suomi • Finnland • Finlande • Finlandia
Location:	Northern Europe
Initials:	FIN
Time:	GMT +2
International Country Code:	☏ 358 (leave the first 0 of area codes)
International Access Code:	☏ 00 or 990 or 994 or 999
Language:	Finnish, Swedish
Area:	338,145 km² / 130,558 sq mi.
Currency:	1 Finnmark (Fmk) = 100 Penniä.
Population:	5,149,242
Capital:	Helsinki/Helsingfors
Religions:	90% Christian
Climate:	Cold moderate subarctic climate, but comparatively mild because of the moderating influences of the North Atlantic Current, the Baltic Sea, and many of lakes.

✱ The laws in Finland have changed towards equality in recent years: age of consent is 16 for homosexuals and heterosexuals. Discrimination against homosexuals is a criminal offence. Partnership law for homosexual couples does not exist yet, but such law is to be introduced by government in 2001. General attitude towards gays and lesbians is tolerant, at least in big cities and among younger people. Every major city has a more or less active gay organisation, which almost all are part of the state-supported national organisation SETA. Travelling in Finland is expensive but, easy with good train and flight connections.

✱ In den letzten Jahren haben sich die Gesetze in Finnland in Richtung Gleichstellung bewegt: das Mündigkeitsalter für Homo- und Heterosexuelle liegt bei 16 Jahren. Die Diskriminierung von Homosexuellen gilt als strafbare Handlung. Ein Partnerschaftsgesetz für homosexuelle Paare existiert noch nicht, soll aber durch die Regierung im Jahr 2001 eingeführt werden. Die allgemeine Haltung gegenüber Lesben und Schwulen ist tolerant, zumindest in den Großstädten und bei jungen Leuten. Jede größere Stadt hat eine mehr oder weniger aktive Gay-Organisation, die fast alle der staatlich unterstützten nationalen Organisation SETA angehören. Reisen in Finnland ist teuer, jedoch aufgrund der guten Zug- und Flugverbindungen leicht und angenehm.

✱ La Finlande a modifié ces dernières années ses lois concernant l'égalité: la majorité sexuelle est fixée à 16 ans pour tous. La discrimination de personnes en regard de leur orientation sexuelle est également considérée comme un délit. Un partenariat pour les couples homosexuels n'existe pas encore, mais devrait être voté en 2001. L'attitude envers les gais et lesbiennes, particulièrement dans les grandes villes et chez les jeunes, est assez tolérante. Dans chaque ville importante du pays on trouve une organisation gaie plus au moins active, généralement une antenne de l'organisation nationale SETA qui est subventionnée par l'Etat. La Finlande possède un bon réseau de trafic ferroviaire et aérien,

ce qui rend les voyages assez aisé même s'ils restent onéreux.

✱ En los últimos años, las leyes finlandeses se han alterado en favor de la igualación y emancipación: la edad de consentimiento de homosexuales y heterosexuales es de dieciseis años. La discriminación de homosexuales es un acto punible. Todavía no hay una ley de parejas para homosexuales, pero su creación está prevista para el año 2001. En general, la postura hacia los gays y lesbianas es tolerante, al menos en las grandes ciudades y entre los jóvenes. Todas las ciudades un poco más grandes tienen una o varias organisaciones gays más o menos activas, todas ellas pertenecientes a la organización nacional SETA, que cuenta con el apoyo del Estado. Viajar en Finlandia no es barato, pero gracias a la buena infraestructura (trenes y aviones) es fácil y agradable moverse por el país.

✱ Negli ultimi anni la legislazione in Finlandia ha fatto dei passi verso l'equiparazione. La maggiore età sia per gli omosessuali che per gli eterosessuali è stata portata a 16 anni e la discriminazione degli omosessuali costituisce un reato. Una legge di unione coniugale per coppie omosessuali non esiste ancora, ma dovrebbe entrare in vigore nel 2001. L'atteggiamento generale nei confronti di gay e lesbiche è caratterizzato dalla tolleranza, almeno nelle grandi città e da parte dei giovani. In tutte le città più grandi esiste un'organizzazione gay più o meno attiva e quasi tutte appartengono all'organizzazione nazionale SETA promossa dallo stato. Viaggiare in Finlandia è costoso, ma comodo grazie agli ottimi collegamenti ferroviari e aerei.

Finland | Helsinki - Uudenmaan Lääni

Lost & Found
BAR · CAFE · RESTAURANT

HIDEAWAY BAR

The Only Hetero Friendly Gay Restaurant with Shows in Helsinki!

Good Food
Fully Licenced
2 Bars in 2 Floors
Frequent Shows
Open till 4 AM Every Night

Annankatu 6, 00120 Helsinki
Mon-Fri 14-04, Sat-Sun 13-04
Tel. 09-680 1010

NATIONAL GAY INFO

■ **Boyztown**
PO Box 18 ✉ 00531 Helsinki 📧 BTlenti@starmail.com
Contact magazine for gay men. Information and debates on gay life. Published quarterly.

■ **SETA (Seksuaalinen Tasavertaisuus ry)** (GLM) Mon-Tue 10-16, Wed 12-18, Thu 10-16, Fri 10-14h
Hietalahdenkatu 2 B 16 ✉ 00180 Helsinki ☎ (09) 612 32 33
🖨 (09) 612 32 66 📧 toimisto@seta.fi 🖥 www.seta.fi
National lesbian, gay, bisexual, transgender organisation. Local SETA member organisations all around Finland.

NATIONAL GROUPS

■ **Dreamwear Club ry** (TV)
PO Box 7 ✉ 33471 Ylöjärvi ☎ (040) 737 9131
📧 dreamwear@seta.fi 🖥 www.user.sgic.fi/~kjl/dreamwear.html
National transvestite organisation.

■ **Finnish AIDS Council** Mon-Fri 10-16 h
Hietaniemenkatu 5 ✉ 00100 Helsinki ☎ (09) 454 20 70
🖨 (09) 454 20 60 📧 hki@aidscouncil.fi 🖥 www.aidscouncil.fi

■ **Sateenkaariperheet** (GLM TV)
🖥 www.seta.fi/rainbow
Rainbow Families is an association for lesbian, gay, bisexual and trans-sexual parents.

■ **TRASEK ry** (TV)
☎ 411 00 171 📧 trasekry@yahoo.com
National transsexual organisation.

Helsinki - Uudenmaan Lääni ☎ 09

GAY INFO

■ **Helsingin seudun SETA ry** (GLM) Mon Tue Thu 10-16, Wed 12-18, Fri 10-14 h
Hietalahdenkatu 2 B 16 ✉ 00100 ☎ 612 32 33 🖨 612 32 66
📧 toimisto@seta.fi 🖥 www.heseta.fi
Very active gay and lesbian rights organization. Ask for their services.

■ **Radio SETA** Thu 18-18.30 h (FM 100,3 MHz)
(capital area only)

■ **SETA-Library** (GLM) Mon Tue Thu 10-16, Wed 12-18, Fri 10-14 h
Hietalahdenkatu 2 B 16 ✉ 00180 ☎ 612 32 33

TOURIST INFO

■ **Helsinki City Tourist Office** May-Sep: Mon-Fri 8.30-18, Sat Sun 10-15; Oct-Apr: Mon-Fri 8.30-16 h
Pohjoisesplanadi 19 ✉ 00100 ☎ 169 37 57

BARS

■ **Con Hombres** (AC B CC dr G LJ MA N OS) Mon-Sun 16-2 h
Eerikinkatu 14 ✉ 00100 ☎ 60 88 26

■ **Escale** (A AC B CC d G MA s) 15-2 h
Kansakoulukatu 1 ✉ 00100 ☎ 693 15 33

■ **Fairytale** (G) 16-02h
Helsinginkatu 7

■ **Lost & Found** (! AC B CC D f GLM MA s) Mon-Fri 14-4, Sat Sun 13-4, Hideaway Bar: 22-4 h
Annankatu 6 ✉ 00120 ☎ 680 10 10

■ **Mann's Street** (AC B cc d f GLM lj MA STV) 16-3 h daily
Mannerheimintie 12 A2 ✉ 00100 *(1st floor)* ☎ 612 11 03

■ **Nalle Pub** (B GLM OS) 15-2 h
Kaarlenkatu 35 ☎ 701 55 43

■ **Terrace** (G) Mon-Sat 9-22h
Pohjois- Esplanadi 41 *(Stockmann Department store, 6th floor)* ☎ 270 60 11

■ **Tom's Club** (B G LJ)
☎ 680 29 48
No club at the moment. Call or email for info.

DANCECLUBS

■ **DTM** (! B D GLM WE YG) 22-04h
Annankatu 32/Kansakoulukatu *(Near bus station)* ☎ 694 11 22
A very trendy disco in Helsinki.

RESTAURANTS

■ **Hercules** Every day 20-04h
Lönrotinkatu 4

SEX SHOPS/BLUE MOVIES

■ **ERIK 10** (G) Mon-Fri 9-18 h, Sat 10-14 h
Eerikinkatu 10 ✉ 00100 ☎ 602 368

■ **Keskusvideo** (G) 9-21, Sun 12-21 h
Eerikinkatu 10 ✉ 00010 ☎ 645 383

■ **King's Sex Video** (g) 9-22, Sat 9-16, Sun 12-16 h
Iso Roobertinkatu 38 ✉ 00120

■ **Sex Center** (g) 10-18, Sat 10-15 h
5 Linja 8 ☎ 773 30 04
Also mail order.

■ **Sex Shop Finland** (g)
Pengerkatu 24 ✉ 00500

■ **Sex 42** (g) 9-18, Sat 9-14 h
Iso Robertinkatu 42 ☎ 62 60 89

LEATHER & FETISH SHOPS

■ **Decadenz** (g)
Forum Shopping Centre
Leather, boots, jackets.

230 *SPARTACUS* 2001/2002

Helsinki - Uudenmaan Lääni ▶ Jyväskylä - Keskisuomen Lääni | Finland

MAIL ORDER
■ **Baffin Books** (GLM)
PO Box 50 ✉ 00240 ☏ 500 96 70 💻 baffin@baffinbooks.com
🖥 www.baffinbooks.com
Scandinavian biggest online gay and lesbian bookstore (Books, videos etc.)

GENERAL GROUPS
■ **OHO-Gay and Lesbian Students of Helsinki University** (GLM YG) Tue 19-21 h
Mannerheimintie 5B ✉ 00100 *(5th floor)* ☏ 612 32 66
🖥 ohory@yahoo.com

FETISH GROUPS
■ **Kinky Club**
PO Box 296 ✉ 00521 💻 kinky.club@sci.fi
🖥 www.kinkyclub.sci.fi
Gay and straight S/M.
■ **MSC Finland** Sat 22-2 h
PO Box 48 ✉ 00531 ☏ 680 29 48 💻 msc@saunalahti.f
🖥 www.saunalahti.fi/~mscfin
Member of ECMC and TOE.
■ **SM-fetisistiryhmä ry**
PO Box 352 ✉ 00531 ☏ (020) 651 1779

HEALTH GROUPS
■ **Helsingin Aids-tukikeskus** Mon, Wed 10-16, Tue & Fri 10-15h
Hietaniemenkatu 5 ✉ 00100 *(4th floor)* ☏ 454 20 70 📠 454 207 60 💻 info@aidscouncil.fi 🖥 www.aidscouncil.fi
HIV testing, information and psycho-social support
■ **Positiiviset ry** Mon-Fri 11-15 Sat 13-15 h
☏ 685 18 45 📠 694 63 87 💻 posy@dlc.fi 🖥 www.positiiviset.fi
Organisation for HIV+ people.

HELP WITH PROBLEMS
■ **Helpline** (GLM TV) Wed Sun 18-21 h
☏ 612 32 55

SPECIAL INTEREST GROUPS
■ **MSC Finland- Tom´s Club** (b DR f G LJ MA P VS)
PO Box 48 ✉ 00531 ☏ 680 29 48 💻 mscfin@sci.fi
🖥 www.sci.fi/~mscfin
MSC Finland has roughly 250 members. They are gay or bi-sexual men who are fetish fans in to leather, boots, uniforms, rubber,motorcycling or bondage/sm-sex.

SWIMMING
-Pihlajasaari (island 15 minutes by boat from Merisatama, the southernmost part of town)
-Tikkurilan uimahalli (in Tikkurila near youth-hostel)
-Uimastadion (g pi sa) (Outdoor pools near the Olympic stadium, open mid May to mid Sep)

CRUISING
-Stockmann department store (2nd & 5th floor)
-Main railway station (Metro-level, where the shops are)
-Mäntymäki AYOR (P) and park near Olympic Stadium)
-Laakso (in the Keskuspuisto/Central park behind the race track, evenings)
-last (P) highway 6 from Porvoo ⇌ Helsinki

Joensuu - Pohjoiskarjalan Lääni ☏ 13

BARS
■ **Molly's Pub** (AC B CC MA N NG)
Torikatu 20 ✉ 80100 ☏ 277 511
■ **Wanha Jokela** (A AC B BF F H MA N NG S)
Torikatu 26 ✉ 88100 ☏ 122 891
Old favorite of the local gays and lesbians. Also popular among intellectuals and artists.

DANCECLUBS
■ **EastWest** (AC B CC D NG WE YG)
Torikatu 20 ✉ 80100 ☏ 277 511
Not exclusively gay but worth a visit. Young and trendy clientele.

SEX SHOPS/BLUE MOVIES
■ **Seksipuoti Soho** (AC NG SNU VS)
Kauppakatu 17 ✉ 80100 ☏ 127 395
Very gay friendly, gay videos for rental and sale, toys, magazines, private shows, etc...

GENERAL GROUPS
■ **Joensuun SETA Demian Klubi ry** (b d GLM MA) Hotline 19-21 h
PO Box 188 ✉ 80101 ☏ 50 362 6865 💻 demian.klubi@sci.fi
🖥 www.seta.fi/demianklubi
Disco and other activities arranged regularly throughout the year at the Aavapirti. Ask or check the website for current information. For the Midsummer weekend in June hundreds of people from all over Finland and abroad gather to celebrate.

HEALTH GROUPS
■ **Red Cross** Tue 17-20 h
Kauppakatu 35 ☏ 226 336
Anonymous and free HIV-testing, support and information

SWIMMING
- Linnulahti (NG, popular beach during summertime, lots of yourng people - see cruising)
- Aavaranta (NG MA, popular beach during simmertime)

CRUISING
- Linnuanlahti (simmertime only, the rocks behind the trees to the right of the beach, very cruisy at sunny weahter)
- Virkistysuimala Vesikko (NG, MA, very cruisy weekday nights)

Jyväskylä - Keskisuomen Lääni ☏ 014

GAY INFO
■ **Jyväskylän Seta • Pink Club ry** (GLM) Thu 19-?, switchboard Wed 19-21, Youths 1st Sat 15-?, Discussions Sun 16-18 h
Yliopistonkatu 26, PO Box 410 40101 ✉ 40101 *(2nd floor.)*
☏ 310 06 60 💻 pinkclub@seta.fi
🖥 www.cc.jyu.fi/~tpkeskit/pink/

BARS
■ **Club Domino** (b g)
Yliopistonkatu 36
■ **Hemingway's** (B f g)
Kauppakatu 32 *(at pedestrian street)*

CRUISING
-Harju Park (in the center)
-Taulumäki (hill beside lake Tuamiojärvi)

SPARTACUS 2001/2002 | 231

Finland — Kotka - Kymenlaakso ▶ Rovaniemi - Lapin Lääni

Kotka - Kymenlaakso ☎ 05

BARS
- **Populus** (NG)
  Kotkankatu 16

GENERAL GROUPS
- **Kymen SETA ry** (GLM)
  PO Box 134 48101 ✉ 48000 ☎ (020) 65 125 65

Kuopio - Kuopion Lääni ☎ 17

BARS
- **Emigrant** (B g)
  Kauppakatu ✉ 70100
- **Henry's Pub** (B g)
  Kauppakatu ✉ 70100
- **Maxim's** (B g)
  Kauppakatu
- **Rosson Pub** (B glm)
  Haapaniemenkatu
- **Tähti** (glm)
  Kauppakatu

DANCECLUBS
- **Gloria**
  Kauppakatu

GENERAL GROUPS
- **Kuopion seudun SETA-Hile ry** (GLM) Wed Thu 18-20 h
  PO Box 213 ✉ 70101 *(3rd floor)* ☎ 261 95 56

SWIMMING
- **Kuopion uimahalli** (NG Pl SA SOL) Mon-Fri -20, Sat & Sun -16 h
  Hannes Kolehmaisen katu 3
  Best on weekdays.

Lahti - Hämeen Lääni ☎ 03

GENERAL GROUPS
- **PH Seta ry** (GLM) Wed 14-21
  PO Box 115 ✉ 15111 *(2nd floor)* ☎ 73 60 993
  ✉ phseta@hotmail.com

CRUISING
- Radiomäki

Mariehamn - Ahvenanmaa Åland ☎ 018

BARS
- **Brittany Bar** (B g WE)
  Norra Esplanaden 3 ✉ 22100
- **Hotel Arkipelag** (B F glm H) Wed F disco, other days orchestra
  31 Strandgatan ✉ 22100 ☎ 140 20
  Expensive.
- **Medley Night Club** (B glm) -3 h
  Ålandsvägen 44 ✉ 22100
- **Pub Adlon** (B g)
  Hamngatan 7

GENERAL GROUPS
- **Vildrosorna** Tue Thu 19-21 h
  PO Box 133 ✉ 22101 ☎ 049-90 73 64

CRUISING
- Lilla Holma Island

Oulu - Oulun lääni ☎ 08

BARS
- **Hilpeä Huikka & Yöhuikka** (B glm) Mon-Sat 17-3 h
  Mäkelininkatu 13 ✉ 90100
- **Madison** (B F g) Sun-Thu 11-1 h Fri, Sat 11-2 h
  Isokatu 18 ✉ 90100

SEX SHOPS/BLUE MOVIES
- **Sex-Market** (g) Mon-Fri 10-18, Sat 10-14 h
  Pakkahuoneenkatu 34 ☎ 375 985
  Gay section with magazines, videos etc.

GENERAL GROUPS
- **Oulun Seta ry** (GLM) Tue 18-20 h
  PO Box 177 ✉ 90101 ☎ 376 932 ✉ ouseta@na.netppl.fi
  🖳 www.netppl.fi/~ouseta/
  Disco twice a month, call for details.

HEALTH GROUPS
- **Oulun AIDS-Tukikeskus** Mon, Wed, 10-16h; Tue, Thu 10-17h
  Kirkkokatu 11 B 23 ☎ 379 398 📠 379 485
  ✉ oulu@aidscouncil.fi

CRUISING
- Oritkari park (3 km south-west of center)
- Hupisaaret (the park on the northern side of center, area behind the Summer Theater.)

Pori - Turun ja Porin lääni ☎ 02

BARS
- **Café Anton** (B g)
  Antinkatu 11 ✉ 28000

GENERAL GROUPS
- **Porin Seudun SETA ry** Helpline ☎ 231 03 35 Wed 18-21 h
  PO Box 261 ✉ 20101 ☎ 0600 902 61
  Parties once a month.

Rovaniemi - Lapin Lääni ☎ 016

BARS
- **Pub Paha Kurki** (B glm)
  Koskikatu 5 ✉ 96100
- **Pub Tupsu** (B glm)
  Hallituskatu 24
- **Roy Club** (B glm)
  Korkalonkatu ✉ 96100

DANCECLUBS
- **Maxim's** (B D glm)
  Koskikatu 11 ✉ 96100

GENERAL GROUPS
- **Rovaniemen SETA ry**
  PO Box 1216 96101 ✉ 96100 ☎ (040) 715 1173
  Parties once a month.

Seinäjoki - Vaasan Lääni ☎ 06

CRUISING
-Törnävänsaari

Tampere - Hämeen Lääni ☎ 03

GAY INFO
■ **Tampereen SETA Ry** (GLM) Mon-Fri 11-15 h, Helpline Tue 20-22 h
PO Box 381 33101, Hämeenpuisto 41 A 47 ✉ 33100 ☎ 214 87 21 ☎ 214 29 69 (helpline) 💻 treseta@sgic.fi
💻 www.treseta.oldhouse.sgic.fi

BARS
■ **Mixei** (B D f GLM OS S VS) Sun Wed Thu 22-3, Fri Sat 22-4 h
Otavalankatu 3 ✉ 33100 ☎ 222 03 64

SEX SHOPS/BLUE MOVIES
■ **Eros** (g) 10-18, Sat 10-15 h
Satamakatu 5
■ **Mansen Video** (g VS) 10-18, Sat 10-14 h
Hämeenpuisto 45
Big gay selection. Also mail order.

HEALTH GROUPS
■ **Tampereen AIDS tukikeskus** Mon-Fri 10-15 h, Hotline: Mon Wed Fri 15-18 h
Aleksanterinkatu 33A ✉ 33101 ☎ 3142 9532 ☎ 3142 9500 📠 3142 9530 💻 Tre@aidscouncil.fi 💻 www.aidscouncil.fi

CRUISING
-Alasenjärvi (surroundings of lake Alasenjärvi)
-Park Eteläpuisto (Park at the southern end of Hämeenpuisto and the area at the lakeside. In the evening.)

Turku - Turun ja Porin Lääni ☎ 02

BARS
■ **Café Bar Pyramid** (B GLM) 12-2 h
Kauppiaskatu 4 ✉ 20501
■ **Jack's and Mike's** (B CC d GLM lj MA s) Mon-Tue 17-2 h, Wed-Thu & Sun 18-3 h, Fri & Sat 21-03h
Humalistonkatu 17 B ✉ 20100 *(Next to railway station)*
☎ 2515 207

RESTAURANTS
■ **Turun kasvisravintola Verso** (F glm) Mon-Fri 11-17 h
Linnankatu 3 *(2nd floor)* ☎ 251 09 56

GENERAL GROUPS
■ **Homoglobiini** 1st & 3rd Mon 19-? h at ➡Jack's and Mike's (not Jun-Aug)
PO Box 288 ✉ 20101 💻 homoglobiini@iname.com
💻 org.utu.fi/tyyala/homoglobiini/
■ **Turun SETA ry** (GLM) Mon-Thu 12-18 Helpline Wed 18-21 h
PO Box 288, 20101, Rauhankatu 1 cB 22 ☎ 250 06 95
☎ 231 03 35 (helpline) 📠 251 29 05 💻 seta@tuseta.fi
💻 www.tuseta.fi

HEALTH GROUPS
■ **Turun AIDS-tukikeskus** Mon Tue 13-19, Wed-Fri 9-15 h Hotline: Mon-Fri 10-15 h
PO Box 850 ✉ 20101 *(4th floor)* ☎ 279 66 55
☎ 233 62 79 (hotline) 📠 279 6553 💻 Turku@aidscouncil.fi

SWIMMING
-Ruissalo Saaronniemi (g NU) (Nudist beach on the Island of Ruissa-lo behind the camping area)
-Samppalinna (g pi sa) (Outdoor swimming pool)
-Turun Ulimahalli (g NU pi sa) (Men only Tue Thu Sat 13-20, best after 17 h, Rehtorinpellontie 4, popular among gays.)

CRUISING
-Urheilupuisto (sporting park, around the ponds and cliffs near the upper sand field. From sunset till late at night.)

Vaasa - Vaasan Lääni ☎ 040

BARS
■ **Café Ernst** (B F glm)
Hietasaarenkatu 7 ✉ 65000
■ **Fondis Street Bar** (B glm) Mon Tue Thu 16-1, Wed Sat 16-3, Fri 16-2 h
Hovioikeudenpuistikko 15
■ **Fontana** (B D glm) 22-3, Wed Sat 21-4 h
Hovioikeudenpuistikko 15
■ **Kleine Olga** (B glm) Mon-Fri 17-2, Sat 14-2, Sun 18-24 h
Vaasanpuistikko 18 *(Hallinkuja)*
■ **Public Corner** (B glm) 12-1 h
Vaasanpuistikko 18
■ **Voho**
☎ 733 76 77

GENERAL GROUPS
■ **Vaasan seudun SETA ry** (GLM) Parties once a month
PO Box 162 ✉ 65101 ☎ 040-521 01 30 💻 vseta@walli.uwasa.fi

CRUISING
-Ahvensaari (behind the Ice Hall)
-Uimahalli (g) (swimming hall, Hietalahdenkatu 8, Tue & Thu evenings best)

France

Name: Frankreich • Francia
Location: Western Europe
Initials: F
Time: GMT +1
International Country Code: ☏ 33 (Do not dial the first "0" of phone numbers)
International Access Code: ☏ 00
Language: French. Regional languages (Basque, Bretton, Alsacian, Catalan, Corsican, Occitanian)
Area: 543,965 km² / 209,971 sq mi.
Currency: 1 French Franc (FF) = 100 Centimes. 1 EURO = 6,55 957 FF
Population: 58, 847,000
Capital: Paris
Religions: 81% Roman Catholic
Climate: Generally summers are mild and winters cool. Along the Mediterranean winters are mild and summers hot.
Important gay cities: Lyon, Marseille, Nice, Paris, Toulouse

✳ France is a country rich in culture and tradition with social tolerance to life and its gay community. Homosexuality is not seen as a crime and the age of sexual consent is generally at 16. Despite impressions to the contrary, the French are a very open and friendly people, even when they are not always able to be perfect in foreign languages. Establishing contact needs some effort, but once contact is made, they will be proud to show you their city and district, turning your holiday into a dream.

In the 80's emerged many gay establishments, such as Bars, Centres, Newspapers and Radio Stations. The gay movement has increased in importance and the Euro Gay Pride took place in Paris in 1997. It is not surprising to see in many public places two women or two men holding hands. A large gay press, channels to establish contact (Minitel, Telephone Networks), Bars, Saunas, a gay film culture, books and events account for the decline in the number of those still closeted. Today major figures in the public eye and also politicians have disclosed their homosexual tendencies. Recognition of same sex relationships, despite many difficulties, has been voted by the Parliament.

France is indeed not only Paris, but also the provinces. There has been the emmergence within the provinces in the last few years of many gay establishments, such as in Lyon, Toulouse or on the Côte d'Azur. Moreover, within the provinces it is possible to get to know the typical French cuisine, bountiful offerings, and friendliness of the locals inhabitants. Even when there are no bars or saunas to be found in the locality there are widespread opportunities to get to know people on the streets, on the beaches and also at events.

✴ Frankreich ist ein Land reich an Kultur und Traditionen. Auch ein tolerantes Land, hier leben und schwul zu sein ist leicht. Homosexualität ist kein Vergehen und die sexuelle Mündigkeit liegt generell bei 16 Jahren. Auch wenn man manchmal den gegenteiligen Eindruck gewinnen könnte, sind die Franzosen charmant und offenherzig, auch wenn sie nicht immer mit Fremdsprachen glänzen können. Zur Kontaktaufnahme muß man schon einmal eine kleine Anstrengung hinnehmen. Habt Ihr aber erst einmal Anschluß gefunden, so lieben die Franzosen nichts mehr, als stolz ihre Stadt und ihre Region zu zeigen: Eure Ferien können schnell zu einem Traum werden!

In den 80er Jahren entstanden viele homosexuelle Einrichtungen: Bars, Zentren, Zeitschriften und Radiosender. Die Schwulenbewegung gewann an Bedeutung und 1997 fand EuroGayPride in Paris statt. Homosexuelle verstecken sich immer weniger. An vielen Orten ist man nicht mehr erstaunt zwei Frauen oder zwei Männer Hand in Hand auf der Straße zu sehen. Eine große schwule Presse, Möglichkeiten des Kennenlernens (Minitel, Telefonnetzwerke, Bars, Saunas), eine schwule Filmkultur, Bücher und Veranstaltungen haben nicht zuletzt zu dieser Aufklärung geführt. Heutzutage stehen auch Personen des öffentlichen Lebens und aus der Politik offen zu ihrer Homosexualität. Die Anerkennung gleichgeschlechtlicher Lebensgemeinschaften, trotz zahlreicher Schwierigkeiten, trat 1999 in Kraft.

Frankreich heißt aber nicht nur Paris. Denn es gibt auch die Provinz. Auch dort haben sich in den letzten Jahren viele schwule Einrichtungn etabliert, in Städten wie Lyon, Toulouse oder an der Côte d'Azur. Eher dort als in Paris könnt Ihr das typische Frankreich kennenlernen, mit seiner Reichhaltigkeit, seiner Gastronomie und der Freundlichkeit. Und, selbst wenn Ihr dort keine Bar oder Sauna vorfindet, gibt es doch überall Möglichkeiten Leute kennenzulernen, auf den Straßen, an den vielen Stränden, auf Veranstaltungen...

✴ La France est un pays riche en traditions et en culture. C'est aussi un pays de tolérance, où vivre et être gai y est facile. L'homosexualité n'est pas un délit et la majorité sexuelle est fixée à 16 ans. Attention toutefois, les autorités sont parfois pointilleuses sur la notion d'"outrage public à la pudeur". Même s'ils donnent souvent l'impression du contraire, les Français sont des gens charmants, ouverts et désireux de faire la connaissance d'étrangers. Cependant, il est vrai qu'ils ne brillent pas par leur connaissance des langues étrangères et un effort est souvent nécessaire pour un premier contact. Mais une fois ce premier pas franchi, vous découvrirez des gens chaleureux, qui adorent faire visiter leur ville, leur région, et vos vacances deviendront vite un rêve.

Les années 80 ont vu la naissance de nombreux lieux où l'homosexualité s'est affichée: bars, associations, presse et radios. Avec l'organisation de la première Gay Pride puis, en 1997, de l'Euro Gay Pride, le militantisme a pris de l'importance. Des moyens de rencontre diversifiés (Minitel, réseaux téléphoniques, internet, bars et saunas), une riche culture cinématographique et littéraire gaie, et de nombreuses manifestations ont contribué à cet essor. On voit aujourd'hui des personnalités publiques revendiquer ouvertement leur homosexualité et il n'est plus rare de croiser dans la rue deux hommes ou deux femmes se tenant par la main. La reconnaissance juridique du couple gai (le PACS) a, malgré de nombreuses difficultés, été enfin voté par l'Assemblée Nationale en 1999.

Mais la France, c'est aussi la province, plus discrète. De nombreux pôles gays s'y sont développés ces dernières années dans des villes comme Lyon, Toulouse, ou sur la Côte d'Azur. C'est là, bien plus qu'à Paris, que vous découvrirez la France typique, généreuse, avec sa gastronomie et la gentillesse naturelle de ses habitants. Vous constaterez d'ailleurs que même s'il n'y a pas de bar, de sauna, ou de clubs, les contacts se lient facilement, que ce soit dans la rue, sur les nombreuses plages naturistes, ou au cours de manifestations locales.

Francia es un país rico en cultura y tradiciones. Sin embargo es un país tolerante, dónde es fácil vivir abiertamente la homosexualidad. Aquí la homosexualidad no es ningún delito y la edad de consentimiento está estipulado en 16 años para ambas orientaciones sexuales. Aunque a veces a uno le podría dar la impression contraria, los franceses son encantadores y abiertos, pero hablar otros idiomas no es precisamente uno de sus méritos más fuertes. Así que para entablar conversacion uno se tiene que esforzar al principio. Pero una vez que se ha establecido contacto, el francés se desvive para enseñaros orgullosamente su ciudad y su región, iasí que vuestras vacaciones se pueden volver en nada de tiempo en un verdadero sueño!

En los años 80 se fundaron innumerables establecimientos gay, entre ellos bares, centros, revistas y emisoras de radio. El movimiento gay ganó importancia y en año 1997 tuvo lugar la primera EuroGayPride en Paris. Las parejas homosexuales se esconden cada vez menos. En muchos sitios ya no se sorprende nadie, cuando dos mujeres o dos hombres pasean cogidos de la mano por las calles. Una amplia prensa gay, posibilidades de encuentro (Minitel, líneas telefónicas, bares, saunas), una cultura cineasta gay, libros y organizaciones han contribuido en gran parte a la acceptación social de la homosexualidad. Hoy en día, hasta famososos y políticos no tienen problemas en reconocer públicamente su ho-

mosexualidad. La acceptación legal de parejas homosexuales está entrará en vigor en 1999.

Pero Paris no es toda Francia, están también las provincias. Aquí también se establecieron en el curso de los últimos años muchas instituciones gay, sobre todo en ciudades como Lyon, Toulouse o por la Costa Azul. Son sitios mucho más adecuados que Paris para conocer la Francia típica, con su variedad, su cultura gastronómica y amabilidad. Y, aúnque a lo mejor allí no encontreís ningún bar o una sauna, existen múltiples posibilidades de conocer a gente, ya bien en las calles o en una de sus numerosas playas o fiestas.

La Francia è un paese ricco di cultura e tradizioni, ma anche un paese tollerante: come gay si può viverci facilmente. L'omosessualità non viene considerata reato, e l'età legale per rapporti sessuali è generalmente dei 16 anni. A volte però si può avere l'impressione opposta, perché i francesi non possono brillare sempre con le lingue straniere, ma a parte questo sono affascinanti ed aperti. Per mettersi in contatto bisogna fare qualche sforzo con la lingua francese. Una volta fatte delle conoscenze, la cosa che i francesi amano di più le far vedere la loro città e la loro regione. E così le vostre vacanze possono diventare un sogno. Negli anni ottanta sono emerse molte istituzioni gay: bar, centri di comunicazione, riviste e stazioni radio. Il movimento gay è diventato sempre più importante, e nel 1997 a Parigi si è svolta l'Euro-GayPride. Gli omosessuali si nascondono sempre di meno. In molti posti non c'è più nulla di speciale vedere due donne o uomini camminare tenendosi per mano. La stampa, le possibilità di conoscersi (Minitel, reti telefoniche, bar, saune), una cultura di film gay, librerie e diversi eventi hanno, tra l'altro, favorito a quest'apertura. Oggi anche persone della vita pubblica si dichiarono omosessuali. La legge per il convivenze tra omosessuali, malgrado alcune difficoltà, è entrata in vigore nel 1999.

Ma con la Francia non si intende solo Parigi: c'é anche la provincia. Anche lì, per esempio a Lyon, a Toulouse o alla Costa Azzurra, si sono aperti molti posti gay. In tali luoghi è più facile conoscere la Francia tipica nella sua ricchezza, gastronomia e gentilezza. Anche se in alcuni luoghi non trovete un bar o una sauna, ci sono dappertutto delle opportunità di conoscere della gente, per esempio per la strada, sulle numerose spiaggie, durante una delle tante manifestazioni o in occasione di spettacoli...

FRENCH LOVER GALLERY
WWW.JNRCPRODUCTION.COM
The Best in France
VIDEO / DVD

France

TÊTU

Le premier magazine gay et lesbien en France

Tous les mois en kiosque 30 F
+ l'agenda de 64 pages

Abonnement : 33 (1) 01 56 80 20 56/www.tetu.com

France

NATIONAL GAY INFO

■ **Agenda Projet X & Projet X Magazine** (G LJ)
PX Presse, Immeuble Métropole 19, 134/290 Rue d'Aubervilliers
✆ 75019 Paris ☎ 01.53.35.98.50 📠 01.53.35.98.80
✉ projetx@projetx.com 🌐 www.projetx.com
Gay SM monthly featuring the European SM and fetish establishments, meetings points and parties. Publisher of the Guide Hard (every two years) featuring all the European gay SM and fetish places.

■ **LSG-Ligue Esperantiste Gay Internationale**
c/o J.E.F.O., 4bis Rue de la Cerisaie ✉ 75004 Paris
Minitél: 3614 CNX, b.a.l. LSG. Gay association communicating in Esperanto (further addresses in Austria, Germany, UK and USA).

■ **Syndicat National des Entreprises Gaies**
44 Rue du Temple ✉ 75004 Paris ☎ 01.44.59.81.01
📠 01.44.59.81.03 ✉ lesneg@easynet.fr 🌐 www.sneg.org
Also coordinates Aids prevention in the Gay and Lesbian community

NATIONAL PUBLICATIONS

■ **Ex Aequo**
99 Rue de la Verrerie ✉ 75004 Paris ☎ 01.48.04.58.00
📠 01.48.04.58.00 ✉ Groupeillico@mail2.imaginet.fr

■ **Guide Gai Pied**
PX Presse, Immeuble Métropole 19, 134/290 Rue d'Aubervilliers
✆ 75019 Paris ☎ 01.53.35.98.50 📠 01.43.57.80.40
🌐 www.guidegay.com
Gay and lesbian guide for France and the French speaking parts of Belgium and of Switzerland. On sale at newstands and bookshops.

■ **Idol**
99 Rue de la Verrerie ✉ 75004 Paris ☎ 01.48.04.58.00
Gay magazine published every two month featuring general and cultural articles, fashion and erotic photos. FRF 35.- About 100 pages.

■ **Nouveau HH. Le** (GLM)
c/o NSP - Nouveau HH, B.P. 669 ✉ 75981 Paris Cedex 20
☎ 01.43.46.57.05
Contact ads gay magazine published 6x/year. FRF 22.-

■ **Pamplemousse** (GLM)
c/o Néopresse, 45bis Boulevard de la Liberté ✉ 35000 Rennes
☎ 02.23.40.49.77 📠 02.99.31.99.83
✉ redaction@neopresse.com
Magazine covering the "Big Lyon" region with news, articles and a gay guide.

■ **Têtu**
2 Boulevard de Magenta ✉ 75010 Paris ☎ 01.48.03.84.30
📠 01.48.03.29.00 ✉ tetu@tetu.com 🌐 www.tetu.com
Glossy, stylish gay newsmagazine.

■ **3. Keller**
3 Rue Keller ✉ 75011 Paris ☎ 01.43.57.21.47 📠 01.43.57.27.93
Monthly magazine of the Paris Gay & Lesbian Centre.

NATIONAL HELPLINES

■ **Ecoute Gaie** Mon-Fri 20-22 h
☎ 01.44.93.01.02
Psychological help for gays.

■ **Sida Info Droit**
☎ (0 800) 636 636 (toll-free)

■ **Sida Info Service**
☎ (0 800) 840 800 (toll-free)

■ **SOS Homophobie** Mon-Fri 20-22 h
☎ 01.48.06.42.41
Help in case of gay bashing.

NATIONAL PUBLISHERS

■ **Collection "Un sur Dix"**
D.L.M. Editions, 3 Rue de Castelnau ✉ 34090 Montpellier
☎ 04.67.72.18.18
Littérature et essais gay, catalogue disponible.

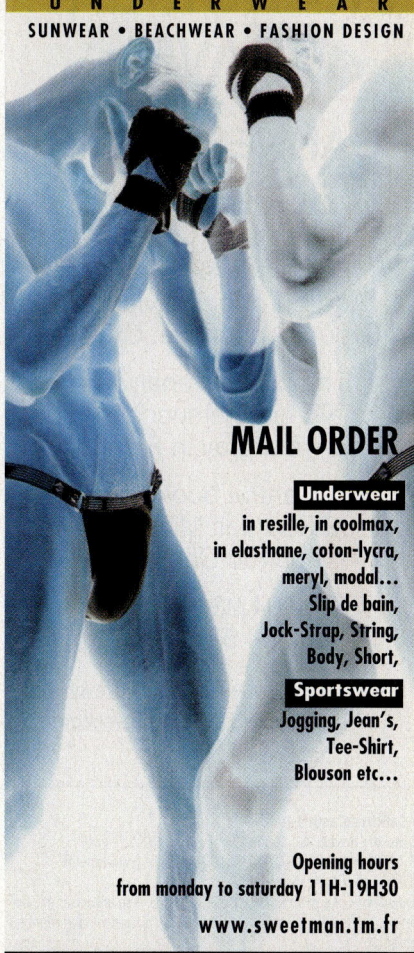

SWEETMAN®
U N D E R W E A R
SUNWEAR • BEACHWEAR • FASHION DESIGN

MAIL ORDER

Underwear
in resille, in coolmax,
in elasthane, coton-lycra,
meryl, modal...
Slip de bain,
Jock-Strap, String,
Body, Short,

Sportswear
Jogging, Jean's,
Tee-Shirt,
Blouson etc...

Opening hours
from monday to saturday 11H-19H30

www.sweetman.tm.fr

TO ORDER SEND YOUR ADRESS. A FREE CATALOGUE
DEMANDEZ GRATUITEMENT NOTRE CATALOGUE

Nom/Name :
Prénom/Surname :
Adresse/Address :
C.P./Zip code :
Ville/City : Pays/Country :

À retourner à/To return : SWEETMAN 36, Bld Sébastopol 75004 Paris
TÉL. : 33 (0)1 42 77 55 00   FAX. : 33 (0)1 42 77 75 65

SPARTACUS 2001/2002 237

France

FRANCE GAY TRAVEL

CANNES PARIS BORDEAUX

For all tours in France
And Europe. Individuals,
Groups, Incentive, Cruises

The professional way
To ensure success
To your stay in France

Central booking:
3 Rue des Mimosas
06400 Cannes

Tél: 04.93.38.16.95
Fax: 04.93.38.28.73

E-mail: noelcastinel@francegaytravel.com
Website: www.francegaytravel.com

■ **GaiKitschCamp** 9-19 h
38 bis Rue Royale ✉ 59800 Lille *(near Rue d'Angleterre)*
☎ 03.20.06.33.91   📠 03.20.78.18.76   ✉ gkc@worldnet.fr
💻 www.gaykitschcamp.com
Rare editions of gay texts. Ask for the catalogue. Also organises the Gay Film Festival in Lille "Question de Genre". Also documentation centre & bookshop.

■ **Groupe David Gerard**
115 Rue du Temple ✉ 75003 Paris ☎ 01.42.71.73.75
Supplier of services télématiques like 3615 GAY, BRONX, TBM, TORSO...

■ **Groupe Gai Pied**
Immeuble Métropole 19, 134/140 Rue d'Aubervilliers
✉ 75019 Paris ☎ 01.53.35.98.50
Publisher of L.F.M., Gai Pied Guide, E.T.R., Projet X and electronic networks.

■ **Illico Groupe**
99 Rue de la Verrerie ✉ 75004 Paris ☎ 01.48.04.58.00
📠 01.48.04.05.92 ✉ e-llico.com
Publishes Illico, Double Face (these two for free at gay venues in Paris) and Idol, Trixx, Fresh and Ex Aequo.

■ **Opale**
B.P. 131 ✉ 59564 La Madeleine Cedex ☎ 03.28.04.08.08
📠 03.28.04.08.01 ✉ first-videomag@first-videomag.fr
💻 www.querel.com
Published of gay erotic magazines & videos: Querel, 1ère Gay, Jeunes Mâles, Lord's Vidéo, Casting Gay, Mâles, France Vidéo Gay, Européan Vidéo Gay, Jeunes Mâles Video, 1ère Gay Vidéo. Production of gay erotic photos & videos: Michel Olivier Productions & First Production. Mail Order company.

■ **RLO** (G)
B.P. 8063 ✉ 34037 Montpellier ☎ 04.67.425.109
📠 04.67.471.149 ✉ rlo@infonie.fr 💻 www.editions-rlo.com
Publisher of contact ads, regional news, erotic photos and places of interest magazines covering the South of France: Guide Gay Lettre Ouverte (yearly), Lettre Ouverte, Journal Lettre Ouverte & Pocket Annonce.

NATIONAL COMPANIES

■ **Comme des Anges Productions** (G VS)
12 Rue Royale ✉ 69001 Lyon ☎ 04.72.98.88.61
📠 04.72.87.02.67 💻 www.commedesanges.com
Producer of gay erotic videos. Mail-order.

■ **Editions Gaies et Lesbiennes**
15 Rue d'Estrées ✉ 75007 Paris ☎ 01.46.33.35.31
📠 01.46.33.35.31 ✉ edigaies@club-internet.fr
💻 www.edigaies.com

■ **French Art**
64 Rue de Rome ✉ 75008 Paris ☎ 01.45.22.57.35
📠 01.42.93.21.17 💻 www.cadinot-films-france.com
The world famous Cadinot film production company.

■ **Gay Boutik** (CC GLM)
Immeuble Métropole 19, 134/140 Rue d'Aubervilliers
✉ 75019 Paris ☎ 01.53.35.98.50 ✉ dbenoist@gaypied.fr
💻 www.gayboutik.com
Minitel 3615 Gayboutik. Gay fiction, videos, erotic books and videos, fashion, gadgets. Mail order.

■ **Hors-Série** (G MA) Mon-Fri 9.30-13, 14-18.30 h
☎ (0803) 103 100 (Paris) ☎ 03.29.96.74.20 (Province)
📠 03.29.96.74.30
Gay travel agency.

■ **Illico IEM Mail Order** 10-19.30 h
PO Box 276 ✉ 75464 Paris Cedex 10 ☎ 01.40.18.51.51
📠 01.40.18.51.50 ✉ iem.mailorder@wanadoo.fr 💻 www.iem.fr
Write for free catalogue. Selection of videos, photobooks, DVDs, leather and latex clothing and accessories, underwear, condoms etc.

■ **Men Store • Groupe Illico**
99 Rue de la Verrerie ✉ 75004 Paris ☎ 01.48.04.58.00
Catalogue in Illico magazine.

■ **New Millenium Production**
5 Rue Frédéric Loliée ✉ 75020 Paris ☎ 01.43.73.23.05
📠 01.43.73.23.05 ✉ new.millenium.prod@mageos.com
X gay film production and distribution company. Also photos. Casting by appointment only / Société de production et de distribution de films X gays. Agence de photos érotiques. Casting sur RDV seulement.

■ **Queerbox.com**
129 Rue du Faubourg St. Antoine ✉ 75011 Paris
☎ 06.09.37.21.23 📠 01.42.46.60.83
E-business, shopping and services, books, travel, art, sex-shop, etc.

■ **SR Films (JNRC)** (G VS)
P.B. 119 ✉ 13443 Marseille Cantini Cedex 06 *(Office and casting: 1, rue Pytheas, 13001 Marseille)* ☎ 06.07.54.99.55 ☎ 04.91.33.42.90
(Casting) ✉ jnrcpacwan.fr 💻 www.jnrcproduction.com
The films of Jean-Noël René Clair. Gay erotic videos.

■ **Tom's Boutic**
8 Allée des Tulistes ✉ 69130 Ecully

Agen ▸ Aigues Mortes — France

NATIONAL GROUPS

■ **Girth & Mirth France**
P.B. 972 ✉ 25000 Besançon Cedex ☎ 03.81.47.01.41
Association for "Bears Daddy's" and other large gays and their friends. Organises meetings and parties in Lyon, Marseille and Nice.

■ **M.E.C. (Mecs en Caoutchouc)**
B.P. 19 ✉ 77191 Dammarie les Lys Cedex
☎ 01.64.87.07.92 (Pascal Bourcier)
☎ 01.42.57.81.00 (Michel-Jean Roupert)
National rubber club. Publishes contact club Magazine "Plan K" with pictures, ads and so on.

■ **Rando's**
B.P. 419 ✉ 75870 Paris Cedex 18
Walking and hiking group.

COUNTRY CRUISING

- A6 Paris ⇄ Lyon
- P de Nemours (direction Paris)
- P de Villabe (between Fontainebleau and Evry, direction Paris) Exit Chalon-sur-Saône, direction Montceau-les-Mines (in the forest/ dans le bois)
- A7 Lyon ⇄ Marseille
- P de la Combe Tourmentée (before Vienne Reventin)
- P de la Grande Combe (at the end near the toilets, evenings)
- P d'Orange (both direction : Le Cres und Coudoulet)
- A8 Aix-en-Provence ⇄ Nice
- P Aire de Briguière
- A9 Nîmes ⇄ Montpellier
- P de Saint-Aunès, km 91.5, direction Nîmes/Montpellier, day and night)
- A31 Lyon ⇄ Metz
- P de Boncourt (between Nuit St Georges and Dijon)
- P de Corgoloin (after Beaune, direction Nancy)
- P de Flagey Echezeaux (between Dijon and Nuit St Georges)
- A43 Lyon ⇄ Grenoble
- P La Tour du Pin
- A50 Marseille ⇄ Nice
- P de Sanary Saint-Cyr
- P de Vidauban
- A61 Toulouse ⇄ Villefranche de Lauragais
- P de Renneville
- P de Bazièges
- RN7 Roanne ⇄ Lyon
- P des Estivaux (8 km from Roanne)
- RN10 Bordeaux ⇄ Paris
- P de Saint Appoline (after Cloyes, direction Chartres)
- P de Maine de Boixe
- P de Bedenac
- RN71 Troyes ⇄ Dijon
- P between Fouchère and Virey sous Bar (evenings)
- RN137 Nantes ⇄ Rennes
- P de Puceul (south of Nozay, both directions)
- P between Rochefort and La Rochelle
- RN141 Limoges ⇄ Angoulême
- P Bourganeuf
- RN147 Mirebeau ⇄ Loudun
- P les Scevolles

Agen ✉ 47000

CRUISING

- Quais de la Garonne
- Jardin Jayan
- Le Gravier
- Bords de la Garonne (after pont du canal)

Aigues-Mortes ✉ 30220

RESTAURANTS

■ **Café de Bouzigues** (AC b CC F glm OS)
7 Rue Pasteur ✉ 30220 ☎ 04.66.53.93.95

■ **Camargue. La** (A AC B CC E F MA N NG OS S) Tue-Sun lunch and dinner
19 Rue de la République ✉ 30220 ☎ 04.66.53.86.88
Cuisine Camargue style.

■ **Goulue. La** (F glm OS) 12-14.30, 19-23 h, closed Oct-Mar
2ter Rue Denfert Rochereau ✉ 30220 ☎ 04.66.53.69.45
Local, international and fish specialties.

■ **Incognito. L'** (CC glm F MA OS WE) 12-14.30, 18.30-22.30 h, Closed Dec-Feb
Place de la Viguerie ✉ 30220 ☎ 04.66.53.94.91

■ **Minos. Le** (E F g OS) 12-14.30, 19-22.30 h
7 Place St. Louis ✉ 30220 ☎ 04.66.53.83.24

HOTELS

■ **Big Ruby's L'Orangerie** (AC B BF CC E F glm H msg nu PI SA SB WH WO)
35 Boulevard Gambetta ✉ 30220 ☎ 04.66.53.10.23
📠 04.66.53.08.72 ✉ france@bigrubys.com 🌐 www.bigrubys.com
All bedrooms have King or Queen beds, heating, phone, cable TV and VCR, fridge, clock radio. Rates low season FF 750-1150, mid-season 950-1400, high season 1400-1800.- incl. bf, complimentary wine and beer. Off street parking, computer facilities, daily shuttle service to the beach.

■ **Royal Hotel** (AC BF F H MA NG OS PI)
Route des Nîmes ✉ 30220 ☎ 04.66.53.66.40

Big RUBYS
GUESTHOUSE

KEY WEST, USA
305-296-2323

LA PLANTACION
MANUEL ANTONIO, COSTA RICA
506-777-1332

L'ORANGERIE
AIGUES-MORTES, FRANCE
33-4-66-53-10-23

1-800-477-7829 USA/CANADA
www.BigRubys.com

France Aigues Mortes ▶ Angers

APARTMENTS
■ **Villafoldeys** (G H MA PI)
La Malamousque ✉ 30220 ☏ 04.67.92.60.40
Studios to rent.

SWIMMING
-Plage de l'Espiguette (take Road D255 to the Phare de L'Espiguette, [P] on the big chargeable at the extreme end, on the beach go to the left, gay after 1.5 km)

Aiguines ✉ 83600

HOTELS
■ **Vieux Château** (B F glm H) 1st of Apr-31st of Oct
✉ 83630 *(core of the village)* ☏ 04.94.70.22.95
📠 04.94.84.22.36 ✉ hotelduvieuxchateau@free.fr
✉ aiguines@fcc.fr

Aix-en-Provence ✉ 13100

BARS
■ **L'Arène** (AC B CC d DR G p s VS YG) 12-2 h
38 Rue des Bernardines ✉ 13100 ☏ 04.42.27.66.90
The gay meeting-place of Aix.

SAUNAS/BATHS
■ **Aix** (AC b DR G MA SA SB SOL VS) 12-20.30, Wed Fri 12-24 h
8bis Rue Annonerie Vieille ✉ 13100 *(between Rue Aude and Rue Bedarrides)* ☏ 04.42.27.21.49
Very discreet sauna on three floors.

TRAVEL AND TRANSPORT
■ **Council Travel Services**
12 Rue Victor-Leydet ✉ 13100 ☏ 04.42.38.58.82

CRUISING
-Cours Mirabeau
-Parc Jourdan (AYOR) (jour et nuit/day and night)

Aix-les-Bains ✉ 73100

CRUISING
-Plage/beach de Brison-St-Innocent
-Parc des Thermes
-Petit-Port
-Esplanade du lac (Avenue du Grand Port)
-Cours Mirabeau
-Parc Jourdan (jour et nuit/day and night)

Albertville ✉ 73200

CRUISING
-Les Trois Etoiles (Avenue des Chasseurs-Alpins, garden)
-[P] at the swimming pool

Albi ✉ 81000

SEX SHOPS/BLUE MOVIES
■ **Eden. L'** (g MA VS) 9-2 h Thu (G)
23 Rue Croix-Verte ✉ 81000 ☏ 05.63.38.76.77

CRUISING
-Place de la Cathédrale (passage)
-Monument aux Morts
-Route D84: woods beyond the quarry on the top of the hill, left side, afternoons

Allauch ✉ 13190

DANCECLUBS
■ **Mare aux Diables. La** (B D G OS s) Fri Sat & evenings before holidays
Chemin de Bon-Rencontre ✉ 13190 ☏ 04.91.68.24.10
Car or taxi necessary.

Ambilly ✉ 74100

SAUNAS/BATHS
■ **King** (B CC DR f G MA p SA SB SOL VS WH) 14-23, Sun -20 h, Tue Fri mixed
39 Rue Jean-Jaurès, Immeuble l'Impérial ✉ 74100 *(in front of the Town Hall)* ☏ 04.50.38.68.12
350 m^2 sauna with beauty shop.

Amiens ✉ 80000

GENERAL GROUPS
■ **GLH d'Amiens**
✉ 80000 ☏ 03.22.91.24.49

HEALTH GROUPS
■ **Centre de Prévention Santé** Mon-9-12, 14-18, Tue-Thu 9-12, 14-17, Fri 9-17 h
16bis Rue Fernel ✉ 80000 *(near St. Leu church)* ☏ 03.22.91.07.70
Free and anonymous HIV testing.

CRUISING
-[P] Montjoie (between Amiens & St-Fuscien)
-The garden at the circus
-Behind Hatoie-Tivoli
-Railway Station

Angers ✉ 49100

BARS
■ **Cordonnerie** (a AC B G MA VS) 14-2 h
6 Rue Boisnet ✉ 49100 *(Place St. Serge)* ☏ 02.41.24.07.07
■ **Variétés. Les** (B G YG) 9-2 h
33 Boulevard Foch ✉ 49100 ☏ 02.41.88.46.62

SAUNAS/BATHS
■ **Maine. Le** (b DR G MA SA SB VS WH) 14-21, Fri Sat -24 h
6 Rue Valdemaine ✉ 49100 *(bus-Ralliement)* ☏ 02.41.20.30.16
Discreet sauna in the centre of the town.
■ **144. Le** (b DR G MA SA SB VS WH) 13-1 h, Mon and Thu mixed
144, 146 Rue Larevellière ✉ 49100 *(Direction St. Barthélémy, opposite Cimetière de l'Est)* ☏ 02.41.60.39.74

MASSAGE
■ **Chiron J.P.** (g MSG)
36 Rue Florent-Cornilleau ✉ 49100 ☏ 02.41.37.53.88
Massage, relaxation.

Angers ▶ Antibes | **France**

HEALTH GROUPS

■ **Dispensaire Gougerot** Mon 17.30-19, Tue 9.30-11, Fri 17.30-19.30 h
Avenue de l'Hôtel-Dieu ✉ 49100 *(near SAMU before the emergencies entrance/près du SAMU avant l'entrée des urgences)*
☎ 02.41.35.32.24

CRUISING

-Railway station
-Jardin des Plantes (day)
-Jardin du Mail
-Place de La-Rochefoucault
-Place du Maréchal-Leclerc
-Place du Tertre
-Château (Esplanades du Pont-Ligny)
-Montée Saint-Maurice (in front of the fountain)

Anglet ✉ 64600

SAUNAS/BATHS

■ **Sauna Le Beau-Lieu** (AC B CC DR f G MA p SA SB SOL VS) 12-24, Fri Sat -4 h
27 Rue Beaulieu ✉ 64600 *(Quatier St-jean, near Biarritz)*
☎ 05.59.58.20.39
Sauna on 500 m² with labyrinth & free SOL incl. entrance fees. Free private parking places available.

SWIMMING

-Plage de Chiberta (be discreet)

Angoulême ✉ 16000

DANCECLUBS

■ **George Sand Club** (AC B D DR Glm MA p S SNU VS) 23-5 h, closed Mon Tue
92 Rue de Limoges ✉ 16000 ☎ 05.45.68.46.15
FAX 05.49.41.77.67.

SAUNAS/BATHS

■ **Bleu Marine** (b DR G MA P SA SB VS WH) Mon Thu 12-20, Wed Fri 14-23, Sat 15-20 h, closed Tue Sun
10 Rue Nesmond ✉ 16000 *(Bus-Maison d'Arrêt)* ☎ 05.45.94.43.11
Small intimate sauna with a mixed crowd.

CRUISING

-Jardin vert (at daytime)
-Place Pablo Cassals (near the barracks, night)
-Place de New York
-Around the theatre
-Les Ramparts
-Forêt de la Braconne (6 km north of Angoulême. Take road 141 to Limoges, turn to the right at second road after passing "Les Rassats". Very busy at daytime.)

Annecy ✉ 74000

BARS

■ **Comédy Café** (AC B CC d G MG) 17-1 h in winter, 17-2 h in summer.
Passage des Sorbiers - 13 Rue Royale ✉ 74000 *Near the Post office.*
☎ 04.50.52.82.83
■ **X.DR** (B DR G LJ OS p P NU VS YG) 20-3 h, closed on Mon
13 Avenue du Rhône ✉ 74000 ☎ 04.50.51.04.20

DANCECLUBS

■ **Happy People** (AC B CC D DR GLM P snu stv tv YG) 23-5 h
48 Rue Carnot ✉ 74000 *(between SNCF station and the old town)*
☎ 04.50.51.08.66
■ **Point G. Le** (B GLM) 22-5 h, closed on Sun
26 Rue Vaugelas ✉ 74000 ☎ 04.50.45.53.38
■ **Stud'. Le** (B D GLM MA P) 23-5 h
9 Avenue du Rhône ✉ 74000 ☎ 04.50.45.01.04

RESTAURANTS

■ **At the Villa** (B BF CC F GLM OS tv YG) 9-1 h
48 Rue Carnot ✉ 74000 *(between SNCF station and the old town)*
☎ 04.50.52.93.25

SAUNAS/BATHS

■ **Oxygène** (b DR G SA SB VS WH) Mon-Thu (G) 13-20 h, Fri-Sun mixed
12 Avenue Mandallaz ✉ 74000 *(Near Banque de France)*
☎ 04.50.51.16.05
300 m² sauna frequented by a mixed age crowd.
■ **Sauna des Romains** (b DR G MA SA SB VS) 14-23, Fri Sat -2 h
15 Rue de Narvik ✉ 74000 ☎ 04.50.57.89.52
Sauna with pool table on 400 m².

SWIMMING

-Pont d'Onnex sur le Fier, Annecy-le-Vieux

CRUISING

-Place des Romains
-Place Tochon
-Place de la Mairie
-Place Stalingrad
-Place de la Visitation
-Jardin de l'Europe
-P at the SNCF station

Annemasse ✉ 74100

SEX SHOPS/BLUE MOVIES

■ **King Video Club & Boutique** (DR G MG VS) 14-23, Sun 14-20 h
39 Avenue Jean Jaurès ✉ 74100 *(opposite Ambilly town hall)*
☎ 04.50.38.68.12

CRUISING

-P in front of cemetery (under Place André)
-Clairière de l'ancien Ball Trap

Annonay ✉ 07100

CRUISING

-Place du Champ-de-Mars
-Post office/La poste

Antibes ✉ 06600

BARS

■ **Rendez-Vous. Le** (B f glm MA) Tue-Sat 18-0.30 (Oct-Apr), Tue-Sun 18-2.30 h (May-Sep)
5 Cours Massena ✉ 06600 ☎ 04.93.34.17.77

DANCECLUBS

■ **Golden Gate** (B D G MA) Thu-Sun
4 Rue Honoré Ferrare ✉ 06600 *(near SNCF station)*
☎ 04.93.74.24.74
Dance sex club. Many theme parties.

SPARTACUS 2001/2002

France | Antibes

SpartacusWorld.com
▶ click and ▶ win!
www.spartacusworld.com

SEX SHOPS/BLUE MOVIES
■ **Eroshop** (AC CC g lj VS) Mon-Sat 10-23 h
6 Rue Vauban ✉ 06600 *(2 minutes from the port, near Place de Gaulle)* ☏ 04.93.34.09.04
The only daytime cruising place. Big screen room and DVDs.

HOTELS
■ **Garoupe. La** (b F g H) 19.45-23 h, 15 Jun-30 Sep
81 Boulevard Francis-Meillant ✉ 06600 ☏ 04.93.61.54.97

■ **Hôtel Méditerranée** (b BF H MA NG OS)
6 Avenue Maréchal Reille ✉ 06600 ☏ 04.93.34.14.84
🖷 04.93.34.43.31
Centrally located. 5 minutes to the beach. Rooms with TV, telephone, bath/WC.

■ **Relais du Postillon. Le** (A B BF CC F glm H MA OS) Restaurant: 8-23 h, closed Sun evening
8 Rue Championnet ✉ 06600 *(In old town, close to post office)*
☏ 04.93.34.20.77
🖷 04.93.34.61.24
✉ postillon@riviera
🖥 relais-postillon.com
Restaurant and hotel.

CRUISING
-The garden of the railway station
-Phare de la Garoupe
-Fort Carré
-Remparts du Port-Vauban (evenings)

EROSHOP
ANTIBES

VIDEOS, GADGETS, MAGAZINES, LEATHER SHOP, CRUISING

**2 FLOORS OF PROJECTION CABINS
PROJECTION ROOM
D.V.DS.**

6,rue Vauban - Antibes
tél.04.93.34.09.04

150 mts from the port

10 H
23 H

Arcueil ✉ 94110

CRUISING
- Quai Gambetta
- Parc Public

Argelès-sur-Mer ✉ 66700

BARS
■ **Pot-Chic. Le** (AC B CC D DR GLM MA OS p SNU TV VS) Fri-Sun and before public holidays 23-? h, Jul-Aug: Mon-Sun
4 Allée des Palmiers ✉ 66700 *(Centre Commercial Costa Blanca)*
☎ 04.68.81.08.86

RESTAURANTS
■ **Crêperie Alexandre** (b CC F glm OS TV YG) 01 Apr-30 Sep 12-1 h
Rue des Roses ✉ 66700 ☎ 04.68.81.41.08

SWIMMING
- Tancande (NU) (between Cap Rederis & Abeille near Banyuls, summer only)
- River Tech (on the street from Argeles Plage Nord to St. Cyprien, P before and after the brigde over the river Tech)

CRUISING
- La Pinède

Argenton-sur-Creuse ✉ 36200

RESTAURANTS
■ **Rive Droite Pizzeria** (AC b CC F glm OS) 19-21.30, closed Sun, Restaurant 12-13.30, 19-21.30 h
8 Rue Ledru-Rollin ✉ 36200
Italian food.

GUEST HOUSES
■ **Manoir des Remparts. Le** (A AC BF CC F glm H lj MA OS s)
14 Rue des Remparts ✉ 36800 ☎ 02.54.47.94.87
✉ willem.prinsloo@wanadoo.fr

Arles ✉ 13200

RESTAURANTS
■ **Tropical** (B BF f glm OS) 10-1 h, closed 15.Nov to 15.Feb
28 Rue Porte de Laure ✉ 13200 ☎ 04.90.96.94.16

APARTMENTS
■ **Provence Camargue Passion** (glm H MA)
B.P. 7 ✉ 13129 *(45 min from Aix-en-Provence, Avignon, Marseille)*
☎ 04.42.86.87.88 04.42.86.86.24
✉ domaine-amerique@free.fr
✉ www.provenceweb.fr/13/domaine-amerique
Located 10 mins from gay nudist beach Piémanson. Apartments and studios in the village. Guest house in Domaine de l'Amérique.

SWIMMING
- Salin de Giraud (NU) (beach of Piémanson, at Rhône mouth)

CRUISING
- Jardin public
- Cimetière
- Quai du Rhône
- Avenue de la gare

Arpajon ✉ 91290

CRUISING
- Forest de la-Roche-Turpin (6 km west of Arpajon)

Arras ✉ 62000

CRUISING
- Le Jardin Minelle (Rue R. Salengro)
- Le Jardin du Gouverneur (Boulevard Crespel)

Arzon ✉ 56640

CRUISING
- Plage naturiste

Asnelles ✉ 14960

SWIMMING
- Les Meuvaines (G) (between Vers-sur-Mer & Asnelles)

Asnières-sur-Seine ✉ 92600

CRUISING
- Swimming Pool
- Quai du Dr-Dervaux
- Métro Station

Auch ✉ 32000

CRUISING
- Jardin Ortholan (WC by day/de jour; P by night/la nuit)
- P RN 124
- Place Denfert-Rochereau

Aups ✉ 83630

SWIMMING
- Plage Naturiste (NU) (Les Salles sur Verdon)

Aurillac ✉ 15000

SWIMMING
- Plage Naturiste (NU) (Use the motorways N 120, D 61, D 18, D 207 direction St-Gérons. At the dam turn the first street left to Rénac-Plage. In front of P follow the right bank)

CRUISING
- Place du Gravier

Auxerre ✉ 89000

SAUNAS/BATHS
■ **Sauna Hommes** (b DR g MA SA VS) Sun-Thu 12-20, Fri (glm) Sat (G) -24 h
21 Avenue de la Tournelle ✉ 89000 *(100 m from SNCF station)*
☎ 03.86.42.76.87

HEALTH GROUPS
■ **Centre Hospitalier d'Auxerre. Dispensaire Antivénérien**
Résidence Saint Germain, B.P. 51 64 ✉ 89000
☎ 03.86.48.47.18
HIV-testing.

France ▶ Auxerre ▶ Avignon

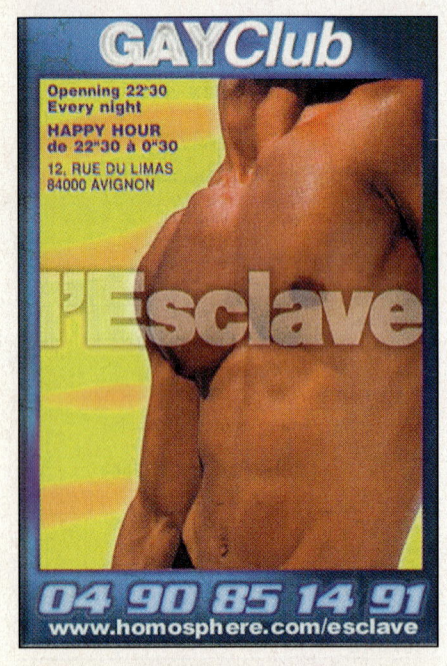

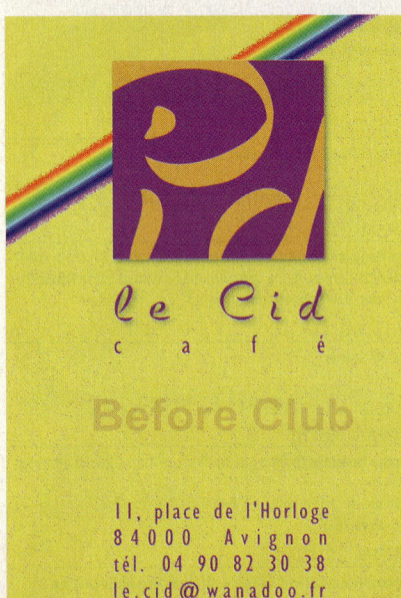

RELIGIOUS GROUPS

■ **David et Jonathan**
B.P. 394 ✉ 89000
Gay christians; monthly meetings

CRUISING

-Passage Soufflot (very busy when it gets dark)
-Near the church St-Pierre (at the little dark place in the centre of town)
-La Passerelle (At the quays of the river Yonne)
-Marché de l'Arquebuse

Avignon ✉ 84000

BARS

■ **Cid Café. Le** (AC B f glm MA OS s) 7-1.30 h
11 Place de l'Horlge ✉ 84000 ☎ 04.90.82.30.38
■ **Esclave. L'** (AC B D G S VS) 22.30-5 h
12 Rue du Limas ✉ 84000 ☎ 04.90.85.14.91
1st floor. Gay videos. Still THE gay place in Avignon.
■ **L.M Café** (B f glm MA OS s) summer 7-1, winter 10-1 h,
Sun afterclub parties 5-12 h
40 Rue des Lices ✉ 84000 ☎ 04.90.86.19.67

DANCECLUBS

■ **Cage. The** (AC B D DR GLM MA P S VS) Fri-Mon 23-5 h
Gare Routière ✉ 84000 *(1st floor of the Bus station/1er étage de la Gare routière)* ☎ 04.90.27.00.84
■ **Kiproko** (AC B CC D GLM p S SNU) Fri Sat Mon 23-? h
22 Boulevard Limbert ✉ 84000 ☎ 04.90.82.68.69
■ **Tison. Le** (AC B CC D DR GLM LJ MA os p PI S SNU TV VS WH)
Thu-Mon 23-5.30, cabaret at 2 h
Avenue de la Gare ✉ 13570 *(5 km from Avignon)*
☎ 04.90.94.94.46
Disco club with garden and pool.

RESTAURANTS

■ **Au Petit Bedon Rose** (A AC CC F g) 12-13.45, 19.30-0 h, closed Sun, Mon/lunch
70 Rue Joseph-Vernet ✉ 84000 ☎ 04.90.82.33.98
■ **Croisière s'amuse. La** (F glm)
Centre Commercial Le Galaxie, Route de Montfaret ✉ 84000
☎ 04.90.87.67.67
■ **Mama Léone** (b F glm) Lunch & Dinner
5 Rue Galante ✉ 84000 ☎ 04.90.82.57.58

SEX SHOPS/BLUE MOVIES

■ **Video Show** (g VS) 10-1 h
15 Rue de la Bourse ✉ 84000 ☎ 04.90.85.47.04
Sex shop and cinema. One is dedicated to gays.

SAUNAS/BATHS

■ **H Club** (AC b DR f G MA SA SB SOL VS) 12-22, Sat -24 h
20 Rue Paul Manivet ✉ 84000 ☎ 04.90.85.00.39
Well equipped and air-conditioned sauna popular in the afternoon.

HOTELS

■ **Lotus Tree. The** (B BF CC G H MA OS PI WO)
La Micocoule ✉ 30630 *(45 min from Avignon, 1 hour from Nîmes)*
☎ 04.66.82.76.09 ✉ booking@thelotustree.com
✉ www.thelotustree.com
6 double rooms, 1 studio, 2 apartments with WC, bath, balcony, phone, Sat TV, radio, safe & own key. Rates FF 300-600.-, weekly discounts. English, French, German, Swedish, Italian spoken. Many sport activities on offer.

Avignon ▶ Bayonne | **France**

THE LOTUS TREE MONTCLUS FRANCE

The elegant new guesthouse in one of the most beautiful valleys in the South of France.
Avignon: 45 minutes
www.thelotustree.com
Tel: +33 4 66 82 76 09

■ **Mas La Bonoty** (b CC F glm H MA OS PI)
Chemin de la Bonioty ✉ 84210 *(20 km from Avignon)*
☎ 04.90.61.61.09 📠 04.90.61.35.14 ✉ bonoty@aol.com
💻 www.bonoty.com

GUEST HOUSES

■ **Loft. Le** (BF G H MA NU OS PI SOL WO)
Chemin Haut Abrian ✉ 84200 ☎ 04.90.34.07.37
📠 04.90.34.07.47 ✉ hotel@homophere.com
💻 www.homosphere.com
In the countryside, easy access to highway, station and historic town of Orange. Large park and pool.

GENERAL GROUPS

■ **Club La Licorne** (A B DR G p VS YG)
B.P. 272 ✉ 84011 ☎ 06.62.49.99.23
💻 pero.wanadoo.fr/clublalicorne
Leisure club for the Provence. Call for dates.

HEALTH GROUPS

■ **Aides Provence**
41 Rue du Portail Magnanen ✉ 84000 ☎ 04.90.86.80.80
📠 04.90.85.96.52 💻 aides-provence.free.fr

SWIMMING

-Piscine de la Barthelasse (on the island of Barthelasse, very popular)

CRUISING

-Between the bridges/entre les ponts de Bompas et de Taracon
-City-wall (between Gate St. Michel and rue de la République)
-Champfleury Park (behind the station; AYOR in summer)
-La Durance (30 mins drive from Avignon)

Bains-les-Bains ✉ 88240

HOTELS

■ **Auberge Chez Dino** (B CC F H OS) closed in Jan, Restaurant 10-2, Mon 10-18 h
Hautemogey ✉ 88140 ☎ 03.29.30.41.87
Rooms with fridge, bathroom, WC, balcony, garden. 30 km from airport, suburb location/chambres avec frigidaire, salle de bains, WC et balcon. Hôtel, hors de ville, avec jardin, 30 km à l'aéroport. Rates FF 250/night, 1500/week.

Bandol ✉ 83150

HOTELS

■ **Auberge des Pins. L'** (b BF CC F glm H MA OS PI) 8.15-15, 18-24 h, closed Sun evening and Mon (low season)
2249 Route du Beausset ✉ 83150 *(Suburb location, 45 min from airport, 5 km from beaches and city centre)* ☎ 04.94.29.59.10
📠 04.94.32.43.46
You'll get a free apéritif on quoting SPARTACUS as your source of accomodation. Private pool reserved for gays.

■ **Hotel Ile Rousse** (AC B CC F E glm MA PI)
17 Boulevard Louis Lumière ✉ 83150 ☎ 04.94.29.33.00
📠 04.94.29.49.49
Luxury establishment with 2 restaurants, private beaches and saltwater pool.

CRUISING

-Aire d'autoroute entre Bandol et Toulon

Barbentane ✉ 13570

RESTAURANTS

■ **Moulin à Huile. Le** (b F g)
Avenue Bertherigue ✉ 13570 ☎ 04.90.95.57.76

Bar-le-Duc ✉ 55000

CRUISING

-Parc (between/entre Rue de la Maréchal-Rue Mgr-Aimond)
-Place des Basques

Barneville-Carteret ✉ 50270

SWIMMING

-Les Moitiers-d'Allonne (NU)

Bayonne ✉ 64100

BARS

■ **Ostadar** (B CC f glm MA OS S) 9-2 h, closed in winter
Avenue Léon Bonnat ✉ 64100 *(opposite public garden)*
☎ 05.59.25.76.22

CRUISING

-[P] St-Léon (also the gardens on the parking/aussi les jardins au-dessus)
-Gare SNCF/railway station
-Château Vieux/old castle
-Sur les remparts et place des Basques

SPARTACUS 2001/2002 | 245

Beaulieu-sur-Mer ✉ 06310
RESTAURANTS
■ **African Queen** (b CC E F glm MA OS) 12-24 h
Port de plaisance ✉ 06310 ☎ 04.93.01.14.60
Popular with gays from Monaco and abroad.
CRUISING
-[P] at the bridge/au pont (direction Monaco)

Beaumont-Hague ✉ 50440
SWIMMING
-Dunes (NU) (D118 towards Biville to Vasteville)
-Plage de la Vieille-Eglise

Beauvais ✉ 60000
CRUISING
-RN 17 (direction de Senlis)
-Table Ronde

Belfort ✉ 90000
CRUISING
-[P] A 36 Séveans ➤ Belfort

Berck ✉ 62600
BARS
■ **Welcome Bar** (B BF glm MA OS) 11-2 h
6 Avenue du General de Gaulle ✉ 62600 ☎ 03.21.09.31.00
SWIMMING
-Beach in the north of the town/plage au nord de la ville (G NU)

Bergerac ✉ 24100
RESTAURANTS
■ **Enfance de Lard. L'** (A CC F glm) Lunch & dinner; closed Tue
Place Pélissière ✉ 24100 ☎ 05.53.57.52.88
French cuisine in 12th century house, on 1st floor, view of 12th century church. Large fireplace and opera music.
CRUISING
-Parc Jean-Jaurès (night)
-Eglise Notre-Dame (WC)
-Rives de la Dordogne (behind the dam, in summer)

Besançon ✉ 25000
DANCECLUBS
■ **Privé. Le** (B CC D GLM MA P S TV VS) 23-4 h, closed Mon
1 Rue Antide-Janvier ✉ 25000 ☎ 03.81.81.48.57
SAUNAS/BATHS
■ **25** (b G MA SA SB VS) 15-20.30, Tue Fri -24 h (closed in summer)
16 Rue Richebourg ✉ 25000 ☎ 03.81.83.23.43
GENERAL GROUPS
■ **Choc. Le (Collectif homo de Franche-Comté)**
B.P. 63 ✉ 25013 ☎ 03.81.83.58.05
Meetings/réunions Centre Pierre Bayle, 27 Rue de la République. Wed 18-20 h. Contact Rosa Hilfe (RFA).

SPECIAL INTEREST GROUPS
■ **Girth & Mirth Alpes Jura** Hotline 10-22 h
B.P. 972 ✉ 25022 ☎ 03.81.88.06.18 ✉ g.m-alpjura@wanadoo.fr
Club for big gay man and their admirers. Monthly events (please call for information).
CRUISING
-Le Parc Micaud (night, at the border of Doubs river/au bord du Doubs)
-Square Elisée-Cusenier
-Parc du centre-ville
-[P] St.Paul (Night)
-Jardin des Senteurs
-[P] Pont de la République (Corner of bridge and avenue Gaulard. Night and day)

Béthune ✉ 62400
CRUISING
-Jardin public (behind la place du Jeu de Paume)
-Parc de Beuvry (Boulevard Poincaré)
-Parc de la Gare-d'Eau

Béziers ✉ 34500
BARS
■ **Kephren** (AC B CC DR G lj MA p s VS) 21.30-2.30 h, closed Mon
5 Rue Nougaret ✉ 34500 ☎ 04.67.49.02.20
■ **Rotonde. La** (B g)
Allée Paul Riquet ✉ 34500 ☎ 04.67.76.35.32
RESTAURANTS
■ **Crèmerie. La** (b CC F glm MA OS s) closed Sun and Mon lunch
1 Place de la Madeleine ✉ 34500 ☎ 04.67.28.54.26
Cheese specialities. Tea shop afternoons.
■ **Madison. Le** (b F g) 20-24 h, closed 1.-8.Jul
5 Rue Louis-Blanc ✉ 34500 ☎ 04.67.31.60.08
■ **Scaramouche. Le** (b F g)
23 Rue Tourventouse ✉ 34500 ☎ 04.67.28.55.39
■ **Storia. La** (b F glm) closed Sun
Rue de l'Argenterie ✉ 34500 ☎ 04.67.28.18.11
SEX SHOPS/BLUE MOVIES
■ **Video Show** (g VS)
5 Rue Víctor Hugo ✉ 34500 *11-23 h* ☎ 04.67.62.37.16
Large sex shop and cinema. One cinema room is dedicated to gays. Underwear, leather, rubber and S/M accessories. 10% for Spartacus readers.
SAUNAS/BATHS
■ **Kheops** (AC B DR f G MA p SA SB VS wo) 12-20 h
5 Rue Berlioz ✉ 34500 (near Allée Paul Riquet) ☎ 04.67.49.31.37
300 m^2 clean and friendly sauna.
HOTELS
■ **Hôtel Alma Unic** (BF CC glm H MA NU OS VS WH) reception -24 h
41 Rue Guilhemon ✉ 34500 ☎ 04.67.28.44.31 📠 04.67.28.79.44
Friendly. Rooms with private bath & WC. Ask for Christian. Free BF with SPARTACUS for two nights & more except Jul & Aug. Nude sunbathing on the terrace.
■ **Revélois. Le** (B BF CC F g H MA) Restaurant closed on Sun
60 Avenue Gambetta ✉ 34500 (near park Plateau des Poètes)
☎ 04.67.49.20.78 📠 04.67.28.92.28

Béziers ▸ Biscarosse | France

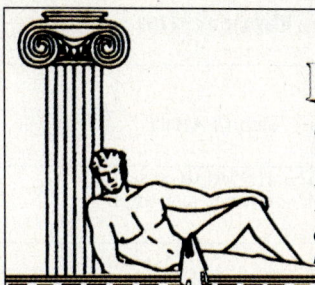

SAUNA (2 niveaux)
LE BEAU-LIEU

Sauna sec - Hammam - Jaccuzi
Cabine de Relaxation - Solarium (offert)
Bar - Salle Vidéo - Salon TV
Petite restauration

Nocturne le Vendredi et Samedi jusqu'à 4 h

TOUTE L'ANNÉE · TOUS LES JOURS
7 jours sur 7 - de 12 h à minuit

entre Bayonne et Biarritz
ANGLET - St-Jean · 27, rue Beau-Lieu · ☏ 05 59 58 20 39 - Fax 05 59 59 27 97

APARTMENTS
■ **Chambres d'Hôte du Moulin** (BF G H NU OS PI)
Domaine Bonne Vigne ✉ 34310 *(5 km from Béziers, 20 km from sea)* ☏ 04.67.49.35.16 ☏ 06.11.32.30.76 📠 04.67.49.35.16
Private naturist pool. 6 rooms with bath. Near the gay naturist beach.

HEALTH GROUPS
■ **Aides**
17 Rue du 4 Septembre ✉ 34500 ☏ 04.67.28.54.82

CRUISING
-Gare SNCF
-Jardin des Bassins réservoirs
-Plateau des Poètes (day/jour)
-Plage à Serigrau (dunes entre camping naturiste et l'arbre)
-Plage à Fleury d'Aude

Biarritz ✉ 64200

BARS
■ **Bakara** (B CC g OS S) 9-3, Jan/Feb Mon-Wed 9-20 Thu-Sun 9-2 h
Place Sainte-Eugénie ✉ 64200 ☏ 05.59.24.05.34
Sea views. Intimate salon.
■ **Caveau. Le** (B D G S) bar 17-5, disco 23-6 h
4 Rue Gambetta ✉ 64200 ☏ 05.59.24.16.17
Also danceclub.
■ **Opera Café** (AC B BF CC d GLM H MA OS p s) Café 12-5, bar 22-5 h
31 Avenue de Verdun ✉ 64200 ☏ 05.59.24.27.85
Also hotel with 21 rooms to rent.

HOTELS
■ **Opera** (AC B BF CC d GLM H MA OS p s)
31 Avenue de Verdun ✉ 64200 ☏ 05.59.24.27.85
📠 05.59.22.21.55
Gay hotel above private gay bar.

■ **Saint Georges. Le** (B BF CC F glm H MA OS s SA SB)
14.30-2 h 9-23 h
closed Nov. 15 - Dec 15
96 Avenue de Biarritz ✉ 64600 *(in Anglet, RN 10 Biarritz direction Bayonne)* ☏ 05.59.41.21.58
Also restaurant & sauna. Special weekend rates.

GUESTHOUSES
■ **Arrostegia** (A AC BF CC F glm H lj MA OS s WH) 9-23 h
closed Nov. 15 - Dec 15
Route d'Arnéguy Lihart-Cize ✉ 64220 *(43 km from Bayonne)*
☏ 05.59.37.06.22 📠 05.59.37.06.22
17th century house nested in an historical village. Guided tour, skiing, piano & painting courses on offer. Whirlpool in the park.

SWIMMING
-Plage du Miramar (towards lighthouse, under cliffs)
-Plage du Port-Vieux

Bidart ✉ 64210

SWIMMING
-Place des 200 marches (D 911)

Biscarosse ✉ 40600

BARS
■ **Bar'Ils** (B D glm) 22-2 h
46 Rue du Grand Vivier ✉ 40600 ☏ 05.58.78.36.30

SWIMMING
-Route d'Arcachon (G NU)

"ARROSTEGIA - chambres d'hôtes" vous reçoit à 43 km de Bayonne, dans un site historique (St-Jean-Pied-de-Port, patrimoine mondial), lieu de villégiature, vignobles, ski, rafting, randonnées pédestres et cyclotouristiques, chasse, pêche...
• Maison du XVIIe siècle avec chambres à thèmes. Petits déjeuners.
• table d'hôtes sur réservation le soir, cuisine traditionnelle Basque
• concerts de piano
• jaccuzzi dans le parc
• antiquités - vente - achat
• stages de confection d'abat-jour, de découvertes historiques du Pays Basque
• Expositions diverses...

N'hésitez pas à nous contacter pour toute information ou réservation au :
00 33 (0)5 59 37 06 22 (téléphone/fax).

ARROSTEGIA

France — Blagnac ▶ Bordeaux

Blagnac ✉ 31700

CRUISING
- Vieux-Pont

Blois ✉ 41000

BARS
■ **Petit Amiral. Le** (AC B CC GLM lj MA OS) 14-3 h
12 Rue du Puit Châtel ✉ 41000 ☎ 02.54.78.81.83

CRUISING
- Jardin des Lices
- Foret de Russy (route de Vierzon)

Bonnieux ✉ 84480

RESTAURANTS
■ **Fournil. Le** (b F g) 12-14.30, 19-22 h, Oct-Feb closed Sun & 5.Jan-15.Feb
5 Place Carnot ✉ 84480 ☎ 90.75.83.62

PRIVATE ACCOMMODATION
■ **Bed & Breakfeast J. C.** (BF G PI)
Route Pont Julien ✉ 84480 *3 km from the village.* ☎ 90.75.86.52

Bordeaux ✉ 33000

BARS
■ **Moyen Age. Le** (B G MA) 22-2 h, closed Tue
8 Rue des Remparts ✉ 33000 *(next to Place Gambetta near Hôtel de Ville)* ☎ 05.56.44.12.87
The oldest gay bar in France. And still popular and gay...
■ **TH. Le** (AC B CC DR G LJ MA s VS) 22-2 h, closed Mon
15 Rue Montbazon ✉ 33000 ☎ 05.56.81.38.16
Theme nights.

MEN'S CLUBS
■ **Traxx** (b DR G LJ MA p VS) 14-3, Fri Sat -7 h
38bis Rue Arnaud Miqueu ✉ 33000 ☎ 05.56.44.03.41
Large fantasy complex with gay shop.

DANCECLUBS
■ **Key West** (B D GLM MA p YG) 22-4
32/34 Rue Cornac ✉ 33000 ☎ 05.56.48.22.13
Bar-Discotheque.
■ **Yellow Moon. Le** (B D DR G MA s VS) 23-4 h
6 Rue Louis Combes ✉ 33000 ☎ 05.56.51.00.79
Two bars, videoroom, three floors.
■ **18. Le** (! AC B CC D G p) 23-4 h
18 Rue Louis de Foix ✉ 33000 ☎ 05.56.52.82.98

RESTAURANTS
■ **Bistrot M.A.P.** (B F glm MA OS) 19.30-2 h, closed on Mon
62 Rue de la Devise ✉ 33000 ☎ 05.56.48.19.92
■ **Cafetière. La** (B F Glm)
14 Rue des Faussetts ✉ 33000 ☎ 05.56.51.66.55
■ **Cave à Jules. La** (AC CC E F g MA) Mon-Sun 12-14 19.30-22.30 h, closed Sat lunch
56 Rue du Mirail ✉ 33000 ☎ 05.56.91.44.69
Cuisine régionale.
■ **Pizza Jacono** (b CC F g) Mon Wed-Sat 12-14, 19.30-23, Sun 19.30-23 h
19 Rue de la Devise ✉ 33000 ☎ 05.56.51.01.48
Credit cards accepted.

SAUNA CLUB LE 137 BORDEAUX
★★★★★

OPEN ALL YEAR
7/7 — 13.30 - 1.00
LATE NIGHT TUES - FRI & SAT

HAVE FUN

© ESPACE DU HA

**THE BIGGEST
THE BEST
THE SEXIEST**

JACUZZI GEANT - FINLANDAIS
HAMMAM - MUSCU - BAR
SOLARIUM (Gratuit) - SNACK
CABINES - 2 SLINGS - BOUTIQUE
LABYRINTHE - MAXI VIDEO

137 QUAI DES CHARTRONS.
TEL : 0556 43 18 49
BUS N°1 STOP : COURS DU MEDOC

SEX SHOPS/BLUE MOVIES

■ **Boîte à Films. La** (glm VS) 10-2 h
26 Rue Rolland ✉ 33000 ☏ 05.56.01.14.26
Videos, magazines, etc.
■ **Love Vidéo** (AC DR CC g VS) 10-1 h
221 Rue Cours de la Marne ✉ 33000 *(train station St. Jean)* ☏ 05.56.91.68.55
Also clothes and accessories.
■ **Love Vidéo** (AC DR CC g VS)
20 Rue G. Bonnac ✉ 33000 ☏ 05.56.44.74.25
■ **Star'x** (CC g MA VS) Special gay movies Tue Fri 11-1 h
46 Cours Alsace Lorraine ✉ 33000 ☏ 05.56.81.81.35

SAUNAS/BATHS

■ **Ferrère** (b f glm MA SA SB SOL VS WH) 12-20, Sat Sun 13-20 h
18 Rue Ferrère ✉ 33000 ☏ 05.56.44.53.01
Newly renovated sauna mixed on the 1st floor, men only on the ground floor.
■ **Sauna Club 137** (AC b DR f G SA SB SOL VS WH WO YG) 13.30-1 h, Tue Fri Sat late nights
137 Quai des Chartrons ✉ 33000 ☏ 05.56.43.18.43
Bordeaux's all gay sauna. Young atmosphere on two floors. Theme nights.
■ **Thiers** (AC b CC DR f G MA PI SA SB SOL VS WH) 13-1, Tue Fri Sat -4 h
329 Avenue Thiers ✉ 33100 *(Bus 2, 4, Pont Saint Emilion)* ☏ 05.56.32.00.63
Friendly sauna busy late afternoons and evenings. Free parking places available.

TRAVEL AND TRANSPORT

■ **France Gay Travel** (GLM)
192 Rue Fondaudege ✉ 33000 ☏ 04.93.38.16.95
📠 04.93.38.28.73 📧 noëlcastinel@airdumonde.com
🌐 www.rivieragaytravel.com
National gay travel agency.

HELP WITH PROBLEMS

■ **SOS Homo** Tue 20-1 h
✉ 33000 ☏ 05.56.81.51.66

CRUISING

-Bois de Bordeaux (de Bruges) (AYOR) (along the lake/vers le lac)
-Les jardins de Mériadeck (night/nuit)
-Ecole de la Santé Navale (park in front of the school/parc face à l'Ecole, Place Renaudel)
-Place d'Arlac (AYOR)
-Parc Bordelais (Cauderan, daytime/de jour)

Bouc-Bel-Air ✉ 13320

CRUISING

-Cimetière/cemetery (in the evening towards the industrial area of Milles)

Boulogne Billancourt ✉ 92100

CRUISING

-Métro station Billancourt (in front of brasserie Rex)
-Quai Quatre-Septembre

Boulogne-sur-Mer ☏ 0321

BARS

■ **Horloge. L'** (B G f) 9-22 h
5 Rue Monsigny ✉ 62200 ☏ 03.21.31.47.29

CAFES

■ **Bistroquet. Le** (B f g) open all day
46 Place Dalton ✉ 62200 ☏ 03.21.30.57.69

DANCECLUBS

■ **Pharaon. Le** (B D CC E glm MA p WE) Thu-Sat 21-6 h
27 Rue du Vivier ✉ 62200 ☏ 03.21.30.03.89

GENERAL GROUPS

■ **Arc-en-Ciel Côte d'Opale**
B.P. 271 ✉ 62204 ☏ 03.21.33.82.95

CRUISING

-Porte Neuve
-Remparts (Ville haute)

Bourg-en-Bresse ✉ 01000

CRUISING

-Champs de Foire
-[P] de la Basilique (behind l'église du Sacre-Coeur)
-La/ Plaine du Bastion
-Le square Bel-Air
-Parc de la Visitation
-Square Joubert
-Square des Quinconces

Bourges ✉ 18000

CRUISING

-RN 76 (20 km-Bourges, direction Moulins)
-[P] Palais des Congrès (le soir/in the evening)
-Parking du Lac d'Oreon
-Place Séracourt

Bray-Dunes ✉ 59123

CRUISING

-In the dunes/dans les dunes (in the summertime/l'été)

Bréhal ✉ 50290

SWIMMING

-Bréville-sur-Mer(beach near the shooting- ground/plage près du champ de tir)
-nudist beach (along golf-course/longer le terrain de golf)

Bressuire ✉ 79300

CRUISING

-Mairie (arcades, evening/le soir)
-Place de la Libération
-Place St.Jacques
-Place St.Jean
-Place de la Brèche
-Rue Gambetta
-Jardin des Plantes

France Brest ▶ Calais

Brest ✉ 29200

BARS
- **Lak-Atao** (B glm MA) 21-1 h, closed Tue
  63 Rue Louis Pasteur ✉ 29200 ☏ 02.99.44.49.84
  Only frequented by gays in the evening.
- **Village Café. Le** (AC B G MA snu VS) 18-1 h
  2 Rue Duquesne ✉ 29200 ☏ 02.98.80.05.22

RESTAURANTS
- **Marina** (b F g) 12-14, 19-23 h
  16 Rue de Siam ✉ 29200 ☏ 02.98.80.09.61
  Menus FF 48. Also Italian food.
- **Vitavi** (B F g) 12-14, 19-23 h, closed Thu
  109 Rue Jean-Jaurés ✉ 29200 ☏ 02.98.43.30.70
  Pizzeria.

HEALTH GROUPS
- **Aides Armor** Call Mon 19.30-22.30 h
  1 Rue de l'Harteloire ✉ 29200 ☏ 02.98.43.18.72

SWIMMING
- Plage de Corsen (25 km de Brest)
- Dunes de Keremna (2 km de Treflez)
- Plage de Trezien

CRUISING
- Jardins Kennedy (AYOR) (day and night)
- Quais du port
- Cours d'Ajot
- Aire du Pont-de-Buis
- Bois de Keroual
- Jardin Beaupré

Briançon ✉ 05100

CAFES
- **Crêperie Hélène Chaix** (AC b CC F glm lj MA) 12-22 h, closed Mon
  40 Grande Rue ✉ 05100 ☏ 04.92.21.11.81
  Restaurant, crêperie, salon de thé.

CRUISING
- P Avenue Vauran
- P du Général Blanchard
- P Place de l'Europe
- Les Bois des Genès
- Parc de la Schappe
- P de la Schappe

Brive-la-Gaillarde ✉ 19100

BARS
- **Nuage. Le** (B CC F g OS P) 18-2, closed Mon
  2 Avenue Jean-Charles Rivet ✉ 19100 ☏ 05.55.87.36.79
  Bar-restaurant.

SEX SHOPS/BLUE MOVIES
- **Ciné Vidéo Shop** (CC g VS) Mon-Thu 14-19.30, 21-23, Fri 10-23, Sat 10-12.30 14-18 h
  44 Avenue Jean-Jaurès ✉ 19100 ☏ 05.55.23.19.49

CRUISING
- Jardins de la Guierle (late afternoon and evening)
- Place Thiers (evening)

Cabourg ✉ 14390

HOTELS
- **Hôtel du Golf** (CC F g H OS PI) Restaurant 12-14, 19.30-24 h
  Avenue de l'Hippodrome ✉ 14390 ☏ 02.31.24.12.34
  Room with WC FF 310/435, bf 45. Menues 98-230.

Caen ✉ 14000

BARS
- **Zinc. Le** (B G MA) 8-2, Fri Sat -4 h, closed on Sun
  12 Rue du Vaugeux ✉ 14000 ☏ 02.31.93.20.30

DANCECLUBS
- **Joy's. Le** (B CC D g MA S) 23-5 h
  12 Passage du Bief ✉ 14000 *(a côte de la FNAC)*
  ☏ 02.31.85.40.40
- **Phil and Bea** (B D G MA) -3 h
  189 Rue St. Jean ✉ 14000 ☏ 02.31.86.60.05

SAUNAS/BATHS
- **Arc-En-Ciel** (b CC d DR G p SA SB VS WH WO YG)
  Men only: 13-22 h, except Fri Sun
  17 rue de Varignon, Impasse Dumont ✉ 14000 ☏ 02.31.93.19.00
  Sauna on 470 m^2 with two video rooms.

HEALTH GROUPS
- **Aides Basse-Normandie** Mon-Fri 14-17 h
  2 Rue du Marais ✉ 14007 ☏ 02.31.84.36.63

CRUISING
- P of the castle/du château
- Place Royale (garden/le jardin)
- Plage de Franceville (à 15 min de Caen, par la route direction Cabourg /15 min from Caen, motorway direction Cabourg)
- Promenade Fossé St-Julien
- Promenade du Long du Cours
- Quartier du Vaugeux

Cagnes-sur-Mer ✉ 06800

RESTAURANTS
- **Entre Cour et Jardin** (b e F glm MA) 19.30-24 h
  102 Montée de la Bourgade ✉ 06800 *(Haut de Cagnes)*
  ☏ 04.93.20.72.27
  An excellent gastronomic halt in the historic old town of Haut de Cagnes.

CRUISING
- Next to castle museum

Cahors ✉ 46000

CRUISING
- Salle des fêtes
- P Gambetta

Calais ✉ 62100

BARS
- **London Bridge** (B F GLM MA) Bar 12-2, restaurant -23 h
  12 Place d'Armes ✉ 62100 ☏ 03.21.85.85.79

Calais ▶ Cannes France

CRUISING
- Citadelle (Boulevard Esplanade, de jour/by day)
- Dunes de Blériot
- Fort Risbau
- Parc Richelieu

Camaret-sur-Mer ✉ 29129
SWIMMING
- Plage de Losmarch

Cannes ✉ 06400
TOURIST INFO
■ **Tourist Info**
Esplanade Président Georges Pompidou 06403 ✉ 06400
☎ 04.93.39.24.53 04.93.99.37.06.

BARS
■ **Vogue Bar** (AC B CC glm MA p) 19-2.30 h, closed Mon
20 Rue du Suquet ✉ 06400 ☎ 04.93.39.99.18
■ **Zanzibar** (AC B CC G MA OS) 18.30-5 h
85 Rue Félix Faure ✉ 06400 ☎ 04.93.39.30.75

RESTAURANTS
■ **Barbarella** (b F glm YG) every evening
14-16 Rue St. Dizier ✉ 06400 ☎ 04.92.99.17.33
■ **Bistro de la Galerie. Le** (A b CC F g) 19.30-23 h, closed Mon
4 Rue Saint Antoine ✉ 06400 ☎ 04.93.39.99.38
French cuisine.

■ **Croisette. La** (b F g) Tue-Sat 12-14.30, 19-22.30, Sun Mon 12.-14.30 h
15 Rue Commandant-André ✉ 06400 ☎ 04.93.39.86.06
Italian cuisine.
■ **Dauphin. Le** (AC F glm MA) 12-14, 19-22.30 h, closed Sun except during Festival
1 Rue Bivouac Napoléon ✉ 06400 *(Near Palais des Festivals)*
☎ 04.93.39.22.73
Popular with gays.
■ **Marais. Le** (AC b CC E F glm MA OS) 19.30-23 h, closed Mon
9-11 Rue du Suquet ✉ 06400 ☎ 04.93.38.39.19
French, English, German, & Italian spoken.
■ **Max** (A AC F glm MA) 12-13.30 h, 22.30 h, closed Mon except Jul. Aug. & holidays.
11 Rue Louis Perissol ✉ 06400 ☎ 04.93.39.97.06
■ **Mirabelle. La** (b E F g MA) 20-23 h, closed Tue & 1.-15.Dec
24 Rue Saint Antoine/2 Rue du Suquet ✉ 06400
☎ 04.93.38.72.75
Reservation necessary.

Hotel ★★ NN
FOR GAY MEN IN CANNES FRANCE

TV SATELLITE
AIR CONDITIONED
FULLY RENOVATED
WITH EN SUITE BATHROOMS

NEAR THE TOWN-CENTER
OLD PORT AND BEACH

LES CHARMETTES
47 avenue de Grasse - Cannes
Tel. 04 93 39 17 13 - Fax 04 93 68 08 41
E-mail: hotelcharmcan@aol.com

France Cannes

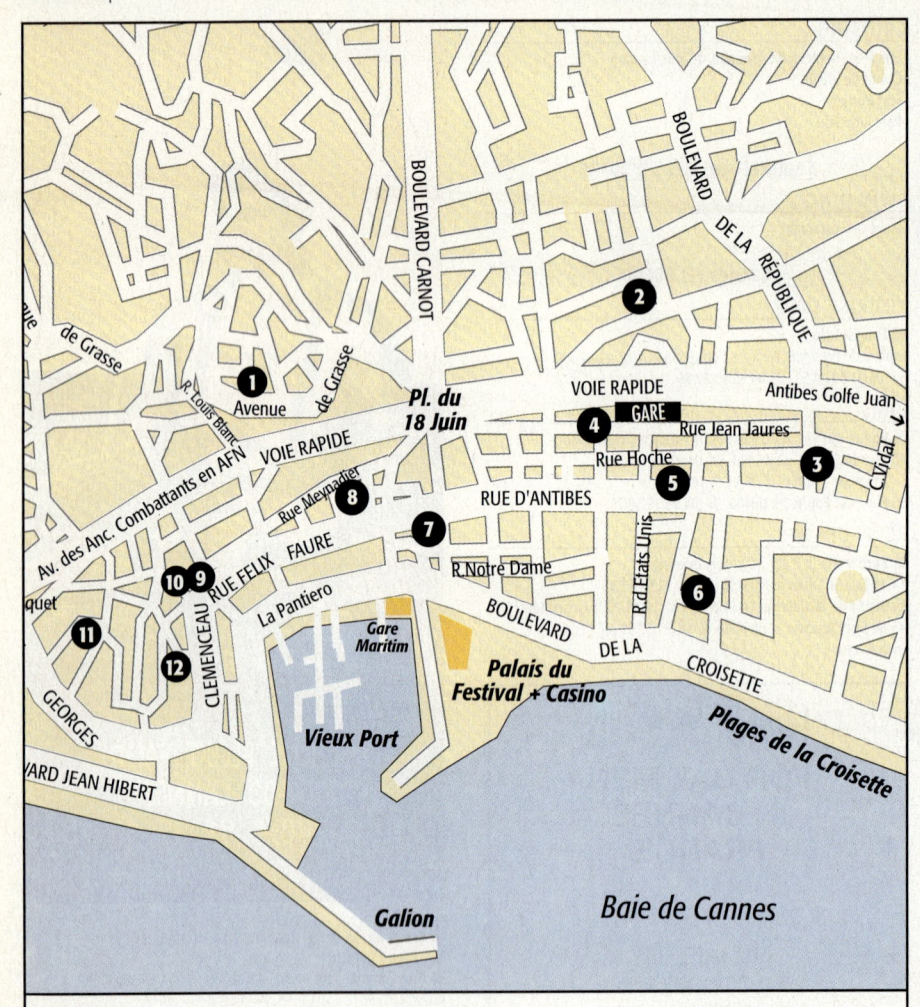

Cannes

1. Les Charmettes Hotel
2. Le Salon Sex Shop
3. France Gay Travel
4. Le Salon Sex Shop
5. Select Hotel
6. La Croisette Restaurant
7. Le Dauphin Restaurant
8. Zanzibar
9. Le Bistro de la Galerie Restaurant
10. Le Marais Restaurant
11. Le 13 Restaurant
12. La Mirabelle Restaurant

Cannes ▶ Carcassonne — France

RESTAURANT AND GARDEN
In 18th Century Stable

Lunch and Dinner

Tél. 04.68.72.04.04

43 Bld Barbès
CARCASSONNE

■ **13. Le** (A CC F glm OS) 19-24.30 h
13 Rue C. Perrissol le Suquet ✉ 06400 *(old town)*
☏ 04.93.39.85.19

SEX SHOPS/BLUE MOVIES
■ **Salon. Le** (CC g VS) 8.30-0.30 h
32 Rue Jean Jaurès ✉ 06400 ☏ 04.93.38.42.59
■ **Salon. Le** (CC g VS) 9.30-12.30, 14.30-19.30 h, closed Sun
13 Rue de Mimont ✉ 06400 ☏ 04.93.68.16.30
■ **Video Sex** (AC CC g VS) 10-24 h
6 Rue Jean Jaures ✉ 06400 ☏ 04.93.68.91.82

TRAVEL AND TRANSPORT
■ **France Gay Travel** (GLM) 9.30-12.30, 14-18.30 h, closed Sat Sun
3 Rue des Mimosas ✉ 06400 *(1st floor, close to centre)*
☏ 04.93.38.16.95 ☏ 04.93.38.28.73
✉ noëlcastinel@airdumonde.com 🖥 www.rivieragaytravel.com

HOTELS
■ **Charmettes. Les** (AC BF CC G H MA OS)
47 Avenue de Grasse ✉ 06400 *(near the town-center, old port and beach)* ☏ 04.93.39.17.13 📠 04.93.68.08.41
📧 hotelcharmcan@aol.com
All rooms with shower or bath, mini-bar, phone, air condition and satellite TV.
■ **Hotel des Allées** (CC g H)
6 Rue Emile-Negrin ✉ 06400 *(central location)* ☏ 04.93.39.53.90
📠 04.93.99.43.25 📧 des-allees@infonie.fr
Rates FF 260-330, 350-430 with bath.
■ **Select** (AC BF glm H MA)
16 Rue Hélène Vagliano ✉ 06400 *(Town center)* ☏ 04.93.99.51.00
📠 04.92.98.03.12.

GENERAL GROUPS
■ **Fierté Gay et Lesbien Côte d'Azur**
11/11 bis Rue Hélène Vagliano ✉ 06400 ☏ 04.93.45.06.37
📠 04.93.45.07.95

CRUISING
-Beach/plage de La Batterie (AYOR at night)
-Beach/plage Ile Ste-Marguerite
-Square Carnot
-Square Frédéric-Mistral (beach)
-Boulevard de la Croisette

Cap-d'Agde ✉ 34300

BARS
■ **Casa Nueva** (B F glm MA NU OS TV) 15 Mar-15 Oct: Mon-Sun, winter: WE 17-3 h
Colline 5, Port Nature ✉ 34300 *(Quartier Naturiste)*
☏ 04.67.26.08.15 *Bar and restaurant.*

■ **Look. Le** (B CC glm NU OS s) Easter-December: 17-2; low season: WE 17-1 h
Village Naturiste ✉ 34300 *(opposite port)* ☏ 04.67.26.30.42
■ **Winch. Le** (b BF CC F glm MA) Apr-Sep 9-3 h
Plage de la Roquille ✉ 34300 ☏ 04.67.01.28.60

DANCECLUBS
■ **Cléopatre** (B D GLM MA stv WE) Fri-Sun 23-6 h, shows on Sun
☏ 04.67.26.93.26

SAUNAS/BATHS
■ **Bain's. Le** (B f G SA SB SOL WH)
2 Avenue Amphitrite, Port Ambonne ✉ 34300 ☏ 04.67.26.35.52

SWIMMING
-Marseillan plage (G NU) (Between Sète and Cap d'Agde, to be reached via N112. Pass junction Cap d'Agde and follow next junction to the right, direction Marseillan plage. When at the beach walk to the right, direction Cap d'Agde, and you will find yourself at the enormous gay nude beach. The access to the dunes is strictly forbidden, frequent police controls)
-Plage de Roche Pongue (at night)

CRUISING
-Bois-Joli (camping)
-Place du Barbecue (late, summer)
-[P] au bord de l'Herault

Cap-d'Ail ✉ 06320

CRUISING
-Beach/Plage des Pissarelles (500 m-Cap-d'Ail)

Cap-Ferret ✉ 33970

RESTAURANTS
■ **Côte Ouest** (B G glm MA)
67 Boulevard de la Plage ✉ 33970 ☏ 05.56.60.66.23

Carcassonne ✉ 11000

BARS
■ **BAR. Le** (B glm) 17-2 h
31 Boulevard Omer Sarrault ✉ 11000 ☏ 05.68..25.90.26

RESTAURANTS
■ **Ecu d'Or. L'** (b CC F g) 12-14, 19-22, closed Tue, Jul-Sept 12-14, 19-22 h, closed 15.Nov-15.Dec
7 Rue Porte-d'Aude, cité Médiévale ✉ 11000 ☏ 04.68.25.88.64
French cuisine à la carte.

France — Carcassonne ▶ Chambéry

■ **Ecurie. L'** (AC b CC E F glm OS) 12-14, 20-22 h, closed Sun
43 Boulevard Barbès ✉ 11000 *(Near Place Général de Gaule)*
☎ 04.68.72.04.04
18th century stable/garden setting.
■ **Saladou. Le** (b CC F glm OS) 12-14.30, 19-23 h, closed Sun evening & Mon in winter
5 Place du Petits Puits ✉ 11000 ☎ 04.68.71.23.56

GUEST HOUSES

■ **Aux Deux Colonnes** (BF glm H MA OS)
3 Avenue de Limoux ✉ 11250 ☎ 04.68.69.41.21
🖶 04.68.69.69.02
Outside Carcassonne, direction Limoux. Open all year.

CRUISING
-Boulevard Marcou (in the evening/le soir)
-Boulevard de Varsovie (in the evening/le soir)

Carcès ✉ 83570

GUEST HOUSES
■ **Mas de Canta-Dié** (A B BF F g H OS PI)
Route de Carcès ✉ 83570 *(2,8 km from Cotignac direction Carcès)*
☎ 04.94.77.72.46 🖶 04.94.77.79.33
✉ mas-de-canta-die@wanadoo.fr
✉ sejour-en-provence.com/canta01.htm

Carnac ✉ 56340

DANCECLUBS
■ **Appalooza. L'** (AC B D DR GLM OS P SNU STV VS) Jul-Aug Tue-Sun 23-5, Sep-Jun Fri-Sun 23-5 h
Route de Auray-Quiberon ✉ 56340 ☎ 02.97.52.16.17
Liveliest gay spot in the south of Brittany. Club on two levels, 2 types of music.

Cassis ✉ 13260

SAUNAS/BATHS
■ **Aqua Douches** (AC B CC f G MA p SA SB VS WH WO)
Open everyday.
34 Rue de l'Arène ✉ 13260 *(30 min from Marseille and 1 h. from St. Tropez. Town centre Cassis)* ☎ 06.14.63.28.19

SWIMMING
-Calanque de Port-Pin (NU)
-La pointe Cacau
-Cap Canaille (NU) (go east from the town, direction Route des Crêtes, there's a non marked steep way to a [P]. On the beach turn east. Gay at the end of the nude beach)

CRUISING
-Autoroute Marseille-La Ciotat

Castillon ✉ 06500

HOTELS
■ **Bergerie. La** (A B d F g H NU OS PI) closed Nov-Mar except for groups
✉ 06500 *(10 km-Menton, Route de Sospel)* ☎ 04.93.04.00.39
About 40km from Airport Nice. Rooms with telephone, bathroom, WC and balcony./Distance à l'aéroport de Nice: 40 km. Téléphone à la chambre, salle de bain, WC et balcon.

CRUISING
-At the old harbour/Au Vieux Port (in the evening/le soir)

Castres ✉ 81100

CRUISING
-Centre culturel
-Gardens of/Jardins de l'Evêché

Cauterets ✉ 65110

HOTELS
■ **Aladin Hotel Club** (B g H PI WE)
Avenue Général Leclerc ✉ 65110 *(Centre)* ☎ 05.62.92.60.00

Cavalaire-sur-Mer ✉ 83240

SWIMMING
-beach in front of/plage en face de "Camping Bon Porteau" (NU)

Cerbère ✉ 66290

SWIMMING
-Criques et Calanques (NU)

Châlons-sur-Marne ✉ 51000

CRUISING
-Grand Jard (in winter/en hiver)
-Petit Jard (in summer; in the surroundings/aux alentours, en été)

Chalon-sur-Saône ✉ 71100

SAUNAS/BATHS
■ **Antheus** (b G MA SA SB) 14-20 h, closed on Sun and in summer
4 Rue des Cornillons ✉ 71100 ☎ 03.85.48.82.68

Chambéry ✉ 73000

DANCECLUBS
■ **Quartier Général** (B CC D GLM LJ MA P p SNU STV VS)
Fri Sat 23-4 h
RN6 St. Cassin ✉ 73000 ☎ 79.69.11.22
Sex Club Dance.

RESTAURANTS
■ **Valentino. Le** (B F glm MA) 10-14.30, 18-23 h
711 Avenue de Lyon ✉ 73000 *(5 min from centre, near the hospital)*
☎ 04.79.69.57.55

GENERAL GROUPS
■ **Groupe d'Actions, d'Information et de Contacts Homosexuels Alpins (G.A.I.C.H.A)** (GLM MA) Fri 20.30-22.30 h
c/o Maison des Associations, Rue Saint-François-de-Salle
✉ 73000 *(salle B 111, 1st floor)*
☎ 04.79.33.95.78 *(answering machine)*
1st Fri general meeting, 2nd Fri young group, 3rd Fri HIV café, 4th Fri women group.

CRUISING
-Railway station/gare SNCF
-Lycée
-Parc Clos Savoiroux
-Parc du Verney
-[P] of the castle
-Place de Genève

Chamonix-Mont-Blanc ▶ Clermont-Ferrand — France

Chamonix-Mont-Blanc ✉ 74400
CRUISING
- Bords de l'Arve
- Hameau Les Bois (à 3,5 km de Chamonix)
- Hôtel de Ville

Charleville-Mézières ✉ 08000
CRUISING
- Pond of Bairon/Étang de Bairon (at the beach/ face à la plage)
- Square Bayard
- Square du Mont-Olympe

Chartres ✉ 28000
DANCECLUBS
■ **Privilège. Le** (B D g) Fri Sat 22.30-? h
1-3 Place Saint Pierre ✉ 28000 ☏ 02.37.35.52.02

GUEST HOUSES
■ **Grange du Bois. La** (BF glm H OS)
34 La Grange du Bois ✉ 28190 (30 km west of Chartres, RN 23 direction Le Mans) ☏ 02.37.37.44.00 📠 02.37.37.44.00
📧 barraka@club-internet.fr 📧 perso.club-internet.fr/barraka

CRUISING
- Bois Paris: woods along RN10 direction Paris, 4 km from Chartres/Bois sur la RN 10 en direction de Paris, 4 km de Chartres
- Facilities at the Theatre/Toilettes près du théâtre
- Lucé post office square/Place Lucé
- near Mainvilliers Town Hall/près de la mairie de Mainvillers

Châteaurenard ✉ 13160
RESTAURANTS
■ **Wagon. Le** (b F g) 20-6 h
Grand Quartier, Parking du Stax ✉ 13160 ☏ 04.90.94.43.24

Château-Thierry ✉ 02400
CRUISING
- Château
- Place de l'Hôtel-de-Ville

Châtel-Censoir ✉ 89660
CRUISING
- Bois d'Arcy

Châtellerault ✉ 86100
RESTAURANTS
■ **Écurie. L'** (B CC F GLM OS) 12-14, 19-24, Sun 12-14 h
141 Avenue Louis-Ripault ✉ 86100 ☏ 05.49.21.24.82
French cuisine.

CRUISING
- Railway station/Gare SNCF

Châtillon-sur-Loire ✉ 45360
BARS
■ **Clin d'Oeil** (B glm MA) Tue-Fri 10.30-24, Sat 13-24 h, closed Sun evening & Mon
17 Grande-Rue ✉ 45360 ☏ 02.38.31.45.86

Chaumont ✉ 52000
CRUISING
- Square Philippe-Le Bon (in front of the SNCF railway station)

Chauvry ✉ 95560
RESTAURANTS
■ **Trèfle à Quatre-Feuilles. Le** (b F glm OS) 12.30-14, 20-22 h, closed Tue Wed
19 Grande Rue ✉ 95560 ☏ 02.39.69.26.00
20 km north of Paris in direction of Enghien.

Cherbourg ✉ 50100
BARS
■ **Freedom Café. Le** (AC B CC d g MA OS)
9-11 Rue Blondeau ✉ 50100 ☏ 02.33.94.08.88
Bar-café.

CRUISING
- Place Napoléon
- Port du Roule

Chinon ✉ 37220
HOTELS
■ **Relais de la Poste** (B BF F glm H OS) restaurant: 12-13.30, 19-20.30 h
Place de l'Eglise ✉ 37190 (16 km from Chinon, direction Azay le Rideau) ☏ 02.47.95.51.16 📠 02.47.95.51.16
Hotel and restaurant. Quote SPARTACUS for free BF.

Cholet ✉ 49300
CRUISING
- Railway station/Gare SNCF
- Jardin du Mail

Clamart ✉ 92140
CRUISING
- Place du Garde (rencontres parfois dans le bois/in the forest)

Clermont-Ferrand ✉ 63000
BARS
■ **Viennois. Le** (B GLM) 8-1, Fri-Sat -2 h
3 Rue Barrière-de-Jaude ✉ 63000 ☏ 04.73.34.12.74

SEX SHOPS/BLUE MOVIES
■ **Erotic Vidéo** (CC g VS) 10-23 h, closed Sun
10-12 Rue Saint Dominique ✉ 63000 ☏ 04.73.37.65.48
■ **Kama Sutra Video** (GLM MA VS)
17 Rue des Tanneries ✉ 63000 ☏ 04.73.77.74.19
■ **Sexy Night** (CC DR glm lj MA msg S VS) 18-? h
6 Rue Sainte Geneviève ✉ 63000 ☏ 04.73.34.25.40

France | Clermont-Ferrand ▸ Corse - Corbara

SAUNAS/BATHS

■ **Edensex** (b cc DR f glm msg Pl SA SOL VS WO YG) 14-? h
16 Rue Ramond ✉ 63000 *(between Place de Jaude and Place des Salins)* ☎ 04.73.93.84.15
Sex shop and sauna. Giant screen video and large fantasy area for a rather young crowd. Nudism parties every week.

■ **Salins. Les** (AC B DR f G MA NU p s SA SB SOL VS WH WO) 14-24, Sat -2 h
1 Rue Montpela-Bujadoux ✉ 63000 *(close to Place des Salins & Bus station)* ☎ 04.73.29.26.10
Clean & friendly sauna on 500 m² with labyrinth. Original decoration, shows on public holidays, lots of young people.

■ **Thermos. Le** (b DR G MA OS SA VS) 13-20 h
77bis Avenue Edouard-Michelin ✉ 63000 *(Gare SNCF)* ☎ 04.73.92.93.25
Hot in winter and pleasantly cool in summer on the nudist terrace.

HEALTH GROUPS

■ **Dispensaire Emile-Roux**
32 Avenue Vercingétorix ✉ 63000 ☎ 04.73.35.12.16
HIV testing.

CRUISING

-Jardin Lecoq
-Place de la Poterne
-Nouvelles Galleries
-Place des Bughes
-Square Blaise-Pascal

Clermont-l'Hérault ✉ 34800

CRUISING

-Lac de Salagou

Clichy ✉ 92110

CRUISING

-Parc Roger-Salengro
-Quai de Clichy

Colmar ✉ 68000

CRUISING

-Parc Rapp (fountain/fontaine)
-Parc du Château d'eau

Colombes ✉ 92700

CRUISING

-Parc de l'île Marante (AYOR)

Compiègne ✉ 60200

DANCECLUBS

■ **Phuture** (B CC D DR G P snu VS YG) 23.30-5 h
10-14 Rue des Boucheries ✉ 60200 *(centre)* ☎ 03.44.86.14.14
In 13th century vaulted crypt. Theme evenings.

CRUISING

-La Faisanderie
-Le Quai Fleurant-Agricola (at the motorway exit Ressons)
-Place du Château
-Ressons-sur-Matz (at the motorway exit in direction of Amiens in the bushes)
-Carrefour du Puits-du-Roy

Concarneau ✉ 29110

CRUISING

-Jardins du Porzou
-Toilettes/facilities de gare routière (at the harbor/sur le port)

Corrençon-en-Vercors ✉ 38250

HOTELS

■ **Caribou. Le** (B CC d F glm H OS Pl SA SOL) Disco Fri 22-2, Sat -3, restaurant 12-14.30, 19-22 h
Le Clos de la Balme ✉ 38250 ☎ 04.76.95.82.82
🖷 04.76.95.83.17
Suburb location. All rooms have private bath. Horse riding in summer, skiing in winter.

Corse

Corse - Ajaccio ✉ 20000

SWIMMING

-Beach next to the airport (Especially in and around the small tower at the end)

CRUISING

-Terre plein de l'aéroport (last parking lot on the right, summer)

Corse - Bastia ✉ 20200

SEX SHOPS/BLUE MOVIES

■ **Extrem' Vidéo** (AC CC g VS) 11-1 h
1 Boulevard Auguste Gaudin ✉ 20200 ☎ 04.95.31.91.44

HEALTH GROUPS

■ **Centre Hospitalier Général Faconaja**
Route Impériale ✉ 20200 ☎ 04.95.55.11.11
HIV-testing.

SWIMMING

-Barcaggio (before villiage, leave D 253 and walk 2 km east)
-Villages naturistes (50 km sur la côte est)

CRUISING

-Café des Platanes -Jardin Romieux -Place De-Gaulle -Place Saint-Nicolas (after 21h, AYOR)

Corse - Bonifacio ✉ 20169

SWIMMING

-Beach/plage "Baie de Stagnolo" (south of/au sud de la plage de Tonara)

Corse - Calvi ✉ 20260

SWIMMING

-Plage de Calvi

Corse - Corbara ✉ 20256

SWIMMING

-Baie de Gienchetu

Corse - Galéria ✉ 20245
SWIMMING
-Caillouteuse (direction Calvi, D 351)

Corse - L'Ile-Rousse ✉ 20220
SWIMMING
-Algajola (north of the beach many gays/beaucoup des gais au nord)

Corse - Propriano ✉ 20110
SWIMMING
-Beach/plage (NU) (between/entre plage du Capu Laurosu & plage de Porto Glio)

Corse - Saint-Florent ✉ 20217
SWIMMING
-Beach at the rocks/plage aux rochers (NU)

Corse - Santo-Pietro-di-Tenda ✉ 20246
SWIMMING
-Anse de Faggiola

Cotignac ✉ 83570
RESTAURANTS
■ **Mas Canta-Dié. Le** (CC F glm OS PI)
Route de Carces ✉ 83570 ☏ 04.94.04.66.57

Cournonsec ✉ 34660
SHOWS
■ **Riviera Show** (B GLM STV) Fri Sat
43 Rue des Barrys ✉ 34660 *(15 min from Montpellier or Sète)* ☏ 04.67.85.30.58

Creil ✉ 60100
CRUISING
-Park/Parc (after 21 h; stay in your car or walk/A partir de 21 h, à pied ou en voiture)

Criel-sur-Mer ✉ 76910
SWIMMING
-Beach/Plage (NU) (under the steep coast between Mesnil-Val-Beach and Criel; be careful at flood-tide/Sous la falaise entre Mesnil-Val-Plage et Criel; dangereux à marée haute)

Dax ✉ 40100
CRUISING
-Allée du Bois du Boulogne (AYOR) (la nuit/at night)
-Cathédrale
-Ancienne Gendarmerie
-Parc des Arènes

Deauville ✉ 14800
BARS
■ **Club 94** (B G) 22-? h
94 Avenue de la République ✉ 14800 ☏ 02.31.98.16.16

CRUISING
-Beach/Plage (3 km-Caen)
-Behind/Derrière le Casino

Dieppe ✉ 76200
SWIMMING
-Plage du Petit-Ailly/Beach (NU)
-Piscine/Swimming Pool(sur la plage le soir/at the beach in the evening)

Dijon ✉ 21000
RESTAURANTS
■ **Concorde. La** (B F g OS) 7-2 h
2 Place d'Arcy ✉ 21000 ☏ 03.80.30.69.43
French cuisine from FF 35-65.

SEX SHOPS/BLUE MOVIES
■ **Librairie Érotique** (CC G VS) 10-24, Sat 10-20 h, closed Sun
64 Rue Berbisey ✉ 21000 ☏ 03.80.30.74.09

SAUNAS/BATHS
■ **Bossuet. Le** (AC b CC DR GLM MA s SA SB VS) 14-1, Sun Mon - 20, glm after 20 h
25 Place Bossuet ✉ 21000 *(near Parvis St Jean Theater)*
☏ 03.80.49.97.45
Very cosy sauna on 200 m² with mirrors and wall paintings. Shows on Fri once a month.
■ **Relaxe. Le** (b DR G MA SA SB VS) 14-20 h
97 Rue Berbisey ✉ 21000 (Bus 5/7/16/19-Hôpital General/1er Mai)
☏ 03.80.30.14.40
Well established sauna existing since 1980.

HEALTH GROUPS
■ **Dispensaire Antivénérien**
1 Rue Nicolas-Berthot ✉ 21035 ☏ 03.80.63.66.00
HIV testing.

CRUISING
-Parc de l'Arquebuse
-Les Allées du parc (Cours du Général-De-Gaulle)
-P du Lac Kir

Dinan ✉ 22100
CRUISING
-Promenade des Douves (below the ramparts/au pied des remparts)
-Cours du Général-De Gaulle
-Parc l'Arquebuse (only in the afternoon)

Diou ✉ 03490
DANCECLUBS
■ **Bataclan. Le** (B CC D glm p S SNU TV VS) Sun 23-4 h
Ecluse de Putay ✉ 03490 ☏ 04.70.42.90.03

Divonne-les-Bains ✉ 01220
CRUISING
-Square municipal
-Route de Crassier

France Dole ▶ Figeac

Dole ✉ 39100
CRUISING
-Parcey (8 km south of Dole at a gravel-pit near river Loue)

Douai ✉ 59500
CRUISING
-Parc Charles-Bertin

Douarnenez ✉ 29100
SWIMMING
-Le Rheum (between/entre la plage de St.Jean & Sables-Blancs; late at night/drague tardive)
-Les/The Dunes (12 km from Douarnenez; during the summer season cruising day and night without interruption; beyond season only from 12 to 14 h /à 12 km de Douarnenez entre 12 et 14 h hors saison, à n'importe quelle heure tout l'été)
-Les Roches blanches (at the edge of the bay, pass along the path of the customs officials; by day also cruising in the wooden huts/Au bord de la baie, le long du sentier des Douaniers; la journée drague dans les blockhaus)

Draguignan ✉ 83300
CRUISING
-Jardin de la Sous-Préfecture (during the day; be discreet)
-Jardin de la gare (day and night)
-Route de Montferrat (sometimes AYOR) (à la sortie du camp militaire de Canjuers (21km) le vendredi soir, soldiers auto stop, be discreet)

Ducey ✉ 50220
RESTAURANTS
■ **Au Rocher de Tombelaine** (B CC F g) 8.30-24 h, closed Oct-Mar
Le Bourg Courtils ✉ 50220 ☎ 02.33.70.96.65

Duclair ✉ 76480
RESTAURANTS
■ **Auberge du Bac. L'** (B CC F g) 12-15, 19-22 h, closed Mon morning
2 Rue Alphonse-Calais, Bac de Jumièges ✉ 76480
☎ 02.35.37.24.16
Menu FF 95-215.

Dunkerque ✉ 59140
HEALTH GROUPS
■ **Tandem**
c/o ADIS, 6 Rue Marengo ✉ 59140 ☎ 03.28.59.19.19
📠 03.28.63.71.14
CRUISING
-behind church/derrière l'église St.Martin
-Passerelle de la Douane (le soir/in the evening)

Durfort ✉ 30170
PRIVATE ACCOMMODATION
■ **Vieille Maison. La** (A BF CC F GLM H msg OS)
✉ 30170 ☎ 66.77.06.46 📠 66.77.55.14
📧 vieillemaison@turqoise.fr 🌐 www.turquoise.fr/vieillemaison
Beautiful old house with 4 rooms to rent dedicated to creativity and art.

Eauze ✉ 32800
CRUISING
-Marché aux Légumes
-Parc Beaulieu

Embrun ✉ 05200
CRUISING
-Garden at the railway station/jardin de la gare
-Postoffice/la poste
-Jardin de l'Archevêché

Epernay ✉ 51200
CRUISING
-Le Jard (in front of the palace of justice/face au palais de justice)
-Covered market/Marché couvert

Epinal ✉ 88000
CRUISING
-Petit Parc (right border between préfecture and Champ de Mars/Rive droite de la "Moselle", entre la préfecture et le Champ de Mars)

Etampes ✉ 91150
CRUISING
-🅿 de Guillervalle

Etretat ✉ 76790
SWIMMING
-Plage du Tilleul (NU) (south of the beach/au sud de la plage)

Evreux ✉ 27000
CRUISING
-Jardin de l'Evêché

Eymoutiers ✉ 87120
RESTAURANTS
■ **Moulin de l'Enfant. Le** (b F g) 12-14.30, 19-? h, closed Mon
✉ 87120 ☎ 05.55.69.24.03

Eze-sur-Mer ✉ 06360
SWIMMING
-Beach/plage de St.Laurent-d'Eze

Fayence ✉ 83440
RESTAURANTS
■ **Pressoir. Le** (b F g s) 12-?, 19.30-? h, Nov-May closed Mon
5 Grande Rue Seillans ✉ 83440 ☎ 04.94.76.85.85
Style of the Fifties.

Figeac ✉ 46100
CRUISING
-Le Celle (facilities and the gardens, in the evening/les toilettes et les jardins, le soir)

Fleury-d'Aude ▶ Grenoble | **France**

Fleury-d'Aude ✉ 11560

RESTAURANTS
■ **Pili Pili. Le** (CC F glm MA OS) 1 Jul-15 Sep every evening, 16 Sep-30 Jun Fri-Sun evening
1 bis Avenue de Beziers ✉ 11560 ☎ 04.68.33.51.30
8 km from Pisse-Vache naturist beach, 16 km from Beziers.

SWIMMING
-Pisse-Vache (NU) (beach between St. Pierre and Les Cabanes de Fleury, 1 km-camping municipal)

Foix ✉ 09000

CRUISING
-behind the postoffice/derrière la poste.

Fontainebleau ✉ 77300

CRUISING
-Croix du Grand-Maître (in the forest and in the surroundings of the bridge/En fôret et vers l'aqueduc)

Fos-sur-Mer ✉ 13270

CRUISING
-the dunes/les dunes (entre/between la pointe St.Gervais et/and la Centrale EDF)

Fouras ✉ 17450

SWIMMING
-Beach/plage de l'Espérance

Fréhel ✉ 22240

SWIMMING
-Plorien (Vieux-Bourg)

Fréjus ✉ 83600

RESTAURANTS
■ **Auberge des Adrets** (BF F g H) Restaurant: 12-14, 19-22.30 h, closed Mon & 11.Nov-14.Dec & 1.-15.Mar
Lieu dit Auberge-des-Adrets, RN7 ✉ 83600 ☎ 04.94.40.36.24

SWIMMING
-Dunes de St-Aygule

Gallargues-le-Montueux ✉ 30660

PROPERTY SERVICES
■ **Agence Yves Lozé** Mon-Fri 9-12, 15-19, Sat 9-12 h
33 Rue de Vergeze ✉ 30660 ☎ 04.66.35.38.56
Property agency.

Gap ✉ 05000

HEALTH GROUPS
■ **Aides Provence** 1st Tue 14-16 h
24 Rue Saint-Arey ✉ 05000 ☎ 04.92.53.43.93 📠 04.92.51.64.41
📧 aides.provence.free.fr

CRUISING
-Jardin de la Pépinière
-La patinoire

Gardanne ✉ 13120

CRUISING
-Place de la République

Gien ✉ 45500

CRUISING
-Place du Château

Gigny-sur-Saône ✉ 71240

DANCECLUBS
■ **Why Not. Le** (AC B CC D GLM OS p PI SNU WE YG) Fri-Sun & before public holidays 23-5 h
Chateau de la colonne ✉ 71240 ☎ 03.85.44.81.71
Garden & swimming pool in summer.

Golf-Juan ✉ 06100

SWIMMING
-Plage de la Batterie (near service station between Cannes and Golf Juan, popular nudist beach)

Gourin ✉ 56110

DANCECLUBS
■ **Starman. Le** (B D DR GLM H MA p s TV) Sat gay 23-5 h
4 Rue de la Gare ✉ 56110 ☎ 02.97.23.66.78
Disco and private hotel.

Grenoble ✉ 38000

BARS
■ **George V** (AC CC D G MA p)
124 Cours Berriat ✉ 38000 ☎ 04.76.84.16.20
■ **Queen's. Le** (B TV VS) 10-1, Sun 18-1 h
62 Cours Jean-Jaurès ✉ 38000 ☎ 04.76.54.13.70
■ **Rutli. The** (AC B CC G MA p) 17-1 h, Sun 18-1, summer 19-1 h, closed Mon
9 Rue Etienne Marcel ✉ 38000 ☎ 04.76.43.21.16
2nd bar upstairs at WE.

SEX SHOPS/BLUE MOVIES
■ **Sexashop** (G VS) 9-22, Sun 15-22 h
2 Rue de Miribel ✉ 38000 ☎ 04.76.46.70.86

SAUNAS/BATHS
■ **Oxygène** (b DR G SA SB VS WH) Mon-Thu 13.30-20.30, Fri -1 h (mixed on WE)
24, Rue Mallifaud ✉ 38100 ☎ 04.76.87.30.00
■ **Saint-Ferjus. Le** (b G SA SOL VS) 14-21, Fri 14-24 h
22 Rue Saint Ferjus ✉ 38000 (next to Place de Verdun)
☎ 04.76.54.13.70
Popular sauna in the centre of the city with free parking places.

HOTELS
■ **Hôtel Rochambeau** (g H) 8-24 h, closed Sun
13 Avenue Rochambeau ✉ 38000 ☎ 04.76.96.05.34
Animals welcome.

France | Grenoble ▶ Ile-du-Levant

HEALTH GROUPS

■ **Aides Dauphiné-Savoie** Mon Wed 19.30-22 h
B.P. 381 ✉ 38015 ☏ 04.76.46.07.58
Help and information about Aids/Entraide et information sur le Sida.

CRUISING

-Piscine Bemat
-Monument des Diables bleus
-Hôtel-de-Ville (night/nuit)
-Parc de l'Ile-Verte
-Rue Malherbe (garden/jardin)
-Champs-sur-Drac (summer)
-Etangs de St-Egrève (summer)
-Monument des Diables bleus
-Parc Paul-Mistral
-Parc Foch
-Place Victor-Hugo

Grignan ✉ 26230

BARS

■ **Greco. Le** (CC D DR GLM MA OS p Pl s VS) Disco: Fri Sat 23-5 h, in summer + Sun
Le Fraysse (Hamlet) on the D4 ✉ 26230 ☏ 04.75.46.51.66
Discotheque, bar, restaurant everyday. Bar & restaurant open only in summer with pool, rooms available.

Gruissan ✉ 11430

RESTAURANTS

■ **Brin de Folie. Le** (CC F G OS) Thu-Mon 12-14, 19-22.30, Apr-Sep Mon-Sun 12-14, 19-23.30 h
Place du Cadran-Solaire ✉ 11430 (At Grazel beach)
☏ 04.68.49.14.08
Thierry and Christian welcome you.

SWIMMING

-Beach/plage (NU) (between/entre Plage de Narbonne & Plage de Gruissan)

CRUISING

-Etang de Mateil

Guérande ✉ 44350

DANCECLUBS

■ **Villa la Grange** (B CC D g MA) Jul-Aug: 23-6, Apr-Sep: Fri Sat 23-6 h
Ch. de la Nantaise ✉ 44350 ☏ 40.60.00.38
Most famous danceclub of La Baune.

Guéret ✉ 23000

CRUISING

-Place Bonhyaud (gare SNCF/railway station)

Herbignac ✉ 44410

RESTAURANTS

■ **Eau-de-Mer. L'** (B F g) 12-15, 19-22 h, closed 1.Oct-1.Mar
Kermoureau-Pompas ✉ 44410 ☏ 02.40.91.32.36

Honfleur ✉ 14600

BARS

■ **Charles V. Le** (B G MA p SNU VS) May-Sep: 12-3, Oct-Apr: 16-3 h closed Tue, some Fri theme parties
25 Boulevard Charles VF ✉ 14600 ☏ 02.31.89.96.70
Bar and small video room.

RESTAURANTS

■ **Au Gai Luron** (CC F glm OS s) closed Wed evening, Thu lunch and dinner, Jul-Aug open every day
20 Place Sainte Catherine ✉ 14600 ☏ 02.31.89.99.90

CRUISING

-Marché aux poissons (behind the fish market, summer only 17-19 h)

Hossegor ✉ 40150

BARS

■ **Tilt. Le** (AC B CC GLM N S YG) 19-3 h
366 Avenue du Touring Club ✉ 40150 ☏ 05.58.41.71.34

RESTAURANTS

■ **Pizzaiol. Le** (AC B CC F glm MA OS) Summer: 12-1, winter: 12-15 19-24 h
376 Avenue du Touring Club ✉ 40150 *(town center next to Hotel Key West)* ☏ 05.58.43.57.04

HOTELS

■ **Key West** (BF CC glm H MA) open all year
366 Avenue du Touring Club ✉ 40150 ☏ 05.58.43.57.04
🖷 05.58.43.65.74 ✉ pizzaiol@wanadoo.fr
Motel style hotel. Reception at restaurant Pizzaiol next-door and bar Le Tilt.

SWIMMING

-Nudist beach/plage naturiste

Houplines ✉ 59116

BARS

■ **Café Brasserie la Nouvelle France** (B g) 7.30-21, Sun 7.30-14 h
84 Rue Carnot ✉ 59116 ☏ 03.20.77.46.82

Hourtin ✉ 33990

SWIMMING

-Hourtin-plage (au sud/in the south)
-Plage du Pin sec (Naujac-sur-Mer. Au nord/in the north)

Hyères ✉ 83400

SWIMMING

-Rochers de Gien (NU) (Côte sud-ouest)
-Plage des Salins (last beach; the restaurant "Chez Pimpin" marks the entrance to the nude section)

Ile-du-Levant ✉ 83400

HOTELS

■ **Chez Valery** (B F glm H NU)
✉ 83400 ☏ 04.94.05.90.83 🖷 04.94.05.92.95
Restaurant and hotel with 8 rooms and 4 bungalows.

Ile-du-Levant ▸ La Rochelle France

■ **Eglantine. L'** (GLM H NU) 1st of May-30th of Sep
Corniche l'Arbousier ✉ 83400 *(6 min form the seaside, 1 min from the village)* ☎ 04.94.05.92.50 📠 04.94.05.92.50
Located in the naturist island in the mediterranean. Rooms & apartments to rent. Simple accomodation in large villa.

CRUISING
-Ile-du-Levant (behind the castle, evening/ derrière le château, le soir)
-Jardin Denis
-Bus station/gare des bus

Ile-sur-la-Sorgue ✉ 84800

RESTAURANTS
■ **Petit Jardin. Le** (F b glm)
19 Place Rose Gouclard ✉ 84800 ☎ 04.90.20.87.67

Issy-les-Moulineaux ✉ 92130

CRUISING
-Pont et Ile de Billancourt
-Parc Henri-Barbusse

Ivry-sur-Seine ✉ 94200

CRUISING
-Parc J.-Coutant
-Piscine municipale (avec sauna ouvert jusqu'à 21 h)

Joue-les-Tours ✉ 37300

DANCECLUBS
■ **Cage. La** (B D g S) 22-4 h
1 Avenue de Bordeaux ✉ 37300 ☎ 02.47.28.81.81
Entrance during shows: FF 50-100.

Juan-les-Pins ✉ 06160

SAUNAS/BATHS
■ **Amadeus** (G MA SA SB VS) 15-22 h, closed on Tue
67 Boulevard Raymond Poincaré ✉ 06160 *(5 min from railway station, Bus-Pauline)* ☎ 04.93.61.03.31
Fun relaxed atmosphere in kitsch decor.

La Barre-de-Monts ✉ 85550

SWIMMING
-Plage des Lays (NU)

La Chaise-Dieu ✉ 43160

RESTAURANTS
■ **Grange. La** (b F glm OS) Jul-Sep 12-24; winter 12-14 19-21 h
Rue St. Martin ✉ 43160 ☎ 04.71.00.02.00

La Ciotat ✉ 13600

SWIMMING
-Rocher du Liouquet (to the left behind Cap Saint-Louis)

La Croix-Valmer ✉ 83420

SWIMMING
-Beach/Plage du Brouis

La Ferté-Gaucher ✉ 77320

GUEST HOUSES
■ **Fontaine aux Loups. La** (BF F glm H OS PI WH)
✉ 77320 *(9 km from La Ferté Gaucher by D215 direction Montmirail)* ☎ 01.64.03.76.76 📠 01.64.03.76.77 ✉ ceranrs@club.internet.fr
Country retreat 1 hour from Paris.

La Grande-Motte ✉ 34280

RESTAURANTS
■ **Brasserie de la Mer/Chez Fabrice** (b CC F g) 12-15, 19-24 h
Quai d'Honneur ✉ 34280 ☎ 04.67.56.75.93
French cuisine. Glossy atmosphere on the harbour. Lunch and dinner.

HOTELS
■ **Hôtel Azur** (H GLM PI) closed 1.Dec-6.Jan
Presqu'île du Port ✉ 34280 ☎ 04.67.56.56.00 📠 04. 67.29.81.26
Beach location. Small bedrooms equipped with AC, mini-bar, telephone, colour TV. Room with shower/WC FF 495, with bath/WC 595, bf 42.

CRUISING
-Le Grand Travers (between Carnon and la Grande Motte)
-Point Zéro

La Plaine-sur-Mer ✉ 44770

SWIMMING
-Criques de Prefailles (beach in front of/ plage en face de camping municipal)

La Rochelle ✉ 17000

BARS
■ **Insolite. L'** (B G MA) 14-2, Sun 17-2 h
12 Rue Bletterie ✉ 17000 *(300 m from the harbour)*
☎ 05.46.41.90.51

DANCECLUBS
■ **Tuxedo Café** (B D G) 21-5 h
Place de la Préfecture ✉ 17000 ☎ 05.46.50.01.22
Bar disco.

HEALTH GROUPS
■ **Centre Hospitalier de la Rochelle. Service de Médecine Interne**
Rue Albert-Schweitzer, B.P. 38 49 ✉ 17019 ☎ 05.46.27.33.33
HIV-testing.

SWIMMING
-Le Marouillet (à 12 km de La Rochelle)
-Plage de St-Jean-des-Sables (NU)(à 8 km de La Rochelle)

CRUISING
-Casino (public garden, evening/jardin public, le soir)
-Rue Thiers (afternoon and evening/l'après-midi et le soir)
-Bridge/pont de Chagnolet
-Le Marché couvert (Rue Thiers)
-Parc d'Orbigny (derrière le casino)
-P de la Tour carrée (a proximité de lar mer/close to the ocean)

France La Roche-sur-Yon ▶ Le Conquet

La Roche-sur-Yon ✉ 85000

HEALTH GROUPS
■ **Aides Vendée** Mon-Fri 16-19 h
Boulevard Branly, Cité des Forges ✉ 85000 *(Bâtiment A, Escalier D, 7e, Porte 106)* ☎ 02.51.46.20.62

SWIMMING
-Beach/plage (NU)

CRUISING
-Cours Bayard
-Railway station/gare SNCF
-Place de la Vendée

La Seyne-sur-Mer ✉ 83500

SWIMMING
-Plage de Fabregas (at night/la nuit)
-Beach/plage du Jonquet (G NU)

La Teste ✉ 33260

SWIMMING
-Nudist beach/plage naturiste

La Tranche-sur-Mer ✉ 85360

SWIMMING
-Conches (beach between/plage entre Longeville & La Tranche)

Lacanau ✉ 33680

SWIMMING
-Wood house of Lion/Maison forestière du Lion
-Le Porge-Océan (Best Jul-Sep)

L'Alpe-d'Huez ✉ 38750

RESTAURANTS
■ **Petite Taverne. La** (b F glm OS) 1 Dec-30 Apr & 1 Jul-31 Aug 8-2 h
Galerie des 4 Soleils, Hameau de l'Eclose ✉ 38750 ☎ 04.76.80.32.25
Mountain specialities. Reservation recommended.

Lamure-sur-Azergues ✉ 69870

GUEST HOUSES
■ **Château de Pramenoux** (BF glm F H OS s)
✉ 69870 ☎ 04.74.03.16.43 📠 04.74.03.16.28
10th-12th century Château in the mountains of Beaujolais. Comfortable rooms and table d'hôtes. Large room for receptions.

Landeronde ✉ 85150

BARS
■ **Damier. Le** (B CC D G) Fri-Sun 22.30-5 h, Jul-Aug Wed-Sun 23.30-5 h
RN 260 ➡ La Roche sur Yon ✉ 85150 *(between La Roche sur Yon and Sables d'Olonne)* ☎ 02.51.34.29.09

Lannion ✉ 22300

SWIMMING
-Beach of/Plage de Beg-Leguer (NU) (between Lannion and Trebeurden; difficult access/entre Lannion et Trebeurden; accès escarpé)

CRUISING
-[P] at the cemetery (in the afternoon)

Lauzerte ✉ 82110

GUEST HOUSES
■ **Jardin Secret. Le** (BF f glm H OS PI SA SB WH)
c/o Maison Tournesol, Rue de la Garrigue ✉ 82110
☎ 05.63.95.72.88 📠 05.63.94.63.41
Small guest house with a garden, pool, sauna and steam room in a medieval town between Montauban & Cahors. 90 km to Toulouse airport.

Laval ✉ 53000

BARS
■ **Vulcain. Le** (B glm) Mon-Sat 18-2 h
32 Grande Rue ✉ 53000 ☎ 02.43.56.09.86

GENERAL GROUPS
■ **WATT!! Les Courants Homosexuels** (GLM) Wed 20-22 h
13 Rue des Béliers ✉ 53000 ☎ 02.43.69.35.08
Gay and lesbian association. Welcoming and information.

HEALTH GROUPS
■ **Centre Hospitalier de Laval. Service de Médecine Interne 7**
37 Rue du Haut-Rocher, B.P. 4280 ✉ 53024 ☎ 02.43.66.50.00
HIV-testing.

CRUISING
-Bois de l'Huisserie
-Basilique d'Avesnières

Lavaur ✉ 81500

BARS
■ **Taverne de la Dame du Plô. La** (AC B CC d f glm H MA OS p s)
18-4 h, Sun afternoon only, closed Mon
5 Rue Père Colin ✉ 81500 ☎ 05.63.41.38.77
Piano Bar and art gallery with accomodation available. In 16th century building. In the middle of the triangle Toulouse-Albi-Castre.

Le Cannet ✉ 06110

CRUISING
-Jardin du Tivoli
-Place Bellevue
-Le Lavoir
-[P] St-Sauveur
-Terminus des bus

Le Conquet ✉ 29217

SWIMMING
-Plage du nord de Lanse des Sablons (take the road D28 direction Ploumguer, then left to Porz Illien)

CRUISING
-Halles St-Louis

Le Croisic ✉ 44490
SWIMMING
-La Turballe (Pen-Bron, beach behind the pyramid/plage après la pyramide)

Le Grau-du-Roi ✉ 30240
SWIMMING
-Plage Port-Camargues
-Plage de l'Espiguette (G NU) (for explanation ⇒ Aigues-Mortes)

CRUISING
-Quai Laperouse

Le Havre ✉ 76600
BARS
▪ **Bar du Bassin** (B CC GLM s) 15-2, Sat Sun 18-2 h
79-81 Quai George V ✉ 76600 ☏ 02.35.41.28.82
Once a month theme night.
▪ **Etage Bar. L'** (B CC G) 19.2 h, closed on Thu
137 Rue d'Etretat ✉ 76600 ☏ 02.35.48.50.59
▪ **Village. Le** (B GLM) 18-2 h
74-76 Rue Voltaire ✉ 76600 ☏ 02.35.42.57.95

RESTAURANTS
▪ **Grignot. Le** (F glm) 12-1 h
53 Rue Racoye ✉ 76600

SAUNAS/BATHS
▪ **Delos. Le** (b DR G MA SA SB SOL VS) 14.30-22 h, closed on Sun
139 Rue Maréchal Joffre ✉ 76600 ☏ 02.35.19.05.39
Little sauna
▪ **Hot Way** (b DR Glm p MSG SA SB VS WH VS) 14-22, Sun 15-22 h
60 Rue Dauphine ✉ 76600 *(neighbourhood St François)*
☏ 02.35.22.58.52
Clean sauna with theme nights first Fri of the month. Rent and sale of videos.

SWIMMING
-Beach/Plage du Ste.Adresse (NU) (at the end near airport/au bout près de l'aéroport)
-Beach/Plage du Tilleul (23 km from Le Havre towards Etretat, after the rocks/23 km du Havre en direction de Etretat, après les rochers)

CRUISING
-Forest of/Forêt de Montgeon (AYOR) (in the surroundings of/aux alentours du Château d'Eau)
-Place Danton

Le Lavandou ✉ 83980
SWIMMING
-Nudist beach/plage naturiste

Le Mans ✉ 72000
BARS
▪ **Arc-En-Ciel Bar** (A B CC GLM MA TV) 17-2 h. closed on MOn
2 Rue Dorée ✉ 72000 *(between Place de l'Eglise and Eglise St. Benoît)* ☏ 02.43.23.80.16

DANCECLUBS
▪ **Limite. La** (B CC D GLM MA p s) 23.30-5 h, closed Mon Tue
7 Rue Saint-Honoré ✉ 72000 ☏ 02.43.24.85.54

SEX SHOPS/BLUE MOVIES
▪ **Sex Shop 72** (AC CC DR GLM MA TV VS YG) 10-22, Sun & public holidays 15-20 h
72 Rue Bourg Belé ✉ 72000 ☏ 02.43.28.51.39

SAUNAS/BATHS
▪ **Nil. Le** (AC b DR f G MA SA SB VS WH) 15-22.30, Mon Wed 15-21 h
36 Rue de Fleurus ✉ 72000 *(close to the train station)*
☏ 02.43.23.26.81

HEALTH GROUPS
▪ **Centre Hospitalier Général. Service de Dermatologie**
194 Avenue Rubillard ✉ 72000 *(Pavillon Duperrat)*
☏ 02.43.43.43.43
HIV-testing.

CRUISING
-Esplanade des Jacobins (night/nuit)
-Jardin de Tesse(avenue de Paderborn)
-Place de Pontlieue (WC)
-[P] Tertre
-[P] Cormier

France — Le Palais ▸ Lille

Le Palais ✉ 56360

BARS
■ **Frégate. La** (B g) 8-2 h, closed Oct-Mar
Quai de l'Acadie ✉ 56360 ☎ 02.97.31.43.76

SWIMMING
-Beach/plage du Dotchau (NU)

Le Pouliguen ✉ 44510

BARS
■ **Petit Navire. Le** (B CC d GLM MA OS P) Jun-Sep 9-3 & Fri Sat Sun in winter; other days 9-1, closed Tue (not Jul Aug)
7 Rue du Gal. Leclerc ✉ 44510 ☎ 02.40.42.41.59

Le Puy-en-Velay ✉ 43000

CRUISING
-Jardin Henry-Vinay
-Place Michelet
-Place du Breuil

Le Touquet ✉ 62520

GUEST HOUSES
■ **Oakland B&B** (BF GLM H MA OS) during holidays
71 Allée des Biches ✉ 62780 *(5 min from Le Touquet)*
☎ 03.21.94.38.14 ✉ www.chez.com/oaklandbb
In the nature, near the forest. Many sport activities possible. Old-style decorated rooms.

CRUISING
-In the dunes

Lens ✉ 62300

CRUISING
-Public garden/jardin public
-Parc de Glissaies (behind the railway station/derrière la gare)

Les Rousses ✉ 39400

CRUISING
-Lake of/Lac des Rousses (behind the rocks in the little wood. Pretty hot in summer/derrière le rocher dans le petit bois. L'été, assez chaud)
-Around the Tourism House, close to the telephone booth/autour de la maison du Tourisme vers la cabine téléphonique

Leucate ✉ 11370

RESTAURANTS
■ **Restaurant Le Clos de Ninon** (A B F glm) 12-15, 19-1, meals -23 €
12 Avenue Francis Vals, Leucate-Village ✉ 11370
☎ 04.68.40.18.16

SWIMMING
-Beach of Leucate/Leucate-Plage (NU) (north of the straight-families' beach/au nord de la plage familiale)
-Northern beach of the villages Ulysse and Aphrodite/Plage du nord commune aux villages naturistes

Levallois-Perret ✉ 92300

CRUISING
-Parc Louis-Rouquier

Lille ✉ 59000

GAY INFO
■ **Lesbian & Gay Pride Lille**
15 Rue Malpart, B.P. 222 ✉ 59002 ✉ LGPLille@apg-tm.com
Organises the city's gay pride.

BARS
■ **Activy. L'** (B GLM MA)
6 Rue Anatole France ✉ 59000
■ **Mam'zelle Fifi** (B GLM MA OS) 11-2 h
59 Jacques Louchard, Les Terrasses Ste Catherine ✉ 59000
■ **Ramponneau. Le** (AC B E glm lj MA N p) Tue-Fri 8-1, Sat-Sun 16-1, Mon 8-20 h
22 Square du Ramponneau ✉ 59800 *(M° Rihour)*, Façade de l'Esplanade ☎ 03.20.74.49.80
■ **The Mum's Bar** (AC B CC G p s SNU YG) 21-2, Sun 16-2 h
4 Rue Doudin ✉ 59000 *(M° Rihour. In the old town)*
☎ 03.20.06.32.22
Look for the gay flag.

DANCECLUBS
■ **Zenith. Le** (B D GLM P) Thu-Sun 23-? h
74 Avenue de Flandre ✉ 59650 *(surbub of Lille)* ☎ 03.20.89.92.29

RESTAURANTS
■ **P'tits Lous. Les** (B F g) Tue-Fri 12-14.30, 19-23.30, Sat 19-.23.30, Sun 12-15 h, 12-25 Aug and 23 Dez-5 Jan closed
4 Place de la Nouvelle Aventure ✉ 59000 ☎ 03.20.57.15.05

SEX SHOPS/BLUE MOVIES
■ **Boîte à Films. La** (DR g MA VS) 10-1 h
39 Rue de Roubaix ✉ 59800 ☎ 03.20.51.29.51
■ **Cinesex** (AC CC glm VS) 10-23, Sun 12-23 h
41 Rue des Ponts-de-Comines ✉ 59000 ☎ 03.20.06.25.83
■ **Golden Boy** (AC CC glm s VS) 10-23 h
14 Rue de la Quenette ✉ 59800 *(M° Gare)* ☎ 03.20.06.34.26
Sex shop and video projection room/Sex shop et salle de projection vidéos.
■ **Sex Center** (AC CC g s VS) 10-24 h
41 Rue des Ponts de Comines ✉ 59800 *(M° Rihour)*
☎ 03.20.06.25.83
Erotic products, videos and DVD's.

SAUNAS/BATHS
■ **Bains. Les** (AC B DR F G msg SA SB SOL VS WH WO YG) 12-24, WE 14-24 h
52 Rue de Cambrai ✉ 59000 *(M°-Porte de Valenciennes)*
☎ 03.20.53.02.02
The gay meeting place of the North on 4 floors.
■ **Lokal. Le** (AC B CC DR F G SA SB SOL VS WH YG) 12-24 h
95bis rue du Molinel ✉ 59800 *(centre)* ☎ 03.20.30.67.85
Many special parties organised.

GENERAL GROUPS
■ **Abou-Nawas Project**
La Bassée 33 ✉ 59480
Support and contact for muslim and arab gays and lesbians. Only by post.

Lille | France

800m²
4 floors
bar
mezzanine plage
double sauna
double hammam
jacuzzi
restaurant
solarium
vidéo

les bains

★★★★★

International Sauna
12-24H
WE 14-24H

www.lesbains.fr

52 rue de Cambrai
Lille
33 (0)3 20 53 02 02

The hottest meeting place of the North

France ▶ Lille ▶ Limoges

le lokal
sauna for men

sauna
whirlpool
steam bath
relax rooms
dark room
video
solarium
snacks
bar
tv

03 20 30 67 85

95 bis, rue du molinel - 59800 lille
(metro gare lille/flandres) - 7/7J-12h/24h

■ **Andromède**
B.P. 1016 ✉ 59011 ☎ 03.20.30.65.54
📧 andromede@minitel.net
Youth group.
■ **Comité pour la Reconnaissance Sociale des Homosexuels (CRSH)**
B.P. 51 ✉ 59008 ☎ 03.20.31.90.67 ✉ sladent@worldnet.fr
Group acting for the recognition of gay rights.
■ **Gai-Kitsch Camp**
B.P. 36 ✉ 59009 ☎ 03.20.06.33.91 ☎ 03.20.78.18.76
📧 GKC@worldnet.fr
Minitel 3615 GKC Organizer of a gay film festival. Also book publishers.
■ **J'en suis - J'y reste** (B d GLM) Tue 18-23, Wed 16-20, Fri 20-23 h
19 Rue de Condé ✉ 59200 (M° Porte d'Arras) ☎ 03.20.52.28.68
📠 03.20.52.28.68
Call for more details on activities. Fri girls only. Includes Les Flamands Roses(GLM), Pourquoi Pas, Au Lieu d'Elles.

HEALTH GROUPS
■ **Aides**
209 Boulevard de la Liberté ✉ 59800 ☎ 03.28.52.05.10
📠 03.28.52.05.11
Minitel 36 15 AIDES.

HELP WITH PROBLEMS
■ **SOS Solitude gaie** 0-24 h
✉ 59000 ☎ 03.20.04.24.17

SPORT GROUPS
■ **Ch'ti Randos**
B.P. 18 ✉ 59008
Organises walking tours and hiking/Gays randonneurs.

CRUISING
-Bois de Boulogne (ayor) (Forest of Boulogne; at the north end, behind the stad. along the canal and in the groves; at night also on the P of the avenue Mathias-Delobel/A l'extrémité nord, derrière le stade, le long du canal, dans les bosquets; la nuit sur le P de l'avenue Mathias-Delobel)
-Bois de Phalempin (Forest of Phalempin, south of Lille, go 15 km on the A1 highway, leave it at exit Seclin and then take the road D8./Au sud de Lille, 15 km par autoroute A1, sortie Seclin, puis route D8)
-Groves in the northern part of town/Bosquets du périphérique nord Boulevard Robert-Schumann (go by car direction St.André; esplanade/en voiture, direction St.André; esplanade)
-Railway station/gare SNCF
-Square de la Porte-de-Roubaix (AYOR)
-Jardin Vauban/Vauban garden
-Stade Gimonprez-Jooris (AYOR; OG)
-University campus/Campus Universitaire (in the surroundings of the library/Autour de la bibliothèque)
-Belgian border/Frontière belge (see/voir Courtrai, Kuurne, Mouscron, Pipaix, Tournai, Bonsecours and/et Willaupuis)

Limoges ✉ 87000

BARS
■ **Café Traxx** (b d glm MG OS) Mon-Fri 12-2, Sat 15-12 h
Place Fontaine des Barres 12 ✉ 87000 ☎ 05.55.32.07.55
■ **Volcanique. Le** (B g) 7.30-2, Sat Sun 5-2 h
51 Ave du Général Leclerc ✉ 87000 ☎ 55.77.41.13
Mixed bar. Mainly gay after 21 h.

266 *SPARTACUS* 2001/2002

Limoges ▸ Luchon France

DANCECLUBS
■ **Panthère Rose. La** (AC BF CC B D DR GLM NU P VS)
Thu-Sun 23-6 h
56 Route du Pont Saint Marial ✉ 8700 ☎ 55.32.27.14

SAUNAS/BATHS
■ **Eros** (AC b CC DR G p SA SB SOL VS WH YG) 14-2, Fri Sat -4 h
8 Rue Jean Jaurès ✉ 87000 ☎ 05.55.32.74.48
Two establishments at the same address, one gay, one mixed. Also sex-shop.

HEALTH GROUPS
■ **Centre Hospitalier R.U. Dupuytren. Service de Médecine A**
2 Avenue Alexis-Carel ✉ 87000 ☎ 05.55.05.66.52
HIV testing.

CRUISING
-Bois de la Bastide (AYOR)
-Garden of/Jardin de l'ancien Palais de l'Évêché
-Champ de Juillet (AYOR R TV)
-P Cora (Route de Paris)
-Place de la Cathédrale (AYOR)

Limoges-Branchard ✉ 70280

HOTELS
■ **Auberge de l'Etape** (F H s)
RN 20 ✉ 70280 ☎ 55.37.14.33 📠 55.37.24.80

Limoux ✉ 11300

HOTELS
■ **Hotel Moderne et Pigeon** (B BF F H OS) Restaurant closed Sat lunch and Mon
1 Place General Leclerc ✉ 11300 ☎ 04.68.31.00.25
📠 04.68.31.12.43
Renovated 18th century mansion. Quote SPARTACUS.

GENERAL GROUPS
■ **Homosexualités Audoises**
B.P. 27 ✉ 11303

Lisieux ✉ 14100

CRUISING
-Public garden/jardin public
-Hôtel-de-Ville
-Railway station/Gare SNCF
-Rue du Char

Loison-sous-Lens ✉ 62318

BARS
■ **Club 175. Le** (B D E GLM MA P stv) Bar: Mon-Thu 22-?, Disco: Fri-Sun 22-? h
175 Route de Lille ✉ 62218 ☎ 03.21.28.05.30

Lons-le-Saunier ✉ 39000

CRUISING
-Public garden/Jardin Public

Lorient ✉ 56100

BARS
■ **Drôles de...** (B GLM MA) Jun-Sep 18-2, Oct-May Mon-Sat 15-1, Sun 18-1 h
26 Rue Jules Legrand ✉ 56100 ☎ 02.97.21.08.73

SEX SHOPS/BLUE MOVIES
■ **Espace Broadway** (AC glm VS) 11-20, Mon 13-23, Fri 11-23 h, closed Sun & Aug
15 Rue Poissinière ✉ 56100 ☎ 02.97.21.81.64
Local gay information available. 10% reduction for Spartacus readers.
■ **Love Love** (g VS) 10-12, 14-23 h, closed Sun
44 Rue Maréchal-Foch
✉ 56100
☎ 02.97.21.29.75

SAUNAS/BATHS
■ **Korosko. Le** (CC b DR f G MA SA SB VS WH) 14-22, Tue -20, Wed Sat -24 h, mixed on Fri
18 Rue Lazare Carnot ✉ 56100 *(near harbour)*
☎ 02.97.35.07.50
Sauna with sling frequented by a mixed age crowd.

CRUISING
-Jardin Le Faoudic (Place Anatole-le-Braz, harbour/port)
-Ile de Groix (beach on the west coast/ plage sur la côte ouest)
-Kaolins (nudist beach/plage naturiste)

Luchon ✉ 31100

HOTELS
■ **Hôtel Panoramic** (b BF CC E F g H MA)
6 Avenue Carnot ✉ 31110 ☎ 05.61.79.30.90
📠 05.61.79.32.84
✉ hotel.panoramic@wanadoo.fr
Quote Spartacus for a 5% reduction.

Luchon, a famous spa resort and Superbagnères, its ski area, in the French Pyrenees, is the place to be for an active holiday in summer and winter time. Nice hotel in the centre of the town, at 300 m from the cable-lifts to go to the ski resort.

Breakfast buffet - private and closed car park - locked storeroom for sports material.

Panoramic hôtel
6, avenue Carnot
F-31110 **Bagnères-de-Luchon**
Tél. +33 (0)561.79.30.90 • fax +33 (0)561.79.32.84
E-mail: hotel.panoramic@wanadoo.fr

Quote Spartacus for 5% reduction!

Lunay ✉ 41360

PRIVATE ACCOMMODATION

■ **Château de la Vaudourière** (BF CC g H MA PI)
✉ 41360   ☎ 02.54.72.19.46   📠 02.54.72.19.46
Antique shop and Bed & Breakfast.

Lunel ✉ 34400

BARS

■ **Zeeboys, Le** (B D GLM OS S YG) 23-?, closed Mon Tue Wed,
Show: Fri-Sun 2.30 h
Route de Nîmes ✉ 34400 *(RN 113)* ☎ 04.67.71.02.01
Disco between Nimes and Montpellier.

Lyon ✉ 69000

TOURIST INFO

■ **Tourist Info**
Place Bellecour, B.P. 2254 ✉ 69214 ☎ 04.72.77.69.69
📠 04.78.42.04.32

BARS

■ **Bar du Centre** (AC B CC G MA p) 8-3, Sun 17-3 h
3 Rue Simon Maupin ✉ 69002 *(M° Bellecour. Opposite Sauna Bellecour.)* ☎ 04.78.37.40.18
■ **Broadway, Le** (AC B CC DR GLM MA p s VS) 21-? h, closed Tue
9 Rue Terraille ✉ 69001 ☎ 04.78.39.50.54
Cocktail bar
■ **Cap Opéra** (AC B G) 14-1 h
2 Place Louis Pradel ✉ 69001 *(near Opera)* ☎ 04.72.07.61.55
■ **Forum Bar** (AC B CC DR GLM lj MA OS p VS) 17-2, Fri Sat -3 h
15 Rue des Quatre Chapeaux ✉ 69002 ☎ 04.78.37.19.74
■ **Lax Bar** (AC B DR f G MA OS p S VS) 14-? h
2 Rue Coysevox ✉ 69001 *(at Rue René Leynard, M° Hôtel de Ville)*
☎ 04.78.27.10.14
Giant screen, cyber café, bar on 200 m². Terrace in summer. Gogo nights.
■ **Motor Men Bar** (AC B DR G lj MA OS) 19-2, Fri Sat 3 h
2 Rue Bellecordière ✉ 69000 ☎ 04.72.56.06.06
■ **Ruche Café, La** (AC B glm MA)
22 Rue Gentil ✉ 69002 ☎ 04.78.37.42.26
■ **Spartac Café** (AC B F GLM MA) 10-1 h
3 Place St. Paul ✉ 69000 ☎ 04.78.28.03.32
■ **Verre à Soi, Le** (A AC B CC GLM MA p WE) 14-3, Sat 19-3 h, closed Sun
25 Rue des Capucins ✉ 69001 *(M° Croix Paquet)*
☎ 04.78.28.92.44
Many theme parties. Happy hour 14-20 h + promotions.
■ **Versus** (A B D GLM VS)
17 Rue René Leynaud ✉ 69001

MEN'S CLUBS

■ **Backstage** (AC CC DR G MA P VS) 14-24 h
1 Rue des Capucins ✉ 69001 *(M° Hotel de Ville)* ☎ 04.78.30.60.44
Sex shop with cruising and video cabin area on 3 floors. Theme nights.
■ **Trou, Le** (AC b CC DR G lj MA p VS) Mon-Thu 19-5, Fri Sat -7, Sun 14-5 h
6 Rue Romarin ✉ 69001 *(M° Hôtel de Ville)* ☎ 04.78.39.98.69
Video labyrinth, sling and dungeon.
■ **1er Sous-Sol** (CC G p VS) 14-3, Fri Sat -7 h
7 Rue du Puits-Guillot ✉ 69001 *(M° Hôtel de Ville)*
☎ 04.78.29.28.87
500 sq.m. of cruising/drague.

Bar-Tapas-Cyber music-Vidéo-Cruising-Soirées
Terrasse-Apéro piano bar-Billard-Gogos night
LAX
à partir de 14h00
WELCOME TO THE FUTURE
www.brick-system.com
2 rue coysevox Lyon 1er

Lyon | France

LE SUMMUN DU SHOPPING GAY

MAJOR VIDEOSTORE

BOUTIQUE

VIDÉOCLUB

N°1 A LYON

2, PLACE DES CAPUCINS - 69001 LYON

premier/sous/sol

Si tu as -de 25 ans
c'est 25 francs
et le mercredi après 20h
c'est gratuit...
PRIX UNIQUE 30F JUSQU'À 22H

7/7 DE 14:00 > 5:00 - VEN./SAM. DE 14:00 > 8:00
7, RUE PUITS-GAILLOT - 69001 LYON TERREAUX

France | **Lyon**

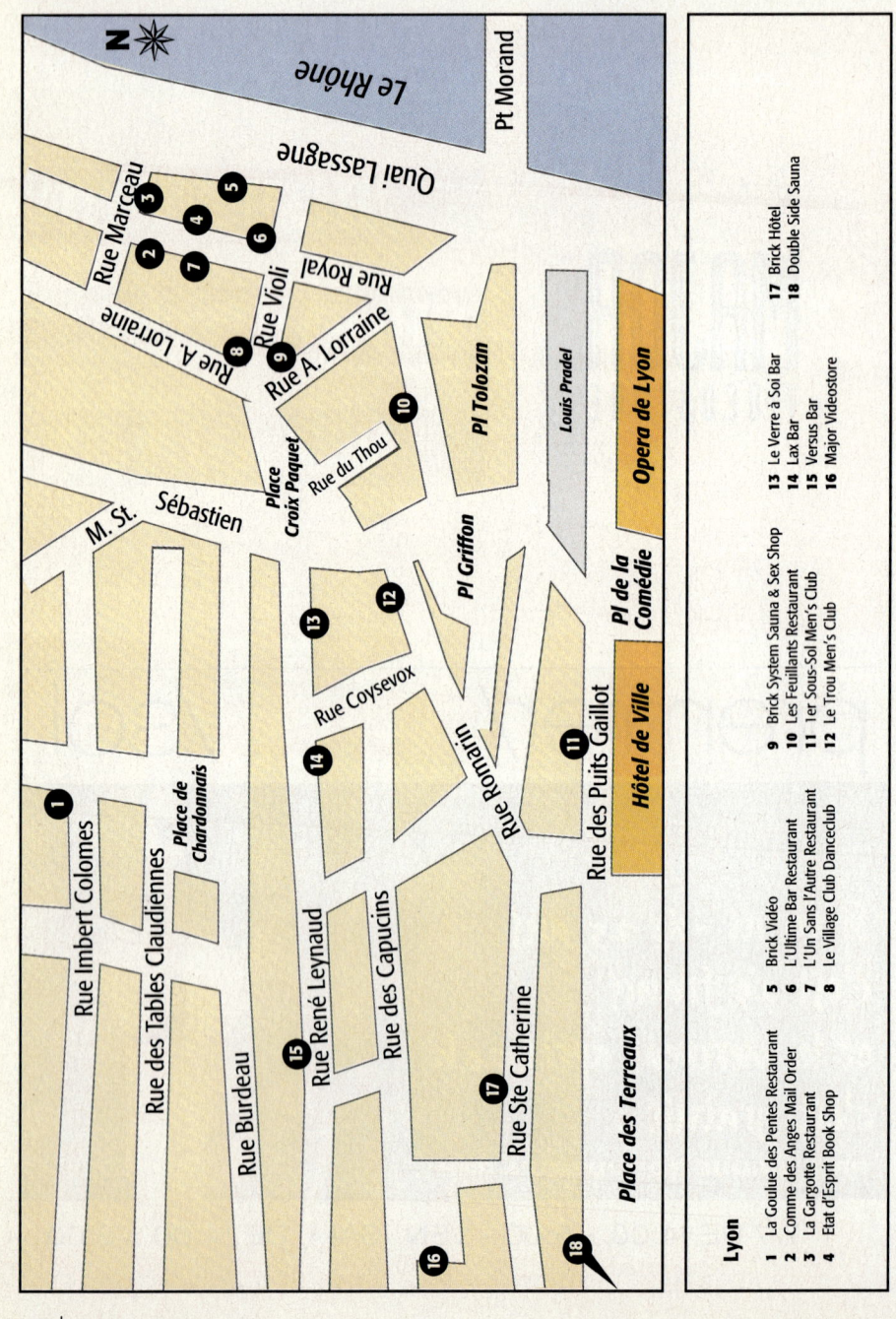

Lyon

1. La Goulue des Pentes Restaurant
2. Comme des Anges Mail Order
3. La Gargotte Restaurant
4. Etat d'Esprit Book Shop
5. Brick Vidéo
6. L'Ultime Bar Restaurant
7. L'Un Sans l'Autre Restaurant
8. Le Village Club Danceclub
9. Brick System Sauna & Sex Shop
10. Les Feuillants Restaurant
11. 1er Sous-Sol Men's Club
12. Le Trou Men's Club
13. Le Verre à Soi Bar
14. Lax Bar
15. Versus Bar
16. Major Videostore
17. Brick Hôtel
18. Double Side Sauna

Lyon | France

France | Lyon

DOUBLE SIDE

Votre centre de plaisir(s) sur 490 m²

**Sauna
Hammam
Bain à remous**

**Cabines
Salles Vidéo
Espace détente**

climatisé

Ouverture du Lundi au Jeudi de 12h à 03h. Le Vendredi, Samedi, Dimanche de 12h à 05h.

8, rue constantine 69001 Lyon 04 78 29 85 22. M° Hôtel de Ville.

DANCECLUBS

■ **Divine Comédie. La** (AC B D glm s) 23-6 h, closed Mon Tue
30 Montée St.Sébastien ✉ 69001 (M° Parquet) ☏ 04.78.30.15.12
■ **Echiquier. L'** (AC B D GLM MA P S SNU) 22-? h, closed Tue
38 Rue de l'Arbre Sec ✉ 69008 (near Hotel de Ville)
☏ 04.78.29.18.19
Karaoké on Mon and Wed. Theme parties.
■ **New Boy** (AC CC D DR GLM lj MA OS p s) Thu-Sun &before public holidays 23-5 h
La Guyonnière, Rue Dieudonné Costes ✉ 42160 *(Outside Lyon, take highway A72 direction Clermont Ferrand, exit 9-Andrézieux, opposite Mc Donald)* ☏ 04.77.55.07.77
With a big park (3000 m²) & private parking.
■ **Village Club. Le** (AC B D GLM YG) 21-3 h
6 Rue Violi ✉ 69001 ☏ 04.72.07.72.62
Popular bar and disco.

RESTAURANTS

■ **Chez les Garçons** (b F glm)
5 Rue Cuviers ✉ 69005 ☏ 04.78.24.51.07
■ **Feuillants. Les** (b CC F glm N YG) 12-13.30 & 19.30-23 h, closed Sun & Mon midday
5 Petite rue des Feuillants ✉ 69001 (M° Hotel de Ville)
☏ 04.78.28.20.50
French cuisine. Popular since 1970.
■ **Gargotte. La** (A b CC F GLM MA)
15 Rue Royale ✉ 69001 (M° Croix -Paquet) ☏ 04.78.28.79.20
Lunch and dinner.
■ **Goulue des Pentes. La** (b F glm)
37 Rue Imbert Colomes ✉ 69000 ☏ 04.78.29.41.80

■ **Grain de Sel. Le** (b F glm)
2 Rue David Girin ✉ 69002 ☏ 04.78.42.77.19
■ **Totila** (F GLM MA)
10 Rue du Pr Weill ✉ 69006 ☏ 04.78.52.95.74
Restaurant Bar Pizzeria. Fun place.
■ **Ultime. L'** (B F GLM MA)
23 Tue Royale ☏ 04.78.27.23.37
Lunch and dinner except Sat Sun dinner only.
■ **Un Sans l'Autre. L'** (b F G) Closed Wed and lunchtime on Sat Sun
20 Rue Royale ✉ 69001 ☏ 04.78.30.43.29

SEX SHOPS/BLUE MOVIES

■ **Boîte à Films. La** (AC CC g MA p VS) 10-1 h
24 Rue Lanterne ✉ 69000 ☏ 04.72.00.83.36
■ **Brick System Shop** (CC G p VS) 12-0.30, WE -5 h
1 Grande Rue des Feuillants ✉ 69001 ☏ 04.72.00.29.57
Sexy clothes, leather & latex, gadgets, magazines etc. Rent and sale of videos.. Call for details.
■ **Brick Vidéo** (AC G VS) 14-23 h
11 Quai Lassagne ✉ 69001 (M° Hôtel de Ville) ☏ 04.72.00.86.24
Cubicles, accessories,...
■ **Major Videostore** (CC G VS) 13-22, Sun Mon 16-22 h
2 Place des Capucins ✉ 69001 (Metro Hôtel de Ville. Near Place des Terreaux) ☏ 04.78.39.09.27
Large selection of videos. Sale and rental. Also accessories and gadgets.

SAUNAS/BATHS

■ **Bellecour. Le** (DR G MA SA SB) 12-22, Fri-Sun -24 h
4 Rue Simon Maupin ✉ 69002 (M° Bellecour, opposite Bar du Centre, 1st floor) ☏ 04.78.38.19.27
Popular welcoming sauna.

BRICK System

LES SAUNAS DE L'EXTREME

Lyon 1er 04.72.00.29.57
1, grande rue des Feuillants

Montpellier 04.67.58.25.27
10, avenue de Lodève

France Lyon

SAUNA LE BELLECOUR

SAUNA-VAPEUR

Heures d'ouverte
De 12 h à 22 h tous les jours
Nocturnes jusqu'à 24 h le vendredi, samedi, dimanche

1st floor
4, rue Simon Maupin
69002 LYON
Tél. 04.78.38.19.27

■ **Brick System Sauna** (AC b cc DR f G p SA SB VS WH WO) 12-3, Fri Sat 0-24 h
1 Grande Rue des Feuillants ✉ 69001 (M° Croix Paquet, near Hôtel de Ville, at Rue Violi) ☎ 04.72.00.29.57
Sauna complex with separate shop & video club. Parties 1st and 3rd Thu of the month. Young nights on Tue 20-3 h. Foam parties on a regular basis.

■ **Double Side** (AC B DR G MA SA SB VS WH) Mon-Thu 12-3, Fri-Sun -5 h
8 Rue Constantine ✉ 69001 (M° Hôtel de Ville, near Place des Terreaux) ☎ 04.78.29.85.22
New sauna on 490 m² frequented by a young and middle aged crowd.

■ **Mandala. Le** (B f G Pl SA SB VS WH WO) 12-24 Fri Sat -6 h
9 Rue Boissac ✉ 69002 (near Place Bellecour) ☎ 04.78.42.74.28
Well equipped sauna on two floors.

■ **Oasis. L'** (B f G SA SB SOL VS WH WO) 13-24 h
10 Quai Jean Moulin ✉ 69001 (M° Hôtel de Ville) ☎ 04.78.39.03.82
Should re-open in July 00 after renovation. Call for information.

BOOK SHOPS

■ **Etat d'Esprit** (A GLM) Mon-Thu 13-20, Fri 13-21 Sat 11-21 h
19 Rue Royale ✉ 69001 (M° Hôtel de Ville) ☎ 04.78.27.76.53
Gay and lesbian community bookshop. Exhibitions of art, discussions, debates. Open to all.

GIFT & PRIDE SHOPS

■ **Kiosque Fleuri. Au** 7.30-20.30 h, closed Mon
Place Maréchal-Lyautey ✉ 69006 (M° Foch) ☎ 04.78.89.57.86
Small gifts.

■ **Veyret**
2 Grande Rue de la Guillotère ✉ 69007 ☎ 04.78.72.23.84

LEATHER & FETISH SHOPS

■ **Tom's Boutic** Mon-Fri 10-12, 14.30-19 h, Sat by appointment only
41 Quai Pierre Size ✉ 69000 ☎ 04.72.00.05.35

MAIL ORDER

■ **Comme Des Anges** (G VS)
1 Rue des Capucins ✉ 69000 ☎ 04.72.00.86.87

HOTELS

■ **Brick Hôtel** (B BF CC GLM H OS)
9 Rue Sainte Catherine ✉ 69001 ☎ 04.78.28.11.01
04.78.28.05.34 www.brick-system.com
Located in the centre of the gay area. Call for rates. Quote Spartacus.

GENERAL GROUPS

■ **Accueil Rencontres Informations Loisirs (ARIS)** (GLM) Mon Fri 19-22 h
16 Rue St. Polycarpe, B.P. 1125 ✉ 69203 (M° Hôtel de Ville)
☎ 04.78.27.10.10 04.78.27.10.10 courrier@aris.asso.fr
aris.asso.fr
Information on the gay life and problems. Meetings of different gay associations.

■ **Forum Gai & Lesbien** (A B GLM MA S) Mon-Fri 18-20 h
17 Rue Romarin (M° A-Hôtel de Ville, Bus 1/6/18/27/44)
☎ 04.78.39.97.72 Forum.gai.lesbien@libertysurf.fr
www.multimania.com/lesgaybb/fgl29
"Café Positif" Café for HIV people Tue 20-22 h, MOOVE young gay and lesbian group Thu from 20 h, organisers or the Lyon Lesbian and Gay Pride.

France & 4 Nations **
BRICK Hôtel lyon
Garden view
open 24h/24
French-breakfast
9 rue Sainte Catherine
Lyon 1° 04 78 28 11 01
The largest gay hôtel in France

274 SPARTACUS 2001/2002

Lyon ▶ Marseille | **France**

FETISH GROUPS
■ **MCRA Lyon**
B.P. 3010 ✉ 69394 ☎ 04.72.33.03.39 💻 yhuneau@imaginet.fr
💻 www.imaginet.fr/~yhuneau/mcra.html
Member of ECMC.

HEALTH GROUPS
■ **Association de Lutte contre le Sida (A.L.S.)** Mon-Fri 10-18 h
16 Rue Pizay ✉ 69169 ☎ 04.78.27.80.80 💻 als@sidaweb.com
💻 www.sidaweb.com
■ **Association de Lutte contre le Sida (A.L.S.)** Mon-Fri 10-18 h
24 Impasse de la Gerbe ✉ 69400 ☎ 04.74.65.92.54
■ **Hôtel Dieu**
71 Quai Jules Courmont ✉ 69002 ☎ 04.78.42.29.26
☎ 04.78.92.20.16
Free HIV-testing.

SPORT GROUPS
■ **Rando's Rhône-Alpes**
B.P. 3173 ✉ 69406 ☎ 04.78.00.54.92
Organises walking tours and hiking/Organise des randonnées pédestres dans la nature.

SWIMMING
-Port Gallaud (left bank, north of the bridge)

CRUISING
-Parc de Parilluy (WE)
-Parc de la Tête d'Or
-Tennis courts in Gerland (22-4 h summers; from avenue Leclerc, drive south, past Mercure Hotel, then straight (3km) to Port Edouard Heriot, park on the left, crawl through holes in fence onto the sports grounds)
-Quais du Rhône (especially in front of sauna on quai Jean Moulin)
-Gare SNCF Pont Dieu
-Parc de Gerland (car park and football field)
-Quai du Rhône (under the bridges)

Mâcon ✉ 71000

GUEST HOUSES
■ **Salamandre. La** (BF CC glm H OS) closed in Feb
Grand Rue ✉ 71250 *(30 km from Mâcon TGV station)*
☎ 03.85.59.91.56 📠 03.85.59.91.67 💻 info@la-salamandre.fr
💻 www.la-salamandre.fr
Dinner possible on reservation.

CRUISING
-Quai Lamartine (above the Saône-river/sur la Saône)

Marmande ✉ 47200

RESTAURANTS
■ **Auberge du Moulin d'Ané** (CC F g OS) Tue-Sat 12-13.45 18.30-0, Sun 12-16 h
D933 Route de Périgueux/Virazeil ✉ 47200 ☎ 05.53.20.18.25

CRUISING
-Place Fiolhe (la nuit/at night)
-Plaine de Loisirs

Marseille ✉ 13000

GAY INFO
■ **Association pour la création du Centre G&L Méditerranén**
1, Rue Chateauredon ✉ 13000 *(Métro Noailles)* ☎ 04.91.33.72.65
📠 04.91.54.00.20
Information about Gay scene, groups and HIV.

PUBLICATIONS
■ **IBIZA News gay information**
c/o Association Gay Information sur le SIDA, 27 Rue ✉ 13006
☎ 04.91.33.24.33 📠 04.91.33.29.60
Available at gay venues. Eight editions a year.

TOURIST INFO
■ **Tourist Info**
4 La Canebière ✉ 13000 ☎ 04.91.54.91.11 📠 04.91.33.05.03

BARS
■ **Eden. L'** (B G) 16-2 h, closed Mon
7 Rue Curiol ✉ 13000 *(M° Le Vieux Port)* ☎ 04.91.47.30.06
■ **Enigme Bar. L'** (AC B CC DR G lj MA OS P p) 19 h-till dawn
22 Rue Beauvau ✉ 13001 *(M° Vieux Port)* ☎ 04.91.33.79.20
Private gay bar. All associations welcome.
■ **MP Bar** (AC BC CC GLM p VS) 18 h-till dawn
10 Rue Beauvau ✉ 13001 *(M° Vieux Port)* ☎ 04.91.33.64.79

MEN'S CLUBS
■ **Entrepôt** (AC DR G MA p VS) 14-2, Fri Sat -6 h
7 Rue Moustier ✉ 13001 *(M° Noailles. Parking Julien)*
☎ 04.91.33.51.70
Huge complex. Fantasies for everyone.
■ **Mineshaft** (B DR G LJ MG p VS) Fri Sat 23-? h
28 Rue Mazagran ✉ 13001 ☎ 04.91.48.49.34
Club with strict dress code.

CAFES
■ **Arcenaulx. Les** (A AC B BF CC F g)
25, Cours d'Estienne-d'Orves ✉ 13000 ☎ 91.54.77.06
Also bookshop.

DANCECLUBS
■ **Mare au Diable. La** (B CC D G OS p s VS WE YG) Fri-Sat and eve of holidays 23-? h
Chemin de Bon Rencontre ✉ 13190 ☎ 04.91.68.24.10
In a suburb of Marseille. Car or taxi required.
■ **New Cancan. The** (AC B CC D DR GLM p VS SNU STV WE) Thu-Mon 23-6 h
3-7 Rue Sénac ✉ 13001 *(M° Réformés/Noailles)* ☎ 04.91.48.59.76
The gay disco of Marseille. Show every night.

RESTAURANTS
■ **Bessonière. La** (B F GLM) 19-24 h
40 Rue Sénac *(M° Noailles, Headquarters of Act up Marseille)*
☎ 04.91.94.08.43
■ **Bistro Venitien** After show service-2h
29, cours Julien ☎ 04.91.47.34.34
Italian food.
■ **Chez Alex** (AC b CC F GLM MG OS stv) 12-14, 18-24 h, closed Sun
43 Rue Curiol ✉ 13000 ☎ 04.91.47.80.12
■ **Pizzeria Phyteas** (b F g) 12-14, 19-23 h, closed Wed, 1.Jun-15.Sep 12-14, 19-23 h
12 Rue Phyteas ✉ 13001 *(M° Vieoux-Port)* ☎ 04.91.33.11.92
■ **Scalino** (b F glm MA OS) 12-15, 19-? h, closed Sun Mon lunch
78 Cours Julien ✉ 13006 *(Centre Ville, Quartier des Artistes)*
☎ 04.91.42.79.69

France | Marseille

ENTREPOT

7/7 - 14:00 > 02:00
fri & sat > 06:00

biggest, best & brightest sex club in france

- 600 m² cruising area
- 5 levels
- 2 cinemas
- 4 darkrooms
- 3 labyrinths
- 12 cabins
- collective showers
- selective movies
- sex shopping
- drinks

ENTREPOT
international gay sex club
7 rue moustier / marseille 13001
04 91 33 51 70

MP SAUNA

82, La Canebière
13001 MARSEILLE
Tél : 04 91 48 72 51

GAY MARSEILLE

Sling — 2 Saunas
2 Jacuzzis — Cabines avec T.V.
Snack Bar — U.V.A.
Salon Vidéo — Labyrinthe
Hamman

OUVERT TOUS LES JOURS de 12h à 24h
(Samedi & Dimanche de 12h à 24h)

P.A.O. GMS Tél: 0442 93 69 79 fax: 0491 72 67 67

Marseille | France

SEX SHOPS/BLUE MOVIES

■ **Eros Center** (AC CC DR g MA VS) 9.30-24 h
5 Boulevard Garibaldi ✉ 13001 (M° Noailles, corner of Canebière/Cours Lieutaud) ☏ 04.91.92.72.30

■ **Sexashop** (g VS) 9.30-24, Sat -20 h, closed Sun
6 Rue Corneille ✉ 13000 (M° Le Vieux Port) ☏ 04.91.33.71.91
Revues, accessoires, magazines, videos.

SAUNAS/BATHS

■ **Aqua Douches** (AC B CC f G MA p SA SB VS WH WO) Open everyday
34 Rue de l'Arène ✉ 13260 (30 min from Marseille and 1 h. from St. Tropez. Towmn centre Cassis) ☏ 06.14.63.28.19

■ **JL Olympic** (B CC G MA SA SB VS) 12-20.30, Tue Fri Sat 12-24 h
28 Rue Jean Roque ✉ 13006 (M° Noailles) ☏ 04.91.47.35.61
Sauna on three floors with a labyrinth frequented by a regular crowd.

■ **M.P. Sauna** (B CC DR f G SA SB SOL VS WH) 12-24 h
82 La Canebière ✉ 13001 (M°-Noailles) ☏ 04.91.48.72.51
One of the biggest saunas in Marseilles.

■ **Palmarium. Le** (B G SA SB VS) 12-20.30, Tue Sat 12-24 h
20 Rue Sénac ✉ 13001 (M° Réformés) ☏ 04.91.47.43.93
2 floors sauna in the core of Marseilles' hottest street.

■ **Salvator** (b DR G SA SB VS WH) 12-20.30 h
20 Boulevard Salvator ✉ 13006 (M° Prefecture) ☏ 04.91.42.99.31
3 floors and more than 300 m².

■ **Sauna Club** (b G OS SA SB VS) 12-20.30, Mon Fri 12-24 h
117 La Canebière ✉ 13001 (M° Les Réformés. Parking Gambetta) ☏ 04.91.64.19.08
Well equipped three floors sauna with a whirlpool on the sun terrace.

HOTELS

■ **Hôtel du Prado** (B g H) 7-1 h
80 Avenue du Prado ✉ 13000 ☏ 04.91.37.55.34

Centrally located, 12 km from the airport. Rooms without bath and tel. Single FF 118-181, double 240. (bf incl.). No bath or telephone in room.

■ **New Hotel Astoria** (AC BF CC g H)
10 Boulevard Garibaldi ✉ 13000 (Métro Noailles)
☏ 04.91.33.33.50 📠 04.91.54.80.75

■ **Saint Ferréol's Hotel** (AC B BF CC glm H WH)
19 Rue Pisancon ✉ 13001 (M° Vieux Port) ☏ 04.91.33.12.21
📠 04.91.54.29.97 ✉ st.ferreol@wanadoo.fr
🌐 www.hotel.stfferreol.com
All rooms with bath, phone, sat TV. Some with whirlpool. Helpful staff. Special rates for Spartacus readers.

■ **Sphinx** (BF g H)
16 Rue Sénac ✉ 13001 (M°Noaille) ☏ 04.91.48.70.59
Central to gay places. Ideal for small budget.

GENERAL GROUPS

■ **Collectif Gai & Lesbien Marseille & Provence** Mon Wed Fri 16-19 h
1 Rue Ferrari ✉ 13005 ☏ 04.91.42.07.48
Organises gay parties from time to time/Organise les Bals Gays de temps au temps.

FETISH GROUPS

■ **F.S.M.C.** (G LJ)
B.P. 70 ✉ 13244

HEALTH GROUPS

■ **Aides Provence**
1 Rue Gilbert Dru ✉ 13002 ☏ 04.91.14.05.15 📠 04.91.14.05.16
✉ aidesprovence@pacwan.fr 🌐 aides.provence.free.fr
Information, prevention, help for people with HIV/AIDS.

■ **Association des Médecins Gais** Tue 20-22 h
✉ 13000 ☏ 04.91.94.19.91

France Marseille ▶ Montauban

SPORT GROUPS
■ **Association Motocycliste Alternative (A.M.A.)** (GLM)
B.P. 212 ✉ 13178 ☎ 04.91.90.70.85
🖳 www.multimania.com/motard
Gay and lesbian bikers of southern France. Headquarters in Marseille, branches in Lyon (☎ 04.37.28.99.54) & Toulouse (☎ 05.34.26.12.02).

SWIMMING
-Le Montrose (direction Ponte Rouge, after Prado beach; follow Avenue Montredon, turn to the right at the chapel to get to the P in front of the beach; to get there by bus, take N° 19)
-Les Gaudes (east of Marseille)
-Le Mont-Rose (gay beach/plage gaie, terminus bus 19)
-Madrague de Montredon (NU) (beach/plage)
-Callelongues (NU) (beach/plage)

CRUISING
-Rue George, Square Sidi-Brahim, bd Sakakini, bd Chave
-Rue Maurice-Bourdet
-Boulevard Voltaire
-Canebière (sex-shop-galerie)
-Railway station/gare SNCF (AYOR)
-Métro Vieux-Port
-Parc Borely (P) IBM)

Martigues ✉ 13500
CRUISING
-Quai du Général-Leclerc
- P Avenue Salvador-Allende (swimming-bath/piscine)
-Rue Verdun(near garden and beach/près du jardin et plage)
-Beach/plage du Ponthau (NU)

Meaux ✉ 77100
CRUISING
-Les quais (at night)

Mende ✉ 48000
CRUISING
-Palais de justice (in the evening/le soir)
- P Stade du Chapitre (day and night)
- P Stade de Mirandol (evenings only)

Mennessis ✉ 02700
BARS
■ **Parilla Club. La** (B D F g) Bar: 16-22, Disco 22- 5h, closed Mon
38 Rue Demosthène-Gauthier ✉ 02700 ☎ 03.23.57.25.08
Bar, restaurant, disco (camping possible).

Menton ✉ 06500
CRUISING
-The high Jetty along the old harbour (especially at night in summer)
-Avenue Winston Churchill (especially at night in summer)

Metz ✉ 57000
BARS
■ **Privilège. Le** (AC B CC D Glm p S SNU TV) 22-5 h, theme nights and shows: Fri Sat, closed Mon
20 Rue aux Ours ✉ 57000 *(near Tribunal)* ☎ 03.87.36.29.29
Disco bar.

RESTAURANTS
■ **Bagatelle. Le** (AC g F) 12-? h
29 Rue du Pont des Morts ✉ 57000 ☎ 87.32.49.08

SAUNAS/BATHS
■ **Blue Club Sauna** (B G SA SB VS) 14-22 h, closed on Tue
8 Rue Sebastien Leclerc ✉ 57000 *(100 m from SNCF station)*
☎ 03.87.18.09.40

HEALTH GROUPS
■ **Centre Hospitalier Beausecours. Service de Dermatologie**
1 Place Philippe-de-Vigneulles ✉ 57038 ☎ 03.87.63.13.13
HIV-testing.

CRUISING
-Bon secours (close to the hospital/près de l'hôpital)
-Ile de Saulcy
-Passage du Sablon
-Square de Luxembourg
-Gare SNCF/railway station
-Ile-aux-Moines
-Rest area "La Croue" (motorway Strasbourg-Paris)

Meudon ✉ 92190
CRUISING
-Bois de Meudon (at the park borderline/aux abords du parc)

Millau ✉ 12100
CRUISING
-At the old bridge of Tarn/Au vieux pont du Tarn
-Jardin de la Gare (Avenue de la République towards Cahors)
-Quai de la Tonnerie (banks of Tarn)

Mimizan ✉ 40200
SWIMMING
-Les dunes Remembert (north side, near the military area)

CRUISING
-Public garden behind the church/Jardin public derrière l'église de Mimizan Bourg (summer only)
- P Remembert (beach, summer only)

Montargis ✉ 45200
CRUISING
-Forest of Montargis/Forêt de Montargis (go in the direction of Nemours; the action is in front of the Château d'Eau)

Montauban ✉ 82000
CRUISING
-Cours Foucault
-Espace Mendès-France
-Gare routière

Montauban ▸ Montpellier France

Le Bar... éternellement nouveau...

les soirées

les **lundis** au soleil les **mardis** surprise

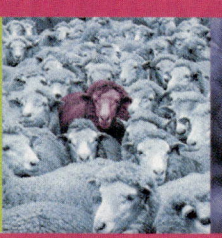

7 jours/7
de 17h à 1h
18 rue de l'aiguillerie
Montpellier
(Hérault)

les **mercredis** PA
les **jeudis** voyages
les **vendredis** sexe
les **Samedis fêtes**
les **dimanches** cultes

chaque soir une ambiance **différente !**
chaque mois un décor **différent !**

-Jardin Montauriol
-Place de la Cathédrale
-Jardin des Plantes

Montbéliard ✉ 25200

CRUISING
-Pool of Brognard/étang de Brognard (in the summertime, along the highway on the right side in direction Montbéliard/l'été, le long de l'autoroute, à droite dans le sens Montbeliard)
-P at the city market/parc du champ de foire (facilities/toilettes)

Montcombroux-les-Mines ✉ 03130

HEALTH GROUPS
■ **Gaillards. Les**
✉ 03130 ☎ 70.99.64.54 70.99.62.89 aristos@cs3i.fr
 www.cs3ifr/abonnes/aristos/index.html
Quiet house that offers palliative care for people with AIDS.

Mont-de-Marsan ✉ 40000

CRUISING
-Rocade Saint-Justin
-P Donjon Lacataye (all night long)

Montélimar ✉ 26200

CRUISING
-Railway station/gare SNCF
-Champ-de-Mars
-Boulevard Marredesmares

Montpellier ✉ 34000

BARS
■ **18. Le** (AC B CC d GLM MA N p S snu) 17-1h (winter) -2 (summer)
18 Rue de l'Aiguillerie ✉ 34000
Piano bar with shows everyday.
■ **Café de la Mer** (B glm MA OS) 8-1, Sun & holidays 15-1, Jul Aug -2 h
5 Place du Marché-aux-Fleurs ✉ 34000 ☎ 04.67.60.79.65
■ **Heaven. Le** (AC B CC G LJ MA) winter: 19-1, summer: 20-2 h
1 Rue Delpech ✉ 34000 *(Place Marché aux Fleurs)*
☎ 04.67.60.44.18

MEN'S CLUBS
■ **Chantier. Le** (AC CC DR G lj MA VS) 15-3 h
25-27 Rue J.-J. Rousseau ✉ 34000 ☎ 04.67.60.91.98

DANCECLUBS
■ **T H T** (AC B D DR GLM MA p VS) 22-? h
29 Avenue de Castelnau ✉ 34000 ☎ 04.67.79.96.17
■ **Villa Rouge** (AC B D DR F G OS) Fri-Sun 22-6? h
Route de Palavas ✉ 34970 ☎ 04.67.06.52.15

RESTAURANTS
■ **Cadran. Le** (B F g)
3 Place St Ravy ☎ 04.67.66.48.26
■ **Pomme d'Or. La** (CC F GLM lj MA OS s) 12-14 19-23.30 h, Sun evening only
23 Rue du Palais-Guilhem ✉ 34000 ☎ 04.67.52.82.62

France | Montpellier

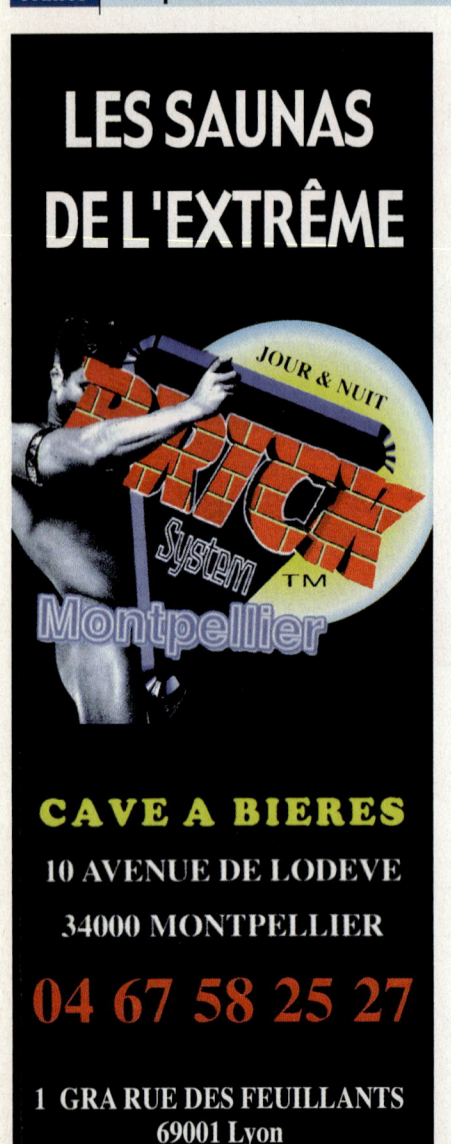

SEX SHOPS/BLUE MOVIES
■ **L'Exotique** (AC g MA VS) 10-22 h
6bis Rue Cope-Combes ✉ 34000
☎ 04.67.60.64.61

SAUNAS/BATHS
■ **Brick System Koncept** (AC B BF CC DR f G MA MSG P p SA SB VS WH WO) winter: 12-1, summer -2 h
10 Avenue de Lodève ✉ 34000 ☎ 04.67.58.25.27
Newest and one the biggest sauna in the region.
■ **Hammam Club** (b g MA msg OS SA SB SOL VS WO) 14-19 h
2 Rue de la Merci ✉ 34000 ☎ 04.67.58.22.06
Steam room with fellinian decor, very modern fitness equipment. Nude sunbathing on the terrace in summer.
■ **Sauna de la Gare** (b CC f G SA SB SOL VS YG) 12-1 h
8 Rue Levat ✉ 34000 *(near the railway station)*
☎ 04.67.58.61.42
Sauna with a sling room. popular within a rather young crowd.

HOTELS
■ **Guilhem. Le** (AC BF CC g H OS)
18 Rue Jean-Jacques Rousseau ✉ 34000 *(bus 2/3/5 /7 stop Henri IV)*
☎ 04.67.52.90.90 📠 04.67.60.67.67
■ **Hotel Ulysse** (BF glm H)
338 Avenue de Saint Maur ✉ 34000 *(near/près du Palais des Congrès)* ☎ 04.67.02.02.30 📠 04.67.02.16.50
Centrally located with underground parking. Shady garden.

GUEST HOUSES
■ **Amairadou. L'** (BF F g H MA OS PI SA SOL WH WO)
620 Chemin de Montpellier ✉ 34400 *(between Nîmes and Montpellier)* ☎ 04.67.86.80.65
Luxury rooms, restaurant, park and pool.

GENERAL GROUPS
■ **Centre Gai & Lesbien (CGL)** (GLM MA)
30 Rue Cardinal de Cabrière ✉ 34000
☎ 04.67.60.37.34
📠 04.67.54.90.77
🖥 www.montpelliergay.com

HEALTH GROUPS
■ **Aides Languedoc-Méditerranée** Mon-Fri 14-18 h
8 Place Roger Salengro ✉ 34000
☎ 04.67.34.03.76
📠 04.67.34.03.78
🖥 aideslm.free.fr
Welcoming, information, orientation, supporting/Accueil, information, orientation, soutien.

SWIMMING
-Beach/Plage (between Théâtre de la Mer and La Corniche)
-Beach/Plage de Grand Travers (between/entre la Grande Motte & Carnou)
-Beach/Plage des Aresquiers/Frontignan (NU) (after parking lot ca. 2km towards Palavas)

CRUISING
-Place des Arceaux (Car cruising/drague en voiture)
-Promenade du Peyrou
-Garden/Jardin des Beaux-Arts
-Le Polygone
-Forest/Forêt des Aresquiers, Vic la Gardiole, Frontignon

Morlaix ✉ 29210

RESTAURANTS
■ **Brocéliande** (b CC F glm MA) 20-23 h, closed Tue
5 Rue des Bouchers ✉ 29600 ☎ 02.98.88.73.78
Mention that you choose the restaurant from Spartacus: Gets you a free aperitif.

CRUISING
-Viaduc (in the evening/le soir)
-Aire Saint-Servais

Moulins ✉ 03000

CRUISING
-Bords de l'Allier
-Square

Moustiers-Sainte-Marie ✉ 04360

HOTELS
■ **Hôtel de la Ferme Rose** (BF CC g H OS) 8-24 h, closed 15 Nov-15 Mar
✉ 04360 (1 km from Moustiers-Ste Marie) ☎ 04.92.74.69.47
📠 04.92.74.60.76
Piano bar in the evening. Superb location.

Mulhouse ✉ 68100

BARS
■ **Latino Cafe** (B CC G MA OS YG) 15-1.30 h
16 Passage du Théâtre ✉ 68100 ☎ 03.89.66.56.52
Latest music in the evening.

DANCECLUBS
■ **Caesar Palace. Le** (AC B CC D DR f glm MA SNU VS) Thu-Mon 22-4 h
192 Rue de la Banlieue ✉ 68110 (Illzach) ☎ 03.89.46.27.88
Late night restaurant and mixed disco complex with several different styles.
■ **Gémeaux. Le** (AC B CC D DR Glm MA p SNU) 23-? h, closed Tue
3 Rue J. Ehrmann ✉ 68100 ☎ 03.89.66.19.60
Centrally located disco bar on two levels.
■ **JH. Le** (AC B CC D Glm MA p stv VS) Thu-Mon 22.30-4 h
1 Rue Sainte Therese ✉ 68200 (near Place du Marché, entrance 32 Quai du Forst) ☎ 03.89.32.00.08

SAUNAS/BATHS
■ **Sauna Club LG** (B DR G MA SA SB VS) Mon Wed Sun 14-21, Tue Thu Sat 14-23, mixed on Tue Thu 20-23 h
69 Rue de Bâle ✉ 68100 ☎ 03.89.36.01.02

HEALTH GROUPS
■ **Centre de Dépistage** Mon 10-13, Tue 16-19, Wed 15-18 h
Hôpital de Moenchsberg, Rue du Dr. R. Laennée ✉ 68100 ☎ 03.89.54.90.33
Gratis and anonymous HIV testing.

CRUISING
-Parc Salvatore (AYOR)

Nancy ✉ 54000

RESTAURANTS
■ **Bistrot de Gilles. Le** (CC F g OS) 12-14.30, 19-23.30 h
31 Rue des Maréchaux ✉ 54000 (near Place Stanislas)
☎ 03.83.35.43.73
French cuisine.

SAUNAS/BATHS
■ **Sauna Club LG** (B DR G MA SA SB VS) 14-23 h, mixed on Tue 20-23 h
5 Rue Alfred Mezières ✉ 54000 ☎ 04.83.36.65.59
Friendly sauna on two floors.

GENERAL GROUPS
■ **Association Homonyme** Mon 18-20 h
✉ 54000 ☎ 03.83.27.91.71
Youth group.

HEALTH GROUPS
■ **Centre Hospitalier R. de Nancy**
29 Rue du Maréchal de Lattre de Tassigny ✉ 54037
☎ 03.83.57.61.61

CRUISING
-La Pépinière

Nantes ✉ 44000

BARS
■ **Amazone. L'** (B TV) 18-2, Jun-Aug 14-2 h
4 Rue des Chapeliers ✉ 44000 ☎ 40.36.61.88
■ **Egout et les Couleurs. L'** (B CC BF GLM OS s YG) 17-2, Fri Sat 17-2, 5-10 h
2 Rue Kervegan ✉ 44000 ☎ 02.40.20.58.58
■ **Ferry. Le** (B G F) 10-15, 17.30-2 h
15 Rue du Bâtonnier Guinaudeau ✉ 44000 *In front of/En face du Pont Anne de Bretagne* ☎ 02.40.73.59.79
Also restaurant.
■ **One Street** (B glm MA)
1 Rue Kervégan ✉ 44000 ☎ 02.40.20.14.20
■ **Petit Marais. Le** (B G MA s) 17-2 h
15 Rue Kervegan ✉ 44000 ☎ 02.40.20.15.25
■ **Plein Sud. Le** (a AC B CC G OS) 17-2 h, closed Mon
2 Rue Premion ✉ 44000 ☎ 40.47.06.03

DANCECLUBS
■ **Temps d'Aimer. Le** (B CC D G) 23-5 h, closed Mon
14 Rue Alexandre-Fourny ✉ 44000 ☎ 40.89.48.60

SEX SHOPS/BLUE MOVIES
■ **Boîte à Films. La** (AC DR glmG MA VS) 10-2, Sun 12-1 h, Tue (G evening), Thu (DR evening)
16bis Allée du Commandant-Charcot ✉ 44000 ☎ 40.37.03.03

SAUNAS/BATHS
■ **Bains du Turenne. Les** (AC b cc f DR G SA SB SOL VS WH WO YG) Mon Tue Thu 12-22, Wed Fri -24, Sat 14-2, Sun and public holidays -22 h
1 Place de la République ✉ 44200 (Bus 42/52, Tram Vincent Gâche)
☎ 02.51.82.37.02
550 m² welcoming sauna and shop on four floors.

France Nantes ▸ Nevers

Les BAINS du TURENNE

www.lesbainsduturenne.com

Sauna Club

THE NUMBER ONE
1, PLACE DE LA RÉPUBLIQUE
44000 NANTES © 02 51 82 37 02

■ **Spartacus Club** (AC B DR MA G SA SB VS WH) 14-21, Fri -23, Sat -24 h
16 Rue Fouré ✉ 44000 ☏ 02.51.82.43.70
Popular sauna on two floors with theme cubicles and other specialities. Check website or call for theme nights.

FITNESS STUDIOS
■ **Gymn'axe** (g SA WO) For men only: Mon 13-21.30, Wed 8.30-21.30, Fri 8.30-22 h
3bis Rue Louis Blanc ✉ 44200 ☏ 40.47.74.17

HOTELS
■ **Grand Hôtel de Nantes**
2 bis Rue de Santeuil ✉ 44000 ☏ 02.40.69.65.90

GENERAL GROUPS
■ **Soeurs de la Perpétuelle Indulgence. Les**
117 Bd Ernest Dalby ✉ 44000 ☏ 51.81.03.53

HEALTH GROUPS
■ **Amitié-Sida**
21 Rue Dufour ✉ 44000 ☏ 02.40.29.12.34
Help for people with HIV or AIDS.
■ **Dispensaire Jean V**
Rue Durant-Gasselin ✉ 44000 ☏ 02.40.73.18.62

RELIGIOUS GROUPS
■ **David et Jonathan** (GLM)
B.P. 12521 ✉ 44215 ☏ 02.40.52.16.86
Gay chrétiens/Christian gays.

SPORT GROUPS
■ **Gay Randonneurs Nantais** (GLM MA)
42 Rue des Hauts-Pavés ✉ 44000 ☏ 02.40.75.25.85
🖥 grn@free.fr 🖥 grn.free.fr/nantes.html
Publishes monthly bulletin. Organises walks, foreign trips and evenings.

CRUISING
-Place Louis-XVI. (Cours St.Pierre, St.André)
-Parc de Procès (night/la nuit)
-Square Elisa-Mercoeur (Allée Baco)
-Beaulieu
-Bords de l'Erdre

Narbonne ✉ 11100

DANCECLUBS
■ **Sapho Club** (B D GLM S SNU) Wed-Sun
39 Avenue de Bordeaux ✉ 11100 ☏ 04.68.42.04.21

RESTAURANTS
■ **Assiette Folle. L'** (B glm F)
c/o Hôtel Le Floride, 66 Boulevard Frédéric Mistral ✉ 11100 ☏ 04.68.90.66.39

HOTELS
■ **Hôtel Le Floride** (B F glm H)
66 Boulevard Frédéric Mistral ✉ 11100 ☏ 04.68.90.66.39

CRUISING
-Pont de l'Avenir
-Jardin du palais du travail
-Cours Mirabeau

Neufchâtel-en-Bray ✉ 76270

RESTAURANTS
■ **Auberge du Bec Fin. L'** (B CC F g MA OS) 12-15, 19-22 h, closed Mon evening
Megnières en Bray ✉ 76270 ☏ 02.35.94.15.15

Neuilly-en-Thelle ✉ 60530

BARS
■ **Corps de Garde. Le** (B D DR F g p s) Fri Sat 20-5 h
4 Rue Driard ✉ 60530 ☏ 03.44.26.72.26

Nevers ✉ 58000

BARS
■ **Petit Marais. Le** (B G MA)
7 Place Guy Coquille ✉ 58000 ☏ 03.86.61.16.64

SAUNAS/BATHS
■ **Y Sauna Club** (b DR G SA SB VS) 12-20 h, closed in Aug
4ter Rue de la Passière ✉ 58000 *(near railway station)*
☏ 03.86.59.55.56

HOTELS
■ **Château Quentin. Le** (BF F glm H OS) open Apr-Oct
Route du Pont ✉ 58110 *(located in Alluy between Nevers and Château Chinon)* ☏ 03.86.84.08.95 📠 03.86.84.08.95
Country retreat. Pick-up at Nevers railway station possible. Special rate for SPARTACUS readers.

Nevers ▶ Nice | **France**

CRUISING
- Park in the centre of town/parc du centre-ville
- Banks of the Loire, chemin du Vert-vert/bord de la Loire, chemin du Vert-vert
- Porte du Croux

Nice ✉ 06000

TOURIST INFO
■ **Tourist Info**
Acropolis Esplanade Kennedy, B.P. 79 ✉ 06000 ☎ 04.93.87.07.07 🖷 04.93.92.82.98

BARS
■ **Bar Le Rusca** (AC B GLM OS p s) 21-2.30 h
2 Rue Rusca ✉ 06300 *(in front of the church on the port)* ☎ 04.93.89.46.25

■ **Castro Street** (AC B CC d DR f G MA VS) 19-2.30 h
18 bis Rue Emmanuel Philibert ✉ 06300 ☎ 04.93.26.35.30
Amercian style bar with pool.

■ **Cherry's Café** (AC B CC d F glm OS s) Fri-Sun private night bar from 20 h
35 Quai des Etats-Unis ✉ 06200 ☎ 04.93.18.85.45
3 floors with sea view.

■ **Chez Michel** (AC B g) 12-24 h
1 Rue Alberti ✉ 06000 ☎ 04.93.85.43.90
Bar-tabac for an early drink.

■ **Latinos. Le** (AC b F GLM MA)
6 Rue Chauvain ✉ 06000 ☎ 04.93.85.01.10
Tapas specialities.

■ **Santiago. Le** (AC B CC F H GLM) 18-2.30 h, closed on Mon
28 Rue Lépante ✉ 06000 ☎ 04.93.13.83.01
Centrally located cocktail bar, restaurant and hotel. French cuisine until 22.30 h.

■ **Tip-Top Bar** (B GLM MA) 21-2.30 h, closed on Wed
30 Quai Lunel ✉ 06000 *(harbour/port)* ☎ 04.93.26.22.88

CAFES
■ **CD. Le** (b F glm) 11-0.30 h
22 Rue Benoit Burico ☎ 04.93.92.47.65

DANCECLUBS
■ **Blue Boy Enterprise (B.B.E)** (AC B CC D G p S YG) 23-5 h
9 Rue J. B. Spinetta ✉ 06000 *(Rue Spinetta is a side street off the Boulevard François Grosso between the Avenue des Orangers and the Rue Bottero)* ☎ 04.93.44.68.24
2 floors, 2 bars.

■ **Klub Le** (B D S)
8 Rue Jules-Gilly ✉ 06300 *(Vieux Nice, behind "Cours Saleya")* ☎ 04.93.80.58.28

RESTAURANTS
■ **Arbalete. L'** (F glm MA) 19-0.30 h, closed on Mon
6 Rue Halevy ✉ 06300 ☎ 06.03.29.70.53

■ **Cave. La** (AC CC F g OS) 12-14, 19-22.30 h
Rue Francis Gallo ☎ 04.93.62.48.46
Good for low prices.

■ **Chez Cyriaque** (b F glm MA) 19-0.30 h
12 Rue Rosetti *(Vieux Nice)* ☎ 04.93.92.68.47
Mediteranian cuisine.

BAR LE RUSCA
Chez Jacques

Where you meet your own kind!

Intimate private gay bar
www.multimania.com/Rusca/
2, rue Rusca (face à l'église du port)
Nice Tel. 04 93 89 46 25
21H à 2H30

HOTEL RESTAURANT
LE GOURMET LORRAIN

7 AVENUE SANTA FIOR
06100 NICE

TEL: 04.93.84.90.78
FAX: 04.92.09.11.25

Quote Spartacus for free Aperitif

France | **Nice**

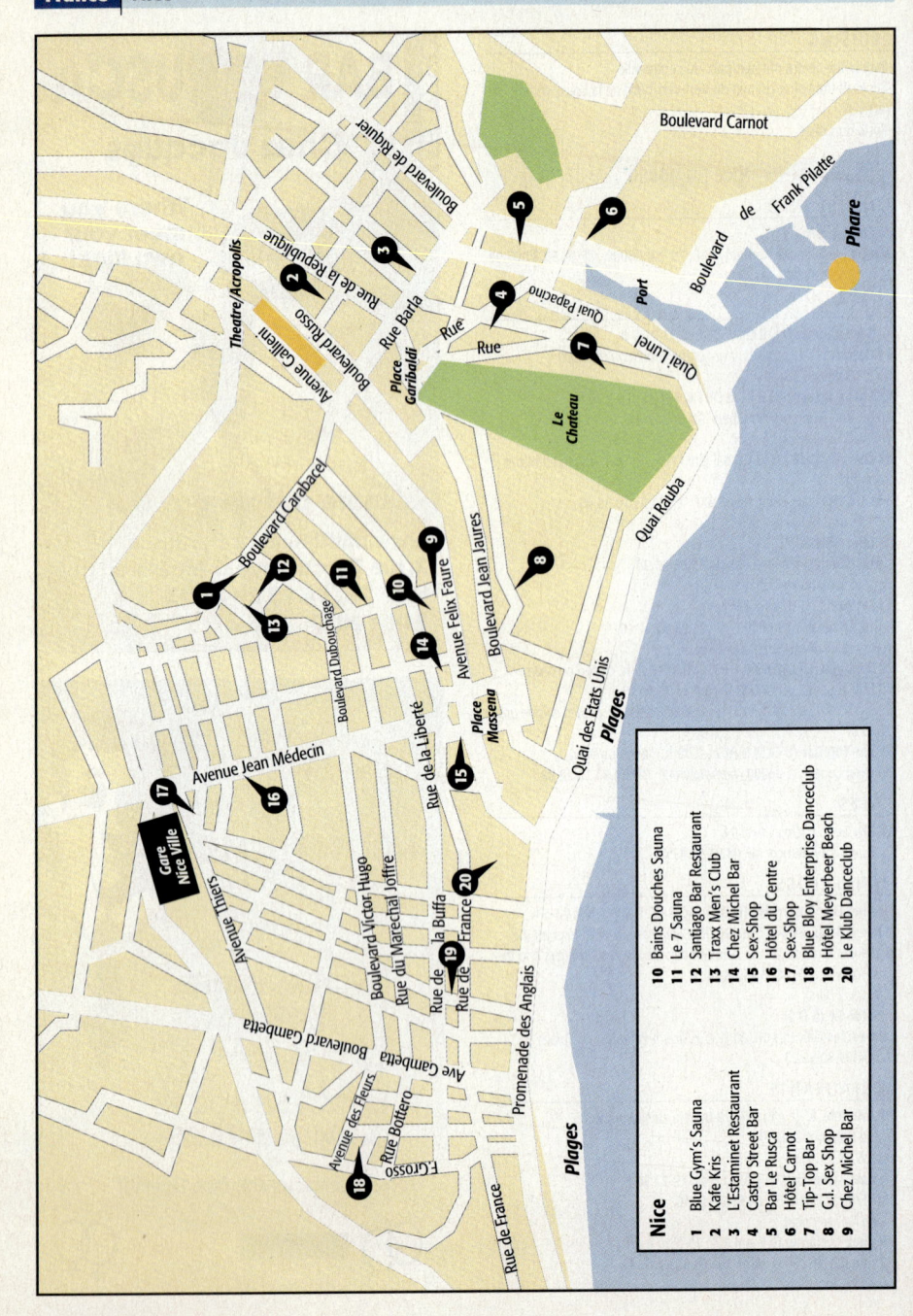

Nice

1. Blue Gym's Sauna
2. Kafe Kris
3. L'Estaminet Restaurant
4. Castro Street Bar
5. Bar Le Rusca
6. Hôtel Carnot
7. Tip-Top Bar
8. G.I. Sex Shop
9. Chez Michel Bar
10. Bains Douches Sauna
11. Le 7 Sauna
12. Santiago Bar Restaurant
13. Traxx Men's Club
14. Chez Michel Bar
15. Sex-Shop
16. Hôtel du Centre
17. Sex-Shop
18. Blue Bloy Enterprise Danceclub
19. Hôtel Meyerbeer Beach
20. Le Klub Danceclub

284 *SPARTACUS* 2001/2002

Edelweiss
DESIGN · 33 (0) 4 93 68 13 13
The Finest Gay Club on the French Riviera
Open 7 days a week
BBE
www.blueboy.fr
Club - Discotheque
BLUE BOY ENTERPRISE
9, rue J. B. Spinetta (angle Bd. Grosso)
06000 NICE / FRANCE
33 (0) 4 93 44 68 24

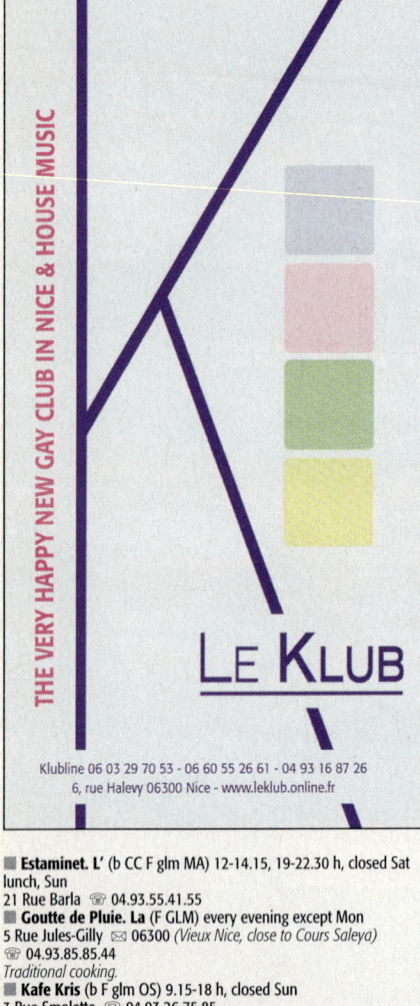

France — Nice

THE VERY HAPPY NEW GAY CLUB IN NICE & HOUSE MUSIC

LE KLUB

Klubline 06 03 29 70 53 - 06 60 55 26 61 - 04 93 16 87 26
6, rue Halevy 06300 Nice - www.leklub.online.fr

BAR TABAC ALBERTI
1, Rue Alberti
06000 NICE
Tél. 04 93 85 43 90
Ouvert de Midi à Minuit

LE LATINOS
RESTO & TAPAS
TEL 04 93 85 01 10
6, RUE CHAUVAIN 06000 NICE

■ **Estaminet. L'** (b CC F glm MA) 12-14.15, 19-22.30 h, closed Sat lunch, Sun
21 Rue Barla ☎ 04.93.55.41.55
■ **Goutte de Pluie. La** (F GLM) every evening except Mon
5 Rue Jules-Gilly ✉ 06300 (Vieux Nice, close to Cours Saleya)
☎ 04.93.85.85.44
Traditional cooking.
■ **Kafe Kris** (b F glm OS) 9.15-18 h, closed Sun
3 Rue Smolette ☎ 04.93.26.75.85
■ **Table Coquine. La** (AC CC F GLM MA OS) closed Mon, Sat (lunch)
44 Avenue de la République ✉ 06000 (near Palais des Congrès)
☎ 04.93.55.39.99

SEX SHOPS/BLUE MOVIES

■ **G.I. Sex Shop** (AC CC DR G lj MA VS YG) 10-24, Sun and public holidays 14-20 h
8 Rue Descente Crotti ✉ 06000 (Place Massena/Vieille Ville/near Palais de Justice) ☎ 04.93.80.29.49
Videos, gadgets and cruising on 4 floors. Big screen cinema and latest DVDs.
■ **Sex-Shop** (g VS) 9-23 h, Sun closed
7 Rue Masséna ✉ 06000

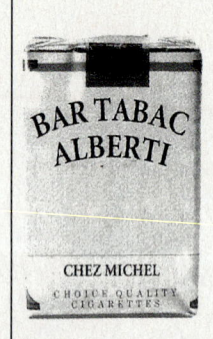

Nice | France

G.F

SEX CLUB - SEX SHOP

4 FLOORS OF CRUISING & STIMULATION
LABYRINTH
PRIVATE CABIN PROJECTIONS
BIG SCREEN CINEMA
LARGE COLLECTION OF VIDEOS & GADGETS

8, Descente Crotti - Nice 04 93 80 29 49

France | **Nice**

LE 7
SAUNA-VAPEUR
HAMMAN
RELAXATION
BAR - T.V.

Ouvert Tous les jours 13H30 - 21 H

Fond Musical

7, rue Foncet - 06000 NICE
Tél. 04.93.62.25.02

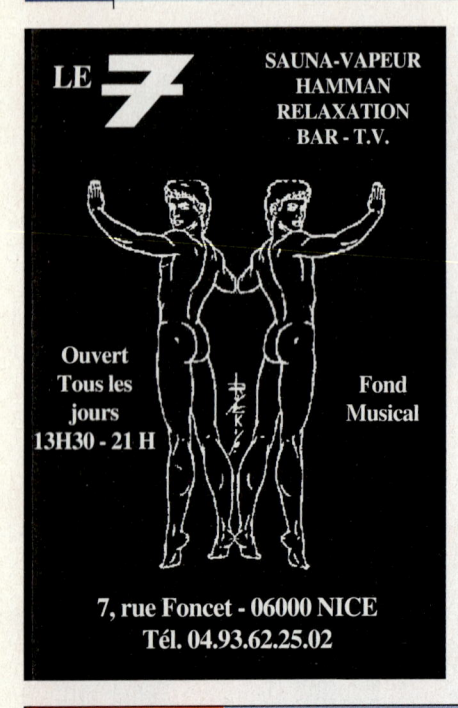

■ **Sex-Shop** (g VS) 9-23 h, Sun closed
23 Rue Belgique ✉ 06000

SAUNAS/BATHS

■ **Bains Douches** (AC B DR f G p SA SB VS WH YG) 13-22 h
7 Rue Gubernatis ✉ 06000 *(Close to Place Massena, Bus-Félix Faure)*
☎ 04.93.80.28.26
Three floors of fun created by Nice's professional gay team (25 years of experience).

■ **Blue Gym's** (AC b f G SA SB SOL VS WH WO) 12-0.30, tea parties Tue Thu 17-18 h
7 Avenue Désambrois ✉ 06000 ☎ 04.93.80.71.11
Cruise sauna with full gym equipment.

■ **7. Le** (b G SA SB SOL WH VS YG) 13.30-21 h
7 Rue Foncet ✉ 06000 ☎ 04.93.62.25.02
Popular sauna on three floors with labyrinth.

HOTELS

■ **Gourmet Lorrain. Le** (AC B BF CC F glm H MA N OS SOL) Restaurant closed Sun evening and Mon, Jan 1st-8th, July 15th-Aug 14th
7 Avenue Santa Fior ✉ 06100 *(North of Nice, St-Maurice, Bus 1/2/23/24-Puget)* ☎ 04.93.84.90.78 📠 04.92.09.11.25
Comfortable quiet hotel. Great food and wine. Quote Spartacus for a free aperitif.

■ **Hôtel Bahia Vista** (AC B F GLM MA VS PI)
Boulevard Napoléon III, Pont St. Jean ✉ 06230 *(between Nice and Monaco)* ☎ 04.93.76.21.50 📠 04.93.01.29.77
Panoramic bar and restaurant with swimming-pool on the roof. Quote SPARTACUS for discount rates (-20%).

■ **Hôtel Carnot** (AC BF CC f glm H MA) 7-23 h
8 Boulevard Carnot ✉ 06300 *(harbour/Port)* ☎ 04.93.89.56.54 📠 04.93.55.48.18
Mixed, but gays are welcome. All rooms with telephone, priv. bath, TV, balcony.

HOTEL DU CENTRE
★★ NN

Conveniently located in the center of Nice. 200 yards from the train station. 500 yards from the sea and the famous "Promenade des Anglais". A friendly staff will welcome you to the Hotel du Centre. The hotel has 28 rooms most with shower or bath and toilet, colour television, telephone and lift. Open year round.

2, rue de Suisse - 06000 NICE - Tél. 04.93.88.83.85 - Fax: 04.93.82.29.80
www.NICE-HOTEL-CENTRE.com

- Gay owned & run
- All rooms with TV, Tel, WC, shower or bath, kitchenette
- Breakfast at any time
- "Gay Pack" for every guest
- Town center, close to the beach (50m) and the gay scene

SPECIAL RATES FOR SPARTACUS GUESTS

★NN

HOTEL MEYERBEER BEACH
15, rue Meyerbeer - 06000 Nice - tel. 04 93 88 95 65 - Fax : 04 93 82 09 25
www.come.to/meyerbeer · e.mail : hotel.meyerbeer.beach@wanadoo.fr

Nice | France

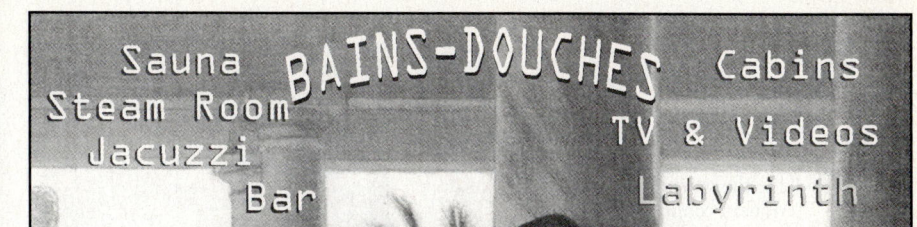

BAINS-DOUCHES

Sauna
Steam Room
Jacuzzi
Bar

Cabins
TV & Videos
Labyrinth

Open Every Day
13.00 - 22.00 h

3 Floors of Fun & More

7, rue Gubernatis - 06000 NICE
Tel : 04 93 80 28 26
Place Masséna Sun Bus Station, Félix Faure

France | Nice ▶ Nîmes

HOTEL BAHIA VISTA ★★★

Overlooking the magnificent Bay of Villefranche.
Modern confortable A.C. rooms
and suites with satellite TV & Videos.
Panoramic restaurant and pool on the 5th floor.
Ideal situation between Nice and Monaco.
Quote Spartacus for special rates (-20%)
Piano Bar & Billiards Room

Best Western
Bd Napoléon III - Pont St Jean - 06230 Villefranche-sur-Mer
Téléphone (33) 04 93 76 21 50 - Téléfax (33) 04 93 01 29 77

■ **Hôtel du Centre** (AC BF H MA OS)
2 Rue de Suisse ✉ 06000 (near train station and "Promenade des Anglais") ☎ 04.93.88.83.85 📠 04.93.82.29.80
📧 hotel-centre@webstore.fr 🌐 www.nice-hotel-centre.com
Gays welcome. Quote Spartacus for a discount. Rooms FF 180-330.-
■ **Hôtel Lyonnais** (BF glm H MA) RReception: 8-22.30
20 Rue de Russie ✉ 06000 ☎ 04.93.88.70.74 📠 04.93.16.25.56
Budget hotel in the centre of Nice.
■ **Hôtel Meyerbeer Beach** (BF F GLM H MA p) 8-12, 15-19 h
15 Rue Meyerbeer ✉ 06000 (50 m from the beach)
☎ 04.93.88.95.65 📠 04.93.82.09.25
📧 hotel.meyerbeer.beach@wanadoo.fr
🌐 www.come.to/meyerbeer
All rooms with kitchenette, TV, telephone, shower, WC. Rates FF 300-350.- BF all day long. "Gay pack" for every guest.

GENERAL GROUPS
■ **Groupe Action Gay Côte-d'Azur (G.A.G)**
53 Boulevard Raimbaldi ✉ 06000 ☎ 04.93.92.34.32
☎ 04.93.92.34.32 📧 gagca@worldnet.net 🌐 gagnice.fr.st
■ **Riviera Gay Community**
c/o Bill Shipley, Les Hauts de Vaugrenier, 10 Allée du Ponson
✉ 06570 ☎ 04.92.02.92.55

HEALTH GROUPS
■ **Accueil Aide aux Malades Information Sida (AAMIS)** Mon-Fri 9-12, 14-17 h
c/o Le Phoenix, 10 Rue de Maeyer ✉ 06300 ☎ 04.93.55.90.35
📠 04.93.55.87.24 📧 aamis_nice@hotmail.com
Help for HIV+ people, their friends and families.
■ **Dispensaire Antivénérien**
2 Rue Edouard Berri ✉ 06000 ☎ 04.93.85.12.62
HIV-testing.

RELIGIOUS GROUPS
■ **David et Jonathan**
B.P. 4221 ✉ 06304 ☎ 04.93.56.97.32

SWIMMING
-Jetée du port (NU)
-Coco Beach/Cap Nice (NU)(Bus at harbour to Coco Beach, small staircase down, climb rocky beach to the left)

CRUISING
-Rue Masséna, avenue Jean-Médecin (afternoon/l'après-midi)

-Around the lighthouse day and evening all year round/Autour du Phare jour et soir toute l'année
-Parc Ferber (R)/Promenade des Anglais
-Parc du Château
-Square Alsace-Lorraine (R)

Nîmes ✉ 30000

DANCECLUBS
■ **Lulu Club** (AC B CC D DR G lj MA P SNU VS) 23-? h, closed Mon-Wed
10 Impasse Curaterie ✉ 30000 (5 mins walk from the station)
☎ 04.66.36.28.20

RESTAURANTS
■ **Ophélie** (AC CC F glm MA OS) 20-23 h, closed Sun Mon
35 Rue Fresque ✉ 30000 (Near Romain Arena) ☎ 04.66.21.00.19
■ **Poulailler. Le** (B F glm)
15 Rue de la Vierge ✉ 30000 ☎ 04.66.36.70.60

SEX SHOPS/BLUE MOVIES
■ **DIPA Sex Shop** (AC CC g VS) 10-20 h, closed Sun
Impasse de la Curaterie ✉ 30000 ☎ 04.66.21.33.33
■ **Hall du K7** (CC G VS) 10-19.30 h, closed Sun
24 Boulevard Courbet ✉ 30000 ☎ 04.66.36.08.12

SAUNAS/BATHS
■ **Nîmes Club Sauna** (AC B CC DR F G MA PI SA SB SOL VS WH) 12-24 h
7/9 Rue Fernand-Pelloutier ✉ 30900 (behind the Carré d'Art)
☎ 04.66.67.65.18
Sauna with shop. Theme nights last week-end of the month 23-7 h.

HEALTH GROUPS
■ **Aides Languedoc-Cévennes** Mon 18-20, Wed 18-22 h
B.P. 183 ✉ 30012 ☎ 04.66.76.26.07

CRUISING
-Boulevard Jean-Jaurès
-Behind the railway station/derrière la gare SNCF
-Jardin La Fontaine (afternoon, evening/après-midi, soir)
-Gorges du Gardon, via motorway Nîmes-Uzès (at P Gardon, Pont St. Nicolas then walk about 1-2 km in direction to the river, also nude bathing)

Paris | France

FRENCH LOVER GALLERY
WWW.JNRCPRODUCTION.COM
The Best in France
VIDEO / DVD

nachts und 5.30 Uhr morgens. Wenn Ihr aus einer Diskothek kommt, nehmt ein Taxi oder den Nachtbus. Was schwule Hotels betrifft, ist Frankreich etwas im Rückstand. Man muß lange Zeit im voraus reservieren, was nicht zuletzt daran liegt, daß in Paris das ganze Jahr Hochsaison ist!

Paris, c'est Paris! Tout simplement. C'est le point de départ idéal pour une découverte du fascinant continent européen et une des premières villes gaies du monde. En plus d'un réseau important de lieux de rencontres, de nombreuses boutiques et entreprises de services pour les gais, tenues par des gais, ont vu le jour ces dernières années. Paris-lumière, Paris la nuit, c'est aussi pour eux. Une vie trépidante anime les bars, les boutiques, les rues du centre, les discothèques, 24 heures sur 24. Le quartier historique du Marais, de la rue Vieille-du-Temple à la rue des Archives en passant par la rue Sainte-Croix-de-la-Bretonnerie, est le centre d'un axe qui va des Halles à Bastille et qui regroupe l'essentiel de la vie gaie. Paris, c'est aussi une vie culturelle intense: expositions, concerts, cinémas, théâtres; consulter le *Pariscope* ou, pour les événements gais et les sorties, les nombreux journaux gratuits disponibles dans presque tous les bars. Attention, les métros ne circulent pas entre une heure à cinq heures trente. En sortant de boîte, il faudra prendre un taxi ou un bus de nuit. En ce qui concerne les hôtels gais, la France est vraiment en retard, il faut réserver longtemps à l'avance quelle que soit la période, car à Paris la saison dure toute l'année.

Se sabe de sobra que Paris es un encanto. Es la ciudad ideal como punto de partida para descubrir el fascinante continente europeo y se ha vuelto una verdadera metrópoli gay. En los últimos años se ha desarollado aquí una vida con muchos bares, restaurantes y tiendas para la clientela homosexual. En los bares, en las calles del centro y en las discotecas se encuentra un ambiente animadísimo tanto de día como de noche. El barrio histórico de Marais, que se extiende de la rue Vielle-du-Temple, sobre rue des Archives hasta la rue Saint-Croix-de-la-Bretonnerie es el centro de la zona gay, que abarca Les Halles y la Bastilla. Paris ofrece además una extensa vida cultural, con exposiciones, conciertos, cine y teatro. Informaciones más detalladas se encuentran en la guía de ocio llamado Pariscope o para actividades o fiestas gay se recomienda echar un vistazo a las númerosas revistas gratuitas, que se pueden consultar en casi todos los bares de la ciudad. Cuidado: Entre la 1 y las 5:30 de la mañana no funciona el métro, así que se tiene que coger un taxi o un autobus nocturno. Paris no se caracteriza precisamente por su gran oferta de hoteles gay. En la mayoría de los casos hay que hacer las reservas con mucho adelanto, ¡entre otras cosas porque Paris está siempre en temporada alta!.

Parigi è sempre Parigi! Come una delle metropoli gay si offre come base ideale per l'esplorazione del continente europeo. Negli ultimi anni si è sviluppata una vita gay con gastronomia, negozi di gay per gay. Un incessante giro pulsante e brillante nei bar, sulle strade e nelle discoteche, tutta la giornata fino all'alba seguente. Il quartiere storico di Marais, tra la Rue Vieille-du-Temple, la Rue des Archives e la Rue Saint-Croix-de-la- Bretonnerie, è anche il centro del quartiere gay, che si estende fino a Les Halles e alla Bastille. Parigi però offre anche un vasto programma culturale: mostre, concerti, cinema, teatro. Più informazioni si trovano nel "Pariscope" o nei numerosi giornali distribuiti gratuitamente nei bar. Attenzione: La Métro è chiusa tra le 1 e le 5.30 del mattino. Uscendo dalla discoteca conviene prendere un taxi o i bus notturni. Per quanto riguarda gli alberghi gay, la Francia è ancora un po' indietro. Bisogna prenotare molto tempo in anticipo, perché a Parigi è sempre alta stagione!

GAY INFO

■ **Centre Gay & Lesbien (CGL)** (GLM) Mon-Sat 12-20 h, Café Positif: Sun 14-19 h
3 Rue Keller ✉ 75011 (M° Bastille/Voltaire/Ledru-Rollin)
☎ 01.43.57.21.47 📠 01.43.57.27.93 🖥 cglparis@cglparis.org
Contact for many gay and gay-lesbian groups. Shop, café, library. Information about HIV and Aids.
■ **Radio FG 98.2** 0-24 h (FM 98,2 MHz)
57 Rue de Rivoli ✉ 75001 ☎ 01.40.13.88.28 📠 01.40.13.88.07
↪ *also introduction France.*

PUBLICATIONS

■ **e.m@le**
Immeuble Metropole 19, 134-140 Rue Aubervilliers ✉ 75019
☎ 01.53.35.98.54 📠 01.53.35.98.80 🖥 emaleredac@netgate.fr
Magazine published by Groupe Gai Pied. Every Thu. Available for free in gay establishments.
■ **Garçons**
8 Rue du Faubourg Poissonière ✉ 75010 ☎ 01.56.56.01.12
📠 01.48.24.95.80 🖥 garcons@wanadoo.fr
Gay magazine for Paris published 11/year. 10 F.
■ **Illico - Double Face**
99 Rue de la Verrerie ✉ 75004 ☎ 01.48.04.58.00
📠 01.48.04.05.92 🖥 groupeillico@mail2.imaginet.fr
e-llico.com
Monthly free news magazine and its supplement. Available in gay establisments.

SPARTACUS 2001/2002 293

France | Paris

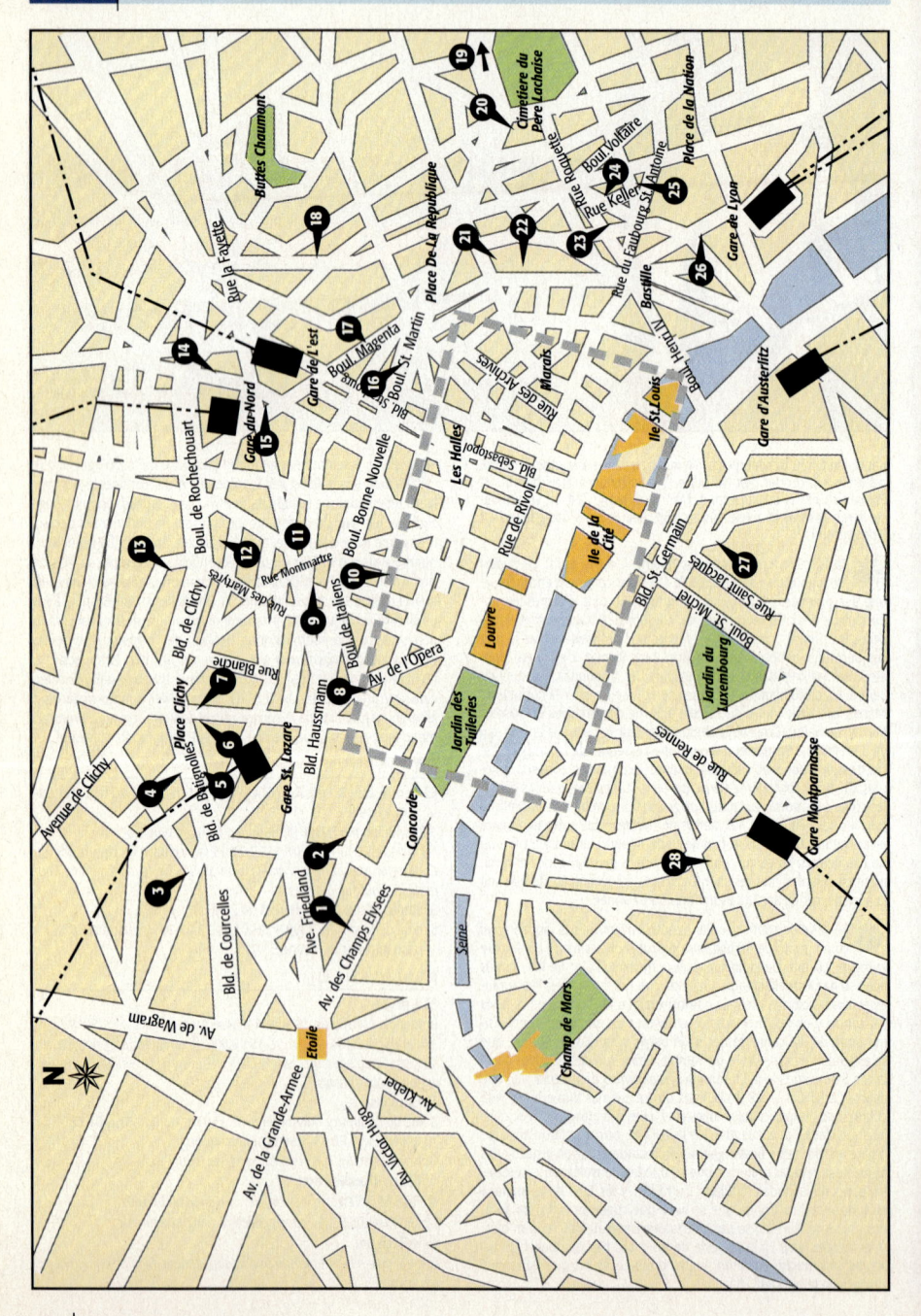

Paris | France

Paris

1. Queen Danceclub
2. Banque Club Men's Club
3. Hôtel des Batignolles
4. King Sauna Night & Day
5. French Art Video Shop
6. IEM Sex Shop
7. Yanko Sex Shop
8. Kiosque des Amis News Stand
9. Le Mandala Sauna
10. Euro Men's Club Sauna
11. IDM Sauna
12. Mec Zone Bar
13. Sauna Mykonos
14. Talisman Video Shop
15. Key West Sauna
16. Hôtel Louxor
17. Station Vidéo
18. IEM Sex Shop
19. Le Riad Sauna
20. La Courtille Restaurant
21. Hôtel Beaumarchais
22. La Station Sex Shop
23. Keller's Bar
24. La Luna Danceclub
25. Bastille Sauna
26. Le Saint-Hubert Hotel
27. Le Petit Prince Restaurant
28. L'Hémis Restaurant

IEM Les Halles
Premier gay store in France!
43, RUE DE L'ARBRE-SEC - 75001 PARIS - MÉTRO LOUVRE - TÉL : 01 42 96 05 74
Ouvert de 11h à 21h - Dimanche de 13h à 21h / Open 11 am to 9 pm - Sunday 1 pm to 9 pm

CULTURE
■ **Stéphane Plassier** (glm) 12-20, Sat 14-22 h
8 rue du Trésor ✉ 75004 (M° Hotel de Ville) ☎ 01.40.29.10.22

TOURIST INFO
■ **Tourist Info**
127 avenue des Champs-Elysées ✉ 75008 ☎ 01.49.52.53.54
🖷 01.49.52.53.00

BARS
■ **Acces Soir Café** (A B CC GLM MG s) 18-2 h
41 Rue des Blancs Manteaux ✉ 75011 ☎ 01.42.72.12.89
■ **Akhénaton Café** (A AC B glm MA) 14-2 h
12 Rue du Plâtre ✉ 75004 (M° Hôtel-de-Ville/Rambuteau)
☎ 01.48.87.02.59
■ **Amnésia Café** (AC B CC f G MA) 10-2, lunch-brunch 12-17 h
42 Rue Vieille-du-Temple ✉ 75004 (M° Hôtel-de-Ville)
☎ 01.42.72.16.94
■ **Arambar. L'** (b f CC glm MA s) 12-2 h
7 rue de la Folie Mericourt ✉ 75011 ☎ 01.48.05.57.79
■ **Au Gobelet d'Argent** (B G lj s TV) 17-? h
11 Rue du Cygne ✉ 75001 (M° Etienne Marcel) ☎ 01.42.33.29.82
■ **Banana. Le** (AC B glm MA OS SNU TV) 16-? h
13 Rue de la Ferronnerie ✉ 75001 (M° Châtelet/Les Halles)
☎ 01.42.33.35.31
■ **Bar du Palmier. Le** (AC B F g OS) 17 h-dawn
16 Rue des Lombards ✉ 75004 (M° Chatelet/Les Halles)
☎ 01.42.78.53.53
Good atmosphere, bar cocktails.

■ **Bar Hôtel Central** (AC B G H MA) 16-2, Sat Sun 14-2 h
33 Rue Vieille-du-Temple ✉ 75004 (M° Hôtel-de-Ville)
☎ 01.48.87.99.33
A friendly, international gay rendez-vous and the only Gay Hotel in Paris!
■ **Bar Le Dépôt** (AC B CC G MA) 12-7 h
10 Rue aux Ours ✉ 75003 ☎ 01.44.54.96.96
■ **Bears' Den** (AC B CC G MG lj VS) 16-2 h
6 Rue des Lombards ✉ 75004 ☎ 01.42.71.08.20
Bears, daddies and friends.
■ **Bunker. Le** (AC B G LJ VS) 21-2 h
23 rue du Temple ✉ 75003 ☎ 01.42.74.05.15
Basement bar under Café Rude.
■ **Café Cox** (AC B G MA OS) 13-2 h
15 Rue des Archives ✉ 75004 ☎ 01.42.72.08.00
■ **Café Rude** (B glm F) 12-2 h
23 rue du Temple ✉ 75004 ☎ 01.42.74.05.15
■ **Cap Horn Bar. Le** (AC B D G WE YG) 16-2 h
37 Rue des Lombards ✉ 75001 M° Châtelet-Les Halles
☎ 01.40.28.03.08
■ **Champmeslé. La** (A B E gLm MA s TV) 12-2 h
4 Rue Chabanais ✉ 75002 (M° Pyramides/Bourse)
☎ 01.42.96.85.20
Shows Thu.
■ **Cirque. Le** (AC B DR glm MA VS) Thu-Sat 22-5, Sun 17-5 h
5/7 Rue de la Ferronnerie ✉ 75001 (M° Chatelet/Les Halles)
☎ 01.40.41.00.10
Three bars, including the Underbar.
■ **Duplex. Le** (A B GLM MA) 20-2 h
25 Rue Michel-le-Comte ✉ 75003 (M° Rambuteau)
☎ 01.42.72.80.86

France | Paris

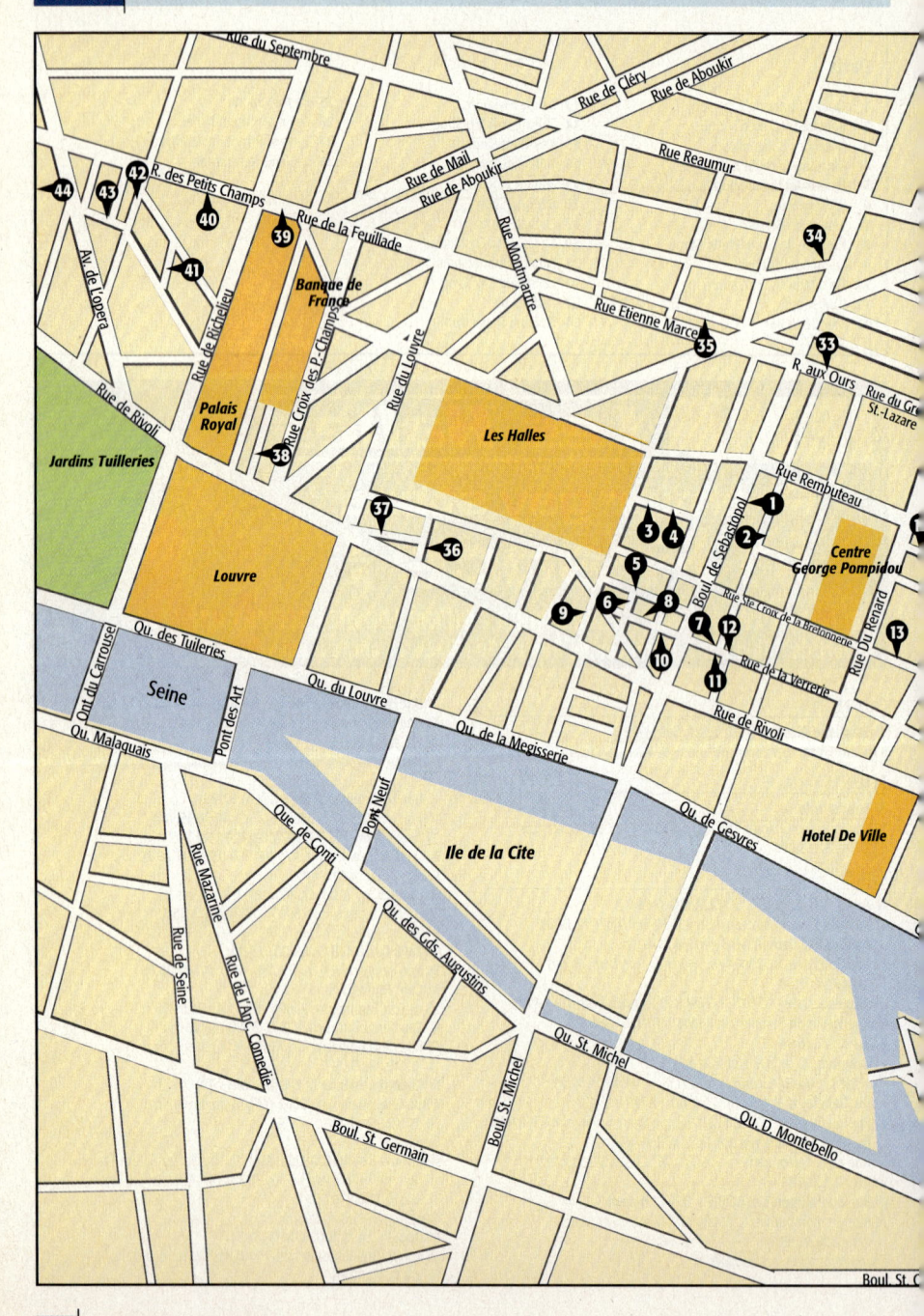

Paris | France

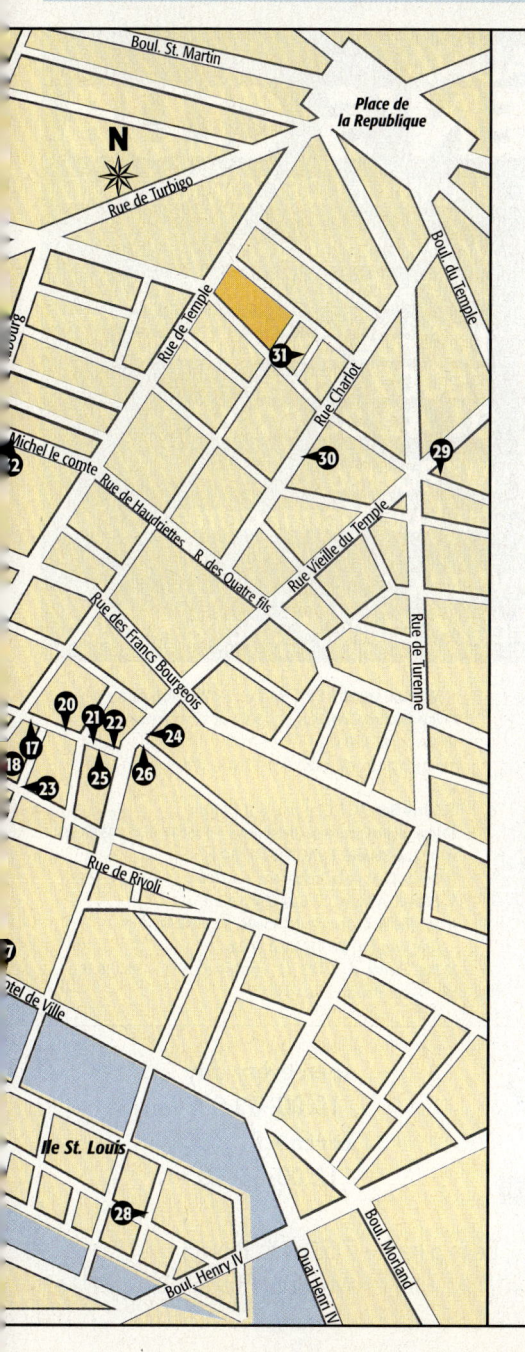

Paris

1. Sweetman Fashion Shop
2. Pause Lecture Book Shop
3. Kiosque Forum News Stand
4. Agora Hotel
5. Le Banana Bar
6. L'Amazonial Restaurant / Le Tropic Café Bar
7. Le Dépôt Bar / X-Bar
8. Au Diable des Lombards Restaurant
9. Chez Max Restaurant
10. Le Club Danceclub
11. Projection Video
12. Le Bar du Palmier
13. Le Gai Moulin restaurant
14. QG Men's Club
15. Le MicMan Bar
16. Le Divin Restaurant
17. Mixer Bar
18. Chez Tsou Restaurant
19. Thermik Bar
20. TTBM Sex Shop
21. Les Mots à la Bouche Book Shop
22. Bar/Hôtel Central Marais
23. Le Quetzal Bar
24. Amnesia Café
25. Boy'z Bazaar Video Shop
26. Okawa Bar
27. L'Arène Men's Club
28. Auberge de la Reine Blanche Restaurant
29. Hôtel Beaumarchais
30. One Way Bar
31. Madame Sans Gêne Restaurant
32. Le Duplex Bar
33. Le Dépôt Bar
34. L'Impact Bar
35. Le Monde à l'Envers Restaurant
36. Yanko Sex Shop
37. IEM Sex Shop
38. Univers Gym Sauna
39. Club 18 Danceclub
40. L'Insolite Danceclub
41. La Champmeslé Bar
42. Le Til't Sauna
43. Le Vagabond Bar
44. Le Transfert Men's Club

SPARTACUS 2001/2002

France Paris

SAUNA EURO MEN'S CLUB
DÉTENTE, CONVIVIALITÉ DANS UN DÉCOR RAFFINÉ

MOINS DE 26 ANS
TARIF RÉDUIT APRÈS 20H30

**10, rue Saint Marc
75002 Paris
01 42 33 92 63**

M° Bourse
ou Rue Montmartre

3 niveaux :
TV bar • cabines • hammam • sauna • piscine • vidéo

■ **Feeling. Le** (B glm MA) 15-2 h
43 Rue Ste.Croix de la Bretonnerie ✉ 75004 ☎ 01.48.04.70.03
■ **Impact Bar. L'** (B G)
18 rue Grenéta ✉ 75002 ☎ 01 42 21 94 24
■ **Interface Bar** (A B CC G MA) 15-2 h
34 Rue Keller ✉ 75011 ☎ 01.47.00.67.15
■ **Keller's** (AC B CC DR G LJ MG p) 22.30-2, Fri Sat -4 h
14 Rue Keller ✉ 75011 (M° Bastille) ☎ 01.47.00.05.39
Pool table. Locker-room and showers. Strict dress-code: Leather or jeans and t-shirt.
■ **Mathis Bar** (B GLM) 21-? h, closed on Sun
3 Rue Ponthieu ✉ 75008 (M° Franklin-Roosevelt)
☎ 01.53.76.01.62
■ **Mec Zone** (AC B G LJ VS) 21-6, Sun 18-6 h
27 Rue Turgot ✉ 75009 (M° Anvers) ☎ 01.40.82.94.18

■ **MicMan. Le** (AC B DR G MA VS) 12-2 WE and holidays -4 h
24 Rue Geoffroy-l'Angevin ✉ 75004 (M° Rambuteau)
☎ 01.42.74.39.80
Friendly atmosphere. Happy hour 19-21 h: 30% reduction on all consumations.
■ **Mixer Bar** (AC B CC d glm VS YG) 16-2 h
23 Rue Sainte Croix de la Bretonnerie ✉ 75004 ☎ 01.48.87.55.44
■ **Oiseau Bariolé. L'** (AC B GLM) 16-2 h
16 Rue St.Croix de la Bretonnerie ✉ 75004 ☎ 01.42.72.37.12
■ **Okawa** (A AC B CC F GLM MA S) 9-2 h
40 Rue Vieille du Temple ✉ 75004 ☎ 01.48.04.30.69
■ **One Way** (AC B G lj MA VS) 17-2 h
28 Rue Charlot ✉ 75003 (M° République) ☎ 01.48.87.46.10
Friendly atmosphere, cruising bar.

---

amnesia café

open every day
10.00–02.00
Lunch – Brunch
12.00–17.00

42, rue Vieille du Temple – 75004 Paris
Tél. 01.42.72.16.94   Métro Hotel de Ville

Paris | France

YOUR GAY GUIDE OF THE SOUTH OF FRANCE

THE GAY LIFE
www.hyzberg.com

SHOPPING, BARS, CLUBS, CONTACTS & MORE...

France | Paris

all about french gay life

e-llico.com

chat
news
guides
erotism
gay scene
entertainment

LE DEPOT
CLUB PARIS
OPEN EVERY DAY
'TILL 8am
1400 m²
Photos : Amir GARGARATCHI
+1000 BOYS A DAY
www.ledepot.com

France | Paris

BAR
HÔTEL CENTRAL

Since 1980
The international
gay rendez-vous
in Paris

33, rue Vieille du Temple
75004 Paris – Métro Hôtel de Ville

01 48 87 56 08   hotelcentralmarais@wanadoo.fr

LE DEPOT
THE BIGGEST CRUISING AREA IN FRANCE
1400 m²
+1000 BOYS A DAY
OPEN EVERY DAY
FROM 2pm TO 8am
Photos : Amir GARGARATCHI
www.ledepot.com

France | Paris

Le Vagabond
Depuis 1956
RESTAURANT - BAR
14, Rue Thérèse 75001 Paris
☎ 01.42.96.27.23

Insolite Club
Discothèque
33, rue des Petits-Champs - 75001 Paris ☎ 01 42 61 99 22

■ **Onix. L'** (B glm OS)
15 Rue des Lombards ✉ 75004
■ **Open Café** (B CC f glm MA OS) 10.30-2 h, brunch 12-17 h
17 Rue des Archives ✉ 75004 ☎ 01.48.87.80.25
■ **Piano Zinc** (AC B CC G MA S) 18-2 h
49 Rue des Blancs Manteaux ✉ 75004 ☎ 01.40.27.97.42
Piano Bar.
■ **Piétons. Les** (B F glm) 11-2 h
8 Rue des Lombards ✉ 75004 ☎ 01.48.87.82.87
■ **Quetzal. Le** (AC B G MA OS) 17-5 h
10 Rue de la Verrerie ✉ 75004 (M° Hôtel-de-Ville)
☎ 01.48.87.99.07
Very popular! Two bars. Games room on the 1st floor.
■ **Rainbow Café** (AC B d G MA s) Tue-Sun 17-2 h
16 Rue de la Verrerie ✉ 75004 ☎ 06.03.34.57.55

■ **Scandaleuses. Les** (AC B gLM VS) 18.2 h
9 Rue des Ecouffes ✉ 75004 *(Marais)* ☎ 01.48.87.39.26
Lesbian bar.
■ **Slider's Bar** (B DR f G lj MA OS) 17-2 h
138 Rue du Faubourg Saint Martin ✉ 75010 *(M° Gare de l'Est)*
☎ 01.43.55.18.34
■ **Stonewall Bar**
46 rue des Lombards ✉ 75001 ☎ 01 40 28 04 05
■ **Sun Café. Le** (AC B BF CC GLM msg SOL) 8-14 h
35 Rue Sainte Croix de la Bretonnerie ✉ 75004 *(M° Hotel de Ville)*
☎ 01.40.29.44.40
Bar with dj, techno and house.
■ **Thermik Bar** (AC B G MA) 16-2 h
7 Rue de la Verrerie ✉ 75004 ☎ 01.44.78.08.18
Theme parties.

ONE WAY
bar — EVERY DAY 17-02 am — vidéo

Happy Hour Everyday · 19⁰⁰ -21⁰⁰
Ambiance Sympa   Air conditioned
Cruising bar   Vidéo en sous-sol

28, rue Charlot – 75003 PARIS – Tél. 01.48.87.46.10 – Métro REPUBLIQUE

Paris | France

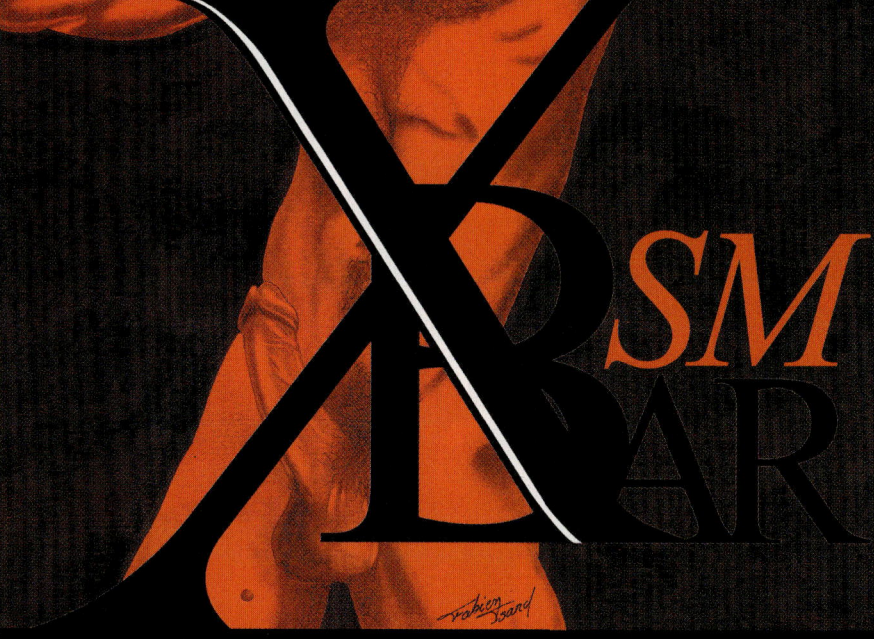

Leather **Latex** *Military* **Bar**
700 m²
9 pm 'till 8 am
MEN ONLY

X BAR 24 - 26, Rue Des Lombards
75004 Paris - France
infos@xbar.fr / www.xbar.fr
Tél : 01 48 87 10 75

www.ledepot.com

France | Paris

LE DEPOT
store
280 F
220 F
Ref 3000003636
H: 22 cm, D: 11 cm
Ref 3000003618
H : 37 cm
75 F
Ref G00003
530g
75 F
Ref G00004
530g
Ref G00001
170g 40F
Ref G00002
170g 40F
60 F
Lubricant Gel 250ml
Ref G00006
40 F
Lubricant Gel 100ml
Ref G00005
Over 1200 Videos titles in stock !
470 F
KEN RYKER
Ref 3000003250
The first true XXX Gay drama
ANIMUS
SERIAL FUCKER
220 F
Ref 1001010010
VHS
Order form on :
www.ledepot.com
ledepotstore@ledepot.com
www.ledepot.com

France — Paris

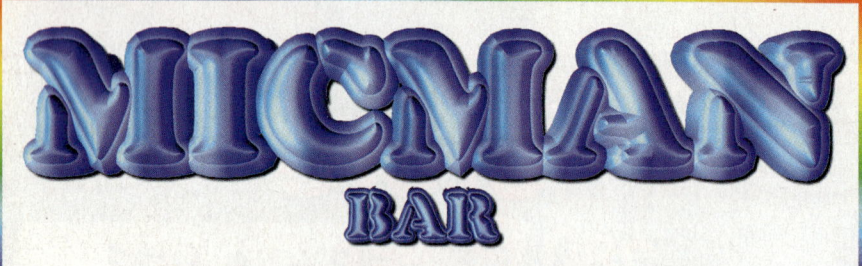

MICMAN BAR

24 rue Geoffroy l'Angevin 75004 PARIS
Tel : 01 42 74 39 80 - Internet : Micman.fr
Ouvert tous les jours de 12 h à 2 h
Week-end et jours fériés jusqu'à...

■ **Tropic Café. Le** (B CC d GLM MA OS TV) 16-4 h
66 Rue des Lombards ✉ 75001 ☎ 01.40.13.92.62
Opposite Amazonial.

■ **Unity Bar** (B gLM MA) 12-1 h
176-178 Rue Saint Martin ✉ 75003 ☎ 01.42.72.70.59
Mostly women, party atmosphere.

■ **Vagabond. Le** (AC B G F lj MA p) 18-4 h, closed Mon
14 Rue Thérèse ✉ 75001 (M° Pyramides) ☎ 01.42.96.27.23
Intimate cocktails, elegant dining and a great bar until late. French cuisine. Oldest gay bar/restaurant in Paris.

■ **X Bar** (G LJ MA) 21-8 h
24-26 Rue des Lombards ✉ 75001 ☎ 01.48.87.10.75

MEN'S CLUBS

■ **Arène. L'** (AC B CC DR G lj P S VS YG) 14-6, WE -7 h
80 Quai de l'Hôtel de Ville ✉ 75004 (M° Hôtel de Ville/Pont Marie)
☎ 01.42.21.03.53
Three floors of fantasy and films. Popular.

■ **Banque Club** (AC B CC DR G lj NU P VS) 16-2, Sun 14-2 h
23 Rue de Penthièvre ✉ 75008 (M° Miromesnil) ☎ 01.42.56.49.26
Three floors. Porno and music videos. Bar and big screen video.

■ **Docks** (AC b G DR LJ MG P VS) 16-2 h
150 Rue St. Maur ✉ 75010 (M°Goncourt) ☎ 01.43.57.33.82

■ **Glove. The** (B DR G LJ nu p) 22-2, Fri Sat -7, Sun 16-6 h
34 Rue Charlot ✉ 75003 ☎ 01.48.87.31.16
2 slings, many special parties: nudist, military, water sports,...

■ **Men's Club** (G P) 17-6 h
34 Boulevard de Clichy ✉ 75018 ☎ 01.42 59 52 24

■ **QG** (AC B CC DR G LJ MG P VS) 17-8 h
12 Rue Simon le Franc ✉ 75004 ☎ 01.48.87.74.18
Dress code leather, jeans, uniform, latex.

■ **Rangers. The** (AC b DR G LJ MA VS) 13-24 h
6 Boulevard St.Denis ✉ 75010 (M° Strasbourg St.Denis)
☎ 01.42.39.83.70

■ **Transfert. Le** (AC B CC DR G LJ MA p VS) 24-till dawn, Fri Sat 17-till dawn
3 Rue de la Sourdière ✉ 75001 (M° Tuileries) ☎ 01.42.60.48.42
Hard cruising bar. Strict dress code leather, uniform, jeans, latex.

■ **Trap. The** (AC B DR G lj MA p SNU VS) 23-4 h
10 Rue Jacob ✉ 75006 (M° Odéon) ☎ 01.43.54.53.53
Good videos. No entry for older people.

CAFES

■ **Coffee de l'Open Café** (CC F GLM OS YG) 12-24 h
15 Rue des Archives ✉ 75004 ☎ 01.48.87.80.25

■ **Coffee-Shop. Le** (A b F G VS YG) 9-2 h
3 Rue Sainte Croix de la Bretonnerie ✉ 75004 (marais)
☎ 01.42.74.24.21

DANCECLUBS

■ **Bains. Les** (AC B F D glm MA s) Gay Sun Mon and certain theme nights
7 Rue de Bourg l'Abbé ✉ 75003 ☎ 01.48.87.01.80

CLUB 18
PALAIS ROYAL
BAR - DISCOTHÈQUE

18, RUE DE BEAUJOLAIS 75001 PARIS • TEL : 01 42 97 52 13

Restaurant Chinois 恒興酒家 *Chinese Restaurant*

CHEZ TSOU

☎ 01.42.78.11.47

16, rue des Archives   75004 Paris

M° Hôtel de Ville – Ouvert tous les jours

■ **Boîte à Frissons au Tango** (D GLM MA s TV WE) Fri Sat 22.30-5 h
13 Rue au Maire ✉ 75003 (M° *Arts et Métiers*) ☎ 01.42.72.17.78
Rétro style dance evening for gays, lesbians and non-homophobic straights.

■ **Club. Le** (AC B D G YG) 23.30-? h
14 Rue Saint-Denis ✉ 75001 (M° *Châtelet/Les Halles*)
☎ 01.45.08.96.25
International, very friendly.

■ **Club 18** (AC B CC D DR G MA P) Thu-Sun & before public holydays 24-till dawn
18 Rue de Beaujolais ✉ 75001 (M° *Palais-Royal*)
☎ 01.42.97.52.13
Shows Wed Fri and Sun.

■ **Déclic. Le** (AC B D G MA p s) 23.30 h-till dawn, closed on Tue
12 Rue Quincampoix ✉ 75004 (M° *Hôtel de Ville*)
☎ 01.40.27.82.67
In an exceptional place dating from the 15th century. Many theme parties.

■ **Dépôt. Le** (AC B CC D DR G SNU VS) 12-7 h
10 Rue aux Ours ✉ 75003 (M° *Etienne Marcel/Rambuteau*)
☎ 01.44.54.96.96
Large disco and sex-club on three floors, with videos and laser shows.

■ **Folies Pigalle** (B D GLM s) 24-?, Black-Blanc-Beur Tea Dance: Sun 18-24 h
11 Place Pigalle ✉ 75009 (M° *Pigalle*) ☎ 01.48.78.25.56

■ **Gibus Club Paris** (D CC GLM MA SNU WE) Wed-Sat 24-7 h
18 Rue du Faubourg du Temple ✉ 75011 (M° *République*)
☎ 01.47.00.78.88

■ **Insolite. L'** (B D G) 23-5 h
33 Rue des Petits-Champs ✉ 75001 (M° *Pyramides*)
☎ 01.42.61.99.22
Good atmosphere.

■ **London. Le** (AC B CC D DR G MA P p VS) 23-7 h, closed on Mon
33bis Rue des Lombards ✉ 75001 (M° *Châtelet*)
☎ 01.42.33.41.45

■ **Luna. La** (AC B D G VS) 23-6 h Mon Tue video bar 22.30-4 h
28 Rue Keller ✉ 75011 (M° *Bastille*) ☎ 01.40.21.09.81

■ **Queen** (B D G lj P S YG) 24-6 h
102 Avenue des Champs Elysées ✉ 75008 (M° *Georges V*)
☎ 01.53.89.08.90
Theme nights and visiting international djs.

■ **Scorp.** (B D DR g lm lj STV YG)
25 Boulevard Poissonière ✉ 75002 ☎ 01.40.26.01.30

RESTAURANTS

■ **Amadéo** (CC F glm MA S) 12-14, 20-23 h, closed Sat lunch & Sun all day
19 Rue François Miron ✉ 75004 ☎ 01.48.87.01.02
Music classic and lyric.

■ **Amazonial. L'** (AC b CC F glm MA OS s SNU TV) Sun-Thu 12-915 19-1, Fri Sat -1.30 h
3 Rue Sainte Opportune ✉ 75001 (M° *Châtelet/Les Halles*)
☎ 01.42.33.53.13
International cuisine, Sat Sun brunch. Soirée cabaret.

LA COURTILLE – CUISINE – **la Courtille** – traditional french cooking
16, rue Guillaume Bertrand
75011 Paris - M° St-Maur tel. 01 48 06 48 34
open daily, closed sat. lunch and sun.
www.lacourtille.com

France | Paris

Restaurant L'Amazonial

You're welcome to **THE GAY** restaurant in Paris

Underground station: Châtelet les Halles.
Open 7/7 for lunch and dinner. Until 1H am, friday and saturday until 1H 30 am.
Brunch, every saturday and sunday morning.

3, rue Ste Opportune
75001 Paris Les Halles
Phone 01 42 33 53 13

and after your dinner finish your night
in the TROPIC CAFÉ - 66, rue des Lombards 75001 Paris
phone 01 40 13 92 62 - Open 7/7 from 4H pm

Le Divin RESTAURANT

Cuisine Traditionnelle et Provençale

41, rue Sainte Croix de la Bretonnerie 75004 Paris

Réservations : 01 42 77 10 20   Fermé le lundi

■ **Au Diable des Lombards** (AC B BF CC F GLM MA) 8-1, brunch daily 10-17 h
64 Rue des Lombards ✉ 75001 (M° Châtelet Les Halles)
☎ 01.42.33.81.84
American restaurant and bar.

■ **Au Tibourg** (AC CC F glm) 12-14, 19-23.30 h
29 rue du Bourg-Tibourg ✉ 75004 ☎ 01.42.74.45.25

■ **Auberge de la Reine Blanche** (AC b CC F glm MA) Mon-Tue 12-15 18-24, Thu 18-24, Fri-Sun 12-24 h, closed Wed, Thu lunch
30 Rue Saint-Louis en l'Ile ✉ 75004 ☎ 01.46.33.07.87

■ **Aux Trois Petits Cochons** (AC b F GLM) 20-1 h
31 Rue Tiquetonne ✉ 75002 ☎ 01.42.33.39.69

■ **Chez Max** (CC F g) 12-14, 20-24 h, closed on Sun
47 Rue Saint Honoré ✉ 75001 ☎ 01.45.08.80.13
"Landaises" specialities. Many artists./Spécialités landaises. Beaucoup d'artistes.

■ **Chez Raymonde** (AC CC d F GLM MA TV) 19.30-? h, closed Mon Tue
119 Avenue Parmentier ✉ 75011 ☎ 01.43.55.26.27
Dinner dance, popular French retro style./ Ambiance ginguette.

■ **Chez Tsou** (F g MA OS)
16 Rue des Archives ✉ 75004 (M° Hôtel de Ville)
☎ 01.42.78.11.47
Chinese restaurant.

■ **Courtille, La** (b F glm MA) closed Sat midday & Sun
16 Rue Guillaume Bertrand ✉ 75011 (M° St-Maur)
☎ 01.48.06.48.34
French traditional cuisine.

■ **Croc Man** (F glm) closed Sat and Sun midday
6 Rue Geoffroy L'Angevin ✉ 75004 ☎ 01.42.77.60.02

SAUNA - STEAM BATH

STAR SAUNA AWARD !

UNIVERS GYM

"The Most Popular in Paris!"

www.univers.net

4 Theme Parties a week !!!

TUESDAY : YOUTH Night
(Under 26: 35 F from 8 PM - I.D. required)

THURSDAY : FOAM Party
(Every 2 weeks from 8 PM)

FRIDAY : TOTAL TOUCH
(Dark Party every 2 weeks from 8 PM)

SATURDAY : LIVE SHOW
(Hot strippers & New video release from 8 PM)

SUNDAY : PARADISE
(Free massage - Just Relax, no sex ! - from 8 PM)

Noon - 1 AM 7/7
(Fri & Sat until 2 am)

- Body Building - High Tech Gym -
- New air Cond. - Sunbeds - Snack Bar -

- Sauna - Jacuzzi - Steam Bath -
- Individual & Group showers -

- Cabines de relaxation - Sling -
- Labyrinth - Glory Holes -
- Giant Screen Video -
- Video rooms -

UNIVERS GYM Paris Special Rate with this coupon !!!

20/22 rue des Bons Enfants
Paris 1er
Métro: Palais Royal / Musée du Louvre (lines 1 & 7)
or Les Halles (line 4 & RER)
Tél.: 01.42.61.24.83

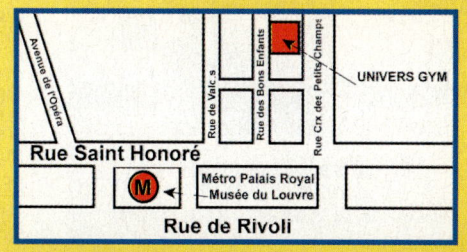

Only 2 minutes' walk from the Louvre Museum (10' from the Marais)

France | Paris

IEM Liège
Premier gay store in France!
33, rue de Liège - 75008 Paris - Métro Liège - Tél : 01 45 22 69 01
Ouvert de 11h30 à 19h30 - Fermé le dimanche / Open 11.30 am to 7.30 pm - Closed on sunday

Photo: Dr. SPRUNG / DICKS STUDIOS / IEM

- **Dénicheur. Le** (b F glm MA) 12-2 h
4 Rue Tiquetonne ✉ 75002 ☎ 01.42.21.31.01
All the furniture and objects are for sale.
- **Divin. Le** (AC CC F G MA) Tue-Sat 19-24, Sun -23.30 h
41 Rue Sainte-Croix-de-la-Bretonnerie ✉ 75004 (M° Hotel de Ville)
☎ 01.42.77.10.20
Charming and intimate. Traditional french and provençal cuisine. Quote Spartacus for a free aperitif.
- **Eclache & Cie** (AC BF cc F GLM MA) 8.30-2 h
10 Rue Saint Merri ✉ 75004 (M° Beaubourg/Hôtel de Ville)
☎ 01.42.74.62.62
Sociable place.
- **Eglantine. L'** (b F G) 11.30-14.30 19.30-23 h closed Sun Mon
9 Rue de la Verrerie ✉ 75004 (M° Hôtel-de-Ville)
☎ 01.48.04.75.58
Traditional cuisine, you'll get a warm welcome from Danielle.

PROJECTION VIDEO
Cabines vidéo au sous-sol
Location K7 et DVD
Accessoires
Lubrifiants
Arômes
Sous-vêtements
CD Rom
Revues
Vidéos
DVD
Cockrings
Vente sur le web: www.bmc-video.com
21, rue des Lombards 75004 Paris
Tél.01 40 27 98 09
Ouvert tlj. de 10h à 2h du matin non-stop

- **Equinox** (A AC CC F glm MA s) 11.30-14.30, 19.30-2 h, closed Mon
33-35 Rue des Rosiers ✉ 75004 ☎ 01.42.71.92.41
Cuisine Québécoise.
- **Fond de Cour** (AC CC F GLM MA OS) 12.30-14, 19.30-24 h
3 Rue Sainte-Croix-de-la-Bretonnerie ✉ 75004 (M° Hôtel-de-Ville)
☎ 01.42.74.71.52
- **Gai Moulin. Le** (CC F GLM) 19-0.30 h
4 Rue Saint-Merri ✉ 75004 ☎ 01.48.87.47.59
- **Hémis. L'** (A B F glm MA S) 9-15, 18-22.30, WE -23.30 h, closed Sat noon, Sun & Mon evening
21 Rue Mademoiselle ✉ 75015 ☎ 01.48.56.80.32
Menus FRF 73-110.-
- **Krokodil** (B F G) 17-2 h
20 Rue de la Reynie ✉ 75004 ☎ 01.48.87.55.67
- **Loup Blanc. Le** (A CC F glm) 20-0.30, Sun brunch 12-17 h
42, Rue Tiquetonne ✉ 75002 ☎ 01.40.13.08.35
- **Madame Sans Gêne** (AC CC F G MA) 12-14, 19.30,24 h, closed Sat Sun lunch
19 Rue de Picardie ✉ 75003 ☎ 01.42.71.31.71
- **Monde à l'Envers. Le** (F G MA) 12-14 20-23.30, Sat Sun 20-23.30 h, closed Mon
35 Rue Tiquetonne ✉ 75002 (M° Etienne Marcel)
☎ 01.40.26.13.91
Traditional cuisine. Good atmosphere.
- **O'2 F** (CC F glm MA) Tue-Thu 20-23.30, Fri-Sun -0.30 h
4 Rue de Roi de Sicile ✉ 75004 ☎ 01.42.72.75.75
- **Petit Picard. Le** (F glm)
42 Rue St. Croix de la Bretonnerie ✉ 75004 ☎ 01.42.78.54.03
- **Petit Prince. Le** (AC b F glm MA) 19.30-0.30 h
12 Rue du Lanneau ✉ 75005 (M° Maubert-Mutualité)
☎ 01.43.54.77.26
Reservation! Very popular, nice atmosphere.
- **Petite Chaumière. La** (CC F glm MG) 19.30-24 h
41 Rue des Blancs Manteaux ✉ 75004 ☎ 01.42.72.13.90
- **Piano Show** (B F g S) 20.30-21 h closed Mon
20 Rue de la Verrerie ✉ 75004 (M° Hôtel-de-Ville)
☎ 01.42.72.23.81
"Diner Spectacle," be sure to get there before 21h when the show starts.
- **Rude. Le** (B F GLM) 19.30-24, Sat -1, Sun brunch 11-16.30 h
23 Rue du Temple ✉ 75004 ☎ 01.42.74.05.15
- **58. Le** (B F glm) 10.30-? h, closed on Sun
58 Rue Saintonge ✉ 75003 ☎ 01.48.04.03.44

SEX SHOPS/BLUE MOVIES
- **Big Shop** (CC GLM VS YG) 10-24 h
2 Rue de la Cossonnerie ✉ 75001 (M° Chatelet-Les Halles)
☎ 01.42.21.47.02
Sex shop, accessories and gadgets. Latex section. Rental and sale of videos. Cinema and cabins.

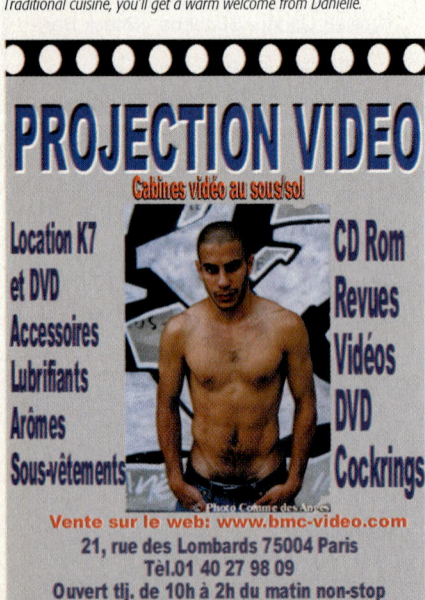

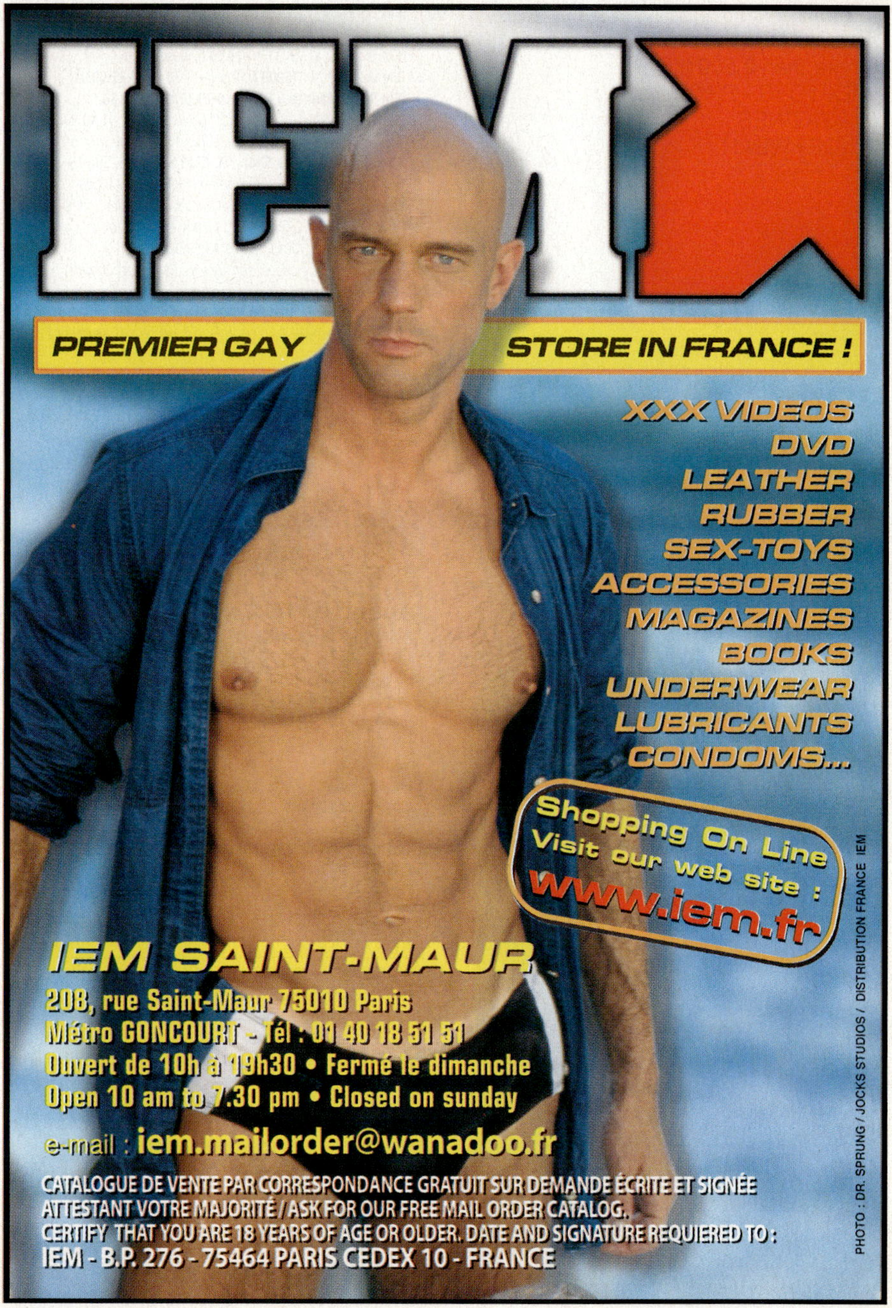
IEM
PREMIER GAY STORE IN FRANCE !
XXX VIDEOS
DVD
LEATHER
RUBBER
SEX-TOYS
ACCESSORIES
MAGAZINES
BOOKS
UNDERWEAR
LUBRICANTS
CONDOMS...
Shopping On Line
Visit our web site :
www.iem.fr
IEM SAINT-MAUR
208, rue Saint-Maur 75010 Paris
Métro GONCOURT - Tél : 01 40 18 51 51
Ouvert de 10h à 19h30 • Fermé le dimanche
Open 10 am to 7.30 pm • Closed on sunday
e-mail : iem.mailorder@wanadoo.fr
CATALOGUE DE VENTE PAR CORRESPONDANCE GRATUIT SUR DEMANDE ÉCRITE ET SIGNÉE
ATTESTANT VOTRE MAJORITÉ / ASK FOR OUR FREE MAIL ORDER CATALOG.
CERTIFY THAT YOU ARE 18 YEARS OF AGE OR OLDER. DATE AND SIGNATURE REQUIERED TO :
IEM - B.P. 276 - 75464 PARIS CEDEX 10 - FRANCE
PHOTO : DR. SPRUNG / JOCKS STUDIOS / DISTRIBUTION FRANCE IEM

France | **Paris**

SALE AND RENT OF VIDEOS & DVD
(more than 2.500 titles)
SEX TOYS - PRODUKTS
MAGAZINES
UNDERWEAR

Men's shop..

YANKO

Mon - Thus: 12 - 20.30
Fri - Sat: 12 - 21.30
Sun & Holidays: 14 - 21.30
54, rue de l'arbre sec (M° CHALET/LOUVRE-RIVOLI)
75001 PARIS ☎ 01.42.60.55.28

YANKO

PLACE DE CLICHY

10, place de Clichy
75009 PARIS

Ground Floor
Boutique
Sale & Rent of
Videos & DVD
Basement
Private video-cabins

Mon-Fri 11h-01h
Sat, Sun, Holidays 15h-01h

Tel. 01 45 26 71 19

■ **IEM Les Halles** (G LJ VS) 11-21, Sun & public holiday 13-21 h
43 Rue de l'Arbre Sec ✉ 75001 (M° Louvre) ☎ 01.42.96.05.74
■ **IEM Liège** (G LJ VS) 11.30-19.30 h, closed Sun
33 Rue de Liège ✉ 75008 (M° Liège) ☎ 01.45.22.69.01
■ **IEM Saint-Maur** (a G LJ VS) 10-19.30 h, closed Sun
208 Rue Saint-Maur ✉ 75010 (M° Goncourt) ☎ 01.40.18.51.51
One of the biggest gay sex shop in Europe. Sometimes gay art exhibits.
■ **Kingdom Gay Men's Shop** (CC GLM VS) 14-23, Sun 15-20 h
19 Rue Keller ✉ 75011 (M° Bastille) ☎ 01.48.07.07.08
Gay men's shop with video room in the basement. Near The Bastille.
■ **La Station** (AC CC G MA VS) 11-20 h, closed Sun
37 Rue Amelot ✉ 75011 ☎ 01.43.55.50.55
Videos, magazines, gadgets and sex toys. 5% reduction with SPARTACUS guide.
■ **Menstore** (CC G) Mon-Fri 9.30-18, Sat 12-18 h
99, Rue de la Verrerie ✉ 75004 (5th. floor) ☎ 01.48.04.57.11
Also mail order.
■ **Projection Video** (AC CC glm MA VS) 10-2 h
21 Rue des Lombards ✉ 75004 (M° Chatelet/Les Halles)
☎ 01.40.27.98.09
Sex shop, sale and rent of videos & DVD, cubicles.
■ **Rexx** (A G lj MA VS) 13-20 h, closed Sun
42 Rue de Poitou ✉ 75003 (M° Saint-Sebastien-Froissart)
☎ 01.42.77.58.57
Leather and latex clothes to measure.
■ **Sex-Shop du Dépôt. Le** (AC CC G MA VS) 12-8 h
c/o Atlantis City Sauna, Impasse Martini, 25 Rue Faubourg Saint Martin ✉ 75010 (M° Etienne Marcel/Rambuteau) ☎ 01.44.54.96.96
■ **TTBM** (AC CC GLM) 12-22, Sun 15-22 h
16 Rue St.Croix de la Bretonnerie, ✉ 75004 (M° Hotel de Ville)
☎ 01.48.04.80.88
Leather/Cuir, Latex, Accesoires. Mail order 3615 TTBM.
■ **Vidéovision** (AC CC G VS) Mon-Sat 11-19 h, closed Sun
62 Rue de Rome ✉ 75008 (M° Europe) ☎ 01.42.93.66.04
■ **Yanko** (G LJ VS) 12-20.30 Fri Sat -21.30, Sun & public holidays 14-21.30 h
54 Rue de l'Arbre Sec ✉ 75001 (M° Chatelet/Louvre-Rivoli)
☎ 01.42.60.55.28
Sale and rent of videos, DVD. Cinema and cubicles.
■ **Yanko** (G VS) 11-1, Sat Sun & public holidays 15-1 h
10 Place de Clichy ✉ 75009 (M° Place de Clichy)
☎ 01.45.26.71.19
Videos, DVD, cinemas and cubicles.

SAUNAS/BATHS

■ **Athletic World** (BF f G SA SB VS WO) 4-1, Tue Wed 12-1 h
20 rue du Bourg-Tibourg ✉ 75004 (M° Hotel de Ville/St. Paul)
☎ 01.42.77.19.78
Gym, sauna and breakfast rendez-vous in the heart of the Marais.
■ **Bains d'Odessa. Les** (b G MA msg SA SB SOL) 9.30-21 h, closed Wed morning & Sun
5 Rue d'Odessa ✉ 75014 (near Montparnasse station)
☎ 01.42.20.91.21
■ **Bastille** (AC b g MA msg SA SB SOL VS WO) 14-24 h
4 Passage Saint Antoine ✉ 75011 (M° Ledru-Rollin)
☎ 01.43.38.07.02
Sign at the entrance door is "BS".
■ **Eden Form-Sauna Victor Hugo** (b f G SA SB SOL) Mon-Sat 12-21, Sun -20 h
109 Avenue Victor-Hugo ✉ 75016 (M° Victor-Hugo)
☎ 01.47.04.41.24

Paris | France

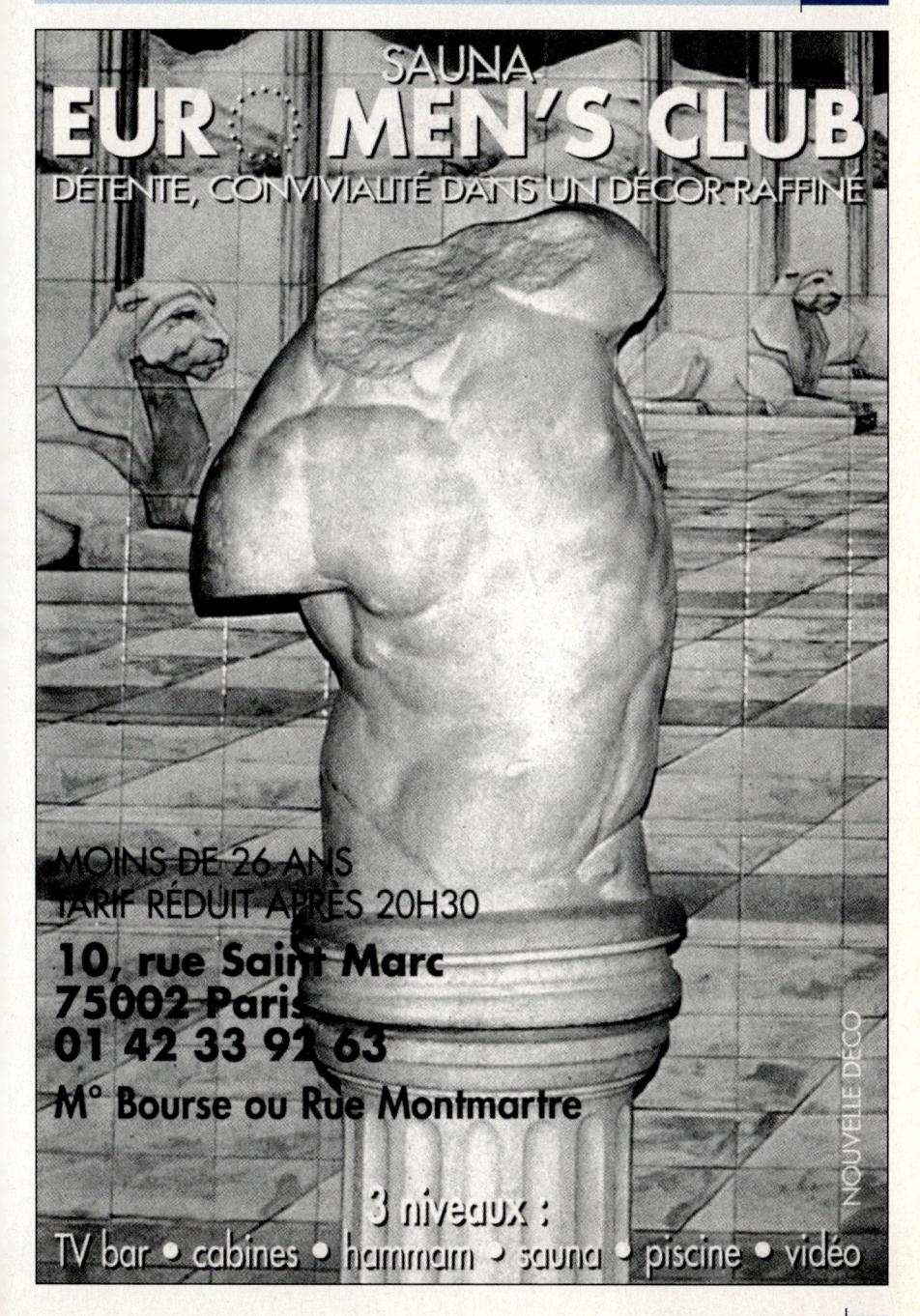

SAUNA
EURO MEN'S CLUB
DÉTENTE, CONVIVIALITÉ DANS UN DÉCOR RAFFINÉ

MOINS DE 26 ANS
TARIF RÉDUIT APRÈS 20H30

**10, rue Saint Marc
75002 Paris
01 42 33 92 63**

M° Bourse ou Rue Montmartre

3 niveaux :
TV bar • cabines • hammam • sauna • piscine • vidéo

NOUVELLE DECO

France | Paris

SAUNA
iDM

4, RUE DU FAUBOURG MONTMARTRE 75009 PARIS
M° GRANDS BOULEVARDS
OPEN EVERYDAY FROM 12H TO 1H AM
EXCEPT ON FRIDAY AND SATURDAY UNTIL 2H AM
TEL. +33 (0)1.45.23.10.03

DOUBLE YOUR PLEASURE !
Buy one admission and get half price on your admission at KeyWest Sauna Club
141, rue Lafayette 750010 Paris - M° Gare du Nord - +33 (0)1 45 26 31 74

Paris | France

KEY WEST
SAUNA CLUB

Open everyday from 12h00 to 1h00 am
except on friday and saturday until 2h00 am
141, rue Lafayette 75010 Paris
+33 (0)1 45 26 31 74 - M° Gare du Nord

DOUBLE YOUR PLEASURE !
Buy one admission and get half price on your admission
at IDM Sauna Club
4, rue du Faubourg Montmartre 75009 Paris - M° Grands Boulevards - +33 (0)1.45.23.10.03

France | Paris

BASTILLE SAUNA
Oriental Hammam
4, Passage Saint Antoine
75011 Paris
01 43 38 07 02

■ **Euro Men's Club** (AC B cc DR f G lj MA PI SA SB SOL VS WH) Mon-Sun 12-23 h
10 Rue Saint-Marc ✉ 75002 (M° Bourse/Rue Montmartre) ☎ 01.42.33.92.63
Lots of action in the afternoon as it is situated in a business area.

■ **IDM Sauna** (B DR f G P SA SB SOL VS WO YG) 12-1, Fri Sat -2 h
4 Rue du Faubourg Montmartre ✉ 75009 (M° Grands Boulevards) ☎ 01.45.23.10.03

■ **Key West** (b f G P SA SB SOL VS WO) 12-1, Fri Sat -2 h
141 Rue Lafayette ✉ 75010 (M° Gare du Nord) ☎ 01.45.26.31.74
Giant jacuzzi gym. CYBEX equipment. Big, beautiful and popular. New aquarium and giant TV screen. For members only.

■ **King Sauna Night & Day** (AC b DR f G MG P SA SB VS) 12-7 h
21 Rue Bridaine ✉ 75017 (M° Rome) ☎ 01.42.94.19.10

■ **Mandala. Le** (B f G SA SB SOL VS WH WO) 12-1, Fri and Sat -6 h
2 Rue Drouot ✉ 75009 (M° Richelieu Drouot) ☎ 01.42.46.60.14
Spacious gym room and sauna.

■ **Riad. Le** (B G PI SA SB MSG VS) 12-1, Fri Sat -2 h
184 Rue des Pyrénées ✉ 75020 (M° Gambetta, 5 min from Porte de Bagnolet) ☎ 01.47.97.25.52
Big hammam (steam bath) traditionally decorated - Morocco style.

■ **Sauna Mykonos** (G MA P SA SOL SB VS WH) 12.30-24 h
71 Rue des Martyrs ✉ 75018 (M° Pigalle) ☎ 01.42.52.15.46
For members only.

■ **Til't** (AC B DR f g MA SA VS) 18-7 h
41 Rue Sainte Anne ✉ 75001 (M° Pyramides, near the Opera) ☎ 01.42.96.07.43
Sauna frequented by the gay club scene.

■ **Top** (G MA SA VS) 11-2, Sun 12-0 h
117 Rue Saint Denis ✉ 75001 ☎ 01.40.13.09.26
Sauna and sex shop.

■ **Univers Gym** (AC b CC DR f G msg p s SA SB SOL VS WH WO YG) 12-1, Fri Sat -2 h
20-22 Rue des Bons Enfants ✉ 75001 (M° Palais Royal, 5 min from Palais Royal) ☎ 01.42.61.24.83
4 theme parties a week. Very popular, young fun crowd. Strip shows on Sat, free massages on Sun.

FITNESS STUDIOS

■ **Body-Gym** (g WO) 8-21.30, Sat 9-19, Sun 10-14 h
157 Faubourg Saint-Antoine ✉ 75012 (M° Faidherbe-Chaligny) ☎ 01.43.73.77.88
Body-building, aerobic, stretching etc.

■ **Club Auteuil** (B f g SA WO) 8-22 h
11 Rue Chanez ✉ 75016 ☎ 01.46.51.88.18

■ **Ken Club** (B F g SA SB WH WO) Mon, Wed, Fri 9.30-21, Tue Thu 7.30-23, WE 9.30-18 h
100 Avenue du Président Kennedy ✉ 75016 ☎ 01.46.47.41.41

BOOK SHOPS

■ **Mots à la Bouche. Les** (A CC GLM) Mon-Sat 11-23, Sun 14-20 h
6 Rue Sainte-Croix-de-la-Bretonnerie ✉ 75004 (M° Hôtel-de-Ville) ☎ 01.42.78.88.30
Paris' famous gay bookshop with the largest stock of gay literature. Ask for catalogue: librairie@motalabouche.com/Librairie gaie réputée de Paris où l'on trouve le plus grand choix de livres gais.

■ **Pause Lecture** (A CC GLM) Mon-Sat 11-24, Sun 13-24 h
61 Rue Quincampoix ✉ 75004 (near Les Halles) ☎ 01.44.61.95.06
New gay bookshop and gallery.

FASHION SHOPS

■ **Sweetman** (AC glm MA) 11-19.30 h, closed Sun
36 Boulevard Sébastopol ✉ 75004 ☎ 01.42.77.55.00
Underwear & sportwear.

Paris | France

Bains Montansier
**SAUNA HAMMAM BAIN A REMOUS
U.V.A. MASSAGES BAR SNACK
VIDEO CLIMATISATION**
Ouvert tous es jours de 12 h à 20 h · Tèl. 01 43 28 54 03
7, rue de Mountreuil - 94 300 Vincennes
M° Château de Vincennes - RER Vincennes
www.montansier.fr

GIFT & PRIDE SHOPS

■ **Dom** (Glm)
21 rue Sainte Croix de la Bretonnerie ✉ 75004 *(M° Hotel de Ville)*
☎ 01.42.71.08.00
Cadeaux and decoration.

NEWS STANDS

■ **Kiosque des Amis** (CC g MA) 10-22.30 h
1 Boulevard des Capucines ✉ 75002 *(M° Opéra)*
☎ 01.42.65.00.94
Big selection of gay magazines plus the usual newspapers, including those in foreign languages. Friendly owner gives latest information about bars and restaurants

■ **Kiosque Forum** (CC glm) 7-23 h
10 Rue Pierre Lescot ✉ 75001 *(RER/M° Châtelet/Les Halles)*
☎ 01.40.26.37.04
International press news stand and a veritable window on the world of gay magazines & newspapers both French and foreign. In the heart of gay Paris. Opposite the Metro/RER.

PHARMACIES

■ **Pharmacie du Village** (CC GLM) 8.30-20.30 h, closed Sun
26 Rue du Temple ✉ 75004 ☎ 01.42.72.60.73

PR & PHOTOGRAPHY SERVICES

■ **Comme des Anges Agency**
80 Rue Legendre ✉ 75017 ☎ 01.42.78.80.00
The only French gay publicity and model agency. Check website under: www.commedesanges.com

■ **Ory's Image** (CC g) 8-19.30 h
23 Boulevard Poissonière ✉ 75002 *(M° Grands Boulevards)*
☎ 01.42.33.05.30
Photographic laboratory.

---

le-riad.com
http://www.

**HAMMAM ORIENTAL
Piscine - Sauna
Exclusivement masculin**

Là où le corps exulte...

le Riad

184 rue des Pyrénées Paris 75020   Téléphone : 01-47-97-25-52   Métro : Gambetta

France | Paris

LES MOTS À LA BOUCHE

The first gay and lesbian bookshop in France

Librairie-Galerie **Les Mots à la Bouche**
6 rue Sainte-Croix-de-la-Bretonnerie
75004 Paris
Métro Hôtel-de Ville
Tel.: 01 42 78 88 23 · fax: 01 42 78 36 41
e-mail: librairie@motalabouche.com
website: motalabouche.com
monday-saturday 11 a.m. - 11 p.m.
sunday 2 -8 p.m.

DATING AGENCIES

■ **Freedhom** (GLM MA) 10-20 h
3 Rue du Faubourg Saint Honoré ✉ 75008 (M° Concorde, 5th floor on the left) ☎ 01.44.94.90.46 📠 01.44.94.90.48
📧 info.freedhom@wanadoo.fr 🖥 www.freedhom.fr
Gay dating agency in Paris since 15 years.

TRAVEL AND TRANSPORT

■ **Eurogays Travel** (CC GLM MA) Mon-Fri 10-19, Sat 12-18 h
23 Rue Bourg Tibourg ✉ 75004 (2nd floor) ☎ 01.48.87.37.17
📠 01.48.87.39.99 📧 eurogays@europgay.com
🖥 www.eurogay.com
One of the biggest gay travel agents in France.
■ **France Gay Travel** (GLM)
18 Avenue G. Clémenceau ✉ 94300 ☎ 04.93.38.16.95
📠 04.93.38.28.73 📧 noëlcastinel@airdumonde.com
🖥 www.rivieragaytravel.com
■ **Voyages de Martine. Les** (gen) Mon-Fri 9-13, 14-20, Sat 10-13 h
247 Avenue Daumesnil ✉ 75012 (M° Michel Bizot)
☎ 01.43.45.75.54 📠 01.43.40.45.24
Ask for Didier

VIDEO SHOPS

■ **Boutique Man** (G) 11-19 h, closed Mon Sun
41 Rue Volta ✉ 75003 (M° Arts & Metiers) ☎ 01.42.78.59.29
■ **Boy'z Bazaar** (CC Glm VS) 15-24 h
38 Rue Sainte Croix de la Bretonnerie ✉ 75004 (M° Hôtel de Ville)
☎ 01.42.71.80.34
Videostore. The best gay videos to rent, in the Marais.
■ **French Art** (AC CC G VS) 10-19 h, closed Sun
64 Rue de Rome ✉ 75008 (M° Rome) ☎ 01.45.22.57.35
Cadinot's famous shop!
■ **Station Vidéo** (g VS) 10-19.30 h
56 Boulevard Magenta ✉ 75010 (M° Gare de l'Est)
☎ 01.43.79.82.82
■ **Talisman** (G VS) 10-19 h, closed Sun
1 Rue de l'Aqueduc ✉ 75010 (M° Gare-du-Nord)
☎ 01.40.36.19.18

HOTELS

■ **Agora** (BF glm H)
7 Rue de la Cossonnerie ✉ 75001 (M° Châtelet/Les Halles)
☎ 01.42.33.46.02
Centrally located. 40 min to the airport. Rooms with priv. bath and telephone.
■ **Hôtel Acacias** (g H)
20 Rue du Temple ✉ 75004 ☎ 01.48.87.07.70
■ **Hôtel Beaumarchais** (AC BF CC glm H)
3 Rue Oberkampf ✉ 75011 (M° Filles du Calvaire/Oberkampf, close to the Marais and the Bastille) ☎ 01.53.36.86.86 📠 01.43.38.32.86
📧 hotel.beaumarchais@libertysurf.fr
🖥 www.hotel.beaumarchais.com
All rooms with bath/shower and WC, satellite TV.
■ **Hôtel Central Marais** (AC B BF CC G H)
33 Rue Vieille-du-Temple ✉ 75004 (M° Hôtel-de-Ville)
☎ 01.48.87.56.08 📠 01.42.77.06.27
The only gay hotel in Paris. Centre of the Marais.
■ **Hôtel des Batignolles** (BF glm H)
26-28 Rue des Batignolles ✉ 75017 (M° Rome) ☎ 01.43.87.70.40
Bath and WC on each floor.
■ **Hôtel des Nations** (BF CC glm H MA)
54 Rue Monge ✉ 75005 (M° Place Monge) ☎ 01.43.26.45.24
📠 01.46.34.00.13 📧 hoteldesnations@compuserve.com
🖥 www.hoteldesnations.com
Quote Spartacus for special reduced rates.
■ **Hôtel d'Estrées** (B BF CC glm H MA OS)
2bis Cité Pigalle ✉ 75009 ☎ 01.48.74.39.22 📠 01.45.96.04.09
■ **Hôtel Louvre-Richelieu** (BF CC glm H)
51 Rue de Richelieu ✉ 75001 ☎ 01.42.97.46.20
📠 01.47.03.94.13 📧 joelgill@club-internet.fr
🖥 perso.club-internet.fr/joelgill
■ **Hôtel Louxor** (BF CC g H) 0-24 h
4 Rue Taylor ✉ 75010 (M° République) ☎ 01.42.08.23.91
📠 01.42.08.03.30 📧 hotel.louxor@wanadoo.fr
🖥 www.hotels-paris-hotel.com
All rooms with bath/shower and WC, satellite TV and phone. Free access to Internet.
■ **Hôtel Moderne du Temple** (BF CC glm H)
3 Rue d'Aix ✉ 75010 (M° Goncourt/République) ☎ 01.42.08.09.04
📠 01.42.41.72.17 📧 vlado.fundarek@libertysurf.fr
🖥 perso.libertysurf.fr/hmt
■ **Hôtel Mondia** (BF CC glm H MA)
22 Rue du Grand Prieuré ✉ 75011 (near Place de la République)
☎ 01.47.00.93.44 📠 01.43.38.66.14 📧 info@hotel.mondia.com
🖥 hotel-mondia.com

France | Paris

7 jours sur 7 jusqu'à minuit - *7 days a week until midnight*

pause lecture ⏸ ▶

La librairie queer nouvelle génération
The new queer bookstore
Livres - books, magazines, CD's, vidéos, photos albums, expos-exhibitions…

Pause Lecture - 61, rue Quincampoix - 75004 Paris
Tél.: 01 44 61 95 06 - www.pauselecture.com
Catalogue sur demande - Tourists informations

■ **Royal Aboukir** (BF CC glm H MA)
106 Rue d'Aboukir ✉ 75002 (M° Sentier) ☎ 01.42.33.95.04
🖨 01.42.33.05.79
Rooms with bath/WC, phone, mini-bar, and TV.

■ **Saint-Hubert. Le** (B BF CC glm H) 0-24 h
27 Rue Traversière ✉ 75012 ☎ 01.43.43.39.16 🖨 01.43.43.35.52
Rooms with phone, bathroom, WC and TV.

■ **55 Guest House. Le** (BF g H)
55 Avenue Reille ✉ 75014 ☎ 01.45.89.91.82 🖨 01.45.89.91.83
Very exclusive apartments in art déco style.

APARTMENTS

■ **Paris Marais Studio Guesthouse** (GLM H)
✉ parismarais@hotmail.com 🖥 www.parismarais.com
A large choice of studios in the centre of Paris to rent for a stay of three days or more. Check website for more information.

■ **RentParis** (G H MA OS)
27 Rue Rossini ✉ 94400 ☎ 01.45.59.07.93 🖨 01.47.26.06.85
✉ RentParis@aol.com 🖥 www.RentParis.com
Studios and apartments to rent in the centre.

Revues françaises - Revues étrangères
Livres/Guides - Vidéos/DVD

1, boul. des Capucines
75002 Paris

www.kiosquedesamis.com

Paris France

■ **Trendy Rentals in Paris** (G H)
7 Rue Berthollet ✉ 75005 ☎ 01.45.35.78.81
💻 www.info@trips-europe.com
Furnished apartments rentals in central/gay Paris. Minimum stay 5 nights. US$ 90-160 per night. Quote Spartacus for a special discount.

PRIVATE ACCOMMODATION

■ **Enjoy Bed & Breakfast** (BF G H MA YG) 16.30-21.00h
☎ +49 (30) 236 23610 📠 +49 (30) 236 236 19
✉ Info@ebab.com 💻 ebab.com
Price 20-25 Euro p.p. Accommodation sharing agency. All with shower & bf.

GENERAL GROUPS

■ **Act Up Paris** 12-17 h
45 Rue de Sedaine ☎ 01.48.06.13.89 📠 01.48.06.16.74
✉ actup@actupp.org
Activist Association fighting AIDS and discrimination. Call for more info.

■ **Atitud-inn** (G H NU OS SA)
129 Rue Faubourg St.Antoine ✉ 75011 ☎ 01.43.46.60.83
💻 www.atitud-inn.com
Association for weekends and holidays in the country.

■ **GBH** (b f glm MA N p s SA VS WO YG) 17-24 h
20 bis Rue Henri Martin, Ivry-sur-Seine ✉ 94200 (M° Léo Lagrange-Ligne 7) ☎ 01.46.70.28.28 📠 01.46.70.08.29
✉ centreGBH@aol.com
Centre de convivialité.

■ **Juristes gais. Les**
B.P. 240 ✉ 75765 ☎ 01.46.31.24.06

■ **Lumière et Justice**
32 Rue Berzélius ✉ 75017 ☎ 01.42.26.70.48

■ **Mâles Fêteurs. Les** (G) Meetings once a month at CGL
P.B. 234 ✉ 75524 ☎ 01.47.00.64.11 ✉ lmf@free.fr
💻 lmf.free.fr

■ **SOS-Homophobie** Mon-Fri 20-22 h
B.P. 117 ✉ 75523 ☎ 01.48.06.42.41 📠 01.43.47.09.63
Association for the fight against homophobia.

FETISH GROUPS

■ **Association Sportive et Motocycliste de France ASMF**
PO Box N2 ✉ 75965 ☎ 01.42.60.69.79
Leather club.

■ **C.L.E.F.**
82 Rue de Rivoli ✉ 75004 ☎ 01.42.70.31.32 📠 01 42 21 09 00
Spanking Club. Meetings 4 times/year at "Keller", Paris. Write for info.

■ **Gai Moto Club de France**
PO Box 94 ✉ 75522 ☎ 01.42.38.15.43

■ **M.E.C. - Mecs En Caoutchouc** (G LJ)
B.P. 19 ✉ 77191 ☎ 01.64.87.07.92 📠 01.64.87.07.92
✉ bottescaoutchouc@free.fr
Association Gay Latex. 15 meetings/year. Publishes a magazine "Plank" 4 times a year.

HEALTH GROUPS

■ **Aides** Mon-Fri 14-17.30 h
247 rue de Belleville ✉ 75019 (Metro Telegraphe)
☎ 01.44.52.00.00 📠 01.44.52.02.01
💻 home.worldnet.fr/aidesidf/
Help for HIV-positive people.

■ **ARCAT-SIDA** Mon-Thu 9-18, Fri -17 h
94 Rue Buzenval ✉ 75020 (M° Buzenual) ☎ 01.44.93.29.29
📠 01.44.93.29.30 ✉ info@arcat-sida.org 💻 www.arcat-sida.org

■ **Association des Médecins Gais (AMG)** We 18-20, Sat 14-16 h
B.P. 433 ✉ 75527 ☎ 01.48.05.81.71
Contact for many gay and gay-lesbian health or medical groups. Contact also possible through C.G.L.

---

3 rue Oberkampf
75011 PARIS
Tél : 01 53 36 86 86
Fax : 01 43 38 32 86

Au cœur de Paris, à deux pas du Marais
et de la place de la Bastille, un tout nouvel hôtel.
In the very heart of Paris, close to the Marais
and Bastille Square, a brand new hotel.

Hôtel Beaumarchais

UN ACCÈS FACILE
EASY ACCESS

Métro : Filles du Calvaire
ou/or Oberkampf
Bus : n° 96 • 20 • 65

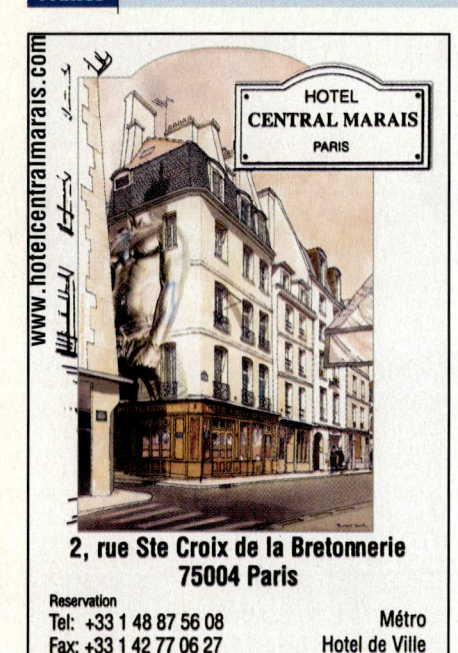

France — Paris

HOTEL CENTRAL MARAIS PARIS
www.hotelcentralmarais.com

2, rue Ste Croix de la Bretonnerie
75004 Paris
Reservation
Tel: +33 1 48 87 56 08
Fax: +33 1 42 77 06 27
Métro Hotel de Ville

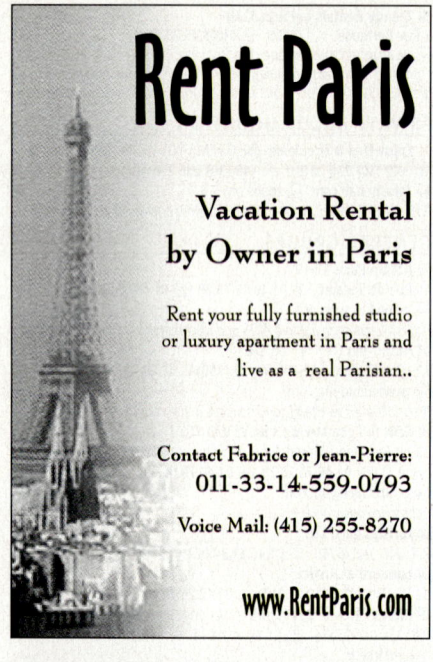

Rent Paris

Vacation Rental by Owner in Paris

Rent your fully furnished studio or luxury apartment in Paris and live as a real Parisian..

Contact Fabrice or Jean-Pierre:
011-33-14-559-0793
Voice Mail: (415) 255-8270

www.RentParis.com

- **Centre de Dépistage Anonyme et Gratuit** Mon-Fri 17-18, Sat 9.30-12 h
218 Rue de Belleville ✉ 75020 ☎ 01.47.97.40.34
- **CRIPS-Centre Régional d'Information et de Prévention du SIDA** Tue-Fri 13-20, Sat 10-17 h
B.P. 53 ✉ 75755 (Tour Montparnasse, 12th floor, 33 Avenue du Maine, Paris 15ème) ☎ 01.56.80.33.33 📠 01.56.80.33.00
✉ info@crips.asso.fr 🖥 www.crisps.asso.fr
CRIPS offers documentation, training and consultation, information, evaluation/assessment, meetings and a newsletter. Also exhibition area on the ground floor: Cyber-crips.
- **Kiosque Info Sida & Toxicomanie** Mon-Fri 10-19, Sa t 14-19 h
36 Rue Geoffroy l'Asnier ✉ 75004 ☎ 01.44.78.00.00
📠 01.48.04.95.30
Information on AIDS, STDs, and drug addiction and prevention. Documents, condoms and lubricants free.
- **Sida Info Droit (SID)** Tue 16-22, Thu -20, Fri 14-18 h
☎ 01.80.16.36.36
National AIDS hotline for legislative questions.
- **Sida Info Service (SIS)**
190 Boulevard de Charonne ✉ 75020
☎ (0800) 84.08.00 (Toll-free in France)
- **Soeurs de la Pérpétuelle Indulgence. Les**
3 Rue Saint Jérôme ✉ 75018 ☎ 01.44.92.06.12
✉ spi.paname@voila.fr
🖥 perso.wanadoo.fr/spi.paname/
- **Vaincre le Sida V.L.S.**
41 Rue Volta ✉ 75003 ☎ 01.44.78.75.50 📠 01.42.77.66.37
Long established institution (since 1983) engaged in the fight against AIDS. Legal, social and psychological help to HIV+ people. Publishes informations.

---

complete offer
see page Germany/Berlin

PARIS — from FRF 150 –
overnight accomodation service
· about 750 beds · more than 28 cities ·

bed & enjoy breakfast

central booking office Berlin ☎ +49-30-236 236 10 4:30-9:00 pm local time
Fax +49-30-23623619 · info@ebab.com · www.ebab.com

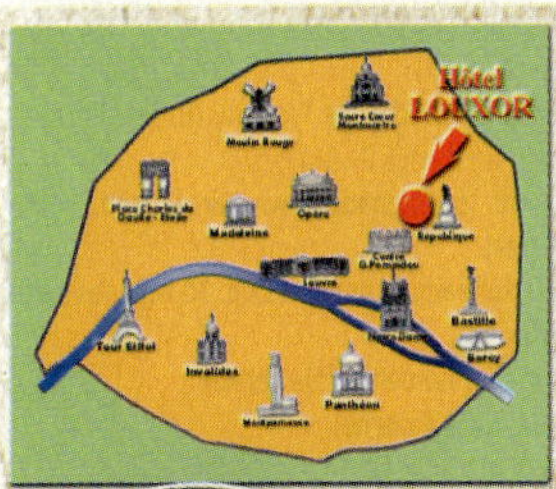

HOTEL LOUXOR

TOURISME ** NN

4, rue Taylor . 75010 PARIS

METRO STATION : REPUBLIQUE

TEL : (33) 01 42 08 23 91 . FAX : (33) 01 42 08 03 30

e mail : hotel.louxor@wanadoo.fr

HOTEL ROOMS FROM $ 19,90 per personn

All rooms with : shower/bath, WC TV and telephone

- **FREE : Access to Internet**
- **Luggage storage**
- **English speaking staff**
- **Credit Card accepted**
- **Booking by fax and E-mail**

WALKING DISTANCE TO :
MUSEUMS, MOVIES THEATRES
BARS AND NIGHT CLUB'S
TOURIST INFORMATION SERVICE

AN IDEAL LOCATION :

In a lively, safe area in the city CENTER of Paris near Marais area and walking distance from les Halles, Bastille, Notre Dame.

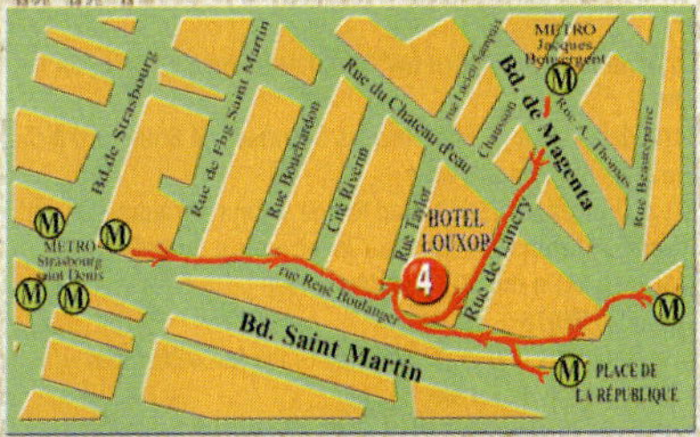

http://www.hotels-paris-hotel.com

France | Paris ▶ Pau

RELIGIOUS GROUPS

■ **Beit Haverim** Wed 20-22 h
B.P. 375 ✉ 75526 ☎ 01.40.40.00.71 📠 01.42.40.53.11
📧 beit-haverim@yahoo.com
Gay and lesbian jewish group, advice, cultural and social activities
■ **David et Jonathan**
92bis Rue de Picpus ✉ 75012 ☎ 01.43.42.09.49
■ **Eglise MCC CEL et CCl** (GLM) MCC: Fri 19-22 h; CCL: Thu + Fri 20-22 h
5 Rue Crussol ✉ 75011 *CCL Thu + Fri 20-22 h Tel.01.48.05.24.48*
☎ 01.48.06.35.15 (MCC) ☎ 01.48.05.24.48 (CCL)
this organisation provides Special services: religious ceremonies for gay and lesbian couples; help and information for sexual minorities.
■ **Eglise MCC (CET et CCL)**
23 Rue Berzelius ✉ 75017 ☎ 01.48.05.24.48 ☎ 01.48.06.35.15

SPECIAL INTEREST GROUPS

■ **Choeur Gai International de Paris C.I.G.A.P.**
c/o C.G.L., 3, Rue Keller ✉ 75011
Auditions every Wed. at 19.30 h, Cathédrale Américaine, ave. George V.
■ **Homo Sweet Home - Association des étudiants gays d'Ile de France** (YG)
29 Blvd Magenta ✉ 75010 ☎ 40400030
Gay student association organising different activities. Call for more information.
■ **MAG - Jeunes Gais et Lesbiennes** (GLM YG) Thu 22-24, Fri 18-22, Sat 14-19 h
106 Rue de Montreuil ✉ 75011 ☎ 01.49.29.15.91
📠 01.43.14.03.18 📧 mag@france.qrd.org
💻 www.france.qrd.org/assocs/mag
Also bar and library. Meeting "accueil" Thu 18-20 h at CGL, 3 rue Keller.
■ **Santé et Plaisir Gai** (G MG msg NU)
B.P. 234 ✉ 75865 ☎ 01.42.72.81.82
📧 sante-plaisir-gai@wanadoo.fr
Organises jack off parties every 3rd Sun 14.45-17 h at "London", 33 Rue des Lombards, 75001 Paris.

SPORT GROUPS

■ **Fédération Sportive Gaie et Lesbienne (CGPIF)** Fri 17-19 h
B.P. 120 ✉ 75623 ☎ 01.48.05.55.17 📠 01.48.05.55.95
📧 cgpif@cgpif.org
Federation of Paris sports groups.

CRUISING

-Jardin des Tuileries/Quai des Tuileries 75001
-Square de la Tour Saint Jacques 75004
-Square Sully Morland 75004
-Champs de Mars 75007 (Near the/vers l'Ecole militaire, nights/la nuit)
-Canal Saint-Martin 75010 (M° Jean Jaurès, on the banks/sur les quais)
-Terre-Plein/Parking 75011 (across from/face 44 Boulevard Richard Lenoir. Nights/La nuit)
-Bois de Vincennes 75012 (Sud Rte de la Tourelle autour de parking)
-Nation 75012 (in the centre/sur le terre-plein central)
-Quai 75013 (On the TGB level/Au niveau de la TGB)
-Trocadéro 75016
-Porte Dauphine 75016 (on the side of the Russian embassy/du côté de l'Ambassade de Russie)
-Square des Batignolles 75017
-Parc des Buttes-Chaumont (AYOR) 75019 (roundabout, nights/aux alentours, la nuit)
-Cimetière di Père Lachaise (southern side/côté sud. Tombe Anna de Noailles)
-Place d'Anvers (ayor R) (at night)
-Place du Paraguay/Place du Maréchal de Tassigny (R) (M° Porte Dauphine. At night)
-Quai du Canal Saint-Martin (promenade downstairs Quai de Valmy, unter the bridge. M° Jaures)
-Bois de la Verrière (NU) Sunbathing and cruising. 30 minutes south of Paris (M° Massy-Verrières)
-Porte de Maillot (near the monument of De Lattre)
-Gare de l'Est 75010 (near Café Taverne)
-Gare du Nord (in front of platform N° 10)
-Gare Saint-Lazare (level -1, besides Metro exit)
-Gare Montparnasse

Pau ✉ 64000

BARS

■ **Gowest. Le** (A AC B CC G MA p s) 16-2, Sun 18-2 h, closed Tue, Jul-Sep 16-3 h
6 Rue René Fournets ✉ 64000 *(near Place Reine Margueritte)*
☎ 05.59.27.71.45
Also men's fashion shop.

RESTAURANTS

■ **Aragon. L'** (B F NG OS)
18 Boulevard dés Pyrénées ✉ 64000 ☎ 05.59.27.12.43
French cuisine, nice view.
■ **Etna. L'** (b CC F g) 12-14.30, 19-0 h
16 Rue du Château ✉ 64000 ☎ 05,59.27.77.94
■ **Mermoz. Le** (b F g OS) 11-14.30, 18-1, closed Tue & Aug
39 Avenue Jean-Mermoz ✉ 64000 ☎ 05.59.32.54.19
Menu FF 70-220. French cuisine.

SEX SHOPS/BLUE MOVIES

■ **Kitsch** (CC G VS) 14-20 h, closed Sun
13 Cours Bosquet ✉ 64000 ☎ 05.59.27.68.67

SAUNAS/BATHS

■ **Centaure. Le** (B DR f G lj MA N p SA SB VS) 13.30-20 h
15 Rue d'Orléans ✉ 64000 *(near Place de Verdun)*
☎ 05.59.27.30.41
Intimate sauna. Friendly welcome with free snack.
■ **Eros** (AC B DR f G MA P SA SB VS WH) 14-2, Fri Sat -4 h
8 Rue René Fournets ✉ 64000 *(Hedas area)* ☎ 05.59.27.48.80
Also a boutique for accessories. Theme evenings.

HELP WITH PROBLEMS

■ **Solidarité Positive** Meetings: Tue 14.30-16.30, Thu 19-21 h
9 Rue Louis-Barthou ✉ 64000 ☎ 05,59.27.63.88
Self-help association for people with HIV and AIDS.

CRUISING

-Bois de Pau (with patience)
-Boulevard Barbanègre
-Cour de la Gare de Marchandises (soldiers!)
-Parc Beaumont
-Parc Nitot
-Place de Verdun
-[P] Souterrain des Halles
-Place Marguerite-Caborde

Périgueux ▶ Pont-Audemer   France

Périgueux ✉ 24000

DANCECLUBS
■ **An des Roys. L'** (AC B CC D GLM lj MA p s TV) Fri, Sat and Holiday Eves 23-5 h
51 Rue Aubarède ✉ 24000 ☎ 05.53.53.01.58
Sauna under construction.

CRUISING
-Garden/Jardin de la Tour de Vesone (daytime only/de jour uniquement)
-Garden/Jardin des Arènes (daytime only/de jour uniquement)
-Parc Aristide-Briand (evening/soir)
-Facilities/Toilettes Rue St-Front

Pernes-les-Fontaines ✉ 84210

HOTELS
■ **Mas La Bonoty** (B CC F glm H Pl OS)
Chemin de la Boniots ✉ 84210 ☎ 04.90.61.61.09

Perpignan ✉ 66000

BARS
■ **Ho Club** (B G MA) 23-5 h
16 Rue Bertrand de Born ✉ 31000 *(near SNCF station)*
☎ 06.61.62.44.44

RESTAURANTS
■ **Doña Maria** (b F glm MA)
23 Rue Jean Payra ✉ 66000 ☎ 04.68.35.00.90
French and Catalane cuisine.

SEX SHOPS/BLUE MOVIES
■ **Défi** (G lj VS) 9-24 h
10 Avenue Leclerc ✉ 66000 ☎ 04.68.52.44.25
Also mail order/également vente par correspondance: B.P. 4051, 66000 Cedex.

SAUNAS/BATHS
■ **Aquatic Club. L'** (AC b CC G MA Pl SA SB VS WH) 15-22 h
13 Rue Rouget de l'Isle ✉ 66000 ☎ 04.68.34.48.50
More than 200 m² sauna frequented by a mixed age crowd.
■ **B.H.** (b DR G SA SB VS WH WO) 14-24 h
1 Quater Rue G. Buffon ✉ 66000 *(near the SNCF station)*
☎ 04.68.55.10.11
New well equipped sauna.
■ **Pharaon. Le** (b f G MA SA SB VS WH WO)
43 Avenue de la Gloire ✉ 31500 *(M° Gare Matabiau)*
☎ 05.61.20.70.90
New luxury sauna on 700 m² and two floors.

BOOK SHOPS
■ **Futur Antérieur. Le** (CC G) 9-12, 14-19 h, closed Sun Mon
8 Rue du Théatre ✉ 66000 ☎ 04.68.34.20.45
Gay bookshop/librairie gaie.

HEALTH GROUPS
■ **Aides**
2 Rue Edmond Roustand ✉ 66000 ☎ 04.68.51.13.93

CRUISING
-Passage Rive-Gauche
-Place Bistan
-Route de Canet (dangerous in the evening!/dangereux le soir!)

Perrignier ✉ 74550

BARS
■ **Ram Dam. Le** (AC B CC D E glm MA OS p WE) Fri Sat 22-5 h
Route de Draillant ✉ 74550 ☎ 04.50.72.40.43

Pinet ✉ 34850

BARS
■ **Echiquier. L'** (AC B D G p) Fri Sat
Domaine de Saint-Jean des Sources ✉ 34850 ☎ 04.67.77.17.51

Plouarzel ✉ 29229

SWIMMING
-Beach/Plage des Charettes (NU on the cliffs/sur les falaises)

Plouescat ✉ 29221

SWIMMING
-Plage/beach Keremna (2 km ➤ Treflez)

Plouharnel ✉ 56640

SWIMMING
-Plage/beach d'Erdeven

Poissy ✉ 78300

CRUISING
-Parc Messonier

Poitiers ✉ 86000

BARS
■ **George Sand Club** (AC B D DR Glm MA P SNU VS YG) 22-5 h
25 Rue Saint-Pierre-le-Puellier ✉ 86000 *(behind the Town Hall)*
☎ 05.49.55.91.58

SAUNAS/BATHS
■ **George Sand** (AC B DR G MA OS Pl SA SB SOL VS WH WO) 13-24 h
56 Boulevard Pont Achard ✉ 86000 *(500 m from the railway station)* ☎ 05.49.41.77.67
Sauna on 500 m² with garden.

CRUISING
-Avenue du Recteur-Pineau (campus Rabelais)
-Garden/Jardin de la Villette (evening/le soir)
-Garden/Jardin des Coloniaux (evening/le soir)
-Parc de Blossac

Pont-Audemer ✉ 27500

HOTELS
■ **Cloches de Corneville. Les** (B BF CC F glm H lj MA OS) closed Mon lunch & Jan-15th Feb
Route de Rouen ✉ 27500 *(Corneville-sur-Risle, 35 km from Honfleur, Rouen and Le Havre)* ☎ 02.32.57.01.04 📠 02.32.57.10.96
💻 www.cloches-de-corneville.fr
Hotel restaurant with garden, terrace, private parking. All rooms with bath, phone and TV.

France Pontcarré ▶ Remoulins

Pontcarré ✉ 77135
CRUISING
-P Forêt d'Armainvilliers

Pont-d'Ain ✉ 01160
CRUISING
-Place des Marronniers
-Market Place/Place du marché
-Along the riverside/Le long des quais (in the evening)

Pont-de-Fillinges ✉ 74250
DANCECLUBS
■ **Athénée. L'** (B D G STV) Fri-Sat 23-5, Sun 19-1.30 h
Route de Boëge ✉ 74250 *(à 15 km de Genève)* ☏ 04.50.36.42.87

Pont-l'Abbé ✉ 29120
BARS
■ **Bar Gavroche** (B g) 17-24 h, closed Mon
46 Rue Victor-Hugo ✉ 29120 ☏ 02.98.82.32.74
SWIMMING
-Beach of/plage de Tréguennec (NU) (between/entre Tronoen et Tréguennec)

Port-Vendres ✉ 66660
SWIMMING
-Beach of l'Ollioulle (B)

Poussan ✉ 34560
DANCECLUBS
■ **Pam. Le** (B D GLM) Fri Sat and Before public holidays 22.30-? h, alos opened on Sun in summer
Parc d'Issanka ✉ 34560 *(Highway exit Sète, direction Gigean then Issanka)* ☏ 04.67.78.71.38

Quimper ✉ 29000
BARS
■ **Carpe Diem** (A B glm) Tue-Sun 18-1 h, closed Mon
54bis Avenue de la Libération ✉ 29000 ☏ 02.98.90.00.21
CAFES
■ **Coffee Shop** (AC B CC DR GLM MA OS p VS) 17-1 h
26 Rue du Frout ✉ 29000 ☏ 02.98.95.43.30
Theme evenings.
SEX SHOPS/BLUE MOVIES
■ **Duo Shop** (CC g MA VS) Mon-Sat 10-1 h
14 Rue de Concarneau ✉ 29000 *(Near the station)*
CRUISING
-Keradennec (forest/bois)
-Public garden of the theatre/Jardin public du théâtre
-Kermoysan (shopping centre in the city/allée du centre commercial)
-P at the Glacière (close to the footbridge/ près de la passerelle)
-Place de La-Tour-d'Auvergne
-Place de la Tourbie (place de l'Ancien-Champ-de-Foire)

-Place de la gare/Station square
-Place du Guéodet
-Place du Nouveau-Champ-de-Foire

Ramatuelle ✉ 83350
CULTURE
■ **Planète. La** (A)
D61, Rouillère Sud ✉ 83350 ☏ 06.07.25.29.09
✉ atelierlaplanete@aol.com 🌐 www.la-planete.com
Art Atelier & Gallery in vineyards.
BARS
■ **CoCo Beach**
Route de l'Epi ✉ 83350 ☏ 04.94.79.83.25
Beach bar in summer/Bar du plage en été.
RESTAURANTS
■ **Aqua Club** (B F g) 10-20.30, Oct-Apr Sat-Mon 10-17 h
Pampelonne Ramatuelle ✉ 83350 ☏ 04.94.79.84.35
SWIMMING
-La Bastide Blanche (G NU) (between/entre Escalet & Pointe de la Douane)
-Baie de Pampelone

Rambouillet ✉ 78120
CRUISING
-Etang de coupe-garage (Route de Saint-Léger, afternoons)

Reims ✉ 51100
DANCECLUBS
■ **Lilas Club. Les** (B D CC G LJ MA P p TV VS WE) 23-4 h, closed 15 days in August
75 Rue de Courcelles ✉ 51100 ☏ 03.26.47.02.81
A video bar and a discotheque.
HEALTH GROUPS
■ **Hôpital Robert Debré** Mon 17-20, Tue 9-12, Wed 14-17, Thu 18-20, Fri 17-19, Sat 9-12 h
Avenue du Général Koenig ✉ 51092 *(Bus A/N/S)*
☏ 03.26.78.79.97 ☏ 03.26.48.45.79 (nurses)
Anonymous and free HIV & Hepatitis C testing. Also skin diseases.
CRUISING
-Low promenades/Basses Promenades (in front of the railway station/face à la gare)
-Place Drouet-d'Erlons
-Railway station/Gare SNCF (opposite facilities/tasses en face)
-Jardins de la Patte-d'Oie (AYOR) (at night/la nuit)
-Parc Léo-Lagrange (in front of the stadium; all day, esp. sat sun morning/face au stade; la journée surtout; samedi et dimanche matin)
-Place du Boulingrin (facilities close to the monument tributing to deads/tasses près du monument aux morts)

Remoulins ✉ 30210
SWIMMING
-Gorges du Gardon
-Beach of Collias

Rennes ✉ 35000

BARS
■ **Bernique Hurlante. La** (B CC glm MA) 16-1 h, closed Sun Mon
40 Rue de St. Malo ✉ 35000 *(Near Place St. Anne)*
☎ 02.99.38.70.09
2nd hand library next to the bar where you can buy or consult over 1500 gay books.
■ **Bon Accord. Le** (B CC f GLM MA S) 16-1 h
45 Rue Duhamel ✉ 35000
■ **Carpe Diem. Le** (B f glm YG) 11-1 h, closed Mon
21 Boulevard de Chezy ✉ 35000
■ **Chat Bleu. Le** (B DR glm MA VS) 17-1 h
36 bis Rue du Pont-des-Loges ✉ 35000 ☎ 02.99.31.86.47
Underground with darkroom and videos/Sous-sol salon avec darkroom, vidéos.

DANCECLUBS
■ **Batchi. Le** (B D GLM) 23-5 h, closed Mon
35 Rue Vasselot ✉ 35000 ☎ 02.99.79.62.27

SAUNAS/BATHS
■ **California** (CC DR G MA NU SA SB SOL VS WH WO) 13-22.30, Wed Sat -1h
7 Rue de Léon ✉ 35000 *(5 min from railway station)*
☎ 02.99.31.59.81
Sauna on 400 m² and three floors. 1st and 3rd Thu of the month foam party, Wed "Stick Fluo" night.

CRUISING
-Le Champ de Mars (roundabout/autour de la Salle omnisports)
-Place des Lices (WC des Halles)
-A Mi-Forêt
-Le Contour de la Motte (square et WC)
-Boulevard Magenta (square and WC near the ex police station/près de l'ex-commissariat)
-Place Le Bastard
-Boulevard Magenta
-Le Thabor (jardin botanique/botanic garden)
-Sauna municipal de la piscine
-Place du Marché/Market Place
-Rue Toullier

Riec-sur-Belon ✉ 29340

GUEST HOUSES
■ **Ferme de Pen-Prat** (BF g lj H MA OS)
✉ 29340 *15 km from Quimperlé. Bus: Quimperlé-Quimper.*
☎ 02.98.06.46.89
Typical farm, bring your own sleeping bag. Leather appreciated (ask Jean-Bernard for more information).

Rochefort ✉ 17300

DANCECLUBS
■ **Cage. La** (B D GLM MA p TV) Fri-Sun 23.30-5 h
34 Rue Denfert Rochereau ✉ 17300 *(Opposite to/En face du Parking du Cour Roy-Bry)* ☎ 05.46.87.01.30

SEX SHOPS/BLUE MOVIES
■ **Sex-Shop** (AC glm VS) 9.30-12, 14.30-20 h, closed Sun, Mon morning
13 Rue Cochon du Vivier ✉ 17300 ☎ 05.46.99.93.63

CRUISING
-Monument Pierre-Loti
-L'ex-Jardin de la Marine (after/après 22 h, stop between/entre Rochefort-BA 721)

Rodez ✉ 12000

BARS
■ **Alibi. L'** (B CC G MA) 17-1 h
48 Avenue Amans Rodat ✉ 12000 ☎ 05.65.68.82.62

CRUISING
-Bus station/station de bus (by day/le jour)
-Place Foch

Romans-sur-Isère ✉ 26100

RESTAURANTS
■ **Charrette. La** (B F g s) 11-2 h, closed Sun
Route de Grenoble ✉ 26100 ☎ 04.75.02.04.25

CRUISING
-Square Marcel-Carné
-Place du Champ-de-Mars
-Place Jules-Nadi
-Quais de l'Isère

Romorantin-Lanthenay ✉ 41200

CRUISING
-Square Ferdinand-Buisson

Roquebrune-Cap-Martin ✉ 61907

SWIMMING
-Beach at the old castle ruin/plage près de la ruine du vieux château (near railway station, take Rue de la Gare)
-Rocks/rochers de Cap-Martin (behind the big house/derrière la grande bâtisse)

Roubaix ✉ 59100

CRUISING
-Avenue Le-Nôtre (behind the Barbieux park in the groves/derrière le parc Barbieux, dans les bosquets)

Rouen ✉ 76000

BARS
■ **Coconuts. Le** (A B CC GLM MA s) 19-2 h, closed on Sun
138 Rue Beauvoisine ✉ 76000 (M° Beauvoisine)
☎ 02.35.07.71.97
Theme parties with DJ.
■ **XXL Bar & Club** (B CC d DR G MA p SNU VS) Café 11-2, Club: 22-4 h, closed Sun Mon
25-27 Rue de la Savonnerie ✉ 76000 *(Near the cathedral)*
☎ 02.35.88.84.00
Monthly theme parties.

DANCECLUBS
■ **Opium** (AC B CC D Glm LJ p S SNU STV YG) Fri-Sun 23-5 h
2 Rue Malherbe ✉ 76100 *(south bank of the river)*
☎ 02.35.03.29.36
Sun transvestite show, Fri male striptease.

France Rouen ▸ Saint-Dizier

RESTAURANTS

■ **Bougainvillier. Le** (CC F MA) 12-14.30, 19-22.30 h, Sun afternoon closed
35 Rue Percière ✉ 76000 (M° Palais de Justice) ☎ 02.35.07.73.32
■ **Gourmandine** (b F g) 11-18, Fri Sat Sun 11-23 h
236 Rue Martainville ✉ 76000 ☎ 02.35.71.95.13
Closed at Christmas.
■ **Molière. Le** (B BF F glm) 7.30-20 h, closed Sun
30 Rue des Angustins ✉ 76000 ☎ 02.35.70.76.11

SEX SHOPS/BLUE MOVIES

■ **Boxx. Le** (CC MA G VS) 12-24 h
8 Rue de la Croix Verte ✉ 76000 *(near Hôtel de Ville)*
☎ 02.35.88.96.50

SAUNAS/BATHS

■ **Square. Le** (B DR G MA p SA VS) 13-20 h, closed Sun
39 Rue St.Nicolas ✉ 76000 *(between town hall and cathedral)*
☎ 02.35.15.58.05
Large video screen and glory holes in darkroom.
■ **Trois Colonnes. Les** (B DR f MA SA SB VS WH WO) 14-22, Tue Fri Sat -24 h
4 Impasse des Hauts Mariages ✉ 76000 *(M° Hôtel de Ville, Quartier St. Maclou)* ☎ 02.32.08.40.66
Two levels sauna on 250 m². Labyrinth with glory holes.
■ **8. Le** (AC B G SA SB SOL VS) 14-23 h
8 Place Saint-Amant ✉ 76000 ☎ 02.35.15.06.29
Renovated sauna with good air conditioning.

HOTELS

■ **Hôtel des Carmes** (BF CC g H)
33 Place des Carmes ✉ 76000 *(between cathedral and town hall)*
☎ 02.35.71.92.31 📠 02.35.71.76.96
Quote SPARTACUS for special rates.

CRUISING

-Woods nearby Novotel (next to Faculté de Médicine, at the southern exit of the city in direction Paris)
-Square Verdrel and rue du Baillage (right in the middle of the city, near rue Jeanne d'Arc)
-Left side of the Seine river/Rive gauche de la Seine (near Jeanne d'Arc bridge/près du Pont Jeaanne d'Arc)
-P Aire parking de Bord
-P Robert-le-Diable
-Forêt de la Londe
-Forêt-Verte
-Port maritime
-Stade Saint-Exupéry
-Rue Henri-Dumont

Royan ✉ 17200

RESTAURANTS

■ **Anjou Restaurant. L'** (B CC F g) 9-24 h, closed Wed
19 Rue Font de Chevre ✉ 17200 ☎ 05.46.05.09.39

SWIMMING

-La Côte sauvage/Plage de la Bouverie
-Plage de la Palmyre
-Plage de la Grande Côte
-At the beach/à la plage Royan
-At the beach/à la plage de la Cèpe

Rue ✉ 80120

SWIMMING

-Dunes (1 km south of Quend-Plage)

Saint-Brieuc ✉ 22000

SWIMMING

-Beach/plage des Rosaires (nu) (at the edge of the Horaine, behind the commune of Plérin. Nudism is tolerated. when reaching the beach, go to the right/pointe de la Horaine, après la commune de Plérin. Le naturisme est toléré. A droite en arrivant sur la plage.)

CRUISING

-Jardins des Remparts/park of the ramparts (in the surroundings of ramparts and in front of the palace of justice/aux alentours des remparts et près du palais de justice)
-Jardin des Promenades
-P du Champs de Mars
-Yffiniac Aire-de-repos

Saint-Chamas ✉ 13250

RESTAURANTS

■ **Bergerie. La** (F g) 12-13.30, 20-21.30 h, closed Sun
Le Gueby Sud ✉ 13250 ☎ 04.90.50.82.29

CRUISING

-Route de Berre

Saint-Cirques-en-Montagne ✉ 07510

HOTELS

■ **Cévènnes. Les** (B F g H) 8-22.30 h
✉ 07510 ☎ 04.75.38.93.73

Saint-Clar ✉ 32380

HOTELS

■ **Hôtel Rison** (B BF F g H) Restaurant 12-13.30, 19-21 h, closed Tue
Place de la Lomagne ✉ 32380 ☎ 05.62.66.40.21

Saint-Denis-de-Jouhet ✉ 36230

BARS

■ **Terre d'Ivry. La** (B D glm) Thu-Mon 23-4 h
✉ 36230 ☎ 02.54.30.77.95
Sun Soirée gaie/Sun Gay evening.

Saint-Dié ✉ 88100

CRUISING

-Place du marché
-Parking de la Pêcherie
-Parc du centre-ville

Saint-Dizier ✉ 52100

CRUISING

-Parc Le Jard (on the P beside the park/sur le P le long du parc)

Saintes ▸ Saint-Laurant-Nouant | **France**

Saintes ✉ 17100

BARS
■ **Salamandre, La** (B CC g MA) 18-2 h
11 Quai de la République ✉ 17100 ☏ 05.46.74.20.33

DANCECLUBS
■ **Grillon, Le** (AC CC D E GLM lj MG P WE) Thu-Sun 23-5, summer: Tue-Sun 23-5 h
12 Rue Pierre Schoeffer, Coucoury ✉ 17100 ☏ 05.46.74.66.98

RESTAURANTS
■ **Borsalino, Le** (b F g) 11.45-15, 18.45-23 h
12 Cours National ✉ 17100 ☏ 05.46.74.31.78

SEX SHOPS/BLUE MOVIES
■ **Sex-Shop** (AC CC glm MA VS) 10-12 14-19.15 h, closed Sun & holidays
9-10 Quai de la République ✉ 17100 ☏ 05.46.74.51.72
Latest gay videos.

HOTELS
■ **Hôtel Climat de France** (BF CC F glm H OS PI) 6-23 h
Route de Royan ✉ 17100 *(35 km from the beach, 5 min from the center of town)* ☏ 05.46.97.20.40 📠 05.46.92.22.54
Hotel-restaurant with an open-air pool in summer, heated and covered in winter.

CRUISING
-Arc de Triomphe
-Palais de Justice
-Charente (at the border/au bord)

Saint-Etienne ✉ 42000

BARS
■ **Bar Le Club** (B CC GLM MA) 19-1.30, Fri Sat 20-1.30 h, closed Sun
3 Place Villeboeuf ✉ 42000 ☏ 04.77.33.56.25

RESTAURANTS
■ **Frascati chez Jacky** (b F g)
24 Avenue du Grand Gonnet *(Place Jacquard)* ☏ 04.77.32.37.27

SAUNAS/BATHS
■ **Libération, Le** (B DR G MA N SA SB VS) 13-20 h
5 Avenue de la Libération ✉ 42000 *(near the post office, Tram-Place du Peuple, Bus-Place Dorian, entrance in the courtyard)*
☏ 04.77.33.53.96
Friendly sauna with a mixed crowd.
■ **130, Le** (AC B DR G MA SA SB VS WH) 13-20, Sun Tue -22 h
3 Rue d'Arcole ✉ 42000 *(Tram-Jean Jaurès, near the Town Hall)*
☏ 04.77.32.48.04

HEALTH GROUPS
■ **Hôpital de Bellevue. Service des Maladies Infectieuses**
Pavillon 1bis Boulevard Pasteur ✉ 42023 ☏ 04,77.42.77.22
HIV testing.

CRUISING
-Jardin des Plantes
-Place Anatole-France
-Place Carnot
-Place Villeboeuf

Saint-Florent ✉ 20217

SWIMMING
-Beach/plage Saint Florent (route Marines du Soleil)

Saint-Germain-en-Laye ✉ 78100

RESTAURANTS
■ **Crêperie de Montardat** (F g) 12-23 h, closed Mon
9 Rue Anesse-de-Montardat ✉ 78100 ☏ 02.39.73.33.83
■ **Crêperie Larcher** (A CC F glm) 12-14.30, 19-23 h
9 Rue Saint-Pierre ✉ 78100 ☏ 01.30.61.51.25

Saint-Gilles-Croix-de-Vie ✉ 85800

SWIMMING
-Beach/plage du Petit-Pont

CRUISING
-Ramblais (close to the/près des cafés)
-Pedestrian street/Rue Piétonne
-Bridge/Pont Jaunay

Saint-Girons ✉ 09200

CRUISING
-Place Guynemer

Saint-Jean-de-Luz ✉ 64500

SWIMMING
-Beach/plage des Deux-Jumeaux

CRUISING
-Promenade Alfred-Pose

Saint-Jean-de-Muzols ✉ 07300

DANCECLUBS
■ **Starnight** (AC B CC D f GLM MA P PI S SNU)
1 Chemin du Passon Frais ✉ 07300 *(15 km from Valence on the riverside)* ☏ 04.75.08.08.62

Saint-Julien-en-Born ✉ 40170

SWIMMING
-Lit-et-Mixte (NU) (plage à 1 km de la plage sud/beach 1 km from south beach)

Saint-Laurant-Nouant ✉ 41220

BARS
■ **Boy's Club, Le** (B CC D DR GLM MA p SNU VS) Fri-Sun & before public holidays 23-5 h
5 Mocquebaril ✉ 41220 *(between Blois & Orléans by autoroute, exit Beaugency)* ☏ 02.54.87.21.39
Theme nights, foam night in summer/Soirées à thème, soirée mousse en été.

HOTELS
■ **Maison du Passant, La** (BF CC glm H MA OS)
La Petite Boulaie ✉ 41220 *(near Château de Chambard)*
☏ 02.54.87.74.03

France Saint-Lô ▶ Saint-Raphaël

Saint-Lô ✉ 50000
CRUISING
-Les Remparts (close to the church /près de l'église Notre-Dame)

Saint-Malo ✉ 35400
SEX SHOPS/BLUE MOVIES
■ **Sex Shop St. Malo** (CC glm MA VS) 11-20 h
4 Rue du Puits aux Braies ✉ 35400 *(old town)* ☏ 02.99.56.01.51
CRUISING
-Parc Bel-Air
-Jardin du Cavalier
-Les Remparts
-Place Vauban
-Square Canada
-Hôtel des Finances (rue Toullier)
-SNCF/Railway station
-Square de la Briantais

Saint-Martin-d'Auxigny ✉ 18100
DANCECLUBS
■ **Mandragore. La** (B CC D G) Fri Sat 22.30-4 h
Vignoux-sous-les-Aix ✉ 18100 ☏ 02.48.64.55.76
Entrance FF 60.

Saint-Martin-de-Jussac ✉ 87200
BARS
■ **Fiacre. Le** (B D g) Fri Sat 22-? h
✉ 87200

Saint-Maur ✉ 36250
CAFES
■ **Terres Noires. Les** (b BF CC g MA N OS) 7-22, Sat -19 h, closed Sun
Route Nationale 20, Exit 14 from A20 ✉ 36250 *(Zone Commerciale CAP SUD)* ☏ 02.54.27.00.64
Cruisy at lunch. Truckers.

Saint-Meloir-des-Ondes ✉ 35350
SWIMMING
-Saint-Coulomb (beach to the east of Chevrets beach/plage à l'est de la plage des Chevrets)

Saint-Même-les-Carrières ✉ 16720
RESTAURANTS
■ **Villageois. Le** (b F g) Wed-Sun 12-14, 19.30-21.30 h
✉ 16720 ☏ 05.45.81.93.03

Saint-Michel ✉ 16470
CRUISING
-Le Jardin vert
-Place Victor-Hugo
-Place de New York
-Place du Théâtre

Saint-Nazaire ✉ 44600
SEX SHOPS/BLUE MOVIES
■ **Exhibi. L'** (AC CC g lj MA TV VS)
19 Bis Rue Cardurand ✉ 44600 *(near the station)*
☏ 02.40.22.15.62
Quote Spartacus for special services.
SWIMMING
-Crique de Chemoulin (NU)
CRUISING
-Hôtel de ville (WC)
-Cirque de Chemoulin (beach between/plage entre St.Marc and Ste.Marguerite)
-Tharon-Plage (beach/plage des Sables d'Or)
-Parcours Vitta Vittel (especially in the evening/particulièrement le soir)
-[P] Parc Paysager
-Avenue de Plaisance (in the evening)

Saint-Paul-de-Vence ✉ 06570
RESTAURANTS
■ **Cocarde. La** (AC CC E F glm MA) 10-22 h
23 Rue Grande ✉ 06570 ☏ 04.93.32.86.17
Culinary innovations. Andreas and Stephan are at your service and will also be delighted to help you organise all your parties.

Saint-Quai-Portrieux ✉ 22410
BARS
■ **Davy's Bar** (B g) Fri-Sun 15-1 h
3bis Place de la Plage ✉ 22410 ☏ 02.96.70.56.91
DANCECLUBS
■ **Étrier-Club. L'** (B D g) Fri Sat 23-5 h
3bis Place de la Plage ✉ 22410 ☏ 02. 96.70.53.42
Open every day in summer/En saison, ouvert tous les soirs.
SWIMMING
-Au Vieux-Bourg (NU) (nudism in a few smaller bays; take the exit to the small village of Pourry/quelques criques naturistes; accès à partir du lieu-dit Pourry)
-Le Val-André (NU) (vast beaches which also welcome nudists; between Pleneuf-Val-André and Ville-Berneuf/vastes plages qui accueillent quelques naturistes; entre Pleneuf-Val-André et Ville-Berneuf)
-Beach/plage de Lortuais (north of the village, behind the cape of Erquy; wonderful landscape/au nord du village, après le cap d'Erquy; plage magnifique)

Saint-Raphaël ✉ 83700
BARS
■ **Pipe-Line** (AC B CC d f glm MA p s TV VS) 22-5 h, Winter: closed Mon
16 Rue Charabois ✉ 83700 *(behind Townhall)* ☏ 04.94.95.93.98
CRUISING
-Place Lamartine

Saint-Romain-en-Viennois ▸ Saxel France

Saint-Romain-en-Viennois ✉ 84110

GUEST HOUSES

■ **Calade. La** (BF H OS)
Rue Calade ✉ 84110 *2 km from the historical village Vaison-la-Romaine.* ☏ 90.46.71.79 90.46.51.82
Charmant house with four bedrooms and a tower with a terrace that overlooks the village, the church and the surrounding hills.

Saint-Sébastien ✉ 23160

BARS

■ **Bastien. Le** (B CC g) 8-1 h, closed Tue
La Goutte-Jean ✉ 23160 ☏ 05.55.63.40.65

Saint-Thibéry ✉ 34630

GUEST HOUSES

■ **7 Avenue de Pezenas** (BF B G H NU OS)
7 Avenue de Pezenas ✉ 34630 *(20 min to Cap d'Agde)*
☏ 04.67.77.91.58 04.67.77.91.58 billnben@net.up.com
 uk.geocities.com/billnben2000
English run gay B&B and self-catering accommodation.

Saint-Trojan-les-Bains ✉ 17370

SWIMMING

-beach/plage (NU) (on the street going to the forest/sur la route d'accès à la forêt)

Saint-Tropez ✉ 83990

DANCECLUBS

■ **Esquinade. L'** (AC D GLM MA P SNU) 23.30-6 h, summer Mon-Sun, winter Fri Sat
2 Rue du Four ✉ 83990 *(near Place de la Mairie)*
☏ 04.94.98.87.45
■ **Pigeonnier. Le** (B D glm MA p tv) 23-? h, closed 20 Jan-15 Mar
13 Rue de la Ponche ✉ 83990 ☏ 04.94.97.36.85

RESTAURANTS

■ **Chez Maggy** (AC B CC F glm MG TV) Pentecote-end Oct 19-? h
7 Rue Sybille ✉ 83990 *(Near town hall)* ☏ 04.94.97.16.12
■ **Chez Nano** (b F g)
Place de l'Hôtel de Ville ✉ 83990 ☏ 04 94.97.01.66
■ **Entrecôte 21. L'** (b F g) 19.30-1 h
21 Rue du Portail-Neuf ✉ 83990 ☏ 04.94.97.40.02
■ **Swing . Le** (b F g TV) Till dawn.
Quai Jean-Jaures
Somptuous Empire decor, theme evenings, gogo dancers.

GUEST HOUSES

■ **Cigognes. Les** (AC BF G H MA NU PI)
803 Chemin du Carry ✉ 83310 ☏ 04.94.54.04.14
 lescicognes@wanadoo.fr
2 double rooms with bath/WC, radio, own key, room service. Open all year.

SWIMMING

-L'Escalet
-Tour des Muscadins et citadelle

CRUISING

-Le Port (L'Escalet, near the maritime cemetery/près du cimetière marin)

Saint-Vivien-de-Médoc ✉ 33590

HOTELS

■ **Résidence les Fougères** (g H) 12-21 h, closed Oct-Feb
Grayan-l'Hôpital ✉ 33590 ☏ 05.56.09.56.38

SWIMMING

-Grayan-et-l'Hôpital (beach/plage)

Salin-de-Giraud ✉ 13129

SWIMMING

- Beach (G NU)

Salon-de-Provence ✉ 13300

CRUISING

-Place Morgan (market-place/place du marché)
-Monument Jean-Moulin (RN 113, direction Avignon)
-Aire de Senas (on the highway/sur l'autoroute)

Sartilly ✉ 50530

SWIMMING

-Genets-Dragery

Saumur ✉ 49400

BARS

■ **Ascot. L'** (AC B CC D glm MA OS) Mon-Sat 19-4 h
15 Rue Molière ✉ 49400 *(centre, near Theater)* ☏ 02.41.67.77.55
Cocktail bar.

CRUISING

-Square Verdun (behind the public library/derrière la bibliothèque municipale)

Savines-le-Lac ✉ 05160

CRUISING

-Round the sea/autour du lac
-Camping (forest/fôret de Boscodon)

Savonnières ✉ 37510

GUEST HOUSES

■ **Prieuré des Granges** (BF H NG OS PI)
15 rue de Fontaine ✉ 37510 *(close to Tours)* ☏ 02.47.50.09.67
 02.47.50.06.43 salmon.eric@wanadoo.fr

Saxel ✉ 74420

RESTAURANTS

■ **Tétras. Le** (B F g)
Super-Saxel ✉ 74420 ☏ 04.50.39.00.70

ATRIUM

A - Decouvrir !!!

Sur deux niveau avec terrasse et jardin

**SAUNA • HAMMAM
SOLARIUM • BAR
TV • RELAX**

Club Gay:
tous le jours à partir de 14 h (Sauf Mardi et Mercredi mixte)

Tarif:
26,50 DM • 95 FF
20 DM off après 20 h ou jeunes de -25 ans

À 5 minutes de STRASBOURG
Schulstrasse 68 • (D) 77694 KEHL
au centre côté église
Tél. 0049 7851 / 48 27 05

Sazaret ✉ 03390

CAMPING
■ **Petite Valette. La** (BF CC F glm H MA msg OS PI) Apr-Oct
La Valette ✉ 03390 ☎ 04.70.07.64.57 📠 04 70.07.25.48
📧 la.petite.valette@wanadoo.fr
55 camping spots on 110 m2. Reasonable.

Sceaux ✉ 92330

CRUISING
-Parc de Sceaux

Sedan ✉ 08200

CRUISING
-Place du Château
-Place du Marché

Seignosse ✉ 40510

SWIMMING
-Plage des Casernes (G)

Sennecey-le-Grand ✉ 71240

DANCECLUBS
■ **Plaka. Le** (AC B CC D G YG) Fri Sat 22.30-4 h
Gigny/Saône-between Chalon sur Saône and Tommans
✉ 71240 (A6/RN6) ☎ 03.85.44.81.71
Situated in a lovely building from the 17th century.

Sens ✉ 89100

CRUISING
-Market place/Place du marché
-Jardin du Clos le Roi

Serignan ✉ 34410

SWIMMING
-Plages naturistes

Sète ✉ 34200

CRUISING
-Quai de la Résistance-Rue F. Mistral
-Beach/plage (théâtre de la Mer-la Corniche)
-Môle Saint-Louis
-Quai du Port

Sevran ✉ 93270

SWIMMING
-Woods of/Bois de Sevran

Soissons ✉ 02220

GUEST HOUSES
■ **Domaine de Montaigu** (BF glm H OS)
16 Rue de Montaigu ✉ 02290 *(near Soissons, 30 min from Compiègne, 40 min from Reims)* ☎ 03.23.74.06.62 📠 03.23.74.06.62
5 guest rooms with old furniture in a 19th century house. Quiet, green and nice. Opening 1st of May 2001.

CRUISING
-Avenue du Mail

Sotteville-les-Rouen ✉ 76300

CRUISING
-Place de la Mairie

Soulac-sur-Mer ✉ 33780

SWIMMING
-Plage de la Négade (NU)

Strasbourg ✉ 67000

BARS
■ **Zoo Bar. Le** (B glm MA)
6 Rue des Bouchers ✉ 67000 ☎ 03.88.24.55.33

RESTAURANTS
■ **Au Coin du Feu** (B CC F glm OS) Tue-Sun 10-14.30 19-23.30 h
10 Rue de la Rape ✉ 67000 *(in front of the cathedral/au pied de la cathédrale)* ☎ 03.88.35.44.85
French cuisine.
■ **Horloge Astronomique** (b F glm OS) 12-14.30, 19-23 h
2 Rue de la Rape ✉ 67000 *(au pied de la cathédrale/at the cathedral)* ☎ 03.88.35.46.37
Next to Hôtel Suisse.
■ **Petit Ours** (CC F GLM) 12-14.30, 19-23 h
3 Rue de l'Ecurie ✉ 67000 *(300 m. from the cathedral)*
☎ 03.88.32.23.21
French cuisine with natural flavours.

Strasbourg ▸ Thonon-les-Bains — France

■ **Petit Tonnelier. Le** (A AC b CC E F glm MA N OS TV) 12-14, 19-23 h, closed Sun lunch
16 Rue des Tonneliers ✉ 67000 *(near the Cathedral)*
☎ 03.88.32.53.54
Pleasant gay welcome. Fresh market products. Last order 23 h.

SAUNAS/BATHS
■ **Equateur** (B CC DR f G MA p SA SB VS) 14-24, Sat -4 h
5 Rue de Rosheim ✉ 67000 *(Bus CT9 10/20-Ste. Aurelie, Tram A-Gare Centrale)* ☎ 03.88.22.25.22
Welcoming sauna frequented by a mixed crowd.
■ **Oasis** (b f G SA SB SOL VS WO YG) 14-24 h
22 Rue de Bouxwiller ✉ 67000 ☎ 03.88.23.03.19
340 m² sauna frequented by a rather young crowd.
↪ See also Germany, Kehl

HOTELS
■ **Hôtel Suisse** (CC F glm H MA OS)
4 Rue de la Rape ✉ 67000 *(Close to the cathedral/près de la cathédrale)* ☎ 03.88.35.22.11 03.88.25.74.23
Centrally located. Nice hotel with 2 stars. Rooms with private bath, SAT-TV, phone.

HEALTH GROUPS
■ **Aides Alsace**
47 Rue de la Course ✉ 67000 ☎ 03.88.75.73.63
 03.88.32.93.12

RELIGIOUS GROUPS
■ **David et Jonathan**
B.P 197 ✉ 67028

SWIMMING
-Bathing lake in Roppenheim (beside the highway Strasbourg ⇒ Lauterbourg, WE and evenings)

CRUISING
-Les Gravières (north of Strasbourg)
-Parc de la Citadelle (AYOR)
-Rue Saint-Arbogast
-Rue Saint-Léon
-Porte Balnche (near rue du Banc de la Roche, besides family garden)
-Little wood (between Route des Roamains and highway besides Parc des Glacis)

Suresnes ✉ 92150

CRUISING
-Railway station/Gare de Longchamp (square attenant/at the park beside)
-Railway station/Gare du Mont-Velérien (derrière la gare/behind the railway station)

Talence ✉ 33400

CRUISING
-Bois de Thouars

Talmont-Saint-Hilaire ✉ 85440

RESTAURANTS
■ **Saint-Hubert. Le** (B F g H) 12-14, 19-21, Tue 12-14 h, closed Wed
Avenue de la Plage-le-Veillon ✉ 85440 ☎ 02.51.22.24.04

Tarare ✉ 69170

CRUISING
-[P] Viaduc
-Railway station/gare SNCF

Tarbes ✉ 65000

RESTAURANTS
■ **Braisière. La** (b F g) 19.30-0.30 h, closed Mon
22 Avenue Bertrand-Barere ✉ 65000 ☎ 05.62.34.10.00

HEALTH GROUPS
■ **Aides Hautes-Pyrénées** Mon-Fri 9-12, 14-19 h
4 Place du Marché Brauhauban ✉ 65000 ☎ 05.62.34.95.14
 05.62.51.31.98 aides.aides@libertysurf.fr

CRUISING
-Massay (le jardin près du musée, le your/the garden at the museum, daytime)
-Place du Foirail (AYOR) (le soir/by night)

Tarnos ✉ 40220

SWIMMING
-Nudiste beach/plage naturiste

Tergnier ✉ 02700

BARS
■ **Parilla Club. La** (B CC D F g) 15-24, Restaurant 16-22, closed Mon, Disco Fri Sat 22-4 h
38 Rue Demosthène-Gauthier Mennessis ✉ 02700
☎ 03.23.57.25.08

Théoule-sur-Mer ✉ 06590

SWIMMING
-La Napoule

Thonon-les-Bains ✉ 74200

BARS
■ **Tiffany's. Le** (B CC glm MA OS p) 18-3 h
6 Place du 8 Mai 1945 ✉ 74200 ☎ 04.50.71.88.91

RESTAURANTS
■ **Restaurant La Tour** (AC B CC E F glm MA OS)
Avenue du Général Leclerc, Port de Rives ✉ 74200 *(View on the Geneva Lake)* ☎ 04.50.71.13.87

SWIMMING
-Geneva Lake/Lac Leman (G NU) (beach 15 min on the pathway after the pool of Thonon-les-Bains, below Château Pipaille/plage à 15 min de distance de la piscine de Thonon-les-Bains, en dessous du château Pipaille)

CRUISING
-Promenade du Belvédère (night/nuit)

France Toulon ▶ Toulouse

Toulon ✉ 83000

BARS

■ **Aqua Bar** (B F glm)
3 Boulevard Pierre-Toesca ✉ 83000 ☎ 04.94.92.01.23
Bar restaurant.

■ **Arlequeen** (AC B BF CC GLM p VS) Winter: 15-1, summer 17-4 h
1 Rue Etienne Dauphin ✉ 83000 *(center of town)*
☎ 04.94.94.95.50

■ **Bar Côté Jardin** (B BF CC E f glm MA OS) 8-2 h
437 Littoral Frédéric-Mistral le Mourillon ✉ 83000
☎ 04.94.41.38.33
Terrace overlooking the sea. Popular with Navy Officers.

■ **Texas** (B G) 16-1, May-Sep -3 h
377 Avenue République ✉ 83000 *(next to the Mairie)*
☎ 04.94.89.14.10

DANCECLUBS

■ **Boy's Paradise** (B D DR G s VS)
1 Boulevard Pierre-Toesca ✉ 83000 *(opposite SNCF station)*
☎ 04.94.09.35.90

■ **Pussy Cat. Le** (B D gLM) Thu-Sun 23-4 h
655 Avenue de Claret ✉ 83000 ☎ 04.94.92.76.91

SEX SHOPS/BLUE MOVIES

■ **Box Vidéo** (g VS)
4 Place Armand Valée ✉ 83000 ☎ 04.94.91.40.25

■ **XXL** (g VS)
3 Avenue de Besagne ✉ 83000 ☎ 04.94.93.11.91

SAUNAS/BATHS

■ **Blue Hot** (b G SA SB MA WO) 13-21, Fri -1 h
16 Place Vincent Raspail ✉ 83000 ☎ 04.94.91.49.55
Friendly sauna on 300 m².

■ **Mouettes. Les** (b G SA NU OS PI SOL VS WO) 14-21 h
87 Chemin de la Pinède ✉ 83000 *(Villa les Mouettes near Tour Royale)* ☎ 04.94.42.38.73
Popular with naturists, here you'll find everything for pleasure in the open air.

HEALTH GROUPS

■ **Dispensaire Antivénérien**
Avenue Lazarre-Carnot ✉ 83000 ☎ 04.94.89.90.42
HIV testing.

RELIGIOUS GROUPS

■ **David et Jonathan** (GLM)
B.P. 5135 ✉ 83093

SWIMMING

-Beach/plage de Fabregas
-Beach/plage du Mourillon

CRUISING

-Avenue Auguste-Berthon
-Railway station/gare SNCF
-Jardin du Mourillon
-Place de la Porte-d'Italie
-Port de Bandol
-La Bedoule (highway/autoroute Toulon-Marseille)
-Square Alexandre-III (garden/jardin centre ville)
-Fort du Cap Brun
-Place du Théâtre

Toulouse ✉ 31000

TOURIST INFO

■ **Tourist Info** winter: 9-18, summer -19 h
Donjon du Capitole ✉ 31000 ☎ 05.61.11.02.22
🖶 05.61.22.03.63 ✉ ottoulouse@mibnet.fr

BARS

■ **Aphrodisiaque. L'** (B glm)
1 Rue des Chalets ✉ 31000 ☎ 05.61.63.81.82

■ **B Machine. Le** (B glm)
37 Place des Carmes ✉ 31000 ☎ 05.61.55.57.59

■ **Beaucoup** (B F GLM MA)
Pont Neuf ✉ 31000 ☎ 05.61.12.39.29

■ **Ciguë. La** (AC B CC D G YG) 18-2, Sat -5 h
6 Rue de la Colombette ✉ 31000 ☎ 05.61.99.61.87

■ **Deux G. Les** (AC B glm) 15-2 h
5 Rue Baronie ✉ 31000 ☎ 05.61.23.16.10

■ **Frescati. Le** (B glm MA)
4 Place Esquirol ✉ 31000 ☎ 05.61.12.40.15

■ **HO Club** (B G MA) 23-5 h
16 Rue Bertrand de Born ✉ 31000 *(near SNCF station)*
☎ 06.61.62.44.44
Bar & sex club.

■ **Imprévu. L'** (B GLM MA) 10-2 h
16 Rue Bertrand de Born ✉ 31000 *(near SNCF station)*
☎ 06.61.62.44.44

■ **Quinquina. Le** (B CC G) 8-22, Sun 18-22 h
26 Rue Peyras ✉ 31000 ☎ 05.61.21.90.73

■ **Scot Tea. Le** (B glm)
35 Rue du Taur ✉ 31000 ☎ 05.61.12.38.48

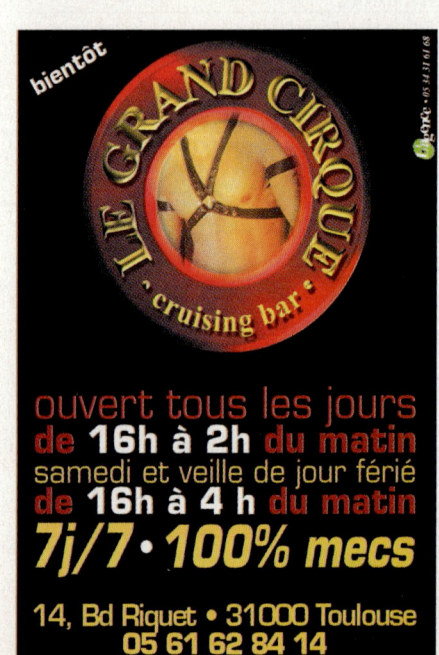

bientôt

LE GRAND CIRQUE
· cruising bars ·

ouvert tous les jours
de **16h à 2h** du matin
samedi et veille de jour férié
de **16h à 4h** du matin
7j/7 · 100% mecs

14, Bd Riquet • 31000 Toulouse
05 61 62 84 14

Toulouse | France

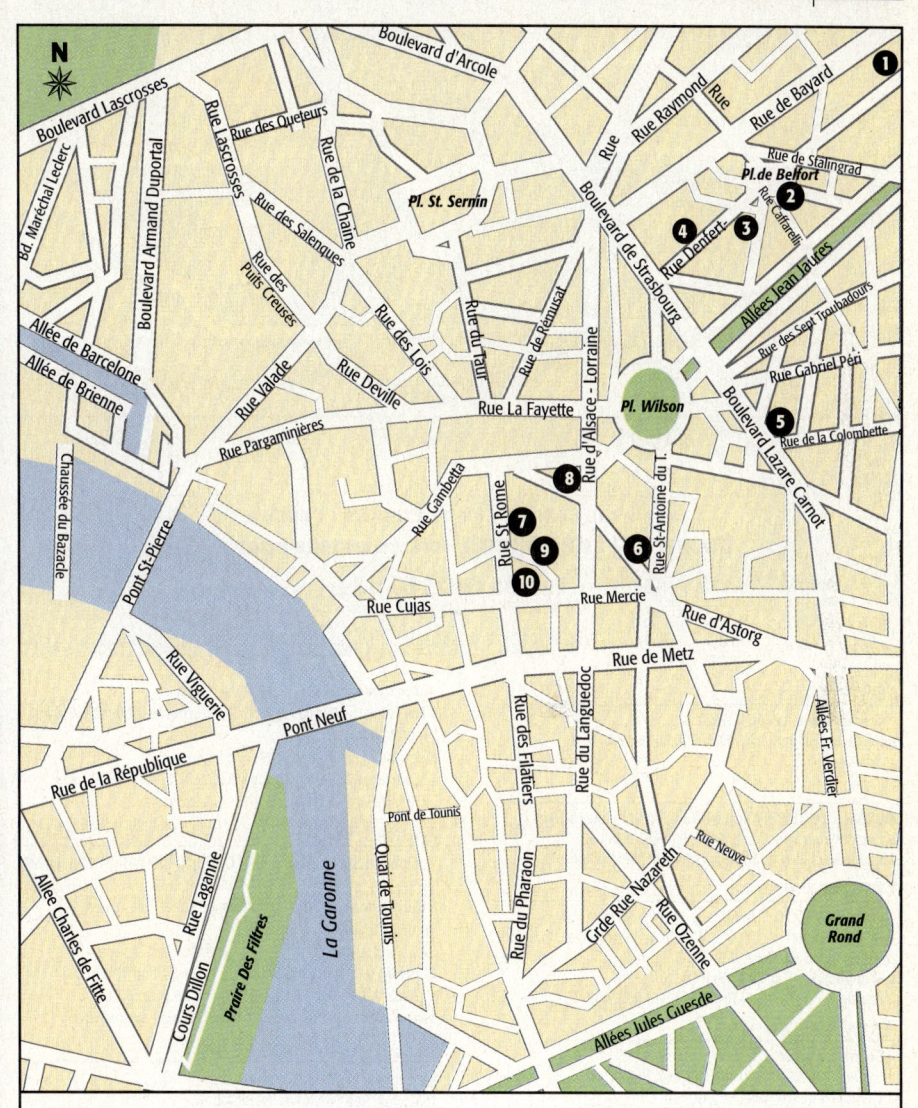

Toulouse

1. Lynx Vidéo
2. Colonial Sauna
3. Spartacus Gay Vidéo
4. Eros Sex Shop/Blue Movie
5. La Ciguë Bar
6. Le Président Sauna
7. Cockpit Danceclub
8. Le Shangai Danceclub
9. Les Deux G Bar
10. Le Quinquina Bar

France Toulouse

Le COCKPIT : 1, rue du Puits Vert - 31000 TOULOUSE
angle rue St Rome - Métro Esquirol / Capitole
Ouvert 7j/7 dès Minuit - entrée gratuite jusqu'à 2H
Tél. 05 61 21 87 53
CLUB GAY

MEN'S CLUBS
■ **Grand Cirque. Le** (AC B G VS)
14 Boulevard Riquet ✉ 31000 ☎ 05.61.62.84.14
Cruising bar.

CAFES
■ **Diables. Les** (b BF F Glm MA) Tue-Sat 8-23, Sun 10-18 h
45 Rue des Tourneurs ✉ 31000 ☎ 05.61.22.11.63
Classical music, busy on Sun afternoons. Also restaurant.

DANCECLUBS
■ **Cockpit** (AC CC D GLM MA p s) 24 h-till dawn
1 Rue du Puits Vert ✉ 31000 (M° Esquirol/Capitole, near Place du Capitole) ☎ 05.61.21.87.53
■ **Shanghai. Le** (B D DR g MA P TV VS) 23-? h
12 Rue de la Pomme ✉ 31000 ☎ 05.61.23.37.80

RESTAURANTS
■ **Bistrot d'Eugène** (B F glm)
3 Rue Delacroix ✉ 31000 ☎ 05.61.62.28.27
■ **Copains d'abord. Les** (B F glm)
38 Rue du Pont de Guilhémery ✉ 31500 ☎ 05.61.20.41.50
■ **Rose Bonbon. Le** (B F glm)
Imp. de la Colombette ✉ 31000 ☎ 05.61.63.48.46
■ **Table d'Aline. La** (B F glm)
7 Quai St.Pierre ✉ 31000 ☎ 05.61.23.24.07

SEX SHOPS/BLUE MOVIES
■ **Boîte à Films. La** (g VS) 10-2 h
23 Rue Denfert-Rochereau ✉ 31000 ☎ 05.61.62.76.75
■ **Eros** (g VS) 13-2 h
22 Rue Denfert-Rochereau ✉ 31000 ☎ 05.61.63.44.72

■ **Lynx Vidéo** (AC CC DR g MA VS) 11-2 h
2 Rue Lafon ✉ 31000 (near SNCF station, at Rue Bertrand de Born)
☎ 05.34.41.63.28
Cinemas (one only gay), videos, accessories,...
■ **Spartacus Gay Vidéo Shop** (CC G MA VS) 10-1 h
29 Rue Héliot ✉ 31000 ☎ 05.61.63.63.59

SAUNAS/BATHS
■ **Colonial Sauna** (AC B cc DR f G MA p SA SB WH VS) 12-1, Fri Sat 14-9 h
8 Place Belfort ✉ 31000 (M° Marengo SNCF/Jean-Jaurès)
☎ 05.61.63.64.11
Sauna on two floors with labyrinth. Reduction for -27 years.
■ **Président. Le** (AC b G SA SB VS) 11-21.30, Sun 12-21.30 h
38 Rue d'Alsace-Lorraine ✉ 31000 ☎ 05.61.21.52.18
Several video rooms and a bar. Original, friendly atmosphere.

TRAVEL AND TRANSPORT
■ **Rainbow Horizon**
15 Grande Rue St. Nicolas ✉ 31300
☎ 05.61.42.70.75
☎ 06.16.27.63.81
Gay cultural guides and interpreters for Toulouse and its region.

HOTELS
■ **Hôtel La Caravelle** (AC BF CC g H)
62 Rue Raymond IV ✉ 31000 (centre, near station SNCF Matabiau)
☎ 05.61.62.70.65 📠 05.61.99.08.67
3 star hotel. All rooms with bath/shower WC, balcony, phone, TV, radio, minibar, safe. Single room FF 240-360, Double 270-320.-

Toulouse | France

spartacus

DVD VIDÉO CUIR LATEX GADGETS...

vente location projection

GAY VIDÉO STORE

STORIX Sexy Store

29, rue Héliot
(métro Jean-Jaurés)
31000 Toulouse
05 61 63 63 59

storix-sexystore.com

OUVERT tous les jours de 11h à 1h

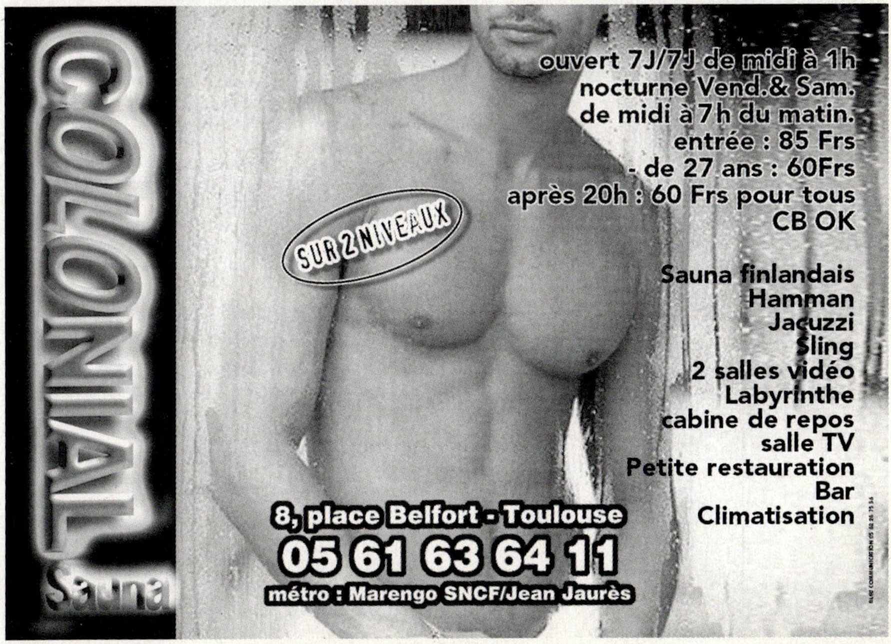

l'agence · 05 34 31 61 61

COLONIAL Sauna

SUR 2 NIVEAUX

ouvert 7J/7J de midi à 1h
nocturne Vend. & Sam.
de midi à 7h du matin.
entrée : 85 Frs
- de 27 ans : 60Frs
après 20h : 60 Frs pour tous
CB OK

Sauna finlandais
Hamman
Jacuzzi
Sling
2 salles vidéo
Labyrinthe
cabine de repos
salle TV
Petite restauration
Bar
Climatisation

8, place Belfort - Toulouse
05 61 63 64 11
métro : Marengo SNCF/Jean Jaurès

France | Toulouse ▶ Tours

lynXvidéo

2 salles de projections vidéos collectives
> écran géant et backroom

cabines de projection individuelles
> DVD ou K7

vente et location
> DVD et K7

boutique : lingerie homme et femme
> accessoires, magazines...

2, rue lafon • toulouse
(angle rue bertrand de born)
05 34 41 63 28

LA CIGUË

bar à musique
ouvert tous les jours

ouvert dès 18h
happy hours 18h30 - 19h30

6, Rue de la colombette• Toulouse
05 61 99 61 87

GENERAL GROUPS
■ **Extra Muros**
B.P. 439 ✉ 31009 ☎ 05.61.33.09.47 📧 bodoc@multimania.com
🖥 www.multimania.com/bodoc/
■ **Gais et Lesbiennes en Marche (GELEM)**
66 Boulevard Maurens, App. 88 ✉ 31270
☎ 06.11.87.38.81
📠 05.61.62.29.49 📧 gelem@altern.org
Organizers of the Gay and Lesbian March of Toulouse.

HEALTH GROUPS
■ **Aides Pôle de Toulouse** Mon-Fri 9-12, 14-18 h
122 Avenue du Général Bourbaki ✉ 31200
☎ 05.34.40.22.60
📠 05.34.40.22.61

RELIGIOUS GROUPS
■ **David et Jonathan** (GLM)
B.P. 4063 ✉ 31029 ☎ 05.61.49.53.51 📧 djtoulouse31@aol.com
🖥 www.multimania.com/djtlse

SPECIAL INTEREST GROUPS
■ **Jules et Julies**
Comité des Étudiants, Université du Mirail, 5 Allée Machado
✉ 31058
Gay and lesbian student group.
■ **Rando's Pyrénées**
B.P. 1332 ✉ 31160
Gay walking and hiking group/gays randonneurs.

CRUISING
-Cours Dillon (AYOR) (very popular; day & night, but especially between 18-23 h/populair; toute la journée, mais surtout de 18 à 23 h)
-Géant Casino Mirail (all day action in the bushes, very mixed/dans les bois, toute la journée; très mélangé)
-Garden of Plants/Jardin des Plantes (in the afternoon/l'après-midi)
-Les Quais (AYOR) (Port de la Daurade, Beaux-Arts)
-Gare SNCF/railway station (rue Compans)
-Place Wilson et Place Roosevelt, Square de Gaulle (AYOR) (at night/la nuit)
-Saint Aubin (21-2 h)
-Ile du Ramier
-Behind Théâtre Garonne (Digne de la Garonne, Rue du Château d'Eau)

Tours ✉ 37000

GAY INFO
■ **Maison des Homosexualités de Touraine (M.H.T.)** 18-22, Fri Sat special parties, disco
1ter Rue des Balais ✉ 37000 *(Vieux Tours, near Place du Grand Marché)* ☎ 02.47.20.55.30 📠 02.47.20.55.30
Association Bar.
■ **Point Gay** Thu 18-20 h
c/o MHT, 1ter Rue de Balais ✉ 37000

BARS
■ **Hélios. L'** (B G) ?-2 h
16 Rue Docteur Fournier ✉ 37000 ☎ 02.47.44.14.14
■ **Lionceau. Le** (B DR g lj OS s) 17-2 h, closed on Sun
55 Rue de Commerce ✉ 37000 *(Vieux Tours)* ☎ 02.47.61.17.13

340 | *SPARTACUS* 2001/2002

Tours ▸ Valence | **France**

■ **Open Bar** (AC b CC f glm MA p s YG) Mon-Fri 17-2, Sat 18-2 h, closed Sun
128 Boulevard Béranger ✉ 37000 *(near the Saint-Elois church)*
☎ 02.47.37.67.60
Theme nights/Soirées thématiques.

DANCECLUBS

■ **Au Club 71** (AC B D GLM MA p s) 22.30-5 h, closed Mon
71 Rue Georges Courteline ✉ 37000 ☎ 02.47.37.01.54

RESTAURANTS

■ **Chez Nello** (B F glm S) 17-2 h
8 Rue Auguste Chevallier ✉ 37000 ☎ 02.47.39.12.11
Cabaret/Shows.

SEX SHOPS/BLUE MOVIES

■ **Miroir des Hommes** (AC DR GLM MA VS) 9-2 h
34 Rue Michelet ✉ 37000 ☎ 02.47.61.13.18
Videos and individual cabins. 8 projection rooms.

SAUNAS/BATHS

■ **Thermes Grammont. Les** (AC b G MA N SA SB VS SH) 14-21 h
22bis Avenue Grammont ✉ 37000 *(near Town Hall and railway station)* ☎ 02.47.05.49.24

HOTELS

■ **Château des Ormeaux** (BF G H PI OS)
Route de Noizay, Nazelles ✉ 37530 *(20 min from Tours)*
☎ 02.47.23.26.51 📠 02.47.23.19.31
📧 chateaudesormeaux@wanadoo.fr
🖥 www.chateaudesormeaux.com
Luxury rooms in a private chateau. Swimming pool, large park. Horse riding.

GENERAL GROUPS

■ **Jeunes et étudiant(e)s homosexuel(le)s de Tours** Tue 20-22 h
c/o MHT, 1ter Rue de Balais ✉ 37000
Youth and student gay and lesbian group.

HEALTH GROUPS

■ **Centre Hospitalier R. de Tours**
2 Boulevard Tonnelé ✉ 37044 ☎ 02.47.34.81.11
■ **Dispensaire Polyvalent**
5 Rue Jehan-Fouquet, B.P. 44 26 ✉ 37000 ☎ 02.47.66.88.41
HIV-testing.

CRUISING

-Quai d'Orléans (AYOR) (around the Library, at night/autour de la Bibliothèque, la nuit)
-Jardin du Musée
-Jardin des Prébendes d'Oé
-Bois de la Ville-aux-Dames (5 km west of Tours direction Montlouis)
-Square Prosper-Mérimée

Trouville-sur-Mer ✉ 14360

RESTAURANTS

■ **Vallée d'Auge. La** (B CC F g OS) Wed-Sun 12-24 h
3-5 Boulevard d'Hautpoul ✉ 14360 ☎ 02.31.88.07.98
French specialities.

Troyes ✉ 10006

CRUISING

-Behind the hospital/Derrière l'hôpital
-La Vallée Suisse/"The Swiss Valley" (the park beside the boulevard

Gambetta, close to the railway station; in the afternoon and at night/ Jardin le long du Blvd Gambetta, près de la gare l'après-midi et le soir)
-Beach of Villepart/Plage de Villepart (On the bank of the river Seine; take road RN 71 in direction to Dijon, exit Bréviande, left hand; wait until the hour when the white collar clerks leave their offices/Bord de Seine, prendre la RN 71, direction Dijon; à la sortie de Bréviande, sur la gauche; heure de sortie des bureaux)
-Tourist office/Syndicat d'Initiative

Tulle ✉ 19000

CRUISING

-au pied de la Cathédrale Notre-Dame

Uzès ✉ 30700

GUEST HOUSES

■ **Marronniers. Les** (BF F glm H MA OS PI)
Place de la Mairie ✉ 30580 *(12 km from the historic town of Uzes, North-West of Avignon)* ☎ 04.66.72.84.77 📠 04.66.72.85.78
📧 les.marronniers@hello.to 🖥 www.hello.to/les.marronniers
Possibility of evening meals.

Valence ✉ 26000

GAY INFO

■ **Agayri Sud-Est France** (GLM) Mon-Fri 14-18 h
100 Avenue Jean Moulin ✉ 26100 ☎ 04.75.72.96.83
📠 04.75.72.96.83 📧 agayri@worldonline.fr
🖥 www.paris-in-love.com/agayri
Information about gay places in the South of France. Only French spoken.

Château des Ormeaux
Guest House ★★★★

Route de Noizay, Nazelles
37530 AMBOISE (France)
Phone : + 33 (0) 247.232.651
Fax : +33 (0) 247.231.931
e-mail : chateaudesormeaux@wanadoo.fr
http://www.chateaudesormeaux.com

Here, there are only gay men to wel-come you in this magnificent place with large park and swimming-pool

France Valence ▶ Vichy

BARS
■ **Ambigu Bar** (AC B D GLM MA) 17-4 h
13 Avenue Gambetta ✉ 26000 ☎ 04.75.56.95.04

SAUNAS/BATHS
■ **Hylas Club Sauna** (AC b DR G MA p SA SB VS WH) 13-21 h, closed Tue
40 Avenue de Verdun ✉ 26000 (Bus 8-Sully, in the Polygone commercial centre) ☎ 04.75.56.03.62
Discreet sauna frequented by a mixed age crowd.

HEALTH GROUPS
■ **Aides**
27 Rue Jeu de Paume ✉ 26000 ☎ 04.75.43.84.38

CRUISING
- Parc Jouvet
- Rue des Musiques
- Rue G.Rey, Jardin de l'Ancienne-Préfecture
- Gorges du Doux
- Barrage de Charmes-sur-Rhône

Valenciennes ✉ 59300

CRUISING
- Aire d'Hordan (both sides of the motorway Valenciennes-Paris/sur l'autoroute Valenciennes- Paris, de chaque côté)
- Parc de la Rhonelle
- Parc Froissart (close to P Charles de Gaulle (22-2 h)
- Soccer field/Terrain de foot de Vauban (22-2 h)
- Aire de Millonfosse

Vallon-Pont-d'Arc ✉ 07150

CRUISING
- Beach/Plage des Templiers

Vals-les-Bains ✉ 07600

CRUISING
- Parc du Casino (very popular in summer/très fréquenté en été)

Vannes ✉ 56000

BARS
■ **Menphis Bar** (CC B G MA) 18-2 h, closed on Mon in winter
33 rue Maréchal Leclerc ✉ 56000 ☎ 02.97.47.00.06

CRUISING
- Le Port P Maison des familles

Vendays-Montalivet ✉ 33930

SWIMMING
- Beach/plage de Montalivet

Vendôme ✉ 41100

BARS
■ **Saint Martin** (B G MA) 12-0-30 h
24 Place St.Martin ✉ 41100 ☎ 02.54.77.23.63

Verdun ✉ 55100

CRUISING
- Rue du Général-Leclerc, Cours Clouet

Verrières-le-Buisson ✉ 91370

GUEST HOUSES
■ **Alain's Bed & Breakfast** (BF glm H MA SA)
4 Sentier des Gatines ✉ 91370 (M° Massy-Verrières)
☎ 01.69.20.67.69
Booking necessary. Owner picks you up at the Métro Station.

CRUISING
- Bois de Verrières (Route A86 Clamart to Créteil; nude sunbathing in summer)

Versailles ✉ 78000

RESTAURANTS
■ **Terrasse. La** (b F glm) 19-2 h
11 Rue Saint Honoré ✉ 78000 (next to the cathedral, close to RER and chateau) ☎ 01.39.50.76.00
South-East specialities. Open late but reservation advised.

CRUISING
- Avenue St. Claud (Beginning of the street opposite the Chateau foot paths/au début de la rue en face des sentiers pédestres du château)

Verteuil-sur-Charente ✉ 16510

HOTELS
■ **Relais de Verteuil. Le** (AC B D F glm H s VS WE) Disco Thu-Sun 20-5 h
RN 10, Les Nègres ✉ 16510 ☎ 05.45.31.41.14 📠 05.45.31.41.40.71

Vichy ✉ 03200

BARS
■ **Saphir. Le** (GLM MA) 18-4, closed on Sun
7 Rue de la Source de l'Hôpital ✉ 03200 ☎ 04.70.96.04.96

SAUNAS/BATHS
■ **Anthares Sauna Club** (AC b DR f G MA p SA SB VS WH) 14-24 h, by theme nights -4 h
164 Avenue des Graviers ✉ 03200 (near Camping d'Abrest)
☎ 04.70.32.89.38
■ **Edensex** (b cc DR G msg SA SOL VS WO YG) 14-3 h
77 Rue Jean Jaurès ✉ 03200 (near the market) ☎ 04.70.96.26.38
Sauna and sex shop on three floors frequented by a rather young crowd. Nudism parties every week.

HEALTH GROUPS
■ **Dispensaire Municipal**
21 Rue d'Alsace ✉ 03200 ☎ 04.70.98.61.89

CRUISING
- Parcs d'Allier
- Pont-Barrage
- Wood/Bois de Serbannes
- Les Iles
- Place de la Poste (Boulevard des Etats-Unis/rue d'Italie)
- Quatre-Chemins (au centre du quartier des cafés/right in the middle of the cafes' area)

Vierzon ✉ 18100

CRUISING
- Abords du Canal
- Jardin de la Mairie
- P Bricolage Service

Vieux-Boucau-les-Bains ✉ 40480

HOTELS
■ **Hôtel d'Alvret** (B F g H) Jun-Nov 9-1 h
Avenue de la Plage ✉ 40480 (Port d'Albret) ☎ 05.58.48.14.09

SWIMMING
- Nudist beach in the north/plage naturiste au nord

Villard-de-Lans ✉ 38250

RESTAURANTS
■ **Caribou. Le** (B D F g H) closed Oct & Nov
Le Clos-de-la-Balme ✉ 38250 (Correncon-en-Vercors)
☎ 04.76.95.82.82
Restaurant 12-14.30 19-22 h. Disco Fri 22-2 Sat -3 h.

Villeneuve-de-Marsan ✉ 40190

HOTELS
■ **Hôtel Restaurant Hervé Garrapit** (BF CC E F glm H MA OS PI WH)
Place de la Boiterie ✉ 40190 (65 km to the North of Pau, 100 km from Biarritz) ☎ 05.58.45.20.08 📠 05.58.45.34.14
✉ hotelrestaurantherveagarrapit@wanadoo.fr
✉ www.ch-demeures.com/garrapit
"Hôtel de charme" and gastronomic restaurant with garden & luxury rooms.

Villeneuve-les-Avignon ✉ 30400

RESTAURANTS
■ **Saint André. Le** (CC F glm OS) Tue-Sun 12-14 19.30-22 h
4bis Montée du Fort ✉ 30400 ☎ 04.90.25.63.23
Trendy crowd. Gastonomic restaurant.

Villeneuve-les-Maguelonne ✉ 34750

SWIMMING
- Beach/Plage Etang de Pierre-Blanche

Villeneuve-Loubet ✉ 06270

CRUISING
- Parc de Vaugrenier (AYOR) (at night)

Villers-sur-Mer ✉ 14640

SWIMMING
- Auberville (G NU)

Villiers-les-Ormes ✉ 36250

BARS
■ **Nicolas II. Le** (B D F G) 22-4 h
✉ 36250 (6 km from/de Châteauroux) ☎ 02.54.36.68.68
Bar-disco 22-4, restaurant Wed-Sun 20-5 h.

Vincennes ✉ 94300

SAUNAS/BATHS
■ **Bains Montansier** (AC B DR f G MA msg p SA SB SOL VS WH) 1 2-20 h
7 Rue de Montreuil, Vincennes ✉ 94300 (M° Château de Vincennes/RER Vincennes) ☎ 01.43.28.54.03
Sauna in East Paris, meeting point for bears and their friends.

HEALTH GROUPS
■ **Dispensaire Municipal**
6 Rue Pierre Brossolette ✉ 94300 ☎ 02.43.28.33.20

CRUISING
- Château (alleys, east side/allées, côté est)

Vitrolles ✉ 13140

CRUISING
- Route de Marignane

Wissant ✉ 62179

SWIMMING
- Beach/plage de Wissant (NU) (in the dunes/dans les dunes)

YOU CAN BE FRANK WITH ME

Ask our Virtual Nurse whatever you want to know about gay sex, safe sex or male bodies and he'll get right back to you by e-mail. Nothing surprises him and with New Zealand AIDS Foundation backing him, you know you can trust his answers. You'll find the Virtual Nurse on our website under 'queeries'.
Frank, anonymous answers to questions about sex.
WWW.NZAF.ORG.NZ/COMMED/QUEERIES.HTML

NEW ZEALAND AIDS FOUNDATION
TE TUUAAPAPA MATE ĀRAIKORE O AOTEAROA

French Polynesia Manihi - Kaina ▸ Tahiti - Papéete

INTENSE
L'APPEL EROTIQUE

INTENSE est un parfum sans odeur qui renforce votre pouvoir de séduction!

INTENSE contient des stimulants sexuels naturels, les phéromones. Avec **INTENSE**, votre propre note sexuelle se trouve renforcée et votre pouvoir de séduction intensifié d'une manière toute naturelle.

INTENSE est inodore. Vous pouvez donc porter sans crainte votre parfum habituel sur **INTENSE** qui est uniquement à base d'eau, d'alcool et de phéromones.

Laissez-vous séduire.
Parfum neutre **INTENSE** aux phéromones naturelles dans un flacon élégant de 63,3 ml. Présentation sous coffret-cadeau.

LA PREMIERE PHEROMONE AU MONDE POUR HOMMES

Revendeurs grossistes/détaillants/informations: Tél. +49.30.610 01 120 · Fax +49.30.615 90 08 · vertrieb@brunogmuender.com

Photo: Steven Underhill

French Polynesia

Name: Polynésie Française • Französisch-Polynesien • Polinesia Francesca
Location: South Pacific
Initials: TAH
Time: GMT -10
International Country Code: ☎ 689 (no area codes)
International Access Code: ☎ 00
Language: French, Tahitian
Area: 3,521 km² / 1,359 sq mi.
Currency: 1 CFP Franc = 100 Centimes
Population: 232,000
Capital: Papéete (Tahiti)
Religions: About 55% Protestants, 24% Roman Catholic
Climate: Tropical, but moderate climate.

✱ Tahiti is the largest of the ca. 115 Polynesian islands. The capital city of Papéete has a population of 30,000. Most tourists come to the island during the Bastille Celebrations, which begin each year on July 14 and last for three weeks. French laws concerning homosexuality are in effect.

✱ Die größte der ca. 115 Inseln Polynesiens ist Tahiti. Die Hauptstadt Papéete hat 30.000 Einwohner. Die meisten Touristen kommen während der "Bastille"-Feiern auf die Insel, die jeweils am 14. Juli beginnen und drei Wochen andauern. Es gelten die französischen Gesetze zur Homosexualität.

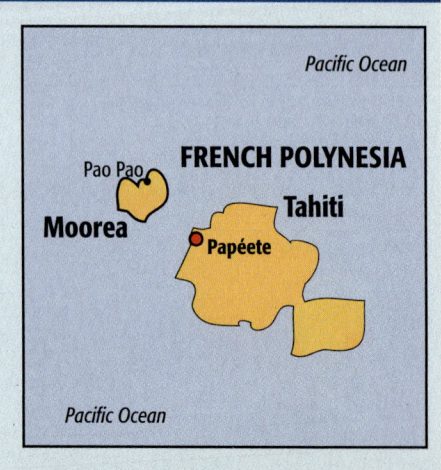

Pacific Ocean
Pao Pao — **FRENCH POLYNESIA**
Moorea — **Tahiti** — Papéete
Pacific Ocean

✱ Tahiti est la plus grande des 115 îles de la Polynésie Française. Papeete, la capitale, compte 30.000 habitants. Les touristes y affluent tous les ans, au 14 juillet, pour célébrer la commémoration de la Prise de la Bastille qui y dure 3 semaines. Même législation qu'en France métropolitaine.

344 SPARTACUS 2001/2002

Tahiti - Papéete ▸ Tahiti - Punaauia / Paea — French Polynesia

Tahiti es la más grande de las 115 islas de la Polinesia Francesa. La capital Papéete tiene 30.000 habitantes. La mayor parte de los turistas visitan esta isla para fiestas como la de la Bastilla que comienza el 14 de julio y dura tres semanas. Aquí rigen las leyes francesas con respecto a la homosexualidad.

Tahiti è la più grande delle 115 isole della Polinesia Francese. La capitale è Papéete (64.000 ab.). Molti turisti arrivano sull'isola durante le celebrazioni per la presa della Bastiglia, che cominciano ogni anno il 14 luglio e durano tre settimane. Anche per quanto riguarda l'omosessualità, qui sono in vigore le leggi francesi.

NATIONAL GAY INFO

■ **Te Anuanua o te Fenua**
PO Box 369, Papeete, Tahiti ☎ 77.31.11
or ☎ & 🖨 45.30.77.

Manihi - **Kaina**

HOTELS

■ **Climat de France Kaina Village** (B F H NG)
PO Box 24 60, Papéete, Tahiti ☎ 42 75 53
Holiday complex-resort. Approximately 90 minutes by air from Tahiti-Faaa. Comprises 16 Polynesian style bungalows. "Fare" of six rooms. All watersports, including scuba diving, deep sea fishing, water skiing, and a visit to pearl oyster beds. Local arrangements can be made in Papeete with most travel agencies. Single CPF 12.345-18.350, double 19.040-29.200 (either with half or full board).

Moorea - **Haapiti**

HOTELS

■ **Club Med** (B F NG PI)
PO Box 10 10 ☎ 56 15 00 🖨 56 19 51

Moorea - **Papetoai**

HOTELS

■ **Refuge du Lézard. La** (AC B BF CC F Glm NU OS PI WH)
PO Box 13 03 22, Punaauia 🖨 58 25 74
First and only gay resort in romantic French Polynesia.

Tahiti - **Mahina**

SWIMMING

-Pointe Vénus (WE) (From the harbour take Le Truck N° 60 to Mahina.)

Tahiti - **Papéete**

BARS

■ **Cave. La / Royal Papeete** (B D NG WE)
Boulevard Pomare ☎ 42 01 29
■ **106. Le** (B D NG WE)
Boulevard Pomare ☎ 42 72 92

RESTAURANTS

■ **Corbeille d'Eau. La** (B F g)
Front de Mer Paofai ☎ 43.77.14
French cuisine.

HOTELS

■ **Beachcomber Parkroyal** (AC B F H NG OS PI)
PO Box 60 14, Faa'a ☎ 42 51 10 🖨 43 61 06
Beach location. All rooms have AC, telephone, fridge, priv. bath, balcony, mini bar, TV. Single US$ 170-200, double 200-230.
■ **Bel Air**
Lagoon Shore, PO Box 354 ☎ 42 82 24
3.5 miles from town.
■ **Hyatt Regency** (AC B F NG OS PI WH)
PO Box 10 15, Matavi Bay ☎ 48 11 22
Expensive and luxurious: US$ 195-500.
■ **Maeva Beach Hotel** (B F H NG)
PO Box 60 08, FAAA ☎ 42 80 42 🖨 43 84 70
■ **Matavai** (AC B F H NG OS PI)
Valle Tipaerui, PO Box 32 ☎ 42 67 67 🖨 42 36 90
Rooms with AC, telephone, priv. bath, balcony, radio. Single FCP 8.800, double 11.700.
■ **Tahiti Budget Lodge** (b f glm H)
Rue de Frere Alain ☎ 42 66 82
Central location. Rates US$ 43 (1 or 2 persons), 48 with shower/WC.

CRUISING

-Beach south of Maeva Beach Hotel (Lots of Mahoos and Raerae)
-The way from the main road to the Bel Air Hotel (bushes on the left)
-Park Bougainville near post-office (MA) (locals in their cars about 21 h)

Tahiti - **Papenoo**

SWIMMING

-Surf Beach (WE YG)

Tahiti - **Punaauia / Paea**

SWIMMING

-White sand beaches

THE GAY MEDIA STORE

Bruno's

www.brunos.de

BÜCHER · MAGAZINE · DVD · VIDEOS · VIDEOVERLEIH

Germany

Name: Deutschland • Allemagne • Alemania • Germania
Location: Central Europe
Initials: D
Time: GMT +1
International Country Code: ☏ 49 (leave away the first 0 of area codes)
International Access Code: ☏ 00
Language: German
Area: 357,022 km² / 138,975 sq mi.
Currency: 1 Deutsche Mark (DM) = 100 Pfennige.
1 EURO = 1,95583 DM
Population: 82,164,000
Capital: Berlin
Religions: 33% Roman Catholic, 34% Protestant
Climate: Moderate and marine climate. Winters and summers are cool, cloudy and wet. In the Alps occasional warm Föhn-winds. The relative humidity is high.
Important gay cities: Berlin, Frankfurt/Main, Hamburg, Köln, München.

✱ The days in which homosexual couples in Germany were mentioned in any legal directives are now history. The German government passed a law in November 2000 for gay men as well as for lesbians who live together as a couple. It covers the central points that apply to the rights of a family and comes into effect in the middle of 2001.
With this law homosexual couples are treated the same as a conventional married couple. The registration at a registry office (the official body which is to undertake this registration has yet to be agreed upon). The changes will cover the laws regarding the changing of names, the right to refuse testimony as a witness, the right to personal or medical information, as well as joint medical and nursing care insurance. On top of this, partners holding a foreign passport are able to apply for a residence and employment permit. Even though aspects such as the right of adoption or the taxation laws are not covered by this new agreement, when one compares Germany internationally, it is as liberal and advanced in this aspect as Holland, France and the Scandinavian countries.
With this new set of laws as well as the lively and well developed gay scene in the large cities, Germany can be regarded as being one of the most liberal countries in the world.
Even though this change which will come into effect in 2001 is a sign of acceptance of homosexuals as people, there is always a differing grade of tolerance with regard to homosexuality.
Although it is possible to lead an open life style in the major cities, such as Berlin, Hamburg, Cologne and Munich, stigmatisation continues in rural and Catholic regions.
Germany provides the tourist with a wealth of possibilities to discover the long history of the country, traditions, customs and of course it's many attractions besides the Berlin Wall or the Heidelberg Castle. Germany has one of the best constructed transport systems of Europe, so it is not necessary to be tied to a car to enjoy the gay scene and also the numerous tourist sights.

★ In Deutschland ist die Zeit der Rechtlosigkeit für homosexuelle Paare vorbei. Der Bundestag hat im November 2000 das Lebenspartnerschaftsgesetz für Schwule und Lesben beschlossen. Es umfaßt den familienrechtlichen Kernbereich und wird zur Jahresmitte 2001 in Kraft treten. Dieses Gesetz bedeutet für die Homosexuellen in Deutschland, daß sie in vielen Bereichen des Alltags Ehepaaren gleichgestellt sind. Die amtliche Eintragung bei einer Behörde, die die einzelnen Bundesländer noch benennen müssen, beinhaltet unter anderem die Gleichstellung in den Bereichen Namensrecht, Zeugnisverweigerungs- und Auskunftsrecht sowie Kranken- und Pflegeversicherung. Zusätzlich bekommen ausländische Lebenspartner und Lebenspartnerinnen künftig eine Aufenthalts- und Arbeitsgenehmigung. Auch wenn Regelungen zu den Bereichen Adoptions- und Steuerrecht in diesem Gesetz nicht enthalten sind, hat Deutschland auf internationaler Ebene Anschluß an Holland, Frankreich und die skandinavischen Länder gefunden. Mit dieser neuen Gesetzgebung und seinen lebendigen Szenen in den Großstädten darf sich Deutschland ohne weiteres zu den liberalsten Ländern der Welt zählen. Doch trotz der im Jahr 2001 in Kraft tretenden gesetzlichen Gleichstellung gibt es in der deutschen Bevölkerung noch immer ein Toleranzgefälle. Während es in den großen Städten möglich ist, die eigene Homosexualität offen auszuleben, gilt sie besonders in ländlichen und katholisch geprägten Gebieten nach wie vor oft als Makel. Viele Schwule und Lesben ziehen deshalb in eine Großstadt, vor allem in die schwulen Hochburgen, wie Berlin, Hamburg, Köln und München. Hier unterscheidet sich Deutschland also wenig von seinen europäischen Nachbarn.
Touristisch gesehen ist Deutschland ein Land der tausend Möglichkeiten: Die mehr als tausendjährige Geschichte hinterließ überall im Land ihre sehenswerten Spuren jenseits von Berliner Mauer und Heidelberger Schloß. Deutschland verfügt über eines der am besten ausgebauten öffentlichen Verkehrsnetze Europas. Deshalb kann man die Szene und die Sehenswürdigkeiten der großen Städte auch ohne Auto problemlos erkunden..

✱ L'époque où les homosexuels n'avaient aucuns droits en Allemagne est désormais définitivement révolu. Le parlement allemand a en effet adopté une loi sur le partenariat enregistré pour gais et lesbiennes en novembre 2000. Cette nouvelle loi comprend les points centraux des droits de la famille et entrera en vigueur au milieu de l'année 2001. Cette loi permet aux couples homosexuels d'être traités dans beaucoup de domaines sur le même pied d'égalité que les couples hétéros. L'enregistrement officiel d'une union auprès d'une autorité administrative, laquelle doit être encore définie

SPARTACUS 2001/2002 | 347

Germany

par chacun des Etats (Bundesland) du pays, garantit l'égalité, entre autres, dans les domaines suivants: le choix du nom de famille, le droit de ne pas témoigner contre son partenaire, l'accès aux informations concernant son partenaire en cas de maladie, l'assurance maladie et de soins complémentaires. De surcroît, des autorisations de séjour et de travail pour les partenaires étrangers seront accordées. Bien que le droit d'adoption et les régulations dans le domaine des impôts ne soient pas compris dans la loi, l'Allemagne se positionne mondialement aujourd'hui au même niveau que les Pays-Bas, la France, ou les pays scandinaves. Grâce à ces avancées législatives et à la vie trépidante des milieux gais de ses grandes villes, l'Allemagne compte aujourd'hui parmi les pays les plus libéraux du monde.

Mais malgré ces reconnaissances légales qui entreront en vigueur en 2001, il existe encore de fortes disparités de tolérance parmi la population allemande. Alors que dans les grandes villes il est possible de vivre ouvertement son homosexualité, ce n'est de loin pas encore le cas dans les régions rurales et catholiques. C'est pourquoi beaucoup de gais s'exilent dans une grande ville, en particulier dans les fiefs homos que sont Berlin, Hambourg, Cologne ou Munich. Ici aussi, l'Allemagne se différencie donc peu de ses voisins européens.

D'un point de vue touristique, l'Allemagne est un pays qui offre mille curiosités: en dehors des célèbres mur de Berlin et château d'Heidelberg, l'histoire millénaire du pays a laissé partout des marques qui méritent un détour. L'Allemagne dispose d'un des réseaux de transport public le mieux structuré d'Europe. On peut donc explorer le milieu gai et les curiosités des grandes villes même sans voiture.

En Alemania, ya ha pasado a la historia la época en que las parejas homosexuales no tenían los mismos derechos que las parejas heterosexuales. En noviembre del 2000, el consejo federal aprobó la ley de parejas de hecho para gays y lesbianas. Se centra en las áreas centrales del derecho familiar y entrará en vigor a mediados del 2001. Esta ley significa que los homosexuales en muchos ámbitos de la vida cotidiana tendrán los mismos derechos que las parejas casadas. El registro oficial ante alguna institución estatal (que todavía debe ser concretizada por parte de los länder) comprende, entre otras cosas, la igualdad en cuanto a la elección del apellido, el derecho de información, la seguridad social, el seguro de invalidez, etc. Además, en el caso de parejas binacionales, los novios procedentes del extranjero tendrán el derecho de estancia y a obtener el permiso de trabajo. Si bien en la nueva ley no figuran regulaciones en cuanto al derecho de adopción y en cuanto al área de los impuestos, con la nueva ley, Alemania se ha unido a países como los Países Bajos, Francia y las naciones escandinavas. Con la nueva legislación y el ambiente gay tan animado en las grandes ciudades, Alemania puede contarse entre los países más liberales del mundo. Pero a pesar de la igualación que entrará en vigor en el 2001, sigue habiendo un cierto desnivel en cuanto a la tolerancia en la sociedad alemana. Mientras que en las ciudades grandes se puede vivir abiertamente la homosexualidad, la situación sigue siendo muy difícil en zonas rurales o con fuerte influencia católica. Por ello, muchos gays y lesbianas fijan su residencia en sitios como Berlín, Hamburgo, Colonia o Munich, que son bastiones homosexuales. En este aspecto, Alemania no se diferencia mucho de sus vecinos europeos.

Desde el punto de vista turístico, Alemania es un país de múltiples posibilidades: Ejemplos de su larga historia dignos de ver no se reducen a la Puerta de Brandenburgo o al castillo de Heidelberg. Alemania dispone de una de las mejores redes de transporte público en toda Europa. Debido a ello, se puede precindir sin problema del coche para visitar los lugares de interés o los sitios de ambiente.

In Germania non vengono più negati i diritti delle coppie omosessuali. Nel novembre 2000 il Bundestag, la Camera bassa del Parlamento tedesco, ha approvato la legge sulle unioni civili per gay e lesbiche. Questa legge si riferisce soprattutto al diritto di famiglia ed entrerà in vigore a metá del 2001 stabilendo pari diritti come per le coppie eterosessuali in tanti settori della vita quotidiana. L'iscrizione delle unioni omosessuali in un registro presso un'autorità che è ancora da definire dai singoli Länder riguarda il diritto dei partner di portare un cognome comune, il possibile rifiuto di testimoniare, il diritto d'informazioni e la copertura assicurativa del partner e dei suoi figli da parte del servizio sanitario nazionale. Per lo più comprende il permesso di soggiorno e di lavoro per i partner stranieri.

Nonostante la mancanza di regolamenti che riguardano il diritto tributario e l'adozione nella legge, la Germania così ha trovato a livello internazionale la coincidenza con l'Olanda, la Francia e i paesi scandinavi. Con le unioni civili e i suoi vivaci ambienti gay nelle grandi città la Germania è senz'altro tra i paesi più liberali del mondo.

Malgrado tutto, però, esiste ancora un dislivello di tolleranza tra la popolazione tedesca. Mentre nelle grandi città è possibile vivere apertamente una vita gay, nei posti di campagna o dominati dal cattolicesimo, l'omosessualità viene ancora vista come una macchia; è per questo motivo che molti gay e lesbiche vanno nelle città, soprattutto nei baluardi gay come Berlino, Amburgo, Colonia e Monaco di Baviera. In questo senso la Germania non si distinguedai suoi vicini europei.

Dal punto di vista turistico, la Germania è un paese dalle mille possibilità. La storia di un millennario del paese ha lasciato, oltre il muro di Berlino e il castello di Heidelberg, le sue tracce. La Germania dispone di una delle migliori reti di comunicazione d'Europa. Così è possibile esplorare l'ambiente gay e le altre bellezze delle grandi città anche senza macchina.

NATIONAL GAY INFO

■ **Freies Tagungshaus Waldschlößchen** Mon-Fri 8.30-12.30, Wed 15-18 h
✉ 37130 Reinhausen *(13 km south east from Göttingen)*
☎ (05592) 382   📠 (05592) 17 92
💻 www.waldschloesschen.org
Tagungshaus mit Workshops, Seminaren und Fortbildungen für Schwule und Lesben. Jahresprogramm anfordern/Conference hotel offering seminars, conferences and workshops for gays and lesbians. Please ask for free program leaflet.

■ **gay-web e.V. - Das Netz für Schwule und Lesben**
Borgweg 8   ✉ 22303 Hamburg   ☎ (0700) 42 99 32 33
💻 stadt.gay-web.de
The German Queer Resources Directory.

NATIONAL PUBLICATIONS

■ **Adam**
c/o Foerster Verlag, Sprendlinger Landstraße 120   ✉ 63069 Offenbach   ☎ (069) 831022/3
📠 (069) 84 59 91
💻 www.foerstermedia.com
National monthly glossy. About 100 pages. DM 15.-

■ **Andere Welt, Die**
Postfach 350 151   ✉ 10210 Berlin
☎ (030) 29 44 90 52
📠 (030) 29 44 90 51
💻 www.die-andere-welt.de
Independant monthly magazine in German covering national and regional news. DEM 42.-/year.

348 SPARTACUS 2001/2002

Linie Charter

URLAUB FÜR UNS
LCR - Linie & Charter Reisen

weltweit
Flugreisen - Individualreisen
Gayhotels - Gruppenreisen

Wir sind täglich für euch da!
Mo. - So. 09.00 - 23.00 Uhr
HOTLINE 0180 - 526 42 35
24 Pf./Min.

LCR - Linie & Charter Reisen
Flughafen Hamburg Terminal 2 - 22335 Hamburg   Tel.: 040 / 50 71 60   -   Fax: 040 / 50 71 624
eMail: info@lcr-reisen.com   Internet: www.linie-und-charter.de

Germany

Germany

■ **Box**
Postfach 29 03 41 ✉ 50525 Köln ☎ (0221) 954 13 12
🖷 (0221) 954 13 11
💻 www.box-online.de
Monthly publication (middle of each month) with regional editions. Featuring news, comments, reports, satire, erotics, scene-gossip, classifieds and dates. Free at gay venues.

■ **Downtown**
c/o Michael Sürth Verlag, Homburger Straße 22 ✉ 50969 Köln
☎ (0221) 360 30 25 🖷 (0221) 360 12 53 💻 downtown@pride.de
Monthly, published last Fri in month. News from the gay scene and classifieds. Free at gay venues.

■ **Du & Ich**
c/o Leine-Verlag, Herrenstraße 15 ✉ 30159 Hannover
☎ (0511) 130 51 🖷 (0511) 17 251 💻 leine@iworld.de
Most traditional of the German gay magazines. Reports on German and international gay scene, entertainment and politics. Lots of personals; is published monthly, DM 15.

■ **Forum Homosexualität und Literatur** Mon-Fri 12-16 h
c/o Uni-GH Siegen, FB 3 ✉ 57068 Siegen ☎ (0271) 74 04 588
🖷 (0271) 74 04 4293
💻 forum-homosexualitaet@germanistik.uni-siegen.de
Research on the aspects of homosexuality and literature.

■ **Freshmen** (G)
Bruno Gmünder Verlag, Leuschnerdamm 31 ✉ 10999 Berlin
☎ (030) 615 00 30 🖷 (030) 615 90 07
💻 info@brunogmuender.com
Bimonthly publication. Introducing erotic photography and stories.

■ **gay-press.de** (GLM)
c/o Bieniek Verlags- und Medien GmbH, Schinkestr. 9 ✉ 12407 Berlin ☎ (030) 78 70 36 30 🖷 (030) 78 70 36 31
💻 www.gay-press.de
Magazine covering the cities of Berlin, Frankfurt and Hamburg.

Die Nummer Eins unter Deutschlands schwulen Magazinen

männer aktuell

von mann zu mann

Einzelheft 14,80 DM

Probeabo: 3 Ausgaben für nur 29,60 DM

Hotline 030-6150030

Mail@maenneraktuell.de

männer aktuell, postfach 61 01 04, 10921 Berlin. Aktuelle Ausgabe: www.brunos.de

**Soap-Star
Laurent Daniels
Exklusiv entblättert**
im Heft 01/2001

Lifestyle, Unterhaltung, Service, Sex:

**Jeden Monat die schärfsten Männer:
Jeff Palmer, Thom Barron, Ken Ryker**

**die neuesten Trends:
Mode, High-Tech, Musik und Bücher**

**die heissesten Reportagen:
Callboys, Schwule Knackis, Gay Manager**

**und die tollsten Promis im Interview:
Guido Westerwelle, Dolce & Gabbana, Stephen Gately**

...und jeden Monat exklusiv einen Ralf-Könic-Comic!

Foto © by Andreas Bitesnich

Germany

GAY MARKT AUSTRIA

VERSANDHANDEL ALLER RICHTUNGEN

VIDEOS · TOYS · KONDOME · APHRODISIACS · CD-ROM & DVD · BÜCHER

LANGJÄHRIGER DISKRETER SERVICE

POSTFACH 161
A-1061 WIEN

WWW.GAYMARKT.AT

Man´s World
Der Versand für Gay Videos, Toys und vieles mehr!

MAN´S WORLD

Fordern Sie jetzt unseren brandneuen Hauptkatalog an!

unsere Adresse:
Man´s World,
Odoakerg. 32
A-1160 Wien
Österreich

Telefon:
0043 1 402 34 62
Mo-Fr. 10-20 Uhr

Fax:
0043 1 408 08 59

mansworld@telering.at
www.mansworld.at

MODELS BY CAZZO FILM BERLIN

■ **Lesbisch-schwule Presseschau, Die** (GLM)
Mehringdamm 61 ✉ 10961 Berlin (U-Mehringdamm, entrance 1st courtyard/Eingang 1. Hof) ☏ (030) 69 40 17 23
🖥 www.lesbisch-schwule-presseschau.de
Monthly magazine reporting gay lesbian themes as published in German media. DM 6,20.

■ **MÄNNERaktuell**
c/o Bruno Gmünder Verlag, Leuschnerdamm 31 ✉ 10999 Berlin
☏ (030) 615 00 30
📠 (030) 615 91 10
✉ MAENNERakt@brunogmuender.com
Monthly publication with news, articles and reviews focusing on society, culture and gay lifestyle with events and happenings in the gay scene. Also includes photographs and personal ads. Over 120 pages.
Monatsmagazin mit aktuellen Informationen, Artikeln und Berichten über Gesellschaft, Kultur und schwulen Lifestyle, mit Hinweisen zu Veranstaltungen in der schwulen Szene. Beinhaltet auch Fotos und Kleinanzeigen. Über 120 Seiten

■ **Queer** Mon-Fri 9-17 h
Pipinstraße 7 ✉ 50674 Köln ☏ (0221) 57 97 60
📠 (0221) 579 76 66 🖥 www.queer.de
National monthly newspaper. Seven regional editions. Contains political news, arts & culture, lifestyle, events, address-listings, classifieds etc. For free at gay venues.

NATIONAL PUBLISHERS

■ **Albino Verlag**
Leuschnerdamm 31 ✉ 10999 Berlin
☏ (030) 615 00 30
📠 (030) 615 90 07
Gay fiction./Schwule Literatur.

■ **Bruno Gmünder Verlag**
Postfach 61 01 04 ✉ 10921 Berlin ☏ (030) 615 00 30
📠 (030) 615 03 37
✉ info@brunogmuender.com
Publisher of SPARTACUS International, National Editions, ...von hinten series, SCHWULE MÄNNER pocket almanac/gay guide, MÄNNERaktuell-magazine, Freshmen-magazine, fiction, non-fiction and photo books.

■ **Foerster Verlag** Mon-Fri 10-18 h
Sprendlinger Landstraße 120 ✉ 63069 Offenbach *(motorway exit-Offenbach-Süd)* ☏ (069) 83 10 22 📠 (069) 84 59 91
🖥 www.foerstermedia.com
Publisher of gay magazines (Adam), gay erotic magazines (Boy oh Boy, Homoh, Kerle), gay videos, fiction books and photography books.

■ **Himmelstürmer Verlag**
Hochallee 114 ✉ 20149 Hamburg ☏ (040) 480 617 18
📠 (040) 48061799
✉ info@himmelstuermer.de

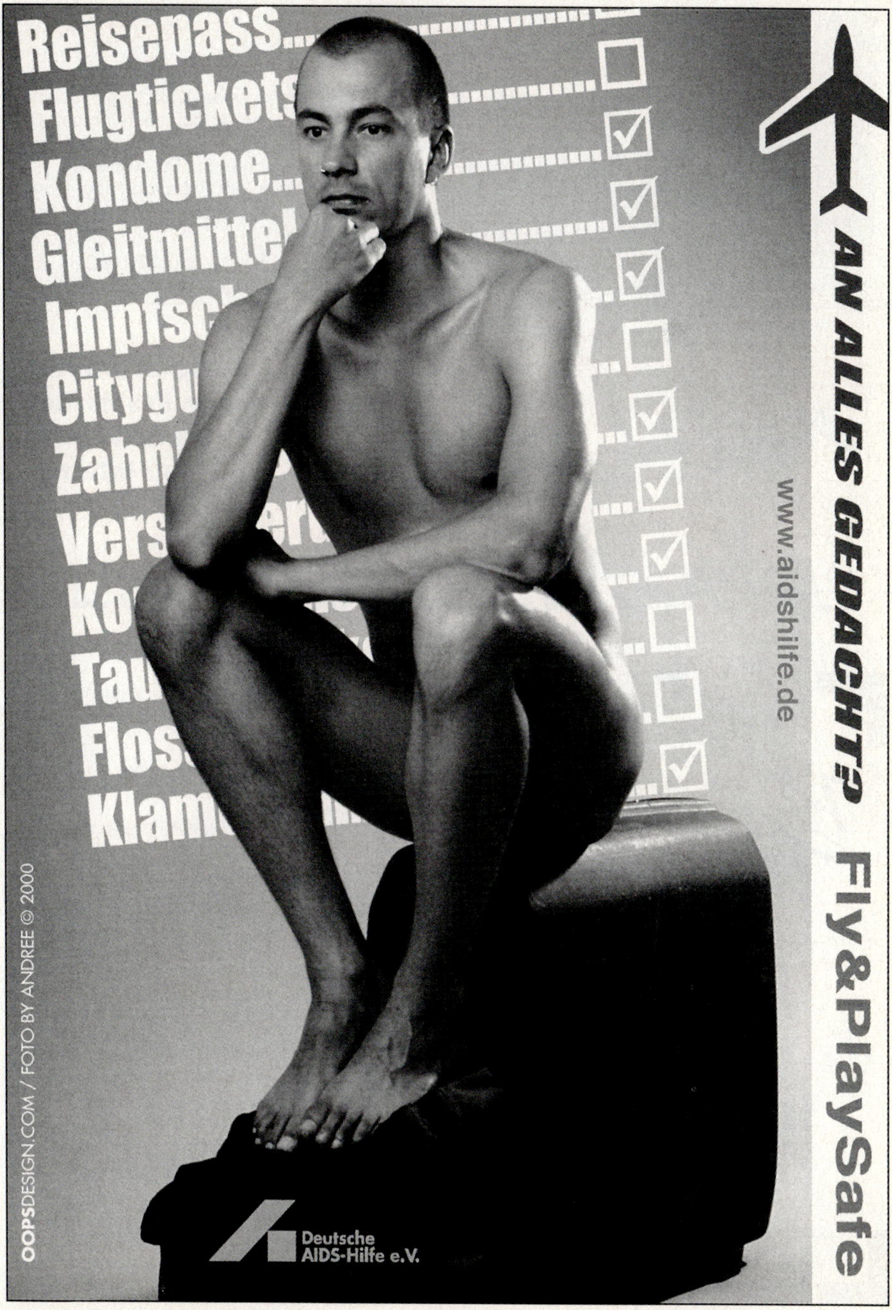
Reisepass...
Flugtickets
Kondome...
AN ALLES GEDACHT?
Fly&PlaySafe
www.aidshilfe.de
OOPSDESIGN.COM / FOTO BY ANDREE © 2000
Deutsche AIDS-Hilfe e.V.

Germany

Rhein-Main/Norddeutschland/NRW/Berlin/Nürnberg/Stuttgart/München/Dresden/Leipzig/Basel/Zürich/Wien/bundes- und europaweit:

Dominanter Er, 34, kräftig, männlich, gut bestückt, aktiv, tabulos, diskret, in diversen Outfits, gibt Dir was Du brauchst von soft bis extrem. Mache vorwiegend Haus- und Hotelbesuche. Auch Reisebegleitung (weltweit) sowie Wäsche- und Fotoversand! Dominant Master, 34 y.o., manly, blond, shaved, uncut only active, discrete, large range of outfits, no tabus. Mainly outcalls. Escort (worldwide)!

Postfach 80 02 80 # 65902 Frankfurt/Main ☎ 0177 / 682 64 36
www.smallboy.sucken.de · eMail: MasterIngo@gmx.net

SIEGESSÄULE
Europas größtes schwullesbisches Stadtmagazin im Internet
>News >Kontakte >Tourist-Information
www.siegessaeule.de

Bruno's
www.brunos.de
THE GAY MEDIA STORE

■ **MännerschwarmSkript**
Neuer Pferdermarkt 32 ✉ 20359 Hamburg ☎ (040) 430 26 50
📠 (040) 430 29 32
💻 www.maennerschwarm.de

■ **Pink Rose Press Verlag**
Lerchenstraße 100 ✉ 22767 Hamburg ☎ (040) 43 18 81 70
📠 (040) 43 18 81 72 ✉ piropr@aol.com
💻 www.gaygermanyguide.de
Publisher of Gay German Guide and different CDroms.

■ **Querverlag**
Akazienstraße 25 ✉ 10823 Berlin ☎ (030) 78 70 23 39
📠 (030) 788 49 50 💻 www.querverlag.de
Publisher of gay and lesbian fiction and non-fiction.

■ **Verlag Erich Scheer** (CC G)
Havelberger Strasse 17 ✉ 10559 Berlin ☎ (030) 396 11 15
📠 (030) 396 11 16 ✉ webmaster@verlag-scheer.de
💻 verlag-scheer.de
Erotic magazines, films, CD-Roms, photo copyrights. Also sex shop.

■ **Verlag rosa Winkel**
Postfach 62 06 04 ✉ 10796 Berlin ☎ (030) 85 72 92 95
📠 (030) 85 72 92 96
💻 www.rosawinkel.de
Publisher of bibliophile gay reprints and general gay literature.

NATIONAL COMPANIES

■ **Adonis Gay Versand** (G)
Bornstraße 14 ✉ 44135 Dortmund ☎ (0231) 57 36 19
📠 (0231) 83 72 23
Leather, toys and accessories. Catalogue for free.

■ **amazon.de mailorder** (CC glm)
☎ (0180) 53 54 990 📠 (0130) 9299
💻 www.amazon.de
Online orders only. Many gay and lesbians titles available.

Germany

saunaguide
& gay bathhouses international

BRUNO GMÜNDER

Sauna Guide & Gay Bathhouses International
252 Seiten/Pages, English / Deutsch / Français, ISBN 3-86187-155-6
DM 26,80 / Sfr 26,- /Ös 196,-

Erhältlich im Buchhandel oder bei www.brunos.de

Germany

www.pride.de
DAS PORTAL DER COMMUNITY
MIT DEM PRIDE GUIDE INTERNATIONAL, DATINGSERVICE UND ÜBER 10.000 SZENETIPPS AUCH PER WAP UND SMS

just_the_way_you_are!

■ **Bruno's Mail Order** 0-24 h
Postfach 61 01 04 ✉ 10921 Berlin ☎ (030) 615 92 03
📠 (030) 615 90 08 🖥 www.brunos.de
Fiction, non-fiction, photo-books, videos, calendars, CDs, etc. Catalogue for free.

■ **Cazzo Film**
Gneisenaustraße 94 ✉ 10961 Berlin ☎ (030) 695 05 245
🖥 www.cazzofilm.com
Producers of high quality German porno films.

Was in keinem Urlaubsprospekt steht...

amnesty international
Das Schweigen brechen
Menschenrechtsverletzungen aufgrund sexueller Orientierung
DM 19,80; sFr 19,80; öS 145

„Der vorliegende Bericht ist bestens geeignet, die schöne bunte Homowelt der westlichen Hemisphäre mit einem Schuß Politik zu beleben."
Siegessäule

www.querverlag.de

■ **DE AH'A-Vertrieb**
Postfach 61 01 49, Dieffenbachstraße 33 ✉ 10921 Berlin *(Kreuzberg)* ☎ (030) 69 00 87 13
📠 (030)69 00 87 42
🖥 www.wetwideworld.de
Sales department of Deutsche AIDS-Hilfe.

■ **homo.de Internet GmbH**
Ritterstr. 12-14 ✉ 10969 Berlin *(Online Shop)* ☎ (030) 61 50 74 79 📠 (030) 69 08 84 16
🖥 www.homo.de
Gay internet book shop and CDs, videos, accessoires & contact ads.

■ **Janssen Versand**
Postfach 15 07 01 ✉ 10669 Berlin ☎ (030) 881 15 90
📠 (030) 881 59 80
🖥 www.galerie-janssen.de

■ **Männer natürlich** (G MA)
Im Mühlenbach 8 ✉ 53127 Bonn ☎ (0228) 25 44 34
📠 (0228) 25 42 19
🖥 www.maenner-natuerlich.de
Tour operator for group-travelling.

■ **Omega- Versand**
Postfach 40 04 35 ✉ 40244 Langenfeld ☎ (02173) 977 952
📠 (02173) 977 953
✉ info@omega-versand.de

■ **Pride Partnerfirmen** (GLM MA) Mon-Fri 9-19, Sat 10-14 h
Höninger Weg 100-100 A ✉ 50969 Köln ☎ (0221) 3680 100
📠 (0221) 3860 111 ✉ company@pride.de 🖥 www.pride.de
A national company network catering for the gay and lesbian community. The Pride Network includes many branch companies and special services. Ask for details.

■ **PRO-FUN Versandhaus** (CC GLM)
Postfach 94 01 32 ✉ 60459 Frankfurt am Main
☎ (069) 70 76 77-0 ☎ (0800) 776 38 61 (freeline)
📠 (069) 70 76 77 11
🖥 www.pro-fun.de
Toys, books, videos, CDs, posters, piercings.

■ **Topversand**
Postfach 11 29 ✉ 85749 Karlsfeld ☎ (08131) 910 50
📠 (08131) 926 69
Clothes, accessories, videos, books, etc.

358 SPARTACUS 2001/2002

Germany

■ **Union Versand**
Postfach 2718 ✉ 55516 Bad Kreuznach ☎ (0671) 324 73
🖥 www.union-versand.de
Books, magazines, videos, toys, leather, rubber, piercing.

■ **Zip Productions** 10-22h
Postfach 103545 ✉ 20024 Hamburg ☎ (040) 736 735 00
📠 (040) 429 11 304 🖥 www.zip-production.de
Producers of the new video series "Men of Istanbul". Turkish/arabic gay erotic videos.

■ **www.spartacusworld.com**
International multilingual community website. Chatpages, event calendar and SPARTACUS – online
International, Mehrsprachig Community Portal mit Chatseite, Event-Kalender und SPARTACUS-Online

NATIONAL GROUPS

■ **BASJ - Bundesarbeitsgemeinschaft Schwuler Juristen**
c/o HS e.V., Postfach 12 05 22 ✉ 10595 Berlin ✉ recht@lsvd.de
🖥 stadt.gay-web.de/basj/
German gay legal professionals group.

■ **Bisexuelles Netzwerk BINE e.V.** (GLM MA) helpline
Mon Wed 17-18 h
Postfach 61 02 14 ✉ 10923 Berlin ☎ (030) 211 74 05
🖥 bine.net
Loosely knit national association of bisexual groups and organizations with many local groups.Information & support, all volunteers.

■ **Bund Lesbischer und Schwuler JournalistInnen e.V.** (GLM MA)
Postfach 30 42 04 ✉ 10724 Berlin ☎ www.gaymedia.de
Federation of gay and lesbian journalists.

■ **Bundesarbeitsgemeinschaft Schwule im Gesundheitswesen**
Warthestraße 70 ✉ 12051 Berlin ☎ (030) 628 37 05
📠 (030) 62 80 44 89
National interest group of gays working in the health system.

■ **Bundesverband der gehörlosen Lesben und Schwulen e.V.**
Meeting every 2nd & 4th Fri / Month from 19 h
Zirkusweg 11 ✉ 20359 Hamburg 📠 (040) 31 79 22 43
✉ bgls_gehoerlos@hotmail.com
🖥 www.home.t-online.de/home/bgls-/index.htm

■ **Cutting Club**
Postfach 10 04 05 ✉ 46524 Dinslaken
✉ cuttingclub@eurocirc.org
Organization for cut gays and those who want to be circumcised.

■ **Deutsche AIDS-Hilfe e.V.**
Dieffenbachstraße 33 ✉ 10967 Berlin (U-Schönleinstraße)
☎ (030) 690087-0 📠 (030) 69 00 87-42 ✉ dah@aidshife.de
🖥 www.aidshilfe.de

■ **Deutscher Beirat für homosexuelle Frauen und Männer bei den Anonymen Alkoholikern**
Postfach 42 08 21 ✉ 12068 Berlin
You can ask for the meetings-list of the gay and lesbian groups in Europe in writing.

■ **EPOA - European Pride Organizers Association** 18-? h
c/o Hartmut Schönknecht, Elberfelder Straße 23 ✉ 10555 Berlin
☎ (030) 392 53 11 📠 (030) 392 43 19
✉ hartmut.schoenknecht@t-online.de
Also the seat of ILGA- information office Berlin and The European Pride Collection. Call or mail for further information.

■ **Feetback** (LJ)
Postfach 10 11 33 ✉ 51203 Leverkusen
✉ andreo61@gmx.de 🖥 www.feetback-club.de
Group for fans of feet, socks, boots, sneakers and tickling. Second-monthly newsletter, meetings and sexparties in several cities. Write for details.

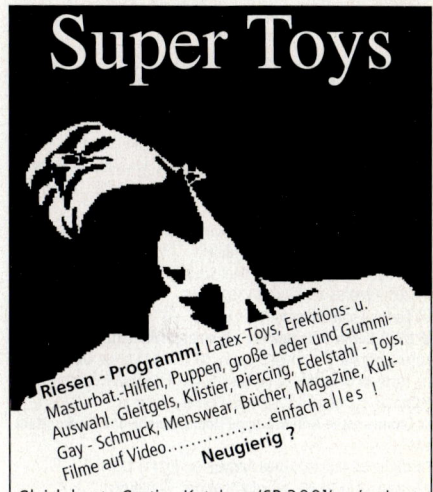

Super Toys

Riesen - Programm! Latex-Toys, Erektions- u. Masturbat.-Hilfen, Puppen, große Leder und Gummi-Auswahl. Gleitgels, Klistier, Piercing, Edelstahl - Toys, Gay - Schmuck, Menswear, Bücher, Magazine, Kult-Filme auf Video..............einfach alles! **Neugierig?**

Gleich heute Gratis - Kataloge 'SP-2001' anfordern
Für Diskret-Briefversand bitte DM 3,-- in Briefmarken beilegen.

**UNION VERSAND, BOX 2718-S
55516 Bad Kreuznach**
Vorab Info: Info@union-versand.de

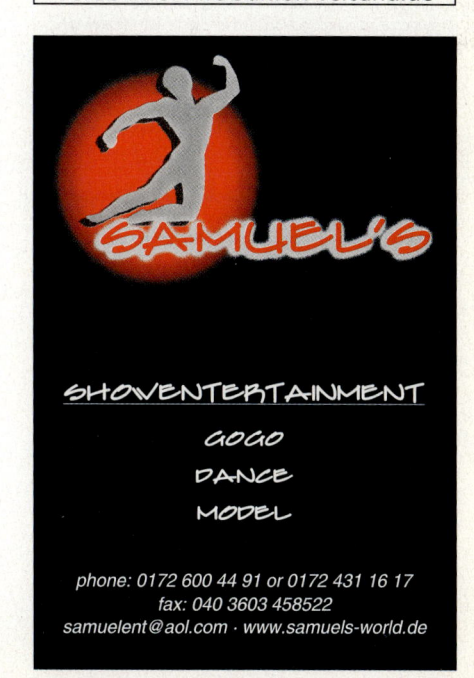

SAMUEL'S

SHOWENTERTAINMENT

GOGO
DANCE
MODEL

phone: 0172 600 44 91 or 0172 431 16 17
fax: 040 3603 458522
samuelent@aol.com · www.samuels-world.de

Germany

■ **Gay Skinhead Movement**
Postfach 10 02 53 ✉ 10562 Berlin
📧 gsmgermany@geocities.com
🌐 www.geocities.com/WestHollywood/Heights/2618
Union of gay skinheads (non racist), no fetish-club, nationwide.

■ **Green Berets International e.V. (GBI)** (G LJ)
Postfach 10 20 17 ✉ 45020 Essen ☎ (0201) 89 144 31
📠 (0201) 83 144 12 📧 gbi_ev@gmx.de 🌐 www.green-berets.de
Group of uniform lovers. Regional groups in different cities in Germany and the Netherlands

■ **International Support Group for Information Transfer and Networking (ISGITN)** by appointment
Elberfelder Straße 23, c/o Hartmut Schönknecht ✉ 10555 Berlin
☎ (030) 392 53 11 📠 (030) 392 43 19
📧 hartmut.schoenknecht@t-online.de

■ **LSVD Berlin-Brandenburg / Bundesgeschäftsstelle**
Katzbachstraße 5 ✉ 10965 Berlin ☎ (030) 44 00 82 40
📠 (030) 44 00 82 41 📧 berlin@lsvd.de 🌐 www.lsvd.de
Information, counselling, addresses, events, programs.

■ **Ökumenische Arbeitsgruppe Homosexuelle und Kirche (HuK) e.V.**
Postfach 500 437 ✉ 52088 Aachen ☎ (0241) 123 46
📠 (030) 42 85 01 28 📧 info@huk.org 🌐 huk.org
The Ecumenical Group Homosexuals and Church (HuK) is a free alliance of men and women that are interested in a critical and constructive examination of the subjects of homosexuality and church. Check website or call for info on regional groups.

■ **Positiv e.V.** aks for details
Waldschlößchen ✉ 37130 Reinhausen ☎ (05592) 382
📠 (05592) 1792 📧 waldschloesschen@t-online.de
Organizer of nationwide get-togethers for people with HIV and AIDS.

■ **Sozialdemokratischer Arbeitskreis gegen die Diskriminierung Homosexueller**
Postfach 22 80 ✉ 53012 Bonn

■ **Völklinger Kreis e.V.-Bundesverband Gay Manager**
Leyendeckerstraße 1 ✉ 50825 Köln ☎ (0221) 546 19 79
Association of gay managers.

■ **Yachad Deutschland**
Müllerstr. 43, c/o SUB ✉ 80469 München 📧 fredf@gmx.net
Nation wide Gay and lesbian Jewish group.

■ **Zentrale Erfassung: Homosexuellendiskriminierung (ZEH)**
c/o HSH, Postfach 47 22 ✉ 30047 Hannover

COUNTRY CRUISING

-A1 (E22) Bremen ⇌ Lübeck Road house "Hamburg-Stillhorn"
-A1 (E31), A3 (E35), A4 (E40) Kölner Ring all (P)
-A1 (E37) Bremen ⇌ Dortmund Raststätte "Münsterland" (Wood behind road house. Leather. Mon only)
-A1 (E37) Bremen ⇌ Osnabrück (P) "Mahndorfer Marsch" after Bremer Kreuz, popular -4 h
-A1 (E37) Dortmund ⇌ Bremen between Hamm-Bergkamen and Hamm-Bockum/Werne
-A1 (E422) Trier ⇌ Saarbrücken 1st resting place ⇌ Saarbrücken (15 min past Trier)
-A2 Bottrop ⇌ Oberhausen (P) between "Bottrop" and "Oberhausen-Sterkrade"
-A2 Hannover ⇌ Minden (P) between "Porta Westfalica-Veltheim" and "Paderborn-Sennelager" (day and night in the wood)
-A3 (E35) Wiesbaden ⇌ Köln (P) past "Niederhausen"
-A3 (E42) Frankfurt ⇌ Nürnberg (P) past "Offenbach" (P) past "Seligenstadt"
-A3 (E42) Frankfurt ⇌ Würzburg Roadhouse "Weiskirchen" Raststätte
-A3 (E42) Wiesbaden ⇌ Würzburg (P) between "Frankfurter Kreuz" & "Frankfurt-Süd"
-A3 Passau ⇌ Regensburg (P) between "Hengersberg" & "Igensbach"
-A4 (E40) Chemnitz ⇌ Glauchau (P) "Rabensteiner Wald" wood behind the road house
-A4 (E40) Köln ⇌ Aachen (P) between "Eschweiler" & "Weisweiler"
-A4 Köln ⇌ Aachen (P) between Kerpen and Buir and between Aachener Kreuz and Aachen-Zentrum)
-A4 Köln ⇌ Olpe (MA) (P) Hasbacher Höhe, 0-24 h)
-A4 Köln ⇌ Olpe (P) Mörkepütz)
-A5 (E35) Darmstadt ⇌ Karlsruhe (P) past "Kreuz Walldorf" (P) past "Bruchsal"
-A5 (E451) Darmstadt ⇌ Frankfurt (P) Langen in both directions after "Langen/Mörfelden"
-A5 Basel ⇌ Karlsruhe (P) before exit Offenburg) (P) Unditz)
-A5 Frankfurt ⇌ Heidelberg (P) Fliegwiese (22-? h)
-A5 Heidelberg ⇌ Mannheim (Weinheim. WC)
-A6 (E50) Saarbrücken ⇌ Kaiserslautern (P) St. Ingbert, Silbersandquelle, Kahlenberg & Homburger Bruch
-A6 Mannheim ⇌ Heilbronn (P) past "Kreuz Walldorf" (P) near Heilbronn
-A6 Saarbrücken ⇌ Mannheim (P) between Landstuhl and Kaiserslautern-Einsiedlerhof)
-A6 Stuttgart ⇌ Heilbronn (1st (P) past Neckarsulm)
-A7 (E45) Kassel ⇌ Fulda (P) between "Guxhagen" & "Melsungen"
-A7 Flensburg ⇌ Hamburg (P) Hüsby between "Schleswig/Schuby" & "Schleswig-Jagel")
-A7 Hamburg ⇌ Kolding (P) "Altholzkrug" & "Handewitter Forst")
-A7 Hamburg ⇌ Flensburg (P) Sielsbrook between "Bad Bramstedt" and "Neumünster-Wittorf"
-A7 Hamburg ⇌ Quickborn (P) "Bönningstedt")
-A8 Saarlouis ⇌ Pirmasens (P) "Kutzhof" between "Kreuz Saarbrücken" & "Heuweiler")
-A9 München ⇌ Nürnberg (P) between "Manching" & "Langenbruck"
-A23 Oldenburg ⇌ Wilhelmshaven (P) Varel
-A24 (E26) Berlin ⇌ Hamburg (P) "Hahnenkoppel" (past "Witzhave". WC & Wald. Leather. Thu)
-A28 (E234) Bremen ⇌ Bremerhaven (P) after the garbage disposal factory
-A29 Oldenburg ⇌ Wilhelmshaven (P) between "Varel-Obenstrohe" & "Varel-Bockhorn"
-A30 (E30) Osnabrück ⇌ Amsterdam (P) between "Lotte" & "Ibbenbüren/Laggenbeck"
-A31 Bottrop ⇌ Schüttorf (P) Dorsten-Holsterhausen
-A33 Paderborn (P) Paderborn-Elsen
-A33 Paderborn ⇌ Bielefeld (P) zwischen Paderborn-Schloß Neuhaus & Paderborn-Sennelager (P) Teutoburger Wald
-All (P) along the A33 between Bielefeld and Paderborn (also in the other direction). Especially the last (P) before the A2 (before the exit Hövelhof). Large cruising area in the woods.
-A42 Bottrop ⇌ Oberhausen (P) between "Bottrop" & "Oberhausen-Sterkrade" (P) "Castrop-Bladenhorst"
-A42 Dortmund ⇌ Gelsenkirchen (P) Castrop-Rauxel-Bladenhorst
-A43 Wuppertal ⇌ Münster Raststätte "Hohe Mark" & (P) "Haltern" & (P) "Speckhorn"
-A44 Aachen ⇌ Düsseldorf (P) Im Tunnel between Aachen-Brand and Aachener Kreuz)

Aachen ▶ Amberg Germany

-A45 [P] Dortmund-Marten (both sides) [P] Dortmund-Hoyensburg (both sides)
-A46 [P] between Kreuz Hilden and Haan-Ost (both sides)
-A48 Koblenz ⇌ Triert (first [P] after Koblenzer Kreuz)
-A48 Trier ⇌ Koblenz ([P] between Kreuz Koblenz and Koblenz Nord, at night only)
-A52 Düsseldorf ⇌ Essen [P] "Ruhrtalbrücke" (between "Kreuz Breitscheid" & "Essen-Haarzopf. In the wood and under the bridge. Day and night. Fri LJ)
-A52 Düsseldorf ⇌ Mönchengladbach Raststätte "Cloerbruch"(on each side at the end in wooded area)
-A57 (E31) Köln ⇌ Neuss [P] past "Köln-Chorweiler"
-A57 [P] Kamp-Lintfort
-A57 Düsseldorf ⇌ Krefeld [P] Geißmühle (abends/evenings)
-A59 [P] between Düsseldorf-Garath and Monheim-Bamberg (both sides)
-A661 Frankfurt ⇌ Darmstadt [P] between "Offenbach-Taunusring" & "Offenbacher Kreuz"
-A67 (E451) Frankfurt ⇌ Mannheim [P] between "Lorsch" & "Viernheimer Dreieck"
-A71 [P] Schmira direction A4. Fri & Sat from 21h
-A73 Nürnberg ⇌ Erlangen [P] past "Eltersdorf" (in the wood)
-A81 (E41) Stuttgart ⇌ Heilbronn [P] "Kälbing" between "Mundelsheim" & "Pleidelsheim"
-A81 (E41) Stuttgart ⇌ Singen [P] "Eschachtal" (AYOR) (between "Rottweil" & "Villingen-Schwenningen". Pedestrian subway)
-A480 (Gießener Ring) Marburg -Kassel-Eisenach [P] "Am Silbersee" (toilets/WC), 1300 m after exit/nach der Ausfahrt "Wettenberg", busy after sunset till dawn (WE -6 h)/populär nach Sonnenuntergang bis in die frühen Morgenstunden (Wochenende -6h)
-A480 (Gießener Ring) Wetzlar-Limburg-Dortmund [P] Car Park "Am Pützenfeld" (toilets/WC), 1800 m before exit, busy after sunset till dawn (WE -6 h)

Aachen ☎ 0241

BARS
■ **Gentlemen** (B D f GLM lj MA OS p s) 20-6 h, Sun Mon closed
Promenadenstraße 31 ✉ 52062 ☎ 401 57 96

RESTAURANTS
■ **P33** (B F g MA N WE) 17-2, Fri-Sat -3 (meals -24 h)
Promenadenstraße 33 ✉ 52062 ☎ 40 37 33

SEX SHOPS/BLUE MOVIES
■ **Filme Video Magazine**
Adalbertsteinweg 1 B ✉ 52070 ☎ 54 19 03
Heterosexual sex shop with a separate gay section.
■ **Sexy Villa Nova** (g VS) Mon-Sat 10-22 h
Heinrichsallee 2, ✉ 52062 ☎ 90 199 12/11
■ **Super Sex Basar** (AC g MA VS) Mon-Fri 9-20, Sat -16 h
Gasborn 17 ✉ 52062 ☎ 20635

BOOK SHOPS
■ **Backhaus Buchhandlung GmbH & CoKG** (g) Mon-Fri 9.30-19, Sat -16 h
Jakobstrasse 13 ✉ 52064 ☎ 212 14
■ **Mayersche Buchhandlung** (g)
Ursulinerstraße 17-19 ✉ 52062 ☎ 477 70

GENERAL GROUPS
■ **Knutschfleck. Jugendgruppe** (YG)
Kasinostraße 37 ✉ 52066 ☎ 281 64
📧 info@knutschfleck-online.de 🖥 www.knutschfleck-online.de
Gay youth group age 15-27.
■ **Rainbow e.V.**
Kasinostraße 37 ✉ 52066 ☎ 401 97 00 📧 Rainbow@gmx.de

HEALTH GROUPS
■ **AIDS-Hilfe Aachen e.V.** Counselling Mon, Tue, Thu 10-16 h, Wed/Fri 10-12 h
Zollernstraße 1 ✉ 52070 ☎ 53 25 58 ☎ 194 11 (helpline)
📠 90 22 32
Gay group Schwule in der AIDS-Hilfe (S.i.d.A.H.).

HELP WITH PROBLEMS
■ **Rosa Telefon** Tue 19-21 h
☎ 346 33
■ **Schwules Überfalltelefon** Tue 19-21 h
☎ 192 28
Gay bashing helpline.

CRUISING
-Saarstraße/"Ehrenmal" (ayor r) Popular.
-Universität, Hauptmensa, Keller/University, Hauptmensa, basement.
-Kármán-Auditorium, unterhalb/below Fo 1
-Bushof und/and Volkshochschule, Petersstraße
-Hauptbahnhof/Main rail station

Ahaus ☎ 02561

HEALTH GROUPS
■ **AIDS-Hilfe Westmünsterland** (GLM MA lj OS p)daily 10-13 & 14-17 h
Marktstraße 16 ✉ 48683 *(100m from town hall)* ☎ 19 411 (helpline) ☎ 96 20 10 📠 96 20 1
📧 info@westmuensterland.aidshilfe.de
📧 westmuensterland.aidshilfe.de
Euregio-Gays meet Wed 20-22 h.

Ahlen ☎ 02382

HEALTH GROUPS
■ **AIDS-Hilfe Ahlen e.V.** Mon 9-12 17-19, Tue Thu 9-12 15-17, Wed Fri 15-17 h
Königstraße 9 ✉ 59227 ☎ 194 11

Altenau ☎ 05328

HOTELS
■ **Haus Waldfrieden** (b BF g H MA SA) Sauna-Club 20-? h (WE)
Bürgermeister-Breyel-Weg 1-3 ✉ 38707 ☎ 14 50 / 252
Hotel with club-bar and sauna. Rooms with balcony. Rates Single DM 45, double 35-55/person (bf incl.)

Amberg ☎ 09621

GENERAL GROUPS
■ **Lederclub Burgfalken Oberpfalz** (B DR G LJ MA p) 1st & 3rd Fri 21 h
Bergstr. 10, Sulzbach-Rosenberg ✉ 92237 *(corner Klostergasse ,historical centre)* ☎ 648 81 📠 648 81
📧 burgfalken@amberg.gay-web.de
🖥 amberg.gay-web.de/burgfalken/index.htm
Meetings in club bar "Falkenhorst" in the centre of Sulzbach.

Germany Amberg ▶ Bamberg

HEALTH GROUPS
■ **AIDS-Hilfe Amberg-Sulzbach** Mon Thu 19-21 h.
Meets 3rd Sun at 14 h
Münzgässchen 3 ✉ 92224 ☎ 49 69 29 💻 aidshilfe@gay-web.de
🖥 www.amberg.gay-web.de/ah
2nd and 4th Fri reunion of gay and bisexual men.

Aschaffenburg ☎ 06021
CAFES
■ **Café ABdaten** (B GLM YG) Thu 20 h
Kirchhofweg 2 *(In youth center / Jugendkulturzentrum)*

Ascha/Straubing ☎ 09961
GUEST HOUSES
■ **Froschauer Hof "Bei Manfred und Werner"** (B BF F G H MA msg NU OS S VS) Mon-Fri 18-24, Sat 15-2, Sun 15-23 h
Froschauer Straße 2 ✉ 94347 *(near Shell filling station)*
☎ 91 04 77 ☎ (0179) 617 61 77 📠 91 04 77
💻 frosch.ascha@t-online.de
🖥 home.t-online.de/home/frosch.ascha
Rates from 40-80 DM. Transfer to station 30 DM.

Augsburg ☎ 0821
BARS
■ **Bistro Giorgio** (B F GLM MA) 15-1 h
Georgenstraße 33 ✉ 86152 ☎ 508 43 14

DANCECLUBS
■ **David's** (D glm) Thu-Sat 17-4, Sun 15-3 h
Prinzregentenstrasse 1 ✉ 86250 ☎ 518718

SEX SHOPS/BLUE MOVIES
■ **Inkognito** (g) 9-24 h
Theaterstrasse 6 ✉ 86152 ☎ 153652
Erotic shop with gay cinema and cubicals

GENERAL GROUPS
■ **ALSO - Augsburger Lesben- und Schwulen-Organisation e.V.**
helpline Thu 19-21h
Neuhäuserstr. 11 ✉ 86154 ☎ 41 51 86 ☎ 58 97 97 97
💻 info@also.org 🖥 also.org
Youth Group meeting Fri 20 h. Call helpline for further details. Thu 19-21 Tel. 58 97 97 97
■ **Schwulen- und Lesbengruppe Augsburg (SCHAU)** Fri 20-22 h
c/o ESG Zentrum, Völkstraße 27 ✉ 86150 ☎ 15 92 42

HEALTH GROUPS
■ **AAH - Augsburger AIDS-Hilfe** Mon-Fri 9-12, Mon-Thu 15-19 h,
☎ Counselling Mon, Tue, Thu 17-19 h
Morellstraße 24 ✉ 86159 ☎ 58 59 08 ☎ 194 11 (counselling)
📠 58 59 05 💻 mail@aidshilfe-augsburg.de
🖥 www.aidshilfe-augsburg.de

CRUISING
-Park "Rotes Tor" 0-24 h
-Wertachbrücke/Wertachstraße (AYOR) 0-24 h
-Meringer Au (lake on the right hand side)

Backnang ☎ 07191
CAFES
■ **Tante Emma** (AC B CC f GLM MA N OS) Mon-Thu 11-24, Fri & Sat 11-1, Sun 14:30-24 h
Willy-Brandt-Platz 3 ✉ 71522 ☎ 954844

Bad Honnef ☎ 02224
HOTELS
■ **Hotel avendi Bad Honnef** (B CC E F glm msg PI SA SOL WH WO)
Hauptstrasse 22 ✉ 53604 *(Bus 566-Kurhaus)* ☎ 18 90
📠 189-189 💻 hotel@avendi.de 🖥 www.avendi.de
rates from DM 135-185 (single) to DM 220-270 (double) incl. bf.

Bad Kreuznach ☎ 0671
BARS
■ **BaLoo** (B CC D G MA s) 20-1, Fri Sat -2 h
Bosenheimer Straße 158 ✉ 55543 ☎ 726 26
■ **Spartacus** (B f GLM lj MA OG s) 20-1, Fri Sat -2 h
Rüsselsheimer Straße 50 ✉ 55545 ☎ 415 35

DANCECLUBS
■ **Hexenkeller** (B D GLM) Wed-Sat 20- ?
Schloßgartenstrasse 29 ✉ 55583 ☎ 06708/66 15 04

CRUISING
-🅿 Konrad-Frey-Straße (at night, near railway station/nachts, nahe Bahnhof)

Bad Tölz ☎ 08041
GENERAL GROUPS
■ **SchuTz-Schwule in Tölz und im Oberland e.V.** (GLM MA)
1st/3rd Fri 20-21.30 h (helpline)
Benediktbeurer Strasse 2 ✉ 83646 ☎ 96 12
call for further information.

Baden-Baden ☎ 07221
BARS
■ **Odeon** (AC B CC D E MA s) Thu-Tue 20-2 h
Balzenbergstraße 41 ✉ 76530 *(Weststadt)* ☎ 280 28

HOTELS
■ **Hotel Regent** (A B BF CC F glm MA s SOL WO)
Eichstraße 2 ✉ 76530 *(central location)* ☎ 90 75-0 📠 256 61
💻 info@regent-hotel-bad-bad.com
🖥 www.regent-hotel-bad-bad.com
22 rooms with shower/WC, TV, telephone. Rates from DM 125.

CRUISING
-Lichtenaler Allee (between Kunsthalle and tennis lawn, best 22-1 h)
-Path between Steigenberger Badischer Hof Hotel and Trinkhalle (best frim 21 h)
-Leopoldsplatz, Kiosk

Bamberg ☎ 0951
BARS
■ **Pausen-Stübla. Zum** (B d F glm MA) 18-1, Sat 20-2, Sun 20-1 h, closed Wed
Martin-Luther-Straße 4 ✉ 96050 ☎ 234 68

Bamberg ▶ Berlin | **Germany**

HOTEL Regent
BADEN BADEN

Ihr Hotel im Herzen
der internationalen
Festspielstadt

Gay owned and operated by:
Jörg Peterson & Brian Cadd

The Regent Hotel is a comfortable and very individual 3 star hotel located in the city centre of Baden-Baden. We are within only a short walking distance of the Congress center, Kur-house, casino, Caracalla and Friedrichs thermal baths, theatre and Opera house.
We offer a high standard of wellness and personal service to make your stay a time to remember.
Our 22 double/single rooms are fitted with satelite TV, telefon, radio and minibar and every floor is reached by elevator. After a good nights sleep, we offer you a lavish complementary breakfast from the buffet.
Come and spend an evening in our wine bar where we serve regional and international cuisine and a vast selection of wines from our local vinyards.
Single room price from DM 125,-
Double room price from DM 160,-
Homepage:www.regent-hotel-bad-bad.com
e-mail:info@regent-hotel-bad-bad.com
Eichstraße 2   Tel.: 07221 - 9075-0
76530 Baden-Baden   Fax: 07221 - 25661
We look foreward to welcoming you in Baden-Baden

■ **Rainbow** (glm)
Innere Löwenstrasse ✉ 96247

GENERAL GROUPS
■ **Uferlos-Schwule und Lesben in Bamberg e.V.** Meetings Thu 19.30 h at Pro familia, Kunigundenruhstraße 24
PO Box 17 42 ✉ 96008 ☏ 247 29
📧 uferlos@bamberg.gay-web.de
🖥 www.bamberg.gay-web.de

HEALTH GROUPS
■ **AIDS-Beratung Oberfranken** Mon-Fri 9-12 h and appointment
Kunigundenruhstraße 24 ✉ 96050 *(near station)*
☏ 279 98
🖨 279 98
📧 aids-beratung-ofr@t-online.de

CRUISING
-Am Kranen (unter den Brücken/under the bridges)
-Tiefgarage/underground garage at Hertie department store
-Stadion-WC (toilets), Pödeldorferstraße

Bansin ☏ 038378

GUEST HOUSES
■ **Villa von Desny** (CC BF g H MA NU OS WH) All year
Strandpromenade 4 ✉ 17429 *(on the island "Usedom")*
☏ 2430 🖨 24324
Beach location. Guest house and Café.

Bayreuth ☏ 0921

GENERAL GROUPS
■ **ECCE Homo**
🖥 www.uni-bayreuth.de/students/eccehomo/ehevents.html
Gay/lesbian student group. See website for more details.
■ **Vereinigung Homosexualität und Gesellschaft e.V. (VHG)** Meetings Mon 20 h at Underground, von-Römer-Straße 15
PO Box 10 12 45 ✉ 95412 ☏ 85 29 28

HEALTH GROUPS
■ **AIDS-Beratungsstelle Oberfranken** Mon-Fri 8.30-13.30, Thu 8.30-17 h
Schulstraße 15 ✉ 95444 *(near the old cinema centre)*
☏ 825 00 🖨 220 82 64 📧 aids-beratung-ofr@t-online.de

HELP WITH PROBLEMS
■ **Rosa Telefon** Mon 18.30-20 h
☏ 85 29 28

CRUISING
-Main rail station/Hauptbahnhof
-[P] Albrecht-Dürer-Straße

Bergisch Gladbach ☏ 02202

GENERAL GROUPS
■ **GayL Bergisch-Gladbacher Gruppe für Schwule, Lesben und Bisexuelle**
PO Box 10 02 48 ✉ 51402 ☏ 0170/961 01 66
🖨 0170/139 61 01 66 📧 GayL@eurogay.net
🖥 www.gayl.notrix.de
Infos, Termine und Beratung per Telefon. Information by telephone

Berlin ☏ 030

✱ Berlin is a city with many different places of interest for its gay visitors and also its gay community. There is a variety of clubs from the West to the East and of course many good-looking men. Many rainbow coloured flags of the gay community are proudly floating in the gay triangle: Wittenbergplatz, Nollendorfplatz and Victoria-Luise-Platz, located in the heart of Schöneberg. In Kreuzberg, and in the whole of Prenzlauer Berg exists a wide range of things to do from sitting in a street cafe to sweating it out in a sauna. The scene in Berlin is much more clear cut than in other German cities. The SNAXX Club has established itself in Europe as a venue for "Hardtrance" and fetish parties. Evening entertainment is well taken care of around the construction sites of the Hackeschen Höfe with numerous assortments of clubs, bars, coffee shops and tea dances. A trend magazine from Japan has given the Sunday parties at the WMF a place in the top ten of the best and most glamorous clubs in the world.

✱ Berlin ist eine Stadt ohne Zentrum. Und das ist gut so: An den unterschiedlichsten Orten öffnen sich hier die Geheimtüren zu angesagten Clubs und schönen Männern. Im Schöneberger Dreieck zwischen Wittenbergplatz, Nollendorfplatz und Viktoria-Luise-Platz wehen den Besucher stolz die Regenbogenfahnen ins Gesicht. Auch in Kreuzberg und im ganzen Prenzlauer Berg ist schwules Leben vom Straßencafé bis zur Sauna gut etabliert. Die Szene steht im Ruf, etwas markiger zu sein als die anderer deutscher Städte. Kein Wunder, daß sich hier mit dem SNAXX Club das Venue aus Hardtrance und Fetischparty Europas überhaupt herausbilden konnte. Doch auch für den Freund gut swingender Abendunterhaltung wird

Germany — Berlin

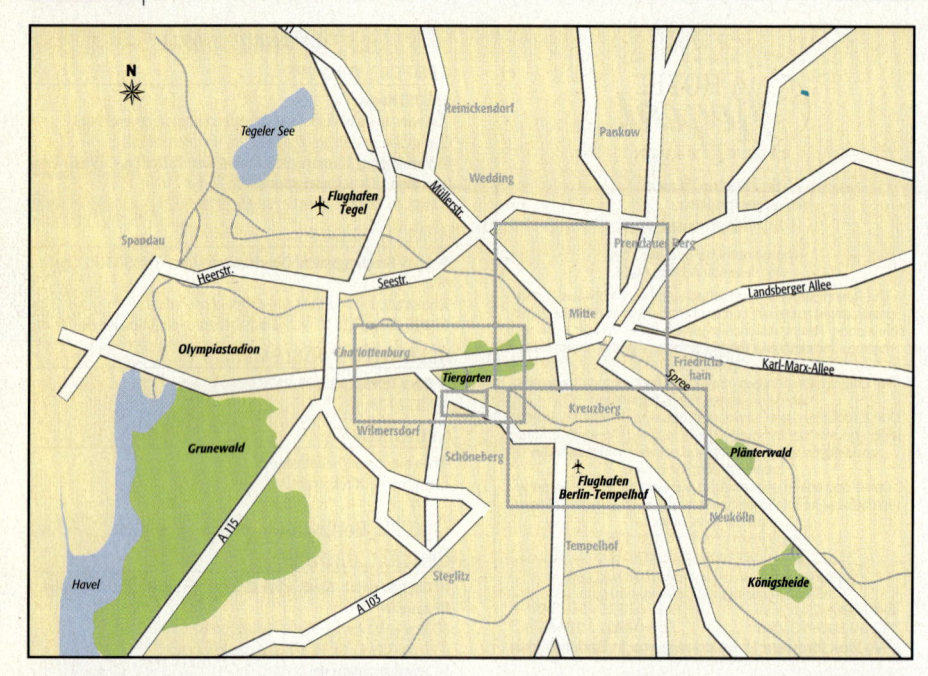

gesorgt. Rund um die Hackeschen Höfe entwickelt sich entlang der vielen Baustellen eine edle, durchaus schwule Clubkultur. So wählte jüngst ein bedeutendes japanisches Trendmagazin die Sonntagsparties im WMF in die Ewigkeits-Top Ten der glamourösesten Dinge der Welt.

★ Berlin est une ville qui n'a pas de centre. Et tant mieux: aux endroits les plus différents s'ouvrent les portes secrètes menant aux clubs et aux beaux hommes. A l'intérieur du triangle "Schöneberg", entre la "Wittenbergplatz", la "Nollendorfplatz" et la "Viktoria-Luise-Platz", des drapeaux aux couleurs arc-en-ciel flottent fièrement au visage du visiteur. Dans le "Kreuzberg" et dans tout le "Prenzlauer Berg", le milieu gai est également bien établi avec de nombreux cafés de rue et saunas. Le milieu a la réputation d'être le plus animé d'Allemagne. Ce n'est donc pas étonnant que l'arrivée en Europe d'un club fétichiste hardtrance ait pu se faire ici avec le "Snaxx Club". Tout autour des "Hackeschen Höfe" s'est aussi développée une culture de sorties, faites de bars, club, cafés et autres thés dansants. Récemment, un important magazine en vogue du Japon a sélectionné le WMF comme un des dix meilleurs club du monde.

⬢ De hecho en la actualidad Berlín no dispone de un solo centro. Pero esto no significa un inconveniente, al contrario, en sitios muy diferentes se abren ahora las puertas secretas de clubs de moda y hombres guapos. En el triangulo del barrio de *Schöneberg*, que abarca *Wittenbergplatz*, *Nollendorfplatz* y *Victoria Luise Platz* el visitante puede contemplar innumerables banderas de arcoiris. Pero también en los barrios de *Kreuzberg* y de *Prenzlauer Berg* la vida gay con sus bares y saunas está bien establecido. El ambiente berlinés tiene fama de ser más duro en comparación con otras ciudades alemanas. Por ello no es de extrañar que precisamente aquí se encuentra el SNAXX Club, el sitio de hardtrance y fetichismo más famoso en toda Europa. Pero también para el amante de la diversión nocturna más moderada Berlín tiene mucho que ofrecer: En los alrededores de los *Hackesche Höfe*, al lado de innumerables obras, surgen nuevos clubs gay. Recientemente una importante revista japonesa de nuevas tendencias tituló las fiestas del domingo en el WMF como una de las cosas más glamorosas de todos los tiempos.

✖ Berlin è una città senza centro. Questo comporta anche dei vantaggi: Nei posti più svariati si aprono le porte segrete per entrare nei club *en vogue* o per godersi i begl'uomini. Nel triangolo di *Schöneberg* tra il *Wittenbergplatz*, *Nollendorfplatz* e *Viktoria-Luise-Platz* le bandiere con i colori dell'arcobaleno sventolano esprimendo l'orgoglio degli abitanti. Anche a Kreuzberg e nell'intero quartiere del Prenzlauer Berg la vita gay si è ben stabilita includendo i bar con terrazze sulle strade e le saune. Si dice che l'ambiente gay sia un po' più estrema rispetto a quello delle altre città tedesche. Non è da stupirsi che qui si è stabilito lo SNAXX Club, *il* posto in Europa per gli amanti di Hardtrance e party di feticcio. Ma anche per coloro che preferiscono una sera più leggera trovano il loro modo di divertimento. Attorno alle Hackesche Höfe lungo i numerosi cantieri si sta sviluppando una cultura di club gay. Recentemente un'importante rivista trendy giapponese ha eletto le feste della domenica nel WMF come le cose più glamour del mondo, così che si sono annoverate per eterno nei luoghi Top Ten.

GAY INFO

■ **aha-Lesben- und Schwulen-Zentrum** Sun 17-22 h (Café)
Mehringdamm 61 ✉ 10961 *(2nd floor. U-Mehringdamm)*
☎ 692 36 00   📠 690 14 041
🖥 www.aha-berlin.de
Different events each month, call for informations.

Berlin –
different every hour.
stündlich neu.

Berlin
Berlin Tourismus Marketing GmbH

We'll arrange your stay in Berlin

Wir organisieren Ihren Berlinaufenthalt

Berlin Tourismus Marketing GmbH
Am Karlsbad 11 · D-10785 Berlin

Information Tel.: 0190-75 40 40
Reservierung Tel.: 030-25 00 25

Calls from abroad: Tel.: +49-1805-75 40 40
Fax: +49-(0)30-25 00 24 24

Fotos: © Doris Padalewski, Dominik Peter, Hanns Joosten, vision photos, Ray Vino – gaystockphotography

www.berlin-tourism.de

Germany | Berlin

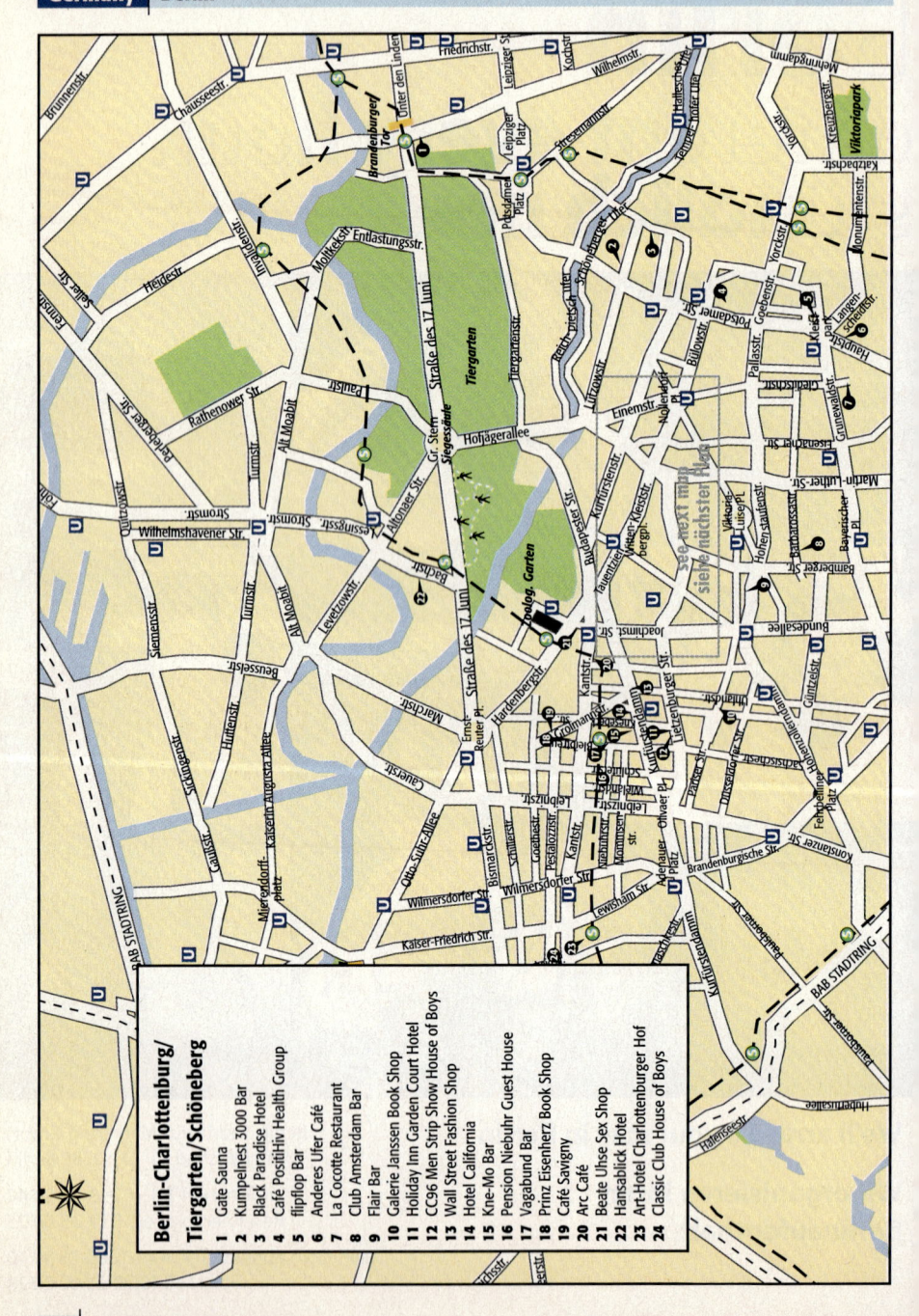

Berlin-Charlottenburg/ Tiergarten/Schöneberg

1. Gate Sauna
2. Kumpelnest 3000 Bar
3. Black Paradise Hotel
4. Café PositHiv Health Group
5. flipflop Bar
6. Anderes Ufer Café
7. La Cocotte Restaurant
8. Club Amsterdam Bar
9. Flair Bar
10. Galerie Janssen Book Shop
11. Holiday Inn Garden Court Hotel
12. CC96 Men Strip Show House of Boys
13. Wall Street Fashion Shop
14. Hotel California
15. Kne-Mo Bar
16. Pension Niebuhr Guest House
17. Vagabund Bar
18. Prinz Eisenherz Book Shop
19. Café Savigny
20. Arc Café
21. Beate Uhse Sex Shop
22. Hansablick Hotel
23. Art-Hotel Charlottenburger Hof
24. Classic Club House of Boys

366 SPARTACUS 2001/2002

Berlin | Germany

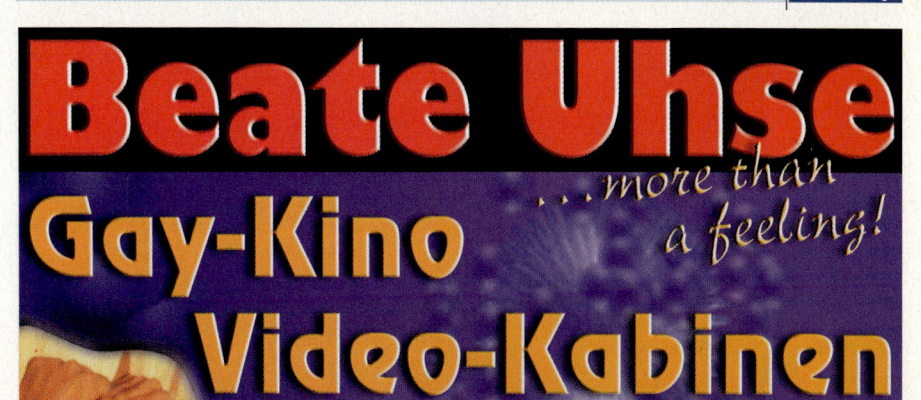

Beate Uhse

...more than a feeling!

Gay-Kino
Video-Kabinen

Täglich von
9h - 24h

Internationale Spitzenfilme

Ständiger Programm-Wechsel

Kinotage
Sonntag und Dienstag
4 Kinos – 1 Preis
11,00 DM
inclusive Getränk!

Berlin · Joachimstaler Str. 4/Ecke Kantstr.

Germany | Berlin

FRENCH LOVER GALLERY
WWW.JNRCPRODUCTION.COM
The Best in France
VIDEO / DVD

■ **Mann-O-Meter e.V.** Berlins schwules Info- und Beratungszentrum (A b G MA) Mon-Fri 17-22, Sat Sun 16-22 h
Motzstraße 5 ✉ 10777 *(U-Nollendorfplatz)* ☎ 216 80 08
☎ 216 33 36 (emergency call) 🖶 215 70 78
🖥 www.mann-o-meter.de
Emergency call/Schwules Überfalltelefon. Health service and help with problems (HIV/AIDS). Also Coffee Shop. Psychologische Beratung, Info+Beratung zu HIV/AIDS. Jugendgruppe.

■ **Sonntags-Club e.V.** (A d GLM MA OS S TV VS) 17-24 h
Greifenhagener Straße 28 ✉ 10437 *(U/S-Schönhauser Allee)*
☎ 449 75 90 🖶 448 54 57
🖥 www.sonntags-club.de
Counselling and information center where parties and exhibitions are held on a regular basis.

SIEGESSÄULE

fon: 030-23 55 39 0
fax: 030-23 55 39 19
e-mail: siegessaeule@berlin.de

Berlin im Blick

Europas größtes schwullesbisches Stadtmagazin
überall in der Berliner Szene und im Internet

www.siegessaeule.de

Berlin | Germany

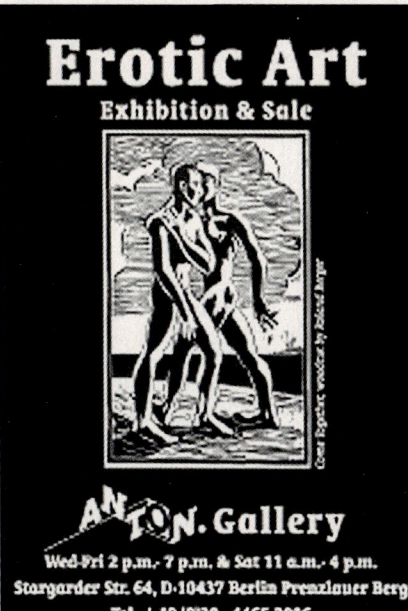

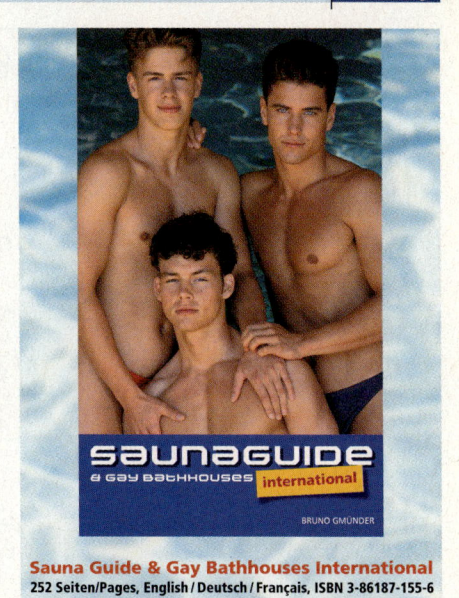

PUBLICATIONS

■ **Berlin von hinten**
c/o Bruno Gmünder Verlag, PO Box 61 01 04 ✉ 10837
☎ 615 00 342 📠 615 91 34
✉ info@spartacus.de
🖳 www.brunos.de
The city guide book about Berlin. Useful general information and lots of addresses with extensive descriptions in English and German. Up-to-date maps. Erotic photos.

■ **Gayinfo Berlin**
Treskowallee 23, Postfach 16 ✉ 10318 ☎ 211 05 80
☎ (0177) 416 47 67 🖳 www.gayinfo.de
Monthly booklet listing all gay and gay-friendly establishments in Berlin. Free at gay venues.

■ **Sergej**
Sergej Medien- und Verlags-GmbH, Kopenhagener Straße 14
✉ 10437 ☎ 44 31 98-0 📠 44 31 98 77
🖳 www.sergej.de
Monthly city gay magazine available for free at gay venues.

■ **Siegessäule** Mon-Fri 10-17 h
c/o Jackwerth Verlag, Kulmerstraße 20a ✉ 10783 *(U7-Kleistpark)*
☎ 23 55 39-0 📠 23 55 39-19
🖳 www.siegessaeule.de
Free monthly gay-lesbian magazine for Berlin featuring news and events.

CULTURE

■ **Anton. Galerie für zimmerfähige Kunst** (A) Wed-Fri 14-19, Sat 11-16 h
Stargader Strasse 64 ✉ 10437 *(U-Schönhauser Allee)*
☎ 44 65 30 06
Art gallery focusing on erotic art: exhibitions and sale.

Germany | Berlin

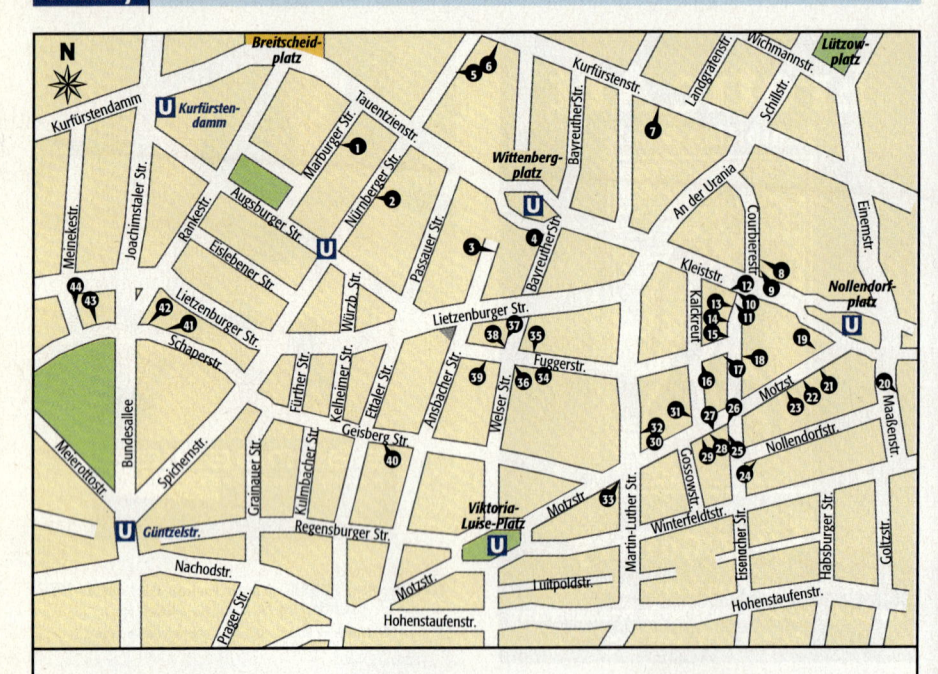

Berlin-Schöneberg Nord

1. Chez Nous Show
2. Bruno's Book Shop
3. Andreas Kneipe Bar
4. Comfort Hotel Auberge
5. Crowne Plaza Hotel
6. Apollo City-Sauna
7. Steam Sauna-Club
8. Playground Sex Shop
9. Movie Bar
10. New Action Men's Club
11. Spot Bar
12. Kleist-Casino Danceclub
13. Lenz... die Bar
14. Blue Boy Bar
15. Fugger-Eck Bar
16. Man's Pleasure Chest
17. Tabasco Bar
18. E116 Bar
19. Omnes Restaurant
20. Café Berio
21. EX! Bar
22. Mann-O-Meter Gay Info
23. Sachsenhof Hotel
24. Mister B Leather & Fetish Shop
25. Tom's House Guest House
26. Tom's Bar Men's Club
27. Hafen bar
28. The Jaxx Club Men's Club
29. Scheune Men's Club
30. Lukiluki Restaurant
31. Pussy-Cat Bar
32. Berlin Connection Café
33. Windows Bar
34. Prinz Knecht Bar
35. City Men Sex Shop
36. Connection Danceclub / Art Connection Hotel / Connection Garage Sex Shop
37. Dreizehn Bar
38. Knast Men's Club
39. Memory's Bar
40. Arco Hotel
41. Pool Berlin Sex Shop
42. Harlekin Bar
43. Kleine Philharmonie Bar
44. Berliner AIDS-Hilfe Health Group

■ **galerie katze 5** (A glm s) Mon-Fri 16-20, Sat 10-16 h
Katzbachstraße 5 ✉ 10965 (U-/S-Yorckstraße, next door to "LSVD")
☎ 78 89 75 51 📠 78 89 75 49
Gay and lesbian artists works often exhibited.

■ **Lesbisch-Schwules Pressearchiv** Mon 19-20 h and by appointment
Mehringdamm 61 ✉ 10961 (U-Mehringdamm, entrance 1st courtyard/Eingang 1. Hof) ☎ 69 24 17 23 🖥 Lesbisch-Schwule-presseschau@t-online 💻 www.lesbische-schwule-presseschau.de

■ **Lila Archiv e.V.** (GLM) by appointment
Choriner Straße 9 ✉ 10119 ☎ 44 85 713 📠 449 22 89
📠 44 85 713 🖥 LilaArchiv@tpp24.net
Gay archives.

■ **Schwules Museum** (! GLM) 14-18, Sat -19 h, Tue closed, Sat 17 h guided tour
Mehringdamm 61 ✉ 10961 (U-Mehringdamm) ☎ 693 11 72
📠 693 40 37 🖥 schwulesmuseum@aol.com
💻 www.schwulesmuseum.de
Exhibitions change on a regular basis. "Capri" is the name of their magazine.

TOURIST INFO

■ **Berlin Tourismus Marketing GmbH**
Am Karlsbad 11 ✉ 10785 ☎ 25 00 25 (reservation)
☎ (0190) 75 40 40 (information) 📠 25 00 24 24
💻 www.berlin-tourism.de

Berlin | Germany

BESENKAMMER BAR
am Alex
Rathausstr. 1
durchgehend geöffnet
Tel. 242 40 83

*Man(n) fühlt sich wohl...
...täglich rund um
die Uhr geöffnet*

BARS

■ **Aah-Haa** (B BF f GLM s OS YG) 17-2 h
Donaustraße 112 ✉ 12043 *(U-Rathaus Neukölln/Hermannplatz)*
☎ 61 30 44 93

■ **Ad Libitum** (B GLM MA OS) 17-5 h
Simon-Dach-Straße 36 ✉ 10245 *(U5-Samariterstraße)*
☎ 29 00 08 72

■ **Adonis** (B BF d f DR G N OS P r S VS) 0-24 h
Pappelallee 32a ✉ 10437 *(S/U-Schönhauser Allee)*
☎ 447 98 88

■ **Altberliner Bierstuben** (B F G lj MA N OS) 12-2 h
Saarbrücker Straße 17 ✉ 10405 *(U8-Senefelder Platz)*
☎ 442 61 30

■ **Amsterdam Café, Restaurant & Pension** (AC B F glm H OS TV YG) Mon-Sat 16-6, Sun 14-6 h
Gleimstraße 24 ✉ 10437 *(U/S-Schönhauser Allee,opposite cinemaxx)*
☎ 44 00 94 54
Café with accommodation available. Daily BF buffet.

■ **Andreas' Kneipe** (! B G lj MA) Sun-Thu 11-3, Fri/Sat 11-4 h
Ansbacher Straße 29 ✉ 10789 *(U-Wittenbergplatz)*
☎ 218 32 57
Popular pub.

■ **Bärenhöhle** (B G lj) 16-2 h
Schönhauser Allee 90 ✉ 10439 *(U-Schönhauser Allee)*
☎ 44 73 65 53
Bar for bears and their friends.

CONNECTION
Club Berlin Fr. & Sa. ab 23 Uhr

GARAGE - SHOP - MOVIE
Leder · Gummi · Toys · Magazine · Piercing · Videos
Mo - Sa 10-1 Uhr · So + Feiertag 14-1 Uhr · Fon 2 18 14 32
www.gayonlinesexshop.de

PRINZKNECHT MÄNNERKNEIPE
Tel.: 23 62 74 44 von 15-3 Uhr

ART HOTEL CONNECTION
"XS66" · Room with open Bath, Cages an more ...
a well packed suitcase with useful tools on request. www.sub-mission.com
16 individually · designed rooms all with TV-VCR, Radio, Minibar, Phone,
Hair dryer an Shower. Located in a old historic building right in the heart
of the city Visit us on www.arthotel-connection.de
Private Appartmen · Livinroom, Bedroom, private Bath and Kitchen,
Hifi, TV-VCR, Minibar, Own key and Entrance

ART HOTEL Connection
030 217 70 28
Phone: +4930/2 17 70 28
Fax: +4930/2 17 70 30

FUGGERSTRASSE 33 · 10777 BERLIN IN SCHÖNEBERG
U-BHF. WITTENBERGPLATZ

Germany | **Berlin**

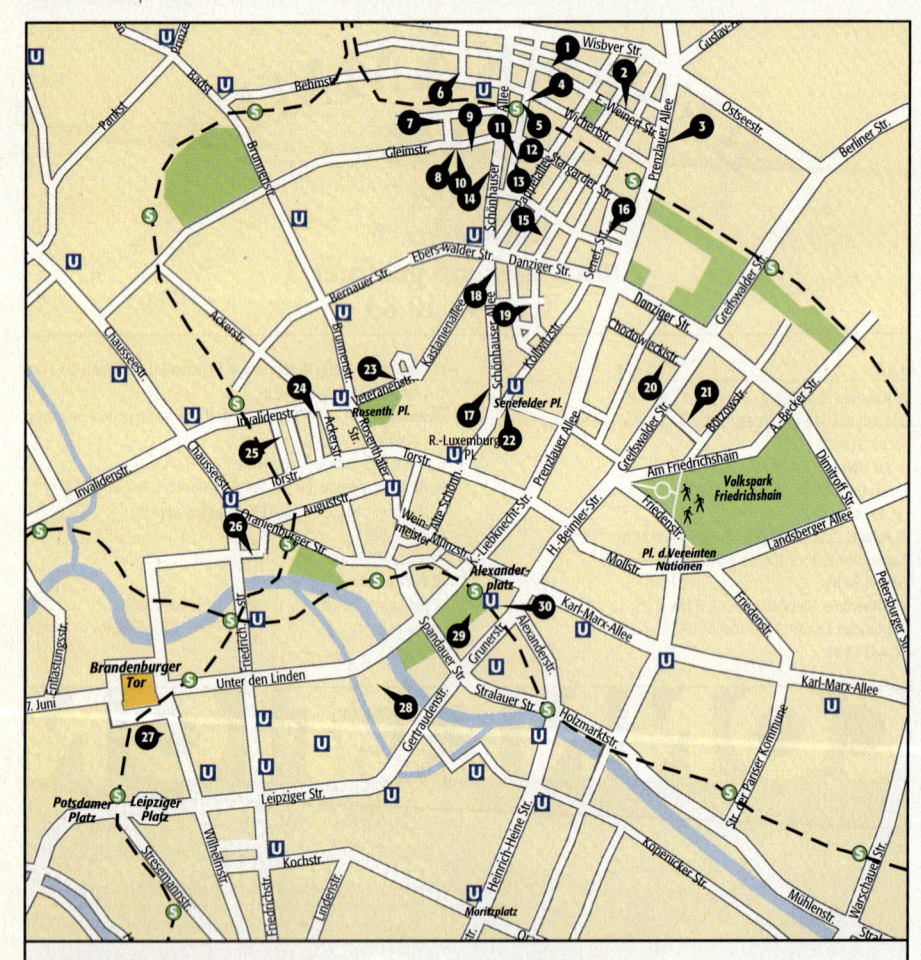

Berlin-Mitte/Prenzlauer Berg

1. Darkroom Men's Club
2. Stiller Don Bar
3. Holiday Inn Hotel
4. Greifbar Men's Club
5. Oxonmagenta Restaurant
6. Black Style Leather & Fetish Shop
7. Sonntags-Club Gay Info
8. Schall & Rauch Bar, Restaurant & Guest House
9. Adam Book Shop
10. Amsterdam Bar, Restaurant & Guest House
11. Guppi Bar
12. Romeo Nachtbar
13. Pick Ab Men's Club
14. Treibhaus Sauna
15. Bad Boy'z Sex Shop
16. Offenbach Stuben Restaurant
17. Transmoderne Narcissen Show
18. Schoppenstube Bar
19. November Bar
20. Flax Bar
21. Sonderbar
22. Altberliner Bierstuben Bar
23. Kapelle Bar
24. Ackerkeller Danceclub
25. Le Moustache Bar & Guest House
26. GMF Gay Tea Dance
27. Gate Sauna
28. BKA Luftschloß Show
29. Oh-ase Bar
30. Besenkammer Bar

372 SPARTACUS 2001/2002

Der **Forever-young-Fitness**-Urlaub

Bewegung hat's in sich. Sie hält jung und setzt Endorphine frei. Glückshormone, die Geist und Körper beflügeln. Wer das neue Körperglück erleben will, bucht am besten Aktivurlaub. Im Club oder bei Veranstaltern mit tollen Sportangeboten. Wenn Sie gerne etwas für den Waschbrettbauch, Muskelaufbau oder die allgemeine Fitness tun möchten, wir beraten Sie gern. Über Urlaub mit Action, Erholung und guter Laune. Besuchen Sie uns. Wir haben super Tipps für Reisen, die in die Beine gehen.
Buchen Sie direkt unter (0 30) 88 75 33 75.

Mein Travel Lounge Lufthansa City Center **Reisebüro**

Hier buchen Sie alles!

Kurfürstendamm 21, am neuen Kranzler Eck, 10719 Berlin, Tel. (0 30) 88 75 38 00, Fax (0 30) 88 75 38 12, Email: info@lccberlin.de

Berlin-Kreuzberg/Friedrichshain/Neukölln

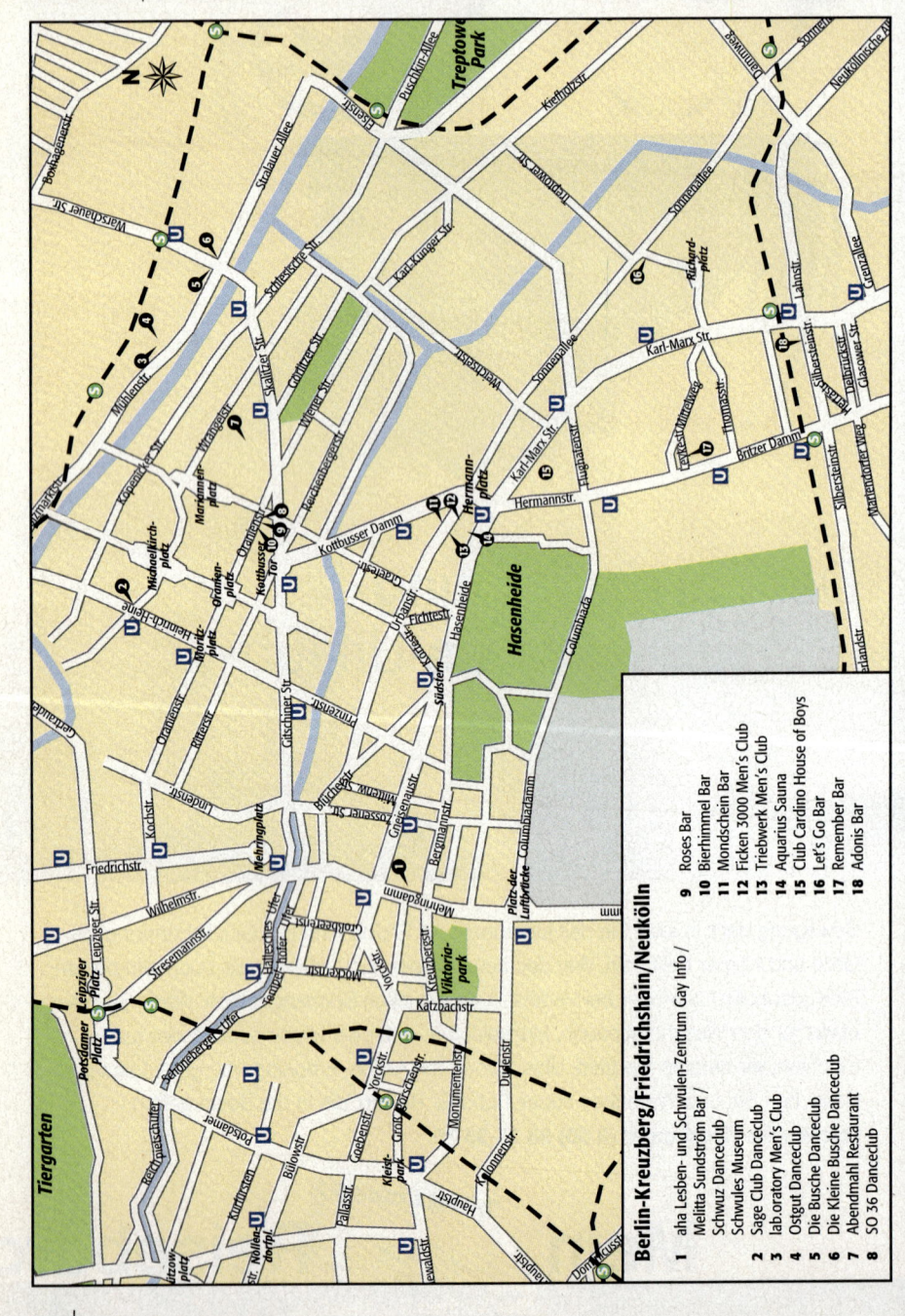

1. aha Lesben- und Schwulen-Zentrum Gay Info /
   Melitta Sundström Bar /
   Schwuz Danceclub /
   Schwules Museum
2. Sage Club Danceclub
3. lab.oratory Men's Club
4. Ostgut Danceclub
5. Die Busche Danceclub
6. Die Kleine Busche Danceclub
7. Abendmahl Restaurant
8. SO 36 Danceclub
9. Roses Bar
10. Bierhimmel Bar
11. Mondschein Bar
12. Ficken 3000 Men's Club
13. Triebwerk Men's Club
14. Aquarius Sauna
15. Club Cardino House of Boys
16. Let's Go Bar
17. Remember Bar
18. Adonis Bar

Berlin | Germany

SAGE
CLUB BERLIN

3 Floors - 4 Bars - 2 VIP Lounges - Pool Area - Limousine Service

Saturdays 11pm
House Expressions
express yourself to the most stylish housesounds.

Sundays 11pm
Niteclub
drags, fags, guys & dolls - for gays and friends.

Sage Club
Köpenicker Straße 76
10179 Berlin - Mitte
(U8 Heinrich-Heine - Straße)

Contact
phone/fax 0049(0)30-2 789 83-0/-20
net: www.sage-club.de
mail: office@sage-club.de

Germany | Berlin

SpartacusWorld.com

► click and ► win!

www.spartacusworld.com

■ **Besenkammer** (B f G MA) 0-24 h
Rathausstraße 1 ✉ 10178 *(U/S-Alexanderplatz under the S-Bahn bridge)* ☎ 242 40 83
■ **Bierhimmel** (B f glm YG) 14-3 h
Oranienstraße 183 ✉ 10999 *(U-Kottbusser Tor)* ☎ 615 31 22
■ **Blue Boy Bar** (B BF f Glm MA p R VS) 0-24 h
Eisenacher Straße 3a ✉ 10777 *(U-Nollendorfplatz, Bus119/N19)* ☎ 218 74 98
Rent bar, best after 3 h.
■ **Blühende Landschaften** (B GLM) Mon-Fri 14-? Sat Sun 17-? h
Samariterstrasse 29 ✉ 10247 *(Friedrichshain)* ☎ 420 137 83
■ **Club Amsterdam** (B G MA og) 19-3 h, Sun closed
Barbarossastraße 38 ✉ 10779 *(U-Güntzelstraße)* ☎ 213 32 32
■ **Club Trommel** (AC B D GLM lj MA N p s TV WE) 21-? h, closed Tue
Thomasstraße 53 ✉ 12055 *(U-Leinestraße)* ☎ 686 73 45
Around for over 26 years - the oldest gay bar in Neuköln
■ **Dreizehn** (B G N OS) 17-5 h
Welserstraße 27 ✉ 10777 *(U-Wittenbergplatz)* ☎ 218 23 63

■ **Eulenspiegel Bar & Pension** (B d G MA p s) 19-3 h
Ebersstraße 58 ✉ 10827 *(S/U-Innsbrucker Platz)* ☎ 782 38 89
Also accomodation
■ **E116** (AC B G MA N OS r) 20-2 h
Eisenacher Straße 116 ✉ 10777 *(U1/2-Nollendorfplatz)* ☎ 217 05 18
■ **Flair** (B f g MA N OS) 6-5 h
Nachodstraße 5, ✉ 10779 *(Eingang/entrance Grainauer Straße)*
■ **Flash** (AC B BF DR G OS R) Mon-Sun 13-7 h
Schönhauser Allee 147a ✉ 10435 *(U2-Eberswalderstraße)*
☎ (0179) 613 72 86
■ **Flax** (AC f B BF GLM OS s) Mon-Fri 17-3, Sat 15-5, Sun 10-3 h
Chodowieckistraße 41 ✉ 10405 *(Prenzlauer Berg, tram Danziger/Greifswalderstr.)* ☎ 44 04 69 88
■ **Fledermaus** (B d G MA N s vs) 12-4, Fri Sat -6 h
Joachimsthaler Straße 14-19 ✉ 10719 *(U-Kurfürstendamm)*
☎ 292 11 36
■ **flipflop** (B f G MA N) 19-2/? h
Kulmer Straße 20a ✉ 10783 *(U-Kleistpark/S/U-Yorckstraße)*
☎ 216 28 25

GAY EAST!
EAST BERLIN HIGHLIGHTS

Berlin | Germany

PEACH CAFÉ·BAR
Thaerstr. 39 · daily 6p.m.-5a.m. · tel. 4202 8531 · Sun brunch 10a.m.
Safer Sex Party every last Sat. of the month 10p.m.

bar café ad libitum
tägl. 17-5 uhr · tel. 29 00 08 72
simon-dach-str. 36

Pickab!
Gay-Bar · Video · Dark-Room
Greifenhagener Str. 16 · 10pm - 6am, 030/4458523

Greifbar — men movies cruising
Wichertstr. 10
at the corner of Greifenhagener Str.
daily 10 pm-6 am · tel. 030/444 08 28

Treibhaus
Schönhauser Allee 132
Monday to Tuesday
from Friday 3 p.m. to Monday
Mon drinks at super prices

Sauna
phone 030 - 448 45 03
3 p.m. - 7 a.m. and
7 a.m. open all weekend
Tue, Wed, Thu: saunaday

SCHALL UND RAUCH
BAR · RESTAURANT · PENSION
GLEIMSTRASSE 23 · 10437 BERLIN
TÄGL: 9 BIS 3 UHR · 030 - 4433970
www.schall-und-rauch-berlin.de

Bar HT Café
Mon-Sun
5 p.m. - 2 a.m.
Kopernikusstraße 23
Tel. 030/29004965

The cheapest accom. in Mitte, 10min from Brandenburg Gate
PENSION & BAR le Moustache
D - 10115 Berlin-Mitte, Gartenstr. 4, Call 030-2817277
www.lemoustache.de · e-mail: pension@lemoustache.de

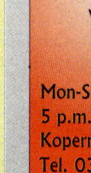

Blühende Landschaften
(Blooming Landscapes)
Bar opens at 2 p.m.
Samariterstr. 29, Friedrichshain

OFFENBAR
Lounge · Cocktails · Weekend Brunch
426-0930
Schreinerstr. 5
U-Bhf Samariterstr.
party & events:
kostl. nutzung unserer räume

ROMEO Gay-Nightbar
Greifenhagener Str.16 · from 11p.m., 4476789

Young? Gay? FLAX!
seating for 70 people inside, for 40 outside
Come in and have some fun with us!
Café Bistro Bar
Chodowieckistraße 41 · Berlin · Call [030] 440 46 988

SPARTACUS 2001/2002 | 377

Germany Berlin

SCHALL UND RAUCH
BAR · RESTAURANT · PENSION · CATERING

GLEIMSTRASSE 23 · 10437 BERLIN / P.BERG
TEL: +49 (0) 30 - 44 33 97 -0
FAX: +49 (0) 30 - 44 33 97 22
e-mail: schall.und.rauch.berlin@talknet.de
http://www.schall-und-rauch-berlin.de

HAFEN BAR
MOTZSTR 19 BERLIN
www.hafen-berlin.de

- **Fugger-Eck** (AC B d f GLM lj MA N OS s) 13-5 h
  Eisenacher Straße 3a, ✉ 10777 (U1/15/12/2/4-Nollendorfplatz)
  ☎ 218 35 06
- **Hafen** (! G s TV YG) 21-?, winter 20- h
  Motzstraße 19 ✉ 10777 (U-Nollendorfplatz) ☎ 211 41 18
  Trendy and popular.
- **Harlekin** (B f G MA N OS) 16-?, Sun 14-? h
  Schaperstraße 12-13 ✉ 10719 (U9-Spichernstraße) ☎ 218 25 79
- **HT** (B) 17-2 h
  Kopernikusstraße 23 (S/U- Warschauer Str.)
  ☎ 29 00 49 65
- **Irrtum** (B G)
  Gabelsbergerstrasse 6 ✉ 10247 ☎ 4201 8000
- **Kapelle** (B BF glm MA) 10-3, WE 10-3/? h
  Zionskirchplatz 22-24 ✉ 10119
- **Kleine Philharmonie** (B G MA N) 18 -?
  Schaperstraße 14 ✉ 10719 (U-Spichernstraße) ☎ 883 11 02
- **Kne-Mo** (B d E f g MA N OS) 15-6 h, Sun closed
  Knesebeckstraße 35 ✉ 10623 (S-Savignyplatz)
  ☎ 883 45 47
- **Kumpelnest 3000** (B d glm MA STV) 17-5 h, weekend open end
  Lützowstraße 23/Potsdamer Straße ✉ 10785 (U-Kurfürstenstraße)
  ☎ 261 69 18
  Very popular on WE, not very gay then. Sun special fuck Barbie night.
- **Lenz...die Bar** (AC B CC G MA OS) 20-? h
  Eisenacher Straße 3 ✉ 10777 ☎ 217 78 20
  Cocktail bar.
- **Let's go** (B f G MA N R) 18-1, Fri Sat -3 h
  Hertzbergstraße 22 ✉ 12055 (U-Karl-Marx-Strasse) ☎ 687 09 34

- **Memory's** (B d F g lj MA OS) 16-? h
  Fuggerstraße 37 ✉ 10777 (U1/15/12/2-Wittenbergplatz)
  ☎ 213 52 71
- **Moustache. Le** (B d DR F G MA s) 20-3/? h, Mon closed
  Gartenstraße 4 ✉ 10115 (U-Oranienburger Tor/Rosenthaler Platz, S-Nordbahnhof) ☎ 281 72 77
- **Movie** (B GLM)
  Courbierstrasse 1 ✉ 10787
- **Neuer Oldtimer** (B G MA) 14-3 h
  Lietzenburger Straße 12 ✉ 10789 (U-Wittenbergplatz)
  ☎ 23 62 03 54
- **November** (a B BF F glm OS WE YG) 10-h ?
  Husemannstraße 15 ✉ 10435 (Prenzlauer Berg, near Kollwitzplatz)
  ☎ 442 84 25
  Brunch Sat, Sun & before public holidays.
- **Offenbar** (B BF G MA OS) 10-2, bf -16 h
  Schreinerstraße 5 ✉ 10247 (U-Samariterstraße)
  ☎ 426 09 30
- **Oh-ase** (B f Glm MA N OS) Mon-Sat 10-2/?, Sun 14-2/? h
  Rathausstraße 5 ✉ 10178 (U/S-Alexanderplatz) ☎ 242 30 30
- **Pinocchio / Boybar** (B G)
  Fuggerstr. 3 ✉ 10777 ☎ 218 57 36
- **Ponyclub**
  Kopernikusstrasse 13 ✉ 10245 ☎ 29 00 32 61
- **Pour Elle** (B d gLM p OS YG) 19-5, Fri Sat 21-5 h
  Kalckreuthstraße 10 ✉ 10777 (U-Nollendorfplatz) ☎ 218 75 33
- **Prinz Knecht** (! B d DR f GLM lj MA OS VS) 15-3 h
  Fuggerstraße 33 ✉ 10777 (U-Wittenbergplatz) ☎ 23 62 74 44
- **Pussy-Cat** (B d f GLM N OS p TV) 18-6 h, Tue closed
  Kalckreuthstraße 7, ✉ 10777 (U-Nollendorfplatz) ☎ 213 35 86

Remember (B G MA N) 14-1 h
Leykestrasse 18 ✉ 12053 (U-Leinestrasse) ☎ 62 70 51 83
Riviera (B G MA N)
Glasower Straße 51 ✉ 12051
Romeo Nachtbar (B f G MA) 23-? h
Greifenhagener Straße 16 ✉ 10437 (S/U-Schönhauser Allee)
☎ 447 67 89
Roses (! B GLM MA TV) 21.30-5/? h
Oranienstraße 187 ✉ 10999 (U-Kottbusser Tor) ☎ 615 65 70
Popular and trashy, best after midnight.
Schall & Rauch-Bar, Restaurant & Pension (! AC B BF F GLM H MA OS YG) Mon-Sat 10-3, Sun 9-3 h
Gleimstraße 23 ✉ 10437 (U/S-Schönhauser Allee) ☎ 44 33 97-0
Schoppenstube (B D DR f G MA OS p s) 22-? h
Schönhauser Allee 44 ✉ 10435 (U-Eberswalder Straße)
☎ 442 82 04
The oldest gay bar in the east part of Berlin.
Sonderbar (B d f GLM MA OS) 20-8 (in summer from 18 h)
Käthe-Niederkirchner-Straße 34 ✉ 10407 (Near/Nähe "Märchenbrunnen") ☎ 42 80 64 25
Spot (B CC f GLM MA OS s) Mon-Fri 16-4, Sat Sun -? h, winter 18-open end
Eisenacher Straße 2 ✉ 10777 (U-Nollendorfplatz) ☎ 213 22 67
Stiller Don (! A B f GLM lj MA OS) 19-? h
Erich-Weinert-Straße 67 ✉ 10439 (S/U-Schönhauser Allee)
☎ 445 59 57
Popular and friendly.
Stonewall (B GLM OS p) 16-2? h
Otto-Suhr-Allee 125 ✉ 10585 (U-Richard-Wagner-Platz)
☎ 347 055 30
Summergarden

LENZ
■■■ DIE BAR

Cocktails and more

ab 20 Uhr

www.lenzdiebar.de

Eisenacher Str. 3
10777 Berlin
Telefon (0 30) 2 17 78 20

NOVEMBER

Husemannstraße 15
10435 Berlin-Prenzlauer Berg
(030) 442 84 25

seit 1993

Täglich ab 10 Uhr Frühstück
Wechselnde Abendkarte
Samstags · Sonntags · Feiertags
Frühstücksbuffet

---

café · bar · weekend club
freitag & samstag dj

GUPPI

gleimstraße 31 (am colosseum)
10437 berlin-prenzlauer berg
fon 030 437 396 11
mo-fr ab 15 uhr geöffnet
Sa/So ab 11 uhr frühstück

Germany | Berlin

APPETIZER
FICKEN 3000
urbanstrasse 70 • berlin-kreuzberg

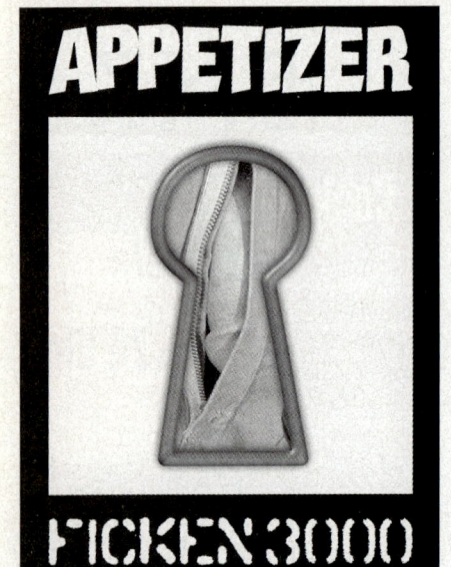

■ **Tabasco** (AC B f G MA p R) 18-6 ?, Fri 18-Mon 6 h, 24h on public holidays
Fuggerstraße 3 ✉ 10777 (U-Nollendorfplatz) ☎ 214 26 36
Well established rent bar.
■ **Toni's** (AC B d f GLM MA N OS) 16-1, Fri Sat -? h, closed Tue
Mecklenburgische Straße 20 ✉ 10713 (U-Heidelberger Platz)
☎ 824 25 45
■ **Treppen Haus** (B F G MA) 19-4/? h
Kollwitzstrasse 89 ☎ 44 05 71 74
■ **Trick** (B GLM MA OS p S STV) 22-6 h
Kleine Präsidentenstr. 3 ✉ 10178 (S/tram-Hackescher Markt)
☎ 280 97 811
■ **Vagabund** (B d G MA OS p) 17-? h
Knesebeckstraße 77 ✉ 10623 (U-Uhlandstraße) ☎ 881 15 06
Very late bar.
■ **Villi's** (B G MA) 17-? h
Greifenhagener Strasse 45 ✉ 19439 (U/S-Schönhauser Allee)
☎ 44 71 90 81
New (2000) beer bar.
■ **Windows Café-Bar-Bistro** (B F GLM MA OS) 14-4 h
Martin-Luther-Straße 22 ✉ 10777 ☎ 214 23 94
Low priced meals.
■ **Zandvoort** (B D G N p s) Mon-Sat 20-? h, closed Sun
Friedrich-Karl-Straße 15 ✉ 12103 (U-Ullsteinstraße) ☎ 752 20 77
■ **808 BarLounge** (B glm) Mon-Fri18-2, Sat Sun 10-3 h
Oranienburger Strasse 42/43 ✉ 10117 (S-Oranienburger Straße)
☎ 28 04 67 27
american cocktail bar

MEN'S CLUBS

■ **Böse Buben e.V.** (B G LJ MA P) Wed 20-22, Fri Sat admittance 21-22h only
Lichtenrader Straße 2 ✉ 12279 (U8-Leinestraße, 2 yard, 1st floor)

☎ 62 70 16 10
S/M, spanking, fetish parties.
■ **Club Culture Houze** (AC B d f G lj MA p VS)
Görlitzer Straße 71 ✉ 10997 (U1-Görlitzer Park) ☎ 61 70 96 69
Bar on 2 floors with video-room, playground and shower. Special event parties: -Mon 19-4 h Naked Sex Party (G) -Wed 20-4 h Adam&Eve (mixed) -Thu 20-4 h SM + Fetish Club (mixed) -Fri 20-5 h Naked Fist Factory (G) -Sat 22-8 h Gay Party -Sun 17-4 h Couple Club (mixed)
■ **Club XS** (B D DR G MA) Thu (G) 23-? h
Glogauer Straße 2 ✉ 10999
Bottoms Up: Gay-dance party.
■ **Crisco** (B DR G LJ) Tue-Thu 21-3, Fri-Sun -5 h
Nollendorfstraße 27 ✉ 10777 (U-Nollendorfplatz) ☎ 21 75 62 82
Strict dresscode: uniform, leather, rubber,...
■ **Darkroom** (B DR G LJ MA) 22-6 h
Rodenbergstraße 23 ✉ 10439 (U/S-Schönhauser Allee)
☎ 444 93 21
■ **Ficken 3000** (d DR G lj MA p tv VS) Mon-Sun 22-? h
Urbanstraße 70 ✉ 10967 (U-Hermannplatz) ☎ 69 50 73 35
■ **Greifbar** (AC B DR G MA p VS) 22-6 h
Wichertstraße 10/Ecke Greifenhagener ✉ 10439 (S/U-Schönhauser Allee) ☎ 444 08 28
■ **Jaxx Club. The** (AC CC DR G VS YG) Mon-Sat 12-3, Sun 13-3 h
Motzstraße 19 ✉ 10777 (U-Nollendorfplatz)
☎ 213 81 03
Popular, especially Tue & WE.
■ **Kit Kat Club** (b D G MA LJ NU) Thu & Sun
c/o Metropol, Nollendorfplatz 5 ✉ 10777 (entrance on the right of the Metropol) ☎ 21 73 68 41
Thu 20 h Soirée nudisme (NU) then 23 h Sexual Danceparty: Sodom & Gomorrha, Sun 21 h naked sex party.
■ **Knast** (AC B DR G LJ MG VS WE) 21-5 h
Fuggerstraße 34/Welserstraße ✉ 10777
 (U-Wittenbergplatz) ☎ 218 10 26
Jail decore.
■ **lab.oratory** (B DR G) Fri & Sat
Mühlenstrasse 26-30 ✉ 10249
*Look out for flyers and special announcements.
Also "Snax-Club" (LJ). The times are irregular.*
■ **Mondschein** (B DR f G LJ MA N) 20-3, Fri Sat -5; Safer Sex Party 2nd & 4th Sun admission 20-22 h
Urbanstraße 101 ✉ 10967 (U-Hermannplatz) ☎ 693 23 55
Home of the "Berlin Leder und Fetisch e.V."
■ **New Action** (! B DR G LJ MA p VS) Mon-Sat 20-?, Sun 13-? h
Kleiststraße 35/Eisenacherstraße ✉ 10787 (U-Nollendorfplatz)
☎ 211 82 56
Very cruisy, best daily after 1 h.
■ **Pick ab!** (B DR G p VS) 22-6 h
Greifenhagener Straße 16 ✉ 10437 (S/U-Schönhauser Allee)
☎ 445 85 23
■ **Scheune** (B DR G LJ MA p VS) 21-7, Fri Sat -9, Naked Sex Party Sun 17.30-21, Rubber Party last Fri 21-2 h
Motzstraße 25 ✉ 10777 (U-Nollendorfplatz) ☎ 213 85 80
Best after midnight.
■ **Stahlrohr** (B DR G lj MA p VS) 20-6 h
Greifenhagener Straße 54 ✉ 10437 (U-Schönhauserallee)
☎ 447 327 47
■ **Tom's Bar** (! B DR G lj MA) 22-6, Fri Sat -? h
Motzstraße 19 ✉ 10777 (U-Nollendorfplatz) ☎ 213 45 70
Very cruisy. Popular Mon (2-4-1). Happy hour daily 22-24 h, Mon all night long.
■ **Triebwerk** (B DR G lj MA N p VS) 22-? h
Urbanstraße 64 ✉ 10967 (U-Hermannplatz) ☎ 69 50 52 03
Tue +Fri Safer Sex Party, Mon 2-4-1.

Berlin | Germany

for successful cruising

Bodies · **Happy Hour** · **Live DJ** · **Darkroom**

TOM'S
http://www.tomsbar.de

Motzstr. 19 · Berlin-Schöneberg · open from 10pm
Happy Hour daily from 10pm – 12pm · Monday all night long

CAFES

■ **Anderes Ufer** (B f GLM MA OS) 11-2 h
Hauptstraße 157 ✉ 10827 (U-Kleistpark) ☎ 78 70 38 00
One of the first openly gay café in Europe,
best in the afternoon and 22-24 h.

■ **Arc** (AC B BF CC F GLM MA OS) Summer 8-2, Winter 11-2 h
Fasanenstraße 81a ✉ 10623 (U/S-Zoologischer Garten/Bus149)
☎ 313 26 25
Café-bar-restaurant in S-Bahn arches.

■ **Café Berio** (BF f glm MA OS TV) 8-1 h
Maaßenstraße 7 ✉ 10777 (U-Nollendorfplatz)
☎ 216 19 46
Popular. Amazing 24h breakfast available.

■ **Berlin Connection Café & Bistro** (! B F G lj MA OS) 14-2 h
Martin-Luther-Straße 19 ✉ 10777
(U-Wittenbergplatz/Nollendorfplatz)
☎ 213 11 16
Good cakes and food at reasonable prices.

SPARTACUS 2001/2002 | 381

Germany Berlin

Advertisement:
Café Berio®
BREAKFAST · SNACKS · DRINKS
Maaßenstraße 8
10777 Berlin-Schöneberg
daily 8-1 h
☎ +49-30 216 19 46
info@berio.de · www.berio.de

■ **Café Savigny** (B BF f g OS) 9-2 h
Grolmanstraße 53/54, ✉ 10623 (S-Savignyplatz) ☎ 312 81 95
■ **EX!** (B GLM MA N OS) Mon-Sun 14-3 h
Motzstraße 5 ✉ 10777 (U-Nollendorfplatz) ☎ 23 63 91 87
■ **Guppi** (B bf d G MA s) Mon-Fri 15-?, Sat& Sun 11-? h
Gleimstraße 31 ✉ 10437 (U-Eberswalder Straße, at Colosseum)
☎ 43 73 96 11
■ **Melitta Sundström** (A B BF f D GLM MA OS TV) 10-4,
Sat 10-Sun 4h
Mehringdamm 61 ✉ 10961 (U-Mehringdamm) ☎ 692 44 14
Best on Sat. Also a gay bookstore.
■ **Peach** (B glm F) 18-5, Sun 10-5 h
Thaerstrasse 39 ✉ 102491 (Friedrichhain)

DANCECLUBS

■ **Ackerkeller** (B D G YG) Tue 22-2, Fri -4 h
Ackerstraße 12, Hinterhaus ✉ 10115 (U-Rosenthaler Platz/U-Oranienburger Tor) ☎ 280 72 16 h
Popular. Entrance Ackerstraße 13.

■ **Busche. Die** (D GLM MA OS s) Wed Sun 21.30-5, Fri Sat 22-6 h, closed Mon Tue Thu
Mühlenstraße 11-12 ✉ 10243 (S/U-Warschauer Straße. Opp. Berlin Wall/East Side Gallery) ☎ 296 08 00
Lots of young people hang around this popular large disco and drift to and from its small twin the "Kleine Busche".
■ **Chantal's House of Shame** (B D G STV YG) Thu 22-? h
c/o Dschungel Club, Dirckensenstraße 37 ✉ 10178 (S/U-Bahn-Hackescher Markt)
Trash drag shows & beautiful people.
■ **Connection** (! B D DR GLM lj MA) Fri Sat 23- open end
Fuggerstraße 33 ✉ 10777 (U-Wittenbergplatz) ☎ 218 14 32
Admission DM 12. Huge cruising area on three floors. Twilight Zone bar integrated in the cellar. ➪ Sex Shop/Blue Movie Connection Garage.
■ **GMF - Gay Tea Dance** (B D G OS p s TV) Sun 22-4 h
c/o WMF, Ziegelstrasse 22 ✉ 10117 (S/U-Friedrichstraße)
☎ 28 04 67 27
One of the most popular party in Berlin. Might shift location in summer 2001. Please call for infos.
■ **Kalkscheune & Basement** (b D GLM)
Johannisstrasse 2 ✉ 10117 ☎ 28 39 00 65
■ **Kleine Busche. Die** (b D GLM) Thu 21.30-5, Fri&Sat 24-9 h
Warschauer Platz ✉ 10245 ☎ 29 60 800
■ **Kleist-Casino-Berlin International** (B D f G MA OS s) Wed-Sun 21- ?, Fri Sat & Sun disco from 22-? h (winter), Thu-Sat 16-?, Fri Sat 22-? h (summer)
Kleiststrasse 35 ✉ 10787 (U-Wittenbergplatz) ☎ 236 219 76
Old fashioned suburban style disco.
■ **Ostgut** (B D DR g MA OS WE) Sat 24-? h
Mühlenstrasse 26-30 ✉ 10243 (U/S-Bahn-Warschauer Straße)
Techno temple in Berlin. 2nd Fri/month: Dance with the Aliens (GLM) 23-? h, Sat (irregular, check website or local press for dates): Snax Club (! G LJ S): fetish party.
■ **Sage Club** (b D glm YG tv) Thu-Sun 23-7 h (G mainly at weekends, not Thu&Fri)
Köpenicker Strasse 76 ✉ 10179 (U8-Heinrich-Heine-Str. corner Brückenstr.) ☎ 27 89 830
■ **SchwuZ** (! AC B D GLM MA S STV TV) Thu 22-?, Fri & Sat 23-? h
Mehringdamm 61 ✉ 10961 (U-Mehringdamm, entrance through café Sundström) ☎ 6950 7892
Newly renovated. Reasonable prices. Mixed crowd.
■ **SO 36** (! AC B D GLM lj MA S TV) Mon 23-?, Wed Sat 22-?, Sun 17-1 h (summer 19-1)
Oranienstraße 190 ✉ 10999 (U-Kottbusser Tor/Görlitzer Bahnhof)
☎ 61 40 13 06
Weekly parties: Mon "Electric Ballroom", Wed "Hungrige Herzen", Sun "Café Fatal". Monthly parties: "Gayhane" (homo-oriental dancefloor), 80ies parties,S oulparties, Bingo, Karaoke, Womens parties, concerts&shows. Call or see webside for details.

RESTAURANTS

■ **Abendmahl** (B F glm OS) 18-1, meals -23.30 h
Muskauer Straße 9 ✉ 10997 (U-Görlitzer Bahnhof) ☎ 612 51 70
Vegetarian and fish meals. Reservation recommended.
■ **Cocotte. La** (B F Glm OS YG) Wed-Mon 18-1 h
Vorbergstraße 10 ✉ 10823 (U-Eisenacher Straße) ☎ 78 95 76 58
French cuisine.
■ **Kern** (b BF CC F GLM) Daily from 10- ?
Fuggerstrasse 18 ✉ 10777 (U - Wittenbergplatz) ☎ 21 96 86 06
Brunch every Sun 10-16 h.
■ **Lukiluki** (AC CC F GLM TV) 18-2 h
Motzstraße 28 ✉ 10777 (U-Nollendorfplatz) ☎ 23 62 20 79
Be served from well-build topless waiters! Shows and special theme evenings make this restaurant unique in Berlin

Berlin | Germany

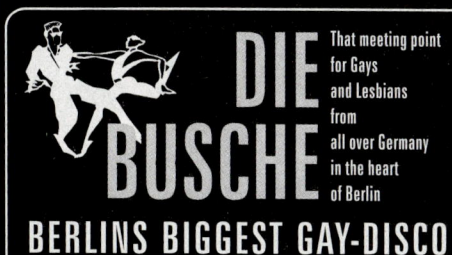

DIE BUSCHE
BERLINS BIGGEST GAY-DISCO

That meeting point for Gays and Lesbians from all over Germany in the heart of Berlin

Mühlenstr. 11-12
Friedrichshain
at Oberbaumbrücke
vis-a-vis
East-Side-Gallery
Wed & Sun 9.30pm - 5am
Fri 9.30pm - 6am
Sat 10pm - 6am

www.diebusche.de

DIE KLEINE BUSCHE
Mühlenstrasse .... 150m.
Warschauer Platz 18, Thu 9.30pm-5am, Fri & Sat 12pm-9am

---

charts — house — classics rock-indie

SchwuZ — **Berlin** — **Mehringdamm 61**

gay-lesbian Disco Club
Entrance thru Cafe Sundstroem
URL: www.schwuz.de
email: info@schwuz.de
call: +49 (0)30 6937025

Do. ab 22h / Thu 10 pm — **Queer** — Fr. & Sa. 23h / Fri. & Sat. 11 pm

lounge — retro — trash — shows

---

café restaurant **KERN**

Neue deutsche Küche. Modern German cuisine.
Frühstück ab 10 Uhr. Breakfast daily from 10 o'clock.
Großes Brunchbuffet jeden Sonntag von 10 bis 16 Uhr.
Brunchbuffet every Sunday from 10am till 4pm.

Open: 10 - ?   Fuggerstrasse 18 · 10777 Berlin · T: 030 - 21 96 86 06

LUKILUKI®
RESTAURANT

Motzstraße 28 · Berlin-Schöneberg · täglich 18-2 Uhr
Tel. 030 - 23 62 20 79 · www.lukiluki.de

Germany | **Berlin**

oxonmagenta

café/restaurant · vegetarian & fish · brunch every sunday

from 10 a.m. daily · www.oxon-magenta.de
greifenhagener str. 48 (prenzlauer berg) Ⓢ Ⓤ schönhauser allee · phone 4473 6482

■ **Offenbach-Stuben** (AC CC F glm) 18-? h
Stubbenkammerstraße 8 ✉ 10437 (S-Prenzlauer Allee/U2-Eberswalder Straße) ☎ 445 85 02
■ **Omnes** (B F GLM) 8-2 h
Motzstrasse 8 ✉ 10777 (U-Nollendorfplatz)
☎ 23 63 83 00
Sat & Sun and before public holidays 9-16 brunch.
■ **Oxonmagenta** (A BF CC F GLM OS) 10-? h
Greifenhagener Strasse 48 ✉ 10437 (S/U - Schönhauser Allee)
☎ 44 73 64 82
Vegetarian and fish meals. Brunch every Sun.
■ **Ribbeck. Zum** Täglich 16-1. warme Küche bis 0 h
Milastraße 4 ✉ 10437 ☎ 44 05 89 00
■ **Steffens** Mo-Fr 11-?h, Sa 17-?h, So & Feiertage ab 10-?h
Potsdamer Straße 131 ✉ 10783 ☎ 215 93 81
■ **Trattoria á Muntagnola** (F glm OS) 18-24 h
Fuggerstraße 27 ✉ 10777 (U-Wittenbergplatz)
☎ 211 66 42
Southern Italian cuisine.
■ **Truxa** (CC F glm MA) Mon-Fri 16-1, Sat Sun& public holidays 10-1 h
Wühlischstr. 30 ✉ 10245 (U/S- Warschauer Str, U-Frankfurter Tor)
☎ 29 00 30 85
Special offers: brunch Sat&Sun 10-16h, fondue

SHOWS

■ **BKA-Luftschloß** (BF d F glm MA OS S)
Shows: Wed-Sun 20-24, Parties: 23-5 h
Schloßplatz ✉ 10178 (S/U-Alexanderplatz. Near Palast der Republik)
☎ 202 20 07
Host of the Oz Party (GLM STV) every 3rd Sat/month.
■ **Chez Nous** (CC STV) Shows 20.30 and 23 h
Marburger Straße 14 ✉ 10789 (U-Wittenbergplatz) ☎ 213 18 10

■ **Transmoderne Narcissens** (B G MA STV) Thu 21-24 h
c/o Goldmund Lounge, Pfefferberg, Schönhauser Allee 178 ✉ 10119 (U2-Senefelderplatz, on the left side of the terrace)
Trash drag show in a tea-room atmosphere.

CINEMA

■ **MonGay @ International** (B GLM) Bar opens 21,
Film starts 22 h Mon only.
Kino International, Karl-Marx-Allee 33 ✉ 10178 (U-Schillingstrasse)
☎ 24 75 60 11
This gay lesbian cult cinema shows gay/lesbian films every Monday night. Often parties held here too.

SEX SHOPS/BLUE MOVIES

■ **Bad Boy'z** (CC G VS YG) Mon-Sat 13-1,
Sun & public holidays 15-1 h
Schliemannstraße 38 ✉ 10437 (U-Eberswalder Straße)
☎ 440 81 65
3rd Sat Safer Sex Party "Youngster's Gay Spartaciade" (check the press for dress code!) Well worth a visit !
■ **Beate Uhse Erotik Museum** (b f g VS)
Joachimsthaler Straße 4 ✉ 10623 (U-Zoologischer Garten)
■ **City Men Shop & Video** (CC G MA VS) Mon-Thu 11-1, Fri Sat -2, Sun 14-1 h
Fuggerstraße 26 ✉ 10777 ☎ 218 29 59
■ **Connection Garage** (CC G lj MA VS) Mon-Sat 10-1, Sun & public holidays 14-1 h
Fuggerstraße 33 ✉ 10777 (U-Wittenberplatz)
☎ 218 14 32
■ **Man's Pleasure Chest** (G lj VS)
10-1, Sun & public holidays 13-1 h
Kalckreuthstraße 15/Fuggerstraße 7 ✉ 10777 (U-Nollendorfplatz)
☎ 211 20 25

Bad Boy'z
Toys Shop Video Cruising

Montags & Samstags Kampftag 7,- DM
Mo - Sa von 13.00 - 1.00 Uhr
So & Feiertags von 15.00 - 1.00 Uhr
☎: 030 / 440 81 65 Schliemannstr. 38 10437 B-Prenzlauer Berg

Berlin | Germany

THE JAXX
Gay Cinema Private Club
Motzstr. 19, Berlin-Schöneberg
daily 12 – 3 h, sundays 13 – 3 h

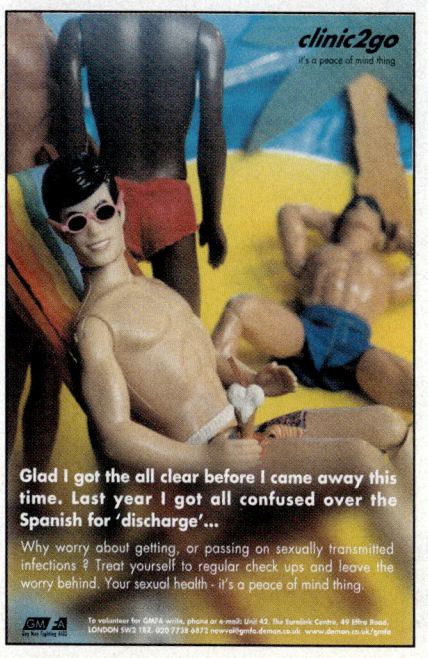

clinic2go
it's a peace of mind thing

Glad I got the all clear before I came away this time. Last year I got all confused over the Spanish for 'discharge'...

Why worry about getting, or passing on sexually transmitted infections ? Treat yourself to regular check ups and leave the worry behind. Your sexual health - it's a peace of mind thing.

GMFA
To volunteer for GMFA write, phone or e-mail: Unit 42, The Eurolink Centre, 49 Effra Road, LONDON SW2 1BZ, 020 7738 6872 renevok@gmfa.demon.co.uk www.demon.co.uk/gmfa

MAN's pleasurechest
Shop & Blue Movies

10777 Berlin • Kalckreuthstr. 15 / Fuggerstr.
10 - 01 Uhr • So + Feiertags 13 - 01 Uhr

SPARTACUS 2001/2002 | 385

Germany | Berlin

- **Videoverleih**
- **Bücher**
- **Condome**
- **Magazine**
- **Toys**
- **Videos**
- **Screening rooms**
- **Cabins etc.**

POOL BERLIN

CLASSIC

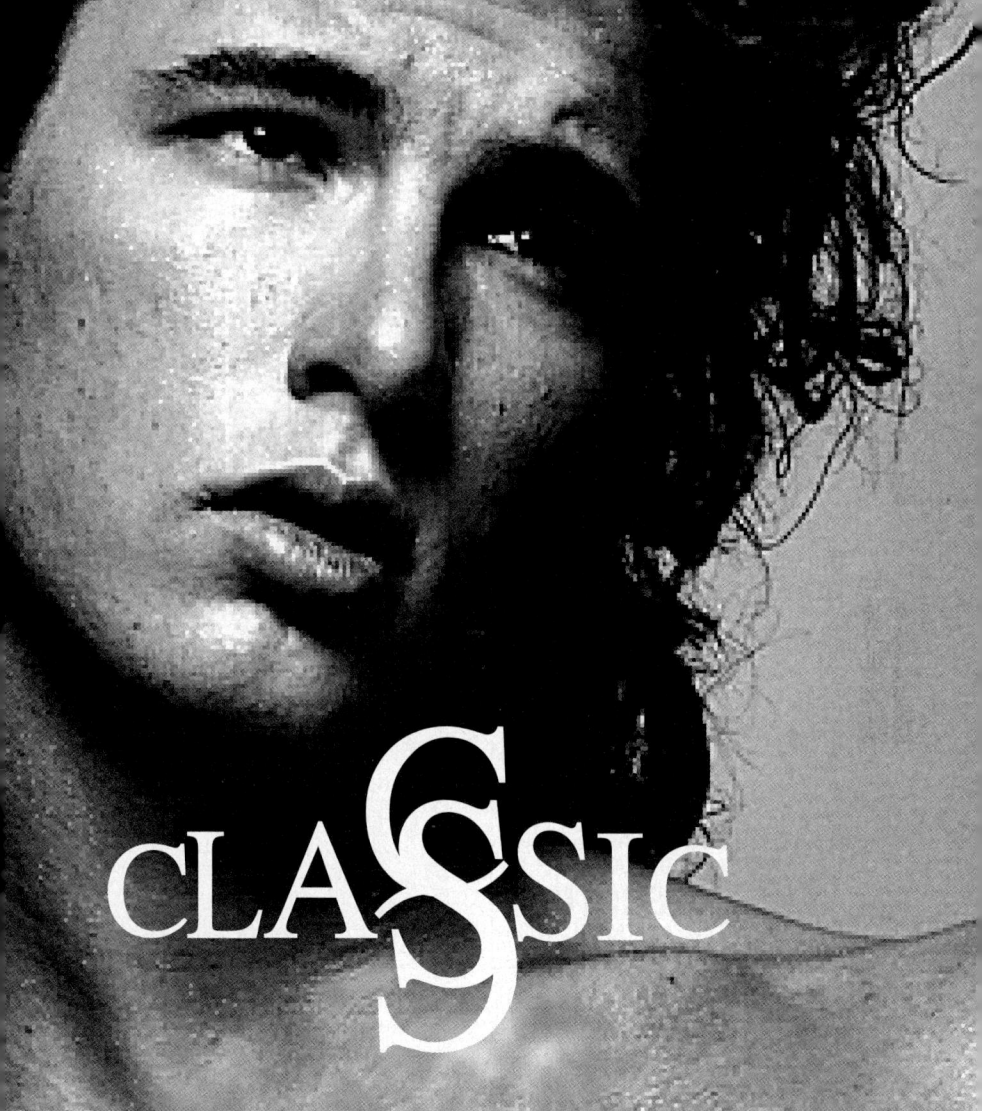

HOUSE OF BOYS
DAILY 8 pm - 5 am

- SUNDAY CLOSED -
D - 10627 Berlin / Charlottenburg
Windscheidstr. 16

ESCORT AGENCY

Phone 030 - 324 44 54
http: // www.ClassicClub.com

Germany | Berlin

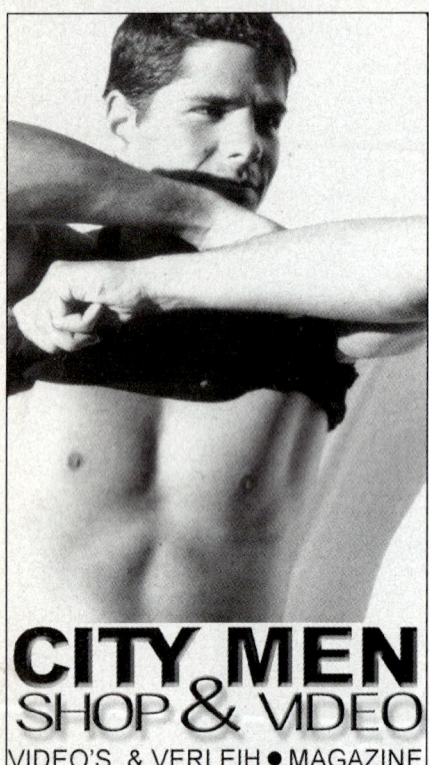

■ **New Man** (AC CC DR G MA r VS) Mon-Sat 10-0.30, Sun 12-0.30 h
Joachimstaler Straße 1-3 ✉ 10623 (U/S-Zoologischer Garten)
☏ 88 68 32 89
Sun all day card 8,- DM.
■ **Pool Berlin** (DR G MA r VS) Mon-Sat 10-22 h
Schaperstraße 11 ✉ 10719 (U-Kurfürstendamm/Spichernstraße)
☏ 214 19 89

ESCORTS & STUDIOS

■ **Classic Agency** (CC G msg)
Windscheidstraße 16 ✉ 10627
☏ 324 44 54
20-30 international men (18-35 years old) of all types.

HOUSE OF BOYS

■ **CC 96 Men Strip Show** (AC B CC d f G MA msg P SNU STV TV VS WH) 20-4 h
Lietzenburger Straße 96 ✉ 10719 (U-Uhlandstrasse, Bus 119/129/229/209) ☏ 883 26 50

■ **Classic Club** (B CC G msg OS R VS) Mon-Sat 20-5h
Windscheidstrasse 16/Kantstrasse
✉ 10627 (S-Charlottenburg/U-Wilmersdorfstrasse)
☏ 324 44 54

SAUNAS/BATHS

■ **Apollo City** (AC B CC DR f G MA msg p SA SB SOL VS WO) 13-7 h
Kurfürstenstraße 101 ✉ 10787 (U-Wittenbergplatz)
☏ 213 24 24
Traditional West Berlin establishment on two floors with extensive sauna facilities. Lively bar.
■ **Aquarius** (A AC B BF d DR F G MA msg SA SB SOL VS WH) 24 h
Hasenheide 13 ✉ 10967 (U-Hermannplatz)
☏ 691 39 20
One of Germany's biggest sauna opening soon. Please call for information or check in the local press for deatils.

Heiße Nächte
in Berlin.
Boys
Men Strip
Fun
Action
and more...
cc96
HOUSE OF BOYS
Lietzenburger Str. 96 · 10719 Berlin
☎ (030) 883 26 50
Täglich 20 – 04 Uhr
www.cc96.de

Germany | Berlin

■ **Gate Sauna** (AC B BF CC DR f G MA msg p SA SB SOL VS WH) 11-7, Fri 11-Mon 7 h
Wilhelmstraße 81 ✉ 10117 (near Brandenburger Tor, U-Mohrenstraße/S-Unter den Linden) ☎ 229 94 30
Intimate atmosphere sauna frequented by a vary diverse crowd. Special days for young, couples, bears, etc...

■ **Steam Sauna-Club** (B BF DR F G lj MA msg p S SA SB SOL VS WH) 11-7, Fri 11-Mon 7 h
Kurfürstenstraße 113 ✉ 10787 (U-Wittenbergplatz/S-Bahnhof Zoo, near KaDeWe) ☎ 218 40 60

Sauna frequented by a mixed age crowd mainly from the leather scene. Numerous parties throughout the year.

■ **Treibhaus** (AC B BF DR f G MA p SA SB SOL VS WH)
Mon-Thu 13-7, Fri 13-Mon 7 h
Schönhauser Allee 132 ✉ 10437 (S/U-Schönhauser Allee/Tram-50/52/53)
☎ 448 45 03
This sauna, with its roomy steam bath and whirlpool areas, is frequented by a young and still young crowd.

saunaguide

SAUNA GUIDE & GAY BATHHOUSES INTERNATIONAL

252 Seiten/Pages,
English / Deutsch / Français,
ISBN 3-86187-155-6
DM 26,80 / Sfr 26,- /Ös 196,-

Erhältlich im Buchhandel oder bei
www.brunos.de

APOLLO CITY SAUNA
Kurfürstenstr. 101 10787 Berlin Germany

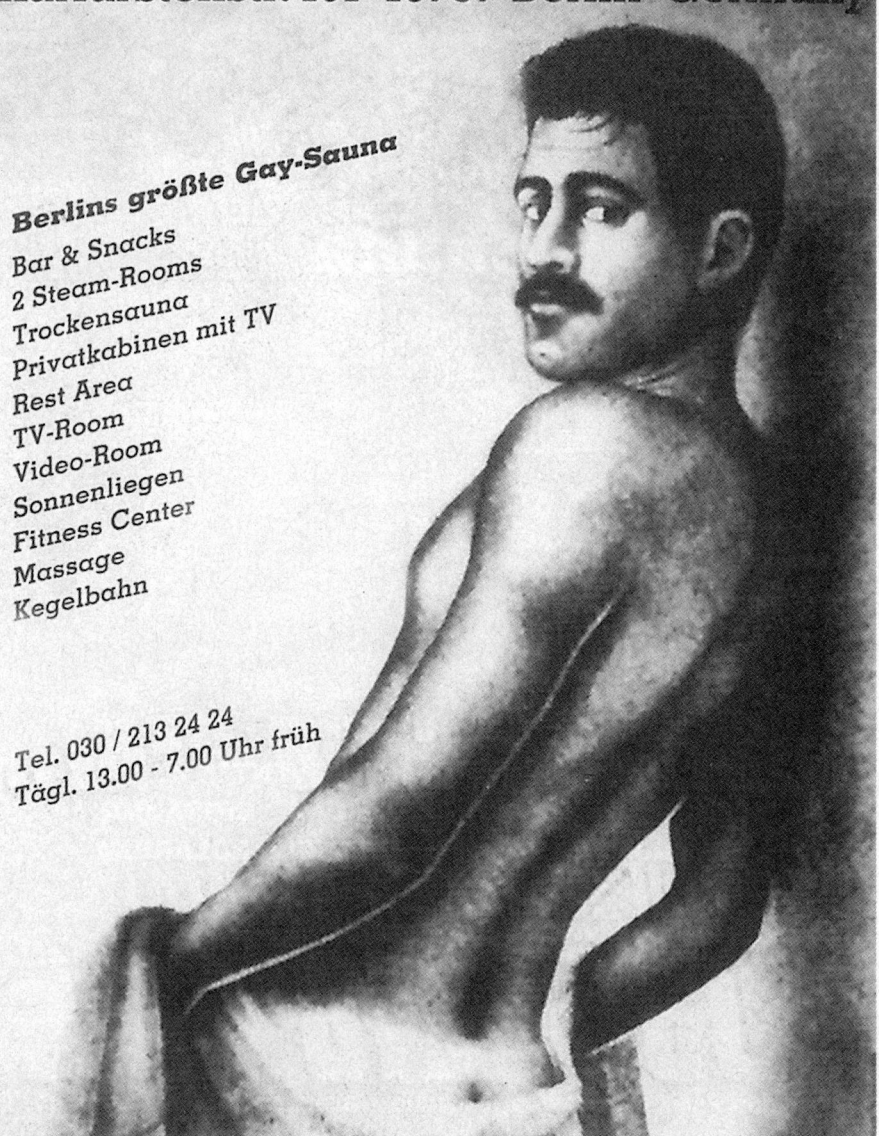

Berlins größte Gay-Sauna

Bar & Snacks
2 Steam-Rooms
Trockensauna
Privatkabinen mit TV
Rest Area
TV-Room
Video-Room
Sonnenliegen
Fitness Center
Massage
Kegelbahn

Tel. 030 / 213 24 24
Tägl. 13.00 - 7.00 Uhr früh

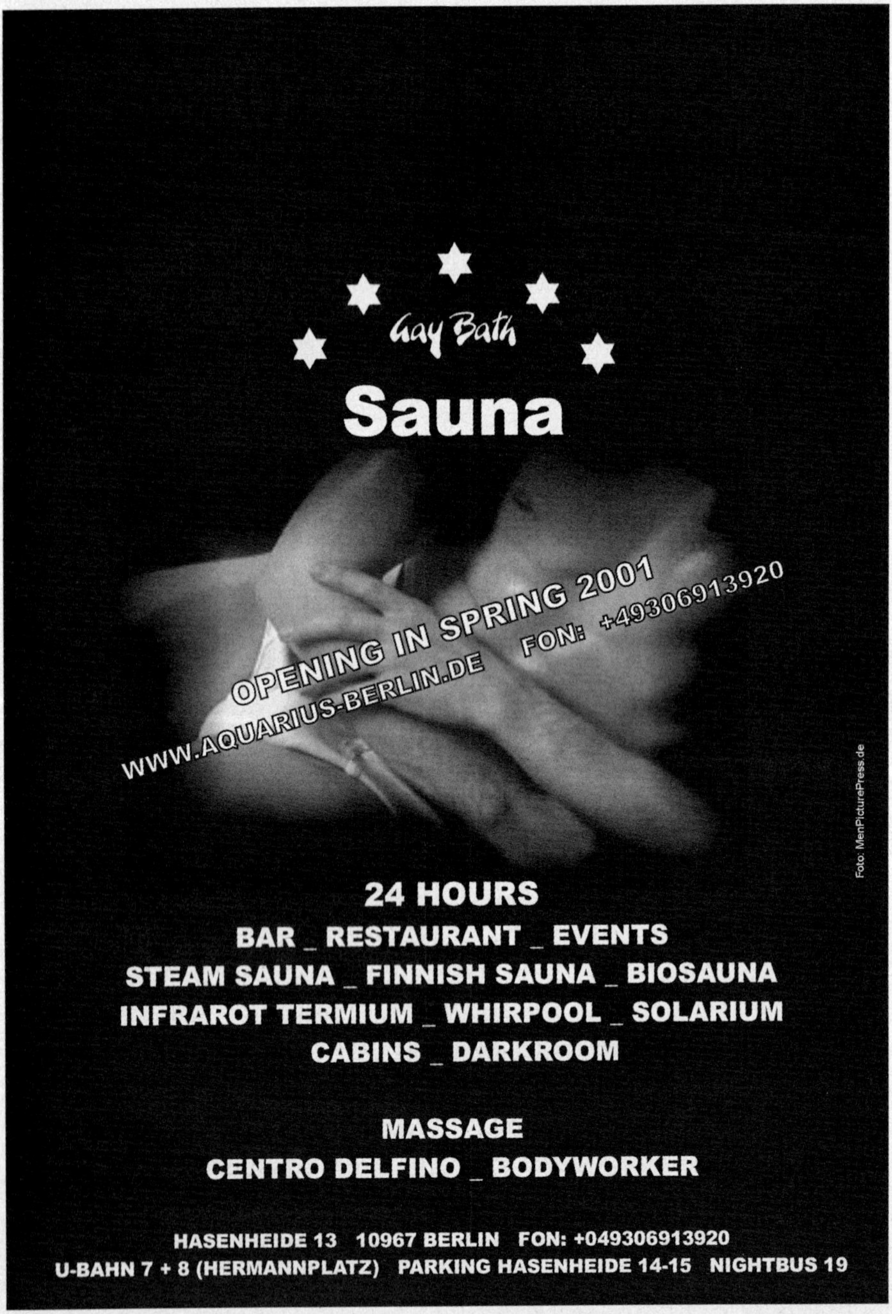
Gay Bath
Sauna
OPENING IN SPRING 2001
WWW.AQUARIUS-BERLIN.DE FON: +4930691392O
Foto: MenPicturePress.de
24 HOURS
BAR _ RESTAURANT _ EVENTS
STEAM SAUNA _ FINNISH SAUNA _ BIOSAUNA
INFRAROT TERMIUM _ WHIRPOOL _ SOLARIUM
CABINS _ DARKROOM
MASSAGE
CENTRO DELFINO _ BODYWORKER
HASENHEIDE 13 10967 BERLIN FON: +049306913920
U-BAHN 7 + 8 (HERMANNPLATZ) PARKING HASENHEIDE 14-15 NIGHTBUS 19

Berlin | Germany

GATE SAUNA
Berlin Mitte • Wilhelmstr. 81
tgl. 11:00 - 7:00 Uhr • Wochenende durchgehend

Specials

Night Special
Mo - Do ab 2h
Eintritt 15,-

Montag & Freitag
Happy Day

Mittwoch
Youngster Tag

Samstag & Sonntag
(7-12h)
Partner Zeit

(030) 22 99 43 0
www.gate-sauna.de

Germany | Berlin

'STEAM'

SAUNA CLUB BERLIN KURFÜRSTENSTR.113 / 10787 BERLIN
030 / 218 40 60
www.steam-sauna.de

SAUNA

STEAM ROOM

SM ROOM
SLING & ANDREASKREUZ

WHIRL POOL

SOLARIUM

PRIVATE CABINS

VIDEO & TV ROOM

REST AREA

BAR & SNACKS

OPENING HOURS:
11-7 FRÜH
WOCHENENDE DURCHGEHEND

c 2000 **OOPSDESIGN.COM**

394 SPARTACUS 2001/2002

Berlin | Germany

Treibhaus Sauna Berlin

jetzt neu mit Massage

Schönhauser Allee 132 · 10437 Berlin
Telefon 030 - 448 45 03
Freitag 13 Uhr – Montag 7 Uhr durchgehend
Montag – Donnerstag 13 bis 7 Uhr

www.treibhaussauna.de

Blauer Montag
Getränke zu Superpreisen
Blue Monday – drinks at super prices

Saunatag
Dienstag · Mittwoch · Donnerstag
Tue · Wed · Thu saunaday

wir empfehlen

EXTRA STARK — LONDON
the original   the condom

Poster | Bücher für Lesben | Zeitschriften | Clothing | Magazine | CDs + Foto-CDs | Bücher + Fotobände | Toys | Video-Verleih | Rainbow-Artikel | Videos | Postkarten

Aus dem Bildband 'Colours Of Men' Janssen Verlag

VIDEO-VERLEIH
nur DM 3,– / Geschäftstag
für alle VHS-Titel:
Cadinot, Cazzo,
Clair, Falcon, ...
Auch DVD-Filme im Verleih!

NEU
BRUNO GMÜNDER DEPOT

JANSSEN

Pariser Straße 45 · 10719 Berlin
direkt am Ludwigkirchplatz
Montag- Samstag 11-20 Uhr
Tel. (+49) 030 - 881 15 90 · Fax 881 59 80
www.galerie-janssen.com

Germany — Berlin

PRINZ EISENHERZ
the gay bookstore
and the first place to visit

BOOKS & MAGAZINES IN ALL LANGUAGES, VIDEOS, CD's, POSTCARDS, RAINBOW ACCESSORIES & MORE

Bleibtreustraße 52 • 10623 Berlin • FON 030 / 313 99 36 • FAX 030 / 313 17 95 • Mailorder!
Mon-Friday 10-19 h, Saturday 10-16 h • Ask for our FREE catalogues! • www.prinz-eisenherz.com

BOOK SHOPS

■ **Adam Buchladen** (CC) Mon-Fri 10-20 h, Sat 10-16 h
Gleimstraße 127 ✉ 10437 (U/S-Schönhauser Allee) ☏ 448 07 67

■ **Bruno`s** (! A CC G) Mon-Sat 10-22 h
Nürnberger Straße 53 ✉ 10789 (U-Wittenbergplatz)
☏ 21 47 32 93 ☏ 21 47 32 95 ✉ brunos.berlin@brunos.de
🖥 www.brunos.de
Also video rental.

■ **Galerie Janssen-men's art gallery and bookshop** (A AC CC) Mon-Sat 11-20 h
Pariser Straße 45 ✉ 10719 (U1/9-Spichernstraße) ☏ 881 15 90

■ **Prinz Eisenherz Buchladen** (! CC GLM) 10-19, Sat -16 h, closed Sun
Bleibtreustraße 52 ✉ 10623 (S-Savignyplatz) ☏ 313 99 36
Ask for their free catalogue. Also Cd's, Magazines, videos and pride articles.

FASHION SHOPS

■ **Wall Street-men's fashion** (AC CC g lj MA s) Mon-Fri 10-20, Sat -18 h
Uhlandstraße 175 ✉ 10719 (U-Uhlandstraße) ☏ 881 16 83
Fashion shop, international designers.

LEATHER & FETISH SHOPS

■ **Black Style** (CC G) Mon-Fri 13-18.30, Thu -20, Sat 10-14 h
Seelower Straße 5 ✉ 10439 (S/U-Schönhauser Allee)
☏ 44 68 85 95
Latex wear creation and mail-order: www.blackstyle.de

■ **Leathers-Lederwerkstatt Berlin** (G LJ) Tue-Fri 12-19.30, Sat 12-16 h
Schliemannstraße 38 ✉ 10473 ☏ 442 77 86
S&M furniture and accessoires.

■ **Mister B Leather & Rubber** (A CC G LJ) Mon-Fri 12-20, Sat 10-16 h
Nollendorfstraße 23 ✉ 10777 (U-Nollendorfplatz) ☏ 21 99 77 04
Branch of the famous Amsterdam institution. Also mail order: www.misterb.com

■ **Playground** (CC G lj VS) Mon-Sat 12-24 h, closed Sun & public holidays
Courbièrestraße 9 ✉ 10787 (U-Nollendorfplatz) ☏ 218 21 64
Tailor-made leather and rubber. Also piercing.

■ **Schwarze Mode** (CC LJ) Mon-Fri 12-19 Sat 10-16 h
Grunewaldstraße 91 ✉ 10823 ☏ 784 59 22
Latex, leather, pvc, toys. Mailorder catalogues available. Call or see website for further information: www.schwarze-mode.de

TRAVEL AND TRANSPORT

■ **Holzfuss Travel Marketing**
Habelschwerdter Allee 14 ✉ 14195 ☏ 49 76 67 12
☏ (0800) 83 22 769 (toll-free) 🖨 49 76 67 13
✉ first@holzfuss.de
Organizes gay travels, sightseeing-tours & accomodation in Berlin and Potsdam. Call for further information.

---

schwarze mode
BERLIN

FASHION FOR ECTASY
LATEX - LEATHER - PVC - TOYS
Design & production
Mailorder Catalogues available - ask for information

Grunewaldstr. 91 · D - 10823 Berlin-Schöneberg
Tel 0049 30 784 59 22 · Fax 0049 30 787 04 533
www.schwarze-mode.de · info@schwarze-mode.de
open: Mo.-Fr. 12:00 - 19:00 und Sa 10:00 - 16:00

THE GAY MEDIA STORE
Bruno's
www.brunos.de
Bruno's in Berlin
Nürnberger Str. 53
Mo - Sa 10 - 22 Uhr
Bruno's in Köln
Friesenwall 24
Mo - Fr 10 - 20 Uhr
Sa 10 - 16 Uhr
BÜCHER · MAGAZINE · DVD · VIDEOS · VIDEOVERLEIH

| Germany | Berlin |

WALL STREET
MEN's FASHION

Designs by:
VERSACE JEANS COUTURE /
D&G JEANS / ARMANI JEANS
GIANFRANCO FERRÉ / J´S EXTÉ /
JUST CAVALLI / JPG JEANS

Schlaf los in Berlin? Sleepless in Berlin?
Ruf an/Call: 030 - 88 11 68 30
0171 - 384 7111

WALL STREET APARTMENTS

Ruhige Apartments direkt am Kurfürstendamm.
Ausgestattet mit Küche, Bad, WC, Telefon, TV, Radio.
DM 140,- bis 170,- pro Nacht

GAYS AUS DEINER STADT!
WARTEN AUF DEINEN ANRUF!
0190-439.150
SKLAVE SUCHT MEISTER:
0190 439.171
NUR 81 Pf/Min!
1 ZU 1 BLITZ KONTAKTE GAYS ONLY
0190-439.166
DEVOTE GAYS! 0190-439.163

■ **Lufthansa City Center** Mon-Fri 10-20, Sat -15 h
Kurfürstendamm 21 ✉ 10719 ☎ 88 75 38 00 🖷 88 75 38 01
LCC-Berlin@t-online.de 🖳 www.lhcc.de/lcc-berlin

■ **Over the Rainbow** Mon-Fri 10-20, Sat -13 h
Knesebeckstraße 89 ✉ 10623 ☎ 31 80 58-0
🖷 31 80 58-8
🖳 info@overtherainbow.de 🖳 www.overtherainbow.de

■ **Schwule Mitfahrzentrale** Mon-Fri 9-20 h, Sat 10-14 h
Yorckstraße 52 ✉ 10965 ☎ 216 40 20 🖷 215 20 67
Gay give-a-lift centre.

HOTELS

■ **Active Hotel Helle Mitte** (BF CC F glm H SOL) 0-24 h
Kurt-Weill-Gasse 7 ✉ 12627 (U5-Hellersdorf) ☎ 99 28 00 0
🖷 99 28 00 333 🖳 active-hotel@t-online.de
🖳 www.active-hotel.de
Single room DM 98.-, double 140-150.-

■ **Arco Hotel** (BF CC glm H MA OS)
Geisbergstraße 30 ✉ 10777 (U-Wittenbergplatz) ☎ 235 14 80
🖷 21 47 51 78 🖳 arco-hotel@t-online.de 🖳 www.arco-hotel.de
All rooms with shower/WC, SAT-TV, phone and safe. Own key. Very central location, right in the gay scene. Rates single DM 110-140, double 140-180 (bf incl.)

■ **Art Connection Cityhotel Berlin** (BF CC GLM H LJ MA msg WO)
Reception: 8-22 h
Fuggerstraße 33 ✉ 10777 (U-Wittenbergplatz) ☎ 217 70 28
🖷 217 70 30 🖳 info@arthotel-connection.de 🖳 www.xs66.de
Located near gay bars. 8 double rooms, 8 single rooms, 1 suite. All rooms with shower/bath, partly WC. TV, phone, radio, minibar, safe, own key. Rates double from DM 170, single from 110. Add. bed DM 60. VCR for rent. Hotel features a leather darkroom.

Berlin | Germany

AMSTERDAM
BV MISTER B LEATHER RUBBER TATTOO PIERCING
WARMOESSTRAAT 89 NL 1012 HZ AMSTERDAM
P ••31(0)20 4220003 F ••31(0)20 6276868
E-MAIL: misterb@mrb.nl WEBSITE: www.mrb.nl

BERLIN
MISTER B GMBH LEATHER RUBBER
NOLLENDORFSTRASSE 23 D 10777 BERLIN
P ••49(0)30 21997704 F ••49(0)30 21997705
E-MAIL: misterb@mrb.nl WEBSITE: www.misterb.com

Mr B LEATHER & RUBBER

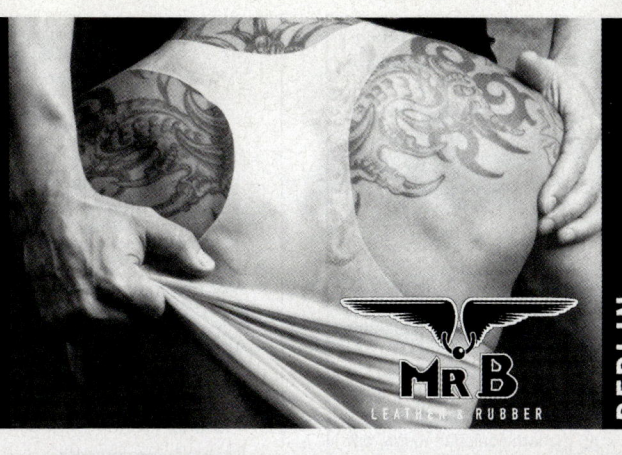

Cataloques
Deutschland DM 12,-
 ind.Versand
Other countries DM 30,-
 incl. p&p

Shop online
www.blackstyle.de
email@blackstyle.de

Credit cards welcome!

BLACK STYLE Shop
Seelower Str. 5
D - 10439 Berlin

Mo-Fr 1.00 - 6.30 p.m.
Thu   1.00 - 8.00 p.m.
Sat   10.00 - 2.00 p.m.

Mailorder
Tel.: +49-30- 44 68 85 95
Fax: +49-30- 44 68 85 94

BLACK STYLE

■ **Art-Hotel Charlottenburg Hof** (A B BF CC F glm H MA OS) 0-24 h
Stuttgarter Platz 14 ✉ 10627 *(U-Wilmersdorfer Straße/S-Charlottenburg)* ☎ 32 90 70 📠 323 37 23
☎ 240 620 📠 240 62 222 ✉ berlin@artotel.de
🖥 www.artotel.de
Central location, close to gay scene. Rooms with shower/WC, cable+Sat TV, phone and safe, some with jacuzzi. Rates single from DM 120-140, double 150-200.

■ **art'otel berlin-mitte** (AC B BF CC E F glm H lj) 24 h
Wallstr. 70-73 ✉ 10179 *(inner city district Mitte, central location)*

■ **Black Paradise Hotel** (b BF CC G H LJ MA OS WH) 24 h
Dennewitzstr. 7 ✉ 10785 *(U1/15 Kurfürstenstr.)* ☎ 29 00 45 41
📠 29 00 45 42 ✉ info@blackparadise.de
🖥 www.blackparadise.de
Centrally located hotel near gay district, 13 doubles, 2 studios. All rooms with bath/WC, telephone, internet access, sling, cage, TV&video, studios with whirlpool & extra toys. Double from 200,- DM, studios 500,- DM bf. incl.

Das Hotel, in dem die Leistung auch den Dienst beinhaltet!

ACTIVE
hotel hellemitte
★★★

47 Zimmer, Dusche/WC, Sat-TV/Radio, Minibar, Telefon und Fax
Fordert unseren Prospekt an!
Kurt-Weill-Gasse 7 • 12627 BERLIN - Hellersdorf

1 ÜN im EZ 98,– DM
incl. Frühstücksbüffet

1 ÜN im DZ 140,–/150,– DM
incl. Frühstücksbüffet

U-Bahn: Linie 5 (vom Alexanderplatz Richtung Hönow bis Hellersdorf) und dann ca. 80m bis zum Hotel
Fon: (030) 99 28 00-0 • Fax: (030) 99 28 00-333
e-mail: active-hotel@t-online.de • www.active-hotel.de

SPARTACUS 2001/2002

Germany | Berlin

ART-HOTEL CHARLOTTENBURGER HOF

Welcome at BERLIN

Tel 00-49-30-32 90 70
Fax 00-49-30-323 37 23
email charlottenburger.hof@t-online.de

close to Kurfürstendamm
close to the scene

SINGLE 120 DM
DOUBLE 150 DM

45 modern equipped rooms with a lot of artwork, all with private bathroom cable-TV, safe, telephone, hair-dryer

in the adjoining Café VOLTAIRE you get breakfast and dinner 24 hrs a day

Here you meet people from all over the world
http://www.charlottenburger-hof.de

HOTEL California

Ihr Zuhause in Berlin
- 50 Komfortzimmer + Suiten Economy – Business – First
- Nichtraucheretage
- Sauna, Solarium, Fitness

Wir freuen uns auf Ihren Besuch und Ihre direkte Reservierung bei uns

Your private home in Berlin
- 50 comfortable rooms + suites Economy – Business – First
- Non-smoking floor
- Sauna, solarium, fitness

We welcome your visit and your direct reservation with us

Kurfürstendamm 35
D-10719 Berlin (Savignyplatz/U-Bhf. Uhlandstr.)

Tel. ++49/30/8 80 12-0 · Fax: ++49/30/ 8 80 12-111
Internet: www.hotel-california.de
e-mail: Info@hotel-california.de

AIRPORT-BUS 109

…nur 50 Schritte in die Szene…
… next to the gay area…

Comfort Hotel Auberge

U-Bahnhof Wittenbergplatz direkt am weltberühmten Kaufhaus „KaDeWe"	Underground-station Wittenbergplatz near the world famous department store "KaDeWe"
29 renovierte und neu möblierte traumhafte Berliner Altbauzimmer mit Dusche/WC, Fön, Telefon, Safe und Kabel-TV	29 renovated and completely new furnished rooms with shower/WC, hairdryer, telephon and cable-TV in a typical old Berlin building with high ceilings and stuckow in most of the rooms

Bayreuther Strasse 10 · D-10789 Berlin
Telefon: (030) 23 50 02-0 · Fax: (030) 23 50 02-99
E-Mail: hotel-auberge@t-online.de
Internet: http://www.hotel-auberge.de

■ **Comfort Hotel Auberge** (BF CC g H)
Bayreuther Straße 10 ✉ 10789 (U-Wittenbergplatz) ☎ 235 00 20
🛏 23 50 02 99 💻 hotel-auberge@t-online.de
💻 www.hotel-auberge.de
Located in the heart of the City, near the reputated ware house KaDe-We and at walking distance to the nearby gay venues. All rooms with shower/WC, telephone, TV, radio, safe and own key. Rates single DM 160, double 210. Additional bed 40. Buffet bf incl.

■ **Connection. Hotel** (BF CC G H)
Fuggerstrasse 33 ✉ 10777 (U-Wittenbergplatz) ☎ 217 70 28
🛏 217 70 30 💻 www.arthotel-connection.de

■ **Crowne Plaza Berlin City Center** (BF H NG)
Nürnberger Straße 65 ✉ 10787 ☎ 210 07-0 🛏 213 20 09
💻 info@crowneplaza.de 💻 crowneplaza.com
4 star superior first class hotel.

■ **Dorint Schweizerhof Berlin** (AC BF CC E F H MA NG pi SA SB WO)
Budapester Straße 25 ✉ 10787 ☎ 26 960 🛏 2696 1000
💻 info.bersch@dorint.de 💻 www.schweizerhof.de
A four star hotel close to the shopping area Ku'damm and the gay scene. Prices from DM 375, in a single room and DM 425, in a double room. Breakfast costs extra.

■ **Hansablick** (b BF CC f g H)
Flotowstraße 6 ✉ 10555 (S-Tiergarten/U-Hansaplatz) ☎ 390 48 00
🛏 392 69 37 💻 reserv@hotel-hansablick.de
💻 www.hotel-hansablick.de
Comfortable hotel near the river Spree in central location. All rooms with shower/WC, hair-dryer, cable-TV, radio and minibar, some with balcony. Rates single DM 135 and double 155-215 bf buffet incl.

Berlin | Germany

SCHWEIZERHOF

DAS GEEIGNETE AMBIENTE FÜR IHREN DESIGNER-KOFFER KÖNNEN SIE IN BERLIN LANGE SUCHEN.

ODER SOFORT BEI UNS FINDEN.

EXPECT MORE

Dorint
★ ★ ★ ★
SCHWEIZERHOF
BERLIN

Ob exklusives Design, viele kulinarische Höhepunkte, entspannende Wellnessangebote oder professionelles Tagungsmanagement – bei uns können Sie jederzeit mehr erwarten. Erfolg und Entspannung im exklusiven Ambiente sind buchbar unter:
Telefon: 030 - 26 96 - 0
Fax: 030 - 26 96 - 1000
Info.bersch@dorint.com
www.schweizerhof.com

Germany | Berlin

Sanfte Massage aus Strom –

Inklusive Video!

SLENDERTONE
LIVING LIFE AND LOVING IT

Perfekte Funktionen für ein Top-Ergebnis:

"Body Matched Impedance"
Eine eingebaute Sicherung gewährleistet, daß Slendertone-Geräte keine erhöhten Spannungswerte erzeugen können, selbst wenn Störungen an den Elektroden auftreten sollten. Diese Technologie bezeichnet Slendertone als "Body Matched Impedance" (Impedanz = Schein-Hautwiderstand).

"Multiplexing"
Eine Mehrfachschaltung bewirkt, daß der Strom immer zwischen dem Elektrodenpaar eines Muskels übertragen wird und nicht auf andere Elektroden, die andere Muskeln stimulieren.

"Safestart"
Vor Beginn einer jeden Anwendung müssen alle Regler auf Minimalstellung gebracht werden, damit nicht mit zu hoher Intensität begonnen wird. Alle Slendertone-Modelle sind mit einer Sicherheitsfunktion ausgestattet, die wir "Safestart" nennen. Das Gerät schaltet erst ein, wenn alle Regler auf Minimalstellung stehen.

Sicherheitspaket
"Safestart" (Sicherheitsstart), "Automatic Shutoff" (automatische Abschaltung), "Multiplexing" (Mehrfachschaltung), "Body Matched Impedance" (Impedanz = Schein-Hautwiderstand).

"Automatic Shutoff"
Nahezu alle Slendertone-Modelle sind mit einer automatischen Zeitschaltuhr ausgerüstet, die gewährleistet, daß Sie Ihre Muskulatur nicht überanstrengen.

DM 499,-/Euro 255,13

Sofort-Lieferung frei Haus!
Bestellen ohne Risiko!
Mit 14 Tage Rückgaberecht

Berlin | Germany

für starke Körper mit Gefühl

Der "Body-Profile" von Slendertone ist das Ergebnis einer bis zur Perfektion gereiften Technologie: "Der Elektronischen-Muskel-Stimulation", kurz EMS. Muskelstimulation mittels Impulsströmen machte man sich früher nur in der Sport-Therapie nach Verletzungen zu Nutze. Inzwischen ist "EMS" weltweit ein Begriff, wenn es um passive Kontraktion der Muskeln geht. Für ein besseres Körpergefühl, Problemzonen-Fitness und Muskel-Kräftigung. Bequem im Sitzen, beim Lesen, Fernsehen, Arbeiten oder einfach nur zum Entspannen und Stimulieren. Für einen strammen, anziehenden Körper von der Brust bis zu den Waden.

Im mobilen Kompaktset mit:

- Slendertone Body Profile Muskelstimulationsgerät (inkl. Batterie)
- Dauerelektroden
- elastische Gurte
- Gürtel zum Anlegen des Body Profile
- Video (mehrsprachig) und eine bebilderte Bedienungsanleitung

Hair Remove -

für schnelles, gründliches Entfernen von Körperhaaren ohne Rasur! Einfach auftragen, wirken lassen, entfernen. Kein Ziepen und lange haarfrei mit

Hair Remove
100 ml nur

DM 19,95/Euro 10,20

zzgl. Porto und Verpackungspauschale von DM 8,95 innerhalb Deutschlands.

! Hair Remove wird von vielen Bodybuilding-Profis wegen seiner unkomplizierten Anwendung vor Wettkämpfen empfohlen!

Info- und Bestell-Hotline:
0180 500 22 20

Koelbel-Trainingsforschung GmbH · Rendsburger Str. 14+16
30659 Hannover

Es gelten die Allgemeinen Geschäftsbedingungen (AGB) der Koelbel-Trainingsforschung, vertreten durch die GF W. Brandt und E. Schlüter

| Germany | Berlin |

Holiday Inn Garden Court
BERLIN-KURFÜRSTENDAMM

CROWNE PLAZA HOTELS · RESORTS
BERLIN CITY CENTRE

Holiday Inn
BERLIN CITY CENTER EAST
PRENZLAUER ALLEE

Stay where the action is in
BERLIN
Europe's leading gay city

Stay at the *Crowne Plaza Berlin City Centre*
centrally located near the renowned Tom's Bar
and just a stone's throw away from Berlin's largest gay sauna *Apollo*
or
if relaxing and sipping coffee is preferred, Café Savigny on Savignyplatz
ist just a short stroll from the
Holiday Inn Garden Court Berlin Kurfürstendamm
or
if you don' want to miss out on the lively scene of Prenzlauer Berg,
the eastern centre of gay Berlin and the hottest spot in town right now, then the
Holiday Inn Berlin City Center East is just the right place for your stay

✳

Crowne Plaza Berlin City Centre
Nürnberger Straße 65 · 10787 Berlin · Telefon (+49) 30 2 10 07-0 · Telefax (+49) 30 2 13 20 09
E-Mail: info@crowneplaza-berlin.de

✳

Holiday Inn Garden Court Berlin – Kurfürstendamm
Bleibtreustraße 25 · 10707 Berlin · Telefon (+49) 30 88 09 30 · Telefax (+49) 30 88 09 39 39
E-Mail: info@holidayinnberlin.de

✳

Holiday Inn Berlin City Center East – Prenzlauer Allee
Prenzlauer Allee 169 · 10409 Berlin · Telefon (+49) 30 44 66 10 · Telefax (+49) 30 44 66 16 61
E-Mail: info@berlin-holidayinn.de

■ **Holiday Inn Berlin City Center East** (H NG)
Prenzlauer Allee 169 ✉ 10249 (S-Bahn Prenzlauer Allee)
☎ 446 610 📠 446 61661 ✉ info@berlin-holidayinn.de
3 Star hotel . Double rooms from 195-224, DM

■ **Holiday Inn Garden Court Berlin** (H NG)
Bleibtreustrasse 25 ✉ 10707 (U-Uhlandstrasse) ☎ 880 30
📠 88 09 39 39 ✉ info@holidayinnberlin.de
3 Star hotel. Double rooms from 195, – to 224, – DM

ARCO HOTEL

Geisbergstraße 30
10777 Berlin
Fon: ++49-30-23 51 48 - 0
Fax: ++49-30-21 47 51 78
E-Mail: arco-hotel@t-online.de
Internet: www.arco-hotel.de

just a few steps from
U-Bahn „Wittenbergplatz"
and the city-center

right in the gay area

- quiet, comfortable rooms, all with private bath, SAT-TV, w. radio and alarm-clock, direct phone and safe
- breakfast buffet until 11.a.m.
- tree-lined garden and terrace

5 Gehminuten
vom KaDeWe
und der City

mitten in der Szene

- ruhige, moderne Zimmer, alle mit Dusche und WC, SAT-TV mit Radio und Weckuhr, eigener Telefon-nummer und Safe
- Frühstücksbuffet bis 11.00 Uhr
- schöner Garten mit Terrasse

Berlin | **Germany**

Unser Weckdienst. Was dem einen zum Wachwerden sein Morgenkaffee, ist dem anderen das herzhafte Müsli. Genießen Sie die freundliche Atmosphäre unseres Hotels, das Ihnen in sehr zentraler aber ruhiger Lage modern eingerichtete Zimmer, Konferenzräume und eigene Parkplätze bietet. Aufgeweckte reservieren am besten gleich. *Nachsaisonpreise im Juli, August und Dezember bis Februar.*

Good morning. Whatever you may prefer – our rich breakfast-buffet offers many delicacies to make your day start much to your taste. Enjoy the friendly atmosphere of our hotel, when you may rest and relax in a beautiful Old-Berlin-House with modern equipment and 24-hour-service – right in the heart of the city. Early birds call for reservations right now. *Low season rates in July, August and December until February.*

Hotel Hansablick · Flotowstr. 6 · 10555 Berlin-Tiergarten
Telefon (0 30) 39 04 80-0 · Fax (0 30) 3 92 69 37
reserv@hotel-hansablick.de · http://www.hotel-hansablick.de

Hotel Garni ★★★ Hansablick

Ab DM 69.- p.P. im DZ

HOLZFUSS
BERLIN

DISCOVER THE NEW
BERLIN
AND OUR HOTELS

first@holzfuss.de

– HOTELS IN BERLIN & POTSDAM
– SIGHTSEEING
– STADTFÜHRER
– TOUREN ZUR SZENE

BITTE FORDERE UNSER HOTELPROGRAMM AN.
WIR SIND FÜR DICH JEDERZEIT UND GERNE DA!

HOLZFUSS TRAVEL MARKETING GMBH
HABELSCHWERDTER ALLEE 14 · 14195 BERLIN
Tel.: 030/49766712 · Fax: 030/49766713

Infos: Freecall 0800 – 83 22 769

SPARTACUS 2001/2002 | 405

Germany | **Berlin**

VARIOUS VOICES 2001

10th European Gay/Lesbian Choir Festival 2001 in Berlin

May 20th - 27th 2001

Come and witness the variety of lesbian and gay choirs for a week. More than 60 of them with about 1,300 singers from all over Europe will perform on Berlin's many stages. Music from all epochs and of different styles mixes with show entertainment, revue, theatre and dance.
Be part of parties and festivities and the Opening Ceremony at the Friedrichstadtpalast – Europe's biggest revue venue. Everybody is welcome.

Various Voices e.V. · c/o fipps oHG
Zossener Str. 55 - 58 (Aufg. D) · 10961 Berlin
Phone +49(0)30 69 53 96 53 · Fax +49(0)30 61 50 73 71
eMail info@various-voices.de · www.various-voices.de
Hotelhotline: 0800-8322769

AB INS GRÜNE

Unser Parkhotel ist in nur 1 Stunde von Leipzig und Berlin aus erreichbar.

- 56 komfortable Zimmer & Suiten
- Restaurant mit Lobby-Bar
- moderner Saunabereich
- kostenloser Fahrrad-Verleih

PARK HOTEL
Wittenberg / Bad Schmiedeberg
RINGHOTELS ...mittendrin ist in!

Dommitzscher Str. 3, 06905 Bad Schmiedeberg
Tel.: 034925/67-0 • Fax: 034925/67-167
www.parkhotel-bad-schmiedeberg.de
email: info@parkhotel-bad-schmiedeberg.de

■ **Hotel California** (B BF CC f H NG SA SOL WO)
Kurfürstendamm 35 ✉ 10719 (U-Uhlandstraße/S-Savigny Platz)
☎ 880 12 0 📠 88 01 21 11 💻 info@hotel-california.de
www.hotel-california.de
4-Star hotel in a very central location on the famous KuDamm boulevard. 50 rooms and suites with shower (bath), WC, hair-dryer, cable and pay-TV, radio, safe, minibar. Junior suites with balcony. Rates single DM 184-275, double DM 214-305 incl. bf. buffet.

■ **Hotel Sachsenhof** (BF CC g H lj) 0-24 h
Motzstraße 7 ✉ 10777 (U-Nollendorfplatz) ☎ 216 20 74
📠 215 82 20 💻 Hotel.Sachsenhof@t-online.de
Central location in gay area. 48 double rooms, 19 single rooms, partly with bath/shower/WC. All rooms with TV, phone and heating. Hotel provides own key. Rates double DM 99-156. single DM 57-120. Add. bed 30, bf DM 10.

■ **Myer's Hotel** (BF CC H OS TV)
Metzer Straße 26 ✉ 10405 ☎ 44 01 40 📠 44 01 41 04
Private hotel in an historic building in the heart of the trendy district Prenzlauer Berg. All rooms with bath/WC, telephone, Fax, TV, radio, hair-dryer. Single rates from 140,- DM, double from 170,- DM bf. incl.

Berlin | Germany

++ www.hotel-transit.de ++

Eröffnung April 2001
opening april 2001

TRANSIT LOFT

INTERNATIONALES JUGENDHOTEL

Greifswalder Straße 219
10405 Berlin-Prenzl.Berg
Tel. (030) 44 05 10 72
Fax (030) 44 05 10 74
loft@hotel-transit.de

In the heart of Berlin:

Find Europes most exciting metropolis right on our doorstep. Spacious loft-styled rooms – make friends from all over the world.
50 large, bright rooms in a converted warehouse. 1 to 5 per room with shower & W.C. plus a fabulous breakfast buffet. Internet access.

„Sleep in": DM 35,–,
EZ/single: from DM 90,–,
DZ/double: from DM 105,–
incl. Frühstücksbuffet/
incl. breakfast.

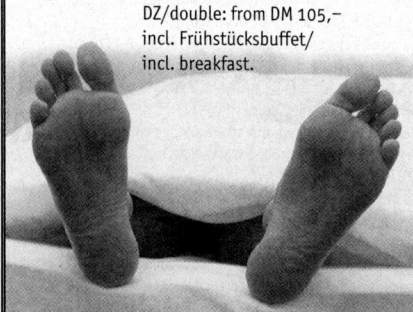

Hotel Sachsenhof

Motzstraße 7 • D- 10777 Berlin

Berlin Schöneberg
In the gay area

single   DM 57,– DM 120,–
double   DM 99,– DM 156,–
breakfast p.P.   DM 10,–

at Nollendorfplatz

Tel : 030/216 20 74
Fax : 030/215 82 20
E-mail: Hotel.Sachsenhof@t-online.de

TOM'S HOUSE

Unter neuer Leitung
Alle Zimmer mit
Dusche/WC und
TV. Kreditkarten-
zahlung möglich.
Hotel • Pension
Eisenacher Str. 10
D-10777 Berlin
Tel. 030/218 55 44
Fax 030/213 44 64

Germany | Berlin

Myer's Hotel Berlin

Zentral gelegen
am historischen Zentrum
von Berlin

Kultur, Kollwitzplatz
Museumsinsel, Kiez

Individuelles, privat geführtes
Hotel mit Flair

Frühstücksbuffet,
Garten, Tearoom,
Lobby-Bar, Lift

Zimmer mit WC/Dusche,
Fön, TV, Telefon,
Radio, tlw. Minibar

Tel.: 030- 44 014 - 0 * Metzer Str. 26 * 10405 Berlin-Prenzlauer Berg * Fax: 030 - 44 014 104

PENSION NIEBUHR

NIEBUHRSTR. 74, 10629 BERLIN
TEL. (030) 324 95 95 FAX (030) 324 80 21
EMAIL INFO@PENSION-NIEBUHR.DE

SCHALL UND RAUCH
BAR · RESTAURANT · PENSION · CATERING

GLEIMSTRASSE 23 · 10437 BERLIN / P.BERG
TEL: +49 (0) 30 - 44 33 97 -0
FAX: +49 (0) 30 - 44 33 97 22
e-mail: schall.und.rauch.berlin@talknet.de
http://www.schall-und-rauch-berlin.de

■ **Transit Loft** (b BF CC g H) 0-24 h
Greifswalder Straße 219 ✉ 10405 *(entrance Immanuelkirchstraße 14)* ☎ 789 04 70 🖨 789 04 77-7 💻 loft@hotel-transit.de
50 loft styled rooms in a converted warehouse.

GUEST HOUSES

■ **Eastside Gayllerie & Guesthouse** (GLM H MA) Mon-Thu 11-20, Fri&Sat 11-22 h
Schönhauser Allee 41 ✉ 10435 ☎ 43 73 54 84 🖨 43 73 54 85
💻 reservations@eastside-gayllerie.de 💻 www.eastside-gayllerie.de
Guesthouse & shop with pride articles, videos, books, dvd´s. Rooms from 69,-DM.

■ **Hotel-Pension Gunia** (BF CC glm H) 8-23 h
Eisenacher Straße 10 ✉ 10777 *(U-Nollendorfplatz, corner Motzstr)* ☎ 218 59 40 🖨 218 59 44 💻 hotelgunia@t-online.de
Spacious rooms, with shower/WC, cable-TV. Rates for a single DM 80-150, double DM 130-180 extra bed DM 50,–

■ **Hotel-Pension Niebuhr** (BF CC glm H MA) 9-21 h
Niebuhrstraße 74 ✉ 10629 *(S-Savignyplatz)* ☎ 324 95 95
🖨 324 80 21 💻 info@pension-niebuhr.de
💻 www.pension-niebuhr.de
Centrally located. Rooms with shower/WC, cable tv, phone, radio or bathroom on corridor. Bf will be served in the room from 7 h. Rates single DM 95-140, double 120-170.

■ **Moustache. Le** (B CC G H) Wed-Sun 20-3 h
Gartenstraße 4 ✉ 10115 *(U-Oranienburger Tor/Rosenthaler Platz, S-Nordbahnhof)* ☎ 281 72 77 🖨 281 72 77
💻 pension@lemoustache.de 💻 www.lemoustache.de
Central location in the east of Berlin. Rooms with fridge and coffeemaker, partly with TV. Rates single from DM 50 double from DM 80.

Berlin | Germany

eastside
gayllery & guesthouse
gay & lesbian store

Zimmer/Rooms ab/from 69,- DM

- videos
- dvd's
- poster
- kunst
- schmuck
- bücher
- rainbow-artikel

- pension

schönhauser allee 41 • 10435 berlin
öffnungszeiten: mo - do 11.00 - 20.00 • fr + sa 11.00 - 22.00
tel.: 030 - 43 73 54 84 • fax: 030 - 43 73 54 85
reservations@eastside-gayllery.de • homepage www.eastside-gayllery.de

Berlin	Hotel Gunia
🐻	Zimmer in Alt-Berliner Architektur mit Dusche, WC, TV Alle Kreditkarten Eisenacher Straße 10, 10777 Berlin Tel.: 0 30/ 2 18 59 40 Fax: 0 30/ 2 18 59 44 eMail: hotelgunia@t-online.de

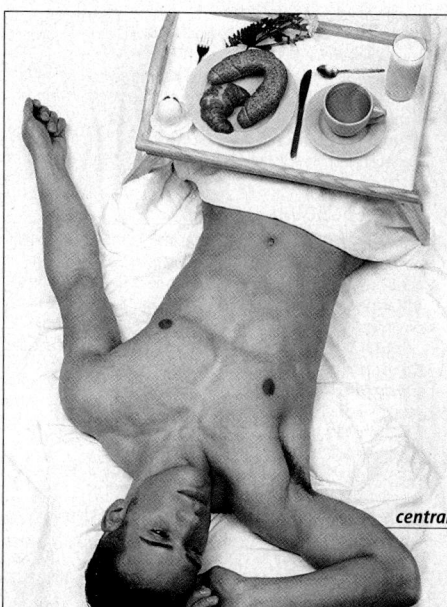

BERLIN

overnight accomodation service
· about 750 beds · more than 28 cities ·

Berlin · Cologne · Hamburg · Munich · Frankfurt
Nuremberg · Hanover · Stuttgart · Leipzig · Lübeck
Oldenburg · Bremen · Dresden · Amsterdam
Barcelona · Gran Canaria (Playa del Ingles)
Cape Town · Kopenhagen · Stockholm · Oslo
London · Lisbon · New York · Boston
San Francisco · Paris · Vienna ...

bed & breakfast enjoy

central booking office 📞 **+49-30-236 236 10**
4:30 pm – 9:00 pm local time
Fax +49-30-236 236 19 · info@ebab.com
www.ebab.com

Germany — Berlin

■ **Schall & Rauch-Bar, Restaurant & Pension** (B BF F GLM H OS) 10-3, Sat 10-3, Sun 9-3 h
Gleimstraße 23 ✉ 10437 (S/U-Schönhauser Allee) ☎ 44 33 970
☎ 44 33 97 22 📠 schall.und.rauch.berlin@talknet.de
🖥 www.schall-und-rauch-berlin.de
All rooms with shower/WC, TV and phone.

■ **Tom's House** (BF CC G H)
Eisenacher Straße 10 ✉ 10777 (U-Nollendorfplatz)
☎ 218 55 44 📠 213 44 64
All rooms with shower, WC and TV.

APARTMENTS

■ **Wall Street Apartments** (CC glm H MA)
Damaschkestr. 7 ✉ 10711 (U7-Adenauerplatz) ☎ 881 16 83
(0171) 384 71 11 📠 886 01 88 📧 wallstreet@snafu.de
At Kurfürstendamm, City West, 5 apartments fully equipped (TV, Tel, Bathroom, Kitchen) for 2 people DM 140-170.-,for 3 p. DM160-190, self-catering only.

PRIVATE ACCOMMODATION

■ **Enjoy Bed and Breakfast** (BF G H MA) 16.30-21 h
Nollendorfplatz 5 ✉ 10777 (U-Nollendorfplatz) ☎ 236 236 10
📠 236 236 19 📧 info@ebab.com 🖥 ebab.de
Accommodation sharing agency. All with shower and BF. 40-45 DM p.p.

■ **Visit Berlin** (BF G)
☎ 26 557 804 📠 26 577 803 📧 bnbinberlin@web.de
Bed and breakfast in the heart of gay Berlin. Close to the clubs and bars.

GENERAL GROUPS

■ **Amnesty International - Aktionsgruppe Homosexualität** Mon 17-19 h
c/o Stephan Cooper, Karl-Stieler-Straße 2 ✉ 12167 ☎ 796 28 74
📠 796 53 40 📧 aim-glc2918@pride.com

■ **Berliner Bären Bartmänner**
c/o Mann-o-Meter, Motzstraße 5 ✉ 10777 ☎ 262 41 61

■ **Gemeinschaft der "verkehrten" Gehörlosen Berlin'85 e.V.** Wed 18-20 h (Schreibtelefon)
Schönhauser Allee 36-39 ✉ 10435 ☎ 440 85 69 📠 440 85 69

■ **Initiative HomoMonument**
c/o Albert Eckert, Fehrbelliner Straße 87 ✉ 10119
☎ 285 34-201 📠 44 34 10 71
📧 eckert@boell.de

■ **KomBi Kommunikation und Bildung vom anderen Ufer** Mon-Thu 10-16 h
Kulmer Straße 11 ✉ 10785 ☎ 215 37 42 📠 26 55 66 34
📧 kombi1@yahoo.de

■ **LSVD-Landesverband Berlin-Brandenburg e.V.** Mon-Fri 10-16 h
Katzbachstraße 5 ✉ 10965 ☎ 44 00 82 40
📠 44 00 82 41
📧 berlin@lsvd.de 🖥 www.lsvd.de

■ **MännerMinne Schwuler Männerchor Berlin**
c/o Olaf Müller, Zillestraße 72 ✉ 10585 ☎ 342 29 73
Gay choir.

■ **Magnus-Hirschfeld-Gesellschaft e.V. Forschungsstelle zur Geschichte der Sexualwissenschaft**
Chodowieckistraße 41 ✉ 10405 ☎ 441 39 73 📠 441 39 73
📧 mhg@magnus.in-berlin.de 🖥 www.magnus.in-berlin.de

■ **MannSbilder Schwuler Foto-Club e.V.** (G) Tue 20-23h
c/o Stadtfestbüro/Regenbogenfonds, Fuggerstraße 7 ✉ 10777
☎ 23 63 81 65 📧 MannSbilder@gaylook.com
🖥 www.geocities.com/~mannSbilder/

■ **MILES and more & Bi-Nats** Mon-Thu 10-18, Fri 10-13 h
Katzbachstraße 5 ✉ 10965 (U-Yorckstraße) ☎ 44 00 82 40
📠 44 00 82 41 📧 berlin@lsvd.de 🖥 www.lsvd.de

■ **Queerstudien**
c/o Institut Kultur- und Kunstwissenschaften der *Humboldt-Uni*
☎ 308 82-246 📠 308 82-258 📧 thinius@rz.hu-berlin.de

■ **Romeo und Julius** Thu 17.30-20 (14-19 yrs), Fri 21 h (20-29 yrs)
c/o Mann-O-Meter, Motzstraße 5 ✉ 10777 ☎ 216 80 08
📠 215 70 78 📧 info@mann-o-meter.de 🖥 www.mann-o-meter.de/jugend/index.html

■ **RosaCaValiere e.V.** (G MA) Meeting/Treffen Mon 19 h at Gemeindesaal Alt-Schöneberg, Hauptstraße 48
c/o Dieter Kremer, Ramlerstraße 21 ✉ 13355 ☎ 464 17 67
☎ 61 65 99 32 (infoline) 📠 61 50 73 71
📧 email@rosacavaliere.de 🖥 www.rosacavaliere.de
Gay Choir/Schwuler Chor.

■ **Schlips e.V.**
PO Box 08 02 25 ✉ 10002 ☎ 651 52 13 📠 651 52 13
📧 eike.stedefeldt@topwave.de.
Gay and lesbian information and press service.

■ **Schwule Internationale Berlin e.V.** every Wed 19.30 at LSVD, 2nd and 4th Fri 20.30 h at Mann-o-Meter, Motzstr.5
c/o LSVD, Katzbachstr. 5 ✉ 10965 ☎ 44 00 82 40 📠 44 00 82 41
📧 SchwuleInternationale@yahoo.de

■ **Verliebte Jungs** Sat 21-0 h
c/o aha-Berlin e.V., Mehringdamm 61 ✉ 10961 (2nd floor)
☎ 692 36 00 📠 690 14 041 📧 jugendgruppe@aha-berlin.de
🖥 www.aha-berlin.de/jugendgruppe
Gay youth group. Hosts the annual meeting "Warmer Winter" for young gays and lesbians between chritmas and new year.

FETISH GROUPS

■ **Berlin Leder und Fetisch e.V.**
Nollendorfstraße 28 ✉ 10777 ☎ 215 00 99 📠 216 10 60
📧 info@blf.de 🖥 www.blf.de

■ **Motorradclub Lederbären Berlin (MCLB)** (G LJ)
c/o Mann-o-Meter, Motzstraße 5 ✉ 10777
☎ 215 14 58 (Wolfgang) 🖥 www.mclb.de
Treffen/meetings 1st Sun 11, 3rd Sat 13 h at parking Hohenzollerndamm/Emserstraße. Bikers only.

■ **Quälgeist Berlin e.V.** call Fri & Sat evening
Merseburgerstraße 3, 2. Hof ✉ 10823 ☎ 788 57 99
SM-group.

HEALTH GROUPS

■ **Berliner AIDS-Hilfe e. V.** (GLM MA) Mon-Thu 12-18, Fri 12-15 h
Meinekestraße 12 ✉ 10719 (U-Spichernstraße) ☎ 88 56 40-0
📠 88 56 40-25 📧 info@Berlin.Aidshilfe.de

■ **Café PositHiv** (a GLM MA) Sun-Fri 15-?, Sat 18-? h
Alvenslebenstraße 26 ✉ 10783 (U-Bülowstraße) ☎ 216 86 54
📠 216 86 55 📧 positiv@berlin.gay-web.de 🖥 berlin.gay-web.de
Please call for detailed information.

■ **Felix Pflegeteam** Mon-Thu 9-17, Fri -16 h
Meinekestraße 12 ✉ 10719 ☎ 887 111-80 📠 887 111-88

■ **H.I.V. (Hilfe, Information, Vermittlung) e.V.** Mon-Fri 9-15 h
Lilienthalstraße 28, ✉ 10965 ☎ 691 80 33
Society for home care and home-nursing, financial help for AIDS-patients and HIV-positives.

■ **Pluspunkt Berlin e.V.** Mon-Fri 11-17 h, Mon 15-17 h counselling
Geifenhagener Straße 6 ✉ 10437
☎ 446 68 80 📠 44 66 88 11 (Detlef)

■ **Prenzelberger AIDS-Projekt-"jederMann e.V."** Mon-Thu 15-20, Fri 15-19 h
Greifenhagener Straße 6 ✉ 10437 ☎ 444 17 64 📠 445 60 00
Counselling ☎ 444 65 55

Berlin ▸ Bielefeld Germany

■ **Schwestern der Perpetuellen Indulgenz Priorei Berlin** 20-23 h
Mehringdamm 65 ✉ 10961 *(Hinterhaus/backyard)* ☎ 788 44 18
🖳 gabi@dieschwestern.org
🖳 www.dieschwestern.org/termine.htm
■ **SUB/WAY berlin e.V.** Mon 11-18, Tue Thu Fri 14-18 h
Nollendorfstraße 31 ✉ 10777 *(U-Nollendorfplatz)*
☎ 215 57 59 📠 217 56 049 🖳 jungs@subway-berlin.de
🖳 www.subway-berlin.de
Help and counselling for hustlers and callboys.
■ **ZiK GmbH-Zuhause im Kiez** Wed 16-19 h and by appointment
Perleberger Straße 27 ✉ 10559 ☎ 398 96 00 📠 398 96 01
🖳 zuhause@zik-gmbh.de 🖳 www.zik-gmbh.de
Living and Nursing projekt for people with HIV and AIDS.
■ **zukunft positiv** Mon-Fri 11-16 h
Mommsenstrasse 45 ✉ 10629 ☎ 32 70 70 70 📠 32 70 30 41
🖳 www.zukunftpositiv.de

HELP WITH PROBLEMS
■ **Infoladen Berlin** Thu 19-21, Wed 19-? h
Kopenhagener Straße 14 ✉ 10437 ☎ 448 21 84
■ **Schwule Hilfe und Beratung** (G MA) Mon-Fri 11-19 h
Mommsenstraße 45 ✉ 10629 ☎ 194 46 📠 32 70 30 41
🖳 schwulenberatung@bln.de 🖳 www.schwulenberatungberlin.de
Schwulenberatung & Kursiv e.V.
■ **Schwules Überfalltelefon Berlin** 18-21 h
c/o Mann-O-Meter, Motzstraße 5 ✉ 10777 ☎ 216 33 36
📠 215 70 78 🖳 sueb@mann-o-meter.de
🖳 www.man-o-meter.de
Hotline for gay victims of violence.

SPECIAL INTEREST GROUPS
■ **Autonomes Schwulenreferat im AStA der FU** (stv YG) Wed 18.30-20 Fri 13-17 h
Otto-von-Simson-Straße 23 ✉ 14195 ☎ 83 90 91-18
📠 831 43 36 🖳 info@gaycampus.de 🖳 www.gaycampus.de
Gay student group.
■ **Heavy Teddies Girth & Mirth Nord-Ost e.V.** (G)
Postfach 44 0 1 10 ✉ 12001 ☎ 40 20 94 40 📠 40 20 94 41
🖳 www.Heavy-Teddies.de
Meetings Fri 20 h at Prinzknecht, Fuggerstrasse 33. Every 4th Sat from 15 h at Gate Sauna, Wilhelmstraße 81.
■ **Long Yang Club Berlin** (GLM MA)
Perleberger Straße 7 ✉ 10559 ☎ 62 73 81 38 📠 21 15 439
🖳 www.longyangclub.org/berlin
Worldwide largest organisation for gay Asian people and their friends.

SPORT GROUPS
■ **Berliner Regenbogenforellen e.V.**
Pflügerstraße 68 ✉ 12047 ☎ 61 70 96 51 🖳 rbf@ecircle.de
Gay and lesbian swimming.
■ **Gaysha-Karate für Schwule und ihre FreundInnen** (MA)
c/o Stephan Bauchwitz, Kaiserdamm 35 ✉ 14057 ☎ 302 85 78
🖳 www.bln.de/gaysha
■ **Kung-Fu-Gruppe**
Kontakt über Dietmar ☎ 611 47 63
■ **Pink-Pong e.V.**
☎ 621 69 94 📠 838 57 16 📠 838 66 25 🖳 www.pinkpong.de
■ **Taktlos Mann Tanzt**
Urbanstraße 21 ✉ 10961 *(U-Prinzenstraße/U-Südstern)* ☎ 693 58 35 📠 96 51 97 18 🖳 manntanzt@taktlos.de 🖳 www.taktlos.de
Ballroom Dancing.

■ **Vorspiel-Sportverein für Schwule und Lesben Berlin e.V.** Mon 17-20, Thu 10-13 h
Friedr.-Ludw.-Jahn Sportpark, Cantianstraße 24 ✉ 10437
☎ 440 5774-0 📠 440 5774-1
🖳 www.vorspiel-berlin.de
Breites Sportangebot, auch Gruppen für HIV-Positive und ältere Menschen. Ausführliches Programm jeden Monat neu in den Szenemagazinen "Siegessäule" und "Queer".

SWIMMING
-Strandbad Müggelsee (S-Friedrichshagen, Tram-Fürstenwalder Damm/ Müggelseedamm)
-Halensee: (S-Halensee; Bus-Rathenauplatz). Not the lido but the lawn beside Halenseestraße at Rathenauplatz)
-Teufelssee (S-Grunewald, than a 15 minutes walk)
-Grunewaldsee (Bus 119 to "Hagenplatz" then take Königsallee to the the lake)
-Tiergarten ("Tuntenwiese") (U-Hansaplatz; Bus 100/187. For sunbathing only.)
-Strandbad Wannsee (! S-Nikolassee, than take bus-shuttle to Strandbad, right behind the nude section)

CRUISING
-Siegessäule/Großer Stern (! between "Hofjägerallee" and "Straße des 17. Juni")
-Grunewald (LJ) (at ⓟ Pappelplatz/Auerbachtunnel)
-Volkspark Wilmersdorf
-Körnerpark (near S/U-Neukölln)
-Preußenpark (U-Fehrbelliner Platz)
-Park U-Turmstraße
-Volkspark Friedrichshain (at "Märchenbrunnen")
-Viktoriapark
-Birkenplatz (Grunewald)

Biberach ☎ 07351

GENERAL GROUPS
■ **Homosexuellen Emanzipationsgruppe Landkreis Biberach (HELB)** (MA)
Postfach 18 10 ✉ 88388 ☎ 803 84
Meeting Thu 20-23 h, Ehinger Straße 19 in Jugendhaus Abseits.

Bielefeld ☎ 0521

GAY INFO
■ **What's up** (GLM)
c/o Aids-Hilfe, Artur-Ladebeck-Straße 26 ✉ 33602 ☎ 12 11 67
📠 13 33 69 🖳 whats-up@gmx.de
Small leaflet-like newsletter for the area.

BARS
■ **Muttis Bierstube** (B d G MA p) Tue-Sun 20-3, Fri & Sat -5h
Friedrich-Verleger-Straße 20, ✉ 33602 ☎ 618 16
■ **Roland's Eck** (B d F G MA OS) 20-5h
Heeper Straße 28 ✉ 33602 ☎ 622 36

CAFES
■ **Café Flutsch** (b G) Mon-Fri 12-14 h
Universitätsstraße 25, ✉ 33615 *(in der Uni)* ☎ 106 34 24
Gallery on 1st floor/Galerie im 1. Stock.
■ **Magnus** (B F GLM MA OS s VS) 18-?
August-Bebel-Straße 126 ✉ 33602 *(Tram 3)* ☎ 629 53
■ **Schäfers Café in der Kunsthalle** (A BF F glm MA OS WE) Tue-Sat 9.30-23 h, Mon closed
Artur-Ladebeck-Straße 5, ✉ 33602 *(Tram 1-Adenauer Platz)*
☎ 17 40 77

Germany Bielefeld ▶ Bocholt

SexPoint BIELEFELD
Kino-Kontaktlandschaft
Video-Verleih topaktuelle Filme (Kristen Bjørn, Cadinot, Falcon, Mustang, Man's BEST etc.)
alle aktuellen Magazine und CD's zu TOP-PREISEN!
Öffnungszeiten:
Mo-Fr 10.00-21.00
Sa 10.00-18.00
Kino DM 10,-
Detmolder Straße 77
33604 Bielefeld
Telefon: 0521/ 67 978
http://151.189.18.61/sexpoint

DANCECLUBS
■ **Hechelei** (B D GLM YG) 1st & 3rd Sat 21-4 h
Heeperstraße 37 ✉ 33607 *(Ravensberger Park)* ☏ 625 58

SEX SHOPS/BLUE MOVIES
■ **Sex Point** (g VS) Mon-Fri 10-21, Sat -18 h
Detmolder Straße 77 ✉ 33604 ☏ 679 78
■ **Shop Intim** (g) 9-24, Sun 13-24 h
Bahnhofstraße 47, ✉ 33602 ☏ 17 95 50

SAUNAS/BATHS
■ **Sauna 65** (B DR f G MA OS SA SB SOL VS WO) 14-24 h, Fri Sat -? h
Niedermühlenkamp 65 ✉ 33604 *(near Youth Centre Kamp)*
☏ 656 59
Sauna very busy on week-ends with a winter garden and terrace.

BOOK SHOPS
■ **Buchladen Eulenspiegel** Mon-Fri 9-18.30, Sat 10-15 h
Hagenbruchstraße 7 ✉ 33602 ☏ 17 50 49

GENERAL GROUPS
■ **Schwusos OWL** (YG)
c/o Jusos, Arndtstraße 8 ✉ 33602 📧 manuel.pinto@gmx.de
📧 www.owl.jusos.org
Gay social democrats.

HEALTH GROUPS
■ **AIDS-Hilfe Bielefeld e.V.** Tue- Fri 10-14, Wed 10-16, Thu 10-20 h
Artur-Ladebeck-Straße 26 ✉ 33602 *(Adenauerplatz)*
☏ 194 11 📠 133369 📧 aids-bielefeld@pride.de
📧 www.bielefeld.aidshilfe.de

HELP WITH PROBLEMS
■ **Schwules Überfalltelefon** Tue 19-21 h
☏ 19 228
Gay bashing helpline.

SPORT GROUPS
■ **Sportverein Warminia Bielefeld**
c/o Kesselbrinkbad, August-Bebel-Straße 91 ✉ 33602
☏ 669 69 📧 warminia@gmx.net
Badminton, Fitness, Volleyball, Schwimmen, Kraftsport, Tischtennis

CRUISING
-Hauptbahnhof (r)
-University Bielefeld (EG, gegenüber/across Cafétéria)
-in Ravensberger Park (evenings)

Bingen
CRUISING
-Rheinanlagen (between Disco Palazzo and KD Schiffahrtsgesellschaft)

Bitterfeld ☏ 03493
GENERAL GROUPS
■ **SchwuLesBische Initiative Bitterfeld-Wolfen** Thu 18.30-?
Hahnstückenweg 4a ✉ 06749 ☏ (0177) 3359032
☏ (0172) 944 49 50 📧 bbz@gux.net.

Böblingen ☏ 07031
BARS
■ **Mirage. La** (d DR MA p VS) 20-2, Fri Sat -4 h
Klaffensteinstraße 12 ✉ 71034 ☏ 23 01 01

SEX SHOPS/BLUE MOVIES
■ **Erotic Video Shop** (g VS) Mon-Sat 9-1, Sun 13-1 h
Klaffensteinstraße 10 ✉ 71032 ☏ 22 74 73
■ **Multi-Video-Show** (g VS) Mon-Sat 9-24, Sun 16-24 h
Wilhelmstraße 27 ✉ 71034 ☏ 22 16 47

GENERAL GROUPS
■ **AIDS-Beratung im Gesundheitsamt**
c/o Albert Mayer, Parkstraße 4 ✉ 71034 ☏ 66 37 77
📧 mayer@lrabb.kdrs.de 📧 www.dr-winter-team.de

CRUISING
-Oberer See (Uferstraße)
-P Schöneicher Straße

Bocholt ☏ 02871
BARS
■ **Old Paddy** (B f g MA) Wed-Sun 21-4 h
Franzstraße 21 ✉ 46397 *(Nähe Bahnhof/near railway station)*
☏ 160 60

SEX SHOPS/BLUE MOVIES
■ **Erotik-World** (g VS) Mon-Sat 10-23 h
Münsterstraße 63 ✉ 46395 *(Close to Stadtring/Nähe Stadtring)*
10 cabins, 2 with gay porns/10 Kabinen, davon 2 mit schwulen Pornos.

Bocholt ▸ Bonn **Germany**

GENERAL GROUPS
■ **Homosexuelle Initiativgruppe und Freunde** Meetings 2nd 4th Fri 20 h
c/o Familienbildungsstätte, Ostwall 39 ✉ 46317 ☎ 36 41

CRUISING
-Langenbergpark
-P Aasee

Bochum ☎ 0234

GAY INFO
■ **Radioprojekt DIN 4 1/2** 105,0 MHz FM/UKW
Ruhrwelle Bochum
Radioproject from and for people that "don't serve as standard".

BARS
■ **Coxx** (B G MA VS) 20-3 h
Ehrenfeldstraße 2 ✉ 44789 ☎ 33 72 96
■ **Freibad** (A B F glm MA N OS) 18-3 h
Clemensstraße 2 ✉ 44789 *(U-Schauspielhaus)* ☎ 31 21 35
■ **Orlando** (A AC BF CC F GLM MA OS) Sun-Thu 10-1, Fri Sat -3 h
Alte Hattinger Straße 31 ✉ 44789 *(Schauspielhaus)* ☎ 342 42

CAFES
■ **Café Zauberhaft** (AC B BF f G lj MA YG) Sun 15-20 h
Kulturzentrum Bhf Langendreer, Wallbaumweg 108
✉ 44892 *(S-Bochum-Langendreer)* ☎ 28 08 22

DANCECLUBS
■ **After Eight** (B D G) Sat 20-1 h
c/o Zwischenfall, Alte Bahnhofstraße 214 ✉ 44892 ☎ 28 76 50
■ **BO-YS** (AC B D F G lj MA OS) 1st Sat 22-4 h
Kulturzentrum Bhf Langendreer, Wallbaumweg 108 ✉ 44892
(S-Bochum-Langendreer) ☎ 194 46
Very popular. Entrance-fee DM 12.
■ **Stargate** (AC D DR G lj S SNU VS YG) Fri Sat and before holidays 23-5 h
Hans-Böckler Straße 10-12 ✉ 44787 *("City-Passage")* ☎ 138 88
Entrance fee DM 9.
■ **Zarah und Leander** (AC B D F GLM LJ MA OS WE) every 4th Fri, 22-4 h
c/o Kulturzentrum Bahnhof Langendreer, Wallbaumweg 108
✉ 44892 *(S-Bahn station Bochum-Langendreer Line 1)* ☎ 28 08 22
■ **Zwischenfall** (A D glm lj S WE) We 22-4, Fr-Sun 22-? h
Alte Bahnhofstraße 214 ✉ 44892 ☎ 287 650

SEX SHOPS/BLUE MOVIES
■ **Sexyland** (g) 9-18.30, Sat -14 h, closed Sun
Humboldtstraße 34/Südring ✉ 44787
■ **Show Center** (DR g lj MA TV VS) 10-24, Wed Fri Sat Sun 10-1
Rottstraße 16, ✉ 44793 ☎ 162 71

HEALTH GROUPS
■ **AIDS-Hilfe Bochum e.V.** Mon & Tue 10-12, Tue & Thu 18-20 h
Bergstraße 115 ✉ 44791 ☎ 519 19 ☎ 194 11 🖶 519 19
🖳 AidshilfeBochum@compuserve.de 🖳 Bochum.aidshilfe.de

HELP WITH PROBLEMS
■ **Rosa Strippe Bochum e.V.** Counselling: Mon 19-21, Wed Thu 18-20, Fri 14-16 h
Eislebener Straße 14 ✉ 44892 ☎ 194 46
🖳 www.rosastrippe.de
Open counselling Wed 16-18 h.

CRUISING
-Main railway station (ayor R)
-Ruhruniversität (Building GA 03 Süd)
-Freiligrathstraße/Bergstraße

Bonn ☎ 0228

GAY INFO
■ **Schwulen und Lesben Zentrum Bonn e.V.** (AC B D GLM s YG) Mon 20-24 (gay café), Tue 20-24 (lesbian café), Wed 19-24 (youth café), Thu 20-24 h (mixed café), 1st Sat 22-? h Party
Am Frankenbad 5 ✉ 53111 *(Altstadt)* ☎ 63 00 39
☎ 19 446 (helpline) 🖶 65 00 50
🖳 www.zentrumbonn.de
Helpline Mon (G) Tue (L) 19-21h. Also Café Z.

BARS
■ **Boba's Bar** (AC B d G MA p) Tue-Sun 21-3 h, Mon closed
Josefstraße 17 ✉ 53111 *(near/nähe Kennedybrücke)* ☎ 65 06 85
■ **Le Copain** (B Glm MA MG) Sun-Thu 17-1, Fri Sat -2 h
Thomas-Mann-Straße 3a ✉ 53111
■ **Sharlie** (AC B CC DR G LJ MA p VS) 19-5 h
Theaterstraße 2 ✉ 53111 *(Tram- Bertha-von-Suttner-Platz)*
☎ 69 07 61
■ **Zarah L.** (B glm MA S) 18-1 h. Mon women only. Wed, Fri, Sat 21.30 & 23 h Show.
Maxstraße 22 ✉ 53111 ☎ 63 46 35

DANCECLUBS
■ **Ysabeau** (AC B D glm MA P s) Café Tue-Thu 22-5, Dance Fri-Sat 22-5, Sun -4 h
Kaiserpassagen, Martinsplatz 2a ✉ 53113 ☎ 65 16 15
Disco with ballroom-dancing.

RESTAURANTS
■ **La Vita** (F g) 12-14.30/18-23.30 h Mon closed
Kessenicher Straße 165 ✉ 53129 *(Tram Dottendorf)* ☎ 23 50 45
Italian Cuisine/Italienische Küche.

HOUSE OF BOYS
■ **Gesellschafter-Team Latour** (G msg P VS) 11-23 h
(Troisdorf) ☎ (0171) 8020860

BOOK SHOPS
■ **Buchladen 46** (glm) Mon-Wed 10-19, Thu Fri -20, Sat -16 h
Kaiserstraße 46 ✉ 53113
☎ 22 36 08

TRAVEL AND TRANSPORT
■ **Bon(n) Voyage Touristik** (GLM MG) Mon-Fri 10-13, 14-18.30, Sat 10-13 h
Thomas-Mann-Straße 56 ✉ 53111 *(nahe/near Hauptbahnhof/Main station)* ☎ 631595 🖶 9851818

GENERAL GROUPS
■ **Autonomes Schwulenreferat im AStA der Uni Bonn** 12-14 h, Sat-Sun closed
Nassestraße 11, Zimmer 11 ✉ 53113
(über Mensa, 1.Etage/1st floor) ☎ 73 70 41 🖶 26 22 10
🖳 schwule@asta.uni-bonn.de
🖳 www.asta.uni-bonn.de

Germany — Bonn ▶ Braunschweig

frankies erotik-shop
Videos
Zeitschriften
Bücher
DVDs
CDs
Kondome
Gleitmittel
Toys
Pride-Artikel

Fallersleber Str. 27
38100 Braunschweig
fon 0531.14774
www.frankies-erotik-shop.de

HEALTH GROUPS
■ **AIDS-Hilfe Bonn e.V.** Mon, Wed & Thu 10-17, Tue 10-14, Fri 10–15 h
Weberstraße 52 ✉ 53113 (tram 61,62-Weberstr.) ☎ 94 90 90
📠 94 90 30 📧 ahb@aids-hilfe-bonn.de
🖥 www.aids-hilfe-bonn.de
Helpline 194 11. Café "Queerbeet" Sun 15-20 h.

HELP WITH PROBLEMS
■ **Schwules Überfalltelefon** Mon, Wed 19-21 h
☎ 192 28
Gay bashing helpline.

SPORT GROUPS
■ **Bonner Hupfdohlen-schwuler und lesbischer Sportverein e.V.**
PO Box 27 34 ✉ 53017 ☎ 65 57 94 📧 hupfdohlen@aol.com

CRUISING
-Hofgarten (ayor)(Hinter der Universität am Rheinufer/behind the university at river Rhine; Straße/street "Am Alten Zoll")
-Dornheckensee (Bonn-Ramersdorf, summer only)

Borken ☎ 02861

GENERAL GROUPS
■ **SchiBo-Schwule in Borken** Tue 20-22 h (ungerade Wochen/uneven weeks)
c/o DRK-Bildungshaus BUG, Burloer Straße 148 ✉ 46325
☎ 633 43 & 652 60

Bottrop ☎ 02041

BARS
■ **Bahnhof Nord** (AC D S) Daily 12.30-1h WE -2h
Kirchhellner Str. 312 ✉ 46240 (Brabus-Allee)

CAFES
■ **Café Schäfer** (AC BF GLM OS) Mon-Thu & Sun 11-1.30h Fri & Sat -3.00h
Pferdemarkt 5 ✉ 46236 (city center between the Martins church and Pferdemarkt)

GENERAL GROUPS
■ **Rainbow on Earth e.V** Counselling telephone Mon 17-18h
Postfach 101723 ✉ 46217 ☎ (0173) 484 04 10
📧 wieczonek@bottrop.de 🖥 www.wieczonek.de
call for information and activities

CRUISING
-Stadtgarten (am Quadrat)

Braunschweig ☎ 0531

BARS
■ **Atelier** (B d f GLM MA) 19 h - open end
Leonhardstraße 7 ✉ 38102 (near/Nähe Stadthalle) ☎ 767 07
■ **Why Not** (B d f GLM lj MA p s STV WE) 20-2, Fri Sat 20-5 h, Sun 15-2 h
Echternstraße 9 ✉ 38102 ☎ 441 66

DANCECLUBS
■ **Exil** (D G) Thu 20-?h
Bohlweg 25
Leather dresscode.

SEX SHOPS/BLUE MOVIES
■ **Boutique intim** (g) Mon-Fri 9-20, Sat -16 h
Friedrich-Wilhelm-Straße 31 ✉ 38100 (opposite/gegenüber Post)
☎ 449 22
■ **Frankies Erotik-Shop** (CC G) Mon-Fri 14-20, Sat 11-17 h, closed Sun
Fallersleber Straße 27 ✉ 38100 (Tram-Fallersleber Tor) ☎ 147 74
■ **Sex Bazar** (g) Mon-Wed, Fri 9-18.30, Thu -20.30, Sat -14, Videoshop: Mon-Sat 9-23 h
Wendenstraße 51 ✉ 38100 ☎ 404 40
■ **Sex intim** (g) Mon-Fri 9-22, Sat -20 h
Malertwete 3 ✉ 38100 (corner Güldenstraße) ☎ 435 41

BOOK SHOPS
■ **Buchhandlung Roters** (glm) Mon-Fri 10-13, 15-18, Sat 10-13 h
Wendenstraße 51 ✉ 38100 ☎ 496 00
■ **Graff Buchhandlung** (cc glm)
Sack 15 ✉ 38100 ☎ 480 89 0

GENERAL GROUPS
■ **Jugendnetzwerk Lambda Niedersachsen e.V.** Mon-Fri 11-16 h
Karlstraße 97 ✉ 38106 ☎ & FAX 34 48 83
■ **VSE-Verein für Sexuelle Emanzipation e.V.** Tue 20-? h, Sun 15-18 h
c/o Andreas Paruszewski, Virchowstraße 5 ✉ 38118 ☎ 280 96 36
📠 280 96 36

HEALTH GROUPS
■ **Braunschweiger AIDS-Hilfe e.V.** Mon Tue Thu 10-16, Fri 10-13 h, helpline Mon Tue&Thu 10-16 h
Eulenstraße 5 ✉ 38114 ☎ 58 00 30 ☎ 19 4 11 (helpline)

Braunschweig ▶ Bremen | Germany

☎ 58 00 330 ✉ ahbs@gmx.de
🌐 www.braunschweiger-aids-hilfe.de
Bisexual group, Youth group. Gay and lesbian café Sun 15-18 h. See website or call for details.

HELP WITH PROBLEMS
■ **Rosa Telefon** Thu 20-22 h
☎ 194 46

SPORT GROUPS
■ **Schwul-lesbischer Sportverein Braunschweig e.V.**
☎ 742 77 (Carsten) -Fitness
☎ 89 65 40 (Holger) -Volleyball
☎ 82 666 (Mark) -Badminton
☎ 790558 (Norbert)

SWIMMING
-Island in Salzgittersee (Lawn on the hill, summer only).
-Kennebad (summer only).
-Bienroder See (nude bathing area).

CRUISING
-Am Rathaus
-Kohlmarkt
-An der Martinikirche
-Wolfenbütteler Straße (near Bürgerpark)
-Kennedyplatz
-Museumspark

Bremen ☎ 0421

GAY INFO
■ **Rat & Tat Zentrum für Schwule + Lesben e.V.** (A B GLM MA N) Mon, Wed (lesbian) & Fri 11-13, Tue 15-18 h (counselling)
Theodor-Körner-Straße 1 ✉ 28203 ☎ 70 41 70 (counselling)
📠 70 00 09
Cafe KWEER Tue Wed Fri 20-1, Sun 15-19 h, Gay and lesbian counselling . Samstagsschwestern meet Sat 15-17.30 h.

BARS
■ **Bienenkorb** (B F g MA r) 10-6, Sat Sun 19-6 h
Rembertistraße 32 ✉ 28203 ☎ 32 72 29
■ **Bronx** (CC DR G LJ MA p VS) 22-? h
Bohnenstraße 1b/Gertrudenstraße ✉ 28203 ☎ 70 24 04
■ **Confession** (B d f GLM LJ MA OS) Tue-Thu 19-2, Fri Sat 21-? h, Sat lesbian and gay only
Humboldtstraße 156 ✉ 28203 ☎ 738 22
■ **David** (B BF F g MA p) Mon-Fri 21-3 h, Sat 21-6 h, Sun 15-? h
Rembertistraße 33 ✉ 28203 ☎ 339 84 18
■ **Leinen los** (B G MA) Tue-Sun 17-? h, closed Mon
An der Weide 24 ✉ 28195 ☎ 32 77 23
■ **Queens** (B G R) 21-5, Fri Sat -? h
Außer der Schleifmühle 10 ✉ 28203 ☎ 32 59 12
■ **Rendezvous. Zum** (B f glm MA N) Tue-Sun 18-2 h, Mon closed
Elisabethstraße 34 ✉ 28217 *(close to steam-sauna)* ☎ 38 31 59
■ **Zone 283** (B G LJ) Fri n& Sat from 22h
Kornstr. 283 ✉ 28201 ☎ 532099
Leather bar.

CAFES
■ **Café 46** (b F GLM)
Waller Heerstr.46 ✉ 28203 ☎ 3876716
■ **Kweer** (A B f Glm MA s) Tue Wed Fri 20-1, Sat 17.30-19.30 h, Sun 15-19 h (YG),
Theodor-Körner-Straße 1 ✉ 28203 ☎ 70 00 08

DANCECLUBS
■ **Monopol** (B D G MA)
Ostertorswallstraße 95 ✉ 28195 ☎ 32 19 40
■ **Tom´s Welt** (B D DR E P R SNU VS) Wed-Sun 22-?
Außer der Schleifmühle 10 ✉ 28203 ☎ 32 54 12
Brandnew. Opened in autumn 2000.

SHOWS
■ **Madame Lothar/Travestietheater im Schnoor** (CC d f p S STV)
Wed-Sat and before holidays 20-? h
Kolpingstraße 9 ✉ 28195 ☎ 337 91 91

SEX SHOPS/BLUE MOVIES
■ **Gay Movie - B1** (G R VS) 10-24, Sun 12-24 h
An der Weide 22 ✉ 28195 *(Near Hauptbahnhof, across post office)*
☎ 337 81 79
■ **Man Video-World** (G VS) 9-24, Sun 13-23 h
Rembertistrasse 56 ✉ 28195 ☎ 32 58 98
■ **Man Video-World** (g VS) Mon-Sat 9-23 h
Pieperstraße 7/Martinistraße ✉ 28195 ☎ 122 85
■ **Men's Seven** (AC b DR G lj MA r VS) Mon-Sat 11-23.30, Sun and public holidays 15-23.30 h
Am Dobben 7 ✉ 28203 *(Tram 1/4/10-Rembertistraße)* ☎ 32 36 87
Blue movie entrance fee DM 14, student 10.

SAUNAS/BATHS
■ **Perseus** (B DR F G MA msg SA SB SOL VS WO) 16-24, Fri -3, Sat 16-Sun 24 h
Waller Heerstraße 126 ✉ 28219 *(near train station)* ☎ 38 51 00
Sauna on 200 m² with fitness and sport room. Nude day - 2nd Fri of the month.

BREMEN VIDEO-WORLD
Shop • Kino • Verleih
Rembertistraße 56
Mo-Sa 9-24 Uhr · So 13-23 Uhr

| Germany | Bremen ▶ Bühl |

BREMEN – from DM 40 –
overnight accomodation service
· about 750 beds · more than 28 cities ·

enjoy bed & breakfast

central booking office Berlin ☎ **+49-30-236 236 10** 4:30-9:00 pm local time
Fax +49-30-23623619 · info@ebab.de · www.ebab.de

complete offer
see page Germany/Berlin

■ **Steam-Sauna-Walle** (B BF DR F G MA MSG OS SA SB SOL VS)
Summer: Tue 12-1 Wed-Fri 18-1, Sat Sun 16-1, Winter: 16-1,
Tue 12-1, Sat 16-Sun 1 h
Steffensweg 157 ✉ 28217 (Tram 2/10-Wartburgstraße, 3-Elisabeth-straße) ☎ 396 60 97
Nice sauna with easy-going clientele, generally young. Grill parties on the terrace in summer.

BOOK SHOPS

■ **Humboldt-Buchhandlung** (g) Mon 13-19 h, Tue-Fri 10-19 h,
Sat 10-16 h
Osterstorsteinweg 76 ✉ 28203 ☎ 777 21
With gay section.

■ **Phönix** (g) Mon-Fri 9-20, Sat -16 h
Sögestraße 46 ✉ 28195 ☎ 17 10 77
General bookstore with gay section.

■ **Wohltat'sche Buchhandlung** (g) Mon-Wed 9.30-19,
Thu 9-20, Sat -16 h
Wenkenstraße 2/Am Brill ✉ 28195 ☎ 143 20

LEATHER & FETISH SHOPS

■ **H M Leder** (CC G LJ MA p s) Tue-Fri 12-20, Sat -16 h, Sun & Mon closed
Neukirchstraße 18 ✉ 28215 (near/nahe Hauptbahnhof)
☎ 37 14 30

PRIVATE ACCOMMODATION

■ **Enjoy Bed and Breakfast** (BF G H MA) 16.30-21 h
Nollendorfplatz 5, 10777 Berlin (U-Nollendorfplatz) ☎ (030) 236 236 10 📠 (030) 236 236 19 💻 info@ebab.de 🌐 ebab.de
Accommodation sharing agency. All with shower and BF. 40-45 DM p.p.

GENERAL GROUPS

■ **Samstagsschwestern** Sat 15-17.30 h
c/o Rat & Tat Zentrum, Theodor-Körner-Straße 1 ✉ 28203
☎ 70 41 70

FETISH GROUPS

■ **LCNW Lederclub Nordwest e.V.** 4th Fri Zone 83, Kornstraße 283
Postfach 103743 ✉ 28237 💻 lcnw@lcnw.de 🌐 www.lcnw.de

HEALTH GROUPS

■ **AIDS-Hilfe Bremen e.V.** Hotline Mon-Fri 11-16 h
Am Dobben 66 ✉ 28203 ☎ 70 28 19 📠 194 11 (counselling)
📠 70 20 12 💻 AHBremen@aol.com

SPORT GROUPS

■ **Wärmer Bremen** (GLM MA)
c/o Rat & Tat Zentrum, Theodor-Körner-Straße 1 ✉ 28203
☎ 70 41 70 💻 waermerbremen@aol.com
🌐 www.waermerbremen.de
Gay and Lesbian sports group.

SWIMMING

-Unisee (southeast the beach, facility, dunes. Evenings: in the northeast bushes/Südöstlich der Strand, Klappe, Dünen. Abends: im Nordosten ein Wäldchen)

CRUISING

-Wallanlagen Diagonally across from Na-Und-sauna, near the pedestrian tunnel/Beim Fußgängertunnel gegenüber Sauna Na Und
-Bürgerpark (ayor) (Entrance/Eingang "Stern", from dusk on/ab Dämmerung, by car enter at/mit dem Auto Einfahrt bei "Parkhotel") Raststätte Mahndorf
-[P] Oldenburger Straße (ayor r) (under the fly over Hochstraße, across/ unter der Hochstraße, gegenüber Arbeitsamt)

Bremerhaven ☎ 0471

BARS

■ **Why Not** (B d GLM lj MA S STV WE YG) 20-? h, closed Mon
Körnerstraße 33 ✉ 27576 (Bus-Körner-/Goethestraße) ☎ 50 15 25

SEX SHOPS/BLUE MOVIES

■ **Erotic Kino & Shop** Mon-Fri 15-23, Sun 17-23, cinema: 15-23 h
Körnerstraße 4 ✉ 27576 ☎ 41 22 26

HELP WITH PROBLEMS

■ **Rosa Telefon** Sun 18-20 h
☎ 440 10

CRUISING

-Weserdeich am alten Leuchtturm.

Bruchsal ☎ 07251

SEX SHOPS/BLUE MOVIES

■ **Sex Shop** (g) Mon-Sat 10.30-19.30 h
Bahnhofsplatz 10 ✉ 76646 ☎ 85 69 99

Bühl ☎ 07223

GENERAL GROUPS

■ **SCHWUBiS- Gruppe für junge und erwachsene Schwule** (G MA) By appointment

BREMEN VIDEO-WORLD
Shop • Verleih • Kabinen
Piperstraße 7 / Martinistraße
Mo-Sa 8-23 Uhr

Postfach 16 14 ✉ 77806 ☎ 88 66 📠 88 76
Meetings, counselling, coming-out, help, info-pool.

Celle ☎ 05141

SEX SHOPS/BLUE MOVIES
■ **MMV-Erotic Shop** (g VS) Mon-Fri 10-18.30, Sat -13 h, closed Sun
Hannoversche Straße 41 ✉ 29221

HEALTH GROUPS
■ **Cellesche AIDS-Hilfe e.V.** Thu 14.30-18 h
Großer Plan 12 ✉ 29221 *near Photo Porst, City Centre* ☎ 236 46
☎ 194 11 (helpline) 📠 236 46
Helpline Mon 19-21, Thu 14.30-18 h.

HELP WITH PROBLEMS
■ **Schwules Beratungstelefon der SchINK e.V.** Thu 17-19 h
☎ 194 46

CRUISING
-Schloßpark
-Mühlenmasch
-Französicher Garten (nights)
-Schloßpark (western part)

Chemnitz ☎ 0371

GAY INFO
■ **CheLSI e.V. - Chemnitzer Lesben und Schwulen Initiative**
(B D GLM LJ MA OS s TV) Tue Thu Fri 15-22, Sat 18-23, Sun 15-23 h
Hainstraße 109 ✉ 09130 *(Bus 21 - Lessingstraße)* ☎ 500 94
📠 558 67 💻 info@chelsi.de 🖥 www.chelsi.de

BARS
■ **Blue Sky** (B DR G MA VS) Sun-Thu 20-2, Fri & Sat -4 h.
Tue closed.
Lessingstrasse 10 ✉ 09130 *(behind the central station)*
☎ 0172/3447451 (mobile)
■ **Casablanca** (B D S SNU STV) Mon-Thur Bar from 20,
Fri & Sat disco from 21 h
Jägerstrasse 5-7 ✉ 09111 ☎ 64 46 201
■ **Fale** 20-?h
Hainstraße 89 ✉ 09130
☎ 402 8446
■ **Man's Point** (CC DR G lj MA p VS) 20-? h
Lessingstr. 10 ✉ 09130 *(Bus 21/22-Lessingstraße)*
☎ 0172/351 94 05

■ **Seventy-four** (AC B CC D F GLM lj MA s WE) Bar: Thu Sun Mon
20-?, Sat Sun 21-?; Disco Fri Sat 23-? h
Blankenauer Straße 74 ✉ 09113 *(Bus 26-Hochhaus Furth)*
☎ 450 31 85
Fri Sat dance-club.

DANCECLUBS
■ **Lait Solair** (B D GLM) Sat 21-? h
Schulstraße 38 ✉ 09125 ☎ 522 82 80
■ **Wo Man's**
Annaberger Straße 354 ✉ 09125

RESTAURANTS
■ **Brosius** (B F glm)
Yorckstraße 9 ✉ 09130 *(Tram-Gablenzplatz)* ☎ 404 06 38

SAUNAS/BATHS
■ **Clubsauna Outside** (B CC DR G MA SA SB SOL VS WH)
15-2, Fri Sat -5 h
Reineckerstraße 64 ✉ 09126 ☎ 520 48 60
Brand new sauna on 500 m^2 and two floors.

BOOK SHOPS
■ **Wittwer Bahnhofsbuchhandlung** (g)
Bahnhofstraße 1 ✉ 09111 ☎ 42 98 65

HEALTH GROUPS
■ **AIDS-Hilfe Chemnitz e.V.** Tue & Thu 15-20, Fri 9-14 h
Hauboldstraße 6 ✉ 09111 *(in the city centre near Mühlenstr./Stadtbad)* ☎ 194 11 ☎ 0371/41 52 23 📠 41 52 23
💻 aidshilfechemn@aol.com

SPORT GROUPS
■ **Sportverein QUEERSCHLÄGER Chemnitz e.V.**
PO Box 825 ✉ 09008
💻 queerschlaeger@hotmail.com
🖥 members.tripod.de/Queerschlaeger/
Volleyball, Swimming, cycling, skiing

CRUISING
-Straße der Nationen/Rathausstraße (At tourist information. Popular.)
-Kaßbergauffahrt (tunnel at Fabrikstraße)
-Central tram stop (Tunnel, 8-18 h)
-Schloßteichpark (Promenadenstraße between Kurt-Fischer-Straße
and Müllerstraße. Popular.)
-Main rail station (from 20 h)

Germany Coburg ▶ Darmstadt

Coburg ☎ 09561

GENERAL GROUPS
■ **COlibri e.V. Coburger Schwulengruppe** Meeting Tue 19.30 h at Spittelleite 40
Postfach 29 10 ✉ 96418 *near Marienkirche* ☎ 55 01 20
✉ COlibri@coburg.gay-web.de ⌘ coburg.gay-web.de
Help line Tue 18.30-19.30 h Tel. 09561-550 120.

HEALTH GROUPS
■ **Aids-Hilfe Coburg/Landkreis e.V.** Mon 10-12, Wed Thu 19-22 h
Neustadter Straße 3 ✉ 96450 ☎ 63 07 40
✉ aidshilfecoburg@aol.com

CRUISING
-Public toilet at Angerparkplatz

Cottbus ☎ 0355

BARS
■ **Café Marie 23** (A B f glm MA OS) 20-? h
Marienstraße 23 ✉ 03046 *(at/am Busbahnhof)* ☎ 79 19 75
■ **Musik Bar Resi** (B D GLM WE YG) Tue-Fri 20-?, Sat 21-? h
An der Werkstatt 99 ✉ 03046 *(near Staatstheater)*
☎ 0355/70 21 25
Disco on Fri Sat.
■ **Resi - Musikbar** (B d GLM) Tue-Fri 20-? h, Sat 21-? h, Sun + Mon closed
An der Werkstatt 9 a ✉ 03046 *(close to Stadttheater - direction Ströbitz)* ☎ 70 21 25
Disco every Friday and Saturday.

CAFES
■ **Cubana** (B F g MA OS) Mon-Sat 10-24, Sun 14-24 h
Stadtpromenade ✉ 03046

GENERAL GROUPS
■ **Lebensart e.V.** Tue 16-20 h
Straße der Jugend 100, PO Box 10 05 17 ✉ 03046 ☎ 232 73
Disco on Fri Sat 21-5 h in "Resi", An der Werkstatt 9 A, Cottbus-Ströbitz

SWIMMING
-Kiesgrube Sachsendorf (g NU) (the side of the forest)
-Badesee Branitz (g NU) (the big lawn. May-Sep)

CRUISING
-Spremberger Straße (21-? h)

Cuxhaven ☎ 04721

GENERAL GROUPS
■ **Cux-Treff** (G MA) 2nd & 4th Tue 20-22 h
c/o Aktions- und Kommunikationszentrum, Bernhardstr. 48
✉ 27472 ☎ 329 48

Damp

CRUISING
-beach in front of Wellenbad (in the evening)
-nude beach (by day)

Darmstadt ☎ 06151

BARS
■ **Harlekin** (A B BF d f Glm MA OS) Mon-Sun 19-3 h
Heinheimer Straße 18 ✉ 64289 ☎ 71 28 81

Video World

Elisabethenstraße 40 • 64283 Darmstadt
Tel. 0 61 51 / 2 51 33
Öffnungszeiten: Montag - Samstag 9.00-01.00 Uhr
Sonntags 13.00-01.00 Uhr

Videokabinen mit 128 Programmen
davon über 40 neueste Gay-Filme
wie z.B. Bel Ami, Falcon, Kristen Bjorn...

Erotik-Komplettprogramm mit Gay-Abteilung
CD-Video-Verleih, 5 Non-stop-Kinos, 1 Großbildleinwand,
Magazine, Hilfsmittel, Videos, **Versand & Verkauf**

Gay Kontakt-Kino + Kabinen!!!
Ihr führender Treff in Süd-Hessen

Elisabethenstr. 40 • 64283 Darmstadt
Tel. 0 61 51 / 2 51 33 • Fax 2 51 38

CAFES
■ **Café Hans** (B f glm) Mon-Sat 9-1, Sun 10-1 h
Dieburger Strasse 19 ✉ 64287 ☎ 42 53 16

SEX SHOPS/BLUE MOVIES
■ **Boy-Shop** (G VS) 8.30-1 h
c/o Dolly Buster Center, Elisabethenstraße 44a ✉ 64283
☎ 224 30
■ **Sex Shop Heguwa** Mon-Fri 9-20 h, Sat 9-16 h
Ludwigstraße 8 ✉ 64283 ☎ 242 33
Video cabins, video rental.
■ **Video World** (AC CC DR MA VS) Mon-Sat 9-01, Sun 13-01 h
Elisabethenstraße 40 ✉ 64283 ☎ 251 33

GENERAL GROUPS
■ **Louisetta Schwul-lesbisches Kulturzentrum** (A GLM MA s) look for city magazines
c/o SchwuF e.V., Mauerstraße 4 ✉ 64289 *(bus stop Alexanderstraße)* ☎ 78 35 15
⌘ 78 35 15
Café and communication centre for events, culture and meetings. Group Pink Purple meets Tue 20-22 h.

HEALTH GROUPS
■ **AIDS-Hilfe Darmstadt e.V.** Mon Tue Thu 9-17, Fri -15, Wed 13-17 h
Saalbaustraße 27 ✉ 64283 ☎ 280 73 ⌘ 280 76
✉ info@darmstadt.aidshilfe.de
⌘ darmstadt.aidshilfe.de

Darmstadt ▸ Dortmund | Germany

CRUISING
- Main station/Hauptbahnhof
- Park Herrengarten (around WC)

Deißlingen ☎ 07420

HOTELS
■ **Die Krone** (BF F g H) 12-13.30, 18-22 h, closed Mon
Hauptstraße 38 ✉ 78652 ☎ 529 🖨 23 03
Nouvelle-German and French cuisine.

Detmold

CRUISING
- Kaiser-Wilhelm-Platz
- Kronenplatz (behind railway station)
- parking garage (near Hospital)

Dillenburg ☎ 02771

SEX SHOPS/BLUE MOVIES
■ **Venus-Erotik-Shop** (DR g MA VS) Mon-Sat 10-22 h
Schelder Au 1 ✉ 35687 *(B 277 near former Frank'sche Eisenwerke)*
☎ 26 17 17

HEALTH GROUPS
■ **AIDS-Hilfe Gießen e.V.-Zweigstelle Dillenburg** Wed 11-13 h
Bismarckstraße 30 ✉ 35683 *(in health office)* ☎ 194 11

Donaueschingen ☎ 0771

SEX SHOPS/BLUE MOVIES
■ **Intim-Shop** (g) Mon-Fri 10-18.30, Sat -13 h, Sun closed
Josefstraße 27 ✉ 78166 ☎ 31 14

SWIMMING
- Kleiner Riedsee (NU) B 33 Donaueschingen ➤ Tuttlingen. In Pfohren ➤ Camping "Riedsee". 🅿 am Camping. 10 min by foot along the wood.

CRUISING
- Schloßpark (at the source of th river Donau on the right side of the castle)

Dortmund ☎ 0231

GAY INFO
■ **KCR-Dortmunder Lesben- und Schwulenzentrum** (GLM MA s)
Mon& Wed-Fri 20-22 h
Braunschweiger Straße 22 ✉ 44145 *(U-Münsterstraße/Lortzingstraße/Brunnenstraße)* ☎ 83 22 63 🖨 83 19 19
📧 info@kcr-dortmund.de 🖥 www.kcr-dortmund.de

BARS
■ **Burgtor Club** (B d G MA s VS) 14-1, Fri Sat -3, Sun 19-1; Show: Sat 22 h
Burgwall 17 ✉ 44135 ☎ 57 17 48
■ **Café Blu** (B BF F glm MA OS) Mon-Sun 18-1 h
Ruhrallee 69 ✉ 44139 *(U-Landgrafenstraße/Stadthaus)*
☎ 12 61 77
■ **Club 64** (AC B d DR f G lj MA p) 21-?, Mon closed (open on/before public holidays)
Rheinische Straße 64 ✉ 44137 *(Bus/Tram-Heinrichstraße,opposite "Westfalenkolleg")* ☎ 14 32 30

■ **Don-Club** (B d G lj MA) Sun-Thu 21-4 h, Fri-Sat 21-open end
Johannisborn 6 ✉ 44135 ☎ 55 32 21
■ **Fledermaus** (B G OS R) Mon-Fri 10-1 Sat-Sun 11-1 h
U-Bahnpassage Hauptbahnhof ✉ 44137 ☎ 14 97 85
■ **Nouvelle** (B G MA OS R) Mon-Sun 0-24 h
Ludwigstraße 9 ✉ 44135 *(At/am Burgwallplatz)* ☎ 57 45 40
■ **Rote Marlene** (AC B d DR G lj MA p) Tue-Sun 21-? h, closed Mon
Humboldtstraße 1-3 ✉ 44137 ☎ 14 95 20
■ **Sidi Club** (B D glm MA) Mon-Thu 20-5, Fri -?, Sat-Sun 20-? h
Burgwall 5 ✉ 44135 ☎ 52 55 59
■ **The Boots Club** (B DR G LJ p VS) Wed Fri Sat 20-3, Sun 15-2 h
Bornstraße 14 ✉ 44135 *(close to main station)* ☎ 558 05 60
Leather bar.

DANCECLUBS
■ **Area Q** (AC B D MA)
Faßstrasse 1 ✉ 44263 ☎ 445 09 00
One of the larger discos in Germany. In an old brewery consisting of two dance floors and many bars.

RESTAURANTS
■ **Kittchen** (AC B BF F g lj MA N s) 11-1 h
Gerichtsstraße 19 ✉ 44135 ☎ 52 44 42
German food/Deutsche Küche.

SEX SHOPS/BLUE MOVIES
■ **Adonis Center** (G) 12-18.30, Sat 10-14 h
Bornstraße 14 ✉ 44135 *(Near/Nähe Hauptbahnhof)* ☎ 57 36 19
■ **Studio X Kino Center** (g LJ MA VS) Mon-Sat 9-23, Sun 14-23 h
Münsterstraße 12 ✉ 44145 *(500 m away from railway station)*
☎ 81 46 39

SAUNAS/BATHS
■ **Fontäne** (AC B CC f G lj MG p SA SB SOL VS) 15-22 h, closed Sat
Gutenbergstraße 50 ✉ 44139 *(S-Bahn-Stadthaus)* ☎ 52 39 99
Modern sauna frequented by a mixed age crowd.
■ **Sauna am Burgwall** (AC B CC DR f G lj MA SA SB SOL VS WH)
15-23, Sat -2 h
Leuthardstraße 9 ✉ 44135 *(5 min from train station)* ☎ 57 46 00
Nice atmosphere. Also gay magazines and books for sale.

BOOK SHOPS
■ **LITFASS Der Buchladen** (CC glm) Mon-Fri 10-20, Sat 10-14 h
Münsterstraße 107 ✉ 44145 *(U-Münsterstraße)* ☎ 83 47 24
General bookshop with gay section.

GENERAL GROUPS
■ **LSVD Ortsverband Dortmund e.V.** Mon 15-17 h, Wed 20-22 h
Braunschweiger Straße 22 ✉ 44145 *(near Nordmarkt)* ☎ 16 48 66
🖨 863 09 80 📧 dortmund@lsvd.de 🖥 www.lsvd.de/dortmund
■ **Schwul-lesbischer Arbeitskreis Dortmund e.V. (SLADO)**
c/o AIDS-Hilfe Dortmund e.V., Möllerstraße 15 ✉ 44137
🖨 168 65 📧 101731.777@compuserve.com
■ **SchwuSos und Andere-Schwule in der SPD** (MA)
c/o SPD Dortmund, Brüderweg 12 ✉ 44135 ☎ 58 56 17
🖨 52 46 79
Meeting/Treffen 2nd Wed 18-? h in KCR, near Nordmarkt, Braunschweiger Straße 22, 44145 Dortmund

FETISH GROUPS
■ **MSC Rote Erde Dortmund e.V.** 3rd Fri 22 h reunion at The Boots Club
PO Box 10 27 39 ✉ 44027
📧 msc.roteerde@dortmund.gay-web.de
🖥 dortmund.gay-web.de/msc-roteerde
Member of ECMC.

Germany Dortmund ▶ Dresden

DRESDEN – from DM 40 –
overnight accomodation service
· about 750 beds · more than 28 cities ·

enjoy bed & breakfast

central booking office Berlin ☏ **+49-30-236 236 10** 4:30-9:00 pm local time
Fax +49-30-23623619 · info@ebab.de · www.ebab.de

complete offer
see page Germany/Berlin

HEALTH GROUPS

■ **AIDS-Hilfe Dortmund e.V.** Mon Tue Thu Fri 8-16, Wed 15-20 h
Möllerstraße 15 ✉ 44137 ☎ 80 90 40 ☎ Counselling 194 11
📠 80 90 425 📧 info@aidshilfe-dortmund
💻 www.aidshilfe-dortmund.de
■ **All Around Aids e.V.** Tue 16-18 h
Hövelstraße 8 ✉ 44137 ☎ 914 37 37 📠 914 37 38
📧 info@aids.de 💻 www.aids.de

HELP WITH PROBLEMS

■ **Schwules Überfalltelefon** Wed 20-22 h
☎ 192 28
Gay bashing helpline.
■ **19446 - Dortmunds Schwule Infoline** Wed 20-22 h
c/o KCR, Braunschweiger Straße 22 ✉ 44145 ☎ 194 46
📧 19446infoline@KCR-dortmund.de

CRUISING

-Westpark (Entrance Ritterhaustr., popular)
-Main Station (ayor)
-Kaufhof, Westenhellweg

Dresden ☎ 0351

GAY INFO

■ **Gerede Dresdner Lesben, Schwule und alle Anderen e.V.** (D GLM MA N OS VS) Info Mon,Tue,Thu 15-17, Tue,Thu,Fri 10-12 h
Prießnitzstraße 18 ✉ 01099 ☎ 802 22 50
☎ 802 22 70 (serviceline) 📠 802 22 60 📧 gerede@gmx.net
💻 www.intercomm.de/gerede
Meeting point for various gay and lesbian (youth) groups, call for details. Helpline Tue Thu 15-17, Fri 20-24 h.

PUBLICATIONS

■ **Gegenpol**
PO Box 10 04 08 ✉ 01074 ☎ 486 77 77 ☎ (0173) 567 09 85
📠 80 33 400 📧 redaktion@gegenpol.net 💻 www.gegenpol.net
The free gay/lesbian magazine for Sachsen/Das gratis SchwuLesbische Mazagine für Sachsen.

BARS

■ **Bunker** (b DR G LJ MA p) Thu 19-23, Fri Sat 22-3 h (Sat - Dresscode)
Prießnitzstraße 51 ✉ 01099 *(Tram-Schauburg)* ☎ 441 23 45
Lederclub/ Leather club.
■ **Cats** (GLM TV) 20-?h
Alaunstr.61 ✉ 01099 ☎ 81 05 660

■ **Down Town** (AC B D G YG) G Mon 21-? h
Katharinenstraße 11-13 ✉ 01099 ☎ 803 64 14
■ **Little Sharlie** (AC B CC G LJ MG) 20-?h, Closed on Mon.
Louisenstraße 11 ✉ 01099 *(Dresden-Neustadt)* ☎ 799 71 47
■ **Queens** (AC B d DR GLM MA S SNU STV) 20-? h
Görlitzer Straße 3 ✉ 01099 ☎ 803 1650
■ **Roberto's** 20-3h
Jordanstraße 2 ✉ 01099 ☎ 899 6880
■ **Roses** (B G MA OS S) 18-5h
Jordanstraße 10 ✉ 01099 ☎ 80 24 264
■ **Scheune** (B glm) 17-2, WE 10-2 h
Alaunstrasse 36/40 ✉ 01099 ☎ 804 55 32
■ **Zeitgeist** (B GLM) Mon-Thu 11-1, Fri & Sat -3, Sun 18-3 h
Großhainer Straße 93 ✉ 01127 ☎ 840 05 10
Art-Bar. Sundays from 18 h gay lesbian night café.

CAFES

■ **Café Flo** (B f glm) Mon-Sat 19- ? h
Louisenstrasse 77 ✉ 01099 ☎ 801 54 55

DANCECLUBS

■ **Riesa efau** (B D glm YG) 1st Fri & 3rd Sat 21-? h
Adlergasse 14 ✉ 01067 ☎ 866 02 11

RESTAURANTS

■ **La Vie en Rose** (B CC F glm MA OS) Mon-Thu 17.30-24, Fri -2, Sat 12-2, Sun -24 h
Alaunstraße 64 ✉ 01099 *(Tram-Albertplatz/Alaunplatz)*
☎ 803 61 61
French restaurant, Café/Bar & wine cellar "La Cave".
■ **Rudi. Der** (B F glm MA) 11-2 h
Fechnerstraße 2a ✉ 01139 ☎ 858 79 90
■ **Walters Café und vegetarisches Restaurant** (CC g) 11-24 h
Königsbrückerstraße 58 ✉ 01099 *(near Albertplatz)* ☎ 826 39 95
Excellent vegetarian cuisine at reasonable prices.

SEX SHOPS/BLUE MOVIES

■ **Gundis Erotik Paradies** (AC g MA VS) 10-20 h, closed Sun
Rudolf-Leonhard-Straße 11 ✉ 01097 ☎ 804 13 97

SAUNAS/BATHS

■ **Man's Paradise** (AC CC DR G MA p PI SA SB SOL VS WH) Sun-Thu 13-2, Fri Sat 13-8 h.
Friedensstraße 45 ✉ 01099 ☎ 802 25 66
Sauna on 640 m² with new S&M area & pool.

BOOK SHOPS

■ **Das internationale Buch** (g) Mon-Fri 9-19, Sat 9-14, 1st Sat -16 h
Kreuzstraße 4 ✉ 01067 ☎ 495 41 90

Dresden ▶ Duisburg | Germany

TRAVEL AND TRANSPORT
■ **Flamingo Reisen** Mon-Fri 10-18 h
Leipziger Straße 139 ✉ 01139 ☏ 849 68 68 🖨 849 68 69

HOTELS
■ **Holiday Inn Dresden** (AC BF CC F H NG)
Stauffenbergallee 25 a ✉ 01099 ☏ 81 510 🖨 8151 333
📧 info@holiday-inn-dresden.de 🖳 www.holiday-inn-dresden.de

PRIVATE ACCOMMODATION
■ **Enjoy Bed and Breakfast** (BF G H MA) 16.30-21 h
Nollendorfplatz 5, 10777 Berlin *(U-Nollendorfplatz)* ☏ (030) 236 236 10 🖨 (030) 236 236 19 ✉ info@ebab.com 🖳 ebab.de
Accommodation sharing agency. All with shower and BF. 40-45 DM p.p.

GENERAL GROUPS
■ **Gerede e.V.**
Prießnitzstraße 18 ✉ 01099 ☏ 802 2250 ☏ 802 2251
📧 gerede@gmx.net 🖳 intercomm.de/gerede

HEALTH GROUPS
■ **AIDS-Hilfe Dresden e.V.** Office: Mon, Wed, Fri 9-14, Tue &,Thu 9-18 h
Bischofsweg 46 ✉ 01099 ☏ 441 61 42 🖨 441 61 42
📧 info@dresden.aidshilfe.de 🖳 dresden.aidshilfe.de
Counselling ☏ 194 11. Mon 9-13+17-19, Tue 9-13, Thu 15-18 h

HELP WITH PROBLEMS
■ **Streetworker der AIDS-Hilfe Dresden e.V.** Thu 14-17 h
Florian-Geyer-Straße 3 ✉ 01307 ☏ 441 61 43

SPECIAL INTEREST GROUPS
■ **Young GAYneration Dresden** (YG) 1st/3rd Sat 16 h at Stadtteilhaus Neustadt
Postfach 16 02 49 ✉ 01288 *(Preißnitzstr. 18)* ☏ 802 2252
Gay youth group.

SWIMMING
-Kiesgrube Dresden-Leuben (NU MA) (Tram2/12-Lasallestraße) Walk the Salzburger Straße up to the P, through the gate, after the second gate to the right. Cruising/Tanning only.
-Auensee (NU MA) (near Moritzburg)
-Tongrube Auer. On the road from Dresden to Großenhain, just after the village of "Neuer Anbau" there is a small parking area. Here you will find a small lake called "Gewandert".

CRUISING
-Altmarkt/Webergasse/Wallstraße (small wood)
-Hauptbahnhof toilets after 21h
-Marienbrücke in summer
-Roßthaler Straße

Duisburg ☏ 0203

BARS
■ **Café Berlin** (B f GLM MA OS p s) 16-2?, Fri-Sat -5? h
An der Bleek 40-42 ✉ 47051 *(U-Steinsche Gasse, exit Sonnewall)* ☏ 242 73
■ **Gaslight** (B d GLM MA) 20-1, Fri Sat -4 h, closed on Mon
Realschulstraße 10 ✉ 47051 ☏ 298 24 06
■ **Harlekin** (B f G h MA p s) Mon-Sat 11.50-? Sun 9.50-? h
Realschulstrasse 16 ✉ 47051 ☏ 262 44
■ **Pilsstübchen** (f G H MA) Mon-Sun 12-1 h
Hohe Straße 24 ✉ 47051 ☏ 28 71 62

SHOWS
■ **Kleinkunstbühne Senftöpfchen** (A AC B d F GLM MA OS S STV WE) Tue-Fri 17-24, Sat Sun 12-24 h, closed Mon
Ziegelhorststraße ✉ 47169 *(Corner of Röttgersbachstraße)*
☏ 50 12 45

SEX SHOPS/BLUE MOVIES
■ **Gay Sex Shop** (g VS) 10-18.30, Sat 10-14 h
Beekstraße 82 ✉ 47051 ☏ 274 40
■ **World of Erotic** (G VS) 9-24, Sun 12-23 h
Kasinostraße 4a ✉ 47051

SAUNAS/BATHS
■ **Gay Sauna Duisburg** (b DR MA p SA SB SOL VS) 15-23, Sat -24 h
Krummacher Straße 44 ✉ 47051 ☏ 244 10
Formerly Club Sauna.
■ **Oasis die Sauna** (B DR f G MA OS p SA VS) 15-23, Sat -3 h
Hamborner Straße 33 ✉ 47179 *(Walsum,tram 903-Striepweg)*
☏ 49 54 08
Friendly sauna with numerous specials: nudism (every Wed), sportwear or underwear parties.

Szene First Class

120 klimatisierte Zimmer
bequemer Shuttleservice
Pool, Sauna, Massage
Fahrradverleih
Restaurant,
Bar, Biergarten

nahe der
Dresdner Szene

Holiday Inn
DRESDEN

Stauffenbergallee 25a • 01099 Dresden
Tel.: 0351/8151-0 • Fax 0351/8151-333

www.holiday-inn-dresden.de
email: info@holiday-inn-dresden.de

Germany | Duisburg ▸ Düsseldorf

oasis
die sauna.

hamborner str. 33 · 47179 duisburg-walsum
telefon: 02 03 / 49 54 08 · e-mail: oasis@bestboy.de

„wir wollen, dass du kommst!"

GENERAL GROUPS
■ **Homosexuelle Kultur Duisburg (HoKuDu e.V.)** 2nd Mon 20-22 h at AIDS-Hilfe, Friedensstraße 100
Postfach 10 07 09 ✉ 47007 ☎ 66 66 33 📠 37 69 35
💻 wulf@hokudu.de 💻 www.hokudu.de
■ **Pink Power e.V.** Meets Wed 20 h, Counselling ☎ Tue 20-22 h, Musfeldstraße 161-163 ✉ 47053 *(entrance downstairs/Eingang über Keller)* ☎ 66 33 83

HEALTH GROUPS
■ **AIDS-Hilfe Duisburg/Kreis Wesel e.V.** Mon 19-21, Tue 11-14, Wed-Fri -16 h
Friedensstraße 100 ✉ 47053 ☎ 66 66 33 📠 699 84
💻 ahdukw@metronet.de

CRUISING
-Rathaus Hamborn (Town Hall Hamborn)
-Ruhrorter Friedhof (Ruhrorter Cemetary)
-main railway station (R)
-Kantpark (behind museum ➤ Realschulstraße)
-Kleiner Park (Mercatorstraße/Hauptbahnhof)

Durmersheim ☎ 07245
MEN'S CLUBS
■ **M + M Club** (b D E f G MA msg P s SA SOL VS WE WH) Thu & Fri 20-? h
Wagnerstrasse 14 ✉ 76248 ☎ (0171) 536 14 14
Between Karlsruhe and Baden Baden. One of the first gay-swinger-club in Germany. Various activities. Call for details.

Düsseldorf ☎ 0211
GAY INFO
■ **Café Rosa Mond e.V.** (A B d GLM MA s)
Oberbilker Allee 310 ✉ 40227 *(S-Oberbilk-Philipshalle)*
☎ 99 23 77 📠 99 23 76 💻 rosa@rosamund.de
💻 www.rosamond.de
■ **Lesben- und Schwulenzentrum Düsseldorf e.V.**
Lierenfelder Straße 39 ✉ 40231 ☎ 737 00 30 📠 737 00 34
💻 info@luszd.de 💻 www.luszd.de

PUBLICATIONS
■ **Köln & Düsseldorf von hinten**
c/o Bruno Gmünder Verlag, PO Box 61 01 04, 10921 Berlin
☎ (030) 615 00 342 📠 (030) 615 91 34 💻 info@spartacus.de
💻 www.brunos.de

The city guide book about Düsseldorf and Cologne. Useful general information and lots of addresses with extensive descriptions in English and German. Up-to-date maps. Erotic photos.

BARS
■ **Bel Air** (B f G MA R) 12-5 h
Oststraße 116 ✉ 40210 *(Nähe Hbf/near central station)*
☎ 16 19 78
■ **Club Flair** (B G MA) Daily from 18 h
Charlottenstraße 62 ✉ 40210 ☎ 164 6086
■ **Comeback** (AC B f G MA R s) 13-5 h
Charlottenstraße 60 ✉ 40210 ☎ *(Entrance/Eingang Bismarckstraße)*
☎ 164 09 78
■ **Five Club** (B d f GLM MA) 17-2 h, Fri-Sat 15-3 h, Sun 15-3 h
Grupellostraße 5 ✉ 40210 ☎ 369 48 16
■ **Harlekin** (B G MA) Mon-Fri 17-5, Sat Sun 20-? h
Corneliusstraße 1 ✉ 40215 *(Tram Luisenstraße)* ☎ 37 46 28
■ **Insider** (AC B f G MA N STV) 11-5 h
Gupellostraße 32 ✉ 40210 ☎ *(U-Oststraße)* ☎ 36 42 18
Thu and Sun - drag show from 22 h.
■ **Le Clou** (AC B f G MA R) Sun-Thu 12-2, Fri Sat -3 h
Grupellostraße 7 ✉ 40210 ☎ 36 43 65
■ **Murphy's Bar-Café** (AC B DR G LJ MA p s) 21-3, Fri Sat -5, Sun 15-3 h
Bismarkstrasse 93 ✉ 40210 *(entrance Karlstrasse)* ☎ 171 0381
Sundays from 15 h - Murphy's pastry party- coffee and cake - DM 7,50 eat as much as you can !
■ **Musk** (! B DR G LJ MA) Thu-Sat 21-5, Sun-Wed 21-3 h
Charlottenstraße 47 ✉ 40210 ☎ 35 21 54
Thu and WE popular.
■ **Nähkörbchen** (B GLM MA) Tue-Fri Sun 18-1 h, Sat -3 h, closed Mon, Sun 15 h coffee and cake
Hafenstraße 11 ✉ 40213 *(Tram Benrather Straße)* ☎ 323 02 65
■ **Relaxx** (B F OS)
Immermannstraße 38 ✉ 40210 ☎ 17 11 580
Cocktail bar & Italian cuisine.
■ **Studio 1** (B f G MG) 17-5 h
Jahnstraße 2 a ✉ 40215 *(S-Bilk)* ☎ 37 87 43
■ **Theater-Stube** (B Glm MA) 13-2, Fri-Sat 13-3 h
Luisenstaße 33 ✉ 40215 ☎ 37 22 44
■ **Wespennest** (B f g MA) 11-1, WE -3 h
Bergerstraße 24 ✉ 40213 *(U-Heinrich-Heine-Allee)* ☎ 32 83 26
■ **Wilma** (B G p) 13-5 h
Charlottenstraße 60 ✉ 40210 ☎ 17 10 373
■ **ZAKK** (A B glm MA OS S WE) Mon-Sat 18-23 h, Disco Fri 21-6 h & Sat 22-4 h
Fichtenstraße 40 ✉ 40233 *(U-Kettwiger Straße)* ☎ 973 00 80

Düsseldorf

1 Motivation Team
2 Sex Messe Sex Shop
3 Gay Sex Messe Sex Shop
4 Murphy's Bar
5 Gerothek Sex Shop
6 Musk Bar
7 Comeback / Wilma Bar
8 Erotik 63 Sex Shop
9 City Appartment Hotel
10 Phoenix Sauna
11 Bel Air Bar
12 Five Club Bar
13 Le Clou Bar
14 Bhaggy Danceclub
15 City Sauna
16 Harlekin Bar
17 Theater-Stube Bar
18 Nähkörbchen Bar
19 Wespennest Bar
20 Café Tom Thomas
21 Ratinger Hof Danceclub

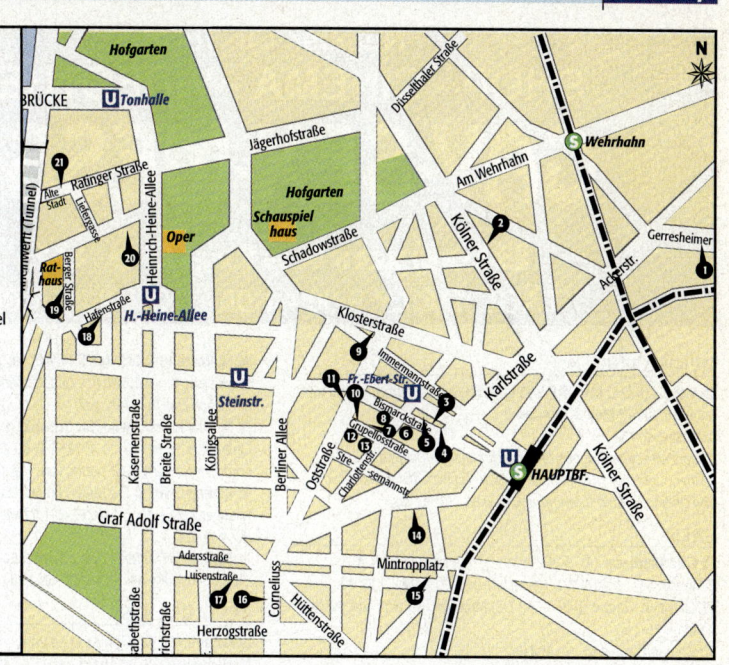

DÜSSELDORFER GAY STATIONEN

RELAXX Cafè Bar
Immermannstr. 38 · 40210 D'dorf
Cocktailbar · Italienische Speisen
Große gepflegte Außenterrasse
Geöffnet täglich von 16°°-1°°h

STATION
Party-House
Charlottenstr. 85
40210 Düsseldorf

Tel. 0211 / 17 11 580

SPARTACUS 2001/2002 | 423

Germany | Düsseldorf

DÜSSELDORF

Number 1 in Town
SHOP - CINEMA - VIDEOTHEK
GAY-SEX-MESSE
Bismarkstraße 88
TÄGL./DAILY 9.00 - 1.00 - SO. 12.00-1.00

Demnächst auch im Internet

MEN'S CLUBS

■ **C.O.K.** (B G LJ MA OS P S VS WE) Fri ,Sun & holidays from 16, Sat from 20 h- ? Mon & Thu closed
Ackerstrasse 137
3 floors with steam sauna& SM underground. Special parties at WE - leather, rubber, or NU. Parties from 20 h. Cubicals, slings, video room and cinema, golden shower room, showers and lockers.

CAFES

■ **Café Balthasar** (AC B BF F g MA OS YG) Mon-Sun 9-1 h
Bolkerstr. 63 ✉ 40213 (U-Heinrich-Heine-Allee) ☎ 32 27 70
■ **Chapeau Claque** (B BF G MA OS) Mon-Sat 10-?, Sun and public holidays 15-? h
Stresemannstrasse 31 ✉ 40210
☎ 171 28 74
■ **Extra Dry. Café** (B F g OS YG) Mon-Sun 17-1 h
Friedrichstraße 125 ✉ 40217 (S-Bilk) ☎ 34 47 01
■ **Strada. La** (A AC f g MA OS YG) daily 11-3 h
Immermannstraße 32 ✉ 40210 (U-Hauptbahnhof)
■ **Tom Thomas in der Mata Hari Passage** (B BF f g MA OS YG) 7.30-1 h
Hunsrückenstraße 33 ✉ 40213 (U-Heinrich-Heine-Allee)
☎ 13 19 71

DANCECLUBS

■ **Bhaggy** (B D g MA we) Thu 22-5, Fri Sat 22 h - open end
Graf-Adolf-Straße 87 ✉ 40210 ☎ 157 60 65 0
Popular on Thu "Club 25" (GLM) .Entry DM 15. Every 3rd Sat "Gay House Club"

■ **La Rocca** (B D GLM MA S TV WE) Sat 22-?
Grünstraße 8 ✉ 40210 (U- Hauptbahnhof) ☎ 83 67 10
Admission DM 18,–. Very gay
■ **Moondance Schwoof für Schwule** (B D G MA OS s VS)
Oberbilker Allee 310 ✉ 40227 ☎ 99 23 77
Locations for SCHWOOF parties vary. Please call for the latest infos.
■ **Ratinger Hof** (B D G MA tv) Fri-Sun 23-5 h
Ratinger Straße 10 ✉ 40213 (U-Tonhalle) ☎ 32 87 77
House music.
■ **Station** (B D G MA S) Disco Fri&Sat 20-5 h, 20 h show
Charlottenstraße 85 ✉ 40210 ☎ 17 11 580

RESTAURANTS

■ **Colopic** (AC CC F g MA) 11.30-24 h
Mertensgasse 5-9 ✉ 40213 ☎ 13 47 40
Italian cuisine.
■ **Tannenbaum** (a F g OS) 17-1 h
Tannenstraße 3/Herrmannplatz ✉ 40476 (U-Frankenplatz) ☎ 454 10 92
■ **Ziegelstübchen** (B F g MA) 17-1, Sun 11-? h
Ziegelstraße 31 ✉ 40468 ☎ 42 72 31

SEX SHOPS/BLUE MOVIES

■ **Erotic 63** (CC g VS) 10-23, Sun 10.30-23.30 h
Bismarckstraße 63 ✉ 40210 ☎ 35 46 01
■ **Gay Sex Messe** (CC G MA VS) Mon-Sat 9-1, Sun 12-1
Bismarckstraße 88 ✉ 40210 (Nähe/near Hauptbahnhof)
☎ 35 25 86
■ **Gay-Video-Markt** (G) 10-24, Sat -21 h, closed Sun
Bismarckstraße 86 ✉ 40210 ☎ 35 67 50

---

complete offer
see page Germany/Berlin

DÜSSELDORF
- from DM 40 -
overnight accomodation service
· about 750 beds · more than 28 cities ·

enjoy bed & breakfast

central booking office Berlin ☎ **+49-30-236 236 10** 4:30-9:00 pm local time
Fax +49-30-23623619 · info@ebab.de · www.ebab.de

424 SPARTACUS 2001/2002

Düsseldorf | Germany

XXL - ESCORTS - XXL - BOYS - XXL - MACHOS

MOTIVATION TEAM
DÜSSELDORF

Unique in Germany Orig.
Big Latin-Lovers
- portfolio available -
top discreet
office location
near central station
power-sex in big rooms -
S/M playroom
home/hotel - bodyguarding
reliable + satisfying
services
all cards acc. mondays +
august closed

www.motivationteam.de

think BIG

0211-361 39 93
straight-acting, mediteranean males always welcome

SPARTACUS 2001/2002

Germany — Düsseldorf

Phoenix Sauna (Advertisement)

Wenn bei anderen das Licht ausgeht, geht es bei uns erst richtig los

ab 12 Uhr • täglich Nachtsauna
werktags bis 13 Uhr Eintritt nur DM 18.-

Düsseldorf • Platanenstr. 11a • Tel: 0211-663638
Köln • Kettengasse 22 • Tel: 0221-2573381
Essen • Viehoferstr. 49

■ **Sex Messe** (g VS) 9-24 h, closed Sun
Kölner Straße 24 ✉ 40211 *(Near/Nähe Hauptbahnhof)*
☎ 35 47 89

HOUSE OF BOYS
■ **Motivation-Team** (AC CC msg p R VS) 13-23 h, closed Mon, closed in august
☎ 361 39 93
Latin lovers in Düsseldorf.

SAUNAS/BATHS
■ **City Sauna** (A AC B BF CC DR F G MA msg N p s SA SB SOL VS WH) 12-1, Fri Sat & before public holidays 12-6 h
Luisenstraße 129 ✉ 40215 *(near Hauptbahnhof)* ☎ 37 39 73
Very large sauna on two floors, incorporating a bar which can also be visited separately.

■ **Phoenix** (! b cc DR f G MA msg p SA SB SOL VS WH) 12-6 h
Platanenstraße 11a ✉ 40233 *(Bus 834-Hermannplatz, Tram 709-Wetterstraße, S-Bahn-Flingern)* ☎ 66 36 38
Very clean sauna on two floors with a decoration full of fantasy.

BOOK SHOPS
■ **Droste Buchhandlung** (cc glm)
Martin-Luther-Platz 26 / Schadow-Arkaden ✉ 40212 ☎ 169 03 17

GIFT & PRIDE SHOPS
■ **Max Seller lifestyle-store** (b CC G) Tue-Fri 11-19 h, Sat 10-16 h
Bahnstraße 48 ✉ 40210 *(between Oststraße & Berliner Allee)*
☎ 02 11/323 08 41
Sexy clothes, toys & tools, books etc.

VIDEO SHOPS
■ **Videothek Tümmers** (g) 0-24 h, closed Sun
Konrad-Adenauer Platz 12 ✉ 40210 ☎ 36 32 29
Angebot an schwulen Filmen/selection of gay films.

PRIVATE ACCOMMODATION
■ **Enjoy Bed and Breakfast** (BF G H MA) 16.30-21 h
Nollendorfplatz 5, 10777 Berlin *(U-Nollendorfplatz)* ☎ (030) 236 236 10 ✉ (030) 236 236 19 ✉ info@ebab.com ✉ ebab.de
Accommodation sharing agency. All with shower and BF. 40-45 DM p.p.

GENERAL GROUPS
■ **Lesben- und Schwulenzentrum Düsseldorf e.V.** (A AC B BF D GLM MA S WE)
Lierenfelder Straße 39 ✉ 40231 ☎ 737 00 30 ✉ 737 00 34
Mon from 20 h - choir "LuSZD-Schrei", Tue from 19 h Ladiescafé, Wed from 19 h Café Total, Thu from 20 h Dance course, Fri from 20 h JuLe, every 2nd Fri/month from 22 h - "Friday Nite Club" - men only . Every 1st 6 & 3rd Sat/month "Crusing" in Schwoof.

FETISH GROUPS
■ **LM Düsseldorf e.V.** Meeting: last/letzten Fri at Club "Musk" 21 h
Postfach 10 20 05 ✉ 40011 *(Charlottenstr. 47)* ☎ 42 50 16
✉ 42 50 16 ✉ Norbyki@aol.com
Member of ECMC and SKVAC.

HEALTH GROUPS
■ **AHD gem. GmbH. Ambulanter Pflegedienst**
Mon-Fri 10-13, 14-16 h
Borsigstraße 34 ✉ 40227 ☎ 72 01 86

■ **AIDS-Hilfe Düsseldorf e.V.** Mon-Fri 10-13, 14-18, Fri -16 h
Oberbilker Allee 310 ✉ 40227 *(U/S - Oberbilk/Philipshalle)*
☎ 77 09 50 ✉ 194 11 ✉ 77 09 527
✉ duesseldorf.aidshilfe.de
Tue 18-22h coming-out group & gay&lesbian youth group Kuchucksei at Loft café. Fri 18-22 group for hiv-positive men. Wed 19-21.30 h, addiction-help.Call for further infos.

HELP WITH PROBLEMS
■ **DGSS-Institut** 9-22 h (call for appointment)
Gerresheimer Straße 20 ✉ 40211 ☎ 35 45 91 ✉ 36 07 77
✉ schwulenberatung@sexologie.org ✉ www.sexologie.org
Counselling. HIV-testing. Gay Switchboard.

■ **Schwules Überfalltelefon** Mon 20-22 h
☎ (0221) 192 28
Gay bashing helpline.

SPORT GROUPS
■ **Düsseldorf Dolphins e.V.**
c/o Hans Georg Saur, Lassallesstraße 9 ✉ 40627 ☎ 27 33 87
Swimming, horseback-riding, fitness/workout, hiking, bicycling, tabletennis, American football.

SWIMMING
- Rheinstadion (stairs)
- Angermunder Baggersee = Kalkumer Baggerloch
- Düsseldorf-Himmelgeist (South of the city), [P] near church, from there 20 minutes walk south to the river Rhine, popular.

CRUISING
- Graf-Adolf-Platz
- Schadowplatz
- Kirchplatz
- Nordpark (until 21 h)

Düsseldorf ▶ Essen Germany

-South cemetery
-Northern cemetery (main entrance)
-Hanielpark (until 16 h)
-Hofgarten, Area Rhein/Inselstraße and Oper (best 22-1 h,popular)
-Schwanenspiegel Elisabethstraße/Haroldstraße (paths around the pond -23 h)

Eisenach ☏ 03691

GENERAL GROUPS

■ **AIDS-Hilfe Eisenach/Wartburgkreis** (GLM MA) Tue 10-15, Thu 14-19, Fri 9-12 h and by appointment
Marienstraße 57 ✉ 99817 (☞ Wartburg, parallel to Wartburgallee)
☏ 21 40 38 ☏ 21 40 38 🖨 info@erfurt.aidshilfe.de
🖳 erfurt.aidshilfe.de
"Wartburg-Café": gay-lesbian café Thu 19-24 h, "Schwules Jugendcafé": gay youth café (-25 yrs) 1st & 3rd Tue 18.30-22 h.

Emden ☏ 04921

CAFES

■ **Alte Post** 1st Sat in month 20-24 h
Cirksenastrasse 2a ✉ 26721 ☏ 872108

GENERAL GROUPS

■ **Schwulen- und Lesbengruppe Emden** Hotline: Mon-Fri 16 h
c/o Aids- und Drogenberatung, Am alten Binnenhafen 2 ✉ 26721
☏ 87 16 65

CRUISING

-park in front of main railway station
-Hesel carpark on the old B75 in the direction Remels - in the woods on both sides of the road.

Erfurt ☏ 0361

GAY INFO

■ **SwiB-Zentrum** (A d f GLM MA s VS) Wed Thu Fri Sun 19-24 h
Windthorststraße 43 a ✉ 99096 (near main station) ☏ 346 22 90
🖨 346 22 98 🖳 info@erfurt.aidshilfe.de
Gay-info-center, switchboard. Home of the SwiB-Café open Wed, Fri & Sun 19-24 h.

BARS

■ **Columbus-Klatsch** (B G MA) Mon-Sun 20-? h
Blumenstraße 78 ✉ 99092 ☏ 260 35 14
■ **Das OX's Clubkeller des Thüringer Lederclub e.V.** (b DR f G LJ MA s VS) Sat 21-4 h
Windthorststraße 43 a ✉ 99096 (near Hauptbahnhof)
☏ 346 22 90

RESTAURANTS

■ **Peters Bergtaverne** (B BF CC d e glm MA OS) Tue-Thu 17-?, Fri-Sun 18-? h,
Brühler Herrenberg 6 ✉ 99092
■ **Wunderbar** (B F glm OS) 11-0 h
Wendenstraße 8 ✉ 99089 ☏ 736 17 43

SEX SHOPS/BLUE MOVIES

■ **Cruising Point** Mon-Sat 10-24h, Sun 15-24h
Papiermühlenweg 3 ✉ 99089
■ **Starlet Erotik** (DR g MG VS) Mon-Fri 9.30-20, Sat -16 h, closed Sun
Thomasstraße 4 ✉ 99084 (Tram-Hauptbahnhof) ☏ 540 39 24

BOOK SHOPS

■ **Haus des Buches-Carl Habel GmbH** (g) Mon-Fri 9-20, Sat -16 h
Anger 7 ✉ 99084 (city centre) ☏ 59 85 80
General book shop with gay section.

GUEST HOUSES

■ **Pension Uferbar** (B BF CC G H lj msg)
Boyneburgufer 3 ✉ 99089 ☏ 566 83 23 🖨 6431403
🖨 5403100 🖳 uferbar@hotmail.com 🖳 www.uferbar.de
Also bar 19- ? h.

FETISH GROUPS

■ **Thüringer Lederclub e.V. (TLC)**
PO Box 124 ✉ 99003 ☏ 731 22 33 🖨 731 24 58

HEALTH GROUPS

■ **AIDS-Hilfe Thüringen e.V.** Tue Wed 10-15, Thu 14-19 h
Windthorststraße 43 a ✉ 99096 ☏ 731 22 33 🖨 346 22 98
🖳 www.aidshilfe.de.

SWIMMING

- Baggersee (quarry) / Stotternheim between Stotternheim and Schwerborn

CRUISING

-Johannesstraße (Kaufmannskirche to Alhambrakino via Hertie) Dangerous but interesting after 23h at WE
-Domplatz- there is a small park nearby
-City park (behing the central railway station)

Erlangen ☏ 09131

DANCECLUBS

■ **Rosa Freitag** (AC B D GLM OS VS YG) 2nd Fri 22-4 h
c/o E-Werk, Fuchsenwiese 1 ✉ 91054 (near main railway station/nahe Hauptbahnhof) ☏ 800 50

GUEST HOUSES

■ **Gasthof Schwarzer Bär** (BF F H)
Innere Brucker Strasse 19 ✉ 91054 ☏ 22872 🖨 20 64 94
🖳 schwarzer.baer.erlangen@topmail.de
Direct in the city center.

CRUISING

-Gerberei (Parking garage)
-Bibliotheque of University (Ground floor)
-Friedrich-List-Straße (Underpass)
-Hugenottenplatz (5-22 h)
-P at Friedrich-List-Straße/Haus des Handwerks

Essen ☏ 0201

BARS

■ **Aerea** (B G) 20.30-5h
Kastanienallee 28 ✉ 45127 ☏ 248 71 33
■ **CARO Sonderbar** (AC B f G MA OS) Sun-Thu 14-1 h, Fri-Sat 14-? h
Vereinstraße 16 ✉ 45127 (near Kennedyplatz)
■ **GO-IN** (AC B f G lj MA p) Tue-Sun 20-5 h
Steeler Straße 83 ✉ 45127 ☏ 23 61 61
■ **Im Büro** (B f G MA R) Mon-Thu 16-4, Fri 16-4, Sat 18-4, Sun 18-? h
Rellinghauser Straße 6, ✉ 45128 ☏ 22 61 51

Germany | Essen

BADESLUST auf 1500 qm
Tel. 0201 - 244 84 03

Phoenix SAUNA
Viehoferstr. 49 • 45127 Essen
U Viehofer Platz Direkt in der Fußgängerzone 10 Min. Hbf
ab 12 Uhr • täglich Nachtsauna • werktags bis 13 Uhr Eintritt DM 18.-

Phoenix Köln • Kettengasse 22 • Tel: 0221-2573381
Phoenix Düsseldorf • Platanenstr. 11a • Tel: 0211-663638

Dax Cocktail Bar
Viehofer Straße 49
Tel.: 24 88 404
daily 10.00 a.m. – 01.00 a.m.

■ **Number Two. Club** (A AC B CC f G lj MA p r) 20-? h
Kleine-Stoppenberger-Straße 17 ✉ 45171 ☎ 831 55 11
■ **Quarterback** (A B CC F glm MA s) Sun-Thu 11-1, Fri-Sat 19-4 h
Alfredistraße 33-35 ✉ 45127 *(near town hall)* ☎ 22 61 04
Musicvideos.

CAFES

■ **Dax** (B f GLM) 10-1 h
Viehofer Strasse 49 ✉ 45127 ☎ 248 84 04

DANCECLUBS

■ **Number One** (AC B CC D DR E GLM N p S WE YG) Mon-Sat and before public holidays 22-5 h
Lindenallee 71 ✉ 45127 *(5 min from railway-station)* ☎ 23 66 82
■ **Power + Glory** (B D G YG) Every 2nd Sat
c/o Jugend & Kulturzentrum Zeche Karl, Hömannstraße 10 *45128 (Altenessen)* ☎ 73 39 20

SEX SHOPS/BLUE MOVIES

■ **Eros-Boutique** (AC DR G MA VS) Mon-Sat 10-22, Sun 16-22 h
Klarastraße 19 ✉ 45130 *(Essen-Rüttenscheid)* ☎ 78 83 21
■ **Man Moviethek** (G VS YG) Mon-Thu 12-1, Fri Sat 12-4, Sun 14-1 h
Vereinstraße 22/Lindenallee ✉ 45127
Entry DM 13,- (4 drinks incl.)/Eintritt DM 13,- (4 Freigetränke inkl.)
■ **Wiscot The World of Him** (G VS) Mon-Sat 10-24 h, Sun 12-24 h
Friedrich-Ebert-Straße 70-72 ✉ 45127 ☎ 208 90

SAUNAS/BATHS

■ **Phoenix** (AC b DR F G MA msg p PI SA SB SOL VS WH) Mon-Fri 12-6, Sat Sun -8 h. Café Dax 9-1 h.
Viehoverstraße 49 ✉ 45127 *(U-Viehoferplatz)* ☎ 244 84 03

Essen ▸ Frankfurt/Main — Germany

Very well equipped sauna. Also offers professional massage and pedicure. Free turkish hamam massage.
- **Ruhrtalsauna** (B DR F G MA OS msg Pl SA SB SOL VS WH WO) 14-24 h
Ruhrtalstraße 221 ✉ 45219 (Kettwig) ☎ 49 46 22
Nice sauna with terrace. Party 1st Sat of the month, free buffet last Fri of the month. Tue 2-4-1.
- **St.Tropez** (A B C DR F G MA msg p s SA SB SOL VS) 12-23 h
Am Freistein 54 ✉ 45141 (U 106-Am Freistein) ☎ 32 25 41
1000 m² sauna with a leather room frequented by a mixed crowd.

BOOK SHOPS
- **Stirnberg Bahnhofsbuchhandlung** (glm)
Hauptbahnhof/U-Bahn Passage ✉ 45127 ☎ 22 30 74

GIFT & PRIDE SHOPS
- **MAX SELLER lifestyle-store** (CC G) Tue-Fri 12-20 h, Sat 10-16 h
Vereinstraße 18 ✉ 45127 (near Kennedyplatz) ☎ 23 60 10
Clothes, toys, tools, books, magazines, videos.

GENERAL GROUPS
- **Fun Project** (G lj) Mon-Thu 17-21, Fri 11-14 h
Borbeckerstraße 4 ✉ 45355 ☎ 68 43 79

FETISH GROUPS
- **LFRR Essen** Meetings 1st & 3rd Wed at Quarterback (Alfredistraße)
Postfach 10 21 04 ✉ 45021 ☎ 23 61 61
✉ lfrressen@gmx.de ✉ essen.gay-web.de
Member of ECMC and SKVdC.

HEALTH GROUPS
- **AIDS-Hilfe Essen e. V.** (g MA) Mon 9-12, Tue 9-12 18-20, Thu Fri 9-12 h
Varnhorststraße 17 ✉ 45127 ☎ 23 60 96, 19411
🖷 20 02 35
Counselling ☎ 19 411.
- **Prävention Projekt Inform e.V.** Mon-Fri 11-16 h, 1st Sat Jack-Off Party at ↦ Sauna St. Tropez (22-23 h)
Postfach 29 03 41, 50525 Köln ☎ (0221) 954 13 13
🖷 (0221) 954 13 11
AIDS prevention.

CRUISING
- Helbingstraße/Frau-Bertha-Krupp-Straße (2 parking lots)
- Hauptbahnhof/Main station (R)
- Uni Essen (Bibliothek, Foyer, Toiletten/library, foyer, toilets)

Esslingen ☎ 0711

CRUISING
- Promenadenweg (Near/Nähe Hauptbahnhof)
- Plienhausbrücke/Neckarstraße (-20 h)
- Kleiner Markt (behind Neues Rathaus. -20 h)
- Marktplatz ↦ Untere Beutau/Geiselbachstraße (underpass -20 h)

Flensburg ☎ 0461

BARS
- **Charly's 4 you** (f GLM MA s) Tue-Fri 20-? h, Sat 21-? h, Sun 20-? h, closed Mon
Speicherlinie 12 ✉ 24937 ☎ 182 42 11
- **Club 69** (B d f G MA) 21-? h, closed Sun
Harrisleer Straße 71 ✉ 24939 ☎ 473 79

DANCECLUBS
- **Schwulen- und Lesbendisco** 2nd Sat 22-4 h
c/o C.u.K. Volksbad, Schiffbrücke 67 ✉ 24939 ☎ 1825462 2 (Info line)

GENERAL GROUPS
- **FLESH** Sun 18h in Jugendkulturhaus
c/o Jugendkulturhaus Exe, An der Exe 25 ✉ 24937 ☎ 182 54 64
☎ 182 56 01 ✉ flesh@gmx.de
🌐 eurogay.net/mitglieder/privat/flesh/index.html
Youth group for young gays and lesbians in Flensburg.

HEALTH GROUPS
- **AIDS-Hilfe Flensburg e.V.** Mon-Thu 10-17, Fri -14 h
Südergraben 53 ✉ 24937 ☎ 255 99 ☎ 194 11 (helpline)
🖷 124 50 ✉ aidshilfe@foni.net 🌐 www.aidshilfe-flensburg.de
Helpline Wed 18-21, Thu 16-19 h.

HELP WITH PROBLEMS
- **Rosa Telefon Flensburg** Tue 18-19 h
☎ 213 47

SWIMMING
- Holnis near Glücksburg (NU) (past Glücksburg 3 km further, then follow the signs to the "Strand".)

CRUISING
- Last parking lot on road BAB 7 before the boarder
- City park after 18h.

Frankenthal ☎ 06233

HOTELS
- **Merkur Post Hotel** (BF glm H)
Eisenbahnstraße 2 ✉ 67227 ☎ (0172) 6241217 🖷 270 26

Frankfurt/Main ☎ 069

GAY INFO
- **AG 36** Counselling: Mon Wed Fri 14-19, Sun 18-21 h; Infocafé: Tue-Thu 19-24, Fri Sat -1, Sun 14-23 h
Alte Gasse 36 ✉ 60313 ☎ 28 35 35 ☎ 194 46 (counselling)
🖷 28 44 01 ✉ ag36@frankfurt.aidshilfe.de
- **Lesbisch/Schwules Kulturhaus** Wed 17-20 h
c/o Emanzipation e.V., Klingerstraße 6 ✉ 60313 ☎ 297 72 96 (G)
☎ 29 30 44 (L) 🖷 29 30 44 ✉ lskh@frankfurt.gay-web.de
🌐 frankfurt.gay-web.de/lskh
Also c/o Lebendiges Lesben Leben e.V.
- **SUB** Mon 20-22, Tue 8-10 h (FM 101.4 MHz, cable 99.85 MHz)
c/o RadioX, Schützenstr. 12 ✉ 60311 (1st floor) ☎ 95 67 80 04
🖷 95 67 80 04 ✉ radioSUB@eurogay.net 🌐 www.radiosub.de

PUBLICATIONS
- **GAB - Das Gaymagazin**
c/o CMC Publishing, Kaiserstr. 72 ✉ 60329 ☎ 274 04 20
🖷 274 04 222 ✉ redaktion@GAB-magazin.de 🌐 GAB.homo.de
Good magazine for gay events in the Frankfurt area.

TOURIST INFO
- **Tourismus + Congress GmbH**
Kaiserstraße 56 ✉ 60329 ☎ 21 23 88 00 🖷 21 23 78 80
✉ info@tcf.frankfurt.de 🌐 www.frankfurt-tourismus.de

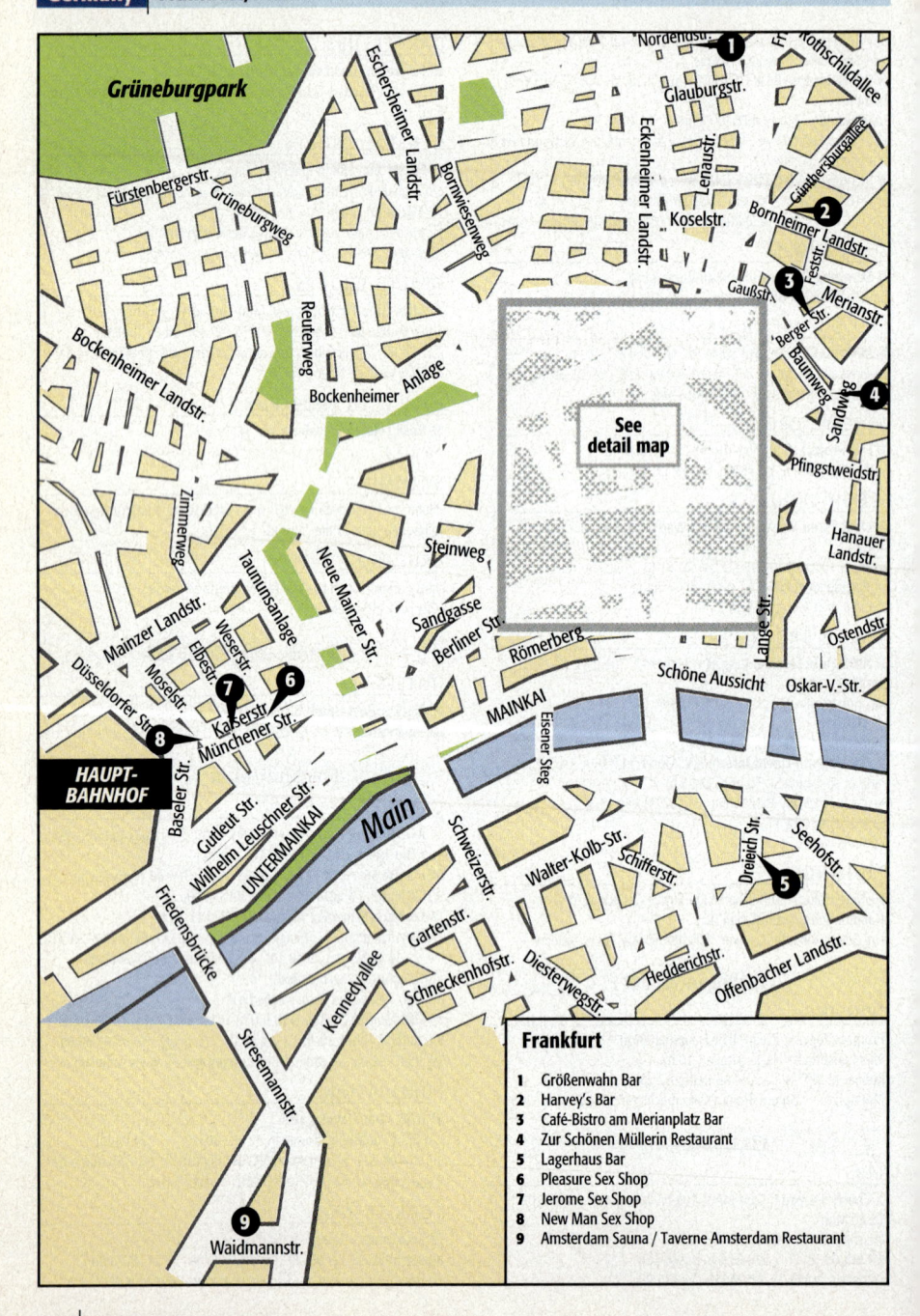

Germany — Frankfurt/Main

Frankfurt

1. Größenwahn Bar
2. Harvey's Bar
3. Café-Bistro am Merianplatz Bar
4. Zur Schönen Müllerin Restaurant
5. Lagerhaus Bar
6. Pleasure Sex Shop
7. Jerome Sex Shop
8. New Man Sex Shop
9. Amsterdam Sauna / Taverne Amsterdam Restaurant

Frankfurt/Main | **Germany**

Club Sauna Amsterdam

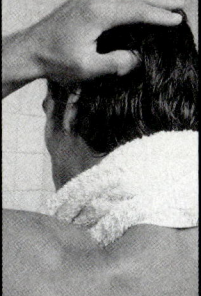

SAUNA
WHIRLPOOL
DAMPFSAUNA
FERNSEHZIMMER
TURBOBRÄUNER
RUHERÄUME
GETRÄNKE
SPEISEN

FEEL YOUR BODY.

14.00 BIS 23.00 UHR
SONNTAG BIS 22.00 UHR
MONTAG RUHETAG

TÄGLICH 23,00 DM
DONNERSTAG 21,00 DM
STUDENTEN 21,00 DM

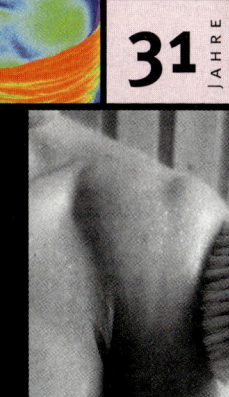

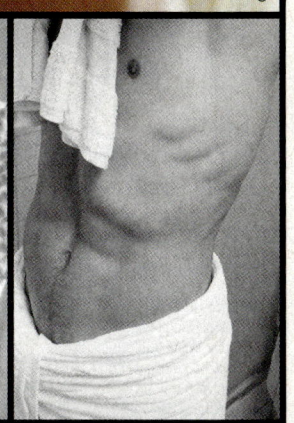

31 JAHRE

© REFORMHOUSE BILDER: VÉRA ATCHOU

60596 FRANKFURT AM MAIN
WAIDMANNSTRASSE 31

(069) 63 13 371

KEINE PARKPLATZPROBLEME!
S-BAHN: S-3 ODER S-4
STATION STRESEMANNALLEE
RICHTUNG DARMSTADT/LANGEN

Germany — Frankfurt/Main

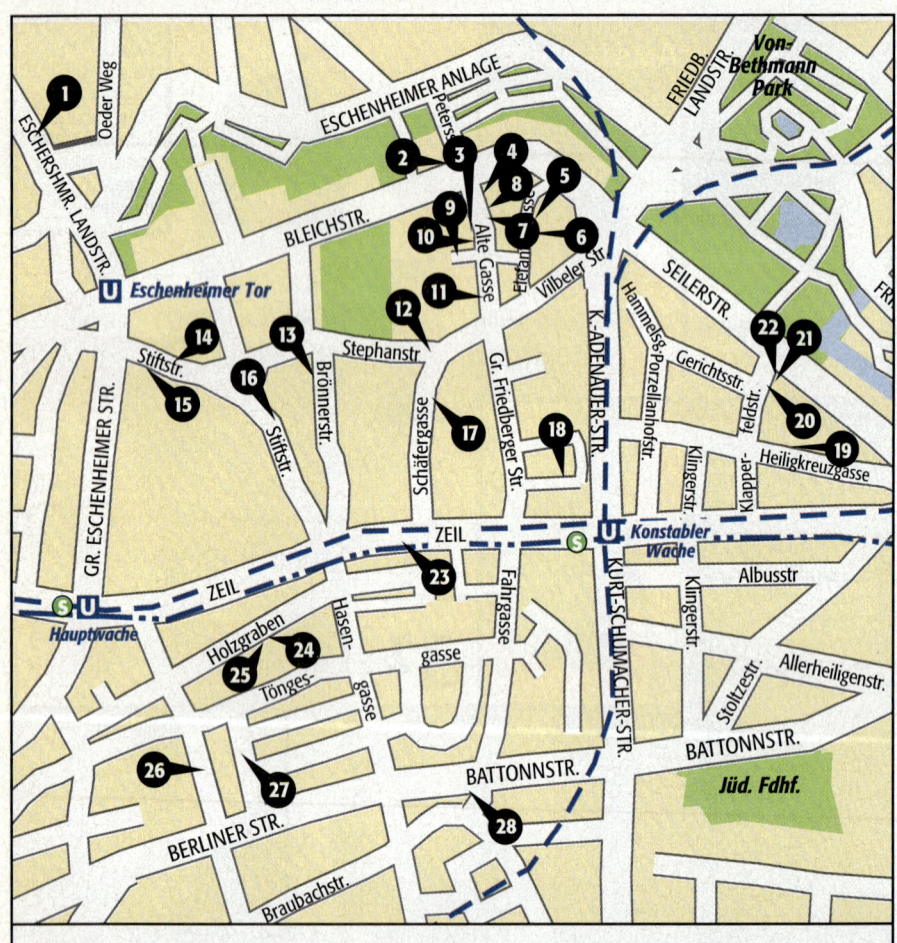

Frankfurt - Innenstadt / City Center

1. Turm Hotel
2. Petras Naomi Bar
3. Oscar Wilde Bookshop
4. Switchboard Gay Info
5. Central Bar
6. Treibhaus Bar
7. Pro Fun Media Store
8. Mr Dorian's Club Bar
9. Comeback Bar
10. KISS - Help with Problems
11. Continental Bathouse
12. Lucky's Manhattan Bar / Sex Shop
13. Blue Angel Danceclub
14. Bannas Bar
15. Tangerine Bar
16. Stall Bar
17. Zum Schweijk Bar
18. Caesar's Bar
19. Why Not Bar
20. Na Und Bar
21. Chapeau Bar
22. Bau Bar
23. Birmingham Pub
24. Heaven Sex Shop
25. City Lights Bar
26. Liliput Café
27. Runset Restaurant
28. Golden Gate Sauna

Frankfurt/Main | **Germany**

WHERE MEN HAVE FUN ...

SCHÄFERGASSE 20 | 60313 FRANKFURT AM MAIN | ☎ (069) 29 31 66

After Business Party

Montags, 16.00 bis 22.00 Uhr
Fun your Monday in City.

ZUM SCHWEJK

FRANKFURT

Die lustige Kneipe.

© REFORMHOUSE BILD: VÉRA ATCHOU

SPARTACUS **2001/2002** | 433

Germany — Frankfurt/Main

SWITCHBOARD
GAY INFO-CAFÉ OF THE FRANKFURT AIDS-FOUNDATION

TUE – THU: 7 PM – MIDNIGHT
FRI + SAT: 7 PM – 1 AM
SUN: 2 PM – 11 PM

ALTE GASSE 36 – 60313 FRANKFURT/M
INFO-LINE +4969 295959
FAX +4969 284401
CAFÉ +4969 283535
infodesk@frankfurt.aidshilfe.de
www.frankfurt.gay-web.de/switchboard

BARS

During the international fairs most bars are open until 4 h.
Während der internationalen Messen haben die meisten Bars bis 4 h geöffnet.

Durant les foires internationales la plupart des bars sont ouverts jusqu'à 4 h.
Durante las ferias internacionales la mayoría de los bares permanecen abiertos hasta las 4 h.
Durante le fiere internazionali la maggior parte dei bar resta aperta fino alle 4 h.

■ **Bannas** (AC B CC e f GLM MA snu stv) 20-4 h
Stiftstraße 34 ⊠ 60313 ☏ 28 89 90
Cocktail & cigarre club, exclusive Whiskeys and Cognacs.
■ **Bau** (AC B Glm LJ MA p s VS WE) Mon-Thu 21-2, Fri & Sat 21-3, Sun 6-? h
Eckenheimer Landstrasse 136 ⊠ 60318
■ **Birmingham Pub** (B f g MA OS p) 21.30-6 h
Zeil 92 ⊠ 60313 *(S/U-Konstablerwache)* ☏ 28 74 71
Gay & popular from 21.30, best after 24 h.
■ **Blue Key** (AC B CC d f GLM MA P r SNU STV TV VS WE) 18-? h
Alte Gasse 26 ⊠ 60313 *(S/U-Konstablerwache)* ☏ 28 37 53
■ **Caesar's - Petit - Palais** (B Glm MA N OS p) 21-? h, Sun closed
Gelbehirschstraße 10 ⊠ 60313 *(S/U-Konstablerwache)*
☏ 13 37 69 53
■ **Café-Bistro am Merianplatz** (B BF g MA OS) Mon-Fri 8-24, Sat 10-24 h Sun closed
Berger Straße 31-33 ⊠ 60316 *(U-Merianplatz)* ☏ 49 38 66
■ **Central** (! AC B GLM YG) Sun-Thu 20-2, Fri Sat -3 h
Elefantengasse 13 ⊠ 60313 *(S/U-Konstablerwache)* ☏ 29 29 26
Trendy "in" bar for students.
■ **Chapeau** (AC B f G N OG) 16-1 Fri Sat -2 h, closed Wed
Klapperfeldstraße 16 ⊠ 60313 *(S/U-Konstablerwache)* ☏ 28 52 23
■ **City Lights** (AC B BF GMA) 6-1, Fri Sat -2 h
Holzgraben 11 ⊠ 60313 *(S/U-Konstablerwache)* ☏ 92 87 08 13
Late night bar.
■ **Comeback** (AC B f G MA R) 13-2, Fri Sat -4 h
Alte Gasse 33-35 ⊠ 60313 *(S/U-Konstablerwache)* ☏ 29 33 45
■ **Größenwahn** (B F glm MA N OS) Mon-Sun 16-1/2 h
Lenaustraße 97/Nordendstraße ⊠ 60318 ☏ 59 93 56
■ **Harveys** (B BF F glm MA OS) Sun-Thu 9-1, Fri & Sat -2 h
Bornheimer Landstraße 64 ⊠ 60316 ☏ 49 73 03
■ **Iks-Bistro-Bar** (AC B f GLM lj MA N OS) 19.30-2, Fri Sat -3 h
Koselstraße 42 ⊠ 60318 *(U-Musterschule, Tram-Friedberger Platz)*
☏ 596 23 89
Meeting place for deaf gay group.
■ **Lagerhaus** (A AC B BF F glm MA N OS s) 10-1, Fri-Sat -2 h
Dreieichstraße 49 ⊠ 60594 *(S-Lokalbahnhof)* ☏ 62 85 52
■ **Maybe** (B DR G VS) Mon-Thu 20-2, Fri & Sat 21-3 h
Elefantengasse 11 ⊠ 60313 ☏ 29 29 50
Bar with dark room and cruising area

434 SPARTACUS 2001/2002

Frankfurt/Main | **Germany**

STALL

23 years
frankfurt's oldest Leatherbar

Frankfurt - Stiftstr. 22
phone 069 / 29 18 80
Sun - Thu 9 pm - 4 am
Fri - Sat 9 pm - ?

where men meet

meeting point for leatherclubs

■ **Mr. Dorian's Club** (B f G MA p R s) Sun-Thu 18-2, Fri & Sat -3 h.
Alte Gasse 34 ✉ 60313 (S/U-Konstablerwache)
☎ 29 45 06
■ **Na Und** (B f Glm MA p) 20-2 h, Fri Sat -3 h
Klapperfeldstraße 16 ✉ 60313 (S/U-Konstablerwache) ☎ 29 44 61

Rh-Main u. überall

Take just the Best
Kevin, 22, blond

0173 / 2141911
eig. App., Hs- u Hotelbes.
Reisebegleitung

■ **Petras Naomi** (B BF F GLM MA OS P s WE) Mon-Thu 17-2, Fri Sat -3, Sun 10-24 h
Bleichstrasse 38 ✉ 60313 (U-Eschersheimer Turm) ☎ 21 99 90 84
Thu Indian night, Wed & Sat cocktail night. German & international cuisine, reservation at WE recommended.
■ **Schwejk. Zum** (! B G lj MA) Tue-Thu 11-1, Fri-Sat -2, Sun 15-1, Mon 16-1 h
Schäfergasse 20 ✉ 60313 (S/U-Konstablerwache) ☎ 29 31 66
Popular and friendly. The number one in Frankfurt.
■ **Stall** (! AC B DR G LJ MA VS) 21-4, Fri Sat -? h, in summer 22-4 h
Stiftstraße 22 ✉ 60313 (U-Eschenheimer Tor) ☎ 29 18 80
■ **Tangerine** (B f Glm MA N) 11-4, Fri-Sat -5/?, Sun 16-4 h
Stiftstraße 39 ✉ 60313 (U-Eschenheimer Tor) ☎ 28 48 79
■ **Tower** (B f glm OS) Mon-Sat 11-4 h
Eschenheimer Turm
Cocktail bar with big terrace in summer.

Petra's Naomi
for gays and friends

Bleichstraße 38
60313 Frankfurt / M.
Telefon 069 - 21 99 90 84

Café - Bar - Bistro
tgl. ab 17 Uhr (Sunday from 10 Brunch)
Inh. Petra Klein

Germany — Frankfurt/Main

Blue Angel Diskothek

Leather + Jeans welcome

täglich 23 h - open end

Brönnerstr. 17 • 60313 Frankfurt/Main • Tel.: 069 / 28 27 72

■ **Treibhaus** (AC B f G MA R VS) Sun-Thu 17-2 h, Fri Sat -3 h
Elefantengasse 11 ✉ 60313 (S/U-Konstablerwache) ☎ 29 12 31
■ **Why Not** (B BF CC f GLM MA N r WE) Mon-Sat 9-4, Sun 17-4 h
Heiligkreuzgasse 24 ✉ 60313 ☎ 9139 6918
■ **Zippo** (B f GLM) Sun-Thu 17.1, Fri & Sat -2 h
Cranachstr.1 ✉ 60596 (Courner of Gartenstrasse) ☎ 61 99 30 90

CAFES

■ **Liliput** (B BF f G MA OS) Daily 9-22 h
Liebfrauenberg ✉ 60311 (Sandhofpassage. S/U-Hauptwache)
☎ 28 57 27
Popular, especially at noon, huge garden area in summer.
■ **Lucky's Manhattan** (! AC B BF CC f GLM OS) 12-1, Fri & Sat -2 h
Schäfergasse 27 ✉ 60313 (S/U-Konstablerwache, in gay district)
☎ 28 49 19
■ **Sunset** (B BF F glm) Daily 10-2 h
Liebfrauenberg 37 ✉ 60313 ☎ 20 23 0
Breakfast every day from 10 h

DANCECLUBS

■ **Blue Angel** (! AC B D G lj p SNU TV VS YG) 23-? h
Brönnerstraße 17 ✉ 60313 (S/U-Hauptwache) ☎ 28 27 72
Frankfurt's traditional danceclub for the past 25 years.
■ **Love Ball** (D DR GLM MA TV) Sat 22-? h
c/o L.O.F.T-house, Hanauer Landstraße 181-185 ✉ 60314
☎ 94 34 48 0
Frankfurt's only big one nighter.

RESTAURANTS

■ **Rosengärtchen** (CC F glm MA OS) Mon-Sun 18-1 h (kitchen open untill 23h)
Eckenheimer Landstr. 71 ✉ 60318 (Nordend, U5 Glaugburstr.)
☎ 59 21 74
French Cuisine
■ **Taverne Amsterdam** (! B F G MA s VS) Tue-Sat 14-24, Sun -23 h, closed Mon
Waidmannstraße 31 ✉ 60596 (S-Stresemannallee) ☎ 631 33 89
Excellent traditional German and Hessian cuisine until 21.30 h. Located in the Amsterdam Sauna.
■ **Schönen Müllerin. Zur** (AC CC f glm MA OS) 16-24 h
Baumweg 12 ✉ 60316 (U-Merianplatz/Zoo) ☎ 43 20 69
Frankfurter und Hessean cuisine.

SHOWS

■ **Gerdas Kleine Weltbühne** (AC glm STV)
Offenbacherstrasse 11 ✉ 63165 ☎ 06108/75841
Please call for details and prices.

SEX SHOPS/BLUE MOVIES

■ **Heaven** (! CC G lj VS) Mon-Sat 11-24, Sun & holidays 13-23 h
Holzgraben 5 ✉ 60313 (S/U-Konstablerwache. Near Zeil)
☎ 29 46 55
Huge selection (5.000) of videos. Europes largest movie all male shop.

JEROME NON-STOP

KINO + KABINEN
SEX-SHOP

Mo – Thu 12 – 23
Fr + Sa 12 – 24
Sun 15 – 23

ELBESTR. 17 • FRANKFURT
4 Min. from Central Station

436 SPARTACUS 2001/2002

Frankfurt/Main Germany

PLAYGROUND FRANKFURT

TOP TEN ESCORTS

Marco · Paolo · Ray · Alex · Phillip · Kai · Roberto · Stefan · Victor

ABSOLUTE DISCRETION ◆ IN-AND OUT-CALLs AVAILABLE ◆
EXKLUSIVE APPARTEMENTS IN FRANKFURT DOWNTOWN ◆
READY TO TRAVEL ◆ ALL CREDITCARDS ARE WELCOME

FON +49(0)69-593906 ◆ http://www.playground-ffm.de

Germany | Frankfurt/Main

Sky...line

Videothek - Shop
Video - DVD - Books - Toys - Fetisch

An der Staufenmauer 5
D-60311 Frankfurt/M.
Phone : +49 69 21 93 93 00

Mo. - Sa. 11^{00} - 23^{00}

Frankfurt/Main Germany

Continental Bathhouse

Da wo MAN(N) schwitzt

Hessen's einzige Nachtsauna

- Dampfsauna
- Fernsehzimmer
- Darkroom
- Massage
- Ruheräume
- Finnische Sauna
- Restaurant
- Shop

Mittwoch
PARTNER-TAG
2 Pers. für
DM 32,-

Donnerstag
MILLENNIUM-DAY
Eintritt pro
Person
DM 21.-

URKUNDE
CONDOMI zeichnet
CONTINENTAL BATHHOUSE
zu einer der TOP 100
Leading Gay Locations
in Deutschland aus.

Köln, 1 Juni 1999
CONDOMI

1.Montag im
Monat
LEDERSAUNA
erm. Eintritt für
FLC, MSC

Dienstag
SINGLE-TAG
Eintritt DM 20.-

Öffnungszeiten:

So. - Do. von 14:00 Uhr - 4:00 Uhr
Fr. +Sa. von 14:00 Uhr - 8:00 Uhr
und vor gesetzlichen Feiertagen.

Continental Bathhouse   Alte Gasse 5   60313 Frankfurt a. Main

Germany — Frankfurt/Main

Oscar Wilde
Buchladen für Schwule und Lesben

Alte Gasse 51
60313 Frankfurt am Main
Telefon 069-28 12 60
Telefax 069-297 75 42
e-mail: shop@oscar-wilde.de

www.oscar-wilde.de

- **Jerome** (AC DR G MA VS) Mon-Thu 12-23, Fri&Sat -24 Sun 15-23 h
Elbestraße 17 ✉ 60329 (S/U-Hauptbahnhof)
☎ 25 39 79
- **New Man** (CC DR G LJ MA VS YG) Mon-Sat 9-24, Sun & holidays 12-24 h
Kaiserstraße 66 ✉ 60329 (S/U-Hauptbahnhof. 1st floor)
☎ 25 36 97
- **Pleasure Sexshop** (AC CC DR g MG OG VS) Mon-Sat 9-24, Sun 12-23 h
Kaiserstraße 51 ✉ 60329 (S/U-Hauptbahnhof)
☎ 23 37 72
4 films in a row in a large cinema
- **Skyline** (G CC lj VS) Mon-Sat 11-23 h
An der Staufenmauer 5 ✉ 60311
☎ 21 93 93 00
Also DVD, boks, toys and fetish-equipment available

ESCORTS & STUDIOS

- **Playground** (AC CC G msg P WH) 14-23 h
(U-Musterschule) ☎ 59 39 06
SM studio on 1st floor. Please call after 11 h for further details.
- **Uniform Master**
Postfach 80 02 80 ✉ 65902
☎ (0177) 68 26 436
Out visits only; nationwide.

HOUSE OF BOYS

- **City Boy's** (CC G msg p) Tue-Sun 12-24 h
(U-Eschersheimer Tor/S-Konstabler Wache) ☎ 91 39 95 16
- **Men's World** (AC CC G msg OS) 14-23 h
(U - Höhenstrasse) ☎ 59 12 82

SAUNAS/BATHS

- **Amsterdam** (B DR F G MA s SA SB SOL WH VS) 14-23, Sun -22 h, closed Mon
Waidmannstraße 31 ✉ 60596 (Sachsenhausen, S-Bahn 3/4, Tram 15/19/21-Stresemannallee) ☎ 631 33 71
Popular and friendly sauna on 4 floors. Very good food. Free buffet every last Fri of the month.
- **Continental Bathhouse** (AC B CC DR F G lj msg p s SA SB SOL VS YG) Sun-Thu 14-4, Fri Sat and before holidays -8 h
Alte Gasse 5 ✉ 60313 (S/U-Konstabler Wache) ☎ 28 27 57
Frankfurt's only night sauna on 700 m². Leather sauna first Mon/month. Young crowd.
- **Golden Gate** (AC B CC DR F G msg P SA SB VS WO YG) 14-1, Fri Sat -3 h
Braubachstraße 1 ✉ 60311 (S/U-Konstablerwache) ☎ 28 28 52
Modern with a large fitness area sauna frequented by a young crowd.

BOOK SHOPS

- **Oscar Wilde Buchhandlung & Mail Order** (A AC CC GLM MA) Mon-Fri 11-20, Sat 10-16 h, closed Sun
Alte Gasse 51 ✉ 60313 (S/U-Konstabler Wache) ☎ 28 12 60
Books, CDs, CD-ROMs, DVDs, videos and accessoires.
- **Wohlthat Cultur-Centrale** (cc glm)
Neue Kräme 14-16 ✉ 60311 ☎ 28 00 64

GIFT & PRIDE SHOPS

- **PRO-FUN media STORE** (CC GLM VS YG) Mon-Fri 11-20, Sat 10-16 h
Alte Gasse 32 ✉ 60313 (S/U-Konstablerwache) ☎ 13 37 70-47

Frankfurt/Main | Germany

GOLDEN GATE
THE BATH

Braubachstr. 1 60311 Frankfurt/Main 069 - 28 28 52

Sauna
Steam Bath
Gym Room
Massage
Solarium
Cabins
TV Lounge
Videoroom
Bar

MEN JUST WANT TO HAVE FUN

Täglich geöffnet von 14 bis 1 Uhr
Freitag/Samstag von 14 bis 3 Uhr
Eintritt 28 DM
Mitgliedschaft ab 75 DM

Daily from 2 pm to 1 am
Friday/Saturday from 2 pm to 3 am
Entry 28 DM
Membership starting from 75 DM

Germany — Frankfurt/Main

pro-fun MEDIA STORE
ALLES ZUM ANFASSEN, ALLES ZUM MITNEHMEN, ALLES ZUM GENIESSEN - BÜCHER, VIDEOS - VON SOFT BIS HART, MUSIK, TOYS, ACCESSOIRES U.V.M. - IMMER TOLLE ANGEBOTE - DAS KOMMEN LOHNT SICH!

ALTE GASSE 32, FRANKFURT/M.
(NEBEN SWITCHBOARD, NÄHE KONSTABLERWACHE)

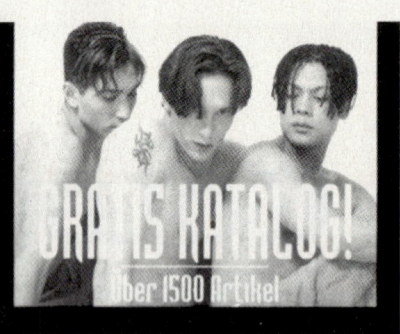

GRATIS KATALOG! Über 1500 Artikel
FORDERN SIE GRATIS UNSEREN VERSANDHAUSKATALOG AN!
PRO-FUN VERSANDHAUS, PF 94 01 32, 60459 FFM
TEL: 069 - 70 76 77 -0, FAX: -11
WWW.PRO-FUN.DE / E-MAIL: PRO-FUN@T-ONLINE.DE

LEATHER & FETISH SHOPS
■ **Fetische-Leder, Latex und Lack** Mon 14-18, Tue-Fri 10-18, Sat 10-13 h
Rotlintstraße 11 ✉ 60316 ☎ 43 91 87

HOTELS
■ **Turm Hotel** (B BF CC f glm H MA) 0-24 h
Eschersheimer Landstraße 20 ✉ 60322 (U-Eschersheimer Tor)
☎ 15 40 50 📠 55 35 78 📧 info@turmhotel-fra.de

TURM HOTEL FRANKFURT ★ ★ ★

Centrally located
Colour-Cable TV
Private Bath/WC
Direct Dial Phones
Trouserpress
Room Service
Collins Bar
Own Parking
Complimentary Buffet-Breakfast
Rates from DM 129 -274

Eschersheimer Landstrasse 20
60322 Frankfurt am Main
Tel. +49 (0)69 15 40 50 Fax: (0)69 55 35 78
E-Mail: info@turmhotel-fra.de
http://www.turmhotel-fra.de

🖳 www.turmhotel-fra.de
Central location in a safe area, 5 min from gay scene. 32 single rooms, 18 twin, 25 double rooms. Rates from 129-274 DM. Bf incl. All rooms with minibar, cable-TV, telephone, modem connection, radio. Gay information available at the reception. No higher rates during fairs. For more information call us or see our web site.

PRIVATE ACCOMMODATION
■ **bed & breakfast** (BF cc G H) Mon-Fri 9-19, Sat -14 h
Postfach 10 05 22 ✉ 60005 ☎ (0177) 2206200 📠 94 59 00 06
📧 bedandbreakfast@gmx.de 🖳 www.bedandbreakfast-ffm.de
■ **Enjoy Bed and Breakfast** (BF G H M Z) 16.30-21 h
Nollendorfplatz 5, 10777 Berlin (U-Nollendorfplatz)
☎ (030) 236 236 10 📠 (030) 236 236 19
📧 info@ebab.com 🖳 ebab.de
Accommodation sharing agency. All with shower and BF. 40-45 DM p.p.

GENERAL GROUPS
■ **LSVD Landesverband Hessen e.V.** Meet 1st Wed/month 20h at Switchboard
Postfach 17 03 41 ✉ 60077 ☎ 62 70 06 01 📠 62 70 06 01
📧 hessen@lsvd.de 🖳 www.lsvd.de/hessen
The group BINATS - gays living in a binational partnership meets here every 3rd Sat / month at 19 h
■ **Schwusos**
c/o SPD, Fischerfeldstraße 7-11 ✉ 60311 ☎ (0179) 6912 969
📧 dirkgent@aol.com
Organisation of gays and lesbians in the SPD. Irregular meetings take place at "Switchboard".
■ **Switchboard. Café & InfoDesk** (A B f G MA s) Tue-Thu 19-24, Fri-Sat -1, Sun 14-23 h (July & August 19-23 h), closed Mon. Infoline Wed-Sat 18-21 h
Alte Gasse 36 ✉ 60313 (U/S-Konstablerwache)
☎ 28 35 35
☎ 29 59 59 (infoline) 📠 28 44 01
📧 infodesk@frankfurt.aidshilfe.de
🖳 www.frankfurt.gay-web.de/switchboard
Info-Café for the AIDS helpgroup. Also meeting point for "Unschlagbar"-project against gay bashing, gropup of gay fathers. Call for details. InfoDesk gives information about various aspects of gay life and is still looking for English speaking volonteers.

Frankfurt/Main | **Germany**

BED & BREAKFAST

Postfach 10 05 22 · 60005 Frankfurt am Main
Tel.: 0177 - 220 62 00 · Fax 069 - 94 59 00 06 o. 0 89 - 14 88 20 37 71
http://www.bedandbreakfast-ffm.de · Email: bedandbreakfast@gmx.de

complete offer
see page Germany/Berlin

FRANKFURT – from DM 45 –
overnight accomodation service
· about 750 beds · more than 28 cities ·

enjoy bed & breakfast

central booking office Berlin ☎ **+49-30-23623610** 4:30 - 9:00 pm local time
Fax +49-30-23623619 · info@ebab.de · www.ebab.de

FETISH GROUPS
■ **FLC Frankfurter Leder Club e.V.**
Postfach 11 13 23 ✉ 60048 ☎ 62 62 75 🖷 62 28 89
💻 flc.frankfurt@pride.de 🖳 frankfurt.gay-web.de/flc

HEALTH GROUPS
■ **Regenbogendienst** 10-13 h, Sat-Sun closed
Eiserne Hand 12 ✉ 60318 ☎ 59 13 93 🖷 59 76 056
Ambulatory nursing care/domestic help.

HELP WITH PROBLEMS
■ **KISS - Kriseninterventionsstelle für Stricher** Mon Wed 14-19,
Thu 16-20 h
Alte Gasse 37 ✉ 60313 *(S/U-Konstablerwache)*
☎ 29 36 71
🖷 29 36 71 💻 kiss@frankfurt.aidshilfe.de
Counselling for hustlers.
■ **Rosa Hilfe Frankfurt** Sun 18-21 h
c/o V.S.B.N., Postfach 11 19 03 ✉ 60054 ☎ 194 46
🖷 469 99 495 💻 rosahilfe@rhein-main.net

SPORT GROUPS
■ **Frankfurter Volleyball Verein e.V. (FVV)**
☎ 70 79 31 33 💻 069441173@t-online.de
🖳 members.aol.com/fvvev/welcome.html
The gay sports club of Frankfurt.

SWIMMING
-**Langener Waldsee (G)** (Take B44 to Mörfelden-Walldorf. Then look carefully for the signs to "Sering-Werk/Regatta/Badesee" and turn left there. Go to the nude area.

Internet Live SEX
Beobachte live nackte Männer!

82 live Kameras

Kameras in: Schlafzimmer, Duschen, Bad, Gay Saunas, Umkleidekabinen, Leder-Keller, Gay Clubs
• Live Amsterdam Sex Shows
• Solo Sex live • Nachtsicht- kameras in Darkrooms • Leder- -Sex live • und, und, und...

**Funktioniert sofort!
Keine Kreditkarte notwendig!**

Gratis Gallerie, Fotos, Tour

www.topgaysex.com

SPARTACUS 2001/2002

| Germany | Frankfurt/Main ▶ Freiburg |

THERMOS CLUB SAUNA

79106 Freiburg • Lehener Str.21
Tel. 0761/27 52 39

Dampfbad, Finnische Sauna
Di.-Fr. 16-23 Sa.-So 14-23
Montag Ruhetag

opening soon

dtm — don't tell mama

CRUISING

- Main railway station (ayor R)
- University (1st floor above Cafeteria)
- Airport (Section C, next to Disco Dorian Gray & behind Dr.Müllers Sex Shop)
- U-Konstablerwache (MA) (B-level, near Entrance U6/U7 direction Heerstraße. 12-21 h)
- U-Nordwestzentrum (MA) (12-16 h)
- U-Alte Oper (by day only)
- Paulsplatz (Paulskirche/Römerberg)
- Friedberger Anlage (ayor)
- Grüneburgpark (at end of August-Siebert-Straße)

Freiberg ☎ 03731

GENERAL GROUPS

■ **G.A.Y.-Schwulesibische Jugendgruppe Freiberg** Meets 2nd/4th Sun 16 h at Begegnungsstätte des DHB e.V., Fischerstraße 38
c/o Andreas Möckel, Postfach 1630 ✉ 09586

Freiburg ☎ 0761

BARS

■ **Garçons. Les** (B BF f glm msg OS YG) Mon-Fri 6.30-1, Sat Sun 9-1 h
Bismarckallee 7-9 ✉ 79098 *(in Freiburg central train station)*
☎ 2927220
Watch out for party flyers.
■ **HaWe's Batzenberg-Stüble**
Adelhauserstr. 7
■ **Sonder Bar** (AC B GLM OS TV YG) Mon-Sat 13-2 Sun 16-1 h
Salzstraße 13 ✉ 79098 *(ca. 50 m vom/from Berthold's Brunnen Richtung/direction Schwaben Tor)* ☎ 339 30

CAFES

■ **Café Légère** (B F g YG) Mon-Sat 10-1, Sun 15-1 h.
Niemenstraße 8 ✉ 79098 *(Near Martins Tor & "McDonalds")*
☎ 328 00
Popular on Sun.
■ **Café Rouge** (d G MA) 18-?h
Oberlinden 4 ✉ 79098 *(Altstadt)* ☎ 290 9253

DANCECLUBS

■ **Divino** (AC B D MA NG P S WE VS YG) Thu & Fri 22-4, Sat 23-5 h
Humboldtstraße 3 ✉ 79089 *(In der Nähe vom/ near Martinstor)*
☎ 345 85
Especially gayfriendly the cream parties Sat 23-5 h.

SAUNAS/BATHS

■ **Thermos** (B F G MA SA SB VS) 16-23, Sat Sun 14-23 h, closed Mon
Lehener Straße 21 ✉ 79106 ☎ 27 52 39

444   SPARTACUS 2001/2002

Freiburg ▶ Fulda Germany

HOTEL AM RATHAUS

RATHAUSGASSE 4-8
79098 FREIBURG TEL: 0761 - 29 61 60 FAX: 0761 - 29 61 666
E-MAIL: HOTEL@AM-RATHAUS.DE

IM ZENTRUM VON FREIBURG ERWARTET SIE EIN MODERNES HOTEL - GARNI MIT ALLEM KOMFORT.
FÜHLEN SIE SICH WOHL!

EZ AB DM 130,-, DZ AB DM 195,-
NICHTRAUCHERZIMMER VERFÜGBAR

BOOK SHOPS
■ **Jos Fritz** (g) Mon-Fri 9-19 h, Sat 10-16 h
Wilhelmstraße 15 ✉ 79098 ☎ 268 77

VIDEO SHOPS
■ **Manhattan No. 1** (g) Mon-Sat 10-22 h
Haslacher Straße 78 ✉ 79115 ☎ 49 92 21
■ **Manhattan No. 1** (CC g) 8-24 h
Christaweg 54 ✉ 79114 ☎ 476 00 80

HOTELS
■ **Hotel am Rathaus** (BF CC g H) Reception 7-24 h
Rathausgasse 4-8 ✉ 79098 *(In pedestrian zone)* ☎ 296 160
🖨 296 1666 🖳 hotel@am-rathaus.de 🖥 www.am-rathaus.de
Nice hotel with comfortable rooms, all with bath or shower/WC, telephone, minibar, own keys. Single DM 120-155, double DM 195, additional bed DM 40, bf buffet incl. Domestic animals allowed. Own garage (DM 15 per day).

GENERAL GROUPS
■ **Rosekids e.V. - schwul-lesbische Jugendgruppe Freiburgs** Wed (G) 19.30-? h
Engelbergerstraße 3 ✉ 79106 ☎ 28 18 74 🖥 www.rosekids.de
Telephone during the meetings./Telefon während der Treffen.
■ **Schwusos-Arbeitskreis Freiburg** Meeting 2nd Thu 19.30 h, call for details.
c/o SPD, Habsburgerstraße 85 ✉ 79108 ☎ 809 57 64
🖨 809 57 64 🖳 kv.freiburg@spd.de
Also Schwusos Baden-Würtemberg (gay and lesbian Social Democrats

HEALTH GROUPS
■ **AIDS Selbsthilfe HIV Positiv e.V.** 18-18.30 h
Postfach 12 27 ✉ 79012 ☎ 231 31
Call for dates of meetings
■ **Beratungsstelle AIDS-Hilfe Freiburg e.V.** Mon-Fri 10-13, Mon Tue Thu 15-17, Wed 17-19 h
Habsburgerstraße 79 ✉ 79104 *(Tram 5/6 - Hauptstraße)*
☎ 27 69 24 ☎ 19 411 (Hotline) 🖨 28 81 12
🖳 AIDS-Hilfe-Freiburg@t-online.de
🖥 www.aids-hilfe-freiburg.de

HELP WITH PROBLEMS
■ **Rosa Hilfe e.V.** café Fri 21-?, helpline Thu 19-21 h
Eschholzstraße 19 ✉ 79106 ☎ 251 61 🖨 251 61
🖳 sifredaktion@freiburg.gay-web.de 🖥 freiburg.gay-web.de

SPECIAL INTEREST GROUPS
■ **Breisgau-Bären Freiburg** 4th Sun 16 h at ➔ Sonderbar
☎ (0781) 227 14 (Jürgen).

SWIMMING
-Baggersee Niederrimsingen (g, NU) (B 31 exit Gündlingen) or Bus-Gündlingen, cruising/action in the wood behind the nude beach)
-Opfinger Baggersee (NU) (in the wood behind the nude area)
-Nimburger Baggersee (NU) (BAB 5 approach Freiburg Nord. The whole lenght of south and west side.)
(all only in summer)

CRUISING
-Colombi Park (opposite of Colombihotel, at night, popular)
-Turmstraße (r)(next to Colombihotel)

Friedberg ☎ 06131

HEALTH GROUPS
■ **AIDS-Hilfe Gießen, Zweigstelle Friedberg** Thu 10.30-12.30 h
Gesundheitsamt, Europaplatz ✉ 61169
☎ 194 11

Friedrichshafen ☎ 07541

GENERAL GROUPS
■ **LesGays**
c/o Jugendhaus Molke, Meisterhofener Str.11 ✉ 88045
☎ 386 725
🖳 lesgays@t-online.de

CRUISING
-Bundesbahnhafen at Seeparkplatz (Ruderclubhaus)

Fulda ☎ 0661

GAY INFO
■ **Regenbogentreff** Wed 20-22 h
Künzeller Straße 15 ✉ 36043 ☎ 901 44 47 🖨 901 44 47
🖥 www.schwulesbi-fulda.de
Information and counselling center. They publish their own magazine called "Gayzette".

BARS
■ **Fleckviehalle** (AC B d f GLM lj MA OS WE) Disco: Mon-Thu 22-1 (Thu G), Fri Sat -3 h, Sun closed, Beer garden: 15-? h
Ruhrstraße 3 ✉ 36043 ☎ 942 89 21

Germany | Fulda ▶ Göttingen

GENERAL GROUPS
■ **SchwuLesBische Organisation Fulda e.V.** (GLM MA)
call for details
Künzeller Straße 15 ✉ 36043 ☏ 194 46 🖷 901 44 47
📧 SchwuLesBi@eurogay.net 🖥 www.SchwuLesBi-Fulda.de
Mon 20-22 lesbian group, Wed 15-16 youth group, 20-22 gay group, Fr 20-22 h "Regenbogencafé".

HEALTH GROUPS
■ **AIDS-Hilfe Fulda e.V.** Mon 11-13, Tue Thu 14-16 h
Friedrichstraße 4 ✉ 36037 *(next to/neben Stadtpfarr Kirche)*
☏ 770 11 🖷 24 10 11 📧 AIDS-Hilfe.Fulda@t-online.de
Helpline Tue 11-13, Mon 14-16 h (Tel 19411). Private counselling Mon 14-16, Thu 11-13 h

HELP WITH PROBLEMS
■ **Informations- und Beratungstelefon** Wed 20-22 h
☏ 194 46

Geislingen ☏ 07331

CAFES
■ **Connexion** (BF d DR F G lj MA r WE) Sun-Thu 6-1, Fri Sat -3
Steingrubestraße 7 ✉ 73312 ☏ 94 40 42

Gelsenkirchen ☏ 0209

BARS
■ **Club "La Mirage"** (B d f G MA s) 21-5 h
Selhorststraße 6-10 ✉ 45879 *(Near/Nähe Hauptbahnhof; Fina Parkhaus)* ☏ 20 11 06

RESTAURANTS
■ **Schwarze Schaf. Das** (B F g) 17-? h, closed Sat
Florastraße 24/Hansemannstraße ✉ 45879 ☏ 261 01

SEX SHOPS/BLUE MOVIES
■ **Gaykino "Höhepunkt"** (DR G LJ MA VS) Mon-Sat 10-22, Sun 16-22 h
Wanner Straße 133 ✉ 45888 ☏ 255 80
Always the latest films. A good place to "come" together.
■ **L.G.S.** (CC glm lj MA) Mon-Fri 9-18.30, Sat -14, 1st Sat -16 h
Bochumer Straße 76 ✉ 45886 ☏ 222 14
Leather, rubber, sexshop. Medical piercing on 1st Sat.
■ **Live Erotika** (g VS) Mon-Sat 9-24, Sun 12-24 h
Augustastraße 11 ✉ 45879

GENERAL GROUPS
■ **Gehörlosen-Club für Schwule & Lesben 1991 e.V.**
Postfach 10 04 29 ✉ 45804 ☏ 20 05 41 🖷 20 16 45
Group for deaf gays/lesbians.
■ **Jugendnetzwerk Lambda NRW e.V. Landesbüro Westfalen**
Wanner Straße 6 ✉ 45879
📧 Jugendnetzwerk.lambda@t-online.de

HEALTH GROUPS
■ **AIDS-Hilfe Gelsenkirchen e.V.** Mon Wed Fri 12-17, Thu 15-17 h
Husemannstraße 39-41 ✉ 45879 ☏ 194 11 🖷 20 91 66
📧 aidshilfege@cww.de
🖥 www.geocities.com/WestHollywood/Heights/1547/index.html
Gay youth group Young connections meets Mon 19-21 h, the bigroup meets Fri 15-17 h, Bi-café 3rd Sun 18.30-21.30h. Call for details.

CRUISING
-Toilets at central train station (OG)
-Schloß Berge
-Toilets at Zeppelinallee.

Gießen ☏ 0641

BARS
■ **Anders als** (B D GLM MA OS s) 20-1, Fri Sat -3 h, Sun closed
Schanzenstraße 9 ✉ 35390 ☏ 781 64
■ **Bonaparte** (A B d f GLM lj MA N OS) Mon-Sun 20-1 h
Liebigstraße 66 ✉ 35390 ☏ 756 49
The oldest gay bar in Gießen

CAFES
■ **Café Einstein** (A B F glm MA OS) 9-1, Sun 10-1, meals -23 h
Mühlstraße 5 ✉ 35390 ☏ 757 53

GENERAL GROUPS
■ **HOMO e.V.** Meeting: 1st & 3rd Wed 19-21 h
Diezstraße 8 ✉ 35390 *(at AIDS-Hilfe)* ☏ 194 46 *(counselling every Wed 19-21 h)* 🖷 394476

HEALTH GROUPS
■ **AIDS-Hilfe Gießen e.V.** Mon Wed Fri 10-14, Thu 14-18 h, closed Tue
Diezstraße 8 ✉ 35390 ☏ 39 02 26 ☏ 194 11 (helpline)
🖷 39 44 76 📧 ah-gi@t-online.de
Helpline Mon 10-14, Thu 14-18 h.

HELP WITH PROBLEMS
■ **Rosa Telefon** Wed 19-21 h
☏ 194 46

CRUISING
-Park an der Ostanlage (opposite Behördenzentrum)

Gladbeck ☏ 02043

CRUISING
-P (opposite post office 1, Bahnhofstr. 82-86, late evenings 22-? h)
-Liebigstraße (opposite Hauptzollamt, late evenings 22-? h)
-Park near Ostanlage (opposite Behördenzentrum (Bus stop Behörden-zentrum), late evenings 22-? h)

Gnandstein ☏ 034344

CAFES
■ **Burg Gnandstein** (B F g H OS WE) Mon Tue closed
04655 *(B95 between Chemnitz and Leipzig, exit Dolzenheim)*
☏ 612 20
12th Century Castle, now hotel, restaurant and café.

Görlitz ☏ 03581

HELP WITH PROBLEMS
■ **schwubs** Wed 18-21 h
Postfach 300 533 ✉ 02810 ☏ 30 69 96 🖷 30 69 87

Göttingen ☏ 0551

DANCECLUBS
■ **Faces** (B D f GLM OS) 19-? h
Nikolaistraße 22 ✉ 37073 ☏ 531 49 49
Minimum consumption DM 10,-Best time later in the evening.

Göttingen ▶ Halle (Saale) Germany

■ **ManDance** (AC B D DR GLM lj s VS YG) 2nd Sat 22-4 h
musa, Hagenweg 2 ✉ 37079 *(behind the "Zollamt")*
☎ (0173)95 15 870
Very sporadical parties events. Watch the press for details.

HEALTH GROUPS
■ **Göttinger AIDS-Hilfe e.V.** Mon-Fri 10-13 h
Obere Klarspüle 14 ✉ 37073 ☎ 437 35 📠 41027
💻 aids-hilfe.goettingen@t-online.de 💻 goettingen.aidshilfe.de

HELP WITH PROBLEMS
■ **Rosa Telefon** Mon 20-22 h
☎ 194 46
■ **Schwulen Hilfe Göttingen S.H.G.**
Postfach 11 51, 37116 Bovenden ☎ 833 55 📠 833 55

SWIMMING
-Badeparadies
-Freibad am Brauweg.

CRUISING
-Jacobi Kirchhof / church yard (between Weender-Jüdenstraße)

Greifswald ☎ 03834

GENERAL GROUPS
■ **Rosa Greif-schwul-lesbischer AK in Vorpommern e.V.** Thu 19.30 (Café), last Fri 21 h (Rosa Schwoof) at St. Spiritus, Lange Str. 49
Postfach 12 03 ✉ 17489 ☎ 89 70 34 📠 89 70 34
💻 rosagreif@gmx.de
Tue 15-17 h, Wed 18-22 h Coming-out group.

CRUISING
- Wallanlagen (between Mühlentor und Fleischerstraße)

Grewesmühlen ☎ 03881

HEALTH GROUPS
■ **Aidshilfe c/o AWO** Thu 12-16 h
Rudolf-Breitscheidt-Straße 27 ✉ 23936 ☎ 71 94 74
📠 (03841) 214 755 💻 wismar.aidshilfe.de

Gummersbach ☎ 02261

GENERAL GROUPS
■ **Schwule Gruppe Oberberg** (GLM MA) Meets every 2nd Wed 20 h
PO Box 31 01 75 ✉ 51616 ☎ 2 54 49
Contact ☎ (02265) 91 52 Joachim

Gütersloh ☎ 05241

GENERAL GROUPS
■ **Coming-Out-Gruppe Gütersloh** Meeting Wed 20 h
c/o Kulturzentrum Alte Weberei, Bogenstraße 1-8 ✉ 33330

Hagen ☎ 02331

BARS
■ **Alaska Bär** (B d f GLM s) Tue-Fri 17-24 h, Sat 17-3 h, Sun 15-3 h, Mon closed
Graf-von-Galen-Ring 13 ✉ 58095 ☎ 204 570
■ **Toleranz** (B f glm MA) Mon-Thu 19-1 h, Fri-Sat 19-3 h, Sun closed
Körnerstraße 47 ✉ 58095 *(Near/Nähe Volkspark)* ☎ 324 26
Formerly "Krönchen".

SEX SHOPS/BLUE MOVIES
■ **Homo-Kino im Sex Shop** (g VS) Mon-Sat 9-24, Sun 13-24 h
Kampstraße 21 ✉ 58095
■ **Venus Kino World** (b DR G MA p VS) Mon-Thu 9.30-23, Fri/Sat - 24h, Sun 13-23h
Hindenburgstraße 22 ✉ 58095 ☎ 37 15 51
Formerly known as "Cine Bar".

GENERAL GROUPS
■ **"aMANNda"** Wed 20.30 h
Kulturzentrum, Pelmkestraße 14 ✉ 58089 ☎ 33 69 67
■ **Elterngruppe homosexueller Söhne und Töchter** every other Tue 19.30 h
c/o VHS-Villa Post, Wehringhauser Straße 38 ✉ 58089
☎ 023 31/207 35 89

HEALTH GROUPS
■ **AIDS-Hilfe Hagen e.V.** Councelling Mon-Fri 9-12 and by appointment
Körnerstraße 82 ✉ 58095 *(Entrance/Eingang C)* ☎ 19 411
📠 20 40 61

HELP WITH PROBLEMS
■ **Gay Line Hagen** Mon 20-22 h
c/o AIDS-Hilfe, Körnerstraße 82 ✉ 58095 ☎ 33 88 33

SPORT GROUPS
■ **SC Moving Man e.V.** (G MA) Tue 21 (Badminton), Thu 20.30 (Volleyball), every 2nd Fri 20 h (Bowling)
c/o Volker Haeske, Unternahmerstr. 47 ✉ 58119 ☎ 934357
📠 934258 💻 moving-men@gmx.de
Badminton at WOS-Eilpe (World of Sports), Eilper Straße. Volleyball at Käthe-Kollwitz-Sporthalle - Bowling at Kegel- & Bowlingcenter Dortmund, Marlinkrodtstraße 212-214.

CRUISING
-Main rail station
-Volkspark
-Johanniskirchplatz

Halberstadt ☎ 03941

HEALTH GROUPS
■ **AIDS-Hilfe Halberstadt e.V.** Mon 8-14h, Tue -22h, Wed -14h, Thu -20h, Fri -13h, Sun 17-20h.
Finckestraße 7 ✉ 38820 ☎ 60 16 66

Halle (Saale) ☎ 0345

GAY INFO
■ **Begegnungs- & Beratungs-Zentrum (BBZ) "lebensart" e.V. schwul-lesbische Interessengemeinschaft** (GLM MA p) office hours 10.30-14.30 h. Various activities in the evening.
Schmeerstraße 22 ✉ 06108 *(Tram-Marktplatz)* ☎ 202 33 85
📠 202 33 85
Call infoline for details.

BARS
■ **Blue Velvet** (B CC d DR f G MA r s STV TV) Mon-Sun 12-1 h, lunch
Alter Markt 29-30 ✉ 06108 ☎ 517 03 59

DANCECLUBS
■ **Easy Schorre** (AC B D f GLM lj s VS YG) Gay disco every 2nd Sun
Philipp-Müller-Straße 77-78 ✉ 06110 *(Tram-Rannischer Platz)*
☎ 21 22 40

Germany   Halle (Saale) ▶ Hamburg

■ **Pierrot** (AC b D DR GLM MA s SNU STV WE) Mon-Thu 18-?, Fri & Sat 20-5 h
Großer Sandberg 10   ✉ 06108   ☎ 290 3331

GENERAL GROUPS
■ **Schwulenverband in Deutschland (SVD) e.V. Landesverband Sachsen-Anhalt: Aussenstelle**
Friedrich-Hesekiel-Straße 22   ✉ 06292   ☎ 775 93 83

HEALTH GROUPS
■ **AIDS-Hilfe Halle e.V.** Mon 14-18, Tue Thu 10-22, Wed Fri 10-14 h
Böllberger Weg 189   ✉ 06110   ☎ 230 90-0   📠 23 09 04
🖥 info@halle.aidshilfe.de   🖥 www.halle.aidshilfe.de
Helpline Tue 19 411. Rainbow breakfast Sat 11 h. Counselling Mon 18-20, Thu 16-20 h

HELP WITH PROBLEMS
■ **Schwules Überfalltelefon** Tue 20-22 h
☎ 192 28
Gay bashing helpline.

SPORT GROUPS
■ **Saaleperlen**
☎ 521 19 30   🖥 www.saaleperlen.de
Gay sports group/ Schwul-Lesbischer Sportverein.

CRUISING
-Stations
-Waisenhausring/Hansering (near Leipziger Turm, -24 h, popular)
-FKK-Kanal/nude swimming (obere Aue, B 80 Angersdorf ➤ Wörmlitz, popular)

Haltern

SWIMMING
-Baggersee (Flaesheimer Straße at Flaesheim)
-Selberseen I & II (Münsterstraße at Sythen)

Hamburg ☎ 040

✱ The atmosphere of a harbour city is ever present in Hamburg. The Red Light District around the Reeperbahn in St. Pauli offered the vast number of sailors in the past a much needed change from long journeys at sea. Today the Reeperbahn is a popular meeting point for the locals and visitors to the city. It's the hub of sexual activity with an endless number of bars, cafés, clubs and prostitution. Certainly not to be missed out on by tourist wanting to strike it lucky. Recommended is to take a trip to the City Park, Elbvorte and Alster to discover several exquisite restaurants serving mouth watering dishes. There are a host of cultural things to do ranging from theatres to museums and city tours.
The gay community has rooted itself in St. Georg, the second Red Light District in Hamburg. In St. Georg many gays walk hand in hand and often visit the most popular gay café: Café Gnosa with it's wide selection of cakes and gâteaux. In this neighbourhood you can also find gay literature, rubber and leather in Mr. Chaps. And not too far from the many sides streets of the district, around the Pulverteich is Tom's or Rudi's Nightclub. Those who travel to Hamburg will discover many different sides of this warm, friendly city, and perhaps those with a little bit more patience an real "Hamburger". Once the heart of a northerner is captured, you will have made a friend for life.

✱ Der Flair einer Hafenstadt ist in Hamburg allgegenwärtig. Das Rotlichtviertel um die Reeperbahn in St. Pauli bot früher den zahlreichen Seemännern reichlich Abwechslung nach einer langen Reise auf hoher See. Heute vertreiben sich die Hamburger und die unzähligen Besucher der Hansestadt ihre Abendstunden in der berühmten Ausgehmeile. Egal ob man auf der Sache nach Bars, Clubs oder käuflichem Sex ist, hier wird der schwule Tourist fündig. Neben dem zweitgrößten Hafen in Europa, bietet die Handelsmetropole Hamburg aber noch mehr. Stadtpark, Elbvororte und Alster sind einen Ausflug wert, exquisite Restaurants bereiten Gaumenfreuden, Theater und Museen bieten kulturelles für jeden Geschmack.
Die Lange Reihe in St. Georg, Hamburgs zweitem Rotlichtviertel in unmittelbarer Nähe des Hauptbahnhofs, hat sich in den letzten Jahren zu einer lebendigen schwulen Umgebung entwickelt. Hier schlendern Schwule Hand in Hand, hier lädt das traditionelle Café Gnosa zu leckeren Torten, hier findet man schwule Literatur im Blendwerk oder Lack und Leder im Mr. Chaps. Von der Langen Reihe ist es auch nicht weit in das ebenfalls in St. Georg gelegene Ausgehviertel um den Pulverteich, wo p.i.t., Tom's oder Rudi's Nightclub ihre schwulen Gäste empfangen. Wer nach Hamburg reist wird schnell feststellen können, wie abwechslungsreich, schön und freundlich diese Stadt ist-auch wenn man vielleicht etwas länger Geduld haben muß einen echten Hamburger kennenzulernen. Wenn man erstmal das Herz eines Nordlichts gewonnen hat, hat man einen Freund fürs Leben.

✱ Partout à Hambourg, on respire l'ambiance d'une ville portuaire. Le quartier chaud autour du "Reeperbahn" à St Pauli offrait autrefois aux nombreux marins beaucoup de distractions après un long voyage en mer. Aujourd'hui, les Hambourgois et les innombrables visiteurs de la ville hanséatique passent leurs soirées dans la célèbre avenue, peu importe que ce soit dans un bar, un club ou un bordel. Le Parc municipal (Stadtpark), les faubourgs au bord de l'Elbe et l'Alster méritent une visite, ainsi que les nombreux restaurants exquis et les théâtres et musées qui offrent de quoi satisfaire tout un chacun.
La "Lange Reihe" à St Georg, le deuxième quartier chaud de Hambourg tout près de la gare centrale, a évolué ces dernières années vers une ambiance gaie animée. Les homos y flânent main dans la main, le traditionnel Café Gnosa invite à déguster de délicieux gâteaux, on trouve de la littérature gaie à Blendwerk ou des articles en latex ou en cuir chez "Mr Chaps". De la "Lange Reihe", on n'est qu'à quelques pas du "Pulverteich" où les clubs gais Tom's or Rudi's se situent. Quiconque vient à Hambourg constatera rapidement combien cette ville est variée, belle et conviviale, même s'il faut avoir de la patience avant de rencontrer un vrai Hambourgeois. Quand on éprouve pour la première fois de la sympathie pour un Allemand du Nord, on a un ami pour la vie.

● El ambiente caracteristico de una ciudad portuaria se hace notar en Hamburgo por todas partes. El barrio St. Pauli en los alrededores de la *Reeperbahn* ofreció en el pasado a innumerables marineros diversión variada después de un largo viaje en alta mar. Hoy en día este districto se ha convertido para los hamburgeses y los numerosos visitantes de la ciudad en una zona de marcha nocturna. El turista gay que busque bares, clubs o sexo pagado, encuentra aquí indudablemente de todo. Hamburgo no solamente es la segunda ciudad portuaria más grande de Europa, sino además un importantísimo centro comercial que tiene mucho más que ofrecer. El parque municipal, los elegantes barrios a orillas del río Elba y también el lago Alster son dignos de ver. Pero también la gastronomía con sus exquisitos restaurantes y la amplia vida cultural con teatros y museos ofrece algo para cada gusto.
En el barrio de *St. Georg*, cerca de la estación central, en la calle *Lange Reihe* se ha desarrollado en los últimos años un animado ambiente gay. Aquí se pasean parejas homosexuales cogidos de la ma-

INTENSE
DER EROTISCHE VERFÜHRER

Jetzt auch bei uns, die erotische Revolution aus den USA. **INTENSE** ist ein geruchsneutrales Parfum, das Ihre erotische Ausstrahlung intensiviert!

Und so funktioniert es: In **INTENSE** sind natürliche sexuelle Stimulantien (Pheromone) konzentriert. Mit **INTENSE** verstärken Sie Ihre eigene „sexuelle Duftnote" und verführen so auf eine völlig natürliche Weise.

INTENSE basiert allein auf Wasser, Alkohol und Pheromonen, ist also geruchsneutral. Sie können unbesorgt Ihr eigenes Parfum über **INTENSE** tragen, ohne die Wirkung zu beeinträchtigen. **INTENSE** wirkt extrem langanhaltend, ist absolut natürlich und 3 Jahre haltbar.

Lassen Sie sich verführen:
INTENSE Parfum mit natürlichen Pheromonen, geruchsneutral. Geliefert im attraktiven Glasflacon (63,3 ml) in Geschenkpackung.
DM 69,95

Erhältlich im Handel oder direkt bei
www.brunos.de

DAS WELTWEIT ERSTE PHEROMON FÜR MÄNNER

Händleranfragen:
Telefon 030/610 01 100
vertrieb@brunogmuender.com

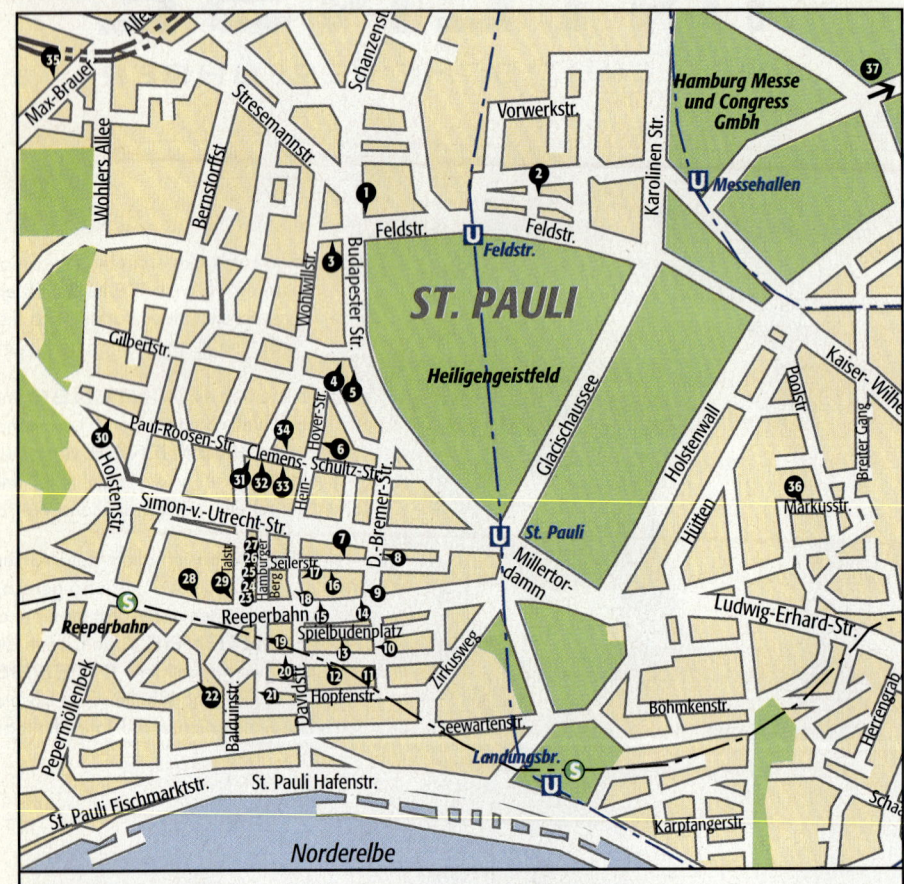

Hamburg - St. Pauli

1. Männerschwarm Bookshop
2. Mess Restaurant
3. Nil Restaurant
4. Spundloch Restaurant
5. Clubika Danceclub
6. Crazy Horst Bar
7. Du & Ich Bar
8. Seagull Bar
9. Fundus Bar
10. Amigo Bar
11. Goldene 13 Bar
12. Schlößchen Restaurant
13. Angies Night Club Bar / Schmidt Theatre
14. Harald's Hotel & Bar
15. Seventh Heaven Sex Shop
16. Sparta Junior Sex Shop
17. Freudenhaus Restaurant
18. Sparta Gay Sex Shop
19. Powderroom at Absolut Danceclub
20. Purgatory Bar
21. E-D-K Danceclub
22. Picadilly Bar
23. Erotic Kino Sex Shop
24. Homo-Kino Hamburg Sex Shop
25. Mystery Hall Bar
26. Wunderbar
27. Sparta Point Sex Shop
28. La Cage aux Folles Danceclub
29. Mystery Hall Sex Shop
30. AIDS-Hilfe Hamburg
31. Toom Peerstall Bar
32. Touché Bar
33. Homo Gay Kino Sex Shop
34. Clements Gift & Pride Shop
35. Apollo Sauna
36. Willi's For You Bar
37. Café Shuh

Hamburg | Germany

Hamburg - St. Georg

- 38 Café Spund
- 39 Blendwerk Bookshop
- 40 Bistro des Artistes Café
- 41 Café Gnosa
- 42 Sparta City Sex Shop
- 43 Café Urlaub
- 44 Mr Chaps Leatherworks Shop
- 45 Pension Sarah Petersen
- 46 Twist Café
- 47 Romeo Bar
- 48 Extratour Bar
- 49 Comeback Bar
- 50 Bajadere Bar
- 51 Black Bar
- 52 My Way Bar
- 53 Adria-Hof Hotel
- 54 Henry's Show Center Sex Shop
- 55 Hotel Village
- 56 Seventh Heaven Erotic Discount Sex Shop
- 57 Hotel Schweriner Hof
- 58 New Man im WOS
- 59 New Man Plaza Sex Shop
- 60 Seventh Heaven Sex Shop
- 61 Mystery World Sex Shop
- 62 Rudi's Night Club Bar
- 63 Bei Franz Bar
- 64 Hein & Fiete Gay Info
- 65 New Man City Sex Shop
- 66 Pulverfaß Caberet Show
- 67 Hotel Königshof
- 68 Male Bar
- 69 Dragon Sauna
- 70 Tusculum Bar
- 71 Salvation Danceclub
- 72 Chaps Bar

SPARTACUS 2001/2002 | 451

Germany Hamburg

Hein & Fiete
hamburg's gay switchboard

pulverteich 21
20 099 hamburg
phone 040 240 333

http://www.heinfiete.de

mo - fr 4 - 9 h p.m.
sa 4 - 7 h p.m.

no y el tradicional *Café Gnosa* seduce con sus buenísimas tartas. La librería *Blendwerk* ofrece una amplia gama de literatura gay y en la tienda *Mr. Chaps* se encuentra de todo hecho de cuero o latex. La *Lange Reihe* no cae lejos de la zona de marcha en las alrededores del *Pulverteich*, también ubicado en el barrio de St. Georg, donde merecen los clubs p.i.t, Tom's o Rudi's una visita. El visitante de Hamburgo notará en seguida que esta ciudad se caracteriza por su variedad, belleza y ambiente hospitalario. Aunque el típico hamburgés tiene fama de ser introvertido, una vez que se haya conquistado el corazón de uno, será una amistad para toda la vida.

✖ L'atmosfera di una città portuale si sente dappertutto ad Amburgo. Una volta il quartiere alle luci rosse attorno alla Reeperbahn in St. Pauli offriva ai numerosi marinai diverse opportunità di svago dopo un lungo viaggio sul mare. Oggi sono gli abitanti ed i turisti della città delle repubbliche marinare tedesche, le Hanse, che passano le loro serate nella famosa strada. Qualunque cosa ci si cerchi, un bar, un club o sesso a pagamento, il turista gay trova di tutto. A parte il porto, che è il secondo in Europa come vastità, la metropoli economica Amburgo offre molto di più. Il parco comunale e i sobborghi lungo i fiumi Elba e Alster valgono la pena di una gita; ristoranti squisiti offrono cibo prelibato; teatri e musei soddisfano ogni gusto.
La via Lange Reihe in St. Georg, il secondo quartiere a luci rosse vicino alla stazione centrale, è diventato negli ultimi anni un vivace ambiente gay. Qui i gay camminano tenendosi per mano. Il tradizionale *Café Gnosa* invita a gustosissime torte, nel *Blendwerk* si trova letteratura gay, nel *Mr. Chaps* si trova lacca e cuoio. Poco distante dalla *Lange Reihe* si trova un quartiere altrettanto situato in *St. Georg* attorno al *Pulverteich* che offre svariate occasioni per uscire di sera come in il *p.i.t, Tom's* o *Rudi's Nightclub*. Il visitatore si renderà velocemente conto della varietà, bellezza e gentilezza della città, anche se

ci vuole un po' di pazienza per fare la conoscenza di un vero nativo d'Amburgo. Ma quando si ha rapito il cuore di "un'aurora boreale", si ha trovato un'amico per tutta la vita.

GAY INFO

■ **Hamburger Gay Information** 8-16 h
Postfach 60 54 20 ✉ 22249 ☎ 46 27 02 📠 460 27 69.
🖥 www.gaycity.de/hgi
Monthly newsletter with advertising and dates of events. Free at gay venues.

■ **Hein & Fiete** (G lj MA s) Mon-Fri 16-21, Sat -19 h, Sun closed
Pulverteich 21 ✉ 20099 (U/S-Hauptbahnhof) ☎ 24 03 33
📠 24 06 75 🖥 www.heinfiete.de
Also meeting point for the gay & lesbian youth group Tom & Jerry (-26yrs). Call or see www.tomjerry.de for further infos. Gay and lesbian excursion group meets every 1st and 3rd Friday at 20.30 h at the info-café.

■ **Magnus Hirschfeld Centrum/Kommunikations- und Beratungszentrum für Homosexuelle** (A b d f GLM) Mon-Fri 16-1, Fri - open end, Sat from 15, Sun from 11 h
Borgweg 8 ✉ 22303 (U-Borgweg) ☎ 27 87 78 00 ☎ 279 00 69 (counselling) 📠 278 778 02 🖥 hamburg.gay-web.de/mhc
Gay center with café and library. Ask for their programme and all the groups meeting here.

■ **Nordgay Radio** every 2nd Sat/month 20-21 h, FM 96,00 MHz (Antenne) & 95,45 MHz (Kabel)

■ **Pink Channel - Radio für Schwule & Lesben** 1st Mon 22-24, 19-20, 1st and 3rd Sat 19-21 & 22-24 h, FM 96.0 MHz
Steindamm 62 ✉ 20099 ☎ 280 51 29-0 📠 280 51 29-1
🖥 www.pinkchannel.net

---

mhc
MAGNUS HIRSCHFELD CENTRUM
Hamburgs Zentrum für Lesben und Schwule
Borgweg 8 · 22303 Hamburg
Tel.: 040/278 778-01 · Fax: -02
Lesbentelefon: 040/279 00 49
Schwulenberatung: 040/279 00 69
Internet: mhc@hamburg.gay-web.de

andersrum · selbstbewußt

Hot Night DISCO FÜR GAYS, LESBIANS & FRIENDS
JEDEN LETZTEN SAMSTAG IM MONAT

feelgood IM MHC CAFE · BAR · BISTRO

emma c. Disco WOMEN ONLY
JEDEN 2. SAMSTAG IM MONAT

Hamburg | Germany

■ **Szene-Guide**
Fun World Studio, Breite Straße 60 ✉ 22767 ☏ 38 41 94
☏ 38 61 07 54 📠 38 87 05 📧 sgh@funworld.com
💻 www.funworld.de
Advertising, maps and some dates of events. Free at gay venues.

PUBLICATIONS

■ **Hamburg Hannover & Sylt von hinten**
c/o Bruno Gmünder Verlag, PO Box 61 01 04, 10921 Berlin
☏ (030) 615 00 342 📠 (030) 615 91 34 📧 info@spartacus.de
💻 www.brunos.de
The city guide book about Hamburg, Hanover & Sylt. Useful general information and lots of addresses with extensive descriptions in English and German. Up-to-date maps. Erotic photos.

■ **Hinnerk** Mon-Fri 9-18 h
Koppel 97 ✉ 20099 ☏ 24 06 45 📠 24 06 50
📧 redaktion@hinnerk.de
Monthly free gay magazine for Hamburg featuring news, reports and addresses.

TOURIST INFO

■ **Tourismus-Zentrale Hamburg GmbH** 8-20 h
Postfach 10 22 49 ✉ 20015 ☏ 30 05 14 29 📠 30 05 13 33
💻 www.hamburg-tourism.de

BARS

■ **Amigo Bar** (B G MA N) 21-? h
Taubenstraße 23 ✉ 20359 *(S-Reeperbahn/U-St.Pauli)* ☏ 31 64 36
■ **Angie's NightClub** (AC B CC GLM NG S WE)
Wed-Sat 22 h-open end
Spielbudenplatz 27-28 ✉ 20359 *(S-Reeperbahn/U-St.Pauli)*
☏ 31 77 88 11
Many cocktails
■ **Bajadere** (B G N R s) 14-4 h
Rostocker Straße 1 ✉ 20099 *(S-Hauptbahnhof)* ☏ 24 01 52
■ **Black** (AC BF D DR G LJ MA VS) 22-4, Fri Sat -6 h
Danziger Straße 21 ✉ 20099 *(U/S-Hauptbahnhof)* ☏ 24 08 04
Dresscode
■ **Can Can** (B F G MA N) 12-4, WE 0-24 h
Danziger Straße 63 ✉ 20099 *(U/S-Hauptbahnhof)* ☏ 24 60 51
■ **Central** (B F g MA OS) Mon-Thu 12-24 , Fri & Sat -2, Sun 15-24 h
Lange Reihe 50 ✉ 20099 *(S/U-Hauptbahnhof)* ☏ 28 05 37 04
The kitchen times are not the same as the opening times. Large selection of vegetarian meals.
■ **Chaps** (B DR G LJ MG VS) Sun-Thu 20-?, Fri-Sat 22-? h
Woltmanstraße 24 ✉ 20097 *(S-Hauptbahnhof)* ☏ 23 06 47
■ **Comeback** (B G MA N TV) Mon-Thu 16-4 h, Fri-Sun -open end
Zimmerpforte 3 ✉ 20099 *(Near Hansaplatz)*
☏ 280 567 89
■ **Crazy Horst** (B BF CC f g MA N) 21-8 h
Hein-Hoyer-Straße 62 ✉ 20359 *(S-Reeperbahn)* ☏ 319 26 33
■ **Diva** (G MA STV TV)
Danziger Straße 51 ✉ 20099 *(S/U-Hauptbahnhof)* ☏ 280 25 12
■ **Du & Ich** (G MG R SNU VS) Sun-Thu 20-4, Fri-Sat 21-? h, closed Wed
Seilerstraße 38a ✉ 20359 *(S-Reeperbahn/U-St.Pauli)* ☏ 31 59 69
■ **Extratour** (B BF CC f GLM MA N OS TV) Mon-Thu 9-4, Fri 9-Sun 4 h
Zimmerpforte 1 ✉ 20099 *(S-Hauptbahnhof)* ☏ 24 01 84
■ **Fehmarn-Stube** (B f G OG) 17-1, Sat 20-? h, closed Sun
Landwehr 35 ✉ 22087 *(U-Wartenau)* ☏ 254 27 54
This rather hidden away bar is open every day except Saturday as most of the regulars visit the city centre at the weekend. During the week the

Wunder Bar

Täglich ab 21 Uhr
Talstraße 14

www.wunderbar-hamburg.de

owner serves along with other delicious dishes a fried potato dish. Mon-Fri 5pm-?, Sun from 6pm
Coffee 2,50; Beer 3,50; Cola 3 DM
■ **Ferdi's** (B G MA) Mon-Thu 11-2, Sun 15-2 h, summer Sun closed
Ferdinandstraße 2a ✉ 20095 ☏ 30 39 27 63
■ **Fundus** (B G MA N OS) 0-24 h
Detlef-Bremer-Straße 54 ✉ 20359 *(S-Reeperbahn/U-St.Pauli)*
☏ 319 17 26
■ **Goldene 13** (B d GLM MA TV) Wed-Sun 21-? h
Hopfenstraße 28 ✉ 20359 *(S-Reeperbahn/U-St. Pauli)* ☏ 31 79 26 05
Nice atmosphere
■ **Hansa Molle** (B f G MA N) 0-24 h
Stralsunder Straße 4 ✉ 20099 *(S-Hauptbahnhof)* ☏ 24 50 05
■ **Jürgens Pub & Bar** (B G N R) Mon-Thu 11-3, Fri Sat 10-?, Sun 12-4 h
Hansaplatz 1 ✉ 20099 *(S-Hauptbahnhof)* ☏ 24 95 92
■ **Male** (B CC DR f G lj MA VS) Mon-Sun 22-3 h, connected to Pit-Disco
Pulverteich 17 ✉ 20099 *(S-Hauptbahnhof)* ☏ 280 30 56
Cocktails and Snacks.

SPARTACUS 2001/2002 | 453

Germany | Hamburg

CAFE Gnosa
LANGE REIHE 93 · 20099 HAMBURG
TEL.: 24 30 34
11-1, FR & SA 11-2, MO 18-1 UHR

■ **Monte Christo** (G MG R)
Detlev-Bremer-Straße 44 ✉ 20359 (S-Reeperbahn, U-St. Pauli) ☎ 31 52 06
■ **My Way** (B G MA OS r) Sun-Thu 19-4
Brennerstraße 2 ✉ 20099 (S-Hauptbahnhof) ☎ 24 08 16
■ **Olli's Down Town** (B d f G MA OS) daily 20-? h
Gustav-Freytag-Straße 9 ✉ 22085 (near Alster) ☎ 22 71 78 51
■ **Piccadilly** (G MA) 20-4 h, closed Thu
Silbersacktwiete 1 ✉ 20359 (S-Reeperbahn) ☎ 319 24 74
■ **Purgatory** (AC d glm MA N WE) Sun-Thu 22-4, Fri-Sat -6 h
Friedrichstraße 8 ✉ 20359 (S-Reeperbahn) ☎ 31 58 07
■ **Rendezvous** (BF f G MA N WE) Mon-Thu 19-2, Fri-Sat -4 h, Sun closed
Pulverteich 18 ✉ 20099 (S/U-Hauptbahnhof) ☎ 28 05 14 37
■ **Romeo** (B CC G R) Mon-Sun 14-3 h
Zimmerpforte 2 ✉ 20099 (S-Hauptbahnhof, Near/Nähe Hansaplatz) ☎ 280 17 38
■ **Rudi's Night Club** (CC f G lj MA R) 18-8, Fri-Sat -?
Steindamm 58 ✉ 20099 (S-Hauptbahnhof) ☎ 24 72 74
■ **Seagull** (B f G MA N s) Mon-Fri 20-?, Sat 20-?, Sun 16-? h
Detlev-Bremer-Straße 37 ✉ 20359 (S-Reeperbahn/U-St.Pauli) ☎ 31 01 28
■ **Seute Dern** (B gLM N) 17-? h
Kohlhöfen 15 ✉ 20355 (Near Großneumarkt) ☎ 34 26 63
■ **Thomaskeller** (BF G MA r)
Rostocker Straße 14 ✉ 20099 (S/U-Hauptbahnhof)
■ **Tolerance** (d G p R)
Rostocker Straße 14 ✉ 20099 (S/U-Hauptbahnhof) ☎ 28 05 38 86
■ **Tom's Saloon** (! A B D G LJ MA VS) 22-? h
Pulverteich 17 ✉ 20099 (S-Hauptbahnhof) ☎ 280 30 56
Very popular not only at the weekend.
■ **Toom Peerstall** (B f G MA) 14-4, Fri-Sat -9 h
Clemens-Schultz-Straße 44 ✉ 20359 (S-Reeperbahn, U-St. Pauli) ☎ 319 35 23
■ **Touché** (B F GLM MA N) Tue-Sat 18-?, Sun from 16 h
Clemens-Schultz-Straße 42 ✉ 20359
■ **Tusculum** (F G MA N OS s) Mon-Sun 0-24 h
Kreuzweg 6 ✉ 20099 (S-Hauptbahnhof) ☎ 280 36 06
■ **Uhlenhorster Stübchen** (B f G MG N) Sun-Thu 20-4 h, Fri-Sat 20-? h
Schenkendorfstraße 3 ✉ 22085 ☎ 227 36 86
■ **Willi's For You!** (B f G lj MA) Daily from 16h
Markusstraße 4 ✉ 20355 (S-Stadthausbrücke/Großneumarkt) ☎ 348 03 88
■ **Wunderbar** (! AC B d G MA WE) Sun-Thu 21-4, Fri Sat -7 h
Talstraße 14 ✉ 20359 (S-Reeperbahn) ☎ 317 44 44
Trendy and popular. Disco at the weekend.

CAFES

■ **Bistro des Artistes** (B BF F G MA OS) 15-?, Sun 11-?, meals 17-23 h, Sun brunch from 11 h
Schmilinskystraße 19 ✉ 20099 (S-Hauptbahnhof) ☎ 24 60 83
■ **Feelgood** (d f GLM MA OS S WE) Mon-Thu 16-1, Fri & Sat open end, Sun 11-22 h
Borgweg 8 ✉ 22303 (near/nahe Stadtpark, U3-Borgweg) ☎ 27 87 78 01
Breakfast only on Sun 11-15 h.
■ **Fradkin. Café** (B BF glm MA) 10-24, Sun 11-24 h
Eulenstraße 49 ✉ 22765 (S-Altona) ☎ 390 31 83
■ **Gnosa. Café** (! A B BF F GLM OS YG) 11-1, Mon 18-1, Fri-Sat -2 h
Lange Reihe 93 ✉ 20099 (S/U-Hauptbahnhof) ☎ 24 30 34
Very popular, an institution.
■ **Magnus. Café** (A B D f GLM MA s) 15-24
Borgweg 8 ✉ 22303 (U-Borgweg) ☎ 27 87 78 01
■ **Mistral. Café** (B F GLM MA N), meals 17.30-23.30 h
Lehmweg 29 ✉ 20251 ☎ 420 77 02
Popular.
■ **Spund. Café** (B G lj MA OS) 10-24 h, Sun 15-24 h
Mohlenhofstraße 3 ✉ 20095 (U-Mönckebergstraße. Near Hauptbahnhof) ☎ 32 65 77
■ **Teatro Nacht Café** (AC B BF CC F glm MA) Daily from 6pm-?, Breakfast from 2am
Pulverteich 12 ✉ 20099 (S/U-Hauptbahnhof) ☎ 24 62 85
■ **Twist. Café-Bar** (b f glm OS) Mon-Sat 8-20, Sun closed
Carl-von-Ossietzky-Platz 1 ✉ 20099 (S-Hauptbahnhof) ☎ 280 17 39
■ **Uhrlaub. Café** (B BF F glm MA OS) 8-2 h
Lange Reihe 63 ✉ 20099 (S-Hauptbahnhof) ☎ 280 26 24
■ **Unter den Linden** (B BF f glm MA OS) 11-1 h
Juliusstraße 16 ✉ 22769 (U-Feldstraße) ☎ 43 81 40
■ **Winterhuder Kaffeehaus** (b BF f glm MA) 9-24, Sun 10-24 h
Winterhuder Marktplatz 16 ✉ 22299 (U-Hudtwalckerstraße) ☎ 47 82 00

DANCECLUBS

■ **Astoria-Frühclub** (B D glm YG) Sun from 5am, entrance 10 DM
Kleine Freiheit 42 ✉ 20359 (S-Reeperbahn) ☎ 31 24 64
■ **Camelot** (B D GLM YG) Fri 22-? h
Hamburger Berg 13, ✉ 20359 (S-Reeperbahn) ☎ 317 44 89
■ **Disco im MHC** (B d f GLM MA) last Sat/month 22-? h
Borgweg 8 ✉ 22303 (U-Borgweg) ☎ 27 877 801
■ **E.D.K.** (AC B D glm MA p s TV)
Fri Sat and before public holydays 0-?h
Gerhardstraße 3 ✉ 20359 (S-Reeperbahn)

454 SPARTACUS 2001/2002

Hamburg | Germany

HOMO-KINO-HAMBURG
JAIL · **OPEN 24 HOURS** · **LOCKERS AVAILABLE!** · **DARKROOM** · **WETROOM** · **SLING**

TALSTRASSE 8

HOMO-KINO-HAMBURG, TALSTRASSE 8
20359 HAMBURG, FON: +49 40 312495
E-MAIL: TALSTRASSE-8@T-Online.de
INTERNET: www.talstrasse-8.de

■ **Gay Factory** (! B D GLM MA s) monthly Sat 22-? h
Fabrik, Barnerstraße 36 ✉ 22765 (S-Altona) ☎ 39 10 70
■ **Gay Oriental Kitchen** (! B D G S MA) Every first Friday in the month from 11pm-?
Stresemannstraße 206 ✉ 22765 c/o Juice Club (S-Holstenstraße) ☎ 24 03 33
■ **Gaylaxy** (B D DR G) irregularly Sat 22-? h
at Pleasure Dome, Anckelmannplatz ✉ 20537 (S/U-Berliner Tor)
Check local press for dates and varying location.
■ **La Cage aux Folles** (! AC CC D G MA SNU STV) Sun 23-6 h
c/o La Cage, Reeperbahn 136 ✉ 20359 (U-Reeperbahn)
☎ 317 90 481
Entrance-fee DM 15.
■ **Paola Club** (B D Glm S) Fri 22 h
Lucky Strike, Nobistor 10 ✉ 22767
■ **P.I.T.** (! AC B D G YG) Wed-Sat 23-? h; connected to cruise bar Male
Pulverteich 17 ✉ 20099 (S-Hauptbahnhof) ☎ 280 30 56
Naked Sex Party on Sundat 18h.
■ **Powderroom at Absolut** (! AC B D glm TV WE YG) Sat 23-6 h (G)
Hans-Albers-Platz 15b ✉ 20359 (S-Reeperbahn/U-St.Pauli)
☎ 317 34 00
One of the best places in town. Entrance fee 10,- DM, excellent DJs (House). Each Friday different events (NG).
■ **Red Club im Cult** (B D G MA) Sun 22h
Große Freiheit 2 ✉ 20359 (S-Reeperbahn)
■ **Salvation** (B D G MA) 2nd/4th Sat 22-? h
c/o Pleasuredome, Anckelmannplatz 3 ✉ 20357 (S-Berliner Tor)
■ **Spundloch** (B CC D f G MA) Wed Thu Sun 21-4 h, Fri Sat 22-? h
Paulinenstraße 19 ✉ 20359 (U-Feldstraße) ☎ 31 07 98

RESTAURANTS
■ **Freudenhaus** (CC F glm MA) Every day from 18- ? h
Hein-Hoyer-Straße 7-9 ✉ 20359 (U-St.Pauli/S-Reeperbahn)
☎ 31 46 42
The only restaurant in St. Pauli serving German cuisine. Interesting.
■ **Opus** (B F glm MA OS) Sun, Tue-Thu 18.30-23, Fri Sat -24 h, closed Mon
Max-Brauer-Allee 80 ✉ 22765 (S-Altona/Holstenstraße)
☎ 389 28 39

■ **Phuket** (B F g MA) 18-24 h, closed Mon
Davidstraße 31 ✉ 20359 (U-St.Pauli/S-Reeperbahn) ☎ 31 58 54
Good Thai cuisine
■ **Schlößchen** (AC B CC F glm MA) Tue-Sat 18-? h
Kastanienallee 32 ✉ 20359 (U-St. Pauli/S-Reeperbahn)
☎ 31 77 88 16
■ **Störtebecker** (B F g MA) Mon-Fri 11-22 h
Bernhard-Nocht-Straße 68 ✉ 20359 (U-St. Pauli/S-Reeperbahn)
☎ 31 54 40
Nice view on the river Elbe. Good food.
■ **Vasco da Gama** (B CC F glm MA) 12-24 h
Danziger Straße 21 ✉ 20099 ☎ 280 33 05
Portugese and spanish cuisine
■ **Weite Welt** (A AC B d F g MA OS) Mon-Thu 18-24 h, Fri-Sat 18-1 h
Große Freiheit 70 ✉ 22767 (S-Reeperbahn) ☎ 319 12 14
Fine dining in a beautiful garden. Reservation advisable.

SHOWS
■ **Pulverfass Cabaret** (B F g STV) Shows 20.30, 23.15, 2; entrance 19.30 h
Pulverteich 12 ✉ 20099 (U/S-Hauptbahnhof) ☎ 247 878
Diner shows. Please call for details.
■ **Schmidt Theater & Schmidts Tivoli** (B f glm OS S)
tickets 12-19 h, Shows daily
Spielbudenplatz 24-28 ✉ 20359 (S-Reeperbahn/U-St.Pauli)
☎ 31 77 88-0

SEX SHOPS/BLUE MOVIES
■ **Dolly Buster by Seventh Heaven** (AC CC DR g MA VS) 9-1 h
Steindamm 14 ✉ 20099 (S/U-Hauptbahnhof) ☎ 28 05 63 92
■ **Dolly Buster by Seventh Heaven** (AC CC DR g MA VS) 0-24 h
Reeperbahn 61 ✉ 20359 (S-Reeperbahn) ☎ 31 12 61
■ **Dolly Buster by Seventh Heaven** (AC CC DR g MA VS) 9-1 h
Steindamm 24 ✉ 20099 (U/S-Hauptbahnhof) ☎ 28 05 38 70
■ **Erotic Kino Shop** (CC DR g MA VS) Sun-Thu 11-4, Fri-Sat 0-24 h
Talstraße 2/Reeperbahn ✉ 20359 (S-Reeperbahn) ☎ 319 37 68
■ **Henry's Show Center** (g VS) 9-2, Fri Sat -4 h
Steindamm 7 ✉ 20099 (U/S-Hauptbahnhof)
■ **Homo Gay Kino und Shop** (g VS) Mon-Sat 10-24, Sun & holidays 12-24 h
Clemens-Schultz-Straße 43 ✉ 20359 (S-Reeperbahn) ☎ 31 50 68

SPARTACUS 2001/2002 | 455

Germany | Hamburg

16 PROGRAMME • MO + DO PROGRAMMWECHSEL • GROSSBILDLEINWAND •

MYSTERY HALL

Shop & Kino
Talstraße 3-5   20359 Hamburg - St. Pauli
Telefon 317 90 570
email   mystery.com@gmx.de
www.mysteryhall.de
rund um die Uhr geöffnet
Kinokarte DM 12 (16 Stunden gültig)

JETZT ONLINE!

Foto: Foerster Media

MYSTERY WORLD

Shop & Kino
Steindamm 26   Hamburg - St. Georg
Telefon 280 30 82
email   mystery.com@gmx.de
www.mysteryhall.de
Mo - Sa 9:30 - 1 Uhr, So 10:30 - 1 Uhr
Kino-Tageskarte DM 12, ab 23 Uhr DM 5

456   SPARTACUS 2001/2002

SEVENTH HEAVEN EROTIC DISCOUNT
STEINDAMM 14   20099 HAMBURG
TELEFON 040 - 280 563 92
TÄGL. 9 - 1 UHR GEÖFFNET

NEU

DOLLY BUSTER BY SEVENTH HEAVEN
REEPERBAHN 61   20359 HAMBURG
TELEFON 040 - 311 261
RUND UM DIE UHR GEÖFFNET

DOLLY BUSTER BY SEVENTH HEAVEN
STEINDAMM 24   20099 HAMBURG
TELEFON 040 - 280 538 70
TÄGL. 9 - 1 UHR GEÖFFNET

DOLLY BUSTER BY SEVENTH HEAVEN
LEDERSTRASSE 2 - 4   23552 LÜBECK
TELEFON 0451 - 70 69 50
MO - SA 9 - 23, SO 12 - 23 UHR

16 PROGRAMME,
2 X PROGRAMMWECHSEL / WOCHE,
DARKROOM, GROSSBILDLEINWAND,
SOLO / DUOKABINEN, SLING ROOM,
KONTAKTLANDSCHAFT

VIDEOS, MAGAZINE, CD-ROMS,
WÄSCHE, DESSOUS, TOYS,
HILFSMITTEL, ACCESSOIRES

KINOS
SHOPS

Germany | Hamburg

Videos & Magazine
Lack & Leder
Stahl & Gummi

Kinos & Shops

G. Kowalski KG

INTERNETSHOP
www.sparta-shops.de

Sparta Gay
Hein-Hoyer-Str. 5-7
HH-St. Pauli
0.00 - 24.00

Sparta Point
Talstr. 18
HH-St. Pauli
0.00 - 24.00

Henry`s Show Center
Steindamm 7
HH-(Hbf)
9.00-2.00/Fr.Sa.-4.00

Sparta City
Lange Reihe 93
HH-St. Georg
10.00-24.00/So.13.00-24.00

Sparta Junior
Seilerstr. 49
HH-St. Pauli
10.00-1.00/Fr.Sa.-6.00

Sparta Shop
Hüxstr. 15
Lübeck
9.00-24.00/Fr.Sa.-4.00

Sparta Shop
Reeperbahn 54
HH-St. Pauli

www.Dragonsauna.de

Hamburg´s most popular sauna

Finish
Steam
Massage
Whirlpool
Bar & Bistro
Solarium
Cruising
Cabins
Video
Sling

Dragon Sauna

Pulverteich 37 ▪ 20099 Hamburg
Tel.: 040 / 240514

Open 12 - 01 Uhr
weekend nonstop

Germany | Hamburg

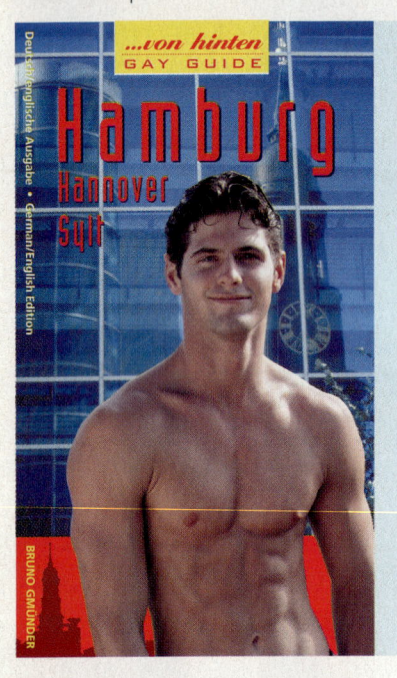

HAMBURG, HANNOVER & SYLT
von hinten.
English/Deutsch,
224 Seiten/Pages, DM 22,80

Erhältlich im Buchhandel oder bei
www.brunos.de

■ **Homo Kino Hamburg** (! AC CC DR G lj MA VS) 0-24 h
Talstraße 8 ✉ 20359 (S-Reeperbahn, U-St.Pauli) ☎ 31 24 95
■ **Mystery Hall** (AC CC DR G lj MA VS) 0-24 h
Talstraße 3-5 ✉ 20359 (S-Reeperbahn) ☎ 31 79 05 70
■ **Mystery World** (AC CC DR G lj MA VS) Mon-Sat 9.30-1,
Sun 10.30-1 h
Steindamm 26 ✉ 20099 (S/U-Hauptbahnhof)
☎ 280 30 82
■ **New Man** (CC G VS) 10-0.30, Sun 11-24 h
Nobistor 38 ✉ 22767 (U/S-Reeperbahn) ☎ 31 27 13
■ **New Man City** (! CC G VS) Mon-Thu 10-0.30, Fri-10 to Sun 0.30 h
Pulverteich 8 ✉ 20099 (Near/Nähe Hauptbahnhof)
☎ 24 01 49
■ **New Man Plaza** (! CC G VS) Mon-Thu 10-0.30, Fri Sat -1.30, Sun 13-0.30 h
Steindamm 21 ✉ 20099 (U/S-Hauptbahnhof) ☎ 24 52 31
■ **Sparta City** (G VS) Mon-Sat 10-24, Sun 13-24 h
Lange Reihe 93 ✉ 20099 (U/S-Hauptbahnhof/Bus108)
☎ 280 27 41
■ **Sparta Gay** (! CC DR G VS) 0-24 h
Hein-Hoyer-Straße 5-7 ✉ 20359 ☎ 319 62 29
■ **Sparta Junior** (DR G VS nu) Sun-Thu 10-1, Fri-Sat -6 h
Seilerstraße 149 ✉ 20359 (U-St.Pauli/S-Reeperbahn)
☎ 31 40 95
1sr & 3rd Sun NU 18-1 h
■ **Sparta Point** (CC DR G VS) 0-24 h
Talstraße 18 ✉ 20359 (S-Reeperbahn)
One of the biggest cinema in St.Pauli.
■ **Sparta Shop** (G VS) 9-2 h
Reeperbahn 54 ✉ 20359

HOUSE OF BOYS
☞ Hotels with the codes "B" and "R".

SAUNAS/BATHS
■ **Apollo** (B G MA msg SA SOL VS) 13-24 h
Max-Brauer-Allee 277 ✉ 22769 (U/S-Sternschanze/Bus112)
☎ 43 48 11
Comfortable sauna on two floors.
■ **Dragon** (AC B CC DR F G msg SA SB SOL VS WH YG) Mon-Thu 12-1, Fri 12-Mon 1 h
Pulverteich 37 ✉ 20099 (U/S-Hauptbahnhof, 2 minutes from station)
☎ 24 05 14
One of the biggest and sauna (680 m^2) in Hamburg popular within a quite young crowd. Free breakfast buffet on Sun morning.
■ **Men's Heaven** (B f G MA msg SA SB SOL VS WH)
Steindamm 14 ✉ 20099 ☎ 280 56 389
Brandnew sauna will open in autumn 2001. Call for details. Also cruisy cinema on 250m^2 with dark&slingroom.

BOOK SHOPS
■ **Blendwerk** (A CC glm) Mon-Fri 10-19, Sat -16 h
Lange Reihe 73 ✉ 20099 ☎ 24 00 03
■ **Buchladen Männerschwarm** (CC GLM MA s) Mon-Fri 10-19, Sat -16 h, closed Sun
Neuer Pferdemarkt 32 ✉ 20359 (U-Feldstraße)
☎ 43 60 93
■ **Stilke Aktuell** (cc glm)
Hauptbahnhof Wandelhalle, Eingang Glockengießerwall
✉ 20095 ☎ 32 17 24

MEN'S HEAVEN

ST. GEORG

by Seventh Heaven

Steindamm 14 • 20099 Hamburg • 040-280 56 389

Hamburg hat's: Eine neue Sauna

ERÖFFNUNG IM HERBST 2001

Trockensauna • Dampfsauna • Whirlpool • Solarium
Massagen • Ruheraum • Fernsehraum • Videoraum
Darkroom • Bar • Restaurant • Shop

NEU

KINO auf 250 qm

16 Programme, 2 x Programmwechsel/Woche, Darkroom, Großbildleinwand, Solo- /Duokabinen, Slingroom, Kontaktlandschaft

Steindamm 14 • 20099 Hamburg • 040-280 56 392
täglich von 9:00 bis 01:00 Uhr geöffnet

Germany | **Hamburg**

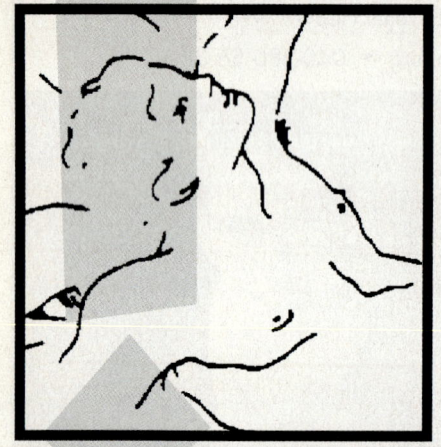

CDs & VIDEOS BÜCHER

ST. PAULI
MÄNNERSCHWARM
Buchladen und Versand

Neuer Pferdemarkt 32 • 20359 Hamburg
Telefon: 040-4302650 / 040-436093
Telefax: 040-4302932

ST. GEORG
BLENDWERK
Lange Reihe 73 • 20099 Hamburg
Telefon/Telefax: 040-240003

www.maennerschwarm.de

MITGLIED DER ARBEITSGEMEINSCHAFT
DIE SCHWULEN BUCHLÄDEN

Montag-Freitag 10.00-19.00 Uhr
Sonnabend 10.00-16.00 Uhr

Online-Shopping: www.clemensHH.de

Geschenke / Gifts — Photobooks — gay T-Shirts — Books — Video & DVD — Rainbow & Pride

clemens GAY STORE

More than 1800 Videos — Toys & Safer Sex — Postcards — Tom of Finland — Keith Haring

NEW: Mail Order - call us for a catalogue!

Hamburg - U 3 St. Pauli
Clemens-Schultz-Str. 77
Mo - Fr 11 - 19 Sa 11 - 16

■ **Thalia Buchhandlung** (cc glm)
Große Bleichen 19 ✉ 20354 ☏ 302 07 01

FASHION SHOPS
■ **Mystery World Men's Bodywear** (CC g) 9.30-1, Sun 10-1 h
Steindamm 26 ✉ 20099 (U-Hauptbahnhof)
☏ 280 30 82

GIFT & PRIDE SHOPS
■ **Clemens Gay Store** (CC G) Mon-Fri 11-19, Sat -16 h, closed Sun
Clemens-Schultz-Straße 77 ✉ 20359 (U-St. Pauli, S/U- Reeperbahn)
☏ 31 79 17 63
Gay shop. Also Mail-Order and Online-Shopping.

LEATHER & FETISH SHOPS
■ **Günter Skarupke** by appointment
Cuxhavener Straße 266 ✉ 21149 ☏ 701 73 88
■ **Mr. Chaps** (G CC LJ) Mon-Fri 11-19, Sat 11-15 h
Gurlittstraße 47 ✉ 20099 (U/S-Hauptbahnhof/Bus108)
☏ 24 31 09
Tailor made fashion in leather and latex. Sales of toys, rubber, leather, rubberboots, gloves and pants.

TRAVEL AND TRANSPORT
■ **Reisebüro am Hellkamp** (CC) Mon-Fri 10-18.30, Sat 10.30-13h
Hellkamp 17 ✉ 20255 (U-Osterstraße)
☏ 40 19 61 86 📠 491 91 00 ✉ hellkamp@aol.com
💻 www.gaytravel.de
■ **Reisepunkt Eppendorf** Mon-Fri 9-18, Sat 10-13 h
Eppendorfer Weg 193 ✉ 20253 ☏ 422 22 61 📠 422 22 81
✉ reisepunkt@startpartner.net
Travel agent.

Hamburg | Germany

John Hamburg
massiert Ihn. HS/Hotel-Escort
Telefon 0175 / 670 90

Live Fummel-Line
Live mitmachen oder zuhören
Hier wird live und scharf gefummelt
0190-80 66 55
www.gratisgayfotos.com
TMG DM 3.63 Min /Live Operator

■ **Ticket Kontor** (CC glm MA) 10-18.45, Sat 11-15 h
Feldstraße 37 ✉ 20357 (U-Feldstraße) ☎ 430 10 75 📠 430 34 58
💻 ticketkont@aol.com 🖥 www.ticketkontor.com

HOTELS

■ **Adria Hof** (g H) 0-24 h
Ellmenreichstraße 24 ✉ 20099 *(100m from the central railway station)* ☎ 24 62 80 📠 24 62 80 💻 Hamburg@gaytel.de
🖥 www.gaytel.de

Single from DM 80, double from 100. All rooms with shower, WC, TV and safe.

■ **Galerie-Hotel Sarah Petersen** (A b BF glm H MA OS s) 8-23 h and by appointment
Lange Reihe 50 ✉ 20099 ☎ 24 98 26 📠 24 98 26
💻 galerie-hotel-sarah-petersen@talkline.de 🖥 www.galerie-hotel-sarah-petersen.de
Centrally located, very close to the gay scene. Newly restaured landmark. Single from DM 85, double from DM 120 All rooms with shower and cable TV.

MEN'S BODYWEAR

UNDERGROUND SHOES

OLAF BENZ undercare

LONSDALE LONDON

MAN store GUYWEAR

MYSTERY WORLD

Steindamm 26   20099 HH - St. Georg   Telefon 280 30 82
email: mystery.com@gmx.de   www.mysteryhall.de

SPARTACUS 2001/2002 | 463

Germany | Hamburg

Galerie - Hotel Sarah Petersen

Hamburgs interessantestes Haus mit Stil, Charme, Geschichte und Komfort

Lange Reihe 50, D-20099 Hamburg
Tel & Fax 040 / 24 98 26
Internet: http://www.galerie-hotel-sarah-petersen.de
E-Mail: galerie-hotel-sarah-petersen@talknet.de

Frühstück
im Salon

Gästezimmer
Chambre Classique

GAYTEL ADRIA HOF

the gayfriendly hotel

Ellmenreichstraße 24
20099 Hamburg

Telefon & Fax
040 / 24 62 80

100 m vom Hauptbahnhof
Zimmer mit Dusche / WC
Kabel-TV / Zimmersafe

Email
Hamburg@gaytel.de

www.gaytel.de

Hamburg | Germany

KINGSIZE? QUEENSIZE?
WHATEVER –
WE HAVE THE SIZE YOU CAN TAKE

HOTEL KÖNIGSHOF HAMBURG

Pulverteich 18, 20099 Hamburg - Germany
Fon +49 40 28 40 74 0 + Fax +49 40 28 40 74 74
e-mail Hotelkhh@aol.com
http://members.aol.com/hotelkhh

HOTEL GARNI
»Schweriner Hof«

traditionell weltoffene, hanseatische Gastlichkeit
in zeitgemäßem Gewand
enjoy traditional hanseatic, cosmopolitan flair
in this modern hotel

- continental breakfast
- Cable-TV
- Shower/WC
- Telephone

Steindamm 19
(2 min. from Central Station and to St. Georg gay scene)
Tel.: 040 / 280 43 23   Fax: 040 / 280 42 24

■ **Harald's Hotel & Bar** (B CC f G H lj MA R SNU) 0-24 h
Reeperbahn 54 ✉ 20359 (S-Reeperbahn) ☎ 31 33 63
📠 31 33 60
Also bar ! Only gay hotel directly on the Reeperbahn. Comfortable rooms. Close to theatres.

■ **Hotel Schweriner Hof** (BF CC glm H) 0-24 h
Steindamm 19 ✉ 20099 *(in the gay scene)* ☎ 280 4323
📠 280 4224   💻 www.funworld.de/Schweriner-Hof
All rooms with cable TV, tel and some with shower/WC. Single rooms DM 65-90.-, double DM 90-125.-, BF 12,50.

■ **Königshof. Hotel** (A BF CC GLM H LJ OS) 7-22 h
Pulverteich 18 ✉ 20099 *(near main station)* ☎ 28 40 74 0
📠 28 40 74 74   ✉ Hotelkhh@aol.com
💻 members.aol.com/hotelkhh
15 double and 6 single rooms with shower/WC. All rooms have phone, cable-TV, Fax, radio, heating. Hotel provides own key and parking. Rates single from DM 80-130, double from DM 140-170 (bf incl.).

■ **Village. Hotel** (BF CC GLM H MA) 24h
Steindamm 4 ✉ 20099 *(at central railway station)* ☎ 24 61 37
☎ 24 59 39   📠 45 03 00 30   ✉ reserv@hotel-village.de
💻 www.hotel-village.de
17 rooms and 4 apartments. Most rooms with shower/WC, balcony, telephone, Fax, Sat-TV, radio, heating, own key. Doubles from DM 95-145, singles DM 80-115 and apartments (information upon request), bf DM 12.

GUEST HOUSES

■ **Ars Vivendi – Gästehaus am Deich** (BF CC H msg PI)
Stormarnstraße 5, Glückstadt ✉ 25348 *(Bus-Marktplatz)*
☎ 04124/937311   📠 93 73 12
✉ ars-vivendi-gaestehausadeich@t-online.de
💻 www.glorylands-palace.com/ars-vivendi.htm
3 rooms and 1 apartment. Shower/WC, phone/fax, TV/video, safe.

HOTEL VILLAGE
the Gay Hotel in the city
directly at the main station

Telefon: 040/24 61 37
Telefax: 040 / 450 300 - 30
www.Hotel-Village.de
20099 HH - Steindamm 4

Germany — Hamburg

overnight accomodation service - from DM 40 -
· about 750 beds · more than 28 cities ·

complete offer see page Germany/Berlin

bed & enjoy breakfast

central booking office Berlin ☏ **+49-30-23623610** 4:30-9:00 pm local time
Fax +49-30-23623619 · info@ebab.de · www.ebab.de

PRIVATE ACCOMMODATION

■ **Enjoy Bed and Breakfast** (BF G H MA) 16.30-21 h
Nollendorfplatz 5, 10777 Berlin (U-Nollendorfplatz) ☏ (030) 236 236 10, (030) 236 236 19, info@ebab.de, ebab.de
Accommodation sharing agency. All with shower and BF. 40-45 DM p.p.

GENERAL GROUPS

■ **Big Spender** Mon-Fri 11-17 h, Sat + Sun closed
Brennerstraße 90 ✉ 20099 ☏ 24 00 62, 24 01 53
big.spender@t-online.de, www.big-spender.de
Organisers of the "Walk against AIDS" and the big "Red, Hot & Dance Party" every December.

■ **International Association for Worldwide Queenism**
c/o Männerschwarm, Neuer Pferdemarkt 32 ✉ 20359
Magazine: Die Putte

■ **LAG Schwulesbenpolitik im Bündnis 90/Die Grünen**
c/o Thomas Mohr, Bahrenfelder Straße 244 ✉ 22765
☏ 280 47 17

■ **Schwule Väter und Ehemänner** Meets 1st/3rd Tue in room 12 at 20 h
c/o Kulturzentrum Rieckhof, Rieckhofstraße 12 ✉ 21073
☏ 765 36 74 (Bernd) or 75 98 35 (Thomas)

■ **Schwulenreferat im AStA der Uni Hamburg** Tue Thu 16-18 h
Van-Melle-Park 5 ✉ 20146 ☏ 45 02 04 37

■ **Schwusos Hamburg** 1st Tue
c/o SPD-Hamburg, Kurt-Schumacher-Allee 10 ✉ 20097
☏ 69 50 798, Schwusos.HH@gmx.de
www.spd-hamburg.de/Schwusos

FETISH GROUPS

■ **LCH Hamburg e.V.** Meets 1st Thu at Chaps, 2nd at Black, 3rd at Toms, 4th at Willi's For You
c/o Reiner Hölscher, Reineckestraße 16 ✉ 22761
☏ 899 12 23, 100773.562@compuserve.com
Every 4th Sun the members meeting takes place at Haus der Jugend, Bei der Schilleroper.

■ **MSC Hamburg e.V.** Meets 2nd/4th Fri at Chaps 22-? ⇒ Bars
Postfach 30 36 83 ✉ 20312, mschamburg@aol.com

HEALTH GROUPS

■ **AIDS-Hilfe Hamburg e.V.** Mon-Thu 9-12 13-16, Fri 9-12 h
Paul-Roosen-Straße 43 ✉ 22767 (St.Pauli) ☏ 319 69 81
☏ 19411 (helpline), 319 69 84, info@aidshilfe-hamburg.de
www.aidshilfe-hamburg.de
Helpline Mon Wed Fri 10-12 19-21, Tue 16-21, Thu 19-21 h, Regenbogen-Café Sun 15-18, Breakfast at Regenbogen Café Wed 10-12 h. Ask for different groups and activities including the LSVD which meets every 2nd Wed/month at 19h

■ **Hamburg Leuchtfeuer AIDS-Hilfe GmbH** Mon-Fri 9-16 h

Unzerstraße 1-3 ✉ 22767 ☏ 38 73 80

HELP WITH PROBLEMS

■ **Basis Projekt e.V.** (BF) Mon Tue Thu Fri 12-16, Wed 15-19 h
St. Georgs Kirchhof 26 ✉ 20099 (Near central railway station)
☏ 280 16 07, 280 518 37, basis-st.georg@t-online.de
www.basis-projekt.de

■ **Beratung für Schwule** Mon-Fri 14-18, Tue Wed 19-22 h
c/o MHC, Borgweg 8, ✉ 22303 ☏ 279 00 69
www.gay-web.de/mhc/beratung

■ **Sexualberatungsstelle der Abteilung für Sexualforschung**
c/o Universität Hamburg, Poppenhusenstrasse 12 ✉ 22305
☏ 47 17 22 25

SPECIAL INTEREST GROUPS

■ **BGLS- Bundesverband der Gehörlosen Lesben & Schwulen e.V.** Meet every Fri 19:00h
Zirkusweg 11 ✉ 20359, 317 927 56, bgls@bgls.de
www.bgls.de
A group for deaf gays and lesbians. Signlanguage courses for gays and lesbians who can hear. Please contact the DSG. Their e-mail address : gebaerden-hh@t-online.de.

SPORT GROUPS

■ **Startschuss-schwul/lesbischer Sportverein Hamburg e.V.** Mon-Fri 16-21, Sat 16-19 h
c/o Hein & Fiete, Pulverteich 21 ✉ 20099 (S/U-Hauptbahnhof)
☏ 24 03 33, info@startschuss-hamburg.de
www.startschuss-hamburg.de
Please call for details.

SWIMMING

-Eichbaumsee (g NU) (Moorfleeter Deich at Allermöhle)
-Boberger See (g NU) (Bergedorfer Straße at Billstedt)

CRUISING

-Blindengarten (Stadtpark)
-U-Ritterstraße
-U-Jungfernstieg
-EKZ Poppenbüttel
-U-Saarlandstraße
-Uni (Philosophenturm, basement, popular)
-Stadtpark (ayor lj MA YG) (U-Borgweg) Popular
-Planten und Blomen (Dammtordamm/Gorch-Fock-Wall))
-Jakobi-Park (Wandsbecker Chaussee, Hamburg-Eilbeck, U-Ritterstraße)
-Gustav-Mahler-Park (BAT)
-Eppendorfer Park, (Bus-Uke/Martinistr.) old entrance, toilets

Hameln ☎ 05151

GENERAL GROUPS
■ **Homosexuelle Initiative "Rosa Hameln"** every other Thu 20 h
c/o Komm'zentrum Sumpfblume, Am Stockhof 2a ✉ 31785
☎ 455 10

CRUISING
-Rathausplatz (on the square and in the underpass)
-Bürgerpark (on the left behind the tourist information -20 h)

Hamm ☎ 02381

BARS
■ **Palazzo** (B GLM MA OS s SNU STV TV) Mon-Wed 17-1, Fri & Sat 17-4 h. Sun closed
Werler Straße 101 ✉ 59063 ☎ 95 32 32
Once a month dragshow,or strip show. Free admission.

SEX SHOPS/BLUE MOVIES
■ **Pegasus** (GLM MG VS) Mon-Fri 13-19, Sat 10-14, closed Sun
Werler Straße 95 ✉ 59063 *(near ev. Krankenhaus)* ☎ 54 02 40
Mail-order.
■ **Sex & Gay Shop** (MG VS) Mon-Fri 10-23, Sat -20, Sun -15 h
Gallberger Weg 37 ✉ 59063 *(head towards Tierpark)* ☎ 518 57

HEALTH GROUPS
■ **AIDS-Hilfe Hamm e.V.** Mon-Fri 9-16, youth group 19.30-? h
Werler Straße 105 ✉ 59063 ☎ 194 11 ☎ 55 75 ☎ 55 76
Also gay and lesbian group "Rosa Engel" & Youth group "LesBiSchwules Dreamteam". Call for further information.

CRUISING
-P at Wasser- und Schiffahrtsamt
-A1 - Exit Bockum-Hövel
-Ostenallee/Exerzierplatz
-Werler Straße/Alleestraße
-Chattanmoga-Platz (across Stadtsparkasse)

Hanau ☎ 06181

BARS
■ **Mutter Courage** (B F G MA) 20-1, Sun 15.30-1 h
Glockenstraße 25 ✉ 63450 ☎ 280 81

HEALTH GROUPS
■ **Aids-Hilfe Hanau e.V.** Mon 9-12 h, Tue 14-20 h, Thu 14-19 h
Alfred-Delb-Straße ✉ 63450 ☎ 310 00 🖨 310 01
■ **Hanauer AIDS-Beratung und Schwulenhilfe Maintal**
Johannisweg 1, 63477 Maintal-Dörnigheim ☎ 491390

CRUISING
-Hauptbahnhof

Hannover ☎ 0511

GAY INFO
■ **HOME-Zentrum** Mon-Fri 11-15 h
Johannssenstraße 8 ✉ 30159 ☎ 36 33 44 ☎ 19 446 (helpline)
☎ 36 33 90 📧 vorstand@home-ev.de 🖥 www.home-ev.de
Different groups and activities, please call for information/verschiedene Gruppen und Aktivitäten, genaue Infos telefonisch erfragen. Also publisher of the "Mimikry" newspaper for Home members. Gays& lesbians meet 2nd-5th Tue 19.30-21.30h. Also helpline Mon-Thu18-20 h and by appointment.

■ **Rosa Leine TV** 1st Fri 21 h at Offener Kanal Hannover
Georgsplatz 11 ✉ 30159 📧 webmaster@rosaleine.de
🖥 www.rosaleine.de
■ **Zentrale Erfassung Homosexuellendiskriminierung (ZEH)**
c/o HSH, Postfach 47 22 ✉ 30047 ☎ 66 10 55

PUBLICATIONS
■ **Hamburg Hannover & Sylt von hinten**
c/o Bruno Gmünder Verlag, Postfach 61 01 04, 10921 Berlin
☎ (030) 615 00 342 🖨 (030) 615 91 34 📧 info@spartacus.de
🖥 www.brunos.de
The city guide book about Hamburg, Hanover & Sylt. Useful general information and lots of addresses with extensive descriptions in English and German. Up-to-date maps. Erotic photos.

CULTURE
■ **Schwullesbisches Archiv Hannover (SARCH)**
Postfach 47 22 ✉ 30047 ☎ 66 10 55
Also seat of the Verein zur Erforschung der Geschichte der Homosexuellen in Niedersachsen.

TOURIST INFO
■ **Hannover Tourist Büro** Mon-Fri 9-19 h, Sat 9.30-15 h
Ernst-August-Platz 2 ✉ 30159 ☎ 30 14 22

BARS
■ **Backstairs** (B DR G LJ MA VS) Wed Fri-Sat 23-? h
Lange Laube 24 ✉ 30159 *(Entrance/Eingang Hausmannstraße; unter/below Vulcano)* ☎ 137 88
■ **Barkarole** (B G OG P) Sun Wed Thu 21-1, Fri Sat -3 h, closed Mon, winter 20- h
Konkordiastraße 8 ✉ 30449 ☎ 44 53 08
■ **Belvédère** (A F GLM MA N OS SNU STV TV) Mon-Thu 17-2, Fri Sat -3, Sun 16-2 h
Gretchenstraße 16 ✉ 30161 *(S-Sedanstraße)* ☎ 388 33 01
■ **Burgklause** (B f G MA N) 18-2, Sat 13-2 h
Burgstraße 11 ✉ 30159 ☎ 32 11 86
■ **Café Caldo** (! B CC f GLM OS YG) Mon-Fri 18-2, Sat 20 -2, Sun 16-2 h
Bergmannstrasse 7 ✉ 30159 *(U - Steintor)* ☎ 15 17 3
Popular cocktail bar and cafe for the young and hip people.
■ **Cage aux Folles. La** (B f Glm N r s) 17-?, Fri-Sun 19-? h
Kronenstraße 4 ✉ 30161
■ **Cup / Factory** (B D f G lj MA) 20-2 h
Escherstraße 11 ✉ 30159 ☎ 161 02 98
Modern and beautiful bar.
■ **Fiacre. Le** (AC B CC DR F G H MA OS R s VS) 11-3, Fri Sat -5 h
Weißekreuzstraße 20 ✉ 30161 ☎ 34 23 37
Guest house included. Rates DM 99-119 (BF and one bottle sparkling wine incl.) Hustlers bar for 25 years.
■ **Hole. The** (B DR G LJ MA VS) Tue 20-? (glm), Wed-Sat 21-3/? h
Franckestraße 5 ✉ 30165 *(U-Werder Straße)* ☎ 352 38 95
2nd & 4th Sun theme and sex parties. Entrance 17-18 h, after the doors are closed.
■ **Kulmbacher Eck** (f glm MA N r) 16-? h, closed Sun
Hallerstraße 6 ✉ 30161 ☎ 348 24 52
■ **Monsieur Melody** (B G N) 19-5 h
Friesenstraße 67 ✉ 30161 ☎ 31 86 89
■ **Odeon Café** (B F g S) 20-5, Fri Sat -7 h
Odeonstraße 5 ✉ 30159 ☎ 144 27
■ **Opus Musik-Café** (B G MA OS) Mon-Fri 18-?, Sat Sun 20-? h
Lange Laube 24 ✉ 30159 *(Entrance/Eingang Hausmannstraße, after 22 h same entrance as Vulcano)* ☎ 138 58

Germany | Hannover

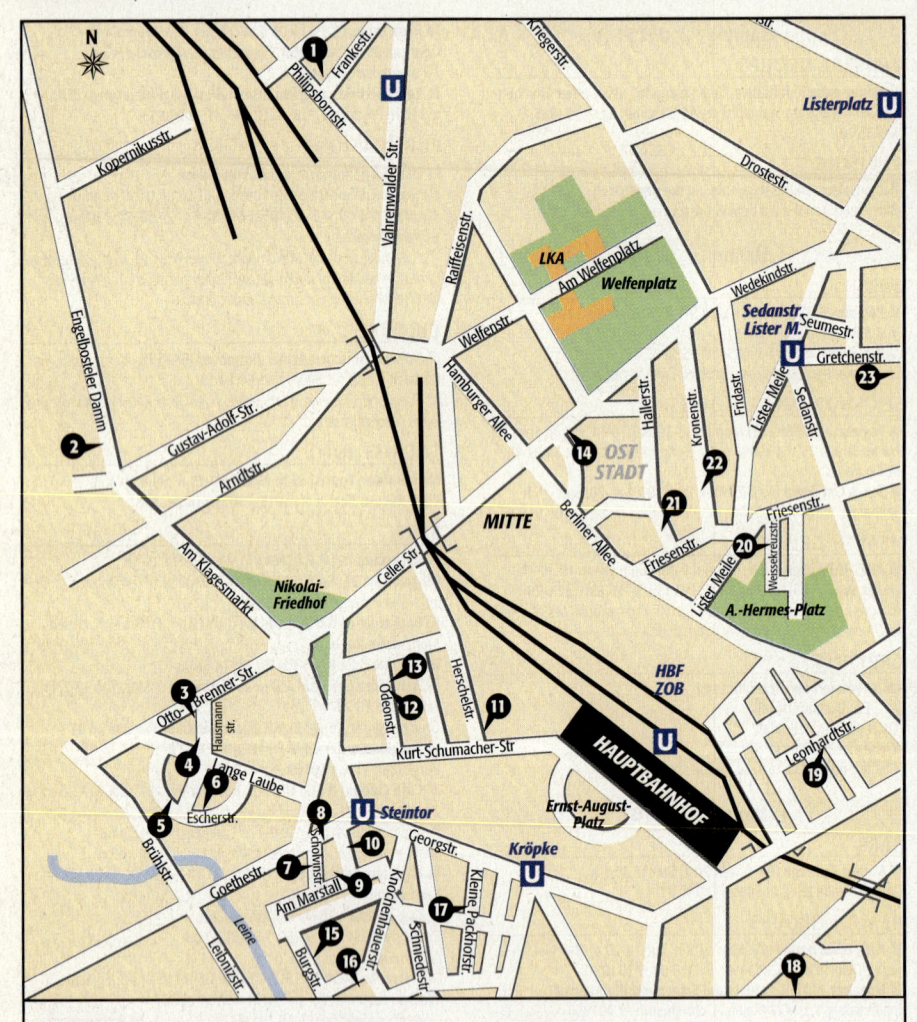

Hannover

1. The Hole Leather Bar
2. Men's Factory Danceclub
3. Vulkan Sauna & Pension
4. Vulcano Danceclub / Opus Musik-Café Bar / Backstairs Bar
5. Cup Bar
6. Café Caldo Bar
7. Kools Sex Shop
8. Men's Point Sex Shop
9. Sex-Palast Sex Shop
10. Irrgarten Sex Shop
11. Video-World Sex Shop
12. Odeon Bar
13. Joe's Dark & Play Rooms Sex Shop
14. Sex Point Sex Cinema
15. Burgklause Bar
16. Café Konrad
17. Beate Uhse Int. Sex Shop
18. HOME-Zentrum Gay Info
19. Alcazar Cabaret Show
20. Le Fiacre Bar
21. Club Oui Bar
22. La Cage Aux Folles Bar
23. Belvedère Bar

world-gay-cruising
www.joesdarkandplayrooms.de
JOE'S®
dark&play
rooms
hannover-city odeonstraße 6

Germany | Hannover

bed & breakfast ?

online-booking:
www.pension-lärchenberg.de

Doppelzimmer mit Dusche
und Kabel TV
incl. Frühstück
DM 100,- !

Pension Lärchenberg Bödekerstraße 37 30161 Hannover
Tel.: 0511 - 34 23 37 Fax: 0511 - 336 04 40

le fiacre

...wo Jungs Herren treffen!

- BAR
- RESTAURANT
- PENSION
- seperate club-room and rooms by hour available

weißekreuzstraße 20
30161 hannover
+49-511-342337
www.lef-hannover.de

DISCO/BAR
MEN'S FACTORY
Engelbosteler Damm / Hannover

■ ALLES CMP.

TÄGLICH AB 20 UHR   ESCHERTSRASSE 11   HANNOVER

Hannover | Germany

CALDO
Wir lassen keinen kalt!

OPEN:
MO - FR AB 18 UHR
SAMSTAG AB 20 UHR
SONNTAG AB 16 UHR

CAFÉ CALDO
BERGMANNSTRASSE 7 · 30159 HANNOVER · TEL (0511) 15173
WWW.CALDO.DE

ALLES UNTER EINEM DACH
IN HANNOVER

Musik-Café Opus
Café • Bar • Bistro

Montag bis Freitag ab 18.00 Uhr
Samstag, Sonntag und Feiertags ab 20.00 Uhr

VULCANO
Diskothek
Mi -Fr- Sa - So ab 22.00 Uhr

FÜR LEDER- UND JEANS-FREUNDE
Backstairs
Mi - Fr - Sa ab 23.00 Uhr

Lange Laube 24,
Eingang Hausmannstraße
30159 Hannover

■ **Oui Club** (B BF f G MA N R) 6-? h
Hallerstraße 30 ✉ 30161 ☎ 388 03 33

CAFES
■ **Café Konrad** (A BF F GLM OS YG) 10-24, Fri & Sat -1 h
Knochenhauer Straße 34 ✉ 30159 *(S-Markthalle)* ☎ 32 36 66

DANCECLUBS
■ **King´s Club** (AC B CC D GLM lj MA s WE) Fri Sat& before public holidays 22-? h
Georgstraße 26 ✉ 30159 *(U-Kröpcke)* ☎ 353 0353
■ **Men's Factory** (! B D DR G lj MA VS) Fri 22-? (g), Sat & before public holidays 22-? (G) h
Engelbosteler Damm 7 ✉ 30167 ☎ 70 24 87
■ **Schwule Sau** (! B d GLM YG) Wed 20-? Sat Sun 21-? h. Café 20-2, closed Mon Thu
Schaufelder Straße 30a ✉ 30167 ☎ 700 05 25
Popular gay and lesbian party. Also café.
■ **Vulcano** (AC B D G MA WE) Wed Fri-Sun 22-? h
Lange Laube 24 ✉ 30159 *(Entrance/Eingang Hausmannstraße)* ☎ 137 88

SHOWS
■ **Alcazar Cabaret** (B d F g MA STV) Wed-Sun 19-5, shows 22.30 and 24, Fri Sat also 3.15 h
Leonhardstraße 11 ✉ 30175 ☎ 34 46 10

SEX SHOPS/BLUE MOVIES
■ **Irrgarten** (B DR G MA VS) Mon-Thu 10-4, Fri 10-Mon 4 h 8 (non-stop)
Reitwallstraße 4 ✉ 30159 *(U-Steintor)* ☎ 363 15 23
Big sex-shop with maze, showers and bar.

■ **Joe's Dark and Play Rooms** (! DR G lj MA VS) 11-1, Fri-Sat -? h
Odeonstrasse 6 ✉ 30159 ☎ 169 06 64
Very large and modern sex shop: showers, bar, SM parties.
■ **Kool's** (CC DR G MA TV VS) Mon-Sat 9-24, Sun 13-24 h
Scholvinstraße 2 ✉ 30159 ☎ 363 15 40
■ **Man Video-World** (G VS) 9-23, Sun 13-23 h
Herschelstraße 1a ✉ 30159 *(Near main station)* ☎ 189 73
■ **Men's Point** (AC b DR G lj MA VS) 10-4 h
Goethestraße 7 ✉ 30169 *(U-Steintor, next to Spielothek)*
☎ 32 47 64
2 cinemas (1 gay).
■ **Reitwall Sex** (g TV VS) Mon-Sat 9-24, Sun 10-23 h
Reitwallstraße 6-7 ✉ 30159 ☎ 32 05 41
■ **Sex Point** (g VS) 11-23, Sun 15-23 h
Celler Straße 32 ✉ 30161 ☎ 319 459
■ **Sex-Palast** (g VS) 10-2h
Reitwallstraße 5 ✉ 30159 ☎ 328734
■ **Videomarkt Cinema** (g VS) Mon-Fri 11-20, Sat 8-20 h
Am Klagesmarkt 9 ✉ 30159 ☎ 177 35

Germany | Hannover

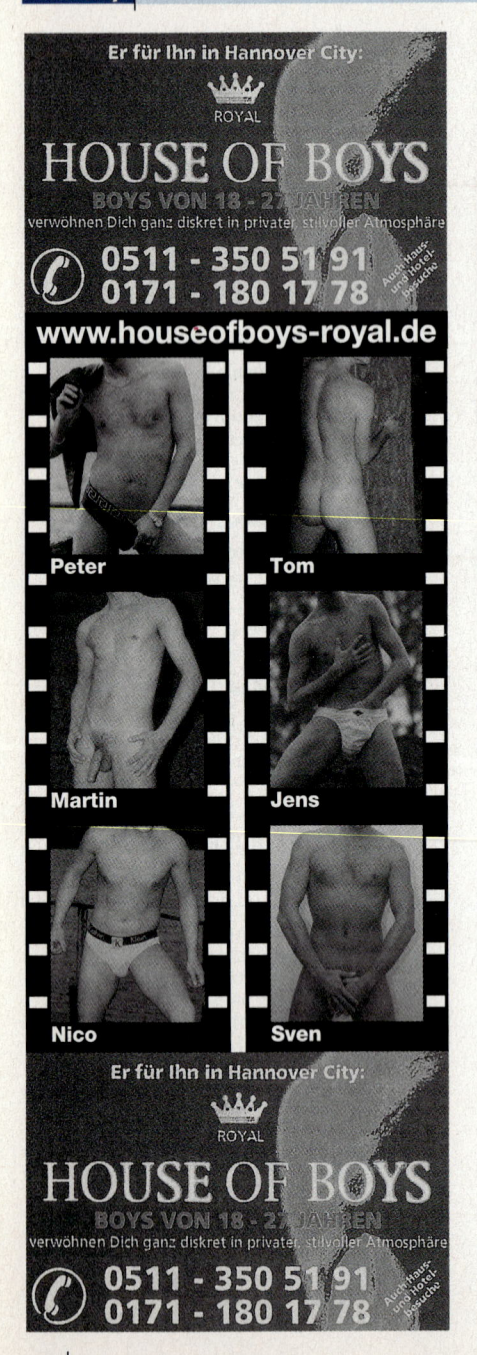

HOUSE OF BOYS
■ **Royal House of Boys**
☎ (0511) 350 51 21
More than 30 young men available.

SAUNAS/BATHS
■ **Vulkan** (B BF DR F G H lj MA p SA SB SOL VS WH) 13-24, Fri 13-Sun 24 h
Otto-Brenner-Straße 15 ✉ 30159 (Tram (HBF) 1-Steintor, near Klagesmarkt, entrance Hausmannstraße) ☎ 151 66
A long tradition sauna recently renovated on 3 floors.

BOOK SHOPS
■ **Buchhandlung Annabee** (glm MA) Mon-Fri 10-19, Sat -14 h
Gerberstraße 6 ✉ 30169 (Bus-Gerberstraße/U-Königswortherplatz)
☎ 131 81 39
Books, magazines and CDs.

FASHION SHOPS
■ **MEC underwear** Mon-Fri 10-20 Sat 9.30-16 h
Galerie Luise ✉ 30159 ☎ 36 32 676

GIFT & PRIDE SHOPS
■ **Masculinum** (AC CC G) Tue-Fri 16-19, Sat 11-15 h
Listerstraße /Baumbachstraße 4 ✉ 30163 (near Lister Platz)
☎ 62 10 24
Erotic shopping for those who love men. A large selection of postcards, books and "rainbow" articles as well as music and CDs.

GUEST HOUSES
■ **Pension Lärchenberg** (BF CC F G H R)
Bödekerstraße 37 ✉ 30161 (near train station) ☎ 34 23 37
🛏 336 04 40

Hannover | Germany

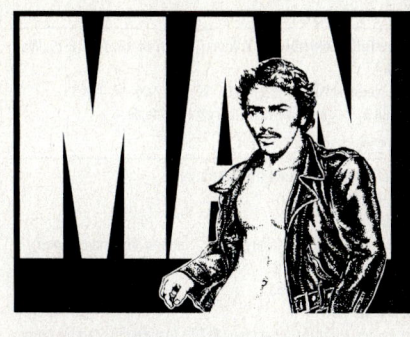

HANNOVER VIDEO-WORLD
Shop • Kino • Verleih
Herschelstraße 1a, nahe Hbf.
Mo-Sa 9-23 Uhr · So 13-23 Uhr

Single DM 40-90, Double 70-100.- BF incl. Also rent by the hour.
■ **Pension Oui** (G R)
Hallerstraße 35 ✉ 30160 ☎ 388 03 33
Rates double DM 90-160, Relax-rooms 40-60 (without/with shower).
■ **Pension Vulkan Sauna** (G H MA p) All year
Otto-Brenner-Straße 15-17 ✉ 30159 (Entrance/Eingang Hausmannstraße) ☎ 151 66 📠 161 38 18 🖥 www.vulkansauna.de
Part of the Vulkan Sauna. Central location. All rooms with shower/WC and TV.

PRIVATE ACCOMMODATION
■ **Enjoy Bed and Breakfast** (BF G H MA) 16.30-21 h
Nollendorfplatz 5, 10781 Berlin (U-Nollendorfplatz)
☎ (030) 236 236 10 📠 (030) 236 236 19 ✉ info@ebab.com
🖥 ebab.de
Accommodation sharing agency. All with shower and BF. 40-45 DM p.p.

GENERAL GROUPS
■ **Schwusos - Schwule Sozialdemokraten Niedersachsens**
☎ 283 42 79 📠 85 82 60 ✉ niedersachsen@schwusos.de
🖥 www.schwusos.de
Gay socialist group. Call or check homepage for further information.

FETISH GROUPS
■ **Leguan e.V.** (LJ) Meets 2nd Tue 19.30 h im Home & 4th Wed 20h im Odeon.
c/o Home, Johannsenstraße 8 ✉ 30159 ☎ 348 23 72
✉ Leguan-Hannover@BikeRider.com
🖥 hannover.gay-web.de/leguan
A club for gay men in leather, rubber, uniform and S/M.
■ **MSC Hannover e.V.** Meets 3rd Sat 21 h at Café Konrad, Knochenhauerstraße 34
Postfach 41 49 ✉ 30041 ✉ mschannover@writeme.com
🖥 www.hannover.gay-web.de/msc
Member of ECMC.

HEALTH GROUPS
■ **Hannoversche AIDS-Hilfe e.V.** Mon-Thu 10-16, Fri -14, Counselling: Mon-Thu 10-16, Thu 18-20 h
Johannssenstraße 8 ✉ 30159 ☎ 194 11 ☎ 13 606 96 0
✉ aidshilfe.hannover@t-online.de
■ **SIDA e.V.-Ambulanter Pflegedienst für AIDS-Kranke**
Mon-Fri 8-16 h
Stolzestraße 59 ✉ 30171 ☎ 66 46 30 📠 623944
✉ SIDA-e.V.Hannover@t-online.de

RELIGIOUS GROUPS
■ **Lazaruslegion-Christenbeistand für AIDS-Kranke und HIV-Infizierte e.V.** (glm p) Mon-Thu 10-16.30, Fri -13h
Podbielskistraße 57 ✉ 30177 ☎ 62 50 41 📠 394 14 53
✉ Lazarusregion.Hannover@gmx.de 🖥 www.nananet.de
Counselling and services for people with HIV and AIDS.

SPORT GROUPS
■ **SLS Leinebagger Hannover e.V.**
c/o Home-Zentrum, Johannssenstraße 8 ✉ 30159 ☎ 306 88 44
📠 306 88 54 ✉ info@leinebagger.de 🖥 www.leinebagger.de
Multi-section gay and lesbian sports club.

SWIMMING
-Ricklinger Kiesteiche (MA NU) (Südlich des/south of Südschnellweg)
-Freiseebad Maschsee

---

complete offer
see page Germany/Berlin

HANNOVER - from DM 40 -
overnight accomodation service
· about 750 beds · more than 28 cities ·

enjoy bed & breakfast

central booking office Berlin ☎ **+49-30-236 236 10** 4:30-9:00 pm local time
Fax +49-30-23623619 · info@ebab.de · www.ebab.de

Germany Hannover ▶ Herne

CRUISING
- Schneiderberg Park (ayor) (nachts/at night)
- Eilenrieder Stadtwald am Zoo/at the zoo (ayor) (nachts/at night)
- P Ricklinger Kiesteiche (Bullenwiese, after dawn)
- Am Klagesmarkt (OG)
- Marktkirche (popular)
- Busumsteige Viergrenzen, Podbielskistraße
- ZOB near Hauptbahnhof/main station

Heide ☎ 0481

HEALTH GROUPS
■ **AIDS-Hilfe Westküste e.V.** Mon 10-13.30, Thu -16 h
Große Westerstraße 30 ✉ 25746 ☎ 76 76 📠 789 08 62
📧 alt-westkueste@t-online.de

Heidelberg ☎ 06221

BARS
■ **Thanner** (AC BF E glm OS YG) Mon-Thu 9-1, Fri Sat -3 h
Bergheimer Straße 71 ✉ 69115 ☎ 16 77 21

DANCECLUBS
■ **Mata Hari** (B D glm MA p) Tue-Sun 22-3 h
Oberbadgasse 10 ✉ 69117 (entrance Zwingerstraße) ☎ 18 18 08

SEX SHOPS/BLUE MOVIES
■ **Beate Uhse International** (AC CC g VS) Mon-Sat 10-1 Sun 14-1 h
Kurfürstenanlage 53 ✉ 69115 (Near/Nähe Hauptbahnhof)
■ **Sex-Shop** (g VS) Mon-Sat 9-23 h
Merianstraße 3/Heugasse ✉ 69117 (Entrance/Eingang Heugasse)
☎ 298 99
Popular sex shop with straight blue movies, gay magazines, videos etc.

BOOK SHOPS
■ **Buchhandlung Wohlthat** (CC) Mon-Fri 9-20, Sat -16 h
Hauptstraße 156 ✉ 69117 (near/nahe Heilig-Geist-Kirche)
☎ 16 27 02
■ **Phönix Buchhandlung** (cc glm)
Hauptstraße 86 ✉ 69117 ☎ 90 57 50

HOTELS
■ **Mayerhof** (CC E F g H OS) 11.30-14 h 17-?
Mon+Sat aftern. closed
Loppengasse 14 ✉ 69226 ☎ (06224) 15 772 📠 (06224) 17 16 08
📧 kontakt@dermayerhof.de ● dermayerhof.de

HEALTH GROUPS
■ **AIDS-Hilfe Heidelberg e.V.** Mon, Tue, Fri 11-13, Tue 16-19, Wed 16-18 h
Untere Neckarstraße 17 ✉ 69117 ☎ 16 17 00 ☎ 194 11
📠 16 88 37 📧 aidshilfe-heidelberg@t-online.de

CRUISING
- Kaufhof department store (Hauptstraße)
- Adenauerplatz (popular)
- Hauptbahnhof
- Universitätsbibliothek (Kellergeschoß, mittags/downstairs, noon)
- Horten department store
- Mensa Neuenheimer Feld
- Alte Brücke Nord
- Park an der/at Kurfürstenanlage (AYOR) (östlich der Stadtbücherei, nachts/east of public library, at night)

Heilbronn ☎ 07131

HEALTH GROUPS
■ **AIDS-Hilfe Unterland e.V.** Mon/Wed 10-16, Thu 13-18, Fri 10-14 h
Wilhelmstraße 3 ✉ 74072 ☎ 194 11 ☎ 890 64
Local gay group meets here Wed 20-22h.

SWIMMING
- Katzenbachsee at Brackenheim

CRUISING
- Alter Friedhof/old cemetery (ayor)
- Hauptbahnhof/Main station
- Rathaus/Town Hall
- Harmonieunterführung

Herdecke ☎ 02330

HEALTH GROUPS
■ **AIDS-Hilfe EN e.V.** Mon 8-13 h
c/o Krisenladen, Hauptstraße 14 ✉ 58313 ☎ 31 53

Herne ☎ 02325

HEALTH GROUPS
■ **AIDS-Hilfe Herne e.V.** Mon 9-11, Thu 16-19 h
Hauptstraße 94 ✉ 44651 ☎ 609 90 ☎ 194 11 (helpline)

---

der *Mayerhof* Hotel Restaurant Terrasse

Komfortzimmer mit Dusche/WC, Kabel-Farb-TV, ISDN Anschluss
Direktwahltelefon, Parkplatz, Tiefgarage, Shuttelservice auf Anfrage

Restaurant mit gehobener deutscher Küche, Terrasse

10 min. bis Heidelberg City, 20 min. bis Mannheim, 5 min. bis Walldorf (SAP)

Loppengasse 14, 69226 Nussloch/Heidelberg
Tel. 06224 / 15772 Fax 06224 / 171608,
www.dermayerhof.de, Kontakt@dermayerhof.de

CRUISING
-Wanner Sportpark, Franzstraße/Rathausstraße
-Bahnhof Herne/Train station
-Saalbau Wilhelmstraße/Stadtgarten

Herten ☎ 02365
CRUISING
-Parking lot Main post office

Hildesheim ☎ 05121
SEX SHOPS/BLUE MOVIES
■ **Beate Uhse Sex Shop** (g VS)
Bahnhofsallee ✉ 31134

GENERAL GROUPS
■ **Kraut und Rüben** (A b d GLM lj MA)
c/o AIDS-Hilfe e.V., Zingel 14 ✉ 31134 ☎ (0177) 2072065
Café: Sun 16-19.30 h at FEZ, Annenstr. 23, party: 3-monthly at Kulturfabrik, Langer Garten 1, call for exact dates.

HEALTH GROUPS
■ **Hildesheimer AIDS-Hilfe e.V.** Mon, Tue, Thu 9-12, Wed 15-17 h
Zingel 14 ✉ 31134 ☎ 194 11 ☎ 05121/133127 📠 13 08 43
📧 info@hildesheimer-aids-hilfe.de
🌐 www.hildesheimer-aids-hilfe.de

SWIMMING
-Tonkuhle (g NU) (Blauer Kamp, at the university/bei der Universität. Summer only/nur im Sommer)

CRUISING
-Ehrlicherpark
-Paul-von-Hindenburg-Platz (PVH)
-Neustädter Markt
-Bohlweg/Pfaffenstieg (am Dom/at the dome)
-Almstor

Hof ☎ 09281
BARS
■ **Schnürsenkel** (B d f g MA OS) 18-2 h, closed Wed
Fabrikzeile 1 ✉ 95028 (near Hofbad) ☎ 446 13

DANCECLUBS
■ **Gay-Bi-Lesbian party at Viva** (AC B D GLM MA) last Sun 21 h
Hohensass 2 ✉ 95030 (Bus5-Hohensass, by car take B 15)
☎ 645 22
Very popular with locals

SEX SHOPS/BLUE MOVIES
■ **Beate Uhse International** (g) Mon-Fri 9.30-18, Sat 9.30-13 h
Brunnenstraße 2 ✉ 95028 ☎ 84499
■ **Sex Shop** (g) Mon-Fri 9-18, Sat 9-13 h
Klosterstraße 30 ✉ 95028 ☎ 2931

CRUISING
-Stadtpark/Stadtbücherei

Hoyerswerda ☎ 03571
GENERAL GROUPS
■ **Men Only Schwulengruppe**
Postfach 34 33 / PA 3 ✉ 02965 ☎ 97 80 89

HELP WITH PROBLEMS
■ **Rosa-Hilfe-Telefon** Tue Thu 17-23 h
☎ 726 67

Husum
CRUISING
-Schloßpark (ayor)
-Bahnhof
-Schloßgang

Ilmenau
GENERAL GROUPS
■ **LSVD Thüringen**
Postfach 01 23 ✉ 98683

Inden ☎ 02465
HOTELS
■ **Gut Merödgen** (A AC B BF CC E F H OS S)
Merödgenerstraße 29 ✉ 52459 ☎ 99 44 0 📠 99 44 77
📧 info@gut-meroedgen.de 🌐 www.gut-meroedgen.de
Hotel and restaurant in the natural reserve Nordeifel between Cologne and Aachen. Walks, tennis, inline-skating, piano music and live entertainment in the restaurant. All rooms with AC, bath/shower, WC, phone, TV, radio. Own keys. Rates single room: 129.-, double 149.-, apartment: single 149.-, double 168.- incl BF.

Ingolstadt ☎ 0841
BARS
■ **Pinocchio** (AC B d f GLM lj MA OS s) Sun, Tue & Wed 18-1, Thu 18-2, Fri Sat 20-3 h, Mon closed
Am Nordbahnhof 4 ✉ 85049 (motorway exit-ingolstadt-nord,at nordbahnhof near Audi) ☎ 91 07 10

SEX SHOPS/BLUE MOVIES
■ **Amor & Co.** (CC g VS) 9-23 h, closed Sun
Höllbräugasse 5 ✉ 85049 (near/nahe Rathausplatz) ☎ 326 24
■ **Erotik-Super-Markt** (g) Mon-Sat 10-23 h, closed Sun
Dollstraße 17 ✉ 85049

GENERAL GROUPS
■ **Romeo und Julius e.V.** Thu 20-22, Counselling ☎ Wed 20-22 h
c/o Bürgertreff "Alte Post", Kreuzstraße 12 ✉ 85049 ☎ 931 19 13
📧 mail@romeo-julius.de 🌐 www.romeo-julius.de

HEALTH GROUPS
■ **AIDS-Hilfe und Arbeiterwohlfahrt**
c/o Thomas Thöne, Postfach 21 09 15 ✉ 85024 ☎ 93 66 33

SWIMMING
-Hirschweiher (G MA NU) (Fuchsschüttweg, only to be reached thru/zu erreichen über Sebastian-Kneipp-Straße and/und Große Zellgasse)

CRUISING
-Hindenburgpark (nach Sonnenuntergang/very busy after sunset)
-Near/Nähe Nordbahnhof
-Franziskanerstraße (OG) (behind/hinter Neues Rathaus -19 h)
-Main railway station/Hauptbahnhof

Germany | Iserlohn ▶ Karlsruhe

Rudolf-Breitscheid-Straße 58 ✉ 67655 *(1st floor)* ☎ 311 44 25

SEX SHOPS/BLUE MOVIES

■ **Pleasure Shop** (AC CC g MA TV VS) Mon-Fri 9-20, Sat -14; cinema Mon-Sat 9-24, Sun 12-23 h
Richard-Wagner-Straße 5 ✉ 67655 *(pedestrian zone, near Fakelpassage)*
■ **VEW Video Erotic World** (g VS) Mon-Sat 9-23, shop: -20 h
Weberstraße 29 ✉ 67655 ☎ 686 89
■ **Video-World** (AC CC glm MA VS) Mon-Sat 9-23, Sun 12-22 h
Rosenstraße 4 ✉ 67655 *(near Hauptbahnhof)* ☎ 89 19 75

SAUNAS/BATHS

■ **Club. The** (b DR f G msg SA SB SOL VS) 15-24, Sat 14-1, Sun 14-23 h
Bännjerstraße 16 ✉ 67655 *(near Westpfalz-Klinikum)* ☎ 253 25
Friendly atmosphere.

HEALTH GROUPS

■ **AIDS-Hilfe Kaiserslautern e.V.** Counselling Mon-Fri 8.30-12.30, Thu 14-16 h
Pariser Straße 23 ✉ 67655 *(entrance Bleichstraße)* ☎ 180 99
☎ 194 11 📠 108 12 💻 aidshilfe@vereine.kaiserslautern.de
💻 www.kaiserslautern.de/shg/aids
Also meeting point for the local gay & lesbian youth group Lauterjungs und -mädels. Wed 20-? h.

CRUISING

- P Frachtstraße *(near station)*
- WC station
- WC Pfalztheater
- WC Karstadt department store

Iserlohn ☎ 02371

BARS

■ **Why Not** (AC D f GLM lj MA SNU STV) Sun-Thu 18-2, Fri Sat -3h
Viktoriastraße 1 ✉ 58636 ☎ 120 02

Jena ☎ 03641

HEALTH GROUPS

■ **AIDS-Hilfe Weimar & Ostthüringen** Office Mon, Wed-Fri 11-15 h, counselling Mon 11-20 h
Rathenaustraße 10 ✉ 07745 ☎ 61 89 98 ☎ 194 11 (counselling)
📠 61 89 98 💻 info@jena.aidshilfe.de

Kaiserslautern ☎ 0631

BARS

■ **Café Sonderbar** (B glm MA) Fri, Sat & Mon 17- ?, Sun 20- ? Tue closed.
Glockenstraße/Mozartstraße ✉ 67655 ☎ 638 06
■ **Kulisse** (B G MA) 20-1, Fri Sat -2 h, closed Tue
Mainzer Straße 6 ✉ 67657 ☎ 669 31
■ **Take-Off** (B G) 20-1, Fri Sat -2 h, closed Mon
Königstraße 3 ✉ 67655 ☎ 180 40

DANCECLUBS

■ **Blue Eye** (D GLM MA p s WE YG) Fri-Sat 22-4 h
Burgstraße 2 ✉ 67659 *(near town hall)* ☎ 958 44
■ **Joy II** (B D f glm MA) Fri Sat 22-4 h
Burgstraße 21 ✉ 67659 *(near town hall/nähe Rathaus)* ☎ 958 44
■ **Nanu** (B D Glm MA VS) Wed-Sun 22-? h, closed Mon Tue

Karlsruhe ☎ 0721

GAY INFO

■ **Radio Rosa Rauschen** Fri 18-19, Sat 12-13 h
(FM 104,8 MHz; cable: FM 100,2)
Steinstaße 23 ✉ 76133 ☎ 38 78 58 📠 38 50 20
The editors meet Tue 20 h.
■ **RoBin-Rosa Bibliothek und Infothek** Mon 19.15-20 h
c/o Gewerbehof, Steinstraße 23 ✉ 76133

BARS

■ **Erdbeermund** (B D Glm MA) 20-1 h, closed Mon Tue
Baumeisterstraße 54 ✉ 76137 ☎ 37 42 42
■ **Miró** (A B BF F G MA OS TV) 16-1 h
Hirschstraße 3 ✉ 76133 *(Entrance Hirschhof. Tram/Bus-Europaplatz)* ☎ 214 32
Popular meeting place.

DANCECLUBS

■ **Club Le Carambolage** (D glm) Thu-Sat 21.30- 3 h
Kaiserstr. 21 ✉ 76131
■ **Club Tropica** (AC B D G GLM MA s) 22-5 h
Bunsenstraße 9 ✉ 76135 *(entrance Kriegsstraße)* ☎ 85 49 80
■ **Stock-Werk** (Ac D g lj MA) Wed 22.30-3 (GLM), Fri Sat (g) -5 h
Waldstrasse 30 ✉ 76133 *(city centre, near pedestrian zone)* ☎ 38 48 174

SEX SHOPS/BLUE MOVIES

■ **Blue Movie** (AC g VS) 9-24, Sun 13-24 h
Kaiserstraße 33 ✉ 76131 *(Multi-Media-Video-Show)* ☎ 37 42 87

---

leathermaster.de

TEL. u. FAX 0721 - 45414
HANDY 0172 - 7229140
Weit mehr als das Übliche
leathermaster with excellent leatherstudio, from soft to hard, bondages, SM, also erotic massage, only Safer SEX, active Top Body
Ich halte, was andere versprechen
Dieter F., Postfach 6527 · 76045 Karlsruhe

www.leathermaster.de
dieter.f@leathermaster.de

Karlsruhe | Germany

miró
Restaurant, Café & Bar

Öffnungszeiten:
Täglich
16 bis 1 Uhr

Inh. Stephan Diedrichs
Hirschstraße 3
76133 Karlsruhe
Telefon 0721/21432
www.cafe-miro.de

HOTEL Regent
BADEN BADEN

Ihr Hotel im Herzen
der internationalen
Festspielstadt

Inhaber: Jörg Peterson & Brian Cadd

Das Hotel „Regent" bietet Ihnen 3 Sterne-Komfort-
Aufenthalt im Herzen von Baden-Baden.
Unser Haus ist nur wenige Schritte vom Kongresshaus, Kur-
haus, Casino, Caracalla-Therme und Friedrichsbad entfernt.
Sie erwartet ein hohes Mass an gemütlicher Behaglichkeit
und persönlichem Service.
Die 22 EZ / DZ mit Sat-TV, Radio, Minibar u. Telefon sind
gemütlich eingerichtet und bequem mit einem Lift zu erreichen.
In unserer Weinstube erwartet Sie ein einzigartiges Ambiente
und ein Zauber von mehr als 70 Spitzenweinen der Region,
verbunden mit den dazu gehörenden Köstlichkeiten.
Einzelzimmerpreis ab DM 125,–
Doppelzimmerpreis ab DM 160,–
www.regent-hotel-bad-bad.com
info@regent-hotel-bad-bad-com

**Herzlich willkommen im schönen Hotel „Regent"
in Baden-Baden**

Saunaland
AQUARIUM

DIE
Sauna in Karlsruhe
auf 500 qm

**Karlsruhe-Mühlburg
Bachstr. 46 / 0721-9553533**
Sa/So/Feiertag 14.00-24.00 h
Di-Fr 16.00-24.00 h   Mo. Ruhetag

www.aquarium-sauna.de

Germany Karlsruhe ▶ Kassel

Sir Nico
das Erlebnis

mit perfekt eingerichtetem Lederstudio mit Klinikbereich.

Von soft bis sadistisch.

Test the Best in Town.

Übernachtungs-möglichkeit.

Karlsruhe
Telefon: 0172 / 635 53 34
www.sir-nico.de

■ **Schwuler Stammtisch** Meeting Mon 20 h
c/o Weißer Stern, Am Künstlerhaus 45
■ **Schwung- Schwule Bewegung Karlsruhe e.V.**
Postfach 60 0 ✉ 76040 (Gewerbehof, Steinstr.23) ☎ 37 09 73
☎ 37 93 52 (helpline) 📠 (07225) 203 17
📧 vorstand@schwung-karlsruhe.de
🌐 www.schwung-karlsruhe.de
Helpline Mon-Fri 19-21 h. See internet or call for further information.

HEALTH GROUPS
■ **AIDS-Hilfe Karlsruhe e.V.** Counselling Mon Wed 15-18, Fri 10-14; Café Regenbogen Thu 16-20
Stephanienstraße 84 ✉ 76133 ☎ 26 26-0
📧 info.ahka@t-online.de
🌐 home.t-online.de/home/ah.karlruhe
Also meeting point for a Coming-out group, the gay youth group Lucky Boy & for gay fathers. Call for details.

HELP WITH PROBLEMS
■ **Rosa Telefon** Mon-Fri 19-24 h
☎ 37 93 52 ☎ 247 44

SWIMMING
-**Epple-See** (g MA NU YG) (7 km ausserhalb nahe Rheinstetten-Forchheim/7 km from the city near Rheinstetten-Forchheim)
-**Baggersee Leopoldshafen** (Nähe/near Eggenstein-Leopoldshafen)

CRUISING
-**Nymphengarten** (AYOR) (Nähe/near Landesmuseum, Kriegsstraße, nachts/ at night)
-**Rheinhafen** (Action findet sich im kleinen Park auf der anderen Seite des P/get to the small park on the other side of P)
-**Main railway station/Hauptbahnhof** (R)
-**Albtalbahnhof**, Straßenbahnhaltestelle/Albtal railway station, tram station (r)

Kassel ☎ 0561

BARS
■ **Bel Ami** (B G MA OS S) Summer: Mon Wed-Thu 16-1, Fri Sat -3 h, Winter: 19-? h, closed Tue
Wilhelmshöher Allee 84 ✉ 34119 ☎ 288 80 90
■ **Mann-O-Mann** (B f G MA) Mon-Thu 19-1, Fri & Sat 19-3 h. Sun - closed
Friedrich-Ebert-Straße 118 ✉ 34119 (Tram-Bebelplatz) ☎ 188 54
■ **Suspekt Café-Bar** (A B GLM MA msg) Tue-Thu Sun 13-1, Fri Sat -2 h, every 1st Sun Rainbow-Breakfast
Fünffensterstraße 14 ✉ 34117 (Near Rathaus) ☎ 10 45 22

DANCECLUBS
■ **Spot** (B D GLM s YG) Sun 21-4 h
Ölmühleweg 10-14 ✉ 34123 ☎ 562 09

SEX SHOPS/BLUE MOVIES
■ **City Sex Shop** (g VS) 10-18.30, Sat 10-14, 1st Sat -16 h
Grüner Weg 10/Sickingenstraße ✉ 34117 ☎ 175 87
■ **Pleasure** (g) Mon-Sat 9-23, Sun 14-22 h
Kölnische Straße 7 ✉ 34117 ☎ 77 44 37
Special area "Gay Point"
■ **Sex Point** (g VS) 10-24, Sun 15-23 h
Kölnische Straße 18 ✉ 34117 ☎ 71 18 41
Gay cinema and shop. Videos for rent, magazines, toys and leather articles for sale.

■ **Erotic Point** (CC g MA VS) 9-24, Sun and holidays 16-23 h
Hardtstraße 21 ✉ 76185 ☎ 55 35 75
■ **Heiner's Shop** (g VS) Mon-Fri 8.30-20, Sat -16 h
Mathystraße 9 ✉ 76133 ☎ 35 83 35
Mixed Sex Shop with selection of gay magazines, books and videos.

SAUNAS/BATHS
■ **Aquarium** (! B DR f G MA p SA SB SOL VS) 16-24, Sat, Sun and holidays 14-24 h, closed Mon
Bachstraße 46 ✉ 76185 (Tram 2/5-Philippstraße, Eingang im Hinterhof, Entrance in the backyard)
☎ 955 35 33
A large sauna in Karlsruhe with over 500 m² , beautiful designed & very popular.
■ **Saunabad der neue Adonis** (B G MA og OS SA SB VS) 15-24 h
Lameystraße 12a ✉ 76185
☎ 955 37 81
Gay bath with small gay shop. Entrance fee 24,- DM/Schwule Sauna mit Shop. Eintritt 25,- DM.

BOOK SHOPS
■ **Buch Kaiser Ta-Bu-La** (g) Mon-Fri 9.30-20, Sat -20 h
Kaiserstraße 199 ✉ 76133 ☎ 209 44
■ **Montanus aktuell** (AC CC g) Mon-Fri 9.30-20, Sat -16 h
Kaiserstraße 127 ✉ 76133 ☎ 38 04 42
general bookstore with gay section.

GENERAL GROUPS
■ **Die Schrillmänner** Meeting Wed 19 h
c/o Gewerbehof, Steinstraße 23 ✉ 76133
Gay chorus/Schwule Gesangsgruppe

478 SPARTACUS 2001/2002

Kassel ▶ Kiel Germany

SAUNAS/BATHS
■ **Haus Lengen** (AC B BF DR f G MA SA SB SOL VS WO) Mon-Thu 15.30-23, Fri Sat -1 h
Erzberger Straße 23-25 ✉ 34117 *(formerly "Uwe's Pferdestall")*
☏ 168 01 📠 78 07 94
Newly renovated and enlarged sauna.

HOTELS
■ **Haus Lengen** (AC B BF DR f G MA SA SB SOL VS WO) Mon-Thu 15.30-23, Fri Sat -1 h
Erzberger Straße 23-25 ✉ 34117 *(formerly "Uwe's Pferdestall")*
☏ 168 01 📠 78 07 94 📧 uwecornelius@gmx.de
🖥 www.haus-lengen.de
Single room from DM 45 and double room from DM 65.

HEALTH GROUPS
■ **AIDS-Hilfe Kassel e.V.** Mon Fri 11-13, Wed 18-20 h
Motzstraße 4 ✉ 34117 ☏ 10 85 15 📠 10 85 69
Counselling ☏ 194 11 Mon Fri 11-13, Wed 18-20 h

HELP WITH PROBLEMS
■ **Rosa Telefon** Fri 18-22 h
c/o Pro Familia, Frankfurter Straße 133a ✉ 34121 ☏ 274 13

SWIMMING
-Bugaseen Fuldaaue (NU) (cruising, too, in bad weather/ Cruising auch bei schlechterem Wetter)

CRUISING
-Weinberg (Henschelgarten)
-[P] Messehallen
-Kulturbahnhof (R)
-Uni (Mensa, at "Menü 2")

Kehl ☏ 07851

SAUNAS/BATHS
■ **Atrium** (AC cc DR F G MA msg OS SA SB SOL VS WO) 14-24, Fri Sat -1 h, Tue Wed mixed
Schulstraße 68 ✉ 77694 *(5 min from Strasbourg, at the Marktplatz, near the church)* ☏ 48 27 05
Nice sauna with terrace.

CRUISING
-between town-hall and police station (zwischen Rathaus und Polizeiwache)

Kempten ☏ 0831

BARS
■ **Le Filou. Club** (B D f GLM MA OS s) 20-1, Fri Sat and before public holidays -3 h
Stuibenweg 1 ✉ 87435 ☏ 268 29

SEX SHOPS/BLUE MOVIES
■ **Inkognito** (AC g lj MA VS) Mon-Sat 9-23
In der Brandstatt 5 ✉ 87435 ☏ 168 69

GENERAL GROUPS
■ **GSC Allgäu** (G MA)
☏ (08321) 222 00 📧 gsc@gmx.de
Contact Wendelin and Andreas. Social activities for gays living in and around Kempten and Sonthofen./2-3 monatliche Veranstaltungen wie Wanderungen, Skifahren oder Radtouren.

SexPoint Kassel

Kino-Kontaktlandschaft
Video-Verleih
topaktuelle Filme
(Kristen Bjørn, Cadinot, Falcon, Mustang, Man's BEST etc.)
alle aktuellen Magazine und CD's
zu TOP-PREISEN!

Öffnungszeiten:
Mo-Sa 10.00-24.00
So 15.00-23.00

Kino DM 10.-

Kölnische Straße 18
34117 Kassel
Tel.: 0561 / 71 18 41
http://151.189.18.61/sexpoint

CRUISING
-Hofgarten (nachts zwischen/nights between "Residenz" & "Orangerie")
-Salzstraße

Kiel ☏ 0431

GAY INFO
■ **HAKI Schwulen- und Lesben-Zentrum** (GLM) Mon 9.30-15, Wed 15-18.30 Thu 9-12 h
Westring 278 ✉ 24116 ☏ 170 90
📠 170 99
📧 haki@kiel.gay-web.de
Meeting point of gay & lesbian youth group Homosexuelle Früherziehung (1st,3rd and 5th Fri/month at 19h) and other groups. Call for futher information.
■ **Queerfunk** 1. Fri 19.15 at OK-TV, Kiel

PUBLICATIONS
■ **HaJo**
c/o HAKI e.V., Westring 278 ✉ 24116 ☏ 170 90 📠 170 99
📧 hajo@kiel.gay-web.de
🖥 www.kiel.gay-web.de
Monthly free gay and lesbian publication of HAKI e.V. for Schleswig-Holstein.

BARS
■ **Alhambra-Bar** (AC B d f GLM MA OS p R) Mon-Sat 19-4 h, Sun closed
Herzog-Friedrich-Straße 92 ✉ 24103 *(near central station)*
☏ 67 64 24

Germany Kiel ▶ Köln

■ **Ca Va** (A B f GLM MA OS) 18-2, Fri Sat -3 h, closed on Mon
Holtenauer Straße 107 ✉ 24105 *(near/neben Schauspielhaus)*
☎ 854 19
Bright and mixed.
■ **Cabinet** (B DR G MA s VS) 18-5, Video rental: Mon-Fri 18-5, Sat - 24 h
Eckonförderstraße 11a ✉ 24116 ☎ 948 93
■ **Harlekin** (B Glm MA VS) 20-4 h
Kirchhofallee 38 ✉ 24114 ☎ 636 48

DANCECLUBS
■ **Pumpe** (B D f GLM MA) 1st, 3rd & 5th Sat 22-3 h
Haßstraße 22 ✉ 24103 ☎ 961 61

SEX SHOPS/BLUE MOVIES
■ **Beate Uhse Sexshop** (g) 9-23.30, Sun 14-? h
Wall 12, ✉ 24103 ☎ 97 08 33
■ **World of Sex-WOS** (g VS) 10-24, Sun 12-24 h
Schuhmacherstraße 31 ✉ 24103 ☎ 932 55
■ **WOS-Markt** (g) 10-24, Sun 12-24 h
Eggerstedtstraße 11 ✉ 24103

BOOK SHOPS
■ **Zapata** (NG) Mon-Fri 9-18, Sat -13 h
Jungfernstieg 27 ✉ 24103 ☎ 936 39

FETISH GROUPS
■ **Kiel gibS/Mir** Meeting 4th Mon at Storchnest,
Gutenbergstraße 66
☎ 130 55
(Couselling and information) Tue 19-20 h.

HEALTH GROUPS
■ **AIDS-Hilfe Kiel e.V.** Mon-Fri 10-13 h (counselling)
Knooper Weg 120 ✉ 24105 ☎ 194 11 ☎ 570 580 📠 570 58-28
📧 info@aidshilfe-kiel.de 🖥 www.aidshilfe-kiel.de

HELP WITH PROBLEMS
■ **Rosa Telefon** Fri 12-14, Sun 19-21 h
☎ 194 46

SWIMMING
-Lindhöft (NU) (Strand in der Eckernförder Bucht 22 km nordwestlich von Kiel. B 503 Ausfahrt "Camping Lindhöft". 200 m nördlich vom Campingplatz. Action in den Büschen./Beach at Eckernförder Bucht, 22 km northwest of Kiel. Leave route B 503 at "Camping Lindhöft", follow road up to the shore. 200 m north of camp ground is the gay area. Action in the bushes.)

CRUISING
-Schrevenpark (popular)

Kirchheim-Teck

SWIMMING
-Bürgerseen (Landstraße Kirchheim-Nürtingen, der kleinste See/smallest lake)

Kitzingen ☎ 09321

FETISH GROUPS
■ **Schwuler Lederclub Franken** 20-? h
Postfach 25 ✉ 97202 ☎ 226 66

Kleve ☎ 02821

HEALTH GROUPS
■ **AIDS-Hilfe Kreis Kleve e.V.** Mon Tue 9-12 13-16, Thu 20-22 h
Lindenallee 22 ✉ 47533 ☎ 76 81 31 📠 76 81 33
📧 ah-kleve@gmx.de
Local gay group meets here Wed 20-22 h.

Koblenz ☎ 0261

BARS
■ **Bistro "Der Zauberlehrling"** (AC d f GLM MA R s)
Mon-Thu 20-1, Fri Sat -2 h, closed Tue
Baedeckerstraße 29 ✉ 56073 ☎ 412 89
■ **ChaCha** (B F glm MA r S TV) Wed Thu 21-3, Fri Sat 21-4 h, once a month gay party
Alte Heerstraße 130 ✉ 56076 *(Horchheim)* ☎ 973 01 16

RESTAURANTS
■ **Rheinzoll-Stube** (B F g MA)
Rheinzollstraße 16 ✉ 56068 ☎ & FAX 177 79

SEX SHOPS/BLUE MOVIES
■ **Dolly Buster Center** (g VS) Mon-Fri 9-21, Sat -16 h
Löhrstraße 10-12 ✉ 56068 ☎ 334 38
■ **Journal** (g VS) 10-21, Sat 10-14 h, closed Sun
An der Liebfrauenkirche 12 ✉ 56068 ☎ 30 97 68
■ **Penny** (g VS) 9.30-22, Sat -14 h, closed Sun
Löhrstraße 65 ✉ 56068 ☎ 366 55

FASHION SHOPS
■ **SOX** (AC CC g) Mon-Fri 9.30-20 h, Sat 9.30-16 h
Löhrcenter, EG ✉ 56058 ☎ & 📠 914 31 16
Men's underwear.

GENERAL GROUPS
■ **SJK-Schwule Jugendgruppe Koblenz** (G s YG) Counselling Thu 19.30-21, Meeting Fri 19.30 h
Rizzastraße 14 ✉ 56068 ☎ 149 91 📠 671 02 53
📧 sjk@RZ-online.de 🖥 www.sjk-online.de

HEALTH GROUPS
■ **AIDS-Hilfe Koblenz e.V.** Mon-Thu 10-15 h
Löhrstraße 53 ✉ 56068 ☎ 194 11 📠 172 35
📧 aidshilfe@rz-online.de 🖥 www.rz-home.de/aidshilfe

CRUISING
-Deutsches Eck (where Mosel and Rhein flow together; evenings)
-Hauptbahnhof/main railway station

Köln ☎ 0221

✱ A summer in Cologne: The smell of the expresso machines, transvestites fighting and drinks being ordered. In Cologne every waiter is a king, every rose seller a fairy tale princess. No where else are there so many warm days to lift the spirits. Moreover, Cologne is ranked after Amsterdam and Sydney as the having most gay inhabitants, and is even ranked before the wonderful city of San Francisco. There are endless trips to be made from the crowded train stations to numerous districts of Cologne. There's a high concentration of cafés, clubs and places to meet in the heart of the city. The city is well known for festivals, such as CSD and Carnival. Hay Market and Rudolfplatz with its trendy locations are only two of the popular places in Cologne.

✱ Ein Sommer in Köln. Das Geräusch der Espressomaschine. Zwei steinalte Transvestiten streiten sich. Jemand bestellt noch

Köln | Germany

ein Getränk. In Köln ist jeder Kellner ein König, jede Rosenverkäuferin eine schöne Fee. Nirgendwo sonst baumelt die schwule Seele derart luftig in den Himmel. Das liegt an den ganz vielen lässig warmen Sommertage. Und daran, daß in Köln- nach den Städten Amsterdam und Sydney- die meisten Leute schwul sind. Und das noch vor, beispielsweise, San Francisco. Führen in Berlin schier endlose Reisen in bauchigen S-Bahnen von einem Stadtteil in den anderen, ist man in Köln schnell von der Altstadt ins Belgische Viertel gelupft. Die hohe Konzentration von Cafés, Clubs und Connections streichelt das Herz -und Konkurrenz belebt das Geschäft. Köln ist aber auch die Stadt der Feste, von CSD und Karneval. Da ist der Heumarkt mit seinem ewigen Vatertag, den gutmütigen Kneipiers. Da ist der Rudolfplatz mit seinen trendy locations.

Un été à Cologne. Le bruit du percolateur. Deux travestis très vieux se disputent. Quelqu'un commande encore une boisson. A Cologne, tout garçon de café est un roi, toute vendeuse de roses une belle fée. L'ambiance gaie ne se balance nulle part ailleurs de façon aussi légère dans le ciel. Ceci est dû au climat (Cologne a beaucoup de journées d'été chaudes et détendues) et au fait qu'à Cologne la plupart des gens sont gais (comme à Amsterdam et à Sydney). Le nombre d'habitants homos dépasse même celui de San Francisco. Si à Berlin des voyages pratiquement interminables dans des RER pleins à craquer conduisent d'un quartier à l'autre, à Cologne on est transporté rapidement de la vieille ville dans le quartier belge. La concentration élevée de cafés, clubs et lieux de contacts caresse le coeur, et la concurrence anime les affaires. Mais Cologne est aussi la ville des fêtes, de la Gay Pride "CSD" et du carnaval. On y trouve le "Heumarkt" avec son éternelle fête des réjouissances, ses bistrotiers d'un bon naturel, la "Rudolfplatz" et ses établissements branchés.

Un verano en Colonia. Se oye el ruido de la máquina de café, alguien pide otra copa. Dos viejos travestis están discutiendo. En Colonia se acepta cualquier estilo de vida, aquí todo el mundo se puede realizar y por ello es el lugar ideal para muchos gays. Por una parte debido al clima, ya que Colonia cuenta con muchísimos días de verano y por otra parte es la ciudad, después de Amsterdam y Sydney, con el mayor número de habitantes homosexuales. Aquí la comunidad gay es más grande que por ejemplo en San Francisco. Mientras en Berlín uno está obligado a pasar horas enteras en transporte público para moverse entre los distintos barrios, en Colonia se llega cómodamente andando desde el casco antiguo al *Belgisches Viertel*. En pocos metros cuadrados encontramos aquí innumerables cafeterías, bares y clubs y desde luego la competencia favorece al negocio. Colonia es también la ciudad de las fiestas, como el Christopher Street Day y carnavales. Durante todo el año merece la pena una visita del *Heumarkt* con sus encantadores bares o del *Rudolfsplatz*, que se caratteriza por sus lugares de moda.

Un'estate a Colonia. Il rumore della macchina espresso. Due travestiti vecchissimi si litigano; qualcuno ordina qualcosa da bere. A Colonia ogni cameriere è un ré, ogni venditrice di rose una fata. In nessun'altro posto l'anima gay emana la sua allegria; è così grazie al clima. Colonia è caratterizzata da molti giorni estivi abbastanza caldi. E perché Cologna, dopo Amsterdam e Sydney, presenta la più alta percentuale di abitanti gay, ancora più alta di quella di San Francisco. Se a Berlino bisogna viaggiare nelle infinite Métro da un quartiere all'altro, a Colonia si arriva con un salto dal centro storico al Belgisches Viertel. L'alta concentrazione di caffè, club e punit d'incontro si fa vero piacere, e la concorrenza stimola gli affari. Ma Colonia è anche la città delle feste, del CSD e del carnevale. Ecco l'Heumarkt con la sua eterna festa del papà, ecco il Rudolfplatz con i suoi "trendy locations".

GAY INFO

■ **anyway - Jugendzentrum für Lesben, Schwule und deren FreundInnen** (GLM YG) Tue 17-21, Wed-Fri -22 h, Wed for women, Thu for men (-23 h)

Kamekestraße 14 ✉ 50672 (tram 5,6,15,17,19 near Friesenplatz)
☎ 510 54 96 ☎ 510 16 95 (infoline) 📠 510 63 44
🖥 anyway-koeln.de
only for people under 26 years

■ **Centrum Schwule Geschichte e.V.** (GLM) Mon& Fri 15-17 h
Vogelsanger Straße 61 ✉ 50823 ☎ 52 92 95
☎ (0171) 899 52 05 📠 52 92 95
gay sightseeing by appointment

■ **Checkpoint** 17-21 h
Pipinstraße 7 ✉ 50667 (U-Heumarkt) ☎ 92 57 68 68
☎ 92 57 68 69 📠 92 57 68 45 🖥 checkup@netcologne.de
Gay and Lesbian Centre for information, health and services

■ **SCHULZ / Schwulen- und Lesbenzentrum Köln** (A B d f GLM MA OS S) Mon-Sat 12-1, Sun 11-1 h
Kartäuserwall 18 ✉ 50678 (near Chlodwigplatz) ☎ 93 18 80 80
📠 93 18 80 85
🖥 www.schulz-cologne.de
4th Fri 22 h Türk Gay Party. Also Cologne feelings 1st Fri at 19h on Bürgerfunk station.

PUBLICATIONS

■ **Köln & Düsseldorf von hinten**
c/o Bruno Gmünder Verlag, PO Box 61 01 04, 10921 Berlin
☎ (030) 615 00 342 ☎ (030) 615 91 34 🖥 info@spartacus.de
🖥 www.brunos.de
The city guide book about Cologne and Düsseldorf. Useful general information and lots of addresses with extensive descriptions in English and German. Up-to-date maps. Erotic photos.

■ **RIK**
Mattei Medien, Norbertstraße 2-4 ✉ 50670 ☎ 390 660
📠 390 66 22 🖥 rik-magazin.de
Monthly magazine for the Rhein area. Featuring gay news, backround information, addresses, classifieds, dates. For free in gay venues.

BARS

■ **?** (! B G lj MA) 19-? h
Schaafenstraße 57-59 ✉ 50676 (Near/Nähe Rudolfplatz)
☎ 24 90 61
Best time 20-23 h. Good music. Formerly known as "Corner".

■ **Anders im Schulz** (A B f GLM MA OS S) 12-1 h, Sun brunch
Kartäuserwall 18 ✉ 50678 (U-Chlodwigplatz) ☎ 93 18 80 22
menu changes daily

■ **Backdoor** (B f G MA N) 11-1 h
Steinweg 4 ✉ 50667 (U-Heumarkt) ☎ 258 14 79

■ **Bei Udo** (B g MA N) Tue-Thu Sun 16-1, Fri Sat -3 h, closed Mon, winter from 17 h
Vor St. Martin 12 ✉ 50667 (Entrance/Eingang Pipinstraße)
☎ 258 23 47

■ **Beim Pitter** (AC B f GLM lj MA N OS) 11-1 h
Alter Markt 58-60 ✉ 50667 (U-Heumarkt) ☎ 258 31 22
Popular bar in downtown Cologne. Largest outdoor area.

■ **Beim Sir** (B f GLM MG N OS) 14-1/?, Fri Sat 14-4 h
Heumarkt 27-29 ✉ 50557 (U-Heumarkt) ☎ 25 68 35

■ **Bilderschreck** (B f g MA OS) Mon-Thu 18-2, Fri-Sun 19-3 h
Königswinterstraße 1 ✉ 50939 (Tram 18/19-Sülzburgerstraße)
☎ 41 78 85

■ **Brennerei Weiss** (AC B F GLM MA OS) Mon-Thu 18-1 Fri-3 Sat 14-3 Sun 11-1 h (kitchen 18-23h)
Hahnenstraße 22 ✉ 50667 (U-Rudolfplatz) ☎ 257 46 38
Sun brunch 11-15 h. Popular meeting place in the afternoon or evening.

■ **Carussel, Le** (B d f G MA N R) 19-4.30 h
Alter Markt 4-6 ✉ 50667 (U-Heumarkt) ☎ 257 69 53

■ **Clip** (AC B G YG) 21-3, Fri Sat -4.30 h
Marsilstein 29 ✉ 50676 (U-Heumarkt) ☎ 240 92 92

Germany | Köln

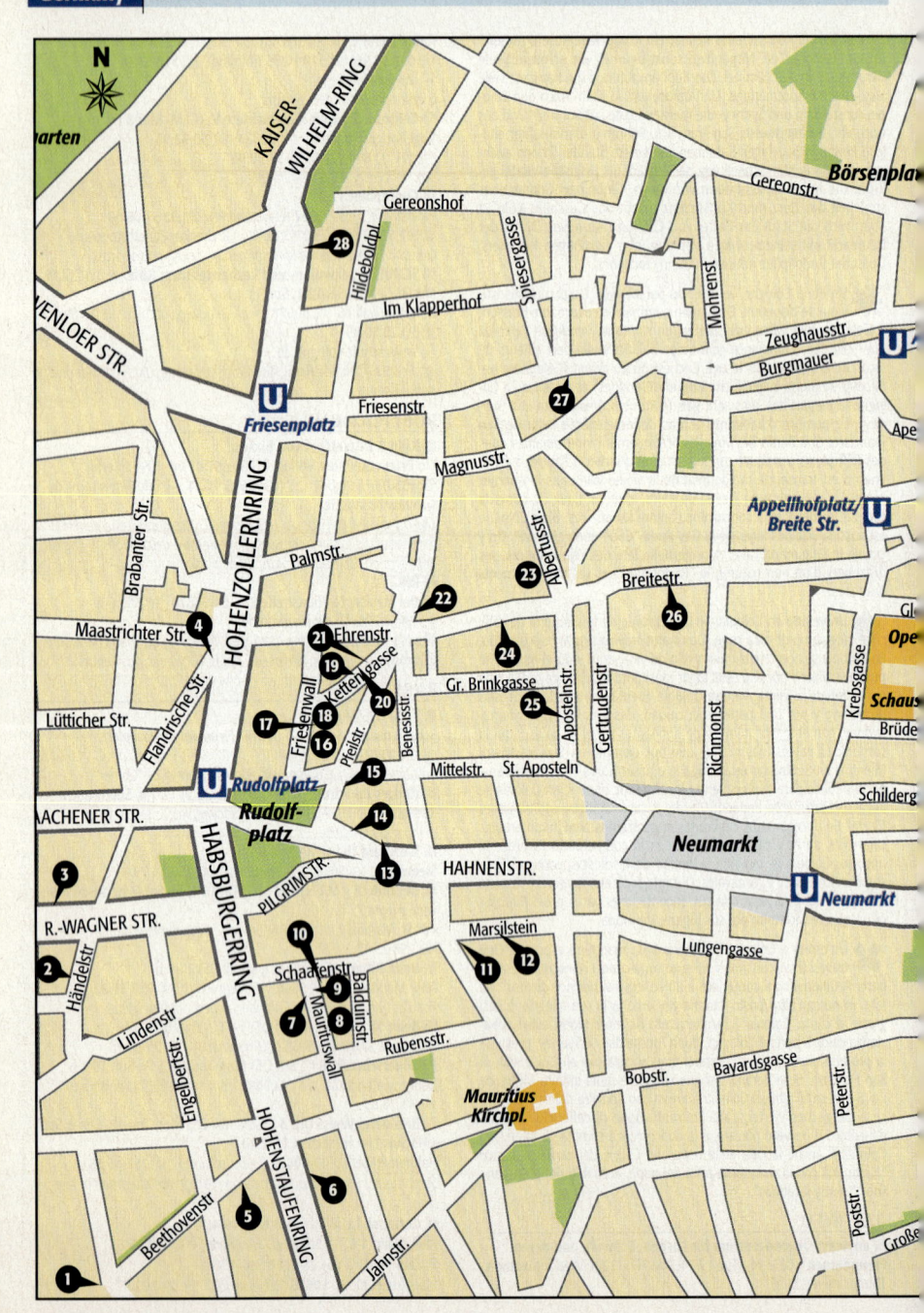

Köln | Germany

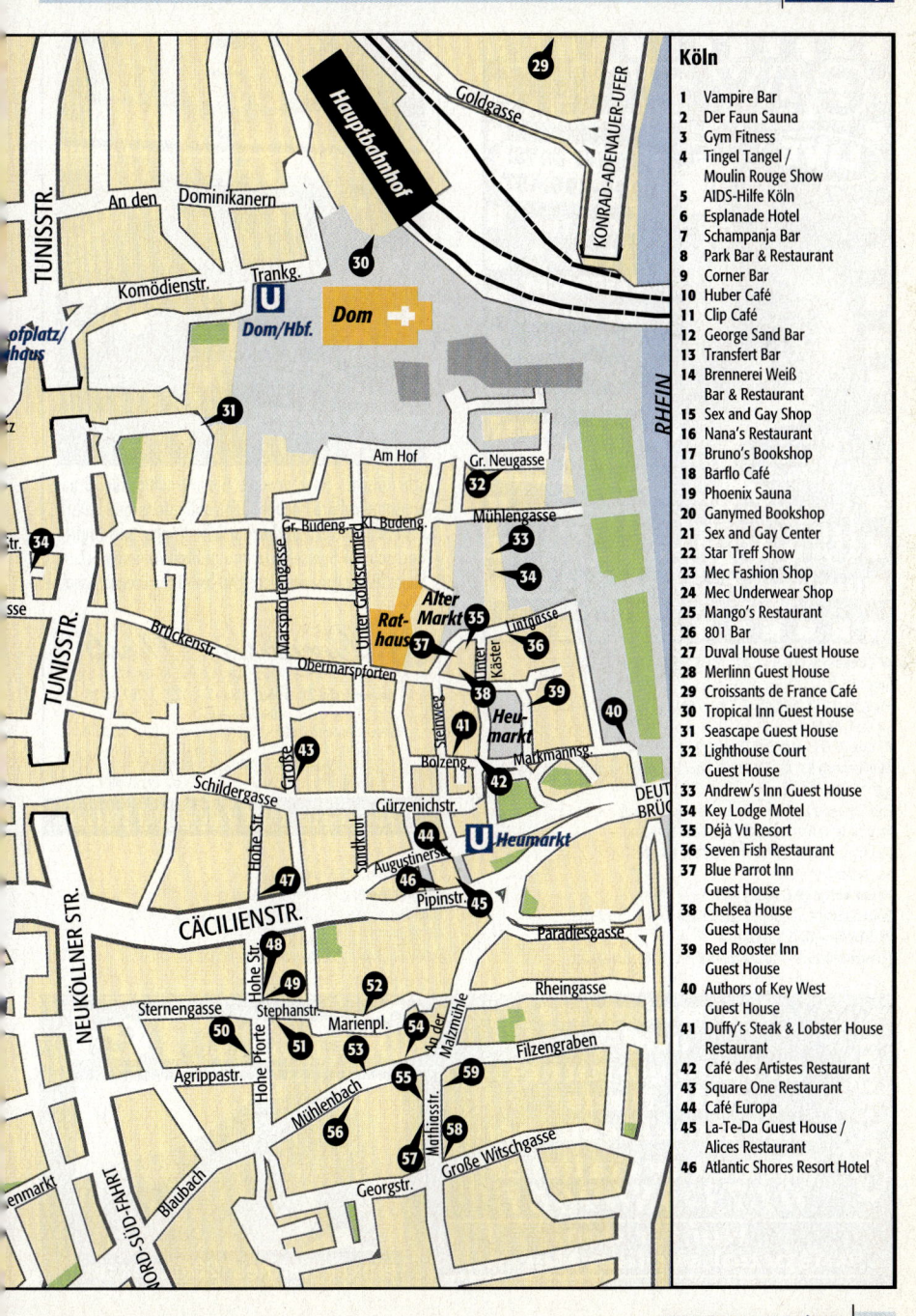

Köln

1 Vampire Bar
2 Der Faun Sauna
3 Gym Fitness
4 Tingel Tangel / Moulin Rouge Show
5 AIDS-Hilfe Köln
6 Esplanade Hotel
7 Schampanja Bar
8 Park Bar & Restaurant
9 Corner Bar
10 Huber Café
11 Clip Café
12 George Sand Bar
13 Transfert Bar
14 Brennerei Weiß Bar & Restaurant
15 Sex and Gay Shop
16 Nana's Restaurant
17 Bruno's Bookshop
18 Barflo Café
19 Phoenix Sauna
20 Ganymed Bookshop
21 Sex and Gay Center
22 Star Treff Show
23 Mec Fashion Shop
24 Mec Underwear Shop
25 Mango's Restaurant
26 801 Bar
27 Duval House Guest House
28 Merlinn Guest House
29 Croissants de France Café
30 Tropical Inn Guest House
31 Seascape Guest House
32 Lighthouse Court Guest House
33 Andrew's Inn Guest House
34 Key Lodge Motel
35 Déjà Vu Resort
36 Seven Fish Restaurant
37 Blue Parrot Inn Guest House
38 Chelsea House Guest House
39 Red Rooster Inn Guest House
40 Authors of Key West Guest House
41 Duffy's Steak & Lobster House Restaurant
42 Café des Artistes Restaurant
43 Square One Restaurant
44 Café Europa
45 La-Te-Da Guest House / Alices Restaurant
46 Atlantic Shores Resort Hotel

SPARTACUS 2001/2002 483

Germany | **Köln**

GAY TALK LIVE

PASSIVE BOYS!
0190-390.457

NONSTOP "1 zu 1" GESPRÄCHE MIT TOLLEN GAYS AUS DEINER UMGEBUNG!

GAYS LIVE AKTION!
0190-390.478

AKTIVE BOYS!
0190-390.413

0190-390.490

Dominante Gays! 0190-355.366
MEGASAT. DM 1,21/Min. 2712

■ **Comeback** (AC B f G MA N OS STV) 15-3, Fri & Sat -4.30, Sun 13-3 h
Alter Markt 10 ✉ 50667 *(Opp. Town Hall/Gegenüber Rathaus)* ☏ 257 76 58
■ **Cox** (B G LJ MA) Sun-Thu 20-2 Fri Sat -3 h
Mühlenbach 53 ✉ 50676 *(U/tram Heumarkt, opposite club 30 sauna)* ☏ 240 04 19
Popular bears and leather pub. Best before 24 h.
■ **Daddy's** (B f G MG N) 18-2, Fri & Sat -3 h
Stephanstraße 2 ✉ 50676 ☏ 240 94 42
Sun brunch 11-15 h.
■ **Em Bölzje** (B G MG) 11-1 h
Bolzengasse 4 ✉ 50667 *(U-Heumarkt)* ☏ 258 23 48
■ **ERA Café** (B G MA OS)
Friesenwall 26 ✉ 50672 *(Rudolf Platz)* ☏ 271 27 25

Brennerei Weiß
DAS BRAUHAUS AM HAHNENTOR

Echt kölsches Essen erwartet Sie in traditioneller Brauhausatmosphäre, neben dem obligatorischen Kölsch vom Faß, unsere gutbürgerliche Küche, mit täglich wechselnder Speisekarte und großen Aktionswochen. Raum für Festlichkeiten jeder Art bietet der Brennereisaal.

Hahnenstraße 22 · 50667 Köln · Tel. 0221 / 257 46 38

Öffnungszeiten:
Montag – Donnerstag 18.00 – 01.00 Uhr • Freitag 18.00 – 03.00 Uhr
Samstag 14.00 – 03.00 Uhr • Sonntag 11.00 – 01.00 Uhr
Warme Küche täglich 18.00 – 23.00 Uhr
Freitag 18.00 – 23.45 Uhr • Samstag 15.00 – 23.45 Uhr

- TRADITIONELLE KALTE UND WARME SPEISEN -

Popular new (2000) café.
■ **Filmdose** (B g MA) Sun-Thu 19-2 h
Zülpicher Straße 39 ✉ 50674 *(U-Dasselstraße/Bhf. Süd)* ☏ 23 96 43
Rather unusual for Cologne: a rather intellectual crowd.

Cologne
Escortservice und Reisebegleitung-
NUR Haus und Hotelbesuche
Signatur Gabriel
0173-5809661
Nur für den Anspruchsvollen Herrn...

Gabriel
e-mail: hermes123@gmx.de

Köln | Germany

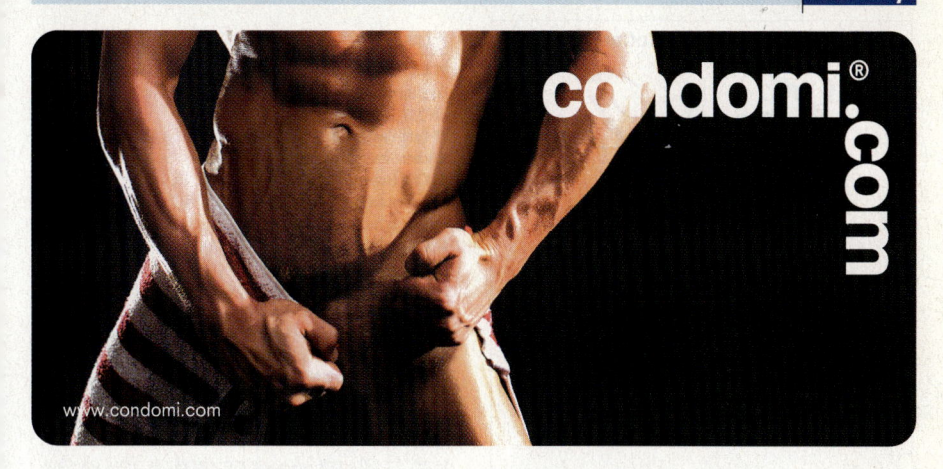

■ **Georg Sand** (B F gLm MA p s) 20-1, Wed Fri Sat -3, 1st Sun from 11.30 h, Mon Tue closed
Marsilstein 13 ✉ 50676 *(U-Heumarkt)* ☎ 21 61 62
■ **Hohenstaufen Klause** (B f glm lj N OS s) Mon-Fri 11-15, 18-1, Sat & Sun 18-1 h
Schaevenstrasse 5 ✉ 50676 *(Rudolfplatz)* ☎ 240 31 02
■ **Hollywood** (AC B f GLM MA OS) 17-4 h
Heumarkt 43 ✉ 50667 ☎ 257 42 19
■ **Hühnerfranz** (AC B BF f G lj MA R TV WE) 7-3 h
Hühnergasse 2 ✉ 50667 *(U-Heumarkt)* ☎ 25 35 36
Early morning breakfast from 7 h.
■ **Kattwinkel** (AC B BF GLM MA N OS s WE) 12-1 (Apr- Oct), 18-1 h (Oct-Mar)
Greesbergstraße 2 ✉ 50668 *(Near/Am Eigelsteintor)* ☎ 13 22 20
Popular terrace in summer.
■ **Monte Christo** (B d G lj MA) 23-6, Sat Sun (D), best time from 1 h
Große Sandkaul 24 ✉ 50667 ☎ 257 68 40
■ **My Lord** (AC B F G oG) 17-3 h, closed Thu
Mühlenbachstraße 57 ✉ 50676 ☎ 23 17 02

■ **Park** (B G YG) Sun-Thu 21-2, Fri Sat -3 h
Mauritiuswall 84 ✉ 50676 *(Near/Nähe Rudolfplatz)* ☎ 21 33 57
Popular with a young crowd.
■ **Rembrandt's** (B d f GLM lj MA r s STV WE) 16-2, Fri Sat -3 h
Lintgasse 4 ✉ 50667 ☎ 257 78 27
■ **Schampanja** (B G MA s) Sun-Thu 20-2, Fri Sat -3 h
Mauritiuswall 43 ✉ 50676 *(U-Rudolfplatz)* ☎ 240 95 44
■ **Teddy Treff** (AC B d GLM lj MA s WE) 20-1, Fri & Sat 20-3 h, Mon closed
Stephanstraße 1 ✉ 50667 *(U-Heumarkt)* ☎ 24 83 10
Various events. Call for information.
■ **Vampire** (A d gLM MA) Tue-Thu 20-1, Fri-Sat -3 h, Sun 20-1 h, Mon closed
Rathenauplatz 5 ✉ 50674 *(U-Rudolfplatz)* ☎ 240 12 11
■ **Verquer** (AC BF f GLM lj MA OS) Mon-Fri 14-1, Sat & Sun 12-3 h
Heumarkt 46 ✉ 50667 *(Altstadt)* ☎ 257 48 10
Sun: breakfast for night crawlers from 6-8 h.
■ **Zille. Der Altstadttreff** (AC B f G lj MA N) 19-3 h
Pipinstraße 5 ✉ 50667 ☎ 258 17 83
■ **Zipps** (AC B f G LJ MA) Mon-Thu 20-2, Fri Sat 15-3, Sun -2 h
Hohe Pforte 15 ✉ 50676 *(U-Heumarkt)* ☎ 240 60 76
Best 22-24 h.

Germany Köln

Altstadt - Treff Coffeethek - Bar

Go-In

24 JAHRE

1977 - 2001

mit großer
Sonnenterrasse

Alter Markt 36 - 42
50667 Köln
☎ **0221 - 258 22 14**

Wochentags
11 - 3 Uhr nachts
Sonntags u. Feiertags
von 13 - 3 Uhr nachts

MEN'S CLUBS

■ **Chains** (AC B d DR G LJ MA VS) from 22-?, Sun from 16 h (special parties)
Stephanstraße 4 ✉ 50676 (U-Heumarkt) ☎ 23 87 30
The largest leather/fetish bar in Cologne. Fri dance party, Sat fetish night.
■ **Hands** (AC B DR G LJ MA WE) 21-2, Fri-Sat -3 h
Mathiasstraße 22 ✉ 50676 (U-Heumarkt)
☎ 24 31 45
■ **Stiefelknecht** (AC B d DR G LJ MA p s VS) 22-4 h
Pipinstraße 9 ✉ 50667 (U-Heumarkt) ☎ 258 07 72
Best late. Leather bar with snooty staff.

CAFES

■ **Barflo** (! AC B BF f GLM OS YG) 10-1 h
Friesenwall 24 d ✉ 50672 (U-Rudolfplatz/Friesenplatz)
☎ 257 32 39
■ **Café Central** (B BF F g MA OS) Sun-Thu 7-3, Fri Sat -4 h
Jülicher Straße 1 ✉ 50674 ☎ 20 71 50
■ **Café Huber** (B f G s YG) Sun-Thu 14-2, Fri Sat -3 h
Schaafenstraße 51 ✉ 50676 (U-Rudolfplatz) ☎ 240 65 30
Popular with a young crowd.
■ **Gloria Café** (A AC B BF D f GLM MA OS S WE) Mon-Thu 10-1, Fri & Sat 9-3, Sun 11-1 h
Apostelnstraße 11 ✉ 50667 (U-Neumarkt) ☎ 258 36 56
Everchanging program, please call for details
■ **Go-In** (B f G MA OS) 11-3, Sun & public holidays 13-3 h
Alter Markt 36-42 ✉ 50667 ☎ 258 22 14
■ **Quo Vadis** (AC b BF CC F GLM LJ MA OS s) Mon-Thu 12-24, Fri -1, Sat 11-1 Sun -24 h
Vor St. Martin 8-10 ✉ 50667 (Entrance/Eingang Pipinstraße)
☎ 258 14 14
seating for 120 people in&outside, many vegetarian dishes, cakes&ice-cream; reservation advisable at the weekend
■ **Transfert** (AC B BF d f G lj MA OS YG) 11-1, Fri Sat -3
Hahnenstraße 16 ✉ 50667 (U-Rudolfplatz) ☎ 258 10 85
Music Café in the center of the Bermuda Triangle

DANCECLUBS

■ **Coconut Gay Special Disco-Party** (B D G lj MA) irregularly 6x/year Sun or before holidays 22-5 h
☎ 13 30 61 *Call for info.*
■ **Gloria Veranstaltungs-Theater** (A AC B D glm S TV YG)
Apostelnstraße 11 ✉ 50667 (U-Neumarkt) ☎ 25 44 33
Popular. Different parties. Check local press for date of "Rosa Sitzung" (Gay and lesbian carnival).
■ **Lulu** (! AC B D DR GLM lj MA s TV VS WE)
Fri Sat & before holidays 23-5 h
Breite Straße 79 ✉ 50667 (U-Appellhofplatz) ☎ 257 54 50
■ **U 27** (b D GLM YG) every 2nd Fri 22.30-3 h
c/o Schulz, Kartäuserwall 18 ✉ 50678 (U-Chlodwigplatz)
For gays, lesbians and friends up to 27.

DIE MISCHUNG MACHT'S
GLORIA
CAFÉ • CLUB • VERANSTALTUNGS-THEATER
APOSTELNSTRASSE 11 • 50667 KÖLN
KARTEN-RESERVIERUNGEN 0221 / 258 36 56

Köln | Germany

KÖLN

Number 1 in Town
SHOP - CINEMA - VIDEOTHEK
GAY-SEX-MESSE
Mathiasstraße 13
Mo–Sat 10:00 – 1:00 · So./Feiertag 12:00 – 1:00
www.KoelnErotik.de

KÖLN

Number 1 in Town
SHOP - CINEMA - VIDEOTHEK
SEX-MESSE
Breite Straße 153
Mo–Sat 10:00 – 1:00 · So./Feiertag 12:00 – 1:00
www.KoelnErotik.de

RESTAURANTS

■ **Alcazar** (B F g MA OS) Mon Tue Thu 12-2, Wed Fri -3, Sat 18-3, Sun 18-2 h
Bismarckstraße 39 a ✉ 50672 *(U-Friesenplatz)* ☎ 51 57 33
Meals 12-14.30, 18-23.30 h.

■ **Anders Ehrenfeld** (B BF F glm MA s) 9-1, bf 9-17, meals 12-15, 18-23 h
Klarastraße 2-4 ✉ 50823 *(U-Körnerstraße)* ☎ 510 14 73
French and local cuisine.

■ **Die Zeit der Kirschen** (A AC B F glm MA OS s) Mon-Fri 11.30-1, Sat 17-1, Sun 10-1 h
Venloer Straße 399 ✉ 50825 *(U-Venloer Straße)* ☎ 954 19 06
Fine international cuisine. Brunch on Sun and public holidays.

■ **Domerie** (b CC E F glm MA OS) Tue-Sat 18-24 h, Sun&Mon closed except fare-times
Frankenwerte 27 ✉ 50667 *(Rheinuferpromenade)* ☎ 257 40 44

■ **Harvey's** (F glm) 18-1, Fri 16-3 h
Weißenburgstraße 58 ✉ 50670 *(U-Reichensperger Platz)*
☎ 72 42 27

THE WEIRD WORLD OF GAY LIFESTYLE

Lulu
BREITE STRASSE 79 50667 KÖLN
WWW.LULU-COLOGNE.DE

Germany | Köln

Gay Erotik Cruising

Die Ultimative, harte
LIVE EROTIK·LINE

Volles Schwitzen
•
volle Gruppen-Action

0190-806644

www.gratisgayfotos.com

TMG DM 3.63 Min/Live Operator

■ **Nana's Restaurant-Bar** (B F g MA) 17-1 h, meals 18-23.15, Fri Sat -0 h
Pfeilstraße 15 ✉ 50672 ☎ 257 30 70

SHOWS

■ **Kaiserhof** (AC B F glm MA S) Shows from Tue-Sun, Ticket Box Tue-Sat 10-20, Sun & holidays 16-20 h, Mon closed.
Hohenzollernring 92 ✉ 50672 *(U-Friesenplatz)* ☎ 139 27 72
■ **Senftöpfchen-Theater** (g STV) Tickets: Mon-Fri 16-20, Sat Sun from 18 h
Große Neugasse 2 ✉ 50667 ☎ 258 10 58
■ **Star-Treff** (B g STV) Wed Thu Sun 19.30-?, Fri Sat -3 h, Wed Thu dinner spectacle
Turiner Strasse 2 ✉ 50668 ☎ 25 50 63
Shows: Wed Thu Sun 20.15, Fri Sat 19.45 & 22.45 h. Admission DM 15.
■ **Timp** (B CC d GLM H MA p SNU STV) 10-5, show at 1 h (free entrance)
Heumarkt 25 ✉ 50667 ☎ 258 14 09
Also Hotel.
■ **Tingel Tangel/Moulin Rouge** (B g MA STV) 20-4.30 h
Maastrichter Straße 6-8 ✉ 50672 ☎ 25 26 01

SEX SHOPS/BLUE MOVIES

■ **Gay Sex Messe** (CC G VS) 10-1 h
Mathiasstraße 13 ✉ 50676 ☎ 24 82 17
■ **Mike Hunter Sexshop** (g VS) Mon-Fri 9-22, Sat 12-1, Sun -24 h
Hohe Straße 2 ✉ 50667 ☎ 240 20 34
Video cabins.
■ **Sex & Gay Shop** (g VS) 9-1, Sun 12-24 h
Pfeilstraße 10 ✉ 50672 *(am/at Rudolfplatz)*
☎ 25 62 78
■ **Sex Discount** (g VS) 9-24 h
Hohe Straße 8 ✉ 50667

---

http://www.valentino.de   Eintritt frei

GAY-CLUB+HOTEL
0221-137079
Valentino
GAY-CLUB+HOTEL

JETZT MIT GRIECHISCH-RÖMISCHEM ZIMMER
Kai, Dein ständiger Ansprechpartner!

Luxuszimmer
Whirlpool
Massagen
Escort-Service
Spontane-Stripshows

Altenberger Str. 13 - Köln (Hinterausgang HBF). So - Do: 15 - 1h, Fr + Sa: 15 - 3h

488 SPARTACUS 2001/2002

Köln | Germany

Wenn bei anderen das Licht ausgeht, geht es bei uns erst richtig los

ab 12 Uhr • täglich Nachtsauna
werktags bis 13 Uhr Eintritt nur DM 18.-

Phoenix SAUNA

Köln • Kettengasse 22 • Tel: 0221-2573381
Düsseldorf • Platanenstr. 11a • Tel: 0211-663638
Essen • Viehoferstr. 49

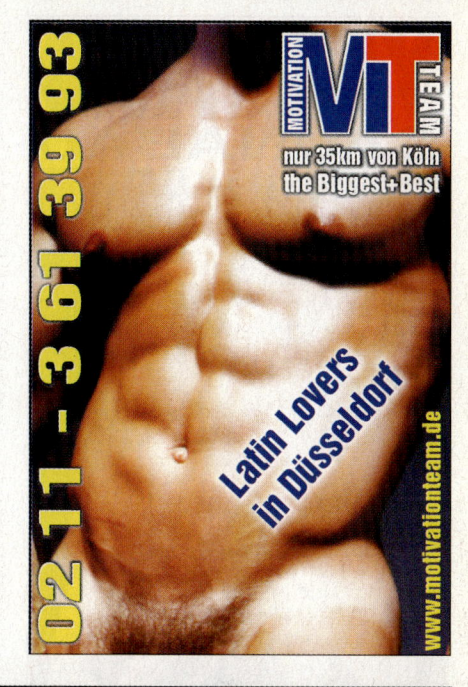

02 11 - 3 61 39 93

MOTIVATION ViT TEAM
nur 35km von Köln
the Biggest+Best
Latin Lovers in Düsseldorf
www.motivationteam.de

the best way to relax

TERRIFIC ATMOSPHERE • LOW PRICES • FANTASTIC GUESTS

DER FAUN
DIE SAUNA · KÖLN
TGL. 12-01 h · FR. + SA. NACHTSAUNA

www.FaunSauna.de

HÄNDELSTR. 31 (RUDOLFPLATZ) · 50674 KÖLN · TEL. 21 61 57

Germany | Köln

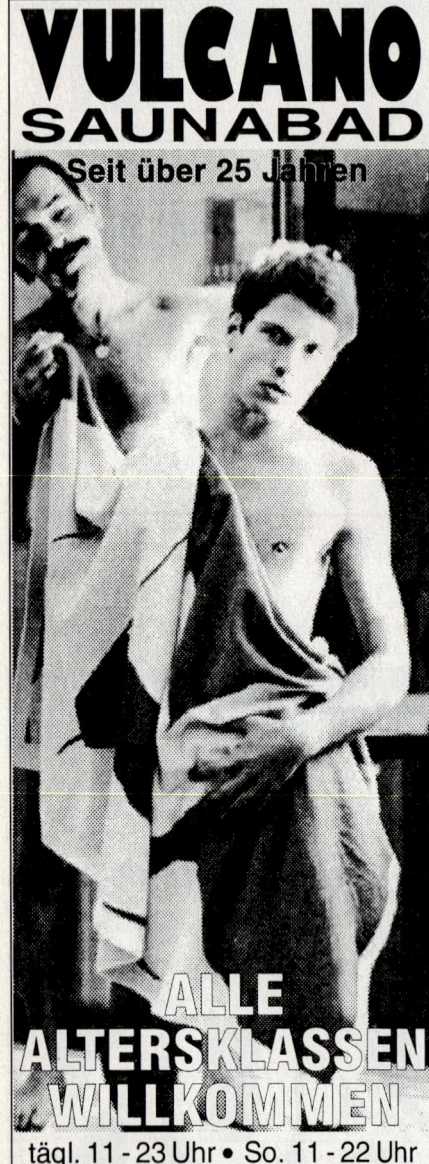

VULCANO
SAUNABAD
Seit über 25 Jahren

ALLE ALTERSKLASSEN WILLKOMMEN

tägl. 11 - 23 Uhr • So. 11 - 22 Uhr
Jeden Samstag Nachtsauna

**Marienplatz 3-5
Tel (0221) 216051**

Badehaus am Römerturm

GAY SAUNA Köln

★ ★ ★ ★ ★

Friesenstr. 23-25 Tel. 0221/257 70 06
www.Badehaus-am-Roemerturm.de

Montag-Freitag 13 - 1 Uhr
Samstags 12 - Sonntag früh
Sonntags 12 - 23 Uhr

Samstags Nachtsauna

■ **Sex Messe** (CC G VS) Mon-Sat 10-1, Sun 12-1 h
Breite Straße 153 ✉ 50667 ☎ 258 17 08
■ **Sex und Gay Center** (G VS) 10-1 h
Mathiasstraße 23 ✉ 50676 ☎ 23 53 01
■ **Sex und Gay Center** (G VS) 10-1 h
Kettengasse 8 ✉ 50672 ☎ 258 09 18

ESCORTS & STUDIOS

■ **Valentino** (AC CC G H MA msg p R SNU VS WE) Sun-Thu 15-1, Fri Sat -3 h
Altenberger Straße 13 ✉ 50668 *(2 min. from central station)*
☎ 13 70 79
Also accomodation available. Strip shows Fri Sat from 20 h.

SAUNAS/BATHS

■ **Badehaus am Römerturm** (! AC B CC DR F G MA msg NU OS p PI SA SB SOL VS WH) Mon-Fri 13-1 Sat 12- Sun 12-23 h
Friesenstraße 23-25 ✉ 50670 ☎ 257 70 06
One of the most beautiful sauna in Europe. Popular on Sun.

Köln | Germany

MEC

men's fashion
shoes
accessories

DKNY GUESS? HUGO
Gianfranco Ferré
Calvin Klein
Gaultier

MEC
underwear

bodywear
beachwear
clubwear

MEC Hugo Boss DKNY
Gianfranco Ferré
Cerutti JOOP!
CK D&G

MEC	Ehrenstrasse 27, 50672 Köln	Tel./Fax: 0221/2581080	Mo-Fr 11-20 Uhr, Sa 10-16 Uhr
MEC underwear	Galerie Luise, 30159 Hannover	Tel./Fax: 0511/3632676	Mo-Fr 10-20 Uhr, Sa 9:30-16 Uhr

Germany — Köln

TEDDY TRAVEL — reisebüro
gay tours

- Individuelle Reiseangebote
- Linien- und Charterflüge
- Pauschalreisen
- Hotel- und Mietwagen-
- Reservierung weltweit

Fordern Sie unseren aktuellen Katalog mit Reisen speziell für gays an

Seit 18 Jahren für Sie da!

www.teddy-travel.de

Mathiasstraße 4-6
D-50676 Köln
Telefon 02 21 - 21 98 86
Fax 02 21 - 24 17 74
e-mail: teddy-travel@t-online.de

Faun. Der (! AC b DR f G msg OS p SA SB SOL VS YG) 12-1, Fri & Sat -8 h
Händelstraße 31 ✉ 50674 (near Rudolfplatz)
☎ 21 61 57
Clean sauna with a relaxing atmosphere and a summer terrace. Tombola on Sun.

Phoenix (! B CC G MA msg p PI SA SB SOL VS) 12-6, Sun and public holidays 12-8 h
Kettengasse 22 ✉ 50672 (U- Rudolfplatz) ☎ 257 33 81
Popular especially late at night and Wed.

Sauna 30 (B F DR G MG SA SB SOL PI WH) 14-23 h
Mühlenbach 30 ✉ 50676 (Tram 1/2-Heumarkt) ☎ 21 73 86

Vulcano (B F G MG msg p SA SB VS) 11-23, Sat -8 h
Marienplatz 3-5 ✉ 50676 (near Kaufhof)
☎ 21 60 51
Intimate atmosphere, sauna established for more than 28 years. Entrance fee 25,- DM

FITNESS STUDIOS

Gym Finess (b f g msg SA WO) Mon-Fri 6-24, Sat 8-23, Sun 10-22h
Richard-Wagner-Sraße 12 ✉ 50674 (U-Rudolfplatz) ☎ 258 11 58

BOOK SHOPS

Bruno's (! A CC G) Mon-Fri 10-20, Sat 10-16 h, closed Sun
Friesenwall 24 ✉ 50674 (U-Rudolfplatz) ☎ 925 26 94
📠 925 25 95 www.brunos.de brunos.koeln@.de
Also video rental.

Ganymed (A CC G MA) Mon-Fri 11-20 Sat -16 h
Kettengasse 18 ✉ 50672 (U-Rudolfplatz) ☎ 25 11 10
Books and CDs.

Mayersche Buchhandlung (cc glm)
Hohe Straße 68-82 ✉ 50667 ☎ 920 10 90
Also in: Köln Galerie, Am alten Posthof.

GYM FITNESS

Open: Mo–Fr   6.00–24.00
       Sa   8.00–23.00
       So   10.00–22.00

daily tickets available

Richard-Wagner Straße 12
50674 Köln (Haltestelle Rudolfplatz)
Tel./Fax 02 21 / 258 11 58

STYLE YOURSELF

Bild: JS Artphot

Köln | Germany

Bruno's

THE GAY MEDIA STORE

www.brunos.de

Bruno's in Berlin
Nürnberger Str. 53
Mo - Sa 10 - 22 Uhr

Bruno's in Köln
Friesenwall 24
Mo - Fr 10 - 20 Uhr
Sa   10 - 16 Uhr

BÜCHER · MAGAZINE · DVD · VIDEOS · VIDEOVERLEIH

Germany | **Köln**

LEATHER & FETISH SHOPS

■ **Cosmic Ware** Mon-Fri 12-18.30, Sat 11-15 h
Engelbertstraße 59-61 ✉ 50674 *(U-Rudolfplatz)* ☎ 240 12 01
Rubber, S/M etc.
■ **Nima Lapelle Lederstudio** Mon-Fri 10-20, Sat -14 h
Wolfsstraße 16 ✉ 50667 ☎ 257 83 15
Fashionable leather and erotic specials./ Ledermode und besondere Erotika.
■ **Secrets** (CC GLM LJ) Mon- Wed Fri 13.30-19, Thu&Fri -20.30, Sat 10-16 h
Marienplatz 1 ✉ 50676 ☎ 24 41 00
Latex.leather,toys,S&M equipment,piercing,rubber,books and cards.

TRAVEL AND TRANSPORT

■ **G-Tours** (cc G) Mon-Fri 10-18.30, Sat 10-16 h
Schwalbengasse 46 ✉ 50667 ☎ 925 89 10 📠 92 58 91 19
■ **Reisebüro im Bazaar de Cologne** 9-18.30, Thu -20, Sat 10-14, 1st Sat -16 h
Mittelstraße 12-14 ✉ 50672 ☎ 257 02 21/22 📠 25 61 50
■ **Teddy Travel** (GLM lj) 9.30-18.30, Sat 10-13 h, Sun closed
Mathiasstraße 4-6 ✉ 50676 ☎ 21 98 86 📠 24 17 74
✉ teddy-travel@t-online.de 🖥 www.teddy-travel.de
Travel agent and tour operator./ Reisebüro und -veranstalter. Own catalogue/Eigener Katalog. Also contact for Raffles Gay Sailing.

HOTELS

■ **Callas am Dom** (BF CC g H msg s)
Hohe Straße 137 ✉ 50667 *(2 min. from Central Station)*
☎ 258 38 38 📠 258 38 39 ✉ callas@aol.com
🖥 www.callas-hotel.de
Single rooms DM 125-290/double rooms 175-390. Special weekend prices. Also Last-Minute from 19 h. Einzelzimmer DM 125-290/Doppelzimmer 175-390. Sonderpreise am Wochenende. Last-Minute ab 19 h.
■ **Esplanade** (A BF CC g H MA SA SOL)
Hohenstaufenring 56 ✉ 50674 *(Near/Nähe Rudolfplatz)*
☎ 921 55 70 📠 21 68 22 ✉ esplanade.hotelcologne@t-online.de
✉ info@e-splanade.de
Centrally located. Rooms with shower/bath/WC, TV, radio and minibar. Single from DM 165, double from 225, Weekend rates (not always available) single from 135, double from 175. Designer hotel.
■ **Gut Merödgen**
☞ See Inden, Germany
■ **Hotel Königshof** (AC BF CC)
Richartzstraße 14-16 ✉ 50667 ☎ 257 87 71 📠 257 87 62
✉ hotel@hotelkoenigshof.com 🖥 www.hotelkoenigshof.com

Nehmen Sie Platz, lehnen Sie sich zurück, seien Sie überrascht, was wir Ihnen zu bieten haben: Eine täglich wechselnde Speisekarte, ein selbstspielendes Piano, Gesang sind nur ein Teil des Erlebnisses. Jedes unserer 16 Hotelzimmer /Appartements ist individuell eingerichtet und bietet Ruhe, Entspannung und Inspiration.

GUT MERÖDGEN
Hotel · Restaurant · Café

Merödgener Str. 29 · 52459 Inden / Altdorf
(In zentraler Lage zwischen Aachen und Köln)
Fon: 0 24 65 / 99 44 -0 · Fax: 0 24 65 / 99 44 77
www.gut-meroedgen.de · info@gut-meroedgen.de

FASHION SHOPS

■ **MEC underwear** (AC CC g) Mon-Fri 11-20, Sat 10-16 h
Ehrenstraße 27 ✉ 50672 *(U-Rudolfplatz)*
☎ 258 10 80
Designer men's wear, shoes, accessoires.

HOTEL LUDWIG

Freundliches 3 Sterne Komforthotel
300 Meter zum Kölner Dom · Für Business und Freizeit

Brandenburgerstr. 24
50668 Köln (Altstadt-Nord)
Fon +49 (0)221 160540
Fax +49 (0)221 16054444
www.hotelludwig.de

KÖLN

Köln | Germany

the new yorker.®

HOTEL

eccentric
ecstatic
egocentric
elevated
eminent
emotional
enchanting
endearing
energetic
enjoyable
entertaining
enthusiastic
erotic
especial
essential
european
exceptional
excessive
exciting
exotic
experimental
exquisite
extraordinary
extreme

WORLDWIDE HOSPITALITY
GOLDEN TULIP
HOTELS

ENJOY THE DIFFERENCE

Cologne's new individual design hotel with 40 rooms, 3 suites.

Shower and WC, some rooms with bathtub and airconditioning, suites with kitchenette, all rooms with analog PC-connection (some ISDN), fax-connection, TV, PayTV, minibar, hairdryer, some with CD-player, garden, sauna, solarium and gym. Close to KölnMesse, KölnArena and Rheinpark.

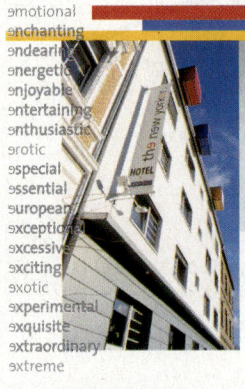

the new yorker® Hotel
Deutz-Mülheimer-Straße 204 • 51063 Köln
Fon: +49(0)221 / 4733-0 • Fax: +49(0)221 / 4733-100
e-Mail: thenewyorkerhotel@netcologne.de
Owner: Johannes Adams • Manager: Ian Folker

Tel: 0221_92 15 57-0

e-splana.de

Hohenstaufenring 56_D-50674 Köln

Privathotel Esplanade wir waren unserer Zeit immer schon voraus.

i-Mac-surfen in der Lobby
Kostenloser Mountainbike- und Kickboard-Verleih

„THE" WELL-KNOWN DESIGN HOTEL
NEXT TO THE BEST GAY BARS (CITY-CENTER)
CHARMING TEAM & COSY ATMOSPHERE
WEEKEND RATES ON REQUEST

e-mail: info@e-splanade.de

Fax 0221_21 68 22

http://www.e-splana.de

Germany | Köln

Restaurant Domerie & Sitanis
Cocktail & Dreams

Die etwas andere Kombination von Restaurant und kölscher Gemütlichkeit

Öffnungszeiten:
Di-Sa 18-01 Uhr
So u. Mo Ruhetag (außer Messen)

Frankenwerft 27 • Buttermarkt 42
50667 Köln • Tel. (0221) 257 40 44
Fax (0221) 257 42 69

ROYAL HOTELS KÖLN

ROYAL HOTEL AM HANSARING
Hansaring 96 · 50670 Köln
Tel. 02 21 / 914 01 8
Fax 02 21 / 914 01 79

ROYAL HOTEL AM AUGUSTINERPLATZ
Hohe Straße 30 · 50667 Köln
Tel. 02 21 / 272 80 20
Fax 02 21 / 272 80 277

ROYAL HOTEL RHEINKASSELER HOF
RESTAURANT WINTERGARTEN
Amandustraße 6-10 · 50769 Köln
Tel. 02 21 / 70 92 70
Fax 02 21 / 70 10 73

---

complete offer see page Germany/Berlin

COLOGNE - from DM 45 -
overnight accomodation service
· about 750 beds · more than 28 cities ·

bed & breakfast enjoy

central booking office Berlin ☏ **+49-30-236 236 10**   4:30-9:00 pm local time
Fax +49-30-23623619 · info@ebab.de · www.ebab.de

GÄSTEHAUS KÖLN
KETTENGASSE
Pfeilstraße 43, Entrance Kettengasse

Günstig übernachten in mitten der Domstadt. Zimmer inkl. Frühstück
Best location in the Gay-Centre of Cologne. Nice & clean rooms. bf served. Your own keys

Infos & Bookings: Tel. +49 (221) 2570950 · E-Mail: GHKoeln@aol.com

Köln | Germany

■ **Hotel Ludwig** (BF H MA NG) closed Dec 22nd-31st
Brandenburgerstraße 24 ✉ 50668 *(300 m from the Cathedral, 200 m from railway station, U-Bahn 5/12/14/16/18, Bus 132/170, S-Bahn-Hauptbahnhof)* ☎ 16 05 40 📠 16 05 44 44
📧 hotel@hotelludwig.com 🖥 www.hotelludwig.com
1 apartment & 55 rooms all with bath/shower, WC, phone, radio, sat-TV, own key, parking place. Rates single: DM 145-270, Double 165-370, Apartment: 250-450.-

■ **New Yorker Hotel. The** (A AC B BF CC glm H msg OS SA SOL VS WO) 0-24 h
Deutz-Mühlheimer-Strasse 204 ✉ 51063 *(station Köln-Deutz/U-Wiener Platz, near foreground)* ☎ 47 33 0 📠 47 33 100
📧 thenewyorkerhotel@netcologne.de
🖥 www.thenewyorkerhotel.com
Design hotel.All 40 rooms with bathromm,(Pay)TV,telephone,minibar,internet access, also conference rooms. Single rates from 180,- DM, double from 220, ask for weekend specials

■ **Royal Hotel am Augustinerplatz** (B BF CC glm H)
Hohe Straße 30 ✉ 50667 *(pedestrian zone, tram-Heumarkt)*
☎ 272 80 20 📠 272 80 277
53 rooms bath/shower,WC,telephone,(Pay)TV,safe,bar, single DM 111-150, double 160-220,- bf buffet incl.

■ **Royal Hotel am Hansaring** (BF CC)
Hansaring 96 ✉ 50670 ☎ 914 018
📠 914 01 79

■ **Royal Hotel Rheinkassler Hof** (BF CC F H)
Amandustraße 6-10 ✉ 50769 ☎ 70 10 70
📠 70 10 73

Wo der Gast noch König ist!

Die perfekte Adresse
im Herzen von Köln
You are welcome!
Relaxed, pleasant atmosphere in smart ambiance.

königshof

D - 50667 Köln/Cologne
Richartzstraße 14 - 16
Phone 0221 / 257 87 71
Fax 0221 / 257 87 62
www.hotelkoenigshof.com
eMail: hotel@hotelkoenigshof.com

bed & breakfast
in Hürth bei Köln

Lichtdurchflutetes Zimmer (31 qm) in Privatwohnung.
1 Person		44,- DM
2-4 Personen	je	39,- DM
5-6 Personen	je	34,- DM
inklusive do it yourself-Frühstück
Info und Reservierung:
02233-70399 oder 0177-6911014
Fax 02233-791271
www.bedandbreakfastkoeln.de
E-Mail bedandbreakfastk@aol.com

Germany   Köln

TRAVESTIESHOW IM HOTEL TIMP
SHOW-TIME

Hier ist garantiert jede Nacht was los !
Travestie-Show tgl. von 1.00 - 4.00h. EINTRITT FREI

Hotel-Timp
Künstler-Klause
Inh.W. Gleno-Geloneck
Heumarkt 25-50667 Köln
Tel.: 0221 / 258 14 09
Fax.: 0221 / 258 45 29
homepage:www.timp.de

GUEST HOUSES

■ **Gästehaus Köln** (BF GLM D) reception by appointment
Pfeilstrasse 43 ✉ 50672 (entrance Kettengasse,gay district Rudolfplatz) ☎ 257 09 50 📠 94 38 380 🖥 GHKoeln@aol.com
Rooms with fridge, clockradio, WC/shower, TV, own keys. Bf incl.

PRIVATE ACCOMMODATION

■ **bed & breakfast Köln** (bf g H)
Luxemburger Str. 380 ✉ 50354 (Hürth, line 18-Hürth-Hermühlheim)
☎ (02233) 703 99 ☎ (0177) 691 1014 📠 (02233) 791 271
🖥 bedandbreakfastk@aol.com 🖥 www.bedandbreakfastkoeln.de
31 m² room in owner's appartment with TV,radio,own WC, shared bath and kitchen. 1 person 44,-, 2-4 ps 39,- each, 5-6 ps 34,- DM each, do-it- yourself bf incl.

■ **Enjoy Bed and Breakfast** (BF G H M) 16.30-21 h
Nollendorfplatz 5, 10777 Berlin (U-Nollendorfplatz) ☎ (030) 236 236 10 📠 (030) 236 236 19 🖥 info@ebab.com 🖥 ebab.de
Accommodation sharing agency. All with shower and BF. 40-45 DM p.p.

■ **Schwule Übernachtungsmöglichkeiten** 17-21 h
c/o Checkpoint, Pipinstraße 2 ✉ 50667 ☎ 92 57 68 68
📠 92 57 68 45 🖥 checkpoint-koeln@gmx.de

GENERAL GROUPS

■ **AK Schwule bei Bündnis 90/Die Grünen**
Ebertplatz 23 ✉ 50668 ☎ 972 78 88 📠 972 78 89

■ **Kölner Lesben- und Schwulentag e.V. (KLUST)**
Rubensstr. 8-10 ✉ 50676 ☎ 47 47 898 📠 47 47 897
🖥 presse@csd-cologne.de 🖥 csd-cologne.de
Organizes CSD (Gay Pride) Cologne.

■ **Iglf-Lesbian & Gay Liberation Front** library Mon Wed 20-22 h
Kartäuserwall 18, c/o SCHULZ ✉ 50678
🖥 lglf.cologne@t-online.de
Contains Lglf-library with over 2000 titels on G&L issues.

■ **LSVD - Lesben- und Schwulenverband in Deutschland e.V.** (GLM MA) Mon-Fri 9-17 h
Pipinstraße 7 ✉ 50667 ☎ 925 96 10 ☎ 192 28 (Gay bashing helpline) 📠 92 59 61 11 🖥 NRW@lsvd.de 🖥 www.lsvd.de
Türk Gay (1st Mon 17 h), Ermis (Greek gay group), Binats (group of binational couples). Emgergency helpline Mon Wed Fri 19-21 h.

■ **Schwusos-Schwule Sozialdemokraten**
c/o SCHULZ, Kartäuserwall 18 ✉ 50678

■ **Türk-Gay** 1st Sat 17, Disco 4th Fri from 22 h in SchULZ
Pippinstraße 7 ✉ 50474 ☎ 925 96 10 📠 92 59 61 11
🖥 svd.nrw@t-online.de
Schwulengruppe für Türken. Türkische Disco im Sch.U.L.Z. jeden 3. Fri.Gay group for Turks

FETISH GROUPS

■ **Leather Friends Cologne United Colours** (G LJ MA) Every 2nd and 4th Mon 20 h at Zipps, Hohe Pforte 13-17
Postfach 451 025 ✉ 50885 🖥 leatherfriends@hotmail.com

■ **MS Panther Köln e.V.** (G LJ MA) Meeting 3rd Sat 20 h at Café Quo Vadis
Postfach 19 03 25 ✉ 50500
Publisher of "Panther Info", monthly. Gay motorcyclers meet every 2nd Fri 19 h at "Quo Vadis".

HEALTH GROUPS

■ **AIDS-Hilfe Köln e. V.** 9.30-18.30 h
Beethovenstraße 1 ✉ 50674 (Tram-Zülpicher Platz) ☎ 20 20 30
📠 23 03 25 🖥 info@koeln.aidshilfe.de 🖥 koeln.aidshilfe.de
Rainbow cafe for PWA, HIV+ and their friends Mon-Fri 10-19, lunch served from 12-14 h, closed Sat&Sun.

■ **AIDS-Hilfe NRW e.V. Landesverband** Mon-Thu 9-12.30 13.30-17, Fri 9-12.30 13.30-15 h
Hohenzollernring 48 ✉ 50672 (U-Friesenplatz) ☎ 925 99 60
📠 925 99 69 🖥 info@nrw.aidshilfe.de 🖥 nrw.aidshilfe.de

■ **SchwIPS - Schwule Initiative für Plege & Soziales** Mon-Fri 10-17 h
Pipinstrasse 7 ✉ 50667 (near Rudolfplatz) ☎ 92 57 68 10
☎ 92 18 30 0 (positiv leben GmbH) 📠 92 18 30 18
The ambulant nursing service "positiv leben GmbH" is based here /Pflege & Betreungszentrum - Rubensstrasse 8-10, 50676 Köln - open from 10-17 h Mon to Fri.

HELP WITH PROBLEMS

■ **HerzensLust-Koordination NRW** Mon-Fri 8-12.30, Mon Thu 13.30-17, Fri 13.30-15 h
c/o AIDS Hilfe NRW e.V., Hohenzollernring 48 ✉ 50672 ☎ 92 59 96-0 📠 92 59 96-9 🖥 Landesverband@AIDS-Hilfe-NRW.org

■ **Sozialwerk für Lesben und Schwule e.V.** (GLM MA) Mon-Fri 10-18 h
Karthäuserwall 18 ✉ 50678 ☎ 93 18 80 81 ☎ 194 46 (counselling) 📠 93 18 80 82 🖥 info@sozialwerk-koeln.de
🖥 www.sozialwerk-koeln.de
Counselling Mon-Fri 16-18, Tue-Thu 20-22 h.

RELIGIOUS GROUPS

■ **MCC Köln** service: Sat 17.30 h at SCHULZ
c/o Schulz, Kartäuserwall 18 ✉ 50678 ☎ 21 33 63
📠 (02551) 83 47 97 🖥 mcc-koeln@gmx.de

■ **Yachad** Mon Fri 16-18, Tue Thu 18-22 h
☎ (0178) 3316417 🖥 YachadKoeln@goldmail.de
Jewish gays and lesbians/Jüdische Schwule und Lesben.

Köln ▶ Krefeld Germany

SPECIAL INTEREST GROUPS
■ **Ford GLOBE** (GLM)
☎ 35537   ✉ FordGLOBEqgmx.de
Gay, Lesbian Or Bisexual Employees working for the motorcar company FORD. Meetings are held every 2nd Mon in the month in SchulZ, Kartäuserwall 18 in Cologne from 19.30h.
■ **Völklinger Kreis e.V.**
Leyendeckerstraße 1   ✉ 50825   ☎ 546 19 79   📠 954 17 57
✉ mail@vk-online.de/   🖥 www.vk-online.de/
Headoffice of the association of gay managers.

SPORT GROUPS
■ **Cologne Hot Balls Schwul-lesbische Squashgruppe** (GLM MA) Tue 20-22 h
c/o Stephan Heller, Moltkestraße 70   ✉ 50674   ☎ 510 3444
✉ stephan.heller@netcologne.de
Every November Rainbow-Cup with 65 participants from different European countries
■ **Sport Club Janus e.V. Köln "Erfrischend anders seit 1980"** (GLM MA) Office Tue 16-19 h
Pipinstraße 7   ✉ 50667 (*Heumarkt*)   ☎ 92 55 930
📠 925 59 31   ✉ info@sc-janus.de   🖥 www.sc-janus.de
Over 53 sport possibilities and sports parties.

SWIMMING
- Bleibtreusee (g NU) (near/Nähe Euskirchen)
- Hallenfreizeitbad Bornheim (g sa) (Rilkestr. 3, 53332 Bornheim)
- Baggersee Köln-Porz/Gremberghoven (an der/on B4)
- Agrippa-Bad (Ha-:llenbad) (Agrippa Straße)
- Aqualand (Wed 18:30-23:00h MA, NU)   🖥 www.aqualand.de

CRUISING
- "Park" Aachener Weiher (AYOR) (Tag und Nacht, populär/day and night, popular.)
- Brühler Landstrasse/Hitzeler Strasse (AYOR; police)
- Cranachwäldchen (nu)
- Mühlheimer Stadtgarten (ayor MG OG)
- Parkanlage Theodor-Heuss-Ring am/at Ebertplatz
- Parkplatz Phantasialand BAB 553 near Brühl (MA LJ)
- Baggersee Köln-Porz/Gremberghoven BAB 4

Königstein ☎ 06174

TRAVEL AND TRANSPORT
■ **Travelman** (GLM MA) 9-18 h Mon-Fri
Im Hainchen 18   ✉ 61462   ☎ 93 18 73   📠 252 90   ✉ travelhouse@t-online.de
Organizer of traveling in gay groups throughout the world./Anbieter schwuler Gruppenreisen weltweit.

Konstanz ☎ 07531

DANCECLUBS
■ **Excalibur** (B D GLM YG) Disco Sun 21-1, Bar 20-1 h (MA)
Blätzleplatz   ✉ 78462 *(Close to "Hertie" department store. Bus-Schnetztor)*   ☎ (0171) 528 47 16

SEX SHOPS/BLUE MOVIES
■ **Film- und Videoshop** (g VS) 10-1/? h
Emmishoferstraße 4   ✉ 78462   ☎ 213 40
Kino und Treffpunkt/meeting place. Magazine, Videos, Vorführungen.
■ **Sexyland** (g VS) Mon-Fri 10-20, Sat -16 h, closed Sun
Kreuzlinger Straße 5   ✉ 78462   ☎ 220 26

SAUNAS/BATHS
■ **Relax-Center Hyperion** (B CC DR f G lj MA msg OS p R SA SB SOL VS WO) 15-22.30 h, Wed closed
Gottlieb-Daimler-Straße 3   ✉ 78462 *(Bus 6/7-Carl-Benz-Straße)*   ☎ 610 61

GENERAL GROUPS
■ **Boys Only** Mon 19 h Schwimmen im Jacobsbad, 21 h Schulze & Schulze Stammtisch
✉ bok@konstanz.gay-web.de
■ **Homosexuelle in Konstanz (HIK)** (b G MA) Tue 20-?, Fri 21.30-? h
Friedrichstraße 21   ✉ 78467   ☎ 645 35
✉ hik@konstanz.gay-web.de   🖥 konstanz.gay-web.de/hik/

HEALTH GROUPS
■ **AIDS-Hilfe Konstanz e.V.** Mon-Tue Thu-Fri 10-12, Tue Thu 16-18 h
Münzgasse 29   ✉ 78462 *(near railway station/nahe Bahnhof)*
☎ 211 13   ☎ 19 411 (helpline)   📠 150 29
✉ aidshilfe.konstanz@t-online.de   🖥 konstanz.aidshilfe.de
Positiven-Café Thu 17-19 h.

HELP WITH PROBLEMS
■ **Rosa Telefon** Mon 20-22 h
☎ 164 46

SPECIAL INTEREST GROUPS
■ **LesBiSchwule Jugendgruppe** (GLM N p YG) Meetings 1st & 3rd Mon 20-? h
☎ (0173) 325 79 39 (Stefan)   ☎ (0179) 505 26 13 (Ute)
call for information

SPORT GROUPS
■ **Gay Outdoor Club Donau-Bodensee** (GLM)
Postfach 10 11 18   ✉ 78411   ☎ 290 72   📠 290 72
Hiking group. Call for dates and further information.

CRUISING
- Stadtpark/municipal park
- Schnetztor underpass (next to Sexyland, popular)/Unterführung am Schnetztor (neben Sexyland, populär)
- Restaurant in/im Hertie (Dept. Store)
- Laube (OG)
- Sternenplatz (selten/seldom)

Korbach ☎ 05631

CAFES
■ **Das T** (A AC BF F glm MA) Mon-Sat 8-18 h, Sun closed
Bahnhofstraße 14-16   ✉ 34467   ☎ 980 92

Krefeld ☎ 02151

BARS
■ **Schickeria** (AC B D f G MA p s VS) 21-5 h
Westwall 33   ✉ 47798   ☎ 288 55
Karaoke/Show on Wed.

DANCECLUBS
■ **Jogis Top Inn** (B D g MA YG) Fri Sat & before holidays 22-5 h
Neue Linnerstraße 85   ✉ 47798   ☎ 236 24

SPARTACUS 2001/2002 | 499

Germany | Krefeld ▶ Leipzig

CLUBSAUNA STARGAYTE™ LEIPZIG

Welcome in a new leading international gay bathhouse.

Otto-Schill-Str. 10 • Leipzig GERMANY
☎ +49 (0)341 - 9614246 • www.stargayte.de

■ **Königsburg** (! AC B CC D F GLM lj MA S TV) 21-5 h (Irregular)
Königstraße 8 ✉ 47798 ☎ 85 06 50
Entrance DM 20,– including cover charge
■ **Tollhaus** (B D GLM YG) Sun 19-? h
Ostwall 4-6 ✉ 47798
19-20 h all drinks half price.

GENERAL GROUPS
■ **Arbeitskreis Schwulenpolitik**
c/o DIE GRÜNEN, Roßstraße 200 ✉ 47798 ☎ 77 73 44

HEALTH GROUPS
■ **AIDS-Hilfe Krefeld e.V.** Mon-Fri 10-13, Wed 19.30-21.30 h
Rheinstraße 2-4 ✉ 47799 ☎ 194 11 📠 78 65 92
💻 info@krefeld.aidshilfe.de 💻 krefeld.aidshilfe.de

SWIMMING
-Elfrather See (Krefeld-Gartenstadt) am Surfsee auf dem Berg/ Elfrather Lake (in Krefeld-Gartenstadt) at surfers lake on the hill.

CRUISING
-Stadtgarten/municipal garden (AYOR)

Kronach ☎ 09261

HOTELS
■ **Schlosshotel Fischbach** (B BF F g H MA NU OS PI S SA)
Fischbach ✉ 96317 ☎ 30 06 📠 31 51
*Rooms partly with TV & phone/Zimmer teilweise mit TV und Telefon.
Rates from DM 50 (bf incl.)*

Landau ☎ 06341

HEALTH GROUPS
■ **AIDS-Hilfe Landau e.V.** Tue 19-21 h
Weißenburger Straße 2b ✉ 76829 ☎ 194 11
or Mon Wed Fri 13-16 h ☎ 886 88.
Rainbow café 1st and 3rd Sun 18 h. Frauencafé 2nd Sun 18 h.

HELP WITH PROBLEMS
■ **Rosa Telefon** Wed 20-22 h
☎ 194 46

CRUISING
-Hauptbahnhof/Main Rail Station
-Schwanenweiher im/in Ostpark (near/Nähe Hauptbahnhof)

Landshut

CRUISING
-Landtorplatz
-Naherholungsgebiet Gretlmühle, 2. Baggersee
-Stadtpark Klinikum Parkhausausgang

Leipzig ☎ 0341

GAY INFO
■ **Grenzenlos** 3rd Sun in uneven months 19.00-19.30 h FM 97,6 MHz, cable 93,6 MHz
c/o Radio Blau, Steinstraße 18 ✉ 04275 ☎ 301 00 97
📠 301 00 07 💻 grenzenlosleipzig@gmx.de
💻 www.freie-radios.de/radio-blau
gay-lesbian broadcast on radio Blau

500 | *SPARTACUS* 2001/2002

2000 sqm. for cruising, wellness and action

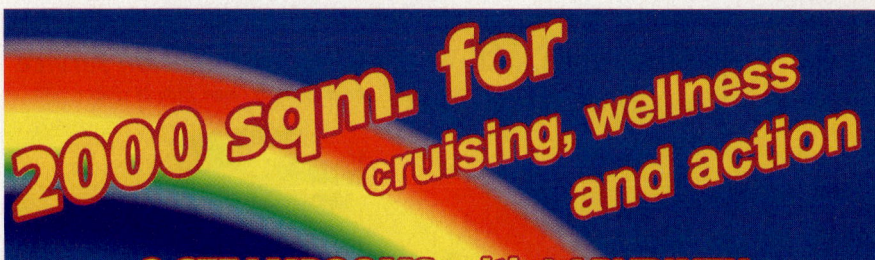

2 STEAMROOMS with LABYRINTH, WHIRLPOOL / JACUZZI, FINNISH SAUNA, BIO-SAUNA, PLAY/POOL, SOLARIUM, CRUISINGLABYRINTH, WINTERGARDEN, SUMMERGARDEN, BODYBUILDING / GYM, VIDEO, CABINS, SHOP, RESTAURANT, BAR

... and of course a lot of men

■ **Querele**
c/o AIDS-Hilfe, Ossietzkystraße 18 ✉ 04277 ☎ 2 32 31 36
📠 2333 968 📧 info@leipzig.aidshilfe.de 🌐 leipzig.aidshilfe.de
Free magazine published by the AIDS-Hilfe Leipzig.

■ **RosaLinde Leipzig e.V.** (A B D GLM MA WE) Café: 17-1 h, Disco: Sat 22-? h
Brühl 64-66 ✉ 04109 *(near train station/nähe Hauptbahnhof)*
📧 kontakt@rosalinde.de 🌐 www.rosalinde.de
Choir "Die Kirschblüten": rehearsals Mon 20 h. Varieté and show: rehearsals Tue 19 h. Dancing lessons: Wed 19 and 20.30 h, Jung group J.u.n.g.s & Jule.

BARS

■ **Black Horse** (B f glm MA) 17-2 h
Roßstraße 12 ✉ 04103 *(near/nahe Hauptpost/Gewandhaus)*
☎ 960 96 05
Irish pub.

■ **Inside** (B glm) 19-? h, Sun closed
Dölitzer Straße 28 ✉ 04277 ☎ 391 13 01

■ **Löwenzwinger** (DR G LJ MA p VS) 3rd Sat 21-? h
(downstairs at AIDS-Hilfe)
Ossietzkystraße 18 ✉ 04347
(Schönefeld; line 17-Gorki-/Ossietzkystr.)
☎ 232 31 26
Leather & fetish party. Guests welcome.

■ **New Orleans** 16-6, Sat & Sun 20-6h
Brühl 56 ✉ 04109 ☎ 960 7989

CAFES

■ **Filou** (B F glm) 14-5h
Lessingstraße 32 ✉ 04105

DANCECLUBS

■ **Blaue Trude** (B D DR glm lj MA OS s TV VS WE) 21-4 h, weekends open end
Katharinenstraße 17 ✉ 04109 *(near Alter Markt)*
☎ 212 66 79
Always free entrance.

■ **Distillery** (b D glm) Gay on Wed, Frio & Sat from 23h
Kurt-Eisner-Straße ✉ 04139

SEX SHOPS/BLUE MOVIES

■ **Erotik-exclusiv** (g)
Kuhturmstraße 6 ✉ 04177

■ **Erotik-Shop** (CC VS) Mon-Fri 10-20, Sat -16 h
Universitätsstraße 18-20 ✉ 04109

SAUNAS/BATHS

■ **Phoenix** (B f DR G msg SA SB SOL VS) Sun-Thu 13-1, Fri-Sat -6 h
Große Fleischergasse 12 ✉ 04109 ☎ 960 79 99

■ **Stargayte** (! AC B CC DR F G MA NU OS p SA SB SOL VS WH WO) Tue-Thu 15-2, Fri 15-8, Sat 15-Mon 2 h nonstop
Otto-Schill-Straße 10 ✉ 04109 *(near Rathaus and Thomas Kirche, Tram 21/24/28/58)* ☎ 961 42 46
One of the most beautiful saunas in the world, very popular. Biggest sauna in the area (2000 m²) and one of the biggest in Germany: 2 floors with 2 steam rooms, 2 whirlpools, 2 dry saunas and a very cruisy large darkroom labyrinth. An absolute must.

BOOK SHOPS

■ **Connewitzer Verlagsbuchhandlung** (CC glm s) Mon-Fri 10-20, Sat -16 h
Schuhmachergäßchen 4 ✉ 04109 *(Speck's Hof)* ☎ 960 34 47

Germany | Leipzig ▶ Lingen

LEIPZIG

overnight accomodation service – from DM 40,-
· about 750 beds · more than 28 cities ·

enjoy bed & breakfast

complete offer see page Germany/Berlin

central booking office Berlin ☎ **+49-30-23623610** 4:30-9:00 pm local time
Fax +49-30-23623619 · info@ebab.de · www.ebab.de

PRIVATE ACCOMMODATION
■ **Enjoy Bed and Breakfast** (BF G H MA) 16.30-21 h
Nollendorfplatz 5, 10777 Berlin *(U-Nollendorfplatz)*
☎ (030) 236 236 10 📠 (030) 236 236 19 ✉ info@ebab.com
🖥 ebab.de
Accommodation sharing agency. All with shower and BF. 40-45 DM p.p.

GENERAL GROUPS
■ **SMILE-Gesprächskreis** 1st Tue 20 h
c/o Café Kleinod

HEALTH GROUPS
■ **abc LEIPZIG e.V.-Verein für Sexualaufklärung und Prävention**
Mon-Fri 12-17 h
Ritterstraße 4 ✉ 04109 *(Theaterpassage between/zwischen Opernhaus and/und Nikolaikirche)* ☎ 961 59 99 📠 961 59 95
✉ abc.leipzig@lycosmail.com 🖥 www.abc-leipzig.de
Information, prevention, condoms. as well as literature.
■ **AIDS-Beratung und Betreuung im Gesundheitsamt** Mon 9-12, Tue 9-18, Thu 12-18.30, Fri 9-12 h
Gustav-Mahler-Straße 1-3 ✉ 04109 ☎ 123 68 91/94
Free and anonymous HIV-testing and Safer Sex counselling.
■ **AIDS-Hilfe Leipzig e. V.** (A f g MA OS) Counselling: Mon Wed 10-18, Tue Thu -21, Fri -1, Cafe: Tue Thu 15-21 h
Ossietzkystraße 18 ✉ 04347 *(Tram-Ossietzkystraße)* ☎ 232 31 27
📠 2333968 ✉ info@leipzig.aidshilfe.de 🖥 leipzig.aidshilfe.de

HELP WITH PROBLEMS
■ **Schwules Überfalltelefon** Tue 19-22, Fri 16-20 h
☎ 192 28
Gay bashing helpline.

SPORT GROUPS
■ **Sport-Club Rosa Löwen e.V.**
Postfach 10 04 34 ✉ 04004 ✉ rosaloewen@gaysport.org
🖥 www.gaysport.org/rosaloewen/

SWIMMING
-Kulkwitzer See (B 87 Leipzig-Markranstädt, northern side/Nordseite)
-Ammelshainer Seen (A 14 ➥ Dresden to "Naunhof", cruising between the two lakes)
-Nauhofer See.

CRUISING
-Clara-Zetkin-Park (am/at Verkehrsgarten -Klingerweg/Nonnenweg, popular)
-Schiller Park

Lemgo

CRUISING
-Ⓟ Regenstorplatz (Regentorstraße, day and night)

Leonberg ☎ 07152

GENERAL GROUPS
■ **SchwuBSi - Schwule Initiative Böblingen Sindelfingen**
c/o Erich Lauer, Neuköllner Straße 9 ✉ 71229 ☎ 90 23 42
✉ schwubsi@boeblingen.gay-web.de
🖥 boeblingen.gay-web.de

Leverkusen ☎ 0214

HEALTH GROUPS
■ **AIDS-Hilfe Leverkusen e.V.** Mon Wed 10-13, Tue Thu 19-21 h
Lichstraße 36a ✉ 51373 ☎ 40 17 66
Betroffeneberatung: Wed 18-20 h

Limburg ☎ 06431

CRUISING
-Bahnhof/railway station
-Stadthalle/Municipal hall (Tiefgarage und Platz davor/Parking garage and square in front of)

Lingen ☎ 0591

SEX SHOPS/BLUE MOVIES
■ **Erotic World** (AC g MA r VS) Mon-Sat 10-23 h
Tecklenburger Straße 2 ✉ 49809 ☎ 15 05

HEALTH GROUPS
■ **AIDS-Hilfe Emsland e.V.** Mon Wed Thu Fr 10-13,
Mon Wed 14-17h
Mühlenstiege 3 ✉ 49808
☎ 54 121
🖥 AH.Emsland@t-online.de
Regenbogenfrühstück Wed 10-12 h. Meeting point for the coming-out group "Newcomer" 1st & 3rd Fri and other groups. Call or see website for details.

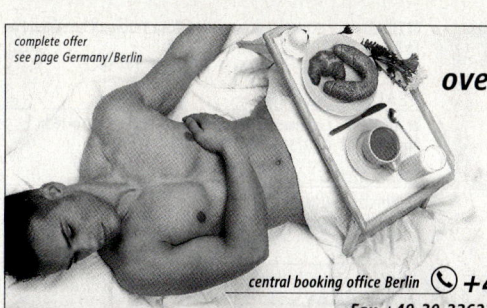

Lippstadt ▶ Lüdenscheid | Germany

LÜBECK – from DM 40 –
overnight accomodation service
· about 750 beds · more than 28 cities ·

bed & enjoy breakfast

complete offer
see page Germany/Berlin

central booking office Berlin ☏ **+49-30-23623610** 4:30-9:00 pm local time
Fax +49-30-23623619 · info@ebab.de · www.ebab.de

Lippstadt

CRUISING
- P hinter dem Bahnhof/behind Train station
- Grüner Winkel
- Bahnhof/Train station

Löbau ☏ 03585

GENERAL GROUPS
■ **Rosa Power e.V.** (b BF D DR f GLM MA SNU STV VS WE) Mon-Fri 10-12 h
Promenadenring 12 ✉ 02708 *(Room 12)* ☏ 40 39 24
Monthly party. Call for details.

Lübeck ☏ 0451

BARS
■ **CC Chapeau Claque** (A B d G GLM MA N s TV WE) Tue-Thu 21-3, Fri Sat -4, Sun 21-2 h, closed Mon
Hartengrube 25-27 ✉ 23552 ☏ 773 71
■ **Flamingo** (B f G H MA OS R N) Mon-Fri 17-?, Sat 20-? h, closed Sun
Marlesgrube 58 ✉ 23552 ☏ 70 48 36
■ **V.I.P. Club** (B G lj MA p) Mon Wed Thu 20-3, Fri Sat -4, Sun 18-3 h, closed Tue
Marlesgrube 61 ✉ 23552 ☏ 79 66 20

SEX SHOPS/BLUE MOVIES
■ **Dolly Buster by Seventh Heaven** (AC CC DR g MA VS) 9-23, Sun 12-23 h
Lederstrasse 2-4 ✉ 23552 ☏ 70 69 50
■ **Sparta Shop** (G VS) 9-24, Fri-Sat -4 h
Hüxstraße 15 ✉ 23552 ☏ 724 53
■ **World Of Sex-WOS** (g VS) 9.30-24, Sun 12-24 h
Wahmstrasse 32 ✉ 23552

BOOK SHOPS
■ **Stilke Aktuell** (cc glm)
Am Hauptbahnhof, Wandelhalle ✉ 23558 ☏ 8 33 45

TRAVEL AND TRANSPORT
■ **Ticketkontor** Mon-Fri 10-13, 14-18 h
Fleischhauerstraße 80 ✉ 23552 *(near Niederegger-Marzipan Shop)* ☏ 702 07 74 🖷 702 07 99
Travel agency with very good service, friendly staff/Reisebüro mit gutem Service

PRIVATE ACCOMMODATION
■ **Enjoy Bed and Breakfast** (BF G H MA) 16.30-21 h
Nollendorfplatz 5, 10777 Berlin *(U-Nollendorfplatz)* ☏ (030) 236 236 10 🖷 (030) 236 236 19 ✉ info@ebab.de 💻 ebab.de
Accommodation sharing agency. All with shower and BF. 40-45 DM p.p.

GENERAL GROUPS
■ **Homosexuelle Initiative Lübeck (HIL)** Wed 20-22 h
c/o ESG, Königstraße 23 III. ✉ 23552 ☏ 746 19 (Wed 20-22h)
■ **Schwule Aktion Lübeck e.V.-SAL**
Postfach 18 23 ✉ 23556 ☏ & FAX 70 58 88

HEALTH GROUPS
■ **Hilfe für HiV-Positive e.V.** Counselling Mon-Fri 10-15 h
Reiferstraße 21 ✉ 23554 ☏ 47 45 95
■ **Lübecker AIDS-Hilfe e. V.** Counselling:Mon-Fri 10-13, Tue Thu 18-20 h (&helpline)
Engelsgrube 16 ✉ 23552 ☏ 194 11 ☏ 725 51 🖷 70 70 218
✉ AIDS-Hilfe-Luebeck@t-online.de
💻 home.t-online.de/home/aids-hilfe-luebeck/home.htm
or Mon-Fri also Tel. 70 41 33.

HELP WITH PROBLEMS
■ **Rosa Telefon** Wed 20-22 h
☏ 798 71 16

SWIMMING
- Brodner Ufer, Travemünde (NU)

CRUISING
- Wallstraße (up to the Holstentor (r) and P at river Trave)
- Katzenberg (ayor r) (between Possehl and Stadtgraben)
- Mühlentorteller
- Burgtorteller (Gustav-Radbruch-Platz)

Lüdenscheid ☏ 02351

SEX SHOPS/BLUE MOVIES
■ **Sex and Gags** (g VS) 9-19, Thu -20.30, Sat 9-14 h
Lessingstraße/Knapper Straße ✉ 58507

HEALTH GROUPS
■ **AIDS-Hilfe im Märkischen Kreis e.V.** Mon 19-21 h
Duisbergweg 3 ✉ 58511 ☏ 232 02

CRUISING
- Parkpalette -18 h Popular.

Germany | Ludwigsburg ▶ Magdeburg

Ludwigsburg ☎ 07141

BARS
■ **Sonny's Club-Bar** (AC B d f G lj MA P s TV WE) 19-3 h, closed Sun
Kirchstraße 30 ✉ 71634 ☎ 90 16 66

SEX SHOPS/BLUE MOVIES
■ **Beate Uhse International** (CC glm MA VS) Mon-Sat 9-22, cabins -23 h, Sun closed
Stuttgarter Straße 56 ✉ 71638 ☎ 90 18 21

CRUISING
-Parking lot/Parkplatz Leonberger Straße 11, corner/Ecke Bahnhofstraße
-Stadtpark/town park "Bärenwiese", Schorndorfer Straße/Fasanenstraße

Ludwigshafen ☎ 0621

BARS
■ **Alter Treffpunkt** (AC B d g MA p STV WE) 20-1, Fri Sat -4 h, closed Mon
Gräfenaustraße 51 ✉ 67063 ☎ 51 13 92
■ **Come Back** (B G MA p) 20-1, Fri Sat -3 h
Welserstraße 10 ✉ 67063 ☎ 51 25 51

SEX SHOPS/BLUE MOVIES
■ **Erotik Dream** (AC cc glm lj MA VS) Mon-Sat 10-23, Sun 14-23 h
Ludwigstraße 10 ✉ 67059 *(pedestrian zone, opposite Mc Donald's)* ☎ 51 03 19
Mixed sexshop with gay section. Only ec-card accepted.
■ **Mike's** (AC DR g MA VS) Mon-Fri 10-23, Sat -1, Sun 14-23 h
Amtsstraße 1 ✉ 67059 ☎ 51 02 12
■ **Sexladen** (g VS) Mon-Sat 9-23 h
Bahnhofstraße 14 ✉ 67059 ☎ 51 72 40

SPECIAL INTEREST GROUPS
■ **Pfundskerle Girth & Mirth Südwest**
c/o Frank Lohöfer, Altholzweg 25 ✉ 67065 ☎ 54 44 26
🖷 54 44 26 💻 Club@Pfundskerle.de 🖳 www.pfundskerle.de
Special club-events: - 2nd Sat/month, 17 h at Butch, Mannheim Sauna-Meeting: - 4th Sat/month, 15 h at Hot House Club, Mannheim

SWIMMING
-Baggersee "Blaue Adria" (on the island/auf der Insel)

CRUISING
-Ebertpark (Haupteingang,links, populär/main entrance, to the left, popular)
-Hauptbahnhof/main railway station

Lüneburg ☎ 04131

BARS
■ **501** (B F GLM) 11-2 h
Bardowicker Straße 20 ✉ 21335

GENERAL GROUPS
■ **Hin & Wech. Schwule lieben in Niedersachsen** (GLM MA) Tue meetings 17.30-19 h
c/o Aids-Hilfe Lüneburg e.V., Am Sande 50 ✉ 21335 *(office near main station)* ☎ 30 34 18 💻 Nds.nordost@hin-und-wech.de
🖳 www.hin-und-wech.de

■ **Lüneburger Schwulengruppe und Rosa Telefon** (Salzsäue) Fri 18 h
c/o AIDS-Hilfe, Katzenstraße 3 ✉ 21335 ☎ 194 46

HEALTH GROUPS
■ **AIDS-Hilfe Lüneburg e.V.** Mon-Fri 9.30-13.30, Tue 14-16 h
Am Sande 50 ✉ 21335 ☎ 194 11 🖷 40 35 50

SWIMMING
-Kalkbruchsee (NU)
-Volgershalle (hinter d. Fachhochschule f. Wirtschaft, Nordwest Ecke)

CRUISING
-Wall/Bardowicker Stadtmauer/Liebesgrund (22-? h)
-Am Werder/Lüner Straße
-Main station/Bahnhof
-Graalwall

Lützensommern ☎ 036041

GENERAL GROUPS
■ **Jugendnetzwerk Lambda e.V. Bundesverband** (GLM YG) Mon-Fri 9-15 h.
Tagungshaus Rittergut ✉ 99955 ☎ 449 83 🖷 44 0 20
💻 bgs@lambda-online.de 🖳 www.lambda-online.de

Magdeburg ☎ 0391

BARS
■ **Gummibärchen** (A AC B BF f GLM MA s) Mon-Fri 13-1, Sat 17-2, Sun 15-1 h
Liebigstraße 6 ✉ 39104 *(Tram2/3/9/10/12-Hasselbachplatz)*
☎ 543 02 99
■ **Tiffany** (B F G MA WE) 20-? h
Sternstraße 29 ✉ 39106 ☎ 543 22 09
Disco on weekend.

SEX SHOPS/BLUE MOVIES
■ **Gay Shop** (DR G MA r VS) Mon-Fri 12-20, Sat 10-16 h
Bernburger Straße 1a ✉ 39104 *(near Hauptstr.)* ☎ 401 52 29

BOOK SHOPS
■ **CloneZone** (CC GLM) Mon-Sat 14-22, Sun 16-22 h video rental only
Liebigstraße 6 ✉ 39104 *(S-Hasselbachplatz)* ☎ 543 16 77

GENERAL GROUPS
■ **LSVD Sachsen-Anhalt** (f G MA) Wed 19-22h
W.-Rathenau-Straße 31 ✉ 39106 *(near Universitätsplatz)*
☎ 543 25 69 ☎ 19 228 (help in case of gay bashing)
🖷 543 25 69
💻 md-lsvd@gmx.de 🖳 www.lsvd.de
Different groups and activities: call for information.

HEALTH GROUPS
■ **Aids-Beratung Caritasverband** Thu 14-18 h
Max-Josef-Metzger-Straße 1a ✉ 39104 *(near central post office,10 min walk from Hauptbahnhof)* ☎ 59 61-208 🖷 59 61-209
■ **AIDS-Hilfe Magdeburg e.V.** Mon-Fri 9-12, Counselling Mon-Fri 12-20 h
Weidenstraße 9 ✉ 39114 ☎ 541 08-49 🖷 541 08 49
💻 AIDS-Magdeburg@t-online.de
Counselling ☎ 194 11..

SWIMMING
-Neustädter See (NU) (S-Rothensee/Eichweiler)

Germany — Magdeburg ▶ Mannheim

CRUISING
- Glacis Anlagen (Sachsenring/Adelheidtring. Popular)
- Bahnhof/railway station
- Haus des Lehrers/Teacher's house

Mainz ☏ 06131

BARS
■ **Jolifante** (AC B F glm MA OS) Mon-Thu 17-1, Fri-Sat -2 h
Leibnizstraße 55 ✉ 55118 ☏ 61 41 30

SEX SHOPS/BLUE MOVIES
■ **Pink Movie** (g vs) Mon-Sat 8-20, Sun 11-18 h
Zanggasse 17 ✉ 55116 ☏ 22 62 62
■ **Stephans Sex Boutique** (g VS) Mon-Wed 9-19, Thu Fri -20, Sat -14 h
Dominikanerstraße 5a ✉ 55116 ☏ 22 16 50

GENERAL GROUPS
■ **Bündnis 90/Die Grünen im Landtag Rheinland Pfalz Arbeitsbereich Lesben- und Schwulenpolitik**
Kaiser-Friedrich-Straße 3 ✉ 55116 ☏ 208 31 58
✉ akll@gruene.landtag.rlp.de 🖥 www.gruene-rlp.de/queer

FETISH GROUPS
■ **MSC Rhein-Main Frankfurt**
c/o Ralf Knöfler, Martin-Josef-Straße 4 ✉ 55129
Member of ECMC.

HEALTH GROUPS
■ **AIDS-Hilfe Mainz e.V.** Office: Mon-Wed 10-16, Thu -19, Fri -13 h
Hopfengarten 19 ✉ 55116 ☏ 22 22 75 ☏ 23 38 72 📠 23 38 74
Meeting point for gay youth group Young companions (-26yrs). 1st & 3rd Thu at 19h. Call for further infos.

CRUISING
- Bahnhof (r)
- Rheinhalle (Grüne Brücke/Green Bridge)

Mannheim ☏ 0621

BARS
■ **Café Klatsch** (AC B f G lj MA OS) 19-3, Sat Sun 16-3 h
Hebelstraße 3 ✉ 68161 (near Nationaltheater) ☏ 156 10 33
■ **Club Ballerino** (AC D f GLM MA r s TV VS) 20-3 h
Friedrichs-Ring 30 ✉ 68161 ☏ 139 48
■ **Jail's** (! B DR G LJ MA) Fri-Sun 21-? h, please call for details
Angelstraße 5-9 ✉ 68199 (next to M&S Connexion) ☏ 854 41 46
300 sq.m. darkroom area.
■ **LC Department** (LJ)
S 6, 12 ✉ 68161
■ **Petit Paris** (AC B BF d F GLM lj MA S STV WE) Tue-Thu 15-1, Fri -3, Sat 5-3, Sun 5-12 h
T3, 2-3 ✉ 68161 ☏ 10 16 96
■ **XS Café Bar** (A AC B BF f G YG) Mon-Sat 11-1, Sun 14.30-1 h
N7, 9 ✉ 68161 (Kunststraße) ☏ 0261/15 23 78
■ **Zelle** (A B G lj MA N) 19-1 h
Schwetzinger Straße 96 ✉ 68165 (Tram-Kopernikusstraße. Near main station) ☏ 40 96 69

CAFES
■ **Café Cortés** (B CC f glm MA) 10-1 h
Passage N6, Kunststraße ✉ 68161 ☏ 12 59 881

DANCECLUBS
■ **Club Action** (B D GLM) Sat & Sun 20-5 h
U5, 13 ✉ 68161 ☏ 15 34 35
■ **M & S Connexion** (! AC B D DR f G lj MA OS s VS) Sat (G) 215, 2nd Sat "Gay Werk" (GLM), Sun (G only) 20-? h
Angelstraße 33 ✉ 68199 ☏ 854 41 44
1st Sun "Macho Time", 3rd Sun Dress Code, admission DM 20. 5 clubs, 7 bars on 3 floors. Germany's biggest disco.
■ **T6** (AC B D DR f GLM lj MA s VS WE) Wed-Sun 21-5 h, Sun special events
T6, 14/16 ✉ 68161 (Near Nationaltheater) ☏ 10 27 79

RESTAURANTS
■ **Spagettioper im Geheimrat** (b F g MA) 17-5 h
K 2, 31 ✉ 68159 ☏ 15 19 64

SEX SHOPS/BLUE MOVIES
■ **Beate Uhse Kino 4** (G VS) Mon-Sat 8-24, Sun 11-24 h
Kaiserring 26-28 ✉ 68161
Another shop at L14, 12.
■ **Binokel Sex Shop** (G VS) Mon-Sat 12-23, Sun 15-22 h
J 2, 18 ✉ 68159 ☏ 221 17
■ **Cruising Point** (g VS) Mon-Sat 12-24, Sun 15-24 h
Mittelstrasse 15 ✉ 68169 (Alter Meßplatz) ☏ 364 07
■ **Erotic Shop** (g) Mon-Fri 9-19, Sat -16 h
M2, 3 ✉ 68161 ☏ 265 80
■ **Studio 7** (AC DR G MA VS) 11-24, Sat 11-6, Sun and public holidays 16-24 h
Heinrich-Lanz-Straße 32 ✉ 68165 (Tram -Tattersaal)
☏ 44 93 06

SAUNAS/BATHS
■ **Galileo City Sauna** (AC B DR f G MA SA SB VS) 14-24 h
O7, 20, Kunststraße ✉ 68161 (near station, tram 2,3,6,7- Wasserturm or Kunsthalle) ☏ 446 57 74
New sauna on three floors in the core of the city. Special attraction steam bath with interesting architecture
■ **Hot House** (AC B DR F G MA msg OS SA SB SOL VS) Wed, Sat, Sun & public holidays 14-23, Thu 16-22 h
Ladenburgerstraße 23 ✉ 68309 (Käfertal) ☏ 73 72 60
Mostly guests around 35 or older enjoy a good meal or relax in the big garden.
■ **Vital Sauna** (AC B DR f G MA msg OS p PI r s SA SB SOL VS) Mon-Fri 16-24, Sat Sun & public holidays 14-23 h
Rheinhäuser Straße 50 ✉ 68165 (7 min from train station, Tram 6- Werderstraße, Tram 1-Kopernikusstraße) ☏ 40 95 36
Sauna with summer garden and swimming pool in winter garden. Many specials in darkroom (sling, chains,...)

BODY & BEAUTY SHOPS
■ **Ars Subcutan** Wed Fri 13-18.30, Thu -20, Sat 10.30-14 h
Alphornstraße 41 ✉ 68169 (Neckarstadt) ☏ 318 91 83
Piercings, Brandings, Cuttings.

BOOK SHOPS
■ **Andere Buchladen. Der** (GLM) Mon-Fri 10-20, Sat -14 h
M 2, 1 ✉ 68161 (Tram-Paradeplatz) ☏ 217 55
Large selection of gay and lesbian books, CDs and videos. Good for information about the local gay scene. Frequent readings.
■ **Prinz Medienhaus** (cc glm)
T1, 1-3 ✉ 68161 ☏ 10 77 145

Germany — Mannheim

FASHION SHOPS
■ **MAN-Store** (CC) Mon-Fri 11-19, Sat 10-16 h
ÖVA Passage P 7, 6-7 ✉ 68161 ☎ 10 37 75

LEATHER & FETISH SHOPS
■ **ERTE-Leder Design** by appointment only
Schwetzinger Straße 116 ✉ 68165 ☎ 40 40 89

TRAVEL AND TRANSPORT
■ **GIV Reisen**
Schwetzinger Strasse 93 ✉ 68165 🖨 44 13 40
📧 info@discustravel.de

GENERAL GROUPS
■ **PLUS - Psychologische Lesben- und Schwulenberatung Rhein Neckar e.V.** call for appointments Tue 17-18, Thu 9-10 h
Alphornstraße 2a ✉ 68169 ☎ 336 21 10 🖨 336 21 86
📧 team@plus-mannheim.de 🖥 www.plus-mannheim.de
counselling for singles, couples and groups.
■ **Quietschboys und Girls** Meeting: Fri 19-? h at Arbeitslosencafé, M 1
Postfach 10 17 11 ✉ 68017 ☎ 19 446
Gay and lesbian youth group of Scham.

FETISH GROUPS
■ **LC Mannheim e.V.** Mon 19-22 h
Postfach 10 21 17 ✉ 68021 ☎ 339 14 47
Meetings: at "Butch" on Thu at 18 h and every 4th Sat at 18 h, at "Zelle" every 1st Sun at 11 h and every 2nd Fri at 19 h.
■ **Mannheim Bären Treff** Meeting last Sunday of the month at 18 h Butch Keller, S6 21 ✉ 68161 ☎ 10 56 61
📧 mannheimbears@geocities.com
Social group for bears and their admirers.
■ **RUBCLUB e.V.** (LJ)
Mannheimer Straße 45 ✉ 68309 ☎ 0172/733 44 44
📧 info@rubclub.de 🖥 www.rubclub.de
Party at "MS Connexion" (Mannheim) every 1st Sat, strictly rubber dresscode. Party at "Chains" (Cologne) at 2nd Sat in Feb,Apr,Jun,Aug,Oct,Dec, stricly rubber dresscode.

HEALTH GROUPS
■ **AIDS-Hilfe Mannheim-Ludwigshafen e.V.** Tue Thu 10.30-13, Wed 15.30-18 h, Counselling Tue Thue 12-13 h
L 10, 8 ✉ 68161 ☎ 28 600 ☎ 194 11 (counselling) 🖨 15 27 64
📧 aids-hilfe@mannheim-net.de 🖥 www.contactpoint.de

HELP WITH PROBLEMS
■ **Rosa Hilfe** Tue 19-21 h
☎ 194 46

SPORT GROUPS
■ **Mannemer Volley Dolls e.V.** 19.30-22 h
Postfach 12 12 02 ✉ 68063 ☎ 262 30
📧 volleydolls@t-online.de   Volleyball and bowling.

CRUISING
-Schloßpark (hinter der Uni auch spät nachts/behind university, late at night too)
-Friedrich-Ebert-Brücke (along the promenade, Neckarufer and -Friedrich-Ebert-Brücke (Tunnel)
-Hauptbahnhof
-Hauptfriedhof-Klinikum (Tunnel)

Marburg ▶ Metzingen | **Germany**

Galileo City Sauna (Advertisement)

Schwule Saunen sind der Untergang von Anstand und Moral.

▶ Jetzt gibt es einen schönen Anlass, trotzdem eine zu besuchen.

Willkommen bei Galileo!

Gay saunas mark the downfall of decency and morality.

▶ Now you have a good reason for visiting one anyway.

Welcome to Galileo!

New!

Mannheim City O7, 20 (Kunststraße) * 4 Min vom Hbf ggüb. Café XS
Täglich 14-24 Uhr * Tel. (0621) 446 577 4 * www.galileo-sauna.de

---

Marburg ☎ 06421

BARS
■ **Havanna Acht** (B GLM YG) 20-2, Sat 21-2 h, GLM only on Sunday
Lahntor 2 ✉ 35037 ☎ 234 32
■ **KFZ** (B GLM YG) Mon 21.30-1 h
Schulstraße 6 ✉ 35037 *(town centre, behind Mc Donald's)*
☎ 68 20 53

BOOK SHOPS
■ **Roter Stern Buchhandlung & Antiquariat** (A BF CC f glm) Mon-Fri 10-19, Sat -16 h, Café: 10-19h

Am Grün 28 ✉ 35037 ☎ 247 87

GENERAL GROUPS
■ **Tuntonia e.V.** Mon-Fri 10-14 h
Bahnhofstraße 27 ✉ 35037 ☎ 68 20 53 📠 624 17
Infoline ☎ 194 46. Call for information on gay sports group, gay fathers and husbands, and group for olders gays.

HEALTH GROUPS
■ **AIDS-Hilfe Marburg e.V.** Mon-Thu 10-13, Mon 14-16, Thu 19-21 h
Bahnhofstraße 27 ✉ 35037 ☎ 645 23 📠 624 14
🖥 info@marburg.aidshilfe.de
🖥 www.aids-hilfe-marburg.de

HELP WITH PROBLEMS
■ **Rosa Telefon** Mon 19-21 h
☎ 194 46
1st Wed 19-21 h, counselling

CRUISING
-Toilet at the central bus station (below the motorway bridge)
-Schülerpark (near railway line and river Lahn)

Memmingen ☎ 08331

GENERAL GROUPS
■ **Homosexuelle in Memmingen (him)** (GLM MA N) Mon 19.30-21 (G), Thu 19.30-21 h (L)
c/o AIDS-Hilfe, Krautstraße 8 ✉ 87700 ☎ 484 57 📠 98 10 89
🖥 aids-hilfe@t-online.de 🖥 www.aids-hilfe.de

Menden ☎ 02373

GENERAL GROUPS
■ **Homosapiens - Gruppe für Schwule** Thu 19.30 h
Am Vollmersbusch 43 *(in der Kindertagesstätte)* ☎ 676 50
🖥 www.freeyellow.com/members/eisbrecher

Metzingen ☎ 07123

BARS
■ **Club Apollo e.V.** (B G MA VS) Wed Fri 21-?, Sat 22-? h, Fri Videotime
Dachsweg 2 ✉ 72555 *(Neuhausen, near Hofbühlhalle)*
☎ 157 25

Germany | Minden ▶ Mülheim a.d.Ruhr

Minden ☎ 0571

BARS
■ **Delfter Stuben** (B d f G lj MA p s) 21-? h, Mon closed
Pionierstraße 1a ✉ 32423 *(Nähe/near Hauptbahnhof)*
☎ 320 18 63

SAUNAS/BATHS
■ **Viktoria** (B DR F G MA OS SA SB SOL VS WH) 15-23 h, closed Mon Tue
Viktoriastraße 22-24 ✉ 32423 *(2 min from railway station, line 442-Bachstraße, rear yard)* ☎ 357 15
Cosy sauna on 4 floors with nudism garden and outside parties in summer.

GENERAL GROUPS
■ **GAYliens** Mon 20 h at "Nähkörbchen", Ritterstraße 1
Postfach 12 22, 31597 Uchte
Gay youth group.
■ **Schwarm e.V.** Meets every Thu 20 h at Kulturcafé Weingarten, Königswall
■ **Schwule Initiative Minden (SchwIM)** (G MA)
c/o BÜZ, Seidenbeutel 1 ✉ 32423 ☎ 88 00 38 (infoline)

CRUISING
-Alter Friedhof (tagsüber/daytime)
-Weserglacis

Moers ☎ 02841

GAY INFO
■ **Pink Channel Duisburg** FM 102.4 MHz

GENERAL GROUPS
■ **DeLSI Demokratische Lesben- u. Schwuleninitiative** Meeting Fri 20.30 h
c/o Jugendzentrum, Südring 2a ✉ 47441 ☎ 256 25
📠 160 82
Jugendzentrum.

HEALTH GROUPS
■ **AIDS-Beratung im Gesundheitsamt** Mon 14-16, 18-19 h
c/o Gesundheitsamt, Mühlenstraße 9-11 ✉ 47441 *(room 32)*
☎ 202 10 32
Anonymous free HIV test and counselling.

CRUISING
-Hauptbahnhof/Main station (links gegenüber/left across the street)
-Schloßpark

Mönchengladbach ☎ 02161

BARS
■ **C'est la vie** (A AC B D f glm MA p S) Tue Thu-Sun 20-?, showtime 24 & 2 h
Gasthausstraße 67 ✉ 41061 ☎ 17 57 64
■ **Germania Stübchen** (AC B Glm MA OS p) 20-2 h
Gasthausstraße 68 ✉ 41061 ☎ 17 66 30

SEX SHOPS/BLUE MOVIES
■ **New Man im WOS-Markt** (G VS) 10-24, Sun 12-24 h
Hindenburgstraße 201 ✉ 41061

GIFT & PRIDE SHOPS
■ **MAN Shop** (CC g MA VS) Mon-Sat 10-24 , Sun & holidays 13-23 h
Hauptstraße 16 ✉ 41236 *(Rheydt-Zentrum)* ☎ 02166/94 45 86

HEALTH GROUPS
■ **AIDS-Hilfe Mönchengladbach/Rheydt e.V.** Mon-Fri 9-17 h by appointment
Rathausstraße 13 ✉ 41061 ☎ 17 60 23 ☎ 194 11
Homophone counselling Sun 18-20 h.

CRUISING
-Hauptbahnhof/Main train station

Montabaur ☎ 02602

GENERAL GROUPS
■ **Schwuler Stammtisch** 1st & 3rd Wed 20-? h at Villa Sonnenschein, Wilhelm-Mangels-Straße 17
☎ 178 84

Moritzburg ☎ 035207

RESTAURANTS
■ **Dreispitz. Zum** (CC F g MA) 11-24 h (meals -23)
Schlossallee 5 ✉ 01468 ☎ 8 22 00
Popular restaurant located in an old house built in 1727. Traditional cuisine.

Mülheim a. d. Ruhr ☎ 0208

DANCECLUBS
■ **Cruise & Queer** (B D GLM) 4th Sat 22.30-5 h
Ringlokschuppen, Am Schloß Broich 38 ✉ 45479 ☎ 412 59 21

GENERAL GROUPS
■ **Enterpride-Schwule Jugendgruppe** (YG) Meeting Mon 18-1 h at Ringlokschuppen, Am Schloß Broich 38
☎ 412 59 22 📠 993 16 13
💻 www.enterpride.de
■ **Sozialverein für Lesben und Schwule e.V.**
c/o Ringlokschuppen, Am Schloß Broich 38 ✉ 45479 ☎ 412 59 21
📠 993 16-13 💻 www.svls.de

HEALTH GROUPS
■ **Herzenslust**
Am Schloss Broich 38 ✉ 45479 ☎ 412 59 20 📠 993 16 13
💻 herzenslust@ruhr-west.de
HIV-prevention fro gays and bisexuals.

HELP WITH PROBLEMS
■ **Beratungsstelle für Lesben,Schwule,Bisexuelle** helpline Mon-Fri 15-18 Wed 19-21 h (G)
c/o Ringlokschuppen, Am Schloß Broich 38 ✉ 45479 ☎ 194 46 (helpline) ☎ 412 59 20 💻 beratung@schwulenberatung-ruhr.de
💻 www.lesbenberatung-ruhr.de
Meeting point for several groups. Call or see webpage for further information."Herzenslust" online councelling www.schwulenberatung.de or irc-net: #schwulenberatung

München / Germany

München 089

Munich is home to the Oktober-Fest where beer is drunk in large quantities or "Maß" as the Germans would say. The beer gardens have become a popular meeting place for gays. Try out the beer garden on the Flaucher. You will find there many handsome Bavarians sitting on one of the numerous wooden benches sipping their beer. Another must is the English Garden. The streets on the Viktualienmarkt and Glockenbach are often frequented by gay men. The proud gay community in Munich strongly contradicts the popular belief that this city is very conservative. Try the local specialties such as "Weißwürst" and "Brezel".

München ist Oktoberfest-Stadt. Und mittlerweile sind hier sogar die Biergärten schwul, wo zu einer verfolgten Minderheit nur gehört, wer ein 0,3-Bier bestellt oder sein Maß mit beiden Händen zum Hals führt. Wir empfehlen besonders den Biergarten am Flaucher. Schöne Bajuwaren machen es sich auf schmalen Holzbänken bequem. Später werden sie auf den taubenetzten Maiwiesen des Englischen Gartens ihr Geheimnis enthüllen. Dann zeigen sie uns das Land der Regenbögen: Es sind die schönen Straßen an Viktualienmarkt und Glockenbach, wo schwule Männer Liebe geben. Damit ist München das Filetstück Bayerns. Doch viele Menschen in Deutschland sagen: Nach Bayern fahre ich nicht, dort ist es mir zu konservativ. Das stimmt nicht. Über all die Jahre hat sich in München ein neues schwules Selbstverständnis entwickelt.

Munich est la ville de l'Oktoberfest. Et entre temps, même les brasseries en plein air sont gaies, là ou on fait partie d'une minorité poursuivie si on commande une bière de 3 décilitres ou si on porte à sa bouche sa chope de bière d'un litre en la tenant à deux mains. Nous recommandons particulièrement la brasserie de plein air "am Flaucher". De beaux Bavarois sont assis confortablement sur des bancs de bois étroits. Plus tard, ils révéleront leurs secrets sur les prés recouverts de rosée du "Jardin anglais". Les belles rues autour du "Viktualienmarkt" et de "Glockenbach" sont aussi des bastions homos. L'image conservatrice de la ville bavaroise s'est beaucoup estompée ces dernières années.

Una gran parte de los turistas viene para ver el Oktoberfest y probar la famosísima cerveza. Ya hay hasta terrazas gay y minorías perseguidas aquí son solo los que piden la típica cerveza en formato "pequeño" de 0,3 l o los que levanten la autentica jarra de un litro con las dos manos. Se recomienda especialmente la terraza al lado del *Flaucher*, donde guapos bavarianos se apiñan en los banquillos. Más tarde se reunen en los *Maiwiesen* del conocido *Englischer Garten*, un parque de la ciudad, donde los amantes del nudismo se exponen al sol en los días de verano. El ambiente gay se concentra en las calles del Viktualienmarkt y Glockenbach. Allí se encuentran sitios encantadores, que distinguen Munich del resto de Bavaria. Pero muchos dicen, que no van a Bavaria, porque les parece un sitio demasiado conservador. Esto no es verdad. Durante los últimos años en Munich se ha desarrollado una nueva autoconfianza gay, que es demostrada con mucho orgullo.

Monaco è la città dell'Oktoberfest. Anche le birrererie all'aperto sono gay, dove viene perseguitato come rappresentante di una minoranza quello che ordina solo una birra da 0,3 litri o leva il boccale da un litro con tutte le due mani. Consigliamo per primo la birreria al *Flaucher* sul fiume Isar, dove i bei bavaresi si accomodano su stretti banchi di legno. Più tardi riveleranno il loro segreto, stendendosi nudi sui prati dei giardini inglesi bagnati di rugiada e ci faranno vedere il paese degli arcobaleni, cioè le belle strade del mercato centrale *Viktualienmarkt* e del quartiere *Glockenbach*, dove i begl'uomini sono pronti adonare il loro cuore. Così Monaco è il posto migliore della Baviera. Ma tanti tedeschi dicono: Non vado in Baviera perché là sono troppo conservativi. Ma non è vero. A Monaco negli ultimi anni si è sviluppata un'atmosfera gay "naturale" che si presenta con orgoglio al pubblico.

GAY INFO

■ **SUB-Schwules Kommunikations- und Kulturzentrum** (A B f G MA s) 19-22, Fri Sat 19-24, Infoservice Mon-Sun 19-22 h
Müllerstraße 43 ✉ 80469 (U-Sendlinger Tor) ☎ 260 30 56
☏ 260 87 90 🖥 www.subonline.org
Center for communication, information, counselling & groups. Call for more information/Kommunikationszentrum, Infothek, Beratung, Gruppen.

■ **Uferlos** (G) Fri 20-21 h on FM 92.4 MHz, FM 96.75 MHz (Kabel)
c/o Münchner AIDS-Hilfe e.V., Lindwurmstraße 71 ✉ 80337
☎ 24 43 67 622 🖨 54 46 47 46
🖥 www.uferlos.lora924.de
Gay radio magazine of radio LORA.

PUBLICATIONS

■ **München & Nürnberg von hinten**
c/o Bruno Gmünder Verlag, PO Box 61 01 04, 10921 Berlin
☎ (030) 615 00 342 🖨 (030) 615 91 34 ✉ info@spartacus.de
🖥 www.brunos.de
The city guide book about Nuremberg and Munich. Useful general information and lots of addresses with extensive descriptions in English and German. Up-to-date maps. Erotic photos.

■ **Our Munich**
Lindwurmstrasse 29 ✉ 80337 ☎ 530 74 30 🖨 530 74 311
🖥 www.ourmunich.de
Gay magazine for Greater Munich. News, events, classifieds. For free at gay venues.

■ **Rosa Seiten** (GLM)
c/o PC-Print GmbH, Adalbertstraße 16 ✉ 80799 ☎ 380 19 10
🖨 34 73 81 🖥 www.rosaseiten.com
Local gay directory. Free at gay venues. Only in German.

■ **Sergej Punkt München**
Adalbert Straße 16 ✉ 80799 ☎ 380 19 119 🖨 380 19 125
✉ sergej.muc@pc-print.com
Monthly city gay magazine available for free at gay venues.

CULTURE

■ **Kunst (B) Handlung. Ausstellungsraum** (A AC CC GLM MA s)
Mon-Fri 12-14+16-19, Sat 11-16 h and by appointment
Müllerstraße 40 ✉ 80469 (U 1/2/3/6/8, near Sendlinger Tor)
☎ 260 53 99
🖥 www.kunstbehandlung.de
Gallery & computerclub.

TOURIST INFO

■ **Fremdenverkehrsamt**
Sendlinger Straße 1 ✉ 80331 ☎ 233 03 00 🖨 233-3 02 33
🖥 www.muenchen-tourist.de

BARS

■ **Adamatschka Bar** (AC B CC f G MG OS R) 10-1-h
Sebastiansplatz 3 ✉ 80331 (U-S-Marienplatz) ☎ 26 02 62 32

■ **Alexander's Bar & Café** (AC B CC f G MA R) 16-1, Fri & Sat -3 h
Utzschneiderstraße 4 ✉ 80469 (U/S-Marienplatz, near/nahe Viktualienmarkt) ☎ 260 54 98
The best R-coded bar in Munich.

Germany — München

München | Germany

OCHSEN GARTEN MÜNCHEN
MÜLLERSTR. 47 - 80469 MÜNCHEN
www.ochsengarten.de

Teddy-Bar München
18–03 open daily
Hans-Sachs-Str. 1
80469 München
Tel. 260 33 59

■ **Spike** (B f G LJ MA OS) 15-1, Fri Sat -3 h
Holzstraße 14 ✉ 80469 *(U- Sendlinger-Tor)*
☎ 26 02 62 37
■ **Sunshine Pub** (B f G MA N r) 6-3 h
Müllerstraße 17 ✉ 80469 *(Tram 17/18/20)*
☎ 260 93 54
■ **Tabasco** (AC B DR f G LJ MA) Tue-Thu 17-1, Fri & Sat -3, Sun 15-1 h
Reisingerstraße 5 ✉ 80337 *(former Löwengrube)*
☎ 232 09941
Also small sex shop

■ **Teddy Bar** (B f G lj MA) Daily 18-3 h, Sun & holidays - brunch from 11 h
Hans-Sachs-Straße 1 ✉ 80469 *(U-Sendlinger Tor)* ☎ 260 33 59
Sun brunch from 11 h, Jan Feb, fashing every WE.
■ **Theaterklause** (B G MG N) 11-1 h, closed Wed
Klenzestraße 30 ✉ 80469 *(Near/nahe Gärtnerplatz, U-Fraunhofer Straße)* ☎ 26 94 93 92
■ **Unantast "Bar"** (B G) 10-22h
Thalkirchner Straße 16 ✉ 80337 ☎ 260 74 69

Café • Bistro • Bar
Prosecco
...einfach was los !
Theklastraße 1 • 80469
München
Telefon 089/260 57 14
täglich 18–04 Uhr
Shows Mo., Mi., Do. 21 Uhr
Eintritt frei

In dem kleinen, feinen Glitzerbistro regiert das glamouröse Ambiente, je nach Motto oder Jahreszeit stets liebevoll und prächtig dekoriert. Man trifft sich zum Gläschen Prosecco, zur kulinarischen Kleinigkeit oder zur Show. Auf Münchens wohl kleinster Bühne steht da schon mal fast leibhaftig die Monroe oder die Leander. Kein Wunder, daß der Funke zum Publikum allabendlich schnell überspringt. Da regnet es schon mal Seifenblasen, da gibt's plötzlich ein riesiges Tischfeuerwerk – und wenn Sie am nächsten Morgen noch bunte Konfetti in der Kleidung haben, dann waren Sie unbestritten nit von der Partie im einzigartigen Bistro – im Prosecco.

Germany München

Zur Feuerwache

80331 München
Blumenstr. 21a   Tel. 089 260 44 30   Fax 089 26 02 37 89

täglich 11 - 1 Uhr   Happy Hour bis 17 Uhr

■ **Zur Feuerwache** (B f G lj MA) 11-1, happy hour 11-17 h
Blumenstraße 21a ✉ 80331 *(U-Sendlinger Tor, Tram 17 +18)*
☏ 260 44 30
A friendly bar to quench your thirst with fun drinks and small snacks. Sat from 11:00h "Weißwürst-bf DM 8,–"

CAFES

■ **Café Glück** (A B BF F gLM OS YG) Mon-Fri 16-1, Sat 14-1, Sun 10-1 h
Palmstraße 4 ✉ 80469 *(U-Fraunhofer Straße)* ☏ 201 16 73
Sun BF from 10-16 h.

■ **My Way** (b f GLM MA s OS) Mon-Sat 10-22 h, Sun 16-22 h
Ligsalzstraße 7 ✉ 80339 *(U4/U5-Schwanthalerhöhe)*
☏ 51 00 91 34

■ **Petit Café** (B G MA N) 15-22 h
Marienstraße 2 ✉ 80331 *(S-Isartor/Marienplatz)*
☏ 29 56 72

■ **Villanis** (BF CC F glm MA OS) 10-1, Sun and public holidays 11-1 h
Kreuzstraße 3b ✉ 80331 *(U-Sendlinger Tor)*
☏ 260 79 72

Leather Levis Uniform Club
http: the-stud.de

the STUD

Thalkirchner Str. 2
80337 Munich Germany
Tel.: 0049 (0)89 2608403
Öffnungszeiten:
Freitag - Samstag 23.00 – 5.00 Uhr
Sonntag 23.00 – 4.00 Uhr

München | Germany

"In einem traditionsreichen
Ambiente
ein gutes Essen geniessen
– vielleicht auch einfach nur
bei einem frisch gezapften Bier
oder einem erfrischenden Cocktail
den Tag ausklingen lassen ..."

"Enjoy a good meal
and select wines enveloped
in a classical atmosphere –
or just come along
and end the day
with fresh draught beer ..."

Tattenbach
BAR & RESTAURANT

· Tattenbachstrasse 6 · 80538 München-Lehel ·
·Tel.: (089) 22 52 68 · U4/U5 Lehel, Tram 17 ·
· Öffnungszeiten: Mo-Do ab 17.00 Uhr, Fr-So ab 19.00 Uhr ·
· Mittagstisch: Mo-Fr 11.30 - 14.30 Uhr ·

DANCECLUBS

■ **Blub Club** (! AC B CC D G S TV YG) every 1st Tue
c/o Park-Café, Sophienstraße 7 ✉ 80333 (U/S-Karlsplatz)
☏ 59 83 13
Very popular party with house music and hot go go boys
■ **Fortuna** (AC B CC D glm MA OS WE) Fri 22:30-6, Sat 23-6 h
Maximiliansplatz 5 ✉ 80333 ☏ 470 76 74
■ **Hossa's** (D GLM) Wed, Thu & Sun 21-3h, Fri & Sat -4h
Müllerstraße 1 ✉ 80469 ☏ 263469
■ **New York** (AC B CC D f GLM MA p) Sun-Thu 23-4 h,
Fri Sat 23-open end
Sonnenstraße 25 ✉ 80331 (U-Sendlinger Tor) ☏ 59 10 56
■ **Soul-City** (AC D f glm S TV VS WE YG) mixed (g): Tue 21-4,
Wed 18-24, Thu 22-6, Fri -4, Gay (GLM): Sat 22-8 h
Maximiliansplatz 5 ✉ 80333 (S/U - Stachus) ☏ 59 52 72
3rd Fri Happy Gays. Best after 2 h. Late night meeting place. DM 10, co-ver charge

Soul-City

CAFE - DISCOTHEK

Maximiliansplatz 5
80333 München
Tel.: 59 52 72
FaxTel.: 55 33 01
Internet:
www.Soul-City.de
email: Dieter.rex@soul-city.de

Germany — München

■ **Stud. The** (! AC B D DR G LJ MA S SNU VS WE) Fri Sat 23-5 Sun-4 h.
Thalkirchner Straße 2 ✉ 80337 (U-Sendlinger Tor)
☎ 260 84 03
Bavarias largest LJ club

RESTAURANTS

■ **Beim Franz** (B F G MA) 18-1 h
Holzstraße 41 ✉ 80469 ☎ 260 75 47
Excellent Bavarian cuisine.

■ **Der Neue Kanzleirat** (AC B BF CC F glm OS) 10-1, meals until 24 h
Oettingerstraße 36 ✉ 80538 (Tram 17-Paradies Straße)
☎ 22 00 84
Traditional Bavarian cuisine.

■ **Orangha Bar & Restaurant** (B F g) Mon-Sun 18-1 h
Klenzestr. 62 ✉ 80469 (U-Fraunhoferstr.,Glockenbachviertel)
☎ 20 23 26 75

■ **Seitensprung** (BF F GLM MA OS) Mon-Thu 12-1, Fri -2, Sat 11-2, Sun -1 h
Holzstraße 29 ✉ 80469 (U-Fraunhofer Straße/Sendlinger Tor)
☎ 26 93 77
Late breakfasts on Sat, Sun & holidays 11-16 h

■ **Tattenbach** (B CC F glm MA OS s) Mon-Fri 11.30-14.30 Mon-Thu also from 17 Fri-Sun from 19 h
Tattenbachstraße 6 ✉ 80538 (U-Lehel)
☎ 22 52 68
Bar and restaurant well known both for its interior design as for its food.

■ **Wirtshaus Zum Isartal** (AC b d F glm MA N OS S STV TV) Mon-Thu 11-2, Fri -3, Sat & Sun 10-3 h
Brudermühlstraße 2 ✉ 81371 (U-Brudermühlstraße)
☎ 77 21 21
Bavarian rustical cuisine with opera and drag shows. Large and popular beer garden open until 3 h.

SHOWS

■ **Bel Étage** (CC g MA S STV) 19.30-1 h
Feilitzschstraße 12 ✉ 80802 (U-Münchner Freiheit)
☎ 33 90 13
Entrance-fee DM 24-35.

■ **Harlekin Sisters** (STV) Sun-Fri 12-18 h
Buttermelcher Straße 4 ✉ 80469 ☎ 26 56 44
Top-class drag shows. One to four artists available./Travestie-Show der Spitzenklasse. Allein oder bis zu vier Künstler buchbar.

SEX SHOPS/BLUE MOVIES

■ **Black Jump** (CC GLM LJ MA p) By appointment only
Orleansstraße 51 ✉ 81667 (S-Ostbahnhof) ☎ 48 00 43 33
Also mail order

■ **Buddy Shop** (G lj VS) Mon-Fri 10-20, Sat -16 h
Utzschneiderstraße 3 ✉ 80469 ☎ 26 89 38

■ **Cornelius Men** (CC G lj VS) Mon-Fri 10-20, Sat -16 h
Corneliusstraße 19 ✉ 80469 (Near/nahe Gärtnerplatz)
☎ 201 47 53
Also two gay cinemas and a large variety of books, leather & toys.

■ **Follow me** (CC G) Mon-Fri 10-20, Sat -16 h
Corneliusstraße 32 ✉ 80469 (U-Fraunhofer Straße)
☎ 202 12 08
Leather, rubber, toys videos to rent / buy.

■ **Gay's Heaven** (G MA) Mon-Fri 10-20, Sat -16 h, Sun closed
Baaderstrasse 82 ✉ 80469 (U/Tram-Frauenhoferstrasse)
☎ 20 00 98 04
Erotic store with books, magazines, toys. Videos to rent or buy.

■ **Sex Point** (AC b CC DR G MA VS) Shop: Mon-Sat 9-23, Cinema: Mon-Sat 11-24, Sun 12-24 h
Sonnenstraße 14 ✉ 80331 (near Stachus and Hbf)
Special price on Mondays. 1 large and 5 small cinemas. Cubicals. Large selection

■ **Sex World** (g MA VS) Mon-Fri 9-22, Sun -16 h, Cinema: Mon-Sat 14-22 h
Sonnenstraße 12 ✉ 80331 (U/S-Karlsplatz) ☎ 55 47 33

■ **Spexter Erotic Store** (A CC DR G LJ MA VS) Mon-Fri 10-20, Sat 10-16 h
Müllerstraße 54 ✉ 80469 (U-Sendlinger Tor)
☎ 26 02 48 64
Centrally located ,popular and well equipped sex-toy-store with a huge selection of leather,rubber and uniform.

■ **Weissblauer Gay Shop** (AC CC G MA VS) Mon Fri 9-20, Sat -18 h
Theresienstraße 130 ✉ 80333 (U2-Theresienstraße)
☎ 52 23 52
2 cinemas, large video and dvd section.

CINEMAS

■ **Atlantik City** (G VS) Mon-Sat 9-1 Sun& on public holidays 11-1 h
Kino 2, Schillerstraße 3 ✉ 80331 (near main station) ☎ 59 42 91
5 cinemas and live strip show in cinema 1.

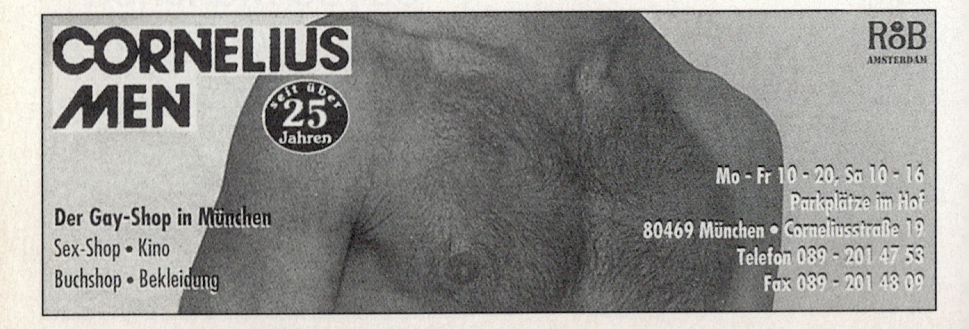

CORNELIUS MEN
seit über 25 Jahren

Der Gay-Shop in München
Sex-Shop • Kino
Buchshop • Bekleidung

RoB AMSTERDAM

Mo - Fr 10 - 20, Sa 10 - 16
Parkplätze im Hof
80469 München • Corneliusstraße 19
Telefon 089 - 201 47 53
Fax 089 - 201 48 09

München | Germany

BUDDY

MÜNCHEN

THE LARGEST GAY-SHOP IN TOWN
Utzschneiderstraße 3
D-80469 München
Tel: 089 / 26 89 38
Fax: 089 / 26 55 58

*2 Non-stop-Cinemas
Videos
Magazines, Books
Toys, Piercing
big choice Leather
and Rubber articles
Jeans and Sportwear*

opening hours: mo-fr 10 am to 8 pm;
sa 10 am to 4 pm

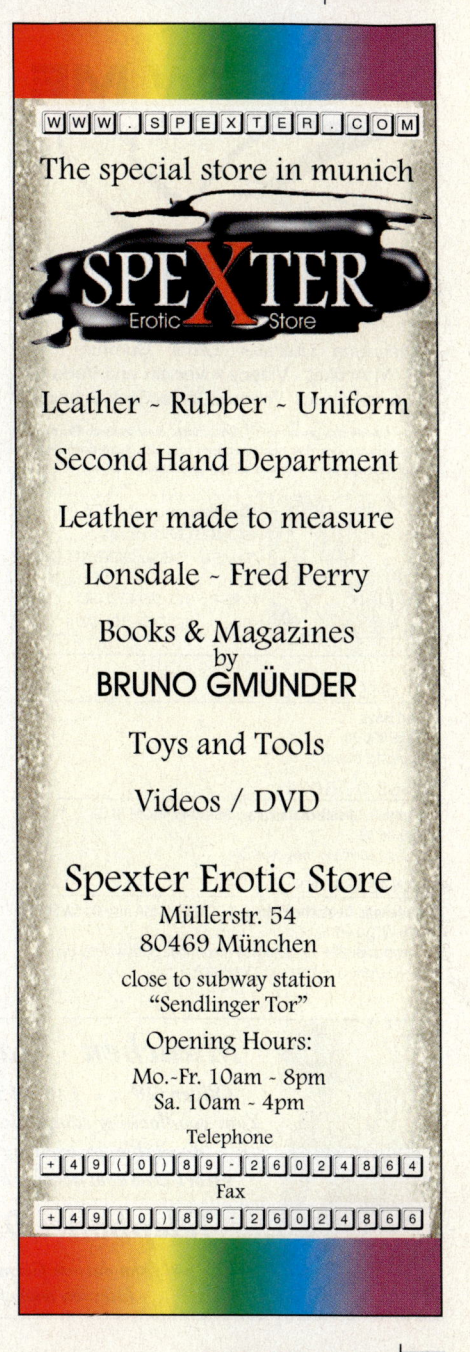

Viktualienmarkt

BUDDY
Utzschneiderstr. 3

Reichenbachplatz

Blumenstr.

Reichenbachstr.

Gärtnerplatz

WWW.SPEXTER.COM

The special store in munich

SPEXTER Erotic Store

Leather – Rubber – Uniform

Second Hand Department

Leather made to measure

Lonsdale – Fred Perry

Books & Magazines
by
BRUNO GMÜNDER

Toys and Tools

Videos / DVD

Spexter Erotic Store
Müllerstr. 54
80469 München
close to subway station
"Sendlinger Tor"

Opening Hours:
Mo.-Fr. 10am - 8pm
Sa. 10am - 4pm

Telephone
+49 (0) 89 - 26 02 48 64
Fax
+49 (0) 89 - 26 02 48 66

Germany München

FOLLOW ME GAY SHOP

Der freundliche Gay-Shop für Preisbewußte

Magazine · Literatur · Leder · Gummi · Toys
S/M Artikel · Videos – Verleih und Verkauf
Intimschmuck · Versand · Verschenk-Schecks

Wir führen das gesamte Sortiment, einschließlich Piercing-Körperschmuck aus hochwertigem medizinischem Edelstahl – Auf Anfrage auch in Edelmetallen und Sondermaßen.

Corneliusstraße 32
80469 München
Tel/Fax 089/202 12 08
Mo-Fr 10.00-20.00
Sa 10.00-16.00

Bruno's
www.brunos.de

THE GAY MEDIA STORE

ESCORTS & STUDIOS
■ **Bad Boys**
☎ 316 990 70
International escorts.

HOUSE OF BOYS
■ **Marcel's Gesellschafterteam München MGM** (B G)
☎ 39 86 39
More than 30 young men available.

SAUNAS/BATHS
■ **Badehaus Deutsche Eiche** (! B CC DR F G MA msg OS SA SB SOL VS WH WO) 14-7 h
Reichenbachstraße 13 ✉ 80469 *(near/nahe Gärtnerplatz, Tram 17/19-Reichenbachplatz)* ☎ 23 11 66 0

Fully equipped sauna with changing decoration. Many special parties organised.
■ **Dom Pedro Gay Club** (B f G MG msg Pl SA SB SOL) 12-24 h, Mon Jack-off-party
Fasanariestraße 18 ✉ 80636 *(Tram 20/21-Leonrodplatz, Tram 12/Bus 33-Fasanariestraße)*
☎ 129 32 76
Small but popular sauna. Jack-off party every Mon from 21 h. Nudism party every Fri from 20 h.
■ **Schwabinger MEN Sauna** (B DR F G MA msg p SA SB SOL VS WO) 15-1 h
Düsseldorfer Straße 7 ✉ 80804 *(U2-Scheidplatz/U3-Bonnerplatz)*
☎ 307 23 42
Infrared cublicles and medidative music. Relaxed, clean and small.

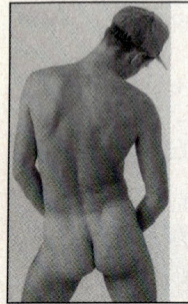

München · GayEscort Munich
*Oliver (28 y. – 176 – 65 – XL-equipped) & friends
Your goodlooking companions in Munich, tops & bottoms, available for exciting massage, hotel visitings, escort & travel accompany & more special services.*

Telephone: 0171 610 46 47
*call from outside Germany: 0049 171 610 46 47
Internet: www.freenet.de/gayescort*

MUNICH - MÜNCHEN

M✰G✰M
Marcel's
Gesellschafterteam
München

MARCEL

RENÉ

JUSTIN

DANIEL

PETER

TIM

absolute discretion !

☆ Luxurious penthouse in the center of Munich
☆ travel-accompany also available international
☆ escort and visiting service to your home or hotel

📞 089/398639   📱 0171/800 11 20

www.mgm-muenchen.de

Germany München

Exxxtrem
Deutschlands schärfster
Dark Room
Sofort ausprobieren
0190-766 725
www.gratisgayfotos.com

TMG DM 2.42 Min / Live Operator

MAX & MILIAN
SCHWULER BUCHLADEN MÜNCHEN
– GAY BOOKSHOP MUNICH –

**lesen.
hören.
schauen.**

Ickstattstr. 2 · 80469 München
Fon 089/260 33 20 · Fax 26 30 59
e-mail: maxundmilian@t-online.de
http://www.gaybooks.de
Mo-Do 10.30-14/15.30-20, Fr 10.30-20, Sa 11-16

BOOK SHOPS
■ **Max & Milian** (CC Glm) Mon-Thu 10.30-14, 15.30-20, Fri 10.30-20, Sat 11-16 h
Ickstattstraße 2 ✉ 80469 (U-Sendlinger Tor/Fraunhoferstraße/Tram-Müllerstraße) ☎ 260 33 20
Large selection of books, magazines, videos and CDs.

GIFT & PRIDE SHOPS
■ **Our Munich Shop** (A CC GLM MA) Mon Tue Thu 11-14.30 Mon-Thu also 15.30-20, Fri 11-20 Sat-16 h
Müllerstraße 36-38 ✉ 80469 (U-Sendlinger Tor) ☎ 260 18 503
In the centre of the gay district. Book shop,CDs,videos,ticket,gay infos for tourists.

LEATHER & FETISH SHOPS
■ **Hard Line** (CC G LJ) Mon-Fri 11.30-19, Sat 11-16 h
Müllerstraße 33 ✉ 80469 ☎ 260 60 17
Professional piercing studio and large selection of rubber, leather and army wear.

TRAVEL AND TRANSPORT
■ **Atlantis Travel GmbH** Mon-Fri 9-20, Sat 9-14 h
Pestalozzistraße 17 ✉ 80469 (U-Sendlinger-Tor-Platz)
☎ 23 66 60-0 ☎ 23 66 60 56 ✉ tom@atlantis-travel.de
🖥 www.atlantis-travel.de
■ **Gaygantic Tours** Mon-Fri 9-18:30h, Sat 9-14 h
Dom-Pedro-Strasse 16 ✉ 80637
☎ 15 91 90 86

HOTELS
■ **Deutsche Eiche. Hotel** (BF CC GLM MA) 0-24 h
Reichenbachstraße 13 ✉ 80469 (S/U-Marienplatz)
☎ 23 11 66 0 ☎ 23 11 66 98
✉ info@deutsche-eiche.com 🖥 www.deutsche-eiche.com
Central location. All rooms with shower/WC, TV, phone. Also restaurant.
■ **Hotel Moosbeck-Alm**
☞ See Rottenbuch
■ **Hotel Nymphenburg Garni** (B BF CC H NG) all year round
Nymphenburger Str. 141 ✉ 80636 (U1-Rotkreuzplatz or Mailingerstr.) ☎ 12 15 97 0 ☎ 18 25 40
✉ info@hotel-nymphenburg.de
🖥 www.hotel-nymphenburg.de
Centrally located 3 star hotel, Rooms with bath or shower/WC, balcony/terrace,telephone,cableTV.Single from 130-230,- DM double 170-290,extra bed 30,-DM, studio/apartment 350-450,- DM bf buffet always incl.
■ **Hotel Seibel** (AC BF F H) all year, 24 h
Theresienhöhe 9 ✉ 80339 (U5 Theresienwiese) ☎ 540 14 20
☎ 54 01 42 99 ✉ Hotel.Seibel@t-online.de
🖥 www.seibel-hotels-munich.de
Three star hotel. 45 rooms with shower/bath/WC, telephone and cable-TV. Own key. Fine Italian cuisine.

Nürnberg ☎ 0911

GAY INFO
■ **Fliederlich e.V.** (A GLM MA s WE) Café Sun 14-21 h
Gugelstraße 92 ✉ 90459 ☎ 42 34 570 ☎ 42 34 5719
📠 42 34 57 20 📧 verein@fliederlich.de 🖥 www.fliederlich.de
Gay and lesbian center. Please call for details or see our web site. Also youth group Ganymed (-25yrs),meets every 2nd and 4th Mon at 19 h; Gelesch, the group for deaf gay and lesbians which meets every 3rd Sat 15-?h. Also g&l sportsclub Rosa Panther.

PUBLICATIONS
■ **München & Nürnberg von hinten**
c/o Bruno Gmünder Verlag, Postfach 61 01 04, 10921 Berlin
☎ (030) 615 00 342 📠 (030) 615 91 34 📧 info@spartacus.de
🖥 www.brunos.de
The city guide book about Nuremberg and Munich. Useful general information and lots of addresses with extensive descriptions in English and German. Up-to-date maps. Erotic photos.
■ **NSP - Nürnberger Schwulenpost**
c/o Fliederlich, Gugelstraße 92 ✉ 90459 ☎ 42 34 57 11
📠 42 34 57 21 📧 redaktion@n-s-p.de 🖥 www.n-s-p.de
Monthly publication, free at gay venues or by subscription.

BARS
■ **Alt Prag** (B G MA) Mon-Sat 11-24, Sun and public holidays 15-24 h
Hallplatz 29 ✉ 90402 ☎ 24 33 41
■ **Amico Bar** (B d f G MA) Sun-Wed 20-2, Fri-Sat -3 h, closed Thu
Köhnstraße 53 ✉ 90478 (Bus 43/44) ☎ 46 32 92
■ **Entenstall. Zum** (B G MA OS SNU VS WE) Mon-Thu 19-1, Fri & Sat -2, Sun 18-1 h
Entengasse 12 ✉ 90402 (U-Weißer Turm/Opernhaus)
☎ 244 84 30
Internet room with 3 Pcs.
■ **King's Pub** (B f g OS) Mon-Fri 11-3, Sat Sun 20-3 h, Summer: Sat 14-3 h
Dr.-Kurt-Schuhmacher-Straße 8 ✉ 90287
☎ 244 77 03
■ **La Bas** (B f G MA OS R) 11-1 h
Hallplatz 31 ✉ 90402 ☎ 22 22 81
■ **Little Hendersen** (B D G H p R OS WE) 22-4 Fri Sat -5, Sat Sun from 6-? h
Frauengasse 10 ✉ 90402 ☎ 241 87 77
Overnight stays possible.
■ **Na und** (B d F GLM lj MA OS r s WE) Mon-Thu 11-14.30, 18-1, Fri Sat 19-3, Sun 18-1 h
Marienstraße 25 ✉ 90402 (near/nahe Hauptbahnhof)
☎ 22 73 20
■ **Petit Café** (AC B C G MA N OS) 18-1 h
Hinterm Bahnhof 24 ✉ 90459 (behind/hinter dem Hauptbahnhof)
☎ 45 41 18
■ **Savoy** (B f G MA TV) Mon-Thu 18-2, Fri Sat 16-3, Sun -2 h
Bogenstraße 45 ✉ 90459 ☎ 45 99 45
■ **Toy Bar** (B DR G MA r VS) 20-4 h
Luitpoldstraße 14 ✉ 90402 ☎ 241 96 00
■ **V 8-Bistro** (B f G MA OS s) 18-1, Fri Sat -3 h
Moltkestraße 2 ✉ 90429 (Entrance/Eingang Deutschherrnstraße)
☎ 28 80 39
■ **Vicking-Club/Babel Bar** (B DR G LJ MA VS) 20-1, Fri-Sat 21-3 h
Kolpinggasse 42 ✉ 90402 (U-Opernhaus) ☎ 22 36 69
■ **Willich** (B BF f glm OS) 17-1, Sat Sun 10-1 h
Volprechtstraße 3 ✉ 90429 (U1-Gostenhof) ☎ 287 90 05

CAFES
■ **Café Max** (B g MA) 17-1 h
Breitscheidstraße 18 ✉ 90459 ☎ 44 59 03
■ **Cartoon** (! B GLM MA OS) 11-1, Sun 14-1 h
An der Sparkasse 6 ✉ 90402 (Near/nahe Lorenzkirche)
☎ 22 71 70
■ **Confetti** (A f GLM MA s vs) Sun 14-21 h
Gugelstraße 92 ✉ 90459 (Near/nahe Christuskirche, U-Maffelplatz, Tram 8) ☎ 42 34 57-12
Cafe of Fliederlich Nuremberg's Gay-Union/Café des Nürnberger Schwulenvereins
■ **Felix** (A B f G OS YG) Mon-Sun 17-2? h
Weißgerbergasse 30 ✉ 90403 (tram 4/6, nightline 10-Hallertor)
☎ 22 42 80
■ **Zur Quetsch'n** (B d f Glm MA) Sun-Thu 17-24, Fri-Sat 15-1 h
Wiesenstraße 85 ✉ 90459 ☎ 450 11 38

DANCECLUBS
■ **DESI Stadtteilzentrum** (B d GLM YG) monthly Sat 21-3 h
Brückenstraße 23 ✉ 90419 (Bus 34-Großweidenmühlstraße)
☎ 33 69 43
■ **Mach 1** (AC B D g MA S) Gay on 1st & 3rd Sun only 22-4 h
Kaiserstraße 1-9 ✉ 90403 (U - Lorenzkirche) ☎ 20 30 30
■ **Twilight** (! AC B D f GLM lj MA s) Fri 22:-4, Sat -5, Sun -3 h, Mon & Tue closed
1st Wed/month & 4th Thu/month 22-2 h
Nimrodstrasse 9 ✉ 90441 (Tram stop - Dianaplatz) ☎ 9414361

RESTAURANTS
■ **Gasthaus im Pegnitztal** (F glm OS) 11-24 h
Deutschherrnstraße 31 ✉ 90429 ☎ 26 44 44
Traditional and vegetarian cuisine. Party service available.
■ **Majorka** (b F g) Tue-Sun 11-14, 17-1 h, closed Mon
Hintere Ledergasse 2 ✉ 90403 ☎ 22 45 14
Italian cuisine
■ **Omas Küche** (B F g MA OS) Tue-Sun 11.30-14, 17.30-22 h, closed Mon
Ostendstraße 97 ✉ 90482 ☎ 54 31 56

SHOWS
■ **Paradies** (B CC glm MA S TV) Shows 20.15, Fri Sat 20, 23 h, closed Mon
Bogenstraße 26 ✉ 90459 (U-Aufseßplatz)
☎ 44 39 91
Plushy ambience. Good shows./Plüschiges Ambiente. Gute Shows. Reservation from 18.30 h.

SEX SHOPS/BLUE MOVIES
■ **Beate Uhse Sexshop** (g) Mon-Fri 9.30-20, Sat 9-16 h
Königstraße 69 ✉ 90402 ☎ 241 89 15
■ **New Man im WOS** (CC DR G MA VS) 10-24, Sun 12-24 h
Luitpoldstraße 11 ✉ 90402 ☎ 20 34 43
■ **Sex Intim Center** Mon-Fri 9-20, Sat -16 h
Hallplatz 21 ✉ 90402 ☎ 205 95 89
Large selection of ladies shoes up to size 46.

SAUNAS/BATHS
■ **Club 67** (b DR G MA p SA SOL VS WO) Mon-Thu 14-24, Fri 14-Sun 24 h
Pirckheimerstraße 67 ✉ 90408 (North of the city, Tram 9, Bus 46/47-Maxfeldstraße, entrance in the court yard) ☎ 35 23 46
Sauna where all nationalities and age groups are welcome. Intimate atmosphere.

Germany | Nürnberg

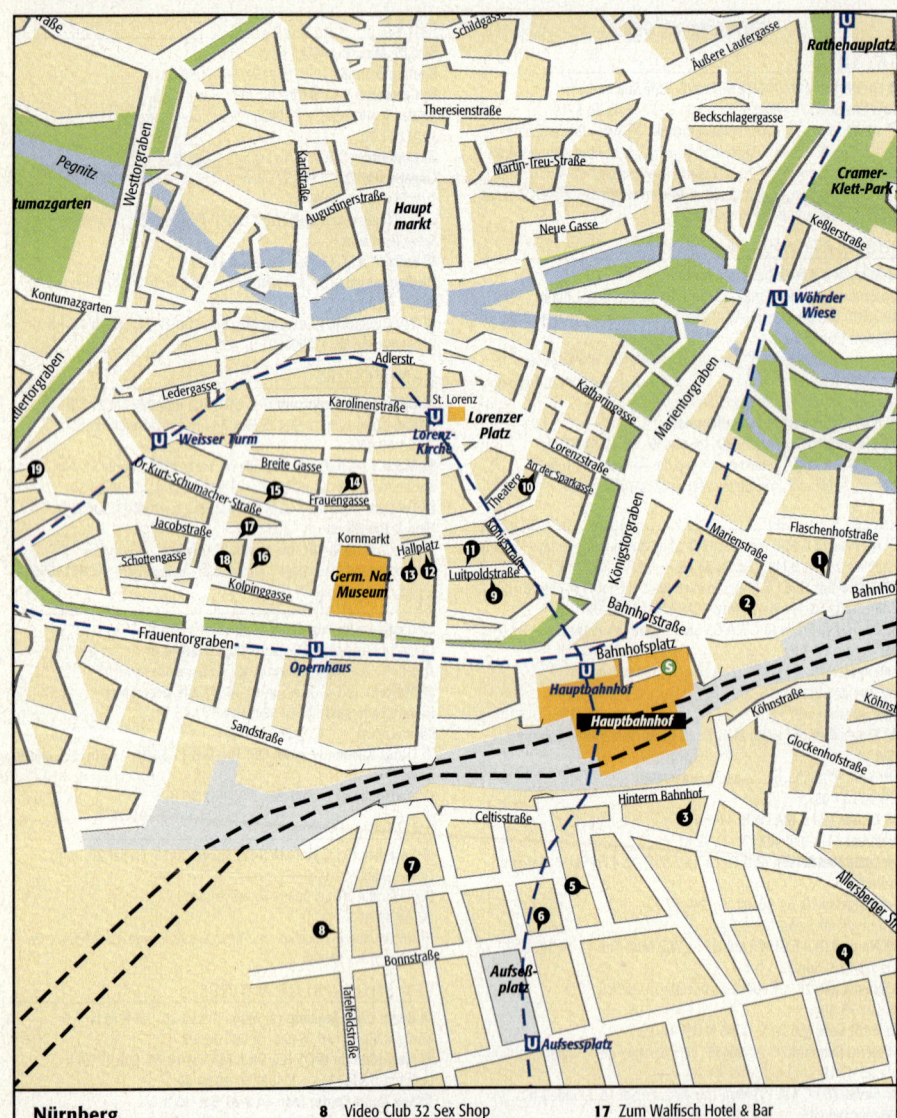

Nürnberg

1. Na Und Bar
2. Nürnberger AIDS-Hilfe Gay Info
3. Petit Café Bar
4. Cafè Max
5. Chiringay Sauna
6. Savoy Bar
7. Paradise Show
8. Video Club 32 Sex Shop
9. New Man im WOS Sex Shop
10. Cartoon Café-Bistro
11. Toy Bar
12. Alt Prag Bar
13. La Bas Bar
14. Little Hendersen Bar
15. King's Pub
16. Zum Entenstall Bar
17. Zum Walfisch Hotel & Bar
18. Vicking Club & Barbel Bar
19. V8 Bar

532 SPARTACUS 2001/2002

Nürnberg ▶ Oberhausen Germany

complete offer see page Germany/Berlin

NUREMBERG

overnight accomodation service - from DM 40 -
· *about 750 beds · more than 28 cities* ·

bed & enjoy breakfast

central booking office Berlin ☏ **+49-30-236 236 10** 4:30-9:00 pm local time
Fax +49-30-23623619 · info@ebab.de · www.ebab.de

BOOK SHOPS
■ **Buchhaus Campe** (glm) Mon-Fri 9-20, Sat 9-16 h
Karolinenstraße 13 ✉ 90402 ☏ 992 08 25

LEATHER & FETISH SHOPS
■ **Sin-A-Matic** (CC GLM LJ) Mon-Fri 12-20, Sat 10-16 h
Ludwigsplatz 1a ✉ 90403 (U-Weißer Turm) ☏ 230 59 86
Professional piercing studio,organiser of the party "Fetish-Revolution".

PRIVATE ACCOMMODATION
■ **Enjoy Bed and Breakfast** (BF G H MA) 16.30-21 h
Nollendorfplatz 5, 10777 Berlin (U-Nollendorfplatz)
☏ (030) 236 236 10 📠 (030) 236 236 19 📧 info@ebab.com
📧 ebab.de
Accommodation sharing agency. All with shower and BF. 40-45 DM p.p

FETISH GROUPS
■ **Nürnberger Lederclub e.V. (NLC)** (b DR G LJ P) 1st Sat 21 h at NLC-Keller
Schnieglinger Strasse 164 ✉ 90427 (U-Muggenhof) ☏ 326 20 01
📠 31 17 58 📧 nlc@nuernberg.gay-web.de
📧 www.nuernberg.gay-web.de/nlc
Dress code leather, rubber, fetish, uniform. Entrance from 21-23 h.
■ **Pegnitzbären Nürnberg**
c/o Dirk Billmann, Am Ruhstein 24, 91054 Buckenhof ☏ 572 64
📠 572 64 📧 Peter.Thung@t-online.de
Group of heavy and hairy men and their fans. Meetings at "Cafe Cartoon" every 3rd Fri 19 h.

HEALTH GROUPS
■ **AIDS-Beratung im Gesundheitsamt** Tue 8-11, 13.30-15.30, Thu 9-11, 13.30-17.30 h
Burgstraße 4 ✉ 90403 (Bus 36-Rathaus) ☏ 231 27 67
📠 231 38 47
Counselling and free and anonymous HIV testing/Beratung sowie kostenloser und anonymer HIV-Test.
■ **AIDS-Hilfe Nürnberg-Erlangen-Fürth e.V.** Mon 15-18, Tue Wed Thu 10-15, Fri -13 h
Bahnhofstraße 13-15 ✉ 90402 (U-Hauptbahnhof) ☏ 230 90 35
(Office) ☏ 194 11 (counselling) 📠 230 903 45
📧 info@aidshilfe-nuernberg.de 📧 www.aidshilfe-nuernberg.de
Counselling, prevention, self-help and community activism. Also café Lichtblick 1st&3rd Sun 14-18 h.
■ **Ambulante Hilfe der AIDS-Hilfe Nürnberg,Erlangen,Fürth e.V.**
Bahnhofstraße 13/15 ✉ 90402 ☏ 23 09 330 📠 230 90 345
📧 ambh@aidshilfe-nuernberg.de
Home-care, support.

HELP WITH PROBLEMS
■ **Rosa Hilfe** Wed 19-21 h
☏ 194 46

SWIMMING
-Birkensee (NU) (along the street from Schwaig to Diepersdorf near/nahe Autobahnkreuz Nürnberg an der Straße von Schwaig nach Diepersdorf)
-Freizeitbad "Palm Beach" (NU)

CRUISING
-Stadtpark/municipal park (nur im Sommer/summer only)
-P Celtisstraße (ayor) (Near/Nähe Hauptbahnhof. Busy/Gut besucht)
-Hauptbahnhof/main railway station (ayor R)
-U-Plärrer
-Hallertor (Brücke)
-U-Frankenstraße

Oberhausen ☏ 0208

GAY INFO
■ **Blitz at six, das schwule Kulturmagazin** Tue 18-19 h (on FM 92,9 MHz or FM 104,0 MHz)

BARS
■ **Maik's** (d g MG) Tue-Thu 16-2, Fri-Sat 16-1, Sun 13-19 h, Mon closed
Stöckmannstraße 36 ✉ 46045 (near station) ☏ 29 09 19
■ **Montparnasse** (B G MA) 20-1, 4-12 h
Helmholtzstraße 7 ✉ 46045 ☏ 20 43 02

SAUNAS/BATHS
■ **Condor** (AC B BF CC DR f G MA msg s SA SB SOL VS WH) 12-23, Fri Sat -6 h
Concordiastraße 32 (Bero-Center) ✉ 46049 *(5 min from railway station, at BERO-Zentrum, right hand side of Eingang Nord 1)*
☏ 80 44 25
Big sauna on 1000 m² frequented by a mixed crowd.

GENERAL GROUPS
■ **ISIT** (YG) Meeting Tue 17-22, Sun 15.30-22 h
John-Lennon-Platz 1 ✉ 46045 ☏ 29 02 09 📠 20 35 84
📧 isit@gmx.net 📧 www.isit.nrw.de

HEALTH GROUPS
■ **AIDS-Hilfe Oberhausen e.V.** Office: Mon-Thu 10-16, Fri 10-14 h
Langemarktstraße 12, ✉ 46045 ☏ 80 65 18 📠 85 14 49
📧 aidshilfe.ob@cityweb.de 📧 oberhausen.aidshilfe.de

Germany Oberhausen ▸ Oldenburg

CRUISING
- Hauptbahnhof/main railway station
- Bero-Zentrum
- Grillopark (Nähe Hauptbahnhof/near main railway station & Schwartzstraße)

Oberstdorf

CRUISING
- Kurpark (near facility and Konzerthaus)

Oberursel

CRUISING
- Near/nahe Stadthalle

Offenbach ☎ 069

BARS
■ **Würtembergische Weinstube** (b F g OS) 18-1h, Fri & Sat -3 h
Taunusstrasse 19 ✉ 63067 ☎ 88 95 35

DANCECLUBS
■ **Club X** (B D glm) Fri 23- ? h
Bierberer Strasse 267 - 269 ✉ 63071

BOOK SHOPS
■ **BAM - Buchladen Am Markt** (glm) 9-19, Sat -15 h
Wilhelmsplatz 12 ✉ 63065 ☎ 88 33 33

HEALTH GROUPS
■ **AIDS-Hilfe Offenbach e.V.** Mon Thu 10-12.30, 13.30-16, Tue 16-20 h, appointments upon request
Frankfurter Straße 48 ✉ 63065 ☎ 88 36 88
🖷 88 10 43
📧 ahilfe2000@aol.com

CRUISING
- Businpark
- Ⓟ A661 Exit before Taunusring

Offenburg ☎ 0781

BARS
■ **Tabu** (AC B D f Glm MA) 20-1, Fri-Sat -4 h, closed Tue
Hauptstraße 102 ✉ 77652 ☎ 742 43

SEX SHOPS/BLUE MOVIES
■ **Erotic-Kino-Center** (AC CC g MA TV VS) Mon-Fri 9.30-24, Sat 9.30-16, Sun and public holidays 16-24 h
Unionrampe 6 ✉ 77652 ☎ 235 53

HEALTH GROUPS
■ **AIDS-Hilfe Offenburg e.V.** (glm) Mon & Tue 10-13, Wed 16-18, Thu 17-20 h
Malergasse 1 ✉ 77652 (Ecke/corner Steinstraße)
☎ 194 11 (helpline) ✉ 0781/771 89 🖷 240 63

SWIMMING
- Burgerwaldsee (g MA NU WE) (☞ Schutterwald)
- Nonnenweirer Baggersee (zwischen Lahr und Rhein)

CRUISING
- Burgerwald (zwischen See und Autobahnparkplatz)

Oldenburg ☎ 0441

GAY INFO
■ **Lesben- und Schwulenzentrum Oldenburg Na Und e.V.** (GML) Wed 19-22 h
Ziegelhofstraße 83 ✉ 26121 ☎ 777 59 23 ☎ 777 59 90 (bar)
🖷 764 78
Also editor of the bimonthly regional magazine "Rosige Zeiten" for gays and lesbians. Editorial meeting every 2nd & 4th Wed 18.30h.

BARS
■ **Hempels Kneipencafé** (A B GLM MA) Mon (G) 20.30-24, Thu (L) 20-23, Fri (GLM) 21-24 h at Lesben- und Schwulenzentrum
Ziegelhofstraße 83 ✉ 26121 ☎ 777 59 90
■ **Schwarzer Bär** (AC B CD DR G lj MA p WE) Bar: Tue-Thu 21-2, Disco: Fri Sat -5, LJ-Party (Dresscode) 1st & 3rd Mon 21 h
Donnerschweer Straße 50 ✉ 26123 (100m from Hauptbahnhof northern exit) ☎ 885 07 37
■ **Zwitscherstübchen** (B G MA OS YG) 21-2, Fri Sat -5, Sun 16-2 h
Bahnhofsplatz 5 ✉ 26122 ☎ 177 53

DANCECLUBS
■ **Club Pulverfaß** (AC B CC D E g MA p SNU) Fri Sat 23-5 h
Kaiserstraße 24 ✉ 26121 ☎ 126 01
■ **Männerfabrik** (D DR G LJ MA) 3rd Sat 22-4/? h
c/o Kulturzentrum Alhambra, Hermannstraße 83 ✉ 26135
☎ 146 72
■ **Rosa Disco** (B D GLM MA) last Sat 22-5 h
Hermannstraße 83 ✉ 26135 (Bus-Nordstraße, in Kulturzentrum)
☎ 777 59 23

RESTAURANTS
■ **Elsässer Restaurant** (AC E glm MA OS) Tue-Sat 18/?, Sun and holidays 12-? h
Edewechter Landstraße 90 ✉ 26131 ☎ 50 24 17
Mon for groups, please request.
■ **Gaststätte Steffmann** (CC F g h MA OS) 11-? h
Kurwickstraße 23-24 ✉ 26122 (pedestrian zone at Waffenplatz)
☎ 260 64

SEX SHOPS/BLUE MOVIES
■ **Intimchen** (g VS) 9-24 h, closed Sun
Kaiserstraße 9-11 ✉ 26122 ☎ 272 91

BOOK SHOPS
■ **Carl von Ossietzky Buchhandlung** (g) Mon-Wed 9.30-19, Thu Fri -20, Sat -16 h
Markt 24 ✉ 26122 ☎ 139 49
General bookstore with gay section.

PRIVATE ACCOMMODATION
■ **Enjoy Bed and Breakfast** (BF G H MA) 16.30-21 h
Nollendorfplatz 5, 10777 Berlin (U-Nollendorfplatz) ☎ (030) 236 236 10 🖷 (030) 236 236 19 📧 info@ebab.com 🖥 ebab.de
Accommodation sharing agency. All with shower and BF. 40-45 DM p.p.

GENERAL GROUPS
■ **Rosa Tanzkurs**
c/o Angela Trautwein, Billungerweg 23 ✉ 26131
☎ 0781/560 01 60
Dance group.

FETISH GROUPS
■ **SMart**
Postfach 1925 ✉ 26009

Oldenburg ▸ Passau Germany

complete offer see page Germany/Berlin

OLDENBURG
overnight accomodation service
· about 750 beds · more than 28 cities ·

bed & enjoy breakfast

central booking office Berlin ☏ **+49-30-23623610** 4:30-9:00 pm local time
Fax +49-30-23623619 · info@ebab.de · www.ebab.de

HEALTH GROUPS
■ **Oldenburgische AIDS-Hilfe e.V.** Mon-Fri 9-12, Mon 14-16, Wed 14-18, Thu 17 h
Bahnhofstraße 23 ✉ 26122 ☏ 145 00 🖨 142 22

CRUISING
-Park hinter den Theater/behind the theater
-Cäcilienpark
-Near/Nähe Theater

Olpe ☏ 02761
GENERAL GROUPS
■ **Schwulen-Selbsthilfegruppe**
Postfach 15 49 ✉ 57445

HEALTH GROUPS
■ **AIDS-Hilfe Kreis Olpe e.V.** Mon 19-21 h
Kampstraße 26 ✉ 57462

Oranienburg
SWIMMING
-Bergwitzsee (6 km from Oranienburg near the Velten autobahn exit. Or take train to Borgsdorf, then 2,5 km by foot. The gay section and cruising area are at the peninsula on the smaller lake side, popular)

Osnabrück ☏ 0541
BARS
■ **K-G** (B d G MA) Mon Wed Thu Sun 20-2, Fri Sat -3 h, closed Tue
Johannisstraße 46/47 ✉ 49074 ☏ 205 17 01
■ **Theo. Bei** (B G MA OS) 20-? h, closed Mon
Pottgraben 27 ✉ 49074 ☏ 20 15 70

DANCECLUBS
■ **New Bivalent** (AC b D f G lj MA p r s TV WE) Sun-Thu 21-3, Fri Sat -5 h
Johannisstraße 131 ✉ 49074 ☏ 982 76 80
■ **Vex** (B D GLM MA) Thu-Mon 21-? h
Bohmter Straße 69 ✉ 17333

SEX SHOPS/BLUE MOVIES
■ **Men's Life** (AC DR G lj MA VS) Mon-Thu 11-23, Fri Sat -24, Sun 14-23 h
Möserstraße 39 ✉ 49074 *(100 m from railway station)*
☏ 2020 846

GENERAL GROUPS
■ **Schwule Coming Out Gruppe** Tue 20.30 h
c/o Lagerhalle, Rolandsmauer/Heger Tor ✉ 49074 ☏ 227 22

HEALTH GROUPS
■ **AIDS-Hilfe Osnabrück e.V.** Mon-Wed 10-14, Tue 14-19 h
Möser Straße 44 ✉ 49074 *(near station)* ☏ 80 10 24 🖨 80 47 88
📧 mail@aidshilfe-osnabrueck.de
🌐 www.aidshilfe-osnabrueck.de
Gay counselling by appointment

CRUISING
-Hauptbahnhof (r)
-Katharinenkirche
-Reifeisenpark (ayor) (Opposite Hauptbahnhof & ⓟ across the street. Popular)
-Gertrudenberg/Bürgerpark (near Hasetorbahnhof around Rosengarten. Popular weekend nights)

Paderborn ☏ 05251
LEATHER & FETISH SHOPS
■ **Master & Servant** (glm LJ MA) Mon-Fri 13-19, Sat 14-18 h
Paderwall 1 ✉ 33102 *(next to hotel Ibis)* ☏ 266 11
Piercing and fetish studio.

HEALTH GROUPS
■ **AIDS-Hilfe Paderborn e.V.** Mon-Thu 10-16, Fri 10-13 h
Friedrichstraße 51 ✉ 33041 ☏ 280293
☏ 0700-44 533 525 (helpline)
Café Jedermann Thu 20-23 h. Call Tel 28 03 19 for further information about interesting locations & the ai-homosexualiy group. The coming-out group meets every Thu 18-20h at the ESG, Am Laugrund 3. Schwip-Schwul meets Thu 20-23 h, radio "Schrillkörper" every 2nd Tue 20h. Ask for details.

Passau ☏ 0851
BARS
■ **Zwickelstube** (B G MA) 20-3 h
Marktgasse 7 ✉ 94032 *(pedestrian zone)* ☏ 374 19

SEX SHOPS/BLUE MOVIES
■ **Beate Uhse** (g) Mon-Fri 10-20, Sat -16 h
Bahnhofstraße 2 ✉ 94032 ☏ 340 70

Germany Passau ▶ Recklinghausen

GENERAL GROUPS
■ **HIP e.V.** Mon & Fri 20-?, Sat 18-21 h
Milchgasse 15 ✉ 94202 ☎ 325 41 🖳 gay_passau@eurogay.net
🖳 www.eurogay.net/mitglieder/gay_passau
Homosexuellen Interessengemeinschaft Passau
-PLC Passauer Leder Club 2nd Sat 20 h
-Youth group 1st & 3rd Sat 20 h

HEALTH GROUPS
■ **AIDS-Beratungsstelle Niederbayern** Mon-Fri 9-13, Thu also 14-19 h
Bahnhofstraße 16b ✉ 94032 ☎ 710 65 🖨 710 66
🖳 aids-passau@t-online.de 🖳 www.aidsberatung-niederbayern.de

HELP WITH PROBLEMS
■ **Rosa Telefon** Fri 20-22 h
☎ 325 41

SWIMMING
-Innstufe between Neuhaus and Mittich

CRUISING
-Schanzelbrücke (below daytime/darunter tagsüber)
-Rathaus
-Nibelungenhalle (rear side)
-Innpromenade (between/zwischen Innsteg & Krankenhaus evenings/abends)

Pforzheim ☎ 07231

BARS
■ **Shadow** (B glm) Tue, Wed & Sat 19-5 h
Westliche 3 ✉ 75172 *(in pedestrian zone)* ☎ 155569

SEX SHOPS/BLUE MOVIES
■ **Multivideoshow & Sexshop** (g VS) Mon-Sat 9-24, Sun 16-24 h
Am Waisenhausplatz 26 ✉ 75172 ☎ 35 67 39
■ **Sex-Shop Maxima** (g VS) 9-24 h
Berliner Straße 12 ✉ 75172 ☎ 10 25 62

GENERAL GROUPS
■ **Schwule Initiative Pforzheim**
Pfälzer Straße 20 ✉ 75177 ☎ 343 84
Call Dominik (18-23 h) for information.

CRUISING
-Hauptbahnhof/main railway station (Bereich Gleis 1/area at platform 1)
-Stadthalle/municipal hall & Theater (Enzufer)
-Park (Landesgartenschaugelände)
-Schloßpark (across/gegenüber Hauptbahnhof)
-Marktplatz/Rathaus
-Turnplatz
-Meßplatz
-Hauptbahnhof/Main train station

Plauen ☎ 03741

BARS
■ **Go-In**
Bergstraße 36 ✉ 08523 ☎ 228 211

SEX SHOPS/BLUE MOVIES
■ **Erotik-Shop** (g) Mon-Fri 9-12.30 13.30-18, Sat 9-12, closed Sun
Bergstraße 30 ✉ 08523

SAUNAS/BATHS
■ **Men's Only** Wed-Sun 18-ßh, Fri/Sat all night sauna
Am Unterer Bahnhof 2 ✉ 08523 ☎ 300 840

Potsdam ☎ 0331

BARS
■ **La Leander** (! A AC B BF F GLM MG OS) 12-2:30 h
Kurfürstenstraße / Bekerstraße ✉ 14467 *(S- Nauener Tor)*
☎ 270 65 78
A wonderful café/bar with home made cakes and great service from the devil himself.

GENERAL GROUPS
■ **Homosexuellen Integrationsprojekt Potsdam e.V.-HIP** Tue 18-19, Thu 17-24, Fri 18-21 h
Berliner Straße 49, Haus der Jugend ✉ 14480 ☎ 29 20 65
🖨 29 20 65
■ **Landesverband Brandenburg Lesben und Schwule BLuS e.V.**
Postfach 60 03 31 ✉ 14403 ☎ 97 08 93 🖨 97 08 93

HEALTH GROUPS
■ **AIDS-Hilfe Potsdam e.V.** Mon, Wed 14-20 h
Berliner Straße 49 ✉ 14467 ☎ 280 10 60 ☎ 194 11 (helpline)
🖨 280 10 70 🖳 info@potsdam.aidshilfe.de
🖳 potsdam.aidshilfe.de

SWIMMING
-Baggersee (Potsdam-Am Stern. Nuthestraße, exit "Am Stern". The lake is located at the end of the street Fichtenallee. Cruising near the railway line.)

CRUISING
-Säulengang an der/colonnade at the Friedenskirche (Park Sanssouci)
-Bassinplatz (bei den Häusern/near the houses)

Ravensburg ☎ 0751

DANCECLUBS
■ **Doala** (GLM) Wed 21-4 h
Pfaumenstiel 31 ✉ 88212

GENERAL GROUPS
■ **SSOS** (GLM MA) Mon 20.30 h in Bärengarten
Postfach 20 03 ✉ 88190 ☎ 168 96 ☎ 490 42
🖳 www.ravensburg.gay-web.de
Disco Wed 21 h (in "Douala, Schubertstr.).Youth group meets Wed 19 (at Aidshilfe,Frauenstr.1)

HEALTH GROUPS
■ **Aids-Hilfe Ravensburg e.V.** Tue-Thu 10-14, Wed 16-18 h
Frauenstraße 1 ✉ 88212 ☎ 194 11 ☎ 35 40 72 🖨 35 40 77
🖳 AIDS-Hilfe.Ravensburg@web.de

SWIMMING
-Rössler Weiher (Weingarten near Ravensburg)

Recklinghausen ☎ 02361

BARS
■ **Chateau** (B f Glm MA) Wed-Sun 18-? h, closed Mon & Tue.
Herner Straße 8a ✉ 45657 ☎ 90 06 99

Recklinghausen ▸ Rostock | **Germany**

SEX SHOPS/BLUE MOVIES
■ **Erotima Videothek** (g VS) Mon-Sat 9-22, Sun 14-22 h
Dortmunder Straße 1-3   ✉ 45665   ☎ 456 01
■ **MEO-Team** (CC G P) Mon-Sat 13-16 h
Henrichenburger Strasse 116   ✉ 45665   ☎ 986 51-0
Bondage and SM toys & fetish products

CRUISING
-Am Neumarkt (Recklinghausen Süd), Toiletten am Marktplatz/toilets at Marktplatz (Bus 205 vom HBF bis Neumarkt/take bus 205 from main railway station to Neumarkt)
-Rathauspark (OG)
-Erlbruckpark (at town hall/am Rathaus)

Regensburg ☏ 0941

BARS
■ **Jeans** (AC B GLM lj MA s) 20-1, Fri Sat -3 h
Glockengasse 1   ✉ 93047   ☎ 517 82
■ **Na Und** (AC B f GLM MA S WE) Mon-Thu 20-2, Fri Sat and public holidays -3 h
Jakobstraße 7   ✉ 93047   *(Jakobstor)*   ☎ 56 57 56
■ **Pegasus** (B DR G MA p VS) 21-4 h
Ladehofstraße 4   ✉ 93047   *(near main railway station/nahe Hauptbahnhof)*   ☎ 467 06 29

CAFES
■ **Allegro** (b BF f glm MA) 10-1, Fri Sat -2 h
Weiße-Lamm-Gasse 1   ✉ 93047   ☎ 527 14

DANCECLUBS
■ **Sudhaus** (B D Glm MA) Thu 23-3 h
Untere Bachgasse 8   ✉ 93047   ☎ 519 33

SEX SHOPS/BLUE MOVIES
■ **Videoworld** (g VS) 9-23 h, closed Sun
Spiegelgasse 5   ✉ 93047   ☎ 541 29

GENERAL GROUPS
■ **RESI e.V.-Regensburger Schwulen- & Lesben-Initiative** (b G MA S VS) Wed Fri Sat 20-1 h
Blaue-Lilien-Gasse 1   ✉ 93047   *(near old townhall)*   ☎ 514 41
🖷 588 39   ✉ info@resi-online.de   🖥 www.resi-online.de

HEALTH GROUPS
■ **AIDS-Hilfe Regensburg e.V.** Counselling Mon & Wed 18-20 h
Wollwirkergasse 25   ✉ 93047   ☎ 79 12 66   🖷 795 77 67
✉ vorstand.ahr@gmx.de   🖥 www.gay-in-regensburg.de/aidshilfe
☎ Counselling 194 11

SWIMMING
-Almer Weiher (bei/near Geisling. B8 Richtung/direction Straubing.)

CRUISING
-Der Wackel (Park at Albertstraße. Near Main railway station. 22-? h/ Park entlang der Albertstraße. Nähe Hauptbahnhof. 22-? h)
-🅿 Neue Bahnhofsstraße/Margaretenstraße
-Vor der Grieb (gegenüber/opposite "Sudhaus", -18 h)
-Main railway station/Hauptbahnhof (r)
-City park/Stadtpark (Prüfeningerstraße, -18 h)
-University/Universität (at/beim Audimax, entrance/Eingang K)
-Vor der Grieb (gegenüber/opposite "Sudhaus", -18 h)
-Main railway station/Hauptbahnhof (r)
-City park/Stadtpark (Prüfeningerstraße, -18 h)
-University/Universität (at/beim Audimax, entrance/Eingang K)

Rendsburg ☏ 04331

SEX SHOPS/BLUE MOVIES
■ **Intim-Boutique** (g)
Oberreiderstraße 16   ✉ 24768   *(Near/Nähe Paradeplatz)*
Gegenüber/opposite Kreiskrankenhaus.

Rheine ☏ 05971

HEALTH GROUPS
■ **AIDS-Hilfe Kreis Steinfurt e.V.** Mon-Fri 9-14 h
Thiemauer 42   ✉ 48431   ☎ 540 23   ☎ 194 11 (helpline)   🖷 540 04
HIV/Aids counselling, prevention, youth and drug counselling.

Rosenheim ☏ 08031

BARS
■ **Jägerstüberl** (b d f GLM lj MA s) 11-2,
Sun and public holidays 18-2h
Nicolaistraße 13   ✉ 83022   *(in town centre)*   ☎ 346 65
■ **Theaterschenke** (B f g) 20-1 h, closed Mon
c/o Theater am Markt, Ludwigplatz 14   ✉ 83022   ☎ 379 73

CRUISING
-Park zwischen Friedhof und Kapuzinerkloster/Park between cemetery and Kapuzinerkloster
-Hauptbahnhof/main railway station

Rostock ☏ 0381

BARS
■ **Aalglatt** (f G MA) Mon 20-1, Tue-Thu 14-1, Fri-Sun 21-1 h
Kistenmacherstraße 17   ✉ 18055   *(Tram-Steintor)*   ☎ 493 42 14
■ **Gerd's Bierbar** (A AC B CC F glm MA OS p) Mon-Thu 11-23, Fri-Sat -2 h, closed Sun
Schnickmannstraße 7   ✉ 18055   *(in Café/Restaurant "Windspiel")*
☎ 493 49 61

CAFES
■ **Sebastian** (b F glm MA OS) 18-2 h
Leonhardstr. 20   ✉ 18057   *(in the Regenbogenhaus)*   ☎ 45 91 407

RESTAURANTS
■ **Kaminstube** (B F g MA OS) Tue-Sat 18-24 h
Am Burgwall 17   ✉ 18055   *(city centre)*   ☎ 313 37
German cuisine.

BOOK SHOPS
■ **Die andere Buchhandlung** (g) 9-18.30, Sat 9-13 h, closed Sun
Ulmenmarkt 1   ✉ 18057   ☎ 492 05 13

HEALTH GROUPS
■ **AIDS-Hilfe im Rat & Tat e.V.** Mon 10-13 15-17, Tue 14-18, Thu 14-19 h
Leonhardstraße 20   ✉ 18057   *(at Regenbogenhaus)*   ☎ 45 31 56
☎ 194 11 (helpline)   🖷 45 31 61   ✉ info@rostock.aidshilfe.de
🖥 rostock.aidshilfe.de

SWIMMING
-Markgrafenheide (! NU) (from Warnemünde take the car ferry to Hohe Düne, from there go 5 km to Markgrafenheide, there go to the camp ground 🅿. Go further by foot ca. 20 minutes, on the beach go 20 min to the east.)

Germany — Rostock ▶ Saarbrücken

-Warnemünde (10 minutes west of tower 6 of the DLRG)
-Elmenhorst (road to the beach, P there, 10 minutes to the west, there's a rocky beach)

CRUISING
-University (in Main building, ground floor/Hauptgebäude, EG; popular)
-Wall (MA) (zwischen/between Kröpeliner Tor & Rosengarten)

Rottenbuch ☎ 08867

HOTELS
■ **Hotel Moosbeck-Alm** (B BF E F glm H MA msg NU OS PI SOL WE WO) 1st Feb-15th Nov +15th Dec-10th Jan
Moos 78 ✉ 82401 *(between Kempten and Munich;1,5 km from Rottenbuch)* ☎ 912 00 📠 91 20 20
📧 hotel.moosbeck-alm.de@t-online.de 🌐 www.moosbeck-alm.de
König-Ludwig-Suite (120m² bed-and livingroom, 2 bathrooms with jacuzzi), tuscany winter garden.Tennis court

Rottweil ☎ 07420

RESTAURANTS
■ **Krone. Die** (BF CC F H OS) Tue-Sat 18-24, Sun 11.30-14 h
Hauptstraße 38 ✉ 78652 📠 07420/5 29
Restaurant and guest-house.

SEX SHOPS/BLUE MOVIES
■ **Esctasy** (g VS) 10-19.30, Sat -13 h, closed Sun
Friedrichsplatz 9 ✉ 78628 ☎ 0741/415 86
■ **Intim-Boutique** (g) 9-12.30/14-18.30, Thu -20, Sat 9-13 h, closed Sun
Königstraße 88 ✉ 78628 ☎ 0741/127 14

CRUISING
- On highway A81 /E41 car park Eschachtal between Rottweil and Villingen-Schwenningen on both sides of the highway.

Rüsselsheim ☎ 06142

CRUISING
-Rail station/Bahnhof
-Karstadt (1st floor)

Saarbrücken ☎ 0681

BARS
■ **Banana Club** (B GLM) 20-5 h
Mainzerstraße 54 ✉ 66211
■ **Black Hole** (B DR f G lj MA p R VS) Mon, Wed, Thu Sun 21-3, Fri,Sat 22-5 h
Schillerplatz 16 ✉ 66111 *(Entrance/Eingang Bleichstraße 4)*
☎ 39 88 57
Darkroom with sling and bathtube. Leather toys etc on sale too
■ **Boots** (B d DR G LJ MA p VS) Mon, Wed, Thu Sun 21-3, Fri Sat -5, Sun -2 h, closed Tue
Mainzer Straße 153 ✉ 66121 ☎ 614 95
■ **Discothek XL** (AC CC D DRf GLM lj MG s SNU WE) 22-5 h
Kohlwaagstraße 1 ✉ 66111 ☎ 317 89
■ **History Bistro** (B F glm) 15-1h, closed Mon.
Obertorstraße 10 ☎ 390 82 82
■ **Hufeisen** (AC GLM MA p TV) closed Tue
Mainzer Straße 27 ✉ 66111

■ **Madame** (B f GLM MA p) Tue-Thu 21-3, Fri & Sat 21-4, Sun 21-2 h
Mainzer Straße 4 ✉ 66111 ☎ 329 63
■ **Mademoiselle** (AC B f G MA s) 21-4 h
Mainzer Str. 8 ✉ 66111 ☎ 390 44 45
■ **Perspektive 1** (A B GLM MA S) Sun-Wed 16.30-1 Thu-Sat -? h
Rotenbergstraße 10 ✉ 66111 *(near S-Landwehrplatz)*
☎ 37 99 313
■ **Teddy Treff** (B G MA p r) 20-3, Fri Sat -5 h
Mainzer Straße 57 ✉ 66121 ☎ 656 08
■ **Tenne** (B F glm MA) Mon-Fri 10.30-24/? h, Sat Sun closed
Eisenbahnstraße 60-62 ✉ 66117 ☎ 563 43

DANCECLUBS
■ **Big Ben** (AC D f GLM MA p s SA STV TV WE) 19-? h, Mon closed
Försterstraße 17 ✉ 66111 *(near/nahe Rathaus)* ☎ 358 55
■ **Cellar. The** (B DR G LJ MA s VS) Fri-Sun 23-5 h
Reichsstraße 10 ✉ 66111 *(Main station/Saargalerie)* ☎ 390 88 22
■ **Warme Nächte** (! AC B D GLM lj MA s TV) 2nd Sat, 22-5 h
c/o Garage, Bleichstraße 11-19 ✉ 66111 ☎ 39 79 91

SEX SHOPS/BLUE MOVIES
■ **Beate Uhse Sexshop** (g VS) Cinema Mon-Thu 9-24, Fri Sat -1, Sun 14-23 h
Bahnhofstraße 74 ✉ 66111 ☎ 354 01
■ **City Live** (CC g MA VS) cinema 10-24, Sun 14-24, Fri-Sat -1; Shop Mon-Fri 10-20, Sat -16 h
Viktoriastraße 26a ✉ 66111 ☎ 390 81 21
■ **Roxy Kino 4** (g VS) 10-24, Sun 14-24 h
Bahnhofstraße 109 ✉ 66111 ☎ 325 44
■ **Showcenter** (g) 11-0.30 h
Kaiserstraße 46 ✉ 66111 ☎ 39 85 23
■ **Video Center** (CC g MA) Mon-Fri 9-19.30, Sat -14, 1st Sat -16 h
Mainzer Straße 11 ✉ 66111 ☎ 39 70 77
■ **Video Dream World** (g) Mon-Thu 9-24, Fri Sat -1, Sun 11-24 h
Bahnhofstraße 17 ✉ 66111 ☎ 390 48 80

BOOK SHOPS
■ **KulTour Buchhandlung** (CC glm) Mon-Wed 9-19, Thu Fri -20, Sat -16 h
Berliner Promenade 12 ✉ 66111 ☎ 365 59
One of the largest gay-lesbian selection in Saarland and Rheinland-Pfalz.

GENERAL GROUPS
■ **Bündnis 90/Die Grünen-LAG Schwulenpolitik**
c/o Patrick G.W. Müller, Parkstraße 1 ✉ 66111 ☎ 39 97 00
■ **Lesben- und Schwulenverband Saar e.V. (LSVD Saar)** Mon-Thu 10-12 h & 13-15 h, Fri 10-12 + 19-21 h
Blumenstrasse 24 ✉ 66028 ☎ 39 88 33 📠 39 88 66
📧 LSVDSaar@aol.com. 🌐 www.LSVD.de/saar

FETISH GROUPS
■ **Leder Club Saar (LC-Saar)** Infos at Boots 21-? h; Meeting last Sun at Boots 20 h
c/o Wachenhausen, Uhlandstraße 2 ✉ 66121 ☎ 68 45 66
📧 rainer.altmeyer@t-online.de
Member of ECMC.

HEALTH GROUPS
■ **AIDS-Hilfe Saar e. V.** Mon Tue Thu 9-12, 14-17, Wed 9-12, 14-20, Fri 9-12 h
Nauwieser Straße 19 ✉ 66111 ☎ 194 11 (helpline) ☎ 311 12
📠 342 52 📧 info@saarbruecken.aidshilfe.de
🌐 saarbruecken.aidshilfe.de
Café Wed 18 h. Saar-Rouge group meets Fri at 19 h.

Saarbrücken ▶ Siegen **Germany**

HELP WITH PROBLEMS
■ **Schwules Überfalltelefon** Mon-Thu 10-12, 13-15, Fri 10-12, 19-21 h
☎ 192 28 ✉ SUT19228@aol.com
Gay bashing helpline.

Saarlouis ☎ 06831
SEX SHOPS/BLUE MOVIES
■ **Video Dream World** (g) Mon-Sat 9.30-23.30, Sun 14-23 h
Zeughausstraße 12 ✉ 66740 ☎ 401 52

Sandförde ☎ 039741
RESTAURANTS
■ **Restaurant Krause** (B BF F CC g H MA OS)
Chausseestraße 9 ✉ 17209 *(on the B 109 between Pasewalk and Anklam)* ☎ 807 03
German cuisine. Also guest house. All rooms with TV and shower, shared WC. Rates: double 90, single 50 (bf incl.)

Schöfflengrund ☎ 06445
TRAVEL AND TRANSPORT
■ **Logo! - Projekt und Reisen** Mon-Fri 10-18, Sat 9-13 h
Zum Waldgraben 18 ✉ 35641 ☎ 92 27 77 📠 92 27 78
✉ info@logo-pur.de 🖥 logo-pur.de

Schöllnach ☎ 09903
HOTELS
■ **Mühle. Die** (B d F G MA OS SA SOL)
Englfing 16 ✉ 94508 ☎ 562 📠 26 14
Rooms with shared bath/WC. Rates half board DM 65/person.

Schwabach
CRUISING
-Stadtpark (summer only/nur im Sommer)
-Hauptbahnhof/Main railway station
-Marktplatz (Tiefgarage/underground garage)

Schwäbisch Gmünd ☎ 07171
HEALTH GROUPS
■ **AIDS-Hilfe Schwäbisch Gmünd e.V.** (b LJ MA) Tue Thu Fri 17-18.30
Bocksgasse 23 ✉ 73525 *(Werdich- Passage)* ☎ 19 411
📠 93 23 44 🖥 AH-GD@t-online.de

Schwerin ☎ 0385
BARS
■ **Absolut. Bierpub** Mon-Sat 20-?, Sun -4 h (Breakfast Buffet)
Münzstraße 36 ✉ 19055 ☎ 581 42 99
■ **Saitensprung** (AC B d DR F GLM MA p VS) 20-? h, Mon closed
Von-Thünen-Straße 45 ✉ 19053 ☎ 71 29 67

DANCECLUBS
■ **Restaurant Casino** (B D GLM YG) Sat 21-3 h
Pfaffenstraße 3 ✉ 19053 ☎ 56 10 43

SEX SHOPS/BLUE MOVIES
■ **Love Line** (g) 9-18 h, closed Sat Sun
Großer Moor 17 ✉ 19055
■ **Sex Shop Erotik-Kaufhaus** (g VS) 9-22 h, closed Sun
Goethestraße 62 ✉ 19053

GENERAL GROUPS
■ **Klub Einblick e.V.** (GLM MA) Mon-Fri 17-23 h
Lübecker Straße 48 ✉ 19053 *(near Marienplatz)* ☎ 55 55 60
📠 581 19 26 ✉ klub_einblick@t-online.de
🖥 www.klub-einblick.de
■ **Landesverband der Lesben und Schwulen in Mecklenburg-Vorpommern-Lambda e.V.**
Wismarsche Straße 190 ✉ 19053 ☎ 53 75 54

HEALTH GROUPS
■ **AIDS-Hilfe Westmecklenburg** Tue 14-20, Thu 10-16 h
Wismarsche Straße 190 ✉ 19053 ☎ 56 86 45
Café Mon 19-? h

SWIMMING
-Schweriner See (Zippendorfer Strand/beach)
-Vorbecker See (Bus 6 von/from Hermann-Duncker-Straße nach/to Vorbeck)
-Kaninchenwerder im/in the Schweriner See (NU) (mit der Fähre der "Weißen Flotte" von der Schloßbrücke oder Tippendorf/take the "Weißen Flotte" ferry from Schloßbrücke or Tippendorf.)

CRUISING
-Westuferpromenade Ziegelsee (Dr.-Hans-Wolf-Straße, evenings/abends)

Siegburg ☎ 02241
BARS
■ **La Playa** (B d f GLM MA OS) Tue-Sun 19-? h, closed Mon; winter: Tue-Fri 19-?, Sat-Sun 19-? h, closed Mon
Frankfurter Straße 85b ✉ 53721 ☎ 59 07 92

Siegen ☎ 0271
GAY INFO
■ **Schwulen Begegnungs Zentrum (SBZ) Siegen** (a B d GLM MA s)
Mon Wed Fri Sun 20-?, counselling Wed 10-12, Thu 16-18 h
Marienborner Straße 16a ✉ 57074 ☎ 532 97 ☎ 194 46 (helpline) 📠 238 35 50 ✉ SiseV@gmx.de 🖥 www.schwul-in-siegen.de
2nd Wed gay/lesbian movies, 1st & 3rd Fri YG (16-25 years) 20-? h, sometimes party on Sat (22-?h).Helpline Wed 19.30-21.30 Thu 16-18 h

BARS
■ **Darling** (B CC D f GLM MA p s STV) Tue-Thu 21-4, Fri-Sun -5 h, closed Mon
Geisweider Straße 4 ✉ 57078 ☎ 834 65
■ **Incognito** (B f GLM MA p) 20-1 h, closed Mon & Sun , last Fri Lesbian
Hundgasse 12 ✉ 57072 ☎ 575 23

HEALTH GROUPS
■ **AIDS-Hilfe Siegen-Wittgenstein e.V.** Tue Thu 20-22 h
Sandstraße 12 ✉ 57072 ☎ 222 22

CRUISING
-Park & P at/am Oberen Schloß (popular/beliebt)
-Rathaus/Town Hall

SPARTACUS 2001/2002 | 539

Germany | Sigmaringen ▶ Stuttgart

Sigmaringen ☎ 07571

GENERAL GROUPS
■ **Romeo & Julius**
Postfach 15 04 ☎ 72486 ☎ 32 68 📠 3331
📧 info@alb.gay-web.de 🌐 www.gay.alb.de
Organise social events (cinema, disco etc), counselling, self-help groups, information and public awareness programs.

Singen ☎ 07731

HEALTH GROUPS
■ **AIDS-Hilfe Konstanz Außenstelle Singen** Wed 11-13 h
Mühlenstraße 17 ☎ 78224 ☎ 684 21

Soest ☎ 02921

HEALTH GROUPS
■ **AIDS-Hilfe Soest e.V.** Mon 16-20, Tue Wed 9-12 h
Siechenstraße 9 ☎ 59494 *(Near/Nähe Hallenbad)* ☎ 28 88
📠 28 83

CRUISING
-An der Reitbahn (accross from the new hall/gegenüber der neuen Stadthalle)

Solingen ☎ 0212

BARS
■ **Café Cobra** (B BF d f g OS s YG)
Merscheider Straße 77-79 ☎ 42699 ☎ 33 25 65
■ **Vogelsang** (B F g MA) 18-2 h
Focher Straße 84 ☎ 42719 ☎ 531 21

HEALTH GROUPS
■ **AIDS-Hilfe Solingen e.V.** Mon-Thu 14-18, café last Sun 15 h
Ringstraße 4 ☎ 42719 ☎ 194 11

Sonthofen ☎ 08321

SPORT GROUPS
■ **Gay Summit Club Allgäu (GSC Allgäu)** (G MG WE YG) 18-22 h
c/o Wendelin Martin, Moltkestraße 8 ☎ 87527 📧 GSC@gmx.de
🌐 www.GSC.home.pages.de
Outdoor activities.

Speyer

CRUISING
-Dompark
-Binsfeld (between Speyer and Ludwigshafen near Waldsee)

Stade ☎ 04141

GENERAL GROUPS
■ **Homosexuelle in Stade (H.i.S.)** Every 1st and 3rd Mon 20 h at DRK-Haus, Poststraße 21 (2nd floor)

St.Ingbert ☎ 06894

BARS
■ **Castro** (B d GLM MA s) Mon-Sat 18-1, Sun and public holidays 15-1h
Ensheimer Straße 1a ☎ 66386 *(opposite the station)* ☎ 69 09

Stralsund ☎ 03831

SEX SHOPS/BLUE MOVIES
■ **Erotic Boutique** (CC glm MA VS) Mon-Fri 10-20, Sat -16 h
Mauerstraße 9 ☎ 18439 ☎ 29 08 69

SWIMMING
-Strand nördlich von/beach to the north of "Alte Fähr"

CRUISING
- Frankenteich (near Bahnhof)

Straubing

CRUISING
-WC at railway station (day)
-Park near railway station (nights)

Stuttgart ☎ 0711

GAY INFO
■ **Weissenburg - Schwul/lesbisches Zentrum** (A AC d f lj MA)
Mon-Fri 17-22, Sun 15-22 h, Sat - call for info.
Weißenburgstraße 28a ☎ 70180 *(U-Österreichischer Platz)*
☎ 640 44 92 ☎ 640 44 94 📠 640 44 95

PUBLICATIONS
■ **Rainbow**
c/o AIDS-Hilfe, Hölderlinplatz 5 ☎ 70193 ☎ 194 11
Three times a year for free in gay venues.
■ **Schwulst**
c/o Buchladen Erlkönig, Bebelstraße 25 ☎ 70193 ☎ 99 14 17
📠 99 14 18 📧 city@schwulst.de 🌐 www.city-mag.de
Free city gay/lesbian magazine published 6x a year.

BARS
■ **Boots** (AC B G lj MA VS) 20-1, Fri Sat -2 h
Bopserstraße 9 ☎ 70180 ☎ 236 47 64
■ **Comix** (AC CC B BF d F GLM OS s YG) 11-1, Fri Sat -6 h
Charlottenplatz ☎ 70173 *(in the metro station/im U-Bahnhof)*
☎ 236 05 72
Large Café-Bar-Theater-Club complex. Danceclub on Fri Sat 23-6 h
■ **Finkennest** (B DR F G MA R) 14-1, Fri Sat -2 h
Weberstraße 11d ☎ 70182 ☎ 24 11 42
■ **Goldener Heinrich** (B F g og) Sun-Thu 10-1, Fri-Sat 10-2 h
Leonhardtstraße 3 ☎ 70182 ☎ 24 58 27
■ **Jakobstube** (B G MA) 10-1, Fri Sat -2, Sun 15-1 h
Jakobstraße 6 ☎ 70182 ☎ 23 54 82
■ **Monroe's Pub** (B F Glm MA OS) Mon-Sat 12-5, Sun 15-5 h
Schulstraße 3 ☎ 70173 *(Nähe/near Rathaus. Upper floor/Obere Etage)* ☎ 226 27 70
■ **Seven** (AC B F G MA OS) Wed Thu Sun 18-3, Fri Sat -5 h, closed Mon Tue
Bolzstraße 7 ☎ 70173 *(Entrance Friedrichstraße 31* ☎ 226 27 54
■ **Treffpunkt Kellergewölbe** (B DR G LJ MA p) last Sat 20-4 h
Blumenstraße 29 ☎ 70182 *(U-Olga-Eck)* ☎ 236 11 26

MEN'S CLUBS
■ **Eagle** (AC B DR f LJ P VS) Sun-Thu 21-1, Fri Sat -2 h
Mozartstraße 51 ☎ 70180 *(U-Österreichischer Platz)* ☎ 640 61 83
2nd Sat "Black leather night", 3rd Sun "S/M Session" (entry 16-17 h only), strict dress code. 1st Fri "Hard Core Night", strict dress code. Every Tue Happy hour from 21 h. Meeting point of LC Stuttgart.

Stuttgart — Germany

Stuttgart

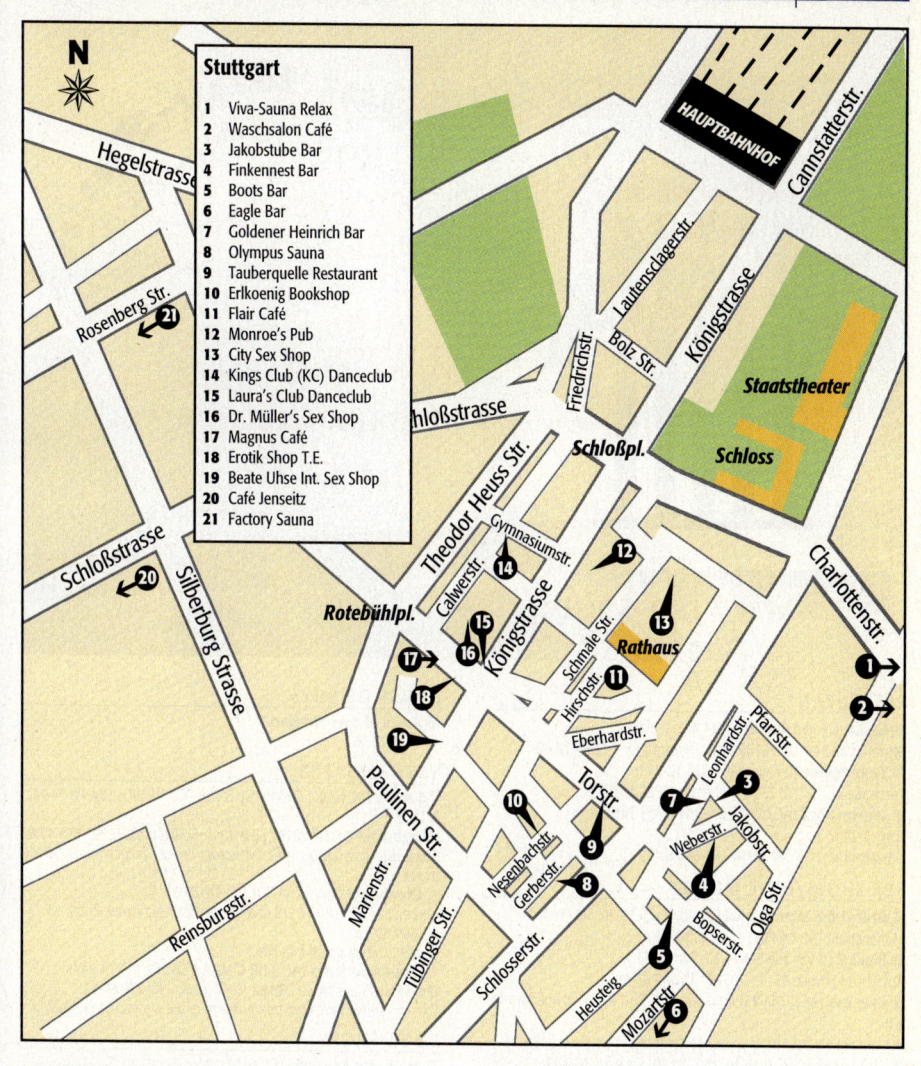

1. Viva-Sauna Relax
2. Waschsalon Café
3. Jakobstube Bar
4. Finkennest Bar
5. Boots Bar
6. Eagle Bar
7. Goldener Heinrich Bar
8. Olympus Sauna
9. Tauberquelle Restaurant
10. Erlkoenig Bookshop
11. Flair Café
12. Monroe's Pub
13. City Sex Shop
14. Kings Club (KC) Danceclub
15. Laura's Club Danceclub
16. Dr. Müller's Sex Shop
17. Magnus Café
18. Erotik Shop T.E.
19. Beate Uhse Int. Sex Shop
20. Café Jenseitz
21. Factory Sauna

CAFES

■ **Café Tocchetto** (BF f glm MA OS) Mon-Fri 10-16 h, Thu 10-20 h
Büchsenstraße 34/36 ✉ 70174 (c/o Aids-Beratungsstelle der ev. Gesellschaft Stuttgart) ☎ 205 43 88
HIV & Aids information available

■ **Flair Café** (AC B f GLM s YG) 18-4 h
Hirschstraße 2 ✉ 70173 (S-Stadtmitte/U-Rathaus) ☎ 226 14 15

■ **Jenseitz. Café** (B BF f GLM MA N) Mon Wed-Fri 11.30-14.30 & 18-1, Tue 18-1, Sat Sun 10-1 h
Bebelstraße 25 ✉ 70193 (U-Schwab-/Bebelstraße) ☎ 63 13 03

■ **Magnus** (B F GLM) 15-3, Fri 15-Mon 3 h
Rotebühlplatz 4/Kronprinzstraße ✉ 10173 ☎ 223 89 95

■ **Waschsalon** (B BF F GLM MA) 11-1, Sat Sun 16-1 h
Charlottenstraße 27 ✉ 70182 (Tram-Olgaeck) ☎ 236 98 96

DANCECLUBS

■ **Gay Tunnel** (B D G MA) 1st & 3rd Fri 22-5 h
Willy-Brandt-Straße 2/1 ☎ 299 14 99
Popular.

■ **Kings Club (KC)** (B D Glm YG) 22-6 h, closed Mon Tue
Calwer Straße 21 ✉ 70173 (Eingang/entrance Gymnasiumstraße) ☎ 226 45 58

■ **Laura's Club** (B D GLM lj MA s) 22-6 h
Rotebühlplatz 4 ✉ 70173 ☎ 29 01 60

Germany | Stuttgart

VIVA

The Real Gay-Sauna
daily open from 14:00 - 24:00 hrs.

Charlottenstrasse 38
70182 Stuttgart
Fon/ Fax: 07 11 – 236 84 62

www.viva-sauna.de

RESTAURANTS

- **Emilie** (b F glm MA OS) 18-24 h, Sun closed
Mozartstraße 49 ✉ 70180 *(near Olgastraße)* ☎ 649 19 00
- **Tauberquelle** (b F glm MA OS s) 12-24 h
Torstraße 19 ✉ 70173 *(U-Rathaus)* ☎ 23 56 56
- **Weißes Rössl** (AC CC d F G lj S STV WE) Tue-Sat 17-1, Sun 12-24 h
Schwabstrasse 32 ✉ 70197 ☎ 615 84 99

SEX SHOPS/BLUE MOVIES

- **Beate Uhse International** (g) Mon-Fri 9.30-20, Sat -16 h
Marienstraße 24 ✉ 70178 ☎ 61 37 48
- **Binokel** (G VS) Tue-Sat 14-23, Sun 16-23 h
König Karl Strasse 85 ✉ 70372 ☎ 549 06 81
- **Blue Box** (AC G MA VS) Mon-Sat 10-1, Sun & public holidays 14-1 h
Steinstraße 15 ✉ 70173 *(opposite Kaufhof carpark)* ☎ 2264076
- **City Sex Shop** (g) 9-18.30, Thu -20.30, Sat 9-14/16/18 h, closed Sun
Bärenstraße 5 ✉ 70173
- **Da capo Sex-Laden** (g VS) Mon-Fri 9-20, Sat -16 h
Blumenstraße 22 ✉ 70182 ☎ 236 47 34
- **Dr. Müller's Sex Shop** (g) Mon-Fri 9.30-20, Sat -16 h
Alte Poststraße 2 ✉ 70173 ☎ 29 55 61
- **Erotik Shop T.E.** (g VS) Mon-Fri 9-20, Sat -16 h
Rotebühlplatz 1, ✉ 70178
☎ 62 53 40
- **New Man** (g VS) Mon-Sat 9.30-21.30, Sun 14-20 h
c/o MAXX, Waiblinger Straße 7 ✉ 70372 *(S-Bad Cannstatt)*
☎ 509 44 00

HOUSE OF BOYS

- **House of Boys Stuttgart**
☎ 236 78 36

SAUNAS/BATHS

- **Factory** (AC b DR f G MA OS p SA SB SOL VS WO) Sun-Fri 14-24, Sat -2 h
Schwabstraße 33 ✉ 70197 *(Bus 42, S–Schwabstraße)* ☎ 615 40 00
Sauna with a skyline bar with a view over the city, predominantly young crowd.
- **Olympus** (B G MA p SA SOL VS) 14-24 h
Gerberstraße 11 ✉ 70178 *(near/nahe Österreichischer Platz)*
☎ 649 89 19
Comfortable sauna on four floors.
- **Viva-Sauna Relax** (AC B DR G MA SA SB SOL VS) 14-24 h
Charlottenstraße 38 ✉ 70182 *(U-Olgaeck)* ☎ 236 84 62
Spacious sauna which can be compared to the big saunas in Zürich.

BOOK SHOPS

- **Buchladen Erlkoenig** (CC GLM s) Mon-Fri 10-20, Sat -16 h
Nesenbachstraße 52 ✉ 70178 *(S/U-Stadtmitte & Österreichischer Platz)* ☎ 63 91 39
Also mail order.
- **Bücherabteilung im Kaufhof** (cc glm)
Königstraße 6 ✉ 70173 ☎ 20 36 0
- **Wittwer Bahnhofsbuchhandlung** (cc glm)
Hauptbahnhof, Wandelhalle *(main station)* ☎ 25 07 235

TRAVEL AND TRANSPORT

- **Flying ticket Reisecenter**
Flamingoweg 1 ✉ 70378 *(Kaufzentrum Neugereut)* ☎ 953 78 20
🖷 539 02 97 🖳 flying@stuttgart.netsurf.de
Gay travel agent

Stuttgart | Germany

EAGLE 2001 Stuttgart
Clublokal des LC Stuttgart e.V.

HARD CORE NIGHT
Jeden 1. Freitag im Monat ab 21 h

BLACK LEATHER NIGHT
Jeden 2. Samstag im Monat ab 21 h

S/M SESSION
Jeden 3. Sonntag im Monat
Einlaß 16 h – 17 h / Auslaß 20 h

eagle.stuttgart@gmx.de
Öffnungszeiten: So. bis Do. 21 - 2 h • Fr. & Sa. bis 3 h
Mozartstraße 51 • 70180 Stuttgart • 0711 / 6406123 • Fax 0711 / 6074436
Spielmann@HP2000/s.mann@topmail.de

OLYMPUS SAUNA

STUTTGART'S GAY SAUNA

SAUNA · BAR · VIDEO
GERBERSTRASSE 11
70178 STUTTGART
TEL. 0711-649 89 19

OPEN 14–24 HRS.

factory — the body obsession
MEN'S SAUNA & FITNESS

Mo+Do Eintritt 15 DM

- Dachterrasse
- Skylinebar
- Dampfbad
- Sauna
- Solarium
- Fitnessraum

factory · Schwabstr. 33 · 70197 Stuttgart-West · Telefon 0711-615 4000
www.factory-sauna.de · Ⓢ Schwabstraße · Open: So-Fr 14-24, Sa 14-2 Uhr

SPARTACUS 2001/2002 | 543

Germany | Stuttgart

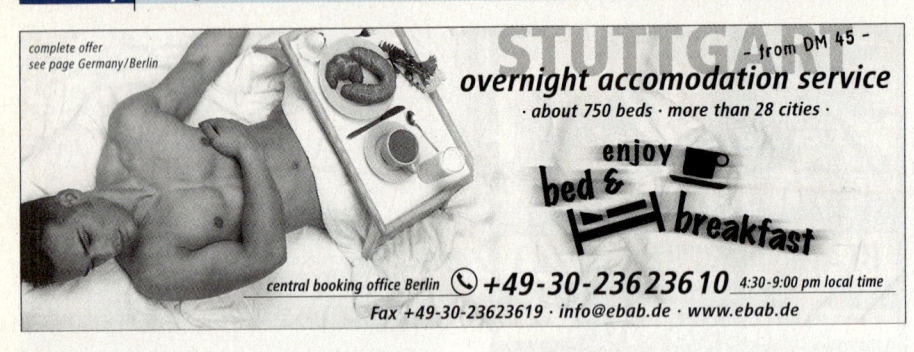

STUTTGART – from DM 45 –
overnight accomodation service
· about 750 beds · more than 28 cities ·

enjoy bed & breakfast

central booking office Berlin ☎ **+49-30-236 236 10** 4:30–9:00 pm local time
Fax +49-30-23623619 · info@ebab.de · www.ebab.de

complete offer see page Germany/Berlin

■ **Gablenberger Reisebüro** (glm MA) Mon-Fri 9.30-13 15-18, Wed 9.30-13, Sat 9.30-12.30 h
Gablenberger Hauptstraße 64 ✉ 70186 *(bus 40/42-Libanonstr.)* ☎ 480 05 35 📠 480 04 34 📧 Gablenberger-Reisebuero@t-online.de. 💻 www.Gablenberger-Reisebuero.de
■ **Reisebüro am Ostendplatz** (glm MA) 9.30-13 15-18, Wed 9.30-13, Sat 9.30-12.30 h
Ostendstraße 69/1 ✉ 70188 *(Ostendpassage,bus 24,tram 4-Ostendplatz)* ☎ 285 90 59 📠 285 90 58
💻 www.Reisebuero-am-Ostendplatz.de

PRIVATE ACCOMMODATION

■ **Enjoy Bed and Breakfast** (BF G H MA) 16.30-21 h
Nollendorfplatz 5, 10777 Berlin *(U-Nollendorfplatz)*
☎ (030) 236 236 10 📠 (030) 236 236 19 📧 info@ebab.com
💻 ebab.de
Accommodation sharing agency. All with shower and BF. 40-45 DM p.p.

buchladen erlkoenig

bücher # cds # postkarten #
kondome # videos # zeitschriften

nesenbachstr. 52
70178 stuttgart
tel: 0711 - 639 139
fax: 0711 - 236 9003

mo-fr 10-20 h # sa 10-16

e: erlkoenig@pride.de
www.buchladen-erlkoenig.de
web-shop: www.gaybooks.de

öpnv: stadtmitte/rotebühlplatz
& österreichischer platz

GENERAL GROUPS

■ **Initiativgruppe Homosexualität Stuttgart e.V. (ihs)** Fri 19-21 h
Weißenburgstraße 28a ✉ 70180 ☎ 640 44 94 📠 640 44 95
📧 ihs@gmx.de 💻 eurogay.net/mitglieder/ihs
Counselling ☎ 0711-19446 Fri 19-21 h. "Schwule Jugendgruppe" Fri 19h c/o Jugendhaus Mitte
■ **LSVD Baden-Württemberg**
Markelstr. 5 ✉ 70193 ☎ 65 93 52 📠 65 93 42
📧 ba-wve@lsvd.de 💻 www.lsvd.de/bw/

FETISH GROUPS

■ **LC Stuttgart e. V.** (G LJ)
Postfach 13 12 16 ✉ 70069 ☎ 607 44 36 📧 info@lc-stuttgart.de
💻 lc-stuttgart.de
Also publish monthly "Blättle" for members of LC Stuttgart (Fax 0711-9469902).

HEALTH GROUPS

■ **AIDS-Beratungsstelle der Ev. Gesellschaft Stuttgart e.V** Mon-Fri 10-16 h
Büchsenstraße 34-36 ✉ 70174 *(S-Stadtmitte)* ☎ 205 43 88
📠 2054 312
Cafe Tocchetto every 2nd and 4th Sun 14-18 h, 1st and 3rd Thu 18-22 (not only) for people with HIV/Aids.
■ **AIDS-Hilfe Stuttgart e.V.** Mon-Thu 10-12, 14-17, Fri 10-12. Helpline Mon Thu Fri 18.30-21 h
Hölderlinplatz 5 ✉ 70193
☎ 224 69-0 ☎ 19 4 11 (helpline)
📠 224 69 99
Positive Wed 18.30-21, every 1st Sun brunch 11-14h

HELP WITH PROBLEMS

■ **Rosa Telefon** Fri 19-21 h
☎ 194 46

SPORT GROUPS

■ **Abseitz Stuttgart e.V.** Wed 19-21 (office)
c/o Weißenburg, Weißenburgstraße 28 A ✉ 70180 ☎ 640 44 90
📠 640 44 95 📧 info@abseitz.de 💻 www.abseitz.de
gay and lesbian sports club

SWIMMING

-Baggersee/Man-made lake Kirchentellinsfurt (NU) (B27 Stuttgart Richtung Tübingen, bei Abzweig Kirchentellinsfurt wenden, Ausfahrt Nürtingen. Vom Hauptsee links. Am hinteren Teil des zweiten Sees./B27 Stuttgart direction Tübingen, turn back at exit Kirchentellinsfurt and take exit Nürtingen. Go left at the first lake. It is the back of the second lake.)

Stuttgart ▶ Tübingen | Germany

CRUISING
-Kursaal-Anlagen (König-Karl-Straße 8/Wildbader Straße in Bad Cannstatt)
-P Planetarium (R)
-Unterer Schloßgarten (near the Rossebändiger/fountain)
-Mittlerer Schloßgarten (near Café am See, by night only)
-TV tower in Stuttgart-Degerloch (behind the news stand/hinter dem Kiosk)
-Klett-Passage
-Bismarckplatz

Suhl ☏ 03681

HEALTH GROUPS
■ **AIDS-Hilfe** Tue Wed 10-15, Thu 10-19, Fri 8-12 h
Am Bahnhof 15 ✉ 98529 ☏ 72 00 84

CRUISING
-Stadtpark (after dusk)

Timmendorfer Strand ☏ 04503

RESTAURANTS
■ **Beiboot** (B F glm s) 16-2 h, Tue closed
Strandallee 204 ✉ 23669 (c/o Hotel Leuchtturm) ☏ 88 19 96

Traunstein

SWIMMING
-Chiemsee (g NU) (A 8 München ⇌ Salzburg, P 2 km after exit/nach Ausfahrt Felden. Through underpass to the lake, path to the right)

CRUISING
-Maximiliansplatz
-Main train station/Hauptbahnhof

Trier ☏ 0651

BARS
■ **Palette** (B f G MG p s) 20-1, Fri Sat -2/? h
Oerenstraße 13b ✉ 54290 ☏ 426 09
■ **Werner's** (AC B f glm OS s WE) 21-3, summer OS 19-24 h
Jüdemerstraße 28 ✉ 54290 ☏ 761 08

CAFES
■ **SchMIT-Z: Café Verkehrt & Schwule Informations- und Beratungsstelle** (A B d f G MA OS s) Café Thu 20-24, Sun 16-20, Helpline Sun 20-22 h
Mustorstraße 4 ✉ 54290 (Bus-Mustorstraße) ☏ 425 14
Helpline Sun 20-22 h. Gay and grey 3rd Sat 18-20, Gayliens (YG) 2nd&4th Sat 17-20 h. Email (beratung@trier.gay-web.de) or call for further information.

DANCECLUBS
■ **HOMOsapiens** (B D GLM MA)
c/o Exil, Zurmaiener Straße 114 ✉ 54292
irregular on Sat 22-? h, look out for flyers.
■ **Treff 39** (B D g MA p vs) 21-3 h
Paulinstraße 39 ✉ 54292 ☏ 124 63

SEX SHOPS/BLUE MOVIES
■ **Erotik Markt** (CC g MA VS) Mon-Sat 10-22 h, closed Sun
Karl-Marx-Straße 70a ✉ 54290 ☏ 423 71

BOOK SHOPS
■ **Gegenlicht** (glm) Mon-Wed 9.30-18.30, Thu Fri -20, Sat 9-16 h
Glockenstraße 10 ✉ 54290 ☏ 765 80

GENERAL GROUPS
■ **Schwulenforum Trier (SchwuFo)** Mon 20 h
Mustorstraße 4 ✉ 54290 ☏ & FAX 425 14

HEALTH GROUPS
■ **AIDS-Hilfe Trier e.V.** Mon Tue Thu 9-16, Wed -19, Fri -13 h
Saarstraße 48 ✉ 54290 ☏ 970 440 📠 970 412
📧 aidshilfe.trier@t-online.de 🌐 www.ahtrier.de
Gay and Grey for gays over 40 Tel. 0651/9740440 and Gayliens - gay youth group Tel. 0651/9704422 (e-mail gayliens@hotmail.de) are also part of the AIDS-Hilfe Trier

HELP WITH PROBLEMS
■ **Beratung im SchMIT-Z** Sun 20-22 h
Mustorstraße 4 ✉ 54290 ☏ 19 446
■ **Rosa Telefon Trier** Sun 20-22 h
☏ 194 46

CRUISING
-Palastgarten between Kurfürstliches Palais and Kaiserthermen (r)
-Nells Park
-Mehringer Höhe

Troisdorf ☏ 02241

HEALTH GROUPS
■ **AIDS-Hilfe Rhein-Sieg e.V.** Mon-Fri 10-12.30 h. Meets 4th/Thu 19 h
Alte Poststraße 31 ✉ 53840 ☏ 97 99 97 📠 979 99 88
📧 info@rhein-sieg.aidshilfe.de 🌐 rhein-sieg.aidshilfe.de
Youth group Tue Thu 14-17 h. Counselling.

Tübingen ☏ 07071

SEX SHOPS/BLUE MOVIES
■ **Erotik-Shop** (glm VS) 10-18, Sat 10-14 h
Collegiumsgasse 4 ✉ 72070 (1st floor) ☏ 271 11

GENERAL GROUPS
■ **LuSchT Lesben und Schwule Tübingen** Cafe: 15-19 h
Herrenberger Straße 9 ✉ 72070 ☏ 448 43
Every Wed: Schwul/lesbische Tacko-Bar at Sudhaus, Hechinger Straße 203 72072 at 21.30. Every Thu: Schwuler Treff in movie theatre Arsenal.

HEALTH GROUPS
■ **AIDS-Hilfe Tübingen-Reutlingen e.V.** Mon Wed-Fri 10-12, Café Wed 16-19 h
Herrenberger Straße 9 ✉ 72070 (opposite Parhaus König)
☏ 499 22 📠 444 37 📧 info@tuebingen.aidshilfe.de
Gay and lesbian group Initiativgruppe Homosexualität Tübingen meets here on Thu 20 h.

HELP WITH PROBLEMS
■ **Rosa Telefon** Fri 20-22 h
Postfach 16 25 ✉ 72006 ☏ 194 46

SPORT GROUPS
■ **Taktlos** Meeting Mon 20-21.30 at Studentendorf Waldhäuser-Ost (big hall), Fichtenweg 5

Germany — Tübingen ▶ Villingen-Schwenningen

SWIMMING
-Strand/beach in Kirchentellingsfurt (NU) (Zwischen/between Tübingen & Nürtingen. Schwule finden sich am kleineren der beiden Seen./There are two lakes. The smaller one is gay.)

CRUISING
-Park am Neckar (Nähe/near Alleenbrücke, nachts/at night)
-Mensaklappe der Mensa 1 (Eingang/entrance Wilhelmstraße, 12-14 h)
-Stadtpark (zwischen/between Derendinger Allee und/and Anlagensee)
-Alter Botanischer Garten/Old Botanical Garden (Wilhelmstraße)
-Busbahnhof/bus station (Unterführung/subway Europaplatz)

Tuttlingen ☎ 07461

GENERAL GROUPS
■ **Kuckucksei**
Postfach 45 22 ✉ 78510 📧 kuckucksei@alb.gay-web.de
🖥 kuckuck.home.pages.de/

HELP WITH PROBLEMS
■ **Rosa Telefon** (Glm)
☎ 16 47 55

Ulm ☎ 0731

BARS
■ **Alten Fritz. Zum** (B f G MA OS YG) Mon Wed Thu 18-2, Fri -3, Sat 19-3, Sun -2 h, closed Tue
Karlstraße 9 ✉ 89073 *(near/nahe Hauptbahnhof)* ☎ 653 00
■ **Wiblinger Eck** (AC B f G MA p r) 16-1 h
Erenäcker 18 ✉ 89079 ☎ 48 21 51

CAFES
■ **Café Viva** (B f glm MA OS) Mon-Thu 11-24, Fri Sat -0.30, Sun 14-24 h
Herdbruckerstraße 20 ✉ 89073 ☎ 602 12 14

DANCECLUBS
■ **Schwullesbische Disco** (B D DR GLM YG) 2x Sat 22-?, 1x Sun 20-2 ? h
c/o Donauturm *(near Maritim Hotel/convention center)*
Watch out for dates published in gay newspapers.
■ **Tangente** (B D G YG) Sun 22.30-? h
Frauenstraße 29 ✉ 89073 ☎ 659 66

RESTAURANTS
■ **Bei Erika** (B G MA) Mon-Sat 17-2 h, Sun and holidays closed
Olgastraße 141 ✉ 89073 ☎ 253 23

GENERAL GROUPS
■ **Rosige Zeiten e.V.** Meeting Mon 20-22 h at "Zum Alten Fritz", Korbstraße 9
Postfach 1252, 89202 Neu-Ulm ☎ & 📠 253 60
Publishers of Mixx, a bi-monthly free newsletter.

HEALTH GROUPS
■ **AIDS-Hilfe Ulm/Neu-Ulm/Alb-Donau e.V.** Mon-Fri 9.30-12.30, Mon Fri 19.30-21 h (helpline)
Furttenbachstraße 14 ✉ 89077 *(corner Furttenbachstr/Zieglerstr)*
☎ 194 11 (helpline) ☎ 373 31 📠 931 75 27
📧 info@aidshilfe-ulm.de 🖥 www.aidshilfe-ulm.de
Coming out group SchwUlm meets Wed & Fri 20-22 h. Ask for details.

CRUISING
-Rosengarten (unterhalb/underneath Adlerbastei from 22 h)
-Donauhalle, Straßenbahnendhaltestelle Line 1 Friedrichsau (tagsüber/ during the day)
-Waldbaggersee Senden (Sommer, ganztags/Summer all day)
-Hauptbahnhof/main railway station
-Herdbrücke
-Donauhalle, Tramlinie/tramline 1, Friedrichsau (tagsüber/during daytime)

Unkel ☎ 02644

GENERAL GROUPS
■ **Die Insel** (GLM MA) Meets 1st/3rd Wed 20 h at "Fritz", Asbacher Straße 25, 53545 Linz
Postfach 02 16 ✉ 53569 ☎ 47 82 ☎ (0172) 74 93 682
🖥 www.lp.info.com/insel

Unna ☎ 02303

DANCECLUBS
■ **Doppelherz** 22 h every 2 months at Kulturzentrum Lindenbrauerei. Call for dates
Massener Straße 33-35 ✉ 59423
☎ 25 11 20

GENERAL GROUPS
■ **Rosa AufSchwUNg** Tue 19.30 h
c/o Kulturzentrum "Lindenbrauerei" Massener Strasse ✉ 59423
☎ (0231) 25 11 20
Gay group

Vechta

CRUISING
-1st [P] B 69 Vechta ▸ Diepholz

Viersen ☎ 02162

HEALTH GROUPS
■ **AIDS-Hilfe Kreis Viersen e.V.** Mon Wed Fri 9-13 h
Gereonstraße 75 ✉ 41747 ☎ 349 87

Villingen-Schwenningen ☎ 07721

BARS
■ **Club 46 a** (A B d Glm lj MA p WE) 21-24, Sat -2 h, closed Mon-Tue, Sat and on public holidays disco
Dauchinger Straße 46 a ✉ 78056 *(in Schwenningen, entrance from backyard nr. 46)* ☎ 639 09
■ **Forum** (B F GLM MA) 18-1, Fri Sat -2, Sun 15-1
Bärengasse 20 ✉ 78050 *(Villingen)* ☎ 50 43 50

SEX SHOPS/BLUE MOVIES
■ **Loveland** (g) 10-13, 14.30-18.30, Sat 10-13 h, closed Sun
Neckarstraße 115 ✉ 78056 *(in Schwenningen)*

SAUNAS/BATHS
■ **Pfeffermühle** (AC B DR f G MA OS p S SA SB VS) 16-22, Sat-Sun 15-22 h, closed Tue
Alte Tuttlinger Straße 4 ✉ 78056 ☎ 07720/56 69
Three floors sauna located in a tasteful Swabian style house. Open air terrace in the garden.

546 *SPARTACUS* **2001/2002**

Villingen-Schwenningen ▶ Westerland - Sylt | **Germany**

HELP WITH PROBLEMS
■ **Rosa Telefon**
☎ (07461) 16 47 55

CRUISING
-Bahnhof/main railway station Schwenningen
-Karl-Marx-Straße (ayor)

Volkenroda ☎ 036025
HOTELS
■ **Deutsche Eiche** (b BF d F glm lj MA OS s WE)
Hauptstraße 24 ✉ 99998 ☎ 503 22 🖨 503 42
Also restaurant.

Völklingen ☎ 06898
CAFES
■ **Sissis Schlössje** (AC f GLM MA s OS) Mon-Wed 14-1,
Thu-Sat -3, Sun 10-1 h
Forbacherpassage 6 ✉ 66333 ☎ 29 78 99

Weiden ☎ 0961
GENERAL GROUPS
■ **HiBISSkus Schwule Initiative Weiden** Thu 19.30-21 h
c/o Diakoniezentrum, Sebastianstraße 18 ✉ 92637 (main entrance,
3rd floor/Haupteingang 3. Stock) ☎ 389 31 72

Weimar ☎ 03643
DANCECLUBS
■ **Felix Disco at Jugendclub Nordlicht** (B D f GLM MA OS s)
1st 3rd 5th Sat 22-3 h
Stauffenbergstraße 20a ✉ 99423 (Bus 7) ☎ 42 78 03

HEALTH GROUPS
■ **AIDS-Hilfe Weimar & Ostthüringen e.V.** counselling Mon Thu
11-15, Wed 11-20 h
Erfurter Straße 17 ✉ 99423 ☎ 85 35 35
☎ 194 11 (counselling)
🖨 85 36 36
Also L.S.D. (Lesbisch-Schwulres Date) café Wed Fri&Sat 20-? h.

CRUISING
-Park an der Ilm (between Burgplatz and Platz der Demokratie)
-Wittumspalais

Wesel ☎ 0281
HEALTH GROUPS
■ **AIDS-Hilfe Duisburg/Kreis Wesel e.V.** (MA G) Tuei 14-17, Wed
19-21, Thu 9-12, Café Sun 16-? h
Herzogenring 4 ✉ 46483 ☎ 29980
The group " Gay nach Wesel" has the same telephone number.
■ **Gesundheitsamt Wesel** Wed 14-15.30 h
Jülicher Straße 6 ✉ 46483 (room 201) ☎ 207 29 81
Anonymous free HIV test and Aids counselling.

CRUISING
-Heuberpark (between Postturm und Hallenbad/between Telecom-
tower and indoor-swimming pool)

Westerland - Sylt ☎ 04651
PUBLICATIONS
■ **Hamburg Hannover & Sylt von hinten**
c/o Bruno Gmünder Verlag, Postfach 61 01 04, 10921 Berlin
☎ (030) 615 00 342 🖨 (030) 65 91 34
✉ info@spartacus.de
🌐 www.brunos.de
The city guide book about Hamburg, Hanover & Sylt. Useful general information and lots of addresses with extensive descriptions in English
and German. Up-to-date maps. Erotic photos.

BARS
■ **Destille** (B f g MA N OS) 19-? h Closed Tue
Norderstraße 11 ✉ 25980 ☎ 220 01
■ **gatz** (B GLM MA OS) 12-? h
Strandstraße 10 ✉ 25980 ☎ 210 06
■ **Nanu** (B g MA s) 21-3 h
Strandstraße 23 ✉ 25980 ☎ 928 01 24

DANCECLUBS
■ **Kleist-Casino (KC)** (AC B CC D GLM lj MA p r s) 22-5/6 h
Elisabethstraße 1a ✉ 25980 ☎ 242 28

RESTAURANTS
■ **Dechters Hüs** (F glm N OS) 12-23 h
Gurtstig 2, 25980 Keitum (near Sylt-Ost) ☎ 318 84
Vegetarian and fish cuisine.
■ **Franz Ganser** (B F g OS) 18-23, Sun 12-14.30, 18-23 h, closed
Mon
Bötticherstraße/Boysenstraße ✉ 25980 ☎ 229 70
French cuisine.

Marin - Hotel - Sylt GmbH
Zimmer mit allem Komfort
DU/WC, Kabel-TV, Mini-Bar
Zimmer-Safe, Telefon
www.marinhotel.de

WESTERLAND/SYLT

Elisabethstraße 1

Ecke Strandstraße

25980 Westerland/Sylt

Tel.: 04651 / 9 28 00

Fax.: 04651 / 9 28 01 50

Bierbar
NANU

Tägl. ab 21 Uhr geöffnet

*Etwas frech,
etwas nostalgisch,
immer gutgelaunt*

Germany | Westerland - Sylt

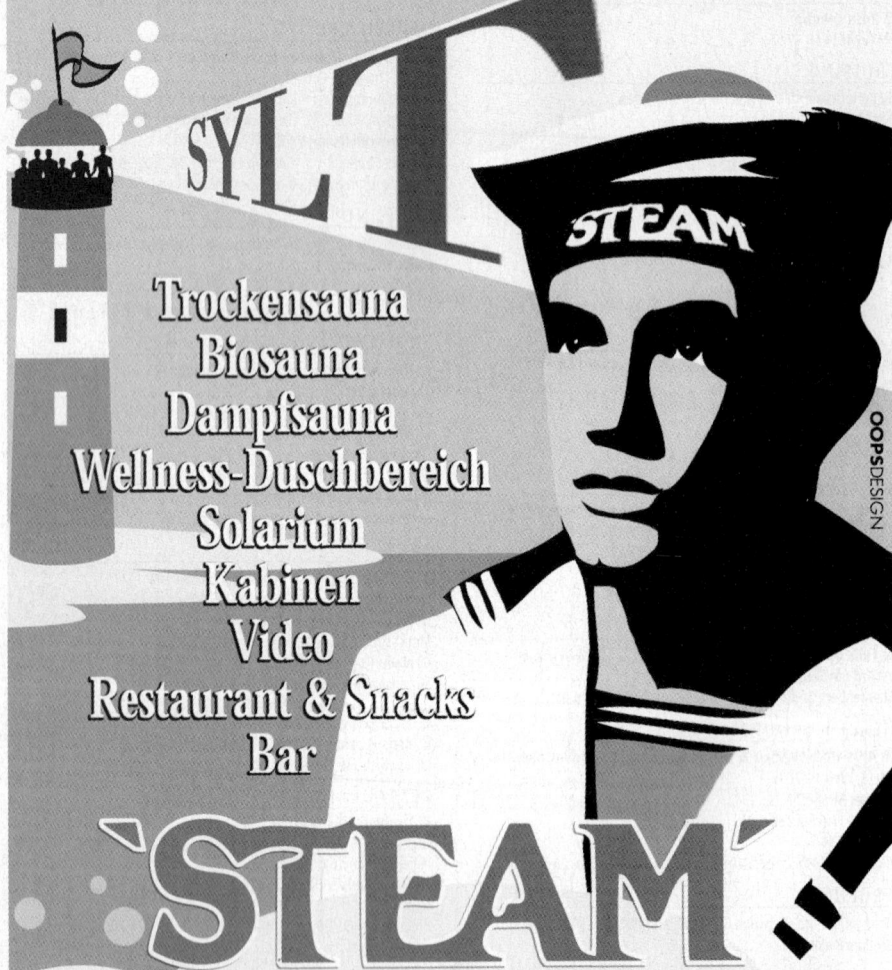

'STEAM'
BEACH CLUB

Trockensauna
Biosauna
Dampfsauna
Wellness-Duschbereich
Solarium
Kabinen
Video
Restaurant & Snacks
Bar

Bötticherstr. 3   25980 Westerland / Sylt
04651 / 83 52 49

Öffnungszeiten: Tgl. 14 - 24 Uhr bei Veranstaltungen 14 - 22 Uhr
www.steam-beach-club.de

OOPSDESIGN

Westerland - Sylt - Wetzlar | **Germany**

SAUNAS/BATHS
■ **Steam Beach Club** (B cc F G MA S SA SB SOL VS) 14-24 h, summer parties -4 h
Bötticherstrasse 3 ✉ 25980 *(5 min from railway station)*
☎ 835 249
New sauna with bio sauna. Many special events in summer.

BOOK SHOPS
■ **Voss Bahnhofsbuchhandlung** (cc glm)
Tinnumer Str. 11 ✉ 25988 ☎ 98 68 0

HOTELS
■ **Marin-Hotel-Sylt** (g)
Elisabethstraße 1 ✉ 25980 *(corner Strandstraße)* ☎ 928 00 🖷 9 28 01 50 💻 marin.hotel@t-online.de 💻 www.marinhotel.de
5km from the airport. Downtown location. Partly equipped with kitchenette, priv. bath/WC, TV and phone. Rates apartments DM 60-210, single 88-165, double 140-304 (bf incl.)

GUEST HOUSES
■ **Haus Hallig** (BF GLM lj MA OS) all year
Danziger Straße 9 ✉ 25980 ☎ 242 13 🖷 242 16
💻 info@haus-hallig.de 💻 www.haus-hallig.de
All rooms with bath/WC. The guesthouse offers a garden. Single from DM 60-100, double from 85-160 (bf incl.) Apartments also available.

APARTMENTS
■ **Hussmann Ferienwohnungen** (g)
Wilhelmstraße 6 ✉ 25980 ☎ 2 20 02 🖷 220 74
💻 hussmannsylt@t-online.de
💻 www.hussmann-sylt.de
40 completely furnished apartments. 1 room app. (max. 2 persons) DM 55-160, 2 room app. (max. 4 persons) 120-200 (low-/high-season). Central location, close to bars.

HEALTH GROUPS
■ **AIDS-Hilfe Sylt - AktHIV für Nordfriesland e.V.** Mon-Fri 10-12, Mon Thu 16-18h
Kjeirstraße 23 ✉ 25980 *(in "Sylter Eck" opposite DRK-Rettungswache)* ☎ 194 11 🖷 92 76 90
Meeting "Klönschnak" 1st & 3rd Thu 19-21 at AIDS-Hilfe-Sylt, 2nd Thu 19-21 Café Kanne (Niebüll), last Thu 19-21 Café Schnack (Bredstedt), 3rd Mon 19-21 h at DRK Reha Klinik (St. Peter Ording).

SWIMMING
-Oase zur Sonne (15 min walk south from Westerland. This spot takes its name from the nearby café which is located in the dunes. You'll need to purchase either a day ticket or a subsription ticket before you are allowed to go on the beach./ Ca. 15 Minuten Fußweg Richtung Süden von Westerland aus. Der Strandabschnitt ist nach dem Café in den Dünen benannt. In der Saison braucht man eine Kurkarte bzw. eine Tageskarte, um an den Strand zu kommen.

CRUISING
-Stephanstraße (Alter Kursaal/Stadtcafé am/on Rathausplatz)
-Bahnhof (r)
-Kurpromenade (near Kurhaus. From dawn to 4 h/ab Dunkelheit bis 4 h)

Wetzlar ☎ 06441

DANCECLUBS
■ **SchwuLesbische Fete** (B D f GLM) Last Fri 22-? h
c/o Harlekin, Güllgasse 9 ✉ 35678

SPARTACUS 2001/2002 | 549

Germany | Wiesbaden ▶ Wismar

Wiesbaden ☎ 0611

BARS
■ **Hauptmann von Köpenick** (B f GLM MA OS r) Sun-Thu 11-1, Fri Sat -2 h
Mauergasse 10 ✉ 65183 ☎ 37 61 02
■ **Joy** (B d GLM YG) 19.30-1, Fri Sat -2, kitchen -23, Fri Sat -24 h
Dotzheimer Straße 37 ✉ 65185 *(Entrance/Eingang Zimmermannstraße)* ☎ 30 75 59
Mon 19.30 meets Smalltown boy group.
■ **Robin Hood** (CC f GLM MA OS r s) 13-1, Fri Sat -3 h
Häfnergasse 3 ✉ 65183 ☎ 30 13 49
Bistro-Bar with internet access.
■ **Spartakus** 20-? h
Mainzer Straße 129 ✉ 65187 ☎ 71 84 32
■ **Trend** (AC B f GLM lj MA N OS) 14-2, Fri & Sat -3, Sun 15-2 h
(Winter - opening times two hours later)
Am Römertor 7 ✉ 65183 ☎ 37 30 40
A comfortable meeting point for locals as well as visitors of all ages.

DANCECLUBS
■ **Mo´ Betta Club** (a AC CC f GLM MA S) Wed Thu Sun 20-2, Fr Sat -3 h.
Saalgasse 9-11 ✉ 65183
☎ 5280 561
Also bar and art performances. Call for details.
■ **Pussy Cats** (B D glm MA p) 22-4 h
Adlerstraße 33 ✉ 65183 ☎ 517 39

SEX SHOPS/BLUE MOVIES
■ **City Video Sex Shop** (g) Mon-Fri 9-20, Sat -16; Cinema Mon-Sat 9-24 h
Mauritiusplatz 1 ✉ 65183 ☎ 30 48 40
■ **Claudia-Sexshop** (g) Mon-Fri 9-18, Sat 9-14 h Sun closed
Augustinerstr. 20 ✉ 97070 *(city centre)* ☎ 546 89

SAUNAS/BATHS
■ **Club-Sauna** (B F G MA p SA SB VS) 15-23, Fri Sat -24 h
Häfnergasse 3 ✉ 65183 *(Drei-Lilien-Platz)* ☎ & FAX 30 55 74
Relatively small but on three floors.

GENERAL GROUPS
■ **Lesbisch-Schwules Netzwerk in Hessen**
c/o Rosa Lüste, Postfach 54 06 ✉ 65044 ☎ 37 77 65 📠 37 77 65
Gay & lesbian helpline Mon 18-21 h.

FETISH GROUPS
■ **MSC Rhein-Main, Frankfurt**
Eleonorenstraße 4 ✉ 65185 ☎ 37 69 65

HEALTH GROUPS
■ **AIDS-Hilfe Wiesbaden e.V.** Mon Tue Thu Fri 10-14, Helpline Mon Fri 19-21, Tue Thu 10-12 h
Karl-Glässing-Straße 5 ✉ 65183 ☎ 30 92 11 (Office)
☎ 194 11 (helpline) 📠 37 72 13
📧 AHWiesbaden@t-online.de
🖥 www.t-online.de/~AHWiesbaden
Breakfast on 1st Fri/month 11-13 h.

HELP WITH PROBLEMS
■ **Gewalt gegen Schwule**
☎ 30 26 86

CRUISING
-Main station/Hauptbahnhof (r)
-Karstadt, Kirchgasse, 2nd floor (YG)
-Hertie, Kirchgasse, 2nd floor (YG)

-Reisinger Anlagen (ayoor r) (am Bahnhof, nachts/in front of railway station, at night)

Wilhelmshaven ☎ 04421

CULTURE
■ **ELCO!** (A CC) 10-20 h, Sun closed
Parkstraße 3 ✉ 26382 *(near/nahe Hauptbahnhof)* ☎ 994 77-6
📠 994 77-9 📧 de_elco@hotmail.com 🖥 elco-shop.de

BARS
■ **mai pen lai** (B G) Sun-Thu 20-2 h, Fri Sat 20-3 h
Ebertstraße 128 ✉ 26382 *(near station)* ☎ 99 54 34
Every 2nd Saturday special event.
■ **My Way** (B f GLM OS) Mon-Thu 21-2, Fri Sat -3, Sun 22-2 h
Bismarckstraße 89 ✉ 26382
☎ 335 94
■ **Sonne. Zur** (B f g MA) 21-5, Sun 18.30-? h
Grenzstraße 21 ✉ 26382 ☎ 215 02
■ **Zoff** (B f glm MA) Mon-Thu Sun 21-2, Fri-Sat -3 h
Bismarkstraße 121 ✉ 26382
☎ 329 78

HEALTH GROUPS
■ **Wilhelmshavener AIDS-Hilfe e.V.** Mon Tue Fri 10-14, Wed Thu 14-18 h
Bremer Straße 139 ✉ 26382 ☎ 211 49 ☎ 194 11
📠 299 39

SWIMMING
-Hooksiel-Campingplatz (g MA NU) (left side/linke Seite, best Sat Sun)
-Klein Wangerooge/Banter See (Coming from the P, take the first path to the left. Best time 12-20 h. In sumer only)(

CRUISING
-Hertie department store
-Adalbertplatz/Köhler Park (r)

Wismar ☎ 03841

GENERAL GROUPS
■ **Na Und e.V.** Mon 19 h
Lübsche Straße 11 ✉ 23966 ☎ 27 43 21
Gay & lesbian group/Schwul-lesbischer Verein
■ **Why Not e.V./AIDS-Hilfe Westmecklenburg** (MG) Mon Thu 9-11.30, Tue 18-20 h
Breite Straße 54 ✉ 23966 *(in the city centre, near station)*
☎ & FAX 21 47 55 📧 aids_hilfe_westmecklenburg@t-online.de
🖥 www.wismar_aidshilfe.de
Café & library Sun 15-20 h.

HELP WITH PROBLEMS
■ **Telefon des Vertrauens** Mon Thu 9-12, Tue 18-21 h
☎ 21 47 55

SWIMMING
-Wohlenberger Wieck
-Ostseebad Boltenhagen
-Insel Poel
-Zierow
-Hohenwieschendorf (Near/Nähe Grankow)

CRUISING
-Am Lindengarten (by day/tagsüber)
-Lindengarten am/at the Rostocker Tor

550 *SPARTACUS* **2001/2002**

Witten ☎ 02302
DANCECLUBS
■ **Werk-Stadt** (B D f G s YG) Mar-Sep 3rd Sat 22-3 h
Mannesmannstraße 2 ✉ 58455
GENERAL GROUPS
■ **Schwule Gruppe Witten** Meets 2nd/4th Sun 15.30 h, later at Cafe Blué, Ruhrallee 69, Dortmund
c/o DPWV, Dortmunder Straße 13 ✉ 58455 ☎ 15 59
Mon Tue 10-12, Wed -15 h. 1st and 3rd Sun social activities, call for details.

Wolfratshausen ☎ 08171
HEALTH GROUPS
■ **AIDS-Projekt Oberland e.V.**
Gebhartstraße 2 ✉ 82515 ☎ 91 00 91 🖨 91 00 91

Wolfsburg ☎ 05361
CAFES
■ **Zum Tannenhof** (A AC BF CC f glm MA N OS WE)
Mon-Thu 12-23, Fri Sat -1, Sun 10-23 h
Kleiststraße 49 ✉ 38440 ☎ 86 15 86
GENERAL GROUPS
■ **Rosa Wolf Wolfsburg e.V.** Mon 17-22, Tue 20-22, Wed 19.30-22, Fri 19-22h, last Sun 15-17h
Schachtweg 5a ✉ 38440 ☎ 29 29 29 ☎ 194 46 🖨 29 29 29
📧 RosaWolfeV@aol.com 💻 www.rosawolf.wolfsburg.de
HEALTH GROUPS
■ **AIDS-Hilfe Wolfsburg e.V.** Mon-Wed 9-15, Thu 9-22, Fri 9-15 h
Schachtweg 5a ✉ 38440 ☎ 194 11 🖨 29 15 21
☎ 133 32 (Office).
CRUISING
-Park am Großen Schillerteich am Betonspielplatz/Park at the Großen
Schillerteich near playground area (abends/evenings)

Wuppertal ☎ 0202
BARS
■ **Keller Club ("KC")** (B GLM MA) 19-? h, closed Wed
Schloßbleiche 32 ✉ 42103 *(Eingang/entrance Wirmhof)*
☎ 45 55 35
■ **Marlene** (B f glm MA N WE) 19-1 h, gay on Wed/Sun, closed Thu
Hochstraße 81 ✉ 42105 ☎ 31 64 28
■ **Schankhaus Merlin's** (B f GLM MA s) 19-3 h, Tue closed
Hochstraße 65 ✉ 42105
☎ 309 79 63
■ **The Number** (B G MA R) Sun-Thu 21-3, Fri Sat -5 h
Gathe 1 B ✉ 42102 ☎ 449 14 93
■ **Wunderbau** Tue-Sun 15-1 h, Mon closed
Calvinstraße 9 ✉ 42103
CAFES
■ **Café Crème** (B BF F g MA) 8.30-1, Sat Sun 10-1 h
Briller Straße 3 ✉ 42105 ☎ 30 43 63

Witten ▶ Würzburg Germany

DANCECLUBS
■ **Börse. Die** (a AC d MA NG S YG)
Wolkenburg 100 ✉ 42119 ☎ 243 220
Local events such as gay tea dance etc. Please call for information
SEX SHOPS/BLUE MOVIES
■ **Starlife Gay** (G) 10-24 h, closed Sun
Höhne 4 ✉ 42275 *(Barmen)* ☎ 59 31 33
■ **Starlife Gay** (G VS) 10-1, Fri Sat -3, Sun 12-22 h
Neumarktstraße 14 ✉ 42103 *(Elberfeld)* ☎ 45 31 06
■ **Videoland** (g) Mon-Fri 6-13 h 15-20 h, Sat 7-18 h, Sun 10-12 h
Westkotter Straße 146 ✉ 42277 *(Bus-Germanenstraße)*
☎ 51 18 06
SAUNAS/BATHS
■ **Theo's Sauna Club** (! B DR F G MA msg OS SA SB SOL VS WH WO) 15-23, Sat 13-1, Sun & holidays -23 h
Uellendahlerstraße 410 ✉ 42109 *(Elberfeld)*
☎ 70 60 59
Friendly sauna with a terrace frequented by a mixed crowd. Lotto on Wed, free buffet at the end of the month.
GENERAL GROUPS
■ **Schwulengruppe Wuppertal** Meeting Wed 20 h
c/o Börse, Raum 5, Viehhofstraße 125 ✉ 42117
Thu 19 h Coming Out Gruppe.
HEALTH GROUPS
■ **AIDS-Hilfe Wuppertal e.V.** Mon-Fri 10-12.30, Mon Tue 14-16, Thu 16-18 h, Wed closed
Hofaue 9 ✉ 42103 *(Elberfeld)* ☎ 194 11 (helpline) ☎ 45 00 09
🖨 45 25 70 📧 aidshilfe@wtal.de 💻 aidshilfe.wtal.de
HELP WITH PROBLEMS
■ **Rosa Telefon** Tue 20-22 h
c/o AIDS-Hilfe, Hofaue 9 ✉ 42107 ☎ 45 00 04
CRUISING
-Adlerbrücke (opposite Opernhaus)
-Neumarkt (evenings)

Würzburg ☎ 0931
GAY INFO
■ **WuF-Zentrum e.V.** (d G lj MA OS VS WE) Thu 20-24, 4th Sat 21 h
Nigglweg 2 ✉ 97082 ☎ 41 26 46 🖨 41 26 47
📧 wuf@wuerzburg.gay-web.de
💻 wuerzburg.gay-web.de/wuf
Youth Group "GayWürz" (16-26 yrs only) meets 1st/3rd Fri 20.30 h.See wuerzburg.gay-web.de/gaywuerz.
BARS
■ **Sonderbar** (B BF f glm MA) 11-2 h
Bronnbachergasse 1/Karmelitenstraße ✉ 97070 ☎ 5 43 25
■ **Warsteiner Treff** (B glm MA) 13-1, Sun 15-1 h, closed Wed
Glockengasse 15 ✉ 97070 ☎ 57 30 03
CAFES
■ **PROSECCO- das Bistro im ÖCO** (B BF CC F glm MA OS) Mon-Sun 10-0 h
Uhlhornsweg 99 ✉ 26129 ☎ 777 0861
DANCECLUBS
■ **Art** (CC E glm MA p s TV WE) Sat 22-5 hBeethovenstraße 1 ✉ 97080 *(Tram-Röntgenring)* ☎ 130 01

SPARTACUS 2001/2002 | 551

Germany — Würzburg ▶ Zwickau

■ **Gay Disco** (B D Glm lj YG) 1st Sat 22-3 h at Dance Hall c/o AKW, Frankfurter Straße 87 ✉ 97082

SEX SHOPS/BLUE MOVIES
■ **Claudia-Sexshop** (g) Mon-Fri 9-18, Sat 9-14 h, Sun closed Bahnhofstraße 3 ✉ 97070 *(near station)* ☎ 143 61

BOOK SHOPS
■ **Neuer Weg** (glm) Mon-Fri 9-20, Sat 9-16 h Sanderstraße 23-25 ✉ 97070 *(Tram-Sandering)* ☎ 355 91-0
Gay-lesbian section

FETISH GROUPS
■ **LC WÜ-Lederclub Würzburg** (G LJ) Meets 2nd/4th Fri 21 h at WuF-Zentrum, Nigglweg 2
Postfach 68 43 ✉ 97018 *(near Nautilandbad)* ☎ 353 85 14
📠 35 38 513 📧 lcwue@wuerzburg.gay-web.de
🌐 wuerzburg.gay-web.de/lcwue
Dresscode nights every 2nd Sat at WuF-Zentrum in the months of Jan, Mat, May, July, Sep and Nov (entry 21-23 h only).

HEALTH GROUPS
■ **AIDS-Beratung der Caritas** Mon-Fri 9-12, 14-17 h Friedrich-Spee-Haus, Röntgenring 3 ✉ 97070 ☎ 32 22 60

HELP WITH PROBLEMS
■ **Rosa Hilfe Unterfranken** Wed 20-22 h, except public holydays
Postfach 68 43 ✉ 97018 ☎ 19 446 📠 41 26 47
📧 rosahilfe@wuerzburg.gay-web.de
🌐 wuerzburg.gay-web.de/rosahilfe

SWIMMING
-Sommerhäuser Badesee (Road B 13 to Ochsenfurth/Ansbach. At Sommerhausen on P Wildpark. Along gardens to the lake (20 min).
- Baggerseen Dettelbach- und Hörblach- approx. 20km east of Würzburg on the B22 motorway. large flooded quarrys (Baggerseen) with nudist area (FKK-Bereich)

CRUISING
-Ringanlagen (Nähe/near Sanderring/Amtsgericht)
-Husarenpark (Ringpark zwischen/between Husarenstraße & Rennweger Ring, nach/after 21 h)
-Hauptbahnhof/Main rail station

Zwickau ☎ 0375

BARS
■ **XXL-Bar** (B d GLM MA p) 18-2 h
Römerstraße 21 ✉ 08056 *(near/nahe Neumarkt)* ☎ 353 15 58

SAUNAS/BATHS
■ **Thermo Club Sauna cTs** (AC B DR f G MA p SA SB SOL VS WH) 15-24, Fri Sat -6 h, closed Tue
Leipziger Straße 40 ✉ 08056 *(Near Neumarkt)* ☎ 29 60 10

HEALTH GROUPS
■ **AIDS-HILFE Westsachsen e.V.** Office hours Mon-Thu 8-12 & 13-15, Tue -20. Helpline Tue 13-20 h and by appointment.
Hauptstraße 10 ✉ 08056 *(near Hauptmarkt)* ☎ 230 44 65
☎ 29 33 00 (helpline) 📠 353 13 70
Gay & Lesbian Youth "Ju.L.S.e.V." group meets Mon 18-23 h.

CRUISING
-Hauptbahnhof/main railway station (after 20 h)
-Kaufhaus Horten (im zentrum/in city centre)
-Schwanenteichanlagen

SpartacusWorld.com
▶ click and ▶ win!
www.spartacusworld.com

Germany

Producer · Wholesaler · Distributor

man's BEST

RISBRIGVEJ 10 A · INDUSTRI III · DK-6330 PADBORG/DANMARK
TEL.: (+45) 73 67 06 00 · FAX: (+45) 73 67 06 11
www.mansbest.com · E-MAIL: sales@mansbest.com

Gibraltar

Location: South Europe
Initials: GBZ
Time: GMT+1
International Country Code: ☏ 350 (no area codes)
International Access Code: ☏ 00
Language: English, Spanish
Area: 6.5 km^2 / 2.5 sq mi.
Currency: 1 Gibraltar Pound (Gib£) = 100 New Pence (p)
Population: 27,000
Religions: 74% Roman Catholic
Climate: Mediterranean climate. Winters are mild, summers warm.

Homosexuality is no longer forbidden in Gibraltar, and the age of consent is 18. No gay scene as such is to be found here; gays meet in each other's homes or go to the Spanish towns along the Costa del Sol. If you are spending your holidays on the Costa del Sol or just passing through, it is worth making a day-trip to Gibraltar for shopping and sightseeing.

Homosexualität ist in Gibraltar nicht mehr verboten. Das Schutzalter ist auf 18 Jahre festgelegt. Eine Szene im eigentlichen Sinne gibt es nicht. Man trifft sich privat oder besucht die spanischen Städte entlang der Costa del Sol. Es lohnt sich eine Tagestour nach Gibraltar zu machen, um die Sehenswürdigkeiten zu besuchen oder einzukaufen, falls man sich an der Costa del Sol aufhält.

A Gibraltar, l'homosexualité n'est plus un délit. La majorité sexuelle y est fixée à 18 ans. Pas de vie gaie à proprement parler. On se retrouve en privé ou on fait un saut dans les stations balnéaires de la Costa del Sol. Gibraltar vaut le détour pour ses magnifiques vues ou pour y faire quelques emplettes.

En Gibraltar la homosexualidad no está prohibida. La edad de consentimiento ha sido fijada en 18 años. Aquí no existe un ambiente gay propiamente dicho. Los gays que viven aquí se reúnen en sus casas o van a las ciudades españolas, situadas a lo largo de la Costa del Sol. Merece la pena hacer una excursión a Gibraltar para hacer una visita turística o para ir de compras.

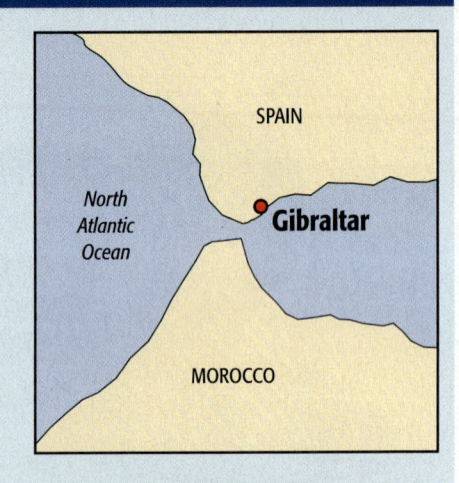

A Gibilterra l'omosessualità non è più proibita. L'età legale per avere rapporti sessuali è di 18 anni. Non c'è una vera vita gay in questa penisola. Gli abitanti gay si incontrano privatamente o vanno nelle città spagnole lungo la Costa del Sol. Se siete in vacanza sulla Costa del Sol o la state visitando, vale però lo stesso la pena di passare un giorno a Gibilterra per fare lo shopping o per dare un'occhiata alle sue curiosità.

BARS

■ **Charles' Hole-in-the-Wall** (AC B g MA) 20-0.30 h WE-1.30
5 Castle Street *(opp Main St. Post Office)* ☏ 753 75

Not gay, but gay-owned and nice. Most of the clients are sailors (British Navy). Before you try to make contacts you should talk with Charles. The wrong approach could get you into trouble here!

Greece

Name: Ellás • Griechenland • Grèce • Grecia
Location: Southeastern Europe
Initials: GR
Time: GMT +2
International Country Code: ☏ 30 (leave the first 0 of area codes)
International Access Code: ☏ 00
Language: Greek
Area: 131,957 km² / 50,949 sq mi.
Currency: 1 Drachme (DR) = 100 Lepta
Population: 10,662,138
Capital: Athina
Religions: 98% Greek Orthodox
Climate: Moderate climate. Winters are mild and wet, summers hot and dry.
Important gay cities: Athina

✱ Welcome to the land of the Gods. Greece is a warm and hospitable nation and in many ways idyllic for gay visitors. It is however steeped in tradition and the Greek Orthodox church has a strong influence on society; hence for residence the picture is not quite so rosy. The age of consent remains at 17 for homosexuals and 15 years for heterosexuals. The handful of active gay groups which exist in Athens and Thessaloniki, lack a certain unity. There is therefore a lack of solidarity between campaigning groups, which might also explain why legislative changes are so slow in coming about.

The gay scene in Athens, Mykonos and Thessaloniki has grown from strength to strength. In recent years and has lead to a greater abundance of openly gay venues, which no longer feel the need to hide behind closed doors. Some of the more attractive islands for tourists such as Santorini and Corfu are catching up fast. Outside of these main focal points gay activities are restricted to cruising. Cruising can be risky, and although there is no outspoken anti-gay legislation, it is recommended that gays cruising carry their passports with them.

Although many gay Greeks feel most comfortable on holiday in Lesbos (and especially lesbians), Mykonos and the surrounding Cyclades, as a visitor to Greece it would be a shame to restrict your choice of holiday destination to the obvious gay hotspots. Greece is a land of untold beauty and charm, and as a visitor you will rarely be made to feel uncomfortable on account of your sexuality.

✱ Willkommen im Land der Götter. Die Griechen sind eine warme und gastfreundliche Nation und Griechenland ist für Gay-Touristen in vielerlei Hinsicht idyllisch. Dennoch ist Griechenland in seinen Traditionen verwurzelt und die Griechisch Orthodoxe Kirche hat großen Einfluß auf die Gesellschaft; daher ist das Leben dort nicht ganz so rosig wie es zu sein scheint. Das Schutzalter bleibt bei 17 Jahren für Homosexuelle und bei 15 Jahren für Heterosexuelle. Eine Handvoll aktiver Gay-Gruppen in Athen und Thessaloniki bilden keine Einheit, woraus ein gewisser Mangel an Solidarität zwischen den beteiligten Gruppen resultiert und vielleicht eine Erklärung dafür ist, weshalb Gesetzesänderungen so lange auf sich warten lassen.

Die Schwulen-Szene in Athen, Thessaloniki und auf Mykonos wurde in den vergangenen Jahren immer größer und führte zu einer größeren Zahl öffentlicher Treffpunkte von Gays, die es nicht mehr länger als notwendig ansahen, sich hinter verschlossenen Türen zu verstecken. Einige der für Touristen attraktiveren Inseln wie Santorini und Korfu haben diesbezüglich sehr schnell aufgeholt.. Außerhalb dieser Hauptanziehungspunkte beschränken sich die Gay-Aktivitäten auf Cruising. Cruising kann ein Risiko darstellen und obwohl es keine Anti-Gay Gesetzgebung gibt, wird cruisenden Gays empfohlen, ihren Pass immer bei sich zu tragen.

Obwohl sich viele griechischen Gays und besonders Lesben auf der Insel Lesbos, Mykonos und den umliegenden Kykladen sehr wohl fühlen, wäre es für den Besucher Griechenlands eine Schande, sich bei der Auswahl des Ferienortes auf die eindeutigen Gay-Hochburgen zu beschränken. Griechenland ist ein Land von sagenhafter Schönheit und liebenswürdigem Charme, und als Tourist wird man bezüglich seiner Sexualität nur selten in unangenehme Situationen geraten.

✱ Bienvenue au pays des Dieux. La Grèce est un pays chaud et hospitalier, et en de nombreux points une destination idyllique pour les touristes gais. Un bémol est toutefois à porter à ce cliché: le pays est bien ancré dans la tradition et l'Eglise orthodoxe grecque a encore une forte influence sur la société. La majorité sexuelle est donc fixée à 17 ans pour les homosexuels alors qu'elle est définie à 15 ans pour les hétérosexuels. La poignée de groupes gais actifs qui existent à Athènes et en Thessalonique manque quelque peu d'unité. Un esprit de solidarité fait défaut dans la manière dont ils mènent leurs campagnes, ce qui explique peut-être pourquoi des changements législatifs mettent autant de temps à entrer en vigueur.

La scène gaie d'Athènes, de Mykonos, et de la Thessalonique prennent cependant toujours plus d'importance. Depuis quelques années, un plus grand nombre de manifestations se sont tenues à jour ouvert. Certaines parmi les plus belles îles touristiques comme Santorini et Corfou rattrapent leur retard. Mais en dehors de ces endroits, l'activité gaie se résume encore à la drague en plein air. Cela peut être parfois risqué et il est recommandé de toujours prendre son passeport avec soi, même s'il n'existe pas de législation homophobe.

Greece Alexandroúpolis ▸ Athina

Bien que la plupart des homosexuels grecs préfèrent se rendre en vacances à Lesbos (plus particulièrement les lesbiennes), à Mykonos, ou dans les Cyclades environnantes, il serait dommage de restreindre un voyage à ces seules destinations. La Grèce est un pays à la beauté et au charme indescriptibles et en tant que touriste gai vous vous sentirez presque toujours partout à l'aise.

Bienvenidos al país de los dioses. Grecia es una nación calurosa y hospitalaria y es, de muchas maneras, idílica para los visitantes gays. Sin embargo, está empapada de tradición y la Iglesia Ortodoxa griega tiene una fuerte influencia sobre la sociedad, por lo que las cosas no están tan bien para quien quiera quedarse a vivir. La edad de consentimiento es de dieciseis años para los homosexuales y de quince años para los heterosexuales. El puñado de grupos gays activos existentes en Atenas y Tesalónica no están muy unidos. Por ello, hay cierta falta de solidariedad entre los grupos que están trabajando en campañas gays, lo que podría explicar la lentitud con que se realizan los cambios legislativos.
En los últimos años, el ambiente gay en Atenas, Mykonos y Tesalónica se ha hecho cada vez más grande lo que conlleva una mayor abundancia de acontecimientos abiertamente gays, pues ya no se siente la necesitad de esconderse trás puertas cerradas. Algunas de las islas más atractivas para los turistas gays, como Santorini y Corfú, están teniendo un rápido auge para igualar quizás a los otros sitios gays. Fuera de estos lugares, las actividades homosexuales muchas veces se limitan a las zonas de cruising. Buscar rollo en lugares públicos puede conllevar ciertos riesgos, y a pesar de que no existen leyes particularmente anti-gays, es recomendable que los gays que estén haciendo cruising lleven sus carnets de identidad o sus pasaportes consigo.
Si bien muchos gays griegos se sienten más a gusto de vacaciones en Lesbos (especialmente las lesbianas), Mykonos y las demás islas Cícladas, sería una vergüenza para cualquier turista gay limitarse a pasar las vacaciones en los puntos gays: Grecia es un país

de increíble belleza y encanto, y al visitante gay normalmente no se le hará sentirse incómodo por sus preferencias sexuales.

✖ Benvenuti nel paese degli dei. La Grecia è una nazione calda e ospitale e per i turisti gay sotto molti aspetti è una terra idilliaca. Ciononostante essa rimane ancorata alle sue tradizioni e la chiesa greco-ortodossa esercita ancora una forte influenza sulla società; di conseguenza la vita qui non è così rosea come potrebbe sembrare di primo acchito. Il limite dell'età protetta è per gli omosessuali di 17 anni, mentre per gli eterosessuali di 15 anni.
Un piccolo numero di gruppi gay attivi non costituisce un'unità coesa, di qui la mancanza di solidarietà tra i vari gruppi e questo spiega anche perché le riforme di legge si facciano così tanto attendere.
L'ambiente gay ad Atene, Tessalonica e Micono ha acquisito negli scorsi anni sempre maggior vitalità e ciò ha contribuito ad aumentare i punti d'incontro per gay, che non sentono più la necessità di nascondersi. Alcune delle isole più attraenti per turisti come nel caso di Santorini e Corfù si stanno velocemente adeguando a questo repentino e progressivo cambiamento. Al di fuori di queste maggiori attrazioni le attività gay si limitano al cruising. Il cruising può essere rischioso e anche se non esiste una legislazione anti-gay, al gay che fanno il cruising si raccomanda di portarsi appresso il passaporto.
Sebbene molti gay greci e specialmente molte lesbiche si trovino a proprio agio sull'isola di Lesbo, Micono e nelle Cicladi circostanti, per il visitatore in Grecia sarebbe comunque una vergogna, limitarsi, nella scelta del luogo di villeggiatura, unicamente alle roccaforti gay. La Grecia è un paese di leggendaria bellezza e d'inesprimibile fascino, e perciò che riguarda la propria sessualità il turista raramente incorre in situazioni spiacevoli.

NATIONAL PUBLICATIONS

■ **a.maze**
122 Tatoiou N. Erythrea ✉ 14671 Athens ☎ (01) 620 65 18
📠 (01) 807 23 97 📧 ozon@compulink.gr
Trendy scene magazine, interesting for gay people. Available free of charge in bars and cafés.

■ **Deon Magazine** Tue Fri 20-23 h
91 Arapaki ✉ 17675 Athina (7th floor)
☎ 097 23 22 988 🌐 www.deon.gr
Magazine and information available. Maily via web. Also organise gay events and parties including gay pride.

Alexandroúpolis ☎ 0551

CRUISING
-Promenade and park at the sea near the Fanar Main Street (close to Hotel Alex)
-Nea Makri Beach

Athina ☎ 01

GAY INFO
■ **To Kraximo**
PO Box 42 28 ✉ 10210 ☎ (01) 52 35 625

📧 www.geocities.com/kraximo
Publish a gay guide to Greece. Useful information to be found on their website.

TOURIST INFO
■ **EOT Tourist Office**
2, Amerikis Street ☎ (01) 33 10 692

BARS
■ **Aiolis** (F glm YG)
Aiolov 23 ☎ 331 28 39
New trendy bar with good DJ's.
■ **Alekos Island** (B F g)
42 Tsakalov Street *(Kolonaki)*
Piano bar with good food and Greek music.
■ **Bee** (AC B CC Glm OS)
Miaovli 6 *(Psiri)*
■ **Floga** (G R)
19 Persefonis Street, Gazi *(2n floor)*
■ **Granazi** (B G MA)
20 Lembessi Street *(Makrigianni)*
Mainly Greek music.
■ **Kirki** (B F glm YG)
31 Apostoulou Pavlou Street *(at Thission Square)*
☎ 346 69 60

Athina

1. Candia Hotel
2. Videorama Sex Shop
3. Cosmopolite Cinema
4. Neon Café
5. Videoland Sex Shop
6. Arion Cinema
7. Gastra Taverna Restaurant
8. Alexander's Bar
9. Hotline Sex Shop
10. Aiolis Bar
11. Bee Bar
12. Multiculti Restaurant
13. Star Cinema
14. Athens Relax Sauna
15. Lizard Bar / Kiriki Bar

Greece Athina

■ **Lizard** (B D GLM)
31 Apostolov Pavlov Street *(Thission)*
■ **Smile** (B f G MA R) ?-3 h
71 Agathoupoleos/Acharnon Street *(near Victoria Square)*
☎ 864 53 98
■ **Sodade** (B G) Daily 18-?, Sun all day.
Triptolemov 10 ✉ 11854 *(Gazi)* ☎ 346 86 57
■ **Ta Paidia-The Guys** (B G MA YG) Sun-Thu 10-3.30, Fri Sat -? h
8 Lempesi Street ✉ 117 42 *(Makrigianni)* ☎ 921 4244
Greek music.
■ **Test Me** (B G R) Mon closed
64 Pipinov Street *(Amerikis Square)*

CAFES

■ **De Profundis** (b f Glm YG) 18-2 h
1 Hajimihali Street *(Plaka)* ☎ 323 17 64
■ **Enydriou Internet Café** (b f glm)
Syngrov Avenue *(Makrigianni)*
■ **Neon Café** (b F g R) ?-2 h
Omonia Square ☎ 522 32 01
■ **Oval Café** (b f glm)
5 Tositsa Street *(near Exarchia Square)*
■ **Peros** (b g YG) 9-3.30 h
Platia Kolonaki 7 *(Kolonaki)* ☎ 364 50 68
One of the several trendy cafés in Kolonaki. Also popular with gays.
■ **Style** (B GLM)
Keitis & Chiou Street *(nearby Larissis railway station)*

DANCECLUBS

■ **Alexander's** (AC B D G STV YG) 23-? h
44 Anagnostopoulou Street, Kolonaki ☎ 364 66 60
Cruisy bar upstairs, disco downstairs. Busy from midnight.
■ **City Club** (B D G S TV) 23-? h
4 Korizi Street ✉ 11743 *(Makriyianni)* ☎ 924 07 40
■ **Factory** (AC B D G SNU) Fri & Sat only
3 Voukourestiou Street *(Syntagma)*
■ **Lambda** (AC B D DR G MA S VS) 11-? h
12 Lembesi Street *(off Sygrou Ave.)* ☎ 922 42 02

RESTAURANTS

■ **Gastra Taverna** (B F glm) 20.30-2 h, closed Sun & Jul & Aug.
1 Dimaki Street *(Kolonaki)* ☎ 360 27 57
Reservation advisable.
■ **Multiculti** (AC B F glm OS)
8 Agias Feklas Street *(Psiri)* ☎ 3244 643

SEX SHOPS/BLUE MOVIES

■ **Emporio private cabins** (G VS)
39 Sokratous Street *(1st floor)* ☎ 522 23 13
■ **Emporio sex video** (G VS)
31 Veranzerou Street *(5th floor)* ☎ 522 72 35
■ **Hotline** (CC glm)
64 Panepistimiou Avenue *(1st floor, Omonia)* ☎ 382 06 60
■ **Videoland** (g VS) Mon-Fri 11-22, Sat -24, Sun 12-18 h
65 Panepistimiou Street *(2nd Floor, Omonia)*
■ **Videorama - Red Lion** Sat 11-18, Sun 12-18h
1, Emmanouil Benaki Street/Stadiou Street *(2nd floor, office 6)*
☎ 321 47 38

CINEMAS

■ **Arion** (g OG VS) 16-24 h
Athenas Street *(near Kotjia Square)*
■ **Athinaikon** (g VS)
11 Kratinov Street *(behind old Town Hall)* ☎ 522 18 26

■ **Averoff** (g VS)
Eolou/Likourgou Street
■ **Cosmopolite** (g VS)
Kotopuli Street *(Omonia Square)*
■ **Laou** (g OG VS) ?-3 h
Megalou Alexandrou Street
■ **Omonia** (g VS) ?-3 h
Santovriandou Street *(behind Omonia Square)*
Mostly gay visitors but straight films shown.
■ **Star** (g VS)
10 Agiou Konstantinou Street *(near Omonia Square)* ☎ 522 58 01
Biggest and most popular.

TRAVEL AND TRANSPORT

■ **Aenaon Travel** (CC g) Mon-Fri 10-19 h, closed Sat Sun
56 Panepistimiou Street ✉ 106 78 *(near Omonia Square)*
☎ 330 49 73 🖷 330 49 75 📧 aenaon@acci.gr
■ **Deon's Travel Services** (GLM)
91 Arapaki Street ☎ 176 75 ☎ 383 90 44 ☎ (097) 232 29 88
(24h service) 📧 travel@deon.gr 📧 deon.gr/travel
■ **Gay Tourism in Greece** (G)
86 Evrou Street ✉ 11527 ☎ 321 03 22 🖷 323 51 25
📧 gaytourism@gay.gr
■ **Yorgos Travel Service** (G) 11-18h
PO Box 30002 ✉ 10033 ☎ 321 03 22 ☎ 097 2265653
📧 gaytravel@yahoo.com

HOTELS

■ **Candia** (AC B F g H Pl)
40 Deligiani Street ☎ 524 61 12
15 km to the airport. Downtown location. All rooms with phone, bath and balcony.
■ **Kissos** (g H)
6 Maisonos Street *(Vathis Square)* ☎ 524 30 11
■ **Olympic Palace** (AC B F H NG Pl)
16 Filellinon Street ✉ 10557 *(Metaxourghion Square)* ☎ 323 76 11
All rooms with telephone & TV.
■ **Plaka** (AC B F H NG)
Mitropolitan Street *(near the cathedral)* ☎ 322 20 96

HEALTH GROUPS

■ **Act Up Greece**
3 Ag. Theodoron Street *(Kapnikareai)* ☎ 701 36 09
☎ 09 444 105 00
Information and support for people with or affected by HIV and AIDS.
■ **AIDS-Hotline**
☎ 722 22 22
■ **Andreas Syngros Hospital** 7-24h
5 Ionos Dragoumi Street *(Ilissia)* ☎ 723 96 11

SWIMMING

-Asteria Beach (take a Voula bus from the city)
-Varkiza-Limanakia Beach (take the Varkiza bus from Zapion N° A2, A3, B2 or B3 from downtown Athens, or A1, B! from Pireaus. Go to Glynda Sq. and change the bus there taking bus 115 or 116 to the 2nd station of Limanakia (exclusively gay) on the left side of the bus-stop is a canteen. From June 15-Sep 15 there is an express E2 from Panepistimiou St and E1 from Piracus going directly to the Limankia gay beach.

Athina ▶ Lesbos - Molyvos   **Greece**

CRUISING
-Kaningos Square (YG) (bus terminus near Omonia Square, from 21 h)
-Dimachia Square (day and night) Kotzia Square.
-Small park near railway station Larissis (AYOR) (opposite Hotel Candia, late)
-Kolonaki Square and surrounding cafés
-Omonia Square (AYOR)
-Pedion Areos Park (southeast section near Kolokotroni Street)
-Zappion Park (AYOR) (between Zappion and Zeus temple)
-Area accross Zappion Park (near the church of Agia Fotini)
-Syngrou Avenue (R TV)
-Athinas Street (R TV)
-Alexandras Avenue (near Katsandoni Street)
-Flower Market, Athinas Avenue (21-23 h)
-Koumoundourou Square (afternoon and night; Piraeus Avenue AYOR, R)
-Kaniggos Square (OG) (day)
-Zappion Park (day and night)
-Pedion Square
-National Park (near the duck pond)

Chios ☎ 0271
CRUISING
-Emporiou (on the beach)
-Daskalopetra (on the beach)
-Around Kara Ali's tomb

Kalamata ☎ 0721
HOTELS
■ **Elite** (B D H NG)
2 Navarinou ☎ 250 15
CRUISING
-Port Authority Park
-Railroad station

Kérkyra - Kérkyra ☎ 0661
CRUISING
-Park (uphill behind the shopping centre)
-Square at the fountain in front of Hotel Astir
-Aleko Swimming Pool

Kérkyra - Mirtiotissa ☎ 0661
BARS
■ **Eros** (AC B G h OS S SNU YG) 17-3 h
✉ 49100 *(Next to Glyfada beach)* ☎ 940 25
GUEST HOUSES
■ **Panorama** (g)
✉ 49100 ☎ 94025
SWIMMING
-Nudist beach (near Pelekas)

Korinthos ☎ 0741
CRUISING
-Central Square
-Railroad station
-Ahilleas Place

Kos ☎ 0242
DANCECLUBS
■ **Limit** (AC B D NG)
6 Al. Diakou *(in bar street)* ☎ 264 84
SWIMMING
-Tingaki gay beach (Take bus from Kos to Tingaki. At sea front drop off point take the left turning by restaurant "Alikes", through the bull bushes to the 1st junction. Turn right down to beach, turn left. Cruising in sand dunes.)
CRUISING
-Harbour (Archway and fortress area)
-Gardens (Taxi area)
-Old ruins behind Taxi area.

Kriti - Iraklion ☎ 081
CAFES
■ **Café Aman** (b F glm)
CINEMAS
■ **Orpheus** (g)
SWIMMING
-Hersonissos, near Knossos Royal Village resort (glm)
CRUISING
-Park of National Resistance (ayor) (next to old city-wall)
–Eleftherias Square

Kriti - Koutsouras ☎ 0843
HOTELS
■ **Okeanis** (B BF CC F H MA NG OS PI) April - November open, Restaurant daily 12-23 h
72055 ✉ 72055 ☎ 516 18 📠 516 18
💻 okeanis.ed@worldonline.nl 🌐 www.c-v.net/hotel/sitia/okeanis
Hotel and apartments with hotel service. Very friendly and clean.

Larissa ☎ 041
CRUISING
-Garden at the Main Square
-Railroad station (café)
-At the river (at night)
-Around football stadium.

Lesbos - Mitilini ☎ 0251
CRUISING
-Park behind and in front of theater
-Beach

Lesbos - Molyvos ☎ 0253
CAFES
■ **Fuego** (glm)
☎ 538 79
SWIMMING
-Eftalou Beach (Bays East of Eftalou, Bus Anaxos-Molyvos-Eftalou. NU glm)

Greece — Mykonos

Mykonos ☎ 0289

✳ After a period of relative inactivity, the island of Mykonos has once again become a paradise for gay tourists from around the world. For this reason a generally young crowd is to be found here, enjoying lots of parties and action. Mykonos can be reached from Athens by boat (6-7 hours) or by plane (1/2 hour). The town of Mykonos itself is idyllic, full of winding streets and charming squares. These streets tend to be devoid of street signs, which makes it difficult to find your way around at first (and explains why the listings below contain descriptions rather than exact addresses). Once you have memorized a few landmarks, though, it becomes much easier.

★ Nach einer Ruhephase ist diese Insel wieder zum Eldorado schwuler Touristen aus aller Welt geworden. Aus diesem Grund findet man hier auch überwiegend jüngeres Publikum, viel Trubel und Action. Von Athen aus per Flugzeug (1/2 Stunde) oder Schiff (6-7 Std.) erreichbar. Die Stadt Mykonos selbst ist eine verwinkelte, idyllische Kleinstadt. Das macht das Zurechtfinden nicht leicht, doch wenn man sich ein paar prägnante Punkte merkt, dann funktioniert auch das.

✳ Après une période creuse ces dernières années, Mykonos est de nouveau le paradis gai qu'elle était il y a 15 ans. La population estivale y est très jeune et ça bouge énormément! On y arrive par avion depuis Athènes (une heure et demie) ou par bateau (6 à 7 heures).
Mykonos elle-même est une charmante petite ville pleine de coins et de recoins sympathiques. Comme les rues n'ont généralement pas de panneaux indicateurs, nous ne pouvons pas vous donner les adresses exactes. On peut cependant s'y retrouver assez rapidement: retenez des points de repères à partir desquels vous pourrez vous orienter.

❋ Despúes de un periodo de silencio esta isla se ha convertido nuevamente en un paraíso para turistas gay de todo el mundo. Esto es en parte la razón por la que se encuentran aquí tantos jóvenes y tanta marcha. Desde Atenas se llega a la isla en avión (media hora de vuelo) o en barco (de 6 a 7 horas de travesía). La ciudad de Mykonos es muy ídilica pero por sus innumerables callecitas no es tan facil orientarse. Por ello damos a continuación más bien descripciones que direcciones exactas de los sitios. Una vez memorizado unos cuantos puntos de referencia de la ciudad, a uno no le cuesta tanto encontrar los lugares indicados.

✖ Dopo un periodo di calma Mykonos è ritornata l'Eldorado dei gay di tutto il mondo. Per questo motivo qui c'è molta azione e molta gente giovane. Mykonos può essere raggiunta da Atene in nave (6-7 ore) o in aereo (1/2 ora). Tipiche dell'isola sono le stradine tortuose, gli edifici bianchi e gli stupendi mulini a vento, il paesaggio è veramente idillico. La città è abbastanza piccola e non avrete problemi ad orientarvi dopo una breve perlustrazione.

THOMAS
BAR glm

relaxed Atmosphere
April 1st – Oct 30th
every night 8 pm – 2 am
Air conditioning

50 m from the shop
of the International Press
near old harbour
Tel. 26866
E-Mail:
tommykonos@hotmail.com

TOURIST INFO
■ **Municipal Information Office**
☎ 222 01 ☎ 239 90 📠 222 29

BARS
■ **Cafe Aristote** (B glm MA)
46 Matoyianni Str. ☎ 234 92
■ **CoCo's** (B F G OS)
(at the gay Super Paradise beach)
■ **Icaros** (! B D G MA OS s) 22-? h
Agia Kiriaki ☎ 227 18
Two bars, roof terrace; gay owned.
■ **Kastro's** (B G MA)
(besides the Paraportiani church) ☎ 230 72
Classical music, relaxed atmosphere. Go during cocktail hour to view the spectacular sunset.

MYKONOS ACCOMMODATION CENTER

**ALL TRAVEL SERVICES and QUALITY ACCOMMODATION
for the INDEPENDENT TRAVELLERS, GAYS and LESBIANS.**
- HOTEL RESERVATIONS, FURNISHED APARTS AND VILLAS
- BOOKINGS FOR SURROUNDING ISLANDS, ATHENS & REST OF GREECE
- AIRLINE TICKETS (INTERNATIONAL AND DOMESTIC)
- WORLDWIDE HOTELRESERVATIONS
- TRAVEL AGENCIES INQUIRIES WELCOME

ADDRESS: Enoplon Dynameon Nr. 10 (upper floor) at the end of Matoyianni street
P.O.Box 58 • 84600 MYKONOS • GREECE • Tel. 00 (from USA: 011) -289-23160 or 23408 • fax 24137
e-mail: mac@mac.myk.forthnet.gr. • web pages at http://mykonos-accommodation.com

Mykonos | Greece

GERANIUM
MYKONOS

Gay owned and runned, located 200 meters from the center of the nightlife of Mykonos town and from the main bus station to all beaches ✖ all rooms, studios and apartments are equipped with fridge, coffee- and teamaking facilities, fan, direct-dial-telephone, color TV, electronic private safe, balconies and terraces private entrance ✖ largest swimming pool in town surrounded by an exotic garden

Geranium ✖ Ano skoli kalon technon ✖ 84600 **Mykonos**/Greece
Phone +30-(0)289 - 22867, 24620, 24144 ✖ **Fax** +30-(0)289 - 24624
WEB-SITE: www.geraniumhotel.com ✖ **e-mail**: info@geraniumhotel.com

■ **Manto's** (AC B GLM OS YG)
Mantoyianni Street *(near Pierro's)*
■ **Montparnasse** (A B glm MA) 11-2 h
24 Ag. Anargyron Street ✉ 84600 *(Little Venice)* ☎ 237 19
Classic music.
■ **Thomas** (AC B glm) ☎ 20866
(near old harbour)

CAFES
■ **Pierro's** (AC B D Glm MA OS s)
Mantoyianni Street ✉ 84600 ☎ 221 77
Pierro's Wild Little Sisters upstairs from Pierro's.

RESTAURANTS
■ **Archaion** (B CC F glm)
19 Dilou Street ✉ 84600 ☎ 792 56
■ **Magic Garden** (! B CC F Glm OS)
✉ 84600 *(Just off Enopion Dynameon Street)* ☎ 62 17
Excellent food served in pleasant surroundings.
■ **Yves Klein Blue** (B CC F glm)
Ag. Saranda ☎ 273 91

TRAVEL AND TRANSPORT
■ **Mykonos Accomodation Center** Sun closed, daily 9-14 h, 17-21 h (summer months open Mon-Sun 8.30-22.30 h)
10 Enoplon Dynameon ✉ 84600 *(1st floor, above Nautical Museum)*
☎ 231 60 ☎ 234 08 ☎ 241 37 🖥 mac@mac.myk.forthnet.gr
🖥 www.mykonos-accommodation.com
Gay friendly travel agency for reservations for all hotels, apartments, villas on Mykonos and travel services for islands in the Cyclades & Athens.

HOTELS
■ **Adonis** (AC B B BF H glm)
PO Box 68 ✉ 84600 ☎ 22434 📠 23749
🖥 mihali@adonis.myk.forthnet.gr
Smart hotel close to town center.
■ **Carrop Tree** (AC B BF cc glm H) 8-24h
PO Box 110 ✉ 84600 ☎ 233 00 ☎ 259 00 📠 221 62
🖥 carroptree@hotmail.com
15 double rooms, 2 single rooms, 2 triple rooms. All rooms with shower/WC, balcony/terrace, heating. Hotel provides own key and car park.

Pierros

Pierros Bar and **Manto Bar** (next door)
For Disco dancing, drag shows on the bar and our outdoor square

Pierros Cafe Bar (upstairs from Pierros)
Techno/trans music and dancing club,
with outdoor veranda overlooking the square

A bit of everthing you've dreamed of.
www.otenet.gr/pierros

Greece | **Mykonos**

Hotel ELYSIUM
- Panoramic views over the old city and the ocean
- Swimming-pool, Jacuzzi, Fitneß Center, Sauna
- All rooms with air condition, Hairdryer, Direct-dial phone, Radio, Refrigerator, Safe Box, Sat-TV
- Snack-bar, Pool Bar, Guest Laundry & Beach Towels.

area scool of fine art
84 600 Mykonos Tel. (0289) 23952 - 23747

■ **Elysium** (B BF CC E f GLM msg OS PI SA WH WO) 0-24 h
Area School of Fine Arts
✉ 84600 *(150m from the central bus station)*
☎ 239 52   📠 237 47   📧 elysium@otenet.gr
🖥 www.elysiumhotel.com
The hotel is built in traditional myconian architecture. Panoramic view over Mykonos city and ocean. 21rooms, 17 suites. All rooms with AC, phone, radio, fridge, safe, Sat-TV. The Elysium has recently been renovated to further improve your comfort level. Breakfast consists of an american buffet. The hotel has a restaurant snack bar and room service.

■ **Geranium** (cc e F Glm H NU OS PI) April-October
Ano Skoli Kalon Technon *(on top of hill of art school)*   ☎ 228 91
☎ 241 44   📠 246 24   📧 info@geraniumhotel.com
🖥 www.geraniumhotel.com

■ **Mantalena** (H g)
PO Box 94   ☎ 229 54   📠 243 24   📠 243 02
Nice hotel with friendly staff, overlooking Mykonos harbour. Rooms and apartments available, rates on request.

■ **Petasos Beach** (AC g H PI)
Plati Yiallos   ✉ 84600   ☎ 226 08   📠 24 101   📧 info@petasos.gr
🖥 www.petasos.gr
Three miles out of the town of Mykonos, located at the seashore of Plati Yiallos, near bus stop. Rooms with phone, TV, minibar and balcony.

■ **Semeli** (BF g H)
Rohari   ☎ 274 66   📠 274 67

■ **Villa Konstantin** (Glm H OS) April-October 24 h
Agios Vassilis   ✉ 84600   ☎ 262 04   ☎ 258 24   📠 262 05
📧 villakonstantin@myk.forthnet.gr
🖥 www.villakonstantin-mykonos.gr
700 m from Mykonos-City, quiet location. Studios and apartments, rates on request. By foot you are 10 minutes from the town and all the night-life. By car or moped it will take you only two or three minutes.

GUEST HOUSES

■ **Pension Maria** (glm H OS)
✉ 84600 *(Close to the bus stop for Plati Yiallos)*   ☎ 249 60

SWIMMING

-Super Paradise (G NU) (Take bus from Mykonos City to Plati Yiallos. From there boats go between 9 and 19.30 h to and fro Super Paradise. You can alos take the direct bus to Paradise Beach. You have to walk 15 mins. along the cliffs.)
-Elia Beach (g) It's a favorite of gay sun worshippers. It can be reached by bus or by boat from the harbor, otherwise take the bus to Plati Yiallos, and from there the little fishing boat will take you.
-Agrari Beach (g)
-Paradise Beach (g)
-Paranga Beach (g) (10 mins. by foot from Plati Yiallos)

CRUISING

-Panorama Beach
-Panagia Paraportiani church (ayor) (sunset 'til sunrise. Popular. Many tourists)

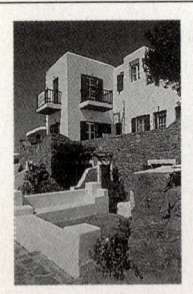

Apartments Studios and Rooms
- Private Bathroom
- AIC
- T.V.
- Kitchen facilities
- Ceiling fans
- Telephone
- Safety deposit box
- Mini Bar
- Balcony with Sea view
- Parking
- Car + Scooter rental
- Internet access
- Free airport pick up

MYKONOS GREECE
Villa Konstantin
Sharon Graham

Tel.: (0289) 25824 / 26204   •   Fax: (0289) 26207
E-Mail: villakonstantin@myk.forthnet.gr
www.villakonstantin-mykonos.gr

Nafplion ☎ 0752

CRUISING
-Promenade along the sea (at the very end)
-Kolokotroni Park

Paros - Naousa ☎ 0284

BARS
■ **Kavarnis Bar & Creperie** (B F glm N OS) Mon-Sun 19.30-?
(near the Post Office at the top of the Square)
■ **Les ZinZins** (A AC B BF d f GLM MA) Easter-End of October, 11-3 h
✉ 84401 ☎ 533 55
■ **To Kyma** (B BF F glm H ma N OS) 9.30-1 h
Ag. Anargiri ✉ 84400 ☎ 520 25
Bar-restaurant-hotel.

HOTELS
■ **Fotilia** (AC B BF CC f glm H MA N OS PI R WH) April-October
✉ 84402 *8150 m from centre of village)* ☎ 525 81 ☎ 525 82
🖨 525 83
■ **Manos** (AC B BF f glm H lj MA OS PI) April-October
✉ 84401 *(350 m form the square of Naoussa)* ☎ 511 14
🖨 517 41 ✉ tzanis@par.forthnet.ger
ww.hotelmanos.gr

GUEST HOUSES
■ **Heaven** (AC E H NG) Apr-Sept.
✉ 84401 ☎ 51549 🖨 51549
10 mins to the beach.

SWIMMING
-Monastiri (Beach on the Bay of Naoussa. Nude sunbathing is permitted, cruising on the left-hand side, when facing the sea)

Paros - Parikia ☎ 0284

BARS
■ **Statues** (B NG)
(on the beach)

RESTAURANTS
■ **Happy Green Cow, The** (F glm)
(Behind National Bank)
Trendy vegetarian restaurant.
■ **Levantis** (B F g OS YG) Closed Nov 1st-Mar 31st
Castro Parikia
☎ 236 13

Paros - Paros ☎ 0284

DANCECLUBS
■ **Chez Leonard** (B D g MA) 23-? h
(at the harbour) ☎ 514 41

SWIMMING
-Langeri Beach (glm, NU).

Pátrai ☎ 061

DANCECLUBS
■ **Ionio** (b glm YG)
(At EOT beach)

CRUISING
-Railway station
-Kalogria Beach (NU)
-Port, by the pier
-Ermis Cinema (toilets)
-Ktel (long distance bus terminal)

Piraeus ☎ 01

BARS
■ **Flying In** (B G STV) Sat STV
34 Harileou Street ☎ 453 39 93

HEALTH GROUPS
■ **State General Hospital Vassilissa Frideriki** 8-11 h
6 Phanariotou/Petrou Rali Street *(Nikea, Piraeus)* ☎ 491 88 40

CRUISING
-Promenade around Passaliami (YG) (19.30-? h).

Ródos ☎ 0241

BARS
■ **Berlin** (B G MA) 21-? h
Orfanidoustreet 47 *(near Alexia Hotel)* ☎ 322 50

RESTAURANTS
■ **Rhobel** (CC F glm OS) 12-24h
G. Leontos 13-15 ✉ 85100 ☎ 759 38
Belgian cuisine.

HOTELS
■ **Via Via** (BF) All year
Pythagora 45, Lisipou 2 ✉ 85100 ☎ 770 27 🖨 770 27
💻 viavia@rho.forthnet.gr

GUEST HOUSES
■ **Pink Elephant** (AC BF CC g H OS)
Irodotou 42 ☎ 224 69 🖨 224 69 ✉ paojegio@otenet.gr
Centrally located, clean, gay-friendly.

SWIMMING
-Faliraki nudist beach (15 minutes by bus from Rhodos; walk to right about 2 km along the beach to third cove)
-Beaches near Thermes Kalitheas (on the rocks near Pinewood area, right side from the small family beach)

CRUISING
-Mandraki Place
-Near Agora
-Between Mandraki Place and post office
-Park opposite Tourist Police
-Park beside St. Francis' Church and Thense Hotel
-Petra Grikov - rocks at the end of the Girkos beach, action in the caves!

Samos ☎ 0273

BARS
■ **Barino** (B BF f g YG) 8-3 h only during summer!
Kokkari Village *(near central Square)*

Greece | Samos ▶ Thira - Thira

RESTAURANTS
■ **Eros Restaurant** (F g)
(located at the habour of Kokkari, near Bar "Barino") ☎ 926 36

CRUISING
-Tsamadou beach (g NU) (Kokkari village, bus from Samos town)

Santorini ☎ 0286
☞ Thira

Skiathos ☎ 0427

BARS
■ **Adagio** (B GLM MA) 22-03 h
Evagelistrias 14 *(Near to post office)* ☎ 210 52
■ **Kalypso** (AC B g) 9-? h
Filokleous Gerogiadou *(near new port)* ☎ 230 51

SWIMMING
-Banana Beach (nudist beach next to Kokounaries Beach; buses from town; take bus to last stop, then walk right over a small hill and through an olive grove)
-Tsougias Island (take the boat from Skiathos, approximately hourly departures).

Spárti ☎ 0731

CRUISING
-Opposite theater

Thessaloníki ☎ 031

CAFES
■ **De Facto** (B glm OS YG)
19 Pavlou Mela Street ☎ 26 36 74

SEX SHOPS/BLUE MOVIES
■ **Laïkon** (g r) 10-2 h
Monastiriou St. 4 *(Near Vardari Square)*
■ **Tower Video** (g VS) 14-22 h
Filikis Eterias Street 3 *(2nd floor)* ☎ 26 90 84

HEALTH GROUPS
■ **AIDS Hotline**
☎ 42 20 21

CRUISING
All are AYOR
-Small park next to Hotel Macedonian Palace
-Sea promenade next to Music Palace behind Luna Park Salaminas and Poseidon swimming pool
-Parking Byzantine museum
-Streets and small park around central train station (Michalikalou Street).

Thira - Firostefani ☎ 0286

RESTAURANTS
■ **Taverna Il Cantuccio** (F g MA) 20-24 h
☎ 220 82
Italian cuisine. In high season reservation recommended.

Thira - Ia ☎ 0286

HOTELS
■ **Zoe House** (g H lj MA OS)
(20 min. from airport) ☎ 714 66
Located in the old village Ia, near the volcano. All rooms with bath, & kitchenette. Rate from DR20.000 per house and night.

CRUISING
-Castle of Ia

Thira - Koloubos ☎ 0286

SWIMMING
-Koloubos (NU) (on the left side)

Thira - Oia ☎ 0286

APARTMENTS
■ **Oia Mare Villas** (glm H)
☎ 710 70 ☎ (0)1-813 76 05 (Nov-Mar)
📠 710 70
Hotel apartments with TV, radio, fully equipped kitchen, private bath and WC. All rooms with private terrace and seaview. Rates upon request. Daily maid service.

Thira - Thira ☎ 0286

BARS
■ **Franco's Bar** (B f MA NG)
Odós Marinatos ☎ 228 81
Closed in winter. Classical music.

HOTELS
■ **Atlas** (BF H NG PI) May-October
Karterados ✉ 84700 ☎ 234 15 📠 234 15
📧 atlas001/otenet.gr
🌐 www.santorini.com/hotels/atlas
■ **Kavalari** (BF CC glm H)
PO Box 17 ✉ 84700 ☎ 224 55 ☎ 223 47
📠 226 03

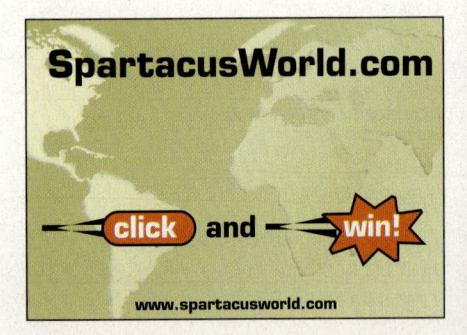

Agaña ▶ Tumon | **Guam**

Guam

Location: Pacific Ocean
Initials: GU
Time: GMT+11
International Country Code: ☎ 1-671 (no area codes)
International Access Code: ☎ 011
Language: English; Chamorro
Area: 549 km² / 212 sq mi.
Currency: 1 US Dollar (US$) = 100 Cents.
Population: 159,000
Capital: Agaña
Religions: 90% Catholic
Climate: Tropical marine climate. Warmth and humidity are moderated by northeast trade winds. The dry season lasts from January to June, the rainy season from July to December. There's little seasonal temperature variation.

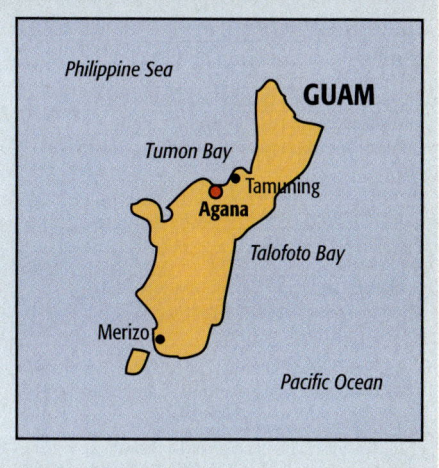

✱ We do not have any information concerning the penal code, but we assume, that homosexuality is open to prosecution.

✱ Zwar liegen uns keine juristischen Informationen vor, aber wir vermuten, daß Homosexualität strafbar ist.

✱ Nous ne disposons d'aucune information concernant la situation des gais face à la loi. Il semblerait cependant que l'homosexualité soit condamnable.

✱ No poseemos informaciones judiciales respecto al trato de la homosexualidad en la isla, pero suponemos que ella es penada.

✱ Non abbiamo informazioni concrete ma presumiamo che qui l'omosessualità sia illegale.

Map: Guam showing Philippine Sea, Tumon Bay, Tamuning, Agana, Talofoto Bay, Merizo, Pacific Ocean.

Agaña

GENERAL GROUPS
■ **Guam Friends**
PO Box 1861 ✉ GU 96910
Gay group

Tamuning

CRUISING
- Bank of Hawaii (AYOR r tv) (rear parking lot, 24-5 h)
- ITC Building (toilets)

Tumon

DANCECLUBS
■ **Onyx, The** (AC B D E glm YG)
San Vitores Road *(at Sand Castle Complex)*
Big and expensive.

CRUISING
- Y'pao beach (ayor G) (near Hilton Hotel, 21-3 h)

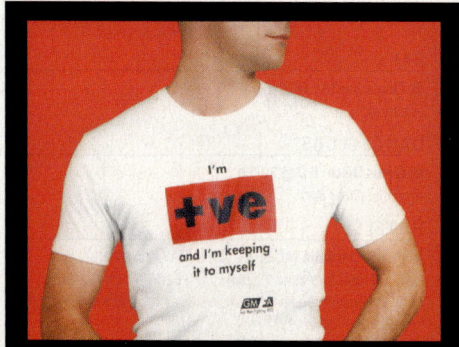

Lots of HIV+ men don't tell

GMFA's campaigns and actions are designed, planned and executed by positive, negative and untested volunteers.
To volunteer for GMFA write, phone or email:
Unit 43, Eurolink Centre, 49 Effra Road, LONDON, SW2 1BZ. 020 7738 6872. newvol@gmfa.demon.co.uk
www.demon.co.uk/gmfa
Registered Charity no. 1076854

GMFA Gay Men Fighting AIDS

Guatemala

Location: Central America
Initials: GCA
Time: GMT -6
International Country Code: ☎ 502 (no area codes)
International Access Code: ☎ 00
Language: Spanish; 23 Indian (Maya-Quiché) languages and dialects
Area: 108,889 km² / 42,042 sq mi.
Currency: 1 Quetzal (Q) = 100 Centavos
Population: 12,007,580
Capital: Ciudad de Guatemala
Religions: 75% Roman Catholic; 25% Protestant
Climate: Tropical climate. The lowlands are hot and humid, the highlands cooler.

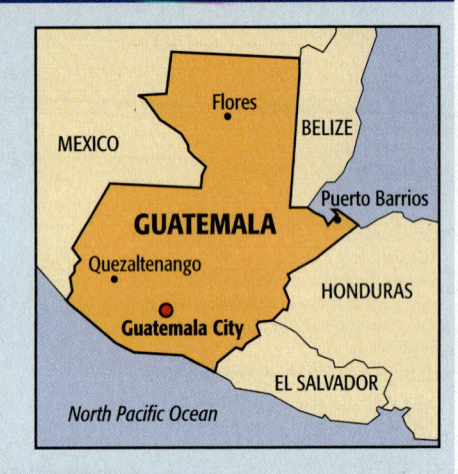

※ Homosexual acts between consenting men over the age of eighteen are legal. However, we have received conflicting reports on the actual social conditions for gays.

※ Einvernehmliche homosexuelle Handlungen zwischen Männern über 18 Jahren sind dem Gesetz nach erlaubt. Allerdings hat gerade die ländliche Bevölkerung ein negatives Bild von Schwulen.

※ Au Guatemala, l'homosexualité n'est pas un délit, à condition que les partenaires soient âgés de plus de 18 ans et consentants. Pour le reste, nous ne disposons que d'informations contradictoires.

※ De acuerdo a la constitución del país, el trato homosexual entre hombres majores de 18 años, si es de acuerdo mutuo, está permitido. Sobre la situación real nos han llegado sin embargo informes contradictorios.

※ Gli atti omosessuali tra uomini maggiorenni e consenzienti sono legali. Comunque, abbiamo ricevuto delle informazioni contrastanti sulla reale condizione sociale dei gay.

NATIONAL GAY INFO

■ **Grupo C'aslen**
4a Avenida 3-39 Zona 1, Ciudad Guatemala

Antigua

CRUISING
- Main Square
- Plaza de Armas
- Earthquake ruins (guides pleasant and helpful)

Guatemala City

GAY INFO
■ **Support Organization for An Integral Sexuality Confronting AIDS (OASIS)**
11 Calle 4-51, zone 1   ☎ 232 33 35   📠 232 33 35
Social centre, infos about gay scene and AIDS.

BARS
■ **Encuentro. El** (B f G) Mon-Sat 17-23h
Cine Los Capitos, 6 Avenida 12- 51 Zona 1 *(3rd floor)*   ☎ 230 4459
Nice and friendly.

DANCECLUBS
■ **Efebus** (B D) Tue-Sat 21-1h
4th Street 5-30 Zona 1   ☎ 253 4119
■ **Pandora's Box** (B CC D DR GLM MA OS P S) Fri 21-1.30, Sat - 2.30 h
Ruta 3 No. 3-08, Zona 4   ☎ 332-2823

■ **Z-Boy** (B D S) Fri & Sat 20-1h
12th Street 6-61, Zona 1   ☎ 220 9916
The most crowded disco/bar, great atmosphere and good shows.

CRUISING
All these places are AYOR and are located downtown
- La Calle del Amor (love street) 7th street between 2nd and 5th Avenues, at night - risky
- Cerrito del Carmen (park) afternoons
- Parque Cenral (central park) afternoons

Panajachel

BARS
■ **Circus Bar** (B F NG) 18-1 h
Live music.

DANCECLUBS
■ **Circus Disco** (B D g) 20-1 h
(opposite Circus Bar)

HOTELS
■ **Chalet Cristinita** (AC BF CC glm H MA OS WE WH)
Calle El Frutal 1-79 zona 2, Sololá   ☎ 762-1184   📠 762-1184
Hotel shuttle from Guatemala City available. Located on shores of the beautiful lake Atitlán.
Single rooms from $ 12, doubles $18.

Puerto Barrios

SWIMMING
-Matias de Calvez beach

Puerto San José

BARS
■ **Hotel Chulamar** (B g WE)

On the beach, ocean front. Fancy beach resort, nice mixed crowd on weekends only.

SWIMMING
-Beaches (many of the lifeguards like action, be discreet)

Honduras

Location: Central America
Initials: HN
Time: GMT -6
International Country Code: ☏ 504 (no area codes)
International Access Code: ☏ 00
Language: Castillian; Spanish; English
Area: 112,088 km^2 / 43,277 sq mi.
Currency: 1 Lempira (L) = 100 Centavos
Population: 5,861,955
Capital: Tegucigalpa
Religions: 90% Catholic
Climate: The climate is subtropical in the lowlands and moderate in the mountains.

There are no specific laws that apply to homosexuality. This however does, not mean, that the situation is very favourable for gays in Honduras. There are no efforts to create any anti-discriminatory regulations, police and military raids are often told of. This situation developed since the outcome of AIDS.

Es gibt keinerlei gesetzliche Regelungen, die sich mit Homosexuellen beschäftigen. Es gibt keinerlei Bestrebungen, Anti-Diskriminierungsregelungen zu treffen. Seit dem Bekanntwerden von AIDS sehen sich Schwule häufig verbalen und physischen Attacken von staatlicher wie auch gesellschaftlicher Seite ausgesetzt. Nach neuesten Informationen hat sich die Situation von Schwulen und Lesben in den letzten Jahren eher noch verschlechtert.

Pas de législation anti-homo aux Honduras, ce qui ne veut pas dire que, là-bas, les gais ont la vie facile. Personne n'est à l'abri des discriminations et des chicanes de la police et de l'armée, par exemple, qui "visitent" régulièrement les lieux gays. Depuis l'apparition de l'épidémie du sida, la situation ne s'est pas améliorée.

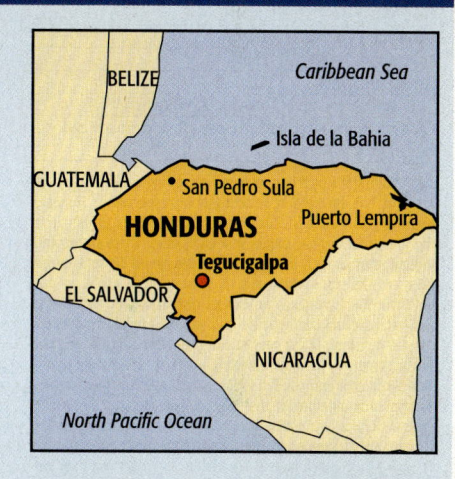

Aunque en Honduras no exista una legislación anti-homosexual, la situación para los gays no es nada favorable. No hay aspiraciones para reformas legislativas y se sabe que los gays son molestados por militares y policías con frecuencia. Esta situación se agravó con la problematica del SIDA.

Non esistono leggi che menzionano l'omosessualità. Tuttavia ciò non significa che la situazione in Honduras sia particolarmente buona. Non esiste neppure il proposito di emanare una legge contro la discriminazione dei gay. Si parla invece di ripetute violenze contro i gay da parte della polizia e dei militari. Questa situazione esiste da quando si conosce l'AIDS.

San Pedro Sula

GENERAL GROUPS
■ **Comunidad Gay Sampedrana**
✉ comunidadgay@mayanet.hn

CRUISING
-Park in center of city (AYOR)
-by the railway tracks (AYOR)

Tegucigalpa

GENERAL GROUPS
■ **Asociación Colectivo Violeta**
PO Box 4053 ☏ 237-6398 📠 237-6398
✉ violeta@hondudata.com
Different activities ranging from HIV prevention to young groups. Call for more details.
■ **Grupo Prisma**
PO Box 45 90 ☏ 232-8342 📠 232-8342
✉ prisma@sdnhon.org.hn

CRUISING
-Parque Central (AYOR) (arround the cathedral)
-Plaza Miraflores (AYOR)
-Mall Multiplaza (AYOR)

Hungary

Name:	Magyar • Ungarn • Hongrie • Hungria • Ungheria
Location:	Central Europe
Initials:	H
Time:	GMT+1
International Country Code:	☎ 36 (leave the first 06 of area codes)
International Access Code:	☎ 00
Language:	Magyar (Hungarian)
Area:	93,033 km^2 / 35,920 sq mi.
Currency:	1 Forint (Ft) = 100 Filler
Population:	10,208,127
Capital:	Budapest
Religions:	64% Roman Catholics; 23% Protestant
Climate:	Moderate climate. Winters are cold, cloudy and humid, summers are warm.

※ During the past few years, an interesting and lively gay scene has emerged in Eastern Europe, especially in Hungary. Also the countryside in Hungary seems to reach a turningpoint: There are monthly gay parties in a lot of cities. There are no anti-sodomy laws as such in Hungary, but the age of consent for gay sex is 18, while for straights it is 14. Same-sex marriage is not possible, but the law makes no explicit distinction between homo- and heterosexual partnerships and gay or lesbian partnerships can get registred. Many gays in Hungary have difficulty acknowledging their gay identity, reflecting a lack of self-esteem due to their social environment. But for all that, Hungarians seem to have no trouble at all enjoying their gay lifestyle. Hungary's gay night spots are typically crowded. Visitors can even find themselves feeling somewhat irritated at Hungarians' frankness with respect to sex, because Hungarian gays are very quick to tell you their wishes and expectations.

★ Innerhalb der letzten Jahre entstand eine lebendige und interessante schwul-lesbische Szene in Osteuropa, insbesondere in Ungarn. Auch auf dem Land tut sich etwas: Monatliche Parties finden vielerorts regelmäßig statt. Schutzalter für schwulen Sex ist 18, für Heterosexuelle 14; Schwule Ehe ist nicht zugelassen, aber das Gesetz macht keinen Unterschied zwischen homo- oder heterosexuellen Lebensgemeinschaften,- eine Registrierung ist möglich. Viele Schwule und Lesben in Ungarn haben ein wenig ausgeprägtes Selbstbewußtsein. In Ermangelung von Jugend- oder Coming-Out-Gruppen übernehmen junge Schwule und Lesben viel zu oft Lebenskonzepte der Älteren. Dennoch sind sie durchaus genußfähig und Ungarns schwule Treffpunkte sind sehr gut besucht. Besucher sind oft erstaunt erstaunt über die Direktheit, mit der mit sexuellen Wünschen und Erwartungen umgegangen wird.

※ Au cours des dernières années, et particulièrement en Hongrie, il s'est développé en Europe de l'Est un milieu gai et lesbien animé et intéressant. Même dans le pays, des fêtes ont lieu régulièrement dans beaucoup de villes provinciales. La majorité sexuelle est fixée à 18 ans pour les gais, et à 14 ans pour les hétérosexuels. Le mariage gai n'existe pas, mais la loi ne fait pas de différence entre les concubinages homosexuels et hétérosexuels et il est ainsi possible de se déclarer pour un partenariat. A cause du climat social, beaucoup de gais en Hongrie ont une image d'eux-mêmes peu valorisante. Cela ne les empêche pas d'apprécier un mode de vie gai comme les nombreux établissements généralement toujours bondés le démontrent. Les visiteurs peuvent être surpris de la franchise des Hongrois en matière de sexe, car ils n'hésitent pas à rapidement parler de leurs désirs et de leurs attentes.

◆ Durante el curso de los últimos años se ha desarrollado un interesante ambiente gay en Europa Oriental, sobre todo en Hungría. Pero incluso en las zonas rurales se nota algo de este cambio, como demuestra la celebración regular de fiestas. La edad de consentimiento para gays es de 18 años, para heterosexuales está estipulada en 14. Aunque el matrimonio homosexual no está permitido, la ley no diferencia entre la orientación sexual de las parejas, así que existe la posibilidad de inscribirse en el registro. Pocos gays y lesbianas húngaros muestran una fuerte autoconfianza, por lo que adoptan con frecuencia modos tradicionales de vida. Esto se debe en gran parte a la escasez de grupos que ayuden y apoyen a los jóvenes en su autodeterminacion sexual. Sin embargo, los húngaros disfrutan el sexo y los sitios de encuentros gay son muy frecuentados. Muchas veces al visitante le sorprende la sinceridad con que se expresan los deseos y expectativas sexuales.

※ Durante gli ultimi anni nei paesi dell'est si è sviluppato un'ambiente lesbico-gay vivace ed interessante, soprattutto in Ungheria. Anche nei posti di campagna sta cambiandosi qualcosa: regolarmente in molti posti vengono organizzati delle feste. L'età legale per avere rapporti gay è di 18 anni, per quelli eterosessuali di 14 anni; il matrimonio gay non è permesso, ma non si fanno distinzioni tra convivenze omosessuali e eterosessuali; è possibile farsi registrare. Molti gay e lesbiche non si dimostrano orgogliosi di se stessi. Per mancanza di gruppi per giovani o di coming out i giovani gay e lesbiche adottano i concetti di vita dell'altra generazione. Nonostante ciò, sono capaci di divertirsi, e i punti d'incontro in Ungheria vengono frequentati in gran numero. Spesso i turisti si stupiscono del modo diretto con cui gli ungheresi trattano i desideri e aspettative che riguardano il sesso.

Budapest | **Hungary**

NATIONAL GAY INFO
- # Gay.hu
- www.gay.hu
Hungary's gay website & internet chat.

NATIONAL PUBLICATIONS
- **Mások**
PO Box 388 ✉ 1461 Budapest ☎ (01) 266 99 59
🖨 (01) 266 99 59 📧 masok@masok.hu 💻 www.masok.hu
Monthly publication featuring news, advertising, photos and classifieds.

NATIONAL COMPANIES
- **Connection Csomagküldő (G)**
Bezerédi utca 5 ✉ 1081 Budapest ☎ (01) 303 61 13
☎ (01) 333 25 85 🖨 (01) 133 25 85
📧 Connection@connectionbt.hu 💻 www.connectionbt.hu
Mail order company: videos, magazines, vibrators, dolls, dildos, etc.

Budapest 01

✳ Budapest ("Paris of the East") has always been known as a gay metropolis in Eastern Europe. Beside bars, dance clubs, the famous baths and the cruising spots, there are gay and lesbian groups doing political activities, counseling and socializing activities, gay orientated AIDS-prevention, publication of gay papers and broad casting gay radio magazines. A Gay Switchboard takes care of the wellbeing of gay tourists before, during and after their stay. Since '97 there is a Gay Pride event every year and in 2001 the Budapest Gay Pride will be an official event of Europride Vienna. Just by occupying during sunset, one of the seats along the Korzo near the Erzsebet bridge and March 15th Square (the most crowded cruising area), you can get a good impression of what gay society in Budapest is like.

✳ Budapest ("Paris des Ostens") war schon immer die schwule Metropole im Osten. Neben Bars, Discos, den berühmten Bädern und den Cruisingplätzen, haben Gruppen und Organisationen politische Aktivitäten und Ansätze einer schwulen Community entwickelt, beraten und machen AIDS-Prävention, verlegen Zeitschriften und produzieren schwule Radiomagazine. Ein "Gay Switchboard" kümmert sich um das Wohlbefinden schwuler Touristen vor, während und nach ihrer Reise. Seit '97 findet jährlich ein Gay Pride statt, und 2001 wird der Budapest Pride offizieller Teil des Europride Wien sein. Einen Eindruck, was schwules Leben in Budapest ist, gewinnt, wer sich kurz vor Sonnenuntergang im Sommer auf einer der Bänke am "Korzo" niederlässt, nahe der Elisabeth-Brücke und dem Platz des 15. März.

✳ Budapest (le "Paris de l'Est") a toujours été la métropole homo à l'Est. En plus des bars, discothèques, bains renommés et lieux de rencontre, des groupes et des organisations ont développé des activités politiques et les prémices d'une communauté homo. Ils conseillent et pratiquent la prévention contre le SIDA, ils publient des revues et produisent des magazines homo à la radio. Un "Gay Switchboard" s'occupe du bien-être des touristes, pendant et après leur voyage. Depuis 1997, un "Gay Pride" a lieu une fois par an et en 2001, le "Budapest Pride" fera partie officiellement de "Europride" à Vienne. Pour se faire une idée de la vie gaie à Budapest, il faut s'asseoir sur un banc au bord du "Korzo" en été, juste avant le coucher du soleil, près du Pont Elisabeth et de la Place du 15 mars.

✳ Budapest, que se conoce también como el París del Este, siempre fue una metrópoli gay en centro Europa. A parte de bares, discotecas, los famosos baños y sitios de cruising han surgido multiples grupos y organizaciones, que defienden los intereses de la comunidad gay, desarrollan actividades políticas, aconsejan, trabajan en la prevención del SIDA, publican revistas y producen programas de radio. Para los turistas homosexuales se creó un "Gay Switchboard", que se encarga del bienestar del visitante, antes, durante y después de su estancia en Hungría. Desde 1997 se organiza anualmente un Gay Pride y en 2001 Budapest formará parte oficial del Europride Viena. Para hacerse una idea como es la vida gay en Budapest se recomienda pasarse en verano poco antes de la puesta del sol por los bancos del Korzo, cerca del puente Isabel y de la plaza del 15 de marzo.

✳ Già da sempre Budapest ("Parigi dell'oriente") è la metropoli gay dell'est. A parte i bar, le discoteche, i famosi bagni e le possibilità per il cruising, gruppi ed organizzazioni hanno sviluppato delle attività politiche e iniziato a stabilire una comunità gay. Tra le diverse iniziative sono da elencare i servizi di consulenza e di prevenzione contro l'AIDS, la pubblicazione di riviste e la mandata in onda di trasmissioni gay nelle radio locali. Un "gay switchboard" si occupa del benessere dei turisti gay prima, durante e dopo il loro viaggio. Dal'97 ogni anno ha luogo un Gay Pride, e nel 2001 il Budapest Pride sarà ufficialmente una parte integrata dell'Europride di Vienna. Un'impressione della vita gay a Budapest si può ricavare sedendosi su uno dei banchi vicino al ponte Elisabeth e alla Piazza del 15 marzo in una sera d'estate poco prima del tramonto.

GAY INFO
- **GayGuide.Net Budapest (GLM)** Hotline daily 16-20 h
☎ +36 309 32 33 34 (from abroad)
🖨 +36 1 351 20 15 (from abroad) 📧 budapest@gayguide.net
💻 www.gayguide.net/Europe/Hungary/Budapest/
Gay tourist information. Information on gay-owned accomodation & gay-operated sightseeing tours. Daily updated Gay Guide Budapest Webpage including news, classifieds, chat, mailing lists & gay dictionary. Hotline every day. All e-mails are replied within 48 hours; English and German spoken.

SPARTACUS 2001/2002 | 569

Hungary — Budapest

TOURIST INFO
■ **Tourinform Budapest** Apr-Sep: daily 9-19, Oct-Mar: Mon-Fri 9-19, Sat Sun 9-16 h
Sütő utca 2 ✉ 1052 *(Metro Deak Ferenc tér)* ☎ 317 98 00
☎ (0680) 66 00 44 *(toll-free)* 📠 317 96 56
✉ hungary@tourinform.hu ✉ www.hungarytourism.hu
German, English, French, Italian, Russian and Hungarian spoken.

BARS
■ **Action** (! AC B DR f G lj MG P VS) 19-4 h
V, Magyar utca 42 ✉ 1053 *(near Hotel Korona. M° Blue Line-Kálvin tér, at number 42 you'll see a yellow A on a black background, but the entrance is 15 meters away from this sign, downstairs)* ☎ 266 91 48
Gay basement bar with Hungary's most frequented backroom & videoroom. Crowded all day. Audience of all age ranges and types of interest. You'll get a consumption card after you've entered the place - payment is at the bar before you leave.

■ **Capella Cafe** (B D f g MA STV) Tue-Sun 21-3 h, Shows: Tue-Thu & Sun at 24, Fri Sat at 23 and 2 h
V, Belgrád rakpart 23 *(Metro Blue Line-Ferenciek tere)* ☎ 318 62 31
The staff is mostly gay, but the Café Capella tries to attract a larger audience. Tue and Wed gay audience (but not only); Disco every day except on Mon. Entrance fees every days except Tue. Minimum consumption 500 Forints.

■ **Chaos Club** (A AC B CC d DR f G M P) 21-5, Oct-Apr 18-5, Gallery Mon-Fri 10-18 Sat 10-13 h
Dohány utca 38 ✉ 1072 *(at Nagydiófa utca)* ☎ 344 48 84
It's cruisy, but not dark. Dance floor & DJ, but it's more a music pub than a dance club. Gallery on the groundfloor their galery, bricks & metal & a huge bar downstairs. You'll need to pay the minimum consumption fee of 500 Forint at the entrance and you'll get a voucher for it.

■ **Darling** (AC B DR G MA P R VS) 19-3 h
V, Szép utca 1 *(M Ferenciek tér & Astoria, Bus 7, Nightbus 78é)* ☎ 267 33 15
Small bar on two levels, centrally located, the oldest gay bar in town. Upstairs videoroom, a darkroom behind the bar.

■ **Mystery Bar & Internet Café** (AC B f G MA p) Mon-Fri 21-4 h
V, Nagysándor József utca 3 ✉ 1054 *(Metro Blue Line-Arany János utca. Near US Embassy)* ☎ 312 14 36
Small bar, good for going there to chat with friends. Go there to check your e-mails and surf the web during your stay in Budapest. Internet 500 Forint per hour; 300 Forint per 1/2 hour.

CAFES
■ **Amstel River Café** (AC B BF F g MA) 11-24 h
V, Párizsi utca 6 ✉ 1052 *(Metro Blue Line-Ferenciek tér; Metro Yellow Line Vörösmarty tér)* ☎ 266 43 34
Café and restaurant. Gays are welcome.

■ **Café Eklektika** (B f glm MA os) Mon-Fri 12-24 Sat Sun 17-24; Summer: Mon-Fri 10-24 h
V, Semmelweis utca 21 ✉ 1052 *(Metro Blue Line-Ferenciek tere, M°Red Line-Astoria, Nightbus 50é/14é/78é)*
☎ 266 30 54
Lesbian and gay friendly café with light meals, colourful cocktails, precious wines, friendly atmosphere, smooth jazz, live concerts on Fri, terrace in the summer. Women's party every 2nd Sat/month at 22 h.

DANCECLUBS
■ **Angel Bar** (! AC B D DR f GLM MA p S STV WE) Thu 22-24 h, Fri-Sun 22-5 h, Fri GLM Sat G
VII, Szövetség utca 33 ✉ 1074 *(Between M Blaha Luijza tér & M Keleti pu; Trolley 74 Almassy tér; Nightbus 78é)* ☎ 351 64 90
Two floors, three bars, restaurant, darkroom, large disco, very popular.

BÁR DARLING
PORN VIDEO — DARK ROOM
Video- Drink Bar
Budapest, V., Szép utca 1.
(Our Bar situated between ASTORIA metro station on the red line and the FERENCIEK TERE metro station on the blue line.)
Phone: +36 (1) 267-3315
OPEN EVERY EVENING
19-03

Angel Privat Club
Bp. VII., Szövetség u. 33.
Theatre, Restaurant, Bar, Disco, Paradise Room
Open:
Thursday 22.00–24.00 drink bar
Friday–Sunday 22.00–05.00 drink bar & disco
**Fridays & Sundays:
TRAVESTI SHOW**
Every show starts at 23.30
Home cooking all night

Budapest | Hungary

Action BAR

ACTION BAR
BUDAPEST, V.
MAGYAR UTCA 42.

OPEN EVERY DAY: 19 – 04

VIDEO
DARK ROOM

Phone: (361) 266-9148
Homepage: www.action.gay.hu
e-mail: action@gay.hu

Hungary | Budapest

Rainbow Quality Male Escorts, Hosts & Tours
Budapest + Prague + All Central Europe!
Plan by e-mail: rain.bow@datanet.hu
Homepage: http://www.gaybudapest.hu
Mobile Telephone: +(36) 209 380 400
(within Hungary dial 06 209 380 400)

RESTAURANTS

■ **Fenyőgyöngye** (B F g H) 12-24 h
II, Szépvölgyi utca 155 ✉ 1025 *(Bus 65/65a from Kolosy tér)*
☎ 325 97 83
Reservation recommended.

■ **Kis Sün** (B F g)
V, Podmaniczky utca 29 ☎ 269 40 72
Restaurant and pub.

■ **Pizzeria Club '93** (B F glm) 12-24 h
VIII, Vas utca 2 ✉ 1087 *(Metro Red Line- Blaha Lujza tér, Bus 7/7a/78, Night bus 78é)* ☎ 338 11 19

SEX SHOPS/BLUE MOVIES

■ **Apollo Video Shop** (G VS) Mon-Fri 10-18 h
VI, Térez Körút 3 *(M° red line-EMKE)* ☎ 342 19 11
Videos, magazines, toys, gay cinema.

■ **Erotic Cinema & Video** (AC g MA VS) 10-2 h
XIII, Hegedus Gyula 1 ☎ 311 80 35

■ **Gloryhole Video Center** (AC DR G VS) 10-1 h
Berkocsis utca 3 *(8th district near Lujza Ter square)* ☎ (30) 275 9287 (mobile)

■ **Intim Lapüzlet és Videotéka** (G VS) Mon-Fri 10-18, Sat 10-14 h
VII, Dob utca 17 *(M° redline-Astoria)* ☎ 312 02 46
Videos, magazines, toys,...

■ **Vénusz Shop** (g VS) Mon-Fri 10-20, Sat 10-14 h
VII, Rákoczi utca 69 ✉ 1081 *(M° redline-Keleti Pu.)* ☎ 313 48 25

ESCORTS & STUDIOS

■ **Rainbow Quality Male** (G msg)
PO Box 701 832 ✉ 1399 ☎ (+36) 209 380 400
Escort & travel services.

SAUNAS/BATHS

■ **Gellért Bath** (g MA MSG OS PI SA SB SOL) Mon-Fri 6-18, Sat Sun -13 h
XI, Kelenhegyi utca 2-6 *(Bus 7, Tram 18/19/47/49)* ☎ 466 61 66
The fountains are over 200 years old. The bath itself was built in 1918 in art nouveau style, and is probably the most famous among all baths in Budapest for its architectural beauty. Gay men go mainly to the thermal baths, but the pool and the outside area during the summner are also cruisy. Massage and other medical services are available. Entrance fees: only for the thermal bath 1100 Forint. Daily ticket valid for all areas: 1600 Forints. Cabin 300-400 Forint (You don't need to pay for a cabin, if you go only to the thermal bath).

■ **Király Bath** (G MA MSG SA SB) Mon Wed Fri 9-21, entrance until 20 h
II, Fő utca 82-86 *(Tram 4, 6, Bus 6, 26 to Margaret bridge, on the Buda side, then walk or take bus 60, 86 for one stop towards Battyány tér.)* ☎ 202 36 88
A more direct & gay atmosphere compared to Gellért bath. Built in the 15th century by Arslan Pasha. Entrance fee 800 Forint.

■ **Rác** (G msg SA SB WO YG) Tue Thu Sat 6.30-19, entrance -18 h
I, Hadnagy utca 8-10 *(Bus 7/8, Tram 18/19, near Elisabeth Bridge)* ☎ 356 13 22
This small bath on the Buda side near Elisabeth bridge, originally built in the 15th century, rebuilt in the last century, is the only one open on Sat afternoons (very crowded from 15 h) Entrance fee 600 Forints.

TRAVEL AND TRANSPORT

■ **Tailored Tours** (G msg)
PO Box 701 832 ✉ 1399 ☎ (+36) 209 380 400 ⎙ 485-0753
✉ rain.bow@datanet.hu 🖥 tailored-tours.com
Escort & travel services.

BUDAPEST-CITY

TOM
Mobile 003620 310 34 87
inside Hungary 0620 310 34 87
also Hotel visiting · escort & travel service

572 SPARTACUS 2001/2002

KM - SAGA

Lónyai utca (Street) 17 • 1093 Budapest • Hungary
III Floor, Door No 1

Tel.: (36) 1-217 1934 • Fax (36) 1-215 6883

Gay-owned, exclusive, discreet Guest-Residence in 1890's enviroment with up-to-date comfort.

■ **Toucan Tourist** (glm) Mon-Thu 9.30-17.30, Fri -13.30 h, Sat Sun closed
Radnoti utca 15/b ✉ 1137 ☎ 329 74 81 🖨 357 54 23
📧 toucantourist@matavnet.hu
Hotel booking, gay map, information and service.

■ **TPG Travel & Air Service** (CC glm) Mon-Fri 9-17.30 h
Váci utca 11b ✉ 1052 ☎ 267 38 05 🖨 267 38 05
📧 gay@tpg.hu 🖥 www.gayhungary.net

GUEST HOUSES

■ **Connection Guest House** (b BF CC G H)
VII, Király utca 41 ✉ 1072 *(M Deák tér, M Opera, Tram 4/6, Trolley 70, 78)* ☎ 267 71 04 ☎ 352 17 03 🖨 352 17 03
📧 guesthouse@connectionbt.hu
🖥 www.connectionbt.hu/guesthouse. htm
6 double and 1 single comfortable rooms with shower/WC, direct phone, SAT-TV, central heating, own key, 24 h. reception service. Central location. Friendly and familiar atmosphere. Rates US$ 30-75. Additional bed US$ 25. Buffet breakfast until 12 h, parking garage nearby.

■ **KM-Saga** (BF glm H MA)
Lonyai Utca, Nr. 17, III Floor, Door Nr 1. ✉ 1093 ☎ 217 19 34
☎ 215 68 83 🖨 215 68 83 📧 bud-kmsaga@gayguide.net
🖥 www.gayguide.net/budapest/Kmsaga/
Gay-owned, exclusive, discreet guest-residence in a 1890s atmosphere with modern comfort. Central location near the National Museum. All rooms with cable TV own key and some with shared baths. 5 rooms in Lonyai utca & 3 rooms in Vámház Körut. Rates 30-60 USD.

■ **Pipacs Guesthouse** (G H)
V, Kossuth Lajos utca 12 ✉ 1053 *(central)* ☎ 317 73 34
🖨 317 73 94 📧 melengay@mail.tvnet.hu
🖥 www.gaybudapest.hu
Free internet and e-mail service, city tours.

APARTMENTS

■ **Dembinszky Street Apartment** (G H)
VII, Dembinszky utca ✉ 1077 ☎ +36 309 32 33 34
📧 demb@gayguide.net
🖥 www.gayguide.net/budapest/Dembinszky/
Apartment for up to 3 persons, close to gay locations.

■ **Lindenmann Apartments** (H)
Klauzál Tér 8 ✉ 1072 ☎ 266 07 79 ☎ +41 76 377 02 10 (mobile)
🖨 266 07 79 📧 klauzal@matavnet.hu
9 apartments in the same building. Rates DM 60-80.- per night. Central location, 5 min to gay scene. Own entrance and key. Very cosy atmosphere. Under Swiss management.

GENERAL GROUPS

■ **Háttér Baráti Társaság a Melegkért** (GLM) info and helpline 18-23 h

PO Box 50 ✉ 1554 ☎ 350 96 50 ☎ 329 33 80 (info and helpline)
🖨 350 96 50 📧 Hatter@hatter.hu 🖥 www.hatter.hu
Support Society for Gays and Lesbians in Hungary. Háttér ('background') is the largest gay and lesbian organization in Hungary founded in 95. It runs several projects: A hotline, which is a psychological-counselling and information line; a HIV/AIDS prevention project (supported by the National AIDS Committee), - a self knowledge group. The group is also the main organiser of the Gay and Lesbian Film and Cultural Festivals and the Pride Marches in Budapest, as well as the Positive Festival and keeps a gay and lesbian archive.

■ **Lambda Budapest**
PO Box 388 ✉ 1461 ☎ 266 99 59 🖨 266 99 59
📧 masok@masok.hu 🖥 www.masok.hu
Gay organisation & publisher of Masok.

CONNECTION
GUESTHOUSE CONNECTION

Central Budapest, close to gay area. Friendly comfortable rooms, some with shower/wc, own key, cable TV, direct dial phones, late breakfast, resident bar/lounge area, central heating parking nearby, open all year. Rooms from £20, most credit cards accepted.

Budapest, Hungaria
Király utca 41.
H - 1072 Budapest
Tel: +036 1 267 7104
fax: +36 1 352 1703
http://homopages.gayweb.com/pansio/index.html
e-mail: guesthouse@freemail.hu

Hungary — Budapest ▶ Debrecen

HEALTH GROUPS
■ **Méta** 10-22 h except Sat
PO Box 44 ✉ 1387 ☎ 247 01 88 ☎ (0620) 93 65 224
(24 h helpline)
Foundation supporting people with HIV/Aids.
■ **PLUSS**
PO Box 29 ✉ 1450 ☎ (06) 60 34 37 73
HIV positives self-help association.

RELIGIOUS GROUPS
■ **Kesergay**
PO Box 50 ✉ 1554
Jewish gay and lesbian group.
■ **Öt Kenyér** meetings on Thu at 19 h
PO Box 25 ✉ 1461 ☎ 329 33 80 ☎ (0630) 210 23 29
🖥 www.otkenyer.hu
Gay catholic group.

SPORT GROUPS
■ **Vándor Mások**
PO Box 926 ✉ 1463 ☎ 446 01 56 📠 329 26 70
🖥 vandorm@freemail.hu 🖥 fules.c3.hu/vandormasok/
Hiking group. Once a month on Sun. Long 4 day hikes take place once a year.

SWIMMING
-**Palatinus Strandfürdö** XIII. Margaret Island (G NU) ☎ 340 45 05
(On the flat roof of the building there is a nudist sun bathing area for men which is almost exclusively visited by gays)
-**Csillághegyi Strandfürdö** II., Pusztakúti út 3 (g NU) ☎ 250 15 33
(Beach with nudist area on the hilltop)
-**Omszki Lake** (just outside Budapest, in the north, reachable by the suburban train "HEV", starting from Batthany tér (direction: Szentendre). Get off at Budakalász. From there it is about 20-30 minutes walk to the lake. There is a nudist area often visited by gays)

CRUISING
-**Promenade** along the Danube on the Pest side (Duna-korzó) (G R) (between Marcius 15. tér and Vigadó tér. Beware of hustlers)
-**The little park** north off Margit bridge on the Buda side
-**Népliget** (Peoples Park) (behind the Planetarium and especially around the area of the old ruins. There is an old abandoned mansion where people go to do everything. Also, near the mansion, a dark park area exists for sex in the warmer months. Also, the road beside the park has lots of cars going by slowly to pick up guys)

Debrecen ☎ 06-52

CAFES
■ **Cafè van Gogh** (glm) 9-24 h
Péterfia utca 146 ✉ 4026 *(Tram 1-Bem tér stop)*
☎ (0630) 20 55 780
Weekly gay parties, but not on a certain day.

DANCECLUBS
■ **Aqua Panziò** (DR Glm H S) 22-4/? h
Sámsoni út 109 ✉ 4033 *(Bus 19 & 6)* ☎ 41 98 42 *(Panzio)*
Parties twice a month: the Sat following the 10th of each month and two weeks later. Accomodation possible for 1300 HUF per person per night.

HEALTH GROUPS
■ **Megyei Bör-Nemibeteggondozó Intézet** Mon-Fri 8-18 h
Bajcsy-Zsilinszky utca 3-5 ✉ 4025 ☎ 41 62 70
Regional institute for skin and venereal diseases.

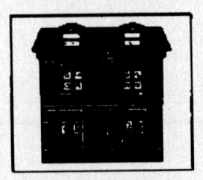

LINDENMANN
APARTMENTS
KLAUZÁLTÉR 8
H-1072 BUDAPEST

4x 1,5 Zimmer-Wohnung mit franz. Bett, TV, eigene Küche, Bad/Toilette
ab 60 DM/Tag

4x 2,5 Zimmer-Wohnung mit je 1 franz. Bett, TV, eigene Küche, Bad/Toilette
ab 80 DM/Tag

Bei uns fühlen Sie sich wie zu Hause! Eigener Wohnungs- und Hausschlüssel! Alle Gay-Lokale zu Fuss innerhalb 5 Minuten erreichbar! Unter Schweizer Führung.

Anfragen & Buchungen:
e-Mail: klauzal@matavnet.hu
tel/fax: 0036-1-2660779
mobil: 0041-76-3770210

Debrecen ▶ Székesfehérvár — Hungary

CRUISING
-Main Railway Station (public toilets)

Eger ☎ 06-36
HOTELS
■ **Köntös Panzió** (BF g H) 0-24 h
Szervita utca 29 ✉ 3300 *(close to Eger's central bus station)*
☎ 41 23 47 📠 41 23 47
Room rates 25-30 DEM. Gay friendly & owned. Monthly gay parties, dates on request.

CRUISING
-Népkert (Park between the bus station and Basilica)

Gyöngyös ☎ 06-37
HEALTH GROUPS
■ **Bugát Pál Kórház Bör-Nemibeteggondozó Intézet** Mon, Tue, Fri 8-14, Wed Thu -17 h
Dózsa György utca 20-22 ✉ 3200 ☎ 312 491
Institute for skin- and venereal diseases at the Bugát Pál Hospital.

Miskolc ☎ 06-46
DANCECLUBS
■ **Pussy Cat Bar** (b D G MA S) last Sat/month
Nagy Lajos király útja 25 *(Tram 1-end station, close to Lugas söröző)*
Pussy Cat Bar is the title of a monthly Party event. Show at midnight. They provide info on gay friendly accommodation, but only on request.

HEALTH GROUPS
■ **Megyei Bör-Nemibeteggondozó Intézet** Mon-Fri 8-14 h
Csabai kapu 9-11 ✉ 3529 ☎ 363 333
Regional institute for skin- and venereal diseases.

CRUISING
-Tapolca swimming pool (in summer)
-Plaza Department Store (In the area of Cafe Woodoo)

Nyiregyháza ☎ 06-42
CRUISING
-Railway station

Pécs ☎ 06-72
CRUISING
-Szent István tér (in front of Dom)
-Barbakán kert (near Dom)

Siófok ☎ 06-84
HEALTH GROUPS
■ **Bör-Nemibeteggondozó Intézet** Mon 8-13, Tue-Wed 13-15, Thu-Fri 8-10 h
Új Rendelő Intézet, Semmelweiss utca 1 ✉ 8600 ☎ 31 05 00
Regional Institute for skin- and venereal diseases.

CRUISING
-Street behind Hotel Europa (near railway station; summer only)

Sopron ☎ 06-99
HEALTH GROUPS
■ **AIDS Segély Alapítvány**
Magyar utca 14, PO Box 217 ✉ 9401 ☎ 33 33 99 📠 33 99 36
✉ aids@matavnet.hu 🖥 www.aidsinfo.hu/
AIDS Support Foundation. Only the first test is anonymous. That means if the result is positive, they cannot do the second (better one) without forwarding your data to the authorities. Go to Vienna for a second anonymous test!

Szeged ☎ 06-62
GENERAL GROUPS
■ **Dél - Alföldi Meleg Baráti Kör (DAMKÖR)** (GLM) Meetings every Sat, info on location on request. Info/helpline daily 21-23 h
PO Box 112
☎ 488 820 (Wed 20-22 h)
☎ (0620) 970 46 62 (Info/helpline)
Circle of gay/lesbian friends living in the South Alföld area.

HEALTH GROUPS
■ **Börklinika** Mon-Fri 8-14.30 h
Korányi fasor 6 ✉ 6720 ☎ 545 260
Skin Clinic.

CRUISING
-Main railway station (2nd floor)
-Széchenyi tér (near Main Post Office)

Székesfehérvár ☎ 06-22
DANCECLUBS
■ **Party** (D Glm S) monthly 20-4/? h
Info about dates & location only on request by phone.

CRUISING
-Main railway station (very seldom)

Iceland

Name: Island • Islande • Islandia • Islanda
Location: near Artic Circle in North Atlantic Ocean
Initials: IS
Time: GMT
International Country Code: ☎ 354 (no area codes)
International Access Code: ☎ 00
Language: Icelandic
Area: 103,000 km² / 39,768 sq mi.
Currency: 1 Icelandic Crown (ISK) = 100 Aurar
Population: 276,000
Capital: Reykjavík
Religions: 93% Protestant
Climate: The climate is moderated by the North Atlantic Current. Winters are mild and windy, summers damp and cool.
Important gay cities: Reykjavik

✱ The age of consent is 16 for both straight and gay people. The gay community in Iceland has gained a remarkable social acceptance and legal rights. With the laws on registered partnership for same sex couples, passed in June 1996, Iceland was the first state in the world to give same sex couples right to common custody of children brought into the partnership. A law on adoption of stepchildren was passed in May 2000. "Sexual orientation" was included in the anti-discrimination clause of the Icelandic code of penalty in 1996. Opinion polls show more tolerance towards gay people in Iceland than elsewhere in the Western World. Along with a strong democratic tradition one reason may be that Icelandic gay people tend to come out to their family which makes almost everybody have gay relatives.
Iceland is a large island; the landscape is wild, rugged and colourful, with black lava, red sulphur, hot blue geysers, rivers, waterfalls and green valleys. Its coastline is richly indented with bays and fjords. More than half the population lives in or around Reykjavík, the capital. Iceland is one of the most volcanically active countries in the world. Hekla, in the south of Iceland, has erupted no fewer than 16 times, and was once described by clergymen as the gateway to Hell. Iceland is a modern country where usage of the Internet and mobile phones is the highest in the world.

✱ Das Mündigkeitsalter für hetero- wie auch für homosexuelle Menschen ist 16. Die isländische Gay Community hat inzwischen eine beachtliche gesellschaftliche Akzeptanz erreicht und viele gesetzlich verankerte Rechte durchgesetzt. So war Island mit den im Juni 1996 verabschiedeten Gesetzen zur eingetragenen Partnerschaft von gleichgeschlechtlichen Paaren der erste Staat der Welt, der es gleichgeschlechtlichen Partnern erlaubte, das Sorgerecht für in die Partnerschaft mitgebrachte Kinder zu übernehmen. Im Mai 2000 wurde dann ein Gesetz zur Adoption von Stiefkindern verabschiedet. Bereits 1996 wurde die Anti-Diskriminierungsklausel des isländischen Strafgesetzbuches durch die "sexuelle Ausrichtung" ergänzt. Bei Meinungsumfragen zeigt die isländische Bevölkerung mehr Toleranz gegenüber Homosexuellen als sonst ein Volk der westlichen Welt. Neben der ausgeprägten demokratischen Tradition könnte ein Grund dafür darin liegen, dass isländische Gays sich ihren Familien gegenüber outen und somit fast jeder Isländer homosexuelle Verwandte hat.

Island ist eine große Insel, die Landschaft ist wild, zerklüftet und farbenprächtig mit ihrem schwarzen Lavagestein, rotem Schwefel, ihren heißen, bläulich schimmernden Geysiren, Wasserfällen, Flüssen und grünen Tälern. Die vielen Buchten und Fjorde machen aus Islands Küste die reinste Zickzacklinie.
Über die Hälfte der Bevölkerung lebt in oder um die Hauptstadt Reykjavík herum. Die Stadt liegt in einer großen Bucht und ist von Bergen umringt. Geotherme (heiße) Quellen in der Gegend wirken wie eine natürliche Zentralheizung und sorgen für eine smogfreie Atmosphäre. Island gehört zu den vulkanisch aktivsten Ländern der Erde. Der im Süden der Insel gelegene Vulkan Hekla ist in den letzten 1000 Jahren nicht weniger als 16 Mal ausgebrochen und wurde von Priestern einst als Tor zur Hölle bezeichnet. Dennoch ist Island ein modernes Land, Internet und Mobilfunktelefone werden hier weltweit am häufigsten genutzt.

✱ En Islande, l'âge de la majorité sexuelle est fixée à 16 ans pour tous. La communauté gaie du pays a gagné une énorme reconnaissance sociale et juridique. Grâce à des lois votées en 1996 sur le partenariat pour couples du même sexe, l'Islande a été le premier pays à reconnaître le droit de garde d'enfants en cas de divorce aux homosexuels. Une loi sur l'adoption des enfants du partenaire est également passée en mai 2000. L'orientation sexuelle a été incluse dans la clause anti-discriminatoire du code pénal en 1996. Les sondages d'opinion montrent une tolérance de la population envers les homosexuels supérieure à celle mesurée dans les autres pays occidentaux. Ceci peut être non seulement expliqué par la longue tradition démocratique du pays, mais aussi par le fait que les jeunes gais ont tendance à faire leur coming out au sein de leur famille : presque chaque habitant de l'île a ainsi un membre de sa famille qui est homosexuel.
L'Islande est une grande île avec des paysages sauvages, escarpés et bigarrés, entre la lave noire et le sulfure rouge, les geysers, rivières et cascades bleutés et les vertes vallées. La côte est édentée par de nombreuses baies et fjords. Plus de la moitié de la population vit dans ou aux alentours de la capitale Reykjavik. L'Islande

Reykjavík | Iceland

est un des pays à l'activité volcanique la plus intense au monde. Le volcan Hekla, au sud du pays, s'est réveillé pas moins de 16 fois et a été décrit un jour par un prêtre comme le passage vers l'enfer. Mais l'Islande est aussi un pays moderne où l'usage de l'Internet et de téléphones portables est le plus répandu du monde.

La edad de consentimiento es de dieciseis años, tanto para heterosexuales como para homosexuales. La comunidad gay de Islandia ha alcanzado una aceptación social notable y derechos constitucionales. Con las leyes de parejas registradas para parejas del mismo sexo aprobadas en junio de 1996, Islandia fue el primer país del mundo que concedió el derecho de custodia conjunta de los hijos de relaciones anteriores a parejas del mismo sexo. En mayo del 2000, se aprobó la ley de adopción de hijastros. La orientación sexual fue incluida en la cláusula de anti-discriminación del código penal islandés en 1996. Encuestas de opinión demuestran que en Islandia la tolerancia hacia las personas gays es más alta que en ninguna otra parte del mundo occidental. Junto a una fuerte tradición democrática, la razón de ello podría ser que los gays islandeses suelen declararse a sus familiares, por lo que prácticamente todas las personas saben de la homosexualidad de algún miembro de su propia familia.

Islandia es una isla muy grande. El paisaje es salvaje, accidentado y lleno de colores con la lava negra, el azufre rojo, los géiseres, ríos y cascadas azules y los valles verdes. El litoral está marcado por un sinfín de bahías y fiordos. Más de la mitad de la población vive en la capital del país, Reykjavík, o en los alrededores de esta ciudad. Islandia es uno de los países con más actividad volcánica. El volcán Hekla, en el sur de la isla, entró en erupción nada menos que dieciseis veces en los últimos mil años, y fue llamado por el clérigo 'la puerta del infierno'. Islandia es un país moderno; el uso del internet y de teléfonos móviles es más generalizado que en ninguna otra parte mundo.

La maggiore età sia per gli omosessuali che per le persone "decenti" è 16 anni. La comunità gay islandese ha raggiunto un notevole riconoscimento sociale ed ha imposto una serie di diritti fissati per legge. Con le leggi sull'unione coniugale registrata per coppie omosessuali, passate nel giugno del 1996, l'Islanda è stata il primo paese del mondo a garantire alle coppie omosessuali il diritto di tutela comune per i bambini portati nell'unione. Nel maggio del 2000 è stata inoltre approvata una legge sull'adozione dei figli del partner. Già nel 1996, "l'orientamento sessuale" è stato incluso nell'articolo contro la discriminazione del codice penale islandese. Nei sondaggi d'opinione pubblica, gli islandesi mostrano più tolleranza nei confronti degli omosessuali di qualsiasi altro popolo del mondo occidentale. Una spiegazione per questo fatto, oltre alla pronunciata tradizione democratica del paese, potrebbe essere che i gay islandesi tendono a rivelarsi alle loro famiglie e quindi quasi tutti hanno parenti gay.

L'Islanda è una grande isola; il paesaggio è selvaggio, frastagliato e variopinto, con la caratteristica lava nera, il solfuro rosso, i blue geyser bollenti, le cascate, i fiumi e le valle verdi. La costa è frastagliata da baie e fiordi. Più della metà della popolazione vive nella capitale Reykjavík e nei suoi dintorni. La città è situata in una grande baia circondata da montagne. Fonti geotermiche nella regione creano un sorta di sistema di riscaldamento centrale naturale e garantiscono un'atmosfera pulita. L'Islanda è uno dei paesi con la più intensa attività vulcanica del mondo. Negli ultimi 1000 anni sul monte Hekla nel sud dell'isola si sono verificate non meno di 16 eruzioni e in passato veniva descritto dai preti come porta all'inferno.

L'Islanda è comunque un paese moderno dove l'uso di Internet e dei cellulari è il più alto del mondo.

Reykjavik

Reykjavík is set on a broad bay, surrounded by mountains. The geothermal hot springs in the area create a natural central heating system and pollution-free environment. It is a busy city combining old-fashioned wooden architecture and modern buildings.
The official website for Reykjavik is www.reykjavik.com

Reykjavík se situe sur une large baie entourée de montagnes. Les sources d'eau chaudes géothermiques des environs permettent d'avoir un système de chauffage central naturel et un environnement peu pollué. C'est une ville très active qui combine des anciennes habitations en bois avec des bâtiments modernes.
Le site Internet officiel de la ville est www.reykjavik.com

Reykjavík está en una bahía grande, rodeada de montañas. Los manantiales calientes geotermales en el área crean un sistema de calefacción central natural y gracias a ello, un entorno libre de contaminación. Es una ciudad activa que combina las antiguas construcciones de madera con edificios modernos.
La página web oficial de Reykjavík es www.reykjavik.com

Reykjavík ist eine geschäftige Stadt, die historische Holzbauten und moderne Architektur in sich vereint. Die offizielle Webadresse von Reykjavík lautet: www.reykjavik.com

Reykjavík è una città operosa dove convivono edifici storici di legno e architettura moderna. Il sito Web ufficiale di Reykjavík si trova all'indirizzo www.reykjavik.com

GAY INFO

■ **Samtökin '78** (GLM)
Laugavegur 3 ✉ 101 Reykjavik *(4th floor)* ☏ 552 78 78
📠 552 78 20
📧 office@samtokin78.is
🌐 www.gayiceland.com
The Icelandic Organization of Lesbians and Gay Men. The national gay rights organization. Runs a Gay Center with café and gay library in Reykjavik. Member of International Lesbian & Gay Association (ILGA).

■ **Samtakafréttir**
PO Box 1262 ✉ 121 ☏ 552 7878
📠 552 7820
📧 ritstjorn@samtokin78.is
🌐 www.samtokin78.is
Monthly newsletter published by Samtökin '78 both in hard copy and on the web

Iceland — Reykjavik

MANNSBAR
gay reykjavík

vegamótastíg 4

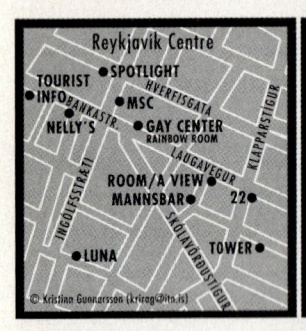

■ **Reykjavik Gay Center** (A b CC GLM MA YG) Office:
Mon-Fri 11-12 h, Center: Mon, Thu 20-23 h, Fri 21-1h Sat 14-18h & 21-2 h
Laugavegur 3 ✉ 100 *(4th floor)* ☎ 552 78 78 📠 552 78 20
💻 office@samtokin78.is 💻 www.gayiceland.com
Rainbow room Café and gay library. Metting place for gay groups: AA group meets Tue 21 h, Parents' supporting group Sat 14 h, Reigious group Sun 17, Youth group Friday nights.

TOURIST INFO
■ **Tourist Information Center**
Bankastræti 2 ☎ 562 3045 📠 562 3057 💻 tourinfo@tourinfo.is
💻 www.tourinfo.is

BARS
■ **Mannsbar** (! AC B CC DR G MA) 17-1, Fri,Sat -5h
Vegamótastígur 4
Very popular and cruisy. Men only Fridays.
■ **Rainbow Room** (! A AC b cc GLM MA s) Mon, Thu 20-23 h, Sat 21-1 h.
Laugavegur 3, 4th floor. Gay Center
Cosy and friendly. Foreigners welcome.
■ **22** (B CC d glm MA) 12-1 h, Fri-Sat 22-5 h disco
Laugavegur 22
Gay friendly.

MEN'S CLUBS
■ **MSC Club** (b CC DR G LJ MA P VS) Sat 22-1 h
Bankastr. 11 *(Entrance from Ingólfsstr.)*
Men only, Dresscode: leather, jeans, uniforms.

CAFES
■ **Nelly's** (B CC d NG) 12-1 h, Fri-Sat 22-3 h disco
Laugavegur/Thingholtsstraeti

DANCECLUBS
■ **Spotlight** (! B CC D GLM S WE YG) Thu 23-1 h, Fri 23-4 h, Sat 23-5 h
Hvefisgata 8-10 ☎ 562 68 12
Large gay disco, very popular.

RESTAURANTS
■ **Jómfrúin** (b CC F glm)
Lækjargata 4 ✉ 101 ☎ 551 01 00
Gay owned. Danish cuisine.
■ **Rex** (B CC F glm)
Austurstræti 9 ☎ 551 9111

SAUNAS/BATHS
■ **Vesturbæjarlaug (Swimming Pool West)** (g Pl SA SB SOL)
Hofsvallagata 107 ☎ 551 50 04
Public swimming pool, but sauna frequented by gays.

FITNESS STUDIOS
■ **World Class** (CC NG SB SOL WO WH)
Fellsmúli 24 ☎ 553 5000

GUEST HOUSES
■ **Good Value** (CC g H)
Ingólfsstræti 12 ✉ 101 ☎ 896 6694 💻 www.guesthouses.is
■ **Guesthouse Luna** (CC g H)
Spítalastígur 1 ✉ 101 ☎ 511 25 00 📠 511 28 01
💻 luna@islandia.is 💻 home.islandia.is/luna
■ **Tower** (CC g H)
Grettisgata 6 ✉ 101 ☎ 552 55 22 ☎ 896 6694 📠 552 55 22
💻 towerguesthouse@hotmail.com
💻 towerguesthouse.homestead.com

APARTMENTS
■ **Room with a View** (CC g H)
Laugavegur 18 ✉ 101 *(6th floor)* ☎ 552 72 62 📠 552 72 62
💻 www.roomwithaview.is
Rates depend on length of stay and season.

GENERAL GROUPS
■ **Different Days**
P.O. Box 1262 ✉ 121 💻 www.this.is/gaypride
Organizers of Gay Pride in Reykjavik the second weekend in August.
■ **FSS Association of Gay, Lesbian and Biseual Students**
Hringbraut ✉ 101 💻 gay@hi.is 💻 www.hi.is/nem/gay
FSS is a social group as well as gay rights association for universities in Iceland. It operates from the University of Iceland in Reykjavik. Meetings regularly, email newsletters available both in icelandic and english. Member of IGLYO.

FETISH GROUPS
■ **MSC Iceland**
PO Box 5321 ✉ 125 ☎ 562 12 80 💻 msc@this.is
💻 www.this.is/msc

HEALTH GROUPS
■ **AIDS Switchboard** Wed 17-18 h
☎ 562 22 80
■ **Alnæmissamtökin**
☎ 552 8586 💻 aids@centrum.is 💻 www.centrum.is/aids
The AIDS Organization of Iceland.
■ **Húd og Kynsjúkdómadeild (Department of Dermatology and Veneral Diseases)**
Thverholt 18 ☎ 560 23 20

CRUISING
-Oskjuhlid (hill with bushes outside Hotel Loftleidir).

Bombay - Maharashtra ▸ Gulbarga - Karnataka | India

India

Name:	Bhárat • Indien • Inde
Location:	South Asia
Initials:	IND
Time:	GMT +5:30
International Country Code:	☎ 91
International Access Code:	☎ 00
Language:	Hindi and English
Area:	3,287,590 km² / 1,269,010 sq mi.
Currency:	1 Indian Rupie (iR) = 100 Paise
Population:	984,003,683
Capital:	New Dehli
Religions:	80% Hindu, 11% Moslem, various religious minorities (Sikhs, Christians, Buddhists)
Climate:	Varies from tropical monsoon climate in the south to moderate in the north.

Gay sex is illegal in India. Article 377 of the Indian penal code forbids "carnal intercourse against the order of nature with man, woman or animal". Article 294 prohibits "obscene behaviour" of any kind in public, and it seems that this law is being used by the police to arrest gays if caught cruising or having sex in public toilets.
A gay movement is slowly beginning to emerge in India, as shown by the fact that gay groups are being formed and demonstrations organized.

Schwule Handlungen sind in Indien illegal. Artikel 377 des indischen Strafgesetzbuches verbietet "carnal intercourse against the order of nature with man, woman or animal" (dt.: "fleischlicher Verkehr gegen die Ordnung der Natur mit Mann, Frau oder Tier"). Artikel 294 beinhaltet "obszönes Verhalten" gleich welcher Art in der Öffentlichkeit. Offensichtlich benutzt die Polizei diesen Artikel, um Schwule beim Klappensex oder Cruisen zu verhaften.
Inzwischen beginnt sich auch in Indien eine Schwulenbewegung zu bilden. Erste Demonstrationen und das Bilden schwuler Gruppen sind Anzeichen dieser Tendenz.

En Inde, l'homosexualité est un délit. L'article 377 du code pénal indien condamne "tout rapport charnel contre nature avec une femme, un homme ou un animal". L'article 294, lui, condamne tout "comportement obscène" en public. Il semble que la police se réfère à cet article pour justifier razzias et descentes dans les toilettes publiques et les lieux de drague.
En Inde, on assiste actuellement à la naissance d'un mouvement d'émancipation homosexuelle. La création d'associations gaies et de premières manifestations dans la rue en sont les premiers signes.

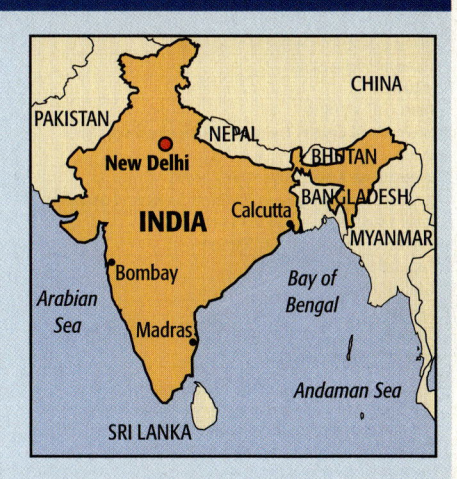

Las relaciones sexuales entre gays son ilegales en la India. El artículo 377 del Códico Penal establece que está prohibida "carnal intercourse against the order of nature with man, woman or animal" ("reclamación carnal con hombre, mujer o animal en contra del orden de la naturaleza"). El artículo 294 hace referencia al "comportamiento obseno" en público de cualquier tipo. Se piensa que la policia utiliza este artículo para detener a gays en los aseos públicos o cuando practican el cruising.
Entre tanto, también en la India se ha comenzado a formar un movimiento gay. Protestas y la fundación de grupos son muestras de esta tendencia.

La pratica omosessuale, in India, è vietata. L'articolo 377 del codice penale indiano proibisce il "rapporto carnale contro natura con uomo, donna o animale". L'articolo 294 punisce "comportamenti osceni" di qualunque genere in pubblico. Ovviamente la polizia ne approfitta per arrestare i gay nei gabinetti e nelle altre zone d'incontro. Nel frattempo anche in India inizia no a formarsi i primi movimenti gay. Alla fine del '92 a Nuova Dehli i gay hanno manifestato, in occasione di una conferenza sull'AIDS, per i loro diritti. L'avvenimento ha ottenuto un grande spazio nella stampa nazionale

---

Bombay - Maharashtra

NATIONAL PUBLISHERS

■ **Pride Publications Private Ltd**
10 Riviera, 15th Road off North Avenue ✉ 400-054 Santacruz, Bombay ☎ 22 640 0128 🖥 www.bombay-dost.com

GENERAL GROUPS

■ **Humsafar Trust, The**
PO Box 69 13 ✉ 400054 ☎ 618 74 76 ☎ 972 69 13 (Helpline)

Gulbarga - Karnataka

GAY INFO

■ **Freedom**
PO Box 80 ✉ 585 102

Indonesia

Name: Indonesien • Indonésie • Indonésia
Location: Southeast Asia
Initials: RI
Time: GMT +7/+8/+9
International Country Code: ☏ 62 (leave the first 0 of area codes)
International Access Code: ☏ 001 or 008
Language: Bahasa Indonesia. English as language of commerce
Area: 1,904,569 km² / 735,354 sq mi.
Currency: 1 Rupiah (Rp) = 100 Sen
Population: 212,941,810
Capital: Jakarta
Religions: 88% Moslem
Climate: Tropical climate that is hot and humid. In the highlands it's more moderate.

※ Homosexual acts are legal. Homosexuality has traditionally been an integral part of Indonesian culture, and many married men also maintain sexual relations with members of the same sex. Only in the country's new, western-style middle class has homophobia taken root. There are, evidently, no laws which specifically deal with HIV or AIDS. Nevertheless, more general regulations provide for the denial of entry or even quarantine of affected persons.

※ Homosexuelle Handlungen werden in Indonesien nicht kriminalisiert und sind traditioneller Bestandteil der indonesischen Kultur. Viele verheiratete Männer pflegen so weiterhin gleichgeschlechtliche Kontakte. Homophobie ist eher ein Kennzeichen der Mittelschicht und der Traditionalisten.
Es gibt offenbar keine indonesischen Vorschriften, die sich konkret mit HIV/AIDS befassen. Die Möglichkeit der Restriktionen gegen betroffene Personen reicht jedoch von der Einreiseverweigerung bis zur Quarantäne.

※ En Indonésie, l'homosexualité n'est pas un délit. Elle ferait même plutôt partie de la culture indonésienne. Les hommes mariés entretiennent fréquemment des relations homosexuelles. Une certaine homophobie se fait sentir au sein de la toute nouvelle couche sociale orientée sur le mode de vie occidental. Apparemment, aucune réglementation concernant le sida et la séropositivité. En revanche, certaines restrictions concernant l'entrée ou le séjour des séropositifs et des sidéens: elles vont du refus du permis de séjour à la quarantaine.

※ Las actividades homosexuales no están criminalizadas y forman tradicionalmente parte de la cultura indonesia. Así que muchos hombres siguen manteniendo contactos sexuales. Sin embargo, las nuevas clases medias del país, más occidentalizadas, se muestran cada vez más homófobas. Según nuestros datos no hay reglamentación que se ocupe concretamente del HIV/SIDA. Las posibilidades de restricciones contra personas afectadas van desde la prohibición de entrada al país hasta la cuarentena.

※ Gli atti omosessuali sono legali. L'omosessualità è parte integrante delle tradizioni culturali dell'Indonesia. Anche gli uomini sposati mantengono delle relazioni sessuali con persone dello stesso sesso. Soltanto nella nuova classe media di gusti occidentali, l'omofobia sta aumentando. Non ci sono ne leggi ne regolamenti che trattano in modo concreto il problema AIDS. Persone infette si aspettino un rifiuto del permesso d'entrata nel paese o l'isolamento se già ci si trovano.

NATIONAL GAY INFO

■ **Buku Seri IPOOS**
IPOOS, PO Box 7631/JKBTN, ✉ 11470 Jakarta
Bimonthly publication of IPOOS. Approximately 52 pages, in Indonesian. Copy US$ 5, annual subscription 30. Free personal ads in Indonesian and English.

■ **Gaya Nusantara** (G) With appointment
Jalan Mulyosari Timur 46, ✉ 60112 Surabaya, East Java
☏ (0)31-593 4924   📠 (0)31-599 3569   ✉ gayanusa@ilga.org
🖥 welcome.to/gaya
Publishes Gaya Nusantara, a monthly publication with 60 pages, in Indonesian with some English. Copy US$ 5, annual subscirption US$ 60- Free personal ads.

■ **Indonesian Gay Society (IGS)** Meeting 2nd Sun 10.30, Karaoke night last Sat 20, Phone hours 16-20 h
PO Box 36/YKBS, Yogyakarta 55281   ☏ (0274) 620 17 (9-13 h)
Publishes Jaka-Jaka.

■ **IPOOS/Gaya Betawi**
PO Box 7631/JKBTN   ✉ 11470 Jakarta   ☏ (0)21-566 05 89
Only Indonesian spoken. Publishes Buku Seri IPOOS.

■ **Jaka-Jaka**
IGS, PO Box 36/YKBS   ✉ 55281 Yogyakarta
Bimonthly publication of IGS. 20 pages, in Indonesian. Copy US$ 3, annual subscription 18. Free personal ads.

NATIONAL COMPANIES

■ **Bali Rainbow Leisure**
Tuban Plaza 12A, Jl By Pass Ngurah Rai   ✉ 80361 Tuban - Bali
☏ (0361) 757 008   📠 (0361) 757 008   ✉ jasbali@inodo.net.id
🖥 www.globalcitizen.tripod.com/bali_rainbow_leisure.html
Gay and lesbian professional tour operator, to arrange accommodation, tours, spa and massages.

Balikpapan - Kalimantan Tinur ▶ Batam - Riau **Indonesia**

BALI & JAVA
Vietnam Cambodia Laos Thailand

local gay guides.
private holidays.
a world of new friends.

www.utopia-tours.com
Asia's gay & lesbian travel pioneers

Utopia Tours
info@utopia-tours.com

■ **Utopia Tours** (GLM)
✉ info@utopia-tours.com 🌐 www.utopia-tours.com

TOURIST INFO
Jawa Barat = West Java
Jawa Tengah = Central Java
Jawa Timur = East Java
Sumatera Utara = North Sumatra
Sumatera Barat = West Sumatra
Sulawesi Selatan = Southwest Celebes
Kalimantan Timur = West Borneo
Kalimantan Selatan = Southwest Borneo
Irian Jaya = New Guinea
Jakarta and Yogyakarta are separate districts on Java
Bengkulu is a separate district on Sumatra

Balikpapan - Kalimantan Timur ☎ 0542

DANCECLUBS
■ **Panorama Disco** Thu from 23h

CRUISING
-Lapangan Monumen
-Jin Jend Sudirman, after 21h
-JL Gunung Pasir after 23h (TV).

Bandung - Jawa Barat ☎ 022

BARS
■ **Marabu Club**
Sunjaraja Street *(near Braga Street)*

DANCECLUBS
■ **LA Dreampalace** (B D g) Wed GLM
Jalan Asia-Africa (Plaza)

HOTELS
■ **Istana** (AC B F g H MA OS PI)
Jalan Lembong 21-44 ☎ 43 30 25
Central location, 15 min to the airport. All rooms have AC, telephone, fridge, priv. bath, balcony. Rates on request.
■ **Kumala Panghegar** (AC B D F g H MA OS PI)
Jalan Asia Afrika 140 ☎ 521 41
First class hotel centrally located, 5 km from the airport. All rooms with priv. bath, TV, radio. Rates on request.

■ **Panghegar** (AC B F H PI SA WO)
Jalan Merdeka 2 ☎ 43 07 88
Convenient location, 20 min to the airport. All rooms with telephone, priv. bath, WC, some with balcony and fridge.
■ **Savoy Homann Panghegar Heritage** (AC B F g H MA OS PI)
Jalan Asia-Afrika 112 ☎ 40262 ☎ 43 22 44 📠 43 61 87
✉ homann@panghegaronline:com
🌐 www.asiatravel.com/savoyhoman
Central to shopping and city centre.

GENERAL GROUPS
■ **Gaya Priangan**
PO Box 1819, ✉ 40018 ☎ 250 43 25

CRUISING
-Taman Badak Putih (G r) (Park with statue of a white rhino, near city hall, Jalan Meredeka, every night)
-Alun-alun Bandung (G r) (Town square, every night)
-Asia Africa Plaza, Wed (GLM)
-Merdeka Stree at night
-Sumatra Street at night
-Taman Balai Kota

Banjarmasin - Kalimantan Selatan ☎ 0511

DANCECLUBS
■ **Bobo Discotik** (g tv) Tue night
■ **Matt Discotik** (g tv) Fri night
■ **Shinta Discotik** (g tv) Wed night

Batam - Riau ☎ 0778

BARS
■ **Club 5-O** (G)
New Holiday Hotel ✉ 29432
■ **Golden Gate Discotik** (glm)
Nagoya Plaza Hotel
■ **Regina Palace Discotheque** (B D G) Sat & Sun nights

DANCECLUBS
■ **Toos 3000** (D)

CRUISING
-Batu Ampar harbour
-In front of BCA from 22-5h
-Plaza 21, Tanjung Pantun-Jodoh 2-22h

SPARTACUS **2001/2002** | 581

Indonesia   Bogor - Jawa Barat ▸ Jember - Jawa Timur

Bogor - Jawa Barat ☎ 0251

BARS
■ **Karaoke Mulia** (B glm) Sat
■ **Taman Topi** (B) Sat nights.
Kaptain Muslihat Street

GENERAL GROUPS
■ **New Friendship Club**
PO Box 2055 ✉ 16020

CRUISING
-Shopping centers and public park and garden
-In front of Hotel Salak
-Internusa Shopping Complex
-In front of the Istana Palace, day and night
-In front of the Radio Republik Indonesia offices
-Tuju Kujang, near guardpost.

Denpasar - Bali ☎ 0361

GENERAL GROUPS
■ **Gaya Dewata** 9.30-15.30 h
Jalan Belimbing Gg Y N°4 ✉ 80231 ☎ 22 26 20

HEALTH GROUPS
■ **Yayasan GAY a Dewata** 9-15 h
Jl. Teuku Umar Gg Maruti/Merati No. 7 ✉ 80231 ☎ 222 620
🖷 235 982 ✉ gayadwata@denpasar.wasantara.net.id
(ATTN: Dr. Tuti Parwati)

Jakarta ☎ 021

BARS
■ **Jalan Jalan** (B d glm stv)
36/F Nenara Imperium Building, Jalan Rasuna Said, *Kuningan*
☎ 835 39 79
Upmarket crowd. Live bands, go-go dancers and sometimes cabaret shows.

DANCECLUBS
■ **Furama Pub & Disco** Tue 22h
Jln Hayam Wuruk Raya 75 *(next to Holland Bakery)*
■ **Kasturi** Mon 22h
10-E Jln Mangga Besar Raya
■ **Klimax Discotheque** (B D G r) Sun 22-2 h
Jln Gayah Mada *(Near New Moonlights)*
■ **Maxtra** (glm) From 22h
Grand Mentang Hotel, Matraman Raya Street
Young gay men on Sat morning.
■ **New Moonlight discotheque** (B D glm MA)
Jalan Hayam Wuruk 120/Jalan Mangga Besar *(Barat, Kota)*
☎ 600 21 62
Small fun disco. Gay at weekends.
■ **Sofian Hotel Diskotik** (B D GLM) Night & day.
Jalan Saharjo
■ **Stardust** (B D g) night & day.
Jalan Pangeran Jayakarta/Jalan Hayam Wuruk *(Jayakarta Tower Building)*
■ **Tanamur Discotheque** (B D glm r)
Jalan Tanah Abang Timur *(Central Jakarta)*
Very popular. Gay section at rear of the dance floor. Most gays are here on Thu, Fri and Sat nights, but busy all week.
■ **Voilà** (B D g) Gay only Sun, 21-2 h
Jalan Rasuna Said, Gedung Patra Jasa *(Patra Jasa Building 4th floor)*

RESTAURANTS
■ **Cafe Batavia** (B g MA S) 0-24 h
Taman Fatahillah ☎ 691 55 31
Seafood and Western cuisine.

MASSAGE
■ **Julian's place** (G MA msg)
Jalan Cikajong 56, Block Q *Kebayoran Baru, Jakarta Selatan 12170*
Massage service.

GENERAL GROUPS
■ **Ikatan Persaudaraan Orang-orang Sehati (IPOOS)/
Gaya Betawi** Mon Wed-Fri 9-18 h
PO Box 7631/JKBTN ✉ 11470 ☎ 566 05 89
■ **Persekutuan WGL Jakarta**
c/o Menteng Beauty Salon, Jalan Gondangdia Lama 28, *Jakarta Pusat 10300*

HEALTH GROUPS
■ **Hotline AIDS Mitra Indonesia** Mon-Fri 15-20 h
Jalan Kebon Kacang 9 N°78, Jakarta Pusat ✉ 10240 ☎ 310 08 55
🖷 310 08 55

CRUISING
-Lapangan Banteng (g R RT) (Park across Hotel Barobudur)
-Taman Suropati (G r) (Park on Jalan Diponegoro, every night)
-Atrium Senen (Monday Atrium) Senen Triangle in front of Studio 21.
-Block M Plaza and Terminal (Kebayoran Bari district)
-Big and Beautiful Market, Block M(Pasaraya Big and Beautiful Blok M) Bathroom on the ground floor, entrance from the parking area. MA day & night)
-Sogo (Plaza Indonesia/Grand Hyatt Hotel/Hotel Indonesia circle. Day & Night)
-Ancol swimming pool (under the waterfall Sun)
-Art Market (Pasar Seni) 20-23 h
-Tugu Senen/Gelanggang (Senen Monument/Arena) R
-Grand Duta/Mulya Agung Movie Theater (Jalan Kramat Raya/Jalan Kwitang) R
-Senen Bus Terminal (R) Si Unyil WC.
-Dangdut Senen (beside the Monday arena opposite bus terminal. R
-Cililitan (outside old bus terminal. Only Sat night!)
-Cinere Movie House (Gedung Bioskop Cinere) Night.
-Ciputat-Sahara Movie House (Gedung Bioskop Sahara) (in the courtyard)
-Sarinah Shopping Centre (ground floor, at McDonalds)

Jayapura - Irian Jaya ☎ 0976

DANCECLUBS
■ **Paramount** Sat and Thu

CRUISING
-Irian Street (g) (in front of shopping complex)
-A. Yani Street (g) (in front of Bintang Mas Store)
-Imbi Park (Taman Imbi) (g tv)
-Taman Pelabuhan Kapal (Dermagea) Park (g tv)

Jember - Jawa Timur

CRUISING
-Town Square (alun-alun) (nighttime tv)
-Small restaurant -The Warung-in alley in front of Station 22-?h.

582 *SPARTACUS* 2001/2002

Kediri - Jawa Barat

DANCECLUBS
- **Sky Disc** (B D g)
c/o Hotel Merdeka
Best Sat.

CRUISING
-In front of the Brawijaya stadium (at night, best on Sat)
-In front of the Kowak swimming pool

Kuta - Bali ☎ 0361

BARS
- **Goa 2001** (B d F g MA R) 20-2 h
Jalan Legian *(Seminyak)*
Very popular meeting place before going on to the disco's. Best after 23 h.
- **Hulu Cafe** (B G MA STV) 17-1 h closed Mondays
J.L. Sahadewa 23 A *(Legian)* ☎ 75 68 48
Show nights Wed, Fri, Sat, Sun.
- **Q Bar and Café** (B CC F G OS MA R)
Jln Dhyanapura, Seminyak ☎ 730 841

DANCECLUBS
- **Double Six** (B G R S YG) Sat 23-4 h
(Located directly at the beach)
- **Double Six 66** (B D glm Pl)
(Seminyak) ☎ 73 12 66

RESTAURANTS
- **La Lucciola Restaurant & Beach Club** (B F g N OS YG) 8-19 h
Jalan Oberoi *(at Pura Petitenget Beach)* ☎ 730 838
Modern cuisine.

BODY & BEAUTY SHOPS
- **Eddy's Hair & Beauty Salon** (g)
Jalan Raya Kartika Plaza ☎ 539 29

TRAVEL AND TRANSPORT
- **Over the Rainbow**
Canggu Resort A5, 100 Berawa Beach Road *(near Kuta)*
☎ 812 3982474 ✉ anasrullah@excite.com
Guest rooms available as well as island tours.

HOTELS
- **Asana Santhi** (G H)
Jalan Tegalwangi 18 ✉ 80361 ☎ 75 12 81 ☎ 75 22 73
🛏 75 26 41
Rates from US$ 30.
- **Bunga Seminyak Cottage** (AC H NG Pl WH)
Jalan Camplung Tanduk, Seminyak ☎ 512 39 🛏 529 05
20 minutes to the airport. 25 minutes to Denpasar. All rooms with bath, telephone, TV, Mini Bar. Rates on request. Credit cards accepted.
- **C-Line Gallery and Art Café** (A B F g H OS)
Kartika Plaza 33 ☎ 512 85
Between Santika Beach and Bali Bintang Hotel. Double with bath US$ 25.
- **Resor Seminyak** (BF H NG)
Jalan Lasmana, Seminyak ✉ 80361 ☎ 73 08 14
Four star hotel.

APARTMENTS
- **Villas. The** (AC cc glm H msg Pl)
Jalan Raya Seminyak 56 ☎ 730 840 🛏 730 840
Rates for single $ 115-145, 3 bedroom villa $ 190-250. Central location.

SWIMMING
-Beach south of Oberoi Hotel in Legian (g R)
-Beach north of where Jalan Pantai meets the beach
-Kuta beach (NU) (Northern part, be discreet)

CRUISING
-Lapangan Puputan (G r tv) (between Surapati & Veteran Streets.
18-23 h Sat later)

Makasar - Sulawesi Selatan ☎ 0411

BARS
- **Donald's Canteen** (B g) 11-22 h
Karunrung
- **Losari Beach Pub & Restaurant** (B F g)
Makassar Golden Hotel

DANCECLUBS
- **Zig Zag Disco**
Makasar Golden Hotel

GENERAL GROUPS
- **Gaya Celebes • Lembayung Celebes • Saensasi Dolls**
Mon 22-2 h
PO Box 1309 90013 ✉ 90000 ☎ 51 09 43
Various organizations including AIDS service.

HEALTH GROUPS
- **Hotline AIDS'PUS-Triple M'** 10-16 h
PKBI, Jalan Landak Baru 55 ✉ 90135 ☎ 871 051

Indonesia

Makasar - Sulawesi Selatan ▶ Semarang - Jawa Tengah

CRUISING
-Karebosi Field (g tv) (nighttime)

Malang - Jawa Timur ☎ 0341

BARS
■ **My Place** (B glm) Sat
c/o Kartika Prince Hotel

CRUISING
-Town Square (alun-alun) (next to Lippobank)
-Next to the station (tv G)
-Next to Brawijaya Museum (Wed night)
-Arjosari Terminal (Sat night)

Manado - Sulawesi Utara

CRUISING
-Pasar 45 (station and terminal complex) (g tv) (21-? h)
-Nearthe Balai Wartawan & Arta Pusara Bank (nighttime)
-People's Unity Park (Taman Persatuan Bangsa) (g tv)

Medan - Sumatera Utara ☎ 061

DANCECLUBS
■ **Dynasty** (B D glm)
c/o Danau Toba International Hotel, Jalan Imam Bonjol 17
Exclusive rendez-vous spot for gay & hetero.
■ **Fire Discotheque** (B D glm)
Istana Plaza
Cruising on the cark park & main floor.
■ **Que Que Discotheque** (B D Glm) Sat
Olympia Plaza
Many Chinese.

RESTAURANTS
■ **TD (Tembakau Deli)** (B F glm)
Jalan Tembakau Deli *(near Deli Plaza)*

CINEMAS
■ **Deli Plaza Theater** (g)

MASSAGE
■ **Tunanetra Sejahtera** (g msg)
Jalan S Parman
Many gay masseurs & meeting point.
■ **Tunanetra Yakestra** (g MSG)
Jalan Sci Wampu
Gay masseurs.

SWIMMING
-Swimming pool at the Tiara Hotel (Jalan Cut Mutia Rp 10,000)

CRUISING
-A. Yani Street
-London Boulevard (at the end of the Post Office PTP)
-Iskander Muda Street (TV)
-Hotel Berlini
-Pal Merah Street (TV)
-Olympia Plaza (top floor, next to the amusement area)

Mojokerto - Jawa Timur

CRUISING
-Town Square (alun-alun) (next to the military police building. Nighttime)

Padang - Sumatera Barat ☎ 0751

CRUISING
-Duta Plaza yard (at night)
-Padang Theater (0-24 h)
-President Music Room
-Taman Melati
-Aditiawarman Museum Complex (near the Utama Theater at the Taman Budaya)

Palembang - Sumatera Selatan ☎ 0711

CRUISING
-Five Days & Five Nights Monument (Tugu Lima Hari Lima Malam) (at night)
-Nusa Indah Park (Taman Nusa Indah) (G TV at night)
-Talang Semut Park (Best Sat night)

Pasuruan - Jawa Timur

RESTAURANTS
■ **Pasar Poncol** (B F glm) at night
Nusantara Street *(beside Himalaja Cinema)*

CRUISING
-North Town Square (alun-alun) (tv G at night)
-Banyubiru baths (17 km from Pasuran, sun daytime)
-Makam Gunung Gangsir, Bangil (TV Fri)

Pekanbaru - Riau ☎ 0761

HEALTH GROUPS
■ **Yayasan Utama**
Jalan Diponegoro 8 ✉ 28111 ☎ 376 45 🖷 376 45

CRUISING
-Atrium of Plaza Citra (21-24 h)
-Café Plaza Citra (glm 20-22 h)
-Jin Cut Nya Dhien (next to the Education & Culture Deepdikbud Building) (21-24 h)

Ponorogo - Jawa Timur

CRUISING
-Town square (alun-alun) (next to the banyan tree on the south side, along the sidewalk between the West & East squares. Best Sat night 20-? h)

Salatiga - Jawa Tengah

CRUISING
-Salatiga Plaza (in front of and across the street, every night, best on Sat night)
-Jalan Sudirman (Sat night)

Semarang - Jawa Tengah ☎ 024

HOTELS
■ **Hotel Candi Indah** (AC B f H NG)
Jalan Dr. Wahidin 112 ☎ 31 25 14 🖷 31 25 15

Semarang - Jawa Tengah ▶ Yogyakarta | Indonesia

CRUISING
- Simpang Lima (G r) (next to the Citraland building site, also generally on the square)
- Jalan Menteri Supeno (G r TV) (Along the street)
- Matahari Department Store (G R) (near the juice bar)

Sidoarjo - Jawa Timur

CRUISING
- Town Square (alun-alun) (near the public telephones beside the Mahkota cinema and the street next to it. Sat night best. G)
- Larangan market

Surabaya - Jawa Timur ☎ 031

BARS
■ **Bongo's African Jungle Bar** (B glm)
Sheraton Hotel, Jalan Embong Malang
Sat best.
■ **Desperado Mexican Bar** (B glm)
Shangri-La Hotel, Jalan Mayjen Sungkono
Fri Sat best.

DANCECLUBS
■ **Borneo Club** (B D glm)
Jalan Tunjungan *(downtown)*
■ **Calypso** (B D glm) Sun
Kenjeran Amusement Park, Panta Ria Kenjeran
■ **Lido Diskotik** (B D glm) Thu Sun after 23 h
Jalan Mayjen Sungkono
■ **Station Top Ten**
6/F Plaza Tunjungan, Jalan Tunjungan
Best Fri Sat.

RESTAURANTS
■ **Indigo**
Mojopahit Mandarin Hotel on Jln Tunjungan
Regional & western food.

SHOWS
■ **Red Top Cabaret** (B glm S)
Jalan Semut
Sat best.

FITNESS STUDIOS
■ **Atlas Clark Hatch**
Jln Dharma Husada Indah
Mostly chinese and locals.

GENERAL GROUPS
■ **DPD Hiwaria MKGR Ja-Tim**
Jalan Kenikir 7 ✉ 60131 ☎ 535 05 17
■ **Gatra Penpals Club**
PO Box 1557 ✉ 60015
■ **Gaya Baya** Meeting 2nd Sun 18h
Jalan Dupak Bangunrejo I/19 ✉ 60179
■ **Gaya Nusantara (GN)**
Jalan Mulyosari Timur 46 ✉ 60112 ☎ 593 49 24 📠 593 90 70
✉ doetomo@server.indo.net.id
■ **Persekutuan Hidup Damai**
Jalan Ngagel Rejo Kidul 113 ✉ 60245 ☎ 588 418
■ **Perwakos (Persatuan Waria Kotamadya Surabaya)** (G TV)
Jalan Kanginan III/10 ✉ 60131 ☎ 517 068
Transvestites.

■ **Yayasan Kemanusiaan**
Jalan Jojoran Gg 3 Perintis N° 10 ✉ 60285 ☎ 594 10 75

SWIMMING
- Water Park Pantai Rai Kenjeran swimming pool, Sun from 16h
- Darmo Grande
- Klub Primalaras.

CRUISING
Warning: some men may expect money.
- Kalifornia (G r tv) (Ketabang Kali. Along the entrance bridge of the Plaza Surabaya complex, after 22 h. Best Thu Sat.)
- Taman Remaja Surabaya (G r TV) (Amusement Park next to Surabaya Mall, Jalan Kusuma Bangsa. Thu 21-22.30 open-air drag show.)
- Texas, Terminal Joyoboyo (G r RT tv) (Along the river at the public transport terminal. Best Sat.)
- Bambu Runcing or SP (espay) (g R) (Park next to Surabaya Post building, Jalan Panglima Sudirman)
- Irian Barat Street (at night)
- Tunjungan Plaza (shopping centre, evening)
- Bungurasih Terminal (back part) at night
- Pasar Complex, Terminal one
- The following Plaza : Surabaya, Tunjungan 3.

Ubud - Bali ☎ 0361

CAFES
■ **Prada-Cafe & Guest House** (AC B BF CC F GLM H MA OS)
JL. Kajeng 80571 Glanyar ☎ 975 122
High standard, US$ 55/night (incl. bf.).

HOTELS
■ **Bali Spirit Hotel & Spa** (B BF G H msg NU OS PI)
At the end of the Post Office Road ☎ 97 40 13 📠 97 40 12

Yogyakarta ☎ 0274

BARS
■ **Borobodur Bar & Restaurant** (B g MA r S) 13-1 h
Jalan Passar Kembang 17 *(Near railway station)*
■ **THR Purawisata** (STV) Show Thu
Jalan Brigjen Katamso

CAFES
■ **Kafe Wayang** (B F GLM TV) 11-01h
JL. Mayjen Sutoyo 67b *(near Prawirotaman tourist area)* ☎ 417 088
Sun are STV, Wed is karaoke night.

RESTAURANTS
■ **Legian Restaurant** (b F g)
Jalan Perwakilan
Garden restaurant with nice atmosphere.
■ **Mirota** (B F g)
Jalan F.M. Noto *(Kotabaru)*
Indonesian fast food.
■ **Panca Ria Terrace** (b F g) best after 21 h
Jalan Malioboro *(in front of Mutiara Hotel)*
■ **Pesta Perak** (b F g)
Jalan Tentara Pelajar
Indonesian cuisine.

Indonesia - Iran | Yogyakarta

HOTELS

■ **Dusun Jogja Village Inn** (AC CC F glm H MA PI)
JL. Menukan N° 5   ✉ 55153 *(in front of Radio Yasika FM-bus N°2 from bus Station)*   ☏ 37 30 31   ☏ 38 44 38   📠 38 22 02
📧 jvigecko@indo.net.id   🌐 www.jvidusun.co.id
Stylish & full of character. Good food including vegetarian. Good selection of movies and music. Manager Paul can provide additional info..

GENERAL GROUPS

■ **Indonesian Gay Society (IGS)**
PO Box 36/YKBS   ✉ 55281   ☏ 56 20 17

HEALTH GROUPS

■ **Lentera**
PKBI, Jalan Tentara Rakyat Mataram Gg kapas Jt. I/705 *55231*
☏ 58 67 67   📠 58 67 67   📧 lentera@ins.healthnet.org

CRUISING

-Alun-Alun Utara (North Square, in front of Sultan Palace)
-In front of Gedong Agung, Benteng Vredeberg & Seni Sono
-Marlioboro Shopping Center

Iran

Name: Îrân • Irán
Location: Middle East
Initials: IR
Time: GMT +3:30
International Country Code: ☏ 98
International Access Code: ☏ 00
Language: Persian (official), Turkic, Kurdish, Luri
Area: 1,648,000 km² / 636,294 sq mi.
Currency: 1 Iranian Rial (IRl) = 100 Dinars
Population: 68,959,931 (1998 est.)
Capital: Tehrän (Teheran)
Religions: 99% Muslim
Climate: Continental climate, although much of the country has a desert climate. Summers are warm to hot. Winters can be extremely cold with cold winds blowing from the northeast.

✱ According to the Islamic penal law, (Chapter 1, Art. 110) "punishment for sodomy is death". Homosexuality is however as common among Iranians as it is with any other nationality. As it is impossible to create an organisation for gay & lesbian Iranians within Iran, HOMAN (a group defending the rights of Iranian gays and lesbians) was founded in 1991 in exile. The group has branches in many countries and contacts with Iranians worldwide and inside Iran.
There is a large exile community of Iranians (estimated at 3-4 million). HOMAN has achieved notable success during the past decade with its work within this community. Iranians in exile are gay friendly and even Iranian political groups (the ecologists) in exile have started talking about gay rights. In August 2000, for the first time in Iran's history, an Iranian political group announced and added to its constitution that they intend to join the struggle for the rights of all people no matter what "their sexual orientation" might be. To get more information regarding the law in relation to homosexuality in Iran, please contact one of the HOMAN organisational offices
Homan Webmaster

★ Nach dem islamischen Strafgesetzbuch, Kapitel 1, Art. 110 "steht auf Analverkehr die Todesstrafe". Dennoch ist Homosexualität unter Iranern natürlich genauso verbreitet wie in jeder anderen Nation auch. Da es unmöglich ist, innerhalb des Irans eine Organisation für Schwule und Lesben zu gründen, wurde 1991 im Exil HOMAN, eine Gruppe, welche die Rechte der Schwulen und Lesben verteidigt, gegründet. Die Gruppe hat Ableger in vielen Ländern und steht nicht nur mit vielen Iranern weltweit als auch innerhalb Irans in Kontakt.
Die iranische Exil-Community wird auf etwa drei bis vier Millionen Personen geschätzt. HOMAN konnte in den letzten zehn Jahren mit ihrer Arbeit innerhalb der Community sehr viele Erfolge verbuchen. Exil-Iraner sind sehr gay-freundlich und sogar sich im Exil befindende und ursprünglich aus dem Iran stammende politische Gruppierungen (eine grüne Partei) haben begonnen, über die Rechte der Schwulen zu sprechen. Im August 2000, geschah es zum ersten Mal in der iranischen Geschichte, daß eine politische Gruppierung ankündigte und zu ihrer Verfassung hinzufügte, daß sie beabsichtigen sich dem Kampf für die Rechte aller Menschen anzuschließen, ganz gleich welche sexuellen Orientierung sie haben. Wenn Sie mehr über die Gesetzgebung bezüglich der Homosexuellen im Iran wissen wollen, dann kontaktieren Sie bitte eine der Dienststellen der Organisation HOMAN.

✱ Selon le Code pénal islamique iranien (chapitre 1, article 110), " la punition pour la sodomie est la mort ". L'homosexualité est cependant aussi répandue parmi les Iraniens que dans

Iran

le reste du monde. Comme il n'est pas possible de créer une association gaie et lesbienne dans le pays, Homan (un groupe défendant les droits des homosexuels iraniens) a été fondé dans des pays d'exil. Le groupe a des ramifications dans plusieurs pays et des contacts avec les Iraniens dans le monde entier, y compris en Iran même.

La diaspora iranienne est très nombreuse (estimée à 3-4 millions de personnes). Homan a gagné depuis une dizaine d'années de nombreuses batailles au sein de cette communauté. Les Iraniens en exil sont devenus plus tolérants vis-à-vis des gais et même un parti politique en exil (les écologistes) a commencé à parler de droits homosexuels. En août 2000, et pour la première fois dans l'histoire de l'Iran, un groupement politique a inscrit dans sa constitution qu'il entendait se battre pour les droits de toute personne, quelle que soit son orientation sexuelle. Pour obtenir plus d'information sur l'homosexualité en Iran au niveau légal, veuillez contacter un des bureaux de Homan.

Homan Webmaster

Según la ley penal islámica (capítulo 1, artículo 110), "sodomía es penalizado con la muerte". No obstante, la homosexualidad es algo tan común entre los iraníes como lo es entre personas de cualquier otra nacionalidad. Como es imposible crear una organización de gays y lesbianas iraníes dentro del Irán, HOMAN, un grupo que defiende los derechos de los gays y lesbianas iraníes, se fundó en el exilio en 1991. El grupo existe en muchos países y reluciona a los iraníes en todo el mundo y dentro del Irán.

Hay una comunidad de iraníes exiliados muy grande (se calcula que se trata de entre tres y cuatro millones). Durante la última década, HOMAN alcanzó éxitos notables con su trabajo en esta comunidad exiliada. Los iraníes exiliados no suelen tener nada en contra de los gays y hasta los grupos políticos iraníes (los ecologistas) en el exilio empezaron a acuparse de los derechos de los gays. En agosto del 2000, por la primera vez en la historia del Irán, un grupo político iraní anunció la intención de luchar por los derechos de todas las personas, "independientemente de su orientación sexual". Para obtener más información acerca de la situación legal de los homosexuales en el Irán, hay que ponerse en contacto con una de las oficinas de HOMAN.

Secondo l'articolo 110 del capitolo 1 del codice penale islamico, è prevista la pena di morte per il rapporto anale. Ciononostante, l'omosessualità tra gli iraniani è altrettanto diffusa quanto nelle altre nazioni. Visto che in Iran è impossibile istituire un'organizzazione per omosessuali e lesbiche, nel 1991 è stato costituito in esilio un gruppo HOMAN, il quale si batte per i diritti degli omosessuali e delle lesbiche. Il gruppo ha diramazioni in svariati paesi e intrattiene contatti non solo con molti iraniani sparsi in giro per il mondo, ma anche con i residenti in Iran. La comunità iraniana in esilio è stimata tra i tre fino ai quattro milioni di persone.

Negli ultimi dieci anni HOMAN ha potuto registrare, con il suo lavoro, molti successi all'interno della comunità. Gli iraniani esiliati sono molto benevoli nei confronti dei gay e addirittura i raggruppamenti politici che si trovano in esilio e che in origine provengono dall'Iran (tra cui un partito dei verdi) hanno iniziato a discutere sui diritti degli omosessuali. Nell'agosto 2000, per la prima volta nella storia dell'Iran è successo che un gruppo politico annunciasse e si prefiggesse, inserendolo nella propria costituzione, di aderire alla lotta per i diritti di tutti gli uomini, a prescindere dal loro orientamento sessuale. Se volete sapere di più sulla legislazione, rispettivamente agli omosessuali in Iran, contattate allora per favore uno dei posti di servizio dell'organizzazione HOMAN.

NATIONAL GAY INFO

Homan on the Web
homan@rocketmail.com www.homan.cwc.net
Information about the organisation, the different sections, the magazine, the Islamic law and personals.

NATIONAL PUBLICATIONS

Homan Magazine
www.homan.cwc.net/magazine.html
In Persian and English. Available from any branch of Homan in the world.

NATIONAL GROUPS

Homan in Germany
c/o Hein & Fiete, Pulverteich 21 20099 Hamburg

Homan in Los Angeles
PO Box 480691 CA 90048 Los Angeles
+1 323 937-4397
homan@yahoo.com

Homan in Norway
c/o IFG, PO Box 2879 0608 Oslo

Homan in Sweden Wed 20-22 h
PO Box 3444 10369 Stockholm +46 31 12 1054

Homan UK
BM Box 7826 WC1N 3XX London

Iran Leathermen (G LJ MA)
sw61@hotmail.com www.iranleathermen.orbix.co.uk

Ireland Baltimore ▸ Cork

Ireland

Name: Éire • Irland • Irlande • Irlanda
Location: West Europe in North Atlantic Ocean
Initials: IRL
Time: GMT
International Country Code: ☏ 353 (leave the first 0 of area codes)
International Access Code: ☏ 00
Language: Irish (Gaelic) and English
Area: 70,284 km^2 / 21,137 sq mi.
Currency: 1 Irish Pound (Ir£ = 100 Pence)
Population: 3,619,480
Capital: Dublin / Baile Atha Cliath
Religions: 93% Roman Catholic, 3% Anglican
Climate: Moderate maritime climate, that is modified by the North Atlantic Current. Winters are mild, summers are cool. There's a consistent humidity and it's overcast about half the time.

North Atlantic Ocean
IRELAND
Galway • Dublin • *Irish Sea* • Limerick • Cork • *United Kingdom*

※ Ireland lies on the edge of Europe, which does however not mean, that its population is especially backward. In contrast to the British mainland the conditions in Ireland are rather progressive. The age of consent is 17 for everybody; there is no special legislation for the military; anti-discriminatory laws are in discussion. Main protagonist of these and more overall social modernisation was the ex-president of Ireland Mary Robinson. By the way: the gay-lesbian newspaper of Ireland, the Gay Community News, is generously supported by the Irish state.

⬢ Irland liegt am Rande des europäischen Kontinents. Das bedeutet aber nicht, daß seine Bewohner besonders rückständig sein. Im Gegensatz zu den benachbarten Briten sind bei den Iren die Verhältnisse recht fortschrittlich: das Schutzalter liegt einheitlich bei 17 Jahren, für das Militär gelten keine Sondergesetze, Anti-Diskriminierungsbestimmungen sind in der Diskussion. Gallionsfigur all dieser und weiterer allgemeingesellschaftlicher Modernisierungen war die ehemalige Präsidentin Irlands, Mary Robinson. Übrigens: Die schwul-lesbische Zeitung des Landes, die Gay Community News wird großzügigerweise vom irischen Staat unterstützt.

✱ L'Irlande est le pays le plus excentré au sein de l'Union européenne, ce qui ne veut pas dire que l'on y est en retard par rapport aux autres. En comparaison avec leurs voisins britanniques, les Irlandais plutôt à la page: majorité sexuelle à 17 ans pour tous (homos et hétéros), armée assez tolérante, législation anti-discriminatoire en préparation. Tous ces changements sont dûs à l'action et l'influence de Mary Robinson, l'ancienne Présidente de la République. Ah oui: le Gay Community News, le seul journal gai du pays, est généreusement subventionné par l'Etat!

⬣ Irlanda está situada al límite del continente europeo, pero esto no quiere decir que sus habitantes tengan una mentalidad cerrada. En comparación con su vecino Inglaterra, la situación en Irlanda es bastante progresiva. La edad de consentimiento es de 17 años, independientemente de la orientación sexual. No existen regulaciones especiales para el servicio militar y la introducción de leyes contra la discriminación gay se está discutiendo. A propósito: La revista gay-lesbiana del país, la *Gay Community News*, está subvencionada generosamente por el estado irlandés.

✕ L'Irlanda è situata ai limiti del continente europeo. Ciò non significa però che i suoi abitanti abbiano una mentalità arretrata. Contrariamente ai vicini del Regno Unito gli irlandesi sono progrediti: la maturità sessuale è di 17 anni per tutti, per il servizio militare non esistono regolamenti particolari e finalmente sono in discussione nuove leggi contro la discriminazione dei gay. Mary Robinson, il presidente precedente irlandese, è stata la promotrice di questi ed altre modernizzazioni sociali. A proposito, il gay community news, il giornale omosessuale nazionale, viene generosamente sovvenzionato dallo stato.

NATIONAL PUBLICATIONS

■ **Gay Community News** (GLM)
6 South William Street Dublin 2 ☏ (01) 671 09 39
☏ (01) 671 90 76 📠 (01) 671 35 49 ✉ gcn@tinet.ie
Irelands gay and lesbian magazine. Monthly free at gay and lesbian venues. Featuring news and events.

NATIONAL GROUPS

■ **Irish Names Quilt**
53 Parnell Sqare Dublin 1 ☏ (01) 873 37 99

Baltimore ☏ 028

HOTELS
■ **Rolf's Holiday Hostel & Restaurant "Café Art"** (A B BF CC glm H MA OS) All year

☏ 202 89 📠 202 89
12 double rooms with shared bath and WC.

Beara ☏ 027

PRIVATE ACCOMMODATION
■ **Island's End B&B** (BF F glm H OS) All year
Rossmackowen, Beara *(Near Glengarriff, Bantry Bay)* ☏ 600 40 📠 600 40
Very friendly B&B. 5 double rooms with spectacular views over the sea and mountains. Rates Ir£ 17 p.p./night (bf incl.) Shower/bath in the hall. Dinner available.

Cork ☏ 021

GAY INFO
■ **Lesbian & Gay Resource Group**
7-8 Augustine Street *(at The Other Place)* ☏ 27 84 70

588 *SPARTACUS* 2001/2002

Cork ▶ Dublin **Ireland**

■ **Other Place. The (Lesbian & Gay Community Centre)**
8 South Main Street *(Entrance via Other Side Bookshop)* ☎ 27 84 70
✉ lesgay@indigo.ie.

BARS

■ **Loafers Bar** (! A B GLM MA N OS) Mon-Sun 17-23.30 h
26 Douglas Street ☎ 31 16 12
Beer garden.

CAFES

■ **Other Side Café. The** (b D F GLM MA) Café Mon-Fri 10.30-17.30, Club Fri Sat 23-2.30 h, 1st Fri women only
8 South Main Street ☎ 27 84 70
■ **Quay Co-op Restaurant and Wholefood Shop** (F glm)
Mon-Sat 9-21 h
24 Sullivans Quay ☎ 431 7026

DANCECLUBS

■ **Other Place Club. The** (B D GLM MA s) Fri-Sat 23-2.30 h
8 South Main Street ☎ 27 84 70

BOOK SHOPS

■ **Other Side Bookshop. The** (GLM) Mon-Sat 11-17.30
8 South Main Street ☎ 27 84 70

HOTELS

⇨ also Skibbereen and Beara, West Cork

GUEST HOUSES

■ **Rolf's Holiday Hostel & Restaurant** (A B BF CC f glm H MA OS)
All year
Baltimore ☎ 028/ 20289 🖷 028/ 20289
Seaside resort with sailing, fishing, waterskiing etc.
■ **Roman House** (BF CC GLM MA msg) All year
3 St. John's Terrace, Upper John Street ☎ 450 3606
✉ rhbb@eircom.net 🖳 www.interglobal.ie/romanhouse
Small, comfortable guest house. Each room with TV and tea / coffee making facilities.
■ **Travara Lodge** (cc g H)
Courtmacsherry ☎ 46493

HEALTH GROUPS

■ **AIDS Helpline Cork** Mon-Fri 10-17, Tue 19-21 h
☎ 27 66 76

CRUISING

-Fitz Patrick park (WE).

Dublin ☎ 01

✸ It may not have the largest gay and lesbian scene in the world, but Dublin is nevertheless a lively cosmopolitan European capital city. A real advantage of the small scene is that almost all places of interest are within 10 minutes walk of one another, many being grouped in and around the South Great George's and Dame Street and across the river Liffey to Ormond Quay.

✸ Auch wenn sie nicht gerade die größte Schwulen- und Lesbenszene der Welt aufweisen kann ist Dublin doch eine lebhafte und weltoffene europäische Hauptstadt. Der größte Vorteil der eher kleinen Szene liegt darin, dass fast alle interessanten Anlaufpunkte nur 10 Gehminuten voneinander entfernt liegen, viele davon in oder in der Gegend der South Great George Street und der Dame Street sowie von der gegenüberliegenden Seite des River Liffey bis zum Ormond Quay.

✸ Dublin ne possède certainement pas la plus grande scène gaie et lesbienne du monde mais est néanmoins une ville cosmopolite européenne très vivante. L'avantage de ce milieu assez petit réside dans le fait qu'il suffit de 10 minutes à pied pour parcourir les endroits intéressants, la plupart se situant autour des South Great George's et Dame streets et de l'autre côté de la rivière Liffey sur le quai Ormond.

✸ No es que tenga el mayor ambiente homosexual del mundo, pero Dublín es, no obstante, una capital europea animada y muy cosmopolita. Una gran ventaja de un ambiente tan pequeño es que todos los sitios de interés se encuentren a diez minutos de distancia - siempre andando. La mayoría de ellos se encuentra en la calle South Great George's and Dame y sus alrededores así como, al otro lado del río Liffey, hacia Ormond Quay.

✸ Anche se non può proprio vantare la più grande scena gay e lesbica del mondo, Dublino è una capitale europea vivace e cosmopolita. Il grosso vantaggio di una scena piuttosto ridotta sta nella distanza minima, ca. 10 min. a piedi, che separa tra loro quasi tutti i luoghi di spicco, molti dei quali si trovano in South Great George Street e in Dame Street o nelle vicinanze immediate, nonché sul lato opposto del River Liffey fino a Ormond Quay.

GAY INFO

■ **Gay Switchboard Dublin** Sun-Fri 20-22, Sat 15.30-18 h
Carmichael House, North Brunswick Street ✉ D 7 ☎ 872 1055
🖳 www.iol.ie/~gsd/

TOURIST INFO

■ **Dublin Tourist Centre**
Suffolk Street ✉ D2 ☎ 605 77 77 🖷 605 77 87

BARS

■ **George. The** (! AC B CC D F G lj STV TV) Wed-Mon 10.30-2.30, Tue -23.30 h
89 South Great George Street ✉ D 2 ☎ 478 2983
The George is both a bar and a club. Normally busy and mostly, but not exclusively, men only.
■ **Globe. The** (AC B f glm YG) Mon-Sat 12-23.30, Sun 16-23 h
11 South Great George Street ✉ D 2 ☎ 671 1220
■ **Out On The Liffey** (AC B D GLM MA STV) Mon-Fri 10.30-0.30, Sat Sun -1.30 h
27 Upper Ormond Quay, ✉ 7 *(Over Capel St. Bridge, besides Ormond Hotel)* ☎ 872 2480

CAFES

■ **Well Fed Café. The** (A AC F glm MA) Mon-Sat 12-21 h
Resource Centre, 6 Crow Street, ✉ D 2 *(Temple Bar area)*
☎ 667 2234

DANCECLUBS

■ **Club Ri'ra** (B D f glm YG) Mon 23.30-3 h (glm)
Dame Court ✉ D 2 *(Behind the Globe bar)* ☎ 671 1220
■ **Kitchen. The** (B D GLM) 23.15- 2.30h
East Sussex Street ✉ D 2 ☎ 677 6178

RESTAURANTS

■ **Juice** (AC CC glm) Sun-Thu 11-22, Fri-Sat 11-24 h
South Great George Street ✉ D 2 ☎ 475 7856
■ **Mark's Bros** (B F glm) 11-23 h
7 South Great Georges Street ☎ 677 10 45
Vegetarian cuisine.
■ **Odessa. The** (B F glm YG) Mon-Sun 12-24 h
13/14 Dame Court ✉ D 2 *(Off Dame Street)* ☎ 670 7634

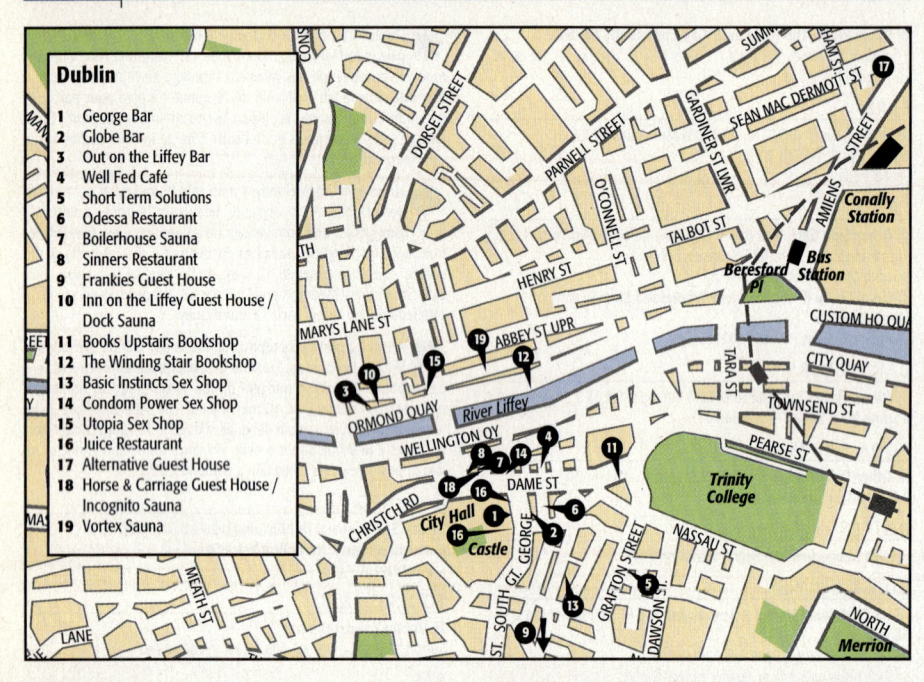

Ireland | Dublin

Dublin

1. George Bar
2. Globe Bar
3. Out on the Liffey Bar
4. Well Fed Café
5. Short Term Solutions
6. Odessa Restaurant
7. Boilerhouse Sauna
8. Sinners Restaurant
9. Frankies Guest House
10. Inn on the Liffey Guest House / Dock Sauna
11. Books Upstairs Bookshop
12. The Winding Stair Bookshop
13. Basic Instincts Sex Shop
14. Condom Power Sex Shop
15. Utopia Sex Shop
16. Juice Restaurant
17. Alternative Guest House
18. Horse & Carriage Guest House / Incognito Sauna
19. Vortex Sauna

■ **Sinners** (CC F glm)
12 Parliament Street ✉ D 2 ☎ 671 9315

SEX SHOPS/BLUE MOVIES

■ **Basic Instincts** (CC g MA) Mon-Sat 10.30-18.30, Thu -20, Sun 12-18 h
56 South William Street ✉ D 2 (Off Grafton Street, near Powers Ct. Shopping Centre) ☎ 671 2223
Large gay video and magazine department as well as rubberwear. Mail order service.

■ **Condom Power** (AC CC glm) Mon-Sat 9-18, Thu-20 h
57 Dame Street ✉ D 2 (Basement. Opposite Rehab Lottery) ☎ 677 8963

■ **Utopia** (CC g) Mon-Sat 9.30-18, Thu -20, Sun 12-18 h
164 Capel Street ✉ D 2 ☎ 872 9045

SAUNAS/BATHS

■ **Boilerhouse. The** (AC b BF CC DR F G MA SA SB SOL VS WH) Mon-Thu 13-5, Fri 13-Mon 5 h
12 Crane Lane (beside Olympia Theatre off Damce St.)
☎ 677 31 30
Popular among all types of clientele.

■ **Dock. The** (AC CC DR f G lj MA r s SA SB VS) 13-5, Fri 13-Sun 5 h
21 Upper Ormond Quay (Same entrance as guesthouse "Inn On The Liffey") ☎ 872 41 72
Intimate sauna with mixed aged visitors.

■ **Incognito** (! b f DR G MA SA SB VS) Mon-Thu 13-5, Fri-Sat & Bank Holiday -9, Sun 14-5 h
1-2 Bow Lane East (Off Aungier Street. Basement of The Horse and Carriage) ☎ 478 3504
Discreet sauna with hotel in the heart of the city with coffee and mineral bar and S+M room. Popular on week-ends.

■ **Vortex** (B DR F G LJ MA S SA SB TV VS) 13-5, Fri 13-Mon 5h, 64 hours at weekends.
1 Great Strand Street (at Capel Street Bridge, city center)
☎ 878 08 98
Sauna and leisure club for men. Café/wine bar, 5 floors of cruising space, fantasy dungeon, mirror rooms, 40 private rest cubicles, maze & pleasure glories. 1st and 3rd Sat of the month: Club Trash fetish party.

BOOK SHOPS

■ **Books Upstairs** (CC glm) Mon-Fri 10-19, Sat -18, Sun (summer) 14-18 h
36 College Green ✉ D 2 (Opposite Trinity College) ☎ 679 6687
A few gay and lesbian books to choose from.

■ **Winding Stair. The** (CC glm) Mon-Sat 10-18, Thu 10-20, Sun 13-17 h
40 Lower Ormond Quay ✉ D 2 ☎ 873 3292

HOTELS

■ **Horse & Carriage** (BF CC GLM H OS SA)
15 Aungier Street ✉ D 2 ☎ 478 3537 📠 478 4010
✉ liamtony@indigo.ie 🌐 indigo.ie/~liamtony.h&c.html
Rates from single IrE 40 per person incl.bf. Free entry to sauna for hotel guests.

GUEST HOUSES

■ **Alternative Guest House. The** (AC CC GLM MA msg VS)
Reception: Mon-Sun 8-23.30 h
61 Amiens Street ✉ D 1 (Near main train / bus station)
☎ 855 3671
Studio rooms with shower/WC, kitchenette and satellite TV.

590 SPARTACUS 2001/2002

Dublin | Ireland

Leisure Club the Vortex and Sauna

Irelands largest, best and most professional Sauna & Leisure Club for men

1, Great Strand Street, (at Capel St Bridge), Dublin 1, Ph: 00-353-1-8780898.

Daily from 13.00 hrs – 0.500 am
Fri 13.00 hrs – Mon 05.00 am (64 hrs open!)

Café / Wine Bar / 5 floors of cruising space

- Sauna / Steam room
- Fantasy Dungeon
- Mirror Rooms
- 40 private rest cubicles

Visit our Website at Basic-Instincts.com

'Club Trash' Fetish Night ... 1st and 3rd Sat of each Month!
Music, Dance and Cruise from 23.00 till 9.00 am, dress code desired)

BASIC INSTINCTS LTD

56, South William Street • Dublin 2 • Tel. 00-353-1-6712223
City Centre location • Open 7 days

Irelands best adult / fetish store   Leather / Rubberwear
Greeting Cards / Novelties
Huge Magazine / Video Section (mail order service)
Designer Underwear / Swimwear (serving all your needs)
Active web-site! D.V.Ds

Ireland | Dublin ▶ Waterford

■ **Fairfield Lodge** (CC G H OS)
Monkstown Avenue, Monkstown, Co. Dublin ☏ 280 3912
📠 280 3912 ✉ jsb@indigo.ie
🖥 indigo.ie/~jsb/webpage/studio.htm
Located 5 km from city centre. Self contained studio apartment. Rates IrE 69 p.p./night, 293 p.p./week.

■ **Frankies** (BF CC GLM H OS) Reception: Mon-Sun 9-23.30 h
8 Camden Place ✉ D 2 *(Off Camden Street)* ☏ 478 3087
☏ 475-2182 (guestline) ✉ frankiesdublin@hotmail.com
🖥 www.frankiesguesthouse.com
Dublin's only exclusive guesthouse for lesbians and gays.

■ **Inn on the Liffey** (BF CC G H MA)
21 Upper Ormond Quay ✉ 7 *(same entrance as Dock Sauna)*
☏ 677 08 28 📠 872 4165 ✉ innontheliffey@hotmail.com
🖥 homepage.eircom.net/~the dock/inn.html
Newly refurbished and under new management. All rooms en-suite. TV in all rooms. Irish breakfast served. Free entrance to "the Dock Sauna"

APARTMENTS

■ **Short Term Solutions** (CC G H MA p WE YG) Mon-Fri 9.30-18 h, closed Sat Sun
85/86 Grafton Street ✉ 2 ☏ 790 59 15 📠 670 96 71
✉ info@shorttermsolutions.com 🖥 www.shorttermsolutions.com
Fully equipped apartments with TV/video, phone and kitchen. Near all bars and clubs.

PRIVATE ACCOMMODATION

■ **Home Bureau**
(near all bars/clubs and saunas) ☏ 679 22 22 📠 670 96 71
🖥 www.shorttermsolutions.com
Apartments & studios, 1/2 beds/studios fully equipped. Weekend rates available.

GENERAL GROUPS

■ **Muted Cupid Theatre Group** Meeting: Tue 19.30 h at 6 South William Street, Dublin 2
■ **Outhave** (GLM) 10-6 h
6 South William Street *(near Trinity College)* ☏ 670 63 77
📠 679 13 06
Dublin's community and resource centre for les-bi-gay and transgender people. Café, library and different groups.

HEALTH GROUPS

■ **AIDS-Helpline Dublin** Mon-Fri 19-21, Sat 15-17 h
☏ 872 4277
■ **Dublin AIDS Alliance** (GLM MA OS) 9-19.30h
The Erin Centre, 53 Parnell Square ✉ 1 *City Centre* ☏ 873 3799
📠 873 3174 ✉ aids-alliance-dublin@hotmail.com
■ **Gay Men's Health Project** (G MA) Tue & Wed 18.30-20h
Baggot Street Clinic, 19 Haddington Road ✉ D 4 *(Next door to Baggot St. hospital)* ☏ 660 2189 📠 668 0050
✉ GMHP2@eircom.net

RELIGIOUS GROUPS

■ **Reach**
PO Box 4625 ✉ D 2
Gay Christian group.

SWIMMING

- "Forty Foot" (g NU)
- Seapoint (g) (close to Forty Foot)
- Dollymount (G NU) (Sand dunes at the far end are quite cruisy)

CRUISING

- Palmerston Park (Best 0.30-6 h)
- Phoenix Park (Very busy at night but AYOR. This park is huge and the most popular cruising areas vary, ask locals for exact location of action.)
- Balbriggan Railway Station (toilets)
- Connolly train station (cruisy toilets)
- Toilets in Killiney Hill Park

Galway ☏ 091

GAY INFO

■ **Gay Help Line** Tue Thu 20-22 h
PO Box 45 ☏ 56 61 34

BOOK SHOPS

■ **Charlie Byrne's Bookshop**
Middle Street ☏ 56 17 66
■ **Pearls of Wisdom** (glm)
4 Quay Street

HEALTH GROUPS

■ **AIDS Help West** Mon-Fri 10-13 and 14-17h
Oznam House, Augustine Street *(Galway City Centre)* ☏ 566 266
📠 564 708 ✉ aidswest@iol.ie

Kilkenny ☏ 056

RESTAURANTS

■ **Motte Restaurant. The** (CC F g MA p) Tue-Sat 19-21.30 h (last orders), closed Sun-Mon
Plas-Newydd Lodge, Inistioge, Co. Kilkenny *(15 miles from city)*
☏ 586 55

Limerick ☏ 061

GAY INFO

■ **Gay Switchboard Limerick** Mon-Tue 19.30-21.30 h
PO Box 151, GPO ☏ 31 01 01 ✉ gsl@eircom.net

Skibbereen ☏ 028

PRIVATE ACCOMMODATION

■ **Mont Bretia B&B** (BF GLM MA p)
Adrigole Townland ☏ 33 663
Farmhouse in the countryside. Rates IrE 20 p.p. (bf incl.) Dinner available, bike hire possible.

Waterford ☏ 051

RESTAURANTS

■ **Haricots** (B F glm)
O'Connell Street
Vegetarian and wholefood.

Ireland

Dublin's Best & Biggest Sauna

CAFÉ

JACUZZI

SAUNA

STEAM ROOMS

SOLARIUM

PRIVATE ROOMS AVAILABLE BY APPOINTMENT

Open Monday to Thursday
13.00 to 05.00

and All Weekend from
Friday 13.00 to Monday 05.00

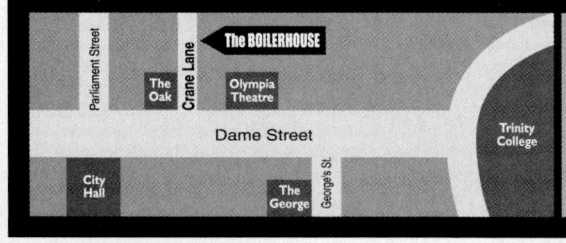

The Boilerhouse
12 Crane Lane, Dublin 2

Telephone (01) 677 3130
Web site www.the-boilerhouse.com

Israel

Name:	Yisra'él/Isra'íl • Israël • Israele
Location:	Middle East
Initials:	IL
Time:	GMT+2
International Country Code:	☏ 972 (leave the first 0 of area codes)
International Access Code:	☏ 00 or 012 or 013 or 014
Language:	Modern Hebrew (Ivrit) and Arabic
Area:	21,946 km² / 8,473 sq mi.
Currency:	1 New Shekel (NIS) = 100 Agorot
Population:	5,643,966
Capital:	Jerusalem (Yerushalayim)
Religions:	82% Jewish, 14% Moslem
Climate:	Moderate climate. Southern and eastern desert areas are hot and dry.

❋ Israel is characterised by a unique combination: a very tolerant society and an advanced legal system on one hand, and a very limited gay scene on the other. Although religious parties have considerable power, recent years have seen great steps toward the full integration of gay men and lesbians into society. The SPPR (Society for the Protection of Personal Rights), the only gay and lesbian organisation in the country, succeeded in pushing through the decriminalisation of anal intercourse (1988), in 1991 there followed an anti-discrimination clause in labour legislation, and in 1993 a sub-committee for homosexual rights was formed in the Knesset. In 1994 a court ruled that employers should treat the partners of gay employees the same as they do the partners of their heterosexual employees.

❋ Die Situation israelischer Schwuler ist durch eine besondere Kombination von Umständen geprägt: eine recht tolerante Gesellschaft mit einer fortschrittlichen Gesetzgebung auf der einen, eine sehr begrenzte schwule Szene auf der anderen Seite. Anfang der 90er Jahre gab es, trotz des großen Einflusses der religiösen Parteien, große Schritte in Richtung einer vollen Integration von Schwulen und Lesben in die Gesellschaft. Die SPPR (Gesellschaft zum Schutz der persönlichen Rechte), die einzige schwullesbische Organisation des Landes, konnte große Erfolge erringen: 1988 die Entkriminalisierung des Analverkehrs, 1991 einen Antidiskriminierungszusatz im Arbeitsrecht, 1993 schließlich die Einrichtung eines Knesset-Unterausschusses für homosexuelle Rechte und Antidiskrimierungsrichtlinien in der Armee. 1994 schließlich entschied ein Gericht, daß ein Arbeitgeber den Lover eines schwulen Mitarbeiters genauso behandeln muß, wie den/die Lebensgefährten/in eines Hetero-Mitarbeiters.

❋ L'état d'Israël propose un mélange peu commun: d'un côté une société tolérante et un système législatif progressiste, mais de l'autre côté un milieu gai très peu développé. D'énormes progrès ont été réalisés en ce qui concerne l'intégration des gais et des lesbiennes dans la société et ce, malgré l'influence encore énorme exercée par les partis religieux. Ces dernières années, la SPPG (Société pour la protection des droits individuels), la seule association gaie du pays a remporté de substantiels succès. En 1988, elle a réussi à faire décriminaliser la pénétration anale. En 1991, elle a fait passer une loi condamnant la discrimination des homosexuels (hommes et femmes) sur leur lieu de travail. En 1993, elle a réussi à mettre en place à la Knesset un groupe de travail qui planche sur les mesures à prendre pour supprimer la discrimination des homosexuels au sein de l'armée. En 1994, finalement, un tribunal a décidé qu'un employeur devait traiter l'amant d'un de ses employés de la même façon que les femmes ou conjointes de ses collègues hétérosexuels.

❋ La situación de los homosexuales israelitas está marcada por una combinación de circunstancias especiales. Por un lado una sociedad tolerante con una legislación progresiva, por otro lado un ambiente gay muy limitado. A pesar de la fuerte influencia de los partidos religiosos, durante los últimos años se consiguieron grandes avances hacía una integración de gays y lesbianas en la sociedad júdia. La S.P.P.R. (Sociedad para la Protección de los Derechos Personales), la única organización gay y lesbiana del país, ha alcanzado grandes exitos; en 1988 la despenalización del coito anal; en 1991 una claúsula de antidiscriminación en la legislación laboral; en 1993 la formación de una comisión para derechos homosexuales en el parlamento y directivas para el ejercito. En 1994 decidió un tribunal, que un empresario está obligado a tratar el amante de un empleado gay del mismo modo que la pareja de un empleado heterosexual.

❋ La situazione dei gay israeliani è marcata da una particolare combinazione di determinanti: una società molto tollerante con una progredita legislazione da una parte, un ambiente gay molto limitato dall'altra. Malgrado la considerevole influenza dei partiti religiosi, negli ultimi anni sono stati fatti grandi passi verso una piena integrazione dei gay e delle lesbiche nella società. La SPPR (società per la protezione dei diritti della persona), l'unica organizzazione omosessuale del paese, ha raggiunto diverse mete: nel 1988 la legalizzazione dei rapporti anali, nel 1991 un paragrafo antidiscriminante nella legislazione del lavoro, infine, nel 1993 un sottocomitato del Knesset per i diritti degli omosessuali e l'antidiscriminazione nell'esercito. Nel 1994 infine un tribunale ha deciso che un datore di lavoro deve trattare il compagno di un suo dipendente gay come il compagno/a di un dipendente eterosessuale.

Beer Sheva ▶ Jerusalem Israel

NATIONAL GAY INFO
■ **Association for Lesbians, Gay Men and Bisexualsj in Israel (The AGUDA)**
PO Box 376 04 ✉ 61375 Tel Aviv ☏ (0)3-629 36 81
🖷 (0)3-525 23 41 💻 sppr@netvision.net.il
💻 www.geocities.com/WestHollywood/hights/8917
National organization of Israel. ⇨ *Tel Aviv and Haifa for their community centers.*
■ **Israel Update**
c/o The Agudah, PO Box 376 04, Tel Aviv 61375
English bulletin of the Israeli group. Published every six months.

NATIONAL GROUPS
■ **Israel AIDS Task Force** Sun-Thu 9-17 h
3 Simra Plonit Street, PO Box 56110 ✉ 61561 Tel-Aviv-Yafo
(between Dizengoff center and Alenby, Bus 25/24/4/5/61/62)
☏ (03) 566 16 39 🖷 (03) 560 23 16
Anonymous testing centre Mon-Wed 17.30-20, Fri 10-13 h

NATIONAL PUBLICATIONS
■ **Hazman Havarod**
PO Box 14595 ✉ 61144 Tel Aviv
☏ (03) 516 7232 💻 zmag@hotmail.com
💻 zmanvarod.co.il
Israels only gay magazine. Monthly with 35 pages. Serious, political and free at gay venues.

TOURIST INFO
The Gaza strip and the West bank cities of Bethlehem, Jenin, Jericho, Kalkiliya, Nablus Ramallah, Tulkarem and partly Hebron are under palestine self-government.
Jerusalem = Yerushalayim
Hefa = Haifa

Beer Sheva ☏ 07

CRUISING
-Gan Ha'atsma'oot/Independence Park (north of Museum of the Negev on Derech Ha'atsma'oot; early evenings)

Eilat ☏ 07

BARS
■ **Nisha** (B glm) 23-? h
Nepton Hotel

CAFES
■ **Cafe Neto** (B F g) 21-24 h
(the mole in front of the sea)

SWIMMING
-Red Rock Hotel (g)

CRUISING
-Ofira Park (near Tedi's Bar)

Haifa ☏ 04

GAY INFO
■ **Haifa Community Center (HCC)**
6 Nordau Street ☏ 867 26 65
Ask for their different activities.

CAFES
■ **Afuch Al Afuh** (B g) 12-? h
2 Hilel ☏ 862 76 93
■ **Cafe Beneinu** (B g) 21.30-1 h, Fri 21.30-6 h
94 Hilel
■ **Cafe Katan** (B F g) Sun-Thu 10-2 h, Fri -18 h
22 Massada *(Hadar)* ☏ 846 04 99
■ **Cafe Neto** (B g) 19:30-2 h
11 Moria (Merkaz Hakarmel) ☏ 836 04 83

DANCECLUBS
■ **Natanzon** (B D GLM) Sat 22.30-? h
10 Natanzon Str. *(Near Paris Square)*
■ **Opera** (B D G) Thu 23-? h
15 Hasnamal

RESTAURANTS
■ **Hotentot** (g F) 9.30-3 h
8 Simatat Amos *(Hadar)*

SWIMMING
-Atlit (G) (summer only, 1 km north of Atlit)

CRUISING
-Gan Ha-Zicaron/Memorial Park (across the street from City Hall, evenings)

Jerusalem ☏ 02

GAY INFO
■ **Jerusalem Open House. The / Ha'Bayit Ha'Patu'ach** Sun Thu 16-23, Tue 10-15, Fri 10-14 h
Ben Yehuda St. 7, PO Box 33107 ✉ 91037 *(3rd floor)* ☏ 625 31 91
☏ 537 39 06 (Infoline) 💻 gayj@hotmail.com
💻 www.poboxes.com/gayj
Jerusalem's intimate and international Gay & Lesbian Centre. Meeting place for groups (transgender, international group (in English), bisexuels, parents, politics, Gay Pride initiatives). Evenings: dance, readings, library, coffee corner.

CAFES
■ **Café del Arte** (B f glm)
28 Hillel St. ☏ 625 02 43
■ **Rif Raf** (B F glm)
Alley between Hilley and Shamai *(beside Mc Donald's)*

DANCECLUBS
■ **Ha'Asiron Ha'Acher / The other 10% organisation** (B D GLM)
Irregular parties. Contact the Jerusalem Open House for infos.
■ **Q Dance** (B D glm) Daily open
1 Yoel Salomon
■ **Shonka** (AC B CC F glm) 12-? h
Ha'Soreg Street 1 *(beside Generali Building)* ☏ 625 70 33
Dance, Bar & Restaurant on 3 floors. Thu evening glm party.

RESTAURANTS
■ **Timol Shilshom** (AC B BF CC F glm) 8-2 h
5 Yoel Salomon St. *(entrance through back alley at Salomon St. 11)*
☏ 623 27 58
Gay owned. Eurpean cuisine (fish & vegetarian). Book shop and a good starting place in the holy city.

Israel Jerusalem ▸ Tel-Aviv-Yafo

GUEST HOUSES
■ **Diana's House** (AC BF H GLM WH)
10 Hulda Ha-Neviah Street, Musrara ✉ 91040
☏ 628 31 31
🖷 628 44 11 📧 dr-adiv@zahav.net.il
Gay B&B 10 min walk to the old city and the main tourist & gay attractions with a spectacular view of Mt. of Olives and Dome on the Rock. Special discount for long stay and reservations by e-mail.

CRUISING
-Gan HaAtzmaut/Independence Park (r) 0-24 h (near Plaza Hotel, popular especially after dusk. Where secular jews or arabs meet orthodox jews and/or tourists. A rare melting point in this city)
-King David Park (behind the hotel, active mainly at dusk)
-Central bus station (pedestrian tunnel -18 h)

Nahariyya ☏ 04
CRUISING
-Park behind the beach (beach patrols are only for security)

Natanya ☏ 09
SWIMMING
-Gaash Beach (NU) (right under the Wingate Institue, summer only)
CRUISING
-Gan Shlomo/King Solomon's Park (behind the movie theater at the sea's edge at the end of Herzl Street; day and night)

Tel-Aviv-Yafo ☏ 03
GAY INFO
■ **Tel Aviv Community Center (TACC)**
28 Nachmani Street ☏ 629 36 81 🖷 525 23 41
📧 sppr@netvision.net.il
Ask for their different activities.

BARS
■ **DIVA** (B F glm, S TV) 12-3 h
The waiters are in drag
■ **He-She** (B f GLM OS TV YG) Mon-Sat 20-? h
8 Hashomer Street *(2nd floor, Nahlat Binyamin area)* ☏ 510 09 14
■ **Minerva Bar Gallery** (A AC B CC F gLm MA OS S) Mon-Sun 21 h-last guest
98 Allenby Street *(Corner of Beit-Hashoeva Alley 20)*
☏ 566 60 51
Also a little book store with magazines, cards and gifts. Art gallery with changing exhibition with full European style bar.
■ **OUT** (AC B CC G MA) 22-? h
45 Nahalat Binyamin Street ☏ 560 23 91
Two floors with 2 bars exclusively designed. Israel's gay scene on a new level.

CAFES
■ **Bazel Cafe** (B CC F g) 7-1 h
42 Bazel Street ☏ 546 18 75
■ **Cafe Bialik** (B F g OS)
1 Bialik Street
Very fashionable.

The only luxurious, Gay Sauna in Israel of international standard.

Jacuzzi
Steam Room
Dry Sauna
Gay movies
Dark-Room
S/M Room
Private Rooms
Strip-Shows on Stage
Pleasure Massage
Bar & Snacks

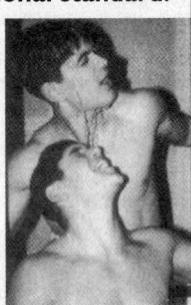

SAUNA-BAR PARADISE

Thursday: Towels Off!
Monday: transsexual masseur at your disposal

Open
Weekdays:
12:00 Noon To 6 am
Weekends:
Friday 19:00
to Sunday 6 am
nonstop

75 Allenby St.,
Tel-Aviv.
Tel: 03-6202188

■ **Café Nordau** (B F glm) Mon-Sun 0-24 h
145 Ben Yehuda Street/Arlozerov Street ☏ 524 01 34
Israeli & International food. Pleasant atmosphere. Bar upstairs.
■ **Café Theo** (AC B BF CC F GLM MA OS S) 8 h-till last guest
1 Lilenbloom Street, Neve Zedek (Bus 4/61/62/18) ☏ 517 63 64
Café & Bookshop
■ **Pet Cafe** (B F glm H) 9-2 h
34 Pinsker ☏ 546 18 75
■ **Sandy Bar-Diner** (b BF f glm) 7-4 h
56 Allenby

DANCECLUBS
■ **Exit Parties** (B D DR GLM MA s STV WE) Thu 24-5h
☏ 516 01 86
Look for information and invitation in Bars Saunas and Sex Shops. they change the location from time to time.
■ **FFF Friendly Fredoom** (! B D DR G MA) Fri 24-8 h
58 Allenby Street
In summer location will change - info in Sexy Shop.

Tel-Aviv-Yafo ▸ Ziqim **Israel**

SAUNA CITY

The Biggest Gay Sauna In The Middle East

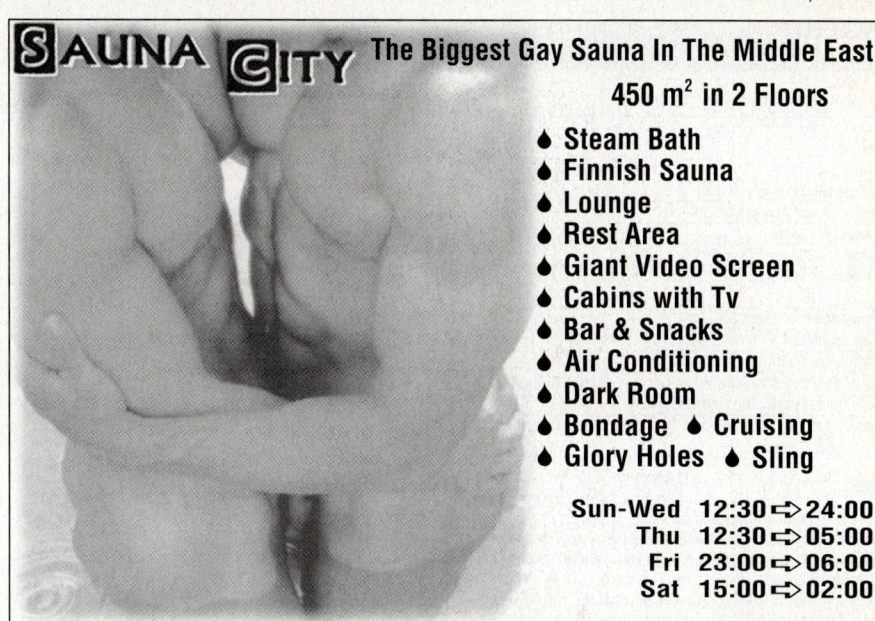

450 m^2 in 2 Floors

- Steam Bath
- Finnish Sauna
- Lounge
- Rest Area
- Giant Video Screen
- Cabins with Tv
- Bar & Snacks
- Air Conditioning
- Dark Room
- Bondage ◆ Cruising
- Glory Holes ◆ Sling

Sun-Wed 12:30 ⇨ 24:00
Thu 12:30 ⇨ 05:00
Fri 23:00 ⇨ 06:00
Sat 15:00 ⇨ 02:00

SAUNA CITY - 113 HaHashmonaim st. Tel Aviv. 972-3-6241148

■ **Mix Morning Parties** (B D glm) Sat 6-13 h
Ask for invitations at Sexy Shop.
■ **Scene** (B D G) Mon 22-? h
56 Allenby Street
■ **Women Parties** (D B L) Thu 10-?
☏ 50 635 604 (Ilana)
Weekly lesbian Parties. Call for more information

SHOWS
■ **Carrousel** (AC B CC f glm MA STV) Mon-Sat 22-3 h, closed Sun
36 Pinsker Street (near Dizengoff Centre) ☏ 620 22 41

SEX SHOPS/BLUE MOVIES
■ **Sexy Shop** (CC DR G VS) Sun-Thu 11-24, Fri 11-16, Sat 18-24 h
150 Dizengoff Street/Gordon Street ☏ 523 17 96
Providing good information for gay tourists. Wide range of magazines, videos, cabins and toys.

SAUNAS/BATHS
■ **City Sauna** (! B DR F G SA SB VS) 12.30-24 h, Thu -5 h, Fri 23-6 h, Sat 15-24 h
113 Hahashmonaim Street ✉ 62965 ☏ 624 11 48
One of the biggest gay saunas in the Middle East on two floors. Oriental style, clean, popular especially in the afternoons & at the WE.
■ **Paradise** (AC B CC d DR f G MA msg p s SA SB VS SDR f) 12-6, Fri 19-Sun 6 h
75 Allenby Street ✉ 61000 (bus 4) ☏ 6202 188
Intimate atmosphere sauna popular among young people.

TRAVEL AND TRANSPORT
■ **Gil Travel** (CC) Sun-Thu 8-18 h, Fri 8-14 h
29 Hamered ☏ 514 00 40 ✉ Russavi@isdn.Net.il

HOTELS
■ **Olympia Hotel** (AC B CC H F msg Pl OS WO)
164 Hayaakon St. ✉ 63415 ☏ 524 21 84 📠 524 72 78
✉ olympia@infolink.net.il

SWIMMING
-Hilton Beach (g) (right under the Independence Park, summer)

CRUISING
-Independence Park (MA r)(The most popular meeting place in Israel. Full especially after dusk)
-Gan Meir (King George Street, south of the Dizingoff Centre, after dark)
-Gan HaRakevet (pedestrian tunnel connecting bus and train stations and in the parks around, 0-24 h)
-Gan HaChashmal (R) (near the old Central Bus Station, parallel to Barzilay, Levontine and HaChashmal Streets, after dark)
-New Center Bus Station (3rd & 6th floor)
-WC Rothschild/Shenkin Streets
-WC Ben Gurion/Shlomo HaMelech Streets

Ziqim ☏ 07

SWIMMING
-Ziqim Beach (By car go from Ashqelon 7 km southward to Ziqim, turn westward to the sea. Or take the bus from Ashqelon to the last stop and walk towards the sea. On the beach turn to the right, to the north for 500m)

Italy

Name: Italia • Italien • Italie
Location: Southern Europe
Initials: I
Time: GMT +1
International Country Code: ☏ 39
International Access Code: ☏ 00
Language: Italian
Area: 301,336 km² / 116,303 sq mi.
Currency: Italian Lira (Lit) = 100 Centesimi. 1 EURO = 1936,27 Lit
Population: 57,589,000
Capital: Roma
Religions: 91% Roman Catholic
Climate: Predominantly Mediterranean climate. Alpine climate in the far north, the south is hot and dry.
Important gay cities: Milano, Torino, Firenze, Roma, Padova, Viareggio, Taormina

※ The Vatican is in Italy, and this continues to have a negative influence on gay life in Italy. The Catholic Church, along with the right-wing opposition party tried preventing the first international Gay World Pride 2000 in Rome. This resulted in a massive immobilisation and solidarity of gays and lesbians, resulting in a new feeling of self-confidence. The Gay World Pride was a big success, with over 300.000 participants. Whether the main CSD parade will take place in Milan is not certain, but sure is that the "International Pride" will take place in Rome this year from the 1st to 8th July (parade on the 7th).

Even in the agriculturally dominated south there seems to have been some influence: an example being the new bath houses/saunas in Pescara and Catania. The Christian parties continue however with their opposition to questions concerning equal rights. Should the right-wing opposition win the elections which are to be held in spring, homosexuals in Italy won't have much to laugh about.

Since 1889 the laws against homosexuality were abolished. The age of consent is set at 14 for all. For young men between the ages of 14 and 18 care should be taken as an accusation of "corruption" can arise when it turns out to be the "first time". Prostitution is legal from the age of 18.

The majority of Italians have their annual holiday in August. Many places are therefore closed until the beginning of September. In the gay-friendly seaside resorts (e.g. Viareggio, Taormina) the discos and bars are logically all open. In many establishments a "Club Pass" is necessary, which can normally be purchased on the spot. The most popular cards are the "Tessera" from Arci Gay.

★ Der Vatikan sitzt in Italien, und diese Tatsache wirkt sich weiterhin negativ auf schwules Leben aus. So versuchte die katholische Kirche zusammen mit der rechten Opposition, den ersten internationalen Gay World Pride 2000 in Rom zu verhindern, was jedoch im Gegenteil zu einer ungeheuren Mobilisierung und Solidarisierung führte und die Lesben und Schwulen zu neuem Selbstbewußtsein verhalf. Der Gay World Pride war mit über 300.000 Teilnehmern ein großer Erfolg und wird nachhaltig in die italienische Gesellschaft wirken. Ob der diesjährige zentrale CSD in Mailand sein wird, ist noch ungewiß, doch findet in Rom in jedem Fall erneut ein "International Pride" vom 1.-8. Juli (mit Parade am 7. Juli) statt.

Auch im agrarisch geprägten und traditionelleren Süden scheint sich etwas zu bewegen, wie z.B. neue Saunen in Pescara und Catania bezeugen. Rechtliche Gleichstellungsmaßnahmen scheitern dennoch weiter am Widerstand der christlichen Parteien. Sollte allerdings die rechte Opposition die Wahlen in diesem Frühjahr gewinnen, haben die italienischen Homosexuellen wenig Erfreuliches zu erwarten, zumal mit offen homophoben Parolen Politik betrieben wird.

Seit 1889 gibt es keine Gesetze mehr gegen Homosexualität. Das Schutzalter liegt einheitlich bei 14 Jahren. Bei Männern zwischen 14 und 18 sollte man vorsichtig sein, da bei ihnen der Vorwurf der "Korrumpierung" zutreffen kann, falls es für jene das "erste Mal" war. Prostitution ist ab 18 Jahren legal.

Die Mehrheit der Italiener hat vor allem im August Ferien. Viele Einrichtungen sind bis Anfang September geschlossen. In den für Schwule interessanten Badeorten (z.B. Viareggio, Taormina) sind die Diskotheken und Bars jedoch gerade dann geöffnet. In vielen Einrichtungen ist ein "Clubausweis" erforderlich, der meistens direkt vor Ort ausgestellt wird. Am gebräuchlichsten ist die "Tessera" des Arci Gay.

※ La vie gaie des Italiens est encore fortement influencée par le Vatican, qui a son siège dans le pays. L'Eglise catholique a tenté avec l'appui des partis d'opposition de droite d'interdire la tenue de la première "Gay World Pride 2000" à Rome mais elle a rencontré une immense mobilisation et solidarité qui a donné un nouveau souffle au mouvement gai. La "Gay World Pride, à laquelle ont participé plus de 300'000 personnes, a été un énorme succès et a certainement créé des répercussions durables sur la société italienne. Il n'est pas encore certain qu'une Gay Pride nationale aura lieu en 2001 à Milan, mais une Gay Pride internationale est à nouveau prévue à Rome du 1er au 8 juillet (avec une parade le 7 juillet).

Même dans le sud agraire plus conservateur les choses commencent à bouger, comme le démontre par exemple l'ouverture de saunas à Pescara et à Catania. L'égalité des droits se bute cependant toujours à l'opposition des partis chrétiens. Si l'opposition de droite qui mène une campagne ouvertement homophobe gagne

Italy

les élections du printemps 2001, les perspectives d'avenir des gais italiens se noirciront rapidement.
Il n'existe en Italie plus de loi contre les homosexuels depuis 1889. La majorité sexuelle est fixée à 14 ans. Il faut cependant se méfier des rapports avec des hommes de moins de 18 ans car on peut être accusé de " corruption ", surtout s'il s'agit d'une première expérience sexuelle. La prostitution est légale à partir de 18 ans.
La majeure partie des Italiens partent en vacances au mois d'août. Beaucoup d'établissements ferment donc jusqu'à début septembre, à l'exception des bars et discothèques des villes balnéaires parfois très intéressantes pour les gais (comme Viareggio ou Taormina).
Beaucoup d'établissements exigent à leur entrée une carte (la plus courante est celle de l'association Arcigay) mais la plus part d'entre eux vous en fourniront une directement sur place.

El Vaticano está en Italia y este hecho sigue teniendo efectos negativos sobre la vida gay. Así, por ejemplo, la Iglesia Católica intentó, junto con la oposición de derechas, impedir el primer Gay World Pride (Fiesta Intenacional del Orgullo Gay) en Roma. Sin embargo, esto llevó a una increíble movilización, muchos se solidarizaron con la causa y los gays y lesbianas ganaron conciencia de sí mismos. Con más de 300.000 participantes, el Gay World Pride fue un gran éxito y tendrá un efecto duradero en la sociedad italiana. Todavía no está seguro si el Día del Orgullo Gay central de este año se celebrará en Milán o no, pero en todo caso, habrá otra Fiesta Internacional del Orgullo Gay en Roma del 1 al 8 de julio de este año (con desfile el día 7 de julio).
También en el sur de Italia, marcadamente agrario y más tradicional que el resto del país, parece que algo está cambiando, como lo demuestran, por ejemplo, las nuevas saunas en Pescara y Catania. Las medidas de equiparación legal de los homosexuales fracasan por causa de la resistencia de los partidos cristianos. En caso de que en las elecciones en primavera gane la oposición de derechas, los homosexuales italianos no pueden esperar nada bueno, ya que se está haciendo política con consignas abiertamente homófobas.
Desde 1889 no hay leyes contra la homosexualidad. La edad de consentimiento es de 14 años para todos. Sin embargo, hay que tener cierto cuidado con hombres entre los 14 y los 18 años, puesto que puede darse el cargo de "corrupción" en caso de que haya sido la "primera vez" para ellos. La prostitución es legal a partir de los 18 años.
La mayoría de los italianos tiene vacaciones en agosto. Muchas entidades y locales están cerrados hasta principios de septiembre. Las discotecas y los bares en los lugares costeros interesantes para los gays (por ejemplo Viareggio,, Taormina) están abiertos precisamente en esta época. En muchos sitios hace falta un carnet o una tarjeta de miembro que se expide en los mismos locales. La más usual es la tessera (tarjeta) de Arci Gay.

La sede del Vaticano si trova in Italia, cosa che influisce ancora negativamente sulla vita gay. La chiesa cattolica naturalmente tentò di impedire insieme all'opposizione di destra il primo 'Gay World Pride 2000' a Roma che comunque ha trovato un'immensa mobilitazione e solidarizzazione creando così una nuova dimensione di orgoglio gay. Il Gay World Pride a cui hanno partecipato più di 300.000 persone, è stato un grande successo, che ha creato sicuramente delle ripercussioni durevoli sulla società italiana. Ancora non è certo se il Gay Pride nazionale del 2001 sarà a Milano, ma in ogni caso avrà luogo un altro 'International Pride' a Roma (1-8 luglio 2001 con la parata il 7 luglio).
Perfino nel Mezzogiorno, più tradizionalista, pare che cambi la situazione per i gay come p.e. testimoniano le nuove saune di Pescara e di Catania. D'altra parte non vengono presi provvedimenti sulla parità di diritti a causa dell'opposizione dei partiti cristiani. Se il centro-destra vincesse le elezioni di questa primavera, non sarebbe sicuramente un fatto positivo per i gay tenendo conto della campagna omofoba da parte di alcuni rappresentanti del Polo della Libertà.
Dal 1889 non esistono leggi contro l'omosessualità; l'età del consenso è in generale di 14 anni, anche se si può essere accusati di aver "corrotto" un ragazzo tra i 14 e i 18 anni nel caso che quest'ultimo non avesse mai avuto rapporti sessuali prima d'allora. La prostituzione dei maggiorenni è legale.
La maggior parte degli italiani vanno in ferie ad agosto. Molti locali sono chiusi fino a inizio settembre. Nei luoghi turistici interessanti per i gay (p.e. Viareggio, Taormina) le discoteche e i bar sono aperti. In molti locali è richiesta una tessera che di solito viene emessa sul luogo. La più usuale tra le tessere è quella dell'Arci Gay.

NATIONAL GAY INFO

■ **ANLAIDS- Associazione Nazionale per la Lotta Contro l'Aids**
Mon-Fri 9-18 h
Via Barberini 3 ✉ 00187 Roma ☎ 06 482 09 99 📠 06 482 10 77
📧 anlaids@anlaids.it 🖥 www.anlaids.it
National coordination of ANLAIDS. Gives information about Aids Organisations in Italy.

■ **Archivio Massimo Consoli**
Via Dario Bellezza 1 ✉ 00040 Frattocchie (Roma)
☎ 06 93 54 75 67 📠 06 93 54 74 83
Available only by appointment to professionals.

■ **Arci Gayline** 0-24 h
✉ 40123 Bologna ☎ 166 117 117
National infoline. Information about gay life in Italy (bars, organizations, etc).

■ **Arcigay Nazionale** Mon-Fri 15-19 h
Piazza di Porta Saragozza 2 ✉ 40123 Bologna ☎ 051 644 70 54
📠 051 644 67 22 📧 arcigl@iperbole.bologna.it
🖥 www.gay.it/arcigay
Head office of Arcigay, the only national organization of Italy with 29 branches nationwide: Information, gay archive, videos, meetings/Arcigay centro nazionale; informazioni, documentazione, convegni, manifestazioni.

■ **Arcitrans (Onlus)** (TV) Infoline Wed 20-23 h
Milano ☎ 02 89 40 17 49 ☎ 0335 560 73 10 (Emergency)
📧 arcitrans@iol.it
National association of transsexuals, transgender and drags.

■ **Coordinamento Omosessuali DS (Democratici di Sinistra)**
c/o Federazione Romana DS, Via del Circo Massimo 7
✉ 00153 Roma ☎ 06 57 30 25 71 ☎ 06 57 30 25 72
📠 06 57 30 25 74

■ **Gay.it** Mon-Fri 9-19 h
Largo Ciro Menotti 19/2 ✉ 50127 Pisa ☎ 050 31 55 51
📠 050 31 55 530 🖥 www.gay.it
Up-to-date information for gay tourists.

■ **Gruppo Di Lavoro Sull'Omosessualitá (G.L.O.) Nel Partito Di Rifondazione Comunista (PRC)**
c/o PRC, Via Tarabochia 3 ✉ 34121 Trieste ☎ 040 63 40 00
☎ 040 63 91 09 📠 040 63 91 03

SPARTACUS 2001/2002 | **599**

Italy

E VI@GGI NEL TUO MONDO
OUT TRAVEL

gay.it

- tourist incoming to Italy
- hotel reservations in any italian town
- farm holidays
- guided tours of the most important italian towns
- cruises

- settimane gay
- prenotazione alberghi gay o gay-friendly
- pacchetti personalizzabili nelle principali località gay e non
- prenotazioni crociere gay ai Caraibi sulle migliori navi
- agriturismo
- prenotazioni voli
- visite guidate delle più importanti città

Web: www.outtravel.it
www.gay.it/outtravel
E-mail: outtravel@gay.it
Tel. nazionale:
al costo di una
840-0583538
telefonata urbana

International phone:
+39.050.97.111.65
Fax: +39.050.31.555.30
Main bureau:
Largo Ciro Menotti, 19/2
56127 Pisa - Italy

Pride

Italy

N°15 SETTEMBRE 2000

PrideGuide Rivista mensile - Autorizzazione del Tribunale di Milano n. 351 del 7-5-1999 - Direttore responsabile Giovanni Dall'Orto Distribuzione gratuita (salvo accordi con edicole).

RIVISTA DI ATTUALITÀ E DI ORGOGLIO GAY

Attualità
Mister Gay Versilia 2000

Personaggi
Piccolo dossier Busi

Interviste
Platinette: sinceramente falsa

Nell'inserto
Guida al sesso sicuro

Inchiesta
Prostituzione maschile parte 2

SPARTACUS 2001/2002 | 601

Italy

www.upcity.it
the best of gay city map

Maps to the most important italian cities are update each month. Maps will be located in all clubs and pubs. Entertainment, clubs parties and events going on in town!

Le mappe delle città più importanti d'Italia con guida aggiornate mensilmente. Le trovate in tutti i locali gay!

For information and publicizing:
Echo communication Via S. Nicolao 10 – 20123 Milano
Tel. 0039 02 89015940-1 Fax 0039 02 89013990

■ **LILA - Lega Italiana Lotta contro l'Aids**
☎ 02 51 00 23
■ **Ministero Della Sanita-Centro Operativo AIDS**
☎ 167 86 10 61 (Free call)
■ **Notizie Omosessuali Italiane (N.O.I.)**
✉ noignet@tin.it 🖥 www.gay.it/noi/
Internet magazine.
■ **Sex Guide International** Mon-Fri 10-20 h
Via Ferentano 48 ✉ 00178 Roma ☎ 06 712 89 564
📠 06 712 79 514 ✉ info@sexy-guide.com
🖥 www.sexy-guide.com

NATIONAL PUBLICATIONS

■ **Babilonia** Mon-Fri 9-18 h
Via Astura 8 ✉ 20141 Milano ☎ 02 569 64 68 📠 02 55 21 34 19
✉ babilonia@iol.it 🖥 www.babilonia.net
National gay magazine of Italy. Featuring news, reports, lifestyle, arts, classifieds and a gay guide. Lit 10.000 at news stands.
■ **Contatti**
Via Aosta 37 ✉ 10015 Ivrea ☎ 0125 490 24 📠 0125 490 24
✉ contatti@contatti.it 🖥 www.contatti.it
Gay, lesbian and straight monthly printed in Italy and distributed in the news-stands all over Italy. Monthly newspaper with hundreds of classifieds and personal ads. Written in Italian. Published by A.C.R.I.
■ **Guide Magazine**
Via Carlo Imbonati 5 ✉ 20159 Milano ☎ 02 66 86 173
📠 02 66 86 173 ✉ guidemagazine@guidemagazine.it
🖥 www.guidemagazine.it
Monthly gay magazine printed in Italy and distributed in the main cities in Europe. Free magazine available in clubs, bars, saunas, restaurants, gay shops. Written in Italian. Published by A.C.R.I.-Edizioni Cassione

■ **Marco**
c/o Edizione Moderne, PO Box 171 82 ✉ 20170 Milano
☎ 02 29 51 74 90
Personal ads and Gay Guide section.
■ **Maschio**
PO Box 171 60 ✉ 20170 Milano ☎ 02 29 51 74 90
Erotic publications, dedicated to the male nude. Single copy Lit 10.000.
■ **Pride**
Via San Nicolao 10 ✉ 20123 Milano ☎ 02 89 09 76 49
✉ 02 789 01 39 90 ✉ direttore.pride@libero.it
Free gay monthly in Italian available for free in all gay venues. Featuring a gay guide of Italy "Pride & Guide". About 80 pages in colors.

NATIONAL PUBLISHERS

■ **Echo Communication** Mon-Fri 9-12.30, 14-19 h, closed in Aug
Via San Nicolao 10 ✉ 20123 Milano ☎ 02 89 01 59 40
☎ 02 89 01 59 41 📠 02 89 01 39 90 ✉ info@echoteam.it
🖥 www.echoteam.it
Publisher of the gay monthly "Up.City".
■ **Edizioni Gruppo Abele (E.G.A.)**
Via Giolitti 21 ✉ 10123 Torino ☎ 011 839 54 44
Books on gay topics. Publisher of Italian gay bibliography.
■ **Omo Edizioni** Mon-Fri 10-20 h
Via Ferentano 48 ✉ 00178 Roma ☎ 06 712 89 564
📠 06 712 79 514
✉ info@sexy-guide.com
🖥 www.sexy-guide.com
■ **RCT - Rainbow Channel Television** (GLM)
☎ 081 87 38 207 🖥 www.rainbowchanneltelevision.com
Gay Sat-TV: Films, documentaries and hard movies every day in all Europe.

UNCONVENTIONAL BEAUTIES
male escorts
http://go.to/ub.com
email: ubag@mail.com
ph: 0347 5510580 (+39.347.5510580)

Italy

DEPURATIVO ANTARTICO

WITH DURVILLEA ANTARTICA

LA DECOTTOPIA DAL 1911 ANTICA BALESTRA & MECH ERBORISTERIA

Durvillea Antartica Algae, Mint, Black Radish, Liquorice, Artichoke, Hosetail, Burdock, Dandelion, Rhubarb, Gentian, Lemon Balm, Chinaroot, Juniper, Spear Grass, Eder, Fucus, Aniseeded, Parsley, Bearberry, Horehound.

NON ALCOHOLIC • SUGAR FREE • NO PRESERVATIVES

The purifying virtues of algae from the ice fields of the Antarctic

Twenty herbs in synergy against the damages of incorrect nourishment. Alginic acid is present among the components (in fact, 48% of *Durvillea Antarctica* is made up of alginic acid): it absorbs poisons such as lead, cadmium and mercury contained in the free radicals that damage the molecules of the cellular membranes. *Purifying and disintoxicating action.* The action of alginic acid is seen in the absorption and elimination of these poisons. *Directions:* one or two measures in a glass of water before breakfast and after lunch and dinner.

Available in 500 and 250 ml bottles and practical single-dose phials at the chemist's and the herbalist's shop

QUALITY BALESTRA&MECH

For further information regarding sales points in your area:
Balestra&Mech via Campistorti 103, 36045 Lonigo (VI) Italy, tel +39 0444 437772 fax +39 0444 430280

www.balestramech.com

SPARTACUS 2001/2002 | 603

Italy — Abano Terme - Padova ▶ Alba - Cuneo

SELENE Viaggi e Turismo
Via Gregorio VII, 96 – 00165 Roma. ITALY
Tel : 0039-06-638 0746 / 635 783 – Fax : 0039-06-633 971
E-mail : seleneviaggi@mclink.it

NATIONAL COMPANIES

■ **Frisco**
Via F. Veracini 15 ✉ 50144 Firenze ☎ 055 35 73 51
🖷 055 35 73 51
Richiedere cataloghi/Ask for catalogue.

■ **Mec Mail Order Italy**
PO Box 67, Frazioen Lunata
✉ 55010 Capannori
☎ 0583 30 32 61
Underwear and fashion bathing-suits.

NATIONAL GROUPS

■ **CIAO - Coordinamento Italiano Atleti Omosessuali**
📧 ciao_italia@hotmail.com
🖥 www.geocities.com/ciaoitalia2001
National gay sport association.

■ **Forum Aids Italia** Tue 21-23 h, Sat 17-20 h
☎ 011 436 50 00 🖷 011 436 86 38
📧 infogay@arpnet.it
National secretariat. Publication: "Forum Aids Italia".

COUNTRY CRUISING

-A1 (E35) Milano ⇆ Roma
[P] Chiaravalle (km 80)
[P] Fontanellato (km 96,5)
[P] Crostolo (km 135)
[P] Castelfranco (km 177)
[P] Firenze Nord (facilities) (km 280)
[P] Scandicci much action, northbound only
-A11 Firenze ⇆ Mare
[P] Altopascio (AYOR, police controls)
service area Versillia nord, direction Firenze
-A31 Padova ⇆ Valdastico
[P] at the exit Thiene
-A4 (E66) Milano ⇀ Torino
[P] at Canale Langosco (1 km west of River Ticino/all'ovest del Fiume Ticino)
-A5 (E 25) Torino ⇀ Aosta
[P] Pietra Grossa (between/fra "Scarmagno" & "S. Giusto")
-A7 Milano ⇆ Genova
[P] Dorno (km 33)
[P] Pavia (km 17) southbound only
[P] Valle Scrivia (km 83)

Abano Terme - Padova ✉ 35031

SWIMMING
-Piscine Termali (-23h)

CRUISING
-Gardens in front of Caffe delle Terme/Giardini di fronte al Caffe delle Terme (Spring and summer/Primavera e estate)

Airole - Imperia ✉ 18030

RESTAURANTS
■ **Nido. Il** (B F g) 18-20 h
Via Roma 1 ✉ 18030 ☎ 0184 20 00 92
Gays are welcome.

SWIMMING
-Fiume Roya Beach (NU) (100 m from Roman bridge/dal ponte romano)

CRUISING
-Via Madonna (only during the summer/solo estate)

Alassio - Savona ✉ 17021

CRUISING
-Torre Saracena (open/aperta April-November)
-La Capannina (in front of the building, street at the lake/ davanti all'edificio, strada al lago)
-Harbour/porto

Alba - Cuneo ✉ 12051

CRUISING
-Railway station/Stazione FS (garden in front of the building/giardino davanti)
-Via Maestra
-Piazzale della S.A.U.B.
-Piazza Savona (near fountain/vicino alla fontana)
-Piazza Tanaro (NU) (on the bank of the river, spring-autumn/riva del fiume, primavera-autunno)

Italy

Nature Fashion

Beauty from Nature

LA RIVOLUZIONE CONTRO I KILI DI TROPPO

The revolution against extra weight

LA REVOLUCIÓN CONTRA LOS QUILOS EN EXCESO

DIE REVOLUTION GEGEN ÜBERGEWICHT

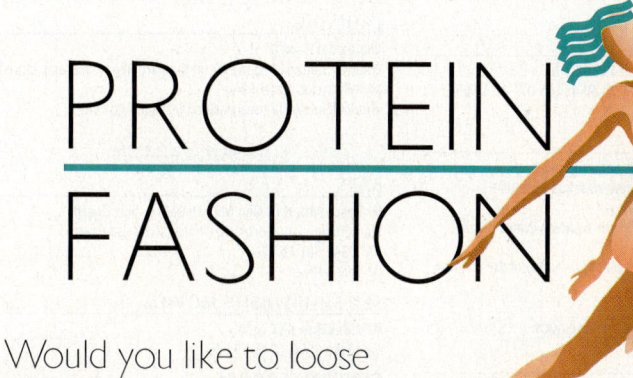

PROTEIN FASHION

Would you like to loose
2/3 kg in only **10 days**?
6/10 kg in only **12 days**?

CHIEDI INFORMAZIONI ALLA TUA ESTETISTA
Contact your beautician for information
PIDE INFORMACIONES A TU ESTETICISTA.
INFORMATIONEN HIERZU ERHÄLST DU BEI DEINER KOSMETIKERIN

For further information regarding sales points in your area and for a personalised diet : NATURE FASHION
Viale Stazione 8, 36054 Montebello (VI) Italy, tel +39 0444 448509, fax +39 0444 440307, www.naturefashion.it

Italy | Alessandria ▶ Aurisina - Trieste

Alessandria ✉ 15100
BARS
■ **Mistraal** (B CC G P S) 21.30-? h
Via Mazzini 40 ✉ 15100 ☎ 0131 68 129

CINEMAS
■ **Cristallo** (g) 20-24 h
Piazza Ceriana 17 ✉ 15100 *(near/vicino Zona Cristo)*
☎ 0131 34 12 72

CRUISING
-Railway station/stazione FS, (also in the gardens in front/anche nei giardini davanti)
-Lungo Tanaro Magenta (by car, at night/in auto, di sera)
-Circonvallazione (truckers/camionisti)

Ancona ✉ 60100
BARS
■ **No Tied Club** (G) Thu Sun 22-? h
Via della Brecciata 25 ✉ 60016 *(Marina di Montemarciano, between Ancona and Senigallia, direction Chiaravalle/tra Ancona e Senigallia direzione Chiaravalle)* ☎ 071 91 52 34

GENERAL GROUPS
■ **Arcigay Arcilesbica Ancona** Wed 19.30-23 h
Corso Mazzini 64 ✉ 60121 ☎ 071 20 30 45 📠 071 20 30 50
📧 Iaconi@arci.it

CRUISING
-Piazza Ciriaco (afternoon and night/pomeriggio e sera)
-Area Passetto (21-? h, panoramic view/zona panoramica)
-Railway station/Stazione FS
-Via XX Settembre, V. G. Marconi (TV) (near/vicino Banca d'Italia)
-Piazza Stamira (R TV)
-Via Panoramica (at the end of the street in direction of the forest/in fondo alla strada, direzione foresta)

Anzio - Roma ✉ 00042
CRUISING
-Riviera di Ponente (mixed, early hours, best in winter/misto, prime ore, meglio d'inverno)
-Piazzale del Porto (best in winter/meglio di inverno)
-Via Fanciulla d'Anzio

Aosta ✉ 11100
GENERAL GROUPS
■ **Arcigay Arcilesbica Aosta**
Via Martinet 4 ✉ 11100 ☎ 0360 48 35 37 📠 0165 32 034

CRUISING
-Railway station/stazione FS (in the gardens in front of the building/giardini antistanti)
-Mura Romane (also at the P on the right of the railway station/e posteggio a destra della stazione ferroviaria)
-Strada per l'autoporto valle d'Aosta (truckers, sometimes police patrols/camionisti, accertamenti Guardia di Finanza)
-Laghetti di Quart/Brissogne (you can see the lakes from the motorway, as you approach the exit (Autostrada A5 Torino-Aosta), near the camping site Du Lac, be careful/ all'uscita del Casello Autostrada A5 Torino-Aosta, si possono vedere dalla strada, vicino al camping Du Lac. Luogo appartato e discreto)

Aprica - Sondrio ✉ 23031
CRUISING
-Public swimming hall/Piscina comunale
-Pineta (behind the camping/dietro il campeggio)

Arezzo ✉ 52100
GUEST HOUSES
■ **Agriturismo Savorgnano** (BF glm H OS)
Loc. I Marzi 5, Savorgnano ✉ 52010 ☎ 0575 42 20 10
📠 0575 42 20 10 📧 info@agriturismosavorgnano.com
🌐 www.agriturismosavorgnano.com
18th century stonewalled country house.
■ **Priello Bed & Breakfast** (BF CC glm OS)
Localita Priello 244 ✉ 52033 ☎ 0575 79 12 18 📠 0575 79 21 18
🌐 www.ruby.he.net/~priello
Historic mountain-top farm house.

CRUISING
- P along Viale Mecenate opposite of the supermarket

Ascoli Piceno ✉ 63100
CRUISING
-Piazza del Popolo
-Railway station/stazione FS (in the gardens/nei giardini, close to Hotel Jolly/vicino Hotel Jolly)
-Rua dell'Industria (near/vicino Piazza S. Agostino)

Asti ✉ 14100
BARS
■ **Boschetto. Il** (B Glm MA) 15-2.30 h, Sun closed
Via Partigiani 34 ✉ 14100 *(highway exit Asti Ovest)*
☎ 0347 581 16 87
Internet service.

SEX SHOPS/BLUE MOVIES
■ **Videoclub XXX** (g VS)
Via Malta 6 ☎ 0141 30 506

GENERAL GROUPS
■ **Coordinamento Gay e Lesbico** (GLM) Fri 17-19 h
c/o Partito della Rifondazione Comunista, Via Toti 5 ✉ 14100
☎ 0141 34 970 ☎ 0349 72 23 867 (infoline)
📧 prcgayasti@hotmail.com

SWIMMING
-Lungo Tanaro (NU) (pass S. Fedele in direction of the bridge, behind the bridge there is a sign-post to the paths, which all end at the beach/oltre S. Fedele, direzione ponte; dietro questo è una freccia per i sentieri, che portano tutti alla spiaggia)

CRUISING
-Bus Station/Stazione Autobus (YG) (police checks)
-Via Artom (close to railway station and along the street, police checks/vicino stazione e lungo la strada, controlli polizia)
-Railway Station/Stazione FS (also in the gardens/anche nei giardini)
-Piazza d'Armi

Aurisina - Trieste ✉ 34011
SWIMMING
-Filtri Beach (NU) (near/vicino Bellariva Restaurant)

Avellino ▶ Bergamo | **Italy**

www.upcity.it
the best of gay city map

Maps to the most important italian cities are update each month. Maps will be located in all clubs and pubs. Entertainment, clubs parties and events going on in town!

Le mappe delle città più importanti d'Italia con guida aggiornate mensilmente. Le trovate in tutti i locali gay!

echo communication
For information and publicizing:
Echo communication Via S. Nicolao 10 – 20123 Milano
Tel. 0039 02 89015940-1 Fax 0039 02 89013990

Avellino ✉ 83100

CRUISING
- Viale Italia (also in the bar nearby/anche nel bar vicino)
- Piazza Kennedy (at night/di notte)
- Villa Communale (Near the toilets/Vicino al WC)

Bareggio - Milano ✉ 20010

CRUISING
- Canale Villoresi (on both sides in the bushes/sui due lati, nei cespugli)

Bari ✉ 70100

SEX SHOPS/BLUE MOVIES
■ **Europa 92** (g) 9-13, 14-19.30 h
Via Pisanelli 16/18 ✉ 70100 *(Stazione Centrale FS)*
☎ 080 54 25 990

SAUNAS/BATHS
■ **Millennium Bath** (AC B DR G P OS SA SB SOL VS WH WO YG)
Tue (L) 16-24, Wed-Sun 15.30-24 h
Via Adriatico 13 ✉ 70100 ☎ 080 53 42 530

NEWS STANDS
■ **Kiosk/Rivendita Giornali** (g) 5.30-21 h
Piazza Aldo Moro ✉ 70100 ☎ 0339 62 25 808

HEALTH GROUPS
■ **Anlaids** Medicalline: 9-12, 16-19 h
Via Osvaldo Marzano 10 ✉ 70124 ☎ 080 50 25 426
☎ 080 50 14 970 (Medicalline) 📠 080 50 22 936
■ **Network Nazionale "Gruppo C" Progetto di Ricerca Aids**
✉ 70100 ☎ 080 76 20 08
Helpline for people with HIV/Aids.

CRUISING
- Lungomare Nazario Saurio (R) (on the pier, in summer, mixed/sul mòlo, estate, misto)
- Piazza Umberto (AYOR)
- Piazza Aldo Moro
- North railway station/Stazione nord (in the evening/sera)
- Central station/Stazione centrale (R)
- Via Sparano and Corso Cavour (at Saicaf Bar in Corso Cavour)
- Fiera del Levante (TV) (by car only)
- Facoltà di Lettere e Filosofia (near post office, behind/dietro Piazza Re Umberto)

- Public park/giardini pubblici (between the universities/fra le università)
- Lungomare (tv) (towards/direzione San Giorgio)
- Lido Marziulli (summer spot/posto estivo)

Bassano del Grappa - Vicenza ✉ 36061

BARS
■ **Bar Nuovo** (B g) ?-1 h
Via Matteotti 42 ✉ 36061 ☎ 0424 32 39 17
■ **Olimpia** (B g YG) 8-22 h
Via Roma 63 ✉ 36061 ☎ 0424 52 40 08

RESTAURANTS
■ **Vecchia Trattoria Gamba** (AC F glm) Wed-Mon 12-15, 19.30-24 h
Strada Cartigliana 273 ☎ 0424 56 60 20
Not gay, but gays welcome, good cooking, reservation appreciated/non gay, ma gay benvenuti, buona cucina, gradita prenotazione.

CRUISING
- Railway station/Stazione FS (also nearby area, e. g. in the gardens during daytime/anche attorno, per esempio, nei giardini di giorno)
- Via Chilesotti (at night/di notte)
- Viale Venezia (barracks area/zona caserma)
- Viale Monte Grappa (R, tv)

Bergamo ✉ 24100

GAY INFO
■ **Arcigay** Tue 17-19, Thu 20-22.30, Sun 15-18 h
Via Baschenis 9/b ✉ 24100 *(bus 4/8-Borgo Palazzo)*
☎ 035 25 86 50
■ **Associazione "Il Triangolo Rosa"** (GLM) Tue 22-23 h
Via Borgo S. Caterina 92 ✉ 24124 *(Bus 2)* ☎ 035 22 65 70

TOURIST INFO
■ **A.P.T.**
Via Vittorio Emanuele 20 24100 ✉ 24100 ☎ 035 21 31 85
📠 035 23 01 84

BARS
■ **Divina Fashion Bar** (B glm YG) Mon-Sat 19-2 h
Via Borgo S. Caterina 1 ✉ 24124 *(near Accademia Carrara)*
☎ 035 21 84 21

SPARTACUS 2001/2002 | 607

Italy | Bergamo

discobar in Bergamo
chiuso il lunedì — venerdì e sabato aperto fino alle 07:00
VIDEO ROOM—DARK AREA
ingresso riservato soci arciUno

Get Up Club
live situation

via Bianzana 46 - Bergamo - tel.0039 035 344460

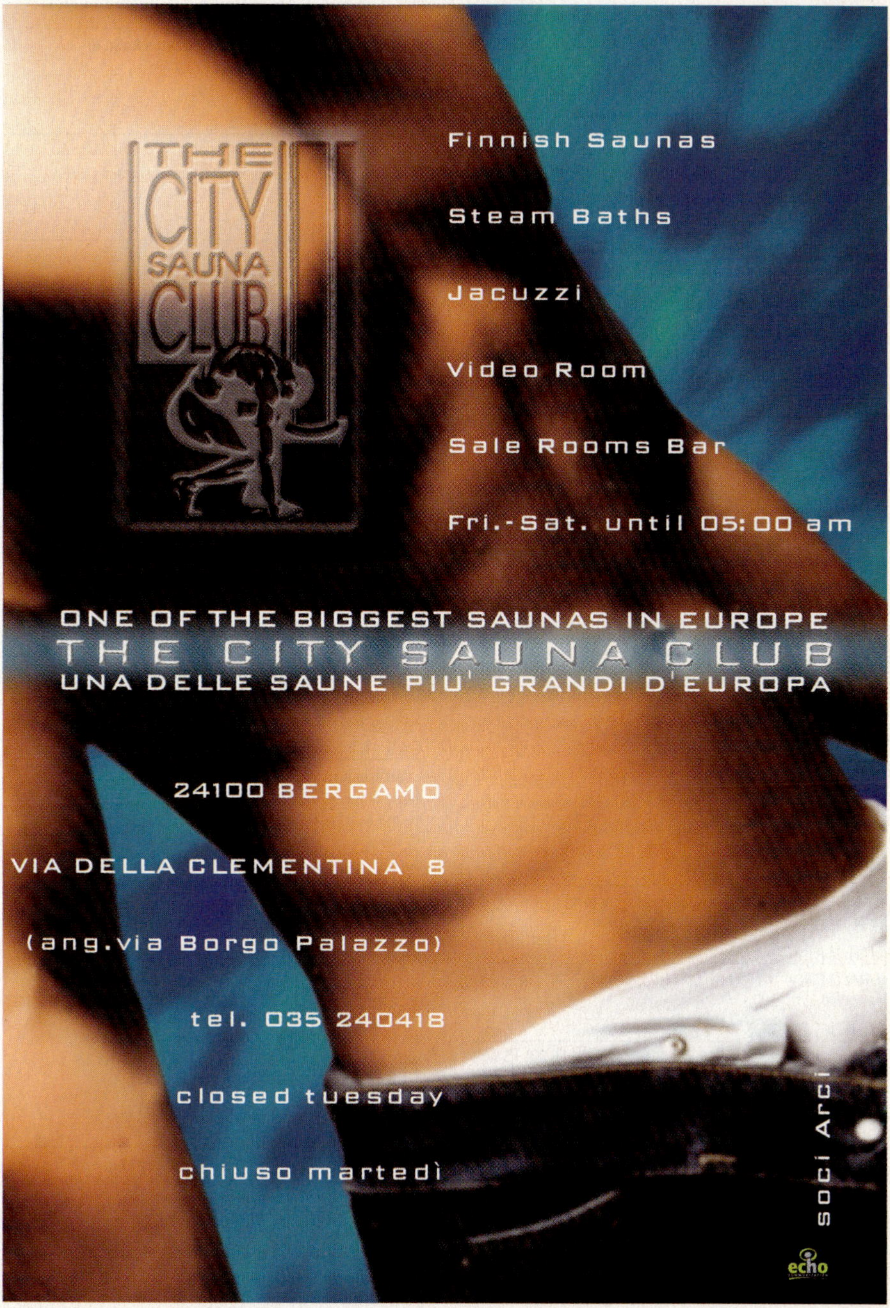
THE CITY SAUNA CLUB
Finnish Saunas
Steam Baths
Jacuzzi
Video Room
Sale Rooms Bar
Fri.-Sat. until 05:00 am
ONE OF THE BIGGEST SAUNAS IN EUROPE
THE CITY SAUNA CLUB
UNA DELLE SAUNE PIU' GRANDI D'EUROPA
24100 BERGAMO
VIA DELLA CLEMENTINA 8
(ang.via Borgo Palazzo)
tel. 035 240418
closed tuesday
chiuso martedì
soci Arci
echo

Italy — Bergamo ▶ Bologna

La tua sauna gay a Bergamo
Your gay Sauna when in Bergamo
Dein gay Sauna wenn in Bergamo
Tu Sauna gay cuando en Bergamo

club 63 fitness & relax

Via S. Lazzaro 63, 24122 Bergamo. Tel. 035-218922
Tutti i giorni dalle ore 15. Domenica dalle 14.
Chiuso il giovedì.
Ogni secondo giovedì del mese: "Naked Party".
Orario d'entrata dalle 21,30 alle 22,30
Every day from 15. Sundays from 14. Thursday closed
Every second Thursday "Naked Party"
Entrance hour 21,30-22,30
www.geocities.com/tuttinudi/tuttinudi.html

DANCECLUBS
■ **Get Up** (AC B BF d DR G lj MA OS P s VS) Tue-Sun 22-?, Fri & Sat -7 h
Via Bianzana 46 ✉ 24124 *(near Rondó delle Valli, bus 2/11/15)*
☎ 035 344 460
4 darkrooms. DJ on Wed, Fri-Sun.
■ **Nite Lite Club** (AC B D DR G P s WE YG) Sat 22-5, Sun -3 h
Via Baschenis 9 ✉ 24122 *(Bus 7, 5 min walk from the railway station)* ☎ 035 24 43 00
Arcigay membership required/Tessera Arcigay.

SEX SHOPS/BLUE MOVIES
■ **Magic America** (CC g p) Closed on Mon morning
Via Fantoni 30 ✉ 24121 ☎ 035 24 92 97

CINEMAS
■ **Ritz** (AYOR g) 14.30-24 h
Via Verdi 8 ✉ 24100 ☎ 035 24 21 24

SAUNAS/BATHS
■ **City Sauna Club** (! AC B CC DR f G MA msg P SA SB SOL VS WH) Sep-May 14-2, Jun-Aug 15-2 h, closed Tue
Via della Clementina 8/Via Borgo Palazzo ✉ 24100 *(Bus 5/8)* ☎ 035 24 04 18
One of Europe's biggest and most comfortable gay saunas/sauna gay tra le più grandi e confortevoli d'Europa; abbonamenti. Free condoms/Preservativi gratis.
■ **Club 63** (AC B DR f MA SA SB VS WH WO) Fri-Sat 15-5, Sun-Wed 15-2, Thu closed
Via San Lazzaro 63 ✉ 24122 *(corner Via Palma Il Vecchio, 5 min from railway station, Bus 7)* ☎ 035 21 89 22
Arcigay membership required. Every 2nd Thu "Naked party" (entrance 21.30-22.30h).

GENERAL GROUPS
■ **Agedo - Associazione Genitori Parenti e Amici di Omosessuali** Tue Thu 14-19 h
✉ 24100 ☎ 035 36 16 74

HEALTH GROUPS
■ **Anlaids**
Casa Accoglienza Oasi di Gerico, Via Conventino 3 ✉ 24100
📠 59 82 71

SPORT GROUPS
■ **Aiuara** (GLM)
Pallavolo Bergamo ✉ 24100 ☎ 0338 29 33 866 (Infoline)
☎ 0347 91 21 892 ✉ alebelotti@hotmail.com
GLM Volleyball group.

CRUISING
-Piazzale Malpensata (TV)
-Piazzale Cimitero (di sera in macchina/in the night by car)

Bibione Pineta - Venezia ✉ 30020
SWIMMING
-Spiaggio Libera (along the dunes/lungo le dune)

Biella ✉ 13051
CRUISING
-Railway station/stazione S. Paolo
-Viale Carducci (behind the hospital/dietro l'ospedale)
-Largo Cusano (Piazza V. Veneto)

Bologna ✉ 40100
GAY INFO
■ **Arcigay Nazionale** Mon-Fri 15-19 h
Piazza di Porta Saragozza 2 ✉ 40123 *(Bus 33, 32)*
☎ 051 64 47 054 📠 051 64 46 722 ✉ arcigl@iperbole.bologna.it
🖥 www.gay.it/arcigay
National headquarters of the Italian gay organisations.
■ **Idea Lavoro**
Via S. Stefano 57 ✉ 40100 ☎ 051 27 12 92 📠 051 27 14 06
✉ staff@idealavoro.com
Recruitment agency. Information on employment opportunities in Italy.

CULTURE
■ **Arcigay Arcilesbica Centro di Documentazione Archivio Videoteca** Mon-Thu 15-19, Mon Wed 22-0.30 h, closed Aug
Piazza di Porta Saragozza 2 ✉ 40123 ☎ 051 64 46 824
📠 051 64 46 252 ✉ dor5142@iperbole.bologna.it
Books, videos, international magazines.

BARS
■ **Cassero. Il** (! B d GLM MA P s YG) Summer 22-2, winter 21.30-1.30 h
Piazza di Porta Saragozza 2 ✉ 40123 *(in the arch in the middle of the square. Bus 20, 33)* ☎ 051 64 46 902
Bar, shows, video shows, exhibitions, debates, parties. Sat Sun disco/Bar spettacoli, proiezioni video, mostre, dibattiti, feste. Dom discoteca. Arcigay membership required/tessera Arcigay.

Bologna | Italy

9th EDITION

1st december 2001

Bologna - Milano

0516.446.902

blowingbubbles@libero.it

www.gay.it/blowingbubbles

BLOWING BUBBLES VIDEOMAKERS & FILMAKERS against AIDS

DANCECLUBS

■ **Cream** (AC B D G P YG) Thu 23-4 h
c/o Kinki Club, Via Zamboni 1 ✉ 40125
☎ 0335 58 54 640 (Infoline)
House music.

■ **Kinki Club** (AC B D glm MA P YG) Fri Sat 23-5, Sun -4 h
Via Zamboni 1 ✉ 40125 ☎ 051 52 22 76
Very mixed in the weekend.

■ **Pachito Club** (! AC B BF CC D DR F G lj MA P s VS) 20-3.30 h,
Fri Sat -6 h, Mon closed
Via Polese 47/C ✉ 40122 ☎ 051 24 39 98
Arcigay membership required/tessera Arcigay. 3rd Sat/month LJ night with show in the "Red Zone".

RESTAURANTS

■ **Ristorante-Pizzeria Speedy** (AC B CC F glm) 12-15, 19-1 h, closed on Mon
Via Saragozza 65/A ✉ 40123 *(Bus 20/32/33/37/38)*
☎ 051 58 50 54

CINEMA

■ **Corallo** (g)
Via Sardegna 15 ✉ 40100 ☎ 051 54 27 01

SEX SHOPS/BLUE MOVIES

■ **Andromeda** (g VS) 9.30-12, 15-19 h, closed Sun
Via San Simone 1/2 ✉ 40126 ☎ 051 22 59 76
Clothes, video, mail order/vendita corrispondenza, video, abbigliamento, novita settimanali.

➢ **P.O.BOX 691**
40100 Bologna
Italy
arcigl@iperbole.bologna.it

Nation wide gay organization for culture, rights, clubs, health care...

ARCIGAY

NATIONAL GAY ORGANIZATION

| Italy | Bologna |

www.upcity.it
the best of gay city map

Maps to the most important italian cities are update each month. Maps will be located in all clubs and pubs. Entertainment, clubs parties and events going on in town!

Le mappe delle città più importanti d'Italia con guida aggiornate mensilmente. Le trovate in tutti i locali gay!

For information and publicizing:
echo communication Via S. Nicolao 10 – 20123 Milano
Tel. 0039 02 89015940-1 Fax 0039 02 89013990

■ **Magic America** (CC g p VS) Closed Mon morning
Via Don Minzoni 4B ✉ 40126 (corner/angolo Piazza dei Martiri)
☎ 051 24 55 04
Large gay section.

CINEMAS
■ **Continental** (OG r) 15-24 h
Via Emilia Ponente 221 ✉ 40100 (near "Ospedale Maggiore")
☎ 051 38 58 71

SAUNAS/BATHS
■ **Cosmos Club** (AC b f G MA p SA SB SOL VS WH) 12-1.30, Sat -3 h
Via Boldrini 22 int. 16 ✉ 40121 (5 minutes from main railway station, in the courtyard through iron gate, look for green light over bell)
☎ 051 25 58 90

■ **New Vigor** (B DR G MA SA SB VS WH YG) Sun-Thu 14-2, Fri Sat -5 h
Via San Felice 6 B ✉ 40100
☎ 051 23 25 07
Arcigay membership required.

BOOK SHOPS
■ **Libreria Feltrinelli** 9-19.30 h, closed Sun
Piazza di Porta Ravegnana
☎ 051 26 13 92
Gay section, Spartacus gay guide.

NEWS STANDS
■ **Kiosk/Rivendita Giornali**
Piazza Porta S. Vitale 1 ✉ 40100

COSMOS CLUB
BOLOGNA • VIA BOLDRINI, 16 INTERNO
(IN THE COURTYARD, THROUGH THE IRON GATE)

TEL. 051 - 255 890

ITALY'S BIGGEST SAUNA, NOW EVEN MORE COMFORTABLE • A FEW MINUTES' WALK FROM THE RAILWAY STATION

SNACKS • AMERICAN BAR • FINNISH SAUNA
TURKISH BATH • SOLARIUM • MUSIC • VIDEO
TV • FILM LOUNGE • READING ROOM
YOUNG WELLKNOWN ATMOSPHERE
AMPLE RELAX FACILITIES • FREE MASSAGES

OPEN EVERY DAY

HYGIENIC, CLEAN AND MAXIMUM PROFESSIONALITY
NO TIME LIMIT

Bologna ▶ Bolzano/Bozen **Italy**

Sporthotel Platz ★★★
Restaurant

PUFELS - BULLA
I-39046 St. Ulrich - Ortisei (BZ)
Gröden - Südtirol - Italien
Val Gardena - Alto Adige - Italy

Tel. (0039) 0471 796935 - 796982
Fax (0039) 0471 798228

Homepage:
www.val-gardena.com/hotel/platz
e-mail: platz@val-gardena.com

The famous Alpe di Siusi - the largest plateau of Europe in the natural park of Scilar – is a sun bathed paradise for cross-country skiers, those who love to walk. Alpine ski and snowboard enthusiasts – but especially for the romantic.

Mountain climbing, ascents, mountain-bike trips, swimming, tennis, skating, paragliding, horse-back riding.

Expert skiers can test their skills on the numerous slopes of the largest skiing area in the world: the DOLOMITI SUPERSKI in the Italian Alps.

…How to get to VAL GARDENA

HOTELS

■ **Guercino. Il** (AC B BF CC g H MA)
Via Luigi Serra 7 ✉ 40129 *(near railway station)* ☏ 051 36 98 93
📠 051 36 98 93 🖳 guercino@guercino.it 🖳 www.guercino.it
Rooms with bath. Rates single Lit 140.000, double 200.000 bf incl. English and French spoken.

■ **Hotel Paradise** (AC CC H)
Vicolo Cattani 7 ✉ 40126 *(close to the railway station)*
☏ 051 23 17 92 ☏ 051 23 45 91
Single room Lit 120-220.000, Double room Lit. 170-340.000 with bf. All rooms with phone and TV.

GENERAL GROUPS

■ **Agedo - Associazione Genitori Parenti e Amici di Omosessuali** Sat 13-17 h
☏ 059 52 53 91

■ **Arcigay Arcilesbica S.C.O.T.** (Servizio Counselling Omosessuale Telefonico) Gay phone: Tue-Fri 20-23, Lesbian line: Mon 20-22 h
Piazza di Porta Saragozza 2 ✉ 40123 ☏ 051 64 46 820
🖳 mixsin@hotmail.com

■ **Arcigay "Circolo 28 Giugno - Il Cassero"** 22-2 h
Piazza di Porta Saragozza 2 ✉ 40123 ☏ 051 64 46 902
📠 051 64 46 252 🖳 cassero@iperbole.bologna.it
Cultural centre, meeting point/Centro culturale, punto d'incontro.

HEALTH GROUPS

■ **Anlaids**
Via Irnerio 53 ✉ 40126 ☏ 051 63 90 727

■ **Arcigay GASP! Gay Aids Prevenzione E Salute** Mon 17-20, Tue 14-18 h
c/o Il Cassero ☏ 051 64 46 820
Closed in Aug.

HELP WITH PROBLEMS

■ **Dott. Pietrantoni Luca**
☏ 0348 85 07 560
Psychologist.

SPECIAL INTEREST GROUPS

■ **Gaya Mater Studiorum** Mon 22-24 h
Via Belle Arti 19/a ✉ 40116 🖳 gayamater@usa.net
Gay students.

SPORT GROUPS

■ **GPB - Gruppo Pesce Bologna**
🖳 gruppo_pesce.bo@libero.it
Swimming group.

CRUISING

-Via Bovi Campeggi (R) *(near facilities/vicino gabinetto)*
-Car park Michelino, Fiera Zone (mainly by car, in the evening/night)

Bolzano/Bozen ✉ 39100

BARS

■ **Centaurus Bar** (B G) Wed, Sat 21-24 h
Talfergasse 1 ✉ 39100 ☏ 0471 97 63 42

SEX SHOPS/BLUE MOVIES

■ **Beathe Uhse International** (CC glm lj) 9-2 h, Sun closed
Via Latemar 10-12 ✉ 39100 *(near railway station)*
☏ 0471 30 12 23

HOTELS

■ **Sporthotel Platz** (B BF CC F H OS PI SA) Closed from 15th Oct-15th Dec & 15th Apr-15th Jun
Bulla - Pufels ✉ 39046 Ortisei/St. Ulrich ☏ 0471 79 69 35
☏ 0471 79 68 2
📠 0471 79 82 28 🖳 platz@val-gardena.com
🖳 www.val-gardena.com/hotel/platz

GENERAL GROUPS

■ **Circolo Arcigay Centaurus** Wed, Sat 21-24, Tue 20-22 h Phone line/servizio telefonico
Via Talvera 1 ✉ 39100 ☏ 0471 97 63 42 🖳 info@centaurus.org
🖳 www.centaurus.org

HEALTH GROUPS

■ **LILA - Lega Italiana Lotta contro l'Aids** Mon-Thu 8.30-12 Fri 8.30-14 h
Via Bari 14/A ✉ 39100 ☏ 0471 93 22 00 📠 0471 93 22 00

HELP WITH PROBLEMS

■ **Rosa Telefon/Linea Gay** Tue 20-22
✉ 39100 ☏ 0471 97 63 42

Italy | Bolzano/Bozen ▶ Camerino - Macerata

TRAP only for man
via Castagna, 55 Brescia
Infoline: 0328 4523880
E-mail: info@trapmad.it
Website: www.trapmad.it
Ingresso riservato ai soci ARCI

SWIMMING
-Stadtbad/Swimming Hall Bozen (NG pi) (just in winter 19-21 h. Via Trieste/Triester Straße)
-Freibad/Lido (g NG pi) (summer 9-19 h near Stadtbad)
-Strand am Talferfluß/beach at river Talvera (G MA NU) (take road to Sarnthein, 2 km from Bozen stop at parking place Sill, from there a short walk down the valley)
-Africa at river Talfer (G MA NU) (take road to Sarnthein/Sarentino, 4 km from Bozen turn off at sign "Bar Seeberger Jausestation" and drive to end of road. From there, walk 500 m up the river.

CRUISING
-Parco Petrarca (neben/near/vicino Piazza Victoria, AYOR)

Bormio - Sondrio ✉ 23023
SWIMMING
-Piscina termale & sauna
-Solarium Di Bormio 2000

Bra - Cuneo ✉ 12042
CRUISING
-Giardini della Rocca

Brescia ✉ 25100
BARS
■ **Re Desiderio** (A B f G YG) 20-1 h, closed Mon
Vicolo Lungo 11 ✉ 25121 ☏ 030 49 499

DANCECLUBS
■ **Out Limits Disco** (AC B D DR f GLM OS VS) Fri Sat 22-5 h
Via Ugo Foscolo 2, Paderno Franciacorta ✉ 25050 *(Highway A4 MI-VE exit "Ospitaletto". 2 km from the exit/Autostrada A4 MI-VE uscita "Ospitaletto". A 2 km dal casello)* ☏ 030 65 75 36
2 dancefloors: House and commercial music. Fri mainly lesbians, Sat mainly gays.

■ **Trap** (B d DR F G lj MA OS P VS) 22.30-2.30, Fri, Sat 23-4 h, closed on Mon and in Aug
Via Castagna 55 ✉ 25100 *(Dogana district)* ☏ 0328 45 23 880 *(infoline)*
Bar, Disco and restaurant in the weekend (20.30-24 h).

SEX SHOPS/BLUE MOVIES
■ **Europa 92** (g)
Via dei Mille 22 ☏ 030 37 58 459
■ **Magic America** (CC g p) Closed on Mon
Oberdan/Via Scuole 20/C ✉ 25100 ☏ 030 39 84 53
■ **Magic America** (CC g p) Closed on Mon morning
Via Lamarmora 146A ✉ 25124 ☏ 030 34 93 94

GENERAL GROUPS
■ **Orlando - Centro Culturale di Iniziativa Omosessuale** Fri 21-24 h
Via San Faustino 38 ✉ 25122 ☏ 030 47 601 🖨 030 494 65
✉ orlandoarci@yahoo.com 🖳 www.geocities.com/orlandoarci

CRUISING
-Breda zone
-Public Garden (Via Ugoni)
-APAM Bus Satation (police)
-Railway Station FS (R TV) (also around the building
-Via Torrelunga and Via Spalto S. Marco (behind the jail)
-Giardini del Castello (AYOR) (in the parks close to S. Pietro church; evening and day)
-Viale Italia (R TV) (after 23 h)
-Zona Industriale (MA YG) (Via Grandi/Via Perotti, by car, weekdays after 21, WE after 13 h)

Brindisi ✉ 72100
CRUISING
-Corso Umberto
-Central Station/Stazione Centrale (R) (also surrounding area/anche dintorni)
-Parco della Rimembranza

Caiolo - Sondrio ✉ 23010
CRUISING
-River Livrio, on Albosaggia-Caiolo road, near Caiolo signpost, follow path to river, summer afternoons on foot or bicycle

Camerino - Macerata ✉ 62032
CRUISING
-Rocca Borghese (gardens, at night/giardini, notte)
-Piazza Principale

M'ama, non m'ama… …indossalo!

NON DARE NESSUNA POSSIBILITÀ ALL' AIDS

Canosa di Puglia - Bari ✉ 70053

CINEMAS
- **D'Ambra** (G)
Via Piave 9 ✉ 70053 ☎ 0883 96 18 97
Action in the corridor.

Capalbio ✉ 58011

SWIMMING
Go to the beach through the parking lot, then walk for 10 minutes towards right. Dunes and busches. Nudity.

Capri - Napoli ✉ 80073

BOOK SHOPS
- **Conchiglia. La** (g)
Via le Botteghe 12 ✉ 80073 ☎ 081 83 76 577

SWIMMING
- L'Arsenale (NU) (occasionally/occasionalmente).

CRUISING
- Via Krupp (also nearby in the park/anche vicino nel parco)
- Piazzetta di Capri

Casale Monferrato - Alessandria ✉ 15053

CINEMAS
- **Poli** (g)
Via Guazzo 13 ✉ 15053 ☎ 0142 45 20 81

Caserta ✉ 81100

TRAVEL AND TRANSPORT
- **Di Matteo Viaggi e Turismo** Mon-Fri 9-13, 16-20, Sat 9-13 h
Via Liberta 94 ✉ 81024 (7 km from Caserta) ☎ 0823 40 59 62
📠 0823 40 59 63 ✉ pinodm@tin.it 🖥 www.dimatteo.it
Specialized in gay travelling.

HEALTH GROUPS
- **Network Nazionale "Gruppo C" Progetto di Ricerca Aids**
✉ 81100 ☎ 0823 23 23 11
Helpline for people with HIV/Aids.

CRUISING
- Palazzo Reale (very AYOR) (in the gardens/nei giardini)
- Piazza Vanvitelli (in the evening; mixed, pleasant atmosphere/di sera; misto, ambiente piacevole)

Cassano d'Adda - Milano ✉ 20062

CRUISING
- River Adda beach, follow paths from Cassano-Rivolta road

Castelfranco Veneto - Treviso ✉ 31033

TRAVEL AND TRANSPORT
- **Alex & Julian Viaggi** (CC) Tue-Sat 9-13, 15-20 h
Piazza Europa Unita 24 ✉ 31033 ☎ 0423 72 31 78
📠 0423 74 44 44

Italy — Castellamare di Stabia - Napoli ▶ Cremona

Castellamare di Stabia - Napoli ✉ 80053
CRUISING
- Villa Comunale (also surrounding area/anche dintorni)
- Railway Station/Stazione Circumvesuviana

Cava dei Tirreni - Salerno ✉ 84013
CRUISING
- Municipio (square in front, cruising by car, at night/piazza davanti, in macchina, di notte)

Cervia Milano Marittima - Ravenna ✉ 48015
CRUISING
- Foce del Canale (day and night/giorno e notte)
- Harbour/Porto (and surrounding area/e dintórni)

Cesena ✉ 47020
GENERAL GROUPS
- **Arcigay Dario Bellezza** Thu 21 h
c/o Arci Nuova Associazione, Via Ravennate 2124 ✉ 47020
☎ 0347 84 69 427 📠 dbellezza@iol.it
🖥 digilander.iol.it/romagnarainbow

Chieuti - Foggia ✉ 71010
SWIMMING
- Chieuti Beach (70 km from Foggia). Walk 2 miles along the beach to the right of the railway station. Take food and drinks with you. Action is in the pine wood

Civitanova Marche - Macerata ✉ 62013
CRUISING
- Piazza Cristo Re (night/notte)
- Via Leonardo da Vinci

Civitavecchia - Roma ✉ 00053
CRUISING
- Terme de "la Ficoncella" (at the highway exit, about 4 km from the city/vicino all'uscita dell'autostrada, circa 4 km dal centro)

Clusone - Bergamo ✉ 24023
CRUISING
- Main Road/Strada provinciale (MA) (woods, all times/pineta, qualsiasi ora)

Cologno Monzese - Milano ✉ 20093
CRUISING
- At the Metro stations/stazioni Metro

Como ✉ 22100
BARS
- **Halloween** (B F glm s)
Piazza S. Rocco/Via Napoleona ✉ 22100
- **Ibiza** (B g)
Via Foscolo 5 ✉ 22100 ☎ 031 30 46 52

CINEMAS
- **Italia**
Via Marchesi 6 *(Ponte Chiasso)* ☎ 031 53 01 35

GENERAL GROUPS
- **Arcigay Arcilesbica Como Circolo "Koiné"** Sun 20.30-22.30 h
c/o LILA, Via Odescalchi 19 ✉ 22100 ☎ 031 30 07 61
📠 031 26 18 08

CRUISING
- Circle around soccer stadium.(+22 h)
- Stazione centrale FS (AYOR)
- Main road between Lomazzo-Turate, wood on the right side/Strada provinciale Lomazzo-Turate, bosco a destra (day and night by car/di giorno e di sera in macchina)

Cosenza ✉ 87100
DANCECLUBS
- **Moana Multiclub** (B D g)
Via Siriomarco, Tortora Marina ☎ 0985 72 325

BOOK SHOPS
- **Domus** (g)
Corso d'Italia ✉ 87100 ☎ 0984 23 110
- **Seme. Il** (g)
Via Nicola Serra/Via Gramsci ✉ 87100
☎ 0984 36 373

HOTELS
- **Grisaro** (g H)
Viale Trieste 38 ✉ 87100 ☎ 0984 27 952
📠 0984 27 838

CRUISING
- Stazione FS/railway station
- Giardini pubblici/public gardens
- Viale Trieste

Creazzo - Vicenza ✉ 36051
SAUNAS/BATHS
- **Rainbow Club** (AC b f g p SA SB MA) 15-1 h
Via Valscura 2/A ✉ 36051 ☎ 0444 52 26 47
Clean and quiet/Locale pulito e tranquillo.

Crema - Cremona ✉ 26013
BARS
- **Charlie Brown** (AC B D G YG) 21.30-1.30 h
✉ 26013 *(5 km east of/est di Crema)* ☎ 0373 78 05 52
Best Thu night/meglio giovedi sera

Cremona ✉ 26100
GAY INFO
- **Arcigay "La Rocca"** Fri 21-23.30 h, closed Aug
Via Speciano 4 ✉ 26100 *(Bus 1, near the Dome)* ☎ 0372 20 484

SEX SHOPS/BLUE MOVIES
- **Adamo ed Eva** (AC CC g VS) Mon 15-20, Tue-Sun 10-20 h
Via Rosario 56 ✉ 26100 *(near Boschetto)* ☎ 0372 23 407
- **Mela Proibita. La** (g) Closed Mon
Galleria Kennedy 12 ☎ 0372 36 118

HEALTH GROUPS

■ **Network Nazionale "Gruppo C" Progetto di Ricerca Aids**
☏ 0372 45 17 55
Helpline for people with HIV/Aids & free HIV test.

CRUISING
-Via Lungo Po Europa (near the camping site, day/vicino campeggio, giorno)
-Foro Boario (near Stadium, by night/vicino Stadio, di notte)

Crotone ✉ 88074

CINEMAS
■ **Apollo** (g)
Via Regina Margherita ✉ 88074

CRUISING
-Viale Regina Margherita

Cuneo ✉ 12100

CINEMAS
■ **Italia** (g)
Via Ponza di San Martino Gustavo 2/B ✉ 12100 ☏ 0171 69 29 51

CRUISING
-Railway Station/Stazione FS (facilities and gardens/stazione, e giardino)
-Viale Marconi (TV) (police)
-Corso Kennedy (R) (police)
-Corso Gesso gardens/giardini

Desenzano del Garda - Brescia ✉ 25015

BARS
■ **Scarabeo** (B g) 18-3 h, closed Tue
Vicolo Duomo 13/A ✉ 25015 ☏ 030 91 40 085

DANCECLUBS
■ **Art Club** (AC B D GLM OS S YG) Wed Fri-Sun 22.30-5 h
Via Mantova 1/A ✉ 25015 *(Highway Milano-Venezia, exit Desenzano, turn left, 300 m)* ☏ 030 99 91 004

RESTAURANTS
■ **Sirenetta. La** (F glm) closed Mon
Lungo Lago Cesare Battisti 59 ✉ 25015 ☏ 030 91 40 524

SEX SHOPS/BLUE MOVIES
■ **Tuttisensi** (g) closed Mon morning
Via le Motta 40 ✉ 25015 ☏ 030 91 21 667
Write/call for free mail oder catalogue/Per ricevere i cataloghi e il listino prezzi tel.

HOTELS
■ **Aquila d'Oro** (AC B BF CC F g OS PI)
Via Francesco Agello 47/49 ✉ 25010 ☏ 030 99 02 353
🖷 030 99 02 263
Hotel and restaurant. Rates from Lit. 180.000 to 240.000.

SWIMMING
-Punta del Vò (rocky beach on road 572, 1 km from the village, daytime only/spiaggia sassosa, SS 572, 1 km dal paese, solo di giorno)
-Rocca di Manerba (G NU) (take the road to Salò, turn off at Moniga del Garda (centro) and follow the signs)
Parco naturale to the end of the road (but don't follow the signs "Manerba del Garda"!) Then take via Marinello on foot to the beach (15 min.)

ART CLUB

EUROPEAN

FASHION

DISCO

ART CLUB DISCOTECA

Via Mantova 1A Desenzano del Garda
25015 Brescia Italy
motor-way Milano-Venezia exit Desenzano
sx 300 mt. Centro Commerciale Garda
phone line +39-030-9991004
fax line +39-030-9120421

www.artclubdisco.com
e-mail art@artclubdisco.com

Italy Deszenzano del Garda - Brescia ▶ Firenze

www.upcity.it
the best of gay city map

Maps to the most important italian cities are update each month
Maps will be located in all clubs and pubs.
Entertainment, clubs parties and events going on in town!

Le mappe delle città più importanti d'Italia con guida aggiornata mensilmente.
Le trovate in tutti i locali gay!

For information and publicizing:
echo communication Via S. Nicolao 10 -- 20123 Milano
Tel. 0039 02 89015940-1 Fax 0039 02 89013990

CRUISING
- Punto del Vò (afternoon above the road, night at P)

Elba, Isola d' - Livorno ✉ 57036
CRUISING
- Harbour/Porto

Empoli - Firenze ✉ 50053
CRUISING
- Viale B. Buozzi (gardens of railway station and in the handicraft laboratories area, by car in the evening)
- Zona Artigianale Carraia

Eraclea Mare - Venezia ✉ 30020
CRUISING
- Isola del Morto (NU) (beach/spiaggia). Very cruisy.

Fabriano - Ancona ✉ 60044
CRUISING
- Stadium/stadio (evening, night/sul tardi)

Fano - Pesaro ✉ 61032
CRUISING
- Viale Buozzi (behind the monument/dietro al Monumento)
- Football stadium/Stadio Calcistico (near entry/presso l'entrata)
- Beach between Fano and Pesaro/spiaggia tra Fano e Pesaro (NU)

Fermo - Ascoli Piceno ✉ 63023
CRUISING
- Between the archs of Lido di Fermo and Lido Tre

Ferrara ✉ 44100
CINEMAS
■ **Mignon** (g)
Porta S. Pietro 18 ✉ 44100 ☎ 0532 76 01 39

CRUISING
- Wall 200 m from railway station/mura 200 m dalla stazione
- Stazione FS

Firenze ✉ 50100
PUBLICATIONS
■ **Giglio Fucsia. Il** (GLM)
📧 pinklily@gay.it 🌐 www.gay.it/pinklily
Free Gay & Lesbian guide for Florence and Tuscany.

TOURIST INFO
■ **A.P.T.** Mon-Sat 8.30-13.30 h
Via Manzoni 16 50121 ✉ 50100 ☎ 055 23 320 📠 055 23 46 286

BARS
■ **Café Cabiria** (B d F glm) 8.30-1, Fri Sat -2 h, closed Tue
Piazza Santo Spirito 4/R ☎ 055 21 57 32
DJ music on Thu-Sun from 22 h.

■ **Crisco** (AC B CC DR f G lj MA P s VS) 22-3.30, Fri Sat -6 h, closed Tue
Via S. Egidio 43/R ✉ 50100 ☎ 055 24 80 580
Shows during the WE/Spettacoli fine settimana.

■ **Piccolo Caffè. Il** (A B GLM MA) 12-? h
Via Borgo Santa Croce 23/R ✉ 50122 *(in town centre)*
☎ 055 24 17 04

■ **Tabasco Bar** (AC B CC D E GLM MA P) 22-6 h
Piazza S. Cecilia, 3r ✉ 50123 ☎ 055 21 30 00

■ **Y.A.G. Bar** (AC B CC GLM S VS YG) 17-2 h
Via de Macci 8R ✉ 50122 *(near Santa Croce church)*
☎ 055 24 69 022
Video & music bar, very crowded. Internet point and huge video screen.

MEN'S CLUBS
■ **Tin Box** (AC CC DR G MA msg)
Via dell'Oriuolo 19/21 R ✉ 50100 *(behind/dietro Duomo)*
☎ 055 24 66 387 ☎ 0348-7091 563 (Infoline)
Cruising place. Internet service with chat zone and web cam.

DANCECLUBS
■ **Flamingo Disco** (A AC B CC D GLM MA P s) 22-6 h, closed in Aug
Via Pandolfini 26/R ✉ 50123 ☎ 055 24 33 56

■ **Timida Gozilla at Auditorium Flog** (D GLM) 2nd. or 3rd.
Sat 22-3 h. Info from Azione Gaylesbica
Via M. Mercati 24 b

RESTAURANTS
■ **Cantina Barbagianni** (AC CC F g) 12.30-14.30, 19.30-23 h, Sun closed
Via Sant'Egidio 13 ✉ 50122 *(Centre)* ☎ 055 24 80 508
Creative cuisine. Nice atmosphere. Close to Crisco and Tin Box.

Firenze | Italy

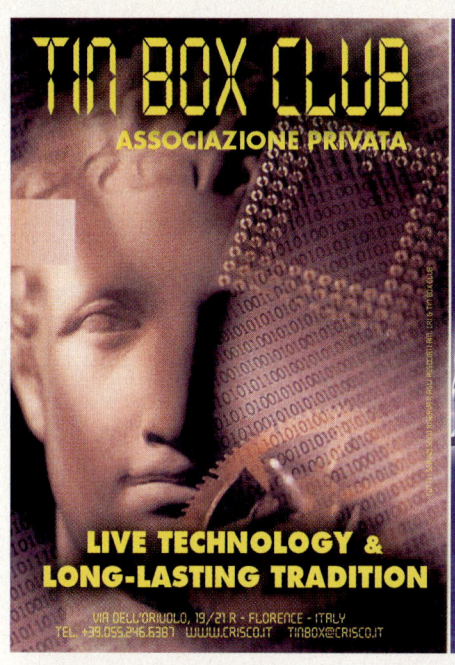

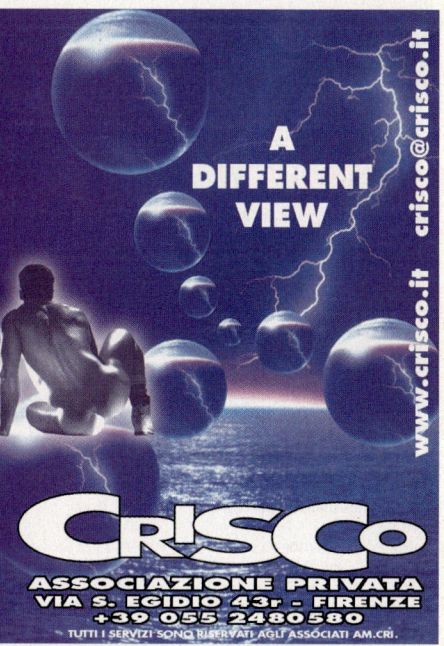

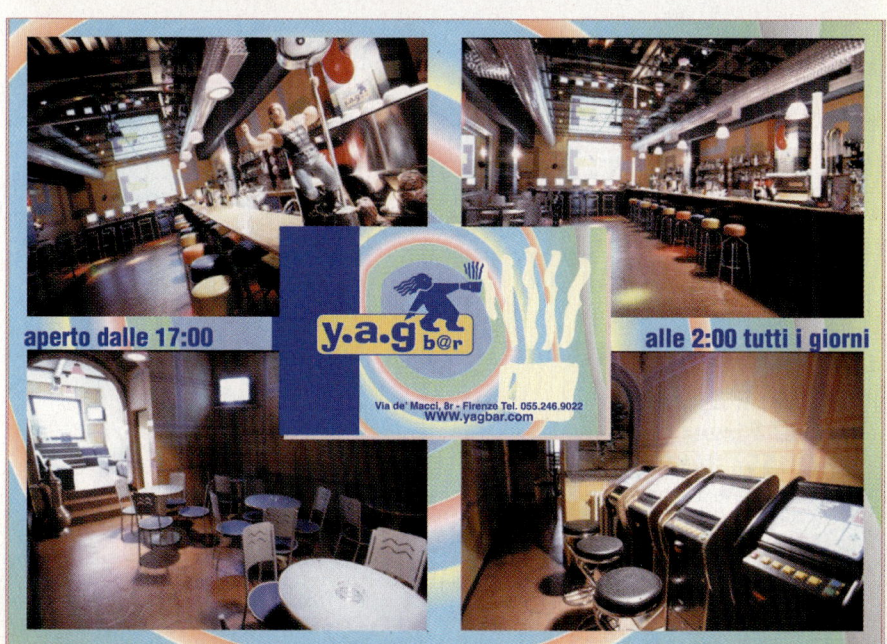

Italy — Firenze

PICCOLO CAFE
florence - italy

Looking for a friendly, cosy, gay/lesbian bar, right in the centre of Florence where you can find out about the local gay scene and meet both locals and tourists? The "Piccolo Cafe" is the place for you. We also offer art shows and good modern music.

email antoniodinapoli@tiscali.it   Open daily: 12:00 am till late

---

- **Osteria Masticabrodo** (F g) 12-15, 19-23 h, Sun closed
  Borgo Allegri 58 R ✉ 50123 *(near Piazza S. Croce)*
  ☎ 055 24 19 20
- **Trattoria San Zanobi** (AC CC F glm) 12-14.30, 19-22.30 h, Sun closed
  Via San Zanobi 33/a R   ☎ 055 47 52 86

SEX SHOPS/BLUE MOVIES
- **Frisco International Import** (G) 9-13, 15.30-19.30 h, closed Sat Sun
  Via Veracini 15 ✉ 50100 *(Bus 17/29/30/35)* ☎ 055 35 73 51
  Mail order, wholesale videos, lubricants, condoms/Vendita per corrispondenza e all'ingrosso di video, lubrificanti, profilattici.
- **Magic America** (CC g p) Closed on Mon morning
  Via Guelfa 87/R ✉ 501   ☎ 055 21 28 40

CINEMAS
- **Arlecchino** (OG R) 15.30-24 h
  Via de' Bardi 47/R ✉ 50100 *(near Ponte Vecchio)* ☎ 055 28 43 32
- **Italia** (g) Gay movies: Wed
  Piazza Alinari   ☎ 055 21 10 69

ESCORTS & STUDIOS
- **Bruno Escorts** 0-24 h
  ☎ 0338 96 43 603

SAUNAS/BATHS
- **Florence Baths** (A AC B CC DR f G MA MSG P SA SB SOL VS WH WO) 14-2, Jun-Sep 15-2 h
  Via Guelfa 93/R ✉ 50123 *(near railway station)* ☎ 055 21 60 50
  Popular extravagant sauna.

---

chiuso la domenica
air conditioned

RISTORANTE CANTINA BARBAGIANNI

...diverso dal solito...

Via Sant'Egidio, 13
50122 Firenze
Tel. 055/ 2480508

www.net-reserve.com/barbagianni.htm

BRUNO'S ESCORTS
MEET MEN IN FLORENCE

SEX HOLIDAYS
ENJOY CHIANTI COUNTRISIDE
WITH US
EXCELLENT ACCOMODATION
DELICIOUS ITALIAN FOOD – CAR SERVICE

TEL. 0039 338 9643603
e-mail: vivabruno@yahoo.it

Firenze | **Italy**

DOMINA
• Hair and Style •

uomo/donna
Via XXVII Aprile, 53-55r
Firenze
Tel. 055.494848

HOTEL CELLAI
FIRENZE

A CHARMING WELCOME
IN THE HEART OF FLORENCE
Via 27 Aprile 14, Firenze - 50129
Tel. +39-55.48 92 91, Fax. +39-55.47 03 87
http://www.hotelcellai.it
E-mail: info@hotelcellai.it

BODY & BEAUTY SHOPS

■ **Domina** (g) 9-18 h, Mon closed
Via 27 Aprile 53-55 R ☎ 055 49 48 48
Hair and style for men and women.

BOOK SHOPS

■ **City Lights** (g) 16-24 h, closed Mon
Via di S. Niccolò 23/R ☎ 055 23 47 882
Gay section. Literature and video festival.

■ **Libreria del Cinema** (CC NG) 9.30-13, 15.30-19.30 h, closed Sun
Via Guelfa 14/R ✉ 50129 (near the Dome/vicino al Duomo)
☎ 055 21 64 16
Cinema specialized book-shop. Also post-cards, photos, magazines and posters.

GIFT & PRIDE SHOPS

■ **Cornice é...** (CC glm) 9.30-19.30 h
Via del Melarancio 15/R ✉ 50123 (Stazione di Santa Maria Novella)
☎ 055 21 58 31

NEWS STANDS

■ **Edicola Balsimelli** (g)
Piazza Santa Maria Novella
Babilonia magazines and gay books. Open till late at night.

TRAVEL AND TRANSPORT

■ **Queer Nation Holidays** (CC GLM) Mon-Fri 9.30-19.30, Sat 10.30-18.30 h
Via del Moro 95/R ✉ 50123 (central/centro) ☎ 055 26 54 587
📠 055 26 54 560 💻 info@queernationholidays.com
🌐 www.queernationholidays.com

Gay travels in Italy and all over the world, gay and gay friendly hotels, flight tickets, tour group with gay guide, information about the Florence and italian gay scene/Viaggi per gay in Italia e nel mondo, hotel gay e gay friendly, biglietteria aerea, pacchetti personalizzati, viaggi di gruppo con accompagnatore gay, info point sulla "scena" gay de Firenze e d'Italia.

HOTELS

■ **Hotel Cellai** (AC B BF CC H OS)
Via 27 Aprile 14 ✉ 50129 (central location) ☎ 055 48 92 91
📠 055 47 03 87 💻 info@hotelcellai.it 🌐 www.hotelcellai.it
Rates Lit single 160.000-250.000, double 230.000-360.000.

■ **Hotel Medici** (B BF CC g H OS)
Via de' Medici 6 ✉ 50123 ☎ 055 28 48 18 📠 055 21 62 02
💻 medici@dada.it
Located in historical center. Rooms with TV and phone, with/without bath. Rates single Lit 70.000-150.000, double 110.000-270.000. bf incl. Roof garden. Appartments on request. Information about gay scene available.

■ **Hotel Morandi alla Crocetta** (AC BF CC g H)
Via Laura 50 (near Piazza della SS. Annunziata) ☎ 055 23 44 747
📠 055 24 80 954 💻 welcome@hotelmorandi.it
🌐 www.hotelmorandi.it
Rates single Lit 170.000, double 290.000. Rooms with bath, TV and phone. Reservation per fax with credit-card only. Garage. Very gay friendly.

■ **Hotel Tina** (CC glm H)
Via San Gallo 31 ✉ 50129 (central located) ☎ 055 48 35 19
📠 055 48 35 93 💻 hoteltina@tin.it
Rates single Lit 70.000-100.000, double 100.000-140.000. Own key at night. Very friendly staff. Information about gay scene available.

Italy — Firenze

QUEER NATION HOLIDAYS
gay travel agency and tour operator

50123 Firenze **(Italy)**
Via del Moro, 95/R
Phone: +39 **0552654587**
Fax: +39 **0552654560**
E-mail: info@queernationholidays.com
Catalogue on-line: www.queernationholidays.com

- Specialized in the main Gay destinations
- Gay accomodations Worldwide
- Gay cruises in Tuscan islands
- Italian Art cities gay packages
- Individual and Group vacations

IGLTA

■ **Hotel Wanda** (BF CC glm H)
Via Ghibellina 51 ✉ 50122 *(near the cathedral/vicino dal Duomo, Bus 14)* ☎ 055 23 44 484 055 24 21 06 055 24 21 06
Single room Lit 120.000-150.000, Double room 150.000-200.000, with/without bath, some with TV and frescoes. 10% discount for gay couples.

■ **Mona Lisa** (BF H NG)
Borgo Pinti 27 ✉ 50100 ☎ 055 24 79 751 055 24 79 755
Very good and well located. Rates single Lit 250.000-300.000, double 380.000-480.000. Buffet bf incl.

GUEST HOUSES

■ **Dei Mori** (AC BF glm MG)
Via Dante Alighieri 12 ✉ 50122 *(between the Duomo and Signoria square)* ☎ 055 21 14 38 055 23 82 216 deimori@bnb.it
 www.bnb.it/deimori

'DEI MORI'
Bed & Breakfast

Florence's First B&B
Internet: www.bnb.it/deimori
deimori@bnb.it
Via Dante Alighieri 12
(between the Duomo and Signoria square)
Phone: 0039-055-211438
Fax: 0039-055-2382216

Rates single Lit 90.000, double 170.000 (bf incl.). Own key. Non smoking hotel. Small and friendly/Ambiente familiare. Early booking advisable/Prenotare in anticipo.

■ **PLP Guest House** (F glm H)
Via G. Marconi 47 ✉ 50131 *(near/vicino Campo di Marte)*
☎ 055 57 20 05
Rates single Lit 50.000-70.000, double 80.000-100.000. Own key at night.

PRIVATE ACCOMMODATION

■ **I.H.S.- Private Accomodation**
(central) ☎ 055 47 52 86 (Sig.a Mariangela) 055 49 65 20
 ihs.apprent@internettrain.it
Appartment with kitchen, TV, bathroom and washing machine/Appartamento con cucina, tv, bagno e lavatrice. Prices on request/ Prezzi da stabilire.

GENERAL GROUPS

■ **Azione Gay e Lesbica "Finisterrae"** (GLM) Mon-Fri 18-20 h
c/o SMS Andrea del Sarto, Via Manara 12 ✉ 50135 *(2nd floor/2° piano)* ☎ 055 67 12 98 ☎ 055 67 13 20 (Hotline) 055 62 41 687 Gaylesbica.Fi@agora.stm.it
 www.agora.stm.it/gaylesbica.fi
Gay and lesbian political association. Meeting, library. Monthly parties, shows. Health consultations. Touristic information/Associazione politica gay e lesbica. Reunioni, Centro di documentazione. Feste mensili, spettacoli. Consulenze sulla salute. Informazioni turistiche.

■ **Coordinamento Queer** Meetings: Wed 21-24 h
c/o Ireos, Via del Ponte all'Asse 7 *(Bus 22)*
☎ 055 35 34 62 ireos@freemail.it
 www.members.tripod.it/ireos/index.html
Informal coordination of gay-lesbian-transgender working groups for social action, culture, tourism and free time, parties, gay film club./Insieme informale di gay-lesbice-transgender per iniziative sociali, culturali, turistiche e ricreative, incontri, feste, gay cineclub.

■ **Ireos - Centro Servizi per la Comunità Queer** Mon-Fri 16-19, Wed 21-24 h
Via del Ponte all'Asse 7 *(Bus 22)* ☎ 055 35 34 62
 ireos@freemail.it
 www.members.tripod.it/ireos/index.html
Gay, lesbian and more association, gay tourist information desk, social action, psychological counseling, courses, workshops, meetings, message board/Associazione di volontariato di e per gay lesbiche e non solo, informazioni, orientamento, messaggi, accoglienza turistica, aggregazione, ascolto psicologico, corsi, gruppi di lavoro, incontri.

Firenze ▶ Genova | Italy

HEALTH GROUPS

■ **Centro AIDS**
Ospedale Santa Maria Annunziata di Ponte Anicicheri
☎ 055 24 96 512

■ **Ireos** Mon-Fri 16-19 h
Via del Ponte all'Asse 7 *(Bus 22)* ☎ 055 35 34 63
✉ ireos@freemail.it 🖥 www.members.tripod.it/ireos/index.html
Free psychological and medical counseling on Mon, free and anonymous HIV test, courses, self-help groups, home-care, physical therapy/Servizi gratuiti: consulenze specialistiche e psicologiche (lun), test HIV anonimo; corsi, gruppi di autoaiuto, assistenza domiciliare, attività psicofisiche.

SPECIAL INTEREST GROUPS

■ **Extramuros**
c/o Ireos, Via del Ponte all'Asse 7 *(Bus 22)* ☎ 055 35 34 63
✉ ireos@freemail.it 🖥 www.members.tripod.it/ireos/index.html
Gay-lesbian hiking, trekking, travelling group/Occasioni d'incontro tra gay e lesbiche e non solo, scoprendo tesori della natura e della cultura: visite, passeggiate, viaggi.

SWIMMING

- Piscina Costoli (swimming pool, facilities and showers/ bagni e docce; best late afternoon/meglio pomeriggio tardi; be discreet/discrezione)

CRUISING

- Viale delle Cascine (AYOR R TV) (P) behind disco Meccanó)
- Campo di Marte stadium/stadio
- Viale Lincoln-Washington(on the bike path from "Ponte della Vittoria" to "Ponte all'Indiano" at night on foot or by bike)
- Highway Florence-Rome A1/autostrada Firenze-Roma A1 (P) between Firenze Sud/Incisa, both directions)
- Gas station Florence North-Florence South A1/aera di servizio Firenze Nord-Firenze Sud A1. "Scandicci", both directions

Foggia ✉ 71100

CINEMAS

■ **Dante** (g) 16.30-23 h
Via Duomo 7 ✉ 71100 ☎ 0881 77 64 39

■ **Garibaldi** (g) 16.30-23 h
Via Garibaldi 80 ✉ 71100 ☎ 0881 74 85 47

CRUISING

- Porta Manfredonia (TV)
- Piazza Cavour (at night/di notte)
- Viale XXIV Maggio
- Railway Station/Stazione FS (R) (also in the gardens/anche giardini and on the square to the right of the station/e nella piazza sulla destra della stazione)
- Viale della Stazione

Forlì ✉ 47100

GENERAL GROUPS

■ **Arcigay Arcilesbica Forlì**
Via Fratelli Bandiera 3 ✉ 47100 ☎ 0543 45 86 66
📠 0543 45 86 65

Gaeta - Latina ✉ 04024

CRUISING

- At the harbour/al porto

Hotel Medici
gives the best view of the city and takes care of you
Rooms with and without bath
Terrace garden with view

Via de Medici, 6 - Firenze
Tel 055/284818 Fax 055/216202
email medici@dada.it
www.hotelmedici.it

Gallipoli - Lecce ✉ 73014

SWIMMING

- Liberia beach/Spiaggia Libera (From Gallipoli go to Ugento. Action in the pine forest on the right 1 km behind the Hotel Costa Brada)

Garda - Verona ✉ 37016

SWIMMING

- Punta S. Viglio at Baia delle Sirene, at the end and on the right side of the nudist beach, action in the evening and in summer only/in località Baia delle Sirene, in fondo a destra spiaggia naturista, solo d'estate, azione di sera (take the APT Bus 62-64, stop at S. Viglio/da VR prendere il Bus APT 62-64 e scendere a S. Viglio)

Genova ✉ 16100

CULTURE

■ **Isola che non c'é. L'** Wed 20-23, Sun 15-17.30 h
☎ 0347 17 92 648 ✉ isola@softhome.net 🖥 www.go.to/isola
Gay culture club. Library with videos. Cinema, parties.

Italy | Genova ▶ Girifalco - Catanzaro

GENOVA - Via Sampierdarena, 167R
Tel. 010 - 645 45 55 - ore 22.00 - 04.00 chiuso lunedì Info 0347 - 357 56 56

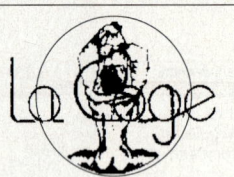

La Cage

AMERICAN BAR - SNACKS - VIDEO - CIRCOLO ARCI GAY

BARS
■ **Aqua Club** (AC B f G MA P VS) 21-3 h, closed Tue
Salita Salvatore Viale 15/R ✉ 16129 *(from Via XX Settembre)*
☎ 010 58 84 89
Uno Club card required.
■ **Cage. La** (AC B BF D DR f G MA P VS) 22-4 h, closed Mon
Via Sampierdarena 167/R ✉ 16131 *(Bus 20/1)* ☎ 0347 35 75 656 (Infoline)
Uno Club Card required.

DANCECLUBS
■ **Altra Notte Extreme. L'** (AC B D DR GLM MA snu WE) Sat & before holidays 23-5 h
Via di Francia 28, 16011 Arenzano (Autostrada Genova ▶ Savona, exit Arenzano, after 100 m on the right, under La Culletta Restaurant. 100 m a destra, sotto ristorante La Culletta) ☎ 0347 35 75 656 (Infoline)

RESTAURANTS
■ **Bruno** (b F g) 12-15. 19.30-22.30 h
Vico Casana 9/1 ✉ 16100 *(first floor)* ☎ 010 24 76 307

SEX SHOPS/BLUE MOVIES
■ **Magic America** (CC g p) Closed on Mon morning
Via Teodosia 7/R ✉ 16129 ☎ 010 31 67 83
■ **Seventeen** (g) 10-13, 15.30-22, Wed -21.30 h
Piazza Verdi 1-4/R ☎ 010 57 00 451
Gay articles, condoms, videos, books & magazines.
■ **Seventeen** (g) 12-24, Wed -21.30 h
Corso Gastaldi 173 ✉ 16131 ☎ 010 52 20 841
Gay articles, condoms, videos, books & magazines.

CINEMAS
■ **Centrale** (g) 14.30-24 h
Via S. Vincenzo 13/R ☎ 010 58 03 80
■ **Cristallo** 14-22 h
Largo della Zecca 1/R ✉ 16100 ☎ 010 25 10 574
■ **Gioiello** (AC g MA tv) Mon-Fri 10.30-24, Sat-Sun 14.30-24 h
Via Balbi 101/R ☎ 010 26 13 51

SAUNAS/BATHS
■ **Aqua Club** (AC B DR f G MA P SA SB VS WH) 15-24 h, closed Tue
Salita Salvatore Viale 15/R ✉ 16129 *(Bus 20, near Via XX Settembre)*
☎ 010 58 84 89
Mixed age sauna with a separate bar.

NEWS STANDS
■ **Kiosk/Rivendita Giornali** (g) 0-24 h
Piazza de ferrari 32/R ✉ 16125

HOTELS
■ **Mini Hotel** (b g H)
Via Lomellini 6/1 ✉ 16124 ☎ 010 24 65 876 ☎ 010 24 65 803
✉ minihotel@tin.it
Rooms with bath, gays welcome/Gay ben accetti.

GENERAL GROUPS
■ **CGIL Liguria - Ufficio Nuovi Diritti Sportello Gay/Lesbico/Trans** Mon Wed Fri 9-13 h
Via San Giovanni d'Acri 6 ✉ 16152 ☎ 010 60 28 213
☎ 010 60 28 200 ✉ liguria.nuovidiritti@mail.cgil.it
🌐 www.liguria.cgil.it/Nuovi%20Diritti/index.htm

HEALTH GROUPS
■ **Anlaids "Alberto Terragna"** Wed 15-18 h
Piazza Embriaci 3/1 ✉ 16123 ☎ 010 25 14 242 📠 010 25 14 242
■ **LILA - Lega Italiana Lotta contro l'Aids** Mon-Fri 10-12, 13-17 h
Via Milano 58/B1 ✉ 16126 ☎ 010 24 62 915 ☎ 010 24 64 543

SPECIAL INTEREST GROUPS
■ **Crisalide - Arcitrans** (TV)
☎ 0339 68 45 584 ☎ 0347 81 05 031
✉ crisalidearcitrans@supereva.it
🌐 www.crisalidearcitrans.tsx.org
Transsexual group.
■ **Liberi.tutti** (G)
☎ 0347 96 63 095 ☎ 0335 54 83 592 ✉ liberi.tutti@inwind.it
Gay & lesbian cultural association/Associazione culturale gaylesbica.

SWIMMING
See Pieve Ligure.
-Spiaggia Nudista-Varigotti (near Savona: from Noli in direction of Varigotti)

CRUISING
-Mura delle Cappucine and Giardini Coco (gardens) (AYOR) (near/adiacente Galliera hospital)
-Via Moresco (on the riverbank by night)
-Punta Vagno (Giardini Govi) (near the water clearing plant Corso Italia by day)
-Via Avio (behind the railway station, r AYOR)
-Via Sampierdarena, near "La Cage" (by car, at night)

Girifalco - Catanzaro ✉ 88024

CINEMAS
■ **Ariston** (g)
Via della Repubblica ✉ 88024 ☎ 0968 74 90 33

624 SPARTACUS 2001/2002

Godega di Sant'Urbano - Treviso ✉ 31010

SAUNAS/BATHS
■ **Hobby One** (AC B DR f G MA MSG P p SA SB SOL VS WH) 16-2, holidays 15-1, summer: 20-2 h
Via Leonardo Da Vinci 4 ✉ 31010 *(Behind "Manhattan" discotheque)* ☎ 0438 38 82 56
Video in the dry heat sauna.

Gorgonzola - Milano ✉ 20064

HEALTH GROUPS
■ **Network Nazionale "Gruppo C" Progetto di Ricerca Aids**
✉ 20064 ☎ 029 51 31 06
Helpline for people with HIV/Aids

Grosseto ✉ 58100

SWIMMING
-Marina di Alberese (wonderful natural landscape, many gays, crowded)
-Marina di Grosseto (along the SS 322 "delle Collacchie", 3 miles south of Castiglione delle Pesciaia, near "Le Marse" camping)

CRUISING
-Around the city wall

Ischia - Napoli ✉ 80070

GUEST HOUSES
■ **Sabina - Bed & Breakfast** (BF H)
Via Campagnano 20 ✉ 80070 ☎ 081 90 11 79 📠 081 99 14 14
Private villa in a lovely location on the island Ischia (near Napoli). Transfer from and to the harbour.

CRUISING
Harbour in Porto on the left side near lighthouse
-Maronti beach behind hotel La Jondola

Isole Tremiti - Foggia ✉ 71040

CRUISING
-Nudist beach/spiaggia nudista (best July, September/meglio luglio/settembre)

Ispra - Varese ✉ 21027

CRUISING
-Beach: follow directions for Diva Venus disco; path on the left (NU)

Ivrea - Torino ✉ 10025

SEX SHOPS/BLUE MOVIES
■ **Videoclub XXX** (g VS)
Via Aosta 35 ☎ 0125 49 328

CRUISING
-Piazza Freguglia
-Piazza del Rondolino, close to/vicino del Cinema Sirio (by car/in macchina)
-Corso Re Umberto, Giardini Lungodora (on foot, evenings/a piedi, di sera)

Jesolo - Venezia ✉ 30020

BARS
■ **Movida** (B D g) Fri-Sun 22-3 h, only in summer
Via Belgio 149 ✉ 30020 ☎ 0421 96 17 19

SWIMMING
-Isola del Morto • Eraclea (Punta Sabbioni, 18km from Jesolo Lido. After "Camping Marina di Venezia" or better between the camping and the lighthouse. Dunes)

CRUISING
-Via Berlino / Via Firenze

La Spezia ✉ 19100

CINEMAS
■ **Diana** (g)
Via Sapri 68 ✉ 19100 ☎ 0187 73 71 79

CRUISING
-Public gardens/Giardini Pubblici (from the Garibaldi monument to the end of the harbour/dal monumento a Garibaldi fino alla capitaneria di porto)

Lanciano - Chieti ✉ 66034

SWIMMING
-Spiaggia Le Morge

L'Aquila ✉ 67100

CRUISING
-Castle/Castello

Latina ✉ 04100

GENERAL GROUPS
■ **Collettivo Di Cultura Omosessuale** Wed 21-23.30 h
c/o PRC, Piazzale Trampolini 33 ✉ 04100 ☎ 0773 66 24 76
Political gay group, telephone helpline.

CRUISING
-Railway Station/Stazione FS (Piazzale del Palazzetto dello Sport)
-Viale Michelangelo
-Via dei Mille

Lecce ✉ 73100

BARS
■ **Nostromo** (B D GLM MA P VS) Sat 23-5, Sun 21-3 h
Via Vincenzo Morelli 25 ✉ 73100 *(500 m from the station, behind the dome/dietro al Duomo)* ☎ 0329 41 75 935 *(infoline)*

SWIMMING
-San Cataldo (Coming from Lecce turn left to "La Darsena")

CRUISING
-Viale Oronzo Quarta (all day)
-Via Petraglione (Car cruising)
-Camera di Commerce (Via Petraglione by night by car)

Lecco ✉ 23900

CINEMAS
■ **Marconi** (g)
Viale Dante 32 ✉ 23900 ☎ 0341 36 27 31

CRUISING
-Railway Station/Stazione FS
-Lungolago (only in summer)

Legnago - Verona ✉ 37045

GENERAL GROUPS
■ **Arcigay Arcilesbica Legnago** Wed 21-23 h
c/o Riccardo Facchin, Piazza della Liberttà 10 ✉ 37045
☎ 036 83 83 72 24
Local section of Arcigay-Arcilesbica, political and cultural activities/sezione locale dell'Arcigay-Arcilesbica, attività politica e culturale.

Legnano - Milano ✉ 20025

CRUISING
-Via Milano and park nearby/e parco vicino

Livigno ✉ 23030

BARS
■ **Art Café** (B glm H) 16-2 h
Via Pozz 20 A ✉ 23030 ☎ 0342 97 08 00
Anche appartamenti turistici in affitto/Also apartments for tourists to rent.

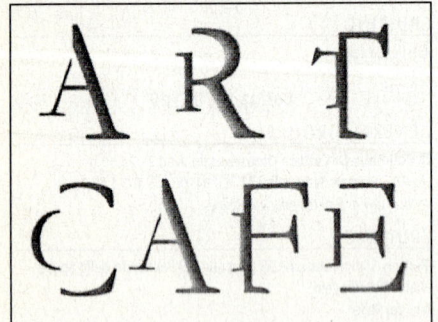

Livorno ✉ 57100

RESTAURANTS
■ **Germoglio. Il** (F g) in the evening only
Via della Campana 31 ✉ 57100 ☎ 0586 88 071
Vegetarian cuisine only.

CINEMAS
■ **Jolly** (g)
Via Michon ✉ 57100
X-rated movies.

SWIMMING
-Sassoscritto (NU) on the cliffs (9 miles south of Livorno, near restaurant Sassoscritto, at km 304 marker on the Aurelia road)

CRUISING
-Piazza Dante (r) (in front of railway station (22-2 h)
-Zona industriale Picchianti (highway exit Livorno Centro. Follow centre indications. At the Circus, drive to Picchianti Industrial Area. In the open area, at night.)
-Lungomare dell'Ardenza (on the seaside, near Bagni Fiume, south of the Naval Academy, in the afternoon and at night, on foot, on the seaside and on the steps)

Lucca ✉ 55100

CINEMAS
■ **Mignon** (g)
Piazza San Quirico ✉ 55100 ☎ 0583 49 65 26
X-rated movies.
■ **Nazionale** (g)
Via Vittorio Emanuele ✉ 55100 ☎ 0583 53 435
Sometimes interesting encounters.

CRUISING
-Hospital, Via Delano Roosevelt e strade adiacenti/and streets nearby (by car at night)
-Porta Elisa (inside of the city walls, near the ramparts, on the right side of the city gate, by foot)

Macerata ✉ 62100

CRUISING
-Sferisterio (summer/estivo)
-Public gardens/giardini pubblici

Malcesine - Verona ✉ 37018

SWIMMING
-Scogli delle Gallerie (State road to Riva del Garda, park your car at the last tunnel before Torbole. Then follow the path and go to the little beaches, nudity, action on the paths, from Verona take the APT Bus 63/Statale per Riva del Garda, scendere per un sentiero all' ultima galleria prima di Torbole; spiaggette per naturisti, azione sui sentieri, da VR prendere il Bus APT 63)

Maleo - Milano ✉ 20076

CRUISING
-Ponte (bridge on the road to Cremona/sul fiume adda strada per Cremona)

Manfredonia - Foggia ▶ Milano | **Italy**

Manfredonia - Foggia ✉ 71043
CRUISING
-Sea coast/Lungomare (near the castle and in the gardens; also on the beach/vicino al castello e nei giardini, anche in spiaggia)

Mantova ✉ 46100
SEX SHOPS/BLUE MOVIES
■ **Tuttisensi** (g MA VS) closed Mon morning
Via Vivenza 70 ✉ 46100 ☎ 0376 26 35 02

HEALTH GROUPS
■ **Network Nazionale "Gruppo C" Progetto di Ricerca Aids**
✉ 46100 ☎ 0376 77 11 60
Helpline for people with HIV/Aids

CRUISING
-Piazzale Palazzo Te (at night/di notte)

Marcelli di Numana - Ancona ✉ 60026
CRUISING
-Foce del Fiume Musone (during the day at the beach and in the forest/di giorno sulla spiaggia e nella foresta)

Marina di Bibbona - Livorno ✉ 13046
SWIMMING
-Nudist beach (G) (2 km south of Marina di Bibbona, near the camping)

Marina di Carrara ✉ 54036
CRUISING
-Tenuta di Marinella, Piazzale Camion (Via G. da Verazzano, along the seaside)
-Pineta (pine tree woods in the docks area)
-Pineta di Villa Ceci (Villa Ceci's pinetree wood, via Marco Polo)
-Scogliera di Levante (between the end of the river Lavello and the Molo di Levante (southernmost harbour). Summer only)

Marina di Cecina - Livorno ✉ 57023
SWIMMING
-Quagliodromo (NU) (beach in the area)

Marina di Pisa ✉ 56013
SWIMMING
-Calambrone (among sand dunes of the shore, half-way between the former children health resorts and the effluent canal. Daytime only)
-Spiaggia Libera Comunale (between Tirrenia and Marina di Pisa, near the US Army beach)

CRUISING
-Pine tree wood (By day only. Get in the first pine-tree wood you find while driving along Bigattiera Road from Pisa)

Marina di Ravenna - Ravenna ✉ 48023
SWIMMING
-Tratto Costiero (between Marina di Ravenna and Punta Marina, among the dunes and in the pine forest. Be discreet!/fra Marina di Ravenna e Punta Marina, fra le dune e nella pineta. Discrezione!)

Merano/Meran - Bolzano/Bozen ✉ 39012
BARS
■ **Ponte Romano** (B YG) 18-1 h, closed Wed
Via Ponte Romano/Sommerpromenade 3 ✉ 39012

SEX SHOPS/BLUE MOVIES
■ **Beate Uhse International** (CC glm) 9-19 h, Sun closed
Via Leonardo da Vinci 32 ✉ 39012 ☎ 0473 27 09 21

CRUISING
-Gardens and avenue around railway station/giardini di fronte alla stazione
-Path between Ponte Romano and Ponte Tappeiner/passeggiata del Passirio (R)

Meransen - Bolzano/Bozen ✉ 39037
HOTELS
■ **Pension Sonnenheim** (BF F g H) All year
Meransen 90 ✉ 39037 ☎ 0472 52 01 57
Rooms with bathroom/WC, balcony, phone & fax

Mestre ✉ 30170
☞ **Venezia**

Milano ✉ 20100

★ The industrial city of Milan is the second largest city in Italy (approx. 1.300.000 inhabitants and over 4.000.000 when including the inhabitants in the outskirts) and also the country's economic centre. Milan is also known as the fashion and media metropolis. Many gay publications come from here. An example is "Babilonoa" and the monthly "Guide Magazine" and "Pride", all to be found in many gay establishments.
Milan is also Italy's gay capital city. The gay scene here is has a more north European influence than any other city in Italy. Very colourful and open minded. The most attractive men in Italy are to be found here!
A gay hotel has recently opened here (unusual for Italy), as well as a gay-lesbian restaurant in the "gay street" Via Sammartini, close to the central station. Many mixed parties are held here and enjoying great popularity. But also the leather and "bear" fans are able to have fun too!
The majority of establishments are able to be reached via the Underground / Subway system. Milan is well worth a visit!

★ Die Industriestadt Mailand ist als zweitgrößte Stadt Italiens (ca. 1.300.000 Einwohner, der Großraum umfaßt jedoch fast 4.000.000 Einwohner) das wirtschaftliche Zentrum des Landes. Doch auch als Mode- und Medienstadt ist die Metropole bekannt. Ein Großteil der schwulen Publikationen wird hier verlegt, wie u.a. das Traditionsmagazin "Babilonia" und die Monatsmagazine "Guide Magazine" und "Pride", die in den meisten schwulen Einrichtungen ausliegen.
Mailand kann getrost als die schwule Hauptstadt Italiens bezeichnet werden. Die schwule Szene wirkt sehr viel "nordeuropäischer" als in den meisten anderen italienischen Städten, sie ist dabei sehr bunt und offen. Die schönsten Männer Italiens tummeln sich hier!
Seit kurzem gibt es auch ein schwules Hotel (nicht unbedingt üblich

Italy — Milano

in Italien) und ein lesbischwules Restaurant in der "Gay Street" Via Sammartini in Bahnhofsnähe. Gemischte Parties mit einem hohen Anteil von Lesben und Schwulen erfreuen sich großer Beliebtheit. Doch auch die "leather"- und "bear"-Liebhaber kommen auf ihre Kosten. Die verschiedenen Lokale sind meist gut mit der U-Bahn erreichbar. Mailand ist also allemal eine Reise wert.

Milan, ville industrielle et poumon économique de l'Italie, est la deuxième plus grande cité du pays (environ 1'300 000 habitants, presque 4'000 000 y compris la banlieue). Elle bénéficie d'une réputation internationale en tant que métropole de la mode et des médias. Une grande partie des publications gaies sont d'ailleurs produite ici, que ce soit le magazine traditionnel "Babilonia" ou les mensuels "Guide Magazine" et "Pride" distribués largement dans les établissements gais.

Milan peut être considérée comme la capitale homosexuelle de l'Italie. La scène gaie, contrairement au reste du pays, s'apparente par sa diversité et son ouverture à celle d'autres villes du nord de l'Europe: ce n'est d'ailleurs pas pour rien que l'on trouve dans la cité lombarde les plus beaux hommes d'Italie!

Depuis peu, on trouve près de la gare dans la célèbre rue gaie, la Via Sammartini, un hôtel et un restaurant pour homosexuels. Les fêtes mixtes avec une majorité de gais et lesbiennes sont ici très courues (par exemple Gasoline ou Magazzini Generali). Ceux qui préfèrent la scène cuir ou "nounours" ne resteront néanmoins pas sur leur faim. Les nombreux lieux gais sont tous bien desservis par le métro. Comme vous le constaterez par vous-même, Milan mérite bien plus qu'un détour.

La ciudad industrial de Milán, segunda ciudad más grande de Italia (ca. 1.300.000 habitantes; el área metropolitana de Milán tiene casi 4.000.000 habitantes), es el centro económico del país, pero también es famosa como ciudad de la moda y de los medios de comunicación.

Una gran parte de las publicaciones gays se editan en Milán, como por ejemplo la revista de tradición "Babilonia" así como las revistas gays mensuales "Guide Magazine" y "Pride", expuestas en la mayoría de las sitios y instituciones gays.

Milán puede llamarse, sin lugar a dudas, 'capital gay de Italia'. El ambiente gay de esta ciudad es mucho más como en el norte de Europa que en el resto de las ciudades italianas, y a la vez es una ciudad multicolor y muy abierta. ¡Los hombres más guapos de toda Italia están aquí!

Desde hace poco hay un hotel gay (algo no realmente habitual en Italia) y un restaurante gay-lesbiano en la 'calle gay', Vía Sammartini, cerca de la estación. están muy de moda las fiestas mixtas con un gran porcentaje de gays y lesbianas. También los amantes del cuero, de los bigotes y los pechos velludos encuentran lo que desean.

A la mayoría de los locales gays de Milán puede irse en Metro. Milán siempre merece un viaje ...

La città industriale di Milano è per grandezza la seconda d'Italia (circa 1.300.000 abitanti, con la periferia arriva ai 4.000.000 di abitanti) e il centro economico del paese. La metropoli è anche conosciuta come città della moda e dei media. Una sostanziosa parte di pubblicazioni gay vengono pubblicate qui, p.e. il famoso mensile "Babilonia", il "Guide Magazine" e il "Pride", che si possono trovare nelle maggior parte dei locali gay.

Milano può essere definita la capitale gay d'Italia. La scena gay assomiglia più a quella nordeuropea rispetto a quella di altre città italiane: qui la scena è molto più variegata e aperta. Gli uomini più belli d'Italia si aggirano da queste parti!

C'è da notare anche un hotel gay (il che non è molto usuale in Italia) e un ristorante gay e lesbico nella "gay street" Via Sammartini, nelle vicinanze della stazione. Molto amati sono i party misti con una alta percentuale di gay e lesbiche. Ma anche per i fans dei "leathers" e dei "bears" (orsi) ci sono buone possibilità. I diversi locali sono ben raggiungibili con la metropolitana. Vale insomma la pena di fare una "capatina" a Milano.

GAY INFO

■ **Altro Martedì. L'** Tue 22-23 h, FM 101,5 and 107,6 MHz
c/o Radio Popolare, Via Stradella 10 ☎ 02 29 52 41 41
■ **Centro di Iniziativa Gay (C.I.G.)** Mon-Fri 17-20 h
Via Bezzecca 3 ✉ 20135 (courtyard/cortile) ☎ 02 54 12 22 25
📠 02 54 12 22 26 ✉ cig_milano@libero.it
Political and cultural activities, conferences, 28th June Festival, international library and archive, anti-Aids programme, coordination with Milan universities gay groups./Attività politiche e culturali, conferenze, festa 28 Giugno, archivio e biblioteca internazionale, attività anti-Aids, punto di conttato per i gruppi gay delle università milanesi.
■ **Speed Demon**
✉ speeddemon@galactica.it
Antagonistic queer 'zine./ Queer 'zine antagonista.
■ **Up City (Gay Map)**
Echo Communication, via San Nicolao 10 ✉ 20123
☎ 02 890 159 401 📠 02 890 139 41 ✉ info@echoteam.it
🌐 www.upcity.it
Gay map. Available in all gay venues/Disponibile in tutti i locali gay.

PUBLICATIONS

■ **Pride**
c/o C.I.G., Via Bezzecca 3 ✉ 20135
Internal newspaper of C.I.G.

CULTURE

■ **Biblioteca, Videoteca, Centro di Documentazione** Wed 21-24 h
c/o C.I.G., Via Bezzecca 3 ✉ 20135
Books videos library & documentation centre.

TOURIST INFO

■ **A.P.T.**
Via Marconi 1 ✉ 20123 ☎ 02 72 52 41

BARS

■ **After Line** (AC B f D GLM YG) 18-2 h
Via G. B. Sammartini 25 ✉ 20100 (Metro Stazione Centrale)
☎ 02 66 92 130
Very busy Disco-bar/ Molto frequentato. Thu 'Single-Party', Fri go-go-boys, Sun striptease.
■ **Argos Bar** (AC B d DR f Glm lj MA P snu VS) 22-3, Fri-Sat-6 h
Via Resegone 1/Via Lancetti ✉ 20158 (Bus 90,91,92/Tram 3/Ferrovia circolare-Lancetti) ☎ 02 60 72 249
Weekly parties, male striptease on Tue, Thu and Sun. Disco bar.
■ **Birreria Uno Alternativa. La** (AC B f GLM YG) 19.30-3 h
Via Borsieri 14 ✉ 20154 (Metro-Garibaldi) ☎ 02 69 00 32 71
"Alternative" pub and internet café.
■ **Cocksucker** (B DR G LJ P VS) Fri Sat 23-4 h
Via Derna 15 ☎ 02 26 82 57 12
Dress code. Sun theme parties. Arcigay membership required. Bar will close in early 2001.
■ **Company Club** (AC B DR G lj P VS) Sun-Thu 22-3, Fri-Sat 22-6 h, Mon closed
Via Benadir 14 ✉ 20132 ☎ 02 28 29 481
Three darkrooms. Arcigay membership required.
■ **Cuore Bar** (A AC B glm MA) 18-2 h
Via Gian Giacomo Mora 3 ✉ 20135 (near Colonne di S. Lorenzo/Tram 3) ☎ 02 58 10 51 26
Very popular, but only few gays.

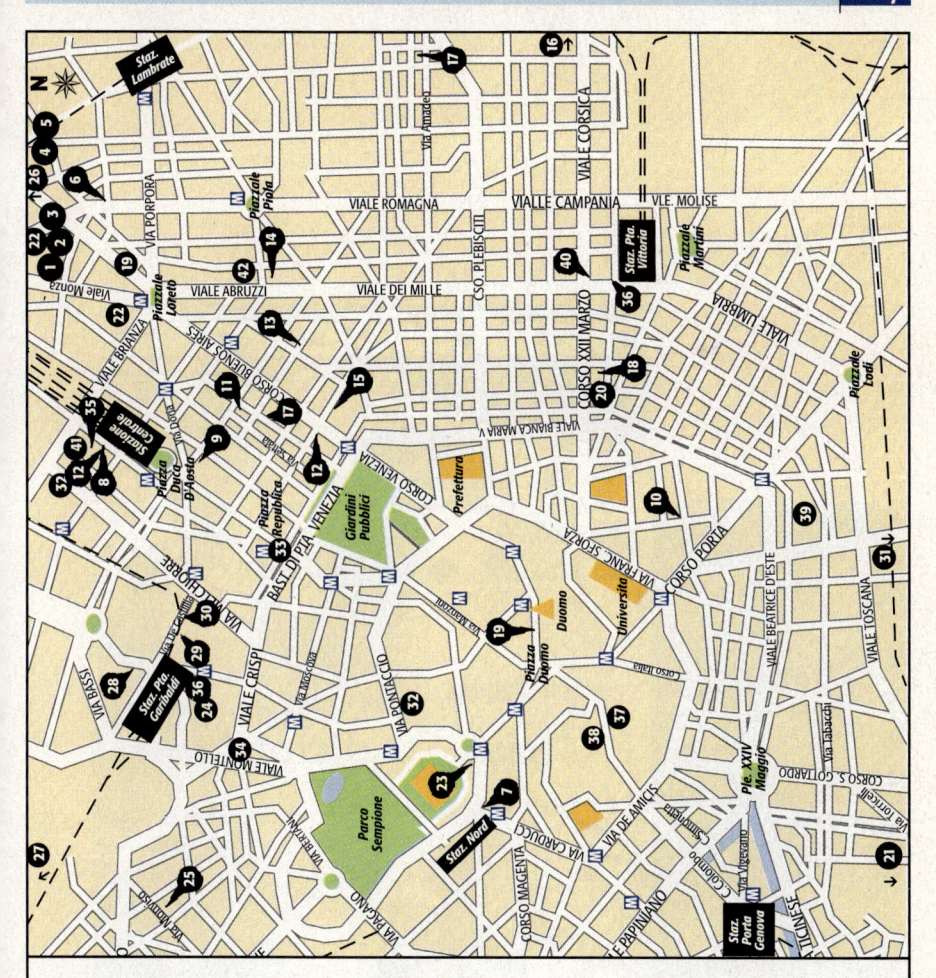

Milano

#	Name	#	Name	#	Name
1	Alexander's Club Sauna	15	Erotika Video & Sex Shop	29	Querelle Bar
2	One Way Danceclub	16	Billy's Holiday Danceclub	30	Nuova Idea Int. Danceclub
3	Company Club	17	HD Danceclub	31	Magazzini Generali Danceclub
4	Transfer Danceclub	18	Thermas Sauna	32	Pape' Sata'n Danceclub
5	Cocksucker Bar	19	Partiqular Danceclub	33	Ricci Bar
6	Hotel Durante	20	Centro d'Iniziativa Gay Switchboard	34	L'Edicolaccia News Stand
7	Libreria & Galleria D'Arte Babele	21	Teddy Sauna	35	Erotika Video & Sex Shop
8	Afterline Bar / Restaurant Hot Line	22	Gate Danceclub	36	Plastic Danceclub
9	Know How Sex Shop	23	Segreta Danceclub	37	Sex Sade Sex Shop
10	Il Girasole Bar	24	Gasoline /G.T.D. Danceclub	38	Gallery -A Fashion Shop
11	Hotel Charly	25	Uiti Bar	39	Castro Gift & Pride Shop
12	Next Groove Café	26	Sauna 13 24	40	Hotel America
13	Magic Sauna	27	Argos Bar	41	Metró Milano Club Sauna
14	Il Sottomario Giallo Danceclub	28	Due Amici Restaurant	42	Cruising Canyon Men's Club

THE FIRST ITALIAN GAY MAGAZINE

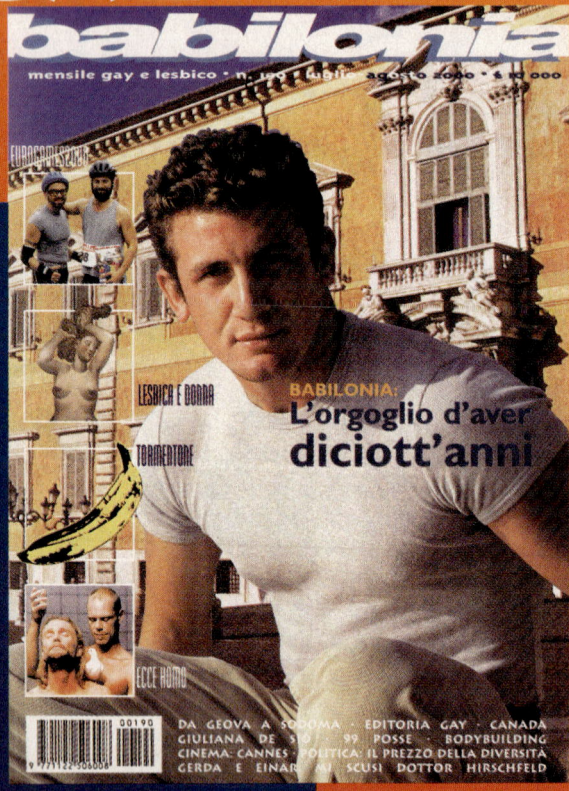

BABILONIA EDIZIONI
Via Astura, 8
I-20141 Milano
Italy

telefono 0039 02 5696468
fax 0039 02 55213419
e-mail babilonia@iol.it
web www.babilonia.net

Milano | Italy

babele*galleria*

**in the centre of milan
a new gay & lesbian space**

cultural events – contemporary art:

— photography
— painting
— sculpture
— performances

for info
www.libreriababele.it
info@libreriababele.it

via San Nicolao 10 - MILANO
(metro 1-2 Cadorna)

■ **Girasole. Il** (A AC B BF F GLM S YG) 7-22 h
Via Lamarmora 19 ✉ 20122 *(near to Porta Romana, Metro Crocetta, Tram 4, Bus 77)*
☎ 0347 89 19 759 *(Infoline)*
Tavola fredda/Sandwiches etc. Happy hour 18.30-21.30 h
■ **Next Groove Café** (A AC B BF f glm YG) 12-2 h
Via Sammartini 23 ✉ 20125 *(metro Stazione Centrale)*
☎ 0328 81 29 338 *(Infoline)*
■ **Querelle** (AC B GLM lj p s) 21-1.30, Fri Sat -3 h, Mon & Tue closed
Via de Castillia 20 ✉ 20100 *(Metro Gioia)*
☎ 02 68 39 00
Cabaret shows on Wed. Arcigay Membership card required/tessera Arcigay.
■ **Recycle** (B GLM S) Wed-Sun 21-1 h
Via Calabra 5 ✉ 20158 *(Bus 90/91/92/Tram 3/Ferrovia circolare)*

Lancetti) ☎ 02 37 61 531
Lesbian discobar, mixed on Wed and Thu. Internet access, cabaret, concert and pool.
■ **Ricci Bar** (B BF f GLM MA YG) 8.30-2 h
Piazza Della Repubblica 27/Via Pisani
   ✉ 20124 *(Metro-Piazza della Repubblica)*
   ☎ 02 66 98 25 36
Popular after 22 h. Trendy bar with DJ.
■ **Uiti Bar** (B G R) 20.30-2 h, Tue closed
Via Monviso 14 ✉ 20100 *(Metro Porta Garibaldi)* ☎ 02 34 51 615
■ **Zelig Café** (AC B f glm MA OS s YG) 21.30-2 h, closed Mon
Viale Monza 140 ✉ 20126 *(Metro-Gorla)* ☎ 02 27 00 13 93
From Oct to May: Dragshow on Fri with very famous comedians, Jazz music on Tue and Latin American music on Thu.

festival
internazionale di cinema
gaulesbico
international lesbian & gay film festival

15th EDITION

MILANO
30/5/01 - 4/6/01

BOLOGNA
4/6/01 - 8/6/01

0516.446.902 | 0254.122.225 | marzig@energy.it | www.cinemagaylesbico.com

Italy | Milano

www.upcity.it
the best of gay city map

Maps to the most important italian cities are update each month. Maps will be located in all clubs and pubs. Entertainment, clubs parties and events going on in town!

Le mappe delle città più importanti d'Italia con guida aggiornate mensilmente. Le trovate in tutti i locali gay!

For information and publicizing:
Echo communication Via S. Nicolao 10 – 20123 Milano
Tel. 0039 02 89015940-1 Fax 0039 02 89013990

MEN'S CLUBS

■ **Cruising Canyon** (AC CC DR G MA) 0-24 h
Via Paisiello 4 ✉ 20124 (Metro Loreto/ Metro Piola)
☎ 02 20 40 42 01 ☎ 0347 - 89 49 419 (Infoline)

Huge cruising area on 3 floors, drinks available. Very popular/Ampio spazio cruising su 3 livelli, molto frequentato. Arcigay membership required.

DANCECLUBS

■ **bar partiqular** (a AC B CC D DR Glm s) Wed 23-4 h
c/o Q, Via Padova 21 ☎ 02 28 00 15 15
House music.

■ **Billy's Holiday** (B CC D G MA OS) Sat 23-5 h, only Jun to Sep
c/o Spider Disco, Via Circonvallazione Idroscalo (near to airport Linate, Bus 73) ☎ 0335 83 27 777 (Infoline)
"Gay happy park": Dancing in a park, animation and cruising.

■ **Gasoline** (AC B CC D glm S YG) Thu 23-5 h
Via Bonnet 11a (Metro Garibaldi) ☎ 0335 66 94 781 (Infoline)
Rock and pop music. Nice place, nice people.

■ **Gate** (AC B DR F G S VS YG)
Via dei Valtorta 19 ✉ 20127 (Metro Turro) ☎ 0339 31 35 712 (Infoline)
Arcigay membership required.

■ **G.T.D. - Gay Tea Dance** (! AC B D CC G S YG) Sun 17-22 h, Closed in Jul-Aug
c/o Gasoline, Via Bonnet 11a (Metro Garibaldi) ☎ 0347 22 01 024 (Infoline)
Mixed music: House, 70s and 80s. Popular with young people.

■ **HD** (AC B D G MA s) 23-3 h, Wed Thu Sun closed
Via Tajani 11/Via Caruso ✉ 20133 (Bus 61, Entrance/entrata in Via Caruso) ☎ 02 71 89 90
Small but nice/piccolo e carino. Men's strip on Mon, Cabaret show on Sat.

■ **Magazzini Generali** (B D glm YG) Fri Sat 23-4 h
Via Pietrasanta 14 ☎ 02 55 21 13 31
Gay night "Jetlag" on Fri/serata gay "Jetlag" venerdì. House music and more.

■ **Nuova Idea International** (AC B D glm MA OS s tv) Thu-Sun 22.30-3, Sat -4 h
Via de Castillia 30 ✉ 20124 (Metro Gioia) ☎ 02 6900 78 59
Two dance halls, one disco and one with band /Due piste, una disco e una di liscio con orchestra. Cabaret, drag shows, striptease on Thu.

■ **One Way Club** (AC b D DR G lj MA P VS) Fri-Sat 23-4.30 h
Via Felice Cavallotti 204, Sesto S. Giovanni (Metro Sesto-Marelli, Sesto Rondo) ☎ 02 24 21 341
Arcigay membership or ID required/tessera Arcigay.

■ **Pape' Sata'n** (! AC B D G YG) Sun 23-4 h
c/o Heaven, Via Fiori Chiari 14 ✉ 20121 (Metro Lanza)
☎ 02 72 02 18 41
Very trendy house party.

COCKSUCKER

the Bar will be closed down beginning 2001

Via Derna, 15 - Milano - Italy
Metro 2 Cimiano

Open every:
Friday & Saturday 23h-4h

ARCI card required

tel (+39)02.26.82.57.12

Milano **Italy**

COMPANY CLUB
WELCOME TO THE
VIA BENADIR Nº 14 - MILANO - 02/28.29.481

■ **Plastic** (B D DR glm MA s SNU TV VS YG) 23.30-4, Fri Sat 24-6 h, closed Mon Wed & Aug
Viale Umbria 120 ✉ 20135 *(Tram 12, 24, Bus 92)*
☏ 02 73 39 96
3 dance floors: garage, pop and easy listening.

■ **Segreta Disco Club** (AC B D DR GLM MA P s) Wed Fri-Sat 22.30-? h, closed Aug
Piazza Castello 1 ✉ 20123 *(Metro-Cairoli)* ☏ 02 86 99 71 42
Tue shows and discobar. Very popular on Sat, quite expensive.

■ **Sottomarino Giallo. Il** (B D GLM p s) 22.30-? h, closed Mon Tue, Wed Thu Fri Sun (GLM), Sat Lesbian only
Via Abruzzi 48/Via Donatello 2 ✉ 20131 *(Metro Loreto)* ☏ 0347 11 02 209 (Infoline)
Shows on Fri, live music on Sun.

■ **Transfer Club** (B D DR lj MA PI VS) Every day 22-5 h bar, Fri Sat 23-6 h disco, Mon closed
Via Breda 158 *(M Villa S. Giovanni)*
☏ 02 27 00 55 65
Arcigay membership required.

RESTAURANTS

■ **Due Amici** (B F g OS) 8-16, 18.30-3, Sat -6 h
Via Borsieri 5 ✉ 20159 *(Metro Garibaldi, exit Gugliemo Pepe)*
☏ 02 66 84 696
Nice garden in summertime.

■ **Hot Line** (AC b BF CC F GLM) 18-2 h, closed on Tue
Via Sammartini 23 ✉ 20125 *(100 m from the railway station/della stazione centrale, Metro Stazione Centrale)* ☏ 02 67 07 20 48
Pub restaurant.

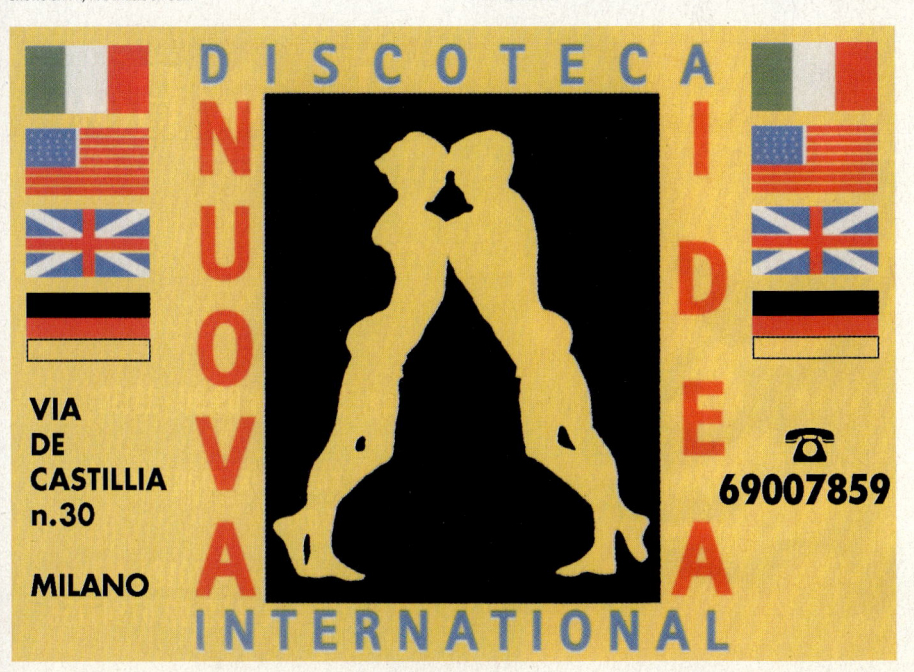

DISCOTECA NUOVA IDEA INTERNATIONAL

VIA DE CASTILLIA n.30
MILANO

☏ 69007859

SPARTACUS 2001/2002

Italy — Milano

sexSade
fetish & fantasy
via s.Maria Valle, 1 ang. via Torino
20123 Milano Italy
Tel. +39 02.80.48.80 www.sexsade.it

mask SM
shoes
lingerie
gadget
leather wear
rubber
PVC
latex

■ **Lady Ristorante** (B F glm H) Tue-Sat 20-24 h, closed Mon Sun
Via Settala 48 *(Metro Lima)* ☎ 02 29 51 06 58
■ **Risotteria. La** (b CC F g) 20-23 h, closed Sun
Via Dandolo 2 ✉ 20122 ☎ 02 55 18 16 94

SHOWS

■ **Alexander Cabaret** (B glm MA S) 23-2 h, Mon striptease, shows Wed-Sun
Via Ronzoni 2 *(Area Navigli)* ☎ 02 89 40 23 30
■ **Sei Favolosa Anche Tu**
Via Carlo Imbonati 5 ✉ 20159 ☎ 0329 45 10 693 (Infoline)
Arts & Show Dario Enriquez & Maurizio Conti. Nation-wide popular cabaret and theatre show with more than 30 of the best drag and theatre actors in Italy. Available every week in the best locations. See gay magazines for dates and addresses.

SEX SHOPS/BLUE MOVIES

■ **CO.Sta.srl** (g) 9-13.30, 14.30-18 h, Sat Sun closed
Via Temperanza 6 ✉ 20127 *(Metro Pasteur)* ☎ 02 28 98 195
Sale only for sex shops/Solo vendita all'ingrosso per sexyshop.
■ **Erotika Video Shop** (G) Mon-Sat 9-21 h
Via Sammartini 21 ✉ 20125
☎ 02 67 38 04 04
■ **Erotika Video Shop** (g) Mon-Sat 9-21 h
Via Melzo 19 ✉ 20129 ☎ 02 29 52 18 49 *(Metro Porta Venezia)*
■ **Europa 92** (g) Mon-Sat 9-19.30 h
Viale G.B. Sammartini 21 *(Metro-Stazione Centrale)* ☎ 02 66 93 217
Gay articles, videos, magazines, rubber and leather articles.
■ **Europa 92** (g) Mon-Sat 9-21 h
Viale G.B. Sammartini 25 *(Metro-Stazione Centrale)*
☎ 02 66 98 24 48
Gay articles, videos, magazines, large offer of rubber and leather articles.

Studio Know How
entertainment

SKH entertainment

l'unico sexy shop interamente gay d'Italia

open: Monday - Saturday 09:30 - 19:30

videos latest releases magazines
toys... and much more

via Antonio da Recanate, 7 - 20124 Milano
tel. +39 02 67391224 - fax +39 02 67847756

Milano | Italy

Accendi il fuoco che è in te!

scegli...

EROTIKA VIDEOSHOP

Videocassette originali da tutto il mondo, articoli erotici, riviste d'importazione, biancheria intima, abbigliamento, vendita per corrispondenza.

20129 Milano, Via Melzo 19 - (zona C. Buenos Aires)
Tel. 02.29.52.18.49 - Fax 02.29.51.06.81
20121 Milano, Via Sammartini 21 - (a fianco Stazione Centrale) - Tel. 02.67.38.04.04
10126 Torino, Via Belfiore 20 - (a 100 mt. Stazione Porta Nuova) - Tel. 011.65.79.44

APERTI TUTTI I GIORNI SABATO COMPRESO DALLE h 9.00 ALLE h 21.00

Italy Milano

SAUNA 13-24

the biggest sauna in milan

via Oropa 3 - Milano - tel. 02 28 51 05 28

Milano | Italy

■ **Maxi Sexy Shop** (g) Mon 14.30-19.30, Tue-Sat 9.30-19.30 h
Via Andrea Doria 48 ✉ 20124 ☎ 02 67 06 420

■ **Sexsade** Mon 15-19.30, Tue-Sat 10-13, 14.30-19.30 h
Via S. Maria Valle 1/Via Torino ✉ 20123 (M Missori, M Duomo, Tram 2/3/14) ☎ 02 80 48 80

■ **Studio Know How Entertainment** (G) Mon-Sat 9.30-19.30 h, Sun closed
Via Antonio da Recanate 7 ✉ 20124 (M° Centrale F. S.)
☎ 02 67 39 12 24
Gay articles, videos; also mail order/Articoli gay, video; anche vendita per corrispondenza.

■ **Yamato Shop** (g)
Via Lecco 2 ✉ 20124 ☎ 02 29 40 96 79
Japanese gay videos and more.

CINEMAS

■ **Ambra** (g) 14-24 h
Via Clitumno/Via Padova ✉ 20123 ☎ 02 26 82 26 10

■ **Roxy** (G r)
Corso Lodi 129 ✉ 20100 ☎ 02 56 92 304

■ **Zodiaco** (g) 14-23.30 h
Via Padova 179 ☎ 02 25 67 602

ESCORTS & STUDIOS

■ **Gianluca Escort** (G msg R) Mon-Fri 17-24, Sat Sun 10-24 h
☎ 0339 50 21 595

■ **Massimo Escort** (G msg R) Mon-Fri 17-24, Sat-Sun 10-24 h
☎ 0339 86 86 633

■ **Stefano Escort** (G msg R) Mon-Fri 17-24, Sat-Sun 10-24 h
☎ 0347 22 05 716

SAUNAS/BATHS

■ **Alexander's Club** (B f G SA SOL WS) 14-1, Fri Sat -2, Fri Sat
Alexander's Bar 2-5 h
Via Pindaro 23 ✉ 20128 (Metro Villa S. Giovanni)
☎ 02 25 50 220
Arcigay card required/Tessera Arcigay. Two floors.

■ **Magic Sauna** (B f G msg SA SB SOL VS) 11-24 h, closed Tue, Summer: 10-24 h
Via Maiocchi 8 ✉ 20129 (4th floor/4° piano) ☎ 02 29 40 61 82
Terrace with bar. In Aug also open on Tue.

■ **Metrò Milano Club** (! AC CC B DR f G P SA SB VS WH YG) 14-2 h
Via Schiapparelli 1 ✉ 20100 (Metro-Stazione Centrale)
☎ 02 66 71 90 89
Popular sauna frequented by a young crowd.

■ **Teddy** (AC b DR f G msg P SA SB VS WH) 11.30-24 h, closed Wed
Via Renzo e Lucia 3 ✉ 20142 (Bus 59/95/Metro-Famagosta)
☎ 02 84 66 148
English, French, German, Spanish spoken. Behind/Dietro Hotel dei Fiori. Monthly meetings of "Magnum" (4th Sat of the month). Arcigay membership required/Tessera Arcigay.

■ **Thermas** (! AC B f DR G SA SB SOL VS WH WO YG) 12-24 h
Via Bezzecca 9 ✉ 20135 (Tram 9/29, Bus 60/73, Metro-Duomo)
☎ 02 54 50 355
Friendly, hygienic, comfortable, young atmosphere.

■ **13 24** (! AC B DR G P SA SB SOL VS WH WO YG) 13-24 h
Via Oropa 3 (Metro Cimiano) ☎ 02 28 51 05 28
3 piani/3 floors. The biggest sauna in Milano. Open since November 2000.

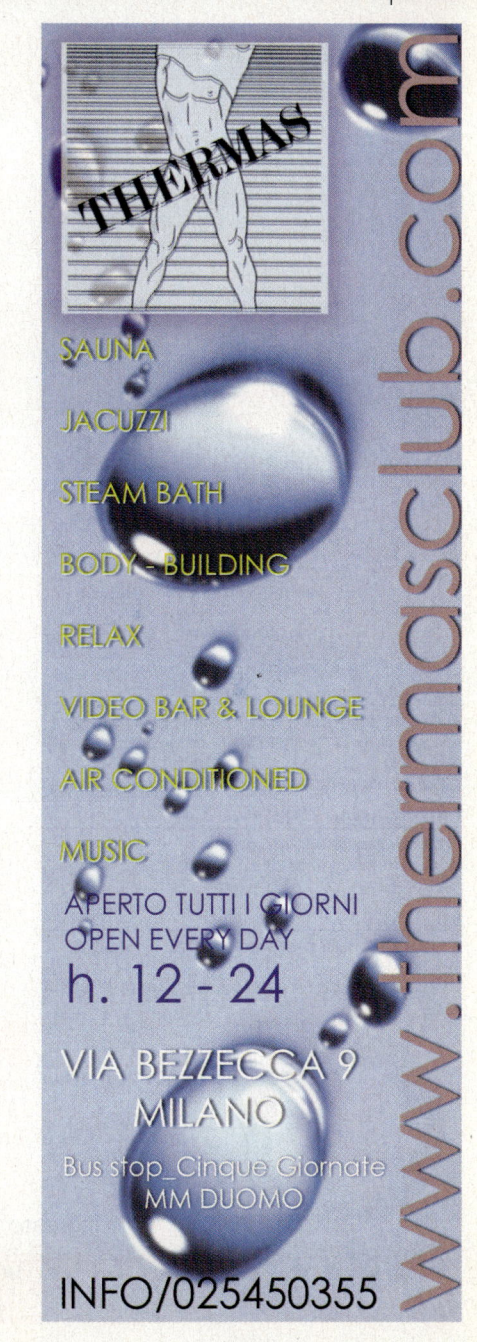

THERMAS

SAUNA
JACUZZI
STEAM BATH
BODY - BUILDING
RELAX
VIDEO BAR & LOUNGE
AIR CONDITIONED
MUSIC

APERTO TUTTI I GIORNI
OPEN EVERY DAY
h. 12 - 24

VIA BEZZECCA 9
MILANO

Bus stop_Cinque Giornate
MM DUOMO

INFO/025450355

www.thermasclub.com

Italy | Milano

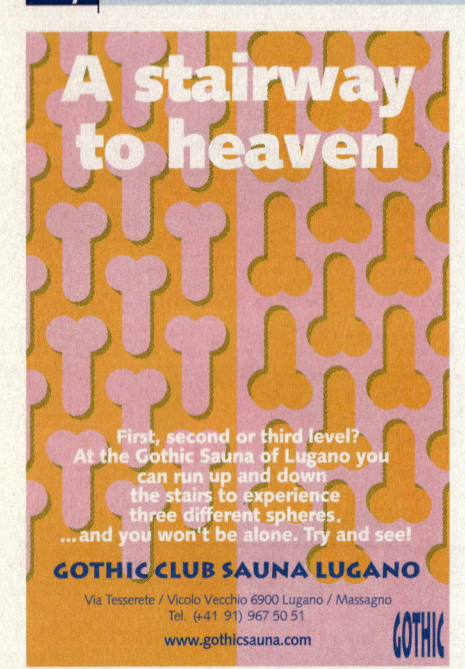

A stairway to heaven

First, second or third level?
At the Gothic Sauna of Lugano you can run up and down the stairs to experience three different spheres.
...and you won't be alone. Try and see!

GOTHIC CLUB SAUNA LUGANO
Via Tesserete / Vicolo Vecchio 6900 Lugano / Massagno
Tel. (+41 91) 967 50 51
www.gothicsauna.com

MASSAGE
■ **Massimo** (GLM MA msg) 11.30-18.30 h, closed Sun and Aug
Via Carlo Goldoni 38 ✉ 20129 *(Metro Porta Venezia)*
☎ 02 70 10 52 77
15% discount for 10 massages./Sconto 15% per 10 massagi.

BODY & BEAUTY SHOPS
■ **Giemme Parrucchieri** Mon-Sat 9-19 h
Via Gian Battista Vico 10 ✉ 20100 ☎ 02 48 19 32 22
Hair dresser.

BOOK SHOPS
■ **Libreria & Galleria d'Arte Babele** (CC GLM) Tue-Sun 10-19, Mon 14-19 h
Via S. Nicolao 10 ✉ 20123 *(Metro Cadorna)* ☎ 02 86 91 55 97

Milan's only completely gay and lesbian book and video shop. English and French spoken. Also order by catalogue. Art gallery in the basement.
■ **Mondadori** (G) Mon-Sat 9.30-23, Sun 10.30-23 h
Corso Vittorio Emanuele 24/26 *(Metro-San Babila)*
☎ 02 76 00 58 33
Large gay section with books and magazines.

FASHION SHOPS
■ **BUBA International Designer** Tue-Sat 9.30-13, 15-19.30 h, Mon 15-19.30 h
Via Spallanzani 6 ✉ 20100 *(Metro Venezia, near to C.so Buenos Aires)* ☎ 02 29 40 96 34
Fashion and accessories.
■ **Gallery-A** (CC g) Mon 15-19.30, Tue-Sat 10-13, 14.30-19.30 h
Piazza S. Giorgio/Via Torino ✉ 20123 *(Near the Dome, Metro Duomo/Tram 2/14/3)* ☎ 02 80 53 252

GIFT & PRIDE SHOPS
■ **Castro Market** (CC GLM) Tue-Sat 9.30-19.30 h
Via San Rocco 5 ✉ 20135 *(Metro Porta Romana)* ☎ 02 58 43 08 98
The only shop with gay & pride merchandise in Italy. Music, cds, videos, underwear, pridewear, guides and magazines.

LEATHER & FETISH SHOPS
■ **Nino Zari** (G)) Tue-Sun 10-19, Mon 14-19 h
Via San Nicolao 10 ✉ 20123 *(inside the bookshop Babele, Metro Cadorna)* ☎ 0333 22 80 719 Laboratory and shop for leather and s/m articles,/Officina hard: articoli pelle, cuoio, metallo personalizzati.

NEWS STANDS
■ **Edicolaccia Edicola e Libreria. L'** (g VS) 0-24 h
Piazza Baiamonti 1 ✉ 20154 ☎ 02 33 60 85 16
Large number of video and imported magazines.

TRAVEL AND TRANSPORT
■ **Arco Turismo** (CC GLM)
Via San Nicolao 10 ✉ 20123 *(Metro Cadorna)* ☎ 02 72 09 42 51
🖨 02 86 46 11 93 💻 arcoturismo@libero.it
Gay & lesbian travel agency in the bookshop Babele.
■ **Ircam Viaggi**
Via de Amicis 44 *(Metro-S. Ambrogio)* ☎ 02 86 91 54 75
🖨 02 86 91 19 37

HOTELS
■ **America** (AC BF CC GLM H)
Corso XXII Marzo 32 ✉ 20135 ☎ 02 73 81 865 🖨 02 73 81 490
💻 info@hotelamericamilano.com
💻 www.hotelamericamilano.com
Single room Lit 50.000-60.000, Double room 80.000-120.000, phone, TV. Central location. The only gay hotel in Milan. Really nice staff. Animation.

METRÒ MILANO
via Schiaparelli, 1 Tel. +39 02 66 719 089

Sauna Finlandese
Bagno Turco / Steam Bath
Idromassaggio / Whirlpool
Camerini Relax / Private rooms

Messagge Serv.
Video X X X
Snack Video Bar
Air Cond.

Ingresso riservato ai soli soci
All Major Credit Cards Accepted — UNO CLUB CARD

www.metroclub.it
SAUNE MILANO · PADOVA · VENEZIA

libreria babele galleria
MILANO — VIA SAN NICOLAO 10
METRO 1-2 CADORNA
www.libreriababele.it
tel. 0039 02 86915597 fax 0039 02 86910001
libreria
book shop
galleria d'arte
art gallery
agenzia viaggi
travel agency
abbigliamento leather
leather shop
gay & lesbian book shop
BOOKS VIDEOS MAGAZINES POSTERS
POSTCARDS GAYGUIDES GADGETS
ARCO TURISMO
TRAVEL AGENCY
IGLTA MEMBER
• MILANO
• ROMA
opening BOLOGNA - TORINO
e-mail: arcoturismo@libero.it
tel. 0039 02 72094251 fax 0039 02 86461193
www.arcoturismo.it
NINO ZARI
leather shop
www.ninozari.it
tel 0039 (0)333 22 80 719

Italy Milano

il primo negozio tutto gay
Castro market

via San Rocco, 5 (MM3 Porta Romana)
MILANO – Tel. 02.58430898
gay pride merchandise • gifts
cd • underwear • clubwear • video
accessories • magazines • bear & leather pride • guide

www.castromarket.it

■ **Hotel Charly** (B BF CC g H)
Via Settala 76 ✉ 20124 *(Metro-Lima, Tram 1/33/60, 3 min from central station)*
☎ 02 20 47 190 📠 02 20 47 190 💻 charlyhotel@mclink.it
💻 www.italaabc.it/az/charly
Rates single Lit 80.000 to 110.000, double 130.000. to 160.00 TV/Video, phone

■ **Hotel Durante** (CC H g OS)
Piazza Durante 30 ✉ 20131 *(Metro Loreto/Pasteur)*
☎ 02 26 14 50 50 ☎ 02 28 27 673 📠 02 26 14 50 50
💻 ycram5@iol.it
All rooms with WC, television and telephone. Single Lit. 80.000 to 90.000, double Lit. 110.000 to 125.000. Nice hotel with small garden.

GENERAL GROUPS
■ **Agedo - Associazione Genitori Parenti e Amici di Omosessuali** Thu 14-17 h
☎ 02 54 12 22 11 💻 agedo@geocities.com
💻 www.geocities.com/WestHollywood/8788

FETISH GROUPS
■ **Leather Club Milano** (G LJ)
PO Box 3750 ✉ 20090 ☎ 0338 81 52 396
💻 lcmilano@leatherinitaly.com 💻 www.leatherinitaly.com
1st Sat every month in the company club. Member of ECMC.

L'edicolaccia

NON STOP 24 ORE SU 24 NON STOP

APERTA TUTTI I GIORNI

Vasta esposizione di videocassette e riviste d'importazione

LIBRERIA   **EDICOLA**

20154 Milano, P.zza Baiamonti 1
Tel. 02.33.60.85.16

Milano | Italy

hotel America

Corso XXII Marzo 32 (4°piano)
tel. 02 7381865 fax. 02 7381490
e-mail: info@hotelamericamilano.com

from Station Centrale FS: bus 60 - 92
from Airport Linate: bus 73
from the center - Terminal Malpensa: tram 27

HOTEL DURANTE

All rooms with shower, telephone and satellite TV

Video on request • Open 24 hours

"MIXED CLIENTELE - GAYS WELCOME"

PIAZZA DURANTE, 30 - 20131 MILANO
TEL./FAX +39/02/26145050, +39/02/2827673

■ **Magnum Club**
PO Box 17140 ✉ 20128 ☎ 0347 43 27 489 (Infoline)
Girth & Mirth/Orsi.

HEALTH GROUPS

■ **Anlaids**
Via Koristka 3 ✉ 20154 ☎ 02 33 60 86 01 📠 02 33 60 86 85
Helpline on Wed 18-20 ☎ 33 60 86 83.
■ **A.S.A. - Associazione Solidarietà AIDS** Mon-Fri 9-19, Sat -14 h
Via Arena 25 ✉ 20125 *(Metro S. Agostino)* ☎ 02 58 10 70 84
📠 02 58 10 64 90 🖳 asa@asamilano.org 🌐 www.asamilano.org
Information, advice, psychological and legal advice, self-help groups for HIV-positives, documentation centre/Informazioni, consulenze, assistenza psicologica e legale. gruppi di auto-aiuto per sieropositivi, centro documentazione.
■ **LILA - Lega Italiana Lotta contro l'Aids** Hotline Mon-Fri 9-13, 14-18 h
Via Tibaldi 41 ✉ 20136 ☎ 02 58 10 35 15 ☎ 02 89 40 08 87
📠 02 89 40 11 11 🖳 lila@ecn.org
🌐 www.ecn.org/flash/lilamilano
Prevention, information, street work project for prostitutes. Legal and psychological counseling, self-help group.

■ **Nucleo Operativo Prevenzione Aids**
Via Fiamma 6 ☎ 02 73 83 370 ☎ 02 73 82 765
HIV test by appointment, psychological support.

HELP WITH PROBLEMS

■ **Dott. Salvi** Mon-Sat 9-20 h
Via Ponte Seveso 39 ✉ 20125 *(Metro Centrale F. S.)*
☎ 02 25 35 385 ☎ 03 30 46 29 11
English spoken, français parlé. Astrology, tarot, indian massage/Astrologia, tarocchi, massaggi indiani, shiatzu.
■ **Istituto Gay Counseling** Mon-Fri
☎ 02 83 23 465
Therapy and counseling for individuals, couples and groups.

RELIGIOUS GROUPS

■ **Gruppo del Guado** Wed 21-23 h
Via Pasteur 24 *(Metro Pasteur)* ☎ 02 28 40 369
Group of gay Christians/gruppo gay cristiani.

SPECIAL INTEREST GROUPS

■ **Joy** Mon 15.30-18.30, Fri 15.30-17.30 h
Università degli Studi, Via Festa del Perdono 3 *(Auletta "A")*
Gay student group.

CRUISING
CANYON
24h/24h
7giorni/7 giorni
open all days
ingresso riservato soci arciUno
VIA PAISIELLO 4
20124 MILANO
INFOLINE:
02 20 40 42 01

Milano ▸ Modena — Italy

FRIENDLY STAFF + COMFORTABLE ROOMS

HOTEL CHARLY MILANO
VIA SETTALA 76

ROOMS WITH SHOWER
T.V. SATELLITE + V.C.R.
DIRECT DIAL TELEPHONES

BAR + COFFEE LOUNGE
CREDIT CARDS ACCEPTED
OPEN 24 HOURS

3 MIN. FROM CENTRAL STATION
METRO 1 - LIMA
METRO 2&3 - STAZIONE CENTRALE

INFO & RESERVATIONS
TEL/FAX + (39) 02.2047190
E-MAIL: CHARLYHOTEL@MCLINK.IT
WWW.ITALIAABC.IT/AZ/CHARLY

■ **Triangolo Silenzioso**
c/o C.I.G., Via Bezzecca 3 ✉ 20135
Deaf gay group.

SPORT GROUPS

■ **A.T.OMO Associazione Tennisti OMOsessuali** Every 1st and 3rd Mon 21-23 h
Piazza Risorgimento 6 ✉ 20129 ☎ 0338 36 64 921 (Infoline)
🖳 info@atomoitalia.org 🖳 www.atomoitalia.org
Gay tennis group.

■ **GATE Volley Milano** Mon & Fri 21-24 h
☎ 0347 263 14 40 (Lucio) 🖳 gatevolley@yahoo.com
🖳 www.geocities.com/gatevolley
Gay volleyball group.

■ **Gruppo Pesce Milano-Milan Swimming Group** Infoline: Mon-Fri 18.30-20.30 h
☎ 0347 25 02 410 (Infoline) 🖳 info@gruppopesce.org
🖳 www.gruppopesce.org

■ **Kaos Milano**
Via Sismondi 6 ☎ 02 70 12 36 07 ☎ 0338 37 62 341 (18-23 h)

🖳 kaosac@tiscalinet.it 🖳 www.tiscalinet.it/kaosmilano
Gay soccer team.

■ **Kukami**
☎ 0347 844 84 51 (Davide)
Running and athletics/atletica e corsa.

■ **SCIG (Sci Milano)**
☎ 02 58 10 03 99 📠 02 83 94 604 🖳 scig_grupposci@yahoo.it
🖳 www.geocities.com/skigroup-it
Gay skiing group.

SWIMMING

- Abbiategrasso-River Ticino (On Milano-Vigevano road, 30 km, [P] at bridge; walk for about 2 km southwards down east bank; action everywhere and NU/Sulla strada Milano-Vigevano, 30 km, [P] prima del ponte. Camminare circa 2 km verso sud sulla sponda est. Azione dapertutto, NU)
- Piscina 'Romano' (Via Ampere, Metro-Piola, in summer; gay zone is between showers and restroom)

CRUISING

- Metro Porta Garibaldi
- Metro Lambrate, Al Bagni della Stazione FS
- Central railway station/Metro Stazione Centrale (ayor r)
- Piazza Trento (R)
- Ortomercato/Via Monte Cimone (by car, at night/sera)
- Via Novara (AYOR) (at Bosco in Città by night)
- Piazza Leonardo Da Vinci (in the garden on the square at night)
- Parco Nord (AYOR) (near Viale Fulvio Testi, by night)
- Idroscalo park (AYOR r) (east side/Lato Est. Segrate, night and day in summer)
- La Fossa (Viale Zola along the northern railway, cruisy day and night, very busy)

Mirandola - Modena ✉ 41037

CRUISING

- Piazzale G. Marconi (behind the/dietro il Teatro Nuovo)
- Via Spagnola (at night, cruising by car/di notte, in macchina)

Modena ✉ 41100

RESTAURANTS

■ **Millemiglia - Formula 3** (B F glm s)
Via S. Paolo 1 ✉ 41100 *(near Parco del Viale)* ☎ 059 21 81 30
Parties or shows on Thu and Sun.

SEX SHOPS/BLUE MOVIES

■ **Magic America** (CC g p) Closed on Mon morning
Via San Giovanni Bosco 212 ✉ 41100 *Near/vicinanza Stabilimento Maserati)* ☎ 059 36 45 58

CINEMAS

■ **Adriano** (g)
Via Selmi/Corso Canalchiaro 57 ✉ 41100 ☎ 059 21 91 41

■ **Odeon** (g)
Piazza Matteotti 9 ✉ 41100 ☎ 059 22 51 35

GENERAL GROUPS

■ **Arcigay Matthew Shepard** Tue 16-19 h
c/o Arci, Via Giardini 476/n ✉ 41100 ☎ 059 35 31 91
☎ 0348 76 69 298 (Infoline) 🖳 arcigaymodena@yahoo.it

Italy | Modena ▶ Napoli

CRUISING
- Railway Station/Stazione FS (also in the gardens/anche nei giardini)
- Giardino Ducale
- A1 Milano ⇌ Roma P Castelfranco at km 177
- Under Cialdino flyover (Viale Monte Kosica, Via Dogali, coach station)
- Via Minutara in front of Aeronautica Militare
- P New Palasport
- Viale dello Sport (facilities outside Iperoop)
- P at public swimming pool Pergolesi

Modica ✉ 97015

HEALTH GROUPS
■ **Anlaids** Medicalline: 9-14 h
Via Fosso Tantillo 14/A ✉ 97015 ☎ 093 27 61 934
☎ 093 29 06 554 (Medicalline) 📠 093 27 61 934

Molfetta - Bari ✉ 70056

CRUISING
- Villa Comunale (especially at night/specialmente di notte)
- Molo del Porto (R) (sometimes harbor workers/alle volte scaricatori del porto)

Monte Isola - Brescia ✉ 25050

HOTELS
■ **Residence Vittoria** (B F glm H OS)
Via Sensole ✉ 25050 ☎ 03 09 88 62 22 📠 03 09 88 62 22
Hotel located directly by the Lago d'Iseo. Nice view. All studio apartments have private bath/kitchenette and balcony overlooking the lake. Own small beach.

Montecatini Terme - Pistoia ✉ 51016

DANCECLUBS
■ **Area Disco Club** (AC B D F GLM H MA OS PI s) Sat 23-4.30 h
Via Pietre Cavate ✉ 51016
☎ 0572 82 016
"Freedom" gay disco night. Week-end ticket: dinner + disco + bed + bf.

CRUISING
- Park around Terme Tettuccio
- In front of railway station

Montesilvano - Pescara ✉ 65016

DANCECLUBS
■ **Alter Ego** (AC B D G) Thu Sat 23-?, last Sun 21-? h
Via Napoli 27 ✉ 65016 ☎ 0854 45 50 37

Monticiano ✉ 53015

CRUISING
- Bagni di Petriolo, Terme d'acqua calda/hot spring water in river itself driving along the National Road 233 from Siena, after 25 km, follow Bagni di Petriolo headings. P near the old Thermal Building, before the bridge on the Farma river. Go down to the river, on the left side of the road (especially gay in the night but staye discreet)

Monza - Milano ✉ 20052

CRUISING
- Piazza Carducci (Centro Elettronico Comunale)
- Viale Reale (WE) (on the left side of the building/all sinistra)
- Railway Station/Stazione FS

Napoli ✉ 80100

DANCECLUBS
■ **Animamia** (B D Glm) Thu 23-? h
c/o Chez-moi, Via del Parco Margherita 13 ✉ 80100
☎ 0347 76 12 337 (Infoline)
Mixed music.
■ **Bar B** (AC B d DR f G MA P s SNU VS) Sat 22.30-5.30 (G), Sun 22.30 h-? (glm)
Via Giovanni Manna 14 ✉ 80133 *(near the university and railway station)*
☎ 081 28 76 81
Disco bar with a video room and a labyrinth.
■ **Exess Disco Club** (AC B D GLM MA S) only in winter, Sun 22-?
Via Martucci 28/30 *(Metro-Piazza Amedeo)*
☎ 0339 54 77 466 (Infoline)
■ **Freezer** (AC B bf CC D f GLM OS P s VS WE YG) Only on Fri, 23-4 h, closed in august
Centro Direzionale Isola G6 ✉ 80100 *(near to the central railway station)*
■ **New Age** (AC B d DR f GLM MA P s VS) 21.30-3 h, closed Mon
Via Atri 36 ✉ 80137 *(centre, Metro Pzza. Cavour)*
☎ 081 29 58 08
Discobar with darkroom.

Napoli | Italy

BLU ANGELS

- LA PRIMA SAUNA PER SOLI UOMINI AL SUD •

LA PRIMA MINIPISCINA IDROMASSAGO IN ITALIA
ALL'INTERNO UN BAGNO TURCO

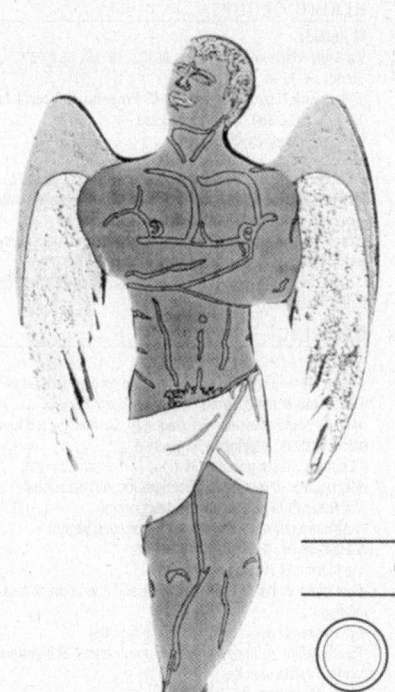

SAUNA FINLANDESE

IDRODOCCIA

BAR

DARK ROOM

2 SALE VIDEO

MASSAGGI RELAX

PULIZIA DEL VISO

LABIRINTO

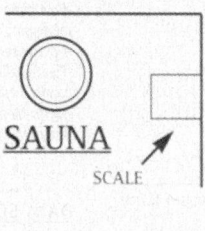

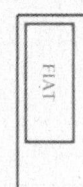

• NAPOLI - CENTRO DIREZIONALE •
ISOLA A/7 - TEL. 081 / 562 52 98

| Italy | Napoli ▶ Nettuno - Roma |

NEW AGE DISCO BAR
Via Atri, 36
NAPOLI
081.295808
0338 3208587
APERTO TUTTO L'ANNO
DA MARTEDÌ ALLA DOMENICA
DALLE 21.00
GIOVEDÌ UNIVERSITY NIGHT

■ **Other Side Group. The** (D)
☎ 0338 6175071
Discoclub on Sat from Jun till Sept. Call for Info.

SEX SHOPS/BLUE MOVIES
■ **Follie d'Amore** (g VS) 10-14, 16-20 h
Via Francesco Ierace 12 ✉ 80129 ☎ 081 57 8 76 12
■ **Sexi Shop-C** (g)
Calata San Marco 2-3 ☎ 081 55 16 353

CINEMAS
■ **Argo** (ayor tv)
Via A. Poerio 4 ☎ 081 55 44 764
■ **Eden** (g)
Via G. Sanfelice 15 ☎ 081 55 22 764
Crowded/Frequentato.
■ **Iride** (g OG tv)
Via A. Poerio 7 ☎ 081 28 79 08
■ **Trianon** (g tv)
Piazza Calenda

SAUNAS/BATHS
■ **Bar B** (AC B DR f G MA msg P SA SB VS WH) May-Sept 14-1, Oct-Apr 12-1, Sat Sun -22 h (after 22h discoclub)
Via Giovanni Manna 14 ✉ 80253 (near the university and railway station) ☎ 081 28 76 81
■ **Blu Angels** (A AC B F G MA msg P S SA SB SOL VS WH WO) 14:30-1, Sat & Mon 10-1 h
Centro Direzionale Isola A/7 ✉ 80133 (Near the railway station/Vicino alla stazione centrale) ☎ 081 56 25 298
Three floors, Labyrinth, Pizzeria service, Info HIV/Aids, Concerts, Books/Tre piani, Labirinto, Servizio pizzeria, Info Aids, Concerti, Libri.

HOTELS
■ **Belvesuvio Inn** (B BF d F glm H OS PI SOL)
Via Panoramica F. 40 ✉ 80040 (5 km from airport, 6 km from the station) ☎ 081 77 11 243 📠 081 57 45 051
Room with bf from USD 40. Ranch with horses and other animals. Beautiful garden. Excursions organised.

GENERAL GROUPS
■ **Agedo - Associazione Genitori Parenti e Amici di Omosessuali** Mon 16-19 h
☎ 081 55 18 293
■ **Arcigay Napoli** Mon-Fri 16-21 h
Via San Geronimo 17-20 ✉ 80139 (tram 1/bus R2, C55)
☎ 081 55 28 815 📠 081 55 18 293
📧 adamoeadamo@hotmail.com

HEALTH GROUPS
■ **Anlaids**
Via Santa Maria in Portico 3 ✉ 80122 ☎ 081 68 07 37
📠 081 66 96 79
■ **Network Nazionale "Gruppo C" Progetto di Ricerca Aids**
☎ 081 76 86 300 ☎ 081 70 63 253
Helpline for people with HIV/Aids.

SWIMMING
-Marechiaro Rocks (!) (from via Posillipo-via Marechiaro; mixed)
-Pozzuoli, in the rocks behind the port
-Scogliera di Mergellina (very central, chaotic, frequent contacts, mixed/molto centrale, caotica, incontri frequenti, ma mista)
-Scogliera di Santa Lucia (mixed, but many opportunities/mista, ma molte possibilità)

CRUISING
-Via Brin (by car, busy)
-Piazza Municipio (R TV) (at night, in the gardens in front of Palazzo S. Giacomo/di notte, anche nei giardini davanti)
-Railway Station/Stazione Ferroviaria (p. Garibaldi, good meeting place, hustlers, anytime)
-"Cumana" Railway Station/Stazione Ferroviara (at night)
-Piazza Carlo III (occasional meetings/incontri occasionali)
-Via Acton (R TV) (in the garden/nei giardini)
-Vesuviano railway station/stazione (facilities/bagno)
-Viale Kennedy (R TV) (at night/di notte)
-Via Marina (R TV) (at night/di notte)
-Capodimonte Park (AYOR) (morning and afternoon/matina e pomeriggio)
-Adiacenze Palasport (R TV) (at night/di notte)
-Piazza Bellini (g) (meeting place in summertime at night/punto d'incontro d'estate di notte)
-Metro Mergellina, WC (AYOR)
-Metro Vanvitelli, WC (AYOR)

Nerviano - Milano ✉ 20014

DANCECLUBS
■ **Cinema Vittoria** (B D DR G VS) 17-0.30, Sun 15-0.30 h
Via Casati 5 ✉ 20014 ☎ 0331 58 61 00

Nettuno - Roma ✉ 00048

CRUISING
-Railway Station/Stazione FS
-Piazzale Santa Maria Goretti

Italy

· DISCO BAR ·
bar b
· SAUNA ·

La vera Megasauna per soli uomini aperta tutti i giorni al centro storico (Borgo Orefici) della tua città il Sabato Sera, dalle 22.30 si trasforma in Disco Bar

Sauna - Disco B.. - Bagno Turco - Sala Video - Sauna Finlandese
Mega Dark Room - 20 Sale Relax & Tunnel b...

MASSAGGI GRATIS

ACCESS FOR ONLY MAN
Art Director: DAVID

B.. B - Via G. Manna, 14 - Napoli - Italy
Infoline: 081.28.76.81 - 0338.840.77.69 - fax 081.553.61.41

Italy Nicotera Marina - Cosenza ▶ Padova

Nicotera Marina - Cosenza ✉ 88034

SWIMMING
-Spiaggetta (between Sabbie d'Oro campsite and the Valtur village; very gay and nice in the summer/fra campeggio Sabbie d'Oro e villagio Valtur; molto gay e piacevole d'estate)

Novara ✉ 28100

CRUISING
-Via Raffaele Sanzio
-Gardens (in front of the police station and around the P/giardini davanti alla polizia e altorno P)

Numana - Ancona ✉ 60026

BARS
■ **Act Up-Seven Up** (B d G WE) Fri-Sat
Plazza del Santuario 15 ✉ 60026 ☎ 071 93 11 756

Orbetello ✉ 58015

SWIMMING
- Giannella (20 miles south of Grosseto, along the road from Albinia to Santo Stefano. Beach and busches, crowded day and night.)

Ortona - Chieti ✉ 66026

CRUISING
-Beach/spiaggia "Lido Riccio"

Paderno Fraciacorta - Brescia ✉ 25050

DANCECLUBS
■ **Out Limits Disco** (B D GLM) Fri (women only) Sat 23-4, Sun 22-3 h
Via Ugo Foscolo 2 ✉ 25050 ☎ 0335 608 92 10

Padova ✉ 35100

PUBLICATIONS
■ **Tralaltro**
Via S. Sofia 5 ✉ 35100
Publication of Circolo Tralaltro. Available in the book-shops Feltrinelli.

BARS
■ **Brief Encounter** (AC B d DR f GLM MA P SNU VS) 21-5 h, closed on Mon
Via Settima Strada 5 ✉ 35100 (Exit Padova Est Zona Industriale Nord) ☎ 049 77 60 73
Disco on Tue Fri-Sun.
■ **Flexo Club** (AC B CC DR f G MA P s VS) Wed-Sun 21.30 h - ?
Via N. Tommaseo 96/B ✉ 35100 (500 m dalla stazione/500 m from the railway station, Uscita/exit A 4 Padova Est) ☎ 049 807 47 07
4 piani/ 4 floors. Clubs Team.
■ **Tartan's Birreria** (B f glm) 19-2 h, closed Sun
Via Cesare Battisti 177 ✉ 35100 ☎ 049 875 66 39
■ **Tiratardi** (AC B f glm) 18-2 h, closed Sun and Aug
Via Palermo 20 ✉ 35142 (Bus 5/near Bassanello) ☎ 049 65 20 83
■ **Tropicana Club** (B d DR G) 21-? h
Via A. Da Bassano 3 ✉ 35100 (near the railway station)
☎ 049 86 41 023
South American music.

DANCECLUBS
■ **Why Disco Club** (AC B D DR GLM MA VS) Fri 22-5, Sat 22-6 h
Viale Navigazione Interna 38/A ✉ 35129 (Zona Industriale Nord)
☎ 049 77 64 14
CSEN card required.

RESTAURANTS
■ **Taverna Nane Della Giulia** (A B F glm MA) 12.30-14.30, 20-1 h, closed Mon
Via Santa Sofia 1 ✉ 35100 ☎ 049 66 07 42

SEX SHOPS/BLUE MOVIES
■ **Magic Top Sex Shop** (g) 9.30-12.30, 15-20, 22-1 h, closed Sun & Mon morning
Via Tommaseo 96/C ✉ 35100 ☎ 049 807 24 14
Gay articles, S/M and leather goods, videos, underwear.

CINEMAS
■ **Ducale** (g) 18-24, Sun 16-24 h
Via Facciolati 34 ✉ 35100 ☎ 049 85 01 41

SAUNAS/BATHS
■ **Metrò Padova Club Sauna** (AC B CC DR f G MA P SA SB VS WH) 14-2 h
Via Turazza 19 ✉ 35100 (Bus 9/18-Piazzale Stanga)
☎ 049 807 58 28
Very popular sauna on 500 m² with a biosauna. Customers are mixed, but generally young.

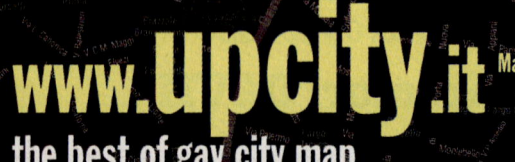

Padova | Italy

METRÒ

PADOVA — via Turazza, 19 Tel. +39 049 807 58 28

- Sauna Finlandese
- Bagno Turco / Steam Bath
- Idromassaggio / Whirlpool
- Camerini Relax / Private rooms
- Messagge Serv.
- Video X X X
- Snack Video Bar
- Air Cond.

Ingresso riservato ai soli soci
All Major Credit Cards Accepted — UNO CLUB CARD

SAUNE MILANO · PADOVA · VENEZIA

www.metroclub.it

Flexo CLUB

PADOVA

- 4 Livelli / levels
- Video bar
- 2 Livelli Darkrooms
- Leather Zone "Bronks"
- Private rooms
- Meeting zone
- Video X X X
- Air Cond.

Ingresso riservato ai soli soci
All Major Credit Cards Accepted — UNO CLUB CARD

VIA N. TOMMASEO, 96b Tel. +39 049 807 47 07

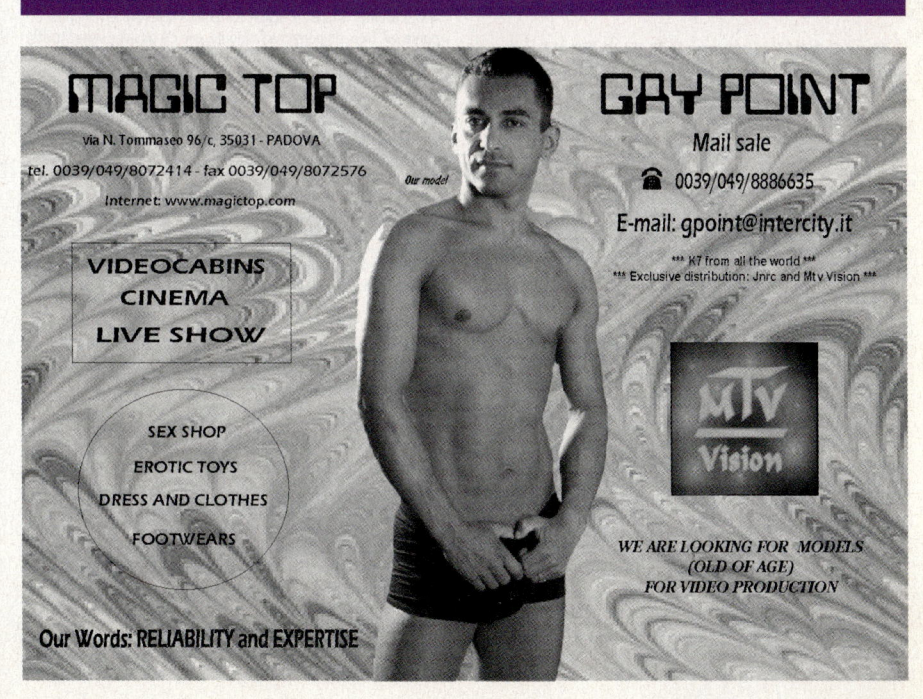

MAGIC TOP

via N. Tommaseo 96/c, 35031 - PADOVA
tel. 0039/049/8072414 - fax 0039/049/8072576
Internet: www.magictop.com

- VIDEOCABINS
- CINEMA
- LIVE SHOW

- SEX SHOP
- EROTIC TOYS
- DRESS AND CLOTHES
- FOOTWEARS

Our Words: RELIABILITY and EXPERTISE

Our model

GAY POINT

Mail sale
☎ 0039/049/8886635

E-mail: gpoint@intercity.it

*** K7 from all the world ***
*** Exclusive distribution: Jnrc and Mtv Vision ***

MTV Vision

*WE ARE LOOKING FOR MODELS
(OLD OF AGE)
FOR VIDEO PRODUCTION*

Italy Padova ▶ Pavia

Miami Club
Aperto tutti i giorni dalle 15.00 alle 1.00
Feste e Spettacoli
A partire da Ottobre
Organizziamo La tua Festa di Compleanno
'Tra i Vapori'
Saune
Massaggi
Solarium
Snack Bar
Via Pellizzo 3 (4° piano) Padova
Tel. 049-776464

■ **Miami Club** (AC B f G MA msg s SA SB SOL VS WH) 15-1 h, closed in Aug
Via Pellizzo 3 ✉ 35128 *(4th floor/bus 15,18)*
☏ 049 77 64 64

BOOK SHOPS
■ **Libreria Feltrinelli**
Via S. Francesco 7 ✉ 35100 ☏ 049 875 46 30

VIDEO SHOPS
■ **Target** (g) 9.30-12.40, 15.30-19.40, Sat -20 h, closed Sun Mon
Piazzale Mazzini 6 ✉ 35137 ☏ 049 876 32 32
Video rental (gay film but no sex videos).

GENERAL GROUPS
■ **Circolo Tralaltro** Meetings Mon 21.30-23, Health counselling Tue 21-23, Youth group Thu 18-20 h
Via S. Sofia 5 ✉ 35100 ☏ 049 876 24 58
📠 049 875 60 05
🌐 www.geocities.com/WestHollywood/2550/pd.htm
Information on HIV, prevention, support. Anonymous free HIV test. Vaccination against hepatitis A B E.

HELP WITH PROBLEMS
■ **Dott. Pasimeni Carmelo**
✉ 35100 ☏ 049 875 87 65
Psychologist.

RELIGIOUS GROUPS
■ **Incontro. L'** Call Tralaltro for information
c/o Evangelic Church, Corso Milano 6 ✉ 35100

CRUISING
- Via Manzoni (AYOR)(Giardini di Pontecorvo)
- Giardinetti di Via Morgagni (AYOR)
- Via Loredan, zona universitaria (TV)
- Via Tommaso Grossi
- Railway Station/Stazione FS (AYOR)

Parma ✉ 43100

DANCECLUBS
■ **Andromeda** (AC B D G MA OS) Sat 22-4 h, closed in Aug
Via Gramsci 5 ✉ 43019 *Soragna (Autostrada A1 Milano-Roma, exit/uscita Fidenza)* ☏ 0335 57 33 604 *(Infoline)*
■ **Boy - Hippopotamus** (AC B D glm s YG) Thu 23-4 h, closed from Jun to Aug
Via E. Lepido 28 ✉ 43100 *(Bus 3, over the/sopra il Bowling Parma)*
☏ 0521 48 38 13

SEX SHOPS/BLUE MOVIES
■ **Magic America** 9.30-12.30, 15.30-20 h, closed Sun and Mon morning
Borgo del Parmigianino 31/D ✉ 43100 *(zona centro vicinanze duomo)* ☏ 0521 20 62 73

CINEMAS
■ **Ritz**
Via Venezia 129 ✉ 43100 ☏ 0521 27 32 72

SWIMMING
- Spiaggia del Taro (after the bridge over the Taro River, walk towards Monte, where the action sometimes takes place/raggiunto il punte sul Taro, dirigerrsi verso Monte, ove c'è qualche volta attività)

CRUISING
- River/fiume Parma (right-hand side)
- Railway Station/Stazione FS (on the square/in piazza)
- Parco Ducale (in summer/d'estate)
- Mercati Generali (R TV) (after 23 h)

Pavia ✉ 27100

BARS
■ **Jolanda** (B f glm MA OS) Mon-Sat 9-24 h *(some gays after 21-24 h)*
Via Rismondo ✉ 27100

HEALTH GROUPS
■ **Network Nazionale "Gruppo C" Progetto di Ricerca Aids**
✉ 27100 ☏ 0382 52 70 67
Helpline for people with HIV/Aids.

SWIMMING
- Lido di Pavia (NU) (P) Lanche)
- Pieve del Cairo (River Agogna: on the road from Pieve del Cairo to Sannazzaro de Burgondi, turn right before bridge over river, continue for 400 m. Beach by the waterfall, mixed.)

CRUISING
- Customs depot/Dogana (AYOR) (Via Donegana, truckers)
- Old railway bridge over river Ticino/Vecchio ponte della ferrovia sul Ticino (until/fino alle 3 h)
- Strada Persa (by car/in macchina until/fino alle 3 h)
- Via Rismondo (around castle at night, on foot and by car/attorno al castello, di notte, a piedi e in macchina)

650 SPARTACUS 2001/2002

Perugia ▶ Piacenza | **Italy**

OASI CLUB SAUNA
APERTO dalle 14.00 alle 24.00
INFOLINE: 085.9500722 – 0335.7022668
PESCARA Marina di Città S. Angelo – Via Saline, 5 – S.S. 16 Adriatica

Perugia ✉ 06100

GAY INFO
■ **Arcigay Arcilesbica "Omphalos"** (B d GLM MA OS P)
Wed, Fri, Sat
Via Fratti 18 ✉ 06123 *(near Piazza IV Novembre)*
☎ 075 57 23 175

BARS
■ **Onphalos** (B D G MA) Wed-Sat 21-? h
Via Fratti 18 ✉ 06100 ☎ 075 57 23 175
Run by Arci Gay

RESTAURANTS
■ **Bocca Mia. La** (A AC CC F NG) 13-14.30, 20-23 h, closed Sun and Aug
Via Rocchi 36 ✉ 06121 ☎ 075 57 23 873

SEX SHOPS/BLUE MOVIES
■ **Paradise Sexy Shop** (g LJ VS) 9.30-13, 15.30-20 h, closed Sun
Via Gerardo Dottori 90, San Sisto ✉ 06100 *(Bus 55, 57)*
☎ 075 52 70 121
Large range of rubber, S/M video./ Vasto assortimento video, gomma, S/M videocassette.

HEALTH GROUPS
■ **Anlaids**
Via Giacomo Matteotti 37 ✉ 06074 ☎ 075 51 71 189

CRUISING
-Piazzale Bellini (in front of/davanti Sant'Anna Station/stazione)

Pesaro ✉ 61100

GENERAL GROUPS
■ **Arcigay Agora** 1st & 3rd Tue 21.30-23.30 h
c/o Verdi, Via Ginevra 11 ✉ 61100 ☎ 0347 33 48 857
☎ 0347 58 75 743

CRUISING
-Piazza Carducci (AYOR) ⓟ at the market)

Pescara ✉ 65100

BARS
■ **Heroes Bar** (B f P)
Via E. Flaiano 21 ✉ 65127 ☎ 085 66 921
Arcigay membership required/tessera Arcigay.

SAUNAS/BATHS
■ **Oasi Club Sauna** (B G MA msg P SA SB VS WH) 14-24 , Sat 14-6
Via Saline 5 ✉ 65013 Marina Città Sant' Angelo *(Highway exit/ Uscita autostrada Pescara Nord, next to/attaccato Sex shop)*
☎ 085 95 00 722
The only gay sauna in this region/ unico locale gay in Abruzzo.

HEALTH GROUPS
■ **Anlaids**
Via Torquato Tasso 29 ✉ 65121 ☎ 085 42 19 428
📠 085 42 20 959

CRUISING
-Porta Nouva station/stazione
-Piazza Salotto
-Piazza Maggio

Piacenza ✉ 29100

DANCECLUBS
■ **Ice** (B CC D DR F GLM OS YG) Sat 23-5 h
c/o Quincy, Via Aguzzafame 87 ✉ 29100 *(highway exit/ uscita autostrada Piacenza Ovest)* ☎ 0349 66 03 914 (Infoline)
■ **Top Secret Club (TSC)** (B d DR Glm MA) Bar: Wed, Thu, Sun 22-?, Disco: Fri Sat 23-? h
Via C. Colombo 87 ✉ 29100 ☎ 0523 60 95 10
Big cruising area in the second floor. Unoclub card required.

CINEMAS
■ **Roma** (g)
Via Capra 48 ✉ 29100 ☎ 0523 32 13 28

GENERAL GROUPS
■ **Agedo - Associazione Genitori Parenti e Amici di Omosessuali**
Mon-Fri 9-17 h
✉ 29100 ☎ 0523 57 10 61
■ **Arcigay Arcilesbica**
Via G. Taverna 137 ✉ 29100 ☎ 0523 49 92 68

SWIMMING
-Beach by the river Po/Spiaggia sul Po (direction Piacenzo-Milano follow signs to C. San Sisto, park your car and walk to the area below the motorway bridges/direzione Piacenza-Milano, seguire frecce C. San Sisto; parcheggiare e raggiungere la zona sotto i ponti dell'autostrada)

Italy | Piacenza ▶ Pisa

SEX & GAY SHOP TENTAZIONI
Pisa Via Rosellini 13 e
Tel. 050 540054

CRUISING
-Girone del Vescovo (under the bridges and motorway-[P], also along the river/sotto i ponti e [P] autostrada, anche lungo il fiume)
-Railway station/Stazione FS (occasional meetings in the garden and in the building/incontri occasionali nell giardino e nell'edificio)
-Piazza della Cittadella
-Bar Bologna (in front of the bar, opposite the railway station/davanti al bar, di fronte all stazione)
-Viale S. Ambrogio
-Monumento al Pontieri (R TV) (on the square/sulla piazzo)
-[P] Fiorenzuola autostrada exit/uscita autostrada
-Lungo Po (meetings between Nino Bixio swimming pool and Via da Feltre/incontri fra piscina Nino Bixio e Via da Feltre)
-Lungo la Foce del Trebbia (YG)

Pinerolo - Torino ✉ 10064

DANCECLUBS
■ **Break** (B D e G MA OS S) Sat 21-3 h
Corso Torino 18 ✉ 10064 ☎ 0121 70 393

SEX SHOPS/BLUE MOVIES
■ **Videoclub XXX** (g VS)
V.le della Rimembranza 32 ☎ 0121 32 30 98

CRUISING
-Piazza Canova (MA)(di sera/evenings

Pisa ✉ 56100

BARS
■ **Absolut** (B GLM s YG)
Via Mossotti 10 ✉ 56100 ☎ 050 55 53 18

RESTAURANTS
■ **Stazione di Ristoro "Leopolda"** (B F glm) 12-14.30, 20-22 h, Sun closed
Piazza Guerrazzi 11 ✉ 56125 *(Near railway station/Vicino alla stazione)* ☎ 050 48 587
Tuscany cuisine/Cucina Toscana

SEX SHOPS/BLUE MOVIES
■ **Tentazioni Sexy Shop** 9.30-13, 16-20 h, closed Sun and Mon morning
Via Rosellini 13/E ✉ 56124 ☎ 050 54 00 54
Biggest gay shop in Tuscany: toys, videos, magazines, leather articles and video cabin.

SAUNAS/BATHS
■ **Siesta Club 77** (AC B DR f G MA P SA SB VS WH) June 1st-10th Sep 20.30-1, 11th Sep-30th May 15-1 h
Via di Porta a Mare 25/27 ✉ 56122 *(500 m from Station/FFSS 500 m circa)* ☎ 050 22 00 146
Sauna on three floors with lots of space to relax. Arci membership required.

BODY & BEAUTY SHOPS
■ **Laura Alberti** Tue-Sat 9-18 h
Via Pardo Roques 4 ✉ 56123 *(near Porta Lucca)* ☎ 050 56 44 84

BOOK SHOPS
■ **Libreria Tra Le Righe**
Via Corsica 8 ☎ 050 83 01 77
Gay books. Bar inside the book-shop. Reductions for ArciGay members.

TRAVEL AND TRANSPORT
■ **Out Travel**
Largo Ciro Menotti 19 ✉ 56127 ☎ 050 31 55 51
🖥 www.outtravel.it
Italian tour operator with online offer in Italy and worldwide.

HOTELS
■ **Royal Victoria Hotel** (B BF CC H OS)
Via Lungarno Pacinotti 12 ✉ 56126 ☎ 050 94 01 11
☎ 050 94 01 80 ✉ mail@royalvictoria.it 🖥 www.royalvictoria.it
Single room Lit 105.000-155.000, Double room 125.000-185.000, bf incl. Historical hotel*** (1837).

GENERAL GROUPS
■ **Info Gay** Wed 21-23, Thu 17-19, 21-23 h
☎ 050 55 56 18
Group for HIV and people with problems. Run by ArciGay Pride!.

Pisa ▶ Porto Recanati - Macerata | **Italy**

HEALTH GROUPS
■ **Anlaids** 9-11-19-22 h
Via Valtriano di Fauglia 40 ✉ 56043
☎ 050 64 41 45 📠 050 64 40 55

SWIMMING
-Tirrenia (g NU) (Beach to the south of Camp Darby's beach/ Spiaggia libera a sud del bagno di Camp Darby)

CRUISING
-Giardini Scotto (G OG) (afternoon)
-Lungarno Guadalongo (along Arno river, by car at night)
-Stazione FS (by day inside the station, at night in the nearby streets as well)

Pistoia ✉ 51100
CRUISING
-Zona industriale Sant'Agostino (by car at night)
-Stazione FS, toilets (AYOR, r)

Poggibonsi ✉ 53036
CRUISING
-[P] at Salceto Area (by night)

Pompei - Napoli ✉ 80045
CRUISING
-Circumvesuviana Railway Station/Stazione FS (R) (police/polizia)
-Villa dei Misteri

Ponsacco - Pisa ✉ 56038
DANCECLUBS
■ **Insomnia** (AC B D GLM OS S) Sat 23-4.30h
Via di Gello ✉ 56038 *(take motorway Firenze-Pisa-Livorno exit Pontedera-Ponsacco)*
☎ 0587 73 39 14

Ponte San Pietro - Bergamo ✉ 24036
CRUISING
-Parco del Fiume Brembo (at the beach on River Brembo/sulla riva del Brembo/last bus of Bus 5/8 from the center of Bergamo AYOR)

Pordenone ✉ 33170
GENERAL GROUPS
■ **Arcigay Arcilesbica Pordenone** Mon Tue (evening)
c/o Casa del Popolo Di Torre, Via Carnaro 10
✉ 33170

CRUISING
-Garden near railway station/giardino vicino alla stazione

Porto Recanati - Macerata ✉ 62017
CRUISING
-Beach (between/fra Porto Recanati and Marcelli di Numana)

HOTEL POSEIDON POSITANO
★★★★

The jewel of the Mediterranean

The swimming pool, sun terrace and outdoor restaurant are surrounded by luscious greenery and overlook one of the most beautiful villages in the world. Our highly trained staff in the Beauty and Fitness Centre will take care of your physical and spiritual well-being.

Via Pasitea 148 • 84017 Positano
Tel. 089/81.11.11 - Fax 089/87.58.33
e-mail: poseidon@starnet.it
Internet: http://www.starnet.it/poseidon

| Italy | Positano - Salerno ▶ Ravenna |

HOTEL VILLA FRANCA POSITANO

WELCOME WELCOME

★★★★

VIALE PASITEA, 318 - POSITANO (SA) ITALY
TEL. (+39) 89 875655 - FAX (+39) 89 875735
INTERNET: http://www.villafrancahotel.it
E-MAIL: hvf@starnet.it

Positano - Salerno ✉ 84017

HOTELS
■ **Hotel Poseidon** (B CC F g H msg OS PI WO) closed Dec-Mar
Via Pasitea 148 ✉ 84017 ☎ 089 81 11 11 📠 089 87 58 33
📧 poseidon@starnet.it 🖥 www.starnet.it/poseidon
Rates double Lit 290.000-330.000 (low-season), 330.000-370.000 (mid-season), 370.000-410.000 (high-season), Also beauty center and gym facilities.

■ **Villa Franca** (AC B BF CC F H msg OS PI SB SOL) closed Nov-Mar
Viale Pasitea 318 ✉ 84017 ☎ 089 87 56 55 📠 089 87 57 35
📧 hvf@starnet.it 🖥 www.villafrancahotel.it
Rates Lit 320.000-400.000.

Potenza ✉ 85100

CRUISING
-Parco Montereale (gardens at the swimming pool and by the Santa Maria barracks, after 21.30 h/giardini alla piscina e alla caserma Santa Maria, da 21.30 h)

Prato ✉ 50047

SEX SHOPS/BLUE MOVIES
■ **Moulin Rouge** (g)
Piazzale Falcone e Borsellino 3 ✉ 50047 ☎ 0574 57 56 92
Over 4000 videos. Underwear and S/M articles.

CRUISING
-Viale Galilei (ayor) (gardens next to the playground/giardini accanto al campo giochi)

-Loc. il Cascido (daytime, between railway and the river Bisenzio/di giorno, fra la ferrovia e il fiume Bisenzio)
-Railway station/Stazione FS (also in the gardens, near Agip Motel/anche nei giardini, vicino al Motel Agip)

Ranzanico - Bergamo ✉ 24060

BARS
■ **Triangolo.Il** (B D g) Fri Sat Sun 21.30-1.30 h (Fri G)
Via Nazionale 5 ✉ 24060
☎ 035 82 91 87

Ravenna ✉ 48100

BARS
■ **Chalet dei Giardini** (B BF F glm OS YG) 7-2 h
Viale Santi Baldini 4 ✉ 48100 *(inside city garden near the station)*
☎ 0544 47 07 58

CINEMAS
■ **Alexander** (g)
Via Bassa del Pignataro 6 ✉ 48100 ☎ 0544 39 787
■ **Roma** (g)
Via Bixio 19 ✉ 48100
☎ 0544 21 22 21

GENERAL GROUPS
■ **Arcigay Arcilesbica "Evoluzione"**
Via G. Rasponi 5 ✉ 48100 *(near/vicino Piazza del Popolo, Bus 4/44)*
☎ 0544 21 97 21 ☎ 0347 8469427 📠 0544 21 97
📧 22arcigay@iol.it

Ravenna ▶ Roma Italy

SWIMMING
- Lido di Classe (NU) (between Ravenna and Cervia, free beach north of the kiosk bearing the same name. Large pine forest. Gay zone of the beach is near the river surrounding the beach itself, in the northern area/fra Ravenna e Cervia. Spiaggia libera al nord dell'edicola omonima. Pineta larga, zona gay vicino al fiume, verso norde)
- Lido di Dante (NU) (free beach beyond the campsites, on the right; dunes and pine trees/spiaggia libera oltre il campeggio, a destra e pineta)

CRUISING
- Railway Station/Stazione FS (late at night, also in the side streets/notte tardi, anche nelle via lateralis)
- Public gardens/Giardini pubblici (ayor R) (Viale S. Baldini, till late/fino a tardi)
- Piazzale and Viale Farini (R)
- Piazza Mameli (R)
- Via Rocca ai Fossi (R)

Reggio Calabria ✉ 89100

CRUISING
- Villa Comunale (good opportunities at night/buone occasioni di notte)
- Via Marina (some meetings at night/alcune incontri di notte)
- Central Station/stazione centrale (main hall and square in front of the building/salone principale e piazzale davanti)

Reggio Emilia ✉ 42100

SEX SHOPS/BLUE MOVIES
■ **Magic America** (g) closed Sun and Mon morning
Via Fabio Filzi 7   ✉ 42100 *(Zona S. Stefano)*   ☏ 0522 30 19 00

CRUISING
- Giardini pubblici/public gardens (AYOR OG) (near/vicino Astoria Hotel)
- Central station/stazione centrale (AYOR R) (also on the square in front of the station/anche nella piazza davanti)
- Porta Santo Stefano (day and night, by car and on foot/giorno e notte, in macchina e a piedi)

Riccione - Rimini ✉ 47838

BARS
■ **Bombo** (AC B BF f GLM MA OS s) Summer: 0-24 h, winter: 6-2 h
Viale Ceccarini 142   ✉ 47838   ☏ 0541 69 03 52

DANCECLUBS
■ **Villa delle Rose. La** (b D G) Fri-Sun -4 h
Villaggio Argentina, Zona Camilluccia   ✉ 47838 *(South of Riccione/verso Misano Adriatico)*   ☏ 0541 60 91 81

SEX SHOPS/BLUE MOVIES
■ **Eros Center** (g)
Viale Dante 116   ✉ 47838   ☏ 0541 64 86 86

HOTELS
■ **Garni Ceccarini 140** (CC glm H MA)
Viale Ceccarini 140   ✉ 47838 *(near station/vicino stazione)*
☏ 0541 69 03 52   ☏ 0541 69 03 70   ✉ garniceccanni@riccione
Rooms with phone, TV, shower/WC, heating. 10% discount to Spartacus readers.

GENERAL GROUPS
■ **Arcigay Alan Turing** Wed 20.30-23.30 h
Viale d'Annunzio 164   ✉ 47638   ☏ 0541 64 86 58
🖷 0541 64 86 58

SWIMMING
- Along the sea/Lungamore Libertà (Viale Ceccarini area)
- Among bathing cabins on the beach/fra le cabine in spiaggia (MA, foreigners/stranieri)

CRUISING
- Behind Hotel Savioli (winter)
- Della Rotonda (Near Hotel Mediterraneo, end of Viale Ceccarini/vicinio Hotel Mediterraneo, in fondo al Viale Ceccarini)

Rieti ✉ 02100

CRUISING
- Railway Station/Stazione FS
- Gardens in front of barracks, Viale dei Flavi
- Facilities under Town Hall

Rimini ✉ 47037

DANCECLUBS
■ **Classic Club** (B D DR G MA P S VS) winter only Sat 23-7 h, June and July WE only, in August every day
Via Feleto 11   ✉ 47037 *(exit highway Rimini Sud, on the right direction Riccione/Ancona, Coriano, San Lorenzo)*   ☏ 0541 73 11 13
Arcigay membership required./Tessera Arcigay.

SEX SHOPS/BLUE MOVIES
■ **Eros Center** (g)
Viale Vespucci 29 A   ✉ 47037
■ **Magic America** (g) closed Thu afternoon
Viale Regina Elena 94   ✉ 47900 *(Lungomare)*   ☏ 0541 39 19 77
Large section of gay videos.

CRUISING
- Grand Hotel (only/solo TV) (gardens, roundabout/giardini e rondò)
- Railway Station (YG)
- South Rimini/Rimini sud (at Miramare, between Centro Talasso Terapico and Colonia Bologna)
- Seafront/Lungomare (among cabins/fra le cabins 73-85)

Riva del Garda - Trento ✉ 38066

BARS
■ **Cascata Varone** (B f g OS) 9-18 h (march-october)
Via Cascata 12   ✉ 38066 *(3 km from Riva del Garda)*
☏ 0464 52 14 21
Best on Sun.

CRUISING
- Beach between "Punta Lido" and "Sabbioni Beach" (at night)
- Cruisy beach (NU)(take road to Torbole-Malcesine. Then take small stairs just at the end of the 5th tunnel behind Torbole.)

Roma ✉ 00100

✻ The majority of tourists in Europe visit the cities of Rome, Paris and London. Tourists can hardly resist the attraction of the city with its multitude of churches, monuments and art treasures.

Italy — Roma

gay>lesbian>bisexual>transgender
INTERNATIONAL PRIDE ROME 2001
FREEDOM AND EQUALITY EVENT

1>8 july
PRIDE PARADE SATURDAY JULY 7

During the week:
- *Uno specchio per Narciso* Fashion show
- *Muccassassina* Pride Parties
- Dance and Theatre
- Movies
- Workshops and debates
- Cinema preview
- Leather Party
- Beach Party

PRIDE VILLAGE
June 28 - July 22

AYOR
ENERGIE

OFFICIAL ORGANIZER
C.C.O. "Mario Mieli"
via Efeso 2/a (Metro **B** S.Paolo) > 00146 Roma
> tel. +39 06.54.13.985 > fax +39 06.54.13.971
> http://www.mariomieli.it > info@mariomieli.it

IN PRIDE WE TRUST!

One has a feeling of being in a massive museum. Also from a gay point of view, this city with its 3 million inhabitants has a lot to offer. It should not however, be compared with Paris or London.
The Gay World Pride last year set some wheels in motion. One result is the street near the Coliseum in which a multitude of openly proud gay-lesbian cafés have sprung up. This is in contrast to the majority of gay-lesbian establishments, which are generally very low key.
The magazine "AUT" offers the newest information regarding gay, lesbian, transsexual and transgender topics. The publishers are "Circolo Mario Mieli". The "International Pride 2001" takes place along with other events from the 1st to the 8th July.
From Rome it is only 30 km to Ostia and the beaches of the Mediterranean Sea which are popular with gay men.

Europaweit zieht Rom zusammen mit Paris und London jährlich die meisten Touristen an. Kaum ein Tourist wird sich der Faszination der ewigen Stadt, seiner unzähligen Kirchen, Monumente und Kunstschätze entziehen können, die den Eindruck vermitteln, sich in einem riesigen Museum zu bewegen. Auch in schwuler Hinsicht hat die 3-Millionen-Einwohner-Metropole einiges zu bieten, doch sollte man Rom hierbei nicht mit Paris oder London vergleichen.
Der letztjährige Gay World Pride scheint in Rom einiges in Bewegung gesetzt zu haben: So gibt es in der Nähe des Kolosseums das erste zur Straße offene lesbi-schwule Café, während die meisten anderen schwulen Kneipen und Diskotheken weiterhin gut von der Öffentlichkeit abgeschirmt sind.
Neben Artikeln zu Kultur und Politik finden sich die neuesten Informationen über das Rom der Schwulen, Lesben, Transsexuellen und "Transgender" im Monatsmagazin "AUT", das vom "Circolo Mario Mieli" herausgegeben wird. Der diesjährige "International Pride" 2001 findet mit diversen Veranstaltungen in der Woche vom 1.bis zum 8. Juli statt.
Von Rom aus sind es nur knapp 30 Kilometer bis nach Ostia und den auch von Schwulen stark frequentierten Sandstränden weiter südlich am Mittelmeer.

Rome est la ville qui, avec Paris et Londres, attire chaque année le plus de visiteurs en Europe. Peu de touristes peuvent résister aux charmes de la Ville éternelle, de ses innombrables églises, des ses riches trésors artistiques et magnifiques monuments qui donnent l'impression de se promener dans un musée à ciel ouvert. Rome a aussi, avec ses plus de trois millions d'habitants, beaucoup à offrir au niveau gai pour autant que l'on ne la compare pas à Paris ou Londres.
La World Pride de 2000 semble avoir fait du bien au milieu gai: le premier bar homosexuel visible de tous depuis la rue a ouvert récemment près du Colisée, alors que les autres établissements restent encore pour l'instant tapis dans l'ombre.
Le mensuel " AUT ", édité par le " Circolo Mario Mieli ", propose, en plus d'articles culturels et politiques, des nouvelles fraîches sur le Rome des gais, lesbiennes et transsexuels. Une " International Pride " se tiendra en 2001 dans la ville du 1er au 8 juillet.
A trente kilomètres seulement de Rome se trouve aussi Ostia, dont les plages de sables méritent un détour tant elles sont assidûment fréquentées par les gais romains.

Roma, París y Londres son las ciudades europeas que más turismo atraen. Pocos visitantes se quedarán inmunes ante la fascinación de la ciudad eterna y sus incontables iglesias, monumen-

Discover Roma (Free tourist Services and reservations)

- Accomodation
- Hotels pensioni
- hostels bed & breakfast
- Scooter, bike and scootcar rent
- Everything you need about Roma
- Emergency aid
- Internet access
- Restaurants
- Laundromat
- Scootcar Tour
- Bike Tour
- Day and dark walking tours
- Disco-pub, night club bar
- Luggage storage
- Free map

International Staff
E-mail: discoverroma@yahoo.it
www.DISCOVERROMA.com
www.holidayinrome.com

For more information contact: **Discover Roma**
Tel 06-49 38 20 80 Fax +390644703154
Address: Via Castelfidardo 50 - 00185 Roma Italy

---

tos y riquezas artísticas que les causarán la impresión de moverse por un enorme museo al aire libre. También desde la perspectiva gay la metrópoli de 3 millones de habitantes ofrece mucho, si bien bajo este aspecto no debería compararse con Londres o París.
El Gay World Pride (Fiesta del Orgullo Gay) en el año pasado parece haber puesto en marcha muchos cambios importantes; así, por ejemplo, cerca del Coloseo hay una cafetería gay y lesbiana abierta hacia la calle, mientras que la mayoría de los locales y discotecas gays siguen bien protegidas de las vistas del público de la calle.
Aparte de artículos sobre cultura y política, en la revista mensual 'AUT', editado por el "Circolo Mario Mieli", se encuentran las informaciones más recientes sobre la Roma de los gays, lesbianas, transsexuales y transgender. Este año, la Fiesta Internacional de Orgullo Gay se celebrará en la semana del 1 al 8 de julio con diversas actividades.
Desde Roma hay sólo alrededor de 30 kilómetros hasta Ostia y, más al sur, hasta las playas de arena del mediterráneo, también muy frecuentadas por los gays.

✖ Roma attrae insieme a Londra e Parigi annualmente la maggior parte di turisti in tutta Europa. Nessun turista può sottrarsi all'attrazione della città eterna con le sue innumerevoli chiese, monumenti e tesori d'arte, che danno l'impressione di muoversi in un immenso museo. Anche per quanto riguarda la vita gay, la metropoli con oltre 3 millioni di abitanti ha qualcosa da offrire. Bisogna però tenere presente che non si deve fare un confronto con Londra o Parigi.
Sembra che il Gay World Pride 2000 abbia provocato degli effetti positivi per i gay: esiste da poco vicino al Colosseo il primo bar gay-lesbico aperto e ben visibile, mentre la maggior parte degli altri locali è ancora ben nascosto al pubblico.
Le informazioni sulla Roma dei gay, delle lesbiche e dei transgender si trovano insieme agli articoli di cultura e politica nel mensile "AUT" che viene pubblicato dal Circolo Mario Mieli. Le manifestazioni dell'International Pride 2001 si svolgeranno dal 1 al 8 luglio.
Da Roma sono solo 30 chilometri per arrivare al lido di Ostia e, un pò più a sud lungo il mare, alle spiagge di sabbia molto frequentate anche dai gay.

GAY INFO

■ **Rome Gay News**
Via Einaudi 33, 00040 Frattocchie RM ☎ 06 93 54 75 67
🖨 06 93 54 74 83
Gay press agency with international news for the Italian mainstream press and national news for the International non-gay press (sent by fax). Sex yellow pages.

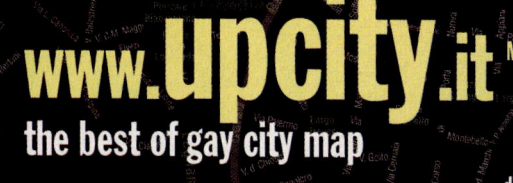

---

www.upcity.it
the best of gay city map

Maps to the most important italian cities are update each month
Maps will be located in all clubs and pubs.
Entertainment, clubs parties and events going on in town!

Le mappe delle città più importanti d'Italia con guida aggiornate mensilmente.
Le trovate in tutti i locali gay!

For information and publicizing:
Echo communication Via S. Nicolao 10 – 20123 Milano
Tel. 0039 02 89015940-1 Fax 0039 02 89013990

Italy | **Roma**

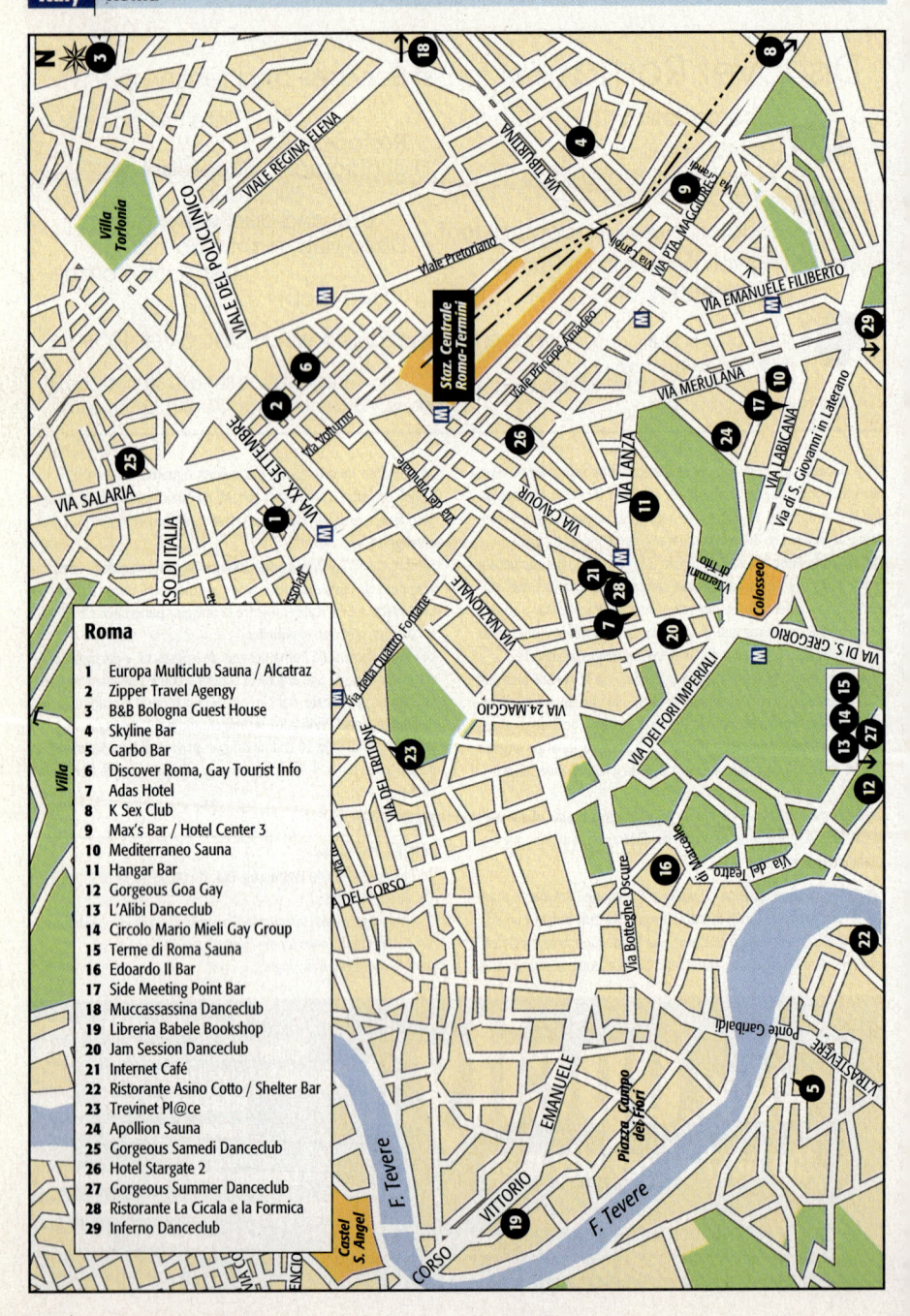

Roma

1. Europa Multiclub Sauna / Alcatraz
2. Zipper Travel Agengy
3. B&B Bologna Guest House
4. Skyline Bar
5. Garbo Bar
6. Discover Roma, Gay Tourist Info
7. Adas Hotel
8. K Sex Club
9. Max's Bar / Hotel Center 3
10. Mediterraneo Sauna
11. Hangar Bar
12. Gorgeous Goa Gay
13. L'Alibi Danceclub
14. Circolo Mario Mieli Gay Group
15. Terme di Roma Sauna
16. Edoardo Il Bar
17. Side Meeting Point Bar
18. Muccassassina Danceclub
19. Libreria Babele Bookshop
20. Jam Session Danceclub
21. Internet Café
22. Ristorante Asino Cotto / Shelter Bar
23. Trevinet Pl@ce
24. Apollion Sauna
25. Gorgeous Samedi Danceclub
26. Hotel Stargate 2
27. Gorgeous Summer Danceclub
28. Ristorante La Cicala e la Formica
29. Inferno Danceclub

mediterraneo
sauna

**Steam Room
Sauna
Jacuzzi
Massage
Solarium
Relax Area
Labyrinth
Dark Rooms
Air Conditioning
Snack Bar
Sandwiches**

message for members

English, French, Spanish and Arab spoken.

**Open sun. trough fri. from 2 pm. to midnight
Saturday from 2 pm. to midnight**

Clean!!! And highest professionality granted

By the way, rush, exciting, attractive hours from 4 to 10 pm.

Have Good Time!

3 floors facilities located in the hearth of the Eternal town about four blocks from the Colosseum and two from St. John in Lateran

ph. Studio Pino

Via Pasquale Villari, 3 - Phone 06/77205934
(Bwn. Via Merulana and Via Labicana)

Italy Roma

SKYLINE

GAY PRIVATE CLUB

membership ARCIGAY required (YOU CAN GET ONE ON THE SPOT)

AMERICAN BAR
VIDEO ROOM
2 DARK ROOMS
SHOWS
LEATHER NIGHT
PARTIES x BEARS x HAIRY MEN
AIR CONDITIONING

Via degli Aurunci 26 - 28
00185 ROMA
Infoline: 06.4440817
E-MAIL: skilineclub@tin.it
sito internet: http://www.skylineclub.it

music bar Edoardo II

00186 Roma - Vicolo Margana,
Tel. 06/69942419 - Fax 06/6797676

Via del Cardello, 13/A (Traversa di Via Cavour)
http://edoardosecondo.web.com

PUBLICATIONS

■ **Aut**
c/o Circolo Mario Mieli, Via Corinto 5 ✉ 00146 ☎ 065 41 39 85
Monthly gay magazine for politics, culture and roman gay scene. Available in gay bars.

■ **Cronache del 2000 - Quotidiano d'Informazione**
Casella Postale 754 ✉ 00187 ☎ 0335 54 57 911
☎ 0349 81 31 181 Fax 77 26 13 59 ✉ cronache2000@libero.it
Free local newspaper with gay ads "Messagi e incontri".

CULTURE

■ **Archivio Massimo Consoli**
Via Dario Bellezza 1 ✉ 00040 *(5 minutes via Appia, 20 km from Roma)* ☎ 06 93 54 75 67 Fax 06 93 54 74 83
The largest Gay and AIDS Archives in Europe. More than 5.000 books, 1.900 in English. Magazines in all languages-English, French, Spanish and Italian spoken. Admission free, by appointment for people with real interest.

TOURIST INFO

■ **Discover Roma**
Via Castelfidardo 50 ✉ 00185 *(2nd floor)* ☎ 06 49 38 20 80
Fax 06 44 70 31 54 ✉ discoverroma@yahoo.it
🌐 www.holidayinrome.com
Offers free services to incoming gay tourists.

■ **E.P.T.**
Via Parigi 5 ✉ 00185 ☎ 06 48 89 92 53 ☎ 06 48 89 92 55
Fax 06 48 89 92 28

BARS

■ **Alcatraz** (AC B d DR G lj MA P s SNU VS) Sun-Thu 15-23, Fri Sat 15-5 h
Via Aureliana 38 ✉ 00187 *(Metro-Repubblica)* ☎ 06 48 23 695
Connected with the sauna "European Multiclub"/Attaccato con la sauna "European Multiclub". Last Sat/ultimo sabato "Leather club".

■ **Apeiron Club** (AC B DR G MA P S VS) 22-3 h, closed Sun
Via dei Quattro Cantoni 5 ✉ 00186 *(Metro Cavour)*
☎ 06 48 28 820

660 SPARTACUS 2001/2002

Roma | Italy

discover italy on **G**

www.gay.it Discover the web-site that talks about you. Chat, books and cds, daily news, lots of reviews, travels, gay-guide of Italy, wap services, free e-mail, gay tv-shows, shop and much more. A universe of goods, for your body and your mind

gay.it

Italy | Roma

FOTO DINO PEDRIALI

AVVISO AI SOCI

HANGAR
BAR VIDEO ROMA
WHERE ROME MEETS THE WORLD
OPEN 22:30 - 02 CLOSED TUESDAY
VIA IN SELCI 69   TELE 064881397
ROME ITALY 00184   FAX 0668309081

■ **Edoardo II** (AC B G MA P S VS YG) 22.30-3 h, Wed 16-21 (Oct-May), closed Mon
Vicolo Margana 14 ✉ 00186 ☎ 06 69 94 24 19
Disco bar with DJ. On Thu & Sun "secret messages" nights/"Biglietti segreti".

■ **Garbo** (AC B f GLM MA) 22-3 h, Mon closed
Vicolo di Santa Margherita 1/A ✉ 00153 *(Trastevere district)*

■ **Gender** (B DR glm MA s TV) 23-3 h
Via Faleria 9 *(Metro-S. Giovanni)* ☎ 06 70 49 76 38
Transgender club.

■ **Hangar Video Bar** (AC B DR G lj MA P r snu VS) 22.30-2 h, closed on Tue
Via in Selci 69 ✉ 00184 *(Metro A Via Cavour/Metro B Piazza Vittorio, vicino al Colosseo/near the Colosseum)* ☎ 06 48 81 397
Striptease on Thu. Rome's first cruising bar.

■ **Incognito 2000** (B F glm MA P R) 14-2 h
Via Casilinia Vecchia 146 ✉ 00167 *(Bus 105, night bus 50, near Via Casilina/going down at the Fiat shop)* ☎ 06 78 43 567

■ **Shelter** (AC B F GLM MA p YG) 21-4 h, Summer: 22-4 h, closed in Aug
Via dei Vascellari 35 ✉ 00153 *(Bus 75, 170, 780/Tram 8)*

■ **Side Meeting Point** (A AC B CC d f GLM s YG) 12-3 h, closed on Wed and in August
Via Labicana 50 ✉ 00184 *(Metro Manzoni/Colosseo, near the Colosseum)* ☎ 0348 69 29 472 *(Infoline)*
Rome's first open gay café and bar. Internet service.

■ **Skyline** (AC B DR G MA P s VS) Tue-Thu 22.30-2, Fri-Sat -3, Sun: Oct-Mai 18.30-2, Jun-Sep 22.30-2 h, Mon closed
Via degli Aurunci 26/28 ✉ 00185 *(San Lorenzo district, near Termini)* ☎ 06 44 40 817
Arcigay membership required; leather, bears &hairy men nights.

Gay Pride

SIDE MEETING POINT

Sala da Tea
Wine Bar
open 16.00 • 04.00
mercoledì chiuso

Roma - Via Labicana, 50 - Tel. 0348.6929472

www.sidemeetingpoint.com

662 SPARTACUS 2001/2002

Roma | Italy

K SEX CLUB

THE BEST IN ROME

- DARK ROOMS - ORGY RROM -
- CABINS - AMATEURS LIVE SEX SHOW -
- **VERY HARD !!!** -

VIA AMATO AMATI, 6 ROMA - ITALY - CASILINA - BUS 105 - 50Night FILARETE STOP -
(10 MINUTE FROM TERMINI STATION) TEL. 03476220462 / 0627800292 fax 062428068

www.ksexclub.com

DESNUDO
NAKED HARD CLUB ONLY FOR MAN
- OPEN EVERY NIGHT -
VIA GAIO MELISSO, 37 - ROMA - TUSCOLANA AREA

INFERNO
THE BIGGEST DISCO PARTY ONLY FOR MAN

EVERY SUNDAY

Via SATURNIA, 18 (SAN GIOVANNI) ROMA

INFOLINE 0349-0063496

MASSIMILIANO BOYS AGENCY
ESCORT SERVICE 24h

SPARTACUS 2001/2002 | 663

Italy — Roma

Max's Bar — ONLY MEN DISCO BAR

VIDEOGIOCHI · MAXISCHERMI
DUE ZONE BAR · LOUNGE AREA

VIA ACHILLE GRANDI 7/A
00185 – ROMA
(PORTAMAGGIORE)
☎ 06 – 70301599
Ⓜ MANZONI – PIAZZA VITTORIO
BUS 105 14 516

MEN'S CLUBS

■ **Desnudo** (AC B DR G LJ MA NU P VS) 22-3 h
Via Gaio Melisso 37 ✉ 00100 *(Metro Porta Furba, Tuscolana district)*
☎ 0349 00 63 496 *(Infoline)*
■ **K Sex Club** (AC B DR G LJ NU P VS YG) 22-5 h
Via Amato Amati 6/8 ✉ 00176 *(10 min from the terminal station, Bus 105, Nightbus 50N)*
☎ 0347 62 20 462 *(Infoline)*

DANCECLUBS

■ **Agatha** (Festa Della Radio Città Futura) Fri 23-? h
Brancaleone, Via Levanna 11 *(Area Montesacro)* ☎ 06 49 14 37 *(Infoline)*
Techno, underground, drum & bass. Mixed party in an alternative cultural centre ("Centro Sociale").

La Cicala e La Formica

CUCINA MEDITERRANEA
Aperto solo la Sera

RISTORANTE
Via Leonina, 17 - 00184 Roma
Tel. 06-48.17.490

DOMENICA CHIUSO

■ **Alibi. L'** (AC B D GLM MA OS S TV) 23.30-4.30 h, closed Mon Tue
Via di Monte Testaccio 39/44 ✉ 00181 *(Metro Piramide)*
☎ 06 57 43 448
In summer OS with VS and soft music/d'estate terrazza con video e musica sottofondo.
■ **Degrado** (AC B D DR f glm MA P s TV) Fri-Sun 23-5 h, closed in August
Via Ignazio Danti 20 ✉ 00100 *(Night Bus 105N, inizio/beginning Via Casilina)* ☎ 06 27 53 508
Mixed erotic discoclub. Entrata/Entrance fee Lit 40.000.
■ **Gorgeous Goa Gay** (AC B D GLM P S YG) Tue 23h, open Oct to May
c/o Goa, Via Libetta 13 ✉ 00100 *(M Garbatella)*
☎ 0347 66 69 547 *(Infoline)*
Trendy party.
■ **Gorgeous Samedi** (B CC D DR GLM P WE YG) Sat 23-5 h, from Oct to Jun
c/o Alien, Via Velletri 13 ✉ 00100 *(near Piazza Fiume/ Porta Pia)*
☎ 0347 66 69 547 *(Infoline)*
3 dancefloors: one for men, one for women, one mixed. House and commercial music. In summertime @ 'Gorgeous Summer'.
■ **Gorgeous Summer** (B CC D DR GLM OS P WE YG) Sat 23-5 h, only from Jun to Sep
c/o Classico Village, Via Libetta 3 ✉ 00100 *(Metro Garbatella/ Metro Piramide)* ☎ 0347 66 69 547 *(Infoline)*
3 dancefloors: one for men, one for women, one mixed. House and commercial music. In wintertime @ 'Gorgeous Samedi'.
■ **Inferno** (B G D DR lj MA S WE) Sun 23-6 h
Via Saturnia 18 ✉ 00100 ☎ 0349 00 63 496 *(Infoline)*
"No cover, no fashion, only really men".
■ **Jam Session** (AC B D DR G MA P s) Wed only 23-4 h
Via del Cardello 13/A ✉ 00186 ☎ 06 69 94 24 19
■ **Max's Bar** (AC B CC D G MA VS) 22.30-? h, closed on Wed
Via Achille Grandi 7A ✉ 00185 *(bus 105,14,516; Portamaggiore, Metro Manzoni, Underneath/sotto Hotel Center 3)* ☎ 06 70 30 15 99
■ **Muccassassina** (B D DR GLM S YG) Fri 22.30-5 h
c/o Qube, Via di Portonaccio 212 ✉ 00100 *(Metro-Piramide)*
☎ 06 54 13 985
Call for information. Very popular.

RESTAURANTS

■ **Asinocotto di Giuliano Brenna** (F glm MA) 20-23 h Sun - lunch, Mon closed
Via dei Vascellari 48 ✉ 00153 *(Tram 8 nearby Piazza Belli in Trastevere)* ☎ 06 58 98 985
Fine and creative mediterranean cuisine.

"MARIO MIELI" CIRCOLO DI CULTURA OMOSESSUALE
CIRCOLO DI CULTURA OMOSESSUALE MARIO MIELI
2001/2002
I SERVIZI
> Gruppo di autoaiuto
> G/L/B/T counselling telefonico
> Assistenza medico/psicologica
> Assistenza domiciliare
> Unita' di strada
> Consulenza legale
LE ATTIVITA'
> Aut magazine
> Muccassassina disco party
> Welcome group
> Cinema & cultura
member of
InterPride
IGLHRC
epoa
GAY AND LESBIAN RIGHTS ARE HUMAN RIGHTS ilga
via Efeso 2/a (Metro S.Paolo) > 00146 Roma > tel. +39 06.54.13.985 > fax +39 06.54.13.971
infoline: dal lunedi' al venerdi' 10.00-18.00 > http://www.mariomieli.it > e-mail:info@mario.mieli.it
-Molly-

maccapop
Il circolo di cultura omosessuale "Mario Mieli" presenta:
muccassassina
MUCCASSASSINA
CIRCOLO DI CULTURA OMOSESSUALE MARIO MIELI
everyfriday 11,00pm > 05,00am
the most popular italian g/l/b/t party
Location info line
+39 06 5413985 > http://www.mariomieli.it > e-mail: info@mariomieli.it

Italy — Roma

RISTORANTE
Asinocotto
di Giuliano Brenna

Enjoy creative Mediterranean cuisine exquisitely prepared by one of Italy's best young chefs. Lively company, a gay and friendly atmosphere. Chef Giuliano Brenna offers memorable dinners and Sunday lunch in his restaurant in the historic centre of Rome. Vast selection of fine Italian wines. Visit Giuliano's web site for menus, wine list, news, and updates of the gay scene in Rome.

Via dei Vascellari, 48, Trastevere - Roma
Tel. 06 589 8985
http://www.asinocotto.com

20:00-23:00 and
Sunday Lunch,
Closed Mondays

■ **La Cicala e la Formica** (AC CC glm MA OS) 19-24 h, closed Sun and in Aug
Via Leonina 17 ✉ 00184 *(Metro Cavour)* ☎ 06 48 17 490
Si consiglia la prenotazione/reservation advisable.
■ **La Piazzetta** (F glm) 12-15, 17.30-21 h, Sun closed
Vicolo del Buon Consiglio 23/A ✉ 00100 *(near Via Cavour)*
☎ 06 69 91 640
■ **La Volpe Rossa** (F glm) 19-23 h, Mon closed
Via Alfieri 4 ✉ 00185 *(Metro Manzoni)* ☎ 06 70 45 35 17
Reservation suggested. Great Roman and Mediterranean cuisine.

SEX SHOPS/BLUE MOVIES
■ **Cobra** (g) Mon-Sat 9-20 h
Via Barletta 23 ✉ 00192 *(Metro Ottaviano)* ☎ 06 37 51 73 50
■ **Cobra** (g) Mon-Sat 9-20 h
Via Giovanni Giolitti 307/313 ✉ 00185 *(Metro-Vittorio)*
☎ 06 44 70 06 36
Underwear, magazines, retail and rental of gay videos/Oggettistica, abbigliamento intimo, riviste, noleggio e vendita di gay video.
■ **Europa 92** (g) Mon 15-19.30, Tue-Sat 9.30-13.30, 15-19.30 h
Via Vitelleschi 38/40 ✉ 00192 *(near Piazza Risorgimento)*
☎ 06 68 71 210
■ **Follie d'Amore** (g) Mon 16-21, Tue-Sat 10-13, 16-21 h
Via Cavour 323 ✉ 00184 ☎ 06 69 92 43 72
■ **Sexy Moon Gay Shop** (GLM) Mon-Sat 10-20 h
Via A. Nobel 38 ✉ 00146 *(Railway station Trastevere)*
☎ 06 55 94 376

CINEMAS
■ **Ambasciatori** (g)
Via Montebello 101 *(Metro Termini)* ☎ 06 49 41 290
■ **Pussycat** (AC g MG R VS)
Via Cairoli 96/98 ✉ 00185 *(Metro Vittorio, near railway station Termini, at via Giolitti)* ☎ 06 44 64 961
No sign outside.
■ **Tiffany**
Via Agostino Depretis ✉ 00184 ☎ 06 48 82 390
Popular.

ESCORTS & STUDIOS
■ **International Escort Service**
☎ 0335 60 51 309
Photo models for studio sessions, shows, publicity etc.
■ **Massimiliano Boys Agency**
☎ 0349 00 63 496 (infoline)
Model & strip-men.

SAUNAS/BATHS
■ **Apollion** (AC DR f G msg p Pl SA SB VS WH YG) 14-23 h
Via Mecenate 59/a ✉ 00184 *(Metro A-Piazza Vittorio/Metro B-Colosseo)* ☎ 06 48 25 389

ROME'S FIRST AND LARGEST GAY BOOKSHOP

LIBRERIA BABELE
GAY BOOK SHOP

00186 ROMA
VIA DEI
BANCHI VECCHI 116
TEL./FAX 06 - 6876628

OPEN FROM MONDAY
TO SATURDAY
FROM 10 A.M.
TO 7,30 P.M.
CLOSED ON SUNDAY

BOOKS-VIDEOS-MAGAZINES-POSTERS-POSTCARDS-GAY GUIDES-GADGETS

Roma | **Italy**

grafic by **With Art**

EUROPA
EMC
multi club
saunas & gym

One of the biggest and most attactive saunas in Europe

E.M.C.
la tua sauna.

1300 mq su tre livelli - Solarium
Mega vasca idromassaggio con cascata
Doppia sauna finlandese - Bagno turco
Camemerini relax con video
Servizio massaggi ed estetica

Un'attrezzatissima palestra
con un fornitissimo bar
video music - sala cinema
Interamente climatizzato.

E.M.C. your sauna
close to Via Veneto
and Termini Station.

Nice atmosfere on three levels
Extra large jacuzzi with waterfall
30 man sauna cabin - Steam room
Free rest rooms with video
Massage available - Solarium

Well equipped gym
with a canfortable
bar on three levels
with video music and cinema.
air conditioning.

OPEN EVERY DAY
14.00 till 02.00
Fri. and Sat. till 06.00

Now, THE CAVE:
Come on!
Every desire
become reality!

GRANDE NOVITA'
LA GROTTA

ENTRA!
ogni tuo desiderio
si esaudirà

Avviso ai soci

Roma - Via Aureliana, 40 - Tel. +39.6.48.23.650

All ages but especially popular with young guys.

SPARTACUS 2001/2002

| Italy | Roma |

HORNY MEN WILL TURN YOU ON

APOLLION
sauna

"THE BEST IN TOWN"

Iacuzzi	Idromassaggio
Steam Bath	Bagno Turco
Sauna	Sauna
Music-Video	Video-Musica
Box Relax	Camerini
Dream Dark Room	Sala Dark
Young People	Frequentata da Ragazzi
Rest Rooms	Frequentato da Militari
American Bar-Snack	American Bar
Massage	Massaggi

Via Mecenate 59a
Roma - Tel.064825389
(Metro P.zza Vittorio)

Roma | **Italy**

INTERNATIONAL ESCORT-SERVICE
www.flesh4free.com/pics/italianmaleescortagency
Email niki27@katamail.com

ROMA ITALY

0335 605 1309

**FOTOMODELLI PER SERVIZI FOTOGRAFICI-VIDEO
ANIMAZIONE SPETTACOLI STRIP-TEASE
ACCOMPAGNATORI PERSONALI PER FESTE-PARTY**

Italy — Roma

TreviNet Pl@ce

INTERNET POINT
near Trevi Fountain
Mon-Sat 10:30-23:00
Sun. 15:00-23:00
LESBIAN OWNED

Via in Arcione 103, Rome
Metro "A", Barberini stop
info@trevinet.com
tel/fax (39) 06699 22320
www.trevinet.com
discounts for glt

Zipper

viaggiare diverso . . .

00185 Roma
Via Castelfidardo 18
Tel. +39064882730
Fax +39064882729

Lun. / Ven. 09.30 – 18.30
Available
Spartacus Gay Guide

Email info@zippertravel.it   Website www.zippertravel.it

TRAVEL AGENCY IGLTA MEMBER

e-mail: arcoturismo@libero.it
www.arcoturismo.it

ARCO TURISMO

Milano: c/o libreriaBabelegalleria
via S.Nicolao 10 (M Cadorna)
tel. 0039 02 72094251 fax 0039 02 86461193
milano@arcoturismo.it

Roma: Arcoturismo Corner c/o A.I.L.
via Laurina 23 (M Spagna)
tel. 0039 06 3219541
roma@arcoturismo.it

Bologna - Torino next opening

■ **Europa Multiclub** (AC B DR f G msg P PI SA SB SOL VS WH WO YG) Mon-Thu, Sun 14-24, Fri Sat and before public holidays -6 h
Via Aureliana 40 ✉ 00178 *(near railway station, Metro-Repubblica)*
☏ 06 48 23 650
Also beauty salon and cinema. Arcigay membership required. Big sauna on 1300 m^2 busy with a young crowd, parties on Fri and Sat at 24 h.

■ **Exess** (AC B CC DR f G msg P SA SB SOL WH YG) Fr-Sat 15-22 h (G)
Via Ombrone 1 ✉ 00198 *(Metro-Policlinico/Tram 19/30)*
☏ 06 85 58 398

■ **Mediterraneo** (AC B DR f G msg P SA SB SOL VS WH YG) 14-24 h
Via Pasquale Villari 3 ✉ 00184 *(Metro A-Manzoni/B-Colosseo, between Via Merulana and Via Labicana)* ☏ 06 77 20 59 34
Sauna on three floors frequented by a young crowd. Arcigay membership required.

■ **Terme di Roma Internazionale** (AC B CC DR G msg SA SB SOL VS WH WO YG) Sun-Thu 13-24, Fri & Sat -2 h
Via Persio 4 ✉ 00178 *(Bus 765 from Metro-Arco di Travertino)*
☏ 06 71 84 378
Sauna with a big labyrinth.

BODY & BEAUTY SHOPS

■ **Jenny di Petta**
Piazza Regina Margherita 3 ✉ 00198 *(close to Porta Pia)* ☏ 06 84 17 561
Hair and style for men and women.

BOOK SHOPS

■ **Libreria Babele** (CC GLM) Mon-Sat 10-19.30 h, closed Sun
Via dei Banchi Vecchi 116 ✉ 00186 ☏ 06 68 76 628
Rome's first and largest gay book and video shop. Wide range of lesbian literature./Prima e più grande libreria gay a Roma. Ampio spazio alla letteratura lesbica.

Roma — Italy

■ **Queer** (CC GLM) Mon 14.30-19.30, Tue-Sat 9.30-19.30 h
Via del Boschetto 25 ✉ 00184 *(close to Via Nazionale)* ☎ 06 47 40 691
The new Rome's GLBT bookshop: books, videos, rainbow gadgets, flags, gifts, t-shirts, reviews, cards./La nuova libreria GLBT a Roma: libri, video, bandiere, idee regalo, t-shirt, riviste, cartoline.
■ **Rinascita** (g) Mon-Sat 10-20, Sun 10-14, 16-20 h
Via delle Botteghe Oscure 2 ✉ 00186 ☎ 06 67 97 460
Large gay section.

NEWS STANDS

■ **Libreria la Bancarella** (g)
Piazza Alessandria 2 ✉ 00198 *(Porta Pia)* ☎ 06 85 30 30 71

TELECOMMUNICATION

■ **Internet Café** (CC) 9-1 h
Via Cavour 213 ✉ 00185 *(near railway station Termini, Metro Cavour)* ☎ 06 47 82 30 51 ✉ clienti_cavour@yahoo.com
Internet café: 20 PCs & internet high speed, scanner, print, bar, change office, Western Union money transfer.
■ **Splashnet**
Via Varese 33 ✉ 00185 *summer 9-1, winter 9-23 h*
☎ 06 49 38 04 50 ✉ splashnet@yahoo.com 🖥 www.splashnet.it
Internet and laundromat near Termini railway station.
■ **Trevinet Pl@ce** (AC CC) Mon-Sat 10.30-23.00, Sun 15-23.00 h
Via in Arcione 103 ✉ 00187 *(Metro Barberini, close to Fontana di Trevi)* ☎ 06 69 92 23 20 ✉ info@trevinet.com
🖥 www.trevinet.com
Internet Point: 40 PC webcam & headsets. Print, scanner, cdr duplication, net to phone calls, computer class, website design & publishing, music compilation. Lesbian owned.

TRAVEL AND TRANSPORT

■ **Arco Turismo** (CC GLM)
Via Laurina 23 ✉ 00100 *(Metro Spagna)*
☎ 06 32 19 541 ✉ arcoturismo@libero.it
Tour operator/Organizzazione viaggi.
■ **Selene Viaggi e Turismo** (CC H)
Via Gregorio VII 96 ✉ 00165 ☎ 06 63 80 746 ☎ 06 63 57 83
✉ SEL.VI.@mclink.it
Hotel and travel agency.
■ **Zipper** (GLM) 9.30-18.30 h, closed Sat Sun
Via Castelfidardo 18 ✉ 00185 *(2nd floor)* ☎ 06 48 82 730
📠 06 48 82 729 ✉ info@zippertravel.it 🖥 www.zippertravel.it
Gay travel agency, tourist service, organization of international gay meetings.

HOTELS

■ **Adas** (AC BF H)
Via Cavour 233 ✉ 00184 *(near Metro Cavour)* ☎ 06 47 41 432
☎ 06 48 20 652 📠 06 47 44 852
Single room 120.000, Double 170.000 with bf, bath, TV and phone.
■ **Cambridge** (AC B BF CC H)
Via Palestro 87 ✉ 00185 *(200 m from the terminal station)*
☎ 06 44 56 821 📠 06 49 38 49 17 ✉ hcambrrm@tin.it
🖥 www.space.tin.it/viaggi/vfuggett
Single room 100.000-160.000, Double room 130.000-230.000 with bf, TV, phone, minibar.
■ **Center 3** (glm H)
Via Achille Grandi 7 ✉ 00185 *(Metro-Manzoni)* ☎ 06 70 30 00 58
📠 06 70 30 00 59
Rates single Lit. 80.000-250.000, double 100.000-320.000. All rooms with shower, WC, TV.
■ **Hotel Labelle** (AC BF CC H MA)
Via Cavour 310 ✉ 00184 *(Metro Colosseo/Cavour)*
☎ 06 67 94 750 📠 06 69 94 03 67
Rates single without shower Lit. 60.000-95.000, with shower 150.000, double without shower 80.000-150.000, with shower 150.000-200.000. Bf not incl.
■ **Hotel Stargate 2** (BF C H)
Via Farini 52 ✉ 00185 *(central, near Stazione Termini)*
☎ 06 47 82 48 44 📠 06 47 88 07 49
✉ informa@stargatehotels.com
🖥 www.stargatehotels.com
Single room Lit. 80-120.000, double room 100-160.000. Ask for the Spartacus' reader discount.
■ **Residence Barberini** (BF E H MA)
Via delle Quattro Fontane 171, 172 ✉ 00184 ☎ 06 420 33 41
📠 06 42 03 34 17 ✉ info@residencebarberini.com
🖥 www.residencebarberini.com
Historical 19th century building. Luxury suites with antique French and English furniture, Bohemian crystal chandeliers and linnengoods.
■ **Scott House Hotel** (AC B BF CC H MA)
Via Gioberti 30 ✉ 00185 *(Stairway A, 4th, near station/Scala A 4°piano, vicino Stazione Termini)* ☎ 06 44 65 379
☎ 06 44 65 392 📠 06 44 64 986 ✉ info@scotthouse.com
🖥 www.italyhotel.com/roma/scotthouse
All rooms with bath, central heating, TV, telephone and safe. Elevator. Fax. 24 hour friendly service. Single room Lit 50.000-200.000, double 60.000-250.000.

INTERNET CAFé

internet surfing - e mail - telnet - scan and print - wester union - change - phone center

CHAT Mirc32 > ICQ > C6
£ 2.000 10min
INTERNETCAFé card £ 6.000 x HOUR
ALL CREDIT CARDS

Open 9:00am 1:00am
7 days a week

Roma Via Cavour, M 213 tel. 06/47823051

Italy Roma

HOTEL STARGATE 2

All rooms with baths, TV and telephones
24 hours friendly service
international staff
Laundromat & Internet access

HOW TO GET TO HOTEL STARGATE:

From the central train station: exit Termini to the left (platform 22) and cross via Giolitti to via Gioberti walk 3 blocks up via Gioberti turn right on via Farini 52

Special price for Spartacus Gay Guide readers

Via Farini n° 52 - 00185 Roma
Tel. +39647824844
Fax -39647880749
E mail: informa@stargatehotels.com
www.stargatehotels.com

GUEST HOUSES

■ **B & B Bologna** (AC bf glm H)
Piazza Bologna 6 ✉ 00162 (Metro Bologna, Bus 61, 62, 93, 309, 310, Nightbus 40N) ☎ 06 44 24 02 44 06 44 23 08 92
 dpajella@tiscalinet.it
 www.beb-bologna.it
English, French, Spanish and Portuguese spoken. Single room Lit 60-75.000, Double room 110-140.000. Own key at night.

■ **Caracalla Hot Springs** (BF GLM H)
Via Matteo Ricci 6 ✉ 00154 (Metro Piramide) ☎ 06 57 57 412
☎ 0338 57 22 623 06 57 57 412 info@caracalla-falls.com
 www.caracalla-falls.com
Own key at night. Lit 49.000/person bf incl.

PRIVATE ACCOMMODATION

■ **Gayopen** (G H)
☎ 06 48 20 013 ☎ 06 48 47 07
 orsogrigio@hotmail.com
 www.angelfire.com/mo/RICLAUDIOHOLYDAYS/
Apartment with TV in the centre. Lit 64.000 per night.

■ **Rainbow Bed & Breakfast** (BF GLM H)
Via Accademia Ambrosiana 41 ✉ 00147
☎ 06 54 05 484
 06 54 05 484
 aimone@hotmail.com
 www.aimone1.com

Rooms with bath, Double from Lit 120.000 incl. BF.

GENERAL GROUPS

■ **Roma Caravaggio**
Via Lariana 8 ✉ 00199 ☎ 06 85 55 522 06 86 32 81 75
Right wing gay organisation. Excluded from arcigays main organisation due to their support of gay world pride opposition./Organizzazione gay di destra. Espulso dall'arcigay per aver sostenuto l'opposizione al gay world pride.

■ **Circolo di Cultura Omosessuale Mario Mieli "WORLD PRIDE 2000 ORGANIZER"** Mon-Fri 9-20 h
Via Efeso 2/a ✉ 00146 (Metro B-San Paolo)
☎ 06 54 13 985
 06 54 13 971 info@mariomieli.it www.mariomieli.it
Call for information on activites.
Federsex federazione mondiale per la tutela dei diritti e delle libertà.
Fax 0349 - 00 63 496

FETISH GROUPS

■ **Leather Club Roma (LCR)** (LJ) Meeting Tue. Leather/fetish parties last Sat/month c/o Alcatraz
 lcrroma@hotmail.com
 www.geocities.com/lcrroma

HEALTH GROUPS

■ **Anlaids** Mon-Fri 10-19 h
Via Dei Mille 6 ✉ 00185 (Termini) ☎ 06 44 70 01 71
☎ 06 44 70 02 29 06 44 70 02 29
Medical information about AIDS ☎ 44 70 01 71
during opening hours.

A GAY HOLYDAY IN ROME

"GAYOPEN"
Bed and breakfast

00185 Roma - Via dello Statuto,44 - apt.18 - 3° piano
Tel. +39-06.4820013
E-Mail: orsogrigio@hotmail.com
www.angelfire.com/mo/RICLAUDIOHOLYDAYS

Bed & Breakfast Bologna
Daniela Pajella Sanguinetti

00162 Roma - P.zza Bologna, 6 - Int. 1
Tel./Fax +39-06.44.24.02.44
E-Mail: d.pajella@tiscalinet.it
www.beb-bologna.it

Roma ▶ San Remo - Imperia | Italy

■ **Associazione Positifs** Mon-Fri 9-17 h
Viale di Valle Aurelia 111 ✉ 00167 ☏ 06 63 80 365 ☏ 06 39 72 25 87 🖷 06 63 80 74 📧 ass.positifs@agora.stm.it
Information on Aids treatment available.
■ **LILA - Lega Italiana Lotta contro l'Aids** Mon-Fri 10-17 h
Via Alessandria 129 ✉ 00198 *(near Piazza Fiume)*
☏ 06 88 48 492 ☏ 06 88 48 451
📧 lilalazio@tiscalinet.it 📧 www.lilalazio.it
■ **Unità HIV** Counselling: Mon Wed Fri 9-21, Tue Thu 15-21 h
c/o Fondazione Villa Maraini, Via Ramazzini 31
✉ 00151 *(near Spallanzzani hospital)*
Information, prevention, assistance. Anonymous free HIV test, self help group .

SPORT GROUPS
■ **GPR - Gruppo Pesce Roma**
📧 parvulus@excite.com
Gay swimming group.

SWIMMING
-Beach south of Ostia/Spiaggia sud di Ostia (nice dunes/belle dune; by car: from Lido die Ostia in direction Anzio, after km-sign 8; by bus: Bus 07 from Ostia till last stop, then on foot for 2 km to km-sign 8, beach bar Stabilimento Balneare Settimo Cielo)
-Spiagga Libera A Cerenova (at km 46 on Via Aurelia)

CRUISING
-Colosseo Quadrato (Metro Magliana, gardens near Palazzo Civiltà del Lavoro/ Giardini vicino al bar Palombini)
-Piazza Belle Arti "Valle Giulia" (in front of National Gallery of Modern Art, opposite hustlers/davanti Galleria Nazionale d'Arte moderna)(r, in macchina/by car, molto frequentato/very busy)
-Monte Caprino (in the evening/night)
-Villa Borghese, Galoppatoio (tardo pomeriggio, sera, molto frequentato/late afternoon, evening, very busy)
-Parco di Piazza Sempione (sera/evening)
-Via dei Colli della Farnesina, Parco di Montemario, dietro/behind il Ministero degli Esteri (during the day)

Rovereto - Trento ✉ 38068
BARS
■ **Chicco Bar** (B g) Daily 8-1 h
Piazza Stazione ✉ 38068 ☏ 0464 43 49 22

Salerno ✉ 84100
SEX SHOPS/BLUE MOVIES
■ **Mediart** (g) 9.30-20 h
Viale Leucosia 91 ✉ 84100 *(zona Mercadello)* ☏ 089 33 05 92

GENERAL GROUPS
■ **Arcigay Arcilesbica Salerno**
Piazza Vittorio Veneto 2 ✉ 84100 ☏ 089 22 06 23
🖷 089 25 32 05

CRUISING
-Railway Station/Stazione FS (occasional/occasionale, daytime)
-Seafront/Lungomare
-Square in front of/piazzo davanti Hotel Jolly (at night/di notte)
-Giardini Teatro Verdi (TV)
-Pineta (12 km from Salerno, summertime in the afternoon/d'estate, pomeriggio)
-Villa Communale

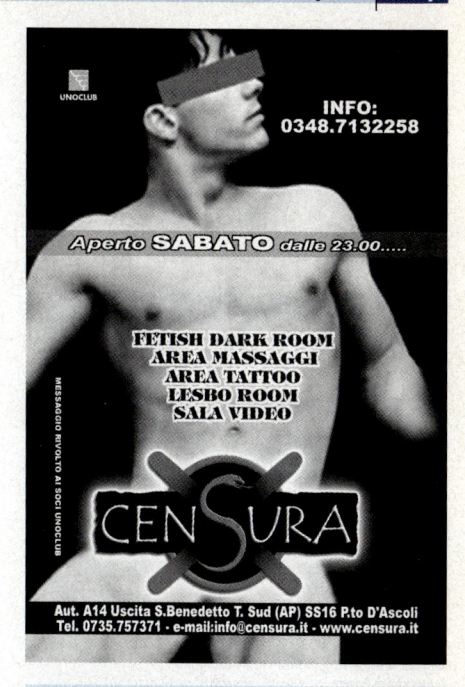

INFO: 0348.7132258

Aperto **SABATO** *dalle 23.00.....*

**FETISH DARK ROOM
AREA MASSAGGI
AREA TATTOO
LESBO ROOM
SALA VIDEO**

CENSURA

Aut. A14 Uscita S.Benedetto T. Sud (AP) SS16 P.to D'Ascoli
Tel. 0735.757371 - e-mail:info@censura.it - www.censura.it

Salsomaggiore Terme - Parma ✉ 43039
HOTELS
■ **Marinella** (F g H OG)
Via Castllazzo 80 ✉ 43039 ☏ 0524 57 82 97
All rooms with phone, private baths and WC. Rates on request.

San Benedetto del Tronto - Ascoli Piceno ✉ 63039
DANCECLUBS
■ **Censura Discoclub** (AC B CC D DR GLM P snu YG) Sat 23 -6 h
Via Pasubio 1/F ✉ 63039 *(Aut. A14-S.Benedetto Sud (AP),SS16 P.to D'Ascoli)* ☏ 0735 75 73 71
Call for info.

CRUISING
-Railway Station/Stazione FS
-Cinema delle Palme (garden behind the cinema/ giardini dietro il cinema)
-Muro del Pianto (garden behind Roxy Hotel/ nei giardini dietro all'Hotel Roxy)
-Pineta (woods at the seashore/sul mare)
-Punta Nina (beach between/spiaggia fra Pevaso and Benedetto, behind/dietro Pensione Il-Contadino)

San Remo - Imperia ✉ 18038
CRUISING
-Park gardens/Giardini del parco (evening/sera)
-Porto Vecchio (in summer, along the pier/in estate lungo il molo)
-Marsaglia (R)
-Railway station/stazione FS (main hall/salone principale)
-Lungo Mare delle Nazzioni

Italy — San Vincenzo - Livorno ▶ Sardegna - Sassari

San Vincenzo - Livorno ✉ 57027

SWIMMING
- La Torraccia (NU) (near the campnig "La Torraccia")

Santa Margherita Ligure ✉ 16038

HOTELS
■ **Hotel La Vela** (BF B g H SOL)
Corso Nicolò Cuneo 21 ✉ 16038 ☎ 0185 28 47 71
☎ 0185 29 00 21 🖳 www.lavela.it
Gays welcome. All rooms with bath, TV and phone.

Sant'Ilario d'Enza - Reggio Emilia ✉ 42049

CRUISING
- Enza river/fiume

Sardegna

Sardegna - Arborea ✉ 09021

CRUISING
- Beach/spiaggia 29 (camping "S'ena Arubia")

Sardegna - Cagliari ✉ 09100

BARS
■ **Circolo Nautilus** (B F GLM MA P) closed on Mon and in summer
Via Basilicata 33 ✉ 09100 ☎ 070 45 41 99
■ **Fico d'India** (B glm MA) Only in summer
Lungomare Poetto ✉ 09100 *(close to Torre Spagnaola)*

DANCECLUBS
■ **Nirvana** (AC B D GLM MA P)
Centro Bellavista, Località Foxi ✉ 09145 ☎ 0360 53 18 923

SEX SHOPS/BLUE MOVIES
■ **Sixtynine Sexy Shop** (G) 10-13, 17-20.30, Mon 17-20.30 h
Via Bayle 69 ✉ 09100 ☎ 070 66 95 50
Toys, videos, clothing, rubber and leathers, gadgets, magazines, CDs.

CINEMAS
■ **Astoria** (g MA)
Via Col di Lana 29 ✉ 09122

GENERAL GROUPS
■ **Kaleidos - Associazione di Cultura Omosessuale** Tue 18-20, Fri Sun 20-22 h
Via Leopardi 3 ✉ 09128 ☎ 0349 26 39 791 (info & helpline)
🖳 aco.kaleidos@tiscali.it

HEALTH GROUPS
■ **Anlaids** Infoline: Mon-Fri 9-13 h
Via Bembo 25 ✉ 09131 ☎ 070 40 20 00 (Infoline)
☎ 070 48 69 70
■ **LILA - Lega Italiana Lotta contro l'Aids**
Via Cilea ✉ 09045 ☎ 070 88 28 28

SWIMMING
- Cala Fighera, Cala Mosca (g NU) (5 km from Cagliari, Bus N°11, under the casern, on the rocks)
- Terra Mala (G NU) (20 km from Cagliari, on the way to Villasimius, last stop of 1Q bus, turn left and walk 700 metres along the shore)
- Piscina Rei (Monte Nai), swimmig pool, on the dunes

CRUISING
- Piazza Matteotti (in front of the railway station, all the day/fronte stazione, tutto il giorno, AYOR)
- ⓟ Stadium S. Elia (after 20 h AYOR)
- ⓟ Fiera, Piazza Marco Polo/via C. Colombo (after 20 h AYOR)
- Via Roma (under the porch, soldiers)
- Lighthouse Cala Mosca (in daytime)

Sardegna - La Maddalena ✉ 07024

BARS
■ **Crystal Bar** (B f DR GLM VS YG) 12-2 h, Thu closed
Via Amendola 8 ✉ 07024 (Ferries) ☎ 0789 73 87 06
Popular
■ **Rolling Rock Cafè** (BF G VS YG) 17-4 h
Via Luca Spano ✉ 07024 *(near Piazza XXIII Febb.)*

Sardegna - Olbia ✉ 07020

RESTAURANTS
■ **Asfodelo. L'** (F glm)
Punta Asfodeli, Porto Rotondo ✉ 07020 ☎ 0789 35 355

SWIMMING
- Porto Ferro (NU) near Arlghero (at the end on the right on the rocks/in fondo sulla destra nelle calette e nelle rocce)
- Maria Pia, Alghero beach/lido (in the last part on the trees side direction Fertilia/nell'ultima parte alla fine degli alberi direzione Fertilia)
- Liscia Ruja (NU) Costa Smeralda (from Olbia direction Arzachena, in a place called Cala di Volpe on the rocks/da Olbia direzione Arzachena, zona Cala di Volpe nelle calette e sulle rocce)

CRUISING
- Harbour/Porto Isola Bianca (at night, after the departure of boats/la notte dopo la partenza delle navi)

Sardegna - Oristano ✉ 09170

SWIMMING
- Marina di Arborea (G MA NU) (Strada mare 29)
- Is Arenas beach/spiaggia (take from Oristano the direction of Cuglieri, turn at the camping Nurapolis, walk around 2 km on the beach at the end of the ⓟ on the left side/Oristiano direzione Cuglieri, bivio camping Nurapolis, dal parcheggio alla fine della strada camminare per ca. 2 km sulla spiaga verso sinistra)

CRUISING
- Torre Grande pine trees wood, after Orbia direction Cagliari/Pineta Torre Grande, dopo Orbia dirrezion Cagliari(by car and on foot/in macchina e a piedi)

Sardegna - Sassari ✉ 07100

BARS
■ **Borderline** (B GLM) Fri, Sun 21-?, Sat 22-? h
circolo Arci Nuova Associazione, via Rockfeller 16/C ✉ 07100
☎ 079 21 90 24

GENERAL GROUPS
■ **Arcigay Arcilesbica** Infoline: Tue, Thu
Via M. Zanfarino 22 ✉ 07100 ☎ 079 27 55 40 ☎ 079 27 51 84
■ **Movimento Omosessuale Sardo** Mon Tue Thu Fri 9.30-13.30, 17.30-20.30, Wed Sun 20.30-22.30 h

Sardegna - Sassari ▶ Sicilia - Agrigento | **Italy**

DISCOTEATRO D'ITALIA
PENSIERO STUPENDO
SENIGALLIA ANCONA

DISCO SHOWS+ANIMATIONS
Sede di:
Premio Internazionale Imprenditoria GAY
Mister GAY Marche
Rassegna Nazionale DISCO TEATRO
pensierostupendo@fastnet.it
premioimprgay@fastnet.it

Info: 03470779266 - 03474758758

MAROTTA — A14 — SS16 — Fiume Cesano — Centro Commerciale — Gay Beach — 7200 mt — SENIGALLIA

Via Rockfeller 16/c ✉ 07100 ☎ 079 21 90 24 🖨 079 21 90 24
📧 movimento.omosessual@tiscalinet.it
Helpline, information on gays and Aids/Telefonico amico e informazione su omosessualità e Aids.

CRUISING
-Corso Giò Maria Angioi (r tv) (from 22 h, on foot or by car)
-Quarto pettine (zona Platamona) (winter by car, summer also by foot)
-Railway station/Stazione FS (and the place in front at night/e nella piazzetta antistanche di notte)
-Alghero (in summer on the seafront between the/d'estate sul lungomare tra il Bar Arca and the Bar de Tramonto, be discreet/discreto)

Sasso Marconi - Bologna ✉ 40037

GUEST HOUSES
■ **Albergo Triana e Tyche** (b BF CC f g H msg NU OS SOL)
Viale J.F. Kennedy 9/2 ✉ 40037 (700 m from station) ☎ 0516 75 16 16 🖨 0516 75 17 02
Special rates for long stays and Spartacus readers.

Saturnia ✉ 58050

CRUISING
-Terme (natural hot waters bathing pools and waterfall (not in the hotel but in the fields of the countryside amidst herds). Drive along the road from Manciano and park immediately past the bridge on the sulphureous stream, near the dilapidated mill. Mostly at night: be discreet)

Savona ✉ 17100

GENERAL GROUPS
■ **Arcigay Arcilesbica Savona** Tue Thu 21-23h
Via Giacchero 22/2 ✉ 17100 ☎ 019 80 74 94 🖨 019 82 57 44
📧 unpostopernoi@virgilio.it 📧 www.gay.it/arcigay/savona

SWIMMING
-Varigotti, castello (up the hill with the small castle besides the tunnel, on the left side to the sea/salire al castello, scendere giù con la corda; il left bay is interesting)

CRUISING
-Loano (seaside from railway station Loano in direction Borghetto, ⓟ ex-railway stop near Piazza del Popolo, at night/Lungomare da stazione FS Loano in direzione Borghetto, ⓟ ex-stazione FS vicino Piazza del Popolo, la notte)

Scandicci - Firenze ✉ 50018

CRUISING
-Outside the building of "Teatro Magazzini"

Senigallia - Ancona ✉ 60019

BARS
■ **Pensierostupendo** (B D glm S) Thu-Sun 21.30 h until Jun 15th, Tue-Sun 21.30 h after Jun 15th
Strada della Bruciata ✉ 60019 ☎ 0347 47 58 758
At residential centre "Le Piramidi" direction Monterado, after 7 km on the left/Centro Residenziale "Le Piramidi" prendere direzione per Monterado, a 7200 mt sulla sx. UNO card required/Ingresso con tessera UNO.

RESTAURANTS
■ **Al Molo** (b F g)
Via Banchina di Levante 6 ✉ 60019 ☎ 071 61 634

CRUISING
-Giardini Morandi (R)
-Railway Station/Stazione FS

Sesto Fiorentino ✉ 50019

SEX SHOPS/BLUE MOVIES
■ **Erotica - La Cosa Sexy Shop** (g) closed Sun and Mon morning
Viale Togliatti 131 ✉ 50019 ☎ 0554 21 64 70
Underwear, S/M articles, gay videos and magazines. Babilonia publications available.

Sibari - Cosenza ✉ 87070

CRUISING
-Beach "Pineta di Thurio" near Foggia Cantinella (best 14-18 h)

Sicilia

Sicilia - Agrigento ✉ 92100

BARS
■ **Galleria, La** (B g R)
Via Atenea 123 ✉ 92100

SPARTACUS 2001/2002 | 675

| **Italy** | Sicilia - Agrigento ▶ Sicilia - Catania |

In un grande complesso storico e pieno di verde, vicino alla stazione centrale, oltre ad una confortevole Sauna, troverai anche Pub-Ristorante e Discoteca.

●

In a storical and full of sap private area, very closed to Catania Central Station, you will find a confortable Sauna, and both a Pub-Restaurant and a Disco.

SAUNA MYKONOS A CATANIA

video bar and lounge
relax rooms
dark room
steam/finnish bath
video gay
air conditioned and music

infoline:
095 531355
0339 7370328
0328 7842210 (english spoken)

Via Platamone, 20 - Catania

RESTAURANTS

■ **Kalos** (B F g R)
Salita Filino 1 ✉ 92100 *(Near railway station/Stazione ferroviaria)*

HOTELS

■ **Colleverde Park Hotel** (AC B BF CC F H OS SOL)
Via Panoramica dei Templi ✉ 92100 *(1 km from station)*
☎ 0922 29 555 🖨 0922 29 012
Rates single Lit. 120.000, double 200.000, incl. bf.
■ **Foresteria Baglio della Luna** (AC B BF CC E F H)
Contradda da Maddalusa ✉ 92100 *(Valle dei Templi)*
☎ 0922 51 10 61
🖨 0922 59 88 02
Upper scale rooms. Rates Lit. 390.000-850.000.

SWIMMING

-Località San Leone (NU)
-Le Dune (last bus stop/capolinea circolare)
-Eraclea Minoa Beach, near Ribera

CRUISING

-Posteggio Autobus/bus parking (behind/dietro Astor cinema)
-Railway station/Stazione FS
-Piazza Vittorio Emanuele (in front of main post office/ davanti alla posta centrale)
-Viale della Vittoria (at bus stop/fermata bus)
-Piazza Fratelli Rosselli (R)
-Villa Communale

Sicilia - Capo d'Orlando ✉ 98071

BARS

■ **Oasis Club** (B g F OS VS) 21-2 h, Closed on Wed and in Aug
Via Forno 51 ✉ 98071 ☎ 0941 90 13 18
Typical sicilian cuisine.

Sicilia - Catania ✉ 95100

BARS

■ **Moon Club Pub** (B gLm) closed Mon
Via Empedocle 66 ✉ 95100
Mainly lesbian.
■ **Nievski** (B F glm MA s) 20-2 h, closed Mon
Scalinata Alessi 15/17 ✉ 95100 ☎ 095 31 37 92
Occasionally concerts and movies/Ogni tanto concerti e rassegne cinematografiche.
■ **SottosopraPub** (B glm MA) Thu-Sun
Via S. Fulci 9 ✉ 95100 ☎ 095 37 72 62

DANCECLUBS

■ **Pegaso's Club** (B D DR G TV VS s) Open from Oct to June only. Thu-Sun 22.30-? h
Via Canfora 9 ✉ 95128 ☎ 0347 72 67 661 (Infoline)
Arcigay card required. Disco on Sat and Sun. Cabaret and dragshow on Sun.
■ **Pegaso's Estate** (B BF D GLM MA OS Pl s) Open from Jun to Sep on Sat and Sun
Via Viale Kennedy 80 ✉ 95100 *(Entrance/Ingresso Lidi Playa)*
☎ 0347 72 67 661 (Infoline)
Shows on Sun. Call for more details.

Sicilia - Catania ▸ Sicilia - Palermo   Italy

SEX SHOPS/BLUE MOVIES
■ **Erotica**
Via Caronda 120   ☏ 095 50 50 10
■ **Tentazione**
Corso delle Province 38   ☏ 095 38 36 00

CINEMAS
■ **Nuovo Sarah** (g OG)
Via A. di Sangiuliano 124   ✉ 95100   ☏ 095 53 98 67

SAUNAS/BATHS
■ **Mykonos Sauna** (AC B d DR F G MA OS P SA SB VS) Thu, Sun 16-24, Fri Sat 17-3 h closed Mon-Wed & July-Aug
Via Platamone 20   ✉ 95131 (near central station/vicino stazione centrale)   ☏ 095 53 13 55
Also pub/restaurant : 19-3h every day, Disco on friday.

HOTELS
■ **Hotel Moderno** (BF H)
Via Alessi 9   ✉ 95124 (Near the Dome)   ☏ 095 32 62 50
🖶 095 32 66 74
Single room Lit 100.000, Double room 150.000 with bath, TV, phone and bf. Discreet gays welcome.

GENERAL GROUPS
■ **Centro di Iniziativa Gay e Lesbica Open Mind** 17-20 h
Via Gargano 33   ✉ 95129 (near Piazza Jouanda)   ☏ 095 53 26 85
🖶 095 53 26 85   🖳 opencatania@tiscalinet.it
Information, Counseling, Library, Cinema, Political campaigns/Informazioni, Telefonico amico, Biblioteca, Rassegne cinema, Iniziative politiche.

HEALTH GROUPS
■ **LILA - Lega Italiana Lotta contro l'Aids**
Via G. Sanfilippo 10   ✉ 95100   ☏ 095 55 10 17

CRUISING
-Piazza Grenoble (only by car)
-Portorossi (touristic harbour behind Piazza Europa-nude beach also)
-Villa Bellini (townpark's toilets, only afternoon)
-Porto (harbour, near the lighthouse, by car)
-Caito (the cliff behind the railway station-nude beach also)

Sicilia - Cefalú   ✉ 90015

CRUISING
-Beach promenade/Lungomare

Sicilia - Enna   ✉ 94100

CRUISING
-Around the Castello Lombardo/attorno al Castello Lombardo

Sicilia - Messina   ✉ 98100

BARS
■ **Haiti** (B G)
Via T. Cannizzaro   ✉ 98100
■ **Select** (B g)
Via T. Cannizzaro   ✉ 98100 (near/vicino university)

CINEMAS
■ **Capitol** (g)
Via N. Bixio 70   ✉ 98100   ☏ 090 29 35 422

HEALTH GROUPS
■ **Anlaids**
Viale Regina Elena 223   ✉ 98121   ☏ 090 46 138

CRUISING
-Harbor area/Zona Porto (R)
-Villetta public gardens/giardini pubblici (Via T. Cannizzaro, behind/dietro Royal Palace Hotel)
-Railway Station/Stazione FS
-Piazza Cairoli (north and south/nord e sud)
-Marittima Railway Station/Stazione
-Viale San Martino (evenings only/solo sera)

Sicilia - Palermo   ✉ 90100

GAY INFO
■ **Arcigay Arcilesbica Palermo** Meetings of Arcilesbica on Wed 21.30 h
Via Genova 7   ✉ 90133   ☏ 091 33 56 88   🖶 091 61 13 245

BARS
■ **Exit** (AC B d f G MA s) 21-3 h
Piazza S. Francesco di Paola 39/40   ✉ 90141 (between/fra il Teatro Politeama and Teatro Massimo)
☏ 0348 78 14 698 (Infoline)
Disco bar.
■ **I Grilli Giu** (A B f glm MA) Mon closed
Largo Cavalieri di Malta 11   ✉ 90133 (historical centre/centro storico)
☏ 091 58 47 47

DANCECLUBS
■ **Feste in discoteca-itineranti "Vannigrilli - Invito a Nocce"** (B D glm s WE YG)
☏ 0360 65 78 58
Call for info. House music club.

RESTAURANTS
■ **Ristorante "I Grilli"** (CC F glm) 20.30-? h, Mon and Jul-Sep closed
Largo Cavalieri di Malta 21   ✉ 90133   ☏ 091 33 41 30
Cosy atmosphere.

CINEMAS
■ **Embassy**
Via Mariano Stabile 223   ✉ 90100   ☏ 091 58 64 94
■ **Etoile**
Via Mariano Stabile 241
■ **Orfeo** (g r)
Via Maqueda 25

BOOK SHOPS
■ **Altroquando** Mon-Sat 9-13.30, 16-19.30 h
Corso Vittorio Emanuele 145   ✉ 90100   ☏ 091 61 14 732
Library with gay and lesbian books, magazines, comics and videos (non porno).

LEATHER & FETISH SHOPS
■ **Cuioa. Le** Mon.Sat 9-13, 16-19.30 h
Via Ponticello 28   ✉ 90133 (historical centre/centro storico)
☏ 091 61 72 831
Traditional work of leather objects/Lavorazione artigianale oggetti di cuoio.

HEALTH GROUPS
■ **Anlaids**
Via Saverio Scrofani 44   ✉ 90143   ☏ 091 62 62 425
🖶 091 62 62 425

SWIMMING
-Balestrate
-Sferracavallo beach/spiaggia (very cruisy)
-Vasca delle Vergine (Barcarello) (on the rocks/rocce)

Italy | Sicilia - Palermo ▶ Sicilia - Taormina

CRUISING
- Railway Station/Stazione FS (6-23.30 h)
- Foro Italico public garden/Giardino publico (days and nights)
- Via Gaetano Daita (TV) (evenings)
- Parco della Favorita, behind/dietro l'Ippodrome (days and nights)
- Giardino Inglese, WC (days)
- Viale Libertà

Sicilia - **Ragusa** ✉ 97100

CRUISING
- Kamarina beach (by/adiacente Club Med)
- Playa Grande (between village and mouth of River Irminio, left of disco La Fazenda, also on the beach below./tra villagio e foce del fiume Irminio)
- square in front of railway station and side streets/piazzale antistante stazione centrale e vie laterali
- Sampieri beach (opposite/contrada Pisciotto)

Sicilia - **Sciacca** ✉ 92019

CRUISING
- Terme Selinuntine

Sicilia - **Siracusa** ✉ 96100

CINEMAS
■ **Capitol** (g)
Via Italia 32 ✉ 96100 ☎ 0931 75 61 11

GENERAL GROUPS
■ **Arcigay Athena** Thu 21-1 h
c/o Verdi, Via Trieste 24 ✉ 96100 ✉ barbiaga@sistemia.it

CRUISING
- Pantheon (gardens/giardini)
- Motel Agip (corso Gelone, gardens/giardini)
- Apollo temple/tempio
- Lido Sayonara (Località Fontane Bianche)

Sicilia - **Stromboli** ✉ 98050

HOTELS
■ **Sciara. La** (B F g H OS Pl SOL)
Via S. Barnao ✉ 98050 ☎ 090 98 60 04
All rooms have telephone, priv. bath and balcony.
■ **Sirenetta Park Hotel** (AC B BF CC F glm H PI) Open from Mar 31st-Oct 31st
Via Marina 33 ✉ 98050 ☎ 090 98 60 25 ☎ 090 98 61 24
✉ lasirenetta@netnet.it ☐ www.netnet.it/hotel/lasirenetta
Beach location, all rooms have phone, priv. bath and balcony.

SWIMMING
- Spiaggia Lunga (in fondo alla Rocca/at bottom of Rocca)

Sicilia - **Taormina** ✉ 98039

BARS
■ **Casanova Bar** (AC B CC f MA N OS) 18-3 h, closed on Wed in winter
Vico Paladini 2/4 ✉ 98039 ☎ 0942 23 945
Cocktail bar, crepes and sandwiches.
■ **Re del Sole** (B f g) May-Oct
Spisone Strada Statale 114 ☎ 0942 62 53 85
Beach bar near the gay beach "Rocce Bianche". Restaurant service until 16 h.
■ **Shatulle** (B f g OS) Mar-Oct: 9-4, closed on Mon, Nov-Feb: daily 18-4 h
Piazzetta Paladini 2 ✉ 98039 ☎ 0942 62 61 75
Cocktail bar and creperie.

ISOCO
GUEST HOUSE TAORMINA

Via Salita Branco, 2
98039 Taormina
Tel.& Fax 0942 23679
E-Mail : info@isoco.it
http://www.isoco.it

All rooms with AC, Cable TV, Radio and Minibar

DANCECLUBS
■ **Discoteca Marabù** (B D g) 23-6 h, summer only
Via Iannuzzo *(near Taormina)* ☎ 0942 65 30 29
Techno house music, many gays on Tue.
■ **Discoteca Taitu** (B g D) 23-6 h, winter only
Via Vulcano 3 *(near Taormina)* ☎ 0942 51 407
Techno house music.

BOOK SHOPS
■ **Edizione Vittorio Malambrí**
Corso Umberto 108 ✉ 98039 ☎ 0942 24 621
Photos, books, videos and calendars on Wilhelm von Gloeden/Collezione fotografica, libri, videocassette, calendri su Wilhelm von Gloeden.

HOTELS
■ **Hotel La Plage** (AC BF H)
Via Nazionale 104 ✉ 98039 ☎ 0942 62 60 95 ☎ 0942 62 58 50
☐ www.laplage.it
■ **Hotel Romantik Villa Ducale** (AC B BF CC E f H MA NG OS WH) Closed Dec 1st -Feb 20th
Via Leonardo da Vinci 60 ✉ 98039 ☎ 0942 28 153
☎ 0942 28 710 ✉ villaducale@tao.it
Rates Lit. 250.000-400.000. Suite 650.000.
■ **Hotel Splendid** (BF B CC F g H PI OS) Closed Nov-Mar except 31st Dec and 1st Jan
Via Dietro Cappuccini ✉ 98039 *(Centrally located)* ☎ 0942 23 500
☎ 0942 62 52 89
Single room Lit 80.000, Double room 140.000 with phone, priv. bath, bf and balcony.
■ **Hotel Villa Schuler** (AC B BF CC H MA msg OS) closed Dec-Feb
Piazzetta Bastione/Via Roma ✉ 98039 ☎ 0942 23 481
☎ 0942 23 522 ✉ schuler@tao.it ☐ www.villaschuler.com
All rooms have priv. bath, balcony with a great sea-view. Rates from Lit 120.000 (single)-230.000 (double).

Italy

Sicilia Taormina ▶ Sorrento - Napoli

in Taormina
Privé LA PLAGE ★★★★
...the privilege for only few

Hotel La Plage
Tel. 0942.626095
Fax 0942.625850
http://www.laplage.it
http://www.sicilyok.com/laplage

A limited part from the Hotel are available for Privé LA PLAGE. With eight different offers to guarantee a holiday for 12 years, every year with a large flexibility.

For further information
800 800 346 PER TELEFONATE
+39.942.620.007 DALL'ITALIA
http://www.laplage.it
http://www.sicilyok.com/laplage

Privé LA PLAGE s.r.l. Via Libertà, 78 - Palermo

■ **Pensione Adele** (BF H g)
Via Apollo Arcageta *(near Porta Catania)* ☎ 0942 23 352
🖨 0942 23 352
Single room Lit 70.000, Double room 136.000, bf and dinner incl. Cosy atmosphere.

GUEST HOUSES
■ **Isoco Guest House** (AC BF CC GLM H msg OS P WO) *open only from Apr to Oct*
Via Salita Branco 2 ✉ 98039 *(Central, near San Antonio church)*
☎ 0942 23 679 🖨 0942 23 679 💻 info@isoco.it 🖥 www.isoco.it
Beautiful view on the coast/Bellissima veduta panoramica sulla costa. Double from Lit 109.000 to 169.000 with TV, minibar, AC and radio.

SWIMMING
-Rocce Bianche (G MA NU) (take any beach/spiaggia bus, the gay beach is at the white rocks between Re del Sole andd Caparena)
-Fondaco Parrino (G MA NU) (Strada Statale 114, near Capo St. Alessio. Take bus direction Messina or Forza d'Argo, step out at Camping Paradise. Cruising)

CRUISING
-Parco Triangolo (in front of Hotel Excelsior)

Sicilia - Trapani ✉ 91100
CINEMAS
■ **Diana** (g) Sat Sun
Via dei Mille ✉ 91100 *(Hall J)* ☎ 0923 21 163

CRUISING
-Beach/spiaggia Scogliera delle Vergini

Siena ✉ 53100
GENERAL GROUPS
■ **Arcigay Arcilesbica Ganimède** Wed 21.30-23 h
Via Massetana Romana 18 ✉ 53100 ☎ 0577 28 89 77
🖨 0577 27 15 38 💻 ganimede@gay.it
🖥 www.gay.it/arcigay/siena
Phone-line, counseling, weekly meetings, shows, exhibitions.

CRUISING
-Railway Station/Stazione FS
-Via Roma
-Giardini La Lizza
-Piazza del Campo
-Fortezza Medicea (at foot of the little garden and along Viale Viattorio Veneto, but only from 22-1 h, and during the day, especially in the afternoon, Viale G. Marconi/al piede del giardinetto e lungo Viale Vittorio Veneto solo 22-1 h, e durante il giorno, specialmente il pomeriggio, Viale G. Marconi)
- P in front of Golden Bar (Via Fiorentina)

Sondrio ✉ 23100
SEX SHOPS/BLUE MOVIES
■ **Magic America** (g) Closed on Mon morning
Via Mazzini 46 ✉ 23100 ☎ 0342 56 72 92

CRUISING
-Via Samaden and Zona Agneda (evenings/sera by car)

Sorrento - Napoli ✉ 80067
SWIMMING
-Bagni Regina Giovanna (NU) (popular/frequentato)

Italy | Sorrento - Napoli ▶ Torino

CRUISING
-Villa Communale (at night; also at the end of the avenue/di notte; anche in fondo al viale)
-Piazzetta V. Veneto (in the gardens/nei giardini)
-Stazione Circumvesuviana (facilities/bagni)
-Piazza del Monumento

Spessa Po - Pavia ✉ 27010
SWIMMING
-Along River Po/lungo il Po (g MA NU r) (afternoons/pomeriggio)

Spresiano - Treviso ✉ 31027
SWIMMING
-Ponte della Priula (NU) (between Treviso and Conegliano, on River Piave; coming from Treviso take the path on the right after Ponte restaurant, just before Ponte della Priula; swimming, action, also in winter/fra Treviso e Conegliano, venendo da Treviso imboccare il sentiero a destra dopo il ristorante Ponte; poco prima di Ponte della Priula; nuoto, azione, anche d'inverno)

Taranto ✉ 74100
CINEMAS
■ **Flamma** (g)
Via Gorizia ✉ 74100
GENERAL GROUPS
■ **Arcigay Arcilesbica Delfino** Mon, Thu 20.30-22.30 h
Via Sannio 25 ✉ 74100 ☎ 099 73 51 710
SWIMMING
-Scogliera delle Donne Maledette (NU) (San Vito - Lido Bruno, 7 km from Taranto, way for 'Sun Bay', romantic spot; also known as Le Conchette/7 km da Taranto, via per 'Sun Bay', posto romantico; anche chiamato Le Conchette)
-Cancello Rosso (NU) (Lama, close to the supermarket/ vicino il supermercato 'Tidy dei fiori', red entry/ entrare nel cancello rosso, 200 m to the left up to the tower/ la scogliera a sinistra fino alla torretta)
CRUISING
-Seafront/Lungomare di Taranto (at night/di notte, AYOR)
-Viale Virgilio (R TV) (at night/di notte)
-Railway Station/Stazione FS
-Parco della Rimembranza and parking nearby/e parcheggio attiguo
-Ponte Punta Penn (TV) (near/vicino Caserma Aeronautica, AYOR at night/di notte)

Tarquinia - Viterbo ✉ 01016
CRUISING
-Piazza Cavour (evenings/sera)
-Tarquinia Lido (near/vicino Porto Clementino, all day in the summer/tutto il giorno d'estate)

Termoli - Campobasso ✉ 86039
CRUISING
-Railway station/stazione FS
-Port, near red lamp/molo del porto, faro rosso

Terni ✉ 05100
CRUISING
-Giardini Via Lungonera Savoia
-Viale Fonderia
-Stadium/stadio Libero Liberati
-Corso Tacito
-Railway Station/Stazione FS

Torino ✉ 10100
GAY INFO
■ **Informagay** Tue 21-23, Sat 17-20 h
Via S. Chiara 1 ☎ 011 43 65 000 🖷 011 43 68 638
✉ infogay@arpnet.it
Telephone help, Aids group, parties, cultural events. National secretariat of Forum Aids Italia.
■ **Maurice - Circolo Culturale Gay E Lesbico** (GLM) Mon-Sat 15-19 h
Via Basilica 3/5 ✉ 10122 ☎ 011 52 11 116 🖷 011 52 11 932
✉ maurice@arpnet.it www.arpnet.it/maurice/
Cultural group, gayline, meetings, information about gay life, entertainment, lesbian group/circolo culturale, linea gay, riunioni, informazioni sulla vita gay, conferenze, spettacoli, gruppo lesbico.
PUBLICATIONS
■ **DiversaMente**
c/o Maurice-Circolo Culturale Gay e Lesbico, Via della Basilica 3/5 ✉ 10122 www.arpnet.it/maurice/DiversaMente
Monthly publication of Maurice-Circolo Culturale Gay e Lesbico.
CULTURE
■ **Fondazione Sandro Penna** Mon-Fri 9-18 h

---

www.upcity.it
the best of gay city map

Maps to the most important italian cities are update each month Maps will be located in all clubs and pubs. Entertainment, clubs parties and events going on in town!

Le mappe delle città più importanti d'Italia con guida aggiornate mensilmente. Le trovate in tutti i locali gay!

For information and publicizing:
echo communication Via S. Nicolao 10 — 20123 Milano
Tel. 0039 02 89015940-1 Fax 0039 02 89013990

680 *SPARTACUS* 2001/2002

Torino | Italy

Via S. Chiara 1 ✉ 10140 ☏ 011 52 12 00 33 🖥 fsp@arpnet.it
💻 www.fondazionesandropenna.org
Library, gay press, cultural centre, archive. Call for appointment.
■ **Maurice - Centro di Documentazione** Thu 16-19 h
Via Basilica 3/5 ✉ 10122 ☏ 011 52 11 116 🖨 011 52 11 132
🖥 maurice@arpnet.it 💻 www.arpnet.it/maurice/
Library and archives, Lectures/Biblioteca e archivio con prestito, Presentazione libri.

BARS

■ **Caffè Lerì** (B d f GLM s) 21.30-3 h, closed Mon
Corso Vittorio Emanuele II, 64 ✉ 10100 ☏ 011 54 30 75
Concerts, piano-bar, cocktails. Cabaret Wed & Sat. Disco on Wed.
■ **Male. II** (B f GLM MA) 20-3, Sat Sun -4 h, closed Tue
Via Lombardore 10/Via Barbania *(Bus 57, Tram 4)* ☏ 011 28 46 17
Single party on Thu. Bears night on Fri.
■ **Radio Kingston** (B d F g s YG) 11-15, 19-2 h, closed Sun
Via Ormea, 78/D ☏ 011 65 02 346
Nice restaurant-Bar with ska music, DJ, theme parties. Only few gays.

CAFES

■ **Les Chats** (AC B BF f glm MA N) 7.30-20 h, closed Sun
Via Carlo Alberto 28 ✉ 10123 *(Bus 61, Tram 18)* ☏ 011 56 25 361

DANCECLUBS

■ **Centralino-Dietrich. II** (AC b D GLM MA s) Fri Sun 24-4 h
Via delle Rosine 16/A ✉ 10100 ☏ 0335 53 49 808 *(Infoline)*
Drag show on Fri, strip on Sun. DJ Superpippo.
■ **Metropolis Club** (AC B D G WE) Sat 0-4 h
Via Principessa Clotilde 82 ✉ 10100 *(near Piazza Statuto)*
☏ 011 48 41 16
Commercial music/Musica commerciale.
■ **Tuxedo** (AC B D GLM MA s SNU) Wed 23-3, Sat 23.30-? h, closed in Aug
Via Belfiore 8 ✉ 10124 *(vicino alla stazione/ close to railway station Porta Nuova)* ☏ 0339 37 51 791 *(Infoline)*

RESTAURANTS

■ **La Reseda** (BF F glm) 6-15, 19-24, Wed 6-15, Sun 18-24 h
Corso Palermo 14bis ✉ 10100 ☏ 011 85 70 74
Ristorante, Pizzeria.

SEX SHOPS/BLUE MOVIES

■ **Drop Out** (g) Mon 13-19.30, Tue-Sat 10-19.30 h
Via Carlo Alberto 41 ✉ 10123 *(in the court)* ☏ 011 81 25 345
Large section with videos, underwear, magazines, accessories (also S/M).

16th edition

DA SODOMA A HOLLYWOOD
TURIN INTERNATIONAL GAY AND LESBIAN FILM FESTIVAL

19/25 April 2001

Office: Piazza San Carlo, 161
10123 Turin - ITALY
ph: +39 011 534 888 - fax: +39 011 535 796
www.turinglfilmfestival.com
info@turinglfilmfestival.com

■ **Erotika** (CC g) Mon 14-20, Tue-Sat 10-20 h
Belfiore 20 ✉ 10125 *(Near railway station Porta Nuova)*
☏ 011 65 79 44
■ **O** (g) Mon 14.30-19.30, Tue-Sat 9.30-12.30, 14.30-19.30 h
Via Sacchi 40 ✉ 10128 ☏ 011 59 15 85
Large gay section.
■ **Temptation Sexy Shop** (glm) Mon-Sat 9.30-20 h
Via San Pio V 7/c *(30 m from railway station Porta nuova)*
☏ 011 66 90 706
Videos to rent and for sale/Vendite e noleggio videocassette in italiano e in lingua originale.

CINEMAS

■ **Hollywood** (MA r) 10.30-1.30 h
Corso Regina Margherita 106 ☏ 011 52 12 385

Discoteca
Tuxedo
"for gays, lesbians and their friends"

il sabato notte ore 24,00
il mercoledí notte ore 23,00

via belfiore, 8 - Torino
vicino Stazione Porta Nuova lato via Nizza
info: Fabietto 0339.3751791

Italy Torino

011 sauna club
piscina riscaldata
bagno turco
sauna finlandese
labirynth
hard-core movies
dark room
sling room
snack video bar
sala giochi e lettura
camerini relax
locale climatizzato

Via Messina 5/d
Torino
(largo Regio Parco)
+39.011 28 42 63

■ **Regina** (g MA r) 15-24 h
Corso Regina Margherita 123 ✉ 10122 *(Near/vicino Porta Palazzo, Tram 3/4/16/Bus 12/50/51/77)* ☎ 011 43 62 092
■ **Roma** (g)
Via San Donato 10/bis ☎ 011 48 77 65
Busy/Frequentato.

SAUNAS/BATHS
■ **Antares** (B DR f G p SA SB VS YG) 13-24 h, Mon closed
Via Pigafetta 73/D ✉ 10129 *(near Largo Orbassano, Bus 64, tram 10,12)* ☎ 011 50 16 45
Small basement sauna in the south of Turin.
■ **Blue** (! b DR F G msg P SA SB SOL VS WO YG) Sun-Thu 12-24, Fri Sat -2 h, Wed closed
Corso Vigevano 41 ✉ 10152 *(Bus 52/46/49/12-Dora)* ☎ 011 24 90 004
Sauna frequented by a young crowd.
■ **San Martino** (G MA SA SB) 15-20 h, closed Tue
Corso S. Martino 8/G ✉ 10122 *(near Porta Susa railway station)* ☎ 011 53 37 94
■ **011 Sauna Club** (! AC B DR f G MA p s SA SB VS WH) Mon-Fri 15-2, Sat -4 Sun -1 h, Aug closed
Via Messina 5/D ✉ 10153 *(Tram 18/Bus 63)* ☎ 011 28 42 63
2nd Fri cruising in clothes, last Fri dresscode leather (sauna closed).

BOOK SHOPS
■ **Libreria Luxemburg** (AC CC g) Mon-Sat 7-19.30 h
Via Battisti 7 ✉ 10123 *(Centro storico)* ☎ 011 56 13 896
International book-shop. Gay friendly information, videos and gay literature.

FASHION SHOPS
■ **Gigolo1** Mon 15.30-19.30, Tue-Fri 9.30-19.30, Sat 9.30-13, 15.30-19.30 h
Via dei Mercanti 11C ✉ 10100 ☎ 011 54 21 69
Underwear for men.
■ **Non Solo Intimo** (CC g) Mon 15-19.30, Tue-Sat 10-13, 15-19.30 h
Via Carlo Alberto 41 ✉ 10123 ☎ 011 83 73 16

NEWS STANDS
■ **Kiosk/Rivendita Giornali**
Corso Vittorio Emanuele II 58 ✉ 10121 *(opposite railway station/di fronte Porta Nuova stazione FS)*

TRAVEL AND TRANSPORT
■ **Blue** (CC GLM) 15-18 h, Wed closed
Corso Vigevano 41 ✉ 10152 ☎ 011 24 90 004 ⌨ 011 28 39 96
Tour operator.

■ **Yag Tours** (CC GLM) Mon-Sat 9.30-12.30, 15-19 h
Via S. Anselmo 2/H ✉ 10100 *(near railway station/vicino stazione Porta Nuova)* ✉ yagtours@xoommail.com

HOTELS
■ **Hotel Napoleon** (B BF CC glm OS)
Via XX Settembre 5 ✉ 10121 ☎ 011 56 13 223 ⌨ 011 54 08 20
Rates single Lit 150.000, double 210.000 (bf incl.). All rooms with bath, TV, fridge. Gays welcome: 30% discount for Spartacus readers.

GENERAL GROUPS
■ **Agedo - Associazione Genitori Parenti e Amici di Omosessuali**
✉ 10100 ☎ 011 52 11 116
Call for information.
■ **Arcigay Michelangelo** Mon-Fri 12-18 h
Corso Vigevano 41 ✉ 10152 ☎ 011 24 90 004
■ **LILA - Lega Italiana Lotta contro l'Aids** Mon 19-22, Wed Fri 18-20 h
Corso Regina Margherita 190/E ✉ 10152 ☎ 011 43 61 043
Information, psychological and legal counselling, home care.

HEALTH GROUPS
■ **Anlaids** Mon Wed Fri 15-19 h
Via C. Botta 3 ✉ 10122 ☎ 011 43 65 541 ⌨ 011 43 65 541
✉ p-anlaids@iol.it
Prevention and information.
■ **Philadelphia** Thu 21-23 h
Via Baretti 8 ✉ 10125 ☎ 011 65 75 82
Gay association for health and against AIDS.

RELIGIOUS GROUPS
■ **Agape-Gruppo Gay Credenti**
✉ 10060 *(Eucumenic centre in Val Germanasca)* ☎ 0121 80 75 14 ⌨ 0121 80 76 90
Summer camp "Faith and homosexuality"/Campo estivo "Fede e omosessualità".
■ **Davide e Gionata - Gruppo Omosessuali Credenti** Tue 21 h
Via Giolitti 21/A ✉ 10100 ☎ 011 88 98 11
Christian meetings, lectures, entertainment.

SPECIAL INTEREST GROUPS
■ **Altra Comunicazione. L'**
☎ 011 53 48 88 ⌨ 011 53 57 96 ✉ glfilmfest@assioma.com
✉ www.turinglfilmfestival.com
Organization of the gay & lesbian film festival.
■ **Linea Trans (Arcitrans)** (TV)
☎ 011 52 11 116

CRUISING
-Corso Marche *(near corner Regina Margherita in gardens, ayor! police checks)*

SPARTACUS 2001/2002

Torino ▶ Varese | Italy

-Lumini, Cimitero Monumentale, Lungo Dora Colletta (by car night and day/in macchina)
-Stazione di Porta Nuova e Porta Susa (r) (police checks/controlli polizia)
-Parco del Valentino (by car, also on foot/in macchina, anche a piedi, Corso Galilei/Viale Marinai d'Italia)
-Corso Palestro (in the public toilet)
-Parco delle Vallere, Moncalieri (by car during the day only)
-Parco Pellerina, Via Pietro Cossa (by car at night AYOR, jogging during the day)
-Piazza d'armi (evenings/de sera)

Torre del Greco - Napoli ✉ 80059

BARS
■ **Makumba** (B D g YG) 22-? h, but gay only Sat night
Via De Gasperi 141 ✉ 80059
Good music/buona musica.

Torre del Lago ✉ 55049
☞ Viareggio

Trento ✉ 38100

GENERAL GROUPS
■ **Arcigay Arcilesbica Trento**
c/o Centro "B. Disertori", Piazza Mostra 19 ✉ 38100
☎ 0461 98 08 71 📠 0461 23 55 81

CRUISING
-Piazza Dante (in front of railway station)(AYOR)
-Piazza de Gaspari

Treviso ✉ 31100

SEX SHOPS/BLUE MOVIES
■ **Magic America** (CC g p) Closed on Mon morning
Via Castello d'Amore 7/9 ✉ 31100 *(Zona Stadio Calcio)*
☎ 0422 30 40 99

SAUNAS/BATHS
☞ Godega di Sant'Urbano

CRUISING
-Little park along the old city walls facing the railway station/Giardinelli lungo le vecchie mura di fronte alla stazione FS

Trieste ✉ 34100

DANCECLUBS
■ **Nepenthes** Sat only
Duino Aurisina *(near Sistiana Costa dei Barbari)* ☎ 040 20 89 93

SEX SHOPS/BLUE MOVIES
■ **Magic America** (CC g p) Closed Mon morning
Viale Miramare 11 ✉ 34135 *(near Stazione Centrale)*
☎ 040 41 27 35

GENERAL GROUPS
■ **Arcigay Arcilesbica Trieste**
Piazza Duca degli Abruzzi 3 ✉ 34100 ☎ 040 39 61 11
📠 040 30 12 16 📧 arcigaylesbica.trieste@poboxes.com
■ **Telefono Amico Gay e Lesbica** Mon 19-22 h
☎ 040 63 06 06 📧 tagl.ts@libero.it

SWIMMING
-Costa dei Barbari (! NU glm) Sistiana (across from the bar Costa dei Barbari. From carpark walk down hill then to the left)

CRUISING
-Railway Station/Stazione FS
-Molo Audace (pier opposite Piazza Unità-late evenings)
-Viale Romolo Gessi (nights only, from Campo Marzio up the hill on viale Romolo Gessi. All the hillside and gardens on the right)

Tropea - Cosenza ✉ 88038

SWIMMING
-Beach at Santa Damenica (rocky beach between spiaggia formicoli and spiaggia riendi)

CRUISING
-Piazza Vittorio Veneto (public gardens/giardini pubblici)
-Corso Vittorio Emanuele (till late at night/fino a tardi)

Udine ✉ 33100

BARS
■ **Camparino. Il** (B glm) until 24 h
Viale Volontari della Liberta 3A ✉ 33100 ☎ 0432 47 01 77

SEX SHOPS/BLUE MOVIES
■ **Magic America** (CC g p) Closed Mon morning
Via Manzini 38/A ✉ 33100 ☎ 0432 29 73 45

CINEMAS
■ **Diana** (g OG)
Via Cividale 81 ✉ 33100 ☎ 0432 28 29 79

GENERAL GROUPS
■ **Arcigay Arcilesbica Udine**
Via Orghi 4/231 ✉ 33100 *(cortile interno/interior courtyard)*
☎ 0432 52 38 38 📠 0432 61 23 37 📧 udinegay@poboxes.com
💻 www.gayfriuli.it
Mon gay bar, gays from the whole region.

CRUISING
-Piazza I Maggio and gardens/e giardini

Varazze - Savona ✉ 17019

CRUISING
-Piani d'Invrea, along the rocks/passeggiata scogliera
-Railway station, inside, outside/stazione, interno e esterno

Varese ✉ 21100

GAY INFO
■ **Arcigay Arcilesbica Varese** Wed 21-23 h
Via Piave 6 ✉ 21100 *(near station)* ☎ 0332 23 59 59
📧 arcigayvarese@hotmail.com

BARS
■ **Magazzino. Il** (B glm) Closed Mon
Via Armellini ✉ 21100

HEALTH GROUPS
■ **Network Nazionale "Gruppo C" Progetto di Ricerca Aids**
☎ 0332 26 43 56
Helpline for people with HIV/Aids.

| Italy | Varese |

FLUG 3343 SAUNA

Via Pradisera, 58
Gallarate (VA)
(near to the Malpensa Airport)
Infoline 03358190705

Varese ▸ Venezia | Italy

VENEZIA
Mestre
via Cappuccina, 82b Tel. +39 041 538 42 99

- Sauna Finlandese
- Bagno Turco / Steam Bath
- Idromassaggio / Whirlpool
- Camerini Relax / Private rooms
- Messagge Serv.
- Video X X X
- Snack Video Bar
- Air Cond.

Ingresso riservato ai soli soci
All Major Credit Cards Accepted — UNO CLUB CARD

www.metroclub.it

SAUNE MILANO • PADOVA • VENEZIA

CRUISING
- Piazzale Kennedy (R AYOR) (police)
- North Railway Station (R AYOR) (police)
- Cimitero di Giubiano-Via Maspero (AYOR)

Varzi - Pavia ✉ 27057

CRUISING
- Piazza della Fiera (evenings/sera)

Venezia ✉ 30100

GAY INFO
■ **Arcigay Arcilesbica "Dedalo"** (! B F GLM MA) Tue 21-23 h, Info-line: Mon 19-21, Thu 21-23 h
Via A. Costa 38/A ✉ 30170 Mestre (2nd floor/2° piano) ☎ 0335 40 70 79 ☎ 041 53 84 151 (Infoline) 🖥 cinema@libero.it
🖥 www.gay.it/arcigay/venezia
Gay center organising lots of cultural events, sometimes shows.

RESTAURANTS
■ **Al Vecchio Borgo** (AC B bf CC F glm H lj OS)
Via Romanziol 27 ✉ 30020 Noventa di Piave (25 km from Venezia. Wed closed)
☎ 0329 21 54 412 (Infoline)
Restaurant & hotel: Single room Lit 60.000, double room 90.000 with Bath room, phone, TV and garage.

SAUNAS/BATHS
■ **Metrò Venezia Club Sauna** (AC B CC DR f G msg MA P SA SB WH YG)
14-2 h
Via Cappuccina 82/B ✉ 35100 Mestre (500 m from the railway station Mestre. Bus 2/7) ☎ 041 53 84 299
New modern sauna on 600 m². Relax cabins. Arcigay membership required.

NEWS STANDS
■ **Kiosk/Rivendita Giornali**
Rialto 10/53

TRAVEL AND TRANSPORT
■ **Venice à la Carte** (CC GLM)
Dorsoduro 3167 ✉ 30123 (Historical centre, next to the Grand Canal, Water bus-Ca' Rezzonico) ☎ 041 27 70 564 📠 001 240 208 72 73
🖥 alvise@tourvenice.org 🖥 www.tourvenice.org
Personalised visits of all interesting and secret aspects of Venetian life. Tailor-made and personalised holidays, adapted to ones own cultural interests (music, antiques, art, historic sites, private houses and gardens, etc.). Accompaniment with a knowledgable, mixed (Venetian &Americ-

an) couple. All daytime expenses include,

HOTELS
■ **Hotel Sardegna** (AC BF CC H NG)
Calle del Forno 2655 ✉ 30100 ☎ 041 72 22 31 📠 041 72 07 14
Single Lit 150.000-180.000, Double Lit 200.000-250.000 with bath, television and phone. Not gay, but discreet gays are welcome./Non gay, ma gay discreti benvenuti.
■ **Lato Azzurro, Il** (A AC BF H MA msg OS)
Via Forti 26 ✉ 30141 S. Erasmo (near Murano) ☎ 041 52 30 642
☎ 0348 44 36 304 📠 041 52 30 642 🖥 other.venice@flashnet.it
🖥 it.fortunecity.com/lunapark/eventi/17/index.htm
Rates Lit 90.000 (double) and 110.000 (triple), with bath/shower, bf at Lit. 5.000. Spanish, French and English spoken.

GENERAL GROUPS

Chiuso il mercoledì

Locanda
Trattoria - Pizzeria

Al Vecchio Borgo

da Graziano e Edoardo

Via Romanziol, 27 - Noventa di Piave (Venezia)
Tel. 0421 65152 - Fax 0421 572807
Info line 0329 2154412 - 0328 4937864

Italy | Venezia ▶ Verona

Centro Culturale di Vacanza
Il lato azzurro
Venezia • Isola di S. Erasmo

A Delightful Alternative in Venice
Via Forti, 26 30141 S. Erasmo Venezia
☎ 041-5230642 (fax/Q)
☎ 041-2444900 / ✆ 0348-4436304
other.venice@flashnet.it
http://it.fortunecity.com/lunapark/eventi/17/index.htm

Located on Venice's "Secret" Garden Island,
with beautiful views across the Lagoon.
All tourist highlights are a short boat ride away.
Relax at nearby beach or tour the island by bike.
Very reasonable rates / All room with private bath
Languages spoken: spanish, french, english

August 2001: italian courses for G&L foreigners
August 1–12: Beginners
August 20–31: Intermediate
August 13–19: Sebastian Week
Gay week looking for the venecian Sebastian

■ **Agedo - Associazione Genitori Parenti e Amici di Omosessuali**
Sun Mon 20-22 h
✉ 30100 ☎ 041 53 40 796

HEALTH GROUPS
■ **Network Nazionale "Gruppo C" Progetto di Ricerca Aids**
Via S. Maria dei Battuti 1/B ✉ 30174 Mestre ☎ 041 98 78 68
💻 me.dipre1@ulss12.ve
HIV-Test: Mon, Fri 9-12, Tue, Thu 14.30-16 h

SWIMMING
- San Marco (along the fence of the Royal Gardens next to the Piazza along the water front. Mostly in warm months from 22 h).
- Rialto (MA) (Public toilets on the side of the market, after dark)
- Under the overpass between Mestre and Marghera (ayor YG) (Via Electricità (off Via Fratelli Bandiera) and side streets, especially near the truck scale, also street along the canal next to the Ship Yard. Busy after dark)
- Via Ca'Marcello, Mestre (occasionally at night by car)

CRUISING
- San Marco (along the fence of the Royal Gardens next to the Piazza along the water front. Mostly in warm months from 22 h).
- Rialto (MA) (Public toilets on the side of the market, after dark)

Ventimiglia - Imperia ✉ 18039
SWIMMING
- Balzi Rossi (Coming from Ventimiglia through the first tunnel, [P] before the gas station, go down, pass under the railway line, to the left)

Vercelli ✉ 13100
CRUISING
- Piazza Mazzini (occasional police patrols/occasionalmente controlli di polizia)
- Railway Station/Stazione FS

Verona ✉ 37100

PUBLICATIONS
■ **PINK**
c/o Arci, Via Nazario Sauro 2 ✉ 37129
Queer magazine published by the local section of Arcigay. Available in gay bars in town. Information about political issues and the local scene./Pubblicato dall' Arcigay di Verona, é disponibile nei bar gay della città. Parla della scena gay-lesbica e di diritti civili.

TOURIST INFO
■ **A.P.T.** Mon-Sat 9-19 h
Piazza Erbe 38 ✉ 37100 ☎ 045 80 68 680 🖨 045 80 68 680

BARS
■ **Bar Al Semaforo** (B G MA r TV) Summer: 20-2, Winter: 19-2 h, closed Mon
Via Unitá d'Italia 100 ✉ 37132 *(in S. Michele)* ☎ 045 97 64 01
■ **Campofiore** (B f glm MA) 9-15, 20-2, Mon 9-15 h, closed Sun
Via Campofiore 35 ✉ 37121 *(near University)* ☎ 045 80 32 534

CAFES
■ **Café Bukowski** (B glm YG) 19-2 h, closed Wed
Vicolo Amanti 6 ✉ 37100 *(near All'Arena)* ☎ 045 80 11 417
Crowded Fri-Sun, Sun mostly gay.

DANCECLUBS
■ **Alter Ego** (B D glm) Fri 23-4, Sat -5 h
Via Torricelle 9 ✉ 37100 *(area Torricelle)*
■ **B Side** (AC B BF D DR f G MA OS P PI s SNU) Sat 23-4.30 h
Via Fontanelle 28, S. Bonifacio ☎ 0368 93 13 09 (Infoline)
Pool with garden Mai-Aug. A4 MI-VE, exit Soave/S. Bonifacio. Outside turn left, direction S. Bonifacio. After 2.5 km right, direction Legnago. After 3 km.
■ **Romeo's Club** (AC B CC d DR f G MA P s VS) Disco: Fri Sat 23-5, Bar: Sun 23-3 h
Via Nicoló Giolfino 12 ✉ 37133 *(area Porta Vescovo-Bus 11/12/13)*
☎ 0338 40 37 781 (Infoline)
Video and disco bar. DJ at week-ends.

Verona | Italy

Finnish Saunas
Steam Baths
Jacuzzi
Video Room
Relax Rooms
Snack Bar
Solarium

THE CITY SAUNA CLUB

Ingresso riservato ai Soci UNO Club

37132 VERONA - Via Giolfino 12 - tel. 045 520009
Www.citysauna.it - e-mail: info@citysauna.it
Chiuso il giovedì

Italy | Verona ▶ Viareggio

RESTAURANTS

■ **Hänsel + Gretel** (B BF F glm OS) 11-15, 18-2, Sat-Sun 11-2 h
Via Corgnano 103 ✉ 37010 ☎ 045 77 33 994

SEX SHOPS/BLUE MOVIES

■ **Europa 92** (g) 9.30-13, 14-19.30 h, closed Sun Mon
Via Scarsellini 30
☎ 045 80 09 714
Videos, condoms, underwear, toys, magazines/Video, preservativi, biancheri intima, accessori, riviste.

■ **Magic America** (CC g p) 9-12.30, 15-19.30 h, closed Mon morning
Via Cantarane 17/A ✉ 37129 *(Zona Porta Vescovo)*
☎ 045 80 05 234
Videos, magazines, toys/video, accessori, riviste.

SAUNAS/BATHS

■ **City Sauna Club** (! AC B CC DR f G MA msg SA SB SOL VS WH)
Sep-May: 14-2, Jun-Aug: 15-2 h, closed Thu
Via Giolfino 12 ✉ 37131 *(Porta Vescovo. Bus 11/12/13)*
☎ 045 52 00 09
Free condoms. Internet café. One of Europes biggest and most comfortable gay-saunas/Sauna gay tra le più grandi e confortevoli d'Europa.

GENERAL GROUPS

■ **Arcigay "Pianeta Urano"** Mon Wed 21-23 h
c/o Arci, Via N. Sauro 2 ✉ 37129 ☎ 0349 17 66 262
🖨 045 80 09 092 💻 pianeta@urano.it 🌐 www.urano.it
Political and cultural activities, meetings, lectures, Aids information, youth group/Attività politiche e culturali, riunioni, conferenze, informazione Aids, gruppo giovani.

■ **Circolo Pink - Centro di Iniziativa e Cultura Gay e Lesbica**
Verona Helpline: Tue Thu 21-23, Sat 15-18 h
Via Scrimieri 7 ✉ 37129 ☎ 045 80 12 854 (Helpline)
☎ 045 80 65 911 💻 pinkverona@tiscalinet.it
Gay and lesbian culture centre. Mon, Thu 21-23 , Sat 16-19 h: Helpline, Info Aids, Presentation of cultural events, films, books and debates/ Telefono amico, info HIV, presentazioni di film, libri, dibattiti. Thu 21-23 h: Lesbian group/Gruppo lesbiche.

HEALTH GROUPS

■ **Anlaids** Infoline: Mon, Wed, Fri, Sat 19-22 h
Interrato Acqua Morta 46 ✉ 37129 ☎ 045 800 50 16 66 (Infoline)
☎ 045 59 25 75
🖨 045 59 29 99

■ **Azalea - Cooperativa Sociale**
Via Brunelleschi 3B ✉ 37138 ☎ 045 57 53 88 🖨 045 57 52 52
Coordination of services for people with Aids/ Coordinamento servizi e assistenza a persone sieropositive o malate di Aids.

■ **Network Nazionale "Gruppo C" Progetto di Ricerca Aids** Mon-Fri 8.30-12.30, Sat by appointment; Hotline 14.30-17, Sat 8.30-12.30 h
Via Germania 20 ✉ 37135 ☎ 045 86 22 232 ☎ 045 86 22 233 (Hotline)
Information on HIV, prevention, psychological support, anonymous free HIV test.

CRUISING

-C. O. N. I. (Via Basso Acquar: streets around the gyms, as far as Alfa Garage, only at night by car/strade attorno palestre, fino al garage Alfa, solo di notte in macchina)
-Borgo Venezia (P) on the left of Vescovo city gate, only at night/sulla sinistra Porta Vescovo, solo di notte)(AYOR)
-Piazzale della Stazione (In front of the railway station, the round street near the church Tempio Vorivo/di fronte alla stazione ferroviaria, la rotonda davanti alla chiesa del Tempio Votivo)(R TV).
-Industrial zone/-Zona Industriale (coming from "Verona Sud" turn left behind "Metro" in direction Alpo, in the tunnel from Via Roveggia at night/proveniendo da "Verona Sud" dopo magazzini Metro girare a sinistra direzione Alpo, sotto il cavalcavia da Via Roveggia, di notte).
-Lazzaretto (a little bit outside from district Porto S. Pancrazio, on the bridge over the Adige, turn left and walk along the Adige to the ruins of the old military hospital, in the afternoon/leggermente fuori città, proveniendo dal quartiere Porto S. Pancrazio si passa il ponte sull'adige e poi si gira a sinistra, proseguendo lungo l'adige; ai ruderi del vecchio lazzaretto, di pomeriggio).
-Porta Vescovo (gardens and parking place near Porta Vescovo, at night/nei giardinetti e nel parcheggio a ridosso della Porta Vescovo, di notte)

Viareggio ✉ 55049

✱ The Mediterranean hotspot of "Friendly Versilia" Viareggio and Torre del Lago are developing into a magnet for gay tourist in the summer. Even though the gay beach "La Lecciona" has been well known and visited for the last 20 years, it is only recently, and with help of the city council, that a gay scene with bars, restaurants, discos and events as well as a few apartments and hotels has been able to develop. From June to August all hell breaks loose (an estimated 10.000 gay men in August last year!), at the beginning and end of the season it is markedly quieter. For those wishing to visit Viareggio during the summer months should reserve accommodation well in advance, otherwise the only remaining possibility will be the camping sites. The annual "Mr gay Versilia" competition attracts attention though out Italy.

Viareggio | **Italy**

Frau Marleen
DISCOCLUB

Venerdì
ingresso con tessera ARCIGAY
Sabato e Domenica
aperto a tutti

Viale Europa - TORRE DEL LAGO (LU) - Tel. 0584/342282 - Fax 0584/352637
www.fraumarleen.com e-mail: fraumarleen@fraumarleen.com

Rugantino
LA PICCOLATRATTORIA

...For a nice meal in a relaxing atmosphere

Viareggio (Lu) Via S. Ambrogio 8 Tel/Fax.: + 39 0584 53598

★ Die Mittelmeerorte der "Friendly Versilia" Viareggio und Torre del Lago entwickeln sich seit einiger Zeit zu einem neuen Anziehungspunkt für schwulen Sommertourismus. Zwar wird der Strand "La Lecciona" schon seit über 20 Jahren von Schwulen besucht, doch entsteht mit Unterstützung der Stadtverwaltung erst seit vier Jahren eine schwule Infrastruktur mit Bars, Restaurants, Diskotheken, Veranstaltungen und allmählich auch mit Appartments und Hotels. Zwischen Juni und August ist inzwischen die Hölle los (10.000 Schwule Mitte August des letzten Jahres), in der Vor- und Nachsaison ist es wesentlich ruhiger. Wer in den Sommermonaten nach Viareggio reisen will, sollte sich also schon sehr frühzeitig um eine Unterkunft bemühen, ansonsten bleibt nur noch die Möglichkeit, auf einem der vielen Campingplätze der Umgebung zu zelten. Jedes Jahr findet die Wahl des "Mr. Gay Versilia" italienweite Aufmerksamkeit.

★ Les stations balnéaires de la "Friendly Versilia" au bord de la Méditerranée, Viareggio et Torre del Lago, deviennent depuis quelques années la destination estivale préférée des touristes gais. La plage "La Lecciona" est fréquentée depuis une vingtaine d'année par les gais mais depuis 4 ans, avec le soutien de la municipalité, une infrastructure plus large s'est développée avec de nombreux bars, restaurants, clubs, et lieux d'hébergement. L'affluence est à son plus haut point entre juin et août (on dénombrait 10 000 gais à la mi-août 2000) pour se calmer à nouveau en basse saison. Il est donc préférable de réserver bien à l'avance si vous compter y passer un séjour en été. Sinon, il vous restera la possibilité de poser votre tente dans un des nombreux campings de la région. Chaque année, l'élection de "Mister Gay Versilia" attire l'attention de tout le pays.

★ Las ciudades del mediterráneo de la 'amable Versilia', Viareggio y Torre del Lago, desde hace algún tiempo se están convirtiendo, poco a poco, en un nuevo imán del turismo estival gay. Si bien la playa de "La Lecciona" cuenta con turistas gays desde hace más de veinte años, sólo hace cuatro años que con el apoyo del ayuntamiento se está creando una verdadera infraestructura gay con bares, restaurantes, discotecas, acontecimientos y, con el tiempo, también apartamentos y hoteles. Ahora, entre junio y agosto la zona está hasta arriba de gays; el año pasado, a mediados de agosto había 10.000 gays! Antes y después de la temporada alta es mucho más tranquilo. Quien quiera viajar a Viareggio durante los meses de verano hará bien en reservar a tiempo, ya que de lo contrario sólo le quedará la posibilidad de acampar en una tienda en uno de los muchos campings de la zona.
Todos los años, la elección del "Mr. Gay Versilia" atrae la atención de toda Italia.

★ I luoghi balneari della "Friendly Versilia" nel Mediterraneo, Viareggio e Torre del Lago, sono diventati negli ultimi anni nuovi punti d'attrazione per il turismo gay estivo. La spiaggia "La Lecciona" è frequentata ormai da una ventina di anni dai gay, da quattro anni però si sta sviluppando con l'appoggio comunale una propria infrastruttura gay con bar, ristoranti, manifestazioni culturali e anche un numero crescente di hotel e appartamenti per gay. Da giugno ad agosto l'affluenza è grandissima (10.000 gay a Ferragosto del 2000), in bassa stagione invece è molto più tranquillo. Chi vuole venire nel periodo estivo dovrebbe quindi prenotare un alloggio con molto anticipo. Nel caso che tutto fosse già esaurito resta solo la possibilità di dormire in tenda in uno dei tanti campeggi circostanti. Ogni anno l'elezione del "Mr. Gay Versilia" richiama l'attenzione di tutt'Italia.

BARS

■ **Bocachica** (B F glm) summer: 12-5; winter: Thu, Fri 22-5, Sat Sun 18-5 h
Viale Europa 1, Torre del Lago ✉ 55640 ☎ 0584 35 09 76
Music bar and cocktails. Also restaurant in the evening, lunch on Sun. Traditional fish food.

TORRE DEL LAGO – VIAREGGIO – ITALY
www.friendsviareggio.it
E-Mail: friends@friendsviareggio.it

FRIENDS HOTEL
Via Mameli 79
55049 Viareggio – Italy
Tel./Fax: ++39/0584-52100
Cell: 0333-4808991 (mario)

MUSICA & SPETTACOLO

MARE & PINETA

RISTORANTE "JACÒ"
Viale Europa
Torre del Lago – Viareggio
Tel.: ++39/0584-350988

■ **Mama Mia** (B Glm YG) Apr/May, Sep/Oct 21-2 h, June to Aug 10-4 h
Viale Europa ✉ 55048 Torre del Lago *(way along the sea/passeggiatta a mare)*
☏ 0584 35 11 11
Crowded bar. Sometimes disco on Sat.

■ **Voice Music Bar** (g)
Viale Margherita 61, Passeggiata a Mare ✉ 55049
☏ 0584 45 814
Open till late.

DANCECLUBS

■ **Barrumba** (B CC D DR F GLM OS P PI s VS M) Fri-Sun 23-6 h, closed Oct-Apr
Viale Kennedy 6 ✉ 55049 Torre del Lago *(near Lecciona beach)*
☏ 0584 35 17 17
Disco, bar and restaurant.

■ **Frau Marleen** (AC B D glm MA tv) Sat Sun 23-4.30 h
Viale Europa, Torre del Lago ✉ 55049 ☏ 0584 34 22 82

■ **Gaya Felix** (AC B D G MA) Fri 23-? h
c/o Frau Marleen, Viale Europa, Torre del Lago ✉ 55049
☏ 050 55 56 18
Party of the Arcigay of Pisa. Free entry.

■ **Kama-Kama** (B D g) Sat 23-4 h
Via per Camaiore/Capezzano Piànore ✉ 55049 *(8 km east of Viareggio)*
Techno, Houseclub.

RESTAURANTS

■ **Ristorante Europa** (B g F) 19.30-22 h
Viale Europa 3 ✉ 55048 Torre del Lago ☏ 0584 35 02 73
Fish specialities, cosy atmosphere.

■ **Ristorante Jacò** (AC B bf CC F GLM OS s)
Viale Europa 7 ✉ 55049 Torre del Lago ☏ 0584 35 09 88
Restaurant and discobar.

■ **Rugantino** (g F) Tue closed
Via S. Ambrogio 8 ✉ 55049 ☏ 0584 53 598
Fresh fish available.

■ **Vignaccio, Il**
Via della Chiesa 26, Santa Lucia Camaiore *(15 km from Viareggio)*
☏ 0584 91 42 00
Typical Tuscany cuisine/Cucina Toscana.

BOOK SHOPS

■ **Libreria Babele** (g)
Viale Marconi 32 ✉ 55048 ☏ 0584 35 20 91
Gay and lesbian section.

HOTELS

■ **CavMare** Mon-Fri 9-13, 15.30-19, Sat 9.30-12 h
Via Matteotti 3 ✉ 55049 ☏ 0584 49 776 ☏ 0584 49 775
Hotel reservation service. For special offers for single and groups, ask for "Friendly Versilia".

Le Rociane

In the Versilian countrysides, only a few kilometres from the sea, a comfortable and relaxing place is available to You

Frazione Pedona, 184   I - 55041 CAMAIORE (Lu)   Tel/Fax: + 39 0584 984387   www.lerociane.it

Viareggio ▶ Vittorio Veneto - Treviso | **Italy**

■ **Friends Hotel** (AC BF CC GLM H OS)
Via Mameli 79 ✉ 55049 *(close to the beaches)* ☎ 0584 52 100
📠 0584 52 100
📧 friends@friendsviareggio.it
Double room Lit 120.000 with BF.
■ **Villa Rosy** (CC bf F H OS)
Viale G. Marconi 315 ✉ 55048 Torre del Lago ☎ 0584 34 13 50
📠 0584 34 13 50 📧 villarosy@viareggio.it
🌐 www.villarosy.viareggio.it
Discreet gays welcome. Also restaurant. Reservations for summer period until Easter (!!). Centrally located/Gay discreti benvenuti. Hotel con ristorante. Prenotazioni per periodo estivo fino a Pasqua (!!).

GUEST HOUSES
■ **Locanda al Colle**
Fraz. Santa Lucia 103 ✉ 55041 Camaiore *(15 mins from the gay beach,30 mins from Pisa airport)* ☎ 0584 91 51 95
📠 0584 91 70 53

APARTMENTS
■ **Le Rociane**
Frazione Pedona 184 ✉ 55041 Camaiore *(15 km from Viareggio)*
☎ 0584 98 43 87 📠 0584 98 43 87 📧 info@lerociane.it
🌐 www.lerociane.it
Hillside holiday villas and appartments for rent/Case e appartamenti per vancaza in collina. Swimming pool and sauna. Prices on request/Tariffe a richiesta. Weekly rentals/Affitti settimanali.

SWIMMING
"La Lecciona" beach, at the end of Viale Europa.

CRUISING
-Via Zara (G R) (by car and on foot by night, also nearby areas, in the pine wood)
-Torre del Lago: at the end of Viale Europa, near the beach in the forest (evening/night)

Vicenza ✉ 36100

CINEMAS
■ **Kursaal** (g OG) 17-24, Sun 16-24 h
Stradella Soccorso Soccorseto ✉ 36100
☎ 0444 32 49 30

FETISH GROUPS
■ **Moto Leather Club Veneto** (G LJ)
c/o Bedin, PO Box 259 ✉ 36100 ☎ 0444 32 12 90
📧 mlcv@geocities.com.
🌐 www.geocities.com/WestHollywood/4081/

HEALTH GROUPS
■ **Arcigay Arcilesbica** 2nd Fri 21-22.30 h
Contrà Fontanelle 5 ✉ 36100 ☎ 0444 50 72 30
AIDS counselling service and free HIV testing.

CRUISING
-Railway Station/Stazione FS (AYOR) (at night-also in nearby areas, e.g. in the Campo Marzio gardens/anche attorno per es. nei giardini di Campo Marzio)
-[P]Largo Bologna (at night ba car or on foot/di notte, in auto e a piedi) -Motorway/Autostrada A31 "Valdastico"
-[P]Villa Tacchi (both sides day & night/sui due lati, notte e giorno)
-[P]Thiene (both sides day & night/sui due lati, notte e giorno)

locanda al colle

Guesthouse

15 minutes from the Gay beach
30 minutes from Pisa airport

Fraz. Santa Lucia 103 - 55041 Camaiore-Lucca-Italy
tel. +39 0584 915195 fax +39 0584 917053

Viterbo ✉ 01100

SEX SHOPS/BLUE MOVIES
■ **Cobra** (g)
Via Cardarelli 59/61 ✉ 01100 ☎ 0761 35 37 48

GENERAL GROUPS
■ **Arcigay Dyonisos** (GLM) Wed 21 h
Via Monte Asolone 4 ✉ 01100 ☎ 0761 32 18 60
📠 0761 32 94 78
📧 arcigayvt@iol.it
🌐 digilander.iol.it/arcigayviterbo

CRUISING
-Railway Station/Stazione FS
-Piazza Gramsci
-Bagnaccio
-Bullicame Park

Vittorio Veneto - Treviso ✉ 31029

CRUISING
-Largo Foro Boario (along the river/e sul lungofiume adiacente)
-Via F. da Milano (beside the "Varietà"-cinema/nei pressi del cinema Varietà)
-Piazza del Popolo (city park, next to the railway station/giardini, davanti alla stazione FS)

Ivory Coast

Name: Côte d'Ivoire • Elfenbeinküste • Costa de Marfil • Costa d'Avorio
Location: Western Africa
Initials: CI
Time: GMT
International Country Code: ☏ 225
International Access Code: ☏ 00
Language: French (official), Baoulé, Bété, Dioula and other dialects
Area: 322,462 km² / 124,502 sq mi.
Currency: 1Franc (CFA) = 100 centimes
Population: 14,492,000
Capital: Yamassoukro (Government), Abidjan (de facto)
Religions: 65% Animists, 23% Muslims, 12% Chistians

✳ Due to the political turmoil and the change of government in Ivory Coast, extreme caution is recommended to gay visitors. At present we have no up-to-date information regarding the legal situation of homosexuals.

✳ Aufgrund der politischen Wirren und dem Regierungswechsel in der Republik Elfenbeinküste, empfehlen wir Gay-Touristen ganz besonders vorsichtig zu sein. Derzeit haben wir keine Informationen bezüglich der rechtlichen Situation von Homosexuellen.

✳ En regard des nombreux troubles politiques et changements de gouvernement en Côte d'Ivoire, nous recommandons la plus grande prudence aux touristes gais. Nous n'avons pas d'information concernant les droits des homosexuels.

✳ Debido a las convulsiones políticas y el cambio de gobierno en la República de la Costa de Marfil recomendamos ser muy cauteloso como turista gay. En este momento no disponemos de información acerca de la situación legal de los homosexuales en este país.

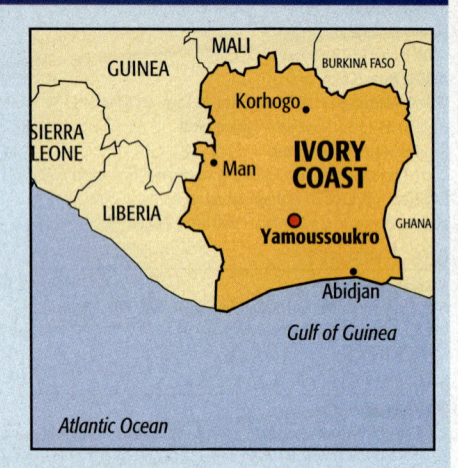

✳ A causa della confusione politica e il cambiamento di governo nella Repubblica della Costa d'Avorio raccomandiamo ai turisti gay viaggiando in questo paese di essere estremamente prudente. Attualmente non disponiamo di informazioni aggiornate per quanto riguarda la situazione legale degli omosessuali

Abidjan

BARS

■ **Factory. Le** (AC B d GLM MA p s) 18-? h
Riviera II, Route d'Attoban ☏ 05.08.76.10
Welcoming place with house music.

Japan

Name: Nippon • Japon • Japón • Giappone
Location: between Sea of Japan & western Pacific Ocean
Initials: J
Time: GMT +9
International Country Code: ☎ 81 (leave the first 0 of area codes)
International Access Code: ☎ 001 or 0061 or 0041
Language: Japanese. English as commercial language
Area: 377,837 km² / 145,831 sq mi.
Currency: 1 Yen ( ) = 100 Sen
Population: 126,410,000
Capital: Tokyo
Religions: 80% Buddhist or Shinto, or a mixture of the two
Climate: The climate varies from tropical in the south to cool moderate in the north.
Important gay cities: Tokyo, Osaka

Homosexual acts are not illegal and also not mentioned in the law. The age of sexual consent is 18. The influence of the gay movement outside Japan has accounted for the emmergence in the 90's of the Lesbian and Gay Parade in Tokyo, the LesBiGay March in Sapporo, as well as the International Lesbian and Gay Film and Video Festival. The question remains open what other influences the emmancipation in the West will have on the development of culture and society in Japan. The older generation in Japan continues to be intolerant of gays. Coming out is difficult because of the pressure to get married imposed by family and society. Many gays are therefore forced to follow a double life style. The group "Occur" and other politically active groups are beginning to set up much more contact with other outside groups, such as prostitutes and transvestites. Unfortunately there are no gay information shops. Besides Tokyo and Osaka there are other gay localities in major cities. However, gay foreigners are often not welcomed in saunas or other establishments because of fear. Gay establishments are often difficult to find. Therefore, we would like to explain the Japanese address system to you. A normal address consists of the district name and a combination of three numbers together. For example, "Shinjuku-ku 2-12-3". The first number is the city district (here No. 2) in Shinjuku-ku, the second number the block in the district (here No. 12) and the third the house number (here No. 3). Street orientation is facilitated by the green signs (for the block -here 2-12) found on the lamp posts and electricity pylons, and the blue signs (for house numbers -here 12-3) on the houses.

Homosexualität ist in Japan nicht illegal, sie wird in Gesetzen nicht erwähnt. Das Schutzalter liegt in Japan bei 18 Jahren. Unter dem Einfluß der im Ausland agierenden Schwulenbewegung finden seit Anfang der 90er Jahre die *Lesbian & Gay Parade* in Tokyo, der *LesBiGay March* in Sapporo sowie das *Tokyo International Lesbian & Gay Film & Video Festival* statt. Jedoch bleibt hier die Frage offen, welche Wirkung diese westlich entwickelte Form der Emanzipation auf die andere Kultur und Gesellschaft Japans hat. Die Einstellung der japanischen Bevölkerung, insbesondere der älteren Generation, gegenüber Schwulen ist intolerant. Ein Coming-out ist schwierig. Immer noch sind der familiäre und gesellschaftliche Druck so groß, daß sich Schwule zur Heirat gezwungen sehen. Sie führen ein Doppelleben. Die Gruppe *OCCUR* und andere politisch aktive Gruppen beginnen sich immer mehr zu vernetzen. Sie arbeiten of mit anderen randständigen Gruppen wie Prostituierten oder Transsexuellen zusammen. Besonders intensiv ist die Zusammenarbeit mit lesbischen Gruppen. Leider gibt es keine schwulen Info-Läden für ausländische Touristen. Neben Tokyo und Osaka findet man auch in anderen größeren Städten schwule Lokale. Jedoch sind Ausländer aus Angst vor kulturellen Unterschieden nicht überall willkommen. Der Zutritt zu den Saunen wird meistens verwehrt. Schwule Lokale sind häufig sehr schwierig für Touristen zu finden. Deshalb möchten wir Ihnen an dieser Stelle das japanische Adreßsystem erklären. Eine normale Adresse setzt sich aus dem Namen des Stadtteils und einer Kombination von drei Zahlen zusammen. Zum Beispiel: "Shinjuku-ku 2-12-3". Dabei gibt die erste Zahl das Stadtviertel (hier Nr.2) im Stadtteil Shinjuku-ku an, die zweite Zahl den Block im Viertel -also Block 12- und die dritte Zahl bezeichnet die Hausnummer -hier Nummer 3. Als Orientierungshilfe im Straßen-Alltag gibt es an den Laternen- oder Strommasten Schilder in weiß auf grün, die die Nummer des Blocks im Viertel angeben (hier: 2-12) und an den Häusern Schilder in weiß auf blau, die die Hausnummer (hier: 12-3) im Block angeben. Oft finden sich an Kreuzungen Pläne des Stadtviertels, aus denen die Nummern der Blöcke ersichtlich sind.

L'homosexualité n'est pas interdite au Japon, elle est simplement ignorée. L'âge de la majorité sexuelle est fixé à 18 ans. Sous l'influence de mouvements homosexuels venant de l'étranger, se tiennent depuis le début des années 90 la *Lesbian and Gay Parade* et le *Tokyo International Lesbian and Gay Film and Video Festival* à Tokyo et la *LesBiGay March* à Sapporo. Mais il reste à savoir quelle est l'influence de cette forme développée d'émancipation occidentale sur la culture et la société si différentes du Japon. L'attitude de la population, surtout de la génération plus âgée, est intolérante vis-à-vis des homosexuels. Il est difficile de faire son coming-out. La pression familiale et sociale reste si forte que les homosexuels se sentent encore obligés de se marier. Ils mènent donc une double vie. De plus en plus, le groupe *Occur* ainsi que d'autres groupes politiquement actifs commencent à établir contact des transsexuels ou des prostitués. Malheureusement, il n'y a pas de lieu d'information pour les touristes gais. Des endroits gais existent pourtant en dehors de Tokyo et Osaka. Les

Japan

étrangers ne sont pas toujours les bienvenus, par peur des différences culturelles. L'accès aux saunas est en général refusé. Les établissements gais sont généralement très difficiles à trouver pour les touristes. C'est la raison pour laquelle nous voudrions vous expliquer le système d'adresses japonais. Une adresse normale est composée du nom du quartier, et d'une combinaison de trois chiffres. par exemple: "Shinjuku-ku 2-12-3" Le premier chiffre indique le quartier, (donc 2), nous allons en l'occurrence le quartier Shinjuku-ku, le deuxième chiffre indique le numéro du pâté de maisons (en l'occurrence 12), le troisième chiffre le numéro de rue, en l'occurrence 3. Pour se retrouver dans la vie de tous les jours, des pancartes vert sur blanc sont accrochées aux poteaux d'électricité, qui indiquent le numéro du pâté de maisons du quartier (ici 2-12), et aux maisons des signes blanc sur bleu qui indiquent le numéro de la maison dans le pâté de maisons (ici 12-3). On trouve souvent aux coins de rues des plans de quartier sur lesquels sont indiqués les numéros de pâtés de maison.

En Japón la homosexualidad no es ilegal y no se menciona en la legislación. La edad de consentimiento es de 18 años. Bajo la influencia de la comunidad gay internacional se organiza desde los principios de los años 90 en *Lesbian & Gay Parade* y el *International Lesbian & Gay Film & Video Festival* en Tokio, como la *LeBiGay March* en Sapporo. Sin embargo, hay que preguntarse, si estas muestras de emanzipación occidentalizadas tengan el mismo efecto sobre la cultura y sociedad tan sumamente diferente en Japón. La actitud de intolerancia de los japonéses hacía los homosexuales, se nota sobre todo por parte de los mayores. Un coming-out es difícil de realizar, ya que la presión de la familia y de la sociedad siguen siendo muy fuertes. Por ello, muchos gays se ven obligados a contraer matrimonio y hacer una vida doble. El grupo *OCCUR* y otras organizaciones muy activas en el campo político estrechan cada vez más su colaboración, incluyendo grupos de marginados como prostitutas y transexuales. Especialmente fructífera es la cooperación con grupos de lesbianas. Desgraciadamente no existen para turistas sitios de información gay. Pero bares de ambiente no se encuentran solamente en Tokio y Osaka, sino también en otras ciudades grandes. Sin embargo, extranjeros no son siempre bienvenidos, tal vez por el miedo a otras culturas. Como consecuencia, escasamente se permite a turistas la entrada en saunas. Aprovechamos la ocasión para explicarle el sistema japonés de direcciones.En general una dirección se compone del nombre del barrio y una combinación de tres números. Por ejemplo: "Shinjuku-ku 2-12-3". La primera cifra indica el barrio (2) en la zona de la ciudad llamada Shinjuku-ku, la segunda determina el bloque del barrio (en este caso el bloque número 12) y el tercer número equivale al número de la calle (3). Para la mejor orientación en la ciudad, los postes de fárolas o de la red éléctrica están provistos con letreros blancos con fondo verde que indican el número de bloque en el barrio correspondiente (aquí: 2-12) y las casas con letreros blancos con fondo azul, que indican el número de casa en el respectivo bloque (en este caso: 12-3). A menudo se encuentran en los cruces mapas de orientación, que informan sobre los números correspondientes de los bloques.

L'omosessualità in Giappone non è vietata e non viene citata nelle leggi. L'età legale in Giappone è di 18 anni. Sotto l'influenza del movimento gay all'estero dall'inizio degli anni 90 anche in Giappone hanno luogo: la *Lesbian & Gay Parade* a Tokio; la *LesBiGay March* a Sapporo e infine il *Tokyo International Lesbian & Gay Film & Video Festival*. Però resta ancora da chiedersi, quale effetto abbia questa forma occidentale d'emancipazione sulla cultura e società giapponese. L'atteggiamento della popolazione e soprattutto della generazione anziana si mostra intollerante verso i gay. Il coming-out diventa difficile. La pressione svolta dalla famiglia e dalla società sui gay fa sì che molti si sentono costretti a sposarsi. Coloro svolgono così una doppia vita. Il gruppo *Occur* e altre associazioni attive in politica cominciano a unificarsi sempre di più. Spesso questi gruppi gay lavorano anche insieme ad altre associazioni di emarginati come gruppi di prostitute o transessuali. La collaborazione tra gruppi di gay e di lesbiche è molto intensa. Purtroppo non esistono centri d'informazione gay per turisti stranieri. Dopo Tokio e Osaka, anche in altre città si trovano diversi locali gay. Però a volte gli stranieri non sono troppo ben venuti a causa della paura delle differenze culturali. L'ingresso alle saune viene perciò molto spesso vietato agli stranieri. I locali gay a volte sono molto difficili da trovare per i turisti, perciò spieghiamo qui il sistema indirizzario giapponese: Un'indirizzo normale consiste dal nome della circoscrizione e una combinazione di tre numeri; per es.: "Shinjuku-ku 2 12-3". La prima cifra (no. 2) indica il quartiere della circoscrizione Shinjuku-ku; la seconda l'isolato (no. 12) e infine la terza (no. 3) il numero di casa. Un'ulteriore aiuto all'orientamento stradale offrono sia i cartelli verdi con la scritta bianca, attaccati ai pali e alle lanterne dell'illuminazione (in questo caso 2-12); come i cartelli blu con la scritta bianca, attaccati ai muri delle case, che indicano il numero (in questo caso 12-3) nell'isolato. Spesso agli incroci si trovano piantine del quartiere, che indicano i numeri degli isolati.

NATIONAL GAY INFO

■ **Badi**
Shinjuku KM Building, 1-14-5 Shinjuku-ku, Shinjuku Tokyo
☎ (03) 3350-3922

■ **Barazoku/Daini Shobo Ltd.**
5-2-11 Daizawa, Setagaya-ku Tokyo 160
☎ (0)3-342 154 62

■ **Gay Help Line**
☎ 5693-4569
Answering machine. Leave message and be sure to give your room number and name, if you are staying at a hotel.

■ **G-Men**
Kasafuka Building 5-4 Araki-cho, Shinjuku-ku Tokyo
☎ (03) 5269-1800

■ **Sabu**
San Building, 26-3 Sanei-cho, Shinjuku-ku, Tokyo 160
☎ (03) 335 923 41

■ **Samson**
Kameikan, PO Box 66, Shitaya Post Office, Taito-Ku, Tokyo *Tokio*
☎ (0)3-384 129 01

■ **The Gay**
T.I.Y. Shuppan, PO Box 209, Shinjuku-ku, Tokyo 160-91
☎ (03) 336 351 97

NATIONAL GROUPS

■ **Bear Club of Japan (B.C.J)** (G)
5-4-2F, Arakicho, Shinjuku-ku ✉ 106-0007 Tokyo
📧 bcj@a1.rimnet.ne.jp
🌐 www.st.rim.or.jp/~lonestar/bcj/
Non-profit (non-commercial) gay semi-social organization with 440 members (Nov.2000).

■ **OCCUR (Association for the Lesbian & Gay Movement)**
Tokyo ☎ (03) 3380-2269

Aomori ▶ Kyoto **Japan**

Aomori ☎ 0177

BARS
- **Frank** (B G)
28-14 Plaza Yasukata, 2nd floor Yasukata ☎ 22-7141

Fukuoka ☎ 092

BARS
- **Bros.** (B f G MA N) 21-4 h, closed Mon
4-9-4 Sumiyoshi, Hakata-Ku ☎ 411-6523
- **Crescent Moon** (B G YG) 20-3 h, closed Mon
2-19-1-1 Haruyoshi, Chuo-ku ☎ 731-0005
- **Hachibankan** (B G) 19.30-3, Sat -4 h, closed Wed
Hakata-ku, Sumiyoshi 2-13-6 (Suminoe Bld. No. 2-103) ☎ 291-2310
- **Plan-B** (AC B G YG) 20-4 h
1-11-36 Haruyoshi, Chuo-ku *(south of Sumiyoshi bridge)* ☎ 724-9007
- **Sichimensho** (B G MA YG) 20-3 h
4-13-15 Sumiyoshi, Hakata-ku ☎ 441-9037

SEX SHOPS/BLUE MOVIES
- **Hakata Anzu-ya** (g) 12-3 h
4-15-3 Sumiyoshi, Hakata-ku ☎ 412 39 25
- **Hakata Budo-ya** (g) 14-24 h
3-9-23-2 Sumiyoshi, Hakata-ku ☎ 272-3628

SAUNAS/BATHS
- **Golgo** (G)
4-15-3 Sumiyoshi, Hakata-ku ☎ 413-5227
- **Hinsenn Kaikan** (G SA) 12-midnight
5-18-18 Sumiyoshi Hakata-Ku ☎ 413-7098
As the staff cannot speak english, visitors should be able to speak Japanese.

GENERAL GROUPS
- **Gay in Fukuoka** (G.I.F.)
☎ 801-1487

CRUISING
- Higashi Koen Park
- Vivre 21 department B 1 toilet
- IWATAYA department 3 f toilet
- Solaria Plaza 5 f toilet
- Shingu Beach (10 mins walkf from Seitetu Shingu station).

Hakodate ☎ 0138

BARS
- **Yorozuya** (B G) 19-2 h
20-9 Matsukaze-Cho ☎ 27-0661

Hamamatsu ☎ 053

SWIMMING
Nakatajima beach, take bus no. 19 from main station, get of at the terminus, walk 20 minutes down the road. At the small hotel called car road turn towards the beach (G, popular at WE in summer).

CRUISING
- Wajiyama Koen (park) after 22 h

Hiroshima ☎ 082

BARS
- **Paul** (B G)
Shintenchi Leisure Building, Shintenchi 1-9, Naka-ku *(2nd floor)* ☎ 243-4087

CRUISING
- Kyohashigawa Ryokudo Park

Kanazawa ☎ 076

BARS
- **Shinjugai** (AC B G YG) 20.30-1.30 h
2F Nozaki Bldg., 1-8-23 Katamachi *(next to Saigawa bridge, walk 5 minutes)* ☎ 233-3002

CRUISING
- Ekimae Cinema
- Spa Dream (5 minutes walk from Nishi Kanazawa station).

Kobe ☎ 078

BARS
- **Taro** (B f g)
Kamitani Building, 4 Kano-cho, Chuo-ku *(3rd floor)* ☎ 332-5443

CRUISING
- Basement of Kobe Shimbun Kaikan Building
- Suma (Shioya Beach)

Kochi ☎ 0888

BARS
- **Katsukazan** (AC B d f G lj MA N TV) 19-1 h
1-3-7 Minami-Harimaya-Cho ☎ 23 -7799

Kokura ☎ 093

BARS
- **P-Man** (B G) 19-3 h, closed Tue
Kita-ku, Konya-machi 10-3, Yamazaki Building *(2nd floor)* ☎ 531-7103

Kumamoto ☎ 096

BARS
- **October 86** (B G)
Isei Building, 1-36 Shinshigai *(4th floor)* ☎ 355-6600
- **Power** (B G MA VS) 19-4 h
1-6-5-2F Shimotori (Arcade St.) *(Line 2, Tram Stop Torichosuzi)* ☎ 354-6712

Kyoto ☎ 075

BARS
- **Accele** (B G YG) 20-4 h
Itou Bld, 3F, Shijo-Kiyamachi Agaru, Nigashigawa *(Hankyu Railways-Kawaramachi Station, near Takashimaya departmentstore)* ☎ 212 40 50
- **Apple** (B G MA) 19-3h
Nakagyo-ku, Kawaramachi, Dori, Shinjo-agaru, Mitsujime, Higashi-iru ☎ 256-0258

SPARTACUS 2001/2002 | 695

Japan   Kyoto ▶ Niigata

■ **C'est bon** (! B G OG) 19-2 h
Shijo Kawara-machi-agaru, Futasujime, Higashi-iru ☎ 211 03 85
■ **Friend** (B G)
Nisi kiyamachi Takoyakushi ugaru ☎ 256-3782
■ **Shu's** (B G MA) 20-2 h
No 13 st., Shijo-Kiyamachi Agaru *(Hankyu Railways-Kawaramachi Station, near Takashimaya departmentstore)* ☎ 251 67 92
■ **V-Zone** (B G YG) 20-4 h
Shjo-Ninshi Kiyamachi 2-suji-Agaru, Ocean Bld 5 F *(Hankyu Railways Kawaramachi St., Takashimaya departmentstore)* ☎ 212 19 33

MEN'S CLUBS
■ **Supporter** 14-8h
☎ 352-8784
Call for more information.

SHOWS
■ **Cine Friends** (G MA S)
Senbon nakadachiori agaru Higashi iru, Kamigyoko *(Bus-Senbon Nakadachiuri)* ☎ 441-1460
From Senbon Nakadachiuri crossing, go north, turn first right, the theater is about 50 m from here on the left.

Matsuyama ☎ 089

BARS
■ **Publick Now** (B G MA) 19-1 h
1-6-7 Nibancho *(close to Matsuyama Washington Hotel)*
☎ 45-7732
Sometimes foreigners.

Nagasaki ☎ 0958

BARS
■ **BanBan** (B g)
Kabashimamachi, Kuraoka Bldg *(2nd floor)* ☎ 822-9703

SAUNAS/BATHS
■ **Kiraku kaikan**
☎ 827-7577

SWIMMING
-Miyazuri beach (30 mins from town by bus).

Nagoya ☎ 052

BARS
■ **Camps** (B G)
(near Kanaya Hotel) ☎ 951-1445
Several blocks away from main gay bar area. Sign in English. Past Tokai TV offices and near Kanaya Hotel; Eastern Building 1st floor.
■ **GI Club** (B G)
Castle Kanko Building ☎ 264-1024
Not military! Initials from owner and former owner. Nice crowd, mixed ages. Sign in English outside the building and by the door on 3rd floor.
■ **Kuriko** (B G MG) 21-4 h
Nishishin Building 2F, 4-4-9 Sakae Naka-ku ✉ 460-0008
(near Tokyu Hotel, subway station Sakae)
☎ 251 01 50
Little hard to find. Sign in English and Japanese. English spoken.
■ **Star Johne** (AC B G WE YG) 19-2, Sat -5 h
Dairokuwako Bldg. Part2 3F, 4-12-24 Sakae, Naka-ku *(close to Chunichi Building)* ☎ 242-5721

MEN'S CLUBS
■ **Pancrace** (G MA)
4-24-26 Naeki Minami, Nakamura-ku ☎ 541-1919

CAFES
■ **Café Allegro** (B CC F glm OS) 11-24 h
4-17 Higashiyama St., Chikusa ☎ 782-0886

Naha ☎ 098

BARS
To the gay snacks take Kokusai Dori Street, then Heiwa Dori Street. At the YanYan-Shop the Street divides in three. Take the very small left one. In the beginning there are some of the listed bar-snacks. If you go to the end of the street turn left then right and you will find the others.
■ **Akira** (B G) 20-4 h, closed Wed
2F ☎ 868-7423
■ **Danke** (B G) 21-4 h
2F ☎ 866-4227
■ **Resort** (B G) 20-4 h, closed 4th Sun
3F ☎ 866-8924
■ **Shiki** (B G)
2F ☎ 867-9966
■ **Shingo** (B G) 22-4 h
(1st on the left side) ☎ 862-4031
■ **Sunset** (B G) 21-5 h, closed Mon
3F ☎ 869-9244
■ **Tayou No Ko** (B G OG) 20-4 h
☎ 861-5570
■ **Umi** (B G) 20-2 h, closed Tue
2F ☎ 867-0433

SWIMMING
-Naminoue beach (near Tomari harbour, recently cruisy)

CRUISING
-Yogi Park (near Naha's prefectural library, hospital and main police office)
-bus terminal (afternoon).

Narita ☎ 03

CRUISING
-Natita JR Station (go out the West Exit. This leads to New Narita-City. Go down the stairs. There are 3 curb-side bus stops. By #2 there is a WC. During the rush hour (18-20 h) a lot of cruising takes place there between train & bus. If you're in a hotel nearby, an invitation might be easily accepted. Alternately go out the east exit, turn left and 20m along the building there is another WC.

Niigata ☎ 0258

BARS
■ **New Shiro** (B G)
7 Kami Okawamae Dori, Sakai Building, 2nd Fl. ☎ 224-1696

RESTAURANTS
■ **Ja Ja** (B F G MA) 20-2 h; closed Tue.
2F Ing. Bld. 1-2-26 Benten *(Near Niigata Station)* ☎ 241-8074

Osaka | **Japan**

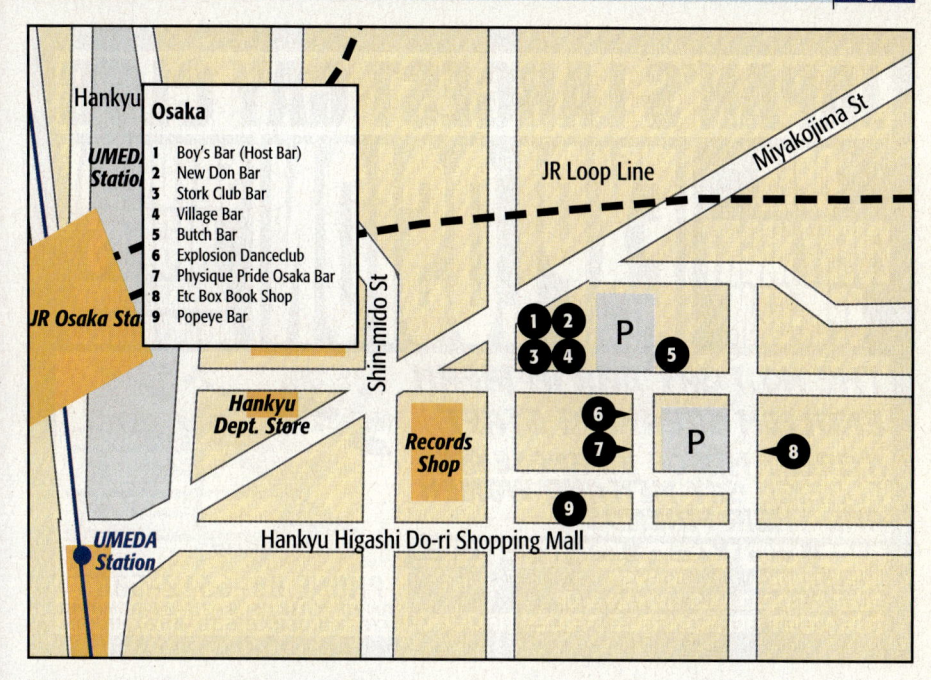

Osaka

1. Boy's Bar (Host Bar)
2. New Don Bar
3. Stork Club Bar
4. Village Bar
5. Butch Bar
6. Explosion Danceclub
7. Physique Pride Osaka Bar
8. Etc Box Book Shop
9. Popeye Bar

Osaka ☎ 06

BARS

■ **Boys** (B G OG) 16-24 h
Doyama-cho 16-19, Kita-ku ☎ 313-4800
■ **Butch Bar** (B G YG) 20-2 h, Sat -4h, Mon closed.
13-4 Juon Doyama Building, Doyama-cho Kita-ku *(5th floor)*
☎ 6363-8731
English spoken. Foreigners welcome.
■ **Garcon Cerkle** (B G) 19-5 h
Minami-ku, Nam-ba 4-3-16, GT Town Building *(3rd floor)*
☎ 643-0541
■ **Hoshi** (B G MA) 19-2 h
Kita-ku, 16-6 Doyama-cho ☎ 312-6741
■ **H2** (B G MA)
Chuo-Ku, Nanba 4-3-16, GT Building 5th floor ☎ 644-0809
■ **Mick's** (B glm MA) 11-21 h
3-3 Banzai-Cho, Kita-Ku *(two blocks from "Explosion")*
☎ 6361-7150
■ **Nagasaki** (B G)
Kita-ku, Doyama-cho 6-14, Shoei Kaikan 104 ☎ 312-6003
■ **New Don** (B G MA) 20-03h
16-5 Doyama-cho, Kita-ku *(2nd floor)* ☎ 315-9312
Call if you need help. Nice place.
■ **Physique Pride Osaka** (! B CC G YG) 20-? h
8-23 Doyama-Cho, Kita-ku ☎ 6361-2430
Friendly gay bar for internationals and their admirers. English spoken.
■ **Popeye** (B G) 16-23.30 h
Kita-ku, Doyama-cho 6-15 *(3rd floor)* ☎ 315-1502
■ **Stork Club** (B d E f G MA)
Stork Building, 17-3 Doyama-cho, Kita-ku *(2nd floor)* ☎ 361-4484

■ **Doorway to Gay Japan Gateway** ■

A casual gay bar, everybody is welcome.

PHYSIQUE
PRIDE
OSAKA

06•6361•2430
www.physiqueprideosaka.com

Japan Osaka ▶ Sapporo

JAPAN'S LARGEST GAY CLUB
EXPLOSION

OPEN EVERY NIGHT 8PM-6AM

SATURDAY NIGHTS 2 DRINKS / 1,500YEN MEN ONLY UNTIL 12:30

THE NO.1 GAY BAR IN JAPAN
ENGLISH SPEAKING STAFF
A GREAT MIX OF JAPANESE AND FOREIGN GAY MEN AND WOMEN AND THEIR FRIENDS

NO COVER CHARGE!
SOFT DRINKS 500YEN
BEER & COCKTAILS 700YEN & UP
THE MOST REASONABLE PRICES AROUND!

PHONE 06-6312-5003
SANYO-KAIKAN 8-23-B1, DOYAMA
KITA-KU, OSAKA, 530-0027, JAPAN

■ **Village** (B G YG)
Pearl Leisure Building 2F Doyama-cho, Kita-ku ☎ 6365-1151
Karaoke bar.
■ **Yacht** (B G VS) 15-18, videos 18-3 h
Minami-ku, Namba 4-7-9, Nanshin Kaikan Building *(2nd floor)*
☎ 643-6734

DANCECLUBS
■ **Explosion** (! B D G s YG) 20-6 h
Sanyo-Kaikan, 8-23-B1, Doyama-cho, Kita-ku ✉ 530-0027 *(Hankyu Umeda or JR Osaka Station)* ☎ 312-5003
Largest gay disco in Japan. English-speaking staff.

SEX SHOPS/BLUE MOVIES
■ **Plaza Apple Inn**
Moto-Machi 1-11-5, Naniwa-ku, Ishimoto Building ☎ 633-4878

SAUNAS/BATHS
■ **Adan** (g SA YG) 0-24 h
Naniwa-ku, Moto-machi 1-7-19 ☎ 631-2350
■ **Hokuokan** (G H SA SB) Open 24h
14-10 Doyama-cho Kita-ku ☎ 6361-2288
Japanese only. Foreigners should be fluent in Japanese.

BOOK SHOPS
■ **Etc Box** 12-23 h
Cosmo Plaza Building, 11-2 Doyama-cho, Kita-ku *(basement)*
☎ 316-0095

HOTELS
■ **Kansai** (AC glm H)
☎ 312-7971
Close to gay area. All rooms with private bath, telephone & WC.

CRUISING
-Under Health Centre (near Sonezaki Police Station)
-Department Store Hankyu (underground)

Sapporo ☎ 011

BARS
■ **Be Be Lu** (B G R)
Minami 5-jo, Nishi 5-chome, Chuo-ku ☎ 512-5392
■ **Bonta** (B g OG)
3rd floor, S.A. Building, Minami-6-jo Nishi-6-chome ☎ 531-1333
■ **Cave. La** (! B G MA) 20-3h
S.A. Builing, Minami 6-jo, Nishi 6-chome *(4th floor)* ☎ 531-6734
■ **Chaplin** (B G) 20-3.30 h
5th floor, S.A. Building, Minami 6-jo, Nishi 6-chome ☎ 531-1434
■ **Crewz** (B g MA) 19-3 h
3rd floor, S.A. Building, Minami-6-jo, Nishi-6-chome ☎ 512-9389
■ **Friend** (B g MA)
3rd floor, Chisan Hotel, Minami-7-jo, Nishi-5-chome ☎ 562-4396
■ **Meeya** (B d DR G MG) 20-5 h
S-A Building, Minami-6-jo, Nishi 6-chome *(3rd floor)* ☎ 521-0683
Orgy bar every Tue. 3.00 plus free drink. Other party nights too.
■ **Ni Zero San (203)** (B g MA) 19-3 h
1st floor, S.A. Building, Minami 6-jo, Nishi 6-chome ☎ 513-1250
■ **Prism** (B g YG) 20-3 h
4th floor, Dai-6, Asahi Kanko Building, Minami 6-jo, Nishi 6-chome
Minami-6-jo, Nishi-6-chome
☎ 512-6790
■ **Shigeru** (B g MA) 19-2 h
4th floor, Dai-6, Asahi Kanko Building, Minami 6-jo, Nishi 6-chome
☎ 531 72 78

Sapporo ▶ Tokyo **Japan**

SAUNAS/BATHS
■ **Men's House Zoo** (G) 17.30-9h, Sat 15-8.30h
7.6 Building 2F Minami 7-jo Nishi 6-chome Chuo-ku ☏ 513 1566

BOOK SHOPS
■ **Shirokuma-do Shoten** (g) 11-23 h
Shinwa Plaza B1, Minami-3-jo, Nishi-9-chome ☏ 261-5406

CRUISING
- Odori Park (Nishi 11-chome)
- Sapporo Railroad Station
- Yuraku Cinema
- Sauna at Basment of Hotel Line

Sendai ☏ 022

BARS
■ **Leo** (B G) closed Tue
Kokubun-cho, 1-6-1, Social Sanro Building B1 *(basement)*
☏ 265-9647
Take a taxi to Kanihachi Restaurant, small side street, downstairs under restaurant. Bar about 3rd door on the right side of hallway. Sign in Japanese.

■ **Taiho** (B g) 2nd & 4th Sun 19-0.30 h
Daisan (No.3) Fujiwara Building, Ichiban-cho *(3rd floor)*
☏ 263-0328

SAUNAS/BATHS
■ **Speed** (G) 14-5h
1-15 Dai 3 Shiratori Building, Room no. 205, Kasuga-cho, Aoba-ku

Tokyo ☏ 03

✱ Tokyo has the largest gay scene of the country. Foreigners can orientate themselves with help of the magazines "Tokyo Classified" and "Tokyo Night Life" both written in English.
Most of the gay bars are located in the district of Shinjyuku-ni-chome. The Japanese are known to be polite and friendly to foreigners. Unfortunately they speak only a little English and often dare not begin a conversation in English.

★ Tokyo hat die größte schwule Szene des Landes. Ausländische Besucher können sich mit Hilfe der englischsprachigen Stadtmagazine *Tokyo Classified* und *Tokyo Night Life* orientieren.
Im Stadtteil Shinjyuku-ni-chome konzentrieren sich die schwulen Bars. Japaner sind aus Prinzip Ausländern gegenüber höflich und freundlich. Bedauerlicherweise sprechen nur wenige Englisch bzw. trauen sich nicht, es zu tun.

✱ Tokyo est la ville avec la plus grande scène gaie du pays. Les visiteurs étrangers peuvent s'orienter grâce à des magazines tels que *Tokyo Classified* et *Tokyo Night Life*.
Dans le quartier de Shinjyuku-ni-chome, on trouve une forte concentration de bars gais. Les japonais sont polis et sympathiques par principe envers les étrangers. Malheureusement, beaucoup ne parlent pas l'anglais ou n'osent pas.

● Tokio dispone del más amplio ambiente gay en todo el país. Para turistas las revistas de ocio *Tokyo Classified* y *Tokyo Night Life*, ambas escritas en inglés, son de gran ayuda para encontrar los lugares interesantes.
Los sitios de ambiente se concentran en el barrio Shinjyuku-ni-chome. En general, los extranjeros son tratados de manera muy amable

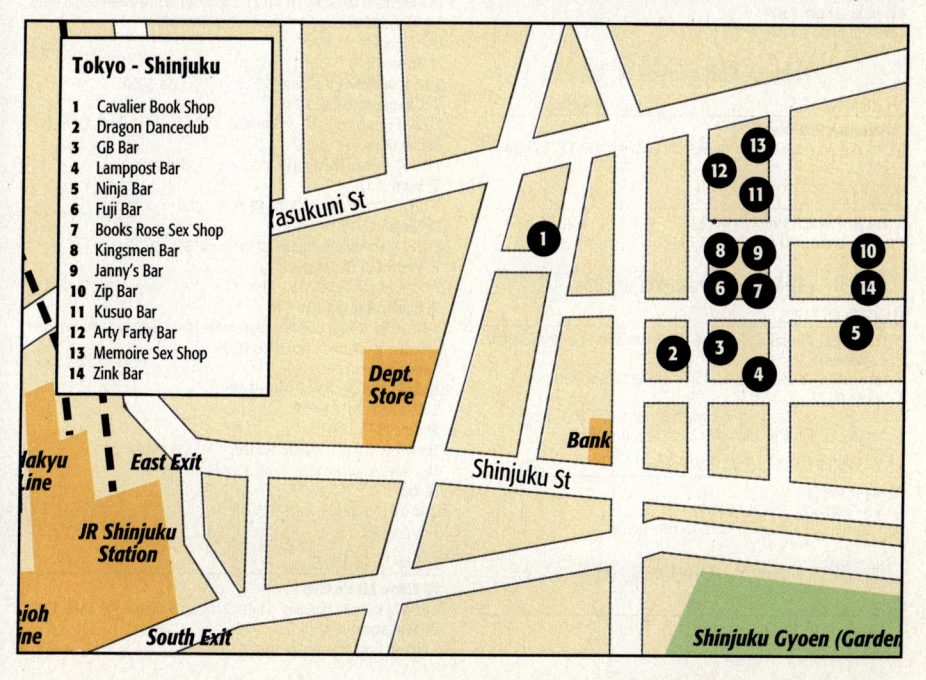

Tokyo - Shinjuku
1. Cavalier Book Shop
2. Dragon Danceclub
3. GB Bar
4. Lamppost Bar
5. Ninja Bar
6. Fuji Bar
7. Books Rose Sex Shop
8. Kingsmen Bar
9. Janny's Bar
10. Zip Bar
11. Kusuo Bar
12. Arty Farty Bar
13. Memoire Sex Shop
14. Zink Bar

Japan — Tokyo - Chiyoda-ku ▶ Tokyo - Shinjuku-ku

y cortés, pero desgraciadamente muy pocos japonéses saben inglés o mejor dicho se atreven a hablarlo.

Tokio vanta del più vasto ambiente gay del paese. I visitatori stranieri si possono orientare con l'aiuto delle due riviste *Tokyo Classified* e *Tokyo Night Life*.
Nel quartiere Shinjyuku-ni-chome si concentrano i bar gay. I giapponesi sono tradizionalmente molto cordiali e amichevoli con gli stranieri. Purtroppo solo in pochi parlano l'inglese o non si azzardano a parlarlo.

TOURIST INFO
■ **Tourist Information Centre**
Tokyo Kokusai Forum B1 3-5-1 Marunouchi, Chiyoda-ku ☎ 3201-3331

GENERAL GROUPS
■ **International Friends Passport**
CPO Box 180, (Chuo Yubin Kyoku) ✉ 100-91 ☎ 5693-4569
Serving all of Japan since 1981 (under various names).

CRUISING
- Ginza Street around Sony Building
- Hibiya and Higashi Park toilets
- Olympic Park (between swimming pool and Akasaka side, at night)
- At Shinbashi Daiichi Building (underground)
- At Higashi Ginza underground station
- Shinagawa Station
- Hakata staion toilet
- Shimbashi Station
- Tabata Railway Station
- Shibuya Station (south exit)
- Bygs Building (basement)
- Jingu Pool (Sendagaya)
- Komazawa Koen Park
- Toilets at Ueno station

Tokyo - Chiyoda-ku ☎ 03

PHARMACIES
■ **American Pharmacy**
1-1 Yurakucho *(at Nikkatsu International Building)* ☎ 32 71 40 34
Drugstore.

HOTELS
■ **Tokyo Y.M.C.A Hotel** (H MA NG)
7 Mitoshiro-cho, Kanda ☎ 293 19 11

Tokyo - Minato-ku ☎ 03

MEN'S CLUBS
■ **Treffpunkt Akasaka** (AC DR G NU P MA) Mon-Sun 12-midnight, Fri 12-Sat 05h
Maeda Bld. 4F, Akasaka 5-4-17 *(Subway Akasaka #7 exit)* ☎ 55 63 05 23
Admission fee 1,700, discount Mon-Fri 12-15h only 1.000. Naked parties on Sat, Sun & holidays. All nationalities welcome.

SEX SHOPS/BLUE MOVIES
■ **Apple Inn** (g)
1-13-5 *(2nd floor)* ☎ 35 74 14 77
Near Shimbashi station. The gay books are upstairs.

Tokyo - Ota-ku ☎ 03

BARS
■ **Mitaka** (B G) 19-2 h
7-60-9 Nishi- Kamata ☎ 3735-6765

Tokyo - Shibuya-ku ☎ 03

BARS
■ **LAX** (B G)
2-8 Fuyo Building *(3rd floor)* ☎ 3496-4190

Tokyo - Shinjuku-ku ☎ 03

BARS
■ **Arty Farty** (B G)
2-17-4 Lily mansion *(1st floor)* ☎ 3356-5388
Popular, inexpensive with a international atmosphere.
■ **Capture** (B CC G) 19-5 h
Watanabe Building 4th Fl., 2-14-7 Shinjuku ☎ 3357-6926
■ **Century** (B G msg R) 12-24 h
2-14-8 Daisan Tenko Building *(6th floor)* ☎ 3356-1628
■ **Fuji Bar** (B G) 19.30-3 h
12-16-2 *(basement No. 104)* ☎ 3354-2707
One of the more popular bars for tourists.
■ **GB Tokyo** (! B G VS MA) 20-2 weekdays, 20-03h at weekends.
2-12-3 Shinjuku Plaza Building *(basement)* ☎ 33 52 89 72
Around the corner from Fuji Bar. Sign "GB" on sidewalk.
■ **Hatten-Hachi (8.8)** (B G)
2-15-13 Shigemi Building *(2nd floor)* ☎ 3354-6695
■ **Janny's** (B G R) 18-3 h
2-18-1 Daiichi Tenko Building *(7th floor)* ☎ 3356-2202
■ **Jiyu-No-Megami** (B G) 18-3 h
2-12-14 New Futami Building *(#302)* ☎ 3351-7214
■ **King of College** (B CC G R) 18-4h
2-14-5 Sakagami Building *(2nd floor)* ☎ 3352-3930
English spoken. Maily host boys.
■ **Kingsmen** (B GLM) Fri Sat 21-5 h, possibly open during the week
2-18-5 Oda Building *(2nd floor)* ☎ 3354-4849
One block from Fuji Bar.
■ **Kusuo** (B G) 19-3 h
2-17-1 Sunflower Building *(3rd floor)* ☎ 3354-5050
■ **Lamppost** (B G) 19-3 h
2-12-15 *(2nd floor)* ☎ 3354-0436
■ **Leo** (B g)
2-14-36 Tsutsui Building *(2nd floor)* ☎ 3354-7699
■ **Maki** (B G)
2-12-15 *(4th floor)* ☎ 3341-8991
■ **Ninja** (B G R) 18-4 h
2-13-7 Nakahara Building *(1st floor)* ☎ 3352-2525
■ **Pierrot** (B G) 18-3 h
2-7-3 *(3rd floor)* ☎ 3352-1939
■ **Poplar Bar** (B G) 18-2 h
2-12-16 Saint Four Building *(basement 103)* *(Subway Marounouchi-Shinjuku Sanchome)* ☎ 33 50 69 29
Foreigners welcome.
■ **Sally`s** (B f g) 20-4 h, closed Mon
2-12-15 ☎ 3356-6409
■ **Zinc** (B G) 18-4 h
Shinjuku 2-14-6, Hayakawaya Bldg. ☎ 3352-6297
New opened cocktail bar. English spoken.
■ **Zip** (B d G YG) 20-5 h
2-14-11 *(1st floor)* ☎ 3356-5029
Very popular.

MEN'S CLUBS
■ **Tokyo Men's Club** (G)
5F Daini-kunisha Building, 11-10 Shinjuku 3-chome ☎ 3355-3389
■ **Treffpunkt** (G)
Chiyoda Line Akasaka 7 exit ☎ 5563-0523

Tokyo - Shinjuku-ku ▶ Yokohama — Japan

DANCECLUBS
■ **Dragon** (B D G) Tue-Thu 21-3, Fri Sat -5 h
In the basement of the building facing GB bar.

SEX SHOPS/BLUE MOVIES
■ **Books Rose** (G) 11-3 h
2-12-15 (basement) ☏ 33 41 06 00
■ **Cavalier** (G) 11-23 h
3-11-2 Muraki Building (basement) ☏ 3354-7976
Porno shop.
■ **Lumiere** (G) 12-7 h
2-17-1 Sunflower Building (1st floor) ☏ 3352-3378
Gifts, books, magazines, videos: large selection.
■ **Memoire** (G) 12-6 h
2-14-8 Tenko Building (1st floor) ☏ 3341-1775
Gifts, postcards, magazines.

SAUNAS/BATHS
■ **Hisen Kaikan**
Sumiyoshi 5-18-18 ☏ 413-7098
■ **Paragon** (G SA SB) 16-12 h
2-17-4 ✉ 160 ☏ 3353-3306
■ **Sky Gym** (G SA YG) 14-11 h
2-5-12 Rashington Palace (10th floor) ☏ 3352-1023
Foreigners welcome.

HEALTH GROUPS
■ **HIV to Jinken Jyoho Centre** 2nd/4th Sun 19-21 h
☏ 5259-0750
■ **Okubo Hospital** 10-18 h, closed Sun & holidays
1-17-10 ☏ 3361-8047
■ **Ugoku Gay to Lesbian no Kai** Tue-Thu 19-22 h
☏ 33 80 22 69

Tokyo - Taito-ku ☏ 03

BARS
■ **Hige** (B F g)
7-7-5 Toho-Building (3rd floor) ☏ 3844-1261
■ **Peppermint** (B G) 19-4 h
4-20-1 Mimasu Building (basement) ☏ 3845-1093
■ **Yuukontei** (B G)
2-21-11 Asakusa (2nd floor) ☏ 3842-6081

SAUNAS/BATHS
■ **Ichijo** (B g H SA) 0-24 h
1-1-5 Negishi (Uguisudani station) ☏ 38 44 45 67

■ **24 Kaikan Asakusa** (B DR F G OG SA SB SOL VS) 0-24 h
2-29-16 Asakusa, Taito-ku ✉ 111-0032 (S Ginza Line-Asakusa, behind Sensoji Temple) ☏ 3841-7806
A friendly sauna for older men. Free condoms available. Foreigners welcome.
■ **24 Kaikan Ueno** (B DR F G SA SB SOL VS WO YG) 24h
1-8-7 Kito-Ueno, Taito-ku ✉ 110-0005 (2 floor - 10th floor, along Showa-doriave)
☏ 3847-2424
Sauna frequented by younger and macho men. Free condoms available. Foreigners welcome.

Tokyo - Toshima-ku ☏ 03

BARS
■ **"X"** (B G LJ) 18-2 h
2-2-7 Daigo Maejima Building (basement) ☏ 3982-8747
S/M backroom; 15 minutes walk from Ikebukuro Station.

MEN'S CLUBS
■ **Club House** (G)
3-25-7 Nishi-Ikebukuro ☏ 3981-8775
Three floors of cruising with erotic theme park.

SAUNAS/BATHS
■ **Jinya** (G SA) 16-12 h
30-19 Ikebukuro Ni-Chome ☏ 5951-0995

Yokohama ☏ 045

BARS
■ **Pegasus** (B F G YG) 17-2 h, closed Wed
☏ 242-9 68
From Sakuragicho Station, leave at Toyoko Line exit and head towards the Key Coffee sign. At the fourth traffic light turn left. At the third street turn right. The bar is one and a half blocks down on the left. The sign is red with white letters.
■ **Tomo** (B G)
Naka-ku, Noge-cho 1-5, Minato-Kosan-Building (2nd floor)
☏ 231-2236

CRUISING
-Isezaki-cho shopping street (1st-2nd section on left; afternoon and evening)

Jordan ▸ Amman ▸ Kerak

Jordan

Name: al-Urdunn • Jordanien • Jordanie • Jordania • Giodania
Location: Middle East
Initials: HKJ
Time: GMT +2
International Country Code: ☏ 962
International Access Code: ☏ 00
Language: Arabic
Area: 89,342 km² / 35,461 sq mi.
Currency: 1 Jordan-Dinar (JD) = 1,000 Fils
Population: 4,563,000
Capital: Amman
Religions: 80% Moslem
Climate: Mostly dry desert climate. The rainy season in the west lasts from November to April.

※ The meeting places listed below are, without exception, mixed. There is no visible gay scene in Jordan. Homosexuality is strictly prohibited and can lead to imprisonment (German embassy, Amman). Although unusual for an Islamic country, hotels and bars in Jordan do serve alcoholic beverages. Inform yourself about the necessary vaccinations before going on your trip.

★ Es gibt in Jordanien keine eingrenzbare schwule Szene: Homosexualität ist streng verboten und mit Gefängnisstrafe bedroht (Deutsche Botschaft, Amman). So können wir im Listing nur gemischte Treffpunkte erwähnen. Ungewöhnlicherweise wird in jordanischen Hotels übrigens Alkohol ausgeschenkt. Wir empfehlen Ihnen, sich vor einer Reise über notwendige Impfungen zu informieren.

✱ Il n'y a pas vraiment de vie gaie en Jordanie. L'homosexualité y est interdite: c'est un délit et on risque la prison. Aucun des lieux mentionnés ci-dessous n'est vraiment gai. Les bars et boîtes sont tous mixtes. En Jordanie, on sert de l'alcool dans les bars et les hôtels, ce qui est inhabituel pour un pays islamique. Avant votre départ, renseignez-vous sur les vaccinations nécessaires.

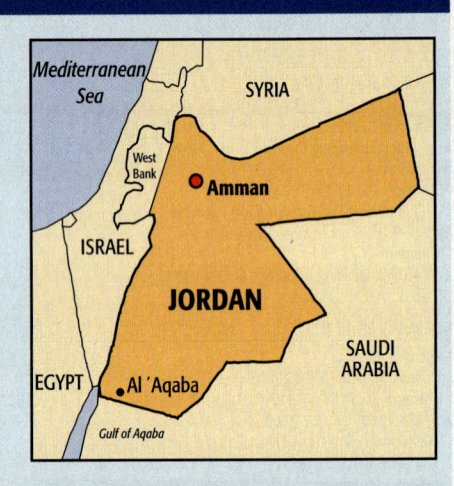

⬢ Los puntos de encuentro que damos a conocer son todos mixtos. En Jordania no hay un ambiente gay, la homosexualidad está estrictamente prohibida y es penada con cárcel. (Segun informaciones de la embajada alemana en Amman). No es costumbre que en bares y hoteles sean servidas bebidas alcohólicas. Antes de un viaje a Jordanía, se recomienda informarse sobre la vacunación necesaria.

✖ Gli atti omosessuali sono proibiti, e puniti con la reclusione (ambasciata tedesca, Amman). Non c'è una vera vita gay e i luoghi d'incontro elencati qui sotto hanno una clientela mista. Nei bar e negli hotel giordani vengono raramente serviti alcolici. Prima di intraprendere il viaggio, informatevi sulle vaccinazioni necessarie.

Amman

BARS

■ **KitKat Bar** (B g MA) 16-23.30 h
Basman Street *(near Hussein Mosque)*
Take a taxi.

■ **Salute Bar** (AC B D F NG MA OS) Thu
Villa d'Angelo Restaurant, Circle Road *(below second circle)*

DANCECLUBS

■ **Scandal Disco** (AC B D g) Thu Fri 22-3 h
Circle Road
From 6 circle behind Amra Hotel in the lower level of Sand Rock Hotel.

RESTAURANTS

■ **Zuwaddeh Restaurant** (B F OS) 13-16 h, 19-24 h
Fuhais *(Fuhais Village)* ☏ 720 677
Fuhais is a small village 10 min. outside of Amman.

CRUISING

- Old Roman Amphitheatre
- On the left of Al Husyni Grand Mosque at Rasheed Al Madai Street
- Hashimiya Square (R) *(in front of amphitheatre and Odeon)*

Kerak

CRUISING

- In the ruin of the old castle

Kazakhstan

Name: Kasachstan • Kazajstán • Kazajistán
Location: Central Asia
Initials: KZ
Time: GMT +6
International Country Code: ☏ 7
International Access Code: ☏ 8 (wait for tone) 10
Language: Kazak
Area: 2,717,300 km² / 1,049,150 sq mi.
Currency: 1 Tenge (T)= 100 Tiin
Population: 16,854,000
Capital: Astana
Religions: 50% Moslem, 50% Russian Orthodox
Climate: Dry continental climate. Winters are cold, summers hot.

✳ Kazakstan has lifted the ban on consenting homosexual intercouse (Article 104.1 of the penal code).

✳ In Kasachstan wurde das Verbot des Geschlechtsverkehrs zwischen Homosexuellen (Paragraph 104 Abs. 1 des Strafgesetzbuches) aufgehoben.

✳ Le Kazakstan a supprimé l'interdiction des pratiques homosexuelles consenties (Article 104.1 du code pénal).

✳ Kazajistán abolió la prohibición de relaciones sexuales de mutuo consentimiento entre homosexuales (104.1 del Código Penal).

✖ In Kazakistan il divieto di rapporto sessuale tra omosessuali (paragrafo 104, art.1 del Codice Penale) è stato abolito.

Almaty ☏ 3272

BARS

■ **XL Bar** (B G)
91 Kalinina ulitsa ☏ 69 11 53

■ **Neytralnaya Zona (Neutral Zone)** (! B d DR F GLM P SNU STV)
51 Nurmakova ulitsa *(at the corner of Sovetskaya street)* ☏ 68 12 91
Recently opened. Strict control at the entrance. Perfect place for an after-work relaxation.

■ **Real** (B d F GLM R OG STV)
Opposite the central entrance of Zeleny bazar (Green market)
☏ 33 55 45

■ **Spartacus** (B d F glm R SNU STV) Mon-Thu 22-4, Fri-Sun 22-4
115 Michurina ulitsa *(at the corner of Kurmangazy street)*

☏ 92 03 74
Believed to be the best gay club of Almaty. Young crowd, drag queens.

RESTAURANTS

■ **Queen** (F GLM MA)
Vinogradova-Rosybakieva ulitsa ☏ 50 94 87
Face control. Cheap and tasty. Entrance fee of 200 Tenge.

GENERAL GROUPS

■ **Kontrast**
PO Box 108 ✉ 96 🖨 33 86 10

CRUISING

-City Park, near the old Orthodox Russian Cathedral

Kenya

Name:	Kenia
Location:	East Africa
Initials:	EAK
Time:	GMT +3
International Country Code:	☏ 254
International Access Code:	☏ 000
Language:	Swahili; English
Area:	580,367 km² / 224,960 sq mi.
Currency:	1 Kenyan Shilling (K.Sh.) = 100 Cents
Population:	29,295,000
Capital:	Nairobi
Religions:	60% African nature religions, 26% Catholic, 7% Protestant
Climate:	The climate varies from tropical along coast to dry in the interior.

Homosexual acts are illegal and harshly punished. Paragraphs 162-165 of the Kenyan penal code declare them to be "carnal knowledge against the order of nature", punishable by a minimum of 5 up to a maximum of 14 years imprisonment. The subject of homosexuality is strictly taboo and is not discussed anywhere in literature, politics or the media. A generally accessible gay infra-structure does not exist to our knowledge. The bars listed below are not gay meeting places but are rather mixed addresses where one has a better chance of meeting gay people.

Homosexuelle Handlungen sind illegal und werden hart bestraft. Die Paragraphen 162-165 des kenianischen Strafgesetzbuches bezeichnen sie als "carnal knowledge against the order of nature" (dt. etwa: "Widernatürlicher Geschlechtsverkehr") und ahnden sie mit Haft zwischen mindestens fünf und höchstens 14 Jahren. Homosexualität als Thema ist in Kenia streng tabu und wird nirgends in Presse, Literatur und Politik diskutiert. Eine allgemein zugängliche schwule Infrastruktur existiert unseres Wissens nicht. Die unten angegeben Bars sind keine Schwulentreffpunkte, sondern gemischte Adressen, wo man eine etwas größere Chance hat, einen Schwulen kennenzulernen.

Au Kénia, l'homosexualité est un délit qui est sévèrement puni. Conformément aux articles 162 à 165 du code pénal kénian, les "actes charnels contre nature") peuvent vous coûter cher: entre 5 et 14 ans de prison. L'homosexualité est un sujet tabou au Kénia. On n'en parle jamais dans la presse, la littérature ou en politique. Il n'y a pas vraiment d'infrastructure gaie.
Les bars mentionnés ci-dessous ne sont pas vraiment des lieux gais.

Ce sont plutôt des adresses mixtes où on aura un peu plus de chance de rencontrer quelqu'un qu'ailleurs.

Las actividades homosexuales son ilegales y son objeto de duras sanciones. Los artículos 162-165 del código penal keniano las califican de "carnal knowledge against the order of nature" (algo así como "actos carnales contra natura") y son sancionados con penas de encarcelamiento que van desde 5 hasta 14 años.
En Kenia la homosexualidad es un tema completamente tabú y no se debate ni en la prensa ni en las obras de carácter literario, ni en la vida política. Que nosotros sepamos, tampoco existe una infraestructura gay. Los bares que citamos a continuación no son sitios de ambiente, sino direcciones mixtas, donde quizás haya posibilidad de algún tipo de contacto.

Gli atti omosessuali sono illegali e duramente puniti. I paragrafi 162-165 del codice penale del Kenya, li definiscono come "conoscenza carnale contro l'ordine della natura" punibili con la prigione da cinque a quattordici anni. L'argomento dell'omosessualità costituisce un tabù mai discusso nella letteratura, dai politici e nei mass-media. Per quanto ne sappiamo, non esiste una infrastruttura gay generalmente accessibile. I bar indicati qui sotto non possono essere considerati dei punti d'incontro gay, ma dei luoghi dove si può avere almeno una piccola possibilità d'incontrare qualcuno.

Kisumu

DANCECLUBS
■ **Club. The** (B D g N P WE YG) Wed Fri Sat 21-? h at Hotel Royal

Mombasa

RESTAURANTS
■ **Fontanella Restaurant** (AC B F NG OS) 8-22.30 h
Moi Avenue/Nyerere Avenue City House ☏ 237 56
International specialties.

■ **Tamarind Restaurant** (B CC F g OS) 12.15-14.30 h, 18.45-22.15 h
Sino Road near Old Nyali Bridge, PO Box 857 85 ☏ 47 17 47
Open-air restaurant serving international and African specialties, especially seafood.

Nairobi

RESTAURANTS
■ **Carnivori** (AC B CC F GLM OS) 12-14.30, 18.45-22.15 h
Langata Road, PO Box 566 85 ☏ 50 17 79
African specialities (roast meats with salads and sauces).

■ **Tamarino Restaurant** (AC B CC F GLM) 12-2, 18.30-22 h
Harambee Avenue, PO Box 744 93 *(National Bank Building)*
☏ 33 89 59
International and African specialties (seafood).

CRUISING
- Kenyatta Avenue
- Back of GPO, Kenyatta Avenue and around Intercontinental Hotel (especially Sun afternoon)
- Sarit Centre (lower ground floor)

Korea-South

Name: Taehan Min'guk • Südkorea • Corée du Sud • Corea del Sur • Corea del Sud
Location: Eastern Asia
Initials: ROK
Time: GMT +9
International Country Code: ☎ 82
International Access Code: ☎ 001 or 002
Language: Korean
Area: 99,313 km^2 / 38,325 sq mi.
Currency: 1 Won (W) = 100 Chon
Population: 46,430,000
Capital: Seoul
Religions: 28% Christian, 21% Buddhist, Confucians (an ethical code, not a religion)
Climate: Moderate climate with rainfall heavier in the summer than in winter.

✳ There are no anti-gay laws in South Korea, but there is still a stigma attached to being gay. Openly gay behaviour is therefore not advisable. Korean men are affectionate and may walk around hand in hand, but this is only a friendly gesture and should not be misunderstood.

✳ Homosexuelle Handlungen zwischen Erwachsenen sollen in Süd-Korea nicht verboten sein. Das Schwulsein aber ist stigmatisiert. Es ist ratsam, sich unauffällig zu verhalten. Koreaner sind herzlich und laufen gerne Hand in Hand mit Freunden durch die Straßen, was aber nicht als eine schwule Geste mißverstanden werden sollte.

✳ Officiellement, l'homosexualité est tolérée en Corée du Sud. Les homosexuels y sont cependant plutôt mal vus. Il est donc conseillé de se faire assez discret. Les Coréens sont chaleureux et aiment bien marcher main dans la main dans la rue. Attention: n'en tirez pas pour autant des conclusions hâtives!

⬢ Las relaciones homosexuales entre adultos no están prohibidas, sin embargo el ser homosexual continua siendo un estigma. Es aconsejable no llamar la atención. Los hombres coreanos muestran su afección tomandose de la mano, esto no tiene mas significado que el de un gesto amable.

✖ In Corea del Sud i rapporti omosessuali tra adulti non dovrebbero essere illegali. L'omosessualità tuttavia non è benaccetta. è consigliabile non ostentare troppo le proprie preferenze. I coreani sono socievoli e passeggiano spesso in strada mano nella mano con i loro amici, questo, però, non deve essere frainteso come un gesto omosessuale.

Pusan

BARS

■ **Telephone** (B G MG)
(Accross from the Samsung Theatre)

CRUISING

Wharves across the bridge.

Seoul

PUBLICATIONS

■ **Chingusai**
Gay magazine, available at gay bars. Published by the group of the same name.

BARS

■ **California** (B D G MA) 12-? h, disco: Fri Sat
72-32 Itaewon Yongsan ☎ 749 77 38
■ **Trance** (B G MA)
Yongsan-gu, It'aewon-dong 136-42 ☎ 797 34 10
■ **Why Not?** (B G MA)
137-4 Yongsan-ku, Itaewon ☎ 795 81 93

DANCECLUBS

■ **Spartacus** (! B D G MA VS)
128-11 Itaewon-Dong, Yongsan-Ku ☎ 749 77 38

CRUISING

-Tapkol Park (popular late afternoon, on right side OG, near monument YG)

Laos | Luang Prabang ▶ Viangchan / Vientiane

Laos

Name:	Sathlanalat Paxathipatai Paxaxôn Lao
Location:	South East Asia
Initials:	LAO
Time:	GMT +7 (Summer +6)
International Country Code:	☎ 856
International Access Code:	☎ 14
Language:	Lao, English
Area:	236,800 km²
Currency:	Kip
Population:	48 49 000
Capital:	Vianchan (Vientiane)
Religions:	58% Buddist, 34% local religions

✱ According to the embassy of Laos in Germany, homosexuality is illegal in Laos and is considered as a violation of traditional rules of conduct.
The local population is very friendly as is the case throughout South East Asia.

✱ Nach Aussagen der laotischen Botschaft in Deutschland, ist Homosexualität in Laos illegal und stellt eine Verletzung der traditionellen Verhaltensregeln dar.
Die einheimische Bevölkerung ist, wie überall in Asien, sehr freundlich.

✱ Selon l'ambassade du Laos en Allemagne, l'homosexualité au Laos est illégale et considérée comme une violation des règles de conduite traditionnelles.
Comme dans le reste de l'Asie du sud-est, la population est cependant très sympathique.

✱ Según informa la embajada de Laos en Alemania, la homosexualidad es ilegal en Laos y se considera una violación de las tradicionales reglas de conducta. La población de este país es muy amable, igual que en los demás países del sudeste asiático.

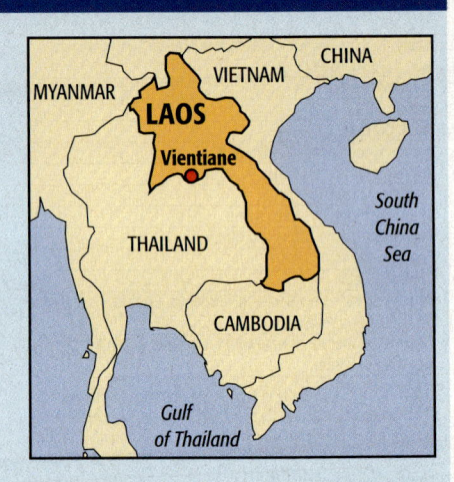

✖ Stando alle dichiarazioni dell'Ambasciata di Laos in Germania, l'omosessualità a Laos è illegale e rappresenta una violazione delle norme comportamentali tradizionali. La popolazione locale è molto gentile, come del resto in tutte le parti dell'Asia.

Luang Prabang ☎ 71

CAFES
■ **Hong's Coffee Shop & Restaurant** (B F glm) 08-02 h
089/3 Baan Vienkeo, Pasaman Road
Excellent food and full bar. Hong speaks english and can arrange accommodation as well as give tips for gay and lesbian travellers.

DANCECLUBS
■ **Hotel Rama** (D g)

Viangchan / Vientiane ☎ 21

CAFES
■ **Kok** (B g) 17-05h
150 Baan Dongpalane Thong (Next door to the Europa restaurant)
☎ 416-598
Around 02h very busy.

DANCECLUBS
■ **Image** (b TV)
Anou Street (on courner near Anou Hotel)
Gay owned and run. Small, loud and lively. At midnight the transvestites arrive who are very friendly and no-one stays alone for very long!

RESTAURANTS
■ **Europa** (b F) -22h
150 Baan Dongpalane Thong
Excellent food and great service. Gay owned and run.

SAUNAS/BATHS
■ **Ajaan Amphone's Herbal Sauna**
Anou Street (one block from the Tai-Pan hotel - direction north east)
Shaolin massage is offered here by Ajaan Amphone, a master in Kong-Fu. His son Inthong is usually called to assist and the result is an amazing massage. Well worth a try.

FASHION SHOPS
■ **New Wave. The**
(near the Nam Phu fountains)
Here is the meeting place where one can find out about the gay life in the city. Ask for Eng.

HOTELS
■ **Anou**
Anou Street (opposite Image Bar/Disco) ☎ 21 36 30
Some of the rooms may need renovating but this hotel in the center of the city is not only reasonably priced but also not a problem when bringing overnight guests.
■ **Novotel Belvedere** (BF g)
Unit , Ban Khountathong, Samsenthai Road, Sikhotabong
☎ 21 35 70 📠 21 35 72
Not in the city center but free transfers available. Room prices include full breakfast.

GUEST HOUSES
■ **Sordadith Guest House**
150 Baan Dong palane Thong *(in same building as Europa Restaurant and Café Kok)* ☎ 413 651   ☎ 412 233   🖷 413 651
Clean, comfortable and centrally located.
■ **Villa Dara** (AC G)
PO Box 4474 *(Near Wat Thatluang Tai)* ☎ 412 628   🖷 412 529

✉ ophilao@laonet.fr   🌐 www.mekongexpress.com
Bed and Breakfast in colonia villa. Airport pickup available.

CRUISING
The whole country is a possible cruising area. Some popular points are:
- The park slong the river, ass well as the well known Nam Phu fountains
- The Nam Phom palace with its fountains

Latvia

Name:	Latvija • Lettland • Lettonie • Letonia • Lettonia
Location:	Northeast Europe
Initials:	LV
Time:	GMT +2
International Country Code:	☎ 371
International Access Code:	☎ 00
Language:	Latvian (official), Russian
Area:	64,589 km² / 24,942 sq mi.
Currency:	1 Lats (Ls) = 100 Santims
Population:	2,450,000
Capital:	Riga
Religions:	55% Protestant, 24% Catholic
Climate:	Continental under the moderating influence of the Baltic Sea.

✳ Homosexuality is legal in Latvia but the age of consent is not clearly defined by the law. Therefore, it's not recommended to have sex with a partner under the age of 18. There are strict rules regarding younger men, especially if a dependence relation is exploited by an older man.

The general attitude towards homosexuality in Latvia varies considerably depending on the location. While people in the capital Riga have a largely tolerant and open-minded attitude, people in rural areas often view it negatively. In the last few years, the public opinion has undergone considerable change. According to a survey, 53% of the population think that homosexual couples should be able to register their partnership.

The scene is concentrated in the Latvian capital - Riga. Many gays from Riga spend their summer holidays on the wonderful gay beaches located outside of Riga.

In 2001, the city of Riga celebrates its 800th anniversary. And in August, at the culmination of the celebrations, Riga will be the European City of Culture for one month. Our tip for Riga is to buy a copy of the city guide "Riga in Your Pocket", which provides good information for tourists, including a small gay section.

Ainars Locmelis - Geju Atbalsta Grupa

✳ Homosexualität ist in Lettland legal, aber das Mündigkeitsalter ist durch das Gesetz nicht eindeutig definiert, und deswegen ist es nicht ratsam Sex mit einem Partner unter 18 Jahren zu haben. Bezüglich jüngerer Männer gibt es strenge Regeln, besonders wenn eine Abhängigkeitsbeziehung von einem älteren Mann ausgenutzt wird.
Die allgemeine Haltung gegenüber Homosexuellen schwankt beachtlich von Ort zu Ort. Während die Menschen in der Hauptstadt Riga eine eher tolerante und offene Haltung gegenüber Homosexuellen einnehmen, sind die Menschen in ländlichen Gegenden diesbezüglich oft sehr negativ eingestellt. In den letzten Jahren gab es jedoch in der lettischen Gesellschaft spürbare Veränderungen, und laut einer Umfrage meinen 53% der Bevölkerung, daß homosexuelle Paare die Möglichkeit haben sollten, Ihre Partnerschaft registrieren zu lassen.
Die Szene konzentriert sich vor allem auf die lettische Hauptstadt Riga. Viele Gays aus Riga verbringen ihre Sommerferien an den wundervollen Schwulenstränden außerhalb von Riga.
Im Jahr 2001 feiert Riga ihr 800jähriges Bestehen, und im August wird Riga einen Monat lang Europäische Kulturhauptstadt sein. Unser Tip für Riga ist, sich den Reiseführer "Riga in Your Pocket" zu kaufen, der sowohl sehr gute Informationen für Touristen als auch ein kleines Kapitel für Schwule beinhaltet

✳ Même si l'âge de consentement n'est pas clairement défini par les lois, l'homosexualité est légale en Lettonie. Il est cependant recommandé de ne pas avoir de relations sexuelles avec un partenaire de moins de 18 ans. Il existe en effet une législation très stricte en ce qui concerne la protection des mineurs, particulièrement si un homme plus âgé exploite une situation de dépendance.
L'attitude des Lettons face à l'homosexualité peut varier considérablement. Si les habitants de la capitale Riga se montrent très tolérants et ouverts d'esprit, il n'en est pas de même pour les régions plus rurale du pays. L'opinion publique a cependant beaucoup évolué ces dernières années. Selon un sondage, 53 % de la population serait en faveur d'un partenariat enregistré pour les homosexuels.
La scène se concentre dans la capitale Riga. Les magnifiques plages gaies en dehors de la ville attirent aussi beaucoup de monde en été. La ville de Riga célèbre son 800ème anniversaire en 2001.

Latvia | Riga

En août, au point culminant des manifestations, Riga sera également pour un mois la ville européenne de la culture. Notre conseil est de se procurer le guide de ville en anglais "Riga in Your Pocket", qui procure de bonnes informations touristiques, y compris sur la scène gaie.
Ainars Locmelis - Geju Atbalsta Grupa

La homosexualidad es legal en Letonia, pero la edad de consentimiento no está claramente definida. Por ello, no es recomendable mantener relaciones sexuales con personas de menos de 18 años. Hay reglas muy estrictas en cuanto a las relaciones con hombres jóvenes, especialmente si un hombre mayor se aprovecha de una relación con un joven dependiente de él.
La postura general hacia los homosexuales en Letonia depende mucho del lugar. Mientras que las personas en la capital, Riga, suelen tener una actitud tolerante y sin prejuicios, las personas que viven en las áreas rurales muchas veces rechazan la homosexualidad. En los últimos años, la opinión pública ha cambiado considerablemente. Según una encuesta, el 53 por ciento de la población cree que las parejas homosexuales deberían tener la oportunidad de registrar su relación. El ambiente gay se concentra en la capital letona. Muchos gays de Riga pasan sus vacaciones de verano en las maravillosas playas 'gays' ubicadas fuera de Riga.
En el 2001, la ciudad de Riga celebra su 800 cumpleaños. Y en agosto, en el momento culminante de las fiestas, Riga será la Capital Europea de Cultura durante un mes. Recomendamos comprar un ejemplar de la guía 'Riga in Your Pocket' ("Riga en tu bolsillo"), pues da mucha información para turistas e incluso tiene un apartado con información para gays.
Ainars Locmelis - Geju Atbalsta Grupa

✖ L'omosessualità è legale in Lettonia, ma la maggiore età non è definita chiaramente dalla legge, e per questo motivo non è consigliabile avere sesso con un partner che non ha ancora compiuto i 18 anni d'età. Per quanto riguarda invece gli uomini più giovani ci sono delle regole molto severe, in modo particolare se in un rapporto di dipendenza chi ne approfitta è un uomo più vecchio. L'atteggiamento generale verso gli omosessuali muta considerevolmente da un posto all'altro. Mentre gli uomini nella capitale Riga assumono un atteggiamento piuttosto tollerante ed aperto nei confronti degli omosessuali, nelle zone rurali le persone si pronunciano a riguardo spesso negativamente. Negli ultimi anni nella società lettone ci sono stati comunque dei cambiamenti percettibili, e secondo un sondaggio, il 53% della popolazione è del parere che le coppie omosessuali dovrebbero avere la possibilità, di poter far registrare la relazione con il proprio compagno. L'ambiente gay si concentra soprattutto a Riga, capitale della Lettonia. Molti gay di Riga trascorrono le proprie ferie in estate sulle splendide spiagge popolate da omosessuali al di fuori di Riga. Nell'anno 2001 la città di Riga festeggia i suoi 800 anni di anniversario e in agosto diventerà per un mese capitale europea della cultura. Il nostro consiglio per chi andrà a Riga è quello di comprarsi la guida turistica "Riga in Your Pocket2, che contiene sia ottime informazioni per i turisti sia un breve capitolo relativo agli omosessuali.
Ainars Locmelis - Geju Atbalsta Grupa

NATIONAL GAY INFO

■ **Latvian Gay And Lesbian Server** (GLM)
✉ gay@gay.lv
🖥 www.gay.lv
Internet site created by the Gay Support Group (GAG). Personals, chat space and city guide. Information in Latvian, Russian or English.

NATIONAL PUBLICATIONS

■ **Elwis** (G) Info in Latvian & Russian 21-21.30,
Info in English 20-21 h
Pastkaste 117 ✉ LV-5674 Dagda
☎ 922 05 30 (Latvian, Russian)
☎ +468 740 42 53 (English)
National gay newsletter with supplement in English. Also penpals club.

■ **Homo Zinas** (GLM)
Pastkaste 65 ✉ LV-1001 Riga
Gay newspaper in Latvian.

NATIONAL GROUPS

■ **Geju Atbalsta Grupa (GAG)** (GLM MA)
Pastkaste 380 ✉ LV-1001 Riga ☎ 959 22 29
✉ gay@gay.lv
🖥 www.gay.lv
Gay support group.

■ **Homoseksualitates Informacijas Centrs (HIC)** (GLM MA)
Pastkaste 65 ✉ LV-1001 Riga ☎ 925 46 10 ✉ jolanta@gay.lv
Homosexuality information center. AIDS information.

Riga ☎ 02

NATIONAL GROUPS

■ **AIDS Centre**
Krijanu iela Riga ☎ 737 22 75 ☎ 52 22 22 (hotline)

TOURIST INFO

■ **City of Riga Information Centre** 9-21 h
Ratslaukums 7 ☎ 704 43 77 ☎ 704 43 78 ✉ tourinfo@latnet.lv
■ **Riga In Your Pocket**
Vokieciu 10-15, 2001 Vilnius, Lithuania ☎ (+370-2) 22 39 78
☎ (+370-2) 22 29 82 ✉ office@inyourpocket.com
🖥 www.inyourpocket.com
Good general guide for Riga and Latvia with a small gay section. Check their website.

CAFES

■ **Santa Lija** (b BF glm MA)
Elizabetes iela 67
■ **Skapis** (b BF glm MA)
Aspazijas bulvaris 22

DANCECLUBS

■ **Purvs** (B D GLM MA S) 21-6 h
Matisa iela 60/62 *(Through the doorway under the rainbow flag lightbox)* ☎ 731 17 17
■ **XXL Club** (AC B CC D DR F G MA P SNU VS) 16-7 h
A. Kalnina iela 4 ✉ LV-1050 *(Near the railway station Marijas iela, in the center)* ☎ 728 22 76
Popular gay club in the centre of town. Decorated with Tom of Finland drawings. Bar and danceclub.

SEX SHOPS/BLUE MOVIES
■ **Labi** (g VS) Gay videos Sun 10-19 h only
Lacplesa iela 61 ☎ 728 66 41
■ **Labi** (g VS) Gay videos Sat 9-5 h only
Elizabetes iela 22
■ **Riga-Berline** (g VS) 0-24 h, Gay videos on Fri and Sun only
Lacplesa iela 47
Two video halls.

DATING AGENCIES
■ **Gay Contact Service** (G)
c/o Gay Support Group, Pastkaste 380 ✉ LV-1001

GUEST HOUSES
■ **Relax Inn Riga** (B BF f G H MA NU OS snu SA VS)
Postfach 13, 72147 Nehren, Germany *(centre Jurmala, near gay beach and not far away from the centre of Riga)*
☎ +49 173 36 36 216 ✉ RelaxInnRiga@aol.com
New guest house opening in spring 2001.

APARTMENTS
■ **Gay Accomodation Service** (G H MA)
✉ accomodation@gay.lv ✉ www.gay.lv/english/cel-viesnicas.htm
Appartments with kitchen, bathroom, hot and cold water, close to gay cruising area Grizinkalns. One night Ls 9.-, one week Ls 57.-, longer stays possible.

HEALTH GROUPS
■ **Agihas**
Pastkaste 391 ✉ LV-1001 ☎ 916 39 13 ☎ 960 73 12
✉ 733 99 54 ✉ agihas@latnet.lv
Support group for people with HIV/AIDS.
■ **Centre for Sexual Diseases**
Briana 2 ✉ LV-1001 ☎ 27 21 98

SWIMMING
-**Kalngale** (g) (take the train direction Saulkrasti and get off at Kalngale, then walk 30 min along the beach to the north)
-**Incupe** (g NU) (take the train direction Saulkrasti and get off at Incupe, then walk 30 min along the beach to the south)
-**Lielupe** (g) (take the train direction Jurmala and get off at Lielupe, then the bus 1 direction Uzvara until the last stop. Walk 20 min to north)
-**Vecaki** (g NU) (take the train direction Saulkrasti and get off at Vecaki, then walk 20 min along the beach to the north)

CRUISING
-**The Square** (in front of the University main building across from Raina bulvaris 19)
-**Esplanade** (Square between Elizabetes, Brivibas, Kalpaka, Kr. Valdemara streets)
-**Arkadijas parks** (AYOR) (Tram 10. Near the toilets)
-**Grizinkalns** (AYOR) (Park on Pernavas street/J Asara street)

Lebanon | Beirut

Lebanon

Name: Lubnan • Libanon • Liban • Libano
Location: Middle East
Initials: RL
Time: GMT +2
International Country Code: ☏ 961
International Access Code: ☏ 00
Language: Arabic
Area: 10,452 km² / 4,015 sq mi.
Currency: 1 Libanese Pound (L£) = 100 Piaster
Population: 4,210,000
Capital: Beirut
Religions: 60% Moslem, 40% Christian
Climate: Mediterranean climate. Winters are mild to cool and wet, summers hot and dry. The mountains can experience heavy winter snowfall.

✱ Homosexuality is illegal.

★ Homosexualität ist illegal.

✱ Au Liban, l'homosexualité est illégale.

⬢ La homosexualidad es ilegal.

✖ L'omosessualità è illegale.

Beirut ☏ 01

BARS
■ **Orange Mecanik** (B D g) Thu-Sat 22-6 h
Hirsh Tabet *(25 min from Beirut)*

SAUNAS/BATHS
■ **Hammam Nuhza** (MG msg NG SA SB) 0-24 h
19 Rue Kasti *(Secteur Sérail)*
Be discreet.

SWIMMING
- Paradise Beach (in the north part of Beirut, between Jounieh and Jbeil (Byblos))
- Summerland (g but still interesting)
- Dbayeh Beach

CRUISING
- Ramlet El-Bayda (popular 21-24 h)
- Dawra Square (stand by the sidewalk and you will be picked up by guys driving a car, 20-24 h)
- The area between Barbir, Mathaf and Aadlieh

SpartacusWorld.com

▶ click and ▶ win!

www.spartacusworld.com

… Schaan | Liechtenstein

Liechtenstein

Location: Central Europe
Initials: FL
Time: GMT +1
International Country Code: ☎ 423 (no area codes)
International Access Code: ☎ 00
Language: German
Area: 160 km² / 62 sq mi.
Currency: 1 Swiss Franc (sfr) = 100 Rappen
Population: 32,000
Capital: Vaduz
Religions: 83% Catholic, 7% Protestant
Climate: Continental climate. Winters are cold and cloudy with frequent snow or rain. Summers are cool to moderately warm, cloudy and humid.

✱ The age of consent in Liechtenstein is 18 for homosexual acts and 14 for heterosexual activity. Here, as in Austria, "promotion of homosexuality" is forbidden. The establishment of gay/lesbian associations is also prohibited (officially, at least).

✱ Das Schutzalter liegt in Liechtenstein bei 18 Jahren für homosexuelle Handlungen, jedoch bei 14 für heterosexuellen Sex. Wie in Österreich ist hier die "Werbung für Homosexualität", genauso wie die Gründung schwul-lesbischer Vereine (zumindest offiziell) verboten.

✱ Au Liechtenstein, la majorité sexuelle est fixée à 18 ans pour les homosexuels et à 14 pour les hétérosexuels. Comme en Autriche, il est interdit de "promouvoir l'homosexualité".

✱ La edad de consentimiento para el sexo homosexual es de 18 años, para el sexo heterosexual es de 14. Al igual que en Austria, aquí también se prohibe oficialmente la "promoción de la homosexualidad", por ejemplo anuncios de contactos, así como fundaciones o asociaciones gay-lesbianas.

✱ L'età legale per i rapporti omosessuali è di 18 anni, quella per i rapporti eterosessuali è invece di 14 anni. Come in Austria anche qui sono vietate campagne a favore dell'omosessualità e organizzazioni gay.

Schaan ✉ 9494

HEALTH GROUPS
■ **AIDS-Hilfe Liechtenstein** Mon 18-20, Thu 8-10 h
Postfach 207 ✉ 9494 ☎ 232 05 20

GENERAL GROUPS
■ **Schwule und Lesben in Liechtenstein und Umgebung (FLAY)**
Postfach 207 ✉ 9494 ☎ 232 05 20

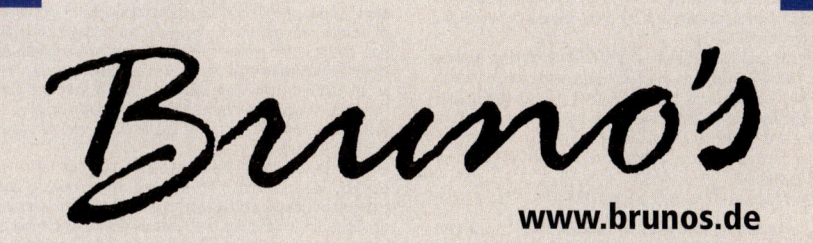

Bruno's
www.brunos.de

THE GAY MEDIA STORE

Lithuania

Name: Lietuva • Litauen • Lituanie • Lituania
Location: Northeast Europe
Initials: LT
Time: GMT +1
International Country Code: ☏ 370
International Access Code: ☏ 8 (wait for tone) 10
Language: Lithuanian. Russian, Polish
Area: 65,3101 km² / 25,174 sq mi.
Currency: 1 Litas (LTL) = 100 Centas
Population: 3,710,000
Capital: Vilnius (Wilna)
Religions: mostly Roman Catholics
Climate: Maritime climate. Winters and summers are moderate.

In Lithuania, male homosexuality was decriminalised in 1993. The age of consent is set up at 18 years for gays, at 14 for heterosexuals and lesbians. Relationships with gays under 18 provide penalties of up to eight years. In Lithuania, there are no laws protecting lesbians and gays against discrimination. Sexual orientation is not included in the Constitution as a criterion for protection from discrimination, but it might appear in the new Penal Code to be adopted in 2000/01. Homophobic hate crimes are treated by courts as "light offence" or hooliganism.

The social prejudice against homosexuals named as perverts (or "pederasts" in common language) - is very strong in Lithuania and based on open anti-gay position of the dominant Catholic church and right wing nationalists. Although gay and lesbian organisations are legally registered and formally recognised by the Government, they are in fact socially marginalised and excluded from state financial support and civil society programmes. Politicians and even human rights organisations do not mention gays and lesbians in their agenda. Private media are the only advocate of gay people, covering local and world news. The first positive coming out stories were published in the biggest daily newspaper in 1995.

There are only two gay discos open at the weekend in the capital of Lithuania, Vilnius. Local communities in the other major cities: Kaunas and Klaipeda socialise in small bars at the weekend alone. Two Internet websites are the most visible examples of the emerging gay sub-culture. The first gay publications hit the streets in 1994, but distribution through public press outlets was banned and went they went bankrupt.

It is worth combining a historic and cultural trip through all three Baltic capitals Vilnius, Riga and Tallinn. You won't find exclusively gay hotels or restaurants, but nightclubbing is expanding. In summer gay men migrate to the male nude beaches along the Baltic coast, especially in Palanga and Lielupe. A good source of information for the visitors are the "In Your Pocket" guides, which include small gay section.

Eduardas Platovas - Lietuvos Geju Lyga (LGL)

In Litauen ist Homosexualität zwischen Männern seit 1993 nicht mehr strafbar. Für Schwule liegt das Mündigkeitsalter bei 18 Jahren, für Heterosexuelle und Lesben jedoch nur bei 14 Jahren. Beziehungen zwischen Gays unter 18 Jahren werden mit einer Gefängnisstrafe mit bis zu acht Jahren bestraft. In Litauen gibt es keine Gesetze, die Lesben und Schwule vor Diskriminierung schützen. Die sexuelle Orientierung ist in der Verfassung als Kriterium zum Schutz vor Diskriminierung nicht eingeschlossen, aber es ist jedoch wahrscheinlich, daß ein diesbezügliches Gesetz im neuen Strafgesetzbuch von 2000/2001 verabschiedet wird. Homosexuellenfeindliche Haßtaten werden von den Gerichten nur als leichte Beleidigung oder Randalieren geahndet.

Die sozialen Vorurteile gegen Homosexuelle, die als Perverse gelten und im Volksmund als Päderasten bezeichnet werden, sind in Litauen sehr stark und basieren auf der offenkundigen feindseligen Haltung gegenüber Schwulen, die von der dominanten katholischen Kirche und dem rechten Flügel der Nationalisten propagiert wird. Obwohl schwul-lesbische Organisationen legal registriert und formal von der Regierung anerkannt sind, stellen sie jedoch eine soziale Randgruppe dar, die keinerlei finanzielle Unterstützung vom Staat erhält und auch von gesellschaftlichen Veranstaltungen ausgeschlossen ist. Politiker und sogar Menschenrechtsorganisationen erwähnen Gays und Lesben nicht in ihrer Agenda. Private Medien sind der einzige Anwalt der Schwulen und bringen regionale und überregionale Nachrichten. Die ersten positiven Coming-out Geschichten wurden 1995 in der größten Tageszeitung veröffentlicht.

In Litauens Hauptstadt Vilnius gibt es nur zwei Gay-Discos, die allerdings nur am Wochenende geöffnet sind; lokale Communities, die jedoch auch nur am Wochenende und in kleinen Bars aktiv sind, gibt es in den größeren Städten Kaunas und Klaipeda. Zwei Websites im Internet sind das zur Zeit sichtbarste Zeichen der aufstrebenden schwulen Subkultur. Die ersten schwulen Veröffentlichungen erreichten 1994 die Öffentlichkeit, aber ihre Verbreitung durch die öffentliche Presse wurde verboten und es kam zum Konkurs.

Die drei Hauptstädte des Baltikums Vilnius, Riga und Tallinn sind dennoch eine Reise wert. man wird keine reinen schwulen Hotels oder Restaurants finden, das Angebot an Nachtclubs nimmt jedoch ständig zu. Im Sommer sind die Nacktbadestrände für Männer entlang der Ostsee ein beliebter Treffpunkt für Gays - dies betrifft besonders die Orte Palanga und Lielupe. Eine gute Informationsquelle für Besucher sind die sogenannten "In Your Pocket" Reiseführer, in denen man einige Zeilen zu Gay-Locations findet.

Eduardas Platovas - Lietuvos Geju Lyga (LGL)

La Lituanie a dépénalisé l'homosexualité masculine en 1993. La majorité sexuelle est fixée à 18 ans pour les gais et à 14 pour les hétérosexuels et les lesbiennes. Les relations avec des par-

Lithuania

tenaires de moins de 18 ans sont passibles de peine d'emprisonnement allant jusqu'à 8 ans. Il n'existe pour l'instant aucune loi antidiscriminatoire protégeant les gais et lesbiennes. L'orientation sexuelle n'apparaît pas dans le texte de la Constitution mais il se peut qu'elle figure dans le nouveau Code pénal qui doit être voté en 2000/01. Les agressions homophobes sont considérées par les cours de justice comme de "légères offenses" ou comme des "actes d'hooliganisme".
La discrimination sociale des homosexuels - souvent nommés "pervers" (ou "pédérastes" dans le langage familier) est très forte et soutenue par la position ouvertement homophobe de l'Eglise catholique et des nationalistes d'extrême droite. Bien que les associations gaies et lesbiennes soient officiellement reconnues par le gouvernement, elles sont dans les faits marginalisées, privées de toute forme de soutien financier et exclues des programmes d'aide sociale. Les politiciens, et même les organisations de défense des droits de l'homme, ne mentionnent pas les gais et les lesbiennes dans leurs agendas. Les médias privés, avec la publication de nouvelles locales et internationales, sont les seuls défenseurs de la cause des gais. Les premiers témoignages positifs de coming-out ont été publiés par le plus grand quotidien en 1995.
Il n'y a que deux clubs gais ouverts le week-end dans la capitale de la Lituanie, Vilnius. Les gais des autres villes majeures du pays, Kaunas et Klapeida, se rencontrent le week-end dans de petits bars. Deux sites Internet sont les exemples les plus visibles de l'émergence d'une culture alternative gaie. Le premier magazine gai, apparu en 94, a vite fait faillite car sa distribution a été interdite dans les lieux de vente publics.
Il est intéressant de combiner une visite culturelle et historique des trois capitales baltiques Vilnius, Riga et Tallinn. On ne trouve pas encore de restaurants ou d'hôtels gais, mais de plus en plus de clubs. En été, beaucoup de gais se rendent sur les plages naturistes pour hommes le long de la côte baltique, en particulier à Palangua et Lielupe. Les guides "In Your Pocket" sont une bonne source d'information pour les touristes et comprennent une petite section gaie.
Eduardas Platovas - Lietuvos Geju Lyga (LGL)

▶ En Lituania, la homosexualidad masculina se legalizó en 1993. La edad de consentimiento se fijó en 18 años para hombres homosexuales y en 14 años para heterosexuales y lesbianas. Las relaciones con personas de menos de 18 años pueden penalizarse con hasta ocho años de prisión. En Lituania no existen leyes antidiscriminatorias para proteger a lesbianas y gays. La discriminación por la orientación sexual no se considera en la constitución, pero podría incluirse en el nuevo código penal que se aprobará en 2000/2001. Crímenes por homofobia son tratados por los tribunales como delitos menos graves o como gamberrismo.
Los prejuicios sociales contra los homosexuales (llamados pervertidos o pederastas en la lengua común) son muy fuertes en Lituania; esta postura tiene sus raíces en la declarada postura homófoba de la iglesia católica, dominante en Lituania, y de los nacionalistas de la derecha. A pesar de que las organizaciones de gays y lesbianas son legalmente registradas y formalmente reconocidas por el gobierno, de hecho son socialmente marginadas y excluidas de los programas de subvenciones financieras y de política social.
Los políticos e incluso las organizaciones de derechos humanos no se ocupan de los gays y lesbianas. Los medios de comunicación privados son los únicos que abogan por las personas homosexuales y cubren las noticias locales e internacionales. Las primeras noticias de coming out positivas se publicaron en 1995 en el mayor diario lituano.
En la capital de Lituania, Vilna (o Vilnius), hay dos discotecas gays que abren los fines de semana. Las comunidades homosexuales de las otras ciudades más grandes del país, Kaunas y Klaipeda, se encuentran en bares pequeños abiertos sólo los fines de semana. Dos páginas web son el ejemplo más visible de una subcultura gay en desarrollo. Las primeras publicaciones gays aparecieron en 1994, pero la distribución a través de los puntos de venta públicos se prohibió, por lo que acabaron por quebrar.
Merece la pena compaginar un viaje cultural e histórico por las tres capitales bálticas Vilnius, Riga y Tallinn. No se encontrarán hoteles or restaurantes gays, pero cada vez hay más clubs y discotecas. En verano, los hombres gays 'migran' a las playas nudistas a lo largo de la costa del mar báltico, especialmente en Palanga y Lielupe. Las guías 'In Your Pocket' ("en tu bolsillo") incluyen un pequeño apartado gay y son una buena fuente de información para el visitante.
Eduardas Platovas - Lietuvos Geju Lyga (LGL)

▶ In Lituania, ormai dal 1993, l'omosessualità tra gli uomini non è più punibile. Per gli omosessuali, la maggiore età si raggiunge a 18 anni; per gli eterosessuali e per le lesbiche invece a soli 14 anni. Le relazioni tra gay al di sotto dei diciotto anni vengono punite con una pena detentiva fino a otto anni. In Lituania non ci sono leggi che proteggano lesbiche e gay dalle discriminazioni. L'orientamento sessuale non è previsto dalla costituzione come criterio per la tutela contro la discriminazione, ma è comunque probabile che venga varata una legge, in merito, nel nuovo codice penale tra il 2000/2001. Gli atti di odio a scapito degli omosessuali sono puniti dai tribunali soltanto come un'offesa leggera oppure come turbativa della quiete pubblica.
I pregiudizi sociali contro gli omosessuali, che vengono visti come perversi e nel linguaggio popolare chiamati pederasti, sono ancora molto forti in Lituania e si basano sull'atteggiamento manifestamente ostile verso gli omosessuali, propagato dalla chiesa cattolica dominante e dall'ala destra dei nazionalisti. Sebbene le organizzazioni dei gay e delle lesbiche siano registrate legalmente e formalmente riconosciute dal governo, rappresentano pur sempre un gruppo sociale emarginato, che non ottiene nessun tipo di finanziamento dallo stato e rimane anche escluso dalle manifestazioni sociali. I politici e anche le organizzazioni per i diritti umani non menzionano i gay e le lesbiche nelle loro agende. I media dei privati sono in definitiva l'unico avvocato degli omosessuali e diffondono le notizie regionali e interregionali. Le prime storie positive sul coming-out sono state pubblicate nel 1995 sul quotidiano più importante.
Nella capitale della Lituania, Vilnius, ci sono solo due discoteche per gay, che però hanno aperto solo il fine settimana; comunità locali, attive tuttavia anche solo il fine settimana e nei piccoli bar, si trovano nelle città più grandi Kaunas e Klaipeda. Due Website in Internet sono al momento il segnale più evidente di una subcultura omosessuale ambiziosa. Le prime pubblicazioni di omosessuali hanno raggiunto il pubblico nel 1994, ma la loro diffusione è stata proibita dalla stampa ufficiale, per cui il tentativo è fallito.
Vale la pena, tuttavia, visitare le tre capitali del Baltico Vilnius, Riga e Tallinn. Non si troveranno di certo hotel o ristoranti esclusivamente per omosessuali, ma l'offerta per quanto riguarda club notturni è continuamente in aumento. In estate le spiagge di nudisti per uomini lungo il Mar Baltico sono il punto d'incontro preferito per gay, in particolare ci si riferisce ai luoghi di Palanga e Lielupe. Una buona fonte d'informazione per i visitatori sono le cosiddette guide turistiche "In Your Pocket", in cui si trovano alcune righe sulle location per gay.
Eduardas Platovas - Lietuvos Geju Lyga (LGL)

Lithuania — Kaunas ▸ Vilnius

NATIONAL GAY INFO
■ **Lithuanian Gay Net** (GLM)
PO Box 2862 ✉ 2000 Vilnius ☎ (2) 33 30 31
📠 lgl@gay.lt
🌐 www.gay.lt
Great internet site in English and Lithuanian featuring community news, chat rooms, personal adverts, and a national gay guide.

■ **Lithuanian Gays & Lesbians Web Page** (GLM)
📠 webmaster@gayline.lt
🌐 www.gayline.lt
Internet site in English and Lithuanian covering community news, a gay and lesbian country guide, personal contact pages, and more.

NATIONAL GROUPS
■ **Lietuvos Geju Lyga (LGL)** (GLM MA)
PO Box 2862 ✉ 2000 Vilnius ☎ (2) 33 30 31 📠 (2) 33 30 31
📠 lgl@gay.lt 🌐 www.gay.lt
The Lithuanian Gay League, which includes SOLIDA LGL lesbian group, works to combat discrimination against lesbians and gay men and to promote their civil rights.

■ **Lithuanian Movement for Sexual Equality** (GLM)
PO Box 720 ✉ 2038 Vilnius ☎ (2) 65 59 40 ☎ (90) 45 939

Kaunas ☎ 7

DANCECLUBS
■ **Ausros Svetaine** (B D GLM MA) Fri, Sat 21-? h
Vytauto pr. 23 ☎ 74 07 24
■ **Mefistofelis** (B D GLM p) Fri-Sat 21-6 h, Summer only Fri
Kalnieciai gatve ☎ 70 05 84

GENERAL GROUPS
■ **Kaunas County Organization of Sexual Equality (Kaslo)** (GLM)
PO Box 1045 ✉ 3042 ☎ 70 57 37
☎ (87) 68 195
📠 robejona@takas.lt

CRUISING
- Laisves Aleja
- Vilniaus Gatve
- Park near bus station
- Ramybes Park
- Azuolynas Park

Klaipėda ☎ 6

BARS
■ **Bolero** (B D F GLM MA WE) Fri, Sat 22-? h
Stadiono gatve 16 ☎ 41 21 74

SWIMMING
- Smiltyne (NU) (male nude beach, left side)

CRUISING
- Skulptury parkas

Vilnius ☎ 2

GAY INFO
■ **Gay Information Line** (G)
c/o LGL, PO Box 2862 ✉ 2000, ☎ 33 30 31
Information about gay organisations, events and accommodation for gay men.

TOURIST INFO
■ **Vilnius In You Pocket**
Vokieciu gatve 10-15 ✉ 2001 ☎ 22 39 78 📠 22 29 82
📠 office@inyourpocket.com
🌐 www.inyourpocket.com
Good general guide for Vilnius and Lithuania with a small gay section. Check their website.

■ **Vilnius Tourist Information Centre** 10-18, Sat -16 h, Sun closed
Pilies gatve 42 ☎ 62 07 62 ☎ 62 64 70
📠 62 07 62
📠 turizm.info@vilnius.sav.lt

DANCECLUBS
■ **Men's Factory** (B D f G snu stv WE) Bar: Wed Thu 19-?, Danceclub: Fri-Sat 22-6 h
Žygimantu gatve 1/8 *(near Cathedral Square)* ☎ 38 40 88
Gay club with one bar, one dance floor and two lounges.

HEALTH GROUPS
■ **Lithuanian AIDS Centre** 8 -16.45, Fri -15.45, closed Sat & Sun, Hotline: Mon-Fri 9-18 h
Kairiukscio gatve 2 ☎ 72 04 65 ☎ 72 03 33 (hotline)

CRUISING
- Pylimo Street (opposite the trolleybus stop "Klaipeda")
- Gedimino prospektas
- Luki kiu Square

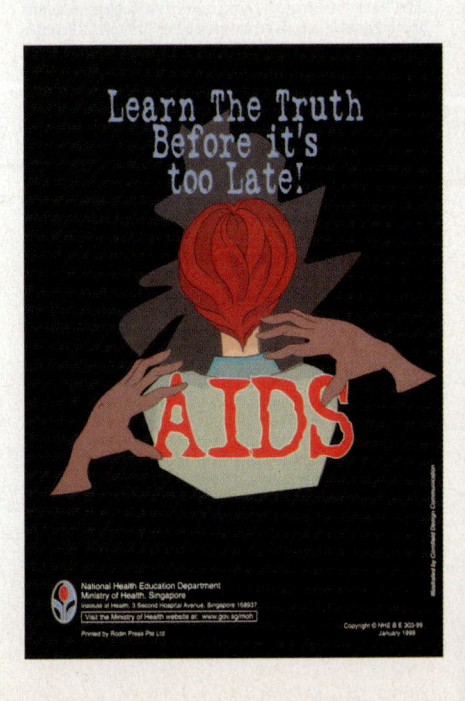

Luxembourg

Name: Letzebuerg • Luxemburg • Luxemburgo • Lussemburgo
Location: Western Europe
Initials: L
Time: GMT +1
International Country Code: ☎ 352 (no area codes)
International Access Code: ☎ 00
Language: French, German, Letzebuergs
Area: 2,586 km^2 / 998 sq mi.
Currency: 1 Lux. Franc (Lfr) = 100 Centimes. 1 EURO = 40,3399
Population: 427,000
Capital: Luxembourg
Religions: 95% Roman Catholic
Climate: Modified continental climate with mild winters and cool summers

The age of consent for both homosexual and heterosexual activity is 16 (Article 372 of the penal code). Luxembourg has a small gay scene centred around the capital.

Das gesetzliche Schutzalter für hetero- wie homosexuelle Handlungen liegt generell bei 16 Jahren (Art. 372 Stgb). Seit dem vergangenen Jahr gibt es auch in Luxemburg ein Anti-Diskriminierungsgesetz, daß eine Benachteiligung aufgrund der sexuellen Orientierung unter Strafe stellt.

Au Luxembourg, la majorité sexuelle est fixée à 16 ans pour tous (article 372 du code pénal). On a vite fait le tour des bars et boîtes gais du Grand Duché.

La edad de consentimiento legal para actividades tanto homo como heterosexual es de 16 años (art. 372 del Código Penal). Desde el año pasado existe una ley prohibe la discriminación de personas a causa de su orientación sexual.

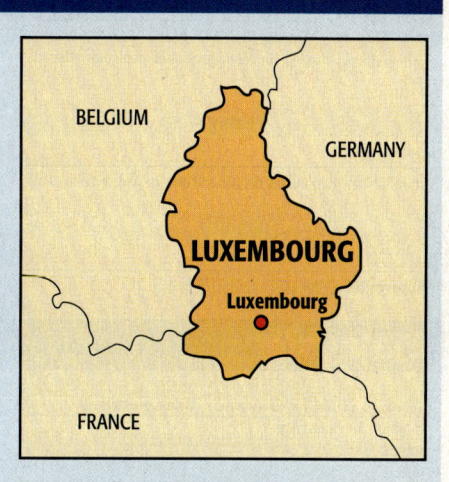

L'età del consenso è di 16 anni (Art. 372 bis del codice penale). Il Lussemburgo è un piccolo paese con una vita gay di dimensioni ridotte concentrata principalmente sulla capitale.

Bettendorf

HOTELS
■ **Hôtel Vallée de la Sûre** (B BF F g H MA) 10-24 h
34 Route d'Echternach ✉ 9355 ☎ 80 30 75 📠 80 37 47

Eich

BARS
■ **Chez Gusty** (B d glm MA N S) Tue-Fri 6.30-1, Sat 6.30-3, Sun 17-1 h
101 Rue d'Eich ✉ 1461 ☎ 43 12 23

Luxembourg

BARS
■ **Café Club David** (B D f GLM MA OS SNU STV) 17-1, Fri-Sat -? h
30 Avenue Emile Reuter ✉ 2420 *(near Place de l'Etoile)*
☎ 45 32 84
Formerly called "Chez Mike".
■ **New Mini Hilton** (B MA N STV) 12-1, Sun 17-1 h
75, Côte d'Eisch ✉ 1450 ☎ 260 942 06

SEX SHOPS/BLUE MOVIES
■ **Boutique Amour** (g VS)
4 Boulevard d'Avranches ✉ 1160
■ **Erotic Shop** (g)
Rue Du Fort Neipperg ☎ 49 36 60

■ **Erotic Video Center** (g VS) 11-24 h, closed Sun
15 Rue de Reims ✉ 2417

SAUNAS/BATHS
■ **Sauna Finlandia** (B CC g msg OS PI SA SB SOL WH) Mon-Thu 12-22, Fri -21, Sat 14-20 h, closed Sun
58 Avenue de la Liberté ✉ 1930 ☎ 48 46 23

HEALTH GROUPS
■ **Aidsberodung Croix-Rouge**
94 Boulevard Patton ✉ 2316 ☎ 40 62 51
📧 henrigoedertz@handitel.lu
📠 40 62 55.
■ **Laboratoire National de Santé**
42 Rue du Laboratoire ✉ 1911 ☎ 49 11 91-1
Free testing.
■ **Onofhängeg AIDS-Hellef Lëtzebuerg Asbl** Organisation Mon 16.30-19.30 Wed Fri 15-18 h.
23 Rue des États-Unis PO Box 917, L-2219 ☎ 49 81 94
📠 29.16.26
■ **Stop Aids Now asbl** (A g)
94 Boulevard Patton ✉ 2316 ☎ 40 62 51
📠 40 62 55.

CRUISING
- City Park/Parc Municipal (near RTL)
- Main railway station/Gare Central
- [P] Patinoire Kokelesheur (AYOR) (evenings, but frequent police controls).

Mondorf-Les-Bains

SWIMMING
-Domaine Thermal (B F g msg NU MA OS PI SA SB SOL WH WO) ☎ 670 11 (Best thermal bath. Many gays at the pool and in the sauna).

Petange

CRUISING
-Parc de la Mairie (around the city hall and into the park, evenings only)

Remich

HOTELS
■ **Auberge des Cygnes** (BF CC F g H s) 10-1 h
11 Esplanade ✉ 5533 *(In front of the river "Moselle" in the middle of the Esplanade)* ☎ 69 88 52 📠 69 75 29 ✉ hpcygnes@pt.lu
All rooms with shower & WC. Rates double Flux 2.200, single 1.700. Also a restaurant.

Rosport

HOTELS
■ **Hotel-Restaurante de la Poste** (BF CC F glm H MA OS) 10-23 h
7 Route d'Echternach ✉ 6580 ☎ 73 50 03

Rumelange

BARS
■ **Cafe Mini's Theaterstuff** (B f glm H MA OS p s) 15-1 h. Thu closed
40 Grand Rue ✉ 3730 ☎ 56 48 26

Malaysia

Name: Persekutan Tanah Malaysia • Malaysie • Malesia
Location: Southeast Asia
Initials: MAL
Time: GMT +8
International Country Code: ☎ 60 (leave the first 0 of area codes)
International Access Code: ☎ 00
Language: Malay, Chinese, English
Area: 329,733 km^2 / 127,320 sq mi.
Currency: 1 Malayan Ringgit (RM) = 100 Sen
Population: 22,180,000
Capital: Kuala Lumpur
Religions: 53% Muslim, 17% Buddhist, 7% Hindu
Climate: Tropical climate. There are annual southwest (April to October) and northeast (October to February) monsoons.

✳ According to our information, homosexuality as such is no longer punishable by law. We were not able to determine the exact legal regulations, but we assume that only sex in public toilets and cruising can lead to problems. Homosexuality is never mentioned in the media (Islam being the state religion) and is considered taboo. For this reason, one should behave with extreme caution. The country is made up mostly of mountains, rain forests and rice fields. In addition, Penang ("The Pearl of the East"), Langkawi, Pangkor, as well as the east coast of the Malayan peninsula, offer some of the most beautiful beaches in the far east.

★ Nach unserem Kenntnisstand stehen homosexuelle Handlungen in Malaysia nicht mehr unter Strafandrohung. Wir konnten zwar keine genauen Rechtsvorschriften ausmachen, aber wir gehen davon aus, daß nur Klappensex und Cruising Probleme bereiten könnten.
In den Medien ist Schwul- oder Lesbischsein tabuisiert, da der Islam in etwa den Rang einer Staatsreligion einnimmt. Schon aus diesem Grund sollte man sich in diesem Land sehr vorsichtig verhalten.
Einen großen Teil des Landes machen Berge, Regenwälder und Reisfelder aus. Darüberhinaus bieten die Inseln Penang ("Perle des Ostens"), Langkawi und Pangkor sowie die Ostküste der malayischen Halbinsel einige der schönsten Strände des Fernen Ostens.

✳ D'après ce que nous savons, l'homosexualité n'est plus un délit en Malaysie. Nous n'avons pas réussi à obtenir de plus amples informations sur la législation en vigueur, mais tout nous donne à penser que la fréquentation des parcs et des toilettes publiques peut vous causer de sérieux désagréments. L'homosexualité est un sujet tabou. Rien d'étonnant à cela, vu que l'Islam est la religion d'Etat. Donc: prudence est mère de sûreté! La majeure partie du pays est faite de montagnes, de forêts tropicales et de rizières. Sur les îles de Penang ("Perle de l'Orient"), de Langkawi et de Pankor, ainsi que sur la côte Est du pays, vous trouverez quelques unes des plus belles plages de l'Extrême-Orient.

⬢ Según sabemos, la homosexualidad ya no es perseguida en Malasia. Aunque no hemos podido obtener informaciones confiables sobre leyes o reglamentaciónes en vigor, suponemos que solamente el sexo en aseos públicos y el cruising pueden traer serios problemas. En los medios de comunicación la homosexualidad es un tema tabú, debido a la fuerte influencia del islam,

Johore Bahru ▶ Penang | **Malaysia**

que se puede considerar como la religión oficial. Por ello, se recomienda un comportamiento muy cauteloso. Una gran parte del país está formado por montañas, selvas y campos arroceros. En las islas Penang ("Perla del Este"), Langkai y Pangkor así como el litoral Este de la península malaya se encuentran las más lindas playas del lejano oriente.

✘ Secondo le nostre informazioni, in Malesia l'omosessualità non è più perseguibile. Non ci sono state presentate nè leggi nè regolamenti, ma possiamo immaginare che possiate avere dei problemi solo cacciando in gabinetti pubblici o in zone simili. Per la stampa e la televisione l'omosessualità resta un tabù. L'islamismo ha quasi assunto il ruolo di religione nazionale, per questo motivo in questo paese ci si deve comportare con molta discrezione. Una larga parte del paese è montuosa con foreste piovose e risaie. Inoltre, Penang ("La perla dell'Est"), Langkawi, Pangkor, così come la costa est della penisola vantano alcune fra le più belle spiagge dell'estremo oriente.

Johore Bahru ☏ 07

CRUISING
-Sungai Segget (near traffic cirlce with fountain and nearby carpark. Late night, weekends)

Kuala Lumpur ☏ 03

BARS
■ **Blue Boy** (B D G MA s) 22-4 h
54 Jalan Sultan Ismail ✉ 50250 (entrance off Jalan Sultan Ismail, behind Pizza Hut) ☏ 242 10 67
Admission M$ 11.
■ **Liquid** (B D CC MA WE) Closed on Sun
Central Market

CAFES
■ **Café Silhouette** (B glm STV) STV 22 h
19A-LGF-12 UOA Centre, Jalan Pinang/Jalan Perak

SAUNAS/BATHS
■ **Babylon KL** (G SB WO)
146 Jalan Batu Estate (off Jalan Segambut) ☏ 621 2139
■ **Hot Top Corner** (G SA SB)
40-6A Jalan Sultan Ismail (near Blue Boy) ☏ 244 96 48
■ **Otot 2** (G SA SB)
7a 2/F Jalan Ipoh Kechil (off Jalan Raja Laut) ☏ 444 33 69
■ **Ryu Member's Sauna** (B DR F G OS SA SB WH WO) 18-24, Sat Sun 15-24 h
56 A&B Jalan Pingai, Taman Pelangi ✉ 80400 (behind Leisure Mall) ☏ 607-333 32 08
Japanese style interior with lots of plants. Open air terrace. Busy with many Singaporeans on WE.

HOTELS
■ **Fortuna Hotel** (AC B F H NG)
87 Jalan Berangan ☏ 241 91 11 📠 241 82 37
■ **Lodge Hotel** (b F H NG Pl)
Jalan Sultan Ismail ☏ 242 01 22 📠 241 68 19
Centrally located. 50 rooms with bath/WC, AC, TV and phone.

GENERAL GROUPS
■ **Pink Triangle** 9.30-17.30, Sun 15-18h
7c Jalan Ipoh Kecil (off Jalan Raja Laut, near Grand Central Hotel)
☏ 4044 46 11 📠 4044 46 22 ✉ isham@pop7.jaring.my

CRUISING
-Sungai Wang Plaza, Jalan Bukit Bintang (commercial centre between Hotel Apoll and Regent Hotel, 3rd floor)
-Kota Raya (shopping complex on Jalan Chen Lock)
-Merdeka Square (AYOR OG) (20-? h)
-Lot Ten Shopping Center (Near Regent Hotel. In front on street level and also on 2nd floor at Deli France)
-Jalan Sultan Ismail (near Regent Hotel and Blue Boy)
-Star Hill Shopping Center (Jalan Bukit Bintang, opposite Regent Hotel)
-KL Plaza (Coffee Bean and Tea Leaf at entrance)

Kuantan ☏ 09

SWIMMING
-Tekluk Cempedak Beach (G WE)

Kuching - Sarawak ☏ 082

HOTELS
■ **Aurora Hotel** (AC B F g)
McDougall Road ☏ 24 02 81
Downtown neighborhood location, all rooms with telephone, frigde, priv. bath, balcony and radio.

CRUISING
-Kuching Plaza Shopping Centre (R TV)
-Merdeka Place (tv) (next to hotel)
-Merdeka Place
-Aurora Hotel

Penang ☏ 04

CAFES
■ **Beach Blanket Babylon** (B f glm YG)
16 Jalan Bishop ☏ 263 81 01

DANCECLUBS
■ **Party Box** (B D g S TV)
Club House No.1, Mar Vista Resort, Batu Ferringghi

HOTELS
■ **Golden Sands** (AC B F H NG OS SA)
Batu Ferringhi Beach ☏ 881 19 11
Beach location, 13 km to the airport. All rooms with bath/wc, telephone, balcony, tea/coffee machine and fridge. Single M$ 140-195, double 165-225.
■ **Lone Pine** (AC B F H NG)
10th Mile, Batu Ferringhi Beach ☏ 881 15 11 📠 881 12 82
Suburb location, 45 min to the airport, all rooms with telephone, fridge, priv. bath and balcony

CRUISING
-Batu Feringghi Beach
-Esplanade.
-Waterfall at Botanical Garden.
-Park next to Dewan Siri Pinang

Malta | Gozo - Gharb ▸ Malta - St. Julians

Malta

Name: Malte
Location: South Europe
Initials: M
Time: GMT+1
International Country Code: ☏ 356 (no area codes)
International Access Code: ☏ 00
Language: Maltese, English
Area: 316 km², / 122 sq mi.
Currency: 1 Maltese Lira (Lm) = 100 Cents
Population: 377,000
Capital: Valletta
Religions: 93% Roman Catholic
Climate: Mediterranean climate. Winters are mild and rainy, summers hot and dry summers.

✻ Homosexuality between adult men is permitted by law and the age of consent is 18. The people in Malta tend to be high-spirited, and are known for their hospitality. Malta is above all a treasure-trove for those interested in archaeology and classical architecture.

✻ Homosexualität zwischen erwachsenen Männern ist dem Gesetz nach erlaubt. Die Schutzaltersgrenze liegt bei 18 Jahren. Die Malteser sind temperamentvoll und ausgesprochen gastfreundlich. Erwähnenswert ist, daß Malta eine wahre Fundgrube für die Freunde antiker Architektur und der Archäologie ist.

✻ A Malte, l'homosexualité entre hommes adultes n'est pas un délit. La majorité sexuelle y est fixée à 18 ans. Les Maltais ont du tempérament et sont très accueillants. A noter: Malte regorge de trésors d'architecture antique et de sites archéologiques splendides.

Mediterranean Sea — Sicilia (ITALY) — Comino — Victoria — MALTA — St. Julian's Bay — Mdina — Rabat — Valleta

⬢ La ley autoriza la homosexualidad entre hombres adultos. La edad mínima legal de consentimiento está fijada en 18 años. Los malteses son un pueblo temperamental y particularmente hospitalario. Es digno de mencionar que Malta es un verdadero i paraíso para los amantes de la arquitectura antigua y de la arqueología.

⬣ L'omosessualità tra adulti di sesso maschile è permessa. L'età legale è di 18 anni. I maltesi sono pieni di temperamento e conosciuti per la loro ospitalità. Desideriamo sottolineare che Malta rappresenta un vero scrigno per tutti coloro che amano l'architettura antica e l'archeologia.

Gozo - **Gharb**

RESTAURANTS

■ **Salvina** (AC BF B CC g F OS PI) Restaurant: daily 12-14.30 h, 18.30-22 h   Bar: 10-15 h, 19-24 h, closed Thu
21 Frenc Ta' L-Gharb Street,   ✉ GRB 102 (near Gharb-Church)
☏ 55 25 05
Closed for a few weeks in Nov and Feb. Courtyard. Friendly atmosphere.

Gozo - **Marsalforn**

SWIMMING

-San Blas Bay (Direction of Nadur. Sometimes NU but then AYOR)
-Ramla Bay (Nadur)

Malta - **Bugibba** ✉ **SPB 05**

BARS

■ **Jambar** (B F GLM OS) 19-23 h
Triq it-Turisti ✉ SPB 05 (1st street behind Boulevard)
☏ 58 34 01

Newly changed mixed gay bar. Good food. Menu Lm 2-5. Ask for Victor or Marco

Malta - **Mriehel**

BARS

■ **Saints Bar** (B TV)
New Street (off Notabile Road, drive along Hamrun Rd into Mrihel and turn left)

Malta - **St. Julians**

BARS

■ **City of London** (B gLm)
Balluta Street
Mainly lesbian crowd.
■ **Lady Godiva** (AC B d GLM MA OS S STV VS YG) Sun-Thu 21-2 h, Fri-Sat 21-5 h
Wilga Street (Paceville) ☏ 39 10 58
Gay Pride takes place outside this bar.
■ **Nix Bar** (B F gLm) 11-15, 18.30-?h, closed Tue
186 Manuel Dimech Street ☏ 340 353

Malta - **Valletta**

BARS
■ **Tom Bar** (B F G) 11.30-14.30 (lunch), 20.30-1 h
1 Crucifix Hill, Floriana ✉ VLT01 *(Floriana)* ☎ 250 780
2 floors. Downstairs is the latest dance/club music.

CINEMAS
■ **City Lights** Mon-Sat 9-22h, Sun 12-22h
St. John Street
Entrance fee 1,40 LM. Very active after 14h.

SWIMMING
-Gnejna Bay (ayor) Take bus 47 from Valletta, from Bugibba bus 51, from Sliema bus 652. Stop off at Ghajin Tuffieha Bay and walk through the narrow passage. NU on rocky plateau, many caves for action.
-White Rocks (active after 14h) Take bus 68 from Valletta to Bahar-lc-Caghaq. Get off at Summerfield Disco and walk from there to right along a narrow road through the tower on the rocks (NU).

CRUISING
-Valletta Bus Terminal (AYOR)
-Republic Street (R)
-Garden around the Commonwealth Air Forces Memorial
-Independence Avenue (bus terminus on the right side of the Phoenicia Hotel)

Mauritius

Name: Maurice • Mauricio
Location: Southwestern Indian Ocean
Initials: MS
Time: GMT +4
International Country Code: ☎ 230
International Access Code: ☎ 00
Language: English
Area: 2,040 km^2 / 794 sq mi.
Currency: 1 Mauritius Rupie (MR) = 100 Cents
Population: 1,160,000
Capital: Port Louis
Religions: 53% Hindu, 30% Christian
Climate: Tropical climate that is modified by southeast trade winds. Winters are warm and dry (May to November), summers anre hot, wet and humid (November to May).

✱ The legal situation is simple: the word "homosexual" does not exist anywhere in the constitution. Nothing is said for or against homosexuals. One can as homosexuals be prosecuted under the law of "good morals" as sodomy is illegal, according to article 250, even with consent, and one can go to prison for up to seven years when convicted.
Gays are looked down upon by society and do not live openly. Some have no other choice than to marry or become priest and lead a double life. Despite this situation, there have been travesties shows in the last few years where most of the people present are "normal" gays. A few gay or bisexual politicians have also been in office. One of which, who was well known, was vice-premier minister for years. None of them ever talk about homosexuality and won't defend the gay cause. To come across drag queens on the street is no longer that unusual. Recently the editor of one of the most important newspaper defended the right of gays although he himself is not gay.
Mauritius is a multicultural and multilingual country. The island is covered with sugar cane. It is surrounded by a coral reef and calm seas - with of course very beautiful beaches. There are two seasons: in Summer the temperature is 30-35C and in Winter 20-25C on the coast. Cyclones are possible from December to February.

✱ Die rechtliche Situation ist ganz einfach: das Wort "homosexuell" taucht in der Verfassung erst gar nicht auf. Nichts wird pro oder contra Homosexualität gesagt. Als Homosexueller kann man, selbst bei freiwilligem Analverkehr, durch das Sittengesetz, Artikel 250, verfolgt werden, da Analverkehr illegal ist. Wird man auf "Tat" überführt, kann man mit einer Gefängnisstrafe bis zu sieben Jahren bestraft werden.
Gays werden von der Gesellschaft von oben herab betrachtet und können nicht offen leben. Vielen bleibt nichts anderes übrig als zu heiraten oder Priester zu werden und somit ein Doppelleben zu führen. Ungeachtet dieser Situation, gab es in den letzten Jahren Travestie-Shows, bei denen die meisten der Anwesenden ganz "normale" Gays waren. Einige schwule oder bisexuelle Politiker waren auch schon im Amt. Einer von ihnen, der auch sehr bekannt war, war jahrelang Vize-Premierminister. Jedoch niemand von ihnen sprach je über Homosexualität und würde niemals für die Sache der Schwulen kämpfen. Drag Queens auf den Straßen zu begegnen ist auch kein ungewöhnliches Bild mehr, und erst kürzlich verteidigte der Herausgeber der wichtigsten lokalen Zeitung die Rechte der Schwulen, und daß, obwohl er selbst nicht schwul ist.
Mauritius ist ein multikulturelles Land in dem viele verschiedene Sprachen gesprochen werden. Mauritius wird vom Zuckerrohranbau eherrscht und liegt von paradiesischen Stränden und einem Korallenriff umgeben, das die Insel vor hohen Wellen schützt, mitten im Indischen Ozean. Es gibt auf Mauritius zwei Jahreszeiten: Im Sommer liegen die Temperaturen zwischen 30° und 35° Celcius und im Winter zwischen 20° und 25° Celsius. Zyklone können von Dezember bis Februar auftreten.

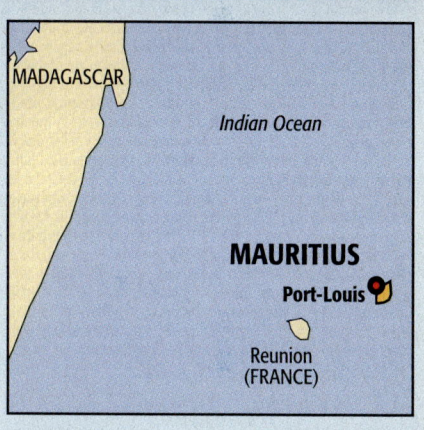

✱ La situation légale des gais sur l'île Maurice est simple: le mot "homosexualité" n'est pas mentionné dans la Constitution. Rien n'est dit pour ou contre les gais. Cependant, on peut toujours être poursuivi en justice car il existe une loi de " bonne morale " et que la sodomie - même consentante - est selon l'article 250 illégale. Les contrevenants risquent une peine allant jusqu'à 7 ans d'emprisonnement.
Les gais, mal perçus dans la société, vivent dans le placard. Certains n'ont pas d'autre choix que de se marier, de devenir prêtre ou de

Mauritius — Curepipe ▸ Trou-aux-Biches

mener une double vie. Malgré cette situation, il existe depuis quelques années des spectacles de transformistes où la majorité du public est composée de gais " normaux ". Certains politiciens gais ou bisexuels ont déjà été au pouvoir. L'un d'eux, très connu, était premier ministre pendant des années. Mais aucun de ces hommes politiques ne parle ouvertement de son homosexualité ou ne défend cette cause. Croiser une drag queen dans la rue n'est plus aujourd'hui chose rare. Et récemment, l'éditeur hétéro d'un des plus grands journal a défendu la cause des gais.
L'île de Maurice est un pays pluriculturel et plurilingue. L'île est couverte de plantations de canne à sucre. Elle est entourée de récifs de coraux et d'eaux tranquilles, avec bien sûr des plages paradisiaques. Il y a deux saisons: l'été, avec des températures entre 30 et 35 °C, et l'hiver, avec entre 20 et 25 °C sur la côte. Des cyclones peuvent déferler entre décembre et février.

La situación legal de los gays es fácil de describir: La palabra "homosexual" simplemente ni siquiera se menciona en la constitución. No se dice nada en contra o en favor de la homosexualidad. El sexo anal, aunque sea voluntario, es ilegal según artículo 250 de la ley moral, por lo que un homosexual puede acabar en la cárcel: En caso de que se "pruebe el delito", la pena es de hasta siete años de prisión. Los gays son tratados con desprecio por lo que no pueden vivir su homosexualidad abiertamente. A muchos no les queda otra salida que casarse o hacer de cura y llevar una vida doble. A pesar de estas condiciones, en los últimos años hubo espectáculos de travestis, en los que la mayoría de las personas en el público fueron gays. Ya hubo algunos políticos gays o bisexuales con cargos públicos, y uno de ellos, relativamente conocido, fue vice del Primer Ministro durante años. Pero nunca nadie de ellos trató el tema de homosexualidad o lucharía por la causa. Pero tampoco es nada extraordinario ya encontrarse con una drag queen por la calle, y hace poco, el editor del periódico local más importante defendió los derechos de los homosexuales (y a pesar de no serlo él mismo). Mauricio es un país multicultural en el que se hablan diversas lenguas. El país vive de la explotación de la caña de azúcar. Se encuentra en medio del océano atlántico y está rodeado de playas paradisíacas y un arrecife coralino que proteje la isla de las olas grandes. Mauricio tiene dos estaciones del año: el verano con temperaturas de entre 30° y 35° C y el invierno con temperaturas de entre 20° y 25° C. Desde diciembre hasta febrero puede haber ciclones.

La situazione giuridica è molto semplice: la parola "omosessuale" non compare affatto nella costituzione. Non viene detto nulla a favore o contro l'omosessualità. Ma siccome il rapporto anale è illegale, in quanto omosessuale si può essere perseguiti anche per il semplice rapporto anale, pur consenziente, secondo la legge sul buon costume, articolo 250. Se è dimostrata la propria colpevolezza, si può essere puniti con una pena detentiva fino a 7 anni. I gay vengono considerati dalla società dall'alto in basso e non possono vivere liberamente. A molti non rimane che sposarsi o diventare preti e in questo modo avere la possibilità di condurre una doppia vita. Tuttavia negli ultimi anni ci sono stati degli show per travestiti, e a questi spettacoli partecipavano in maggioranza gay che erano del tutto normali. Addirittura alcuni omosessuali o bisessuali erano politici in carica. Uno di loro, molto noto, è stato per lunghi anni vice- primo ministro. Però nessuno di loro ha mai parlato di omosessualità apertamente e tanto meno sarebbe disposto a battersi per la causa degli omosessuali. Incontrare sulle strade dei drag queens non è più così insolito. Recentemente l'editore del giornale locale più importante ha difeso i diritti degli omosessuali, pur non essendo gay.
L'isola Mauritius è un paese caratterizzato da una molteplicità di culture, nel quale vengono parlate diverse lingue. L'isola è coperta interamente dalla coltura della canna da zucchero ed è circondata da spiagge paradisiache e da una barriera corallina che protegge l'isola, in mezzo all'Oceano Indiano, dalle onde alte. Sull'isola Mauritius ci sono due stagioni: in estate la temperatura va dai 30 fino ai 35 gradi centigradi mentre in inverno la temperatura oscilla tra i 20 e i 25. Cicloni possono presentarsi tra dicembre e febbraio.

Curepipe

CRUISING
-Toilet at Jan Palach Sud Bus Station (daytime)
-Area around Jan Palach Arcade (AYOR) (evening)

Grand Bay

DANCECLUBS
■ **Number One** (B D g YG) 22-? h – Royal Road

Perybere

SWIMMING
-Perybere Public Beach

Port Louis

HEALTH GROUPS
■ **Prevention Information Lutte contre le Sida (PILS)**
Mon-Fri 9-16.30h
06 rue d'Artois ☏ 210 7075 ☏ 210 7047 🖨 210 7034
🖳 pils@internet.mu

Trou-aux-Biches

SWIMMING
-Trou aus Biches Public Beach (next to Trou aux Biches Hotel)

Visiting Mauritius?
Appatments, bungalows, cars for rent
Tel 00-230-7556322
Fax 00-230-2615500
E-mail: gchowree@hotmail.com

Mexico

Name:	México • Mexique • Messico
Location:	Southernmost Country in North America
Initials:	MEX
Time:	GMT -6/ -7 /-8
International Country Code:	☎ 52
International Access Code:	☎ 00
Language:	Spanish
Area:	1,953,162 km² / 756,061 sq mi.
Currency:	1 Mexican Peso (mex$) = 100 Centavos
Population:	95,842,000
Capital:	Mexico City (Ciudad de México)
Religions:	90% Roman Catholic
Climate:	The climate varies from tropical to desert.
Important gay cities:	Acapulco, Mexico City, Monterrey, Puerto Vallarta

✱ Mexican federal law does not mention homosexuality. Laws governing "public morality" are often arbitrarily enforced against homosexuals throughout Mexico. Homosexuals enjoy much more freedom in the capital, Mexico City. Here, for example, gays and lesbians were confident enough to hold a large Gay Pride demonstration as early as 1982. Since then, gay liberation groups have been set up in all Mexican cities, such as "Lambda Mexico", organisers of the only gay and lesbian centre in the city, and the radical "Frente Homosexual de Acción Revolucionaria/FAHR". The "Grupo Orgullo Homosexual de Liberación/GOHL" has done important work in the city of Guadalajara for gay rights.

✱ Das Schutzalter liegt in Mexico bei 18 Jahren. In ganz Mexiko werden oft die gesetzlichen Bestimmungen über die "Erregung öffentlichen Ärgernisses" nach Belieben gegen Homosexuelle angewandt.
Relativ liberal geht es in der Hauptstadt Mexiko-City zu. Hier trifft man selbstbewußte Schwule und Lesben, die sich schon vor über einem Jahrzehnt offen mit einer großen Gay-Pride-Demonstration auf die Straße wagten.
Mittlerweile existieren in allen mexikanischen Metropolen schwule Organisationen: z.B. in Mexiko-City die gemäßigte "Lambda Mexico" -sie ist Trägerin des einzigen Schwulen- und Lesbenzentrums- und die radikalere "Frente Homosexual de Acción Revolucionaria/FAHR". In der Stadt Guadalajara leistet die "Grupo Orgullo Homosexual de Liberación/GOHL" einen wichtigen Beitrag zur Emanzipation schwuler Männer.

✱ Le code pénal mexicain ne se prononce pas directement sur l'homosexualité. Dans tout le pays, on a recours à des lois répriman "l'offense publique à la pudeur" comme moyen d'action contre les gais qui auraient l'audace de s'afficher en plein jour.
Dans la capitale, la situation est en revanche normale. Les gais y sont à l'aise. Voilà déjà 10 ans que, pour la première fois, ils sont descendus dans la rue pour fêter la Gay Pride avec leurs copines, les lesbiennes. Il y avait 4.000 personnes dans la rue. Depuis, il y a une association ou un groupe gais dans chaque grande ville mexicaine. A Mexico-City, c'est la "Lambda Mexico" qui gère le seul centre homo-lesbien du pays. Le "Frente homosexual de acción revolucionaria/FAHR" est, lui, plus engagé. A Guadalajara, le groupe "Grupo Orgullo Homosexual de Liberación/GOHL" travaille à l'émancipation des homosexuels.

✱ Las leyes federales mexicanas no mencionan la homosexualidad. Sin embargo, las disposiciones referente al "escandalo público" se aplican frecuentemente contra los homosexuales, sin ningún tipo de criterio. Por el contrario, en la Ciudad de México se difruta de un ambiente relativamente liberal, donde el orgullo gay se demuestra abiertamente. Aquí se organizó ya en 1982 la primera manifestación de Gay-Pride. Así mismo, han ido surgiendo en todas las metrópolis mexicanas organizaciones de liberación gay: por ejemplo la moderada "Lambda México", en Ciudad de México, que es la iniciadora del único centro para gays y lesbianas, o la más radical "Frente Homosexual de Acción Revolucionaria/FAHR". En la ciudad de Guadalajara, el "Grupo Orgullo Homosexual de Liberación"/GOHL" presta una importante contribución para la emancipación de los gays.

✱ Le leggi federali del Messico non includono l'omosessualità. Le leggi che proteggono "la pubblica moralità" vengono spesso usate in maniera arbitraria contro i gay riconoscibili su tutto il territorio del paese. Nella capitale, Mexico City, l'omosessualità è vista con occhi più liberali. Per esempio, nel 1982, le lesbiche e i gay dichiarati hanno organizzato la prima Manifestazione dell'Orgoglio Omosessuale con 4.000 partecipanti. Da allora si sono formati vari gruppi di liberazione gay in tutte le città messicane, come "Lambda Mexico", una delle più attive organizzazioni a Mexico City o il più radicale "Frente Homosexual de Acción Revolucionaria/FAHR". Nella città di Guadalajara il "Grupo Orgullo Homosexual de Liberaciòn/GOHL è molto attivo nella lotta per l'emancipazione dei gay.

Mexico | Acapulco - Guerrero ▶ Aguascalientes - Aguascalientes

NATIONAL GAY INFO
■ **Mexicanos Contra el SIDA, Confederación de Organismos no Gubernamentales, A.C.**
Calzada de Tlalpan 613, Col. Alamos, Mexico City-D.F. 03400
☎ 530 27 71 ☎ 530 25 49

NATIONAL PUBLICATIONS
■ **Sergay** (G)
c/o American Trade Magazine, Morelos Sur 1211B Cuernavaca
☎ (015) 5110414 ✉ trade@df1.telmex.net.mx
💻 sergay.com.mx
National bi-weekly gay magazine featuring cultural and social news and a listing of gay venues. In Spanish. About 60 pages.

Acapulco - Guerrero ☎ 74

BARS
■ **Bar. El** (B f G s) 12-24 h
Avenida Las Conchas 155 (poolside at the Las Palmas Hotel)
☎ (74) 87 08 43
Popular bar with great city and bay views. English spoken.

■ **Plaza Las Mariachis** (B f G MA N OS) 24 hours
Avenida Juan Escudero (Zócalo)
Becomes more gay from 1-6 h, jukebox, beer US$0.75, check out pool hall next door and taxi-washing boys in parking lot (AYOR)

DANCECLUBS
■ **Diferencia. La** (B D G S)
Costera M. Alemán, Plaza Condesa ☎ 84 04 1

■ **Disco Demas** (B D GLM S) 22-? h.
Privada Piedra Picuda 17 (Behind Carlos & Charles) ☎ 84 13 70
Shows on the WE.

■ **Relax** (AC B D G R snu TV VS) 22-5 h
Lomas del Mar 4 (off Costera M. Aleman near Denny's Restaurant)
☎ 84 04 21
Tourists pay entry US$ 10 including 1 drink. Best on Sat night. Thu/Sat Strip shows.

RESTAURANTS
■ **Beto's Beach restaurant** (B F glm)
Ave. Costera Miguel Alemán 99 (at Condesa Beach)
☎ (74) 84 04 73

■ **Le Bistroquet** (b CC F glm OS) 18-23.30 h
Andrea Doria 5, Costa Azul (opposite the Oceanic 2000 building, 1/2 block from Main Ave) ☎ 84 68 60
International cuisine

CINEMAS
■ **Dorado 2000** (NG)
Plan de Ayala 1-6 (Col. Progreso)

HOTELS
■ **Acapulco Las Palmas** (AC B BF CC F G H msg NU OS PI WH) 0-24 h
Avenida Las Conchas 155, Fracc. Farallon ✉ 39690 ☎ 87 08 43
📠 87 12 82 ✉ bobbyjoe@acapulco-laspalmas.com
💻 www.acapulco-laspalmas.com
2 minutes from Condesa Gay Beach and bars. Airport pick-up. 15 premier rooms and suites. Clothing optional. Air conditioned rooms and suites.

■ **Luna del Mar Hotel** (H NG)
Costera Miguel Aleman/de la Cosa ☎ 84 00 71

■ **Villa Costa Azul** (! AC GLM H MA OS PI) 15.Nov-15.May
Fdo. Magallanes 555, GRO 39850 ☎ 84 54 62

ACAPULCO "LAS PALMAS"
THE ONLY GAY RESORT HOTEL IN ACAPULCO

★★★★★
DELUXE

● Tranquil A/C
● Suites & Rooms
● Pool • Restaurant
● Near Gay Beach
● Bars • Shopping
● 24 Hour Security

RESERVATIONS
011•52•7•(487•08•43)
FAX
011•52•7•(487•12•82)
FREE COLOR BROCHURE

ACAPULCO LAS PALMAS

bobbyjoe@acapulco-laspalmas.com
www.acapulco-laspalmas.com

CLOTHING OPTIONAL

"THE HOT GAY MECCA OF MEXICO"

VISA MasterCard

Also visit!
www.gaymexicoguide.com

■ **Villa Tiffany** (CC G H MA PI)
Calle Villa Vera 120 ☎ 294 78 49
In gay area, close to bars and gay beach.

GUEST HOUSES
■ **Villa Roqueta** (AC B BF CC F G H msg NU OS p PI SA WH WO)
All year / 24h
24 San Marcos, Las Playas ✉ GRO 393600 (on the cliffs of Acapulco)
☎ 294 7849 📠 294 7849 ✉ van4@prodigy.net
💻 www.acavio.com/roqueta2.htm
Former Gloria Gaynor Estate now a luxury guesthouse non the cliffs. All rooms with ocean view. Pool and bar 11 double rooms with shower/WC. Rates from US$ 125, Suites rom US$250. Free airport transfers.

CRUISING
- Beto's Beach (near Condesa, Chichifos)
- Pie de la Questa (BA Beach about 13 km south)
- Plaza Alvares/Zocalo (R, AYOR)
- Flecha Roja (AYOR) (bus station)

Aguascalientes - Aguascalientes ☎ 49

BARS
■ **Circulo. El** (B G)
Calle del Horneado s/n

DANCECLUBS
■ **Mandiles** (D GLM p) Fri Sat 22-3 h
Blvd Lopéz Mateos 730 (near Convención de 1914, between Chabacano and Aguacate) ☎ (49) 15 32 81

Aguascalientes - Aguascalientes ▶ Ciudad de Mexico - D.F. | **Mexico**

RESTAURANTS
■ **Mitla** (b F g OS)
Calle Madero 220
■ **Wolworth** (B F GLM)
5 de Mayo/Victoria
Best after 20 h.

FITNESS STUDIOS
■ **Ojo Caliente** (g SA WO)
Carretera Aguascalientes-San Luis Potosi

CRUISING
-Plaza Principal (YG, AYOR)
-Jardin de San Marcos (AYOR)

Arriaga - Chiapas ☏ 966
GENERAL GROUPS
■ **Gruppo Pisis**
6a Sur/5a Avenida, Poniente 522 ✉ 30450

Campeche - Campeche ☏ 981
CRUISING
-Plaza Principal/Plaza de Independencia

Cancún - Quintana Roo ☏ 98
BARS
■ **Karamba** (B D G snu YG) Tue-Sun 22-6 h
Avenida Tulum 9 *(Downtown, across the street from city hall, above Bananas restaurant)* ☏ 84 00 23
■ **Picante Bar** (! B d GLM MA VS) 21.30-3, Fri -4h , Sat&Sun-? Mon closed
Avenida Tulum 20 *(Plaza Galerias)* ☏ 84 09 57
■ **Risky Bar** (B g) 24 h
Ave Tulum *(at Coba Ave)*
Gets really gay&cruisy on WE in the early morning. Check out the bathrooms.

DANCECLUBS
■ **Backstage** (AC B D G MG SNU VS) 21-3 h
Avenida Tulipanes 30, Centro *(at Avenida Tulum)*

RESTAURANTS
■ **Ajua** (B CC F GLM MA s) 15-?
Calle 4 *(City center, beween Ave 5 &10)*
■ **Over the Rainbow** (F G OS) 9-19 h
Avenida Tulipanes 30 B, Centro ☏ 87 91 06

FASHION SHOPS
■ **Pierro's Boutique** (g) daily 10–21 h, closed on Sun
Plaza Bonita 10-E *(Centre-near Market 28)*

SWIMMING
-The Mirador (across from the Ruinas del Rei)
-Beach near Club Med (AYOR)
-Playa Chac Mool (r)
-Beach at Sheraton
-Playa del Carmen (g) (50 min. by bus, walk left along the beach north)
-Caesar Park Beach (G)

CRUISING
-Avenida Tulum (late)
-Beach between hotels Camino Real & Caribe Hilton
-Palapa Park (opposite Cinema Blanquita, at night)

Chihuahua - Chihuahua ☏ 14
BARS
■ **Bar Gambrinus** (B G)
Trias 300 *(around the corner from Hotel Posada Tierra Blanca)*
■ **Chindos** (B G) -23 h
Calle 6, 30 *(to the right of Hotel Maceyra)*

CRUISING
-Plaza de la Constitución
-Plaza Hidalgo

Ciudad de Mexico - D.F. ☏ 5

★ The gay scene in this vast city of 20 million, is concentrated in the "Zona Rosa": Paseo de la Reforma, Avenidas Insurgentes, Liverpool, Londres, Hamburgo, Florencia, Amberes and especially in the Avenidas Genova and Niza. This is also the area where most of the prostitutes, male and female, are to be found.

★ Die Schwulenszene dieser 20 Millionen Einwohner zählenden Großstadt ist konzentriert in der "Zona Rosa": Paseo de la Reforma, Avenidas Insurgentes, Liverpool, Londres, Hamburgo, Florencia, Amberes und ganz besonders in den Avenidas Genova und Niza. In dieser Gegend arbeitet auch das Gros der mexikanischen Prostituierten, ob männlich oder weiblich.

★ Les quartiers gais de cette métropole de 20 millions d'habitants sont connus sous le nom de "Zona rosa": Paseo de la reforma, Avenidas Insurgentes, Liverpool, Londres, Hamburgo, Florencia, Amberes et surtout la Avendia Genova et Niza. C'est dans ce coin que travaillent aussi la plupart des prostitués mexicains, hommes et femmes.

● El ambiente gay de esta gran ciudad de 20 millones de habitantes está concentrado en la "Zona Rosa": Paseo de la Reforma, Avenidas Insurgentes, Liverpool, Londres, Hamburgo, Florencia, Amberes y sobre todo en las Avenidas Génova y Niza. Es la bona clave de prostitución.

● La vita gay in questa grande città di 20 milioni di abitanti, è concentrata nella "Zona Rosa": Paseo de la Reforma, Avenidas Insurgentes, Liverpool, Londres, Amburgo, Amberes e soprattutto nelle Avenidas Genova e Niza. Questa è anche la maggiore area di prostituzione maschile e femminile della città.

PUBLICATIONS
■ **Boys & Toys**
Paseo de la Reforma 269, Torre B-301, Col. Cuauhtémoc ✉ 06500
Mexico City ☏ (5) 525 18 25 ☏ (5) 796 00 04
Gay monthly; Latin America's largest Gay publication.

GAY INFO
■ **Canal Amigo** (GLM MA)
Ave Lázaro Cárdenas 228, #102 *(Colonia Obrera)* ☏ 588 19 93
Call for infos.

TOURIST INFO
■ **Mexico City Tourism Office**
Amberes 54 ✉ 06600 ☏ 525 93 81 🖷 525 93 87

Mexico Ciudad de Mexico - D.F.

BARS

■ **Ansia. El** (B D G MA SNU STV) Wed-Sat
Algéciras 26, Col. San José Insurgentes ☎ 611 61 18
■ **Anyway, Exacto, The Door** (! AC B D GLM S WE YG) 21-4 h
Calle Monterrey 47, Col Roma *(near Metro Insurgentes)*
☎ 533 16 91
Very good, 3 floors, 3 clubs, friendly and relaxed.
■ **Box** (B D G MA S) Sat 23-? h
Versalles 64-68, Col. Juaréz ☎ 566 74 76
■ **Butterflies** (AC B D GLM MA R S TV WE) Mon-Sun 21-4 h
Izagaza 9/Eje Central *(Metro Salto del Agua, right of the church)*
☎ 761 18 61
All kinds of music, mostly modern, pop & folkoric Mexican. Crowded WE. Large place.
■ **Cantina del Vaquero** (B D DR G LJ SNU VS) 17-? h
Algéciras 26, Col Insurgentes Mixcoac ☎ 559 821 95
■ **Caztzi** (B D G S) Thu- Sat
Carlos Arellano 4, Cd. Satélite
■ **Clandestine** (B G s VS) 18-3, WE- 5 h
Calle Colón 1 ☎ 518 19 91
Stripshow Thu-Sat.
■ **Dark Room** (B G SNU VS YG) 20-4 h
Calle Bajio 339 *(Insurgentes Sur)* ☎ 518 19 91
■ **La Estación** (B G LJ MA) Mon-Sun 16- ? h
Hamburgo 234 *(Col Juarez)* ☎ 514 47 07
Leather bar.
■ **Milan** (B g) 21-1 h Sun closed; Wed G
Calle Milán 18, Col. Juarez ☎ 592 00 31
■ **Paseo. El** (B f G OG) 13-2 h, closed Sun
Paseo de la Reforma 148, Col Juárez *(Zona Rosa)* ☎ 546 51 24
Piano bar.
■ **Privata** (B D G MA SNU VS) 21-3 h
Av. Universidad 1909, Coyoacán ☎ 661 59 39
■ **Tom`s** (B D g lj snu) Tue-Sun 21-2 h
Insurgentes sur 357, esq. Hermosillo
■ **Viena** (B G) 11-23 h
República de Cuba 3 *(Centro Historico)*
Beer bar, crowded in the evening.
■ **33. El** (B f G N r tv) 22-2 h
Ave Lázaro Cárdenas 19 *(Eje Cental, at Republica del Perú)*

MEN'S CLUBS

■ **Casita I .La** (B DR G lj p VS YG WO) 24 h
Viaducto M. Aleman 72, Col Algarin ☎ 519 88 42
Only men under 35.

DANCECLUBS

■ **Alquimia** (D G TV R S SNU)
Calle Ponciano Arriaga 31 ☎ 566 43 01
Salsa music.
■ **Amsterdam Club** (D G MA R SNU)
Calle Dinamarca 24
Disco on 3 levels with regular stripshows.
■ **Antro. El** (B D glm MA S) Wed-Sat
Londres 77 *(Zona Rosa)* ☎ 551 116 13
■ **Baron. L'** (D G S YG) 21-4, Fri&Sat - 8 h
Ave Alvaron Obregón 85-B, Col. Roma ☎ 208 63 85
■ **Enigma** (B D G S) Tue-Sun 21-5 h
Calle Morelia 111 *(Colonia Roma, Zona Rosa)* ☎ 207 73 67
Drag shows. Cover M$20.00 with 1 drink.
■ **Kao's** (B D G STV) Wed-Sun 21-4 h
Querétaro 217/Medellín *(Colonia Roma)* ☎ 264 25 67

■ **Privata** (D G s SNU YG) Wed-Sat 21-3 h
Ave Universidad 1909, Col Copilco *(between Ave Copilco & Calle Miguel Ángel de Quevada)* ☎ 661 59 39
■ **Rosales. Los** (B D Glm STV)
Calle Pensador Mexicano 11 *(Centro)*
■ **Spartacu' s** (B D G STV) Fri-Sat 21-5 h
Avenida Cuaúhtemoc 8 *(Colonia Maravillas Ciudad Neza)*
☎ 763 80 28
Rough neighborhood.
■ **Taller. El** (AC B CC D f G lj MA SNU VS) 21-3 h Tue-Sun
Florencia 37A , ✉ 03740 *(Zona Rosa, Metro Insurgentes)*
☎ 533 49 84
Friendly staff, good music. Strip shows Wed/Thu. Admission

RESTAURANTS

■ **Vips del Angel** (B F glm)
Reforma/Florencia *(Zona Rosa, Metro Insurgentes or Sevilla)*
☎ 546-1567

CINEMAS

■ **28 de Marzo** (g)
República de Colombia 88 *(Centro)*

ESCORTS & STUDIOS

■ **An Executive´s Choice** (CC GLM msg) 24 h
Barracuda 37, Penthouse, SM 3 MZA 20 ✉ 77300 ☎ 884 49 86

SAUNAS/BATHS

■ **Baños Casita. La** (G P VS YG WO) 24 h
Viaducto Miguel Alemán 72, Col. Algarin ☎ 519 88 42
Ages 18-25 only. La Casita II (YG) at Insurgentes Sur 228 (Col. Roma, Tel. 514 46 39).
■ **Baños Finesterre** (g MA msg SB) 6-21, Sun 6-16 h
Manuel Maria Contreras 11, Col. San Rafael ✉ 06140 *(Metro Cosme)* ☎ 535 35 43
Recommended.
■ **Baños Señorial** (b G msg SA SB) Mon-Sat 6-20 h, Sun 6-15 h
Isabel la Católica 92/Calle Regina *(Centro-Metro Isabel la Católica)*
☎ 709 07 32
■ **Baños Torre Nueva** (G MA msg SA SB) 6-21 h
Alvaro obregón No. 42, Col Roma ✉ 1500 *(Condesa. Metro Cuauhtémoc)* ☎ 574 81 31
Not very clean.

GIFT & PRIDE SHOPS

■ **Vaquero. El (Querelle)** Tue-Sat 15-1 h
Insurgentes Sur 1231 *(Local Isla)*
Mags, videos, etc.

TRAVEL AND TRANSPORT

■ **Viajes Bru** 10-19 h
Kepler 92, D.F. 11590 *(near Anzures)* ☎ 545 25 76
Travel agent.

HOTELS

■ **New Hotel Ambar** (H)
San Jeronimo 105, Esq. Pino Suarez, Centro ✉ 06090
☎ 522 01 05
Gay-friendly hotel.

GENERAL GROUPS

■ **Alianza-Gay and Lesbian entrepreneurs**
PO Box 6-962 ✉ 06602 ☐ 74563.2046@compuserve.com
■ **Circulo Cultural Gay**
AP 75-237, CP ✉ 06760

Ciudad de Mexico - D.F. ▸ Cuernavaca - Morelos | Mexico

■ **Colectivo Sol**
Avenida Universidad 1900, Edificio 2, Departmento 402
(PO Box 13-320, 03500) ☎ 666 68 49 📠 606 72 16
Operates a non-profit gay archive.

HEALTH GROUPS

■ **AMAC**
Bolivia 5, Centro ☎ 772 07 78
or ☎639 9195.

■ **Ser Humano AC**
Fray Servando Teresa de Mier 104, Col. Centro ✉ 06740 *(2 blocks from Metro-Isabel La Católica)* ☎ 2 55 88 76 29 📠 2 55 88 76 29
✉ serhumano@serhumano.org.mx 🖥 www.serhumano.org.mx
Non governmental organisation founded in 1992 to provide professional medical and psychological services and support for people living with HIV/AIDS and their families.

HELP WITH PROBLEMS

■ **Alcohólicos Anónimos Gay**
Culiacán apt. 122-Altos, Colonia Hipódromo, Condesa

RELIGIOUS GROUPS

■ **MCC-ICM**
PO Box 7-1423, 06700

CRUISING

-Alameda Parque (ayor), Avenida Juarez
-Chapultepec Bosque (Park), Castle Hill
-Zona Rosa (best at: Calle Genova, Calle Londres, Calle Niza, Avenida Insurgentes, Pasaje Jacaranda and Pasaje Toulouse)
-Metro Insurgentes
-Metro Chapultepec
-Metro Universidad
-Metro Sevilla
-Metro Balderas Hidalogo (near Alameda Park)
-Parque Hundido (ayor)

Ciudad del Carmen - Campeche ☎ 938

DANCECLUBS

■ **Umma-Guma Palace** (B D glm)
Calle 26 y 55 *(opposite Puerto Pesquero)*
Local music.

RESTAURANTS

■ **Tropical Guacamayos** (B F glm)
Calle 55 y 26 *(opposite Puerto Pesquero)* ☎ 201 02

Ciudad Juarez - Chihuahua ☎ 16

BARS

■ **Club Luz. La** (B D GLM S YG)
Calle 1, Mariscal N
■ **Club Padrino** (B D GLM)
Calle Santos Degollado N
■ **G&G** (B d g)
Lincoln 1252
■ **Madelon. La** (B D GLM STV)
Santos Degollado 771 *(Centro)*
■ **Nebraska** (B F glm r)
Calle Mariscal 251 *(Centro)*
Rough neighborhood.
■ **Olímpico** (B GLM)
Avenida Lerdo 210 Sur *(Centro)*

■ **Quijote. El** (B g TV)
Calle Mariscal 721 *(Centro)*
■ **Rex Bar** (B D glm)
Calle Mariscal 186 Norte *(Centro)*
■ **Ritz** (B GLM)
Ignacio de la Peña
■ **Sarawak** (B D g)
Avenida Juárez Norte *(Centro)*

DANCECLUBS

■ **MN'MS** (B D g STV)
Avenida Juárez Norte *(opposite X.O. Laser)*
■ **Omare** (B D G)
Ignacio de la Peña y Rámon Corona *(Centro)*
■ **X.O.Laser** (B D g)
Avenida Juárez 832 Norte *(Centro)*

RESTAURANTS

■ **Coyote Invalido** (B F g)
Avenida Lerdo, Pasaje Continental *(Centro)*
■ **Escondida. La** (B F GLM)
Calle Ignacio de la Peña 366 *(around the corner from Olímpico)*

SAUNAS/BATHS

■ **Baños Roma** (g)
Calle Ignacio Mejia 881 Oriente *(at Calle Constitutión)*
☎ (16) 12 77 32

Colima - Colima ☎ 331

BARS

■ **Terraza Azul. La** (B GLM) 20-? h
Gabino Barreda y Avenida Francisco I. Madero *(on top of Hotel Flamingo)*

CINEMAS

■ **Micro 2001** (NG)
Maclovio 47-A/Venustiano Carranza *(Centro)*

Córdoba - Veracruz ☎ 271

BARS

■ **Salon Bar El Metro** (B D GLM)
Ave 7 No 117-C, 1

CRUISING

-Mercado/Market Juarez, Calles 7 & 9 (WE YG)
-Sidewalk cafés on El Portal Zevallos

Cuernavaca - Morelos ☎ 73

BARS

■ **Shadeé** (B D G S) Fri-Sun, show Sat.
Avenida Adolfo López Matéos *(across from the DIF gas station)*
☎ 12 43 67
■ **Terraza. La** (B glm)
Calle Salazar 1, local 5

CAFES

■ **Parroquia** (b f g OG OS)
Guerrero
■ **V.I.P.S.** (B g YG)
Boulevard Juarez *(near Cuauhnahuac Museum)*

SPARTACUS 2001/2002 | 725

Mexico | Cuernavaca - Morelos ▸ Guadalajara - Jalisco

DANCECLUBS
■ **Scala** (B D G) 21-2 h
Ave Plan de Alaya 100 (at Ave Lopéz Mateos)

GENERAL GROUPS
■ **Grupo Encuentro de Amigos**
PO Box 1-1161 ✉ 6200

HEALTH GROUPS
■ **Cadena Contra el Sida A.C.**
Francisco Leyva 403, Colonia Centro ☎ 18 45 76

RELIGIOUS GROUPS
■ **Iglesia de la Comunidad Metropolitana (ICM) Renovación Cuernavaca** Wed-Sun 18-? h.
Leandro Valle 524-A

CRUISING
-Zocalo/Plaza Morelos/Jardín Juarez
-Mercado/market (Sun)

Culiacan - Sinaloa ☎ 67

BARS
■ **Don Quijote** (B g s)
Boulevard Madero 507

GENERAL GROUPS
■ **Grupo Culiacán Gay**
PO Box 884, 8000

CRUISING
-Plaza Obregon/Zocalo (AYOR YG)

Durango - Durango ☎ 181

BARS
■ **Arthur's** (B D g STV)
Bruno Martinez 134 Sur
■ **Eduardos** (B F glm)
20 de Noviembre 805

CRUISING
-Zocalo (20 de Noviembre & Juarez)

Ensenada - Baja California Norte ☎ 667

BARS
■ **Coyote Club** (B.D GLM MA VS) Tue-Sat 21-3, Sun 18-2 h
1000 Boulevard Costero N°4 & 5/Diamante (near Corona Hotel)
■ **Hola Verde** (B D G YG) 16-3 h
2nd Street (1st floor)
Crowded Fri Sat after 23 h.

DANCECLUBS
■ **Club Ibis** (B D G S) Thu-Sun 21-2 h
Blvd Costero/ Ave Sangines
Cover charge.

SAUNAS/BATHS
■ **Baños Los Arcos** (AYOR g)
Calle 2, 1357 (between Calles Gustelum & Miramar, next door to Dugout bar) ☎ (68) 78 26 08

Guadalajara - Jalisco ☎ 3

BARS
■ **Botanero. El** (B G S TV) Tue-Sun 19-23 h.
Javier Mina y la 54
Wed & Sat admission fee.
■ **Caudillos** (B D F G YG) 14-3 h
Calle Prisciliano Sánchez 407 (at Ocampo) ☎ (3) 613 54 45
Bar & restaurant.
■ **Chivas** (B f G MA) 8-5 h
Calle Degollado 150/Avenida López Costilla ☎ 613 16 17
■ **Gerardo** (B F G MA OS) 21-2, -4 on WE
Ave de la Paz 2529 (Sector Juaréz) ☎ (3) 616 12 07
■ **Kumbala TV** (B G tv S) Tue-Sun 20-2 h
Calle Galeana 159
Transgender friendly; Thu-Sun drag shows.

CAFES
■ **Máscaras** (! B f G MA) 8-2 h
Calle Maeztranza 238/Priscilliano Sánchez (2 blocks from Degollado Theater) ☎ 614 81 03
■ **Pancho Jr. Los** (B D glm MA r) 8-2 h
Calle Galeana 180 A (2nd floor) ☎ 613 53 25

DANCECLUBS
■ **Angel's** (AC B CC D E F G MA S SNU WE) Disco 22-4
(F 19-1,B -3 h)
Lopez Cotilla 1495-B, Colonia Americana (between Ave. Chapultepec & Marsella) ☎ 615 25 25
■ **Malinche. La** (B D glm MA YG) 22-2 h Tue-Sun
Alvaro Obregon 1230 (Sector Libertad) ☎ 643 65 62
■ **Monica's** (B D f glm S TV YG) 22-12 h
Ave Álvaro Obergón 1713 (Sector Libertad, between Calles 68 &70)
Popular. Drag & strip shows Fri-Sun.
■ **Punto G** (D G MA SNU) Thu-Sun 21-2 h
Calle Morelos 859 ☎ (3) 825 74 99
Thu-Sun stripshow.
■ **SOS Club** (D GLM OS S) 21-3 h, Mon closed
Ave La Paz 1413 (Sector Juaréz) ☎ (3) 826 41 79
■ **Taller. El** (! B D G S ma S YG) 22-12 h
Calle 66 #30, Sector Reforma

SAUNAS/BATHS
■ **Baños Galeana** (AYOR b g SA SB) 7-20 h
Galeana 159 (near Lopez Catilla Street) ☎ 613 62 86
Action in steam room mostly.

HEALTH GROUPS
■ **Ser Humano**
Francisco I. Madero 540, Zona Centro ✉ 44100
☎ (52) 361 36 000 361 36 200
📧 funserjal@serhumano.org.mx
Non governmental organisation founded in 1992 to provide professional medical and psychological services and support for people living with HIV/AIDS and their families.

CRUISING
-Avenida Juarez (AYOR)
-Plaza de los Mariachis (AYOR)
-Pedro Moreno Street

Guanajuato - Guanajuato

BARS
■ **Lola. La** (B F g) 13-2 h, Mon closed
Ancha de San Antonio 31, San Miguel de Allende ☎ (415) 2 40 50

CRUISING
-Zocalo (Jardin de la Union opposite Teatro Juarez)
-Calle Pedro Moreno / Calle Morelos / Avenida Chaputepec / Avenida Donato Guerra

Irapuato - Guanajuato ☎ 462

BARS
■ **Blanco y Negro** (B D g) Thu-Sun
Ave Ejército National 890 ☎ (462) 4 23 81

Ixtapa Zihuatanejo - Guerrero ☎ 753

BARS
■ **Splash** (B f g MA VS) 12-24 h
Calle Ejido Esquina/Calle Vicente Guerrero *(in front of Comermex Bank)* ☎ 408 80

Jalapa - Veracruz ☎ 281

BARS
■ **Mansion. La** (B D G S TV) Fri Sat
Highway toward Banderillas
Drag shows.
■ **Strago's** (B F G OG)
Ave Américas 354 *(between Calles Niños Héroes & Laureles)*

DANCECLUBS
■ **DKché** (D GLM MA S) Fri&Sat 22- ?h
Calles Zaragoza / Prolongatión

CRUISING
-Parque Juarez

La Paz - Baja California Sur ☎ 682

BARS
■ **Intimo** (B glm)
Calle 16 de Septiembre
■ **Talizman** (B glm)
Belisario Dominguez/5 de Mayo

Leon - Guanajuato ☎ 47

BARS
■ **Amigo, El** (B g) -24 h
Belisario Dominguez 423 P.B.
■ **Bagoas** (AC B D GLM S SNU) Fri&Sat only
Mar Baltico 1332 *(at Alfredo Valadez / Col Rinconada del Sur)* ☎ 71 01 53
■ **Movida. La** (B G) 10-24 h
Belisario Dominguez 417 *(2nd floor)* ☎ (47) 14 21 41

CRUISING
-Mercado/market (Mon Tue)
-Zocalo

Manzanillo - Colima ☎ 333

BARS
■ **OK** (B D G s) Thu-Sun only
Independencia 42 *(in the towm center)*

CRUISING
-Plaza Santiago and Playa Santiago
-La Perlita
-El Jardín
-Plaza San Pedrito
-Zona Roja

Mazatlan - Sinaloa ☎ 69

BARS
■ **Pepe Toro** (AC B D E GLM MA S SNU WE) Thu-Sat
Avenida de las Garzas 18 ✉ 82100 *(Zona Dorada)* ☎ 14 41 76

CAFES
■ **Panama Restaurant Pasteleria** (b f glm)
Ave de las Garzas / Ave Camerón Sábalo

CRUISING
-Beach walk from Valentino's to the El Pollo Soco restaurant.

Mérida - Yucatan ☎ 99

DANCECLUBS
■ **Kabukis** (B D glm MA TV) open Thu, Fri, Sat
Ave Jacinto Canek 381 *(ext. of Calle 59A, west of Calle 124, along the Corralón)*
Drag shows

HOTELS
■ **Casa San Juan** (AC BF Glm H)
Calle 62 #545A, 69 x 71, Centro ✉ 97000 ☎ 23 68 23
🖷 86 29 37 ✉ csjuan@pibil.finred.com.mx
■ **Pantera Negra** (BF glm H) 24 hours
547 B Calle 67 x 6470 ✉ 97000 *(close to main bus station)*
☎ 24 02 51 ✉ caracterint@hotmail.com
🌐 www.panteranegra.com
■ **Posada 49** (A AC H OS) 8-24 h
Calle 49 N°514A ✉ 97000 *(between 62 and 64)* ☎ 24 54 39
🖷 24 54 39
Centrally located. Rates US$ 15-25.

CRUISING
-Zoccalo (Parque Centrale)
-Santa Lucia Park (after 16 h)
-Calle 60 (between Zoccalo and Santa Lucia Park)
-Cinema Premiere

Mexicali - Baja California Norte ☎ 65

BARS
■ **Cantine Tare** (B G MA N s) -2 h
Calle Uxmal / Ave Jalisco
■ **Linterna. La** (AYOR B g N OG) 13-1 h
Blvd Juárez *(between Calle Azeta&Altamirano)*
■ **Taurino. El** (B D GLM MA)
Ave Juan de Zuazua 480 *(at Ave José Maria)*
Late bar.

Mexico — Mexicali - Baja California Norte ▶ Orizaba - Veracruz

■ **Trigal, El** (B D G MA) 17-3 h
Ave José Maria Morales 348 (zona centro)

CRUISING
-Chapultepec Park (downtown)
-San José Steam Baths (AYOR)

Monterrey - Nuevo Leon ☎ 8

BARS
■ **Kloster, El** (B g N YG) G after 22 h
Ave Benito Juárez 916 (between Calle Arteaga& Madero)
■ **Napoleón** (B G VS) 22-? h, closed on Sun
Calle Garibaldi 727 S (between Matamoros& Padre Mier)
☎ 342 68 36
Cruisy bar.
■ **Taurus, El** (B G N YG WE) 11-1 h
Calle Arteaga 117, Poniente (between Colegio Civilo&Juárez)

DANCECLUBS
■ **Extremo** (G D MA S) 19-2 h, closed Wed&Thu
Ave Fidel Velazques 318 (200 m North of Pulga Mitras)
Stripshows on Sat.
■ **Vongole** (! AC B D GLM MA N S SNU WE) Wed Fri Sat 22-3 h
Avenida Constitucion (at Santa Barbara, down "Cenno de las Mitnas" mountain) ☎ 336 03 35
Best in Northern Mexico, modern music, excellent environment.

SAUNAS/BATHS
■ **Baños Orientales** (G MA R) 7-22 h
Calle Hidalgo Oriente 310 (Southeastern suburb of Monterrey)
☎ 367 28 43

NEWS STANDS
■ **Revistería Johnny**
Aramberri 807

GENERAL GROUPS
■ **Abrazo**
México 224, Colonia Azteca, San Nicolas de los Garza 44100

SWIMMING
-Baños Del Norte (Mercado del Norte)

CRUISING
-Zona Rosa-Plaza Hidalgo (from 17-21 h)
-Sanborns Zona Rosa News Stand
-Galerias Monterrey Shopping Mall (Public Bath)
-Padre Mier Street/Juarez Ave
-Padre Mier Street/Cuauthemoc Ave
-Villa de Santiago (WE) (La Boca Lake area)
-Morales Street

Morelia - Michoacan ☎ 43

BARS
■ **Aka Bar Florida** (B G MA) 21-3 h, Sun closed
Ave Morelos 161-B (2nd floor of Hotel Florida) ☎ 12 18 19
■ **Eloines, Los** (B D G STV SNU) 21-3 h, closed on Sun
Avenida Madero Ote. 5039 ☎ 14 28 19
Thu-Sat drag and strip shows.

DANCECLUBS
■ **Con la Rojas** (b D G MA) 23-2 h, closed Sun-Wed
Aldama 343 ☎ 12 15 78

■ **No Que No** (B D G S TV) 22-3 h, Mon closed
Periférico República 7551, Col. Sindurio ☎ 11 14 25

SAUNAS/BATHS
■ **Baños Mintzicuri** (g MA)
Calle Vasco de Quiroga 227 (enter through the Hotel Mintzicuri)
☎ 12 06 64
The gay area of the sauna is marked through "Ruso general" at the door.

CRUISING
-Bus station
-Plaza de los Martires/Zocalo (AYOR YG)

Naucalpan de Juarez

CRUISING
-Plaza Satelite

Nuevo Laredo - Tamaulipas ☎ 87

BARS
■ **Gambrinus** (B g)
Avenida Ocampo y González
■ **Gusano** (B g) -2 h
Calle Dr. Mier 2908 ☎ 2 20 75

Oaxaca - Oaxaca ☎ 951

BARS
■ **Arcos, Los** (B D GLM)
20 de Noviembre
■ **Cascada, La** (B F g N) - 1 h
Calle Bustamente 843 (North of Periférico) ☎ 2 31 33

DANCECLUBS
■ **Snob** (B D g MA) Wed 22-? h (G)
Calzada Niños Héroes de Chupultepec (One block west of bus station)
■ **502 / Numerito, El** (B D g TV YG) 20-? h
Calle Portirio Diaz 502

RESTAURANTS
■ **Jardin, Del** (B CC F glm OS) 7.30-0.30 h
Portal de Flores 10 (on the Zocalo) ☎ 620 92
Mexican specialties.

SAUNAS/BATHS
■ **Baños del Jardin** (g MA) 6-19.30 h
Calle Melchor Ocampo 509 ☎ 645 30

CRUISING
-Alameda (across from cathedral)
-Zocalo (with its arcade)
-Mercado (AYOR) (Sat is market day)

Orizaba - Veracruz ☎ 272

BARS
■ **Sky Drink** (B D g) Wed-Sat
Madero Norte 1280

DANCECLUBS
■ **Tukanes Bar** (B D G S) 21-?
Madero Norte 1280
Wed/Fri no admission. Sat strippers.

Orizaba - Veracruz ▶ Puerto Vallarta - Jalisco | Mexico

CRUISING
-Plaza Principal

Patzcuaro - Michoacan
CAFES
■ **Escudos. Los** (b g OS)
Portal Hidalgo 73

CRUISING
-Mercado/market (Fri)
-Plaza Principal/Plaza Grande

Playa del Carmen ☎ 954
HOTELS
■ **Aventura Mexicana Resort** (AC B BF CC F H MA PI OS s WH)
Avenida 10 y Calle 22 ☎ (98) 73 18 76 📠 (98) 73 18 76
✉ Hotelaventura@playadelcarmen.com 🖥 aventuramexicana.com
Comfortable gay-friendly resort.
■ **Global Cooling** (AC B CC GLM H PI)
C/10 Norte bis # 20 Y 25 AV. ✉ 77710 ☎ 305 37

Puebla de Zaragoza - Puebla ☎ 22
BARS
■ **Cigarra. La** (B G MA s) 18-3 h
Calle 5, Poniente 538 *(at Calle 7 Sur)*
Beer bar.

DANCECLUBS
■ **Jaleo's** (B D G S WE) Fri-Sat 22-3 h
Reforma Sur 3121S, Col. La Paz
■ **Keops** (B D GLM SNU STV YG) Thu-Sun 22-3 h
14 Poniente No. 101 San Andreas Cholula *(12 km from Puebla)*
☎ 47 03 68

SAUNAS/BATHS
■ **Club Las Termas** (G msg SA SB SOL WH) 7-19 h, closed Mon
Calle 5 de Mayo 2810 ✉ 72260 ☎ 32 95 62

CRUISING
-Zocalo/Plaza de la Constitution
-CAPU (bus station)
-Casa de la Cultura (5 oriente No. 5)

Puerto Vallarta - Jalisco ☎ 322
BARS
■ **Kit Kat Bar** (B GLM s) 17-1.30 h
Pulpito 120 ☎ 300 93
■ **Lio's** (B F glm) 10-2 h
264 Ignacio L. Vallarta/Lázaro Cárdenas ☎ 240 60

CAFES
■ **Este Café** (b glm) 8-22 h, Sun closed
Libertad 336 *(near Flea Market)* ☎ 2 42 61
Espresso and juice bar.
■ **Marilyn's** (B F GLM MA OS) 8.30-23 h
Isla Rio Cuale ☎ 221 48
FAX 221 48

Aventura Mexicana
Playa del Carmen (Near Cancun)

A Gay Friendly Resort In Mexico
Near city center & two blocks from the beach, 5 min to gay nude beach. Rooms & suites all with A/C, ceiling fans and private bathrooms, Suites w/refrigerator & TV. Large Pool, Jacuzzi, in tropical surroundings. Restaurant & Bar.
Call For Reservations
In Mexico: Aventura Mexicana
Ph & Fax (52) 987-31876
In U.S.: The Eternal Sun
ph: 954-462-6035 Fax: 954-525-1204
E-mail: HOTELAVENTURA@PLAYADELCARMEN.COM
www.aventuramexicana.com

■ **Tito's (Blue Chairs)** (B F G MA)
Los Muertos beach (south) *(At the gay beach)*

DANCECLUBS
■ **Balcones. Los** (! B D GLM SNU) 21-3 h
Juárez 182/Libertad ☎ 246 71
■ **Club Paco Paco** (D F G MA OS S) 15-6 (disco 22-?h)
Ignacio L Vallarta 278 ☎ 2 18 99
Patio with live piano music.
■ **Paco's Ranch** (B G LJ MA S SNU VS) 20-6 h
Calle Venustiana Carranza 239 *(Entrance through Paco Paco)*
■ **Porqué No** (AC B D glm) 17-4 h
Morelos 101 Plaza Rio ☎ 303 03
Bar upstairs, disco in the basement.

RESTAURANTS
■ **Adobe Café** (CC F glm) 18-23 h, closed Tue
Basilio Badillo 252 ☎ 26 720
Mexican food.
■ **Cuiza** (B F glm) 9-24 h, Tue closed
Isla Rio Cuale 3, West Bridge *(upstairs)* ☎ 256 46
Live jazz music.
■ **Lunatics** (B F glm) 18-23 h
Ignacio L. Vallarta 179 *(Col. Emiliano)* ☎ 261 42
Restaurant and bar.
■ **Ristorante Romano** (B CC F glm) 13-23 h, sat dinner only
☎ 207 25or 📠 204 94. Italian food.

Mexico — Puerto Vallarta - Jalisco ▶ Tijuana - Baja California Norte

■ **Santos** (B F glm MA) Mon closed
Francisco Rodriguez 136
international cuisine.

FITNESS STUDIOS

■ **Tito's Gym** (b g SB WO) Mon-Fri 6-23, Sat 8-20, Sun 10-14 h
Calle Enrico 287-1 *(Near flea market, at Cuale river)* ☏ 222 77

TRAVEL AND TRANSPORT

■ **Amadeus Tour's** Tours on Thu & Sun
Olas Altas 449 ✉ 48380 *(Col. Emiliano Zapata)* ☏ 328 15
📠 235 20
Organizes gay excursions.
■ **Gay-Day-Bay-Cruise / Amadeus Tours** Call for further infos
Muertos Pier ☏ 3 28 15
■ **P.V. Journeys** Tours on Wed & Fri
☏ 476 27
Organizes horseback rides.
■ **Rainbow Cruise** Tours on Sat
☏ 260 59
Organizes gay tours.

HOTELS

■ **Casa Dos Comales**
Calle Aldama 274 ☏ 320 42
Gay-friendly B&B.
■ **Casa Panoramica** (BF G H PI)
Crratera a' Mismaloya ☏ 236 56
■ **Quinta Maria Cortez**
132 Calle Sagitario ☏ 153 17
Rates.US$ 75-240 (depending on room and season).
■ **Vallarta Cora's** (AC B GLM H MA msg NU OS PI R) 14-22h
Calle Pilitas 174 ☏ 328 15 💻 coragay@pvnet.mx
Hotel & popular bar.
■ **Villa Blanca** (g H)
Amapas 349 *(Col. Emiliano Zapata)* ☏ 261 90
Near the gay beach. Rates on request.

SWIMMING

-Playa Los Muertos

CRUISING

-Beach opposite Océano Hotel
-Playa del Sol Beach
-Near Piano Bar
-Dorado Beach

Queretaro - Queretaro ☏ 42

BARS

■ **Villa Jardin / Bar Oz** (B D G MA) Sat only
Blvd Bernardo Quintana 556, Col Arboledas *(across Cinemark)*
☏ 24 13 96

CRUISING

-Alameda (AYOR)
-Zocalo/Plaza Obregon/Plaza de la Constitución (AYOR)

Reynosa - Tamaulipas

CRUISING

-Plaza opposite America Hotel (19-22 h)

Saltillo - Coahuila

CRUISING

-Parque Alameda
-Plaza de Armes
-Transportes del Norte (bus depot)

San Luis Potosi - San Luis Potosi ☏ 48

BARS

■ **Sheik** (B D G GLM SNU STV) Fri-Sat
Prolongación Zacatecas 347 *(Fracc. San Juan)* ☏ 12 74 57
Strip&drag shows.

Tampico - Tamaulipas ☏ 12

BARS

■ **Bilbao** (B glm)
West of Calle Francisco I, Madero Oriente / A Serdan Sur
■ **Clandestin** (B D G SNU) Thu-Sat 21-? h.
Avenida Hildalgo y Violetas 3400 *(Colonia Las Flores)*
■ **Tropicana** (B glm)
Calle de General López de Lara Sur

CRUISING

-Liberty Plaza -Plaza de Armas

Tijuana - Baja California Norte ☏ 66

GAY INFO

■ **Gay & Lesbian Info Line**
☏ 88 02 67

BARS

■ **Bar D.F.** (B GLM)
Plaza Santa Cecilia 781 *(near Calle Tercera)*
Late bar.
■ **Noa Noa** (B D GLM R STV) 22-? h
Calle 1/Avenida D 150 *(2 blocks east of avenida Revolución)*
☏ 86 22 07
■ **Ranchero Bar** (B f G N YG) 10-3 h
Plaza Santa Cecilia 769 *(Near Calle Primera)*
■ **Taurino, El** (B G YG) 15-2 h
Avenida Niños Heroes 579 *(Zona Norte between 1st Street and Coahuila)* ☏ 85 24 78
■ **Terraza 9** (B G S TV) Thu-Sun 20-5 h
Calle 6, 8150 *(at Ave Revolución)* ☏ 85 35 34

DANCECLUBS

■ **Equipales. Los** (B D g S TV) Mon-Sun
Calle 7 2024/Avenida Revolución *(Zona Centro)* ☏ 88 30 06
■ **Mike's** (B D G S SNU TV VS) 15-6 h
Avenida Revolución 1220 *(at Calle 6)* ☏ 85 35 34

SAUNAS/BATHS

■ **Baños San José** (AYOR g MA)
Ave Negrete 1637 *(at Calle 8)*

GENERAL GROUPS

■ **Y Que!**
PO Box 904 ☏ 80 99 63

RELIGIOUS GROUPS

■ **ICM Tijuana**
MCC of Tijuana services Sun 17 h at Calle Tercera 1810-11
(P America).

SWIMMING

-Rosarita Beach, B.C.N. (half an hour south of Tijuana)
-along the coast from Playas Tijuana to Punta Bandera

CRUISING

-Near Noa Noa & El Taurino
-Park at Amerika parking (in heart of Zona Norte at 1981 Calle 3a, 3rd Street)
-Revolución (from 2nd to 8th Street)
-4th Street (from Constitución across Revolución to Maderos)
-7th Street (from Revolución to Maderos)
-Zona del Rio
-Plaza Santa Cecilia (AYOR) (by night)
-Plaza Rio Shopping Centre (WE YG) (area near central arcade cafeteria)

Tlaquepaque - Jalisco ☎ 3

HOTELS

■ **Casa Domingo** (B BF E F H MA NG OS)
Calle Morelos 288　☎ 657 38 46　🖷 657 38 46
Tlaquepaque is an "outskirt" of Guadalajara.

Toluca De Lerdo - Mexico ☎ 72

BARS

■ **Bar El Conde** (B F g)
Pasaje Curi Norte 201 E
■ **Bar El Jardín** (B GLM)
Avenida Hidalgo Oeste 100 D
■ **Cafe del Rey** (B F NG)
Portal 20 de Noviembre
■ **Vip's Toluca** (B glm MA)
Paseo Tollocán / Blvd Isidoro Fabela

CRUISING

-Mercado (Fri)
-Zocalo/Plaza de Los Martires

Tuxpan - Veracruz ☎ 783

CRUISING

-Avenida Juárez (near hotels)

Tuxtla Guiterrez - Chiapas ☎ 961

BARS

■ **Olas** (B D GLM)
Calle 9 Sur Oriente 1498
■ **Sandy's Bar** (B glm TV)
Calle 9 Sur / 8 Poniente

CRUISING

-Plaza Belisario Dominguez

Veracruz - Veracruz ☎ 29

BARS

■ **Cid. El** (B F glm S)
Américo Vespucio 178 (opposite Estadio Pirata Fuente)　☎ 37 77 14

DANCECLUBS

■ **Club Mediterraneo** (B D) Thu-Sat
Avenida Veracruz 927　☎ 24 01 47
■ **Deeper** (B D G SNU) Thu-Sun 21-4 h
Calle Idaza 1005 (between Victoria and Revillagigedo)　☎ 35 02 65
Fri&Sat stripshows.
■ **Hip-Pop-Potamus** (B glm STV WE YG) 21-6 h, closed Mon-Wed
Calle 11, Col. Costa Verde (Centro)
■ **Vieu Carre** (D G S) Thu-Sat 21-4 h
Ave Independencia Norte 19-A (at Calle Padilla)　☎ 30 60 60
Go-go-boys.

SAUNAS/BATHS

■ **Baños El Edén** (AYOR g) -21 h
Ave Hidalgo 1113, Centro　☎ 32 44 00
Buy tickets at the rear counter of music store.

Villahermosa - Tabasco ☎ 93

BARS

■ **Yardas** (B GLM)
1318 Ave 27 de Febrero　☎ 13 43 62

CRUISING

-Central Camionera de Primera (A.D.O. Bus Station)
-Plaza Hidalgo (opposite cathedral)
-Plaza de Armas

Zacatecas - Zacatecas ☎ 492

DANCECLUBS

■ **Escálando** (D GLM MA S) Fri&Sat 21-3 h
Esplanada La Feria　☎ 4 14 76

CRUISING

-Plaza Hidalgo
-Plaza de las Armas

Zihuatanejo/Ixtapa - Guerrero ☎ 753

BARS

■ **Casita. La** (B G MA S) Bar 18-24 h
Camino Escenico a Playa La Ropa　✉ 40880 (across from restaurant Kontiki)　☎ 445 10

DANCECLUBS

■ **Roca Rock** (b D glm S YG)
Calles 5 de Majo / Nicolas Bravo

RESTAURANTS

■ **Splash** (B F GLM) 12-24 h
Calle Ejido / Vincente Guerrero　☎ 4 08 80
Restaurant&bar.

Mongolia

Name: Monggol Ulus • Mongolei • Mongolie
Location: Central Asia
Initials: MNG
Time: GMT +7 / +8 / +9
International Country Code: ☏ 976
International Access Code: ☏ 00
Language: Khalkha Mongol
Area: 1,565,000 km² / 604,247 sq mi.
Currency: 1 Tugrik (Tug) = 100 Mongo
Population: 2,584,000
Capital: Ulaanbaatar (Ulan Bator)
Religions: 90% Buddhist

✱ Homosexuality is illegal in Mongolia. According to sub-paragraph 113 of the penal code, homosexuality is defined as "immoral satisfaction of sexual desires". No further information on the legal or social situation of homosexuals is available. There is no gay scene in Mongolia.

★ Homosexualität ist in der Mongolei illegal. Gemäß des Unterparagraphen 113 des Strafgesetzbuches wird Homosexualität als "unmoralische Befriedigung sexuellen Verlangens" definiert. Bezüglich der sozialen und legalen Situation von Homosexuellen liegen uns keinerlei Informationen vor. In der Mongolei gibt es keine Gay-Szene.

✱ L'homosexualité est illégale en Mongolie. Selon le sous-paragraphe 113, l'homosexualité est définie comme une " satisfaction immorale des désirs sexuels ". Pas plus d'information sur la situation sociale et légale des homosexuels n'est disponible. Il n'y a pas de milieu gai en Mongolie.

⬢ La homosexualidad es ilegal en Mongolia. En subartículo 113 de la ley penal, homosexualidad es definido como "satisfacción inmoral de deseos sexuales". No es posible obtener informaciones acerca de la situación legal o cultural de los homosexuales en Mongolia, y no hay un ambiente gay en este país.

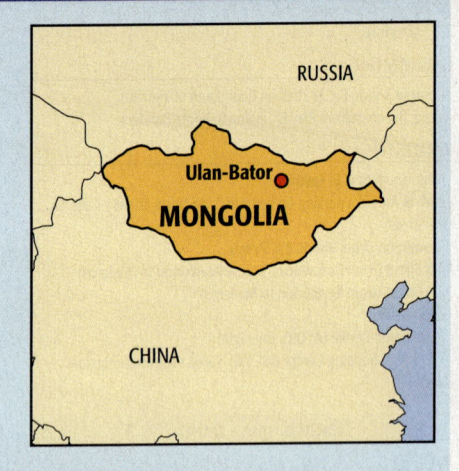

✖ In Mongolia l'omosessualità è illegale. Secondo il subparagrafo 113 del codice penale l'omosessualità viene definita come "soddisfazione immorale dei desideri sessuali". Per quanto riguarda la situazione legale e sociale degli omosessuali, non disponiamo di ulteriori informazioni. In Mongolia non vi esiste una scena gay.

NATIONAL GROUPS

■ **Tavilan** (GLM)
PO Box 405 ✉ 210644 Ulaanbaatar

First gay group in the Central Asian Republic of Mongolia set up in the spring of 1999.

Morocco

Name: Al-Magrib • Marokko • Maroc • Marruecos • Marocco
Location: Northwestern Africa
Initials: MA
Time: GMT
International Country Code: ☏ 212
International Access Code: ☏ 00 (wait for tone)
Language: Arabic, Berber Dialects, French
Area: 458,730 km^2 / 172,413 sq mi.
Currency: 1 Dirham (DH) = 100 Centimes
Population: 27,775,000
Capital: Rabat
Religions: 90% Sunnite Moslem (state religion)
Climate: Mediterranean climate, becoming more extreme in the interior.

※ Homosexual acts are reportedly illegal and punishable under Article 489 of the penal code with a penalty of 6 months to 3 years imprisonment and a fine of 120 to 1,200 Dirhams. It is becoming increasingly apparent that affluent Western tourists and their demands are not always welcome. Islamic fundamentalists have also become noticeably more aggressive towards gays in recent years; no doubt due in some degree to prostitution, which is rigorously combatted. According to our information, Agadir and Marrakech are (especially for gays after nightfall) downright dangerous!

※ Homosexualität ist dem Vernehmen nach illegal und wird gemäß Artikel 489 des Strafgesetzes mit 6 Monaten bis 3 Jahren Haft und einer Geldbuße von 120 bis 1200 Dirhams bestraft. Die Abneigung gegen den westlichen Wohlstandstourismus und seine manchmal peinlichen Auswüchse vergrößert sich zunehmend. Auch ist der fundamentalistische Islam in den vergangenen Jahren immer feindseliger gegen Schwule vorgegangen. Dazu trug offensichtlich auch die enorme Prostitution bei.

※ Au Maroc, l'homosexualité est un délit (article 489 du code pénal). On s'expose à des peines de prison allant de 6 mois à 3 ans et à des amendes de 120 à 1.200 dirhams. Le tourisme à l'occidentale (et ses conséquences souvent fâcheuses) est de plus en plus décrié. Ces derniers temps, les fondamentalistes de l'Islam prennent position de plus en plus durement contre les homosexuels et utilisent les méfaits de la prostitution que l'on combat, par ailleurs, assez vigoureusement, pour discréditer l'homosexualité. On nous a rapporté qu'à Agadir et Marrakech, les touristes gais, surtout, feraient mieux de ne pas sortir après la tombée de la nuit.

※ La homosexualidad es ilegal y es perseguida según el artículo 489 del Código Penal con una sentencia a prisión desde 6 meses hasta 3 años y una multa de 120 a 1200 dinares. Se nota cada vez más, que los turistas ricos de los paises de Occidente y sus demandas no son siempre bienvenidas. En los últimos años ha incrementado la agresión de los fundamentalistas islámicos contra los gays, sobre todo a causa de la prostitución proliferante, que está perseguida rigurosamente. Segun nuestras informaciones las ciudades de Agadir y Marrakesch son para turistas (especialmente en la oscuridad y en solitario) no son recomendables, en absoluto.

※ L'omosessualità è illegale ed è punita dal paragrafo 489 del codice penale con la prigione da sei mesi a tre anni e una multa da 120 a 1.000 dirahms. Si fa sempre più chiaro il concetto che i turisti occidentali, con le loro richieste, non sono benvenuti. Si sa che, negli ultimi anni, il fondamentalismo islamico è diventato più aggressivo verso i gay; senza dubbio, questo è dovuto, in qualche modo, alla prostituzione che viene rigorosamente combattuta. Secondo le nostre informazioni Agadir e Marrakesch sono città poco consigliabili ai turisti (soprattutto se gay e soli).

Agadir ☏ 08

DANCECLUBS
■ **Moon Disco** (B D glm MA r) 22-5 h
Hotel Agador

RESTAURANTS
■ **Via Veneta** (F g OS) 12-23.30 h
Avenida Hassan II *(near Dome Bar)*

APARTMENTS
■ **Ray and Dave Apartments** (g H)
PO Box 12 95, Tamraght
18 km from Agadir. Car rental adviced. Superb location. Gay owned.

PRIVATE ACCOMMODATION
■ **Chez Manou et Henri** (g H MA OS)
9 rue de Paris, Ville Nouvelle ✉ 80 000 ☏ 82 83 44
🖳 www.chez.com/lamar/
Close to the sea and the city center.

SWIMMING
-**Inezgane** (8 km from Agadir; beach at mouth of River Sousse; main beach between P.L.M. Hotel Dunes d'Or and la Douche; municipal showers)
-**Tarhazoute** (NG) (go with the green busses 12 or 14 from Avenue Mohammed to the north. You will reach a quiet beach with camping area)

Morocco — Agadir ▶ Marrakech

Guest House Marrakech

Réservation:
506, Rue Amrou Ben Salma Issil — Marrakech — MAROC
Tél. mobile (212) 1.24.38.62 · B: (212) 4.31.18.71

http://www.cybernet.net.ma/maisonhotes/
E-mail lachgarridouane@voila.fr

CRUISING
-in front of all the cinemas (afternoons are best)
-along Avenue Hassan II (late evening)

Asilah ☎ 09

CRUISING
-There is a well-known market every Sunday in a village about 3 km from the coast where many of the young men will make it very clear that they are ready, willing and able.

Beni Mellal ☎ 03

BARS
■ **Cafe Restaurant du Rif** (F NG)

Casablanca ☎ 02

BARS
■ **Café de France** (B g)
Rue P. Sorbier *(across the square from Hotel Casablanca)* ☎ 236 79

SWIMMING
-Plage Ain Diab

CRUISING
-Souterrain/Subway (YG) (Place Mohamed V)

El Jadida ☎ 03

HEALTH GROUPS
■ **Centre de Santé** mornings

CRUISING
-The three principal cafés facing the Municipal Theatre in Place Mohamed V
-Beach 2 km north of the Hotel Maharba
-Street from Place Mohammed V to Hotel Bruxelles
-Beach road to Houzia Beach (about 3 to 4 km north from El Jadida)

Essaouira ☎ 04

RESTAURANTS
■ **Minzah. El** (A B F NG) 8-23 h
3 Avenue Oqba Ibn Nafia *(near Jardins du Mechouar)* ☎ 47 23 08
Fish specialities.

HEALTH GROUPS
■ **Centre de Santé** mornings

CRUISING
-Bus Station, Place Hassan II
-The Beach (dunes to the south of the bay)

Fes ☎ 05

BARS
■ **Café de Florence** (B F g)
Avenue Hassan II
■ **Café de la Renaissance** (B g)
Avenue Mohamed V
■ **Café de la Resistance** (B g)
Avenue des Etats-Unis/Avenue Hassan II

CRUISING
-Boulevard Gardens in the Medina (near the Bartha Museum)

Marrakech ☎ 04

BARS
■ **Renaissance Bar** (B g)
Avenue Mohamed V *(near Hotel les Ambassadeurs)*
Very cruisy.

CAFES
Any cafe overlooking Square El F'naa. Sit and have coffee, you will soon be approached.

RESTAURANTS
■ **Poêle d'or. La** (B F NG) 12-15, 19.30-23.30 h
Rue Allal Ben Ahmed *(Centre Ville Europeenne)* ☎ 44 81 20
French cuisine.

GUEST HOUSES
■ **Guest House Marrakech** (AC g H OS PI SOL)
506, Rue Amrou Ben Salama Issil ☎ 61 24 38 62 (mobile)
☎ 44 31 18 71 ✉ lachgarridouane@voila.fr
🖥 www.cybernet.net.ma/maisonhotes/
Réception à votre arrivée à l'aéroport. Proximité du centre ville dans quartier Issil à 10 mn de la place JAMÂA EL FNAA et des souks. Possibilité acompagnement pour excursion et visite de la ville. Can be met at the airport. Close to the center of the city in Issil which is 10 min from the JAMÂA EL FNAA square. Guided tours can be arranged.

SWIMMING
-Douche Medina (200 meters from Grand Place)

CRUISING
-Avenue Mohamed V
-Place Jemma El Fnaa
-Piscine Municipale (behind Hotel Palais Badia)
-Piscine de la Koutoubia

Rabat ☎ 07
BARS
■ **Florida Bar** (B g)
Avenue Al'lal ben Abdul'lah
CRUISING
-Sidi Moussa Beach (by day)

Tangier/Tanger ☎ 09
BARS
■ **Balima Hotel Bar** (B g H r)
12 Rue Magellan ☎ 393 46
Best between 21-1 h. Rooms by the hour in the same house.
■ **Café Pilo** (B NG)
Rue de Fés
Crowded around dawn.
SWIMMING
-Atlas Beach
-Coco Beach
-Mustapha Beach Club

-Neptuno
-In front of Café Sherazade
-In front of Soleil Lounge

CRUISING
-All the cafés in the Petit Socco, a small, lopsided square in the Medina, particularly the Café Central. The whole length of the sea front (Avenue d'Espagne and Avenue des F.A.R.). Safe enough by day but has become a very dangerous area by night and should be avoided (muggings). It is also advisable not to visit the Medina area unaccompanied at night.
-Bazaar Kinitra
-Rue du Mexique (especially the bottom part, 19-? h)

Tetouan ☎ 09
CRUISING
-Place Hassan II (in front of Palace of the Khalifa)

Tiznit ☎ 08
CRUISING
-Main Square (in the evening)

Zagora
CRUISING
-Around Grand Hotel (in the evening)

Myanmar

Name: Myanma Pye
Location: Southeast Asia
Initials: MYA
Time: GMT +6.30
International Country Code: ☎ 95 (no area codes)
International Access Code: ☎ 0
Language: Burmese, English
Area: 676 552 km^2 = 261,969 sq mi.
Currency: 1 Kyat (K) = 100 Pyas
Population: 43,893,000
Capital: Yangon (Rangoon)
Religions: 87% Buddist, 6% Christian, 4% Muslim, 4% other
Climate: Mid may to late Oct is the monsoon and rainy season. Nov to Mar is dra season and Mar to May is hot and dry

✱ We have no information regarding the legal situation of homosexuals in Myanmar. The military regime based in Yangon (Rangoon) is totally corrupt and the legal situation for visitors can change without notice. The local population is very friendly and hospitable.
Once having passed immigration, one is obliged to exchange US$ 300 (or a similar amount in other major currencies) for Foreign Exchange Certificates (FEC). In most places in Yangon the FECs are accepted by hotels, large businesses and are exchangeable with local currencies.
Neither Myanmar currency nor FEC can be taken out of the country. FECs exceeding US$ 300 can be exchanged back to US$ - hence it is advisable to keep all exchange slips.

✱ Zur rechtlichen Situation von Homosexuellen in Myanmar liegen uns keinerlei Informationen vor. Das in Yangon (Rangoon) ansässige Militärregime ist durch und durch korrupt, die Rechtsvorschriften für Besucher können sich jederzeit und unvorhergesehen ändern. Die Bevölkerung ist sehr zuvorkommend und gastfreundlich.

Myanmar — Yangon

Sobald man den Zoll passiert hat, ist man verpflichtet, 300 US-Dollar (bzw. einen gleichwertigen Betrag in einer anderen größeren Währungen) in sog. Foreign Exchange Certificates (FEC) zu wechseln. Diese FEC werden von den meisten Hotels und größeren Geschäften in Yangon akzeptiert und können in Landeswährung umgetauscht werden. Weder myanmarische Währungen noch FEC dürfen ausgeführt werden. FEC im Wert von über 300 US-Dollar können jedoch in US-Dollar rückgetauscht werden. Es ist daher ratsam, die Nachweise über den Geldwechsel aufzubewahren.

✳ Nous ne possédons pas d'information sur la situation légale des homosexuels à Myanmar. Le régime militaire basé à Rangoon est totalement corrompu et la situation pour les touristes peut changer à tout moment sans préavis. La population est très sympathique et hospitalière.
Une fois passé la frontière, vous êtes obligés d'échanger 300 dollars (ou un montant similaire dans une autre devise) contre des " Foreign Exchange Certificates " (FEC). Ces FEC sont acceptés à Rangoon dans la plupart des hôtels, grands magasins et peuvent s'échanger contre de la monnaie locale.
Il est interdit de sortir du pays des devises locales ou des FEC. Il est conseillé de garder vos coupons d'échange car les FEC excédant un montant de 300 dollars peuvent être échangés à nouveau.

✳ No disponemos de información acerca de la situación legal de los homosexuales en Myanmar. El régimen militar con base en Rangún (o Yangon, como también se llama la capital del país) es totalmente corrupto y la situación legal de los visitantes del país puede cambiar repentinamente y sin previo aviso. La populación local es muy amable y hospitalaria.
Una vez pasado por aduana, el visitante es obligado a cambiar 300,00 dólares americanos (o una suma equivalente en otras monedas internacionalmente importantes) por Certificados de Cambio (FEC). Estos son aceptados en los hoteles y en los negocios más grandes de Rangún y pueden cambiarse por monedas locales.
No está permitido sacar del país ni la moneda de Myanmar ni los FEC. Todos los FEC que excedan los 300,00 dólares americanos pueden recambiarse por dólares, por lo que es recomendable conservar los recibos de cambio.

✖ Non abbiamo alcuna informazione sulla situazione legale degli omosessuali in Myanmar. Il regime militare di Rangoon è completamente corrotto e la situazione legale dei visitatori può cambiare all'improvviso. Dopo aver passato la dogana, si è obbligati a cambiare 300 dollari (o una somma dello stesso valore di un'altra valuta forte) in Foreign Exchange Certificates (FEC). Nella maggior parte dei posti in Yangon, gli FEC vengono accettati dai alberghi e dai negozi più grandi e sono cambiabili in valuta locale. Né la valuta di Myanmar né gli FEC possono essere esportati. FEC del valore superiore ai 300 dollari possono però essere ricambiati in dollari, perciò è raccomandabile conservare tutti i tagliandi del cambio.

Yangon ☎ 01

DANCECLUBS
■ **Pioneer** (g)
Yuzana Garden Hotel *(at Yuzana Garden Hotel)*

HOTELS
■ **Central** (AC B BF F)
335 Bogyoke Aung San Lan ☎ 241 007

■ **Equatorial** (AC B BF F PI)
33 Alan Pya Paya Lan ☎ 250 388
Most of the hotels will accept neatly dressed guests in one's room during the day, and with due disrection maybe for the night too. This does not imply that any of the hotels are gay friendly!

■ **Pansea** (NG)
☎ 228 260 ✉ pansea@myanmars.net
No problem bringing guests back to your room. Known locally as the "pansy".

Namibia

Name: Namibie
Location: South West Africa
Initials: NAM
Time: GMT +2
International Country Code: ☏ 264
International Access Code: ☏ 09
Language: English, Afrikaans, native languages & German
Area: 824, 292 km² / 318,694 sq mi.
Currency: 1 Namibia Dollar (N$) = 100 Cents
Population: 1,662,000
Capital: Windhoek
Religions: 62% Protestant, 20% Catholic
Climate: Desert climate that is hot and dry. Rainfall is sparse and erratic. April to September would be the best time to visit Namibia. However, if you prefer cool with rain, (not unpleasant at all) then December to March would be just as good.

✴ Namibia has a progressive Constitution, to date does not have laws in place that outlaws sodomy. LGBT (lesbian, gay, bisexual and transgendered) people in Namibia have no rights. Here I refer to laws with regard to the adoption of children, marriage and immigration of partners. Furthermore, politicians frequently engage in hate speech. However, it needs to be noted that in the ten years of Namibia's independence, no-one has been prosecuted with regard to sodomy or gay-related charges.
Namibia has beautiful resorts and breathtaking scenery which travellers would and could enjoy at their leisure and in safety.
The Rainbow Project.

★ Namibia hat zwar eine fortschrittliche Verfassung, und es gibt bis heute kein Gesetz, das Analverkehr für widerrechtlich erklärt. LGBT (Lesben, Schwule, Bisexuelle und Transsexuelle) haben in Namibia keine Rechte. Ich beziehe mich hier auf Gesetze, die im Zusammenhang mit Adoption, Heirat und der Immigration von Partnern stehen. Außerdem halten Politiker des öfteren Hetzreden. Man kann dennoch sagen, daß in den zehn Jahren seit der Unabhängigkeit Namibias niemand aufgrund seiner Homosexualität oder Gay-Aktivitäten strafrechtlich verfolgt wurde. Namibia hat wundervolle und atemberaubende Landschaften, die Reisende durchaus sicher und in Muße genießen können.
The Rainbow Project.

✴ La Namibie a une Constitution plutôt progressive qui ne mentionne à ce jour aucune interdiction concernant la sodomie. La communauté gaie, lesbienne, bisexuelle et transsexuelle du pays n'a pourtant aucun droit en ce qui concerne l'adoption d'enfants, le mariage et l'immigration des partenaires. De plus, il n'est pas rare d'entendre des politiciens prononcer des discours homophobes. Cependant, depuis l'indépendance du pays il y a dix ans, personne n'a été poursuivi pour des raisons liées à son homosexualité.
La Namibie possède de magnifiques plages et de splendides paysages que les voyageurs peuvent apprécier en toute quiétude et sécurité. The Rainbow Project

⬢ Namibia tiene una constitución progresiva, y en la actualidad no tiene leyes que ilegalicen relaciones sexuales anales. Lesbianas, gays, bisexuales y transsexuales no gozan de derechos particulares en cuanto a la adopción de niños, matrimonio e inmigración de la pareja. Además, muchos políticos de este país suelen dar discursos airados en contra de la homosexualidad. Sin embargo, hay que decir que en los diez años desde la independencia de Namibia, no ha habido procesamientos por cargos relacionados con la homosexualidad o relaciones sexuales anales.
Namibia tiene maravillosos lugares para pasar las vacaciones y paisajes impresionantes donde los viajeros podrán disfrutar en seguridad de su tiempo libre.
The Rainbow Project.

✴ Namibia ha una costituzione progressista, e a tutt'oggi non esistono leggi che vietino la sodomia. Lesbiche, gay, bisessuali e transessuali non godono in Namibia di alcun diritto. Qui mi riferisco a leggi che riguardano l'adozione di bambini, il matrimonio e l'immigrazione del partner. In più, i politici spesso si esibiscono in discorsi pieno d'odio. Bisogna comunque annotare che nei dieci anni d'indipendenza della Namibia nessuno è stato perseguito per sodomia o altri delitti legati all'omosessualità.
La Namibia ha dei bellissimi parchi nazionali e un paesaggio da mozzare il fiato di cui i viaggiatori possono godere appieno senza dover temere per la propria sicurezza.
The Rainbow Project.

NATIONAL GROUPS

■ **Rainbow Project (TRP)** 1st Wed 18 h at 84, Burg Street, Windhoek PO Box 26 122 Windhoek ☏ 230 710 ☏ 230 760 📠 240 765
✉ trp@mweb.com.na
Committed to equality and human rights for all lesbian, gay, bisexual and transgender people of Namibia. Contact for all further information on the scene in Namibia.

Windhoek ☏ 61

BARS

■ **Casablanca Bar** (B D F Glm OS YG) 22-4 h
Nelson Mandela Drive/Sam Nujoma Drive
■ **Luigi and the Fish** (B g)
132 Sam Nujoma Drive, Klein Widhoek *(Upstairs Bar)*

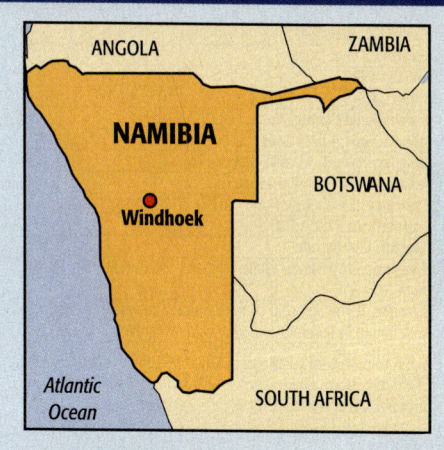

DANCECLUBS

■ **Equinox** (D g)
Lazarett Steet, Auspanplazt
Techno music.
■ **La dee da's** (D g)
McAdam Street, Auspanplatz
■ **Sessions** (D g)
Lazarett Street, Auspanplatz

RESTAURANTS

■ **Plaza Bistro. The** (f g)
Centaurus Road, Maerua Park

CRUISING

-in front of Kalahari Sands Hotel (bus station)
-at Wernhil shopping center upper level toilets.

Nepal

Name:	Nepál • Népal
Location:	Central Asia
Initials:	NEP
Time:	GMT+5
International Country Code:	☏ 977
International Access Code:	☏ 00
Language:	Nepali, Maithili, Bhojpuri (Bihari)
Area:	147,181 km² = 54,363sq mi.
Currency:	1 Nepalese Rupee (NPR) = 100 Paisa
Population:	22,851,000
Capital:	Kathmandu
Religions:	90% Hindu (state religion), 5% Buddist, 3% Muslim
Climate:	Three different climate zones. The valleys have a hot climate in Summer and very cold in Winter.

✱ Homosexuality is illegal in Nepal. We do not have any further information regarding the social or legal situation of homosexuals in Nepal.

★ Homosexualität in Nepal ist illegal Es liegen keine weiteren Informationen über die soziale oder rechtliche Situation von Homosexuellen in Nepal vor.

✱ L'homosexualité est illégale au Népal. Nous n'avons pas pu obtenir d'autres informations concernant la situation sociale ou légale des gais dans le pays.

⬢ Homosexualidad es ilegal en Nepal. No disponemos de informacionesacerca de la situación cultural o legal de los homosexuales en Nepal.

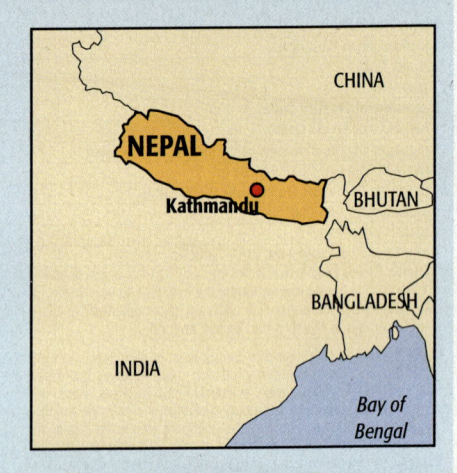

✖ Secondo quanto sappiamo, l'omosessualità in Népal é illegale. La società népal é relativamente ancora poco aperta e si mostra sfavorevole agli omosessuali.

Kathmandu ☏ 01

RESTAURANTS

■ **Ying Yang** (F NG)
CCHA 2/393, Thamel ☏ 425 510
Excellent Thai food.

CRUISING

-Along the same street as Yin Yang. Young men may approach you and offer a "massage".

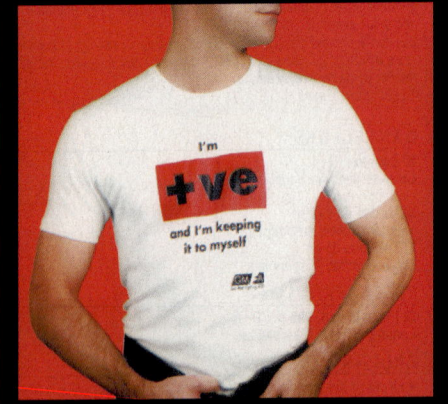

Netherlands

Name: Nederland • Niederlande • Pays-Bas • Paises Bajos • Paesi Bassi
Location: Western Europe
Initials: NL
Time: GMT +1
International Country Code: ☎ 31 (leave the first 0 after area codes)
International Access Code: ☎ 00
Language: Dutch, Frisian
Area: 41,526km^2 / 16,164 sq mi.
Currency: 1 Dutch Guilder (hfl) = 100 Cents. 1 EURO = 2,20371 hfl
Population: 15,698,000
Capital: Amsterdam, Den Haag (Government and Royal Residence)
Religions: 36% Roman Catholic, 26% Protestant
Climate: Moderate and marine climate. Summers are cool, winters mild.
Important gay cities: Amsterdam, Rotterdam, Den Haag

✱ The senate and the Queen still have to agree, but its almost sure that from January the 1st 2001 it will be legal in The Netherlands for people of the same sex to marry. The Netherlands is known for its tolerant and progressive attitude. Especially the capital Amsterdam, which has to keep up a world wide reputation in this respect. In the Netherlands homosexuality has been legal since 1911. The age of consent for homosexuals and heterosexuals is 16. Since the beginning of 2000, the many brothels have been legalised (which means: they now have to pay taxes). Selling and using "soft" drugs has been legal (and controversial) for a long time. The heart of the city Amsterdam is a sparkling centre of festivities. Especially during summer, when gays and straights go wild together. But as far as the local council is concerned, things had become a bit too cosy in Amsterdam. So rules have been sharpened under the guidance of mayor Patijn. One of them concerning frontal nudity during the Gay Pride. Up till now this feast was held every first weekend of August, but because of this and several other restrictions (i.e. no loud music after midnight) the organisation is considering moving to the 'second Gay Capital' in the Netherlands: Rotterdam.
As in other countries, there is quite a difference between the big cities and the countryside in respect to the general view on homosexuality. Nevertheless the majority of the "down-to-earth" Dutch have a positive (or indifferent) attitude towards the subject. And as far as Patijn is concerned: he has threatened to quit his job on the same day gay marriage becomes a reality. So with a bit of luck, Queensday (30 April) will be a party with classical quality.
Expreszo magazine

✱ Der Senat und die Königin müssen ihr Einverständnis noch geben, aber es ist so gut wie sicher, daß Gays in den Niederlanden ab 1. Januar 2001 heiraten dürfen. Die Niederlande sind für ihre tolerante und fortschrittliche Haltung bekannt. Besonders die Hauptstadt Amsterdam genießt diesbezüglich einen weltweiten Ruf. In den Niederlanden ist Homosexualität seit 1811 nicht mehr illegal. Das Schutzalter für Homosexuelle und Heterosexuelle liegt bei 16 Jahren. Seit Anfang des Jahres 2000 wurden viele Bordelle legalisiert, was im Klartext heißt, daß sie auch besteuert werden. Der Verkauf und Genuß von weichen Drogen war eine lange Zeit legal, aber auch kontrovers. Die pulsierende Metropole bietet gerade in den Sommermonaten, wenn Gays und "Heten" zusammen auftreten, eine Reihe von Festen. Aber was den Stadtrat betrifft, ging es ihm in Amsterdam etwas zu gemütlich zu, und so wurden die Regeln unter Bürgermeister Patijn verschärft. Eine Einschränkung war dabei die frontale Nacktheit während der Gay Pride. Bis jetzt fand das Fest am ersten Wochenende im August statt, aber wegen dieser und vielen anderen Einschränkungen (z.B. keine laute Musik mehr nach Mitternacht) erwägt die Organisation die Veranstaltung in die Gay-Hauptstadt Nummer zwei, nämlich nach Rotterdam, zu verlegen.
Wie in anderen Städten auch, gibt es bezüglich der Einstellung zu Homosexuellen einen eklatanten Unterschied zwischen Großstädten und dem Leben in der Provinz. Dennoch hat die Mehrheit der bodenständigen Niederländer eine positive Einstellung zu diesem Thema. Und was Patijn betrifft, hat er gedroht sein Amt an dem Tag niederzulegen, an dem eine Gay-Hochzeit zur Realität wird. Und mit ein bißchen Glück kann der Queensday (30. April) wieder ganz klassisch gefeiert werden.
Expreszo magazine

✱ Le Sénat et la reine doivent encore donner leur consentement, mais il est à peu près certain qu'à partir du 1er janvier 2001, les gais seront autorisés à se marier aux Pays-Bas. La Hollande, et plus particulièrement Amsterdam, est réputée mondialement pour son esprit progressif et tolérant. L'homosexualité a été dépénalisée en 1911 déjà. La majorité sexuelle est fixée à 16 ans pour tous. Depuis début 2000, les nombreux bordels ont été légalisés (ce qui signifie entre autres qu'il doivent s'acquitter d'impôts). La vente et la consommation de drogues douces ont été, non sans controverses, depuis longtemps dépénalisées. Le centre ville d'Amsterdam est en ébullition continue, particulièrement en été, lorsque gais et hétéros font la fête. Ce n'est pas du goût du gouvernement municipal qui pense que les libertés vont trop loin à Amsterdam. De nouveaux règlements ont donc été édités sous l'égide du maire Patijn. L'un d'eux concerne l'interdiction de se montrer nu de face pendant la Gay Pride, qui se déroulait jusqu'à présent chaque année le premier week-end d'août. A cause de cela - et d'autres chicaneries telle que l'interdiction de

Netherlands

passer de la musique forte après minuit - les organisateurs hésitent à déplacer la parade dans la deuxième ville gaie des Pays-Bas, Rotterdam.
Comme dans les autres pays, il existe une différence dans la manière dont les gais sont perçus à la ville ou à la campagne. Cependant la majorité des Hollandais, très terre à terre, ont une opinion positive ou indifférente des homosexuels. Pour ce qui est du maire Patjin, il a promis de démissionner le jour où le mariage gai entrera en vigueur. Avec un peu de chance, la fête de la reine " Queensday " le 30 avril sera l'occasion de célébrer cela en une grande fête.
Expresso magazine

El senado y la reina todavía tienen que dar su acuerdo pero es casi seguro que a partir del uno de enero del 2001, en los Países Bajos será legal el matrimonio entre personas del mismo sexo. Los Países Bajos son conocidos por su actitud tolerante y progresiva. Especialmente la capital, Amsterdam, se ha ganado reputación mundial por ello. En los Países Bajos, la homosexualidad es legal desde 1911. La edad de consentimiento es de dieciseis años. A principios del 2000 fueron legalizados muchos de los burdeles (lo que significa que ahora tienen que pagar impuestos. Vender y consumir drogas 'suaves' es legal (y motivo de polémica) desde hace mucho tiempo. El corazón de Amsterdam es un centro animado de festividades, especialmente durante el verano cuando homosexuales y heterosexuales juntos se ponen frenéticos. Pero para el consejo local de Amsterdam, las cosas se han convertido en algo demasiado íntimo, por lo que las reglas se hicieron un poco más estrictas bajo la dirección del alcalde Patjin. Una de las reglas concierne la 'desnudez frontal' durante la fiesta del orgullo gay. Hasta el momento, esta fiesta siempre se celebró el primer fin de semana de agosto, pero por esta y unas cuantas restricciones más (como, por ejemplo, la prohibición de música alta después de media noche), los organizadores están pensando en mudarse a la 'segunda capital gay' de los Países Bajos, a Rotterdam.
Igual que en otros países hay bastante diferencia entre las grandes ciudades y el campo en cuanto a las actitudes generales hacia la homosexualidad. Sin embargo, la mayoría de los neerlandeses realistas tiene una actitud positiva o indiferente hacia la cuestión.

Y en cuanto a Patijn: Amenazó con dejar su trabajo el mismo día en que el matrimonio homosexual se convierta en realidad. Así, con un poco de suerte, el 30 de abril, día del cumpleaños de la Reina, habrá una fiesta como siempre.
Expresso magazine

Il Senato e la Regina devono ancora sancire alla legge ma è quasi sicuro che nei Paesi Bassi a partire dal 1 gennaio del 2001 diventa legale il
matrimonio tra gay. I Paesi Bassi sono conosciuti per la loro attitudine tollerante e progressista. Questo vale soprattutto per la capitale Amsterdam che ha una reputazione internazionale quanto all'omosessualità. Nei Paesi Bassi, l'omosessualità è legale dal 1811. L'età minima legale per rapporti sessuali sia per omosessuali che per eterosessuali è 16 anni. All'inizio del 2000 tanti bordelli sono stati legalizzati il che vuol dire che vengono anche tassati. Per molti anni, vendere e consumare delle droghe leggere era nello stesso momento legale e controverso. Il cuore della città è un centro vivace dove hanno luogo molte festività. Questo vale soprattutto per i mesi estivi quando c'è un forte caos tra gay ed eterosessuali. Il consiglio municipale però considera che ad Amsterdam, le cose sono diventate un po troppo intime. Perciò, sotto il sindaco Patjin le regole sono state inasprite. Una di queste regole riguarda la nudità frontale durante il Gay Pride. Finora il Gay Pride si festeggiava il primo fine settimana in agosto ma a causa di questa ed altre restrizioni, ad esempio il divieto di musica ad alto volume dopo mezzanotte, l'organizzazione prende in considerazione di trasferirsi nella seconda capitale gay dei Paesi Bassi e cioè a Rotterdam.
Come in tutti gli altri paesi del modo, c'è una differenza enorme tra le grandi città e la vita in provincia relativa all'attitudine generale nei
confronti degli omosessuali. Ma nonostante ciò l'attiudine della maggior parte degli Ollandesi relativo a questo oggetto è indifferente o positiva. E per quanto riguarda Patijn, egli ha annunciato che rinuncerà alla sua carica il giorno stesso quando il matrimonio gay diventa realtà. E con un pò di fortuna il Queensday, il compleanno della Regina il 30 aprile, sarà festeggiato come si deve.
Expresso magazine

NATIONAL GAY INFO

■ **COC Nederland** 9-16 h
Postbus 3836 ✉ 1001 AP Amsterdam *(Visiting address: Rozenstraat 8, Tram 13/17/14/20-Westermarkt)* ☏ 020/623 45 96
☏ 020/620 75 41 (deaf people) 📠 020/626 77 95 ✉ info@coc.nl
💻 www.coc.nl
Largest gay and lesbian organisation in the Netherlands "for the integration of homosexuality". Founded in 1946, publisher of XL, Expresso, central office of local COC organisations around the country. Tries to influence the political debate in the Netherlands. Wide range of activities including help for mentally retarded, young, deaf and old gays among others.

■ **Homodok-Lesbisch Archief Amsterdam** (GLM) Mon-Fri 10-16 h
Nieuwpoortkade 2a ✉ 1055 RX Amsterdam ☏ 020/606 07 12
📠 020/606 07 13 ✉ info@homodok-laa.nl
💻 www.homodok-laa.nl
Archives, library and info-center.

■ **Netherbears**
PB 15495 ✉ 1001 ML Amsterdam

■ **Stichting Homo-Monument**
Westerstraat 16 ✉ 1015 MJ Amsterdam *(Monument location: On Westermarkt, near Anne Frank House and Western Church, Tram 1/2/5/13/17/20)* ☏ 020/626 71 65
The monument for gays and lesbians was erected in 1987 by the whole Dutch gay community. Originally aimed to be a place for remembrance and for warning, it is also nowadays a place for mourning about deceased friends, a place to meet, and a symbolic place for tourists to express their belonging to the gay community.

■ **www.gaysite.nl**
✉ info@gaysite.nl
Up-to-date information on bars, events and gay life in the Netherlands.

NATIONAL PUBLICATIONS

■ **Ami en Marcel**
PB 427 ✉ 3300 AK Dordrecht
Gay porno magazine.

■ **Binky**
Herengracht 24a ✉ 2511 EJ Den Haag
Bi-monthly publication with 60 pages, hfl. 6.95. Macho magazine with photographies, stories and personal ads.

Netherlands

gaydar.nl
what you want, when you want it

■ Centurion
PB 93506 ✉ 2509 AM Den Haag
S/M magazine; 4 times a year. 100 pages with photographies and personal ads. hfl 9.95.

■ Circuit (G. Leather)
Diepenbrockstraat 14 ✉ 6044 SH Roermond
Monthly magazine of Rurals Motorclub. Some English texts.

■ Culture and Camp
Gerard Doustraat 160 F ✉ 1073 VZ Amsterdam ☎ 020/679 91 88
Lifestyle magazine for free on 30 pages.

■ Drummer
RoB, Weteringschans 253 ✉ 1017 XJ Amsterdam
☎ 020/625 46 86 📠 020/627 32 20
💻 webmaster@drummer.com 🌐 www.drummer.com
One of the world's leading fetish magazine for gay males.

■ Expreszo 9-17 h
c/o COC Netherlands, PO Box 3836 ✉ 1001 AP Amsterdam (visiting address: Rozenstraat 8, Westermarkt) ☎ 020/623 45 96
📠 020/626 77 95 💻 info@expreszo.nl 🌐 www.expreszo.nl
Bimonthly 30 pages magazine aimed at young gays and lesbians.

■ Freshmen (G) Mon-Thu 8.30-17, Fri -12.30 h
c/o Gay Krant, P.O. Box 10 ✉ 5680 AA Best ☎ 0499/39 10 00
📠 0499/39 06 06 💻 red@gaykrant.nl 🌐 www.gaykrant.nl
Bimonthly gay erotic magazine published in co-operation with Bruno Gmünder Verlag. 68 pages in full color.

■ Gay Krant.De
c/o Best Publishing Group, PB 10 ✉ 5680 AA, Best
☎ 0499/39 10 00 📠 37 26 38 🌐 www.gaykrant.nl
Biweekly publication. Approx. 40 pages: Gay information with reports about gay life, society, politics and the arts. Focus on gay life in the Netherlands.

■ Gay News
PB 76609 ✉ 1070 HE Amsterdam ☎ 020/679 15 56
📠 020/675 38 61
Completely English-Dutch newspaper with reports and reviews from all aspects of gay life. Large cultural section. Free publication, complete listing of gay places in the Netherlands.

■ MaGAYzine
c/o Best Publishing Group, PB 10 ✉ 5680 AA Best
☎ 0499/39 10 00 📠 0499/39 06 03
Bimonthly publication with pin up models for Hfl 15.

■ Regenbooggids (GLM) Mon-Thu 8.30-17, Fri -12.30 h
Hoofdstraat 64-63 ✉ 5683 AG Best ☎ 0499/39 10 00
📠 0499/39 06 03 💻 gaykrant@gaykrant.nl 🌐 www.gaykrant.nl
Annual gay yellow pages for the Netherlands and Belgium.

■ Squeeze
PB 1372 ✉ 1000 BJ Amsterdam ☎ 20 584 90 20
📠 20 584 90 50 🌐 www.sQueeze.nl
Bimonthly gay glossy with lots of fashion, interviews, beauty and gay items.

■ XL 9-17 h
PB 3836 ✉ 1001 AP Amsterdam (Visiting address: Rozenstraat 8, Tram 13/17/14/20-Westermarkt) ☎ 020/623 45 96
📠 020/626 77 95 💻 xl@coc.nl 🌐 www.coc.nl
Bimonthly magazine featuring reports and reviews about all relevant topics of gay and lesbian life. Very interesting international reports. Informations about all COC activities (member groups are listed). Approx. 48 pages (Hfl 6,95).

NATIONAL HELPLINES

■ Gay and Lesbian Switchboard (GLM) 10-22 h
PB 11573 ✉ 1001 GN Amsterdam ☎ (020) 623 65 65
💻 info@switchboard.nl 🌐 www.switchboard.nl
Information and Helpline.

NATIONAL COMPANIES

■ Delta Boek
PB 92 ✉ 2980 AB Ridderkerk
Books.

■ Expectations
Warmoesstraat 32 ✉ 1012 JE Amsterdam
Leather and rubber.

■ Gay Business Amsterdam
Lijnbaansgracht 210h ✉ 1016 XA Amsterdam

■ Gay Holland Mailorder
Kasteellaan 98 ✉ 7325 RS Apeldoorn ☎ 055/360 22 50
📠 055/360 22 51 💻 sales@gayholland.com
🌐 www.gayholland.com
Mail-order.

■ Gay Safe c/o Central Middelen Depot
Nieuwe Molstraat 6 ✉ 2512 BK Den Haag ☎ 070/346 56 00
📠 070/361 51 77 🌐 www.condoom.com

■ Gayway.nl Mail Order
PO Box 11186 ✉ 2301 ED Leiden ☎ 071/576 92 23
📠 071/572 19 03 🌐 www.gayway.nl
Mail order company for gays. Sell almost anything from underwear to poppers.

■ Intermale
Spuistraat 251 ✉ 1012 VR Amsterdam
☞ Bookshops (A'dam).

■ P+E Postorders (G)
PB 6102 ✉ 3002 AC Rotterdam ☎ 010/474 83 60
Leather, rubber and films.

■ SandMark (G LJ)
Postbus 76561 ✉ 1070 HD Amsterdam ☎ 020/777 81 44
🌐 www.hardgay.org/visit/sandmark
S/M articles and publications. Mail order from Netherlands.

Netherlands — Alkmaar

■ **Stichting Safe Service**
PB 3836 ✉ 1001 AP Amsterdam ☎ 020/623 37 94
📠 020/624 96 91 📧 janleer@x54all.nl
🌐 www.coc.nl/safeservice.html
Condoms and lubricants.

■ **Video Post Service (VIPS)**
PB 583 ✉ 2700 AN Zoetermeer ☎ 079/342 62 16
Mail order.

NATIONAL GROUPS

■ **Empowerment Lifestyle Services**
Troelstralaan 220 ✉ 2624 GB Delft ☎ +31(0)20-662 42 06
☎ +31(0)20-682 91 01 📧 empower@xs4all.nl
Advisors and consultants for gay and lesbian emancipation on Dutch and European levels.

■ **Hanzeplak Spanking** (G LJ) 2nd Sun in month 14-19h
Oude Holterweg 18 ✉ 7416 WG Deventer ☎ 0570/62 93 81
Spanking Club.

■ **Roze Gebaar**
PB 15511 ✉ 1001 NA Amsterdam 📠 020/470 56 31
Gay and lesbian deaf group.

■ **SAD-Schorerstichting** Mon-Thu 10-17 h
P.C. Hooftstraat 5 ✉ 1071 BL Amsterdam *(tram 2/5)*
☎ 020/662 42 06
📠 020/664 60 69 📧 helpdesk@sadschorer.nl
🌐 www.sadschorer.nl
Expert center for lesbian and gay- specific health issues.

■ **Sjalhomo**
PB 2536 ✉ 1000 CM Amsterdam ☎ 020/683 50 73
☎ 020/690 09 79
Jewish gay organization with some local branches.

■ **Stichting De Kringen**
Kanaalweg 21 ✉ 3526 KL Utrecht ☎ 030/288 86 36 (evenings)
📧 infoqkringen.nl 🌐 www.kringen.nl
With over 200 participants monthly - a group for men, women and young adults from all over the country. English spoken.

■ **VSSM-Vereniging Studiegroep Sado-Masochisme** (g LJ)
PB 3570 ✉ 1001 AJ Amsterdam ☎ 592/40 71 63
📧 info@vssm.nl 🌐 www.vssm.nl
S/M group and S/M-party organizer in all the country. Also publishes a magazine "Kerfstok" in Dutch on themes relative to S/M practices, as well as some brochures and books. Call or visit the website for details.

COUNTRY CRUISING

Route A1 (E8)
-Hengelo-Amersfoort-Amsterdam 28.9 km (Section betweeen Baarn and Huizen. De Witte Bergen. Take the exit for Soest at 28.9 km, but continue on the parallel road towards Amsterdam, until you see the sign for the motel-restaurant, turn left at top of exit road, park at the end of the short road. Walk through the area of trees and sand on the left at the end of the road.)
-21.6 km (Section near Naarden. [P] without name. In cars and adjacent bushes, mainly at night, but some daytime possibilities.)
-Amsterdam-Amersfoort-Hengelo 20.6 km ([P] without name. Section near Naarden. In cars and bushes, day and evening. Not very busy.)
-27.8 km (Section between Huizen and Baarn. De Witte Bergen. Take the exit for the motel-restaurant, turn left of top of exit road, drive over the bridge crossing the motorway, park at the end of the short road. Walk through the area of trees and sand on the left at the end of the road.)
Route N2 (E9)
-Liege-Utrecht (De Baan behind Makro, Gagel, in section Eindhoven-Best) Route A4 (E10)
-Amsterdam-Den Haag (at Amsterdam end of motorway, Nieuwe Meer, beach behind Eurohotel, days and evenings)
Route A27 (E37)
-Breda-Almere, [P] Bosberg, 90.2 km (Section near Hilversum. In cars, and in adjacent forest. Main area is in the trees ahead of [P]-area, turn left after you climb through hole in fence.)
-96.8 km (De Witte Bergen. Section Hilversum-Almere. Take exit onto A1, direction Amsterdam. Take next exit from A1 (restaurant). Turn left at stop of exit road, park at the end of the short road. Walk through the area of trees and sand on the left at the end of the road.)
Route A28 (E35)
-Amersfoort-Zwolle-Groningen, Laakse Strand (Take exit Nijkerk and follow direction Lelystad-Almere. Over the bridge, and turn into loop road which takes you under the same bridge. 2.5 km further turn left at sign Laakse Strand. At end of road you will find cruising in the big [P]; evenings. Same [P] is also good for nude beach (NG) in the daytime.)
-Strand Horst (Follow "Strand" direction. At several [P]s, left or right, is cruising. Evenings best)
-[P] Section Zwolle-Harderwijk (near Zwolle)
-[P] Glimmermade (Section Assen-Groningen, 7 km south of Groningen, off northbound carriageway) Route A58
-Breda-Tilburg [P] Leikant (near Gilze, follow pathway to wooded area, very popular)
Route A67 (E34)
-Antwerpen-Duisburg, Section in the Netherlands. Formerly E3, now with new number E34, 46.2 km, [P] Leysing (Parked cars, and a hole in the fence leading to forest area, day and night)
-[P] Oeienbosch, 15.2 km (Parked cars, and adjacent forest area, day and night)
-9.5 km, E3 Strand (Leave motorway and follow sign-boards either E3 Strand or E3 Plas. You have to pay to go in. Sunbathing, swimming, cruising. Mixed. Sunny days only.)
-[P] Beerze, 0.2 km (Parked cars, and adjacent forest. This is the last [P] in the Netherlands before the Belgian frontier. Day and night)
Route A79
-Maastricht-Aachen, [P] Keelbos
-Aachen-Maastricht, [P] Ravenbos
Route N228 (E37)
-Amersfoort-Maarn (Section to south of Amersfoort, near Leusden. Den Treek recreation area, by Trekerpunt, day and evening, before dark. Leave N228 at 4.9 km and follow the [P] signs. Use either [P] or explore woodland area.) Route A12 (E35)
-Arnheim ⇌ Utrecht, [P] 't Ginkelse Sand
-117.2 [P] Grysoord (between Arnhem and Ede, northside)
Route A1
-81.3 [P] (Southside)
-N345 [P] Bussloo (turn left at km 7.7, 9km east of Apeldoorn)
-48.4 on N31 (Southside, between Appelscha and Smilde, 15-20 h)
Route A29 Rotterdam ⇌ Bergen op Zoom
-[P] between exits Numansdorp and Oud-Beyerland
A 28 (E232) Zwolle ⇌ Meppel
-[P] between exists Ommen and Nieuwleusen

Alkmaar ☎ 072

BARS

■ **Shippertje. 'T** (B glm) Thu-Sun 21-2, Wed 22-2 h
Kanaalkade 77 ☎ 515 02 92

Alkmaar ▸ Amsterdam **Netherlands**

DANCECLUBS
▪ **De Kleine Unie** (B D glm) Sun 17-2 h
Koorstraat 12

SEX SHOPS/BLUE MOVIES
▪ **Eros** (CC glm) Mon 13-18, Tue Wed Fri 10-18, Thu 10-21, Sat 10-17 h, closed Sun
Luttik Oudorp 112 ✉ 1811 MZ *(near Chees Market)* ☏ 512 15 51
▪ **Erotheek** (g VS) 11-22 h, closed Sun
Koningsweg 17 ✉ 1811 LK ☏ 515 77 15
▪ **H. T.** (G VS lj) 11-23 h
De Laat 6 ✉ 1811 EJ ☏ 515 66 17

GENERAL GROUPS
▪ **COC-Alkmaar** (glm) Bar: 1st Fri (YG) 15-18, 1st Sat (D) & 4th Sat (D YG) 22-2.30 h
PB 1040 ✉ 1801 KA *(Bierkade 14 A)* ☏ 511 16 50

CRUISING
- Molen van Piet
- P "Geestmerambacht" (Alkmaar-Schagen, southern parking, take paths to nudist beach area, sunset and after dark, be discreet)

Almere ☏ 036

CAFES
▪ **Gay Café M'N EX** (B GLM MA WE) Fri & Sat 22-2, Sun 16-21h
Noordeinde 162 ✉ 1334 BC

CRUISING
- Zilverstrand (NU) (at Hollandse Brug, take exit Muiderzand direction Zilverstrand from Route A6. Last part of nudist area is gay)

Alphen aan de Rijn ☏ 0172

BARS
▪ **Luzern** (B glm) 12-18, Thu 12-21, Fri Sat 12-?, Sun 12-17 h.
Hooftstraat 102

Ameland ☏ 0519

HOTELS
▪ **Hotel 't Honk** (H glm)
J.W. Burgerstr. 4 ☏ 55 42 56

Amersfoort ☏ 033

BARS
▪ **WHAM** (B d GLM MA s) Wed 21-24, Sat 22-2 h
Hendrik van Viandenstraat 13ab ✉ 3811 CB ☏ 461 26 54

GENERAL GROUPS
▪ **Anti-discriminatie meldp.**
Zuidsingel 45 ☏ 472 87 28

CRUISING
- Den Treek recreation area (road Amersfoort-Maarn, near Trekerpunt)
- Plantsoen-West (between Koppelpoort and Stadthuis)
- Birkhoven (at the sand pits)

Amsterdam ☏ 020

❋ Amsterdam has, without a doubt, earned the title of the gay capital of Europe, leaving the other metropoles far behind. In no other city has the gay scene been so actively involved in combatting AIDS and its consequences. No other town has so prominently honoured its gay citizens victims of the nazis (*Gay monument*, Westermarkt/ Keizersgracht). No other city has such a liberal attitude towards prostitution and drug-consumption. So it is no wonder that Amsterdam has formed such an intensive and compact gay scene. You will find 3 gay centres on a stretch of 1.5 kilometres: *Warmoesstraat*, *Rembrandtplein* and *Kerkstraat*. Just a walk along the canals *Grachten* will give you insights into the sizzling gay life. The Dutch sociability *gezelligheid* is a guarantee for a worthwhile and friendly stay. Also one date not to forget: on April 30th the Dutch celebrate their queens birthday in the streets and thousands of gays take part in the festivities, celebrating their own personal *Koninginnedag*.

★ Ohne Zweifel: Amsterdam verdient vor allen anderen Metropolen den Titel der schwulsten Hauptstadt Europas. Keine andere Stadt war in der schwulen Szene so aktiv, um die Krankheit AIDS und ihre Folgen bekämpfen zu können. Keine andere Stadt hat ihre von den Nazis ermordeten schwulen Mitbürger so prominent geehrt (*Homomonument*, Westermarkt/Keizersgracht). Und kaum eine andere Stadt Europas sieht Prostitution und Drogengebrauch so liberal wie Amsterdam.
Kein Wunder also, daß sich in Amsterdam eine derart intensive und dichte Szene gebildet hat. Auf einer Laufstrecke von eineinhalb Kilometern liegen gleich drei schwule Zentren: *Warmoesstraat*, *Rembrandtplein* und *Kerkstraat*. Schon ein solcher Spaziergang sagt sehr viel über das brodelnde schwule Leben zwischen den *Grachten*. Dabei sorgt die niederländische *gezelligheid* dafür, daß ein Besuch in Amsterdam immer sehr übersichtlich und menschlich bleibt.
Einen Tag, den man im internationalen schwulen Jahresablauf nicht vergessen sollte: Am 30. April eines jeden Jahres feiern die Niederländer auf den Straßen des Landes den Geburtstag ihrer Königin. Und in Amsterdam feiern dann Tausende von Schwulen ihren ganz persönlichen *Koninginnedag*.

❋ Pas l'ombre d'un doute: Amsterdam est LA capitale gaie de l'Europe! Aucune autre ville n'a su combattre aussi activement et efficacement le Sida. Aucune autre ville n'a su rendre hommage aussi sincèrement aux homosexuels victimes de la discrimination et de la barbarie nazies ("Homomonument", Westermarkt/Keizergracht). Aucune autre ville d'Europe ne règle les problèmes liés à la drogue et la prostitution d'une façon si libérale. Tout ça, c'est Amsterdam! Rien d'étonnant à ce qu'Amsterdam soit la Mecque gaie d'Europe. Les hauts-lieux gais sont dans la "Warmoestraat", la "Keerkstraat" et sur le "Rembrandtplein". On peut tout faire à pied: c'est une jolie promenade le long des canaux ("Grachten"). L'hospitalité et la gentillesse des Hollandais rendront votre séjour à Amsterdam encore plus agréable. Le 30 avril est un jour important dans le calendrier gai hollandais: c'est l'anniversaire de la reine Béatrix. Tout le monde est dans la rue pour faire la fête. Les gais sont de la partie et ne sont pas en reste: eux aussi fêtent leur "Koninginnedag".

● No hay duda: Amsterdam se ha guanado, delante de las otras ciudades europeas, el título de capital gays europea. Ninguna otra comunidad gay fué y sigue siendo tan comprometida en la activa lucha contra el SIDA. Además es una de las pocas ciudades que recuerda sus victimes homosexuales durante la dictadura nazi en un sitio tan importante (*Homomonument, Westermarkt/Keizersgracht*) Amsterdam mantiene una postura muy liberal hacia la prostitución y el consumo de drogas y se ha desarollado un intenso y compacto ambiente gay. En un trayecto de 1,5 kilometros se encuentran tres

SPARTACUS 2001/2002 | **743**

Netherlands | Amsterdam

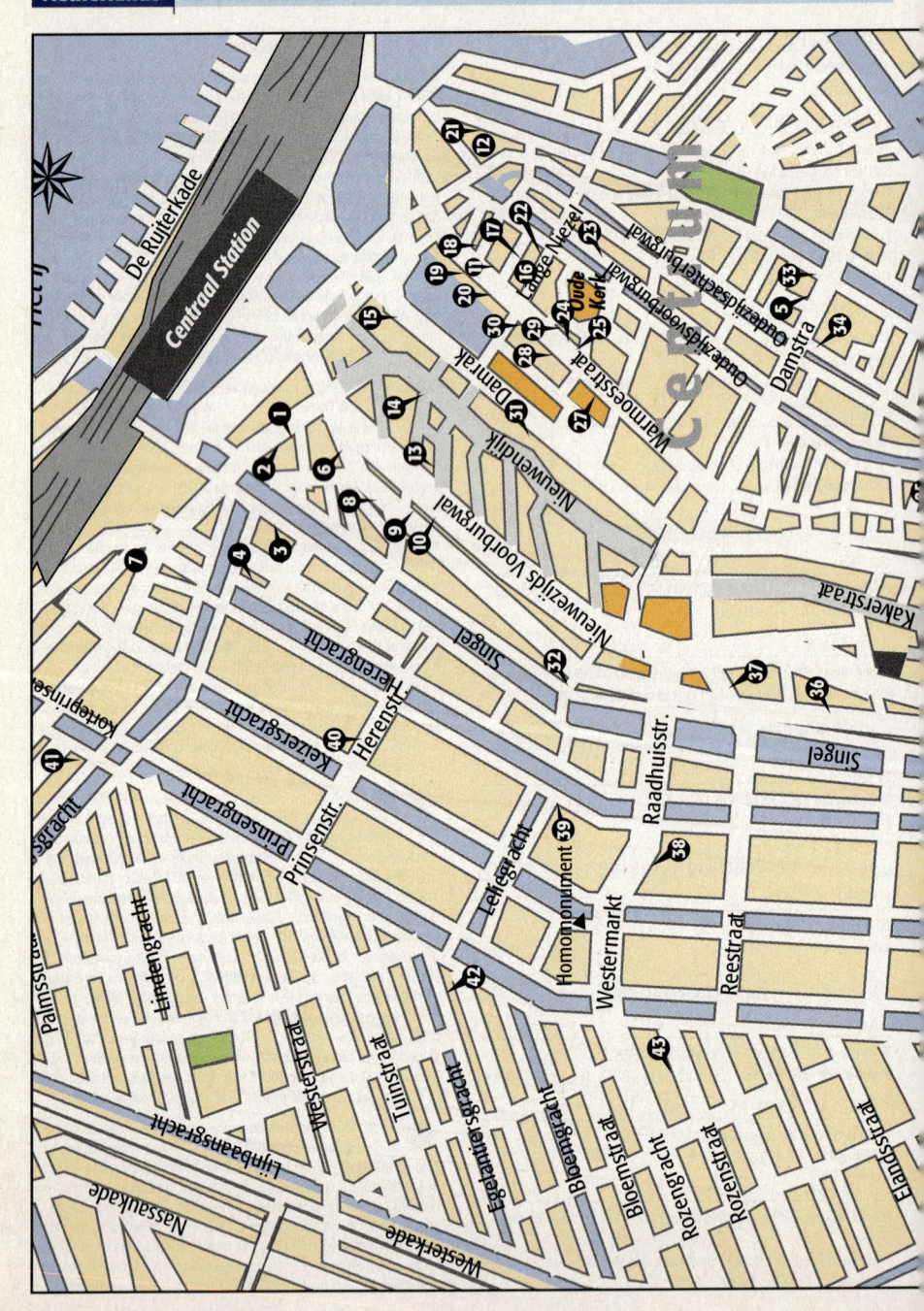

Amsterdam — Netherlands

Amsterdam

1. Alfa-Blue Sex Shop
2. William Higgins Le Salon Sex Shop
3. E & D City Amsterdam Apartments
4. New York Hotel
5. Body Manipulations
6. Club Boys for Men
7. Barangây Guest House
8. Krua Thia Restaurant
9. Man to Man Sex Shop / Boysclub 21
10. Why Not Bar / Blue Boy Bar
11. Getto Café
12. Queens Head Bar
13. Cuckoo's Nest Bar
14. The Web Bar
15. Museum of Sex
16. Boomerang Sauna
17. Centre Apartments Amsterdam
18. Stable Master Bar & Hotel
19. Mister B Leather / Fetish Shop
20. Casa Maria Bar
21. Black Tulip Hotel
22. Monico Bar
23. Anco Bar & Hotel
24. Club Jaques Bar
25. Argos Bar
26. RoB Leather / Fetish Shop
27. Cockring Danceclub
28. The Eagle Bar
29. Mister B Leather / Fetish Shop
30. Dirty Dicks Bar
31. Drake's Of LA Sex Shop
32. 't Sluisje Restaurant
33. Gay Krant Reisservice Travel Shop
34. Homodok Documentation Center
35. Upstairs Pancake House Restaurant
36. Intermale Bookshop
37. Vrolijk Bookshop
38. Rainbow Palace Hotel
39. Sunhead of 1617 Guest House
40. Maes B&B Guest House
41. Doll's Place Bar
42. Jordan Canal House Hotel
43. COC Café, Danceclub & Info Centre
44. Robin & Rik Leather / Fetish Shop
45. Thermos Day Sauna
46. Prinsen Hotel
47. Quentin Engeland Hotel
48. Hotel Quentin
49. Freeland Hotel
50. Cuts & Curls - Body & Beauty Shop
51. Back Body Leather / Fetish Shop
52. Mandate Fitness
53. Orfeo Hotel
54. Flightbrokers Travel & Transport
55. De Spijker Bar
56. Cosmo Bar
57. Thermos Night Sauna
58. Meia Meia 66 Bar
59. The Bronx Sex Shop
60. Camp Café
61. Golden Bear Hotel
62. D.O.K. Danceclub
63. Saturnino Restaurant
64. Havana Bar
65. Havana Club Danceclub
66. Exit Danceclub
67. Downtown Café
68. April Bar
69. Mantalk Fashion Shop
70. American Book Center
80. Monmartre Bar
81. Entre Nous Bar
82. Le Monde Restaurant
83. Lellebel Bar
84. IT Danceclub
85. De Krokodil Bar
86. Sluizer Restaurant
87. Orlando Hotel
88. ITC Hotel
89. Frederik Park House Hotel

any time, any place, any type

the leading gay escortservice
020-662 99 90
24 hours a day
Internet: http://www.peoplemale.com

PEOPLE™
male escorts
amsterdam

Amsterdam | Netherlands

Your Gay Way to Amsterdam

Gay News Amsterdam:
monthly gay publication in both English and Dutch. The largest bilingual gay publication in the Netherlands. With all the latest information, parties etc. For sale in the better bookshops, Hfl. 4.95 or on-line.

The Amsterdam Gay Map:
complete map with all the Amsterdam Gay Venues, completed with an extensive listing and additional information. A valuable source for every gay tourist. Available for free around town in all the gay (friendly) venues.

Gay Amsterdam On-Line:
Amsterdam's on-line Gay Resource: extensive and huge tourist guide, hotel-guide, events/ agenda, maps, general info, classifieds, and much much more. Over 4 miljon visitors each year.

For inquiries please dial +31 20 679 15 56 or fax +31 20 675 38 61

Web: http://www.gayamsterdam.com

SPARTACUS 2001/2002 | 747

Netherlands | Amsterdam

HOMO ESCORT

24 hours a day
boys in any type
cards accepted
020- 662 31 42

Call now! You'll come back to us.

CallBoys ESCORTS
Black & White

body builders, leather,
sm-masters, spanking,
students and much,
much more...

020 - 679 50 98

24 hrs, all cards acc.

AA Boys escort

A Great Time
Guaranteed by
the Very Best Boys
in Amsterdam

Home & Hotel visits
Dinner dates and
attractive rates
for the entire night

020 - 675 57 50
24 hours a day,
cards accepted

Amsterdam | Netherlands

centros gays: *Warmoesstraat, Amstelstraat/Halvemaansteeg* y *Regulierschwarsstraat*. Un paseo por esta zona da una buena impresión de la marcha de ambiente entre los *Grachten* (canales). Los holandeses son famosos por su *gezelligheit* (sociabilidad) que junto con su musica popular garantizan una estancia agradable. Hay dos fechas claves para la comunidad gay de esta ciudad: El 30 de abril se celebra el cumpleaños de la reina Beatrice, en este día la ciudad entera se convierte en una gran fiesta, con innumerables puestos en la calle, espectáculos, grupos de musica y muchisimos gays que celebran su *Koninginnedad* (día de la reina) de manera muy particular. En agosto tiene lugar anualmente la Amsterdam Pride. Uno no debería perderse la impresionante Canal Parade, donde docenas de barcos decorados fantasticamente pasan por los *Grachten*.

✖ Amsterdam merita senza dubbi il titolo di capitale gay europea. Nessun'altra *gay comunity* fa tanti sforzi nella lotta contro l'AIDS e le sue conseguenze. Inoltre non c'è un'altra città che abbia eretto un monumento per le vittime del nazismo (l'*Homo monument al Westermarkt/Keizersgracht*). E nessun'altra città è così aperta verso la prostituzione e l'uso di droghe leggere. Quindi non c'è da stupirsi che ad Amsterdam è sorto un grande ambiente gay. In un distretto lungo 3 kilometri si trovano tre centri gay: la *Warmoesstraat, l'Amstel/Halvemaansteeg* e la *Reguliersdwarsstraat*. E la *gezelligheid* (cordialità/accoglienza) olandese con la tipica musica vi dà la garanzia di un bellissimo soggiorno. Ci sono due date che bisogna segnarsi nel calendario gay: il 30 aprile quando gli olandesi festeggiano il compleanno della regina Beatrice, e la città diventa un crogiolo di mercati giganteschi, di navi, di shows spettacolari e di tanti gay che festeggiano il loro proprio *Koninginnendag* (giorno della regina). Ogni anno in agosto ha luogo l'Amsterdam Pride. Un dovere assoluto è il *Canal Parade*, una sfilata di dozzine di navi decorate in modo bello ed elegante che si svolge per i tanti canali.

PUBLICATIONS

■ **Culture and Camp**
Gerard Doustraat 160 F ✉ 1073 VZ ☏ 679 91 88 🖨 679 91 88
📧 cultureandcamp@iname.com
Monthly gay art and lifestylee magazine.

■ **Gay & Night**
PO Box 10757 ✉ 1001 ET ☏ 427 48 11 🖨 624 65 97
📧 welcome@gay-night.nl 🖳 www.gay-night.nl
Monthly free newspaper focusing on entertainment, travel, film, interviews, music and sex. Bilingual (English/Dutch) with a complete listing of gay activities. Also publisher of Gay Map G.B.A.

■ **Gay News Amsterdam**
PO Box 76509 ✉ 1070 HE ☏ 679 15 56 🖨 675 38 61
🖳 www.gayamsterdam.com
Popular free gay publication with monthly listing of events, parties, and activities. Bilingual (English and Dutch).

GAY INFO

■ **MVS-Radio** 18-21 h on FM 106.8, on cable 103.8
PB 11100 ✉ 1001 GC ☏ 620 02 47
■ **Pink Television** Mon 21-22 h on local Amsterdam TV
■ **Wilma TV** (Glm) Mon 20-21 h on local Amsterdam TV

CULTURE

■ **Museum of Sex**
Damrak 18
Entry hfl 3.75. Presentations of prostitution. homosexuality, heterosexuality and various fetishes.

■ **Stichting IHTA** (A GLM STV) Tue Thu Fri 14-17 h
1e Helmershaat 17BG ✉ 1054 CX ☏ 676 36 26 🖨 676 36 26
📧 ihta@wxs.nl 🖳 home.wxl.nl
International gay and lesbian art projects.

---

the leading gay escortservice
020 - 662 99 90
24 hours a day

home/ hotel visiting service
reliable and discreet

Visit our internet site:
www.peoplemale.com
e-mail: info@peoplemale.com
cards welcome

PEOPLE™
male escorts
amsterdam

SPARTACUS 2001/2002

Netherlands | Amsterdam

EUROPE

Amsterdam	+ 31 (20) 427 47 00
Berlin	+ 49 (30) 895 413 50
Köln	+ 49 (221) 935 66 55
London	+ 44 (171) 717 00 00
Manchester	+ 44 (161) 833 99 99
München	+ 49 (89) 447 600 50
Paris	+ 33 (1) 40 16 56 56

THE NUMBER

USA

Atlanta	+ 1 (404) 237 37 00
Chicago	+ 1 (312) 840 90 00
Dallas	+ 1 (214) 760 77 07
Ft. Lauderdale	+ 1 (954) 454 66 00
Houston	+ 1 (713) 523 89 89
Los Angeles	+ 1 (213) 625 33 66
Miami	+ 1 (305) 654 77 77
New York	+ 1 (212) 355 10 00
San Francisco	+ 1 (415) 392 84 00
Seattle	+ 1 (206) 548 15 48

Lowest prices for your

LIVE TALK ● BULLETIN BOARDS

GROUP CONVERSATIONS ● SERVICES

Amsterdam | Netherlands

INTERNATIONAL & OUTCALLS

10 years of reliability

escorts

PEOPLE

☏ 020- 662 999 0
24 hours a day, cards welcome

http://www.boysescort.com
extensive interactive website available

Carefully selected boys in any type, selected on a.o. looks and personality

The Leading Gay Escortservice
gay owned & gay operated
Reliable & Discreet
Home/ Hotel visiting service

The largest collection of boys in the country

SPARTACUS 2001/2002

Netherlands | Amsterdam

THE CUCKOO'S NEST

EUROPE'S LARGEST PLAYROOM

NIEUWEZIJDS KOLK 6
AMSTERDAM
PHONE :
020-6271752

trance X-press

smartproducts
aphrodisiacs

visit the other site at
www.trance-xpress.com

Amsterdam | Netherlands

Every first weekend of August

AMSTERDAM GAY PRIDE

The famous and outrageous Canal Parade will be held on the first Saturday of August. Organized by the Gay Business Amsterdam.

www.amsterdampride.nl

SPARTACUS 2001/2002 | 753

Netherlands Amsterdam

ARGOS

sun-thu 22-3
fri/sat 22-4

Warmoesstraat 95
1012 HZ AMSTERDAM
tel.   + 31 20 622-6595
fax.   + 31 20 627-1024
e-mail: leather@argosbar.demon.nl

TOURIST INFO

■ **VVV Amsterdam Centraal Station** 9-17 h
Stationsplein 10 ✉ 1012 AB ☎ 06 340 340 66 625 28 69

BARS

The Amsterdam Bars often close one hour later during the summer months and on Fri/Sat night.
Die Öffnungszeiten der Amsterdamer Bars, Cafés etc. beziehen sich auf gewöhnliche Wochentage. Normalerweise sind sie an den Wochenenden, und meist auch in den Sommermonaten, eine Stunde länger geöffnet.
En été, les bars amstellodamois ferment une heure plus tard; de même, vendredi et samedi tous les clubs et bars ferment une heure plus tard.
Los horarios de apertura de los locales en Amsterdam se refieren a los días laborales. Los fines de semana y durante los meses de verano están abierto normalmente una hora mas.

■ **Amstel Taveerne** (! B G OS S) Sun-Thu 16-1, Fri Sat 15-2 h
Amstel 54/Halvemaansteeg ✉ 1017 AB ☎ 623 42 54
One of the oldest Dutch bars.

■ **Anco Bar** (B BF f G H LJ MA) 9-22, happy hours 16-18 h
Oudezijds Voorburgwal 55 ✉ 1012 EJ ☎ 624 11 26

■ **April** (! A B GLM MA VS) Sun-Thu 14-1, Fri Sat 14-3 h
Reguliersdwarsstraat 37 ✉ 1017 BK ☎ 625 95 72
Modern, trendy. Live TV-Connection with "Exit". Renovated, with spinning bar. Happy hour Mon-Sat 18-19h, Sun 18-20h.

■ **Argos** (! AC B DR G LJ) Sun-Thu 22-3, Fri Sat -4 h
Warmoesstraat 95 ✉ 1012 HZ (Near central station) ☎ 622 65 95
Oldest leather bar in Europe and the only one with a host. Very friendly staff, check for special events.

■ **Biecht. De** (B G MA TV S) 21-4 h
Kerkstraat 346 ✉ 1017 JA ☎ 420 80 74

■ **Café de Huyschkaemer** (AC B CC d F GLM MA) 15-1, 15-3 h weekend
Utrechtsestraat 137 ✉ 1017 VM ☎ 627 05 75
International cuisine, not expensive.

■ **Café de Steeg** (! AC B G S) Sun-Thu 17-1, Fri Sat 16-3 h
Halvemaansteeg 10 ✉ 1017 CR ☎ 620 01 71

■ **Café Lellebel** (AC B glm MA OG STV TV) Mon-Thu 21-3, Fri Sat 20-4, Sun 20-3 h
Ultrechtsestraat 4 ✉ 1017 VN (tram 4, 9 and 14 stop Rembrandt-Square) ☎ 427 51 39
Drag-Travestie Café with shows, karaoké and other in-house specialities.

■ **Camp Café** (B BF CC F G MA N OS) Breakfast 8-12, 12-1h, (meals -10-23.30h)
Kerkstraat 45 ✉ 1017 GB ☎ 622 15 06
Daily menu, Dutch cuisine, more popular in the evenings.

■ **Casa Maria** (B G lj MA OS tv) 12-1, Fri Sat -3 h
Warmoesstraat 60 ✉ 1012 JG ☎ 627 68 48
This bar - where drinks are cheap - is popular with the Gay community. Snacks on Sun from 15 h.

■ **Club Jacques** (AC B DR LJ MA) Sun-Thu 20-3, Fri Sat 21-4 h
Warmoesstraat 93 ✉ 1012 HZ ☎ 622 03 23
Best after 24 h.

■ **Cosmo Bar** (AC B CC G MA N) 24-3, Fri Sat -4 h
Kerkstraat 42 ✉ 1017 GM (Trame 1/2) ☎ 624 80 74

■ **Cuckoo's Nest** (AC B DR G lj MA OS VS) Sun-Thu 13-1, Fri Sat 13-2 h
Nieuwezijds Kolk 6 ✉ 1012 PV ☎ 627 17 52
Best in the afternoon. A good place to start a horny day.

Amsterdam | Netherlands

BOYS CLUB 21

Sexy Boys!

Why waste words? Our quality speaks for itself !

Spuistraat 21
Amsterdam
Phone:
(020) 6228828

Netherlands Amsterdam

GETTO
FOOD & DRINKS
Cocktails, home cooking and more
Cocktail Lounge 17-19:00 (Cocktail Happy Hour)
Wed/Sat: 16-01.00 Sun: 16-24.00 Tues: 19-01.00 (women only) Mon: Closed
WARMOESSTRAAT 51, 1012HW AMSTERDAM tel: 421 51 51

■ **Dirty Dicks** (B DR G LJ p) Mon-Thu 22-3, Fri/Sat 22-4h
Warmoesstraat 86 ✉ 1012 JH ☎ 627 86 34
■ **Doll's Place** (B glm MA N) 21-3, Fri Sat 21-4 h
Vinkenstraat 57 ✉ 1013 JM ☎ 627 07 90
■ **Eagle. The** (B G LJ MA) 22-4, Fri Sat 22-5 h
Warmoesstraat 90 ✉ 1012 JH ☎ 626 86 34
■ **Entre Nous** (B G MA WE) 20-3, Fri Sat -4 h
Halve Maansteeg 14 ✉ 1017 CR ☎ 623 17 00
■ **Gaiety** (B G MA YG) 16-1, Fri-Sat -2 h
Amstel 14 ✉ 1017 AA ☎ 624 42 71
Nice atmosphere. Popular with young people.
■ **Getto** (A AC B CC F GLM lj MA VS) Tue 19-1, Wed-Sat 16-1, Sun -24 h, closed Mon
Warmoesstraat 51 ✉ 1012 HW ☎ 421 51 51
Tue women only, Thu bingo, Fri-Sun DJs, Happy hours 17-19 h. 1st Mon/month Karaoke night (5 Hfl.). Also restaurant with international cuisine, also vegetarian dishes. Prices from Hfl 18.50.
■ **Havana** (! AC B D GLM s YG) 16-1, Fri-3, Sat 14-3, Sun 14-1h
Reguliersdwarsstraat 17-19 ✉ 1017 BJ ☎ 620 67 88
Elegant.
■ **Krokodil Bar. De** (B G OG s) 16-2 h
Amstelstraat 34 ✉ 1017 DA ☎ 626 22 43
Oldest bar in Amsterdam. Sun afternoon very popular (!). Pub atmosphere.
■ **Meia Meia 66** (AC B G MA N OS s) 14-1, Fri Sat -3 h
Kerkstraat 63 ✉ 1017 GC ☎ 623 41 29
■ **Milord** (B G MA) 18-1, Fri Sat -3 h
Amstel 102 ✉ 1017 DA ☎ 622 83 35
■ **Mix** (AC B GLM MA) Sun-Thu 20-3, Fri Sat -4 h
Amstel 50 ✉ 1017 AB ☎ 622 52 02

■ **Monico Bar** (B glm MA N r) 12-2 h
Lange Niezel 15 ✉ 1012 GS ☎ 623 74 41
■ **Montmartre** (! B GLM lj s YG) 17-1, Fri Sat 16-3 h
Halvemaansteeg 17 ✉ 1017 CR ☎ 620 76 22
Beautiful wallpaintings by Eppo Doeve.
■ **Music Box. The** (AC B CC G MA R) 21-3, Fri-Sat -4 h, Mon closed
Paardenstraat 9 ✉ 1017 CX *(Near Rembrandtplein)* ☎ 620 41 10
Hustler bar.
■ **Night Life** (B G R) 20-3, Fri Sat -4 Sun 17-3 h
Paardenstraat 7 ✉ 1017 CX ☎ 420 92 46
Hustler Bar.
■ **Queens Head. The** (B G lj MA tv s) 17-1, Fri Sat 16-3 h
Zeedijk 20 ✉ 1012 AL ☎ 420 24 75
Bingo night on Tue hosted by Dusty, English pub decoration.
■ **Reality** (B G MA) Sun-Thu 20-3, Fri Sat -4 h
Reguliersdwarsstraat 129 ✉ 1017 BL ☎ 639 30 12
Popular meeting place for black men and their friends.
■ **Shako. Le** (AC B G MA N OS) 22-3, Fri Sat -4 h
's Gravelandseveer 2 ✉ 1011 KM *(opposite Amstel Taveerne)* ☎ 624 02 09
Very social talkcafé, friendly owner. Popular on Tue.
■ **Soho** (AC B d GLM s YG) Sun-Thu 20-3, Fri Sat -4h
Reguliersdwarsstraat 36 ✉ 1017 BM *(near the flower market)* ☎ 330 44 00
Classy bar on two floors. 1st floor: British pub, 2nd floor American style. Happy hour Mon-Thu 24-1h.
■ **Spijker. De** (B DR f G lj MA vs) 13-2, Fri Sat -3 h
Kerkstraat 4 ✉ 1017 GL ☎ 620 59 19
Western and leather bar.

APRIL AMSTERDAM
sunday till thursday
2 pm - 1 am
friday & saturday
2 pm - 3 am
REGULIERSDWARSSTRAAT 37

Amsterdam | Netherlands

REGULIERSDWARSSTRAAT 5H
1017 BJ AMSTERDAM-C
TEL: 020-6390102

Saturnino

SIMPLY THE FINEST ITALIAN FOOD

SATURNINO

OPEN FROM 12.00-24.00 O'CLOCK

■ **Man-to-Man** (CC DR G MA VS) 11-1 h
Spuistraat 21 ✉ 1012 SR *(near Central Station)* ☎ 625 87 97
■ **William Higgins Le Salon** (AC CC G VS YG) 9-24h, Sun 12-24h
Nieuwendijk 20-22 ✉ 1012 ML ☎ 622 65 65
Over 16 years in the William Higgins tradition. Store with books, magazines, videos, cinema, peep shows, etc. Gay and leather movies as well as video cabins, many with added ventilation.

CINEMAS

■ **Filmtheater Desmet** (B GLM MA WE)
Plantage Middenlaan 4A ✉ 1010 DD ☎ 627 34 34
Call for dates of Gay art films at WE.

ESCORTS & STUDIOS

■ **AA Boys Escort** (CC) 0-24 h
☎ 675 57 50
■ **Call Boys** (CC G lj)
☎ 679 50 98
■ **City Boys** (G)
☎ 400 44 55
■ **Homo Escorts** (G)
☎ 662 31 42
■ **Michael's Boys Escort** (CC G) 0-24 h
☎ 618 18 24
High quality long established escort service.
■ **People male escorts** (CC G LJ) 0-24 h
☎ 662 99 90
Very well-known, long established gay escort service. Home and hotel visits.

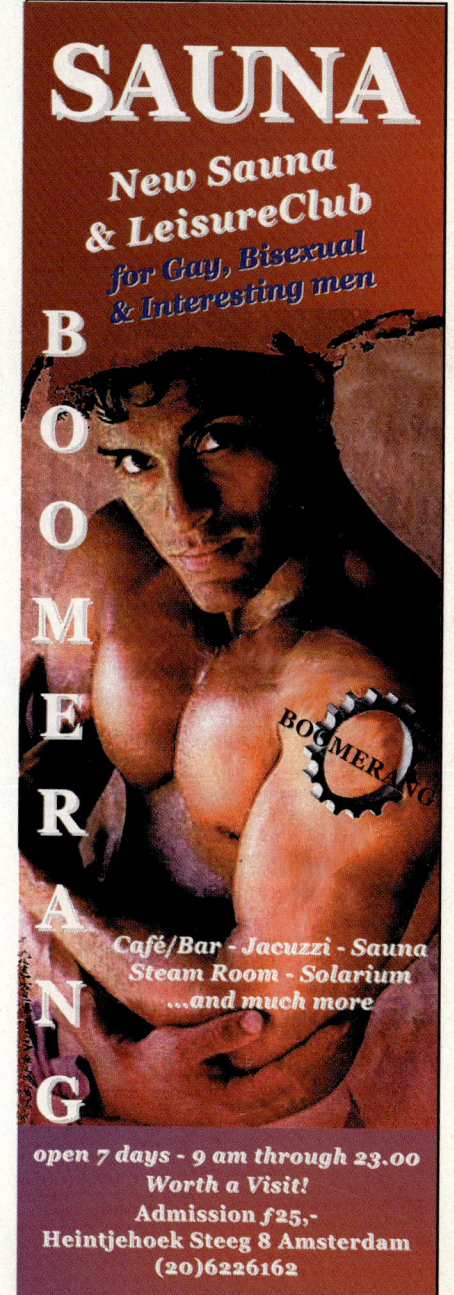

SAUNA

New Sauna & LeisureClub
for Gay, Bisexual & Interesting men

BOOMERANG

Café/Bar - Jacuzzi - Sauna
Steam Room - Solarium
...and much more

open 7 days - 9 am through 23.00
Worth a Visit!
Admission ƒ25,-
Heintjehoek Steeg 8 Amsterdam
(20)6226162

Netherlands — Amsterdam

INTER@CTIVE @S EVER!!

drake's

NO.1 GAY

STORE | CINEMA

☎ +31 20 6279544

DAMRAK 61 AMSTERDAM
(200 MTRS. SOUTH OF CENTRAL STATION)

WILLIAM HIGGINS' LE SALON

Amsterdam's no.1 **sEX**

- TOYS
- VIDEOS
- MAGAZINES

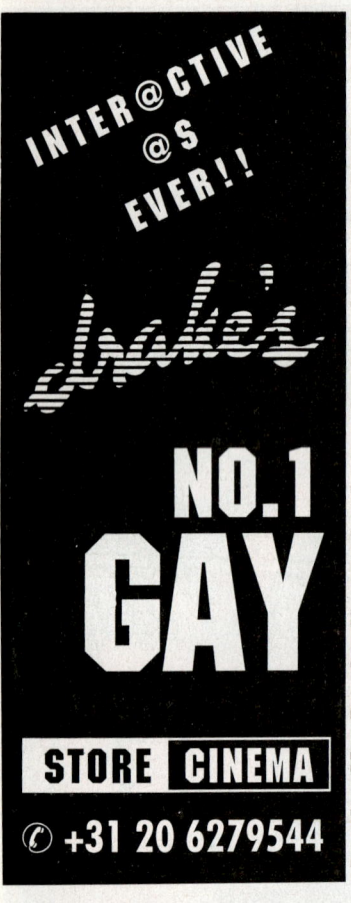

NIEUWENDIJK 20-22
(CLOSE TO CENTRAL STATION)

HOUSE OF BOYS

■ **Boys. The** (G STV) Sun-Thu 17-3, Fri Sat -4 h
Amstel 140 ✉ 1017 AE ☎ 622 80 36

■ **Boysclub 21** (AC B CC G SNU VS msg) 12-2, Fri Sat -3 h
Spuistraat 21 ✉ 1012 SB (above Man to Man) ☎ 622 88 28
International boys, 4 standard rooms, 1 VIP room with spa.

■ **Club Boys for Men** (AC B CC G msg P R SNU VS) 15-2 h
Spuistraat 44b ✉ 1012 TV ☎ 638 15 12
Nice, polite student types, relaxed atmosphere in a cosy and clean place.

■ **Try It** (B CC G msg N p R VS) 13-24 h
Kuiperstraat 86 ✉ 1074 EN ☎ 662 70 91
Small establishment in cellar out of the city centre.

■ **Why Not** (AC B CC G msg R SNU VS) 12-2 h
N.Z. Voorburgwal 28 ✉ 1012 RZ ☎ 627 43 74
The oldest and largest house of boys in Amsterdam. 15-20 boys on premises, more available on portfolio.

SAUNAS/BATHS

■ **Boomerang** (B CC DR f G SA SB SOL VS WH) 9-23 h
Heintje Hoeksteeg 8 ✉ 1012 GR (alley opposite to police station, just off Warmoestraat) ☎ 622 61 62
New sauna opened in summer 99, busy early in the morning. Mostly young crowd. Tue & Wed underwear party.

■ **Modern** (b DR G OG SA SOL VS) 12-18 h, closed Sun & holidays
Jacop van Lennepstraat 311 ✉ 1053 JJ ☎ 612 17 12
Especially for older gays.

■ **Thermos Day** (! AC B CC DR F G MA msg OS PI s SA SB SOL VS WH) 12-23, Sat & holidays -22 h, Sun 11-23h
Raamstraat 33 ✉ 1016 XL (Tram 5/2/1-Leidseplein) ☎ 623 91 58
Huge sauna on 5 floors with à la carte restaurant, roof terrace, sun beds, beauty salon, hair dresser. Very clean and friendly, free condoms avalaible.

■ **Thermos Night** (AC b CC DR f G MA SA SB VS WH YG) 23-8, Sat -10 h
Kerkstraat 58-60 ✉ 1017 GM (Tram 5/2/1-Keizergracht) ☎ 623 49 36
Spacious and clean sauna in the heart of the city.

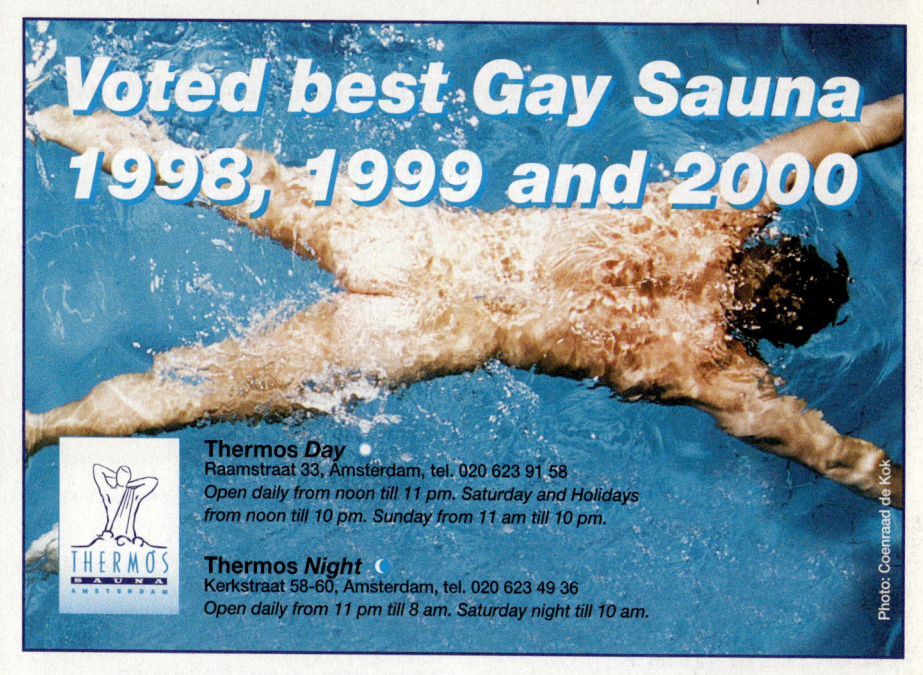

Amsterdam | **Netherlands**

Voted best Gay Sauna 1998, 1999 and 2000

THERMOS SAUNA AMSTERDAM

Thermos *Day*
Raamstraat 33, Amsterdam, tel. 020 623 91 58
Open daily from noon till 11 pm. Saturday and Holidays from noon till 10 pm. Sunday from 11 am till 10 pm.

Thermos *Night*
Kerkstraat 58-60, Amsterdam, tel. 020 623 49 36
Open daily from 11 pm till 8 am. Saturday night till 10 am.

Photo: Coenraad de Kok

FITNESS STUDIOS
■ **Mandate Gay Gym** (AC b G SA SOL WO) 11-22, Sat 12-18, Sun 14-18 h
Prinsengracht 715 ✉ 1017 JW *(Trams 1/2/3)* ☏ 625 41 00
Day ticket Hfl 20.

BODY & BEAUTY SHOPS
■ **Body Manipulation** (CC glm MA) Mon- Wed 12-18, Thu -21, Fri Sat -19, Sun 17 h
Oude Hoogstraat 31 ✉ 1012 CD *(near Nieuwmarkt)* ☏ 420 80 85
Piercing studio. Many languages spoken.
■ **Cuts and Curls Hairstyling** (A CC GLM LJ MA) Mon, Tue, Wed 10-20, Thu -21, Fri 10-19, Sat 10-16.30 h
Korte Leidsedwarsstraat 74 ✉ 1017 RD *(near Ryksmuseum)*
☏ 624 68 81
Hairstylist and barber for rough types.
■ **Thermos Beautysalon** (CC glm msg) 12-20 h
Raamwarstraat 5 ✉ 1016 XL *(entrance trough Thermos sauna day or from the street)* ☏ 623 91 58
Hairstyling, body and facial cosmetics, waxing, massage.

BOOK SHOPS
■ **American Book Center. The** (CC g) Mon-Fri 10-20, Thu -22, Sun 11-19 h
Kalverstraat 185 ✉ 1012 XC *(Near Muntplein)* ☏ 625 55 37
English language gay section downstairs, literature, magazines, travel books.
■ **Intermale** (G) 10-18, Thu -21 h, closed Sun
Spuistraat 251 ✉ 1012 VR ☏ 625 00 09
Wide selection of gay literature, magazines and non-porn videos.

Boekhandel Vrolijk
Gay & Lesbian Bookshop

Behind the palace of the Queen you 'll find two floors filled with gay books, magazines, video's, travelguides, postcards, erotica, and more!

Or visit our virtual store at
http://www.xs4all.nl/~vrolijk

Bookshop Vrolijk, Paleisstraat 135, 1012 ZL, Amsterdam tel. +31(0)20 6235142 fax 6383807

SPARTACUS 2001/2002 | 763

Netherlands — Amsterdam

In the ♥ of Amsterdam:
We're More Than a Bookshop with an Attitude!

We carry a big collection of gay & lesbian fiction and non-fiction and … loads of juicy mags for fags!

The American Book Center
Kalverstraat 185, 1012 XC Amsterdam - tel: 020-6255537
Check out Pink Camp, the gay page on www.abc.nl

■ **Boekhandel Vrolijk** (GLM) Mon-Fri 10-18, Thu -21, Sat 10-17 h
Paleisstraat 135 ✉ 1012 ZL *(near the Royal Palace)* ☎ 623 51 42
Gay books in many languages, soft porn magazines, art films. Also mail order.

■ **Zwart Op Wit** (glm) 9.30-19, Sat -18, Sun 12-18 h
Utrechtsestraat 149 ✉ 1017 VM ☎ 622 81 74
Small gay section (Dutch and English).

CONDOM SHOPS

■ **Condomerie Het Gulden Vlies** 10-18 h
Warmoesstraat 141 ✉ 1012 JB *(city center)* ☎ 6274174
For all sorts, colors, tastes and sizes of condoms as well as lubricants.

FASHION SHOPS

■ **Man Talk** (G) 10-18, Thu -21 h, closed Sun
Reguliersdwarsstraat 39 ✉ 1017 BK ☎ 627 25 25
Big selection of underwear and swimwear.

LEATHER & FETISH SHOPS

■ **Black Body** (AC CC G LJ) Mon-Fri 10-18.30, Sat 11-18 h, closed Sun
Lijnbaansgracht 292 ✉ 1017 RM *(Tram 6/7/10 stop Rijksmuseum/Spregelstraat)* ☎ 626 25 53
Specialized in rubber. More than 500 rubber clothing models in stock. Also large leather collection. Call for catalogue. Also mail order.

■ **Demask** (A g LJ TV) 10-19, Thu -21, Sun 12-17 h
Zeedijk 64 ✉ 1012 MB ☎ 620 56 03
Rubber and leather shop with gallery.

■ **Mister B Leather & Rubber** (A CC G LJ) Mon-Wed Fri 10-18.30, Thu -21, Sat 11-18, Sun 13-18 h
Warmoesstraat 89 ✉ 1012 HZ *(City center, near central train station)* ☎ 422 00 03
Leather and rubber wear, toys, tatoos and piercings. Magazines and cards. Also mail order www.misterb.com

■ **RoB** (CC G LJ) Mon-Fri 11-18.30, Sat -17 h, closed Sun
Weteringsschans 253 ✉ 1017 XJ ☎ 625 46 86
Handmade leather and rubber clothing. Very good reputation. Toys, videos, cards. Also mail order. Catalogue for hfl 25.

■ **RoB Accessories** (CC G LJ) 13-19, Sat -20, Sun 14-18 h
Warmoesstraat 32 ✉ 1012 JE *(2 min from station)* ☎ 420 85 48
2nd RoB shop in Amsterdam.

■ **Robin and Rik Leermakers** (CC G) Mon 13-18.30 Tue-Sat 11-18.30 h
Runstraat 30 ✉ 1016 GK ☎ 627 89 24
Hand-made own leather collection.

TRAVEL AND TRANSPORT

■ **Flightbrokers** (CC GLM) Mon-Fri 9-20, Sat 10-17 h
Lange Leidsedwarsstraat 96 ✉ 1017 NM *(near Leidseplein, Tram 1/2/5)* ☎ 420 28 14 ☎ 420 28 17 ✉ info@flightbrokers.nl
🖳 www.flightbrokers.com
Travel agent and internet place.

AMSTERDAM
BV MISTER B LEATHER RUBBER TATTOO PIERCING
WARMOESSTRAAT 89 NL 1012 HZ AMSTERDAM
P ••31(0)20 4220003 F ••31(0)20 6276868
E-MAIL: misterb@mrb.nl WEBSITE: www.mrb.nl

Mr B LEATHER & RUBBER

BERLIN
MISTER B GMBH LEATHER RUBBER
NOLLENDORFSTRASSE 23 D 10777 BERLIN
P ••49(0)30 21997704 F ••49(0)30 21997705
E-MAIL: misterb@mrb.nl WEBSITE: www.misterb.com

Amsterdam | **Netherlands**

CUTS and Curls
HAIRSTYLING

A salon with an atmosphere and interior like you've never experienced (the Village People would be jealous). Check it out yourself. Three remarkable professionals, who work without appointment, no matter if your visit is for a great crew cut, long hair styling, colouring or a total new you. Just walk in and check out your/our possibilities.

The new longer opening hours are very convenient:
Monday   from 10. til 20.   Tuesday   from 10. til 20.
Wednesday   from 10. til 20.   Thursday   from 10. til 21.
Friday   from 10. til 19.   Saturday   from 10. til 16.30.
appointments only mon-fri between 09.00 and 10.00 (if possible)

Please note that near closing time, we might not be able to help you anymore. To avoid disappointments try to be in on time!
CUT or UNCUT, WE WOULD LIKE TO WELCOME YOU TO OUR SALON.
KORTE LEIDSEDWARSSTRAAT 74 · 1017 RD AMSTERDAM
TEL: 020 62 46 88 1 · FAX 020 42 13 49 8 · info@cutsandcurls.A2000.nl

---

EUROPE'S INTERNATIONAL GAY BOOKSTORE
INTERMALE

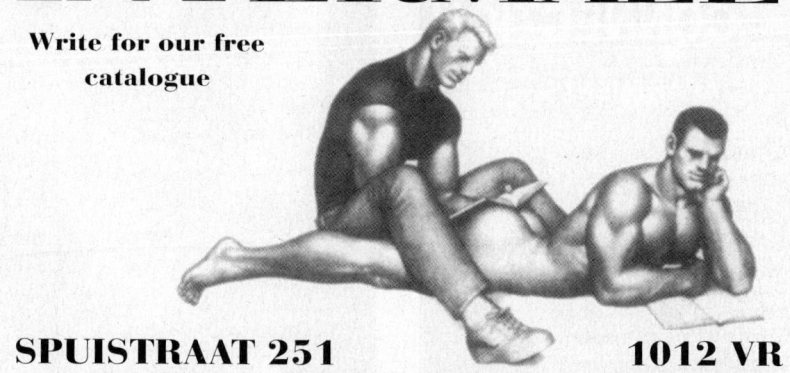

Write for our free catalogue

SPUISTRAAT 251   **1012 VR**
AMSTERDAM
telephone: (020) 6250009 fax: (020) 6203163
internet: http://www.intermale.nl e-mail: info@intermale.nl
open: mon.-sat. 10.00 AM - 6.00 PM (thurs. until 9.00 PM)

Netherlands — Amsterdam

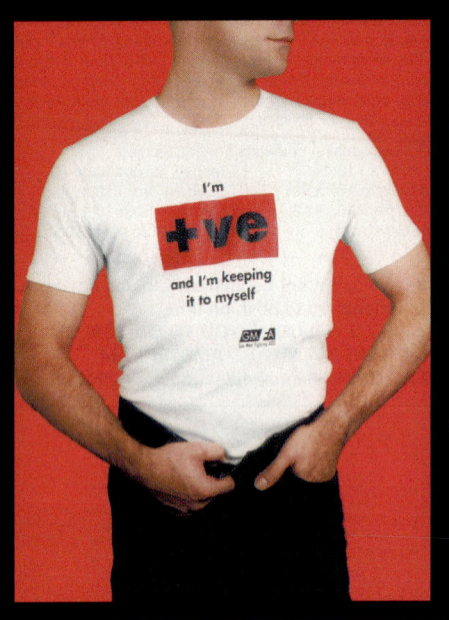

Lots of HIV+ men don't tell

I'm +ve and I'm keeping it to myself

GMFA's campaigns and actions are designed, planned and executed by positive, negative and untested volunteers.
To volunteer for GMFA write, phone or email:
Unit 43, Eurolink Centre, 49 Effra Road, LONDON, SW2 1BZ.
020 7738 6872. newvol@gmfa.demon.co.uk
www.demon.co.uk/gmfa
Registered Charity no. 1076854

GMFA
Gay Men Fighting AIDS

AMSTERDAM CONNECTION

APARTMENTS

Furnished Apartments available in the Gay Capital of Europe - Amsterdam

Situated in the centre of the city and only minutes away from your favourite bars.

Apartments include shower, WC, cable TV, Music and Kitchen facilities and own key. Apartments available now from HFl 110- per night

For information & Booking Call David or Eric

+(31) 20 625 74 12

SPECIALISTS IN RUBBER !!!
CALL, FAX OR E-MAIL FOR CATALOGUE

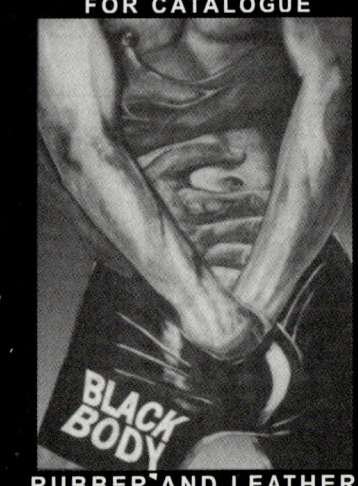

BLACK BODY

RUBBER AND LEATHER
LIJNBAANSGRACHT 292 (OPPOSITE RIJKSMUSEUM)
1017 RM AMSTERDAM THE NETHERLANDS
TEL + FAX : + 31 - (0)20- 6262553
MON - FRI 10:00 TO 18:30 SAT 11:00 TO 18:00
E-MAIL : WELCOME@BLACKBODY.NL

Amsterdam | **Netherlands**

amsterdam ANCO
hotel bar

Welcoming leathermen from all over the world

O.Z. Voorburgwal 55
1012 EJ Amsterdam
tel (31 20) 624 1126
fax (31 20) 620 5275
Info@ancohotel.nl
www.ancohotel.nl

FREELAND ◦ HOTEL

**MARNIXSTRAAT 386
1017 PL AMSTERDAM
CENTRAL (LEIDSENPLEIN) TRAMS 1·2·5**

- ALL ROOMS WITH SHOWER-TOILET OR BATH
- COLOUR TV (FREE)
- ALL ROOMS WITH DIRECT DIAL TELEPHONE
- YOUR OWN KEYS
- FULL DUTCH BREAKFAST
- ALL CARDS WELCOME
- RESERVATION 020 622 75 11
- GUESTS 020 627 75 78
- FAX 020 626 77 44

Netherlands — Amsterdam

RoB 25
LEATHERRUBBERTWISTEDGEAR

RoB of Amsterdam / Weteringschans 253/ 1017 XJ Amsterdam
www.rob.nl / info@rob.nl / phone: 020-625.46.86 / fax: 020.627.32.20

■ **Gay Krant Reisservice** Mon 14-18, Tue-Fri 10-18, Sat 10-16 h
Kloveniersburgwal 140 ✉ 1012 CW (*city center*) ☎ 421 00 00
🖨 620 62 17 🖳 travel@gaykrant.nl 🖳 www.gaykrant.nl/reizen
Travel agent and De Gay Krant shop.

VIDEO SHOPS
■ **Gay Rental Video** 13-1 h
N. Z. Voorburgwal 51 ✉ 1012 RD ☎ 622 52 20

HOTELS
■ **Amsterdam House Hotel** (b BF CC glm H MA)
's Gravelandveer 3-4 ✉ 1011 KM ☎ 624 66 07 🖨 624 13 46
🖳 amshouse@euronet.nl 🖳 www.amsterdamhouse.com
Central location near Rembrandt plein. All rooms en-suite, with TV, phone, safe, VCR. Hotel provides own key. Rates per room from hfl 175 (bf incl.).

■ **Black Tulip** (BF CC G H IJ MA)
Geldersekade 16 ✉ 1012 BH (*close to Central Station*)
☎ 427 09 33 🖨 624 42 81 🖳 www.blacktulip.nl
All rooms with private bath, phone, minibar/fridge, safe. All rooms with sling and bondage hooks. Hotel provides additinal leather and S/M equipment, own key. Rates from Euro 95,–

AMSTERDAM
hotel Orfeo
an all gay guest house

- GAY AND CENTRAL
- PARKING FACILITIES NEARBY
- FRIENDLY ATMOSPHERE
- FULLY LICENSED BAR
- LAUNDRY SERVICE
- CREDIT CARDS ACCEPTED
- OWN KEYS
- DAILY RATES
- SPECIAL WEEKLY RATES IN WINTER, EXCEPT CHRISTMAS AND EASTER
- DIRECT CALLS FROM ROOMS
- ALL ROOMS WITH PRIVATE SAFE AND COLOR TV

LEIDSEKRUISSTRAAT 14
1017 RH AMSTERDAM
HOLLAND
FAX (NOT FOR INFORMATION): ++ 31 (0) 20 620 23 48
TEL (RESERVATIONS ONLY): ++ 31 (0) 20 623 13 47

BLACK TULIP

A LEATHER HOTEL LIKE NEVER BEFORE

- exclusively gay, located in the leather district
- 2 minutes from central railway station, other public transport, restaurants, shops and bars
- stylish 16 th century building on a canal

WITH LUXURY

- all rooms with private bathroom (some with a whirlpool), TV-VCR, direct dial telephone/voice mail, minibar/fridge, tea/coffee making facility and safe deposit box • your own keys • convenient check out times and breakfast hours
- friendly lounge and patio

AND LUST

- all rooms with a sling, bondage hooks • beautifully crafted fun equipment: different pieces per room, such as St. Andrew's cross, bondage chair, stocks, metal cage • special rooms: XL guestrooms with additional fun equipment • kinky videos available • boots rental service for the light traveller if requested in advance

- Rates: Euro's 95–170 including breakfast buffet •major credit cards accepted • public parking garages in neighbourhood

Geldersekade 16
1012 BH Amsterdam
the Netherlands
tel. +31(0)20-427.0933 fax +31(0)20-624.4281
www.blacktulip.nl

Netherlands — Amsterdam

■ **Freeland Hotel** (BF CC G H)
Marnixstraat 386 ✉ 1017 PL ☎ 622 75 11 (reservations)
☎ 627 75 78 (for guests) 📠 626 77 44
Most rooms en-suite, all with color TV, telephone, full bf.

■ **Golden Bear. The** (A b BF CC GLM lj H MA N) Reception: 8-23 h
Kerkstraat 37 ✉ 1017 GB (central, Line 1/2/5-Pinsengracht)
☎ 624 47 85 📠 627 01 64 📧 hotel@goldenbear.nl
🖥 www.goldenbear.nl
Comfortable. Friendly staff. Rates hfl 105-215 incl bf. All rooms with tel, tv, video with/without shower/WC.

■ **Hotel Anco** (B BF CC f G H lj MA) Bar 9-22 h
Oudezijds Voorburgwal 55 ✉ 1012 CJ ☎ 624 11 26 📠 620 52 75
📧 info@ancohotel.nl 🖥 www.ancohotel.nl
Very near leather bars. Own key. Dormitory NLG 70,- single rooms NLG 105,- double rooms 150,- all with shared shower / WC. Studio NLG 195,-. All rooms with cable TV and 24 hours gay videos.

■ **Hotel Orlando** (B CC g H)
Prinsengracht 1099 ✉ 1017 JH (near Rembrandtplein / tram 4 stop Utrechtsestraat) ☎ 638 69 15 📠 625 21 23
Luxury hotel in a 17th century canal house. Centrally located (near the Amstel river). 5 beautifully decorated rooms with bath/shower, tv, mini-bar and tel. Friendly staff. Own key for guests. Single hfl. 130-200, double 160-275 incl. bf.

■ **Hotel Prinsen** (B BF glm OS)
Vondelstraat 36-38 ✉ 1054 GE ☎ 616 23 23 📠 616 61 12
📧 manager@prinsenhotel.demon.nl
🖥 www.prinsenhotel.demon.nl
Central location. All rooms with phone, shower, WC, TV, some with bath, balcony and safe. Rates single hfl 200, double 250.

ITC HOTEL

Centrally located in historical canal house close to main gay areas - CTV, telephone and private safe in all rooms - your own keykards - breakfast buffet till noon - lounge and bar

»ITC Hotel has the prettiest location of any of the gay-oriented hotels in Amsterdam.«
(Fodor's Gay-Guide to Amsterdam)

PRINSENGRACHT 1051
1017 JE   AMSTERDAM
res.:   +31 20 6230 230
fax: +31 20 624 5846

web site: http://www.itc-hotel.com

e-mail:office@itc-hotel.com

Gay Guesthouse drakes

- Modern rooms with shower
- In room colour TV w/ gay adult movies
- Direct dial telephones
- Private safe in each room
- Private key
- Free city gay map
- English speaking staff

Fax or Call for reservations
Most credit cards accepted

Damrak 61
1012 LM AMSTERDAM
TEL 00-31-20-638-2367
FAX 00-31-20-420-0518

WEBSITE:
www.drakes.nl
EMAIL :
drakes@drakes.nl

NOT just a HOTEL .....
in the center of Amsterdam

IGTA

ENJOY THESE GREAT
BED & BREAKFAST IN AMSTERDAM

Maes B&B

Relax in a cosy home ambience in residential townhouse. In historical city centre, a short walk from the Central Station, Museums and shops. Near all Gay nightlife and sauna's.

Ken Harrison and Vladimir Melnikov
Herenstraat 26   Amsterdam
Tel:+31 20 427 5165/ Fax:+31 20 427 5166

Email:maesbb94@xs4all.nl
http://www.xs4all.nl/~maesbb94

SUNHEAD OF 1617

Stay in a charming 400 year old canal house along Amsterdams's most beautiful canal the Herengracht. We offer fabulous central location and cosy, spacious rooms all with en sulte bathroom/shower/wc, fridge, microwave, tea/coffee facilities, cable TV. Own keys. See for yourself on our webside www.sunhead.com

To reserve send e-mail: carlos@sunhead.com
or call +3120 626 18 09

Sunhead of 1617, Herengracht 152, 1016 BN Amsterdam

BED & BREAKFAST barangây

Quiet rooms in colonial style, coffee/tea making facilities. TV, fridge, radio alarmclock. We serve a wonderful breakfast in your room.

Right in the old centre, you'll find shops, bars, canals and more just around the corner.
Only 5 min. walk from the nearest gay scene.

WIMMO & GODWIN
DROOGBAK 15

Tel. +31 20 777 99 15
Tel. +31 62 504 54 32
Fax +31 20 770 62 99
www.BARANGAY.nl
barangay@chello.nl

Your tropical hide-away just 3 min. from Central Station

Netherlands Amsterdam

Hotel Quentin

20 rooms with a beautiful view on the canals of Amsterdam

The Hotel is situated in the heart of Amsterdam, close to all the gay and lesbian bars, clubs and events.
We are a small friendly hotel providing rooms with/without bath.
All rooms have colour-cable TV and direct dial telephone.
You have your own private key.
To insure that you have an enjoyable stay, our bar and reception is 24 hours open with drinks, snacks and information.
We have a nice garden.

**Hotel Quentin, Leidsekade 89
1017 PN Amsterdam
Tel.: 0031 - 20-6262187
Fax.: 0031 - 20-6220121**

Prices: single-rooms start at 67,50 hfl

---

clinic2go
it's a peace of mind thing

Glad I got the all clear before I came away this time. Last year I got all confused over the Spanish for 'discharge'...

Why worry about getting, or passing on sexually transmitted infections? Treat yourself to regular check ups and leave the worry behind. Your sexual health - it's a peace of mind thing.

Hotel Orlando

A ROOM OF ONE'S OWN

Designhotel in 17th century canal house in the heart of Amsterdam. 5 rooms each tastefully appointed. Prinsengracht 1099 1017 JH Amsterdam - Tel. (020) 638 69 15

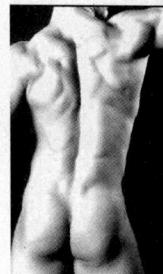

WEST END HOTEL

right in the gay centre of Amsterdam

Kerkstraat 42 - 1017 GM Amsterdam - Reservations: +31 (0) 20 624 80 74

HOTEL THE GOLDEN BEAR

(formerly Hotel Unique)

The central, comfortable, friendly hotel you're looking for

tel: +31 20 624 4785
fax: +31 20 627 0164
e-mail: hotel@goldenbear.nl
www.goldenbear.nl

Kerkstraat 37
1017 GB AMSTERDAM

Netherlands Amsterdam

RAINBOW PALACE HOTEL

Near the Queens Palace
All Comfort

Rooms with and without shower
All the rooms with radio, TV, telephone and minibar
Your own key

since 1958

Your hosts Cor and Bram

Raadhuisstraat 33
1016 DC Amsterdam
Tel.: 31-(0) 20 625 43 17
Fax: 31-(0) 20 420 54 28

TONY STAR WELCOMES YOU TO

THE STABLEMASTER HOTEL
HOTEL • APARTMENTS • BAR

Rooms with cable TV,
coffee-making facilities.
Two minutes from leather bars.
Warmoesstraat 23
1012 HT Amsterdam
Phone   00-3120-625-0148
FAX   00-3120-624-8747

STABLEMASTER BAR
JACK-OFF PARTIES

Mon+Thu 20.00 - 01.00
Fri + Sat 20.00 - 02.00
Sun 20.00 - 01.00
Tue + Wed closed
Admission Hfl. 10,-

Warmoesstraat 23
1012 HT
Amsterdam

■ **Hotel Quentin** (B BF CC glm H MA OS)
Leidsekade 89 ✉ 1017 PN *(Tram 1/2/5/11-Leidseplein)*
☎ 626 21 87   626 22 01 21

Centrally located, 30 mins. by bus to the airport. All rooms with TV and phone, some with bath. Hotel provides own key. Rates from single hfl 67.50-110, double 110-240, triple 165-260. Recommended.

The Jordaan Canal House

"Amsterdam's worst kept secret"

An enchanting 17th century canal house, exclusively gay and simply unique. Centrally located in the historic quarter of the Jordaan, known as "The Garden of Amsterdam", the gay centre and most visitor attractions are all within a pleasant short walk. The Jordaan Canal House is excellently appointed, in a quiet location, enjoying local shopping, restaurants and weekly markets. Rates from Hfl 195 per room per night, all inclusive. All rooms with private facilities. Contact Hans Tel: (0031) 20. 6201545. Fax: 6385056. E-mail Hanspluygers@csi.com

Amsterdam Netherlands

■ **Hotel Quentin Engeland** (b BF CC g H MA OS)
Roemer Visscherstraat 30 ✉ 1054 EZ ☎ 689 23 23 685 31 48
Downtown location, 15 km to the airport. Hotel with garden. Rooms en suite/shared facilities. Single hfl 85-145, double 110-175, triple 170-240.
■ **Hotel Sander** (B BF CC glm H MA OS WO)
Jacob Obrechtstraat 69 ✉ 1071 KJ ☎ 662 75 74 679 60 67
📧 htlsandr@xs4all.nl www.xs4all.nl/~htlsandr/
All rooms en-suite, with TV, phone, radio, safe. Rates single hfl 145-185, double 185-225, triple 260-320.
■ **ITC Hotel** (B BF CC GLM H MA)
Prinsengracht 1051 ✉ 1017 JE ☎ 623 02 30 624 58 46
📧 office@itc-hotel.com www.itc-hotel.com
Nice hotel centrally located. Late bf, personal attention and own front door keys.
■ **New York Hotel** (B BF CC GLM H)
Herengracht 13 ✉ 1015 BA ☎ 624 30 66 620 32 30
16 min. by train from the airport. Quiet downtown location, 10-20 min from local gay bars. All rooms with priv. bath, TV and phone. Rates single hfl 150, double 200-250 (bf incl.) Garages availabe for 35. Recommended.
■ **Orfeo** (B BF CC G H)
Leidsekruisstraat 14 ✉ 1017 RH ☎ 623 13 47 620 23 48
Rooms with telephone (direct calls). Single Hfl 90-195, double 120-195 (incl. bf). Weekly rate incl. 1 night free. Special off season rates. Running for 30 years now.
■ **Rainbow Palace Hotel** (BF g H MA)
Raadhuisstraat 33 B ✉ 1016 DC ☎ 626 70 86 ☎ 625 43 17
 420 54 28
Centrally located. All rooms with TV, radio, phone, minibar, partly with shower. Hotel provides own key. Rates from hfl 90.
■ **Stable Master Hotel** (B f G H LJ MA VS) Bar 20-1, Fri-Sat 20-2 h, closed Tue-Wed
Warmoesstraat 23 ✉ 1012 HT ☎ 625 01 48 624 87 47
Double (Hfl 185) and single rooms with colour TV, fridge, own key. Apartments available from Hfl 200.
■ **Westend** (AC BF CC G H) 24h
Kerkstraat 42 ✉ 1017 GM ☎ 624 80 74 622 99 97
📧 westendhotel@yahoo.com
Newly renovated gay hotel with private and shared bathrooms.

GUEST HOUSES

■ **Barangây B&B** (BF CC G lj)
Droogbak 15 ✉ 1013 CG *(3 min from Central Station)*
☎ (062) 504 5432 770 62 99 📧 barangay@chello.nl
 www.barangay.nl
Bed and breakfast.
■ **Chico's Guesthouse** (bf GLM H)
St. Willibordusstraat 77 ✉ 1073 VA ☎ 675 42 41 675 42 41
■ **Drake's Guest House** (CC G H VS)
Damrak 61 ✉ 1012 LM ☎ 638 23 67 420 05 18
📧 drakes@drakes.nl www.drakes.nl
■ **Frederik Park House** (A BF CC glm H OS)
Frederiksplein 22 ✉ 1017 XM *(central, Tran 4-Frederiksplein)*
☎ 420 77 26 ☎ 06/29 06 04 60 620 78 79
📧 frederik.park.house@wxs.nl
Hotel guesthouse with rooms 40 m² from Hfl 200 incl. bf. Different decorations. Quiet, next to a park with bars and restaurants at the corner. Personal attention and insight guide to Amsterdam.
■ **Jordaan Canal House** (BF CC G H MA OS)
Eglantiersgracht 23 ✉ 1015 RC ☎ 620 15 45 638 50 56
📧 Hanspluygers@csi.com
Canal side quiet and cosy hotel in the old city centre. All rooms with bathrooms, tv and hifi. Advance booking advised. Rates from hfl 195 per room per night.

Prinsen✭✭✭ Hotel

★ The recently renovated »Prinsen« Hotel in the »Vondelstraat« street offers the friendly atmosphere of a three-star hotel, where personal contact and service are a matter of course.

★ All our hotel rooms feature direct dual telephone, television, hair dryer and safe.

★ The lively »Leidseplein« Square with bars, discos, shops, the Casino, the National Museum and the Van Gogh Museum are at a stone's throw and most gay-bars and saunas within 500 m distance.

**sgl. from Hfl 200,-
dbl. from Hfl 250,-**

all credit-cards accepted

**Vondelstraat 36 - 38
1054 GE Amsterdam
Tel. 020 - 616 23 23
Fax 020 - 616 61 12**

e-mail:
manager@prinsenhotel.demon.nl

homepage:
http://www.prinsenhotel.demon.nl

Netherlands Amsterdam

E & D CITY APARTMENTS AMSTERDAM
1015 AA Singel 34
2 person apartments for the leather boy and his friend.
Minimum stay 3 nights.
Info and reservations:
Tel.: 00 31 20 624 73 35 • Fax: 00 31 20 428 48 30
nicehew@worldonline.nl

AMSTERDAM - from hfl 40 -
complete offer see page Germany/Berlin
overnight accomodation service
· about 750 beds · more than 28 cities ·
bed & enjoy breakfast
central booking office Berlin **+49-30-236 236 10** 4:30-9:00 pm local time
Fax +49-30-23623619 · info@ebab.com · www.ebab.com

■ **Maes Bed & Breakfast** (BF CC GLM MA)
Herenstraat 26 ✉ 1015 CB ☎ 427 51 65 🖷 427 51 66
💻 maesbb94@xsall.nl 💻 www.xs4all.nl/~maesbb94
In the Jordaan area. All rooms are nicely decorated and en suite. Non-smoking establishment. Rates hfl 125-175.

■ **Sunhead of 1617** (BF CC GLM H MA)
Herengracht 152 ✉ 1016 BN ☎ 626 18 09 🖷 626 18 23
💻 carlos@sunhead.com 💻 www.sunhead.com
Central, but quiet location. Mostrooms with shower/WC, all with tv, fridge, coffee/tea facilities and microwave. Own key. Rates Nlg 235-255 for a double, two room suite ngl 355 (rates exclude 5% city tax).

■ **Truelove** (CC G H M)
Prinsen Straat 4 ✉ 1015 DC ☎ 624 1881 🖷 320 6897
💻 truelove@zonnet.nl 💻 www.truelove.nl

APARTMENTS

■ **Amsterdam Connection** (G)
Lijnbaansgracht 252 ✉ 1017 RK ☎ 625 74 12 🖷 624 8257
Comfortable apartments all with shower, TV, radio, kitchenette and own key. Rates start at hfl 110.

■ **Amsterdam House** (AC CC glm H MA)
Amstel 176a ✉ 1017 AE ☎ 626 25 77 🖷 626 29 87
Self catering apartments and house boats. Rates from Hfl 125 one person, double 225, triple 285.
US Reservations: ☎ (904) 677-5370 or ☎ (800) 618-1008 (toll-free), FAX (904) 672-6659.

■ **Centre Apartments Amsterdam** (G H LJ MA)
Heintje Hoeksteeg ✉ 1012 GR ☎ 627 25 03 ☎ 06 537 13452 (mobile) 🖷 625 11 08 💻 caa-gd@wxs.nl
💻 www.gay-apartments-amsterdam.nl

Fully furnished self catering apartments with tv, hifi, video (to rent) and safe. Rates: 1-3 people Hfl 295, studios 245 (1-2 people), extra bed 50.per person.

■ **E&D City Apartments Amsterdam** (G H LJ)
Singel 34 ✉ 1015 AA ☎ 624 73 35 🖷 428 48 30
💻 nicehew@worldonline.nl
Centrally located in the Jordaan quarter. 2 people apartments for the leather man and his friend. Minimum stay 3 nights.

PRIVATE ACCOMMODATION

■ **Enjoy Bed and Breakfast** (BF G H MA) 16.30-21 h
Nollendorfplatz 5, 10777 Berlin - Germany ☎ +49 (30) 236 236 10
🖷 +49 (30) 236 236 19 💻 info@ebab.com 💻 ebab.com
Accommodation sharing agency. All with shower & bf. Price 20-25 Euro.

■ **Gelerse Neel B&B** (BF CC GLM H MA)
Gelerse Kade 75 ✉ 1011 EL *(neat central station)* ☎ 422 33 38
🖷 422 35 66 💻 gelneel@hotmail.com

■ **Rubens B&B**
Rubensstraat 38 bv ✉ 1077 MS ☎ 6629187 🖷 6629187
💻 info@rubensbb.com 💻 www.rubensbb.com
All guest rooms are all non-smoking, as is the rest of our apartment.

GENERAL GROUPS

■ **Gay and Lesbian Association (GALA)** (GLM)
PO Box 158 15 ✉ 1001 NH ☎ 616 19 79
Organises factory parties and other gay festivals.

■ **Gay and Lesbian Studies** (GLM)
Oude Achterburgwal 185 ✉ 1012 DK *(Dam Square)* ☎ 525 22 26
🖷 525 26 14 💻 hekma@pscw.uva.nl
💻 www.pscw.uva.nl/internationalschool

776 SPARTACUS 2001/2002

Amsterdam — Netherlands

■ **Homogroep VSSM**
PB 3570 ✉ 1001 AJ ☎ 420 21 78

FETISH GROUPS

■ **Leather Pride Netherlands** (DR G LJ)
PO Box 2674 ✉ 1000 CR ☎ 422 37 37 🖷 422 37 37
🖳 info@leatherpride.nl 🖳 www.leatherpride.nl
Organise leather/rubber/fetish parties for gay men.

■ **Master Terry's SM Society & School**
Pienemanstraat 46 ✉ 1072 KV *(Tram 25)* ☎ 671 06 82
S&M instruction for gay & bisexual males only.

■ **MS Amsterdam**
PO Box 35 40 ✉ 1001 AH 🖳 www.msamsterdam.org
Monthly meeting every first Sun in the month at Café "West-Indie".

HEALTH GROUPS

■ **Aids Fonds** Helpline Mon-Fri 14-22h
Keizersgracht 390-392 ✉ 1016 GB ☎ 626 62 669
☎ 0800 022 22 20 (Helpline) 🖷 627 52 21
🖳 aidsfonds@aidsfonds.nl
🖳 www.aidsfonds.nl

■ **A.I.D.S.-Infolijn** Mon-Fri 14-22 h
☎ 06/022 22 20

■ **Fight for Life Foundation**
Sarphatiestraat 310 ✉ 1017 ET ☎ 627 50 93

■ **HIV-Café 4 US**
Rozenstraat 14 ✉ 1016 NX ☎ 623 40 79

■ **HIVnet Computernetwork for HIV and Aids**
Van Limburg Stirumstraat 22A ✉ 1051 BB ☎ 684 19 69
🖷 681 15 04

■ **HIV-Vereniging Nederland** Mon, Wen, Fri 13-16, Tue, Thu 20-22.30, Sat 20-0.30
1e Helmersstraat 17 ✉ 1054 CX ☎ 616 01 60 🖷 681 15 04
🖳 www.hivnet.org
Association that safeguards the interests of people who are carriers of hiv (medical, welfare, juridical, social, assistential, representational). Saturday HIV-Café.

■ **Stichting Duc d'Alf**
PB 1331 ✉ 1000 BH ☎ 618 25 95

■ **Venereal disease Clinic GG & GD** Mon-Fri 8-10.30, 13.30-15.30 h
Groenburgwal 44 ☎ 555 58 22 ☎ 020/555 52 70 🖷 555 57 51
Free testing for EC citizens. AIDS testing anonymous if wanted NOT free of charge: Nieuwe Achtergracht 100

HELP WITH PROBLEMS

■ **HIV-Plusline** Mon Wed Fri 13-16, Tue Thu 20-22.30 h
☎ 685 00 55
Assistance service.

■ **Project Jongens Prostitutie** (G YG)
N. Z. Voorburgwal 38 ☎ 555 54 62 ☎ 020/555 52 90

RELIGIOUS GROUPS

■ **CHJC, Society of Christian gay's and lesbians** (GLM)
Pusbus 14722 ✉ 1001 LE ☎ (06) 53 23 45 16 🖳 www.chjc.nl

SPECIAL INTEREST GROUPS

■ **Gay Bridge Club** (B GLM MA) Wed 19-midnight
Lijnbaansgracht 185 ✉ 1016 XA ☎ 420 6988
🖳 www.gaybridge.nl

■ **Gay Garden Club. The** (G)
PB 15672 ✉ 1001 ND ☎ 688 12 43 🖷 688 12 43
🖳 ancion@wolmail.nl 🖳 www.gaygardenclub.nl
Europe's only pink club for green fingers. Monthly meeting in Holland, trips abroad, lectures....

SPORT GROUPS

■ **Amsterdam Stetsons. The** (GLM) Mon 19.30-22.30, Tue 20-23 h
c/o The Cruise Inn, Zeeburgerdijk 271 ☎ 419 98 51 ☎ 693 57 54
Country and western line dancing and instruction.

■ **Gay Swim Amsterdam** (GLM)
☎ 625 20 85

■ **Tijgertje** (glm)
PB 10521 ✉ 1001 EM ☎ 673 24 58
Sports organization including self defense, (karate), basketball, wrestling, joga, fitness-training, aerobics, badminton, volleyball and swimming.

SWIMMING

☞ Zandvoort

CRUISING

-Vliegenbos, Meeuwenlaan (AYOR) (Amsterdam Noord)
-Vondelpark (very popular at night)
-Oosterpark
-Sarfatipark (busy at night)
-Nieuwe Meer. Take tram 2 and stop before the last stop then walk direction north. popular in summer, daytime
-Oosterdok (next to main post office by C.S.)
-Bilderdijkpark (busy at night)

WEEKEND — **HOLIDAY**

TAKE SUPERBLY FURNISHED

APARTMENTS OR STUDIOS

Absolutely private and just five minutes from
Central Railway Station and around the corner of
the Warmoesstraat Leather Bars.

CENTRE APARTMENTS
AMSTERDAM
HEINTJE HOEKSSTEEG

Corr.: P.O. Box 15889 · 1001 NJ Amsterdam,
The Netherlands
Telephone: +31 - 20 - 627 25 03 · Fax: + 31 - 20 - 625 11 08
Mobile: +31 - 6 - 537 134 52
E-mail: caa-gd@wxs.nl
Website: http://www.gay-apartments-amsterdam.nl

Netherlands — Apeldoorn ▸ Best

Apeldoorn ☎ 055

BARS
■ **Schouw. De** (AC B d DR GLM MA OS WE) Fri 22-2, Sat 23-4, Sun 14-19, Mon 20-24 h (doors close at 21.30 h)
Spadelaan 8 ✉ 7331 AL ☎ 541 70 35
Special sex parties. Call for dates.

SEX SHOPS/BLUE MOVIES
■ **Christine Le Duc** (CC g VS) Mon-Fri 10-22, Sat -17.30 h
Asselsestraat 131 ✉ 7311 EJ ☎ 522 51 04
■ **Cinema Shop Station** (DR g MA VS) Mon-Sat 10-18 h
Stationsdwarsstraat 20 ✉ 7311 NW *(near station)* ☎ 522 11 81
■ **Station** (DR g MA r VS) 10.30-18 h
Stationsdwarsstraat 20 ✉ 7311 NW ☎ 522 11 81
■ **Tutti Frutti** (B DR f G MA SA VS) 10-24, Sun 13-24 h
Marktstraat 15 ✉ 7511 LH *(near market place)* ☎ 522 42 73
Shop, sauna, movie place.

GENERAL GROUPS
■ **COC-Apeldoorn** (GLM)
PB 15 ✉ 7300 AA ☎ 533 22 32
Call for info on activities.

CRUISING
-Oranjepark

Arnhem ☎ 026

BARS
■ **Brazzon** (B GLM YG) 17-1 Thu-Sun -2 h
Nieuwstraat 66 ✉ 6811 HX ☎ 370 34 60
■ **Café Noir** (B GLM)
Coehoornstraat 8 ✉ 6811 LA ☎ 442 80 72
HIV+ café on Wed.
■ **Diva** (B GLM) Mon Wed 17-1 Thu Sun -2 h. closed on Tue
Rodenburghstraat 63 ✉ 6811 HX ☎ 370 34 84
■ **Entre Nous** (AC B d f GLM lj STV TV) Fri-Sun 22-4 h
Sweerts de Landasstraat 65 ✉ 6814 DB ☎ 445 06 52
■ **Yentl** (A B d GLM MA S) Tue-Sun 17-1, Thu-Sat -4 h, closed Mon
Nieuwe Keyebergseweg 158 ✉ 6811 BV *(Next to theatre)*
☎ 370 42 03
Bar and art gallery.

CAFES
■ **Café Spring** (B f GLM MA OS) Wed-Sat 16-2, Sun-Tue 16-1 h
Bovenbeekstraat 5 ✉ 6811 CV *(near central station)* ☎ 442 50 36
■ **Keldercafé Dwars** (AC B GLM MA s) Wed-Sat 22-4 h
Sweerts de Landasstraat 65 ✉ 6814 DB *(behind central station)*
☎ 445 06 52
In the basement of the club Entre Nous.

SEX SHOPS/BLUE MOVIES
■ **Christine Le Duc** (CC g VS) Mon-Fri 10-22, Sat 10-17.30 h, closed Sun
Walstraat 55 ✉ 6811 BD ☎ 445 65 77

GENERAL GROUPS
■ **COC-Midden Gelderland** (GLM) Wed Fri 13-18, Thu 13-18, 19-21 Sat 13-17 h
Postbus 359 ✉ 6800 AJ ☎ 442 31 61 ✉ mail@diverzo.nl
💻 www.diverzo.nl
Advice, information and shop for gays and lesbians. Call for info on activities.

HEALTH GROUPS
■ **Aidsoverleggroep**
c/o GG & GD, Broerenstraat 55 ✉ 6811 EB

CRUISING
-Park Sonsbeekpark (near westside entrance at Zijpendaalseweg, evenings and nights)
-Rozendaalsebos
-Railway station

Assen ☎ 0592

CRUISING
-Asserbos 15-20 (city park, directly behind ice stadium)
-Parking space Snelweg (Assen-Noord/Assen-West, by small petrol station off Assen-West)
-A28 (E35) Assen-Groningen (parking space Glimmenade, 7km south of Groningen, off north-bound carriageway)
-De Moere (NU) (12 km southeast of Assen, lake on west-side, 14-20 h)

Baarle Nassau ☎ 013

SEX SHOPS/BLUE MOVIES
■ **Fun House** (g VS) 10-22 h
Nieuwstraat 22 ✉ 5111 CW ☎ 507 91 62

Beek (Ubb) ☎ 024

SAUNAS/BATHS
■ **Azzurra** (AC B DR F G SA SB snu SOL VS WH YG) 14-24, Fri-Sat -2 Sun -24 h, closed on Wed
Kerkberg 22 ✉ 6573 DN *(Near Nijmegen, Bus 6, behind the church)*
☎ 684 18 08
Sauna frequented by a young crowd (20-35).

Bergen aan Zee ☎ 072

CRUISING
-Beach near Pile 36 and nude area between piles 31 and 32

Bergen op Zoom ☎ 0164

BARS
■ **Café Dwars** (B GLM MA s) Mon-Thu 20-2, Fri 17-2.30, Sat 20-2.30, Sun 16-2 h
Engelsestraat 14 ✉ 4611 RR ☎ 23 08 16
■ **COC-Café** (B D GLM MA) Fri-Sat 22-2.30, Last Sun/month 16-22 h
Blokstallen 4 ✉ 4611 WB *(close to Gevangenpoort)* ☎ 25 42 35
Bar Disco. Special parties are organised on a regular basis.

GENERAL GROUPS
■ **COC-Bergen op Zoom** (GLM)
PB 590 ✉ 4600 AN ☎ 25 42 35
Call for info on activities.

Best ☎ 0499

BARS
■ **Manus** (B G MA) 11.30-2 h
Nieuwstraat 92

CRUISING
-De Baan (behind Makro, Gagel)
-Route E9 (Eindhoven/Best)

Den Haag ▶ Ede | **Netherlands**

fides GAY SAUNA

sauna - 2 stoombaden
non stop video - bar
Veenkade 20
2513 EG Den Haag
070 - 346 39 03

■ **Bellevue** (g H)
Stationsweg 80 ✉ 2515 BP ☎ 380 17 51
Rooms per hour.

GENERAL GROUPS
■ **COC-Haaglanden** (GLM) Bar: (B d GLM MA) Wed 17-24, Thu 21-2, Fri Sat -1.30 h, Sat: women only
Scheveningseveer 7 ✉ 2514 HB *(next to the Queen's palace "Noordeinde")* ☎ 365 90 90 🖥 coc@dehaag.demon.nl 🖥 www.coc.nl

HEALTH GROUPS
■ **AIDS Spreekuur** Tue Thu 19-21 h
Van Beverningstraat 134 ✉ 2582 VL ☎ 354 16 10

CRUISING
-Het Haagsebos-Leidsestraatweg (AYOR R) (near station)
-De Scheveningsebosjes-Jacobsweg (safe, between the trees, very busy)

Den Helder ☎ 0223

BARS
■ **Chez Nous** (B D G) 22-2 Fri Sat -4 h closed Mon Tue
Emmastraat 105 ✉ 1782 PC ☎ 61 44 45

GENERAL GROUPS
■ **COC-Kop von Noord-Holland** (GLM)
Vismarkt 5 ✉ 1781 DA ☎ 61 87 38
Cal for info on activities.

SWIMMING
-Strandslag Droogeweert (G NU) (by the small firewatch tower in the dunes)

CRUISING
-Kennedypark

Deventer ☎ 0570

SAUNAS/BATHS
■ **Ero Visie** (B D R f G MA SA SOL VS) Mon-Fri 11-23, Sat -19 h
Grote Overstraat 24 ✉ 7411 JC *(Near Brink Market Place)*
☎ 64 91 76
New sauna with sex shop just opened in April 00.

GENERAL GROUPS
■ **COC-Ijsselstreek** (GLM)
Assenstraat 151 ✉ 7411 JZ ☎ 61 91 49
Call for info on activities.

Doetinchem ☎ 0314

BARS
■ **Mi Ami** (B D glm) Thu-Sat 20-2, Sun 16-2 h
Dr Hubernoodtstraat 50 ✉ 7001 DX ☎ 32 68 78

GENERAL GROUPS
■ **Stichting Homoseksualiteit Achterhoek** (GLM)
PO Box 8031 ✉ 7000 DE ☎ 36 08 11

Domburg ☎ 0118

APARTMENTS
■ **Jonathan Appartments** (H)
Domburgseweg 30 ✉ 4357 NH *(500 m from village/200 m from beach)* ☎ 58 37 10 📠 58 37 10

Dordrecht ☎ 078

CAFES
■ **Nickolson** (B g) Sun 21-1 h
Voorstraat 426 ✉ 3311 CX ☎ 613 37 88

GENERAL GROUPS
■ **COC-Dordrecht** (GLM)
PB 934 ✉ 3300AX *(Dolhuisstraat 4)* ☎ 613 17 17
Call for info on activities.

CRUISING
-De Merwelanden (near Spaarbekken)
-Weizigtpark (close to central station)

Ede ☎ 0318

BARS
■ **Feestje. 'T** (B D GLM MA) Fri Sat 21-3, Sun 21-2h
De Halte 7A ✉ 6711 NZ *(Centre)* ☎ 69 44 51

SPARTACUS 2001/2002 | **781**

Netherlands — Eindhoven ▸ Enschede

Eindhoven ☎ 040

BARS
■ **Charlies Pub** (AC B d F g MA OS) Wed-Sun 17-2 h
Dommelstraat 36 ✉ 5611 CL *(round the corner from De DansSalon)*
☎ 243 88 04
■ **Club Funki Bizniz** (B G MA) 19-2, Fri-Sat 14-2, Sun 16-2 h, Mon closed.
Stratumsedijk 35
■ **Nephews** (AC B d f glm MA OS p s) 21-4 h
Stratumsedijk 14 ✉ 5611 ND *(Bus 6/7/8 Stratumsedijk)*
☎ 211 80 13
Micky Mouse decoration.
■ **Pêcheur. Le** (AC B D f GLM YG) 21-2 h Fri Sat -4 h closed Tue
Stratumsedijk 37A ✉ 5611 NB ☎ 211 91 03
■ **Queen's Pub** (B GLM MA) 20-2, Sun 16-2 h, closed Thu
Lambertusstraat 42 ✉ 5615 PH ☎ 244 25 06
■ **Shakespeare** (B G MA) 20-2 h
Kloosterdreef 108
■ **Tolerant** (B glm MA) 22-2 h, closed on Mon & Thu
Stratumsedijk 103A *(15 min from the station)* ☎ 212 59 19
■ **Vagevuur** (B BF DR G LJ MA P WE)
Kanaaldijk Noord 11 ✉ 5612 LD ☎ 244 27 44

CAFES
■ **Café Boschdijk** (B GLM MA) Tue-Sun 12-2 h
Boschdijk 229 ☎ 243 91 42

DANCECLUBS
■ **Danssalon. De** (AC B D GLM MA s stv) Sun 21.30-3h
Stationplein 4 ✉ 5611 AB ☎ 245 63 77
Black Party every last Sun in the month. Dress code: Black rubber and leather.

SEX SHOPS/BLUE MOVIES
■ **Christine Le Duc** (CC g VS) Mon-Fri 10-22, Sat 10-17.30 h, closed Sun
Willemstraat 33 ✉ 5611 HB ☎ 243 90 81

SAUNAS/BATHS
■ **Jaguar** (AC b f DR G MG OS s SA SB VS) 12-24, Sun 13-20 h
Ledeganckstraat 1 ✉ 5615 KC ☎ 251 12 38
Sauna with a terrace frequented by a mixed age crowd.
■ **Royal** (B F DR G H PI SA SB SOL VS WH) Mon-Thu 12-24, Fri-Sun 12-8 h
Stratumsedijk 23f ✉ 5611 NA *(8 min from station)* ☎ 211 08 40
Renovated and clean sauna. Also hotel.

HOTELS
■ **Hotel Royal** (BF CC G H)
Stratumsedijk 23F ✉ 5611 NA ☎ 212 13 30 ⌨ 211 65 93
Single Hfl 112.50, double room Hfl 125 incl. bf and parking place. All room with shower/WC, tel, TV.

GENERAL GROUPS
■ **COC-Eindhoven** (GLM) Café (B f GLM MA OS): Mon-Fr 10-16, Tue Thu Fr 21-1, Sun 15-22 h
PB 206 ✉ 5600 AE *(Prins Hendrikstraat 54)* ☎ 245 57 00
Lesbian 1st & 3rd Wed 21-? h.
■ **De Kringen** (B GLM MA) 2nd 4th Sat 20.30-1 h
PO Box 6323 ✉ 5600 HH ☎ 244 35 87
✉ post@kringen-eindhoven.myweb.nl
🖥 www.kringen-eindhoven.myweb.nl
At Studentenbunker, room Eskafé, Kennedylaan/v.d. Heuvellaan.

SPORT GROUPS
■ **Eindhoven Stetsons. The** (GLM) Thu 19.30-23 h
c/o Zaab Hofzicht, Hofstraat 85b ✉ 5641 TB ☎ 2813226
⌨ 8440617 ✉ stetsons@worldmail.nl
🖥 members.tripod.com/~stetsons/
Dutch Gay & Lesbian country dance Club.

CRUISING
-Dommelplantsoen (Elzentlaan/Jan Smitzslaan/Anna Frank Plantsoen)
-"E3 plas" (NU) (between Eersel and Vessem)
-De Hut van Mie Pils, Waalre (moors between Eindhoven and Leende)
-De Baan (behind Makro; Gagel, E9 Eindhoven)

Emmen ☎ 0591

SWIMMING
-De Kleine Rietplas (g NU) (in summer on WE or week days late)

CRUISING
-Marktplein (near Stadthuis)
-Bargeresbös (right and left side)

Enschede ☎ 053

GAY INFO
■ **COC Mediatheek** Thu 19-21 h
Walstraat 12-14 ✉ 7511 GH
Here is the home of Stonewall Café.

BARS
■ **For You** (AC B D f GLM MA S WE) Mon-Sun 21-4h
Molenstraat 22 ✉ 7514 DK *(near station)* ☎ 432 03 01
■ **Poort van Kleef** (B f glm OS) 10-2 h
Oude Markt 19 ☎ 432 37 02
■ **Stamcafé De Hofhouding** (B f GLM MA)
Stadsgravenstraat 16 ✉ 7511 ES ☎ 433 6610

CAFES
■ **Café Stonewall** (AC B d g GLM MA OS S) Thu 19.30-23.30 (YG) Fri -2, Sat 15.30-2, Sun -20.30 h
Walstraat 12-14 ✉ X ☎ 431 70 14
■ **'t Bölke** 21-4h
Molenstraat 6-8 ✉ 7514 DK ☎ 434 1341

DANCECLUBS
■ **'t Bölke** (AC B D DR f GLM MA S) Fri 24-4h, Sat 23-4h
Molenstraat 6-8 ✉ 7414 DK *(close to station)* ☎ 434 13 41
Gay disco.

RESTAURANTS
■ **Hans & Heinz Bistro** (B F NG) 17-1 h closed Wed
Walstraat 5 ✉ 7511 GE ☎ 432 52 62
■ **Petite Bouffe. La** (A AC CC E glm MA OS) 17.30-22 h, closed Mon Tue
Deurningerstraat 11 ✉ 7514 BC ☎ 435 85 91
French cuisine.

SEX SHOPS/BLUE MOVIES
■ **Amsterdam** (G VS) Daily 12-23h
Molenstraat 14-16 ✉ 7514 DK ☎ 433 74 01

Netherlands

ROYAL

SAUNA

Telephone INT+31-40 211 08 40

Bar
Petit Restaurant
Cinema
Whirlpool
Swimmingpool
Steambath
Sauna
Solarium
Fitness room

Open: mon-thu 12-24
fri/sat/sun 12-8
In- and out-walks allowed
In-en uitlopen toegestaan

HOTEL

Telephone INT+31-40 212 13 30

15 Comfortable double rooms
1 Luxurious suite
All rooms with:
bathroom
shower
telephone
colour TV

In the center of Eindhoven
Close to all the gays places
Creditcards, PIN and chip-card accepted

STRATUMSEDIJK 23f, EINDHOVEN
Fax INT+31-40 211 65 93

Netherlands Enschede ▸ Gouda

CINEMAS
■ **Eroticaland** (DR G MA VS) Every day 12-23h
Deurninger Straat 24 ✉ 7514 BJ ☏ 430 18 65

SAUNAS/BATHS
■ **'t Bölke** (AC B DR F G MA msg PI SA SB VS WH WO) 14-24, Fri Sat -2 h
Molenstraat 6-8 ✉ 7514 DK *(near railway station)*
☏ 434 13 41
Classic design and friendly atmosphere sauna with all facilities.

GENERAL GROUPS
■ **COC-Twente/Achterhoek** (GLM) Mon 14-14 (L)
Wed 10-11.30 Fri 13-14 h
PB 444 ✉ 7500 AK *(Walstraat 12-14)* ☏ 430 51 77
Call for info on activities.

CRUISING
-Volkspark
-Vliegveld, Veldschoterweg
-Het Rutbeek (5 km southwest of Enschede, follow cycle-path east side, 15-20 h)

Epen ☏ 043

HOTELS
■ **Vier Jaargetijden. De** (B BF F g H MA OS)
Wilhelminastraat 43 ✉ 6285
☏ 455 21 77
Downtown neighborhood location, 20 min from Maastricht airport. All rooms with priv. bath. Single hfl 45-50, double 90-100 (bf incl.).

Gemert ☏ 0492

GENERAL GROUPS
■ **Stichting Homo Groep Gemert** (B GLM MA YG) Mon 20-24, last Sun 15-18 h
Ruyschenberghstraat 3, PO Box 167 ✉ 5420 AD
☏ 36 68 94

Goes ☏ 0113

BARS
■ **Kelderbar** (B g) Tue-Wed 20-2, Thu-Sat -4 h
Blauwe Steen 5

CRUISING
-Poelbos
-Oostendestraat

Gouda ☏ 0182

SEX SHOPS/BLUE MOVIES
■ **Bureau 700** (g VS) 13-18 h, closed Sun
Raam 66 ✉ 2801 VM ☏ 51 43 81
■ **Erotheek** (g VS) 10.30-22.30, Sat -21 h
Waluisstraat 9 ✉ 2802 SB
☏ 58 23 02

VIDEO SHOPS
■ **Liberty** (g) 10-22 h
Vredebest 22 ✉ 2801 AS ☏ 58 53 90

't Bölke

SAUNA
Sun-Thu 14.00-24.00
Fri-Sat 14.00-02.00

CAFÉ
Daily 21.00-04.00

DISCO
Fri 24.00-04.00
Sat 23.00-04.00

't Bölke
GAY CENTER ENSCHEDE

Molenstraat 6-8
7514 DK Enschede
Tel: (0031)-(0)53-4341341
URL:Http://www.bolke.nl
Email: info@bolke.nl

Gouda ▸ Groningen | **Netherlands**

Stamcafé De Hofhouding

Stadsgravenstraat 16, Enschede
openingstijden: zie vermelding
Kijk op www.dehofhouding.nl
voor verdere informatie.

Gezellig bruin café, koninklijke
allure, rode pluche. Met name
Nederlandse en Duitse muziek.
Amsterdamse sfeer in Twente!

GENERAL GROUPS
■ **COC-Gouda** (GLM) Fri-Sun 21-1h
Postbus 3026 ✉ 2800 CC *(Spieringstraat 113 A)*
☎ 52 46 34
Call for info on activities.

CRUISING
-Bus station
-Railway station
-Houtmansplantsoen, near band stand
-Ysselpark

Groningen ☎ 050

BARS
■ **Bite Me** (A B f G OS s) 15-2 h, closed Tue
A-Kerkstraat 20   ☎ 313 59 60
■ **El Rubio** (B GLM MA OS s TV) Sun-Fri 16-?, Sat 15-? h
Zwanestraat 26 ✉ 9700 ☎ 314 00 39
■ **Koningin. De** (B gLM MA)
Boteringstraat 60
For lesbians and their friends.
■ **Mac. The** (AC B D R F Glm lj MA SNU VS YG) 23-?, Sun 17-? h, closed Mon-Wed
Hoge der A 3
☎ 312 71 88

■ **Rits. De** (B G) 16-1, Fri Sar -2 h
Pottenbakkersrijge 2
☎ 318 01 66
Small coffee bar.

DANCECLUBS
■ **Golden Arm. De** (B D DR GLM P) Thu-Sun 23-6 h
Hardewikerstraat 7 ✉ 9712 GR ☎ 313 16 76

RESTAURANTS
■ **Twee Dames. De** (F glm MA p S) 18-23 h, closed Sun Mon
Ged. Zuiderdiep 64 ✉ 9711 HK *(next to Pathé Cinema)*
☎ 314 20 52
Cabaret/piano/entertainment every evening. Show starts at 21 h.

SEX SHOPS/BLUE MOVIES
■ **Videotheek 3000** (G VS) 11-23, Sat 13-19, Sun 17-22.30 h
Ged. Zuiderdiep 130 ✉ 9711 HM
☎ 314 42 21

SAUNAS/BATHS
■ **Pakhuisje. 'T** (B f DR G MA SA SB SOL VS) Mon-Thu 14-24,
Fri 14-Sun 20 h
Schuitemakersstraat 17 ✉ 9711 HW ☎ 312 92 88

HOTELS
■ **Friesland** (g H)
Kleine Pelsterstraat 4   ☎ 312 13 07

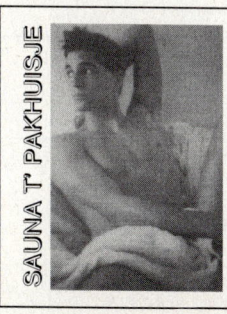

SAUNA 'T PAKHUISJE

De GaySauna van het noorden

Stoomsauna
Finse Sauna
Kabines
TV - Video
Zonnebank
Warme en koude keuken
Gezellige bar

Geopend: Maandag t/m donderdag
van 14.00 tot 24.00 uur

Vrijdag van 14.00 tot Zondag 20.00 uur
doorlopend geopend.

Half weekeinde 24 uur:
Fl 45.00 incl. 1 x ontbijt

Schuitemakersstraat 17
9711 HW Groningen
Postbus 1262
Telephon 050-319288, Fax 050-3134914

Netherlands | Groningen ▸ Hilversum

GENERAL GROUPS
■ **COC-Groningen** (GLM)
PB 144 ✉ 9700 AC *(Kraneweg 56)* ☎ 313 26 20
Call for info on activities.

CRUISING
-Behind Main Post Office
-Noorderplantsoen
-[P] "Glimmermade" E35 (A28) Assen (Groningen, north-bound)
-Hoornseplas (south, near road Haren, Groningen)
-Nude beach (action until late)
-Stadspark

Haarlem ☎ 023

BARS
■ **Gay Café Wilsons** (B d f G MA s) Wed Thu Sun 20-2, Fri Sat 22-4, closed Mon Tue
Gedempte Raamgracht 78 ✉ 2011 WK ☎ 532 58 54
■ **Jeltes** (B glm) 16-2, Fri Sat 16-4, Sun 17-2 h
Schagelstraat 15
■ **Justesse. La** (B G MA) 20-2, Fri Sat 17-4 h, closed on Mon & Tue
Ged. Oudegracht 127 ☎ 532 40 52

DANCECLUBS
■ **Lounge Stalker** (B D GLM MA) last Sat
Kromme Elleboogsteeg 20
Hosted by famous Dutch transvestite Dolly Bellefleur.

SEX SHOPS/BLUE MOVIES
■ **Christine Le Duc** (CC g VS) Mon-Fri 10-22, SSat -17.30 h, closed Sun
Generaal Cronjéstraat 77 ✉ 2021 JC ☎ 525 97 35

CINEMAS
■ **Gay-Sex Cinema** (DR G VS) 12-24 h
Turfsteeg 2 ☎ 531 11 00
■ **Roxy Sex Theater** (DR G VS) 12-24 h
Kleine Houtstraat 77 ☎ 532 51 39

BOOK SHOPS
■ **Agora** (glm) Mon 13-18, Tue Wed Fr 10-18, Thu -21, Sat -17 h
Zijlstraat 100 ✉ 2011 TR ☎ 531 31 82

GENERAL GROUPS
■ **COC-Kennemerland** (B GLM) Thu 19.30-22.30, Fri 17-02, Sat 22-03h
Postbus 342 ✉ 2000 AH *(Gedempte Oudegracht 24)* ☎ 532 54 53
🖥 coc.haarlem@multiweb.nl 🖥 go.to/coc.haarlem
Call for info on activities.

CRUISING
-Haarlemmerhout (park, Hertenkamp) after dark
-Bolwerk (behind the station) after dark

Heerlen ☎ 045

BARS
■ **Bodytalk** (AC B d G LJ MA s) Tue-Thu 21-2, Fri-Sun -3 h, closed on Mon
Gringelstraat 3 ✉ 6412 AK *(near railway station)* ☎ 572 74 63
■ **Gay Cocktail** (B DR G LJ MA P VS) Mon, Wed & Thu 20-02, Fri -Sun -03h. Tue closed
Oude Kerkstraat 7 ✉ 6412 XD ☎ 570 92 27

■ **Splash N.Y Café** (AC D G MA N p S YG) Tue-Thu 21-2, Fri Sat -3, Sun 15-3 h, Mon closed
Kemkensweg 7 ✉ 6412 AV ☎ 572 83 26

DANCECLUBS
■ **Splash N.Y.** (AC D GLM S TV YG) Sun 21-3 h
Pancratiusstraat 44 ✉ 6411 KC ☎ 571 12 66

SEX SHOPS/BLUE MOVIES
■ **Christine Le Duc** (CC g VS) Mon 13-18.30, Tue-Sat 9-18.30 h, closed on Sun
Dautzenbergstraat 5 ✉ 6411 LA ☎ 571 75 53
■ **Funhouse** (CC DR G MA S VS) 10-22, 2nd Mon Gay party 21-24 h
Willemstraat 13 ✉ 6411 KX ☎ 571 06 87

'S Hertogenbosch/Den Bosch ☎ 073

BARS
■ **Café Joost** (AC B G MA) Mon Thu Fri 19-2, Sat -3, Sun -2 h
Postelstraat 10 ✉ 5211 EA ☎ 614 14 79
■ **Club Chez Nous** (AC B D GLM MA s) 22-4 h
Vughterstraat 158 ✉ 5211 GH ☎ 614 25 92
■ **COC-Café The Cockpitt** (B D GLM MA) Thu 20-1, Fri-Sat -2, Sun 15-1 h
Vughterstraat 277 ✉ 5211 EA ☎ 614 16 75
■ **Kings** (B glm) Fri Sat 22-4 h
Vughterstraat 99A ☎ 613 44 79

CAFES
■ **Stamineeke. 'T** (B GLM MA OS) Tue Wed 12-1, Thu Fri -2, Sat Sun 14-2 h
le Korenstraatje 16 ✉ 5211 EJ ☎ 614 36 46

SEX SHOPS/BLUE MOVIES
■ **Christine Le Duc** (CC g VS) Mon-Fri 10-22, Sat -17.30 h, closed Sun
Vughterstraat 62-64 ✉ 5211 GK ☎ 612 31 76

VIDEO SHOPS
■ **Cinetex Video Verhuur BV** (CC g MA VS) Mon-Sat 11-22 h
Vughterstraat 111 ✉ 1017 CL ☎ 614 34 86

GENERAL GROUPS
■ **COC-'s Hertogenbosch** (GLM)
Postbus 1420 ✉ 5200 BL *(Vughterstraat 277)* ☎ 614 16 75
🖥 info@denbosch.coc.nl 🖥 www.coc.nl/denbosch/
COC is a national group for gays and can be found in many cities throughout the Netherlands.

HEALTH GROUPS
■ **Buddyproject**
☎ 642 12 21 📠 642 12 21
Help for people with AIDS.

CRUISING
-Tennisbaan-Heekellaan (evening)
-Railway station (r)

Hilversum ☎ 035

BARS
■ **COC-Café Happe Tappe** (AC B d F GLM lj MA s snu) 22-1 h
Naarerstraat 43 *(15 min from station)* ☎ 697 03 70

Hilversum ▸ Maastricht — Netherlands

■ **So What** (AC B GLM MA OS) 16-1, Fri-Sat -2 h
Noorderweg 72 ✉ 1221 AB ☏ 683 10 03

SEX SHOPS/BLUE MOVIES
■ **Black & White Sexshop** (g MA VS) 10-22, Sun 13-20h
Vaartweg 24c ☏ 621 97 85
gay film video cabines

GENERAL GROUPS
■ **COC't Gooi en omstreken** (GLM)
PB 1631 ✉ 1200 BP (Tagrijn, Koninginnewg 44) ☏ 697 03 70
Call for info on activities.

CRUISING
-Route A27 (E37) Breda (Almere, at km 90.2)
-[P] Bosberg (near Hilversum)

Hoek van Holland ☏ 0747

CRUISING
-Nudist beach between piles 116110 and 116360 (Rechtzeestraat, between two camping areas opposite 's Gravenzande).
-Maasvlakte (opposite road to first Overslag service)

Hoogeveen ☏ 0528

CRUISING
-N37 ⇒ Emmen (1st [P] after Hoogeveen)

Hoorn ☏ 0229

CRUISING
-[P] De Koggen (A7 from Purmerend to Hoorn)
-[P] ABC (after 16 h)
-Westerdijk (near De Hulk; summer only)

Hulst ☏ 0114

GENERAL GROUPS
■ **Stichting Tent**
Wilhelminastraat 1 ✉ 4564 AC ☏ 31 59 20
Help with coming out problems.

Ijzendijke ☏ 0117

BARS
■ **Homotel Queen** (A CC f G H MA OS p SA WH) 19-5 h
Landpoortstraat 10 ✉ 4515 CB ☏ 30 23 27
■ **Mercury Gay Bar** (B CC D p S VS YG) 19-5 h
Landpoortstraat 10 ✉ 4515 CB ☏ 30 23 27

Leeuwarden ☏ 058

GAY INFO
■ **Anna Blaman Huis** (AC GLM p) Mon-Fri 9-17, Sat 14-17h
Postbus 40 62 ✉ 8901 EB ☏ 212 18 29 ≞ 213 91 31
✉ anna.blaman.huis@worldonline.nl
Intercultural information-place.
■ **COC Friesland Gay Switchboard/ Service Center** (GLM)
Mon-Fri 13-17 h
Maria Anna Straat 5-7 ✉ 8921 GD (5 min from the station)
☏ 212 49 08 ≞ 212 49 08 ✉ info@friesland.coc.nl
✉ www.friesland.coc.nl

BARS
■ **COC Friesland Café** (B d GLM MA s) Mon-Fri 13-17h, Fri & Sat 21-1h
Maria Annastraatje 5-7 ✉ 8911 HP (5 min from station)
☏ 212 49 08
2nd Sat/month: women only; 4th Sat/month (YG) -30 years.
■ **Incognito** (B D GLM) 22.30-3 h
Noordvliet 13 ☏ 212 60 82
■ **Koningin. De** (B GLM MA) Sun-Thu 20-2, Fri Sat 16-4 h
Tuinen 3 ✉ 8911 KB ☏ 213 74 87

CRUISING
-Ringerspark
-[P] Groningsestraatweg
-Citypark (near museum Prinsentuin, evenings and nights)

Leiden ☏ 071

GAY INFO
■ **Holland Centraal** (GLM MA p) 24 hour broadcasts, Office 9-21 h
Oude Rijn 57 ✉ 2301 CA (old town centre, within close range of everything) ☏ 512 75 15 ≞ 512 75 83
Local Radio Station incl. TV Newletter, Teletekst.

BARS
■ **Odessa** (B F GLM OS YG) Thu 22-1 h
Hogewoerd 18 ☏ 512 33 11

GENERAL GROUPS
■ **COC-Leiden** (GLM)
PB 11101 ✉ 2301 EC (Langegracht 65) ☏ 522 06 40
Call for info on activities.

CRUISING
-Plantsoen
-Vlietlanden (NU)

Maastricht ☏ 043

BARS
■ **COC-Café Rose** (B d GLM MA s) Fri 14-17, Fri-Sat 21-2, Thu Sun 20-2 h
Bogardenstraat 43 ☏ 321 83 37
■ **Falstaff** (B G MA) 10-2 h
Amersplein 6
■ **Ferme. La** (B d G MA p) Mon Wed Thu 20-2, Fri Sat 21-3, Sun 16-2 h, closed on Tue
Rechtstraat 29 ✉ 6221 EG ☏ 321 89 28
■ **Gare. La** (AC B D E GLM p s WE) 22-5 h, closed on Mon
Spoorweglaan 6 ✉ 6221 BS ☏ 325 90 90
■ **Rembrandt** (B G MA) 20-2 h
Markt 32

DANCECLUBS
■ **Kadans. De** (AC B D g OS s YG) Sun-Tue 10-2, Wen-Sat 10-5
Kesselskade 62 ✉ 6211 EN ☏ 326 17 00

RESTAURANTS
■ **Pieterspoort. De** (b F g) 12-22 h, closed Tue
Sint Pieterstraat 8a ☏ 325 00 74
■ **Suhnothai Restaurant** (! CC F g MA OS) 17-? h Mon closed
Tongersestraat 54 ✉ 6211 LP (across the university) ☏ 321 79 46

Netherlands | Maastricht ▶ Nijmegen

SEX SHOPS/BLUE MOVIES
■ **B-1** (g) 10-24 h
Kommel 3 ☏ 314 56 41
Also sexshop.

BOOK SHOPS
■ **Tribune** (g) 9-18 h, closed Sun Mon
Kapoenstraat 8 ☏ 325 19 78

GENERAL GROUPS
■ **COC-Maastricht** (AC B GLM MA) Thu & Sat 21-02, Fri 12-02, Sun 16-0h (café),
Wed & Fri 14-17h, Thu 19-21h (info-center)
Bogaardenstraat 43 ✉ 6211 SN ☏ 321 83 37 📠 321 83 37
💻 coczl@xoommail.com 💻 members.xoom.com/coczl
Call for info on activities.

CRUISING
-Mgr. Molenpark (at St. Lambertuslaan in Villapark)
-Oudenhof

Middelburg ☏ 0118

GENERAL GROUPS
■ **COC-Midden-Zeeland** (GLM)
Lange Noordstraat 52 ✉ 4331 CE ☏ 61 22 80
Call for info on activities.

CRUISING
-Park Molenwater

Naarden ☏ 035

DANCECLUBS
■ **Club Kogh** (AC B d DR GLM lj MA msg P S SA SOL VS)
Binnenhof 327 ✉ 1412 LA *(3 min from station)* ☏ 678 12 79
Entertainment house parties, Playroom, Video shows. Different locations.

GENERAL GROUPS
■ **Homo Ontmoetingen/Homo Initiatieven Nederland/Homo 2000** (GLM)
Binnenhof 327 ✉ 1412 LA *(3 min from station Naarden-Russum)*
☏ 678 12 79 💻 Jelle@Duckie.neep.net
Holds special meetings, projects for friendships / contacts worldwide.

Niekerk ☏ 0594

CAMPING
■ **Heerenborgh. De** (G MA NU PI) Ap-Sep
Niekerkerdiep 1 ✉ 9822 AH *(between Grootegast and Zuidhorn, end of Havenstraat)* ☏ 50 34 46 📠 50 34 46
💻 heeren.borgh@worldonline.nl
💻 home-2.worldonline.nl/~301161/
Caravan and camping place for gay men only.

Nieuwegein ☏ 030

CRUISING
-Park Oudegin (near tramstop Merwestein)
-Ⓟ 300m to Plofsluis

Nijmegen ☏ 024

BARS
■ **Bakkertje. 'T** (AC B D GLM MA P s) Wed-Sat 20-?, Sun 19-? h, closed Mon Tue
Van Welderenstraat 65 ✉ 6511 MD ☏ 080/323 13 48
■ **Café de Plak** (A B D F g MA OS YG) 11-1, Thu 22.30-? h
Bloemerstraat 90 ☏ 322 27 57
■ **Chaps** (AC B DR G LJ MA p VS) Mon-Sun 21-? h, closed Tue & Wed.
2e Walstraat 96 ✉ 6511 LW ☏ 360 42 72
Mon & Thu dress code : underwear, shoes or t-shirt only.
■ **Eend. d'** (B G MA) 12-2, Sun 14-2 h
Van Welderenstraat 87
■ **Mets** (B d GLM MA N) 12-2, Sun 14-2 h
Grotestraat 7 ✉ 6511 VB *(centre)* ☏ 323 95 49
■ **Revolutie. De** (B G MA) Sat 23-5, Sun 5-10 h
Parkweg 98
Late night café.
■ **Verjaardag. De** (B g) 20-2 h
Van Welderenstraat 77 ☏ 360 61 66

DANCECLUBS
■ **Gay Club Nijmegen** (B D GLM) Fri Sat 23-5 h
Graafseweg 32-34
■ **Mythe. De** (B D f GLM MA s) Bar Thu 20-4, Fri 21-4, Sat 21 -5, Sun 16-2; Disco Thu Fri 23-4, Sat -5 h
Platenmakersstraat 3 ✉ 6511 TZ *(centre)* ☏ 322 01 55
Popular mixed male/female bar & disco.

RESTAURANTS
■ **Steiger. De** (A b E F glm MA) 17-24 h, closed Mon Tue
Reguliersstraat 59 ✉ 6511 DP ☏ 322 90 77

SEX SHOPS/BLUE MOVIES
■ **B-1** (g) 9.30-24, Sun 14-23 h
Bloemenstraat 37 ☏ 323 74 53
■ **Christine Le Duc** (CC g VS) Mon-Fri 10-22, Sat -17.30 h
Bloemerstraat 78 ✉ 6511 EM ☏ 360 56 14

BOOK SHOPS
■ **De Feeks-Boekhandel** (GLM) Mon 13-18, Tue Wed Fri 10-18, Thu 10-21, Sat 10-17 h
Van Welderenstraat 34 ✉ 6511 ML *(accross Het Bakkertje)*
☏ 323 93 81
Gay and lesbian bookshop. Free catalogue on request.

FASHION SHOPS
■ **Bofkont!** (CC g SOL) Mon-Sat 9.30-18, Thu -21h
Strikke Hezelstraat 28 ✉ 6511 JX ☏ 360 45 25
Male underwear and gay solarium.

GENERAL GROUPS
■ **COC-Nijmeren** (GLM) Mon 13.30-16, Tue-Fri -17h, Thu evenings 19-21.30h
Postbus 592 ✉ 6500 AN *(Villa Lila, In de Betouwstr. 9)*
☏ 323 42 37 📠 323 37 17 💻 info@pinknijmegen.nl
💻 www.pinknijmegen.nl
Call for info on activities.

HEALTH GROUPS
■ **SVG**
☏ 322 61 41

Nijmegen ▸ Rotterdam Netherlands

CRUISING
-Hunerpark
-Kelfkenbosch (near Traianusplein)
-Goffertpark (only evenings)
-De Elsthof-forest along grootstalseweg (only daytime)

Noordwijk ☎ 071

CRUISING
-NU beach north of Langevelderslag near Zandvoort
-N 206 near Rijnsburg

Numansdorp ☎ 0186

SWIMMING
Haringvlietbrug (parallel road to A 29, beach near Haringvlietsluijses)

Ommen ☎ 0529

CRUISING
-N48 Ommen ⇌ Raalte (1st P after Ommen)

Oostkapelle ☎ 0118

SWIMMING
-Beach (The beach to the right of the path is frequently visited by gays)

Oss ☎ 0412

GENERAL GROUPS
■ **COC-Brabant-Noordoost** (GLM)
PO Box 551 ✉ 5340 AN *(Sint Barbaraplein 6)* ☎ 62 66 66
Call for info on activities.

Prinsenbeek ☎ 076

LEATHER & FETISH SHOPS
■ **Rimba. Factory of leather SM articles** 08-17h
PO Box 33 ✉ 4840 AA ☎ 541 44 84

Purmerend ☎ 0299

GENERAL GROUPS
■ **COC-Purmerend** (GLM)
Postbus 786 ✉ 1440 AT *(Wijkcentr. "Vooruit", Wilhelminalaan 1 A)*
☎ 42 03 70 ✉ info@cocpurmerend.nl 🖥 www.cocpurmerend.nl
Call for info on activities.

Roermond ☎ 0475

BARS
■ **Mix. De** (A B CC E f G MA OS s) 16-2, Fri-Sat -3 h
Venloseport 3 ✉ 6041 CG ☎ 31 58 50
■ **Sjinderhannes** (A AC B G LJ MA s) 21-2 Fri Sat -3 h closed Tue
Swalmerstraat 42 ☎ 33 31 19
-1st Sat Rubbermens-club
-2nd & last Sat MSC Limburg
-3rd Sat Black Angels Köln
-last Sun 15 h VSSM

SEX SHOPS/BLUE MOVIES
■ **B-1** (G VS) 10-24 h
Kraanpoort 6 ☎ 32 97 10
Also blue movies.
■ **Climax** (g VS) 10-18 h
Willem II Singel 22a
Also blue movies.

SAUNAS/BATHS
■ **Dingeman** (! B G MA OS SA SB SOL VS WH) 13-24 h
Willem II Singel 14 ✉ 6041 GH *(near railway station)* ☎ 33 62 36
Sauna with a terrace. Parties are from time to time organised.

Roosendaal ☎ 0165

BARS
■ **Déjà-Vu** (AC B D E GLM MA P S SNU TV) Mon Thu 19-1
Fri Sat 19-2 Sun 16-2 h closed Tue Wed.
Damstraat 101-103 ✉ 4701 GM *(near railway station and inner city)*
☎ 54 86 78
Bar, café and disco.

CRUISING
-Emile van Loonpark *(near city-center, 16-23 h)*

Rotterdam ☎ 010

GAY INFO
■ **Apollo** (B GLM s YG) Fri 18-2 h
PO Box 1490 ✉ 3000 BL ☎ 436 14 44 ✉ apollohj@dds.nl
Visitors address: Van Oldebarneveldstraat 116.

PUBLICATIONS
■ **David Boy (voor de leerboys) en Boy Smile**
PB 3061 ✉ 3003 AB
Lots of information about the Rotterdam scene.

BARS
■ **AbFab**
Van Oldebarneveldstraat 88
■ **Bak. De** (A f G DR lj MA OS s) 16-2 h
Schiedamse Vest 146 ✉ 3011 BG *(U-Churchill plein)* ☎ 433 47 83
Showtime (STV) Thu 22, Happy Hour Sun 17-18 h, then free food.
■ **Beetje Vaag** (B DR G lj MA)
Brandersplaats 32 ✉ 3011 EV
■ **Bonaparte** (B GLM d) 14-4, Fri Sat 14-5 h
Nieuwe Binnenweg 117 ☎ 436 74 33
■ **Cosmo Bar** (B G DR lj VS tv WE) 20-2 h
Schiedamsesingel 133 ☎ 412 36 68
Multicultural crowd.
■ **De Doos** (B GLM WE)
W.Boothlaan 7A ✉ 3012 VG ☎ 4137646
■ **Havenzicht** (GLM) Every Sunday-evening
Hillelaan 52 ✉ 3072 JE
■ **Heren op de Hoek** (G OS) Fri/Sat 15-2, Sun-Thu 15-1h
Mauritsstraat 1 ✉ 3012 CE ☎ 4135120
■ **Keerweer** (AC B f GLM p s YG) Mon- Thu 17-5, Fri Sat 16-5
Keerweer 14 ☎ 413 12 17
Sociable drinking place located in a small alley around the corner of Binnenwegplein. Best after 1h.
■ **Loge'90** (AC B G) 12-4, Fri Sat -5 h
Schiedamsedijk 4 ☎ 414 97 45
Happy hour every day from 17-18h.

SPARTACUS 2001/2002 | 789

Netherlands Rotterdam

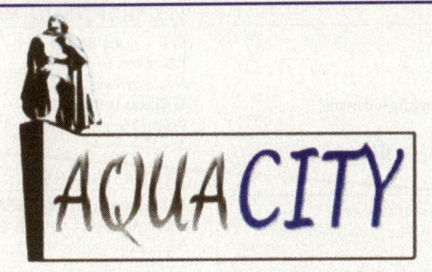

AQUACITY
'S Gravendijkwal 4 · 3014 EA
Tel (10) 436 0104
Open every day from 13h to 1h · Trendy gay sauna in the heart of Rotterdam
www.Aquacity.nl

■ **Shaft** (B DR G LJ MA P VS) 21-2, Fri Sat 23-5 h, closed on Wed
'S Gravensdijkwal 137 ☎ 414 14 86
Special themes/dresscodes throughout the week.
■ **Soap** (B GLM WE YG) Sun-Thu till 4h, Fri/Sat till 5h
Witte de Withstraat 14 ✉ 3012 BP ☎ 516 333 333
■ **Strano** (B GLM) Mon-Thu 15-2, Fri -3, Sat 14-3, Sun -2, happy hour Mon-Sun 18-19 h
Van Oldebarneveldtstraat 154 ✉ 3012 GX ☎ 412 58 11

DANCECLUBS
■ **Gay Palace** (B D GLM) 23-4, Fri Sat -5 h
W.Boothlaan 7A ☎ 414 14 86
Being renovated and temporay moved to this address.
■ **Nighttown** 22-5 h, ask for special gay events
Gouvernestraat 4C ☎ 436 40 54
■ **Stats** (D GLM YG)
Schiedamsevesthof 21 *(entrance under Cinerama cinema)*
■ **Vibes** 1st Sun 22-? h
Westersingel 50 ☎ 436 63 89

SEX SHOPS/BLUE MOVIES
■ **Cano** (A AC B DR f glm LJ MA VS) 12-24 Sun 12-18 h
Proveniersingel 130 ✉ 3033 EL *(near Central Station and centre)*
☎ 467 6348
■ **Christine Le Duc** (CC g VS) Mon-Fri 10-22, Sat -17.30 h, closed Sun
Schieweg 108 ✉ 3038 BC ☎ 467 95 27
■ **Hans Sexshop**
Oranjeboomstraat 267 ✉ 3071 SM ☎ 4859079

HOUSE OF BOYS
■ **Boys Factory. The** (CC G msg) 14-1, Fri Sat 14-2 h
'S Gravendijkwal 92 ✉ 3014 EH ☎ 225 17 25
Also Escort service.

SAUNAS/BATHS
■ **Aquacity** (AC B GLM f G MA OS p SA SB VS WE) Every day 13-1h
'S Gravendijkwal 4 ✉ 3014 EA *(% minutes frim Central Station)*
☎ 436 0104
■ **Cosmo** (B F DR G msg OS SA SB SOL VS WH) 13-23, Fri Sat -8 h
Schiedamse Singel 133 ✉ 3012 BA *(next to Eaye Hospital)*
☎ 412 36 68
This sauna with terrace is decorated in a classical style.

■ **Finland** (B DR G MA msg PI SA SB SOL VS WH WO) 13-23.30, Fri Sat -2 h
Grondherendijk 7 ✉ 3082 DD ☎ 429 70 29
Sauna offering extensive facilities and frequented by a mixed age crowd.
■ **Spartacus** (B F DR G MA SA SB SOL VS WH) 13-6, Sat Sun 14-6 h
'S Gravensdijkwal 130 ✉ 3015 CC ☎ 436 62 85
Intimate sauna which was renovated in summer 00.

LEATHER & FETISH SHOPS
■ **Massadshop** (g LJ MA TV) 9-18, Fri -21, Sat -17 h, closed Sun-Mon
Zaagmolendrift 35-41 *(Tram6/9)* ☎ 466 43 68
Leather and rubber equipments, magazines.

HOTELS
■ **Bagatelle** (g H MG p) 8-23 h
Provenierssingel 26 ✉ 3033 EL ☎ 467 63 48 🖨 467 63 48
Single Hfl 50, double 80-100 (bf incl.)

GUEST HOUSES
■ **Pension Matras** (BF GLM OS) All year
(Train station Rotterdam Noord - 5 minutes walk) ☎ 184 97 161
🖨 (0842) 114 314 ✉ pension.matras@planet.nl
🖳 home.planet.nl/~pension.matras
Rates: 1 person HFL 40,-/night; 2 persons HFL 75,-/night including breakfast.

GENERAL GROUPS
■ **COC-Rotterdam** (GLM) Wed & Thu 20-22 h
Schiedamsesingel 175 ✉ 3000 AT *(Schiedamsesingel 175)*
☎ 414 15 55 🖨 414 65 17

FETISH GROUPS
■ **MS Rotterdam**
PO Box 221 84 ✉ 3003 DD 🖳 www.duko.demon.nl
Member of ECME. Meeting every Sunday in bar "De Bak".

HEALTH GROUPS
■ **HIV-Café Rotterdam** Every Tue from 20-23h
Westersingel 103 ✉ 3015 LD *(Ron Wichmanhuis)* ☎ 4365034

Rotterdam ▸ Terneuzen | Netherlands

SPARTACUS
Gaysauna and more
S'Gravendijkwal 130
Rotterdam
Tel. 010-4366265
7 days a week
Nights a week
Mo-Fri 1300-0600
Sa-Sun 1400-0600

Rotterdam

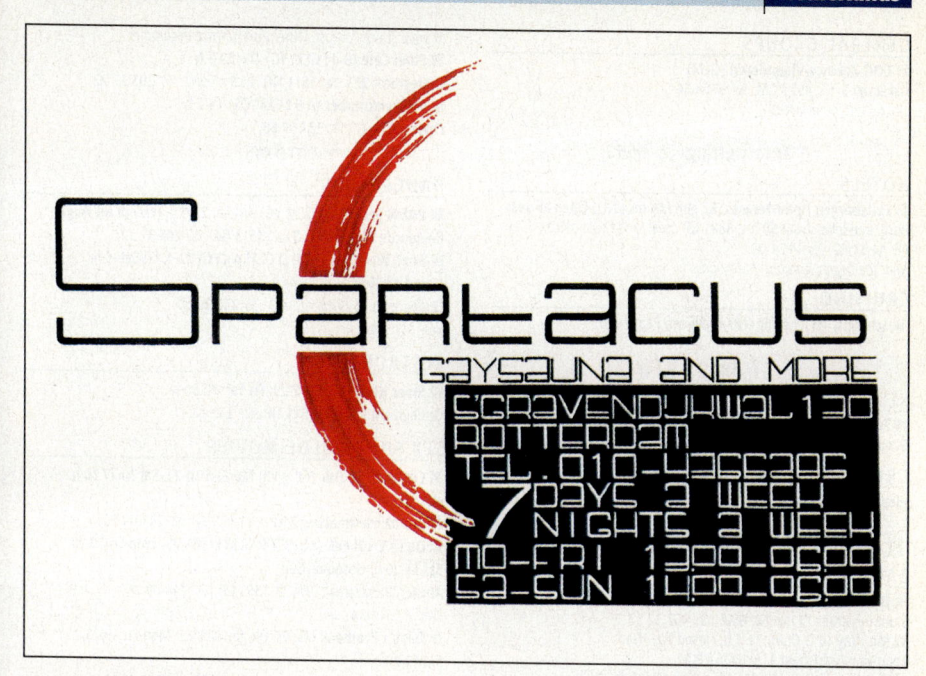

HELP WITH PROBLEMS
■ **Rotterdam Verkeert** (GLM)
Batavierenstraat 1 3 ✉ 3014 JH ☎ 414 86 20
Professional psycological help for gays and lesbians.

SPORT GROUPS
■ **Gay Sports Club Ketelbinkie** (GLM MA)
☎ 4145538 ✉ ketelbinkie@geocities.com
Swimming, volleyball, gay-choir.

CRUISING
-Kralingsebos
-Museumpark (rozentuin) (AYOR)
-Behind railway station, Statenpad (R)
-under Willemsbrug
-Zuiderpark
-Het Park
-Nudist beach and dunes Hoek van Holland.

Schagen ☎ 0224

GENERAL GROUPS
■ **Pink Café**
PB 106 ✉ 1740 AC ☎ 21 31 99

Scheveningen ☎ 070

DANCECLUBS
■ **Glitz Gay-Nite (Club Exposure Danceclub)** (B D DR G SNU VS)
Every 3rd Fri of the month 22.30-? h
Westduinweg 232 ✉ 2583 AK ☎ 354 33 56

Schiedam ☎ 010

BARS
■ **Mallemolen. De** (B f g OS) 17-1, Fri-Sat 16-4.30, sun 16-1, closed Mon
Vlaardingerstraat 17 ☎ 426 34 47
■ **Melody** (AC B G s) Tue-Thu 19-1, Fri -2 Sat 16-2, Sun -1 h
Singel 230 ☎ 427 07 65

CRUISING
-Ⓟ & Sportspark Harga near Novotel Schiedam

Sneek ☎ 0515

RESTAURANTS
■ **Stoofje. 'T** (B CC F g MA) 17-24 h, Mon closed
Oude Koemarkt 9-11 ✉ 8601 EH ☎ 41 74 38

St. Anthonis ☎ 0485

RESTAURANTS
■ **Heksenboom. De** (AC B CC F glm MA OS) Fri/Sat 11-?
Sun 10-?,Apr-Sept Tue-Thu 11-?,Oct-Mar Wed 12-18 Jul/Aug 10-? h
Bosweg 40 ✉ 5845 EB ☎ 38 28 03
Also possible to make reservations on closed days with minimum of 15 guests.

Terneuzen ☎ 0115

CAFES
■ **Uientuin. De** (B G MA)
Nieuwstraat 6

SPARTACUS 2001/2002 | 791

Netherlands Terneuzen ▶ Veghel

GENERAL GROUPS
■ **COC-Zeeuws-Vlaanderen** (GLM)
Dijkstraat 3 ✉ 4531 CM ☎ 630 654
Call for info on activities.

Terschelling ☎ 0562
HOTELS
■ **Spitsbergen Appartments** (BF glm MA msg NU) Open all year
Burg. Reedekerstraat 50 ✉ 8881 CB (next to the post office)
☎ 44 31 62 44 31 62
Near the beach, harbour and woods.

CRUISING
-Beach West Terschelling (NU)(between Paal 7 & 8)

Texel ☎ 0222
RESTAURANTS
■ **Taveerne. De** (AC B D E F GLM MA) 16.30-2 h
Dorpstraat 119 ☎ 31 75 85

CRUISING
-Beach (NU)(between pile 26.4 and 27.4)

Tilburg ☎ 013
BARS
■ **Dynasty. Le** (B GLM) Mon-Fri 21-24, Sat 16-3, Sun -24 h
Stadthuisstraat 17 ✉ 5038 XZ ☎ 467 22 57
■ **My Way** (B D GLM) 21-3 h, closed Tue-Wed
Leon van Vechtstraat 1 ☎ 536 78 27
■ **Popcorn** (B D GLM lj MA OS p S tv) 18-?, Sat 14-? h
Paleisring 19 ✉ 5038 WD ☎ 543 32 18

SEX SHOPS/BLUE MOVIES
■ **Candy Shop** (g) 10-midnight, Sat 14-midnight
Korvelseweg 215 ☎ 543 23 94
Also house with boys; S/M.
■ **Gay Cinema Candy** (G VS) 10-midnight, Sun 14-midnight
Korvelseweg 217 ☎ 543 23 94

GENERAL GROUPS
■ **COC-Tilburg** (GLM)
Stadshuisplein 344 ✉ 5038 TH ☎ 535 90 50
Call for info on activities.

CRUISING
-Wilhelminakanaal Biest-Houtakker
-A58 Breda-Tilburg, P Leikant (near Gilze)
-Wilhelminapark
-Luis Bouwmeesterplein

Utrecht ☎ 030
GAY INFO
■ **COC-Midden-Nederland** (B D GLM MA) Disco: 20-1, Fri-Sat 21-2, Sun 20.30-2 h
Posbus 117 ✉ 3500 AC (Oude Gracht 221) ☎ 231 88 41
✉ info@coc-utrecht.demon.nl

BARS
■ **Bodytalk** (! AC B D DR f G lj MA OS p s VS) Mon-Thu 20-3, Fri Sat 16-5, Sun 16-4 h
Oudegracht 64 ✉ 3511 AS (Centre, near main railway station)
☎ 231 57 47

Regular special events. Water front Terrace in summer.
■ **Pann Café** (B d f GLM YG) Thu 22-3 h
Oudegracht 221 ✉ 3511 NH (water level) ☎ 293 37 22
■ **Wolkenkrabber** (A B f GLM OS) 16-2 h
Oudegracht 47 ☎ 231 97 68
Popular bar, friendly atmosphere.

DANCECLUBS
■ **PANN Fest** (B D f GLM YG) 3rd Sat 22-4 h. (except Jul, Aug)
Bemuurde Weerd W.Z. 3 ✉ 3513 BH ☎ 293 37 22
■ **Roze Wolk. De** (AC B D GLM p s YG) 22-4, Fri Sat -5 h, closed on Mon
Oudegracht 45 (Water Level) ☎ 232 20 66
Very popular.

RESTAURANTS
■ **River Kwai** (B g F) 17-22, Fri Sat -22.30 h
Oudegracht 184 ✉ 3511 NP ☎ 232 18 51

SEX SHOPS/BLUE MOVIES
■ **Christine Le Duc** (CC g VS) Mon-Fri 10-22, Sat 10-17.30 h, closed Sun
Amsterdamsestraatweg 310 ✉ 3551 CT ☎ 243 69 56
■ **Dali's Erotheek** (AC CC DR GLM LJ MA VS) Mon-Fri 10-23, Sat 11-20 h, closed on Sun
Amsterdamsestraat 197 ✉ 3351 CB ☎ 244 09 75
Wed & Fri is gaynite.
■ **Davy's Erotheek** (AC CC DR glm MA VS) Mon-Fri 10-23, Sat 12-20
Amsterdamsestraat 197 ✉ 3351 CB ☎ 243 68 15

BOOK SHOPS
■ **Rooie Rat. De** (g) 9-18, Thu -21, Sat -17
Oudegracht 65 ✉ 3511 AD ☎ 231 789
Leftist bookshop with gay/lesbian department.

HOTELS
■ **Bed & Breakfast Memory** (BF CC)
Prinses Markgrielstraat 5a ✉ 3554 GA ☎ 242 07 37 244 40 72
✉ pension.memory@utrecht-hotel.nl www.utrecht-hotel.nl
Friendly hotel with good bf and low prices.

GENERAL GROUPS
■ **ILGA Support Group Utrecht**
Herenweg 93 ✉ 3513 CD ☎ 234 09 12
■ **Orpheus** (GLM)
PB 14121 ✉ 3508 Se ☎ 020/639 07 65
✉ www.xsall.nl/~orpheus

CRUISING
-Museumbrug, Prinsesselaan
-Sterrenwacht (at the end of Nieuwegracht)
-Hogelandse Park (near Museumlaan, 19-24 h)

Veghel ☎ 04130
HEALTH GROUPS
■ **SVG** Mon-Fri 9-17 h
☎ 679 15

Venlo ☎ 077

SEX SHOPS/BLUE MOVIES
■ **B-1** (g VS) 10-23 h
Havenkade 12   ☎ 334 83 38
Also blue movies.

GENERAL GROUPS
■ **COC-Noord-en-Midden-Limburg** (GLM)
PB 611   ✉ 5900 AP   ☎ 351 84 12
Call for info on activities.

CRUISING
-Park opposite railway station (northern part, evenings and nights)

Vlaardingen ☎ 010

CRUISING
-Likkebaardboss (NU) (first P from Vlaardingen)

Vlissingen ☎ 0118

HOTELS
■ **Admiraal Logies** (BF g H NU OS)
Badhuisstraat 201   ✉ 4382 AM   ☎ 41 37 52   📠 41 37 52
All rooms with shower, WC and TV.

SWIMMING
-Nollestrand

CRUISING
-Nollebos

Vrouwenpolder ☎ 010

SWIMMING
-Beach (Path at campingsite Oranjezon to the beach. Some gays on the right)

Waalre ☎ 040

BARS
■ **Hut van Mie Pils. De** (B g) 11-18, Fri-Sun -23 h
Leenderweg 1

Wageningen ☎ 0317

GENERAL GROUPS
■ **Homogroep Wageningen** (B D GLM S YG) Fri 21.30-3 h at De Wilde Wereld, Burgstraat 1, disco 1st & 3rd Fri
Burgtstraat 1   ✉ 6701 DA   ☎ 42 28 35   📧 hgw@freemail.nl
📧 huizen.ddsw.nl/bewoners/hgw

Winschoten ☎ 0597

SEX SHOPS/BLUE MOVIES
■ **De Pottekijker** (CC g VS YG) Mon-Fri 15-21, Sat 12-17 h
Pottebakkerstraat 27   ✉ 9671 LD   ☎ 41 24 85
Sex shop + mail orders.

Zandhuisen ☎ 0561

CAMPING
■ **Vlegel. De** (G MA NU OS PI) Apr 1-Okt 1
Oldeberkoperweg 23   ✉ 8389 TE   ☎ 43 31 13
Homo-camping.

Zandvoort ☎ 023

BARS
■ **Adonis** (B G MA OS) 20-3 h, closed Mon Wed
20 'tjerk Hiddestraat   ☎ 571 31 10
■ **Joy** (B G MA) Sept-Apr: Thu-Sat 22-3, Sun 15-1; May-Aug Mon-Sat 20-3, Sun 15-3 h
Stationstraat 17   ✉ 2042 LD   ☎ 573 10 09

CAFES
■ **Eldorado** (B glm) 8-24 h (summer only)
Zuidstrand 6   ☎ 571 82 29
Little bar on the beach.

HOTELS
■ **Hotel Hoogland** (A B BF CC F g OS SOL)
Westerparkstraat 5   ✉ 2042 AV *(near beach and city center)*
☎ 571 55 41   📠 571 42 00   📧 info@hotelhoogland.nl
🌐 www.hotelhoogland.nl
All rooms with shower/WC, TV, radio, CDplayer, room safe and phone. Rates single Hfl 60-100, double 120-160 (bf incl.)

SWIMMING
-Zuidstrand (go by bike or 40 min by foot along the beach. The gay beach is near the nude beach. Cruising in the dunes behind the beach)

Zeist ☎ 030

SEX SHOPS/BLUE MOVIES
■ **Dali's Erotheek** (AC CC DR GLM LJ MA VS) Mon-Fri 10-23, Sat 11-20 h, closed on Sun
J. v. Oldenbarneveltlaan 82   ✉ 3705 HG   ☎ 699 23 32

Zoetermeer ☎ 079

GENERAL GROUPS
■ **COC-Zoetermeer** (GLM)
Frankrijklaan 35   ✉ 2711 CV *(Van't Hoffplein 1)*   ☎ 343 33 36
Call for info on activities.

Zwolle ☎ 038

GAY INFO
■ **COC-Zwolle** (B D GLM MA) Tue 21-24, Thu 20-24h (YG only), Fri -02, Sat 22-03h
Kamperstraat 17   ✉ 8011 LJ   ☎ 421 00 65   ☎ 422 44 03
📠 422 56 45

HEALTH GROUPS
■ **HIV Vereniging**
☎ 455 16 03

CRUISING
-Rode Toren Plein
-Railway station
-Potgietersingel (evenings and nights)

New Caledonia

Name: Nouvelle Calédonie • Neukaledonien • Nueva Caledonia
Location: Nouvelle-Calédonie
Initials: NC
Time: GMT +11
International Country Code: ☏ 687 (no area codes)
International Access Code: ☏ 00
Language: French
Area: 19,103 km² / 7,358 sq mi.
Currency: 1 Franc (CFP)= 100 Centimes
Population: 204,019
Capital: Nouméa
Religions: 59% Catholic, 17% Protestant
Climate: Tropical climate that is hot and humid. It's modified by southeast trade winds.

✱ The French penal code is in effect here (⇒France).

★ Es gelten die Strafbestimmungen ⇒Frankreichs.

✱ Actuellement, même législation qu'en ⇒France.

⬢ El Código Penal francés (⇒ Francia) es vigente en Nueva Caledonia.

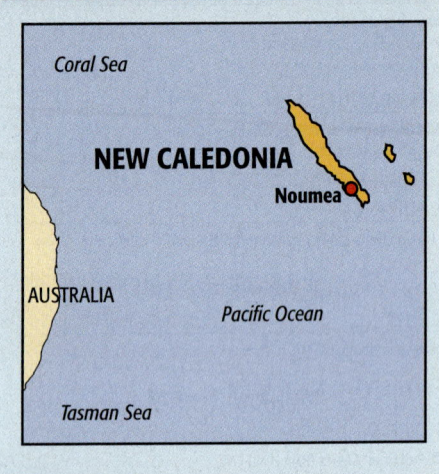

✖ E'in vigore il codice penale francese (⇒Francia).

Nouméa

BARS
▪ **Bilboquet Village** (B F g)
(city center near Berheim Library) ☏ 28 43 30
▪ **Byblos. Le** (B D g YG)
44 Rue Anatole France ☏ 28 14 36
▪ **Café de Paris** (B D E F g YG) 22-4 h
Rue de Sébastopol/Rue de la Somme
Barman speaks English. Meeting place for tourists, airline personnel etc., who can give leads to local scene, parties, etc..
▪ **DS Bar** (AC B CC f G MA) Mon-Thu 19-1, Fri Sat -2, Sun 20-24 h
15 Rue Auguste Brun ☏ 28 19 70
▪ **Metropolis** (B D g S YG) 22-4 h
Rue Surleau, Immeuble "Le Surcouf" (opposite cathedral) ☏ 27 17 77
▪ **Paris Club. Le** (B D g YG)
45-47 Avenue de Sebastopole ☏ 28 28 29
▪ **St.Hubert** (B F r)
Place des Cocotiers/Sébastopol ☏ 27 21 40
Cruisy.
▪ **421 New Center Club** (B D g YG)
c/o New Center, Route 1, 7km ☏ 28 57 00

DANCECLUBS
▪ **Star Struck** (B D g YG)
Anse Vata

SWIMMING
-Plage de Nouville (G NU) (between Cimetiere de Nouville and Kuendu Hotel)

CRUISING
-Baie des Citrons
-Around Brandshell (late evenings)
-Quartier Latin (AYOR R TV)

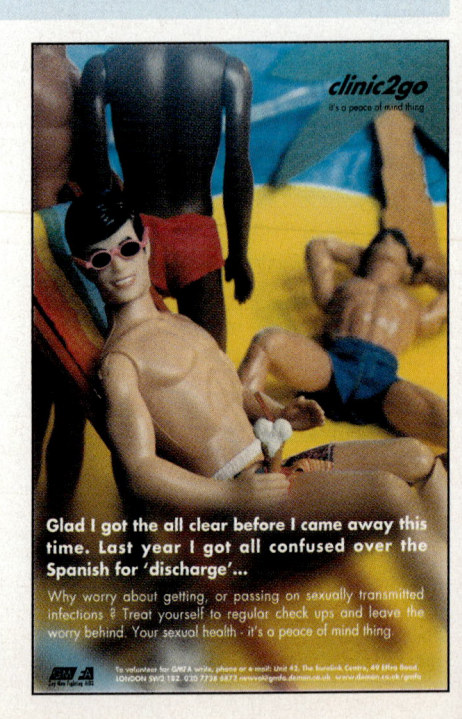

New Zealand

Name: Neuseeland • Nouvelle Zélande • Nueva Zelandia • Nuova Zelanda
Location: Oceania
Initials: NZ
Time: GMT +12
International Country Code: ☏ 64 (leave the first 0 of area codes
International Access Code: ☏ 00
Language: English, Maori
Area: 270.534 km² / 104,628 sq mi.
Currency: 1 New Zealand Dollar (NZ$) = 100 Cents
Population: 3,792,000
Capital: Wellington
Religions: 61% Christian, Maori religions
Climate: Moderate climate with dramatic regional contrasts.
Important gay cities: Auckland, Christchurch & Wellington

New Zealand is an extremely scenic country with a small but friendly population and a rich Polynesian culture among its indigenous Maori people. Volcanic and thermal activity offers spectacular sights on the North Island, while the South Island boasts beautiful mountains, glaciers and forests. Rotorua and the Bay of Islands on North Island, Queenstown and Franz Josef on South Island are favourite tourist destinations. Both islands have excellent ski slopes as well as world-class beaches for surfing.
In New Zealand sex between men over the age of 16 is permitted. Discrimination due to sexual orientation is prohibited under the laws of Human Rights. It is also one of the few countries in the world to grant residency to same-sex partners. The partnership must be four years old however.
Ever since the laws on homosexuality were reformed in 1986 a small gay scene has developed in the cities and visitors will find a variety of clubs, bars, guesthouses, restaurants, and saunas. A major gay festival called "Hero", a major gay festival is held each year in mid-February : overseas visitors can conveniently attend this on their way to Sydney's Gay and Lesbian Mardi Gras.

Neuseeland ist vor allem ein Land mit wunderbaren kontrastreichen Landschaften. Zwar ist seine Bevölkerung klein, doch dafür ist die mannigfaltige polynesische Kultur der Maori sehr lebendig.
Auf der Nordinsel wird das Bild vor allem von Thermalquellen und vulkanischer Aktivität bestimmt, während auf der Südinsel Berge, Gletscher und Wälder vorherrschen. Beliebte Touristenziele sind Rotorua und die "Bay of Islands" auf der Nordinsel, Franz Josef und Queenstown auf der Südinsel.
Seit 1986 (damals wurden die gesetzlichen Bestimmungen zur Homosexualität reformiert) hat sich in den Städten eine beachtliche schwule Szene entwickelt. Als Tourist hat man die Wahl zwischen einer ganze Reihe von Clubs, Bars, Unterkünften, Restaurants und Saunen. Eine besonders günstige Gelegenheit bietet sich im frühen Februar, denn da läßt sich auf dem Weg zum "Sydney Gay and Lesbian Mardi Gras" bequem ein Abstecher zum größten schwulen Fest Neuseelands- "Hero"- machen.
Sex ist in Neuseeland zwischen Männern über 16 Jahren erlaubt. Dem gleichgeschlechtlichen Partner wird hier das Aufenthaltsrecht gewährt. Damit ist Neuseeland eines der wenigen Länder mit solcher Rechtspraxis, auch wenn dafür die Partnerschaft bereits vier Jahre bestehen muß.

La Nouvelle Zélande est un pays splendide, très peu peuplé et de culture polynésienne. Les indigènes s'appellent les Maoris. Dans le nord de l'île, on trouve des volcans et des sources thermales. Le sud, lui, est fait de montagnes, de forêts et de glaciers. Les hauts-lieux touristiques sont, dans le nord, Rotorua et Bay of Islands et Queenstown et Franz Josef, dans le sud.
Depuis la réforme du code pénal en 1986, les choses ont commencé à bouger pour les homosexuels, dans les grandes villes surtout où on trouve maintenant de nombreux clubs, bars, pensions, restaurants et saunas gais. Tous les ans, début février, a lieu le "Hero", un festival gai qui attire les foules. Les touristes européens peuvent combiner cet évènement avec le Gay et Lesbian Mardi Gras de Sydney, en Australie.
L'homosexualité entre hommes adultes (plus de 16 ans) n'est pas un délit en Nouvelle Zélande. C'est un des rares pays au monde qui reconnaît les relations entre personnes du même sexe. Pour cela, il faut prouver que la relation tient depuis au moins 4 ans.

Nueva Zelanda es sobre todo un país con paisajes maravillosos. La afable población es poca númerosa y sigue manteniendo viva la rica cultura de sus indígenos, los Maori. El país está formado por dos islas: la norteña está caracterizada por sus fuentes termales y volcanes, mientras en la sureña predominan montañas, glaciares y bosques. Roturua y los "Bay of Islands" son los sitios más frecuentados por turistas en la isla del Norte, mientras en el sur Franz Josef y Queenstown atraen a muchos visitantes. Desde 1986 (el año cuando se llevaron a cabo las reformas legislativas referente a la homosexualidad) se ha desarrollado en las ciudades un ambiente gay muy considerable. El turista puede elegir entre varios clubs, bares, hoteles, restaurantes y saunas. Al principios de Febrero es muy buena fecha para hacer una visita: Quien participe en el "Sydney Gay and Lesbian Mardi Gras" debería aprovechar la oportunidad para hacer una pequeña excursión a la fiesta gay más grande de Nueva Zelanda, llamada "Hero". Aquí el sexo entre hombres mayores de 16 años está permitido. Nueva Zelanda es uno de los pocos paises que concede a la pareja de un homosexual el permiso de residencia, siempre y cuando la relación tenga más de cuatro años de antigüedada.

New Zealand — Akaroa

La bellezza della Nuova Zelanda è in rapporto diretto con la cordialità della sua popolazione e con la ricchezza della cultura polinesiana, tenuta viva dagli indigeni Maori. Sulla North Island Vulcani e getti termali offrono una vista spettacolare mentre montagne, foreste e ghiacciai sono le particolarità della South Island. Le destinazioni favorite dai turisti sono: Roturua e Bay of Islands sulla North Island e Queenstown e Franz Josef sulla South Island. Da quando, nel 1986, sono state modificate le leggi contro l'omosessualità, nelle varie città sono sorti locali di ogni tipo, come bar, discoteche, ristoranti e saune. Ogni anno all'inizio di febbraio ha luogo un festival chiamato "Hero": i visitatori d'oltre oceano possono assistere a questa manifestazione facendo scalo durante il loro viaggio verso il Mardi Gras di Sydney. In Nuova Zelanda sono permessi i rapporti omosessuali tra maggiori di 16 anni. Inoltre questo paese è uno dei pochi al mondo a concedere il permesso di residenza a compagni stranieri dello stesso sesso: tuttavia bisogna dimostrare che la relazione esiste da almeno quattro anni.

NATIONAL GAY INFO

■ **HERO Project Trust Board** (GLM)
PO Box 68287, Newton Auckland ☎ (0)9 360 9391
🖷 (0)9 360 9392 ✉ info@hero.org.nz 🌐 nz.com/Queer/HERO/
HERO is the major G&L event in NZ. It is comprised of a three-week arts, cultural and sporting festival, culminating in the HERO parade and dance party in mid-February. This is Auckland's equivalent of Sydney's Gay and Lesbian Mardi-Gras.

■ **Lesbian & Gay Archives of New Zealand (LAGANZ)**
Manners Street, Wellington ☎ (04) 474 3000
Research library and national lesbian/gay archives. Curator: Phil Parkinson.

■ **NZ Gay & Lesbian Tourism Association Inc.**
Private Bay MBEP 255 ✉ 6001 Auckland ☎ (0)9-303 42 62
🖷 (0)9-303 42 62 ✉ info@nzglta.org.nz 🌐 nz.com/aglb/nzglta

■ **NZ Quilt Project. The**
PO Box 7024, Wellesley St, Auckland ☎ (0)9-302 7632
🖷 (0)9-302 23 38 ✉ mbancroft@xtra.co.nz
Promoting AIDS awareness and remembrance through memorial quilts.

■ **Rights Right Now**
Auckland ☎ (0)9 358 6544
National political gay/lesbian/bi lobby group.

NATIONAL PUBLICATIONS

■ **Express - New Zealand's Newspaper of Gay Expression**
Mon-Fri 9-17 h
c/o Cornerstone Publications, PO Box 47 514, Ponsonby Auckland 2 (ground floor) ☎ (0)9 361-0190 🖷 (0)9 361-0191
editor@expressnewspaper.co.nz 🌐 gaynz.com/express
New Zealands bi-weekly read gay and lesbian publication. Free at gay venues. NZ$ 2 from newsagents.

■ **OUT! Magazine** (CC G) Mon-Fri 9-18 h
3rd Floor, OUT! Centre, 39 Anzac Avenue Auckland (2nd floor)
☎ (0)9-377 90 31 🖷 (0)9-377 77 67 ✉ out@nz.com
🌐 www.outnz.net.nz
New Zealand's national gay magazine with news, features, personals, mailorder and venue information, NZ$ 5.

NATIONAL HELPLINES

■ **AIDS National Hotline** 0-24 h
☎ (0)800-802-437
AIDS counselling & information

NATIONAL PUBLISHERS

■ **Lawrence Publishing Co. (NZ) Ltd.**
Private Bag 921 26, 3rd Floor, OUT! Centre, 39 Anzac Ave Auckland 1 2nd floor ☎ (0)9-377 90 31 🖷 (0)9-377 77 67 ✉ out@nz.com
Publisher OUT! MAGAZINE New Zealand's gay magazine and distributors of gay magazines and books.

NATIONAL COMPANIES

■ **Gaylink Tours** (CC GLM)
Level 4, Willbank House, 47 Willis Street ✉ 6001 Wellington
☎ (04) 498 0063 🖷 (04) 498 0063 ✉ reznz@gaylinktours.co.nz
🌐 www.gaylinktours.com
Providing semi-structured independent, small group and chauffeur tours for New Zealand, Australia and South Pacific.

NATIONAL GROUPS

■ **Deaf Gays & Lesbians in New Zealand**
PO Box 15 07 69 New Lynn Auckland ☎ (0)9-827 0542

■ **Gay Sport New Zealand**
PO Box 90778, Auckland ☎ (0)9-625 75 97
✉ tquayle@outnet.co.nz
National umbrella group for gay and lesbian sports groups and clubs.

■ **NZ AIDS Foundation (National Office)**
31-35 Hargrave Street, Ponsonby, Auckland ☎ (09) 303-3124
FAX 309-3149. E-Mail: nzaf@iconz.co. Prevention/education, anonymous, confidential, free HIV testing and counselling, support services for people living with HIV/AIDS.

Akaroa ☎ 03

GUEST HOUSES

■ **Totara Vale Retreat** (BF CC G MA NU OS pi WH)
Dawbers Road, Le Bons Bay ☎ 304 71 72 🖷 304 71 82
✉ erik.russell@xtra.co.nz
Located 90 min. from Christchurch 15 min from Akaroa by car. For backpackers.

OUT!
NEW ZEALAND'S National GAY Magazine

NEWS
PERSONALS
SCENE
REPORTS
FEATURES

Informative and Entertaining
Single copy $5 (+$2 Post Airmail)
Subscription $60 Airmail

OUT! MAGAZINE
Private Bag 92126 Auckland 1
Ph 64+9+377 9031 Fax 64+9+377 7767
Email:out@nz.com
http://www.outnz.net.nz

Auckland ☎ 09

Auckland is the largest city in New Zealand and has a large Polynesian population. It is a clean, modern city with excellent restaurants, hotels and tourist services. Auckland is built around two harbours and a number of extinct volcanic hills with lush greenery and fine beaches. The inner city suburbs of Ponsonby, Grey Lynn, Mt. Eden and Parnell have significant gay populations. Ponsonby is well known for its restaurants and wine bars.

Auckland ist die größte Stadt Neuseelands. Das Straßenbild wird auch durch den hohen polynesischen Bevölkerungsanteil geprägt. Sauber und modern ist diese Stadt, die exzellente Restaurants, Hotels und touristische Dienstleistungen bietet. Mehrere erloschene Vulkane und erstklassige Strände umgeben Auckland, daß an zwei Buchten entstand. Die Vororte Ponsonby, Grey Lynn, Mt. Eden und Parnell haben einen beachtlichen Anteil an schwuler Bevölkerung. Ponsonby selbst ist sehr bekannt für seine Restaurants und Weinstuben.

Auckland est la plus grande ville de Nouvelle Zélande. La majorité des Aucklandais est d'origine polynésienne. La ville est moderne, propre et jouit d'une excellente infrastructure touristique (hôtels, restaurants, services...). Auckland a été construite sur d'anciennes collines volcaniques, au bord de deux baies. Les arrondissements du centre-ville Ponsonby, Grey Lynn, Mont Eden et Parnell revêtent un intérêt particulier pour le touriste gai. Ponsonby est réputé pour ses excellents restaurants et ses nombreux bars à vin.

Auckland es la ciudad más grande de Nueva Zelanda. Lo primero que llama la atención es la gran concentración de población polinesia. La ciudad es limpia y moderna y ofrece excelentes restaurantes, hoteles y servicious turísticos. Auckland se encuentra entre encantadoras playas y varios vólcanes, que ya no son activos. Los barrios del cinturón de la ciudad como Ponsonby, Grey Lynn, Mt. Eden y Parnell poseen un considerable número de habitantes gay. Ponsonby mismo es famoso por sus restaurantes y tabernas.

Auckland, la più grande città della Nuova Zelanda, ha una grande comunità polinesiana. è una città moderna e pulita con eccellenti ristoranti, hotel e servizi turistici; è costruita intorno a due porti ed a numerose colline vulcaniche, in mezzo ad una vegetazione lussureggiante ed a spiagge incantevoli. I distretti centrali Ponsonby, Grey Lynn, Mt.Eden e Parnell hanno una rilevante comunità gay. Ponsonby è conosciuta per i suoi ristoranti e per le sue enoteche.

GAY INFO

■ **Gay/Lesbian Welfare**
2nd Floor, OUT! Centre, 39 Anzac Avenue ☎ 303 35 84
Counselling, information, person to person support.

■ **Gayline/Lesbianline** Mon-Fri 10-22 h Sat Sun 17-22 h
☎ 303 35 84
Information, support, counselling, referral.

■ **QYC-Queer Youth Chronicle**
PO Box 5426, Wellesley Street
Bimonthly youth update.

■ **Rainbow Youth Hotline** 0-24 h
☎ 376 41 55
Information line for gay and lesbian youth.

■ **The Pride Centre** 10-16.30 h
281 Karangahape Road ☎ 302 05 90 📠 303 2042
Gay, lesbian, bisexual, transpeople centre for social contact and information.

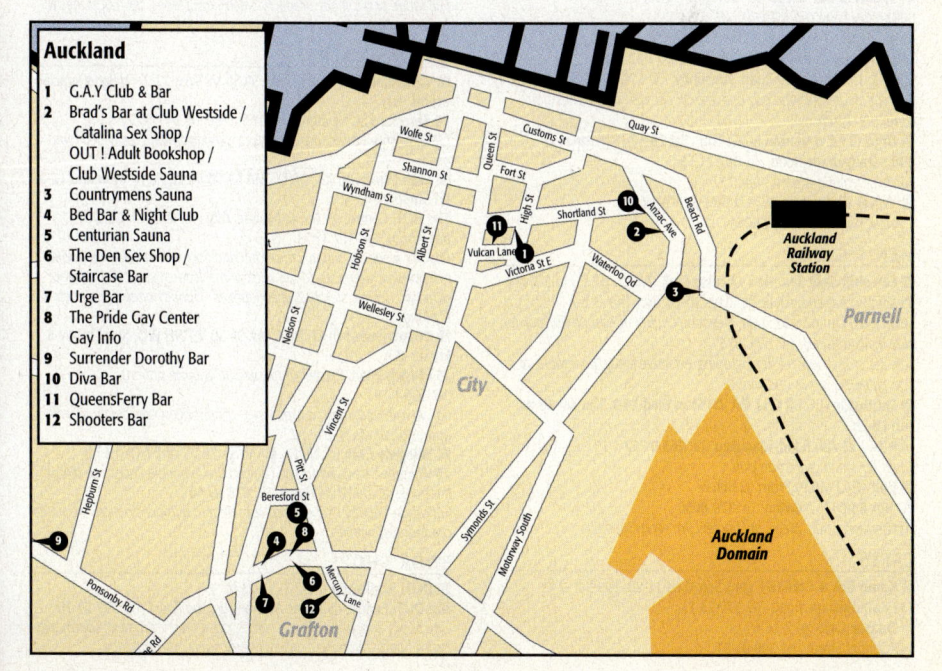

Auckland

1. G.A.Y Club & Bar
2. Brad's Bar at Club Westside / Catalina Sex Shop / OUT ! Adult Bookshop / Club Westside Sauna
3. Countrymens Sauna
4. Bed Bar & Night Club
5. Centurian Sauna
6. The Den Sex Shop / Staircase Bar
7. Urge Bar
8. The Pride Gay Center Gay Info
9. Surrender Dorothy Bar
10. Diva Bar
11. QueensFerry Bar
12. Shooters Bar

New Zealand — Auckland

■ **Triangle Community Television Ltd.**
PO Box 78034, Grey Lynn ☎ 376 5867
Community access TV.
■ **Triangle Productions (Gays & Lesbian TV)**
☎ 377 4142 📧 Q@triangle.org.nz 🌐 www.triangle.org.nz
Producers of gay and lesbian programmes for broadcast on Triangle TV.

TOURIST INFO

■ **Auckland Visitor Centre**
287 Queen Street *(behind Civic Theatre)* ☎ 979 23 33
📠 979 23 34 📧 reservations@auckland.nz.com
🌐 www.aucklandnz.com

BARS

■ **Bed Bar & Night Club** (B D glm) 22-?h
324 Karangahape Road
■ **Brad's Bar at Club Westside** (B f G MA NU SA SB WH) 12-2, Fri Sat 0-24 h
The OUT! Centre, 39 Anzac Avenue *(above OUT! bookshop, 1st floor)*
☎ 377 77 71
Bar with accompanying gay sauna.
■ **Diva** (! B G d STV) 18-?h
1 Anzac Avenue ☎ 357 09 64
Gay/mixed friendly bar and café.
■ **Phoenix Club** (B d G MA s) Thu-Sat 19-? h
St. George Tavern, Wallace Road, Papatoetoe ☎ 277 99 55
South Auckland's only gay bar.
■ **Queens Ferry** (B G MA) 16-1.30h and 3.30-06h
Vulcan Lane, City
New inner-city gay drinking spot.
■ **Shooters Bar & Café** (B CC F glm) 12-? h
5 Mercury Lane *(off K'Road)* ☎ 303-2323
Venue for VOLT leather club every Sat.
■ **Surrender Dorothy** (B f glm) Tue-Sat 17-12.30h
Shop 3, 175 Ponsonby Road, Ponsonby ☎ 376 44 60
Popular neighbourhood gay and lesbian bar with an emphasis on camp and kitsch.
■ **Urge** (B CC C d GLJ MA N VS) Thu - Sat 20-3 h, Sun 18-24 h
490 Karangahape Road ☎ 307 21 55
Leather/denim gay men's bar.
■ **Velvet Underground** (B D DR F S MA) 18-?h
1 Anzac Avenue ☎ 357 9064

MEN'S CLUBS

■ **Lateshift Safe Sex Men's Cruise Club** (AC CC DR f G LJ MA N p VS WE) Fri Sat and public holidays 20-10, Sun-Thu -3 h
Level 2, 25 Dundonald Sreet, Newton *(Couner of Basque Rd, look for blue lights outside)* ☎ 373 26 57
Safe sex cruise club, fetish playrooms, extensive maze, pool table, pinball, cable TV, drinks and snacks.
■ **Southside** (CC DR G LJ MA VS) Mon-Wed 18-2, Thu-Sat 16-04, Sun 16-2h
Unit 3A / 23 Ash Road, Manukau ☎ 263 01 22
South Auckland gay cruize club.
■ **Volt** (G LJ MA P) From 22:00h-?
PO Box 68-087, Newton ☎ 379 8058
Leathermen's club. Meets at Shooters Bar every Sat night.

CAFES

■ **Kamo Bar & Café** (B F glm) Sun-Wed 11-20, Thu-Sat -2 h
382 Karangahape Road ☎ 377 23 13
■ **Quasar Café** (g) 7-16 h
3 O'Connel Street ☎ 309 01 51

■ **Salsa Bar & Café** (B CC E F glm MA) 15-23.30 h
137A Richmond Road, Ponsonby ☎ 378 81 58
Popular local bar & café.

DANCECLUBS

■ **G.A.Y. Club & Bar** (B D G OS R S STV) Thu-Sat 21-4 h (G)
5 High Street *(Entrance - High St)*
Very popular inner-city gay dance club and bar.
■ **Sinners** (B D glm s WE) Wed-Sun 20-? h
373 Karangahape Road, Newton ☎ 308 99 85
Late night dance club and bar.
■ **Staircase** (AC B CC D glm MA s STV)
340 Karangahape Road, Newton ☎ 374 42 78
Newly refurbished gay/mixed dance venue and bar. Drag shows Fri-Sat.

RESTAURANTS

■ **Bayou Cafe** (B F glm) 17.30-? h
422 Richmond Road *(Greylynn)* ☎ 376 70 55
Bring your own alcohol. Best on Sun.
■ **Wagamamas** (B F glm) 12-15 h, 18-?
173 Karangahape Road, Newton ☎ 373 32 99

SEX SHOPS/BLUE MOVIES

■ **Catalina Video Distributors (NZ)**
The OUT! Centre, 39 Anzac Avenue *Bag, 921 26 Auckland 1*
☎ 377 90 31
Retailer/distributor of gay videos.
■ **Den. The** (DR G VS) Mon-Sun 11-? h
348 Karangahape Road ☎ 307 91 91
Gay magazines, videos, leather, adult toys and more.
■ **OUT! Gay Adult Bookshop** (G) Mon-Sat 11-22, Sun 13-22 h
The OUT! Centre, 39 Anzac Avenue, City *(ground floor)*
☎ 377 77 70
Full range of adult gay products: videos, toys, lubes, sex magazines & books and more. Inner city location.

SAUNAS/BATHS

■ **Centurian** (b CC DR f G MA SA SB VS WH) 12-2, Fri Sat & special events -6 h
18 Beresford St, Newton *(Off Pitt Street)* ☎ 377 55 71
Classical style bath house with maze, sling room and two video lounges.
■ **Club Westside** (CC DR f G MA SA SB VS WH WO) Mon-Thu 12-3, Fri-Sun 0-24 h
The OUT! Centre, 39 Anzac Avenue, City *(1st floor, above OUT! bookshop)* ☎ 377 77 71
Popular inner-city sauna, cruise club and licensed bar. New international standard premises. Maze, bunkrooms, leather playroom, workout gym, spa, sauna, steam, 2 video lounges. "Sunday afternoons- Jocks & G Strings"
■ **Countrymens** (b CC DR G MA SA SB VS WH WO) Sun-Thu 12-6, Fri Sat -8 h
151 Beach Road, Parnell *(opposite Shell service station)*
☎ 366 17 81
Sauna with pool table, a wide range of light beers and computer with games or access to internet.
■ **Wingate Club** (cc DR f G MA Pl SA SB VS WH WO) 12-? h
76 Wingate Street, Avondale *(behind the Avondale Racecourse along the banks of the Whau River)* ☎ 828 09 10
Suburban Country club atmosphere. Heated outdoor pool and secluded outdoor sun bathing.

BOOK SHOPS

■ **OUT! Bookshop** (! CC G) 11-23 h
The OUT! Centre, 45 Anzac Avenue *(ground floor)* ☎ 377 77 70
Gay books, magazines, cards, videos, adult toys, video hire. Community notice board. Auckland's only fully exclusively gay bookshop.

Auckland — New Zealand

TRAVEL AND TRANSPORT

■ **Dolphin Travel** (CC GLM) 8.30-17 h
20 Georgina Street, Freemans Bay *(Bus-College Hill)* ☏ 376 66 11
🖷 376 66 16 ✉ inbound@dolphin-travel.co.nz
🖳 www.dolphin-travel.co.nz

■ **Grey Lynn Travel** Mon-Fri 9-18, Sat 10-16 h, closed Sun
555 Great North Road, Grey Lynn ✉ 1002 *(Western Springs Bus-Surrey Crescent Shops)* ☏ 376 35 56 🖷 376 63 63.
🖳 glt@greylynntravel.co.nz.

■ **Travel Desk New Zealand** (GLM) Mon-Fri 9-17 h
The OUT! Centre, 39 Anzac Avenue ✉ 92126 *(2nd floor above OUT! Bookshop)* ☏ 377 90 31 🖷 377 77 67 🖳 traveldk@ihug.co.nz
Gay owned and operated.

HOTELS

■ **Darlinghurst Quest Inn** (BF CC glm H)
52 Eden Crescent ✉ 1001 ☏ 366 32 60 🖷 366 32 69
🖳 qrc@questapartments.com.au 🖳 www.questapartments.com.au

GUEST HOUSES

■ **Awatea** (Glm H)
☏ 378 63 95
B & B homestay in Ponsonby.

■ **Brown Kiwi Travellers Hostel. The** (B CC glm MA OS): Office: 8-20 h
7 Prosford Street, Ponsoby *(Link Bus-Redmonds Street)*
☏ 378 01 91 🖷 378 01 91 🖳 enquiries@brownkiwi.co.nz
Cosy travelers hostel in renovated two-storey colonial home located 5 minutes from the beach. Accommodation in 4 to 6 beds dormitories with lockers or four double rooms. Shared bath. Kitchen with cooking and eating utensils. Coin operated laundry.

■ **Herne Bay B&B & Serviced Apartments** (GLM H)
4 Shelley Beach Road, Herne Bay ☏ 360 03 09 🖷 360 03 89
🖳 brianross@xtra.co.nz 🖳 herne-bay.co.nz
5 rooms and 4 apartments with shower/WC, fax, minibar and kitchenette. Own key.

APARTMENTS

■ **Pacific Westmount Serviced Apartments** (AC BF CC F glm H MA OS)
23 Upper Queen Street ☏ 356 7211
FAX 356 7116. Email: andreas@dynpac.co.nz. Rates from NZ$ 135.

GENERAL GROUPS

■ **Auckland Gay & Lesbian Welfare Group** Office hours: Mon-Fri 10-17 h
The OUT! Centre, 39 Anzac Avenue *(2nd floor)* ☏ 303 35 84
🖳 aglw@xtra.co.nz
Counselling and support, local and national information.

■ **Auckland Lesbian & Gay Lawyers Group**
PO Box 5918, Wellesley Street
Support & networking for lawyers and law students.

■ **Auckland University Gay Students Association** Fri 17-19 h
c/o Student Union Auckland University, Room 114 *(Exec. lounge, 1st floor)*
Social group for gay & bisexual students & friends, on & off campus.

■ **Bears**
c/o KUBS Wellesley St.
Support and social group for hairy men, friends and admirers.

■ **Couples (Auckland) NZ**
PO Box 6251, Wellesley St. ☏ 627 23 38
For gay couples in relationships. Friendship/support/social activities.

■ **Gay Auckland Business Association (GABA)** (GLM)
PO Box 30 92 ☏ 636 98 92 🖷 636 97 26
🖳 membership@gaba.org.nz 🖳 www.gaba.org.nz
Association of gay and lesbian business & professional people.

■ **Gay Diners** (G)
☏ (021) 613 136
Wine and dine and meet new people. Gay Matchmaking Club.

■ **Mercury Motorcycle Club** Meets 3rd Fri of month.
PO Box 26-335, Epsom ☏ 479 79 20

■ **Parents of Lesbian & Gays Support Group**
☏ 846 78 89
Contact/support group for parents of gays & lesbians.

■ **Rainbow Youth Inc.** (YG)
PO Box 5426 Wellesly Street ☏ 376 41 55 ☏ 376 66 50 (24-hour info line) 🖷 376 66 50 🖳 info@rainbowyouth.org.nz
🖳 www.outnet.co.nz/RainbowYouth/
Meetings held every Sun at Kamo Café, for those under 26.

■ **Transexual Outreach (TOPS)** Mon-Fri 9-16 h
c/o PO Box 68 501 ☏ 09/366-6106
Education, health, referral service.

■ **Whakapuakitanga**
☏ 309 45 72
For young Maori Men.

HEALTH GROUPS

■ **A.D.I.O.-Needle Exchange**
227a Symonds Street ☏ 309 85 19

■ **AIDS-Hotline** 0-24 h
☏ 358 00 99
Information and counselling.

■ **Auckland Sexual Health Service**
Building 16, Auckland Hospital ☏ 307 28 85
Free and confidential testing.

■ **Body Positive / 12 on 12 Group** Mon-Fri 12.30-16h
3 Poynton Terrace, Newton ☏ 309 39 89 🖳 bp_nz@ihug.co.nz
HIV positive men's support group, drop-in centre, 12-on-12 peer support groups.

■ **Cairnhill Health Centre** Mon-Fri 8.30-17h
95 Mountain Road, Epsom ☏ 630 95 07

■ **Community AIDS Resource Team (CART)**
76 Grafton Road ☏ 367 74 36
Health support for those living with AIDS/HIV at home. Education and counselling.

■ **Herne Bay House**
☏ 376 11 92
Long and short term accommodation for people with AIDS/HIV. 24 hr cover by registered nurses.

■ **NZ AIDS Foundation Burnett Ctr/Auckland Support Service**
Mon-Tue 8.30-16.30, Wed-Thu -17 Fri -15.30 h
3 Poynton Terrace, Burnet Centre, Newton ☏ 309 55 60
🖷 302 23 38 🖳 burnettc@ihug.co.nz
Free confidential HIV testing. Gay related counselling & practical support for people living with HIV/AIDS.

HELP WITH PROBLEMS

■ **Aquarius Gay & Lesbian Alcoholics Anonymus** Meeting: Tue 19.30-20.30 h at the Pride Centre, 281 Karangahape Rd, Newton.
☏ 815 24 66

■ **Icebreakers for Men** (YG)
☏ 376 66 33
☏ 303-3584 (Gayline), ☏ 376-4155 (Rainbow Youth) Social Support for men under 26 who think they are gay or bisexual.

New Zealand — Auckland ▶ Christchurch

■ **Lesbian & Gay Narcotics Anonymous** Mon 19-? h
All Saints Church Hall, Ponsonby Road ☏ 303 14 49

RELIGIOUS GROUPS
■ **Ascent** Mass 1st Wed 19.30 h, gathering 3rd Wed
PO Box 47465, Ponsonby *(at St Benedicts, Newton)* ☏ 849 78 09
Gay Catholic group.
■ **Auckland Community Church** Service Sun 19.30 h
St.Matthews in the City, Hobson Street *Wellesley Street*
☏ 638 77 96
A Christian service of worship particularly serving those who are gay.
■ **Evangelical Gay/Lesbian Network**
Wellesley Street
■ **Universal Fellowship of Metropolitan Churches (MCC)** Meets Sun 19.30 at Methodist Church, Pitt St/Group discussion Tue 19.30 h
PO Box 3964 ✉ 1001 ☏ 629 09 27 🖷 636 80 86
🖳 nz.com/nz/queer/mccauckland/index.html
Serving the spiritual needs of the gay, lesbian, bisexual and transgender community.
■ **Zen 2000 Buddhist Association**
PO Box 6132, Wellesley Street ☏ 373 45 28

SPORT GROUPS
■ **Auckland Gay Bowling Organization**
PO Box 90-779, Auckland Mail Centre ☏ 849 36 53
■ **Gay Sport New Zealand / Team Auckland**
PO Box 90778 ☏ 625 75 97 🖳 tquayle@outnet.co.nz
Multi sports group.

SWIMMING
-St. Leonard's Beach (Catch bus to Takapuna, e.g. Long Bay Bus 839, and walk south; walk down the steps at the end of St. Leonard's Road; left is the predominately gay swimming area)
-Long Bay (30 km north of the city, reached by Long Bay Bus 839; gay area is 5 min. walk around rocks at the northern end, labelled Pohutakawa Bay)
-Ladies Bay (Catch 769 Glendowie bus along waterfront to St Heliers, ladies Bay is next beach to South. Follow road along cliff until you reach path heading down to beach)

CRUISING
-All AYOR
-Student Union Building (basement)
-Avondale (Roxbard Road-extreme caution suggested)
-Newton Road (New North Road at shopping centre)
-Kingsland (New North Road at shopping centre)
-Parnell Rose Gardens
-Cheltenham Beach
-High Street (below car park)
-Albert Park
-Domain (around Winter Gardens area)
-Ladies Bay (in bushes behind the beach)
-Long Bay/Pohutakawa Bay (most cruising in bushes around cliff at north end of the beach).

Bay of Islands/Northland ☏ 09

HOTELS
■ **Kaitia Hotel** (H NG)
☏ 408 03 60 🖷 408 03 61
Gateway to Northland/Cape Reinga, large

GUEST HOUSES
■ **Orongo Bay Homestead** (F g H)
Aucks Road, RD 1, Russell ☏ 403 75 27 🖷 403 76 75
🖳 orongo.bay@clear.net.nz
Luxury accomodation in historic house with fine dining. 4 rooms with bath/WC en suite, fax, hair-dryer and heating.

Blenheim ☏ 03

PRIVATE ACCOMMODATION
■ **Blenheim Gay Homestay** (BF GLM OS)
PO Box 62 ☏ 578 22 59 🖳 ewood@mlb.planet.gen.nz

CRUISING
-Alfred Street
-Scott Street (by Olympic Pool)
-All AYOR

Charleston ☏ 03

GUEST HOUSES
■ **Pyramid Farm** (BF F G H OS)
Highway 6, Westport ☏ 789 8487 🖷 789 8487
🖳 dkl23@yahoo.com
Guest house, wet coast. 3 bedroomed house.

Christchurch ☏ 03

GAY INFO
■ **Dextours** (AC BF GLM MA)
c/o Rainbow House, 9 The Crescent, St Martins ✉ 8002
☏ 337 14 38 🖳 mfraser.rainbowhouse@clear.net.nz.
■ **Ettie Rout News**
PO Box 21-285, Edgeware ☏ 379 19 53 🖷 365 24 77
Monthly local gay info.
■ **Gayline Christchurch** Mon 20-21, Sat 19.30-22 h
PO Box 25-165 ☏ 379 39 90 (24 h)
Info about local places and events for lesbians and gays. Also contact for:
-Futures Forum (LGB activist group)
-Icebreakers (Support group for young gays & lesbians)
-Men loving men-Oral history project
■ **Loud & Queer** Wed 18-19 h (RDU 98.3 FM-student radio) Gay show.
c/o Canterbury Students Association, Private Bag

BARS
■ **UBQ Southern Boys** (AC B CC D f G MA N S) 19-? h
88 Lichfield Street ✉ 8001 *(opposite "Dick Smith Electronics" store)*
☏ (0)21-379 29 10
Special Feature & drag show nights.

DANCECLUBS
■ **Ministry** (B CC D f G)
18 Lichfield Street
Fri featuring G.A.Y. @Ministry. Outdoor cruising area. Gay members have free entry on Fri/Sat nights.
■ **Platinium** (B D GLM)
78 Lichfield St. ☏ 377 78 91

SAUNAS/BATHS
■ **Colombo** (CC DR f G MG P SA VS WH) 11-23 h
661 Colombo Street *(upstairs)* ☏ 366 73 52
A boutique bathhouse catering to mature and non-scene gay and bisexual men. See website for weekly special events. Including an OUT! bookshop.
■ **Menfriends** (b cc DR f G lj P SA SB VS WH YG) Sun-Thu 12-2, Fri Sat -6 h
83 Lichfield Street *(upstairs)* ☏ 377 17 01
Sauna, cruise club and shop on two floors frequented by a young crowd. Lots of special feature nights.

BOOK SHOPS
■ **Davids Book Exchange** (g VS)
181 High Street ☏ 366 20 57
Gay magazines, books and videos.

Christchurch ▶ Dunedin — New Zealand

■ **Kate Sheppard Bookshop** (glm)
145 Manchester Street ☎ 379 07 84
■ **OUT! Bookshop** (G) Open until 23:00h
At Colombo Healthclub, 661 Colombo Street ☎ 366 73 52
Huge selection of reading material and full range of American WET lube as well as videos, adult toys, poppers.
■ **Scorpio Books** (AC CC glm) Mon-Thu 8.30-17.30, Fri -21, Sat 9.30-16, Sun 12-16 h
79 Hereford Street/Oxford Terrace ✉ 8015 ☎ 379 28 82

TRAVEL AND TRANSPORT
■ **Settlers Travel Ltd.** (CC) Mon-Fri 8.30-17.30 h
26 New Regent Street ☎ 379 51 87 📠 379 86 29

GUEST HOUSES
■ **Dorothy's** (B BF BB glm)
2 Latimer Square ☎ 365 60 34 📠 365 60 35
■ **Rainbow House Bed & Breakfast** (BF GLM H)
9 The Crescent ✉ 8002 *(off the ends of Hillsborough Terrace)*
☎ 337 14 38 📠 337 14 96
✉ mfraser.rainbowhouse@clear.net.nz
✉ members.tripod.com/~martin_fraser/index.htm
Located 8 minutes from downtown Christchurch. Rates NZ$ 30-40. Additional bed 15. Bf incl.
■ **Ross's Homestay** (BF GLM OS)
410 Oxford Terrace, Avonloop ☎ 336 0962 📠 336 0384
✉ rossed@xtra.co.nz
Quiet home overlooking the Avon river. Easy walk to central city and all venues.

PRIVATE ACCOMMODATION
■ **Glendurgan Homestay** (BF G)
☎ 329 41 04
Private home with great views 30 mins. from city.
■ **NZ Gay Hospitality Exchange** 10-20h
386 Oxford Terrace ✉ 8001 ☎ 379 94 93
✉ gic_chchnz@excite.com
Accommodation exchange for gay overseas visitors. To be arranged before traveling.

GENERAL GROUPS
■ **Campus Queers**
c/o University of Canterbury Students' Association *Ilam Road*
☎ 348 70 69
■ **Gay Information Line** 24 h
PO Box 25-165 ✉ 8030 ☎ 379 39 90 ✉ gic_chchnzqexcite.com
■ **Gays & lesbians in business (GLIB)**
PO Box 22-099 ☎ 366 33 12 📠 381 01 73 ✉ glib@xtra.co.nz

HEALTH GROUPS
■ **HIV Support Group**
☎ 379 19 53
(Contact Terry, NZ AIDS Foundation, Ettie Rout Centre)

HELP WITH PROBLEMS
■ **Gayline** Mon 20-21, Sat 19.30-22 h
PO Box 25-165 ✉ 8002 ☎ 379 47 96
Phone couselling and information.

RELIGIOUS GROUPS
■ **All Saints Metropolitan Community Church** Sun 11 h
PO Box 13 468 ☎ 389 32 35
■ **Ascent** Meetings 3rd Thu of month
PO Box 22-718 ☎ 355 85 76
Support group for gay Catholics.

SPORT GROUPS
■ **Avon Mens' Netball Club**
☎ 338 11 03
■ **Gay Sport New Zealand Team Christchurch**
c/o Dan Knowles, PO Box 212 85 ☎ 385 10 01
✉ ettie@ihug.co.nz.

CRUISING
-North Hagley Park (next to Rolleston Avenue)
-Waimairi Beach (1km north of the Surf Club in dunes)
-Spencer Park (along the sand dunes)
-All AYOR
-All are (AYOR)
-Arts Centre (Relleston Avenue)
-Brighton Pier (New Brighton Beach)
-Denton Park (Sports Pavillion)
-Hagley Park (Armagh Street Entrance of changing shed)
-Jellie Park (Greers Road)
-Malvern Park (Innes Road)
-Manchester Street Car Park (Manchester Street)
-North Beach Surf Pavillion (in changing shed)
-St. Albans Park (Madras street around changing shed)
-Wordsworth Street (next Colombo Street Corner)

Dunedin ☎ 03

GAY INFO
■ **Dunedin Gay Radio•One** Tue Thu 18-19 h (FM 91 MHz)
☎ 477 19 69
Thu "Tea with the Boys", Tue "Lesbian show"
■ **Gayline** 0-24 h Answering machine. Wed 17.30-19-30
Fri 19.30-22.30 h
PO Box 1382 ☎ 477 20 77
Info & support for gays, friends and family.
■ **Otago Gaily Times**
Private Bag 6171 ☎ 474 77 32
Monthly local gay info.

CAFES
■ **Powder @ Fusin Café**
Frederick Street
Sat nights: mixed gay crowd.
■ **Tangenté Café** (A AC BF CC F glm MA WE) 8-15.30 h
111 Moray Place ☎ 477 02 32
■ **Zambesi** (b f g MA) 2nd & 4th Fri
Moray Plaace *(next to Fortune Cafe)* ☎ 477 20 77

SAUNAS/BATHS
■ **Bodyworks Club** (cc DR G MA P SA SB VS) Mon Tue Thu 17-24, Wed Sun 12-24, Fri Sat 12-2 h
284 Princes Street ✉ 9001 ☎ 477 82 28
Private men's club.

BOOK SHOPS
■ **Modernway Books** (g)
331 George Street ☎ 477 66 36
Stocks OUT! magazine.
■ **Southern Books** (NG)
225 King Edward Street
Stocks OUT!Magazine

TRAVEL AND TRANSPORT
■ **Otago Campervans** (G) 0-24 h
40 Franklin Street ☎ 473 09 36 📠 473 09 46
Fully self-contained 2-berth campervans.

New Zealand — Dunedin ▶ Hastings

GENERAL GROUPS
■ **Gay/Bi Boys On Campus** Meets every 2nd week Wed 13-14 h in Otago Room.
c/o OUSA, PO Box 1436 ☎ 477 20 77
Clubs and socials organized.
■ **Icebreakers**
c/o Gayline, PO Box 1382 ☎ 477 20 77
Social group for gays under 25 years.
■ **Queerspace** Thu 19.30-23 h
Tangente Café, Upper Money Race
Queer social space / companionship.
■ **Tuatua**
PO Box 1382 ☎ 477 20 77
Social group for men over 30.
■ **Youth Esteem Services (YES)**
☎ 473 97 20
Youth Group for those under 25. Contact Gayline.

HEALTH GROUPS
■ **NZ AIDS Foundation Otago**
154 Hanover Street ☎ 474 02 21 📠 474 76 31
■ **Sexual Health Clinic**
☎ 474 95 65
Free STD info and treatment.

HELP WITH PROBLEMS
■ **Gayline** Wed 17.30-19.30 Fri 19.30-22.30 h
PO Box 13 82 ☎ 477 20 77
For information and help.

RELIGIOUS GROUPS
■ **Ascent Dunedin**
PO Box 5328, Moray Place ☎ 477 20 77
Catholic-based gay and lesbian group. All welcome.

SPORT GROUPS
■ **Gay Sports New Zealand Team Dunedin**
Libby Knight, 30 Chambers Street ☎ 472 55 99
Multi sports group.

CRUISING
-Jubilee Park (Queens Avenue)
-Smailles Beach
-St. Clair Beach (at sand dunes and by Barnes Memorial Lookout)
-All AYOR
-Dowling Street (opposite Queens Gardens)
-Upper Botanic Gardens
-Albany Street (near George Street)
-All AYOR

Fielding ☎ 04

GUEST HOUSES
■ **Westward Bed & Breakfast** (g H)
☎ 323 93 77

Gisborne ☎ 06

PRIVATE ACCOMMODATION
■ **Gisborne - Gay Villa** (GLM)
☎ 863 04 13 ☎ (025) 736 544
Bed and breakfast accommodation.

Hamilton ☎ 07

GAY INFO
■ **Different Strokes** Sun 20-22 h (89 FM)
Private Bag 3059 ☎ 838 44 40

■ **Social Tendencies BBS** 0-24 h
☎ 846 26 03
Social bulletin board service on Internet. Use system password m2m1 when logging on for the first time.

BARS
■ **Next Door Bar** (B GLM) Wed-Sun 17.30-3 h
10 High Street, Frankton ☎ 847 86 35

SAUNAS/BATHS
■ **10 High** (b f G MA SA SB VS) 17.30-1.30 h
10 High Street, Frankton ☎ 847 86 35

GENERAL GROUPS
■ **Parents of Gay Waikato**
☎ 827 49 35
Supportive parents group.

HEALTH GROUPS
■ **NZ AIDS Foundation (Waikato)**
3/17 Ohaupo Road ☎ 838 35 57 ☎ 838 35 11 📠 838 35 14

HELP WITH PROBLEMS
■ **Waikato Gay and Lesbian Support and Information Service**
(GLM MA) Wed 20-22 h (drop-in centre)
4 Te Aroha St. (Link House) ☎ 855 54 29
24 h telephone answer phone, message regulary updated

RELIGIOUS GROUPS
■ **MCC Waikato** (GLM) Sun 17 h
PO Box 52 17, Frankton ☎ 855 06 51

SPORT GROUPS
■ **Team Hamilton/Cambridge**
☎ 827 58 67

CRUISING
All are AYOR!
-Garden Place
-City Square
-Memorial Park (also known as Parana Park)
-Victoria Lake (near miniature railway)
-Towpath near Waikato River

Hastings ☎ 06

MEN'S CLUBS
■ **Embassy Cruise Club** (G b f MA VS) Tue 11-14, Wed-Thu 16-1, Sat, 16-3, Sun 17-21 h
King St/Heretauna St. ☎ 870 71 11

BOOK SHOPS
■ **Stortford Lodge Bookshop** (g)
1102 Heretaunga Street

GUEST HOUSES
■ **Providencia Country House** (AC BF CC glm H msg)
225 Middle Road, R.D. 2, Hawkes Bay ☎ 877 23 00
🖳 nz.comwebnz/tpac/gaynz/Prov.dencia.html
Beautiful historical house in the middle of a prosperous wine region. Three rooms with bath/WC.

CRUISING
-Cornwell Park

Hokitika ▶ Nelson **New Zealand**

Hokitika ☏ 03

PRIVATE ACCOMMODATION
■ **Beachhouse Hostel** (B CC F H NG OS)
139 Revell Street ✉ 7900 *(Main street on seafrontage)*
☏ 755 63 349   📠 755 63 49   💻 beachhouse1999@hotmail.com
Accommodation for backpackers.

GENERAL GROUPS
■ **Wild Wild West Gay Club**
☏ 768 03 66

Invercargill ☏ 03

GAY INFO
■ **Gayline** (GLM) Gayline: Wed 17.30-19.30 Fri 19.30-22.30 h
☏ 477 20 77

MEN'S CLUBS
■ **Haven Cruise Club. The** Phone for hours.
115 Spey Street ☏ 214 13 37

CRUISING
All AYOR
-Town Hall (back of Tay Street)
-Queens Park Gardens (Kelvin Street side)

Kaitaia ☏ 09

HOTELS
■ **Kaitaia Hotel** (B g H)
☏ 408 03 60   📠 408 03 61
Historic Hotel near 90 mile beach at Bay of Plenty.

PRIVATE ACCOMMODATION
■ **Awanui Homestay** (G)
☏ 406 77 70
Retreat for men, NZ$20 per night.

Levin ☏ 04

SAUNAS/BATHS
■ **Woolshed. The** (DR G MA SA)
153 Waihou Road ☏ 368 58 48
Mens sauna and cruise club.

GENERAL GROUPS
■ **Rainbow Club** Meetings last Sat of month.
PO Box 134, Otaki Railway ☏ 293 71 77
Friendship & social contact group for Kapiti/Harawhenuc area.

Masterton ☏ 06

GUEST HOUSES
■ **Koeke Lodge** (E G H)
"Koeke" Upper Plain Road ☏ 377 24 14
💻 koekelodge@ytra.co.nz
4 rooms with shower/WC, radio. Rates single NZ$ 75, double 95-120. Additional bed 30. Half-board.

Mount Maunganui ☏ 07

CAFES
■ **Muffin Boutique** (BF F glm) 8-16h
195 Mt. Maunganui Road *(Mount shopping area)* ☏ 575 8674

GENERAL GROUPS
■ **Fabulous Group (Social Men Grop)**
☏ 577 04 33

CRUISING
-Papamoa Beach (nude bathing in the sand dunes)
-Soundshell (Marine Parade/Grace Avenue)
-The Mall (Harbourside-Changing Sheds)

Napier ☏ 06

GUEST HOUSES
■ **Cornucopia Lodge** (BF CC F GLM pi) All year
361-367 State Highway 5 R.D. 2 Eskdale ✉ 4021 ☏ 836 65 08
📠 836 65 18   💻 info@cornucopia-lodge.com
🖥 www.cornucopia-lodge.com
■ **Decor City Motor Lodge** (CC g H)
308 Kennedy Rd. ☏ 843 43 42   📠 423 75 65
💻 decocity@xtra.co.nz

GENERAL GROUPS
■ **Club 80**
PO Box 8341
Social/support Group for men over 30.
■ **Regal**
☏ 835 74 82
Social group: Meeting 3rd Sat at Baycity Club, Milton Road.

HELP WITH PROBLEMS
■ **Gayline/Icebreakers** Mon-Sun 17-20 h
☏ 835 74 82

CRUISING
-Soundshell
-Marine parade (near coloured fountain)
-Anderson Park (Auckland Road-Greenmeadows)
-Spriggs Park (Hardinge Road).

Nelson ☏ 03

RESTAURANTS
■ **Ribbetts Restaurant** (F g)
20 Tahunanvi Drive ☏ 548 69 11

HOTELS
■ **Te Puna Wai Lodge** (BF CC f GLM LJ MA OS)
24 Richardson Street, Port Hills ✉ 7001 ☏ 548 76 21
📠 546 76 21   💻 richardhewetson@clear.net.nz
Restored historic colonial villa, sea & mountain views. Languages: english, german, spanish, french, danish, polish, portuguese, russian. From NZ$ 115.

GUEST HOUSES
■ **Old Cederman House Bed & Breakfast**
Main Road, Riwaka reservation *(near Able Tasman national Park)*
☏ 528 44 84
■ **Palmgrove Guest House** (BF CC g H MA OS) All year
15 Tasman Street ☏ 547 28 27   📠 545 07 97
💻 kevin@ts.co.nz or ntilly@xtra.co.nz.   🖥 www.ts.co.nz/kevin
Central location. 2 double rooms, 4 single rooms, partly with WC/bath. All rooms with balcony, telephone, TV, radio, heating, own key. Rates single NZ$ 35-45, double 70-85. Additional bed 15. Bf incl.

New Zealand Nelson ▶ Rotorua

PRIVATE ACCOMMODATION
■ **Golden Bay Homestay** (BF G H)
C/- H Harries NZ Post, Takata ☏ 525 97 81
Homestay accomodation.
■ **Nelson Famestay** (BF H)
☏ 522 44 84
Short or long country farm stays.

CAMPING
■ **Autumn Farm** (NU)
R.D. 1, Golden Bay ✉ 7172 (*Golden Bay at the top of the South Island*) ☏ 525 9013 ✉ stay@autumnfarm.com
💻 www.autumnfarm.com
Set in 15 acres of secluded woodlands. Communal bathhouse, kitchen and laundry plus comfortable guest house.

GENERAL GROUPS
■ **Nelson Countrymens Group** (over 30's Social Group)
☏ 548 64 70
■ **Spectrum (Nelson) Inc.** (G MA) Thu 19.30-22.30 h
PO Box 40 22, Nelson South *(Meets at 42 Franklyn Street)*
☏ 548 2390 ✉ spectrumnelson@hotmail.com
Social and support group.
■ **Spectrum Drop-In Centre** Thu 19.30-22.30 h
42 Frankly Street

RELIGIOUS GROUPS
■ **Ascent**
138 Vanguard Street ☏ 355 85 76
Catholic gay support group.

CRUISING
-At the Cathedral
-Tahuna Beach
-Rabbit Island (Beach)

New Plymouth ☏ 06
GENERAL GROUPS
■ **Taranaki Pride Alliance**
PO Box 6074, Moturoa
Gay, lesbian, bi and transperson contact and publishers of the Rainbow Times.

SWIMMING
-Back Beach (behind Paratutu, New Plymouth during summer.

CRUISING
-By the State Hotel

Palmerston North ☏ 06
BARS
■ **Club Q (Manawatu Lesbian & Gay Rights Association)** (B D GLM MA S) Sat 20-? h
PO Box 14 91 ☏ 358 53 78
Contact Gayline for address and schedule of events.

GUEST HOUSES
■ **Bed and Breakfast** (g H)
☏ 323 93 77

GENERAL GROUPS
■ **Manawatu Chapter Gay Couples**
☏ 323 93 77
■ **Manawatu Lesbian and Gay Rights Association**
Fri 20 Sat 21.30 h
PO Box 14 91 ☏ 358 53 78

Social/Welfare group for gay men, lesbians and bisexuals. Club Q (behind Square Edge shopping complex, upstairs) opens Fri 20-?, Sat 21-? h.

HELP WITH PROBLEMS
■ **Gayline/Lesbianline** 0-24 information, Wed Fri 19-22 h counselling
☏ 358 53 78
Also contact for Icebreakers (Support group for gays under 26)

SPECIAL INTEREST GROUPS
■ **Club Farout** Thu, Fri & Sat from 20:00h

CRUISING
-City Square
-Fitzroy Park
-Milverton Park

Queenstown ☏ 03
GUEST HOUSES
■ **Coneburn** (BF CC G NU SA WH)
PO Box 274 ☏ 442 23 81
Guest house in rural setting.
■ **Wahine House Bed & Breakfast**
31 Lomond Crescent ☏ 441 81 83

GENERAL GROUPS
■ **Queer Queenstown**
PO Box 1215 ☏ 025 334 187 ☏ 441 81 83 📠 441 81 83
✉ wahinehouse99@hotmail.com

CRUISING
-Waterfront Jetty (city center)

Rotorua ☏ 07
GAY INFO
■ **Gayline Information & Support** Tue 19-21 h
☏ 348 35 98
Confidential support, friendship and info for gays & bisexuals.
■ **Rotorua Gay Information/What's On**
☏ 348 01 93

GUEST HOUSES
■ **Devon Homestay** (BF F GLM MA OS p YG)
Devon Street ☏ 348 01 93 ☏ (0)621 388 311 📠 348 01 93
✉ parkhill@wave.co.nz
■ **Troutbeck-Homestay and Bed & Breakfast** (BF CC F GLM H MA)
PO Box 242, 16 Egmont Road, Ngongotaha ☏ 357 47 95
📠 357 47 80 ✉ troutbeck@troutbeck.co.nz
💻 nz.com/webnz/troutbeck
Homestay (bf incl.) accomodations. Rates NZ$ 50 for a single, NZ$ 80 for a kingsize double. Dinner NZ$15 p.p.

PRIVATE ACCOMMODATION
■ **Ascott Villa** (H)
7 Meade St. ☏ 348 48 95 ☏ 348 83 84 💻 www.ascottvilla.co.nz
Superior Bed & Breakfast. Gay owned. Member ILGTA. Historic house and gardens with elegant charm.

CRUISING
-The Domain (Lakeside Park)
-Kerosene creek (natural hot water stream and swimming pool)
Kuirau Park, lake front.

804 | *SPARTACUS* 2001/2002

Takaka - Golden Bay ☎ 03

GUEST HOUSES
■ **Autumn Farm** (BF F G H NU OS p) All year
Central Takaka Road ✉ 7172 ☎ 525 90 13
💻 stay@autumnfarm.com 💻 www.autumnfarm.com

Taupo ☎ 07

PRIVATE ACCOMMODATION
■ **Boulevard Spa Motel** (H NG)
261 Waihi Rd.   ☎ 800-369 000   📠 578 32 68
Gay owned accommodation

CRUISING
-Small public garden near new library (SH1, central Taupo)
-Waterfront (public toilets)

Tauranga ☎ 07

GAY INFO
■ **Tauranga Gayline** 2nd & 4th Wed in Month 14-20:00h
all other Wed. nights 18-22:00h
☎ 577 0481
New information and helpline.

PRIVATE ACCOMMODATION
■ **Boulevard Spa Motel** (H NG)
261 Waihi Road   ☎ 800-369 000   📠 578 32 68
Gay owned accommodation.

GENERAL GROUPS
■ **Guys Nite Out**
PO Box 9125   ☎ 577 04 33
Monthly social group.

CRUISING
-Memorial Park
-Tauranga Domain (Hamilton/Cameron Road).

Timaru ☎ 03

GENERAL GROUPS
■ **Aoraki Lesbian/Gay Group**
PO Box 59   ☎ 684 7016
Social gatherings and information.

CRUISING
-Central Stafford Street (underground)
-Caroline Bay (near rail viaduct and Loop Road)

Waikanae

SWIMMING
-Peka Peka (NU OG) (5 km North of Waikanae. Turn left off SH1 into Peka Peka Road. The gay area is about 200 m north along beach)

Wanganui ☎ 06

HEALTH GROUPS
■ **Wanganui HIV/AIDS Co-Ordinator**
c/o Youth Advice Centre, 58 Dublin St.   ☎ 347 13 83

CRUISING
- P -area of the Olympic Swimming Pool (by the yacht harbor)
-Uretiti Beach (NU) (go onto the beach from the car P and turn right, keep walking until you are out of the mixed area)

Wellington ☎ 04

✱ The capital of New Zealand is located at the southern tip of the North Island and because of the fresh breezes is called "Windy City". Wellington is not surprisingly a bit conservative owing to it being the centre for government administration with many governmental authorities located there. Wellington is worth visiting because of it's mild climate and wonderful position between ocean and mountains and not forgetting it's small lively gay scene.

✱ Die Hauptstadt Neuseelands liegt am Südzipfel der Nordinsel und wird nicht zu Unrecht "windy city" genannt, weht hier doch eigentlich immer eine frische Brise.
Wellington ist das Verwaltungszentrum des Landes und Sitz diverser Behörden und so wundert es nich, daß man sich hier etwas konservativer im legeren Auckland gibt. Doch das ausgeglichene und milde Klima, die wunderschöne Lage zwischen Ozean und Bergen, sowie eine kleine aber lebendige Szene, machen einen Stop auf jeden Fall lohnenswert.

✱ La capitale de la Nouvelle Zélande se trouve à la pointe sud de l'île du nord, et n'est pas nommée pour rien "windy city", même si c'est toujours une brise fraiche qui souffle ici. Wellington est le centre administratif du pays et le siège de nombreuses administrations, et il n'est donc pas surprenant que les gens soient un peu plus conservateurs qu'à Auckland. Mais le climat doux et équilibré, la situation géographique magnifique, entre l'océan et les montagnes, et un milieu gai petit mais vivant font qu'un arrêt dans cette ville en vaut la peine.

● La capital de Nueva Zelanda se encuentra en el más extremo sur de la isla norteña y su apodo es, y con mucha razón "windy city", ya que aquí siempre corre una suave brisa. Wellington es el centro administrativo del país y la sede de varios ministerios y oficinas estatales. Por ello, no es de extrañar que la gente de aquí se muestre más conservadora en comparación con el liberal Auckland. Pero un visita merecerá sin duda la pena, no solo por el agradable clima, sino también por la situación impresionante de Wellington entre oceano y montañas y su pequeño, pero muy animado ambiente.

✱ La capitale della Nuova Zelanda è situata sul punto meridionale della permanente brezza è comprensibile che la città venga nominata la "windy city". Wellington è il centro amministrativo e la sede di diverse istituzioni. Quindi non c'è da stupirsi che qui l'atmosfera è un po' più conservativa in rispetto ad Auckland, dove la vita è più facile. Però il clima mite ed equilibrato, la posizione meravigliosa tra oceano e montagna, e un'ambiente gay piccolo ma vivace, valgono la pena di fermarvisi.

GAY INFO
■ **Awhina Newsletter**
PO Box 7287, Wellington South   ☎ 389 31 69
Information about Aids.
■ **Gay Broadcasting Collective** Sat 11.15-12.15 h (AM 783 kHz)
PO Box 24-165 Manners St   ☎ 385 87 83
■ **Gay Switchboard** 19.30-22 h
PO Box 11 372   ☎ 473 78 78
Information about events, venues, gay groups & accommodation.

BARS
■ **£ (Pound Sterling)** (A AC B bf CC D F Glm MA N)
Tue-Sun 11-3 h, Mon closed
The Oaks Building, Cnr Dixon St & Cuba Mall *(Upstairs)*
■ **Bojangles** (B D F GLM MA S)
60 Dixon St.   ☎ 384 84 45
■ **Chad's Bar @ Club Wakefield** (B F G) 12-? h
15 Tory St.
Bar is part of Club Wakefield Sauna & Cruise Club.

New Zealand — Wellington

MEN'S CLUBS
■ **Sanctuary** (CC DR G LJ MA P) Tue Sun 20-24, Wed Thu -2, Fri Sat -6 h, Mon closed
39 Dixon Street ✉ 6001 (3rd floor) ☎ 384 15 65
Cruise Club, $ 8 beofrer 20 h and $ 12 after 20 h. Tue/Wed 2 for 1 night, Sunday free for students with I.D.
■ **Valve** Wed 20.30- ?
154 Vivian Street ☎ (0800) 4 213 2699
For bisexual and gay men. Also skinheads, levis, uniforms, leather and bears fans. Gay on Wed. only.

CAFES
■ **Eva Dixons Place** (F g)
35A Dixon Street ☎ 384 10 00

SEX SHOPS/BLUE MOVIES
■ **Out! Bookshop** (G) Mon-Sat 11-23 h
15 Tory Street *(same building as Wakefield Sauna)* ☎ 385 44 00
Gay magazines, books, videos, adult supplies. Wellington's only gay adult shop. Also Wellington office of OUT! Magazine. Community notice board and info.

ESCORTS & STUDIOS
■ **Adam Male Escorts**
☎ 384 85 15
Incalls and outcalls available.
■ **Imaginations**
☎ 387 73 40
■ **Wellington Gay Escorts**
☎ 386 22 29

SAUNAS/BATHS
■ **Checkmate** (CC DR f G MA SA SB VS wh) Sun-Thu12-2, Fri Sat -6 h. 364 days.
20 Garrett Street, City *(Three private street entrances from Cuba Street; through Glover Park; or down Bute Street)* ☎ 385-6356
With lounges, billiard table, computer, chess & backgammon.
■ **Club Wakefield** (B DR f G MA SA SB VS WH WO) 12-2, Thu- 3, Fri Sat -6 h
15 Tory Street *(near Museum of New Zealand, next to OUT! bookshop)* ☎ 385 44 00
Long established popular men's sauna & cruise club, incorporates "Chad's " licensed bar.

FITNESS STUDIOS
■ **Les Mills World of Fitness** (NG WO)
2/52 Taranaki Street ☎ 384 88 98
Inner city gym popular with gay men.

BOOK SHOPS
■ **Unity Books** (GLM)
57 Willis Street ☎ 499 42 45

TRAVEL AND TRANSPORT
■ **Gaylink Tours** (CC GLM)
Level 4, Willbank House, 47 Willis Street ✉ 6001 ☎ 498 0063
☎ 385 7735 ✉ reznz@gaylinktours.co.nz
🖥 www.gaylinktours.co.nz
Providing semi-structured independent, small group and chauffeur tours for New Zealand, Australia and South Pacific.
■ **Rainbow Rentals** (CC G)
PO Box 11-462 ✉ 6001 ☎ 384 18 65 📠 384 18 35
✉ reznz@rainbowrentals.co.nz
🖥 webnz.com/tpac/gaynz/Rainbow
Providing rental car and campervan hirer throughout New Zealand.

PRIVATE ACCOMMODATION
■ **Koromiko Homestays** (CC GLM)
11 Koromiko Road, Highbury ☎ 938 6539 📠 (021) 553 370
✉ gaystay@paradise.net.nz
Accommodation for gay men and their friends.

GENERAL GROUPS
■ **Gays of the Hutt**
☎ 385 06 74
Local neighbourhood fellowship.
■ **Icebreakers**
PO Box 9247 ☎ 473 78 78 ✉ ice-breakers@geocities.com

HEALTH GROUPS
■ **AIDS/HIV Hotline** 24 hrs
☎ 0800 802 437
Counselling and information service.
■ **Area Health Board Aids Programme Co-Ordinator**
☎ 472 56 79
■ **Body Positive**
PO Box 7287, Wellington South ☎ 389 31 69 📠 389 42 07
■ **NZ AIDS Foundation Wellington (Awhina Centre)**
Mon-Fri 9-17h
45 Tory Street, PO Box 9247 ☎ 381 66 40 📠 381 66 41
✉ nzaf.org.nz
Confidential HIV testing and counselling.

HELP WITH PROBLEMS
■ **Counselling Services**
☎ 384 55 49
(John Mayesm) private counsellor.
■ **Narcotics Anonymous Lesbian & Gay Group** Mon 18 h
St Andrews on the Terrace, 30 The Terrace

RELIGIOUS GROUPS
■ **Ascent** (GLM MA)
PO Box 276 ☎ 387 32 05
Support group for gay lesbian catholics, monthly mass and social activities.
■ **"Galaxies" - Lesbian, Gay & Bisexual Christian Group** "Galaxies" Meets 1st & 3rd Sun 19.30 h each month at St. Andrews on theTerrace.
PO Box 5203 Wellington ☎ 472 9211
✉ standrews.ontheterrace@xtra.co.nz
🖥 nz.com/NZQueer/Galaxies

SPORT GROUPS
■ **Capital Walking Group** 1st Sun each month
☎ 473 10 19
■ **Gay Sports New Zealand Team Wellington**
Kerri Swinn, 14 Akatea Street, Berhanpore *South* ☎ 389 38 30
■ **Wellington Gay Cycling Group**
☎ 389 49 41

SWIMMING
-Breaker Bay (at Wellington Harbor entrance; catch bus 3 to last stop and walk either up through Pass of Branda or take coast trail around Point Dorset)
-Paekakariki Beach (20 mins. out of Wellington North (State Highway 1). entrance to QEII park opposite railway crossing. Drive down to beach- P 6)

CRUISING
-Oriental Parade (sunny days)
-Paekakariki Beach
-Lower Hutt (near the river)
-Lower Hutt (near Council offices and park)
-Thorndon Road

806 **SPARTACUS** 2001/2002

West Coast ▸ Whangarei | **New Zealand - Nicaragua**

GAYLINK TOURS

AUSTRALIA, NEW ZEALAND AND THE PACIFIC'S MOST EXPERIENCED TOUR PLANNER

For detailed itineraries and secure online bookings:

www.gaylinktours.com

Independent travel package, ski and small group tour specialists – Travel Agents most welcome

IGLTA	NZGLTA	GALTA	TIANZ	ITOC
Member International Gay & Lesbian Travel Association	Member New Zealand Gay & Lesbian Tourism Association	Member Gay and Lesbian Tourism Australia	Member Tourism Industry Association New Zealand	Member Inbound Tour Operators Council of New Zealand

West Coast ☎ 03

GAY INFO
■ **Gayline Westport** Wed Fri 19-20.30 h
PO Box 185 ☎ 789 60 27
Information and help

Whangarei ☎ 09

GAY INFO
■ **Gay Help** Tue Thu 19-21.30 h
PO Box 7 ☎ 37 76 20
Support, counselling & information.

GENERAL GROUPS
■ **Gay Noth Social Group**
PO Box 1081 ☎ 21-864 ✉ john@merlin.ne.nz
🖳 nzco.co.nz/NZ/Queer/GayNorth/

HEALTH GROUPS
■ **Northland Health HIV/AIDS Network**
PO Box 10173, Te Mai ☎ 430 41 01

SWIMMING
-Uretit Beach (MA NU) (Travel 30 km south from Whangerei. Uretiti is well signposted on the East Coast. Gay section is at south end of beach)

Nicaragua

Location: Central America
Initials: NIC
Time: GMT -6
International Country Code: ☎ 505 (no area codes)
International Access Code: ☎ 00
Language: Spanish; English
Area: 120,254 km² / 50,456 sq mi.
Currency: 1 Córdoba (C$) = 100 Centavos
Population: 4,794,000
Capital: Managua
Religions: 90% Roman Catholic
Climate: Tropical climate in the lowlands, cooler in the highlands.

✱ The Nicaraguan president Violeta Chamorro passed a law (article 204) in the summer of 1992 by which anyone convicted of "committing" anal intercourse can be sentenced to up to 3 years in prison. Homosexual activities are considered acts of sodomy.

✱ Der Präsident Nicaraguas, Violeta Chamorro, hat im Sommer 1992 ein Gesetz verabschiedet (Artikel 204), das vorsieht, daß jeder, der beim "Vergehen" Analverkehr überführt wird, mit einer Gefängnisstrafe von bis zu drei Jahren bestraft werden kann. Homosexuelle Aktivitäten werden mit Sodomie gleichgesetzt.

✱ En 1992, la présidente du Nicaragua, Violeta Chamorro, a fait passer une loi (article 204) qui permet d'inculper toute personne s'adonnant à la sodomie et lui infliger une peine allant jusqu'à 3 ans d'emprisonnement. L'homosexualité tombe sous le joug de cette loi.

✱ En verano de 1992, la presidenta de Nicaragua, Violeta Chamorro, aprobó una ley (artículo 204) según la cual las personas declaradas culpables de 'cometer' relaciones sexxuales anales puede ser condenadas a hasta tres años de prisión. Las actividades homosexuales se consideran actos de sodomía.

✱ In estate del 1992, il presidente del Nicaragua, Violeta Chamorro, ha approvato una legge (articolo 204) che prevede che una persona che pratica rapporti anali può essere punita con una reclusione fino a tre anni. Inoltre, le attività omossessuali vengono equiparate con la sodomia.

SPARTACUS 2001/2002 | 807

Nicaragua - Nigeria — León ▶ Managua

León

BARS
■ **Taquezal** (B F NG) 12-1h, Closed mon.
Frente al Teatro Municipal 205 ☎ 74278

CRUISING
- Central Park at night (ayor)

Managua

BARS
■ **Pacu's** (B D f GLM MA) 19-? h
1 Cuadro a Lago, 1/2 cuadro Arriba *(Puente el Eden)*
■ **Somos** (B D GLM S) Sat
Gonzalez Paso-1 "a lago" *(in front of Parque de las Palmas)*

DANCECLUBS
■ **Discotecha Medianoche** (! AC B D f G S YG) Fri-Sun 19-6 h
35 Avenida Linda Vista ☎ 266 34 43

CRUISING
- Cinema Gonzalez
- Park near A.C. Sandino Stadium (sidewalks around Laguna di Tiscapa)
- Plaza de la Revolucion
- Inside the ruins of the cathedral Las Ruinas de la Cathedral (ayor)
- Near mausoleum of Carlos Fouseca (AYOR)
- Gardens near Ruben Dario Teatro
- Camino de Oriente (Fri-Sun between Lobo's Jack and Infinito)
- Parque de las Piedrecitas (AYOR) (at night)

Nigeria

Location: West Africa
Initials: WAN
Time: GMT+1
International Country Code: ☎ 234 (leave the first 0 of area codes
International Access Code: ☎ 009
Language: English, Kwa-Languages Yoruba, Igbo
Area: 923,768 km^2 / 356,668 sq mi.
Currency: 1 Naira (N) = 100 Kobo
Population: 120,817,000
Capital: Abuja
Religions: 45% Muslim, 26% Protestant, 12% Catholic, 11% Nature Religions

✱ Homosexuality in Nigeria is illegal according to paragraph 214 as well as 217 of the Nigerian penal code and can be punished by imprisonment of up to 14 years. Nigeria is a conservative country and gay people are advised to be discrete. As with most large, developing countries, it is not advisable to walk around at night, but rather to take a taxi to and from your destination Nigeria is often described as the "Giant of Africa". The country has had a troubled history dominated by military rule which is only now beginning to shake off. Nigerians are extremely friendly and welcoming to foreigners who come to Nigeria, mainly on business. Lagos has however, acquired a reputation as being one of the most dangerous cities in Africa. In actual fact, most travellers who venture out of their air-conditioned hotels are often surprised at how friendly Lagosians are and how much the city has to offer. Lagos is probably the most vibrant city in Sub-Saharan Africa (outside of South Africa). The new democratic government has brought about a revival of nightlife in Lagos with bars, clubs and restaurants springing up everywhere.

★ In Nigeria ist Homosexualität nach den Paragraphen 214 und 217 des nigerianischen Strafgesetzbuches gesetzwidrig und kann mit Gefängnisstrafen bis zu 14 Jahren bestraft werden. Nigeria ist ein konservatives Land. Daher ist Schwulen anzuraten, sich unauffällig zu verhalten. Wie in den meisten Entwicklungsländern ist es auch hier nicht ratsam, nachts zu Fuß unterwegs zu sein, besser man fährt mit dem Taxi.
Nigeria wird oft als der "Riese Afrikas" bezeichnet. Das Land blickt auf eine schwierige, von Militärregierungen beherrschte Geschichte zurück, die es erst jetzt abzuschütteln beginnt. Die Nigerianer sind ein extrem freundliches Volk und gelten als sehr gastfreundlich. Lagos hat den Ruf, eine der gefährlichsten Städte Afrikas zu sein. Tatsache ist jedoch, daß die meisten Reisenden, die sich aus ihren klimatisierten Hotelzimmern wagen, überrascht feststellen, wie freundlich die Einwohner von Lagos ihnen begegnen und wieviel die Stadt zu bieten hat. Lagos ist wahrscheinlich die lebendigste Stadt im subsaharischen (außerhalb von Südafrika liegenden) Afrika. Die neue demokratische Regierung hat ein Wiederaufblühen des Nachtlebens in Lagos mit sich gebracht, Bars, Clubs und Restaurants schießen überall wie Pilze aus dem Boden.

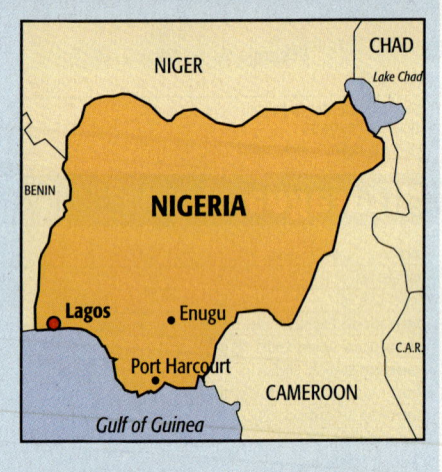

✱ L'homosexualité est illégale au Nigeria et peut être punie par une peine d'emprisonnement allant jusqu'à 14 ans selon les paragraphes 214 et 217 du Code Pénal. Le Nigeria est un pays conservateur et il est recommandé de rester très discret. Comme dans la plupart des pays en voie de développement, il est préférable de ne pas se promener dans les rues la nuit mais d'utiliser les taxis.

Lagos Nigeria

Le Nigeria est souvent surnommé le " Géant de l'Afrique ". L'histoire tumultueuse du pays, dominée par les régimes militaires, ne s'est apaisée que depuis peu. Les Nigérians sont très sympathiques et accueillent chaleureusement les étrangers qui viennent dans le pays, en général pour des raisons professionnelles.
Lagos a la réputation d'être une des villes les plus dangereuses d'Afrique. En fait, la plupart de voyageurs qui se risquent à sortir des hôtels climatisés sont surpris par la chaleur de ses habitants et par ses richesses. Lagos est probablement la ville la plus active de l'Afrique sub-saharienne (en dehors de l'Afrique du Sud). La vie nocturne de la ville s'est redynamisée depuis l'élection démocratique d'un nouveau gouvernement et de nombreux bars, clubs et restaurants se sont ouverts.

✘ En Nigeria, segun los artículos 214 y 217 del código penal nigeriano, la homosexualidad es ilegal y puede ser castigada con prisión de hasta 14 años. Nigeria es un país conservador y se aconseja a las personas gays moverse con la máxima discreción. Como en la mayoría de los países grandes en vías de desarrollo, es mejor no andar por las calles durante la noche: siempre es mejor ir y volver en taxi. Nigeria muchas veces se ha descrito como 'El Gigante de África'.. El país tiene una historia turbulenta, predominada de una dictadura militar de la que sólo ahora parece poder deshacerse. Los nigerianos son extremadamente agradables y cordiales con los extranjeros que, mayoritariamente por razones de negocio, visitan el país.
Sin embargo, Lagos, la capital, se ha hecho con la reputación de ser una de las ciudades africanas más peligrosas. De hecho, la mayoría de los viajeros que osan salir de sus hoteles al estilo occidental y con aire acondicionado, suelen quedar sorprendidos con el trato agradable y amistoso de los habitantes de Lagos y con la cantidad de posibilidades que la ciudad les . Lagos es, probablemente, la ciudad más animada del África subsahariano (fuera de Sudáfrica). El nuevo gobierno democrático ha producido un renacimiento de la vida nocturna de Lagos, con un sinfín de bares, clubes y restaurantes que abren en todas partes.

✘ In Nigeria l'omosessualità secondo i paragrafi 214 e 217 del codice penale nigeriano è illegale e può essere punita con delle pene detentive fino a quattordici anni di reclusione. La Nigeria è un paese tradizionalista, per cui si raccomanda agli omosessuali di comportarsi con discrezione. Come nella maggior parte dei paesi in via di sviluppo anche qui non è consigliabile girare a piedi di notte, è meglio spostarsi in taxi.
La Nigeria spesso viene definita come il "Gigante dell'Africa". Il paese ha avuto un passato difficile che ha visto la dominazione di governi militari e solo ora ha iniziato a liberarsene. I nigeriani sono un popolo estremamente gentile, e accolgono i visitatori, che il più delle volte vanno in Nigeria per motivi d[1] affari, a braccia aperte. Lagos gode la fama di essere una delle città più pericolose dell'Africa. Sta di fatto che la maggior parte dei viaggiatori che osano uscire dalle loro stanze d[1] albergo climatizzate, devono constatare con stupore, quanto gli abitanti di Lagos siano invece gentili e disposti ad andare loro incontro e quanto la città abbia da offrire. Lagos è probabilmente la città più vivace dell[1] Africa subsahariana (ad eccezione del Sudafrica). Il nuovo governo democratico ha favorito il rifiorire della vita notturna a Lagos, bar, club e ristoranti spuntano dappertutto come funghi.

Lagos ☞ 01

BARS
■ **Atlantic** (AC B D F NG)
14B Adeola Hopewell Street ☎ 610 584
■ **Boyle's Bar** (AC B NG)
6 Boyle Street, Onikan *(Entrance on Military Street)*
■ **Thistle** (AC B F NG)
899 Balarabe Musa Crescent ☎ 619 122
■ **Timmy's Place** (B F N R)
Open air barbecue on Bar Beach opposite the Intercontinental Merchant Bank (IMB) building.
■ **Tribes Bar & Grill** (AC B D F NG)
20-24 Ozumba Mbadiwe Street ☎ 262-4948

RESTAURANTS
■ **After Hours** (AC B BF F NG)
Plot 8, Eleke Crescent ☎ 262 0954
Very pleasant indoor/open-air restaurant overlooking the Lagos lagoon.
■ **Double 4** (AC BF F NG)
44 Awolowo Road ☎ 269 2689
■ **Tarzan's Bar & Restaurant** (B F NG WE)
Lekki - Epe Expressway *(On left after Mobiil Complex driving out of Epe)*
Open air thatched restaurant. Best on Sun evenings when there is live Congolese music.

FITNESS STUDIOS
■ **Eko Hotel Gymnasium** (AC NG SA WH WO)
Adotokunbo Ademola Street

HOTELS
■ **Eko** (B BF F NG PI)
Adetokunbo Ademola Street ☎ 262 4600 ☎ 261 4444
One of the best hotels in Lagos with great views, overlooking the Bar Beach.

SWIMMING
-Airpot Hotel swimming pool (B, F; N; NG, R) in Lagos,(Ikeja). especially Sun. afternoon
-Sheraton Hotel pool, 30 Mobolaji Bank-Antony Way, Lagos (Ikeja).

CRUISING
-Bar Beach (AYOR, R)
-Tarkwa Bay (AYOR R WE) to get there hire a small boat from Federal Palace or from Tarzan's Restaurant.

Norway

Name:	Norge • Norwegen • Norvège • Noruega • Norvegia
Location:	Northern Europe
Initials:	N
Time:	GMT +1
International Country Code:	☎ 47 (no area codes)
International Access Code:	☎ 00
Language:	Norwegian
Area:	323,759 km² / 125,049 sq mi.
Currency:	1 Norwegian Kroner (nkr) = 100 re
Population:	4,432,000
Capital:	Oslo
Religions:	89% Protestant (Lutheran state Church)
Climate:	Moderate climate along the coast, modified by North Atlantic Current. The interior is colder. The west coast is rainy all year round.
Important gay cities:	Oslo, Bergen and Trondheim

The age of consent in Norway is 16 years of age. Legislation was passed in 1981 which protects gays and lesbians from discrimination, and in 1993 a law was passed recognising the partnerships of homosexual couples. The legal situation resembles that in Denmark, giving gays and lesbians exactly the same status as heterosexuals (with the exception of adoption rights).

The Norwegian scene is concentrated in the cities of Oslo, Bergen and Trondheim, and here you will find exclusively gay bars. In smaller towns it is common for the discos to hold a gay/lesbian night once a week. The atmosphere here is, however, so gay-friendly that gays and lesbians are socialising more and more with straight people, to the point that mixed meeting places are gradually becoming the norm.

Norway has two decidedly interesting and professional gay publications: "Løvetann" (= 'dandelion') dealing with sexual politics, and the news & entertainment magazine "Blikk".

In Norwegen liegt das Schutzalter bei 16 Jahren. Für Schwule und Lesben gibt es gesetzlichen Schutz vor Diskriminierung (seit 1981) und ein Gesetz zur registrierten Partnerschaft für homosexuelle Paare (1993). Das Gesetz ist dem dänischen sehr ähnlich und stellt Hetero- und Homopaare -bis auf das fehlende Adoptionsrecht- gleich.

Die Szene des Königreiches konzentriert sich auf die Städte Oslo, Bergen und Trondheim. Hier gibt es reine Schwulenkneipen. Ansonsten, in den kleineren Städten, ist es nicht unüblich, daß allgemeine Discos einen wöchentlichen "Schwulen- und Lesbentag" pflegen. Da jedoch das gesellschaftliche Klima so schwulenfreundlich ist, gibt es kaum Berührungsängste zwischen Schwulen, Lesben und Heteros, und allmählich werden gemischte Treffpunkte die Regel.

Norwegen hat zwei außerordentlich interessante und professionelle Zeitschriften für Schwule: Das sexualpolitische Fachblatt "Løvetann" (dt.: "Löwenzahn") und das populäre Nachrichten- und Freizeitmagazin "Blikk".

En Norvège, la majorité sexuelle est fixée à 16 ans. Les gais et les lesbiennes norvégiens ont la loi de leur côté: loi antidiscriminatoire (1991) et loi sur le "concubinage enregistré" (1993). La législation norvégienne sur les droits des homosexuels s'inspire largement de la législation danoise: les couples homosexuels jouissent des mêmes droits que les couples hétéros, sauf en ce qui concerne l'adoption d'enfants.

Oslo, Bergen et Trondheim sont les principales villes gaies du pays. On y trouve des bars exclusivement gais. Sinon, dans les petites villes, les boîtes de nuit organisent une fois par semaine une "soirée gaie et lesbienne". La Norvège est un pays homophile où on peut vivre vivre sa différence au grand jour. Résultat: les gais et les lesbiennes sont de plus en plus intégrés au reste de la population. Les lieux de rencontre mixtes sont devenus la règle. En Norvège, il y a 2 excellentes revues gaies: le "Løvetann" ("Dent de lion") (sexe et politique) et le magazine d'information et de divertissement "Blikk".

Homosexuales y heterosexuales son iguales ante la ley. Desde 1981 existe una ley contra la discriminación que protege esta igualdad de derechos. Existe también desde 1993 un registro de noviazgo homosexual, esta ley es muy parecida a la danesa, situa a parejas homosexuales al mismo nivel de las heterosexuales incluso en cuestiones de adopción.

El "ambiente" gay del reinado noruego se concentra en las ciudades de Oslo, Bergen y Trondheim-en estas ciudades hay bares gay "puros". Por lo demás, es bastante habitual que discotecas de ciudades pequeñas organicen un "Día de los gays y lesbianas" una vez por semana. Por otro lado el clima social noruego es de lo más afable para con los homosexuales. Los gays y las lesbianas suelen mezclarse cada vez más con los heterosexuales y lentamente sitios de reunión mixtos son los más habituales.

Noruega tiene dos revistas para gays extraordinariamente bien hechas e interesantes: La revista especializada en temas de contenido político sexual "Løvetann" (en español: "diente de león") y la revista de actualidades y entretenimiento "Blikk".

L'età legale per aqvere rapporti omosessuali è di 16 anni. Dal 1991 le leggi norvegesi proteggono i gay e le lesbiche da discriminazioni legate alla sessualità. Dal 1993 le coppie omosessuali possono registrare legalmente le loro relazioni. Questa legislazione, molto simile a quella danese, uguaglia gli omosessuali agli eterosessuali anche nel diritto di adozione. La vita gay norvegese si concentra nelle città di Oslo, Bergen e Trondheim, dove troverete dei locali esclusivamente gay. Altrimenti, nelle piccole città, è spesso abitudine, per le discoteche, di avere una notte alla settimana per gay e lesbiche. Da quando l'atmosfera generale in Norvegia è così favorevole ai gay e pochi di essi nascondono la loro omosessualità, i gay e le lesbiche si uniscono sempre di più e con sempre meno difficoltà agli eterosessuali e i luoghi d'incontro misti stanno diventando sempre più comuni. La Norvegia vanta due riviste gay molto interessanti e valide: la pubblicazione politico/sessuale "Løvetann" (Bocca di Leone) e la rivista di notizie e intrattenimento "Blikk".

Ålesund - Møre og Romsdal ▶ Bergen - Hordaland | Norway

NATIONAL GAY INFO
■ **LLH•Landsforeningen for lesbisk og homofil frigjøring** Mon-Fri 9-16 h
St.Olavsplass 2, PO Box 68 38, 0130 Oslo ☎ 22 36 19 48
FAX 22 11 47 45. *The national gay/lesbian rights organization. Local groups spread nationwide.*
■ **Ungdomstelefonen**
☎ 90 10 02 77
Help line for young gays.

NATIONAL PUBLICATIONS
■ **Blikk** (! GLM)
St. Olavsplass 2 ✉ 0130 Oslo ☎ 22 99 22 80 🖨 22 99 22 99
📧 post@blikk.no 💻 www.blikk.no
Monthly newpaper, approx. 50 pages, Reports on Norwegian and international topics, cultural reports, guide. Some personal ads.
■ **Exit**
Osterhaus'gate 5 ✉ 0183 Oslo ☎ 22 20 80 16 🖨 22 20 82 28
📧 exit@image.no
High profile, glossy gay magazine for Norway.
■ **Killkontakt** (! G)
PO Box 96 56, Grønland ✉ 0133 Oslo ☎ 22 20 37 36
🖨 22 49 15 24
Norwegian/Swedish sex/contact magazine. (A lot of personal ads/phone ads).
■ **LEK** (glm)
PO Box 7123, Homansbyen ✉ 0307 Oslo ☎ 22 56 55 10
Monthly sex/contact magazin.
■ **Løvetann** (GLM)
PO Box 6745, St. Olavsplass ✉ 0130 Oslo ☎ 22 36 00 78
🖨 22 20 61 75
Bimonthly publication. Six copies 165 kroner. About 60 pages. Political and cultural reports, reviews and essays of a high standard.

NATIONAL GROUPS
■ **FPE-NE (Forening for transvesitter)** (TV)
PO Box 1968, Vika, ✉ 0125 Oslo
■ **SMIL-Sadomasochitisk Forening** (IJ)
PO Box 3456 ✉ 0406 Oslo ☎ 22 17 05 01

Ålesund - Møre og Romsdal

BARS
■ **Sjøhuset** (B D g)
Notengsgt 1
■ **Studenten** (B g)
Keiser wilhelms g 2b ☎ 70 15 25 22

GENERAL GROUPS
■ **LLH Nordvestlandet**
PO Box 665, Sentrum ✉ 6001 ☎ 94 40 50 62

CRUISING
-Borgernes vei (tour path behind the town mountain Aksla)
-Byparken (Town park)
-Kaiområdene (Harbor areas)
-Bus station/Rutebilsentralen
-Town hall square/Rådhusplassen

Alta - Finnmark

GENERAL GROUPS
■ **Landsforeningen for Lesbisk og Homofil frigjøring (LLH), Finnmark lag**
PO Box 12 07 ✉ 9501 ☎ 78 43 08 05

Åndalsnes - Møe og Romsdal

CRUISING
-Gatekjøkkenet (during the day at the harbor)
-Railway station/Jernbanestasjonen

Bergen - Hordaland

BARS
■ **Fincken. Café** (A B f glm MA) Mon Tue 12-23, Wed-Thu -2, Fri Sat -3, Sun 18-23 h
Nygårdsgate 2a ☎ 55 32 13 16
In the afternoon more a café.

CAFES
■ **Kafé Permanenten** (B f glm) Tue-Fri 11-17, Sat Sun 12-17
Nordahl Bruns gatan 9 ☎ 55 31 05 02
■ **Opera. Café** (b f glm)
Engen 24 ☎ 55 23 03 15

SAUNAS/BATHS
■ **Tropic Sauna** (f G MA SA SOL VS WH) Wed 16-21 h
Nye Sandviksvei 48 A ✉ 5035 ☎ 55 32 65 33
Sauna established since November 85. Gay only Wed.

GENERAL GROUPS
■ **Landsforeningen for Lesbisk og Homofil Frigjøring (LLH)** Wed 19-21 h
Nygårdsgate 2a, PO Box 312, ✉ 5001 *(2nd floor)* ☎ 55 31 21 39
🖨 55 96 12 10
■ **Støttegruppa for homofile og deres familier.**
☎ 55 12 25 81
■ **Uglesett-Gay and Lesbian Student Group**
PO Box 11 16 ✉ 5001
Student group. Phone HBB for info.

FETISH GROUPS
■ **LMC Bergen**
PO Box 44 18 ✉ 5028 ☎ 91 14 18 32

HEALTH GROUPS
■ **Helseutvalget for Homofile**
PO Box 318, Nygårdsgaat 2a, ✉ 5001 ☎ 55 32 16 20
🖨 55 96 12 10
■ **HIV/AIDS Info**
☎ 55 20 00 88

RELIGIOUS GROUPS
■ **Guds Løvetenner**
c/o Kvarteret, Olav Kyrres gatan 53 ✉ 5015
Open church group for lesbians and gays.

SPORT GROUPS
■ **Bardots/LLH** (GLM)
PO Box 312 ✉ 5001
Volleyball.

CRUISING
-Fløyen
-Fish market/Fisketorget
-Rasmus Meyers Allé
-Skoltegrunnskaien (near ships)

Bodø - Nordland

BARS
■ **Piccadilly Pub** (B glm)
Storgata 4B *(At Norrøna Hotel)* ☏ 75 52 55 50

GENERAL GROUPS
■ **Landsforeningen for Lesbisk og Homofil frigjøring (LLH) (GLM)** Café Tue 21-23
Hålogalandsgate 7 ✉ 8001 ☏ 75 52 27 75

HEALTH GROUPS
■ **Rådgivningskontoret for HIV/AIDS**
Biskop Kroghs gt. 15, ✉ 8017 ☏ 75 53 43 58

Drammen - Buskerud

BARS
■ **Børsen Musikkbar** (B g)
Bragernes Torg 13 ☏ 32 89 41 15

CAFES
■ **Kafé Unique** (B g)
Bragernes Torg 5 ☏ 32 83 17 00

HEALTH GROUPS
■ **Smittevernkontoret** Mon-Sat 8-15 h
Gamle Kirkeplass 2 ✉ 3019 ☏ 32 80 63 73

CRUISING
-Spiraltoppen (by WC and the old cannons)
-P by Damtjern.

Follo

DANCECLUBS
■ **Reenskaug disko** (B D glm)
Storgate 3, Drøbak ✉ 1440 *(In Reenskaug Hotel)*

GENERAL GROUPS
■ **As homofile og lesbiske studentforening**
PO Box 12 48, 1432 Ås-NLH
■ **LLH Folloavdelinga**
PO Box 48, Hebekk ✉ 1406

SPORT GROUPS
■ **LLH-Follos Volleyball**
☏ 64 93 95 38

Førde - Sogn og Fjordane

DANCECLUBS
■ **Treskeverket** (B D E F g H MA)
c/o Sunnfjord Hotel, Storehagen 2, ✉ 6800 ☏ 57 82 16 22

GENERAL GROUPS
■ **LLH Nordvestlandet**
PO Box 367 ✉ 6801 ☏ 90 68 06 67

Frederikstad - Østfold

BARS
■ **Punktum** (B glm MA)
Nygaardsgatan

GENERAL GROUPS
■ **LLH østfold**
PO Box 1119, Gamle ✉ 1631 ☏ 69 32 44 69. 🖨 69 32 44 69.

HEALTH GROUPS
■ **Rågivningskontoet mot aids** 18-20 h
Hassinveien 34 ✉ 1604 ☏ 69 39 46 69

CRUISING
-Tollbodbrygga (by the river from the library to the Ferra to Gamblebyfergen)

Gjøvik - Oppland

GENERAL GROUPS
■ **Ungdomsgr i Oppland**
☏ 61 13 22 26 📧 uioppland@usa.net

CRUISING
-Resting place at the Biri-side of the Mjøs-bridge (Mjøsbrua)
-Roof of the Domus-toilets

Grimstad - Aust-Agder

BARS
■ **Skyline** (B glm MA)
Jyskestredet

Hamar

GENERAL GROUPS
■ **Åpen Kirkegr/LLH**
☏ 61 19 51 52

Harstad - Nordland

GENERAL GROUPS
■ **LLH Sør-Troms og Ofoten-lag**
PO Box 20 97, Kanebogen ✉ 9405 ☏ 77 06 59 48

Haugesund - Rogaland

BARS
■ **Flytten Pub** (B g)
Smedasundet 87 ☏ 52 71 73 03

HELP WITH PROBLEMS
■ **Opplysningstelefon** Mon-Fri 17-22 h
☏ 90 93 21 17

Helegeland - Nordland

GENERAL GROUPS
■ **LLH Nordland lag, avdeling Helgeland**
PO Box 439, Sandnessjøen ✉ 8801 ☏ 75 04 36 98

Indre Troms

GENERAL GROUPS
■ **Aktivitetsgr for homsern**
☏ 77 83 33 37
■ **Støttettelefon for homofile og lesbiske**
☏ 77 83 86 37

Kongsvinger

GENERAL GROUPS

■ **Stjerneskudd, gr. for bifile, lesber og homser**
PO Box 537 St.sida ✉ 2201 ☎ 91 15 11 50
■ **Villskudd-Kongsvinger, ungdomsgr.**
PO Box 282 ✉ 2201 ☎ 92 80 95 28 💻 Villskudd@hotmail.com
💻 www.geocities.com/WestHollywood/Village/2103/

Kristiansand - Vest-Agder

BARS

■ **Kafe Kilden** (B glm MA)
Rådhugate 11 ☎ 38 02 96 20
■ **Markens** (B d glm MA) Disco Fri Sat
Markengate 13

GENERAL GROUPS

■ **LLH Kristiansand lag** Tue 11-13, Thu 16-18 h
PO Box 45 98 Grim ✉ 4602 ☎ 38 02 00 48

HEALTH GROUPS

■ **PLUSS Sørlandet**
PO Box 239, Sentrum ✉ 4604 ☎ 38 02 84 08

Kristiansund - Møre og Romsdal

BARS

■ **Endestasjonen** (B e f g H MA)
Storgate 41-43 ☎ 71 67 64 11
■ **Pontongen** (B f g H MA)
Berndorffstr. 1 ☎ 71 67 30 11
■ **Tordenskiold** (B e f g H MA)
Hauggaten 16 ☎ 71 67 40 11

CRUISING

-Storsand (summer only)

Lillehammer - Oppland

BARS

■ **Ludvig ølstue** (B glm MA)
Wiesesg 2 ☎ 61 25 89 60

GENERAL GROUPS

■ **LLH Hedmark og Oppland lag**
PO Box 423, ✉ 2601 ☎ 61 19 51 52

Molde - Møre og Romsdal

BARS

■ **Alexis** (B D E f g H MA)
Storgate 1-7 ☎ 71 25 11 33
■ **Dockside** (B f g MA)
Torget 1 ☎ 71 21 50 33

GENERAL GROUPS

■ **Guds Anemoner**
PO Box 71 ✉ 6400
■ **LLH Nordvestlandet**
PO Box 71 ✉ 6400

Kongsvinger ▶ Oslo Norway

Oslo

✱ Norways capital city is the starting point to a spectacular landscape. The train ride from Oslo to Bergen is reputed to be of special scenic beauty. But even from the city of Oslo you can reach untouched nature (Oslofjord, Sognsvann, Holmenkollen a.s.f.) in the shortest of time by public transport. Oslo is a very modern city, surprisingly multicultural, and it offers everything you expect from a modern metropolis. In the short months of the summer, life is enjoyed to the maximum. On weekends the whole of Oslo seems to be up and about. The gay scene is small but very friendly and, contrary to other european metropolises, very unpretentious.
Our tips:
- Vigelandpark, with its expressive granite- and bronce-sculptures depicting lifes cycle.
- Vikings ships on the peninsula Bygdøy (boat ride!)

✱ Norwegens Hauptstadt ist der Ausgangspunkt in eine spektakuläre Landschaft. Die Eisenbahnfahrt von Oslo nach Bergen gilt dabei als landschaftlich besonders reizvoll. Aber selbst von Oslo aus ist man innerhalb kürzester Zeit per öffentlichem Verkehrsmittel in unberührter Natur (Oslofjord, Sognsvann, Holmenkollen etc.) Oslo ist sehr modern, überraschend multikulturell, und hat alles, was man von einer modernen Großstadt erwartet. In den kurzen Sommermonaten wird das Leben in vollen Zügen genossen, und ganz Oslo scheint am Wochenende unterwegs zu sein.
Die Schwulenszene ist zwar klein, aber ausgesprochen freundlich und im Gegensatz zu anderen europäischen Großstädten sehr unprätentiös.
Unsere Tips:
-Vigelandpark mit ausdrucksstarken Granit- und Bronzeskulpturen, die den Lebenskreislauf darstellen
-Wikingerschiffe auf der Halbinsel Bygdøy (Bootsfahrt!)

✱ Un paysage spectaculaire vous attend aux portes d'Oslo! Prenez le train d'Oslo à Bergen, vous découvrirez les splendeurs du paysage norvégien, au chaud depuis votre compartiment. Depuis Oslo, on est vite en plein coeur de la nature, une nature sauvage accessible par les transports en commun: Oslofjord, Sognsvann, Holmemkollen... La capitale norvégienne est moderne et étonnement multiculturelle. Elle a tous les avantages d'une grande ville. Les Norvégiens profitent au maximum des quelques beaux mois d'été qui leurs sont donnés et, les week-ends, on a l'impression que tout Oslo est dans la rue. L'infrastructure gay d'Oslo peut sembler assez peu développée, mais notez bien que les gens y sont bien plus souriants et ouverts que dans certaines autres grandes villes d'Europe. A voir absolument:
- le Vigelandpark et ses impressionnantes sculptures de bronze et de granit représentent les différentes étapes de la vie et
- les drakkars des Vikings sur la presqu'île de Bygdøy (prenez le bâteau!).

● La capital noruega es el punto ideal de partida para visitar paisajes espectaculares. El trayecto en tren entre Oslo y Bergen está considerado una maravilla. Desde Oslo con transporte público y sin necesidad de recorrer grandes distancias podemos visitar parques naturales intactos como Oslofjord, Sognsvann, Holmenkollen etc. Oslo es moderna, sorprendentemente multicultural y cuenta con todo lo que se espera de una gran ciudad. En los meses de verano la vida se disfruta al máximo, los fines de semana da la impresión de que toda la ciudad se encuentra de paseo. El ambiente gay es pequeño pero muy afable y al contrario que en a otras ciudades europeas muy poco pretencioso. Nuestros consejos:
- El parque Vigeland, muestra esculturas de granito y bronce que representan el ciclo de la vida.
- Barcos vikingos en la península Bydoy (viaje en barco).

SPARTACUS 2001/2002 | 813

Norway — Oslo

La capitale della Norvegia è un punto di partenza per raggiungere una campagna spettacolare. Il percorso ferroviario da Oslo a Bergen è particolarmente stimolante. Da Oslo con i mezzi pubblici si arriva in poco tempo a luoghi in cui la natura è ancora intatta (Oslofjord, Sognsvann, Holmenkoller ecc.). Oslo è molto moderna, sorprendentemente multiculturale e offre tutto ciò che ci si aspetta da una grande città. Durante i corti mesi estivi le giornate vengono vissute intensamente, e la fine settimana tutta Oslo esce a passeggio. L'ambiente gay è piccolo ma molto cordiale. Al contrario delle altre città europee Oslo è naturale e sincero. I nostri consigli:
- Vigelandpark con espressive sculture in granito e in bronzo che rappresentano il ciclo della vita;
- Navi vichinghe sulla penisola Bygdoy (viaggio in traghetto).

TOURIST INFO
■ **Oslo Promotion A/S**
Grev Wedels plass 4   ✉ 0151   ☎ 22 33 43 86

BARS
■ **Bakgård'n Pub** (AC B CC DR G MA OS) Sun-Thu 14-2, Fri-Sat 14-4 h
Teatergt 3 ✉ 0158 *behind the courthouse* ☎ 22 20 62 99
Lowest beer prices in town.
■ **London Pub** (! B d GLM MA) 18-4, Sat-Sun 15-4 h
C.J. Hambros Plass 5 ✉ 0164 *(entrance in Rosenkrantzgate. Also entrance for "Chairs")* ☎ 22 70 87 00
Popular, best after 23 h. Billard. Pub-style atmosphere. Choose your favourite tunes from the juke box. Piano Bar.
■ **Naboens Mat & Vinhus** (B F glm MA OS) 11-1, Sun 12-1 h
Smalgangen 31 *(Grønlands torg)* ☎ 22 17 50 53
■ **Spartacus** (stv) Thu, Fri, Sat & Sun 22-03.30h,
Pilestredet 9
Thu 18 year olds allowed, Fri - Sun 20 and over.

CAFES
■ **Coco Chalet** (b f g)
Prinsensg 21   ☎ 22 33 32 66
Charming café.
■ **Habibi Café** (b f g)
Storgt 14 *(Grønland square)*   ☎ 22 17 98 31
Middle-eastern cuisine. Inexpensive.
■ **Kafe Jonas** (AC B CC d F GLM MA OS) Sun-Thu 15-0, Fri 15-2, Sat 11-2 h
Teatergt 3 ✉ 0158 *Behind the courthouse* ☎ 22 20 62 99
Dinner is also served. Homemade cakes.
■ **Tin Kafé** (B f GLM MA) Sun 18-21, Wed 19-22 h
Olavs plass 2   ☎ 22 11 33 60

DANCECLUBS
■ **Castro** (! B D G s YC) Tue-Sun 21-4 h
Kristian IV gate 7-9   ☎ 22 41 51 08
1st floor Disco (70's/80's), 2nd floor Club mix, 3rd floor chill-out lounge. Occasional drag shows and go-go boys. Very popular.
■ **Potpurriet** (B F gLM D MA OS s) Sun-Thu 16-2, Fri-Sat 16-6 h
øvre Vollgate 13   ☎ 22 41 14 40

RESTAURANTS
■ **Chairs** Every day 20-03h
C J Hambros plass 5 *(entrance Rosenkrantz - next to "London Pub")*

SEX SHOPS/BLUE MOVIES
■ **Gay International** (G) 10-19, Sat -15 h
Rostedsgate 2, Grønland ✉ 0133   ☎ 22 20 37 36
Selection of videos, that's about all.
■ **Man Fashion** (G) Mon-Fri 12-19, Sat 11-16 h
Möllergt. 47, ✉ 0179   ☎ 22 36 06 03
A lot of leather and toys.

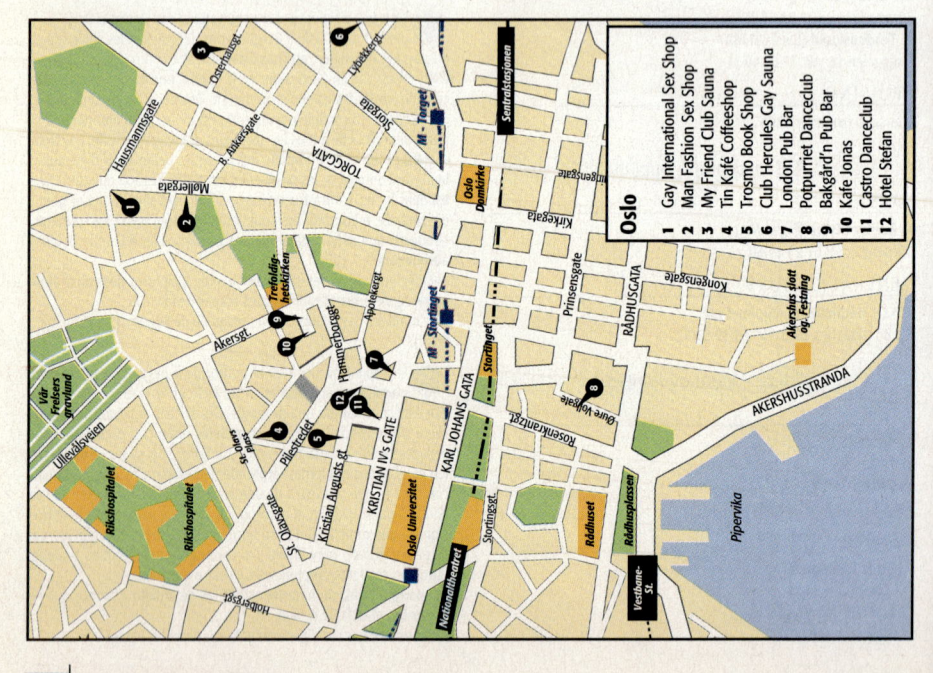

Oslo
1 Gay International Sex Shop
2 Man Fashion Sex Shop
3 My Friend Club Sauna
4 Tin Kafé Coffeeshop
5 Trosmo Book Shop
6 Club Hercules Gay Sauna
7 London Pub Bar
8 Potpurriet Danceclub
9 Bakgård'n Pub Bar
10 Kafe Jonas
11 Castro Danceclub
12 Hotel Stefan

Oslo — Norway

OSLO overnight accomodation service
· about 750 beds · more than 28 cities ·
enjoy bed & breakfast

complete offer
see page Germany/Berlin

central booking office Berlin ☎ **+49-30-236 236 10** 4:30-9:00 pm local time
Fax +49-30-23623619 · info@ebab.de · www.ebab.dk

SAUNAS/BATHS
■ **Boy's Club** (DR G SA SOL VS WO)
Parkveien 62 ✉ 0254 *(near Royal Castle)* ☎ 22 35 50 51
■ **Club Hercules** (AC b CC DR f G MA msg SA SB SOL VS WH)
Sun-Thu 15-2, Fri-Sat -8 hClub
Storgate 41 ✉ 0182 ☎ 22 11 11 13
Just moved to a new renovated building in December 99. Nice atmosphere, big steam bath, opening of a swimming pool in 2000.
■ **My Friend Club** (AC DR G MA SA SOL VS) Sun-Thu 11-2, Fri-Sat 11-8h
Calmeyergate 15 B ✉ 0183 ☎ 22 20 36 67

BOOK SHOPS
■ **Tronsmo Bøker & Tegneserier** (GLM) 10-17, Thu -18, Sat -15 h, closed Sun
Kristian Augustsgate 19, 0130 ☎ 22 20 25 09
Limited range of gay and lesbian books. Friendly staff.

HOTELS
■ **Hotel Stefan** (b BF CC F NG)
Rosenkrantz Gate 1 ✉ 0159 *(Opposite London Pub)*
☎ 22 42 92 50 🖷 22 33 70 22
Comfortable, clean and friendly hotel close to the gay scene. All rooms with shower/WC, TV and telephone. Restaurant famous for lunch buffet. BF imcluded in room rate.

PRIVATE ACCOMMODATION
■ **Enjoy Bed and Breakfast** (BF G H MA)
☎ +45 32 960 206 info@ebab.dk ebab.dk

GENERAL GROUPS
■ **Cabarosa (LLH-Oslo)**
☎ 22 38 51 06
Cabaret group.
■ **Den norske homofenien av 1990 (LLH)**
☎ 22 35 49 95
Choir.
■ **Drillarguri**
☎ 22 33 70 15
Twirling group.
■ **Fri Utblåsning (LLH)**
☎ 22 44 90 91
Music group.
■ **Homofile Og Barn**
PO Box 68 38, St.Olavsplass, ✉ 0130 ☎ 22 55 55 65
Group for gays with children.
■ **Homoversitas Osloensis**
PO Box 87, Blindern, ✉ 0314
Student group.
■ **Informationgroup for the School**
☎ 22 67 57 77

■ **LLH Sentralt Landsforeningen for lesbisk og homofil frigjøring** Mon-Fri 9-16 h
PO Box 68 38, St.Olavsplass ✉ 0130 *(Close to the National Art Gallery)* ☎ 22 36 19 48 🖷 22 11 47 45 llh@czi.net
 www.llh.no
The gay/lesbian rights organization. Umbrella organization for various interest groups.
■ **Manneguppa i SMil Norge** Tue 18-20.30 h
PO Box 34 56, Bjølsen, ✉ 0406 ☎ 22 30 27 58
S/M group for gay men.
■ **Oslo Gay Naturists**
☎ 22 37 84 98
■ **Skeive Filmer**
PO Box 68 38, St.Olavsplass, ✉ 0130 ☎ 22 20 19 60
🖷 22 20 19 60 sfilmer@sn.no
■ **Ungdomsgruppa (LLH-Oslo)** (GLM YG)
PO Box 6838, St.Olavsplass ✉ 0130 ☎ 90 10 02 77
 www.login.eunet.no/~janda/
Youth group.

FETISH GROUPS
■ **SLM Oslo**
PO Box 703, Sentrum ✉ 0106 ☎ 22 17 40 90
 slm@newmedia.no home.newmedia.no/slm/

HEALTH GROUPS
■ **Aksept (Kirkens Bymisjon)**
☎ 22 71 55 22
Contact center for HIV-positive.
■ **Helseutvalget for homofile** Mon-Fri 9-15 h
øvre Slottsgate 29 ✉ 0157 ☎ 22 33 70 15
Health organization for gays. Offices spread nationwide.
■ **Helseutvalget for homofile** Mon-Fri 10-16 h
øvre Slottsgate 29 ✉ 0157 ☎ 22 33 70 15
 www.helseutvalget.no
■ **LMA · Landsforeningen mot aids**
Universitetsgt 20 ✉ 0162 ☎ 22 42 37 90
■ **Olafiaklinikken** Mon 12-17, Tue-Fri 8-11 h
Olafiagangen 7 ☎ 22 08 29 50
Center for preventative medicine. Councilling service for gays and lesbians.
■ **PLUSS**
PO Box 835, Sentrum ✉ 0104 ☎ 22 33 01 60
Organization for HIV-positives.
■ **Pluss (HIV-positive)**
PO Box 835, ✉ 0130 ☎ 22 33 01 60

RELIGIOUS GROUPS
■ **Åpen Kirkegruppe for homofile og lesbiske**
PO Box 68 38, St.Olavsplass, ✉ 0130 ☎ 22 11 59 79
Christian group.

Norway Oslo ▸ Vesterålen - Nordland

SPORT GROUPS
■ **Klatregruppe**
c/o LLH ☏ 22 18 27 48
Climbing group.
■ **Raballder**
c/o LLH ☏ 22 35 71 05 ☏ 92 28 77 68 (Handball).

SWIMMING
-Langøyene (!,NU) Take the boat from Vippetangen to Langøyene, then go straight til you pass a kiosk. Take the small path to the gay nude area.
-Gay Beach (!,NU) Close to Paradisbukta. Take Bus 30 from downtown to the last stop (Bygdøy). Go along the small path on the right side of the parkinglot.
-Svartskog (NU) Close to Sognsvann.

CRUISING
-Galgeberg (Jordalsgate, near Jordal Amfi. Take bus 37 from downtown. Best around midnight.)
-Sognsvann (Toilets and outdoors. Take the subway, 2nd car park from station, day and night)
-Frognerparken
-Smalgangen (Grønlands torg)
-Stensparken

Sandefjord - Vestfold
BARS
■ **Bennigan Pub** (B g)
Torggata 1 ☏ 33 46 68 50
■ **Byefly** (B g)
Torggata 1 ☏ 33 46 68 50
■ **Sir James Pub** (B g)
Søbergtorget ☏ 33 46 19 00
■ **Speitet** (B g MA)
Kvartal 19 ☏ 33 46 02 02

Skien - Telemark
GENERAL GROUPS
■ **LLH Telemark lag** Wed 20-22 h (Helpline and café)
PO Box 407, Kongensgate 10 ✉ 3701 ☏ 35 52 98 30
✉ llh.telemark@go.to ✉ go.to/llh.telemark

Stavanger - Rogaland
GAY INFO
■ **LLH Rogaland** Mon 18-20, Café Sat 13-15 h
Jelsgat 34, PO Box 1502, Kjelvene ✉ 4004 ☏ 51 53 14 44
✉ 51 53 65 01 ✉ www.powertech.no/~bjornto/llhrogaland.html
BARS
■ **Gyldene Fontene. Den** (B g)
St. Olaf ☏ 51 53 05 88
■ **Sting** (B glm MA)
Valbjerget 3 ✉ 4006 ☏ 51 53 24 40
CRUISING
-Skansekaien (from Victoria Hotel to Hurtigbåtterminalen)
-Bjergstedskaien (from Englansterminalen to the parking place by the grove, after dark)

Tønsberg - Vestfold
BARS
■ **Kaptein Krok** (B g)
Rådhusgt 30 ☏ 33 31 92 67

■ **Lauritz** (B g)
Nedre Langg 30 ☏ 33 31 23 20
CAFES
■ **LLH Vestfold** Wed 19-22 Sat 14-17 h
Halfdan Wilhelmsensallé 2B
GENERAL GROUPS
■ **LLH Vestfold lag**
PO Box 557 ✉ 3101 ☏ 33 31 06 10

Tromsø - Troms
BARS
■ **Mirage. La** (B G) 12-4 h
Storgata 42 ☏ 77 68 76 70
■ **Prelaten** (B g) 11-2 h
Sjøgate 12 ☏ 77 68 20 85
GENERAL GROUPS
■ **Homopolaris**
Hovedgården, Uitø, ✉ 9037 ☏ 77 64 64 53
Gay/lesbian/bi student group.
■ **LLH-Troms lag** (B D GLM)
Vestregt 2, ✉ 9008 *(1st floor)* ☏ 77 68 56 43
HEALTH GROUPS
■ **Pluss Nord-Norge**
Søndre Tollbug. 9 ✉ 9008 ☏ 77 62 04 85
■ **Rådgivningstjenesten for homofile og lesbiske i Tromsø**
Mon 19-21 h
☏ 77 68 56 43
■ **Tromsø komm. Helsekontor**
☏ 77 62 04 85

Trondheim - Sør-Trøndelag
BARS
■ **Café Remis** (B CC D F GLM MA) Tue Wed 20-2, Fri 22-2.30, Sat 12-16 22-3 h
Kjøpmannsgate 12, PO Box 937 ✉ 7001 ☏ 73 52 05 52
GENERAL GROUPS
■ **LLH Trondheim**
Kjøpmannsgate 12, ✉ 7001 *(Entrance Erling Skakkes g)*
☏ 73 52 42 26
Gay center, café, bookshop, various activities.
HEALTH GROUPS
■ **Helseutvalget for homofile**
Olafv Trygvasons g 15 ✉ 7011 ☏ 73 52 45 57 ✉ hu-trd@sn.no
■ **Infeksjonshelsetjenesten Miljøardelingen**
Prinsensgate 61 ✉ 7011 ☏ 72 54 73 81 ✉ 72 54 61 67
RELIGIOUS GROUPS
■ **Åpen Kirkegrupe (LLH)** 1st Tue 19 h
PO Box 937 ✉ 7001
CRUISING
-Brattøra
-Jernbanestasjonen
-Sentralbadet

Vesterålen - Nordland
GENERAL GROUPS
■ **LLH Nordland lag, avd Vesterålen**
PO Box 435, 8401 Sortland ☏ 76 12 27 80

Panamá City | Panama

Panama

Location: Southern Central America
Initials: PA
Time: GMT -5
International Country Code: ☏ 507 (no area codes)
International Access Code: ☏ 0
Language: Spanish; English
Area: 75,517 km² / 29,761 sq mi.
Currency: 1 Balboa (B/.) = 100 Centésimos
Population: 2,764,000
Capital: Panamá City
Religions: 96% Roman Catholic
Climate: Tropical climate that is hot, humid and cloudy. There is a prolonged rainy season from May to January and a short dry season that lasts from January to May.

※ Homosexual acts are not mentioned in Panamanian law.

★ Homosexuelle Handlungen werden in der Gesetzgebung Panamas nicht erwähnt.

※ Le code pénal panaméen ne fait pas état de l'homosexualité.

⬢ La legislación panameña no contempla en ningún momento to actos o actividades de carácter homosexual.

✕ Gli atti omosessuali non sono menzionati dal codice penale panamense.

Panamá City

BARS

■ **Bar Discotequa** (B D G MA)
Avenida J/Calle 9

■ **Bar Tropical** (ayor B G) -23 h
Calle 12 *(Old city)*

■ **Boys Bar (Garage)** (! B D GLM P MA TV WE) Fri-Sun 22.30-? h
Avenida Industrial, Esperanza, Tumba Muerto *(Edificio Sefame #2, Driveway beside the company "IHRE")*

■ **Ecos Bar** (ayor B D GLM WE) Sat 22-6 h
Avenida de los Martires *(Close to Parque Legislativo)*

■ **La Deivi** (B D G MA)
Via Tansistmica *(across from Sony)*

■ **La Madrid** (B G)
Calle 12

■ **La Mami** (B D G MA)
Calle 50 *(across from Mansion Dante)*

■ **Michelle's (Hidalgo)** (B D GLM P MA AC) Thu-Sun 21.30-4 h
Via Brasil *(across from Texaco gasstation, 2 blocks from Via España)*

CINEMAS

■ **Cine El Dorado** (g)
Avenida Central

■ **Cine Tropical** (g)
Calle Monteserrin/Calle I

■ **Cine Variedades** (g)
(close to Cine El Dorado)

HOTELS

■ **Residencial Turistico El Volcan**
Calle 29 *(between Avenida 1 Sur &Avenida 2 Sur)*
Guests no problem

CRUISING

-Via Espana (from Via Argentina to El Panama Hotel)
-Parque Legislativo (around the corner from Plaza 5 de Mayo)
-Avenida Cuba (R) (from Calle 29 to Calle 42).

Paraguay

Location:	Central South America
Initials:	PY
Time:	GMT -4
International Country Code:	☏ 595 (leave the first 0 of area code)
International Access Code:	☏ 00
Language:	Spanish, Guaraní (mostly bilingual)
Area:	406,752 km^2 / 157,047 sq mi.
Currency:	1 Guaraní (G) = 100 Céntimos
Population:	5,219,000
Capital:	Asunción
Religions:	94% Roman Catholic
Climate:	Varied climate from moderate in the east to quite dry in the far west.

✱ We have been told that homosexuality as such is not illegal in Paraguay. If however a judge considers the accused to be "perverse" because of his homosexuality, this can have an influence on his sentence. Here, as in many so-called macho countries, there are no visible signs of an emerging gay movement. Society's attitude toward gays ranges from indifference to tolerance, providing that their homosexuality is not made public.

✱ Unseres Wissens nach stellt Homosexualität an sich in Paraguay keinen Straftatbestand dar. Allerdings kann wohl ein Richter, wenn er das Schwulsein eines Täters als "pervers" eracht, diesen Umstand als strafverschärfend werten. Das Verhalten der Gesellschaft Schwulen gegenüber bewegt sich zwischen Gleichgültigkeit und Toleranz zumindest solange diese ihr Schwulsein nicht öffentlich machen.

✱ On nous a fait savoir qu'au Paraguay l'homosexualité en tant que telle n'est pas considérée comme un délit. Cependant, si un juge décide qu'un accusé est "pervers" en raison de son homosexualité, il pourra utiliser cet état de fait pour en rajouter et alourdir le verdict. Comme dans tous les pays machistes, pas le moindre signe d'émancipation homosexuelle. Les gens sont, en général, plutôt tolérants ou indifférents à l'homosexualité. On fiche la paix aux homosexuels, à condition qu'ils ne se fassent pas trop remarquer.

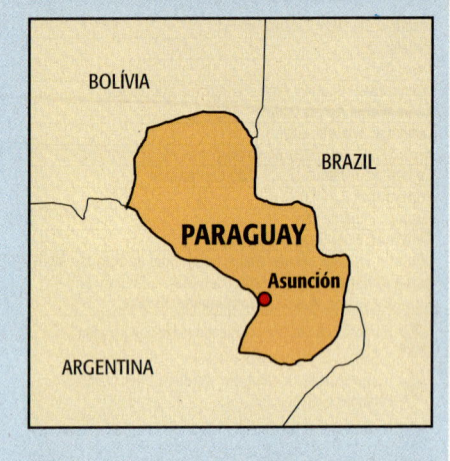

✱ Nos han informado que en Paraquay la homosexualidad no es un objeto penal. Sin embargo, si un juez considere la orientación homosexual de un acusado como algo pervertido, esto puede influir negativamente en la sentencia. Al igual que en otros países machistas, en Paraguay no existen los principios para el desarrollo de una organización homosexual. Siempre y cuando el comportamiento homosexual no sea muy evidente, la población paraguaya se comporta tolerantemente.

✱ Abbiamo saputo che in Paraquay l'omosessualità in sè non è un reato, benchè un giudice possa tenerne conto come aggravante se considera l'omosessualità dell'accusato una perversione. Come in molti altri paesi maschilisti, neanche in Paraguay esistono le premesse per la nascita di un movimento gay. La società resta indifferente o tollera fintanto che i gay non manifestano la loro omosessualità.

Asunción ☏ 021

BARS
■ **Audace** (B G MA)
Ayolas/Manduvirá
■ **La Barca** (B D GLM) Tue-Sat
Presidente Franco 564 *(Next to Hotel Embajador)*
Best on Sat.
■ **Stop** (B d G)
14 de Mayo, 477

DANCECLUBS
■ **Spider** (B D G MA)
Perú 568/ Azará

HOTELS
■ **Guarani** (AC B D E F H NG OS PI SA SB SOL)
Oliva/Independencia Nacional *(ground floor)* ☏ 911 31
11 km to the airport. Centrally located. All rooms with telephone, bathroom and WC. Single US$ 114.

CRUISING
-Plaza de los Heroes (after dark)
-Streets near Hotel Guarani

Arequipa ▶ Lima **Peru**

Peru

Name: Perú • Pérou
Location: Western Coast of South America
Initials: PE
Time: GMT -5
International Country Code: ☏ 51 (leave the first 0 of area codes)
International Access Code: ☏ 00
Language: Castillan, Quechua
Area: 1,285,216 km² / 496,222 sq mi.
Currency: 1 New Sol (S/.) = 100 Centimos
Population: 24,801,000
Capital: Lima
Religions: 89% Roman Catholic
Climate: Varied climate from tropical rainforests in the east to arid regions in the west.

❋ Homosexual acts among consenting adults are legal. An exception is made for all military and police personnel, who can be punished with between 60 days to 20 years imprisonment or discharge from the forces. Homosexuality can also be used as grounds for separation or divorce. Laws meant to protect "public morals" are often used against lesbians and gays. Society's attitude towards homosexuals is generally hostile and is heavily influenced by the Catholic Church. In the 1980's the founding of the organisation "Movimiento Homosexual de Lima" (MHOL) managed to bring about at least a slight change in the way the media treated homosexuality.

❋ Homosexualität ist unter Einverständnis zwischen Erwachsenen legal. Eine Ausnahme besteht für Angehörige des Militärs und der Polizei, die bei homosexuellen Handlungen eine Strafe von 60 Tagen bis 20 Jahren Gefängnis erhalten oder aus dem Amt entlassen werden. Homosexualität wird als Trennungs- und Scheidungsgrund anerkannt. Gesetze, die die "öffentliche Moral" betreffen, werden oft gegen Lesben und Schwule angewandt. Die allgemeine Einstellung der Bevölkerung gegenüber den Schwulen ist feindselig und wird zusätzlich von der katholischen Kirche beeinflußt. Die Gründung der Organisation "Movimiento Homosexual de Lima" (MHOL) hat in den 80er Jahren zumindest einen leichten Wandel zu einer wohlwollenderen Darstellung gleichgeschlechtlicher Lebensweisen in den Medien bewirkt.

❋ Au Pérou, les relations sexuelles entre adultes consentants ne sont pas un délit, sauf pour les membres de la police ou de l'armée qui, eux, risquent, selon les circonstances, 60 jours à 20 ans de prison, accompagnés d'un licenciement sec. L'homosexualité est une raison officielle de séparation ou de divorce. Les lois protégeant la "morale publique" sont fréquemment utilisées contre les gais et les lesbiennes.
Les Péruviens sont, dans l'ensemble, plutôt homophobes et l'Eglise catholique ne fait rien pour arranger les choses. Le MHDL, "Movimiento Homosexual de Lima" a été fondé au début des années 80.

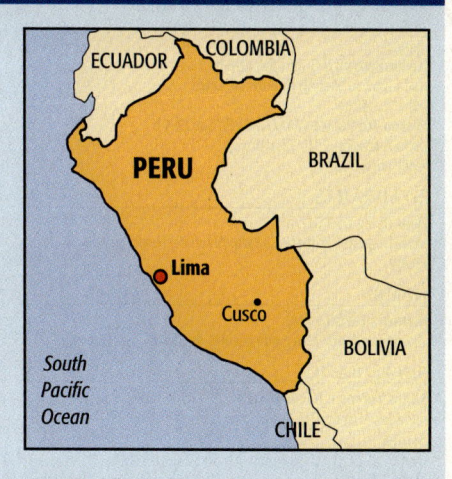

C'est grâce à lui que les choses ont pu bouger, surtout dans les médias.

● Las relaciones homosexuales por acuerdo mutuo entre adultos son legales. Se excluyen a miembros de las fuerzas armadas y de la policia, que pueden ser condenados desde 60 días hasta 20 años de cárcel o pueden ser separados del cargo. La homosexualidad es reconocida como motivo de separación o divorcio. También se aplican leyes con respecto a la "moral pública" en contra de las lesbianas y los gays. La opinión pública es generalmente hostil e influenciada sobre todo por la iglesia católica. El "Movimiento Homosexual de Lima (MHOL)" inició en los años 80 por lo menos un cambio leve en la representación de formas de vida homosexuales en los medios de comunicación.

❋ Gli atti omosessuali fra adulti consenzienti non sono illegali. Un'eccezione viene fatta per appartenenti alle forze militari e alla polizia, dove l'omosessualità può essere punita con la reclusione da 60 giorni fino a 20 anni o l'espulsione dal corpo. L'omosessualità può anche essere usata per le cause di separazione o di divorzio. Le leggi concernenti la "pubblica moralità" vengono spesso usate contro persone lesbiche e gay. Il comportamento generale della società verso gli omosessuali è ostile e pesantemente influenzato dalla presenza della Chiesa Cattolica. La costituzione del "Movimiento Homosexual de Lima (MHOL)" negli anni ottanta ha contribuito a cambiare l'opinione dei mass-media riguardo allo stile di vita di coppie dello stesso sesso

Arequipa ☏ 054

SWIMMING
- Jaime Baños (pi) (Golfo 208, Miraflores. ☏ 213 06.)

Lima ☏ 01

BARS
■ **Barcelona** (B glm)
Plaza Larco Mar, Miraflores
■ **Kitch** (B GLM)
Avenida Bolognesi, Barranco

CAFES
■ **Bohemia** (F g YG)
Ovalo Gutiérrez, Miraflores *(San Isidro)*
■ **Café Café** (! BF CC F g MA OS)
250 Avenida Mártir Olaya *(At Parque de Miraflores)* ☏ 445 1165
■ **Twist** (b glm)
Avenida Diagonal, Miraflores

DANCECLUBS
■ **Calle Berlin 231**
(Near Kennedy park - Miraflores)
■ **Eden** (B D glm)
Las Caobas 114, Sotano, La Molina

Peru - Philippines | Lima

■ **Gitano** (! B D GLM S) Wed & Thu 23-ß, Fri & Sat -3h. Shows Thu-Sat.
Schell, 8th block *(Near Parque Kennedy. Miraflores)*
Wed is ladies night, but also glm. Entrance fee from US$ 7-25, Sun free of charge.

■ **Hedonismo** (B d G) Fri Sat 22-6 h
Avenida Ignacio Merino Cuadra 17, Lince
Entrence fee 6 US$

■ **Perseo-Ice Palace** (B D G MA) Fri Sat 22-4 h
Avenida Avicación 2514 *(San Borja)*
Entrence fee 6 US$

RESTAURANTS
■ **Haiti** (B F g OS YG)
Avenida Diagonal/Primera Cuadra *(Miraflores, opposite Parque Kennedy)*

CINEMAS
■ **Colmena** (AYOR g MA).
Av. Comena cuadra 7, Avenida Nicolás de Piérola ☎ 428 45 25

SAUNAS/BATHS
■ **Baños Turcos J. Pardo** (AYOR B g OG SA SB WH WO)
Avenida José Pardo 192 *(Near Plaza Kennedy. Miraflores)*
Be discreet!

■ **Oupen** (A AC B CC f G MA msg SA SB VS) 14-23 h
Av 28 de Julio 171 *(Near Gran Hotel Miraflores, downtown Miraflores)*
☎ 242 30 94
Clean sauna along with art gallery renovated in 99.

TRAVEL AND TRANSPORT
■ **Explora Peru** (GLM)
Francisco de Zela 1580 ☎ 265-9524 ☎ 266-0953 📠 471-5287
✉ explora@computextos.com.pe

HOTELS
■ **Hotel Domeyer** (glm H MA)
Domeyer 296, Barranco ☎ 247 14 13 📠 247 11 13
✉ believeinc@correo.dnet.com.pe

GENERAL GROUPS
■ **Germinal**
Barcelona 417, Pueblo Libre ☎ 462 47 13
■ **Moviemento Homosexual de Lima (MHOL)** Mon-Fri 9-13, 16-20 h
Mariscal Miller 828 Jesús María ☎ 433 63 75 ☎ 33 55 19
Please write to: MHOL, PO Box 110289, Lima 11

HEALTH GROUPS
■ **Via libre**
☎ 433-0003
AIDS-hotline.

SWIMMING
-Beaches in the Miraflores area (best near Restaurant "Costa Verde")

CRUISING
-Avenida Nicolás de Piérola (also known as Colmena)
-Plaza San Martín (AYOR R)
-Parque El Olivar (AYOR R TV) (near library)
-Avenida J. Prado Oeste cuadra 1, San Isidro
-Parque Kennedy, Avenida Benavides cuadra 4, Miraflores
-Parque Pedro Ruiz Gallo, Lince
-Parque de Miraflores/Parque Kennedy (between the church and the Municipal Hall, late on weekends, especially Sun)
-Parque Salazar (at the end of Av. Larco, Miraflores)

Philippines

Name: Pilipinas • Philippinen • Filipinas • Filippine
Location: Southeastern Asia
Initials: RP
Time: GMT +8
International Country Code: ☎ 63 (leave the first 0 of area codes)
International Access Code: ☎ 00
Language: Pilipino. English
Area: 300,000 km^2 / 115,830 sq mi.
Currency: 1 Phillipine Peso (P) = 100 Centavos
Population: 75,174,000
Capital: Manila
Religions: 84% Roman Catholic
Climate: Tropical and marine climate. The northeast monsoon lasts from November to April, the southwest monsoon from May to October.

✳ Homosexuality is permitted in the Philippines, and the age of consent is 18. Our information is at present contradictory. The Philippines are known to have had anti-gay tendencies in the past, but their embassy in Germany tells us a different story: "Gays lead a normal life, are accepted and even respected in their jobs. Gay organisations are of a purely social nature."

★ Homosexualität ist auf den Philippinen nicht illegal; das Schutzalter liegt bei 18 Jahren. Unsere Informationen sind zum jetzigen Zeitpunkt allerdings uneinheitlich. Aus der Vergangenheit sind schwulenfeindliche Tendenzen auf den Philippinen durchaus bekannt. Allerdings erklärte die Botschaft der Philippinen in Deutschland: "Schwule führen ein normales Leben, sind akzeptiert, in ihren Berufen gar respektiert. Die schwulen Organisationen des Landes haben rein sozialen Charakter."

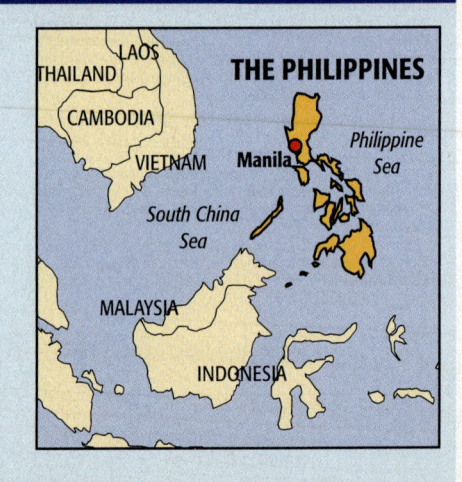

Bacolod - Negros ▸ Manila — Philippines

L'homosexualité n'est pas un délit aux Philippines. La majorité sexuelle y est fixée à 18 ans. Les informations dont nous disposons actuellement sont contradictoires. Nous avons toujours entendu dire qu'il était plutôt mal vu d'être homosexuel aux Philippines. L'Ambassade des Philippines en Allemagne nous a fait savoir, en revanche, que "les homosexuels mènent une vie tout ce qu'il y a de plus normal, qu'ils sont bien intégrés dans la société et estimés et respectés au niveau professionnel". Les organisations gaies aux Philippines auraient, en outre, avant tout une vocation sociale.

La homosexualidad en Filipinas no es ilegal, la edad de consentimiento es de 18 años. Nuestras informaciones son un poco contradictorias; del pasado sabemos de las tendencias hostiles contra los gays, a pesar de ello la embajada de las Filipinas nos ha informado que "los homosexuales llevan una vida normal, son aceptados por la sociedad, e incluso en sus trabajos son respetados. Las organizaciones homosexuales del país poseen un caracter puramente social".

Le nostre informazioni sulla situazione attuale sono discordi. Mentre in passato ci era stato riferito che i gay nelle Filippine non conducono una buona vita e che i bar gay sono stati chiusi nel corso di una campagna contro il turismo di sesso e la prostituzione minorile, intrapresa dal governo, l'ambasciata delle Filippine a Bonn ci presenta un'altro quadro del paese: "i gay conducono una vita normale e vengono accettati e rispettati anche nel mondo del lavoro. Le organizzazioni gay sono apolitiche e hanno solo un carattere sociale. Solo l'accademia militari discrimina con il suo rifiuto i gay e le lesbiche, mentre dal 1993 accetta le donne".

NATIONAL GAY INFO

■ **Buy and Sell**
PO Box 2181 MCPO, Makati, Metro Manila ☎ 35 35 35 ☎ 35 35 31 📠 35 21 55
Classified Ads magazine. Penfriend service for men.

Bacolod - Negros ☎ 034

BARS
■ **Spectrum Disco** (B D F g H) 20-1 h
c/o Sea Breeze Hotel, San Juan Street ☎ 245 71

CRUISING
-City Plaza (mainly on the right side; gays often sit under "the gay tree" in the evening)

Baguio - Luzon ☎ 074

HOTELS
■ **Venus Parkview Resort Hotel** (g H)
19-A Kisad Road, Burnham Park ☎ 442 64 52 or ☎ 442 55 97. *Good food.*

CRUISING
-Mines View Park (day or evening)
-Sessions Road

Boracay Island ☎ 0632

BARS
■ **Cafe Duo** (B f G H MA) 18-? h
Manggayad, Malay Aklan ✉ 5608 *(near Lorenzo Beach Resort)* ☎ 634 26 39
■ **Coco Loco Bar** (B F g OS) 10-24
Malay Aklan ✉ 5608 *(near Boracay Beach)* ☎ 288 30 28

HOTELS
■ **Nigi Nigi Nu Noos** (B BF CC F msg NG S)
PO Box 4258 ☎ 288 31 01 📠 288 31 12
✉ niginigi@pworld.net.ph
Resort directly located at the beach. 20 rooms all with shower/WC, balcony/terrace and safe. Room service and own key available. Scuba diving and sailing possible.

CRUISING
-Southern part of the white beach where the rocks are (daytime).

Caloocan City - Luzon

DANCECLUBS
■ **Club Maginoo** (B D glm)
BMTC Building

Cebu - Cebu ☎ 032

CINEMAS
■ **Ultravistarama Theatre** (G)
Legaspi Street ☎ 964 26

HOTELS
■ **Cathay** (AC B F H NG)
Colon Street/Pelaez Street ☎ 976 21
Central location, all rooms have AC, telephone, priv. bath.

CRUISING
-Around University of the Visayas, Colon Street
-South Expressway Bus Terminal (late at night)
-Pelaez/Colon interesection (day and evening; also arcade nearby)(tv)
-Public market
-Maroco Beach, Dumlob, Talisay (13 km from Cebu; rent a cottage; the swimming pool nearby can be fairly gay)
-Marigandon beach, Vanu Resort, Mactan
-Cebu Coliseum Roller Skating (afternoon and evening)
-Fuente Osmena (circular skating rink downtown, night)
-Boulevard Pub (22-? h)

Davao - Mindanao ☎ 082

HOTELS
■ **Apo View Hotel** (H NG)
J Camus Street, *(15 minutes from airport)* ☎ 748 61

Manila ☎ 02

TOURIST INFO
■ **DOT Director for National Capital Region**
Room 207, DOT Bldg., Rizal Park ☎ 587 902

BARS
■ **Adam's & Adam's** (AYOR B D f G r s tv)
Claro M. Recto/Evangelista, Santa Crus
■ **Bassilica** (B g S)
1855 Pilar Hidalgo Lim Street, Malate

Philippines — Manila ▶ Zamboanga del Sur - Mindanao

■ **Chico's** (AC B D g SNU) 20-1 h
Timog Avenue, Quezon City ☎ 79 96 34
Beware of cheating, high prices.
■ **Cine-Café** (AC B f G MA)
Roces Avenue, Quezon City
■ **Club 690** (AC B D glm MA OS SNU TV) 20-2 h
690 NS Amoranto Street, Quezon City ☎ 712 36 62
One of the most popular bars in Manila.
■ **Joy** (B G MA WE) Tue-Sun 17-2h, Fi & Sat -4h
1808 Maria Orosa Street, Malate ☎ 525 0863
Hosts annual Gay Celebtation.
■ **Library. The** (AC B F g S YG TV) 18-3 h
1779 Adriatico Street, Malate ☎ 522 24 84
■ **Mr. Piggy's** (B D G MA WE)
Adriatico Street, Malate *(near Library Bar)*
■ **Stop Over** (AYOR B D G YG) 21-4 h
1608 Mayhaligua/Rizal Avenues Santa Cruz ☎ 711 74 54

CAFES

■ **Jefz Café** (B G)
c/o New Solanie Hotel, 1811 Leon Guinto Street, Malate

RESTAURANTS

■ **Adriatico** (AC B CC F G OS) 11-6 Sun 11-4 h
1790 M. Adriatico Street ☎ 58 40 59
Continental Spanish cuisine.
■ **Igorot** (B D F g MA R S) Gay Sat-Sun
West Avenue, Quezon City *(close to EDSA)*

CINEMAS

■ **Alta Theater** (G R)
Aurora Boulevard Cubao
■ **Capitol Theater** (G R)
Escolta Street
■ **Ginto Theater** (G R)
Quiapo Boulevard
■ **Grace Theater** (G R)
16th Avenue, Caloocan City
■ **Joy Cinema** (G R)
Libertad Street, Pasay City
■ **Pearl Theater** (G R)
Avenida Street
■ **Times Theater** (G R)
Quiapo Boulevard

MASSAGE

■ **Datu (NY5) Therapy Massage** (G MA msg R) 0-24 h
1823 FMSG Building, E. Rodriguez Street/New York Street
(white gate) ☎ 721 10 32
Call for appointment.

TRAVEL AND TRANSPORT

■ **Round World Booking Service** (g)
c/o New Solanie Hotel, 1811 Leon Guinto Street, Malate
✉ diving4u@pacific.net.ph

HOTELS

■ **Nigi Nigi Nu Noos 'e' Nu Nu Noos** (B BF CC glm H msg)
PO Box 4258 ☎ 288 31 01 🖷 288 3112
✉ niginigi@world.net.ph 🖳 pworld.net.ph/user/niginigi
■ **Palmas. Las** (AC F g H PI WH)
1616 A. Mabini Street, Malate ☎ 50 66 61 🖷 522 16 99
Very low prices and convenient situation.

■ **Pension Kanumayan** (b BF cc H Pl)
2284 Taft Avenue, Malate *(Quirino LRT Station and Vito Cruz LRT Station)* ☎ 521-1161 to 66 ✉ Kanumayan@netasia.net
Roms from US$ 26 to 64 per day.
■ **Tropicana Apartment Hotel** (AC B g H msg Pl SA)
1630 L.M. Guerrero Street, Malate ☎ 59 00 81
Highly recommended by several readers.

HEALTH GROUPS

■ **ClinicoMed**
470 San Andres cor Del Pilar Street, ☎ 521 54 99 ☎ 536 08 40
Gay friendly.
■ **Manila Doctor's Hospital**
669 United Nations Avenue, Ermita ☎ 50 30 11
Initial consultation fee in the Emergency Section pesos 25, specialists start at 200.

CRUISING

- Harrison Plaza Shopping Center, 2nd floor (R YG) (14-20 h, students)
- Amihan Gardens (Makati; in the evening)
- Robinson's Commercial Center (AYOR) (M. Adriatico Street)
- Makati Stock Exchange (AYOR)
- Old Mill Theatre (in the lobby, afternoon)
- Mehang Gardens (AYOR) (evenings)
- Aurora Gardens (opposite Congress Building in Rizal Park)
- Greenbelt Cinemas in Makati (daytime)
- At side of Delta Theater (R) (Quezon Avenue, Quezon City)
- Around Araneta Coliseum at Cubao (R) (Quezon City)
- Ali mall shopping center (R) (Quezon City)
- Farmer's market shopping center (R) (Quezon City)
- S.M.City (West Avenue, Quezon City)
- Eliptical Rd., Quezon City Memorial Park (AYOR) (near Aristocrat Rest., parking lot)
- Quezon Memorial Circle (AYOR) (Quezon City, after midnight)

Puerto Princesa - Palawan ☎ 048

HOTELS

■ **Kiao Sealodge** (F glm H) Dec-Jul
Uyunis Garden, Circulation Road ✉ 5300 ☎ 433-3500
6 cottages with shower/WC, terrace. Hotel provides own key. Rates cottage US$ 25, full-board US$ 25. Lots of nature, trekking in rainforest possible.

Quezon City - Luzon ☎ 02

BARS

■ **Butterfly Blue Bar** (B glm)
28 Scout Tobias *(at Timog Avenue)*
■ **Gigolo** (B glm)
76 A Timog Avenue
■ **Notary Public** (B glm)
109 G. Araneta Avenue
■ **Steel Bar** (B glm)
Scout Tobias *(at Timor Avenue)*

Zamboanga del Sur - Mindanao ☎ 062

BARS

■ **Rancho. El** (B D F g S)
(in the city)
Bar, disco & restaurant.

Poland

Name: Polska • Polen • Pologne • Polonia
Location: Eastern Europe
Initials: PL
Time: GMT +1
International Country Code: ☏ 48 (leave the first 0 of area codes)
International Access Code: ☏ 0 (wait for tone) 0
Language: Polish
Area: 312,685 km² / 120,727 sq mi.
Currency: 1 New Zloty (Zl) = 100 Groszy
Population: 38,666,000
Capital: Warszawa
Religions: 91% Roman Catholic
Climate: Moderate climate. Winters are cold, grey and severe with frequent snow or rain. Summers are mild to warm with frequent showers and thundershowers.

Homosexuality is not mentioned in Polish legislation and the general age of consent is set at 15. As in the Czech Republic and in Hungary, the first debates about registered relationships are beginning to take place. The influence of the Catholic church is evidently diminishing. The society is becoming more open and tolerant and a gay scene is gradually developing in the main cities.

Homosexualität findet im polnischen Strafgesetzbuch keine Erwähnung. Die allgemeine Schutzaltersgrenze liegt bei 15 Jahren. Die konservative Regierung unter Führung der Gewerkschaftsbewegung Solidarnoscz hat bis jetzt aber nicht erkennen lassen, daß sie an einer weiteren Liberalisierung der Gesetzgebung interessiert ist. Der Einfluß der katholischen Kirche geht nur langsam zurück. Allerdings läßt sich zumindest bei der städtischen Bevölkerung eine zunehmende Offenheit und Toleranz gegenüber Schwulen erkennen und so wundert es nicht, daß man- wenn auch nur in den Großstädten- Ansätze einer sich entwickelnden Schwulenszene erkennt.

Le code pénal polonais ne fait pas état de l'homosexualité. En Pologne, la majorité sexuelle est fixée à 15 ans. En Pologne, comme en République Tchèque et en Hongrie, on commence à envisager l'éventualité d'un contrat d'union civile. Ici aussi, l'Eglise est en perte de vitesse: les mentalités évoluent et les Polonais sont de plus en plus ouverts et tolérants. Et peu à peu, une scène gaie se développe dans les grandes villes.

En el Código Penal polaco, la homosexualidad no es mencionada. La edad de consentimiento es de 15 años. Al igual que en la Rep. Checa y Hungría también en Polonia se están llevando a cabo los primeros debates sobre el registro de noviazgos. La influencia de la iglesia católica ha experimentado en los últimos años una disminución. La sociedad se ha vuelto más abierta y tolerante. Esta circunstancia ha permitido un cierto tipo de desarollo de un ambiente gay en las grandes ciudades.

La legge polacca non fa menzione dell'omosessualità. La maturità sessuale è per tutti di 15 anni. Come nella Repubblica Ceca ed in Ungheria anche in Polonia vengono cautamente aperti i primi dibattiti sulle relazioni registrate. L'influenza della chiesa cattolica sta retrocedendo palesemente e la società sta diventando sempre più aperta e tollerante. Così lentamente nelle grandi città polacche si stanno formando ambienti gay.

NATIONAL GAY INFO

■ **GayGuide.Net Warsaw & Crakow** (GLM)
✉ warsaw@gayguide.net ■ gayguide.net/Europe/Poland/
Gay tourist information. Information on gay owned/friendly accommodation. Daily updated Gay Guide Webpage including news, classifieds, chat, mailing lists. English spoken.

NATIONAL PUBLICATIONS

■ **Filo Gay & Les Magazyn**
PO Box 733 ✉ 80-958 Gdansk 50 ☏ (058) 301 98 28
■ **Gejzer** (G)
PO Box 158 ✉ 00-975 Warsawa 12 *(Krakowiakow 16)*
☏ (022) 868 54 17 ⌨ (022) 868 42 78
Monthly gay magazine with general news, articles, contact ads, a country gay guide in English and Polish, and numerous erotic photos. Published by Pink Press. About 70 pages. Zt 11.95

■ **Inaczej** 10-16 h
c/o Softpress, PO Box 84 ✉ 60-971 Poznan 59 ☏ (061) 853 76 55
■ **Nowy Men**
PO Box 158 ✉ 00-975 Warsawa 12 *(Krakowiakow 16)*
☏ (022) 868 54 17 ⌨ (022) 868 42 78
The most popular gay magazine in Poland. Lots of solo and action pictures of Polish boys and men. Stories, ads, video reviews, gay guide to Poland in Polish and English. Updated monthly.

NATIONAL PUBLISHERS

■ **Pink Press**
PO Box 158 ✉ 00-975 Warsawa 12 ☏ (022) 868 54 17

Bedzin ☏ 032

DANCECLUBS

■ **Pod Blacha** (B D G h S YG) Fri 21-? h
Ulica Sportowa 4 ✉ 42 500 *(in the sport stadium)* ☏ 267 33 92
Guestrooms available (double with shower) Zl 70.-

Poland Bielsko-Biala ▸ Kraków

Bielsko-Biala ☏ 033

CRUISING
-In front of railway station

Chalupy ☏ 058

SWIMMING
-Beach on the Hel Peninsula (AYOR g NU) (Drive to [P] C4 or C5. The beach is on the side towards the sea not towards the bay. Action in the bush near the beach)

Chorzów Batory ☏ 032

SAUNAS/BATHS
■ **Therma Silesia** (B CC DR G p SA SB VS WO YG) Sun-Thu 15-23, Fri -1, Sat -8 h
Ulica Lesna 10 ✉ 41 506 *(entrance from ulica Żelazna, 5 km from Katowice)* ☏ (0) 602 76 30 26
Sauna on 250 m² with cubicles and internet café.

Czestochowa ☏ 034

CAFES
■ **Ty i Ja** (B D GLM) 17-? h, Fri-Sat disco
Ulica 1 Maja 40 B ☏ 368 14 79

Debki ☏ 058

SWIMMING
-Beach of Debki (ayor G NU YG) (nearly 65 km from Gdansk, the road ends in the village of Debki and from there walk west through the woods, over a covered wooden bridge and on for approx. 2 km along the beach)

Gdansk ☏ 058

BARS
■ **Kogiel Mogel** (B D GLM) Mon-Thu 20-2, Fri-Sun 20-5 h
Ulica Kolobrzeska 39F
■ **Piatka** (B DR G) 16-? h
Ulica Malachowskiego 5

GENERAL GROUPS
■ **Inicjatywa Gdanska** Wed 17.30-19.30 h
PO Box 34 ✉ 80-250 ☏ 348 91 91

HEALTH GROUPS
■ **Wojewódzka Przychodnia Skórno-Wenerologiczna**
Mon-Thu-13 h Fri-12 h
Ulica Dluga 84/85 *(Old Town)*
HIV & STD tests. Room 5.

SWIMMING
-Stogi (AYOR NU) (Tram Nr. 8 to the roundabout in Stogi. Walk along the beach about 1500 m to the right. Gay beach is right after the nude one)
-See also Chalupy/Debki

CRUISING
-Main railway station Gdansk-Glowny
-Railway Station Gdansk-Wrzeszcz
-Small park at the student's club "Zak" (corner of Waly Jagiellonskie/Hucisko-evenings and nights AYOR)

Gdynia ☏ 058

RESTAURANTS
■ **Pizzeria Solo** (B D F G) Restaurant (NG) 14-21, Gay parties on Fri Sat 21-? h
Ulica Szarych Szeregów 3

CRUISING
-All are (AYOR)
-Railway station Gdynia-Glówna
-Station Gdynia-Orlowo (walk on main street in direction to Zoppot, there is a gas station and opposite to it a [P]; walk straight ahead about 200 m and you will find a forest and lawn area)
-Gdynia-Kolibki (NU) (take the City-train to Sopot/Kamienny Potok, walk approx. 300 m in the direction of Gdynia, past a camping ground to the gas station then take the path on the right to the sea)
-Plac Kaszubski
-Skwer Kosciuszki (near the cinema, in front the White Fleet Harbor)
-Skwer Plymouth

Jelenia Góra ☏ 075

BARS
■ **Galery** (B D F g) Disco Fri-1 Sat-? h (other days regular Restaurant hours)
Ulica Wroclawska 67 ☏ 752 16 94

CRUISING
-Park near railway station (AYOR) (evenings)

Katowice ☏ 032

BARS
■ **Tropicana Club** (B d DR F GLM) 12-2, Disco Fri-Sat 21-4 h
Ulica Mariacka 14 ☏ 206 94 10

CRUISING
-Andrzeja Place
-In front of Café Monopol (underground)
-New railway station

Kielce ☏ 041

CRUISING
-Railway station Dworzec PKP (evenings)

Koszalin ☏ 094

BARS
■ **Oscar** (B DR G) 17-? h Parties on Sat
Ulica Matejki 5 ☏ 346 24 45

CRUISING
-Main railway station (city underpass)

Kraków ☏ 012

BARS
■ **Hades Nightclub** (B D GLM MA YG) Tue-Thu 20-1, Fri-Sat 20-5 h, Mon closed
Ulica Starowislna 60 *(basement of house in front of Club Sindy)*
☏ 21 93 69

824 *SPARTACUS* 2001/2002

Kraków ▶ Poznan | Poland

SPARTAKUS
Sauna & Fitness
Kraków, ul. M. Konopnickiej 20, tel. 48 (012) 266 60 22

■ **Hali Gali** (B d G stv) 18-? h
Ulica Karmelicka 10 *(entrance form the gate)*
Sat disco and drag show.

SAUNAS/BATHS
■ **Spartakus** (AC b DR f G MA SA SB SOL WO) 11-23, Sun 14-21 h
Ulica Konopnickiej 20 ✉ 30-302 *(opposite Wawel Castle)*
☎ 266 60 222
Friendly atmosphere sauna frequented by a mixed age crowd.

GENERAL GROUPS
■ **Lambda Kraków** Wed 19-20 h
PO Box 249 ✉ 30-960 ☎ 56 24 56

CRUISING
-Planty (Park around the old town)

Łódź ☎ 042

BARS
■ **Mercury** (B D DR GLM) Sun, Tue-Thu 18-?, Fri-Sat 20-5 h (disco)
Ulica Pilsudskiego 158a
Fri, Sat Disco from 20 h, new large danceclub with two halls.
■ **Narraganset** (B D DR GLM) Mon-Thu 16-24 h, Fri-Sat 20-5 h (disco)
Ulica Kosciuszki 93 ☎ (0) 601 31 77 58

DANCECLUBS
■ **Ganimedes** (B d GLM) Fri, Sat 21-? h
Ulica Piotrkowska 138/140 ☎ 637 29 33
Fri, Sat disco from 21h

SEX SHOPS/BLUE MOVIES
■ **Erotic Land** (AC b CC DR G MA VS) Mon-Sat 10-21 h, Sun closed
Ulica Piotrkowska 48 ✉ 90-265 *(left doors)* ☎ 630 26 91

SAUNAS/BATHS
■ **Parys** (AC B CC d DR f G MA P s SA SOL VS WO)
Mon-Wed 13.30-23, Thu-Sat -1, Sun -22 h
Ulica Piotrkowska 46 ✉ 90-265 *(near Fabryczna railway station)*
☎ 630 39 94
Nice sauna with a very mixed age clientele. Organisation of many special events like for example "Mister Gay" competitions.

CRUISING
-Ulica Zielona 5-7 (near Cinema Mloda Gwardia)
-Ulica Narutowicza (especially in summer)
-Dworzec Kolejowy railway station

-Main railway station Lódz Fabryczna
-Park Zdrowie (Al. Unii)
-Park Moniuszki (Ulica Nartowicza/Ulica Armi Ludowej)

Lublin ☎ 076

SWIMMING
-O.W.-Marina (AYOR) (Bus 8. Pass through the nudist beach. Behind is the gay meeting point)

CRUISING
-Plac Litewski

Olsztyn ☎ 089

GENERAL GROUPS
■ **Lambola-Olsztyn** Thu 18-19 h
PO Box 377 ✉ 10-959 *(Ulica Kajki 3, Monar Organization)*
☎ 27 22 09
Please enclose an IRC.

CRUISING
-Olsztyn Glowny (main railway station)

Opole ☎ 077

CRUISING
-Ulica Krakowska, Rynek
-Opole Gtowny (walk straight into Ulica Krakowska)

Piotrków Trybunalski ☎ 044

CRUISING
-Park (AYOR) (Ulica Kopernika, by night)
-Railway station/Dworzec PKP (evenings)

Poznan ☎ 061

GAY INFO
■ **Gay Center & Help Line** Fri 17-19 h
☎ (0) 604 384 089

BARS
■ **Cafe 2000** (B D GLM) Fri and Sat disco
Ulica Nowowiejskiego 8

Poland Poznan ▸ Warszawa

DANCECLUBS
■ **Skorpio Pub** (AC B D DR f GLM MA p SNU stv VS)
Mon-Wed 19-2 (bar), Thu-Sat (disco) 21-? h
Ulica Garbary 62 ✉ 61-758 *(entrance from ulica Mostowa)*

SAUNAS/BATHS
■ **Amigo** (B DR f G p SA SB SOL VS) 16-22, Fri-Sat -24 h, Sun closed
Osiedle Lecha 120 ✉ 61-298 *(Back side of drugstore)*
☎ (0) 601 941 700

SWIMMING
-Biskupice (g NU) *(from Poznan go to Gniezno to the lake of Kowalkie)*

CRUISING
-Park K. Marcinkowskiego (AYOR) *(by night)*

Radom ☎ 048

CRUISING
-Park Ulica Zeromskiego
-Park Kosciuszk

Rzeszow ☎ 017

GENERAL GROUPS
■ **International Gay Friendship Club**
c/o T. Czeslaw, PO Box 258 ✉ 35-959

Sopot ☎ 058

DANCECLUBS
■ **Enzym** (B D glm YG) 20-? h, closed Mon closed, Sun (G)
Ulica Al. Mamuszki 21 *(Lazienki Pólnocne, 500 m north from molo and Grand Hotel)*
Mixed young and trendy crowd.

Swinoujscie ☎ 091

SWIMMING
-Ferry Boat Pier and beach

Szczecin ☎ 091

BARS
■ **Incognito** (B d G) daily 21-? h
Ulica Wojska Polskiego 20
■ **No Problem** (B D GLM) 17-2 h
Ulica Dworcowa 2

DANCECLUBS
■ **To Tu** (B D GLM) Pub: 16-?, Club: 21-? h
Ulica Wojska Polskiego *(corner of Boguslawa)*

CRUISING
-Plac Brama Portowa & Planty *(near Plac Zwyciestwa)*

Torun ☎ 056

DANCECLUBS
■ **Underground** (B D GLM) Fri Sat 20-5 h
Ulica Lazienna 9 ✉ 87-100

CRUISING
All are (AYOR)
-Plac Rapackiego
-Park near Club Wodnik *(evenings)*

Walbrzych ☎ 074

CRUISING
-Railway station Walbrzych Miasto *(evenings)*

Warszawa ☎ 022

GAY INFO
■ **Rainbow Gay Centre** (GLM MA) Mon-Fri 10-17 h
Czerniakowska 178/16 ✉ 00-440 *(Entrance marked by rainbow)*
☎ 628 52 22 ✉ lambdawa@polbox.com
Support groups, helpline, sport groups, religious groups, etc.

BARS
■ **FanTOM Club** (B d DR G lj MA SNU VS) 14-1, Fri -2, Sat -4, Sun 16-24 h
Ulica Bracka 20 A ✉ 00-028 *(Tram 7/9/25-Smyk shopping centre, in the yard on the right gate, 3rd door)* ☎ 828 54 09
Bar, Sex shop, cinema. Parties on Sat from 22 and Sun from 18 h. Last Sunday of the month - Leather/Uniform/SM parties. Very popular on weekdays, crowded at the WE. Foreigners welcome.
■ **Mykonos** (B G MA)
Ulica Jana Pawla II 73 *(near Hotel Maria)*

DANCECLUBS
■ **Delos** (B D DR GLM S) Fri-Sat 22-? h
Ulica Jana Pawla II 71 ☎ 838 04 77
■ **Paradise** (B D Glm YG) Fri Sat 22-5 h
Wawelska 5 *(near stadium)*

---

fanTOM
...SIMPLY THE BEST

20a, Bracka st. Warsaw, Poland ☎ (22) 828-54-09
(celler in Brzozowski Palace, 3rd entrance from left gate)
open daily 2PM-1AM, Fridays 2PM-2PM, Saturdays 2PM-4AM

www.gejteb.pwp.pl

Warszawa ▶ Zakopane | Poland

RESTAURANTS
■ **Miedzy Nami** (b F glm YG) 11-22, Fri Sat -24, Sun 16-20 h
Bracka 20
Trendy cafe/restaurant for young/progressive crowd. Very popular, gay friendly, membership cards available.

ESCORTS & STUDIOS
■ **Gay Secret** (b G SNU) 0-24 h
☎ (0) 601 240 308
Home and hotel visits. The longer established service in Warsaw with studio in the centre of town.
■ **Studio Adam** (b G SNU) 0-24 h
☎ (0) 603 44 77 79
Home and hotel visits. Studio with minibar in the centre of Warsaw available.

SAUNAS/BATHS
■ **FanTOM Sauna** (B DR G MA MSG p SA SB VS YG) 14-1, Fri Sat -2, Sun 16-24 h
Ulica Bracka 20 A ✉ 00-028 *(Tram 7/9/25-Smyk shopping centre, in the yard on the right gate, 3rd door)* ☎ 828 54 09
Sex shop, cinema, sauna and fitness centre. Popular with a very mixed age clientele. Best time from 18-22 h. Complimentary free entrance to FanTOM club. Foreigners welcome.
■ **Galla** (b DR G MA msg p SA WO) 14-23, Sat -1 h
Ulica Ptasia 2 *(Polish Travel Building)* ☎ 652 19 86
Men and women on Sun, men only the rest of the week.

HEALTH GROUPS
■ **Stowarzyszenie Woluntariuszy Wobec AIDS** Tue, Wed, Fri 18-21 h
c/o Rainbow Gay Centre, Czerniakowska 178/16 ✉ 00-440
☎ 628 52 22
AIDS Helpline.

RELIGIOUS GROUPS
■ **Christian Gay Group** Tue 18-21 h
c/o Rainbow Gay Centre, Czerniakowska 178/16 ✉ 00-440
☎ 628 52 22

SWIMMING
-Beach Blota (G NU) (20 km from Warszawa, walk from Blota 500 m in direction of Wisla (nude area), then to your left)

CRUISING
All are (AYOR)
-Park Skaryszewski-Praga
-Central railway station (WC)
-Plac Trzech Krzyzy (Park close to Ulica Ksiazeca, night)

Wroclaw ☎ 071

GAY INFO
■ **Gay Forum** 11-17 h
c/o Remick, PO Box 195 ✉ 50-900 ☎ 72 39 25

DANCECLUBS
■ **Klub Scena** (D glm OS p YG) Thu (g), Fri-Sat (G) 20-? h
Ulica Kazimierza Wielkiego 43 ✉ 50-077 *(Opera-Tram 3/5/10/12/23 Bus K/E/M, entrance from the side street accross the backyard, look for the pink triangle, second floor)* ☎ 44 45 31

GENERAL GROUPS
■ **Dolnoslaska Grupa Gejów i Lesbijek**
PO Box 879 ✉ 50-950

HELP WITH PROBLEMS
■ **AIDS Telefon Zaufania** Tue 17-21 h
☎ 21 05 52

SWIMMING
-Opatowicka Isle (behind zoological garden)

CRUISING
-Ulica Swidnicka (opposite of opera)
-Opposite Palaca of Justice
-Hanka Sawicka Park
-Wzgórze Polskie (near Panorama Raclawicka)

Zabrze ☎ 032

DATING AGENCIES
■ **Contact**
PO Box 90 ✉ 41-800

Zakopane ☎ 018

CRUISING
-Kropowki Ulica

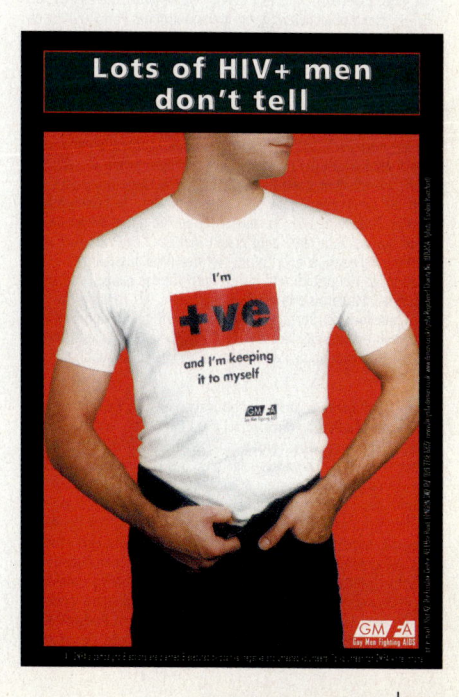

Portugal

Name: Portogallo
Location: Southwest Europe
Initials: P
Time: GMT
International Country Code: ☏ 351 (no area codes)
International Access Code: ☏ 00
Language: Portuguese
Area: 92,345 km² / 35,671 sq mi.
Currency: Escudo (Esc) = 100 Centavos. 1 EURO = 200, 482 Esc.
Population: 9,968,000
Capital: Lisboa
Religions: 90% Roman Catholic
Climate: Maritime and moderate climate. The north is cool and rainy, the south warmer and drier.
Important gay cities: Lisboa

The age of consent in Portugal is 16. Ever since joining the EC in 1986, the situation for gays and lesbians has improved considerably. The level of acceptance however of homosexuality in the cities as well as in rural areas is still not as high as that in other western European countries. The Catholic Church continues to play a significant role in the community. The past years have been important for the gay movement in Portugal. On the 28th June 1997 the first Gay Pride took place in Lisbon and in 1998 the organisation of the world exhibition EXPO in Lisbon led to a modernisation of Portugal. It is slowly developing into an interesting destination for gays, especially the classic holiday destinations: the Algarve, the flower island of Madeira, the northern metropolis Porto and the capital city Lisbon.

Das Schutzalter liegt in Portugal generell bei 16 Jahren. Seit dem Beitritt zur EG im Jahre 1986 hat sich die Situation für Schwule und Lesben erheblich verbessert. Dennoch ist die Akzeptanz von Homosexualität sowohl in den Städten als auch auf dem Lande noch nicht so hoch wie in anderen Ländern Westeuropas. Die katholische Kirche spielt in der portugiesischen Gesellschaft nach wie vor eine große Rolle. Die letzten beiden Jahre jedoch waren für die Schwulenbewegung insbesondere in Lissabon von großer Bedeutung. Wie in vielen Metropolen schon längst üblich, fand am 28. Juni 1997 zum ersten Mal ein Gay-Pride-Day statt. 1998 war Lissabon Ausrichtungsort der (Weltausstellung) EXPO, die für die Hauptstadt und nicht zuletzt für das ganze Land einen enormen Modernisierungsschub bedeutete. Als Paradies für Homosexuelle kann Portugal zwar noch nicht gelten und dennoch scheinen Urlaubsklassiker wie die Algarve, die Blumeninsel Madeira, die Nordmetropole Porto oder die Hauptstadt Lissabon auf gutem Wege.

La majorité sexuelle au Portugal est en général à 16 ans. depuis l'adhésion du Portugal à la CE en 1986, la situation des gais et lesbiennes s'est considérablement améliorée. Mais l'acceptance vis-à-vis de l'homosexualité n'est pas aussi grande que dans les autres pays d'Europe de l'Ouest, que ce soit à la ville ou à la campagne. L'Eglise catholique joue encore un grand rôle dans la société portugaise. Mais deux années furent, surtout à Lisbonne, particulièrement importantes: pour la première fois, une journée de la Gay-Pride eut lieu le 28 juin 1997, comme dans beaucoup d'autres métropoles. En 1998, Lisbonne fût le lieu d'exposition d'EXPO (exposition universelle), ce qui a été symbole de modernisation pour la ville, mais aussi pour tout le pays. Le Portugal n'est pas un paradis pour homosexuels. Mais certains lieux de vacances classiques comme Algarve, l'île des fleurs de Madère, la métropole du nord Porto ou même la capitale Lisbonne sont sur le bon chemin.

La edad de consentimiento está estipulada en 16 años, independientemente de la orientación sexual. Desde que Portugal entró en la Comunidad Europea en 1986, la situación para lesbianas y gays del país mejoró notablemente. Sin embargo, la aceptación de la homosexualidad en la sociedad no es muy alta, ni en las ciudades y naturalmente menos en zonas rurales. La situación es peor que en otros país de Europa Occidental, en parte debido a la fuerte influencia de la iglesia católica. Pero los dos últimos años han sido de mucha importancia para el movimiento gay: El 28 de junio de 1997 tuvo lugar por primera vez un Gay-Pride-Day en Lisboa y por supuesto la Expo en 1998 significó un gran impulso de modernización para el país entero y tuvo también una repercusión muy positiva para la comunidad gay. Aunque todavía Portugal está lejos de ser denominado un paraíso para homosexuales, parece ser que sitios como la zona de Algarve, la isla de flores Madeira, la metrópoli del norte Porto y la capital Lisboa están en buen camino.

L'età legale in Portogallo è di 16 anni ugualmente per etero e omosessuali. Dal 1986, l'anno dell'adesione del Portogallo alla CE, la situazione dei gay e delle lesbiche è migliorata notevolmente. Nonostante ciò né in città né in posti di campagna l'omosessualità viene accettata nella stessa misura come in altri paesi dell'Europa occidentale. La chiesa cattolica svolge ancora una notevole influenza. Gli ultimi due anni però hanno avuto una grande importanza per il movimento gay soprattutto a Lisbona. Mentre in molte metropoli il "Gay Pride Day" è già usanza comune, a Lisbona si è svolto per la prima volta il 28. luglio 1997. Nel 1998 a Lisbona è stata effettuata l'esposizione mondiale, l'EXPO, che ha portato con sè una spinta di modernizzazione non solo per la capitale, ma anche per tutto il paese. Il Portogallo non può essere detto un paradiso per omosessuali, ma sembra che i posti classici per il turismo come l'Algarve, l'isola di Madeira, la metrópoli del Nord Porto o la capitale Lisbona siano in via di miglioramento.

NATIONAL PUBLICATIONS

■ **Korpus**
PO Box 22868 ✉ 1147-501 Lisboa ☎ 96 5086300
📠 21 353 0711 💻 revistakorpus@hotmail.com
The national gay magazine of Portugal. Many articles, listing of gay bars and associations, contact ads. Published 3 timesyear.

NATIONAL GROUPS

■ **Gorduxos Girth & Mirth Portugal** (G LJ)
Apartado 52131 ✉ 1700 Lisboa ☎ 93 635 4040
■ **ILGA-Portugal** (B GLM MA) 16-20 h, Sun closed
Rua de São Lázaro, 88 ✉ 1150 Lisboa ☎ 21 887 3918
📠 21 887 3922 💻 www.ilga-portugal.org
Organiser of Gay Pride and Gay Film Festival. The Lesbian and Gay Community Center has legal, medical and psychological counselling (appointment necessary) as well a small bookstore, cafeteria and internet acess document center, and HIV counselling. All are welcome. O Centro Comunitário Gay e Lésbico põe à sua disposição aconselhamento jurídico, médico, e psicológico gratuito(com marcação), um centro de documentação, uma pequena livraria, acesso à internet, aconselhamento sobre o VIH e uma cafetaria. Todos são bem vindos!
■ **Liga Portuguesa Contra a Sida**
Rua Crucifixo, 40, 2° ✉ 1100-183 Lisboa*(2nd floor)* ☎ 21 322 5575
☎ 21 322 5576
■ **Opus Gay Associação/Association** (GLM)
Rua da Ilha Terceira, 34, 2 andar ✉ 1000-173 Lisboa *(2nd floor)*
☎ 21 315 1396 📠 21.3170797 💻 anser@netpac.pt
💻 www.opusgayassociation.com
Opus Gay Association was the organiser of the first Gay and Lesbian Summer University and the founder of the first owned GLBT Travel department, ILGTA and ATL (Lisbon Tourism Association) Member! Opus Gay Association has Legal, Psychological, Religious Assistance, as well as tarot consultations, Internet, bar, laundry, Dog and Cat Sitter! A Opus Gay Associação organizou pela primeira vez em Portugal a Universidade de Verão de Estudos Gays e Lésbicos, bem como criou o 1 Departamento de Viagens GLBT em Portugal, Opus Gay Turismo-membro da ILGTA(International Lesbian and Gay Travel Association) e da ATL(Associação de Turismo de Lisboa). A Opus Gay Associação põe à sua disposição aconselhamento jurídico, psicológico, bem como Assistência Religiosa(Casamentos), Tarot, Internet, Bar, Lavandaria, Dog and Cat Sitter !

Albufeira - Algarve

BARS

■ **Dream's** (AC GLM s) 21-3 h Closed Mon & Tue.
Avenida Sá. Carneiro, Centro Comercial Isamar - Loje 13-14
✉ 8200 *(Montochoro)* ☎ 289 58 7441
Shows on Wed, Fri & Sat at 1h.
■ **Espehlo Bar** (B GLM)
Avenida Sá Carneiro 6, Montechoro

SWIMMING

-Bicas Beach- Lagoa de Albufeira.

Almancil - Algarve

RESTAURANTS

■ **Memories** (F GLM)
En.125 ✉ 8135 *(National road-125)*

Armação de Pêra - Algarve

CRUISING

-Sand Dunes
-Praia Grande(Big Beach)
-Praia da Galé(Galé Beach)

Aveiro - Beira

BARS

■ **Café Ria** (B g)
Club Galitos 5/6 ☎ 3800

HEALTH GROUPS

■ **Centro de Saude** Tue Thu Sat 10-12 h
Avenida Dr. Lourenço Peixinho 138-140 ✉ 3800 ☎ 234 23 381
■ **Hospital distrital de Aveiro**
Avenida Artur Ravara ✉ 3800 ☎ 234 378300

SWIMMING

-Costa Nova beach (behind the camping site)

Braga - Minho

BARS

■ **Copacabana** (B glm)
Avenida da Liberdade ✉ 4700
■ **Deslize** (glm)
Rua da Sé

DANCECLUBS

■ **Club 84**
Galerias Hotel Turismo, Praça João XXI
■ **Club 90** (B D g)
Centro Comercial Galecia, Praça de Maximinos ✉ 4700

RESTAURANTS

■ **A Toca** (b F g)
Rua do Souto ✉ 4700

HOTELS

■ **Parque. Do** (AC B g H)
Parque do Bom Jesus do Monte ✉ 4700 ☎ 253 22 048
Downtown neighbourhood location, hotel with garden. All rooms with telephone, priv. bath and WC.

FETISH GROUPS

■ **Club Marquis du Sade** 21-24, WE 15-24 h
Apartado 110 ✉ 4702 ☎ 253 27 9296

HEALTH GROUPS

■ **Dispensario de Higiene Social** Mon-Fri 9-12 h
Larrgo Poulo Osorio ✉ 4700 ☎ 253 27 041
Ask for AIDS Help Group.

CRUISING

-Bon Jesus do Monte (in the park)
-Centro Comercial GOLD-Center (especially when there are blue movies)
-Sta. Barbara Gardens
-Avenida des Combatentes (Avenue)

Portugal — Bragança - Tras-os-Montes ▶ Figueira du Foz - Beira

Bragança - Tras-os-Montes

RESTAURANTS
■ **Snack Bar Leal** (b F G)
Avenida João Cruz 16 ✉ 5300

HEALTH GROUPS
■ **Dispensario de Higiene Social** Mon-Fri 10-12 h
Delegação de Saude, Avenida João da Cruz 144 ✉ 5300
☎ 273 103

Carvoeiro - Algarve

GUEST HOUSES
■ **Casa Marhaba** (b BF G H MA OS PI)
Rua de Benagil, Alfanzina ✉ 8400-427 ☎ 282 35 87 20
☎ 282 35 87 20 💻 casamarhaba@hotmail.com

Cascais - Extremadura-Lisboa

CRUISING
-Railway station (Summer)
-Beaches at Poente
-Amusement Arcade - Rua da Palmeira, 4E

Coimbra - Beira

BARS
■ **Mil Olhos** (B D g p YG)
Santa Clara ✉ 3000

CAFES
■ **Café International** (b f g)
Avenida Navarro ✉ 3000 (in front of railway station)
■ **Pigalle** (B g r)
Avenida Sá da Bandeira 123/125 ✉ 3000
■ **Santa Cruz** (B g OS)
Praça Santa Cruz ✉ 3000
■ **Sing Sing** (B F g OS YG)
Rua Castro Matoso ✉ 3000

DANCECLUBS
■ **Via Latina** (AC B D NG) 23-4, best after 1 h
Rua Almeida Garrett 1 ✉ 3000

CRUISING
-Sereia Garden(near kiosk at night)
-Ralway station
-Shopping Center Sofia
-Praça da República.

Espinho - Porto

SWIMMING
-Beach (between New Golf Hotel and town)

Estoril - Extremadura-Lisboa

BARS
■ **Café Yate** (g MA OS PI)
Arcadas de Casino ✉ 2765 (below casino)
■ **John's Bar** (B f g)
Rua Jeaquin ✉ 2765 (near Aparthotel Nino Pilipe)

CRUISING
-Terrace near clock and above restaurant on promenade
-Behind railway station

Faro, Ilha de - Algarve

SWIMMING
-In beach island of Faro (extreme right end).

CRUISING
Jardim Manuel Bivar(Garden)- near the Marina
-Café Allianca
-Also near the Miracoles(gambling house).

Figueira da Foz - Beira

BARS
■ **Brisma Mar** (B g)
Praia de Leinos, Marinha das Ondas ✉ 3080
■ **La Belle Epoque** (AC B g MA OS p) 16-4 h, closed Tue
Rua Capitão Argel de Melo 20, Alto do Forno - Buarcos ✉ 3080
(near the camp site) ☎ 233 43 4888
■ **Pôr do Sol** (B g)
Rua dos Pescadores 60 ✉ 3080 (Praia de Buarcos)

CRUISING
-Around the Casino and adjacent streets
-Buarcos Beach
-Beaches to the south.

Casa Marhaba
ALGARVE

Our friendly private guest house in the sun is close to beaches and bars. Nestling in quiet countryside, it's the perfect place for a relaxing, carefree holiday at unbeatable value

✻

En-suite Bedrooms, Pool, Bar, Gardens, Sun Terraces, Sat TV and Video

✻

Car Rental Available

✻

"Marhaba" means "Welcome" – we mean to make you just that!

✻

For our Brochure and full details call Tony direct on Tel/Fax:
00 351 282 358720
e-mail: casamarhaba@hotmail.com

Funchal - Madeira ▶ Lagos - Algarve **Portugal**

Funchal - Madeira
BARS
■ **Apolo Café and Funchal Café** (B f g r)
Situated in the Largo da Sé on either side of a square where the Madeira youth gather most of the day. Decreation is called for. Many hustlers!
■ **Beerhouseto Marina** (B g MA) 10-4 h
Xarambinha, Largo Corpo Santo 29
■ **Café do Theatro** (B F glm MA OS) 15-24 h
Avenida Arriaga *(in Theatre building)*
■ **Crazy Sailor** (B F g)
Marina ✉ 9000

HEALTH GROUPS
■ **Associação Abraco**
Rua Direita 21 ✉ 9050 *(2nd floor)* ☎ 291 23 6700

CRUISING
-Santa Catarina Park (AYOR) (at Avenida do Infante)
-Avenida Arriaga (ayor) (stay in the lighted areas)
-Municipal Park
-Along the sea wall
-Beach Poças do Governador

Ilhavo - Beira
BARS
■ **Opção** (B G MA)
Av. Fernandes Lavrador 214 ✉ 3830 *(Barra)* ☎ 234 36 0519

Lagoa - Algarve
HOTELS
■ **Casa Marhaba** (g H)
Rua de Benagil, Alfanzina ✉ 8400 ☎ 282 35 8720
🖳 casamarhaba@hotmail.com

Lagos - Algarve
GAY INFO
■ **Gay News**
Apartado 687, Rua dos Carmachinhos 40 ✉ 8600-725
☎ 282 782 059 📠 282 782 058 🖳 gaynews@clix.pt
🖳 gaynews.tripod.com
Information service, room referral and car rental.

**RESIDENCIAL/GUESTHOUSE
RUBI - MAR**
AN 8 BEDROOM GUESTHOUSE SITUATED
IN THE CENTRE OF LAGOS. ONLY 2
MINUTES FROM NEAREST BEACH AND 10
MINUTES BY CAR
TO GAY NUDIST BEACH
COMFORTABLE ROOMS WITH PRIVATE
OR SHARED BATHROOM SOME ROOMS
WITH SEA VIEWS AND BALCONIES.
BREAKFAST IS INCLUDED AND SERVED
TO YOU IN BED
OWN KEY NO RESTRICTIONS
INFORMATION OR RESERVATIONS
DAVID OR TONY
RUA DA BARROCA 70-1,
8600-688 LAGOS
TEL: +351 282 763165
FAX: +351 282 767749
MOBILE; +351 91 4119569
E-MAIL: rubimar01@hotmail.com

HIDEAWAY BAR
The best bar on the Street
Trav 1 de maio No 9
This friedly bar is
Co-Owned by the Rubi-Mar
Great Cocktails/Wines/Beers
& much, much more
Bar Food avaible till 01.30am
Bar open from 6pm till 2am Daily

A private,
peaceful,
small
and clean
residencial.

All rooms with private terrace
to the wonderful garden, own
bathroom, WC and Sat-TV and
private safe

Pleasant lounges, pool, own key.
Breakfast until 11.00 a.m.
Car rental available.

Call or write to Werner at:
Quatro Estradas – Apartado 689
P-8601-908 Lagos/Algarve
Phone: 00351 282 763642
Fax: 00351 282 761914
e-mail: werner.zaiser@oninet.pt

Portugal — Lagos - Algarve - Beira ▸ Lisboa

BARS

■ **Eclipse Bar** (A AC B f G MA p vs YG) 21-2 h
Rua Lançarote de Freitas 30A ✉ 8600 ☎ 282 76 8219
■ **Hideaway** (B F glm MA N) 18-02h
Trav 1 de maio No. 9 ✉ 8600 ☎ 282 767203
Info service. Room referral. English, German & Portuguese spoken.
■ **Luisol** (B E G MA p) 19-2 h
Rua de São José 21 ✉ 8600 ☎ 282 76 1794

RESTAURANTS

■ **Kalunga** (CC F g MA) 18-23h
Rua Marquês de Pombal 26 ✉ 8600 *(1st floor)*

GUEST HOUSES

■ **Residencial Guest House Rubi-Mar** (BF CC g H MA) 0-24 h
Rua da Barrocia 70 ✉ 8600 *(1st floor)* ☎ 282 76 3165
☎ 91 4119569 (mobile) 📠 282 76 7749
📧 rubimar01@hotmail.com
■ **Ai que Bom** (g H)
☎ 91 922 1931 📠 282 76 4705
Cottages and rooms.
■ **Casa Pequena** (BF b F GLM H MA NU PI WH) 0-24 h
Apartado 133, Praia da Luz ✉ 8600 ☎ 282 78 9068
📠 282 78 9068
Praia da Luz is a beach village 5 km west of Lagos. 2 double rooms with private bath, terrace, telephone, Sat-TV, radio and video. Minimum stay 3 nights.
■ **Gay Guest House** (B BF G H msg OS VS)
Rua dos Camachinhos 40 ✉ 8600 ☎ 282 76 4907
📠 282 76 4907
Centrally located. Some rooms with own bath.
■ **Oasis do Sul** (BF g H MA NU OS PI) Mar-Oct 0-24 h
Quatro Estradas-Apartado 689 ✉ 8601-908 ☎ 282 76 3642
☎ 282 76 1914 📧 werner.zaiser@oninet.pt
All rooms with private terrace to the wonderful garden, own bathroom, WC, SAT-TV and private safe. Pleasant lounges, own key. Breakfast until 11h. Car rental available. Call or wite to Werner.
■ **Residência Gil Vicente** (B BF CC GLM H OS)
Rua Gil Vicente 26 ✉ 8600-596 ☎ 282 762 982 ☎ 282 762 836
📠 282 762 832 📧 ggh@dix.pt 🌐 gaynews.tripod.com
■ **Terramar** (glm MA OS)
Urbanização Terramar-lote 30-Torralinha ✉ 8600
☎ 282 78 2716
Friendly atmosphere in a private house. Big roofterrace, close to nude beaches. 2 doubles with shared bathroom, 1 with balcony.

CRUISING

- Promenade along the river
- Beach at the end of Meia Praia by the dunes (NU)

Leiria - Beira

BARS

■ **Dórius Bar** (B GLM MA STV) 21-2h Tue-Sun
Rua D. Alfonso Henriques, 26 ✉ 2400-081 ☎ 96 573 0427
Drag Show every Fri & Sat 1h and Sun at 23h.

CRUISING

- Parque de Jardim central

Lisboa

Lisbon with it's population of 680,000 is split between tradition and the modern age. The Portuguese metropole is a mixture of old charm and modern living. With the world exhibition EXPO, Portugal has succeeded to counteract it's reputation as the back yard of Europe. With this development the gay community has clearly gotten better. A year ago the first AIDS Solidarity Demo took place along side Gay Pride, as well as a Gay-Lesbian Film Festival. In Lisbon homosexuality still remains somewhat closed to general conversation. This might be due to the mentality of the Portuguese, who are slow to accept change. Everyone can form his own opinion of Lisbon, whether it be a stroll through the Park Princip Real after a pub crawl, or a day spent on beach Nr. 17 (the Cost de Caprica) in the bushes behind the sand dunes.

Lissabon mit seinen 680 000 Einwohnern meistert den Spagat zwischen Tradition und Moderne. Die portugiesische Metropole, der einst ein Weltreich zu Füßen lag, hat sich viel von seinem alten Charme bewahrt, der sich heute mit modernem Großstadtleben mischt. Mit der (Weltausstellung) EXPO ist es in der Stadt ganz am Rande des westlichen Europa gelungen, seinem Ruf als Hinterhof Europas entgegenzuwirken. Mit dieser Entwicklung hat sich auch die Situation für Homosexuelle deutlich verbessert. Schon ein Jahr zuvor fanden neben dem Gay-Pride-Day die erste AIDS-Solidaritätsdemonstration sowie ein schwulesbisches Filmfestival statt. Über Homosexualität wird hier längst nicht so offen gesprochen wie in anderen europäischen Metropolen, was vielleicht auch an der Mentalität der Portugiesen liegt, die Dinge nicht allzu methodisch anzugehen. Für Lissabon jedoch gilt: Stille Wasser sind tief. Und davon kann sich jeder selbst ein Bild machen, sei es nach einer nächtlichen Kneipentour im Park Principe Real oder am nächsten Morgen am Strand Nr. 17 der Costa de Caparica, dessen Gebüsche sich hinter den Dünen erstrecken.

Lisbonne est une ville qui, avec ses 680 000 habitants, essaie de trouver un compromis entre tradition et modernité. La métropole portugaise, autrefois à la tête d'un royaume, a beaucoup gardé de son ancien charme, qui se mélange aujourd'hui avec la vie de la grande ville. Avec l'exposition universelle EXPO, la ville la plus à l'ouest de l'Europe a réussi a combattre sa réputation de cour arrière de l'Europe. Cette amélioration a aussi profité à la situation des homosexuels. Un an auparavant, un festival du film gai et lesbien ainsi que des manifestations de soutien aux malades du SIDA eurent lieu en addition à la Gay Pride. Mais ici, on ne parle pas d'homosexualité si facilement que dans les autres grandes métropoles européennes, ce qui tient peut-être à la mentalité des portugais qui n'ont pas une approche très méthodique des choses. Mais à Lisbonne une chose est vraie: ne vous fiez pas à cette impression! et chacun peut s'en convaincre soi-même, que ce soit en faisant une tournée nocturne des bars du Park Principe Real ou le lendemain matin sur la plage no.17 de la Costa de Caparica, dont les buissons s'étendent derrière les dunes.

Lisboa con sus 680 000 habitantes es la combinación perfecta entre tradición y modernidad. La metrópoli portuguesa, en el pasado soberana de un imperio, ha sabido conservar mucho de su antiguo encanto que hoy en día se mezcla con la vida moderna de una gran ciudad. Desde que se organizó la Expo, Lisboa ha demostrado ejemplarmente que no es una ciudad atrasado en el extremo de Europa occidental, sino una capital de modernidad y progreso. De este desarrollo positivo también se ha beneficiado la comunidad gay, que ya organizó en 1997 el Gay-Pride-Day, manifestaciones de solidaridad con infectados de SIDA, así como un festival de cine gaylesbiana. Aquí el tema de la homosexualidad no se discute tan abier-

Lisboa — Portugal

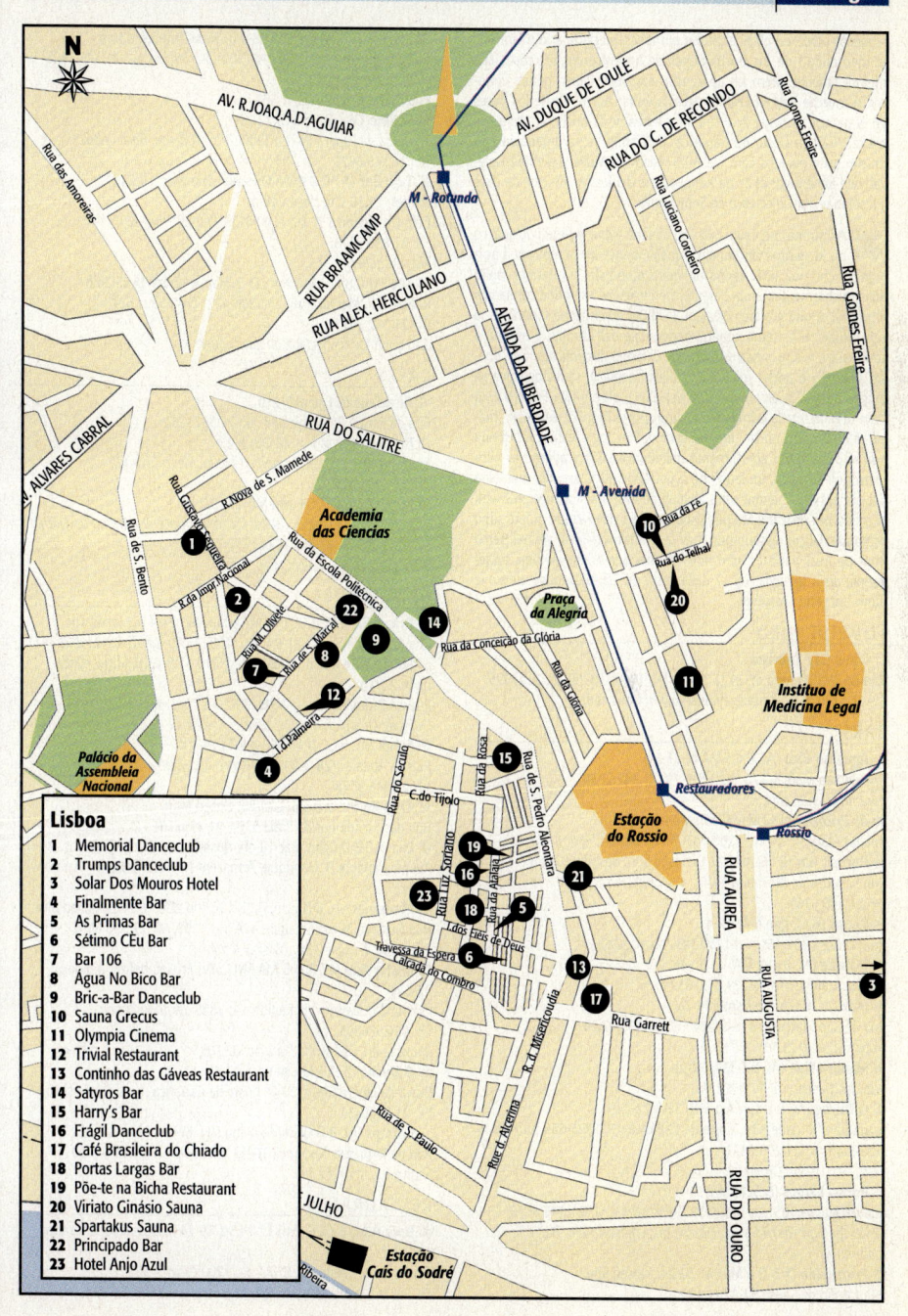

Lisboa

1. Memorial Danceclub
2. Trumps Danceclub
3. Solar Dos Mouros Hotel
4. Finalmente Bar
5. As Primas Bar
6. Sétimo Céu Bar
7. Bar 106
8. Água No Bico Bar
9. Bric-a-Bar Danceclub
10. Sauna Grecus
11. Olympia Cinema
12. Trivial Restaurant
13. Continho das Gáveas Restaurant
14. Satyros Bar
15. Harry's Bar
16. Frágil Danceclub
17. Café Brasileira do Chiado
18. Portas Largas Bar
19. Põe-te na Bicha Restaurant
20. Viriato Ginásio Sauna
21. Spartakus Sauna
22. Principado Bar
23. Hotel Anjo Azul

SPARTACUS 2001/2002 | 833

Portugal | Lisboa

tamiente como en otras capitales europeas, en parte a lo mejor por la mentalidad de los portugueses de no enfrentar las cosas tan metódicamente. !Pero las apariencias engañan! Quien quiera conocer la marcha gay en Lisboa, debería visitar por la noche los bares en el parque Principe Real o a altas horas de la noche la playa número 17 de la Costa de Caparica. En Lisboa ya se organizan con mucho exito eventos como la AIDS-March en Mayo y el Pride Festival, que tiene lugar el 27 de Junio, aparte del festival de cine de gays y lesbianas que se celebra en Septiembre.

A Lisbona con i suoi 680.000 abitanti viene superato lo spacco tra lo spirito tradizionale e quello moderno. La metropoli portoghese che una volta regnò un'imero mondiale, si è tenuta molto del suo charme dei tempi passati, che oggigiorno si fonde con la vita moderna di una grande città. Con l'EXPO, l'esposizione mondiale, la città situata al estremo confine occidentale dell'Europa, è riuscita a contrastare la sua antica reputazione di luogo dimenticato. Con questo sviluppo è anche migliorata notevolmente la situazione per gli omosessuali. Già un'anno prima dell'EXPO, oltre il Gay-Pride-Day, è stata organizzata la prima manifestazione per la solidarietà con i malati di AIDS come anche una rassegna di film gay e lesbici. A Lisbona non si parla tanto apertamente dell'omosessualità quanto in altre metropoli europee, un fatto che si potrebbe attribuire alla mentalità dei portoghesi, che non sono abituati ad avvicinarsi ai loro problemi in modo organizzato. Ma per Lisbona vale a dire: acque quiete sono profonde. Di ciò ognuno può farsi la sua propria idea, sia nel parco Principe Real dopo un giro notturno nei bar o alla mattina susseguente nella spiaggia No. 17 della Costa de Caparica, dove, dietro le dune, sorgono i cespugli.

TOURIST INFO

■ **Opus Gay Tourism**
Rua da Ilha Terceira, n 34, 2 andar ✉ 1000.173 ☏ 21.3151396
☏ 21.3170797 ✉ opusgayturismo@hotmail.com

BARS

■ **Água no Bico** (AC B f G MA p) 21-3 h
Rua de São Marçal, 170 ✉ 1200 ☏ 21 347 2830
Bar and internet café.
■ **As Primas** (B f GLM MA WE) Mon-Sat 22-4 h
Rua da Atalaia, 154 ✉ 1200-043 *(Metro-Baixa-Chiado)*
■ **Harry's Bar** (B f G MA) 22-6, closed Sun. Best time 2-4 h
Rua S. Pedro de Alcântara 57/61 ✉ 1200 *(Bus 58/15)*
☏ 21 346 0760
■ **Keops** (B CC glm MA) 19-4 h
Rua da Rosa 157-159 ✉ 1200-383 *(Bairro Alto)*
■ **Majong** (AC B glm MA) 21.30-4h
Rua da Atalaia, n 3 ☏ 21 3421039
■ **Max** (AC B G MA p s snu) 20-2h
Rua de São Marçal, n 5 ✉ 1200 ☏ 21 395 27 26
Happy hour 20-23.30h.
■ **Mistura Fina** (AC B G MA) 21-2h
Rua das Gáveas, 15-17 ☏ 1200
■ **O Duche** (AC B D G MA p SNU STV) 22-4 h
Praça da Liberdade 33 c, Costa de Caparica ✉ 2825-355 *(outside of Lissabon)* ☏ 21 290 0431
Disco bar. Fri-Sun Dragqueen shows.
■ **Portas Largas** (B GLM MA) 20-4 h
Rua da Atalaia 105 ✉ 1200-038 *(Bairro Alto)* ☏ 21 346 6379
Under the sign: Record. Very popular, ancient Bairro Alto-Bar, often fado-music.
■ **Principado** (A B G p MA) 21.30-2 h, closed Sun
Rua Cecílio de Sousa 94-A ✉ 1200

■ **Satyros** (B G MA p STV) 23-4 h, Show Thu-Sat 2.30 h
Calçada da Patriarcal, 6-8 ✉ 1200 *(Bus 58/15)* ☏ 21 342 1525
■ **Sem Nome** (glm)
Rua Diário de Noticias, n 132
■ **Sétimo Céu** (B G s YG) 22-2 h
Travessa da Espera 54 ✉ 1200 *(Metro-Chiado, Barrio Alto)*
☏ 21 346 6471
■ **Tejo Bar** (A AC B g MA OS s WE) Summer: 16-2 h, Winter: 21.30-2 h, closed Mon
Belo Do Vigário 1-A ✉ 1100-613 *(Alfama, Tram-28)*
☏ 21 886 8878
Also art gallery.
■ **106** (! AC B f GLM MA p) 21-2, Happy hours 'til 23:30 h
Rua de São Marçal, 106 ✉ 1200-422 *(Bus 100 or 58)*
☏ 21 342 7373
Also good for information on gay venues.

CAFES

■ **Alsaciana** (B F glm) 7-21h
Rua da Escola Politécnica 88 ☏ 21.3963362
■ **Brasileira** (B bf F g MA OS) 8-2 h
Rua Garrett 120 *(near Largo do Chiado. Metro-Chiado)*
☏ 21 346 9541
■ **Rosso Café** (B CC F glm MA OS) 9-2 h
Rua Ivens 53-61 (patio) *(Metro-hiado, entrance also from Rua Garrett 19 to patio)* ☏ 21 347 1524
More gay people at night time.

DANCECLUBS

■ **Bric-a-Bar** (AC B CC D G MA p snu stv) 21-4 h, Closed Tue.
Rua Cecílio de Sousa, 82-84 ✉ 1200 *(Metro Rato)* ☏ 21 342 8971
■ **Finalmente** (AC B D GLM MA p SNU STV) 23-6, Show every night 2.30 h
Rua da Palmeira 38 ✉ 1200-313 *(Bus 100)* ☏ 21 347 2652
Daily very popular. Monday-amateur night.
■ **Frágil** (AC b CC D MA NG p WE) 23-4 h
Rua da Atalaia, 128 ✉ 1200 *(Bairro Alto, Metro-Chiado)*
☏ 21 346 9578
■ **Kremlin** (AC B D glm) 24-8h, closed Mon.
Rua das Escadinhas da Praia 5 ☏ 21.3957101
■ **Lux** (AC B D f glm) Bar-18-4h. closed Mon, Disco- Thur-Sat 24-6h.
Avenida Infante D. Henrique- Armazém A/ Warehouse A *(Warehouse A)*
■ **Memorial** (AC B D gLm S) 23-4 h, Sun also 16-20 h, closed Mon
Rua Gustavo Matos Sequeira 42A ✉ 1200 ☏ 21 396 8891
Show Thu, Fri, Sun 2.30 h. Mainly lesbians.
■ **Mister Gay** (AC B D G MA SNU STV) Fri-Sat, before holidays 22-5 h
Quinta da Ilveira - Vía Rápida ✉ 2825 *(outside Lisbon)*
☏ 96.2586803
Shows every Friday and Saturday 02.30h.
■ **O Duche** (B D G MA snu stv) 22-4h
Praça da Liberdade, n 33 D, Costa da Caparica *(outside of Lisbon)*
☏ 21.2900431
■ **Trumps** (AC B D GLM MA p snu stv) 23-6 h, Mon closed
Rua da Imprensa Nacional, 104-B ✉ 1200 ☏ 21 397 1059
Shows Sun & Wed 2.30h.

RESTAURANTS

■ **Bota Alta** (B CC F glm) 12-14.30, 19-24 h, closed Sat afternoon and Sun
Travessa da Queimada 35-37 ✉ 1200 *(Bairro Alto)*
☏ 21 342 7959

Lisboa | Portugal

KORPUS

P.O.BOX 22.868
1147-501 LISBOA
FAX: +351-21-3530711

THE ONLY PORTUGUESE GAY MAGAZINE
Trimestral. Information, news, interviews, cronicles, debates, footage, small ads, short stories, artistic and erotic fotos, Gay Guide... ANUAL SUBSCRIPTION: 4.000$00 (in Portugal), 5.640$00 (in Europe), 6.400$00 (outside Europe)

LISBOA

Bar

ANB
ÁGUA NO BICO

OPEN EVERY DAY 21.00-03.00 H

INTERNET@ACCESS

RUA DE SÃO MARÇAL,
170 1200-LISBOA

TEL: 21-3472830   FAX: 21-9608054

http://www.agua-no-bico.com
E-Mail: anb@mail.pt

■ **Cantinho das Gáveas** (B CC F glm) 13-15 and 19-23h. Closed Sat. for lunch & all day Sun.
Rua da Gáveas, 82/84
Portuguese cuisine.

■ **Casanostra** (B CC F glm) 12-24 h, closed Sat afternoon Mon
Travessa do Poço da Cidade 60 ✉ 1200 *(Bairro Alto)*
☎ 21 342 5931
Italian cuisine.

■ **Chez Degroot** (A B CC E F NG MA)
Rua Dq. Bragança, 4   ☎ 21 347 2839
International/Portuguese cuisine.

■ **Chiado** (B F g) 10-2h, closed Sun.
Largo no Picadeiro, 11/13 ☎ 21.3423040

■ **Consenso** (B CC F glm MA) Lunch Mon-Fri 13-15,
Dinner Thu-Fri 19.30-23.30, Sat -0.30 h

Rua da Academia das Ciências 1-1 A ✉ 1200-003 *(Metro-Baixa-Chiado/Bus-5/100/Tram-28)* ☎ 21 346 8611
Portuguese cuisine.

■ **Fidalgo** (F g MA) 12-16 and 19-24h closed Sunday.
Rua da Barroca 27 ☎ 21 342 2900
Very reasonably priced food.

■ **Pap'Açorda** (B CC F g) 12.30-14.30, 20-23 h, closed Sun & Mon.
Rua da Atalaia, 57-59 ✉ 1200 *(Bairro Alto)* ☎ 21 346 4811
International food.

■ **Põe-te na Bicha** (B CC F G MA) 19-24h
Travessa da Água da Flor, 36 ✉ 1200 *(Bairro Alto)* ☎ 21 342 5924
Portuguese and international cuisine.

■ **Promotora Choop** (AC B CC F g MA s WE) 11-2 h, closed Sun
Largo do Calvário 3 ✉ 1300 *(Alcântara)* ☎ 21 362 3102

■ **Tacão Pequeno** (B F glm)
Travessa da Cara, 3-A ☎ 21 347 2848

7°
SÉTIMO CÉU BAR

Travessa da Espera, 54 • LISBOA • Tel. 21 346 64 71
BAIRRO ALTO

Portugal | Lisboa

BRICABAR
your favourite!

Rua Cecilio de Sousa 84
Open from 10 p.m. to 4 a.m.
closed Tuesday
TEL: 21 342 89 71

Lisbon-Portugal

TRUMPS
CAFÉ • BAR • DISCOTECA

RUA DA IMPRENSA
NACIONAL N° 104-B

OPEN FROM 23 - 6 h
MON closed

SHOW
SUN and WED   2.30 h

TEL: 21 397 10 59
www.trumps.pt

Lisboa | Portugal

Lisbon's most popular sauna

sauna spartakus

Finnish Sauna Cabins
 Solarium

Steam B*aths* *Labyrinth*

Video
Jacuzzi **Dark Rooms**
Bar

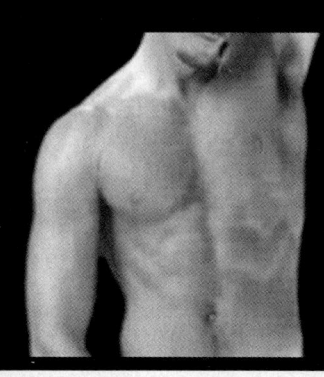

Largo Trindade Coelho N.º 2
Tel. 21 3225022
spartakus@netc.pt

Portugal | Lisboa

LISBOA
Bar 106

Rua de São Marçal

Open every day 21.00-02.00

HAPPY HOUR UNTIL 23.30
(Pay 1, Drink 2)

PARTY NIGHTS - CABLE TV
INFORMATION CENTRE

RUA DE SÃO MARÇAL, 106 — 1200-422 LISBOA
TEL.: 213427373   FAX 213950151
www.bar106.com   e-mail: bar106@bar106.com

LISBOA
FINALMENTE CLUB

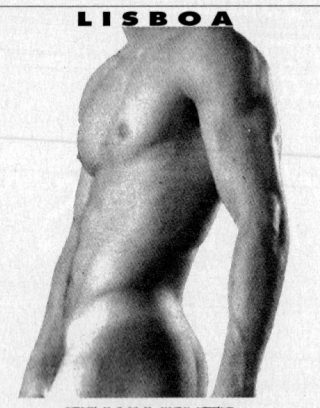

OPEN EVERY DAY 23.00 - 06.00
EVERY NIGHT TRAVESTY SHOW

RUA DA PALMEIRA, 38
1200-313 LISBOA, PORTUGAL
TEL: 21 347 26 52

Portas Largas BAR

Rua da Atalaia, 105 (BAIRRO ALTO)
1200 - 038 LISBOA TEL. 21 346 63 79

■ **Trivial** (B CC F g MA) 12.30-15, 20-23.30h, Sun closed
Rua da Palmeira 44A ☎ 21 347 35 52
Portugese cuisine - reservation recommended.

SEX SHOPS/BLUE MOVIES

■ **Contra Natura** (g) 10-0.30h
Rua dos Correieros 163-169 *(near Rua Augusta)* ☎ 21 343 0786
■ **Erótica** (g) 10-24h
Rua Quirino da Fonseca, 7B ☎ 21 8465972
■ **Espaço Lúdico Sex Shop** (g) Mon-Sat 10-14, 15-1.45h, Sun 17-24 h
Rua do Conde Redondo 82 ☎ 21 3155094

CINEMAS

■ **Olympia Cinema** (g MA r) Best time 16-18h
Rua dos Condes 13 ✉ 1200 *(near Avenida de Liberdade)*
☎ 21 342 5309
Best time 16-18 h in these heterosexual porno cinemas with gay cruising.

SAUNAS/BATHS

■ **Descan** (b G og SA) Tue-Sat 9-21h
Avenida da República, 83-6 *(Metro Campo Pequeno)*
☎ 21 7979602

Lisboa | Portugal

SERTORIO
sauna club

2ª aSábado - 15h / 08h · Domingo - 15h / 24h

Calçada da Patriarcal, 34 - 1250-182 Lisboa
(Jardim Príncipe Real) - Telef: 21 347 03 35

**SAUNA•BANHO TURCO
SOLÁRIO•MASSAGEM
PISCINA•GINÁSIO
CABINES DE RELAX•CINEMA
BAR**

2ª a 5ª - 13h / 02h · 6ª e Sábado 13h / 05h
Domingo - 13h / 24h

Rua do Telhal, 4-B - 1150-346 Lisboa
Telef: 21 342 94 36

HOTEL ANJO AZUL

Lisbon's first and friendliest gay hotel
located in central gay Bairro Alto
20 Bedrooms – 24 Hour Reception

Rua Luz Soriano, 75
Tel/Fax: 21-3478069
E-Mail: anjoazul@mail.telepac.pt

Opus Gay Association

Rua da Ilha Terceira, nº 34, 2º andar
1000.173 Lisboa
Telephone: 00.351.21.3151396
Fax: 00.351.21.3174035
Mobile: 96.2400017
Metro Station: Saldanha/Arroios

Daily except Sundays from 4 pm to 8 pm

Email: anser@netpac.pt
Site: www.opusgayassociation.com

**Legal counselling, Religious
counselling, Psychological counselling,
Laundry Service, Tarot, Dog + Cat Sitter!**

**Opus Gay Association Tourism
Department-ILGTA and Lisbon Tourism
Association Member**

Daily except Saturdays and Sundays from
09.30 am to 13.30 pm
Email: opusgayturismo@hotmail.com

Portugal — Lisboa

■ **Grecus** (b G MA og SA) 12-24 h, closed Sun
Rua do Telhal 77-4° ✉ 1150 *(4th floor/Metro-Avenida)*
☎ 21 346 6259
■ **Oasis** (b G MA SA SB VS) 12-23, Sun & public holidays 14-21 h
Rua do Salitre 85 ✉ 1250 *(Metro Avenida)* ☎ 21 352 4626
Yellow sign. Frequented by many businessmen after work.
■ **Sertório** (b DR G msg SA SB SOL VS) Mon-Sat 15-8, Sun -24h
Calçada da Patriarcal, 34 ✉ 1250-182 *(Garden / Jardim Principe Real)* ☎ 21 347 0335
■ **Spartacus** (AC B DR f G MA SA SB VS WH wo YG) 15-9 h
Largo Trindade Coelho, 2 ✉ 1200 *(Bairro Alto)* ☎ 21 322 5022
No sign at the door! Best times 16-20 h, and later on WE.
■ **Viriato Ginásio Sauna** (! B DR f G MA msg Pl SA SB SOL wo vs)
Mon-Thu 13-2, Fri Sat -5 h, Sun-24h
Rua do Telhal, 4-B ✉ 1150-346 *(Metro Avenida)* ☎ 21 342 9436
One of the biggest steam bath in Portugal. Interior in art-deco style.

BOOK SHOPS
■ **A Esquina cor de Rosa** (A CC GLM MA) Tue-Sat 15-20, 21-24h
Travessa do Monte Carmo 1 ✉ 1200-276 *(Metro-Rato)*
☎ 21 324 0346

FASHION SHOPS
■ **M de M** (G) Mon-Thu 11-20, Fri -23, Sat 15-23, Sun -20h
Rua Dom Pedro V, 21 ☎ 21 3974792

HOTELS
■ **Anjo Azul** (GLM H) 24h
Rua Luz Soriano, 75 ✉ 1200-246 *(Bairro Alto)* ☎ 21 347 8069
🖷 21 347 8069 ✉ anjoazul@mail.telepac.pt
■ **Impala Hotel-Apartments** (b CC g H MA)
Rua Filipe Folque 49 ✉ 1000 ☎ 21 314 3853 🖷 21 314 8914
🖷 21 357 5362
■ **Pensão Alegria** (glm H MA)
Praça Alegria 12 esquerda ✉ 1250 ☎ 21 322 0670
🖷 21 3478070 ✉ pensao.alegria@mail.telepac.pt
All rooms with shower and phone.
■ **Pensão Londres** (BF CC H glm)
Rua D. Pedro V. 53 ✉ 1250 ☎ 21 346 2203 🖷 21 346 8739
Located near the gay bars. Rooms with phone.
■ **Solar Dos Mouros** (AC CC G H)
Rua de Santo António, 4/8 ✉ 1100-351 ☎ 21 888 0155
🖷 21 888 0155
Deluxe hotel.

GUEST HOUSES
■ **Carlos Alberto Freire Cabaço Home Guest** (BF G MG)
Rosa Damaceno N° 9 1°Andar ✉ 1900 ☎ 21 951 2767

■ **Monumental** (g H)
Rua da Gloria 21 ✉ 1200 *(near Av. de Liberdade)* ☎ 21 346 9807
Simple, basic pension. Rooms with shower or bath, WC, phone, TV.
■ **Sintra Auberge** (glm H) 14-? h
Quinta da Capela ☎ 21 992 0170 🖷 21 929 9425
✉ sintracapela@teleweb.pt
Rooming house with large garden 25 km outside of Lisbon.

PRIVATE ACCOMMODATION
■ **Enjoy Bed and Breakfast** (BF G H MA) 16.30-21 h
Nollendorfplatz 5, 10777 Berlin - Germany ☎ +49 30 236 236 10
🖷 +49 30 236 236 19 ✉ info@ebab.com ✉ ebab.com
Accommodation sharing agency. All with shower and BF. 20-25 Euro p.p.

HEALTH GROUPS
■ **Associação Abraco** 10-13 & 15-20h
Rua da Rosa 243-1 ✉ 1200 *(Bairro Alto)* ☎ 21.3421647
🖷 21 343 2499 ✉ abraco.esoterica.pt
Help for people with HIV/AIDS.
■ **Centro de Saúde** 18-22 h
Rua de São Ciro , 36 ☎ 21 3957993
HIV/AIDS Tests and Counselling. Easier for EC nationals with health cards.
■ **Centro de Testes Confidenciais e Anónimos do VIH**
c/o Fundação N° Sra. Bom Sucesso, Avenida Dr. Mário Moutinho
☎ 21 303 1427
Anonymous HIV testing.
■ **Grupos Apoio e Auto-Ajuda** 14-20h
Rua de São Paulo, 216, 2° ✉ 1200-429 *(2nd floor)* ☎ 21 342 2976
✉ positivo@esterica.pt

SWIMMING
-Praia do Meco (g NU) (30 km south of Lisboa in direction Lagoa de Albufeira. Then the road to Alfarim, right into the village. Follow the bad road to Aldeia do Meço.)
-Costa da Caparica (! AYOR G NU)Get the Bus in Praça de Espanha to Costa da Caparica and then the small train to the 17/19 beach
-Praia dos Pescadores (g)
-Praia do Tamariz-Tamariz Beach and surroundings-/Estoril-glm
-Praia do Albano-Albano's Beach(Cascais).

CRUISING
Shopping Centers : Amoreiras, Monumental(Metro Saldanha), Espaço Chiado(Metro Baixa-Chiado), Atrium Saldanha (Metro Saldanha), Saldanha Residence(Metro Saldanha) & Vasco da Gama.
All parks of Lisboa are dangerous! AYOR. Not recommended:
Campo Grande Park (Metro: Entrecampos-best place near the pool)

Moskva ▶ St. Petersburg **Russia**

Yaroslavsky railway stations), in the WC.
- Izmailovsky park (Metro Izmailovsky par, two paths which leading to the clearing).
- Paveletsky railway station. (Metro Belorusskaya), in the WC.
- Kursky railway station (Metro Kurskaya), in the WC.

Murmansk - Russia/Murmansk Region ☏ 08152
GENERAL GROUPS
■ **Murmansk Regional Public Association "Krug"**
PO Box 70 33 ✉ 183 018 💻 gay.polarcom.ru
Member of ILGA.

HEALTH GROUPS
■ **AIDS Center**
47 Tralovaya ulitsa ✉ 183 038

CRUISING
- Zolotoy Lev Café (Samoylovoy Ulitsa)
- Logovo Bar

Nizhny Novgorod - Russia/Nizhegoroskaya Region ☏ 08312
DANCECLUBS
■ **Pyramida Club** (B D f NG) Fri-Sun 23-5.30 h
29 Timiryazeva ulitsa *(dormitory of Architecture and Construction Academy, Vokzalfollow Timiryazeva street from Lyadova square)*

GENERAL GROUPS
■ **Public Association "Drugoi Bereg"/ Human Rights Society**
PO Box 233 ✉ 603 000 💻 plas@osi.nnov.ru

CRUISING
- Ploschad Minina (the alley to the right from the Dmitievskaya tower of the Novgorod Kremlin)

Novokuznetsk - Russia/Kemerovo Region ☏ 03843
GENERAL GROUPS
■ **Gay Information Center** (GLM)
PO Box 220 ✉ 654 032

Novosibirsk - Russia/Novosibirsk Region ☏ 03832
GAY INFO
■ **Gay Novosibirsk Web Site**
💻 www.gaynovosib.da.ru
Guide to gay Novosibirsk. Russian only.

CRUISING
- Square in front of the Opera Theatre.
- Beach on Obskoye More in Akademgorodok.

Omsk - Russia/Omsk Region ☏ 03812
BARS
■ **Bar 9** (B f G MA R) 12-6 h
14 Lenina ulitsa *(Lyubinsky prospekt)*

GENERAL GROUPS
■ **Omsk Center for Support of Sexual Minorities "Favorit"**
Helpline on Tue and Sat 14-18 h (Moscow time)
PO Box 2861 ✉ 644 033 ☏ 631 727 💻 ocpsm@mail.ru
■ **Sibirskaya Alternativa**
PO Box 2875 ✉ 644 033 💻 www.sibalt.da.ru

CRUISING
- Square in front of the Drama Theater.

Rostov-na-Donn - Rossia/Rostov Region ☏ 08632
DANCECLUBS
■ **Duncan Club** (B D glm) Tue 20-23 h
45 Temernitskaya ulitsa *(close to the central market)*

GENERAL GROUPS
■ **Lyubov Sistem**
PO Box 1143 ✉ 344 091
LGB support group. Pen friend service.
■ **SKGK**
PO Box 6161 ✉ 344 023
North Caucasian Gay Club.

Sochi - Rossia/Krasnodar ☏ 08622
CRUISING
All are AYOR
- Cherry (Vishenka) Café (located in Lunapark, behind the flower shop on Kurortny prospekt)
- Lakomka Café (also in Lunapark)
- Pauk (Spider) Café (located in Maurice Taurez Sanatorium, Ordzhonikidze street)
- Sputnik Beach (NU) (shuttle bus 4 or 4C from the main bus station, Maly Akhun)
- "Alley of Love" (from Winter Theater to Hotel Leningrad)
- Underground in park near Stereo Kino (evenings)
- Beach Teatralny (NU) (opposite Hotel Magnolie)

St. Petersburg ☏ 0812
GAY INFO
■ **All-In-One Reference Guide to Gay St. Petersburg**
💻 spb_guide@gay.ru 💻 www.gay.ru/english/travel/rtf/
Easy to use condensed guide to all St. Petersburg gay and lesbian venues. Free of charge.
■ **St. Petersburg Gay Website**
💻 www.gayrussia.msk.ru/spb.htm
Exhaustive info in English about St. Petersburg.
■ **St. Petersburg's Gay Web Site**
💻 xs.gay.ru
Review of gay venues in St. Petersburg, news, info on the city.

BARS
■ **Monroe** (B D DR F G YG) 16-23 h
8 Griboyedova kanal *(Metro Nevsky prospekt)* ☏ 312 13 31
A stylish bar just off Nevsky. Russian pop/Eurodance music. Egyptian, Greek and Oriental halls.

CAFES
■ **Zazu-Lizu** (A B F G s) Sun & Mon 20-6 h
48 Shpalernaya ulitsa *(Metro 1-Tchernishevskaya)* ☏ 110 09 28
Gay art café with erotic shows.

DANCECLUBS
■ **Cabaret** (B D DR f GLM MA S STV WE) Thu-Sat 23-6 h
5 Ploschad Truda *(The Sailor's Club)* ☏ 312 09 34
■ **Club Sinners** (B DR D G SNU)
Kan. Griboedova nab. 28/1 ☏ 219 42 91
■ **Djungli** (AC B D DR f GLM MA S WE) Fri-Sat 24-6 h
8 Blochina ulitsa *(Metro Gorkowskaya/Sportivnaya)* ☏ 238 80 33
Entrance fee US $ 2, Shows begin at 1.30 h.

SPARTACUS 2001/2002 853

Russia — St. Petersburg ▸ Yuzhno-Sakhalinsk

■ **Greshniki** (B D DR G SNU YG) 18-6 h
1/28 Griboyedova kanal *(Metro Nevsky Pospekt)* ☎ 219 42 91
Full strip shows at 2 h.

■ **Island** (B D DR S SNU SA) Every Sun 23-6 h
Leitenanta Shmidta emb., 37 ☎ 323-3824
A complex with bars, darkrooms and a sauna.

■ **Metro Club** (AC B CC D DR F GLM MA) 22-6 h
174 Ligovsky prospekt *(Metro Ligovsky prospekt)* ☎ 166 02 11
New trendy club in Factory style. Speed garage/progressive house music. Full and amateur striptease.

■ **Mono** (AC B BF D GLM MA S) 22-6 h
4 Kolomenskaya ulitsa *(Metro Vladimirskaya/Dostoyevskaya)*
☎ 164 36 78
Entrance fee US $ 2-4, Mon men only.

■ **Club 69** (! AC B CC D DR F GMA SNU STV VS) Tue-Thu, Sun 22-6, Fri-Sat 21-7 h
6 Vtoraya Krasnoarmeyskaya ulitsa ✉ 198 005 *(Metro Teknologitchesky Institute)* ☎ 259 51 63
The oldest gay-club in St. Petersburg, frequently visited by foreign tourists. Disco after 22, 2 bars, video hall, dark sex room. Entrance fee US$1-3. Special parties: Tue "Male Night", Thu, student parity "Sexydance", Fri, Sat, "Crazy Male Strip".

SAUNAS/BATHS
■ **Narcisse** (B DR f G MA msg P PI R SA VS) Tue-Sun 18-6 h
7/9 Krasnich Teckstil'tchikov ulitsa *(Near Smol'ninskie bani, 1st floor, left side, Metro Ploschad Vosstania)* ☎ 110 09 50

TRAVEL AND TRANSPORT
■ **Blue Angel** (G) Mon-Fri 11-19, Sat Sun 12-17 h
Baskov per., 6 of 18 ✉ 196 066 *(at Mayakovskaya ulitsa)*
☎ 279 00 80 📠 279 00 80 💻 www.blueang@comset.net
Travel and tour operator.

■ **Inter-Male** (G MA) Mon-Fri 9.30-19.30, Sat 11-16 h
18 Bronnitskaya ulitsa ✉ 198 013 *(Metro Teknologuitcheski Institute, not far from Club 69)* ☎ 316 20 45 📠 316 20 45
💻 inter-male@gay.com
Gay travel agency.

GENERAL GROUPS
■ **Krilija (Wings)**
c/o Aleksander Kukharsky, PO Box 108 ✉ 191 186 ☎ 312 31 80
📠 312 31 80 💻 krilija@ilga.org
ILGA-member. Gay and lesbian association, tourist agency providing information and help for accommodation.

HEALTH GROUPS
■ **City Anti-AIDS Center**
179-a Obvodnil Canal *(Metro Baltiskaya)* ☎ 259 94 05

SWIMMING
- Beach at old Finnish border. (Take train from Finland Railway Station (Finliandsky Vokzal) to Sestroretsky Kurort Station. From the station ca. 30 min. by foot along the sea side to the right up to the nudist beach)

CRUISING
- Moskovyky Railway Station (Metro Vokzalnaya Ploschad, main hall, WC as well as WC at the other four city railway stations)
- Small park near to the monument to Catherine the Great. (Metro Gostiny Dvor)
- Bolshoi Michailovsky Sad (Park behind the Russian Museum, Moika River embankment, Metro "Nevsky Prospekt, during daytime)
- WC at Sosnovsky Park (Metro "Tchernaya Retchka", bus 94/98 until Svetlanovsky Prospekt)
- WC at TSPKO (Kirov Recreation Park, Metro "Tchernaya Retchka)

Twjer - Rossija/Twjer ☎ 0822

GENERAL GROUPS
■ **All Colors of the Rainbow**
PO Box 2321 ✉ 170 023
Gay penfriends club.

CRUISING
- Kazakov Square (on Sovetskaya ulitsa)
- Medical Academy Square (on Ploschad Revolutsii)

Vladivostok - Primorsky krai ☎ 04232

GAY INFO
■ **Gay Vladivostok**
💻 www.gay.ru/vladivostok
Info on gay life and venues in Vladivostok.

BARS
■ **Mandarin Club** (B D f GLM) 18-3 h
51a Krasnogo Znameni prospekt ☎ 25 56 09
Entrance fee US $ 2.

Voronezh - Russia/Voronezh Region ☎ 0732

HEALTH GROUPS
■ **AIDS Center**
109 Moskovsky Prospekt ✉ 39053 ☎ 145 440

Yuzhno - Sakhalinsk ☎ 0424

CRUISING
- Ariran café in the Gagarin municipal park
- Benches on the railway station Komsomolkaya

Blue Angel

* Accomodation service
* Tour guide / interpreter
* Boat trips on rivers and canals
* Sightseeing (city and its suburbs)
* Meeting at the airport and taxi-service during all the time on your visit.

196066, Russia Saint-Petersburg
PO Box 110 "Blue Angel"
blueang@comset.net
www.blueang.spb.ru www.gay.spb.ru

Russia

THESE ARE NOT MODELS. THIS IS A STAFF

ISLAND

★ Bars
★ Disco
★ Downfalling dance floor
★ Rainfall
★ Darkroom
★ Shows
★ Beach party
★ Mail Strip
★ Sauna

Every Sunday from 23 p.m. till 6 a.m.
Leitenanta Shmidta emb., 37, St. Petersburg
Tel/Fax: +7 (812) 323-3824
E-mail: ostrov@mail.lanck.net
www.ostrovpiter.com

Остров

Senegal

Name: Sénégal
Location: Northwestern Coast of Africa
Initials: SN
Time: GMT
International Country Code: ☏ 221
International Access Code: ☏ 00
Language: Wolof and French
Area: 196,722 km^2 / 76,593 sq mi.
Currency: 1 Franc (CFA) = 100 Centimes
Population: 9,039,000
Capital: Dakar
Religions: 94% Muslim, 5% Christian
Climate: Hot and humid tropical climate. Rainy season (strong southeast winds) lasts from December to April, dry season from May to November.

✱ According to article 319, paragraph 3 of the code of law in Senegal, homosexuality is said to be an " immoral and unnatural act" and is illegal. It is punishable with imprisonment for up to five years.

★ Nach Artikel 319, Paragraph 3 des senegalesischen Strafgesetzbuches ist Homosexualität ein "unmoralischer widernatürlicher Akt" , damit illegal und kann mit einer Freiheitsstrafe von bis zu fünf Jahren bestraft werden.

✱ Selon l'article 319, Paragraphe 3 du Code pénal sénégalais, l'homosexualité, considérée comme "immorale et contre nature" est illégale et est passible de peines d'emprisonnement allant jusqu'à 5 ans.

⬢ Según artículo 319 párrafo 3 de la ley penal de Senegal, la homosexualidad es un "acto inmoral y perverso", es ilegal y puede ser castigada con condenas de prisión de hasta cinco años.

✖ Secondo l'articolo 319, alinea 3 del codice penale senegalese l'omosessualità è considerato un "atto immorale contro natura" ed è illegale. La trasgressione di questa legge può essere punita con un massimo di cinque anni di pena carceraria.

Thiaroye

BARS

■ **Flamboyent. Le** (B d F g OS) Tue-Sun 11-2 h
Route de Rufisque, km 21, Grand M'Bao *(20 km from Dakar)*
☏ 863 28 31
Bar & restaurant.

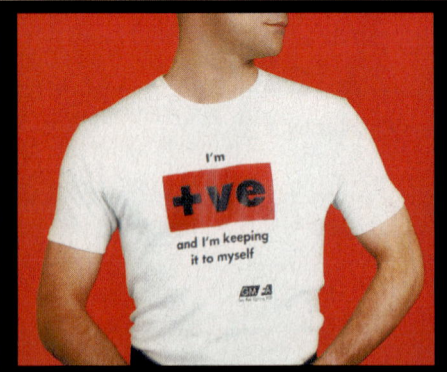

Lots of HIV+ men don't tell

GMFA's campaigns and actions are designed, planned and executed by positive, negative and untested volunteers.
To volunteer for GMFA write, phone or email:
Unit 43, Eurolink Centre, 49 Effra Road, LONDON, SW2 1BZ. 020 7738 6872. newvol@gmfa.demon.co.uk
www.demon.co.uk/gmfa
Registered Charity no. 1076854

GMFA — Gay Men Fighting AIDS

Mahé | **Seychelles**

Seychelles

Name: Sesel • Seychellen • Seicelle
Location: East Africa
Initials: SY
Time: GMT +4
International Country Code: ☏ 248
International Access Code: ☏ 00
Language: Kreolish, English, French
Area: 454 km^2
Currency: 1 Seychellen -Rupie(SR) = 100 Cents
Population: 79,000
Capital: Victoria (Mahé)
Religions: 90% Catholic, 8% Anglican
Climate: The country consists mainly of flat desert. To the east are the mountains of Oman. Hot and dry climate.

✱ Homosexuality is Illegal in the Seychelles. No reliable information regarding the legal situation is available.

✱ Auf den Seychellen ist Homosexualiät strafbar. Uns liegen keine weiteren verläßlichen Informationen zur aktuellen Situation vor.

✱ L'homosexualité est illégale au Seychelles. C'est tout ce que nous pouvons dire à ce sujet.

✱ La homosexualidad está prohibida en Secel. Lastimosamente no poseemos informaciones legales más exactas.

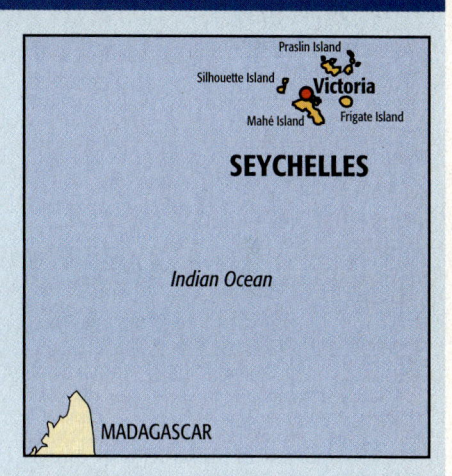

✖ In Seicelle l'omosessualità è illegale. Non abbiamo a disposizione informazioni legali più precise.

SEYCHELLES

Praslin Island
Silhouette Island
Victoria
Mahé Island   Frigate Island

Indian Ocean

MADAGASCAR

Mahé

CAFES

■ **Splash** (BF F) 9-17h (closed in the evening)
Baie Lazare (near Plantation Club Resort & Casino) ☏ 361500

SpartacusWorld.com

▶ click and ▶ win!

www.spartacusworld.com

SPARTACUS 2001/2002 | 857

Singapore

Name: Singapur • Singapour
Location: Southeast Asia
Initials: SGP
Time: GMT +8
International Country Code: ☎ 65 (no area codes)
International Access Code: ☎ 001
Language: Malay, Mandarin, Tamil and English
Area: 647 km² / 239 sq mi.
Currency: 1 Singapore Dollar (S$) = 100 Cents
Population: 3,164,000
Capital: Singapore
Religions: 32% Buddhists, 22% Daoists, 15% Moslems, 13% Christians
Climate: A hot and tropical climate, humid and rainy. There are frequent thunderstorms - especially in April.

Section 377 of the penal code punishes "offences against the order of nature" with 10 years to life imprisonment, and section 377a prohibits "gross indecency" between males, in public or private, with a maximum penalty of two years in prison. According to our information, the conduct of the police is prejudiced. Singapore's population is relatively young, as is the appearance of the city itself. It is characterised by high, modern buildings, as well as by streets and buildings which seem typically English. All the addresses listed below are straight-and-gay mixed. Favourite meeting places for Singaporean gays are Scotts Road and Orchard Road.

Artikel 377 bestraft "Vergehen gegen die Natur" mit zehn Jahren bis zu lebenslanger Haft, und Abschnitt 377a sieht für öffentlich oder privat stattfindende "grobe Unzucht" zwischen Männern eine Gefängnisstrafe von bis zu zwei Jahren vor. Nach unseren Informationen verhält sich die Polizei diskriminierend.
Die Bevölkerung von Singapur ist relativ jung. Ebenso jung ist das Stadtbild: Es wird geprägt durch moderne, hohe Bauten, aber auch durch Straßen und Gebäude, die sehr stark an England erinnern. Die unten angegebenen Adressen sind allesamt schwul-heterosexuell gemischt. Die Schwulen treffen sich in der Stadt bevorzugt in der Scotts Road sowie der Orchard Road.

A Singapour, l'homosexualité est un délit. Tout "crime contre nature" est puni de peines de prison allant de 10 ans à la perpétuité (article 377 du code pénal). On risque 2 ans de prison maximum pour "actes obscènes" entre hommes, en public comme en privé. D'après ce que nous savons, la police de Singapour fait tout pour rendre la vie impossible aux homosexuels et aux travestis.
Singapour est une ville jeune, aussi bien dans sa population que dans son architecture: gratte-ciels modernes, mais aussi quartiers rappelant étrangement l'Angleterre. Les adresses indiquées ci-dessous sont mixtes. Les gais de Singapour se retrouvent avant tout dans Scott Road et la Orchard Road.

Artículo 377 del código penal castiga las "relaciones carnales contra la natura" con una pena desde 10 años de cárcel hasta cadena perpétua. El artículo 377 castiga "indecencias" entre hombres con una pena de hasta dos años de cárcel. Según nuestras informaciones, la policía se comporta de manera discriminatoria. La población de Singapur es relativamente joven. Igualmente joven es la imagen de la ciudad: está marcada por construcciones modernas y altas pero también por calles y edificios que recuerdan fuertemente a Inglaterra. Las direcciones citadas a continuación son de carácter mixto: frequentados por gays y heteros al mismo tiempo. Los gays de Singapur tienen su punto de reunión favorito tanto en las cercanías de la Scotts Road, como en la Orchard Road.

La sezione 377 del codice penale punisce il "rapporto carnale contro natura" con la reclusione da 10 anni fino all'ergastolo, e la sezione 377a proibisce "l'indecenza volgare" fra uomini, in pubblico o in privato, con una pena massima di due anni di prigione. Secondo le nostre informazione la polizia discrimina i gay. La popolazione di Singapore è relativamente giovane. Anche il profilo architettonico della città è abbastanza giovane, connotato da palazzi alti e moderni, ma anche da strade ed edifici che ricordano molto all'Inghilterra. Tutti gli indirizzi qui sotto indicati sono di locali a clientela mista. I gay di Singapore amano incontrarsi nell'area di Scotts Road come in quella di Orchard Road.

Singapore

BARS

■ **Babylon Karaoke** (AC B d f G N YG) Mon-Thur 19- 02, Fri, Sat -03h, Sun closed.
52 Tanjong Pagar Road ✉ 0208 *(Tanjong Pagar Metro Station)* ☎ 227 74 66
Karaoke.

■ **Inner Circle** (AC B G N YG) Mon-Thur 19-01, Fri,Sat -02h, Sun closed.
78 Tanjong Pagar Road ☎ 2228462
Karaoke.

■ **Vincent's Lounge** (AC B G) Weekdays 19-1h, Fri & Sat -2h
304 Orchard Road, 06-05 Lucky Plaza ✉ 238863 *(opp Orchard MRT station)* ☎ 736 13 60
Ask Vincent for all the latest happenings in Singapore.

858 SPARTACUS 2001/2002

Singapore

■ **Why Not** (AC B d f G MA)
Tras Street
Why Not now operates as a Karaoke Mon-Thurs and as a Disco Club on Fri,Sat.

CAFES
■ **Crossroads** (B f g)
Scotts Road *(Marriot Hotel)*
■ **Niche** (AC B f D G YG) Opening Hours see "Taboo"
32A Pagoda Street ✉ 059191 ☎ 323 6063
■ **Spinelli's** (B f g)
Scotts Road (The Heren Building) *(opposite Mandarin Hotel)*
■ **Taboo** (AC B G YG) Mon & Tues19-0, Wed-Thur -02, Fri & Sat - 03h Sun closed.
21 Tanjong Pagar Road ✉ 088440 *(Tanjong Pagar metro station)* ☎ 225 6256

DANCECLUBS
■ **Velvet Underground** (B D F g OS YG) Thu-Sat
17, 19, 21 Jiak Kim Street ✉ 0316 ☎ 738 29 88
■ **Venom** (AC B D E G STV YG) Only on Sun 21-3
Pacific Plaza/ Scotts Road ☎ 734 7677
Admission $18 includes first drink. Parties every Sun 22-3h, STV and non-stop dance musik.

RESTAURANTS
■ **Picnic. The** (B F NG)
Scotts Shopping Centre *(basement)*

SAUNAS/BATHS
■ **Rairua** (AC b CC G MA P S SA SB VS WH WO) Sun,Tue,Wed,Thu 17-23 Fri,Sat, 17-1h
118 Neil Road *(near Tanjong Pagar MRT)* ☎ 324 62 56
Members only.
■ **Stroke Spa & Gym** (AC b CC G MA P S SA SB SOL VS WH WO)
Tue-Sun 12-19h
22 Ann Slang Road ☎ 222 12 26
Theme nights.

HOTELS
■ **Bencoolen** (AC B F H OS)
47 Bencoolen Street ☎ 336 08 22
Downtown location, 20 min to the airport. Hotel with garden. All rooms (accessible without passing reception) are equipped with telephone, bathroom, and WC. Rates single from S$ 60.
■ **Sea View Hotel** (AC B D F g H PI SA SOL)
Amber Close, Katong ☎ 345 22 22
Suburban location, 15 min from Gay Beach. There are no problems taking somebody into the rooms, which are equipped with telephone, kitchenette, priv. bath and balcony.

HEALTH GROUPS
■ **Action for Aids** 10-16.30 h
c/o DSC STD Clinic # 02-16, 31 Kelantan Lane ✉ 200031
(Balestier/Whampoa area) ☎ 254 01 12 🖷 256 59 03
✉ afa@pacific.net.sg 🌐 www.afa.org.sg
Aids information & education. Anonymous HIV testing.

HELP WITH PROBLEMS
■ **AIDS Helplines and Counselling Line** Mon-Fri 8-17 h
☎ 254 16 11 (Helpline) ☎ 252 13 24

SWIMMING
-East Coast Parkway Beach (G) (near "Singapore Crocodilarium" Go towards the end of the East Coast Park Service Road and look for the large storm water drainage canal which has green railings. At the end of the canal there is a notice besides a well-worn path saying "State Land - keep out". Don't take notice of the panel and follow the path through the woods until you reach the beach. particularly active with Singaporians on Sundays)
-Clark Hatch in Regent Hotel
-Westin-Stamford Hotel gym/sauna (Sat Sun 17-20 h. Be very discreet)
-The River Valley Swimming Pool - River Valley rd. (opposite Hotel New Otani) Mon-Sun 8-21h.

CRUISING
All cruisings are AYOR
-Centrepoint, Orchard Road (cruisy Sat and Sun afternoon)
-Far East Plaza, Scotts Road
-Park Lane Shopping Mall, Selegie Road (Sun afternoon on all levels with a Singaporian crowd)
-River Valley Swimming Pool (opposite Liang Court Shopping Complex; be discreet!)
-Raffles City shopping lobby (near Westin Hotel)
-Raffles Place (called "The River, Chulia and Market Street, late)
-River Valley Swimming Pool (opposite Diamaru Shopping Centre)
-Takashimaya Shopping Centre (Orchard Road near the indoor waterfall area, Sat Sun afternoons)
-Orchard MRT station (evenings)
-Weston Hotel
-City Hall
-Fort Road

Slovakia Bratislava

Slovakia

Name: Slovensko • Slowakei • Slovaquie • Slovachia
Location: Central Europe
Initials: SK
Time: GMT +1
International Country Code: ☏ 421 (leave the first 0 of area codes)
International Access Code: ☏ 00
Language: Slovakian
Area: 49,034 km² / 18,932 sq mi.
Currency: 1 Koruna (Sk) = 100 Halierov
Population: 5,391,000
Capital: Bratislava
Religions: 60 % Roman Catholic
Climate: Moderate climate. Summers are cool, winters cold, cloudy and humid.

Homosexuality is not illegal, and the legal age of consent is fifteen. In the last few years, the public opinion concerning homosexuality has undergone a considerable change. Following the establishment of gay and lesbian groups and organisations based on the western model, more is heard about homosexuality in the media.

Homosexualität ist nicht illegal. Das Schutzalter liegt bei 15 Jahren. Die öffentliche Meinung hinsichtlich schwuler Themen hat sich in den letzten Jahren positiv gewandelt. Nach der Gründung schwul-lesbischer Organisationen und Vereine nach westlichem Vorbild wird jetzt auch in den Massenmedien zunehmend über Homosexualität berichtet. Die rechtliche Situation der Schwulen hat sich allerdings noch nicht verbessert.

En Slovaquie l'homosexualité n'est pas un délit. La majorité sexuelle y est fixée à 15 ans. L'opinion publique est devenue beaucoup plus tolérante face aux homosexuels. Grace à la création d'associations et de groupes sur le modèle occidental, les médias abordent le sujet de plus en plus ouvertement.

La homosexualidad es legal. La edad de consentimiento es de 15 años. La opinión pública en relación a la homosexualidad ha experimentado un cambio radical en los últimos años. Ahora, el tema de la homosexualidad se trata con más frecuencia en los medios de communicación, debido a la fundación de organizaciones gay y lesbianas, siguiendo modelos occidentales.

L'omosessualità non è illegale. L'età legale per avere dei rapporti sessuali è di 15 anni. Negli ultimi anni la gente ha cambiato di molto la propria opinione sugli omosessuali. Dopo la fondazioneà di organizzazioni gay e lesbiche secondo il modello occidentale, la stampa e la televisione trattano questo tema con crescente frequenza.

NATIONAL GAY INFO

■ **Ganymedes**
PO Box 4, Pošta 3 ✉ 83000 Bratislava ☏ (07) 25 38 88

Bratislava ☏ 07

BARS

■ **Dunaj Pub** (B D G)
Beblavého 1 ☏ 27 27 05

GENERAL GROUPS

■ **Ganymedes Bratislava** Mon Thu 17-20 h
Beblavého ulica 1 ☏ 25 38 88

■ **H-plus - Občianske Združenie**
Jungmanova 8 ✉ 851 01 ☏ 62 24 51 17 🖥 hplus@nextra.sk
🖥 home.nextra.sk/anex/hplus/

HEALTH GROUPS

■ **Laboratory for AIDS-Institute of preventive and clinical medicine**
Limbova 14/Kramáre ☏ 37 35 60

SPECIAL INTEREST GROUPS

■ **HaBiO - Občianske Združenie**
PO Box 233 ✉ 810 00 🖥 habio@mailbox.sk
🖥 home.nextsk/habio/
Gay student group.

SWIMMING

-Lake in Rusovce near Bratislava
-Lake in Rovinka near Bratislava

CRUISING

-Main railway station
-Hviezdoslavovo námestie
-Old Danube Bridge/university building/safarikovo námestie
-Jesenského Boulevard
-Kyjevské námestie
-Park in front of Slovakian Philharmony "Reduta", near Slovak National Theatre (small park around, very busy)
-Park at State Hospital (Americké námestie) "Avion"

Dubnica nad Váhom ▸ Lubljana | Slovakia - Slovenia

Dubnica nad Váhom ☏ 0827
GENERAL GROUPS
■ **Ganymedes Dubnica**
PO Box 38/89-23 ✉ 018 41 ☏ (0905) 126 987
📧 bazo.milan@bb.telecom.sk

Košice ☏ 095
BARS
■ **RG - Café Galéria** (Vyagra) (A AC B d f GLM MA P STV) 19-? h
Rooseveltova 12 ✉ 040 01 *(city center)*
☏ 625 59 01
Café-gallerie with disco on Sat.

RESTAURANTS
■ **Restaurant Pod Bankou** (B F NG) Mon-Sun 20-? h
Kovácská ulica ✉ 04001

GENERAL GROUPS
■ **Ganymedes Košice**
c/o Mars A & E, PO Box B-18 ✉ 040 98 📧 levan@pobox.sk
🌐 www.gay.sk/index.html

Prievidza ☏ 0862
GENERAL GROUPS
■ **Ganymedes Prievidza**
PO Box 47, 97251 Handlová

Žilina ☏ 089
BARS
■ **Harley Pub** (B D g) G on Sat
Horny Val 22

Slovenia

Name: Slovenija • Slowenie n • Slovénie • Slovenia
Location: Southeastern Europe
Initials: SLO
Time: GMT +1
International Country Code: ☏ 386 (leave the first 0 of area codes)
International Access Code: ☏ 00
Language: Slovenian
Area: 20,253 km² / 7,819 sq mi.
Currency: 1 Tolar (SIT) = 100 Stotin
Population: 1,982,000
Capital: Ljubljana
Religions: 71% Catholic
Climate: Mediterranean climate on the coast, continental climate with mild to hot summers and cold winters in the plateau's and valleys to the east.

✱ In Slovenia, the general age of consent is set at 14 years of age.

✱ In Slovenien liegt das Schutzalter allgemein bei 14 Jahren.

✱ En Slovénie, la majorité sexuelle est fixée à 14 ans pour tous.

✱ En Eslovenia la edad de consentimiento es de 14 años.

✖ In Slovenia l'età legale per dei rapporti sessuali è di 14 anni.

NATIONAL GROUPS
■ **Roza Klub**
Kersnikova 4 ✉ 1000 Ljubljana ☏ (061) 130 47 40
📠 (061) 329 185 🌐 www.ljudmila.org/siqrd/rk-e.html
Roza klub is an independent political organisation for gays and lesbians living in Slovenia.

Bled ☏ 064
CRUISING
-Beach between Toplice Hotel and the entrance to the bathing-place beneath Bled castle
-Beach on camping site Sobec

Celje ☏ 063
CRUISING
-Mestni Park (across the Savinja river)
-Railway station

Ljubljana ☏ 061
CAFES
■ **Cafe Galerija** (A B g) 10-24 h
Mestni trg 5 *(Old town)*
■ **Magnus Café** (A B GLM S) Fri Sat 20-? h, Wed, Thu, Sun -24 h
Metelkova

Slovenia — Lubljana ▶ Ptuj

DANCECLUBS
■ **Klub K 4** (AC B D GLM MA S YG) Sun 22-4 h, Aug closed
Kersnikova 4 ☎ 132 40 89

GENERAL GROUPS
■ **SKUC-Magnus**
Kersnikova 4 ✉ 61000 ☎ 329 185

SWIMMING
-Beach on the Sava river (500m away from the Zagar Restaurant on the left bank. Popular in Jul/Aug)

CRUISING
-Park (AYOR) (by the railway behind the petrol station on the Tivolska cesta)
-Tivoli Park P (AYOR) (evenings)
-Railway station
-Old Town

Maribor ☎ 062

BARS
■ **Stop** (B glm MA) 18-23 h, Sun 15-23 h.
Mlinska ulica *(at the bus station)*

CRUISING
-Park Ribnik (AYOR) (between the facility and the aquarium; 18-22 h)
-Railway station

Piran ☎ 066

SWIMMING
-Beach from Piran to Strunjan (nu)

CRUISING
-Coast walk (at night)
-Main street along coast in Portoroz (at night)

Ptuj ☎ 062

CRUISING
-City Park (epecially near Ribič)

Lots of HIV+ men don't tell

I'm +ve and I'm keeping it to myself

GMFA — Gay Men Fighting AIDS

All GMFA's campaigns & actions are planned & executed by positive, negative and untested volunteers. To volunteer for GMFA write, phone

South Africa

Name: Suid-Afrika • Südafrika • Afrique du Sud • Africa del Sur • Sud Africa
Location: Southern Africa
Initials: ZA
Time: GMT +2
International Country Code: ☏ 27 (leave the first 0 of area codes)
International Access Code: ☏ 09 or 091
Language: English, Afrikaans, African languages
Area: 1,219,080 km^2 /471,442 sq mi.
Currency: 1 Rand (R) = 100 Cents
Population: 41,402,000
Capital: Cape Town (legislative capital); Pretoria (administrative capital)
Religions: 78% Christians
Climate: Mostly quite dry climate. Along the coast it's subtropical, days are sunny, nights are cool.
Important gay cities: Capetown

※ South Africa is the only country of the world where it is a punishable offence to discriminate against someone on grounds of his or her sexual orientation. In contrast to other statesmen in the neighbouring states, such as Robert Mugabe from Zimbabwe who claims that "homosexuals are lower than pigs" and Sam Nujoma from Namibia who purports that homosexuals are "white perverts". Nelson Mandela has explicitly indicated in his vision of a "Rainbow Generation" that gays and lesbians have an equal standing in South Africa. It only remains a matter of time for the changes in South Africa to become legally recognisable.
However, the age of consent is fixed at 16 years of age for heterosexuals and 18 for homosexuals The A.N.C. supports equal rights and it will be even possible for gays and lesbians soon to get married. This positive development has lead naturally to a more visible gay scene and the emmergence of many new bars and clubs, particularly in the larger cities, such as Johannesburg, Pretoria, Cape Town and Durban.

★ Als bisher einziges Land der Welt hat Südafrika in seiner Verfassung ausdrücklich auch die Diskriminierung aufgrund der sexuellen Orientierung unter Strafe gestellt. Im Gegensatz zu anderen Staatsmännern in den Nachbarstaaten wie Robert Mugabe (Zimbabwe), der behauptet hat "Homosexuelle seien niedriger als Schweine" und Sam Nujoma (Namibia), der Homosexuelle als "weiße Perverse" beschimpfte, hat Nelson Mandela die Schwulen und Lesben Südafrikas ausdrücklich als gleichberechtigte Bürger in seine Vision einer "Regenbogennation" mit einbezogen.
Noch müssen sich diese postiven Entwicklungen in Gesetzen niederschlagen, doch scheint es nur eine Frage der Zeit zu sein, bis dies geschieht. Zur Zeit liegt das Schutzalter bei Heterosexuellen bei 16 und bei Homosexuellen bei 18 Jahren.
Der ANC will sich aktiv für die gesetzliche Gleichberechtigung von Homosexuellen einsetzen. Schwule und Lesben sollen sogar heiraten dürfen. Dieses positive Umfeld hat natürlich dazu geführt, daß die schwule Szene immer sichtbarer wird, viele neue Bars und Clubs öffnen und Schwule und Lesben organisieren sich zunehmend in Gruppen, um ihre Interessen besser durchsetzen zu können. Diese Entwicklung ist aber momentan noch auf die größeren Städte wie Johannesburg, Pretoria, Kapstadt und Durban be-schränkt.

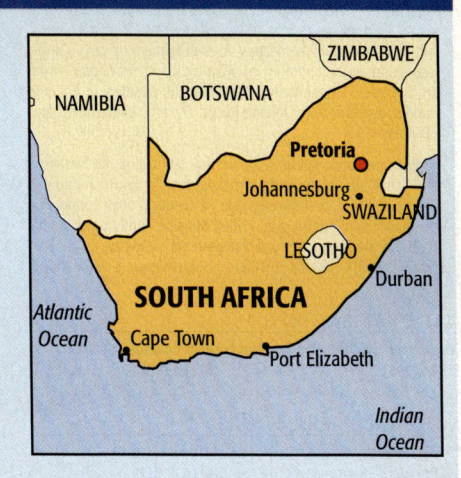

※ L'Afrique du Sud est le seul pays au monde jusqu'à présent à inclure expréssement dans sa constitution un article visant la condamnation de la discrimination en raison des inclinations sexuelles. A l'inverse, d'autres chefs d'États de pays voisins comme Robert Mugabe (Zimbabwe), qui a déclaré que "les homosexuels sont plus bas que des porcs" et Sam Nujoma (Namibie) qui traite les homosexuels de "pervers blancs", Nelson Mandela a inclu les gais et lesbiennes d'Afrique du Sud dans sa vision d'une Nation "arc-en-ciel" en tant que citoyens égaux en droits. Ces décisions positives doivent encore être transformées en lois, mais cela ne semble être qu'une question de temps pour que cela se fasse. La majorité sexuelle est fixée à 16 ans pour les hétérosexuels et à 18 ans pour les homosexuels.
L'ANC veut s'engager activement pour l'égalité des droits des gays et lesbiennes. Ceux-ci devraient même avoir le droit de se marier. Tout cela mème au fait que la scène gaie est devenue de plus en plus visible, que de nombreux bars et clubs ouvrent, et que les gays et lesbiennes s'organisent et se rassemblent en groupes pour mieux défendre leurs intérêts. Cette évolution ne concerne pour le moment que les villes de Johannesburg, Pretoria, Le Cap et Durban.

⬢ Sudáfrica es el único país en el mundo que prohibe en su legalización expresamente la discriminación de personas por causa de su orientación sexual. Mientras los presidentes de los estados vecinos rechazan los gays por completo, como por ejemplo Robert Mugabe (Zimbabue) quien dijo que los homosexuales "esten en un nivel más bajo que los cerdos" o Sam Nujoma (Namibia) que los insulta al ser "blancos pervertidos", su hómologo Nelson Mandela ha incluido los gays y lesbianas expresamente como ciudadanos con los mismos derechos en su concepto de la nación sudáfricana. Aunque todavía este desarollo positivo no se refleja en la legislación, parece ser solamente una cuestión de tiempo. La edad de consentimiento es de 16 años para heterosexuales y de 18 años para homosexuales.
El ANC afirmó su intención de luchar por los mismos derechos pa-

South Africa | Barrydale - Westerrn Cape ▶ Bloemfontein - Orange Free State

ra gays y lebianas ante la ley, hasta se habló de la posibilidad de matrimonios homosexuales. Por esta base positiva el ambiente gay en las ciudades se hace notar cada vez más. Muchos bares y clubs han abierto últimamente y un gran número de gays y lesbianas se organizan ahora en grupos para hacer prevalecer mejor sus intereses. De momento este desarollo positivo se limita a grandes ciudades como Johanesburgo, Pretoria, Ciudad del Cabo o Durban.

✖ Come unico paese al mondo la costituzione del Sudafrica contiene un paragrafo che condanna la discriminazione a seconda dell'orientamento sessuale. Al contrario degli uomini politici di altri stati africani, p.es. Robert Mugabe (Zimbabwe) che ha affermato che gli omosessuali siano inferiori ai maiali, e Sam Nujoma (Namibia) che ha insultato gli omosessuali chiamandoli "perversi bianchi"; Nelson Mandela ha incluso esplicitamente nella sua visione di una "nazione arcobaleno" i gay e le lesbiche sudafricani. Questi positivi sviluppi non trovano ancora riscrontro nelle leggi vigenti del paese, ma è solo questione di tempo fino a che questo avverrà. L'età legale per rapporti eterosessuali è di 16 anni, per quelli omosessuali di 18 anni.

L'ANC si sta adoperando attivamente per l'equiparazione legale degli omosessuali. Secondo questo progetto, in futuro i gay e le lesbiche si potranno sposare. Quest'atmosfera positiva ha fatto sì che l'ambiente gay diventi sempre più visibile, che si aprono molti bar e club e che molti gay e lesbiche si uniscano sempre più numerevoli in gruppi per far valere i loro interessi. Al momento questo sviluppo si limita alle città più grandi come Johannesburg, Pretoria, Kapstadt e Durban.

NATIONAL GAY INFO

■ **National Coalition for Gay and Lesbian Equality (NCGLE)**
PO Box 27811, Joubert Park 2044 ☎ (011) 487 3810
🖷 339-7762. ✉ coalgr@iafrica.com

NATIONAL PUBLICATIONS

■ **Exit Newspaper**
PO Box 28827, Kensington 2101 ☎ (011) 622 2375
☎ (011) 622 2175. ✉ exitnews@iafrica.com. Monthly gay and lesbian newspaper, published mainly in English. Information about events, venues, travel etc. Personal ads at US$ 10.

■ **Gay Pages**
PO Box 1050 ✉ 2109 Melville ☎ (011) 726 1560
🖷 (011) 726 6948
✉ gaypages@iafrica.com
Bi-annual magazine & business directory.

■ **Outright**
PO Box 2431 ✉ 2118 Cresta ☎ (011) 276 1453
🖷 (011) 482 6139 ✉ www.outright.co.za
Monthly glossy magazine, alternative lifestyles.

NATIONAL COMPANIES

■ **Bare Wear**
PO Box 1251, Scottburgh 4180
Men's underwear, swimwear, casualwear. Catalogue R 10.

■ **CCCC**
PO Box 1942, Cape Town 8000
☎ (021) 462 4019. Photographic books, calendars, magazines and novels. Catalogue for free.

■ **Travel Services SA** (G) Mon-Fri 08.30-17h
PO Box 629, Somerset West   Cape Town✉ 7129 ☎ 853 0117
🖷 854 6322 ✉ info@travelservicessa.com
✉ www.tripmanagement.com
Holiday planning, accommodation and car hire in South Africa.

Barrydale - Western Cape ☎ 028

GUEST HOUSES
■ **Greenman Cottage** (BF g msg)
1 Keerom Street ✉ 6750 ☎ 572 16 85
■ **Tradouw Guest House** (B bf glm OS)
46 van Riebeeckstraat ✉ 6750 ☎ 572 14 34

Benoni - Gauteng ☎ 011

BARS
■ **W@nc** (D G GLM MA)
Woburn Str / Swan Street ☎ 082 531 9094 (mobile)

CRUISING
-Kleinfontein Dam (Warm Stream) (access can be gained via Swan Street; park car and walk through bushes and trees, very nice during late summer evenings)
-Benoni Plaza (WE evenings)
-Bus terminal

Bloemfontein - Orange Free State ☎ 051

BARS
■ **Club Buzerant Estate** (B D G MA SNU)
Orange Grove Farm, Ferreira Road

•• ★ gaydar.co.za
what you want, when you want it

864 SPARTACUS 2001/2002

Cape Town | South Africa

www.galacttic.co.za...where to start planning your holiday and to stay in South Africa and Cape Town

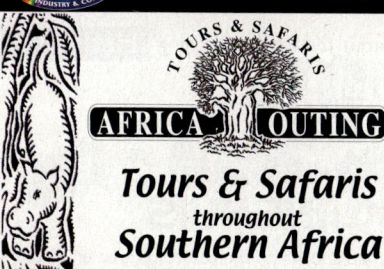

AFRICA OUTING
Tours & Safaris throughout Southern Africa

Based in Cape Town, gay capital of Africa AND the "GAY way to Africa," **AFRICA OUTING** offers customized tours throughout the region and handles all travel arrangements.

Tel: (+27-21) **671 4028** Fax: (+27- 21) 683 7377
e-mail: afouting@iafrica.com   www.afouting.com

Yesterday was Europe & America. Now discover Africa!

An Africa Dream...
MAXES
Personal Gay Travel Consultants

All travel in and around Southern Africa & The Indian Ocean Islands

Accommodation • Safaris • Transport • Tours

Tel: (+27-21) 782 6979   Fax: (+27- 21) 782 3499
e-mail: info@maxes.co.za
Website: www.maxes.co.za

Wilderness

Palms Wilderness

Palms Wilderness
"A place of style"

Come and enjoy incredible natural beauty along the world famous Gardenroute.

Christoph, Italo, Tom and Urs welcome you...out of town ensuring a memorable stay.

Swiss owned and managed...
Guest House
Restaurant - Bar, Pool, SatTV, Telephone

Palms Wilderness Guest House Restaurant, Box 372, 6560 Wilderness
Phone: ++27 44 877 1320   Fax   ++27 44 877 1422
mailto: palms@pixie.co.za   visit us: www.palms-wilderness.com

---

Cape Town

Blackheath Lodge
simply because you deserve it !

Stylish Victorian Villa, situated in a quiet residential area, it offers all you need for a great holiday.

Run by Rick and Roland, it is one of the most popular guesthouses in Cape Town, so make your bookings on time !!
e mail: Blackheathlodge@iafrica.com
www.blackheathlodge.co.za

6 Blackheath Road 8005 Sea Point Cape Town
Tel+27(0)21-439 2541 Fax +27-(0)21-439 9776

South Africa | Cape Town

www.galacttic.co.za.....where to stay on your holiday in Cape Town and around South Africa

Clarence House
Your gay getaway in Cape Town

Luxurious accommodation each with sat.-TV, phone, mini-safe, mini-bar, heater/aircon and private bathroom. In-house Restaurant and Bar, Continental and English breakfast till noon.
Panoramic view of Table Mountain and close to Kirstenbosch Botanical Gardens. Best access to all gay venues. Swiss management.
Your hosts Freddy & Armin

6 Obelisk Rd., Claremont 7708, Cape Town
phone: +27(0)21-683-0307
fax: +27(0)21-683-0355
e-mail: chc@chchouse.co.za
website: www.chchouse.co.za

Famous for whale watching — **Hermanus**

SKUINSHUIS

Lie in bed and watch the sea from three en-suite bedrooms with private entrances.
Jacuzzi on balcony with magnificent mountain and sea views.
Small intimate beach around the corner.
Intriguing selection of gay art & literature.

Afrikaans & German hosts.
Niel le Roux 083 309 4821
Thomas Höhnke 083 380 4128

67 Kandelaar Street, Vermont Hermanus
Tel/Fax: +27 (028) 316 2213

e mail: skuinshuis@hermanus.co.za
website: www.bluecape.co.za/skuinshuis

THE QUARTERS
Guest House
**Cape Town
South Africa**

Exclusively Gay in Gay Village

Next to gay bars, clubs,
steam bath and restaurants and walking distance to the famous
waterfront and centre of Cape Town.

Rooms-en-suite equipped with television, telephone, bar fridge.

Coffee & Tea - 24 hours
Laundry service, e-mail on request
Airport shuttle
Assistance with day tours, Car rental

76 Waterkant Street, De Waterkant
Cape Town, South Africa, 8001
Tel: 00 27 21 **419 - 1479**
Fax: 00 27 21 421 - 5914
e-mail: quarters@iafrica.com
www.thequarters.co.za

Wilderness

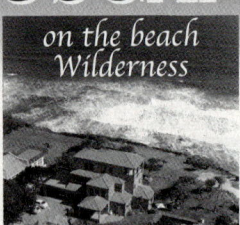

The TUSCANY
on the beach
Wilderness

Come and relax in luxury with a cocktail after a day filled with water skiing, horse riding, hang-gliding, golfing, hiking or just lounging around the pool or at the seaside!

Call Vaughan or Dirk on (044) 8770748/082 5661 529
e mail tuscany@cyberhost.co.za
www.tuscany.co.za

Cape Town | South Africa

www.galacttic.co.za.....where to stay on your holiday in Cape Town South Africa

Experience one of the Cape's *trendiest destinations*

The gay village of South Africa lies in the historical Bo Kaap area of beautiful Cape Town which was built to house freemen and slaves in the 1700's. Trendy and fashionable it is compared to Greenwich Village with its quiet tree-lined streets, elegantly restored cottages, spectacular views and friendly village atmosphere.

- Private, exclusive and secure.
- 50 luxurious self-catering, fully serviced cottages with splash pools and roof terraces.
- Gay clubs, bars and steam houses.
- Minutes from the V&A Waterfront, Table Mountain and dazzling white beaches.

De Waterkant VILLAGE

Call **Village & Life** Central Reservations at **+27 21 422 2721**
No 1 Loader Street, De Waterkant, Cape Town • Website: www.dewaterkant.com

the BUNK-HOUSE

BUDGET ACCOMMODATION

23 Antrim Road,
Three Anchor Bay, Cape Town,
8005, South Africa.
tel: +27-21 434 5695
mobile: +27-82 546 9662
fax: +27-21 434 5695
e-mail: bunkhouse@new.co.za
website: www.bunkhouse.co.za

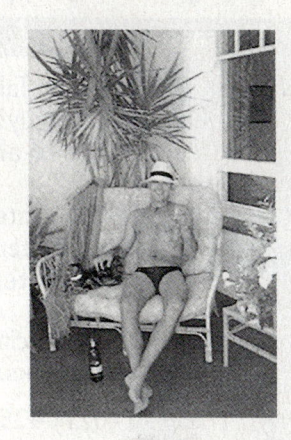

Richborough Villa

The Best
Gay Guest House
in Cape Town

www.richborough.co.za

5 Highworth Road Seapoint
Cape Town
South Africa

Telephone +27 (21) 434 6550
Fax +27 (21) 434 8459
tim@richborough.co.za
Cellular 083 457 4905
PO Box 27542 Rhine Road 8050

(Formerly Bay Lodge)

---

www.galacttic.co.za.....where
Cape Town

Open noon to 2am weekdays,
24 hours weekends and
public holidays.

STEAMERS
HEALTH AND LEISURE CLUB

corner of Solan and
Wembley Roads
Tel/Fax:+27(0) 21 461 6210

info@steamers.co.za
steamers.co.za

Absolute Discretion Guaranteed • Private
& Upmarket •Strippers • Doubles • Travel
• Credit cards accepted

All Men All Night
All Week All Ways

Knights

Ultimate M2M Indulgence

Tel:[27][21](021) 434 0428/434 4759
e-mail: ctknight@mweb.co.za

SPARTACUS 2001/2002 | 871

South Africa — Cape Town

THE BARRACKS
Massage and Escort

In House or Take out
Hot, diverse guys
available to cater to all your
needs
cnr Highfield & Waterkant
Street Greenpoint
(entrance in Waterkant)

e-mail: thebarracks@excite.com
www.thebarracks.co.za

Phone (021) 425 4700

Established 1994
cafe manhattan

Tel: (27 21) 421 6666
Fax: (27 21) 418 7843

e-mail:
madhatte@iafrica.com

74 Waterkant St
Cape Town
800...

We will take care of all
your booking needs in the
Western Cape, South Africa.

We ONLY use accredited airlines and approved
car hire and accommodation establishments.

Tel: 27 21 853 0117
Fax: 27 21 854 6322
info@tripmanagement.com
www.tripmanagement.com

We are driven by YOUR quest for excellence.

A member of
Cape Town Tourism

TripManagement

TOURIST INFO

■ **Cape Town Tourism**
The Pinnacle - Corner Burg & Castle Streets ✉ 8001 ☎ 426-4260
📠 426-4266 💻 info@cape-town.org 🌐 www.cape-town.org
Cape Town Tourism is the official Visitors' Centre for Cape Town, the Gayway to Africa. Come play down South. Contact us for details of accommotion, tours and events happening in Cape Town.

GAY INFO

■ **GALACTTIC** (GLM)
💻 george@dotco.co.za 🌐 www.galacttic.co.za
Provides all infos about the gay life in Cape Town
■ **Pink Map. The**
☎ 685-4260 📠 685-3682 💻 acmaps@iafrica.com
The gay guide to Cape Town & Surrounds, and Johannesburg, Pretoria & Surrounds. Part of a series of special interst map guides for the informed traveller.

BARS

■ **Bar Code** (! B DR G LJ OS P S VS) Sun - Thu 21-01 Fri - Sat 22-3h
16 Hudson Street ☎ 421-5305
Cape Town's most popular leather bar, located in the Gay Village. A definite must for all leather/jeans men. Very friendly staff. Check for special events.
■ **Bar 89** (B f g MA N)
89 Roodebloem Road, Upper Woodstock ☎ 4470-982
Relax, chat and watch the locals & tourists.
■ **Bronx Action Bar** (B D GLM MA OS) 20-? h, daily
Somerset Street, Green Point *(Corner of Sommerset & Napier Stree)*
☎ 419 85 47
Three bars, very popular.
■ **Soho** (B f GLM MA) 12- 2h
21 A Somerset Road, Green Point ☎ 419-5599

CAFES

■ **Aladin's Coffee Shop** (b BF CC F glm OS) Mon-Fri 8-17h, Sat - 13.30h
Nedbank Centre, Kloof Road, Sea Point ☎ 439-4428
Best breakfast in town, all day long! Sit back, relax and watch Sea Point go by.
■ **Café Manhattan** (A B CC F GLM MA OS)
74 Waterkant Street, De Waterkant ☎ 421-6666
Opened in 1994 in the heart of Cape Town's gay village; come and enjoy the relaxed home-away-from-home vibe of the oldest gay owned and operated bar and restaurant in Cape Town.
■ **Obz Café** (B BF F glm OS) Mon-Sat 9.30-23.30 h, Sun 18-22.30 h
115 Lower Main Road, Observatory ☎ 448 55 55

DANCECLUBS

■ **Angel's** (B D GLM YG) Fri-Sat22-? h
27 Somerset Road, Green Point ☎ 419 85 47
DETOUR is upstairs. Large dancefloor with balcony and deck.
■ **Club 55** (B D DR GLM S STV TV) 10h - late
22 Somerset Road, Green Point ☎ 083 479-9532 (Mobile)
Drag shows Tue, Thu and Sun, very popular in the early hours of the morning.
■ **Detour** (B D G) Fri, Sat, public holidays 24-? h, in high season open every night.
27 Sommerset Road, Green Point ☎ 419-9216
Cape Town's top DJ's playing international techno and uplifting house.

RESTAURANTS

■ **Café Manhattan** (A B CC F GLM MA OS)
74 Waterkant Street, De Waterkant ☎ 421-6666
Opened in 1994 in the heart of Cape Town's gay village; come and enjoy the relaxed home-away-from-home vibe of the oldest gay owned and operated bar and restaurant in Cape Town.
■ **Food Affair** (B F glm OS)
247 Main Road, Sea Point ☎ 439-6988
Upmarket crowd, seating for 60 people.
■ **L'Orient**
50 Main Road, Three Anchor Bay ☎ 439-6572
Gay owned malasian restaurant. Traditional Malay decor and food. Well worth a visit.
■ **On Broadway** (CC F NG MA S STV)
1st Floor, 21 Somerset Road, Green Point ☎ 421-6668
Cape Town's hippest cabaret restaurant established in 1997 and home to the South Africa's hottest talents including the drag sensation "Mince"; situated in Cape Town's gay village.
■ **Robert's Café and Cigar Bar** (B CC F GLM MA)
72 Waterkant Street ☎ 425 2478
Fine restaurant in the heart of the gay village, friendly bar.
■ **245 on Main** (B F g MA)
245 Main Road, Three Anchors Bay ☎ 439-7283

SEX SHOPS/BLUE MOVIES

■ **Adult World** (AC CC DR g MA VS) Mon-Sun 9-0 h
174 Main Road, Claremont ☎ 683 44 14
■ **Adult World** (AC CC DR g MA VS) Mon-Sat 9-? h, Sun 12-? h
36 Riebeek Street ✉ 8001 ☎ 418 74 55
■ **Adult World** (AC CC DR g MA VS) Mon-Sat 9-? h, Sun 12-? h
22 Spin Street, Parow Industria ☎ 933 20 29
■ **Wet Warehouse** (CC DR G SNU VS) Mon-Sat 9.30-19 h
1 Sea Street ☎ 419 04 58

Cape Town — South Africa

ESCORTS & STUDIOS

■ **Knights** (G msg R) 0-24 h
Atlantic Seaboard ☎ 434 04 28
Good looking studs for massage and escorting. Strippers available, Upmarket, discreet, shower facilities, in/out and overnight service, secure parking.

■ **Other Side. The** (G msg P TV VS)
Private Bag X7 ☎ 462-1411
Exclusively for sexually liberated connoisseurs. Luxurious relaxed adult entertainment studios and overnight accommodation. Only Cape Town number needed.

■ **Barracks. The** (G msg Vs SNU R) 24 h
Charlemont House, Greenpoint (Corner of Highfield & Waterkant streets) ☎ 425-7400
Cape Town's foremost upmarket m2m studio. Hot, diverse guys available to cater to all your needs, located in "gay village".

SAUNAS/BATHS

■ **Hot House - Steam & Leisure** (! AC B BF CC DR F G MA OS p SA SB VS WH) Mon-Thu 12-2 h, Fri 12-Mon 2 h
18 Jarvis Street, De Waterkant ☎ 418 38 88
Luxurious double volume lounge with 2 bars, restaurant, fireplace & satellite TV, 2 spas and a labyrinth. Spectacular views from sundeck.

■ **Steamers** (CC f G DR MA VS) Mon-Thu 12-2, Fri 12-Mon 2 h
Wembly Road/Solar Road, Gardens ✉ 8000 ☎ 461 62 10
Steam, sauna, sun bed, indoor pool, Jacuzzi's, lounges, private cabins, maze, dark room, glory holes, bar, light meals, internet café.

BODY & BEAUTY SHOPS

■ **ABACA Hair design** (CC glm)
371A Main Road, Sea Point ☎ 434-6725

TRAVEL AND TRANSPORT

■ **Africa Outing** (CC GLM MA)
5 Alcyone Road, Claremont ✉ 7708 ☎ 671 40 28 ☎ 683 7377
✉ afouting@iafrica.com 🖥 www.afouting.com
Gay tour operator in Cape Town - tours throughout southern Africa, travel arrangements, car hire and reservations.

■ **Maxes** (CC G)
PO Box 37546, Valyland ✉ 7978 ☎ 782-6979 📠 782-3499
✉ info@maxes.co.za 🖥 www.maxes.co.za
Gay travel agent for Southern Africa & the Indian Ocean Islands.

■ **Trip Management** (CC GLM)
9 Marais Street, Strand ✉ 7140 ☎ 853 0117 📠 854 6322
✉ info@tripmanagement.com 🖥 www.tripmanagement.com
Travel specialists for the Western Cape.

GUEST HOUSES

■ **Amsterdam Guest House** (! A ac BF CC G NU OS PI SA SB VS WH WO)
19 Forest Road ✉ 8001 ☎ 461 82 36 📠 461 55 75
✉ info@amsterdam.co.za 🖥 www.amsterdam.co.za
Centrally located with stunning views. Exclusively gay. 9 double rooms with bath, WC, TV, video, phone and own key. Entertainment area (clothing optional). Full breakfast 'til noon. One of the most popualr gay guest houses in Cape Town. Early reservations recommended. Laundry service as well as transfer from the airport possible.

■ **Bantry Bay B&B** (BF g pi)
103 Kloof Road ☎ 439-4067 📠 439-7439 ✉ tdacpt@iafrica.com

■ **Bayview Bed & Breakfast** (BF g H OS)
12 Harrington Road, Simon's Town/Seaforth, Cape P. ✉ 7995
☎ 786 33 87 📠 786 33 87 ✉ bayview@yebo.co.za
🖥 www.peninsulainfo.co.za/bayview

This exclusive guest house is located close to the rushing waves and fresh air of the Sea Point Promenade.

KINNERET
Guest House
SEA POINT

Each room is fitted for your comfort with private bathroom, TV, M-NET, fridge, tea and coffee making facilities and telephone.
Light breakfasts are served in the delightful breakfast room.
The bustling Victoria & Alfred Waterfront development with its restaurants and live entertrainment is just a few minutes' drive away.
We cater for corporate clients and holiday makers.

Kinneret Guest house:
11 Arthurs Road • Sea Point • Cape Town
South Africa
Tel: (021) 439 9237 • Fax: (021) 434 8998

45 km south of Cape Town. 2 rooms, 1 with private bath/WC, 1 room with shared bath. Both rooms with TV and a terrace with bayview. Beaches in walking distance. Rates single ZAR 110-150 and double ZAR 160-240 (bf incl.). Weekly rates available.

■ **Black Heath Lodge** (BF CC OS pi MA NG)
6 Blackheath Road, Sea Point ✉ 8005 ☎ 439 2541 📠 439- 9776
✉ blackheathlodge@iafrica.com 🖥 www.blackheathlodge.co.za
This luxurious gay owned guesthouse is situated in a quiet residential area, yet close to the city centre and beaches. With its secluded garden and swimmingpool, and 7 lovely rooms, it really is a home away from home. Rick and Roland will see to your every need, and make sure you will have the holiday of a lifetime.

■ **Britford House** (BF g OS pi) 24 hours
15 Oliver Road/Beach Road, Sea Point ✉ 8005 (Opposite Graaf's Pool) ☎ 439 0257 ✉ popkissm@iafrica.com
🖥 safarinow.com/go/BritfordHouse

■ **Bunk House. The**
23 Atrium Road, Three Anchor Bay ✉ 8005 ☎ 434 5695
☎ (082) 546 9662 (mobile) 📠 434 5695
✉ bunkhouse@new.co.za 🖥 www.bunkhouse.co.za
Backpackers accommodation.

South Africa | Cape Town

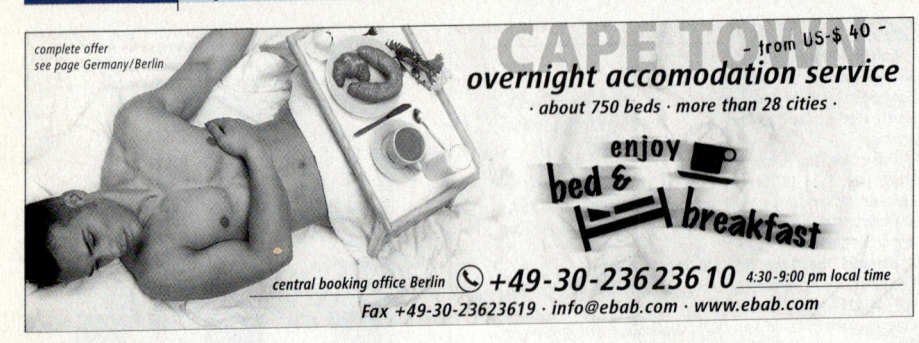

CAPE TOWN
overnight accomodation service
· about 750 beds · more than 28 cities ·
– from US-$ 40 –
enjoy bed & breakfast

central booking office Berlin **+49-30-23623610** 4:30–9:00 pm local time
Fax +49-30-23623619 · info@ebab.com · www.ebab.com

■ **Clarence House** (AC B BF CC F g H MA OS Pl)
6 Obelisk Rd., Claremont ✉ 7708 ☎ 683 0307 🛏 683 0455
📧 chc@chchouse.co.za 🖥 www.chchouse.co.za
Luxurious gay accommodation at reasonable rates. Magnificent view on Table Mountain. Fully licensed with restaurant and bar. Swiss management. Easy Access to all gay venues.

■ **Huijs Haerlem** (ac BF CC H OS M)
25 Main Drive, Sea Point ✉ 8005 ☎ 434-6434 🛏 439-2506
📧 haerlem@iafrica.com 🖥 users.iafrica.com/h/ha/haerlem
Gay owned luxury Guest House with spectacular sea views. Some rooms with private balconies. Five minutes from everywhere.

■ **Kinnert & Oliver Guest Houses** (BF CC H MA NG OS) 0-24 h
11 Arthurs Road, Sea Point ✉ 8005 ☎ 439 92 37 🛏 434 89 98.
Victorian style guest house. All rooms double. Close to Victoria & Alfred waterfront, olympic sized pool close to hotel. Prices on request.

■ **Lady Victoria** (BF g H)
1 Kelvin Street, Upper Gardens ✉ 8001 ☎ 233-814
All rooms with en-suite bathroom, TV, phone, radio. Rates on request.

■ **@Lantic B&B** (BF glm)
12 Fir Avenue, Bantry Bay ☎ 434-7226 🛏 434-7366
📧 peachm@iafrica.com
4 en-suite rooms.

■ **Liberty Lodge** (ac BF CC F MA g OS H) 24 hours
33 De Lorentz Street, Tamboerskloof ✉ 8001 ☎ 423 2264
🛏 423 2274 📧 liberty@capetowncity.co.za
🖥 www.capetowncity.co.za
Warm-hearted hospitality, well-equipped rooms decorated with great character and style. Walk to the city and restaurants.

■ **Little Lemon, The** (BF H glm MA OS pi)
9 Antrim Road, Green Point ✉ 8001 ☎ 439 19 90 🛏 434 42 09
📧 little-lemon@iafrica.com 🖥 www.little-lemon.co.za
Central location. Close to gay clubs etc.

■ **Newlands Guesthouse** (bf)
4 Alcis Road, Newlands ☎ 686-0013 🛏 686-9216
📧 garth@newlandsguest.co.za

■ **Norman Road Guest House, The** (bf glm)
Norman Road, Green Point ☎ 434-7055 🛏 434-7066
📧 normangh@iafrica.com 🖥 www.normanroad.com
Closer to clubs and Victoria & Albert Waterfront complex.

■ **Observatory Guest House** (CC bf F g OS pi SA SB w)
47 Williams Street, Observatory ☎ 448 20 14 🛏 448 20 14
📧 obsguesthouse.cape@new.co.za

■ **Parker Cottage** (BF CC g H OS)
3 Carstens Street, Tamboerskloof ✉ 8001 ☎ 424 64 45
🛏 424 64 45 📧 info@parkercottage.co.za
🖥 www.parkercottage.co.za
Accommodation in gracious Victorian home. Four imaginatively decorated bedrooms. Continental/Health breakfast. Personal service, central location. Close to gay locations. Rates double from R 195/single R 280 per person per night.

■ **Quarters, The** (AC bf G H MA p)
76 Waterkant Street, De Waterkant ✉ 8001 ☎ 419 14 79
☎ 082-5570824 (mobile) 🛏 421 59 14
📧 quarters@iafrica.com 🖥 www.thequarters.co.za
Centrally located in the gay scene. Rooms with bath/WC, TV, phone and mini-bar.

■ **Richborough Villa** (BF CC G H MA OS) All year
5 Highworth Road, Sea Point ✉ 8001 (2 mins to beach, 7 mins to Pink Triangle, 20 mins to Sandy Bay) ☎ 434 6550 🛏 434 8459
📧 tim@richborough.co.za 🖥 www.richborough.co.za
Exclusively Gay. Central location. All rooms en suite, telephone, TV,tea/coffee.own keys. Walk to beach, nude swimming, shops and restaurants.

■ **Twenty Nine** (BF CC E f g MA Pl OS SA WO)
29 Atholl Road, Camps Bay ✉ 8005 ☎ 438 3800 🛏 438 3801
📧 info@twentynine.net 🖥 www.twentynine.net
Whatever you desire, they attend to everything so that you can just let yourself go.

■ **Underberg Guest House**
Tamboerskloof Road, Tamboerskloof (courner of Carstens St.)
☎ 426-2262 🛏 424-4059 📧 underberg@netactive.co.za

■ **Verona Lodge** (BF CC g H OS)
11 Richmond Road, Three Anchor Bay ✉ 8005 ☎ 434 94 77
🛏 434 94 77 📧 info@veronalodge.co.za
🖥 www.veronalodge.co.za
Five rooms with shower/WC, phone, fax, TV, video, own key. Rates: single R210-320 double: R320-500.

■ **30 Fiskaal Road** (ac BF CC g H MA OS Pl)
30 Fiskaal Road, Camps Bay ✉ 8005 ☎ 438 1206 🛏 438 1206
📧 seroy@mweb.co.za 🖥 home.mweb.co.za/se/seroy
Luxury Mediterranean style guest house overlooking the world famous Camps Bay beach. Finalists in the AA Guest House of the year 2000 Accommodation Awards.

■ **65 Kloof** (BF G MA OS Pl WO)
65 Kloof Road, Sea Point ☎ 434-0815 🛏 434-0815
📧 65kloof@netactive.co.za 🖥 www.web.netactive.co.za/~65kloof
Stylish, premium location under the gaze of Lions head. Sparkling pool, relax and enjoy.

APARTMENTS

■ **De Waterkant Village** (bf g H MA pi)
☎ 422 2721 🛏 426 5088 📧 karyn@hvc.co.za
🖥 www.dewatercant.com
60 Luxurious, self catering, serviced cottages, splash pools and roof terraces. In the heart of the gay village. Fashionable village atmosphere.

PRIVATE ACCOMMODATION
■ **Enjoy Bed and Breakfast** (BF G H MA) 16.30-21 h (Central European Time)
Nollendorfplatz 5, 10777 Berlin - Germany ☏ +49 30 236 236 10
☏ +49 30 236 236 19 ✉ info@ebab.com 🖳 ebab.com
Accommodation sharing agency. All with shower and BF. 20-25 Euro p.p.

■ **Le Freak**
☏ +34-971-39 58 84 (international)
Private Guest House.

■ **Richborough Villa Country Retreat** (AC B bf CC G MA N NU OS pi) All year
Hof Street, ✉ 7306 (90 km outside of Cape Town in the vinelands)
☏ 022/461 2289 📠 022/461 2335 ✉ Jackie@richborough.co.za
🖳 www.Richborough.co.za
Self catering or B&B (meals on request). All rooms ensuite with bath/shower and WC, TV, AC. Secluded pool. 90 km from central Cape Town in Riebeeck Valley winelands. Restaurants and pubs nearby. Wine tasting on surrounding wine farms possible.

HEALTH GROUPS
■ **ATIC (Aids Training Information Counselling Centre)**
☏ 400 34 00
■ **Triangle Project** 9-17 h
Community House, 41 Salt River Road, Salt River ✉ 7925
☏ 448 38 12 📠 448 40 89 ✉ triangle@icon.co.za
Health information, couselling & support.

HELP WITH PROBLEMS
■ **Gay/Lesbian/Bisexual Helpline** Daily from 13 - 21 h
☏ 422 2500

RELIGIOUS GROUPS
■ **Gay Christian Community** Sun 17.30 h at Quaker House, Hornsey Road/Rye Roda, Mowbray 7700
PO Box 36 137, Glosderry ✉ 7702 ☏ 61 27 50

SPORT GROUPS
■ **Cape Organization for Gay Sports (COGS)**
☏ 557 71 95

SWIMMING
-Graaff's Pool (NU g) (Sea Front Road, Sea Point. Opposite Winchester mansions Hotel, men only swimming area)
-Sandy Bay Beach (G NU) Cold water!(Take M6 to Hout Bay and leave in Llangdudno)
-Clifton 3rd Beach (very nice beach).

CRUISING
-Sandy Bay, Llandudno. In the bushes on the far right hand side of Sandy Beach (!)
-Beach and promenade along ocean in Sea Point (all night long, especially around Graaf's pool)
-Toilets in Waterfront Centre
-Adelphi Centre, Main Rd., Sea Point
-Blouberg beach toilets near Saddles. After dark from 21-02h Also the very end of Beach Road 4km from Dolphin Beach.
- Beach Road private beach near Putt Putt center. Take R44 off the N2 highway towards Strand.
-Waterfront - end toilet at the back end facing Bertie's Landing behind Den Anker (a small glory hole between last two toilet booths)
-Tygervalley toilets in the Missippi detour area
- Kenilwoth Cnetre toilets - upper level
-Rocklands beach in Sea Points toilets.

Durban - Kwazulu/Natal ☏ 031

BARS
■ **Axis** (B D dr Glm SNU)
4 Rutherford Street/Gillespie ☏ 32 26 03
■ **Late Night Galleon** (AC B BF d DR F G MA S) 9-4 h
Shop 5B, Nedbank Circle, 577 Point Road ☏ 32 46 89

CAFES
■ **Garth`s Place** (B f G MA) 10-24 h, Mon closed
Avonmore Centre, 9th Avenue/Clarence ☏ 23 73 28

DANCECLUBS
■ **Pandora's** (B D Glm YG) 21-? h
27 Hunter Street

SEX SHOPS/BLUE MOVIES
■ **Adult World** (AC CC DR MA VS) Mon-Thu 9-23, Fri & Sat -24, Sun 12-22h
114 West Street ✉ 4000 ☏ 332 1376
■ **AVN x-rated cinema** (MA)
Woodford Grove, Morningside
" small cinemas. One is gay. Lots of movement between the two cinemas. Action in back rows and toilets.
■ **Fantasies** (GLM)
320 West Street, Shop 113, 4001 (1st floor) ☏ 304 14 08
Sex toys and condoms. Ask for mail-order catalogue.

GENERAL GROUPS
■ **Gayline Durban**
PO Box 11744, Marine Parade ✉ 4056 ☏ 37 57 84
■ **KwaZulu-Natal Provincial Coalition for Gay and Lesbian Equality**
PO Box 30890, Mayville ✉ 4058 ☏ 260 11 49

HEALTH GROUPS
■ **AIDS Foundation KwaZulz/Natal**
☏ 21 33 03
■ **Open Door**
Room 1116, Colonial Towers, 332 West Street ☏ 304 67 01
HIV/Aids drop-in centre.

RELIGIOUS GROUPS
■ **Grace MCC**
☏ 23 04 05

SWIMMING
-Battery Beach (opposite Blue Waters Htl., especially WE- AYOR)
-Beachwood (7 km north, turn off Northern Freeway at Beachwood sign, follow sign to Nature Reserve, turn left to dunes, very active)
-Rachael Finlayson Baths (g WE) (in the showers)
- Toilets in Technikon - Botanic Gardens Road.
-Marine Parade - in front of the reserve military base.
-Privateet - bottom end of Davenport Rd. last road before Umbilo, entrance via the back. Tuesdays after 21h.

CRUISING
-Beach by Ocean Cinema (AYOR) (opposite Holiday Inn; night only)
-Battery Beach (opposite Blue Waters Hotel and down the beach to the Snake Park, 24 hrs, AYOR)
-City Square (AYOR)(opposite city hall)
-Toilets in Beach View Mall (opposite Killarney Hotel)
-Beachfront (from Addington to North Beach, esp. at night, AYOR)
-Toilets in "The Workshop" shopping centre (near City Hall)
-Beachwood beach (carpark, beach, toilets and dunes, NU, R, AYOR)

South Africa | East London - Eastern Cape ▶ Johannesburg - Gauteng

East London - Eastern Cape ☎ 043

BARS
■ **Star Lites** (d Glm MA WE) 21: - ?
9 Dyer Street, Arcadia (behind Wap) ☎ 722 1109
Fri & Sat gay disco.
■ **Thumpers** (B d g MA)
Recreation Road

GUEST HOUSES
■ **Mikes Guest House** (glm)
22 Clifford Street, Quigney ☎ 743 3647 ☎ 743 0308
22 en-suite rooms - 100 m from the beach.

PRIVATE ACCOMMODATION
■ **Castle. The** (OS PI)
13 Acacia Drive, Beacon Bay ✉ 5241 ☎ +27 83 504 0888 (mobile) ☎ 748 3293 ✉ lekla@iafrica.com
Self-catering apartments.

HELP WITH PROBLEMS
■ **St. Mary's Home for PWA's**
☎ 43 75 17

CRUISING
-Eastern Beach (entire beachfront)
-Esplanade area especially opposite the Quanza Marine Hotel or Osner Hotel
-Blue Lagoon Hotel carpark in Nahoon - after 16h as well as Nahoon Reef parking lot Fri & Sat around midnight
- Vincent Park Center - upstairs toilet

Franschhoek - Western Cape ☎ 021

HOTELS
■ **Dieu Donné Guest Farm** (g H)
PO Box 569 ✉ 7690 ☎ 876 21 31 ☎ 876 37 76
50 min. from Cape Town. 30 min. from Stellenbosch. 20 min. from Paarl.

Hanover - Karoo ☎ 053

GUEST HOUSES
■ **Darling Street Guest House** (glm)
3 Darling Street ☎ 643 0254 ☎ 083 777-1947 (mobile)
✉ darlingst3@icon.co.za
Victorian Karoo-style house. In the heart of the Karoo. Ideal for a stop over between Johannesburg and Cape Town.

Hermanus ☎ 028

GUEST HOUSES
■ **Buçaco Sud** (BF CC glm MA OS PI WE)
☎ 272 9750 ☎ 083- 5141015 (Mobile) ☎ 272 9750
✉ bucaco@bucacosud.co.za ☎ www.bucacosud.co.za
Situated on the spectacular whale coast, close to Cape Town and winelands, great decor, stunning views.
■ **Seemeeue. Die** (BF F GLM H MA OS PI)
60 Ghwarrieng Crescent, Vermont, Onrus River *(5 km from Hermanus, 110 km from Cape town.)* ☎ 316 24 79 ☎ (0)83-763 65 72 (mobile) ☎ 316 24 79 ✉ seemeeue@seemeeue.co.za
☎ www.seemeeue.co.za
Cosy guesthouse, wide views over sea and mountains; beaches and nature-reserves of unspoilt beauty; whale-viewing; affordable tariff's.

■ **Skuinshuis B&B. Die** (BF F CC g MA OS wh)
67 Kandelaar Street, Vermont ☎ 3162213 ☎ 083 309 4821 (mobile) ✉ skuinshuis@hermanus.co.za
☎ www.bluecape.co.za/skuinshuis
Lie in bed and watch the sea. En-suite bedrooms with private entrances. Intimate beach around corner. German host.

Johannesburg - Gauteng ☎ 011

BARS
■ **Balcony Bar. The** (B DR f G MA msg OS p SNU STV VS)
1st floor, 430 Commissioner Street, Fairview *(100m from Kensington Fire Station)*
■ **Connections** (B f g MA R) 11-2 h
1 Pretoria Street, Hillbrow *(in Hillbrow between Clarendon and Klein Street)* ☎ 642 85 11
■ **Gotham City/58** (! B D DR G MA S VS WE) 11-? h
58 Pretoria Street, Hillbrow
■ **Jeb`s Leather Bar** (B DR lj MA)
2 Carnarvon Road, Bertrams
■ **Rainbows** (AYOR B D F GLM R)
Wolmarans/Rissik Streets, Braamfontein *(Old Academy Theatre)*
☎ 725 26 97
Dangerous
■ **Skyline** (B G MA R)
Harrison Reef Hotel, Pretoria Street, Hillbrow
Black scene.
■ **Stonewall** (B g MA N OS VS)
Rockney Street, Yeoville
■ **Zoo** (B DR lj MA SNU VS)
Hopkins Street, Yeoville
Jack-off parties at weekend.

RESTAURANTS
■ **Caffe della Salute** (B F g MA OS)
Sandton Square
■ **La Contadina Restaurant** (B CC F GLM MA OS) Mon-Thu 11-20, Fri Sat -23, Sun 9-17 h
12 Gleneagles Road, Greenside ☎ 486 26 26
■ **Mea Culpa** (B F g MA)
12 Keyes Avenue/Tyrwhitt, Rosebank ☎ 447 45 43
■ **Thin Lyzzeez** (B F g lj s)
Langermann Drive, Kensington
Pool table, bikers.

SHOWS
■ **Market Theatre**
☎ 834 20 46
Gay plays are sometimes featured. Call for information

SEX SHOPS/BLUE MOVIES
■ **Adult World**
Jan Smuts Avenue, Craighall Park
■ **Esteem Books** (VS)
Gleneagles Road, Greenside *(off Barry Herzog St)*
5 video cubicals.
■ **Garage Video Den** (G VS) 12.30-19 h
54 Nottingham Road, Kensington ☎ 622 22 75
■ **The Love Inn** (G)
212 Lower Level, Carlton Centre, Commissioner Street ☎ 331 9531
■ **Luv Land** (g) Mon-Fri 8.30-18, Sat 9-15 h
Valley Centre, 396 Jan Smuts Avenue, Craighall Park *(Lower Level)*
☎ 789 81 03

Robertson ▶ Wilderness | **South Africa**

Robertson

GUEST HOUSES

■ **Fraai Uitzicht 1798 - Historic Wine & Guestfarm** (A b BF CC F glm MA OS Pl) 12-22h
Klass Voogds East (R60) ✉ 6705 *(Central located in Robertson Wine Valley, near Hotsprings, between Robertson and Ashton)* ☎ 626 61 56 🖥 fraai.uitzicht@lando.co.za
💻 www.lando.co.za/fraaiuitzicht
Rates: double B&B ZAR 430, single ZAR 290 and self catering apartments R 150 + R 90 per person. All rooms are with WC/shower, TV.

Stellenbosch - Western Cape ☎ 021

GUEST HOUSES

■ **Amaryllis** (AC BF CC glm H MA Pl)
106 Jonkerhoek Road ✉ 7600 ☎ 887 2305 ☎ 082 779 1727 (mobile) 📠 887 2305 🖥 amaryllis@new.co.za
💻 www.amaryllis.co.za
Enjoy comfort and warm hospitalaty amid spectacular mountains and famous vineyards just 35 minutes from Cape Town.

■ **Evergreen Lodge** (BF CC H NG pi) Office: 07-19h
Cnr. Bosman & Murray Streets, ✉ 7612 *(Historic center of Stellenbosch)* ☎ 886 68 32 📠 883 84 49. 🖥 evergrn@global.co.za
Five bedrooms.

Wilderness ☎ 044

GUEST HOUSES

■ **Palms Wilderness** (B BF CC glm F H Pl) All year. Restaurant closed June/July
Owen Grant Street 1 ✉ 6560 ☎ 877 14 20 📠 877 14 22
🖥 palms@pixie.co.za
💻 palms-wilderness.com
Gay owned. Located in Wilderness National Park, 2 min. from the beach.

■ **Tuscany. The** (b BF CC f g MA OS Pl)
☎ 877-0748 ☎ 082 566-1529 (mobile)
🖥 tuscany@cyberhost.co.za 💻 www.tuscany.co.za
Gay owned. Come and enjoy the best S.A. hospitality in the Garden Route. Beachwalks and BBQ.

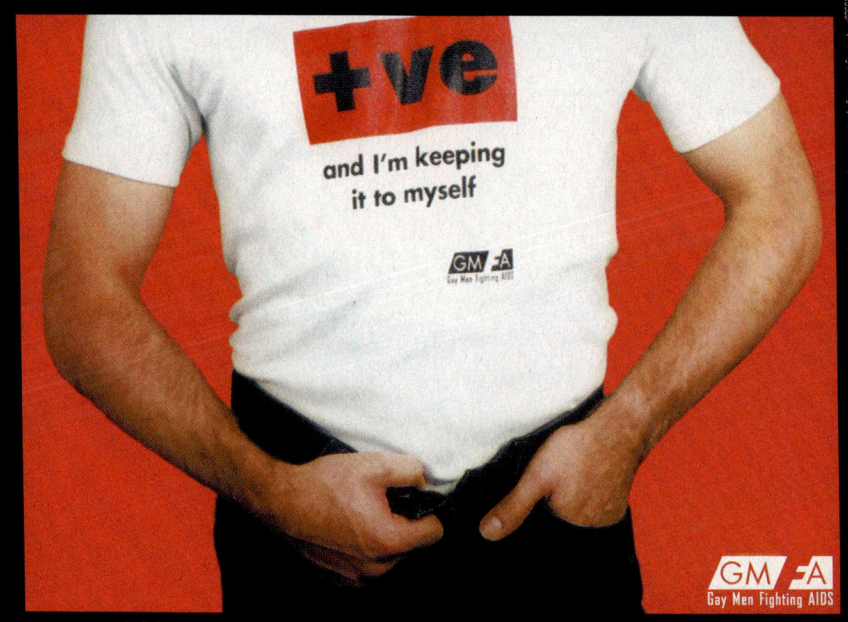

South Africa

Spain

Name: España • Spanien • Espagne • Spagna
Location: Southwest Europe
Initials: E
Time: GMT +1
International Country Code: ☎ 34
International Access Code: ☎ 07 (wait for tone)
Language: Castilian, Catalan, Basque, Galician (Gallego)
Area: 504,782 km² / 194,884 sq mi.
Currency: 1 Peseta (Pta). 1 EURO = 166,386 Ptas
Population: 38,873,000
Capital: Madrid
Religions: 96% Roman Catholic
Climate: Moderate climate. Summer in the interior is clear and hot, more moderate and cloudy along the coast. Winters are cloudy and cold in the interior, partly cloudy and cool along coast.
Important gay cities: Madrid, Barcelona, Ibiza, Sitges, Playa del Inglés (Gran Canaria), Torremolinos, Benidorm, Sevilla and Valencia

✱ The general age of consent is 16 years. However, to avoid any trouble with the law, you should steer clear of men under the age of 18 if you yourself are above it. Spain today lies right in the cultural centre of Europe. To this, the autonomy of the Spanish provinces, as well as hosting major international events, has contributed much. Gay Spaniards have become very self-confident, and the gay scene is very communicative, open and interesting. Madrid and Barcelona are, of course, the centres of activity, but a number of beach resorts are also of importance: Sitges, Ibiza, Torremolinos, Palma de Mallorca, Benidorm and Lloret de Mar. In winter, a favourite meeting place for gays is Playa del Ingles on Gran Canaria. After all, Spain is Europe's number one holiday spot!

✱ Zwar liegt das allgemeine Schutzalter bei 16 Jahren; wer aber keinerlei rechtliche Gefahren eingehen möchte, sollte, wenn er über 18 Jahre ist, Männer unter 18 Jahren meiden. In Madrid gibt es ebenso wie in Katalonien eine eingetragene Partnerschaft. Allerdings hat dies nur Auswirkungen auf Rechte, die in die Kompetenz der Provinz fallen wie z.B. Erbrecht, Mietrecht und Vertretungsrecht. Auf Landesebene ist ein ähnlicher Gesetzesentwurf bisher am Widerstand der konservativen Regierung gescheitert.
Doch die schwulen Spanier sind sehr selbstbewußt geworden, und die Szene präsentiert sich interessant, kommunikativ und frei.
Barcelona und Madrid sind die Zentren dieser Entwicklung. Bedeutend sind aber auch eine Reihe von Badeorten: Ibiza, Sitges, Torremolinos, Palma de Mallorca, Benidorm und Lloret de Mar. Im Winter trifft man sich in Playa del Ingles auf Gran Canaria-schließlich ist Spanien Europas Reiseland Nr. 1!

✱ En Espagne, la majorité sexuelle est fixée à 16 ans. Soyez quand même prudents avec les mineurs de moins de 18 ans, si vous voulez éviter des ennuis. L'Espagne a retrouvé sa place au sein des grandes nations culturelles d'Europe, et ce grâce à la volonté et au tempérament de chacune de ses provinces et aux nombreuses manifestations culturelles ou sportives internationales. Les gais espagnols ont acquis une certaine assurance, les lieux gais sont intéressants, variés et animés. Madrid et Barcelone se disputent le titre de capitale gaie du pays. Mais n'oublions pas non plus les stations balnéaires gaies de Sitges, Ibiza, Torremolinos, Palma de Mallorca, Benidorm et Lloret de Mar. En hiver, on se retrouve à la Playa del Ingles sur Gran Canaria. L'Espagne est la destination touristique gaie numéro 1 en Europe!

✱ Aunque la edad de consentimiento es de 16 años, para evitar problemas, se deberían evitar relaciones con jovenes menores de 18 años. En Madrid es posible el registro de parejas homosexuales. Estas "parejas de hecho", parecidas al matrimonio, no pueden ser comparadas con las de los paises del Norte de Europa, ya que tienen poco valor legal.
Los homosexuales españoles tienen hoy en día mucho más autoconfianza, y el ambiente es muy interesante, comunicativo y libre. Madrid y Barcelona son los centros gay del país. Importantes son también los centro turísticos de Sitges, Ibiza, Torremolinos, Palma de Mallorca, Benidorm y Lloret de Mar. En invierno los gays se reunen en la Playa del Inglés en Gran Canaria. Yaque España se ha convertido en el país turístico número 1 de Europa.

✱ L'età legale per avere dei rapporti sessuali è di 16 anni, chi è già diciottenne però per evitare ogni pericolo dovrebbe scegliersi compagni maggiorenni. La Spagna si trova oggi nel centro culturale dell'Europa. A ciò hanno contribuito l'ostinatezza delle provincie spagnole per l'organizzazione di grandi avvenimenti internazionali. I gay spagnoli si sono emancipati e l'ambiente si presenta interessante, comunicativo e libero. Madrid e Barcellona sono naturalmente i centri più importanti, sono però di grande interesse anche alcuni centri balneari: Sitges, Ibiza, Torremolinos, Palma de Mallorca, Benidorm e Lloret de Mar. In inverno ci si incontra sulla playa del ingles alla Gran Canaria. In Europa la Spagna è la meta turistica numero uno.

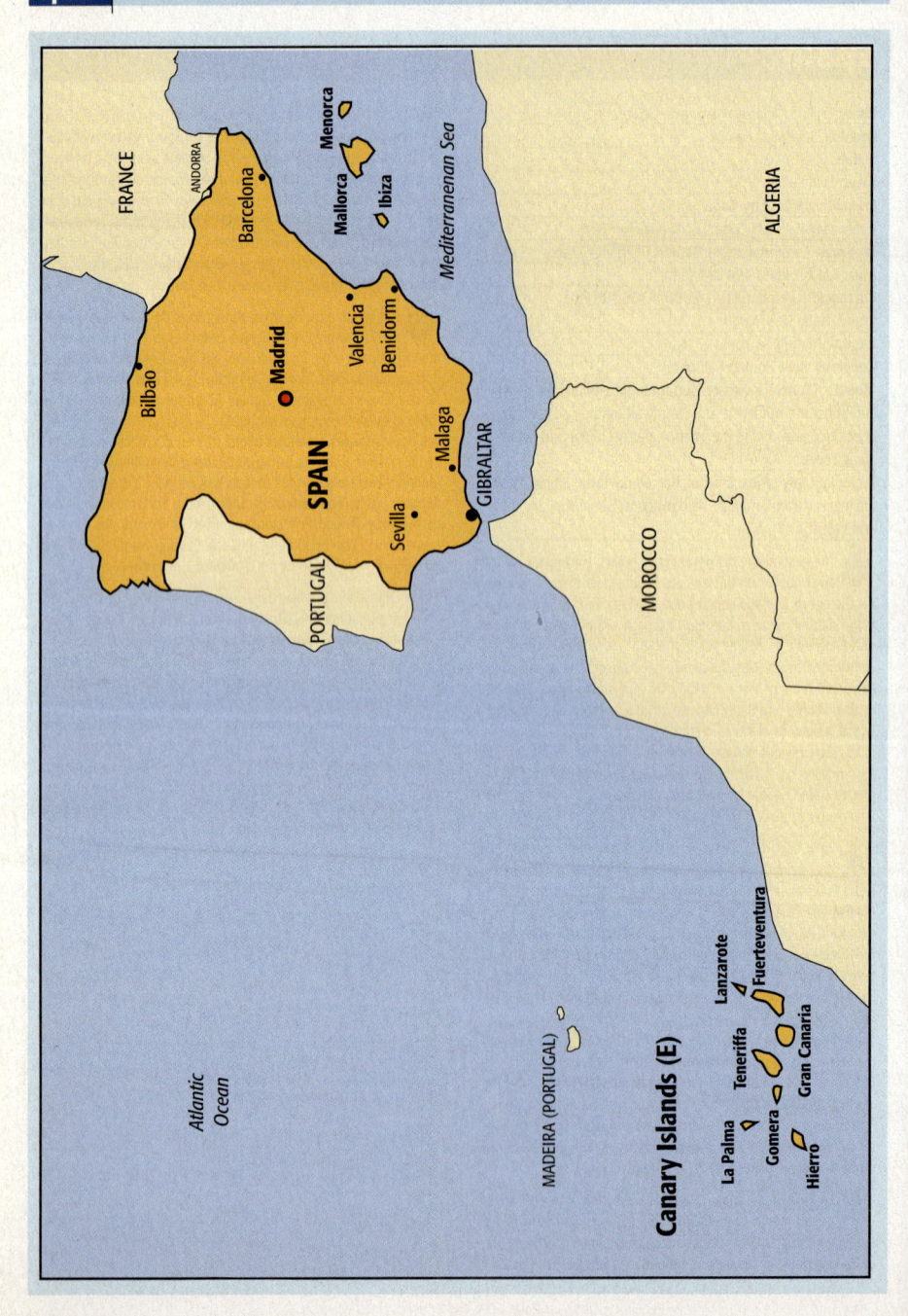

Spain

zero

EL CINE MÁS ATREVIDO
nuevos directores de cortos

IMMA BATTAGLIA
la pasionaria lesbiana

MODA DE OTOÑO
todas las tendencias

VIAJES
florencia, palma

EL PRIMER MILITAR GAY
EL TENIENTE CORONEL SÁNCHEZ SILVA ROMPE EL SILENCIO EN EL EJÉRCITO

INCLUYE: GUIA COMPLETA • OCIO • SERVICIOS • NOCHE • ANUNCIOS PERSONALES

Spain — Aguadulce ▸ Alicante/Alacant

Your mind's gym

la primera librería gay en internet en español
ENVÍOS A TODO EL MUNDO

first internet gay bookstore in spanish
WE SHIP ANYWHERE IN THE WORLD

www.tulibro.com

NATIONAL PUBLICATIONS

■ **Atrevete**
c/o Chavez, C/ Quintana 20, 3 ✉ 28008 Madrid ☎ 91 542 54 03 📠 91 542 89 28
The Spanish gay travel magazine. Published quarterly. For free in gay venues.

■ **Mensual - La Revista y Guia Gay de España**
S.L., PO Box 20 28 ✉ 08080 Barcelona ☎ 93 412 53 80 📠 93 412 33 57 ✉ correo@mensual.com 🌐 www.mensual.com
Listings and maps from Spain, every year, about 60 pages, and a monthly magazine including photos, small ads, listings from Spain.

■ **Odisea**
C/ Espiritu Santo, 33 ✉ 28004 Madrid ☎ 91 523 21 54 ☎ 91 522 74 83 📠 91 522 74 83 ✉ odisea@ctv.es 🌐 www.revistaodisea.com
Free gay monthly newspaper.

■ **Shangay**
PO Box 40 23 ✉ 28080 Madrid ☎ 91 308 45 39
Biweekly gay newspaper. Distributed nationwide, special focus on Madrid and Valencia. Free at gay venues.

■ **ZERO**
Pza Sta Ma Soledad Torres Acosta, 2 ✉ 28004 Madrid ☎ 91 701 00 89 📠 91 531 51 17 ✉ zero@zeropress.com 🌐 www.zero-web.com
Monthly magazine on gay information and life styles in Spanish language.

NATIONAL COMPANIES

■ **Las Lagrimas de Eros**
Apto. 3008 ✉ 46080 Valencia ☎ 96 382 49 38 📠 96 382 53 88
National mailorder company.

Aguadulce

BARS

■ **Milenium** (B DR G MA VS) 22.30-4 h
Av. Carlos III (Centro Commercial Neptuno) ☎ 950 34 80 31

■ **Neptuno** (B d DR G MG OG VS) 21-03 h, winter closed Mon
Av. Carlos III *(Neptuno Centre)* ☎ 950 34 73 90

■ **Sire. El** (B d G MA p) 22-4.30 h, closed Mon
Nacional 340 *(1st floor, ca. 12 km from Almeria)* ☎ 950 34 14 02

Albacete

SEX SHOPS/BLUE MOVIES

■ **Sex Shop** (g)
C/ Pedro Coca, 2 ✉ 02080

GENERAL GROUPS

■ **Grupo Regional de Gays, Lesbianas y Transexuales del PSOE (GLM tv)**
C/ Pedro Coca, 19 ✉ 02004 ☎ 967 22 55 50 ☎ 967 50 84 72 ✉ psoealbacete@teleline.es

■ **Jovenes Gais Albacete JOGAL** 18-21 h
PO Box 627 ✉ 02080 ☎ 96 65 62

Algeciras

SEX SHOPS/BLUE MOVIES

■ **Intimate** (CC g VS) 11-14h, 16-22h, sun closed
Ed. Plaza Alta, local 7, pasaje ☎ 956 65 76 15

Alicante/Alacant

BARS

■ **Boys** (AC B DR G MA VS) 22-? h
C/ César Elguezábal, 11

■ **Canibal Pub** (AC B d G MA S snu stv) 22-?h, Sun closed
C/ César Elguezábal, 26 ✉ 03001

■ **Desfici** (AC B CC D GLM MA WE) Wed-Sat 22-5 h
C/ Bazán 18 ✉ 03001

■ **Enigma** (! AC B DR G MA p VS YG) 21-3, Fri Sat 21-4, winter Sun 17-3 h
C/ Arquitecto Morelli, 23

■ **Horus-Pub** (AC B d g MA STV) 21-h ?
C/ Cesar Elguezábal, 11 ✉ 03001

■ **Jardineto. El** (AC B DR G MA r VS) 20-?
C/ Barón de Finestrat, 5 ☎ 96 521 17 36

■ **Missing** (! AC B d DR G MA s VS) 22-3.30 h
C/ Gravina, 4 ✉ 03002 ☎ 96 521 67 28

■ **Montecristo** (B G OG p vs) 22-3 h
C/ Ab-El-Hamet, 1 ✉ 03003 ☎ 96 512 31 89

■ **Tres Rombos** (AC B G MA R) 20-3h, WE-6h
C/ Santa Marta, 1 ✉ 03001 *(near Plaza Gabriel Miró)*

■ **Trompa. La** (AC B d DR G MA r VS) 20-4h
C/ Baron de Finestrat, 3

CAFES

■ **Or y Ferro** (A AC B f G MA s) 16-24 h, WE-2 h
C/ Belando, 12 ✉ 03004 ☎ 96 521 54 61

DANCECLUBS

■ **Enigmas Disco** (! AC B DR Glm MA OS s YG) Fri-Sun 1-?, summer daily 1-? h
Ctra. Villafranqueza ▸ Tángel, km 5 ☎ 96 517 97 79
Very large, two floors.

Alicante/Alacant ▸ Balearic Islands - Ibiza Spain

■ **Venial Club Alicante** (AC B D G MA s snu stv VS WE)
Thu-Sun 1-?h
Av. Condes de Soto Ameno, 16 ✉ 03005
Thu dragshow, Sun stripshow, 3h.

SEX SHOPS/BLUE MOVIES
■ **Cosmopolitan** (g VS)
C/ Rafael Altamira, 5 ☎ 96 514 48 22
■ **Portugal-3** (g VS)
C/ Portugal,3
■ **Quintana** (g VS) 10-14 h, 17-21
C/ Poeta Quintana, 41 ✉ 03004 ☎ 96 521 49 81
■ **Sex Shop** (g VS) 10-3 h
C/ Pintor Lorenzo Casanova
■ **Sexyland** (g VS)
C/ Segura, 18 ✉ 03004 ☎ 96 520 08 26

SAUNAS/BATHS
■ **Asia** (B DR G MA SA SB VS) 15.30-21h
C/ Cardenal Payá, 17
■ **Ipanema Termas** (! AC B DR f G p SA SB VS WH yg) 15-23h
C/ Espronceda, 12 ✉ 03013 ☎ 677 840 119
■ **Sauna 26** (B DR G MA SA SB VS) 15.30-21.30 h
C/ Poeta Quintana, 26 ✉ 03004 ☎ 96 521 98 25

GIFT & PRIDE SHOPS
■ **Canibal Shop** (CC GLM) 10-14h, 17-20.30h
C/ Colón, 16 ✉ 03001 ☎ 965 20 25 23

HOTELS
■ **Casa Rural L´Almasera** (A AC B BF CC g MG OS msg SA WH)
Reception: 9-13.30 h, 17-21.30 h
C/ Ciabadia, 20 ✉ 03828 ☎ 96 551 42 32 📠 96 551 43 14
✉ almasera@wanadoo.es

GUEST HOUSES
■ **Residencia Mariola** (g H)
C/ Hércules, 9 bajo ✉ 03006 ☎ 96 510 16 88

GENERAL GROUPS
■ **Lambda**
Apto 1088 ✉ 03080

HEALTH GROUPS
■ **Centro de'Informacia i Prevencio de la SIDA (CIPS)**
Plaza España, 6 ☎ 96 523 05 63

SWIMMING
-Cabo de Las Huertas (NU) (take bus S)
-Carabasi Beach (NU) (12 km south of Alicante, late afternoons and evenings)
-Marina o Camino del Rebollo (NU) (Entrance at Camping International de la Marina and Club Michel)
-Urbanova (NU) (Go to the direction of the airport. Entrance of the beach at Altet)
-Las Canas between Play de Altet and Urbanova (dunes between parking and beach)

CRUISING
-Coast (2 km) between Postiguet Beach and La Albufera (especially in summer)
-Calle de Isabel / Avenida de Elche / Calle del Doctor Just / Calle Quintiliano (this block and back, at night carcruising)

Almeria

DANCECLUBS
■ **Abakos** (B D Glm MA SNU STV YG) 23-6 h, closed Mon
C/ Dr. Araez Pacheco, 8
■ **Dracena** (B g) 16-14h
C/ Rafael Alberti, s/n *(Oliveros)*

SWIMMING
-Playa del Rio (g)
-Playa Serena, Urbanización Roquetas de Mar (g NU) (19 km from Almeria)
-Playa Nudista, Vera (g NU) (93 km from Almeria)

CRUISING
-Paseo Maritimo (at night, mostly with car, opposite Gran Hotel Almeria and filling station Elf)

Avila

GENERAL GROUPS
■ **Colectivo Gay de Avila**
PO Box 105, ✉ 05080

Aviles

SEX SHOPS/BLUE MOVIES
■ **Internacional Sex-Shop** (g VS) 11-14, 16-21 h
C/ Periodista Pruneda, 2 ✉ 33400 ☎ 985 556 77 96

SWIMMING
-Dunas de Espatal/Playa San Juan

Badajoz

BARS
■ **Athos Club** (B D DR G MA S) 22-? h
C/ Joaquín Sama, 11 *(Plaza Chica)* ☎ 924 25 81 55

Balearic Islands

Climate: Mild winters, not colder than 10°C, and dry and hot summers with sometimes 45°C.
Important gay cities: Ibiza, Palma de Mallorca.

Balearic Islands - Formentera

BARS
■ **Claro! En Cán Gavinu** (B F GLM OS) 20-? h
Km 3,3 Ctra. San Francisco - La Mola ☎ 971 32 24 21

SWIMMING
-Platja de Llevant (G NU) (Take the boat from Ibiza to Formentera. Rent a bike and go towards Es Pujols around the saltwater lake Estany Pudent. 150 m after the "Tanga Bar" turn left and follow the path to the beach.)

Balearic Islands - Ibiza

※ Ibiza belongs to the most important gay beach resorts of Europe. While the Canarian Playa del Ingles is visited mainly in winter, and Sitges has the near Barcelona to offer, Ibiza (ibizian: Eivissa) is the top summer destination for gays from May to mid-September. One of Ibizas strong sides is its intensive heterosexual club-

Spain Balearic Islands - Ibiza

Ibiza

1. Monroe's Café / Hotel Marigna / Café Central / Magnus Café
2. Casa Campo Hotel
3. Privilege Danceclub (8km)
4. El Olivo Restaurant
5. Dalt Vila Restaurant
6. Anfora Disco
7. El Portalon Restaurant
8. El Bistro Restaurant
9. Angelo Bar
10. Dome Bar
11. Studio Restaurant
12. Waunas Bar
13. Pheno'Men Bar
14. Samsara Showbar / Indira Bar
15. Foc i Fum Bar
16. Exis Bar
17. JJ Bar
18. Teatro Bar
19. Galeria Bar
20. GC Bar
21. Leon Bar
22. Capricho Bar
23. La Muralla Bar
24. La Scala Restaurant
25. Incognito Bar

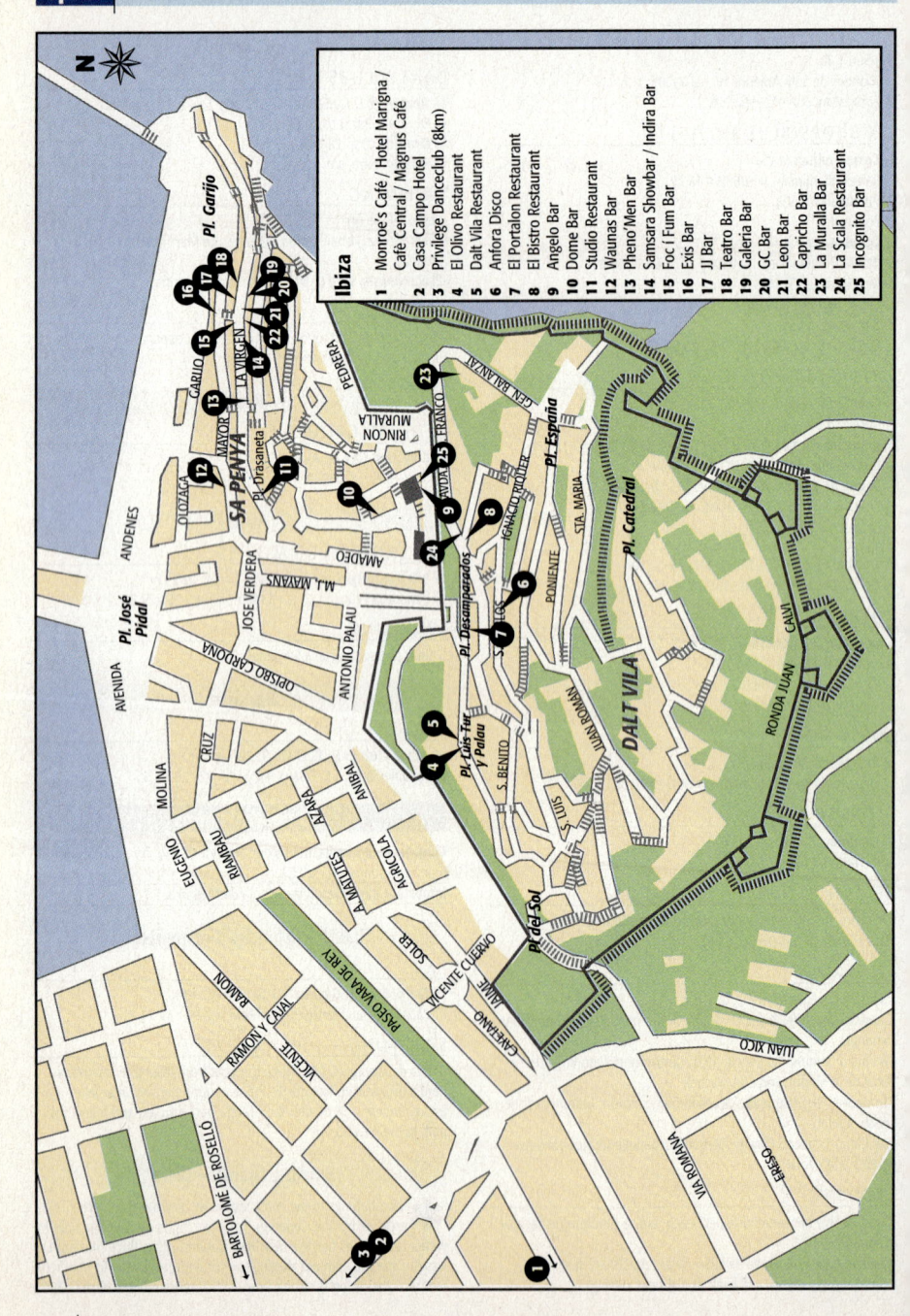

Balearic Islands - Ibiza | Spain

nightlife, which is open and friendly towards gays. Moreover, the gay beach Es Cavallet and the extremely short distances of the gay scene, are a delight. Note, that the 'gay round' begins after supper at about 11-12 p.m. in C/. de la Virgen. After a stopover on the city walls (C/. Santa Lucia), you move up to Dalt Vila for dancing and cruising. If you stay outside Ibiza-town, hiring a car -which is however expensive- is rewarding. Nevertheless, the public bus transport is dense and includes the routes to the gay beach. A tip: If you crave for a quiet day on a really beautiful beach, go to Formentera with the ferry (60 minutes ride). Marvellous!

Ibiza gehört zu den wichtigsten schwulen Badeorten Europas. Während die kanarische Playa del Inglés vor allem ein Winterziel ist und Sitges zusätzlich das nahe Barcelona bietet, ist Ibiza (ibizenkisch: Eivissa) ein absolutes Sommer-Topziel von Mai bis Mitte September.
Eine von Ibizas Stärken ist sein intensives Hetero-Disco-Nightlife, in dem auch Schwule getrost mitmischen können. Dazu kommt der schwule Traum-Strand Es Cavallet und die extrem kurzen Wege der schwulen Szene. Dabei ist zu beachten, daß die „schwule Runde" nach dem Essen gegen 23/24 h in der C/. de la Virgen beginnt. Über eine Zwischenstation an der Stadtmauer (C/. Santa Lucia) geht's dann hinauf nach Dalt Vila zum Tanzen und Cruisen.
Gerade wenn man außerhalb von Ibiza-Stadt wohnt lohnt ein -allerdings teures- Mietauto. Das Busnetz ist allerdings dicht und reicht bis an den schwulen Strand.
Zum Schluß noch ein Tip: bei Lust auf einen ruhigen und richtig schönen Strand-Tag fährt man in 60 Minuten mit der Fähre nach Formentera. Herrlich.

Ibiza est l'île gaie numéro 1 d'Europe. Si Playa de Ingles, sur les Canaries, est avant tout une destination pour l'hiver et si Sitges offre l'avantage d'être à proximité de Barcelone, Ibiza (les autochtones disent "Eivissa") est, elle, le must touristique de la saison estivale. Une des principales attractions d'Ibiza sont les boîtes de nuit hétéros que fréquentent aussi les gais. A voir absolument: la plage gaie "Es Cavallet". L'avantage d'Ibiza, c'est qu'on peut tout faire à pied. Le soir, ça commence à bouger aux environs de minuit, après le dîner, dans la C. de la Virgen. Passez par les remparts (C. Santa Lucia), puis montez à Dalt Vila pour aller danser et draguer. Ceux qui logent à l'extérieur d'Ibiza auront toujours intérêt, même si cela revient cher, à louer une voiture. La ville et ses environs sont bien desservis par les bus qui vous conduisent même jusqu'à la plage gaie. Ceux qui auront envie de passer une journée au calme et au soleil, prendront le bac pour Formentera (une heure de trajet) et passeront une journée inoubliable.

Ibiza es uno de los balnearios gay más importantes de Europa. Mientras la Playa del Inglés de las Islas Canarias es sobre todo interesante en invierno y Sitges ofrece la cercanía a Barcelona, Ibiza es el destino veraniego ideal para gays entre los meses de Mayo hasta mediados de Septiembre. La isla se distingue por su fuerte y animada marcha nocturna heterosexual, donde los gays son siempre bienvenidos. No debe quedar sin mencionar la playa gay de ensueño "Es Cavallet", y la ventaja de la cercanía entre sí de todos los establecimientos gay. El llamado tour gay (ronda gay), empieza después de la cena entre las 23 y 24:00 horas en la calle de la Virgen. Después de una parada en la muralla de la ciudad en la calle Santa Lucia, se sube en dirección Dalt Vila para bailar e ir de cruising. Para los que residan fuera de la ciudad merece la pena alquilar un coche (aúnque es bastante caro). Sin embargo, la red de transporte público es densa y los autobuses llegan hasta las playas gay. Un consejo: Para disfrutar un día tranquilo en la playa, se recomienda una excursión a la encantadora isla de Formentor (approx. 1 hora en barco).

Ibiza fa parte delle stazioni balneari più importanti d'Europa. Mentre la playa del inglés delle Canarie è una meta squisitamente invernale e Sitges, per la prossimità a Barcellona, rientra nel turismo urbano-culturale, Ibiza è in assoluto una meta estiva fiorente da maggio fino a metà settembre. Una carta vincente di Ibiza è la vita notturna nelle discoteche per eterosessuali, nelle quali anche i gay si mescolano armoniosamente. A ciò si aggiungono l'onirica spiaggia gay Es Cavallet e le viette della zona gay. Ricordatevi che il giro gay inizia dopo cena tra le 23 e le 24 nella c. de la Virgen. Dopo una pausa alla cinta muraria (c. Santa Lucia) si sale a Dalt Vila a ballare e a cercare compagnia. Se si vive fuori da Ibiza paese conviene, anche se è costoso, noleggiare un'auto. Il servizio degli autobus è efficiente e raggiunge la spiaggia gay. Infine ancora un consiglio: se avete voglia di trascorrere una giornata su una spiaggia bella e tranquilla Formentera è a solo un'ora di traghetto. Favoloso!

TOURIST INFO

■ **Oficina de Turismo**
Passeig Vara del Rey, 13 ✉ 07800 ☎ 971 30 19 00

BARS

■ **Angelo** (AC B G lj MA OS) 22-4 h, closed Mid Oct-Apr
C/ Vía Alfonso XII, 11 ✉ 07800 ☎ 971 31 03 35
■ **Atrium. L'** (B g OS YG) 22.30-4 h, Winter only WE
C/ Vía Alfonso XII, 3 ✉ 07800
Trendy and popular.
■ **Bar J. J.** (B G lj MA OS) 22-3 h, closed Mid Oct-Apr
C/ de la Virgen, 79 ✉ 07800 ☎ 971 31 02 47
Terrace to observe the people, balcony overlooking the harbour.
■ **Bar Teatro** (B G MA OS) 22-? h, closed Oct-Apr
C/ de la Virgen, 83 ✉ 07800 ☎ 971 31 32 25
A very nice terrace to see and be seen.

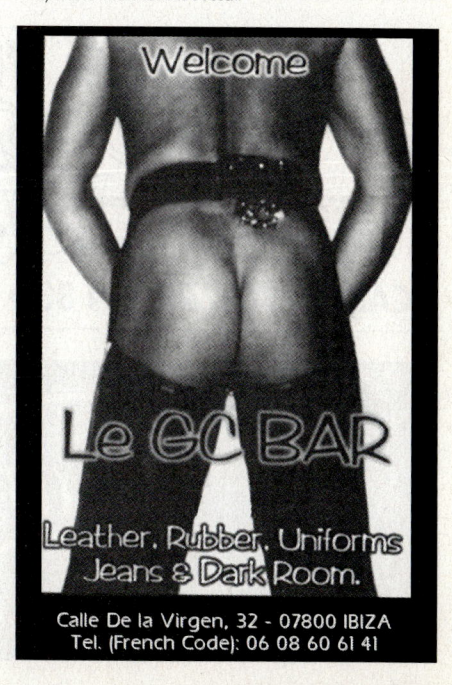

Welcome

Le GC BAR

Leather. Rubber. Uniforms
Jeans & Dark Room.

Calle De la Virgen, 32 - 07800 IBIZA
Tel. (French Code): 06 08 60 61 41

Spain | Balearic Islands - Ibiza

Pheno' Men

Night Bar

Terrace - Dance Floor

Dark Room

Calle de la Virgen 22
IBIZA

Gran Canaria - Torremolinos - Sitges - Benidorm
Mykonos - Fort Lauderdale - Key West - San Francisco - Orlando
Amsterdam - London - Wien - Berlin - Hamburg - Sydney - Kapstadt

IBIZA

www.discustravel.de

Tel.: + 49 (0)6 21 - 40 96 27
Fax: + 49 (0)6 21 - 44 13 40
e-Mail: info@discustravel.de

GiV- Reisen / Discustravel
Schwetzinger Str. 93
D - 68165 Mannheim - Germany

BAR TEATRO

CALLE DE LA VIRGEN 83 • IBIZA • TEL. 971 - 31 32 25

Bar J.J.

C/.de La Virgen, 79 - tel 971 31 02 47 - 07800 - Ibiza - Baleares

Balearic Islands - Ibiza **Spain**

BAR LA MURALLA

SA CARROSSA, 3
DALT VILA

IBIZA
TEL. 971 30 18 83

---

beach bar and restaurant
open every day

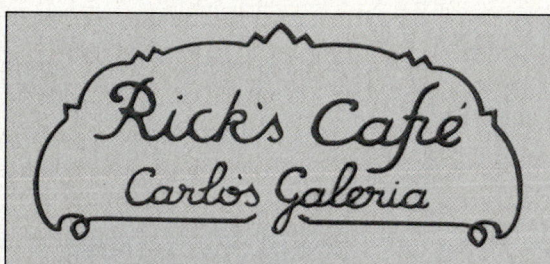

Chiringay

PLAYA ES CAVALLET

Rick's Café
Carlos Galeria
Restaurant-Bar

Calle Valladolid 5
Port Des Torrent
07830 San Agustin-San Jose

Tel. 971 34 76 54
Fax 971 34 69 11

■ **Camp Nonsense** (AC B G OS) Open all year 22-4 h,
Sa Carossa, 4 ✉ 07800 *(Dalt Vila)*
■ **Capricho Bar** (B G MA OS) 22-4 h
C/ de la Virgen, 42 ✉ 07800 ☎ 971 19 24 71
■ **Chiringay** (! B F G MA) Apr-Oct 9.30-21 h
Platja Es Cavallet ✉ 07800 ☎ 971 18 74 29
■ **Dome** (B g OS YG) 22.30-4 h, closed Oct-Apr
C/ Via Alfonso XII, 5 ✉ 07800 ☎ 971 31 14 56
Trendy and popular.
■ **Es Passadis** (AC B G MA OS) 22-4 h, in winter only WE
C/ des Passadis 5, bajos ✉ 07800 ☎ 971 316 358
Carribean music and coctails.
■ **Exis** (B G MA OS) Apr-Oct 22-4 h
C/ de la Virgen, 57 ✉ 07800
■ **Fabu ! Velvet** (A B G MA OS s) 21-? h
C/ de la Virgen, 72 ✉ 07800 ☎ 971 31 11 29
Specialized in coctails, apartments also available.

■ **Foc í Fum** (B G MA OS) 21-4 h, closed in winter
C/ de la Virgen, 55 ✉ 07800 ☎ 971 31 33 80
■ **Galeria** (A B G MA OS) 21.30-3 h, closed 20.Oct-Apr
C/ de la Virgen, 64 ✉ 07800
Bar and art gallery.
■ **GC Bar** (B DR G LJ MA s VS) 22 h-?
C/ de la Virgen, 32 ✉ 07800 ☎ +31 608 60 61 41
Leather, uniform, rubber & jeans bar.
■ **Incognito** (B G MA OS) 21.30-4 h
C/ Santa Lucia, 23-21 ✉ 07800 ☎ 971 19 13 15
■ **Indira** (A AC B CC G MA OS)
C/ de la Virgen, 40 ✉ 07800
■ **Joey's** (AC B DR G lj MA OS s) 23-4 h
Sa Carossa 4, Dalt Vila ✉ 07800 ☎ 971 31 20 49
Open all year. From June to September Joey's Surprise Night at 0100.
■ **Leon Bar** (B G MA OS) 22-? h
C/ de la Virgen, 62 ✉ 07800

Spain — Balearic Islands - Ibiza

El Portalón
CASA DE COMIDAS
AÑO MCMLXXII
Plaza Desamparados, nos. 1 y 2
Teléfonos: 971 30 39 01 - 971 30 08 52
Ibiza - Baleares

RESTAURANTE Can den parra
Calle San Rafael, n°3 - Dalt Vila
IBIZA
Teléfonos 971 39 11 14 - 971 30 39 01

■ **Muralla. La** (AC G MA OS) 22-4 h
Sa Carossa, 13 ✉ 07800 ☎ 971 30 18 83
■ **Nada. La** (AC f G MA OS) 20-4 h, closed Jan
C/ de la Virgen, 10 ✉ 07800 ☎ 971 31 12 26
■ **Pheno'Men** (AC B D DR G MA OS) 21.30-4 h
C/ de la Virgen, 22 ✉ 07800
■ **Rick's Café** (A B F GLM)
C/ Valladolid 5, Port Des Torrent, San Augustin ✉ 07830 (San Jose) ☎ 971 34 76 54
■ **Waunas** (B G MA OS) 20-?h, Thu-Tue also 12-15h
C/ d'Enmig, 9 ✉ 07800 ☎ 971 31 56 60

CAFES

■ **Bandidos** (A BF F G OS) 10-2h, Nov-Apr closed
Sa Carossa, 11 ✉ 07800
■ **Bistro. El** (ACB BF CC F G OS) 8-23 h, Sun closed
Av Isidoro Macabitch, 23 ✉ 07800 (Opposite bus station to Salinas and airport) ☎ 971 39 98 60
■ **Central** (B BF f g MA) 8.30-20.30 h, closed Nov-Apr
C/ Galicia, 6 ✉ 07800 (Figueretas) ☎ 971 30 17 26
Home-made German cakes and food.
■ **Kitsch** (B BF F G MA OS) 12-3h
C/ Ramón Muntaner, 26 ✉ 07800 (Figueretes) ☎ 971 39 90 13
■ **Magnus** (AC B BF F G MA OS) 10-3h, Nov-Mar closed
Paseo Marítimo ✉ 07800 (Figueretas) ☎ 971 39 25 65
Hot meals all day.
■ **Monroe's** (AC B BF CC F glm MA) 9.30-3 h
C/ Ramón Muntaner, 33 bajo ✉ 07800 (Figueretas)
☎ 971 39 25 41
Drag shows Wed Fri sun 22.30 h. Home-made English food.

DANCECLUBS

■ **Anfora Discoteca** (! AC B D DR G lj MA s VS YG) 0-6 h, Sun shows, closed 12.Oct-30.Apr
C/ San Carlos, 7 ✉ 07800 (Dalt Vila) ☎ 971 30 28 93
2 floors. Shows.
■ **Privilege** (B D f g YG) 22.30-8 h, Fri one big gay part in the disco, closed Oct-May
(San Rafael) ☎ 971 30 40 81
Also on Mon many gays. Special party nights frequently advertised all over Ibiza. Admission Ptas 6.500. Best from 5, Fri from 3.30/4 h.
■ **Space** (B D g OS MA) 8-till late afternoon; Tue, Thu, Sun also by night
(Playa d'en Bossa, Sant Josep) ☎ 971 39 67 93
Techno. Sat Gay only.

RESTAURANTS

■ **Bistro. El** (F g H MA OS) 20-1 h, closed Nov-Mar
C/ Sa Carossa, 15 ✉ 07800 (Dalt Vila) ☎ 971 39 32 03
French cuisine. Also studios & apartments available.
■ **Can Den Parra** (b CC F g MA OS) 20-1 h, closed in winter
C/ San Rafael, 3 ✉ 07800 (Dalt Vila) ☎ 971 39 11 14
Has a nice terrace from which you can watch people going to and from the bars of Dalt Vila. Fresh fish and grilled meat specialities.

CAN DOMINGO DE CAN BOTJA RESTAURANT

Carretera d'Eivissa a Sant Josep, km. 9,800
07830 Sant josep - Eivissa
Tel. 971 80 01 84

Balearic Islands - Ibiza | Spain

El Bistro

Restaurante
Plaza Sa Carossa, 15 · Dalt Vila
Ibiza
Tel. 971 393203

Café
Av. Isidoro Macabitch, 23
Tel. 971 399860

Studios – Apartments
Ibiza

RESTAURANTE EL OLIVO

PLAÇA DE VILA
TEL. 971 - 30 06 80

IBIZA

RESTAURANTE Beda's la Scala

Joachim & Beda
Sa Carrossa, 7 • Dalt Vila
Teléfono 971 - 30 03 83 • IBIZA
beda_s_lascala@hotmail.com

■ **Can Domingo de Can Botja** (AC B CC F g MA OS) 20-24 h
Carretera d'Eivissa a Sant Josep, km 9.800 ✉ 07830 *(Restaurant in an old finca in the countryside)* ☎ 971 800 184
Cocina mediterránea, ca 5000 ptas per person for dinner.

■ **Dalt Vila** (B CC F g MA OS) Apr-Oct 20-1 h
Plaça de Vila, 3-4 ✉ 07800 *(Dalt Vila)* ☎ 971 30 55 24
Basque and catalan cuisine.

■ **Images of China** (B CC F G) 19.30-23.30h
C/ Isidoro Macabitch, 3 *(20 min by car from Ibiza town)*
☎ 971 33 92 82
Ken from Hongkong prepares original chinese food. reservation recommended.

■ **Olivo. El** (b F g MA OS) 19-1 h
Plaça de Vila, 7 ✉ 07800 *(Dalt Vila)* ☎ 971 30 06 80
International cuisine; prices are surprisingly reasonable for the quality offered.

■ **Plaza Santa Gertrudis. La** (F g MA) 20-0.30 h closed Nov-Mar
Plaça Santa Gertrudis ✉ 07800 *(Santa Gertrudis)* ☎ 971 19 70 75
Bus from Ibiza City to San Miguel ca. 20 minutes.

■ **Portalón. El** (B CC F g MA OS) 12-16, 20-1 h
Plaza Desamparados, 1-2 ✉ 07800 *(Dalt Vila)* ☎ 971 30 39 01
Local and international cuisine.

■ **Rocky's. Restaurante** (b F g MA OS) 19-2 h, Nov-Easter closed
C/ de la Virgen, 6 ✉ 07800 ☎ 971 31 01 07
International food, specialist for Paellas.

■ **Scala. La** (B F G MA OS) 20-1 h, winter Mon Tue closed
C/ Sa Carrossa, 7 ✉ 07800 *(Dalt Vila)* ☎ 971 30 03 83
Swiss & international cuisine. Nice terrace with fresh flower decoration.

■ **Studio** (b F g MA OS) 19.30-1.30 h
C/ de la Virgen, 4 ✉ 07800 *(2nd entrance: Plaça de Sa Drassaneta, 12)* ☎ 971 31 53 68
Fresh quality produce used for à la carte, set and vegetarian menus.

Spain — Balearic Islands - Ibiza

Aparthotel NAVILA

Pepita Ferrer Ferrer
GERENTE

San Luis, 1 - Tels. 971 39 05 73 - 971 30 39 01
Fax 971 30 08 52   07800 IBIZA

HOTEL MARIGNA IBIZA

ABIERTO TODO EL AÑO / GANZJÄHRIG GEÖFFNET / ALL YEAR OPEN

Calle Al Sabini 18 - Figueretas - E - 07800 Ibiza - Baleares

44 HABITACIONES / ROOMS / ZIMMER CON / WITH / MIT SAT-TV

DELUXE CON / WITH / MIT AIRCONDITION

HOTEL - BAR

DESAYUNO - BUFFET
BREAKFAST - BUFFET
FRÜHSTÜCK - BÜFETT
9'00 — 13'00

TERRAZA CENITAL
ROOF TERRACE
DACH TERRASSE
CON / WITH / MIT
JACUZZI / WHIRLPOOL
SAUNA

Tel. +34 971 304 912 · Fax: +34 971 304 689
E-Mail: hotelmarigna@ctv.es · www.hotelmarigna.com

SHOWS

■ **Samsara** (B g MA OS STV) Mar-Sep 21-3h. Show 0.30 h.
C/ de la Virgen, 144 ☎ 07800 ☎ 619 631 634 (mobile)
International shows.

SAUNAS/BATHS

■ **Hamman Meeting Point** (B DR F G msg SA SB VS)
C/ Galicia 1 (Figueretas) ☎ 971 39 44

FASHION SHOPS

■ **Ovlas**
C/ de la Virgen, 7 ☎ 07800 ☎ 971 19 29 20

PROPERTY SERVICES

■ **Exclusive Ibiza Properties** (G H PI) Mon-Fri 10-14, 17-20h
PO Box 1133 ☎ 07800 ☎ 971 33 65 36 ☎ 670 83 80 06 (Mobile)
☎ 971 30 35 84 ✉ michaelholtz@ole.com
Houses in the countryside of the island with swimming-pool and apartments on the sea front in Ibiza city. Special properties are rented in the absence of the owners.

HOTELS

■ **Can Romanica** (BF glm H MA OS PI SOL)
Ctra Sant Josep km 4, Puig Gros ✉ 07819 *(PO Box 49, St. Jorge)*
☎ (908) 63 81 28 (mobile)
☎ 971 30 25 66
Rates Double Ptas 10.500-14.500. Six spectacular decorated rooms in mountainside villa. 10 minutes by car to Ibiza city and gay beach.

■ **Casa Alexio** (AC B BF G H MA PI WH)
Barrio Ses Torres 16, Jesus ✉ 07819 *(Talamanca)*
☎ 971 31 42 49 ☎ 639 632 522
☎ 971 31 26 19
✉ alexio@alexio.com
🌐 www.alexio.com
Beautiful and luxurious gay house. Rooms with bath, AC and sat-TV. Rental cars available for guests and with a car only 5 minutes to the gay bars.

■ **Casa Campo Guest House** (BF Glm H MA OS PI)
Club San Rafael, 18 ✉ 07816 *(San Rafael)* ☎ 971 19 82 01
☎ 971 19 80 53
Location 5 min from Ibiza town. Guest house in country style, beautifully furnished.

Balearic Islands - Ibiza **Spain**

- A private and peaceful place
- Only 5 minutes away from the Gay Bars
- Marvellous view to Ibiza town, to the sea and Formentera island
- 2 minutes from the beach
- Air-condition
- Whirlpool
- T.V. in all rooms

CASA ALEXIO

BARRIO SES TORRES, 16
APDO.: N° 10.062
07819 JESUS - IBIZA
TEL: (0034) 971 314 249
Movil: (0034) 639 632 522
FAX: (0034) 971 312 619
E-mail-alexio@alexio.com
www.alexio.com

Spain — Balearic Islands - Ibiza

Sauna Hammam "meeting point"

new in Ibiza

- CUARTO OSCURO - DARKROOMS
- CABINAS - RELAX ROOMS
- SAUNA - FINNISH SAUNA
- BAÑO DE VAPOR - HAMMAM (TURKISH BATH)
- BAR/RESTAURANTE
- SALA VIDEO - VIDEO ROOM
- MASAJE - MASSAGE
- CERCA APARCAMIENTO - NEAR PARKING ZONES

Hammam "meeting point"
Calle Galicia n·1 (figueretas) Ibiza
tel/Fax - 971 39 44 90

Balearic Islands - Ibiza ▶ Balearic Islands - Mallorca | Spain

La Finca Ibiza

Gästehaus oberhalb Ibiza Stadt /
Guesthouse near Ibiza Town

3 km v. Ibiza Stadt ★ Romantic Garden ★ Pool
★ Sauna ★ Fitnessgeräte ★ Sonnenterrassen

App. mit Du/WC ★ Airconditon ★ Salon ★ Sat-TV
Kaminzimmer ★ Frühstück bis 13 Uhr ★ kleine Küche
Oase zum Wohlfühlen

La Finca, C./del Cabussó 11, 07817 Sant Jordi /
IBIZA
Tel/Fax 0034 971 301004
Handy Deutschl. 0172-411 63 81

■ **Don Quijote** (b BF g H MA PI)
C/ Pais Basc, 10 ✉ 07800 *(Figueretas)* ☏ 971 30 18 69
📠 971 34 13 58
Near the Beach. All rooms with bath, telephone and most with terrace.

■ **Finca Ibiza. La** (! AC B BF E f G H OS SA PI WO) 0-24 h
C/ del Cabussó 11, Sant Jordi ✉ 07817 *(3 km for Ibiza city center)*
☏ 971 30 10 04
📠 971 30 10 04
Double rooms & suites. Airport pickup. Wonderful breakfasts.

■ **Hotel Canonigo** (B g H MA)
C/ Mayor, 8 ✉ 07800 *(Dalt Vila)* ☏ 971 30 38 84
📠 971 30 78 43 📧 hotelcanonigo@ctv.es
Elegant, renovated hotel in a 14th century building.

■ **Hotel Marigna** (AC B BF CC f G H lj OS PI SA WH) All year
C/ Al Sabini, 18 ✉ 08700 *(Figueretas, 100m from the beach)*
☏ 971 39 99 42 ☏ 971 30 49 12 ☏ 971 30 46 89
📧 hotelmarigna@ctv.es
🌐 www.hotelmarigna.com
44 rooms with bath/shower, phone, sat-TV. 24 h reception. Bar open 10-1 h.

■ **Navila Aparthotel** (AC b g H MA OS PI) All year
C/ San Luis, 1 ✉ 07800 *(Dalt Vila)* ☏ 971 39 05 73
☏ 971 30 39 01
📠 971 30 08 52
All rooms with bath, WC, phone, satellite TV, kitchen and big terraces with sea view.

APARTMENTS

■ **Apartamentos El Olivo** (AC CC G) Apr-Oct
C/ Manuel Sora, 16 ✉ 07800 *(Close to the gay scene)*
☏ 971 19 13 65 📠 971 19 13 65 📧 ick2@retemail.es
With bath/shower, kitchen, balcony, own key. cleaning service available.

■ **Casa Galería** (GLM H) May-Sep
C/ Montblanc 2, Sant. Jorgi ✉ 07817 *(On the bus-route Ibiza-Salinas, 200 m from the nearest bus stop).* ☏ 971 39 64 64
☏ 639-81 12 54 *(mobile)*
Two double rooms with Bath/WC, Sat-TV, radio, hair-dryer, own key, room service. With car park and garden.

■ **Cenit Apartements** (g H PI)
Los Molinos, Figueretas ✉ 07800 ☏ 971 30 14 04
📠 971 30 07 54
Rates Ptas 9.000 (high season).

■ **Chiringay Casa** (G H)
Platja Es Cavallet ✉ 07800 ☏ 971 18 74 29
For 3-6 persons. For reservation ask in Café Chiringay.

■ **Delfin Verde Apartments** (G H)
C/ Garigo, 2 ✉ 07800
☏ +31/20/421 00 00
Reservations through "De Gay Krant Reisservice".

■ **Pepita Apartamentos** (G H)
c/o El Portalón Restaurant, Plaça Desamparados, 1-2 *(Dalt Vila & Figueretas)* ☏ 971 30 39 01
☏ 971 30 08 52 📠 971 30 08 52
All with bath/shower, WC, some with balcony/terrace.

■ **Ripoll. Apartments** (g H)
C/ Vincente Cubruo, 10/14 ✉ 07800
☏ +31/20/421 00 00
Reservation through "De Gay Krant Reisservice", Amsterdam, NL.

■ **Rucar Apartments** (CC g) Open all year
☏ 971 39 11 41 📠 971 39 11 41
All with bath/wc/kitchen/television/own key.

SWIMMING

Nude bathing is permitted everywhere outside of town, where signs reading "Playa natural" show the way to the beach.
-**Platja Es Cavallet** (G NU) (from Ibiza-Town follow the signs to the airport, then to Platya Es Cavallet. P possible at the beach. Walk along the beach or the dunes to the far end with the bar Chiringay. Action is going on in the bushes behind the bar towards the other side of the peninsula).

CRUISING

-Southwest corner at top of old city walls (above La Muralla Bar on opposite side of the street)
-Playa Figueretas (nights and early mornmings after barhopping)
-Rocas (entrada: Tunel frente al Ayuntamento/ entrance: tunnel oppostite of the townhall)

Balearic Islands - Mallorca - **Cala Millor**

CRUISING

Natural Parc "Punta de Amer" between Cala Millor and Sa Coma, at the Castle.

Spain | Balearic Islands - Mallorca

Son Sebastian

Apartado de correos 332
Codigo postal 07620
Llucmajor
Mallorca > Baleares > Spain
Tel: 0034-971120935 · fax: 0034-971669073
From Germany and England tel: 0034-670701591

E-mail: sonsebastian@navegalia.com · Web: www.sonsebastian.com

Privately situated in the beautiful Mallorcan countryside only 20 minutes from the city of Palma and from the best beaches on the island, Son Sebastian combines isolation and accessibility with a choice of luxurious suites or double bedrooms to offer the best gay accommodation on Mallorca. An ideal Holiday destination. We can't always guarantee the weather but we can guarantee the warmest and friendliest atmosphere.

To make your reservation or to receive more information about Son Sebastian please call, E-mail or visit our web site. We look forward to hearing from you.

Balearic Islands - Mallorca - **Llucmajor**

HOTELS

■ **Son Sebastian** (BF GLM)
Apartado de Correos 332 ✉ 07620 ☎ 971 12 09 35
📠 971 66 90 73 📧 sonsebastian@navegalia.com
🌐 www.sonsebastian.com
Luxurious suites and double bedrooms on the countryside only 20 min from Palma. Call, e-mail or check website for more info.

Balearic Islands - Mallorca - **Palma de Mallorca**

BARS

■ **Abaco** (B E g MA) 21-2 h
C/ San Juan, 1 ✉ 07012 *(close to old stock market Lonja)*
☎ 971 72 49 39
Best from 22 h, nice patio in historic building, classic music.

■ **Africa** (B GLM MA N) 12-15, 18.30-24 h, closed Tue and Sun lunch
C/ Robert Graves 17, El Terreno ✉ 07015 *(100 m from Plaza Gomila)* ☎ 971 731 548
Small but friendly.

■ **Aries Pub** (B DR G MA VS) 22-8 h, WE 23-8h.
C/ Porras, 3 ✉ 07015 *(at Av. Joan Miró)* ☎ 971 73 78 99
Darkroom with cabins.

■ **Boy. El** (AC B d G MA OS s) 21-4h
Plaza Gomila ✉ 07015 *(Terrace Plaza Gomila, 2nd floor, entrance: C/ Bellver, 3)*
Great terrace with outdoor-bar, happy hour 21-22.30h.

■ **Flesh** (AC B d G MA s VS) 22-4 h
Av. Joan Miró, 68 ✉ 07015 ☎ 971 455 146

Marcus PUB

DISCO PUB

CUARTO OSCURO
PANTALLA GIGANTE
SALA DE VIDEO

ABIERTO DE 22 h A ...

Joan Miró, 54
Palma de Mallorca Telf. 971286144

http://members.xoom.com/marcuscb

Balearic Islands - Mallorca | **Spain**

HOTEL

- COMPLETLY NEW RENOVATED
- NEW MANAGEMENT
- FRIENDLY STAFF
- 24 – HOURS – RECEPTION
- ROOMS WITH: INDIVIDUAL, DOUBLE & SUITES CABLE TV, FRIDGE

SAUNA

FINNISH SAUNA
STEAM BATH
JACUZZI

RELAX ROOM
DARK ROOM

BAR

MOST CRUISY BAR IN TOWN
DARKROOM, CABINS, PORNO
NEWEST MUSIC

C/Porras, 3 (Gomila) – Palma
Tel.: 00-34-971-73 78 99
Fax: 00-34-971-78 06 36
Special Low Season Prices

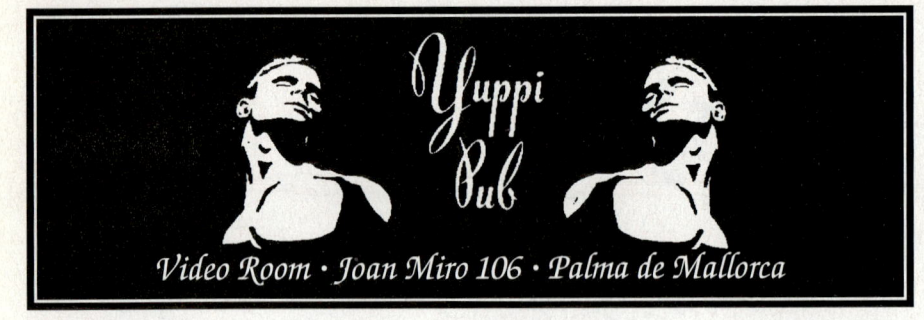

Spain | Balearic Islands - Mallorca

Yuppi Pub
Video Room · Joan Miro 106 · Palma de Mallorca

■ **GE** (AC d DR G LJ MA VS) 24-4 h
Av. Joan Miró, 73 bajo ☎ 639 304 008 (mobile)
■ **Marcus Pub** (AC B CC D DR G MA r snu VS WE) 22-? h
Av. Juan Miró 54 ✉ 07015 ☎ 971 286 144
■ **Querelle** (AC B G MA SNU stv VS) 23-4 h, show 24 h
Av. Joan Miró, 52 ✉ 07015
■ **Status Pub** (AC B E G MA) 22-4 h
Av. Joan Miró 38, Gomila ✉ 07014 ☎ 971 45 40 30
Popular & elegant with beautiful, fresh flowers - new milenium, new decoration.
■ **Yedra. La** (AC B glm MA YG) 23-? h, closed Sun
Av. Joan Miró 47 ✉ 07015
Popular late bar for all kind of people. Best from 6 h.
■ **Yuppi Club** (AC B DR G p VS YG) 22-6?, Fri Sat -8 h
Av. Joan Miró 106 ✉ 07015 ☎ 639 71 90 85
Popular.

CAFES
■ **Sarao** (A AC B bf F g MA OS s W) Mon-Fri 11.30h-?h, Sat 18-?h
C/ Costa Llobera, 15F ✉ 07005 *(Near Plaza Espanya)*
☎ 971 46 21 64
■ **Tasca. La** (AC B f GLM MA OS VS) 18-4 h, Sun closed
Av. Joan Miro 41 ✉ 07014 ☎ 971 45 04 68

DANCECLUBS
■ **Black Cat** (! AC B D DR G MA S VS YG) 24-7 h, best from 2 h,
Show 3.30 h, winter: closed Mon
Av. Joan Miró 75 ✉ 07015
Good show, very popular.

RESTAURANTS
■ **Casita. La** (AC B CC F G) Every day.
Av. Joan Miró, 68 ✉ 07015 *(Near Plaza Gomila)* ☎ 971 737 587
French cuisine, newly renovated and enlarged.

STATUS PUB
Joan Miró, 38 - Gomila
Tel. 971 454 030
07014 Palma de Mallorca

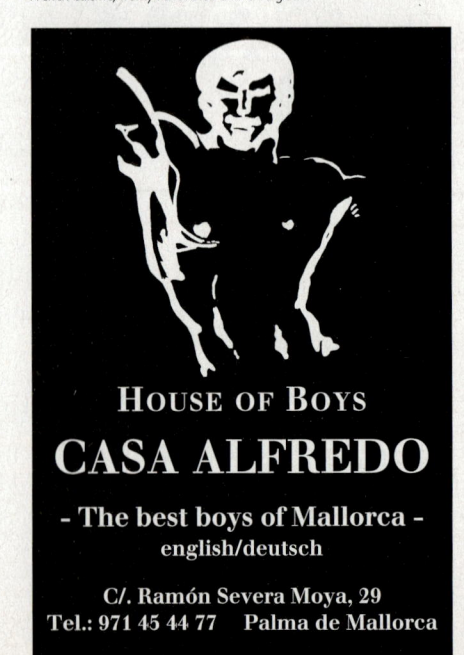

HOUSE OF BOYS
CASA ALFREDO
- The best boys of Mallorca -
english/deutsch

C/. Ramón Severa Moya, 29
Tel.: 971 45 44 77   Palma de Mallorca

Balearic Islands - Mallorca **Spain**

MALLORCA

CLEAN & COMFORTABLE
ALL ROOMS EN-SUITE
ATTRACTIVE BAR WITH
GARDEN TERRACE
CONTINENTAL BREAKFAST
UNTIL MIDDAY
24HR RECEPTION
IN THE MIDDLE OF
THE GAY SCENE

HOTEL ROSAMAR

Avenida Joan Miró, 74
Palma de Mallorca
07015 Spain

Tel: 00 34 971 732723
Fax: 00 34 971 283828
e-mail: rosamar@ocea.es
URL: http://illes.balears.net/rosamar/

CB
La mejor selección de chicos para tu relax
Antoni Ribas nº 42 - Bajos / Tel. 971 460 825
http://www.mallorcaservice.com/clubboys

■ **Fred's Bistro** (B F g) 19-?, Tue closed
C/ Virgilio, 21 (Ca'n Pastilla) *(Near gay beach, bus 15)*
☎ 971 74 36 83
■ **Jardin. El** (B F GLM OS) Tue-Sat 19:30-?, Sun lunch 12.30-16h
Passatge C'an Fustera, 10 ✉ 07184 (Calvia, 20 min from Palma)
☎ 971 67 08 40
A new restaurant bar in a wonderful setting. Outdoor terrace with classical music. Bar open til late.

SEX SHOPS/BLUE MOVIES
■ **Amsterdam** (g VS) 11-22 h, Sun closed
Av. Argentina, 34 ✉ 07011 ☎ 971 73 97 34
■ **Erotic Toy Stories** (CC G VS) 10-21 h, Sun closed
Passatge Maneu, 10 ✉ 07002 ☎ 971 72 78 65

■ **Master's Sex Shop** (g VS) 10.30-20.30 h, closed Sun
C/ Gabriel LLabrés,11 *(near Plaza Saint Antonio)* ☎ 971 24 82 09
■ **Non Stop** (g VS) Mon-Sat 11.30-14, 16-22 h, closed Sun
Av. Joan Miró, 38 ✉ 07015 *(Local 8)* ☎ 971 45 63 40
■ **Sex Shop Amsterdam II** (g VS) 11-14, 17-22, Sun 17-21 h
Av. Joan Miró, 15 ☎ 971 45 73 70
Video cabins, videos for sale, books and magazines

HOUSE OF BOYS
■ **Casa Alfredo** (B CC G PI R VS) 15-3 h
C/ Ramón Servera Moya, 29 ✉ 07014 *(Near Plaza Gomila)*
☎ 971 45 44 77
■ **Club Boys** (A AC CC G MG msg p R VS) 0-24 h
C/ Antonio Ribas 42 ✉ 07006 ☎ 971 46 08 25

El Jardín

"El Jardin" A 200 year old farmhouse in a beautiful garden setting. Opposite the Town Hall in delightful Calvia. Dine in our elegant Dinning room with log fires and romantic music, or in the summer, on our large terrace.
Enjoy superb food from our Award winning Chef;
Tel. (0034) 974 67 08 40 or Fax (0034) 974 67 03 93

Spain — Balearic Islands - Mallorca

**SAUNA FINLANDESIA - SAUNA DE VAPOR
GIMNASIO - PISCINA CLIMATIZADA
SOLARIUM FACIAL - SALA DE VIDEO**

- In retirement For Sale, to rent or exchange possible -

SPARTACUS SAUNA

A must for the international tourist!
Santo Espiritu, 8 bajos
Tel. 971 72 50 07 - 07002 Palma de Mallorca

www.espanet.com/spartacus/

SAUNAS/BATHS

■ **Aries** (B DR f G MA msg SA SB VS WH) 16-24 h
C/ Porras, 3 ✉ 07015 *(near Plaza Gomila, entrance in Hotel Aries)*
☎ 971 73 52 97
Part of a gay bar and hotel complex. Admission 1.500 Ptas, cabins & large screen television.

■ **Spartacus Sauna** (! B DR G MA PI SA SB SOL VS WO) 16-22 h
C/ Santo Espiritu, bajos ✉ 07002 *(near Plaza Mayor)*
☎ 971 72 50 07
Recently renovated, nicely decorated with art and sculptures. Admission 1.400 Ptas.

TRAVEL AND TRANSPORT

■ **Gay Friendly - Club de Viajes** (CC G) Mon-Fri 9-14h, 16-20h
C/ Bartomeu Sureda i Miserol, 4A ✉ 07011 ☎ 971 60 94 42
📠 97160 94 55 ✉ gay-friendly@balear.onenet.es

HOTELS

■ **Aries** (B BF g H MA OS wh) Sauna 16-0, Pub 23-? h
C/ Porras, 3 ✉ 07015 *(at Av. Joan Miró)* ☎ 971 73 78 99
📠 971 73 27 94
Rates Ptas 6.000-12.500 (bf incl., with shower, cable-tv). Newly renovated.

■ **Casa Miramar** (G H)
C/ Miramar, 5 ✉ 07001 ☎ 971 72 59 98 📠 971 72 59 98
5 apartments, one maisonette and one luxury suite for four persons.

■ **Palau Sa Font** (ac B CC g PI)
C/ Apuntadores, 38 ✉ 07102 ☎ 971 712277 📠 971 712618
✉ palausafont@atlas-iap.es ✉ www.palausafont.com

■ **Rosamar** (B BF G H OS) Closed Nov 31st-Mar 1st
Av. Joan Miró 74 ✉ 07015 ☎ 971 73 27 23 📠 971 28 38 28
✉ rosamar@ocea.es ✉ illes.balears.tsh/rosamar/
Rooms with bath, WC, phone and terrace. Rates: double 7.500-8.000.

GENERAL GROUPS

■ **Ben Amics-Agrupació Gai i Lesbiana** Information
Mon-Fri 19-21 h
C/ Imprenta 1, 1°, 1A (centro) ✉ 07001 ☎ 971 72 30 58
✉ benamics@oem.es ✉ www.espanet.com/benamics

-*Teléfon Rosa* ☎ 900 601 601 18-22 h
-"Ben Amics" -bimonthly paper with articles, informations, gay scene listings of Mallorca, classified ads and photographies. Free in gay venues. Carnet GL for reduction in bars and shops available. Meetings all week. Mo: newspaper group, Tue: Aids prevention, Wed: Grupo de Amistad, Thu: Youth group, Fri: Lesbian group Beverages and snacks available.

HEALTH GROUPS

■ **Asociación de Lucha anti-sida de Mallorca ALAS**
Mon-Fri 10-13, 18-19, café Fri 19-22 h
C/ Cecilio Metelo 11, esc B, 2°,1A ✉ 07003 ☎ 971 71 55 66
☎ 971 71 44 88 📠 971 71 44 88 ✉ alas@espanet.com
✉ www.espanet.com/alas
■ **Conselleria de Sanitat** Mon-Fri 9-10.30 h
C/ Cecili Metel, 18 ☎ 971 17 68 68
HIV testing anonymous and for free.
■ **Escuela de Salud, Sida y Convivencia - FASE**
Pça. Peixetería, 4, 2° ✉ 07001 ☎ 971 72 75 80 ☎ 900-111 000
✉ fase@idecnet.com ✉ www.idecnet.com/fase

SWIMMING

-Es Trenc (! g NU) (Take road to Campos del Puerto, then direction Colonia de Sant Jordi. Near restaurant El Ultimo Paraíso. Ca. 50 km from Palma)
-Playa de Illetas (g OG) (gay at the end, bus 3)
-Playa del Mago (NU) (in Portas Vells at the rocks. Popular)
-Playa San Juan de Dios in Ca'n Pastilla (r NU)
-Playa Cala Aguua (NU) (rocky part north of the beach, cruisy in the forest)
-Ca'n Picafort (g) (Playa de Muro, action in the dunes between the two west side towers)
-Playa Cala Grand in Cala D'Or Centre (G)
-Playa San Carlos (g)
-Playa y Dique del Oeste (Porto Pi), Bus EMT n°1 (directo), 3 y 21
-Es Carnatge (Ca'n Pastilla), Bus EMT n°15
-Cala Blava (Final S'Arenal), Bus EMT n°23
-Playa de Muro (Ca'n Picafort) Inca, Autocares Bellver

Balearic Islands - Mallorca ▶ Barcelona | Spain

CRUISING

-Promenade at city walls beneath Cathedral (AYOR) (steps and gardens)
-Plaça de Espanya (ayor) (R)
-Passieg del Borne
-Dique del Oeste (G) 24 h. Bus 3. At end of Paseo Maritimo, also cruising by car, no swimming)
-Camino de Jesus (R) (near river, by car)
-El Bosque (S'Arenal), Bus EMT n°15

Balearic Islands - Mallorca - **Playa de Palma**

BARS

■ **Estil** (AC B G MA) 21.30-3.30h, winter: 21-1h
C/ Lisboa *(Between balneario 1 and yacht-harbour)*
■ **Miguel Cafeteria** (B F g) 11-15, 18-23, winter 10.30-18.30 h
C/ Trasimeno, 69, El Arenal ✉ 07600 *(Balneario 1, Bus 15)*
☎ 971 26 47 47
■ **Sa Bota** (B d DR G lj MA VS) summer 22-4, winter 21-1 h
C/ de Trasime 73, El Arenal ✉ 07600 *(Near Balneario 1, 2nd line)*
☎ 971 44 44 29
■ **Töff Töff** (B f G lj MA) 17-?h
C/ Lisboa, 4b ✉ 07600 *(between balneario 1 and yacht-harbour)*

RESTAURANTS

■ **Teide** (B g F MA)
C/ Berga 3

Barbate de Franco

SWIMMING

-Los Caños de Meca (behind the rocks)

Barcelona

✱ Barcelona has been the secret capital of Spain for centuries, at least in economic and cultural terms, a fact shown by numerous sights, such as charming old city quarters, palaces, museums and churches. The administrative capital Madrid has only started catching up with Barcelona over the past few years. The urban renewal prompted by the 1992 Olympic Games helped give Barcelona a new face, but the old one has nonetheless been retained. Barcelona's "Modernismo" buildings, like Park Güell, Palais Güell, Casa Mila and the cathedral Sagrada Familia, are feasts for the eyes. "Modernismo" is the Catalonian version of art nouveau. The gay scene offers everything you might expect from a metropolis of over 2 million: two of the best gay discos in Europe, interesting saunas, bars, mixed restaurants; in short, everything your heart desires. You may find street signs and official notices confusing, especially if you have learned Spanish and are expecting it to be used here. In Barcelona, Catalan is spoken, and the language is considered an expression of their sovereignty. Even the flyers and leaflets of local gay groups are in Catalan; nevertheless everyone can speak and understand "Castillian", which is what Spanish is called here.

★ Zumindest in kultureller und wirtschaftlicher Hinsicht war Barcelona über Jahrhunderte hinweg die heimliche Hauptstadt Spaniens. Davon zeugen eindrucksvolle Altstadtviertel, Paläste, Museen und Kirchen. Erst seit einigen Jahren holt die Verwaltungshauptstadt Madrid wieder auf.

| Spain | Barcelona |

Barcelona

1. Roma Cinema
2. Espai-Magic Bar
3. Cafè de la Calle Bar
4. Nois Quina Nit Bar
5. Bahia Bar
6. Eagle Bar
7. Martin's Bar
8. New Chaps Bar
9. La Luna Danceclub
10. Topxi Bar
11. Sauna Bruch
12. Satanassa Danceclub
13. Este Bar
14. Punto BCN Bar
15. Sauna Casanova
16. Metro Danceclub
17. Thermas Sauna
18. Dietrich Bar
19. Sauna Galilea
20. Arena Sala Classic Danceclub
21. Arena Danceclub
22. Tatu Danceclub
23. Nostromo Sex Shop
24. Monaco Bar
25. Cyber Bar
26. Castro Restaurant
27. Eterna Restaurant
28. La Diva Restaurant
29. Nois Gay Info
30. Alternativ Café
31. Guia Global Fashion Shop
32. Hostal Que Tal Guest House
33. Café Miranda
34. Nerón House of Boys
35. Z:eltas Bar / Medusa Bar
36. Cosmopolita Restaurant
37. Madness Bar

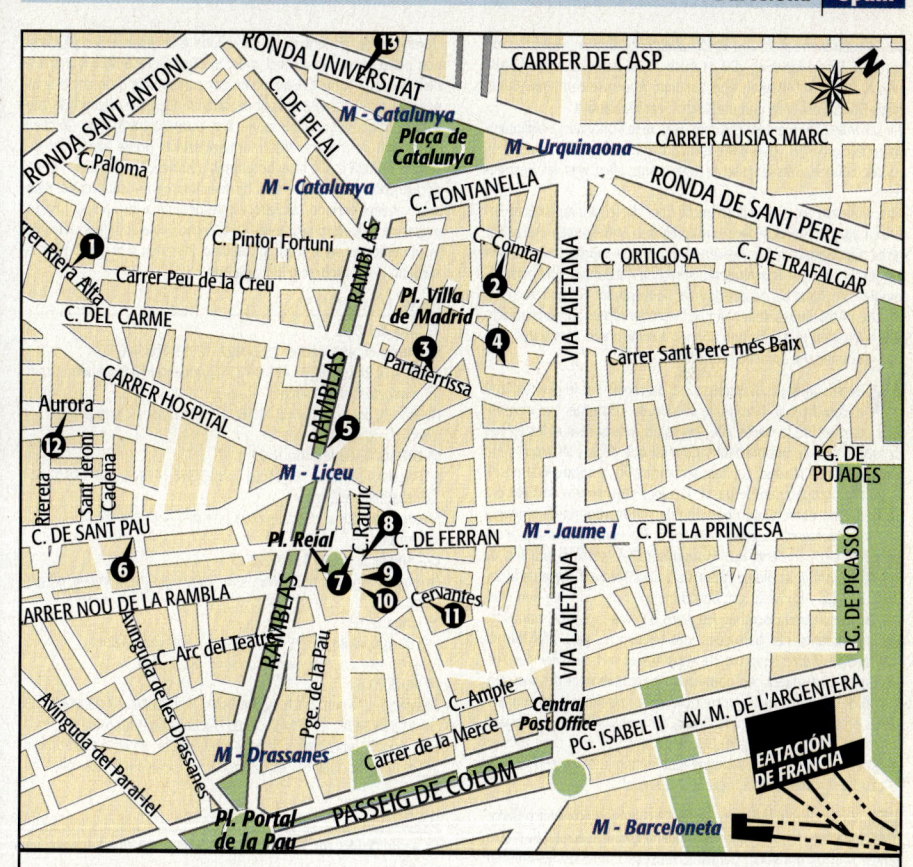

Barcelona - Ramblas

1. Zeus Gay Shop
2. Sauna Condal
3. Ovlas Fashion Shop
4. Regencia Colon Hotel
5. Café de la Opera
6. Marsella Bar
7. Hotel California
8. Padam Padam Bar
9. Sestienda Gay Shop
10. Dickens Bar / EA3 Bar
11. Cómplices Bookshop
12. Aurora Bar
13. American Boys House of Boys

Spain | Barcelona

Die Olympischen Spiele von 1992 haben der Stadt ein neues Gesicht gegeben. Doch daneben gibt es auch Altes. Barcelonas Modernismo(i.e. Jugendstil)-Bauten sind absolute Augenweiden: Park Güell, Palais Güell, Casa Milá und die Kirche Sagrada Familia.
Die schwule Szene entspricht dem, was man von einer 2-Millionen-Metropole erwartet: Zwei der besten schwulen Discos Europas, interessante Saunen, Bars, gemischte Restaurants: alles, was das Herz begehrt.
Bitte wundern Sie sich jedoch nicht über die eigenartigen Schreibweisen von Straßenschildern und amtlichen Mitteilungen. Auch wer gerne sein Spanisch zur Anwendung bringen möchte, wird etwas enttäuscht sein: Die Barcelonesen sprechen Katalanisch und betrachten dies durchaus als Ausdruck ihrer Souveränität. So sind auch die örtlichen Mitteilungsblätter der Schwulengruppen auf katalanisch. Aber verstehen und sprechen können natürlich alle "Kastilisch", wie man die spanische Sprache hier nennt.

✱ Depuis toujours, Barcelone est, au moins sur le plan culturel et commercial, la capitale secrète de l'Espagne. Les magnifiques quartiers de la vieille ville, les palais, les musées et les églises en sont la preuve incontestable. Ce n'est que depuis le retour de la démocratie que Madrid, capitale administrative, a retrouvé la position qu'elle occupait dans le passé. Les Jeux Olympiques de 1992 ont été l'occasion d'une vaste opération de construction et de rénovation. Modernisme et tradition donnent à Barcelone son visage d'aujourd'hui. Les bâtiments du "Modernismo" -la version catalane de l'art-déco- sont splendides: Park Güell, Casa Mila et l'église de la Sagrada Familia. Au niveau gai, Barcelone n'est pas en reste non plus: une des meilleures discothèques gaies d'Europe, un des saunas les plus intéressants, des bars cuirs, des restaurants gais, bref tout ce qu'il faut pour être heureux! Ne vous laissez pas dérouter par l'orthographe particulière des panneaux de circulation et des inscriptions officielles. Ceux qui voudront mettre en pratique leurs connaissances en espagnol devront repasser, car tout Catalan qui se respecte parle autant sa langue. Les Magazines gais sont donc tous en catalan. Bien sûr, en Catalogne tout le monde comprend et parle le "castillan", comme on appelle ici l'espagnol.

✱ Al menos desde el punto de vista cultural y económico Barcelona fue durante siglos la capital española secreta. Impresionantes barrios antiguos, palacios, museos e iglesias testimonian ésto. Pero hace algunos años Madrid, la capital administrativa ha vuelto a recobrar terreno. Los juegos olímpicos de 1992 dieron una nueva cara a la ciudad que se conjuga a la perfección con las edificaciones antiguas ya existentes. Las construcciones modernistas de la ciudad son un deber: Parque Güell, Palacio Güell, Casa Milá y la iglesia de la Sagrada Familia. El ambiente gay responde a lo que se exige de una metrópoli de 2 millones de habitantes: dos de las mejores discotecas europeas, saunas muy interesantes, bares con clientela portadora de prendas de cuero, bares frecuentados por prostitutos, restaurantes gay, en fin, todo lo que a uno le apetece. El orgullo nacional de Catalunya también se refleja en el idioma: Aqui todos los letreros de las calles y las señalizaciones oficiales están escritas en catalán y los barceloneses usan poco el castellano. Por eso también los periódicos locales de las organizaciones gay están escritos en catalán. Pero por supuesto también se entiende y se habla el castellano.

✱ Per secoli, Barcellona è stata la capitale segreta della Spagna, almeno per ciò che riguarda la cultura e l'economia. Ci sono molte attrazioni che confermano ciò, per esempio gli affascinanti vecchi quartieri della città, i palazzi e i musei. Madrid è riuscita a raggiungere Barcellona solo da pochi anni. Le olimpiadi del 1992 hanno cambiato il volto della città, senza cancellare le tracce del passato.

L'architettura modernista di Barcellona è un piacere per gli occhi, non perdetevi il parco Güell, palazzo Güell, la casa Milá e la chiesa della Sagrada Familia. L'ambiente gay corrisponde a ciò che ci si aspetta da una città di 2 milioni di abitanti: due delle migliori discoteche d'Europa, interessanti saune, bar, ristoranti misti, tutto ciò che il cuore può desiderare. Non meravigliatevi di fronte alle scritte dei cartelli stradali e alle insegne ufficiali. Chi desidera praticare un po' di castigliano ("spagnolo" è un termine improprio) sarà un po' deluso: i catalani parlano catalano e considerano la loro lingua una espressione della loro sovranità. Così anche i volantini informativi del movimento gay sono scritti in catalano. Però non scoraggiatevi, il castigliano viene capito e parlato da tutti.

PUBLICATIONS

■ **Guía del Ocio**
C/ Muntaner, 492, baixos ✉ 08022 ☎ 93 418 50 05
☎ 93 418 28 09 ☎ 93 417 94 71 🖂 guiaocio@idrup.ibernet.com
💻 www.guiadelociobcn.es
Weekly city guide in spanish.125 Pts Great source of information on what's going on in the city.
■ **INFOGAI** Meeting: Fri 18-21 h
C/ Paloma,12, baixos ✉ 08001 ☎ 93 318 16 66 ☎ 93 318 16 65
🖂 cgb@olemail.com
Free monthly gay paper issued by Col.lectiu GAi de Barcelona.
■ **Lambda**
C/.- Ample, 5 ☎ 93 412 72 72
Free quarterly publication. News from the group Casal Lambda, the gay scene, cultural and political articles, addresses, and personal ads.
■ **Línea G** (G)
☎ 93 200 80 88 ☎ 93 200 02 08 🖂 edito@lineag.net
Free monthly gay paper with a personal ads section.
■ **NOIS** (! G)
Diputació, 174 entl. 1er A, Apdo. 94015 ✉ 08080 ☎ 93 454 38 05
☎ 93 454 38 05 ☎ 93 454 38 05 🖂 nois@alehop.com
Free monthly gay paper in Spanish listing all the venues and attractions in gay Barcelona. Acurate city map. Available in every gay bar and stores.

BARS

■ **Acido Oxido** (AC B d DR G lj MA VS WE) 22-2.30 & 5-9, Sat&Sun -10.30 h
C/ Joaquín Costa, 61 ✉ 08001 (Metro Universidad)
☎ 93 412 09 39
■ **Aire** (A AC B G MA s) 23-3 h, Sun&Mon closed
C/. Valencia, 236 ✉ 08007 ☎ 93 451 84 62
■ **Aurora** (A AC B g p s WE YG) 21-2.30, Fri-Sun & public holidays also 6-12 h
C/. Aurora, 7 ✉ 08001 (Metro Liceo / San Antonio)
☎ 93 442 30 44
■ **Bahia** (A AC B d gLm MG WE) 22-3.30 h
C/. Séneca, 12 (Metro Diagonal/Fontana)
■ **Barbarella** (AC B CC F G MA) 21-3 h, Mon closed
C/ Calabria, 142-144 ✉ 08015 (Metro Rocafort) ☎ 93 423 18 78
■ **Blended 04** (B G MA r) 19-3 h
C/. Marià Cubí, 55 (Metro Fontana) ☎ 93 200 71 26
■ **Bunker** (AC B DR G LJ MA S VS) 21-2.30, WE-3.30 h
C/ Entenca, 46 ✉ 08015 ☎ 93 426 93 92
Large darkroom with cabins and sling. Popular early mornings when the discos close.
■ **Café de la Calle** (AC B f Glm YG) 18-3 h
C/. Vic, 11 ✉ 08000 (Metro Fontana) ☎ 93 218 38 63
■ **Caligula** (AC B d G MA s) 22-3h
C/ Consell de Cent, 257 ✉ 08011 (M° Universidad)

Barcelona | Spain

z:eltas
casanova 75

■ **Cyber** (A AC B D G MA S WE) Wed-Mon 20-3, 5-10 h, closed Tue
C/. Urgell, 84 ✉ 08011 *(Metro Urgell)*
■ **Dickens** (B G MA N) 20-3 h
C/. Rauric, 21 *(Metro Liceu)*
■ **Dietrich** (! AC B d f G STV YG) 22-3 h
C/. Consell de Cent, 255 ✉ 08011 *(Metro Universidad, between Muntaner and Aribau)* ☎ 93 451 77 07
Daily drag shows.
■ **Eagle** (AC B DR G LJ MA P S VS WE) Sun-Thu 22-2.30, Fri Sat -3 h
Passeig -Sant Joan, 152 ✉ 08037 *(Metro Verdaguer)*
☎ 93 207 58 56
■ **EA3-Bar** (B g MA R) 20-3 h
C/. Rauric, 23 *(Metro Liceu)* ☎ 93 412 05 84
■ **Espai-Magic** (AC B d DR G lj MA R SNU STV VS WE) 21-3 h
C/. Sant Marc, 18-20 ✉ 08006 *(Metro Fontana)* ☎ 93 415 36 10
21-24h karaoke

■ **Este Bar** (A AC B Glm YG) 22-03 h
C/. Consell de Cent, 257 *(Metro Universidad)*
■ **Madness** (AC B D DR G MA s VS) 22.30-3, Mon-Fri also 6-8.30h
C/. Balmes, 88 ✉ 08008 *(Mº Diagonal)* ☎ 93 216 00 38
DJs on WE.
■ **Marsella** (AC B glm lj MA s) 21-2.30, Fri Sat -3.30 h
C/. Sant Pau, 65 *(Metro Liceu)*
■ **Medusa** (A AC B d G MG s WE) 17-3 h
Casanova 75 ✉ 08011 *(Metro Gran Via/Urgell)* ☎ 93 454 53 63
Bar and cafeteria.
■ **Monaco** (A AC B CC d DR G MA STV VS WE) Mon-Thu 20-2, Fri-Sat -3, Sun 18-2 h
C/. Diputació, 210 ✉ 08011 *(Metro Universidad)*
■ **New Chaps** (AC B DR G LJ MA s VS WE) 21-3, WE -3.30 h
Av. Diagonal, 365 *(Metro Diagonal)* ☎ 93 215 53 65
Leather bar, Sun 19-22h happy hour.

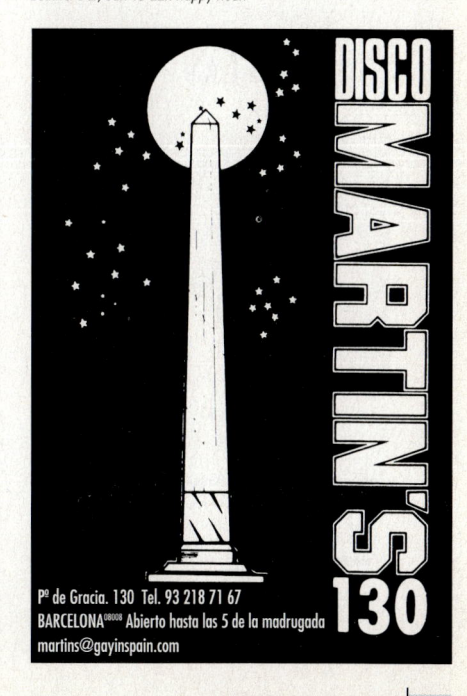

SPARTACUS 2001/2002 | 907

Spain — Barcelona

■ **Nois Quina Nit** (B G D S VS) 22-3 h
Riera de Sant Miguel, 59 ✉ 08006
■ **Padam Padam** (A AC B g MA) 10-15, 19-3 h, closed Sun
C/. Rauric, 9 ☏ 93 302 50 62
Classical music.
■ **Punto BCN** (! A AC B e G MA) 18-2.30 h
C/ Muntaner, 63 *(Metro Universidad)* ☏ 93 453 61 23
■ **Remix** (B d g) Mon-Sun 19-3 h
C/. Lleida, 23 *(Pça. España)*
■ **Rosa. La** (B gLM MA) Thu-Sun 20-3 h
C/. Brusi, 39 ✉ 08006 *(Entrance Augusta and San Elias)*
☏ 93 414 61 66
■ **Six** (AC B CC G MA s WE) 21-3h, Mon closed
C/ Muntaner, 6 ✉ 08011 ☏ 93 453 00 75
Wed-Sat different DJs.
■ **Theseo Bar** (A B BF F g MA) 8.30-2.30, closed Sun; best evenings
C/ del Comte Borrell, 119 ☏ 93 453 87 96
■ **Topxi** (AC B d DR G MA STV VS) 22-5, Show Mon-Thu 1.45, Fri-Sun 1.45, 4 h
C/. Valencia, 358 ✉ 08000
■ **Z:eltas** (AC B d G MA s) Wed-Sun 22.30-3 h
C/ Casanova, 75 ✉ 08011 *(Metro Gran Via / Urgell)*

CAFES

■ **Alternativ** (B G OS s YG) 22-3h
C/ Villarroel, 71 ✉ Barcelona *(M° Urgell)*
Café de nuit.
■ **Antonious Libreria-Café** (A b BF CC GLM s) Mon-Fri 10.30-14, 16.30-21, Sat 12-14, 16.30-21 h, Sun closed
C/. Josep Anselm Clavé, 6 ✉ 08002 *(Metro Drassanes, between Ramblas and C/ Ample)* ☏ 93 301 90 70
Bookshop and café.

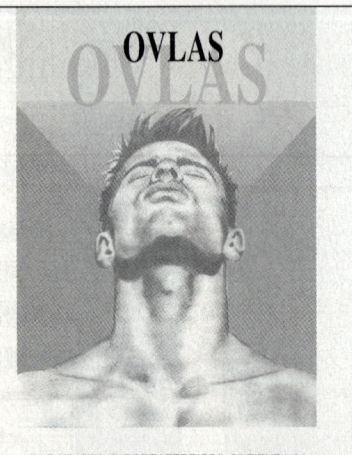

■ **Café de la Opera** (B f NG OS) 10-2 h
Rambla, 74 ✉ 08000 *(Metro Liceu)*
■ **G-Café** (A AC f G MA OS) 18-2 h, WE-3 h
C/ Muntaner, 24 ✉ 08013 *(Metro Universidad)* ☏ 93 451 65 36
■ **Oui Café** (AC B f G MA OS VS) 17-2 h, WE-3 h
C/ Consell de Cent, 247 ✉ 08011

DANCECLUBS

■ **Arena Sala Classic** (AC B D G MA VS YG) Fri Sat 0.30-5 h
C/. Diputació, 233 ✉ 08007 *(Metro Universidad)* ☏ 93 487 83 42
Spanish music.
■ **Arena Sala Dandy** (AC B D G MA) Fri, Sat 1-6.30h
Gran Vía de les Corts Catalanes, 593 ✉ 08011 *(Metro Catalunya / Universidad)*
newest disco of the arena-group, house music.
■ **Arena Sala Madre** (AC B D G MA VS) 0.30-5h
C/ Balmes, 32 ✉ 08007 *(Metro Universidad)* ☏ 93 487 83 42
special theme parties Wed, Thu, Sun.
■ **Arena Sala V.I.P.** (! AC B D G MA VS YG) Fri Sat 1-6.30 h
C/.Gran Via de les Corts Catalanes, 593 ✉ 08011 *(Metro Universidad)*
■ **Luna. La** (B D DR G MA snu VS) 21-3, WE -4, winter Show Sun 1 h
Av. Diagonal, 323 ✉ 08000 *(Metro Verdaguer)*
■ **Martin's** (AC B D DR GLM lj MA r s VS) 0-5 h
Passeig de Gràcia, 130 ✉ 08008 *(Metro Diagonal)*
☏ 93 218 71 67
■ **Metro** (! AC B D DR G MA S STV SNU VS) 24-5, Sun also 19-22.30 h
C/. Sepúlveda,185 ✉ 08011 *(Metro Universidad)* ☏ 93 323 52 27
Sat nights at 2am - folk dancing on one dance floor.
■ **Salvation** (AC B D G MA SNU STV VS WE) Thu-Sat 24-6 h
Ronda Sant Pere, 19-21 ✉ 08010 *(Metro Urquinaona)*
☏ 93 318 06 86
■ **Satanassa** (AC B D glm MA s) 22.30-3 h
C/. Aribau,27 ✉ 08011 *(Metro Universidad)* ☏ 93 453 61 41
Popular.
■ **Tatu** (AC B D G DR MA S VS) 22-4.30, Sun 19-4.30 h
C/. Cayo Celio, 7 ✉ 08014 ☏ 93 425 33 50
Popular. Entry Ptas 500 incl. 1 drink. Show Thu, Fri, Sat 1.30, Sun also 21 h

RESTAURANTS

■ **Café Miranda** (! b F G MA S) 21-1 h
C/. Casanova, 30 ✉ 08011 *(near Gran Via)* ☏ 93 453 52 49
Mediterranean cuisine in a nice atmosphere.
■ **Cafeti. El** (F g MA) 13.30-15.30, 20.30-23.30 h, closed Mon & Sun evening
C/. Sant Rafael, 18 ☏ 93 329 24 19
Spanish cuisine.
■ **Castro Restaurant** (AC B CC F G lj MA s WE) 13-16, 21-24 h, closed Sun
C/. Casanova, 85 ✉ 08011 *(Metro Urgell)* ☏ 93 323 67 84
Menu at 1200 Pts (cocina del mercado), menu à la carte at 3000 Pts.
■ **Comsopolita** (AC B CC F G s) 13-16, 20.30-23.30h, Mon evening closed
C/ Muntaner, 6 ✉ 08011
lunch menu 1150 ptas, Thu-Sat DJs for dinner.
■ **Diva. La** (AC B CC F g MA STV) Tue-Sun 13-15.30 21-0.30 h, closed Mon
C/. Diputación,172 ✉ 08011 *(Metro Universidad/Urgell)*
☏ 93 454 63 98
Drag shows, cabaret.

Barcelona | Spain

CASTRO RESTAURANT

CASANOVA, 85
08011 BARCELONA
TELEFON 93 323 67 84

La DIVA

gay restaurant

Diputación 172 / 08011 Barcelona
tel. 93 454 63 98

CAFÉ miranda
gay restaurant

Casanova 30, 08011 Barcelona (entre Sepúlveda - Gran Via)

gay teatro café — DIETRICH

Consell de Cent 255 (entre Muntaner y Aribau)

Spain Barcelona

**GAY INFORMATION CENTER.
GAY SHOP
RIERA ALTA, 20
TEL.: 93 442 97 95
08001 BARCELONA**

SESTIENDA
EL PRIMER GAY-SHOP DE LA HISTORIA EN ESPAÑA
DESDE 1981 AL SERVICIO DE LA COMUNIDAD
GAY INFORMATION CENTRE
www.sestienda.com
CALLE RAURIC, 11. 08002 BARCELONA
PLANO GAY DE BARCELONA GRATIS   FREE GAY CITY MAP

■ **Eterna** (CC F g) 13-16, 21-24 h
C/ Casanova, 42 ☏ 93 453 17 86
■ **Fuse** (AC B CC F G MA stv) Thu-Sat 21-4 h
C/ Roger de Lluria, 40 ✉ 08009 *(Metro Urquinaona / Passeig de Gràcia 9)* ☏ 93 481 31 74
Diner spectacle with DJs.
■ **Little Italy** (F g MA) Mon-Sat 13.30-16, 21-24 h
C/. del Rec, 30 ✉ 08003 *(near P. del Born)* ☏ 93 319 79 73
Wed & Thu live jazz music.
■ **Mexico Lindo** (B F g MA) 13-16, 20.30-1 h
C/. Regás, 35 *(Metro: Fontana, Passeig de Gràcia)* ☏ 93 218 18 18
Mexican cuisine.
■ **Ovlas Cafe Restaurante** (AC B BF CC F G MA s STV) 9.30-20.30 h, Sun closed
C/. Portaferrissa, 15 ✉ 08002 *(Gralla Hall)* ☏ 93 412 38 36
Italian food, menu del día, Sat 17-20 Show.

SEX SHOPS/BLUE MOVIES

■ **Blue Box** (g VS) 10-24 h
C/. Aragó, 249
■ **Blue Star** (g VS) Mon-Fri 9-23 h, Sat-Sun 10-23 h
Av. de Roma, 2-4 *(Edificio Torre Catalunya)* ☏ 93 426 32 16
■ **Kitsch** (g VS) 10-22, Sun 17-22 h
C/. Muntaner,17-19 *(At Gran Vía)* ☏ 93 451 20 48

■ **Nostromo** (AC CC G VS) 12-22, Sun 17-22h
C/ Diputació 208 ✉ 08011 ☏ 93 323 31 94
Very cruisy cabins.
■ **Sestienda Gay Shop** (CC G VS) 10-20.30 h, closed Sun
C/. Rauric, 11 ✉ 08002 *(Metro Liceu)* ☏ 93 318 86 76
Ask for information.
■ **Sexgold** (AC CC E g VS WE) 11-22, Sun & public holidays 16-22 h
C/. Balmes,180 ✉ 08006 ☏ 93 217 26 29
■ **Skorpius** (g VS)
Gran Vía de les Corts Catalanes, 384-390
■ **Zeus** (AC CC G MA VS) 10-21 h, closed Sun
C/. Riera Alta, 20 ✉ 08001 *(Metro Sant Antoni)* ☏ 93 442 97 95
Gay shop & information center.

CINEMAS

■ **Arenas** (b G OG) 15.30-23.30 h
C/. Tarragona, 5-7 *(Metro España)* ☏ 93 423 11 69
■ **Cine Diorama** (AC DR G MA OG) 10.30-22 h
Placa Buensuceso, 5 ✉ 08000 *(Metro Cataluña)* ☏ 93 318 12 91
Walking down the Ramblas, 2nd street to the right. Popular in the evening. Entry Ptas 700.
■ **Roma** (g)
C/. Aragó, 197 ✉ 08000 *(between Aribau and Muntaner)*
■ **Urquinaona Cinema** (g MA) 10.30-22.30 h
Placa Urquinaona, 5 ☏ 93 301 70 94

AMERICAN BOYS

CHICOS DE COMPAÑIA ***** ALTO STANDING

TEL.: 93 412 75 33

- **EXCLUSIVE MODELS**
  (10 BOYS FROM 18 TO 28 AWAIT FOR YOU)
- **LUXURY SUITES WITH BATH, YACUZZI, VIDEO AIR CONDITION.**
  STREAPTEASE, FREE DRINK.
- **COME AND SEE US.**

PLAZA CATALUNYA
RONDA UNIVERSIDAD 23 3º 2B
PERMANENT SERVICE 12H - 24H
ESCORT SERVICE
VISA - MASTERCARD

- WE SPEAK ENGLISH, FRANÇAIS, ITALIANO ...
HTTP://WWW.SEXOLE.COM/AMERICANBOYS.COM

Spain | Barcelona

NERÓN

VARONES MASCULINOS EXCLUSIVOS

Instalaciones de lujo únicas en España.
Bañera, jacuzzi, Cama redonda.
Servicio desde 11 horas hasta 5 madrugada

Salidas Hotel y Domicilio.   Discreción.   VISA

EXCLUSIVE MALE

Instalation's of luxury unique in Spain.
Bathtub, jacuzzi, round bed.
Service of 11 a.m. to 5 early morning

Outset Hotel and Home   Discretion.   VISA

TL. 93 451 10 28

Consejo de ciento, 185 3º 1ª
BCN   www.neronboys.com

HOUSE OF BOYS

- **American Boys** (AC CC G R SNU VS WH) 12-24 h
Ronda Universidad, 23, 2B ✉ 08007 (Metro Catalunya, 3rd floor)
☎ 93 412 75 33
- **Nerón** (CC G R tv VS WH) 11-5 h
C/. Consell de Cient, 185 3º 1-a ✉ 08006 (Metro Urgell)
☎ 93 451 10 28

SAUNAS/BATHS

- **Bruch** (B G MA msg SA SOL WH VS WO) 11-23 h
C/. Bruc, 65 ✉ 08009 (Metro Girona) ☎ 93 487 48 14
Two floors with labyrinth.
- **Casanova** (B DR F G MA msg SA SB SOL VS) 0-24 h
C/. Casanova, 57 ☎ 93 323 78 60
- **Condal** (B CC F msg SA SB VS WH) 12-6, Fri Sat 0-24 h
C/. Espolsasacs, 1 ✉ 08002 (Metro Cataluña. C/. Espolsasacs is a very small street !) ☎ 93 301 96 80
Cold whirlpool in the hot steam room - great !
- **Corinto** (B CC F G MA r SA SB SOL VS WH) 12-2, Fri Sat 0-24 h
C/. Pelai, 62 ✉ 08001 (near Pl. Catalunya) ☎ 93 318 64 22
- **Galilea** (! B CC DR F G MA msg SA SB VS) 12-24, Fri-Sat 0-24 h
C/. Calabria, 59 ✉ 08015 (Metro Rocafort) ☎ 93 426 79 05
- **Lesseps** (B G MA msg SA SB VS) 10-22, Sun 15-22 h
C/ Mauricio Serrahima, 9 ✉ 08012 (Metro Lesseps)
☎ 93 218 05 92
- **Thermas Barcelona** (AC B CC DR F G MA msg PI R SA SB SOL VS WH wo) 10-2, Fri 10-Sun 2 h
C/. Diputación, 46 ✉ 08015 (Metro Rocafort) ☎ 93 325 93 46
Also bar and restaurant offering Spanish cuisine. hairdresser service.

despierta a la nueva dimension de

SAUNA GALILEA

o...sigue soñando

CALABRIA, 59 - Tel. 93 426 79 05
08015 BARCELONA

LAS MEJORES SAUNAS DE ESPAÑA
THE BEST SAUNAS IN SPAIN

BARCELONA

CASANOVA
C/ Casanova, 57
Tel. 93 323 78 60

CONDAL
Espolsasacs, 1
(C/ Condal)
Tel. 93 301 96 80

CORINTO
Pelayo, 62
Tel. 93 318 64 22

VALENCIA

MAGNUS
Av. del Puerto, 27
Tel. 96 337 48 92

OLIMPIC
Vivons, 17
Tel. 96 373 04 18
(en obras)

SEVILLA

HISPALIS
C / Céfiro, 3
(Calle Luis Montoto)
Tel. 95 458 02 20

GRUPO PASES — SAUNAS MASCULINAS
CONDAL BARCELONA · PÁDUA BARCELONA · OLIMPIC VALENCIA · CORINTO BARCELONA · CASANOVA BARCELONA · HISPALIS SEVILLA · MAGNUS VALENCIA

SAUNAS PASES
para lo que deseas
make your wishes come true — what ever you want, what ever you need

---

LITTLE ITALY RISTORANTE

Cocina mediterránea de calidad
Mon - Sat 13 - 16 h, 21 - 24 h
Reservations: 93 319 79 73
C/Rec, 30 Pº del Borne, 08003 Barcelona
Wed & Thu night live jazz music

Dinner spectacle until 1:30
Thu - Sat 21 - 4 h
Reservations: 93 481 31 74
C/Roger de Lluria, 40, 08009 Barcelona
dinner with DJ, disco until 4 h

fuse

Spain | Barcelona

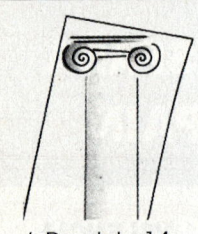

HOTEL CALIFORNIA

H ★★

AIRE ACONDICIONADO
BAÑO COMPLETO - TV. - TELEFONO
(en todas las habitaciones)

c/. Raurich, 14
(esq. Fernando)

Tel. 93- 317 77 66 - Fax 317 54 74
08002 BARCELONA (España)
www.seker.es/hotel_california

complete offer
see page Germany/Berlin

overnight accomodation service — from ESP 4.000
· about 750 beds · more than 28 cities ·

enjoy bed & breakfast

central booking office Berlin ☎ **+49-30-236 236 10** 4:30-9:00 pm local time
Fax +49-30-23623619 · info@ebab.com · www.ebab.com

ENJOY THE CHARMS OF GOTHIC QUARTER

With the advantages of an excellent location, next to the Cathedral, in the heart of th Gothic Quarter and only five minutes far from both Catalunya Square and Barcelona's Harbour, it is the perfect starting point for your visit to the city. You can find Las Ramblas, the main museums and monuments, and the comercial streets after a short and pleasant walk.

HOTEL REGENCIA COLÓN ★★★ Barcelona

C/. Sagristans, 13/17 - Tel.: 93 318 98 58

BOOK SHOPS

■ **Antinous** (A B BF CC GLM) Mon-Fri 10.30-14, 16.30-21, Sat 12-21 h, closed Sun
C/. Josep Anselm Clavé, 6 ✉ 08002 *(Metro Drassanes)* ☎ 93 301 90 70
Books, magazines, videos, post cards, posters. Also mail-order.
■ **Cómplices** (GLM) Mon-Fri 10.30-20.30, Sat 12-20.30 h
C/. Cervantes, 2 ✉ 08002 *(Metro Liceu)* ☎ 93 412 72 83
Also very good for information about the gay scene.
■ **Tulibro.com** (CC G)
C/ Llacuna, 162 ✉ 08018
librería en internet para gays - gay internet bookstore in Spanish.

CONDOM SHOPS

■ **Condoneria** Mon-Sat 10.30-14.00 16.30-20.30 h, closed Sun
Placa Sant Josep Oriol, 7 *(near Placa del Pi; Metro Liceu)* ☎ 93 302 77 21

FASHION SHOPS

■ **Ovlas**
C/ Portaferrissa, 25 ✉ 08002 ☎ 93 412 12 52

HOTELS

■ **Hostal Que Tal** (bf G H)
C/. Mallorca, 290 ✉ 08037 *(M° Catalunya)* ☎ 93 459 23 66
☎ 93 459 23 66
10 double and 3 single rooms. Rooms partly with bath/WC.
■ **Hotel California** (AC BF CC Glm H)
C/. Raurich, 14 ✉ 08002 *(Fernando. Metro Liceu)* ☎ 93 317 77 66
🖷 93 317 54 74 💻 www.seker.es/Hotel_California
Centrally located. Rooms with bath, AC, phone and tv. Rates Ptas 6.750-11.500 (bf incl.).
■ **Hotel Regencia Colón** (AC B BF CC F g H wo)
C/. Sagristans 13/17 ✉ 08002 *(Metro Jaume I)* ☎ 93 318 98 58
🖷 93 317 28 22 📧 info@hotelregenciacolon.com
💻 www.hotelregenciacolon.com
3 star-hotel. Located in the Gothic quarter, only a few steps from the Ramblas. 55 rooms with bath, sat-TV, telephone, mini bar, AC, safe. Rates single Ptas 9.500, double 16.000, bf 1.200. Special discount for SPARTACUS-readers 10%.

Barcelona | Spain

THERMAS BARCELONA SAUNA

Las instalaciones mas grandes de España.
20 años de experiencia
Diputación, 46 • Tel. 93 325 93 46
BARCELONA

HOSTAL ** QUE TAL

c/Mallorca 290-BCN
Tel/Fax: +34-93 459 23 66
EN EL CENTRO DE BARCELONA
Just a few minutes away from gay-bars.
We will be happy to help you plan
your stay in Barcelona.

■ **Villa Francesca. La** (B BF glm MA OS PI SOL)
Av. España 5, Canyelles ☎ 93 897 35 82 📠 93 879 35 92

GUEST HOUSES
■ **Hostal Centro** (g H) 10-20h for reservations
C/ Balmes, 83 *(M° Passeig de Gràcia)* ☎ 93 453 91 82
📠 93 453 91 82 🖳 www.gayinspain.com/hostalcentro
■ **Natalia's Guest House** (g H)
C/ Cervantes, 7, 2° ✉ 08002 *(near the Gothic Quarter)*
☎ 93 654 238 161 📠 93 302 07 52
■ **Villa Francesca. La** (B BF glm MA OS PI SOL) May-Oct
Av. España, 5, Canyelles ✉ 08811 *(10 km from Sitges)*
☎ 93 897 35 82 📠 93 897 35 82
3 double rooms with TV, radio and bath. Rates from ESP 10 000 to 14 000.-

PRIVATE ACCOMMODATION
■ **Enjoy Bed and Breakfast** (BF G H MA) 16.30-21 h
Nollendorfplatz 5, 10777 Berlin - Germany ☎ +49 30 236 236 10
📠 +49 30 236 236 19 🖳 info@ebab.com 🖳 ebab.com
*Accommodation sharing agency. All with shower and BF.
20-25 Euro p.p.*

GENERAL GROUPS
■ **Casal Lambda** Café Mon-Fri 17-21, Sa 17-23 h
C/. Ample, 5, baixos ✉ 08002 *(Metro Drassanes)* ☎ 93 412 72 72
🖳 info@lambdaweb.org 🖳 www.lambdaweb.org
■ **Col.Lectiu Gai de Barcelona (C.G.B.)** Mon-Fri 19-21 h
C/. Paloma, 12 ,baixos ✉ 08008 *(PO Box 32.016 08080; near Zeus Sexshop)* ☎ 93 318 16 66 📠 93 318 16 65

FETISH GROUPS
■ **Associació Gai d'Òssos i Admiradors de Catalunya - BEARcelona** (G)
c/o CGB, Ptge. Valeri Serra, 23 ✉ 08011 ☎ 93 54 31 25
📠 93 23 04 46 🖳 bearcelona@bearcave.org
🖳 www.geocities.com/bearcelona

HEALTH GROUPS
■ **Actua!** Mon-Fri 9-14, 16-19 h
C/ Gomis, 38, baixos ✉ 08023 ☎ 93 418 50 00 📠 93 418 89 74
🖳 info@interactua.net 🖳 www.interactua.net
Magazine for and about people living with AIDS.

SPARTACUS 2001/2002 | 915

Spain | Barcelona ▸ Benidorm

■ **Asociación Ciudadana Anti-Sida de Catalunya** Mon-Fri 10-14, 16-21 h
C/ Junta del Comerc, 23 baja ✉ 08000 ☎ 93 317 05 05
📠 93 301 41 82
Information and services concerning AIDS.

■ **Departamento de Sanidad**
Av. Drassanes, 17-21 ✉ 08000 *(Metro Universidad)* ☎ 93 441 29 97
HIV-testing.

HELP WITH PROBLEMS

■ **Teléfono Rosa** 18-22 h
☎ 900 601 601

PRIVATE ACCOMMODATION

■ **Enjoy Bed and Breakfast** (BF G H A) 16.30-21 h
Nollendorfplatz 5, 10777 Berlin - Germany ☎ +49 30 236 236 10
📠 +49 30 236 236 19 ✉ info@ebab.com 🌐 ebab.com
Accommodation sharing agency. All with shower and BF. 20-25 Euro p.p.

RELIGIOUS GROUPS

■ **Gays Cristianes de Cataluña** Mon Sat 19.30-22 h
PO Box 854 ✉ 08080 ☎ 93 398 16 84
Meeting: C/. Escudellers 53, 1,2 (Metro Drassanes).

SWIMMING

-Platja de Chernobil (g NU) (beside Barcelona near the Olympic City) in S. Adrian de Besos. Metro Sant Roc. The beach is behind the TAGRA-factory. No bushes. Very popular. In winter car-cruising!
-Platja Mar Bella (g NU) (Metro Ciudadela, then 2 km by foot)
-Platja de la Barceloneta (g)

CRUISING

All are AYOR
-Station/Estación de Sants (very popular)
-San Andrés/Arenal Estación
-El Corte Ingles-Shopping Centre, Placa Catalunya
-Parque de Montjuic ! (especially between Palau Nacional and C/ Lleida. Popular day and night)
-Placa de Catalunya (R)
-Estación del Norte

Benidorm

✱ Benidorm is the jewel of the Costa Blanca, as it is famous for it's beautiful beach Poniente, which is considered to be one of the best seven beaches in the world by the U.N.O. The gay area is concentrated in the old village close to the beach. The mild climate all year round (even in winter an average daytime temperature is above 20°C), the varied gay scene (365 days a year) and a full spectrum of leisure make Benidorm a perfect holiday destination throughout the year. Enjoy yourself on the sandy beaches, the small nudist bays, cosy or modern gay bars, visit the large outdoor gay disco, stay in a simple hostal or at the exclusive gay resort a little way from the centre. Since August 2000 you can visit Terra Mitica, one of the biggest themeparks in Europe, where you can experience a fascinating journey through the Mediterranean's five most legendary civilisations. Gay Benidorm - a real alternative.

✱ Benidorm ist das Juwel der Costa Blanca und berühmt für den wunderschönen Strand Poniente, den selbst die UNO als einen der sieben schönsten Strände der Welt bezeichnet. Die schwule Szene konzentriert sich in der Altsîn unter 20°C), die abwechslungsreiche und ganzjährig geöffnete Schwulszene, sowie ein riesiges Spektrum an Freizeitangeboten machen Benidorm zu einem idealen Reiseziel. Man(n) vergnügt sich am Sandstrand, der kleinen Nudistenbucht, in angestauten Plüschschuppen, oder in der Outdoordisco, wohnt im einfachen Hostal in der Altstadt oder im stilvollen Guesthouse ein wenig außerhalb. Seit August 2000 ist Benidorm durch Terra Mitica, den größten Themepark des Mittelmeerraumes, um eine Attraktion reicher. Wer das authentische Spanien sucht, muß nicht weniger Kilometer ins Landesinnere und befindet sich wunderschönen spanischen Bergdörfern, fernab des Massentourismus. So ist Benidorm für den Spanienliebhaber eine wahre Alternative.

✱ Benidorm est le joyau de la Costa Blanca, surtout connu pour sa magnifique plage Poniente considérée par l'ONU comme l'une des 7 meilleures plages du monde. La scène gaie se concentre dans le vieux village, pas loin de la plage. Le climat doux toute l'année (la température moyenne en hiver est de 20 °C), la scène gaie diversifiée (365 jours par an) et l'offre nombreuse en loisirs font de Benidorm une destination de choix toute l'année. Vous pourrez y apprécier les plages de sables, les baies naturistes, les bars confortables et modernes ou un grand club en plein air, que se soit en séjournant dans un petit hôtel ou dans un établissement exclusivement gai à l'écart de la ville. Depuis août 2000, il est également possible de visiter Terra Mitica, un des plus grands parcs d'attraction d'Europe, qui propose un merveilleux voyage à travers 5 civilisations légendaires de la Méditerranée. Pour résumer: Benidorm mérite plus qu'un détour.

✱ Benidorm es la perla de la Costa Blanca y famosa por la playa maravillosa de Poniente, considerado por la ONU una de las siete playas más bellas del mundo. El ambiente gay se concentra en la ciudad vieja cerca de la playa. El clima benigno durante el año entero (en invierno hay pocos días con menos de 20°C), el ambiente gay muy variado y abierto durante los doce meses del año así como una gran variedad de ofertas para pasar bien el tiempo de ocio convierten Benidorm en un destino ideal para pasar las vacaciones. El turista puede divertirse en la playa de arena, en la pequeña bahía de nudistas, en algún local kitsch o en una discoteca al aire libre, y vive en algún hotelito sencillo en la parte vieja de Benidorm o en la elegante casa de huéspedes Guesthouse en las afueras. Desde agosto del 2000, Benidorm tiene una nueva atracción, Terra Mítica, el mayor parque temático del mediterráneo. Quien quiera conocer la España auténtica sólo tiene que desplazarse unos kilómetros hacia el interior y encontrará las bellísimas aldeas de las montañas, lejos del turismo de masa. De esta forma, Benidorm es una verdadera alternativa para el turista enamorado de España.

✱ Benidorm, gioiello della Costa Blanca, è famosa per la sua meravigliosa spiaggia Poniente, definita anche dalla stessa ONU come una delle sette spiagge più belle del mondo. L'ambiente gay si concentra nella parte vecchia della città, nei pressi della spiaggia. Il clima, mite tutto l'anno, (in inverno la temperatura scende raramente sotto i 20°), l'ambiente omosessuale così vario e aperto ininterrottamente, così come il tempo libero rendono Benidorm una meta turistica ideale. Ci si diverte sulla spiaggia di sabbia, della piccola baia dei nudisti, nel capannone impolverato dagli arredamenti in velluto, oppure nella discoteca all'aperti; si vive, senza grandi pretese, nell'ostello della città vecchia o altrimenti nella raffinata pensione, un po' al di fuori dell'abitato. A partire dall'agosto 2000 Benidorm vanta un'attrazione in più grazie alla Terra Mitica, il più grande Themepark dell'area mediterranea. Chiunque sia alla ricerca di una Spagna autentica, deve percorrere solo pochi chilometri verso l'interno per ritrovarsi poi tra gli splendidi paesi di montagna, lontano dal turismo di massa. Così, per l'amante della Spagna, Benidorm si presenta come una vera alternativa.

BARS

■ **Arcos Bar** (AC B G MA) Summer: 19-3 h. Winter: 18-2 h, Mon closed
C/. Sta Faz, 31 ✉ 03500
■ **Blue Moon.The** (AC B BF F g MA VS) 11-1 h, Wed 20-1 h
C/ de la Palma 23 ✉ 03500
Englisch breakfast, lunch and dinner.
■ **Blue's Bar** (AC B d DR G MA stv snu VS) 22-5h
C/ Santa Faz, 35 ✉ 03500 ☎ 96 27 80 25 40
Sun& Thu dragshow, Fri stripshow, 1.30h.
■ **Chaplin** (AC B G MA) 22.30-3 h
C/. San Vicente, 16 ✉ 03500
Popular.
■ **Company Bar** (B G BF f LJ OS) 10-1 h
C/. San Miguel, 16 ✉ 03500 ☎ 96 586 87 13
■ **Diosa Bar. La** (AC B G MA s) Summer 22-4 h, Winter 17-4 h
C/ San Vicente, 17 ✉ 03500
■ **Eros** (AC B CC DR G LJ MA S SNU VS) 0.30-6 h
C/. Santa Faz, 24 ☎ 96 585 37 06
■ **Hectors** (AC B F f g MA) 20-2.30h
C/. Alicante, 11 ✉ 03500 ☎ 655 952 255
ex-Dieter's Café Bahía now downtown!

916 SPARTACUS 2001/2002

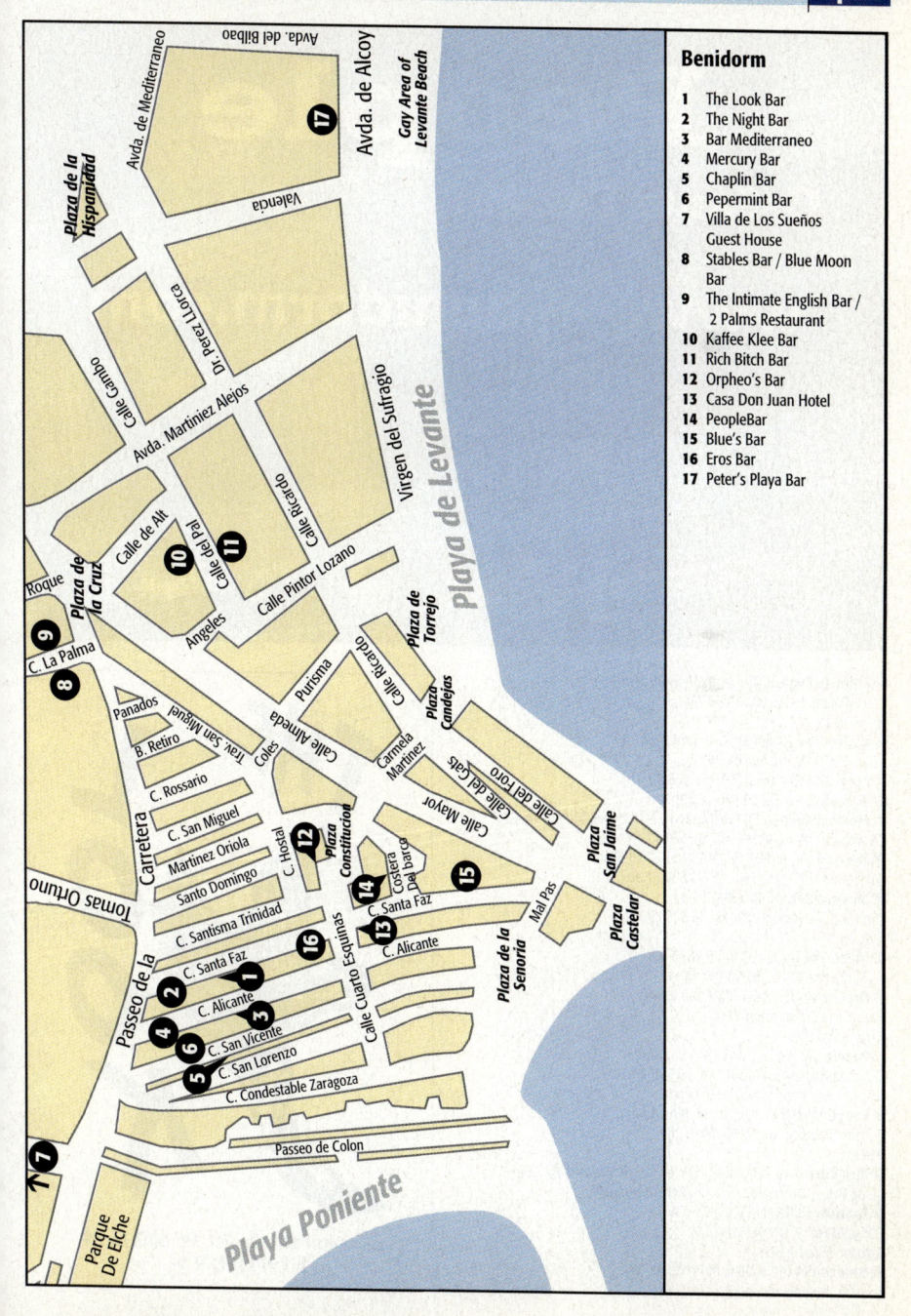

Benidorm Spain

Benidorm

1. The Look Bar
2. The Night Bar
3. Bar Mediterraneo
4. Mercury Bar
5. Chaplin Bar
6. Pepermint Bar
7. Villa de Los Sueños Guest House
8. Stables Bar / Blue Moon Bar
9. The Intimate English Bar / 2 Palms Restaurant
10. Kaffee Klee Bar
11. Rich Bitch Bar
12. Orpheo's Bar
13. Casa Don Juan Hotel
14. PeopleBar
15. Blue's Bar
16. Eros Bar
17. Peter's Playa Bar

Spain Benidorm

People
C/Santa Faz 29.

www.gaybenidorm.com

■ **Intimate English. The** (B g MA S) 20.30-2 h
C/. La Palma, 6 ☏ 96 680 38 76
Shows at 23 h.
■ **Kaffee Klee** (B glm S) 17-3 Sat 21-3 h
C/. de Pal, 9 ☏ 96 585 64 76
■ **Look. The** (B d DR G MA VS) 23-5.30 h
C/. Santa Faz, 12 ☏ 96 680 16 89
■ **Mediereáneo** (AC B G H MA VS) 22- h, closed Mon in winter
C/. Alicante 18 ✉ 03500 ☏ 96 585 67 60
■ **Mercury** (AC B d DR G lj MA s VS) 22.30-5h
C/. Alicante, 10 ✉ 03500 ☏ 96 680 67 30
■ **Minerva Bar** (AC B G MA) 22-4 h
Carretera San Vicente, 22 ☏ 96 585 87 15
Popular.
■ **Night. The** (AC B d G MG S VS) 3-9 h
C/. Santa Faz 10 ☏ 96 680 82 85
■ **Orpheo's** (AC B d DR G MA VS) 22-4 h
Plaza de la Constitución,12
Popular late bar.
■ **People** (AC B d DR GLM lj MA VS) 22-4 h
C/. Santa Faz, 29 ✉ 03500 ☏ 96 586 00 92
Popular, very friendly and good service.
■ **Peppermint** (B G MA) 22-3?, Mon Show 1 h
C/. San Vincente,11 ☏ 96 586 07 89
Popular.
■ **Rich Bitch** (AC B d G MA S STV TV) 21-?, shows daily 22-1 h
C/. de Pal, 4 ✉ 03500 ☏ 666 055 906 (mobile)
■ **Zanzibar** (B DR G STV VS) 23-6 h
C/. Santa Faz, 7 ☏ 96 586 78 07
Popular. STV at 1.30 h.
■ **42nd Street** (AC B DR G MA r VS) 21-3 h
Avenida Uruguay (*under Hiper-Condor*)

THE LOOK
C/. Santa Faz, 12 - Tel. 96 680 16 89
BENIDORM

Benidorm | Spain

VILLA DE LOS SUEÑOS

- The only Gay Men Guesthouse on the Costa Blanca
- Relaxed holidays in private + exclusive atmosphere
- Spacious + tastefully decorated designer rooms with luxury baths
- Scenic seaviews, tropical garden with swimming pool, whirlpool, gym + BBQ
- Only 5 min to gay-bars, beaches + Oldtown or to the untouched countryside
- 2 km to the biggest theme park of the Mediterranean

A PRIVATE GAY MEN'S GUESTHOUSE ~ BENIDORM, COSTA BLANCA
TEL: (0034) 96 586 8824 ~ FAX: (0034) 96 586 2106 ~ email: villadelossuenos@ctv.es
www.villadelossuenos.com

CAFES
■ **Peter's Playa Bar** (AC B GLM MA N) 10-22 h
Levante Beach, Edificio Iberia ☎ 96 681 24 78
Only day-time gay bar in Benidorm. Cozy and friendly atmosphere.

DANCECLUBS
■ **Terraza, La** (AC B CC D DR GLM lj OS MA s SNU STV WE) 2-8 h, Sept-June only WE
Av. - Severu Ochor 31 ✉ 03500 *(In front of Benidorm Palace)*

RESTAURANTS
■ **Casa Abdul** (B F g) 12-15, 19-24 h, Wed closed
C/. La Palma, 13 ✉ 03500 ☎ 96 585 39 35
International cusine with a French/Morrocan touch.
■ **Gigi** (b F glm MA)
C/. La Palma, 12 ✉ 03500 ☎ 96 585 05 85
■ **Hierbas** (F g MA) 19-23.30 h , Tue closed
C/. Purisima, 4 ☎ 96 586 86 32
International - English cuisine.
■ **Secret Gardens, The** (B F g MA) 19.30-? h
C/. Condestable Zaragozá 21 ☎ 96 680 69 18
French cuisine.
■ **Two Palms** (F g MA) 19.30-23 h, Tue closed
C/. La Palma, 30 ☎ 96 680 18 07
International - English cuisine.
■ **Vagabund Restaurant, The** (F g OS) Winter: 19.30-22.30, Summer 20-24 h
C/. Bon Retiro, 4 ☎ 96 680 81 66
International cuisine.

SHOWS
■ **Molino** (B g MA STV) 22-?, Show 22.30 h
Av. Beniardá, 2 *(El Cruce)* ☎ 96 680 23 08

■ **Sabrina** (B g STV) 22-?, show 22.45 h
Av. Jaime, I 9 *(in the basement of Hotel Sirena)* ☎ 96 585 36 06

SEX SHOPS/BLUE MOVIES
■ **Sex Shop Benidorm** (g MA VS) 10.30-13.30, 16-21.30 h, Sun closed
C/. San Roque, 6 ☎ 96 586 67 46
■ **Show Center Sexyland** (g VS) 10-24 h
C/. Marqués de Comillas, 2 ☎ 96 680 64 00

SAUNAS/BATHS
■ **Adonis** (AC B G MA msg SA SB VS) 15.30-21.30 h
C/. Venezuela 4 ✉ 03500 *(Edificio Narcea, near Gasolinera Isleta, Avenida Jaime I)* ☎ 96 585 79 58
■ **Scorpios** (B G MA msg SA SB VS WH) 15.30-22 h
C/. Ruzafa ✉ 03500 *(next to bike shop)*

HOTELS
■ **Casa Don Juan** (B bf G H OS) 11-15, 19-2 h
C/. Santa Faz, 28 ✉ 03500 ☎ 96 680 91 65 📠 96 680 48 86
✉ casadonjuan@mixmail.com
5 double and 2 single room some with shower/WC, TV and terrace; apartments available. Also popular Bar-Café.

GUEST HOUSES
■ **Villa de los Sueños** (BF CC f G H msg NU OS PI WH WO)
Carretera Finestrat 5 ✉ 03500 *(3 km above Benidorm in a quiet surrounding)* ☎ 96 586 88 24 ☎ (619) 108 341 (mobile)
📠 96 586 21 06 ✉ villadelossuenos@ctv.es
🖥 www.villadelossuenos.com
8 double rooms and 2 suites incl. bf buffet. Rooms with Bath/WC, TV and ceiling fan. Car rental, excursions, aiport service, half board available. Close to the new theme park.

Spain — Benidorm ▶ Bilbao

APARTMENTS

■ **Front Line Apartments**
Benipark, Av. Armada Española, 4 ✉ 03500 *(Block 2, Apt. 6-7)*
☎ 96 586 51 29   ☎ 670 593 891 *(mobile)*
Swimming Pool, Tennis, Privat Parking Rates Jul-15 Sep Ptas 70.000/week, low season 45.000. 20 luxury apartments.

HEALTH GROUPS

■ **Asociacion Civica a Afectados del HIV • SIDA, Amigos Benidorm, Marina Baixa** 9-13, 17-21 h
C/. Gambo 6, 2, 6   ☎ 96 680 44 44   ☎ 96 654 45 02 95

SWIMMING

-La Cala (g NU MA) (Playa Poniente, by the rocks at the end of the beach. Popular, but dangerous.)
-Rincon de Loix (g) (at the end of the beach)
-Playa Levante, in front of "Peter's Playa Bar (Popular)
-Playa Campomanes, ca. 10 km north of Benidorm (g NU) (near 03590 Altea, take road Altea-Calpe, before tunnel, under Pueblo Mascarat.)
-Playa Racó Conill (g NU) (bus to playa Finestrat, then walking in direction Alicante, up the hill and down to the beach and further on)
-Playa Poniente

Bilbao

BARS

■ **Convento. El** (B Glm d MA) 21-? h
C/. Esperanza, 11
■ **Heaven Club** (B DR G MA VS) 22-3, WE -4.30 h
C/. Dos de Mayo, 6   ☎ 94 416 17 10
■ **High** (B d DR G MA VS) 20.30-3.30, WE -4 h
C/. La Naja, 5
■ **Kasko** (AC B CC d F G MA S)
C/. Santa Maria, 16 ✉ 48005 *(Casco Viejo)* ☎ 94 416 03 11
It's also a restaurant, dinner with piano music.
■ **Mykonos** (AC B DR G MA s SNU VS) 20-? h
C/. General Castillo, 4 ✉ 48003
■ **Otxoa** (B d g TV) 20-3, WE -4 h
C/. Lersundi, 10 *(Calle Heros)* ☎ 94 424 18 48
■ **Santurio** (B DR G MA R VS) 19-? h
C/. Lamana, 5   ☎ 94 415 94 96
■ **Sperma** (B DR G MA r VS) 20-3, WE -4 h
C/. Dos de Mayo, 6
■ **Tabernville** (B DR G MA) 21-3.30, WE -6 h
C/. Hernani, 18 ✉ 48003 ☎ 94 415 35 76
■ **Txoko Landa** (B D GLM p s WE) Fri-Sat 23-2.30 h
Escalinatas de Solokoetxe, 4 ✉ 48005 *(Metro Casco Viejo)*
☎ 94 415 07 19
Bilbao's gay movement bar.
■ **28** (B gLM) 21-3 h
C/. Hernani, 3

CAFES

■ **Biziztu** (B glm OS)
C/. la Torre / Casco Viejo
■ **Bristol** (B BF f G MA OS) 11-2 h, WE 19-4 h
Plaza Venezuela, 1 ✉ 48001 *(Entrance via C/Principe)*
☎ 94 424 55 98
■ **Ekklesía** (B f glm MA) 10-15, 17-23, WE -2 h
C/. Hernani, 3
■ **Lamiak** (B f GLM s) 19-1, Wed -2. Winter 16.30-24, WE -2.30 h
C/. Pelota, 8   ☎ 94 416 17 65

■ **Nervion. El** (B f G r) 19-3 h
C/. Dos de Mayo, 1
■ **Sorgiñe** (B f GLM OS) 19-1 h
C/. Pelota, 4

DANCECLUBS

■ **Bailongo** (AC B D glm S STV) 20-3, WE -4.30 h
C/. Henao, 6 ✉ 48001 ☎ 94 424 70 03
Gay only on Thu and Sun for show 22.30 an 1 h.
■ **Congreso** (B D g) 24-4 h
C/. Uribitarte, 8
■ **Conjunto Vacio** (B d g) 22-4 h
Muelle de la Merced, 3
■ **Distrito 9** (! B D g WE) Fri Sat 1-? h
C/. Juan de Ajuariaguerra, 17
■ **Enigma** (B D glm MA) 20-5 h, WE (G)
C/. Luis Iruarrizaga, 7
■ **Key** (B D G STV) WE show 1 & 3 h
C/. Cristo, 3
■ **La Cantora** (AC B D glm MA S STV) 20-4, WE -6 h
C/. Henao, 25 ✉ 48009 ☎ 94 423 77 18
Shows Wed and Sun 22.30 h and 1.30 h.

RESTAURANTS

■ **Arrebato** (A AC B CC D F glm MA S WE) 11-1.30 h
Muelle Marzana, 4   ☎ 94 416 41 81
■ **Deliciosa. La** (B F g MA) 19-23 h
C/. Jardines, 1   ☎ 94 416 35 90
■ **Ruedo. El** (B F G MA) 10-22 h, closed Sun
C/. García Salazar, 6   ☎ 94 422 11 35
Good, cheap lunch.
■ **Txiriboga** (B F glm) 13-15, 19-23 h
C/. Santa María, 11
Bocadillos.
■ **Txomin Barullo** (B F g) 18.30-23.30 h
C/. Barrenkalle, 40

SHOWS

■ **Tiffany's** (AC B CC d e g MA S SNU STV TV) 23-6, Show 1.30-3.30 h
C/. Francisco Macia, 11 ✉ 48008 *(Near Museo Guggenheim)*

SEX SHOPS/BLUE MOVIES

■ **American's** (g VS) 10-3, Sun 10-14, 16-3 h
C/. Nicolás Alcorta 5 *(Galería Centro Zabalburo, 1st floor)*
■ **Internacional** (g VS) 10-2
C/. Nicolás Alcorta, 7 *(Galería Centro Zabalburo; 1st floor)*
☎ 94 444 68 51
■ **Sex Shop** (g VS) 10-14, 15.30-22.30 h
C/. Ledesma, 2   ☎ 94 424 40 23

SAUNAS/BATHS

■ **Oasis** (B DR f G MA SA SB SOL VS WO) Mon-Thu 17-22, Fri -8, Sat 17-Sun 22 h
C/. Atxuri, 43 ✉ 48006 *(tram-Euskotren, Bus 77-27)*
☎ 94 433 66 30
■ **XQ 28** (B cc DR f G MA SA SB SOL Pl VS) 17-23, Fri Sat -8 h
C/. Nicolas Alcorta, 5 ✉ 48003 *(near Plaza Zabalburu)*
☎ 94 422 39 20
Condoms, lubricant and poppers on sale.

BOOK SHOPS

■ **Libreria De Babel** 10-14, 17-21 h.
C/. de la Pelota, 6 ✉ 48005 ☎ 94 416 85 83

Bilbao ▶ Canary Islands - Gran Canaria | **Spain**

GENERAL GROUPS
■ **Aldarte** Mon-Fri 10-13 , Mon-Thu 17.30-20,30 h
C/. Barroeta Aldamar, 7 ✉ 48001 (2nd Floor, Metro Albaudo)
☎ 94 423 72 96 📠 94 423 72 96
Center for information, help with problems, archives.
■ **EHGAM** Mon-Fri 20-22 h
Escalinetas des Solokoetxe, 4 ✉ 48005 ☎ 94 415 07 19
Gay library and archives. Publisher of "Gay Hotsa". Friendly help with all sorts of problems.

■ **T-4 Asoc. Ciud. lucha contra el sida**
Alameda Gregorio de Revilla, 36 ✉ 48080 ☎ 94 422 12 40
📠 94 422 24 65 📧 autopoyot4@mx3.redestb.es

HEALTH GROUPS
■ **Comisión Ciudadana Anti Sida de Bizkaia** Mon-Fr 9-13, 16-20 h
C/. Bailén, 6 ✉ 48003 ☎ 94 416 00 55
Information and services concerning AIDS.
■ **Gays por la Salud de Euskadi-T 4** 10-23 h
C/. Autonomía, 56,3 ✉ 48012 ☎ 94 422 12 40
■ **Servicio Vasco de Salud (ETS)** Mon-Fri 9-12 h
C/. Coctor Arcilza, planta baja
☎ 94 441 25 00
HIV-testing.

SWIMMING
-Playa Larrabastera (La Salvaje)
-Playa Arrigunaga (Algorta)

CRUISING
-Azkorri
-Park Casilda Iturriza

Blanes

SWIMMING
-Playa los Pinos (NU) (cruising at the end of the beach.)

Burgos

BARS
■ **Sebastian** (AC B G MA OS S) 17-2.30, WE-4 h, Mon closed
C/. Trinidad, 16 ✉ 09001 *(Near Palacio Capitanía)*
☎ 947 27 86 52
Sat shows or special events.
■ **Trastienda. La** (B glm) 20-2 h
Plaza de la Isla

CRUISING
-Pirazes de Cortez (day and evening)
-El Empecinado (park at the river, gardens of La Isla)

Cadiz

BARS
■ **Café de Levante** (B f glm YG) 20-1, Fri Sat -2 h
C/. Rosario

SEX SHOPS/BLUE MOVIES
■ **Internacional** (g VS) 10-22 h
C/. Pintor Murillo, 2
☎ 956 26 20 00

GUEST HOUSES
■ **Pension "Torre Mar"** (BF F H glm) 24 h
C/. Cordoba, 30 ✉ 11550 *(50 m to the beach, 5 min. to the center)*
☎ 956 976 126 📠 956 976 126 📧 ehlershd@aol.com
4 double rooms with WC/bath, Sat-TV

SWIMMING
-Playa El Chato (NU)(on the way from Cadiz direction San Fernando)

CRUISING
-Playa de Cortadura (from the Edificio Alfa over the beach wall to the beginning of the beach; night and late night)
-Maritim Promenade (Victoria Beach; nights)
-Callejón del Blanco

Canary Islands

Time: GMT
Climate: subtropical sea climate, under the influence of the dry northeasterly winds which keep the temperatures at a pleasant level. Short winter rainy season.
Important gay cities: Playa del Ingles/Maspalomas (Gran Canaria), Las Palmas (Gran Canaria).

Canary Islands - **Fuerteventura**

BARS
■ **Freedom 41B** (B GLM MA S) 21.30-2.30 h
C.C. Atlantico, Corralejo ☎ (676) 15 89 93

HEALTH GROUPS
■ **Hospital Seguridad Social**
Street to the Airport km 1 *(in Puerto del Rosario)* ☎ 922 85 04 99
☎ 922 85 05 45

SWIMMING
-Dunas de Corralejo (g NU) (between Puerto del Rosario and Corralejo; sometimes)
-Playa Castillo, Caleta de Fuste (g MA NU)

Canary Islands - Gran Canaria - **Las Palmas**

BARS
■ **Iron Bridge** (B G MA SNU) 22-3 h, Show Thu
C/. Mariana Pineda, 17
Recently renovated, new image.
■ **Lady Pepa** (B G MA) 21.30-3 h
C/. Sargento Llagas, 32
■ **Miau** (! AC B d G MA s) 22-4h
C/ Secretario Artiles, 51, 1° ✉ 35007 *(near Parque Sta Catalina)*

CAFES
■ **Magic** (B BF f GLM OS) 9-4 h
Plaza Feray, 6 ✉ 35007 *(Zona Puerta)*
■ **Nuevo Rio** (! B F G MA OS r) 8-2 h
Parque Santa Catalina ☎ 928 20 30 48
Newly renovated, very popular.

DANCECLUBS
■ **Faunos** (AC B D G MA r VS WE) 23-? h
C/. Dr. Miguel Rosas, 37, bajo ✉ 35007 ☎ 928 264 758
■ **Flash** (B D G STV VS WE YG) Tue-Sun 0-8, show Sun 2 h
C/. Bernardo de la Torre, 86 *(near Parque Santa Catalina)*
Popular.

Spain — Canary Islands - Gran Canaria

RESTAURANTS
■ **Casa Pablo** (B F g) Mon-Sat 13-16.30, 20-0.30 h
C/. Tomas Miller, 73 ☎ 928 26 81 58
■ **Menina** (AC B jCC g MA S) 21-1 h, Mon closed
C/. Diderot, 15 ✉ 35007 *(near by the port)* ☎ 928 269 546
Dinner Show
■ **Rincón Vasco. El** (A AC B CC F g MA) 13-16, 20-24 h, closed Sun evenings and Mon
C/. Hierro, 4 ✉ 35009 *(near Playa Canteras)* ☎ 928 27 74 63

SEX SHOPS/BLUE MOVIES
■ **Jomato'G** (g VS) Mon-Sat 10-2, Sun 10-24 h
C/. Dr. Miguel Rosas, 4 ☎ 928 22 15 02
■ **Sala X** (g VS) 11-0 h
C/. Tomás Miller, 51, bajo ✉ 35007 *(Zona Puerto)*

SAUNAS/BATHS
■ **Cómplice Sauna** (AC B DR G MA p s SA VS WH) 16-24h, Mon closed
C/ Joaquín Costa, 48, bajo ✉ 35007 *(near Parque Sta. Catalina)*
☎ 928 22 43 97
Private cubicles with TV and 4 porn channels.
■ **Portugal** (AC B DR G MA msg N P SA SB VS) 16-24 h
C/. Portugal, 27 ✉ 35010 *(Near by La Playa de las Canteras)*
☎ 928 227 284
■ **Trebol** (B DR f G MA msg SA SB VS) 16-24 h
C/. Tomas Miller, 55 ✉ 35007

HOTELS
■ **Hotel Guacamayo** (g H)
C/. Dr. Miguel Rosa, 9

GENERAL GROUPS
■ **Collectivo de Gays y Lesbianas de Gran Canaria, GAMÁ**
Mon-Fri 18-21h
C/ Buenos Aires, 53, bajo ✉ 35002 *(near Parque San Telmo)*
☎ 928 433 427 🖨 928 433 427

CRUISING
- Parque Santa Catalina/Calle Ripoche (r)
- Parque Doramas
- Playa de las Canteras el Balneario
- Roques Muelle Deportivo
- Parque San Telmo
- Estación de Guaguas
- Toilets San Telmo

Canary Islands - Gran Canaria - Playa del Inglés

✳ What can be said about some other gay holiday spots, can be said particularly about Playa del Ingles: It's on the edge. On the outer edge of Spain, of Europe. It could be said that its part of Africa. Playa lies in the utmost south of Gran Canaria, and the gay beach is found, naturally, in the utmost corner between Playa and Maspalomas. Gay nightlife offers the other extreme. Most but not all of the gay establishments like cafés, bars, discos, saunas and sex shops are in the *Yumbo Center*. This is very convenient. The venues range from dusky leather-bars to buzzling discos. The distances are no problem at all. The only reason you could need a car is if you want to make a trip round the island, which however can be also made by bus. And if you stay in one of the bungalows of Maspalomas, the nightly trips to and fro by taxi are easily affordable.

✳ Was für manchen anderen schwulen Urlaubsort gilt, gilt für Playa del Inglés ganz besonders: Es liegt am Ende. Am äußersten Ende Spaniens, ja Europas, eigentlich ein Teil Afrikas. Playa liegt im äußersten Süden, und der schwule Strand liegt natürlich in der äußersten Ecke zwischen Playa und Maspalomas.
Das schwule Nightlife bietet genau das andere Extrem. Im *Yumbo Centro* finden sich die meisten, wenn auch nicht alle, Cafés, Bars, Discos, Saunen, Sex Shops. Das ist sehr praktisch. Und dabei reicht die Palette wirklich von der schummrigen Lederbar bis zur heftigen Disco.
Die Wege sind in Playa kein Problem. Wer dort wohnt, benötigt ein Wagen höchstens für die Inselrundfahrt, die man aber auch per Bus unternehmen kann. Und selbst für die abendlichen und nächtlichen Fahrten von und nach Maspalomas -so man dort in einer Bungalowanlage wohnt- reichen die äußerst günstigen Taxen.

✳ Playa del Ingles est un vrai paradis gai. Cette station balnéaire est à l'extrême sud de l'Europe, déjà en Afrique. La plage gaie se trouve entre Playa et Maspalomas, au bout du monde pour ainsi dire. La vie gaie nocturne, c'est avant tout le "Yumbo Centro" où l'on trouve la plupart des cafés, bars, boîtes, saunas et sex shops, ce qui a l'avantage d'être pratique. Il y en a pour tout le monde: de la pénombre du bar cuir aux lasers des boîtes de nuit. Ici aussi, on peut tout faire à pied: pas besoin de voiture, sauf pour faire le tour de l'île, si une excursion en bus ne vous dit rien. Vous n'aurez pas besoin de voiture même pour les trajets de nuit depuis et jusqu'à Maspalomas, car les taxis sont bon marché.

✳ Lo que es valedero para otros centros turísticos gay, vale también para Playa del Inglés. Se encuentra geograficamente casi escondida y es el punto más alejado de España e incluso de Europa, en realidad es parte de Africa. La playa se localiza en el más extremo sur de la isla y los gays se reunen sobre todo en la parte de la playa más próxima a Maspalomas. La vida nocturna gay se concentra en el otro extremo de la isla. En *Yumbo Center* se encuentra la mayoría (no todos) de los cafes, bares, discos, saunas, sex shops etc.. La variedad de los sitios de ambiente es sorprendente: Aquí se encuentran desde oscuros bares de cuero hasta discotecas marchosas. Las distancias no suponen ningún problema. Un coche de alquiler se necesita solo para un recorrido de la isla, que se puede hacer hasta en autobus. A los turistas que vivan en Maspalomas recomendamos el taxi para sus salidas nocturnas, ya que es bastante económico.

✳ Ciò che vale per alcuni luoghi turistici gay vale particolarmente per la playa del Inglès: è il massimo. Il limite estremo della Spagna, dell'Europa, a dire il vero dell'Africa. Playa è situata all'estremo sud, e la spiaggia gay in un angolo estremo tra Playa e Maspalomas. La vita notturna gay offre naturalmente l'estremo opposto. Nel *Yumbo centro* si trovano, se non tutti, la maggior parte dei bar, delle discoteche, delle saune e dei sex shop. É molto comodo, e la gamma va dal più sordido bar sado-maso alla più vivace discoteca. A Playa le distanze non sono un problema, chi ci vive ha bisogno dell'auto solo per fare il giro dell'isola, che si può fare anche in autobus. Se vivete in un villaggio turistico ricordate che per le escursioni da e per Maspalomas i taxi sono particolarmente economici.

BARS
■ **Adonis** (B G MA OS) 19-?
Yumbo Centro, ✉ 35100 *(1st Floor)*
Popular.
■ **Ana Lupez - Punto de Encuentro** (B GLM MA OS s TV VS)
22-4 h, Sun closed
Yumbo Centro ✉ 35100 *(2nd floor)*
El rincón romántico - Fri/Sat live music.

Canary Islands - Gran Canaria | Spain

Wir bringen dich ans Ziel.
Gran Canaria   Ibiza
    Mykonos
         Sitges

Neuen Prospekt kostenlos anfordern!
www.atlantis-travel.de
089/23 666 00

ATLANTIS
THE TRAVEL COMPANY

Pestalozzistr. 17 · 80469 München
Fax 23 666 056 · tom@atlantis-travel.de

NEW SAUNA PORTUGAL

Finland Sauna
Steam Sauna
Dark room
Free Cabins
Video X
Massage
Bar

C/ Portugal, 27   LAS PALMAS
16:00 - 24:00   928 227 284

VILLAS BLANCAS
THE BEST AND LARGEST EXCLUSIVELY GAY COMPLEX ON THE ISLAND

ALL VILLAS WITH SEPARATE BEDROOM / PATIO / SUN TERRACE / BATH + TOILET / KITCHENETTE / SATELLITE-TV.
ALLE VILLEN MIT SEPARATEM SCHLAFZIMMER / PATIO / SONNENTERRASSE / BAD / WC / KITCHENETTE / SATELLITEN-TV.

- BEAUTIFUL SWIMMING-POOL WITH POOL-BAR AND BISTRO SURROUNDED BY TROPICAL GARDENS.

  SCHÖNER SWIMMING-POOL MIT POOL-BAR UND BISTRO IN GEPFLEGTER TROPISCHER GARTENANLAGE.

- QUIET AREA NEAR YUMBO, BEACH AND SAND DUNES.

- BISTRO WITH DAILY MENU AND WEEKLY BARBEQUE WITH SHOW - FRIENDLY PERSONAL SERVICE.

  BISTRO MIT TAGESMENU UND WÖCHENTLICHEM BARBEQUE MIT SHOW - FREUNDLICHE PERSÖNLICHE ATMOSPHÄRE.

- RUHIGE LAGE, NÄHE YUMBO, STRAND UND DÜNEN.

INFORMATION AND RESERVATIONS:
TELF: + 34.902.168.169 FAX: +34.902.268.269 vb@boesweb.com

Spain — Canary Islands - Gran Canaria

GRAN CANARIA

Ibiza - Torremolinos - Sitges - Benidorm
Mykonos - Fort Lauderdale - Key West - San Francisco - Orlando
Amsterdam - London - Wien - Berlin - Hamburg - Sydney - Kapstadt

www.discustravel.de

Tel.: + 49 (0)6 21 - 40 96 27
Fax: + 49 (0)6 21 - 44 13 40
e-Mail: info@discustravel.de

GiV- Reisen / Discustravel
Schwetzinger Str. 93
D - 68165 Mannheim - Germany

CRUISE
LEATHER - UNIFORM BAR
YUMBO CENTER
2ª Planta - Local 11 - 12 - 13
FROM 11 p.m. till ...
Ab 23:00 bis ...
PLAYA DEL INGLES

■ **Bärenhöhle** (AC B DR G LJ MA OS VS) 20-3 h
Yumbo Centro ✉ 35100 ☎ 928 769 692
■ **Berlin Cafe Bar** (B f G MA OS) 10-3 h closed Sun
Yumbo Centro (Planta 3a)
■ **The Block** (B DR G LJ MA OS s VS) 21-3 h
Yumbo Centro ✉ 35100 (Planta 1)
■ **Buddies** (B f G MA OS s) 19-3 h
Yumbo Centro (Planta 1)
■ **Casablanca** (B G MG OS S) 19-3h
Yumbo Centro, Local 111-113 ✉ 35100 (1st Floor)
Travestie show 4 x per week
■ **Centre Stage** (! B G lj MA OS stv) 22-3, WE -3.30 h,
Thu Leather & Feather Party
Yumbo Centro (Planta 2)
■ **Construction** (B DR G LJ MA OS SNU VS) 20-? h

Yumbo Centro ✉ 35100 (basement) ☎ 928 14 30 75
Leather Bar
■ **Contact** (B DR G LJ MA VS) 23-4 h
Yumbo Centro (Planta 2)
■ **Cruise** (AC B DR G LJ MA VS) 23 h- ?
Yumbo Centro, Local 11-12-13 (2nd floor/Planta 2) ☎ 928 76 34 53
■ **Diamonds** (B G MA OS STV) 21-? h
Yumbo Centro (Planta 1)
■ **Dicke Ei. Das** (AC B D G MA STV) 20-4 h
Cita Centro, planta baja ✉ 35100 (underground level)
☎ 928 76 50 98
Daily shows beginning at 22 h.
■ **Du & Ich Wunderbar** (AC B G MA OS s) 19-3 h
Yumbo Center, Local 151-02 ✉ 35100 (1st floor/Planta 1)
More than 80 different cocktails.

Coffee-House & Bar Hummel Hummel

*for all ages we offer:
2 Dark-Rooms, Video,
Shows (Strip & Drag)
300 m² largest Gay-Bar
in town, open 19.30 - 3.00*

924 SPARTACUS 2001/2002

Canary Islands - Gran Canaria **Spain**

Du & Ich WunderBar

- über 80 Cocktails
- 12 internationale Biersorten

Yumbo Center
1ª Planta
Local 151-02
Playa del Ingles

PUB NESTOR

**GREAT ATMOSPHERE · FABULOUS MUSIC
STYLISH DECOR · REALISTIC PRICES · SHOWS**

* THE PLACE TO BE FOR A FUN NIGHT OUT *
* THE FRIENDLIEST STAFF*

GROUND FLOOR ... YUMBO CENTRE.
PLAYA DEL INGLES ... GRAN CANARIA
Tel. 928 766266. ... e.mail...STUTBAR@twice.net

DONT FORGET
Every Wednesday & Saturday our very own Gay Game Show. „Open the Box"

Open every day
7.00 to 2.30

■ **Eden** (B g MA OS s) 19-2.30h
CC Yumbo, planta 1 ✉ 35100 ☎ 928 76 66 78
■ **First Lady** (B D gLM OS s) 20-3 h, Thu closed
Yumbo Centro ✉ 35109 ☎ 928 50 11 18
■ **Flip** (AC B G MA OS s VS) 23-3.30, Sun 6-?h
CC Yumbo, planta 4 ✉ 35100
Occasionally after hour.
■ **Gran Café Latino** (B f G MA OS YG) 16-2.30, summer: 19-2.30 h
Yumbo Centro *(Planta 1)* ☎ 928 76 12 69
■ **Hollywood** (B d G MA OS VS) 21-3 h, Sun closed
Yumbo Centro, Local 131-14 ✉ 35100
Music videos.
■ **Hummel Hummel** (B DR G MA OS snu stv VS) 19.30-3 h
Yumbo Centro ✉ 35100 *(1st floor)*
2 darkrooms, one for the young men, one for the elderly.
■ **Ibiza** (B G MA OS) 20-?h
CC Yumbo, local 111-05 ✉ 35100
■ **Klapsmühle** (AC B f G MA OS R VS) 22-6h
CC Yumbo, planta 2 ✉ 35100 ☎ 649 738 483

■ **Lux** (B G MA OS) 18-3 h
Yumbo Centro ✉ 35100 *(ground floor)* ☎ 928 77 60 54
Original Italian ice creams.
■ **Mykonos** (B d DR G MA OS VS YG) 22-3 h
Yumbo Centro *(Planta 4)*
■ **Na Und** (B d G MA og OS) 21-3 h
Yumbo Centro *(Planta 1)*
■ **Nachtcafé Moonlight** (B G MA OS stv) 21-4 h
Yumbo Centro *(Planta 1)* ☎ 928 77 90 35
■ **Pajaro Loco. El** (B d G MA OS) 22-? h
Yumbo Centro *(Planta 2)*
■ **Peppermint** (B G MA OS) 20-3 h
Yumbo Centro *(Planta 1)*
■ **Prison Bar** (B DR G LJ MA OS VS) Summer: 0-5 h, Winter: 23-5 h
Yumbo Centro ✉ 35100 *(2nd floor/Planta 2)*
■ **Pub Nestor** (B G MA OS S) 19-2.30 h
Yumbo Centro ✉ 35100 *(1st floor/Planta 1)* ☎ 928 76 62 66
Wed & Sat Gay Game show.

Spain | Canary Islands - Gran Canaria

DaLi's
Eddy & Gary's
Gay CAFE - Restaurante

Cuisine International – Française

cc Yumbo
2e PLANTA

en façe/über/in font
La Belle (2e etage)

Cuisine open/overt
14u - 24u
Domingo 17u - 24u

Tel./Fax 928/77 11 73

Welkom - Welcome - Bienvenu - Willkommen

Playa del Inglés **Gran Canaria**

SAUNA NILO

☎ 928 76 54 64

2 FINLAND SAUNAS
1 WITH SHOWER INSIDE
T.V. IN ALL PRIVATE CABINS
MASSAGE
SNACK BAR, VIDEO ROOM
300 m² - BIGGEST SAUNA
IN PLAYA DEL INGLES
VERY CLEAN
SAFE ENVIRONMENT

FOR MEN

C.C. NILO, PLAYA DEL INGLES

Valentine's

THE ONLY GAY RESTAURANT
IN YUMBO - CENTER

Open all year
19.00 - 24.00

■ **Spartacus** (B G MA OS) 20-2.30 h
Yumbo Centro *(Planta 1)* ☎ 928 76 65 40
■ **Terry's Show** (B G MA OS STV) 22-? h
Yumbo Centro *(Planta 2)*
Daily 0-1 show with frequent guest star Batusi Pérez Prado from Tropicana, Cuba.
■ **Toby's Bar** (AC B glm MA s stv) 12.30-3.30 h
Yumbo Centro
Three times a week Dragqueen-Show.
■ **Tubos** (B G MA OS VS) 22-3, WE -3.30 h
Yumbo Centro *(Planta 4)*
■ **Typisch Kölsch** (AC B G MA r) 18-1 h
CC Metro, 2nd Floor ✉ 35100
■ **Why Not** (AC B G MA VS) 22-? h
Yumbo Centro *(Planta 4)*
■ **1. September** (AC B G MG) 20.30-? h
Yumbo Centro, Local 131-01 *(1st Floor)*
English, German and Spanish spoken.

Canary Islands - Gran Canaria | **Spain**

Lux

BAR • CAFÉ • PUB

original italian icecreme

C.C. YUMBO
Groundfloor
Playa del Inglés
Gran Canaria
www.bar-lux.de
e-mail: info@bar-lux.de
Tel.: 0034 928 77 6054

PRISON BAR

of GRAN CANARIA
PLAYA DEL INGLÉS
YUMBO CENTER

FOR MEN

XL CLUB — MEN'S

HAVE A LOOK ON THE REST
AND THEN GO FOR THE BEST

The one and only LASER-SHOW!
Best Sound & Light System!!!!!!!!!
Latest imported records!!!!!!!!!!!!!!!!
Special events every 2. night!!!!!!!!

Gran Canaria - Playa del Ingles - Yumbo Center - below mainroad

Spain — Canary Islands - Gran Canaria

GRAN CANARIA À LA CARTE:

VILLAS BLANCAS
BEACH BOY BUNGALOWS
PASION TROPICAL
VISTA BONITA

... und natürlich auch:
IBIZA, SITGES, MYKONOS, FLORIDA, NEW YORK, LONDON, KAPSTADT ...

Reisebüro am Hellkamp
Hellkamp 17 · 20255 Hamburg · Tel. (040) 40 19 61 86 · Fax (040) 49 19 00
hellkamp@aol.com · www.gaytravel.de: Über das „Buchungsportal" online buchen
Katalog mit Sonderprospekten gegen 3 DM in Briefmarken

---

complete offer
see page Germany/Berlin

GRAN CANARIA – from ESP 4.000,-
overnight accomodation service
· about 750 beds · more than 28 cities ·

enjoy **bed & breakfast**

central booking office Berlin ☎ **+49-30-236 236 10** 4:30-9:00 pm local time
Fax +49-30-23623619 · info@ebab.com · www.ebab.com

CAFES

■ **Gourmet Café** (AC B bf CC F G OS) 11-1h
CC Yumbo, planta 2 ✉ 35100 ☎ 928 77 29 24
Breakfast & cakes during daytime, gourmet dinner.

■ **Mambo N°5** (B bf f g OS) 8-19h, Sun closed
Av. de Tirajana, 3 ✉ 35100 (opposite Hotel Rey Carlos)
☎ 676 249 184
breakfast, cakes, sandwiches

■ **Marlene** (B CC G MA OS s) 10.30-1 h
CC Cita, Planta 2 ✉ 35 100 ☎ 928 768 514

■ **Strand Apo-Theke** (B F g) Mon-Fri 11-20, Sat Sun 15-? h
Oasis Centro Maspalomas ☎ 928 14 12 96
Follow the beach towards the fare, see the rainbow flag.

■ **Café Wien** (B f g OS) 9.30-23 h
Cita Centro (Planta 2) ☎ 928 76 03 80

DANCECLUBS

■ **Kings Club** (B D DR G MA OS V) 24-? h
Yumbo Centro, Planta 2 ✉ 35100

■ **Metropol** (AC B D DR G MA OS SNU SG V) 23-5, Sun 6-?h
CC Yumbo, planta 4 ✉ 35100
occasionnally after hour.

■ **XL Men's Club** (B D G OS SNU SG V) 22.30-5, WE -6, Show Tue Thu Sun 1.45 h
Yumbo Centro (Planta 2; below mainroad)

RESTAURANTS

■ **A. Gaudi** (CC B F g) Fri-Wed 18-24 h
C/. Cuba, 3, El Tablero de Maspalomas ☎ 928 14 14 85

■ **Bei Lelo** (B CC F G OS) Thu-Tue 11-24 h
Yumbo Centro ✉ 35100 (Planta 2a) ☎ 928 77 29 24

■ **Dali's** (B CC F G OS) 14-24, Sun 17-24 h
Yumbo Centro ✉ 35100 (2nd floor) ☎ 928 77 11 73
Café-restaurant with international & French cuisine from 19 h.

■ **Merlin** (B F G OS Pl) 12-24 h
Av. de Tirajana 18 ✉ 35100 ☎ 928 76 95 01

■ **Monroe** (B F G MA OS) 22-4.30 h
Yumbo Center (2nd floor)
Fastfood restaurant, café and bar.

■ **Ola** (B CC F g MA OS) 18-2 h, Thu closed
Yumbo Centro ✉ 35100 (Planta 2) ☎ 928 76 46 15

■ **Valentine's** (B F G OS) 19-24 h
Yumbo Centro ✉ 35100 (2nd floor/Planta 2) ☎ 928 77 06 48
International cuisine.

■ **Zürich** (AC B CC e F g OS) Winter: 17-23 h. Summer: 18-24 h, Sun closed
CC Cita, Local 268 ✉ 35100 ☎ 928 774 697

SHOWS

■ **Westphalia** (B g OS STV) 21-1 h
Cita Centro (Planta 1) ☎ 928 76 13 51

SEX SHOPS/BLUE MOVIES

■ **Man's Garage** (AC CC G MA VS) 19.30-3.30 h
Yumbo Center 4th floor ☎ 928 76 42 86
Darkroom with sling, all cabins with video.

■ **Man's Plaza** (AC CC DR G MA VS) 16.30-3.30 h
Yumbo Centro (1st Floor)

■ **Sexyland** (AC CC g MA VS) 16-8 h
Yumbo Center, planta Caja 131

Canary Islands - Gran Canaria | Spain

Always Fun!

Beach Boy Bungalows - Gran Canaria

GAY MEN ONLY!

BEACH BOY BUNGALOWS
Los Robles Campo Internacional

Call for information and reservations:
De GAY Krant Travel
Kloveniersburgwal 40 - 1012 CW Amsterdam
tel +31 (0)20 421 00 00 - fax +31 (0)20 620 62 17
email: travel@gaykrant.nl - Internet: http://gaykrant.nl
Also your address for any trip throughout the world, including Amsterdam, Paris, London, Berlin, Barcelona, Sitges, New York, Mykonos, Brazil, Florida, California and Mexico.

The IGLTA
Gays & Lesbians Unite in World Travel

Spain — Canary Islands - Gran Canaria ▸ Canary Islands - Lanzarote

SAUNAS/BATHS
■ **Hot House** (AC B CC DR G MA OS msg SA SB VS) 16.30-3.30 h
Yumbo Centro ✉ 35100 (1st floor) ☎ 928 76 42 86
Sauna frequented by a mixed gay crowd.

■ **Sauna Nilo** (B f G MA msg p R SA VS WO) 21-3 h
Nilo Centro ✉ 35100 ☎ 928 76 54 64
Easy to find: when entering the Nilo straight at the end of the aisle. 14 cabins with TV, 2 dry saunas. Special prize Wed Sat 2 for 1. Safe area, clean facilities.

FITNESS STUDIOS
■ **Enigma Victoria** (b g SA SB WH WO) 9-21 h
Av. Gran Canaria 55 ✉ 35100 (Hotel Enigma Victoria)
☎ 928 762 500

GIFT & PRIDE SHOPS
■ **D.G.'s Pride Shop** (A AC CC G lj OS) 20-1 h
Yumbo Centro ✉ 35100 (1st floor)
Drugstore & men's art gallery.

TRAVEL AND TRANSPORT
■ **Doris' Gay-Jeep-Safari** (BF F G) Tour Wed Fri 9 h
☎ 928 751 902 📠 928 751 902
Jeep Safari: Ptas 6.500.

■ **Sun Fun - Dieter's Motorbike Rental** (G) Mon-Fri 9-19, Sat 9-14, Sun 11-14 h
CC Gran Chaparral 161 ✉ 35100 ☎ 928 76 38 29
☎ 619-18 50 66 (mobile) 📠 928 76 38 29
💻 sunfun@ctv.esHomepage
Also bikes available, Rates from Ptas. 2000 for a motor bike per day.

APARTMENTS
■ **Pasion Tropical** (BF B GLM H PI SOL WH WO)
Calle las Adelfas 6, San Agustin ✉ 35100 ☎ 928 77 01 31
📠 928 77 37 71 💻 www.pasion-tropical.com
Sat-TV in all bungalows, seaview, open-air jacuzzi, sundeck terrace, recently renovated. Relaxed and exotic atmosphere. Rates per bungalow Pts 9.000 (low season), 12.000 (high season), BF incl.

■ **Robles. Los** (B BF f G H MA NU OS PI VS)
Av. de Finnmatkat, 8 ☎ 928 76 38 71 ☎ 20 421 00 00 (mobile)
📠 928 76 38 71
Reservation through "De Gay Krant Reisservice", Amsterdam, Netherlands. Fully equipped apartments.

■ **Tenesor** (CC g H MA OS PI)
Av. de Tirajana ☎ 928 770 122 📠 928 770 302
1 and 2 bedroom apartments in central Playa del Inglés near to Yumbo Center.

■ **Villa Mareu** (CC g NU OS PI)
C/. Raqueta, 3 ☎ 928 770 122 📠 928 770 302
Luxurious villa with two bedrooms, two bathrooms for individual rental close to dunes and beach.

■ **Villas Blancas** (B BF CC F G NU OS PI S VS)
Av. T.O. Tjaereborg, Campo Internacional ✉ 35100
☎ 902 168 169 📠 902 268 269 💻 vb@boesweb.com
The bungalows, swimming pool and bar are surrounded by tropical gardens. Accomodation is self-contained and has twin bed rooms, bathrooms, living rooms are open to fitted kitchens. All bungalows are with terraces, satellite TV, VCR. The bistro restaurant serves breakfast, lunch and dinner. Also Bistro from 18-22h.

■ **Vista Bonita Villas** (B BF CC f G H MA NU OS PI VS) 9-23 h
C/. Carmen Laforet, ✉ 35100 (Urbanización Sonnenland)
☎ 928 142 969 📠 928 142 969
💻 info@freedom-maspalomas.com
💻 www.freedom-maspalomas.com
Good quality and economically priced accomodation. 20 fully equipped poolside villas and two penthouse apartments, all with private balconies, terraces, satellite TV, VCR, in house video channel.

PRIVATE ACCOMMODATION
■ **Enjoy Bed and Breakfast** (BF G H MA) 16.30-21 h
Nollendorfplatz 5, 10777 Berlin - Germany ☎ +49 30 236 236 10
📠 +49 30 236 236 19 💻 info@ebab.com 💻 ebab.com
Accommodation sharing agency. All with shower and BF. 20-25 Euro p.p.

HEALTH GROUPS
■ **Amigos contra El Sida (A.C.S.)** Mon-Fri 10-14, 17.30-20 h
Nilo Centro, Local 120 (Planta Satano 1) ☎ 928 76 48 49
Help and assistance for any questions concerning AIDS in Spanish, English, French, German, Dutch.

SWIMMING
-Beach in front of Beach Bar No. 7 (! G NU)

CRUISING
-Cita Centro (toilet below Café Marlene)
-Yumbo Centro (from 0 h (ayor, r))
-Maspalomas Sand Dunes (AYOR) (in the small bushes, very popular)
-P Charco Maspalomas (Car-cruising 19-4 h)

Canary Islands - La Palma - **Puntagorda**

GUEST HOUSES
■ **Mar y Monte** (BF glm H OS)
C/. Pino de la Virgen, 7 b ✉ 38789 ☎ 922 49 30 67
📠 922 49 30 67 💻 www.la-palma.de/marymonte
Rates from Ptas. 2.700,- per day & person.

Canary Islands - La Palma - **Santa Cruz de la Palma**

APARTMENTS
■ **Apartamentos La Fuente** (g H MA OS SOL) Mon-Fri 9-12, 17-20, Sat 9-12 h
C/. Perez de Brito, 49 ✉ 38700 (in the historic centre)
☎ 922 415 636 📠 922 412 303 💻 lafuente@infolapalma.com
💻 www.la-fuente.com
Fully equipped apartments. Price for two persons Ptas 4.600-7750, additional bed 1.200. 10 apartments and rental of further houses in the countryside and in the city as well as cars.

SWIMMING
-Playa Los Cancajos (g MA NU) (South of Santa Cruz. Walk along the beach from Los Cancajos to the south in direction of the airport, climb over the rocks. After about 30 minutes you reach the beach.)
-Playa Cuatro Monjas (g MA NU) (South of Playa Naos. Follow road to south just behind Puerta Naos. Leave car near banana plantations, follow path to the sea.)

Canary Islands - Lanzarote - **Arrecife**

BARS
■ **Tambo. El** (B g MA) 20-2 h
C/. Luis Morote

Spain

The only gay complex at the side of the sea!

PASION TROPICAL

Beachfront Bungalows

- **20 meters** from the sea.
- Solar panels **heated swimming pool.**
- Open air **whirlpool.**
- **Buffet breakfast** in the garden included.
- Big **panoramic roof top sun terrace.**

- Open air **gym.**
- **Free satellite TV** in each room.
- Tropical gardens.
- Music in pool and garden.
- Clothing optional.
- Car hire service.
- **Quiet area.**

Calle Las Adelfas, 6 San Agustin - Playa del Ingles - Gran Canaria
Tel.: +34-928-770131 Fax: +34-928-773771
e-mail: info@pasion-tropical.com **www.pasion-tropical.com**

A Different Style!

Spain
Canary Islands - Lanzarote ▶ Canary Islands - Tenerife

GUEST HOUSES
■ **La Molina** (B gLm H) open all year
Av. Guanarteme, 67 ✉ 35558 *(near National Park in the centre of the island, 7km from the beach)* ☎ 928 52 92 66 🖷 928 52 92 66
📧 lamolina@eresmas.com
7 rooms with bath/shower/wc/own key.

HEALTH GROUPS
■ **Hospital General** 24 h
Carretera San Bartolomé s/n ☎ 928 80 16 36

CRUISING
-Castillo (from 23 h)

Canary Islands - Lanzarote - **Puerto del Carmen**
BARS
■ **Black & White** (B d G MA) 21-4 h
Atántico Centro, Av. de la Playa, 38
■ **Free** (B G MA stv) 21-3 h
Calle detrás del C.C. Atlántico
Show Fri & Sat

RESTAURANTS
■ **Sardinero** (F NG) 12-23 h
C/ Nuestra Señora del Carmen, 2 ☎ 928 51 19 33

SEX SHOPS/BLUE MOVIES
■ **JOMATO´G** (g) 11-14, 16-20 h, Sun closed
CC Atlántico ✉ 35100 *(Downstairs)* ☎ 928 511 331

SWIMMING
-Playa Guasimeta (g nu) (behind the airport)
-Playa del Papagayo

Canary Islands - Tenerife - **La Laguna**
BARS
■ **Consulado** (B g stv) Tue-Sun 20-2 h
C/ Antonio Torre Edward, 45
■ **Nashville Pub** (B g) Sun-Thu 18.30-2, Fri Sat 18.30-4 h
C/ Dr. Antonio Glez, 11

HEALTH GROUPS
■ **Unapro**
C/ Marqués de Celada 70, local 2 ☎ 922 25 96 54
HIV/AIDS-Group.

CRUISING
-Estación de Guaguas

Canary Islands - Tenerife - **Los Realejos**
GUEST HOUSES
■ **El Madroño** (BF CC F G PI SA SOL) Open all year
Camino La Cumbre 21, Palo Blanco ✉ 38315 *(Valle de Orotava,20 mins from Puerto de la Cruz, and 30 mins from Santa Cruz)*
☎ 922 353 633 🖷 922 353 633
📧 hotelitomadrono@hotmail.com
🌐 www.aloe-consulting.com/hotelito
This guest house, made up of two flats and an intimate lounge with fireplace, library and kitchen is surrounded by lush gardens.

HOTELITO de montaña El Madroño

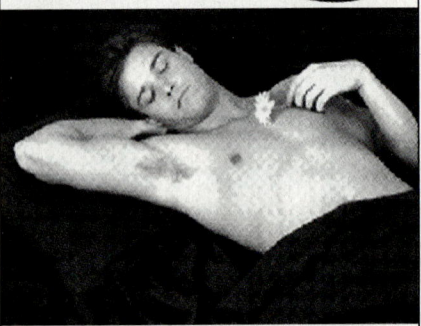

MOUNTAIN LITTLE HOTEL EL MADROÑO
"A quiet place for friends"
Reservations: 00 34 922 35 36 33
hotelitomadrono@hotmail.com
http://www.aloe-consulting.com/hotelito
TENERIFE-CANARY ISLANDS

Canary Islands - Tenerife - **Playa de las Americas**
BARS
■ **Chaplin's Bar** (AC B D DR G MA STV TV VS) 23-? h
C.C. Sayltien *(Souterrain)*

SWIMMING
-Los Christianos (NU) (reachable from Santa Cruz by bus)
-Playa de la Tejita (g NU) (very popular day and night; between El Medano and Los Abrigos)

CRUISING
-Playa de las Americas (after dark)

Canary Islands - Tenerife - **Puerto de la Cruz**
BARS
■ **Anderson Club** (B d DR G MA OS) 22.30-6, Sat Sun 8-13 h
Av. Generalísimo, 24 *(Edificio Drago)*
■ **D'Espanto** (B d DR G MA OS vs) 23-4 h
Av. Generalísimo, 24 *(Edificio Drago)*
■ **Incognito** (B G MA) 21-5 h, closed Mon
Av. Generalísimo *(Edificio Centro Avenida)*
■ **Jim's** (B G MA OS) 17-3, Fri Sat 17-5 h; summer 21-3, Fri Sat 21-5 h
Av. Generalísimo, 24, bajo *(Edificio Drago)*
■ **Tabasco** (B DR G MA vs) 21.30-8, summer 22.30-8 h
Av. Generalísimo, 15

Canary Islands - Tenerife ▶ Córdoba — Spain

DANCECLUBS
■ **Anderson** (B D G MA) 23-6 h
Av. Generalísimo, 24, bajo *(Edificio Drago)*
■ **Despanto** (B D G MA)
Av. Generalisimo, 24 *(Edificio Drago)*
■ **Vampi's Discoteca** (B D E G MA P VS) Thu-Sun 24-8, Show 1.30 h
Av. Generalisimo, 24 *(Edificio Drago)*

RESTAURANTS
■ **Casa Europa** (B F g) Tue-Sun 18-24 h
Urbanización Montalmar, 38250 Bajamar n8

SAUNAS/BATHS
■ **Laurent** (b DR G MA SA VS WH) Sun-Thu 14.30-23, Fri Sat -5 h
C/ Iriarte, 37 ✉ 38400 *(near shopping mall Martianez)*
☎ 922 31 97 77

GUEST HOUSES
■ **Villa Maspalmeras** (B BF CC f GLM H OS PI WO) all year round
Vista Panoramica, 20 ✉ 38398 ☎ 922 302 607
Small and stylish guest house in beautiful gardens in hills overlooking Puerto De La Cruz.

SWIMMING
-Playa de los Patos (4 km east of town)

CRUISING
-Estación de guaguas
-Montañas del Amor
-Playa Martiánez
-Avenida de Colón (day and night)
-Plaza del Charco
-Playa Jardín/Castillo San Felipe

Canary Islands - Tenerife - **Santa Cruz**

BARS
■ **Blue Dreams Bar Suenos Azules** (B G MA vs) 21-3 h
C/ San Miguel, 14 ☎ 922 27 45 06

CAFES
■ **Cloe Café-Restaurant** (A B F g) Mon-Sat 12-2, Sun 18-2 h
C/ San Francisco Javier, 36 ☎ 922 28 32 01

SEX SHOPS/BLUE MOVIES
■ **Luna Sex Shop** (AC CC g MA p VS) Mon-Sat 10-22, Sun 17.30-22 h
C/ Vincente Ferrer, 75, bajos *(near Parque Garcia Sanabria)*

HEALTH GROUPS
■ **Centro Dermatologico** Fri-Wed 8.30-13 h
C/ San Sebastian, 75 ☎ 922 27 93 97
Information and help concerning AIDS.
■ **Unión para la Ayuda y Protección de los Afectados por el SIDA**
C/ Marqués de Celada,70, ✉ 38202 ☎ 922 25 96 54
☎ 922 63 32 23 🖥 unapro@redkbs.com

SWIMMING
-Las Gaviotas (15 km from Santa Cruz, left side of the beach)
-Las Teresitas (take bus 914)
-Dársena Pescadora (Los Rusos)
-Benijos

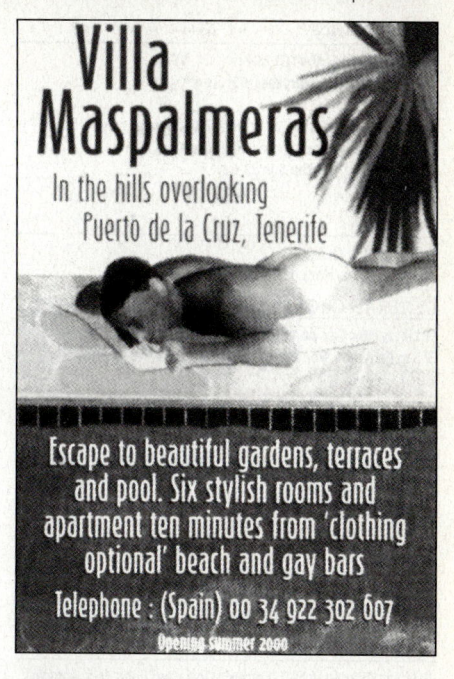

Villa Maspalmeras
In the hills overlooking Puerto de la Cruz, Tenerife

Escape to beautiful gardens, terraces and pool. Six stylish rooms and apartment ten minutes from 'clothing optional' beach and gay bars

Telephone : (Spain) 00 34 922 302 607

Opening summer 2000

CRUISING
-Estación de guaguas
-Plaza del Principe de Asturias
-Parque García Sanabria (r)
-Avenida Anaga (R)
-La Rambla del General Franco (between Parque Sanabria and Plaza de la Paz)

Canillas De Albaidas

HOTELS
■ **Aparthotel Bar Los Chicos** (B BF CC d F g H MA OS PI) 9-2 h
Cómpeta/Torrox ✉ 29755 *(behind Sayalonga-bus from Tore del Mar to Competa)* ☎ 95 255 35 95 🖨 95 255 35 95
10 holiday apartments for 2-3 pers/4-6 pers.7500-16000 Pts. 3 singles/3 doubles 4400-8300 pts.

Cartagena

SEX SHOPS/BLUE MOVIES
■ **Sexyland** (g)
C/ Sagasta, 55 ☎ 968 52 60 87

SWIMMING
-Playas de Calblanque (g NU) (between Cartagena and Cabo de Palos)

Córdoba

BARS
■ **Siena** (B BF F g MA OS) 19-0.30/1 h
Plaza las Tendillas s/n ☎ 957 47 30 05

Spain — Córdoba ▸ Gijón

DANCECLUBS
■ **A 85** (B D GLM MA YG) 23-? h
Poligono Industrial Pedroches, 85
Very popular.
■ **Kiss** (B d gLm OS YG) 21-?, Mon closed. Winter only Fri Sat 21-? h
Carrertera de Almaden (near Club Azland)
■ **Plató** (B D g YG) Thu-Sun 23-6 h
C/ Gongora

CINEMAS
■ **Góngora** (g OG)
Palacio del Cine/Plaza de las Tendillas

GENERAL GROUPS
■ **Liberación Gay de Córdoba (LGC)** Tue 19-21 h
C/ San Fernando, 68 ☏ 957 47 37 60 📠 957 48 44 59

CRUISING
-Parks Victoria (northern part) and Diego de Rivas (popular day and night) (MA)
-Park at Guadalquivir, Avenida del Alcazar (at San Rafael bridge; popular)
-Plaza de las Tendillas
-Ferial (near Calle Teresa de Córdoba y Hoces; at night carcruising)
-Los Naranjos (at Mesquita, some man, days only)
-Main railway station, Ronda de Cercadilla

Denia

SWIMMING
-Cala San Antonio (g NU) (Entrance Denia and Cabo de S. Antonio)

Estepona

BARS
■ **Cheers** (B GLM MA) 22-3 h
C/ Caravaca, 32 ✉ 29680 (Market-Old Town) ☏ 939 80 41 05
■ **Kiss** (B glm MA) 19.30-4 h
C/ Victoria ☏ 939 56 82 16

RESTAURANTS
■ **Robbies** (B CC F glm)
C/ Jubrique, 11 ✉ 29680
Gay owned restaurant; excellent food.

SWIMMING
-Costa Natura (NU,MA) (southern end gay, cruising in bushes) On N340 4km from Estepona, direction Algeciras. NudeCamp: Costa Natura.

Figueres

BARS
■ **Natural Men Bar** (B D DR GLM MA OS s VS WE) 22-6 h
Centre Aduana, Poligono Enporda, Vilamalla ✉ 17369 ☏ 972 52 60 39

RESTAURANTS
■ **Jalisco** (B F glm) 12-0 h
C/ Tapis, 21 ✉ 17600 ☏ 972 50 53 52
Mexican cuisine.

SAUNAS/BATHS
■ **Sparta** (AC B DR G MA SA SB VS) 16-22 h
C/ Sant Pau, 82 ✉ 17600 (near the railway station)
☏ 972 51 17 05
Sauna existing for 15 years and attracting a lot of French people.

HOTELS
■ **Hostal Androl y Camping Pous** (AC B BF CC F g H) 7.30-24 h
Carretera Nacional II A, km 8.5 ✉ 17600 ☏ 972 67 54 96
☏ 972 67 50 57
Also camping facilities.

Fuengirola

BARS
■ **Stuart's Bar** (AC B D GLM MA OS) 21-? h
C/ Martinez Catena, Complejo Las Palmeras, Locales 38 & 39
✉ 29640 (in the backarea of Citröen Car Garaje & Hot Shot)
☏ 610 827 549 (mobile)

RESTAURANTS
■ **Casa Vieja. La** (CC F glm MA OS) 19-?, Sun also 12-16 h, closed Mon
Av. de Los Boliches, 27 ✉ 29640 ☏ 952 266 44 07

GUEST HOUSES
■ **Rio del Sol** (B BF F G H PI)
C/ Cactus,14, Torreblanca del Sol
Near Torremolinos and the nudist beaches Torrequebrado and Las Dunas in Cabo Pino. 3 rooms, one with bath. Private swimmingpool and Bar/Restaurante (NG)

CRUISING
-Paseo Marítimo (between Caracola Restaurant and London Pub, including new elevated promenade accross from London Pub; especially in summer)
-Right from the Old Castle near the obsolete hotel facing the sea

Gandia

RESTAURANTS
■ **San Roc i Ec Gos. Restaurante Aleman** (A AC CC F glm WE)
Tue-Sat 12-16, 21-0, Sun 12-16 h, closed Mon
C/ Hospital, 10 ✉ 46700 ☏ 96 287 34 21

Gijón

BARS
■ **Escalera 7** (AC B DR G MA VS WE) 21-8 h
C/ Ezcurdia, 40, bajo ✉ 33202 ☏ 98 534 21 80
■ **Pipos** (B DR G MA r VS) 20-8 h
Plaza San Augustí, 2 ☏ 98 517 13 79

CAFES
■ **Dindurra** (B f NG) 8-24 h
Paseo de Begoña (Teatro Jovellanes)
Best 19-21 h.

DANCECLUBS
■ **Eros** (AC B D DR G MA S SNU) 0-7 h
C/ la Playa, 17 ✉ 33202 ☏ 98 513 17 19

934 SPARTACUS 2001/2002

Gijón ▶ Jaén **Spain**

SEX SHOPS/BLUE MOVIES
- **Fantasías** (g VS) Mon-Sat 10-3, Sun 10-14, 16-3 h
C/ Ezcurdia, 49
- **Sex Shop** (g VS) 10-14, 15.30-23 h
Av. Pablo Iglesias, 20 ☏ 98 536 28 85

HEALTH GROUPS
- **Comité Ciudadano Anti Sida de Asturias** 9-14 h
C/ Ramon y Cajal, 39, bajo ☏ 98 533 88 32
Information and services concerning AIDS.

SWIMMING
-Playa de Peñarrubia/La Providencia

CRUISING
-Parque de Isabela la Católica
-Estación Renfe
-Statue La Madre de los Emigrantes
-Paseo de la Playa de San Lorenzo

Girona

BARS
- **Big-Hit** (B D g)
Av. Ramón Folch, 11

CRUISING
-Estación de Renfe
-Plaza de la Independcia
-La Rambla

Granada

BARS
- **Al Pie de la Vela** (B G MA) 21.30-4, We -5 h
C/ del Darro, 35, bajo *(near Alhambra)* ☏ 958 22 85 39
- **Ambient XXL** (AC B d DR G MA s VS) 21-4h
C/ Montalbán, 13 ✉ 18002
- **Fondo Reservado** (B G MA YG) 22.30-4 h, closed Mon
Cuesta de Sta. Inés,4 *(Placeta de Santa Ines)*
- **Perfil** (A AC B d f g MA S) 17-5 h
C/ Rosario,10
- **Puerta del Vino** (A AC B BF F glm MA OS WE) Summer: 18-2 h,
Winter: 12-2 h
Paseo de los Tristes, 5 ✉ 18010 ☏ 958 210 026
- **Ricon de San Pedro. El** (B g MA) 21-4, Fri Sat -? h
C/ del Darro, 12
Bar de copas in the center of Granada.
- **Sal. La** (B gLM MA) 22-5 h
C/ Santa Paula, 11
- **Tic Tac** (B DR G MA VS) 17-4.30, Fri Sat -5 h
C/ Horno de Haza, 19

CAFES
- **Lisboa. Café** (B BF f g MA) Mon-Thu 8-22, Fri-Sun -3 h
C/ Reyes Catalocicos / Plaza Nueva ✉ 18010 ☏ 958 21 05 79

DANCECLUBS
- **Angel Azul. El** (B D DR G p S SNU STV VS YG) 22-6, Fri Sat -?.
Show Fri Sat 2 h
C/ Lavadero de las Tablas, 15

SAUNAS/BATHS
- **Boabdil** (B G MA SA VS) 17-23 h, Tue & Aug closed
Carretera de la Sierra, 34 ✉ 18008 *(El Trevenque)* ☏ 985 22 10 73

BOOK SHOPS
- **Librería G & L** (CC GLM) summer: Mon-Fri 10.30-14, 17.30-21,
winter: Mon-Sat 10-14, 16-20 h
Palacio de Congresos, local 1 ✉ 18006 *(next to the river Genil)*
☏ 958 13 57 57

GENERAL GROUPS
- **Asociación Andaluza de Gays y Lesbianas (NOS)**
Mon-Fri 1.30-13.30, 17.30-20.30, Sat 17-22 h
C/ Lavadero de las Tablas, 15 ✉ 18002 ☏ 958 200 602
📠 958 200 602
"Triángulo" is the publication of the group. Every three months for free in gay venues with articles and a gay guide of Southspain.

HEALTH GROUPS
- **Bisagra. La**
C/ Chueca, 8, 1b ✉ 18004 ☏ 958 52 13 52
Group for people with HIV/AIDS.

CRUISING
-Paseo de Basilios (at the border of the river Genil (popular car cruising at night)
-Los Jardines del Triunfo
-Estación de Renfe
-Estación de autobuses
-Camino de Puchil, near "Puleva" factory (car cruising or by bike, by day only)

Huesca

BARS
- **Candanchú** (B f G)
C/ Coso Alto
- **Papillón** (B F G)
C/ San Lorenzo

DANCECLUBS
- **Tránsito** (B D g)
Plaza de San Voto

CRUISING
-Estación de autobuses (Calle del Parque)
-Parque Municipal
-Zona del Hospital Provincial

Jaén

BARS
- **Noche. La** (AC B D g GLM p S SNU STV WE) 22-6 h
Av. de Andalucía, 22 ✉ 23002 ☏ 953 27 30 34

SEX SHOPS/BLUE MOVIES
- **Amsterdam** (g)
C/ Salido, 23 *(near C/ San Clemente)*

GENERAL GROUPS
- **28 de Junio • Asociación Pro Derechos de los Homosexuales**
Meeting Wed Sat 20-22
PO Box 443 ✉ 23080 ☏ 953 27 04 20

CRUISING
-Parque de la Victoria

Spain | Javea ▶ Lloret de Mar

Javea

SWIMMING
-Torre d'Ambolo (g NU) (C/. al cabo de la Nau)
-Playa de la Cumbre del Sol (g NU)

La Coruña/A Coruña

BARS
■ **Café Alfama** (A AC B d GLM MA WE) Tue-Fri 20-2, Sat Sun -3 h, closed Mon
R. Orzán,87, bajo ✉ 15006 ☎ 981 20 46 21
■ **Fibonacci** (AC B glm MA)
R. Pasadizo do Orzán, 2
Very gay.
■ **Laberinto** (AC B DR G MA p VS)
R. Magistrado Manuel Artime, 6
Very large place.
■ **Marítimo** (B G MA) 23.30-3.30 h
Av. de la Marina s/n

SEX SHOPS/BLUE MOVIES
■ **Fantasías** (g VS) Mon-Sat 10.30-22.30, Sun 10.30-14, 16-22 h
R. Rosalia de Castro, 4

GENERAL GROUPS
■ **Milhomes**
PO Box 24 ✉ 15080

SWIMMING
-Praia de Bastiagueiro (on the rural road to the north, towards El Ferrol, halfway between Santa Cristina and Santa Cruz.)

CRUISING
-Xardíns de Méndez Núñez and the port nearby

León

BARS
■ **Capote** (B G MA)
C/ Lancia, 3

CAFES
■ **Gran Café** (A AC d g lj MA N S WE) 15.30-3.30 h
C/ Cervantes, 9 ✉ 24003 ☎ 987 27 23 01

DANCECLUBS
■ **Chasis** (AC D g YG)
C/ Lancia, 5

RESTAURANTS
■ **Girola. La** (A AC B CC d F glm lj MA OS WE) 13.30-16, 21-23.30
C/ Ave Maria, 2, esquina C/ San Lorenzo, 5 ✉ 24007 ☎ 987 27 05 69

SEX SHOPS/BLUE MOVIES
■ **Internacional** (g) 10-22 h
C/ General Sanjurjo, 5 ☎ 987 24 85 72

CRUISING
-Jardines del Paseo de Papalaguinda
-Railway & bus station
-Plaza del Ganado

Lleida

DANCECLUBS
■ **Big Ben** (B D F g)
Carretera de Mollerussa
20 km from Lérida. Large entertainment center with bars, discos, gambling halls and restaurants. Not exclusively gay but very popular.

CINEMAS
■ **Cine Xenon**
Av. Alcalde Rovira Rouve, 3, Sala 1

CRUISING
-Campos Elíseos
-Campo Escolar
-Castillo
-Estación de Renfe
-Plaza Noguerola
-Parque La Mitjana
-Estacion Autobuses

Lloret de Mar

BARS
■ **El David** (AC B G YG) 23-3 h, in winter closed on Mon
C/ Migdian, 53 ☎ 972 36 23 10
■ **Incógnito** (AC B G MA VS) 22-3 h, closed Oct-Mar
C/ Migdia, 44 ☎ 972 36 71 89
■ **Tortuga Bar** (AC B G MA) 22-3 h, closed in winter Tue
C/ Santa Teresa, 5 ☎ 972 37 05 69

CAFES
■ **Manila** (AC B G MA s) 12-3 h
C/ Venecia, 60 ✉ 17310 ☎ 972 36 25 44

DANCECLUBS
■ **Bubu. La** (AC B D DR G MA) 23-3.30 h
C/ L'Areny, 33 ☎ 972 36 71 89

RESTAURANTS
■ **Restaurant Valls** (F g) closed in winter
C/ Santa Teresa, 11 ☎ 972 36 43 89
Spanish and international cuisine.

SEX SHOPS/BLUE MOVIES
■ **Lloret Sex Center** (AC glm VS) Summer: 10-22, rest of the year: Mon-Sat 10-13.30, 14-20.30 h
C/ San Tomàs, 19 ✉ 17310 ☎ 972 37 04 43

HOTELS
■ **Hostal Valls** (F G H)
C/ Santa Teresa, 11 (near Bar Tortuga) ☎ 972 36 43 89
Near to the gay scene. Single Ptas 2.000, double Ptas. 4.000. All room with bath/WC

APARTMENTS
■ **Bubu Apartamentos** (G H)
C/ L'Areny, 33 (near La Campaña) ☎ 927 36 71 89
Large apartments. Rates Ptas 2.000-3.000, Jun Aug 4.000-5.000.
■ **Tortuga Rooms** (G OS)
C/ Santa Teresa, 5 ✉ 17310 ☎ 972 37 05 69
25 km to the airport. Central location. A few steps to the local gay scene. Most units with kitchenette, priv. bath and access to balcony. Rates Ptas 2.500-3.500.

Lloret de Mar ▶ Madrid **Spain**

SWIMMING
-Boadella beach (g NU) (Busy and cruisy. There is a ferry from the town hall to this mixed beach. Gay part is on the left side of the docks. Mixed on the right side)
-Passeig Maritim/Trav. Venecia (Mixed beach in front of the bars)
-La Aguadilla (Take the boat to Blanes 1 station. No sand, but many cliffs and rocks. The cruising starts after the last ferry has left.)

CRUISING
-Around the castle
-Busstation (daytime)

Madrid

The majestic capital of Spain has impressive buildings, lots of sightseeing, and a truly wild gay scene. The gay scene is concentrated mainly in the area around the metro station Chueca, and if you look at the map, you will see that most of the gay bars are in walking distance from there. Expect a wild time in Madrid! You can do your sightseeing during the morning, perhaps spend the afternoon at a gay sauna, then move on to the cafés in the early evening, and at around 9 pm choose one of the many restaurants in the gay village for an inexpensive but delicious meal. The gay bars start getting lively around midnight, discos fill up around 3 and then stay packed all night.

Die majestätische Hauptstadt Spaniens mit herrlichen Gebäuden, einer Menge Sehenswürdigkeiten und einer wirklich wilden schwulen Szene. Die schwule Szene konzentriert sich im Gebiet um die Metro Chueca. Betrachten Sie den Stadtplan und Sie werden sehen, daß die meisten der schwulen Bars zu Fuß erreichbar sind, wenn Sie in Chueca ankommen. Es erwartet Sie eine aufregende Zeit in Madrid! Besichtigen Sie die Sehenswürdigkeiten am Vormittag, verbringen Sie Ihre Nachmittage in den schwulen Saunen, gehen Sie am frühen Abend in die Cafés, und wählen Sie gegen 21 Uhr eines der vielen Restaurants in der schwulen Zone aus, um - nicht teuer, aber vorzüglich- zu Abend zu essen. Das Nachtleben beginnt gegen 24 Uhr in den Bars, ab 3 Uhr in den Discos. Das schwule Leben tobt dann bis zum frühen Morgen!

Majestueuse capitale de l'Espagne: splendides édifices, innombrables sites touristiques et vie gaie trépidante. Le quartier autour de la station de métro Chueca est le bastion gai de la ville. Etudiez le plan et vous verrez que la plupart des bars gais sont accessibles à pied depuis cette station. A Madrid, vous passerez des vacances sauvages! Réservez vos matins pour le tourisme, passez vos après-midi au sauna, allez au café en début de soirée et, vers 21 h, choisissez l'un des nombreux restaurants du quartier gai pour un repas bon marché, mais délicieux! Les bars n'ouvrent qu'à partir de minuit et ne désemplissent qu'aux aurores.

Capital majestuosa de España con edificios bonitos, una cantidad de lugares interesantes para visitar y un ambiente gay verdaderamente loquísimo. Los locales gay se concentran en el area de la estación de Metro Chueca
. Fíjese en el mapa y verá Ud. que desde la paras Chueca, a la mayoría de los bares se puede llegar andando. Le espera una estancia turbulenta. Visite los lugares de interés durante las mañanas, pase las tardes en las saunas gay, en la temprana noche vaya a los cafés, y a eso de las 21 horas elija uno de los restaurantes de la zona gay, para tomar una cena no cara, pero deliciosa. La vida nocturna comienza a eso de las 24 horas y sigue toda la noche hasta la madrugada.

La meravigliosa capitale della Spagna, con degli splendidi edifici, innumerevoli luoghi turistici e una vita gay molto attiva. La vita gay è concentrata soprattutto nell'area intorno a Metro Chueca. Osservate la cartina e capirete che tutti i bar gay possono essere raggiunti a piedi, una volta arrivati a Chueca. Potete aspettarvi un soggiorno selvaggio a Madrid. Visitate la città il mattino, passate i pomeriggi nelle saune gay, trasferitevi nei caffè la sera presto, circa alle 21, scegliete uno dei ristoranti della zona gay per una cena deliziosa e poco costosa. La vita gay nei bar comincia ad animarsi verso le 24 e prosegue praticamente per tutta la notte.

GAY INFO
■ **Gay Inform COGAM** Mon-Fri 17-21h
C/ Fuencarral, 37 *(Metro Tribunal/Gran Via)* ☎ 91 523 00 70
Answers to nearly all questions concerning gay life.

PUBLICATIONS
■ **Entiendes**
c/o COGAM, PO Box 18165 ✉ 28080
Bimontly publication, about 64 pages. Cultural information and a gay guide of Spain. Ptas 500. At some newsstands and bars.
■ **Mapa Gay de Madrid**
c/o Berkana, C/ Gravina, 11 ✉ 28004 ☎ 91 532 13 93
📠 91 532 13 93
Free gay city map issued by the gay bookshop "Berkana".
■ **Shangay**
PO Box 4023 ✉ 28080 ☎ 91 308 11 03 ☎ 91 308 66 23
📠 91 310 17 11 ✉ shangay@ctv.es
Free bimontly gay paper listing all sites and venues in gay Madrid. Great information source on what's going on in the city.

LEATHER CLUB
PELAYO, 42
MADRID

Spain — Madrid

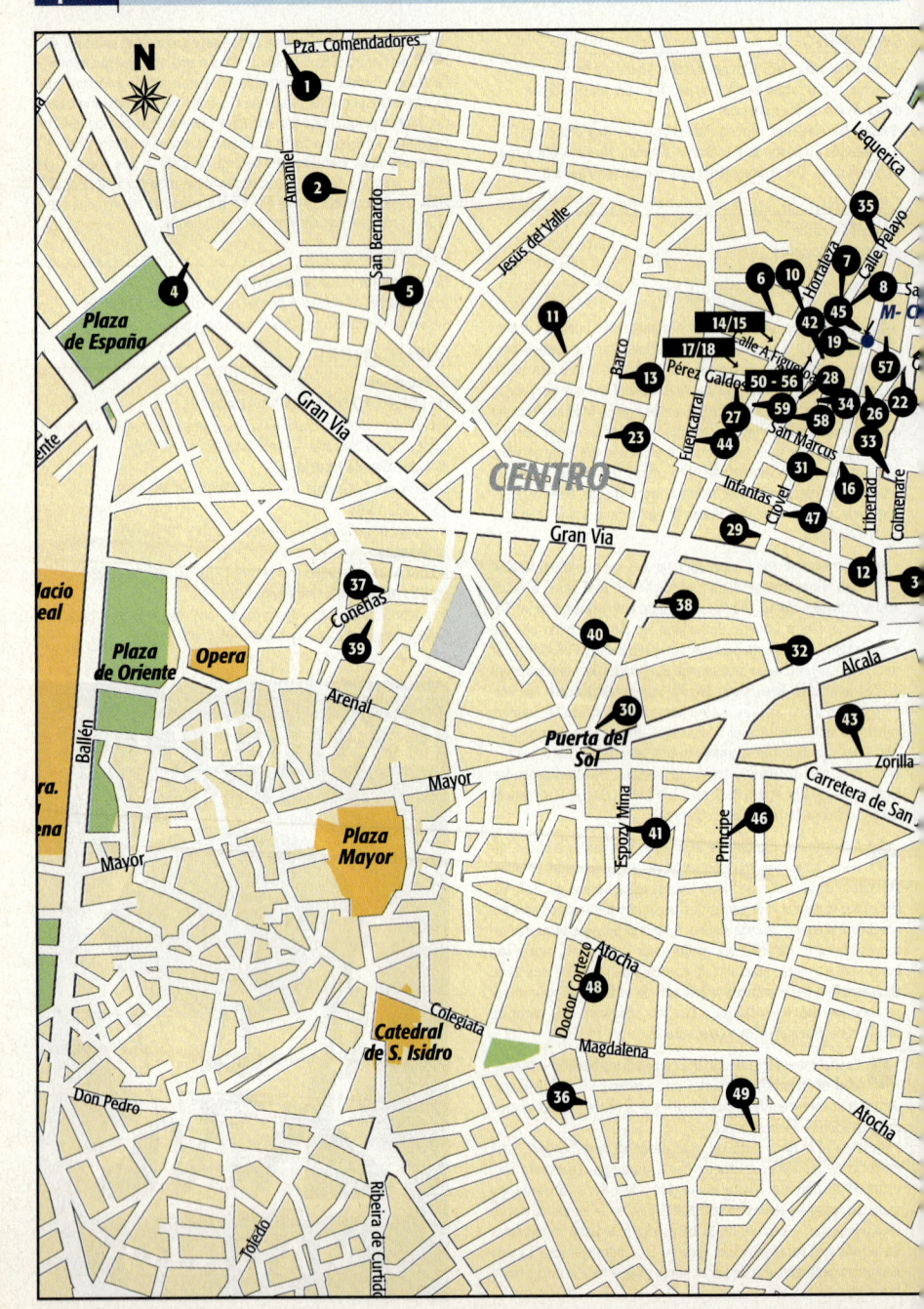

Madrid Spain

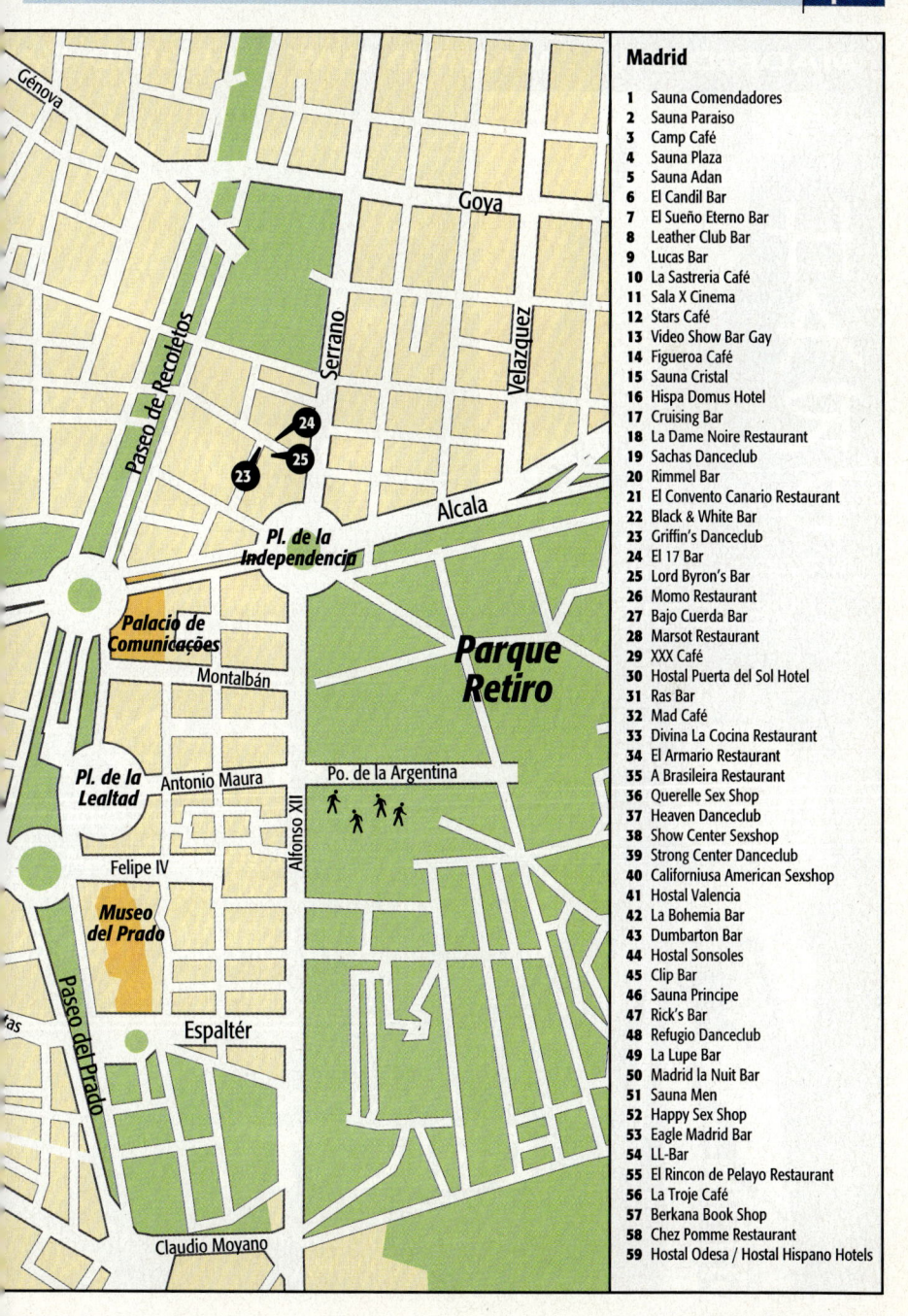

Madrid

1. Sauna Comendadores
2. Sauna Paraiso
3. Camp Café
4. Sauna Plaza
5. Sauna Adan
6. El Candil Bar
7. El Sueño Eterno Bar
8. Leather Club Bar
9. Lucas Bar
10. La Sastreria Café
11. Sala X Cinema
12. Stars Café
13. Video Show Bar Gay
14. Figueroa Café
15. Sauna Cristal
16. Hispa Domus Hotel
17. Cruising Bar
18. La Dame Noire Restaurant
19. Sachas Danceclub
20. Rimmel Bar
21. El Convento Canario Restaurant
22. Black & White Bar
23. Griffin's Danceclub
24. El 17 Bar
25. Lord Byron's Bar
26. Momo Restaurant
27. Bajo Cuerda Bar
28. Marsot Restaurant
29. XXX Café
30. Hostal Puerta del Sol Hotel
31. Ras Bar
32. Mad Café
33. Divina La Cocina Restaurant
34. El Armario Restaurant
35. A Brasileira Restaurant
36. Querelle Sex Shop
37. Heaven Danceclub
38. Show Center Sexshop
39. Strong Center Danceclub
40. Californiusa American Sexshop
41. Hostal Valencia
42. La Bohemia Bar
43. Dumbarton Bar
44. Hostal Sonsoles
45. Clip Bar
46. Sauna Principe
47. Rick's Bar
48. Refugio Danceclub
49. La Lupe Bar
50. Madrid la Nuit Bar
51. Sauna Men
52. Happy Sex Shop
53. Eagle Madrid Bar
54. LL-Bar
55. El Rincon de Pelayo Restaurant
56. La Troje Café
57. Berkana Book Shop
58. Chez Pomme Restaurant
59. Hostal Odesa / Hostal Hispano Hotels

Spain — Madrid

MADRID GAY . MADRID GAY . MADRID GAY

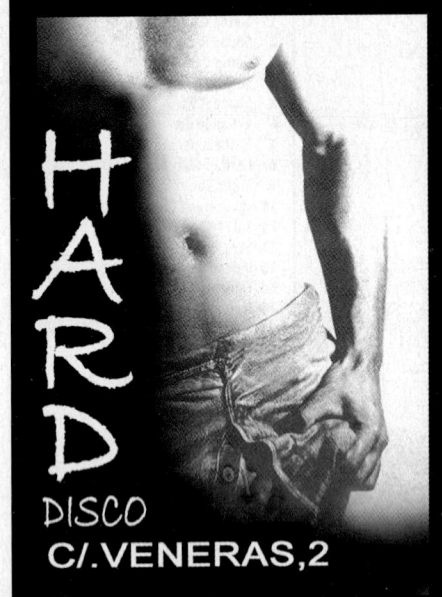

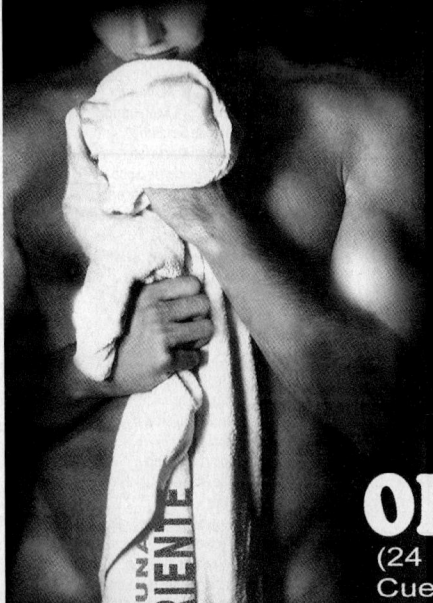

HARD
DISCO
C/. VENERAS, 2

disco
Strong Center
C/. TRUJILLOS, 7

SAUNA PLAZA
Gran Vía 78 (Edif. España)
Cabinas privadas, bar, sauna, baños de vapor, peluqueria, gimnasio.
BOYS ESPECIAL MASAJES
Abierto de 10 a 22 h.

SAUNA ORIENTE
(24 Horas)
Cuesta Sto. Domingo, 1
METRO OPERA

Madrid | Spain

MADRID GAY . MADRID GAY . MADRID GAY

manstore
C/. B. PEREZ GALDOS, 1

CRUISING BAR
C/. B. Perez Galdós, 5

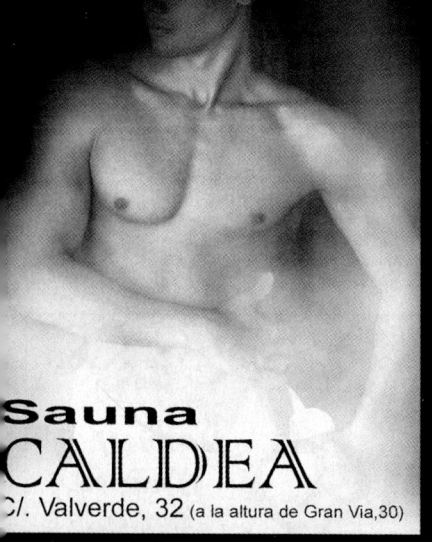

Sauna **CALDEA**
C/. Valverde, 32 (a la altura de Gran Via, 30)

A NOITE
Espectáculos diarios
C/. HORTALEZA, 43

AMERICAN'S FOOD
RTALEZA, 37

HUDSON PIZZA & AMERICAN'S FOOD
C/. HORTALEZA, 37

HUDSON PIZZA & AMERICAN'S FOOD
C/. HORTALEZA, 37

SPARTACUS 2001/2002 | 941

Spain | Madrid

dumbarton bar
ZORRILLA, 7
TEL. 91. 429 81 91 MADRID-14
abierto todos los dias a partir de las 19h

BARS

■ **A Noite** (AC B d DR G MA R SNU STV VS) 20-6; show 0.30h
C/ Hortaleza, 43 ✉ 28004 *(M° Chueca)* ☎ 91 531 07 15
■ **Bajo Cuerda** (AC B DR G MA SNU VS) 21-?; SNU Fri Sat 1 h
C/ Perez Galdos, 8 *(Metro Chueca)*
■ **Black & White** (AC B D G SNU YG) 20-5, Fri Sat -6. Show Thu-Sun after 2 h.
C/ de la Libertad, 34 *(Metro Chueca)* ☎ 91 531 11 41
Popular. Dance floor downstairs.
■ **Bohemia. La** (AC d E g MA OS P WE) Mon-Sun 20-? h
Plaza de Chueca, 10 ✉ 28004 *(Metro Chueca)*
■ **Caldós** (AC B d DR G MA snu) 19-2, WE -3.30 h
C/ Pérez Galdós, 1 and C/ Fuencarral, 36 ✉ 28004 *(Metro Chueca/Gran Via)* ☎ 91 532 12 86
■ **Candil. El** (AC B g STV VS) 20-2, Fri Sat -2.30; TV-Show Mon Fri Sat 0.30 h
C/ Hernán Cortés, 21 *(Metro Chueca)* ☎ 91 522 71 48
■ **Cantina COGAM** (A B GLM MA) Mon-Thu 17-0, Fri Sat -1, Sun 12-0h
C/ Fuencarral, 37 ✉ 28004 *(M° Gran Via, Tribunal)*
■ **Clip** (B G MA) 20-2 h
C/ Gravina, 8 *(Metro Chueca)*
■ **Cruising** (! AC B D DR G lj MA VS) 19-3h, Fri Sat -3.30 h
C/ Pérez Galdós, 5 ✉ 28004 *(Metro Chueca)* ☎ 91 521 51 43
■ **Dumbarton** (B G MA p) 19-2 h
C/ Zorrilla, 7 ✉ 28014 *(Metro Sevilla)* ☎ 91 429 81 91
■ **Eagle Madrid** (B BF DR G LJ MA P VS) 14-2.30, Fri-Sat -3.30 h
C/ Pelayo, 30 ✉ 28004 *(Metro Chueca)* ☎ 91 531 62 96
■ **Fragola** (a AC B G MA) 21.30-3 h, Mon closed
C/ Buenavista, 42 ✉ 28012 *(Metro Chueca)* ☎ 603 97 12
Cocktail-bar.

■ **Freedom** (AC B d G MA s VS) 22.30-3.30 h, Mon closed
C/ Infantas, 12 ✉ 28004 ☎ 91 523 45 38
■ **Hot** (AC B DR G lj MA p VS WE WO) 18-3, Fri Sat -4 h
C/ Infantas, 9 ✉ 28004 *(Metro Chueca, Gran Via)*
■ **Leather Club** (! B d DR G lj MA VS) 18-3, Sat -3.30 h
C/ Pelayo, 42 *(Metro Chueca)* ☎ 91 308 14 62
■ **Liquid** (AC B CC d G MA VS WE) 21-3, WE -4 h
C/ Barquillo, 8 ✉ 28004 ☎ 91 532 74 28
Video bar
■ **LL Bar** (B DR G MA S VS) 18-?, Show 23.30 h
C/ Pelayo, 11 ✉ 28004 *(Metro Chueca)* ☎ 91 523 31 21
Popular. Two floors with two bars. Cabins. Recently renovated.
■ **Lord Byron's** (B e G MA) 22-4, WE -5 h
C/ Recoletos, 18 *(Metro Banco)* ☎ 91 575 00 00
During daytime cafeteria-restaurant. Wed bingo.
■ **Lucas Bar Mix** (AC B d GLM MA s) 20.30-3.30 h
C/ San Lucas, 11 *(Metro Chueca)*
■ **Lupe. La** (B f g s YG) 17-2, Fri Sat -3.30, Sun 13-2 h
C/ Torrecilla del Leal 12 *(Metro Antón Martín)* ☎ 91 527 50 19
■ **Mad. Café-Club** (! A AC BF CC D F g MG OS S) Mon-Wed 10-2, Thu -4, Fri Sat -5, Sun 13-0 h
C/ Virgen de los Peligros, 4 ✉ 28013 ☎ 91 532 62 28
■ **Madrid La Nuit** (AC STV) 20-1 h
C/ Pelayo, 31 ✉ 28004 *(Metro Chueca)* ☎ 91 522 99 78
■ **Medium** (AC B d G MA s STV) 17-2, Fri Sat -4 h
C/ Reina, 17 ✉ 28004 *(Metro Chueca, Gran Via)* ☎ 91 523 02 25
Only esoteric bar in Spain, tarot lectures.
■ **Mojito. El** (A B Glm MA) 21-2.30, Fri Sat 21-3.30 h
C/ Olmo, 6 *(Metro Antón Martín)*
■ **Moskito Bar. The** (AC B d GLM MA) 20-3 h
C/ Torrecilla del Leal, 13 ✉ 28012 *(Metro Antón Martín)*

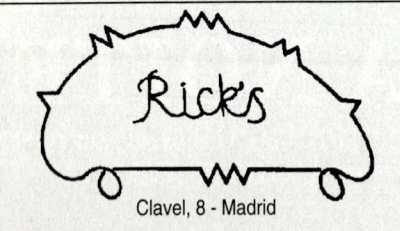

Rick's
Clavel, 8 - Madrid

A tope - todos los días del año
Super atmosphere - every day of the year

Ras
Fundado 1980
Barbieri, 7
Madrid
Tlf.: 91 522 43 17

Veinte años dando lo mejor para vosotros
The last 20 years we have given our best for you!

Madrid Spain

■ **PK 2** (B d DR G MA VS) 20-? h
C/ Libertad, 28 ☏ 91 531 86 77
■ **Ras** (AC B g s WE YG) 21-4, Fri Sat -4.30 h, Sun closed
C/ Barbieri, 7 ✉ 28004 *(Metro Chueca)* ☏ 91 522 43 17
■ **Regine's Terraza** (B g YG) Summer only 21-? h
Paseo de la Castellana, 56 *(near Plaza Emilio Castelar)*
Best time 0-3 h.
■ **Rick's** (B d g p YG) 23-5, Fri Sat -? h
C/ Clavel, 8 *(Metro Chueca)* ☏ 91 531 91 86
■ **Rimmel** (! B DR G VS YG) 19-3 h
C/ Luis de Góngora, 2 *(Metro Chueca)*
■ **Sueño Eterno. El** (B g MA) 20-3 h
C/ Pelayo, 37 *(Metro Chueca)*
■ **Tabata** (B G YG) 22.30-5 h
C/ Vergara, 12 *(Metro Opera)* ☏ 91 547 97 35
■ **Troyans** (AC B DR G LJ MA p VS) 21.30-3, Fri Sat 22.30-4 h, closed Mon
C/ Pelayo, 4 *(Metro Chueca)*
3 bars. Very friendly and highly recommended. Headquarters of MSC Madrid.
■ **Truck** (B D G MA) Tue-Sun 22-5.30 h
C/ Libertad, 28 ☏ 91 531 18 70
■ **Video Show Bar Gay** (AC B G MA S SNU VS) 16-24, SNU Sun 21.30 h
C/ Barco, 32 ✉ 28004 *(Metro Gran Vía/Tribunal)* ☏ 639 20 87 16
Also video cabins.
■ **Why not?** (B g MA) 22-4 h
C/ San Bartolomé, 7 *(Metro Gran Vía)*
■ **17. El** (B G MA) 21.30-3, WE -4 h
C/ de Recoletos, 17 *(Metro Banco)* ☏ 91 577 75 12

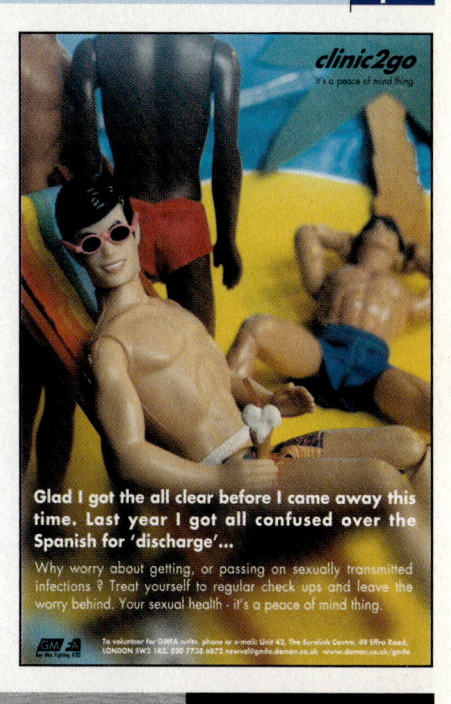

Spain | Madrid

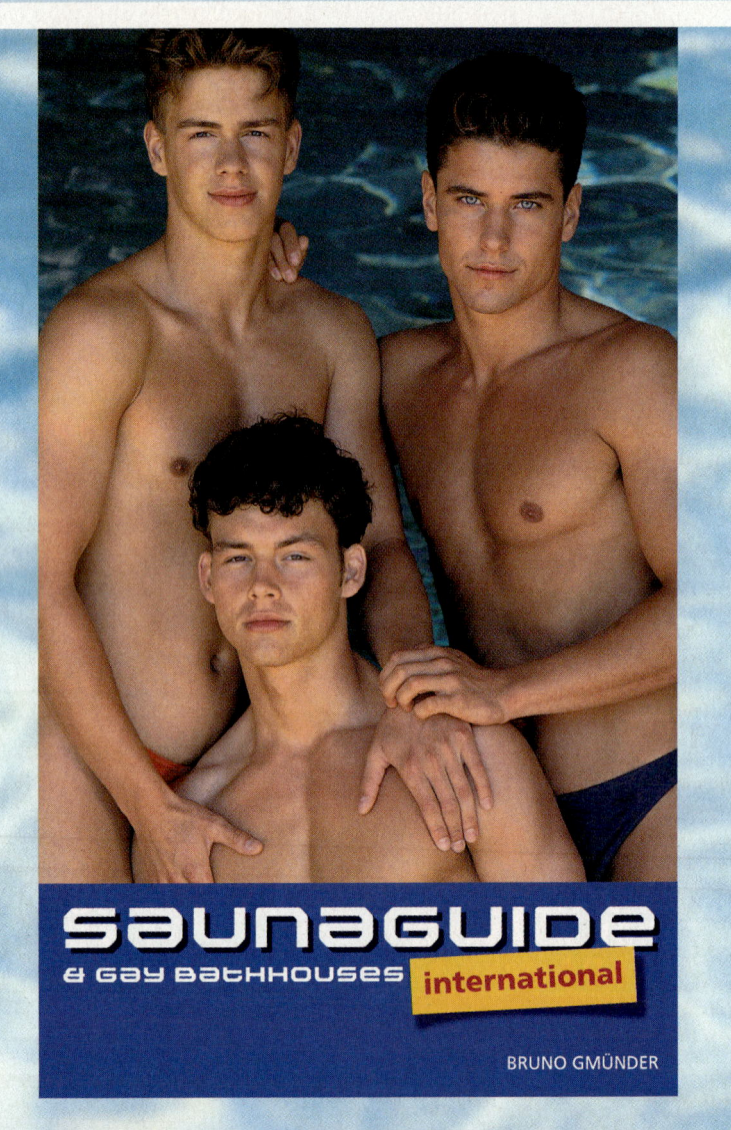

sauna guide
& gay bathhouses *international*

BRUNO GMÜNDER

Sauna Guide & Gay Bathhouses International
252 Seiten/Pages, English / Deutsch / Français, ISBN 3-86187-155-6
DM 26,80 / Sfr 26,- /Ös 196,-
Erhältlich im Buchhandel oder bei www.brunos.de

- coffee
- restaurant
- drinks
- lunch menu everyday
- music
- internet

la sastrería

915 320771

c/ hortaleza, 74. 28004 madrid - chueca

Spain | Madrid

CAFES

■ **Acuarela Café** (A B glm MA) 15-3, Sat Sun 11-3 h
C/ Gravina, 10
■ **Camp** (AC B bf CC d F glm MA VS WE) 10-3h
C/ Marqués de Valdeiglesias, 6 ✉ 28004 (M° Banco)
☏ 91 532 60 99
lunch & dinner menus, mostly gay at WE.
■ **Color** (AC B f G MA) 15-24, WE 17-3 h
C/ Augusto Figueroa, 11 ✉ 28004 *(Metro Chueca, Gran Vía)*
☏ 91 522 48 20
Tapas, cakes & milkshakes.
■ **Figueroa. Café** (! B f Glm MA) 12-1.30, Fri Sat -2.30 h
C/ Augusto Figueroa, 17/C/ Hortaleza *(Metro Chueca)*
☏ 91 521 16 73
■ **Jardin. El** (AC B BF f G MA) 10-2, Fri Sat Sun -3 h
C/ Infantes, 9 ✉ 28004 *(Metro Gran Vía)* ☏ 91 521 90 45
■ **Sastrería. La** (AC B BF e F g MA WE) Mon-Thu 10-2, Fri-Sun 11-3 h
C/ Hortaleza, 74 ✉ 28004 *(Metro Chueca)* ☏ 91 532 07 71
Popular designer cafe, public internet access.
■ **Star's Café-Dance** (A AC B BF CC D F G snu YG) Mon-Thu 20-2, Fri -3, Sat -4 h ,Sun closed
C/ Marqués de Valdeiglesias, 5/C/ Infanta ✉ 28004 *(Metro Banco)*
☏ 91 522 27 12
■ **Troje. Café La** (A B Glm MA) 16-2, WE -3 h
C/ Pelayo, 26
■ **Underwood** (AC B CC f G YG) 12-1.30, Fri Sat -2.30 h
C/ Infanta, 32 ✉ 28004 *(Metro Banco)* ☏ 91 532 82 67
International newspapers and magazines.
■ **XXX Café** (AC B BF CC f G MA s) Sun-Thu 13-2, Fri Sat 17-1h; Show Thu 23.30h
C/ Clavel/C/ Reina *(Metro Gran Vía)* ☏ 91 532 84 15

DANCECLUBS

■ **Escape** (AC B D GLM MA s) Thu 23-4.30, Fri Sat 1-7 h, Sun-Wed closed
C/ Gravina, 13 ✉ 28004 *(Metro Chueca)*
■ **Griffin's** (AC D E G MG S) Sun-Thu 0-4.45, Fri -5.30, Sat -5.45 h
C/ Villalar, 8 ✉ 28001 *(Metro Banco)* ☏ 91 576 07 25
■ **Heaven** (AC B D dr G MA STV vs YG) 1.30-8, Fri Sat 2-10 h. Show Mon-Wed 3 h
C/ Veneras 2 *(Metro Santo Domingo, next to Strong Center)*
☏ 91 548 20 22
Popular WE early in the morning. Heaven-Techno-Gothic-Club Fri Sat 21-2 h
■ **Ohm** (B D G MA) Fri-Sat 0-6h
Plaza Callao, 4
■ **Olimpo** (AC B DR G MA S VS WE) Tue-Fri 23-6, Sat 23-7 h
C/ Advana, 21 ✉ 28004 *(Metro Gran Vía)* ☏ 91 531 16 95
Wednesday: underwear party, very popular
■ **Polana** (AC B CC D g glm MA S) 23-?h
C/ Barbieri, 10 ✉ 28004 *(M° Chueca / Gran Vía)* ☏ 91 532 33 05
cantantes, teatro, lecturas, etc.
■ **Priscilla** (AC B CC D g MA) 19-3, Fri Sat -5 h
C/ San Bartolomé, 6 ✉ 28004 *(Metro Gran Vía)*
■ **Refugio** (AC B D DR G MA S VS WE) Wed-Sun 0-? h
C/ Dr. Cortezo, 1 ✉ 28012 *(Metro Sol, under Teatro Calderón)*
☏ 91 369 40 38
■ **Sachas** (AC B D GLM OS r STV) Disco Thu-Sun 20-5, Bar next door also Mon-Wed 20-3 h
Plaza Chueca, 1 *(Metro Chueca)*

CAFÉ Miranda
GAY RESTAURANT
BARQUILLO, 29 — 28004 MADRID
CASANOVA, 30 — 08011 BARCELONA
RESERVAS MADRID .91 52129 46
RESERVAS BARCELONA 93 453 52 49
ABIERTO TODOS LOS DIAS A PARTIR DE LAS 21H.
Lunes - Domingo 21 - 01 (o más tardes)

DIVINA la cocina
Jose Luis de Castanedo
Executive Chef
colmenares, 13
esq. san marcos
28004 madrid
tel. 91 531 37 65
divina@retemail.es

946 SPARTACUS 2001/2002

Madrid   Spain

■ **Shangay Tea Dance** (B D Glm S YG) Sun 22-3 h
c/o Pasopoga, Gran Vía, 374 *(Metro Callao)* ☎ 91 521 50 27
Very popular.
■ **Strong Center** (! B D DR G lj MA SNU) 0-6, Show 3.30 h
C/ Trujillos, 7 *(Metro Santo Domingo)* ☎ 91 541 54 15

RESTAURANTS

■ **Al Natural** (F G) 13-16, 21-24h
C/ Zorilla, 11 ☎ 91 369 47 09
Health Food restaurant. Menu at 1.450 Pts
■ **Armario. El** (A AC CC F GLM MA WE) 13.30-16, 21-24 h
C/ San Bartolomé, 7 ✉ 28004 *(Metro Chueca)* ☎ 91 532 83 77
■ **Brasileira** (F g MA) 13-16, 20-24 h
C/ Pelayo, 49 *(Metro Chueca)* ☎ 91 308 36 25
Brasilian cuisine.
■ **Cafe Miranda** (AC CC F G MA S WE) 21-1 h
C/ Barquillo, 29, bajo ✉ 28004 ☎ 91 521 29 46
■ **Castro de San Francisco, El** (AC B CC F G) 11.30-2h, Sun closed
C/ Hernán Cortés, 19 ✉ 28004 *(M° Chueca / Tribunal)*
☎ 91 531 27 40
Equilibrated healthy Spanish cuisine.
■ **Chez Pomme** (F g MA) 13.30-16, 20.30-23 h
C/ Pelayo, 4 *(Metro Chueca)* ☎ 91 532 16 46
Vegetarian restaurant.
■ **Convento Canario, El** (AC B CC F G) 12-16, 20-24, WE-1h
C/ Valverde, 6 ✉ 28004 *(M° Gran Vía)* ☎ 91 532 01 88
Typical Spanish (Canarian) cuisine.
■ **Cornucopia** (AC CC F g MA) Tue-Sun 13.30-16, 21-0 h
C/ Flora, 1 ✉ 28013 *(Metro Opera)* ☎ 91 547 64 65
Reservation recommended.
■ **Dame Noire. La** (AC b CC F G) 21-1, Fri Sat -2 h
C/ Pérez Galdós, 3 ✉ 28004 *(Metro Gran Vía)* ☎ 91 531 04 76
■ **Divina, la cocina** (AC CC F GLM MA WE) Mon-Sat 13.30-16,
Tue-Thu 21-0, Fri Sat 21-1 h
C/ Colmenares, 13 /San Marcos ✉ 28004 *(Metro Chueca, Gran Vía)*
☎ 91 531 37 65
■ **Dolce Vita. La** (AC B CC F g MA) 13.30-16, 21-24 h
C/ Cardenal Cisneros, 58 *(Metro Quevedo, Bus 16, 61, 149)*
☎ 91 445 04 36
Classic italian cuisine.
■ **Gula Gula** (AC CC F g MA s STV) 13-17, 21-3 h
Gran Vía, 1 ✉ 28013 ☎ 91 522 87 64
Buffet-salad bar.
■ **Hudson** (AC b F G MA) 11.30-3 h, Mon closed
C/ Hortaleza, 37 ✉ 28004 ☎ 91 532 33 46
Pizza & fast food
■ **Marsot** (b F g MA) 13-16, 20.30-24 h, closed Sun
C/ Pelayo, 6 *(Metro Chueca)* ☎ 91 531 07 26
Good, cheap and very typical.
■ **Momo** (AC CC F glm MA) 13-16, 21-24 h
C/ de Augusto Figueroa, 41 ✉ 28004 *(Metro Chueca)*
☎ 91 532 71 62
■ **Rincon de Pelayo. El** (CC F G MA) 12.30-16.30, 20.30-1 h
C/ Pelayo, 19 ✉ 28004 *(Metro Chueca)* ☎ 91 521 84 07
■ **Sarrasin** (A AC CC glm MA WE) 13-16, 21-24 h
C/ Libertad, 8 ✉ 28004 *(Metro Chueca)* ☎ 91 532 73 40

SEX SHOPS/BLUE MOVIES

■ **B 43 Gay Shop** (CC G MA p) Mon-Sat 11-14, 16-22 Sun 16-22,
summer 11-14, 17-21, Sun 17-22 h
C/ Barco, 43 *(Metro Gran Vía)* ☎ 91 531 49 88
■ **Californiusa/American** (g VS) 10-23 h
C/ Montera, 13 *(Metro Sol)* ☎ 91 531 35 05
Cruisy.

C/. San Bartolomé, 7
28004 MADRID
Reservas: (91) 532 83 77

■ **Libería Sexologica** (g) 10.30-14.30, 17-21 h
C/ Hortaleza, 38 ✉ 28004 *(Metro Gran Vía)* ☎ 91 532 81 91
Books, magazines, comics, fotos, etc.
■ **Querelle** (AC DR MA VS) Mon-Sat 22-3h, Sun 19.30-3h
C/ Lavapiés, 12 ✉ 28012 *(M° Tirso de Molina)* ☎ 91 528 38 60
Very darkroom! Wed sexparty, 2nd Sat fleshparty
■ **Sex Center Mundo Fantastico** (g VS) 10-4 h
C/ Atocha, 80 *(Metro Antón Martín)*
■ **Show Center** (g VS) 10-24 h
C/ Montera, 30 *(Metro Gran Vía)* ☎ 91 521 87 15
■ **Showcenter Hollywood** (g VS) 10-4 h
C/ Atocha, 70 *(Metro Antón Martín)* ☎ 91 528 25 84
■ **TVX** (CC g MA VS) 10-22, Sun 12-21 h
Mejia Lequerica,16 ✉ 28004 ☎ 91 447 73 73

CINEMAS

■ **Sala X** (g VS) 10.30-23 h
C/ Duque de Alba, 4 *(Metro Tirso de Molina)* ☎ 91 369 18 65
■ **Sala X** (g VS) 10.30-21.30 h
C/ Corredera Baja de San Pablo, 37 *(M° Callao / Gran Vía)*
☎ 91 522 81 09

Spain — Madrid

ESCORTS & STUDIOS
■ **Antonio** (CC msg) 24 h
C/ Arturo Savia 267, 2°A ✉ 28033 ☎ 619 17 14 03 (mobile)

HOUSE OF BOYS
■ **Angel's** (CC G msg R VS WH) 0-24 h
C/ Triana, 53 ✉ 28016 *(M° Pio XII)* ☎ 91 350 76 32

SAUNAS/BATHS
■ **Adan** (B DR G MA msg Pl R SA SB VS) 0-24 h
C/ San Bernardo, 38 ✉ 28015 *(Metro-Santo Domingo/Noviciado)*
☎ 91 532 91 38
■ **Alameda** (DR G msg OG SA SB) 13-23 h
C/ Alameda, 20 ✉ 28015 *(Metro-Atocha)* ☎ 91 429 87 45
Small sauna on two floors, patronised largely by older men. Drinks at the entrance, cabins, darkroom and showers downstairs.
■ **Caldea** (B f G msg SA SB SOL WO) 0-24 h
C/ Valverde, 32 ✉ 28004 *(Metro Gran Vía, Chueca, Tribunal)*
☎ 91 522 99 56
■ **Comendadoras** (B G MA msg SA SB VS) 24 h
Plaza de las Comendadoras, 9 ✉ 28015 *(Metro Noviciado/San Bernardo, near Plaza de España)* ☎ 91 532 88 92
■ **Cristal** (b DR G MA msg r SA VS) 15-3 h
C/ Augusto Figueroa, 17 ✉ 28004 *(Metro Chueca)*
☎ 91 531 44 89
■ **Men** (B DR G MA SA SB VS) 15-8, Fri 15.30-Mon 8 h
C/ Pelayo, 25 ✉ 28004 *(Metro Chueca)* ☎ 91 531 25 83
■ **Paraiso** (! AC B G msg SA SB VS YG) 15-1 h
C/ Norte, 15 ✉ 28015 *(Metro San Bernardo/Noviciado)*
☎ 91 522 42 32
Beautiful sauna with old faience.

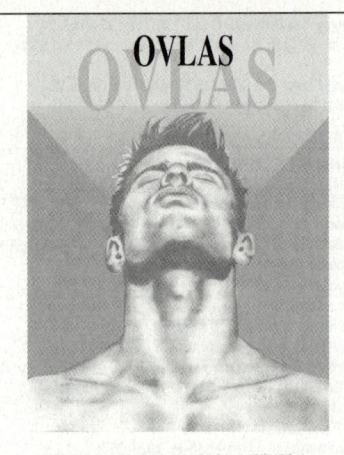

OVLAS

MADRID C/ AUGUSTO FIGUEROA, 1 (CHUECA)
Tel. 91 522 73 27

BARCELONA C/ PORTAFERRISSA, 25 TIENDA 34
(Hombre)Tel. 93 412 52 29 (Mujer) Tel.93 412 12 52
GAL. GRALLA HALL

BAR - RESTAURANTE C/PORTAFERRISSA,25
Tel. 93 412 38 36 GAL.GRALLA HALL (BARCELONA)

SITGES SAN FRANCISCO, 22 Tel. 93 894 15 21
PASEO VILAFRANCA,3 Tel. 93 894 73 20
SITGES - BARCELONA

IBIZA C/ LA VIRGEN, 7
Tel. 971 19 29 20

ADAN
SAN BERNARDO 38
METRO » NOVICIADO

ALAMEDA
ALAMEDA 20
METRO » ATOCHA

SAUNAS

MADRID

COMENDADORAS
PZA. COMENDADORAS 15
METRO » NOVICIADO

CRISTAL
AUGUSTO FIGUEROA 17
METRO » CHUECA

DO YOU KNOW WHERE THE TRUES
PARTIES ARE GOING ON
IF YOU HAVE NEVER BEEN IN **MADRID**,
YOU DON'T UNDERSTAND WHAT IS A
TRUE NIGHT LIFE
MADRID IS MOVING 'ND GROOVING
MADRID IS PARTY 24 HOURS A DAY
¡¡ LET'S GO !! STAY IN THE CENTRE OF **MADRID**
THE TOURISM AND THE SCENE ARE HERE

GET THE BEST !

HOSTAL PUERTA DEL SOL

TEL: 0034 91 522 51 26
FAX: 0034 91 522 98 15
e-mail : puertadelsol@retemail.es
www.hostalpuertadelsol.com

OVERLOOKING THE SQUARE
SINGLE ROOM 5.000-6.000-8.000
DOUBLE ROOM 8.000-10.000-12.000
BREAKFAST INCLUYED
FOR MORE OF THREE DAYS FULL BOARD

PUERTA DEL SOL 14, 4º   28013 MADRID

Spain — Madrid

HISPA DOMUS PENSION

San BARTOLOMÉ, 4 – 2° Izq.
28004 MADRID
telf. +34 915238127 fax. +34 917010114
http://www.hispadomus.com

NEW
DEVOTED TO MEN
INNOVATIVE DECORATION
7 COMFORTABLE ROOMS
UNIQUE KIND OF ACCOMODATION
AT THE HEART OF CHUECA'S

HOSTAL HISPANO ☆☆

- HABITACION CON BAÑO
- HILO MUSICAL
- TELEFONO
- TELEVISION

HORTALEZA, 38 - 2° • 28004 MADRID • TEL. 531 48 71 - FAX 521 87 80

■ **Plaza** (G MA msg R SA SB SOL WO) 10-22 h
Plaza de España ✉ 28013 (Gran Vía 88, Edificio Plaza España) ☎ 91 548 37 41
Discreet sauna in oldfashioned style.

■ **Príncipe** (AC B f G MA msg SA SB VS) 10-1 h
C/ Príncipe, 15 ✉ 28012 (Metro Sol/ Sevilla) ☎ 91 429 39 49
Clean and cruisy.

BOOK SHOPS

■ **Berkana** (CC GLM) Mon-Fri 10.30-14 ,17-20.30, Sat 12-14, 17.30-20.30 h, closed Sun
C/ Gravina, 11 (Metro Chueca) ☎ 91 532 13 93
Also very good information point for the gay scene. Free gay map of Madrid. Catalogue on request.

■ **Different Life, A** (CC GLM) 11-14, 17-22h
C/ Pelayo, 30 ✉ 28004 ☎ 91 532 96 52

FASHION SHOPS

■ **Ovlas**
C/ Augusto Figueroa, 1 (M° Chueca) ☎ 91 522 73 27

LEATHER & FETISH SHOPS

■ **SR** (CC G LJ) Mon-Thu 11-14.30 17-21, Fri Sat 11-14.30 17-22 h, closed Sun
C/ Pelayo, 7 ✉ 28004 (Metro Chueca) ☎ 91 523 19 64
Leather, rubber, uniform, skin, army, industrial.

TRAVEL AND TRANSPORT

■ **Lambda Viajes** (CC glm) Mon-Fri 9.30-14.30 h, 16.30-20, Sat 10-14 h
C/ Fuencarral, 43 ✉ 28004 (Metro Chueca/Tribunal)
☎ 91 532 78 33 📠 91 532 51 62

■ **Navegaytour Agencia de Viajes** (GLM) Mon-Fri 9.30-14, 16-19, Sat 11-14 h
Gran Vía 80, 1° - 1 ✉ 28013 (Metro Plaza Espana)
☎ 91 542 78 35 📠 91 541 00 99 ✉ navegaytur@menet.es

HOTELS

■ **Hispa Domus** (CC G H)
C/ San Bartolomé, 4, 2°, izq. ✉ 28004 (M° Chueca/Gran Vía)
☎ 91 523 81 27 📠 91 701 01 14 ✉ hdomus@wanadoo.es
🖥 www.hispadomus.com
All rooms individually furnished and with bath/wc/telephone/television.

■ **Hispano Hostal** (g H)
C/ Hortaleza, 38, 2° ✉ 28004 (Metro Chueca, Gran Vía; Bus 3,7,40, 2nd floor) ☎ 91 531 48 71 📠 91 521 87 80
Centrally located. 21 rooms with bath/wc, telephone and TV. Ask for prices.

■ **Hostal Odesa** (G H MA)
C/ Hortaleza, 38, 3°izq. ✉ 28004 (Metro Chueca, Gran Vía; Bus 3, 7,40, 3rd floor) ☎ 91 521 03 38 📠 91 532 08 28 📠 91 521 03 38
✉ sonsodesa@retemail.es 🖥 personal2.iddeo.es/sonsodesa
Gay hotel. Centrally located. Rooms with shower/WC and TV, own key. Rates single Ptas 4.000, double 5.500 (tax incl.)

■ **Hostal Puerta del Sol** (BF G H OS)
Puerta del Sol 14, 4° ✉ 28013 (4th floor) ☎ 91 522 51 26
📠 91 552 98 15 ✉ puertadelsol@retemail.es
🖥 www.hostalpuertadelsol.com
Rates single: ptas 5.000-8.000, Double 8.000-12.000.-

■ **Hostal Sonsoles** (CC glm H)
C/ Fuencarral,18, 2° Derecha ✉ 28004 (Metro Gran Vía / Chueca)
☎ 91 531 75 25 📠 91 532 75 22
✉ sonsodesa@retemail.es 🖥 personal2.iddeo.es/sonsodesa
Rooms with bath, WC, balcony or terrace, telephone, fax, TV, radio and room service. Internet access.

Madrid ▸ Málaga **Spain**

HOSTAL odesa ★★
also apartments available
EXCLUSIVELY GAY
T.V. EN TODAS LAS HABITACIONES
TV IN EVERY ROOM
CAJA FUERTE INDIVIDUAL
Metro: Gran Via y Chueca
Bus: 3 - 7 - 40
28004 MADRID
Hortaleza, 38, 3º Izda.
Tels. 91-521 03 38 / 91-532 08 28
Fax: 91-521 03 38
E-MAIL:sonsodesa@retemail.es
http://personal2.iddeo.es/sonsodesa

HOSTAL sonsoles ★★
• HABITACON CON BAÑO • TELEFONO
• HILO MUSICAL • TELEVISION
CAJA FUERTE INDIVIDUAL
Fuencarral 18, 2º Dcha.
28004 Madrid
Teléfs. 91-532 75 23 – 91-532 75 22
Fax 91-532 75 22
http://personal2.iddeo.es/sonsodesa
E-MAIL:sonsodesa@retemail.es
internet access for the clients

GUEST HOUSES
■ **Valencia. Hostal**
C/ Espoz y Mina, 7, 4º Derecha ✉ 28012 ☏ 91 521 18 45

APARTMENTS
■ **Apartamentos Galdos** (GLM H OS)
C/ Pérez Galdós, 6 ✉ 28004 *(Metro Gran Vía)* ☏ 91 531 28 98
🖷 91 531 28 98
Appartment with double room.
■ **Apartamentos Odesa** (AC CC G)
C/ Hortaleza, 38, 3°, izq. ✉ 28004 *(Mº Chueca / Gran Vía)*
☏ 91 521 03 38 🖷 91 521 03 38 💻 sonsodesa@retemail.es
All apartments with bath/wc/television.

PRIVATE ACCOMMODATION
■ **EG´s City Apartments** (glm H) all year
C/ Conde de Ramanones, 2 ✉ 28012 *(4th floor)* ☏ 619 44 02 32
🖷 91 420 00 90
2 studios and 2 apartments in the city center with bath/WC or shower/WC, TV, Kitchenette, heating, Minibar and radio. Rates from Pts. 8.500 per night (max. 2 persons)

GENERAL GROUPS
■ **Colectivo Gays y Lesbianas de Madrid (COGAM)**
Mon-Fri 17-21, Cafe 17-24 h
C/ Fuencarral, 37 *(Metro Chueca / Gran Vía)* ☏ 91 522 45 17
🖷 91 524 02 00 💻 cogam@ctv.es 💻 www.cogam.org
Ask for their different groups.

FETISH GROUPS
■ **MSC Madrid**
C/ Pelayo, 4 ✉ 28004
Member of ECMC.

HEALTH GROUPS
■ **Centro de Promoción de la Salud** Test Mon-Thu 9.30-10.30 h
C/ Navas de Tolosa, 10 *(Metro Callao / Sto. Domingo)*
☏ 91 532 23 67 🖷 91 532 98 02
Free and anonymous HIV-testing.
■ **Entender en Positivo (COGAM)** Sun 17-21 h
C/ Fuencarral, 37 *(Metro Chueca/Gran Vía)* ☏ 91 523 00 70
Confidential group.
■ **Fundación para la Formación e Información sobre tratamientos SIDA** Mon-Fri 9-14, 16-20h
C/ Sandoval, 4, 2° ☏ 91 591 20 19 🖷 91 591 20 19
💻 fitpeio@jet.es 💻 www.fit.es
Information about AIDS treatment.

RELIGIOUS GROUPS
■ **Cohesión**
PO Box 510 57
Christian gays.

SWIMMING
- Piscina del Lago (Casa del Campo, Mº Lago)

CRUISING
-Estación de Chamartin (r)
-Estación de Atocha, Cercania-station,WC entrepiso (very popular)
-Cortes Ingles Shopping Center 1.Sol, 2.Goya, 3.Castellana
-La Vaguada Shopping Centre (downstairs, next to the Disney shop. Metro Barrio del Pilar. Popular)
-Legazpi,(polígono industrial / C/ del Ricardo)
-Parque del Retiro (near sports zone; popular daytime; at night AYOR; Metro Atocha-Renfe)
-Plaza de la Lealtad (in front of Ritz Hotel, after 1h)
-Calle del Almirante (R)
-Calle del Prim (R)
-Plaza de Toros, Monumental, Parking (Metro Ventas, Carcruising from 22 h, very popular)
-Avenida de America (Calle de Cartagena, out of town, right side. Car-cruising from 22 h, popular)
-Parque Atenas (at night)
-Templo de Debod (at night)
-Casa de Campo (in the surrounding wood of Teleférico (cable railway) ground parking. 24 hours; at night: ayor)

Málaga

BARS
■ **Kiss** (AC B D GLM MA stv) Tue-Sat 0-6h
C/ Madre de Diós, 11 ✉ 29002 *(near Plaza de la Merced)*
Thu dragshow.
■ **Sobrelamesalastazas** (B bf f GLM) 10-3h
Plaza de la Merced, 1 ✉ 29008
■ **Telon** (AC B bf f G MA OS) 10-3h
Plaza de la Merced, 18 ✉ 29008

CAFES
■ **Calle de Bruselas** (AC B BF f g MA OS) 10-4 h
Plaza de la Merced, 16 ✉ 29012 ☏ 95 260 39 48
■ **Flor de Lis** (A AC B BF f G MA OS) 9.30-4 h, Sun 12-4 h
Plaza de la Merced, 18 ✉ 29008 ☏ 95 260 98 19

Spain | Málaga ▸ Murcia

DANCECLUBS
■ **Sodoma** (AC B D G MA stv) Tue-Sat 0-6h
C/ Juan de Padilla, 15 ✉ 29008 ☎ 952 21 01 38
Sat 4h dragshow
■ **Torrero** (AC B D G MA) 23-5 h
Plaza San Francisco, 7 ✉ 29000

SEX SHOPS/BLUE MOVIES
■ **Amsterdam** (AC g VS)
C/ Duquesa de Parcent, 1
■ **Cosmopolitan** (g VS) 10-24 h
C/ Muelle de Heredia, 12 ☎ 95 222 15 83
■ **Hamburgo** (g VS)
C/ Casa de Campo, 11
■ **Sex Shop** (g VS)
Plaza Bailén 2

SAUNAS/BATHS
■ **Thermi Sauna** (AC B CC DR f G lj MA msg P SA SB SOL VS WE WH) 16-24 h
C/ Pito, 3 ✉ 29008 *(near Plaza de Uncibay)* ☎ 95 213 222
4 floors.

GUEST HOUSES
■ **Finca Lería**
Partido los Anéales ✉ 29500 ☎ 95 2112 703
📧 info@fincaleria.com 🖥 www.fincaleria.com

CRUISING
-Paseo del Parque (AYOR) (nights)
-Jardines de Puerta Oscura (ayor r)
-Campo de Golf beach (8 km from Málaga and Torremolinos, car cruising at night)
-Train station (ayor, r)

Marbella

BARS
■ **Boccacio Inn** (B G MA VS) 23.30-? h
C/ Puerto del Mar, 7
■ **Ojo** (B G MA p S VS YG) 23.30-3, WE -? h, Show Sat
C/ Puerto del Mar, 9 ☎ 95 277 16 79

RESTAURANTS
■ **Finca Besaya** (b F g s) 20-2 h
Rio Verde Alto ☎ 95 286 13 86
Telephone reservation only. 3-course menu Ptas 4.500.
■ **La Comedia** (B F g MA) Mon-Sat 19-?
C/ San Lazaro, 3 *(Plaza de la Victoria)* ☎ 95 277 64 78
Restaurant and Bar in the heart of the old town of Marbella.
■ **Le Biarritz** (CC F G MA OS) 13-16, 20-24 h
C/ Ribera, 122, Puerto Banus ✉ 29600 *(2nd line of seafront)*
☎ 95 281 12 48

SWIMMING
-Cabo Pino (Follow the coastal highway N-340 towards Torremolinos about 5 km to the km-marker 194, shortly after the Hotel Artola. Take the first right into the unmarked road, then the third left all the way to the end, then right down to the beach. Walk over the dunes, the beach bar "Las Dunas" is to your left and reach the most popular nudist beach on the Costa del Sol. The bus from Marbella to Fuengirola stops near Hotel Artola, from there by foot as above.)

CRUISING
-Paseo de Maritimo (at night some people)

FINCA LERÍA, ÁLORA, COSTA DEL SOL, SPAIN

A converted farmhouse set in its own orange grove with swimming pool and beautiful mountain views. Ideal for that relaxing `get away from it all´ holiday or as a base to explore the surrounding area yet only 45 minutes from Torremolinos and the gay scene.
B&B or half board available.
**Phone Roger or Martin on
00 34 95 2112 703 or
e-mail: info@fincaleria.com
www.fincaleria.com**

Merida

BARS
■ **Athos Club** (AC B D DR GLM lj MA p s VS WE) 21.30-? h
C/ Baños, 23, bajo *(near Roman Theatre and Museum)*
☎ 924 33 05 74

Murcia

GAY INFO
■ **No te Prives** Meeting Fri 20 h
c/o Colectivo Gai de Murcia, PO Box 776, ✉ 30008
☎ 968 29 54 84
10-page monthly newsletter. For free at gay venues.

BARS
■ **Bacus** (AC B DR G MA p STV VS) 19-2.30 h, Tue closed, Sun 21.30 show
C/ Isidoro de la Cierva, 5, B3 *(Galería Muñoz)*
■ **Blaky Disco Pub** (AC B DR G MA p s VS) 22.30-4.30 h. Show Sun.
C/ San Antonio, 1 *(Galería Muñoz)* ☎ 968 21 23 36
Popular, modern music bar.
■ **Odeon** (B f GLM MA) 16-?, winter Sat Sun also 6-10 h (bf)
C/ Fuensanta, 5 ☎ 968 22 16 41
■ **Piscis Disco Bar** (AC B D DR Glm MA p s VS) 22-4 h, Show Sun
C/ Enrique Villar, 13 / Trav. Santo Domingo 6 *(near Cathedral)*
☎ 968 23 89 62
Disco, video, surprise shows. Recommended and popular.
■ **Vie en Rose. La** (AC B DR G MA VS) 20-3 h
Rincón del Santo Domingo 7 *(Near Plaza Santo Domingo)*
☎ 600 416 253 (mobile)

Murcia ▶ Pamplona/Iruña | **Spain**

■ **5 Mentarios** (AC B CC d G MA STV VS WE) 22-? h, Mon closed, Fri, Sat, Sun 6-? afterhour
C/ Torre de Romo, 52 ✉ 30011 ☎ 968 346 122
Show Fri, Sat 1 h, Sun games and contests.

DANCECLUBS

■ **Metropol** (AC B D DR Glm MA S VS YG) Fri-Sun 2-6, Show Sun 3 h
C/ San Andrés, 14 ☎ 968 28 39 23

SEX SHOPS/BLUE MOVIES

■ **Internacional Sex-Shop** (g VS) 10-22, Sun 10-14 h
C/ Enrique Villar, 7 ☎ 968 24 82 15
■ **Master's** (g VS) 10-14, 16-22 h
C/ Mariano Ruiz Funes, 5 ☎ 968 24 28 57
■ **Sexyland** (g VS) 10.30-1 h
C/ Los Bolos, 1 ☎ 928 28 30 90

SAUNAS/BATHS

■ **Nordik Sauna Masculina** (! B DR G MA SA SB VS) 15-22 h
C/ Cartagena, 72 ✉ 30002 ☎ 968 25 91 20
■ **Ulises** (B G MA msg SA SB SOL VS wo) 15-23, Sat -4 h
C/ Madre Elisea Oliver Molina s/n ✉ 30002 ☎ 968 93 30 55

GUEST HOUSES

■ **Villa Aya** (G H NU OS pi)
Urb. Rusticana, 16, Mazarron ✉ 30879 ☎ 968 592094
Exclusively gay. All en-suite rooms. Lounge. Secluded pool and satellite TV.

HEALTH GROUPS

■ **Comité Ciudadano Antisida de la región Murcia (CASMU)**
☎ 968 29 88 31 (helpline) 📧 casmu@lix.intercom.es
AIDS-helpline.
■ **Consejería de Sanidad** Mon-Fri 9-14 h
Ronda de Levante, 11 *(Main floor)* ☎ 968 23 51 41
Anonymous HIV-testing.

CRUISING

-Main rail station
-Bus station
-El Corte Inglés - Shopping Centre, 3rd floor
-Paseo del Malecón (ayor) (and gardens; popular after sunset)
-Calle de Luis Fontes Pagan (car cruising)

Nerja

BARS

■ **Blanco y Negro** (B g MA)
C/ Pintada, 35 ☎ 95 252 47 55

EDUCATION SERVICES

■ **Giralda Center Languages**
C/ Jaen, 7 ✉ 29780 ☎ 95 52 33 98 📠 95 52 33 98
📧 gircenternerja@arrakis.es 💻 www.giraldacenter.com
Language school.

SWIMMING

-Playa Catarijan (on the road from Malaga -N 340- to Nerja, between Nerja and Herradura. Turn of just before tunnel at the signs of Cerro)

Oviedo

BARS

■ **Valentinos** (B D DR G VS YG) 20-4 h
C/ Hermanos Pidal, 28
■ **Versace** (AC B DR E G MA S SNU STV WE) Mon-Thu 21-4, Fri-Sun 21-7 h
C/ Campo Amor, 24 bajos ✉ 33001 ☎ 98 521 83 11

CAFES

■ **Santa Sede** (B G MA) 20-1 h
C/ Altamirano, 6
■ **Tamara** (B f glm YG) 11.30-15.30, 19-?; Aug only 19-? h
C/ Altamairano, 6

SEX SHOPS/BLUE MOVIES

■ **Internacional** (g VS) 10-14, 16-22 h
C/ González del Valle, 6 *(Galerías Pidal)* ☎ 98 525 24 99

SAUNAS/BATHS

■ **Finalmente Sauna** (B G msg PI SA SB SOL VS) 17-23, Fri Sat 17-8 h
C/ Alvarez Lorenzana, 22 ✉ 33006 ☎ 98 523 82 52

GENERAL GROUPS

■ **Xente Gai Astur (XEGA)**
PO Box 1397, C/ Gascona,12, 3° ✉ 33080 ☎ 98 522 40 29

HEALTH GROUPS

■ **Centro de Orientación sobre el SIDA**
Hospital Monte Naranco, C/ Vázquez de Mella s/n ☎ 98 523 07 50

CRUISING

-C/ Dr. Fleming/C/ Marqués de Mohías (after dark)
-Santullano Park (WE) (at night)

Pals

SWIMMING

-Bay of Pals (G NU) (10 minutes walk from Pals or the Gold Club, located near the installation of Radio Liberty)

Pamplona/Iruña

BARS

■ **Alakarga** (AC B GLM MA) 24-6 h
Plaza Monasterio de Azuelo, 1 ☎ 948 26 60 05
■ **M40** (AC B DR G MA VS) 23-4 h
Plaza San Juan de la Cadena, 2

SEX SHOPS/BLUE MOVIES

■ **Amsterdam Sex-Center** (AC CC glm VS) 10-22 h
C/ Virgen del Puy, 9 ✉ 31011 *(y Trasera)* ☎ 948 25 23 19
■ **Haizegoa Amsterdam Sex Centre** (g VS) 10-15, 17-22 h
Sancho Ramirez, 35 *(Bus 7, near planetarium)* ☎ 948 17 72 99
■ **Sex Mil 1** (AC CC glm VS) 10-22 h
C/ Virgon del Puy, 9 ✉ 31011 *(near by Juzgado)* ☎ 948 25 23 19

HEALTH GROUPS

■ **Comisión Ciudadana Anti Sida de Navarra**
C/ Calderería, 16, bajo ☎ 948 21 22 57

SPARTACUS 2001/2002 | 953

Spain — Pamplona/Iruña ▸ San Sebastian

■ **Comunidad Foral de Navarra**
☎ 948 24 53 00
HIV-testing.

CRUISING
-Parque de la Taconera
-Plaza del Castillo
-Bus station (AYOR)

Pedreguer

BARS
■ **Villa Romana Bar** (AC B D Glm lj MA OS S) 23-? h
C/ Partidá La Sella, 23 *(Crta. de Ondara a Gata km. 194,5)*

SWIMMING
-Playa in Pedreguer (NU)

Platja d'Aro

BARS
■ **Chapó** (B G MA) 21-3 h, Mon closed
Víctor Catalá s/n ☎ 972 82 52 50

SWIMMING
Cala del Pi (G NU) (from Platja d' Aro coming take the Camino de Ronda. After 15 min take the tunnel uphill.)

Pontevedra

HEALTH GROUPS
■ **Comité Ciudadano Anti Sida de Pontevedra**
PO Box 603 ✉ 36080

CRUISING
-Jardines de la Alameda

Reus

BARS
■ **Odeon** (AC B D E GLM MA P s WE) 22-4 h, Sat -6 h
C/ Boule, 7 , bajos ✉ 43201 ☎ 619 800 380 (mobile)

Rota

SWIMMING
-Beach and dunes at the Hotel "Playa de la Luz"

Sabadell

BARS
■ **Atic. L'** (B DR GLM MA S VS) 20-3 h, closed Mon
C/ Maria Aguilo, 22 ✉ 08203
■ **Divinae Alternative Bar** (AC B F G MA SNU STV) Tue-Sun 20-3 h
Les Planes 13-15 ✉ 08202 ☎ (696) 20 84 95
■ **Laundry** (B G MA) 20-3 h
C/ Can Viloca, 62 *(La Creu de Barberá)*

Salamanca

BARS
■ **Boston** (B g MA r)
Plaza de San Justo

■ **Sarao** (AC B DR G MA p S SNU STV VS) 23-4.30 h
Paseo de Carmelitas, 11-21 ✉ 37002

GENERAL GROUPS
■ **Unión pro derechos de Gais y Lesbianas de Castilla-León IGUALES**
PO Box 4004 ✉ 37080
Publish their own bimonthly gay-lesbian magazine "Entre Iguales".

HEALTH GROUPS
■ **Comité Ciudadano Anti Sida de Salamanca**
PO Box 819 ✉ 37080 ☎ 923 21 15 77
Information and services concerning AIDS.

CRUISING
-Parque de Alamedilla (AYOR)
-Estación Renfe
-Estación de autobuses
-Calzada de Medina, at the end of Paseo de la Estación (car cruising in the evening)

Salou

BARS
■ **Pou. El** (B G MA VS) 20-3 h
C/ Ramón Llull, 4
■ **Tres Coronas** (B G MA S) 23-4 h; Show Fri Sat
C/ del Sol, 72 *(near Plaza Venus)* ☎ 977 38 14 99

DANCECLUBS
■ **New Chatelet** (B G MA)
C/. Bruselas s/n

San Sebastian

BARS
■ **Trigono** (AC B d G YG) 23-3 h
C/ del General Lersundi, 6
■ **Txirula Pub** (AC B d g) 19-4 h
C/ San Martin, 9 ✉ 20007

DANCECLUBS
■ **Kontra** (B D GLM MA) 20-? h
C/ Manterola, 4 ☎ 945 473 609
■ **Rotonda. La** (B D glm) 23-3 h
Paseo de la Concha s/n

SAUNAS/BATHS
■ **Von Con Men** (AC B DR f G MA p SA SB VS) 11-23, WE 24h
C/ General Jauregui, 8 ☎ 943 44 61 16

GENERAL GROUPS
■ **GEHITU** (GLM MA)
Arrasate 51-3 ✉ 20005 ☎ 902 200 096 🖥 infasis@gehitu.net
🖥 www.gehitu.net

SWIMMING
-Playa de la Concha (daytime)

San Sebastian ▸ Sevilla — Spain

CRUISING
- Paseo del Urumea
- Playa de la Concha (at night)
- Roques de Mompas

Santa Cristina d'Aro
DANCECLUBS
■ **Mas Marco** (A AC B CC D DR GLM MA OS r SNU STV VS) Summer 22-5. Winter -3 h, Sat & Sun -5 h
Ctra. Roca de Malvet Km. 1 *(1 km from Opel Garage at Costa Brava, 32 km north of Lloret de Mar)* ☏ 972 837 790
Free entrance.

Santander
BARS
■ **Luna Pub. La** (B g MA) -2 h
C/ Gran Mola

DANCECLUBS
■ **Cuic** (B D g WE) 1-6 h
C/ Panamá
■ **Pacha Disco** (B D g) Thu-Sun -3.30 h
C/ Gran Mola

SWIMMING
- Playa del Puntal (Travel round the bay to Somo and walk the rest or take the ferry from Santander to Somo. The beach is a long isthmus with sand dunes along its length. Most gay activity is to be found approximately half the way along.)
- Playa de Valdearenas/Dunas de Liencres (10 km west of Santander, between Liencres and Boó, on the south side of the land spit in the dunes by the river Pas. You can reach it by bus from Santander)

CRUISING
- Paseo Pareda (after 24 h)
- Jardin Pareda (AYOR)
- Bus station/Estación de Autobuses
- Jardines de Piquío (nights)

Santiago de Compostela
GENERAL GROUPS
■ **Colectivo Gai de Compostela**
PO Box 191 ✉ 15780

HEALTH GROUPS
■ **Comite Antisida de Santiago**
C/ Fuente de San Miguel, 2, bajo ☏ 981 57 34 01

Segovia
BARS
■ **Amarote** (B g MA)
C/ Escuderos, 5 ☏ 911 43 02 15

GENERAL GROUPS
■ **Asociación Gay de Segovia (A.G.S.)**
PO Box 285 ✉ 40080

CRUISING
- Train station
- bus station
- at the border of the river Eresma in the outskirts of the city

Sevilla
BARS
■ **Arte** (B G N OG) 22.30-3? h, closed Sun
C/ Trastamara, 19
■ **Barón Rampante. El** (A B G MA OS) 16-4 h
C/ Arias Montano, 3 ✉ 41002
■ **Bosque Animado. El** (B f g MA OS S) Winter: Mon-Sat 16-?, Sun 12.30-?, Summer: 20-? h
C/ Arias Moutano, 5 ✉ 41002 *(Near Alameda de Hercules)*
■ **Cafelito Muero Petri** (A B F glm MA OS s) Summer: 20-? h, Winter: 17-? h
C/ Peral, 1 ✉ 41002
Specialized in different types of coffee
■ **Frenessi** (A AC B d G MA S STV VS WE) 19? h
Pasaje Amor de Dios, 2 ☏ 95 490 81 12
■ **Galeria-Torneo** (A AC B CC g MA S VS WE) 19-4.30 h
C/ Torneo, 64 ✉ 41002
Designer bar.
■ **Habanilla Café** (A AC d F G GLM S TV WE) 11-5 h
Alameda de Hércules, 63 ✉ 41002 ☏ 95 490 27 18
Old café from 1928.
■ **Hombre y el Oso, El** (AC B DR G LJ MA VS) 22-4h
C/ Amor de Diós, 32 *(near Alameda de Hercules)*
2 Bars where the bears meet...
■ **Isbiliyya Café-Bar** (B G MA OS YG) 20-5, winter 19-4 h
Paseo de Colon, 2 ☏ 95 421 04 60
Popular.
■ **Mirada. La** (AC B DR G MA og r VS) 22-5 h, closed Sun
C/ Luis de Vargas s/n
■ **Mundo. El** (B D g MA S WE) 22.30-? h
C/ Siete Revueltas, 5 ✉ 41004 *(Near by Plaza del Salvador/Zona Alfalfa)*
Disco-Bar
■ **O. D. C. - Opción Delitto e Castigo** (A AC B f G OS s) Winter: Mon-Sat 16-? h, Sun 14-?, Summer: 19-? h
Alameda de Hercules, 79 b ✉ 41003
■ **Paseo Bar. El** (B g MA OS) 20-22
Paseo Colon, 2 ☏ 95 422 50 34
Best in the evenings.
■ **27 . El** (AC B DR G MA R VS) 22-7 h, Mon closed
C/ Trastamara, 27 ✉ 41001 ☏ 95 422 40 98
Rooms for rent.

CAFES
■ **Café del Mar** (AC B glm f s) 20-4h
C/ Jesús del Gran Poder, 83 ✉ 41002 *(near Alameda de Hercules)*
☏ 95 490 75 03
■ **Cafe Hercules** (B f G MA OS) 9.30-2 h
C/ Peris Mencheta, 15 ✉ 41002 *(between Alameda de Hercules and C/ Fería)* ☏ 95 490 21 98
■ **Central. Café** (AC B F g MA OS) 11-4 h
Alameda de Hércules, 64 ✉ 41002 ☏ 95 438 73 12

DANCECLUBS
■ **Itaka** (! AC B D DR G MA STV VS) 22.30-?h
C/ Amor de Diós, 31 ✉ 41002 *(near Alameda de Hercules)*
Wed & WE show 1h
■ **Monnalisa** (AC B D G s WE YG) Thu-Sat and before holidays 24-? h
C/ Arjona, 15 ✉ 41001 *(Next to Estación de Córdoba)*
☏ 95 422 81 53

Spain | Sevilla ▸ Sitges

RESTAURANTS

■ **Los Munditos** (AC CC g MA) Mon-Sat 13.30-16.30, Thu-Sat 21.30-23.30 h
C/ Carlos Canal, 40 ✉ 41001 *(Near Plaza Nueva)*
☎ 95 422 67 43
Sevillan cuisine.

■ **Sopa Boba. La** (AC F MA s) Mon- Sat 13.30-16, 21-23.30, Fri, Sat -24 h, closed Sun & Mon nights
C/ Bailén, 34 ✉ 41001 ☎ 95 456 48 84

■ **Tel Aviv** (F g) 14.30-16, 20-1, Fri Sat -2 h
C/ Vírgen de la Estrella, 23 ☎ 95 445 76 33

SEX SHOPS/BLUE MOVIES

■ **Intimate** (AC CC g VS) 11-1 h
C/ Monsalvez, 5 ✉ 41001 *(at corner C/ Saucera)* ☎ 95 421 07 82
Video cabins for 2 or more.

■ **New Sex-Shop** (g VS) 10-22 h
C/ Sierpes, 48 ☎ 95 456 45 97

■ **Sex Shop Intimate** (CC g) 11-14, 16-22 h, closed Sun
C/ Gravina, 86

■ **Sex Shop S.T.** (g VS) 10.30-14.30, 17.30-22 h, Sun closed
C/ Trajano, 29 *(near Alameda)*

SAUNAS/BATHS

■ **Hispalis Sauna** (AC B CC F G MA p PI SA SB SOL VS WE WH) 11-24, Fri 11-7, Sat 14-7, Sun 14-24 h
C/ Céfiro, 3 ✉ 41018 *(Bus 21, 24, 32: Corte Inglés Nervión)*
☎ 95 458 02 20
Admission Ptas 1.500, Tue Thu 1.200, under 26 years daily 1.000.

■ **Nordik** (AC B F G MA PI SA SB SOL VS WH) Mon-Thu 11-23, Fri -7, Sat 15-7, Sun 13-23 h
C/ Resolana, 38 ✉ 41009 *(Bus C 1-4, C 13, C 14)* ☎ 95 437 13 21

BOOK SHOPS

■ **Librería Jano** (CC GLM) Mon-Sat 10-14, 17-21h
C/ Padre Tarín, s/n *(between Plaza Gavidia and C/ Jesús del Gran Poder)* ☎ 95 490 30 24

TRAVEL AND TRANSPORT

■ **Passion Tours** (G) Mon-Fri 9-14h, 17-21h
☎ 95 456 32 45   95 450 08 15 ✉ passiontours@teleline.es
Guides city tours, gay itineraries in Spanish, English, French & Italian.

GUEST HOUSES

■ **Casa Emililio** (g H)
(7km from Sevilla) ☎ 95 561 07 63
Rates single 2.000, double 4.000.

HEALTH GROUPS

■ **Comité Ciudadano Anti-Sida** Mo-Fri 10-14, 18-21 h
C/ San Luis, 50 ✉ 41003 ☎ 95 437 19 58
Information and services concerning AIDS. Free condoms.

CRUISING

-El Corte Ingles department store, Plaza del Duque, El Nervión
-Santa Justa rail station (right side)
-Bus station (Calle Torneo)
-Parque de Maria Luisa (!) (evenings, also car-cruising)
-Plaza del Duque de la Victoria (r) (in front of El Corte Ingles)
-Parque del los Príncipes (until 21 h, than AYOR) (at the end of Avenida Rep. Argentina)
-Paseo de Colon (until 21 h, then AYOR)
-Parque del Alamillo (between former AVE-train-station of the EXPO92-ground and the river Guadalquivir)

Sitges

Despite the large tourist industry, Sitges has managed to keep something of its old-world charm. Few places can boast such a high concentration of excellent gay hotels and apartments, so many busy gay bars, and a wide range of gay beaches. From May to the beginning of October, as well as in February, the gay scene in Sitges is vibrant and colourful. Gay men flock here from all over Europe, and as far as North America and Australia. Sitges offers everything from small friendly bars and cafés to huge discotheques and first-class gay and gay friendly restaurants. Barcelona, the Catalan capital, is nearby and can easily be reached by train.

Trotz des Tourismus hat Sitges es geschafft, etwas von seinem alten Charme beizubehalten. Wenige Plätze haben eine solche Konzentration an ausgezeichneten schwulen Hotels und Apartmenthäusern, so viele betriebsame schwule Bars und eine Auswahl an schwulen Stränden.
Von Mai bis Anfang Oktober sowie während der Faschingszeit ist die schwule Szene von Sitges vibrierend und kunterbunt. Schwule aus ganz Europa und sogar aus Nordamerika und Australien strömen hierher. Es bietet alles: von kleinen, netten Bars und Cafés, riesigen Diskotheken bis hin zu schwulen und gemischten Restaurants erster Klasse.
Und für alle Fälle liegt ja Barcelona, die katalonische Metropole, fast vor der Haustür und ist in kürzester Zeit per S-Bahn erreicht.

Malgré le boom touristique des dernières années, Sitges a su préserver son petit charme d'autrefois. Rares sont les stations balnéaires où les hôtels, les locations, les bars et les plages où le rapport qualité/prix est si intéressant. De surcroît, Sitges est très bien fréquentée, surtout de mai à octobre et pendant le carnaval, où ça bouge beaucoup. Tous les gays d'Europe semblent s'y donner rendez-vous et on y vient même d'Amérique et d'Australie, pour les les petits bars sympas, les cafés intimes, les méga boîtes de nuit et les restaurants gays ou mixtes de première classe. Barcelone, la métropole catalane, est à deux pas d'ici. On y va en prenant les transports en commun.

A pesar de la gran cantidad de turistas, Sitges ha sabido conservar algo de su viejo encanto. Pocos lugares ofrecen tal concentración de excepcionales hoteles, apartamentos, bares o variedad de playas gay. Desde Mayo hasta Octubre, y otra vez durante el Carnaval, la comunidad gay de Sitges se muestra vibrante y alegre. De toda Europa y hasta desde Norteamérica y Australia vienen hombres gay a Sitges. Ofrece todo: desde pequeños y acogedores bares y cafés, hasta enormes discotecas y restaurantes gay y mixtos de primera categoría. A Barcelona, la capital catalana, se puede llegar en muy poco tiempo con la ayuda del tren regional.

Sebbene l'industria del turismo sia enormemente sviluppata, Sitges è riuscita a conservare il suo fascino di antica città. Poche località hanno una così alta concentrazione di ottimi hotel gay ed appartamenti da affittare, un'enorme quantità di bar animati e una grande varietà di spiagge gay. Da maggio a ottobre e ancora durante il carnevale, la vita gay di Sitges è vibrante e variata; i gay vengono da tutta Europa, perfino dall'America e dall'Australia. C'è di tutto. Dai piccoli bar e caffè alle grandi discoteche e ai ristoranti gay e misti di prima categoria. In ogni caso la capitale catalana si trova a due passi ed raggiungibile in poco tempo con un treno metropolitano.

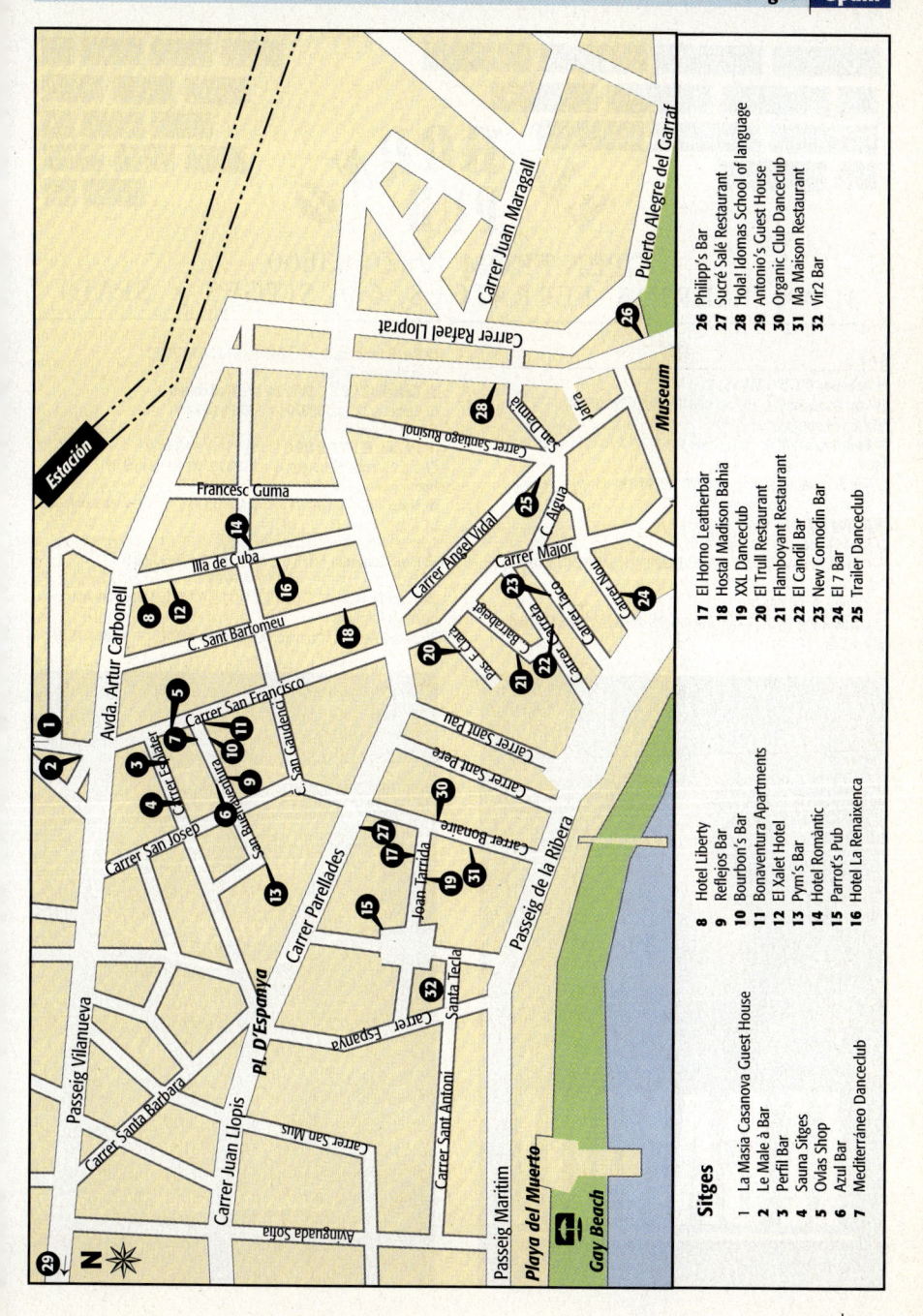

Sitges — Spain

Sitges

1. La Masia Casanova Guest House
2. Le Male à Bar
3. Perfil Bar
4. Sauna Sitges
5. Ovlas Shop
6. Azul Bar
7. Mediterráneo Danceclub
8. Hotel Liberty
9. Reflejos Bar
10. Bourbon's Bar
11. Bonaventura Apartments
12. El Xalet Hotel
13. Pym's Bar
14. Hotel Romàntic
15. Parrot's Pub
16. Hotel La Renaixença
17. El Horno Leatherbar
18. Hostal Madison Bahia
19. XXL Danceclub
20. El Trull Restaurant
21. Flamboyant Restaurant
22. El Candil Bar
23. New Comodin Bar
24. El 7 Bar
25. Trailer Danceclub
26. Philipp's Bar
27. Sucré Salé Restaurant
28. Hola! Idomas School of language
29. Antonio's Guest House
30. Organic Club Danceclub
31. Ma Maison Restaurant
32. Vir2 Bar

Spain | Sitges

EL HORNO PUB
OPEN FROM 17h30-03h00
JUAN TARRIDA FERRATGES, 6 • SITGES • SPAIN

BARS

■ **Azul Bar** (AC B G MA VS) 21-3 h
C/ Sant Bonaventura, 10 ✉ 08870 ☎ 93 894 76 34
Popular. Happy Hour 21-24 h.

■ **Bourbon's** (! AC B CC D G MA VS) 22.30-3.30 h, in winter only Sat
C/ San Bonaventura, 13 ✉ 08870 ☎ 93 894 33 47
Lively ambience. Very popular.

■ **B.Side** (AC B DR G MA s) 18-3h
C/ Sant Gaudenci, 7 ✉ 08870

■ **Candil. El** (! AC B D DR G MA VS) 22-3, Fri Sat -3.30 h, closed Oct-Jan
C/ Carreta, 9 ✉ 08870

■ **Casablanca** (A AC B Glm MA OG) 20.30-3 h, Winter: Closed Mon &Tue

C/ Pau Barrabeig, 5 ✉ 08870 ☎ 93 894 70 82
Art gallery on 1st floor

■ **Castell** (B CC F G MA) 20-2 h, Wed closed
C/ Carreta, 21 ✉ 08870 ☎ 93 894 33 49
Bar & restaurant.

■ **Horno. El** (! AC B DR G LJ MA VS) 17.30-3 h
C/ Juan Tarrida Ferratges, 6 ✉ 08870 ☎ 93 894 09 09
Happy Hour 17.30-19 h.

■ **Male à Bar. Le** (AC D DR f G MA OS VS) 19-3 h, winter only WE
CC Oasis, Local 28 ✉ 08870
Terrace with salad bar, disco from 22 h.

■ **New Comodín** (AC B d G MA) 22-3, Fri Sat -3.30 h
C/ Tacó, 4 ✉ 08870 ☎ 93 894 16 98

■ **Parrot's Pub** (AC B Glm lj MA OS s) 17-3 h, closed Nov-Mar, open on Carnaval
Plaza Industria, 2 / Primero de Mayo ✉ 08870 ☎ 93 894 78 81

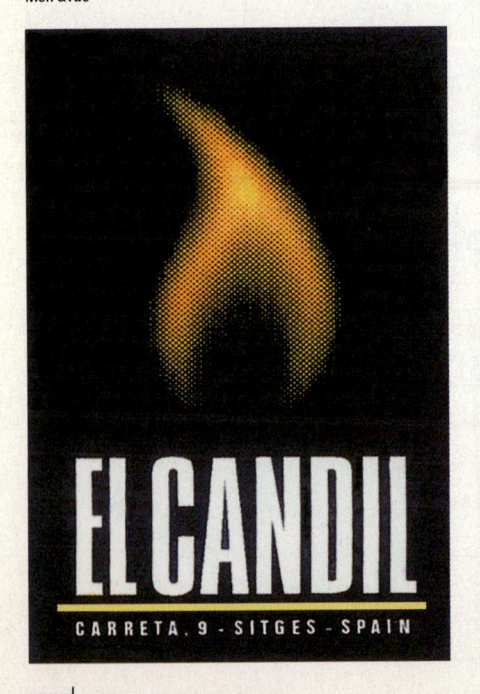

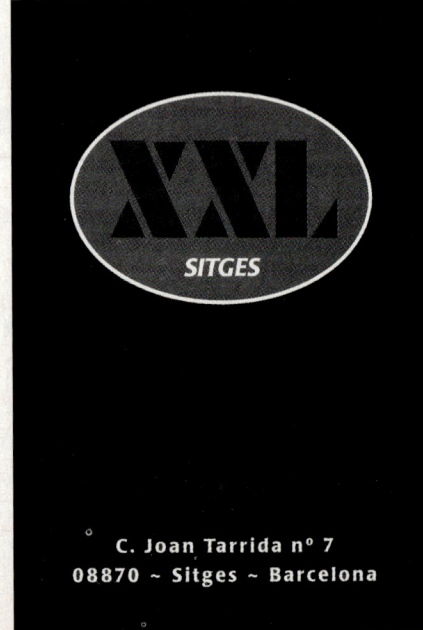

EL CANDIL
CARRETA, 9 - SITGES - SPAIN

XXL SITGES
C. Joan Tarrida nº 7
08870 ~ Sitges ~ Barcelona

Sitges | Spain

■ **Perfil** (B d DR G lj MA VS) 22.15-3 h
C/ Espalter, 7 ✉ 08870 ☎ 656 376 791 (mobile)

■ **Philipp's Bar** (B f g MA OS) 10.30-3, Fri Sat -3.30 h, closed Nov-Feb
C/ Puerto Alegre, 10 (at the beginning of Plata de San Sebastian)
☎ 93 894 97 43

■ **Prinz Bar** (AC d G MA s) 22-3h, winter only WE
C/ Nou, 4 ✉ 08870

■ **Pym's Bar** (AC B d GLM MA OG s) 20.30-3 h,, closed Nov-Apr
C/ Sant Bonaventura, 37 ✉ 08870
Friendly bar, no loud music.

■ **Reflejos** (! AC B d G YG) 22.30-3, Fri Sat -3.30 h, closed in November
C/ Sant Bonaventura, 19 ✉ 08870

■ **VIR 2** (AC B CC d G lj MA s VS) 20-3 h
C/ Santa Tecla, 6 ✉ 08870

■ **XXL** (! B d DR G MA VS) 23-3.30 h, in winter only WE
C/ Juan Tarrida Ferratges, 7 ✉ 08870

■ **7. El** (AC B G MG s) 22-3 h, in winter only WE
C/ Nou, 5

CAFES

■ **Locacola, La** (B bf f G MA) 10.30-14, 17.30-3h
C/ Bonaire, 35 ✉ 08870

DANCECLUBS

■ **Bourbon's** (! AC B CC D G MA VS YG) 22.30-3.30 h, in winter only Sat
C/ Sant Bonaventura, 13 ☎ 93 894 33 47

■ **Mediterráneo** (! AC B D G MA YG) 22-3.30 h, Easter-May only Fri Sat, closed Oct-Carneval
C/ Sant Bonaventura, 6 ✉ 08870
Very large bar, popular.

■ **The Organic Club** (! AC B D BR G MA stv YG) 24-6 h, winter only WE
C/ Bonaire, 15 ✉ 08870
Show WE 2 and 4 h.

■ **Trailer** (! AC B D G MA YG) 24-6 h, closed Oct-Mar, but open Carneval, Apr/May & Easter week only WE
C/ Angel Vidal, 36 ✉ 08870
Very popular.

SAUNA SITGES RELAX

- SAUNA FILANDESA
- YACUZZI / SPA POOL
- UVA
- MASAJE
- SALÓN TV / VIDEO
- CABINAS RELAX
- BAR
- LABERINTO
- SLING

FOAM PARTY · FIESTA DE LA ESPUMA · SCHIUMA
FETE DE LA MOUSSE · SCHAUM PARTY
FRIDAY · VIERNES · FREITAG · VENDREDI
SATURDAY · SABADO · SAMSTAG · SAMEDI

ABIERTO TODO EL AÑO
OBERT TOT L'ANY
OPEN ALL YEAR
OVERT TOUTE L'ANNÉE
Horario 16.00/4 PM — 8.00/8 AM

C/ ESPALTER, 11 · TEL. 93 894 28 63 · SITGES

RESTAURANTS

■ **Al Fresco** (B Glm MA)
Pau Barrabeitg, 4 ✉ 08870 ☎ 93 894 06 00

■ **Alma** (B CC F GLM OS s) 20-?h, winter Sun-Tue closed
C/ Tacó, 5 ✉ 08870 ☎ 93 894 63 87
French cuisine, menu 1400 ptas.

■ **Chez Jeanette** (AC F g MA) 13-16, 19.00-23.30 h, closed Nov & Dec.
C/ Sant Pau, 23 ✉ 08870 ☎ 93 894 00 48

RE/MAX
La Estación
Sant Francesc, 38
08870 - SITGES

ALEX DEKKER
INDEPENDENT REAL ESTATE AGENT
Tel. **+ 34 - 639 60 81 85**

AN OPEN DOOR TO THE BEST REAL ESTATE!!

ALEX DEKKER, your Real Estate agent in Sitges and surroundings. English, German, Dutch and Spanish spoken.

Tel. + 34 639 60 81 85 - + 34 639 34 10 81 - Fax. + 34 93 894 42 66
e-mail: bpmw@arrakis.es - internet: www.remax.es

Spain | Sitges

Spanish in Sitges

- INTENSIVE COURSES AND PRIVATE CLASSES
  (www.holasitges.com)
  since 180 euros per week
- APARTMENT FOR RENT:
  (www.holasitges.com/apartment)
  since 210 euros per week

Hola! idiomas

Francisco Gumá 25 - Sitges
Ph.: ++34-93-894-1333
Fay: ++34-93-894-9621
e-mail: evila@holasitges.com

RAS — Room Advice Service

Tel. +34-607149451
Tel. +34-667904484
Fax. +34-938944272
11 - 14h, 17 - 20h (local time)

- reservations of hotels in Sitges & Barcelona
- reservas de hoteles en Sitges & Barcelona
- English, French, German & Spanish spoken

Raservice@yahoo.es
www.raservice.com

■ **Flamboyant** (B F G MA OS) 20-23.30 h, closed Oct-Mar
C/ Pau Barrabeig, 16 ✉ 08870 ☎ 93 894 58 11
International cuisine.

■ **Ma Maison** (B F G MA OS) 20.30-1, Sat Sun 13.30-15.30, 21-0.30 h, closed Nov
C/ Bonaire, 28 ☎ 93 894 60 54

■ **Racó de la Carreta. El** (F G MA) 20.30-0.30 h
C/ Carreta, 7

■ **Sucré Salé** (F g) 13.30-15.30, 20.30-0.30 h, Tue closed.
C/ San Pablo, 39 ✉ 08870 ☎ 93 894 23 02
Crêpes and salads.

■ **Trull. El** (! A AC CC E F G GLM MA MG) 19.30-?
C/ Mossén Félix Clará, 3 ✉ 08870 ☎ 93 894 47 05
International cuisine.

SAUNAS/BATHS

■ **Sauna Sitges Relax** (B DR f G MA msg SA SOL VS WH WO) 16-8 h
C/ Espalter, 11 ✉ 08870 ☎ 93 894 28 63
Free condoms and lube on entering. Foam parties on Fri & Sat.

EDUCATION SERVICES

■ **Hola! Idiomas**
C/ Francesc Gumà, 25 ✉ 08870 ☎ 93 894 13 33 ☎ 93 894 96 21
✉ evila@holasitges.com 💻 www.holasitges.com
Language school. Learn Spanish in Spain !

FASHION SHOPS

■ **Ovlas**
Paseo Vilafranca, 3 ✉ 08870 ☎ 93 894 73 20
■ **Ovlas** 10.30-14, 17-21.30 h
C/ San Francisco, 22 ✉ 08870 ☎ 93 894 15 31

Clothes and accessories, sell their own creations. Also in Passeig Vilafranca, 3; same opening hours (tel. 93 894 73 20).

PROPERTY SERVICES

■ **Fincas Paradis**
Passeig de Vilanova, 10 ☎ 93 894 38 18 ☎ 93 607 300 896
📠 93 894 37 83 💻 www.fincasparadis.com

■ **ReMax - Alex Dekker** (glm) 10-14, 17-20 h
C/ Sant Francesc, 38 ✉ 08870 ☎ 639 60 81 85 ☎ 639 34 10 81
📠 93 894 42 66 ✉ bpmw@arrakis.es 💻 www.remax.es
Real estate agent for Sitges and surroundings. English, German, Dutch and Spanish spoken.

TRAVEL AND TRANSPORT

■ **Room Advice Service - RAS** (H) 11-14, 17-20 h
☎ 60 714 94 51 ☎ 66 790 44 84 📠 93 894 42 72
✉ Raservice@yahoo.es 💻 www.raservice.com
Reservations of hotels in Sitges & Barcelona. English, French, German & Spanish spoken.

HOTELS

■ **Hotel de la Renaixenca** (B BF CC E G H MA) 21.3.-31.10.
C/ Illa de Cuba, 13 ☎ 93 894 83 75 📠 93 894 81 67
Recommended - mostly gay. Bar also open to non-residents 19-23 h. High season is August. Dress appropriately!

■ **Hotel Liberty** (AC b BF CC G H OS)
C/ Illa de Cuba, 45 ✉ 08870 ☎ 93 811 08 72 ☎ 93 894 16 62
✉ hotelliberty_sitges@hotmail.com
Centrally located & completely renovated. Own key. Breakfast until 12 h. All rooms with satelite TV, phone, hifi and mini-bar. Bar and garden. Rates single Ptas 8.000-13.000. Double 9.500-13.000.

Hotel Liberty

- Just few steps from the gay bars.
- 14 rooms with sat-tv, minibar, hifi, telephone, air conditioning, own key
- Hotel bar with patio.
- Breakfast until 12 pm
- Apartments also available

Illa de Cuba 45,   Sitges 08870,   Spain
Tel: 34-93-8110872 • Fax: 34-93-8941662
e-mail: hotelliberty_sitges@hotmail.com
open all year

HOTEL Romàntic

SANT **I**SIDRE, 33
SITGE**S** 08870
BARCELON**A**
TEL.   **+34 - 93 - 894 83 75**
FAX.   **+34 - 93 - 894 81 67**
          +34 - 93 - 811 41 29

e-mail: romantic@arrakis.es

HOTEL LOS GLOBOS

NEW FRENCH OWNERS PHILIPPE & ANDRÉ

THE MOST QUIET AND RESIDENTIAL PLACE IN SITGES

- ONLY 50 MTS FROM THE BEACH
- JUST A FIVE MINUTES WALK TO THE GAY AREA
- BREAKFAST ON THE TERRACE
- ALL 22 ROOMS WITH PRIVATE BATH AND TERRACE
- VIEW OF THE SEA AND THE MOUNTAINS

AVDA.NTRA.SRA DE MONTSERRAT S/N
08870 SITGES
PHONE-FAX
00-34-93 894 36 92

Antonio's

—Exquisite Guesthouse—
& Apartments

Passeig Vilanova, 58
08870 Sitges

Telephone: 93 894 9207
Fax: 93 894 6443

Email: antonios_sitges@hotmail.com

open all year

Property Consultancy Service Available

Spain | Sitges

LA VILLA FRANCESA
LUXURIOUS PRIVATE GUEST HOUSE

Chambres independantes
Bains - Jardin Piscine
La tranquilité à 5 minutes de Sitges dans un village
medieval. Accés Facil.

AV. ESPAÑA nº5 (reception), 08811 CANYELLES · BARCELONA - SPAIN Tel.-Fax 93 897 35 82

■ **Hotel Los Globos** (AC B BF CC H MA OS) Open form Carnaval to Nov
Av. Ntra. Sra de Montserrat S/N ✉ 08870 ☎ 93 894 36 92 📠 93 894 36 92
22 rooms with private bath and terrace. Beautiful view to sea and mountain. BF on the terrace. Rates: Jul-Aug Ptas 10'000, Low season 6'000-8'000.-

■ **Hotel Romàntic** (! B BF CC E g H MA SOL)
C/ Sant Isidre, 33 ✉ 08870 ☎ 93 894 83 75 📠 93 894 81 67
✉ romantic@arrakis.es
Convenient location. Beautiful ancient mansion, romantic garden. Mainly gay. Bar also open to non-residents 7-1 h. 18 Single Ptas 7.500-8.900, 40 double 10.400-13.000 (bf buffet 900). High season is August. Rooms with bath/WC or shower, (some with) balcony or terrace, telephone, safe and ventilators.

■ **Hotel Sumidors** (AC B bf CC F g H OS PI SA) all year
Carretera de Vilafranca km 24 *(7km from Sitges,3 km from Sant Pere de Ribes direction Vilafranca del Penedés)* ☎ 93 896 20 61
📠 93 896 20 61 ✉ sumidorshtl@retemail.es
17th century countryhouse with 9 rooms, all with shower/wc/telephone, in quiet green hills. Also restaurant.

■ **Hotel Madison Bahia** (AC b BF CC g H OS SOL) 24 h
C/ de Parellades, 31-33 ☎ 93 894 00 12 📠 93 894 00 12
25 double rooms with private bath/wc, 14 rooms with balcony or terrace, phone, satelite TV, heating.

■ **Hostal Pension Madison** (g H)
C/ Sant Bartomeu, 9 ✉ 08870 ☎ 93 894 61 47 📠 93 894 00 12
Rooms with private shower/WC, van or heating, refrigerator, safe and balcony/terrace. Additional bed possible.

■ **Xalet. El** (F g H MA OS PI)
C/ Illa de Cuba, 35 ✉ 08870 ☎ 93 894 55 79 📠 93 811 00 70
Rooms with TV, phone, bath/WC, Minibar.

GUEST HOUSES

■ **Antonio's** (CC Glm H)
Passeig Vilanova, 58 ✉ 08870 ☎ 93 894 92 07 📠 93 894 64 43
✉ antonios_sitges@hotmail.com
5 double rooms with bath/WC, balcony, TV, fridge and rental of bikes.

■ **Masia Casanova. La** (CC G H NU OS PI VS)
c/o Bourbon's Music Club, C/ San Buenaventura, 13 ✉ 08870

☎ 93 818 80 58 📠 93 818 80 58
All suites with bath/WC, colour satellite TV and safe.

■ **Villa Francesa. La** (B bf g H OS PI) May-Oct & Carnaval, winter on demand
Av. Espanya, 5 *(Canyelles,10km from Sitges direction Vilafranca)*
☎ 93 897 35 82 📠 93 897 35 82
2 rooms, 1 suite all furnished with antiques within an italian style garden.

APARTMENTS

■ **Apartments Bonaventura** (G H MA SOL)
C/ Sant Bonaventura, 7 ✉ 08870 ☎ 93 894 97 62
📠 93 894 97 62
6 fully equipped apartments. Rates Ptas 6.500-13.500/day.

■ **Phillip's Appartments** (glm H)
C/ Port Alege, 10 ✉ 08870 ☎ 93 894 97 43 📠 93 894 97 43
All apartments with Bath or Shower & WC, kitchenette, some with TV and balcony. Room service available. Rates from Ptas. 6.000 per day

■ **Sisitges** (g H)
☎ 693 53 4979 (mobile) ☎ 93 894 31 56 ✉ sisitges@yahoo.es
Only reservation of apartments. spanish, english, dutch, german spoken.

■ **Sitges Holiday Apartment**
C/ Pau Benazet, 7, 3°, 1a ✉ 08870 ☎ 93 894 13 33
One apartment with bath/shower/WC, balcony or terrace, SAT-TV, radio, kitchen, room service. Weekly rates Oct-May Ptas 35.000, Jun-Sep 42.000, Jul Aug 49.000.

SWIMMING

-Beach in front of Calipolis Hotel
-Playas del Muerto (G NU) (Two small beaches between Sitges and Vilanova i la Geltru. There is a shuttle bus from the Cathedral to Golf Terramar. Then take the road to the old Guardia Civil Headquarters and walk along the railway. First beach is mixed but the second is gay. At the side of the railway there is a forest with all kinds of possibilities)
-Playa El Espigón (ayor) (between Restaurant Picnic and Hotel Terramar, late at night and in the morning)

CRUISING

-C/. Primero de Mayo, C/. Marqués de Montroig (especially Café Mont Roig)

Sitges | Spain

LA MASIA CASANOVA
GUEST HOUSE

On top of a hill with superb views. Just 11 kmts. from Sitges

- Luxurious rooms all with on-suite bathrooms, satellite-color TV, safes and queen size beds.
- Large swimming pool (nude sun-bathing permited).

◆ English, french and german spoken   ◆ Personal and friendly service
◆ For more information and reservation, fax or phone Eric or Carlos of the BOURBON'S CLUB in Sitges-Spain: (93) 818 80 58

BOURBON'S MUSIC CLUB: C/ San Buenaventura, 13 - SITGES

Sisitges

apartment reservations

Tel: +34 639 53 4979 Fax: +34 93 894 3156
sisitges@yahoo.es

Dutch, English, German and Spanish spoken

APARTMENTS BONAVENTURA
Sant Bonaventura, 7 E-08870 SITGES
Tel. & Fax: (34) 93.894.9762

The best apartments in the liveliest gay area.
Every comfort: solarium, satellite TV, safe box...

Spain | Tarragona ▶ Torremolinos

Tarragona

BARS
■ **Meson El Candil Café-Bar** (B g YG)
Placa de la Font, 15 ✉ 43080

GENERAL GROUPS
■ **Front d'Alliberament Gai de Catalunya**
PO Box 11 17, 43080 ✉ 43080
Publishers of gay newsletter "Tarraco Gai".

Torrelavega

BARS
■ **Don "D"** (B d G)
C/ Marqués de Valdecilla, C/ Pelayo, 6

SWIMMING
-Dunas de Liencres

Torremolinos

BARS
■ **Abadia** (B G MA OS VS) 23-4 h
La Nogalera 521
■ **Anfora** (B GLM MA OS) 23-? h
La Nogalera 522
■ **Arcos Pub** (AC B e G p R SNU VS) 22.30-2, WE- 3 h
La Nogalera, C/ Danza Invisible, 12 ✉ 29620 *(1st floor)*
With 2 comfortable & clean relax rooms and showers.
■ **Bar Bacchus** (AC B G LJ MA WE) 22-3 h
La Nogalera, Local 712
Bears meeting point.
■ **Boys "R" Us** (AC B DR G MA OS VS) Nov-May 17-?, Jun-Oct 20-? h
La Nagalera 19 ✉ 29620
■ **Bubu. La** (B G MA OS) 21-3, WE -4, winter only Fri-Sun
La Nogalera, 203
■ **Candelero, El** (B d G MA OS stv) 23-7 h
La Nogalera, Local 405 ✉ 29620
Fri & Sat show after 1.30 h.
■ **Chessa** (AC B G og OS) 22-3, WE -4 h
La Nogalera 408
■ **Chicos Pub** (B G MA) 10-3, Fri Sat -4 h
Plaza Andalucia *(Pasaje Pizarro bajo)* ☎ 95 237 22 43
■ **Contacto** (AC B DR G MA OS S VS) 22-4 h
La Nogalera 204
Popular.
■ **Gorila. La** (B g OS YG) 21-3, WE -4 h
Pueblo Blanco 33
■ **In & Out Plaza** (B glm MA OS WE) 20-? h
La Nogelera, Local 701 ☎ 639 95 34 68
■ **Malú** (B GLM MA OS) 20.30-3 h
La Nalanera 1103, C/ Danza Invisible *(1st floor)*
■ **Men's Bar** (B DR G lj MA VS) 22-5 h
La Nogalera, 714 ☎ 95 238 42 05
Popular cruisy place. Offers also apartment rental service (ask for Frank).
■ **Morbos** (B G MA OS STV SNU) 23-6 h
La Nogalera 113
Show 2 h
■ **Pempinel** (B G MA p R) 18-3 h
C/ Skal / Pueblo Blanco, local 19
■ **Pourquoi Pas?** (B GLM OG) 21-3, Fri Sat -4 h
La Nogalera 703
■ **Salsipuedes** (B G MA OS s) 22-5 h, Mon closed
C/ Casablanca, Pueblo Blanco, Local 28 ✉ 29620
■ **Soho** (B d G YG) 22-6 h
La Nogalera 502
Popular.
■ **Tensión** (AC B DR G lj MA OS VS) 22-3 h
La Nogalera 524
Also Video- and Sex Shop. Popular.
■ **Zatanazza** (B G MA OS) 5-? h
La Nogalera 306

CAFES
■ **Café El Atrio** (B GLM MA OS) summer: 19-?, winter: 17-?h
C/ Casablanca / C/ Danza Invisible ✉ 29620 *(La Nogalera)*
■ **Nogalera Café** (! B BF F g MA OS) 11-1.30 h
La Nogalera 519, C/ Danza Invisible
■ **Poseidon** (! B BF CC F g MA OS) 9.30-24, winter 9.30-18 h
Paseo Maritimo, Playa del Lido 3 *(at the gay beach)*
☎ 95 238 00 40
Popular.

TORREMOLINOS - LA NOGALERA
EMPORIO
www.discoemporio.com

Torremolinos | Spain

ARCOS PUB
...the best boys for gentlemen. New boys always welcome.

ARCOS PUB
La Nogalera
C/Danza Invisible, 8
29620 TORREMOLINOS
Tel. 00-34-952.37.17.38

DANCECLUBS
■ **Emporio** (AC B D G MA s) 24-6 h
C/ Casablanca, La Nogalera ✉ 29620 *(at C/ Danza Invisible, bloque 6, downstairs)* ☎ 95 205 30 03
■ **Parthenon** (! B D DR G MA OS VS YG) 22-4?, WE -5 h
La Nogalera, 716
Bar and disco. Very popular. Happy hour 22-24 h.
■ **Passion** (AC B D DR G MA S SNU STV WE) 3-8 h, winter only WE
C/ Palma de Mallorca, Local 16 ✉ 29620

RESTAURANTS
■ **Comedor. El** (b F g MA OS) 20-24 h, closed Wed
Urb. Pueblo Blanco, C/ Casablanca ☎ 95 238 38 81
International Cuisine.
■ **Crema. La** (AC CC F g OS) 18-24 h, closed Thu
C/ Skal, 19 ✉ 29620 ☎ 95 238 13 94
Spanish and international cuisine.
■ **Escalera. La** (CC E F glm) 19-? h
C/ Cuesta del Tajo, 12 ✉ 29620 *(end of C/ San Miguel)* ☎ 95 205 80 24
■ **Mousetrap. The** (B bf F g MA OS) 10-16, 19-0 h, closed Mon
C/ Skal *(back of Pueblo Blanco, 1st floor)*
■ **Nogalera Café** (! B bf F g MA OS) 11-1.30 h
La Nogalera 519, C/ Danza Invisible
■ **Noray** (b F g) 12-16, 20-24 h
Puerto Marina, Benalmadena Costa ✉ 29620 *(near Torremolinos)* ☎ 95 614 76 14
Bar-Restaurant. Meeting point for local gays.
■ **Poul's Steak House** (B F g OS) 12-? h
C/ Skal, 2 *(back of Pueblo Blanco)*

SEX SHOPS/BLUE MOVIES
■ **Supersex** (g VS) 11-1 h
Av. Manantiales, Edificio Tres Torres
■ **Venus** (g) 11-23 h
C/ Hoyos, Edificio Congreso, bajos *(near bus terminal)*

SAUNAS/BATHS
■ **Termas Miguel** (AC B DR f G MA msg PI SA SB VS WH WO) 16-24 h
Av. Carlota Alessandri, 166 ✉ 29620 *(10 min from centre of the town)* ☎ 95 238 87 40
Sauna on 1240 m² and two floors with a labyrinth, rates 1600 ptas, cabin 2300 ptas. Tue & Thu 1000 ptas.

HOTELS
⇒ See also Canillas de Albaidas
■ **Guadalupe** (B CC F G H OS) Restaurant: 12-16, 19-23 h, winter closed Wed

C/ Peligro, 15 ✉ 29620 *(Bajondillo, down at the beach)*
☎ 95 238 19 37 95 238 19 37
10 rooms with bath. Rates single Ptas 3.000-6.000, double 4.000-8.000 (bath/WC in room). Sunny roof patio.
■ **Hostal Loreto** (CC B BF G H)
C/ del Peligro 9, Playa Bajondillo ✉ 29620 ☎ 95 237 08 41
 95 205 23 98 loreto@raro.net.es
Rooms with bath/shower and WC, wash basin, balcony/terrace, apartments also with SAT-TV, radio, video, kitchen and waterbed on request.

GUEST HOUSES
■ **Finca Lería** (BF F G H msg PI)
Partido Los Anéales, Álora ✉ 29500 ☎ 95 211 27 03
 95 211 27 03 info@fincaleria.com www.fincaleria.com
45 minutes from Torremolinos and the gay scene, B&B or half board available. Converted farmhouse with mountains views.

GUADALUPE

Bajondillo,
Calle Peligro 15
Torremolinos 29620
Malaga, Spain
Tel/Fax 952 38 1937

Hostal • Restaurante
✶✶
A charming, spanish style hostal
& public restaurante & café
✶✶
Next to the beach at Torremolinos
& the gay scene
✶✶
Ten rooms with private bathrooms,
also a sunny roof patio in Andalusian style
✶✶
Very helpful english, spanish owners

Spain | Torremolinos ▶ Valencia

TERMAS S MIGUEL

Finnish Sauna, Steam Bath Jacuzzi, Relax Cabin

OPEN EVERY DAY
FROM 16 TO 24 H.

Av. Carlota Alessandri, 166
29620 TORREMOLINOS
Tel.: 952 38 87 40

APARTMENTS
■ **Apartamentos Buendia** (H g) 24 h
Urb. Los Naranjos, Plaza Alpujarras 4 ☎ 95 238 65 17
Centrally located. Rates: Summer: single Ptas 4.500, double Ptas 6500. Winter: single Ptas 3.000, double Ptas 5.000

SWIMMING
-Playamar at Restaurant/Bar El Poseidon (G)
-Campo de Golfo, near Hotel Guadalmar (G) (between Torremolinos and Malaga -ca. 8 km from Torremolinos- daytime some cruising in the bushes; car cruising at night)
-Torrequebrado (g NU) (Beach after the casino between Torremolinos and Fuengirola in Benalmádena, first exit after casino and go back to the beach. There (G) at the right side)
-Las Dunas (G NU) (20 miles west of Torremolinos, just past Cabo Pino. Narrow stony beach, but busy dunes and wood at the end of the beach in direction Marbella. Parking at bar (F g) "Las Dunas")

CRUISING
-Calle San Miguel (the shopping mall with the sidewalk cafes: "Heladería San Miguel" & "Bar El Toro")
-Plaza Andalucia (R)
-In front of the bus station (r)

Torrevieja

BARS
■ **Coliseo** (AC d DR G MA OS) 19-3 h
C/ San Pablo, 12 ✉ 31800

SEX SHOPS/BLUE MOVIES
■ **Eros** (AC CC GLM VS) 10-1 h
Av. Purisima 31, Playa del Cura ✉ 03180 ☎ 96 670 46 46

Valencia

PUBLICATIONS
■ **Paper Gai**
c/o Colectivo Lambda de Valencia, PO Box 1197 ✉ 46080
Free bimontly publication. News from the gay scene, cultural and political articles on 24 pages.

BARS
■ **ADN** (AC D GLM MA s WE) 22.30-3.30 h
C/ Angel Custodi, 10, Barri del Carme ✉ 46003 ☎ 96 391 79 88
Disco-Pub.
■ **Contramano** (B d G MA) 22-3 h
C/ Murillo, 12

■ **Guerra. La** (AC B DR G MA VS) 20-3, Fri Sat-4, Sun -3.30 h
C/ Quart, 47 ☎ 96 391 36 75
Five floors with different ambiance, large darkroom.
■ **North Dakota Saloon** (B G lj MA) 20-3 h
Plaza Margarita Valldaura 1 ☎ 96 357 52 50
■ **Nuncadigono** (AC B DR G LJ MA VS) 17-3, WE-4 h
C/ Dr. Montserrat, 24 ✉ 46008 *(near Torres de Quart)*
■ **OH! Valencia** (B D DR OG STV VS WE) 22-4, Show Fri-Sun 1.30 h, Tue closed
C/ Rumbau, 6
■ **Romeo** (AC B DR G MA R SNU) 20-3 h
C/ del Mar, 45 / Calle de Bonaire ☎ 96 391 09 54
Also accomodation.
■ **Studio 17** (AC B D G p YG) 19-1.30, Sun 18-2 h, closed Tue
C/ Cerrajeros 17 / Plaza Redondo ☎ 96 391 82 03
Popular disco bar, best Fri-Sun.

NUNCADIGONO BAR
LEATHER - CRUISING
7/7 A las 17h.
Dr. MONSERRAT, 24
VALENCIA

966 SPARTACUS 2001/2002

Valencia | Spain

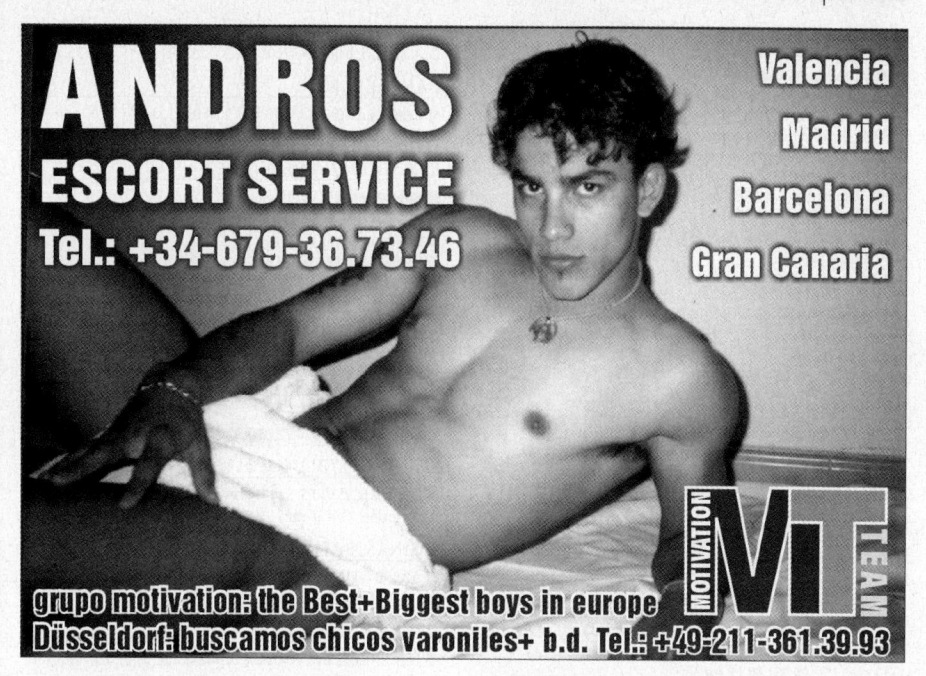

ANDROS ESCORT SERVICE
Tel.: +34-679-36.73.46

Valencia
Madrid
Barcelona
Gran Canaria

grupo motivation: the Best+Biggest boys in europe
Düsseldorf: buscamos chicos varoniles+ b.d. Tel.: +49-211-361.39.93

MOTIVATION VT TEAM

■ **Xandro's. Pub** (AC B G MA p R VS) 18-2 h, closed Mon
C/ Derechos, 30 ✉ 46001
Also accomodation.

CAFES

■ **Café de la Seu** (A AC B d f G MA OS s) 16-2 h, Tue closed
C/ Santo Cáliz, 7 ✉ 46001 ☏ 96 391 57 15
■ **Cafe de las Horas** (A AC B f glm MA s) Winter: 16-?, Summer: 18-? h
C/ Conde de Almodóvas, 1 ✉ 46003 *(Near Plaza Virgen)*
☏ 96 391 73 36
■ **Cafe Infanta** (A AC B d g MA OS) 19-3 h
Plaza Tossal, 3 ✉ 46001 ☏ 96 392 16 23
■ **Espai Obert** (A B d f GLM MA OS s) Mon-Wed 17-22, Thu Sun -0, Fri Sat -2 h
C/ Salvador Griner, 9 ✉ 46003 ☏ 96 391 20 84
■ **Café Sant Miquel** (AC B G MA OS) 19.30-3, Fri Sat -4.30 h, Mon closed
Plaza Sant Miguel, 13 ✉ 46003 ☏ 96 392 45 96

DANCECLUBS

■ **Goulue. La** (AC B D G MA S) Wed-Sun 22-4 h
C/ Quart, 32 ✉ 46003
■ **Metal** (b D GLM MA p) Sat Sun 6-12 h
Piazza Picadero Marqués de Dos Aguas 3
After hours disco.
■ **Venial** (! B D Glm S VS YG) 0-5, Fri Sat -6. Show Thu Sun 2.30 h
C/ Quart, 26 ☏ 96 391 73 56
■ **Victor's** (B D DR Glm MA S) 1-5, Fri Sat -6. Summer daily -6. Show Fri Sat 3.30 h
C/ D. Monserrat, 23 ☏ 96 391 70 81

RESTAURANTS

■ **Amanida** (AC b CC F g MA)
C/ Quart, 17 ✉ 46001 ☏ 96 392 41 77
Salad bar & 2nd dish for Ptas. 1.700.
■ **Boulevard Corinto** (AC B BF CC F G H MA OS) 8.30-24 h
Urbanisacion Corinto 1 46529 Sagunto, Va *(20 min. from Valencia at seaside)* ☏ 96 260 89 11
■ **De Pas** (F g) 20-2 h, Tue closed.
C/ Sant Calze, 7
Sandwiches.
■ **Oficio de Boca** (AC B BF CC F G OS) 12-16, 20-2 h, WE 20-2 h, Mon closed
C/ Corretgeria, 33 ✉ 46001 ☏ 96 392 50 13
■ **TasKeta** (A B glm MA s) 19-? h
Plaza Santa Margarita, 1 ✉ 46003 ☏ 96 392 35 91
■ **Turangalila** (AC B C F G S) summer: 14-15.30, 22-?, winter: 14-15.30, 21.30-1.30h
C/ del Mar, 34 ✉ 46003
Dinner spectacle, reservation recommended.

SEX SHOPS/BLUE MOVIES

■ **Afro** (g) 9.30-22.30 h, closed Sun
Gran Vía Germanías 53 / C/ Cuba ☏ 96 341 11 02
■ **Blue Sex Factory** (g VS) 9.30-22.30 h
C/ Bailen, 28 ☏ 96 342 38 68
■ **Erotic Planet**
C/ Castellón, 12 ✉ 46004 ☏ 96 3940 649
■ **Erotik Planet King Video**
Av. Peres y Valero, 48 ✉ 46006 ☏ 96 33 432 70
■ **European Center** (g VS) 11-14, 16.30-21.30 h
Av. Constitución, 26 ☏ 96 347 44 27

Spain | Valencia ▸ Vitoria

■ **Evadán** (g) 9.30-22.30 h
C/ Matías Parelló, 14 ☎ 96 374 20 65
■ **Moncho Internacional** (g) 9.30-22.30 h
C/ Dr. Zamenhof, 15 *(near "Nuevo Centro")* ☎ 96 382 33 49
■ **Sala X** (g R VS) 11-20 h
C/ Alcoy, 3 *(behind station and Plaza de toros)*
Nice men from the "barrio".
■ **Sex Hollywood** (g VS) 9.30-22.30 h
C/. Dr. Zamenhoff, 5 ✉ 46008 ☎ 96 382 14 67
■ **Spartacus** (DR G VS) 9.30-22.30 h
C/ Flassaders, 8 ✉ 46001 *(near Plaza Merced)* ☎ 96 352 56 62
Gay cabins upstairs.

SAUNAS/BATHS
■ **Magnus Termas** (! B DR f G msg SA SB SOL VS WH WO) 10-24 h
Av. del Puerto 27 ✉ 46023 ☎ 96 337 48 92
■ **Olimpic** (G MA SA SB)
Vívons, 17 ☎ 96 373 04 18

APARTMENTS
■ **Torre Corinto** (AC B BF CF g H N NU OS PI WO)
Summer: 9-24 h, Winter: 9-20, Sat Sun -24 h
Urbanización Corinto, 1, 46529 Sagunto, Va *(20 min. from Valencia on seaside)* ☎ 96 260 89 11 ☎ 96 260 70 75
✉ conver@torrecorinto.com
Also restaurant.

HEALTH GROUPS
■ **Asociació Valenciana Contra la SIDA (AVACOS)** Mon-Fri 10-13, Wed Thu also 17-19 h
C/ Cuba, 61, bajo,izq. ✉ 46006 ☎ 96 380 07 37
■ **Comite Ciudadano Anti-Sida** 10-14 h
C/ Flora, 7 ☎ 96 361 88 11, ext 26

SWIMMING
-Playa del Saler (NU) (take bus from Plaza Porta del Mar to the end of the bus line, approximately 15 km south of Valencia. Walk south on beach for 1 to 2 km. It's very cruisy nearby the forest)
-Playa de la Casa Negra (NU) (On the same bus line at the golf course resort hotel)
-Playa de Malvarosa de Corinto (G NU) 20 mins. from Valencia to Sagunto, near Hotel Torre Corinto

CRUISING
-Billares Colon, Calle Lauria (R)
-Jardines del Turia (near Paseo de la Alameda)
-Paseo Alameda (also by car, at night)
-Calle Joaquín Ballester (r tv) (also by car, at night)
-Bus station/Estación de autobuses (near the "Ballkiss-Disco" in the park, best after 1 h, (r tv))
-Main train station/Estación de trenes central (ayor R)

Vall de Ebo / Alicante

HOTELS
■ **Molino. El** (A AC B F glm H OS) Wed-Sun 12.30-17-30, Sat 19.1 h
Carretera Pego, km. 8 ✉ 03789 ☎ 96 597 72 82
In Pego follow the sign "Cova del Rull-La Vall de Ebo". 15 minutes to the beach. Also camping. Laid in the hills.

Valladolid

BARS
■ **Planet Café** (B GLM MA N WE) 19-3 h
Calle Alegria 7 *(near Piaza de España)*

■ **Pub de Eddi 1900** (AC B D g MA snu VS WE) 20-4 h
C/ Alarcón, 3, bajo ✉ 47001 *(Near Plaza Mayor)* ☎ 983 35 35 90

DANCECLUBS
■ **Reserva. La** (B D GLM YG WE) 23-4 h
Calle Correos

SEX SHOPS/BLUE MOVIES
■ **International** (g VS) 10-3 h
C/ San Blas, 19 ☎ 983 26 18 37
■ **Sex Shop** (g VS) 10-22 h
C/ San Blas, 17 ☎ 983 25 66 20

Vigo

BARS
■ **Roy Bleck** (B D DR G MA VS) 24-4 h
Rúa Oporto, 12 ☎ 986 22 30 46
■ **7.4** (B g OS YG)
Rúa Arenal, 74 ☎ 986 22 78 05

SEX SHOPS/BLUE MOVIES
■ **Pikante** (g VS) 10-3, Sun -14, 16-3 h
Rúa Príncipe, 22 *(Galerías)* ☎ 986 43 21 55

SAUNAS/BATHS
■ **Azul** (B G MA SA SB WO) 16-4 h
Rúa Roupeiro, 67 ☎ 986 22 82 92

GENERAL GROUPS
■ **Legais - Colectivo de Gais e Lesbianas de Vigo** (GLM MA) Tue 19-21, Fri 20-22 h
Rúa Marques de Valladares, 9 ✉ 36201 *(2nd floor)*
☎ 696 03 77 20 📠 696 03 77 20

SWIMMING
-Samil Beach/Praia Samil (G nu) (at the rocks)
-Barra Beach/Praia Barra (g NU)

CRUISING
-Garden at Club Náutico
-Gardens at Arenal (behind Comandancia de Marina)
-Estación Renfe (railway station)
-El Corte Inglés (WC)

Vitoria

BARS
■ **Moët & Co** (AC B GLM MA) Sun-Thu 19-3 Fri Sat -3.30 h
C/ Los Mantelli, 1 *(junto a Calle Los Herrán 46)* ☎ 945 28 93 33

SEX SHOPS/BLUE MOVIES
■ **Cosmopolitan Sex Shop** (g)
C/ Manuel Iradier, 42
■ **Sex Shop** (g)
C/ Tintoreria, 51

SAUNAS/BATHS
■ **Querelle** (B DR f G MA SA VS) Tue-Thu, Sun 17-22, Fri -7, Sat -10, in winter Sat 17-Sun 22 h
C/ Paraguay, 30 , bajo ✉ 01008 ☎ 945 12 00 82
Bar also accessible without entering the sauna.

Vitoria ▶ Zaragoza **Spain**

GENERAL GROUPS
■ **Gaytasuna Colectivo Gay de Alave** Mon-Fri 9-14, 16-20h
C/ San Francisco, 2 - 1° ✉ 01001 ☎ 630 244 314
🖷 945 25 78 66

HEALTH GROUPS
■ **Comisión Ciudadana Anti-Sida de Alava** Mon-Fri 9-14, 16-20 h
C/ San Francisco, 2 - 1° ✉ 01001 ☎ 945 25 78 66
🖷 945 25 77 66 💻 sidalava@jet.es

Zaragoza

BARS
■ **Mick Havanna** (B DR G MA VS) 16-3, WE 16-5 h
C/ Ramón Pignatelli, 7 /Avda. Cesaraugusto ☎ 976 28 44 50
■ **Sandor** (B DR G MA VS) 21-4 h
C/ Loscos, 13 ☎ 976 39 82 02
■ **Urano** (AC B G MA s VS) 18-? h
C/ Fita, 8-14 ✉ 50005 ☎ 976 222 167

CAFES
■ **Madalena. La** (B F GLM MA OS)
C/ Mayor, 48 ✉ 50001 ☎ 976 391 952
■ **Recalada. La** (A AC B G lj MA s)
C/ Madre Sacramento 20 ✉ 50004
☎ 976 211 517

DANCECLUBS
■ **Boy´s** (AC B D G MA s VS) Thu-Sun 22-5 h
C/ Dato, 18 ✉ 50005 ☎ 976 228 402
■ **Boy´s** (AC B D G MA s SNU STV WE) Thu-Sun 22-4 h
C/ Dr. Horno, 25 ✉ 50004 ☎ 976 226 876
■ **Oasis** (AC B g MA S STV TV WE) 24-8 h
C/ Boggiero, 28 ✉ 50003
Show Fri & Sat from 1.30 h on, Special events for e.g. gay liberation day.

■ **Sphinx** (B D Glm MA) 22.30-6 h
C/ Madre Rafols, 2 ✉ 50004 ☎ 976 44 10 11

RESTAURANTS
■ **Flor Restaurante** (AC B CC F G OS) 13.30-16, 20.30-24 h,
Sun closed, Mon only evenings
C/ del Temple, 1 ✉ 50003
☎ 976 39 49 75

SEX SHOPS/BLUE MOVIES
■ **Pignatelli** (g VS) 10-22 h
C/ Ramón de Pignatelli, 44 ✉ 50004 ☎ 976 43 71 99
■ **Sexshop** (G VS) 10-22 h
C/ José Anselmo Clavé *(opposite train station)*
■ **Tubo. El** (G VS) 10-22 h
C/ Cuarto de Agosto, 15 *(Near Bar El Plata)*

SAUNAS/BATHS
■ **Nordik Sauna** (AC B G MA SA SB SOL VS) 15-22 h
C/ Andrés Gurpide, 4 ☎ 976 59 45 36
Recommended. Entry Ptas 1.400.

GENERAL GROUPS
■ **Lesbianas y Gays de Aragón (LYGA)** Mon 19-22, Fri 19-22 h
(Youth group)
C/ San Vicente de Paul, 26, 2° ✉ 5001
☎ 976 39 55 77
🖷 976 39 73 73 💻 lyga_aragon@yahoo.es

SWIMMING
-Rio Ebro (NU)/(Between Avenida de Francia and Puente de la Almozara. In winter car-cruising at night.)

CRUISING
-Plaza de los Sitios (at night)
-Estación El Portillo (at night)

Sri Lanka

Location: South Asia
Initials: CL
Time: GMT +6
International Country Code: ☎ 94
International Access Code: ☎ 00
Language: Sinhalese, Tamil, English
Area: 65,610 km^2 = 25,332 sq mi.
Currency: 1 Sri Lanka Rupee (LKR) = 100 Cents
Population: 18,778,000
Capital: Colombo
Religions: 69% Buddhist, 15% Hindu, 8% Muslim, 8% Christian

✱ According to paragraph 365a, homosexuality is illegal in Sri Lanka. Gay men can be imprisoned for up to ten years when prosecuted.

✪ In Sri Lanka ist Homosexualität verboten. Nach Paragraph 365a können Männer wegen dieses "Vergehens" mit einer Haftstrafe von bis zu zehn Jahren verurteilt werden.

✱ L'homosexualité est illégale au Sri Lanka. Selon le paragraphe 365a, les contrevenants risquent jusqu'à 10 ans d'emprisonnement.

⬢ La homosexualidad está prohibida en Sri Lanka. Según artículo 365a, hombres gays pueden ser castigados con hasta diez años de prisión.

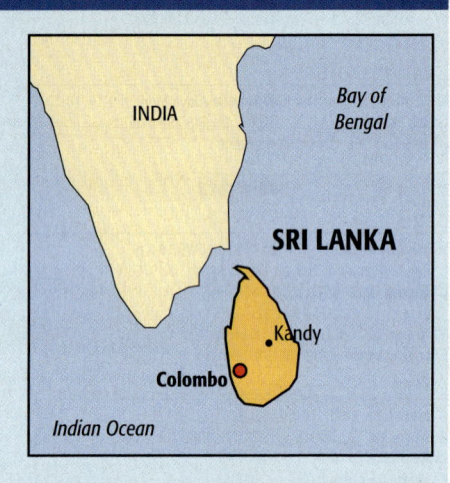

✖ In Sri Lanka l'omosessualità è illegale. Secondo il paragrafo 365a uomini perseguiti possono essere puniti con una reclusione fino a 10 anni.

Colombo ☎ 1

HOTELS
■ **Windsurf** (g H)
15a De Soyza Avenue ☎ 73 22 99

CRUISING
-On the beach across from the Hotel Windsurf

Lots of HIV+ men don't tell

GMFA's campaigns and actions are designed, planned and executed by positive, negative and untested volunteers. To volunteer for GMFA write, phone or email:
Unit 43, Eurolink Centre, 49 Effra Road, LONDON, SW2 1BZ. 020 7738 6872. newvol@gmfa.demon.co.uk
www.demon.co.uk/gmfa
Registered Charity no. 1076854

GMFA Gay Men Fighting AIDS

Sweden

Name: Sverige • Schweden • Suède • Suecia • Svezia
Location: Northwest Europe
Initials: S
Time: GMT +1
International Country Code: ☏ 46
International Access Code: ☏ 00
Language: Swedish
Area: 449,964 km² / 173,731 sq mi.
Currency: 1 Swedish Crown (skr) = 100 Öre
Population: 8,863,000
Capital: Stockholm
Religions: 89% Protestant
Climate: Moderate climate in south with cold, cloudy winters and cool, partly cloudy summers, the north is subarctic.
Important gay cities: Stockholm, Göteborg & Malmö

※ There are no specific laws against male or female homosexuality in Sweden. The age of consent (15 years) is the same for both gays, lesbians and heterosexuals. Social opinion is markedly tolerant and many Swedish gays are open about their homosexuality. Even so, it can be difficult to be openly homosexual in smaller towns and in rural areas. Since 1994, "registered partnerships" are also recognized in Sweden: this is not the same as marriage, but it does give homosexual couples a similar legal status to that of heterosexual marriages. Anti-discrimination laws have been in force for some time, and each year public funds are made available for the financial support of gay organizations. Most of the gay venues are in the cities, but the scene is much smaller than might be expected in such a liberal country. It has become mandatory to notify officials of a positive HIV test result.

※ Es gibt in Schweden keine speziellen Gesetze gegen männliche oder weibliche Homosexualität. Das Schutzalter liegt für Schwule/Lesben und Heteros gleichermassen bei 15 Jahren. Die Einstellung der Bevölkerung ist bemerkenswert tolerant und viele schwedische Schwule sind sehr offen mit ihrer Sexualität. Aber es gibt noch immer Schwierigkeiten, besonders in den Kleinstädten und auf dem Land. Hier ist Offenheit nicht immer möglich.
Seit 1994 gibt es in Schweden die "registrierte Partnerschaft", die zwar keine Ehe im herkömmlichen Sinne ist, aber homosexuellen Paaren eine rechtliche Stellung gibt, die der heterosexuellen Ehe sehr nahe kommt. Schon seit längerem gibt es ein Anti-Diskriminierungsgesetz. Außerdem stellt der schwedische Staat jährlich eine Summe zur Unterstützung homosexueller Organisationen zur Verfügung.
Die meisten schwulen Einrichtungen sind in den größeren Städten, aber die Szene ist viel kleiner, als man es in so einem liberalen Land erwarten würde. Bei einem positives HIV-Test-Ergebnis besteht in Schweden für die Bevölkerung den Behörden gegenüber Meldepflicht.

※ En Suède, il n'existe aucunes lois spéciales contre l'homosexualité masculine ou féminine. La majorité sexuelle est à 15 ans, pour les gais, les lesbiennes et les hétéros. Les suédois sont étonnamment tolérants et de nombreux homos suédois sont très ouverts sur leur sexualité. Mais bien sûr il y a encore des problèmes, à la campagne et dans les petites villes. Là, l'ouverture n'est pas possible. Depuis 1994, il y a en Suède le "partenariat registré", qui n'est pas un mariage au sens propre, mais qui donnent aux couples homosexuels une situation juridique très proche de la situation des couples hétérosexuels mariés. Depuis longtemps existe une loi anti-discrimination. De plus, le gouvernement met à la disposition chaque année une somme d'argent pour le soutien des organisations homosexuelles. La plupart des infrastructures gaies se trouvent dans les grandes villes, mais il faut remarquer que pour un pays si libéral, le milieu gai est plus petit que ce que nous attendions. En cas de test de dépistage VHI positif, il faut le signaler immédiatement aux autorités.

※ En Suecia no hay leyes especiales contra la homosexualidad femenina o masculina. La edad de consentimiento es de 15 años, independientemente de la orientación sexual. La población sueca reacciona muy tolerantemente; gran cantidad de homosexuales viven su homosexualidad abiertamente. Sin embargo en las ciudades pequeñas así como en los pueblos del interior del país esta apertura sigue siendo difícil.
Desde 1994 existe también en Suecia el llamado "Registro de Parejas de Hecho" que aunque no es un matrimonio, les dá a los gay una base legal que se asemeja a la de los heterosexuales. Desde hace ya mucho tiempo existe una ley de antidiscriminación. El estado sueco pone a disposición cada año una determinada suma de dinero para el apoyo de organizaciones gay. La mayor parte de la infraestructura gay se encuentra en las grandes ciudades. Para un país tan liberal como este, el ambiente gay es sorprendentemente pequeño. En caso de ser HIV-positivo, es obligatorio comunicárselo a las autoridades.

※ In Svezia non esistono leggi specifiche contro l'omosessualità maschile o femminile. L'età legale è di 15 anni ugualmente per etero e omosessuali. L'atteggiamento della popolazione è notevolmente tollerante, e molti gay svedesi si comportano molto apertamente per quanto riguarda la loro sessualità. Esistono ancora difficoltà nelle piccole città e nei paesi di campagna. Qui non è sempre possibile comportarsi apertamente. Dal 1994 in Svezia esiste la "registrazione ufficiale delle coppie di fatto", che non è l'equivalente del matrimonio, ma che garantisce alle coppie omosessuali una situazione legale molto vicina a quella delle coppie sposate eterosessuali. Già da molto tempo esiste una legge antidiscriminatoria. Inoltre lo stato svedese mette a disposizione ogni anno una certa somma alle organizzazioni omosessuali. La maggior parte dei centri gay si trova nelle città più grandi, ma l'ambiente è più ristretto di quanto si possa credere per un paese così liberale. Oggigiorno è d'obbligo mostrare il risultato positivo del test HIV alle autorità.

Sweden — Borås - Västergötland ▸ Göteborg - Bohuslän

NATIONAL PUBLICATIONS

Kom Ut!
Box 350 ✉ 101 26 Stockholm ☎ (08) 736 02 17
📧 komut@rfsl.se 🌐 www.rfsl.se/komut
Members magazine of the RFSL.

Privée (G)
Box 873 ✉ 251 08 Helsingborg ☎ (736) 24 94 20
📧 privee@spry.se 🌐 go.to.privee
Gay Swedish magazine with free personal ads, porn videos reviews, articles, interviews in Swedish. About 40 pages. Skr 100.-.6 issues per year.

QX (GLM)
Box 17 218 ✉ 104 62 Stockholm ☎ (08) 720 30 01
📠 (08) 720 38 70 📧 redaktionen@qx.se 🌐 www.qx.se
Free monthly gay-lesbian magazine for Sweden. Featuring articles, dates. In Swedish. About 30 pages.

Straight (G)
Box 172 18 ✉ 104 62 Stockholm ☎ (08) 720 30 01
📠 (08) 720 38 70 📧 info@straight.st 🌐 www.straight.st
Quarterly gay lifestyle magazine in Swedish. SEK 200.- for one year subscription.

NATIONAL COMPANIES

Istberger (G P snu stv YG)
Box 873 ✉ 251 08 Helsingborg ☎ (0736) 24 94 20
📧 privee@telia.com 🌐 go.to/privee
Gay video production, mail order, wholesale, publishing of Privée magazine, party organisation & gay artist management.

NATIONAL GROUPS

DGN - Nät för Gayföretagare
c/o Det Glada Nätet, Box 4053 ✉ 182 04 Enebyberg
📧 m8796@abc.se
Network for gayfriendly companies and managers.

Förenignen Homosexuella Läkare
c/o Sven Grützmeier, Venhälsan, Södersjukhuset Stockholm
📧 sven.grutzmeier@mailbox.swipnet.se
Swedish Gay and Lesbian Physicians Association for gay and lesbian physicians, dentists and medical and dental students.

Gaymoderaterna-Gay Conservatives Tue Sun 18-21 h
Saltmätargatan 18 ✉ 11359 Stockholm ☎ (08) 34 44 56
Gay conservateurs.

Homosexuella Liberaler (GLM)
Box 3444 ✉ 10369 Stockholm ☎ (08) 31 41 27
📧 homosexuella.liberaler@liberal.se 🌐 www.folkpartiet.se/hl/
Gay liberals.

Homosexuella Socialdemokrater
Saltmätargatan 18 ✉ 113 59 Stockholm
Gay social-democrats.

Homosexuella Socialister
Box 170 ✉ 101 23 Stockholm ☎ (08) 32 03 39
Gay socialists.

Regnbågen Stockholm
Box 350 ✉ 101 26 Stockholm ☎ (08) 31 47 01
"The Rainbow" Group for deaf gay people.

RFTS-Stockholm (TV)
Box 9083 ✉ 102 71 Stockholm 📧 mail@rfs.a.se
🌐 www.rfts.a.se/
National organisation for transsexuals.

Borås - Västergötland ☎ 033

SEX SHOPS/BLUE MOVIES

Erocenter (g VS) 11-22 h
Sturegatan 29

GENERAL GROUPS

RFSL-Borås (GLM MA) Pub Fri 21-1 h, Party last Sat 22-2 h
Magasinsgatan 1 ✉ 50311 ☎ 10 69 70 📠 12 72 42
📧 boras@rfsl.se 🌐 www.rfsl.se/boras/

Eskilstuna - Södermanland ☎ 016

GENERAL GROUPS

RFSL-Eskilstuna (GLM MA) Café Wed 19-21, Disco occasionally, call for info
Klostergatan 3 ☎ 51 00 69 📧 eskilstuna@rfsl.se
🌐 www.rfsl.se/eskilstuna

CRUISING

- Ⓟ Mc Donald's Drive through
- Main road E20 Ⓟ Rabyhed, 10 km west of town
- Klippberget, 1 km north of Mc Donald's, direction Torshalla

---

Falun - Dalarna ☎ 023

GENERAL GROUPS

RFSL-Dalarna
Box 401 ✉ 79128 ☎ 16725 📧 dalarna@rfsl.se
🌐 www.rfsl.se/dalarna
Café Wed 19-21h & Sun 16-19h, Trotzgatan 35. Disco 4th Fri 22-2h in "The Club".

Gävle - Gästrikland ☎ 026

GENERAL GROUPS

RFSL-Gävleborg Counselling Sun 19-21 h
Fjärde Tvärgatan 55 *(close to Staffan Chruch, in Brynäs)* ☎ 18 09 67
☎ 18 77 18 📠 18 77 18 📧 gavleborg@rfsl.se
🌐 www.rfsl.se/gavleborg

Göteborg - Bohuslän ☎ 031

GAY INFO

RFSL-Göteborg Hellmans café Wed&Thu 17-21, Sun 15-21, Youth café Mon 19-22 h
Karl Johansgatan 31 ✉ 4033 *(Bus 85)* ☎ 775 40 10 📠 775 40 29
📧 goteborg@rfsl.se 🌐 www.rfsl.se/goteborg/
Local branch of The Swedish Federation for Gay and Lesbian Rights (RFSL). Call or see webside for further infos.

BARS

Next (B D F G MA P S)
Karl Johansgatan 31 ✉ 4033 ☎ 775 40 10
Call or email for further infos.

Park Lane (B g)
c/o Park Aveny Hotel, Aveny

Satyros (B F D G MA S WE)
Karl Johansgatan 6 *(near Sjöfartsmusseet)*
☎ 12 95 70

DANCECLUBS

Matahari (B D GLM)
Drottninggatan 35 ✉ 41135 *(Brunnsparken)*

RESTAURANTS

Gretas Bar (B CC F GLM MA S STV) Mon-Thu 16-2, Fri&Sat -3, Sun 17-2 h

Göteborg - Bohuslän ▶ Helsingborg - Skåne Sweden

GRETAS
Café Bar Restaurant

The only gay bar in Gothenburg open 7 days a week.

Drottninggatan 35
Gothenburg, Sweden
Telephone
+ 46 31 13 69 49

including the nightclub
MATAHARI

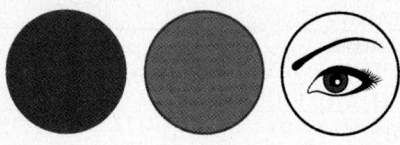

Drottninggatan 35 ✉ 41135 *(Brunnsparken)*
☎ 13 69 49
Two bars with a restaurant & nightclub with regular prices in the town center.

SEX SHOPS/BLUE MOVIES
■ **Blue Video** (G MA VS)
Andra Långgatan 32 *(Tram 3/4/9-Masthuggstorget)*
■ **Future Erotica Nyhavn** (G MA VS) 11-22 h
Lilla Drottninggatan 3
☎ 711 19 63
■ **Videoshopen** (G MA VS) Mon-Sat 10-23, Sun 12-23 h
Gamla Tuvev. 10 *(at the island Hisingen, near Vågmästareplatsen)*
☎ 50 80 55

FETISH GROUPS
■ **SLM Göteborg** (B DR G LJ P) See website
Box 5220 ✉ 402 24 ☎ 46 47 85 📠 91 80 20
💻 mail@slmgbg.nu 💻 www.slmgbg.nu
Member of ECMC.

HEALTH GROUPS
■ **Gayhälsan** Mon 17-19 h
Sahlgrenska Sjukhuset, Gröna stråket 16 ☎ 342 34 42 📠 411 584
Health-clinic for gay men.
■ **Positiva Gruppen Väst** Tue-Thu 11-15, Wed 18-21, Sat 12-16 h
Nordhemsgatan 50 ☎ 14 35 30 📠 14 35 30
💻 positiva.gruppen.vast@mailbox.swipnet.se
For HIV+/Aids people and their friends and families.

RELIGIOUS GROUPS
■ **EKHO-Göteborg**
Karl Johansgatan 31 ☎ 775 40 27 📠 775 40 28
💻 ekho@goteborg.mail.telia.com 💻 www.go.to/ekhogbg
Ecumenical christian gay group.

SWIMMING
-Saltholmen (g NU) (Nude coldbath house. Seperate departments for men and women)
-Smithska udden (G)
-Stora Amundön (g) (Nudist beach, in summertime only)

CRUISING
-Slottsskogen Park (day and night, only in the summer)
-Kungsparken (night, only in the summer)

Götene - Skaraborgs län
CRUISING
-Blomberg (outdoor bath)
-Kungsparken (at nighttime)
-Slottsskogen Park Cruising day and night

Halmstad - Halland ☎ 035
GAY INFO
■ **Gay Radio** Mon 20.30-21.30 h (FM 88,6 MHz)

SEX SHOPS/BLUE MOVIES
■ **Erocenter** (g VS) 11-22 h
Laholmsvägen 25

GENERAL GROUPS
■ **RFSL-Halland** (GLM MA) Mon Wed 19-21,
Youth group Wed 19-22 h
Lyckåkersgatan 7 ☎ 21 48 00 📠 21 48 00 💻 halland@rfsl.se
💻 www.rfsl.se/halland/

HELP WITH PROBLEMS
■ **Gay Jouren** Mon Wed 19-22 h
☎ 12 07 22

SWIMMING
-Vilshärads Beach (NU)
-Heden, Hagön (NU)

CRUISING
-Norrekatts Park
-Heden, Hagön

Helsingborg - Skåne ☎ 042
BARS
■ **Empire** (B D f GLM MA stv TV WE) Café Mon-Fr 11-17, Pub Fri 22-2, Disco Sat 23-3 h
Pålsgatan 1 *(near theater and concert hall)* ☎ 12 35 32

Sweden | Helsingborg - Skåne ▸ Lund - Skåne

SEX SHOPS/BLUE MOVIES
■ **Erocenter** (CC g VS) 11-22 h
Järnvägsgatan 27 ☏ 137 172
■ **Kosmos Movie** (DR VS) 11-21 h
Furutorpsgatan 73 ☏ 14 16 16
Videos also on sale as well as DVD's, magazines and sex toys.

HOTELS
■ **Hotell Kärnan** (BF glm SA)
Järnvägsgatan 17 ✉ 25224 ☏ 12 08 20 🖷 14 88 88
28 double rooms, 22 single rooms. All rooms with shower/WC, phone, satellite TV, radio, own key. Hotel provides car park amd TV room. Rates double skr 690-1.045, single 595-910, add. bed 175 (bf incl.)

GENERAL GROUPS
■ **RFSL-Helsingborg** (GLM) Mon-Fri 11-17 h
Pålsgatan 1 *(close to theater and concert hall)* ☏ 12 35 32
☏ 28 13 99 🖳 helsinborg@rfsl.se 🖳 www.rfsl.se/helsingborg/
Youth group, HIV/AIDS support project.

CRUISING
-Rosenträdgården (in the evening around the old fortress Kärnan)
-Knutpunkten (innercity terminal on 2nd floor)

Jönköping - Småland ☏ 036
SEX SHOPS/BLUE MOVIES
■ **Erocenter** (g)
Vilhelm Thams gatan 24

GENERAL GROUPS
■ **RFSL- Jönköping** (B D GLM MA)
Västra Halmgatan 14 🖳 jonkoping@rfsl.se
🖳 www.rfsl.se/jonkoping
Café Thu 19-22, disco every 2nd Sat/month 21-2, pub every 4th Sat 20-1 h.

CRUISING
-Östra torget
-Idas park (Friardalen)

Karlskrona ☏ 0455
CAFES
■ **Café Tre G** (A BF g MA OS) Mon-Fri 9-20 h, Sat 9-18 h, Sun 10-18 h
Landbrogatan 9 ✉ 371 34 ☏ 251 65

GENERAL GROUPS
■ **RFSL-Blekinge** (GLM MA)
Box 266 ✉ 371 24 ☏ 105 56 🖳 blekinge@rfsl.se
🖳 www.rfsl.se/blekinge/

Karlstad - Värmland ☏ 0454
GENERAL GROUPS
■ **RFSL-Värmland** (B d GLM MA)
Lantvärnsgatan 12 ☏ 15 20 90 🖳 varmland@rfsl.se
🖳 www.rfsl.se/varmland/
Party once a month, café Wed 19-21.30h Call for information.

HEALTH GROUPS
■ **Noaks Ark**
☏ (0570) 112 22

SWIMMING
-Skutberget (GLM OG) (westbound of the city)

Kristianstad - Skåne ☏ 044
GENERAL GROUPS
■ **RFSL-Kristianstad** (GLM) Café Fri 19-12 h
Norra Kanalgatan 2 ☏ 10 65 90 🖳 kristianstad@rfsl.se
🖳 www.rfsl.se/kristianstad/

SWIMMING
-Yngsjö Naturbad (in summer only)

CRUISING
-Tivoliparken (between theater and baths, northern section at night all year round)

Lidköping - Skaraborg ☏ 0510
CRUISING
-Nude beach (in summer only)
-Truve (outdoor bath)

Linköping - Östergötland ☏ 013
GENERAL GROUPS
■ **RFSL-Linköping** (GLM MA) Café Tue 19-22, Wed Thus 13-16, Pub Fri even weeks 21-24, Disco Sat even weeks 22-2.30 h
Nygatan 58 ✉ 58102 *(behind Hotel Brask)* ☏ 13 20 22
☏ 31 03 33 🖳 linkoping@rfsl.se 🖳 www.rfsl.se/linkoping/

HEALTH GROUPS
■ **Noaks Ark**
☏ 19 10 00

HELP WITH PROBLEMS
■ **Gayjour** Tue 19-22 h
☏ 31 03 33

CRUISING
-Simhallen
-Rydskogen (P behind Folkets Park)

Luleå - Norrbotten ☏ 0920
SAUNAS/BATHS
■ **Badhuset** (g)
Bastugatan 6-8

HELP WITH PROBLEMS
■ **Gayjouren** Sun 19-22
☏ 170 55

SWIMMING
-Lulvikens Beach (gay to the right; you can pitch a tent in the forest)

Lund - Skåne ☏ 046
GAY INFO
■ **Homo Sapiens**
Gay Radio. Channel AF 99,1 MHz. Organized by gay student group in Lund.

Lund - Skåne ▶ Norrköping - Östergötland — Sweden

BARS
■ **Petri bar** (B e F glm OS)
Petri Kyrkogata 7 ☎ 13 55 15
■ **Smålands Pub** (B glm)
Kastanjegatan 7

GENERAL GROUPS
■ **Gaystudenterna i Lund & Malmö** During termtimes Thu 17-19h c/o Akademiska föreningen, Sandgatan 2 ✉ 223 50 *Meets weekly at "Hic's",Kattesund 8.* ☎ 15 71 34 💻 info@gaystudenterna.nu 🌐 www.gaystudenterna.nu/lund
Call or see webside for details.

HEALTH GROUPS
■ **Venhälsan**
☎ 10 11 65

RELIGIOUS GROUPS
■ **EKHO-Syd**
c/o Studentprästerna, Krafts Torg 12 ✉ 223 50 ☎ 040/30 38 53

SWIMMING
-Lomma (nudist beach, 11 km west of Lund, north of Lomma; between a square artificial lake and the sea)
-Högevalls badet (Stadsparken)

CRUISING
-Stadsparken

Malmö - Malmöhus län ☎ 040

GAY INFO
■ **Identity Malmö**
☎ 611 99 23

DANCECLUBS
■ **Fyran** (B G MA) 23-3 h
Snapperupsgatan 4 ☎ 23 03 11
Thu 21-0, "Blue Boys Bar". 2nd, 4th Fri 23-3, "The temple". 1st, 3rd Fri 23-3 h (Swedish Leather Men).
■ **Indigo** (B D GLM LJ MA S) Wed 21-24, Thu 21-24, Fri Sat 22-2 Sun 22.30-2 h
Monbijougatan 15 ✉ 211 53 *(3rd floor. near Folkets Park)*
☎ 611 99 62

RESTAURANTS
■ **Gustav Adolf** (A AC B BF CC F glm MA OS) 9-1 h
Gustav Adolfs Torg 43 ✉ 203 13 ☎ 611 22 72
Gay run and owned. Friendly staff
■ **No Name** (CC B F glm) 11.30-24 h, Sun closed
S. Vallgatan 3 ✉ 212 98 ☎ 121 298
Quality food at reasonable prices.

SEX SHOPS/BLUE MOVIES
■ **Taboo** (g VS) Mon-Fri 11-22, Sat & Sun -18h
Södra Förstadsgatan 81 ☎ 976 410

SAUNAS/BATHS
■ **Vattenpalatset Aq-Va-Kul** (g SB) Mon-Thur 9-21, Fri 9-20, Sat-Sun 9-18 h
Regementsgatan 24 ☎ 30 05 40
Municipal bathhouse.

HOTELS
■ **Hotel Pallas** (BF glm H MA)
Norra Vallgatan 74 *(in front of railway station)* ☎ 611 50 77
🖷 97 77 77
Centrally located. Single skr 295, double 395.

GENERAL GROUPS
■ **RFSL-Malmö** Pub Wed 21-24 h
Monbijougatan 15 ☎ 611 99 62 ☎ 611 99 23 💻 malmo@rfsl.se
🌐 mila.landskrona.se/rfslmalmo/
Local branch of The Swedish Federation for Gay and Lesbian Rights (RFSL).

FETISH GROUPS
■ **SLM Malmö** (G LJ)
Amiralsgatan 14, Suite 112 ✉ 21155 ☎ 30 18 93
💻 snl864q@tninet.se 🌐 www.come.to/slm.malmo/
Member of ECMC.
■ **ToE Secretariat**
Slussgatan 21 ✉ 211 30 💻 oerjan-schoenberg@ebox.tninet.se
ECMC's Nordic/Scandinavian Club's secretariat.

HEALTH GROUPS
■ **Noaks Ark**
Södergatan 13 ✉ 211 34 ☎ 611 52 15 🖷 611 29 58
Group for people with HIV+/Aids.
■ **STD Mottagningen & Infektionskliniken** (G)
MAS Universitetssjukhuset, Ingång 45 ☎ 33 17 67 ☎ 33 13 25
Infectious diseases section.

HELP WITH PROBLEMS
■ **RFSL Rådgivningen Skåne** (G)
Drottninggatan 36 ☎ 611 99 50 ☎ 611 99 51 🖷 97 12 18
💻 radgivningen.malmo@rfsl.se 🌐 www.safe6.nu
Information and counselling.

SWIMMING
-Ribersborg (on the west part of the beach, close to the harbor for small boats)
-Ribersborgs Kallbadhus (NU pi) (summer only, 9-19 h)
-Aq-va-kul (pi) (10-21 h. Regementsgatan, opposite Slottsparken. Ask for Turkish bath-sauna in 2nd floor.) Mon-Thu 9-21, Fri 9-20, Sat-Sun 10-18 h. ☎ 30 05 40

CRUISING
-Gustav-Aolfs-Torget
-[P] Stortorget
-Nobeltorge (WC)
-West part of Ribersborg beach-park (at the far end of the bycicle track towards Limnann, turn right into the woods after passing "Båskytteklubben". Daytime in summer only.)
-East part of Ribersborg beach-park (in the bushes east of Ribersborgs Kallbadhus. Summer only from 22-? h)
-Slottsparken (by the tennis-courts. All year round at night)
-Öresundsparken
-Pildammsparken
-Södra/Östra promenaden
-Tivoliparken Kristianstad

Norrköping - Östergötland ☎ 011

DANCECLUBS
■ **Brittas** (B D glm)
Drottninggatan 36
Best Sat

SPARTACUS 2001/2002 | 975

Sweden | Norrköping - Östergötland ▸ Stockholm

GENERAL GROUPS
■ **RFSL-Norrköping** (GLM MA) Café Wed 18-21 h
Sjötullsgatan 3 ☏ 23 81 50 🖷 18 00 40 ✉ orrkoping@rfsl.se
💻 www.algonet.se/~rfsl011/

CRUISING
-Karl Johansparken
-Järnvägsparken

Nyköping - Södermanland ☏ 0155
GENERAL GROUPS
■ **RFSL-Nyköping** (GLM MA TV) Café Thu 18-21 h
PO Box 2012 ✉ 61102 *(Behing"Expert Photo Shop")* ☏ 21 02 29
🖷 21 02 29 ✉ nykoping@rfsl.se 💻 wwww.rfsl.se/nykoping/

Örebro - Närke ☏ 019
GENERAL GROUPS
■ **RFSL-Örebro** Café Mon-Fri 13-16, Tue 19-22, Disco Sat 21-2 h
c/o Orlando, Slottsgatan 19b ☏ 14 42 32 ✉ orebro@rfsl.se
💻 www.rfsl.se/orebro/

Östersund - Jämtland ☏ 063
BARS
■ **Lokalen** (B f d GLM MA)
Gränsgatan 13 ☏ 100 668
Cafe Wed 19-22, party 1st Sat 22-2 h. Call for further Info.

SAUNAS/BATHS
■ **Storsjöbadet** (f g SA SB SOL WH WO) Mon-Fri 10-21,
Sat-Sun 10-17 h
Krondikesvägen 94
Take Bus 2,6 or 9 from central bus station, southern direction to bus stop "Fritidsbyn". Behind Scandic Hotel. Interesting are 1st floor jacuzzi and men's side sauna/steam bath. Popular. Be discreet because it's a public bath.

Piteå - Norrbotten ☏ 0911
RESTAURANTS
■ **Pigalle** (B CC d F glm MA)
Sundsgatan 36 ☏ 118 75

GENERAL GROUPS
■ **RFSL-Piteå** (B d f GLM MA s WE)
Aronsgatan 11 *(in the yard)*
☏ 925 70 ☏ 144 40 🖷 925 70 ✉ polarstar@ilga.org
💻 www.rfsl.se/pitea

HELP WITH PROBLEMS
■ **Roggbiv Skellefteå. Group for Gays and Lesbians** (GLM)
Sun 19-21 h
Box 155 ✉ 94121 ☏ (0912) 303 00 ☏ (0910) 722 222
🖷 925 70

Skövde - Skaraborg ☏ 0500
GENERAL GROUPS
■ **RFSL-Skaraborg** (GLM MA) Café Thu 18-22, Disco 1st Sat 21 h
Storgatan 12 A ☏ 41 06 63 ☏ 41 06 69 🖷 41 06 63
✉ skaraborg@rfsl.se 💻 www.rfsl.se/skaraborg

Stockholm ☏ 08

❋ Stockholm gets its name from the many islands which are to be found in this city - "holm" being the Swedish word for "island". The Swedish capital city is an artwork, formed by nature and architecture. In this wonderful city you can go from the bustling city centre into splendid forests within fifteen minutes. We especially recommend a visit during the bright summer months, when the Swedes -usually quite reserved people- enjoy the long nights. A calm and relaxed rhythm then prevails in Stockholm and in the small gay scene. Tips:
- Party on Sundays on the old boat "Patricia"
- A boats ride to the castle of "Drottningholm"
- A boats ride through the waters of the "Schären", the island group opposite to Stockholm, e.g. to Vaxholm.
-"Propaganda" parties (Sat).

★ Stockholm hat seinen Namen von den vielen innerhalb der Stadt liegenden Inseln erhalten. Das schwedische Wort "Holm" steht nämlich für "Insel". Die schwedische Hauptstadt ist ein von der Natur und Architektur geformtes Kunstwerk. In dieser wundervollen Stadt kann man innerhalb von 15 Minuten aus dem lebendigen Stadtzentrum in die umliegenden Wälder gelangen. Wir raten, Stockholm in den hellen Sommermonaten zu besuchen, wenn die Schweden, die normalerweise eher reserviert sind, die langen hellen Nächte genießen. Dann herrscht in Stockholm mit seiner kleinen Gay-Szene ein richtig relaxtes Klima. Und hier noch einige Tips:
- Parties auf dem alten Boot "Patricia", Sonntags
- Eine Schiffahrt zum Schloss Drottningholm
- Eine Schiffahrt zu den Schären, die Stockholm gegenüberliegende Inselgruppe, z.B. nach Vaxholm.
- "Propaganda" Parties, Samstags.

❋ Stockholm tient son nom des nombreuses îles que contient la ville, "holm" signifiant île en suédois. La capitale suédoise est une uvre d'art à elle seule, un étroit mélange entre nature et architecture. Il est possible, en un quart d'heure de marche, de quitter le centre ville pour se retrouver au beau milieu des forêts. Bien sûr, il est plus agréable de découvrir Stockholm en été, saison où les Suédois revivent littéralement. Les nuits y sont longues, l'atmosphère est sympathique et décontractée. C'est aussi valable pour lieux gais qui malgré leur petit nombre sont très accueillants et chaleureux. A faire absolument:
- les fêtes sur l'ancien bateau "Patricia", le dimanche,
- une excursion en bateau au château de Drottningholm,
- ou dans les eaux de " Schären ", un groupe d'îles en face de Stockholm, par ex. à Vaxholm,
- les fêtes de Propaganda, le samedi.

● El nombre de Estocolmo viene de las numerosas islas que se encuentran en esta ciudad: "holm" es la palabra sueca para "isla". La capital sueca es una obra de arte creada por la naturaleza y la arquitectura. En esta ciudad maravillosa, sólo se tarda quince minutos en llegar desde el bullicioso centro de la ciudad a los bosques espléndidos en las afueras. Recomendamos especialmente una visita durante los meses más claros de verano que es cuando los suecos (personas normalmente más bien un poco reservadas) disfrutan de las noches largas. Entonces, en la ciudad de Estocolmo y en su pequeño ambiente gay predomina un ritmo tranquilo y relajado. Recomendaciones:
- Los domingos, fiesta en el barco antiguo "Patricia"
- Un viaje en barco al castillo de "Drottningholm"

Stockholm | Sweden

- Un viaje en barco por las aguas de las islas "Schären", un grupo de islas enfrente de Estocolmo, por ejemplo a Vaxholm.
- Los sábados, las fiestas "Propaganda".

✖ La città di Stoccolma ha avuto il suo nome dalle tante isole che si trovano al suo interno. Infatti la parola "Holm" in svedese significa "isola". La capitale svedese è un'opera d'arte risultante dal connubio tra natura ed architettura. Dal centro cittadino pieno di vita di questa meravigliosa città si possono raggiungere le bellissime foreste vicine, in soli 15 minuti. Vi suggeriamo di visitare Stoccolma soprattutto durante i luminosi mesi estivi, quando gli svedesi, solitamente persone piuttosto riservate, si rallegrano delle lunghe notti chiare. Ed è proprio in questo periodo che a Stoccolma e nel piccolo ambiente gay regna un'atmosfera calma e rilassata. Vi consigliamo:
- le feste sulla vecchia barca "Patricia", di domenica;
- un giro con il battello al castello di Drottningholm;
- un giro con il battello verso le "Schären", un gruppo di isole situate di fronte a Stoccolma, come per esempio Vaxholm;
- le feste "Propaganda", di sabato.

GAY INFO
■ **TGT • The Gay Telegraph**
☎ 32 32 32
Modem settings: 300, 1200, 2400 (8, N, 1).

TOURIST INFO
■ **Stockholm Information Service**
Kungsträdgården ✉ 10383 ☎ 789 24 00 📠 789 24 50
💻 stoinfo-se 💻 www.stoinfo.se

BARS
■ **Bottle & Glass** (B f g MA) Mon-Fri 16-1, Sat-Sun 14-1 h
Hornsgatan 136 (T- Hornstull.) ☎ 84 56 10
Thirty different kinds of beer. Pool-table, Black jack, Dart.

■ **Hjärter Dam** (B F g lj MA N OS tv) Wed-Sun 16.30-23.50, Kinky Bar Fri Sat 20.30-1 h
Polhemsgatan 23/Hantverkargatan (T-Rådhuset)
☎ 653 57 39
In the evenings: P.

■ **Junkyard Bar** (B F g) Wed 21-1 h
Birkagatan 10 (T- Eriksplan, Trainstation Karlberg) ☎ 34 88 87
Bar and restaurant.

■ **Mandus** (B CC F GLM MA OS) 15-24 h, Mon closed
Österlånggatan 7 ✉ 111 31 (T-Gamla Stan) ☎ 20 60 55
Gay bar and restaurant with a friendly atmosphere in the old town.

■ **Side Track** (B CC F G MA) 18-1, Jun-Aug 20-1 h
Vollmar Yxkullsgatan 7 ✉ 11850 (T-Mariatorget)
☎ 641 16 88
Also restaurant.

■ **SLM • Scandinavian Leather Men** (B D G LJ MA P VS)
Wed Fri Sat 22-2 h
Wollmar Yxkullsgatan 18, PO Box 17 241 ✉ 104 62 (T-Mariatorget).
Entrance at garage door) ☎ 643 31 00

■ **Torget** (AC B CC F GLM MA OS) 11-1h daily.
Mälartorget 13 (T- Gamla Stan)
☎ 205 560
New gay bar in the heart of the old town, near the royal castle.

CAFES
■ **Café Albert** (b f g) Mon-Thu 7.45-1, Fri-Sat -5, Sun 9-1 h
Birger Jarlsgatan 5 ☎ 611 33 11
Mixed café in the city area. Perfect for checking out the city-crowds.

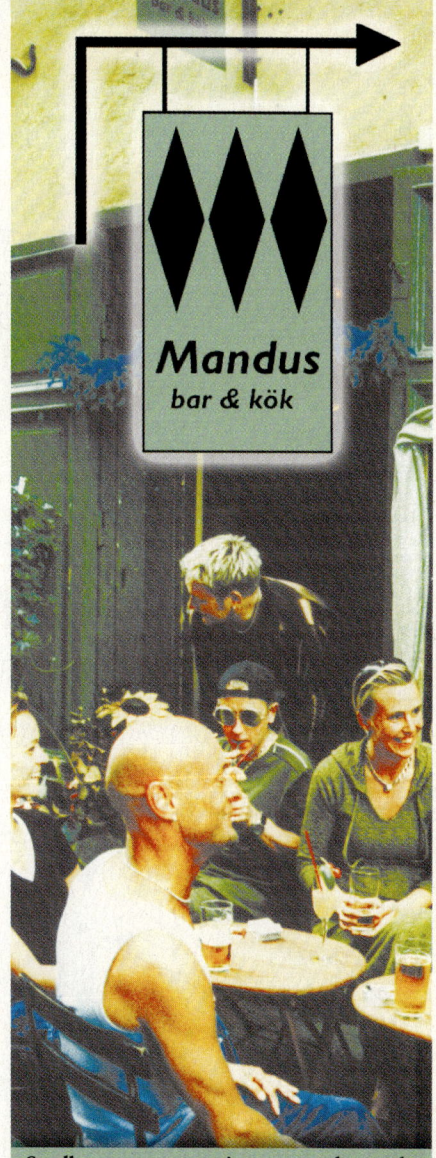

Mandus
bar & kök

Small, cosy restaurant, just next to the royal palace, voted "Restaurant of the Year '99".
Österlånggatan 7, Old Town
Phone 08-20 60 55
Open: Seven daily from 17-24. Welcome!

SPARTACUS 2001/2002 977

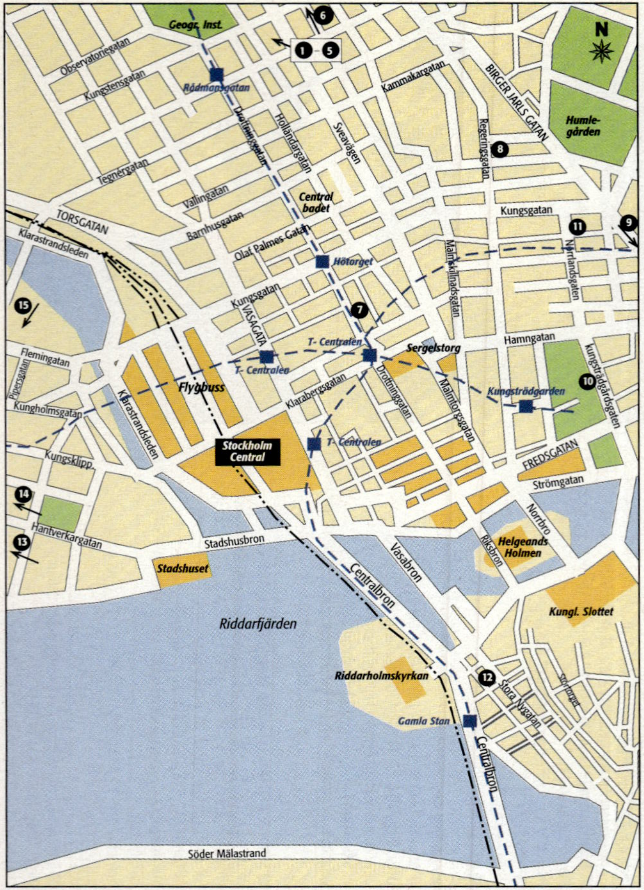

Sweden | Stockholm

Stockholm - Center

1. Stockholm Gay Center
2. RFSL-Stockholm Group
3. Rosa Rummet Bookshop
4. Tip Top Danceclub
5. Tip Top Restaurant
6. Berlin Sex Shop
7. Element Café
8. US Video Blue Movies
9. Café Albert
10. Piccolino Café
11. Fatale-Hair Dressing Center
12. Nitty Gritty Fashion Shop
13. Manhattan Blue Movies
14. Hjärter Dam Bar
15. Spisa Hos Helena Restaurant

Stockholm - Södermalm

1. Häcktet Danceclub
2. Patricia Danceclub
3. Side Track Bar
4. The Muscle Academy Fitness Club
5. Bottle & Glass Bar
6. SLM Bar
7. The Basement Blue Movies
8. Revolt Sex Shop
9. Pensionat Oden Guest House

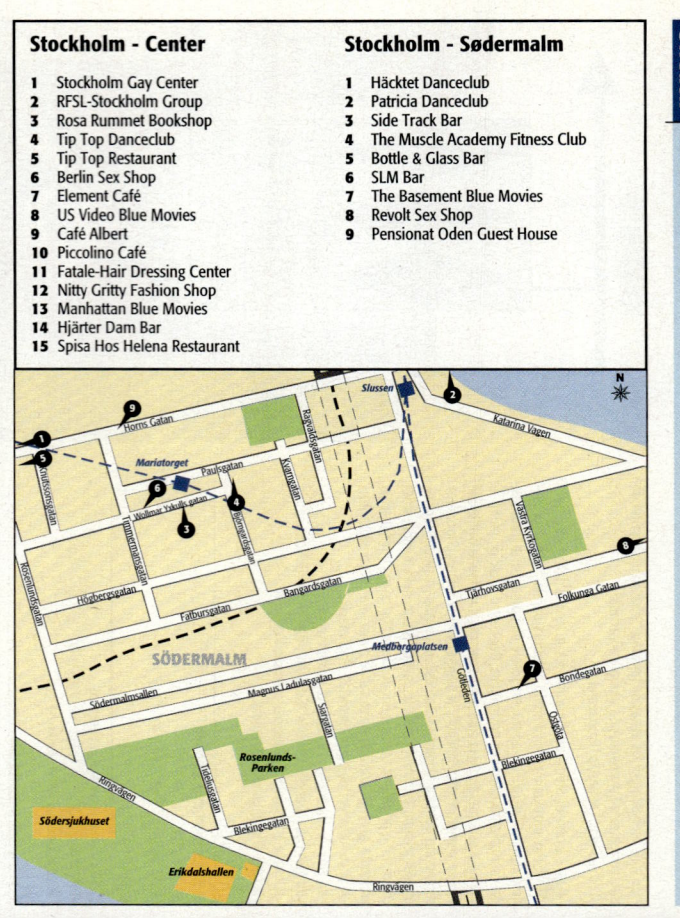

Stockholm — Sweden

torget

Mälartorget 13, Old Town, 08- 20 55 60

Newly opened and already a favorite livingroom-like hangout for Stockholm's gay crowd in the heart of Old town. Beautiful bar and restaurant with all sorts of drinks and coffe + hot dishes. Fabulous wall decorations and a spinning crystal crown in the ceiling. Mixed music ranging from N.Y house to Judy Garland. One minute's walk from subway station Gamla Stan.
Open daily 11-01 a.m.

DJURGÅRDS terrassen

Sirishovsvägen 3, 08- 662 62 09

Cosy outdoor café at Djurgården, Stockholm's royal green park. All sorts of beverages, pastry, food and home-made ice cream served by the lovely staff in this oasis with a stunning view.
Open from 10 am til late from 15 april to 30 september.
Turn left after bridge Djurgårdsbron, then ten minutes' walk.

Sweden | Stockholm

OLD TOWN
STORTORGET 18
CHOKLADKOPPEN
COFFEE / CHOCOLATE / CAKES / SANDWICHES / OUTDOOR SEATING

+46 (0)8 20 31 70

■ **Chokladkoppen** (A AC BF F GLM MA OS) 9-23h every day. Stortorget 18, Gamla Stan ✉ 12289 *(Subway station Gamla Stan)* ☎ 203170
Beautiful in and outdoor seating. Close to the Royal Palace, in the heart of the historic old town. Cosy atmopshere, delicious cakes, sandwiches and coffee/hot chocolate. Voted "Gay Cafe of the Year" in '98 and '99 by QX Readers.

■ **Djurgårds Terassen** (B BF CC F GLM MA OS) 15 April - 30 Sept from 10-24h
Sirishovsvägen 3, Djurgården ☎ 662 62 09
Cafe & restaurant. Outdoor seating only in a natural setting, close to the water.

■ **Element** (A AC BF F GLM OS YG) 8-22 h
Drottninggatan 73c *(T-Centralen, close to shopping area)* ☎ 22 56 66
Spacious café with minimalistic, interesting architecture. Delicious meals. Recommended.

DANCECLUBS

■ **Häcktet** (AC B CC D F GLM MA OS) Wed Fri 19-1 h
Hornsgatan 82 ☎ 84 59 10
Popular mixed gay bar.

■ **Patricia** (! AC B CC D F GLM MA OS S) Sun 18-3 h gay
Stadsgårdskajen 152 ✉ 116 45 *(T-Slussen)* ☎ 743 05 70
On a ship, very popular. Good restaurant, all meals half price, free entrance in disco after restaurant visit.

■ **Propaganda** (! B CC D F G lj MA s) Sat 22-3 h
Teaterbaren, Sergels Torg *(T- Centralen)*
Scandinavia's leading gay disco.

■ **Tip Top** (AC B CC D F GLM MA OS) 16-3 h
Sveavägen 57-59 *(T-Rådmansgatan)* ☎ 32 98 00
Bar, café, restaurant and danceclub.

PATRICIA

Restaurantboat
with a great view of Stockholm
Restaurant- Nightclub-
Casino and 4 bars

Summer time:
Big outdoor deck with 2 bars

Open:
Sundays 18-03
All meals half price

Welcome aboard!

PATRICIA
STADSGÅRDSKAJEN T-SLUSSEN 08/743 05 70

PROPAGANDA
STOCKHOLM

SCANDINAVIAS LEADING GAYDISCO

AT TEATERBAREN, SERGELS TORG
22-03 EVERY SATURDAY

WWW.PROPAGANDA.NU

Stockholm | Sweden

sideTRACK bar
& restaurant

THE GAY STAFFED BAR IN STOCKHOLM
OPEN 7 NIGHTS
WOLLMAR YXKULLSGATAN 7
WWW.SIDETRACK.NU

Sweden | Stockholm

RESTAURANTS

■ **Bakfickan** (B F g OS) Mon-Fri 11-22 h, Sat 17-22 h
Folkungatan 126 ✉ 116 30 *(T-Södermalm)* ☎ 641 33 87
Genuine Swedish restaurant. Outdoor seating.

■ **Spisa hos Helena** (B CC F glm MA N OS) Mon-Thu 11-24, Fri -1, Sat 17-1 h, Sun closed
Scheelegatan 18 ✉ 112 28 *(T-Rådhuset)* ☎ 654 49 26
International cuisine. Main course skr 100-230. Also cocktail bar.

SEX SHOPS/BLUE MOVIES

■ **Basement. The** (G MA VS) 12-6 h
Bondegatan 1 b ☎ 643 79 10
Popular.

■ **Berlin** (g VS)
Luntmakargatan 76 ☎ 612 09 76

■ **Eros Video** (DR G MA VS)
Hornsgatan 67 ✉ 118 49 *(T- Zinkensdamm), Söder* ☎ 11-6 h

■ **Foxy** (g) 10-22, Sun 12-22 h
Tomtebogatan 13 *(T-St. Eriksplan)*

■ **Haga Video** (G MA VS) Sun-Thu 11-4, Fri Sat -6 h
Hagagatan 56 *(T-Odenplan)* ☎ 33 55 44

■ **Kino** (g VS) 0-24 h
Döbelnsgatan 4 *(T-Rådmansgatan)* ☎ 24 41 41
Homepage http://www.clubkino.com

■ **Manhattan** (DR G MA VS) 12-6 h
Hantverkargatan 49 ✉ 11220 *(T-Rådhuset)* ☎ 653 92 10
Very popular!

■ **Red Light-Video**
Roslagsgatan 32

■ **Revolt Shop** (G VS) Mon-Thu 11-22, Fri -20, Sat 12-18, Sun 14-19 h
Nytorgsgatan 21 A *(T-Medborgarplatsen)* ☎ 643 79 50
Rending of videos possible.

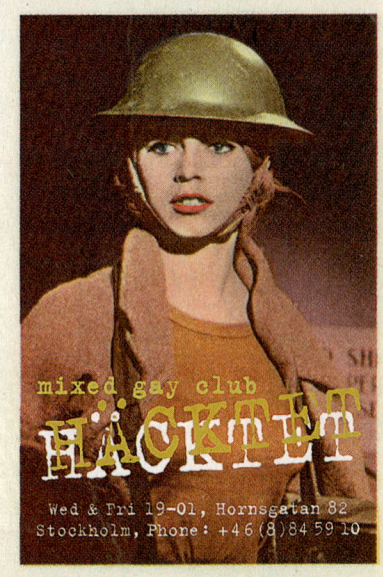

---

mixed gay club
HÄCKTET
Wed & Fri 19-01, Hornsgatan 82
Stockholm, Phone: +46(8)84 59 10

B 127 Brigitte Bardot

Manhattan
Cruise Stockholm at Manhattan
Hantverkarg. 49
Opening hours:
always from 12 a.m. to 6 a.m.
http://www.ix.nu/manhattan

THE BEST NONSTOP IN TOWN
U.S.VIDEO — **SEX SUPERMARKET**
INTERNET SEXSHOP
www.usvideo.nu
24.000 VIDEO FILMS
OPEN 24HOURS   REGERINGSGATAN 76 STOCKHOLM

---

982 SPARTACUS 2001/2002

Stockholm — Sweden

The Muscle Academy

Björngårdsgatan 1 B
118 52 Stockholm
Mon-Fri 13.00-22.00

Tel. 08-642 6306
Ⓣ Maria Torget
Sat-Sun 16.00-20.00

**gym • sauna • massage
cardio • tanning • relax**

www.the-muscle-academy.com   info@the-muscle-academy.com

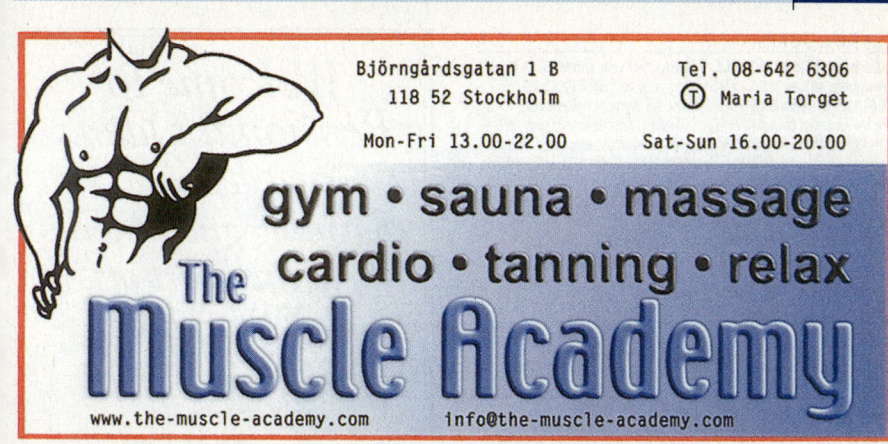

■ **Roslags Video** (g)
Roslagsgatan 43
■ **US Video** (AC b CC DR G MA VS) 24 h
Regeringsgatan 76 ✉ 111 39 (T- Hötorget) ☎ 10 42 53
Popular darkroom. Large selection.
■ **Video Staden** (g)
Roslagsgatan 25 ☎ 165 953

SAUNAS/BATHS
■ **Eriksdalsbadet** (b F MA NG PI SA SOL WO) 6-16, Sat Sun -13 h
Gräsgatan/Ringvägen (T-Skanstull)
Outdoor in summer.
■ **Storkyrkobadet** (NG MA pi SA) Tue Fri 17-20 h
Svatmannagatan 20-22 (T-Gamla Stan) ☎ 20 90 27
Small pool in medieval vaults.
You won't find any gay baths/saunas in Sweden. They all have been closed down.

FITNESS STUDIOS
■ **Muscle Academy. The** (CC f G MA msg p SA SOL WO) 13-22, Sat&Sun 16-20 h
Björngårdsgatan 1B ✉ 118 52 (T-Mariatorget) ☎ 642 63 06
Day pass for tourists available.

BODY & BEAUTY SHOPS
■ **Fatale - Hair Dressing Center** (g) Mon 9-18, Tue-Fri 9-20, Sat 10-14 h
Norrlandsgatan 22 (T- Hötorget, T- Östermalmstorg) ☎ 611 54 54
Hair dresser in the city center.

BOOK SHOPS
■ **Rosa Rummet** (CC GLM) Mon-Thu 12-20, Fri -18, Sat-Sun 13-16 h
Sveavägen 57 ✉ PS 10369 (T- Rådmansgatan) ☎ 736 02 15
Selling of books, magazines, videos, pins, rainbowflags, etc. Good information on gay Stockholm. Also mail order: www.rfsl.se/rosarummet/

FASHION SHOPS
■ **Nitty Gritty** (g) Mon-Fri 11-20, Sat 11-16 h
Stora Nygatan 7 (old town) ☎ 240 044
London style clothing.

LEATHER & FETISH SHOPS
■ **Läderverkstan** (CC G LJ) Mon-Fri 12-18 h
Rosenlundsgatan 30 A ✉ 104 62 (T-Mariatorget) ☎ 442 30 35
Leather and toy store, repairs etc.

MAIL ORDER
■ **M&D Video**
Kihlgrens Väg 3 ✉ 192 79 ☎ 594 702 10 🖷 594 702 11
✉ mdekonomi@usa.net
Gayvideo mailorder

TRAVEL AND TRANSPORT
■ **Resebutik Noble Travel** (CC glm MA) 10-18 h
Björngårdsgatan 1B ✉ 118 52 (T-Bana Mariatorget) ☎ 644 74 56
🖷 644 24 23 ✉ noble@bahnhof.se

---

complete offer
see page Germany/Berlin

STOCKHOLM
overnight accomodation service
· about 750 beds · more than 28 cities ·

bed & enjoy breakfast

central booking office Berlin ☎ **+49-30-2151666** 4:30-9:00 pm local time
Fax +49-30-23623619 · info@ebab.de · www.ebab.dk

Sweden — Stockholm

GUEST HOUSES

■ **Pensionat Oden** (AC bf CC G H MA) All year round, 9-21 h
Odengatan 38 ✉ 113 51 *(T-Rådmansgatan)* ☎ 612 43 49
📠 612 45 01 📧 info@pensionat.nu 🌐 www.pensionat.nu
Centrally located boarding house. 1 single, 8 double rooms with bath/WC on the corridor. All rooms with satellite TV, minibar. Hotel provides own key, car park. Rates double skr from 595-875, single skr from 495-550.

■ **Pensionat Oden Söder** (AC bf CC G H MA) Open all year, 9-21 h
Hornsgatan 66b ✉ 11849 *(T-Mariatorget)* ☎ 612 43 49
📠 612 4501 📧 info@pensionat.nu 🌐 www.pensionat.nu
5 single and 10 double rooms. All with sat.TV, own key and car park. Singles from 795-895, doubles from 895-995.

PRIVATE ACCOMMODATION

■ **Enjoy Bed and Breakfast** (BF G H MA) 16.30-21 h
☎ +45 32 960 206 📧 info@ebab.dk 🌐 ebab.dk

GENERAL GROUPS

■ **Bikupan**
Box 3444 ✉ 10369

■ **Gay Studenterna**
c/o Studentkårens Sociala Utskott, PO Box 50006 ✉ 104 05
☎ 16 55 03
University student group.

■ **Gaytek**
📧 gaytek@ths.kth.se 🌐 www.gaytek.home.ml.org/
Student group at the Royal Institute of Technology.

■ **GLIS-Grupo Latinoamericano por la Iqualidad Sexual**
Meeting Wed 18 h at Gay Center

■ **RFSL-Stockholm** (GLM MA) Mon-Fri 10-15 h
Sveavägen 57 *(Subway- Rådmansgatan)* ☎ 736 02 12 📠 30 47 30
📧 stockholm@rfsl.se

■ **Stockholm Rubber Mens Club**
c/o SLM, PO Box 17 241 ✉ 104 62 ☎ 643 31 00

FETISH GROUPS

■ **SLM Stockholm**
Box 172 41 ✉ 104 62 📧 slm@slm.a.se 🌐 www.slm.a.se
Member of ECMC.

HEALTH GROUPS

■ **AIDS-Jouren**
☎ (020) 78 44 40

■ **Noah's Arc- Red Cross Foundation. The**
Drottninggattan 61 ✉ 111 21 ☎ 700 46 00 📠 700 46 10
📧 info@noahsark.redcross.se 🌐 www.noahsark.redcross.se
Centre for HIV/AIDS prevention and care.

■ **Posithiva Gruppen** Tue-Thu 15-23, Fri -2, Sat 20-2, Sun 15-19 h, Mon closed
Magnus Ladulåsgatan 8 ✉ 100 64 ☎ 720 19 60 📠 720 10 48
The Swedish organization for HIV+/AIDS gay men. Editor of the magazine "T cellen".

■ **Riksförbundet för HIV-positiva (RFHP)**
Gotlandsgatan 72 ✉ 11638 ☎ 714 54 10 📠 714 04 25
📧 rfhp@mbox300.swipnet.se
🌐 www.home2.swipnet.se
National organization for the hiv-positive.

■ **Venhälsan** Tue-Thu 17-20.30h
c/o Södersjukhuset Hospital, Ringvägen 52 ☎ 616 25 00
📠 616 25 09
Anonymous hiv-testing & councelling free of charge.

HELP WITH PROBLEMS

■ **Anonyma Alkoholister, Gay Group** Tue 19, Sat 17 h
Sveavägen 57 *(1st floor, Gan Room)*

■ **Brottsofferjour för Homosexuella** Mon-Fri 19-23 h

Welcome to Pensionat Oden's two genuine, charming guest houses in the heart of Gay Stockholm

- CENTRALLY LOCATED
- PRIVATE ROOMS FOR SHORT OR LONG STAYS
- OWN KEY
- CENTURY-OLD STYLE

Pensionat Oden
STOCKHOLM CITY

SOUTH Hornsgatan 66b NORTH Odengatan 38
BOOKINGS Phone +46(0)8-612 43 49,
Fax +46(0)8-612 45 01, E-mail info@pensionat.nu
WWW.PENSIONAT.NU

ENJOY YOUR STAY IN STOCKHOLM

Stockholm ▶ Västerås - Västmanlands län Sweden

☎ 08 34 13 16
Gay bashing helpline
■ ☎ 24 74 65
■ **Linje 59** (G YG) Mon Wed 19-22 h
☎ (020) 59 59 00
Gay youth switchboard.
■ **PH-Center** Mon Wed-Fri 8.30-16 h, Tue 10-16 h
Wollmar Yxkullsgatan 25 ✉ 118 91 *(3rd floor)* ☎ 616 55 00
🖨 616 55 11
Medical center, with a psychosocial approach, for gay and bisexual men. No charge.
■ **P.L.U.S.** Every other Sun.
c/o SLM, PO Box 172 41 ✉ 104 62 ☎ 643 31 06
Party for HIV-positives.
■ **RFSL Rådgivningen** (G) Mon 9-21, Tue-Fri 9-16 h
☎ 736 02 10
Councelling service.

RELIGIOUS GROUPS
■ **EKHO** every 2nd Fri 19-23 h
Katarinavägen 19, PO Box 19047 ✉ 104 32 *(T-Slussen)*
☎ 643 74 45   ☎ (020) 78 77 76 *(helpline)*
Ecumenical Christian gay group.
■ **Galej-Homosexuella Judar**
Box 350 ✉ 101 26 ☎ 736 02 11
Gay and Lesbian Jewish Organisation.

SPECIAL INTEREST GROUPS
■ **Gay Opera Lovers** (GLM MA)
☎ (70) 76 23 685 🖂 rogerwallen@hotmail.com
🖳 www.rfsl.se/stockholm/ob
Opera lovers who meet to talk, to go to the opera together or to meet artists. For more info e-mail or call RFSL Stockholm.
■ **Homosexuella Pensionärer** (OG)
Box 170 ✉ 101 23 ☎ 20 90 20
Group for older gays.

SWIMMING
-**Frescati** (G NU) (T-Universitetet, over the railway, left and through the woods)
-**Långholmen** (G NU) (T-Hornstull, west side, on the hill above the café)
-**Solsidan** (g NU) (T-Slussen, then train to Solsidan-Stop. Walk along Vårgårdsvägen until its end, then over the hill)
-**North end of Kärsön Island** (G NU) (bus from T-Brommaplan, get off at first stop after first bridge and walk around wheat field, then uphill through forest. Warm summer days until about 20 h. Plenty of action)

CRUISING
-**Stadshusparken** (small park by the water just north of the city hall)
-**Skinnarviksparken** (T-Zinkensdamm)
-**Frescati** (Near university, walk through tunnel under the motorway straight ahead through the park to the lake. One the left hand there is a rocky hill. Popular in summer!)

Sundsvall - Medelpad ☎ 060

GENERAL GROUPS
■ **RFSL-Sundsvall** (B D GLM) 20-22 h, Disco: 2nd/last Sat 22-2, Café Wed 20-22 h
Skolhusallén 23 ✉ 850 03 ☎ 17 13 30

CRUISING
-**Badhusparken**
-Ⓟ **Norrmalms**

Trollhättan - Västergötland ☎ 0520

GENERAL GROUPS
■ **RFSL-Trestad** (b d f GLM MA) Café Wed Thu 18-22(YG), Disco last Sat 21-2 h
c/o Regnbågen, Stridsbergsgatan 8 ☎ 41 17 66 🖨 41 17 66
🖳 trestad@rfsl.se 🖳 www.rfsl.se/trestad/

HELP WITH PROBLEMS
■ **Gay Jouren**
☎ 806 07   ☎ 42 61 56 (women)

Umeå - Västerbotten ☎ 090

GENERAL GROUPS
■ **RFSL-Umeå** Café: Wed 19-22 h, Disco: 1st/3rd Sat
Box 38 ✉ 901 02 ☎ 77 47 10

Uppsala - Uppland ☎ 018

DANCECLUBS
■ **Sten Sture** (B D GLM MA) GLM only Sun
Nedre Slottsgatan 3

GENERAL GROUPS
■ **RFSL-Uppsala** Wed 18-20 h
Whitehouse, Torsgatan 10 ☎ 69 23 96

HELP WITH PROBLEMS
■ **Gayjouren** Mon 19-21 h
☎ 69 25 89

RELIGIOUS GROUPS
■ **EKHO Uppsala** (GLM) 2nd Sun 13 h at Pasoralinstitutet, Linnégatan 1
PO Box 1915 ✉ 751 49 ☎ 26 02 21
Gay and lesbian Christian group.

SPECIAL INTEREST GROUPS
■ **Föreningen Uppsala Gaystudenter (FUGS)** (GLM YG) Meetings on Tue in a pub at Kalmar nation
PO Box 30276 ✉ 750 03

SWIMMING
-**Fjällnora** (NU) (beach to the right)
-**Centralbadet** (NG pi sa)

CRUISING
-**Stadsparken** (public park northern part behind Flustret and next to Nedre Slottsgatan)

Västerås - Västmanlands län ☎ 021

GENERAL GROUPS
■ **RFSL-Västmanland** (GLM MA)
Mimersgatan 6 ☎ 410 375 🖳 vastmanland@rfsl.se
🖳 www.rfsl.se/vastmanland
Café every Tue 19-22 h. Call or see webside for futher information.

HELP WITH PROBLEMS
■ **Telefonjour** Wed 19-22 h
☎ 11 80 41

SWIMMING
-**Kristiansborgsbadet**
-**Lögaränsbadet** (in summer)

Switzerland

Name: Schweiz • Suisse • Svizzera • Suiza
Location: Central Europe
Initials: CH
Time: GMT +1
International Country Code: ☎ 41 (leave the first 0 of area codes)
International Access Code: ☎ 00
Language: German, French, Italian, Rhaeto-Romanic
Area: 41,284 km² / 15,943 sq mi.
Currency: 1 Swiss Franc (CHF) = 100 Centimes/Rappen
Population: 7,106,000
Capital: Bern
Religions: 46% Roman Catholic, 40% Protestant
Climate: Moderate climate that varies with the altitude. Winters are cloudy and rainy or snowy. Summers cool to warm, cloudy and humid with occasional showers.
Important gay cities: Basel, Genève, Zürich

✳ In 1992, the age of consent in Switzerland was set at 16 years of age. Sexual relations between persons under 16 are not punishable by law. (Male) prostitution is permitted. The scene in Switzerland is concentrated around 3 cities: Basel, Geneva and Zurich.

✪ Das Schutzalter liegt in der Schweiz seit 1992 bei 16 Jahren. Kontakte zwischen unter 16jährigen bleiben straffrei. (Männliche) Prostitution ist erlaubt. Die Szene der Schweiz konzentriert sich auf die drei Großstädte Basel, Genf und Zürich.

✳ L'homosexualité entre personnes adultes n'est pas un délit en Suisse. Depuis 1992, la majorité sexuelle y est fixée à 16 ans. La prostitution masculine est tolérée. Bâle, Genève et Zurich sont les principales villes gaies du pays.

⬡ Desde 1992 la edad de consentimiento es de 16 años. Relaciones sexuales entre menores de 16 años permanecen libres de pena. La prostitución masculina está permitida. El ambiente gay en Suiza se concentra en las tres grandes ciudades del país: Basilea, Ginebra y Zurich.

✖ Dal 1992 in Svizzera i giovani sono sessualmente maggiorenni a 16 anni. I rapporti tra minori di 16 anni non vengono puniti. La prostituzione maschile è legale. L'ambiente gay in Svizzera è concentrato nelle 3 maggiori città: Zurigo, Ginevra e Basilea.

NATIONAL GAY INFO

■ **Chaps Club** (G LJ)
Case Postale 67 ✉ 1000 Lausanne 20
☎ (078) 619 69 69
🖥 www.chaps.ch
News internet magazine for the army-leather-rubber scene in Europe.

■ **Pink Elephant, The** 1st Thu 21.20 h (UHF-Kanal 54)
c/o Dream Team Productions, Postfach 128 ✉ 8957 Spreitenbach
☎ (01) 850 50 20
Videos can be ordered by mail.

NATIONAL PUBLICATIONS

■ **A/K Anderschume/Kontiki - Das Schweizer Magazin für den schwulen Mann**
Postfach 7979 ✉ 8023 Zürich ☎ (01) 272 84 40
📠 (01) 272 84 40 🖥 www.planetgay.ch
Bimonthly Swiss-german magazine for gays. Interesting reports and comments about all topics regarding gay liberation and life style. Many book reviews, b/w art photographs. Commercial and classified ads. Text in German only. You can find additional English texts on the internet-homepage.

■ **Coming In**
C.P. 246 ✉ 1211 Genève 1 ☎ (022) 329 93 09
📧 info@swissgay.com 🖥 www.swissgay.ch
Free booklet on the gay scene in Switzerland.

■ **Cruiser/Cruiser KonAction**
c/o Zbiro GmbH, Postfach 2363 ✉ 8031 Zürich
☎ (0878) 88 18 88 📠 (01) 400 08 87 📧 info@cruiser.ch
🖥 www.cruiser.ch
Bimonthly gay newspaper (50 pages) with information about the Swiss-German gay scene. Reports, Party guide and more. CHF 7.50, free in gay establishments.

■ **Dialogai Infos**
C.P. 69 ✉ 1211 Genève 21
☎ (022) 906 40 40
📠 (022) 906 40 44
Bimonthly gay publication for the gay French speaking community of Switzerland. Free at gay venues.

■ **Kontakt**
c/o Belami Verlag AG, Postfach 8252 ✉ 8050 Zürich ☎
(01) 313 15 05 📠 (01) 311 44 75 📧 kontakt@belami.ch
Published every six weeks, approx. 100 pages, price Sfr 6, free in all gay establishments. Consists of classified and commercial ads, mostly from people offering friendship and/or sex.

■ **Play Mec**
Postfach 556 ✉ 3000 Bern 25
☎ (031) 302 11 33
📠 (031) 302 11 33
Gay magazine with free personal ads and city-guide in German and French/Schwules Magazin mit kostenlosen Kontaktanzeigen und Stadtführer.

Switzerland

■ **360°**
C.P. 2117 ✉ 1211 Genève 2 ☎ (022) 789 18 62
🖥 www.360.ch
The most important Swiss gay magazine in French. Good photos, interesting articles, funny and serious at the same time. Bimonthly. Available everywhere in Switzerland and at the border in France. Sfr 6.

NATIONAL HELPLINES

■ **Rainbow Line** 0-24, counselling Sun-Fri 19-21 h
☎ (0848) 80 50 80
Information on homosexuality, bisexuality, coming-out, young gays, authorities, groups, meeting points, parties, safer sex,...

NATIONAL PUBLISHERS

■ **Arcados Verlag**
Rheingasse 69, Postfach 4411 ✉ 4002 Basel ☎ (061) 681 31 32
Publishes books about Swiss gay history, literature, catalogues, etc.

■ **Belami Verlag**
Postfach 8252 ✉ 8050 Zürich ☎ (01) 313 15 05
🖨 (01) 311 44 75
Publisher of "Kontakt".

■ **Kaos Editions**
C.P. 246 ✉ 1211 Genève 4 ☎ (022) 329 93 09
Publisher of Swiss gay and lesbian guide "Coming in".

NATIONAL COMPANIES

■ **ELC-Verlag**
Postfach 493 ✉ 8280 Kreuzlingen
Gay video films.

■ **Euro-Business Services Inc.** (A CC G LJ) Mon-Fri 8-18 h
Schwaendi 63 ✉ 6170 Schüpfheim *(Bahnhofstraße Bar Russia)*
☎ (041) 485 70 87 🖨 (041) 485 70 85
Immigration Services, consulting, leather/latex goods, travel guides, Gay Hospitality Exchange and more. For info send a self-addressed envelope with two international reply-coupons.

■ **Gero-Schweiz Video Versand** (CC G VS)
Postfach 856 ✉ 8045 Zürich ☎ (01) 451 26 16 🖨 (01) 451 26 65
📧 info@gero.ch 🖥 www.gero.ch
Sale of videos, books and magazines.

■ **Ikarus Entertainment**
Postfach 50 ✉ 4153 Reinach 📧 ikarus@bluemail.ch
🖥 www.ikarus-entertainment.ch
Gay porno videos production company active in Switzerland and Europe.

■ **Kontiki Versand**
Postfach 14 ✉ 8501 Frauenfeld ☎ (052) 720 24 02
📧 mail-order@planetgay.ch
🖥 www.playnetgay.ch/versand
Sale of erotic male photo books, coming out books and videos. Catalogue on internet.

■ **Librairie du Centaure**
C.P. 44 ✉ 1211 Genève 19 ☎ (022) 733 98 33 🖨 (022) 733 98 33
📧 rolandjean@hotmail.com
🖥 www.gayromandie.ch/centaure
Mail order only gay bookshop.

■ **www.kink.ch** Internet shop for leather, all kind of fetish and piercing
📧 info@kink.ch 🖥 www.kink.ch
Internet shop for leather, all kind of fetish and piercing

NATIONAL GROUPS

■ **Aids-Hilfe Schweiz (AHS)** 8.30-12, 14-17 h
Konradstrasse 20 ✉ 8005 Zürich ☎ (01) 447 11 11 🖨 (01) 447 11 12 📧 aids@aids.ch 🖥 www.aids.ch
Prevention, information, and counselling for people with HIV/AIDS.

■ **Bartmänner Schweiz**
Postfach 7560 ✉ 8023 Zürich 📧 info@swissbears.ch
🖥 www.swissbears.ch
Group for hairy, bearded men and their admirers.

■ **COSMA - Coordination Suisse des Ministères Sida et Aids-pfarrämter**
c/o Aids-Pfarramt beider Basel, Peterskirchplatz 8 ✉ 4051 Basel
☎ (061) 262 06 66 🖨 (061) 261 07 69
Swiss coordination of the Aids/HIV+ people assistance religious groups.

■ **Lacets roses. Les** (G MA)
c/o Heinz Rubin, Mittelstraße 68 ✉ 3012 Bern ☎ (031) 302 21 04
Swiss-German walking and hiking group.

■ **Loge 70**
Postfach 725 ✉ 8025 Zürich 📧 loge70@gayleather.ch
🖥 www.gayleather.ch/loge70
Swiss leather group. Member of ECMC. Publisher of a Info-magazine on the leather scene in Switzerland.

■ **MediGay - Schwule und Lesben im Gesundheitswesen**
Postfach 8107 ✉ 3001 Bern 📧 medigay@bboxbbs.ch
🖥 www.bboxbbs.ch/home/medigay
Information network for gay- and lesbian-friendly doctors.

■ **Network - Verein für Schwule Führungskräfte**
Postfach 417 ✉ 8027 Zürich
Gay managers and CEOs.

■ **Organisation suisse des enseignants et éducateurs/trices homosexuels (OSEHH)**
C.P. 894 ✉ 1212 Grand-Lancy 1
Swiss gay teachers and educators organisation.

■ **Pink Cross. Schwulenbüro Schweiz**
Postfach 7512 ✉ 3001 Bern *(Zinggstraße 16)* ☎ (031) 372 33 00 (office hours) 🖨 (031) 372 33 17 📧 office@pinkcross
🖥 www.pinkcross.ch
The Swiss national gay organsation.

---

die schwule Schweiz.

www.planetgay.ch
www.e-gay.ch

Entdecke die schwule Schweiz: Bei planetgay.ch gibt's topaktuelle News, Adressen und Veranstaltungshinweise. Ausserdem findest du hier aK, das Schweizer Magazin für den schwulen Mann, und den Buch- und Videoversand e-gay.ch.

News · Reportagen · schöne Männer · Buchversand

Switzerland

Cruiser-KonAction – the newspaper for the Swiss Gay Community – with a large agenda of Switzerlands gigs and parties. Available at newsstands and for free in most bars and discos.

For further information contact: ZBIRO GmbH
Cruiser-KonAction
P.O.Box 2363
CH-8031 Zurich
e-Mail: info@cruiser.ch

www.cruiser.ch

Information and News for Gays in Switzerland ...

■ **Stiftung "Stonewall"**
Postfach 2115 ✉ 4001 Basel
📧 info@stonewall.ch
📧 www.stonewall.ch
Charity-group which supports gay-lesbian projects. Post-Account: PC 40-23202-2 Bank-Account: Basler Kantonalbank Konto: 59.785.90

■ **Swiss Gay and Lesbian Sports**
Postfach 2004 ✉ 8051 Zürich
National coordination of gay sport groups. Member of Federation of Gay Games/EGLSF.

■ **XLarge**
Postfach 6018
✉ 8023 Zürich
☎ (01) 994 17 83
Club for bears, bulls, chubbies and those who like them. Offers power and combative sports.

COUNTRY CRUISING

- N1 Winkeln ⇆ Feldli Reitbahn [P] Moosmüli
- N1 Richtung/direction Baden-Zürich, vor/in front of Zürich [P] Oberengstringen
- N1 Genève ⇆ Lausanne [P] between/zwischen "Morges" & "Aubonne"
- N12 (E27) [P] behind/nach "Matran"
- N14 Luzern ⇆ Zug, zwischen/between Emmen-Süd & Gisikon Root [P] St.Katharina
- N2 Chiasso ⇆ Basel [P] Lugano Sud/Nord (both sides)
- N2 Chiasso ⇆ Basel [P] Mendrisio (both sides)
- N2 Chiasso ⇆ Basel [P] Ceneri Sud/Nord (both sides)
- N20 Nordring Zürich, both sides/beidseitig [P] Büsisee
- N9 Brig ⇆ Lausanne, exit 1 km before Sion [P] in summer 17-24 h

www.escortboys.ch
Boys warten auf Dich
+41-79-478 26 03

988 SPARTACUS 2001/2002

Aarau ▶ Basel **Switzerland**

Aarau ☎ 062

GENERAL GROUPS
- **Aargay**
Postfach 11 ✉ 5616 ☎ (056) 667 35 74 📠 (056) 667 35 74
💻 info@aargay.ch 🌐 www.aargay.ch

HEALTH GROUPS
- **Aids-Hilfe Aarau** Mon 8-12, Wed 15-19 h
Entfelder Straße 17 ✉ 5000 ☎ 824 44 50

CRUISING
- Schulpark am Ententeich/park of the school by the duck lake
- Bahnhofsunterführung/subway at the railway station

Arbon ☎ 071

BARS
- **Sternen Bar** (B G)
St. Gallerstraße 32 ✉ 9320

Basel ☎ 061

GAY INFO
- **Pink Tube**
c/o Arcados Verlag, Rheingasse 67 ✉ 4058 ☎ 681 31 32
Weekly leaflet with informations and dates.

Switzerland — Basel

Club-Sauna
MAWI BASEL

St. Alban-Vorstadt 76
061/272 2354
tägl. offen ab 12 bis 23 h
www.gay-Sauna-mawi-basel.ch
e-mail: mawi@balcab.ch

EIN STUECK FERIEN IM ALLTAG

TOURIST INFO
■ **Basel Tourismus** Mon-Fri 8.30-18, Sat 10-16 h
Schifflände 5 ✉ 4001 ☎ 268 68 68 📠 268 68 70

BARS
■ **Dupf** (B f GLM MA OS) Sat-Thu 16-1, Fri -3 h
Rebgasse 43 ✉ 4058 *(Kleinbasel, right of river Rhine)* ☎ 692 00 11
■ **Elle et Lui** (B f Glm MA N OS) Mon-Sat 19-3 h
Rebgasse 39 ✉ 4058 *(right of river Rhine)* ☎ 692 54 79
■ **Zisch-Bar** (B GLM OS) Tue 19-1 h
Klybeckstraße 1b ✉ 4057
Im Foyer der Kulturwerkstatt-Kaserne.

CAFES
■ **Café Florian** (B BF f glm MA) Mon-Fri 6-19, Sat-Sun 8-18 h (brunch)
Totentanz 1 ✉ 4051 *(Tram11-Predigerkirche)* ☎ 261 57 54

DANCECLUBS
■ **Isola Club** (AC B D GLM MA s) Fri 21-2, Sat (G) 22-3 h
Gempenstraße 60 ✉ 4002 *(Gundeldingen, behind the railway station)* ☎ 361 91 07

SEX SHOPS/BLUE MOVIES
■ **Gerothek** (CC G MA) Mon-Fri 11.30-19.30, Sat 11-18 h, closed Sun
Holeestraße 15 ✉ 4054 *(Tram 2/bus 36/37-Zoo Dorenbach)* ☎ 421 48 88
Videos, toys, magazines, body wear and DVDs.
■ **Partout L'Amour** (A CC GLM LJ MA msg snu stv VS) 12-22 h
Dornacherstraße 63 ✉ 4053 *(Tram 16-Bahnhofunterführung)* ☎ 361 73 32

SAUNAS/BATHS
■ **Mawi** (B CC f G MA OS PI SA SB SOL VS) 12-23 h
St. Alban-Vorstadt 76 ✉ 4052 *(near River Rhine left site, Wettsteinbrücke, Grossbasel)* ☎ 272 23 54
Popular two floors sauna on 460 m². Reduced entrance fee after 19.30 h.
■ **Sauna Brunnhof** (f G msg OS SA SB) Mon-Sat 11-20.30 h, closed Sun
Brunngässlein 8 ✉ 4052 ☎ 271 10 81
■ **Sunnyday** (AC B CC DR F G MA msg p SA SB SOL VS WH WO) 12-23, Fri -5, Sat Sun & public holidays 14-23, in summer opens everyday at 16 h
Grenzacherstraße 62 ✉ 4058 *(near River Rhine, right side, Wettsteinbrücke, in the basement of the building with the supermarket Migros)* ☎ 683 44 00
Beautiful modern and clean sauna with a mixed, younger gay crowd & shop with books, postcards, calendars, pride articles, toys, videos, swim- and underwear.

BOOK SHOPS
■ **Arcados Buchladen** (CC GLM) Sep-Apr: Mon-Fri 12.30-19, Sat 11-16 h, Mai-August closed Mon
Rheingasse 67 ✉ 4058 *(Tram 6-Rheingasse/2-Wettsteinplatz)* ☎ 681 31 32
Videos and books. Mail order service.

HOTELS
■ **White Horse** (g H)
Webergasse 23 ✉ 4058 ☎ 691 57 57 📠 691 57 25

Basel ▶ Bern Switzerland

GENERAL GROUPS
■ **Homosexuelle Arbeitsgruppen Basel-Stadt (HABS)** Wed 20-22, Fri 17-20, Sat 14-18 h
Postfach 1519 ✉ 4001 ☏ 692 66 55 (helpline)
📧 info@habs.ch 💻 www.habs.ch

FETISH GROUPS
■ **Brutus Basel**
Lindenberg 23 ✉ 4058
Regular leather parties, visitors welcome.

HEALTH GROUPS
■ **Aids-Beratungsstelle Kantonshopital Basel**
Hebelstrasse 2 ✉ 4056 ☏ 265 24 31
■ **Aids-Hilfe beider Basel**
Clarastrasse 4 ✉ 4058 ☏ 692 21 22 📠 692 50 75
■ **Ökumenisches AIDS-Pfarramt beider Basel** Mon-Wed, Fri 9-12, Thu 14-17 h
Peterskirchplatz 8 ✉ 4051 (near University) ☏ 262 06 66
📠 261 07 69
📧 info@aidspfarramt.ch
💻 www.aidspfarramtbs.ch
Offer pastoral and spiritual assistance to people with HIV/Aids and their relatives and friends.

RELIGIOUS GROUPS
■ **Homosexuelle und Kirche (HuK)**
Postfach 1049 ✉ 4001

SPECIAL INTEREST GROUPS
■ **Rose. Die** (G YG) Mon 19.30-? h
Elsässerstr. 11 ✉ 4002 (between tram 11-Johannstor & tram 1/11-Voltaplatz) ☏ (0848) 80 50 80 📧 info@rose.ch 💻 www.rose.ch
Group for gay and bisexual youngsters. Counselling/Beratung Wed 20-22 h (telephone). See webside or call for further information.
■ **SLUG - Schwul-lesbische Unigruppe** 2nd Wed 19.30 h at Kaffi Schlappe, Klybeckstraße 1B
c/o Habs, Postfach 1519 ✉ 4001 ☏ 692 66 55
📠 692 66 55
📧 SLUG@ubaclu.unibas.ch
💻 www.unibas.ch/uni/dienste/gruppierungen

SPORT GROUPS
■ **Lesbian and Gay Sport Regio Basel** (GLM)
Postfach 467 ✉ 4021
Write for info on activities (from beach volleyball to swimming).

SWIMMING
-Northern shore of river Rhine (NU g) (between ferry station St. Alban and facility at the Solitude, Schaffhauserrheinweg)

CRUISING
-Barfüßerplatz (Underpass/Unterführung)
-Rheinweg (AYOR) (unter der mittleren Rheinbrücke an beiden Flußseiten an der Treppe/under the middle brigde on both sides of the river at the stairs)
-Wettsteinbrücke (AYOR r) (Nähe/near Park)
-SBB-station (near the French railways)
-Schützenmatt Park (AYOR) (Hinterseite des Bundesplatzes und Nähe der Straßenbahnhaltestelle/back part of Bundesplatz and near tram station)

Bellinzona ☏ 091

SAUNAS/BATHS
■ **Al Ponte** (AC B CC DR F G MA msg P p snu stv SA SB SOL TV VS WH WO) 12-1, Sun 14-24 h
Via Cantonale ✉ 6593 (5 min from railway station) ☏ 858 37 85
Big sauna with shows on Fri and Sat.

Bern ☏ 031

PUBLICATIONS
■ **Berner Gay Agenda**
c/o HAB, Postfach 312 ✉ 3000 ☏ 311 63 53
📧 redaktion.gayAgenda@bluemail.ch
Social, political and news magazine published 6/year for the region of Bern and Switzerland.

TOURIST INFO
■ **Offizielles Verkehrs- und Kongreßbüro Bern** Jun-Sep: 9-20.30, Oct-May: Mon-Sat 9-18.30, Sun 10-17 h
Bahnhof/Postfach ✉ 3001 (at the train station) ☏ 328 12 12
📠 312 12 33 📧 info-res@bernetourism.ch
💻 www.bernetourism.ch

BARS
■ **Comeback** (AC B CC f GLM MA s) Sun Mon 18-0.30, Tue-Thu -2, Fri Sat -3.30 h
Rathausgasse 42 ✉ 3011 (near Rathaus) ☏ 311 77 13
■ **Petits Fours** (B G YG) 17-0.30 h
67 Kramgasse ✉ 3011 ☏ 312 73 74
■ **Samurai. The** (B D GLM MA OS) 17-2.30, Fri-Sat -3.30 h
Aarbergergasse 35 ✉ 3011 ☏ 311 88 03

CAFES
■ **anderLand. Schwul-lesbisches Begegnungszentrum** (A B BF D F GLM s YG) Mon-Fri 14-18 h
Mühlenplatz 11 ✉ 3011 (centre, in Matte, 5th floor) ☏ 311 11 97
Email bhr@bluewin.ch.

DANCECLUBS
■ **House of Tolerdance - H.O.T** (B D GLM YG) 4th Sat 22-4 h
c/o ISC Club, 10 Neubrückstraße ✉ 3012 ☏ 302 52 36
■ **ISC Club** (B D glm) Thu 21-1, Fri Sat 22-0.30, Sun 21-? h
Neubrückstraße 10 ✉ 3012
■ **Klappe** (B D G YG) 4th Sun 18-24 h
c/o Comfort Bar, 6 Casinoplatz
Gay tea dance.

RESTAURANTS
■ **Amis. Les** (B F g MA OS) Mon-Thu 11-0.30, Fri -3, Sat 9-3 h, c losed Sun
Rathausgasse 63 ✉ 3011 ☏ 311 51 87
■ **Beaujolais. Le** (CC glm F OS) Mon-Fri 10-23.30 h, closed on WE
Aarberggasse 50/52 ✉ 3011 (2 min from Samurai-Bar)
☏ 311 48 86
French cuisine.

SEX SHOPS/BLUE MOVIES
■ **Loveland Videos** (CC g VS) 9.30-18.30, Thu -21, Sat -16, Sun closed
Gerechtigkeitsgasse 41 ✉ 30011 ☏ 311 45 33

Switzerland | Bern

František, Liebesbriefe, 99

LOVELAND XXX-STORE, MOVIE-RENT, MINI-CINEMAS
Gerechtigkeitsgasse 41, Parterre und Keller, Bern

SAUNAS/BATHS

■ **Al Peter's Sundeck** (! B CC F G MA OS SA SB SOL VS WH WO) 12-23 h
Länggassstraße 65 ✉ 3012 *(Entrance/Eingang Schreinerweg 14)*
☎ 302 46 86
One of the biggest and best gay baths in Switzerland. Biosauna and sundeck.

■ **Studio 43** (B G lj MA OS SA SB SOL VS WO) 14-23, last Sat -8 h
Monbijoustraße 123 ✉ 3007 *(Tram9-Wander)* ☎ 372 28 27
Popular sauna with bio-sauna and terrace in courtyard.

HOTELS

■ **Belle Epoque** (A B BF CC E f glm OS)
Gerechtigkeitsgasse 18 ✉ 3011 *(20 min from the station)*

☎ 311 43 36 📠 311 39 36 📧 info@belle-epoque.ch
💻 www.belle-epoque.ch
Hotel and bar with precious Art Nouveau decoration.

GENERAL GROUPS

■ **Homosexuelle Arbeitsgruppen Bern (hab)** (GLM MA) Mon-Fri 14-18 h
Mühlenplatz 11 ✉ 3000 ☎ 311 63 53 📠 311 63 53
📧 hab@gay-bern.ch 💻 www.gay-bern.ch
Gay and Lesbian organisation for the region of Bern. Publisher of the "Berner Gayagenda" and "hab-info". Call or check website for more info on activities.

■ **Jugendgruppe Coming Inn** 1st, 3rd Mon 19.30 h at anderLand
c/o HAB, Postfach 312 ✉ 3000 💻 www.datacomm.ch/cominginn
Gay youth group.

Fitness und Sauna — Monbijoustr. 123, 3007 Bern
Öffnungszeit: Jeden Tag ab 14.00 Uhr
Tram 9 (Wabern) Station Wander
Tel. 031 372 28 27

Inh.: Renate Meier

STUDIO 43

Bern ▶ Brig Switzerland

HEALTH GROUPS
■ **AIDS-Hilfe Bern/Aide Sida Berne** Mon Wed-Fri 9-12, 14-17 h, Tue 9-12 h
Monbijoustraße 32 ✉ 3001 ☎ 390 36 36 (German)
☎ 390 36 38 (French) 📠 390 36 37 ✉ mail@aidshilfe-bern.ch
🖥 www.aidshilfe-bern.ch
Prevention, information, and counselling for people with HIV/AIDS.
■ **Oekumenisches Netzwerk Kirche und Aids**
Postfach 5461 ✉ 3001 ☎ 385 17 17 📠 385 17 20
Offer pastoral and spiritual assistance to people with HIV/Aids and their relatives and friends.

RELIGIOUS GROUPS
■ **HuK - Homosexuelle und Kirche** Thu 19.30 at anderLand
Postfach 100 ✉ 3604

SPECIAL INTEREST GROUPS
■ **Schwule Berner Sänger SCHWUBS** Wed 19 h at Aula Seminar Marzili HMM, Brückenstraße 71
Gay choir.
■ **Schwul-lesbische Unigruppe (SCHLUB)** Brunch 3rd Sun 11 h at anderLand
c/o SUB, Lerchenweg 32 ✉ 3009

SPORT GROUPS
■ **Gay and Lesbian Sport Bern (GLSBE)** (GLM)
Postfach 254 ✉ 3000 ✉ glsbe@rainbow.ch
🖥 www.gay.ch/glsbe
Write or check website for info on activities.
■ **Rainbow Biker Bern/Gay Bikers** 1st Wed 19.30 h at anderLand
☎ 971 89 31
Call for info on activities.

CRUISING
-Allmend
-Rosengarten
-Grosse Schanzen-Promenade (!) (vor der Universität, Eingang Schanzenstrasse/in front of university, entrance in Schanzenstreet)
-Casinoplatz (R) (underpass/Unterführung)
-Metro Parkhaus Waisenplatz
-Waisenhausplatz (R) (underpass/Unterführung)

Biel/Bienne ☎ 032

CAFES
■ **Willi's Café** (B g MA) Sun-Thu 6.30-22.30, Fri Sat 6.30-0.30 h
Neumarktstraße 14 ✉ 2500 ☎ 322 42 44

RESTAURANTS
■ **Restaurant Seeland** (BF CC F g OS)
Bahnhofsplatz 7 ✉ 2502 ☎ 322 27 11
Café-restaurant.

SAUNAS/BATHS
■ **Mawi** (AC B DR F G MA p SA SB VS) 13.30-21 h
Bahnhofsplatz 11 ✉ 2502 *(4th floor)* ☎ 323 88 21
■ **Sun Beach** (CC DR f GLM MA msg p s SA SB SOL VS) Wed Thu 14-22, Sat 15-? h
Dufourpassage 12 ✉ 2502 *(Bus 4, opposite to shopping mall EPA, 3rd floor)* ☎ 323 23 63
Intimate atmosphere sauna with a mixed age crowd. Also open Tue Fri & Sun but for women and men.

CRUISING
-P SMH
-Centralplatz
-Marktplatz/market place

Boll-Sinneringen ☎ 031

RESTAURANTS
■ **Rössli/Thai-In** (CC F glm MA OS) Tue-Thu 8.30-23.30, Fri -0.30, Sat 9-0.30, 17-22 h
Bernstraße 32 ✉ 3067 ☎ 839 24 28
Thai and Swiss specialties.

Brig

CRUISING
-WC, railway station, platform 1

REFRESHINGLY DIFFERENT
AL PETER'S
SUN DECK
SAUNA- UND FITNESS-CLUB
Länggass-Str. 65, CH-3012 Bern, Tel. +41 (0)31 302 46 86
Entrance rear of the bldg., Bus no. 12, stop «Uni Tobler»
Open daily from noon to 11 p.m.   **Male only!**

Switzerland | Brunnen ▶ Fribourg/Freiburg

Brunnen ☎ 041

HOTELS

■ **Hôtel Bellevue au Lac** (BF CC F g H OS SOL) from Apr-Oct
Axenstrasse 2 ✉ 6440 *(direct at Vierwaldstättersee)* ☎ 820 13 18
🖨 820 38 89 💻 bellevue@email.ch 🖥 www.bellevue-brunnen.ch

Bulle ☎ 029

SEX SHOPS/BLUE MOVIES

■ **Planet X**
67 Grand Rue ✉ 1630

CRUISING

-Place du Marché

Chur ☎ 081

BARS

■ **Sonderbar** (B glm)
Im Palace, Masanserstrasse 14 ✉ 7000 ☎ 253 33 56

CAFES

■ **Café-Teria** (b f glm)
Poststraße 6 ✉ 7000 ☎ 252 82 47

GENERAL GROUPS

■ **Capricorn - schwul und lesbisch in Graubünden**
Postfach 380 ✉ 7002 💻 capricorn@freesurf.ch
🖥 www.spin.ch/homepages/Capricorn
Check homepage for details.

MAWI
CLUB-SAUNA BIEL-BIENNE

TÄGLICH GEÖFFNET AB 13.30 H
TOUS LES JOURS OUVERT DES 13.30 H
BAHNHOFPLATZ 11 11, PLACE DE LA GARE
LIFT 4. ETAGE 032 - 323 88 21

HEALTH GROUPS

■ **AIDS-Hilfe Graubünden**
Loestraße 8a ✉ 7002 ☎ 252 49 00

HELP WITH PROBLEMS

■ **Rosa Telefon** Tue 19-21 h
☎ 253 67 66

CRUISING

-Quader (Park)

Delémont ☎ 032

GENERAL GROUPS

■ **Juragai** (GLM)
C.P. 459 ✉ 2800 ☎ 422 65 58 ☎ 423 06 88

HEALTH GROUPS

■ **Groupe SIDA Jura** Mon & Wed 13-17 h
23 Faubourg des Capucins, C.P. 2201 ✉ 2800 ☎ 421 80 89
🖨 421 80 81

Engelberg ☎ 041

GUEST HOUSES

■ **Pension St. Jakob** (BF CC f g H WH)
Engelbergstraße 66 ✉ 6390 ☎ 637 13 88 ☎ (079) 232 31 31
(mobile) 🖨 637 15 11
Rates Sfr 36-75 incl. BF.

Frauenfeld ☎ 054

GENERAL GROUPS

■ **Homosexuelle Organisation Thurgau (HOT)** Tue 19.30-23 h at Vereinslokal
Postfach 355 ✉ 8501 ☎ (052) 233 41 55 🖨 (052) 233 41 55
💻 hot-tg@swissonline.ch
Meetings, sportgroup, choir. Call or see webside for more info.

Fribourg/Freiburg ☎ 026

PUBLICATIONS

■ **Gay News**
c/o Sarigay, C.P. 282 ✉ 1709

SEX SHOPS/BLUE MOVIES

■ **Exodus** (g)
33 Rue Pierre Aeby ✉ 1700
■ **Point X** (g LJ VS) Mon-Fri 10.30-19, Sat 10.30-16.30 h
27 Rue Pierre Aeby ✉ 1700 ☎ 322 51 21

SAUNAS/BATHS

■ **Maxim** (b f G MA SA SB SOL VS) Mon-Thu 14-21.30, Fri Sat 14-6, Sun 14-20 h
18 Grand-Places ✉ 1700 ☎ 322 72 25

GENERAL GROUPS

■ **Sarigai - Association Homosexuelle Mixte** Tue Fri 20-? h
33 Route des Neiges, C.P. 282 ✉ 1709 ☎ 481 67 89
🖨 481 67 89 🖥 www.sarigai.ch
E-mail sarigai@bluewin.ch

Fribourg/Freiburg ▶ Genève | **Switzerland**

HEALTH GROUPS

■ **Empreinte - Centre d'Information, d'animation et de soutien**
57 Boulevard de Pérolles ✉ 1700 ☎ 424 24 84
■ **Info SIDA** Mon-Fri 9-20 h
CP 181 ✉ 1709 ☎ 426 02 99

CRUISING

- Grand-Place
- Place du Comptoir

Genève 022

GAY INFO

■ **Dialogai - Association homosexuelle** (AC B f G lj MA) Tue-Fri 15-18, Wed -22, Sun (in winter) 11-15 h
11-13 Rue de la Navigation ✉ 1211 (Bus 1-Zürich/Bus 4-Navigation)
☎ 906 40 45 (information on activities) ☎ 906 40 40 (office)
📠 906 40 44 📧 dialogai@hivnet.ch ● www.hivnet.ch/dialogai
Organises many activities on a range that goes from leather to choir. Also health service. Parties every Sat (call for info). Publishers of a guide on the gay scene in the french-speaking part of Switzerland "Dialogai Infos".
■ **Espace 360** Sun 16-21 (GLM), Thu 19-22 h (TV)
Case postale 2217 ✉ 1211 ☎ 0878 878 360
Helpline for lesbians, gays, bi and transsexuals.

TOURIST INFO

■ **Office du tourisme de Genève** Mon-Sat 9-18 h
3 Rue du Mont-Blanc ✉ 1201 ☎ 909 70 00
FAX 788 81 70.

BARS

■ **Bretelle. La** (B GLM MA s) 17-2 h, Thu-Sat live music
17 rue des Etuves ✉ 1201 (Below Cornavin railway station)
☎ 732 75 96
■ **Chez Brigitte** (B D GLM MA)
12 Rue Prévost-Martin ✉ 1205 (Tram12/13-Pont d'Arve/Bus1/ 5-Hôpital) ☎ 320 50 44
The alternative bar of Geneva.
■ **Concorde. La** (B F G MA OS R) Mon-Fri 7-2, Sat 9-2, Sun 15-2 h
3 rue de Berne ✉ 1201 (Below Cornavin railway station)
☎ 731 96 80
■ **Excuse. L'** (AC B f g MG s) 4-2 h
11 rue des Etuves ✉ 1201 (below Cornavin railway station)
☎ 738 99 24
■ **Inside Bar** (B D DR G WE) Fri-Sat 23 h-till dawn
13 Rue de la Navigation ✉ 1201 (Bus 1-Zürich/Bus 4-Navigation)
☎ 906 40 47
Live DJs, free entry.
■ **Loft. Le** (! AC B BF CC D F GLM MA OS S) 5-2 h
20 Quai du Seujet ✉ 1201 (Tram13/Bus1-St.Gervais/Bus11-Seujet)
☎ 738 28 28
Popular disco-bar-restaurant. Transvestites shows at 22.45 h.
■ **Nathan** (B Glm MA OS) 15-2 h
6 rue Baudit ✉ 1201 (behind the Cornavin railway station)
☎ 733 78 76
■ **Oxford** (B glm) 9-2 h
Rue de Montbrillant 26 ✉ 1201 ☎ 734 08 88
■ **Phénix Bar** (B G) 16-2, Sun 18-2 h
6 Confédération Centre ✉ 1204 2nd floor ☎ 311 90 01

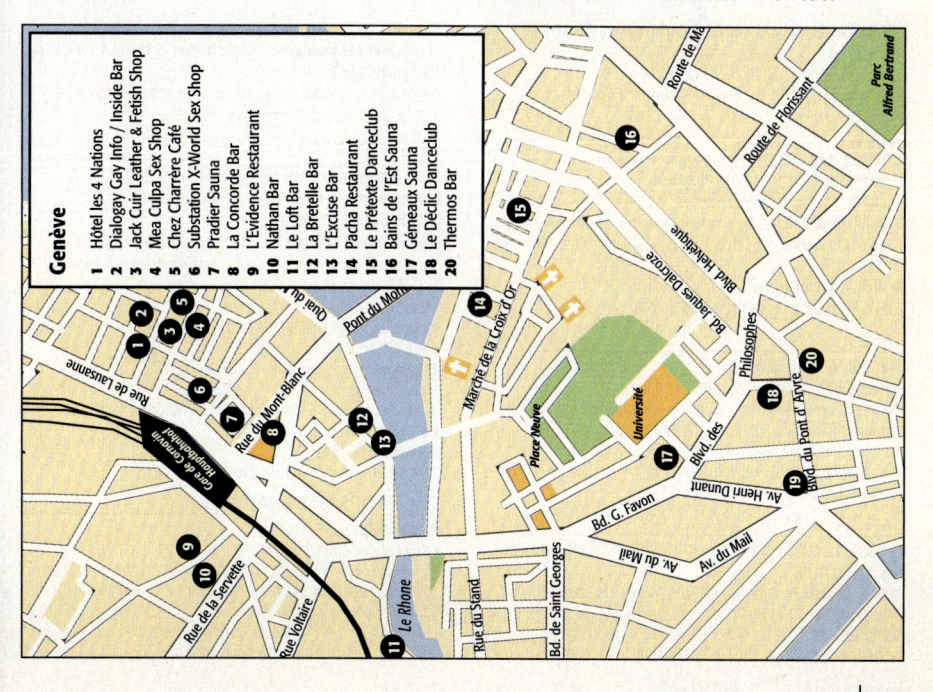

Genève
1 Hôtel les 4 Nations
2 Dialogai Gay Info / Inside Bar
3 Jack Cuir Leather & Fetish Shop
4 Mea Culpa Sex Shop
5 Chez Charrère Café
6 Substation X-World Sex Shop
7 Pradier Sauna
8 La Concorde Bar
9 L'Evidence Restaurant
10 Nathan Bar
11 Le Loft Bar
12 La Bretelle Bar
13 L'Excuse Bar
14 Pacha Restaurant
15 Le Prétexte Danceclub
16 Bains de l'Est Sauna
17 Gémeaux Sauna
18 Le Déclic Danceclub
20 Thermos Bar

Switzerland | Genève

SUBSTATION / X-WORLD

X-store | Vidéoclub
Cabines vidéo | Cruising area !
www.subinfo.com
022/900 14 69

Welcome to the hottest place in Geneva !

250 m² on 3 level !

Lundi > samedi
11:00 > minuit

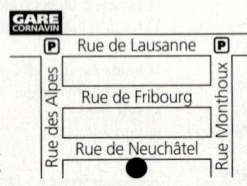

14, rue de Neuchâtel - Genève

■ **Terrasse d'Eté. La** (B CC f Glm MA OS) 17-1 h, Fri-Sat -2 h, summer only
9 rue Goetz-Monin ✉ 1205 ☎ 329 93 09
■ **Thermos** (B CC d DR G MA) Tue-Thu 19-2, Fri-Sat 21-2 h
10 Rue Goetz-Monin ✉ 1205 ☎ 320 72 65
Popular.
■ **Trappe. La** (AC B F g MA p) 4-2, Sat Sun 4-10 h
13 Rue Sismondi ✉ 1201 ☎ 732 87 98
Best when discos close, night-restaurant.
■ **Unplugged. The** (AC B f glm MG) Mon-Fri 17-2, Sat Sun 21-2 h
3 Rue de l'Université ✉ 1205 (Tram 12, 13-Rond-Point de Plainpalais)
☎ 329 82 98
■ **Walldorf' Café** (B glm)
Rue du Cendrier 10 ✉ 1201 ☎ 732 68 68

CAFES

■ **C. Dubois** (BF b glm)
Carrefour de Villereuse 4 ✉ 1207 ☎ 736 80 64
■ **Chez Charrère** (BF f glm) Wed-Sun 6.30-18.30 h
21 rue des Pâquis ✉ 1201 ☎ 731 87 12
Baroque style café popular with gays on Sun.
■ **Yves Quartier** (BF glm) Tue-Sun 7-19 h
24 Rue Voltaire ✉ 1201 ☎ 344 53 21

DANCECLUBS

■ **Déclic. Le** (AC B CC D GLM s VS YG) Mon-Fri 17-2 h, Sat 21-2 h, Sun closed
28 Boulevard du Pont d'Arve ✉ 1205 (Bus1/44-4/Tram12/13-Pont d'Arve) ☎ 320 59 14
■ **Prétexte. Le** (! AC B CC D dr GLM MA p s) 22-5 h
9-11 Rue du Prince ✉ 1204 ☎ 310 14 28

The most popular gay club of Geneva.
■ **Une nuit par mois avec... Angie Becker** (B D DR Glm tv vs) 1st Thu/month, 23-5 h
c/o Rêve d'O, Quai des Forces-Motrices ✉ 1205 ☎ 329 01 33
Popular gay night with the best local DJs.

RESTAURANTS

■ **Au Platane** (F glm OS) Mon-Fri 8-24, Sat 18.30-24 h
91 Boulevard de la Cluse ✉ 1205 ☎ 329 71 98
■ **Café Gallay** (CC F glm)
Boulevard Saint-George 42 ✉ 1205 ☎ 321 00 35
Popular café restaurant with a mixed crowd. Reservation advised on WE.
■ **Certitude. La** (B CC F GLM) Mon-Fri 7-2, Sat Sun 16-2 h
7 Rue Rossi ✉ 1201 ☎ 738 27 26
■ **Esquisse. L'** (B F glm) Mon-Fri 10-1, Sat 18-1 h
7 Rue du Lac ✉ 1201 ☎ 786 50 44
■ **Evidence. L'** (B glm MA) 6-1, Sat-Sun 11-1 h
13 Rue des Grottes ✉ 1201 ☎ 733 61 65
■ **Nid'Poule. Le** (B F glm) closed Sat Sun midday, Mon all day
Rue Adrien-Lachenal 26 ✉ 1207
■ **Pacha** (BF F glm)
22 Rue Neuve-du-Molard ✉ 1204 ☎ 312 08 88

SEX SHOPS/BLUE MOVIES

■ **Mea Culpa** (G VS) 10-24 h
8 Rue Charles-Cusin ✉ 1201 ☎ 783 01 73
■ **Substation X-World** (AC B CC DR G lj MA VS) Mon-Sat 11-24 h
14 Rue de Neuchâtel ✉ 1201 (5 min from the station)
☎ 900 14 69
250 m² sex-shop and videoclub on three floors, basement 100% gay with giant screen, cubicles and labyrinth.

SPARTACUS 2001/2002

Genève | Switzerland

SAUNAS/BATHS
■ **Avanchets. Les** (AC B cc DR f G MA msg SA SB SOL VS WH)
12-24, Fri -1, Sat -2 h
Avenue de Baptista, Avanchets-Parc ✉ 1220 *(5 min. from airport.*
Bus 10, 15, 23-Avanchets, near the shopping centre Balexert)
☎ 796 90 66
International meeting point near Geneva airport.

■ **Bains de l'Est** (! B BF CC DR f G msg SA SB SOL WH VS WO YG)
12-1, Fri-Sat -6, Sun 14-1 h, Tue Fri mixed
3 Rue de l'Est ✉ 1207 *(Tram12/Bus1/6/8-Terrassière)* ☎ 786 33 00
Very popular sauna frequented by a rather young crowd.

■ **Gémeaux** (b f G OG SA SOL) 11.30-22, Sat Sun 15-22 h
4bis Rue Prévost Martin ✉ 1205 *(Entry Rue des Sources)*
☎ 320 04 63
Popular with an older clientele.

■ **Pradier** (b G MG SA SB VS WH) 11.30-21 h, Sun 13-20 h
8 Rue Pradier ✉ 1201 *(Near Cornavin railway station)*
☎ 732 28 57
Popular with the more mature crowd.

LEATHER & FETISH SHOPS
■ **Jack Cuir** (g LJ) 10-19, Sat -17 h, closed Sun
40 Rue de Monthoux ✉ 1201 ☎ 731 89 15

NEWS STANDS
■ **Kiosk 3** (g) Mon-Fri 7.30-19, Sat 8-17 h
3 Rue des Pâquis ✉ 1201 ☎ 731 05 66
A good choice of gay magazines.

DATING AGENCIES
■ **Exception** (GLM) Mon-Fri 14-20 h
2 Rue de La Faucille ✉ 1201 ☎ 734 89 41

TRAVEL AND TRANSPORT
■ **Cameleon Travel** Mon-Fri 8-18 h
10b rue Emile Young ✉ 1205 *(near hospital)* ☎ 839 81 88
FAX 839 81 90. Email cameleontravel@hotmail.com

HOTELS
■ **Hôtel les 4 Nations** (H glm)
43 Rue de Zurich ✉ 1201 ☎ 732 02 24 🖨 731 21 41
■ **Hôtel Luserna** (BF CC g H)
12 Avenue de Luserna ✉ 1203 *(between the station and the airport)* ☎ 345 46 76 ☎ 345 45 45 🖨 344 49 36
📧 info@hotel-luserna.ch
📧 www.hotel-luserna.ch
Gays are welcome.

GENERAL GROUPS
■ **Pink Cross. Secrétariat Romand**
Case postale 49 ✉ 1211 ☎ 738 02 00
🖨 738 02 00
French speaking office of the gay political association.

HEALTH GROUPS
■ **Groupe Sida Genève (GSG)** 9-17 h
17 Rue Pierre-Fatio ✉ 1204 ☎ 700 15 00
Support association for HIV/AIDS people, call for more information.
■ **Hôpital Cantonal, Policlinique de Médecine** Mon Wed Fri
10-18, Sat 8-10 h
24 Rue Michel-du-Crest ✉ 1204 *(2nd floor)* ☎ 372 96 17
☎ 372 95 25
HIV testing.

NEW IN GENEVA

SAUNA „LES AVANCHETS"
ONE OF THE LARGEST GAY PLACES OF SWITZERLAND

BIG SAUNA - STEAM BATH - WHIRLPOOL
ICE POOL - CINEMA - SOLARIUM - 2 BARS
4 DARK-ROOMS LABYRINTH - GAY PRESS
VIDEO ROOMS - CRUISING AREA - AND MORE...

4 MINUTES FROM GENEVA AEROPORT
LES AVANCHETS (COLORS HOUSES).
AV DE BAPTISTA. NEXT FROM SHOPPING
CENTER „BALEXERT" TEL: 796.90.66

Switzerland   Genève ▶ Lausanne

■ **Ministère SIDA**
5 Place Jargonnant ✉ 1207 ☏ 736 24 26 736 70 10
Offer pastoral and spiritual assistance to people with HIV/Aids and their relatives and friends.
■ **PVA Genève**
35 Rue des Pâquis ✉ 1201 ☏ 906 40 30
HIV+ people group.

SWIMMING
-Bains des Pâquis (Strand/beach very popular in summer)

CRUISING
-Parc des Bastions (ayor)
-Perle du Lac (parc)
-Parc Geisendorf
-Parc Bertrand
-Rue du Mont-Blanc (AYOR)
-St.Gervais (AYOR)

Hergiswil am See ☏ 041

HOTELS
■ **Pilatusblick** (BF CC F glm MA NU OS PI WH)
Bergstraße ✉ 6052 *(Lake of Lucerne)* ☏ 630 11 61 630 00 65
✉ info@pilatusblick.ch ✉ www.pilatusblick.ch
Situated above the Lake of Lucerne, 20 minutes from the city of Lucerne with a spectacular view, this hotel offers quiet and comfortable rooms all with bath or shower/WC/radio/TV and minibar.

Hinwil ☏ 01

GENERAL GROUPS
■ **Klick - Schwulengruppe Zürcher Oberland and Oberer Zürichsee** (G MA)
Postfach 174 ✉ 8340 ☏ 938 04 08
Call or write for information on activities.

Interlaken ☏ 033

SAUNAS/BATHS
■ **Club Sauna Horn** (AC B G MA msg p VS) Mon 18-22, Sat 14-22 h (G)
Postfach 76, Harderstraße 35 ✉ 3800 ☏ 822 60 02

CRUISING
-Vor dem Hauptpostamt/in front of the main post office
-Bahnhof/railway station Interlaken West

Lausanne ☏ 021

BARS
■ **Art Zoo** (A AC B F glm MA OS) Mon-Thu 17-1, Fri Sat -2, Sun 14-1 h
27 Rue du Petit-Chêne ✉ 1003 *(In Les Galleries du Cinéma)*
☏ 340 05 12
■ **Fourmi Rouge. La** (B D F Glm MA) 17.30-1, Fri Sat -2 h, Mon closed
Chemin du Martinet 29 ✉ 1007 *(near Avenue Tivoli)* ☏ 625 78 80
■ **ML 16** (AC B CC DR F G MA OS) Mon-Thu 6.30-1, Fri Sat 16-2, Sun -1 h
16 Avenue Mon Loisir ✉ 1006 ☏ 616 32 98
Bar-restaurant.

■ **Saxo. Le** (B E F g) Tue-Sun 18-2 h
3 Rue de la Grotte ✉ 1003 ☏ 323 46 83

MEN'S CLUBS
■ **Cage Club - Sex Club for Uniform Men's** (AC B DR f G LJ NU P VS) Last Fri of the month 21-?
7 Avenue de Tivoli ✉ 1007 *(Entrance in the Pink Beach Sauna)*
☏ 311 06 05

DANCECLUBS
■ **Balcon. Le** (B D glm MA) Fri Sat 23.30-5 h
c/o D! Club, Rue Centrale ✉ 1003 ☏ 351 51 42
More gays on the first floor.
■ **Jungle Gay Party** (! A B CC D DR f GLM MA OS SNU) 22-5 h, only on public holidays
c/o MAD, 23 Rue de Genève ✉ 1003 ☏ 312 29 19
Very popular for ten years. A meeting point for all Swiss boys. Call or check website for exact dates.
■ **Trixx Gay Dance-Bar** (! B CC D GLM OS P YG) Sun 23-5 h
c/o Le Mad, 23 rue de Genève ✉ 1003 ☏ 311 29 18
Best world DJ's playing. Happy hour 2for1 from 23-24 h.

RESTAURANTS
■ **Ma Mère m'a dit...** (A AC B BF CC F GLM MA OS s VS) Mon-Fri 6.30-2, Sat-Sun 5.30-2 h
8 Avenue de Tivoli ✉ 1007 *(in front of Pink Beach Sauna)*
☏ 311 06 70
Bar/restaurant in the gay street of Lausanne.

SEX SHOPS/BLUE MOVIES
■ **Garage. Le** (AC B CC DR G LJ MA NU VS) 11-23 h
22b Avenue de Tivoli ✉ 1007 *(in front of Sauna Pink Beach)*
☏ 320 69 69

SAUNAS/BATHS
■ **New Relax Club** (b f glm OG OS SA SB SOL VS WH) Mon-Thu 12-24, Fri-Sun 12-5 h
Galerie St. François ✉ 1000 ☏ 312 66 78
■ **Pink Beach** (! AC B BF CC DR f G MA msg p SA SB SOL VS WH WO) Sun-Thu 12-23, Fri -2, Sat -8 h
7 Avenue de Tivoli ✉ 1007 *(5 min from railway station)*
☏ 311 06 05
Very popular sauna in centre of the town which is currently being renovated after a fire. Check website or call for re-opening date.
■ **Top Club** (! b f G MA msg SA SB SOL VS WH WO) 14-23, Sat -4 h
6 Rue Bellefontaine ✉ 1003 ☏ 312 23 66
Friendly sauna with a big whirlpool.

LEATHER & FETISH SHOPS
■ **Garage. Le** (CC G lj MA VS) Mon-Sat 10-19
22a Avenue de Tivoli ✉ 1007 ☏ 320 69 69

GUEST HOUSES
■ **Rainbow Inn** (CC G H MA VS)
22 Avenue de Tivoli ✉ 1007 ☏ 312 92 98 311 06 70
✉ pinkinfo@cyberlab.ch

GENERAL GROUPS
■ **Vogay** (B GLM MA)
13 Avenue des Oiseaux ✉ 1000 ☏ 646 25 35 646 29 29
✉ vogay@worldcom.ch ✉ www.vogay.ch
GLB association for the Vaud canton. Young group, HIV prevention, help with problem and bar every Sun evening. Call or check website for details.

Lausanne | Switzerland

THE GAY STREET AVENUE DE TIVOLI LAUSANNE

Lausanne, the cultural center of the French speaking part of Switzerland has everything to seduce you by day and by night !

Its privileged situation on the edge of Lake Geneva gives Lausanne an unique and irresistible charm.

Lausanne, the City you will enjoy... !

See you in Lausanne

PINK BEACH
PINK BEACH
The hottest & biggest Sauna in Switzerland
Avenue de Tivoli 9
☎ + 41 21 311 69 69

Grand Opening 2001

MA MÈRE M'A DIT
MA MÈRE M'A DIT
Ideal for fine dining or just having a drink
Avenue de Tivoli 8
☎ + 41 (0)21 312 69 69

LE GARAGE
LE GARAGE
X Shop, blue movies and cruising area
Avenue de Tivoli 22
☎ + 41 (0)21 320 69 69

CAGE CLUB
CAGE CLUB
The land of masters and slaves. No limits !
Avenue de Tivoli 3
☎ + 41 (0)78 619 69 69

RAINBOW INN
RAINBOW INN
The cosy guesthouse in the centre
Avenue de Tivoli 8
☎ + 41 (0)21 312 69 69

AROBASCITY
AROBASCITY
For hot Internet surfing & e-mailing
Avenue de Tivoli 3
☎ + 41 (0)21 351 59 69

www.avenuetivolilausanne.ch

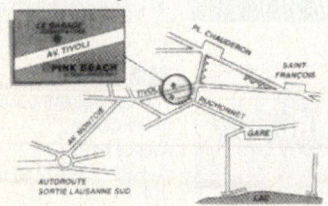

Switzerland   Lausanne ▸ Lugano

HEALTH GROUPS
■ **Ministère SIDA**
9 Pré-du-Marché ✉ 1004 ☎ 320 35 33 📠 320 35 35
Offers pastoral and spiritual assistance to people with HIV/Aids and their relatives and friends.

SWIMMING
-Beach (1 km from Morges reached through the forest)

CRUISING
-Parc du Denantou (Near/près Tour Haldimand)
-Promenade du Lac
-Parc de Montriond
-Passage souterrain Place St-François
-WC Theater Charles Monnard

Locarno ☎ 093

HOTELS
■ **Hôtel-Ristorante Piazza** (BF CC F g H OS)
Piazza Motta 29, 6612 Ascona ☎ (091) 791 11 81
📠 (091) 791 27 57 ✉ welcome@hotel-piazza-ascona.ch
🌐 www.hotel-piazza-ascona.ch

SWIMMING
-Delta della Maggia (G NU) (between Locarno and Ascona river Maggia, summer)

CRUISING
-Park near tennis court (Rright and left side of the road along the Lago Maggiore)
-Ponte Brolla Grotten (summer AYOR g NU) (2km out of Locarno in direction Centovalli-Valle Maggia, at Ponte Brolla in front of Maggia bridge to the right, path to the grotten)
-Forest between stadium and city center (21-24 h)
-Railway station
-Small park around Casinotheatre

Lugano ☎ 091

GAY INFO
■ **Centro informazione gay Ticino** 10-24 h
Via Stazio 8 ✉ 6900 *(Massagno)*
☎ 968 17 17
✉ spaziogay@ticino.com

MEN'S CLUBS
■ **R-Axxion** (B D DR G lj MG p s VS) Fri Sat 23-4 h, 1st & 3rd Sun/month afternoon party (entrance 15-16 h)
Via Cantonale ✉ 6915
☎ (079) 406 05 71
Tourists welcome. Temporary membership available.

SAUNAS/BATHS
■ **Gothic** (B CC DR F G MA p SA SB SOL VS) Mon-Thu 15-24, Fri Sat and before holidays -1, Sun 14-24 h
Via Tesserete 7 ✉ 6900 *(400 m from Lugano railway station, entrance Vicolo Vecchio 3)* ☎ 967 50 51
Very clean and popular sauna on three floors with original decoration.

Lugano ▶ Luzern **Switzerland**

GENERAL GROUPS
■ **Comunità Gay Svizzera di Lingua Italiana (CGSI)**
Fermoposta ✉ 6901 ☏ 53 35 00

HEALTH GROUPS
■ **Progetto MSM di Aiuto AIDS Svizzero** 10-24 h
Via Stazio 8 ✉ 6900 *(Massagno)* ☏ 23 17 17

CRUISING
-Piazza al Forte (P) behind PTT central post office)
-Campo Marzio (Lugano-Cassarate close to the Lido)
-Parco Civico/Ciani (behind Mövenpick, closed 22.30 h)
-Parco Tassino (behind Main railway station, closed 22.30 h)
-Parking UBS City
-Central station (platform 1)

Luzern ☏ 041

CULTURE
■ **Gemeinschaft Interesse für Theater (GIfT)**
Postfach 7304 ✉ 6000 📧 gift.luzern@gmx.ch
🌐 www.kreuz-und-queer.ch
Gay and lesbian theater group and choir.

BARS
■ **Bar-Capitol-Café** (B glm OS YG) Mon-Fri 16-0.30, Sat Sun 14-0.30 h
Zentralstrasse 45a ✉ 6003 ☏ 210 96 36
■ **Heaven** (AC B CC DR GLM MA) 17-? h
Burgerstrasse 21 ✉ 6002 *(in front of Parkhaus Kesselturm)*
☏ 210 41 43
■ **Schwul-lesbisches Zentrum Uferlos** (B D GLM MA WE)
Sat 22-4 h, 2nd Sat/month (L)
Geissensteinring 14 ✉ 6005 *(Bus 6-Hauptnahnhof)*
☏ 811 49 62
■ **Widder** (A AC B CC F GLM MA OS s) Tue-Sat 11.30-14, 17-0.30 h
Steinstrasse 2 ✉ 6004 ☏ 410 43 73
Bar-restaurant. Good Swiss and Austrian food.

SEX SHOPS/BLUE MOVIES
■ **Erotic-Shop** (CC g VS)
Bireggstrasse 20a ✉ 6003 ☏ 362 05 62
■ **Erotic-Shop** (CC g VS)
Kramgasse 3 ✉ 6004 *(in front of Spengler)* ☏ 410 60 62

SAUNAS/BATHS
■ **Discus** (! AC B DR f G MA SA SB SOL VS WO) Mon-Fri 13-23, Sat -2, Sun -22, 2nd Sat -6 h
Geissensteinring 26 ✉ 6002 *(Bus 4/5-Tiefe)*
☏ 360 88 77
Sauna on 400 m² which attracts a mixed age crowd. Tourists are welcome.
■ **Tropica** (f DR G MA p SA SB SOL VS) 14-23, Fri -6 h
Neuweg 4 ✉ 6003 *(7 min from train station)* ☏ 210 11 50
More than 20 years of activity. Attracts a mixed age crowd.

GENERAL GROUPS
■ **HALU** Helpline: Mon 19-21 h
Postfach 3112 ✉ 6002 ☏ 811 49 62 ☏ 0848 80 50 80 (helpline)
📠 811 49 31 📧 halu.sekr@bluewin.ch
🌐 www.gay.ch/halu

Switzerland | Luzern ▶ Monthey

DISCUS CLUB SAUNA

A Place even the Greeks would have loved !

Geissensteinring 26
6002 Luzern
Phone: +41 (41) 360 88 77
www.werbeecke.ch

Reductions for under 25!

Mon–Fri 13–23
Saturday 13–02
Sunday 13–22

Nightsauna 1st Satury every month:
open till 6 am

Sauna, Steambath, Fresh-Air Room, Bar, TV
Cabins with Video, Solarium, Shop and Gym

HEALTH GROUPS
■ **AIDS-Hilfe Luzern** Helpline: Mon 17-19 Wed 9.30-11.30 Thu 15-17 h
Wesemlinrain 20 ✉ 6006 ☎ 410 68 48

SPECIAL INTEREST GROUPS
■ **Why Not** (d G YG) meeting Thu 20 h at restaurant Engelsgruss, Engelgrussstraße 2
Postfach 2304 ✉ 6002 🖥 w.whynot@gmx.ch
🖥 www.gay.ch/whynot
Gay youth group.
■ **Zentralschweizer Schwulen-Motorrad-Club (ZSMC)**
Postfach 2231 ✉ 6002
Please write for information.

SWIMMING
-Öffentliches Bad am See/public baths at the lake (Strandbad mit Sonnenbaden auf dem Sonnendach/bathing enclosure with sun bathing area on the sun decks, Nähe/near Hauptbahnhof/central station & Hotel Palace)

CRUISING
-Haldenstrasse (seitlich des/by the side of Grand Hotel National)
-Inseli Promenade, Park Aufschütte am See (Nähe Badeanstalt/close to bath)

Monthey ☎ 024

SEX SHOPS/BLUE MOVIES
■ **Love-X-Video** (AC CC g) Mon-Fri 13-18.30, Sat 10-17 h
3b Rue de Venise ✉ 1870 ☎ 472 16 49

SAUNA TROPICA

Neuweg 4
LUZERN
041/210 11 50

jeden TAG offen

Freitag **Nachtsauna**
bis Samstag morgens

Oeffnungszeiten
Montag – Sonntag 14.00 – 23.00 h
Freitag – Samstag morgens

Montreux ▶ Solothurn | **Switzerland**

Montreux ☎ 021

BARS
■ **Il Baretto** (B CC f g MA OS) Tue-Sun 17-1 h
1 Rue du Marché ✉ 1820 ☎ 963 27 37

DANCECLUBS
■ **Back Stage** (B D glm) Tue-Sat 11-5 h
100 Grand Rue ✉ 1820

SWIMMING
-Villeneuve (NU) (at the end of the beach)

CRUISING
-Quai des fleurs (between Casino & Hotel Excelsior)
-[P] Bus stop "Bon-Port"
-Railway station (ticket office hall)

Morges ☎ 021

CAFES
■ **Metropolis Café** (B BF CC F glm MA) Mon-Thu 6.30-1, Fri Sat 6.30-2, Sun 9-1 h
20-22 Rue Louis-de-Savoie ✉ 1110 (near Geneva Lake)
☎ 803 23 33

Neuchâtel ☎ 032

GENERAL GROUPS
■ **Homologay** 2nd and last Thu of the month 20.30-23 h
C.P. 1719 ✉ 2002 (meeting at Rue Ph. Godet in Case à Chocs)
☎ (079) 292 66 94 ⌨ homologay@isuisse.com
⌨ homologay.isuisse.com
Call or check website for more information.

HEALTH GROUPS
■ **Groupe Sida Neuchâtel** Mon-Fri 8-11.30
6 Rue de Verger ✉ 2034 ☎ 737 73 37

CRUISING
-Jeunes Rives (path along the lake between university and harbour)
-Avenue de la Gare
-Place de la Poste (at harbour)

Olten ☎ 062

BARS
■ **Rainbow Bar** (B GLM MA) Wed-Sat 21.30-0.30 h
Rosengasse 1 ✉ 4600 (behind railway station, in the basement Restaurant Isebähnli) ☎ (076) 321 77 39

SEX SHOPS/BLUE MOVIES
■ **Menzone - Der Gay-Discounter** (b G MA) Thu-Fri 17-21, Sat 10-12, 13.30-17 h
Klarastraße 1 ✉ 4600 (Bus 1-Bifang) ☎ 296 56 53 (24 h)
Discount prices/used videos.

CRUISING
-Bahnunterführung, öffentliche WCs beim Ausgang zur Aare/railway underpass, public toilets near the exit for Aare

Samedan ☎ 081

APARTMENTS
■ **Chesa Macun Ferienwohnung** open Dec-Apr & Jul-Sep
✉ 7503 (near/nahe St. Moritz)
☎ 854 34 44 🖷 854 34 44
⌨ dediou@gmx.ch

Schaffhausen ☎ 052

HEALTH GROUPS
■ **AIDS-Hilfe Thurgau/Schaffhausen**
Rathausbogen 15 ✉ 8200 ☎ (053) 25 93 38
■ **Les Homos**
Postfach 3176 ✉ 8201
☎ 624 68 60

CRUISING
-Bahnhof/Main Station
-Kiosk & Toiletten Bahnhofsunterführung/Toilets at the station

Sion ☎ 027

GENERAL GROUPS
■ **Alpagai** Thu, 2nd & 4th Fri 20-23, Hotline Sun 19-22 h
Route de Loèche 41 ✉ 1950 ☎ 322 10 11
Homosexual association (gay and lesbian). Information, counselling, bar, library.

HEALTH GROUPS
■ **Antenne SIDA du Valais Romand**
14 Rue de Condémines ✉ 1951 ☎ 322 81 85 🖷 322.99.73
⌨ antenne.sida@vsnet.ch ⌨ www.antenne.sida.vsnet.ch
Counselling, information for people with HIV/Aids and their families.

CRUISING
-Gardens near Banque Cantonale du Valais
-Near Église St. Guérin.
-WC in public garden (rue du Chanoine-Berchtold behind the bank, evenings)
-WC/in underground [P] of Planta (rue de Lausanne, afternoons)
-Tourist office (under the office)

Solothurn ☎ 065

BARS
■ **Bigoudi** (B g MA) Tue-Sat 17-0.30 h, closed Sun Mon
Kronengasse 10 ✉ 4500 (underneath/unterhalb Barockkirche)
☎ 622 25 29

GENERAL GROUPS
■ **Sogay** (b G MA p) Mon 20-? h
Oberer Winkel 2 ✉ 4502

HEALTH GROUPS
■ **Aids-Hilfe Solothurn**
Postfach 155 ✉ 4502 ☎ 622 94 11

Switzerland St. Gallen ▸ Yverdon

St. Gallen ☏ 071

BARS
■ **Club Seventy-seven** (B CC F G MA OS) 16-? h
Linsenbühlstaße 96 ✉ 9003 *(Bus 1-Neudorf)* ☏ 222 72 22
■ **Felice** (B glm OS S)
Rickenstraße 2 ✉ 9014 ☏ 277 34 18
■ **Peppermint-Bar** (B CC d G YG) Mon-Sun 18-1 h
St. Jakobstraße 103 ✉ 9000 *(Bus 3-Olma)* ☏ 245 24 98

DANCECLUBS
■ **Ozon** (AC B CC D G) Sun 21-3 h
Goliathgasse 28 ✉ 9000 ☏ 244 81 24
Gay Tea Dance on Sundays: Peppermint goes Ozon.

RESTAURANTS
■ **Obelisco** (CC F glm) Mon closed
Bahnhofstraße 23 ✉ 9100 *(10 min from St. Gall)* ☏ 351 57 57
Japanese restaurant.
■ **Restaurant Gutenberg** (CC F g) Tue Wed closed
Hagenbuchstraße 28 ✉ 9000 *(Kinderspital)* ☏ 245 66 66

SAUNAS/BATHS
■ **Augustinergasse** (b DR G SA SB SOL VS) Mon-Fri 11.30-22, Sat-Sun 10-22 h, Tue-Thu (glm)
Augustinergasse 19 ✉ 9000 *(near main station and Marktplatz)* ☏ 230 14 85
■ **Olympic** (B g SA) Mon-Sat 14-22 h, closed Sun
Torstraße 17 ✉ 9004 *(near Parkhaus Brühltor)* ☏ 245 44 24

HEALTH GROUPS
■ **AIDS-Hilfe St. Gallen** Mon-Thu 9-12 h
Postfach 8 ✉ 9001 *(Tellstraße 4)* ☏ 223 38 68
🖳 ahsga@hivnet.ch 🖳 www.hivnet.ch/ahsga

SPECIAL INTEREST GROUPS
■ **Bären Club** (G N)
Postfach 255 ✉ 9001 🖳 baerenclub@bluewin.ch
🖳 mypage.bluewin.ch/baerenclub
Write or check website for info on activities.

CRUISING
-Bahnhof/railway station
-municipal park/Stadtpark *(Nähe/near Theater)*

St. Moritz ☏ 081

BARS
■ **Graffiti Bar** (AC B CC f G MA p) 19-2 h
Plazza dal Mulin 2 ✉ 7500 ☏ 361 88
Open/Geöffnet Summer 01.07.-31.08. Winter 01.12.-15.04.

Thun ☏ 033

RELIGIOUS GROUPS
■ **Homosexuelle und Kirche Schweiz**
Postfach 100 ✉ 3604
Publication/Vereinszeitung: Schildkrott.

CRUISING
-Bahnhof/railway station
-Aare Promenade
-Park Thunerhof

Uster ☏ 01

BARS
■ **Uschteria 77** (B CC D g MA N) Tue -0.30 h
Zürichstraße 1 ✉ 8610 *(in shopping-centre/im Einkaufszentrum)*
☏ 940 70 44

CRUISING
-Municipal park/Stadtpark
-Quay/Schiffanlegestelle Niederuster
-Lido/Strandbad Uster am Greifensee

Vevey ☏ 021

HEALTH GROUPS
■ **Sid'Action Vevey**
10 Rue Tillents ✉ 1800 *(3rd floor)* ☏ 923 91 91

CRUISING
-Place du Marché
-Bois d'Amour
-Passage souterrain Placette

Visp ☏ 027

HEALTH GROUPS
■ **Aids-Hilfe Oberwallis**
St. Martiniplatz 1 ✉ 3930 ☏ 346 46 68

Winterthur ☏ 052

GAY INFO
■ **Derwisch** (b f GLM) Sat 18-24 h
Badgasse 8 ✉ 8400 ☏ 213 81 88

GENERAL GROUPS
■ **WISCH - Winterthurer Schwule** (G)
Postfach 294 ✉ 8401 ☏ 213 81 88
Call for info on activities.

HEALTH GROUPS
■ **Aids Infostelle Winterthur**
c/o Haus zur Einsamkeit, Lagerhausstraße 5 ✉ 8401 *(2nd floor)*
☏ 212 81 41
FAX 212 80 95

CRUISING
-Stadtpark/municipal park (19-22 h)

Yverdon ☏ 024

CRUISING
-Ⓟ in front of railway station
-Plage d'Yvonnard (3 km direction Estavayer-le-Lac)

Zürich | Switzerland

saunaguide
& gay bathhouses international

BRUNO GMÜNDER

Sauna Guide & Gay Bathhouses International
252 Seiten/Pages, English / Deutsch / Français, ISBN 3-86187-155-6
DM 26,80 / Sfr 26,- /Ös 196,-
Erhältlich im Buchhandel oder bei www.brunos.de

Switzerland — Zürich

Zürich 01

Zurich is the financial metropolis of Europe. There has developed over the past few years in the older part of the city a small gay scene with bars, cafés and hotels reflecting the charm and comfort of Switzerland. Zurich has many gay saunas offering friendliness and warmth. The old proverb about Swiss cleanliness shows it's self from it's best side in the playful cruising areas of the saunas.

Die etwas verträumte Bankenmetropole Europas hat auch dem schwulen Touristen Einiges zu bieten. In den letzten Jahren hat sich in der Altstadt eine kleine Szene entwickelt. Hier findet man Bars, Cafes und Hotels, die den Charme und die Gemütlichkeit der Schweiz widerspiegeln. Zürich hat zudem besonders viele Saunaclubs zu bieten. Ein Besuch lohnt immer, da neben besonderer Freundlichkeit auch angenehm große und freundlich gehaltene Naß- und Schwitzbereiche angeboten werden. Zum großen Teil bieten die Saunen verspielte Cruising- und Entspannungsmöglichkeiten, und die schon sprichwörtliche Schweizer Sauberkeit zeigt sich von der allerbesten Seite.

Cette métropole banquière quelque peu rêveuse a aussi de quoi satisfaire le touriste gai. Au cours des dernières années, un petit quartier gai s'est crée au coeur de la vieille ville. On y trouve des bars, des cafés et des hôtels, qui reflètent le charme et le comfort de la Suisse. Zürich a par ailleurs de nombreuses saunas. Une visite vaut la peine, car en plus de la sympathie du personnel on trouve plusieurs grands espaces bien aménagés et la renommée de la propreté suisse montre ici son côté le plus plaisant.

La metrópoli bancaria europea algo dormida, pero romántica también tiene mucho que ofrecer al turista gay. En los últimos años se desarrolló un pequeño ambiente gay en la ciudad vieja de Zúrich donde el visitante encuentra bares, cafés y hoteles que reflejan el encanto y la atmósfera de Suiza. La ciudad además tiene muchos sauna-clubs, y visitarlos siempre merece la pena, ya que aparte de la extrema amabilidad también se goza de piscinas y saunas grandes y de un diseño interior muy agradable. La mayoría de las saunas ofrecen posibilidades de cruising y zonas de relax muy diversas, y en estos establecimientos, la ya famosa limpieza suiza puede convencer a cualquier visitante.

Nella alquanto romantica metropoli bancaria di Zurigo, il turista gay vi trova abbastanza possibilità per divertirsi. Negli ultimi anni nel centro storico si è creato un piccolo ambiente gay. Qui si trovano dei bar, caffé ed alberghi, che danno una buona immagine dell'attrattività e dell'intimità della Svizzera. Vale la pena andare in una delle numerose saune, perché oltre alla gentilezza del personale offrono ampi e piacevoli spazi per impianti sanitari e saune. Molte saune dispongono di aree carine per il cruising e per il riposo, e la proverbiale pulizia degli Svizzeri mostra qui il meglio di sé.

GAY INFO

Homosexuelle Arbeitsgruppen Zürich (HAZ) (GLM MA)
Mon-Fri 19.30-23 h
Sihlquai 57, Postfach 7088 ✉ 8005 *(near central station)*
☏ 271 22 50   📠 271 22 50   ✉ haz.ch@haz.ch   🖥 www.haz.ch
Meeting point, library, counselling.

CULTURE

Schwulenarchiv Schweiz
Postfach 6311 ✉ 8023   ✉ beat-und-peter@bluewin.ch
Swiss gay archives.

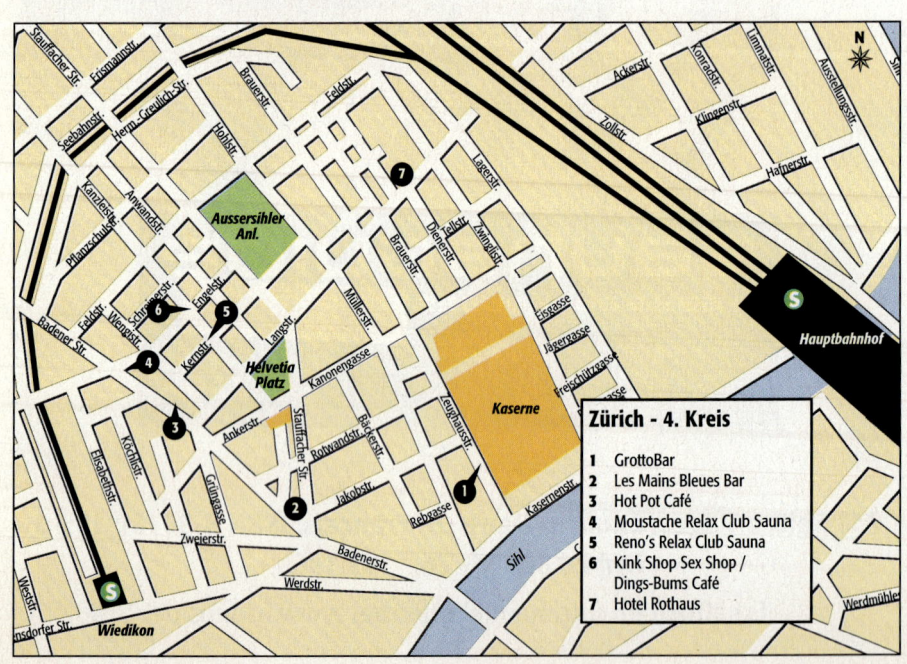

Zürich - 4. Kreis

1. GrottoBar
2. Les Mains Bleues Bar
3. Hot Pot Café
4. Moustache Relax Club Sauna
5. Reno's Relax Club Sauna
6. Kink Shop Sex Shop / Dings-Bums Café
7. Hotel Rothaus

Zürich Switzerland

① INTERcomestibles
Brauerstrasse 87
Getränkelieferungen:
Tel. 01-291 46 15
Laden:
Tel. 01-242 75 65

② Reno's Relax-Club
(gay only)
Kernstrasse 57
Tel. 01-291 63 62

③ Andy's Tierhüüsli
am Helvetiaplatz
Molkenstrasse 17
Tel. 01-240 33 20

④ Kutscherhalle
gutbürgerliches
Speise-Restaurant
Müllerstrasse 31
Tel. 01-241 53 15

⑤ kink shop & body
Fetisch-Shop/Piercing
Engelstrasse 62 a
Tel. 01-241 32 15 (shop)
Tel. 01-241 32 30 (body)

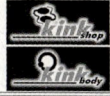

⑦ Blumen
Zamboni + Bachmann
Dienerstrasse 72
Tel. 01-241 48 45

⑧ Daniel H.
fine food & catering
Müllerstrasse 51
Tel. 01-241 41 78

⑨ dings-bums
books, media, gifts,
coffee-bar
Engelstrasse 62 c
Tel. 01-241 32 31

⑩ Paracelsus
Apotheke & Drogerie
Langstrasse 122
Tel. 01-240 24 05

⑪ Wengihof
Apotheke & Drogerie
Kernstrasse 8
Tel. 01-240 23 33

GAY-Life im Chreis 4 Zürich

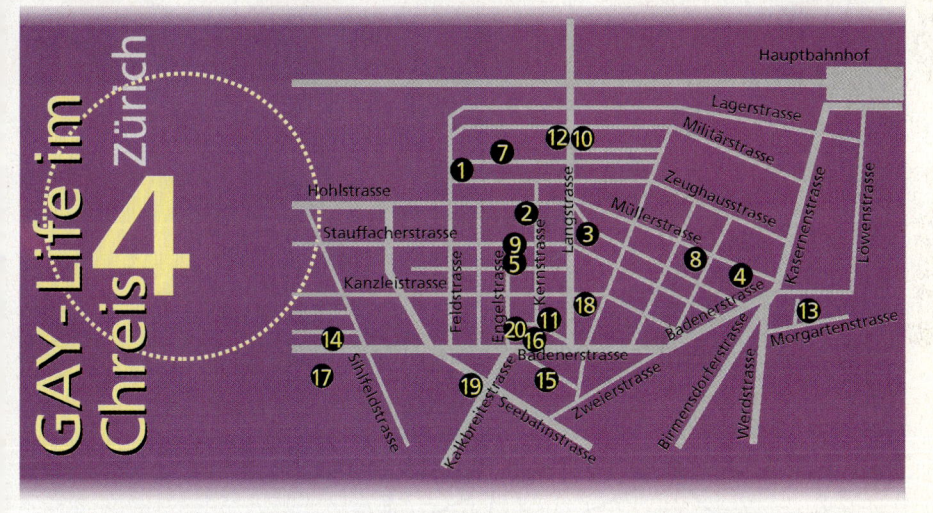

⑫ Hotel Rothaus
Sihlhallenstrasse 1
Ecke Langstrasse
Tel. 01-241 24 51

⑬ Kosmos
Schmuckschmiede
Werdgässchen 25
Tel. 01-242 41 21

⑭ Erotic Factory
Badenerstrasse 254
Tel. 01-241 11 61

⑮ Body-Care für Sie + Er
Rücken-Therapien
Massagen
Köchlistrasse 25
Tel. 01-242 41 57

⑯ Hot Pot Café, Bistro
Badenerstrasse 138
Tel. 01-241 11 18

⑰ The Hairdresser
Zentralstrasse 138
Tel. 01-462 72 21

⑱ Body Electric,
Werner B.
Massagen für Männer
Einzel und Kurse
Kanzleistrasse 63
Tel. 01-242 77 74

⑲ Sauna Mylord
Seebahnstrasse 139
Tel. 01-462 44 66

⑳ Moustache Relaxclub
(gay only)
Badenerstrasse 156/
Eingang Engelstrasse 4
Tel. 01-241 10 80

KICK Institut für Coaching und Kommunikation
Postfach
8021 Zürich
Tel. 01-291 61 60
Fax 01-291 61 61

www.chreis4.ch
powered by:
InternetService
Tel. 01-310 26 26

Switzerland | Zürich

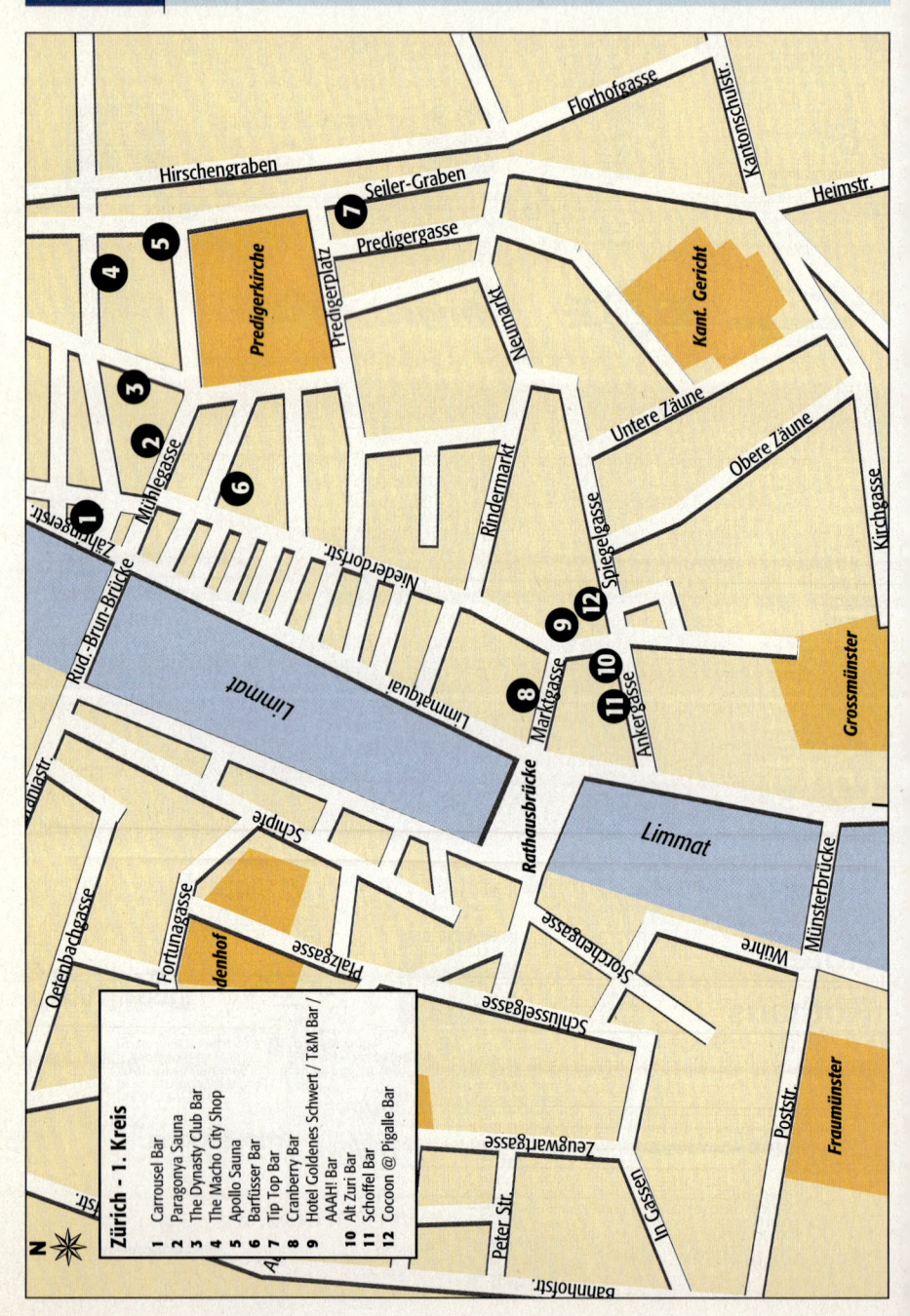

Zürich - 1. Kreis

1. Carrousel Bar
2. Paragonya Sauna
3. The Dynasty Club Bar
4. The Macho City Shop
5. Apollo Sauna
6. Barfüsser Bar
7. Tip Top Bar
8. Cranberry Bar
9. Hotel Goldenes Schwert / T&M Bar / AAAH! Bar
10. Alt Zuri Bar
11. Schoffel Bar
12. Cocoon @ Pigalle Bar

Zürich | Switzerland

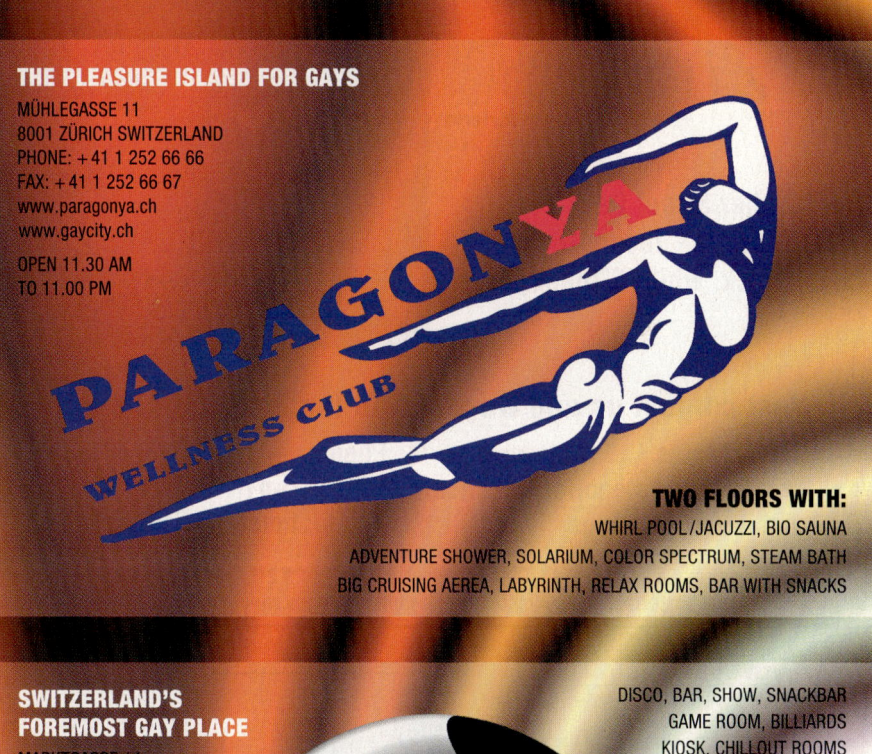

THE PLEASURE ISLAND FOR GAYS

MÜHLEGASSE 11
8001 ZÜRICH SWITZERLAND
PHONE: +41 1 252 66 66
FAX: +41 1 252 66 67
www.paragonya.ch
www.gaycity.ch

OPEN 11.30 AM
TO 11.00 PM

PARAGONYA WELLNESS CLUB

TWO FLOORS WITH:
WHIRL POOL/JACUZZI, BIO SAUNA
ADVENTURE SHOWER, SOLARIUM, COLOR SPECTRUM, STEAM BATH
BIG CRUISING AEREA, LABYRINTH, RELAX ROOMS, BAR WITH SNACKS

SWITZERLAND'S FOREMOST GAY PLACE

MARKTGASSE 14
8001 ZÜRICH SWITZERLAND
PHONE: +41 1 266 18 89
FAX: +41 1 266 18 88
www.gaybar.ch
www.gaycity.ch

OPEN 9 PM
TILL LATE

DISCO, BAR, SHOW, SNACKBAR
GAME ROOM, BILLIARDS
KIOSK, CHILLOUT ROOMS
GOGO DANCER, TV ROOM
ROOMS FOR RENT, TOILET
WITH SHOWER & BATH
CRUISING AEREA ETC.

T&M
The foremost gay place

© A MEMBER OF MEKDAENG'S

| Switzerland | Zürich |

zürich
downtown switzerland

Christopher Street Day
Street Parade - Techno-Event
Many black, white & foam parties

Just contact us and we will find the ideal hotel for you!

- special rates
- hotels of all categories in Zürich and its surroundings

Phone +41 1 215 40 40
Fax +41 1 215 40 44
E-mail: hotel@zurichtourism.ch

Zürich Tourism, Bahnhofbrücke 1, CH-8023 Zürich • Phone +41 1 215 40 00 • Fax +41 1 215 40 99
E-mail: information@zurichtourism.ch • Internet: www.zurichtourism.ch

TOURIST INFO

■ **Zürich Tourismus** summer: 8.30-20.30, Fri-Sun -18.30, winter 8.30-19, Fri-Sun 9-18.30 h
Bahnhofbrücke 1 ✉ 8023 *(main railway station, centre)*
☎ 215 40 00 📠 215 40 44 💻 information@zurichtourism.ch
🌐 www.zurichtourism.ch
Hotel information and reservation: hotel@zurichtourism.ch

BARS

■ **AAAH!** (A AC B CC D DR F G LJ VS YG) 14-4 h
Marktgasse 14-16 ✉ 8001 *(Tram 4/15-Rathaus)* ☎ 266 18 89
Every Sun club parties with house music and techno at 17 h.

■ **Angels** (AC B G MA OS)
Kurzgasse 4 ✉ 8004 *(near Helvetiaplatz)* ☎ 240 58 76

■ **Bar im Restaurant** (B f glm MA OS s) Mon-Fri 17-24.30, Sat 18-24.30, closed Sun
Lägernstrasse 37 ✉ 8037 ☎ 367 07 07

■ **Barfüsser** (AC B CC F G lj MA OS r s) 14-0.30 h
Spitalgasse 14 ✉ 8001 ☎ 251 40 64
Switzerlands' longest existing gay bar and restaurant.

■ **Carrousel** (AC B CC F G MA OS R) Sun-Thu 16-2, Fri Sat -4 h, Zähringerstraße 33 ✉ 8001 ☎ 253 62 02
Warm meals til 02 and WE 'til 03:30h/ Warme Küche bis 02:00, WE bis 03:30h.

■ **Cocoon @ Pigalle** (AC B f GLM) 17.30-? h
Marktgasse 14 ✉ 8001 ☎ 266 18 77
BARstelle im Pigalle opening in March 2001.

■ **Cranberry - The Juice & Booze Bar** (AC B CC GLM MA OS) Sun-Tue 17-24.30, Wed Thu -1, Fri Sat -2 h, Wed (YG)
Metzgerstraße 3 ✉ 8001 *(Tram 4/15-Rathaus)* ☎ 261 27 72
Very popular American cocktail bar.

CARROUSEL BAR-CLUB

Spring' über Deinen Schatten
und sei Du selbst.

Zähringerstrasse 33 . 8001 Zürich

ZURICHS PLACES
gaycity.ch

Zürich | Switzerland

THE DYNASTY CLUB Zähringerstrasse 11, www.dynastyclub.ch
CARROUSEL BAR-CLUB Zähringerstrasse 33, www.johanniter.com
APOLLO SAUNA Seilergraben 41
LEONHARDS APOTHEKE Stampfenbachstrasse 7
MACHO CITY SHOP Häringstrasse 16, www.macho.ch
CRANBERRY BAR Metzgergasse 3, www.cranberry.ch
TGM BAR DISCO Marktgasse 14, www.gaybar.ch
HOTEL GOLDENES SCHWERT Marktgasse 14, Tel. 0041-01-266 18 18
PARAGONYA WELLNESS CLUB Mühlegasse 11, www.paragonya.ch
AAAH! Marktgasse 14-16, www.aaah.ch
SCHOFFEL schoffelgasse 7, 8001 zürich, www.schoffel.ch
BARFÜSSER BAR RESTAURANT Spitalgasse 14, www.barfuesser.ch
TIP TOP BAR Seilergraben 13, www.swiy.ch/tiptop
ALT ZÜRI Schoffelgasse 11 & Ankergasse 6
COCOON @ PIGALLE Marktgasse 14, www.coon.ch

STRICTLY GAY
STRAIGHT & GAY, GAYFRIENDLY

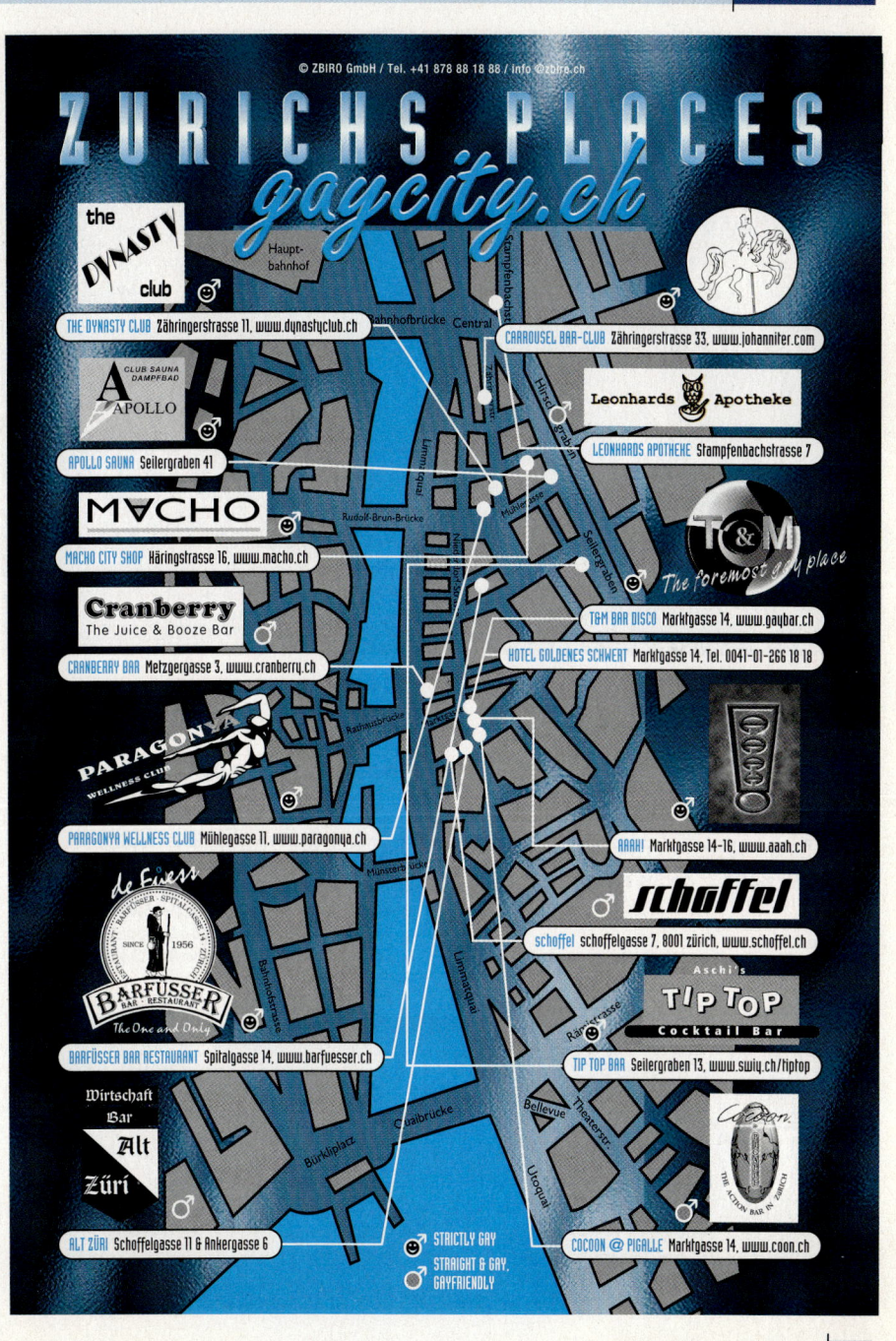

SPARTACUS 2001/2002 | 1011

Switzerland | Zürich

LABYRINTH CLUB

FOR GAYS • MEMBERS • FRIENDS

EVERY FRIDAY AND SATURDAY
FROM 23.00 – TILL LATE
HOUSE
– PROGRESSIVE
– TRANCE
3 BARS – DARKROOM –
CHILL-OUT –
OUT-DOOR-AREA

LABYRINTH CLUB - PFINGSTWEIDSTRASSE 70 - 8005 ZÜRICH
PHONE 0041 1 440 59 80
WWW.LABY.CH – MAIL. INFO@LABY.CH

■ **Dynasty Club.The** (AC B CC G f MA OS r) 16-2 h
Zähringerstraße 11 ✉ 8001 *(near central station)* ☎ 251 47 56
■ **Grotto Trübli Bar** (B CC F glm OG OS) 14-24 h
Zeughausstraße 67 ✉ 8004 ☎ 242 87 97
Also restaurant.
■ **Kafi Schoffel** (B BF F glm MA OS) 9-24, Sun 10-22 h
Schoffelgasse 7 ✉ 8001 *(Tram 4/15-Rathaus)* ☎ 261 20 70
Bar Restaurant.
■ **Mains Bleues. Les** (AC B CC F G MA) 17-24, meals -23 h
Kanzleistraße 15 ✉ 8004 *(near/nahe Stauffacher)* ☎ 241 73 78
■ **Predigerhof Bistro** (B CC G OG OS) 14-2, Fri Sat -4 h
Mühlegasse 15 ✉ 8001 *(after the Post office on the left side)*
☎ 251 29 85
Backyard garden.
■ **Tip Top** (B CC f GLM s YG) Sun-Thu 16-2, Fri Sat -4 h
Seilergraben 13 ✉ 8001 *(Tram 3/Bus 31-Neumarkt)* ☎ 251 78 22

■ **Velvet Bar** (B glm MA)
Schneggengasse 8 ✉ 8001 ☎ 252 27 37

MEN'S CLUBS

■ **Phoenix Club** (AC b d DR G LJ MA P p WE) Fri 22.30-3,
Sat 22.30-4, every two weeks Sun 18-23 h
Postfach 605 ✉ 8902 *(located in the industrial area Bergermoos
West at the end of the A4 highway)* ☎ 734 24 69
*Privat club for fetish friends (leather, latex, uniform). Strict dress code
on Sat (call for info). ECMC Members welcome.*
■ **Sector C** (B DR G LJ MA VS WE) Fri 23-4, Sat -5 h
c/o Rage, Wagistraße 13 ✉ 8952 *(In a suburb of Zurich, Bus 31-
Wagonfabrik, Train-Schlieren, 1st floor of Rage Club)* ☎ 773 38 43
Fetish club. Dresscode: leather, rubber, army etc.

Dancearena Darkrooms
Rage Club
Wagistr. 13
8952 Schlieren/Zurich
www.rage.ch   info@rage.ch

Zürich Switzerland

CELEBRATE HAPPYNESS

A very special place for gay people to meet eachother, drink, eat, talk, play. Don't miss it.

already open at 12.00 lunchtime

AAAH! Marktgasse 14-16
(Tram 4/15 Rathaus)
8001 Zürich/Switzerland
Internet: www.aaah.ch
open 12.00 am till late

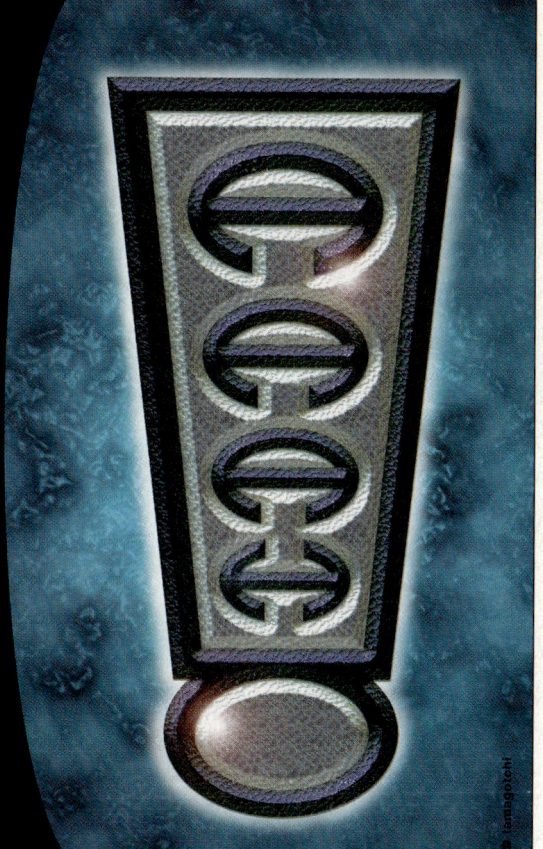

CAFES

■ **Café Bistro Marion** (AC B BF CC F g MA R) Mon-Fri 6-23, Sat Sun 5-18 h
Mühlegasse 22 ✉ 8001 *(old town)* ☎ 261 27 26
■ **Dings-Bums** (A b CC GLM OS) Tue-Fri 12-20, Sat -17 h
Engelstraße 62c ✉ 8004 *(tram 8- Helvetiaplatz, tram 2/3- Kalkbreite)* ☎ 241 32 31
Also bookshop & bar.
■ **Hot Pot Café** (A b BF F glm OS) Mon-Fri 6.45-22.30, Sat 8-16 h, Sun closed
Badenerstraße 138 ✉ 8004 *(Tram2/3-Kalkbreite)* ☎ 241 11 18
Also restaurant.
■ **Odeon Café** (B BF F g MA OS) Mon-Thu 7-2, Fri Sat -4, Sun 11-2 h
Limmatquai 2 ✉ 8001 *(near/Nähe Bellevue)* ☎ 251 16 50

DANCECLUBS

■ **Aera** (! D DR Glm lj MA s WE) Sat 23-? h
Albulastraße 38/40 ✉ 8048 *(behind the shopping mall Letzipark, Tram 2-Kappeli/Tram 33-Luggwegstrasse)*
Underground club, trance and progressive house music.

■ **At the T&M** (AC B CC D DR E GLM MA OS R S SNU STV) 20-4 h
Marktgasse 14 ✉ 8001 *(Tram 4/15-Rathaus)* ☎ 266 18 89
Since 14 years one of the foremost gayplaces in Zurich.
■ **Labyrinth-Club** (AC B D DR glm lj MA P SNU VS WE)
Thu 22.30-6, Fri Sat 23-late, Sun 21.30-6 h
Pfingstweidstraße 70 ✉ 8005 *(Tram-Escher-Wyss-Platz)* ☎ 440 59 80
Many special parties with international DJs. Check website or flyers for more info. More gays (G) late (around 4 h)
■ **Rage** (! B D DR G lj MA WE) Wed Thu Sun 21-2, Fri 22-4, Sat -5 h
Wagistrasse 13 ✉ 8952 *(In a suburb of Zurich, Bus 31-Wagonfabrik, Train-Schlieren)* ☎ 773 38 33
Very cruisy; house and trance music.
■ **Spidergalaxy** (! AC B D DR GLM MA P s) Fri-Sat 23-? h
c/o Supermarket Club, Geroldstraße 15 ✉ 8005 *(1 min from Bahnhof Hardbrücke)*

RESTAURANTS

■ **Barrique Weinrestaurant** (B F glm)
Marktgasse 17 ✉ 8001 ☎ 252 59 41

SPARTACUS 2001/2002 | 1013

Switzerland | Zürich

kink shop

leather - rubber - uniform - toys

s/m - media - video

mail-order - internet-shopping

best selection - best prices

kink shop
engelstrasse 62
8004 zürich
switzerland

fon 01-241 32 15
fax 01-241 32 19

www.kink.ch

YES, please send me your free mail-order-journal:
name/first name:
address:
zip/place/country:
with my signature I certify that I'm of legal age in my country

RENOS RELAX

Grosses Dampfbad · Bio-Sauna mit Lichtspektrum und Finarium · Finnische Sauna · Solarium · Massage · Dark-Room · Aufenthalts- und Ruheräume · Kabinen mit Video · Sling-Room · Grossbild TV · Bar mit alkoholischen Getränken · Snacks · Magazine · **Exklusiv: Schaum-Bad**

www.renosrelax.ch

Kernstrasse 57, 3. Stock, 8004 Zürich - beim Helvetiaplatz, Tel. 01-291 63 62
Jeden Samstag Nachtsauna - jede Woche neue Gay-Videos

Preisermässigung bis 26 Jahre

Montag-Donnerstag: 12.00 - 23.00 Uhr
Freitag-Samstag: 12.00 - 07.00 Uhr
Sonn- und Feiertage: 14.00 - 23.00 Uhr
RENOS RELAX CLUB SAUNA

moustache

Junioren-Bonus:
16 – 25 Jahre!
Dampfbad
Biosauna mit Lichtspektrum
Finnische Sauna
Tauchbecken
Solarium
Ruheraum mit Kabinen
Bar, TV/Video
Massage nach Vereinbarung

Relaxclub für Gays
Badenerstrasse 156 b, CH-8004 Zürich
Eingang Engelstr. 4, Tel. 01 241 10 80
http://www.moustache.ch
info@moustache.ch
Tram 2 / 3 oder Bus 32 bis Kalkbreite
7 x in der Woche von 12 h – 23 h

Zürich | Switzerland

MACHO CITY SHOP
Häringstr. 16 · 8001 Zürich · 01/251 12 22

- Erotic-Art Books
- Postcards
- Magazines
- Books
- Underwear — OLAF BENZ / BODY ART / MENSTORE
- Videos VHS/DVD
- Toys

www.macho.ch
online shopping — worldwide delivery

■ **Restaurant** (A CC F glm MA OS VS) Mon-Fri 11.30-14, 19-24, Sat 18-24, closed Sun
Lägernstrasse 37 ✉ 8037 ☎ 361 07 07

■ **Sunset Thai** (CC F g OS) 12-14, 18-0.30 h
Birmensdorferstraße 488 ✉ 8055 *(Tram9/14-Triemli)* ☎ 463 65 70

SEX SHOPS/BLUE MOVIES

■ **BS-Laden** (G LJ MA VS) Mon-Fri 14-18.30, Sat 11-16 h, closed Sun
Anwandstraße 67 ✉ 8004 *(Tram 8-Helvetiaplatz)* ☎ 241 04 41
Videos, books, magazines, leather, rubber.

■ **Erotik Video Discount** (AC CC G VS YG) 11-23 h
Sihlfeldstraße 58 ✉ 8003 *(Tram 2/3-Lochergut)* ☎ 451 21 01

■ **Kink Shop** (CC DR G LJ s) Mon-Fri 12-20, Sat -17 h
Engelstraße 2 ✉ 8004 *(Tram 3-Kalkbreite)* ☎ 241 32 15
Leather, rubber, army, toys, videos, bodypiercing.

■ **Macho City Shop** (CC GLM) 11-20, Sat 10-16 h, closed Sun
Häringstraße 16 ✉ 8001 *(Near Central Station/Nähe Hauptbahnhof)*
☎ 251 12 22
Books, magazines, CD's, videos.

ESCORTS & STUDIOS

■ **Escortboys**
☎ (079) 478 26 03
Escort service Switzerland wide.

IKARUS Entertainment
P.O. Box 50, CH-4153 Reinach 2 / Switzerland

Gay Video Production

www.ikarus-entertainment.ch

| Switzerland | Zürich |

moustache
Relaxclub für Gays

Junioren-Bonus:
16 – 25 Jahre!
Dampfbad
Biosauna mit Lichtspektrum
Finnische Sauna
Tauchbecken
Solarium
Ruheraum mit Kabinen
Bar, TV/Video
Massage nach Vereinbarung

Badenerstrasse 156 b, CH-8004 Zürich
Eingang Engelstr. 4, Tel. 01 241 10 80
http://www.moustache.ch
info@moustache.ch
Tram 2 / 3 oder Bus 32 bis Kalkbreite
7 x in der Woche von 12 h – 23 h

SAUNAS/BATHS

■ **Adonis** (b DR f G MG p SA VS) Mon-Fri 13-21, Sat -19 h, closed Sun
Mutschellenstraße 17 ✉ 8002 *(near Wollishofen, S-Bahn-Brunau)*
☎ 201 64 16
Small sauna with a more elderly crowd.

■ **Apollo** (b G MG SA SB VS) 12-22, Sat-Sun & holidays 14-21 h
Seilergraben 41 ✉ 8001 *(5 min from railway station)* ☎ 261 49 52
Small sauna frequented by middle aged men.

■ **Moustache** (! A AC B CC DR f G MA MSG p SA SB SOL VS) 12-23, Oct-May Sat -2 h
Badenerstraße 156b (IV) ✉ 8004 *(Entrance Engelstraße 4, Tram 2/3, Bus 32-Kalkbreite)* ☎ 241 10 80
Offers bio-sauna, plunge pool. A popular spot for bears and the bearded but attracts also a wider crowd.

■ **Mylord** (b f DR G msg N OG P SA VS) 11-24 h
Seebahnstraße 139 ✉ 8003 *(near station Zürich-Wieclikon, Tram2/3, Bus 32-Locherguß)* ☎ 462 44 66
Small and intimate sauna existing since 1972, renovated in 97. Gay, bi mixed local crowd.

■ **Paragonya** (! AC B CC DR f G P p SA SB SOL VS WH YG) 11.30-23 h
Mühlegasse 11 ✉ 8001 *(near main station/nahe Hauptbahnhof, near river Limmat, in the Post Office Building PTT)* ☎ 252 66 66
Two floors for this popular sauna on 440 m² with bio-sauna. Attracts a young crowd.

■ **Reno's Relax** (! AC B DR f G MA MSG p SA SB SOL VS)
Mon-Thu 12-23, Fri Sat -7, Sun 14-23 h
Kernstraße 57 ✉ 8004 *(Tram 8/Bus 32-Helvetiaplatz)* ☎ 291 63 62
Popular sauna with foam room, bio sauna, two slings, "lovers swing"...

DOWNTOWN ZURICH

ZIMMER ZU VERMIETEN

An der Spitalgasse 3, möblierte Zimmer mit Dusche und Lavabo zu vermieten. WC und Küche auf dem Gang. Miete von 950.– bis 1400.– Fr. pro Monat. Kurzfristige Miete ab 10 Tagen möglich. Bitte ruf an für einen Besichtigungstermin.

ROOMS TO LET

In Zurich town centre, only 4 minutes from central station, at Spitalgasse 3, furnished rooms with shower and wash-basin to let between CHF 950.– and 1400.–. WC and kitchen in corridor. Short-term lettings from 10 days also available. Please call for a viewing.

CHAMBRE À LOUER

Dans le centre de Zurich, à 4 minutes seulement de la gare centrale, Spitalgasse 3, nous proposons des chambres meublées à louer de 950.–à 1400.– CHF. Douche et lavabo dans la chambre. WC et cuisine dans le couloir. La location est également possible pour de courtes périodes de 10 jours au moins. Vous pouvez nous appeler pour convenir d'une visite.

HABITACIONES PARA ARRENDAR

En el centro de Zurich, a cuatro minutos de la estación central de ferrocarriles, en la Spitalgasse 3, arrendamos habitaciones amuebladas con ducha y lavabo dentro de las mismas, a partir de CHF 950.– hasta 1400.–. WC y cocina en el corredor. También son posibles arrendamientos de corto tiempo a partir de 10 días. Por favor, llámenos para una visita.

QUARTOS PARA ALUGAR

No centro de Zurich, a 4 minutos da estação central do caminho de ferro, na Spitalgasse 31 alugamos quartos mobilados com ducha e lavatório dentro dos mesmos, a partir de CHF 950.– até 1400.– . WC e cozinha no corredor. Também são possíveis aluguéres de curto tempo. Por favor, chame-nos para uma visita.

POKOJE DO WYNAJĘCIA

W centrum Zurychu, 4 minuty od Dworca Głównego, Spitalgasse 3, umeblowane pokoje do wynajęcia w cenie od 950.– do 1400.– franków szwajcarskich, wyposażone w prysznic i umywalkę. WC i kuchnia na korytarzu. Możliwość wynajmu również na krótki okres - od 10 dni. Prosimy o telefoniczne umawianie się na oglądanie.

TELEFON 01 266 18 18
(HOTEL GOLDENES SCHWERT)

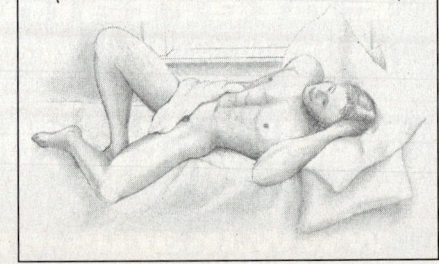

Zürich | Switzerland

the gay & lesbian paradise...

books
postcards
gifts
rainbow-stuff
and...

...Zurich's coziest coffeeplace

check out
www.dings-bums.com
for more

dings bums

Engelstrasse 62c, 8004 Zürich, 01-241 32 31, Fax 01-241 32 19
Tue-Fri 12.00-18.00, Sat 12.00-17.00

■ **Sauna Zentral** (B f G MA msg p SA SB VS) Mon-Sat 9-22, Sun 13-20 h
Zentralstraße 45 ✉ 8003
☏ 463 34 38
Once a month special vacuum pumper night.

BODY & BEAUTY SHOPS
■ **Kink Body** (CC GLM) Tue-Fri 12-20, Sat-17 h
Engelstrasse 62 ✉ 8004 *(Tram 3-Kalkbreite)*

☏ 241 32 15
Body manipulation & piercings.

BOOK SHOPS
■ **EBS Erotic Book Store** (CC glm) Mon 14-18.30, Tue Wed Fri 11-18.30, Thu -21, Sat 10-16 h
Klingenstraße 33 ✉ 8005
☏ 272 83 13
No admittance if you are under age of 16.

THE REAL GAY-HOTEL IN SWITZERLAND

Goldenes Schwert

© A MEMBER OF MEKDAENG'S

E-mail: hotel@rainbow.ch
Internet Online:
http://www.gaybar.ch

Marktgasse 14
8001 Zürich/Switzerland
Phone 41.1.266 18 18
Fax 41.1.266 18 88

SPARTACUS 2001/2002 | 1017

Switzerland | Zürich

Hotel Rothaus

Ihr **-Hotel im Zentrum (Vergnügungsviertel) von Zürich. 10 Min. zu Fuss vom Bahnhof und von der Shopping-Area. Alle Zimmer mit Dusche, WC, TV und Direktwahltelefon. Sehr Gay-freundlich. Infos über Nightlife durch den Geschäftsführer.

Sihlhallenstrasse 1, CH-8004 Zürich, Tel. +41/1/2412451, Fax +41/1/2910825
E-Mail:uhk@swissonline.ch, www.cd-hotel.com/ch/rothaus.htm

■ **Sec 52 Buchladen** (g) 10.30-18.30, Sat -16 h, closed Sun
Josefstraße 52 ✉ 8005 ☎ 271 18 18

TRAVEL AND TRANSPORT

■ **Pink Cloud Travel Service** (CC glm) Mon-Fri 9-12.30 13.30-18 h Sat&Sun closed
Albisstr. 33 *(Adliswil, 15 min from Zurich with SZU)* ☎ 712 30 01
📠 712 30 03   📧 pinkcloud@dorado.ch   💻 www.pinkcloud.ch
The ultimate travel-service for the lesbian and gay community and their friends. See website or call for further information.

HOTELS

■ **Goldenes Schwert** (BF CC f G MA)
Marktgasse 14 ✉ 8004 *(central, in Zurich old town)* ☎ 266 18 18
📠 266 18 18   📧 hotel@rainbow.ch
Located in the middle of the gay scene. All rooms with shower or bath/WC, TV, video, safe, phone.

■ **Hotel Adler** (BF B CC F H NG) 0-24 h
Rosengasse 10 ✉ 8001 *(at/Am Hirschenplatz)* ☎ 266 96 96
📠 266 96 96   📧 info@hotel-adler.ch   💻 www.hotel-adler.ch
Centrally located & new renovated hotel in the heart of the old town. All rooms have barth/shower, direct dial phones without any extra charges, TV, radio, minibar, BF buffet in the price included. Single room CHF 120-140.-, double 210-290.-

■ **Hotel Rothaus Zürich** (CC g H) Reception 7-0.30 h
Sihlhallenstraße 1 ✉ 8004 *(Near Helvetiaplatz. Bus31-Militärstraße)*
☎ 241 24 51   📠 291 09 95   💻 www.cd-hotel.com/ch/rothaus.htm
43 rooms with shower/WC, phone, TV and own key. Price in double room CHF 98-120.- 3/4 bedded rooms 120-152.-

PRIVATE ACCOMMODATION

■ **Intakt Zimmervermittlung** (BF G H)
Kirchweg 22 ✉ 8102 *(in Zurich and surroundings)*
☎ (079) 441 33 03   📧 info@intakt.ch
💻 www.intakt.ch
Gay private accomodation. Singles from CHF 42.-, doubles from 66.- Fee per reservation 15.-, BF 7.50. Full use of kitchen and bathroom.

FETISH GROUPS

■ **Leder- und Motorradclub Zürich (LMZ)**
Postfach ✉ 8026   📧 info@lmz.ch   💻 www.lmz.ch

HEALTH GROUPS

■ **Oekumenisches Aidspfarramt**
Universitätstrasse 46 ✉ 8006 ☎ 255 90 55 📠 255 44 10
📧 mail@aidspfarramtzh.ch
💻 www.aidspfarramtzh.ch
Offers pastoral and spiritual assistance to people with HIV/Aids and their relatives and friends.

■ **Zürcher AIDS-Hilfe** Mon-Fri 9-13, 14-17 h, Helpline: Mon-Fri 14-17 h
Birmensdorferstraße 169 ✉ 8003 *(Tram 9/14-Schmiede Wiedikon)*
☎ 455 59 00   📠 455 59 19   📧 mail@zah.ch
💻 www.zah.ch

HELP WITH PROBLEMS

■ **Act-HIV** Tue 9-13 h, Wed 19-22 h
Hallwylstraße 78 ✉ 8004 ☎ 291 37 20

HOTEL ADLER
★★★

Rosengasse 10, Zürich
www.hotel-adler.ch   info@hotel-adler.ch
Tel +41 1 2669696   Fax +41 1 2669669

Genießen Sie Schweizer Gastfreundschaft und modern ausgestattete Zimmer in unserem neurenovierten, im Herzen der Altstadt gelegenen Hotel

Enjoy modern & well equipped rooms in our newly renovated century old hotel in the heart of Zurich's historical centre

Preise / prices: single 140–180,– CHF; double 210–290,– CHF

Zürich ▶ Zug | **Switzerland**

■ **Beratungsstelle für männliche Opfer sexueller Gewalt-Zürcher Sozialprojekte** Mon-Fri 10-17, Wed-Thu -19 h
Hallwylstraße 78, Postfach 8155 ✉ 8036 ☎ 291 37 80
📠 291 23 88
Counseling in case of sexual violence.
■ **Projekt Herrmann** (G R) Tue-Fri 14-17 h
Müllerstraße 37 ✉ 8004 ☎ 291 00 15 📠 291 00 15
📧 projektherrmann@freesurf.ch 🌐 www.malesexwork.ch
Information, counselling and meeting point for hustlers/Information, Beratung und Treffpunkt für Stricher.

RELIGIOUS GROUPS

■ **HuK Zürich-Ökumenische Arbeitsgruppe Homosexuelle und Kirche**
Postfach 7013 ✉ 8023 ☎ 311 73 12

SPECIAL INTEREST GROUPS

■ **Spot 25 - Jugendgruppe** (GLM YG) Wed 19.30-22 h
Posfach 4363 ✉ 8022 *(Sihlquai 67, 3rd floor)* ☎ 273 11 77
📧 info@spot25.ch 🌐 www.spot25.ch
Youth gay and lesbian group.
■ **Zart und Heftig - Schwules Hochschulforum von Uni und ETH Zürich** (GLM YG) Thu 16.30-17.30 h
Rämistraße 66 ✉ 8001 *(3rd floor)* ☎ 252 46 32
🌐 www.zundh.unizh.ch
Gay and lesbian student group. Meeting last Thu/month at the "Centro, Sihlquai 67, 3rd floor, 19.30 h

SPORT GROUPS

■ **Gay Bikers Zürich**
Postfach 71 ✉ 5014 🌐 www.datacomm.ch/gaybikers
■ **Gay Sport Zürich**
Postfach 3312 ✉ 8021

SWIMMING

-Werdinsineli (G NU) (Beach on a small island in the middle of River Limmat. Take tram 4 or Bus 80/89 to Tüffenwies. Go to the coloured wheel then to the end of the island)

CRUISING

-Beckenhofpark (closes at 21 h)
-Einkaufszone/shopping mall "Shop Ville"
-Seepark Mythenquai/Park Arboretum (! YG) (evenings)
-Waffenplatzpark (AYOR LJ) (after midnight)
-Schaffhauserplatz
-Kreuzplatz
-Sihlpromenade (Sihlhölzli)
-Aussersihlanlage/Bäckeranlage (very AYOR)

Zug ☎ 042

HEALTH GROUPS

■ **AIDS-Hilfe Zug** Mon 14-17, Tue 9-13, Wed 12-16, 17-21, every 1st Sat 9-15 h

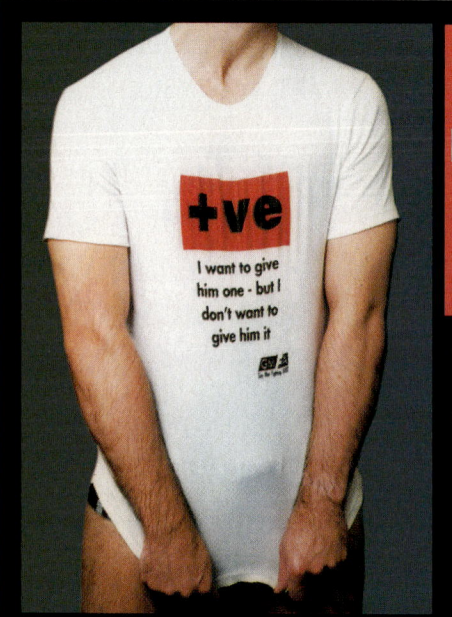

Taiwan

Name: T'ai-wan
Location: Off Mainland China
Initials: RC
Time: GMT +8
International Country Code: ☎ 886 (leave the first 0 of area codes)
International Access Code: ☎ 002
Language: Chinese
Area: 36,981 km² / 14,275 sq mi.
Currency: 1 New Taiwan Dollar (NT$) = 100 Cents
Population: 21,871,000
Capital: T'aipei
Religions: 43% Buddhists, 34% Daoists, 6% Christians
Climate: Tropical and marine climate. The rainy season during southwest monsoon lasts from June to August. All year round cloudiness is persistent and extensive.

✱ Neither the term "homosexuality" nor the concept of an age of consent exist in Taiwanese legislation. Marriage is legal from the age of 18, and that too is the age people become fully accountable to law. Yet, legally, people become of full age only when they are 20 years of age. Death penalty threatens when being seduced to homosexual acts while serving in the army.

✱ Es gibt in den taiwanesischen Gesetzen weder den Begriff "Homosexualität", noch ein Konzept, das ein "Schutzalter" beinhaltet. Man darf zwar ab 18 heiraten und wird dann auch vollständig strafmündig, rechtlich volljährig wird man aber erst mit 20. Wer sich in der Armee zu homosexuellen Handlungen verführen lässt, wird mit der Todesstrafe bedroht.

✱ A Taïwan, la législation ne connaît pas le mot "homosexualité" et de restriction concernant la majorité sexuelle. Passé 18 ans, on peut se marier et on devient majeur pénal. Ce n'est qu'à partir de 20 que l'on est considéré comme majeur face à la loi. A l'armée, les rapports entre personnes de même sexe sont passibles de la peine de mort.

✱ En las leyes de Taiwan no aparec la palabra "homosexualidad", tampoco existe reglamentación alguna respecto a edades de consentimiento. El matrimonio esta permitido a patir de los 18 años, pero la mayoría de edad se alcanza a los 20. Quien mantenga relaciones homosexuales en el ejército está amenazado con la pena de muerte.

✱ Le leggi di Taiwan non menzionano nè l'omosessualità nè la maggiore età sessuale. I cittadini di questo paese sono maggiorenni a 20 anni, a 18 però si possono sposare e sono maggiorenni penalmente. Chi nell'esercito si abbandona a rapporti omosessuali viene minacciato con la pena di morte.

Kaohsiung ☎ 07

BARS
■ **Bolivia** (B D YG)
10F. 80, Da jen Rd. ☎ 521-7032
■ **Colour Plate** (B G MA)
Tayou Street 5 *(2nd floor)* ☎ 551-3757
■ **Encounter** (B MA)
49, Wu Fu 4th Rd. ☎ 551-9090
■ **Men's Talk** (b d G) 20-5 h
B1 32, Ming Shing St. ☎ 211-7049
D on Sat.
■ **Private Life** (B g MA)
278, Chi Hsien 3rd Rd. *(Basement)* ☎ 561-1100

MASSAGE
■ **Han Chin** (msg)
101, Hou Nan 2nd Rd. ☎ 216-7073
■ **Michael Angelo** (msg)
12F. 21, Gee Kuan St. ☎ 216-9052

CRUISING
-Kaohsiung Main railway station
-Lover River (near burned down shopping center)

Taichung ☎ 04

BARS
■ **Ai Chiao** (B g MA)
216, Chen Kung Rd. ☎ 221-1975
■ **Celestial** (B g MA)
3F 12, Tzi Yu Rd. Sec.2 ☎ 223-2348
■ **Eternal Love** (B g MA)
8F-3 12, Tzu Yu Rd. Sec.2 ☎ 222-4336
■ **Hollywood** (B g YG)
141, Chung San Rd. *(Basement)* ☎ 222-2863
■ **King Fu Restaurant**
Chi Kuang Street ☎ 223-2534
■ **Molin Violet** (B D g MA)
60, Chung Shan Rd. *(Basement)* ☎ 220-2126
■ **Sparrowlet** (B g MA)
28, Ming Tzu Rd. *(Basement)* ☎ 223-4467

CRUISING
-Main railway station
-Taichung park

Taiwan

Tainan ▶ Taipei/Taipeh

Tainan ☎ 06

BARS
■ **China Town** (B D MA)
11F 72, Huan Ho South St. ☎ 06/220-8800

MASSAGE
■ **Male Massage**
PO Box 1350 ☎ 07/33 91 974
Pager 060732985.

CRUISING
-Main railway station facilities.

Taipei/Taipeh ☎ 02

BARS
■ **Art** (B g OG)
2F 147 Lin Sen North Rd. ☎ 571-3540
■ **Buffalo Town** (B D WE YG)
289 Linsen North Road *(12th floor)* ☎ 564-1172
■ **Casablanca Pub** (AC B D G MA)
N° 22, Lane 33, Section 1, Chung Shan North Road ☎ 563 78 95
Friendly staff. Karaoke.
■ **Funky** (! AC B D G YG)
B1, No.10, Sec.1,Han Chou Rd. S *(basement)* ☎ 394-2162
or ☎ 394-2290. Very popular on WE. Karaoke.
■ **Jupiter** (AC B G MA)
154 Po Ai Rd. *(basement)* ☎ 311-8585
■ **President** (AYOR B G R)
9 Teh Hwei Street ☎ 595-1251
■ **Source. The** (AC B d f G MA N) 19-3 h
192 Nancheng Road, Sec. 2 *(near downtown)* ☎ 368 87 97
■ **Traffic Fish** (B g OG)
5 Chun Shan N. Rd., Sec.2 Lane 6 *(basement)* ☎ 562-7123
■ **1/20** (B g YG)
137 Chon Hwa Rd. ☎ 382-0218

CAFES
■ **Game Box** (AC b f G P S YG) Tue-Sat 19-24h
No.181, 40 Lane 216, Sec.4 Chung-Hsiao East Road ☎ 277 272 31

RESTAURANTS
■ **Cupid Restaurant & Pub** (AC B D F G MA) 20-4.30 h
154 Po Ai Rd. *(at new Garden Park)(Xin Gongyuan)* ☎ 311 85 85
■ **Our Place** (G F) 10-21 h
☎ 341-1057
Homestyle restaurant. Call for directions.

SAUNAS/BATHS
■ **Da Fan** (AC G MA msg SA VS WH) 0-24 h
5F, 195, Chung-Shiao West Road, Section 1 ☎ 381-1859
Very busy! Private rooms at no extra charge.
■ **Hans Men's Sauna** (AC G MA msg SA WH) 0-24 h
2F, 120 Hsi-Ning South Road ☎ 311-8681
■ **Hilton Hotel Sauna** (g msg SA SOL WH WO) 10-20 h
(Basement)
Local and foreign gays.
■ **Nong Lai** (AC G MG msg SA VS) 0-24 h
5F, 155, Shih-Ning South Road ☎ 381-0891
Private rooms at no extra charge.
■ **Royal Palace (Huang-Kong)** (OG msg SA SB VS) 0-24 h
20, Hsi Ning South Rd. ☎ 381-5900

BOOK SHOPS
■ **Gin Gin's** (AC b f G YG)
No.7-14 Alley, 8 Lane, 210 Sec.3 Roosevelt Rd ☎ 236 420 06

HOTELS
■ **Brother** (AC B F H NG)
255 Nanking East Road, Section 3 ☎ 712-3456
Downtown location, 40 min to the airport. All rooms with telephone, fridge, priv. bath, WC. Single NT$ 2.800-3.500, double 3.300.

CRUISING
-New Garden Park (Xin Gong Yuan)(best place is Pagoda Pond, 18-21 h)
-YMCA behind Hilton Hotel
-Lobby of Hilton Hotel
-Little park in New Peitou (suburb af Taipei)
-Hung Lou Hsi Yuan (Red Building Theater Movie House)
-Yuan Huan Movie House (near Yuanhuan Road Circus, Chungking North Road)
-Kuang Hua Shang Chang (Basement of Kuang Hua Market on

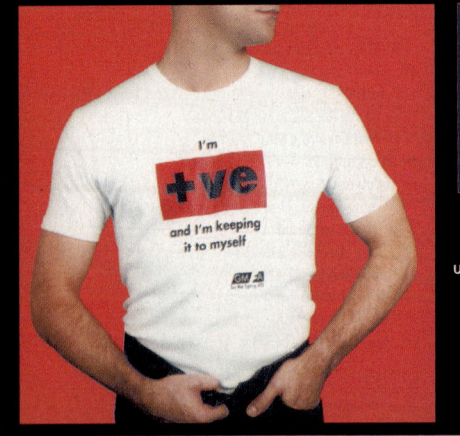

Lots of HIV+ men don't tell

GMFA's campaigns and actions are designed, planned and executed by positive, negative and untested volunteers. To volunteer for GMFA write, phone or email:
Unit 43, Eurolink Centre, 49 Effra Road, LONDON, SW2 1BZ. 020 7738 6872. newvol@gmfa.demon.co.uk
www.demon.co.uk/gmfa
Registered Charity no. 1076854

GMFA Gay Men Fighting AIDS

Thailand

Name: Prathet Thai • Thailande • Tailandia
Location: Southeast Asia
Initials: THA
Time: GMT +7 (Summer +6)
International Country Code: ☏ 66
International Access Code: ☏ 001
Language: Thai, English
Area: 513,115 km² / 198,114 sq mi.
Currency: 1 Baht (B) = 100 Stangs
Population: 61,201,000
Capital: Bangkok (Krung Thep)
Religions: 94% Buddhists
Climate: Tropical climate. The rainy, warm and cloudy southwest monsoon lasts from mid-May to September, the dry and cool northeast monsoon lasts from November to mid-March.
Important gay cities: Bangkok, Chiang Mai, Pattaya, Phuket

※ Homosexual acts have never been forbidden and the age of consent is 18. Threats of punishment for legal contravention have considerably increased in the past few years.
The blending of West European lifestyle and Buddhism reflects in the acceptance of gays by Thais. Astonishingly there is no stigma about prostitution in Thailand.
As in other neighbouring countries in South Asia there is a gay-lesbian movement, but in contrast to its neighbours there is no restrictiveness to the flourishing gay scene. Bangkok is the gay capital of the South and Pattaya is the only gay bathing resort of Asia.

※ Es gab in Thailand nie ein gesetzliches Verbot homosexueller Handlungen. Das Schutzalter liegt bei 18 Jahren. Die Strafdrohungen für Zuwiderhandlungen, vor allem im Bereich der Prostitution, wurden in den vergangenen Jahren erheblich verschärft.
In Thailand vermischen sich westlich-europäische Einflüsse mit den buddhistischen Traditionen des Landes. Entsprechend liberal verhalten sich die Thais - zumindest in den großen Städten - Schwulen gegenüber. Ganz erstaunlich ist dabei, daß Prostitution absolut nicht stigmatisiert ist.
Wie in den Nachbarstaaten in Südostasien gibt es auch in Thailand nur ansatzweise eine schwul-lesbische Bewegung. Aber im Gegensatz zu den restriktiven Nachbarstaaten, hat sich in Thailand eine blühende schwule Szene entwickelt. Bangkok ist die schwule Hauptstadt Süd- und Südostasiens. Pattaya ist der einzige schwule Badeort Asiens.

※ En Thaïlande, l'homosexualité n'est pas interdite par la loi. La majorité sexuelle est fixée à 18 ans. Les condamnations pour non-respect de ces lois, surtout dans le domaine de la prostitution, se sont renforcées considérablement au cours des dernières années.
En Thaïlande, les influences occidentales et européennes se mélangent à la tradition bouddiste du pays. Surtout dans les grandes villes, les thaïlandais se comportent de manière libérale à l'égard des homosexuels. Il est ainsi très surprenant de voir que la prostitution n'est pas du tout stigmatisée.

Tout comme dans les autres pays de l'Asie du Sud-Est, le mouvements gay et lesbien est encore embryonnaire. Mais contrairement à ses pays voisins plus restrictifs, la Thaïlande a développé un milieu gay florissant. Bangkok est la capitale gaye de l'Asie du Sud et du Sud-Est. Pattaya est la seule ville balnéaire gaye de l'Asie.

※ En Tailandia nunca han estado prohibidas las actividades homosexuales. La edad de consentimiento es de 18 años. Sobre todo en el campo de la prostitución y han sido intensificado las penas por contra vención.
En Tailandia se mezclan la influencia europea con las tradiciones budistas del país. De igual forma (liberal) se comportan los tailandeses homosexuales de las grandes ciudades. Es de admirar que la prostitución no es estigmatizada.
Al igual que los países vecinos del Asia menor, existen solamente los despuntes de un posible movimiento gay-lesbiano. A pesar de ello, en Tailandia se ha desarrolllado un colorido ambiente gay. Bangkok es la capital gay del Asia menor. Pattaya es el único balneario gay de Asia.

※ In Tailandia non è mai esistita una legge contro gli atti omosessuali. L'età legale è di 18 anni. Negli ultimi anni sono cresciuti gli avvisi di condanna per le trasgressioni in special modo nel campo della prostituzione minorile.
In Tailandia si fondono influssi culturali europei con le tradizioni buddiste del paese. Perciò l'atteggiamento della popolazione tai almeno nelle grandi città si mostra molto liberale verso i gay e è anche molto sorprendente che la prostituzione non venga additata dalla popolazione.
Come negli altri paesi del Sud-Est asiatico anche in Tailandia si ha solo un principio di un movimento politico gay e lesbico. Però al contrario dei più severi paesi confinanti, in Tailandia si è sviluppato un vivace ambiente gay. Bangkok è la capitale gay del Sud e Sud-Est asiatico. Pattaya è l'unica gay del paese.

Thailand — Bangkok/Krung Thep

Hsinsheng South Road)

NATIONAL GAY INFO

■ **Internet addresses**
-Dragon Castle: http://dragoncastle.com
-Dreaded Ned: http://www.dreadedned.com (Search Engine)
-GAMTH: http://www.geocities.com/westhollywood/heights/2999/eindex.html (Gay Asian Men of Thailand)
-Gay Asian Links: http://members.aol.com/apxrds/gal.html
-Mens Club Publishing: http://www.chamon.com (Gay magazine in Thai and English)
-Pink Ink: http://www.khsnet.com/pinkink - E-mail: pinkpage@hotmail.com (Monthly newsletter)
-Utopia (!): http://www.utopia-asia.com (Interesting and colourful site about gay Thailand and other Asian countries)

NATIONAL PUBLICATIONS

■ **Grace, Male**
P.O. Box 156, Dusit ✉ 10300 Bangkok
Magazines in Thai. But the pictures are internationally understood.

■ **Men of Thailand, The**
Floating Lotus, PO Box 44, Ratchawithi Post Office ✉ 10408 Bangkok 🖥 books@floatinglotus.com 🖥 http://www.floatinglotus.com
Publishers of books interesting for gays, along with the best-selling guide to Thailand.

■ **Midway**
PO Box 599, Phra Kanong ✉ 10110 Bangkok
Bilingual gay magazine (English and Thai). Many beautiful pictures.

■ **Mithuna Magazine**
P.O. Box 586, Phra Khanong ✉ 10110 Bangkok
Gay Thai magazine.

■ **Thai Guys** (!)
☎ 02/6 74 27 51 🖥 thaiguys@loxinfo.co.th 🖥 http://www.thaiguys.org
New gay English magazine covering all Thailand. Featuring the main meeting points and information about the scene, contact and stories about gay life-style. Bimonthly.

NATIONAL PUBLISHERS

■ **Gay Media Group**
☎ 02/6 79 79 85 ☎ 01/6 10 95 81 ☎ 02/6 79 79 86
🖥 Info@gay-media.com 🖥 www.gay-media.com

NATIONAL COMPANIES

■ **Utopia Tours** (GLM) 10-18 h
Tarntawan Place Hotel, 119/5-10 Surawong Road, Bang Rak ✉ 10500 Bangkok/Krung Thep *(between Patpong 1 and Soi Than Thawan)* ☎ (02) 2383227 🖥 info@utopia-tours.com 🖥 www.utopia-tours.com
Asia's gay travel pioneers. They will arrange your stay in Thailand and your tour to other Asian countries. Go there for information on the gay scenes.

Bangkok/Krung Thep ☎ 02

※ For those who have never experienced before tropical cities with populations in the millions, will feel overwhelmed on landing in a city of tropical temperatures, enormous crowds in the streets, noise, and motorisied conjestion in a city of over 6 million inhabitants. To over come this overwhelming experience it helps to relax, and to take in all sights and pleasures that this city has to offer. The city has a large number of palaces and temples, over crowded markets and the Chao Pyra River (the river of the King), which is the traditional transport artery and is still a rich pageant of life. Bangkok far surpasses other countries for it's turbulent colourfulnes. Shopping is a must! There is a varied selection of clothes, silk, jewellery and objects of art.
In Bangkok there are fundamentally three gay centres. Firstly, *Patpong* is regarded as the night life address for heteros and gays, especially two soi (or lanes) Patong I and Patong II that run between *Silom Road* and *Suriwong Road*. The gays concentrate themselves around soi 2, 4 and 6. It is suggested to avoid touts at the entrance to the gay soi. The second most important area is *Sukhumwit Road* and *Siam Square*. In contrast to Patong this area has the largest number of hotels and international restaurants. The third area is *Sapan Kwai*, which is further towards the airport. This is an area to meet Bangkokers or tourists looking for a break from the hustle and bustle of the inner city.

★ Wer tropische Millionenstädte nicht kennt, wird sich im Moment der Ankunft überwältigt fühlen: vom tropischen Klima, vom Menschengewirr in den Innenstadtgassen, vom dem enormen Verkehr, der mit kaum öffentlichem Nahverkehr und überlasteten Hauptstraßen in einer sich motorisierenden 6-Milionen-Metropole auskommen kann. Da hilft nur entspannen, noch mal hinsehen und genießen. Die Stadt bietet Paläste und Tempel in Hülle und Fülle. Die schwimmenden Märkte und der "Chao Pyra" (Fluß der Könige, das traditionelle Transportader der Stadt) sind an turbulenter Buntheit nicht zu übertreffen. Und Schoppen muß man! Bekleidung, Seide, Schmuck, Kunstobjekte lohnen jeder Besuch.
In Bangkok gibt es im wesentlichen drei schwule Zentren. Das *Patpong* ist ganz allgemein Die Nightlife-Adresse, auch für Schule. Benannt ist die Gegend nach den beiden Wegen (oder "Patpong") zwischen der *Silom Road* und der *Suriwong Road*. Dabei konzentrieren sich die schwulen Lokalitäten auf die soi Silom 2, 4 und 6. Von den Schleppern am Eingang der schwulen soi sollte man sich tunlichst fernhalten. Da zweite wichtige schwule Areal ist die Gegend um die *Sukhumvit Road* und den *Siam Square*. Im Gegensatz zum Patpong ist dies eher das Viertel der großen Hotels und der internationalen Restaurants. Ein weiteres Gebiet ist *Sapan Kwai*, etwas außerhalb Richtung Flughafen gelegen. Hier trifft man eher Bangkoker an, oder Touristen, die sich einen Abend lang etwas Ruhe vor Volldampf der Innenstadt gönnen.

✱ Ceux qui ne connaissent pas les villes tropicales de plusieurs millions d'habitants seront très impressionnés en arrivant à Bangkok. Impressionnés par le climat, par la foule dans les rues étroites, par la circulation massive, marquée par la quasi inexistance de transports en commun et par des rues principales surchargées dans lesquelles les 6 millions d'habitants motorisés doivent circuler. Tout ce qui reste à faire est de se détendre, d'observer, et d'en profiter. La ville offre une quantité de palaces et de temples. Les marchés flottants et le Chao Pyra (fleuve des rois, l'artère du transport traditionnel de la ville), ne pourraient être plus colorés. Et le shopping est un must! On y trouve d'innombrables vêtements, de la soie, des bijoux, des objets d'arts.
A Bangkok il y a trois grands centres gays. Le *Patpong* est l'adresse nocturne par excellence, y compris pour les homosexuels. Ce quartier a été nommé d'après les deux grands chemins (ou "patpong") entre la *Silom Road* et la *Suriwong Road*. Les endroits gays sont concentrés sur les soi Silom 2, 4 et 6. Il vaut mieux rester à l'écart des ramasseurs à l'entrée des soi gays. Le second quartier gay est celui des *Sukhumvit Road* et de *Siam Square*. Au contraire du Patpong, c'est plutôt le coin des grands hôtels et restaurants internationaux. Le troisième quartier est le *Sapan Kwai*, à l'écart et situé dans la direction de l'aéroport. Ici, on rencontre surtout des thaïlandais, mais aussi des touristes qui veulent se reposer pour un soir des tumultes du centre ville.

● Quien no conozca ciudades tropicales con millones de habitantes, se sentirá en el momento de su llegada abrumado por el clima tropical, las masas de gente en las callejuelas del centro de la ciudad, el enorme tránsito vial que casi no posee red de servicio público y también por las abarrotadas calles principales de una metrópoli motorizada que cuenta con 6 millones de habitantes. Lo úni-

THAI GUYS

www.thaiguys.org

Asian News Connection

Subscribe to Thai Guys magazine. Just send your credit card details (Visa or MasterCard, name, number, date of expire, reason of payment). The subscription for 12 issues is 2,000 Baht (about 50 US$).
e-Mail: subscription@thaiguys.org

www.thaiguys.org
No, no, no: org does *not* stand for orgy!

Thailand — Bangkok/Krung Thep

V club

"The Pinnacle of Pleasure. Number one in Bangkok and certainly one of the top in the world"

Steam, Gym, Restaurant, Erotic Massage by models and men in uniform.
Sky Train: Ari Station, go into Soi Ari, no. 52/1
For Taxi: วี คลับ สุดซอยอารีย์ พหลโยธิน 7 หน้ากรมสรรพากร
http://www.chamon.com/vclub e-mail: vclub@chamon.com

Fitness & Sauna Chakran

Welcome to The Spice of Life, the newest and most trendy sauna, Jacuzzi, erotic steam, sauna, and heated pool with Jacuzzi behind waterfall. Poolside Lounge, sun decks, bar & Restaurant, aerobic & gym. Theatre & Sexy Rooms, Fantasy maze & Dark Rooms, Exotic Roof Top Garden.

A Place dedicated to intemperance pleasure and intimate relations.

Tel: +66 - 2 - 279-1359, 279-5410
Sky Train: Ari Station, go into Soi Ari, turn left at Soi Ari 4, no. 34
http://www.chakran.com   V CLUB MANAGEMENT

---

co que puede ayudar es relajarse, tratar de encontrarle diversión al asunto y gozarlo. La ciudad ofrece gran cantidad de palacios y templos para visitar. Los mercados flotantes de Chao Pyra ("Río de los Reyes", vía de transporte tradicional de esta ciudad) son de un colorido turbulento que en ningún lugar del mundo encuentran un igual. Puedes ir de compras, adquirir prendas de vestir, seda, joyas y artículos de arte para hacer que una visita a esta ciudad se justifique.
En Bangkok hay tres centros homosexuales. El *Patpong* es considerado el centro nocturno homosexual. Esta región, es la loacalizada entre la *Silom Road* y la *Suriwong Road*. las localidades gay se concentran sobre todo en soi (callejuelas) Silom 2, 4 y 6. Es aconsejable no dejarse llevar al interior de ellas. La segunda región homosexual de importancia son los alrededores de la *Sukhumvit Road* y la *Siam Square*. En contraposición a Patpong este es un sector que se caracteriza por los grandes hoteles y restaurantes internacionales. El otro sector homosexual es *Sapan Kwai*, situado en las afueras de la ciudad de camino al aeropuerto. Este es visitado sobre todo por nativos y turistas que intentan escapar del alocado ritmo de la ciudad.

✖ Per chi non conosce ancora metropoli tropicali, verrà sopraffatto al momento dell'arrivo: dal clima tropicale, dalle affollatissime strade del centro, dall'enorme traffico stradale, carente di mezzi pubblici adeguati e dalle sovracariche strade principali in una sempre più motorizzata città di oltre 6 milioni di abitanti. In questo caso è consigliabile di prendere tutto con calma, guardarsi attorno e godere l'atmosfera eccezionale. La città offre tantissimi palazzi e templi. I mercati sull'acqua e il Chao Pyra ("il fiume dei re", la tradizionale arteria principale di trasporto della città) sono insuperabili per la loro vivace turbolenza. E lo shopping! Ogni visita merita per l'abbigliamento, la seta, i gioielli e gli oggetti d'arte.
A Bangkok si trovano più che altro tre centri gay. La zona *Patpong* è generalmente conosciuta come il migliore indirizzo notturno, anche per clientela gay. La zona prende il nome dalle due strade (in tailandese "patpong") tra la *Silom Road* e la *Suriwong Road*. I locali gay si concentrano nelle soi Silom 2, 4 e 6. Si consiglia di tenersi a distanza dei cosiddetti accompagnatori all'inizio dei "soi" gay. La seconda area gay d'importanza è quella attorno alla *Sukhumvit Road* e alla *Siam Square*. Al contrario del Patpong, questa è la zona dei grandi alberghi e dei ristoranti internazionali. Un'altra zona è il *Sapan Kwai* situata fuori città in direzione dell'aeroporto. Qui è più facile incontrare nativi di Bangkok, o anche turisti che per una sera si vogliono riposare dalla frenesia della città.

GAY INFO

■ **Bangkok Gay Festival**
🖥 www.khsnet.com/bgf
All the information about the next Bangkok Gay Festival on November 4th, 2001.

PUBLICATIONS

■ **Guide of Bangkok with Pink Page**
19/32 Sukhumvit Road, Soi 65, Khlong Toey ✉ 10110 ☎ 3900307
📠 3918060 📧 pinkpage@hotmail.com
🖥 www.geocities.com/westhollywood/5752
Monthly free newspaper with gay pages compiled by Trident. E-mail version available.

■ **This Week**
Free weekly magazine. Its supplement "Afterdark" presents a gay guide.

TOURIST INFO

■ **Tourism Authority of Thailand (TAT)**
Le Concorde Office Building, 202 Ratchadapisek Road, Huay Khwang
✉ 10310 ☎ 6941222 📠 6941220 📧 info1@tat.or.th

Bangkok/Krung Thep - Sapan Kwai — Thailand

■ **Tourist Assistance Center**
4 Ratchadamnoen Nok Avenue, Pom Prap Sattru Phai, Praprachai
✉ 10100 ☎ 282 1143 📠 280 1744
Touristic information. Not gay.

Bangkok/Krung Thep - Sapan Kwai
☎ 02

BARS

■ **Adam** (AC B G S) 20-2 h
6/7-8 Pradiphat Soi 20 (Soi Kaw Toey), Sapan Kwai ✉ 10400
☎ 2781191
One of the oldest go go bars in the area. Small but friendly.

■ **Aladdin** (B D G N S) 19.30-3 h
218/3 Pradiphat Soi 18 (Soi Sahavaree 2), Sapan Kwai ✉ 10400
☎ 2712154
Small bar with go go dancing mainly for Thai customers. Go there, to meet the customers...

■ **Apache Boy** (B G S) 20-2 h
1407/13-14 Soi Laleewan, Phahon Yothin Road, Sapan Kwai
✉ 10400 *(soi between Phahon Yothin Soi 13 and Pradiphat Road)*
☎ 2782756
Go go boys wearing tiny Indian costumes. Draws more and more foreigners.

■ **Be High Bar** (B G S)
11/1 Soi Laleewan, Phahon Yothin Road, Sapan Kwai ✉ 10400 *(soi between Phahon Yothin Soi 13 and Pradiphat Road)* ☎ 2796382
Small and quiet go go bar.

■ **Belami** (B E G N S) 19-2.30 h
971/29 Phahon Yothin Road, Samsennai, Phaya Thai ✉ 10400
☎ 2791434
Nice, elegant bar with hosts mainly for neighbourhood crowd.

■ **Charmming** (AC B G)
2 Pradiphat Soi 17 (Soi Thawan Sak), Sapan Kwai ✉ 10400
☎ 2791437
Indeed a charming place.

■ **Climax** (B G S)
11/2 Soi Laleewan, Phahon Yothin Road, Sapan Kwai ✉ 10400 *New bar, next to Be High Bar*

■ **Cruise Park** (AC B G S)
6/10 Pradiphat Soi 20 (Soi Kaw Toey), Sapan Kwai ✉ 10400

■ **Hippodrome** (AC B CC G MA) 20-3 h
18 Pradiphat Soi 12 (Soi Santi Sewi), Sapan Kwai ✉ 10400 *(Behind Mido Hotel)* ☎ 2780413
Karaoke, pub and hosts. Where friends meet.

■ **King's Heaven and Paradise Cocktail Lounge** (B F G)
466/12 Phahon Yothin Road, Sapan Kwai ✉ 10400 *(soi beside Government Savings Bank, opposite Soi 13)* ☎ 2710602
Small bar and restaurant.

■ **Lucky Boy** (B D G)
169/25-26 Pradiphat Road, Sapan Kwai ✉ 10400 *(in front of Elisabeth Hotel)* ☎ 2781103

■ **Oasis** (B G S)
11/19 Pradiphat Soi 20 (Soi Kaw Toey), Sapan Kwai ✉ 10400
☎ 2785058
Small go go bar and restaurant with karaoke.

■ **Peak Point Entertainment '41** (B G)
1019/4 Phahon Yothin Road, Phaya Thai ✉ 10400 *(in the alley beside Thai Farmer Bank)* ☎ 6170862
Hosts and karaoke in a small bar.

■ **Seven Nights** (B G S)
6/2-3 Pradiphat Soi 20 (Soi Kaw Toey), Sapan Kwai ✉ 10400
☎ 2799399
Karaoke.

■ **Stax Boy und Stax Karaoke Lounge** (B G S STV) Fri + Sat ladyboy show at 1h
9 Pradipat Soi 20 (Soi Kaw Toey), Sapan Kwai ✉ 10400 *(soi Embassy Hotel)* ☎ 2784018
Two bars with drag shows and karaoke.

■ **Street Boy** (B G)
6/1 Soi Pradiphat 20, Sapan Kwai ✉ 10400 ☎ 2784739
Small new bar with boys and beer.

■ **Water Boy** (B G S) 18-2 h
6/5-6 Pradiphat Soi 20 (Soi Kaw Toey), Sapan Kwai ✉ 10400
☎ 6 18 73 24

SAUNAS/BATHS

■ **Adonis II** (G msg SA SB) Mon-Fri 16-23, Sat, Sun 13-23 h
169/44 Pradiphat Road (Soi Suthisarn), Sapan Kwai ✉ 10400 *(soi of Elizabeth Hotel)* ☎ 6184130
Sauna mainly for Thais, who never the less will appreciate the visit of the few farangs (foreigners). Entrance 140 Baht.

Thailand — Bangkok/Krung Thep - Sapan Kwai ▶ Silom Road/Surawong Road

■ **Chakran** (G msg wh WO)
34 Soi Ari 4, off Phahon Yothin Soi 7 (Soi Ari), Phaya Thai ✉ 10400 ☎ 79 13 59
The new massage place of V Club with sauna, jacuzzi, heated pool and waterfall. Right opposite the traditional V Club.

■ **V Club** (F G msg WH WO)
52/1 Phahon Yothin Soi 7 (Soi Ari), Phaya Thai ✉ 10400 *(right side behind Soi Ari 4)* ☎ 2793322
One of the best saunas in Bangkok. Very friendly, nice location and well trained men for massage. They look like models because most of them also work as models. So do not close your eyes during your massage...

FITNESS STUDIOS

■ **G.G. (Grey Gymnastics Men's Club)** (AC B G MA msg WO)
16-23 h
1155/1 Ronachai Soi 2, Nakorn Chaisri, off Rama 6 Road, Phaya Thai ✉ 10400 ☎ 2793807
Sauna, gym, steam, massage, coffee-shop. Popular with local Thais and some foreigners only.

HOTELS

■ **Elizabeth Hotel** (glm H)
169/51 Pradiphat Road, Sapan Kwai ✉ 10400 *(between Soi 15 and 17)* ☎ 2710204 📠 2712539
Close to all gay venues in the area.

■ **Liberty Garden** (glm H)
215 Pradiphat Road, Sapan Kwai ✉ 10400 *(between Soi 19 and 21)* ☎ 2785018 ☎ 2799756
Close to all gay venues in the area.

■ **Paradise 2** (AC BF B F G H msg OS S SB VS WH)
42/1 Phahon Yothin Soi 11, Sapan Kwai ✉ 10400 ☎ 2795609 ☎ 01/6357786 (Mobile)
Guest house, Titanic cocktail lounge with hosts, cabaret, weekend special shows. Also restaurant with Thai and Vietnamese food and Leonardo Club Sauna.

■ **Pradiphat Hotel** (AC B BF CC F g H MA)
173/1 Pradiphat Road, Sapan Kwai ✉ 10400 ☎ 2781470 ☎ 2781477 📠 2781478
Cheapest hotel in this area.

CRUISING

- JJ Park
- Chatuchak Park

Bangkok/Krung Thep - Siam Square/Pattunam ☎ 02

BARS

■ **Planet Hollywood** (B F glm) 11-2 h
Gaysorn Plaza, 999 Phloen Chit Road / Ratchadamri Road, Lumpini, Pathumwan ✉ 10330 ☎ 6561358
Mixed club and restaurant with excellent bands.

■ **Saxophone** (AC B CC F g MA) 18-3 h
3/8 Phayathai Road, Victory Monument, Phaya Thai ✉ 10400 *(at the Victory Monument, close to Mr. Donut and KFC)* ☎ 2465472
Beautiful pub with excellent life jazz & blues every night. Mixed.

CAFES

■ **Colour**
645/25-26 Petchburi Road Soi 17 (Soi T.S. Apartment), Pattunam ✉ 10330 ☎ 2529221

SHOWS

■ **Calypso Cabaret** (B glm S STV) Shows at 20.15 and 21.45 h
Asia Hotel, 296 Phaya Thai Road, Pathumwan ✉ 10330 ☎ 2616355 (9-18 h)
Hundreds of tourists come with buses every night, only to find out, that the most beautiful women in Thailand are men.

SAUNAS/BATHS

■ **Angelo Sauna** (glm N SA SB) Mo-Fri 16-23.30h, Sat, Sun, Holiday 14-23.30h
1025/10-11 Ploenchit Road, Pathumwan ✉ 10330 ☎ 2529176
Sauna, steam, video & gym. Mainly for local crowd.

HOTELS

■ **Opera** (glm H)
16 Petchburi 11 (Soi Somprasong 1) Petchburi Road, Phaya Thai ✉ 10400 ☎ 2524031 ☎ 2524032 📠 2535360
Popular with gays.

■ **Reno Hotel** (glm H)
40 Soi Kasem San 1, Rama 1, Pathumwan ✉ 10330 ☎ 2150026

GUEST HOUSES

■ **Ban Thai**
108 Ratchawithi Road Soi 6 (Soi Santisuk), Phaya Thai ✉ 10240 ☎ 2453946 📠 (06) 44 53 64

CRUISING

National Stadium P (Rama 1 Road, Pathumwan)

Bangkok/Krung Thep - Silom Road/Surawong Road ☎ 02

✱ All roads lead to Patong, but the taxis alone create a traffic chaos. This fun centre is named after the two streets Patong 1 and Patong 2, which connect the Li Lom Road with the parallel Surawong road. The night market is renowned for its bargains, bartering is compulsory, watches are cheap and fake, silver often reasonably priced and the real thing.
The gay scene comes to life in the evening in Si Lom Soi 4, going through the many bars and shows in the Si Lom Soi 6, Than Thawan or Duangthwee Plaza and ends in the discos in the Si Lom Road from Soi 2 to Soi 10.

✱ Alle Wege führen nach Patpong, schon die Taxis alleine verursachen hier allabendlich einen hoffnungslosen Verkehrschaos: Dieses Vergnügungszentrum ist benannt nach den beiden Straßen Patpong 1 und Patpong 2, welche die Li Lom Road mit der parallelen Surawong Road verbinden. Der Nachtmarkt ist berühmt für seine günstigen Gelegenheiten, Handeln ist Pflicht, Uhren sind billig und alle falsch, Silber meistens preiswert und echt.
Das schwule Leben beginnt am frühen Abend in Si Lom Soi 4, streift dann durch die Bars und Shows in Si Lom Soi 6, Soi Than Thawan oder Duangthawee Plaza und endet nachts in den Diskotheken der Si Lom Road von Soi 2 bis Soi 10.

✱ A Bangkok, toutes les routes mènent à Patong et rien ne se taxis créent chaque soir des embouteillages monstres. Ce centre de divertissements a été nommé d'après les rues Patong 1 et Patong 2, qui connectent la Li Lom Road avec la rue parallèle, la Surawong Road. Le marché de nuit est connu pour ses occasions uniques, le marchandage y est de mise, les montres sont bon marché, l'argent est souvent vrai et offert à des prix raisonnables.
La scène gaie s'éveille le soir dans la Si Lom Soi 4, se déplace ensuite dans les nombreux bars et spectacles de la Si Lom Soi 6, Than Thawan et Duangthwee Plaza, pour finir la nuit dans les clubs de la Si Lom Road, du Soi 2 au Soi 10.

Bangkok/Krung Thep - Silom Road/Surawong Road — Thailand

Todos los caminos llevan a Patpong, donde todas las noches ya sólo los taxis causan un increíble caos de tráfico. Esta zona de recreación tiene su nombre de las dos calles Patpong 1 und Patpong 2, que unen la Li Lom Road con la calle paralela Surawong Road. El mercado nocturno es famoso por las ofertas económicas; hay que regatear. Los relojes son baratos (y siempre falsificados), la plata suele tener precios atractivos (y ser plata de verdad).
La vida gay empieza por la tarde en Si Lom Soi 4, después se desplaza a los bares y espectáculos de Si Lom Soi 6, Soi Than Thawan o Duangthawee Plaza y termina en la noche en las discotecas de Si Lom Road entre Soi 2 y Soi 10.

Tutte le strade portano a Patpong. Qui bastano già i taxi da soli a provocare tutte le sere ingorghi insolubili di traffico. Questo centro di divertimenti prende il nome dalle due strade Patpong 1 e Patpong 2, che collegano la Li Lom Road con la parallela Surawong Road. Il mercato notturno è famoso per le sue favorevoli occasioni d'acquisto, contrattare è d'obbligo, gli orologi si vendono a basso prezzo e sono tutti falsi, l'argento e quasi sempre a buon mercato ed è vero.
La vita gay comincia in prima serata in Si Lom Soi 4, poi passa per i night-club e gli show in Si Lom Soi 6, Soi Than Thawan o Duangthawee Plaza e finisce in nottata nelle discoteche della Si Lom Road da Soi 2 a Soi 10.

BARS

■ **Balcony. The** (! AC B F G MA N OS) Sun-Thu 19-2 h, Fri-Sat 19-3 h
86-88 Si Lom Road Soi 4 (Soi Jaruwan), Bang Rak ✉ 10500
☎ 2355891
One of the very popular night spots for eating, drinking and meeting. For sure the most reasonable prices in the gay night life.

■ **Blue Star** (! AC B CC D F G MA msg S SNU VS) 20-2 h, show every hour
Duangthawee Plaza, 38/6 Soi Pratoochai, at 38 Surawong Road, Bang Rak ✉ 10500 ☎ 2332121
Sexy circus. Large go go bar with cute hosts and party every night. Lots of handsome dancers, colourful randy shows. Completely renovated.

■ **Boys Bangkok. The** (! AC B CC G MA S SNU STV) 20-2h, shows 22.30h, 24h, 1h
Duangthawee Plaza, 894/12-13 Soi Pratoochai, at 38 Surawong Road, Bang Rak ✉ 10500 ☎ 2372006
One of the best go go bars in town. Crowded every night. Lots of dancers and three special shows every night.

■ **Café de Maru-Ya** (B G)
944/18 Rama IV Road, Bang Rak ✉ 10500 (Next to My Way)
Karaoke bar mainly for Thais.

■ **Dream Boy Barbeir** (! AC B G MA S SNU) 20-2 h. Shows 22.30h + 0.30h
35/3-5 Surawong Road, Bang Rak ✉ 10500 (opposite Duangthawee Plaza) ☎ 2340830
Not only one of the largest, but for sure one of the best go go bars in Thailand. Dream Boy shows on two stages are usually packed crowded every night, colourful and exciting.

■ **Eve House** (B G)
18-18/1 Surawong Road, Bang Rak ✉ 10500 (Opposite Soi Thaniya)
☎ 2336506
Karaoke for Thais and their friends. Mainly interesting in the after hours.

■ **Future Boys** (B G S)
Duangthawee Plaza, 894/5-6 Soi Pratoochai, at 38 Surawong Road, Bang Rak ✉ 10500 ☎ 6 37 05 07

■ **Golden Cock** (B G S SNU) 13-1h
39/27 Soi Rajanakarindra 1 (Soi Anuman Rajadhon) Surawong Road, Bang Rak ✉ 10500 (Off Si Lom Soi 6, off Soi Than Thawan)
☎ 2363859
Small but interesting go go bar. Opens already in the afternoon.

PUB FOOD KARAOKE

HAPPY HOURS AND SPECIAL OFFERS DAILY

The Balcony

VOTED Bangkok's #1 Gay Pub & Restaurant again in 2000 internet survey

86~88 Silom Soi 4, Bangkok Tel: 235-5891
http://www.balconypub.com

---

the only **ultimate** gay zone in THAILAND
HTTP://WWW.DJ-STATION.COM

diSco Disco D.J. STATION SILOM SOI 2 BKK THE JJ PARK

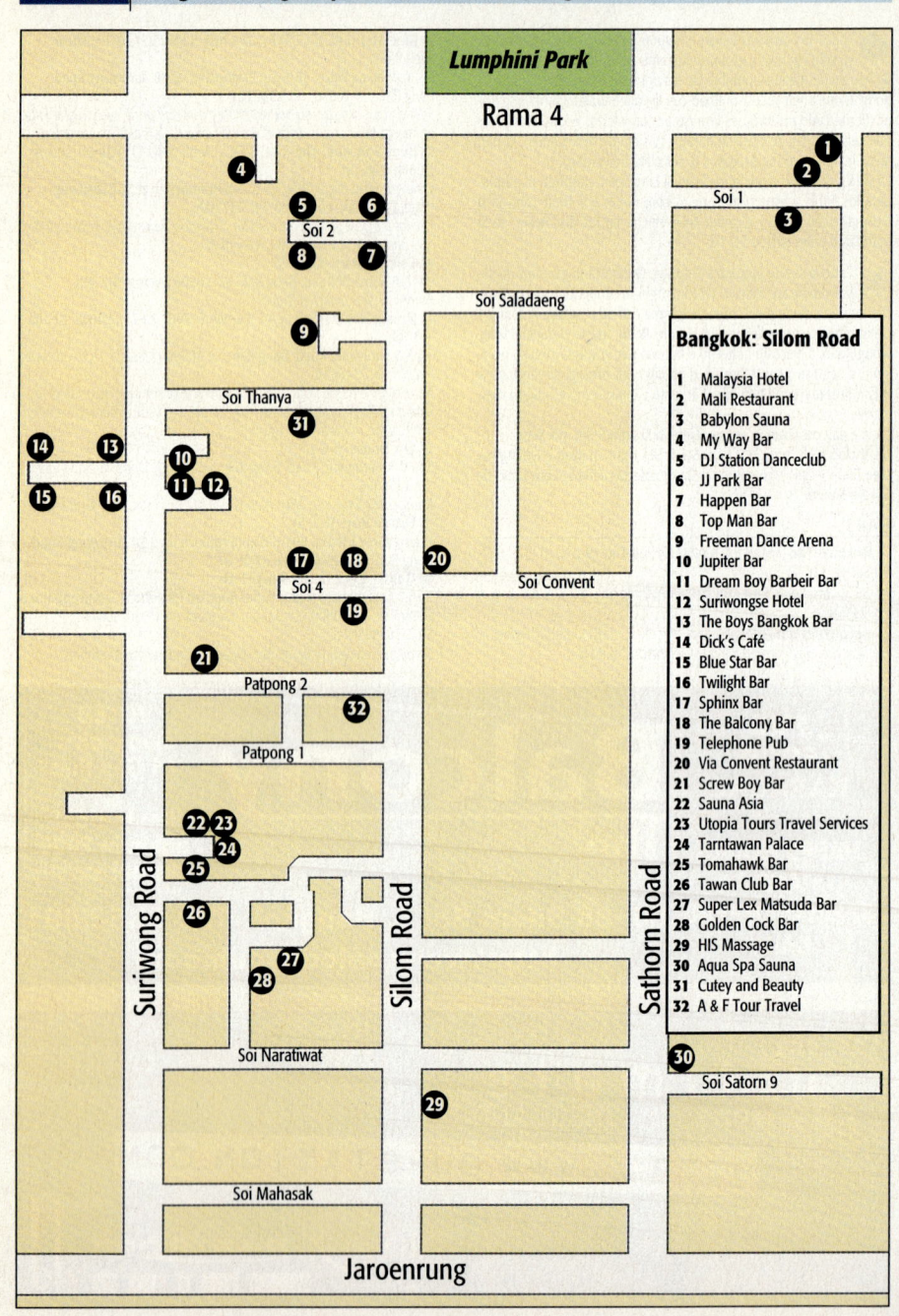

Thailand — Bangkok/Krung Thep - Silom Road/Surawong Road

Bangkok: Silom Road

1. Malaysia Hotel
2. Mali Restaurant
3. Babylon Sauna
4. My Way Bar
5. DJ Station Danceclub
6. JJ Park Bar
7. Happen Bar
8. Top Man Bar
9. Freeman Dance Arena
10. Jupiter Bar
11. Dream Boy Barbeir Bar
12. Suriwongse Hotel
13. The Boys Bangkok Bar
14. Dick's Café
15. Blue Star Bar
16. Twilight Bar
17. Sphinx Bar
18. The Balcony Bar
19. Telephone Pub
20. Via Convent Restaurant
21. Screw Boy Bar
22. Sauna Asia
23. Utopia Tours Travel Services
24. Tarntawan Palace
25. Tomahawk Bar
26. Tawan Club Bar
27. Super Lex Matsuda Bar
28. Golden Cock Bar
29. HIS Massage
30. Aqua Spa Sauna
31. Cutey and Beauty
32. A & F Tour Travel

Bangkok/Krung Thep - Silom Road/Surawong Road — **Thailand**

TAWAN CLUB

The exculusive club for men only

Muscle shows

Special show Time 10.30 p.m. to 1 a.m.
2/2 Soi Than Thawan, Surawong Road
Bang Rak, Bangkok 10500 Thailand
Open 8 p.m. to 2 a.m.
☎ +66 - 2 - 234 5506

BLUE STAR sexy circus

Boys ★ Show ★ Fun ★ Party

Very special special shows
Duangthawee Plaza
38/6 Surawong Rd. Bangkok
http://bluestar.thaiboy.net
☎ +66-2-233 21 21

DREAMBOY BARBEIR

Bangkok's most popular Go Go Boy Bar
Show time every night 22.30 and 0.30h
100 sexy hosts on two stages!
With very special shows!

Don't miss the DREAMBOY experience
where your dreams come true.

35/3-4 Surawong Road, Bangkok 10500
next to Suriwongse Hotel ☎ 234-0830
for Taxi: DREAMBOY BARBEIR
35/3-4 ถ.สุริวงค์ หน้า โรงแรม สุริวงค์

| Thailand | Bangkok/Krung Thep - Silom Road/Surawong Road |

Freeman Dance arena

60/18-21 Silom Road, Bangrak, Bangkok, Thailand, 10500.
Telephone : 632-8033 Fax : 632-8033
http : // www.freemanclub.com email : info@freemanclub.com

Disco-vdotheque
Cabaret show
Relaxing area
Cruising area

HAPPEN!
8/14 SILOM RD.,
SOI 2, BANGRAK
BANGKOK 10500
THAILAND
TEL 66 2 2352552

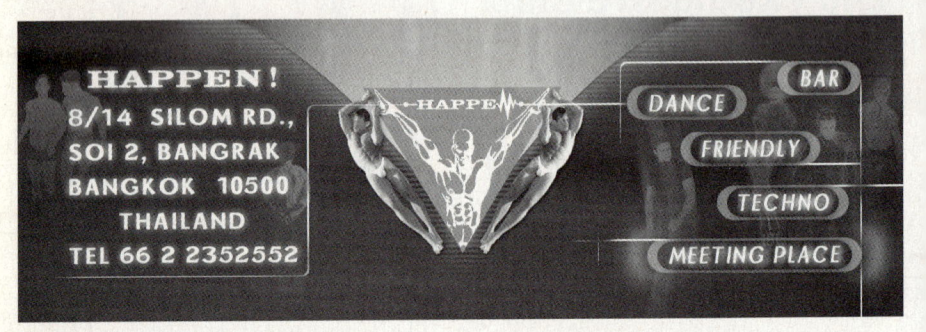

BAR / DANCE / FRIENDLY / TECHNO / MEETING PLACE

■ **Happen** (AC B d G s) 21-4 h
8/14 Si Lom Soi 2, Bang Rak ✉ 10500 ☎ 2352552
A friendly bar

■ **JJ Park** (AC B f g YG) 21-3 h
8/3 Si Lom Soi 2, Bang Rak ✉ 10500 ☎ 2351227

■ **Jupiter** (AC B G MA S) 20-2 h
31/1-33 Surawong Road (Soi Thaniya 2), Bang Rak ✉ 10500 *(Next to Suriwong Hotel)* ☎ 2374050
Big bar with shows.

■ **Krua Mama** (B F G)
39/16 Soi Rajanakarindra 1 (Soi Anuman Rajadhon) Surawong Road, Bang Rak ✉ 10500 *(Off Si Lom Soi 6, off Soi Than Thawan)*
Karaoke and restaurant mainly for Thais.

■ **My Way** (AC B G S VS) 16-1, Sat Sun 13-1 h
944/4 Rama IV Road, Bang Rak ✉ 10500 *(in small sub-soi off Rama IV Road between Si Lom Road and Suriwong Road)* ☎ 2339567
One of the oldest go go bars in Bangkok. Small and intimate place.

■ **P.M. Karaoke** (B F G)
39/19 Soi Rajanakarindra 1 (Soi Anuman Rajadhon) Surawong Road, Bang Rak ✉ 10500 *(Off Si Lom Soi 6, off Soi Than Thawan)*
Karaoke and restaurant mainly for Thais.

■ **Sanctuary Bar** (B G)
34/17 Soi Si Bumphen, Sathorn ✉ 10500 *(Near Malaysia Hotel)*
☎ 2871670
Nice little outside bar run by Pom.

■ **Screw Boy** (AC B G SNU) 20-2 h
Patpong 2 Road, 37/3-17 Surawong Road, Bang Rak ✉ 10500
(Next to Pink Panther, opposite KFC) ☎ (01) 6555055 (Mobile)
The only gay go go bar directly on Patpong among hundreds of straight places.

■ **Sphinx** (B F G) 18-2 h
100 Si Lom Soi 4 (Soi Jaruwan), Bang Rak ✉ 10500 ☎ 2347249

Good food and friendly staff. The place for a dinner with your friend. Upstairs Pharaoh's Karaoke.

■ **Super Lex Matsuda** (AC B CC f G MA OS S SNU TV VS) 20-2 h
39/14-16 Soi Rajanakarinda 1 (Soi Anuman Rajadhon), Surawong Road, Bang Rak ✉ 10500 *(Off Si Lom 6, off Soi Than Thawan)*
☎ 2361633
Go-go bar with popular shows and outdoor seating.

■ **Tawan Club (The Sun)** (! AC B G lj msg NU S SNU VS WO)
20.30-2 h
2/2 Soi Than Thawan, Surawong Road, Bang Rak ✉ 10500 *(Corner of Surawong Road, Si Lom Soi 6)* ☎ 2345506
Muscles, muscles and more muscles. One of the oldest and best maintained bars in Bangkok. Exciting shows.

■ **Telephone Pub** (! AC B F G MA OS) 19-2 h
114/11-13 Si Lom Soi 4 (Soi Jaruwan), Bang Rak ✉ 10500
☎ 2343279
Wait for a call or call up a new friend from the telephone on your table. Excellent food (Thai and Western). Probably the most famous gay pub in Bangkok. Completely renovated.

■ **Tomahawk Bar** (AC B G S SNU)
7/3 Soi Than Thawan, Surawong Road, Bang Rak ✉ 10500 *(Corner of Surawong Road, Si Lom Soi 6)* ☎ 2362865
Go go bar in high-tech style and very cute and friendly staff.

■ **Top Man Bar** (AC B CC G MA S VS) 20-2 h, show 22.30 h.
8/9 Si Lom Soi 2, Bang Rak ✉ 10500 *(2nd floor)* ☎ 6328934
Go go bar.

■ **Twilight Bar** (AC B G S VS) 19.30-2 h
Duangthawee Plaza, 38/40 Soi Pratoochai, at 38 Surawong Road, Bang Rak ✉ 10500 ☎ 2361944
Go go bar with cabaret shows every night.

■ **Up2 Bar** (B G OS S SNU) 20.30-2 h
928-930 Rama IV Road, Bang Rak ✉ 10500 ☎ 2353876
Most shows include muscle men, bodypainting, candle shows.

Bangkok/Krung Thep - Silom Road/Surawong Road — Thailand

CAFES

■ **Banana Café** (B F G OS)
Duangthawee Plaza, 894/14-15 Soi Pratoochai, at 38 Surawong Road, Bang Rak ✉ 10500
Open air bar and restaurant.

■ **Bangkok Tootsie Terrace** (B bf CC F G MA OS) 24 hours daily
34 Soi Nantha, South Sathorn Soi 1 (Soi Atthakan Prasit), Sathorn ✉ 10120 ☎ 79 79 85
New coffee shop.

■ **Dick's Café** (! A B F G) 11-5 h
Duangthawee Plaza, 894/7-8 Soi Pratoochai, at 38 Surawong Road, Bang Rak ✉ 10500 ☎ 6370078
The pleasant coffee oasis directly in the heart of the gay scene. Excellent cappuccino and beautiful ambience. You will meet nice people all day, all night. They also have Thai food, sandwiches and cakes.

■ **Espresso, The** (B G MA)
8/10-11 Si Lom Soi 2, Bang Rak ✉ 10500
New coffee shop run by D.J. Station.

■ **Grace Café** (B F G) 10.30-15, Dinner 17-2 h
942/51 A. Charn Isara Building 1, Rama IV Road, Bang Rak ✉ 10500 ☎ 2672099
Gay owned café and restaurant.

■ **Kitsch**
8/14 Si Lom Soi 2, second floor, Bang Rak ✉ 10500 ☎ 25 25 52
Funky café, decorations, costumes, paintings, gifts.

DANCECLUBS

■ **Babylon Sound Factory** (AC B CC D DR G MA VS WE) Fri, Sat 23h-late
34 Soi Nantha, South Sathorn Soi 1 (Soi Atthakan Prasit), Sathorn ✉ 10120 ☎ 79 79 85
New dancefloor with dark corner.

■ **diSco Disco** (B D G)
8/12-13 Si Lom Soi 2, Bang Rak ✉ 10500 ☎ 2346151
Bar and disco. The Thai alternative to DJ Station.

■ **D.J. Station** (! AC B D G MA S VS) 23h-3h
8/6-8 Si Lom Road, Soi 2, Bang Rak ✉ 10500 ☎ 2664029
Best and most popular gay disco in Southeast Asia! Three floors packed crowded every night. Every night at midnight show with Puppet String and famous Miguel!

■ **Freeman Dance Arena** (! AC B CC D DR G MA OS S STV) 22-3 h
60/18-21 Si Lom Road, Bang Rak ✉ 10500 (Small soi between Thanya Road and Si Lom Soi 2, opposite Si Lom complex. Sky train: Saladang) ☎ 6328032
Bangkok's pleasant new gay disco with excellent shows and darkroom on the top floor. Cheerful crowd every night.

■ **Gay Pub** (AC B D f G MA S VS)
Duangthawee Plaza, 38/5 Soi Pratoochai, at 38 Surawong Road, Bang Rak ✉ 10500
Disco & Karaoke. May change to a go go bar soon.

■ **Oi**
144/9-10 Si Lom Soi 10, Bang Rak ✉ 10500
Small disco and karaoke with all gay Thai crowd. Go there late after the big discos close, to be one of the few foreigners. Do not expect to meet a new friend.

RESTAURANTS

■ **Mali** (F glm)
43 South Sathorn Soi 1 (Soi Atthakan Prasit), Sathorn ✉ 10120 ☎ 6798693
Thai and international cuisine.

■ **Mango Tree** (F glm OS)
37 Soi Rajanakarindra 1 (Soi Anuman Rajadhon) Surawong Road, Bang Rak ✉ 10500 (Off Si Lom Soi 6, off Soi Than Thawan) ☎ 2362820
Traditional Thai restaurant in a beautiful mango tree yard. Sometimes Thai life music.

■ **Pi Lek** (F glm OS)
39/13 Soi Rajanakarindra 1 (Soi Anuman Rajadhon) Surawong Road, Bang Rak ✉ 10500 (Off Si Lom Soi 6, off Soi Than Thawan) ☎ 2361636
Eat simple food outdoors and see the most colourful crowd.

■ **Via Convent** (F glm) 11.30-14, 18-23 h, Sat, Sun + Holiday dinner only
1 Convent Road, Bang Rak ✉ 10500 ☎ 2667162
One of the finest restaurants in the heart of Bangkok's night life. Italian and international food. And be sure, here they cook the spaghetti al dente, the steak rare or medium.

SAUNAS/BATHS

■ **Aqua Spa**
K. S. Building, 11/4-5 South Sathorn Soi 9, Bang Rak ✉ 10120 ☎ 2864535
New sauna with steam, jacuzzi, gym, massage.

■ **Babylon 2000. The** (! AC b CC DR F G MA OS PI s SA SB WH WO) 12-24 h
34 Soi Nantha, South Sathorn Soi 1 (Soi Atthakan Prasit), Sathorn ✉ 10120 (Moved 200 m down the soi) ☎ 6797985
Bangkok's world famous and most popular sauna bath moved in the new millenium 200 meters down the soi to a new location with pool and hotel.

■ **C.O.A. City of Angels** (AC b CC DR F G MA SA SB VS WO) 15-23, Fri, Sat, Holiday 14-24 h
Si Lom Center Building, (Robinson Si Lom), Bang Rak ✉ 10500 (17th floor, lift on the right side of Robinson Department Store) ☎ 6328027
A recreation centre for men only.

■ **Heaven** (AC B D R F G MA msg OS SA SB VS WO) 15-24 h
Warner Building, 4th floor, 119 Soi Mahesak, Bang Rak ✉ 10500 (Between Si Lom Soi 32 and 34) ☎ 2669092
Sauna with a rooftop garden together with Eden massage.

■ **K-Why** (b CC DR F G MA S SA SB VS WO) 16-24, Fri-Sun 14-24 h
942/51 A. Charn Isara Building 1, Rama IV Road, Bang Rak ✉ 10500 (1st floor, behind Grace Café) ☎ 2672098
Totally renovated in December 99, this sauna organises many special events.

■ **Sauna Asia** (b G SA SB WO)
Tarntawan Place Hotel, 119/5-10 Surawong Road, Bang Rak ✉ 10500 (between Patpong 1 and Soi Than Thawan) ☎ 2362929
New sauna in the heart of the gay night life. Steam, sauna, gym, cabins, restaurant, bar.

MASSAGE

■ **Eden** (G msg)
Warner Building, 4th floor, 119 Soi Mahesak, Between Si Lom Soi 32 and 34, Bang Rak ✉ 10500 ☎ 6359017
Oil and other special massages.

■ **Eve House** (glm msg)
18-18/1 Surawong Road, Bang Rak ✉ 10500 ☎ 2663846
Traditional Thai Massage.

■ **HIS** (G msg wo) 12-24 h
Si Lom Plaza, 2nd floor, 491/10-11 Si Lom Road, Bang Rak ✉ 10500 (5 mins from Silom Soi 4) ☎ 2340063
Oil and cream massage, body scrub, gym and cafe.

Thailand — Bangkok/Krung Thep - Silom Road/Surawong Road

A & F TOUR TRAVEL

For all your travel needs in *Thailand, Laos, Cambodia and Burma*.
Contact us and discover Southeast Asia in your favorite way.
Check and See that we have the best price.

Pattaya Bangkok Phuket Samui Chiang mai Angkor Wat

Check out our website: www.gayasiantravel.com
Phone: +66 - 2 - 266 5105-6 Fax: +66 - 2 - 267 0364
We are convenient located: 120 Si Lom Road, Bangkok
aandftour@hotmail.com

Cutey Beauty HAIR SALON

3rd floor Thaniya Plaza
52 Si Lom Road
Bangkok 10500
☎ +66 - 2 - 231 2315
Website: www.cuteybeauty.com

BODY & BEAUTY SHOPS

■ **Cutey and Beauty** (AC CC) 11-20h
Thaniya Plaza, 3rd floor, 52 Si Lom Road, Bang Rak ✉ 10500
Hair designer. Speciality: Face Massage with oxygen. Staff trained with Vidal Sassoon and Toni + Guy in London. Gay owned and operated.

TRAVEL AND TRANSPORT

■ **A & F Tour Travel**
Kasemkij Building, 120 Si Lom Road, Bang Rak ✉ 10110
☎ 2670369 📠 2670364
📧 aandftour@hotmail.com
New gay travel agent. Convenient located 1 minute away from the gay night live around Patpong.

■ **Utopia Tours** (GLM) 10-18 h
Tarntawan Place Hotel, 119/5-10 Surawong Road, Bang Rak
✉ 10500 (between Patpong 1 and Soi Than Thawan)
☎ 2383227 📧 info@utopia-tours.com
🌐 www.utopia-tours.com
Asia's gay travel pioneers. They will arrange your stay in Thailand and your tour to other Asian countries. Go there for information on the gay scenes.

HOTELS

Most of the hotels in Bangkok are gay friendly and there is normally no problem to bring your friend(s) upstairs. Many hotels are concerned for your security and will hold your visitor's ID Card during your stay. Only few luxury hotels charge extra

■ **Babylon Barrack** (AC b BF CC F G H MA PI)
34 Soi Nantha, South Sathorn Soi 1 (Soi Atthakan Prasit), Sathorn
✉ 10120 (Same building as the new Babylon Sauna) ☎ 6797985
📠 6797986 📧 info@babylonbkk.com 🌐 www.babylonbkk.com
New gay hotel opened 2000. 40 rooms from 800 Baht/day.

■ **Malaysia Hotel** (B F g H PI)
54 Soi Ngam Duphli, Rama IV Road, Sathorn ✉ 10120
☎ 6797127 ☎ 02/6797136 📠 2871457
📧 malaysia@ksc15.th.com 🌐 ksc15.co.th/malaysia
Located near the famous Babylon sauna and close to the gay nightlife, this budget friendly hotel is most popular among gay travellers.

■ **Suriwong**
33/1-33 Surawong Road (Soi Thaniya 2), Bang Rak ✉ 10500
☎ 66 82 57-60 📠 66 82 61
Gay friendly low budget hotel with famous 24h coffee shop. Beware of hustlers.

■ **Tarntawan Place** (! AC B BF CC F GLM H msg)
119/5-10 Surawong Road, Bang Rak ✉ 10500 ☎ 2382620
📠 2383228 📧 tarntawan@tarntawan.com
🌐 www.tarntawan.com
Bangkok's best gay hotel in the heart of the gay night life. Among many other services the Tarntawan offers 24 hour Business centre, lobby lounge and bar, safe deposit boxes, meeting rooms, karaoke, internet - e-mail access, tour desk and the gay travel agency Utopia Tours. Special discount rates for Spartacus Readers!

■ **Tower Inn** (g H PI SA WH WO)
533 Si Lom Road, Bang Rak ✉ 10500 ☎ 2378300
☎ 02/2378304 📠 2378386 📧 towerinn@bkk.a-net.net.th

TARNTAWAN PLACE HOTEL

The **Tarntawan Place Hotel** is a new boutique hotel and the best choice for gay business men and tourists. Gay owned and managed, the Tarntawan Place Hotel offers great value for your money.

The **Tarntawan Place Hotel** is the #1 gay hotel in Bangkok. It is within walking distance to all the best gay nightlife venues as well as the shopping and commercial centre.

Tarntawan Place Hotel
119/5-10 Surawong Road
Bangkok 10500, Thailand
Tel: +66 - 2 - 2 38 26 20
Fax: +66 - 2 - 2 38 32 28
Mail: tarntawan@tarntawan.com
Website: www.tarntawan.com

Dick's Café Bangkok

Duangthawee Plaza, 894/7-8, Soi Pratoochai, Surawong Road, Bangkok 10500
Tel: (+66-2) 637-0078, Website: http://www.dickscafe.com

Thailand Bangkok/Krung Thep - Silom Road/Surawong Road ▸ Sukhumvit Road

GUEST HOUSES

■ **Aquarius Guest-House** (AC B BF CC F G H MA OS VS) Bar open 19-1 h
243 Soi Hutayana, South Satorn Soi 3 (Soi Suanplu), Sathorn
✉ 10120 ☏ 2860217 ☏ 6793180 🖷 2862174
💻 aquarius@bangkok.com 💻 bangkok.com/mypage/aquarius
Gay guest house in residential area in a converted cosy house with garden. The nice owner speaks English.

■ **Win's Guesthouse** (AC B BF G H MA msg)
21/8 Soi Ngam Duphli, Thanon Rama IV ✉ 10120 (Sathorn)
☏ 287-1345 💻 www.angelfire.com/ky/winbkk
14 double rooms , shared showers and WC. Good breakfasts not included in room rate. No hot meals.

HEALTH GROUPS

■ **Anonymous Clinic, Thai Red Cross Society** Mon-Fri 12-19, Sat 9-12 h
1871 Rama IV Road, Bang Rak ✉ 10500 *(At the Saowapha Institute, the Snake Farm)* ☏ 2564109
Anonymous HIV testing.

■ **Surawong Medi-Clinic** Mon-Fri 8.30-21, Sat 12-21 h
37/4-5 Surawong Road, Soi Surawong Plaza, Bang Rak ✉ 10500
HIV testing.

SWIMMING

-Malaysia Hotel (the hotel pool is open for public use for small fee and is a favourite cruising place).

CRUISING

-Lumpini Park (6-20 h inside the Park, after dark around Rama IV monument. Corner of Rama IV/Si Lom Road. The most popular Bangkok cruising. Beware of hustlers)
-Robinson Department Store (Cruising around all entrances and toilets. Beware of hustlers).

Bangkok/Krung Thep - Sukhumvit Road ☏ 02

★ The business center of Bankok has a number of attractive gay places. These are however, not all concentrated in one area, but dispersed along the rather long Sukhumvit Road. Few tourist cross you path, instead more business people and foreigners who live here.

★ Das Geschäftszentrum von Bangkok hat auch eine ganze Reihe attraktiver schwuler Plätze. Sie liegen allerdings nicht konzentriert sondern eher verstreut über die ganze Länge der Sukhumvit Road verteilt. So trifft man weniger Touristen und eher den Geschäftsmann, den ortsansässigen Ausländer, den Dauergast.

★ Le centre des affaires de Bangkok a de nombreux endroits gais à offrir. Ceux-ci ne sont pas concentrés en un point mais éparpillés tout le long de la grande Sukhumvit Road. Ici, on ne croise que peu de touristes, mais plutôt des hommes d'affaire ou des étrangers établis dans la ville.

★ En el centro económico de Bangkok también hay unos cuantos lugares gays. No están concentrados en una zona en concreto sino que están esparcidos a lo largo de la Sukhumvit Road. Por ello, es menos probable encontrarse con otros turistas, pero sí con hombres de negocios o extranjeros que viven y trabajan en Bangkok.

★ Il centro commerciale di Bangkok dispone di una ricca serie di posti attraenti per omosessuali. Tuttavia non sono così vicini l'uno all'altro ma distribuiti lungo tutta la Sukhumvit Road. In questo modo s'incontrano meno turisti e, più di frequente, l'uomo d'affari, lo straniero residente, il cliente permanente.

BARS

■ **Jet Set**
32/19 Sukumvit Soi 21 (Soi Wirot), Khlong Toey ✉ 10110
☏ 58 43 11
Karaoke mainly for Thais.

■ **Mercury** (B G MA msg)
116/1 Sukhumvit Soi 23 (Soi Prasan Mit), Khlong Toey ✉ 10110 (2nd floor) ☏ 6623021
Karaoke, pub and massage.

■ **Silver Fox** (AC AYOR B G MA S TV VS) 12-1h.
1/11 Sukhumvit Soi 24, Khlong Toey ✉ 10110 *(Behind Nimitr Restaurant)* ☏ 2585372

■ **Turning Point** (AC B CC d f G MA msg S SB STV) 20.30-2.30, show Fri Sat 23-23.30 h
120/19-20 Sukumvit Soi 23 (Soi Prasan Mit), Khlong Toey ✉ 10110
☏ 6621103
One of the finest host bars in town. Go there for karaoke and special entertainment. They have now steam bath and massage available.

■ **Two Thirds (2/3)** (B G H MA msg) 18-2 h
2/3 Sukhumvit Soi 34, Khlong Toey ✉ 10110 *(near Rex Hotel)*
☏ 2599619

To be a hot man in a hot place and get your basic life

HERO
Men's Fitness club

Oil Massage   VIP Rooms
Tora: Massage with body
Sanshiro: Massage and Scrub with steam

65 Soi Sukhumvit 11
Bangkok, Thailand
☏ 251-1033, 651-2358-9
http://www.herosauna.com

Open Daily 15h, Sauna Section till 2h, Massage Therapy Section till 24h

Bangkok/Krung Thep - Sukhumvit Road — **Thailand**

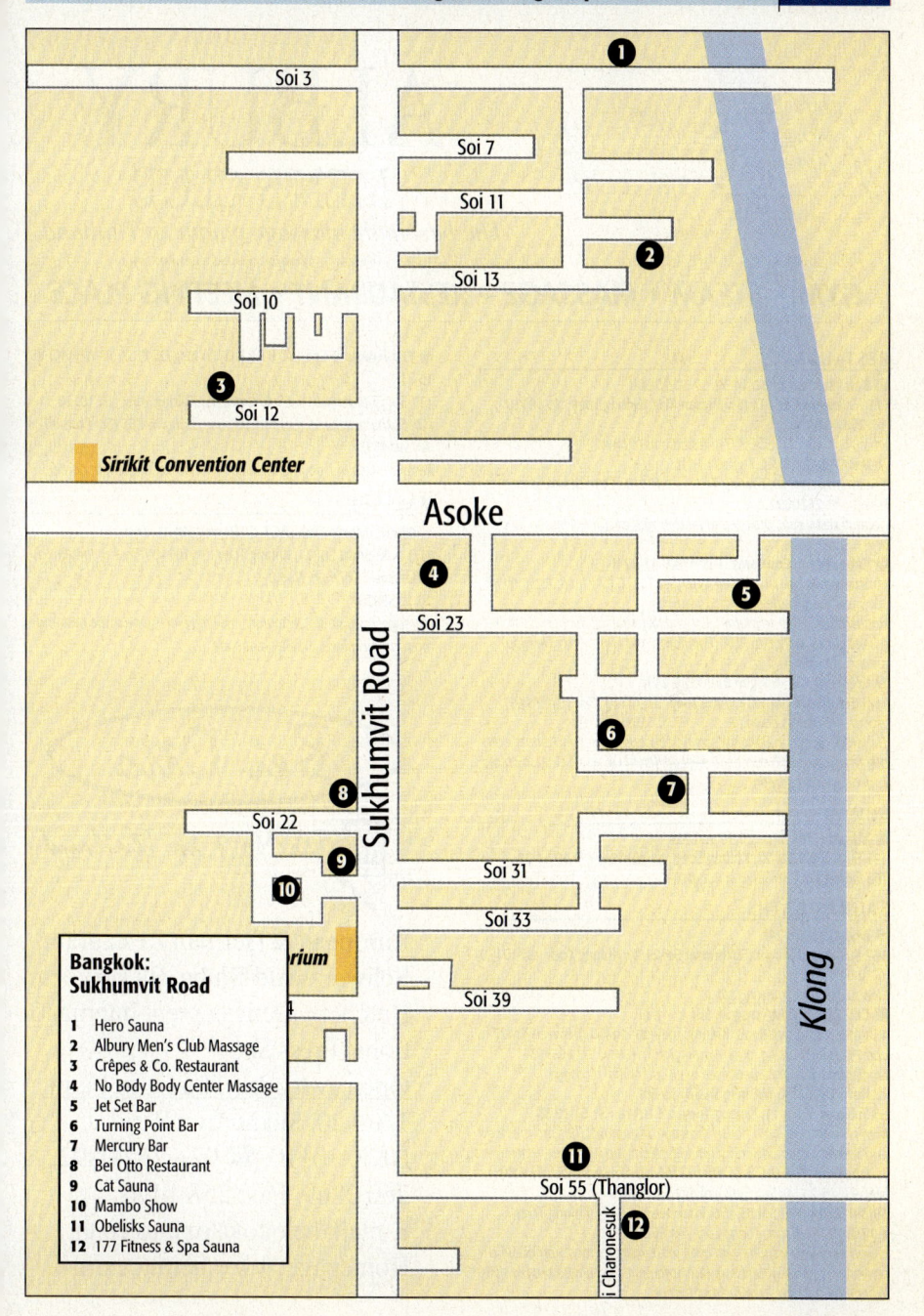

Soi 3
Soi 7
Soi 11
Soi 13
Soi 10
Soi 12
Sirikit Convention Center
Asoke
Sukhumvit Road
Soi 23
Soi 22
Soi 31
Soi 33
Soi 39
Soi 55 (Thanglor)
Charonesuk
Klong

Bangkok: Sukhumvit Road

1. Hero Sauna
2. Albury Men's Club Massage
3. Crêpes & Co. Restaurant
4. No Body Body Center Massage
5. Jet Set Bar
6. Turning Point Bar
7. Mercury Bar
8. Bei Otto Restaurant
9. Cat Sauna
10. Mambo Show
11. Obelisks Sauna
12. 177 Fitness & Spa Sauna

SPARTACUS 2001/2002 | 1037

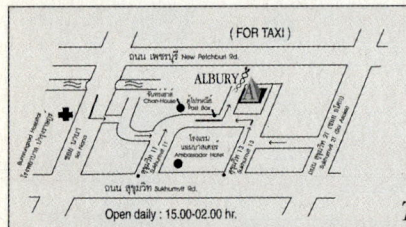

Thailand Bangkok/Krung Thep – Sukhumvit Road

ALBURY
MEN'S CLUB
The best male massage palour in Thailand

71/1 SUKHUMVIT 11, BANGKOK, THAILAND TEL: 2558920, 2554768

Open daily : 15.00-02.00 h.

GYM • STEAM • MASSAGE • RESTAURANT • MEETING PLACE

RESTAURANTS

■ **Ban Mai San** 11.30-14.30, 17.30-23.30h
4/11 Sukhumvit Soi 23 (Soi Prasan Mit), Khlong Toey ✉ 10110
☏ 258 40 34
Small, but one of the best Thai restaurants in town.

■ **Bei Otto** (AC B CC F glm) 11-1h
1 Sukhumvit Soi 20, Khlong Toey ✉ 10110 *(Opposite Windsor Hotel)* ☏ 2620892
German restaurant, bakery and butcher with exclusive German food, beer & apple wine.

■ **Cabbages & Condoms** (F glm MA) 11-22 h
10 Sukhumvit Soi 12, Khlong Toey ✉ 10110 *(Sky train: Asok. About 300 meters down the soi)* ☏ 2294610
Handycrafts & Thai restaurant. Eat and love safe: All the benefits from the restaurant will go to PDA (Population and Community Development Association).

■ **Crêpes & Co.** (b F glm MA OS) 9-24 h
18/1 Sukhumvit Soi 12, Khlong Toey ✉ 10110 *(Sky train: Asok. About 400 meters down the soi)* ☏ 6533990
The only crêperie in Bangkok serving delicious brunch and dinner every day (more than 100 savoury & sweet different crêpes). Set up in an old Thai house and garden.

SHOWS

■ **Mambo** Showtime 20.30 and 22h
496 Sukhumvit Soi 22, Khlong Toey ✉ 10110 ☏ 2 59 51 28
The largest Cabaret Show in Bangkok.

SAUNAS/BATHS

■ **Body Line** 13-24h
167 Sukhumvit Soi 19 (Sukhumvit Soi 21/3), Khlong Toey ✉ 10110
☏ 2 04 13 18
Steam, massage, meeting place.

■ **Cat** (AC B F G MA msg SA SB) 15-12 h
450-452 Sukhumvit Road, Khlong Toey ✉ 10110 *(Between Soi 22 and 24, in the parking lot of Washington Theatre)* ☏ 6634031
Small bar and sauna specialised in oil and herbal massage.

■ **Hero** (AC B F G MA msg SA SB) 15-2h
65 Sukhumvit Soi 11, Khlong Toey ✉ 10110 ☏ 51 10 33
Men's fitness club, bath house, massage, restaurant. The Tora massage and Sanshiro massage and scrub with steam you will never forget.

■ **Obelisks, The** (AC B CC DR F G MA NU OS SA SB VS WH WO)
Mon-Fri 15-23.30, Sat, Sun, Holiday 13-23.30 h
39/3-4 Sukhumvit Soi 53, (Soi Bhai Dee Ma Dee), Khlong Toey
✉ 10110 *(Sky Train: Thong Lor)* ☏ 6624377
Eleven story luxury sauna with gym, jacuzzi, steam, food, karaoke in a converted apartment building. Rich ornamental decorated marble style. Wonderful city view from the roof terrace.

■ **177 Fitness & Spa** (AC B DR F G MA msg OS PI SA SB WH WO VS) 15-? h
117 Soi Charoensuk, Soi Sukhumvit 55, Khlong Toey ✉ 10110
(Off Sukhumvit Soi 55 (Soi Tonglor) and Sukhumvit 63 (Soi Ekamai))
☏ 3914393
Restaurant, sauna, pool, gym, massage in a cosy house with garden.

MASSAGE

■ **Albury Men's Club** (AC F G MA msg SB) 15-24 h
71/1 Sukhumvit Soi 11, Khlong Toey ✉ 10110 *(Close to the Ambassador Hotel. Sky train: Nana)*
☏ 2558920
Massage, gym, steam, restaurant, meeting place. One of the best and most famous places to relax your body.

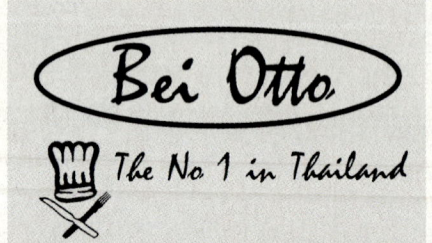

Bei Otto
The No 1 in Thailand

European & German Restaurant Schwarzwald-Stube, Bakery, Butchery, Delicatessen, International Press Shop
Open every day 11 a.m. to 1 a.m.
1 Soi 20, Sukhumvit Road, BKK 10110, ☏ 02 - 262 0892, 260 0869, Fax: 258 1496
E-mail: beiotto@loxinfo.co.th
Homepage: www.beiotto.com

BABYLON
SAUNA-BARRACKS

OPENING HOURS
SUN - THU
12.00 - 01.00
FRI - SAT
12.00 - 06.00

BABYLON BANGKOK The NAME says it all!

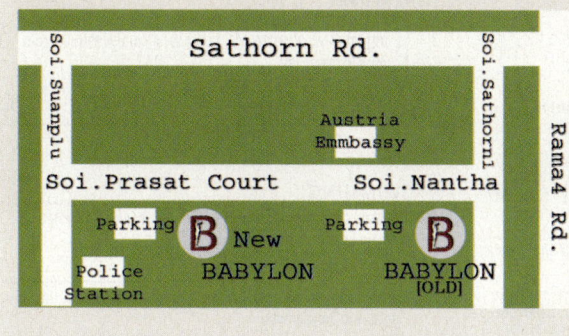

Map showing: Sathorn Rd., Soi Suanplu, Soi Sathorn1, Austria Emmbassy, Soi Prasat Court, Soi Nantha, Rama4 Rd., Parking, New BABYLON, Parking, BABYLON [OLD], Police Station

BABYLON BANGKOK
- 24hr. Coffee Shop
- Barber & Massage
- Barracks & Hotel
- Gym
- Jaguzzi
- Restaurant Dining
- Sound Factory
- Steam & Dry Sauna
- Swimming Pool

WWW.BABYLONBKK.COM
info@babylonbkk.com
Tel: 213-2108, 679-8212
Office: 679-7985 Fax: 679-7986

OBELISKS SAUNA
Bangkok

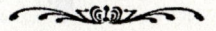

39/3-4 Sukhumvit Soi 53
Bangkok 10110, Thailand

Bangkok's most magnificent sauna in an 11 floor complex. Rich ornamental decorated in marble grand style. Super clean.

Nice restaurant, karaoke, well and modern equipped gym. Warm jacuzzi, steam bath, hot sauna, mysterious starry darkroom, video room and plenty of private rooms for your pleasure.

Roof top garden with refreshment bar, where you can enjoy the magnificent view over Bangkok, the roof jacuzzi and steam room in the midst of palm trees under the sky.

Imagine, how much you can enjoy! A place to meet hundreds of new friends in private and comfortable atmosphere.

Tel: (+66 2) 6 62 43 77, 6 62 43 78, Fax: 6 62 43 79

Open daily:	Mon – Fri 15.00 – 23.30 h
	Sat, Sun, Holiday 13.00 – 23.30 h
Admission:	Mon – Fri 200 Baht
	Sat, Sun, Holiday 220 Baht
Sky Train:	Thong Lor Station
For Taxi:	39/3-4 ถนน สุขุมวิท ซอย 53

Thailand   Bangkok/Krung Thep - Sukhumvit Road ▶ Chiang Mai

■ **Ambassador Hotel Health Centre** (g msg) Mon-Fri 7-21, Sat Sun 9-21 h
171 Sukhumvit Road, Khlong Toey ✉ 10110 *(Near Soi 11)*
☎ 2540444
Massage with a bang. Ask for a man if you prefer.
■ **Macho Men Club. The** (G msg) 15-24 h, 24 hour out service
316/18 Sukhumvit Soi 22, Soi Sainamthip, Khlong Toey ✉ 10110
☎ 2597247
Oil massage for men by men.
■ **No Body Body Center** 12-23h
1 Ban Chang Glas Haus Building, Sukhumvit Soi 25, Wattana, Khlong Toey ✉ 10110 *(Basement)* ☎ 2 60 60 16
Massage, gym.

HOTELS
■ **Nana**
Sukhumvit Soi 4, Soi Nana Thai, Khlong Toey ✉ 10110
☎ 2 52 01 21   📠 2 55 17 69
Rates 900 - 1,200 Baht.
■ **Regency Park** (AC g H PI)
12/3 Sukhumvit Soi 22, Soi Sainamthip, Khlong Toey ✉ 10110
☎ 2597420   📠 2582862   💻 utopia@best.com
🖥 www.utopia-asia.com/acchotel.shtml
Utopia guest house. For discount booking send e-mail only. Internet access.
■ **Rex Hotel** (BF g H)
762/1 Sukhumvit Road, Khlong Toey ✉ 10110 ☎ 2590106
All rooms have phone, fridge, bath, WC and balcony.
⇒ *also Si Lom/Surawong for comment.*

HEALTH GROUPS
■ **British Clinic. The** 8-12, 14-16, Sat 8-12 h
109 Sukhumvit Road, Khlong Toey ✉ 10110 *(between Soi 5 & 7)*
☎ 2528056   ☎ 02/2529179
■ **Raja Clinic**
6/20 Sukhumvit Soi 3/1, Khlong Toey ✉ 10110 *(North Nana)*
☎ 2535678
■ **Samitivej Hospital**
Sukhumvit Soi 49, Khlong Toey ✉ 10110 ☎ 3920911

Bangkok/Krung Thep - Other Areas ☎ 02

BARS
■ **Mon Copain** (B G)
1091/74 Petchaburi Soi 33, Pathumwan ✉ 10330 ☎ 2552976
■ **Sperm Entertainment** (B G)
223/1 Soi 3, Pacharachbumpen Road, Huay Khwang ✉ 10320
☎ 6926025
New entertainment centre far outside the gay scene.

SAUNAS/BATHS
■ **Abacus** (B F PI SA WO) 15-24h, Fri-Sat -2.30h
3141/2 Soi Ram, between Soi 81and 83, Ramkhamhaeng Road, Bang. api ✉ 10240 *(Opposite Ramkhamhang Hospital)*
Sauna, gym, pool, restaurant, cyber corner.
■ **David de Bangkok** (G msg OS SA SB WO) 16-3h, Fri,Sat - 6h
Ratakosin Mansion, 1 Chao Fa Road, Phra Pin Klao Bridge, Pranakorn ✉ 10200 *(opposite National Theatre, close to Khao San Road)*
☎ 6290429
Sauna, steam, gym, roof garden and massage.
■ **Sukhothai Health Club** (G msg SA WO)
383 Sukhothai Road Soi 4, Dusit ✉ 10300 *(near corner of Soi 4)*
☎ 2413385
Sauna, gym, massage.

■ **Uomo** (G SA SB) Mon-Thu 16-23, Fri-Sun 16-24 h
549 Rama IX Road, Soi 49, Sounlong ✉ 10250 ☎ 7183666

FITNESS STUDIOS
■ **Hercules Health Club** (B F G SB WO) Mon-Thu 16-23, Fri-Sun 12-24 h
91/194 Siam Park City, Sukhapiban 2 Road, Siam Park Avenue, Bangapi ✉ 10230 *(near Fashon Island)* ☎ 9199609
Gym, sauna, steam, restaurant, escort.

TRAVEL AND TRANSPORT
■ **99 Travel**
99/1 Moo 6, Srinakarin Road, Nongbon, Prawet ✉ 10260
☎ 7218160   ☎ 7218165   📠 7218169   💻 info@99travel.com
🖥 www.99travel.com
Tour and travel management.

GENERAL GROUPS
■ **Mituna Club**
573/21 Samson Road, Dusit ✉ 10300 ☎ 2824244

SWIMMING
The Mall, shopping centre in Thonburi (many gays come here to swim and cruise, afternoons).

CRUISING
-Sanam Luang (large open field between Wat Phra Keow, the Royal Palace, and Banglamphu)

Cha Am ☎ 032

HOTELS
■ **Jolly & Jumper** (glm H)
273/3 Ruamchit Road, Petchburi ✉ 76121 ☎ 433887 📠 433887
Country western guest house with steak house.
■ **Novotel Gems** (glm H)
251 Chao-Lai Road, Petchburi ✉ 76121 ☎ 434060 ☎ 434079
📠 434002 🖥 www.hotelweb.fr
■ **Regent Cha Am** (glm H)
849/21 Petchkasem Road, Cha Am Beach, Petchburi ✉ 76120
☎ 471480   ☎ 032/471486   📠 471491

Chiang Mai ☎ 053

✴ This northern city was, for many centuries, the capital of an autonomous kingdom. Chiang Mai is very much smaller and quieter than the metropolis Bangkok. It is thus ideal for escaping the hectic life of the capital and the southern resorts. The old city walls are still intact in some places, and you will also find ancient temples, good shopping, beautiful scenery and excellent northern Thai cuisine. Despite an explosive increase in the number of gay bars two years ago, the gay scene in this city is still small. It reflects the culture and pace of the wider Chiang Mai community. Most bars look more like an extension of a living room: you sit on traditional cushions, enjoy a drink, talk, watch a show, all in an unhurried manner. All in all a unique experience, and well worth the journey.

✴ Über viele Jahrhunderte war die nordthailändische Stadt die Hauptstadt eines autonomen Königreiches.
Chiang Mai ist sehr viel kleiner und stiller als die Metropole Bangkok. Es eignet sich hervorragend für's Ausspannen vom Trubel der Großstadt oder der südlichen Ferienorte.
Die Stadtmauern sind noch zum Teil intakt. Es gibt alte Tempel, eine schöne Landschaft, gute Einkaufsmöglichkeiten und exzellente nordthailändische Küche.

Chiang Mai — Thailand

Auch wenn es vor zwei Jahren eine regelrechte Explosion der Anzahl der schwulen Bars gab, ist die schwule Szene doch noch recht klein. Sie ist wie ein Spiegel der Stadt Stadt und ihrer Umgebung: Bars wirken eher wie eine Erweiterung des Wohnzimmers. Man sitzt auf traditionellen Kissen, geniesst einen Drink, unterhält sich, betrachtet die Show. Und das alles auf äußerst ruhige Weise. Alles in allem ein einzigartiges Erlebnis, das die Reise wert ist.

✱ Située dans le nord du pays, Chiang Mai est l'ancienne capitale du royaume. Tout y est beaucoup plus calme qu'à Bangkok. C'est donc un endroit idéal pour souffler après le stress de la capitale ou l'agitation des stations balnéaires du sud.
Fortifications encore intactes, temples magnifiques, paradis du shopping, paysages splendides, cuisine excellente: tout y est! En revanche, encore peu de lieux gays, même après le boom des dernières années. Les bars gays sont souvent une sorte de prolongement de la salle de séjour du propriétaire. Assis sur des coussins, on sirote une boisson en papotant ou en regardant un show. Tout cela dans une ambiance bon enfant! Rien que pour ça, Chiang Mai vaut le détour!

● Esta ciudad norteña fue durante muchos siglos la capital de un reinado autónomo. Chiang-Mai es mucho más pequeña y tranquila que Bangkok. Chiang Mai es una excelente alternativa a Bangkok o a los centros turisticos del Norte del país. La muralla de la ciudad se encuentra casi intacta. Hay templos, buenas posibilidades para ir de compras, un lindo paisaje y la excelencia de la cocina tailandesa norteña. A pesar de que hace dos años hubo una explosión de bares gay, el ambiente homosexual es pequeño, es el reflejo de la ciudad y sus alrededores. La mayoría de los bares son como una extensión de una sala de estar. Aquí te sentarás sobre almohadas, beberás algo, hablarás con alguien, observarás el ambiente y disfrutarás del show de una forma muy amena. Es una experiencia que vale la pena vivir.

✱ Questa città del nord è stata per molti anni la capitale di un regno indipendente. Chiang Mai è molto più piccola e calma di Bangkok; è un ideale punto intermedio tra la frenetica Bangkok e le stazioni balneari del sud. Le mura della città si sono in parte conservate, vi sono vecchi templi da visitare, altrimenti si possono fare compere, visitare la campagna circostante o gustare l'eccellente cucina tailandese. L'ambiente gay è ancora ristretto, malgrado il boom di due anni fa che ora sta svanendo. L'ambiente gay riflette la cultura di tutti i giorni di questa regione: la maggior parte dei bar ha un aspetto casereccio, sembrano essere il soggiorno dell'abitazione del proprietario. Ci si siede su tradizionali cuscini, si beve qualcosa si chiacchera e si guarda uno spettacolo in tranquilla compagnia piacevole. Questa simpatica singolarità è per sè un buon motivo per fare il viaggio.

BARS

■ **Adam's Apple** (AC B CC F G MA msg SNU STV VS) 22-1.30, show 23.30 h
1/21-22 Soi Viengbua, Chotana Road, Chang Peuak ✉ 50300 (Opposite Lotus Hotel) ☏ 220380
Go go bar.

■ **Circle Pub** (AC B G MA S) 20-2 h
161/7-8 Soi Erawan, Chang Phuek Road, Chang Peuak ✉ 50300
☏ 214996

■ **Coffee Boy. The** (B G MA S) 20-2 h
248 Thung Hotel Road, Amphur Muang ✉ 50000 (Soi to Chiang Mai Arcade) ☏ 244458
Located in a beautiful ancient teak house.

■ **Jungle Bar** (B G) 20-1 h
Night Bazaar, Chang Klan Road, Chang Klan ✉ 50100

■ **Macho** (AC B G MA S) 20-2, Show at 22 h
8 Nantharam Soi 1, Hay-Ya, Amphur Muang ✉ 50000 (opposite Wat Taht Kam) ☏ 200904
Go go bar with cabaret show located in acient teak home.

■ **Man's Bar. A** (B G) 20-24 h
Night Bazaar, Chang Klan Road, Chang Klan ✉ 50100
☏ 01/6022551 (Mobile)

■ **Marlboro Bar** (B G) 18-1 h
Night Bazaar, Chang Klan Road, Chang Klan, Chiang Mai ✉ 50100
(North side of Night Market)

■ **My Way** (AC B G MA S) 20-1 h
3/5-6 Hatsadee Sewee Road, Chang Peuak ✉ 50300 ☏ 404361

■ **New Lanterns'** (B G MA OS S)
25/1 Rajchichaen Road Soi 2, Amphur Muang ✉ 50000
☏ 271022
Go go bar and escort.

■ **Nice Illusions Pub** (B NG)
Opposite Somphet Market, Amphur Muang ✉ 50000
Kruatek style, loud music, people tend to dance around the tables and Thai food can be ordered.

■ **69** (B G) 20-1h
Night Bazaar, Chang Klan Road, Chang Klan ✉ 50100

CAFES

■ **Hot Shot** (NG)
Porn Ping Hotel, Jaroen Prathet Road, Chang Klan ✉ 50100
Kruatek style, loud music, people tend to dance around the tables and Thai food can be ordered. Not gay, but many young men go there.

SPAROMA MEN'S SAUNA www.sparoma.com

Open 15.00-23.00 hrs.
Bali-style
pool & sun deck
Sauna & gym
Steam
Jacuzzi
Dark room
massage

RESORT SAUNA

9/4 Moo 3 Padad Rd. T.Padad A.Meung
Chiangmai Thailand Tel.053-812900

For Taxi: 9/4 ถ.ป่าแดด ต.เมือง เชียงใหม่เลยบ้านใหม่(ป่าแดด) ฝั่งตรงข้าม

Thailand — Chiang Mai

SOUVENIR
Guest House & Wildflowers Restaurant
118 Caaroen Prathet Road
Chiang Mai 50100, Thailand
Phone/Fax: +66 - 53 - 81 87 86
E-mail: souvenirguesthouse@hotmail.com

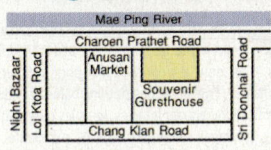

Map: Mae Ping River, Charoen Prathet Road, Anusan Market, Souvenir Gusthouse, Chang Klan Road, Night Bazaar, Loi Ktoa Road, Sri Donchai Road

DANCECLUBS

■ **Bubble Disco** (B D glm)
c/o Porn Ping Hotel, 46-48 Charoen Prathet Road, Chang Klan ✉ 50100 *(located near the river and the Night Bazaar)* ☏ 270099
Popular disco for gays and straights.

RESTAURANTS

■ **Fascination** (B F g S STV)
99 Suthep Road, Amphur Muang ✉ 50000 ☏ 810549
Has also cabaret shows.

■ **Gallery. The** (B F glm) 12-24 h
25-27 Jaremsrad Road, Amphur Muang ✉ 50000 *(On the River)* ☏ 248601

■ **Garden Bar** (B F g MA N OS) 19h till late
2/25 Soi Viengbua, Chotana Road, Chang Peuak ✉ 50300 ☏ 215462

■ **Gi-Gi** (B F glm MA)
Lampoon Road, Amphur Muang ✉ 50000
Kruatek style, loud music, people tend to dance around the tables and Thai food can be ordered.

■ **Grand Canyon** (F glm)
Kad Sua Kaew Shopping Complex, 2nd floor, Huay Kaew Road, Amphur Muang ✉ 50000

■ **J. J. Restaurant & Bakery. The** (F glm OS) Shows at 23 h.
Montri Hotel, 2-6 Ragdammen Road, Chang Klan ✉ 50100 *(Opposite Tapae Gate)* ☏ 211069

■ **Riverside** (F glm)
9/11 Jaroenrat Road, at Nakhorn Ping Bridge, Amphur Muang ✉ 50000 ☏ 243239

■ **Romantic Restaurant & Pub** (AC B CC F G MA) 19.30 h till late
1/21-22 Soi Viengbua, Chotana Road, Chang Peuak ✉ 50300 ☏ 220380

■ **Swai Riang** (F glm)
Soi 8 Chiang Mai - Lampoon Road, Saraphi, Amphur Muang ✉ 50000 ☏ 322061
Gay owned and operated.

■ **Tha-Nam** (B F glm)
River Front, Amphur Muang ✉ 50000 ☏ 275125
Northern Thai cuisine. Mixed.

■ **Wildflowers** (B bf F GLM MA OS) 7.30-22h
Souvenir Guest House, 118 Charoen Prathet Road, Amphur Muang ✉ 50100 ☏ 81 87 86
Thai, American and European dishes for very reasonable prices.

SAUNAS/BATHS

■ **House of Male** (B CC DR F G MA msg OS PI SB VS WO) 12-24 h
19 Sirimangklajarn Road Soi 3, Tambol Suthep, Amphur Muang ✉ 50200 *(last house in the soi)* ☏ 894133
Sauna set in a traditional Thai house with an outdoor pool. Sat barbeques from 17 h.

■ **Sparoma Sauna** (DR F G MA msg PI SA SB WH WO) 15-23 h
9/4 Moo 3, Padadd Road, Amphur Muang ✉ 50000 *(7th floor. Near Wat Padadd)* ☏ 812900
Sauna, steam, gym,Bali style pool, tropical garden, restaurant, massage and nice balcony with view over Chiang Mai. Fun and friendly place.

HOTELS

■ **Cherry House** (AC b F G H MA msg SOL)
21/7-8 Soi Ratchapruk, Huay Kaew Road, Amphur Muang ✉ 50000 ☏ 215207 🖷 053/405244 📧 servmind@chmai.loxinfo.co.th
Gay hotel. Rooms from 750 Baht, suites from 1,200 Baht. No charge for overnight guests. Massage possible. All rooms with shower/WC, balcony or terrace, telephone, Satellite TV, minibar, air-conditioning.

■ **Coffee Boy Cottages** (G H)
248 Toonghotel Road, Amphur Muang ✉ 50000 ☏ 247021 🖷 247021

■ **Lotus Hotel** (AC B BF CC G H MA msg OS)
2/25 Soi Viengbua, Chotana Road, Chang Peuak ✉ 50300 ☏ 215376 🖷 221340 📧 mohamad@loxinfo.co.th
📧 www.angelfire.com/biz/lotushotel
One of the first gay hotel of Chiang Mai, located close to the bars in the north and part of the largest gay complex in the city. Rooms have bathroom, TV, fridge, mini bar. Rates about 800 Baht/night. The bar is the only streetside gay bar in Chiang Mai. Same management as Adam's Apple.

GUEST HOUSES

■ **New Connection** (AC B BF d F G H MA msg OS s) Restaurant 17-24, Pub 16-2 h
155 Rajmanraka Road, Phrasing Road, Amphur Muang ✉ 50200 *(Near Felix City Inn Hotel)* ☏ 276161 ☏ 814123
📧 connection-cnx@gmx.net
Guest house, bar and restaurant. Room rates 150 - 490 Baht. Gay taxi service, pick up from airport or railway station.

■ **Souvenir** (AC B bf F glm H MA msg OS) 7.30-22h
118 Charoen Prathet Road, Amphur Muang ✉ 50100
📧 souvenirguesthouse@hotmail.com
Shared or private bathrooms, fans or air-con - 130 - 430 Baht. Restaurant wis excellent food.

Chiang Mai ▶ Koh Samui **Thailand**

CRUISING
- Taepae Gate (r, after 21 h)
- Narawat Bridge (evenings)
- Park opposite market near Post office
- Nong Buak Hat Park
- Huay Kaew Waterfall (daytime)
- Huay Kaew recreational park (Arboretum near zoo, Huay Kaew road opposite police station, evenings)
- Railway station (park in front)
- Bus station
- Fitness Park Chamgmai University International Centre (Nimmanhemmin Road, evenings)

Chiang Rai ☏ 053

BARS
■ **Lobo Boy Boy** (B g S)
528/25 Thaiwiwat-U-Thid Road, Amphur Muang ✉ 57000 ☏ 752516

Hat Yai ☏ 074

BARS
■ **Buddy Pub** (B F G msg S) 11-2 h
37/2 Sriphuvanart Road, Song Khla ✉ 90110 ☏ 420944
Go go boys, massage, food and drinks.
■ **Jacks Pub. The** (B G S)
Soi 16 Rath-U-Thit, Pracha-U-Thit Road, Song Khla ✉ 90110 ☏ 425408

DANCECLUBS
■ **Dance Zone** (B D glm)
92/11 Petchakasem Road, Song Khla ✉ 90110 ☏ 365876

HOTELS
■ **Hansa Hotel and Café** (B BF glm H)
361 Sutti Hansa Road, Song Khla ✉ 90110 ☏ 359601 ☏ 359603

Hua Hin ☏ 032

BARS
■ **Boys Red Indian. The** (B G)
Hua Hin Bazar, Prachuapkhirikhan ✉ 77110 *(opposite Hotel Sofitel)* ☏ 01/8472673 (Mobile)
■ **Doi Boy Cabaret** (B G S)
53-54 Am Nuoi Sin Road, Soi Tana Vit Condo, Prachuapkhirikhan ✉ 77110 ☏ 515782
■ **Guys Bar** (B G)
58 Amnuay Sin Road, Prachuapkhirikhan ✉ 77110 *(opposite Supmitra Hotel)* ☏ 530170

DANCECLUBS
■ **Doodle's Disco** (B D g)
Melia Hotel, 33/3 Naretdamri Road, Prachuapkhirikhan ✉ 77110
■ **Voice** (B D g)
Hua Hin Grand Hotel, 22272 Petchakasem Road, Prachuapkhirikhan ✉ 77110

RESTAURANTS
■ **Muay Thai Gardens** (F g)
Poonsak Road, Prachuapkhirikhan ✉ 77110

HOTELS
■ **Mechai Hotel** (H g)
57/2 Phetkasem Road, Prachuapkhirikhan ✉ 77110 *(Facing Chatchai Market)* ☏ 511035
■ **Melia** (g H)
33 Naresdamri Road, Prachuapkhirikhan ✉ 77110 ☏ 511612 ☏ 511614 ☏ 511135
■ **Sofitel Central** (G H)
1 Damnernkasern Road, Prachuapkhirikhan ✉ 77110 ☏ 512021 ☏ 512038 ☏ 511014

GUEST HOUSES
■ **All Nations** (B F glm H)
10/1 Deachanuchit Road, Prachuapkhirikhan ✉ 77110 ☏ 512747 ☏ 530474
■ **Ken Diamond Travel & Parichart Guesthouse** (CC G H MA)
Travel office: 9-22 h
162/6 Naresdamri Road, Prachuapkhirikhan ✉ 77110 *(150 m from the beach)* ☏ 513863 ☏ 513870 ☏ 513863
✉ soe@prachuab.a-net.net.th
Rooms: Fan 150 Baht/night, 2000 Baht/month, AC: 300 Baht/night, 4500 Baht/month. Toilet and shower inside the rooms. Gay owned and operated.
■ **Pattana** (b BF F glm H MA OS)
52 Naretdamri Road, Prachuapkhirikhan ✉ 77110 *(close to beach and centre)* ☏ 513393 ☏ 530081
Café and restaurant. Traditional Thai teakwood house, 3 minutes walk from the beach. Roomrates 300 to 600 Baht. European breakfast.

CRUISING
- Monkey Temple

Koh Samui ☏ 077

✹ Koh Samui is one of the most attractive holiday resorts which is not over-crowded. A gay scene is slowly developing and is concentrated at the Chaweng Beach area.

✹ Koh Samui ist eines der schönsten Ferienresorts und noch nicht überlaufen. Das schwule Leben ist gerade im Entstehen und konzentriert sich auf Chaweng Beach.

✹ Koh Samui est une des plus belles station balnéaire qui n'est pas encore envahie de touristes. Une scène gaie se développe peu à peu, concentrée autour de la plage de Chaweng.

✹ Koh Samui es uno de los lugares de vacaciones más bonitos y todavía no desbordado de turistas. La vida gay está empezando a desarrollarse y se concentra en Chaweng Beach.

✹ Koh Samui è un vero paradiso per le vacanze e non è ancora affollato. La vita gay è in via di formazione sta e si concentra sulla spiaggia Chaweng Beach.

BARS
■ **Christie's** (B glm OS S STV)
Chaweng Beach Road, Opposite Centre Point, Surat Thani ✉ 84320
Mixed outside bar with drag shows 23 and 1h.
■ **Club, The**
Chaweng Beach Road, Centre Point, Surat Thani ✉ 84320
■ **Free Way** (B G)
Chaweng Beach Road, Centre Point, Surat Thani ✉ 84320 *(Next to Kelly's)*
■ **Reggae Pub**
Soi near the lake, Surat Thani ✉ 84320
Pub and disco.

Thailand   Koh Samui ▶ Pattaya

■ **Roxy Bar** (B G)
Chaweng Beach Road, opposite Centre Point, Surat Thani ✉ 84320
(Besides Full Circle)

DANCECLUBS
■ **Full Circle** (B D glm) 22-3h
Chaweng Beach Road, Surat Thani ✉ 84320 *(at the end of the Soi next to Centre Point)*
■ **Green Mango** (B D glm)
Chaweng Beach Road, at the end of the Soi next to Centre Point, Surat Thani ✉ 84320

RESTAURANTS
■ **Ban Thai Sea Food** (F g)
Chaweng Beach Road, Surat Thani ✉ 84320
■ **Chai Thalee Seafood** (F g)
440/1 Thanon Maret, Surat Thani ✉ 84320 *(on the main road, after Lamai, before Hua Thanon)* ☎ 233267
■ **Oriental Gallery/Upstairs** (A B F g) 14-1 h
39/1 Moo 3, Bophut, Surat Thani ✉ 84320 ☎ 422200
Asian arts, restaurant and music lounge.

TRAVEL AND TRANSPORT
■ **D. J. Paradise Tour** (CC) Mon-Sat 12-20 h
Papillon Resort, 1 & 2 Chaweng Beach Road, Surat Thani ✉ 84320
(at the very north end of Chaweng Beach) ☎ 231169
☎ (01) 9826372 (Mobile) 📠 231169 ✉ djparadi@smart.co.th
🌐 www.djparadisetour.com
Gay owned and operated. Go there for information. Tours, hotel reservations, ticketing, diving excursions.
■ **Saai Travel Service**
124/1 Chaweng Beach Road, Surat Thani ✉ 84320 ☎ 230477

HOTELS
■ **Baan Samui Resort** (E g H)
Chaweng Beach, Surat Thani ✉ 84320 ☎ 422415 📠 422412
Mixed and expensive.
■ **Central Samui Hotel** (g H)
38/2 Moo 3, Bor Phud, Chaweng Beach, Surat Thani ✉ 84320 ☎ 230500
■ **Long Island Resort** (g H)
24/2 Moo 4, Lamai Beach, Surat Thani ✉ 84320 ☎ 424202
■ **Montien House** (g H)
5 Moo 2, Chaweng Beach, Surat Thani ✉ 84320 ☎ 422169
📠 422145
■ **Papillon Resort** (AC B BF CC F g H MA OS PI WH) 6-24 h
1 & 2 Chaweng Beach Road, Surat Thani ✉ 84320 *(at the very north end of Chaweng Beach)* ☎ 231169 📠 231169
✉ djparadi@smart.co.th
Bungalow resort with new pool and French restaurant, bar, dive center, travel agency. Gay managed. No problem to bring your friend to your room. 20 bungalows with AC, mini bar, sat TV, video channel, shower, WC, phone. Rates: Low season from 1,490 Baht to 2,990 Baht, high season 2,000 Baht to 3,490 Baht.

SWIMMING
- Chaweng Beach
- Volley ball games (beach behind Christie's)

Lopburi ☎ 036

HOTELS
■ **Lopburi Tai Pei Hotel** (g H)
24/6-7 Surasangkram Road, Amphur Muang, ✉ 15000 ☎ 411524

Nong Khai ☎ 042

HOTELS
■ **Isan Orchid Guest Lodge** (AC B bf G H MA msg)
87/9 Gaowarawud Road, Thabo ✉ 43110 ☎ 43 16 65
📠 43 16 65 ✉ isnorchd@nk.ksc.co.th
Bed 'n' Breakfast at the gateway to Indo China" on the Mehkong River, across from Vientiane, Laos. Experience Thailand as it was before the tourist boom in a farming community. Prehistoric park, archaeological site. Rates: 1,200-1,300 Baht. English outside the hotel not spoken. Bar "Black & White".

Pattaya ☎ 038

✱ During the Vietnam War, this formerly sleepy fishing village (about two hours drive from Bangkok) was transformed into an American base providing GI's with rest and recreation before returning to combat. This past has somewhat tarnished its reputation somewhat but Pattaya has now developed into an international resort of considerable charm, particularly for gays. Foreign and local venue owners in Pattaya go to great lengths to augment the standards of gay entertainment and accommodation. The main gay section is concentrated in a small but lively area of South Pattaya which should not be left out. Pattaya is famous for its drag acts, which are particularly popular with straight tourists.

✱ Zwei Stunden von Bangkok entfernt befindet sich dieses ehemalige Fischerdorf, daß sich während des Vietnam-Krieges überraschend in ein Erholungszentrum der US-Amerikaner verwandelt sah. Die Vergangenheit hat den Ruf dieser Stadt etwas ramponiert (unter anderem auch, weil der vordere Strand wegen der Verschmutzung nicht benutzbar ist). Doch inzwischen ist Pattaya ein internationaler Urlaubsort von ganz beträchtlichem Charme, besonders für Schwule. Die ausländischen und heimatlichen Barbesitzer geben sich große Mühe, den Standard schwuler Unterhaltung und Unterbringung anzuheben.
In einem kleineren, aber lebhaften Gebiet Süd-Pattayas findet sich das Zentrum schwulen Lebens. Aber auch eine kleinere Zahl von guten Bars im Norden der Stadt sollte nicht ausgelassen werden. Pattaya wurden durch seine Travestie-Shows bekannte. Sie sind besonders bei Hetero-Touristen sehr beliebt.

✱ Pendant la guerre du Vietnam, cet ancien petit port de pêche (à environ deux heures de Bangkok) était une base américaine où se "reposaient" les GI's avant de retrouver au combat. La réputation de la ville en a beaucoup souffert. Après la guerre, la saleté de ses plages n'a pas aider à améliorer cette image. Aujourd'hui Pattaya est une station balnéaire de réputation internationale, particulièrement appréciée des gays. Les propriétaires d'établissements thaïlandais et étrangers ont particulièrement travaillé à améliorer la qualité en matière de divertissement et d'hébergement. Le quartier gay se trouve dans le sud de la ville, mais le nord a aussi quelques endroits intéressants à offrir. Pattaya est particulièrement réputée pour ses spectacles de transformismes dont raffolent les hétéros.

✱ Este antiguo pueblo pesquera se convirtió en un centro de descansa para Norteamericanos durante la guerra de Vietnam. Se encuentra a dos horas de viaje desde Bangkok. A pesar de que en su playa principal esta prohibido bañarse (debido a la contaminación) se ha desarrollado - y sobre todo para los homosexuales - una centro vaccacional internacional. Los dueños extranjeros y nativos de los bares gay de Pattaya han sabido mantener el grado de comfort y elegancia de sus locales. El ambiente gay está concentrado en una región pequeños bares gay en el Norte que no deberían dejar de ser vistados. Pattaya tiene fama por sus shows de travestíes, muy frecuentados por el público heterosexual.

Pattaya - Jomtien Beach ▶ Pattaya - North & Central | Thailand

Durante la guerra del Vietnam questo villaggio di pescatori, distante due ore da Bangkok, è stato trasformato in centro di ripaso per americani. La rinomatezza della città è stato prò compromessa del suo sporchissimo litorale. Negli ultimi anni però Pattaya è diventata un'amata meta turistica internazionale visitata anche da molti gay. I proprietari tailandesi e stranieri dei localistanno migliarando notevolmente lo standard, i confort e le infrastrutture alberghiere e di divertimento che Pattaya può offrire ai turisti. La parte più gay della città si trova in un piccolo ma vivace quartiere al sud di Pattaya. Tutavia non bisogna perdersi gli interessanti bar situati nella parte nord. Pattaya è famosa per i sui spettacoli di travestiti, molto amati dai turisti eterosessuali.

GAY INFO
■ **Internet addresses**
🖳 www.pattayagay.com

TOURIST INFO
■ **Tourism Authority Of Thailand (TAT). Central Region Office**
8.30-16.30 h
609 Moo 10, Pratamnak Road, Chon Buri ✉ 20260 *(up the hill, close to the sundial)* ☏ 427167 ☏ 428750 🖶 429113
🖳 tatpty@chonburi.ksc.co.th 🖳 www.tat.or.th

Pattaya - Jomtien Beach ☏ 038

BARS
■ **Bamboo's Bar** (B G MA) 12-24 h
410/35 Thapaya Road (Jomtien Road), Chon Buri ✉ 20260
☏ 232315
Open host bar.

■ **Nuttawut Café** (B G MA OS)
410/37 Thapaya Road (Jomtien Road), Chon Buri ✉ 20260

MASSAGE
■ **Friendz** (B G msg)
410/32-34 Thapaya Road (Jomtien Road), Chon Buri ✉ 20260

GUEST HOUSES
■ **Tui's Place** (! AC B BF F G H MA OS) 8-21 h
318/77 Moo 12, Tambon Nongprue, Banglamung, Chon Buri
✉ 20260 ☏ 25 14 32, ☏ 23 10 45 🖶 37 01 36
🖳 tui_69@hotmail.com
The only gay guest house, bar & restaurant right on Jomtiens beach, 20 meters to the gay seating. All rooms with AC, TV, phone, fridge, separate bath room. Very clean, so take off your shoes. Rooms 500 to 1,250 Baht/night. Take a shower here after swimming at the beach.

SWIMMING
-Jomtien Beach (Take the open taxi to Jomtien (10 Baht for foreigners), get off when you arrive at the beach, and use the brand new walkway to the right about 500 meters. You reach the gay area when you can see Tui's Place, the only gay hotel on Jomtien Beach. Rent a deckchair and wait for the things to happen)

Pattaya - North & Central ☏ 038

RESTAURANTS
■ **Balcony, The** (B F g)
151/35 Moo 5, Soi Ananthakul, North Road, Chon Buri ✉ 20260
(opposite city hall) ☏ 411429

Le Café Royale
Hotel, Restaurant & Piano Bar

An „Oasis" in the heart of Boystown

Le Café Royale offers guests:
* Standard, Superior and Superior Deluxe rooms and Suites, all of which are quiet;
* furnished with one double Queen size bed;
* en-suite, with all facilities;
* efficient air-conditioning; room safe;
* mini-bar with wide range of beverages;
* IDD telephone in all rooms; e-mail service;
* colour satellite TV & movie channel
* 24 hour room service with no service fee;
* 24 hr Restaurant and Coffee Shop;
* Piano Bar and Restaurant open 7.30 p.m. to 4 a.m. with music and entertainment.

Le Café Royale:
* is situated in the very heart of Pattaya's gay night life and within a few minutes walk of a score of Go-Go Bars;
* caters exclusively to a gay clientele;
* is only 100 metres from Pattaya Beach;
* is close to the main shopping thoroughfares;
* & Jomtien Beach is but a short taxi ride away.

**325/102-105 Pattayaland Soi 3,
Sth. Pattaya, Chonburi 20260, THAILAND**
Tel: [++66] (38) 423 515, 428 303
Fax: [++66] (38) 424 579
E-Mail: reservations@caferoyale-pattaya.com

SEND FOR INFO PACK
Refer details at the foot of our internet home page at http://www.caferoyale-pattaya.com

Thailand | Pattaya

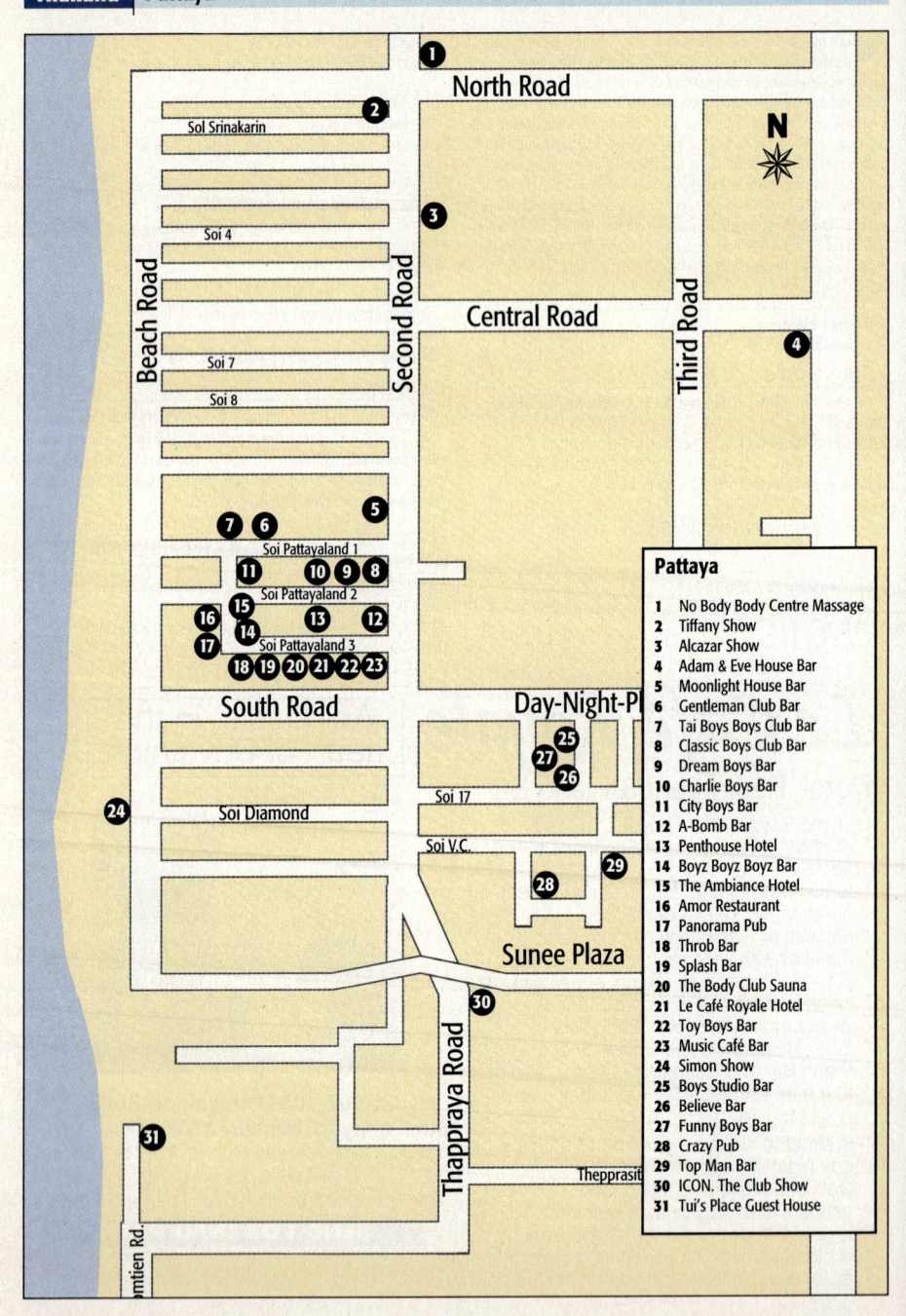

Pattaya

1. No Body Body Centre Massage
2. Tiffany Show
3. Alcazar Show
4. Adam & Eve House Bar
5. Moonlight House Bar
6. Gentleman Club Bar
7. Tai Boys Boys Club Bar
8. Classic Boys Club Bar
9. Dream Boys Bar
10. Charlie Boys Bar
11. City Boys Bar
12. A-Bomb Bar
13. Penthouse Hotel
14. Boyz Boyz Boyz Bar
15. The Ambiance Hotel
16. Amor Restaurant
17. Panorama Pub
18. Throb Bar
19. Splash Bar
20. The Body Club Sauna
21. Le Café Royale Hotel
22. Toy Boys Bar
23. Music Café Bar
24. Simon Show
25. Boys Studio Bar
26. Believe Bar
27. Funny Boys Bar
28. Crazy Pub
29. Top Man Bar
30. ICON. The Club Show
31. Tui's Place Guest House

"Dreams Do Come True .... In Pattaya"

View Talay Villas Jomtien Beach

Check out our GAY website at:
www.exclusivelygay.com

Whether renting or buying, a stunning high-rise condominium or a spacious villa, the promise of five star luxury is now a reality in Pattaya. Just 300 meters from Pattaya's "in vogue" location, Jomtien Beach, "View Talay Villas" and "View Talay Condominium 2" are absolutely unique.

View Talay Villas (above) offers stunning 1 & 2 bedroom villas all with private pools. This unique resort boasts absolute 5 star hotel facilities.

View Talay Condominium 2. If you prefer an apartment, the decor of the foyer and hall ways on the "Executive Floors" (levels 16 & 17) is of highest international standard. Each luxury Condo features breathtaking ocean views.

For Sales Enquiries with exceptional investment potential, call Rob Astbury 66-1-8519718. It's so simple to own your own property in Pattaya, for as little as 20,000 Baht ($500 US) deposit, with a guaranteed annual return of 14% minimum for five years.

For the holiday you have dreamt about ... Visit our web site www .pattayaproperties.com Or telephone: (66) 38-756640-7

PATTAYA PROPERTIES
"Pattaya's Premier Property Developers"

Shop E.1. P.K. Shopping Centre, Beach Road, Sth Pattaya, THAILAND 20260.
Phone: 66 (038) 710443, 410661 Fax: 038-410661
Email: pattprop@loxinfo.co.th Website: www.pattayaproperties.com

Rob Astbury

Our quality workmanship will satisfy the most discerning buyer.

View Talay Condominium 1 & 2 offer stunning sea views and huge swimming pools.

Thailand | Pattaya - North & Central ▸ Pattaya - South Pattaya

THE PREMIER GAY VENUE IN PATTAYA
The best looking and frendliest boys

BOYS STUDIO great fun Go-Go
JOLLY BOYS for discerning
BELIEVE for a legendary Turkish Bath
STUDIO FOOD for French and Thai food
STUDIO SUITES for a happy hotel experience
and they are all in one place!

The one-stop-shop for gay enjoyment in Pattaya
Soi Day-Night II
off Pattaya South Road
Tel: +66 (0) 38 723-118
www.gaypattaya.com

■ **Bavaria House II** (AC B CC F g)
Central Shopping Arcade, 216/62 Second Road, Chon Buri ✉ 20260 *(opposite Mike Shopping Mall)* ☎ 427790
German beer garden. Gay owned and operated.

■ **Bruno's Restaurant & Wine Bar** (! AC CC E F glm MA N) 18-24 h, closed Mon
436/77 Sri Nakhon Centre, Chon Buri ✉ 20260 *(soi Regent Marina, corner of Second Road)* ☎ 361073
This gay owned restaurant has a great selection of international and Thai cuisine, an outstanding wine card. Bruno gives the place a personal touch of decent luxury.

■ **Little Italy** (AC B CC E F glm MA N) 16-24 h
215/68 Second Road, Chon Buri ✉ 20260 *(opposite Royal Garden Plaza)* ☎ 466152
Italian cuisine. Gay owned and operated.

■ **PIC Kitchen** (B F NG) 8-24 h
Soi 4 / Soi 5 Beach Road, Chon Buri ✉ 20260 ☎ 422774
Classical Thai cuisine in a beautiful Thai garden. Not gay but worth a visit.

SHOWS

■ **Alcazar** (! AC B glm S STV) 18.30, 20 and 21.30, Sat also 23 h
78/14 Second Road, Chon Buri ✉ 20260 *(opposite Soi 5)* ☎ 410505
The most famous show in Thailand. The Miss Alcazar Thailand contest every year in April always selects a man as the most beautiful woman.

■ **Malibu** (B g OS S STV)
Second Road, Chon Buri ✉ 20260 *(corner of Soi Post Office)*
Very popular (straight) cabaret with kathoey show.

■ **Tiffany** (B glm S STV)
464 Second Road, Chon Buri ✉ 20260 ☎ 421700
The biggest silicon breasts of Thailand.

SAUNAS/BATHS

■ **Sport Man Studio Sauna** (G SA SB WO)
151/ Moo 5, Soi Ananthakul, North Road, Chon Buri ✉ 20260 *(opposite city hall)* ☎ 410673

MASSAGE

■ **No Body Body Center** (msg) 13-23 h
151-151/1 Moo 5, Soi Ananthakul, North Road, Chon Buri ✉ 20260 *(opposite city hall)* ☎ 370170
Many different types of massage by men.

Pattaya - South Pattaya ☎ 038

BARS

■ **Adam & Eve House** (AC B F G msg SNU tv) 11-22.30, club 20-2, show at 0.30 h
42/10 Sabajai Village, Sukhumvit Road, Chon Buri ✉ 20260 ☎ 427413
This Thai restaurant, club and massage moved from Soi 2 to a more residential area.

DANCECLUBS

■ **Marine Disco** (AC B D glm)
Beach Road, Chon Buri ✉ 20260 *(Walking Street - The Strip)* ☎ 428583
Very mixed disco. Here everybody meets when the bars close.

SHOWS

■ **ICON. The Club** (AC B CC D f G MA N S SNU) Wed-Sun and Holiday Mondays 21-2 h
146/8 Thappaya Road (Jomtien Road), Chon Buri ✉ 20260 *(between South Pattaya and Jomtien)* ☎ 250300
Dance shows and live singer every night, featuring their own dancing group "The ICONs".

Pattaya - South Pattaya | **Thailand**

Experience the Splendors of a Kingdom

EXOTIC Thailand

Come to Paradise and Stay at the Fabulous

now open: THE BODY CLUB
- Sauna & Steam Center
- Gym • Massage

Ambiance HOTEL

THE HEART OF PATTAYA'S BOYZTOWN

52 Luxurious Rooms and Suites each fully appointed with:
- Ensuite Shower Room
- Air-Conditioning
- Satellite T.V.
- Queen Size Beds
- Mini-bar
- El Safes
- Direct Dial Telephones
- 24 Hour Room Service
- 24 hour Coffee Shop offering Thai and International Cuisine
- Mercedes Limousine Service available to and from Bangkok and Airport

For brochure or reservations contact:
The Ambiance Hotel, 325/89-93 Pattayaland Soi 3, Pattaya City, Chonburi 20260 Thailand
Tel: (66-38) 424099 & 425145 • Fax: (66-38) 422824 & 424626
or e-mail: ambiance@loxinfo.co.th
Visit our Website: www.ambiance-pattaya.com

Come feel the warmth of our hospitality, and relax in the luxury of our legendary hotel.
NOW CATERING TO THE DISCERNING TRAVELER FOR OVER 12 YEARS.
A special place for special people where you can feel the "Ambiance".

INCORPORATING THE WORLD FAMOUS

Boyz Boyz Boyz
NIGHT CLUB

Open: 9pm to 3am

Cabaret Show Nightly

"Where your fantasies become reality"

LOCATED IN BOYZTOWN PATTAYALAND SOI 3
Visit our websites at: www.boyzboyzboyz.com
FOR TAXI : 325/89 พัทยาแลนด์ ซอย 3 พัทยาใต้ ชลบุรี

Thailand — Pattaya - South Pattaya ▶ Pattaya - South Pattaya/Boyz Town

■ **Simon** (AC B G MA S)
325/11 Beach Road, Chon Buri ✉ 20260 *(Walking Street - The Strip)*
☎ 429647
Kathoey shows. Same owner as Simon in Phuket.

PROPERTY SERVICES

■ **Pattaya Properties**
E.1. P. K. Shopping Arcade, Beach Road, Chon Buri ✉ 20260
☎ 41 06 61 📠 41 06 61
✉ pattprop@loxinfo.co.th
🌐 www.pattayaproperties.com
Pattaya's leading realtor and property developer, specialized in apartments/condos and luxurious 1 and 2 bedroom villas each with beautiful very private swimming pool close to the Gay beach. Fife star international standard.

TRAVEL AND TRANSPORT

■ **Taxi Services**
In Front of Cerry Hotel, 270 Pratamnak Road, Chon Buri ✉ 20260
Ask at the reception for a limousine or take a taxi in front of the hotel. Pattaya-Bangkok about 1,000 Baht.

HOTELS

■ **ICON Boutique Hotel** (AC B bf CC F f G H OS pi)
146/8 Thappaya Road (Jomtien Road), Chon Buri ✉ 20260 *(between South Pattaya and Jomtien)* ☎ 250300 📠 250838
✉ iconhotel@ine.inet.co.th 🌐 www.iconhotel.com
Elegant and exclusive gay hotel between Pattaya City and Jomtien Beach. Beautiful rooms and pool.

Pattaya - South Pattaya/Boyz Town ☎ 038

BARS

■ **A-Bomb** (AC B G msg)
325/75-76 Pattayaland Soi 2, Chon Buri ✉ 20260 *(corner of Pattaya 2nd Road)* ☎ 429043

■ **Boyz Boyz Boyz** (! AC B CC d f G MA S STV VS) 21-3 h
325/89-91 Pattayaland Soi 3, Chon Buri ✉ 20260 ☎ 421910
The No. 1 bar in Pattaya. Handsome boys, freelancers, local crowd, tourists, party and disco mix with sexy kathoey shows after midnight to a unique cocktail of fun and entertainment.

■ **Charlie Boys** (AC B G MA) 21-2 h
325/48-49 Pattayaland Soi 1, Chon Buri ✉ 20260

■ **City Boys** (AC B G MA)
325/52 Pattayaland Soi 1, Chon Buri ✉ 20260

■ **Classic Boys Club** (AC B G MA)
325/42 Pattayaland Soi 1, Chon Buri ✉ 20260 ☎ 429868

■ **Dream Boys** (AC B G MA)
325/44-45 Pattayaland Soi 1, Chon Buri ✉ 20260

■ **Gentleman Club** (AC B G msg) 20-? h
325/27 Pattayaland Soi 1, ✉ 20260 ☎ 429867
Pattaya's oldest go go bar, since Oktober 13, 1982.

■ **Moonlight House** (AC B G MA S) 21-2 h
325/120-121 Second Road, Chon Buri ✉ 20260 *(north around the corner of Pattayaland Soi 1)* ☎ 423595

■ **Music Café** (B F G OS)
325/161 Pattayaland Soi 3, Chon Buri ✉ 20260 *(corner of Pattaya Second Road)* ☎ 426914
Open bar with German food. No go go.

JR Penthouse

BEAUTIFUL ROOMS
IN THE ♥ OF PATTAYA'S GAY NIGHTLIFE !

Double rooms from 19 US$ to 109 US$ with King size bed, some with multi showers, play bath or jacuzzi, A Go Go stage and mood lightening, red lights, balcony. Restaurant, breakfast buffet, Teddy, condoms.
Pattaya**fun**land Soi 2, Chon Buri, Pattaya 20260, Thailand
Phone +66 - 38 - 429-639 Fax 421-747, 428-928
http://www.penthousehotel.com mail: penthous@loxinfo.co.th

Pattaya - South Pattaya/Boyz Town ▶ Pattaya - Sunee Plaza/Day & Night Plaza | Thailand

■ **Muttley's Bar** (B G MA OS) 14-3h
Moo 10, 103/6-7 Soi 14, Chon Buri ✉ 20260 ☎ 424846
Outside bar with very reasonable prices.

■ **My Life Boys**
325/109 Pattayaland Soi 3, Chon Buri ✉ 20260
Go go bar.

■ **Od's Spot** (B G MA OS)
Sophon Court, Moo 10, 103/14 Soi 15, Chon Buri ✉ 20260
☎ 710 321
Small outside host bar.

■ **Panorama Pub** (AC B F G MA OS S) 12-3 h
244/10-11 Pattayaland Soi 3, Chon Buri ✉ 20260 ☎ 710597
See and be seen. No go go boys.

■ **Serene Pub**
325/110 Pattayaland Soi 3, Chon Buri ✉ 20260
Open pub with hosts.

■ **Splash** (AC B CC f G MA msg Pl VS) 21-3 h
325/107 Pattayaland Soi 3, Chon Buri ✉ 20260 ☎ 710578
Erotic swimming shows.

■ **Star Boys Boys** (AC B G MA)
194/23-24 Soi Welcome Plaza, Second Road (Soi Toyota Karaoke),
Chon Buri ✉ 20260 *(opposite Pattayaland Soi 2)* ☎ 249852

■ **Tai Boys Boys Club** (AC B G MA S)
325/25-26 Pattayaland Soi 1, Chon Buri ✉ 20260

■ **Throb** (! AC B d G MA S SNU) 21-3 h
325/108 Pattayaland Soi 3, Chon Buri ✉ 20260 ☎ 424099
Nightly male revue at 23.30 h.

■ **Toy Boys**
325/100 Pattayaland Soi 3, Chon Buri ✉ 20260 ☎ (01)9037578
(Mobile)

CAFES

■ **Ambiance Coffee Shop. The** (AC B G MA) 0-24 h
325/89-91 Pattayaland Soi 3, Chon Buri ✉ 20260 ☎ 424099

RESTAURANTS

■ **Amor** (B F G OS) 17-1h
244/15 Pattayaland Soi 3, Chon Buri ✉ 20260 ☎ 710680
Good food along with the best overview of boyz town. Try their hamburger - you will never go to fast food restaurants again. Greatest selection of desserts.

■ **Café Royale. Le** (! AC B BF CC F G MA N OS S) 0-24 h
325/102-5 Pattayaland Soi 3, Chon Buri ✉ 20260 ☎ 423515
Most popular eating place in Boyz Town. Sit outside to see and be seen, have your breakfast in the sun or your dinner with candle light. The Piano Bar is the place to go for your dinner, to meet your friends and for sure the place to go after all other bars are closed.

■ **Ice Café Berlin** (AC BF F g MA OS) 17-2 h
25/1-2 South Road, Chon Buri ✉ 20260 ☎ 710188
Gay owned and operated.

SAUNAS/BATHS

■ **Body Club. The** (AC B CC f G MA msg SA SB WH WO) 10-22 h
325/106 Pattayaland Soi 3, Chon Buri ✉ 20260 *(opposite Boyz Town)* ☎ 424099
Fully equipped gym and 5 private massage rooms. Food available.

HOTELS

Most of the hotels in Pattaya are gay friendly and there normally is no problem to bring your friend(s) upstairs. Many hotels are concerned for your security and will hold your visitor's ID Card during his stay. Only a few luxury hotels charge extra.

■ **Ambiance Hotel. The** (! AC B BF CC d F f G H MG msg OS SA SB)
325/89-91 Pattayaland Soi 3, Chon Buri ✉ 20260 ☎ 424099
☎ 425145 📠 422824 📧 ambiance@loxinfo.co.th

📧 www.ambiance-pattaya.com
Exclusively high standard gay hotel and coffee shop in the centre of gay bars. Beautiful maintained rooms from 1,200 Baht/night, suite2,100 Baht/night, 2-bedroom suite: 2,300/night.

■ **Café Royale Hotel. Le** (! AC B BF CC F G H MA OS) 24h
325/102-5 Pattayaland Soi 3, Chonburi ✉ 20260 ☎ 428303
☎ 423515 📠 424579 📧 reservations@caferoyale-pattaya.com
📧 www.caferoyale-pattaya.com
Exclusively gay hotel in the heart of Boyz Town. Well appointed quality accommodation. Room rates from 900 Baht, Suites from 1,950 Baht.

■ **Penthouse Hotel** (AC B BF CC D F f glm H MA msg OS VS WH)
Pattayafunland Soi 2, Chon Buri ✉ 20260 ☎ 429639 📠 421747
📧 penthoun@loxinfo.co.th 📧 www.penthousehotel.com
Mixed clientele, many gays and a unique place in the centre of the gay nights. Red lights, condoms and teddy supplied in the rooms. Some with multi showers, play bath or jacuzzi, a go go stage and mood lightening, balcony. Restaurant, breakfast buffet. Rates: Double rooms for 19-109 US$.

CRUISING

-Beach Road (after dark underneath the trees along the beach close to Boyz Town)

Pattaya - Sunee Plaza/Day & Night Plaza
☎ 038

BARS

■ **Believe** (AC B G MA) 20.30-2h
20/49 Moo 10, South Road, Day & Night Plaza Soi 2, Chon Buri
✉ 20260 ☎ 72 32 38
*Go go bar with a collection of the most beautiful hosts in town.
No shows, but the men are show enough.*

■ **Boys Studio** (AC B G MA) 20.30-2h
20/49 Moo 10, South Road, Day & Night Plaza Soi 2, Chon Buri
✉ 20260 ☎ 72 32 38
*Go go bar with a collection of the most beautiful hosts in town.
No shows, but the men are show enough.*

■ **Country Club** (AC B G MA OS)
273/45 Moo 10, Sunee Plaza, Chon Buri ✉ 20260

■ **Crazy Pub** (! AC B G MA S SNU)
273/66-68 Moo 10, Sunee Plaza, Chon Buri ✉ 20260 *(between Soi VC Hotel and Soi Yensabai)* ☎ 713190
Realy a crazy pub. The oldest bar on Sunee Plaza. Randy shows on the central stage.

■ **Forest House** (AC B G MA)
273/94 Moo 10, Soi VC Hotel, Sunee Plaza, Chon Buri ✉ 20260
Corner bar to have a drink and meet a friend even when most of the other bars have closed.

■ **Full Monty's Café Night Spot. The** (B bf F G MA OS S STV) 9-2h
273/83 Moo 10, Sunee Plaza, Chon Buri ✉ 20260
Open Bar with shows every night set up by Monty and his cute staff.

■ **Funny Boys** (AC B G MA)
20/10-11 Moo 10, South Road, Day & Night Plaza Soi 1, Chon Buri
✉ 20260 ☎ 723055

■ **Jack-In-The-Box** (B G MA N OS) 15-2.30 h or later
273/56-57 Moo 10, Sunee Plaza, Chon Buri ✉ 20260 *(between Soi VC Hotel and Soi Yensabai)* ☎ 713 269
Open bar with hosts.

■ **Jolly Boys** (AC B G MA) 20.30-2h
20/49 Moo 10, South Road, Day & Night Plaza Soi 2, Chon Buri
✉ 20260 ☎ 72 31 92
Go go bar. The name says it all: Jolly.

SPARTACUS 2001/2002 1051

Thailand — Pattaya - Sunee Plaza/Day & Night Plaza ▶ Phuket

■ **K. Boys** (AC B CC d G MA OS s VS) 21-2 h
273/90-91 Moo 10, Soi VC Hotel, Sunee Plaza, Chon Buri ✉ 20260
☎ 713479
New go go bar.
■ **Lek's Bananas** (B G)
273/69-70 Moo 10, Sunee Plaza, Chon Buri ✉ 20260
■ **Lek's Beer Bar** (AC B G MA)
273/58 Moo 10, Sunee Plaza, Chon Buri ✉ 20260 *(between Soi VC Hotel and Soi Yensabai)*
■ **Minou** (AC B G MA OS)
273/43 Moo 10, Sunee Plaza, Chon Buri ✉ 20260 *(between Soi VC Hotel and Soi Yensabai)* ☎ 713471
Open bar.
■ **My Place** (AC B G MA)
273/93 Moo 10, Soi VC Hotel, Sunee Plaza, Chon Buri ✉ 20260
Beer bar.
■ **Pineapple** (AC B G MA OS)
273/46 Moo 10, Sunee Plaza, Chon Buri ✉ 20260 *(between Soi VC Hotel and Soi Yensabai)*
■ **Redgy's Place** (AC B G MA OS)
273/44 Moo 10, Sunee Plaza, Chon Buri ✉ 20260 *(between Soi VC Hotel and Soi Yensabai)*
■ **Super Boys** (AC B G MA S SNU)
273/81-82 Moo 10, Sunee Plaza, Chon Buri ✉ 20260 *(between Soi VC Hotel and Soi Yensabai)* ☎ 42 46 05
■ **Top Man** (AC B CC E G MA STV) 20-3 h, show 23.45h
273/95-96 Moo 10, Soi VC Hotel, Sunee Plaza, Chon Buri ✉ 20260
☎ 713228
Elegant bar with go go boys and cabaret show every night.
■ **White Night** (AC B G MA OS)
273/97 Moo 10, Soi VC Hotel, Sunee Plaza, Chon Buri ✉ 20260
Open bar.

DANCECLUBS
■ **Hollywood** (B D glm MA)
32/64 Moo 10, South Road, Day & Night Hotel, Chon Buri ✉ 20260
☎ 424975
Mixed Thai disco with life band. No cruising, so bring your friend(s) and you will have a lot of fun. If you come too late, all tables will be gone.

RESTAURANTS
■ **Butcher Hans Pub** (AC B F g MA N OS) 18-? h
273/32-33 Moo 10, Sunee Plaza, Chon Buri ✉ 20260 *(between Soi VC Hotel and Soi Yensabai)* ☎ 01/8338139 (Mobile)
Rainbow International Gay Pub. Here the gay butcher cooks personally. Good food and nice atmosphere.
■ **Casserole. La** (AC B bf F G MA OS) 18-2h
20/49 Moo 10, South Road, Day & Night Plaza Soi 2, Chon Buri
✉ 20260 ☎ 72 33 26
Restaurant and pub with French and Thai food.
■ **Eldorado** (AC B BF F G H MA OS) Restaurant 9-24 h, Bar 16-3 h
273/84-85 Moo 10, Sunee Plaza, Chon Buri ✉ 20260 *(between Soi VC Hotel and Soi Yensabai)* ☎ 713259
■ **Seven Bar** (AC BF F G MA OS)
273/37-38 Moo 10, Sunee Plaza, Chon Buri ✉ 20260 *(between Soi VC Hotel and Soi Yensabai)*
Open restaurant where the waiters will help you, to enjoy your food. Best overview of Sunee Plaza.

BODY & BEAUTY SHOPS
■ **Boy Design**
257/11 Moo 10, Soi V.C., Pratamnak Road, Nongprue, Banglamung, Sunee Plaza, Chon Buri ✉ 20260 *(between Soi VC Hotel and Soi Yensabai, two Sois behind Sunee Plaza)* ☎ 01/9454764 (Mobile)
Diplom hair designer, trained in Paris and for sure very gay.

HOTELS
■ **Studio's Suites** (AC B bf FG H MA msg OS S VS)
20/49 Moo 10, South Road, Day & Night Plaza Soi 2, Chon Buri
✉ 20260 ☎ 72 33 26 ☎ 72 31 92 📠 72 31 25
📧 micros@loxinfo.co.th 🌐 www.gaypattaya.com
Nice and comfortable hotel at very reasonable prices. All gay accomodation.

GUEST HOUSES
■ **Tropy Guest House** (AC B BF F G H OS)
273/84-86 Moo 10, Sunee Plaza, Chon Buri ✉ 20260 ☎ 713480
☎ 713481
Small guest house in the heart of Sunee Plaza. Rooms from 390 Baht/day to 5.500 Baht/month (low saison, 500 Baht/day, 7000 Baht/month high saison. Gay owned and operated.

Phitsanuloke ☎ 055

DANCECLUBS
■ **Studio 54** (B D g)
38 Borom Trilokant Road, Amphur Muang ✉ 65000 *(in the basement of Pailyn Hotel)*

Phuket ☎ 076

★ This large island (about the size of Singapore) is connected to the mainland by a causeway, and is located to the west of the narrow neck of land which connects Thailand to Malaysia. Formerly a series of unspoilt beaches with thatched hut cottages, it has now become a dependency of the international hotel chains. There are still enough of its beautiful beaches, however, to allow the tourist to find one to his liking. Patong is a good base from which to visit the beautiful islands of the Surin and Similan National Parks. The town of Phuket itself may be the commercial centre, but the main tourist and gay area is Patong Beach. Here you'll find superb watersports- and golfing facilities. The German and Italian influence is strong in Patong, so visitors from these countries will find their languages spoken and even their food available. Patong's gay scene is still searching for its identity: some bars copy the kind of place that you find in Pattaya or Bangkok, while others are trying to create something distinctly local and worthwile. The 'outdoor beer bars' are a typical feature of Patong, and the city is developing its own particular cabaret style.

★ Diese große Insel (in etwa der Größe Singapurs) ist über einen Damm mit dem Festland verbunden und liegt auf der Westseite der Landenge, über die Thailand in Richtung Malaysia verläuft.
Aus einer unzerstörten Strandlandschaft mit Strohdachhütten ist ein Filialort internationaler Hotelketten geworden. Seinen Lieblingsstrand kann man sich natürlich trotzdem noch aussuchen. Und übrigens ist Phuket eine ideale Ausgangsbasis für Besuche auf den schönen Inseln der Nationalparks Surin und Similan.
Die Stadt Phuket selbst ist das kommerzielle Zentrum, aber das Hauptgebiet für Touristen und Schwule ist Patong Beach. Ein optimales Wassersport- und Golf-Revier. Deutscher und italienischer Einfluß sind stark in Patong, so daß Besucher aus diesen Ländern ihre Muttersprachen und sogar heimatliche Küche vorfinden.
Patongs schwule Szene ist noch auf der Suche nach ihrer Identität: einige Bars reflektieren nur Pattaya oder Bangkok, andere aber versuchen etwas eigenes und wertvolles zu schaffen. Dazu kommen die Patong-typischen "Outdoor beer bars" und die Entwicklung eines eigenen Kabarett-Stils.

Phuket — Thailand

Pour aller à Phuket (île de la taille de Singapour), on passe par la digue qui la relie au continent. Phuket se trouve sur le côté ouest de l'isthme qui mène de la Thaïlande à la Malaisie. Il y a quelques années, on n'y trouvait encore que des plages et des huttes de paille. Aujourd'hui, les grands hôtels internationaux se suivent les uns les autres. Une consolation: les plages, elles, sont toujours aussi belles!

Phuket est le point de départ idéal pour aller découvrir les splendides îles Surin et Similan, parc naturel protégé. Phuket est le premier centre commercial de la région, mais les gays et les touristes préféreront certainement Patong Beach, ses terrains de golf et ses sports nautiques. Patong fourmille d'Allemands et d'Italiens, à tel point qu'on y parle la langue de Goethe et de Dante et qu'on y sert saucisses et pizzas. Les établissements gays de Patong n'ont pas encore de caractère propre. Certains bars se contentent de recréer l'atmosphère de Pattaya ou de Bangkok, d'autres essayent d'innover et de créer un style particulier, plus recherché. A ne pas manquer, les "Outdoor beer bars" et les boîtes style cabaret que vous ne trouverez nulle part ailleurs.

Phuket, casi del mismo tamaño que Singapur, está unida a tierra firme por un dique. Phuket se encuentra al oeste del istmo que une Tailandia con Malasia. Esta gran isla, que se distinguió antes por sus playas tranquilas con los típicos chiringuitos de palma, se ha convertido hoy en día en uno de los lugares preferidos de las grandes cadenas hoteleras. De cualquier forma quedan todavía suficientes bellas playas, donde cada uno puede elegir su sitio preferido. Phuket es un buen punto de partida para visitar las lindas islas y a la vez parques nacionales de Surin y Similian.

El centro comercial de la isla es Phuket-Ciudad, sin embargo para los turistas gays la región Patong Beach es de mayor atracción. Esta región tailandesa es famosa por las posibilidades de la práctica de deportes acuáticos y los cursos avanzados de golf. En Patong hay una fuerte influencia alemana e italiana, por lo que turistas de estos países se podrán comunicar en su idioma materno y encontrarán también la comida típica de su país.

El ambiente gay de Patong busca aún su propia identidad. Algunos bares imitan Pattaya o Bangkok, otros intentan desarrollar sus propias ideas. Aquí encontramos los en Patong típicos "Outdoor beer bars", así como el desarrollo de un estilo propio de cabaret.

Questa grande isola (grande quanto Singapore) è raggiungibile attraverso una diga che la collega al continente; è situata sul lato occidentale dell'istmo che conduce dalla Tailandia alla Malesia. Da un susseguirsi di spiagge incontaminate con capanne di paglia si è giunti a catene di filiali di hotel internazionali. Tuttavia le bellissime spiagge sono rimaste alla libera scelta del turista. Phuket è un punto di partenza ideale per un'escursione sulle splendide isole Surin e Similan, che sono un parco naturale protetto. Phuket è anche il primo centro commerciale della regione, ma la zona preferita dei gay è Patong Beach, dove vi sono campi da golf di importanza internazionale e la possibilità di fare sport acquatici. Patong è stata influenzata molto dagli italiani e dai tedeschi: i turisti di questi paesi dunque potranno parlare la propria lingua e gustare la propria cucina. L'ambiente gay di Patong è ancora alla ricerca della propria identità. Alcuni bar imitano l'ambiente di Pattaya e di Bangkok, altri invece cercano di creare un'atmosfera propria, più ricercata. Tipici di Patong sono gli "Outdoor beer bars" e i locali stile cabaret.

GAY INFO
■ **Internet addresses**
Gay Patong: http://www.beachpatong.com (site with many gay Phuket links. Up-to-date)
Gay Phuket: http://www.gayphuket.com

TOURIST INFO
■ **Tourism Authority Of Thailand (TAT)**
73/75 Phuket Road, Amphur Muang ✉ 83000 ☏ 211036 ☏ 212213 🖷 213582

BARS
■ **Black & White Music Factory** (AC B D G S SNU) 20-2, show at 24 h
133/5-6 Rath-U-Thit Road, Paradise Complex, Patong Beach ✉ 83150 *(3rd soi, middle walkway)* ☏ 340758
■ **David's Bar** (B G MA OS S) 17-3 h
133/8 Rath-U-Thit Road, Paradise Complex, Patong Beach ✉ 83150 *(3rd soi, middle walkway)* ☏ 340312
Beer bar with cute hosts and very nice manager.
■ **F1** (B G MA S)
123/2 Rath-U-Thit Road, Paradise Complex, Patong Beach ✉ 83150 *(1st soi, way in)*
■ **Heaven** (B G MA) 20-3h
133/14 Rath-U-Thit Road, Paradise Complex, Patong Beach ✉ 83150 *(2nd soi, north walkway)* ☏ (01) 893 6437
■ **J & B** (B G H MA) Bar 20-3h, guesthouse 8-3h
141/15 Rath-U-Thit Road, Paradise Complex, Patong Beach ✉ 83150 *(5th soi, way out)* ☏ (01) 893c6437
Bar and guesthouse.
■ **James Dean Bar** (AC B CC G H MA OS) 15-3 h
125/10 Rath-U-Thit Road, Paradise Complex, Patong Beach ✉ 83150 *(1st soi, way in)* ☏ 344215
One of the oldest gay beer bars. Overnight stays possible.

Connect
Bistro & Bar
with Guesthouse
http://www.beachpatong.com/connect/

- 11 rooms on-line
- Internet
- Laundry
- Motorbikes
- Phone & Fax
- Thai & Euro food

+ 66 (0)76 294 195

Thailand | Phuket

KENYA'S RESTAURANT AND GUEST HOUSE

FINE STEAKS AND PHUKET LOBSTER

Kenya's is a fine restaurant located fifty meters from the Andaman Sea in Patong Beach on Phuket Island, specializing in fine steaks, fresh local lobster and continental cuisine.

- Above the restaurant is ***Kenya's House***, a guest house, owned and operated by Mister Kenya. The rooms are spacious and well designed with A/C, private baths, cable TV, stereo, telephone and the hospitality Kenya is famous for.

78/13-14 Permpong Soi 3, (next to Wattana Clinic), Patong Beach, Phuket, Thailand 83150
telephone: 66 (76) 345 783-4   fax: 66 (76) 345 785   e-mail: kenya@phuketkenya.com

Map labels: Soi Bangla • Banana Disco • Post Office • Soi Post Office • Starbucks • Soi Permpong 3 • Sea Hag • Kenya's Restaurant • Holiday Inn — PATONG BEACH / Thaveewong Road (Beach Road)

RENDEZ-VOUS HOTEL

A place to meet, a place to stay

143/14-15 Paradise Complex, Patong Beach, Phuket 83150
Tel: (66-76) 342433, 342032, Fax: (66-76) 342033
E-mail: boonco@loxinfo.co.th, Website: boontarika.com

■ **My Way** (! AC B G S) 14-2 h
125/15-17 Rath-U-Thit Road, Paradise Complex, Patong Beach ✉ 83150 *(1st soi, way in)* ☏ 342163
Without any doubt the best go go bar and show in town. Many beautiful hosts and special shows every night.

■ **Passport** (B G MA S) 14-2 h
125/3 Rath-U-Thit Road, Paradise Complex, Patong Beach ✉ 83150 *(1st soi, way in)* ☏ 344266

■ **Patong A Go Go Boys** (B G MA S) 21-? h
123/6-7 Rath-U-Thit Road, Paradise Complex, Patong Beach ✉ 83150 *(1st soi, way in)* ☏ 341305

■ **Pink Cadillac** (B G MA OS S SNU) Show between 23-1 h
135/6 Rath-U-Thit Road, Paradise Complex, Patong Beach ✉ 83150 *(3rd soi, middle walkway)* ☏ 01/2701906 (Mobile)

■ **Tangmo** (B G MA S)
141/24-26 Rath-U-Thit Road, Paradise Complex, Patong Beach ✉ 83150 *(opposite the 5th soi, way out)*

■ **Uncle Charly's** (AC B f G MA msg OS S STV VS) 20-3 h
77/64 Hat Patong Road, Aroomson Plaza, Patong Beach ✉ 83150 ☏ 342865

CAFES

■ **Connect Bistro and Bar** (AC B BF CC f GLM MA OS J) 10-24 h
125/8-9 Rath-U-Thit Road, Paradise Complex, Patong Beach ✉ 83150 *(1st soi, way in)* ☏ 294195
Very friendly owners and staff, reliable internet service. Come here to get information on the gay life.

DANCECLUBS

■ **Boat Bar. The** (! AC B CC D DR GLM MA S STV) 21-? h
125/19-20 Rath-U-Thit Road, Paradise Complex, Patong Beach ✉ 83150 *(1st soi, way in)* ☏ 341237
The only gay disco in Phuket and a place where you have to go. Most friendly owner, great shows and many cute boys.

RESTAURANTS

■ **Bicycle** (B F G MA N OS) 16-? h
5/16 Hat Patong Road, Aroomson Plaza, Patong Beach ✉ 83150 *(Near Andaman Beach Suites)* ☏ 342927
Thai and German food served by nice hosts.

■ **Bingo** (B F G)
125/5 Rath-U-Thit Road, Paradise Complex, Patong Beach ✉ 83150 *(1st soi, way in)* ☏ 342176
Gay owned German restaurant and pub.

■ **Kenya's** (AC B CC F GLM H MA OS s STV)
78/13-14 Soi Permpong 3 (Soi Wattana Clinic), Thaveewong Road (Beach Road), Patong Beach ✉ 83150 ☏ 34 57 83
New restaurant and guesthouse run by Kenya from "Sea Hag" restaurant.

■ **Sea Hag** (! AC B CC F glm MA N) 11-24 h
78/5 Soi Permpong 3 (Soi Wattana Clinic), Thaveewong Road (Beach Road), Patong Beach ✉ 83150 *(50 meters inside the soi)* ☏ 341111
One of the best restaurants in town. Gay owned. A small place to really enjoy your dinner. Call for reservation. Price Range: 200-400 Baht/person.

■ **Siam Restaurant** (B F glm)
135/8 Rath-U-Thit Road, Paradise Complex, Patong Beach ✉ 83150 *(3rd soi, middle walkway)*

Sea Hag Restaurant

Khun Kenya has brought his artistic talents to an exquisite Thai restaurant in Patong Beach. Sit back and enjoy the soft music while savoring the unusual atmosphere of his tastefully decorated restaurant with traditional, quality Thai cuisine prepared only with the finest ingredients. The Sea Hag is more than just a place to eat, but a place to return again and again.

Sea Hag Restaurant
78/5 Permpong Soi III, Thaweewong Road
Patong Beach, 83150 Phuket, Thailand
Open from 11.00 to 24.00   Reservations: Tel: (076) 341111   Fax: (076) 340888

Soi Bangla — Banana Disco
Soi Post Office — Post Office, Mc Donald's, Ban Thai Hotel
PATONG BEACH — Clinic, KFC, Holiday Inn, Ocean Plaza, Merlin, Soi Thaweewong, Sea Pearl

■ **Thiphaluck** (B F G)
125/7 Rath-U-Thit Road, Paradise Complex, Patong Beach ✉ 83150 (1st soi, way in)
Thai food and beer.

SHOWS

■ **Queen Andaman Show** (B g STV)
Middle Soi off Bangla Road, Amphur Muang ✉ 83000 (middle Soi off Soi Bangla)
Male drag shows every night in a very, very straight area.

■ **Simon Cabaret** (B D g S STV) Shows 19.30, 21.30 h
8 Sirirat Road, Katoo, Patong Beach ✉ 83150 (2 km south of Patong) ☎ 342011
One of the best female impersonator show in Thailand. Popular among foreign straight tourists but also gays.

MASSAGE

■ **Alkazar Garden** (B msg)
135/14-15 Rath-U-Thit Road, Paradise Complex, Patong Beach ✉ 83150 (4th soi, south walkway) ☎ 292588

TRAVEL AND TRANSPORT

■ **Sykinn Travel & Tours** (AC CC glm MA)
62/012 Patong Condotel, Rath-U-Thit Road, Patong Beach ✉ 83150
☎ 342476 ☎ 01/89347769 (mobile) 🖷 342476
Very reliable service, friendly and well informed.

HOTELS

■ **Beach Resortel, The** (B CC F g H OS)
37 Moo 3, Thaweewong Road (Beach Road), Patong Beach ✉ 83150 (behind the gay beach...) ☎ 340544 🖷 340848
✉ beach@loxinfo.co.th
Friendly gay owned hotel right on the beach. Rooms 1,200 Baht low season, 1,800 Baht high season.

■ **Club Bamboo Resort** (AC CC F glm H msg pi SA wh WO) 24h reception
247 / 1-8 Nanai Road ✉ 83150 ☎ 345 285 🖷 345 099
✉ Info@clubbamboo.com www.clubbamboo.com
Gay owned and managed upscale hotel with 10 bungalows, 20 deluxe rooms, 4 suites, 3 penthouses. All rooms with cable tv, refrigerator, telephone.

■ **Kalama Bay Terrace Resort**
16/12 Moo 6, Tambon Kamala, Amphur Kathu ✉ 83120
☎ 27 08 01 🖷 27 08 18 ✉ room@kamala.co.th
 www.kamalabay.com
123 bedrooms and suites

■ **Monte Carlo** (AC B BF CC F G H MA OS)
135/9-11 Rath-U-Thit Road, Paradise Complex, Patong Beach
✉ 83150 (3rd soi, middle walkway) ☎ 340815 🖷 340814
✉ montecarlo@phuket.a-net.net.th
Nearly always booked out. Best coffee in town. Princess Grace Restaurant.

■ **Phuket Cabana** (AC B F g H MA PI)
41 Thaweewong Road (Beach Road), Patong Beach ✉ 83150
☎ 340138 ☎ 342100 🖷 340178 ✉ cabana@samart.co.th
 www.impiana.com
Luxury hotel right on the beach. Rates between 3,200 Baht (May - October) and 6,800 Baht (November - April). Straight place but gay friendly.

■ **Rendez-vous** (AC B G g H)
143/14-15 Rath-U-Thit Road, Paradise Complex, Patong Beach
✉ 83150 (5th soi, way out) ☎ 342433 🖷 342033
✉ boonco@loxinfo.co.th www.boontarika.com
Newly renovated and new location. Beautiful rooms, well maintained. Rates from 500 Baht. Motorbike rental.

■ **Sky Inn** (AC B F G H MA)
62 Patong Condotel, Rath-U-Thit Road, Patong Beach
✉ 83150 (9th floor) ☎ 342486 ☎ 340380 🖷 340576
Very friendly staff. Close to night life area.

GUEST HOUSES

■ **Connect** (AC B BF CC F GLM H MA OS) 10-24h
125/8-9 Rath-U-Thit Road, Paradise Complex, Patong Beach
✉ 83150 (1st soi, way in) ☎ 294195 🖷 294195
✉ connect@beachpatong.com www.beachpatong.com/connect
Nice and very friendly guest house in the heart of the gay night life. Come here and feel at home. Motorbike service (200 Baht). Laundry. 11 rooms with fan, AC or penthouse room low season (May-Oct) 200 - 800 Baht, high season (Nov-Apr) 300 - 1,350 Baht, peak season (15 Dec-15 Jan) 400 to 1,450 Baht.

■ **Home Sweet Home** (AC G H)
70/179-180 Rath-U-Thit Road, Paradise Complex, Patong Beach
✉ 83150 (at the corner of 1st soi, way in) ☎ 340756 🖷 340757
🖷 340757
Lovely rooms with bath, phone, fridge and TV. Rates around 1,000 Baht. Enter through the Dow Wow Pub. Gay owned.

■ **200 Years** (G H MA)
141/8-9 Rath-U-Thit Road, Paradise Complex, Patong Beach
✉ 83150 (5th soi, way out)
New gay owned guest house.

Thailand - Tunisia Phuket ▸ Tunis

SWIMMING
- Freedom Beach (South part of Patong Beach)
- Patong Beach (The gay beach is right in front of the Beach Resortel. Beware of hustlers)

Sukhothai ☎ 055
HOTELS
■ **Northern Palace Hotel** (AC H)
43 Singhawat Road, Amphur Muang ✉ 64000 ☎ 611194
Rooms with phone and private bath.

CRUISING
- Bridge in centre of Sukhothai (17-24 h)
- Night market and open-air café (22-? h)

Trang ☎ 075
GUEST HOUSES
■ **Chai's** (BF G H MG NU OS)
22/3 Moo 3 T. Khuanpring, Amphur Muang ✉ 92000
☎ 01/6774031 (Mobile) 📠 222909
Country-side location 20 min. from Trang. Beautiful garden and delicious fish cuisine. Ideal for nature lovers.

Udon Thani ☎ 042
DANCECLUBS
■ **High Tech Music World** (B D g)
2272 Chammusorn, Amphur Muang ✉ 41000 ☎ 241330
■ **Yellow Bird** (B D g)
Charoen Hotel, Pho-Sri Road, Amphur Muang ✉ 41000

Tunisia

Name: Tunis • Tunesien • Tunisie
Location: North Africa
Initials: TN
Time: GMT +1
International Country Code: ☎ 216
International Access Code: ☎ 00
Language: Arabic, French
Area: 163,610 km / 63,170 sq mi.
Currency: 1 Tunesian Dinar = 1,000 Millimes
Population: 9,335,000
Capital: Tunis
Religions: 99% Muslim
Climate: In the north the climate is Mediterranean with hot, dry summers and rain in winter. In the south begins the Sahara desert.

✱ Homosexuality is illegal in Tunesia and may lead up to 3 years imprisonment.

★ Homosexualität ist in Tunesien illegal und kann mit bis zu drei Jahren Gefängnis bestraft werden.

✳ L'homosexualité est illégale et est passible de peines d'emprisonnement allant jusqu'à 3 ans.

◆ La homosexualidad es ilegal y puede ser castigada con condenas de prisión de hasta tres años.

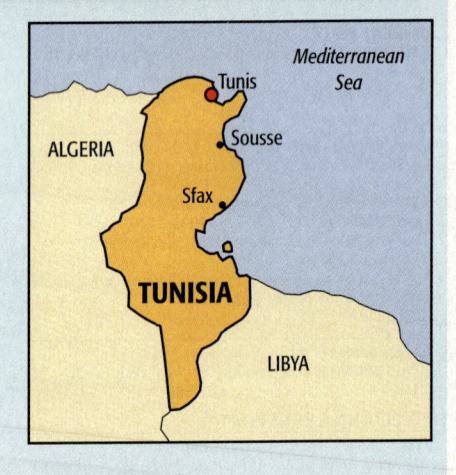

✖ L'omosessualità è illegale. La trasgressione di questa legge può essere punita con un massimo di tre anni di pena carceraria.

Sousse
BARS
■ **Topkapi** (AYOR B MA R WE)
Avenue Habib Bourguiba
Bad reputation.

CAFES
■ **Sirene. La** (g MA OS)
Hotel Abou Nawas Boujaffar, Avenue Habib Bourguiba/Couniche

CRUISING
The Courniche (street along the beach) is very busy during the summer months. AYOR.
CAUTION: Never go with locals on the beach at night. The police are in civil clothing and are everywhere.

Tunis
CAFES
■ **Café de Paris** (B f g MA R OS) 7-23h
Avenue Habib Bourguiba/ Av. de Carthage
AYOR. Meeting point for hustlers at midday. Busy except during Ramadan.
■ **Café-Terrace in Hotel Africa** (B f g MA R OS)
Avenue Habib Bourguiba
Well known and busy café.

CRUISING
Aveune Habib Bourguiba- the locals will want to talk. Try to find a streetside café where you will not be disturbed.

Turkey

Name: Türkiye • Türkei • Turquie • Turquia • Turchia
Location: Southeastern Europe
Initials: TR
Time: GMT +2
International Country Code: ☏ 90 (leave the first 0 after area codes)
International Access Code: ☏ 00
Language: Turkish
Area: 779,452 km^2 / 300,946 sq mi.
Currency: 1 Turkish Pound (TL.) = 100 Kurus
Population: 63,451,000
Capital: Ankara
Religions: 99% Moslems
Climate: Moderate climate. Summers are hot and dry, winters are mild and wet. The interior is harsher.

※ There are no legal restrictions which are directed against homosexuals in Turkey. The general age of consent is 18. There is one article in the law which can be used against homosexuals, and this is the law protecting moral standards. More important than any laws is the local social climate, which is due to the influence of religion, antihomosexual. Along with this the typical roles of men and women need to be taken into consideration. Homosexual acts are considered particularly repugnant when a man allows anal intercourse. It is more common in Turkey than in the rest of Europe for men with a passive sexual preference to undergo a sex change operation and make their money as a prostitute, along with transvestites, who are generally social outcasts but often very popular with many men.
In the last few year s a small gay scene has developed in Istanbul, under surveillance from the police, but nevertheless able to organise a CSD (Christopher Street Day Parade). A homosexual subculture based on the west European model has made its mark in Istanbul, Ankara and Izmir. At the same time the public opinion in respect to homosexuality has slowly started changing. In the large cities you will find more men who openly admit to being gay. Along with the European-like scene there is also a local scene developing in which men can meet (e.g. in Hammams, the Turkish baths) without the fear that they may be considered gay. One should not expect to find west European standards at any of the mentioned bars, clubs. Most of the locals in these establishments do not even consider themselves as gay. Cruising is seldom that which it is in Europe and one has to find a local hotel in which one can "come together". For reasons of security, you should never use your own hotel! All cruising areas are AYOR, where one can often find sex for money.

※ Es gibt in der Türkei keine gesetzlichen Vorschriften, die sich gegen Homosexuelle richten. Das allgemeine Schutzalter liegt bei 18 Jahren. Lediglich ein Artikel des Strafgesetzes zum Schutz der öffentlichen Moral kann gegen Homosexuelle angewendet werden. Entscheidender als die gesetzlichen Vorschriften ist diesbezüglich das gesellschaftlich vorherrschende Klima, das auch religiös bedingt eher gegen Homosexualität eingestellt ist. Im Zusammenhang damit kann auch das Verständnis von Homosexualität, respektive Männer- und Frauenrollen betrachtet werden. Homosexuelle Handlungen gelten besonders dann als verwerflich, wenn ein Mann sich penetrieren läßt. Deutlich häufiger als in Europa ziehen passive Homosexuelle unter diesen Bedingungen eine Geschlechtsumwandlung in Betracht, auch um als Transsexuelle, die gesellschaftlich zwar verachtet, von vielen Männern jedoch begehrt werden, mit Prostitution Geld zu verdienen.
In den letzten Jahren hat sich eine kleine Schwulenbewegung entwickelt, die vorerst in Istanbul einen von der Polizei zwar mißmutig beobachteten, jedoch geduldeten CSD organisiert hat. Eine homosexuelle Subkultur westeuropäischer Prägung beginnt sich vorsichtig in Istanbul, Ankara und Izmir zu entwickeln. Gleichzeitig damit beginnt sich das Bild von Homosexuellen zu verändern. In den Großstädten finden sich nunmehr auch Männer, die sich als "gay" bezeichnen. Neben der sich entwickelnden europäisierten Szene existiert seit je her eine "Szene", in der Männer mit Männern in Kontakt treten können (z.B. in den Hammams, den türkischer Bädern), ohne dass diese sich jedoch selbst als Homosexuelle definieren. Gleichwohl empfiehlt es sich, keine westeuropäische Standards an die hier genannten Adressen und Orte zu legen. Bars und Clubs, und die in ihnen verkehrenden Gäste werden sich auf Nachfrage selbst oft nicht als schwul bezeichnen, Cruising ist an den wenigsten angegebenen Orten mit dem Cruising in europäischen Park- oder Pornokinoanlagen zu vergleichen, läuft ungleich dezenter ab und immer wird man ein Hotel oder eine Pension aufsuchen müssen, um "zur Sache" zu kommen. Man sollte aus Sicherheitsgründen nie ins eigene Hotel gehen. Alle Cruising-Orte sind AYOR, oft gilt dort auch die Devise: "Sex for money".

※ Il n'existe pas en Turquie de législation contre l'homosexualité. La majorité sexuelle est fixée à 18 ans pour tous. Seul un article du Code pénal qui défend la morale publique peut être appliqué contre les gais. Mais bien plus que la législation, c'est le climat social très influencé par la religion qui est en général homophobe. Ceci peut être mieux compris en regard des rôles précis que la société turque confère aux hommes et aux femmes. Un homosexuel est d'autant plus diffamé s'il se laisse pénétrer. Bien plus que dans le reste de l'Europe, les gais au comportement sexuel passif, rejetés par la société mais très appréciés de beaucoup d'hommes, se décident à changer de sexe ou se travestissent et se prostituent.

Turkey

Ces dernières années, un maigre mouvement gai s'est développé sous le surveillance étroite de la police qui a quand même toléré la tenue d'une première Gay Pride à Istanbul. Une culture homosexuelle basée sur le modèle ouest européen commence lentement à se développer à Istanbul, Ankara et Izmir. En outre, l'image des homosexuels dans la société (qui distingue les "Ibne", au comportement sexuel actif, des "Latscho", hommes ou femmes au comportement sexuel passif) évolue peu à peu. Plus en plus d'hommes vivant dans les grandes villes se déclarent ouvertement gai.
En dehors de la scène copiée sur le modèle occidental, il existe aussi une scène locale (par exemple dans les hammams) où les hommes peuvent se rencontrer en toute intimité sans pour autant se définir comme homosexuel. Il est préférable de ne pas comparer les bars et clubs que nous vous mentionnons avec les modèles occidentaux, car la plupart de ces établissements ne se définissent pas comme gai. Les lieux de drague publics comme les cinémas porno et les parcs existent également mais, pour des raisons de décence, un acte sexuel n'est envisageable que dans un hôtel ou une pension. Pour des raisons de sécurité, il est préférable des ne pas amener son partenaire dans son propre hôtel. Tous les endroits de drague sont à vos risque et péril et sont aussi fréquentés par des gigolos.

En Turquía no hay diposiciones legales en contra de los homosexuales. La edad de consentimiento, tanto para hombres como para mujeres, es de 18 años. Solamente un articulo de la ley penal para la protección de la moral pública puede aplicarse contra homosexuales. Sin embargo, en cuanto a la homosexualidad es más importante el clima que domina en la sociedad: ya por razones religiosas predomina una actitud más bien negativa hacia los homosexuales. Esto también explica la manera de entender la homosexualidad y el papel que han de desempeñar hombres y mujeres. Las prácticas homosexuales se consideran especialmente vituberables si un hombre se deja penetrar. En estas circunstancias, homosexuales pasivos consideran un cambio de sexo mucho antes que los homosexuales en Europa, también para poder prostituirse como transversales, puesto que los transsexuales, si bien son despreciados por la sociedad, son mucho más deseados por los hombres. En los últimos años se desarrolló un pequeño movimiento gay que hasta el momento organizó un Día del Orgullo Gay en Estambul, permitido, pero bien observado por una policía más bien malhumorada.
Una subcultura homosexual de estilo occidental empieza a desarrollarse muy tímidamente en Estambul, Ankara e Izmir. Con ello, a la vez empieza a cambiar la imagen predominante de los homosexuales: por un lado está la Ibne, que es penetrado (o penetrada), por otro lado está el Latscho, que es el que penetra (y da igual que penetre a hombres o a mujeres). En las grandes ciudades empieza a haber hombres que se llaman a sí mismos 'gays'. Aparte del ambiente de carácter europeizado, desde siempre hubo un 'ambiente' en el cual hombres pueden entrar en contacto con hombres (por ejemplo en los Hammam, los baños turcos) sin que se definan a sí mismos como homosexuales.
Sin embargo, es recomendable no medir los lugares alistados aquí con el estándar de Europa occidental. Tanto bares y clubs como su clientela no se autodefinirían como gays si se les preguntase, y el cruising en los lugares que mencionamos aquí normalmente no puede compararse con el cruising en parques o cines europeos. El cruising es muchísimo más discreto y siempre habrá que irse a un hotel o a una pensión para 'meter mano'. Por razones de seguridad es mejor no llevar estos ligues al propio hotel. Todos los sitios de cruising son AYOR y en muchos de ellos se puede encontrar sexo por dinero.

In Turchia non ci sono norme di legge che proibiscono l'omosessualità. In generale il limite dell'età protetta va fino ai 18 anni. Solamente un articolo del codice penale per la tutela della morale pubblica può essere invocato contro gli omosessuali. Più determinante delle stesse norme di legge è a questo proposito il clima socialmente predominante, che è orientato, anche per un fatto religioso, contro l'omosessualità. Ciò premesso la comprensione dell'omosessualità dovrà tenere presente l'opinione comune relativa ai ruoli delle donne e degli uomini nella società.
Le pratiche omosessuali sono ritenute riprovevoli soprattutto nel caso in cui un uomo si lascia penetrare. Qui gli omosessuali passivi, più spesso che in Europa, date le condizioni, considerano seriamente l'idea di cambiare sesso. Lo fanno al fine di guadagnare soldi con la prostituzione anche come travestiti, che, sebbene socialmente disprezzati, sono comunque desiderati da molti uomini. Negli ultimi anni si è sviluppato un piccolo movimento di omosessuali a Istanbul, che ha dato vita ad un CSD, in un primo momento osservato con sospetto dalla polizia, in seguito però tollerato. Lentamente si sta sviluppando una subcultura omosessuale d'impronta europea occidentale che si sta espandendo cautamente ad Istanbul, Ankara, Izmir. Contemporaneamente l'immagine degli omosessuali sta cambiando (qui l'Ibne, che subisce una penetrazione, là un uomo, o Latscho, che penetra, indifferentemente che si tratti di uomini o donne). Nelle grandi città si possono trovare oramai uomini che si definiscono "gay". Accanto all'ambiente che si sta sviluppando e adeguando ai canoni europei, esiste da tempo un ambiente, dove gli uomini possono entrare in contatto con altri uomini (per esempio nei bagni turchi, i cosiddetti Hammams), senza però che quest'ultimi si definiscano omosessuali. Allo stesso modo si raccomanda di non applicare gli stessi standard occidentali ai seguenti indirizzi e luoghi. Bar e club e i rispettivi clienti, se glielo si chiede, il più delle volte non si definiscono omosessuali, la pratica del cruising nei posti indicati è difficilmente paragonabile al cruising dei parchi o dei cinema porno europei, essa avviene in modo diverso con più discrezione e si dovrà cercare sempre un hotel o una pensione, per poi arrivare "al dunque". Non si dovrebbe mai tornare nel proprio hotel per ragioni di sicurezza. Tutti i posti dove si pratica il cruising sono AYOR, e in alcuni si può anche fare commercio di sesso.

NATIONAL PUBLICATIONS

■ **Express GL**
Tarlabasi Bulvari 60, Taksim Istanbul ☎ (212) 256 11 50
A weekly political magazine. It has a gay and lesbian page which is edited by Lambda istanbul. Sold at newsstands and bookstores in major cities.

■ **KAOS GL**
PK 53, Cebeci, Ankara ☎ (0312) 363 90 41 ✉ kaosgl@ilga.or
The first gay and lesbian (underground) magazine. Monthly, containing political news. Sold in Istanbul at Pandora bookstore near Taksim square.

■ **Playgay**
CC 351, Mecidiyeköy ✉ 80303 Istanbul ☎ (212) 251 12 84
☎ (212) 251 12 83
Soft-core porn magazine with some coverage of the political issues. Personal ads. Sold at newsstands in major cities.

Istanbul/Estambul ▶ Izmir   Turkey

■ **Cihangir** (b sa sb msg) 9-20h
Altipatlar Sok. 14, Cihangir ☎ 243 0693
Owners try to stop gay sex, nevertheless this takes place in the cubicles when you are discreet.
■ **Çukurcuma Hamami** (b MA msg PI SB) 15-22 h
Çukurcuma cad. 57, Siraselviler *(Taksim)*
Gay action possible. Dark cubicle used as darkroom.
■ **Kösk Hamami** (MA msg SB) 13-22 h
Çatalçesme sok. *(near Alayköskü, Sultanahmet)*
■ **Park Hamai** (SB msg) 9-18h
Divanyolu, Dr. Emin Pasa Sok, Sultanahmet *(Near the blue Mosque)*
Discrete action possible.
TIP: a Hamam is not a gay place in Turkey. It is however possible for men to have sex with other men here.

FITNESS STUDIOS

■ **Flash Gym** (g WO)
Istiklal Cad. Aznavur Pasaji 4, Taksim. ☎ 249 53 47
■ **Vakkorama** (glm WO)
Vakkorama Center, Taksim. *(Basement of the Marmara Hotel)*
☎ 251 15 71
Expensive.

BOOK SHOPS

■ **Mephisto** (g)
Istiklal Cad. Taksim.
Kaos GL available.

FASHION SHOPS

■ **Seker Portakali**
Atlas Pasaji 2.Kat., Beyoglu.
In the Atlas Pasaji in Istikal Cad. there are a few fashion shops, like this one, which are often frequented by local gay men.

MAIL ORDER

■ **Royal Ltd.** (glm)
CC 58 80303, Mecidiyeköy. ☎ 418 65 32 ☎ 418 65 33
Sex toys, condoms, etc.

HOTELS

■ **Eris** (H NG)
Istasion Arkasi Sokagi No. 9, Sirkece, Eminönü ✉ 34360 *(Behind the railway station)* ☎ 511 36 70 ☎ 527 89 51 ☎ 511 59 06
Friendly. A great view of the city in this well cared for hotel.

GUEST HOUSES

■ **Rose of Istanbul** (B BF glm H MA OS)
Ishakpasa Mah. Aksanal, Sok 20, Kücük Ayasofya Sultanahmet *(500 m. from historical point)* ☎ 518 97 04
✉ roseofistanbul@yahoo.com 🖥 www.roseofistanbul.com
Rates single (without shower) from $15, double (without shower) from 20.- (with shower) from 25.-

HEALTH GROUPS

There is no anonymous test in Turkey yet, but in most of the private clinics and major hospitals, taking a HIV test is possible without showing an ID, giving a false name.

SPORT GROUPS

■ **Gay Outdoor Group**
MBE 113, Taksim ✉ 80096 ☎ 256 6818

SWIMMING

-Florya Plajlari beach (three popular beaches within reasonable distances from the city; all quietly cruisy, especially Günes plaji)
-Küçük Cekmeçe Plaj/beach (NU) (Take subway from European Railway Station called Galata to Kanarya)
-Kilyos (beach at European part of the city, extending 3 km along Black Sea)
-Sile (beach at European part of city, extending 8km along the Black Sea, hidden bays in evening)

CRUISING

-Istiklal Cad., well hidden but as this road coming from the Taksim square leads to many gay bars, it is popular with many gays and hustlers
-Katiköy Park, from early evening
-Park opposite the blue mosque, evenings in summer after the "light show" taking place at the blue mosque
-Taksim Park, day and night. This is the most active cruising area in the city. Also popular with hustlers. Making contact is quite easy. For your own safety, one should not try to do anything outdoors, or in a dark courner, but rather in a small hotel nearby.

Izmir ☎ 0232

✱ For reasons of security, one should not choose budget or low class hotels in Izmir, rather the better class hotels such as the Hotel Nil, in which one can bring visitors too. The houses in the streets of Izmir are not always numbered. As there is no numerical system evident, one should ask for assistance (but never ask a taxi driver, as he will tell you it is far away and drive you all over the place).

✱ Man sollte in Izmir aus Sicherheitsgründen nicht die Hotels der untersten Kategorie, sondern etwas bessere Hotels nehmen (z.B. Hotel Nil), um dort mit einer neuen Bekanntschaft ein Ständchen zu verbringen. Die Straßen in Izmir sind teils nur numeriert. Da die Numerierung eine Systematik vermissen läßt, sollte man fragen. (Doch nie einen Taxifahrer, er wird immer erzählen, die Straße sei weit weg, und endlose Umwege zur gleich um die Ecke liegenden Bar nehmen.)

✱ Pour des raisons de sécurité, il est préférable de ne pas choisir un lieu d'hébergement bon marché à Izmir, mais plutôt un hôtel de classe supérieure comme l'hôtel Nil, où il est également possible de recevoir de la visite. Les rues d'Izmir ne sont parfois que numérotées. Comme ce système numérique n'est pas évident à comprendre, n'hésitez pas à demander votre chemin aux passants (plutôt qu'aux chauffeurs de taxi qui vous affirmeront que c'est très loin et vous proposeront une course).

✱ Por razones de seguridad, es mejor no alojarse en hoteles de la categoría más baja sino en un hotel algo mejor (por ejemplo en el hotel Nil) para pasar un buen rato con algún amigo recién conocido. En algunas partes de Izmir, las calles sólo llevan números. Como no es posible entender el sistema de numeración, es mejor preguntar por el camino. Es recomendable no preguntárselo a los taxistas, ya que siempre dirán que el lugar buscado está demasiado lejos como para andar - para poder dar mil rodeos en taxi hasta el bar ubicado detrás de la siguiente esquina.

✱ Ad Izmir per motivi di sicurezza non bisognerebbe scegliere gli hotel della categoria più bassa, ma cercare di alloggiare in un hotel migliore (come per esempio l'Hotel Nil), per trascorrere dei bei momenti in nuova compagnia. Le strade ad Izmir sono numerate solo in parte e siccome la numerazione manca di una certa sistematicità, si raccomanda di chiedere. (Mai rivolgersi ad un taxista, perché ti dirà sempre che la strada è molto distante, e ti consiglierà di prendere scorciatoie infinite per arrivare poi al bar che sta praticamente all'angolo.)

Turkey - Ukraine Izmir ▶ Kusadasi

BARS

■ **Bonçuk** (B g R)
Fevzipasa Bulevard, Basmane *(Near train station and next to Nil hotel)*
Here men with moustaches and effeminate men wait for their lucky day.

■ **Papirus** (B d g tv YG) 22-4h
1445 Sokak 5, Alsancak *(From Mc Donalds on a parallel street to the harbour edge, the street is just before the small parking lot, on the right.)*
Entrance at the weekend approx. US$5, -including one free drink.

■ **Yüzbinyüz** (B d g) 22-4h
1471 Sokak 45/A *(Near the station Alsancak, brightly lit pink building)*
☎ 463 46 43
Entrance at the weekend US$5, including one free drink.

CINEMAS

■ **Büyük Sinamasi**
Gaziler Cad., Tepecik-Yenisehir

■ **Saray Sinamasi**
Kapilar, Basmane

■ **Saray 2 - Sinamasi**
Iki Cesmelik, Mezarlik Basi, Cankaya

SAUNAS/BATHS

■ **Istanköy Hamami**
916 Sokak 6, Salepcioglu Camii Arkasi *(Near Konak, a small sign on a grey building shows the way)*

■ **Yeni Sark Hamami**
Gazi Osman Pasa Bulevari 39c

SWIMMING

- Çesme (touristic town (the biggest) 7 km from Izmir)
- Karaburun (Bus from Altay Meydane)
- Sigacek
- Pamucak
- Sifne

CRUISING

- Fuar Kültürparki faregrounds. One has to pay a minimal entrance fee, there is a small park here. Interesting from 22h
- Waterfront Bopulevard Kordon 1 - Atatürk Caddesi. At night.
- The traffic circle near the entrance to the faregrounds Fuar, at night.
- Konak, Townhall park at the clock, day and night (R).

Kusadasi ☎ 0256

BARS

■ **Z Bar** (B g) 10-? h (in summer only)
17 Camikebir Mahallesi Tuna Sok. ☎ 614 81 72

HOTELS

■ **Elit** (B g H)
Cifuk Yapi Koop, Dogan Sk. ☎ 15 128

CRUISING

- Tea Garden

Ukraine

Name: Ukraïna • Ukraine • Ucrania
Location: East Europe
Initials: UA
Time: GMT +2
International Country Code: ☎ 38 (leave the first 0 after area codes)
International Access Code: ☎ 8 (wait for tone) 10
Language: Ukrainian
Area: 603,700 km² / 233,089 sq mi.
Currency: 1 Gryvna (UAH) = 100 Kopeks
Population: 50,295,000
Capital: Kiev (Kyiv)
Religions: mostly Russian Orthodox also Roman Catholic
Climate: Moderate continental climate. Mediterranean only on the southern Crimean coast. The west and north are areas with the highest precipitation. Winters vary from cool along the Black Sea to cold farther inland. Summers are warm across the greater part of the country, hot in the south.
Important gay cities: Kiev, Kharkov

✱ Homosexuality between consenting adults is legal. The general age of consent is set at 16 for both gays and straights.

★ Einvernehmliche Homosexualität zwischen Erwachsenen ist legal. Das Schutzalter liegt für Hetero- wie Homosexuelle gleichermaßen bei 16 Jahren.

✱ En Ukraine, l'homosexualité entre adultes consentants n'est pas un délit. La majorité sexuelle est fixée à 16 ans pour tous.

⬡ La homosexualidad por acuerdo entre adultos es legal. La edad de consentimiento es de 16 años, independientemente de la orientacion sexual.

✖ L'omosessualità tra adulti conseziente e legale. La maturita sessuale e di 16 anni per tutti.

1062 SPARTACUS 2001/2002

Cherkassy ▶ Kharkov — Ukraine

NATIONAL GAY INFO

■ **Gay.Ru**
P.O. Box 1, 109457 Moscow Moscow ⌂ www.gay.ru/
Russian National website for gays, lesbians, bi- and transsexuals. The most comprehensive web site covering all aspects of gay life in all Republics of the former USSR, including Ukraine. Reliable, exhaustive and up-to-date. English version available.

■ **Our World (Nash Mir) Gay and Lesbian Center** (GLM)
PO Box 62 ✉ 91051 Lugansk ☎ (0642) 53 06 99
☎ (0642) 47 94 22 ☎ (0642) 53 06 99 ⌂ ourworld@cci.lg.ua
⌂ www.gay.org.ua
Official Ukrainian gay and lesbian organisation. Conferences, events, advice etc. Information about the Ukrainian gay scene in English & Ukrainian on their website.

NATIONAL PUBLICATIONS

■ **Nash Mir**
PO Box 62 ✉ 91051 Lugansk ☎ (0642) 47 94 22
⌂ www.geocities.com/Westhollywood/2118/
Quarterly publication by Nash Mir gay and lesbian centre.

■ **Odyn Z Nas**
30 Kominterna vulitsa ✉ 01001 Kyiv ☎ (044) 239 38 53
☎ (044) 239 38 52 ⌂ (044) 239 38 52
⌂ www.geocities.com/WestHollywood/Cafe/7177/
Monthly magazine in Russian and Ukrainian featuring articles on contemporary Ukrainian gay life, inteviews, personals, discussions etc.

NATIONAL GROUPS

■ **International Friendship Club** (GLM) 12-22 h ask for Vladimir
PO Box B-451 ✉ 01001 ☎ (044-94) 65709 (International)
☎ (8 294) 657709 (Local calls) ⌂ (044-94) 65709 (International)
International contacts, penpals, exchange visits, work as photo models. Information, meetings, massage, entertainment. Please send us ICRs.

Cherkassy ☎ 0472

NATIONAL GROUPS

■ **Gay Club**
P.O. Box 1821 ✉ 18015

CRUISING

- Ledovoye pool near the Central stadium
- Faggot Bar (195 Schevchenko Boulevard)
- Interspace Café (44 Smelyanskaya ulitsa)
- Bagration Bar (corner of Schevchenko Boulevard and Lenina vulitsa)
- Square near the railway station
- Square near the main bus station
- Beach in the district Mytnitsa-2: the extremety of the sand beach opposite the city center

Dnepropetrovsk ☎ 0562

BARS

■ **Sterling Bar** (B D F G) Wed 20 h
32 Petrovskogo ☎ 52 51 46 (private)

GENERAL GROUPS

■ **Alter Ego**
P.O. Box 141 ✉ 320069 ⌂ club_int@hotmail.com

CRUISING

- Park Shevchenko

Donetsk ☎ 062

GENERAL GROUPS

■ **Nash Mir**
PO Box 860 ✉ 86132 ⌂ dgluck@mcn.skif.net
⌂ www.gay.org.ua
Donetsk regional representative office of the Our World Gay and Lesbian Center in Lugansk.

CRUISING

- Square opposite the Pchelka café
- Square near the Krupskaya library
- Park near the Yuzhny (Southern) bus station

Kaniv ☎ 04736

GENERAL GROUPS

■ **Kaniv Group** (GLM MA) 18-22 h
PO Box 34, Post Office N2 ✉ 19002 *(next to Kyiv)* ☎ 420 42
A service of acquaintance for gays & lesbians.

Kharkov ☎ 0572

PUBLICATIONS

■ **Simona**
PO Box 8410 ✉ 61105 ☎ 14 85 92 ⌂ itl568@online.kharkov.ua
Quarterly bulletin of some interest for gays.

■ **Zvezdy**
PO Box 4627 ✉ 310022
(Zvezdy = the Stars) Weekly newspaper with news on the gay and bi scene, free contact ads.

BARS

■ **Oscar Bar** (B glm r)
31 Petrovsky vulitsa *(Metro Pushkinskaya)*
Luxurious "cowboy" sallon like in American westerns with an old piano. Expensive cocktails and light food served.

■ **Sofi** (B glm) 11-22 h
5 Lenin Prospekt *(Metro Nauchnaya)*
Small cafe for romantic atmosphere for gay couples.

■ **Zolotoye Runo** (b F G) 11-22 h
37 Sumskaye vulitsa *(Metro Universtitet)*
The oldest and most well-known gay cafe in Kharkov (since 1987), no alcoholic drinks (but visitors are allowed to bring some with if they eat), excellent Russian and Ukrainaian food for low budget. The gay meeting point in the evening.

DANCECLUBS

■ **City** (B D G SNU STV) Thu 22-7 h
Sovetskaya square *(the back entrance to Ditchi Svit supermarket)*
Cosy place to meet and chat.

■ **Contra** (B D G STV) Fri 21-6 h
25 Mironositskaya vulitsa ☎ 40 21 50
Expensive gay disco with techno music, shows and male dancers.

■ **Drive** (B D G SNU STV) Wed-Sun 21-6 h
Rudneva square *(Dom Kultury - DK Stroiteley)*

Ukraine Kharkov ▸ Simeiz

■ **Hobo** (B D f G) Fri 21-6 h
120 Akademika Pavlova vulitsa *(Metro Akademika Pavlova)*
☎ 26 97 63
The most popular gay disco of the city.

■ **Joy** (B D G SNU STV) Thu and Sun 21-6 h
26 Petrovsky vulitsa *(Metro Pushkinskaya)* (no sign board outside, ask for the architect atelier "interior design")
Most popular gay disco with pop music, transvestites shows and male stripers.

CRUISING
- Svodoby ploschad (freedom Square) (YG) (near the Lenin Monument)
- Central Railway station (Metro Yuzhnyi Vokzal, platform 5 near faciltities)
- Hydropark, Shevchenko vulitsa (Tram 15, 16, and 26) (WC near the entrance) and gay nude beach (cross two central bridges, turn right and walk at the end of the island, summer only)
- Kharkov State University, 4 Svobody ploschad' (WC on the 6th, 7th and 8th floor, cafe at the entrance of the library on the 7th floor)
- Gorky Park, Sumskaya vulitsa, (benches on the central alley and public faciltities near the tennis court)

Kyiv ☎ 044

BARS
■ **Stary Kyiv** (B glm)
52 Kreschatik vulitsa *(across Bessarabsky market)*

DANCECLUBS
■ **Big Boys Club** (B D f G OG R) 19-6 h, closed Mon
26/2 Garmatna vulitsa *(Metro Shulyavskaya)* ☎ 435 06 13
■ **Brodyachaya Sobaka** (AC B D DR f G MA P R OS SNU TV WE)
10 Nesterovsky pereulok *(near Lvovskaya ploschad)* ☎ 441 44 32
(Brodyachaya Sobaka = Stray Dog).
■ **Kletka** (AYOR B D DR f G R) 22-6 h, closed Mnn
3 Kutuzova pereulok ☎ 573 88 48

GENERAL GROUPS
■ **Gay Wagon** 19-23 h
P.O. Box 250 GW ✉ 252150 ☎ 491 27 43

HEALTH GROUPS
■ **We Are With You**
9-201 Georgievsky pereulok ✉ 252034 ☎ 228 73 85
AIDS support group.

CRUISING
- Khreshchatyk vulitsa (from the metro station to the Bessarabsky market)
- Park T.Shevchenko (across the main red building of the Kiev State University)
- Main railway station

Lutsk ☎ 03322

SWIMMING
- Beach on the island of Sty river

CRUISING
- Bistro on Peremogy prospekt (near the stadium)
- Neofit cafe on Lesyi Ukrainki vulitsa
- WC in the metro near Dom Byta on Leyi Ukrainiki vulitsa

Lviv ☎ 0322

CRUISING
- Pingvin cafe on Svodoby prospekt
- Kofeynaya on Armyanskaya vulitsa
- Alley in the front of the Opera House
- Bodrost' public bathhouse (35 Turgeneva vulitsa)

Nikolayev ☎ 0512

GENERAL GROUPS
■ **LIGA**
P.O. Box 66 ✉ 327002
Gay, lesbian and bisexual association of Nikolayev.

Odessa ☎ 048

DANCECLUBS
■ **Hollywood** (B D glm WE) Fri, Sat 22-6 h
Deribassovskaya vulitsa *(at the corner of Sadovaya vulitsa)*
☎ 24 61 91
■ **Parnas** (B D glm) 21-6 h, closed Mon
48 Grecheskaya vulitsa *(1st floor of the Russian Drama Theater)*
☎ 26 37 65
■ **69 Night Club** (B D GLM) Wed-Sun 22-6 h
32 Troitskaya vulitsa ☎ 21 40 00

SWIMMING
- Beach of Chkalov sanatorium

CRUISING
- Gambrinus bar on Deribassovskaya vulitsa
- Pushkin monument on Frantsuzsky boulevard
- City garden along Deribassovskaya vulitsa

Poltava ☎ 0532

CRUISING
- Slavy Park (near the moonument to Poltavskaya bitva)

Sevastopol' ☎ 0692

CRUISING
- Admirala Ushakova square (near Sailors' House)

Simeiz ☎ 0600

SWIMMING
- Beach under the Koshka mountain (30 km from Yalta by Bus 26 or 43, then direction Lenin Sanatorium, 50 meters ahead and down the sea, right after the rock overlooking the sea (Simeiz is a well-known gay resort in summer)

CRUISING
- Ezhiki (Hedgwhogs) Café

Simferopol' ▶ Zhitomir | **Ukraine**

Simferopol' ☎ 0652
CRUISING
- Gurman cafe (11 Pushkina vulitsa)
- Square between the main post office and the Crimean Parliament
- Square near the new stage of Russian Groky Theater

Yalta ☎ 0692
CRUISING
- near Yubileiny concert hall

Zaporizhzhe ☎ 0612
CRUISING
- Velikoy Otechestvennoy Voiny ploschad' (across the City hall building)

Zhitomir ☎ 0412
GENERAL GROUPS
■ **Gay Initiative Group**
PO Box 32 ✉ 262012 💻 lgbt_zhitomir@yahoo.com

He loves me, he loves me not... ...use them!

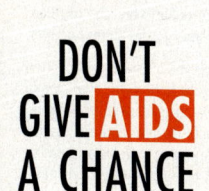

DON'T GIVE AIDS A CHANCE

United Kingdom

Name:	Great Britain • Großbritanien • Grande Bretagne • Gran Bretaña • Gran Bretagna
Location:	Northwestern Europe
Initials:	GB
Time:	GMT
International Country Code:	☎ 44 (leave the first 0 of area codes)
International Access Code:	☎ 00
Language:	English
Area:	242,100 km2 / 93,451 sq mi.
Currency:	1 Pound Sterling (£) = 100 Pence
Population:	58,970,000
Capital:	London
Religions:	57% Anglicans, 15% other Protestants, 13% Catholics
Important gay cities:	London, Manchester, Brighton, Edinburgh

✱ Ever since the new Labour government has taken power in the United Kingdom, gay rights have been back on the UK political agenda. The age of sexual consent has been equalised at 16, gays can serve in the military and sexuality education courses are now permissable in schools. There are 3 openly gay cabinet members and a few more openly gay members of parlament. Attitudes have been changing rapidly since Mrs Thatcher departed and though there is still some way to go, especially outside London, things have improved greatly. The scene in the UK is large and confident and is based mainly in London, Manchester, Edinburgh and Brighton, though wherever you go you will probably find some bar or club. There is an extensive local media and gay programmes and characters on television are now common. However this is still Britain, so sex in public places is frowned upon and too much public affection is not liked, gay or straight. British men are not generally into holding hands in the street or lots of public kissing and tend to be a little reserved at first, but get them back to your hotel room and you will find them as anyone else!

★ Das Schutzalter liegt bei 16 Jahren. Analverkehr und S/M-Sex können als illegal betrachtet werden. Beim Besuch von Klappen und dem öffentlich Austausch von Zärtlichkeiten ist Vorsicht geboten, die Polizei kann dies als "public offence" (öffentlicher Moralverstoß) verfolgen.
Ebenso gilt weiterhin die Clause 28, die es den Behörden untersagt, Homosexualität zu fördern oder entsprechendes Material zu veröffentlichen, Homosexualität an Schulen oder Universitäten als gleichwertig darzustellen und/oder für solche Zwecke Gelder zur Verfügung zu stellen. Weiterhin können Schwule und Lesben wegen ihrer Homosexualität aus der Armee entlassen werden.
Offensichtlich aber führt gerade dieses Maß an juristischer Repression zu einer Szene, die so facettenreich kaum irgendwo sonst in Europa anzutreffen ist. London besitzt eine der besten Szenen der Welt. Die Gay Prides, die britischen CSDs, sind jährliche Demonstrationen homosexuellen Selbstbewußtseins, mit mehreren Hunderttausend Teilnehmern- mit steigender Tendenz.
Die Medien beschäftigen sich intensiv mit dem Thema Homosexualität und schwule Prominente gehen offen mit ihrer geschlechtlichen Identität um. Außerdem werden in Großbritannien einige der besten schwulen Filme und TV-Serien produziert.

✱ Depuis que le gouvernement travailliste a pris le pouvoir au Royaume-Uni, les droits des homosexuels ont enfin repris une place dans le calendrier politique anglais. L'âge de la majorité sexuelle (16) a été revue au même niveau pour tous, les gays peuvent servir dans l'armée et les cours d'éducation sexuelle sont maintenant autorisés dans les écoles. Trois membres du Cabinet ainsi que plusieurs parlementaires sont ouvertement gays. Les attitudes ont rapidement évoluées depuis le départ de Margaret Tatcher même s'il reste encore du chemin à faire, particulièrement en dehors de Londres. La scène du Royaume-Uni est grande et bien implantée et se concentre principalement dans les villes de Londres, Manchester, Edimbourg et Brighton, bien que l'on trouve aujourd'hui un peu partout des bars ou clubs gays. De nombreux journaux locaux, des programmes de radio, et une présence télévisuelle gays participent à la diversité de cette scène. Même si l'on reste en Angleterre, pays où les rapports sexuels dans les lieux publiques sont interdits et où une attitude trop affectée n'est que peu appréciée, que ce soit d'ailleurs de la part des hétéros ou des homos. Les Britanniques ne se tiennent que rarement par la main et ne s'embrassent que peu en public mais, une fois dans l'intimité, se révèlent tout aussi semblable que les autres hommes.

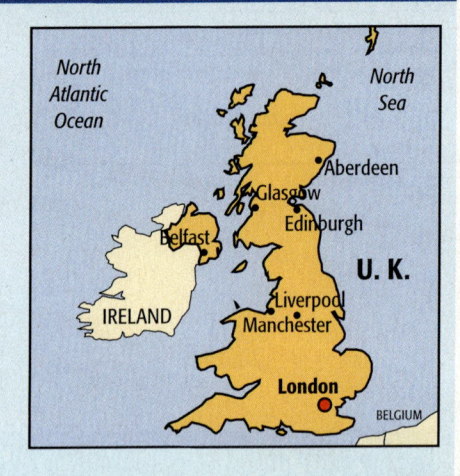

✱ Desde que el nuevo gobierno Labour está en el poder en Gran Bretaña, los derechos gays han vuelto a la agenda política del Reino Unido. La edad de consentimiento se ha fijado en dieciseis años, independientemente de la orientación sexual. Gays pueden servir en las Fuerzas Armadas, y en las escuelas se permiten clases de educación sexual. Hay tres miembros de ministerio abiertamente gays y algunas personas abiertamente gays más en el parlamento británico.
Las actitudes han cambiado rápidamente desde la despedida de Margaret Thatcher, y si bien, especialmente fuera de Londres, todavía hay un buen trazo por andar, las cosas han mejorado considerablemente.
El ambiente gay en el Reino Unido es grande y orgulloso y se encuentra sobre todo en Londres, Manchester, Edinburgo y Brighton, pero vayas donde quieras, lo más probable es que siempre encuentres algún bar o club.

United Kingdom

Existen muchos medios de comunicación locales, y programas o personajes gays en la televisión son comunes en la actualidad. Sin embargo, Gran Bretaña sigue siendo Gran Bretaña, por lo que sexo en lugares públicos no está bien visto, como tampoco lo es mostrar los sentimientos en público, sea entre homosexuales o entre heterosexuales. Los hombres británicos no suelen ir cogidos de la mano por la calle o besarse mucho en público, y tienden a ser algo reservados al principio; pero llévatelos a tu hotel y conocerás su verdadera naturaleza

⚠ En Gran Bretagna la maggiore età sessuale è di 16 anni per tutti. I rapporti anali e sado-maso possono essere puniti legalmente così come i rapporti sessuali consumati nei gabinetti pubblici possono essere perseguiti dalla polizia come "public offence" (offesa alla pubblica morale). Resta inoltre in vigore la clausola 28 che vieta alle istituzioni pubbliche di sostenere l'informazione sull'omosessualità, di pubblicare materiale sopra il tema, a fini pedagogici, di presentare nelle scuole e nelle università l'omosessualità come normale orientamento sessuale e o di utilizzare denaro pubblico per tali scopi. Gay e lesbiche possono ancora essere espulsi dall'esercito a causa della loro omosessualità. Tale repressione a livello giuridico ha condotto tuttavia allo sviluppo di un ambiente gay molto sfaccettato come non esiste in nessun altra città europea. La vita gay di Londra è una delle più articolate del mondo. Il Gay Prides e CSD sono manifestazioni di centinaia di migliaia di partecipanti che dimostrano consapevolezza del loro stato sociale. I mezzi di comunicazione di massa trattano spesso il tema dell'omosessualità; molti personaggi dello spettacolo omosessuali non nascondono la propria identità sessuale e a partire da quest'anno vi sarà anche un'emittente per gay e lesbiche.

NATIONAL GAY INFO

■ **Campaign for Homosexual Equality (CHE)**
PO Box 342 ✉ WC1X 0DU London ☎ 0402/326 151
🖨 (020) 8743 6152

■ **Gay and Lesbian Penfriends** 9-17 y.
36, Edwalton Avenue ✉ PE3 6ER Peterborough
☎ (01733) 76 7242 📧 penfriends@base2promotions.demon.co.uk

■ **Gay Business Association (GBA)**
Unit 10 Eurolink Centre, 49 Efra Rd, ✉ SW2 1BZ London
☎ 07002 255 422 🖨 (020) 7737 3571

■ **Pride Scotland**
58a Broughton Street, ✉ EH1 3SA Edinburgh
☎ (0131) 556 8822

■ **Stonewall Lobby Group (GLM)**
46-48 Grosvenor Gardens ✉ SW1 WOEB London
☎ (020) 7881 9440 🖨 (020) 7881 9444
📧 info@stonewall.org.uk 🌐 www.stonewall.org.uk
National lobby group working for legal equality& social justice for lesbians ans gays in the UK. Call for further information.

The following free publications can be found in most gay bars / clubs etc.
-Boyz. (Free, weekly, colour newspaper with complete scene listings and reviews (plus weekly pin-up!))
-QX.(The scene and music magazine)
-DNA. (Monthly gay, satirical, sexy magazine)
See also National Publications.

NATIONAL PUBLICATIONS

■ **Attitude**
Northern & Shell Tower, City Harbour, ✉ E14 9GL London
☎ (020) 7308 5090 🖨 (020) 7308 5075
Monthly colour magazine for £ 2.20. Over 100 pages of fashion, films, arts, nightlife and music. Glossy and light-hearted. Available at most good newsagents.

■ **BOYZ**
Cedar House., 72 Holloway Road ✉ N7 8NZ London
☎ (020) 7296 6000 🖨 296-0026.
Free weekly scene guide with news, reviews (plus a hot pin-up). Two versions: London/Brighton and the national edition. Available at most gay venues in London and throughout the UK.

■ **DNA Magazine**
14a Newman Street ✉ W1P 3HD London ☎ (020) 7631 0955
🖨 (020) 7323 4253 📧 dna.magazine@virgin.net.
Witty and funny magazine distributed nationwide.

■ **EuroBoy**
c/o Millivres Press, 3 Broadbent Close ✉ N6 5GG London
☎ (020) 7482 2576 🖨 (020) 7284 0329 🌐 www.gaytimes.co.uk
Monthly pin-up magazine featuring young, cute models. Price £ 4.99, available in gay shops or by mail-order.

■ **Gay Times (GLM)**
Millivres Ltd., Ground Floor, 116-134 Bayham St., ✉ NW1 London (Worldwide House) ☎ (020) 7482 2576 🌐 www.gaytimes.co.uk
Monthly glossy full of news, reviews, interviews as well as comprehensive listings for Great Britain and Ireland. Availabe in all good newsagents in London and gay friendly outlets throughout the U.K.

★ **gaydar.au.com**
what you want, when you want it

SPARTACUS 2001/2002 | 1067

United Kingdom — Aberdeen - Grampian ▶ Ashford - Kent

■ **Gay to Z** (see web or call for details)
41 Cooks Road ✉ SE17 3NG London ☎ (020) 7793 7450
🖨 (020) 7820 1366 📧 info@gaytoz.com 🌐 www.gaytoz.com
This phone directory of over 100 pages is bulging with telephone numbers of UK based gay and gay-friendly businesses and organisations and over 6000 listings at www.gaytoz.com.

■ **Outcast**
42 Birch Grove ✉ W3 9SS London ☎ 0906/20 10 028
🌐 www.outcast.co.uk
Queer current affairs magazine

■ **Pink Paper. The**
Cedar House, 72 Holloway Rd. ✉ N7 8NZ London
☎ (020) 7296-6210 🖨 (020) 7957-0046
Long running free weekly newspaper available throughout the UK at most gay venues and establishments. Covers all aspects of gay life from culture and entertainment to political issues and other news stories.

■ **QX**
Firststar, 24 Denmark Street, ✉ WC2H 8NJ London
☎ (020) 7379-7887 🖨 (020) 7379-7325 📧 qxmag@dircon.co.uk
🌐 www.qxmag.co.uk
Club news, music, lifestyle, contacts.

■ **Scots Gay** (GLM)
Pageprint Ltd., PO Box 666, ✉ EH7 5YW Edinburgh
☎ (0131) 539 0666 🖨 (0131) 539 299
📧 editorial@scotsgay.co.uk 🌐 www.scotsgay.co.uk
Monthly magazine, covering all aspects of gay life in Scotland including comprehensive scene listings. Price £ 1.00, free in most gay venues.

NATIONAL PUBLISHERS

■ **Axiom Publishers**
73 Collier Street,, London ✉ N1 9BE ☎ (020) 7833-3399
🖨 (020) 7837-2707 🌐 www.axiomgay.com
Publisher of the monthly gay magazine „Axiom" – a glossy lifestyle magazine with around 130 pages!

NATIONAL COMPANIES

■ **Clone Zone**
37/39 Bloom Street, ✉ M1 3LY Manchester ☎ (0161) 236 1398
Mail order company with shops in London, Manchester, Brighton and Blackpool. Jocks, clothes in leather and denim, swim wear, exotic wear, rubber, greeting cards, books etc. Catalogue for free.

■ **Dangerous to know**
17 A Newman Street ✉ W1P 3HB London ☎ (020) 7255 1955
🖨 (020) 7636 5717

■ **Fantasy Erotique**
PO Box 1019, ✉ PE31 6PJ Dersingham ☎ (01485) 544 884
📧 bubo@compuserve.co.uk
Mail order only. Catalogue for free by phone, E-mail or SAE. Leather, rubber and toys.

■ **Gay Times Book Service**
Camden High Street ✉ NW1 7BX London ☎ (020) 7267 0021
Worldwide mailorder of quality books

■ **Honour** (mo)
86 Lower Marsh, Waterloo, ✉ SE1 7AB London
☎ (020) 7401 8219
Leather, rubber, toys. Catalogue for £ 5 (refunded on order).

■ **QSoft Consulting Ltd**
PO Box 113 ✉ TW3 5FB Twickenham ☎ (208) 896-9550
🖨 (208) 893 9553 📧 info@qsoft.co.uk 🌐 www.qsoft.co.uk

NATIONAL GROUPS

■ **Bears Club UK**
188 Main Road, ✉ DA14 6RL Sidcup

■ **British Gay and Lesbian Sports Federation**
c/o Central Station, 37 Wharfdale Road, ✉ N1 9SE London
📧 teamUK@gaygames.org

■ **Gay Nudist Group** (G MA NU) mainly evenings
GNG BM.2 Box 372 ✉ WC1N 3XX London
☎ (020) 01376-503112 📧 GNG@digdab.freeserve.co.uk

■ **Terrence Higgins Trust** Daily 12-22 h
✉ WC1N 3XX London ☎ (020) 7242 1010 (helpline)
📧 info@tht.org.uk 🌐 www.tht.org.uk

■ **Total Rubber Coverage (TRC)** (G LJ P)
PO Box 9945 ✉ W6 8WW London *(occasional parties are held at The Hoist in London)* 📧 TRC@greyhanky87.freeserve.co.uk
Further information can be requested via email or post.

■ **Lesbian & Gay Christian Movement** 10-18 h
Oxford House, Derbyshire Street, ✉ E2 6HG London ☎ (0207) 739 8134 🖨 (0207) 739 1249 📧 lgcm@aol.com
🌐 members.aol.com/lgcm

Aberdeen - Grampian ☎ 01224

GAY INFO
■ **Grampian Lesbian, Gay & Bisexual Switchboard** Wed Fri 19-22 h
PO Box 174, Crown Street ✉ AB11 5UZ ☎ 212 600 🖨 212 442

DANCECLUBS
■ **62 Shiprow** (D p) 21-2h
62 Shiprow, off Market Street ☎ 596999

HOTELS
■ **Jasmine Guest House** (glm H MA)
27 Jasmine Terrace ✉ AB2 1LA ☎ 64 14 10
Central and convenient for the scene. B&B rates single from £ 15, twin £ 12.00 per person

HEALTH GROUPS
■ **AIDS Helpline** Tue Fri 19-21 h
☎ 57 40 00

Aberystwyth - Dyfed ☎ 01970

DANCECLUBS
■ **Treehouse** (B f glm MA) (GLM) 2nd Tue/month 19-21.30 h
2 Pier Street ☎ 61 57 91

Aldershot - Surrey ☎ 01252

BARS
■ **South Western Hotel** (AC B D GLM MA N SNU STV YG)
11-23.30 h, 12-22 h
Station Road ✉ 9U11 1HT *(Opposite BR train station)* ☎ 31 80 91

Ashford - Kent ☎ 01233

DANCECLUBS
■ **Pink Cadillacs** (B D f GLM lj MA OS SNU STV WE)
Wed Fri-Sat 20.30-2 h
Canterbury Road, Charing ✉ TN27 OEY *((A252) at the Woodland Country Club)* ☎ 71 37 31

Ashton-Under-Lyne - Greater Manchester ▶ Bath - Avon | United Kingdom

Ashton-Under-Lyne - Greater Manchester ☎ 0161

BARS
■ **Blues Fun Bar** (B D F glm MA STV TV VS) Mon-Sat 22-2 h
211/215 mStamford Street, Stalybridge ✉ OL6 7QB ☎ 330 32 12

Aviemore - Highland ☎ 01479

HOTELS
■ **Auchendean Lodge Hotel** (B BF CC F glm H MA OS) 24 h
Dulnain Bridge ✉ PH26 3LU ☎ 85 13 47 🖷 85 13 47
📧 hotel@auchendean.com 💻 www.auchendean.com
Located in a beautiful countryside. The 7 bedrooms are comfortably furnished, all with private toilets and bath or shower. All rooms have central heating, heated towel rails, tea / coffee making facilities, radio colour TV, handbasins and shaver sockets. Full Scottish breakfast and dinner served. Prices from £25-84 p/p.

Aylesbury - Buckinghamshire ☎ 01296

CAFES
■ **Good and Plenty. The** (glm) Mon-Sat 08:45-17:00h
17 Cambridge Street ☎ 485258

Ayr - Strathclyde ☎ 01292

GUEST HOUSES
■ **Daviot Guest House** (H)
Queens Terrace ✉ KA7 1DU ☎ 269678

Bangor - Gwynedd

SWIMMING
-Llanddwyn Beach (g). (Easiest access by car (parking fee £ 2). From Newsborough on W. coast of Anglesey follow signs for beach parking through forest. On the beach itself, turn left and walk for 15-20 minutes to where the dunes are highest.)

Barnsley - Yorkshire ☎ 01226

BARS
■ **Baker Street** (B g MA) (G) Tue 19-23, Thu 19-24 h
Sheffield Road ☎ 78 16 74

SAUNAS/BATHS
■ **Greenhouse Health Club** (B DR CC f G SA SB SOL VS WH WO) 11-23, Fri Sat -2, Sun 12-23 h
56 Sheffield Road ✉ S70 1HS (Junction 36. M1) ☎ 73 13 05
Popular sauna frequented by a mixed age clientele.

Barnstaple - Devon ☎ 01392

GAY INFO
■ **Devon Gay & Lesbian Switchboard** Mon 19:30-22:00h
☎ 422016 💻 www.egrorian.internetfci.com/~daved
Helpline and Switchboard.

Bath - Avon ☎ 01225

BARS
■ **Bath Tap. The** (B D GLM MA SNU STV) Mon-Sat 12-23, Sun -22.30 h
19 St. James Parade ✉ BA1 1U2 ☎ 40 43 44

Historic 16th Century farmhouse near Bath

Leigh House

Tasteful en-suite rooms. Home-cooked meals.
Converted old bakehouse available as self-catering cottage.
On the edge of beautiful Bradford-on-Avon, an historic woollen town.
Good base for exploring Bath, Bristol, Cheddar, Glastonbury,
Longleat, Stonehenge, Wells and many National Trust properties.

Contact Alan or Peter

**Leigh Road West,
Bradford-on-Avon, Wiltshire, BA15 2RB
Tel: 01225 867835**
http://business.virgin.net/leigh.house
e-mail: leigh.house@virgin.net

■ **Green Room in Garrick's Head** (B f glm MA) 11-23,
Sun 12-22.30 h
St. John's Place, Sawclose (next to Theatre Royal)

HOTELS
■ **Kennard Hotel. The** (BF CC glm)
11 Henrietta Street ✉ BA2 6LL ☎ 31 04 72 🖷 46 00 54
📧 kennard@dircon.co.uk 💻 www.kennard.co.uk
Each room has colour TV, direct-dial telephone, hairdryer and beverage facilities. Rates single £ 48, double 88-98. Full English or Continental bf incl.

GUEST HOUSES
■ **Guesthouse** (BF F G MA p)
10 Hawarden Terrace, Larkhall ✉ BA1 6RE ☎ 31 01 18
Bed & Breakfast accommodation for gay men only. Naturists welcome.
■ **Leigh House** (BF F GLM H lj MA) all year round
Leigh Road West ✉ BA15 2RB (near Bath, train station Bath/Bradford-on-Avon) ☎ 86 78 35 📧 leigh.house@virgin.net
💻 business.virgin.net/leigh.house/
All rooms with bath/WC, own key, Rates from £ 55-62 (double), 33-37 (single).

GENERAL GROUPS
■ **Bath Gay Nudist Group**
☎ 31 01 18
(Colin and Ian)

HEALTH GROUPS
■ **Gay Men's Health Project Bath & Western Wilshire**
c/o St. Martins Hospital, Midford Road ✉ BA2 2RP
☎ 83 39 00 🖷 83 39 00
Information about HIV and AIDS.

SPARTACUS 2001/2002 | 1069

United Kingdom Bath - Avon ▶ Birmingham - West Midlands

HELP WITH PROBLEMS
■ **Students Lesbian and Gay Line** Tue 18-19.30 h
☎ 46 57 93

Bedford - Bedfordshire ☎ 01234
BARS
■ **Barley Mow. The** (B d GLM) Mon-Thu 12-15, 19-23:00h,
Fri & Sat 12-23:00h
72 St. Layes Street ☎ 35 93 55
Gay run pub. Disco Fri and Karaoke Sat.

DANCECLUBS
■ **Clarence Hotel** (B D GLM MA S SNU) 11-23 h
13 St. John Street ✉ MK42 0AH ☎ 35 27 81

Belfast - Antrim ☎ 01232
BARS
■ **Crow's Nest. The** (B F glm MA) Mon-Wed 11.30-23,
Thu 11.30-24.30, Fri Sat 11.30-1 h
Skipper Street/High Street ☎ 32 54 91
■ **Kremlin** (AC B D GLM S VS YG) 21-3 h
96 Donegal Street ✉ BT1 2GW ☎ 80 97 00
Three bars, many special feature nights.
■ **Parliament Bar** (AC B D F glm MA S) Mon-Sat 11.30-1.30,
Sun 12-15, 19-23 h
2-6 Dunbar Street *(next to Albert Clock)* ☎ 23 45 23

SEX SHOPS/BLUE MOVIES
■ **Mystique** (glm) Mon-Thu Sat 9.30-16, Sun 12-17 h,
until late Thu-Fri
27 Gresham Street ✉ BT1 4QN *(back of Castle Court Shopping Centre)* ☎ 31 20 43
Videos, toys, cards and magazines.

BOOK SHOPS
■ **Soho Books**
18 Church Lane ✉ BT1 4QN ☎ (07720) 009866

HEALTH GROUPS
■ **GUM Clinic** (STD Clinic) Mon, Wed & Fri 8.30-12, 13.30-15.30,
Tue Thu 8:30-11 h
Royal Victoria Hospital, Infirmary Road ☎ 894 777
■ **Rainbow Project**
33 Church Lane ✉ BT1 4QN ☎ 31 90 30 📠 31 90 31
Drop-in center.

Bideford - Devon ☎ 01237
GUEST HOUSES
■ **Bocombe Mill Cottage** (BF F G H NU OS)
Bocombe, Parkham ✉ EX39 5PH *(Will collect you from the station)*
☎ 45 12 93 📠 45 12 93 💻 info@bocombe.co.uk
💻 www.bocombe.co.uk
Small B&B in beautiful setting close to the sea. All rooms with shower, TV and radio. Gourmet Dinner (five courses) £ 30 p.p. served. Room rates single £ 45 and 68 incl. English bf.

Birmingham - West Midlands ☎ 0121
GAY INFO
■ **Lesbian & Gay Switchboard West Midlands** 19-22 h
PO Box 3626 ✉ B5 4LG ☎ 622 65 89
Helpline for lesbians and gays and everyone who needs it.

BARS
■ **Fountain Inn. The** (AC B CC DR G H LJ MA N OS s SNU)
Mon-Fri 17-23, Sat & Sun 13-23h
102 Wrentham Street ✉ B5 6QL *(New Street station)* ☎ 622 1452
Comfortable rooms with TV above this gay pub in the gay village. All rooms are en suite and the substantial full english breakfast is served downstairs in the bar area. Rates: Single from £ 25, Double £ 45.
■ **Fox. The** (B gLM MA OS) Mon-Sat 19-23, Sun 19-22.30 h
17 Lower Essex Street ✉ B5 6SN ☎ 622 1210
■ **Jester. The** (AC B G MA N) 12-23 h
Holloway Circus, Queensway ✉ B1 1EG *(Opposite Dome Nightclub)*
☎ 643 0155
■ **Missing** (B d F G MA SNU STV) Mon-Sat 12-23, Sun 16-22.30 h
48 Bromsgrove Street ✉ B5 6NU ☎ 622 42 56
■ **Partners Bar** (AC B D GLM MA SNU STV) 13-23 h
27-35 Hurst Street ✉ B5 4BD *(Next to Hippodrome Theatre)*
☎ 622 4710
■ **Route Two** (AC B C D F GLM STV TV YG) Mon-Sat 19-02:00,
Sun 17-22.30 h
139-147 Hurst Street ✉ B5 6JD ☎ 622 3366
■ **Village. The** (B CC D GLM H MA N OS S SNU TV WE)
Mon-Sat 16-23, Sun 14-22.30 h
152 Hurst Street ✉ B5 6RY ☎ 622 4742

DANCECLUBS
■ **Nightingale Club. The** (AC B CC D F GLM lj MA OS SNU STV WE)
Tue Wed 22-2, Fri Sat 21-3.30, Sun 21-1 h
Essex House, Kent Street ✉ B5 6RD *(city center in the gay village)*
☎ 622 1718
Fittings leather bar 18-22.30 h.
■ **Subway City** (AC B BF D F GLM lj MA P SNU STV TV)
Thu 22-3.30, Fri 22-4, Sat 22-4.30, Sun 21.30-2 h
Livery Street ✉ B3 *(Under the archways by the Post Office Tower)*
☎ 233 0310

RESTAURANTS
■ **Woodloft. The** (A AC B BF CC E F GLM lj MA OS s) 8-2 h,
closed Mon
18 Kent Street ✉ B5 6RO *(Next to Nightingales)* ☎ 622 6717

SAUNAS/BATHS
■ **Looking Glass. The** (CC DR f G MA SA SB SOL VS WE WH WO)
12-23, Fri Sat -6 h
Unit 5, Kent House, Gooch Street North ✉ B5 6QF *(Train Station-New Street)* ☎ 666 7529
Spacious sauna and fitness centre in the heart of the gay village.
■ **Spartan Health Club** (b f G MA OS P SA SB SOL VS WO) 12-23,
Sun 13-22 h
127 George Road, Erdington ✉ B23 7SH ☎ 382 3345
Friendly sauna with outdoor sitting and on site parking.

GIFT & PRIDE SHOPS
■ **Clone Zone** (GLM) Mon-Wed 10.30-19, Thu-Sat 10.30-21,
Sun 12-18 h
84 Hurst Street ✉ B5 4TD ☎ 666 6640
Extensive range of magazines, books, videos, clothing, leather, rubber, toys and more.

HOTELS
■ **Monument Gardens** (BF CC DR glm H lj msg p)
266 Monument Road, Edgbaston ✉ B16 8XF ☎ 455 9459
📠 454 7307 💻 sebshouse@aol.com
Each room has TV, video, direct dial telephone, refrigerator, tea/coffee facilities. Some en-suite rooms. Rates single from £ 26, double 35, en-suite 45.

1070 SPARTACUS 2001/2002

Birmingham - West Midlands ▶ Blackpool - Lancashire | United Kingdom

■ **Village Inn** (B BF f GLM H MA OS)
152 Hurst Street ✉ B5 6RY ☎ 622 4742
Bright and spacious rooms available in this B&B. Ideally located above the very popular bar in the centre of the "Gay Village".
Rates: Single £ 25, Double £ 38.50 incl. bf.

GENERAL GROUPS

■ **Central Central Rainbow, Deaf Gays & Lesbians** (GLM MA) 3rd Sat 20.30-23.00 h at "The Fox"
PO Box 4036 ✉ B30 1AT (Lower Essex St.) ☎ 478 0562
🖷 478 0562 ✉ centralrainbow@tinyworld.co.uk

FETISH GROUPS

■ **Midland Link MSC Birmingham** meetings 1st 3rd Sun at 8.30pm at The Fountain Inn, Wrentham St.
✉ midland.link@virgin.net ✉ midlandlink.tsx.org
Member of ECMC.

RELIGIOUS GROUPS

■ **Quest (L&G catholics)** 20-22:00h
☎ 608 9153

SPORT GROUPS

■ **Gay Outdoor Club** 19.30-21.30 h
☎ 01902/757 624 ☎ 0958/403 931
Walking & swimming group

CRUISING

- Kennedy Gardens (AYOR) (Near Colmore Circus)
- Canal bank (AYOR) (Rear of Jug)
- Manzoni Gardens (AYOR) (Bull Ring)

Blackburn - Lancashire ☎ 01254

DANCECLUBS

■ **C'est La Vie** (B D GLM MA) Sun 20-24, Tue 21-2 h
11-15 Market Street ☎ 69 18 77

Blackpool - Lancashire ☎ 01253

✱ The weather in Blackpool can sometimes be good enough for swimming, but even if the weather isn't the best you will love the fish and chips and the drag and karaoke shows. The main landmark of Blackpool is the 158 meter high "Tower". At its feet you'll find the hustle and bustle of gambling halls on the piers, cinemas and fairs. Just let yourself go. The friendly people of Blackpool will charm you too.

✱ Blackpool ist kein Seebad im klassischen Sinne. Das Wetter ist einfach nicht mild genug. Aber dafür kommen hier die Fans britischer Trashkultur bei Fish'n Chips, Travestie und Karaoke voll auf ihre Kosten. Wahrzeichen der Stadt ist "The Tower" (158 m hoch). Zu seinen Füssen tobt das wahre Leben: Spielhallen auf den Piers, Kinos, Vergnügungsparks und so fort. Lassen Sie sich einfach vom Urlaubstrubel anstecken.

✱ Un temps clément vous permettra peut-être de vous baigner à Blackpool mais, même en cas d'intempéries, vous allez adorer les "fish and chips", les soirées karaoké et les spectacles de transformistes qu'offre cette ville. C'est au pied de la "Tower" (attraction principale de ville, une tour 158 m de haut) que la fête bat son plein: les salles de jeux y côtoient cinémas et autres parcs d'attraction. Il ne vous restera qu'à vous laisser emporter et surtout à vous laisser charmer par la gentillesse des habitants de ce lieu.

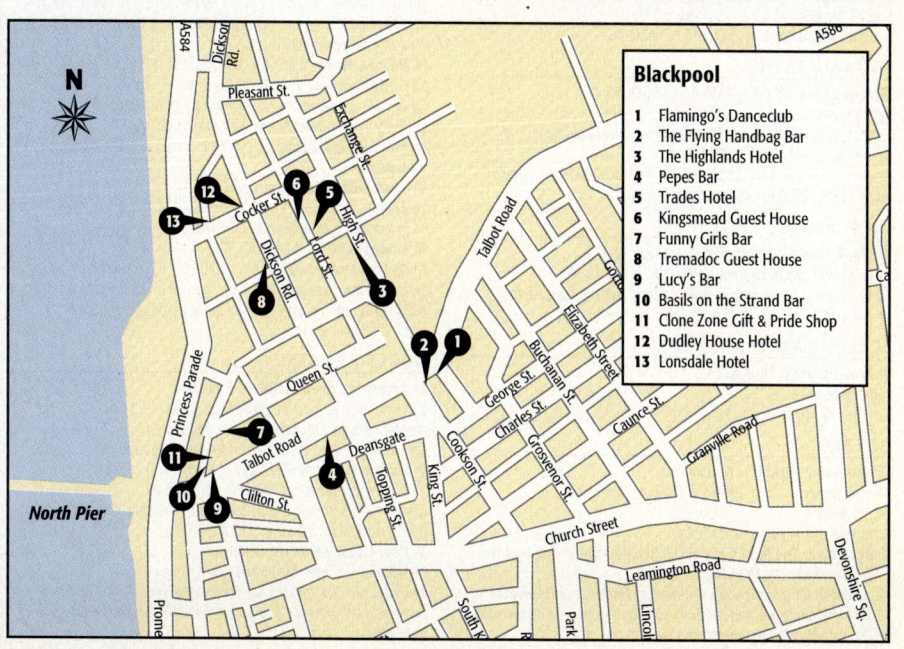

Blackpool

1. Flamingo's Danceclub
2. The Flying Handbag Bar
3. The Highlands Hotel
4. Pepes Bar
5. Trades Hotel
6. Kingsmead Guest House
7. Funny Girls Bar
8. Tremadoc Guest House
9. Lucy's Bar
10. Basils on the Strand Bar
11. Clone Zone Gift & Pride Shop
12. Dudley House Hotel
13. Lonsdale Hotel

United Kingdom — Blackpool - Lancashire

Blackpool no es un balneario en el sentido clássico, simplemente porque su clima no es suficientemente bueno. Sin embargo, los "fans" de la cultura trash inglesa pueden disfrutar aquí al máximo del Fish'n chips, espectáculos de travesti y karaoke. El monumento característico de la ciudad es "The Tower" (la Torre) con sus 158 metros de altura. A sus pies la vida vibra: casinos, cines, parques de atración etc. ¡Dejate simplemente llevar por la marcha!

Blackpool non è una stazione balneare in senso tradizionale, poichè il tempo non è sufficientemente mite. Ciononostante gli appassionati della cultura trash britannica trovano il modo di spendere qui i loro soldi in fish'n chips, spettacoli di travestiti e karaoke. "The tower" (158 m.) è il simbolo della città. Ai suoi piedi vi è una vita spumeggiante: casin, cinema, luna park etc. Lasciatevi contagiare dall'euforia delle vacanze.

BARS

■ **Basil's on the Strand** (! AC B D f GLM MA SNU STV VS) 12.30-0.30, Thu, Fri & Sat -02:00h, Sun 12-22.30 h
9 The Strand ✉ FY1 2DW *(Walk towards North Pier)* ☎ 29 41 09
■ **Flying Handbag. The** (B d F GLM MA N SNU STV VS) Mon-Sat 11-23, Sun 12-22.30 h
170/172 Talbot Road ✉ FY1 3AZ *(next to Flamingo)* ☎ 255 22
■ **Funny Girls** (B glm STV) Mon-Sun 11-23 h
1-7 Queen Street ✉ FY1 1NL ☎ 0125/29 11 44
■ **Lucy's Bar** (AC B D f GLM MA S SNU STV VS) Mon-Sat 20-2, Sun 20-22.30 h
Talbot Square ✉ FY1 1LB *(Below Rumours)* ☎ 29 32 04
■ **Pepes Bar** (B D f GLM MA SNU) Mon-Fri 12-1, Sat Sun 12-2 h
94 Talbot Street ✉ FY1 1LR ☎ 266 91

DANCECLUBS

■ **Flamingo's** (! B D f GLM MA S YG) Mon-Sat 22-2.00, Sun 21-24:00 h
170-176 Talbot Road ✉ FY1 3AZ ☎ 6249 01

SAUNAS/BATHS

■ **Acqua** (AC b CC DR F G MA P SA SB SOL VS WH) 12-2, Sat 12-Sun 22 h
25-27 Springfield Road ✉ FY1 1QW *(near Metropole Hotel; Train Station-Blackpool North)* ☎ 29 41 13
Modern bathhouse with lots of pine, bright colours, subdued lighting and a mixed age clientele. Regular theme nights.

GIFT & PRIDE SHOPS

■ **Clone Zone** (GLM) Mon-Sat 11-18, Sun 12-17 h
3 The Strand, North Shore ✉ FY1 1NX ☎ 29 48 50
Extensive range of magazines, books, videos, clothing, toys, leather, rubber and more.

TRAVEL AND TRANSPORT

■ **Progress Taxis Limited** 24 h
158 Talbot Road ☎ 23 411
Gay friendly taxi service.

HOTELS

■ **Abbeyville** (GLM H LJ MA) all year
39 High Street, ✉ FY1 2BN *(6 doors from main station)* ☎ 75 20 72
Rates from £ 12-15 per person incl. bf.
■ **Belvedere. The** (B BF F glm H OS) Reception: Mon-Sun 8-24 h
77 Dickson Road ✉ FY1 2BX ☎ 247 33
📧 belvhotel@btinternet.com 🌐 www.gay-hotels.co/belvedere
Small, immaculate licensed hotel providing quality en-suite accomodation. Rooms with TV & refreshment trays. Rates from £ 16 incl. bf.
■ **Brooklyn Hotel. The** (b F glm H OS SA) Reception: Mon-Sun 7-23 h
7 Wilton Parade, ✉ FY1 2HE *(North Shore)* ☎ 627 003
📠 624 622 📧 enquiries@brooklyn-hotel.co.uk
🌐 www.brooklyn-hotel.co.uk
En suite hotel, with sea view, serving evening meals where vegetarians are well catered for. The rooms have colour TV. Rates: from £ 20 incl. bf.
■ **Colins Hotel** (BF G H OS)
9-11 Cocker Street ✉ FY1 1SF ☎ 205 41
Large guest house, some rooms en suite. Rates: £ 10-15, incl. bf.
■ **Dudley House Hotel** (BF GLM)
27 Cocker Street ☎ 6209 88
13 rooms, some en suite rooms available. Rates: £ 15 p.p, incl. bf.
■ **Hertford Hotel** (B BF CC f glm H MA OS) All year
18 Lord Street ✉ FY1 2BD ☎ 292 931 📠 292 933
📧 hertford@ceges.dircon.co.uk
Small gay owned hotel. Rooms en suite.
■ **Highlands. The** (b BF CC F glm H MA)
46-54 High Street, ✉ FY1 2BN ☎ 75 22 64
All rooms have satellite TV, and most are en suite. Bar with a pool table. Rates from £ 15, incl. bf.
■ **Kingsmead Guest House** (BF CC glm H MA msg OS) 8-24 h
58 Lord Street ✉ FY1 2BJ ☎ 62 44 96 📠 62 15 99
📧 kingsmead@redhotant.co.uk 🌐 www.kingsmead.co.uk
Member of Blackpool Accomodation for Gays.
■ **Lonsdale Hotel** (b BF CC F glm H MA) 8-24 h
25 Cocker St. ✉ FY1 2BZ ☎ 6216 28
📧 stephen@lonsdalehotel.freeserve.co.uk
🌐 www.lonsdalehotel.freeserve.co.uk
Small hotel with private parking. All rooms en suite. Rates: from £ 16 incl. bf.
■ **Mardi Gras. Hotel** (B BF CC f G H MA)
41-43 Lord Street ✉ FY1 2BD ☎ 75 10 87 📠 01253/75 10 88
This hotel is also exclusively gay. All rooms are en suite with satellite TV. Bar is open until the early hours of the morning. Rates: Single from £ 14, Double from £ 28 incl. bf.
■ **Nevada. Hotel** (B BF CC f GLM H LJ MA N WE) all year
23 Lord Street ✉ FY1 2BD ☎ 29 07 00 📠 62 27 49
📧 nevada@gaybeds.co.uk 🌐 www.gaybeds.co.uk
Centrally located guest-house, with a liscenced bar. All rooms with TV, and some en suite rooms are available. Late licensed bar. Vegetarian bf. available.
■ **Sunnyside Hotel. The** (BF g H MA)
16 Charles Street ✉ FY1 3HD ☎ 6229 83
Most rooms are en suite and all with TV.
■ **Trades** (B BF f G H lj MA SA SOL)
51-55 Lord Street ✉ FY1 2BJ ☎ 264 01 📠 6231 79
Exclusively gay hotel with 32 rooms, some of which are en suite. The bar is open until the early hours of the morning. All rooms with TV. The accomodation is basic.

GUEST HOUSES

■ **Arendale Private Hotel** (BF F glm H)
23 Gynn Avenue ✉ FY1 2LD ☎ 35 10 44 📠 31 84 33
Small hotel with 7 rooms en-suite or with shared bath, all with radio. Rate from £ 19 incl. bf, dinner £ 6.50 extra. TV room.
■ **Carlton House** (B BF E F glm H MA OS WE) May-Nov
77 Abbington Street ✉ 7Y1 1PP ☎ 62 86 87
Near the gay scene. Rooms with TV, central heating, in this friendly guest-house. Rates from £ 15 incl. bf.
■ **Cosy Guest House** (BF GLM H)
26 Milbourne Street ☎ 251 63
Very cosy with just 2 bedrooms! The friendly landlady makes you feel at home and she gives you free access to the kitchen and lounge. Rates: from £10 p.p incl. bf.

Blackpool - Lancashire ▸ Bournemouth - Dorset | United Kingdom

■ **Sandolin Guesthouse** (BF glm H MA OS) 8-? h
117 High Street ✉ FY1 2DW *(Pink canopy over front door/Rosa Baldachin vorm Eingang)* ☎ 75 29 08
Gay-friendly guest house, all rooms with TV. Rates: from £ 12.50 p.p, incl. bf.

■ **Sandylands Guest House** (BF glm H lj)
47 Banks Street, North Shore ✉ FY1 2BE ☎ 29 46 70 🖷 29 46 70
✉ sandylands@blackpool.net
✉ www.ndirect.co.uk/~sandylands/accom.htm
8 rooms with TV, tea/coffee, shower/WC on corridor. Rates from £ 12-15 incl. English bf.

■ **Sheron House** (BF CC F glm H MA OS) Jan closed
21 Gynn Avenue ✉ FY1 2LD ☎ 35 46 14
✉ sheronhouse@amserve.net
✉ www.usefulblackpool.com/ghouses/sheron.html
Small hotel with 6 rooms. Recently refurbished all rooms en suite. English bf included. TV lounge.

■ **Tremadoc Guest House** (B BF F G H MA) 24h
127-129 Dickson Rd., North Shore ✉ FY1 2EU ☎ 6240 01
✉ tom@tremadoc.com ✉ www.tremadoc.com
All rooms with Satellite TV. Rates: £ 12-16, incl.bf.

■ **Willowfield Guest House** (BF CC glm MA N OS)
51 Banks Street ✉ FY1 2BE ☎ 623406
✉ www.gayhotels.com/willowfield.html

PRIVATE ACCOMMODATION

■ **Chaucer House** (BF G H MA VS) All year
59 High Street ✉ FY1 2BN *(close to railway station & flamingos)* ☎ 29 90 99
Small B & B, some rooms are en suite. Rates: from £ 10 p.p incl. bf.

CRUISING
- Bethesda Square
- Lytham Road/station road opposite Grand Hotel
- Bond Street (back of the pleasure beach)
- North and Central Piers
- Silcocks amusement arcade (top of the building)
- Winter Gardens (AYOR) (downstairs, busy)
- Bust station Talbot Road
- Reuoe Park (summer only)
- Starr gate (Tram Terminus)
- Middle walk (AYOR RT) (busy)
- Middle walk (north of Metropole Hotel below the tram tracks. Busy in summer. Nights ayor)

Bolton - Greater Manchester ☎ 01204

BARS

■ **Absolutely Fabulous** (B GLM MA STV) 17-23 h
Clarence Street ☎ 39 37 05

■ **Star. The** (B d f GLM MA) Mon-Wed 17-23:00h, Thu, Fri & Sat 13-23:00h, Sun 12-22:30h
11 Bow Street ✉ BL EQ *in town center*

DANCECLUBS

■ **Church Hotel** (B d GLM s) please call for info
174 Crook Street *(Opposite British Rail station)* ☎ 52 18 56

GENERAL GROUPS

■ **LGB Friendship National Pen Pals**
PO Box 2000, Horwich ✉ BL6 7PG ☎ 66 77 47
✉ www.lgb.org.uk

Bournemouth - Dorset ☎ 01202

BARS

■ **Bakers Arms** (AC B D f GLM MA S) 12-23, Sun -22.30 h
77 Commercial Road ✉ BH2 5RT *(back to back with Triangle Club)*
☎ 55 55 06

■ **Triangle Club. The** (B D GLM MA SNU STV) Tue-Thu 21.30-2, Fri Sat -3 h closed Sun&Mon
29/30 The Triangle ✉ BH2 5SE *(town center)* ☎ 29 76 07

■ **Xchange Wine Bar** (! AC B D F G MA S) Mon-Sun 12-1 h
4 The Triangle ✉ BH2 5RY ☎ 29 43 21

CAFES

■ **Legends Café Bar** (B BF CC F glm MA N OS) 10-23 h
53 Bourne Avenue ✉ BH2 6DW ☎ 31 01 00

SEX SHOPS/BLUE MOVIES

■ **Cerebus** (CC g) Mon-Sat 9.30-17.30 h
25 The Triangle, ✉ BH2 5SE ☎ 29 05 29

SAUNAS/BATHS

■ **Spa. The** (b DR G MA SA SB) 13-20 h
121 Poole Road, Westbourne ✉ BH4 9BG *(directly opposite "Anglo-World" language school)* ☎ 75 75 91
Nice sauna with friendly local clientele. Price includes towels and refreshments.

HOTELS

■ **Chine Beach Hotel. The** (B BF CC d F GLM MA N OS p Pl S SA SOL STV WE) All year
14 Studland Road, Alum Chine ✉ BH4 8JA *(close to town & scene, 1 min from beach)* ☎ 76 70 15 🖷 76 12 18
✉ thechinebeachhotel@btinternet.com
Large hotel, 25 comfortable rooms all of which are en suite and equipped with satellite TV. As well as the large pool there is direct access onto the Chine via the hotel garden. Rates: from £30 p.p. Lunch & dinner available. 24h drinks licence, 2 bars and 2 lounges. 3 crown award (tourist board recommemded).

■ **Creffield Hotel. The** (b BF G H MA OS)
7 Cambridge Road ✉ BH2 6AE ☎ 31 79 00
All rooms are en-suite with TV and hair dryers. It is very centrally located and there is a large private car park.

■ **Orchard Hotel. The** (B BF CC f G H MA)
15 Alumdale Road, Alum Chine ✉ BH4 8HX ☎ 76 77 67
✉ orchard@orchard.co.uk ✉ www.orchardweb.co.uk/orchard
20 mins. walk to the town centre. Accomadation includes five en suite rooms and five rooms with shared facilities. Rates: from £ 15-20.50 per person

GUEST HOUSES

■ **Bondi Hotel** (BF F G H MA OS)
43 St. Michael's Road ✉ BH2 5DP ☎ 55 48 93 🖷 55 48 93
✉ colin+malcom@bondihotel.freeserve.co.uk
Small smart guest house, offering 7 bedrooms with TV and private bathroom or en-suite. Ask about the self-catering apartment. The local gay bars and clubs are just around the corner. Rates from £14 p.p, incl. bf.

HEALTH GROUPS

■ **Body Positive** Mon 10-17, Tue Thu 13-17 h
c/o Drop in, 136 Commercial Road ☎ 29 73 86

SPARTACUS 2001/2002 | 1073

United Kingdom — Bournemouth - Dorset ▸ Brighton - East Sussex

HELP WITH PROBLEMS
■ **Dorset L&G Helpline** Mon-Fri 7.30-10.30 h
PO Box 316 ✉ BHI 4HL ☏ 31 88 22

SWIMMING
-Shell Beach.

CRUISING
-Alum Chine (Nights)
-Sea front (Busiest at night but may be worth taking a pleasant stroll during the day. 100-200 m either side of the pier)
-Park in centre of Bournemouth (Crusiest at night. Go to the quieter side of the square walking with the pier behind you in the direction of Westbourne until you reach the tennis courts.)
-Boscombe Gardens (Drive to Eastcliffe and walk down through the woody area to the gardens)

Bradford - West Yorkshire ☏ 01274

BARS
■ **Bavaria Tavern** (B D g) Mon-Thu 19-23, Fri-Sat 12-23, Sun 12-22.30 h. (L) Tue. Disco: Sat
Church Street, Heaton ☏ 48 76 81
■ **Sun Hotel. The** (AC B D f GLM H MA N OS STV WE) Thu-Sat 12-24 h
124 Sunbridge Road ✉ BD1 2ND ☏ 73 77 22
Accommodation available. All rooms with tea / coffee making facilities and TV.

CRUISING
-Manningham Park (by Lister Statue)
-Sunbridge Road
-Peel Park

Bridgwater - Somerset ☏ 01278

BOOK SHOPS
■ **Bookworm** (CC glm)
25 St. John Street ☏ 42 35 12

HOTELS
■ **Old Vicarage Hotel** (B CC F glm H)
41-51 St. Mary's Street ☏ 45 88 91
Rates from £ 47.50

Brighton - East Sussex ☏ 01273

✱ Only 45 minutes from central London by train or car, Brighton is the biggest and most popular bathing area on the south coast. Its tranquility is a welcome change to the London bustle. You shouldn't miss seeing the Royal Pavillion, an indian-style palace built in 1823. Of course Brighton is at its best in summer but even in winter Brighton is well worth a visit. A very gay friendly atmosphere.

✱ Von London aus ist man in nur 45 min in Brighton, dem größten und beliebtesten Seebad an der Südküste. Die Szene hier ist eine willkommene Alternative zum Londoner Trubel. Am den Gay Pride Veranstaltungen nehmen im Mai jeden Jahres auch viele Londoner teil. Wer allerdings Strandleben an sich sucht, wird erst außerhalb der Ortes fündig werden, in Brighton selber ist das Baden kein Vergnügen. Wenn man nicht gerade auf dem Palace Pier die Urlaubskasse verzockt, sollte man nicht den im indischen Stil erbauten Royal Pavillon von 1823 versäumen.

✱ A seulement 45 minutes du centre de Londres en train ou en voiture, se trouve Brighton, la station balnéaire la plus prisée

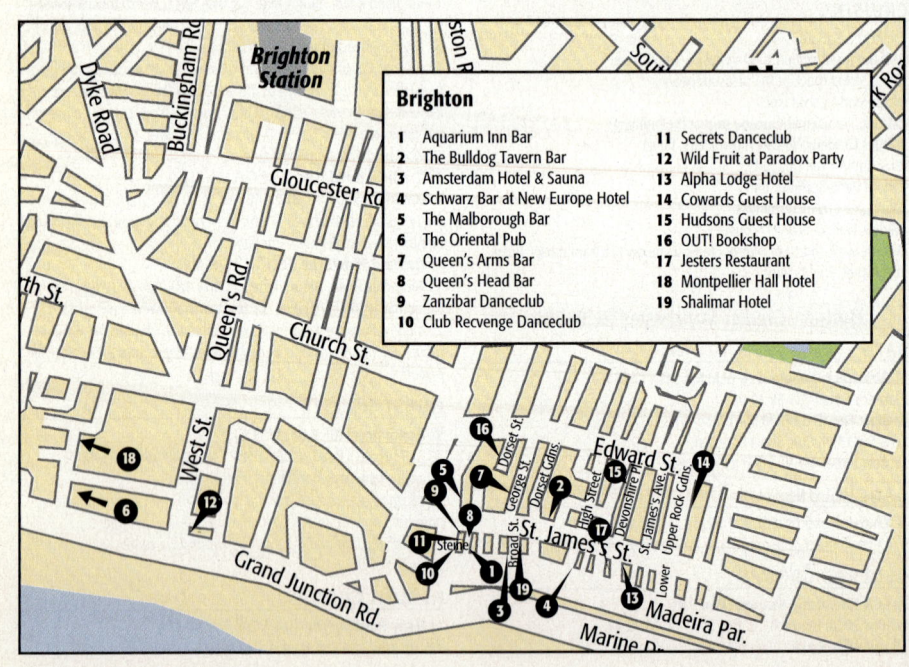

Brighton

1. Aquarium Inn Bar
2. The Bulldog Tavern Bar
3. Amsterdam Hotel & Sauna
4. Schwarz Bar at New Europe Hotel
5. The Malborough Bar
6. The Oriental Pub
7. Queen's Arms Bar
8. Queen's Head Bar
9. Zanzibar Danceclub
10. Club Recvenge Danceclub
11. Secrets Danceclub
12. Wild Fruit at Paradox Party
13. Alpha Lodge Hotel
14. Cowards Guest House
15. Hudsons Guest House
16. OUT! Bookshop
17. Jesters Restaurant
18. Montpellier Hall Hotel
19. Shalimar Hotel

Brighton - East Sussex | **United Kingdom**

de la côte sud britannique. Ici, vous trouverez un calme bienfaisant en comparaison de la vie tumultueuse de la capitale. La visite du "Royal Pavillion", un palace de style indien qui date de 1823, n'est à ne manquer sous aucun prétexte. Même si Brighton est évidemment mieux en été, une visite en hiver ne vous décevra cependant pas. Vous y trouverez toute l'année une ambiance très chaleureuse où les gais sont bienvenus.

El balneario más grande de la costa sur se encuentra a solo 45 minutos de distancia de Londres y ofrece una agradecida alternativa al ritmo acelerado de la capital. Pero quien busque la vida de las playas se tiene que trasladar a las afueras de Brighton, ya que tomarse un baño en la ciudad misma no es precisamente muy aconsejable. Si no te estás jugando tu dinero en el Palace Pier, no te pierdas el Royal Pavillon, construido en 1823 en estilo hindú.

Da Londra si raggiunge Brighton in soli 45 minuti. Nella stazione balneare più grande e più amata della costa meridionale la vita gay è una benvenuta alternativa alla confusione londinese. Chi però cerca solo la vita da spiaggia in sè dovrebbe uscire dal paese visto che fare il bagno a Brighton non è piacevole. Se non avete già svuotato il portafoglio al Palace Pier non perdetevi il Royal Pavilion costruito in stile indiano nel 1823.

NATIONAL PUBLICATIONS
■ **G Scene**
PO Box 2200 ✉ BN3 3QS Hove - East Sussex ☎ 749947
📠 726518
Magazine for Brigton and Hove

GAY INFO
■ **Brighton Gay Switchboard** Mon-Sat 18-22, Sun 20-22 h
☎ 69 08 25 ☎ 204050
Write to: IB/Lambda, PO Box 449, Brighton, BN1 1UU.
■ **Scene 22** (B G) 10-18:00h, Fri, Sat & Sun -19:30h
129 St. James Street ✉ 62 66 82
Brightons only gay shop & coffee bar.

TOURIST INFO
■ **Tourist Information Centre**
10 Bartholomew Square ✉ BN1 1JS ☎ 29 25 99

BARS
■ **Aquarium Inn** (AC B G MA s STV YG) Mon-Sat 11-23, Sun 17-22.30 h
6 Steine Street ✉ BN2 1TE *(Opposite Secrets)* ☎ 60 55 25
■ **Black Horse. The** (B F GLM MA OS STV) Mon-Sat 11-23, Sun 12-22:30 h
112 Church Street ✉ BN1 1UD *(Opposite Dome)* ☎ 60 68 64
■ **Bulldog Tavern. The** (AC B G MA VS) Mon-Sat 11-23, Sun 12-22.30 h
31 St. James Street ✉ BN2 1RF ☎ 68 40 97
Happy Hour Mon-Fri 15-18 h.
■ **Harlequin. The** (B GLM S TV) Mon-Sat 7-2 h, Sun closed
43 Providence Street ☎ 620 630
■ **Legends Bar at New Europe Hotel** (B f GLM p)
Mon-Sat 12-23:00h, Sun 12-22:30h.
31-32 Marine Parade ✉ BN2 1TR ☎ 62 44 62
■ **Marlborough. The** (B f GLM MA MG s) Mon-Sat 12-23, Sun 12-16, 19-22.30 h
4 Princes Street *(Opposite Royal Pavilion)* ☎ 57 00 28
■ **Oriental Pub. The** (B GLM MA S STV) Mon-Thu 12-15, 19-23, Fri Sat 12-23, Sun 12-22.30 h
5/6 Montpelier Road ✉ BN1 2LQ ☎ 72 88 08

■ **Queens Arms** (B d f GLM MA STV) 11.30-23, Sun 12-22:30h
7 George Street ✉ BN2 1RH *(Off St. James Street)* ☎ 69 68 73
■ **Queens Head** (AC B BF D F GLM MA N STV) Mon-Sat 12-23, Sun -22.30 h
10 Steine Street ☎ 60 29 39
Happy Hour 15-18 h.
■ **Schwarz Bar** (AC B DR G LJ MA WE) Fri Sat 22-2 h
31/32 Marine Parade ✉ BN2 1TR *(Basement of New Europe Hotel)*
☎ 62 44 62

DANCECLUBS
■ **Gayte Club** (D glm)
75-76 Grand Parade ☎ 242927
■ **Revenge. Club** (AC B D Glm MA SNU STV) Mon-Thu 22.30-2, Fri-Sat 22-2 h, closed Sun
32-34 Old Steine Street ✉ BN1 1EL *(Opp. Palace Pier)* ☎ 60 60 64
■ **Secrets Club** (AC B D G MG N S) Mon-Sat 22-2 h
5 Steine Street ☎ 60 96 72
■ **Wild Fruit at Paradox** (! B D f GLM YG) 1st Mon/month 22-2 h
78 West Street ☎ 32 16 28

BRIGHTON'S LONGEST ESTABLISHED EXCLUSIVELY GAY HOTEL

Free Steam Room
(Residents only)
Wed, Fri, Sat evenings
MANY SINGLE ROOMS

ALPHA LODGE PRIVATE HOTEL
19 New Steine
Brighton BN2 1PD

Ring DERRICK

Tel: (01273) 609632
Fax: (01273) 690264
Email: alphalodge@cwcom.net
Website: www.alpha-lodge.net

United Kingdom | Brighton - East Sussex

BRIGHTON'S UNIQUE GAY COMPLEX

AMSTERDAM Brighton
BAR • HOTEL • SAUNA

LARGE SEA VIEW THEMED ROOMS
FULLY-EQUIPPED, ALL WITH BATHS, TVS ETC.

SAUNA OPEN 18.00 - 06.00 - IN SUMMER
HALF-PRICE FOR RESIDENTS

BRIGHTON'S BIGGEST EURO-STYLE
CRUISE BAR
COMPLETE WITH LARGE CRUISE PATIO
OVERLOOKING THE FAMOUS PALACE PIER

BAR - HOTEL - SAUNA
11 - 12 MARINE PARADE BRIGHTON BN2 1TL
TEL: +44 (0)1273 688825 TEL: +++ 688828
EMAIL & WEB PAGE • www.amsterdam.uk.com
• *more than just another hotel* •
100% GAY-OWNED • FEEL FREE TO BE YOURSELF

■ **Zanzibar** (AC B D GLM MA P S VS YG) Mon-Sat 14-2, Sun 16-22.30 h
129 St. James Street ✉ BN2 1TH *(Just off the "Old Stein")*
☎ 62 21 00

RESTAURANTS
■ **Capers** (F)
27 Garden Street ☎ 675550
■ **Fudges** (AC CC F glm OS) 11-15:00 and 18-24:00h, Sun 11-15:00h
127 King's Road ✉ BN1 2FA ☎ 20 58 52
FAX 74 68 42 English seafront restaurant.
■ **Jesters** (AC B CC F glm MA TV) Mon-Sun 12-23 h
87 St.James Street ✉ BN2 1TP ☎ 62 42 33

SAUNAS/BATHS
■ **Amsterdam** (B CC DR f G SA SB VS) 14-4, Fri-Sat -6 h
11-12 Marine Parade ✉ BN2 1TL *(on seafront)* ☎ 68 88 25
Sauna steam complex together with a hotel. Popular late night/early morning.
■ **Bright'n Beautiful** (b DR f G MA SA SB SOL VS) 12-22 h
9 St. Margaret's Place ✉ BN1 2FE *(opposite Sussex Height's)*
☎ 32 83 30
Sauna established since 1975 with a friendly mixed age clientele.
■ **Brighton Oasis** (AC CC DR f G msg CPI SA SB SOL WH YG)
Mon-Thu 12-22.30, Fri -4, Sat -6, Sun -24 h
75/76 Grand Parade ✉ BN2 2JA *(5 min from railway station, opposite the Royal Pavillon)* ☎ 689966
Egyptian themed sauna frequented by a young crowd. Best time late Fri & Sat night.

■ **Unit One** (AC b DR F G MA msg PI SA SB) 11-23 h
St. Margarets Flats, High Street ✉ BN2 7HS *(10 min east of Brighton along the coast road. Look for the "White Horse" pub in Rottingdean. Turn right here and the sauna is 50 m further on towards the sea, Bus 27/271-White Horse pub)* ☎ 30 72 53
Sauna established since 68. Very clean and relaxed atmosphere with a large heated pool.

BOOK SHOPS
■ **OUT! Brighton** (CC GLM) Mon-Thu 10-18, Fri Sat 10-19, Sun 11-17 h
4&7 Dorset Street ✉ BN2 1WA *(opposite the Law Courts)*
☎ 62 33 56

TRAVEL AND TRANSPORT
■ **Cruising in Style** (CC GLM H MA) 9-18 h
36 Marine Parade ✉ BN2 1TR ☎ 60 53 16 📠 60 53 16
📧 buoys@dircon.co.uk
Selling gay group cruises on various deluxe ships or exclusive gay cruises. Also accomodation in self-catering, non-smoking apartments in "Eastcliff House" (OS). Weekly lets. Ask for details.

HOTELS
■ **Alpha Lodge Private Hotel** (BF CC f GLM H MA SB) All year
19 New Steine ✉ BN2 1PD ☎ 60 96 32 📠 69 02 64
📧 alphalodge@cwcom.net 🌐 www.alpha-lodge.net
Located close to the gay scene, this hotel caters well for the single traveller (many single rooms available). All rooms with radio and TV. Rates: single/shared bath £ from 22, en-suite up to 53 and double rooms £ 44-60. Steam room for free for guests on Wed, Fri and Sat. Full English bf served. TV room.

1076 SPARTACUS 2001/2002

Brighton - East Sussex — United Kingdom

■ **Amsterdam. The** (AC b CC G MA OS SA SB) Bar :
Mon-Sat 11-23:00, Sun 12-22:30, Sauna : all day 'til 06:00h
11-12 Marine Parade ✉ BN2 1TL
(In the heart of "gay village" Opposite Pier.) ☎ 688825 🖷 688828
🖳 www.amsterdam.uk.com
Hotel with bar and sauna. Large victorian seafront hotel. Large well appointed hotel. All rooms ensuite. Fabulous sea views. Prices include breakfast. Rooftop patio. Brightons largest cruise bar with a terrace. Sauna half price for residents. All usual facilities. Large 20 man steam & dry sauna areas.

■ **Ashley Court Guest House** (AC BF CC glm H) 0-24 h
33 Montpelier Road ✉ BN1 2LQ ☎ 73 99 16
Small centrally located guest house, all rooms have TV and tea / coffee making facilities. Rates: Single £ 18, Double £ 32 incl. bf.

■ **Court Craven Hotel** (B BF f GLM H lj MA)
2 Attlingworth Street ✉ BN2 1PL (Off St James's Street)
☎ 60 77 10
Situated just off the main gay street this hotel offers rooms with showers, T.V, and tea / coffee making facilities.

■ **Cowards Guest House** (BF CC G H MA) all year round
12 Upper Rock Gardens ✉ BN2 1QE (bus 7 or taxi from station; near gay district) ☎ 69 26 77
Centrally located gay only guest house in which most rooms are en suite (2 have shower only). All rooms have tea / coffee making facilities and TV. Rates: Single £ 21-25, Double £ 42-55 bf. incl.

■ **Hudsons Guest House** (BF CC GLM H MA OS) all year 8-2h
22 Devonshire Place ✉ BN2 1QA (50 yds to next bus stop)
☎ 68 36 42 ☎ 69 60 88 🖳 hudsons@brighton.co.uk
🖳 www.brighton.co.uk/hotels/hudsons
The only gay guest house in the UK recommended by the Consumers Association, 3 diamond hotel. All rooms with showers, some with toilet, telephone, radio, hospitality tray. Full English or vegetarian. bf included. Rates £ 42-70 (double) single from £ 24. Apartment 250-300 p/w.

■ **Montpellier Hall** (BF e F GLM H lj MA OS) All year round
17 Montpellier Terrace ✉ BN1 3DF (Town Center) ☎ 20 35 99
🖷 70 60 30
Lovely Regency house with "grand" rooms and a beautiful walled garden. Private car park

■ **New Europe Hotel** (B BF CC GLM H MA p) 0-24 h
31-32 Marine Parade ✉ BN2 1TR ☎ 62 44 62
This is the largest gay hotel in Brighton. Bars open until the early hours of the morning. The rooms are en suite and have T.V and tea / coffee making facilities.

■ **Shalimar Hotel** (B BF CC E f GLM H MA) 8-23 h
23 Broad Street ✉ BN2 1TJ (Bus 7 from station) ☎ 694 314
Each room has central heating, TV, telephone, clock/radio, hairdryer, tea/coffee facilities, most have ensuite shower/bath/WC and are serviced all day. Full English or vegetarian bf. Closed over Christmas. Rates nightly per person £ 25-28. Discount for Spartacus readers.

GUEST HOUSES

■ **Avalon Guesthouse** (B BF CC GLM H MA) all year round
7 Upper Rock Gardens ✉ BN2 1QE ☎ 69 23 44 🖷 69 23 44
🖳 avalongh@aol.com
All rooms with bath/shower, WC, radio. Rates double from £ 40 (winter) £ 45 (summer) incl. bf. Bicycle hire, TV room and bar.

■ **Catnaps Private Guest House** (BF GLM H MA) 8.30-23 h
21 Atlingworth Street ✉ BN2 1PL ☎ 68 51 93 🖷 62 20 26
Centrally located guest house with a variety of rooms on offer, some with shower. Rates: up to single £ 18, double 36, twin £ 35 incl. bf.

HEALTH GROUPS

■ **Brighton Body Positive** 10-17, Sat 11-16 h, closed Sun
PO Box 1317 ✉ BN2 2ZU ☎ 69 32 66 🖷 62 20 06
🖳 info@bodypositive.co.uk 🖳 www.bodypositive.co.uk
Drop-In Centre, alternative therapies, information, support for people affected by HIV.

Montpellier Hall
Montpelier Terrace, Brighton BN1 3DF
Tel: 01273-203599 Fax: 01273 706030

Come and stay at our beautiful Grade II historic italianate style Regency Villa in the centre of Brighton, lived in by two past mayors of the town.
Spacious rooms overlooking the spectacular walled garden. Relax in the grand drawing room, or dine in our period dining room in an atmosphere of another age.
All rooms have colour TV and tea / coffee making facilities. Private car parking.
Functions and parties also catered for.
Easy walk to clubs, restaurants and the sea.
Summer barbecues in the garden weather permitting.

**Bed and full English breakfast
from £ 30+VAT per person**

HUDSONS

The only gay hotel in the UK recommended by which? Hotel Guide
English Tourist Council.◊◊◊

Small, friendly, central exclusively gay guest house with high standards.

All our spacious rooms have:
Showers, some have WCs;
Direct dial telephones; Unlimited tea + coffee;
Double glazing; central heating
& Patio garden; and are furnished by NEXT Interior.

Frank and Graham welcome you to:

AMEX 22 Devonshire Place, VISA
Brighton BN21QA
Tel : (01273) 683642 · Fax: (01273) 696088
e-mail: hudsons@brighton.co.uk
http://www.brighton.co.uk/hotels/hudsons

Town centre one bedroom flat available

United Kingdom | Brighton - East Sussex ▶ Bury St. Edmunds - Suffolk

SWIMMING
-Telscombe Cliffs (G) (Take a bus to Saltdean. This is a very cruisy picnic venue at the weekends)
-Shoream Beach (g nu) (This is an unofficial nudist beach located opposite the old power station chimney)
-Angle Beach (G)(Located on the Brighton / Hove border this is the place to tan on a hot summer's day. It can also get quite cruisy when the clubs are closed)

CRUISING
-The Amsterdam Bar - Brightons only outside cruise terrace.
-Dukes Mound (Pathways through the bushes on the sand banks leading to the official nudist beach near the Marina at the end of Madeira Drive. Most interesting after clubs, but some action during the day too.)

Bristol - Avon ☎ 0117

GAY INFO
■ **Bristol Lesbian & Gay Switchboard** 20-22:00h
BLAGS, PO Box 49, Green Leaf Bookshop, 82 Colston Street BS1 SBB
☎ 942 08 42

BARS
■ **Elephant. The** (B GLM MA s STV YG) Mon-Fri 10.30-23, Sat 12-23, Sun 12-22.30, happy hour 12-18 h
20 St. Nicholas Street ✉ BS1 1UB (City centre) ☎ 949 99 01
■ **Griffin. The** (B GLM lj MA) Mon-Sat 12-23, Sun 12-22.30 h
41 Colston Street, BS1 5AP (just up from Colston Hall) ☎ 927 24 21
■ **Pineapple. The** (B D F GLM MA S SNU STV YG) 12-23, Sun 12-22.50 h
37 St. Georges Road ✉ BS1 5UU
☎ 907 1162
Friendly bar, sometimes Karaoke and Pop Quiz Night.
■ **Queens Shilling. The** (B D F GLM MA SNU STV) Mon 19-23, Tue-Sat -2, Sun 17-22.30 h
9 Frogmore Street ✉ BS1 5NA ☎ 926 43 42

DANCECLUBS
■ **Castro** (B D GLM LJ WE YG) Mon-Thu 22-? Fri & Sat 22-6, Sun 22-3h
72 Old Market ☎ 9220774
■ **Lakota** (AC B F glm P S WE) Fri 22.30-5, Sat 21.30-4 h
6 Upper York Street ✉ BS2 8QE (Town Centre)
☎ 942 62 08

RESTAURANTS
■ **Michael's Restaurant** (F glm) Tue-Sat 19-?. Lunch: Tue-Fri 12.30-15.30 h
129 Hotwell Road, Clifton BS8 4RU ☎ 927 61 90
International cuisine.

BOOK SHOPS
■ **Green Leaf Bookshop** (CC g) Mon-Fri 9.30-17.30, Sat 10-17 h
82 Colston Street ✉ BS1 5BB ☎ 921 13 69

HOTELS
■ **Abbotswould Bristol** (BF f G H MA msg)
102 Abbotswoody, Yate ✉ BS17 4NE ☎ (01454) 324 324
✉ headmanray@bt.internet.com
Courtesy car from Rail Station. Discount for stays of more than 3 days.

GUEST HOUSES
■ **Longreach** (BF GLM H MA WH) 6-23 h
1 Uplands Road, Saltford ✉ BS18 3JQ (between Bath & Bristol)
☎ (01225) 874724 ✉ weng@longreach-bath.co.uk
✉ www.longreach-bath.co.uk
Elegant detached house with great garden & views. Exclusively gay & very friendly. All rooms with TV, tea trays, radio. Complimentary pick up from the station.
■ **Woodstock** (BF CC e glm H lj MA OS WE)
534 Bath Road, Brislington ✉ BS4 3JZ ☎ 987 1613 📠 987 1613
✉ woodstock@cableinet.co.uk
✉ www.homestead.com/wstock/
Small guesthouse in an 1800's Victorian home. Rates single £ 30 and double 45 incl. full English bf.

GENERAL GROUPS
■ **Black Lesbian & Gay Group (SAFAR)**
PO Box 10, 82 Colston Street ✉ BS1 5BB
■ **Gay Men's Chorus** Meets: Wed
☎ 968 42 84

HEALTH GROUPS
■ **Gay Men's Team of Terrence Higgins Trust**
8-10 West St., Old Market ✉ BS2 0BH ☎ 955 10 00
Offer information on HIV/Aids/sexual health and safer sex. Free condoms and lube. Info on gay scene and gay-friendly services available. Also Young Men's group&Married Men's group.

CRUISING
-The Promenade (Clifton; bushes and woodland, twilight)
-Sea Walls/Circular Road (AYOR) (Clifton; walk along Circular Road towards Sneyd Park; very busy at all times, police)
-Eastville Park (near Lake)
-Clifton Downs (AYOR) (near observatory, after dark, police)
-Berrow Sands (AYOR) (coast north of Burnham-on-Sea 20km from Bristol)
-Ashton Park (opposite Bristol City football ground)
-Stapleton Road (end of Fishponds Road)
-Redcross Street (near Old Market, Mon-Fri daytime only)

Burnham-on-Sea - Somerset

SWIMMING
-Berrow Beach (NU) (Activity in the dunes)

Burnley - Lancashire ☎ 01282

BARS
■ **Garden Bar. The** (B d GLM) 11-23, Sun 12-22.30 h. (D) Fri-Sat
133 St.James Street ☎ 41 48 95

Bury St. Edmunds - Suffolk
☎ 01638

GUEST HOUSES
■ **Pear Tree House** (BF F GLM H N OS)
Chapel Road, West Row, Mildenhall ✉ IP28 8PA ☎ 71 11 12
📠 71 11 12
Restored 240 year old house. All rooms with TV, tea / coffee making facilities and hairdryers. Reductions for longer stays. B&B from £ 17.50 p/p.

1078 **SPARTACUS** 2001/2002

Cairnryan - Dumfries & Galloway ▶ Cheltenham Spa - Gloucestershire | United Kingdom

Cairnryan - Dumfries & Galloway ☏ 01581

HOTELS
■ **Merchant's House. The** (B BF CC F glm H MA WE) 9-1 h
Main Street, Cairnryan, Wigtownshire ✉ DG9 8QX *(Near Stranraer)*
☏ 20 02 15
Gay owned guest house and restaurant. Short distance from P&O Ferry Terminal (Ferries to Northern Ireland). Most rooms with sea view. B&B £ 16p.p. (£ 14p.p. in winter).

Cambridge - Cambridgeshire ☏ 01223

BARS
■ **Town & Gown Pub** (B CC d F GLM MA) 12-14.30, 19-23, Sun 12-22.30 h
Northampton Street, Pound Hill ✉ CB3 0AE ☏ 35 37 91

DANCECLUBS
■ **Dot Cotton Club** (D GLM YG) Last Sat/month 22-3 h
The Junction, Clifton Road ☏ 511 511
■ **Tasty at Q Club** (B D GLM MA TV) 2nd/4th Thu/month 22-1 h
Hills Road ☏ 51 59 57

GUEST HOUSES
■ **Pear Tree House** (BF CC F GLM MA OS) All year.
Chapel Road, West Row, Mildenhall ✉ IP28 8PA *(Rail-Cambridge)*
☏ 01638/711112 🖨 01638/711112 📧 peartree@hello.to
🌐 www.peartree.hello.to
250 year old former village inn. Quality accomodation. English Tourist Board 4 Diamond rating& silver award winner.

GENERAL GROUPS
■ **Cambridge Uni LGB Society** Bar: Mon 21-23 h at University Centre
c/o CUSU, 11-12 Trumpington Street ☏ 740777

RELIGIOUS GROUPS
■ **Lesbian and Gay Christian Movement**
☏ 57 38 53

CRUISING
-Opposite Four Lamps (Victoria Avenue, near Midsummer's Green)

Canterbury - Kent ☏ 01227

GAY INFO
■ **East Kent Friend and Switchboard** Tue 19.30-22 h
PO Box 40 ✉ CT1 2YE ☏ 01843
☏ 58 87 62

Cardiff - South Glamorgan ☏ 029

GAY INFO
■ **Cardiff & District**
c/o 30 Glamorgan St., Canton ☏ 2064 02 87
(Mark) Self-Help-Group.

BARS
■ **Exit Bar** (B d GLM MA OS STV YG) Wed-Sun 6-24, Mon Tue - 2 h
48 Charles Street, ✉ CF1 4EF *(Opposite Club X)* ☏ 2064 57 21
■ **King's Cross. The** (! B F GLM MA) Mon-Sun 11-23 h
Hayes Bridge Road/Caroline Street ☏ 20649 891
■ **Minskys** (! B d F glm MA STV WE) Mon-Sun 11-23 h
42 Charles Street *(Entrance in Cathedral Walk)* ☏ 23 31 28

DANCECLUBS
■ **Club X** (AC B D f GLM lj MA s SNU) Wed-Sat 22-2 h. WOW Club Wed-Sat.
39 Charles Street, ✉ CF1 4EB *(Opposite Exit Bar, below Atlantica Café Bar)* ☏ 2064 57 21

SAUNAS/BATHS
■ **Locker Room** (F DR G MA SA SB SOL VS WH) 13-23, Sat -8, Sun -22 h
50 Charles Street ✉ CF10 2GF ☏ 2022 03 88
Modern gay sauna frequented by a mixed age crowd.

HOTELS
■ **Courtfield Hotel** (B BF CC glm H MA N)
101 Cathedral Road ✉ CF1 9PH *(near Cardiff castle/city centre)*
☏ 20 22 77 01 🖨 20 22 77 01 📧 courtfield@ntlworld.com
🌐 www.courtfieldhotel.co.uk
This renovated Victorian house has comfortable rooms with radio, TV, tea/coffee making facilities, some en-suite. Rates single (shared bath) £ 25 and double (en-suite) £ 55 incl. bf.

GENERAL GROUPS
■ **Cardiff Students Lesbian, Gay & Bisexual Society**
c/o University Union Cardiff, Park Place ✉ CF1 3ON ☏ 2039 89 03

HEALTH GROUPS
■ **Cardiff AIDS Helpline** Mon-Fri 10-20 h
PO Box 304, ✉ CF1 9XA ☏ 0800 074 3445 (freeline)
🖨 20 666 467 📧 aidshelpline@celtic.co.uk

CRUISING
-Bute Park (AYOR) (Day and night. Busiest at rear of music college.)

Carlisle - Cumbria ☏ 01228

SAUNAS/BATHS
■ **Acqua** (AC B CC DR F G MA P SA SB SOL VS WH) 12-22 h
Atlas House, Nelson Street ✉ CA2 5ND *(10 min from railway station, Denton Holme District)* ☏ 52 3328
New bathhouse set in the basement of an old mill and themed around a Mediterranean fishing village, with houses and lanterns and stars on the ceiling. Regular theme nights.

HELP WITH PROBLEMS
■ **Outreach Cumbria**
☏ 60 30 75
Helpline for men.

Chelmsford - Essex ☏ 01245

BARS
■ **Army & Navy** (B g) (G) Wed 19-23, Sun 19-22.30 h only
Roundabout, Parkway ☏ 35 41 55

Cheltenham Spa - Gloucestershire ☏ 01242

BARS
■ **Phoenix Inn** (AC B CC d f GLM lj MA MA OS S SNU STV tv VS)
Mon-Fri 18-24, Sat 19-24, Sun 12-23.30 h
36 Andover Road ✉ GL50 2TJ ☏ 52 94 17
Door closes Mon-Sat 23, Sun 22.30 h.

SPARTACUS 2001/2002 | 1079

United Kingdom — Cheltenham Spa - Gloucestershire ▸ Crewe - Cheshire

■ **Pride of Leckhampton Inn** (B F GLM MA s YG)
33 Shurdington Road ✉ GLS3 OHY ☎ 52 77 63
■ **Sherbets** (AC B BF CC F glm MA OS) Mon-Sat 11-14.30, 18-22.30, Sun 12-22.30 h
36 Andover Road ✉ GL50 2TJ *(rear of Phoenix Inn)* ☎ 52 94 17
Sun Lunch from £ 2.75, Sat bf from £ 1.95.

DANCECLUBS

■ **Racecourse Disco** (B D g) Sat 21-2 h
Prestbury Race Courcе ☎ 529417
Once a month "Handbag at the Racecourse" party on Sat. Free buffet. Theme nights.

HOTELS

■ **B&B Heron Haye** (BF glm H MA OS)
Petty Lane, Cleeve Hill ✉ GL52 3PW ☎ 67 25 16 📠 67 25 16
4 miles out of Cheltenham, which is 20 miles from Stratford-upon-Avon. 2 doubles and 1 single room. Rates incl. bf £ 20 p.p..

PRIVATE ACCOMMODATION

■ **Heron Haye** (GLM MA OS p) 8-22 h
Petty Lane, Cleeve Hill ✉ GL52 3PW ☎ 672 516
📧 dick.whellamore@virgin.net
Rural location, 4 miles outside Cheltenham, 80 miles from London, 20 from Stratfort/Avon.

CRUISING

-College Road
-Post Office Lane
-Old Bath Road (truckers)
-By town hall

Chester - Cheshire ☎ 01244

BARS

■ **Liverpool Arms** (AC B glm MA N) 11-23, Sun 12-22.30 h
79 Northgate Street ✉ CH1 2HQ *(within the city wall at the North Gate)* ☎ 314 807

GENERAL GROUPS

■ **Clwyd and Cheshire Gay Group** Meet alt Tue
Call for info
☎ (01978) 29 10 08 (Nigel)

Chesterfield - Derbyshire ☎ 01246

BARS

■ **Basement** (B D GLM) Wed 20-23 h
Cavendish Street *(below Bluebell Inn)* ☎ 20 18 49
■ **Manhattan Bar** (B GLM s) (GLM): Sun-Wed 20-? h, (glm) Thu-Sat
50 Saltergate ☎ 23 20 42
■ **Marsden's** (B d glm MA) Mon-Fri 13-15, 19-23, Sat 19-23, Sun -22.30 h
13 Marsden Street ✉ S40 1JY *(Off Saltergate)* ☎ 23 26 18

Chichester - West Sussex ☎ 01243

BARS

■ **Bell Inn. The** (AC B CC F g MA OS) 11.30-15 17-23, Sun 12-22.30 h
3 Broyle Road ☎ 78 33 88
Bar and restaurant.
■ **Bush Inn. The** (B CC d f GLM MA OS S) 10.30-23:00h, Sun 12-22:30h
16 The Hornet ✉ PO19 4JG ☎ 782939

Colchester - Essex ☎ 01206

GAY INFO

■ **Colchester Gay Switchboard and AIDSline** (GLM MA TV)
Mon-Fri 19-22. Drop in: Tue 18-20 Thu 19-22 Sat 10.30-13 h
The Outhouse, 19 East Hill ✉ CO1 2QX *(town centre, close to bus station)* ☎ 86 91 91 📠 87 13 94 📧 gay.essex@ukonline.co.uk
🖥 www.gayessex.org.uk

BARS

■ **Forbidden Gardens at the Minorios Café Bar** (A B F GLM MA OS)
Mon 19-23:00h
The Minorios Café Bar, East Hill ✉ CO1 1VE *(Next to bus station)*
☎ 500169
■ **Fox & Hounds** (B D f GLM MA OS SNU) Wed 19-24, Thu 20-24, Fri-Sat -2, Sun 12-15, 20-22.30 h, closed Mon-Thu
Bentley Road, Little Bromley ✉ CO11 2PL *(Off A 120, 5 miles from Colchester)* ☎ 39 74 15

HEALTH GROUPS

■ **HIV/Aids Helpline** Mon-Fri 19-22 h
c/o Switchboard, ☎ 869191

Conwy - North Wales ☎ 0142

SAUNAS/BATHS

■ **Jacks Hydro** (B DR F G MA OS SA SB SOL VS WH) 12.30-22.30 h
Pennant Hall, Beach Road, Penmaenmawr ✉ LL34 6AY *(3 min from railway station)* ☎ 62 28 78
Friendly sauna attached to hotel with sun terrace food and beverages served all day. Check website for special events.

HOTELS

■ **Pennant Hall** (B BF CC DR F GLM H MA N NU OS P SA SB SOL VS WE WH) Health Spa & Sauna: 12.30-22.30 h
Beach Road, Penmaenmawr ✉ LL34 6AY *(Near railway station)*
☎ 62 28 78
Hotel & bar ideally situated for excursions to the coast and Snowdonia National Park. All rooms en-suite. Just 400 mtrs to the beach.

Coventry - West Midlands ☎ 01230

HEALTH GROUPS

■ **HIV Network**
10 Manor Road ✉ CU1 2LH ☎ 22 92 92 📠 63 42 48
Volunteer-led organisation to promote greater awareness HIV and AIDS and provide support for people living with HIV. Buddy service. Body Positive Grup.
■ **MESMEN (Health project for men)** Mon-Fri 10-17 h
c/o Terrence Trust, 10 Manor Road ✉ CV1 2LH ☎ 7622 92 92
☎ (01203) 22 40 90 📠 (01203) 63 42 48
📧 info@thtmidlands.org.uk
HIV prevention and care.

CRUISING

-Cathedral walls

Crewe - Cheshire ☎ 01270

GENERAL GROUPS

■ **Crewe Gay Social Group Men** Meets: 2nd Tue/month 19.30 h
☎ 21 14 55
(John)

Crewe - Cheshire | United Kingdom

THE GREENHOUSE HEALTH CLUBS

For Gay and Bisexual men only

Opening times: Mon-Fri 12 noon
until 11.00pm
Saturday: 12 noon all night
untill 8am Sunday
Sunday: 1pm until 11pm

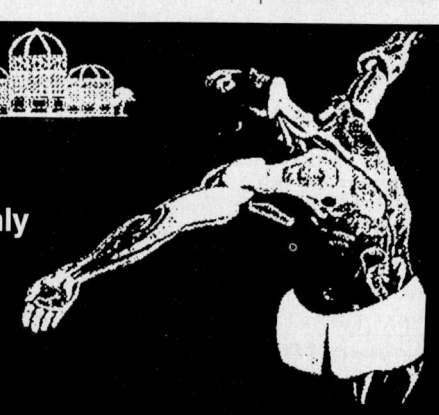

FACILITIES IN ALL PREMISES
SAUNA • STEAM ROOM • JACUZZI • TV LOUNGE • REST ROOMS

For further details telephone:

BARNSLEY
01226 731305
Junction 36. M1.

DARLASTON
0121 568 6126
Junction 9. M6.

NEWPORT
(GWENT)
01633 221172
Junction 27. M4.

LUTON
01582 487701
Opening times: Sun - Thur 11am - 12 noon
Fri: 11am - All night til 8am Sat
Sat: 12am - 8am Sun
LUXURY HOTEL ROOMS ALSO AVAILABLE

United Kingdom
Croydon - Greater London ▸ Eastbourne - East Sussex

Croydon - Greater London ☎ 020

GAY INFO
- **Croydon Friend** Mon Fri 19.30-21.30 h
PO Box 464 ✉ SE25 4TT ☎ 8683 42 39

GENERAL GROUPS
- **Croydon Area Gay Society**
PO Box 464 ✉ SE25 4AT ☎ 8656 9802
David

Darlaston - West Midlands ☎ 0121

SAUNAS/BATHS
- **Greenhouse Health Club** (b CC DR G OS PI SA SB SOL VS WH WO)
10-2, Fri -6, Sat 12-8, Sun -2 h
Willenhall Road ✉ WS10 8JD *(Junction 9/10, M6)* ☎ 568 61 26
Big sauna with a new roof top garden play-maze, 2 secure car parks, 2 TV rooms - 1 smoking & 1 smoking free.

Darlington ☎ 01325

GAY INFO
- **Gay Advice Darlington** Mon & Sat 19-22 h
PO Box 307 ✉ DL3 6YH ☎ 24 73 55 📧 admin@g-a-d.fsnet.co.uk
🖥 www.g-a-d.fsnet.co.uk
Information, support and advice around safer sex/HIV.

Derby - Derbyshire ☎ 01332

GAY INFO
- **Derby Friend** Wed 19-22 h
☎ 34 93 33

BARS
- **Curzons Nightclub** (B d F GLM MA N P S TV) Thu 20-2 (cabaret), Fri-Sat 20-2 (disco)
25 Curzon Street ✉ DE1 1LH ☎ 36 37 39
- **Freddies Bar** (AC B d f GLM MA s TV VS) Mon-Sat 19-23:30h Sun 19-22:30h
101 Curzon Street ✉ DE1 1LH ☎ 20 42 90
- **Gallery. The** (AC B F GLM MA N) Mon-Thu 19-23, Fri-Sat 13-23, Sun 13-22.30 h
130 Green Lane ✉ DE1 1RY *(Next to Little City car park)*
☎ 36 86 52

HEALTH GROUPS
- **Derbyshire Body Positive** Office hours Mon-Fri 14-17, Wed 14-19.45 h drop-in
PO Box 124 ✉ DE1 9NZ ☎ 29 21 29 29 21 29

CRUISING
- Fish Market (known to the trade as "Fish Cottage")
- Bus station

Derrygonnelly - Fermanagh ☎ 01365

GUEST HOUSES
- **Pierce's Folly** (BF glm H)
Dresternan ✉ BT93 6FF ☎ 64 17 35

Doncaster - South Yorkshire ☎ 01302

BARS
- **Vine. The** (B D GLM SNU STV) 19-2 h
2 Kelham Street, Balby ✉ DN1 3RE ☎ 364 096

Douglas - Isle of Man ☎ 01624

GENERAL GROUPS
- **Ellan Vannin Gay Group**
PO Box 195 ☎ 62 87 72
Information, Campaigning, Social. Contact Alan after 18:00h

Dumfries - Dumfries & Galloway ☎ 01387

GAY INFO
- **Dumfries & Galloway Lesbian & Gay Phoneline**
Thu 19.30-21.30 h
c/o PO Box 1299 ✉ DG1 2PD ☎ 26 91 61

GENERAL GROUPS
- **Dumfries and Galloway Lesbian & Gay Group**
PO Box 1299, ✉ DG1 2PD ☎ 26 18 18
Thu 19.30-21.30. Regular social meetings every Thu. Call for details.

Dundee - Tayside ☎ 01382

GAY INFO
- **Dundee LGB Switchboard** Mon 19-22 h
PO Box 53 ✉ DD1 3YG ☎ 20 26 20

BARS
- **Charlie's Bar** (B D f glm MA)
75 Seagate ☎ 226840

DANCECLUBS
- **Liberty Nightclub** (B D GLM SNU VS YG) Wed-Sun 23-2.30 h
124 Seagate ✉ DD1 2HB ☎ 20 06 60

Durham ☎ 919

GENERAL GROUPS
- **Durham University LGB Association** Meets weekly
Durham Students Union, Dunelm House, New Elvet ✉ DH1 3AN
☎ 0191/374 3310 ☎ 0191/374 3313   0191/374 3328
🖥 www.dur.ac.uk/LGB

Eastbourne - East Sussex ☎ 01323

BARS
- **Hartington. The** (B D f GLM MA S SNU STV) 11-23:00h
89 Cavendish Place ✉ BN21 3RR ☎ 64 31 51
Various theme nights.

GUEST HOUSES
- **Freedom Guest House** (BF GLM H MA) All year
105 Cavendish Place ✉ BN21 3TY ☎ 41 10 01

Edinburgh - Lothian ☎ 0131

✱ Edinburgh is the capital city of Scotland and one of the most beautifully situated cities in the world. The gay scene is mainly located in Newton and in Broughton Street, which depicts the tolerant atmosphere of the city and the relaxed lifestyle of the Edinburgh gays. Best month for sightseeing (the castle, old town center, museums) is in August, when the annual Arts Festival is celebrated.

★ Edinburgh ist das Zentrum und die Hauptstadt Schottlands. Und es ist eine der am schönsten gelegenen Städte der Welt. Die schwule Szene konzentriert sich in Newtown und in der Broughton Street. Dort spiegeln sich auch das tolerante Klima der Stadt und die relaxte Stimmung der Schwulen wider. Ein optimale Gelegenheit, dieses Klima und die Sehenswürdigkeiten der Stadt (Schloß, Altstadt, Museen) kennenzulernen, bietet das jährlich im August stattfindende Festival.

✱ Edimbourg, centre et capitale de l'Ecosse, compte parmi les plus belles villes du monde. Les lieux gais sont concentrés dans le quartier de Newton, principalement dans la Broughton Street. Les gens ici sont calmes, détentus et il y règne un agréable climat de tolérance. Profitez de l'occasion qu'offre le Festival d'Edimbourg pour découvrir les curiosités touristiques de la vieille ville (château, vieux quartiers, musées) et goûter à l'atmosphère de cette agréable ville britannique.

★ Edimburgo es centro y capital de Escocia y una ciudad privilegiada por su situación. Los locales gay se encuentran en Newtown y en la Broughton Street. Aquí se refleja el tolerante clima de la ciudad y el relajado ambiente gay. La fecha óptima para conocer este clima y los sitios de interés (castillo, ciudad antigua, museos etc.) es en Agosto, cuando se celebra anualmente el famoso festival de Edimburgo.

✱ Edimburgo, centro e capitale della Scozia, è una delle città meglio situate del mondo. La zona gay si concentra a Newtown e nella Broughton street dove si rispecchia il clima tollerante della città e l'atmosfera rilassante dell'ambiente gay. Il festival di Edimburgo, che ha luogo ogni anno in agosto, può essere un'occasione per visitare la città e le sue bellezze (il palazzo, il centro storico ed i musei).

GAY INFO

■ **Edinburgh Lesbian, Gay & Bisexual Community Centre**
(b BF f GLM MA msg YG)
58-60 Broughton Street ✉ EH1 3SA ☎ 557 1662
🖨 558 1683.
■ **Lothian Gay & Lesbian Switchboard** Mon-Sun 19.30-22 h
PO Box 169 ✉ EH1 3UU ☎ 556 4049 🖨 556 8997
📧 mail@lgls.org 🌐 www.lgls.org

TOURIST INFO

■ **Edinburgh & Scotland Information Centre**
3 Princes Street ✉ EH2 2QP ☎ 473 3800
■ **Edinburgh Gay Escorts**
19a Albany Street ☎ 558 1011
📧 enquiries@edinburghgayescorts.co.uk
🌐 www.edinburghgayescorts.co.uk
Gay and lesbian escorts throughout Scotland offering tours of Edinburgh and surrounding areas.

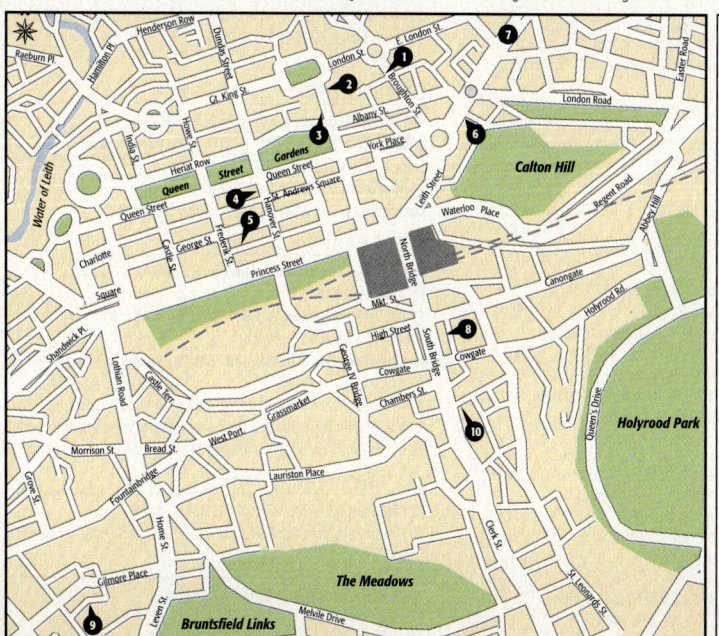

Edinburgh

1 Blue Moon Café
2 Mansfield House Hotel
3 The New Town Bar
4 Cyberia Café
5 Hott Stuff Bar
6 CC Blooms Bar
7 No. 18 Sauna
8 Bo's Restaurant
9 Amaryllis Guest House
10 Fantasies Sex Shop

United Kingdom — Edinburgh - Lothian

EDINBURGH
- for a full online guide visit www.gayscotland.com

scotland's largest gay TOWNHOUSE sauna & gym
steamroom, large jacuzzi, 20 man sauna
'Kruze' video zone, fully licenced bar
tanning booth, internet cafe
gymnasium, massage

sun - thu: noon - 11pm
fri & sat: noon - midnight

53 East Claremont Street
Edinburgh 0131 556 1116
www.townhouse-sauna.co.uk

ALVA HOUSE guesthouse for gay men
- Non-smoking house
- Reasonable rates
- In-room TV and VCR with video tape library
- Walk to gay bars and nightlife

45 Alva Place
Edinburgh EH7 5AX
Tel 0131 558 1382 Fax 0131 556 8279
www.gayscotland.com/alvahouse

gayscotland.com — the definitive online guide…
- accommodation
- bars / nightclubs
- chat / personals

BARS

■ **CC Blooms** (AC B D GLM MA s SNU) Mon-Sat 18-3, Sun 16-3 h
23 Greenside Place ✉ EH1 3AA *(Next to Edinburgh Playhouse Theatre)* ☎ 556 9331
Disco every night from 22:30h. Thu-Sun Karaoke, Sun stippers from 16.30h.

■ **Holyrood Tavern** (B glm)
9a Holyrood Road ☎ 556 5044

■ **Hot Stuff** (B glm s) 12-1h
89 Rose Street Lane North ☎ 225 7651
Karaoke on Wed.

■ **New Town Bar. The** (AC B D G lj M A N) Mon-Thu 12-1, Fri&Sat -2 Sun 12.30-1 h
26b Dublin Street ✉ EH3 6NN ☎ 538 7775
Basement leather & fettish bar open Thu-Sun.

■ **Planet Out** (AC B F GLM MA N S) Mon-Fri 16-01:00h, Sat & Sun 12:30-01:00h
66 Baxter's Place ✉ EH1 3AF ☎ 524 0061

■ **Stag & Turret. The** (B F GLM MA SNU STV) 12-02:00 h
1-7 Montrose Terrace ✉ EH7 5DJ ☎ 478 7231

CAFES

■ **Blue Moon Café** (! A AC B BF F GLM MA) Bar: Mon-Thu 7-0.30, Sun 9-0.30 h. Café Sun-Thu -24, Fri-Sat -0.30 h.
1 Barony Street/36 Broughton Street ✉ EH1 3SB ☎ 556 2788

■ **Cyberia** (b f glm) 10-22:00h, Sun 12-19:00h
88 Hanover Street ☎ 220 4403
Cybercafé.

■ **Nexus Cafe Bar** (A AC B BF F GLM MA N) 11-23 h
60 Broughton Street ✉ EH1 3SA ☎ 478 7069
Nice cafe which is located in the LGB centre.

■ **Web 13** (B f glm MA) Mon-Fri 9-22:00h, Sat -20:00h, Sun 11-20h
13 Bread Street ☎ 229 8883
Cybercafé

DANCECLUBS

■ **Joy** (! AC B D GLM MA WE) 4th Sat 22.30-3 h
Wilkie House, 207 Cowgate ✉ EH1 1JD ☎ 467 2551
Friendly club with house music.

■ **Mingin'** (B D G MA) Every 2nd Sat 22.30-3h
c/o Studio 24, 24 Calton Road *(upstairs)* ☎ 467 2551

RESTAURANTS

■ **Bo's Vegetarian Restaurant** (CC F glm MA) 18-22:00h, Fri & Sat 12-14:00h
57-61 Blackfriars Street, ✉ EH1 1NB ☎ 557 6136
Charming vegetarian restaurant.

■ **Claremont Bar & Restaurant. The** (B F GLM lj MA N) 11-1, Sun 12.30-1 h
133-135 East Claremont Street ✉ EH7 45N ☎ 556 5662
Scotland:s only Science Fiction theme pub. Different groups meet here. 1st Sat in month from 20h for leather & rubber fans.

SEX SHOPS/BLUE MOVIES

■ **Fantasies** (glm) Mon-Sat 10-21, Sun 12-21 h
8b Drummond Street, EH8 9TU *(by the Festival Theatre)* ☎ 557 8336

ESCORTS & STUDIOS

■ **Capital Gay Escorts** (G) 12-23 h
☎ 556 5094
Sexy young guys for home and hotel visits available.

Edinburgh - Lothian | United Kingdom

SAUNAS/BATHS

■ **No.18** (AC DR f G MA p SA SB WH) 12-22 h
18 Albert Place ✉ EH7 5HN *(10 min from train and bus stations, entrance off Leith Walk)* ☎ 553 3222
Clean and friendly sauna with a social club atmosphere. Known to locals as "The Steamie".

■ **Townhouse** (B DR F G MA msg SA SB SOL VS WH WO)
Sun-Thu 12-23, Fri&Sat -24 h
53 East Claremont Street ✉ EH7 4HU *(close to gay district)*
☎ 556 6116
Scotland's largest gay sauna and gym on 4 floors. Popular and friendly.

BOOK SHOPS

■ **Bobbies Bookshop** (g) Mon-Sat 10-17.30 h
220 Morrison Street ✉ EH3 8EA *(near Haymarket)* ☎ 538 7069

GIFT & PRIDE SHOPS

■ **Atomix** (CC GLM) Mon-Sun 11-19 h
60 Broughton Street ✉ EH1 3SA ☎ 558 81 74
Exclusive fetishware and clubware&videos.

■ **Out of the Blue** (GLM) Sun-Wed 12-19:00h Thu-Sat 12-20:00h
1 Barony Street, Broughton ✉ EH3 6PD *(basement)* ☎ 478 7048
Magazines, books, cards, videos, gifts, toys, body, swim & underwear.

HOTELS

■ **Mansfield House** (AC BF CC GLM H MA)
57 Dublin Street ✉ EH3 6NL ☎ 556 7980 🖷 446 1315
✉ mansfieldhouse@cableinet.co.uk
Gay guest house: All the rooms are spacious and elegantly decorated; one room is en suite and all have TV and tea / coffee making facilities. It is located within easy walking distance of the local gay pubs / clubs. Rates: single from £ 30 and twin (en suite) 70.

■ **Thistle Court Hotel** (H)
5 Hampton Terrace ✉ EH12 5JD ☎ 3135500 🖷 3135511
✉ thistle@clansman.demon.co.uk

GUEST HOUSES

■ **Alexander Guest House** (cc BF E H glm) all year
35 Mayfield Gardens ✉ EH9 2BX *(on the A 701,bus 3,7-9,30,31,36,69,80,81,87)* ☎ 258 40 28 🖷 258 12 47
✉ alexander@guest68.freeserve.co.uk
💻 smoothhound.co.uk/hotels/alexand3.html

■ **Alexander Palms Guesthouse** (BF GLM H MA VS)
63 Brunswick St. ✉ EH7 5HT *(close to gay district)* ☎ 558 1382
🖷 556 8279
Exclusively GLM guesthouse,TV and video in all rooms,own keys.Rates £ 29 (single), 39-49 (double).

■ **Alva House** (BF G H MA VS)
45 Alva Place ✉ EH7 5AX *(close to gay district)* ☎ 558 1382
🖷 556 8279 ✉ alvahouse@gayscotland.com
💻 www.gayscotland.com/alvahouse
Gay men only guesthouse,TV and video in all rooms,own keys.Rates GBP 29 (single), 39-49 (double).

■ **Amaryllis Guest House** (BF CC glm H MA) all year
21 Upper Gilmore Place ✉ EH3 9NL ☎ 229 32 93 🖷 229 32 93
✉ ghamaryllis@aol.com
Comfortable guest house furnished to a high standard. Easily accessible to the gay scene by public transport. All rooms have T.V and tea / coffee making facilities. Rates Vary seasonally from £ 20-30 incl. bf and p.p.

■ **Ardmor House** (BF CC glm H MA) All year, 24h
74 Pilrig Street ✉ EH6 5AS *(10 minutes walk from city center)*
☎ 554 4944 🖷 554 4944 ✉ robin@ardmorhouse.freeserve.co.uk
💻 www.ardmorhouse.freeserve.co.uk
Stylish victorian town house decorated to a fine standard. All rooms en suite & with TV, tea/coffee making facilities. Gay owned, non-smoking.

■ **Garlands Guest House** (BF CC glm) all year
48 Pilrig Street ✉ EH6 5AL ☎ 554 4205 🖷 554 4205
✉ bill@garlands.demon.co.uk 💻 www.garlands.demon.co.uk

HEALTH GROUPS

■ **Solas Café at SOLAS** (A B F glm MA) Mon-Tue Thu-Fri 11-16, Wed 17-21 h
2/4 Abbeynoury ✉ EH8 8EJ ☎ 661 0982

CRUISING

- Calton Hill (Day or night AYOR)
- Regent Road (Night AYOR. Park car or yourself along side of the road.)
- Warrington cemetery (Night AYOR)

CC BLOOMS

23 GREENSIDE PLACE, EDINBURGH, SCOTLAND (NEXT TO THE PLAYHOUSE)
0131 556 9331

MON - SAT 6PM - 3AM
SUN 3PM - 3AM
(NO DOOR CHARGE)
KARAOKE THURS & SUN FROM 11PM
DJ EVERY NIGHT FROM 11PM
MALE STRIPPER ON SUN FROM 5PM

United Kingdom — Elgin - Grampian ▶ Glasgow - Strathclyde

Elgin - Grampian ☎ 01343

GAY INFO
■ **Moray LGB Switchboard** Fri 19-22 h
PO Box 5763 ✉ IV30 2ZE ☎ 54 11 88

GENERAL GROUPS
■ **Pride of Moray Firth LGB Social Group** (GLM MA) Meets 2nd and 4th Wed from 20 h in the Georgian Suite, Park House Hotel, South Street.
PO Box 5866 ✉ IV36 1WG ☎ 54 11 88 📧 PofMF@aol.com

Exeter - Devon ☎ 01392

GAY INFO
■ **Devon L&G Switchboard** Mon 19.30-22 h
PO Box 178 ✉ EX4 1TY ☎ 42 20 16
📧 glswitchboard.sw@zetnet.co.uk
Information&advice helpline.

BARS
■ **Loft at Bart's Tavern. The** (B D F Glm s) Mon-Thu 20-24, Fri-Sat 21-1, Sun 12-22.30 h
53 Bartholomew Street West ☎ 275 623

DANCECLUBS
■ **Boxes on Tuesday** (B D GLM MA YG) Tue 21-1 h
35/37 Commercial Road, The Quay

HEALTH GROUPS
■ **Positive Action South West (PASW)** Helpline: Mon-Fri 9-17 h
Palace Gate House, Palace Gate ✉ EX1 1HX ☎ 494441
☎ 0800 328 3508 (helpline) 📠 436097
📧 info@devonaids.freeserve.co.uk
PASW is a voluntary organisation which offers a wide range of services for people affected by HIV and AIDS.

Farnham - Surrey ☎ 01252

DANCECLUBS
■ **Ralph's Cellar** (AC B D f G lj MA N OS P s) Fri 21.30-1.30, Last Sat/month 21-3 h
33 Shortheath Road ✉ GU9 8SH ☎ 71 58 44
Private venue. Call for details.

Folkestone - Kent ☎ 01303

BARS
■ **Portland Hotel** (B f glm MA) 11-23, Sun 12-22.30 h
2-4 Langhorne Gardens (Opposite Leas Cliff Hall) ☎ 251444

HEALTH GROUPS
■ **South Kent Health Info for g&b men** Tue 16-19 h
☎ 22 88 13
(Richard)

SWIMMING
-Warren (NU) (45 minutes walk from East Cliff towards Dover. Small secluded unofficial bay. Popular)
-Sandwich (NU) (far end of the beach near the golf course)

CRUISING
-The Leas (AYOR)
-Warren

Galashiels - Scottish Borders ☎ 01896

CAFES
■ **Green's Diner** (A AC B CC f glm MA N WE) Tue-Sat 10-22:00h. Closed Sun & Mon.
4 Green Street ✉ TD1 3AE next to Tescos supermarket ☎ 75 76 67

Gateshead - Tyne & Wear ☎ 0191

HELP WITH PROBLEMS
■ **Stag Project**
☎ 490 1708
Confidential advice and information.

Glasgow - Strathclyde ☎ 0141

GAY INFO
■ **Glasgow Gay and Lesbian Centre** (B CC F GLM MA) 10-24:00h
11 Dixon Street (near to St. Enoch's Shopping Mall) ☎ 221 7203
📠 221 7203
📧 gglc@gglc.org.uk
■ **Glasgow University LGB Society** Meets weekly in QM Union
LGB Convener c/o John McIntyre Building ☎ 339 8541
■ **Strathclyde Gay & Lesbian Switchboard** 19-22 h
PO Box 38 ✉ G2 2QF ☎ 332 8372

BARS
■ **Court Bar. The** (AC B BF glm MA N WE) Mon-Sat 8-24, Sun 12.30-24 h
69 Hutcheson Street (Close to Bennets) ☎ 552 2463
Straight until mid-evening
■ **Delmonica's** (AC B CC d GLM MA N s) 12-24 h
68 Virginia Street ✉ G1 ☎ 552 4803
■ **MacSorley's** (B F)
42 Jamaica Street ☎ 248 8581
■ **Victoria Bar** (B glm MA) Mon-Sat 11-24
157-159 Bridgegait ☎ 552 6040
Real Ale bar
■ **Waterloo. The** (B f GLM MA STV) 12-24 h
306 Argyle Street (Central Station) ☎ 229 5891

CAFES
■ **Caffe Latte** (AC B CC F glm MA) Mon-Sat 11-24:00h, Sun 12-24:00h
58 Virginia Street ✉ G1 INU ☎ 553 2553
■ **GLC Café/Bar** (B BF CC F GLM MA S) 11-24 h
11 Dixon Street ✉ G1 4AL (Side entrance with gay flag)
☎ 400 1008

DANCECLUBS
■ **Bennets** (AC B D f GLM MA S STV TV) Wed-Sun 23:30-03:30h
80-90 Glassford Street ✉ G1 1UR (near George Square)
☎ 552 5761
■ **Polo Lounge and Club. The** (B CC D GLM MA) 12-1, Fri-Sun -3 h
84 Wilson Street, Merchant City ✉ G1 1UZ ☎ 553 1221
Largest gay bar and club in Scotland. Very popular.

SAUNAS/BATHS
■ **Centurion Health Club** (CC f DR G SA SB SOL WH WO) 12-22, Sat -7 h
19 Dixon Street ✉ G1 4AL (St. Enoch Square Shopping Center, 2nd floor) ☎ 248 4485
One of Scotland's largest (13000 sq feet) sauna. Free hot food and beverages.

1086 SPARTACUS 2001/2002

Glasgow - Strathclyde ▶ Herne Bay - Kent | United Kingdom

BOOK SHOPS
■ **Centre Books at GLC** (CC GLM) Mon 11-18, Tue-Sat 11-21, Sun 12-17 h
11 Dixon Street *(In the GLC)*
Call GLC, Dixon Street.

HOTELS
■ **Berkely. The** (BF glm H) reception 8-20 h
63 Berkely Street ✉ G3 *(next to Mitchel Library)* ☎ 221 7880
Twins £ 23.50, dormitory 10.50.

GUEST HOUSES
■ **Glasgow Guest House** (BF glm MA)
56 Dumbreck Road ✉ G41 5NP *(Near Burrell Collection)*
☎ 427 0129 427 0129 brian.muir@ukonline.co.uk
3 double, 3 twin, 1 single room, 1 apartment, all rooms ensuite. Rates from £ 20. Five minutes to the city centre. Relaxed & friendly atmosphere.

HEALTH GROUPS
■ **Body Positive** Mon-Thu 11-20:00h, Fri 11-17:00h
3 Park Quadrant ✉ G3 6BS *(U-Kelvinbridge)* ☎ 332 5010
 332 4285
Support for those who are HIV+ or have AIDS.
■ **PHACE West** Mon-Fri 9-17 h
49 Bath Street, ✉ G2 2DL *(Corner of Renfield Street)* ☎ 332 3838
HIV/AIDS charity offering services and information; free condoms and lubricant.
■ **Steve Retson Project** Tue 17.30-21 h
Sandyford Initiative, 6 Sandyford Place, Sauchiehall St. ✉ G31 2NP
(1st floor, Sandyford initiative) ☎ 211 8601 211 8630
 www.steverretsonproject.org.uk
Free confidential advice and treatment for all sexual health issues concerning gay men; free condoms and lube.

SPORT GROUPS
■ **Gay Outdoor Club (GOC)**
PO Box 16124 ✉ G12 9YT ☎ 342 4088 (07840) 536 004
(Julie, for women's contact) 342 4088 goc@bi-org
 bi-org/~goc
Events organized throughout UK (£13 p.a. membership). Walking, climbing, mountaineering, cycling, snowboarding, swimming. Call for details.

CRUISING
- Queens Park (Night AYOR; the most interesting area is the section closest to Victoria Road.)
- Kelvin Grove Park (Walk to the statue in the middle, but watch out for police.)

Gloucester - Gloucestershire

DANCECLUBS
■ **Hysteria at Crackers Night Club** (B D G) Mon 21.30-2 h
Bruton Way ☎ 01452/30 02 89

GUEST HOUSES
■ **Yew Tree Cottage** (BF GLM MA OS)
Bradley Hill, Soudley ✉ GL14 2UQ *(In Forrest of Dean, 15 miles from Gloucester)* ☎ 01594/824 823 82 43 17
Nice B&B in beautiful location. Rate from £ 17.50-20 p.p.

Grimsby - Humberside ☎ 01472

HELP WITH PROBLEMS
■ **Gay Helpline** Tue Thu 19-21 h
☎ 25 18 18

Guildford - Surrey ☎ 01483

BARS
■ **Elm Tree. The** (B D F GLM OS YG) Mon-Sat 11-23, Sun 12-10.30 h
13 Stoke Fields ✉ GU1 4LS ☎ 44 00 06
■ **Spread Eagle** (B GLM STV) 12-23 h
46 Chertsey Street ✉ GU1 4HD ☎ (01252) 53 50 18

GENERAL GROUPS
■ **Guildford Area Gay Society** Meets: Wed 20-22 h
☎ 37 08 09 (Simon)

Gunby - Lincolnshire ☎ 01754

BARS
■ **Kings Head** (B F D glm MA) 11-23:00h
Gunby Courner *(Near Spilsby and Skegness)* ☎ 89 06 38

Harlow - Essex ☎ 01279

GAY INFO
■ **Lesbian and Gay Switchboard** Mon-Fri 20-22:00h
☎ 63 96 37

Harrogate - North Yorkshire

CRUISING
- Harlow Moor Road/Cornwall Road

Hastings - Sussex ☎ 01424

BARS
■ **Club ID** (AC B G Ij MA N p S SNU STV) Thu-Sat 20-23, Sun 19:30-22.30 h, closed Mon-Wed
18-20 Prospect Place ✉ TN34 1LN ☎ 72 22 40

HOTELS
■ **Sherwood Hotel** (B BF CC g MA NU)
15 Grosvenor Crescent, St. Leonards-on-Sea TN38 0AA ☎ 43 33 31
Five min driving from Hastings centre. All rooms with colour TV. Some rooms with private shower and toilet. Rates from £ 16.

Hebden Bridge - West Yorkshire ☎ 01422

BARS
■ **Nelson's Wine Bar** (A B d F glm MA) Mon 19-23:00h, Tue-Sun 16-23:00h
Crown Street ✉ HX1 8AH ☎ 84 47 82

Hereford - Hereford and Worcester ☎ 01432

DANCECLUBS
■ **Club Impulse at The Old Harp** (B D G) Wed 21-1 h
54 Widemarsh Street *(Opp. multi-storey car park)* ☎ 27 73 30

Herne Bay - Kent ☎ 01227

GUEST HOUSES
■ **Foxden Bed & Breakfast** (BF glm H MA)
5 Landon Road ✉ CT6 6HP ☎ 36 35 14 36 35 14
Gay owned, high quality B&B in quiet area close to sea and town centre. Rates single from £ 20 and double 40 incl. full English bf.

United Kingdom | Hove - Sussex ▶ Isleworth - Middlesex

Hove - Sussex ☏ 01273

CAFES
■ **Lizzie's** Mon-Sat 08-16:00h
61 Blatchington Road ☏ 731193

RESTAURANTS
■ **PJ's**
117 Western Road ☏ 773586

SAUNAS/BATHS
■ **Denmark** (b f G MA msg SA SB WH) 12-22 h
84-86 Denmark Villas ✉ BN3 3TJ *(near Hove station)* ☏ 72 37 33

Huddersfield - West Yorkshire
☏ 01484

GAY INFO
■ **Lesbian and Gay Switchboard** Sun 19-21, Tue 19-21 h
c/o KCVS, PO Box 293 ✉ HD1 1WB ☏ 53 80 70

BARS
■ **Greyhound Hotel. The** (B D GLM H lj MA) Mon-Sat 19-23,
Sun 12-22.30 h
16 Manchester Road ☏ 42 07 42
Disco on Wed & Sun.

Hull - Humberside ☏ 01482

GAY INFO
■ **Humberside Friend** Mon Thu 20-22, Sat 19-21 h
c/o CVS, 29 Anlaby Road ✉ HU1 2PG ☏ 44 33 33
Men's group (Sun 19-21) and Youth group (Sun 18.30-21).
☏ 58 97 42.

BARS
■ **Polar Bear. The** (B gLM WE)
229 Spring Bank *(Front bar only)* ☏ 32 39 59
■ **Vauxhall Tavern. The** (B D Glm S) 11-23, 12-22.30 h
1 Hessle Road *(Near Alexander Hotel)* ☏ 32 03 40

DANCECLUBS
■ **Alexandra Palace Club Hotel** (B D glm H s) 11-0.20,
Sun -22.30 h. (D) Fr & Sa (G)
69 Hessle Road ☏ 32 74 55
Accomodation available. Only Gay on Fr & Sa.
■ **Silhouette Club** (B D glm)
Park St. ☏ 320 584

SAUNAS/BATHS
■ **Blue Corner** (b DR G MA P SA SOL VS WH) Mon-Thu 12-22,
Fri Sat -4, Sun 13-22 h
43 High Street ✉ HU1 1PT *(just off High St.)* ☏ 620 775
Relaxed, friendly atmosphere sauna in the city centre.

BOOK SHOPS
■ **Page One Books** (GLM)
9 Princess Avenue ☏ 01428/34 19 25

HEALTH GROUPS
■ **Aids Action in Humberside** Mon-Fri 9.30-4.30 h
Cornerhouse, 29 Percy St. ✉ HU2 8HL ☏ 32 70 44 ☏ 32 70 60
☏ 58 07 29 ✉ user@aidsaction.karoo.co.uk
HIV & AIDS &sexual health awareness, support, information and advice agency. Gay mens drop-in open Tue 19.30-22 h.

Inverness - Highland ☏ 01463

BARS
■ **Nico's Bar/Bistro** (B f glm MA N) Wed Fri 19-23 h
c/o Glen Mhor Hotel, Ness Bank ☏ 23 43 08
■ **Royal Highland Hotel** (B F glm H)
Station Square, 18 Academy Street ✉ IV1 1LG
Smart hotel bar.

GENERAL GROUPS
■ **Gay Outdoor Club**
☏ 751 258

CRUISING
-Bus station (AYOR)
-Railway station (AYOR)

Ipswich - Suffolk

GENERAL GROUPS
■ **Gay Group**
PO Box 63IP4 2RB ☏ 01473/(01206)
☏ 57 81 65 (Brian)

HEALTH GROUPS
■ **AIDS Helpline** Tue Fri 19.30-22 h
☏ 01473/23 20 07

Isle of Mull - Strathclyde
☏ 01688

HOTELS
■ **Ardbeg House Hotel** (AC B BF d F g H msg s SA WE WH)
Dervaig, Isle of Mull ✉ PA75 6QJ ☏ 40 02 54 ☏ 40 02 54
Picturesque village hotel.

Isle of Wight - Ryle ☏ 01983

BARS
■ **Tin Tin's** (B d f GLM MA) Mon-Sat 11-23:00h, Sun 12-22:30h
9 Anglesea Street, Ryde ✉ PO33 2JJ ☏ 56 78 33

HOTELS
■ **Dorset Hotel. The** (B BF CC F glm H PI WE) all year
31 Dover Street ✉ PO33 2BW ☏ 56 43 27 ☏ 56 43 27
✉ hoteldorset@aol.com ☏ www.thedorsethotel.co.uk
Very central too all amenities. All rooms en-suite. Rates £ 19.50 p.p., discount for SPARTACUS readers available.

Isle of Wight - Shanklin ☏ 01983

BARS
■ **Plough & Barleycorn** (B f GLM MA s) Fr 19-23:00h
4 North Road ☏ 86 28 82

Isleworth - Middlesex ☏ 0208

FETISH GROUPS
■ **Leather Hands**
22 Morton Avenue, Osterley ✉ TW7 4NW
Member of ECMC.

Isleworth - Middlesex ▶ Leeds - West Yorkshire | United Kingdom

BARS
■ **George. The** (B d G MA OS s) Mon-Sat 17-23, Sun 12-22.30 h, Cabaret Fri Sat
114 Twickenham Road ✉ TW7 7DJ *(Opposite War Memorial/ buses 37 and 267)* ☎ 8560 14 56

Jersey - St. Helier ☎ 01534

CAFES
■ **Café des Artistes** (A AC B CC d f glm MA) Tue-Fri 12-15:00h 17-01:30 h , Sat 17-01:30h , Closed Mon
58-60 St. Saviour's Road ✉ JE2 4AL ☎ 630811

CRUISING
-Liberation Square
-Snow Hill
-Minden Place
-Broad Street
-The Weighbridge (ayor) (around the carpark, near the toilets, by night only)
-Portler Common (by day)
-The Rocks (an area of rocks near Green Street, looking to the sea, the rocks on your right reached by a short walk, watch the tide though, by day action)
-Portelet Beach (Summer months)
-Victoria Avenue (1st layby)
-Parade Gardens (after dark)

Kidderminster - Hereford and Worcester

SPORT GROUPS
■ **G.B.M.C.C.**
☎(01299) 896177
(Stuart) Gay bikers group

King's Lynn - Norfolk ☎ 01553

BARS
■ **Hob-in-the-Well. The** (B glm WE) Thu-Sat 20.30-23 Sun- 22.30 h
Littleport Street *(close to town centre)* ☎ 77 44 04

Kingston - Surrey

GENERAL GROUPS
■ **Kingston University LGB Society** Weekly (Term time)
Room 241, Pernhyn Road ☎ 8255 555

Kirkcaldy - Fife ☎ 01592

GAY INFO
■ **Fife Friend** Fri 19.30-22.30 h
PO Box 19 ✉ KY1 3JF ☎ 26 66 88
Small voluntary phoneline offering support, advice and information. Monthly disco, weekly pub night.

Lampeter - Dyfed ☎ 01570

GENERAL GROUPS
■ **LG&B support group** Meets weekly
c/o Students Union, Lampeter Uni ☎ 42 26 19
Social events/trips. Ask for welfare LGB officer.

Lancaster - Lancashire ☎ 01524

GAY INFO
■ **L&G Switchboard** Thu Fri 19-21 h
☎ 84 74 37
Gay Men's Social group meets 1st Fri. Lesbian & gay youth group for all under 21 meets Thu 18.30-21 h.

BARS
■ **Dukes. Theatre/Cinema Bar** (A B CC glm) Mon-Sat 18-23, Sun 19-22.30 h
Moor Lane ✉ LA1 1QE ☎ 674 61
🖷 84 68 17.
■ **Navigation** (B F glm MA N OS) Summer 11-23, winter 17-23 h
Penny Street, Bridge Wharf ✉ LA1 1XN *(Rear Thurnham Street car park)* ☎ 84 94 84
Draught German beers, superb wine& A-Z beer list.

CAFES
■ **Single Step Co-Op** (B f GLM)
78a Penny Street ✉ LA1 1XN ☎ 630 21

GENERAL GROUPS
■ **Lancaster University LGB Society** Meets: Wed 17 h in Harrington Building (termtime only)
☎ 258 382

HEALTH GROUPS
■ **Positive Action for HIV** 10-16:00h 'til 18:00h on Th.
Unit 10, Lanc. Enterp. Workshops, White Cross ✉ LA1 4XH
☎ 424 117 🖷 419 597

Leeds - West Yorkshire ☎ 0113

GAY INFO
■ **Leeds Switchboard** 19-22 h, closed Tue
☎ 245 35 88

BARS
■ **Bridge Inn. The**
(B F glm MA MG N s STV W WE) 11-23 h
1-5 Bridge End ✉ LS1 7HG ☎ 244 47 34
■ **Fibre** (B F GLM)
Queen's Court, Lower Briggate ✉ LS1 6NA
■ **New Penny. The** (B glm MA s STV) Mon-Fri 13-23, Sat 12-16, 19-23, Sun 12-15, 19-22.30 h
57 Call Lane, ✉ LS1 7BT
■ **Old Red Lion** (B f glm MA s) Mon-Thu 11-15, 19-23, Fri, Sat 11-23, Sun 12-15, 19-22.30 h
2 Meadow Lane, ✉ LS11 5BJ ☎ 242 67 79

DANCECLUBS
■ **Nato** (B D GLM MA YG) Red Raw: 1st Tue 21-2, Queer-doo: Sun 21-2 h
Walk 34, Middletown Road ☎ 238 0999
Popular venue
■ **Queen's Court** (AC B CC D F GLM MA SNU STV) Mon-Sun 11-23 (Cafe-Bar), Mon-Sat 22-2 h (Nightclub)
Queen's Court, Lower Briggate ✉ LS1 6NA ☎ 245 94 49
🖷 245 8826.

RESTAURANTS
■ **Metz** (B CC F GLM MA) Mon-Thu 12-23, Fri-Sat -24, Sun-22.30 h
Baker House, Cavern Quarter ✉ L2 6PT ☎ 0151/227-2282

United Kingdom — Leeds - West Yorkshire ▶ Liverpool - Merseyside

SAUNAS/BATHS
■ **Spartan Mantalk** (b f G MA SA SB VS WH) Mon-Sun 0-24 h
72 Bayswater Road, Harehills ✉ LS8 5NW ☎ 248 77 57
Comfortable sauna on two floors.

HOTELS
■ **Central Hotel** (B BF CC H MA)
35-45 New Briggate, ✉ LS2 8JD ☎ 294 1456 🖷 294 1551
Hotel with a variety of rooms to suit all budgets, situated in the city centre. All rooms have T.V and tea / coffee making facilities and many are en suite. Rates from: Single £ 26-38, Double (en suite) £ 38-46 incl. continental breakfast.

RELIGIOUS GROUPS
■ **Yorkshire MESMAC**
PO Box 172 ✉ LS7 3BZ ☎ 244 42 09 🖳 leeds@mesmac.co.uk
🖳 www.mesmac.co.uk
Gay & bisexual Mens sexual health project.

Leicester - Leicestershire ☎ 0116

GAY INFO
■ **Leicester Lesbian Gay & Bisexual Centre** (F GLM OS) Mon-Sat
45 King Street ✉ LE1 6RN ☎ 254 74 12
Telephone Helpline Mon-Fri 9-17 h. Youth Group Thu 19.30-22 h.
■ **Lesbian and Gayline** Mo-Th 19.30-22 h
☎ 255 06 67

BARS
Bossa (B glm)
110 Granby St. ☎ 275 54 00
■ **Dolly's** (B CC D E GLM MA OS S VS YG) 11-15.30, 18.30-23 h. (D) Wed, Fri-Sun
34 Dover Street *(Off Granby Street)* ☎ 255 05 61
■ **Pineapple Inn. The** (! B D f G h MA S) Sun-Thu 12-15, Fri-Sat 12-16, Mon-Wed 19-24, Thu-1, Fri Sat-2, Sun-22.30 h
27 Burleys Way ☎ 262 33 84
Cabaret Fri, stripper Sun, Sun lunch, accomodation available.
■ **Streetlife @ Leicester Place** (B D GLM YG) Wed 20.30-2.30, Fri&Sat -3 h
24 Dryden Street *(Off Lee Circle)* ☎ 251 07 85

DANCECLUBS
■ **Knight Life at The Pineapple Inn** (! B D G MA S) Fri-Sat -2 h
27 Burleys Way ☎ 262 33 84
■ **Rapture in the Asylum** Fortnightly Fri 21-2 h
c/o Leicester University S.U., University Road ✉ LE1 7RH
☎ 223 11 11
■ **Shag** (B D GLM)
De Montefort Student Union Arena ☎ 255 55 76
Monthly Club. Call Uni LGB group for dates.

GENERAL GROUPS
■ **Leicester Gay Group**
☎ 251 58 10
(Neil) or ☎ (01509) 55 28 32 (Chris)
■ **Leicester Lesbian and Gay Action**
25 Walton St. ✉ LE3 ODX ☎ 255 34 36
Campaign & lobbying grouzp

HEALTH GROUPS
■ **AIDS Support Services** Mo-Fr 09:30-16:30h
c/o Michael Wood Centre, 53 Regent Road ✉ LE1 6YF
☎ 255 99 95

■ **Men's sexual health project** 12-16 h
15 Wellington Street ✉ LE1 6RN ☎ 254 17 47 🖷 251 87 55

CRUISING
-Abbey Park (Abbey Lane near Canal Side, evenings)
-Tugby Picnic Area (AYOR MG) (A47 8 miles east of Leicester, daily)

Lincoln - Lincolnshire ☎ 01522

GAY INFO
■ **Lincoln Switchboard** Sun, Thu 19-22 h
PO Box 99 ✉ LN4 2SD ☎ 53 55 53

HEALTH GROUPS
■ **AIDS-Helpline** Tue, Thu 9-17.30, Mon, Wed, Fri -19 h
☎ 51 39 99
■ **Health Shop** Mon-Fri 9-16.30 h
Portland House, 3 Portland Road ☎ 52 92 22
Drop-in center dealing with sexual health, alcohol and drug use.

Little Bromley - Essex ☎ 01206

BARS
■ **Fox & Hounds** (AC B D f GLM MA S) Wed &Thu 19-24, Fri & Sat 20-2, Sun 12-15 & 20-22.30 h
Bentley Road ✉ CO11 2PL *(off A 120)* ☎ 39 74 15

Liverpool - Merseyside ☎ 0151

GAY INFO
■ **Merseyside Switchboard** 19-22 h
☎ 708 95 52
■ **Meryside Friend** General helpline: 19-22 h Mon-Sun, (Tue&Thu L)
36 Bolton St. ☎ 708 95 52 (general help line) ☎ 708 02 34 (women's line)

BARS
■ **Baa Bar** (AC B BF F glm OS s YG) Mon-Sat 10-2, Sun 14-20 h
43-45 Fleet Street ☎ 708 6810
■ **Brunswick Vaults. The** (B glm MA) 11-23 h
69 Tithebarn Street ☎ 284 3258
■ **Curzon Club** (B D f GLM MA SNU STV TV VS YG) Mo-Sa 12-02:00h, Su closed.
8 Temple Lane ✉ L2 5RQ *(Off Victoria Street)* ☎ 236 5160
■ **G-Bar** (B GLM YG) Thu-Sat
Eberle Street *(Opposite Garlands)* ☎ 258 1230
Popular before and after Garlands
■ **Lisbon. The** (B glm MA YG) 11-23 h, best Sun
36 Victoria Street ✉ L1 6BP ☎ 286 5466
■ **Masquerade. The** (B f GLM MA s) 12-23 h
10 Cumberland Street ✉ L1 6BU ☎ 236 7786
■ **Pacos** (B G MA r) Mo-Sa 12-23.00h. Su -22:30h
25 Stanley Street ✉ L1 6AA ☎ 236 9737

CAFES
■ **Café Tabac** (A B F glm YG) Mon-Sat 9.30-23, Sun 10.30-17 h
126 Bold Street ☎ 709 3735

DANCECLUBS
■ **Escape/E2. The** (B D GLM MA S VS) Tue Thu 22-4, Fri Sat 22-6 h
41-45 Paradise Street ✉ L1 3BP
■ **Garlands** (B D GLM PI SNU TV YG) Thu-Sat 21-2 h
8-10 Eberle Street ✉ L2 2AG ☎ 236 3307

Liverpool - Merseyside ▶ London — United Kingdom

RESTAURANTS
■ **Greenbank** (B F glm MA) Tue-Sun
332-338 Smithdown Rd. ☎ 734 4498
Wine bar / vegetarian restaurant.
■ **Metz** (B CC F GLM MA) Mon-Thu 12-23, Fri-Sat -24, Sun-22.30 h
New York Street *(Exchange Quarter)*

BOOK SHOPS
■ **News From Nowhere Bookshop** (AC CC glm) Mon-Sat 10-17.45 h
96 Bold Street ✉ L1 4HY *(City centre shopping centre)* ☎ 708 7270

HOTELS
■ **Feathers Hotel** (B BF CC F H MA)
119-125 Mount Pleasant ☎ 709 9555
Large, comfortable gay friendly hotel located in Liverpool city centre. All rooms have TV, telephone and tea / coffee making facilities. Rates: Single £ 44.95, Double £ 59.95 incl. full buffet breakfast.

GENERAL GROUPS
■ **LGB Soc at Liverpool University** Meets every Tue 20 h
(termtime) at Lisbon Bar, Victoria St.
☎ 794 41 22 ☎ 794 41 73
■ **Wirral Penninsulana Group** Meets Wed 29-1 h at Queens Royal, Marine Promenade, New Brighton
☎ 630 6251 ☎ 638 6371

HEALTH GROUPS
■ **Healthwise** Daily 10-22 h (free phone)
☎ (0800) 83 89 09
Health information/advice
■ **Maryland Centre** Mon-Tue Thu 9.30-17.30, Wed -21, Fri -18.30, Sat 11-17 h
8 Maryland St. *(off Hope St.)* ☎ 709 22 31
HIV testing, advice & info.

CRUISING
- Ainsdale Dunes (summer, nu)
- Otterspool Promenade (AYOR)
- Waterloo Marina, gardens and car parks in Crosby area (ayor)

Llandrindod Wells - Powys ☎ 01597

HEALTH GROUPS
■ **Powys Aidsline** Wed Sat 20-22.30 h
PO Box 24 ✉ LD1 I22 ☎ 82 42 00
or ☎ (0800) 45 43 91

Llandudno - Conwy ☎ 01492

DANCECLUBS
■ **Broadway Boulevard** (B D G S) every other Mon 20.30-0.30 h
Mostyn Brdwy ☎ 87 96 14

London ☎ 020

✱ The capital city of the United Kingdom and without doubt the gay capital too. In the last ten years the gay scene has exploded with many new bars and clubs opening accross the city. The gay scene is centered around Old Compton Street in SoHo, right in the heart of the city, this is where you will find all the theatre shops, cafés, cinemas and many gay bars and clubs. However do not feel that this is the only area to see. Many of the interesting bars, clubs and saunas are to be found outside the centre. London is a very cosmopolitan city and you will find young gay people from all over the world who have come to settle here for a time to make use of the excellent club and bar scene that is rivalled anywhere else in Europe. The underground system is extensive but be warned it does not operate after 22:30h. Alternatives such as night busses or taxis are available. Please remember the underground map bears very little relation to the geography of the city. Enjoy your time in vibrant London !

✱ Herzlich willkommen in der Hauptstadt "Cool Britannias". In London boomt es, denn diese Stadt ist immer angesagt. Am besten kommen Sie nach London zu den "Summer Rights" oder zu "Gay Pride" im Sommer, oder Sie werfen sich einfach in den Weihnachtstrubel im Winter. Unbedingt sehenswert sind dabei *Portobello Market, Camden, Harvey Nichols* und *Selfridges*. Schwules Leben spielt sich hauptsächlich in Earls Court und um Compton Street ab, dem sogenannten *Gay Village*. Das heißt aber nicht, daß man unbedingt im Westen Londons unterkommen muß. Besonders der Norden, Süden und Osten stellen eine erfrischende Alternative dar. Die neuesten Informationen zu der sich ständig wechselnden Club-Szene sind in den kostenlosen Magazinen, wie dem BOYZ, zu finden. Sie sind überall in den schwulen Lokalen erhältlich. In der britischen Hauptstadt findet man wohl die größte Auswahl an kulturellen und kulinarischen Möglichkeiten Europas. Doch alles hat schließlich auch seinen Preis: Machen Sie sich also auf knappen und preislich eher gehobenen Hotelraum gefaßt.

✱ La capitale du Royaume-Uni fait sans aucun doute également office de capitale gaie du pays. La scène homosexuelle a littéralement explosé ces dix dernières années et on a pu assister à l'ouverture, à travers toute la ville, d'une multitude de nouveaux bars et clubs. Plus particulièrement autour de Old Compton Street, dans le quartier de SoHo, vous trouverez une concentration de théâtres, de cafés, de cinémas, mais aussi de bars et clubs gais en plein coeur de la ville. Ce n'est cependant pas le seul quartier intéressant et beaucoup de saunas, bars et clubs se trouvent aussi en dehors du centre. Londres est une ville très cosmopolite et vous serez peut-être amenés à rencontrer un de ces nombreux jeune gai, venu récemment s'installer dans la capitale pour profiter pleinement d'une offre en sorties qui reste encore inégalée en Europe. Soyez attentifs au fait que les cartes de métro ne respectent pas forcément la géographie de la ville et que le réseau du métro, bien que très développé, ne dessert pas en delà de 22 heures 30. Des bus de nuits et taxis sont heureusement aussi disponibles partout. Il ne nous reste plus qu'à vous souhaiter un heureux séjour dans cette ville palpitante !

✱ Bienvenido a la capital de *Cool Britannia*. Londres es una ciudad en pleno auge que siempre está en temporada alta. Las mejores ocasiones para una visita son el Gay Day en verano o los dias antes de navidad para hacer compras (Recomendamos por ello especialmente Portobello Market, Camden, Harvey Nichols y Selfridges). El ambiente gay se concentra sobre todo en Earls Court y la calle Compton y sus alrededores (llamada también Gay Village). Pero no solo la parte oeste de Londres es interesante para el turista gay: las otras zonas también ofrecen sitios prometedores. Informaciones detalladas sobre los clubes de ambiente que están de moda se encuentran en revistas gratuitas (por ejemplo BOYZ) que hay en casi todos los sitios de ambiente. Londres es probablemente uno de los sitios más cosmopolitas de Europa y ofrece una amplia gama de posibilidades culturales y culinarias que no tienen comparación. En está ciudad el mundo está a tus pies...aunqúe a un cierto precio: hoteles son siempre difíciles de encontrar y en general bastante caros.

United Kingdom | London

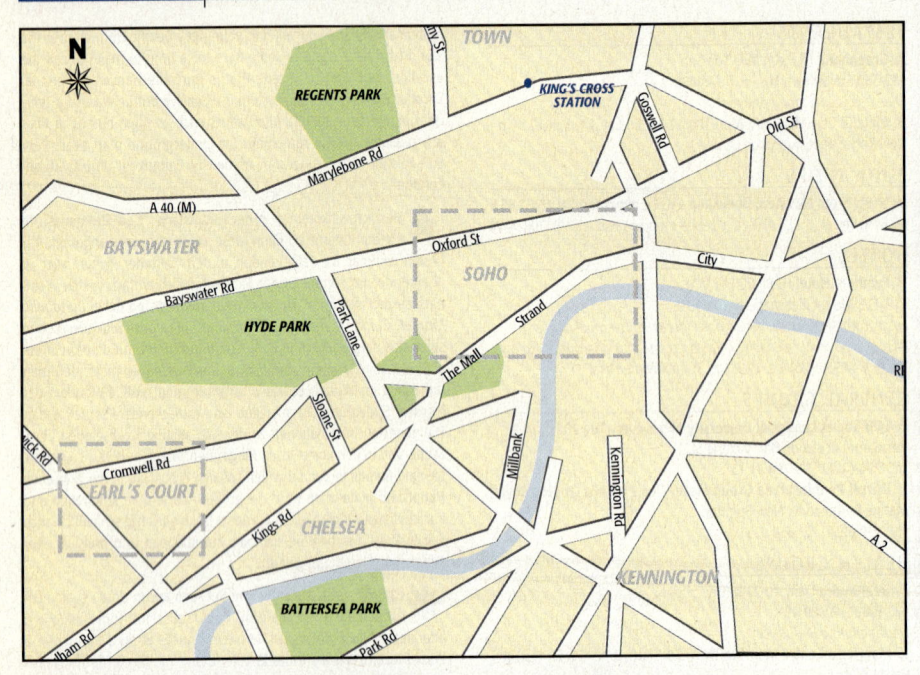

Benvenuto nella capitale del *Cool Britannia* Londra è sempre Londra. + consigliabile andarci per i *Summer Rights* o per il *Gay Pride* che hanno luogo in estate, o ci si tuffa nella vivace atmosfera dello shopping natalizio. In ogni caso sono da vedersi il *Portobello Market, Camden, Harvey Nichols* e *Selfridges*. I centri della vita gay sono l'Earls Court e la zona intorno alla Compton Street, il cosiddetto *Gay Village*. Ciò però non significa che si deve alloggiare per forza nella parte occidentale di Londra, perché tutta Londra offre delle alternative adeguate. Le ultime informazioni sul mondo dei club che cambia in continuazione, si trovano nelle riviste gratuite come il BOYZ esposte in tutti i locali gay. Nella capitale britannica viene offerta la più grande scelta culturale e culinaria d'Europa. Ma tutto ha il suo prezzo: è bene sapere che i pochi posti-letto degli alberghi londinesi hanno prezzi abbastanza elevati.

NATIONAL COMPANIES

■ **Regents Park Clinic** Mo-Fr 09-18:00h, Sa 10-17:00h, Su 10-16:00h
184 Gloucester Place ✉ NW1 6DS London *(U-Baker Street)* ☎ 7402 2208
London's foremost private clinic for sexually transmitted diseases.

GAY INFO

■ **London Lesbian and Gay Switchboard** (GLM p) 24 h
PO Box 7324 ✉ N1 9QS ☎ 7837 7324 📠 7837 7300
✉ admin@llgs.org.uk 🌐 www.llgs.org.uk
Excellent, round-the-clock telephone helpline, providing support, advice and information for lesbians & gays.

■ **Time Out**
251 Tottenham Ct. Rd., ✉ W1P 0AB ☎ 7813 3000
This weekly city guide can be bought at all newsagents and newstands. It has a comprehensive gay section as well as news on all other aspects of life in the capital.

TOURIST INFO

■ **London Tourist Board and Information Centre** 08-18:00h
Victoria Station Forecourt ✉ SW1V 1JU ☎ 7932 2000

BARS

■ **Admiral Duncan. The** (AC B CC f G GLM MA)
Mon-Sat 11-23:00h, Sun 12-22:30h
54 Old Compton Street, SoHo ✉ W1V 5PA *(U-Piccadilly)*
☎ 7437 5300
Refurbished after the SoHo bombing.
Very busy bar especially evenings.

■ **Angel. The** (AC B F GLM MA s YG) Mon-Sat 12-24, Sun 12-23.30 h
65 Graham Street ✉ N1 *(U-Angel. Next to canal)* ☎ 7608 2656

■ **Artful Dodger. The** (B d f Glm M) Th,Fr & Sa 14-02:00h, Su 13-24:00h Mo-We 14-24:00h
139 Southgate Road ✉ N1 *(U-Highbury/Angel)* ☎ 7226 0841
We- Towel Party. Su - Underwear Night. Gym & Sauna in Basement.

■ **Backstreet. The** (B G LJ MA P) Thu-Sat 22-3, Sun 21-1 h.
Wentworth Mews ✉ E3 SAP *(U-Mile End.Off Burdett Road.Look out for light above entr.)* ☎ 8980 8557
Leather and rubber club with strict dress code.

■ **Bar Aquda** (B F GLM MA) 12-23, Su -22.30 h
13-14 Maiden Lane ✉ WC2 *(U-Covent Garden)* ☎ 7557 9891

■ **Barcode** (A AC B d G MA) Mon-Sat 12-1, Sun 12-22.30 h
3-4 Archer Street ✉ W1 *(U-Piccadilly Cicus)* ☎ 7734 3342

■ **Black Cap. The** (AC B BF CC F GLM MA OS STV TV)
Mon-Thu 12-2 h, Fri Sat 12-3 h, Sun 12-22.30 h
171 Camden High Street ✉ NW1 *(U-Camden Town)* ☎ 7428 2721
Drag/cabaret pub.

1092 SPARTACUS 2001/2002

London United Kingdom

Next stop Amsterdam?
Call PEOPLE MALE ESCORT
the leading gay escortservice in the Netherlands
from Amsterdam, Europe's Gay Capital
Meet the hottest boys of Amsterdam

We offer first class healthy reliable boys (and men). Reasonable all-in prices. Pleasure and satisfaction assured, discretion guaranteed. 24 hours service. In Amsterdam, just 30 minutes from your phone call, you'll be with your ideal boy.

+31-20-662 99 90
visit our internet-site and browse our database (pictures available) at http://www.peoplemale.com
e-mail: info@peoplemale.com
International outcalls possible: minimum 12 hours, prepaid airplane ticket required, attractive night-rates.

PEOPLE™
male escorts amsterdam

■ **Black Horse. The** (AC B d G MA S SNU STV) Mon-Sun 20-2 h, Fr & Sat 20-02:00h
168 Mile End Road ✉ E1 4LJ *(U-Stepney Green. Opposite Globe Centre)* ☎ 7790 1684
Gay cabaret bar.

■ **Box. The** (A AC B BF CC d F GLM MA OS) Mon-Sat 11-23, Sun 12-22.30h
32-34 Monmouth Street, Covent Garden ✉ WC2 9HA *(U-Leicester Square/Covent Garden. Opp. Cambridge Theatre.)* ☎ 7240 5828

■ **Brief Encounter** (AC B D G lj MA OS s YG) Mon-Sat 11-23, Sun 12-22.30 h
41 St. Martin's Lane ✉ WC2 4EA *(U-Leicester Square/Charing Cross. Next to London Coliseum)* ☎ 7240 2221

■ **British Prince.** (AC B G S SNU VS) Mon-Sat 12-23.30, Sun 12-22.30 h
49 Bromley Street, Stepney ✉ E1 *(U-Limehouse)* ☎ 7790 1753

■ **Bromptons** (! AC B D G lj MA S) 18-2, Sun 20-24 h
294 Old Brompton Road ✉ SW5 *(U-Earls Court, Exit Warwick Road)* ☎ 7370 1344
Very popular on weekends, cruisy atmosphere.

■ **Cafe Goya** (B BF CC F glm MA N OS WE) Mon-Sat 17-23, Sat & Sun 11-17 h (brunch).
85 Acre Lane ✉ SW2 5TN *(10 min walk from Victoria Line, Brixton)* ☎ 7274 3500
Also grill restaurant.

■ **Central Station** (A AC B CC D F G LJ MA OS SNU STV VS) Mon-Wed 17-2, Thu -3, Fri -4, Sat 13-4, Sun 13-24 h
37 Wharfdale Road ✉ N1 *(U-King's Cross)* ☎ 7278 3294
Three floors. UK's only gay sports bar. Cabaret bar, nightclub, and roof terrace.

■ **Champion. The** (AC B d G MA N OS s) 12-?, Sun 12-22.30 h
1 Wellington Terrace, Bayswater Road ✉ W2 *(U-Notting Hill/Queensway)* ☎ 7229 5056

■ **Coleherne. The** (AC B G LJ MA) 12-23, Sun 12-22.30; Detour Bar Fri-Sun 21.30-24 h
261 Old Brompton Road ✉ SW5 *(U-Earl's Court)* ☎ 7244 5951

■ **Comptons of Soho** (! AC B CC F G LJ MA) 12-23, Sun 19-22.30 h
53 Old Compton Street ✉ W1 *(U-Picadilly)* ☎ 7437 4445

■ **Crash** (AC B D G MA) Mon-Thu 22.30-3h
66 Albert Embarkment, Vauxhall ✉ SW8 1SQ *(Opposite MI6 building, U-Vauxhall)* ☎ 7820 1500
Cruisy bar with video and theme nights.

■ **Due South** (B G MA) Mon-Fri 16-?, Sat Sun 13-? h, Thu women only
35 Stoke Newington High Street ✉ N16 ☎ 7249 7543

■ **Duke of Wellington. The** (B F glm MA N WE) 12-24, Sat 13-24, Sun 13-22.30 h
119 Balls Pond Road ✉ N1 *(U-Highbury/Islington)* ☎ (0171 254 4338

■ **Edge. The** (A B CC D F GLM MA) 12-1, Sun 12-22.30 h. Evenings (G).
11 Soho Square ✉ W1V 5DB *(U-Tottenham Court Road)* ☎ 7439 1313

■ **Escape** (B D F GLM MA) 16-3, Sun 16-22.30 h
8 Brewer Street ✉ W1R 3FP *(U-Leicester Square)* ☎ 7734 2626

■ **Gate Club. The** (B CC G MA N) Mon-Sat 10-01:00h, Sun 22-24:00h
68 Notting Hill Gate ✉ W11 3HT *(U-Notting Hill Gate)* ☎ 7229 0161

■ **George. The** (B F Glm MA STV OS) 17-23, Sun 12-22.30 h
114 Twickenham Road, Isleworth *(U-Hounslow East, plus a good walk)* ☎ 8560 1456
Good Cabaret

SPARTACUS 2001/2002 | 1093

United Kingdom — London

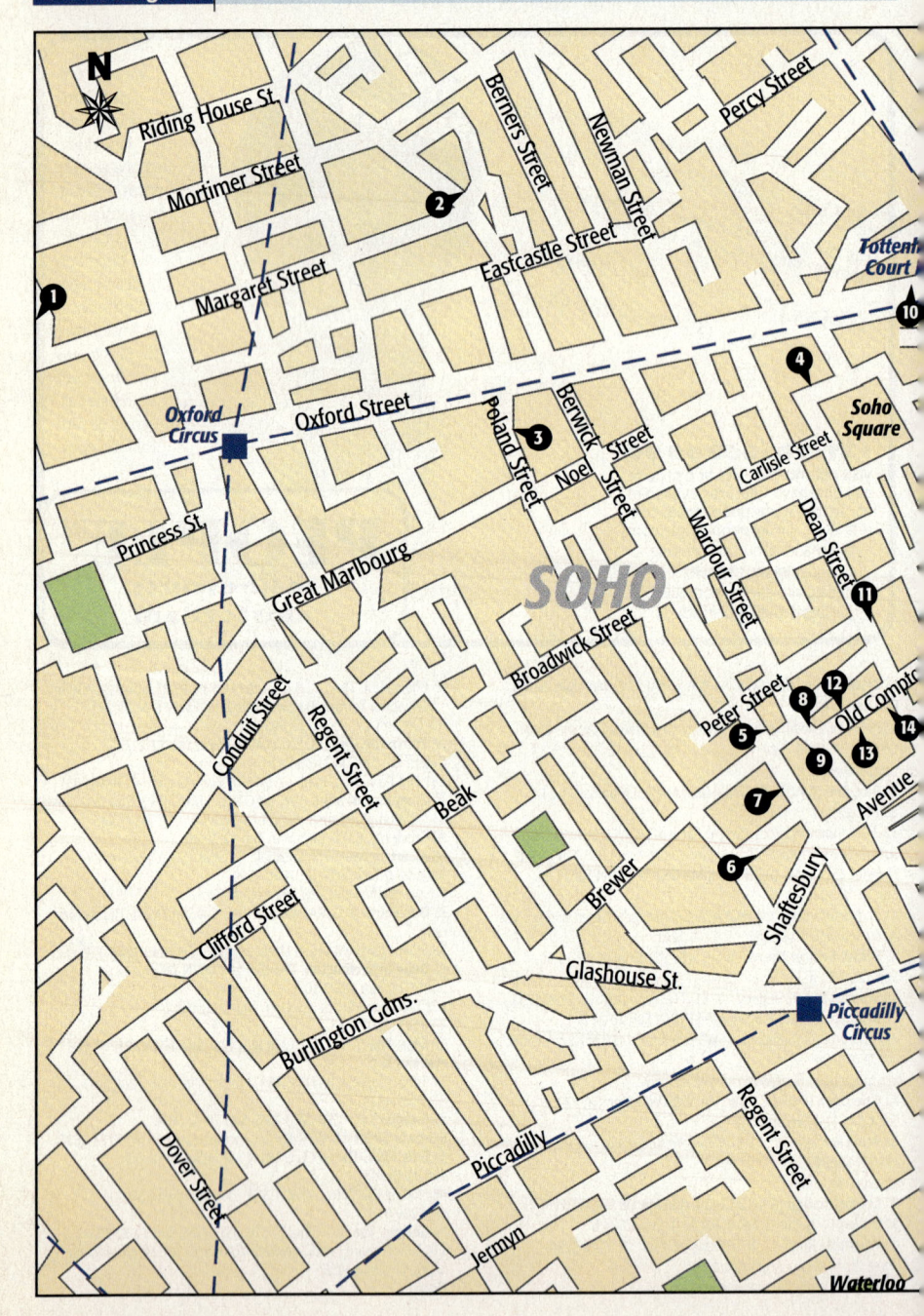

London – Soho / Holborn

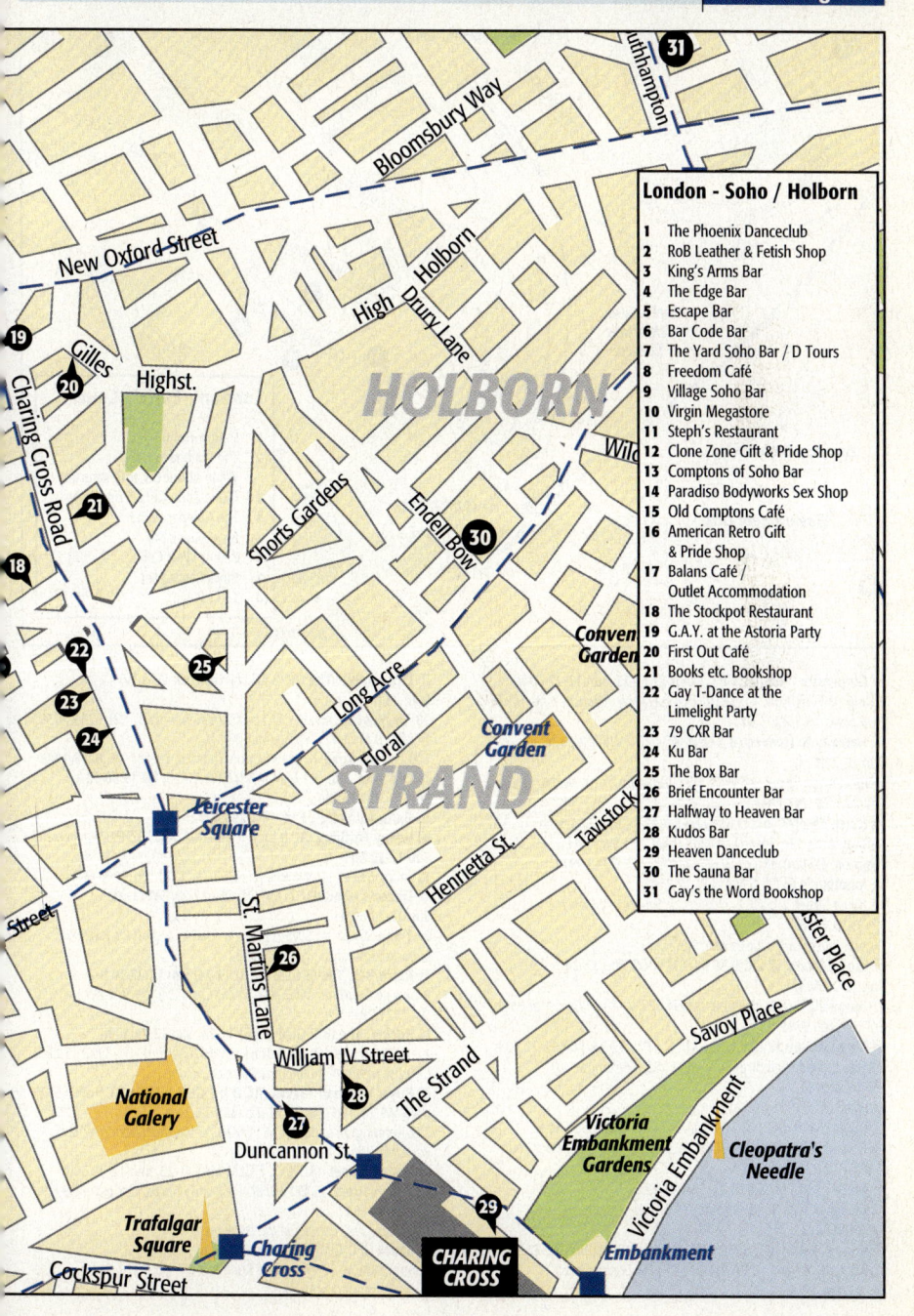

1. The Phoenix Danceclub
2. RoB Leather & Fetish Shop
3. King's Arms Bar
4. The Edge Bar
5. Escape Bar
6. Bar Code Bar
7. The Yard Soho Bar / D Tours
8. Freedom Café
9. Village Soho Bar
10. Virgin Megastore
11. Steph's Restaurant
12. Clone Zone Gift & Pride Shop
13. Comptons of Soho Bar
14. Paradiso Bodyworks Sex Shop
15. Old Comptons Café
16. American Retro Gift & Pride Shop
17. Balans Café / Outlet Accommodation
18. The Stockpot Restaurant
19. G.A.Y. at the Astoria Party
20. First Out Café
21. Books etc. Bookshop
22. Gay T-Dance at the Limelight Party
23. 79 CXR Bar
24. Ku Bar
25. The Box Bar
26. Brief Encounter Bar
27. Halfway to Heaven Bar
28. Kudos Bar
29. Heaven Danceclub
30. The Sauna Bar
31. Gay's the Word Bookshop

United Kingdom — London

London - Earle's Court

1. Halifax Hotel
2. The Philbeach Hotel / Wilde About Oscar Restaurant
3. Clone Zone Gift & Pride Shop
4. The Coleherne Bar
5. Brompton's Bar
6. Balans West Café
7. Roy's Restaurant
8. Ted's Place

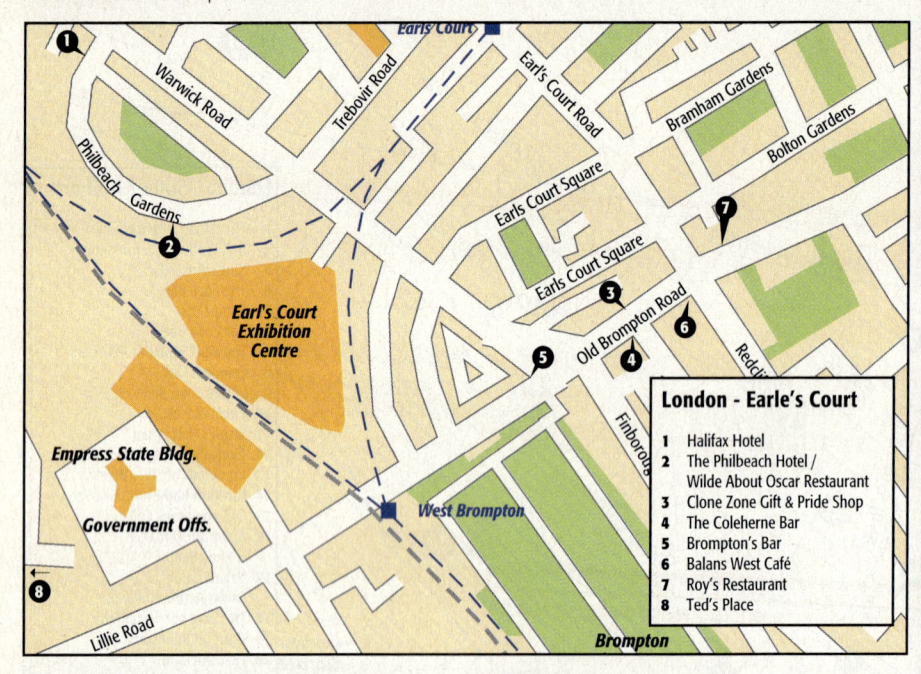

Gloucester. The (B CC F G MA N S) 11-23, Sun 12-22.30 h
1 King William Walk ✉ SE10 (BR-Greenwich. Opposite Greenwich Park gates) ☏ 8293 6131

Halfway to Heaven (B d GLM MA S STV WE) 12-23 h, Sun 12-22.30 h
7 Duncannon Street ✉ WC2 4JF (U-Charing Cross. Next to Trafalger Square) ☏ 7930 8312

Hoist. The (AC B G LJ MA) Fri-Sat 22-3 , Sun 21-1.50 h
Railway Arch 47c, South Lambeth Road, ✉ SW8 IRH (opposite U-Vauxhall, Exit One, in arches) ☏ 7735 9972

Jonathan's (B CC G MA N P) 17-23 h
16 Irving Street ✉ WC2 (U-Leicester Square. 1st Floor) ☏ 7930 4770
Gay members club. Guests welcome.

King Edward VI (AC B BF F G MA N OS WE) 12-24, Sun 12-22.30 h
25 Bromfield Street, Islington ✉ N1 0PZ (U-Angel.Corner of Parkfield St.) ☏ 704 0745

King William IV (B F Glm lj MA N STV) 12-23, Sun 12-22.30 h
77 Hampstead High Street ✉ NW3 1RE (U-Hampstead) ☏ 7435 5747
Not far from cruising area Hamstead Heath.

Kings' Arms (AC B C F G MA s) 11-23, Sun 12-22.30 h
23 Poland Street ✉ W1V 3DD (U-Oxford Circus/Tottenham Court Road) ☏ 7734 5907

Ku Bar (B GLM YG) 12-23, Sun 13-22.30 h
75 Charing Cross Road ✉ WC2H ONE (U-Leicester Square) ☏ 7437 4303

Kudos (A B CC d F G MA s VS) Mon-Sat 11-23, Sun 12-22.30 h
10 Adelaide Street ✉ WC2N 4HZ (BR/U-Charing Cross) ☏ 7379 4573

Little Apple. The (AC B CC D F GLM MA OS s TV) 12-24, Sun -23 h
98 Kennington Lane ✉ SE11 4XD (U-Kennington) ☏ 7735 2039

LJ's (B D GLM STV) Tue-Sun 20-? h
140 London Road, Kingston-Upon-Thames, Surrey ☏ 8288 1448

Old Ship. The (B f GLM MA N STV) 18-23, Sat 19.30-23, Sun 13.30-22.30 h
17 Barnes Street ✉ E14 ☏ 7790 4082

Penny Farthing (AC B CC d F GLM MA N OS S STV WE) 12-2, Sun 12-22.30 h
135 King Street ✉ W6 9JG (U-Hammersmith) ☏ 8600 0941

Queen's Head (B F G MA OG OS) 12-23, Sat 11-23, Sun 12-22.30 h
27 Tryon Street ✉ SW3 (U-Sloane Square. Just off the King's Rd. opposite Safeways) ☏ 7589 0262

Retro Bar. The (B GLM MA s) 12-23, Sun 12-22.30 h
2 George Court ✉ WC2 (U-Charing Cross. Off the Strand) ☏ 7321 2811

Rocket. The (B D GLM MA S) 11-23, Sun 12-22.30 h
11-13 Churchfield Road, Acton ✉ W3 (U-Acton) ☏ 8992 1545
One bar with cabaret and one more cruisy one.

Royal Vauxhall Tavern (AC B D f GLM lj MA r RT S SNU STV u VS W) 20-24/1, Fri Sat 21-2 h, Sun 12-24 h
372 Kennington Lane ✉ SE11 5QH (U-Vauxhall. Near river and Vauxhall Viaduct.) ☏ 7582 0833

Rupert Street (AC B CC F G GLM MA) 11-23, Sun 12-22.30 h
50 Rupert Street ✉ W1V 7HR (U-Picadilly Circus. Opposite The Yard) ☏ 7734 5164
Stylish bar. Very popular in the evenings.

Shoot (B D G MA) 2nd Sun 18-24 h
Central Station, 37 Wharfdale Road ✉ N1 ☏ 7278 3294
Strict dresscode : sportswear .

1096 SPARTACUS 2001/2002

London | United Kingdom

LONDON'S FOREMOST PRIVATE CLINIC FOR SEXUALLY TRANSMITTED DISEASES

Screening & treatment for all sexually transmitted diseases
HIV testing / results in 15 minutes
Impotence

Professional · Discreet · Efficient · Gay Friendly

Open 7 days per week & most Bank Holidays

Information Lines (60p per min)
09068 172 316 HIV information, testing and prevention
09068 172 317 AIDS diagnosis, treatments and staying well
09068 172 318 Hepatitis B information and vaccination
09068 172 323 Erectile Dysfunction

184 Gloucester Place, London NW1 6DS
Phone: 020 7402 2208 / Fax: 020 7262 0675
e-mail: info@regentsparkclinic.com
internet: www.regentsparkclinic.com

THE *Regent's Park* CLINIC
Established 1985

Derek Smith, co-ordinator at the Regent's Park Clinic

United Kingdom | London

SOHO'S BUSIEST LATE BAR

79

HAPPY HOURS EVERY DAY FROM 20.00 TO 22.00

OPEN WEEKDAYS TO 2am - FRI & SAT TO 3am

79 CHARING CROSS ROAD WC2

barcode

barcode

SOHO
3/4 ARCHER ST
LONDON W1V 7HE
TEL 020 7734 3343
FAX 020 7734 2329
1PM-1AM MON-SAT
1PM-10.30PM SUN

SOHO'S LARGEST GAY BAR

bc

■ **SubStation South** (AC B D GLM lj MA) Mon 22-?, Tue Thu 10.30-2, Wed -3, Fri 22-5, Sat 22.30-6, Sun 21-3 h
9 Brighton Terrace, Brixton ✉ SW9 (U-Brixton) ☎ 7737 2095
Different theme nights. Cruisy and popular.
■ **Ted's Place** (B D DR G MA P STV TV VS) Mon-Fri 19-late. Last Sun/ month 16-23:00h
305a Northend Road ✉ W14 9NS (U-West Kensington/ U-West Brompton) ☎ 7385 9359
Mon,Tue,Fri & Sun - men only.
■ **Tube. The** (B D GLM MA) 22-?, Fri-Sat -5 h
Falconberg Court ✉ W1 (U-Tottenham Court Road, behind Astoria)
■ **Two Brewers. The** (AC B D GLM MA N S STV VS WE)
Mo-Th 12-02:00h, Fr & Sa -03:00h, Su -24:00h
114 Clapham High Street ✉ SW4 7UJ (U-Clapham Common)
☎ 7498 4971
■ **Underground** (AC B CC D F G lj MA S SNU STV YG) 17-2, Thu-3, Fri-5, Sat 12-5, Sun 12-24 h
37 Wharfdale Road ✉ N1 (U-Kings Cross) ☎ 7833 8925
See Central Station.
■ **Village Soho** (AC B CC F G YG) Sun 12-22.30, weekdays 16-1 h.
81 Wardour Street ✉ W1V 3TG (U-Piccadilly Circus. At the top of Old Compton Street) ☎ 7434 2124
Weekend GoGo Boys.
■ **West Central** (B GLM MA)
29-30 Lisle Street ✉ WC2 (Subway-Leicester Square) ☎ 7479 7981
Large, Busy gay bar on three floors
■ **White Hart. The** (B f glm MA S) 19-24, Sun 12-23.30 h
51 Station Road ✉ N15 (U-Tottenham Hale. In front of Blockbuster Video.) ☎ 8808 5049

Europes hottest gay chat and date service!

GAY CHAT!

Connect live 1-2-1 with guys from across Europe!

From the UK dial:
0870 333 5050

From outside the UK dial:
+44 870 333 5050

0870 CALLS COST 2P PER MIN CHEAP RATE 8P PER MIN PEAK RATE. +44870 CALLS ARE CHARGED AT STANDARD INTERNATIONAL RATES. WHEN MAKING A DATE BE SAFE AND SECURE. MEET IN A PUBLIC PLACE AND TELL A FRIEND

chat to men

CHAT AND MEET GUYS ON THE INTERNET OR OVER THE PHONE!

- join 4 free
- create your own web profile page
- browse for guys
- personals
- contacts
- text messaging
- voice messaging
- connect 1-2-1
- events calendar
- club listings
- jobs
- accomodation
- 100's of guys online

www.chattomen.com

United Kingdom | London

suited*and*booted

stunning educated guys
great personalities & friendly attitude
~
one call to us
and we make all the arrangements
~
we can visit you with our portfolio
online portfolio at
www.suited*and*booted.com
email service also available
~
telephone: +44 (0)20 7723 8788
email: info@suited*and*booted.com

■ **White Swan. The** (AC B CC D G MA OS SNU STV VS) Mon 21-1, Tue-Thu -2, Fri Sat 21-3, Sun 17:30-24 h
556 Commercial Road ✉ E14 7JD *(U-Aldgate East / Limehouse Docklands Light Railway)* ☎ 7780 9810
Sun Original Tea Dance with Latin music.

■ **Yard. The** (! A B CC F GLM MA OS) 12-23, meals 12-17, Sun 12-22.30 h
57 Rupert Street ✉ W1V 7HN *(U-Piccadilly Circus / Tottenham Court Road)* ☎ 7437 2652
FAX (0171) 434 0344

■ **79CXR** (AC B G MA) Mon-Thu 13-02, Fri & Sat -3, Sun -22:30h
79 Charing Cross Road, Soho ✉ WC2H ONE *(U-Leicester Square. Cambridge Circus intersection)* ☎ 7734 0769
Popular late bar. Happy hour daily and all day on Sun. DJ Thu to Sat.

CAFES

■ **Balans West** (AC B BF CC F GLM OS YG) 8-1 h
239 Old Brompton Road ✉ SW5 9HP *(U-Earl's Court)* ☎ 7244 8838

■ **First Out Café Bar** (A B BF F GLM MA OS) 10-23, Sun 11-22.30, Fri 20-23 h Women's night
52 St. Giles High Street ✉ WC2 *(U-Tottenham Court Road. Next to Center Point.)* ☎ 7240 8042

■ **Freedom** (A B F glm MA S YG) 11-3, Sun -24 h
60-66 Wardour Street ✉ W1 ☎ 7734 0071

■ **Old Compton Cafe** (AC BF F GLM MA OS) 0-24 h
34 Old Compton Street ✉ W1 *(U-Piccadilly Circus / Tottenham Court Road)* ☎ 7439 3309

■ **Patisserie Valerie** (b f NG) 8-20, Sun 10-17.30 h
44 Old Compton Street ✉ W1 *(U-Leicester Square)*

Bill Glen & Adams *As seen on BBC TV*
Celebrating our 25th year

Covering the United Kingdom and beyond. Let our fit, good-looking guys introduce themselves!
09069-526979 75p all times
Our friendly staff will be happy to speak to you at any time.
Bookings/Enquiries 0044 (0) 20 8530 1050 or 07850 469255 24hrs, CC's
If you'd like to join us ask for Peter
www.billglens.com

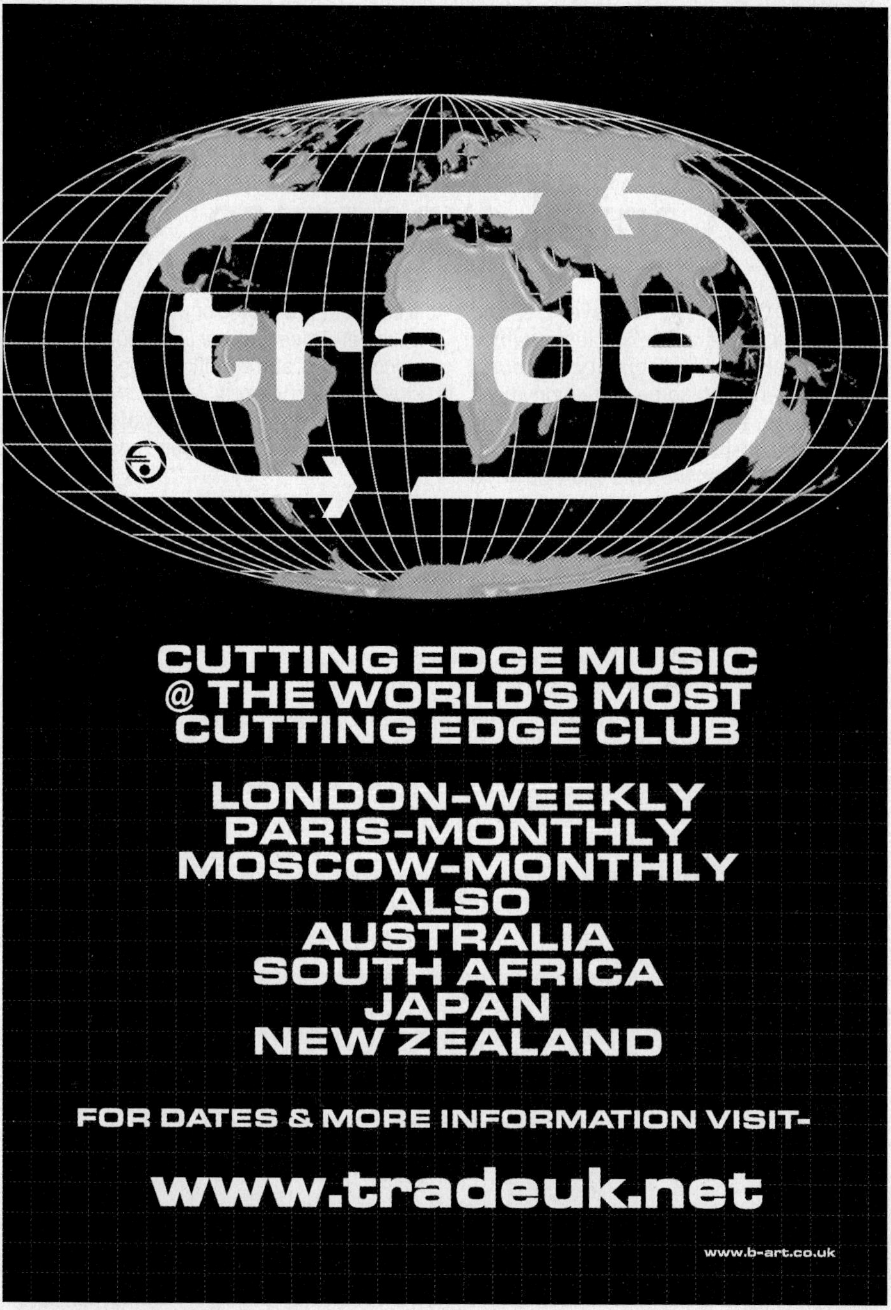
trade
CUTTING EDGE MUSIC
@ THE WORLD'S MOST
CUTTING EDGE CLUB
LONDON-WEEKLY
PARIS-MONTHLY
MOSCOW-MONTHLY
ALSO
AUSTRALIA
SOUTH AFRICA
JAPAN
NEW ZEALAND
FOR DATES & MORE INFORMATION VISIT-
www.tradeuk.net
www.b-art.co.uk

United Kingdom | London

When you choose an escort agency, make sure it's a Capital experience.

At Capital we believe it's the quality of *our* experience which guarantees the quality of *yours*. We're not some big anonymous company, but a small, long established consultancy which really takes the time and trouble to listen to your needs.

We're friendly, professional and totally discreet. Whether you want a companion at home or abroad, for a brief meeting or a longer encounter, Capital will arrange it quickly, efficiently and with pleasure. That's why so many of our clients return to us again and again.

So why risk a disappointing experience, when you could have a Capital one? Call us today and find out why *nobody does it better*.

- Hotel or home visits, dinner evenings, theatre trips, sightseeing, weekends or longer.
- Visit our central London offices to see the Capital portfolio of London's most attractive young escorts and masseurs.
- Carefully vetted to be friendly, educated and good company.
- Escorts are London-based and are happy to travel throughout the UK, Europe and further.

Capital
London's most exclusive escort agency
020 7630 7567

AMERICAN EXPRESS VISA MasterCard

All major credit cards accepted

SPARTACUS 2001/2002

London — United Kingdom

VILLA GIANNI

Why not visit our sumptuous and elegant new premices in Central London?

Alternatively, we can arrange for an attractive escort to visit you.

Absolute discretion assured.

☎ +44 (0) 20 7244 9901   +44 (0) 20 7259 2529

WWW.VILLAGIANNI.COM

Open daily 11.00am *till late*

United Kingdom | London

INTENSE
THE EROTIC SEDUCER

Wholesaler/Retailer Inquiries: Phone +49.30.610 01 120 · Fax +49.30.615 90 08 · vertrieb@brunogmuender.com

INTENSE is a non-fragrant, man for man pheromone developed to intensify your erotic appeal!

INTENSE contains concentrated natural sexual stimulants (pheromones). Reinforce your own individual "sexual charisma" with **INTENSE** and seduce in a perfectly natural way.

INTENSE is based purely on water, alcohol and pheromones and is therefore odourless. This means that you can wear your favourite perfume on top of **INTENSE** at any time.

Let yourself be seduced: **INTENSE** perfume with natural pheromones is odourless and comes in an attractive 63.3 ml glass bottle as a gift set.

THE WORLD'S FIRST PHEROMONE FOR MEN.

Photo: Steven Underhill

DANCECLUBS

■ **ATELIER** (AC B D GLM YG) Thu 9-3.30 h
18 West Central Street ✉ WC1A 1JJ (U-Tottenham Court Road)
☎ 7419 9199

■ **Benjys 2000** (AC B D GLM s YG) Th-Sa 22-03:00h, Sun 21-1 h
562a Mile End Road ✉ E3 (U-Mile End) ☎ 8980 6427

■ **Club Travestie** (AC B D GLM MA STV TV) 2nd/4th Sat 20.30-2 h
Stepney Nightclub, 373 Commercial Road ✉ E1 (U-Aldgate East. Entrance on Aylward St., off Jubilee St.) ☎ 8788 4154
This TV/drag which has been running for the last nineteen years, attracts a mixed crowd. Every other Sat.

■ **Club V** (AC B D GLM s YG) 2nd Sat 21-03:00h
20-22 Highbury Corner ✉ N1 (U-Highbury and Islington. Upstairs at the Garage.) ☎ 7607 1818

■ **Duckie at the Vauxhall Tavern** (AC B D GLM lj S VS) Sat 21-2 h
372 Kennington Lane ✉ SE11 (U-Vauxhall) ☎ 7582 0833

■ **G.A.Y. at the Astoria** (AC B D GLM MA s) Mon Thu Pink Pounder 22.30-4, Fri Camp Attack 23-4, Sat G.A.Y. 22.30-5 h
157 Charing Cross Road ✉ WC2 (U-Tottenham Court Road)
☎ 7734 6963
Mon Thu admission just GBP 1.

■ **Gay Tea-Dance at The Limelight** (! AC B D GLM MA YG)
Sun 18-23 h
136 Shaftesbury Avenue ✉ W1 (U-Leicester Square) ☎ 7437 0572

■ **Heaven** (AC B CC D f GLM MA S STV) Mon-Thu 22-3, Fri Sat -6, Sun 17-24 h
Under the Arches, Villiers Street ✉ WC2N 6NG (U-Charing Cross/Embankment) ☎ 7930 2020
Events changing from night to night.

■ **Love Muscle at The Fridge** (! AC B BF D F GLM MA OS s WE YG)
Sat 22-6 h, Sun - Fridge Bar 20-12:30h
Town Hall Parade, Brixton Hill ✉ SW2 (U-Brixton. Next to Brixton Town Hall) ☎ 7326 5100
Mixed crowd with muscle boys and disco dykes. Fantastic lighting.

■ **Phoenix. The** (AC B D GLM MA STV YG) Fri Sat 22.30-3 h
37 Cavendish Square ✉ W1 (U-Oxford Circus) ☎ 8551 1987

■ **Reflex 2** (B D GLM MA) Fr & Sa 21-03:00h
184 London Road, Kingston-Upon-Thames, Surrey K2
☎ 8549 9911

■ **Sundays at home** (AC B D f glm MA s STV VS WE YG) (G)
Sun 16:-0:00h
1 Leicester Square ✉ WC2H In SoHo U-Leicester Square.
☎ 964 2073
7 floors, 5 bars, 3 clubs. The bst sound system. Exclusive members bar & restaurant with terrace.

■ **Trade** (b D GLM P YG) Sun 4-13 h
Turnmills, 63b Clerkenwell Street ✉ EC1 (U-Farringdon)
☎ 7250 3409
Call for membership before going to the club

■ **Tube. The** (B D GLM MA) 22-4 h
Falconberg Court ✉ W1 (U-Tottenham Court Road, behind Astoria)
☎ 7287 9608

■ **West Central** (B D GLM MA) We-Sa 22:30-03:30h
29-30 Lisle Street ✉ WC2 (U-Leicester Square. Beneath the Polar Bear) ☎ 7479 7981

RESTAURANTS

■ **Amazonas** (AC B CC F glm MA OS YG) 19-23, Sat Sun 12-15, 19-23 h
75 Westbourne Grove ✉ W2 4UL (U-Queensway/Bayswater. Behind Whiteley's Shopping Centre.) ☎ 7243 0090
Mouth-watering Brazilian / South American food at reasonable prices

London — United Kingdom

■ **Atlantic Bar and Grill** (AC B CC F glm) 12-2, Sun 19-23.30 h
20 Glasshouse Street ✉ W1 *(U-Piccadilly Circus)* ☎ 7734 4888
■ **Balans** (! B BF CC F GLM MA OS S TV WE YG) Mon-Thu 8-4, Fri-Sat -6, Sun -1 h
60 Old Compton Street ✉ W1V 5PA *(U-Leicester Square/Piccadilly Circus)* ☎ 7437 5212
■ **Dome. The** (b BF F glm) 9.30-? h
57-59 Old Compton Street ✉ W1 *(U-Piccadilly)* ☎ 7287 0770
■ **Drawing Room & Sofa Bar. The** (AC B BF CC glm) 12-24, Sat 11-24, Sun -18 h
103 Lavender Hill, Battersea ✉ SW11 5ZL ☎ 7350 2564
Restaurant with seperate bar. Lunch and dinner served daily, brunch on weekends.
■ **Ground Floor** (B F glm MA)
186 Portobello Road ✉ W11 *(U-Notting Hill Gate)* ☎ 7428 9931
Good food
■ **Kavanagh's Restaurant** (B F glm N) Tue-Fri 12.30-14.30, 19-22.30, Sat 19-22.30, Sun 12-15.30 h
26 Penton Street, Islington ✉ N1 *(U-Kings Cross/U-Angel)* ☎ 7833 1380
Friendly restaurant. Good and reasonably priced cuisine.
■ **Le Gourmet** (AC CC F g MA) 18.30-23.30, Sun 13-15.30, 19-23 h
312 Kings Road ✉ SW3 *(U-Sloane Square. 10 mins. walk down King's Road.)* ☎ 7352 4483
International cuisine.
■ **Roy's Restaurant** (AC B CC F G MA s) 18.30-23.30 h (last orders)
234 Old Brompton Road ✉ SW5 0DE *(U-Earl's Court)* ☎ 7373 9995
■ **Steph's** (B CC E F GLM MA) Mon-Thu 12-15, 17.30-23.30, Fri Sat -24 h, cabaret brunch 1st Sun of month
39 Dean Street ✉ W1V 5AP *(U-Tottenham Court Road/Leicester Square)* ☎ 7734 5976
Experience english cuisine at its best.

■ **Stockpot. The** (AC F MA NG) Mon-Tue 11.30-23.30, Wed-Sat 11.30-23.45, Sun 12-23 h
18 Old Compton Street ✉ W1V 5PE *(U-Tottenham Court Road)* ☎ 7287 1066
Cheapest restaurant in central London.
■ **Wilde about Oscar** (b BF CC E F GLM MA OS p) 19-22.30 h
30-31 Philbeach Gardens ✉ SW5 *(U-Earl's Court; at Philbeach Hotel)* ☎ 7835 1858
Conservatory restaurant, serving lovely french food. Newly renovated.

SHOWS

■ **Madame Jo Jo's** (AC B CC D E g MA STV) Mon-Sat 22-3 h
8 Brewer Street ✉ W1R 3FP *(U-Piccadilly Circus)* ☎ 7734 2473
FAX (0171) 434 1616

SEX SHOPS/BLUE MOVIES

■ **Man to Man** (G MA) Mon-Sat 10-19.30 h
57 Pembridge Road ✉ W11 *(U-Notting Hill Gate)* ☎ 7727 1614
■ **Paradiso Bodyworks** (CC glm MA TV) 11-21 h
41 Old Compton Street ✉ W1V 5PN *(U-Piccadilly Circus / Tottenham Court Road)* ☎ 7287 2487
FAX (0181) 348 9352 T.V. friendly fetish boutique in the centre of Soho selling a wide selection of fetish clothing, S&M equipment, toys, lingerie, kinky boots (large sizes) and body jewellry.
■ **Pink Triangle** (b CC G MA) 10-24, Sun 12-23 h
13 Brewer Street ✉ W1 *(U-Piccadilly Circus)* ☎ 7734 0455
■ **Zipperstore** (AC CC G MA) 10.30-18.30 h
283 Camden High Street ✉ NW1 7BX *(U-Camden Town. Next to Camden Lock Market)* ☎ 7284 0537
Wide selection of European and American gay magazines, books, cards, leather articles, rubber, toys, leisurewear and underwear.

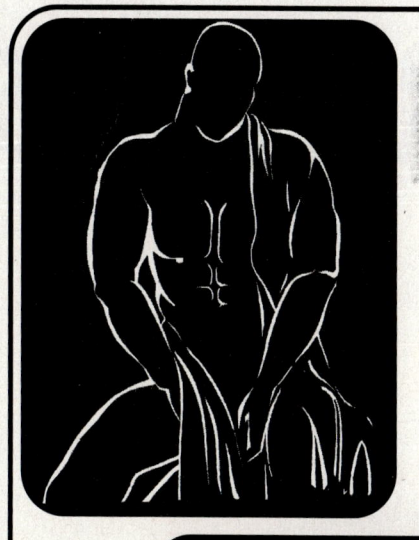

---

saunabar

Luxurious lounge area
Fully licensed bar
30 man spa
20 man sauna
Steam room
5 rest rooms
Shower Area
Masseurs

Monday-Sunday 12.00-24.00

29 Endell Street Covent Garden London WC2H 9BA
tel: 020 7836 2236   www.thesaunabar.com

United Kingdom | London

Chariots

London | United Kingdom

Chariots 1

Englands BIGGEST & Friendliest Sauna
25,000 SQ Ft of hedonistic decadent Roman Sauna

- 2x 30-man steam rooms
- 2 x 20 man sauna cabins
- Fabulous heated pool
- A host of private rooms
- 2 large hot bubbly jacuzzis
- Large fully equiped gym
- Genuine qualified massage
- Huge screen TV Lounge
- Complimentary tea & fruit juice bar
- High powered sunbeds
- 400 locker changing room
- Complimentary towels & toiletries
- Mens Grooming Service
- Snack Bar/Restaurant Specialising in Health Food

Opening Times:
Monday To Saturday: 12 noon - 9am
Sunday: 12 noon - midnight

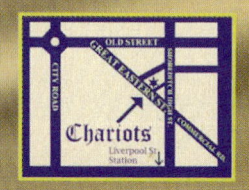

ENTRY £12

Chariots House, Fairchild Street, London EC2A 3NS
Tel 020 7247 5333
Web Site: www.gaysauna.co.uk

Chariots 11

Open 7 days a week:
Monday-Thursday 12 noon - midnight
Weekends Friday 12 noon - Sunday midnight

- Saunas
- Large Steam Room
- Hot Bubbling Jacuzzis
- Rest Rooms
- TV Lounge/Snack Bar
- Free Refreshments
- High Powered Sunbed
- Showers & 150 Locker Room Capacity
- Complimentary towels & toiletries

Attitude Free Zone

Tuesdays: BARE for big boys
& bear cubs every second saturday
of the month BEAR 2000

Rear of) 292 Streatham High Rd SW16
Tel: 020 8696 0929

Chariots 111
Farringdon

Directly opposite Farringdon tube station

- Large Sauna
- Large Steam Room
- Rest Rooms
- TV Lounge
- Free Refreshments
- (Complimentary Tea & Fruit Juice Bar
- Snack Bar
- High Powered Sun Shower
- Complimentary Towel & Toiletries

'NON STOP'

Same day return pass
Farringdon Only
for a limited period.

Entry
Mon-Fri b4 4pm £8
After £10
All Weekend £10

NEW OPENING TIMES
11am-11pm Mon-Thurs
11am-3am Fri & Sat
11am-11pm Sun

57 Cowcross St, London EC1 Tel: 020 7251 5553

United Kingdom — London

ESCORTS & STUDIOS

■ **Bill Glens** (CC G MSG) 24 h
☎ 8530 1050
■ **Capital Services** (CC G msg) Bookings -2 h
☎ 7630 7567
Portfolio service available by appointment.
■ **Suited & Booted** (CC G msg)
27 St. James St. ✉ W1M 5HY *(U-Bond St.)* ☎ 7723 8788
Situated in the centre of London in the busy Westend.
■ **Villa Gianni** (AC b G msg p) 11-2 h
☎ 7244 9901

SAUNAS/BATHS

■ **Chariots II** (AC CC DR F G lj MA N SA SB SOL WE WH)
Mon-Thu 12-24, Fri 12-Sun 24 h
292 Streatham High Road ✉ SW16 6HG *(BR-Streatham, the left, rear of the building)* ☎ 8696 0929
No attitude sauna which offers a relaxed atmosphere. Tue and 2nd Sat of the month: Bear 2000 parties. Also shop with leather goods. Reduced price for students.
■ **Chariots III** (AC B CC DR F G MA SA SB SOL WO) 11-23 h
57 Cowcross Street ✉ EC1 *(U-Farringdon)* ☎ 7252 5553
The City executive spa on 4000 sq ft.
■ **Chariots Roman Spa, Chariots House** (AC BF cc DR F G MA msg N PI SA SB SOL VS WE WH WO) 12-9, Sun 12-24 h
201-207 Shoreditch High St. ✉ EC1 6LG *(U-Liverpool Street)*
☎ 7247 5333
Large popular sauna (20 000 sq ft) in Roman style with heated pool. Complimentary tea & fruit juice, towel and toiletries. Bar accessible without entering in the sauna (open 11-23 h). Restaurant specialized in veg/health food, recently refurbished, charity evenings.
■ **Health Club. The** (b DR f MG SA SB WH) 13-0 h
800 Lea Bridge Road ✉ E17 9DJ *(U-Leytonstone)* ☎ 8556 8082
Newly refurbished relaxation area. Middle aged clientele.
■ **H.P.S 156** (f G MA SB SOL WH WO) 11.30-23.30 h
156 Shepherds Bush Shopping Centre ✉ W12 8PP *(U-Shepherds Bush. Shepherds Bush Green, opposite Boots)* ☎ 8743 3264
Big sauna on three floors frequented by a mixed age crowd. H.P.S. stands for Holland Park Sauna.

■ **Locker Room. The** (DR f G MA SA SB SOL VS) 11-1, Fri 11-Sun 24 h
8 Cleaver Street, Kennington ✉ SE11 *(Close to Kennington Tube)*
☎ 7582 6288
■ **Pacific 33** (AC b f G MA P SA SB) Mon-Thu 10-24, Fri 11-Sun 24 h
33 Hornsey Road ✉ N7 7DD *(U-Holloway Road. Next to college)*
☎ 7609 8133
Soft drinks, towels, toiletries, cakes and fruits included in price.
■ **Pleasure Drome Central** (b CC DR G MA SA SB WH) 0-24 h
125 Alaska Street ✉ SE1 4JB *(U-Waterloo)* ☎ 7633 9194
Newly refurbished. Complimentary soft drinks available.

Gay's The Word
lesbian & gay bookshop

UK's widest selection of lesbian and gay books – over 2000 titles to choose from! We also sell a great range of cards, videos and magazines. So come and visit.

66 Marchmont Street · London
WC1N 1AB
Russell Square Underground

Mo–Sat 10–18.30h Sun 14–18h
Tel. 020 7278 7654
sales@gaystheword.co.uk
www.gaystheword.co.uk

CENTAURUS
Central London Gay Store & More

youthful male image specialist
Videos + Books + Photos
100 OLD STREET. LONDON. EC1V 9AY
Old Street tube Exit 6.
Mon~Sat 10~18.30
FREE MAIL ORDER CATALOGUES
Tel. 020 7251 3535 Fax. 020 7251 3536
e-mail. spartacus@centaurus.co.uk
www.centaurus.co.uk

PHOTO GALLERY
WWW.STARBOY.CO.UK

London | United Kingdom

REGULATION LTD

Opening Times
Monday - Saturday 10.30am - 6.30pm
Sunday 12.00am - 5.00pm

17a St.Albans Place
Islington Green
London, N1 0NX
UK

Tel No. +44 (0) 020 7226 0665
Fax No. +44 (0) 020 7226 0658

Catalogue Available
£2.50 uk, £5.00 overseas

www.regulation-ltd.co.uk
e-mail payne@regulation-ltd.co.uk

THE ART OF CONTROL

RUBBER - LEATHER - BONDAGE - TOYS

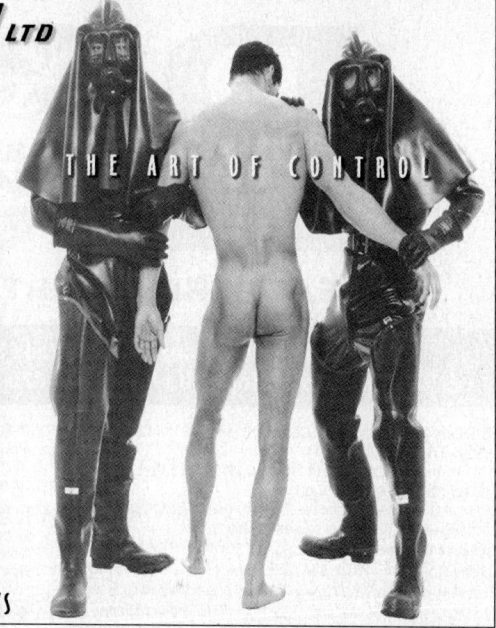

---

75 Great Eastern Street, London EC2A 3RY
Telephone: 0171-739 0292

e-mail: sales@expectations.co.uk
Visit our web site at:
www.expectations.co.uk

Opening times:
Monday - Friday 11-7;
Saturday 11-8; Sunday 12-5

Catalogue now available,
£8 UK, £10 overseas
– refundable on first order

We dare you...
EXPECTATIONS
London's largest leather & rubber store

United Kingdom | London

R25B

LEATHERRUBBERTWISTEDGEAR

RoB of Amsterdam / 24-25 Wells Street / London W1P3FG
www.rob.nl / info@rob.nl / phone: 020-7735.7893 / fax: 020-7637.4510

■ **Sailors** (AC f G MA SA SB SOL VS WH) Mon Tue Thu 12-24, Wed -6, Fri 12-Sun 24 h
574 Commercial Road ✉ E14 7JD (near the "White Swan" U-Limehouse DLR-Line) ☎ 7791 2808
Big sauna on 4 floors in three buildings with cinema lounge, spacious changing rooms, 12 dry heat saunas, 12 steam rooms.

■ **Sauna Bar. The** (B f G MA msg SA SB SOL WH) 12-24 h
29 Endell Street ✉ WC2H 9BA (U-Covent Garden) ☎ 7836 2236
Beautifully decorated health spa in the heart of London, 5 minutes walk from Old Compton St. with one of the biggest whirlpools in Europe. Licensed to sell alcoholic drinks. Rest rooms and friendly staff.

■ **Star Steam** (b DR f G MA OS SA SB SOL VS) 12-24, Sun 12-23 h
38 Lavender Hill ✉ SW11 5RL (BR-Clapham Junction) ☎ 7924 2269
Sauna with terrace frequented by a mixed age clientele.

FITNESS STUDIOS

■ **Centre Point Gym** (b f G MA SA SOL WH WO)
Mon-Fri 12-21:00h, Sat Sun 12-18:00 h
New Oxford Street ✉ WC1 (U-Tottenham Court Road. Under Centre Point.) ☎ 7240 6880

■ **Chelsea Sports Centre** (glm MA PI SOL WO)
Chelsea Manor Street ✉ SW3 (U-Sloane Square) ☎ 7352 6985

TRAVEL by Gianni

THE EXCITING NEW NAME IN GAY TRAVEL

VISITING LONDON? — SUPERB HOLIDAYS FEATURING VIP CLUB ADMISSIONS

WORLDWIDE TRAVEL? — ESCORTED TOURS TO PRAGUE, BARCELONA, CAPETOWN, SYDNEY & RIO - PLUS MANY MORE EXCITING "HOT SPOTS"

LOOKING FOR COMPANY? — OUR UNIQUE "COMPANIONS PROGRAMME" FEATURING GOOD LOOKING YOUNG MEN.

TRAVEL BY GIANNI - IT'S THE ONLY WAY

☎ +44 (0) 20 7370 2116
Or visit us online at www.travelbygianni.com

London — United Kingdom

■ **London Central YMCA** (b f glm MA PI SA) 07-22:30h,
Sa & Su 10-21:00h
112 Great Russel Street ✉ WC1 (U-Tottenham Court Road)
☏ 7637 8131
■ **Paris Gym** (AC CC G MA SA SOL WO) Mo, We & Fr 14-22:00h,
Te & Th 10-22:00h, Sa 10-20:00h, Su 15-20:00h
Arch 73, Goding Street ✉ SE11 5AW (U-Vauxhall. Behind Vauxhall Tavern) ☏ 7735 8989
■ **Soho Athletic Club** (b BF CC f glm MA SOL WO) Mon-Fri 7-22,
Sat 10-22, Sun 12-18 h
10/14 Macklin Street ✉ WC2B 5NF (U-Holborn) ☏ 7242 1290
FAX (0171) 242 1099.

BOOK SHOPS

■ **Books etc.** (CC glm) 9.30-20, Tue 10-20, Sun 12-18 h
120 Charing Cross Road ✉ WC2 (U-Tottenham Court Road)
☏ 7379 6838
Other centrally located branches include
-66 Victoria Street, SW1 ☏ (0171) 931 0677
-16 Whiteley's of Bayswater W2 ☏ (0171) 229 3865
-28 Broadway Shopping Centre, Hammersmith W6
☏ (0181) 746 3912
-Level 2, Royal Festival Hall, South Bank Centre SE1
☏ (0171) 620 0403
■ **Gay's the Word** (CC GLM) Mon-Sat 10-18:30, Sun 14-18:00h
66 Marchmont Street ✉ WC1N 1AB (Russell Square Underground)
☏ 7278 7654
The largest gay&lesbian bookstore in the UK.
■ **Soho Original Bookshop** (see webside for details)
23/25 Leather Lane ✉ EC1

GIFT & PRIDE SHOPS

■ **American Retro** (CC GLM) Mon-Fri 10.30-19.30, Sat 10.15-19 h
35 Old Compton Street ✉ W1V 5PL (U-Piccadilly Circus /Tottenham Court Road) ☏ 7734 3477
Clothes, books, cards, fashion accessories, and great gifts from Alessi and other contemporary designers.
■ **Centaurus** (A CC G) 10-18.30 h, Sun closed
100 Old Street, Clerkenwell ✉ EC1V 9AY (Opposite St. Lukes Church. U-Old Street, exit 6) ☏ 7251 3535
Gay shop & video producers. B&B also available.
■ **Clone Zone** (GLM) Mon-Sat 19-21, Sun 12-18 h
266 Old Brompton Road ✉ SW5 9HR (U-Earls Court. Opposite Colherne Pub) ☏ 7373 0598
Extensive range of magazines, books, videos, clothing, toys, leather, rubber and more.Another store at 46 Old Compton Street, W1.
■ **Obsession** (glm) Mon-Fri 9.30-18.30 h
18 Blomfield Street ✉ EC2M 7AJ ☏ 7638 7491
■ **Prowler Soho** (CC) Mon-Thu 11-22.30, Fri-Sat 11-24,
Sun 12-20 h
3-7 Brewer Street ✉ W1 (behind the bar Village and opposite The Yard) ☏ 7734 4031
(0800) 45 45 66 (mail order service).
Clothes, books, fashion and videos, big gift and music section.

LEATHER & FETISH SHOPS

■ **Expectations** (CC G MA) Mon-Fri 11-19, Sat 11-20, Sun 12-17 h
75 Great Eastern Street ✉ EC2A 3RY (U-Old Street, Exit 3)
☏ 7739 0292
Full made to measure and design service. Good selection of leather, rubber, and army surplus. Catalogue See web.

---

outlêt
est.95

**HOLIDAY ACCOMMODATION
in and around SOHO**

Residential accommodation also available throughout London

- Double Rooms
- Studio Flats
- 1 Bedroom Flats
- 2 Bedroom Flats
- 3 Bedroom Flats

Studio flat for 4 people from
£19.95*pppn

Double rooms for 2 people from
£19.95*pppn

*prices based on one weeks accommodation with maximum occupancy
pppn - per person per night

Two bedroom flat for 4 people from
£23.21*pppn

(W) **www.outlet.co.uk**
VISIT, VIEW AND BOOK your holiday accommodation on our interactive website. See photos, read descriptions and make your reservation on line!

(T) **0207 287 4244**

Information & Advice Centre

Whatever your enquiry - we are here to help and look forward to meeting you!

(E) holidays@outlet.co.uk
(F) 0207 734 2249
(☺) 32 Old Compton Street, Soho, London
(🕐) Mon - Fri 12noon to 6pm, Sat 12noon to 5pm

United Kingdom — London

CENTRAL LONDON BED & BREAKFAST

LARGE COMFORTABLE ENSUITE ROOM SINGLE/DOUBLE/TRIPLE from £35 - £55

Private Penthouse B&B

A RANGE OF ROOMS IN A LUXURY APARTMENT. LARGE TERRACE. EVERYTHING TO MAKE YOUR STAY IN LONDON COMFORTABLE AND SECURE

from £35 - £45 - £55 - £65

Call Mike on
+44 (0)20 7251 3535
Fax: +44 (0)20 7251 3536
e-mail mike@centaurus.co.uk
full details on our website
www.GayAccom.co.uk

■ **Honour** (LJ) Mon-Fri 10.30-19, Sat 11.30-17 h, closed Sun
86 Lower Mash, Waterloo ✉ SE1 7AB (U-Waterloo) ☎ 8450 6877 FAX 450 6899. Email: honour@honour.co.uk.
Homepage: http://www.honour.co.uk. Fetish wear, rubber, leather, toys.

■ **Regulation** (LJ) Mon-Sat 10.30-18.30, Sun 12-17 h
17A St.Albans Place,Angel,Islington ✉ N1 ☎ 7266 0665
Largest collection of rubber and leather wear, plus toys and assecoires for every taste.Catalogue £ 2,50.

■ **RoB London** (CC LJ) Mon-Sat 10.30-18.30, Sun 12-17 h
24 Wells Street ✉ WIT 3PH (U-Oxford Circus) ☎ 7735 7893
Excellent selection of leather, rubber, toys and bondage gear for the serious fetish lovers.

■ **Studio 218**
Bon Marché Centre,241-251 Ferndale Rd. ✉ SW9 8BJ
☎ 77 33 16 20

TRAVEL AND TRANSPORT

■ **D Tours Ltd.** (CC GLM) Mon-Fri 9.30-18 h, closed Sat Sun
59 Rupert Street ✉ WIV 7HN (U-Piccadilly Circus) ☎ 494 4988
🖨 494 4997 📧 info@dtours.co.uk
Tour operator.

■ **Freedom Cars** (GLM) 24 h
2nd Floor, 52 Wardor Street ✉ W1V 3HL ☎ 7734 1313
🖨 74390399 📧 freedom.cars@virgin.net
London's biggest Lesbian and Gay cab company. Also parcel service worldwide.

■ **Man Around** (CC GLM) Mon-Sat 9.30-18.00, Sat 10-14 h
89 Wembley Park Drive, Wembley ✉ HA9 8EH (U-North Wembley)
☎ 8902 7177 🖨 8903 7257

■ **Travel By Gianni Ltd**
Flat 79, 44 Warwick Road ✉ SW5 4PL ☎ 370 2176
📧 www.travelbygianni.com

HOTELS

■ **Accommodation Outlet** (CC GLM MA) Mon-Fri 10-19, Sat 12-17 h
32 Old Compton Street, Soho ✉ W1D 4TP ☎ 7287 4244
🖨 7734 2249 📧 holidays@outlet.co.uk. 🌐 www.outlet.co.uk
Offering a large selection of accommodation on and around Old Compton Street. Cable TV and CD player, dining table, seating and shared kitchen come as standard in most rooms. With photos and extensive description of each property on our interactive website, you can view and reserve accommodation online.

■ **Halifax Hotel** (BF CC G H MA) All hours
65 Philbeach Gardens, Earl's Court ✉ SW5 9EE (U-Earl's Court, Warwick Rd. exit near Earl's Ct. Exhibition Centre.) ☎ 7373 4153
Just a few minutes walk to the local gay scene. All rooms with radio, intercom unit and TV. A few rooms have showers and/or toilets, but in any case there are showers and toilets on each floor. Rates single £ 30-45, double 50-60. Bf incl.Reservation recommended.

■ **Montague on The Gardens** (H)
15 Monatgue Street, Bloomsbury ✉ WC1B 5BT (U-Russell Square, U-Holborn, close to Euston & Kings Cross) ☎ 7637 1001
🖨 7637 2516
Very comfortable and exclusive hotel. All rooms with bath/shower, WC, telephone/Fax, telephone, radio, hair-dryer, TV, suites have minibar, safe and air-condition.

■ **Philbeach Hotel. The** (A B BF CC d F GLM H MA OS S TV) All year 24h
30-31 Philbeach Gardens, Earl's Court ✉ SW5 9EB (U-Earl's Court. Behind Earl's Ct. Exhibition Centre) ☎ 7373 1244 🖨 7244 0149
🌐 www.philbeachhotel.freeserve.co.uk
A well established gay hotel, with a late-opening bar and restaurant, Wilde about Oscar, which has just been refurbished; garden, laundry, TV lounge, 24 hour room service, TV and telephone.

GUEST HOUSES

■ **Centaurus** (GLM)
100 Old Street ✉ EC1V 9AY ☎ 251 3535 🖨 251 3536
📧 mike@centaurus.co.uk 🌐 www.centaurus.co.uk/b&b
A range of rooms in a luxury apartement.

■ **Mentone Hotel** (BF H glm) all year round
54-56 Cartwright Gardens ✉ WC1 H9EL (Bloomsbury,U-Russell Square or Kings Cross/Euston) ☎ 7387 3927 🖨 7388 4671
📧 mentonehotel@compuserve.com 🌐 mentonehotel.com

■ **Noel Cowards Hotel** (B CC GLM H MA msg) 07:30-23:00h
111 Ebury Street, Belgravia ✉ SW1W 9QU (U-Victoria)
☎ 7730 2094 🖨 0171/730 8697 📧 sirncoward@aol.com
🌐 www.members.aol.com/sirncoward/noel.htlm
Former home of Sir Noel Coward. Central gay guest house

■ **Number Seven Guesthouse** (AC BF CC GLM H MA p)
7 Josephine Avenue ✉ SW2 2JU ☎ 86741880 🖨 86716032
📧 hotel@no7.com 🌐 www.no7.com

APARTMENTS

■ **Accommodation Outlet** (CC GLM MA) Mon-Fri 10-19, Sat 12-17 h
32 Old Compton Street, Soho ✉ W1D 4TP ☎ 7287 4244
🖨 7734 2249 📧 holidays@outlet.co.uk. 🌐 www.outlet.co.uk
A large selection of shared & self-contained accommodation for holidays or long-term stays available to lesbians and gays in and around the Old Compton Street. Studio apartments from GBP 80, – per night. View and reserve accommodation online. Ask for other services available such as luggage storage, airport taxis, gay tour guides etc.

■ **Central London Apartments** (AC CC GLM) 9-22 h
(U-Tottenham Court Road) ☎ 0973/167 103 🖨 797 7000
Superior 1 & 2 bedroom fully-furnished self catering flats with fully-

London | United Kingdom

The Philbeach Hotel
london's biggest and most popular gay hotel

35 Rooms

TV and internet Lounge

24 Hour Reception

All Rooms Direct Dial Phones

Tea and Coffee facilities

Now Welcoming
New York Hotel Guests
0044 (0) 20 7244 6884

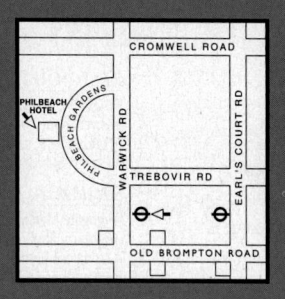

Wilde About Oscar

GARDEN RESTAURANT
Open Mon, Wed-Sat
6pm - 11pm

"Probably the best gay
Restaurant in town."
Time Out

Appleby's Bar

6pm - Late
Ideal For Private Functions

30/31 Philbeach Gardens, Earl's Court, London SW5 9EB
RESERVATIONS 020-7373 1244
Fax: 020-7244 0149   www.philbeachhotel.freeserve.co.uk

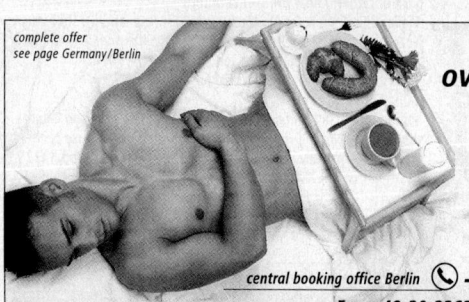

---

complete offer
see page Germany/Berlin

LONDON - from £ 30 -
overnight accomodation service
· about 750 beds · more than 28 cities ·

enjoy
bed & breakfast

central booking office Berlin **+49-30-236 236 10** 4:30-9:00 pm local time
Fax +49-30-23623619 · info@ebab.com · www.ebab.com

Number Seven GuestHouse
BEST UK GAY HOTEL · THE PINK PAPER
7 Josephine Avenue · LONDON SW2 2JU

Tel: +44 20 8674 1880
Fax: +44 20 8671 6032
USA Fax: +1 707 885 2959
Email: hotel@no7.com
Internet: http://www.no7.com

United Kingdom — London ▶ Loughborough - Leicestershire

equipped kitchens, lounge/dining rooms and balconies. Spec incl fitted mirrored wardrobes, dimmer switches, tel/fax lines, video-entryphone and 2 lifts. Rates £ 100-225 per night (min 3 nights). Discounts for 1-3 month stays (TAC 5-20%).

■ **Visit Berlin**
Berlin, Germany (BF G) ☎ +49 30 26 557 803 💻 bnbinBerlin.de
Bed and breakfast in the heart of gay Berlin. Close to the clubs and bars.

GENERAL GROUPS

■ **Albany Trust**
Balham High Rd. ✉ SW17 7AL ☎ 8767-1827
Counselling service.

■ **Croydon Area Gay Society**
PO Box 464 ✉ SE25 4AT
☎ (0181) 771 1814 or ☎ (0181) 651 0292.

■ **Ealing Gay Group** (G MA)
PO Box 130 ✉ W5 1DQ ☎ 8998 6708
💻 www.jkh.dircon.co.uk/egg.html

■ **Kingston and Richmond Area Gay Society (KRAGS)**
PO Box 158 A, Surbiton ✉ KT6 6RS ☎ 8397 4903
(David)

■ **Notting Hill Lesbian & Gay Youth Group** Thu 19.30-22 h
☎ 7229 3266

■ **West London Group for Homosexual Equality**
☎ 7229 0481

FETISH GROUPS

■ **London Blues. The (TLB)** Meets Wed 20 h at STAG,
15 Bressenden Place SW1E 5DD
BM London Blues ✉ WC1N 3XX ☎ 7607 8064
💻 londonblues@geocities.com
💻 www.peterjd.demon.co.uk/tlb/index.html
Member of ECMC.

■ **MSC London**
BM Box MSCL ✉ WC1N 3XX ☎ 7675 0634 📠 7675 0521
💻 msc_london@hotmail.com
💻 www.leatherbear.demon.co.uk/MSC_London
Meeting at "Jubilee Tavern", 79 York Road, Waterloo, SW1 every 3rd Fri 21-22.30 h

■ **Rubber Man's Club** Meets last Fri 21-2 at 37 Wharfdale Road, Kings Cross
BCM RMC ✉ WC1N 3XX
Member of ECMC.

■ **SNC London** Meets 2nd Fr 21:00h at Jubilee Tavern, 79 York Road, Waterloo.
BM SNC ✉ WC1N 3XX 💻 sixtynineclub@btinternet
Member of ECMC.

HEALTH GROUPS

■ **Aids Helpline** Mon-Sun 15-22 h
☎ 7242 1010

■ **Body Positive Gay Men's Group** Mo 18-21:00h
14 Greek Street ✉ W1 (U-Picadilly Circus) ☎ 7287 8010

■ **Gay Men Fighting AIDS** 10:30-16:30h
☎ 7738 6872

■ **Metro Sexual Health** (CC) 0-24 h
10 Harley Street ✉ W1N 1AA (Central London) ☎ 8264 0143
📠 7886 6468 💻 metrosex@aol.com 💻 www.metrosexual.co.uk
Specialist nurse practioner service offering private primary health care for gay men, including HIV testing, STI screening.

HELP WITH PROBLEMS

■ **Alcoholics Support Group** 19.30-22.30
c/o London Friend ☎ 7837 3337

■ **Blenheim Project. The** Mon-Fri 10-17 h
☎ 8960 5599
Advice & counselling for drug addiction.

■ **Jewish Lesbian and Gay Helpline** Mon Thu 19-22 h
BM Jewish Helpline ✉ WC1N 3XX ☎ 7706 3123
💻 www.jglg.org.uk

■ **London Friend** 19.30-22 h (helpline)
86 Caledonian Road ✉ N1 9DN (5 min from Kings Cross Station)
☎ 7837 3337 📠 7278 3119 💻 office@londonfriend.org.uk
💻 www.londonfriend.org.uk
An organization to help gays seeking an alternative to the scene and/or somebody to talk to. Has social groups for different ages, genders and interests+ helpline.

■ **Turning point**
☎ 7837 3337
For men who think they might be gay and want to meet others.

RELIGIOUS GROUPS

■ **QUEST Group for Gay and Lesbian Catholics** Fr 19-22 h & 24h answerphone
PO Box 25 85 ✉ WC1N 3XX ☎ (0808) 808 0234
💻 quest@dircon.co.uk

SWIMMING

- Highgate Men's Pond (U-Hampstead Heath)
- Highbury Pool (U-Highbury and Isllington)
- Oasis Pool (Endell St. WC2, ☎(0171) 831 1804; one indoor and one outdoor pool)
- Tooting Bec Lido (U-Tooting Bec)
- University of London Pool (Malet St.WC1
☎(0171) 636 2818; host to "Out to Swim".

CRUISING

- Hampstead Heath (Activities 24 h, but most popular at WE and in evenings)
- Brompton Cemetry (Busy in the daytime (esp. lunchtime), near the back of cemetery near the crematorium)
- Holland Park Walk (ayor) (Busy after 23 h (esp. at WE). Start your walk the Holland Park Road junction, walk to the middle of the walk near the school, and jump the fence on the park side)
- Russel Square (ayor) (Anytime of night)
- Soho Square (summer)
- Public Toilets (attention should be taken due to police and camera surveillance. Notting Hill Gate / Tottenham Ct. Rd. are busy central favourites, especially at lunchtime and the afternoon rush-hour (17 h))
- Charing Cross British Railways Station at the toilets (on evenings)

Londonderry - Derry ☎ 01504

GAY INFO

■ **Foyle Friend** Mon-Fri 9-17 h
37c Clarendon Street (2nd floor) ☎ (028) 7126 3120

DANCECLUBS

■ **Hennessey's Nightclub** (B D GLM MA) Thu 22-1.30 h
64 Strand Road

■ **Magee University** (B D GLM MA) Alternate Fri
☎ & 📠 26 84 64
Contact Rainbow Project for further information.

BOOK SHOPS

■ **Bookworm**
16 Bishop Street ☎ 26 16 16

Loughborough - Leicestershire ☎ 01509

DANCECLUBS

■ **Rickencampers at Rickenbackers American Bar**
(B d GLM MA STV) Tue 19-23 h
Granby Street ☎ 21 62 20

1114 **SPARTACUS** 2001/2002

Lowestoft - Suffolk ☏ 01502

HOTELS

■ **Royal Court Hotel** (B BF CC f g H MA NU WE) All year
146 London Road South ✉ NR33 0AZ ☏ 56 89 01 📠 56 89 01
📧 royalcourt@hotels.activebooking.com
Fully-licenced hotel and bar open to non-residents. B&B from £ 17.50 p.p.

Luton - Bedfordshire ☏ 01582

BARS

■ **Shirley's Temple** (B glm MA N OS s SNU STV) Mon-Wed 19-23, Thu 16-23, Fri-Sun 12-23 h
1 Liverpool Road ✉ LU1 1RS ☏ 725 491
Popular.

SAUNAS/BATHS

■ **Greenhouse Health Club** (b CC f DR G MA SA SB SOL WH) Su-Thu 11-12, Fri -8, Sat 12-8h
23 Crawley Road ✉ LU1 1HX *(1/4 mile from railway station)*
☏ 48 77 01
Hotels rooms also available. Special events for bears and bears lovers

Lynton - Devon ☏ 01598

BARS

■ **Ye Olde Cottage Inne** (B BF CC F glm H lj MA msg N OS) Mon-Sat 12-23, Sun -22.30 h
Lynbridge ✉ EX35 6NR ☏ 75 35 70
Also room to let. Rates £ 20-25.

HOTELS

■ **Mayfair Hotel. The** (B BF CC glm)
Lynway ✉ EX35 6AY ☏ 75 32 27
Ensuite rooms. Rates £20-25.

Maidenhead - Berkshire ☏ 01628

BARS

■ **Custom House** (B G MA) 11-23, Sun 12-22.30 h
90 Morrbridge Road ☏ 220 42

Maidstone - Kent ☏ 01622

BOOK SHOPS

■ **Books & Mags Shop** (glm)
46 Sandling Road ☏ 66 15 04

Manchester ☏ 0161

For a long time Manchester was seen as a symbol for the rise and fall of the british industry. Today Manchester is back and going strong. Big business, banks, insurance agencies and high-tech industries show a strong presence. Most visible symbol of this process is the congress center G-Mex. But even sightseeing is possible in Manchester: the terribly terribly mancunian soap opera *Coronation Street* is produced in the Granada tv-studios; you can dine excellently in Chinatown and the industrial past can be studied in the *Museum of Science and Industry*. The *Gay Village* is located around *Canal Street*. Manchesters gay scene is the best and most diverse next to London. The colourful hustle and bustle in the summer months is quite astonishing.

Lange galt Manchester als eines der Symbole für den Aufstieg und Fall der britischen Industrie. Heute ist Manchester wieder da und obenauf.
Die Industrie hat mit Banken und Versicherungen, mit Hi-Tech (z.B. Siemens oder IBM) wieder Tritt gefasst. Sichtbarstes Symbol ist das Kongreßzentrum G-Mex.
Selbst Sightseeing ist in Manchester möglich: In den Granada TV Studios wird die ur-britische Soap *Coronation Street* gedreht, in *Chinatown* lässt es sich bestens speisen und die industrielle Vergangenheit betrachtet man im *Museum of Science and Industry*.
Das *Gay Village* der Stadt hat sich rund um die *Canal Street* gebildet. Die Szene Manchesters ist nach der Londoner die beste und vielfältigste. Gerade in den Sommermonaten ist das bunte Treiben hier ganz erstaunlich.

Manchester a longtemps symbolisé la grandeur et décadence de l'industrie britannique. Aujourd'hui, Manchester s'est refait une sacrée santé et ce, grâce aux banques, aux compagnies d'assurances et aux industries high-tech (Siemens ou IBM). Le bâtiment symbole de ce renouveau est le centre de congrès G-Mex. Côté tourisme, allez voir les studios de TV Granada où on tourne le sempiternel soap opera "Coronation Street". Allez aussi faire un tour à "Chinatown" et au "Museum of Science and Industry". Le quartier autour de "Canal Street" est aujourd'hui le bastion gai de Manchester qui est, après Londres, la deuxième ville gaie du pays. Profitez des mois d'été pour visiter Manchester!

Durante mucho tiempo Manchester fue el símbolo del auge y de la caida de la industria britanica. Pero hoy en día la ciudad se ha recuperado y ocupa de nuevo un puesto líder en el país. Aquí se establecieron bancos, compañias de seguro y industrias de alta tecnología (como Siemens o IBM). El simbolo visible de este progreso es el centro de congresos G-Mex. Pero también desde el punto de vista turistico Manchester tiene mucho que ofrecer: En los estudios de televisión Granda se realiza el rodaje de la famosa telenovela inglesa *Coronation Street*; en *China Town* se come estupendamente y el *Museum of Science and Industry*. El *Gay Village* de la ciudad se concentra en los alrededores de la *Canal Street*. El ambiente de Manchester es después de Londres uno de los mejores y de los más varidos del país. Especialmente durante los meses de verano, la marcha aquí es sorprendente.

Per molto tempo Manchester è stata un simbolo dell'ascesa e della decadenza dell'industria britannica. Oggi questa città è di nuovo a galla: l'industria si è ripresa con l'alta tecnologia (Siemens e IBM), le banche e le assicurazioni. Il centro-congressi G-Mex ne è il simbolo più palese. Manchester è interessante anche come città turistica: negli studi Granada si gira il mitico teleromanzo *Coronation street*, a *Chinatown* vi sono molti ristoranti e nel *Museum of Science and Industry* si può ammirare il passato industriale della città. Il *gay village* si è creato intorno alla *Canal street*. L'ambiente gay di Manchester è, prescindendo da quello di Londra, il migliore ed il più vario di tutta l'isola britannica; durante i mesi estivi è colorato più che mai.

GAY INFO

■ **Manchester Gay Centre** (b GLM)
49-51 Sydney Street, All Saints *(next to Mandella Building)*
☏ 274 3990 📠 274 3990
Free accommodation service. Provides meeting places for various specialist groups. Further information and details
☏ 274 3999.

United Kingdom Manchester

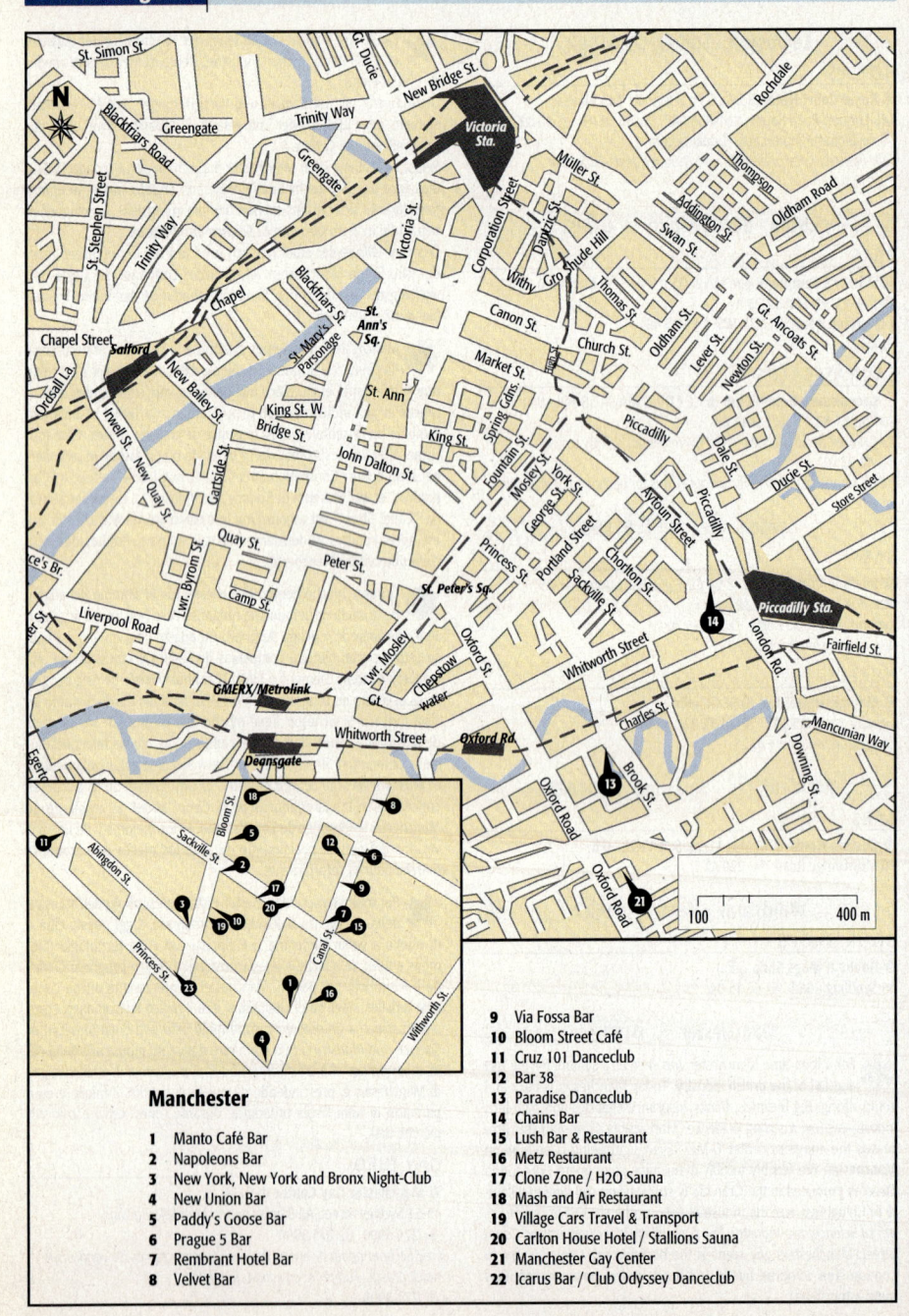

Manchester

1. Manto Café Bar
2. Napoleons Bar
3. New York, New York and Bronx Night-Club
4. New Union Bar
5. Paddy's Goose Bar
6. Prague 5 Bar
7. Rembrant Hotel Bar
8. Velvet Bar
9. Via Fossa Bar
10. Bloom Street Café
11. Cruz 101 Danceclub
12. Bar 38
13. Paradise Danceclub
14. Chains Bar
15. Lush Bar & Restaurant
16. Metz Restaurant
17. Clone Zone / H2O Sauna
18. Mash and Air Restaurant
19. Village Cars Travel & Transport
20. Carlton House Hotel / Stallions Sauna
21. Manchester Gay Center
22. Icarus Bar / Club Odyssey Danceclub

Manchester — United Kingdom

■ **Manchester Switchboard** 16-22 h
PO Box 153 ✉ M60 1LP ☎ 274 3999

TOURIST INFO

■ **Tourist Information Centre**
Town Hall Extension, Lloyd Street ✉ M6O 2LA ☎ 234 3157
📠 236 99 00

BARS

■ **Bar Confidential** (AC B G LJ MA R)
Whitworth Street ✉ M1 5WV (near "Chains") ☎ 950 5777
MSC meets Fr. Cruise Bar

■ **Bar 38** (AC B BF CC d E F GLM MA S) 11-24, Fri Sat -2.30,
Sun -22.30 h
38 Canal Street

■ **Chains** (B D f G LJ N MA SNU WE) Mon, Tue, Thu 22-02:00h,
Fri 22-02:30h, Sat -03:00h. Sun closed
4-6 Whitworth Street ✉ M1 3QW (near Picadilly Railway Station)
☎ 236 0335
Host to specialist parties.

■ **Company** (AC B F G LJ MA P) Mon-Sat 16-2, Sun 15-22.00 h.
28 Richmond Street ✉ M1 3NB (Opposite Blue Restaurant)
☎ 237 9329
1st Sun MSC meeting, 3rd Sun bears.

■ **Dickens** (B GLM N TV) Mon-Sat 22-2 h
74a Oldham Street ☎ 236 4886

■ **Icarus** (! A AC B CC d F GLM MA s) Mon-Wed 12-24, Thu 12-2 h
100 Bloom Street ☎ 236 39 95
Café and bar with live DJs.

■ **Manto** (! A AC B CC d F GLM MA s) 12-23, Sun 11-22.30,
Fri-Sat also 2.30-6 h (chill-out)
46 Canal Street ✉ M1 3WD ☎ 236 2667

■ **Napoleons** (B D G MA MG TV) 21-2 h, closed Sun
35 Bloom Street / Sackville Street ✉ M1 3LY ☎ 236 8800

■ **New Union** (AC B CC D f GLM MG OS SNU STV TV WE YG)
Mon-Wed 11-1, Thu-Sat 11-2, Sun 12-22.30 h
111 Princess Street ☎ 228 1492

■ **New York, New York and Bronx Night-Club** (AC B D f GLM lj
MA SNU STV TV) 12-2, Sun 12-23 h, Night Club 20-bar closing.
98 Bloom Street ☎ 236 6556

■ **Paddy's Goose** (B glm MG) 12-23, Sun 12-22.30 h
29 Bloom Street (Behind coach station) ☎ 236 1246

■ **Prague** (A AC B CC D F GLM ME YG) 11-24 h
Canal Street ✉ M1 3HY (at the corner of Canal/Chorlton St.)
☎ 236 9033

■ **Rembrandt Hotel Bar** (B CC F G H LJ MA OS) Mon-Wed 11-23,
Thu-Sat -1, Sun 12-22.30 h
33 Sackville Street (city centre, in the gay village) ☎ 236 1311

■ **Velvet** (B BF CC F GLM MA OS) 11-23 h
2 Canal Street ✉ M1 3DE ☎ 236 9003

■ **Via Fossa** (AC B CC d E F GLM MA S) Mon-Wed 11-24, Thu -1,
Fri-Sat 11-2, Sun 11-22.30 h
28-30 Canal Street ✉ M1 3EZ ☎ 236 8132

CAFES

■ **Bloom Street Café** (b f GLM MA) Mon-Sat 9-18 h
39 Bloom Street ✉ M1 3LY ☎ 236 3433

■ **Café Hollywood** (F GLM MA) Mon-Sun 0-24 h
100 Bloom Street ✉ M1 6DD ☎ 236 6151
The exclusively gay hotel "The Hollywood Heights Hotel" will open in
April on the same premises.

DANCECLUBS

■ **Club Odyssey** (AC B D f GLM YG) Tu & Sa 22-02:00h
100 Bloom Street ☎ 236 3995

■ **Cruz 101** (AC D f G MA P YG) Mo-Sa 22-2 h. Closed Tu & Su
101 Princess Street ✉ M1 6DD (Train Station-Piccadilly)
☎ 237 1554

■ **Paradise Factory. The** (AC B D F GLM YG) Fri 22-2.30, Sat 22-3 h
112-116 Paradise Street ✉ M1 7EN (Corner of Charles Street)
☎ 273 5422

RESTAURANTS

■ **Lush Bar & Restaurant** (AC B CC F glm MA) Sun 12-22.30,
Mon-Sat 12-23 h
27 Sackville Street ✉ M1 3LZ ☎ 288 7800
Californian and mediterranean cuisine.

■ **Mash and Air** (B F glm)
Canal Street/Chorlton Street ☎ 661 6161
Expensive and highly select plush bar and restaurant. Formal dress for
dining.

■ **Metz** (B CC F GLM MA OS) Mon-Thu 12-23, Fri-Sat -24, Sun-22.30 h
Amazon House, 3 Brazil Street ✉ M1 3PJ ☎ 237 9852

SHOWS

■ **Hollywood Showbar** (AC B D F GLM MA P R S SNU TV)
Mon-Sun 17-2 h
100 Bloom Street ✉ M1 6DD ☎ 236 6151
Leisure complex with bars and restaurants. Members only. An exclusively gay hotel to open here soon.

SAUNAS/BATHS

■ **Basement.The Sauna Complex** (B f G MA pi SA SB VS WH WO)
24 h, daily
18 Tariff Street MCR ☎ 237 9996

■ **Eurosauna** (! AC B D f G MA SA SB VS) 13-21 h
202 Hill Lane, Higher Blackley ✉ M9 6RG (off Victoria Avenue)
☎ 740 5152
One of the oldest gay saunas in the UK - established in 1973.

■ **H2O Zone** (b cc DR f G SA SB SOL VS WH) 12-23, Fri Sat -7,
Sun -22 h
36-38 Sackville Street ✉ M1 3WA ☎ 236 3876
Numerous specials and parties organised. 1st Sat of the month Cocks &
Jocks night.

■ **Nero's Roman Spa** (AC b CC DR F G MA SA SB SNU SOL VS WH
WO) 12-24
Whitelegg Street, Bury ☎ 764 2576
Sauna with maze and one of the largest steam bath in the UK.

BOOK SHOPS

■ **Libertas** (AC CC GLM) 11-19, Sat 12-18, Sun 12-16 h
105-107 Princess St.

GIFT & PRIDE SHOPS

■ **Clone Zone** (GLM) Mo-Th 11-22:00h Fr & Sa 11-23:00h,
Su 13-19:00h
36-38 Sackville Street ✉ M1 ☎ 236 1398
An extensive range of magazines, books, videos, clothing, leather, rubber, toys and more.

TRAVEL AND TRANSPORT

■ **Village Cars** 24 h
Bloom Street ☎ 237 3383
Very gay friendly taxi service, licensed by Manchester City Council, offering a reliable and competitive service (no extra charge after midnight).

SPARTACUS 2001/2002 | 1117

United Kingdom — Manchester ▶ Middlesbrough - Cleveland

HOTELS

■ **Carlton House Hotel** (B BF CC GLM)
153 Upper Chorlton Road, Whalley Range ✉ M16 7SH
☎ 881 4635
Comfortable hotel approximately 2 km south of the city centre. Rates: Single £ 25, Double £ 40 incl. bf. En suite rooms are also available for £ 45. Includes Stallions Sauna, discount for hotel guests.
■ **Merchants** (B BF g)
1 Back Piccadilly ☎ 236 2939
Rates: Single £ 15, Double £ 25.
■ **Monroes** (B BF F g H)
38 London Road *(opposite Main Station)* ☎ 236 0564
Hotel on top of a pub which also attracts a certain number of gay customers. Rates: Single £ 18, Double £ 30 incl. bf.
■ **New Union Hotel. The** (b BF CC f GLM H MA)
111 Princess Street ✉ M1 6JB ☎ 228 1492
This hotel with its popular bar, has been renovated and extended providing quality accommodation at a reasonable price. Rates: Single from £ 35, Double £ 45.

APARTMENTS

■ **Clone Zone Apartments** (GLM)
39 Bloom Street ✉ M1 3LY ☎ 236 1398
Modern accomodation equipped with colour T.V., telephone, tea / coffee making facilities and a shared bathroom. Situated in the heart of the Gay Village. Rates frome £ 35.
■ **Visit Berlin** (BF G)
Berlin, Germany ☎ +49 30 26 577 803 📧 bnbinBerlin@web.de
Bed and breakfast in the heart of gay Berlin. Close to the clubs and bars.

GENERAL GROUPS

■ **Gay Manchester Professionals** 1st Thu
☎ 474 7585
Social/dining group for professional people in Manchester.
■ **Long Yang Club (Gay Western & Oriental friends)**
PO Box 153 ✉ M60 1LP ☎ 366 7655
(David)
■ **Manchester Deaf Gay Group "Triangle"**
PO Box 153 ✉ M60 1LP

FETISH GROUPS

■ **Manchester Super Chain MSC** Meet at Company Bar, Richmond Street - 1st Su 20:30h and 3rd Fr 22:00h
PO Box 104 ✉ M60 1GY
📧 mscmsc@dircon.co.uk
📧 www.users.dircon.co.uk/~mscmsc. *Member of ECMC.*

HEALTH GROUPS

■ **Body Positive Group N W** Tue/Thu 19-22 h
BP Center, 3rd Floor, Fairways House, 18 Tariff St. ✉ M1 2EP
☎ 237 9717
■ **Healthy Gay Manchester**
Ducie House, 37 Ducie St. ✉ M1 2JW ☎ 236 7600
📠 236 7611. *Gay men's health project. Regular benefit parties at Chains.*
■ **Manchester Royal Infirmary**
Oxford Road ☎ 276 5200
STD and HIV testing.

RELIGIOUS GROUPS

■ **MCC** Meets Sun 16.45, Tue 13.05 h at St. Peter's House, Oxford Road
PO Box 153 ✉ M60 ILP ☎ 273 1567 📧 revandy@easynet.co.uk
📧 www.easyweb.easynet.co.uk/~revandy
(Rev Andy Braunston)
■ **Quest L&G Catholic Group**
☎ 976 1210 *(Ian)*

CRUISING

- Piccadilly Gardens (Market Street side)
- Piccadilly Lock (Night AYOR. Go under the bridge at Rochdale Canal, entrance via Dale Street, a small stone doorway leading to a stairway)
- Rhodes Lodges (A 567 at Middleton)
Near Wilmslow:
- Styal Country Park (ayor) (bushes left and right of the river near the small bridge. Be discreet)
- Readsmear Lake (between Congleton and Alderney, after 350 m picnic area to the left, on the paths. Be discreet)
Near Handforth:
- Alderley Edge (Take a road off A34, turn right, Wizard Restaurant, woods on the right)
- V.I.P. cinema (Oxford Rd.) straight porno cinema with very interesting possibilities in back row seats

Mansfield - Nottinghamshire ☎ 01623

SAUNAS/BATHS

■ **Zeus @ 71** (DR F G MA SA SB SOL VS WH) 12-24, Fri -2 h
71 Ratcliffe Gate ✉ NG18 2JB *(10 min from train station, near Mansfield Brewery)* ☎ 42 22 57
Sauna located in a converted coaching inn dating back to 1677 which has kept a lot of old surprising features that make the place interesting.

GENERAL GROUPS

■ **Under 26 L&G Group** Youth Line Mo 19-20:00h
The Folk House, Westfield Lane ☎ 428459

HEALTH GROUPS

■ **MAPS (Mansfield & Ashfield Positive Support Group)**
PO Box 3 ✉ NG16 1QT ☎ 64 23 04
(Sarah) or ☎ 225 15 ext 4552 *(Shaun)*

Margate/Ramsgate - Kent ☎ 01843

BARS

■ **New Inn** (B d g s) Mon-Sat 17.30-23 h. Disco Wed Sat
New Street ☎ 22 37 99

SEX SHOPS/BLUE MOVIES

■ **Pillow Talk** (g) Mo-Sa 10-18h
13 Marine Drive ☎ 29 40 69
See webside for further information.

Middlesbrough - Cleveland ☎ 01642

BARS

■ **Cassidy's Club** (B D f G) 11-23:00h Su 12.-22:30h
Grange Road ☎ 654411

DANCECLUBS

■ **Strings** (B D GLM) Th & Fr 22-02:00h, Sa 21-02:00h
47a Linthorpe Road ☎ 231 353

GENERAL GROUPS

■ **Friend** Meets Tue & Fri 19.30-21.30, drop-in 2nd Sat 15-17 h
St. Mary's Centre, Corporation Road ☎ 24 88 88
(Minicom)
■ **University of Teeside LGB Group**
c/o Students Union, Borough Rd. ✉ TS1 3BA ☎ 34 22 34
FAX 34 22 41

Middlesbrough - Cleveland ▶ Northampton - Northamptonshire — United Kingdom

HEALTH GROUPS
- **Cleveland AIDS Support (CAS)**
  ☎ 25 45 98

RELIGIOUS GROUPS
- **Metropolitan Community Church** Meets 1st Sun 15 h at St. Mary's Centre
  PO Box 18, St. Mary's Centre, Corporation Road

Milton Keynes - Buckinghamshire ☎ 01908

GAY INFO
- **Milton Keynes Lesbian & Gay Switchboard** Th 19:30-21:30h
  PO Box 153, Dawson Road ✉ MK1 3AA ☎ 66 62 26

Newcastle-upon-Tyne - Tyne & Wear ☎ 0191

BARS
- **Barking Dog** (B F glm MA S STV) Tue-Sat 11-23, Sun 12-22.30, Upstairs from 20 h
  Marlborough Crescent ✉ NE1 4EE (Central Station) ☎ 221 0775
- **Heavens Above** (B GLM YG) Mon-Thu 20-23, Fri-Sat 19.30-23, Sun 20-22.30 h
  2 Scotswood Road ✉ NE4 7JH (Above Courtyard) ☎ 261 0488
- **Rockies** (B d GLM MA OS S SNU STV) 19.30-23, Sun -22.30 h
  78 Scotswood Road ✉ NE4 7JH (at Newcastle end of Redheugh Bridge) ☎ 232 6536
- **Village. The** (B D GLM)
  Sunderland Street ☎ 261 8874
- **Yard. The** (B GLM MA N S STV) Mon-Sat 13-23, Sun- 22.30 h
  78 Scotswood Road ✉ NE4 7JB (Central Station) ☎ 2322 037

DANCECLUBS
- **Powerhouse. The** (B D f GLM MA S) Mon-Sat 22-2, Tue-Wed -1 h
  Waterloo Street ✉ NE1 4DD (Central Station) ☎ 261 8874
- **Rock' N ' Doris at Live Theatre** (B D GLM s YG)
  C/O Pink Planet Promotions, P.O. Box 58, Heaton ✉ NE6 5YS
- **Rockshots 2** (AC B D f glm MA N) Wed 23-2.30 (GLM), Thu 22-2.30 Fri&Sat-3 h
  Alfred Wilson House, Waterloo Street ✉ NE 1 4DE (Central Station / Metro station) ☎ 232 9648

SAUNAS/BATHS
- **Blue Corner** (AC b DR f G MA P SA SB SOL VS) 11-22, Sun 13-20 h
  164b Heaton Park Road, Heaton ✉ NE6 5AP (near Heaton Library)
  ☎ 240 01 22
  Relaxed, friendly atmosphere sauna near the city centre.

HOTELS
- **Cheviot View** (B BF CC GLM)
  194 Station Road, Wallsend ✉ E28 8RD ☎ 230 3662
  📱 07788 197011
  Gay and lesbian guest-house. All rooms have TV and tea / coffee making facilities.
- **Hedgefield House** (BF CC f GLM H MA msg OS) All year
  Stella Road, Blaydon-upon-Tyne ✉ NE21 4LR ☎ 413 73 73
  📠 413 73 73
  Beautiful country hotel in an old Georgian Residence close to Newcastle. All rooms are comfortably furnished. Rates standard room £ 42, kingsize room 50 and rooms with private bathroom or en-suite 60 incl. cont. bf.

GENERAL GROUPS
- **MESMAC North-East** Mon-Fri 10-17 h
  3rd floor, 11 Nelson Street ✉ NE1 5AN ☎ 233 1333 ☎ 233 2112 (textphone) 📠 233 1551 ✉ all@mesmacnortheast.com
  www.mesmacnortheast.com
  Works with groups and individuals to increase positive choices arouund safer sex, and to offer general support to gay and bisexual men.
- **Newcastle University Lesbian, Gay, & Bisexual Soc.**
  c/o Porters Lodge, Union Building, Newcastle University
  ☎ 232 8402
  ext. 136 (ask for LGB Officer)
- **Tyneside Young Gay & Bisexual Men's Group** Tue 19.15-21 h
  ☎ 233 1333
  (Lee/Chris)
- **University of Northumbria Globe** Meets Thu 19.50 (term-time)
  Porter's Lodge, Students' Union, Sandyford Road ☎ 227 4757

HEALTH GROUPS
- **BPNE**
  ☎ 232 6411 ☎ 221 2277 (Helpline)
  Confidential service offering information, advice and support on all aspects of HIV infection to people either infected or affected by HIV / AIDS.

CRUISING
- **Copthorne Gardens** (OG) (Close to Central Station; the cruisiest area is near the entrance on the same side as the Copthorne Hotel.)

Newport - Gwent ☎ 01633

BARS
- **Log Box. The** (B glm)
  Carpenter's Lane, High Street (Side entrance to Hall of Fame)
  ☎ 26 63 54
  Back bar

DANCECLUBS
- **Cotton Club** (B D G) 2nd Tue/month
  Cumbrian Road ☎ 252 973
  Gwent AIDS Support Group disco

SAUNAS/BATHS
- ■ **Greenhouse Health Club** (b CC DR F G MA SA SB SOL WH WO) 11-23, Fri -2, Sat -2.30, Sun 13-23 h
  24 Church Street ✉ NP9 2BY (Junction 27 on M4) ☎ 22 11 72
  Very crowded on week-ends.

HEALTH GROUPS
- **Gwent Aids Helpline** Wed evening
  ☎ 223 456

Newton Abbot - Devon ☎ 01647

HOTELS
- **White Hart Hotel** (B BF E F H MA NG) 7-0 h
  The Square, Moretonhampstead ✉ TQ13 8NF ☎ 44 04 06
  Rates for a double £ 65 and for a single £ 43 incl. bf.

Northampton - Northhamptonshire ☎ 01604

GAY INFO
- **Gay Line c/o Northamptonshire Lesbian & Gay Alliance**
  Tue 19-22:00 h
  1st floor, Charles House, 61-69 Derngate ✉ NN1 1UU ☎ 635 975
  Call for details of LGB group meetings.

SPARTACUS 2001/2002 | 1119

United Kingdom Nottingham - Nottinghamshire ▶ Oxford

BARS
■ **K2** (B D e GLM MA) Disco Fr & Sa, Karaoke on Su.
39 Sheep Street ✉ NN1 2NE ☎ 228 22

Norwich - Norfolk ☎ 01603

GAY INFO
■ **Norwich Gayline** Mon 20-22 h (term time only)
☎ 59 25 05

BARS
■ **Lord Raglan, The** (AC B BF f G H MA N OS s TV) 12-14, 19-23, Sun 12-15, 19-22.30 h
30 Bishop Bridge Road ✉ NR1 3ET *(Close to Norwich Station)*
☎ 62 33 04
B&B available.
■ **Lord Rosebery** (B gLM S) Mon-Thu 19-23, Fri 12-14, 19-23, Sat 12-15, 19-23, Sun 12-22.30 h
94 Rosebery Road ☎ 48 61 61
■ **Woolpack** (B glm MA) 11-23, Sun 12-22.30 h
Muspole Street ☎ 61 11 39

DANCECLUBS
■ **Jigsaw Club at The Talk** (B D gLM MA) Fri 22-2 h
Oak Street ☎ 660 220
■ **Loft Nightclub, The** (AC B D glm lj MA s STV) Mon-Sat 21-2 h (Thu+Sat gay).
80 Rose Lane ✉ NR1 1PT ☎ 62 35 59

RESTAURANTS
■ **Bailey's Bistro** (B F glm) Mon-Sat 12-14.30, 17.30-?, Sun 19-? h
6 Pottergate *(City centre)* ☎ 62 67 63

BOOK SHOPS
■ **Bookmark** (CC) 9.30-17.30, Sat 9-17 h, cosed Sun
83 Unthank Road ✉ NR2 2PE ☎ 76 28 55
■ **Green City Central** (glm) Tue-Sat 10-17 h
42-46 Bethel Street ☎ 631007
Shop & information center inc. gay publications

HEALTH GROUPS
■ **AIDS Helpline** Tu & Th 20-22:00h, Sa 10-13:00h
☎ 61 58 16

Nottingham - Nottinghamshire ☎ 0115

GAY INFO
■ **Nottingham L & G Switchboard** Mon-Fri 19-22 h
7 Mansfield Road ✉ NG1 3FB ☎ 934 8485

BARS
■ **Admiral Duncan** (AC B CC d f GLM MA SNU STV)
Mon-Sat 21-24 h, closed Sun
74 Lower Parliament Street ✉ NG1 1EH ☎ 950 2727
■ **Forresters Inn** (AC B d f GLM MA N OS) 11-15:30h, 17:30-23:00h Su 11-23:00h
183 Huntingdon Street NG1 3NL ☎ 941 96 79
■ **The Central** (B f G) 11-15, 17.30-23, Sun 12-14, 19-22.30 h
Huntingdon Street ☎ 950 53 23
■ **The Mill** (B GLM MA) 11:30-16:00h, 19:-24:00h Su 12-22:30h
Woodpack Road ✉ NG 1 1 QA ☎ 964 4341

DANCECLUBS
■ **Revolution at Ocean** (B D GLM) 1st Mon 21-2 h

Greyfriar Gate ☎ 958 05 55

BOOK SHOPS
■ **Soho Books** (G)
147 Radford Road ☎ 978 35 67

GENERAL GROUPS
■ **Eastern Rainbow (Deaf lesbian & gay group)**
☎ 927 97 04
(Kevin-minicom).

HELP WITH PROBLEMS
■ **GAI Project** Mon-Fri 9-17 h
Health Shop, Broad Street ✉ NG1 3AL ☎ 947 54 14
🖨 955 49 90
Sexual health drop-in which offers free & confidental sexual health services, including condoms, lubricant, HIV testing& needle exchange.
■ **The Chameleon Group** Thu 20-23 h
Wollaton Grange Community Centre, Tremayne Road ✉ NG8 4HQ
☎ (01159) 289 479 *(during group hours only)* 🖨 953 8485
Self help group for TV/TS.

RELIGIOUS GROUPS
■ **Lesbian and Gay Christian Movement**
☎ 925 55 14
(Paul)

Oldham - Greater Manchester ☎ 0161

GAY INFO
■ **Oldham & Rochdale Switchboard** Tue 17-19 h
☎ 678 94 48

BARS
■ **Iguana** (B glm) Mo-Sa 22-02:00h
171 Union Street, Rhodes Bank ☎ 652 56 62

SAUNAS/BATHS
■ **Pennine** (b DR F G MG SA SB SOL) Sat Sun 13-21, Mon -20, Wed 12-21 h
96 Rochdale Road, Shaw ✉ OL2 7SB *(Junction 21, 62, next to bakery)* ☎ 01706/ 84 20 00
Long established sauna frequented by a mature crowd. Home-made food available.

Ormskirk - Lancashire ☎ 01772

HEALTH GROUPS
■ **Heal**
PO Box 26 ✉ L39 2WE ☎ 55 55 25
Support service for people living with HIV/Aids.

Oxford ☎ 01865

GAY INFO
■ **L&G Centre** (G) Thu 20-23, (L) Fri 20-1 (D), Sat 12-16, 21-2 (B D GLM), Sun 19.30-22.30 h
North Gate Hall, St. Michale's Street ☎ 20 00 30

BARS
■ **Jolly Farmers, The** (B CC F GLM MA OS s) 12-23 h, Sun 12-22.30 h
20 Paradise Street ✉ OX1 1LD *(Near Westgate Centre)* ☎ 79 37 59
■ **Royal Blenheim** (B CC f GLM MA N) 12-23, Sun -22.30 h
13 St. Ebbes ✉ OX1 1PT ☎ 72 64 84

1120 *SPARTACUS* 2001/2002

Oxford

BOOK SHOPS
■ **Inner Bookshop** (glm) Mon-Sat 10-17.30 h
111 Magdalen Road ✉ OX4 1RQ ☎ 24 53 01

GENERAL GROUPS
■ **Gay Oxford** (G MA N)
PO Box 144 ✉ OX1 1SX ☎ (01869) 34 09 92
🖷 (01869) 34 09 92 📧 gayoxford@lineone.net
A group of gay men to support the gay community.
■ **LGB Professionals Network**
c/o Oxford Health Promotion ☎ 226042

HELP WITH PROBLEMS
■ **Oxford Friend** Tue Wed Fri 19-21 h
c/o Inner Bookshop, 111 Magdalen Street Road ✉ OX4 1RQ
☎ 72 68 93

RELIGIOUS GROUPS
■ **MCC Oxford**
☎ 714 838

SPORT GROUPS
■ **Swimout** Meets: Mon 21 h at Marston Ferry Pool
☎ 24 33 89

CRUISING
-Angel Meadow (off St. Clements, Oxford, access via rear of car park, signposted)
-Hinksey Park (off Abingdon Road)

Paisley - Strathclyde ☎ 0141

GENERAL GROUPS
■ **Paisley Forum** 2nd & 4th Sun 20.30-22.30 h
Workshop Room, Paisley Arts Centre, New Street ☎ 887 26 49
(Sandra)

Penmaenmawr - Gwynedd ☎ 01492

HOTELS
■ **Jack's Health Hydro** (B BF CC DR F G H MA N NU OS P SA SB SOL WE WH WO) 12.30-22.30 h
Beach Road ✉ LL34 4AY *(Off A55/400m from Railway Station)*
☎ 622 878 🖷 622 875 📧 terry@gaypennanthall.co.uk
🌐 www.gaypennanthall.co.uk
11 bedrooms from £24 (incl. bf.) £7 sauna fee (9 visitor fee). Restaurant with full menu, bar open to non-residents. Coastal/Mountain area with many attractions.
■ **Pennant Hall** (B BF CC d F GLM H MA OS P S SA SB SOL VS WH)
Beach Road ✉ LL34 6AY ☎ 622878 🖷 622875
🌐 www.gaypennanthall.co.uk
Exclusively gay country hotel.

Penzance - Cornwall ☎ 01736

HOTELS
■ **Glencree Hotel** (b CC BF F glm H)
2 Mennaye Road ✉ TR18 4NG ☎ 362 026 🖷 362 026

Peterborough - Cambridgeshire ☎ 01733

BARS
■ **Bridge. The** (B d GLM MA) 19-23:00h Closed on Tu.
London Road ☎ 31 21 92

Plymouth - Devon ☎ 01752

BARS
■ **Clarence** (B glm) 11-23, Sun 12-22.30 h
31 Clarence Place, Stonehouse ☎ 60 38 27
■ **Swallow. The** (B f GLM MA N) 11-23, Sun 12-22.30 h
59 Breton Side ☎ 225 17 60

DANCECLUBS
■ **Zeros Nightclub** (B D f GLM MA G) Mon-Sat 21-2, Sun 20-24 h, closed Tue
24 Lockyer Street ☎ 66 23 46

BOOK SHOPS
■ **In Other Words Ltd.** (CC glm) Mon-Fri 9-18, Sat- 17.30 h
64 Mutley Plain ✉ PL4 6LF ☎ 66 38 89
Large range of gay & lesbian books, magazines, rainbow&pide merchandise, notice board,also mailorder. Ask for details about Plymouth Pride Forum.

PRIVATE ACCOMMODATION
■ **Twoways B&B** (BF G H MA) all yer round except 14.12-4.1.
234 Saltash Road, Keyham ✉ PL2 2BB *(2 miles from the city, bus and train station nearby)* ☎ 56 95 04
📧 petetwowaysbandb@talk21.com
Two double rooms and one twin room in a Victorian house. Own key, TV and AC. Small and cosy.

GENERAL GROUPS
■ **Allfellas** Wed 19.30 h
☎ 556 192
Social group.

HEALTH GROUPS
■ **Eddystone Group** Mon Wed Fri 19-21, Tue Thu 10-1 h
☎ 25 16 66
Support group for people with HIV/AIDS.

Portsmouth - Hampshire ☎ 023

BARS
■ **Martha`s** (AC B CC D F GLM MA SNU STV) Bar 11-23, Sun 12-22.30, Disco Mon-Sat 22-2 h
227 Commercial Road ✉ PO1 4BJ *(Town centre)*
☎ 9285 29 51
■ **Old Vic** (B F GLM MA) 11-23, Sun 12-22.30 h
104 St. Paul's Road, Southsea PO5 4AQ ☎ 92297013

DANCECLUBS
■ **1 Above**
227 Commercial Road

SAUNAS/BATHS
■ **Tropics** (f G MA OS SA SB SOL VS) Mon-Sat 12-22 h, closed Sunday and bank holidays
2 Market Way ✉ PO1 4BX *(central, 5 min from railway station)*
☎ 92 29 61 00
Sauna on three floors with a roof garden open from May to Oct. Towels and robes supplied.

HEALTH GROUPS
■ **Gay Men`s Health Project** Mon-Fri 10-17:00h
☎ 9265 50 77

United Kingdom | Preston - Lancashire ▶ Sheffield - South Yorkshire

Preston - Lancashire ☎ 01772

BARS
■ **Fruit Machine. The** (B D f GLM)
28 Croft Street *(Off Marsh Lane)*
■ **Oblivion** (b GLM MA STV) 20-23:00h
12-14 Grimshaw Street

RESTAURANTS
■ **Cannons Restaurant** (B F glm) Tue-Sat 11-14, 19-23 h
37 Cannon Street ☎ 561 741

HEALTH GROUPS
■ **Community AIDS Support Team**
PO Box 17 ✉ PR1 4UG

Reading - Berkshire

BARS
■ **Wynford Arms. The** (B GLM) Mon-Fri 19.30-23, Sat 12-23, Sun -22.30 h
110 Kings Road ✉ RG1 3BY ☎ 0118 958 9814

GENERAL GROUPS
■ **Reach Out**
PO Box 75 ✉ RG1 7DU ☎ 0118 959 7276
Social group for gay youths.

HELP WITH PROBLEMS
■ **Reading Helpline/Friend** Tue Wed Fri 19.30-21.30 h
PO Box 75 ✉ RG1 7DU ☎ (0118) 959 7269
A helpline for support, advice, places of interest in the local area, local events, general information, HIV/AIDS information, safer sex advice and much more.

RELIGIOUS GROUPS
■ **Metropolitan Community Church (MCC)**
☎ 01734/(01202) 763 609
(Rev. Stewart Harrison)

Redcar - Cleveland ☎ 01642

BOOK SHOPS
■ **Books and Magazines** (glm) Mon-Sat 9.30-17.15 h
5 Station Road ✉ TS10 1AH ☎ 47 41 44

CRUISING
-Promenade from Granville Terrace towards Marske
-Sanddunes opposite blastfurnace at British Steel

Redhill/Reigate - Surrey ☎ 01737

HEALTH GROUPS
■ **St. Peters House Project** Mon-Fri 10-17:00h
☎ 24 10 44
Helpline for questions concerning HIV/AIDS. Home care support service provided.

Richmond - Greater London ☎ 020

BARS
■ **Richmond Arms. The** (AC B f G N OS S) Wed 11-23, Thu 11-24, Fri & Sat 11-1, Sun 12-22:30 h
20 The Square *(BR/U-Richmond, off Princes Street)* ☎ 8940 2118

Rochdale - Greater Manchester ☎ 01706

GAY INFO
■ **Oldham & Rochdale Switchboard** Tue 17-19 h
☎ (0161) 678 94 48

Rochester - Kent ☎ 01634

BARS
■ **Ship Inn. The** (AC B BF D F GLM lj MA N STV) Mon-Sat 11-23, Sun 12-22.30 h
347 High Street ✉ ME1 1DA *(Close to Chatham & Rochester railway station)* ☎ 84 42 64
Sun open for lunch, disco from Thu-Sun.

Runcorn/Halton - Cheshire ☎ 01928

BARS
■ **Canalside** (B F glm MA) Mon 16-23:00h, Tue & Wed 17-23:00h, Thu -Sun 12-23:00h
45 Canal Street ☎ 58 06 69

Salisbury - Wiltshire ☎ 01722

CAFES
■ **Shout!** (b f G)
☎ 42 19 51

HEALTH GROUPS
■ **Gay Men's Health Project**
Greencroft House, 42-46 Salt Lane ✉ SP1 1EG ☎ 42 19 51
HIV information.

Sandbach - Cheshire ☎ 01270

BARS
■ **Market Tavern** (B d G MA) (G) only Thu evening
The Square ✉ CW11 1AT ☎ 76 20 99

Scarborough - North Yorkshire ☎ 01723

HOTELS
■ **Interludes Hotel** (BF CC glm H)
32 Princess Street ✉ YO11 1QR ☎ 36 05 13 📠 368597
✉ interludes@cwcom.net 🖥 www.interludes.mcmail.com
Nice Georgian building located in the heart of the Old Town. All rooms with hairdryer, colour TV, radio, central heating, most en-suite and with seaview. Non-smoking rooms only. No children. Dining room and bar for residents only. Elegant atmosphere.

CRUISING
-North Side Promenade (June-September)

Scunthorpe - Humberside ☎ 01724

HELP WITH PROBLEMS
■ **Helpline** Wed Fri 19-21 h
☎ 27 16 61

Sheffield - South Yorkshire ☎ 0114

GAY INFO
■ **Shout Centre** Tue 16-19, Thu 18.30-21.30,
14-18 West Bar Green *(next to Fire Museum)* ☎ 267 0843
Gay/bi men's health & community centre. Ring for details.

1122 | SPARTACUS 2001/2002

Sheffield - South Yorkshire ▶ Southend-on-Sea - Essex | United Kingdom

BARS
■ **Bar-celona** (B GLM lj OS STV) Mon-Thu 12-14, 19.30-23, Fri 12-23, Sat 19.30-23, Sun 20-22.30 h
387 Attercliffe Road ✉ S9 3QU *(Opposite The Club. Bus 30, 52, 71)*
■ **Cossack. The** (B F G lj MA) Mon-Sat 12-23, Sun 12-22.30 h
45 Howard Street ✉ S1 2LW *(Opposite railway station)*
Food daily from 12-18, happy hour Mon-Fri 17-19 h. Popular.
■ **Norfolk Arm's** (B D GLM MA SNU VS YG) 20-24, Fri-Sun 19.30-24, 2nd Fri X-loungers (glm) 20-? h
195 Carlisle Street ✉ S4 7LT *(Near Meadow Hall/Bus 93 stops outside)* ☏ 275 24 69
■ **Rutland Arms. The** (B glm) 11-23, Sun 12-22.30 h
86 Brown Street ☏ 272 90 03

DANCECLUBS
■ **Climax** (B D GLM)
University of Sheffield Union, Fusion & Foundry ☏ 228 8777
Please call or check webside for details.
■ **Club Xes** (B D f GLM lj MA OS S SNU TV) Mon-Thu 21-1, Fri & Sat 20-24, Sun -22.30h
Carlisle Street ✉ S4 7LJ ☏ 2752469
■ **Planet** (B D G) Wed-Sat 10-2, Sun 10-1 h
429 Effingham Road ☏ 244 01 10

GUEST HOUSES
■ **Brockett House** (BF F G H MA msg P SA VS) All year
1 Montgomery Road ✉ S7 1LN *(bus no. 22 from city center)*
☏ 258 8952 📠 258 8952 ✉ brocketthouse@yahoo.com
🖳 www.brocketthouse.com
Non-smoking B&B with comfortable&elegant guest rooms. Each room has tea/coffee facilities, TV, video, hairdryer, fan &.internet access. Rates with shared shower from £ 30-50.

GENERAL GROUPS
■ **Bears Club** Meets 1st Fri/month "The Norfolk Alms"
☏ 255 45 29

HEALTH GROUPS
■ **Sheffield Centre for HIV and Sexual Health** Mon-Fri 09-17:30h
☏ 267 8806
Ask for Rob or Anthony.

HELP WITH PROBLEMS
■ **Gayphone** Mon-Wed 19.30-21.30 h. Social groups meets Mon 20-22 h
☏ 258 81 99

Shepton Mallet - Somerset ☏ 01749

BARS
■ **Waggon and Horses. The** (A B CC E F MA NG OS) 11-15, 18-23.15, Sun 12-15, 19-23 h
Frome Road, Doulting Beacon ✉ BA4 4LA ☏ 88 03 02

CRUISING
-Church car park

Shrewsbury - Shropshire ☏ 01743

CAFES
■ **Fruit Bowl Coffee Shop. The** (f GLM MA OS) Sat 12-16, Tue 12-14, Thu 19-21 h
The Wyle Cop Centre, Unit 3, 1a Wyle Cop ✉ SY1 1UT *(Next to the Chinese Medicine Centre)* ☏ 34 41 79
Run by and for lesbian, gay & bisexuals.

RESTAURANTS
■ **Peach Tree. The** (b F glm)
21 Abbey Foregate ☏ 35 50 55

HEALTH GROUPS
■ **Shropshire and Telford Gay Mens Health Project** Mon-Fri 12-16 h
Unit 4, 1a Wyle Cop ✉ SY1 1UT ☏ 34 41 79 📠 34 42 69
Interaction L+G youth group meet Wed 16.30-19.30 h.

Sidmouth - Devon ☏ 01395

GENERAL GROUPS
■ **EDGAR-East Devon Gay Advice & Recreation**
☏ 03195/51 51 31
(John)

Slough/Uxbridge - Berkshire ☏ 01753

BARS
■ **Greyhound. The** (B D f GLM MA OS SNU STV) 12-15, 19-2, Sat 12-15, 19-3, Sun 19.30- 24 h
Colnbrook, Bypass A4 *(Junction 5 off M4)* ☏ 68 49 20

Southampton - Hampshire ☏ 01703

GAY INFO
■ **Switchboard & AIDS Helpline** Mon Tue Thu-Fri 19.30-22 h
PO Box 139 ✉ SO14 0G2 ☏ 8063 73 63

BARS
■ **Atlantic Queen** (B f GLM MA STV) 11-23:00h
Bugle Street
■ **Edge** (B D G MA) 12-02:00h. Fri & Sat : The Box at Edge nightclub (D) -02:00h
St. Mary's Road ☏ 366 163
■ **Magnum** (AC B D f GLM lj SNU STV YG) Mon-Thu 21:30-02:00h, Fri & Sat 22-03:00h
113 St. Mary's Road ✉ SO14 0AN
■ **Smugglers Arms** (B D G MA) 21-23:00h, Sun 12-22.30 h
Bernard Street
■ **Victoria. The** (B GLM MA S) 17-23:00h, Sat 12-23:00h, Sun 12-22:30h
Northam Road, Northam ✉ SO14 0PD *At end of Northam Road in cul-de-sac* ☏ 0703/33 3963

BOOK SHOPS
■ **October Books** (glm) Mon-Sat 9-18 h, closed Sun
4 Onslow Road ✉ SO14 0JB ☏ 8022 44 89

GENERAL GROUPS
■ **Breakout** Thu 19.30-21.30 h
☏ 22 33 44
Youth project for under 26's.
■ **Southampton Gay Community** Meets: Mon 20 h
☏ 8067 88 63
(Bob).

Southend-on-Sea - Essex ☏ 01702

BARS
■ **Cliffs** (B f g h STV) 11-23, Sun 12-22.30 h
48 Hamlet Road ☏ 34 44 66

SPARTACUS 2001/2002

United Kingdom Southend-on-Sea - Essex ▸ Stoke-on-Trent - Staffordshire

DANCECLUBS
■ **Eclipe at the Jack of Clubs** (B D glm MA) 21:-02:00h
Lucky Road *(next to TOTS)* ☎ 467305
Eclipse disco- last Sat. every month and Bliss disco last Fri. every month.

FETISH GROUPS
■ **Essex Leather MSC** Meet 1st Sat 21:00h at Cliffs,
48 Hamlet Road.
PO Box 184 ✉ SS2 6SD 🖳 bill@tramline.demon.co.uk
Member of ECMC.

HEALTH GROUPS
■ **Southend Aids Helpline** Mon-Fri 18-22.00 h
☎ 39 17 50

HELP WITH PROBLEMS
■ **South Essex Switchboard** Helpline Mon Thu 19-22 h
PO Box 5324 ✉ SS2 1BF ☎ 344 355 (helpline) 📠 344 056
🖳 lesbigay@freenet.co.uk 🖳 www.southessexswitchboard.org.uk
Helpline for gays, lesbians and bisexual people.

Southport - Merseyside ☎ 01704

DANCECLUBS
■ **Hellbent at Underworld** (B GLM) Sat 22-2 h
4-6 Coronation Walk *(Off Lord Street)* ☎ 500 466

GENERAL GROUPS
■ **Southport Gay Infoline** Mon & Fri 11-18:00h
☎ 543 612

St. Albans/Hatfield - Hertfordshire ☎ 01727

BARS
■ **Spritzers** (B D f GLM LJ MA OS SNU STV) Mon-Wed 19-23,
Thu-Fri -2, Sat -4, Sun 12-16, 19-24 h
Redbourn Road, Redburn ✉ AL3 6RP ☎ 01582/794 053

FETISH GROUPS
■ **Verulam MSC** Meets: last Thu21 h at " Load of Hay" - Watford
PO Box 158 ✉ AL2 3UQ
Member of ECMC.

HEALTH GROUPS
■ **Crescent Support Group. The** Mon-Thu 11-19, Fri- 17,
HIV-testing Wed 8.30-11 h
c/o HIV Centre, 19 Russel Avenue ✉ AL3 5ES *(opposite multi-storey)*
☎ (842 532 📠 848 908
🖳 director@thecrescent.org.uk 🖳 thecrescent.org.uk

St. Helens - Merseyside ☎ 01744

BARS
■ **Flex 2** (B D glm MA STV) Wed 20-23.30, Sun 20-22.30 h
Tolver Street

HELP WITH PROBLEMS
■ **L&G Helpline** Mon Wed 19-21:00h
PO Box 135 ✉ WA10 1JD ☎ 45 48 23

St. Ives - Cornwall ☎ 01736

GUEST HOUSES
■ **Barkers** (BF GLM MA p) All year exept Christmas time
11 Seaview Terrace ✉ TR26 2DH ☎ 79 67 29
From £ 22/person. Lovely Edwardian house, overlooking harbour, near gay beach and town centre. Television lounge, full English breakfast. Tea / coffee making facilities.

St. Leonards on Sea ☎ 01424

HOTELS
■ **Sherwood Guest House** (B BF CC f g NU)
15 Grosvenor Crescent ✉ TN38 OAA *(BR-Mastings Station)*
☎ 43 33 31 📠 43 33 31
Hotel in seafront location. All rooms with TV, tea/coffe making facilities, some en-suite. Rates incl. bf from £ 16.50per person.

Stamford - Lincolnshire ☎ 01780

RESTAURANTS
■ **Three Towers. The** (B BF CC E F g MA N OS) Tue-Sat 19-23:00h,
Sat 12-15:30h
39 Broad Street ✉ PE9 1PX *(Opposite Brounes Hospital)* ☎ 755751
Gay owned restaurant with B&B in the center of town.

Stirling - Central Region ☎ 01786

BARS
■ **Barnton Bistro** (B f glm YG) Mon-Thu 10.30-23.45,
Fri-Sat 10.30-0.45, Sun 12-23.45 h
3½ Barnton Street *(Near railway station)* 1 46 16 98

Stockport - Greater Manchester ☎ 0161

BARS
■ **New Inn** (AC B GLM MA N) 19-23, Fri-Sat 12-15, 19-23,
Sun 12-22.30 h
93 Wellington Road South ✉ SK1 3SL *(Corner John Street/next to town hall)* ☎ 480 40 63
Wed is Quiz Night, Fri Karaoke.

Stoke-on-Trent - Staffordshire ☎ 01782

GAY INFO
■ **North Staffs Lesbian, Gay and Bisexual Switchboard** Mon Wed
Fri 20-22 h
57-59 Piccadilly, Hanley ☎ 26 69 98

BARS
■ **Club. The** (B D G s) Mon-Sat 21-2 h
14 Hillcrest Street, Hanley ☎ 20 18 29
■ **Queen and Crumpet. The** (B GLM MA OS) Tue-Fri 12-16, 19-23,
Sat 12-23, Sun 13-22:30 h
5 Hope Street, Hanley ☎ 28 99 25
■ **Three Tuns. The** (AC B D F GLM MA STV) 14-16, 19-23,
Sun 13-22.30 h
9 Bucknall New Road, Hanley ✉ ST1 2BA ☎ 21 34 08

DANCECLUBS
■ **Ruby's** (B D GLM MA) 19.30-2 h
14 Hillcrest Street, Hanley ☎ 20 18 29

1124 *SPARTACUS* 2001/2002

Stoke-on-Trent - Staffordshire ▶ Torquay - Devon — United Kingdom

SPORT GROUPS
■ **Mustangs. The** Tue 19.30 h
c/o The Club, 14 Hillcrest Street, Hanley ☎ 630 681
dancing group.

Stourbridge - West Midlands ☎ 01384
SAUNAS/BATHS
■ **Heroes Health Club** (B DR f G MA SA SB SOL WH) Sun-Thu 12-23, Fri Sat -2 h
4 Lower High Street ✉ DY8 1TE ☎ 44 20 30
Sauna with darkroom maze.

Stratford-Upon-Avon - Warwickshire ☎ 01623
BARS
■ **The Monastery** (B GLM STV S MA) Mo-We 20-02:00h, Th-Sa 20-02:00h & Su 19-22:30h
Watling Street, Fenny ☎ 373 018

Stroud - Gloucestershire ☎ 01452
GENERAL GROUPS
■ **Gloucestershire Gay Community** Mon-Fri 19.30-22 h (helpline)
☎ 30 68 00

Sunderland - Tyne & Wear ☎ 0191
GENERAL GROUPS
■ **Liberal G&L Campaign**
☎ 528 28 13

HEALTH GROUPS
■ **Wear Body Positive**
☎ 548 3144

Sutton in Ashfield - Nottinghamshire ☎ 01623
HOTELS
■ **Central Private Hotel** (AC BF CC F g H MA msg)
Bar & Restaurant 18-21, Sun 12-14 h
1 Station Road ✉ NG17 5FF *(Close to M1 J28)* ☎ 55 23 73
🖨 44 31 06
B&B. Laundry service. Special meals for vegetarians available.

Swansea - West Glamorgan ☎ 01792
BARS
■ **Champers** (B GLM MA) 11-23, Sun 12-22.30 h
210 High Street ☎ 65 56 22
■ **Station Inn** (B GLM) 12-23:00h Sun -22:30h
63-64 High Street ☎ 457 977

HEALTH GROUPS
■ **AIDS Helpline** Thu 15-20 h
☎ 45 63 03

HELP WITH PROBLEMS
■ **Advice Line** Tue 18-21 h
☎ 45 63 03

Swindon - Wiltshire ☎ 01793
BARS
■ **Cricketer's Arms. The** (B G) 12-14.30, 19-23 h, Sun 12-22.30 h
14 Emlyn Square *(Near BR station)* ☎ 52 37 80
■ **London Street** (B D GLM YG) Mon-Wed 19-23:00h, Sun 19-22:30h
1 London Street ☎ 497 774
■ **Red Lion** (B f glm)
3 The City, Melksham ☎ 01225)/70 29 60.

HEALTH GROUPS
■ **SPACE (Swindon Project for Aids Counselling & Education**
Mon-Thu 09-17:00h, Fri 09-16:30h
Frampton Villa, 9 Devizes Road ✉ SN1 4BH ☎ 42 06 20
🖨 48 48 79

Telford - Shropshire ☎ 01734
GAY INFO
■ **Shropshire Switchboard** Tue , Wed & Fri 20-22 h
PO Box 41, Wellington ✉ TF1 1YG ☎ 232393

Torquay - Devon ☎ 01803
BARS
■ **Ibiza** (B D GLM MA) Mon-Sat 21-1, Sun 20-22.30 h
3-4 Victoria Parade *(Under Queens Hotel)* ☎ 21 43 34
■ **Meadfoot Inn. The** (AC B f G MA N) 12-16, 19-23, Sun 12-15, 19-22.30 h
7 Meadfoot Lane ✉ TQ1 2BW *(Near the harbour)* ☎ 29 71 12
Gay owned. A small intimate bar within walking distance of all gay hotels and clubs.
■ **Rockies** (B D DR f GLM MA N OS P VS) Sun-Thu 22-1, Fri & Sat 22-2 h
Rock Cottage, Rock Road ✉ TQ2 5SP *(Town centre, next to main post office)* ☎ 29 22 79

HOTELS
■ **Cliff House Hotel. The** (B BF CC f G MA msg N NU OS s SB SOL WH WO) All year
St Marks Road, Meadfoot Beach ✉ TQ1 2EH ☎ 294656
☎ (0800) 328 28 13 (toll-free) 🖨 211983
📧 alan@cliffhousehotel.com 📧 www.cliffhousehotel.com
Exclusively Gay. Hotel with bar and gym area (steam room).
■ **Ocean House Hotel. The** (B BF CC F GLM H MA N OS PI SB SOL WO)
Hunsdon Road ✉ TQ1 1QB ☎ 29 65 38 🖨 29 99 36
📧 cshore@dircon.co.uk 📧 www.oceanhouse.co.uk
Very comfortable hotel situated in a beautiful garden. Rates from £ 29.50 p.p.
■ **Oscars Restaurant & Hotel** (B BF CC F GLM H MA)
56 Belgrave Road ✉ TQ2 5HY ☎ 29 35 63 🖨 29 66 85
📧 reservations@oscars-hotel.com 📧 www.oscars-hotel.com
Good food at reasonable prices. Quiet candlelight cellar restaurant. Vegetarians welcomed. 38 seats.B&B accomodation. Comfortable rooms. Full English or vegetarian bf. Completely renovated. Close to all gay venues and rail station.
■ **Ravenswood Hotel** (B BF CC glm MA OS)
535 Babbacombe Road ✉ TQ1 1HQ ☎ 29 29 00 🖨 29 29 00
Private car parking. Close to beaches and gay bars. Rates £ 14-18 in winter and £ 16-20 in summer p.p. incl. bf. 4 course dinner optional.

SPARTACUS 2001/2002 | 1125

United Kingdom | Torquay - Devon ▶ Woking - Surrey

Torquay

GUEST HOUSES
■ **Rainbow Villa** (BF CC f G H OS) All year
24 Bridge Road ✉ TQ2 5BA ☎ 21 28 86 📠 21 28 86
📧 rainbow@globalnet.co.uk 🌐 rainbowvilla.co.uk
Three double rooms with shower & WC, TV, heating, own key. Rates double from £ 45-55, single 30-34.50 (bf incl.) Luxury home stay (B&B).

GENERAL GROUPS
■ **Torbay Gay Community**
☎ 29 20 55
(Ronnie).

SWIMMING
-**Petittor Beach** (7 km from the city in the suburb of St.Marychurch. Take bus from the beach to St. Marychurch or Modell Village. Then follow Petittor Road to the end.)

Truro - Cornwall ☎ 01726

HOTELS
■ **Trewirgie House** (BF F G H OS) Mar-Nov
Trewirgie Road, Redruth ✉ TR15 2SX ☎ (01209) 212831 📠 (01209) 212 831
B&B located in fine period house and close to beaches. Beautiful garden. Rates £ 18-22.
■ **Woodbine Villa** (b BF DR F G H MA NU p SA VS) Men only sauna open to non-residents Wed Sun 18-22 h
Fore Street, Grampound ✉ TR2 4QP *(Next to Guild Hall)*
☎ 88 20 05
Friendly B&B in an old 18th century building, which is furnished with lots of antiques. Rates for a double from £ 21 p.p. and for a single from £ 23 p.p. incl. bf, shared bath. 5 miles to nude beach.

Tunbridge Wells - Kent ☎ 01892

GENERAL GROUPS
■ **Turnbridge Wells Ind Gay Group (TWIGG)** Meets: Fri 20-24 h at Calverley Hotel, Crescent Rd. 8-12
☎ (01580) 75 36 68 (Keith)

Wakefield - West Yorkshire ☎ 01924

BARS
■ **Dolphin Public House. The** (B D GLM MA SNU STV OS)
Mon-Sat 12-16, 19-24, Sun 19-24 h; Wed-Sun shows/cabaret
6 Lower Warrengate ✉ WF1 1SA *(Near Cathedral)* ☎ 20 17 05

HEALTH GROUPS
■ **HIV Centre**
c/o Clayton Hospital ☎ 36 41 44

Wallasey - Merseyside ☎ 01051

SAUNAS/BATHS
■ **Dolphin. The** (AC f G MA SA SB SOL WH) 14-21.30 h
129 Mount Road ✉ CH45 9JS *(5 min from New Brighton railway station)* ☎ 630 1516
Friendly sauna frequented by a mixed crowd.

Walsall - West Midlands ☎ 01922

BARS
■ **Golden Lion. The** (AC B d DR GLM MA p S VS) Tue Thu 20.30-2, Fri Sat 19.30-2, Sun 19.30-24 h
41 Birchills Street ✉ WS2 8NG ☎ 610977
Weekend lunch, disco.

Warrington - Cheshire ☎ 01925

HEALTH GROUPS
■ **AIDS Helpline** Mon Wed 19-22 h
☎ 41 71 34

HELP WITH PROBLEMS
■ **Warrington LGB Helpline** 2Tue 19-21:00h
☎ 24 19 94

Wells-Next-The-Sea - Norfolk ☎ 01328

BARS
■ **Three Horseshoes. The** (B BF F glm H MA N) Pub: 11.30-15, 18-23 h
Bridge Street, Warham ✉ NR23 1NL ☎ 71 05 47
Hotel with bar, located in rural area next to sea and gay beach.

Weymouth - Dorset ☎ 01305

HEALTH GROUPS
■ **DASH Dorset Aids Support and Help** Mon-Fri 9-17 h
5 Belle Vue ✉ DT4 8DR ☎ 77 92 24

Whitby - North Yorkshire ☎ 01947

HOTELS
■ **Sandbeck Hotel** (BF CC H MA NG)
West Cliff ✉ YO21 3EL ☎ 60 40 12
Small luxury hotel with 16 rooms, all en-suite. Hotel faces sea front. Rates incl. bf from £ 20 p.p. (low season) and £ 27.50 (high season).

Winchester - Hampshire ☎ 01962

GENERAL GROUPS
■ **King Alfred's College LGB Society**
c/o Students Unio, Sparkford Road ✉ SO22 4NR ☎ 85 31 44
■ **LGB Group** Meets: Thu 19.30-22.30
☎ 85 26 91 (Ken) ☎ (01730) 26 29 17 (Paul)

HEALTH GROUPS
■ **Gay Men's Health Project**
☎ 863511 ext 484

Windermere - Cumbria ☎ 015394

GUEST HOUSES
■ **Lingmoor Guest House** (BF F glm H MA WE) All year
7 High Street ✉ LA23 1AF *(Very close to bus and train stations)*
☎ 449 47

Windsor - Berkshire ☎ 01753

CRUISING
-**Public toilets** at Bachelor's Acre, central Windsor. Best time 13-16:00h weekends 14-17:00h.
- **Public toilets** in St Luke's Road, Old Windsor, times as above.

Woking - Surrey ☎ 01483

GENERAL GROUPS
■ **LGB Support Group** 1st/3rd Thu 19-21 h
Crescent Project, Heathside Crescent

HELP WITH PROBLEMS
■ **Outline** Tue 19.30-22 h
☎ 72 76 67

Wolverhampton - West Midlands ☏ 01902

BARS
■ **White Hart. The** (B f GLM lj MA OS S) Mon-Fri 11-16, 19-23.30, Sat -24, Sun 14-22.30 h
66 Worcester Street ✉ WV2 4LQ ☏ 42 17 01

GENERAL GROUPS
■ **Gay Men`s Group** Meets alternate Sun
☏ 820 626
■ **Gay Nudist Group** Meet 20th of each month
☏ 84 41 85 (Neil)

HEALTH GROUPS
■ **AIDSline** Mon Tue Thu 9-17, Wed Fri 9-12 h
☏ 64 48 94
■ **Reach-HIV and AIDS Support group** Mon-Thu 18-20.45 h
242-244 Bond House, Bond St. ✉ WV2 4AS ☏ 425 702 (helpline) ☏ 310 231 (office) 🖨 310 231
📧 feedback@reach-hiv.demon.co.uk
🖥 www.reach-hiv.demon.co.uk

CRUISING
-West park, Chapel Ash (AYOR, police)

Worcester - Hereford & Worcester
☏ **01905**

GAY INFO
■ **Hereford & Worcester L&G Switchboard** Tue, Wed & Thu 19.30-22 h
PO Box 156 ✉ WR5 1BP ☏ 72 30 97
🖥 101234.1637@compuserve.com.
Disco on every 1st Tue.

DANCECLUBS
■ **Surrender** (B D f GLM s) 1st Tue/month 21.30-2 h (G)
c/o Images Night Club, The Butts, PO Box 156 ✉ WR5 1BP
☏ 72 30 97

GENERAL GROUPS
■ **Gay Outdoor Club**
☏ 278 42

York - North Yorkshire ☏ 01904

BARS
■ **The Bay Horse**
54 Gillygate ✉ YO3 7E0 ☏ 62 76 79

■ **York Arms.The** (B g MA) 11-23, Sun 12-22.30 h
26 High Petergate *(Near York Minster)*

RESTAURANTS
■ **Churchill Hotel** (B F glm)
Bootham ☏ 64 44 56

HOTELS
■ **Astley House Hotel** (AC BF CC glm H MA msg)
123 Clifton ✉ YO3 6BL ☏ 63 47 45 🖨 62 13 27
Small and friendly hotel close to the historic center of York. All rooms are en-suite with SAT-TV, radio alarm, tea / coffee making facilities, hairmdryers and direct dial telephones. Free car park.

GUEST HOUSES
■ **Bull Lodge** (cc f glm H MA)
37 Bull Lane, Lawrence Street ✉ YO10 3EN *(1 km from city centre, on quiet side-street off A1079)* ☏ 41 55 22 🖨 41 55 22
📧 stay@bullodge.co.uk 🖥 www.bullodge.co.uk
Rates £ 17-23 depending on season and length of stay.Visa&Mastercard only.

GENERAL GROUPS
■ **One in Ten Project** Meets: Tue 19-21:00h
c/o Community House, 10 Priory Street ✉ YO1 1EZ ☏ 61 26 29
Youth group under 21.
■ **York Gay Group** Mon 20-21:00 h
The Workshop, Marygate Lane ✉ YO3 7BT ☏ 61 36 39

HEALTH GROUPS
■ **Yorkshire M.E.S.M.A.C.** Mon-Fri 10-13 h
PO Box 549 ✉ YO30 7GX ☏ 62 04 00 🖨 6620444
📧 northyorkshire@mesmac.co.uk 🖥 www.mesmac.co.uk
Service and groups for gay men and bisexual men who have sex with men. Counselling service available. Free condoms.

CRUISING
-Riverbank adjacent to Museums Gardens to Clifton Ings.
-Lay by on A166 Bidlington Road (5 miles out of the city centre)
-Train station
-Bus station
-Wiggington Road (accross from hospital)
-Parking at Haxby Road (Gillygate Road)
-Museum Gardens (daytime)
-Toft Green (daytime)

+++ register now +++ constantly updated +++ all current info

Lifestyle

Shopping

Personals

Adult Entertainment

Gay Chat

www.SpartacusWorld.com

Events

Travel

Spartacus Gay Guide

Free newsletter

Entertainment

Launch date: 1st May 2001!

As purchaser of the jubilee edition of SPARTACUS International Gay Guide 2001/2002, after I have registered myself, I have the possibility to use and research in the SPARTACUS address data bank free of charge until the 31st December 2001.

The registration card should be completed in full, signed and sent off by post to:
SpartacusWorld.com GmbH
P.O. Box 17 01 23 • 10203 Berlin • Germany

Your personal password will be sent to you promptly.

+++ all current information +++ register now +++ constantly

United States of America

Name: Vereinigte Staaten • Etats-Unis • Estados Unidos • Stati Uniti
Location: North America
Initials: USA
Time: See each state
International Country Code: ☎ 1
International Access Code: ☎ 011
Language: English, (Spanish)
Area: 9,809,155 km^2 / 3,615,102 sq mi.
Currency: 1 US Dollar (US$) = 100 Cents
Population: 270,299,000
Capital: Washington D.C.
Religions: 26% Catholic, 16% Baptists, 6% Methodists
Climate: Mostly moderate climate. Hawaii and Florida are tropical, Alaska is arctic. The great plains of the Mississippi are quite dry, the Great Basin of the southwest is very dry. The low winter temperatures in the northwest are ameliorated occasionally in January and February by warm chinook winds from the eastern slopes of the Rocky Mountains.
Important gay cities: Atlanta, Boston, Chicago, Dallas, Houston, Key West, Los Angeles, New York City, New Orleans, Palm Springs, Philadelphia, Provincetown, San Diego, San Francisco, Washington.

It is true to say that the USA is known for its diversity. The spectrum ranges from the large gay communities in many of the major cities down to the small towns with a bar and a bookstore. Equally diverse is the legal situation. The US-constitution gives the right to each state to make its own laws. On the one hand there are several states in which oral and anal intercourse, be it hetero- or homosexual, is prohibited; on the other hand we find several states with anti-discriminatory legislation. The age of consent is not laid down federally but does not exceed the age of 18 anywhere. In most of the states the penal code is based on a draft which was drawn up in the sixties. This decriminalises private sexual acts between consenting partners. In an attempt to provide information on the laws regarding sodomy we have indicated the situation as it is at present in a pictorial form. Please refer to the map of the entire USA. We have also included the age of consent in the form of a list. Comprehensive information was however difficult to obtain.
Due to the complex legal situation in each of the 51 states, we suggest you take particular care when visiting the USA. In particular, care should be taken when having sex in public places.
All cities the USA are not alphabetically listed, but are to be found under the respective state name.

ie USA sind vor allem für ihre Vielfalt bekannt. Das Spektrum reicht von großen Gay-Communities in den Großstädten bis zu den kleinen Städten, in denen es nur eine Bar und einen Buchladen gibt. Dementsprechend unterschiedlich ist die rechtliche Situation. Die Verfassung der Vereinigten Staaten verleiht jedem einzelnen Bundesstaat das Recht, seine eigenen Gesetze zu verfassen. Einerseits gibt es verschiedene Staaten in denen Oral- und Analverkehr sei es unter Homo- oder Heterosexuellen, verboten ist und andererseits gibt es jedoch einige Staaten, die sogar ein Antidiskriminierungs-Gesetz haben. Das Mündigkeitsalter ist nicht genau fest geschrieben, es liegt jedoch in keinem Bundesstaat über 18 Jahren. In den meisten Bundesstaaten basiert das Strafgesetzbuch auf einem Gesetzesentwurf aus den 60er Jahren wodurch private sexuelle Handlungen zwischen einvernehmenden Partnern nicht strafbar sind. Bei dem Versuch, Informationen über die Rechtslage bezüglich des Analverkehrs zu liefern, haben wir die aktuelle Situation in den USA illustrativ dargestellt und beziehen uns auf die Landkarte der USA. In einer Tabelle außerdem haben wir versucht, die Situation bezüglich des Mündigkeitsalters tabellarisch darzustellen. Dennoch war es nicht leicht zu diesen Themen weitreichendere Informationen zu erhalten.
Aufgrund der komplexen rechtlichen Situation in den 51 Bundesstaaten empfehlen wir, bei einer Reise in die USA besonders vorsichtig zu sein. Besonders aufpassen sollte man bei Sex an öffentlichen Orten. Alle Städte der USA sind hier nicht alphabetisch aufgelistet, können aber unter dem entsprechenden Namen des Bundesstaates gefunden werden.

Entre les larges communautés gaies des grosses métropoles jusqu'aux petites villes avec un bar et une librairie, les Etats-Unis sont avant tout connus pour leur diversité. Ceci est aussi valable au niveau légal, la Constitution américaine laissant le droit à chaque état de proclamer ses lois. Il existe donc plusieurs états ou les rapports sexuels anaux et oraux sont interdits mais aussi d'autre états qui ont des lois anti-discriminatoires. La majorité sexuelle est également variable mais n'excède jamais les 18 ans. La plupart des codes pénaux date des années soixante et décriminalise les relations entre adultes consentants. Pour une vue d'ensemble des lois concernant la sodomie dans chaque état, vous pouvez vous référer à la carte générale des Etats-Unis au début du listing. Nous y avons ajouté une liste qui indique la majorité sexuelle dans chaque état, même si des informations précises à ce sujet sont difficiles à obtenir.
A cause de la situation légale complexe du pays, nous vous recommandons d'être particulièrement prudent, surtout en ce qui concerne le relations sexuelles dans les lieux publics.
Le villes ne sont pas classées par ordre alphabétique, mais respectivement sous le nom de l'état où elles se situent.

Los Estados Unidos son conocidos por su gran diversidad. El abanico abarca desde las grandes comunidades gays en muchas de las mayores ciudades hasta las villas pequeñas con nada más que un bar y una librería. También la situación legal es muy diversa en los diferentes Estados. La constitución estadounidense concede a todos los Estados el derecho de crear sus propias leyes. Por un lado, hay varios Estados donde el sexo oral y anal, sea entre heterosexuales, sea entre homosexuales, está prohibido; por otro lado, existen varios Estados con una legislación con leyes contra la discriminación por la orientación sexual. La edad de consentimiento no está regulada por una ley federal, pero excede los dieciocho años en ninguno de losEstados. En la mayoría de los Estados, el código penal está basado en una versión elaborada en los años sesenta que legaliza los actos sexuales voluntarios entre dos personas adultas. Para dar información acerca de las leyes acerca de las prácticas de sexo anal, indicamos la situación actual en una ilustración en un mapa de los enteros Estados Unidos. También incluimos la edad de consentimiento en

United States of America

forma de una lista. De todas formas, no es fácil obtener información más amplia.
Debido a la complexa situación legal de los 51 estados, recomendamos tener mucho cuidado al visitar los Estados Unidos. Es particularmente importante tener mucho cuidado al tener sexo en lugares públicos.
Las ciudades de los Estados Unidos no estan ordenadas por alfabeto, sino que se se encuentran ordenadas bajo los estados respectivos.

Si può dire che gli Stati Uniti sono famosi per la loro diversità. Lo spettro delle diversità va dalle grandi comunità gay in molte delle città più importanti a quelle delle piccole cittadine con bar e negozi di libri. Ugualmente varia è la situazione legale. La costituzione degli Stati Uniti dà ad ogni stato la facoltà di legiferare in merito all'argomento dell'omosessualità. Da un lato esistono parecchi stati in cui il rapporto orale e anale, sia etero- che omosessuale, è proibito; dall'altro lato troviamo invece molti stati con delle leggi antidiscriminatorie. La maggior età non è stata stabilita a livello federale ma non supera comunque da nessuna parte i diciotto anni. I codici penali della maggior parte degli stati si basano su una bozza redatta negli anni sessanta che depenalizza gli atti sessuali privati tra partner consenzienti. Nel tentativo di fornirvi informazioni sulle leggi riguardanti la sodomia, abbiamo rappresentato l'attuale situazione in forma illustrativa e facciamo riferimento alla carta geografica di tutti gli Stati Uniti. Abbiamo riassunto inoltre in una tabella la situazione relativa all'età consentita. Non è comunque facile ottenere informazioni più esaurienti in merito.
A causa della complessa situazione legale in ciascuno dei 51 stati, vi raccomandiamo di fare molta attenzione quando visitate gli Stati Uniti: state particolarmente attenti quando fate del sesso nei luoghi pubblici! Non tutte le città degli Stati Uniti figurano nell'elenco alfabetico, ma si possono trovare sotto il nome del rispettivo stato.

NATIONAL GAY INFO

■ **American Educational Gender Information Service (AEGIS)**
PO Box 33144 ✉ GA 30033-0724 Decatur ☎ (770) 939-0244
🖷 (770) 939-1770 📧 aegis@mindspring.com
■ www.spartacusworld.com
International multilingual community website. Chatpages, event calendar and SPARTACUS – online

NATIONAL PUBLICATIONS

Almost every large city of the U.S. offers free publications (available in bars or other gay venues) with calendar of events, personal and classified ads, and other features.
In fast jeder US-amerikanischen Großstadt gibt es in den Bars oder anderen schwulen Einrichtungen kostenlose Zeitschriften mit einem Terminkalender, wichtigen Adressen, Kleinanzeigen und anderen Inhalten.
Dans chaque grande ville des Etats-Unis, on trouve dans les bars et autres lieux gais des revues gratuites qui contiennent un agenda, des petites annonces et autres.
En casi todas las ciudades importantes de los E.U. se distribuyen en los bares u otros establecimientos publicaciones gay que contienen informes sobre los acontecimientos mensuales, avisos personales, publicitarios y otras temáticas.

In quasi tutte le grandi città statunitensi si trovano nei bar o in altri locali gay le riviste gratuite con l'agenda, gli indirizzi importanti, annunci e altro.

■ **Advocate. The**
c/o Liberation Publication Inc., 6922 Hollywood Boulevard, Suite 1000 ✉ CA 90028-6148 Los Angeles ☎ (323) 871-1225
🖷 (323) 467-0173 📧 info@advocate.com ■ www.advocate.com
The national gay-lesbian news magazine. Featuring national and international news coverage from all areas that are of interest to the gay and lesbian community.

■ **Alternative Family Magazine (Gay & Lesbian Parenting Magazine)**
PO Box 7179 ✉ CA 91409 Van Nuys ☎ (818) 909-0314
🖷 (818) 909-3792 📧 editor@altfammag.com
■ www.altfammag.com
■ **A&U**
25 Monroe Street, Suite 205 ✉ NY 12210-2743 Albany
☎ (518) 426-9010 ☎ (800) 841-8707 🖷 (518) 436-5354
📧 inbox@aumag.org ■ www.aumag.org
Monthly Aids magazine. US$ 4.95

FRENCH LOVER GALLERY
WWW.JNRCPRODUCTION.COM
The Best in France
VIDEO / DVD

United States of America

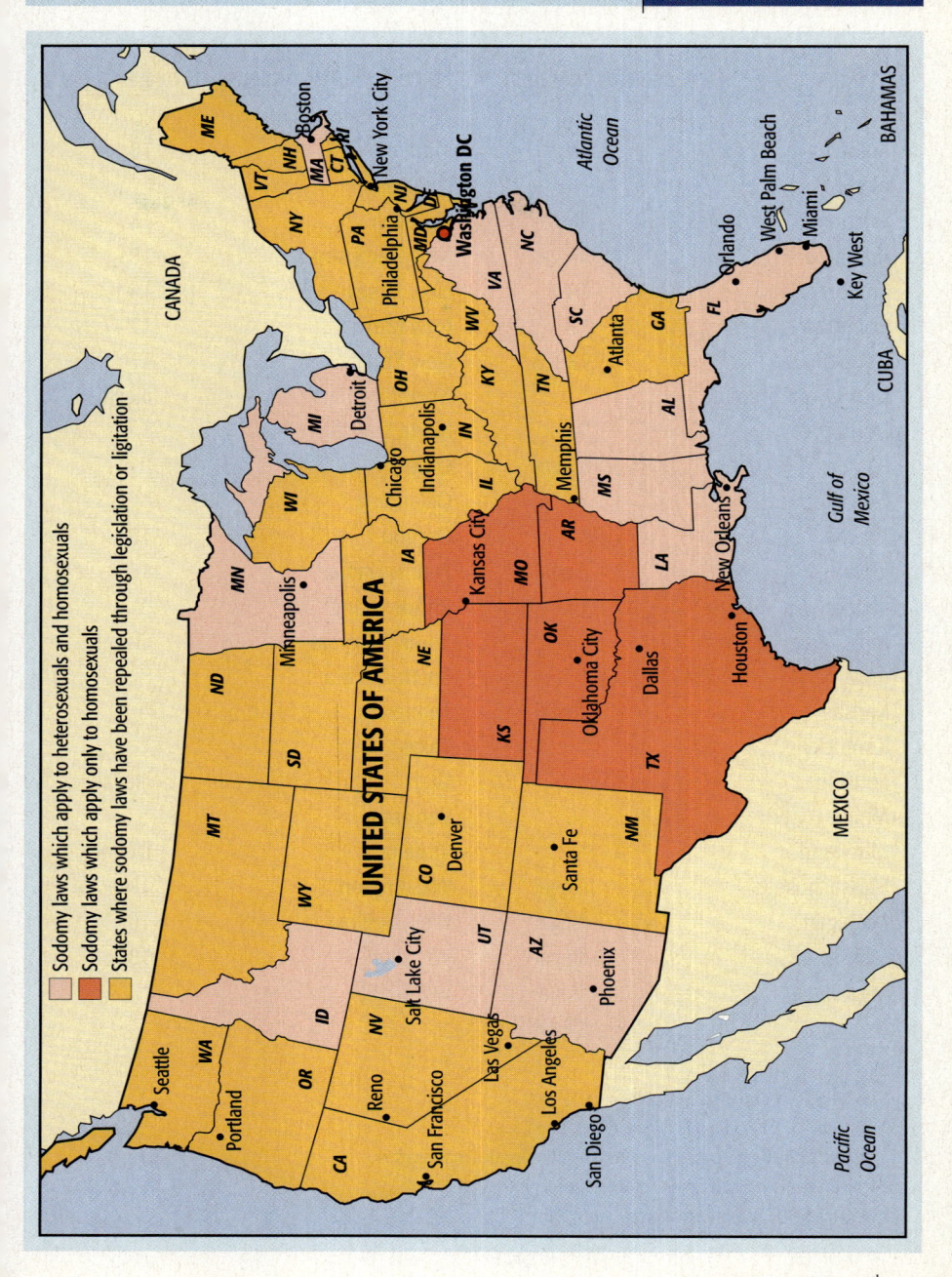

- Sodomy laws which apply to heterosexuals and homosexuals
- Sodomy laws which apply only to homosexuals
- States where sodomy laws have been repealed through legislation or litigation

SPARTACUS 2001/2002 | 1131

United States of America

State	Age of consent for gay men	State	Age of consent for gay men
Alabama	illegal	Montana	18
Alaska	16	Nebraska	*
Arizona	illegal	Nevada	18
Arkansas	illegal	New Hampshire	18
California	18	New Jersey	16
Colorado	17	New Mexico	17
Conneticut	18 (*)	New York	17
District of Columbia	*	North Carolina	illegal
Delaware	*	North Dakota	*
Florida	illegal	Ohio	*
Georgia	16	Oklahoma	*
Hawaii	*	Oregon	18
Idaho	illegal	Pennsylvania	16
Illinois	17	Rhode Island	*
Indiana	16	South Carolina	illegal
Iowa	*	South Dakota	*
Kansas	illegal	Tennessee	*
Kentucky	*	Texas	*
Lousiana	*	Utah	illegal
Maine	16	Vermont	*
Maryland	*	Virginia	illegal
Massachusetts	illegal	Washington	18
Michigan	illegal	West Virginia	18 (*)
Minnesota	illegal	Wisconsi	18
Missisippi	illegal	Wyoming	*
Missouri	illegal		

* no reliable information available
* Aucune information fiable n'est à disposition
* Lastimosamente no poseemos informaciones legales más exactas
* Non abbiamo a disposizione informazioni legali più precise
* Keine verläßlichen Informationen verfügbar

United States of America

■ **Curve Magazine**
One Haight Street, Suite B ✉ CA 94102 San Francisco
☎ (415) 863-6538 📠 (415) 863-1609 📧 curvead@aol.com
💻 www.curvemag.com

■ **Cybersocket**
7510 Sunset Boulevard Suite 1203 ✉ CA 90046 Los Angeles
☎ (323) 650-9906 📠 (323) 650-9926
📧 editor@cybersocket.com 💻 www.cybersocket.com
Bimonthly gay web magazine.

■ **Damron Travel Guides**
Damron Co., PO Box 42 24 58 ✉ CA 94142 San Francisco
☎ (415) 255-0404 ☎ (800) 462-6654 💻 www.damron.com
Addresses books covering mainly USA, Canada, Caribbean, Mexico. Also publisher of Road atlases and Accommodations books.

■ **Drummer** (LJ)
PO Box 410390 ✉ CA 94141-0390 San Francisco
☎ (415) 252-1195
Monthly men's leather, S/M erotic magazine with related articles, fiction, commissioned art work, reviews, short stories, classified ads, and an abundance of photographs. 100 pages, published monthly by Desmodus Inc.

■ **Ferrari Guides**
Ferrari International Publishing, Inc., PO Box 378 87 ✉ AZ 85069 Phoenix ☎ (602) 863-2408 📧 ferrari@q-net.com
💻 www.q-net.com
Gay addresses books covering the USA and the world.

■ **Fodor's Gay Guide to the USA**
Fodor's Travel Publications, 201 E. 50th Street ✉ NY 10022 New York
Features ca. 30 cities and resorts in the US.

■ **Friction**
Monumentum Publishing, 462 Broadway, Suite 4000 ✉ NY 10013 New York ☎ (212) 966-8400
Monthly gay erotic (novel) magazine, male nude drawings, some photos. Approximately 80 pages.

■ **Gay USA**
First Books, Inc., PO Box 57 81 47 ✉ IL 60657 Chicago
☎ (312) 276-5911
Features ca. 20 big cities and gay resorts.

■ **Gayellow Pages**
Renaissance House, PO Box 533, Village Station ✉ NY 10014-0533 New York ☎ (212) 674-0120
One of the best and most complete gay guides of the USA. With accommodations, bars, businesses, churches, health care, lawyers, organizations, publications, switchboards etc.

■ **Genre Magazine**
7080 Hollywood Boulevard #1104 ✉ CA 90028 Los Angeles
☎ (323) 467-8300 📠 (323) 467-8365
📧 genresubs@GenreMagazine.com 💻 www.genremagazine.com
Monthly glossy lifestyle magazine.

■ **Guide, The**
c/o Fidelity Publishing, PO Box 990593 ✉ MA 02199-0593 Boston
☎ (617) 266-8557 📠 (617) 266-1125
📧 theguide@guidemag.com 💻 www.guidemag.com
Monthly magazine (US$ 3.50) featuring gay travel, entertainment, politics etc.

■ **HERO**
451 North La Cinega Boulevard, Suite 1 ✉ CA 90048 Los Angeles
☎ (310) 360-8022 📠 (310) 360-8023
📧 feedback@heromag.com 💻 www.heromag.com
Glossy and stylish magazine for gay men.

■ **Instinct Magazine**
11638 Ventura Boulevard ✉ CA 91604-2613 Studio City
☎ (818) 505-9205 📠 (818) 505-9875 📧 mail@instinctmag.com
💻 www.instinctmag.com
Monthly gay lifestyle magazine.

■ **International Directory of Gay & Lesbian Periodicals**
The Oryx Press, 1250 West Grace ✉ IL 60611 Chicago *(1st floor)*
Guide to Gay and Lesbian periodicals (international, which appears every two years.

■ **Joey Magazine**
11901 Santa Monica Boulevard, Suite 598 ✉ CA 90025 Los Angeles
☎ (888) 550-5639 📠 (310) 388-1139
📧 feedback@joeymag.com 💻 www.joeymag.com
Gay magazine for the young men.

■ **Lambda Book Report**
PO Box 73910 ✉ DC 20056 Washington D.C. ☎ (202) 462-7257
📠 (202) 462-7257 📧 lbreditor@aol.com
💻 www.lambdalit.org/lbr
Book reviews.

■ **Mavity Group Erotic Magazines**
462 Broadway ✉ NY 10013-2697 New York *(4th floor)*
☎ (212) 966-8400 📠 (212) 966-9366
Erotic gay magazines published by the Mavity Group:
-All Man: 💻 www.allman.com
-Black Inches: 💻 www.blackinchesmag.com
-Honcho: 💻 www.honcho.com
-Latin Inches: 💻 www.latininches.com
-Mandate: 💻 www.mandatemag.com
-Play Guy: 💻 www.playguy.com
-Torso: 💻 www.torsomag.com

■ **Men Magazine**
7060 Hollywood Boulevard., Suite 1010 ✉ CA 90028 Los Angeles
☎ (323) 960-5400 📠 (323) 960-1163
📧 letters@menmagazine.com 💻 www.menmagazine.com
Monthly erotic publication. See website for details.

■ **Odysseus**
PO Box 1548 ✉ NY 11050 Port Washington ☎ (516) 944-5330
📠 (516) 944-7540 📧 odyusa@odyusa.com 💻 www.odyusa.com
Accommodation and travel guide with detailed and updated information about the USA and other countries.

■ **Our World International Gay & Lesbian Travel Magazine**
1104 North Nova Road, Suite 251 ✉ FL 32117 Daytona Beach
☎ (904) 441-5367 📠 (904) 441-5604
📧 info@ourworldmag.com 💻 www.ourworldmag.com
Gay & lesbian international monthly travel magazine. Monthly. US$ 4.99

■ **Out**
110 Greene Street Suite 600 ✉ NY 10012-3838 New York
☎ (212) 334-9119 ☎ (800) 792-2760 📠 (212) 334-9227
📧 letters@out.com 💻 www.out.com
Magazine published 12x/year featuring real advice on jobs, relationships, staying healthy, and getting fit, fashion. On-target reviews of the best movies, music, and books. Articles on travel, grooming, personal finance, the arts. US$ 4.95

SPARTACUS 2001/2002 | 1133

United States of America

■ **Out & About. The Gay Travel Newsletter** Mon-Fri 9-17 h
c/o PlanetOut Corp, 657 Harrison Street ✉ CA 94107 San Francisco
☎ (415) 486-2591 🖷 (415) 229-1793
💻 comments@outandabout.com 🖳 www.outandabout.com
Gay and lesbian travel magazine published 10x/year. US$ 4.95.
■ **POZ**
349 West 12th Street ✉ NY 10014 New York ☎ (212) 242-2163
🖷 (212) 675-8505 💻 poz-editor@poz.com 🖳 www.poz.com
Monthly publication providing information to HIV positive persons for whom it could extend or improve the quality of their lives.
■ **XY Magazine**
4104 24th Street ✉ CA 94114 San Francisco ☎ (415) 552-6668
🖷 (415) 552-6664 💻 xymag@aol.com 🖳 www.xymag.com

NATIONAL HELPLINES

■ **Gay and Lesbian National Hotline** Mon-Fri 16-24, Sat 12-17 h (Eastern Standard times)
San Francisco ☎ (1-888) 843-4564 🖷 (415) 552 0649
💻 glnh@glnh.org. 🖳 www.glnh.org.
Nationwide information, referals and couseling to the gay, lesbian, bisexual and transgender community. A non-profit organisation.

NATIONAL PUBLISHERS

■ **Desmodus Inc.**
2354 Market Street ✉ CA 94114 San Francisco *(top floor)*
☎ (415) 252 1195 🖷 (415) 252-8284
Publisher of Drummer Magazine, Drummer Hardcore, Drummer Touch Customers.
■ **Gay and Lesbian Yellow Pages**
4200 Montrose Boulevard, Ste. 480 ✉ TX 77006 Houston
🖳 www.glyp.com
Publisher of annual telephone directories for the gay, lesbian, bisexual and trangender community.
■ **Persona Productions**
PO Box 14022 ✉ CA 94114-0022 San Francisco
☎ (415) 775-6143 💻 personapro@aol.com
Publisher of gay novels and nonpronographic videos.
■ **Pridetime Productions**
105 Charles Street, Suite 283 ✉ MA 02114 Boston
☎ (617) 723-5130
Travel info on gay/lesbian life on video.
■ **Streetlife Video**
PO Box 1872 ✉ NY 10013 New York ☎ (212) 253-6034
🖷 (212) 477-7729 💻 webmaster@streetlife.com
Black and latino videos.
■ **Tom of Finland Company**
PO Box 26716 ✉ CA 90026 Los Angeles ☎ (800) 334-6526
Publisher of magazines, postcards, posters etc. with Tom's drawings. Catalogue available for US$ 10.

NATIONAL COMPANIES

■ **A Different Light** (GLM) 10-24 h
151 West 19th Street ✉ NY 10011 New York *(at 7th Avenue)*
☎ (212) 989-4850 ☎ (800) 343-2002 (toll free)
🖷 (212) 989-2158
Books. Ask for free catalogue.

■ **Bijou Video** 0-24 h
1349 North Wells ✉ IL 60610 Chicago ☎ (312) 943-5397
■ **Colt Studio**
PO Box 16 08 ✉ CA 91614 Studio City ☎ (818) 985-7751
💻 info@coltstudio.com 🖳 www.coltstudiostore.com
Videos, magazines, calendars, posters, and more.
■ **Different Drummer Tours**
PO Box 528 ✉ IL 60137 Glen Ellyn ☎ (708) 993-1716
International Tours.
■ **Dragonfly (OUT-er Wear)**
19 South West 2nd Street ✉ FL 32601 Gainesville *(Upstairs)*
☎ (904) 375 2144
Mail order line of clothing geared to the gay/lesbian community.
■ **Falcon Studios** (G VS)
PO Box 880906 ✉ CA 94188-0906 San Francisco
☎ (415) 431-7722 ☎ (1-800) 227-3717 (toll-free)
🖳 www.falconstudios.com
Producers of porno films and magazines etc.
■ **Gay Entertainment Television**
7 East 17 Street ✉ NY 10003 New York ☎ (212) 255-8824
Three gay TV-shows: Party Talk, Inside/Out and Makostyle.
■ **Jaybird's Toybox** (LJ)
PO Box 74 66 ✉ FL 33338 Fort Lauderdale
Leather and erotica collection.
■ **Lambda Rising**
1625 Connecticut Avenue ✉ DC 20009-1013 Washington D.C.
☎ (202) 462-6969 ☎ (800) 621-6969 🖷 (202) 462-7257
💻 lambdarising@his.com
🖳 www.lambdarising.com
■ **Malibu Sales** 9-17 h
PO Box 4371 ✉ CA 90078 Los Angeles ☎ (800) 533-8567
Mail order company of Advocate. Videos, magazines, etc.
■ **Oscar Wilde Memorial Bookshop**
15 Christopher Street ✉ NY 10014 New York ☎ (212) 255-8097
Ask for free catalogue.
■ **Picture This! Home Video** (CC)
7471 Melrose Avenue, Suite # 7 ✉ CA 90046 Los Angeles
☎ (1 888) 604-8301 (toll-free) 💻 gaypicture@aol.com
🖳 www.PictureThisEnt.com
Home video distributor.
■ **SVP**
PO Box 1807 ✉ CA 92022 El Cajon ☎ (619) 440-1020
Mail order for spanking videos.
■ **Vista Video International Inc.**
PO Box 370706, Miami, Florida ✉ FL 33137 USA ☎ 754-5717
☎ 877-845-5628 (toll free) 🖷 754-2988 🖳 www.vistavideo.com
See the latest Vista men. Visit their site www.vistamen.com.

NATIONAL GROUPS

■ **Able-Together**
PO Box 460153 ✉ CA 94146 San Francisco ☎ (415) 522-9091
🖳 www.well.com/user/blaine/abletog.html
Non-for-profit organization for bisexual and gay men with and without disabilities.
■ **Affirmation**
PO Box 1021 ✉ IL 60204 Evanston ☎ (847) 733-9590
💻 umaffirmation@yahoo.com 🖳 www.umaffirm.org
United Methodists for gay, lesbian, and bisexual concerns. Call or check website for regional groups.

Birmingham ▶ Hunstville Alabama/USA

American Foundation for AIDS Alternatives
11684 Ventura Boulevard, Studio City ✉ CA 91604 Los Angeles
☏ (818) 780-7093 ☏ (877) 922-5483 (toll-free)
🖨 (818) 780-5483 📧 nto@aliveandwell.org
💻 www.aliveandwell.org
Free monthly forums with acclaimed speakers; books, tapes and studies challenging HIV/AIDS hypothesis. Call for dates and locations of meetings.

Dignity USA
1500 Massachussetts Ave. North West, Suite #11 ✉ DC 20005-1894 Washington ☏ (202) 861-0017 ☏ (800) 877-8797
🖨 (202) 429-9380 📧 dignity@aol.com 💻 www.dignityusa.org
Dignity is one of the largest and most progressive US lay movement of lesbian, gay, bisexual and transgender (GLBT) Catholics, including families and friends. Check website or call for information on local groups.

Gay and Lesbian Medical Association
211 Church Street, Suite C ✉ CA 94114 San Francisco
☏ (415) 255-4547 📧 AGLPNAT@aol.com
💻 members.aol.com/aglpnat/homepage.html

Integrity
1718 M Street North West, PM Box 148 ✉ DC 20036 Washington
☏ (202) 462-9193 🖨 (202) 588-1486 📧 info@integrityusa.org
💻 www.integrityusa.org
Integrity is a nonprofit organization of lesbian, gay, bisexual, and transgendered Episcopalians and straight friends. Check website or call for local groups.

International Gay Rodeo Association (IGRA)
900 East Colfax Avenue ✉ CO 80218 Denver ☏ (303) 832-4472

Lesbian and Gay Immigration Rights Task Force
PO Box 7741 ✉ NY 10116-7741 New York ☏ (212) 802-7264
Provides assistance to lesbian & gay immigrants including those seeking asylum through a national campaign of advocacy, support, education and outreach.

Lutherans Concerned
PO Box 10461, Ft. Dearborn Station ✉ IL 60610-0461 Chicago
📧 luthconc@aol.com 💻 www.lcna.org
Lutherans Concerned stands as a community of faith, modeling the gospel within the church and within the lesbian and gay community. Call or check website for regional groups.

Military and Police Club, Int.
1286 University Avenue #142, ✉ CA 92103-3392 San Diego
📧 mpcted@aol.com 💻 www.mpcint.com

Names Project Foundation. The
310 Townsend Street, Suite 310 ✉ CA 94107 San Francisco
☏ (415) 882-5500 🖨 882-6200 💻 www.aidsquilt.org

National Foot Network (NFN)
P.O. Box 150790 ✉ NY 11215 New York
A correspondence club for men into feet, footwear and related scenes.

National Gay & Lesbian Task Force Mon-Fri 9-19 h
1700 Kalorama Road North West ✉ DC 20009-2624 Washington D.C. ☏ (202) 332-6483 🖨 (202) 332-0207 💻 www.ngltf.org
NGLTF is a national progressive organization working for the civil rights of gay, lesbian, bisexual and transgendered people.

Seventh-Day Adventists Kinship Int., Inc.
PO Box 7320 ✉ CA 92677 Laguna Miguel ☏ (714) 248-1299
📧 sdkinship@aol.com 💻 www.sdakinship.org

Universal Fellowship of Metropolitan Community Churches - UFMCC (GLM)
8704 Santa Monica Boulevard ✉ CA 90069- 4548 West Hollywood (2nd floor) ☏ (310) 360-8640 🖨 (310) 360-8680
📧 info@ufmcchq.com 💻 www.ufmcc.com
MCC, also referred to as UFMCC is a Christian denomination with a primary, affirming ministry to gays, lesbians, bisexuals and transgendered persons and their friends and families. Check website or call for different location & groups throughout the USA.

USA-Alabama

Location: Southeast USA
Initials: AL
Time: GMT -6
Area: 135.775 km^2 / 55,532 sq mi.
Population: 4,319,000
Capital: Montgomery

Birmingham ☏ 205

PUBLICATIONS

Alabama Forum
205 32nd Street South, Ste 216 ✉ AL 35233 ☏ 328-9228
📧 alforum@aol.com
Alabama GLM paper.

CULTURE

Barnes Memorial Library
516 27th Street South ✉ AL 35205 ☏ 326-8600
Largest gay/lesbian library in Alabama. Gay Center also here. Mon-Fri 18-22 h.

BARS

Club 21 (B D glm) Thu-Sat 22-4 h
117 1/2 21st Street North ✉ AL 35203 ☏ 322-0469
Misconceptions Tavern (B F G VS)
600 32nd Street South ☏ 322-1210
Quest (B D GLM OS) 0-24 h
416 24th Street South ✉ AL 35233 ☏ 251-4313

BOOK SHOPS

Lodestar Books (GLM) 10-18, Sun 13-17 h
2020 11th Avenue South, ✉ AL 35205 ☏ 939-3356

CRUISING

-Rushton Park (AYOR)

Huntsville ☏ 256

GAY INFO

Pink Triangle Alliance 9-21 h
☏ 539-4521

SPARTACUS 2001/2002 | 1135

USA/Alabama - Alaska | Hunstville ▸ Fairbanks

BOOK SHOPS
■ **Rainbow's Ltd.** (glm) Mon-Sat 11-21, Sun 13-18 h, closed Tue
522 Jordan Ln NW ✉ AL 35805-2626

Mobile ☏ 334

BARS
■ **B-Bob's** (B D F GLM VS)
6157 Airport Boulevard No. 201 Plaza de Malaga ✉ AL 36608
☏ 341-0102
■ **Exit** (B D glm)
9 North Jackson Street ✉ AL 36611 ☏ 694-0909
■ **Gabriel's Downtown** (AC B CC d GLM MA OS) Mon-Thu 17-?,
Fri-Sat 19-?, Sun 15-? h
55 South Joachim Street ✉ AL 36602 *(Downtown)* ☏ 432-4900
■ **Society Lounge** (! B d GLM)
51 South Conception Street ✉ AL 36602 ☏ 433-9141
■ **Zippers** (B d GLM)
215 Conti Street ✉ AL 36602 ☏ 433-7346
Oldest gay bar in town

DANCECLUBS
■ **Baton Rouge Dance Club** (AC CC D GLM lj MA) Thu-Sun 21- ?
213 Conti Street ✉ AL 36602 ☏ 433 2887

GIFT & PRIDE SHOPS
■ **Rainbow Printing** (glm)
1379 Smokerise Drive ✉ AL 36695 ☏ 607-0041
Cards, envelopes, rubber stamps, announcements etc.

HEALTH GROUPS
■ **Mobile AIDS Coalition**
☏ 432-AIDS
Information and referral line.

SPECIAL INTEREST GROUPS
■ **Gay and Lesbian Student Alliance**
University of South Alabama, University Center ✉ AL 36688

CRUISING
-Downtown area
-Bel Air Mall (AYOR) (Sears restroom)
-Springdale Mall
-University of South Alabama (Restrooms in the University Center, Library and Humanities Bldg.)
-I-10 (P) between Mobile and Pensacola, FL)
-Speedway gas station (Restrooms, truck drivers and adjacent streets, take I-65 North, exit at Moffet Rd., turn right, pass under the I-65, the first gas station on your right is Speedway)

Montgomery ☏ 334

BARS
■ **Hojons** (B D Glm S) 20-?, Sat -2 h, closed Sun-Mon
215 N. Court Street ☏ 269-9672
■ **Jimmy Mac's** (B D GLM P) 19-2 h
211 Lee Street ☏ 264-5933

USA-Alaska

Location: Northern America
Initials: AK
Time: GMT -9
Area: 1,700,138 km^2 / 695,356 sq mi.
Population: 609,000
Capital: Juneau

Anchorage ☏ 907

PUBLICATIONS
■ **Anchorage Press**
702 West 32nd Street, #203 ☏ 561-7737 🖷 561-7777
Alternative GLM magazine.

BARS
■ **O'Grady's** (B f glm MA)
6901 East Tudor Road ☏ 338-1080
■ **Raven** (B GLM lj MA OG) 11-?, Sun 12-? h
618 Gambell Avenue ☏ 276-9672

SEX SHOPS/BLUE MOVIES
■ **Cyrano's Bookstore & Café** (b F glm S) 10-22 h
413 D Street ☏ 274-2599

HOTELS
■ **Aurora Winds Resort B&B** (BF CC g WH wo)
7501 Upper O'Malley ✉ AK 99516 ☏ 346-2533 🖷 346-3192

GUEST HOUSES
■ **Alaska Bear Company B&B** (BF G H)
535 East 6th Avenue ✉ 99501-2639 ☏ 277 2327
🖥 www.alaska.net/~akbearco
Convenient downtown location, smoke free B&B. True Alaskan hospitality. Ask for Ted D. Bear and tell him you have his address from SPARTACUS!
■ **Cheney Lake B&B** (BF glm H)
6333 Colgate Drive ☏ 337-4391
■ **Pink Whale. The** (BF glm H)
3627 Randolph Street ☏ 561-9283

HELP WITH PROBLEMS
■ **Gay/Lesbian Helpline**
☏ 276-3909 ☏ 258-4777

Fairbanks ☏ 907

HOTELS
■ **Fairbanks Hotel** (CC glm H)
517 Third Avenue ✉ AK 99701 ☏ 456-6411 🖷 456-1792
🖥 fbxhotl@alaska.net
Located in the center of Downtown Fairbanks.

Juneau ☏ 907

GUEST HOUSES
■ **Pearson's Pond** (AC BF CC f H MA msg OS WH)
4541 Sawa Circle ✉ AK 99801-8723 ☏ 789-3772 🖷 789-6722
✉ pearsons.pond@juneau.com
🖥 www.juneau.com/pearsons.pond
Serene, private retreat on the banks of a peaceful pond.

USA-Arizona
Location: Southwest USA
Initials: AZ
Time: GMT -7
Area: 295,276 km² / 120,768 sq mi.
Population: 4,555,000
Capital: Phoenix

Flagstaff ☏ 520

GAY INFO
■ **Gay and Lesbian Info Line**
☏ 525-1199

BARS
■ **Charlie's** (B glm)
23 North Leroux Street

BOOK SHOPS
■ **Aradia Books** 10.30-17.30 h, closed Sun
116 West Cottage Avenue, AZ 86001 ☏ 779-3817

CRUISING
-Thorp Park (AYOR) (sunset & on WE)

Glendale ☏ 602

HOTELS
■ **Arrowzona Casitas** (AC BF cc g H msg NU OS PI SA SB WH WO) all year
PO Box 11253 ✉ AZ 85318-1234 *(located NW of Phoenix/Scottsdale)*
☏ 561-1200 🖷 561-1200
Located not far from downtown Phoenix. 17 condos with bath/shower/WC, balcony/terrace, phone, satellite TV, VCR, minibar, full kitchen, safe, own key. Provides car park, bicycle hire, riding. Rates from US$ 99 per night per condo (bf incl.)

Phoenix ☏ 602

GAY INFO
■ **Community Center, The** (GLM MA) 10-21 h
24 West Camelback Road, Suite C ✉ AZ 85013 ☏ 265-7283
🖷 234-0873 ✉ info@phxcenter.org
Gay, lesbian and bisexual community center.

PUBLICATIONS
■ **Echo Magazine**
PO Box 16630 ✉ AZ 85011-6630 ☏ 266-0550 🖷 266-0773
✉ editor@echomag.com 🖥 www.echomag.com
General GLM interests magazine published every second week.

■ **Phoenix's Gay Community Yellow Pages**
c/o Outwest Publications ☏ 277-0105 ☏ (800) 849-0406 (toll-free)
🖷 277-1065
■ **Spectrum Weekly**
PO Box 16430 ✉ AZ 85011 ☏ 252-7077 🖷 252-7077
✉ editor@spectrumweekly.com 🖥 www.spectrumweekly.com
Weekly newspaper covering regional and national GLM news.

TOURIST INFO
■ **Phoenix & Valley of the Sun Convention & Visitor Bureau**
400 E. Van Buren ✉ AZ 85004 ☏ 254-6500 🖷 253-4415

BARS
■ **Apollo's** (B d CC G lj) 8-1 h
5749 N. 7th Street ☏ 277-9373
■ **Charlie's** (B D G MA N) 12-1 h
727 W. Camelback Road ✉ AZ 85007 ☏ 265-0224
Country/Western dance bar with patio.
■ **Country Club Bar** (B GLM MA N) Mon-Sat 11-1 h
4428 N. 7th Avenue ☏ 264-4553
■ **Cruisin' Central** (AYOR B G LJ N R SNU) 6-1 h
1011 N. Central ☏ 253-3376
Downtown neighborhood pub. Thu night strip shows.
■ **Harley`s 155** (B D GLM) 12-1 h
155 W. Camelback Street ☏ 274-8505
Also: back bar The Cell (B G LJ).
■ **J.C.'s Fun One Lounge** (B GLM) 11-1 h
5542 N. 43rd Avenue, Glendale ☏ 939-0528
■ **Marly's** (AC B d GLM MA N s) 15-1 h
15615 N. Cave Creek Road ✉ AZ 85032 ☏ 867-2463
■ **Nu Towne Saloon** (B f G LJ) 10-1 h
5002 E. Van Buren Street ☏ 267-9959
■ **Wink's** (! B BF f GLM S) 11-1
5707 N. 7th Street ☏ 265-9002
Popular.

SEX SHOPS/BLUE MOVIES
■ **Castle Superstore** (g VS) 0-24 h
300 East Camelback Road ✉ AZ 85012 ☏ 266-3348
Leather, lingerie, magazines, books, DVD's, toys and more.
■ **Castle Superstore** (g VS) 0-24 h
8802 North Black Canyon Highway ✉ AZ 85051 ☏ 995-1641
Leather, lingerie, magazines, books, DVD's, toys and more.
■ **Castle Superstore** (g VS) 0-24 h
8315 East Apache Trail ✉ AZ 85207 ☏ 986-6114
Leather, lingerie, magazines, books, DVD's, toys and more.

SAUNAS/BATHS
■ **Chute** (AC b DR f G LJ NU P SB VS WO) 0-24 h
1440 E. Indian School Road ✉ AZ 85014 *(West Entrance)*
☏ 234-1654
Private club for bears and leathermen.
■ **Flex** (b G MA OS P PI SA SB VS WH WO) 0-24 h
1517 South Black Canyon Highway ✉ AZ 85009 ☏ 271-9011
Under new management. Heated outdoor pool, full gym equipment and many special rooms. Free condoms. Member specials. Mon Levi&leather night, Tue Gym ID-day, Wed 1/2 price room day, Thu military, Fri student ID-day.

USA/Arizona — Phoenix ▸ Tucson

BOOK SHOPS
■ **Obelisk** (GLM) Mon-Sat 10-22, Sun 12-20 h
24 W. Camelback, Suite A ✉ AZ 85013 ☎ 266-2665
Books, cards, videos, music, magazines, t-shirts and more.

GIFT & PRIDE SHOPS
■ **Unique on Central** (GLM) 10-20 h
4700 N. Central, Suite 105 ✉ AZ 85012 ☎ 279-9691
Pride shopping.

LEATHER & FETISH SHOPS
■ **Tuff Stuff** (LJ) 10-18, Sat -15 h, closed Sun Mon
1714 E. McDowell Road *(near 17th Street)* ☎ 254-9561

TRAVEL AND TRANSPORT
■ **First Travel** Mon-Fri 8-18 h, closed Sat Sun
4700 North Central Avenue #205 ✉ AZ 85012 ☎ 265-0666
📠 265-0135
Full service travel agency serving the Gay Community since 1984.

GUEST HOUSES
■ **Arizona Sunburst Inn** (AC BF CC G msg NU OS PI WH) all year
6245 N. 12th Place, AZ 85014 ✉ AZ 85014 ☎ 274-1474
📠 264-3503 ✉ sunbrstinn@aol.com
✉ members.aol.com/sunbrstinn/index.htm
7 rooms with TV, partly with bath. Guest house provides TV room. Rates double US$ 79, single 69.

■ **Larry's Bed & Breakfast** (AC BF GLM H MA NU OS PI WH)
502 West Claremont Avenue ✉ AZ 85013 ☎ 249-2974
✉ kenezz@earthlink.net
European style B&B in residential area, private home since 1988. Close to gay scene&airport. Rates: $50-70 per day. Rooms with private phone.

■ **Windsor Cottage** (AC BF CC glm MA NU PI OS)
62 West Windsor ✉ AZ 85003 ☎ 264-6309
Bath, cable-TV, refrigerator, microwave, laundry facilities. Rates single US$ 65-95, double 85-125. Addtional bed 15.

APARTMENTS
■ **Arizona Royal Villa Resort** (AC CC G H NU PI WH WO)
1110 East Turney Avenue #8 ✉ AZ 85014 ☎ 266-6883
☎ (888) 266-6884 📠 279-7437 ✉ azroyalvil@aol.com
✉ www.royalvilla.com
7 double rooms and 8 apartments with bath/shower, telephone, TV, minibar, kitchenette, heating and own key. 15 minutes from the airport, convenient location, close to most valley bars.

FETISH GROUPS
■ **Arizona Rangers MC**
PO Box 130 74, AZ 85002

HEALTH GROUPS
■ **AIDS-Info Line**
☎ 234-2752

CRUISING
- Papago Park
- Camelview Plaza Mall
- Fiesta Mall
- Kiwanis Park

Sedona ☎ 520

GUEST HOUSES
■ **Casa Tiigaua B & B** (A AC BF CC GLM MA msg NU OS PI WH)
PO Box 405 ✉ AZ 86339 *(Uptown Sedona)* ☎ 203-0102
☎ (888) 844-4282 (toll-free) 📠 204-1075
✉ tiigaua@sedona.net ✉ www.casatiigaua.com
6 suites. All rooms with jetted tub, fireplace, private decks/patios.

Tucson ☎ 520

GAY INFO
■ **Wingspan Community Center**
422 N. 4th Avenue ☎ 624-1779

PUBLICATIONS
■ **Observer** Mon-Fri 9-16 h
PO Box 50733 ✉ AZ 85703 ☎ 622-7176 📠 792-8382
✉ info@tucsonobserver.com
✉ www.tucsonobserver.com
Gay and lesbian weekly newspaper for Tucson and Greater Arizona.

BARS
■ **IBT's** (B D GLM OS S) 12-1 h
616 N. 4th Avenue/5th Street ☎ 882-3053

■ **Stonewall Eagle** (AC B D f GLM MA N OS S SNU STV WE) 12-? h
2921 North 1st Avenue ✉ AZ 85719 ☎ 624-8805
Monthly changing parties and events.

■ **Venture-N** (B f G lj OS) 6-1, Sun 10-1 h
1239 N. 6th Avenue ✉ AZ 85705 ☎ 882-8224

CAFES
■ **Rainbow Planet Coffee House & Bistro** (BF F GLM MA OS)
Mon-Fri -23, Sat Sun -24 h
606 North 4th Avenue ✉ AZ 85705 ☎ 620-1770
Tucson's only gay coffee house.

DANCECLUBS
■ **Congress Hotel** (A B BF CC D F g H MA OS s)
311 East Congress ✉ AZ 85701 ☎ 622-8848
■ **Rita's** (B F GLM)
3455 East Grand Road ☎ 327-3390

SEX SHOPS/BLUE MOVIES
■ **Speedway Books & Videos** (g MA) 10-15, Fri Sat 10-17 h
3660 East Speedway Boulevard, AZ 85716 ☎ 795-7467
■ **Tropicana Adult Bookstore** (g) 0-24 h
617 West Miracle Mile, AZ 85705 ☎ 622-2289

HOTELS
■ **Hacienda del Sol** (G H PI)
5601 North Hacienda del Sol Road, AZ 85718 ☎ 299-1501
■ **Sun Catcher** (BF g H PI)
105 N. Avenida Javalina ✉ AZ 85748 ☎ 885-0883
☎ (800) 835-8012 (toll-free)

GUEST HOUSES

■ **Catalina Park Inn** (AC BF CC glm MA OS)
309 East 1st Street ✉ AZ 85705 ☎ 792-4541
📧 CPInn@flash.net 🌐 www.catalinaparkinn.com
6 rooms with private bath, phone, TV, some with fireplace. Gourmet BF.

■ **Tortuga Roja B&B** (AC BF CC GLM MA NU PI WH)
2800 East River Road ✉ AZ 85718 ☎ 577-6822
☎ (800) 467-6822 (toll-free) 📧 carl@arizona.edu
2 double rooms, 1 cottage with shower/bath/WC, phone, TV, radio, kitchenette, heating, own key. Hotel provides car park and TV room.

FETISH GROUPS

■ **Desert Leathermen**
PO Box 15 86, AZ 85702

HEALTH GROUPS

■ **AIDS-Hotline** 10-24 h
☎ 326-2437

USA-Arkansas

Location: Southern USA
Initials: AR
Time: GMT -6
Area: 137,742 km² / 56,337 sq mi.
Population: 2,553,000
Capital: Little Rock

Eureka Springs ☎ 501

RESTAURANTS

■ **Jim's & Brent's Bistro** (AC CC F glm MA OS s) 16-24 h, closed Tue-Thu
173 South Main ✉ AR 72632 *(on Planer Hill)* ☎ 253-7457

GUEST HOUSES

■ **Woods Resort, The** (AC CC GLM MA msg WH)
50 Wall Street ✉ AR 72632 ☎ 253-8281
🌐 www.eureka-usa.com/woods
One and two bedroom cottages. TV, VCR, full kitchen.

Fort Smith

CRUISING

-6th and Garrison Street (AYOR)
-Fort Smith, Creekman and Tiles Park

Little Rock ☎ 501

BARS

■ **Backstreet** (AC B D G MA P WE) 21-? h
1021 Jessie Road *(near Discovery III)* ☎ 664-2744
Private Club, but ask someone at the entrance to be their guest.

■ **Discovery III** (B D GLM S) Thu 21-2, Fri Sat 21-5 h, closed Sun-Wed
1021 Jessie Road ☎ 664-4784
Popular.

USA-California

Location: Southwest USA
Initials: CA
Time: GMT -8
Area: 424,002 km² / 173,417 sq mi.
Population: 32,268,000
Capital: Sacramento
Important gay cities: Long Beach, Los Angeles, Palm Springs, Russian River, San Diego, San Francisco

California is likely to be the most interesting of the US-states for gay men, which is not only due to the immense gay scene here, but also to the relaxed atmosphere in the *golden state*, the most populated of the US-states. There may be some politically conservative corners in California, but all consenting and non-aggressive sexual acts are legal and anti-discriminatory legislation can be found locally. San Francisco, although its scene has been diminished by AIDS, is a gay capital, a rainbow city, and provides a worthwhile stay. The gay holiday resort *Russian River* is situated in Guerneville, a short trip to the north. On the (car)ride to Los Angeles in the south, you'll pass the region of *Monterey* with its historical missions and scenic landscapes, which are popular tourist destinations. Onward to *Los Angeles*, or to be more precise, to *West Hollywood*, an embodiment of the american dream (or nightmare) of car fetishism, class distinction und body culture. A paradise for visitors delighting in body and bodies. *Disneyland* in Anaheim, Orange County and the seaside town *Laguna Beach*, well loved by artists and gays are situated to the south In *Palm Springs* visitors are presented with incomparably grandiose desert and mountain scenery. To the southwest, lying on the coast, is *San Diego*, a large city with a small reputation. But still the big military presence, boosts the local economy, and a lively gay scene.

USA/California — Allegany ▸ Anaheim

Kalifornien dürfte für schwule Männer der interessanteste US-amerikanische Staat sein. Das liegt nicht nur an der großen Szene des bevölkerungsreichsten US-Staates, sondern einfach auch an der lockeren Atmosphäre im *golden state*.
San Francisco ist, auch wenn AIDS die Szene zeitweise sehr schwächte, eine Rainbow-City und absolut sehenswert. Von dort ist es nur eine kurze Fahrt nordwärts nach Guerneville, dem Zentrum des schwulen Ferienreviers *Russian River*.
Auf dem (Auto-)Weg ins südlich gelegene Los Angeles liegt die bei allen Touristen als Zwischenstop beliebte Gegend von *Monterey* mit ihren historischen Missionen und Naturschönheiten.
Weiter also nach *Los Angeles*, oder genauer gesagt nach *West Hollywood*, dieser Verkörperung des amerikanischen (Alp-)Traums von Autowahn, Statusdenken und Körperkult. Für Körpersüchtige also ein himmlisches Paradies. Südlich davon liegen im Orange County *Disneyland* bei Anaheim und der ebenso bei Künstlern wie bei Schwulen beliebte Badeort *Laguna Beach*.
Mit Unmengen von Wasser, die Luft und Boden feucht halten, wird mitten in der Wüste das Ferienzentrum *Palm Springs* am Leben gehalten. Der Besucher wird hier mit einer unvergleichlich grandiosen Wüsten- und Bergszenerie verwöhnt. Südwestlich davon, an der Küste, liegt *San Diego*. Keine Stadt, die sonderlich von sich reden macht. Aber eine der größten Städte der USA, mit dem Militär als wesentlichem Wirtschaftsfaktor und mit einer lebhaften schwulen Szene.

La Californie est certainement l'état américain le plus intéressant pour le touriste gai, grâce à la qualité de l'infrastructure gaie du plus peuplé des états américains et aussi et à l'atmosphère particulière du "Golden State". En Californie aussi, à trouvera des coins et recoins plutôt conservateurs et rétrogrades, mais sachez bien que les relations sexuelles de tout genre, si elles sont placées sous le signe du consentement et de la non-violence, ne sont pas poursuivies par la loi. Certaines municipalités ont même pris des arrêtés anti-discriminatoires qui mettent homos et hétéros sur le même pied d'égalité.
San Francisco reste la "rainbow city" des Etats-Unis, même si le sida y a causé d'irréparables dégâts. Au nord de San Francisco, on trouve Guerneville et la station banéaire gaie par excellence "Russian River".
Sur la route de Los Angeles, au sud, on peut faire une pause dans la région de Monterey pour y visiter les missions catholiques historiques et jouir des merveilles de la nature.
En descendant encore plus bas, sur Los Angeles, on arrive à West Hollywood, l'incarnation même du rêve/cauchemar américain: le paradis des body-builders, de l'argent et de la voiture. Plus au sud encore, on arrive à Orange County avec son Disney Land (près de Anaheim) et à la station balnéaire de Laguna Beach qui est très prisée par les gais.
En plein coeur du désert, Palm Springs, ville artificielle maintenue en vie par des hectolitres d'eau, offre aux touristes des paysages grandioses et inoubliables. Au sud-ouest de Palm Spring, il y a San Diego, une ville qui fait rarement parler d'elle, mais une des plus grandes du pays. L'Armée y est un des premiers employeurs. L'infrastructure gaie y est assez bien développée.

California es el estado norteamericano más interesante para los homosexuales. Esto no se debe solo a la gran comunidad gay, sino también al relajado ambiente en el *Golden State*. Aunque California no esté libre de aspectos conservadores, aquí toda relación sexual por acuerdo mutuo y sin violencia está permitida. A nivel estatal existen incluso reglamentos de antidiscriminación. A pesar de que el SIDA la debilitó un poco, San Francisco continua teniendo un ambiente gay excepcional, su Rainbow-City tiene que ser visitada. Desde aquí y en dirección hacia el norte se llega al centro vacacional gay llamado *Russian River*. Si se viaja en coche hacia el sur en dirección Los Angeles se puede hacer una pausa en la región de *Monterey* que cuenta con mansiones coloniales de interés histórico así como bellezas naturales. Continuando se llega hasta *Los Angeles* o mejor dicho hasta el *West Hollywood*, ejemplo del típico sueño americano (o la pesadilla); el estatus social, el culto al cuerpo y el automovil como segunda vivienda. Si lo que te gusta es lucir tu cuerpo entrenado, estás aquí en tu paraíso. Más hacia el sur se encuentra en el Orange County *Disneyland* y en las cercanías de Anaheim se localiza el balneario *Laguna Beach* que es muy visitado por artistas y homosexuales. Con grandes cantidades de agua, se mantienen humedos el aire y los suelos de *Palm Spring*. Este centro vacacional en medio del desierto ofrece un paisaje de cadenas montañosas de especial belleza. Hacia el suroeste se encuentra *San Diego*. Esta ciudad a pesar de pasar un poco desapercibida, es una de las más grandes de los E.E.U.U., donde el ejercito ocupa un papel determinante en el ámbito económico y el ambiente gay se muestra bastante interesante.

La California dovrebbe essere lo stato più interessante per i gay. Ciò non dipende solo dal vasto ambiente gay dello stato più popolato della federazione, ma anche dall'atmosfera distesa di *golden state*. In raltà anche in California vi sono angoli conservatori, tuttavia in questo stato non sono punibili i rapporti sessuali non violenti praticati tra consenzienti e a livello locale esistono persino leggi contro la discriminazione. Anche se per un certo tempo l'AIDS ha indebolito l'ambiente gay, *San Francisco* è una città arcobaleno che merita di essere vista. Il viaggio verso Guerneville, al nord, è breve. In poco tempo potete raggiungere la zona di villeggiatura per gay Russian River. Sul tragitto per Los Angeles si trova la zona di *Monterey*, tappa amata da tutti i turisti per le sue missioni storiche e per le bellezze naturali. Si segue poi per *Los Angeles* o, più precisamente, per *West Hollywood*, la materializzazione del sogno americano, maniaco per le auto, lo status sociale e per il culto del corpo. Per chi dà molto valore all'aspetto fisico, dunque, è un vero paradiso. Più a sud nella contea di Orange si trovano *Disneyland* presso Anaheim e la stazione balneare di *Laguna Beach* amata da gay ed artisti. Con ingenti quantità d'acqua, che coferiscono umidità al suolo ed all'aria, viene mantenuto in vita, nel mezzo del deserto, la città turistica di Palm Springs. Qui il visitatore può godere un grandioso ed incomparabile paesaggio desertico e montano. A sud ovest sulla costa si trova San Diego, una delle più grandi città degli USA caratterizzata da basi militari (che costituiscono il fattore economico principale) e da un vivace ambiente gay.

Allegany ☎ 916

HOTELS

■ **Kenton Mine Lodge** (F GLM H)
PO Box 942 ✉ CA 95910 ☎ 287-3212
Open durings season. Call for dates and room rates.

Anaheim ☎ 714

HOTELS

■ **Anaheim A Penny Inn Motel** (AC CC g H PI)
1800 West Lincoln Boulevard ✉ CA 92801 ☎ 774-0950
🖷 497-8598

1140 *SPARTACUS* 2001/2002

California/USA

clinic2go
it's a peace of mind thing

Glad I got the all clear before I came away this time. Last year I got all confused over the Spanish for 'discharge'...

Why worry about getting, or passing on sexually transmitted infections ? Treat yourself to regular check ups and leave the worry behind. Your sexual health - it's a peace of mind thing.

GMFA
Gay Men Fighting AIDS

To volunteer for GMFA write, phone or e-mail: Unit 42, The Eurolink Centre, 49 Effra Road, LONDON SW2 1BZ. 020 7738 6872 newvol@gmfa.demon.co.uk www.demon.co.uk/gmfa

SPARTACUS 2001/2002 | 1141

USA/California — Auburn ▸ Forestville

Auburn ☎ 916
CRUISING
-Nude Beach on American river (downstream)

Bakersfield ☎ 661
BARS
■ **Casablanca Club** (B D GLM) 18.30-2 h
1030 20th Street ✉ CA 93301 ☎ 324-1384
■ **Cellar, The** (B D GLM YG) 17-2 h
1927 K Street ✉ CA 93301 ☎ 322-1229

GENERAL GROUPS
■ **Friends** 18.30-23 h
PO Box 304 ✉ CA 93302 ☎ 323-7311
Support group & community outreach.

CRUISING
-Beach Park (21st Street/Oak Street nights AYOR)

Berkeley
GAY INFO
☞ San Francisco

Boonville ☎ 707
RESTAURANTS
■ **Boont Berry Farm Store** (b F glm) 10-18 h, closed Sun
Highway 128, Santa Rosa-Ukiah ✉ CA 95415 ☎ 895-3576

HOTELS
■ **Toll House Bed and Breakfast** (b BF F glm H WH) Thu-Tue
Highway 253, Santa Rosa-Ukiah ✉ CA 95415 ☎ 895-3630
♿ 895-3632

Buena Park ☎ 714
BARS
■ **Ozz Restaurant** (B CC D F GLM MA S)
6231 Manchester Boulevard ☎ 522-1542
Popular with Disneyland employees. Piano player & disco. Call for details.

Burbank ☎ 818
FETISH GROUPS
■ **Iron Tigers MC**
PO Box 70 91 ✉ CA 91510
Harley-Davidson owners.

Carmel ☎ 831
GAY INFO
☞ Monterey

Castroville ☎ 408
BARS
■ **Franco's Norma Jean Bar** (B D F G S)
10639 Merritt Street ✉ CA 95012 ☎ 633-2090

Cathedral City ☎ 760
GAY INFO
☞ Palm Springs

Cerritos ☎ 562
RESTAURANTS
■ **Avenue 3 Cafe and Catering** (AC CC F glm MA) 11-21 h
12612 South Street ✉ CA 90703 ☎ 865-9215

Chico ☎ 530
GAY INFO
■ **Gay Hotline**
☎ 891-5718

Clear Lake ☎ 707
HOTELS
■ **Blue Fish Cove Resort** (GLM Pl)
10573 East Highway 20 ✉ CA 95422 ☎ 998-1769

CRUISING
-Austin Beach Park (Clear Lake Highlands)
-Kneeling Park
-Library Park (Lakeport)

Cloverdale ☎ 707
HOTELS
■ **Vintage Towers B&B** (BF glm H)
302 North Main Street ✉ CA 95425 ☎ 894-4535

Costa Mesa ☎ 714
BARS
■ **Tin Lizzie Saloon** (B G N) 12-2 h, WE 14-2 h
752 St. Clair Street ✉ CA 92626 ☎ 966-2029

DANCECLUBS
■ **Lion's Den** (B D G MA)
719 W. 19th Street ✉ CA 92627 ☎ 645-3830

Eureka ☎ 707
BARS
■ **Club Triangle** (B D glm) 21-2 h, Sun Gay
535 5th Street ✉ CA 95501 ☎ 444-2582
■ **Lost Coast Brewery Pub** (AC B CC F gLm MA N) 11-1 h
617 4th Street ✉ CA 95501 ☎ 445-4480
Lesbian brewpub.

BOOK SHOPS
■ **Booklegger**
402 2nd Street ✉ CA 95501 ☎ 445-1344
Some Gay titles.

HOTELS
■ **Carter House** (BF H)
301 L Street ✉ CA 95501 ☎ 444 8062

Forestville
GAY INFO
☞ Russian River

Fresno ▶ Laguna Beach | California/USA

Fresno ☎ 209

GAY INFO
■ **Community Link Inc.**
1130 North Wishon ✉ CA 93728 ☎ 264-6973
Call for drop-in hours.
■ **G.U.S. Inc.** Mon-Fri 8-17 h
1999 Tuolumne, Suite 625 ✉ CA 93701 ☎ 268-3541
Counselling and referrals.

BARS
■ **Cave. The** (B G LJ MA OS s) 16-2 h
4538 East Belmont Street ✉ CA 93702 ☎ 251-5972
■ **Express. The** (B F D glm OS S VS) 17-2, Sun 15-2 h
708 North Blackstone ✉ CA 93701 ☎ 233-1791
■ **Palace** (B glm S) 15-2 h
4030 East Belmont Street ✉ CA 93702 ☎ 264-8283
■ **Red Lantern** (B g N) 14-2 h
4618 East Belmont Street ✉ CA 93702 ☎ 251-5898

SEX SHOPS/BLUE MOVIES
■ **Only For You** (glm) 12-22 h
1468 N. Van Ness Avenue ✉ CA 93728 ☎ 498-0284
Video shop
■ **Wildcat Book Store** (g MA VS) 9-24, Sun 12-24 h
1535 Fresno Street ✉ CA 93705 ☎ 237-4525
Erotica, magazines and videos.

BOOK SHOPS
■ **Fig Garden Bookstore**
5148 North Palm Avenue, ✉ CA 93704
Gay/lesbian section.

FETISH GROUPS
■ **Knights of Malta MC**
PO Box 41 62 ✉ CA 93744

CRUISING
-Redeo Park (1st Street & Clinton Street)
-Roeding Park
-Tower District (Olive Street/Wishon Street)
-Woodward Park

Fullerton ☎ 714

SEX SHOPS/BLUE MOVIES
■ **Errogeneous Zone**
343 N. State College Boulevard ✉ CA 92631 ☎ 879-3270

Garden Grove ☎ 714

GAY INFO
■ **Orange County Gay and Lesbian Center** 12-20 h, WE 18-22 h
12832 Garden Grove Boulevard ✉ CA 92643 ☎ 534-0862

BARS
■ **Happy Hour** (B GLM)
12081 Garden Grove Boulevard ✉ CA 92643 ☎ 537-9079
■ **Nick's** (B D G VS)
8284 Garden Grove Boulevard ✉ CA 92644 ☎ 537-1361

DANCECLUBS
■ **Frat House. The** (B D GLM VS) 21-2 h
8112 Garden Grove Boulevard ✉ CA 92644 ☎ 897-3431
Popular.

Glenhaven ☎ 707

HOTELS
■ **Lake Place Resort** (AC glm H SA)
9515 Harbor Drive ✉ CA 59443 ☎ 998-3331
Suburb location, 2 1/2 hours from San Francisco. All rooms with priv. bath/WC, kitchenette and balcony.

Hermost Beach ☎ 310

CAFES
■ **Java Man Coffeehouse** (A BF F GLM WE) Mon-Fri 6-22 h, Sat+Sun 6-23 h
157 Pier Avenue ✉ CA 90254 *(two blocks from beach)*
☎ 379 72 09
Oldest Coffeehouse in Hermost Beach in a Landmark beach house.

RESTAURANTS
■ **Ocean Diner** (AC BF CC F glm WE) Mon-Fri 6-14 h, Sat+Sun 7-15 h
959 Aviation Blvd ✉ CA 90254 *(next to Quality Inn Hotel)*
☎ 372 3739

Huntington Beach ☎ 714

TRAVEL AND TRANSPORT
■ **Golden Eagle Travel**
7238 Heil Avenue ✉ CA 92647 ☎ 848-9090

HOTELS
■ **Colonial Inn Youth Hostel** (glm H)
421 8th Street ✉ CA 92648 ☎ 536-3315 📠 714-536-9485
Forty minutes south of Los Angeles International Airport. Weekly rates available.

Idyllwild ☎ 909

HOTELS
■ **That Special Place** (BF G H)
PO Box 21 81 ✉ CA 92349 ☎ 659-5033
Bed & breakfast inn with individually decorated guest rooms with priv. baths and decks (some with fireplaces), and unsurpassed mountain views.

Laguna Beach ☎ 714

BARS
■ **Boom Boom Room** (! B CC D G YG) 10-2 h
1401 Pacific Coast Highway ✉ CA 92651 *(Mountain Road)*
☎ 494-7588
■ **Hunky's Video Bar and Disco** (AC B CC D glm VS YG) 10-2 h
1401 South Coast Highway ✉ CA 92651 *(at Coast Inn)*
☎ 494-7588
Latest music videos and progressive house music.
■ **Main Street** (B GLM MA)
1460 South Coast Highway ✉ CA 92651 ☎ 494-0056
Cozy piano bar.
■ **Woody's** (AC B CC F GLM MA) 17-01:00h
1305 South Coast Highway ✉ CA 92651 ☎ 376 8809

CAFES
■ **Cafe Zinc Market**
350 Ocean Avenue ✉ CA 92651 ☎ 494-6302

SPARTACUS 2001/2002 | 1143

USA/California | Laguna Beach ▸ Long Beach

Laguna Beach, California

THE COAST INN
BOOM BOOM ROOM

Ocean Front Rooms • Restaurant • Two Bars & Disco
949-494-7588 • 1-800-653-2697
www.boomboomroom.com

■ **Laguna Café, "Woodys"** (B CC G MA WE) 24 hrs- internet gay sitcom
278 Glenneyre Street, # 182 ✉ CA 92651 ☎ (800) 866-8154
Internet gay café. Sitcom filmed there.

RESTAURANTS
■ **Cottage Restaurant** (B BF F g MA OS WE) 7-15, 17-22 h
308 North Coast Highway ✉ CA 92651 ☎ 494-3023
American cuisine.
■ **Mark's** (B F glm)
858 S. Coast Highway ✉ CA 92651 ☎ 494-6711

BOOK SHOPS
■ **Different Drummer Books** (CC glm) 10-20 h
1294 South Coast Highway ✉ CA 92651 ☎ 497-6699
Bestsellers, spirituality

GIFT & PRIDE SHOPS
■ **Gay Mart** (! B CC G) 11-24 h
168 Mountain Road ✉ CA 92651 *(across the street from Boom Boom Room)* ☎ 497-9108
Gifts, video rentals and club wear.

VIDEO SHOPS
■ **Video Horizons** (CC glm) Mon-Thu 11-21, Fri Sat -22, Sun 13-21 h
31678 South Coast Highway ✉ CA 92677 ☎ 499-4519

HOTELS
■ **By The Sea Inn** (AC G H Pl SA SB WH)
475 North Coast Highway ✉ CA 92651 ☎ 497-6645
☎ (800) 297-0007 (toll free) 🖷 497-9499
Garden, downtown neighborhood location, 1,6 km from all gay bars, 20 min to the airport. All rooms with telephone, priv. bath, jacuzzi, some with kitchenette and balcony.
■ **Carriage House** (H G OS)
1322 Catalina Street, ✉ CA 92677 ☎ 494-8945
Centrally located, 1 1/2 hours from L.A. airport. All rooms with kitchenette, priv. bath and balcony.
■ **Coast Inn** (B d f G H)
1401 South Coast Highway ✉ CA 92651 ☎ 494-7588
☎ (800) 653-2697 (toll free)
Also bar "Boom Boom Room".
■ **Hotel Firenze** (H G)
1289 South Coast Highway ✉ CA 92651 ☎ 497-2446
■ **Tides Motor Inn** (AC CC glm H OS Pl)
460 North Coast Highway ✉ CA 92651 ☎ 494-2494
🖷 497-8598.

SWIMMING
-West Street Beach (at the south end of the laguna)

Lake Tahoe ☎ 619
GAY INFO
☞ Tahoe Paradise, California and Lake Tahoe, Nevada
HOTELS
■ **Bavarian House B&B** (BF GLM H)
PO Box 62 45 07 ✉ CA 96154 ☎ 916/544-4411
☎ (800) 431-4411 (Toll free)

Lancaster ☎ 805
BARS
■ **Back Door** (B D GLM) 18-2 h
1255 West Avenue I ✉ CA 93534 ☎ 945-2566

Long Beach ☎ 562
GAY INFO
■ **Long Beach Gay & Lesbian Community Center** (CC GLM MA S) 9-22, Sat 9-18 h
2017 East 4th Street ✉ CA 90814 ☎ 434-4455 🖷 433-6428
✉ center@millenia.com 🖳 millenia.com/~center
BARS
■ **Brit** (B D G MA N) 10-2 h
1744 East Broadway Avenue ✉ CA 90802 ☎ 432-9742
Happy hour 16-19 h
■ **Broadway** (B G MA N) 10-2 h
1100 East Broadway Avenue ✉ CA 90802 ☎ 432-3646
■ **Club Broadway** (B D gLM MA N) 11-2 h
3348 East Broadway Avenue ✉ CA 90803 ☎ 438-7700
■ **Club 5211 / Inspiration** (AC B CC f GLM MA N S STV TV WE) 8-2, Fri-Sat after hour club 2-4/? h
5211 North Atlantic Avenue ✉ CA 90805 ☎ 423-9860
Happy hour daily 8-20 h
■ **Crest. The** (B G LJ MA OS) 14-2 h
5935 Cherry Avenue ✉ CA 90805 ☎ 423-6650
■ **Executive Suite** (B D GLM MA SNU) 20-2 h, Tue closed
3428 East Pacific Coast Highway ✉ CA 90804 ☎ 597-3884
■ **Falcon. The** (AC B CC G MA N) 09-02:00h
1435 East Broadway ✉ CA 90802 ☎ 432-4146
Friendly cruise bar.
■ **Fennel and Hops** (B F glm)
1800 E. Broadway ✉ CA 90802 ☎ 590-8773

Long Beach ▶ Los Angeles | California/USA

■ **Floyd's** (B D G) 18-2, Sun 14-2 h, Mon closed
2913 East Anaheim Street ✉ CA 90804 *(Entrance on Gladys Street)*
☏ 433-9251
■ **Mineshaft. The** (B G LJ MA) 10-2 h
1720 East Broadway Avenue ✉ CA 90802 ☏ 436-2433
Happy hour 16-19 h. Popular.
■ **Pistons**
2020 Artesia Boulevard ✉ CA 90805 ☏ 422-1928
■ **Ripples** (! AC CC D G MA S VS YG) 12-2 h
5101 East Ocean Boulevard ✉ CA 90803 *(across street from beach)*
☏ 433-0357
Two levels, two bars, two dance floors, upstairs bar has a panaramic view of the Pacific Ocean, smoking patio in club.
■ **Silver Fox** (AC B G MA N VS) 16-2 h
411 Redondo Avenue ✉ CA 90814 ☏ 439-6343
Happy hour is very popular.
■ **Styx**
5823 Atlantic Avenue ✉ CA 90805 ☏ 422-5997
■ **Sweetwater Saloon** (B G MA N) 6-2 h
1201 East Broadway Avenue ✉ CA 90802 ☏ 432-7044
Cruisy atmosphere

DANCECLUBS

■ **Que Sera Sera** (AC B D GLM MA S STV) Mon-Fri 17-2,
Sat-Sun 14-2 h
1923 E. 7th Street ✉ CA 90813 ☏ 599-6170

RESTAURANTS

■ **Babouch Moroccan Restaurant** (AC CC E F glm MA S) Tue-Sun 17-24 h, closed Mon
810 S. Gaffey Street, San Pedro ✉ CA 90731 *(Harobor Freeway (110) South to San Pedro)* ☏ (310) 831-0246
Exotic male & female belly dancers.
■ **Birds of Paradise** (B F GLM MA S) 10-1 h
1800 E. Broadway ✉ CA 90802 ☏ 590-8773
Happy hour 16-19 h
■ **Madame JoJo** (b F GLM) 17-22 h, Sun-Mon closed
2941 Broadway Avenue ✉ CA 90803 ☏ 439-3672

SEX SHOPS/BLUE MOVIES

■ **Hot Stuff** (g)
2121 East Broadway ✉ CA 90803 ☏ 433-0692

SAUNAS/BATHS

■ **1350 Club** (b CC G MA OS S SA SB VS WO) 0-24 h
510 West Anaheim Street ✉ CA 90744 *(Los Angeles-Wilmington)*
☏ (310) 830-4784
Big bathhouse newly remodelled. Outside patio with redwood deck, water fountain and a maze. Free condoms. Sun 16 h Barbecue.

Los Angeles ☏ 213

✱ Nowhere in the US does the dream of stardom, wealth and luxury come more true than in Los Angeles. And nowhere else can the corresponding nightmare of highway congestions, brutal race riots and a gigantic city without urbanity be more vividly seen. Speaking of gay L.A. means in reality speaking of the autonomous city of *West Hollywood*, one of the gayest centers of north America. Santa Monica Boulevard could also be called Rainbow Boulevard. The gay center of Los Angeles is in *Silverlake* to the north of *Downtown*. Smaller centers of gay life are in the Valley to the north of Los Angeles conurbation, on the beaches to the west and in Long Beach to the south. A car is indispensable. With it you can reach the gay resort *Laguna Beach* in 90 minutes. A lot, which seems to be gay, is only a facade, but what can one expect in the city, where façades are produced for films. And looking behind the façade of Hollywood is nearly impossible; production halls are not that impressive. Small glimpses of the myth can be gotten on the *Walk of Fame* on Hollywood Boulevard or in the *Universal Studios* on Hollywood Freeway. But one product of Los Angeles is not just façade: the charity for AIDS-victims. Events like the *California AIDS Ride* (on bycicle) or the *AIDS Walk LA* bring large amounts of money for the AIDS-stricken, plus the opportunity to exhibit yourself and keep fit. An activity, which can also be done beautifully in *Venice* on the coast. More reasons for visiting L.A. are the pride-events or the gay days at *Disneyland*.

✱ Nirgendwo sonst kommen die USA dem Traum von Starruhm, Reichtum und Luxus näher. Und nirgendwo sonst ist der dazugehörige Alptraum eindrucksvoller zu erleben: Stundenlange Autobahnstaus, gewalttätige Rassenunruhen, eine Riesenstadt ohne jegliche Urbanität.
Spricht man von schwuler Hinsicht von L.A., dann meint man am ehesten die eigenständige Stadt *West Hollywood*, eine der schwulsten städtischen Gegenden Nordamerikas. Der Santa Monica Boulevard könnte ebensogut Rainbow Boulevard heißen. Los Angeles' schwules Zentrum findet sich in *Silverlake*, nördlich des *Downtown*.
Kleinere Ballungen schwuler Adressen finden sich auch im Valley (im Norden des Ballungsraumes), an den Beaches (im Westen) und in Long Beach (im Süden). Bei diesen Entfernungen ist ein Auto unerlässlich, mit dem man den recht schwulen Badeort *Laguna Beach* im Süden in etwa 90 Minuten erreicht.
Natürlich ist vieles, was so schwul erscheint, nur Fassade. Doch wie sollte es anders sein in der Stadt, in der sich die Fassade *Hollywood* befindet. Zu sehen ist von der allerdings nicht viel, Produktionshallen machen eben keinen Eindruck. Kleine Einblicke in den Mythos erlangt man dennoch am *Walk of Fame* am Hollywood Boulevard oder den *Universal Studios* am Hollywood Freeway. Ein Besuch des neuen Paul Getty Museums ist nicht nur für Kunstfreunde ein Muß.
Eines jedoch ist ganz sicherlich nicht aufgesetzt: Charity, Wohltätigkeit, für die Opfer von AIDS. Veranstaltungen wie der *California AIDS Ride* (per Rad) oder der *AIDS Walk LA* (per pedes) generieren Unsummen für die Betroffenen. Und damit ideale Gelegenheiten, sich sowohl zu zeigen, als auch fit zu halten. Eine Tätigkeit, die sich übrigens auch in *Venice* am Ozean vorzüglich betrachten lässt.
Weitere Gelegenheiten für einen Besuch LAs sind die Pride-Veranstaltungen oder die schwulen Thementage im *Disneyland* in Anaheim.

✱ Nulle part ailleurs aux Etats-Unis, vous ne verrez ce que peut être le rêve américain: gloire, célébrité, luxe. Et aussi le cauchemar que ça peut être: embouteillages monstres, violentes émeutes raciales, ville énorme sans aucune urbanité et tutti quanti...
Quand on parle de Los Angeles gai, on pense plutôt à West Hollywood, un des bastions gais d'Amérique du Nord. Le Santa Monica Boulevard est aux mains des gais. Le centre gai de Los Angeles se trouve à Silverlake au nord de Downtown.
Les quartiers nord (Valley), ouest (Beaches) et sud (Long Beach) valent également le détour. Vu les distances, une voiture est nécessaire. Pour aller à Laguna Beach, par exemple, il faut environ une heure et demie. Attention: tout ce qui a l'air gai ne l'est pas forcément! Comme beaucoup d'autres choses, tout est façade ici. Hollywood en premier lieu. D'Hollywood, on ne voit pas grand chose, si ce n'est que le "Walk of Fame" sur le Hollywood Boulevard ou les "Universal Studios" sur le Hollywood Freeway.
Une chose au moins n'est pas du cinéma: la "Charity" pour les victimes du sida. Le "California AIDS Ride" (course de bicyclette) et le "AIDS Walk LA" (course à pied) sont des manifestations qui rappor-

USA/California — Los Angeles

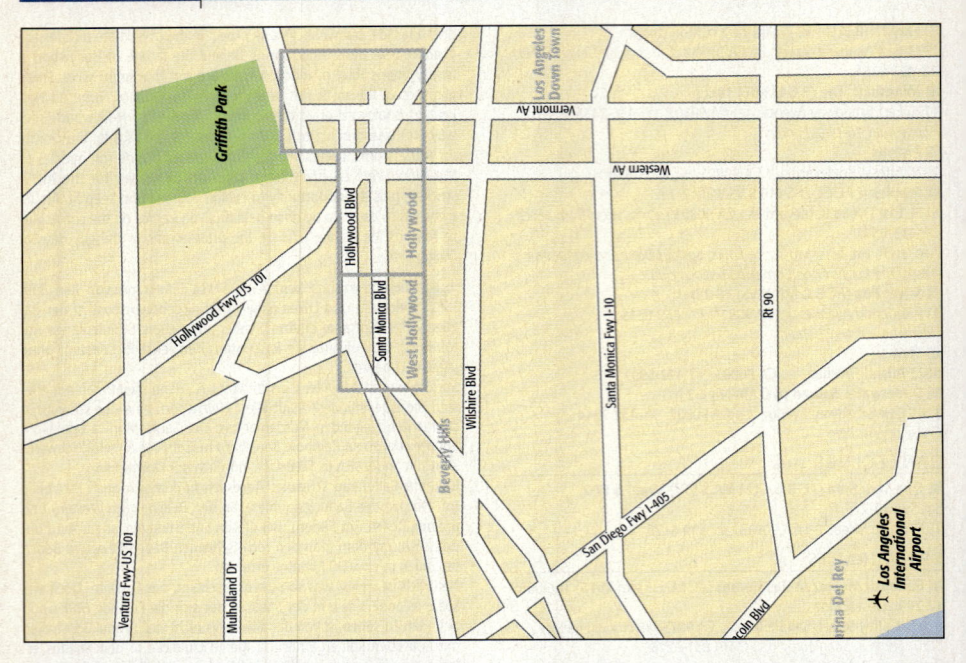

tent d'importantes sommes d'argent que l'on distribue aux malades. Deux bonnes occasions de se montrer et de se maintenir en bonne santé. Les amateurs de culturisme se donnent rendez-vous à Venice Beach.

Profitez de la "Gay Pride" ou des journées gaies de Disney Land (Anaheim) pour découvrir Los Angeles.

En ningún otro lugar de los E.E.U.U. se deja palpar el sueño de éxito, riqueza y lujo, pero tampoco en ningún otro lugar se pueden vivir en carne propia las pesadillas de los enormes congestionamientos viales, violentas disputas rasistas y la falta de sentido de urbanidad. Si se quiere hablar del ambiente gay de L.A. se debe hacer mención inmediata de la ciudad autónoma *West Hollywood*. El Santa Mónica Boulevard podría también llevar el nombre de Rainbow Boulevard. El centro gay de L.A. se encuentra en *Silverlake* al norte de *Downtown*. Pequeñas agrupaciones de direcciones gay se encuentran en Valley (al norte de la aglomeración urbana), en las playas (en el oeste) y en Long Beach (en el sur). Un coche es de vital importancia, debido a las grandes distancias que se deben recorrer. A *Laguna Beach* en el sur, se llega alcanzar en cuestión de 90 min.. Muchos sitios que parecen a primera vista ser gays, lo son solamente de fachada. Pero que se puede esperar de una ciudad que se dedica a la producción de ilusiones. No hay mucho que visitar de esta fábrica de suenos, ya que las salas de producción no provocan pasiones. Un pequeño vistazo en el mito que envuelve a esta ciudad se puede recibir en el *Walk of Fame* en el Hollywood Boulevard o en el *Universal Studios* en Hollywood Freeway. Las obras de caridad para los afectados de SIDA son de especial mención. La organización de eventos como *California AIDS Ride* (en bicicleta) o *AIDS Walk L.A.* (a pie) generan grandes cantidades de dinero para los afectados así como la oportunidad ideal para mostrarse y mantenerse en forma.

Otras oportunidades ideales para visitar L.A. son las fiestas de Pride Gay (orgullo gay) o los días de tematización de la cuestión homosexual en *Disneyland* en Anaheim.

In nessun luogo gli Stati Uniti si avvicinano tanto al sogno di gloria, ricchezza e lusso come in questa città, e da nessuna parte è possibile vivere l'impressionante incubo concomitante il sogno: code stradali interminabili, violenti conflitti razziali e una città senza urbanità. Chi parla della vita gay di Los Angeles intende *West Hollywood*, la zona urbana più gay del Nordamerica. Il boulevard Santa Monica potrebbe chiamarsi boulevard dell'arcobaleno. Il centro gay di Los Angeles si trova a *Silverlake* a nord di *Downtown*. Concentrazioni più piccole di indirizzi gay si trovano anche a Valley (a nord della zona densamente abitata), alle Beaches (ad ovest) e a Long Beach (a sud). Considerate le grandi distanze è indispensabile un'automobile: potrete raggiungere così in 90 minuti la stazione balneare di *Laguna Beach*. La vita gay è molto influenzata dalle apparenze, ma come potrebbe essere altrimenti ad Hollywood. Qui non vi è molto da vedere, considerato che i capannoni di produzione non sono un grande spettacolo. Potrete ottenere piccole impressioni sul mito di Hollywood al *Walk of fame*, sull'Hollywood Boulevard o negli *Universal Studios* sull'Hollywood Freeway. Una cosa però non è artificiale: charity, la beneficenza per le vittime dell'AIDS. Manifestazioni come *California AIDS ride* (in bicicletta) o *AIDS Walk LA* (a piedi) raccolgono ingenti somme e creano occasioni per mostrarsi e per mantenersi in forma; è possibile fare sport anche a *Venice* sull'oceano. Altre occasioni per visitare L.A. sono le manifestazioni Pride e i giorni dei temi gay a *Disneyland* ad Anaheim.

GAY INFO

■ **Gay & Lesbian Community Center** 8.30-22, Sat 9-22 h
1625 N. Schrader Boulevard ✉ CA 90028 ☎ 993-7400

Los Angeles | California/USA

■ **Reactions**
PO Box 12 70, Studio City, ✉ CA 91614-0270 ☎ (818) 877-1000 ☎ (818) 980-8800.

PUBLICATIONS

■ **Center News. The**
c/o Gay and Lesbian Community Center, 1625 North Hudson ✉ CA 90028 ☎ 464-0029
A bimonthly publication of the Los Angeles Gay & Lesbian Community Services Center.

■ **Community Yellow Pages** (GLM) Mon-Fri 10-18 h
2305 Canyon Drive ✉ CA 90068 ☎ 469-4454
Complete gay & lesbian guide to L.A. Annual.

■ **Edge**
6434 Santa Monica Boulevard ✉ CA 90038 ☎ (323) 962-6994
Magazine published biweekly. Edge features reports and articles about the local gay community, cultural events, classified ads.

■ **Fab!**
6363 Wilshire Boulevard # 350 ✉ CA 90038 ☎ (323) 655-5716
🖨 (323) 655-1408 📧 editor@gayfab.com 💻 www.gayfab.com
Biweekly magazine availbale for free at gay venues feating clubs/bars listing.

■ **Frontiers Newsmagazine** Mon-Fri 9-18 h
7985 Santa Monica Boulevard, #109, West Hollywood ✉ CA 90046
☎ 848-2222 🖨 656-8784 📧 gaynewsla@aol.com
💻 www.frontiersweb.com
Biweekly magazine. Features gay related news, political reports, community events, reviews, guide to Southern California, and classified ads.

■ **Leather Journal. The**
7985 Santa Monica Boulevard, Suite 109, West Hollywood ✉ CA 90046
Club News Calendar with listing of upcoming activities, Interviews of prominent individuals in the leather/S&M community, Reviews of major S&M/ leather communities in the U.S.A., classified ads.

■ **Odyssey Magazine**
7985 Santa Monica Boulevard #447 ✉ CA 90046
☎ (323) 874-8788
Everything on the gay party scene in LA.

CULTURE

■ **Tom of Finland Foundation**
1421 Laveta Terrace ✉ CA 90026 ☎ 250-1685 🖨 481-2092
📧 tomfound@earthlink.net 💻 www.eroticsarts.com
Non-profit archives established to collect, preserve, exhibit and publish Tom's drawings. Publishers of a newsletter "Dispatch" relating the activities and programms of the Foundation.

TOURIST INFO

■ **Los Angeles Convention & Visitor Bureau**
633 West Fifth Street, Suite 6000 ✉ CA 90071 ☎ 624-7300
🖨 624-9746.

TRAVEL AND TRANSPORT

■ **David Tours**
310 Dahlia Place, Suite A ✉ CA *(Corona del Mar)*
☎ (949) 723-0699 ☎ (888) 723-0699 (toll-free)
🖨 (949) 723-0666 📧 info@DavidTours.com
💻 www.DAvidTours.com
Call or see webside for details.

GENERAL GROUPS

■ **Black & White Men Together**
7985 Santa Monica Boulevard ✉ CA 90046 ☎ (818) 250-0904

■ **One. Institute and Archives** by appointment only
909 West Adams Boulevard ✉ CA 90007 *(downtown LA, near the campus of the University of Southern California)* ☎ 741-0094
📧 oneigla@usc.edu 💻 www.oneinstitute.org
Oldest gay/lesbian organization in USA. Education, research; largest library on male and female homosexuality, bisexualiy & transgendered persons in America.

HEALTH GROUPS

■ **AID for AIDS**
6985 Santa Monica Boulevard, Suite 109-171 ✉ CA 90038
☎ 656-1107
Nonprofit organization that provides direct financial assistance to people with AIDS or ARC.

■ **Coalition of People with AIDS/L.A.**
☎ (818) 989-7085 ☎ (818) 662-1213
A group whose purpose is to promote self-empowerment of people with AIDS or ARC. With social, political and personal goals, the association is open to all people with AIDS or ARC.

■ **Special Health Education Programm (SHEP)**
☎ 274-7437
Information resource for gay or bisexual men administered by the Shanti AIDS Project. SHEP provides a seminar and support group, both of which address high-risk sexual practices, stress and stress managment, feelings about AIDS, and adjusting to safe sex.

HELP WITH PROBLEMS

■ **Alcoholics Together Center**
☎ 663-8882

■ **Positive Living for US (PLUS)**
☎ 885-0640 ☎ 852-1480
Support for HIV-positives.

■ **Sex Information Helpline**
☎ 653-1123

SPECIAL INTEREST GROUPS

■ **Gay and Lesbian Latinos Unidos**
1625 Hudson Street ✉ CA 90038 ☎ 780-9943

SPORT GROUPS

■ **Golden State Gay Rodeo Association Greater Los Angeles Chapter**
8033 Sunset Boulevard, Ste. 41 ✉ CA 90046 ☎ (310) 498-1675

CRUISING

- Griffith Park (AYOR) (by golf course and Ferndale loop parking lot)
- Beverly Center
- De Longpre Park (AYOR)
- Santa Monica Boulevard (anywhere in West Hollywood)
- Main Street
- Area around block by Gauntlet II
- Sunset Drive (near Vista Theater)
- Encino Park (AYOR)
- Griffith Park (near Sonora and Victory)
- Sepulveda Dam Recreation Area (West end of parking lot)
- Valley Plaza Park

Los Angeles - Downtown ☎ 213

BARS

■ **Red Head. The** (B GLM MA N SNU) 14-2 h
2218 East 1st Street ✉ CA 90033 ☎ 263-2995

■ **Score** (B D G N) 10-2 h
107 West 4th Street ✉ CA 90013 ☎ 625-7382
Popular with Latinos.

USA/California — Los Angeles

DANCECLUBS

■ **Jewel's Catch One** (B D GLM S YG) 15-2, Fri-Sat -4, Thu-Sat from 21 h dancing
4067 West Pico Boulevard ✉ CA 90019 ☏ (323) 734-8849
Popular club which attracts a diverse crowd. Special theme nights.

SAUNAS/BATHS

■ **Midtowne Spa** (B G MA OS PI S SA SB VS WH) 0-24 h
615 South Kohler Street ✉ CA 90021 *(near 6th and Central Streets)*
☏ 680-1838
Big bath house with a redwood sauna and private sundeck with view of LA. Free condoms. Mon 21 h & Sun 15 h Strip parties, Sun 16 h Barbecue party.

Los Angeles - East L.A.

BARS

■ **Plush Pony** (D GLM S)
5261 Alhambra Avenue ✉ CA 90032 *(El Sereno)*
☏ (213) 224-9488
Mainly Latino clientele.

HOTELS

■ **The Whittier House** (AC F GLM MA OS)
12133 South Colima Road, Whittier ✉ CA 90604
☏ (562) 941-7222
Near Disneyland. Early-Callifornia/Spanish style, antique furnishings, fireplace, TV. Two night minimum stay on weekends or holidays. Rates US$ 65-70, double $75-90 (bf incl.).

Los Angeles - Hollywood ☏ 213

BARS

■ **Blacklite. The** (B GLM N) 6-2 h
1159 North Western Avenue ✉ CA 90029 ☏ 469-0211

■ **Faultline. The** (! B G lj MA OS VS) Mon closed, Thu-Thu 16-2, Fri-Sun -4 h
4216 Melrose Avenue ✉ CA 90029 ☏ (323) 660-0889
Popular. Sun afternoon beer bust. Also Faultline store (tel. (323)-660-2952).

■ **Ming's Dynasty** (B G MA s) Tue-Sun 20-2 h
5221 Hollywood Boulevard ✉ CA 90027 ☏ 462-2039

■ **Orbit** (B D G MA VS) Sat 21-? h
6655 Santa Monica Boulevard ✉ CA 90038 ☏ (323) 462-1291

■ **Rawhide** (AC B CC D f GLM LJ MA N os s VS) Mon-Sat 13-2, Sun 14-1 h
10937 Burbank Blvd ✉ CA 91601 *(1 block from intersection of Vineland & Burbonk Boulevard in North Hollywood)* ☏ (818) 760-9798
Oldest classic country/western gay bar in LA. A landmark known for line dancing, two-stepping, handsome cowboys. Famous for Sunday beer bust.

■ **Spit** (B D glm MA) every 3rd Sat 21-3 h
4216 Melrose Ave *(in Faultline)* ☏ (323) 969-2530

■ **Spotlight** (B G N R) 6-2 h
1601 North Cahuenga Boulevard ✉ CA 90028 ☏ 467-2425

■ **Study. The** (! B G MA N) 11-2 h
1723 North Western Avenue ✉ CA 90027 ☏ (323) 464-9551
Friendly neighborhood cocktail lounge. Popular with an African-American crowd.

MEN'S CLUBS

■ **M-B Club** (CC DR G lj MA P VS) Mon-Thu 16-4, Fri -5, Sat 15-5, Sun -4 h
4550 Melrose Avenue ✉ CA 90029 ☏ (323) 663-2241

DANCECLUBS

■ **Circus. The** (! B D G MA VS S) Tue &Fri 21-2 h
6655 Santa Monica Boulevard ✉ CA 90038 ☏ (323) 462-1291
Mainly Latino and African-American crowd.

■ **Club 836** (! AC B D G LJ P) Sat 21- 9 h
836 North Highland Avenue ✉ CA 90028 ☏ (323) 692-5657
Best AC, best music and best bodies in LA. Please be prepared to show your bare chest. Membership US$ 20-25.

■ **Tempo** (! B D G s) 20-2, Fri-Sat -4 h
5520 Santa Monica Boulevard ✉ CA 90038 ☏ 466-1094
Inexpensive and very friendly. GLM on Wed and Thu, L on Sun. Latino nights Tue.

RESTAURANTS

■ **La Poubelle** (b F glm) Mon-Thu 17.30-23.15, Fri Sat 17.30-24 h
5907 Franklin Avenue ✉ CA 90028 ☏ 462-9264
French cooking.

■ **Mexico City** (B F glm MA)
2121 Hillhurst Avenue ✉ CA 90027-2003 ☏ (323) 661-7227
Mexican cuisine.

SHOWS

■ **Cinegrill** (AC B CC E f glm H MG S) 2 shows each night
Roosevelt Hotel, 7000 Hollywood Boulevard ✉ CA 90028
☏ 466-7000
Cabaret.

SEX SHOPS/BLUE MOVIES

■ **Casanova's East**
1626 1/2 Cahuenga Boulevard ✉ CA 90028 ☏ 465-9435

■ **Highland Books Inc.** (g VS) 0-24 h
6775 Santa Monica Boulevard ✉ CA 90028 ☏ 463-0295

■ **Le Sex Shoppe** 0-24
6315 1/2 Hollywood Boulevard ✉ CA 90028 ☏ 464-9435

■ **Pit Shop** 14-2 h
1064 Myra Avenue ✉ CA 90029 ☏ 660-0343

SAUNAS/BATHS

■ **Flex** (b CC f G MA OS P PI SA SB VS WH WO) 0-24 h
4424 Melrose Avenue ✉ CA 90029 ☏ (323) 663-5858
Outdoor heated swimming pool and whirlpool, full gym equipment, tropical foliage on the deck, maze and many rooms. Free condoms.

■ **Hollywood Spa** (! AC B F G MA P SA SB VS WH WO) 0-24 h
1650 Ivar Street, Hollywood ✉ CA 90028 ☏ (323) 463-5169
ID required. Popular.

HOTELS

■ **Chateau Marmont** (AC b g H PI)
8221 Sunset Boulevard West ✉ CA 90046 ☏ 656-1010
Very luxurious; 20 minutes from downtown Los Angeles, 30 min to the airport. All rooms with priv. bath/WC, telephone, kitchenette, balcony.

■ **Coral Sands Hotel** (AC bf G H lj PI SA WH)
1730 North Western Avenue ✉ CA 90027 ☏ (323) 467-5141
📠 (323) 467-4683 📧 www.coralsands-la.com
Located in the heart of Hollywood. All rooms with fridge, bath/WC, TV, telephone, safe, hair-dryer and room-service. Rates single from US$ 58, double 68 (+ tax) incl. BF.

■ **Saharan Motor Hotel** (AC CC f glm H MA N OS PI)
7212 Sunset Boulevard ✉ CA 90046 ☏ 874-6700 📠 874-5163
📧 Sahara-Jaco@worldnet.att.net 📧 www.saharanmotel.com
Located in the heart of Hollywood, 30 minutes to the airport. All rooms with phone, TV, bath/WC.

N
Los Angeles - Hollywood
1 Spotlight Bar
2 Circus Disco
3 Tempo Danceclub
4 The Blacklite Bar
5 Coral Sands Hotel
6 The Study Bar
7 Flex Sauna
Highland Ave.
N. Highland Ave.
Wilshire Country Club
Cahuenga Blvd
N. Vine St.
Franklin Ave.
Lexington Ave
Hollywood Blvd.
Melrose Ave.
Paramount Studios
N. Van Ness Ave.
Sunset Blvd.
Western Ave.
101
Santa Monica Blvd.
Normandie Ave.
Fountain Ave.
Rosewood Ave.
L.A. City College
Barnsdell Park
Vermont Ave.
1
2
3
4
5
6
7

USA/California — Los Angeles

CORAL SANDS HOTEL
www.coralsands-la.com

1730 NORTH WESTERN AVENUE, HOLLYWOOD, CA 90027
FEATURING: HEATED POOL, SAUNA, SPA
OFF STREET PARKING,
FREE CONTINENTAL BREAKFAST
CALL (323)467-5141 FAX (323) 467-4683
TOLL FREE: CA (800) 367-7263 CONT. (800) 421-3650

GUEST HOUSES

■ **Hilltop House. The** (AC BF G H Pl WH)
3307 Bonnie Hill Drive ✉ CA 90068 ☎ 883-0073 📠 969-0073
💻 81235@aol.com.

Los Angeles - San Fernando Valley ☎ 818

BARS

■ **Bananas** (B CC D G MA OS S SNU) 15-2 h
7026 Reseda Boulevard, Reseda ✉ CA 91335 *(south of Sherman Way)* ☎ 996-2976
Special events every week, Good WE crowd. Cute young staff. Popular.

■ **Bullet. The** (B G LJ MA OS) 12-2 h, happy hour Mon-Sat 12-20 h
10522 Burbank Boulevard, North Hollywood ✉ CA 91601
☎ 760-9563

■ **Escapades** (! B D GLM MA N S) 13-2 h
10437 W. Burbank Boulevard, North Hollywood ✉ CA 92601
☎ 508-7008
Pool tables. Popular.

■ **Gold 9** (B D G MA N S) 11-2 h
13625 Moorpark Street, Sherman Oaks ✉ CA 91423
☎ 986-0285

■ **Jox** (B G N S) Mon-Fri 16-2, Sat-Sun 12-2 h
10721 Burbank Boulevard, North Hollywood ✉ CA 91601
☎ 760-9031

■ **Lodge. The** (! B D G N S) 14-2, -4 h at WE
4923 Lankershim Boulevard, North Hollywood ✉ CA 91601
☎ 769-7122
*Neighborhood bar with fireplace. Popular.
Various theme nights.*

■ **Mag Lounge** (B D G YG) 11-2 h
5248 Van Nuys Boulevard, Van Nuys ✉ CA 91401
☎ 981-6693
Popular dance bar.

■ **Oasis** (B G OS VS) 14-2 h
11916 Ventura Boulevard, Studio City ✉ CA 91604
☎ 980-4811
Cozy piano bar with a relaxed atmosphere.

■ **Oxwood Inn** (B D gLM) 15-2, Fri Sun 12-2 h
13713 Oxnard Street, Van Nuys ✉ CA 91401
☎ 997-9666

■ **Queen Mary** (! B g S STV) Wed Sun 17-2 h
12449 Ventura Boulevard, Studio City ✉ CA 91604
☎ 506-5619
King's Den Bar on premises. Popular. Shows at weekends.

■ **Rawhide & Shooterz** (AC B CC D f G LJ MA N OS)
Mon-Fri 18.30-2, Sat&Sun 14-24 h
10937 Burbank Boulevard, North Hollywood ✉ CA 91601
☎ 760-9798
Country western style.

■ **Silver Rail** (AC B G lj MA VS YG) Sep-May: Mon-Fri 16-2, Sat Sun 12-2 h, Jun-Aug: 10-2 h
11518 Barbork Boulevard, North Hollywood ☎ 980-8310

DANCECLUBS

■ **Apache Territory** (B D G lj MA S) Mon-Thu 20-2, Fri Sat 20-4, Sun 16-2 h
11608 Ventura Boulevard, Studio City ✉ CA 91604
☎ 506-0404
Popular.

Los Angeles — California/USA

RESTAURANTS
■ **Venture Inn** (B CC F GLM MA N WE) 11-2 h
11938 Ventura Boulevard, Studio City ✉ CA 91604 ☎ 769-5400

SEX SHOPS/BLUE MOVIES
■ **Big Apple Video**
10654 Magnolia Boulevard, North Hollywood ✉ CA 91601
☎ 769-0325
■ **Le Sex Shoppe**
4539 Van Nuys Boulevard, Sherman Oaks ✉ CA 91403
☎ 501-9609
■ **Twisted Video Rental & Sales**
10530 Burbank Boulevard, North Hollywood ✉ CA 91601
☎ 508-0559
■ **Video West**
11376 W. Ventura Boulevard, Studio City ✉ CA 91604
☎ 760-0096
■ **Video'n Stuff**
11612 Ventura Boulevard, Studio City ✉ CA 91604 ☎ 761-3162

SAUNAS/BATHS
■ **North Hollywood Spa** (b CC F G p S SA SB SOL VS WH WO) 0-24 h
5636 Vineland Avenue, North Hollywood ✉ CA 91601
☎ (800) 772-2582
Upscale bath house with many parties (check website or call).
■ **Roman Holiday Health Club** (B f G msg Pl SA SB WH) 0-24 h
14435 Victory Boulevard, Van Nuys ✉ CA 91401 ☎ 780-1320

HOTELS
■ **L.A. Tura Motel** (AC g H)
11745 Ventura Boulevard, North Hollywood ✉ CA 91604 *(Studio City)* ☎ 762-2160
Gay bars within walking distance, downtown L.A. Rooms with color TV.

Los Angeles - Santa Monica & West L.A. ☎ 310

BARS
■ **Annex Club** (B G N) 12-2 h
835 South La Brea, Inglewood ✉ CA 90301 ☎ 671-7323
■ **Caper Room** (B G S) 11-2 h, Sun Mon 14-2 h
244 South Market Street, Inglewood ✉ CA 90301 ☎ 677-0403
■ **The Friendship Bar** (B G MA N OS) 12-2 h
112 West Channel Road, Santa Monica ✉ CA 90402 *(across the street from gay beach)* ☎ 454-6024
■ **Gauntlet II** (AC B G LJ MA) 16-2, Sat 14-2, Sun 15-2 h
4219 Santa Monica Boulevard ✉ CA 90029 ☎ (323) 669-9472
Leather bar.
■ **Roosterfish** (B G N OS) 11-2 h
1302 Abbot Kinney Boulevard ✉ CA 90291 *(Venice)* ☎ 392-2123
Very popular with a diverse crowd.

RESTAURANTS
■ **Golden Bull Restaurant** (AC B CC F GLM MA OS) Mon-Sat 16.30-24, Sun 11-24 h
170 West Channel Road, Santa Monica ✉ CA 90402 ☎ 230-0402

SAUNAS/BATHS
■ **Roman Holyday Health Club** (g msg SA WH) 0-24 h
12814 Venice Boulevard ✉ CA 90066 *(Mar Vista)* ☎ 391-0200

SWIMMING
-Santa Monica Will Rogers State Beach (Entrada Drive/Pacific Coast Highway)
-Venice beach (Near Westminster Avenue/Ocean Front Walk. By lifeguard stand 15)

Los Angeles - Silverlake ☎ 213

BARS
■ **Cuffs** (! B G LJ MA) 16-2 h
1941 Hyperion Avenue ✉ CA 90027 ☎ (323) 660-2649
Popular.
■ **Detour** (B G lj MA N) 14-2 h
4100 Sunset Boulevard ✉ CA 90029 *(near Sunset Boulevard)*
☎ 664-1189
Cruisy western bar.
■ **The Faultline** (B G LJ MA) Wed-Sat 18-2 h, Sun 14-24 h
4216 Melrose Avenue/Vermont ✉ CA 90029 ☎ 660-0889
Popular with Latinos.
■ **The Garage** (B d G MA) 14-2 h
4519 Santa Monica Boulevard ✉ CA 90029 ☎ 662-6802
■ **Gauntlet II** (B G LJ MA) 16-2 h
4219 Santa Monica Boulevard ✉ CA 90029 ☎ (323) 669-9472
Pool table. Popular.
■ **Houston's Cabaret** (B F G MA s) 11-2 h
2538 Hyperion Avenue ✉ CA 90027 ☎ 661-4233
Food available, Sun brunch.
■ **Hyperion Bar** (! B D G N MA s) 11.30-2, Sat -4 h
2810 Hyperion Avenue ✉ CA 90027 ☎ (323) 660-1503
Popular.
■ **Le Bar** (B D G SNU)
2375 Glendale Boulevard ✉ CA 90039 ☎ 660-7595
Mainly Latino clientele.
■ **Little Joy** (B G N OG) 16-2 h, Sat-Sun 11-2 h
1477 Sunset Boulevard West ✉ CA 90026 ☎ 250-3417
Neighborhood bar with pool tables and jukebox. Popular with Latinos.
■ **Mr. Mike's Piano Bar** (B G OG s) 11-2 h
3172 Los Feliz Boulevard ✉ CA 90039 ☎ 669-9640
■ **Silverlake Lounge** (B d G N S) 10-2 h
2906 W. Sunset Boulevard ✉ CA 90026 ☎ 663-9636
Mainly Latino crowd.

MEN'S CLUBS
■ **Basic Plumbing** (G P) Mon-Fri 20-4 h, Sat Sun 20-5 h
1924 Hyperion Avenue ✉ CA 90027 ☎ 953-6731
Popular. ID required.
■ **Prowl** (B G lj VS) Wed-Sat 22-?, Sun 18-? h
1064 Myra Avenue ✉ CA 90029 ☎ 662-4726
Membership available.

CAFES
■ **Tsunami Coffee House** (A AC f glm lj MA OS S) Tue-Sun 10.30-22 h
4019 Sunset Boulevard ✉ CA 90029 ☎ 661-7771

DANCECLUBS
■ **Dragstrip 66** (B D G MA S) call for infos
2500 Riverside Dr ✉ CA 90039 *(at Rudolpho's)* ☎ (323) 969-2596
■ **Rudolpho's** (b D glm OS S) 20-2
2500 Riverside Drive ✉ CA 90039 ☎ (323) 669-1226
Salsa music.

RESTAURANTS
■ **Casita del Campo** (b F GLM OS) 11-22 h
1920 North Hyperion Avenue ✉ CA 90027 ☎ (323) 662-4255
Mexican food.
■ **Cha Cha Cha** (b F glm) 11-23 h
656 North Virgil Avenue/Sunset ✉ CA 90026 ☎ 953-9991
Delicious Carribean cuisine.

USA/California — Los Angeles

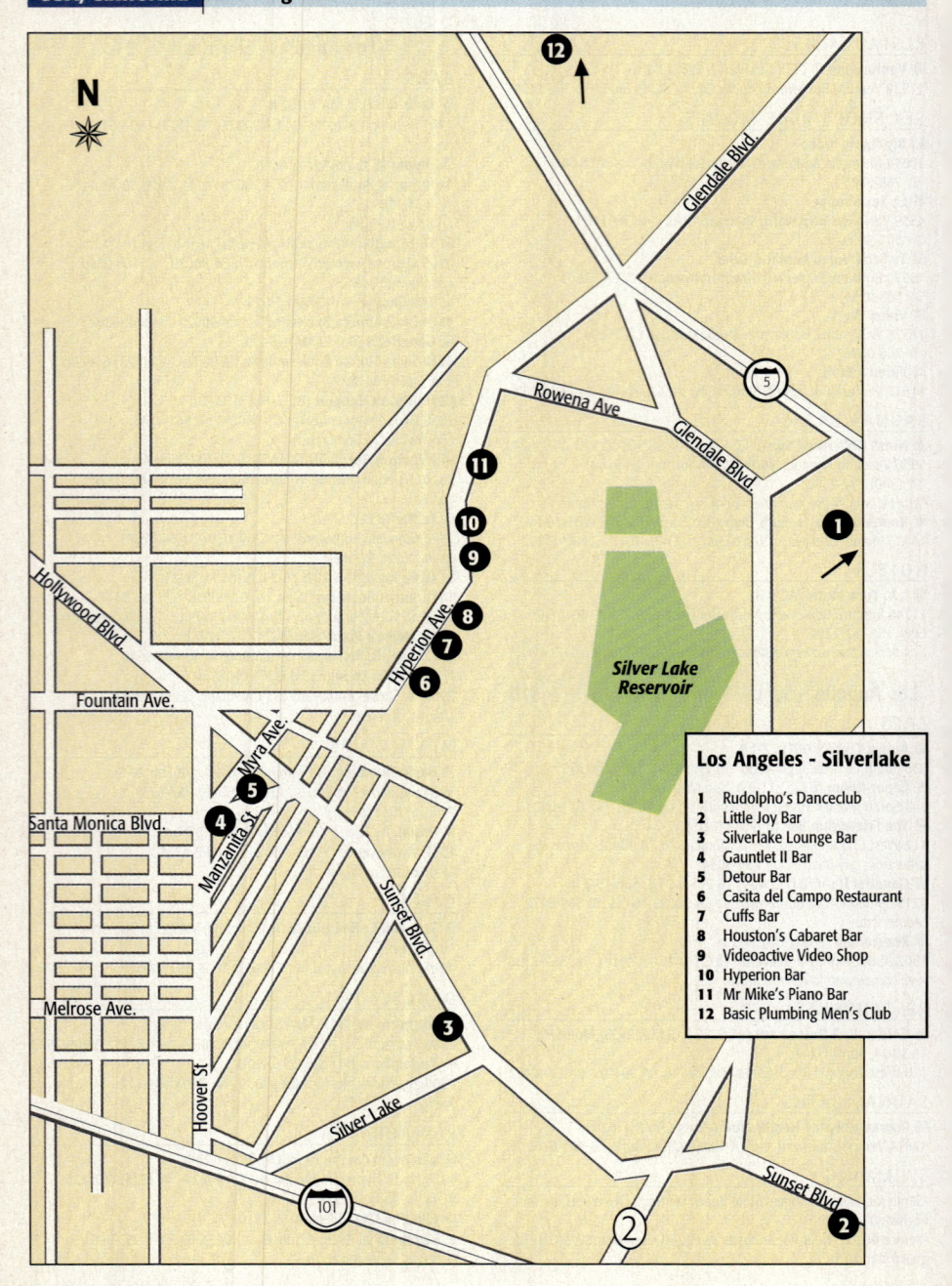

Los Angeles - Silverlake

1. Rudolpho's Danceclub
2. Little Joy Bar
3. Silverlake Lounge Bar
4. Gauntlet II Bar
5. Detour Bar
6. Casita del Campo Restaurant
7. Cuffs Bar
8. Houston's Cabaret Bar
9. Videoactive Video Shop
10. Hyperion Bar
11. Mr Mike's Piano Bar
12. Basic Plumbing Men's Club

Los Angeles | California/USA

■ **Cobalt Cantina. The** (A AC B CC F GLM N OS WE) 11-23 h
4326 Sunset Boulevard ✉ CA 90029 ☏ (323) 953-9991
Very busy Fri evening, 2 for 1 prices until 19 h. Californian/Mexican food.
■ **Crest Coffee Shop**
3725 Sunset Boulevard ✉ CA 90026 ☏ 660-3645
■ **El Conquistador** (AC B CC F GLM MA N OS s) 11-23.30 h
3701 Sunset Boulevard ✉ CA 90026 ☏ 666-5136
Mexican restaurant.
■ **Peloyan's** (b F NG) closed Sun
1806 ½ Hillhurst Avenue ✉ CA 90027 ☏ 663-0049
Armenian cuisine.

SEX SHOPS/BLUE MOVIES
■ **Circus of Books** (g) 6-2 h
4001 Sunset Boulevard ✉ CA 90029 ☏ 666-1304
Retail bookstore with large selection of gay videos and magazines, aromas, lubes, toys.

FITNESS STUDIOS
■ **Body Builders Gym** (g MA WO) Mon-Fri 6.30-21.30 h, Sat Sun 9.30-17.30 h
2516 Hyperion Avenue ✉ CA 90027 (at Griffith Park Blvd)
☏ (323) 668-0802

BOOK SHOPS
■ **Tom of Finland World Headquarters**
1601 Griffith Park Boulevard ✉ CA 90026

VIDEO SHOPS
■ **Video Journeys**
2730 W. Griffith Park Boulevard ✉ CA 90027 ☏ 663-5857
■ **Videoactive** (A AC CC GLM MA) 10-24 h
2522 Hyperion Avenue ✉ CA 90027 ☏ 669-8344

HOTELS
■ **David & Daniel's Delight** (BF g H) 24 h telephone
1353 Elysian Park Drive ✉ CA 90026 ☏ 250-5967
Intimate guest house, central location.

Los Angeles - South Bay ☏ 310

GAY INFO
■ **South Bay Lesbian and Gay Community Organization** (GLM)
Mon- Fri 19.30 -22 h
2009-A Artesia Boulevard, PO Box 2777 ✉ CA 90278 ☏ 379-2850
🖥 southbaycenter.cjb.net
Offers Men's Group, Gay AA Group, Youth Group, Out Dining, Lesbian Group, Bi Social Group, and organizes fund raising events.

RESTAURANTS
■ **Buona Vista Ristorante** (B F glm)
425-439 Pier Avenue, Hermosa Beach, ✉ CA 90254 ☏ 372-2433
■ **Local Yolk. The** (BF CC F g YG)
3414 Highland Avenue, Manhattan Beach ✉ CA 90266
☏ 546-4407
■ **Ocean Diner** (B F GLM)
959 Aviation Boulevard, Hermosa Beach ✉ CA 90254
☏ (562) 372-3739

GUEST HOUSES
■ **Palos Verdes Inn** (AC B CC F glm H MA PI S WO)
1700 S. Pacific Coast Highway, Redondo Beach ✉ CA 90277 (3 blocks from beach) ☏ 316-4211 🖷 (1-800) 421-9241 (toll-free)
🖳 316-4863

RELAX.

(OR NOT)

Swim in our Pool, Play Volleyball,

Rollerblade, Enjoy our free Bikes,

Walk on the Ocean Front, Shop,

Run on the Beach, or Surf.

Sea View Inn
at the beach

3400 Highland Avenue
Manhattan Beach, CA 90266
310.545.1504   310.545.4052 fax
www.seaview-inn.com

■ **Sea View Inn** (AC CC glm H OS PI WO) Office 8-22 h
3400 Highland Avenue, Manhattan Beach ✉ CA 90266 (10 minutes to Los Angeles International Airport) ☏ 545-1504 🖷 545-4052
🖳 seaview@ix.netcom.com 🖥 www.seaview-inn.com
Located two blocks from the ocean with ocean view.

SWIMMING
-Beach at 32nd Street

Los Angeles - West Hollywood ☏ 213

TOURIST INFO
■ **West Hollywood Convention and Visitors Bureau**
☏ (800) 368-6020
Toll Free information about the general & gay scene and West Hollywood.

BARS
■ **Gold Coast** (! B D G MA N VS) 11-2 h, Sat Sun 10-2 h
8228 Santa Monica Boulevard ✉ CA 90046 (at La Jolla)
☏ 656-4879
Popular video bar with cocktail hours. Cruisy atmosphere.

USA/California | Los Angeles

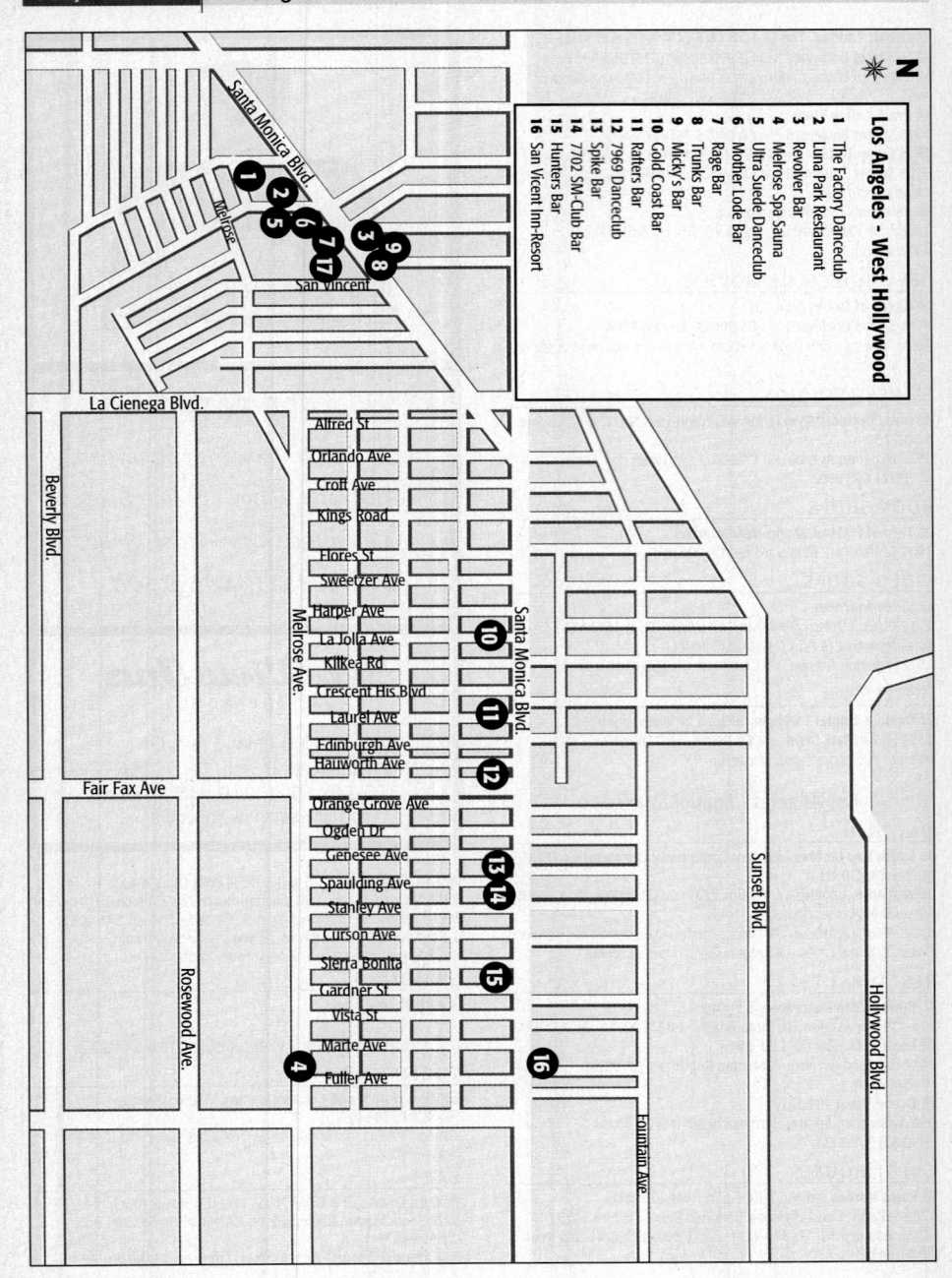

Los Angeles - West Hollywood

1. The Factory Danceclub
2. Luna Park Restaurant
3. Revolver Bar
4. Melrose Spa Sauna
5. Ultra Suede Danceclub
6. Mother Lode Bar
7. Rage Bar
8. Trunks Bar
9. Micky's Bar
10. Gold Coast Bar
11. Rafters Bar
12. 7969 Danceclub
13. Spike Bar
14. 7702 SM-Club Bar
15. Hunters Bar
16. San Vicent Inn-Resort

Los Angeles | California/USA

■ **here Lounge** (B GLM YG)
696 No. Robertson, Santa Monica ✉ CA 90069
New lounge opening in 2001.
■ **Hunters** (B G N R) 19-2 h, Sat Sun 6-2 h
7511 Santa Monica Boulevard ✉ CA 90046 ☏ 850-9428
Pool table.
■ **Micky's** (! AC B D F GLM OS SNU VS YG) 12-2 h
8857 Santa Monica Boulevard ✉ CA 90069 *(Sta.Monica Blvd/San Vicente)* ☏ (310) 657-1176
Popular. Various theme nights.
■ **Mother Lode** (! B G lj MA N VS) 12-2 h
8944 Santa Monica Boulevard ✉ CA 90046 *(at Robertson)*
☏ (310) 659-9700
Cocktail hours, pool table. Popular.
■ **Numbers** (B F G MA) 17-2 h
8741 St Monica Blvd *(at Hancock, 2nd floor)* ☏ 652-7700
■ **Rafters. The** (B G N VS) 12-2 h
7994 Santa Monica Boulevard ✉ CA 90046 ☏ 654-0396
■ **Rage** (! A AC B CC D MA S VS WE) 13-2 h
8911 Santa Monica Boulevard ✉ CA 90069 ☏ (310) 652-7055
Very popular.
■ **Revolver** (! B G VS YG) 16-2, Fri-Sat -4, Sun 14-2 h
8851 Santa Monica Boulevard ✉ CA 90069 *(corner San Vicente)*
☏ (310) 659-8851
Sun beer bust popular.
■ **Spike** (AC B G LJ MA OS s VS) Mon-Fri 15-2, Sat Sun -4 h
7746 Santa Monica Boulevard ✉ CA 90046 ☏ 656-9343
Popular on weekends after 2 h when all the other bars are closed. Various theme nights. Cruisy.
■ **Trunks** (B G N VS) 13-2 h
8809 Santa Monica Boulevard ✉ CA 90069 ☏ (310) 652-1015
■ **7702 SM-Club** (B D G LJ N YG) 6-2 h, Fri-Sat 0-24 h
7702 Santa Monica Boulevard ✉ CA 90046 ☏ 654-3336
Popular after hour club after 6 h on weekends.

CAFES

■ **Big Cup**
7965 Beverly Boulevard ✉ CA 90048 *(Los Angeles)* ☏ 653-5358
■ **Buzz Coffeehouse** (b glm)
8200 Santa Monica Boulevard ✉ CA 90046 ☏ 876-4910
Popular
■ **Greenery Café. The** (B f GLM YG)
8945 Santa Monica Boulevard ✉ CA 90069 ☏ 275-9518
■ **Mel n Rose's**
8344 Melrose Avenue ✉ CA 90046 *(Los Angeles)* ☏ 655-5557
■ **Stonewall Gourmet Coffee Company** (b f GLM MA s) Sun-Wed 7-24, Thu-Sat -3 h
8717 Santa Monica Blvd ☏ (310) 659-8009
■ **Weho Lounge** (f glm)
8861 Santa Monica Boulevard ✉ CA 90069 ☏ (310) 360-0430

DANCECLUBS

■ **Factory. The** (! AC B CC D GLM SNU VS YG) 21-2h, closed Mon-Tue. Wed Latino, Fri (L), Sat (G)
652 N. La Peer Drive North ✉ CA 90069-5602 *(Corner of Santa Monica)* ☏ (310) 659-4551
Largest Danceclub in West Hollywood.
■ **Ultra Suede** (! AC B CC D G MA S VS) 21-2.30 h, closed Mon
661 N. Robertson Boulevard ✉ CA 90069 *(behind Axis Nightclub)*
☏ (310) 659-4551
Theme events nightly.
■ **7969** (B D GLM stv) 21-2h
7969 Santa Monica Boulevard ✉ CA 90046 *(Courner of Fairfax Ave)*
☏ (323) 654-0180
Dragshows Mon & Fri.

OPENING 2001

YOU ARE

here
WEST HOLLYWOOD

696 No. Robertson @ Santa Monica
West Hollywood, CA 90069

SPARTACUS 2001/2002 | 1155

USA/California   Los Angeles ▶ Modesto

RESTAURANTS

■ **Abbey. The** (AC B BF CC F GLM MA N OS) 7-3 h
692 North Robertson Boulevard ✉ CA 90069 ☎ (310) 289-8410
Very popular & cruisy, reservation advisable. Famous for martinis and desserts.

■ **Caffe Luna** (b F glm) 8-3, Fri-Sat -5 h
7463 Melrose Avenue ✉ CA 90046 ☎ 655-8647
Popular bistro cuisine.

■ **Cobalt Cantina** (A AC B CC F GLM N OS WE) Mon-Fri 12-23 h, Sat 11-23 h, Sun 10-23 h
616 N. Robertson Boulevard ✉ CA 90069 ☎ (310) 659-8691
Mexican food.

■ **Figs** (b F glm)
7929 Santa Monica Boulevard ✉ CA 90046 ☎ 654-0780
Home style, tasty and reasonably priced food.

■ **French Quarter** (! b BF CC F GLM OS) 7-24, Fri Sat -3 h
7985 Santa Monica Boulevard ✉ CA 90046 ☎ 654-0898
Good food at reasonable prices. Popular Sun for brunch.

■ **Hoy's Wok** (b F glm) 12-23 h, Sun 16-23 h
8163 Santa Monica Boulevard ✉ CA 90069 ☎ 656-9002
Good chinese cuisine. Many vegetarian dishes.

■ **Luna Park** (AC B CC d E F glm MA OS S) 18-2 h
665 N. Robertson Boulevard ✉ CA 90069 ☎ (310) 652-0611
Bar, restaurant, nightclub. Great shows.

■ **Marix Tex-Mex** (b F glm) 11-24 h
1108 North Flores Street ✉ CA 90048
Texas cuisine.

■ **Mark's** (AC B CC F G MA OS) Mon-Fri 18-22, WE -23 h
861 North La Cienega Boulevard ✉ CA 90069 ☎ (310) 652-5252

■ **Yukon Mining Co.** (AC F GLM OS OS) 24 h
7328 Santa Monica Boulevard ✉ CA 90046 ☎ 851-8833
American steaks, seafood. Friendly staff.

SEX SHOPS/BLUE MOVIES

■ **Casanova's West** 10-1.45 h
7766 Santa Monica Boulevard ✉ CA 90046 ☎ 650-9158

■ **Circus of Books** (g) 6-2 h
8230 Santa Monica Boulevard ✉ CA 90029 ☎ 656-6533
Retail bookstore with large selection of gay videos, magazines, books, aromas, lubes, toys.

■ **Drake's Melrose** (! AC CC G MA VS) 0-24 h
7566 Melrose Avenue ✉ CA 90046 (at Curson) ☎ 651-5600
Originally designed, overwhelming selection of videos and magazines.

■ **Drake's West Hollywood** (AC CC G MA) 10-02.30 h
8932 Santa Monica Boulevard, ✉ CA 90069 (one block west of San Vicente Boulevard) ☎ (310) 289-8932
Videos for sale / rent. Condoms, lube, magazines, guides on sale.

■ **Pleasure Chest. The** (g LJ) 10-23 h
7733 Santa Monica Boulevard ✉ CA 90046 ☎ 650-1022
Erotic department store. Certainly one of the largest selections of leather goods and novelties. Call (800) 753-453 for toll free mail order.

SAUNAS/BATHS

■ **Melrose Spa** (! B G OS S SA VS WH) 0-24 h
7269 Melrose Avenue ✉ CA 90046 ☎ 937-2122
Popular sauna with free condoms. Sun 14 h Barbecue.

FITNESS STUDIOS

■ **Athletic Club** (AC BF CC F G MA msg OS PI SA SB SOL WH WO) 5.30-23, Sat Sun 7-21 h
8560 Santa Monica Boulevard ✉ CA 90069 ☎ (310) 659-6630
Very popular.

BOOK SHOPS

■ **A Different Light** (A AC CC GLM MA S) 10-24 h
8853 Santa Monica Boulevard ✉ CA 90069
☎ (310) 854-6601
In the heart of West Hollywood's gay neighbourhood. Thousands of titles, magazines, videos, gifts, cards etc

■ **Unicorn Bookstore** (GLM) 10.30-22, Fri Sat 10-24 h
8940 Santa Monica Boulevard, ✉ CA 90069
☎ (310) 652-6253
A big choice of gay and lesbian books; newsstand.

EDUCATION SERVICES

■ **New American Language Institute**
P.O. Box 691153 ✉ CA 90069 ☎ (310) 657-5440
📠 (310) 854-6699

GIFT & PRIDE SHOPS

■ **Dorothy's Surrender** (CC G) 10-23.30 h
7985 Santa Monica Boulevard ✉ CA 90046 ☎ 650-4111
Gay gift shop.

LEATHER & FETISH SHOPS

■ **Wayne's Leatherack**
4216 Melrose Avenue ✉ CA 90029 ☎ 913-3530

HOTELS

■ **Le Parc Suite Hotel** (AC B BF CC E F glm H msg N OS PI SA WE WH) 24 h
733 North Knoll Drive ✉ CA 90069 (near Santa Monica Boulevard)
☎ (310) 855-8888 📠 (310) 659-8508 ✉ leparcres@aol.com
🖥 www.leparcsuites.com

GUEST HOUSES

■ **Le Montrose** (AC BF f g H WH PI wo)
900 Hammond Street ✉ CA 90069 ☎ (310) 855-1115
☎ (800) 776-0666 (toll-free) 🖥 www.travelweb.com

■ **San Vincente Inn-Resort** (! AC bf CC f G H MA msg NU PI SB SOL WH WO) All year
845 North San Vincente Blvd ✉ CA 90069 ☎ (310) 854-6915
📠 (310) 289-5929 ✉ infodesk@sanvincente.com
🖥 www.sanvincenteinn.com
Friendly and only gay guesthouse in West-Hollywood. Excellent location. Most rooms have AC .Rates from US$ 59-US$ 199

Modesto ☎ 209

BARS

■ **Brave Bull** (B G LJ) 19-2 h, Sun 16-2 h
701 South 9th ✉ CA 95354 ☎ 529-6712

■ **Mustang Club** (B D GLM S) Mon-Thu 16-2, Fri-Sun 14-2 h
413 North 7th Street ✉ CA 95354 ☎ 577-9694

CAFES

■ **Espresso Caffe** (AC b BF CC F glm MA OS) Mon-Thu 7-23, Fri -24, Sat 10-24, Sun -22 h
3025 McHenry Avenue ✉ CA 95350 ☎ 571-3337
Also restaurant.

LA and West Hollywood's Only Gay Resort

Acknowledged as "one of the 10 best Gay Bed & Breakfasts in North America, and recipient of Out and About "Editor's Choice Award" for the past five years.

Come relax, meet new friends, and enjoy a friendly Gay clothing optional, tropical paradise in the heart of the city. Located mere steps from WeHo's vibrant entertainment & shopping..gyms, restaurants, clubs and more.

- Heated Pool, Jacuzzi & Steamroom
- Complimentary Continental Breakfast
- A/C and TV w/VCR's in each room
- Private telephones with Voice Mail
- Open 24 hours per day

A variety of rooms and suites are available from $ 69-259/night single occupancy; added guests $30/person/night, plus tax. parking additional.

West Hollywood Executive Suites
Adjacent to the Inn, fully furnished and equipped apartments are available for stays of 30 days or more. See wwwgayresort.com for details or call 310-854-6915 Extension 217

San Vicente Inn Resort
845 N. San Vicente Blvd. West Hollywood, CA 90069
Tel. 310-854-6915 • Fax: 310-289-5929
Email: infodesk@sanvicente.com • www.sanvicenteinn.com

USA/California — Monte Rio ▶ Palm Springs

Monte Rio

GAY INFO
☞ Russian River

Monterey ☎ 831

BARS
■ **After Dark** (B D GLM OS VS) 20-2 h
214 Lighthouse Avenue ✉ CA 93940 ☎ 373-7828

RESTAURANTS
■ **Lighthouse Bar & Grill** (B F GLM MA)
281 Lighthouse Avenue ✉ CA 93940 ☎ 373-4488

SWIMMING
-Garrapata Beach, Carmel (g NU WE)
-Carmel Park Beach (from dunes to North end)

CRUISING
-Veteran's Park (bushes & restroom, NG OG AYOR)

Oakland ☎ 510

PRIVATE ACCOMMODATION
■ **Mi Casa Su Casa** (GLM)
PO Box 10327 ✉ CA 94610 ☎ 531 4511
☎ (800) 215 2272 (toll free) 📠 531 4517
📧 homeswap@aol.com 🖥 www.well.com/user/homeswap
International home exchange and hospitality network.

Oceanside ☎ 619

BARS
■ **Capri Lounge** (AC B CC GLM MA)
207 North Tremont ✉ CA 92054 *(Oceanside, 3 blocks from the beach)* ☎ 722-7284

SEX SHOPS/BLUE MOVIES
■ **Midnight Books** 0-24 h
316 3rd Street ✉ CA 92054 ☎ 757-7832

Palm Springs ☎ 760

✱ Just imagine: You leave Los Angeles on the Interstate 10, driving through the desert. And suddenly, at the foot of its majestic mountain ranges, appears out of nothing a green oasis: Palm Springs. Palm Spring itself is only the biggest town of a whole string of towns, for who its name is a sort of trade mark. Here, gay live concentrates in Palm Springs, south of downtown, and in the six kilometres distant *Cathedral City* on Cathedral Canyon Drive.
Following the boomyears of the eigthies, tourism slackened a bit. This baisse has, nevertheless, made Palm Springs more interesting for people with a smaller income. The peak times of Palm Springs are in March/April, when the *Dinah Shore golf tournament*, a popular sporting event attended by many lesbians takes place; in November with the popular *Gay Rodeo*; and at Easter, when the *White Party* with thousands of gay guests takes place. For further information look into one of the local magazines.
Now, don't imagine Palm Springs to be a big city. There is no public transport, so that you'll still need at least a bycicle, if not a car. Yet, too much sightseeing cannot be done as the variety of scenic attractions, which merit leaving the gay resorts, is limited. The dessert comes alive in the interesting *Living Desert Museum*, Indian culture and roots are found in the *Agua Caliente Cultural Museum* and *Mount San Jacinto* is visited by taking the *Palm Springs Aerial Tramway*. Palm Springs offers spectacular holidays for reasonable prices with relaxed recreation.

★ Man stelle sich vor: von Los Angeles aus (in gleicher Entfernung auch von San Diego) fährt man auf der Interstate 10 durch die Wüste. Und inmitten dieser Ödnis mit ihren majestätischen Gebirgszügen taucht völlig unvermutet eine grüne Oase auf: Palm Springs. Dies ist allerdings nur bedingt richtig, denn der größte Ort Palm Springs fungiert nur als "Markenname" für eine ganze Reihe von weiteren Orten. Das schwule Leben konzentriert sich zum einen in Palm Springs südlich der Downtown, zum anderen im etwa sechs Kilometer entfernten *Cathedral City* am Cathedral Canyon Drive.
Nach dem Boom der 80er Jahre hat sich das Tourismus-Geschäft etwas beruhigt. Diese Baisse macht Palm Springs allerdings auch wieder interessant für Leute mit schmalerem Geldbeutel. Weiterhin aber hat Palm Springs seine Spitzenzeiten: das *Dinah Shore Golfturnier* (Ende Mär/Anfang Apr) beschert der Stadt das größte lesbische Fest Amerikas, Ende November gibt es das *Gay Rodeo* (sehr beliebt) und zu Ostern die *White Party* mit Tausenden schwuler Partygäste. Weitere Informationen entnimmt man einem der schwulen Magazine vor Ort.
Nun darf man sich diesen Ort nicht sonderlich groß vorstellen. Es gibt keinen öffentlichen Nahverkehr, so daß man zumindest ein Fahrrad benötigt, vielleicht aber auch ein Auto. Allerdings wird man dieses nicht übermäßig häufig für's Sightseeing einsetzen. Die Auswahl an Attraktionen, die den Weg aus dem schwulen Resort lohnen, ist begrenzt. Die Wüste lebt im interessanten *Living Desert Museum*, die indianischen Ursprünge finden sich im *Agua Caliente Cultural Museum* und per *Palm Springs Aerial Tramway* fährt man auf den Mt. San Jacinto. Palm Springs heißt nicht spektakulär urlauben sondern günstig und ohne großen Szenestreß erholen.

✱ Imaginez un peu: vous venez de Los Angeles, vous traversez le désert sur la "Interstate 10" et au beau milieu du désert et des impressionantes chaînes montagneuses, vous apercevez tout d'un coup un mirage, une oasis. Vous êtes à Palm Spring!
Palm Spring, c'est plusieurs lieux regroupés sous le même nom. Les endroits gais intéressants sont à Palm Spring même (au sud de Downtown) et à Cathedral City (environ 6 km), au bord du Cathedral Canyon Drive.
Le boom touristique des années 80 est terminé. Palm Spring est aujourd'hui plus abordable, moins chère. Profitez des manifestations gaies et lesbiennes pour découvrir la région, p. ex.: fin mars/début avril ("Dinah Shore Golfturnier", la plus grande fête lesbienne du pays), Pâques ("White Party", fête gaie très courrue) et, enfin, novembre ("Gay Rodeo", très populaire). Pour de plus amples informations, consultez les magasines gais locaux.
Palm Spring n'est pas très étendue. Les transports en commun sont inexistants. On a donc besoin d'un vélo ou d'une voiture.
Côté tourisme, il n'y a pas grand chose à faire. A voir cependant: le "Living Desert Museum", la "Agua Caliente Cultural Museum" (Histoire indienne) et le Mont San Jacinto (prenez le "Palm Springs Aerial Tramway" pour y aller). Rien de bien excitant, somme toute! Palm Spring n'est pas le lieu où vous passerez de folles vacances, mais plutôt un endroit où vous pourrez vous remettre du stress et des fatigues des grandes métropoles californiennes.

● El oasis verde de Palm Springs se encuentra en medio del desierto aproximadamente a la misma distancia de L.A. que de San Diego. El nombre Palm Springs es tan solo la denominación de una gran cantidad de lugares. La vida gay se concentra por un lado

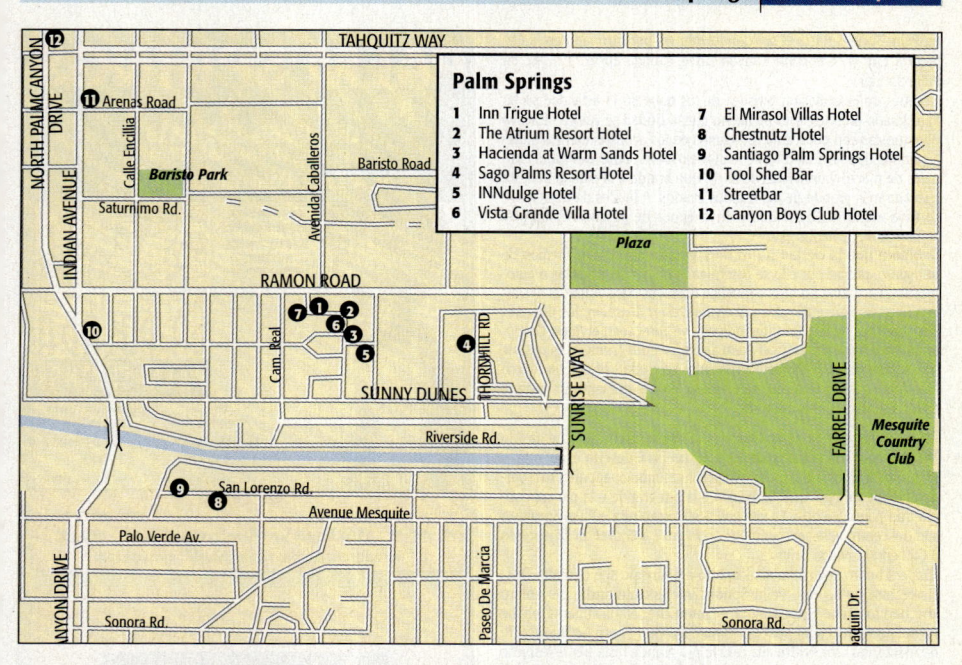

Palm Springs — California/USA

Palm Springs

1. Inn Trigue Hotel
2. The Atrium Resort Hotel
3. Hacienda at Warm Sands Hotel
4. Sago Palms Resort Hotel
5. INNdulge Hotel
6. Vista Grande Villa Hotel
7. El Mirasol Villas Hotel
8. Chestnutz Hotel
9. Santiago Palm Springs Hotel
10. Tool Shed Bar
11. Streetbar
12. Canyon Boys Club Hotel

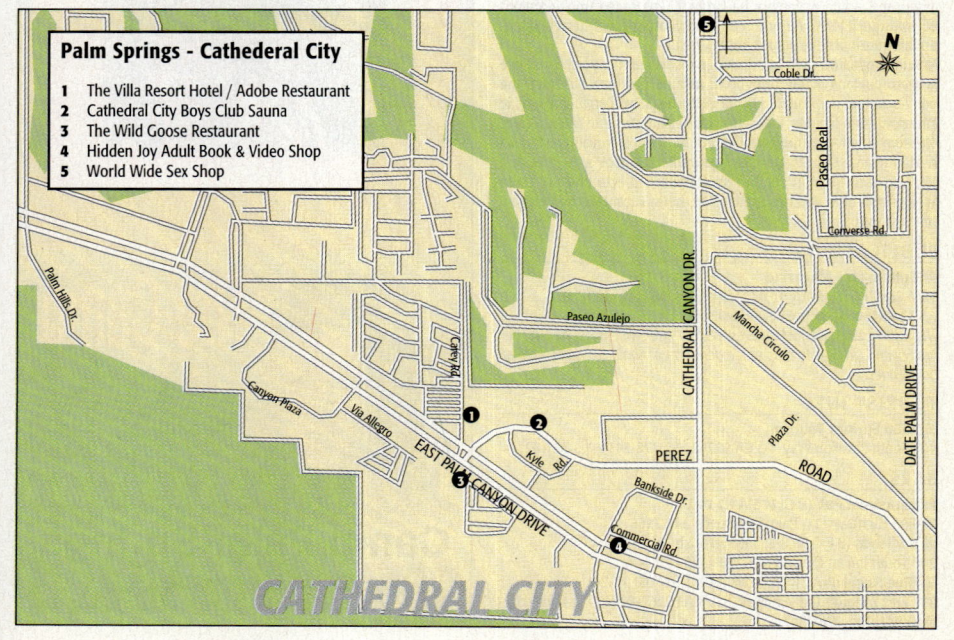

Palm Springs - Cathederal City

1. The Villa Resort Hotel / Adobe Restaurant
2. Cathedral City Boys Club Sauna
3. The Wild Goose Restaurant
4. Hidden Joy Adult Book & Video Shop
5. World Wide Sex Shop

USA/California — Palm Springs

en Palm Springs hacia el sur del downtown, por otro lado en la *Cathedral City* en Cathedral Canyon Drive, situada aprox. a 6 km. de Palm Springs.

Después de la explosión turistica de los años 80 la actividad se ha apaciguado un poco, esto ha hecho que la ciudad se vuelva atractiva para turistas con poco dinero. Algunos de los acontecimientos anuales en los que la ciudad se llena son el *Dinah Shore Golfturnier* (finales de marzo y principios de abril) que brinda a la ciudad la fiesta lesbiana más grande de los Estados Unidos. A finales de noviembre se lleva acabo el *Gay Rodeo* y en la época de pascua *White Party* con miles de invitados gay.

Debido a que la ciudad no es muy grande no existen medios de transporte public, por ello se recomienda el uso de bicicletas o automoviles. La ciudad no ofrece muchos objetivos para visitar. El desierto se puede experimentar en el *Living Desert Museum*, los origenes y costumbres de la población indigena se aprecia en el *Agua Caliente Cultural Museum* y con el *Palm Springs Aerial Tranway* es posible trasladarse hasta el Monte San Jacinto. La ciudad ofrece un marco ideal para gays que se quieran recrear en un ambiente sin ningún estrés y a precios muy comodos.

✖ Immaginatevi: da Los Angeles (a stessa distanza anche da San Diego) con la Interstate 10 si attraversa il deserto e, nel mezzo di questa solitudine dal maestoso profilo montano, appare l'oasi verde di Palm Springs. Questa località è la più grande e la più conosciuta tra i paesi dell'oasi. La vita gay si è concentrata a Palm Springs a sud del centro ed a sei chilometri di distanza a *Cathedral City* presso il Cathedral Canyon Drive.

Dopo il boom degli anni 80 il settore del turismo si è calmato. Questa recessione ha reso Palm Springs interessante anche per coloro che hanno meno disponibilità economiche. Naturalmente anche Palm Springs ha i suoi periodi animati: il *Dinah Shore Golfturnier* (fine marzo/iniz. apr.) offre alla città la più grande festa per le lesbiche americane, a fine novembre ha luogo il *Gay Rodeo* (molto amato) ed a pasqua il *White Party* con migliaia di ospiti gay. Otterrete ulteriori informazioni nelle pubblicazioni locali.

Non immaginatevi però questo luogo molto grande: poichè non vi è la metropolitana avrete bisogno di un'auto o di una bicicletta; ma non le userete per visitare la città visto che, salvo l'ambiente gay, le attrazioni sono limitate. Il deserto vive nell'interessante *Living Desert Museum* e nell'*Agua Caliente Cultural Museum* si trovano resti della civiltà indiana. Con la *Palm Springs aerial tramway* si raggiunge il Mt. San Jacinto. Non sembra spettacolare? Certo che no! Palm Springs non offre vacanze spettacolari, bensì vacanze economiche e senza stress.

PUBLICATIONS

■ **Bottom Line Magazine**
1243 North Gene Autry Tr #121 ✉ CA 92322 ☎ 323-0452
☎ 323-8400 ✉ botmline69@aol.com
The Bottom Line is published every second week with local news, scene articles and Guide with map to the desert area. About 52 pages. Free at gay venues.

TOURIST INFO

■ **Palm Springs Tourism**
401 South Pavillion Way ✉ CA 92262 ☎ 778-8415 🖨 323-8279

BARS

■ **Backstreet Pub** (B GLM MA N) 14-2 h
72-695 Highway 111, Palm Desert ☎ 341 7966
■ **Badlands** (B F G N) 8-2, Sat-Sun 6-2 h
200 South Indian Canyon ☎ 778-4326
■ **Blue Angel** (A AC B CC GLM MA N OS S YG) 17-2 h
777 East Tahquitz Canyon Way, ✉ CA 92262-6781 *(The Courtyard, Suite 341)* ☎ 778-4343

PALM SPRINGS
CALIFORNIA
Call 1-760-323-8813
Toll Free (1-888-866-2744)
For A Free Colorful Gay Guide.

Out & About's
EDITOR'S CHOICE
& FOUR PALMS AWARDS
3 Years Running

PHOTO ©JEFF PALMER

LA POSADA
PALM SPRINGS

Upscale Accommodations — Exclusive Las Palmas Neighborhood
Large Sparkling Pool & Jacuzzi — Spectacular Mountain Views
Clothing Optional — Continental Breakfast

★★★★ 888-411-4949
120 W. Vereda Sur • Palm Springs, CA 92262 IGLTA
www.laposada.com • laposada@laposada.com

NUDE SUNBATHING
Mirage • Vista Grande • Atrium • Avalon

760-322-2404
800-669-1069 • FAX 760-320-1667
3 pools • 3 spas   www.mirage4men.com

The Camp
Frisky
Clothing Optional
29 Luxury Rooms
Day & Weekend Night Passes Available

Camp Palm Springs
800-793-0063 • 760-322-2267
www.camp-palm-springs.com

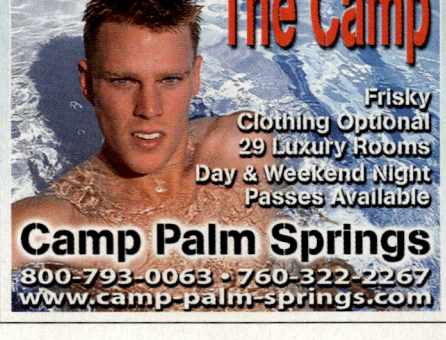

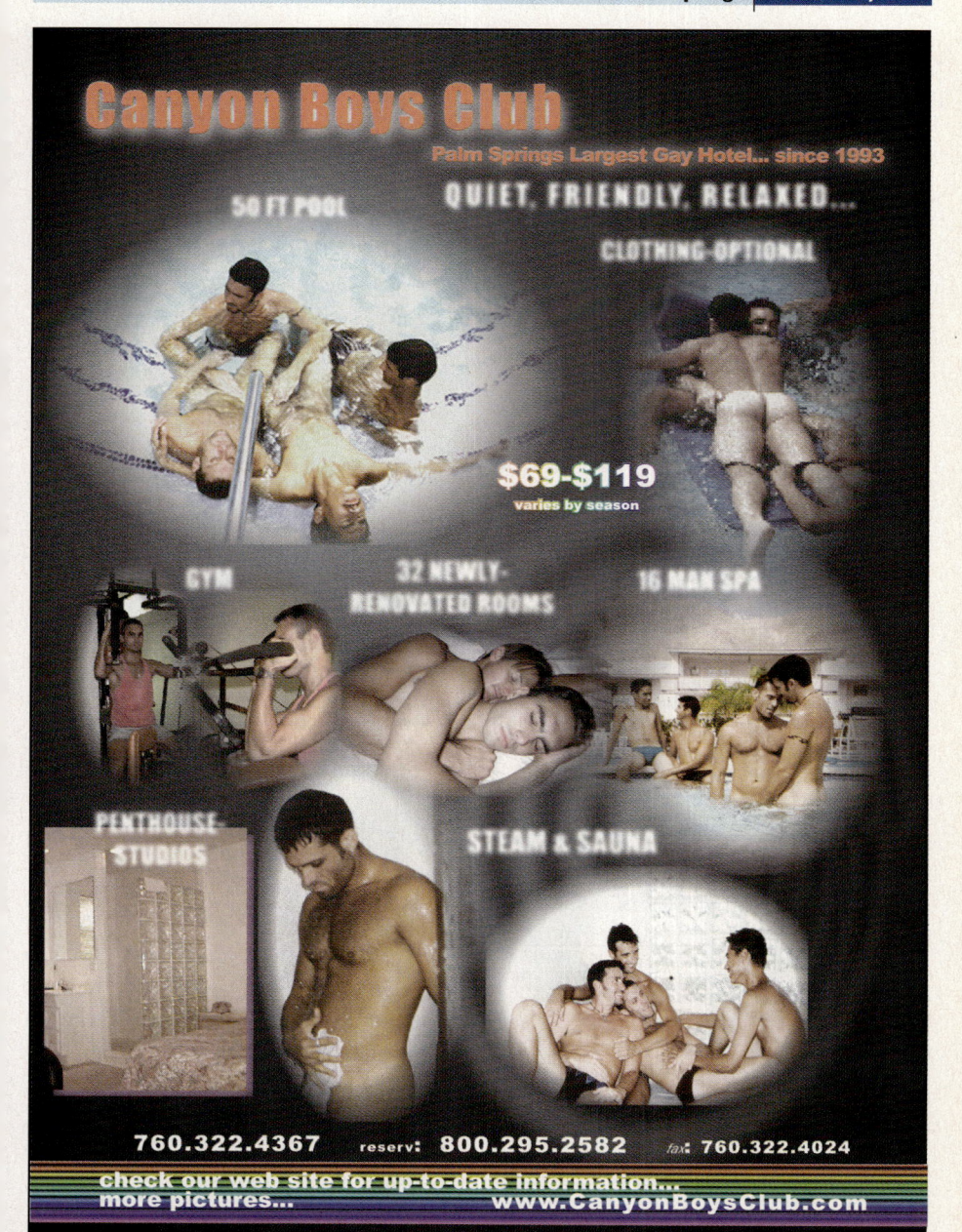

Palm Springs | California/USA

Canyon Boys Club

Palm Springs Largest Gay Hotel... since 1993

QUIET, FRIENDLY, RELAXED...

CLOTHING-OPTIONAL

50 FT POOL

$69-$119
varies by season

GYM   32 NEWLY-RENOVATED ROOMS   16 MAN SPA

PENTHOUSE STUDIOS

STEAM & SAUNA

760.322.4367   reserv: 800.295.2582   fax: 760.322.4024

check our web site for up-to-date information...
more pictures...   www.CanyonBoysClub.com

USA/California — Palm Springs

■ **CC Construction** (AC B CC D DR GLM MA S VS WE) Wed-Fri 19-2, Sat -4, Sun 16-2 h
1775 E. Palm Danyon Drive ✉ CA 92264-1613 *(Smoketree Center, Suite G)* ☏ 778-1234

■ **Dates Bar at the Villa** (AC B BF CC F GLM MA OS PI VS) 11-24, Sat Sun 9-24 h
67-670 Carey Road, Cathedral City ✉ CA 92234 ☏ 328-7211

■ **Ground Zero** (B D GLM S) Mon-Sun 14-2 h
36-737 Cathedral Canyon Road, Cathedral City ☏ 321-0031
Happy hour is from 14-20 h daily. Dance bar with Karaoke Mon, Wed, Fri and Sun starting at 21 h. Sat. country western. Thu Jock night.

■ **Hunter's Video Bar** (B G lj VS) 10-2 h
302 East Arenas Road ☏ 323 0700

■ **Rainbow Cactus Cafe** (AC B F GLM s) 11-2 h
212 South Indian Canyon ✉ CA 92262 *(at Arenas)* ☏ 325-3638
Restaurant & piano bar.

■ **Streetbar** (AC B GLM MA N s OS) 14-2 h
224 E. Arenas Rd. ✉ CA 92262 ☏ 320-1266
Happy hour daily 14-19 h.

■ **Sweetwater Saloon** (B F GLM S) 11-2 h
2420 North Palm Canyon ☏ 320 8878

■ **Tool Shed** (B G LJ) 10-? h
600 East Sunny Dunes Road ✉ CA 92264 ☏ 320-3299

■ **Wolf's Den** (B D G LJ) 16-2 h
67-625 Highway 111, Cathedral City ☏ 321-9688
Cruise bar.

DANCECLUBS

■ **Millennium 2001** (B D GLM) 14-2, Sat-Sun 17-2 h
68-449 Perez Road, Cathedral City ☏ 202 9649

RESTAURANTS

■ **Adobe** (AC BF CC) Mon-Fri 9-3, 18-22 h
67-670 Carey Road, Cathedral City ☏ 328-7211
Reservations highly recommended. Brunch on Saturday and Sunday from 8-15 h.

■ **Red Pepper & Red Tomato** (B CC F glm) 17-22 h
68-748 Est Palm Canyon, Cathedral City *(at Highway)* ☏ 328-7518
Pizza & Pasta.

■ **Wild Goose, The** (AC CC B F GLM s) 17.30-23.30 h
67-938 Highway 111, Cathedral City ✉ CA 92234 ☏ 328-5775
Continental cuisine with entertainment.

SEX SHOPS/BLUE MOVIES

■ **Hidden Joy Adult Book and Video** (g)
68-424 Commercial Road ✉ CA 92234 ☏ 328-1694

■ **World Wide**
68-300 Ramon Road, Cathedral City ✉ CA 92234 ☏ 321-1313

SAUNAS/BATHS

■ **Cathedral City Boys Club** (G MA N P SA SB SOL VS WH WO) 0-24 h
68-369 Sunair Road, Cathedral City ✉ CA 92234 *(at Cathedral Canyon Drive)* ☏ 324-4588

HOTELS

■ **Alexander Resort** (AC BF CC G H nu OS PI WH)
598 Grenfall Road ✉ CA 92264 ☏ 327-6911 ☏ (800) 448-6197 (toll free)
All rooms with priv. bath, TV, some with kitchenette. Rates US$ 79-99. downtown location, 10 minutes to gay bars.

■ **Atrium Resort, The** (AC CC G H MA nu OS PI SOL WH)
981 Camino Parocela ✉ CA 92234 ☏ 322-2404
☏ (800) 669-1069 (toll free) ☏ 320-1667
Three km to the airport. Centrally located. One and two bedroom apartments with priv. bath and TV. Rates US$ 79-165. Check-in is at 574 Warm Sands Drive (Vista Grande).

In the Heart of Warm Sands

INNdulge
PALM SPRINGS

"to pamper, pleasure, or gratify oneself"

22 poolside rooms
Continental breakfast
24 hour pool & Jacuzzi
Poolside happy hour
Gym on site
Rates from $85
Special Summer Discounts
CLOTHING FOREVER OPTIONAL

(800)833-5675 ▼ (760)327-1408
www.inndulge.com
info@inndulge.com

Fax (760)327-7273
601 Grenfall Road, at Parocela
Palm Springs, CA 92264

IGLTA

Palm Springs | California/USA

Bacchanal (AC BF CC G H NU OS PI WH) all year
589 Grenfall Road ✉ CA 92264 ☎ 323-0310 ☎ (800) 806-9059
(toll-free) 📠 416-4107 💻 bacchanal9@aol.com
💻 www.bacchanal.net
Located in the Warm Sands enclave - within walking distance of restaurants and night clubs.

■ **Canyon Boys Club Hotel** (AC BF G H NU PI SA SB OS WH WO)
Office: 9-23 h
960 North Palm Canyon Drive ✉ CA 92262 ☎ 322-4367
☎ (800) 295-2582 📠 322-4024 💻 info@CanyonClub.com
💻 www.CanyonClub.com
On pool clothing is optional. All rooms with TV, video and refrigerator. 50ft pool and 16 man spa. See web site for more details.

■ **Cathedral City Boys Club** (AC bf cc G H NU PI s SA WH)
68-369 Sunair Road, Cathedral City ✉ CA 92234
☎ 324-1350 💻 ccbc@earthlink.net
💻 www.ccbc-gay-resort.com

■ **Chestnutz** (AC BF CC G MA msg NU OS PI VS WH)
641 San Lorenzo Road ✉ CA 92264 ☎ 325-5269
☎ (800) 621-6973. 📠 320-9535 💻 chestnutz@aol.com.

■ **Columns Resort** (AC BF CC G MA NU PI SA WH) Office 8-22 h
537 Grenfall Road ✉ CA 92264 ☎ 325-0655 📠 325-1436
💻 rescolumns@aol.com
A tropical paradise in Warm Sands.

■ **Desert Knight** (BF CC G H PI)
435 Avenida Olancha ✉ CA 92264 ☎ 325-5456

■ **Desert Palms Inn** (AC B BF CC F G H MA OS PI S WH) Reception 0-24, Cafe: 9-15, Wed-Sun 18-22, Bar: 10-24 h
67-580 Highway 111, Cathedral City ✉ CA 92234 ☎ 324-3000
☎ (800) 801-8696 (toll free) 📠 770 5031
💻 dpinn@desertpalmsinn.com 💻 www.desertpalmsinn.com
Special events held throughout the year, across the street from the largest gay disco in Palm Springs. 29 rooms overlooking beautifully landscaped gardens. See web site for more details. Also bar and restaurant.

■ **Desert Paradise Hotel** (BF G H NU PI WH) Office: 8-20 h
615 Warm Sands Drive ✉ CA 92264 ☎ 320-5650
☎ (800) 342-7635 (toll-free)

■ **El Mirasol Villas** (AC BF CC f G H PI SB WH)
525 Warm Sands Drive ✉ CA 92264 ☎ 327-5913
☎ (800) 327-2985 📠 325-8931 💻 mirasolps@aol.com
💻 www.elmirasol.com
All rooms with phone, kitchenette, private bath/WC.

■ **Inn Exile** (AC b BF CC G H MA NU PI WH WO) 24 h
545 Warm Sands Drive ✉ CA 92264 ☎ 327-6413
☎ (800) 962-0186 (reservations) 📠 320-5745
💻 innexile@earthlink.net 💻 www.innexile.com
Popular Warm Sands area of Palm springs.

■ **INNdulge** (AC BF CC G H msg NU PI WH WO) All year / 24h
601 Grenfall Road ✉ CA 92264 (at Parocela) ☎ 327-1408
☎ (800) 833-5675 📠 327-7273 💻 info@inndulge.com
💻 www.inndulge.com
20 poolside rooms, clothing optional. Afternoon happy hour. 24 hour pool and jacuzzi. See website for more details.

■ **Inntimate** (AC BF CC G H NU OS PI) Office: 8-20 h
556 Warm Sands Drive ✉ CA 92264 ☎ 778-8334
☎ (800) 695-3846 (tollfree) 📠 778-9937
Rates US$ 75-105 per room/night.

■ **Mirage** (CC G H NU PI WH)
555 Grenfall Road ✉ CA 92264 ☎ 322-2404 ☎ (800) 669-1069
📠 320-1667 💻 www.mirage4men.com
3 pools and 3 spas. See our web site for further details.

■ **Posada. La** (AC BF CC f G H NU PI)
120 West Vereda Street ✉ CA 92262 ☎ 323-8813
☎ (888) 411-6599 💻 www.laposada.com
"Editors Choice Award '99" from "Out & About".

USA/California — Palm Springs ▸ Redwood City

■ **Sago Palms Resort** (AC BF CC G H MA NU PI WH WO)
Office 9-22 h
595 Thornhill Road ✉ CA 92264 ☏ 323-0224 ☏ (800) 626-7246 (toll-free) ✉ sagopalmca@aol.com
🖥 www.webworkps.com/sago/
Suites with kitchen and fireplace.

■ **Santiago Palm Springs** (BF F G NU OS PI WH WO)
650 San Lorenzo Road ✉ CA 92264 ☏ (800) 710-7729
🖨 416-0347 ✉ santiagops@earthlink.net
🖥 www.prinet.com/santiago

■ **Versailles. Hotel** (AC BF CC G H MA msg PI SOL WH)
288 Camino Monte Vista/Indian Avenue ✉ CA 92262 ☏ 320-2888
Ten min to the airport (free pick up). Centrally located. Gay bars within walking distance. All units with priv. bath, color TV, some with kitchenette. Rates US$ 75-150.

■ **Villa Resort. The** (CC GLM msg PI SA WH)
67-670 Carey Road, Cathedral City ✉ CA 92234 ☏ 328-72 11
🖨 321 14 63 ✉ reservations@thevilla.com 🖥 www.thevilla.com
All rooms with bath/shower and WC, wash-basin, telephone, Satellite TV, radio, air-conditioning. Double and single room rates $49-130 incl. continental breakfast.

■ **Vista Grande Villa** (CC G H NU PI WH WO)
574 Warm Sands Drive ✉ CA 92264 ☏ 322-2404
☏ (800) 669-1069 (toll-free) ✉ mirage4men@aol.com
All rooms with phone, TV/VCR, private baths.

■ **Warm Sands Villas** (B CC G H NU PI VS WH) Office: 9-21 h
555 Warm Sands Drive ✉ CA 92264 (2 miles from airport)
☏ 323-3005 ☏ (1-800) 357-5695 (toll-free) 🖨 323-4006
Exclusively gay resort, open all year. Bilingual (English/German) staff, free parking.

■ **550. The** (BF CC G H lj MA nu PI WH)
550 Warm Sands Drive ✉ CA 92264 ☏ 320-7144
☏ (1-800) 669-0550 (toll-free)
Rates on request.

GUEST HOUSES

■ **Hacienda at Warm Sands. The** (AC BF CC G H MA NU PI WH)
586 Warm Sands Drive ✉ CA 92264 ☏ 327-8111
☏ (800) 359-2007 🖨 778-7890 🖥 www.thehacienda.com
Located in a residential area only minutes away from most gay bars. 7 One bedroom apartments. Luxuriously equipped. Rates please call or see our web site.

■ **InnTrigue** (AC BF CC G H MA NU OS PI WH WO) All year
526 Warm Sands Drive ✉ CA 92264 ☏ 323-7505
☏ (800) 798-8781 🖨 323-1055 ✉ Inntrigue@Earthline.net
🖥 www.gaytravelling.com/inntrigue
Rooms with microwave, coffe makers and fridge. See web site for more info.

■ **Triangle Inn. The** (AC BF CC G H MG msg nu PI WH)
555 San Lorenzo Road ✉ CA 92264 ☏ 322-7993
☏ (800) 732-7555 🖨 322-0784 ✉ triangleinnps@earthlink.net
🖥 www.triangle-inn.com
9 beautiful private rooms. Rates US$ 104-219.

Pasadena ☏ 626

BARS

■ **Boulevard. The** (B D G VS) 11-2 h
3199 East Foothill Boulevard ✉ CA 91107 ☏ 356-9304

■ **Club 3772** (B D G S) 16-24, Fri 12-2, Sat Sun 14-2 h
3772 East Foothill Boulevard ✉ CA 91107 ☏ 578-9359

■ **Nardi's** (AC B CC d f GLM MA OS S) Mon-Thu 15-2, Fri & Sat 13-2 h
162 N. North Sierra Madre Boulevard ✉ CA 91732 ☏ 449-3152

CAFES

■ **Equator Coffee House**
22 Mills Place ✉ CA 91105 ☏ 564-8656

SEX SHOPS/BLUE MOVIES

■ **Le Sex Shoppe** 0-24 h
45 E. Colorado Boulevard ✉ CA 91105 ☏ 578-9260

HEALTH GROUPS

■ **AIDS Service Center**
126 W. Del Mar Boulevard ✉ CA 91105 ☏ 796-5633

CRUISING

-Raymond Avenue Park (AYOR)

Pomona ☏ 909

GAY INFO

■ **Gay/Lesbian Hotline** 18.30-22 h
☏ 824-7618

BARS

■ **Alibi East & Back Alley** (B D GLM MA OS VS) 10-2, Fri Sat -4 h
225 South San Antonio Avenue ✉ CA 91766 ☏ 623-9422

■ **Mary's** (AC B d F GLM MA N S STV) 17 2, Fri-Sun 15-2 h
1047 East Second Street ✉ CA 91766 ☏ 622-1971

■ **Robbie's** (B d F GLM S) Fri-Mon 17-2 h, Mon men only
390 2nd Street ✉ CA 91766 ☏ 620-4371

CAFES

■ **Haven Coffee House & Gallery**
296 W. Second Street ✉ CA 91766 ☏ 623-0538

SEX SHOPS/BLUE MOVIES

■ **Mustang Adult Books** (g) Mon-Thu 8-1, WE 0-24 h
959-961 North Central Avenue, Upland ✉ CA 91786 ☏ 981-0227

SAUNAS/BATHS

■ **Pleasure Spa** (G P SA)
1284 South Garey Avenue ✉ CA 91766 ☏ 622-0951

Red Bluff

CRUISING

-Dog Island Park (days)
-Park along river (early evenings)

Redding ☏ 530

SEX SHOPS/BLUE MOVIES

■ **Adult Bookstore** 0-24 h
2131 Hilltop Drive ✉ CA 96002 ☏ 222-9542

CRUISING

-Clear Creek Road (4 miles East of old 99, nude beach, summer)
-Lake Redding Park (near boad ramp, AYOR)

Redwood City ☏ 650

BARS

■ **Shouts Bar and Grill** (B D e GLM N) 11-2 h
2034 Broadway ✉ CA 94063 ☏ 369-9651
Safe and friendly place. Recommended.

Redwood City ▸ Sacramento — California/USA

SEX SHOPS/BLUE MOVIES
■ **Golden Gate Books** 0-24 h
739 El Camino Real ✉ CA 94063 ☎ 364-6913

Reseda ☎ 818

BARS
■ **Bananas !** (B CC D G MA OS s SNU) 15-2 h
7026 Reseda Boulevard ✉ CA 91335 *(San Fernando Valley)*
☎ 996 2976

Riverside ☎ 909

DANCECLUBS
■ **V.I.P. Club** (B D F GLM) Mon-Thu 16-2 h, Fri Sat -4 h, Sun 11-2 h
3673 Merril Avenue ✉ CA 92506 ☎ 784-2370

SEX SHOPS/BLUE MOVIES
■ **Le Sex Shoppe** 0-24 h
3945 Market Street ✉ CA 92501 ☎ 788-5194

Russian River ☎ 707

BARS
■ **Rainbow Cattle Co.** (B D GLM) 6-2 h
16220 Main Street, Guerneville ✉ CA 95446 ☎ 869-0206
Popular

HOTELS
■ **Camelot Resort** (F GLM H OS PI)
PO Box 467 ✉ CA 95446 *Guerneville* ☎ 869-2538
Conveniently located. Accomodations consist of attractive rooms, spacious cabins and deluxe 2 bedroom apartments.
■ **Dew Drop Inn** (B BF CC F g H MA N WH)
205 Main Street, Point Arena ✉ CA 95468 *(29 miles north of Russian River)* ☎ 882-3027 ☎ (888) 338-9977
Located on the old Highway 1.
■ **The Estate** (B BF E F glm H PI)
13555 Highway 16 ✉ CA 95446 *Guerneville* ☎ 869-9093
Elegant accommodation for people seeking comfort and luxury. All rooms with priv. bath, color TV, telephone. Distance to gay bars: 5 min drive. Rates US$ 75-150 (American bf incl.), meals available.
■ **Fife's** (B BF CC D F glm H lj MA msg OS PI s WE) ask for info
16467 River Road ✉ CA 95446 *(Guerneville)* ☎ 869-9500
☎ (800) 734-3371 🖷 869-0658 💻 info@fifes.com
💻 www.fifes.com
A classic country resort on the Russian River surrounded by redwood forests and meadows.
■ **Highland Dell Inn** (BF CC GLM H PI) Closed in Jan
PO Box 370 ✉ CA 95462 *(Monte Rio)* ☎ 865-1759
☎ (800) 767-1759 (toll free) 💻 highland@netdex.com
💻 www.netdex.com/~highland
Located directly on Russian River.
■ **Highlands Resort** (BF GLM H MA msg NU PI WH)
14000 Woodland Drive ✉ CA 95446 *(Guerneville)*
☎ 869-0333 🖷 869-0370 💻 travel.org/HighlandResort
Convenient location, 20 min to the airport. All rooms with kitchenette, priv. bath. Other facilities: hot tub, campgrounds, TV lounge.
■ **Paradise Cove Resort** (BF GLM H PI)
14711 Armstrong Woods Road ✉ CA 95446 *Guerneville*
☎ 869-2706
Suburb location, in the heart of local gay area. All rooms with kitchenette, priv. bath, WC, color TV and balcony.

■ **Rio Villa Beach Resort** (CC g H OS) all year
20292 Highway 116, Monte Rio ✉ CA 95462 *(Russian river)*
☎ 865-1143 🖷 865-0115 💻 riovilla@sonic.net
💻 www.riovilla.com
■ **Russian River Resort** (B BF CC F G H lj MA msg NU OS PI S VS WE WH) Bar 9-2 h, restaurant 9-21 h
16390 4th Street, Guerneville ✉ CA 95446 ☎ 869-0691
☎ (800) 417-3767 (toll free) 🖷 869-0698
💻 tripleRRR@wclynx.com
■ **Willows. The** (BF GLM H OS)
15905 River Road ✉ CA 95446 *Guerneville* ☎ 869-2824
Downtown neighborhood location, 5 min to local gay bars. All rooms with priv. bath and WC.

GUEST HOUSES
■ **Jacques' Cottage** (GLM H NU PI)
6471 Old Trenton Road, Forestville, ✉ CA 95436 ☎ 575-1033
🖷 573 8911 💻 acques@wco.com

SWIMMING
-Guerneville (NU) (Beach on Russian River at Wohler Bridge)

Sacramento ☎ 916

PUBLICATIONS
■ **Mom Guess What Newspaper** (GLM YG) Mon-Fri 9-18 h
1725 L Street ✉ CA 95814 ☎ 441-6397 🖷 441-6422
💻 info@mgwnews.com 💻 www.mgwnews.com
GL bimonthly newspaper.
■ **Outword Newsmagazine**
709 28th Street ✉ CA 95816-4116 ☎ 329-9280 🖷 498-8445
💻 editor@outword.com 💻 www.outword.com
Biweekly news magazine.

BARS
■ **Depot. The** (B G OS vs) 14-2 h
2001 K Street ✉ CA 95814 ☎ 441-6823
■ **Faces** (AC B CC D GLM MA OS S VS) 14-2 h
2000 K Street ✉ CA 95814 ☎ 448-0706
Bar & disco.
■ **Mercantile Saloon** (B G OG r) 10-2 h
1928 L Street ✉ CA 95814 ☎ 447-0792
■ **Mirage. The** (B GLM N) 11-2 h
601 15th Street ☎ 444-3238
■ **Townhouse** (B F G N) 15-2, WE 10-2 h, Fri Sat dinner, Sun brunch
1517 21st Street ☎ 441-5122

SEX SHOPS/BLUE MOVIES
■ **Adult World** (g)
5138 Auburn Boulevard ✉ CA 95841 ☎ 344-9976

BOOK SHOPS
■ **The Open Book** (A AC CC f GLM MA) Sun-Thu 10-23, Fri Sat -24 h
910 21st Street ✉ CA 95814 *(between I and J Streets)* ☎ 498-1004

GUEST HOUSES
■ **Hartley House B&B Inn** (AC BF CC glm MA msg OS WH) All year
700 22nd Street ✉ CA 95816-4012 ☎ 431 78 55
☎ (800) 831-5806 (toll free) 🖷 431 7859
💻 randy@hartleyhouse.com 💻 www.hartleyhouse.com
Downtown location, 15 min. to airport. B&B inn with garden and deck are for sunbathing. Five rooms with bath/WC, phone, fax, TV, video, radio, own key.

USA/California Sacramento ▶ San Diego

GENERAL GROUPS
■ **Lesbian & Gay Alliance**
6000 J Street ✉ CA 95819 ☎ 451-5725

San Bernardino ☎ 909

BARS
■ **Lark. The** (B D GLM) 12-2 h
917 Inland Center Drive ✉ CA 92408 ☎ 884-8770
■ **Prime Time Food & Spirits**
127 W. 40th Street ✉ CA 92407 ☎ 881-1286

SEX SHOPS/BLUE MOVIES
■ **Bearfacts Adult Bookstore** 0-24 h
1434 East Base Line ✉ CA 92410 ☎ 885-9176

San Diego ☎ 619

GAY INFO
■ **Lesbian & Gay Men's Community Center**
3909 Centre Street ☎ 692-2077
Many activities and groups. Call for info.

PUBLICATIONS
■ **Gay & Lesbian Times**
3911 Normal Street ✉ CA 92103 ☎ 299-6397 🖷 299-3430
💻 editor@uptownpub.com 💻 www.gaylesbiantimes.com
Weekly news magazine.
■ **Update**
2801 4th Avenue ✉ CA 92103 ☎ 299-0500 🖷 299-6907
💻 updateed@aol.com 💻 www.sandiegogaynews.com
Weekly newspaper for Southern California.

CULTURE
■ **Lesbian and Gay Historical Society of San Diego. The**
PO Box 40389 ✉ CA 92164 ☎ 260-1522

TOURIST INFO
■ **San Diego Convention & Visitor Bureau**
401 B Street ✉ CA 92101 ☎ 232-3101 🖷 696-9371

BARS
■ **Bourbon Street** (AC B CC f G MA OS S VS) 14-2, Sat Sun 11-2 h
4612 Park Boulevard ✉ CA 92116 *(University Heights, bus stop in front)* ☎ 291-0173
Entertainment every night. Happy hour Mon-Fri 14-19 h. Popular.
■ **Brass Rail** (B D G stv VS) 10-2 h, Thu Latino night
3796 5th Avenue ✉ CA 92103 *(Hillcrest)* ☎ 298-2233
One of the oldest gay bar in town still popular.
■ **Caliph. The** (B g S) 11.30-2 h
3100 5th Avenue ✉ CA 92103 ☎ 298-9495
Piano bar.
■ **Chee Chee Club** (B G MA N r) 6-2 h
929 Broadway ✉ CA 92101 ☎ 234-4404
■ **Cheers** (B G MA N) 10-2 h
1839 Adams Avenue ✉ CA 92116 *(University Heights)* ☎ 298-3269
■ **Flame. The** (B D gLM s) 17-2, Fri 16-2 h
3780 Park Boulevard ✉ CA 92103 ☎ 295-4163
Lesbian bar. Boys Tue.
■ **Flicks** (B G VS YG) 14-2 h
1017 University Avenue ✉ CA 92103 ☎ 297-2056
Popular on Sun pm.

■ **Hole. The** (B CC F G LJ) 14-2, Sat-Sun 12-2 h
2820 Lytton Street ✉ CA 92103 *(Point Loma)* ☎ 226-9019
Mainly military clientele.
■ **Kickers** (B D F G LJ S) 19-2 h
308 University Avenue ✉ CA 92103 *(Hillcrest)* ☎ 491-0400
■ **Loft. The** (! AC B CC G MA N) 10-2 h
3610 5th Avenue ✉ CA 92103 ☎ 296-6407
■ **Matador. The** (B D g) 12-2 h
4633 Mission Boulevard ✉ CA 92109 *(Pacific Beach)* ☎ 483-6943
Beach bar.
■ **Moby Dick's** (AC B G MA N OS s VS) 12-22 h
642 West Hawthorn Street ✉ CA 92101 *(Harbour area)* ☎ 338-9966
■ **North Park Country Club** (AC B GLM MA N) 13-2 h
4046 30th Street ✉ CA 92104 *(North Park)* ☎ 563-9051
Popular beer bar
■ **Number 1 Fifth Avenue** (AC B G N OS VS) 12-2 h
3845 5th Avenue ✉ CA 92103 *(between Robinson and University Avenue, no sign)* ☎ 299-1911
Smoke friendly patio.
■ **Numbers** (! AC B CC D f G lj MA OS P S VS) 12-2 h
3811 Park Boulevard ✉ CA 92103 *(Hillcrest)* ☎ 294-9005
Popular bar with a new dance floor.
■ **Pecs** (B G lj MA) 12-2 h
2046 University Avenue ✉ CA 92104 *(North Park)* ☎ 296-0889
Popular & cruisy.
■ **Redwing Bar & Grill** (B F G MA N WE) 10-2 h
4012 30th Street ✉ CA 92104 ☎ 281-8700
■ **Shooterz** (B D G VS) 12-2 h
3815 30th Street ✉ CA 92104 *(North Park)* ☎ 574-0744
Pool tables and darts. Cruising atmosphere.
■ **SRO** (B CC GLM MA N) 10-2 h
1807 5th Avenue ✉ CA 92101 *(Uptown)* ☎ 232-1886
■ **Wolf's** (B G LJ)
3404 30th Street ✉ CA 92104 *(North Park)* ☎ 291-3730
■ **Zone. The** (B G LJ N) 16-2 h
3040 North Park Way ☎ 295-8072

CAFES
■ **Big Kitchen. The** (BF f GLM OS) 6-14 h, WE 7-15 h
3003 Grape Street ✉ CA 92102 ☎ 234-5789
Snacks and bf from US$ 3-5.50.
■ **David's Place** (f GLM MA OS) 7-24, Fri-Sun 0-24 h
3766 Fifth Avenue ✉ CA 92103 *(at Robinson Street)* ☎ 296-4173
Nice and friendly place.
■ **Euphoria** (A BF f GLM OS YG) 6-1, Sat-Sun -3 h
1045 University Avenue, ✉ CA 92103 *(near Rich's Rainbow Block)* ☎ 295-1769

DANCECLUBS
■ **Club Montage** (B D F G OS VS YG) 20-2, Fri Sat -4 h, Mon-Wed closed
2028 Hancock Street ✉ CA 92110 ☎ 294-9590
■ **Rich's** (B D G VS YG) Thu-Sat 21-2, Sun 19-2 h
1051 University Avenue ✉ CA 92103 *(Opposite shopping-mall)* ☎ 497-4588
Popular.

RESTAURANTS
■ **California Cuisine** (A AC CC F g MA OS WE) Tue-Fri 11-22, Sat Sun 17-22 h
1027 University Avenue ✉ CA 92103 ☎ 543-0790

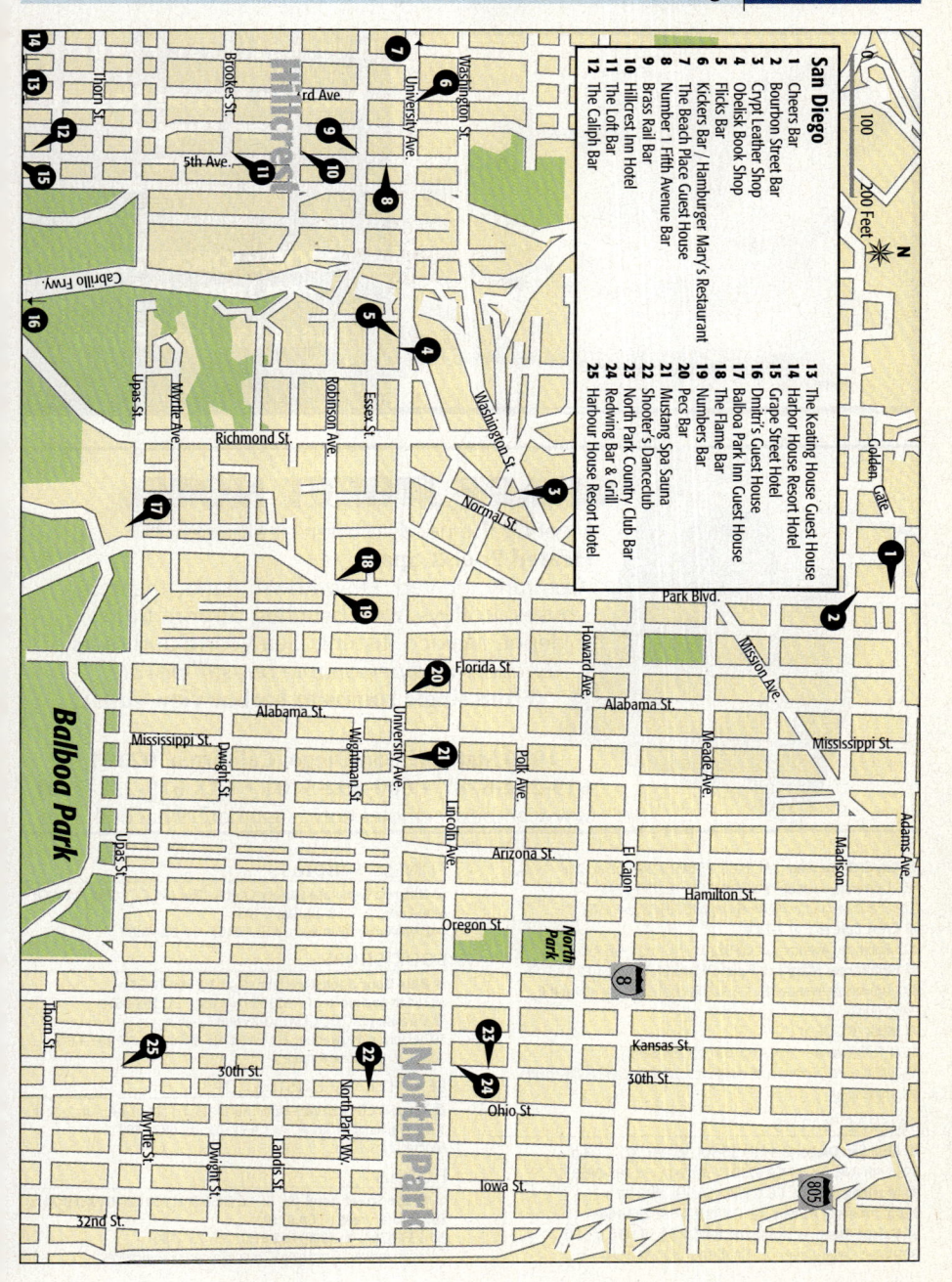

San Diego — California/USA

1. Cheers Bar
2. Bourbon Street Bar
3. Crypt Leather Shop
4. Obelisk Book Shop
5. Flicks Bar
6. Kickers Bar / Hamburger Mary's Restaurant
7. The Beach Place Guest House
8. Number 1 Fifth Avenue Bar
9. Brass Rail Bar
10. Hillcrest Inn Hotel
11. The Loft Bar
12. The Caliph Bar
13. The Keating House Guest House
14. Harbor House Resort Hotel
15. Grape Street Hotel
16. Dmitri's Guest House
17. Balboa Park Inn Guest House
18. The Flame Bar
19. Numbers Bar
20. Pecs Bar
21. Mustang Spa Sauna
22. Shooter's Danceclub
23. North Park Country Club Bar
24. Redwing Bar & Grill
25. Harbour House Resort Hotel

SPARTACUS 2001/2002 | 1167

USA/California — San Diego

International Favorite
Harbor House Resort San Diego
Jacuzzi, Decks,
Tropical Gardens • Walking Distance To All.

Featuring

MOBY DICK'S Bar
Pool Table • Videos

1-619-338-9966 Phone

GRAPE STREET HOTEL
Meeting the needs of men of all ages.
Heated Pool & Spa
Centrally located. Downtown, parks, theaters, buses, trolleys, zoo, beaches, airport, train depot, Mexico, fishing, Sea World and tours
Friendly and personable but still private.
(From single rooms to harbor view suits)

1970 State St., San Diego, California 92101
619-234-6787 • 800-692-5101 • FAX 619-231-3501
www.grapestreethotel.com • gayhotel@pacbell.net

- **City Delicatessen** (! AC CC F GLM) 7-24, Fri Sat -2 h
535 University Avenue ✉ CA 92103 ☎ 295-2747
Large restaurant offering American and Jewish specialties.
- **Crest Café** (B F g) 7-24 h
425 Robinson Avenue ✉ CA 92103 (Hillcrest) ☎ 295-2510
- **Hamburger Mary's** (b F glm OS) 10-22, Fri-Sat 10-23 h
308 University Avenue ✉ CA 92103 (Hillcrest) ☎ 491-0400
Very popular.
- **MiXX** (B CC F g)
3671 Fifth Avenue ✉ CA 92103 ☎ 299-6349
Mix of different cuisines such as Mexican, Italian, French. Reservations recommended.

SAUNAS/BATHS
- **Club San Diego** (B d f SA SB SOL VS WH WO) 0-24 h
3955 4th Avenue ✉ CA 92103 (Hillcrest) ☎ 295-0850
- **Mustang Spa** (AC CC G P PI r SA SOL WH) 24 h
2200 University Avenue ✉ CA 92104 ☎ 297-1661
- **Vulcan Steam & Sauna** (AC B f G P SA SB WH) 0-24 h
805 West Cedar Street ✉ CA 92101 ☎ 238-1980

FITNESS STUDIOS
- **Hillcrest Gym and Fitness Center. The** (AC CC f GLM MA WO)
Mon-Fri 6-22, Sat 8-20, Sun 8-18 h
142 University Avenue, ✉ CA 92103 ☎ 299-7867

BOOK SHOPS
- **Blue Door Bookstore** (glm) 9-21.30, Sun 10-21 h
3823 5th Avenue ✉ CA 92103 (Hillcrest) ☎ 298-8610
- **Obelisk** (! AC CC GLM) 10-23 Sun 12-20 h
1029 University Avenue ✉ CA 92103 (Hillcrest) ☎ 297-4171
Books, cards, music & more.

LEATHER & FETISH SHOPS
- **Crypt** (! CC GLM WE) Mon-Thu 11-23, Fri Sat 11-24, Sun 2-22 h
1515 Washington Street ✉ CA 92103 ☎ 692-9499
Leather & novelties.

HOTELS
- **Grape Street Hotel** (AC BF CC DR G H LJ MA NU PI WH) 0-24 h
1970 State Street ✉ CA 92101
☎ 234-6787 ☎ (800) 692 51 01 🖨 231-3501
Centrally located. From single rooms to harbor view suites.

San Diego ▶ San Francisco | California/USA

Southern California's Host
to the Gay and Lesbian Community

Near Everywhere You Want to Be
Bars, Shops, Zoo, Balboa Park

San Diego's Hillcrest Inn
International Hotel

San Diego, CA
Fax (619) 293-3861
Toll Free (800) 258-2280

■ **Harbor House Resort** (AC BF CC G H nu p WH WO YG)
642 West Hawthorn ✉ CA 92101 ☎ 338-9966 ☎ 888-338-9966 (toll-free) 🖷 338-9177 🖳 HarborHouseUSA@aol.com
🖳 www.harborhouseresort.com
Open all year long. Walking distance to all venues.

■ **Hillcrest Inn** (CC G H lj WH) 8-24 h
3754 5th Avenue ✉ CA 92103 ☎ 293-7078 ☎ (800) 258-2280 ☎ 293-3861 🖳 hillcrestinn@juno.com
In the heart of Hillcrest gay area. Rooms with phone, TV, fridge, priv. bath.

GUEST HOUSES

■ **Balboa Park Inn** (AC BF CC GLM H MA OS WH)
3402 Park Boulevard ✉ CA 92103 *(next to San Diego Zoo)*
☎ 298-0823 ☎ 800-938-8181 (toll free) 🖷 294-8070
🖳 info@BalboaParkInn.com 🖳 www.balboaparkinn.com
Complex of four Spanish colonial buildings, centrally located. Each suite with queen-sized bed, fridge, phone, some also with kitchen and jacuzzi.

■ **Beach Place, The** (AC CC G H NU VS WH)
2158 Sunset Cliffs Boulevard ✉ CA 92107 *(4 blocks to beach)*
☎ 225-0746 🖷 421-2972 🖳 beachplace@webtv.net
🖳 www.beach.place.cc
Fully equipped small apartments.

■ **Dmitri's Guesthouse** (BF G lj MA msg NU PI WH)
931 21st Street ✉ CA 92102 ☎ 238-5547 🖳 dmitriBB@aol.com
Central location, airport pick-up. Priv. bath. Rates from $ 75-110/room/night.

■ **Harbor Lights Inn** (AC BF CC f G H MA msg p PI WH)
505 West Grape Street ✉ CA 92101 ☎ 234-6787
☎ (800) 692-5101 (toll free) 🖷 231-3501
🖳 HarbrHouse@aol.com
Great view over San Diego. Heated pool.

■ **Keating House, The** (AC BF F glm H)
2331 2nd Avenue ✉ CA 92101 *(Banker's Hill)* ☎ 239-8585
☎ (800) 995-8644 🖷 239-5774 🖳 inn@keatinghouse.com
🖳 www.keatinghouse.com
Conveniently located Victorian residence. 3 km to the airport and to gay bars. Shared baths.

PRIVATE ACCOMMODATION

■ **Kasa Korbett** (BF F GLM msg OS WH) All year
1526 Van Buren Avenue ✉ CA 92103-2419 ☎ 291-3962
🖳 kasakorbett@hotmail.com
Free transport to aiport / train station. Bed and breakfast with kitchen use.

SWIMMING

-Black's Beach (G NU) (In the north of San Diego take direction of La Jolla and University of California San Diego then follow route to Torrey Pines Hang Gilder Park. [P] in front of the beach. Gay section is at the north side. Action in the dunes.) AYOR police.

CRUISING

-Balboa Park (along 6th Ave., south of Quince Street, best afternoons)

San Francisco ☎ 415

✱ "San Francisco punished!" was the heading of a Los Angeles newspaper after the big earthquake of 1906. It seems that the more conservative south of California was able to see a positive side to the disastrous events. This is not too astonishing. San Franciso is the perfect example of what the Americans call *liberal*, what can best be transcribed as open-minded. Without this open-mindedness an ethnically diverse city like this could not operate smoothly. And without it San Francisco would never have become the capital of the gay community. In the seventies *Castro Street* became a refined, very 'upmarket' looking center of gay-lesbian America. Also of importance are the areas around *Polk Street* with a grand view from nearlying Nob Hill and *SoMa*, South of Market, a very fashionable part of the city with nice clubs and cultivated shopping facilities. It is presumed, that the foundation of San Franciscos gay tradition was laid in the licentious era of the gold rush. In the fifties the first gay and lesbian groups and organisations were founded. But the gay boom came in the sixties, when the police warned the public of the 70.000 gays and lesbians in the city. This warning sounded, for many, more like an invitation and the run on S.F. began. With success came crises. Harvey Milk, an openly gay member of the city council was shot by another of its members. Following the mild sentence of the murderer, riots spread, which showed, how brittle the ghetto-paradise Castro Street really was. The eighties were the era of AIDS, which plunged the *gay community* of the city into one of its deepest crisis. Even today, every second gay is presumed to be hiv-positive. The AIDS-crisis has led to a profound change in the gay scene. Lesbians have often filled the posts left behind by stricken gays, and have engaged themselves in service groups for HIV-positives and AIDS-sufferers. Today lesbians are present everywhere, more than in most other cities. A car is not needed in S.F. You can reach every corner with the subway (BART), daylight trains (MUNI) and bus, however it can take time, as public transport is not very well coordinated. San Francisco is larger than it may seem. San Francisco is worth a visit, but don't expect warm weather in summer and the typical San Francisco fog means it can get quite cold in the mornings and evenings.

USA/California — San Francisco

★ "San Francisco bestraft!", so lautete nach dem großen Erdbeben von 1906 die Schlagzeile einer Zeitung in Los Angeles. Offensichtlich gewann man der Tragödie im konservativen Süden Kaliforniens durchaus eine positive Seite ab. Erstaunen muß daß nicht, denn San Francisco ist wirklich ein Musterbeispiel für das, was US-Amerikaner *liberal* nennen. Etwas, das man am ehesten mit tolerant übersetzen könnte. Ohne Toleranz könnte eine ethnisch dermaßen vielfältige Stadt sicher nicht reibungslos funktionieren. Und ohne sie wäre San Francisco wohl nie eine der Hauptstädte der schwulen Welt geworden. In den 70er Jahren hat sich die *Castro Street* zu einem heute sehr gepflegt, sehr *upmarket* wirkenden Zentrum des schwul-lesbischen Amerika entwickelt. Ebenfalls von Bedeutung sind zum einen die Gegend um die *Polk Street* (tolle Aussicht vom nahen Nob Hill) und SoMa, South of Market, eine sehr angesagte Ecke mit tollen Clubs und anspruchsvollem Shopping. Es wird vermutet, daß die ersten Grundsteine für San Franciscos schwule Traditionen bereits in der als zügellos geltenden Goldgräberzeit gelegt wurden. In den 50er Jahren wurden die ersten schwulen und lesbischen Gruppen und Organisationen gegründet. Zu einem regelrechten Run auf die Stadt kam es in den 60er Jahren, als die Polizei vor den 70.000 Schwulen und Lesben in der Stadt warnte(!); eine Warnung, die auf viele Schwule auf dem Land wie eine Einladung wirkte. Mit den Erfolgen kamen die Krisen. Harvey Milk, offen schwuler Stadtrat in den 70ern, wurde von einem Stadtratsmitglied erschossen. Auf das milde Urteil folgten Unruhen, die offenbarten, wie zerbrechlich das Ghetto-Paradies Castro war. Die 80er Jahre wurden zum Zeitalter von AIDS und haben die *gay community* der Stadt in eine ihrer tiefsten Krisen gestürzt. Noch heute gilt jeder zweite Schwule als HIV-positiv. Doch gerade die AIDS-Krise hat zu einer tiefgreifenden Wandlung der Szene geführt: oftmals haben Lesben die Funktionen erkrankter Schwuler eingenommen, haben sich in Hilfsgruppen für Positive und an AIDS Erkrankte eingesetzt. Heute sind Lesben in San Francisco so sichtbar wie an kaum einem anderen Ort. Wer in diese Stadt kommt, benötigt kein Auto. Mit BART (U-Bahn), MUNI (S-Bahn) und Bus kommt man gut durch die Stadt, auch wenn es wegen mangelnder Abstimmung lange dauern kann. Übrigens ist San Francisco nicht so klein, wie es den Anschein hat. San Francisco ist immer eine Reise wert, einen warmen Sommer aber sollte man nicht erwarten, den im sommerlichen Nebel morgens und abends kann es recht kühl werden.

✱ "San Francisco punie!" titrait un quotidien de Los Angeles le lendemain du grand tremblement de terre de 1906. Le sud conservateur de la Californie s'est réjoui de cette terrible catastrophe et cela ne surprend personne, car San Francisco est, a toujours été, une ville progressiste et tolérante. "Liberal" disent les Américains, ce qu'on pourrait traduire par "large d'esprit". Et c'est bien tolérance et cette ouverture d'esprit qui permet à la ville de fonctionner comme elle fonctionne: mélange des races et des cultures et, en plus, capitale mondiale des gais. Depuis les années 70, Castro Street est le bastion gai/lesbien des Etats-Unis. C'est aujourd'hui un quartier très soigné, très "upmarket". A voir également: autour de Polk Street (vue magnifique depuis la Nob Hill toute proche) et South Market ("SoMa"), très mode, avec de nombreux clubs et de jolies boutiques. On dit qu'à l'époque des chercheurs d'or, San Francisco avait déjà acquis ses lettres de noblesse gaies. Dans les années 50, on y a fondé les premières associations gaies et lesbiennes du pays. Ce n'est que dans les années 60 qu'a eu lieu le "rush" gai sur la ville. La police n'a rien trouvé de mieux que d'affoler les touristes en criant haut et fort que 70.000 gais et lesbiennes vivaient à San Francisco. Inutile de dire que, dans le reste du pays, certaines personnes n'ont eu vite fait de prendre cette mise en garde pour une invitation! Toute médaille a ses revers et les problèmes ont vite surgi.

Dans les années 70, Harvey Milk, conseiller municipal qui vivait ouvertement son homosexualité, a été assassiné par un autre membre du conseil municipal. Le jugement indulgent prononcé par la Justice a déclenché une vague d'émeutes à Castro. Le paradis gai de Castro Street a su se montrer rebelle et combatif. Avec l'épidémie de sida dans les années 80, la ville a plongé dans une des plus profondes crises de son histoire. Aujourd'hui encore, on dit qu'un gai sur deux est séropositif. La crise déclenchée par la maladie a permis aux gais de se retrouver et de se restructurer. Dans de nombreux cas, ce sont les lesbiennes qui ont pris la relève des gais malades ou morts pour les remplacer dans leurs fonctions. Elles se battent aujourd'hui pour les groupes d'aide et de soutien aux malades du sida. A San Francisco, les lesbiennes font aujourd'hui partie du décor, comme nulle part ailleurs aux Etats-Unis. Aujourd'hui pas besoin de voiture pour visiter San Francisco. Le métro, le tram et le bus sont les moyens de transport les plus pratiques, même si les changements de lignes sont souvent peu pratiques et mal coordonnés. Notez bien que San Francisco n'est pas si petite qu'elle en a l'air! San Francisco est intéressante toute l'année. Attention, l'été y est relativement frais. Le matin et le soir, il ne fait pas chaud, surtout les jours de brume.

✱ "¡San Francisco castigado!" ese fue el titular de un periodico de Los Angeles después del gran terremoto de 1906. Por lo visto el sur más conservador de California era capaz de ver hasta un lado positivo de esta tragedia. Y no es de extrañar, ya que San Francisco representa todo, lo que llaman los norteamericanos *liberal*, que se traduce mejor como tolerante. Y la tolerancia es imprescindible para hacer funcionar la convivencia en una ciudad que dispone de una multiplicidad étnica como San Francisco. Sin ella San Francisco no se habría convertido en una de las capitales mundiales gay. En la década de los '70 la *Castro Street* se convirtió en el centro gay-lésbico de E.E.U.U., hoy en día se ha convertido en el centro elegante y *upmarket* de la cultura homosexual. De mucha importancia lo son los alrededores de la *Polk Street* y SoMa South of Market, lugar en el que se encuentran atractivos clubs y tiendas de compra de gran estilo. Se cree que la base de la tradición gay de San Francisco fue cimentada en los desenfrenados tiempos de la busqueda de oro. En los años '50 se formaron los primeros grupos gay y lesbianos de la ciudad. En los años '60 la ciudad comenzó a tomar auge cuando la policia advertia sobre los más de 70.000 gays y lesbianas de la ciudad. Esta advertencia fungió como una invitation para gran cantidad de homosexuales de las zonas rurales. Junto con los éxitos llegaban también las crisis. Harvey Milk miembro del ayuntamiento de la ciudad, fue asesinado por uno de sus colegas debido a su orientación sexual. A la suave pena jurídica siguieron grandes desordenes que dejaron ver que delicado era el Paraíso-Ghetto Castro. La década de los '80 se convertieron en los tiempos del SIDA y condujeron a la *Gay Community* de la ciudad a una de las crisis más grandes de su historia. Aún hoy en día uno de cada dos homosexuales está infectado con el virus del SIDA. Pero la crisis del SIDA condujo a un cambio radical en el ambiente gay de la ciudad. Con frecuencia fueron lesbianas que pasaron a ocupar los puestos de los gays enfermos. En pocos sitios se encuentra una presencia tan masiva de lesbianas como en San Francisco. La ciudad se puede visitar sin la necesidad de tener que alquilar un coche. El transporte publico con el BART (metro), el MUNI (tren) y buses ofrecen un buen servicio. San Francisco vale la pena, sin embargo no se debe esperar que el verano sea caliente.

✖ "San Francisco punita", questo fu il titolo di un quotidiano di Los Angeles dopo il grande terremoto del 1906. Ovviamente il sud della California, molto conservatore, scoprì nella tragedia un lato positivo. Non c'è da sorprendersi poichè San Francisco è veramente un'esempio di ciò che gli americani chiamano *liberal*. Ma senza tale atteggiamento liberale una città così vasta etnicamente avrebbe molto più conflitti e non sarebbe mai divenuta una delle capitali gay mondiali. Negli anni '70 la *Castro street*, oggi molto curata,

San Francisco — California/USA

molto *up market*, è divenuta il centro dell'America omosessuale. Altrettanto importanti sono le zone intorno alla *Polk Street* (con vista spettacolare dalla vicina Nob Hill) e a *SoMa*, South of Market, un angolo molto alla moda con ottime discoteche e negozi di lusso. Si presume che le fondamenta della tradizione gay siano state gettate durante la disinibita epoca dei cercatori d'oro. Negli anni '50 del nostro secolo sono stati fondati i primi gruppi e le prime organizzazioni di gay e lesbiche. Ma il grande afflusso di omosessuali è avvenuto negli anni '60, quando la polizia, con un avviso d'allarme, ha reso nota la presenza di 70.000 gay e lesbiche nella città. Per i gay americani questo avviso è stato piuttosto un invito. Ma dopo il successo venne la crisi: Harvey Milk, assessore gay, negli anni '70 venne assassinato da un membro del consiglio comunale. In seguito ad una condanna troppo leggera vi furono dei disordini che rivelarono la fragilità di Castro, il ghetto paradisiaco. Negli anni '80 si aprì l'epoca dell'AIDS che trascinò la *gay community* in una profonda crisi. Malgrado la profilassi si suppone tutt'oggi che un gay su due sia positivo. L'AIDS ha introdotto radicali cambiamenti: spesso donne omosessuali hanno rimpiazzato gay ammalati, si sono formati gruppi di positivi e gruppi di assistenza per i malati. In nessun luogo come a San Francisco le lesbiche sono così emancipate. Chi visita la città non ha bisogno di un'auto, si può spostarsi con il BART (metrò), il MUNI (tram) e gli autobus, anche se spesso perderà tempo a causa di una imprecisa coordinazione delle linee.

PUBLICATIONS

■ **BAR - Bay Area Reporter**
395 9th Street ✉ CA 94103-3831 ☎ 861-5019 📠 861-7230
📧 barpaper@aol.com 💻 www.ebar.com
Weekly newspaper for the greater Bay area, about 48 pages, free at delivery points in Bay Area. News, sports & entertainment of interest to the gay community.

■ **Odyssey Magazine**
584 Castro Street, # 302 ✉ CA 94114 ☎ 621-6514
📠 (323) 874-8782 📧 odysseyz@pacbell.net
Free bi-weekly magazine available at gay venues.

■ **QSF - Q San Francisco**
584 Castro Street, Ste 521 ✉ CA 94114 ☎ 764-0324 📠 626-5744
📧 qsf1@aol.com 💻 www.qsanfrancisco.com
Bimonthly gay entertainment and trends magazine.

■ **San Francisco Bay Times**
3410 19th Street ✉ CA 94110 ☎ 626-0260 📠 626-0987
📧 sfbaytimes@aol.com
Biweekly magazine covering the Bay Area scene.

■ **San Francisco Frontiers Newsmagazine** Mon-Fri 9-18 h
2370 Market Street ✉ CA 94114 *(2nd floor)* ☎ 487-6000
📠 487-6060 📧 sfeditor@frontiersweb.com
💻 www.frontiersweb.com
Biweekly magazine. Features gay related news, political reports, community events, reviews, guide to San Francisco, and classified ads.

BARS

■ **Aunt Charlie's Lounge** (B G N OG tv) Sun-Thu 6-24, Fri-Sat -2 h
133 Turk Street ✉ CA 94102 *(Between Taylor and Jones Streets)*
☎ 441-2922

■ **Badlands** (! AC B G LJ MA VS) 11.30-2 h
4121 18th Street ✉ CA 94114 *(Between Castro and Collingwood)*
☎ 626-9320
Cruisy atmosphere.

■ **Bar on Castro, The** (B G MA N) 15-2 Sat&Sun 12-2
456 Castro St. ☎ 626-7220

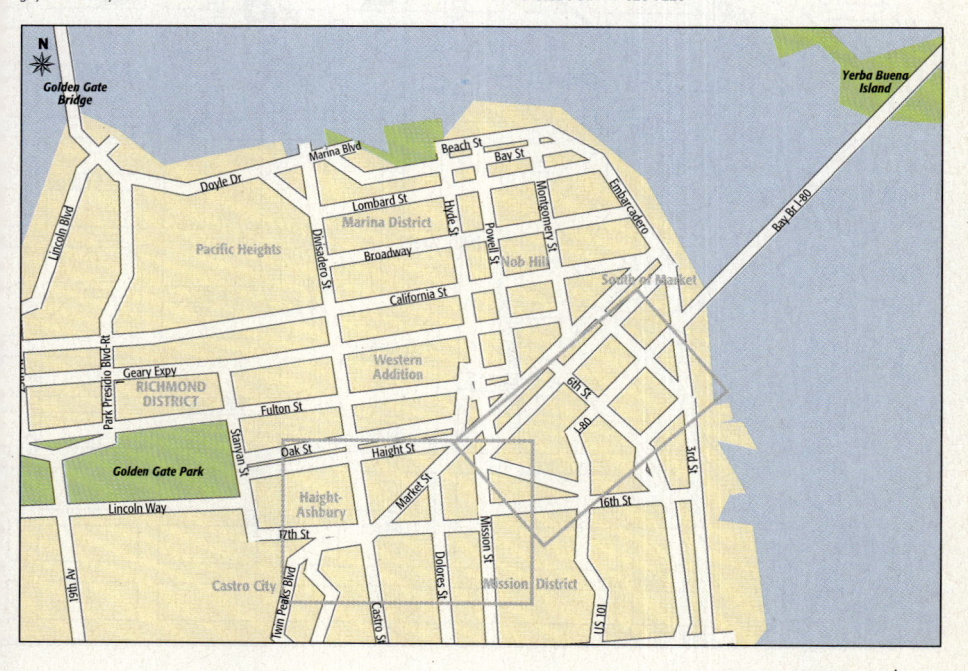

USA/California | San Francisco

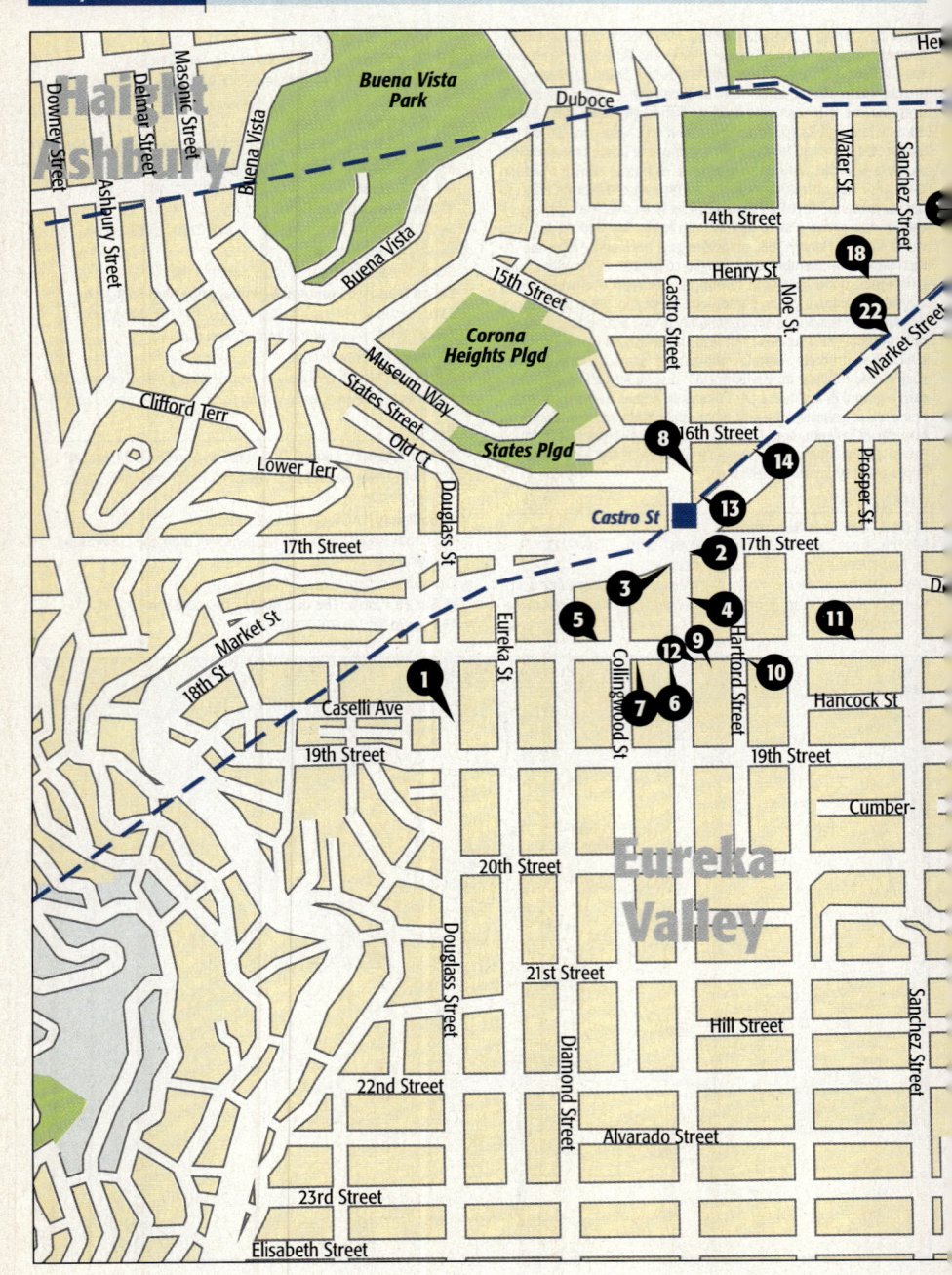

San Francisco — California/USA

San Francisco - Castro Area

1. Belvedere Guest House
2. Twin Peaks Bar
3. Daddy's Bar
4. A Different Light Bookshop
5. The Pendulum Bar
6. Badlands Bar
7. The Eagle Bar
8. Inn on Castro Guest House
9. Midnight Sun Bar
10. Moby Dick Bar
11. Men's Room Bar
12. Uncle Bert's Place Bar
13. The Café Bar
14. Pasta Pomodoro Restaurant
15. Pilsner Inn Bar
16. Transfer Bar
17. Willows B&B Inn Guest House
18. 24 Henry Guest
19. Dolores Park Inn Guest House
20. The Inn San Francisco Guest House
21. Baby Judy's Discoteque
22. Thai House Bar & Restaurant
23. Eros Men's Club
24. The Mint Bar
25. Andora Inn Guest House
26. The Parker House Guest House

USA/California | San Francisco

San Francisco — California/USA

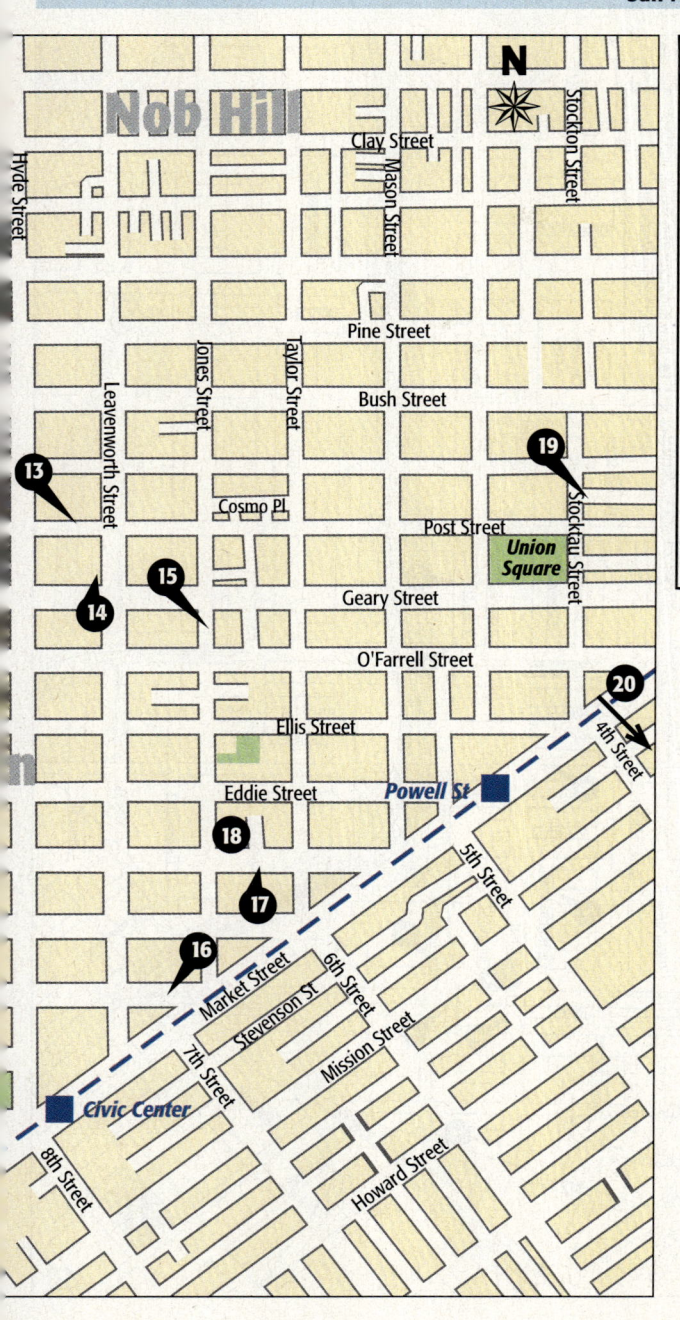

San Francisco - Hayes Valley / Polk Street Area / Downtown

1. Marlena's Bar
2. The Clinch Bar
3. N'Touch Bar
4. Polk Rendevous Bar
5. The Kimo's Bar
6. Grubstake Restaurant
7. Reflections Bar
8. Quetzal Café
9. Divas Nightclub
10. Old Rick's Gold Room Bar
11. The Gangway Bar
12. Atherton Hotel
13. Pensione International Guest House
14. The Hob Nob Bar
15. Dottie's True Blue Café
16. Renoir Hotel / Café do Brasil
17. Aunt Charlie's Lounge Bar
18. New Meat Campus
19. Allison Hotel
20. Steamworks Bathouse Berkeley Sauna

USA/California — San Francisco

San Francisco - South of Market

1. Power Exchange Mainstation Men's Club
2. Eagle Tavern Bar
3. Lone Star Saloon Bar
4. Powerhouse Leather Club
5. My Place Bar
6. The Stud Danceclub
7. Hole in the Wall Saloon Bar
8. Rawhide II Bar
9. The EndUp T-Dance Danceclub
10. Blow Buddies/Golden Shower Buddies/Leather Buddies Men's Club

San Francisco — California/USA

■ **Cable Reef** (B d GLM MA SNU) 12-2 h
2272 Telegraph Ave, Oakland ✉ CA 94612 *(Near Grand Avenue)*
☎ 451-3777
Different theme nights.

■ **Cafe Mars** (B d glm YG) Mon-Sat 17-2 h
798 Brannan Street/7th Street ✉ CA 94103 *(SOMA)* ☎ 621-MARS
Formerly frequented mostly by gays, now straight guys and girls party here too.

■ **Café. The** (B D GLM) 12.30-2 h
2367 Market Street ✉ CA 94114 *(Between 16th and 17th Streets)*
☎ 861-3846
Popular

■ **Cinch Saloon. The** (B G MA N OS) 6-2 h
1723 Polk Street ✉ CA 94109 *(Between Washington and Clay Streets)* ☎ 776-4162

■ **Club Rendezvous** (A AC B D GLM MA S SNU) open until 02:00h
1312 Polk Street ✉ CA 94109 *(At Bush Street)* ☎ 673-7934
Newly opened in Nov. '99. Male strippers

■ **Comfort Zone** (B GLM YG) 21-2 h
581 5th Street, Oakland ✉ CA 94607 ☎ 510/ 869-4847
Predominately afro-american crowd and their friends.

■ **Daddy's** (B G LJ MA N) 6-2 h
440 Castro Street ✉ CA 94114 *(Between Market and 18th Streets)*
☎ 621-8732
Popular

■ **Detour. The** (B G MA N s) 14-2 h
2348 Market St ☎ 861-6053
Gogo-boys on Saturday.

■ **Eagle Tavern. The** (AC B CC f G LJ MA N OS S) 12-02:00h
398 12th Street ✉ CA 94103 *8 Courner of 12th and Harrison streets)*
☎ 626-0880
Heated outdoor patio.

■ **Edge. The** (B G LJ MA N) 12-2 h
4149 - 18th Street ✉ CA 94114 *(One block from U- Castro-Muni)*
☎ 863-4027

■ **El Rio** (B D f GLM MA S OS) 15-2, Mon -24 h
3158 Mission Street/Precita ✉ CA 94110 ☎ 282-3325
Live entertainment. Nice backyard with lots of plants. Popular. Mixed white and Latino crowd.

■ **Expansion Bar** (B GLM MA N) 10-1 h
2124 Market Street ✉ CA 94114 *(Between 14th and 15th Streets)*
☎ 863-4041

■ **Gangway. The** (B G N OG) 6-2 h
841 Larkin Street ✉ CA 94109 *(Between O'Farrell and Geary Streets)*
☎ 885-4441

■ **Ginger's Too** (B G N OG) 10-2 h
43 6th Street ✉ CA 94103 *(Between Market Street and Mission Streets)* ☎ 543-3622

■ **Ginger's Trois** (B f G N) Mon-Fri 10-22 h, closed Sat-Sun
246 Kearny ✉ CA 94108 *(In Financial District, between Sutter and Bush Streets)* ☎ 989-0282

■ **Giraffe. The** (B D Glm MA) 8-2 h
1131 Polk Street ✉ CA 94109 *(Between Post and Sutter Streets)*
☎ 474-1702
Popular

■ **Hob Nob. The** (B G N OG) 6-2 h
700 Geary Street/Leavenworth ✉ CA 94109 ☎ 771-9866

■ **Hole in the Wall Saloon** (B G LJ MA N) Tue-Thu 12-2, Fri-Mon 6-2 h
289 8th Street ✉ CA 94103 *(Between Folsom and Howard Streets)*
☎ 431-4695
Very popular bar. Friendly predominantly biker and leather crowd.

■ **Kimo's** (AC B CC d Glm MA N STV) 8-2 h
1351 Polk Street/Pine Street ✉ CA 94109 ☎ 885-4535

■ **Lone Star** (! B G LJ N MA OS) 12-2, Sat-Sun 6-2 h
1354 Harrison Street ✉ CA 94103 *(Between 9th and 10th St.)*
☎ 863-9999
Popular. Lots of bears. Nice patio.

■ **Marlena's** (B GLM MA N STV) 12-2, Sat-Sun 10-2 h
488 Hayes Street ✉ CA 94102 *(Between Octavia and Gough Streets, Hayes Valley)* ☎ 864-6672
Fri at 24 h drag show.

■ **Martuni's** (B G MA N P) 16-2 h
4 Valencia St ☎ 241-0205
Piano bar famous for its martinis.

■ **Men's Room** (B G MA N) 12-2 h. Cocktail hour 16-19:00h Mon, Thu & Fri.
3988 18th Street ✉ CA 94114 *(Between Noe and Sanchez Streets)*
☎ 861-1310
Friendly atmosphere.

■ **Metro. The** (B F GLM OS YG) 14-1 h, restaurant 17.30-23 h
3600 16th Street ✉ CA 94114 *(Between Noe and Market Streets)*
☎ 703-9750
Tue karaoke night. Popular on weekends. Nice terrace overlooking Market Street.

■ **Midnight Sun. The** (! B G VS YG) 12-2 h
4067 18th Street ✉ CA 94114 *(Between Castro and Noe Streets)*
☎ 861-4186
Oldest video bar in town. Cruisy atmosphere.

■ **Mint. The** (B F GLM MA OS S) 11-2 h
1942 Market Street ✉ CA 94102 *(Between Haight and Duboce Streets)* ☎ 626-4726
Best karaoke bar in SF. Karaoke hours Mon-Fri 19-2, Sat Sun 16-2 h. Also restaurant.

■ **Moby Dick** (B Glm N YG) 12-2 h
4049 18th Street/Hartford ✉ CA 94114
Friendly and relaxed atmosphere

■ **Motherlode** (B glm S TV) 6-2 h
1085 Post Street ✉ CA 94109 ☎ 928-6006
The place to go for transvestites and transsexuals and their fans.

■ **My Place** (B G LJ MA) 12-2 h
1225 Folsom Street ✉ CA 94103 *(Between 8th and 9th Streets)*
☎ 863-2329
Most diverse crowd in the city.

■ **N'Touch Bar** (B D G SNU STV YG WE) 15-2 h
1548 Polk Street ✉ CA 94109 ☎ 441-8413
For those who fancy Asian men.Cruisy atmosphere.

■ **Old Rick's Gold Room** (B G N OG) 6-2 h
939 Geary Boulevard ✉ CA 94109 *(Between Polk and Larkin Streets)*
☎ 441-9211
Small neighbourhood bar.

■ **Pendulum. The** (! B G MA) 6-2 h
4146 18th Street ✉ CA 94114 *(Between Collingwood and Castro Streets)* ☎ 863-4441
Where black and white men meet. Very popular. Good R&B music.

■ **Pilsner Inn** (B G N OS) 9-2 h
225 Church Street ✉ CA 94114 *(Between Market and 15th Streets)*
☎ 621-7058

■ **Powerhouse** (! B G LJ) 16-2, Sat-Sun 12-2 h
1347 Folsom Street/Dore Alley ✉ CA 94103 *(Between 9th and 10th Streets)* ☎ 552-8689
Definitely a must for all leather men. Thu they host the Sissy Bar. Lots of tattoed and pierced guys enjoy the relaxed atmosphere. Go-go boys.

■ **Rawhide II** (B D Glm MA) 16-2, Fri-Sun 12-2 h
280 7th Street ✉ CA 94103 *(Between Folsom and Howard Streets)*
☎ 621-1197
Country/Western music, popular.

USA/California — San Francisco

■ **Reflections** (B f G OG R) 6-2 h
1160 Polk Street ✉ CA 94109 *(Between Post and Sutter Streets)*
☎ 771-6262
Good snacks

■ **Transfer** (B Glm MA N WE) 11-2, Sat-Sun 6-2 h
198 Church Street/14th Street ✉ CA 94114 ☎ 861-7499

■ **Trax** (B GLM MA N) 12-2 h
1437 Haight Street ✉ CA 94117 *(Between Masonic and Ashbury Streets)* ☎ 864-4213
Popular and only gay bar in the Haight/Ashbury district.

■ **Twin Peaks** (B GLM MA N OS) 6-2 h
401 Castro Street/Market Street ✉ CA 94114 ☎ 864-9470
No bottled beer available. Always busy, it has a nice interior terrace from where you can overlook what's going on on Market Street.

■ **Uncle Bert's Place** (B GLM MA N OS) 6-2 h
4086 18th Street ✉ CA 94114 *(Between Castro and Noe Streets)*
☎ 431-8616
Relaxed atmosphere

■ **White Horse** (B CC D GLM lj MA N) Mon-Tue 15-2, Wed-Sun 13-2 h
6551 Telegraph Avenue Oakland ✉ CA 94609 ☎ (510) 652-3820
Oldest gay bar west of the Mississippi. Popular.

MEN'S CLUBS

■ **Blow Buddies** (! DR G MA NU P) Thu 19.30-3, Fri & Sat 21-4, Sun 18-24 h
933 Harrison Street ✉ CA 94017 *(at 5th Street)* ☎ 863-4323
Other clubs at the same location: -Golden Shower Buddies (2nd Wed / month) -Underwear Buddies (3rd Wed / month) -Leather Buddies (4th Wed/ month). Call for info.

■ **Eros** (CC DR G MA msg SA SB SOL STX) Sun-Thu 16-22, Fri-Sat -4 h
2051 Market Street ✉ CA 94114 *(at Church Street)* ☎ 864-3767
Softly lit playrooms featuring video pits, bunk beds, cages, glory holes and sling.

■ **Power Exchange Mainstant** (DR G MA VS)
74 Otis Street ✉ CA 94103 *(Between S. Van Ness and Gough Street)*
☎ 487-9944
Admission fee.

■ **Rubber Corps** (G LJ) 1st Sat/month 21-2 h
(call for location) ☎ 552-7979

■ **Steam Works** (! AC DR G MA msg P SA SB VS WH WO YG) 0-24 h
2107 4th Street/Addison, Berkeley ✉ CA 94710 *(Near University Avenue in Berkeley)* ☎ (510) 845-8992
Take the Bay-Bridge direction Oakland, than exit University Avenue from Interstate N° 80. ID with photo required. Popular gay bath.

CAFES

■ **Dottie's True Blue Cafe** (b BF f GLM) 7.30-14 h
522 Jones Street ✉ CA 94102 *(Between Geary and O'Farrell Streets)*
☎ 885-2767
The perfect place to enjoy a delicious breakfast. Very popular on weekends for brunch.

■ **Flore. Cafe** (F GLM OS) 7-23 h
2298 Market Street/Noe Street ✉ CA 94114 ☎ 621-8579
Popular. Rather mixed in the evenings.

■ **Harvey's** (B BF F GLM MA S) 11-2, WE 9-2 h
500 Castro Street/18th Street ✉ CA 94114 ☎ 431-4278
Cute and friendly staff.

■ **Jumpin' Java** (b f glm YG) 7-22 h
139 Noe St./14th St. ✉ CA 94114 ☎ 431-5282

■ **Quetzal** (AC b BF F GLM MA OS s VS) 6-23 h, Sat, Sun 7-23 h
1234 Polk Street ✉ CA 94109 ☎ 673-4181

DANCECLUBS

■ **Baby Judy's Discotheque and Leisure Lodge at the Casanova** (B D GLM YG) Wed 22-2 h
527 Valencia Street ✉ CA 94110 *(Between 16th and 17th Streets)*
Popular dance club which attracts a young and very mixed non-mainstream crowd.

■ **Chulo** (b D G MA S) 4th Sun 21-? h
2925 16th St. ☎ 248-1616
Go-go-Boys.

■ **Club Asia** (AC B D G MA s WE) 2nd/4th Fri 22-? h
174 King Street ✉ CA 94107 *(Between 2nd and 3rd Streets)*
☎ 285-2742
Lots of cute young Asian girls and boys who enjoy themselves. Very cute go-go dancers.

■ **Divas** (AC b D G MA S STV TV YG) 06-02 h. Dancefloor Wed-Sat 22-02 h
1081 Post Street ✉ CA 94109 ☎ 474-3482

BLOW BUDDIES
San Francisco
a private club
415-863-HEAD
www.blowbuddies.com

San Francisco | California/USA

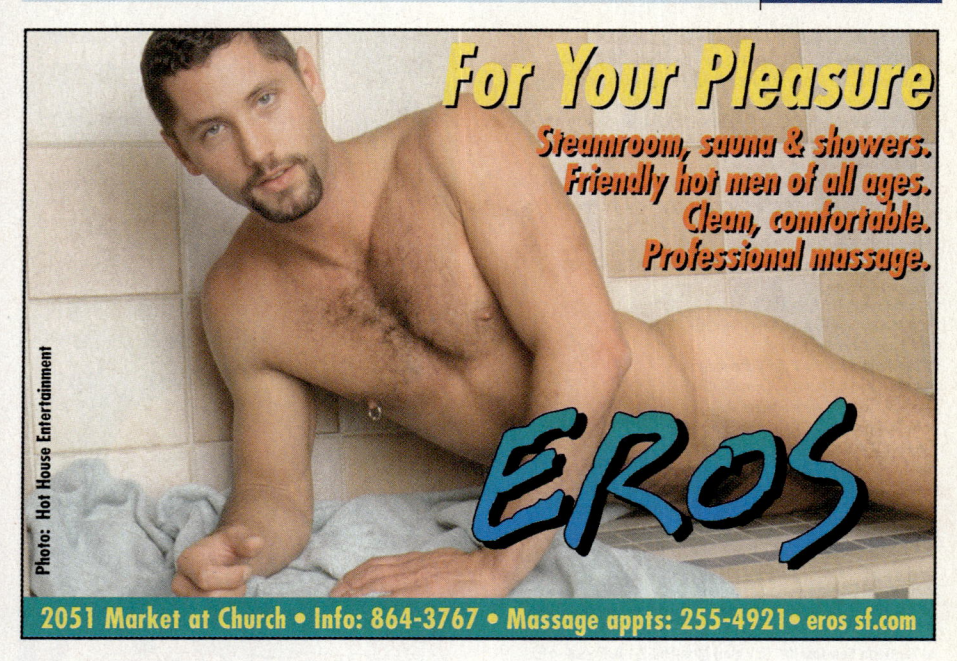

For Your Pleasure

Steamroom, sauna & showers.
Friendly hot men of all ages.
Clean, comfortable.
Professional massage.

EROS

Photo: Hot House Entertainment

2051 Market at Church • Info: 864-3767 • Massage appts: 255-4921 • eros sf.com

■ **EndUp T-Dance** (B f GLM MA s TV) Fri 20-Sat 16 h, Sat 20-2.30 h, Sun 5.30-2 h
401 6th Street ✉ CA 94103-4706 ☎ 896-1095
This place gets packed on Sun mornings. For all non-stop party-goers this is the place to be.
■ **Fag Fridays at the Endup** (! B D Glm OS YG) Fri 22-5.30 h
401 6th Street/Harrison ✉ CA 94108 ☎ 263-4850
Popular alternative dance club. Very relaxed atmosphere. Nice patio.
■ **Funk & Soul Nights** (D G MA YG) Mon 21-2 h
399 9th St. (in "The Stud") ☎ 252-7883
■ **Futura at the King St. Garage** (AC B D G LJ MA s WE) 2nd and 4th Sat 22-3 h
174 King Street ✉ CA 94107 (Between 2nd and 3rd Streets)
☎ 665-6715
Popular gay Latino dance club, which attracts some Black and White boys too. Not every Sat, check dates.
■ **King Street Garage** (AC B D glm lj MA s WE) 1st/3rd Fri/month 0-6 h
174 King Street ✉ CA 94107 (Between 2nd and 3rd Streets)
☎ 947-1156
■ **Metropolis** (D G MA) every 3rd Sat 22-6 h
550 Barneveld St. (off Bayshore) ☎ 646-0890
■ **Pleasuredome at Club Townsend** (AC B D G LJ MA s WE) Sun 21-6 h
177 Townsend Street ✉ CA 94107 (Between 2nd and 3rd Streets)
☎ 974-1156
Lots of a hungry guys dance to the latest tunes. This is a must!
■ **Stud. The** (! B D G STV YG) 17-2 h, Thu dykes only
399 9th Street/Harrison Street ✉ CA 94103 ☎ 252-7883
Mon popular Funk Night which attracts a mixed black and white crowd (21-3 h). Every Tue The Stud hosts the popular Trannyshack club for Trannies and their admirers. The drag show at 24 h is a must (22-3 h).

Wed Midweek beer-bust. Highly recommended. Sun 80 Something alternative club attracts a very relaxed crowd (21-2 h).
■ **Sugar** (b d G YC) Sat 21-5 h
399 9th St. ☎ 252-7883
■ **Sundance Saloon at The King Street Garage** (AC B D GLM LJ MA WE) Sun 18-23 h
177 Townsend Street ✉ CA 94107 ☎ 974-1156
Two-stepping and line dancing.
■ **Universe at Club Townsend** (AC B D GLM LJ MA s WE) Sat 21.30-7 h
177 Townsend Street ✉ CA 94107 (Between 2nd and 3rd Streets)
☎ 974-1156
The place to be on a late Sat night. Very busy after 2 h when a mixed crowd, among them lots of hunky bare chested guys, enjoy themselves and the cute go-go dancers dance to the hottest House and Techno music. Cruisy atmosphere.
■ **Vertigo at the Endup** (B D GLM OS YG) Sat 23-4 h
401 6th Street/Harrison ✉ CA 94103 ☎ 703-7172
Popular dance club. Nice outdoor patio.

RESTAURANTS

■ **Baghdad Café** (BF F GLM MA OS) 0-24 h
2295 Market Street/16th Street ✉ CA 94114 ☎ 621-4434
Inexpensive and good food. Busy late at night. They serve vegetarian dishes too.
■ **Blue** (F G MA) 17-23 h
2337 Market St ☎ 863-2583
■ **Cafe Akimbo** (b CC F glm MA) Mon-Thu 11.30-15, 17.30-21, Fri-Sat 11.30-15, 17.30-22 h, closed Sun
116 Maiden Lane ✉ CA 94108 (near Grant, Union Square)
☎ 433-2288
Elegant but casual restaurant serving Californian cuisine.

SPARTACUS 2001/2002 | 1179

USA/California — San Francisco

■ **Café do Brasil** (b BF F glm MA s) 7.30-21.30 h
1106 Market Street ✉ CA 94102 (at 7th Street) ☎ 626 6432
Exotic brunch. Thu-Sun Churrasco (Brazilian barbecue). Specialities from Bahia, seafood, Feijoada and vegetarian dishes.

■ **Grubstake** (AC BF F GLM MA) Mon-Fri 17-4, Sat-Sun 10-4 h
1525 Pine Street ✉ CA 94109 (Between Polk and Van Ness Avenue) ☎ 673-8268
Hamburgers, chili, steaks and breakfast. Highly recommended, friendly service. Meeting place after the bars are closed. Popular Portuguese dinner Sat night.

■ **Hot'n Hunky** (B f G) 11-24 h
4039 18th Street near Hartford ✉ CA 94132 ☎ 621-6365
Hamburger restaurant.

■ **JohnFrank** (B F Glm MA)
2100 Market Street ✉ CA 94114-1319 ☎ 503-0333
Californian-American cuisine.

■ **La Mediterranée** (F glm) closed Mon
288 Noe St. ✉ CA 94114 (near Market) ☎ 431-7210
Good and inexpensive food, nice staff

■ **Millennium** (b CC F GLM MA WE) Tue-Fri 11.30-14.30 h (lunch), Tue-Sun 17-21.30 h (dinner)
246 McAllister Street ✉ CA 94102 (Civic center, 10 mins from the Castro) ☎ 487-9180
Award winning vegetarian cuisine in a fine dining and romantic atmosphere.

■ **Pasta pomodoro** (! b F GLM) ?-24 h
2304 Market Street ✉ CA 94114 (Castro) ☎ 558-8123
This popular and always busy restaurant offers great inexpensive Italian food. It attracts a very gay crowd which doesn't mind to wait to get a table.

■ **Taqueria San Jose #1** (b F glm) Mon-Thu 7-1 h, Fri-Sat -4 h, Sun -3 h
2830 Mission Street ✉ CA 94110 (Between 24th and 25th Streets) ☎ 282-0203
Very cheap and delicious Mexican food.

■ **Thai House Bar & Café** (F glm)
2200 Market Street/Sanchez ✉ CA 94114 ☎ 864-5006
Inexpensive and delicious Thai food.

■ **Valentine's Cafe** (! b CC F GLM) Wed-Thu 11-14.30 h, 17.30-21.30 h, Fri -22 h, Sat-Sun 8-15.30, 18-22 h
1793 Church Street ✉ CA 94131 (Between 29th and 30th Streets) ☎ 285-2257
Great vegetarian food at reasonable prices.

■ **Without Reservation** (b BF F glm) 7.30-2.30 h
2451 Harrison Street ✉ CA 94114 (Between Market and 18th Streets) ☎ 861-9510
Breakfast, lunch and burgers.

■ **Zuni Café** (B F glm)
1658 Market Street ✉ CA 94102 ☎ 552-2522
Very trendy place, nice staff, reservation advisable.

SHOWS

■ **New Meat Campus Theater** (A AC DR G MA SNU VS) Sun-Thu 11-24, Fri & Sat -2 h
220 Jones Street ✉ CA 94107 (off Market street at 6th street) ☎ 673 3384
Male strip club, Multi xxx screen cinema, Video arcade. 12-14 live nude shows daily. All day pass only US$ 10.

■ **Theatre Rhinoceros** Performances Wed-Sun
2926 16th Street, ✉ CA 94103 (Mission District) ☎ 861-5079
America's oldest and foremost theatre devoted only to gay and lesbian issues.

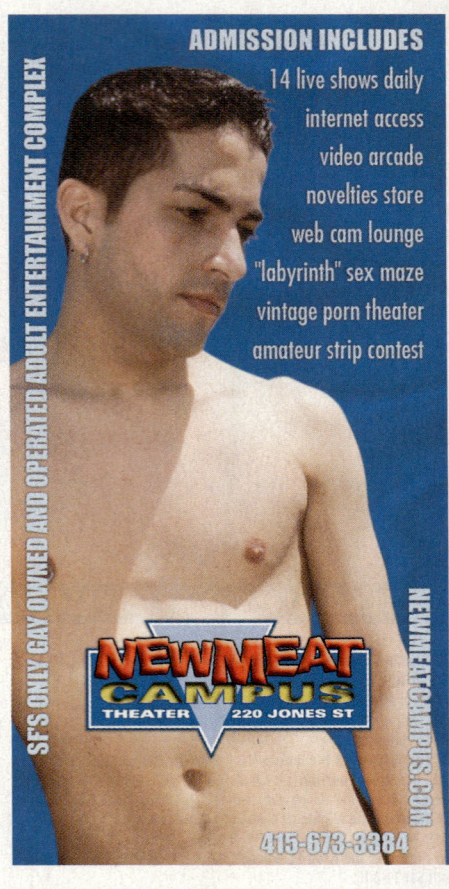

SEX SHOPS/BLUE MOVIES

■ **Campus Cinema** (G SNU VS)
220 Jones/Turk Street ✉ CA 94102

■ **Circle J Cinema** (G S VS) 10-24 h
369 Ellis Street ✉ CA 94102 ☎ 474-6995
Admission fee.

■ **City Entertainment**
960 Folsom Street ✉ CA 94107 ☎ 543-2124

■ **Folsom Gulch**
947 Folsom Street ✉ CA 94107 ☎ 495-6402

■ **Frenchy's**
1020 Geary Street ✉ CA 94109 ☎ 776-5940

■ **Good Vibrations** (GLM) Sun-Thu 11-19, Fri Sat -20 h
1210 Valencia Street ✉ CA 94103 ☎ 550-7399
Popular, well-equipped sex toy store, also mail-order.

■ **Jaguar** Sun-Thu 10-23, Fri Sat -24 h
4057 18th Street ✉ CA 94114 ☎ 863-4777

San Francisco | California/USA

take the pressure off

STEAMWORKS
BERKELEY CA CHICAGO IL SAN JUAN PR **24/7 MEN'S BATHHOUSE**
2107 4th Street / Berkeley / 510.845.8992 / www.SteamworksOnLine.com

■ **Nob Hill Cinema** (G R S VS) 11.45-1.30 h
729 Bush Street/Powell, ✉ CA 94108-3402 ☏ 781-9468
■ **Tearoom Theater, The** (G MG S VS SNU) 9-2, Fri&Sat-22 h
145 Eddy Street ✉ CA 94102 ☏ 885-9287

SAUNAS/BATHS
■ **Steamworks Bathhouse Berkeley** (! AC DR f G MA msg NU P SA SB VS WO) 24 hours daily
2107 4th Street, Berkeley ✉ CA 94710 ☏ (510) 845 89 92
Very popular steam bath.

FITNESS STUDIOS
■ **Market Street Gym** (GLM WH WO YG) Mon-Fri 6-22, Sat Sun 9-20 h
2301 Market Street ✉ CA 94114 ☏ 626-4488
Daily membership possible.
■ **Muscle System** (g MA WO)
2275 Market Street ☏ 863-4700
Daily membership pass available.
■ **Pacific Heights Health Club** (GLM)
2358 Pine Street/Fillmore Street ✉ CA 94115 ☏ 563-6694

BOOK SHOPS
■ **A Different Light** (! CC GLM we) 10-24 h
489 Castro Street ✉ CA 94114 ☏ 431-0891
■ **Cody's Books** (glm)
2454 Telegraph Avenue ✉ CA 94704 *Berkeley* ☏ 845-7852

GIFT & PRIDE SHOPS
■ **Does your Mother know...** (CC GLM) 9.30-22 h
4079 18th Street, ✉ CA 94114 *(Castro Street)* ☏ 864-3160

LEATHER & FETISH SHOPS
■ **A Taste of Leather** 12-20 h
317-A 10th Street/Folsom Street ✉ CA 94103 ☏ 252-9166
Also catalogue available for US$ 3.
■ **Stormy Leather** Tue-Sun 12-18 h, Fri 12-19 h
1158 Howard Street, CA 94103 ✉ CA 94103 *(between 7th and 8th)*
☏ 626-1672

TRAVEL AND TRANSPORT
■ **Joie de Vivre Hotels, Inc.** (GLM)
246 McAllister Street ✉ CA 94102 ☏ 1-800-738-7477
🖷 861-0954
Hotel reservation service for gays & lesbians.
■ **Now, Voyager Travel** Mon-Fri 10-18, Sat 11-17 h
4406 18th Street, ✉ CA 94114 *(Castro)* ☏ 626-1169
☏ (800) 255-6951 (toll free) 🖷 626-8626
🖳 www.nowvoyager.com
Specialist in Gay/Lesbian Travel since 1984.
■ **SFGayTours.com** (CC G MA MG)
173 Elsie Street ✉ CA 94110 ☏ 648 7758
🖳 www.sfgaytours.com
Gay tours of San Fransisco and bay area (gay clubbing, dining, theatre, shopping and gay weddings).

VIDEO SHOPS
■ **Captain Video** (g)
2358 Market Street ✉ CA 94114 ☏ 552-0501
Home delivery service for videos.
■ **Captain Video** (g)
2398 Lombard Street ✉ CA 94123 ☏ 921-2793

USA/California | San Francisco

The Hotel Atherton

Experience the history & charm of San Francisco. Dowtown location.
1 blk to polk St., 15 mins. to Castro.
Abbey Room Bar & Atherton Grill
$99 - $149 single/double

685 Ellis Street, San Francisco, CA 94109
Tel. 415-474-5720/Fax 415-474-8256
Res. 800-474-5720
www.hotelatherton.com/
reservations@hotelatherton.com

Proudly Serving Our Community For 19 Years

$119-$149 single/double $175-$250 suite

Renoir Hotel
Downtown San Francisco

- Gay-friendly boutique hotel in a historical landmark building
- Near Cable Cars, Union Square, theaters and shopping
- Walking distance to Folsom St. / SOMA bars and clubs, 15 min. to Castro
- Access to all public transportation in front of hotel
- 135 rooms, café, bar, Brazilian restaurant "Café do Brasil"
- Best view of SF Gay Pride Parade from our Market St. rooms and suites (last Sunday in June)
- Ideal location for "Folsom Street Fair", one of the world's biggest leather events. (last weekend in September)
- Come stay with us for the International Lesbian & Gay Film Festival (10 days preceding the SF Gay Pride Parade), "Dore Alley-Up your Alley Fair" (leather event last weekend in July), "Castro Street Fair" (first weekend in October), "Halloween in the Castro" (October 31)

45 McAllister at Market St., San Francisco, CA 94102
Tel: 415-626-5200 www.renoirhotel.com
Reservations: 800-576-3388 Fax: 415-626-0916

IGLTA

HOTELS

■ **Allison Hotel** (BF CC glm H MA) 24 h
417 Stockton Street ✉ CA 94108 (1 block to Union Square,China Town and cable car line) ☎ 986-8737 ☎ (800) 628-6456 (toll free) 📠 392-0856 💻 info@allisonhotel.com 💻 www.allisonhotel.com
All rooms with color cable TV, some with private baths. Continental bf incl. in price.

■ **Amsterdam Hotel. The** (G)
749 Taylor Street ✉ CA 94108 ☎ 673-3277
20 minutes to the airport. Central location. 12 minutes walk from gay bars. All rooms with phone, some with bath/WC.

■ **Atherton Hotel** (B CC F GLM H MA)
685 Ellis Street/Larkin Street ✉ CA 94109 ☎ 474-5720
☎ (800) 474-5720 (toll-free) 📠 474-3356
💻 reservations@hotelatherton.com 💻 www.hotelatherton.com
Nineteen km to the airport. Centrally located in the Civic Center district. 21 double rooms, 54 single rooms with priv. bath/WC, phone, satellite TV, radio, safe, heating.

■ **Civic Center Hotel** (G H)
20 12th Street/Market and Van Ness Streets ✉ CA 94103
☎ 861-2373
Daily US$ 20 and up, weekly US$ 70 and up.

■ **Ivy Hotel** (G H)
539 Octavia Street ✉ CA 94102 ☎ 863-6388
■ **Mosser Victorian Hotel** (B F GLM)
54 Fourth Street ✉ CA 94103 (South of Market area) ☎ 986-4400
☎ (800) 227-3804 📠 495-7653
All rooms with TV.
■ **National Hotel** (GLM H)
1139 Market Street ✉ CA 94103 ☎ 864-9343
Convenient location. Rates US$ 20-30.
■ **Renoir Hotel** (B BF CC F glm H MA) 0-24 h
45 McAllister ✉ CA 94102 (F-line stops in front of the hotel; downtown at Market St., only three blocks north of Folsom St.) ☎ 626-5200
☎ (800) 576-3388 (toll free) 📠 626-0916
💻 sales@renoirhotel.com 💻 www.renoirhotel.com
Friendly cosmopolitan boutique hotel with multilingual gay-friendly staff. Close to all gay neighbourhoods. 133 rooms and 2 suites all with private bath/ telephone, cable TV and many other extras.Café, Brazilian Restaurant. See website or call for special rates. Super location to watch GAY PRIDE parade !
■ **Union Square Hotel** (B BF GLM H)
114 Powell Street ✉ CA 94102 ☎ 397-3000
Downtown location. 10 min by subway to Castro District. All rooms with telephone, TV, bathroom, WC. Rates US$ 68-70.

San Francisco | California/USA

CASTRO DISTRICT
CASTILLO INN

48 Henry Street, San Francisco, CA 94114

Just steps to Castro and major transportation to Downtown-Wharf-GG Bridge from $60.00 to $80.00
Continental Breakfast
Refrigerator-Microwave
Also ask about our two bedroom apt.
Long term rates
Try us, you'll like us.

VISA/MC/Amex
(for reservations call)
1-800-865-5112
415-864-5111
Fax: 415-641-1321
Rates subject to change

SAN FRANCISCO

The **Andora Inn** is an 1875, fully restored Victorian Manor located in the heart of San Francisco's oldest and most colorful district, the "Mission", which is now one of the hippest neighborhoods in the country filled with wonderful art galleries & gift shops, bookstores & cafés and a thriving nightlife with a multitude of lounges, bars & restaurants, including the new cinematic sensation, **Foreign Cinema** (www.foreign cinema.com) and SF's very own **Beauty Bar** (www.beautybar.citysearch.com), both located 1 block away from the elegant Andora Inn, which is also located on a main bus & B.A.R.T line. For more information on Mission/Castro and SOMA night-life, special events and more, please log on to www.sfstation.com

Amenities include:
- Expanded Continental Breakfast Buffet
- 15 minute walk to Castro/SOMA
- Five Star Serta Mattresses
- Color TV With remote & VCR
- AM/FM Alarm Clock Radios
- Pleasant Garden Sun Deck
- Automated voice/phone system w/internet access.

— RATES: —
European Guest Rooms $79 to 119
Deluxe Rooms & Suites $119 to 249
*discounted rates for extended stays (add 14% hotel tax)
All rates are per night, upon availability & subject to change without notice.

(415) 282-0337 or 1 (800) 967-9219
FAX (415) 282-2608
website: www.andorainn.citysearch.com
e-mail: AndoraSF@aol.com
2438 Mission Street
San Francisco, California 94110

GUEST HOUSES

■ **Andora Inn** (b BF f GLM H OS)
2438 Mission Street ✉ CA 94110 ☎ 282-0337
☎ (800) 967-9219 (toll-free) 📠 282-2608 💻 AndoraSF@aol.com
🖥 www.andorainn.citysearch.com
B&B in a restored Victorian home located in the thriving Mission District just a few blocks from the Castro. All rooms with TV, video and radio. Rates double/shared bath USD79-119 and double/suites with private bath 199-249 incl. expanded continental bf. Elysium Café & Bar located on the first floor.

■ **Baby Bear's House** (BF CC GLM H) All year
1424 Page Street ✉ CA 94117 ☎ 255-9777
💻 babybear@babybearshouse.com 🖥 www.babybearshouse.com
2 rooms and a studio with bath/WC, telephone/fax, TV, VCR, own key. See web site or call for more information.

■ **Belvedere House** (BF e GLM H WH)
598 Belvedere Street ✉ CA 94117 (near the Castro, the Haight-Ashbury and Golden Gate Park) ☎ 731-6654 📠 681-0719
💻 BelvedereHouse@mindspring.com
🖥 www.GayBedAndBreakfast.net
Small, reasonably priced guest house.

■ **Bock's Bed and Breakfast** (BF GLM H MA OS)
1448 Willard Street ✉ CA 94117 (two blocks from Golden Gate Park)
☎ 664-6842 📠 664-1109 💻 bedandbreakfast.com
Lovely Edwardian residence in the Parnassus Heights area. Convenient location. Non-smoking. Ask for details.

■ **Castillo Inn** (bf cc H)
48 Henry Street ✉ CA 94107 ☎ 864-5111
📠 641-1321

■ **Edwardian San Francisco Hotel** (CC BF F GLM H MA)
1668 Market Street ✉ CA 94102 (6 blocks east of Castro St.)

☎ 864-1271   ☎ (888) 864-8070 (toll free)   📠 861-8116
🖥 www.edwardiansfhotel.com
Rooms with bath. Rates on request.

■ **Inn On Castro. The** (! BF GLM H MA) Office: 7.30-22.30 h
321 Castro Street/Market Street ✉ CA 94114 ☎ 861-0321
Located in the heart of San Francisco gay area. No smoking indoors. Rates $155.00 double $125.00 single.

■ **Inn San Francisco. The** (BF CC g H MA OS WH) Office: 7-23 h
943 South Van Ness Avenue ✉ CA 94110 ☎ 641-0188
☎ (800) 359-0913 (toll free) 📠 641-1701
💻 innkeeper@innsf.com 🖥 www.innsf.com
Restored 1872 Victorian Mansion in Mission neighborhood location. All rooms with phone, fridge, priv. bath (2 rooms with shared bath), color TV and radio. All rooms very nicely furnished. Rates US$ 85-215. Healthy bf buffet. Hot tub in the beautiful garden. Hosts Marty and Fred make sure you enjoy your stay.

■ **Parker House. The** (BF CC G H MA OS SB) All year
520 Church Street ✉ CA 94114 (Castro District) ☎ 621-3222
📠 621-4139 💻 info@parkerguesthouse.com
🖥 www.parkerguesthouse.com
Rooms with private bath, cable TV, telephone/modem. Very comfortable. Library and large gardens. See web site for more information. Awarded Out&About's "Five Palms" award for each of the last three years.

USA/California | San Francisco

SAN FRANCISCO'S PREMIER GAY GUEST HOUSE

IGLTA

THE PARKER HOUSE
"Guest House and Gardens"

"Highest Rating"
–DAMRON, FODOR'S and OUT & ABOUT

- Perfect Castro location
- Well appointed public rooms, gardens & steam spa
- Complete business and leisure traveler amenities

VISIT OUR WEBSITE AT: www.parkerguesthouse.com
OR CALL US AT: 1-415-621-3222

520 CHURCH STREET SAN FRANCISCO, CA 94114

INN ON CASTRO
A BED & BREAKFAST GUEST HOUSE
INDIVIDUALLY APPOINTED ROOMS
WITH PRIVATE BATHS. NO SMOKING INDOORS
321 CASTRO ST. SAN FRANCISCO 94114 (415) 861-0321

18th INN CASTRO
Bed and Breakfast
4515 18st San Francisco CA 94114
Telephone/fax (415) 252-7192

e-mail us at: The18thInnCastro@aol.com
all rooms with private bath & full breakfast
walk to bars and cafes in heart of the Castro!
Spanish & French spoken for our international guests
visit our web site at: 18thinncastro.com

complete offer
see page Germany/Berlin

SAN FRANCISCO – from $ 50 –
overnight accomodation service
· about 750 beds · more than 28 cities ·

enjoy bed & breakfast

central booking office Berlin ☎ **+49-30-236 236 10** 4:30-9:00 pm local time
Fax +49-30-23623619 · info@ebab.com · www.ebab.com

San Francisco | California/USA

BELVEDERE HOUSE
Bed and Breakfast
A place to be and let be.

toll free **1.877.BandBSF**
phone 415.731.6654 fax 415.681.0719
email **BelvedereHouse@mindspring.com**
www.GayBedAndBreakfast.net

Your popular gay stay in The City.
Located right above the Castro –
Walk to the bars, restaurants, shops and all the fun
Overlooking Golden Gate Park and the Pacific Ocean
Walk to the Haight-Ashbury and UCSF

Wir sprechen DEUTSCH

Continental breakfast
Afternoon refreshments
Laundry service available

10% DISCOUNT
for bookings made
four weeks in advance *

Rooms from $85.00 to $120.00
Private bath, private half-bath, shared bath available

*some restrictions apply

Gay owned
and operated

USA/California — San Francisco ▶ San Jose

THE WILLOWS INN
San Francisco

Homey atmosphere and personal friendly service
Voicemail/modem jacks
Complimentary breakfast/evening beverage
Visit our website for specials

Tel: 415-431-4770
www.WillowsSF.com
Fax: 415-431-5295

Your Haven within the Castro since 1981

■ **Phoenix Inn. The** (A AC B BF F g H MA msg N OS Pl)
601 Eddy Street ✉ CA 94109 ☎ 776-3109 ☎ (800) 2489-466 (toll free) 🖶 885-3109
Renovated and newly opened restaurant and bar, Backflip.

■ **Willows Inn. The** (BF CC GLM H MA) Daily 9-21 h
710 14th Street ✉ CA 94114-1106 ☎ 431-4770 🖶 431-5295
📧 Vacation@WillowsSF.com 🌐 www.WillowsSF.com
Located in the Castro district, 25 min. to the airport. All non-smoking rooms with voice mail phones. Rates from US$ 85-125 (bf incl.).See webside for specials and many links.

■ **18th Inn Castro** (bf H GLM M)
4515 18th Street ✉ CA 94114 ☎ 252-7192 🖶 252-7192
📧 the18thinncastro@aol.com 🌐 18thinncastro.com
Friendly B&B; all rooms with bath full bf. incl. French&Spanish spoken.

■ **24 Henry Guesthouse & Village House** (BF CC GLM H MA)
24 Henry Street ✉ CA 94114 *(in the town centre)* ☎ 864-5686
☎ (800) 900-5686 (toll free) 🖶 864-0406
📧 HenrySt24@aol.com 🌐 www.24Henry.com
Two guesthouses in the Castro district. All rooms are non-smoking.

PRIVATE ACCOMMODATION

■ **Enjoy Bed and Breakfast** (BF G H MA) 16.30-21 h (Central European Time)
Nollendorfplatz 5, 10777 Berlin - Germany ☎ +49 30 236 236 10
🖶 +49 30 236 236 19 📧 info@ebab.com 🌐 ebab.com
Accommodation sharing agency. All with shower and BF. 20-25 Euro p.p.

■ **Friends** (BF GLM H msg)
PO Box 460795 ✉ CA 94146 ☎ 826 5592 🖶 642 3700
📧 staywithfriends@pacbell.net
🌐 home.pacbell.net/donoharm/friends.htm
Private bed and breakfast accommodation. In-house masseur. Please call or see web site for details.

GENERAL GROUPS

■ **Affiliated Bigmen's Club**
584 Castro Street, Suite 139J ✉ CA 94114 ☎ (800) 501-3090
📧 abc@chubnet.com
Meeting once a year on Labor Day.

■ **Alice B. Toklas Lesbian/Gay Democratic Club**
PO Box 113 16, ✉ CA 94201

■ **Committee to Preserve our Sexual & Civil Liberties**
PO Box 42 23 85 ✉ CA 94142-2385

FETISH GROUPS

■ **California Eagles MC**
PO Box 146 65 ✉ CA 94114-0665 ☎ 267-0560

■ **Society of Janus. The**
PO Box 67 94 ✉ CA 94101
Non-profit educational and social organization for adults with S/M interests.

HEALTH GROUPS

■ **San Francisco City Clinic** Mon Thu 9.30-18, Tue Wed Fri 8-16 h
356 7th Street ☎ 864-8100

RELIGIOUS GROUPS

■ **Congregation Sha'ar Zahav** Mon-Fri 9-15 h
220 Danvers Street, ✉ CA 94114 *(in upper Castro district)*
☎ 861-6932 📧 shaarzahav@igc.apc.com
Jewish gays & lesbians.

SWIMMING

-Seal Rock Beach (Enter El Camino del Mar at the west end of Geary street and go from P downhills)

CRUISING

-Ocean beach (between Dutch windmill on Fulton street and Murphy windmill on Lincoln Way)
-Lafayette Park (nights, around the tennis courts)
-Buena Vista Park

San Jose ☎ 408

BARS

■ **A Tinkers Damn** (B d G)
46 North Saratoga Avenue, Santa Clara ✉ CA 95051 ☎ 243-4595

■ **Renegades** (B G LJ MA OS) 11-2 h
393 Stockton Avenue/Cinnabar ✉ CA 95126 ☎ 275-9902
Cruise bar.

■ **Stockade at Bucks Saloon** (B G LJ) 12-2 h, WE 0-24 h
301 Stockton Street/Julian Street ✉ CA 25126 ☎ 286-1176

■ **641 Club** (B d G OS) 14-2 h, WE 11-2 h
641 Stockton Avenue ✉ CA 95216 *(Between Villa and Schiele Ave)*
☎ 998-1144

SPARTACUS 2001/2002

San Jose ▶ Stockton | California/USA

SAUNAS/BATHS
■ **Watergarden** (AC CC G MA P OS SB SOL VS WH WO) 0-24 h
1010 The Alameda/Atlas Street ✉ CA 95126 ☏ 275-1215
Very nice garden with a big whirlpool. Relaxed atmosphere. Check website for special nights.

LEATHER & FETISH SHOPS
■ **Leather Masters** (LJ)
969 Park Avenue ✉ CA 95126 ☏ 293-7660

San Luis Obispo ☏ 805
GIFT & PRIDE SHOPS
■ **Twisted Orbits** (CC GLM YG) daily 11-19 h
778 Marsh Street ✉ CA 93401 ☏ 782 02 78

San Pedro ☏ 310
RESTAURANTS
■ **Babouch Moroccan Restaurant** (AC CC E F g lj MA S) Tue-Sun 17-22 h
810 South Gaffey Street ✉ 90731 ☏ 831-0246

Santa Barbara ☏ 805
GAY INFO
■ **Pacific Pride Foundation** Mon-Fri 9-17 h
126 East Haley Street, #A-11 ✉ CA 93101 ☏ 963-3636
963-9086
Social Service Agency with community center. Gay and Lesbian Resource Center.

RESTAURANTS
■ **Chameleon Restaurant And Bar** (A B CC d F GLM STV VS) Seasonal: Summer 7 days a week, Winter closed Mon-Tue
421 East Cota Street ✉ CA 93101 ☏ 965-9536
Drag-shows on Saturday.

SEX SHOPS/BLUE MOVIES
■ **For Adults Only** (glm) 0-24 h
223 Anacapa ✉ CA 93101 ☏ 963-9922

SWIMMING
-Cabrillo Beach (East of wharf)
-East Beach (NU)
-Padero Lane Beach (Summers AYOR)

Santa Cruz ☏ 831
GAY INFO
■ **Lesbian/Gay/Bisexual Center** Call for hours
1328 Commerce Lane ✉ CA 95060 ☏ 425-5422

BARS
■ **Blue Lagoon** (B D GLM S VS) 16-2 h
923 Pacific Avenue ✉ CA 95060 ☏ 423-7117

CRUISING
-Beer Can Beach (AYOR)
-Bonney Doon Beach (8 miles North on Highway 1)

Santa Rosa ☏ 707
BARS
■ **Santa Rosa Inn** (B D GLM) 12-2 h
4302 Santa Rosa Avenue ✉ CA 95407 ☏ 584-0345
Piano Bar Fri 17-20 h.

CAFES
■ **Aroma Roasters** (GLM) 7-24 h
95 5th Street ✉ CA 95401 ☏ 576-7765

SEX SHOPS/BLUE MOVIES
■ **Santa Rosa Adult Books**
3301 Santa Rosa Avenue ✉ CA 95407 ☏ 542-8248

BOOK SHOPS
■ **Sawywer's News** Sun-Thu 7-21 h, Fri Sat 7-22 h
733 4th Street ✉ CA 95404 ☏ 542-1311

TRAVEL AND TRANSPORT
■ **Holidays by Land & Sea Travel Club** (CC) 9-17 h
1605 Fourth Street ✉ 95404-4019 ☏ 573-9988 📠 568-0446
✉ holidays@sonic.net 🖥 www.holidaysbylandandsea.com
Gay Australia, Europe, cruises, resorts.
■ **Santa Rosa Travel**
542 Farmers Lane ✉ CA 95405 ☏ 542-0943 ☏ (800) 227-1445
(Toll free)
■ **Sun Quest**
1208 4th Street ✉ CA 95404 ☏ 573-8300 ☏ (800) 444-8300
(toll free)

Sausalito
CRUISING
-Black Sand Beach (off Lookout Road)

Sherman Oaks ☏ 818
BARS
■ **Gold 9** (AC B d G MA) 11-2 h
13625 Moorpark Street ✉ CA 91423-3722 ☏ 986-0285

Sonoma ☏ 707
GUEST HOUSES
■ **Sonoma Chalet Bed & Breakfast** (AC BF CC H)
18935 Fifth Street West ✉ CA 95476 ☏ 938-3129 📠 996-0190
✉ sonomachalet@cs.com 🖥 www.sonomachalet.com
Swiss-style farmhouse and country cottages in the wine country north of San Fransisco.

Stanford ☏ 415
GAY INFO
■ **Lesbian, Gay and Bisexual Community Center** (LGBCC)
Firetruck House *(across from Tresidder Union, 2nd floor)*
☏ 725-4222

Stockton ☏ 559
BARS
■ **Paradise** (B D GLM S YG) 18-2, WE 16-2 h
10100 North Lower Sacramento Road ☏ 477-4824

USA/California - Colorado — Stockton ▸ Breckenridge

BOOK SHOPS
■ **Adult Books**
332 North California ✉ CA 95202 ☎ 941-8607

Tahoe Paradise ☎ 530

HOTELS
■ **Driftwood Cafe** (b F glm H) 8-15, winter 7-15 h, closed Wed
4115 Laurel Avenue ✉ CA 95708 ☎ 544-6345
■ **Ridgewood Inn** (GLM H)
1341 Emerald Bay Road ✉ CA 95708 ☎ 541-8589
■ **Silver Shadows Lodge** (GLM H PI WH)
1251 Emerald Bay Road ✉ CA 95708 ☎ 541-3575

GUEST HOUSES
■ **Black Bear Inn** (BF CC glm)
1202 Ski Run Boulevard ✉ CA 96150 ☎ 544-4411 544-7315
✉ info@TahoeBlackBear.com www.TahoeBlackBear.com
A luxury lodge with 5 guest rooms plus three cabins. All rooms with private bath, fireplace, kingsize beds TV and full breakfast.
■ **Sierrawood Guest House** (AC BF F GLM H MA N NU VS WH) 0-24 h
3374 Grass Lake Road, ✉ CA 96155-0194 *(near South Lake Tahoe)*
☎ 577-6073 527-4739 ✉ swooddave@aol.com
 www.q-net.com/sierrawood

Upland ☎ 909

SEX SHOPS/BLUE MOVIES
■ **Mustang Adult Books & Videos**
959-961 N. Central Avenue ✉ CA 91786 ☎ 981-0227

Vallejo ☎ 707

BARS
■ **Nobody's Place** (AC B CC d f GLM OS) 12-2 h
437 Virginia Street ✉ CA 94590 ☎ 645-7298

Ventura ☎ 805

BARS
■ **Club Alternatives** (B D GLM) 14-2 h, WE 12- h
1644 East Thompson Boulevard ✉ CA 93001 ☎ 653-6511
■ **Fathom** (B CC D GLM OS S VS) Wed - Sat 18-2, Sun 16-2 h
2815 East Main Street ✉ CA 93003 *(Midtown Ventura between Telegraph and Cabrillo, near five points)* ☎ 643-7200

SEX SHOPS/BLUE MOVIES
■ **Three Star Adult News** 0-24 h
359 East Main Street ✉ CA 93001 ☎ 653-9068

CRUISING
-Bates Beach (between Ventura & Santa Barbara, AYOR)
-Emma Wood Street Beach

Victorville ☎ 619

BARS
■ **West Side 15** (b GLM) 12-2 h
16868 Stoddard Wells Road ✉ CA 92394 ☎ 243-9600

SEX SHOPS/BLUE MOVIES
■ **Oasis Adult Department Store**
14949 Palmdale Road ☎ 241-0788

CRUISING
-Pebble Beach Park (AYOR)

Walnut Creek ☎ 925

BARS
■ **Club 1220** (B d GLM) 16-2 h
1220 Pine Street ✉ CA 94596 ☎ 938-4550
■ **JR's** (B D GLM) Sun-Thu 17-2 h, Fri-Sat -4 h
2520 Camino Diablo ✉ CA 94596 ☎ 256-1200
Lesbian night every Sat. Popular.

West Sacramento ☎ 916

HOTELS
■ **Continental Hotel** (F glm H PI)
1432 West Capital Avenue, ✉ CA 95691 ☎ 371-3660

USA-Colorado

Location: Western USA
Initials: CO
Time: GMT -7
Area: 269,618 km^2 / 110,274 sq mi.
Population: 3,893,000
Capital: Denver

Aspen ☎ 970

GENERAL GROUPS
■ **Aspen Gay and Lesbian Community Fund** 9-17 h
520 East Cooper, Suite 16 81611 ✉ CO 81612 ☎ 925-4123
☎ 925-9249 (24 h hotline) 925-4146 ✉ aspengay@rof.net
Call for more iformations about events such as Aspen G&L Ski Week and Summerfest.

CRUISING
-Hyman Street Mall

Boulder ☎ 303

BARS
■ **Yard. The** (AC B d GLM MA N s) Mon-Fri 16-2 h, Sat-Sun 14-2 h
2690 28th Street, Unit C ✉ CO 80301 ☎ 443-1987
Friendly atmosphere.

SEX SHOPS/BLUE MOVIES
■ **The News Stand** 9-1 h, Sun 10-12 h
1720 15th Street ✉ CO 80302 ☎ 442-9515

CRUISING
-Chataquea Park
-Pearl Street Mall
-University of Colorado (men's locker room at recreation center)

Breckenridge ☎ 970

HOTELS
■ **Bunkhouse Lodge. The** (b BF CC G H MA SA VS WH)
13203 Hwy 9 ✉ CO 80424 ☎ 453-6475 453-3977
✉ bhlodge@colorado.net www.bunkhouselodge.com
■ **Mountain House** (GLM H PI SA)
PO Box 6 ✉ CO 80424 ☎ 453-6475
Priv. & shared bath, all rooms with telephone, TV. Kitchenette.

1188 SPARTACUS 2001/2002

Colorado Springs ▶ Denver Colorado/USA

Colorado Springs ☎ 719

BARS
■ **David's** (B D F GLM MA S)
2125 East Fountain Boulevard ☎ 444-0400
■ **Hide & Seek Complex. The** (B CC D F GLM lj MA OS S SNU) 10.30-? h
512West Colorado Avenue ✉ CO 80905 ☎ 634-9303
5 bars & restaurant.

HOTELS
■ **Pike's Peak Paradise** (BF GLM H)
PO Box 57 60, Woodland Park, CO 80866 ☎ 697-6656
In the outskirts of Colorado Springs.

CRUISING
-Palmer Park (Sections called "Lazy Lane" and "South Canyon")

Denver ☎ 303

GAY INFO
■ **Gay and Lesbian Community Center of Colorado** 10-22 h
1245 East Colfax ✉ CO 80218 ☎ 831-6268
Data Call/Colorado Athletic Exchange/Library Information/referral/ support groups/meeting space/peer counselling/outreach speaker's bureau /women's committee.
■ **Gay, Lesbian and Bisexual Community Center of Colorado**
Mon-Fri 10-19 h
☎ 837-0166

PUBLICATIONS
■ **Lesbian & Gay Pink Pages**
2785 North Speer Street #202 ✉ CO 80211 ☎ 837-8663
■ **Out Front**
244 Washington Street ✉ CO 80203 ☎ 778-7900 📠 778-7978
✉ outfrontc@aol.com
Published every other Fri, Colorado's No.1 gay publication. Features national news, reports and articles about the gay community, calendar of events, bar specials and classifieds.
■ **Quest Magazine** Mon-Fri 8-16 h
1115 Broadway #105 ✉ CO 80203 ☎ 534-4342 📠 524-4407
✉ questh@aol.com
Monthly publication. Features articles on movies, book reviews, gay events, ads. Approximately 40 pages. Supplement H Ink magazine on the party scene.

BARS
■ **BJ's Carousel** (AC B CC F G lj MA N S STV) 12-2, Sat-Sun 10-2 h
1380 S. Broadway ✉ CO 80210 ☎ 777-9880
Sun bf
■ **Bricks** (B f G N)
1600 East 17th Avenue ✉ CO 80218 ☎ 377-5400
■ **Charlie's** (B CC d F G LJ MA OS S) 10-2 h
900 East Colfax Avenue ✉ CO 80218-1915 ☎ 839-8890
Country/western style dance bar. Rated one of top 5 bars in the state (regardless of sexual orientation).
■ **Club Stud** (B G LJ MA)
255 South Broadway ✉ CO 80209 ☎ 733-9398
■ **C's** (B D GLM MA) 16-24 h, Fri Sat 16-2 h, Sun 14-2 h
7900 East Colfax Avenue/Trenton ✉ CO 80220 ☎ 322-4436
Happy hour 7 days a week 16-19 h.
■ **Den. The** (B F GLM N OS) 10-2 h
5110 West Colfax Avenue ✉ CO 80219 ☎ 534-5346
Restaurant: Mon-Thu 11.30-14 h, 17.30-22 h, Fri Sat 17.30-22.30 h, Sun brunch 10-15 h.

■ **Detour** (B F gLM N) Tue Men's night.
551 East Colfax Avenue ✉ CO 80203 ☎ 861-1497
■ **Grand Bar** (B CC E GLM MA OS VS) 11-2 h
538 East 17th Avenue ✉ CO 80203 ☎ 839-5390
Mostly business clientele.
■ **Highland Bar** (B GLM N)
2532 15th Street ✉ CO 80211 ☎ 455-9978
■ **Mike's** (AC B d GLM LJ MA N STV VS) 11-2 h
60 South Broadway ✉ CO 80209 ☎ 777-0193
■ **R&R Denver** (AC B f GLM MA N s WE) Mon-Fri 11-2, Sat-Sun 9-2 h
4958 East Colfax Avenue ✉ CO 80220 ☎ 320-9337
Happy hour Mon-Fri 11-13 h, Sat-Sun 9-12 h
■ **Snake Pit** (! B D f Glm S) 17-2 h
614 E 13th Avenue ☎ 831-1234
■ **Triangle Denver** (AC B CC d f G LJ MA s) 15-2, Sun 11-2 h
2036 Broadway ✉ CO 80220 ☎ 293-9009
■ **Wrangler** (B G LJ MA)
1700 Logan ✉ CO 80203 ☎ 837-1075
Cruise bar.
■ **Zippz** (AC B f G MA N SNU STV) 10-2 h
3014 East Colfax Avenue ✉ CO 80206 ☎ 321-6627

CAFES
■ **Dad's** (b f GLM N)
282 South Pennsylvania Street ✉ CO 80209 ☎ 744-1258

DANCECLUBS
■ **Club Proteus** (B D GLM)
1669 Clarkson Street (at 17th) ☎ 869-4637
■ **Compound. The** (AC B D G LJ MA N YG) Mon-Sat 7-2, Sun 8-2 h.
Dancing 21-2 h
145 Broadway ✉ CO 80203 ☎ 722-7777
■ **Foxhole at Centerfield Sports Bar** (AC B CC d f GLM MA N OS)
Sun 15-2 h
2936 Fox Street ✉ CO 80216 ☎ 298-7378
Every Sunday on the patio all summer.
■ **Maximilian's** (B D f glm OS) Fri Sat after hour
2151 Lawrence Street ✉ CO 80205 ☎ 297-0015
■ **Tracks 2000** (AC B CC D f GLM MA N OS STV TV VS WE) Thu 20-1.45 h, Fri 21-1.45 h, Sat, Sun 21-? h
2975 Fox Street ✉ CO 80216 ☎ 292-6660
Large gay nightclub, on Wed sometimes special events, Thu & Sun until 23 h 16+, Fri ladies night, Sat Circuit.

RESTAURANTS
■ **Club 404** (B F glm)
404 Broadway ☎ 778-9605
Restaurant and bar
■ **Nobody's Business** (B F glm N)
800 Decatur Street (I-25 and 8th Avenue) ☎ 825-4521

SEX SHOPS/BLUE MOVIES
■ **Heaven Sent Me** (AC CC MA WE) 10-22 h
482 South Broadway ✉ CO 80206 ☎ 331-8000
Gay gift items and rainbow merchandise.

SAUNAS/BATHS
■ **Denver Swim Club** (AC CC f DR G MA NU P PI SB VS WH WO) 0-24 h
6923 East Colfax Avenue ✉ CO 80220 (Bus 15) ☎ 321-9399
Nude sunbathing possible. Many special rooms. Free condoms and lube.

SPARTACUS 2001/2002 | 1189

USA/Colorado - Connecticut — Denver ▸ Hartford

■ **Midtowne Spa** (b CC G MA OS S SA SB VS WH) 0-24 h
2935 Zuni Street ✉ CO 80211 ☎ 458-8902
Bath house with a sundeck, a dungeon room, sling and more. Free condoms. Mon leather night, Wed young night (1/2 price).

■ **Triple C. The** (AC CC DR G MA P S SA SB VS WH WO) 0-24 h
2151 Lawrence Street ✉ CO 80205 *(2 blocks east from Coors Field downtown)* ☎ 257-2601
Relaxed atmosphere frequented by a mixed age crowd. Patio and in-house deli. Parties every month.

FITNESS STUDIOS

■ **Broadway Bodyworks** (glm WO)
160 South Broadway ✉ CO 80209 ☎ 722-4342

BOOK SHOPS

■ **Category Six Books** (AC CC G MA WE) Mon-Sat 10-18, Sun 11-17 h
42 South Broadway ✉ CO 80209 *(RTD bus route, 2 blocks south of Mayan Theatre)* ☎ 777-0766
Gay bookshop. 15% discount on all hardback books.

■ **Isis Bookstore** (glm)
5701 East Colfax Avenue ✉ CO 80220 *(at Ivanhoe)* ☎ 321-0867

GUEST HOUSES

■ **Elyria's Western Guest House** (AC BF CC GLM H NU OS WH)
4700 Baldwin Court ✉ CO 80216 ☎ 291-0915 📠 296-9892
📧 JamesE.Klismet@usa.net
🌐 www.bestinns.net/usa/co/rdewgh.html
Small B&B. Rooms with shared bath, radio and TV. Rates single US$40 and double $50 incl. cont. bf.

■ **Twin Maples B&B** (AC CC G H msg) Open all year
1401 Madison Street ✉ CO 80206 ☎ (888) 835-5738
📠 394-4776 📧 twinmaples@boytoy.com
🌐 boytoy.com/twinmaples.htm
Located in the heart of historical Denver. 3 double rooms with facilities on the corridor, all rooms with balcony, phone, TV, radio, heating. Hotel provides TV room.

■ **Victoria Oaks Inn** (AC BF E CC F glm)
1575 Race Street ✉ CO 80206 ☎ 355-1818 📠 331-1095
📧 Vicoaksinn@aol.com
9 rooms with private and shared baths. All with minibar, cable TV and VCR, some with kitchenette. No pets, no kids.

GENERAL GROUPS

■ **Auraria Lesbian & Gay Alliance**
1006 11th Street ✉ CO 80204 ☎ 556-3317

■ **Coming Out/Being Out Group**
☎ 831-6268

■ **Girth & Mirth of the Rockies**
PO Box 2351 ✉ CO 80201 ☎ 211-8269
📧 girthmirthotr@usa.net 🌐 www.chubnet2.com/gmotr
Meeting 1st Sat at Capital Hill Community Center, 13th Williams at 19.30 h

■ **Parents and Friends of Lesbians & Gays**
☎ 333-0186

FETISH GROUPS

■ **Knights of Malta**
PO Box 98 36 ✉ CO 80209 ☎ 744-6340

HEALTH GROUPS

■ **Colorado AIDS Project (CAP)**
☎ 837-0166

RELIGIOUS GROUPS

■ **Congregation Tikvat Shalom**
PO Box 66 94 ✉ CO 80206 ☎ 331-2706
Jewish gays. and lesbians.

CRUISING

- Berkley Park
- Chessman Park
- Danish World (R) (upper level arcades, Grant & Sherman between 13th and 14th Street)
- May D.& F. Store (AYOR) (downtown and Aurora Mall)
- 16th Street Mall
- Royal Host Motel (area around)
- Stapleton International Airport (AYOR) (mezzanine level & change rooms, behind mosaic)
- "The Point" (AYOR) (north west of I-70 and Sheridan Road)
- UCD (East Classroom Building, 3rd floor)
- U of D (Boettcher Hall, downstairs & library)

Durango ☎ 970

HOTELS

■ **Leland House / Rochester Hotel** (AC BF CC f glm H MA OS)
721 E. Second Avenue ✉ CO 81301 *(located in the historic downtown)* ☎ 385-1920 ☎ (800) 664-1920 (toll free) 📠 385-1967
📧 leland@rochesterhotel.com 🌐 www.rochesterhotel.com
All rooms with private bath, radio and TV, studios with kitchenette. Rates studio US$75-109, single $95-159, double $105-199 incl. bf buffet.

Woodland Park ☎ 719

HOTELS

■ **Pikes Peak Paradise** (BF GLM H MA OS) 8-22 h
PO Box 57 60 ✉ CO 80866 ☎ 728-8282
Northwest of Colorado Springs. Bed & Breakfast in comfortable rooms. A full "all-you-can-eat" breakfast buffet is offered as well as light snacks and beverages.

USA-Connecticut

Location: Northeast USA
Initials: CT
Time: GMT -5
Area: 14,358 km² / 5,872 sq mi.
Population: 3,270,000
Capital: Hartford

Hartford ☎ 860

PUBLICATIONS

■ **Metroline**
495 Farmington Avenue ✉ CT 06105 ☎ 231-8845 📠 233-8338
📧 info@metroline-online.com 🌐 www.metroline-online.com
Community monthly news magazine.

BARS

■ **Chez Est** (B D G OS) 15-1 h, Sun 12-1 h
458 Wethersfield Avenue ✉ CT 06114 ☎ 525-3243
Popular.

■ **Nicks** (B G)
1943 Broad Street ✉ CT 06114 ☎ 522-1573

Hartford ▶ Rehoboth Beach — Connecticut - Delaware/USA

RESTAURANTS
■ **Summit Hill Cafe** (B F GLM)
Zion Street/Summit Street ✉ CT 06106 ☎ 547-1921

BOOK SHOPS
■ **Reader's Feast Bookstore & Cafe** (b GLM)
529 Farmington Avenue ✉ CT 06105 ☎ 232-3710

New Haven ☎ 203

GAY INFO
■ **Gay Switchboard** Mon-Thu 20-23 h
☎ 624-6869

BARS
■ **Partners** (B D GLM MA p s VS YG)
365 Crown Street ☎ 776-1014
■ **168 York Street Café** (B GLM) 14-1 h
168 York Street ☎ 789-1915

SEX SHOPS/BLUE MOVIES
■ **Video Expo and Magazine Center** (glm)
754 Chapel Street ☎ 562-3299

CRUISING
-Chapel Street (from York to park)
-East Rock Park
-Yale University (Woolsey Hall and library)
-New Haven Information Pavillion
-Parking areas between Route 95 and shore line-night car cruising.

USA-Delaware

Location: Northeast USA
Initials: DE
Time: GMT -5
Area: 6,448 km² / 2,637 sq mi.
Population: 732,000
Capital: Dover

Rehoboth Beach ☎ 302

GAY INFO
■ **Camp Rehoboth** (CC GLM MA OS) 10-19 h
39 Baltimore Avenue ✉ DE 19971 ☎ 227-5620 📠 227-5604
✉ info@camprehoboth.com ⌂ www.camprehoboth.com
Community center publishing a bi-weekly magazine.

BARS
■ **Blue Moon** (B F GLM) Thu-Mon 18-22, Sat -23, Sun brunch 11-15 h
35 Baltimore Avenue ✉ DE 19971 ☎ 227-6515
Popular.

DANCECLUBS
■ **Renegade** (B F GLM) Sun-Tue 11-2 h, Wed-Fri 16-2 h, Sat 11-3 h
4274 Highway One ✉ DE 19971 ☎ 227-1222

RESTAURANTS
■ **Adriatico Ristorante** (b F g)
North 1st Street ✉ DE 19971 ☎ 227-9255
Italian food.
■ **Black Porch Cafe** (B F GLM)
21 Rehoboth Avenue ✉ DE 19971 ☎ 227-3676
■ **Cloud Nine** (B F g)
234 Rehoboth Avenue ✉ DE 19971
Creative menu.

■ **La La Land** (b F g)
22 1/2 Wilmington Avenue ✉ DE 19971 ☎ 227-7244
■ **Palms Restaurant** (B F GLM) Thu-Sun 15-2 h, dinner 18-22 h, Sun brunch 10-15 h
234 Rehoboth Avenue ✉ DE 19971 ☎ 227-0800
■ **Sydney Sidestreet** (b F g)
25 Christian Street ✉ DE 19771 ☎ 227-1339
■ **Tijuana Taxi** (b F GLM)
207 Rehoboth Avenue ✉ DE 19771 ☎ 227-1986
Mexican cuisine.

BOOK SHOPS
■ **Lambda Rising** (AC CC GLM MA VS) Summer 10-24 h, winter -20 h
39 Baltimore Avenue ✉ DE 19971 ☎ 227-6969
Gay, lesbian, bisexual and transgender books, videos, magazines and gifts. Free local guides.

HOTELS
■ **Beach House** (g H Pl)
15 Hickman Street ✉ DE 19971 ☎ 227-7074
Heated pool with private sundeck, color cable TV in each room.
■ **Guest Rooms at Rehoboth** (G H)
45 Baltimore Avenue ✉ DE 19771 ☎ 227-8355
Downtown, reasonable rates.
■ **Paper Nautilus** (GLM H)
42 1/2 Baltimore Avenue ✉ DE 19971 ☎ 227-1603
■ **Rams Head Inn. The** (BF G H MA NU PI SA WH WO)
Road 2, PO Box 509 ✉ DE 19971 ☎ 226-9171
Rates US$ 35-110. Call ahead for reservations.
■ **Rehoboth Guest House** (AC BF CC GLM) 8.30-21 h
40 Maryland Avenue ✉ DE 19971 ☎ 227-4117
☎ (800) 564-0493 ✉ reho@guesthse.com
10 double rooms, 3 kings- 1 queenapartment, in 100 years old renovated Victorian Beach house. All rooms with balcony/terrace, bath/shower/WC, heating, own key.
■ **Renegade Resort** (AC B F G H Pl s)
4274 Highway One ✉ DE 19971 ☎ 227-1222
Private bath, TV. Very cruisy.
■ **Southside Suites** (G H)
45 Deleware Avenue ✉ DE 19771 ☎ 227-8355
Downtown, reasonable rates.
■ **Valhalla Resort** (AC BF CC H MA msg OS PI WO)
8 Anna B Street, ✉ DE 19971 ☎ 226-1408 📠 226-0134
Completely enclosed complex with total privacy and parking. Resort offers courtesy transportation to beach, restaurants and bars.

GUEST HOUSES
■ **Shore Inn. The** (AC BF CC G MA PI WH) closed Ja
703 Rehoboth Avenue ✉ DE 19971 ☎ 227-8487
☎ (800) 597-8899 ✉ horeinn@ce.net
⌂ beach-net.com/shoreinn.html
14 rooms with private bath, refrigerator, tea/coffee facilities, TV and telephone in centrally located house.
■ **Silver Lake Guest House** (AC BF CC GLM H MA OS)
133 Silver Lake Drive ✉ DE 19971 ☎ 226-2115
☎ (800) 842-2115 📠 226-2732
✉ info@silverlakeguesthouse.com
⌂ www.silverlakeguesthouse.com
Beautifully located on the Silver Lake near Gay Ocean beach. 13 double rooms, 2 apartments with kitchen, shower/bath/WC. All rooms with private bath, TV, heating, AC, own key, most with balcony. Guest house provides car park. Rates from $80 to $350 according to season and room/apartment.

USA/Delaware - District of Columbia | Reboboth Beach ▸ Washington D.C.

SWIMMING
-Poodle Beach (at the end of Queen Street)
-Cape Henlopen State Park (North Shores)

Wilmington ☏ 302

BARS
■ **Roam** (A AC B CC D F GLM MA N S STV WE) Fri 17-2, Sat-Thu 18-2 h
913 Shipley Street ✉ DE 19801 ☏ 658-7276

RESTAURANTS
■ **Anthonys on Shipley Street** (A AC B CC E F g N WE) 17-22, Fri Sat -23, Sun -21 h
913 Shipley Street ✉ DE 19801 ☏ 652-7797
American/Italian fine dining.

■ **814 Club** (B F G)
814 Shipley Street ✉ DE 19801 ☏ 657-5730

USA-District of Columbia

Location: East USA
Initials: DC
Time: GMT -5
Area: 177 km² / 72 sq mi.
Population: 529,000

Washington D.C. ☏ 202

✱ Leonard Matlovich's tombstone reads: 'They gave me a medal for killing a man, and discharged me for loving one'. This symbolizes very well the ambivalent face of Washington, a face which makes it a first class travel destination. The *District of Columbia* (D.C.) comprises only the city of Washington. Containing only 600.000 inhabitants in a conurbation of a population of 4 million, it is surprisingly small. This shows Washington being no buzzing *business town*; Washington is the federal government and politics is business here. Seen under this perspective, the business center of Washington is the *Mall*, which is lined by many political institutions and US symbols like the *White House* or the *Vietnam Memorial*, or by museums like the *Holocaust Museum*. The Mall is most beautiful in March and April when the cherry trees blossom. The gays have learned to live with the presence of the federal institutions. Accordingly there is lobbying for gay interests, with which not only the gay scene is preoccupied, but also the gay town newspaper, the *Washington Blade*. When going out, the Washingtonians favour the area around the *Dupont Circle*, northwest of the White House. No car is needed for expeditions here or to other city quarters. The subway is fast und will transport you savely to (nearly) any destination. Nevertheless: Where gay nightlife is not in the vicinity of Dupont Circle, always take a taxi. Two attractions must be mentioned: the impressive *Union Station*, the giant railway station, now a shopping and restaurant center, and *Mount Vernon*, the pittoreske dwelling of George Washington. The gay resort *Rehoboth Beach*, situated two hours distant in Delaware, is worth the trip.

★ Es existieren keine einschränkenden Gesetze einvernehmlichen Sex betreffend. 1977 wurde ein *Anti-Discrimination Law* verabschiedet. Seit 1992 gilt im D.C. ein *Domestic Partnership Law*. Es wurde bis jetzt noch keine *Anti-Marriage Bill* eingebracht. Der *District of Columbia* (D.C.) besteht nur aus der Stadt Washington.

Mit ca. 600.000 Einwohnern in einem 4-Millionen-Ballungsraum ist er erstaunlich klein. Das zeigt, daß Washington selbst keine quirlige *business town* ist. Washington ist die Bundesregierung. Politik ist das Geschäft dieser Stadt. So gesehen ist das "Geschäftszentrum" die *Mall*, an der entlang sich viele politische Institutionen und US-amerikanische Symbole wie *Weißes Haus* oder *Vietnam Memorial* finden. Dazu gehören auch zahlreiche Museen wie das *Holocaust Museum*. Die schönste Zeit ist übrigens, wenn entlang der Mall im März/April die Kirschbäume blühen. Die Schwulen Washingtons haben sich mit der massiven Präsenz des Bundes eingerichtet. Es wird entsprechender Lobbyismus für schwule Interessen betrieben. Womit sich, neben der Szene auch die schwule Zeitung der Stadt, die *Washington Blade*, beschäftigt. Und wenn sie denn ausgehen, die Washingtonians, dann tun sie das bevorzugt in der Gegend um den *Dupont Circle*, nordwestlich des Weißen Hauses. Um diese und andere Gegenden innerhalb der Stadt zu erkunden, benötigen Sie kein Auto. Die Washingtoner U-Bahn bringt Sie schnell und sicher (fast) überall hin. Trotzdem: dort, wo schwules Nightlife abseits des Dupont Circle liegt, nachts ein Taxi benutzen. Zwei Attraktionen sollen noch erwähnt werden: die beeindruckende *Union Station*, der zum Shopping- und Restaurantkomplex umgestaltete, gewaltige Bahnhof der Stadt und *Mt. Vernon*, der pittoreske Wohnsitz George Washingtons. Als Ausflugsziel empfiehlt sich schließlich der schwule Badeort *Rehoboth Beach*, zwei Stunden entfernt in Delaware gelegen.

✱ Sur la pierre tombale de Leonard Matlovich, on peut lire: "L'Armée m'a décerné une médaille pour avoit tué un homme. L'Armée m'a viré pour en avoir aimé un autre". Washington est la ville des contradictions. C'est donc une ville qu'il faut absolument avoir vue. Le District of Columbia ("D.C."), c'est la ville de Washington. Elle ne compte que 600.000 habitants, mais se trouve au coeur d'une agglomération de 4 millions d'habitants. Washington n'est pas une ville d'affaires, Washington, c'est le gouvernement fédéral. Le business, ici, c'est la politique. L'artère vitale de Washington, c'est le Mall, le long duquel on trouve les symboles et les institutions des Etats-Unis: la Maison Blanche, le Mémorial de la Guerre du Vietnam, le Musée de l'Holocauste... En mars et avril, les cerisiers qui bordent le Mall sont en fleur. C'est le moment idéal pour visiter Washington! Les gais de Washington ont pris leur parti de la présence des institutions politiques et s'attachent à défendre leurs intérêts, ce que fait "Washington Blade", le magazine gai de la ville. Quand les gais de la capitale sortent, c'est dans le quartier autour de Dupont Circle, au nord-ouest de la Maison Blanche. Pas besoin de voiture pour découvrir Washington: prenez le métro! Il est rapide et sûr. Enfin, presque partout. Si vous sortez le soir, en dehors du Dupont Circle, il est plus prudent de prendre un taxi. Ne passez pas à côté de Union Station (ancienne gare transformée en un méga centre commercial) et de Mont Vernon (pittoresque résidence de George Washington). Pour une excursion hors de la capitale, allez à Rehobotho Beach. Cette station balnéaire gaie se trouve dans l'Etat du Delaware, à deux heures de voiture de Washington.

▪ La lápida de Leonard Matlovich tine la siguiente inscripción: "Me concedieron una medalla por matar a un hombre y me despidieron por amar a uno". Washington posee muchos de esos conceptos disonantes y precisamente eso es lo que la hace valiosa como destino turístico de primer clase. El *District of Columbia* (D. C.) y la ciudad de Washington son la mismacasa y con aprox. 600.000 habitantes y con 4 mill. si se incluyen los habitantes de sus alrededores es sorprendentemente pequeña. Washington es el *business town* de la nación. Washington es el gobierno federal y el pan diario de

Washington D.C. — District of Columbia/USA

Washington, DC

1. JR's Bar and Grill
2. Straits of Malaya Restaurant
3. The Brenton Guest House
4. Leather Rack Sex Shop
5. Lambda Rising Book Shop
6. Escalanos Bar
7. Radisson Barceló Hotel
8. Badlands Bar
9. The Fireplace Bar
10. Mr. P's Bar
11. The Childe Harolde Restaurant
12. Cafe Berlin Restaurant
13. Two Quail Restaurant
14. D.C. Eagle Bar

SPARTACUS 2001/2002 | 1193

USA/District of Columbia | Washington D.C.

esta ciudad es la política. Visto desde este punto de vista, el centro de negocios lo es el *Mall* en el que se situan muchas de sus instituciones políticas y símbolos norteamericanos como *La Casa Blanca* o el *Vietnam Memorial*. También se encuentran gran cantidad de museos como el *Holocaust Museum*. Una visita al Mall en los meses en los que sus cerezos florecen (marzo y abril) es muy recomendable. Los gays de Washington han aprendido de vivir con la presencia masiva federal. Dentro del ayuntamiento hay representantes de los gays que velan por sus intereses. El periódico *Washington Blade* apoya también estos intereses. El centro gay de la ciudad se encuentra sobre todo en los alrededores de *Dupont Circle* al lado noroeste de la Casa Blanca. Para visitar estos sitios y otros dentro de la ciudad no es necesario el uso de automovil. El metro te transporta rápido y seguro a casi todo lugar. Pero quien sale en las afueras del Dupont Circle, deberta coser sin falta un taxi. Dos atracciones son de especial mención. El asombroso *Union Station*, la enorme estación de trenes que fue convertida en un complejo de compras y restaurantes, asi como *Mt. Vernon* el pintoresco lugar de habitación de George Washington. En Delaware a 2 horas de distancia aconsejamos el balneario gay *Rehoboth Beach*.

Sulla lapide di Leonard Matlovich's vi è un epitaffio: "Mi conferite una medaglia per aver ucciso un uomo e mi congedate per averne amato un altro." Sono proprio questi numerosi tratti contradditori a fare di Washington una meta di prima classe. Il *District of Columbia* (D.C.) è costituito unicamente dalla città di Washington; è sorprendentemente piccolo: ha 600.000 abitanti con una periferia di 4.000.000. Ciò prova che Washington non è una movimentata *business town*. Rappresenta il governo federale e la politica costituisce l'anima commerciale di questa città. Così è considerato il centro commerciale, *Mall*, lungo quale si trovano istituzioni politiche, simbolo degli Stati Uniti, come la *Casa Bianca*, il *Vietnam Memorial* e numerosi musei come l'*Holocaust Museum*. Il periodo più bello per una visita è in marzo-aprile, quando lungo il Mall fioriscono i cigliegi. I gay di Washington si sono adattati alla massiva presenza del governo: mediante associazioni cercano di difendere i propri interessi, appoggiati dal giornale locale *Washington Blade*. Gli abitanti di Washington escono con preferenza nella zona intorno al *Dupont Circle* a nord ovest della Casa Bianca. Per conoscere questa ed altre parti della città non avrete bisogno di un'auto poichè la metropolitana vi porta ovunque velocemente e (quasi) senza rischi. Tuttavia nelle zone esterne al Dupont Circle non rinunciate mai ad un taxi; é d'obbligo in fine menzionare due attrazioni: l'imponente *Union Station*, trasformata in un centro commerciale, ricca di ristoranti e negozi e *Mt. Vernon*, la pittoresca residenza di George Washington. Vi consigliamo inoltre un'esursione a Rehoboth Beach, una stazione balneare gay situata a Delaware a due ore da Washington.

GAY INFO

■ **Gay and Lesbian Switchboard** (GLM) 19.30-22.30 h
☎ 387-4348

PUBLICATIONS

■ **Metro Weekly**
1012 14th Street NW, Suite 615 ✉ DC 20005 ☎ 638-6830
🖷 638-6831 🖳 rshulman@metroweekly.com
Gay and lesbian weekly distributed free every Thu throughout the DC Metropolitan area.

■ **Washington Blade**
1408 U Street North West ✉ DC 20009-3916 *(2nd floor)*
☎ 797-7000 🖷 797-7040 🖳 news@washblade.com
🖳 www.washblade.com
Weekly G&L news magazine.

TOURIST INFO

■ **Washington DC Convention & Visitor Bureau**
1212 New York Avenue NW, Suite 600 ✉ DC 20005 ☎ 789-7000
🖷 789-7037

BARS

■ **Back Door Pub** (B G) 17-? h
1104 8th Street South East ✉ DC 20003 *(second floor at Bachelor's Mill)* ☎ 546-5979
■ **Badlands** (! AC B D f GLM MA N s VS YG)
1415 22nd Street North West ✉ DC 20037 ☎ 296-0505
■ **Brass Rail. The** (B D F G) 11-2 h
476 K Street North West ✉ DC 20001 ☎ 371-6983
■ **D.C. Eagle** (B G LJ) 12-2 h, Fri Sat -3 h
639 New York Avenue NW ✉ DC 20001 ☎ 347-6025
■ **Escandalo** (B F GLM r S) 16-? h
2122 P Street North West ✉ DC 20037 ☎ 822-8909
Friendly piano bar and restaurant.
■ **Fireplace. The** (! B G VS YG) 13-2 h
2161 P Street North West ✉ DC 20037 ☎ 293-1293
■ **Hung Jury** (B GLM)
1819 H Street North West ✉ DC 20006 ☎ 785-8181
■ **J.R.'s Bar & Grill** (AC B CC F G lj R VS) 11-2, Fri Sat -3 h
1519 17th Street North West ✉ DC 20036 ☎ 328-0090
■ **La Cage aux Follies** (B d G S SNU) Mon-Thu 19.30-2 h, Fri Sat -3 h
1354 Capital Street South East ✉ DC 20003 ☎ 554-3615
■ **Larry's Lounge** (AC B CC GLM MA N OS) 17-2 h
1840 18th Street North West ✉ DC 20009 ☎ 483-1483
■ **Mr. P's** (B D f G STV VS) 15-2 h, Fri Sat -3 h, Sun 12-2 h
2147 P Street North West ✉ DC 20037 ☎ 293-1064
■ **Nob Hill** (B G MA)
1101 Kenyon Street North West ✉ DC 20010 ☎ 797-1101
■ **Omega DC** (AC B G s VS) Sun-Thu 16-2 h, Fri -3 h, Sat 20-3 h
2123 Twining CT North West ✉ DC 20037 *(Dupont Circle)*
☎ 223-4917
■ **Remington's** (AC B CC d GLM LJ MA N S STV VS) Mon-Thu 16-2, Fri Sat -3, Sun 12-2 h
639 Pennsylvania Avenue South East ✉ DC 20003 *(Metro-Eastern Market)* ☎ 543-3113
New beautiful oak bar addition to 2nd floor.

MEN'S CLUBS

■ **Crew Club. The** (CC DR G P VS WO) 0-24 h
1321 14th Street North West ✉ DC 20005 *(Metrorail Red Line-Dupont Circle/Blue or Orange Line-McPherson Square)* ☎ 319-1333
Smoke, alcohol and drug free. Coming soon: steam, sauna, additional cabins.

Washington D.C. — District of Columbia/USA

■ **GHC - The Gloryhole** (G VS) 0-24 h
24 O Street South East ✉ DC 20001 ☎ 863-2770

DANCECLUBS

■ **Bachelor's Mill** (B D G s) 22-? h, closed on Mon
1104 Eight Street South East ☎ 544-1931
African-American clientele.

■ **Edge. The** (B D F G snu VS) 22-5, Fri Sat 23-5 h, Sun closed
56 L Street South East *(at Half Street)* ☎ 488-1200

■ **Tracks** (B D f G MA s WE) Thu Sat 21-? h, Fri 22-? h, Sun 17-22.30 h
1111 1st Street South East ✉ DC 20003 *(Metro-Navy Yard)* ☎ 488-3320
Thu is college night, Sun country/western tea dance.

■ **Ziegfeld's** (B D GLM STV)
1345 Half Street South East ✉ DC 20003 ☎ 554-5141

RESTAURANTS

■ **Boss Shepherd's** (B F GLM OS) Sun 11-16 h brunch
1527 17th Street North West ✉ DC 20036 ☎ 328-8193

■ **Bradshaw's** (B F G)
2319 18th Street North West ✉ DC 20009 ☎ 462-8330

■ **Café Berlin** (AC B CC F GLM MA OS) Mon-Thu 11-22, Fri -23, Sat 12-23, Sun 16-22 h
322 Massachusetts Avenue, NE ✉ DC 20002 ☎ 543-7656
German and continental cuisine. Casual dress. Patio dining in season.

■ **Café Japon** (B F G)
2032 P Street North West ✉ DC 20036 ☎ 223-1573

■ **Cafe Luna** (A B BF F glm OS YG) 11-2 h
1633 P Street North West ✉ DC 20036 ☎ 387-4005
Italian cuisine.

■ **Childe Harolde Restaurant and Saloon** (! AC B CC F glm MA N OS) Sun-Thu 11.30-2, Fri Sat 10.30-3 h
1610 20th Street North West ✉ DC 20009 *(metro Dupont Circle-Q Street exit)* ☎ 483-6700
One of the oldest restaurants in Washington, full menue, great seafood and steaks, lots of sandwiches, best burger in DC. Private room available.

■ **La Fourchette** (B F GLM)
2429 18th Street North West ✉ DC 20009 ☎ 332-3077

■ **Lauriol Plaza** (b F g) 12-24 h, Sun 11-24 h
1801 18th Street North West ✉ DC 20009 ☎ 387-0035

■ **Louis** (B F G lj)
476 K Street North West ✉ DC 20001 ☎ 371-2223

■ **Lucy's and Fred's** (B F GLM YG) 18-22 h
56 L Street South East ✉ DC 20003 *(at Lost & Found)* ☎ 488-1200

■ **Mr. Henry's** (AC B CC F GLM MA N OS) Mon-Sat 11.30-2, Sun 10-2 h
601 Pennsylvania Avenue S.E. ✉ DC 20003 ☎ 546-8412

■ **Pan Asian Restaurant** (B F g)
2020 P Street North West ✉ DC 20036 ☎ 872-8889

■ **Paramount Steak House** (AC b CC F glm OS) 10.30-24 h, Fri Sat -? h
1609 17th Street North West ✉ DC 20009 ☎ 232-0395
Steaks and seafood.

■ **Perry's** (AC B F glm OS YG)
1811 Columbia Road North West ✉ DC 20009 ☎ 234-6218
Japanese and nouvelle cuisine.

■ **Ribs and More** (AC b F G)
2122 P Street North West ✉ DC 20037 ☎ 822-8909

■ **Sala Thai Restaurant** (B F g) Mon-Fri 11.30-23, WE 12-23.30
2016 P Street North West ✉ DC 20037 *(Dupont Circle)* ☎ 872-1144

■ **Skewers** (b F g)
1633 P Street North West ✉ DC 20036 ☎ 387-7400

■ **Straits of Malaya** (AC B CC F glm MA N OS) Mon-Fri 12-14, 17.30-2 h
1836 18th Street North West ✉ DC 20017 *(Dupont Circle)* ☎ 483-1483
Malaysian cuisine.

■ **Trio** (AC b F GLM OS)
1537 17th Street/Q Street ✉ DC 20002

■ **Two Quail** (AC CC E F glm MA) 11.30-14.30, 17-23 h
320 Massachusetts Avenue North East ✉ DC 20002 *(M-Union Station)* ☎ 543-8030

■ **Zapata's** (B F g)
601 Pennsylvania Avenue South East ✉ DC 20003 ☎ 546-6886
Mexican food.

SEX SHOPS/BLUE MOVIES

■ **Follies Theater** 0-24 h
24 O Street South East/Half Street ✉ DC 20003 ☎ 484-0323
Pornos, male burlesque and Sun buffet. Videos also for sale.

■ **Pleasure Place** (AC GLM MA) 10-22, Wed-Sat -24, Sun 12-19 h
1063 Wisconsin Avenue North West ✉ DC 20007 *(Georgetown-bus & subway Foggybottom)* ☎ 333-8570
Erotic boutique, leather, fetish wear, toys, condoms, etc.

■ **Pleasure Place** (AC GLM MA) Mon-Tue 10-22, Wed-Sat -24, Sun 12-19 h
1710 Connecticut Avenue NW ✉ DC 20009 *(Dupont Circle-bus & subway)* ☎ 483-3297

SAUNAS/BATHS

■ **Club Washington** (G P SA) 0-24 h
20 O Street South East ✉ DC 20003 ☎ 488-7315

BOOK SHOPS

■ **Lambda Rising** (AC CC GLM MA VS) 9-24 h
1625 Connecticut Avenue North West ✉ DC 20009 *(Metro-Dupont Circle)* ☎ 462-6969
Gay books, videos, magazines and gifts. Free local guides.

GIFT & PRIDE SHOPS

■ **Outlook** 10-22, Fri Sat -23 h
1706 Connecticut Avenue North West ✉ DC 20009 ☎ 745-1469
Cards T-shirts, jewelry and accessories for gay guys.

LEATHER & FETISH SHOPS

■ **Leather Rack. The** (G LJ)
1723 Connecticut Avenue North West ✉ DC 20009 ☎ 797-7401
Leather accessories, cards, and T-shirts designed exclusively for gay men.

USA/District of Columbia — Washington D.C.

You are *always* welcome at the Bed and Breakfast at the

WILLIAM LEWIS HOUSE
Washington' finest
Friendly, Warm, Convenient • Close to 17th St. & Dupont Circle
Minutes from the Mall • Close to Metro
Great Restaurants Nearby
Gay Owned and Operated
(202) 462-7574 •• (800) 465-7574
Http: www.wlewishous.com • Fax (202)462-1608

■ **S&M Leathers** 16-24 h
628 New York Avenue North West ✉ DC 20001 ☎ 682-1160

HOTELS

■ **Carlyle Suites Hotel. The** (AC B BF CC glm H N)
1731 New Hampshire Avenue ✉ DC 20335 *(in the heart of Dupont Circle)* ☎ 234-3200 322-1488
✉ reservations@carlylesuites.com
🖥 www.carlylesuites.com
Lovely Art deco hotel welcoming gay visitors. Rates from US$ 89.

■ **Monticello** (F glm H)
1075 Thomas Jefferson Street ✉ DC 20007 *(Georgetown)*
☎ 337-9100 ☎ (800) 388-2410 (toll-free)
🖥 www.hotelmonticello.com
Conveniently located hotel with comfortable rooms & internet access. Call or see website for details.

■ **Radisson Barceló Hotel** (AC B BF CC F H OS PI WO)
2121 P Street North West ✉ DC 20037 *(1 block from subway Dupont Circle)* ☎ 293-3100 ☎ (800) 333-3333 (toll-free)
 857-0134
4 star European hotel (Spanish owned) in the heart of the gay community.

■ **Savoy Suites Hotel** (AC B BF F glm H PI WH)
2505 Wisconsin Avenue North West ✉ DC 20007-4575
☎ 337-9100 ☎ (800) 944-5252 337-3644
Many rooms with kitchen and jacuzzi. Rates US$ 65.

GUEST HOUSES

■ **B&B at the William Lewis House** (AC BF CC G H WH)
1309 R Street N.W. ✉ DC 20009 ☎ 462-7574 ☎ (800) 465-7574
 462-1608 info@wlewishous.com
🖥 www.wlewishous.com
Located near gay bars and tourist attractions. 10 rooms with shared bath, rooms with phone, heating, own key. Guest house provides safe and TV room. Rates $ 75-85 bf. incl.

■ **Brenton. The** (AC BF CC G H MA) Office 13-21 h
1708 16th Street North West ✉ DC 20009 *(4 blocks from Dupont Circle)* ☎ 332-5550 ☎ (800) 673-9042 (toll free) 462-5872
Victorian townhouse near Dupont Circle. 8 doubles all with shared bath/WC, phone, radio, heating, own key. Hotel provides bar and TV room. Rates US$ 85 per room, suite $109 (en-suite, kitchen, TV/VCR), bf incl.

■ **Capitol Hill Guest House** (AC BF CC glm H) Open all year
101 5th Street N.E. ✉ DC 20002 ☎ 547-1050 547-1050
Located in the historic district of Capitol Hill. 6 doubles, 2 singles, 1 apartment. Rooms partly with bath/WC. Rates double US$ 55-100, single $45, apartment $115-125 (bf incl.)

■ **Kalorama Guest House at Woodley Park** (AC BF glm MA OS)
9-21 h
2700 Cathedral Avenue North West ✉ DC 20008 ☎ 328-0860
 328-3827

GENERAL GROUPS

■ **Gay People's Alliance** (GLM)
George Washington University ✉ DC 20006 *800 21st Street North West, Room 420, DC 20006* ☎ 676-7590

Hotel Monticello
OF GEORGETOWN

The Monticello provides accommodations that discriminating world travelers expect: refined and comfortable. Located in Georgetown, convenient to Washington's business centers and tourist attractions, the Monticello's suites feature: rich linens, bath amenities, computer access ports, voicemail, TVs, microwaves, and coffeemakers.

1075 Thomas Jefferson St., NW • Washington, DC 20007
202/337-0900 • 800/388-2410
www.hotelmonticello.com

Washington D.C. | District of Columbia - Florida/USA

FETISH GROUPS
- **Centaur Motorcycle Club**
PO Box 341 93, Martin Luther King Station ✉ DC 20043-4193
- **FFA, Washington DC**
PO Box 461 ✉ DC 20044
- **Highwaymen TNT**
PO Box 545 ✉ DC 20044-0545
- **Lost Angels**
901 5th Street NE ✉ DC 20002

HEALTH GROUPS
- **AIDS Action Council**
☎ 547-3101
- **AIDS Information Line**
☎ 332-2437
- **Whitman Walker Clinic**
1407 S Street North West ✉ DC 20009 ☎ 797-3500 ☎ 833-3234
(Hotline 19-23 h)

HELP WITH PROBLEMS
- **Gay Hotline** 19-23 h
☎ 833-3234
General information, referral, peer counselling, crisis intervention.

USA-Florida

Location: Southeast USA
Initials: FL
Time: GMT -5
Area: 170.314 km^2 / 69.658 sq mi.
Population: 14,654,000
Capital: Tallahassee
Important gay cities: Fort Lauderdale, Key West, Miami, Miami Beach, Orlando, St. Petersburg, Tampa

Florida is today the prime state for gay holidaymakers. Of course, this development did not appear out of nothing. The sinking prices for interstate and oversea flights, the presence of Florida in the media or the everlasting popularity of gay classics like Fort Lauderdale or Key West have contributed to it. By the way: when on a (south) Florida trip, don't miss a ride in a convertible along the Florida Keys to Key West. In inner Florida the Walt Disney Corporations gay-friendly stance is impressively shown by their favours granted to gay employees and the *Gay Day at Disneyworld*. This fun-park and the others around Orlando are only a few hours drive to the fun-and-thrill-park where everything is for real, the *John F. Kennedy Space Center* at Cape Canaveral. The most important center, around which the gay part of Floridas tourism industry revolves, is *South Beach*, the southern tip of Miami Beach. Its Art-Deco buildings with their pastel shade façades, the palm trees, the beautiful people-all of this blends to create *the* trendy holiday destination of the nineties.

Florida ist das Reiseland Nr. 1 in den USA. Die große Präsenz in den schwulen Medien oder auch die traditionelle Popularität schwuler Klassiker wie Fort Lauderdale oder Key West. Überhaupt: wenn möglich sollte in einem (Süd-)Florida-Urlaub nie die Cabrio-Fahrt entlang der Florida Keys nach Key West fehlen. In Mittelflorida setzt die Walt Disney Corporation schwulenfreundliche Firmenpolitik eindrucksvoll in Vergünstigungen für die schwulen Mitarbeiter und den *Gay Day at Disneyworld* um. Dieser Vergnügungspark und die übrigen um Orlando sind nur einige Stunden Fahrt vom realen "Theme Park" *John F. Kennedy Space Center* am Cape Canaveral entfernt. Wichtigster Dreh- und Angelpunkt für den schwulen Teil von Floridas Tourismusindustrie ist derzeit *South Beach*, die Südspitze von Miami Beach. Die pastellfarbenen Art-Deco-Gebäude, die Palmen, die schönen Menschen- all das vermengt sich zum trendgemäßen Urlaubsziel der 90er Jahre.

La Floride est aujourd'hui la destination vacances numéro 1 des gais américains, ce qui n'est pas le fruit du hasard. Les vols nationaux et internationaux bon marché, la présence de la Floride dans les média et le cinéma, la popularité des stations balnéaires de Fort Lauderdale et Key West ont fait de cet état fédéral un des hauts-lieux touristiques des Etats-Unis. A faire absolument: descendre la côte en direction de Key West en décapotable! La Walt Disney Corporation met en pratique une politique plutôt homophile: avantages pour les employés gais et "Gay Day at Disneyworld" pour les visiteurs. Ce parc d'attractions est, comme les autres autour d'Orlando, à quelques heures de voiture d'un autre parc bien plus réel: Cape Canaveral. South Beach, la pointe sud de Miami Beach, est le haut-lieu du tourisme gai en Floride. Les bâtiments art-déco dans les couleurs pastel, les palmiers, la beauté et la jeunesse des gens: voilà pourquoi la Floride est la destination touristique "in" des années 90.

Florida es hoy en día uno de los destinos turísticos gay número 1 de los E.E.U.U.. A este hecho han contribuido los baratos costos de vuelo (dentro de los E.E. U.U. y a través del Atlántico), la presencia de Florida en muchos medios de comunicación o bien la tradicional popularidad de los lugares clásicos gay (Fort Lauderdale y Key West). En Florida central el *Gay Day at Disneyworld* se ha convertido en una atracción, en el que la Corporación Walt Disney afirma su política gay en la medida en la que los trabajadores gay de la empresa obtienen descuentos. Este parque de diversiones y los restantes en los alrededores de Orlando estan tan solo a unas cuantas horas del "Theme Park", *John F. Kennedy Space Center* en Cabo Cañaveral. El sitio clave para el turismo gay de Florida es por el momento *South Beach* en el más extremo sur de Miami Beach. Los colores pasteles de las edificaciones Art-Deco, las palmeras y la gente guapa hacen de este lugar el destino turístico de moda de los años '90. A propósito: turistas el (en sur) de Florida deberían aprovechar para hacer una excursión en un descapotable por los Florida Keys hacía Key West.

La Florida, in USA, è la meta turistica numero uno; ciò non è casuale, bensì dipende dalla diminuzione del prezzo dei voli (interni e d'oltre Atlantico), dalla presenza della Florida nei mass media e dalla fama di luoghi gay come Fort Landerdale o Key West. Se siete in vacanza nel sud della Florida non perdetevi in nessun caso un giro in decappottabile a Key West lungo la Florida Keys. Nella Florida centrale la Walt Disney Corporation attua una politica aziendale a favore dei gay, con agevolazioni per i dipendenti gay e con il *Gay Day at Disneyworld*. Questo parco divertimenti ed altri presso Orlando distano poche ore d'auto dal "Theme Park" *John F. Kennedy Space Center* presso Cape Canaveral. Attualmente il punto centrale del turismo gay della Florida è *South Beach*, all'estremità meridionale di Miami Beach. Gli edifici art decò color pastello, le palme e la bella gente si mescolano e creano la meta turistica più alla moda degli anni '90.

USA/Florida — Bradenton ▶ Fort Lauderdale

Bradenton ☎ 941

SEX SHOPS/BLUE MOVIES
■ **C&J Adult Center**
4949 14th Street West ✉ FL 34207 ☎ 755-9076

CRUISING
-Coquina Beach

Clearwater ☎ 727

BARS
■ **Lost & Found** (B GLM) Open 7 days from 16-02h
5858 Roosevelt Boulevard ✉ FL 34620 ☎ 539-8903
Gay owned & operated. Proper ID required.
■ **Pro Shop** (AC B CC f G MA N OS WE) Mon-Sat 11:30-02:00h, Sun 13-02:00h
840 Cleveland Street ✉ FL 33755 ☎ 447-3459

DANCECLUBS
■ **Triangles** (AC B D E G OS S SNU VS YG)
5858 Roosevelt Boulevard ✉ FL 34620 ☎ 539-8903

HEALTH GROUPS
■ **VD-Clinic** (glm)
310 North Myrtle ✉ FL 34615 ☎ 461-2727

Cocoa Beach ☎ 407

BARS
■ **Mango Tree** (b F GLM) Dinner. Closed Mon.
118 North Atlantic Avenue ✉ FL 32921 ☎ 799-0513
Fine dining.

Dade City ☎ 352

PRIVATE ACCOMMODATION
■ **Sawmill Campground** (AC cc G H lj msg NU OS Pl)
21710 US Highway 98 ✉ FL 33523 *(45 min north of Tampa, 1 hour west of Orlando)* ☎ 583-0664 🖷 583-0896 ✉ flsawmill@aol.com
🖥 www.flsawmill.com
Entertainment on WE. US$ 49 (2 people) 59 (4 people).

Daytona Beach ☎ 904

BARS
■ **Barndoor** (B F G N) 11-3 h
615 Main Street ✉ FL 32118 ☎ 252-3776
■ **Beachside Club** (B D G S) 12-3 h
415 Main Street ✉ FL 32118 ☎ 252-5465
■ **Club Xess** (B D Glm lj) Mon-Sat 17-3, Sun 16-3 h
952 Orange Avenue ✉ FL 32114 ☎ 254-3464
■ **Hollywood Complex** (B D GLM S) 11-3h, Dancing Fri Sat.
615 Main Street ✉ FL 32118 ☎ 252-3776

HOTELS
■ **Oasis Beach Motel** (glm H)
3169 South Atlantic Avenue ✉ FL 32118 ☎ 967-8862
Rates on request

GUEST HOUSES
■ **Villa. The** (AC BF CC E f glm H MA msg OS p Pl VS WH WO) 8-22 h

801 North Peninsula Drive ✉ FL 32118 *(1 h drive to St. Augustine)*
☎ 248-2020 🖷 248-2020 ✉ thevilladaytona@aol.com
🖥 www.thevillabb.com
All rooms with color TV-VCR, tub/shower Tile Baths, A/C + Heat in an historical Spanish mansion. Continental breakfast, newspaper, T.V. Lounge, Game Room, complimentary coffee & soft drinks, non-smoking. Prices from US$ 50-140.

CRUISING
Boardwalk & beach (AYOR) (in front of sightseeing tower & by bandshell)

Fort Lauderdale ☎ 954

GAY INFO
■ **Gay Lesbian Community Center of South Florida** (AC GLM MA) Mon-Fri 10-22, Sat 13-22 h, closed Sun
1717 N. Andrews Ave. ✉ FL 33311 ☎ 563-9500 🖷 563-9007
✉ glccftl@aol.com

PUBLICATIONS
■ **Hot Spots**
5100 North East 12th Avenue ✉ FL 33334 ☎ 928-1862
🖷 772-0142 ✉ hotspots1@aol.com
🖥 www.hotspotsmagazine.com
"Florida's most entertaining gay publication" with ads and calendar of events. Weekly publication.
■ **Outlook Magazine**
2410 Wilton Drive ✉ FL 33305 ☎ 567.1306 🖷 567.1309
✉ publisher@outlookflorida.com 🖥 www.outlookflorida.com
Weekly gay and lesbian magazine.
■ **Scoop Magazine**
2219 Wilton Drive ✉ FL 33305 ☎ 561-9707 🖷 956-8418
🖷 561-5970 ✉ scoop@scoopmag.com 🖥 www.scoopmag.com
Weekly gay news and entertainment magazine covering Florida.

TOURIST INFO
■ **Greater Fort Lauderdale Convention & Visitor Bureau**
1850 Eller Drive #303 ✉ FL 33316 ☎ (800) 22-78669, ext. 922
☎ 983-4668, ext. 922 🖷 765-4467 🖥 www.sunny.org

BARS
■ **Bill's Filling Station** (AC B G MA N)
1243 North East 11th Avenue ☎ 525-9403
■ **Boots** (B G LJ MA N OS) 12-2, Sat 8-3 h
901 South-West 27th Avenue, ✉ FL 33312 ☎ 792-9177
■ **Bushes. The** (AC B CC G MA N S) 9-2 h
3038 North Federal Highway, ✉ FL 33306 ☎ 561-1724
■ **Cathode Ray** (B GLM N OS VS YG) Sun-Fri 14-2, Sat 14-3 h
1301 East Las Olas Boulevard ✉ FL 33301 ☎ 467-3266
■ **Chainz** (AC B D DR G LJ MA N) Sun-Thu 13-2, Fri Sat -3 h
1931 South Federal Highway ✉ FL 33316 ☎ 462-9165
■ **Chaps** (AC B G LJ MA) 14-? h
1727 North Andrews Extension ☎ 767-0327
■ **Eagle. The** (AC B d G LJ MA VS) Sun-Thu 15-2, Fri Sat -3 h
1951 North West 9th Avenue ✉ FL 33311 ☎ 462-7224
Popular. Leather bar
■ **Everglades in Chainz** (AC B d G LJ MA N) Sun-Thu 15-2 h, Fri-Sat 15-3 h, in Winter open from 13 h
1931 S. Federal Highway ✉ FL 33316 ☎ 462-9165
■ **Georgies Alibi** (AC B glm MA) Sun-Fri 11-2, Sat -3 h
2266 Wilton Drive ✉ FL 33305 ☎ 565-2526
FAX 565-2527.

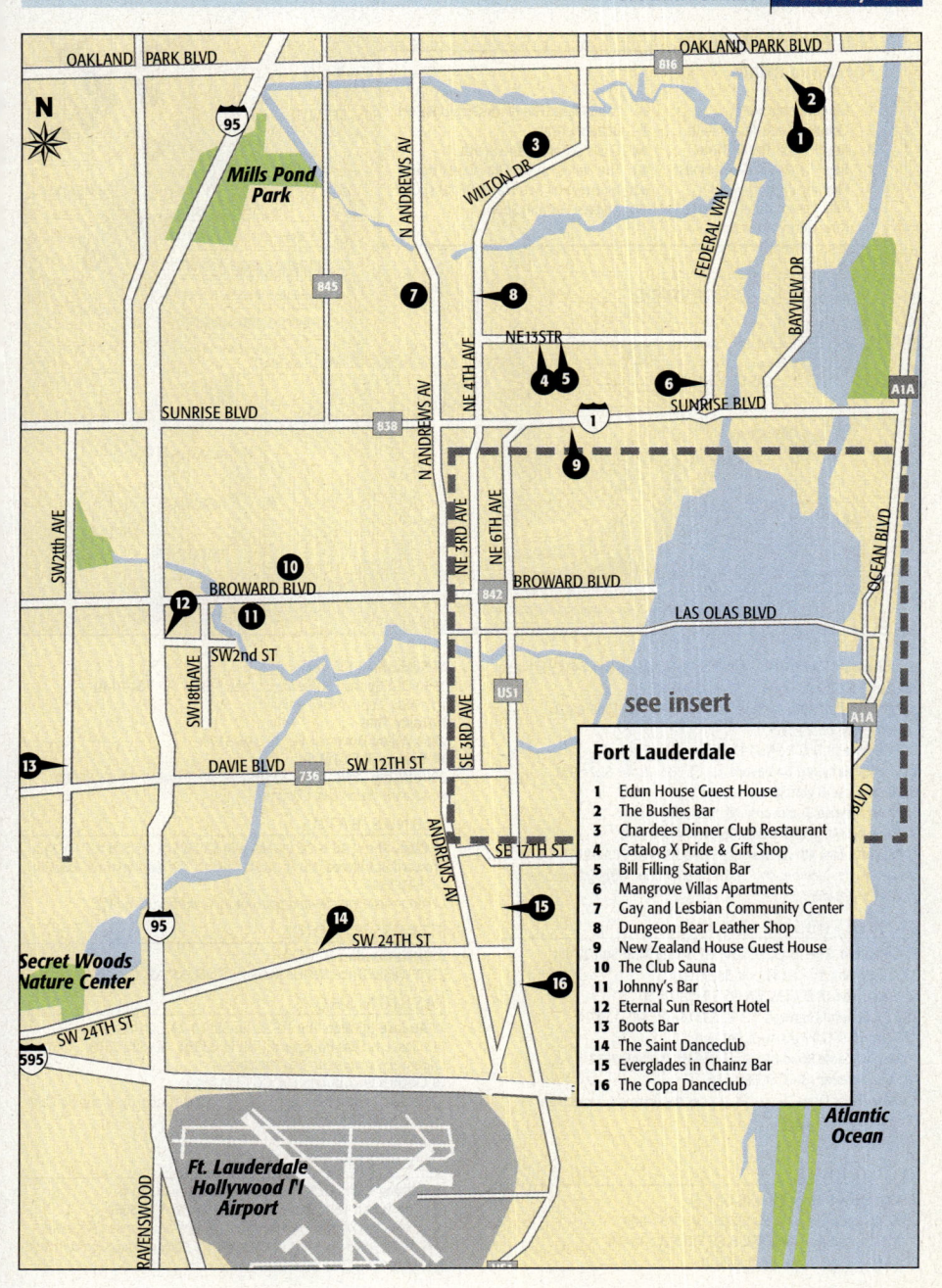

Fort Lauderdale — Florida/USA

Fort Lauderdale

1. Edun House Guest House
2. The Bushes Bar
3. Chardees Dinner Club Restaurant
4. Catalog X Pride & Gift Shop
5. Bill Filling Station Bar
6. Mangrove Villas Apartments
7. Gay and Lesbian Community Center
8. Dungeon Bear Leather Shop
9. New Zealand House Guest House
10. The Club Sauna
11. Johnny's Bar
12. Eternal Sun Resort Hotel
13. Boots Bar
14. The Saint Danceclub
15. Everglades in Chainz Bar
16. The Copa Danceclub

USA/Florida — Fort Lauderdale

Fort Lauderdale

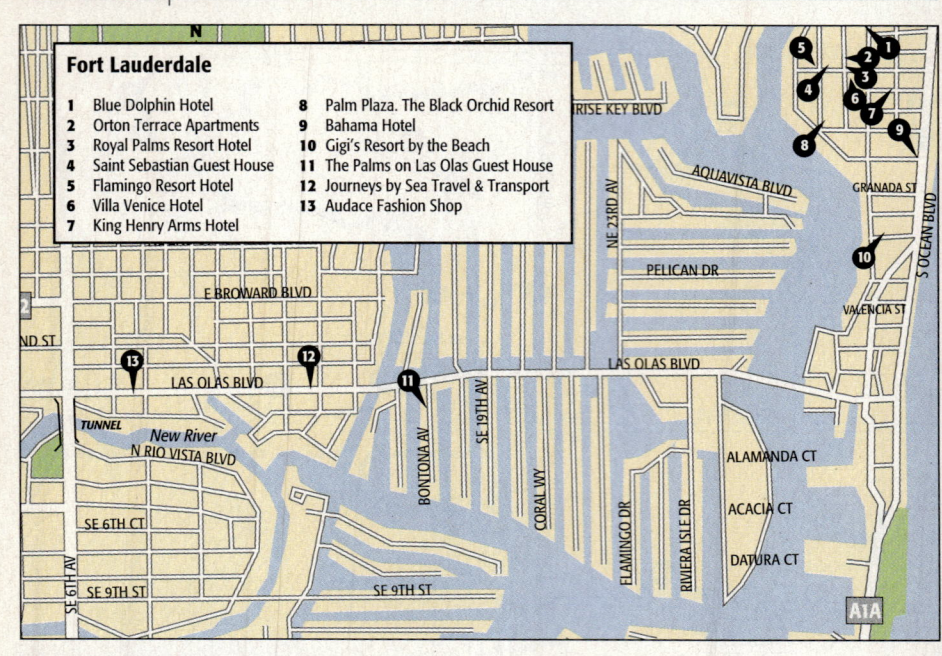

1. Blue Dolphin Hotel
2. Orton Terrace Apartments
3. Royal Palms Resort Hotel
4. Saint Sebastian Guest House
5. Flamingo Resort Hotel
6. Villa Venice Hotel
7. King Henry Arms Hotel
8. Palm Plaza. The Black Orchid Resort
9. Bahama Hotel
10. Gigi's Resort by the Beach
11. The Palms on Las Olas Guest House
12. Journeys by Sea Travel & Transport
13. Audace Fashion Shop

■ **Hideaway. The** (AC B G MA N S OS VS) Mon-Thu 14-02, Fri & Sat -03, Sun 15-02:00h
2022 North East 18th Avenue, ✉ FL 33304 ☏ 566-8622
Cozy, friendly, pool table.

■ **Johnny's** (B D G R SNU) 12-2, Sat 12-3 h
1116 West Broward Boulevard ✉ FL 33312 ☏ 522-5931

■ **Monas** (AC B glm MA)
502 East Sunrise Boulevard ☏ 525-6662

■ **Ramrod** (AC B d G LJ MG OS SNU VS) 3-14 h
1508 North East 4th Avenue ✉ FL 33304 ☏ 763-8219
Dresscode (levi, leather and uniform) after dark. Happy hour daily 15-21 h. Very popular.

DANCECLUBS

■ **Coliseum. The** (B CC D GLM MA S WE) Mon-Sun 22-? h
2520 S. Miami Rd. ✉ FL ☏ 832-0100

■ **Copa. The** (B D GLM MA OS S TV) 21-4 h
2800 S. Federal Highway ✉ FL 33316 ☏ 463-1507

■ **Saint** (B D G lj MA) 16-2, Sat -3 h
1000 West State Road 84 ✉ FL 33315 ☏ 525-7883

■ **Sea Monster** (B CC D GLM WE)
2 S New River Drive W. ✉ FL (under the Andrews Drawbridge, Downtown) ☏ 463-4641
Very popular on Sunday.

RESTAURANTS

■ **Chardees Dinner Club** (B CC F g)
2209 Wilton Drive, ✉ FL 33305 ☏ 563-1800

■ **Mustards Bar - Grill** (AC B CC F G MA) 11-? h
2256-60 Wilton Drive ☏ 564-5116

■ **Sukhothai** (B F glm)
1930 East Sunrise Boulevard ✉ FL 33304 ☏ 764-0148
Thai food. Popular with gays.

■ **Tasty Thai**
2254 Wilton Drive ✉ FL ☏ 396-3177

■ **Tropics** (B F GLM S)
2004 Wilton Drive ✉ FL 33305 (NE 4th Avenue) ☏ 537-6000
Restaurant, Biano Bar, Cabaret

SAUNAS/BATHS

■ **Club. The** (! AC b CC f G MA p PI SA SB SOL VS WH WO) 0-24 h
Broward Boulevard ✉ FL 33312 (across the road from old location)
☏ 525-3344
Outdoor patio with heated pool. Poolside barbecues on WE.

FITNESS STUDIOS

■ **Better Bodies** (G WO)
2270 Wilton Drive, Wilton Manors ✉ FL 33305 ☏ 561-7977

FASHION SHOPS

■ **Audace** (g) Mon-Thu 10-22, Fri-Sat 10-24, Sun 10-22 h
813 East Las Olas Boulevard, ✉ FL 33301 ☏ 522-7503
Underwear, swimwear, and sportswear.

■ **Clothes Encounters** (AC CC GLM MA)
1952 East Sunrise Boulevard ✉ FL 33304 (Gateway Shopping Centre) ☏ 522-2228
T-shirts.

GIFT & PRIDE SHOPS

■ **Catalog X** (AC GLM) 9-22, Sat 10-21, Sun 10-19 h
850 North East 13th Street ✉ FL 33304 ☏ 524-5050
Huge selection of clothing, swimwear, magazines, dance CD's, adult toys, lubes, pipes & papers, greeting cards, pride products, custom leather shop, and videos for rent or sale.

Fort Lauderdale | Florida/USA

LOG ONTO
WWW.GAYTRAVELING.COM
FOR MORE INFORMATION ON
THESE ACCOMMODATIONS

FORT LAUDERDALE'S FAVORITES!

The Cabanas
At Wilton Manors
NEW GUESTHOUSE!

A new and fresh approach...
Fun and relaxed with a touch of sophistication. Just like home.

2209 N.E. 26th Street, Wilton Manors, FL 33305
Phone/Fax 954.564.7764
www.TheCabanasGuesthouse.com

---

the other *fabulous* gay guesthouse on Ft. Lauderdale Beach!

Saint Sebastian
(954) 568-6161

2835 Terramar St.,
Ft. Lauderdale FL 33304

800-425-8105
FAX: (954) 568-6209

www.saintsebastianhotel.com

"Richard Says: Sleep Cheap & Dine Fine"

Richard's Inn
Fort Lauderdale's Largest and Hottest All-New Men's Resort

A Secluded private paradise nestled in the heart of gay Fort Lauderdale
• Complimentary Tropical Breakfast
• Rooms, Suites and Apartments
• Large Heated Pool and Nude Sundeck
• Charming Courtyard with Intimate Hideaways
• Friendly Elegant and Affordable

1025 Northeast 18th Av., Fort Lauderdale, FL 33304
(954) 563-1111 • (800)-516-1111
Fax (954) 764-1111
www.richardsinn.com

INNLEATHER.COM
GUESTHOUSE

• Cable, Fridge
• Microwave
• Private Bath
• Hot Tub
• Clothing-Optional
• Heated Pool
• Dungeon + Slings

610 SE 19th St. Ft. Lauderdale, Florida
954-467-1444 / 877-532-7729
WWW.INNLEATHER.COM • EMAIL JDHANGER@BELLSOUTH.NET

GEMINI HOUSE

A 1/2 Acre Enclosed Tropical Paradise.
The Place To Stay In Ft. Lauderdale
Where Clothing is *NOT* An Option!

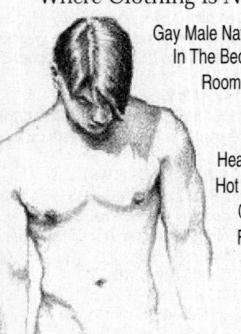

Gay Male Naturist Vacation Rentals
In The Bed & Breakfast Tradition
Rooms with Cable TV, VCR,
All Cotton Linens,
Oversized Towels,
Heated Pool, Sun All Day,
Hot Tub, Outdoor Shower,
Gym, Free Local Calls,
Fresh Squeezed Juice,
Starbucks® Coffee,
Off-Street Parking

"Like Staying With Friends"
Your Host John

PHONE: 954-568-9791
FAX: 954-568-0617   IGLTA

GeminiHse @ aol.com • www.geminihse.com

USA/Florida — Fort Lauderdale

LEATHER & FETISH SHOPS
■ **Dungeon Bear Leather** (LJ) Mon-Thu 20-2, Fri Sat 18-3, Sun -2 h
1508 NE 4th Avenue ✉ FL 33339 ☎ 523-1035
■ **Wicked Leather** (CC G MA)
2422 Wilton Drive ✉ FL 33305 ☎ 564-PLAY
Selection of leather, rubber, toys and bondage. Full made to measure and design service.

PR & PHOTOGRAPHY SERVICES
■ **Blue Door Productions Inc**
515 Seabreeze Boulevard, Suite 228 ✉ FL 33316 ☎ 713-8126
Web site design, gay stock photography, graphic design and photography services.

TRAVEL AND TRANSPORT
■ **Journeys by Sea. Inc.** (AC B BF F GLM MA NU)
1402 East Las Olas Boulevard, Suite 122 ✉ FL 33301 ☎ 522-5865 ☎ (800) 825-3632 (toll-free) 📠 522-5836
📧 info@journeysbysea.com 💻 www.journeysbysea.com
Gay yacht vacations in the Caribbean are all-inclusive. All meals, bar and port taxes are included.

HOTELS
■ **Bahama Hotel** (AC BF B CC F G H msg OS PI WH WO)
401 North Atlantic Boulevard (A-1-A) ✉ FL 33304 ☎ 467-7315
☎ (800) 622-9995 📠 467-7319 📧 bahama@bahamahotel.com
💻 www.bahamahotel.com
Hotel with patio bar at poolside, parking palce, large tanning deck, heated swimming pool. Rates rooms: US$ 85-153, efficiency 115-179.
■ **Blue Dolphin Hotel** (AC BF CC G H MA msg PI)
725 North Birch Road ✉ FL 33304 ☎ 565-8437
☎ (800) 893-2583 (toll free) 📠 565-6015
📧 dolphinftlaud@aol.com 💻 www.bluedolphinhotel.com
Heated pool. Close to gay clubs, bars and restaurants.
■ **Brigantine. The** (AC BF b CC G H NU OS PI) Office: 8-20 h
2831 Vistamar Street ✉ FL 33304 (beach area) ☎ 565-6911
☎ (877) 565-6911 (toll-free) 📠 565-8911
📧 info@brigantinehotel.com 💻 www.brigantinehotel.com
All rooms with fridge, microwave, coffee maker, phone. A fully equipped kitchen is in addition available for apartments and efficiencies. Heated pool and guest laundry room. Rates: rooms US$ 65-115, efficiencies 85-145, apartments 105-175.
■ **Embassy Suites** (AC B BF F NG H PI WO)
1100 SE 17th Street ✉ FL 33316 ☎ 527-2700 ☎ (800) 3622779 (toll-free) 📠 760-7202 📧 reservations@embassysuitesftl.com
💻 www.embassysuitesftl.com
■ **Eternal Sun Resort** (AC CC G H MA NU OS PI WH)
1909 South West 2nd Street ✉ FL 33312 ☎ 462-6035
📠 522-2764 📧 MrIbiza@aol.com 💻 www.EternalSun.Org
Formerly Kelly's Guesthouse. All rooms have cable TV, phones, refrigerator and microwave. Tropical garden with pool.
■ **Grand Resort. The** (AC CC G H OS PI WH WO)
539 North Birch Road ✉ FL 33304 ☎ 630-3000
☎ (800) 818-1211 (toll-free) 📠 630-3003
💻 www.grandresort.net
Rooms, suites or villas with cable TV, VCR, voice-mail, fridge, coffee maker. Call for rates.
■ **King Henry Arms** (AC BF CC GLM H NU OS PI)
543 Breakers Avenue ✉ FL 33304-4129 ☎ 561-0039
☎ (800) 205-5464 (toll-free) 📠 563-1246
💻 www.kinghenryarms.com
Single rooms US$ 61-95, double 76-108, studio 90-121, apartment 97-135, all with private bath, refrigerators and some with kitchens. Continental bf included.

■ **Palm Plaza. The Black Orchid Resort** (AC BF CC G H lj MA NU OS p PI WH)
2801 Riomar Street ✉ FL 33304 ☎ 260-6568 ☎ (888) 954-7300 (toll free) 📠 566-4948 📧 palmplazaresort@aol.com
💻 www.palmplazaresort.com
New ownership.upgraded rooms with cable TV,phone,most with kitchen.Tropical garden, steps to beach. LJ on special weekends.
■ **Richard's Inn** (e F G H MA OS PI)
1025 Northeast 18th Avenue ✉ FL 33304 ☎ 563-1111
☎ (800) 516-1111 📠 764-1111 💻 www.richardsinn.com
■ **Royal Palms Resort** (AC BF CC G H MA msg NU OS PI)
2901 Terramar Street ✉ FL 33304 ☎ 564-6444
☎ (800) 237-7256 (toll free) 📠 564-6443 📧 ryalpalms@aol.com
💻 www.royalpalms.com
Double rooms and appartments with showers, WC, phone, fridge, cable TV, cd-players. Rates for 2 people US$ 125-269 incl. bf. Also 10 man Spa &business centre. Rated one of the best gay accomodations in the USA by "Out&About".
■ **Sun n' Spalsh** (AC BF CC G H NU OS PI WO)
1129-35 North Victoria Park Road ✉ FL 33304 ☎ 467-2669
☎ (888) 842-9352 (toll-free) 📠 467-1385 💻 www.GAY-FLA.com
Home of "Fort Lauderdale's Gay Men's Nude Swim Club". All rooms with TV and VCR and free telephone with unlimited computer connection. Call for rates.
■ **Venice Beach Guest Quarters** (AC BF CC G H msg OS p PI VS WH) 8.30-20.30 h
552 North Birch Road ✉ FL 33304 (just 180 yds. from the beach)
☎ 564-9601 ☎ (800) 533-4744 (toll-free) 📠 564-5618
📧 veniceqtrs@aol.com 💻 www.veniceqtrs.com
Studios and suites with bath, full kitchen, phone, cable TV, radio, AC. Stereo, VCR in addition for suites. Guest computer station available, guest laundry, sundeck, heated pool, video library. Rates rooms: US$ 65-95, studios 75-135, suites 85-165, extra person 15.
■ **Villa Venice Hotel** (AC BF CC GLM LJ MA msg NU OS PI) 8.30-18 h
2900 Terramar Street ✉ FL 33304 ☎ 564-7855
☎ (877) 284-5522 (toll-free) 📠 564-7859
📧 villaven@bellsouth.net 💻 www.villavenice.com
Heated pool.

GUEST HOUSES
■ **Cabanas. The** (G H MA OS PI)
2209 North East 26th Street, Wilton Manors ✉ FL 33305
☎ 564-7764 📠 564-7767 📧 info@thecabanasguesthouse.com
💻 www.thecabanasguesthouse.com
■ **Coral Reef** (A AC BF CC G PI WH WO) Office: 8-20 h
2609 North East 13th Court ✉ FL 33304-1505 ☎ 568-0292
☎ (888) 365-6948 (toll-free) 📠 568-1992 📧 Coralref@aol.com
💻 www.coralreefguesthouse.com
Rates in-season US$ 79-119, off-season 81-105.
■ **Edun House** (BF G H NU OS PI)
2733 Middle River Drive ✉ FL 33306 ☎ 565-7775 📠 565-7912
📧 Edun2733@aol.com 💻 members.aol.com/edunhouse
Guest house with swimming pool, fitness room, massage possible, nude sunbathing/nude bathing possibility, clothing always optional. All rooms with bath/WC, telephone, Satellite TV, radio, air-conditioning. Rates from US$ 79-159 incl. Continental breakfast.
■ **Gemini House** (AC BF G H msg NU OS PI WH WO)
☎ 568-9791 📠 568-0617 📧 GeminiHse@aol.com
💻 www.geminihse.com
Gay Male Naturist Vacation in Bed and Breakfast tradition.

Fort Lauderdale | **Florida/USA**

GREATER FORT LAUDERDALE

Rolling out the rainbow carpet.

Feel the warmth and excitement of Greater Fort Lauderdale's gay-friendly hotels and guest houses. Discover the shops, fine restaurants, museums, theaters and clubs. Enjoy the unparalleled hospitality that is the essence of Greater Fort Lauderdale. The only thing missing on the rainbow carpet is you. For your Free Vacation Planner or Vacation Package reservations, call 800-22-SUNNY, ext. 922 (US & Canada) or 954-983-4668, ext. 922. Or visit us at www.sunny.org, and click on the rainbow icon. **IGLTA**

Voted Destination of the Year by *Out and About.*

GREATER FORT LAUDERDALE *Immerse yourself.*

USA/Florida Fort Lauderdale

GREATER FORT LAUDERDALE

The Worthington Guest House

In the Heart of Ft. Lauderdale Beach
Guest Rooms, Studios, & Suites
Sunny Private Courtyard
400' to the Beach
Newly Renovated
Clothing Optional
Large pool

543 N. Birch Rd. - Ft. Lauderdale Beach, FL 33304
800-445-7036 / 954-563-6819
www.worthguesthouse.com

Villa Venice

COMFORTABLE ACCOMMODATIONS

(Toll Free) **877-284-5522**
954-564-7855 • FAX 954-564-7859
www.villavenice.com
email: villaven@bellsouth.net

Heated Pool,
Walk to The Beach,
In The Heart Of
Gay Ft. Lauderdale.

2900 Terramar St.,
Ft. Lauderdale, FL 33304

IGLTA

Fort Lauderdale | Florida/USA

GREATER FORT LAUDERDALE

Fort Lauderdale's Ultimate Tropical Oasis

THE ROYAL PALMS

Luxury. Charm. Magic.

- Luxurious Rooms • Private Tropical Paradise • Clothing Optional
- 10 Man Spa • Steps To The Beach

Out & About 2000 "Editor's Choice Award" and "5 Palm" Rating.
1997 City of Fort Lauderdale Award for Excellence

2901 Terramar St. Ft. Lauderdale, FL
Tel: 954-564-6444 • 1-800-237-7526 • Fax: 954-564-6443
E-Mail: ryalpalms@aol.com • http://www.royalpalms.com

IGLTA

SPARTACUS 2001/2002 | 1205

USA/Florida — Fort Lauderdale

GREATER FORT LAUDERDALE

THE BLUE DOLPHIN
FORT LAUDERDALE
1-800-893-BLUE
WWW.GAYWIRED.COM/BLUEDOLP.HTM

Call FREE From England & Germany

England Dial:
0800 89 0011 800 893 2583

Germany Dial:
0800 225 5288 800 893 2583

725 North Birch Road
Fort Lauderdale,
Florida 33304

IGLTA

954-565-8437
FAX 954-565-6015

The Blue Dolphin - A tropical retreat for the discerning gay traveler. Our superior and well appointed amenities such as VCR, Voice Mail, Data Ports plus CD players in the efficiencies and suites. Our rooms are equipped with refrigerators and coffee service and our efficiencies and suites are complete with fully equipped kitchens, reflecting the highest standards of comfort and cleanliness.

Enjoy a complimentary continental breakfast around our heated pool and later relax and enjoy your vacation sunbathing in our private courtyard. We have been established for over 6 years and our commitment to excellence reflects our extremely high percentage of satisfied repeat clientele. Remember, SERVICE IS OUR SIGNATURE. Our goal is to provide you with a memorable vacation experience.

800-893-BLUE

E-Mail: dolphinftlaud@aol.com - http://www.bluedolphinhotel.com

Fort Lauderdale | Florida/USA

GREATER FORT LAUDERDALE

EMBASSY SUITES®

GREAT LOCATION. IT'S THAT SIMPLE.

- Spacious two room suite • Free American breakfast, daily • Manager's Reception, nightly
- Complimentary airport shuttle • Outdoor pool & fitness center

1100 SE 17th Street, Fort Lauderdale, FL 33316   (954) 527-2700 Ph   •   (954) 760-7202 Fax

1-800-EMBASSY

Email: reservations@embassysuitesftl.com • www.embassysuitesftl.com

IGLTA

Direct (954) 565-6911 • Fax (954) 565-8911
2831 Vistamar Street, Fort Lauderdale, FL 33304
www.brigantinehotel.com

The BRIGANTINE
FORT LAUDERDALE

GREATER FORT LAUDERDALE
The newest and grandest resort
for the discriminating gay traveler.
Our oceanview sundeck,
heated pool, spa, club and fitness rooms
are just a few of the amenities that
await you.
TEL: 954-630-3000
FAX: 954-630-3003
The Grand Resort
Fort Lauderdale Beach
1-800-818-1211
www.grandresort.net
IGLTA

Fort Lauderdale | Florida/USA

GREATER FORT LAUDERDALE

Coral Reef GUESTHOUSE

A quaint guesthouse amidst lush tropical surroundings. Spacious accomodations. Walk to the beach and shopping.

"Warm, friendly ambiance, scrupulously clean...merits a 4 Palm Rating" · Out & About

For Info/Reservations (365--6948)
1-888 ENJOY IT
954-568-0292

2609 NE 13 Court, Ft. Lauderdale, FL 33304
www.coralreefguesthouse.com
email: Coralref@aol.com

IGLTA

FLAMINGO RESORT
FORT LAUDERDALE, FLORIDA

INTIMATE ART DECO TROPICAL RESORT ON FORT LAUDERDALE BEACH

- Luxury Hotel Rooms, Studios & Suites • Private Courtyard with Heated Pool • Clothing Optional
- Continental Breakfast • Steps to Beach

800/ 283/4786 • 954/561/4658
2727 Terramar St, Ft. Lauderdale, FL 33304
www.TheFlamingoResort.com

IGLTA

USA/Florida — Fort Lauderdale

GREATER FORT LAUDERDALE

A Luxury Guesthouse in Ft. Lauderdale

WHERE THE BOYS ARE!!!

"Fort Lauderdale was named the #1 gay destination".
"One of the finest luxury gay guest houses in the world..."

Clientele: Gay Men
Type: Luxury, Key West/Victorian, Lush Tropical Gardens, Private, & Clothing Optional.
Nearby Attractions: Shopping & Gay Bars/Restaurant, Disney World, Miami Beach, Key West, Daytrips to Bahamas, Beach, Everglades National Park, & International Airport.
Amenities: Heated Pool, Secluded SPA, Bikes, Continental Breakfast, Happy Hour, Guest Computer w/ Internet Access, Videos, & Books.
Rooms: Non-Smoking, King Beds, Private Bath, A/C, Bahama Fans, Robes, Refrigerator, TV/VCR, CD/Cassette, Full-Kitchen, & Private Decks.
Rates: $140-$195 May-Nov. $179-$239 Dec - Apr.

"A stunning addition to the hospitality industry...Phil & Judd will be happy to show their diamond."-Scoop Mag.-Dec.99

PINEAPPLE POINT

Toll Free: 888.844.7295
954.527.0094
www.pineapplepoint.com

315 NE 16th Terrace,
Ft. Lauderdale, FL 33301 USA

ON BEAUTIFUL FORT LAUDERDALE BEACH
THE ALL NEW
King Henry Arms

New rooms by Gallant Interiors

(954) 561-0039

Enjoy a sun-drenched, heated pool and the ocean beach just one block away.

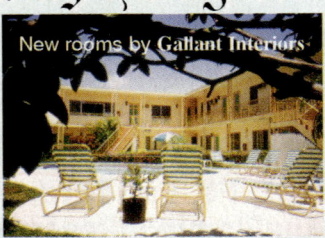

1-800-205-KING

543 BREAKERS AVENUE
FORT LAUDERDALE, FL 33304

www.kinghenryarms.com

IGLTA

Fort Lauderdale | Florida/USA

GREATER FORT LAUDERDALE

Orton Terrace

Call About Our Affordable Rates
800-323-1142
US, Carib, CAN

606-Orton Ave., Ft. Lauderdale, FL 33304
954-566-5068 • FAX 954-564-8646
e-mail: orton@ortonterrace.com
Web: www.ortonterrace.com

- Guest Rooms
- 1 & 2 Bedroom Apartments
- All with Refrigerators, Microwave Cable TV/Videos/VCR

- Clothing Optional Heated Pool
- Barbeque Grill
- Continental Breakfast
- Steps to the Beach

IGLTA

PARADISO
TROPICAL GUEST COTTAGES
1-800-644-7977

KING BEDS
CLOTHING OPTIONAL SUNBATHING
FREE BREAKFAST
FULL KITCHENS
954-764-8182

1115 TEQUESTA STREET
FORT LAUDERDALE, FL 33312
http:www.paradiso-FTL.com email at: Paradisoresort@aol.com

STAY AT FORT LAUDERDALE'S ONLY HISTORIC BED AND BREAKFAST

New Zealand House

gay male guesthouse
clothing optional heated pool

- cable tv, vcr, a/c
- refrigerator, microwave
- private bath
- private entrance
- continental breakfast

888-234-5494 • 954-523-7829
908 N.E. 15th Avenue • Fort Lauderdale, FL 33304
www.newzealandhouse.com

USA/Florida   Fort Lauderdale

GREATER FORT LAUDERDALE

Venice Beach
Guest Quarters

Ft. Lauderdale's Newest Boutique Hotel

California Inspired
Heated Pool
Clothing Optional Sundeck
Guest Lounge
200 Yards to the Beach

954-564-9601
800-533-4744

www.veniceqtrs.com
552 N. Birch Rd (at Terramar) • Fort Lauderdale, FL 33304

www.blackorchidresort.com
PALM PLAZA
featuring
THE BLACK ORCHID RESORT
(954)260-6568   fax(954)5664948
POOL — tropical garden near beach — SPA
2801 Riomar, Ft Lauderdale

Fort Lauderdale | Florida/USA

Gigi's RESORT BY THE BEACH

THE CLOSEST GAY RESORT TO THE GAY BEACH IN FORT LAUDERDALE

- Rooms & Suites w/Kitchens
- Private Bath • Cable TV • Ceiling Fan
- AC • Minibar • Daily Maid Service
- Clothing Optional Jacuzzi & Sun Deck
- Telephone Answering Machine
- Barbeque • Continental Breakfast
- Tropical Courtyard • Steps To Gay Beach

1-954-463-4827
US & CAN 1-800-910-2357

FAX: (954) 524-4649
E-mail: GigisResort@aol.com
http://www.GigisResort.com

3005 ALHAMBRA ST.
FORT LAUDERDALE, FLORIDA 33304 USA

IGLTA

■ **Gigi´s Resort by the Beach** (AC BF GLM H NU OS VH WH) all year round, 9-22 h
3005 Alhambra Street ✉ FL 33304 *(2mins walk to the gay beach)*
☎ 463-4827 📠 524-4648 ✉ GigisResort@aol.com
🖥 www.GigisResort.com
All rooms with private bath, AC cable TV, minibar, daily maid service telephone/answerphone some with kitchenette and fax. Tropical garden. From $ 49 to $ 199/night.

■ **Innleather.com** (G H LJ NU PI)
610 South East 19th Street ☎ 467-1444
✉ jdhanger@bellsouth.net 🖥 www.innleather.com

■ **New Zealand House** (AC BF CC G H msg NU OS p PI)
908 North East 15th Avenue ✉ FL 33304 *(1,5 miles from the beach)*
☎ 523-7829 ☎ (888) 234-5494 (toll-free) 📠 523-7051
✉ imakiwi@worldnet.ott.net 🖥 www.newzealandhouse.com
Rooms from US$ 69-150 (double).

■ **Paradiso Tropical Guest Cottages** (AC b BF CC G MA msg NU OS PI WH) 9-21 h
1115 Tequesta Street ✉ FL 33312 ☎ 764-8182
☎ (800) 644-7977 (toll-free) 📠 462-0066
✉ paradisoresort@aol.com 🖥 www.paradiso-ftl.com

■ **Pineapple Point** (AC E G H NU PI)
315 North East 16th Terrace ✉ FL 33301 ☎ 527-0094
☎ (888) 844-7295 (toll-free) 🖥 www.pineapplepoint.com
Call or see website for details.

■ **Saint Sebastian Guest House** (AC BF CC G H msg PI)
Office: 8-18 h
2835 Terramar Street ✉ FL 33304 *(3 blocks to the beach)*
☎ 568-6161 ☎ (800) 425-8105 (toll-free) 📠 568-6209
🖥 www.saintsebastianhotel.com
Rooms with private bath, refrigerator, TV, telephone, some with kitchen.
Rates US$ 59-179.

Fort Lauderdale's Best Kept Secret.

EDUN House

Out & About – 4 Palm Winner

- Friendly, intimate accommodations for the gay male traveler.
- Heated Pool at your doorstep.
- Casual Courtyard & Indoor Lounge

CLOTHING ALWAYS OPTIONAL

2733 Middle River Dr., Fort Lauderdale, FL 33306
Phone: 954-565-7775 • FAX 954-565-7912
E-mail: Edun2733@aol.com
http://members.aol.com/edunhouse

USA/Florida | Fort Lauderdale ▶ Fort Myers

Eternal Sun Resort
www.EternalSun.Org
Ft. Lauderdale's Hidden Treasure for Gay Men
A 21 Room "Men Only" resort spread over 3 acres of Paradise where Clothing is always an Option anywhere on the property. Large pool & deck area. Close to gay bars & restaurants. 10 minute drive to Gay Nude Beach. Hotel Rooms, Studios & apartments. Voted second best resort in Ft. lauderdale by the gay travel magazine "Out & About"
954-462-6035 • Fax: 954-522-2764
1909 SW 2nd Street, Ft. Lauderdale, FL 33312
e-mail: MrIbizia@aol.com

■ **Sea Grape House Inn and Cabanas** (AC B BF CC G H NU OS VS W) 9-21 h
1109 NE16th Place ✉ FL 33205 *(5 blocks from gay Wilton Dr bars)*
☎ 525-6586 ☎ (800) 447-3074 code 44 (toll-free) 📠 525-0586
💻 CGrapeHse@aol.com 💻 www.seagrape.com
All rooms with TV, VCR and phone. 2 pools and spa.Clothing optional. Call for rates.

■ **Worthington, The** (AC G bf H NU OS PI)
543 North Birch Road ✉ FL 33304 ☎ 563-6819
☎ (800) 445-7036 💻 www.worthguesthouse.com
Guestrooms, studios & suites all with AC, bath,fridge, TV,VRC, in the heart of the gay beach area and just a few steps to the ocean. Clothing is optional.

APARTMENTS

■ **Flamingo Resort** (AC BF CC G MA msg NU OS p PI WO) 8-19 h
2727 Terramar Street ✉ FL 33304 *(tropica Art-deco resort)*
☎ 561-4658 ☎ (800) 283-4786 📠 568-2688
💻 flamingors@aol.com 💻 www.theflamingoresort.com
Heated pool. Call for rates. Apartments with fully equipped kitchens, just a few steps to the beach.

■ **JP's Beach Villas** (AC CC GLM H OS PI)
4621 North Ocean Drive (A-1-A) ✉ FL 33308 ☎ 772-3672
☎ (888) 992-3224 (toll-free) 📠 776-0889
💻 info@jpsbeachvillas.com 💻 www.jpsbeachvillas.com
All apartments and efficiencies with cable TV and phone and fully equipped kitchens. Heated pool. Near shopping, clubs and restaurant. Rates from US$ 100-175.

■ **Mangrove Villas** (AC CC G H NU PI)
1100 North Victoria Park Road ✉ FL 33305 *(central)* ☎ 527-5250
☎ (800) 238-3538 (toll free) 📠 764-1968 💻 villasftl@aol.com
💻 www.mangrovevillas.com
Each villa is a small house with bedroom, bath, living, dining and fully equipped kitchen. Daily houseman service. Rates US$ 89-169 (high season), 70-125 (low season).

■ **Orton Terrace** (AC BF CC f GLM A NU OS PI VS)
606 Orton Avenue ✉ FL 33304 ☎ 566-5068 ☎ (800) 323-1142 (toll free) 📠 564-8646 💻 orton@ortonterrace.com
💻 www.ortonterrace.com
One and two bedroom apartments with fridge, microwave, cable TV, VCR, continental bf included. Community room with computer including internet access. Very close to the beach.

■ **Villa Torino** (AC CC glm H)
3017 Alhambra Street ✉ FL 33304 ☎ 527-5272
💻 www.VillaTorino.com
Apartments for rent daily, weekly or monthly. Call for info and rates.

GENERAL GROUPS

■ **South Florida Gay Pride Committee**
PO Box 2048 ✉ FL 33303 ☎ 523-3737

HEALTH GROUPS

■ **Health Link / Wansiki Foundation** Mon Wed Fri 10-18, Tue Thu -20h closed Sat&Sun
3213 N. Ocean Boulevard, Suite 7 ✉ FL 33308 ☎ 565-8284
📠 565-8289 💻 wansiki@aol.com
Primary medical care, free HIV-testing, emgergency HIV/AIDS medication.

SWIMMING

-Fort Lauderdale beach (g) (In front of Sebastian street, and in front of Terramar Street)
-Beach opposite of North-East 18th Street (One mile north of Sunrise Boulevard) - cruisy at night.
-Lloyd Beach State Recreation Area (Take U.S. 1 to Dania Beach Boulevard, east to A1A. Follow signs to park entrance. First parking lot on right. Admission charge. Caution: Undercover police in T-rooms)
- NEW gay beach - Terramar street and A1A (Ocean)

CRUISING

-Holiday Park (South side of Sunrise Boulevardat North-East 12th Avenue. Check out parking area)

Fort Myers ☎ 941

GAY INFO

■ **Gay Switchboard** 0-24 h
PO Box 546 ✉ FL 33902 ☎ 275-1400

BARS

■ **Bottom Line, The** (AC B CC D f GLM MA OS S VS) 15-2 h
3090 Evans Avenue ✉ FL 33901 ☎ 337-7292

California Dream Inn.

"...Tucked away...right on the beach. The California Dream Inn reminds us of some other time, some other place, somewhere redolent of your dreams..."
SOUTH FLORIDA MAGAZINE

California DREAM INN
AAA Diamond Rating

300-315 Walnut Street
Hollywood, FL 33019
(954) 923-2100

Superior Small Lodging Award Of Excellence

www.californiadreaminn.com

RESTAURANTS
■ Oasis. The (B F glm)
2222 McGregor Boulevard ✉ FL 33901 ☎ 334-1566

HELP WITH PROBLEMS
■ AIDS-Hotline
☎ 337-AIDS

SWIMMING
-Bunch Beach (John Morris Parkway. South end of beach AYOR)

Fort Walton Beach ☎ 904

BARS
■ Choo Choo's Pub (AC GLM LJ S) 20-2 h
223 Highway 98 East ✉ FL 32548 (adjacent to Frankly Scarlet)
☎ 664-2966
■ Frankly Scarlet (AC B D GLM LJ MA S STV) Thu-Sat 20-4 h, Sun&Mon closed
217 Highway 98 East ✉ FL 32548 (adjacent to Choo Choo's Pub)
☎ 664-2966

Gainesville ☎ 904

GAY INFO
■ Gay Switchboard (GLM) 18-23 h, computer system 23-8 h
PO Box 12002 ✉ FL 32604-0002 ☎ 332-0770

BARS
■ Melody Club. The (! B D GLM OS SNU STV) 20-2 h
4130 North-West 6th Street ✉ FL 32609 ☎ 376-3772
■ Oz (B G)
7118 West University Avenue/Tower Road ✉ FL 32609 (I-75)
■ Phil's Bar and Resort (B GLM)
County Road 316, Reddick, Ocala ✉ FL 32686 (1.5 miles west of State Road 25 A) ☎ 591-9924
Call about membership.
■ Quake. The (AC B D F GLM MA OS S WE YG) 16-2 h
7118 West University Avenue ✉ FL 32607 ☎ 332-2553
■ University Club (B GLM STV)
18 East University Avenue ✉ FL 32601 ☎ 378-6411
■ Wild Angels (B G LJ) 16-? h
4130 North-West 6th Street ✉ FL 32609 ☎ 376-3772

HEALTH GROUPS
■ Alachua County Public Health Unit
730 North-East Waldo Road ✉ FL 32601 ☎ 336-2356 ext.153 or 154

HELP WITH PROBLEMS
■ AA Gay New Life (glm) 20 h Sun.
☎ 332-0700 ☎ 372-8091

CRUISING
-Newman's Lake (AYOR)
-Park at North East 16th Avenue/Main Street (days)
-Bivens Arm Park
-Lake Alice (at the University)

Gulfport ☎ 727

BARS
■ Sharp A's Lounge (AC B CC d f GLM MA N S SNU STV) 16-2 h
4918 Gulfport Boulevard South ✉ FL 33707-4940 ☎ 327-4897
Gay bar with liquor store.

Hallandale ☎ 305

BARS
■ Underpass (B D G S) Tue-Sun
100 Ansin Boulevard ✉ FL 33009 ☎ 547-8800

Holiday ☎ 727

BARS
■ Lovey's Pub (AC B d f GLM MA s) Mon-Sat 10-2, Sun 13-2 h
3338 U.S. Highway 19 ✉ FL 34691 ☎ 849-2960

Hollywood ☎ 323

HOTELS
■ California Dream Inn (BF GLM H OS)
300 - 315 Walnut Street ✉ FL 33019 ☎ 923-2100
✉ info@californiadreaminn.com 🖳 www.californiadreaminn.com
Named one of the best hideaway hotels by South Florida Magazine. Fort Lauderdale Airport and nightlife is less than three miles away. The Miami International Airport and the South Beach/Art Deco district are just twenty minutes by car.

USA/Florida Jacksonville ▸ Key West

Jacksonville ☏ 904

BARS
■ **Bootrack Saloon** (B G lj OS) 14-2 h
4751 Lenox Avenue ✉ FL 32205 ☏ 384-7090
■ **Bo's Coral Reef** (B D G)
201 North 5th Avenue ✉ FL 32250 *(Jacksonville Beach)*
■ **Club Carousel** (B D F glm S) Sat (G) 19-2 h
8550 Arlington Expressway ✉ FL 32211 ☏ 725-8282
■ **Junction Tavern. The** (A AC b f GLM MA N OS S) 14-2 h
1261 King Street ✉ FL 32204 ☏ 388-3434
■ **Metro** (AC B CC D f GLM LJ MA N S SNU STV WE) Mon-Fri 16-2,
Sat 18-3, Sun -24 h
2929 Plum Street ✉ FL 32205 ☏ 388-8319
■ **Park Place Lounge** (B G N)
931 King Street ✉ FL 32204 ☏ 389-6616
■ **Third Dimension 3D** (AC B CC D f G MA SNU STV TV VS)
Mon-Fri 15-3, Sat 16-3, Sun 17-3 h
711 Edison Avenue ✉ FL 32204-2904 ☏ 353-6316
18-21 years old allowed after 21 h.
■ **616** (AC B CC d f GLM lj MA OS S SNU) 16-2 h
616 Park Street ✉ FL 32204 ☏ 358-6969

SAUNAS/BATHS
■ **Club Jacksonville** (G MA PI SB WH OC) 0-24 h
1939 Hendricks Avenue ✉ FL 32207 *(12 blocks frrom downtown in the San Marco Area)* ☏ 398-7451
Friendly atmosphere to meet people from 18 to 80 or just to relax and enjoy the facilities.

SWIMMING
-Beach in the Jacksonville area (G) (25 miles south of Jacksonville on A1A at the end of South Ponte Vedra Beach. The entrance has to be found at the Guano River Boat Ramp. Once across the sand dune, go to the right about 200 yards. There is some dune activity but can be rather risky as the police regularly patrol the beach)

CRUISING
-Boone Park
-Friendship Park (AYOR)
-Hemming Park (AYOR)

Jasper ☏ 850

HOTELS
■ **Mystic Lake Manor** (AC BF F G MA PI WH OC) 8-24 h
PO Box 1623 ✉ FL 32052 *(8.4 miles off 1-10 in Northern Florida)*
☏ 973-8435
Located on a 30 acre lake. Boating and fishing. Private rooms with private baths, private rooms with shared baths and dormitory.
■ **Swan Lake B&B**
238 Route 129, PO Box 1623 ✉ FL 32052 ☏ 904/792-2771

Key West ☏ 305

✱ Key West is at the most southern point of the U.S.A. The best way to get there is by hire car from Miami or to take the shuttle bus from Miami International Airport. The scenic trip across the US 1 to Key West takes roughly three hours and offers the best impression of the island. For those who are not able to wait - take a direct flight from Miami. In Key West you will find a very open minded crowd. Gays are so intrigated in the community that they are almost not noticeable in every day life. Duval Street, known as the "longest street of the world" connecting the Atlantic with the Gulf of Mexico, is the main shopping district. But watch out for the shops bearing the rainbow flag, many of these are tourist traps. The "Fantasy Fest" takes place every year in October, which is the largest attraction of Key West. At this time of year this small island seems to almost bursts with gays and lesbians gathering here from all corners of the globe. After indulging in a sight seeing trip, including the Ernest Hemingway Home, one of the best things to do is to relax by the pool at your guest house. The early evening starts with a cocktail (normally complimentary in all good guest houses). Most action takes place in the early hours of the morning in the hot tub ! The best time to travel to Key West is in the winter when there are still tropical temperatures.

✱ Key West ist der südlichste Punkt der Vereinigten Staaten. Die letzte Insel der Florida Keys besucht man am besten, indem man sich auf dem Festland einen Wagen mietet oder am Miami International Airport den Bus-Shuttle nimmt. Über die US 1 gelangt man -ohne es zu verpassen- innerhalb von drei Stunden nach Key West. Somit erhält man gleich die besten Eindrücke dieses Eilands. Diejenigen, die es kaum erwarten können, nach Key West zu gelangen, sollten direkt von Miami ein Flugzeug nehmen. In Key West erwartet einen das aufgeschlossenste Völckchen, das man sich vorstellen kann. Homosexuelle werden so offenherzig in die Gemeinde aufgenommen, daß sie im Alltag kaum auffallen. *Duval Street*, die liebevoll "die längste Straße der Welt" genannt wird, da sie den Atlantik mit dem Golf von Mexico verbindet, stellt die Einkaufsmeile Key Wests dar. Man hüte sich aber vor den Geschäften, die zwar mit der Regenbogen-Flagge getarnt sind, sich jedoch als reine Schwulen-Fallen herausstellen. Im Oktober findet jährlich die größte Attraktion Key Wests statt: das *Fantasy Fest*. Zu diesem Zeitpunkt scheint die kleine Insel aus allen Nähten zu platzen, pilgern doch aus aller Welt Schwule und Lesben hierhin. Da es neben Attraktionen, wie das *Ernest Hemingway Home*, kein wirklich touristisches Muß gibt, kann man in seinem *guest house* gnadenlos am Schwimmingpool entspannen. Abends beginnt das alles mit einem Cocktail (in guten Gästehäusern normalerweise im Preis inbegriffen). Das interessante findet früh morgens im Hot Tub statt ! Ideale Reisezeit für Key West ist der Winter, denn dann herrschen hier noch tropische Temperaturen.

✱ Key West est le point situé le plus au sud des États-Unis. La meilleure façon de visiter cette île, la dernière des keys de Floride, est de louer une voiture ou de prendre une navette de l'aéroport. En environ trois heures, en passant par la US 1, vous arriverez à Key West avec en prime une vue imprenable d'ensemble. Les plus impatients d'entre vous peuvent cependant s'y rendre en avion depuis Miami. A Key West, vous trouverez la population la plus ouverte qui soit. Les homosexuels sont si bien intégrés à la communauté que l'on ne les remarque presque pas. La *Duval Street*, surnommée "la plus longue rue du monde", car elle relie l'Atlantique au Golf du Mexique, est la rue marchande de la ville. Mais méfiez-vous des magasins qui arborent les couleurs de l'arc-en-ciel! Ce sont des véritables attrape-nigauds. Chaque année, en octobre, a lieu à Key West le plus grand événement de l'année: la *Fantasy Fest*. Pendant cette péride, l'île est véritablement surpeuplée de gais et lesbiennes venus en pèlerinage des quatre coins du globe. A l'exception de cet événement, l'île n'offre pas beaucoup d'activités, hormis peut-être la visite de la maison d'*Ernest Hemingway*. Il vous restera donc à vous prélasser au bord de la piscine de votre maison d'hôtes. Le début de soirée commence avec un cockail (normalement gracieusement offert par tout *guest house* de ce nom). Le moment le plus palpitant de la journée se situera aux premières heures du matin lorsque que vous vous plongerez dans votre jacuzzi. L'hiver est la saison idéale pour se rendre à Key West, car les températures y sont encore tropicales.

Key West | Florida/USA

Key West

1. Rooftop Cafe Restaurant
2. Kelly's Caribbean Bar Grill Restaurant
3. Papa's of Key West Restaurant
4. Harbour Inn Guest House
5. Simanton Court Hotel
6. Pilot House Guest House
7. Café Marquesa Restaurant
8. Coconut Grove Guest House
9. Oasis Guest House
10. Fleur de Key Guest House
11. Island House for Men Guest House
12. Alexander's Guest House
13. Flaming Maggie's Bookshop
14. Coral Tree Inn Guest House
15. Curry House Guest House
16. Equator Guest House
17. Heron House Guest House
18. La Trattoria Venezia Restaurant
19. Big Ruby's Guest House
20. Leather Master's Shop
21. Antonia's Restaurant
22. Dim Sum Restaurant
23. Diva's Danceclub
24. New Orleans House Guest House
25. Mango's Restaurant
26. 801 Bar
27. Duval House Guest House
28. Merlinn Guest House
29. Croissants de France Café
30. Tropical Inn Guest House
31. Seascape Guest House
32. Lighthouse Court Guest House
33. Andrew's Inn Guest House
34. Key Lodge Motel
35. Dèjà Vu Resort
36. Seven Fish Restaurant
37. Blue Parrot Inn Guest House
38. Chelsea House Guest House
39. Red Rooster Inn Guest House
40. Authors of Key West Guest House
41. Duffy's Steak & Lobster House Restaurant
42. Café des Artistes Restaurant
43. Square One Restaurant
44. Café Europa
45. La-Te-Da Guest House / Alices Restaurant
46. Atlantic Shores Resort Hotel

USA/Florida — Key West

Key West está situado en el más extremo sur de los Estados Unidos. La mejor manera de visitar la última isla de los Florida Keys es alquilando un coche en tierra firme o cogiendo el autobus que parte del aeropuerto de Miami. Por la autopista US 1 se llega en tres horas a Key West. De esta manera se puede apreciar la belleza natural de esta isla. Si se tiene prisa, se debe coger el avión directamente en Miami. Los habitantes de Key West son abiertos y afables. Los homosexuales están tan integrados en la comunidad, que en la vida cotidiana pasan casi desapercibidos. La *Duval Street*, que se llama también cariñosamente la "calle más larga del mundo", y que une el Atlantico con el Golfo de México, es la calle comercial de Key West. Un consejo: Cuidado con las tiendas que intentan atraer clientela con la bandera de arcoiris, ino son más que trampas para homosexuales! En Octubre se celebra anualmente la mayor atración de Key West: El "Fantasy Festival". En estas fechas la isla se llena de gays y lesbianas, que vienen de todas las partes del mundo para participar en estas festividades. Aparte del *Hemingway Home*, no hay muchos sitios de visitar y por ello uno puede dedicar sus vacaciones completamente al relax en los *guest houses*. El invierno es la fecha óptima para visitar Key West, ya que en esta temporada se pueden disfrutar aquí todavía temperatures tropicales.

Key West è il punto più al sud degli USA. L'ultima isola del Florida Keys è da visitare alla meglio con una macchina a noleggio che ci si può procurare sulla terraferma o con il servizio navetta dell'aeroporto di Miami (International Airport Bus Shuttle). Dalla US 1 si arriva senza sbagliarsi nel giro di tre ore a Key West. Cosi si raggolgono già le prime impressioni di quest'isola. Per coloro che non vedono l'ora di arrivare a Key West è consigliabile prendere un volo diretto da Miami. A Key West ci aspetta la popolazione più aperta che si possa immaginare. Gli omosessuali vengono accolti cosi apertamente nella società del posto che non danno più nell'occhio nella vita quotidiana. La *Duval Street* viene chiamata amorevolmente la strada più lunga del mondo, perché congiunge l'Atlantico con il Golfo del Messico e rappresenta anche la zona shopping di Key West. Si avverte però di fare attenzione ai quei negozi che mettono in mostra la bandiera dell'arcobaleno, ma che poi risultano una truffa per la clientela gay. Ogni anno in ottobre ha luogo l'avvenimento più importante per Key West: il *Fantasy Fest*. In questo periodo la piccola isola sembra scoppiare dalla moltitudine di "pellegrini" gay e lesbiche provenienti da tutto il mondo. Siccome oltre a certi punti d'attrazione come la Ernest Hemingway Home non esistono mete propriamente turistiche è possibile oziare perennemente nel suo *guest house*. Il periodo ideale per un viaggio a Key West è l'inverno, perché si ha un clima tropico.

PUBLICATIONS

■ **Celebrate!**
1315 Whitehead Street, PO Box 247 ✉ FL 33041 ☎ 296-1566
📠 296-0458 ✉ editor@celebrate-kw.com
🌐 www.celebrate-kw.com
Weekly magazine.

■ **Gay Guide to Key West**
☎ 294-4603 ✉ keywestgay@aol.com
Colour guide and map to Key West.

■ **Southern Exposure Guide**
819 Peacock Plaza, Suite 215 ✉ FL 33041 ☎ 294-6303
📠 295-9597 ✉ jon@gaykeywest.net 🌐 www.gaykeywest.net
Monthly guide to Key West area. Complete map of Old Town, calendar of events and local information.

BARS

■ **Bourbon Street Pub** (B GLM MA) 12-4 h
730 Duval Street ✉ FL 33040 ☎ 296-1992

■ **801 Bar** (B GLM N OS) 11-4 h
801 Duval Street ✉ FL 33040 ☎ 294-4737
Hosts Dan's bar every day after 21 h.

CAFES

■ **Court Cafe at Lighthouse Court** (b BF CC F glm) 9-16 h
902 Whitehead Street ✉ FL 33040 ☎ 294-9588

■ **Croissants de France** (b CC F glm) ?-23 h, closed Wed
816 Duval Street ✉ FL 33040 ☎ 294-2624

DANCECLUBS

■ **Diva's** (B D glm STV) Mon-Sun 12-4 h
711 Duval Street ☎ 292-8500

RESTAURANTS

■ **Alice's on Duval** (B CC F glm OS)
1114 Duval Street ✉ FL 33040 ☎ 292-4888
Tropical atmosphere with open air (but indoor) dining.

■ **Antonia's** (AC B CC F glm) 18-23 h
615 Duval Street ✉ FL 33040 ☎ 294-6565
Regional Italian cuisine.

■ **Café des Artistes** (B CC F glm) 18-23 h
1007 Simonton Street ✉ FL 33040 ☎ 294-7100

■ **Café Europa** (F GLM OS) 8-22 h
1075 Duval Street C-13 (Duval Square) ✉ FL 33040 (Duval Sq.)
☎ 294-3443
Restaurant with European & Island cuisine. German beer & wine. All occasion cakes.

■ **Camille's** (BF CC F G MA)
703 ½ Duval Street, u FL 33040 1 296-4811
Sunday brunch.

■ **Caribe Soul** (CC F glm) 11-15 h & 18-21 h
1202 Simonton Street ✉ FL 33040 ☎ 296-0094
Gay owned and operated. Homestyle food infused with spices of the Caribbean.

■ **Dim Sum** (b CC F glm) 18-23 h, closed Tue
613 ½ Duval Street ✉ FL 33040 1 294-6230
Asian cuisine.

■ **Duffy's Steak and Lobster House** (B CC F glm) 11-23 h
1007 Simonton Street ✉ FL 33040 ☎ 296-4900
American cuisine.

■ **El Siboney** (B CC F glm)
900 Catherine Street ✉ FL 33040
Best Cuban food in Key West.

■ **Kelly's Carribbean Bar Grill & Brewery** (B CC F glm)
301 Whitehead Street ✉ FL 33040 ☎ 293-8484
American and Carribean cuisine. The establishment is owned by actress Kelly McGillis.

■ **Mango's** (B CC F glm) 7-24 h
700 Duval Street ✉ FL 33040 ☎ 292-4606
International cuisine.

■ **Marquesa. Cafe** (B CC F glm) 18-24 h
600 Fleming Street ✉ FL 33040 ☎ 292-1244

■ **Michael's** (B CC F glm)
532 Margaret Street ✉ FL 33040 ☎ /295-1300
Chicago Style Steak House, very expensive.

■ **Papa's of Key West** (b CC F glm) 11-24 h
217 Duval Street ✉ FL 33040 ☎ 293-7880
American and Italian cuisine.

■ **Pepe's** (CC F glm) 6.30-23 h
806 Caroline Street ✉ FL 33040 ☎ 294-7192

■ **Rooftop Café** (B CC F glm) 9-1 h
310 Front Street ✉ FL 33040 ☎ 294-2042

1218 SPARTACUS 2001/2002

Key West | Florida/USA

You're among friends.

For color guide & map call **(305)294-4603** or email at **keywestgay@aol.com**

fabulous the gay destination **KEY WEST**

■ **Seven Fish** (B CC F glm)
632 Olivia Street ✉ FL 33040 ☎ 296-2777
A favorite with the gay community.
■ **Square One** (B CC F glm)
1075 Duval Street ✉ FL 33040 *(Duval Square)* ☎ 296-4300
American cuisine.
■ **Trattoria Venezia. La** (B CC F glm) 18.30-23 h
524 Duval Street ✉ FL 33040 *(Old Town)* ☎ 296-1075
Italian cuisine; seafood.

BOOK SHOPS
■ **Flaming Maggie's Books, Art & Coffee** (GLM) Mon-Sun 10-18 h
830 Fleming Street (at Margaret) ✉ FL 33040 ☎ 294-3931

LEATHER & FETISH SHOPS
■ **Leather Master Key West** (CC LJ) 11-23, Sun 12-18 h
418 Appelrouth Lane ✉ FL 33040 ☎ 292-5051

PR & PHOTOGRAPHY SERVICES
■ **Key West Business Guild**
PO Box 1208 ✉ FL 33041 ☎ 294-4603
Local information, maps etc.

TRAVEL AND TRANSPORT
■ **Hanns Ebensten Travel, Inc.** (G) Mon-Fri 9-17 h, closed Sat Sun
513 Fleming Street, ✉ FL 33040 ☎ 294-8174 📠 292-9665
Operator of Tours, cruises and expeditions for men.

HOTELS
■ **Atlantic Shores Resort** (AC B BF CC d F GLM H lj MA NU OS PI s)
510 South Street ✉ FL 33040-3118 ☎ 296-2491
☎ (888) 414-4102 (toll free) 📠 (305) 294-2753
✉ atlshores@aol.com
✉ www.atlanticshoresresort.com
Rates US$ 110-150 (high-season), US$ 80-100 (off-season).
■ **Blue Parrot Inn** (AC BF CC g H nu OS PI)
916 Elizabeth Street ✉ FL 33040 ☎ 296-0033 ☎ (800) 231-BIRD (Toll-free)
Ten minutes to the airport. Two blocks from gay scene. All rooms with priv. bath/WC.
■ **Chelsea House** (AC BF CC glm H PI)
707 Truman Street ✉ FL 33040 ☎ 296-2211 ☎ (800)-845-8859 (toll free) 📠 296-4822
Rooms with priv. bath.
■ **Douglas House** (AC BF CC g H MA OS PI WH) 8-23 h
419 Amelia Street ✉ FL 33040 ☎ 294-5269 ☎ (800)833-0372 (toll free) 📠 292-7665
■ **Eaton Lodge Historic Inn and Gardens** (BF g H OS PI WH)
Office: 8-21 h
511 Eaton Street ✉ FL 33040 ☎ 292-2170 ☎ 800 294-2170 (toll free)
Pool, lush landscaping, bf incl. Full bar during hospitality hour.
■ **Habitation. L'** (AC BF CC GLM H OS)
408 Eaton Street ✉ FL 33040 ☎ 293-9203 📠 296-1313
Double rooms US$ 52-109, studio 72-109, incl. breakfast.
■ **Harbor Inn** (AC BF G H OS)
219 Elizabeth St ✉ FL 33040 ☎ 296-2978 📠 294-5858
■ **Heron House** (AC BF CC g H MA OS PI) 24 hours
512 Simonton Street, ✉ FL 33040 ☎ 294-9227
☎ 1-800-294-1644 (Toll Free) 📠 294-5692
Downtown location. All rooms with priv. bath/WC, balcony. Rates US$ 85-220.

Key West
FLORIDA
THE ORIGINAL GAY DESTINATION STILL IS.

CALL 305-294-4603 (800-535-7797)
FOR YOUR 56 PAGE COLOR GAY GUIDE.
WWW.GAYTRAVELING.COM
IGLTA

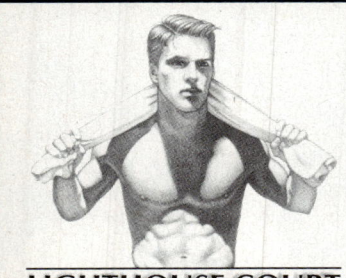

LIGHTHOUSE COURT
GUESTHOUSE RESORT

Lighthouse Court Guesthouse Resort, Old Town's Largest All-Male Premier Resort Compound, at the Historic Key West Lighthouse. 42 cottages, cabanas, rooms and suites with Café, Bar, Health Club, Heated Pool & Jacuzzi. One block from the Duval St. action & a few blocks from the gay beach. Across from the Hemingway House.

902 Whitehead St., Key West, FL 33040
(305) 294-9588

---

724 DUVAL • KEY WEST
THE NEW ORLEANS HOUSE
Key West's Premier Guesthouse for Gay & Lesbian Travelers

heated pool & spa
off - street parking

305.293.9800 • Fax 305.293.9870
www.NewOrleansHouseKW.com

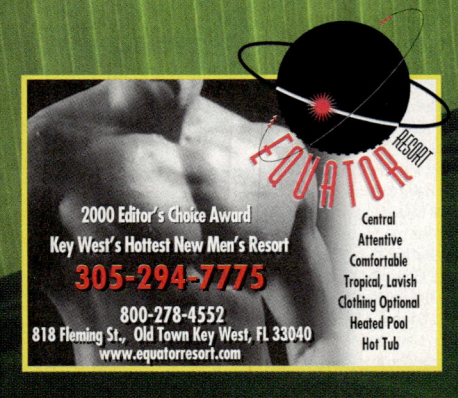

Big RubyS
GUESTHOUSE

KEY WEST, USA
305-296-2323

LA PLANTACIÓN
MANUEL ANTONIO, COSTA RICA
506-777-1332

L'ORANGERIE
AIQUES-MORTES, FRANCE
33-4-66-53-10-23

1-800-477-7829 USA/CANADA
www.BigRubys.com

EQUATOR RESORT

2000 Editor's Choice Award
Key West's Hottest New Men's Resort
305-294-7775

800-278-4552
818 Fleming St., Old Town Key West, FL 33040
www.equatorresort.com

Central
Attentive
Comfortable
Tropical, Lavish
Clothing Optional
Heated Pool
Hot Tub

Formerly the Brass Key

"One of Key West's most impressive & refined lodgings."
The Advocate

FLEUR DE KEY GUESTHOUSE

412 Frances St • Key West, FL 33040-6950
305-296-4719 • 800-932-9119
Fax 305-296-1994
www.fleurdekey.com

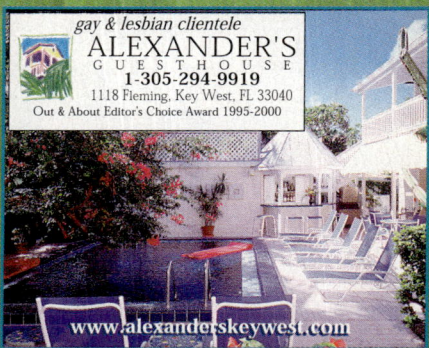

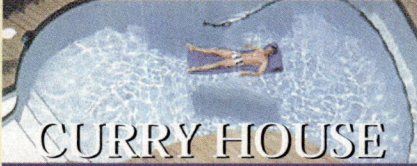

---

gay & lesbian clientele
ALEXANDER'S GUESTHOUSE
1-305-294-9919
1118 Fleming, Key West, FL 33040
Out & About Editor's Choice Award 1995-2000

www.alexanderskeywest.com

CURRY HOUSE
Key West's original exclusively-male bed & breakfast for over 20 years.
Friendly. Relaxed. Affordable. Clothing Optional.
Large Pool & Jacuzzi. Full Breakfast.
(305) 294-6777
(800) 633-7439 • 806 Fleming St., Key West, FL 33040
www.gaytraveling.com/curryhouse

Central Location • Private Parking
Large Pool, Jacuzzi & Gym

305-294-5188 • 800-995-4786
Fax: 305-296-7143
www.seaisleresort.com

Sea Isle Resort
915 Windsor Lane
Key West, FL 33040

USA/Florida — Key West

Key West's Only Oceanfront Alternative Resort

Clothing Optional Pool and Pier
Wave Runners, Hobie Cats, Snorkel & Scuba Trips
Thursday Night "Cinema Under the Stars"
Sunday Evening "Tea By The Sea"
DINER SHORES for Breakfast, Lunch & Cocktails
POOL BAR AND GRILL for Sun, Fun and Frolic

ATLANTIC SHORES RESORT · KEY WEST
305-296-2491
U.S. TOLL FREE 888-414-4102
Check Out Our Live Cam @ www.atlanticshoresresort.com

■ **Key Lodge Motel** (AC CC glm H OS Pl) 8-22 h
1004 Duval Street ✉ FL 33040 ☎ 296-9915 ☎ (800) 458-1296 (toll free)
Rooms with phone, private bath/WC, some with kitchenette. Rates US$ 70-163.

■ **La-Te-Da** (AC B BF CC d F GLM H lj MA msg N OS Pl S STV WH)
1125 Duval Street ✉ FL 33040 ☎ 296-6706 ☎ 296-0438
✉ latedakw@aol.com
Hosts the popular Tea Dance. Good restaurant (Alices) and barbecue outdoors.

■ **Lighthouse Court** (AC B CC F G H Pl WH WO)
902 Whitehead Street ✉ FL 33040 ☎ 294-9588 ☎ 294-6681
All rooms with fridge and priv. bath, some have kitchenette and balcony. Health club, video bar and café on the premises. Rates US$60-235.

■ **Rose Lane Vacation Rentals** (CC glm H Pl)
524 Rose Lane ✉ FL 33040 ☎ 292-6337 ☎ (800)654-2781 (toll free) ☎ 294-6500
Rates US$ 96-107.

■ **Sea Isle Resort** (AC BF CC G H NU Pl WH WO)
915 Windsor Lane ✉ FL 33040 ☎ 294-5188 ☎ (800) 995-4786 (toll free) ☎ 296-7143 ✉ www.seaisleresort.com
All rooms with fridge, private bath, cable TV and telephone. Rates US$ 75-250 incl. bf.

■ **Seascape** (AC BF CC g H OS Pl WH)
420 Olivia Street ✉ FL 33040 (located in old town) ☎ 296-7776
☎ (800) 765-6438 (Toll-free) ☎ 296-7776
✉ seascapekw@aol.com
All rooms with private bath, queen size beds and color TV.

■ **Simonton Court** (AC B CC BF GLM H OS Pl WH) 8.30-18 h
320 Simonton Street ✉ FL 33040 ☎ 294-6386
☎ (800) 944-2687 (toll free) ☎ 293-8446
Downtown location. All rooms with kitchentte, priv. bath, TV. Rates US$ 100-350.

■ **Tropical Inn** (CC glm H)
812 Duval Street ✉ FL 33040 ☎ 294-9977
Rooms with priv. bath, sundecks, some with TV, kitchenette, spa. Rates US$ 70-140.

GUEST HOUSES

■ **Alexander Palms Court** (AC CC glm OS Pl WH)
715 South Street ✉ FL 33040 ☎ 296-6413 ☎ (800) 858-1943 (toll free) ☎ 292-3975

■ **Alexander's Guest House** (AC BF CC GLM OS Pl WH)
1118 Fleming Street ✉ FL 33040 ☎ 294-9919 ☎ 295-0357
✉ info@alexghouse.com ✉ www.alexanderskeywest.com
Centrally located. All rooms with private bath/WC, fridge, some with balcony. Rates US$ 80-300.

■ **Andrew's Inn** (AC B BF CC g H MA OS Pl) 8-22 h
Zero Whalton Lane ✉ FL 33040 (900 Block of Duval Street)
☎ 294-7730 ☎ 294-0021
Oldtown location. All gay bars within three blocks. All rooms with private baths, private entrances. Rates US$ 98-158, incl. bf.

■ **Authors, Key West** (A AC BF CC glm H lj MA OS Pl) Office: 9-19 h
725 White Street ✉ FL 33040 (central, entrance on Petronia St.)
☎ 294-7381 ☎ (800) 898-6909 (Toll-free) ☎ 294-0920
✉ lionxsx@aol.com ✉ www.authors-keywest.com
Convenient location, 10 min to gay bars. All rooms with cable, priv. bath/WC, kitchenette. Summer rates US$ 129-175, winter rates 149-249. Home of the Alexander Project, international male-oriented art organisation (www.alexanderproject.com).

Key West Florida/USA

■ **Big Ruby's Guesthouse** (AC BF CC GLM H MA OS PI WH)
409 Applerouth Lane ✉ FL 33040 *(1/2 block off Duval Street)*
☎ 296-2323 ☎ (800) 477-7829 (toll free)
🖥 keywest@bigrubys.com 🖥 www.bigrubys.com
Full breakfast included, complimentary wine + beer, heated swimming pool, gay/lesbian clientele. All rooms with shower/WC, wash-basin, air-conditioning, TV.

■ **Coconut Grove Guest House** (AC BF CC G OS PI WH WO)
817 Fleming Street ✉ FL 33040 ☎ 296-5107 ☎ (800) 262-6055
🖥 296-1584 🖥 cocgro@ibm.net
🖥 www.coconutgrovekeywest.com
All rooms with kitchenette, priv. bath/WC, and balcony. Rates US$ 55-220.

■ **Coral Tree Inn** (B CC G H MA nu OS PI WH) Office: 8-22 h
822 Fleming Street ✉ FL 33040 ☎ 296-2131 ☎ (800) 362-7477 (toll free) 🖥 296-9171 🖥 oasisct@aol.com
🖥 www.coraltree.com
Rooms with priv. bath, AC, coffee makers, fridge, TV, VCR, and phone. Out & About Editor's Award.

■ **Curry House** (AC BF CC E G H MA nu OS PI WH) 8-20 h
806 Fleming Street ✉ FL 33040 ☎ 294-6777
☎ (800) 633-7439 (toll free) 🖥 www.gaytraveling.com/curryhouse
All rooms with fridge, balcony, bath/WC. Rates US$ 75-150.

■ **Cypress House** (AC BF CC g H PI) 8-20 h
601 Caroline Street ✉ FL 33040 ☎ 294-6969 ☎ (800) 525-2488 (toll free) 🖥 296-1174 🖥 CypressKW@aol.com
Downtown location. Two block from gay bars. Some rooms with kitchenette, priv. bath/WC. Rates US$ 99-300.

■ **Déjà Vu Resort** (BF G H NU PI WH)
611 Truman Ave. ✉ FL 33040 ☎ 292-9339

■ **Duval House** (AC BF CC glm H PI) 8.30-22.30 h
815 Duval Street ✉ FL 33040 ☎ 292-9491
Rates US$ 75-250 (high-season), US$ 75-150 (off-season).

■ **Equator Resort** (! AC CC BF G H MA NU OS PI WH)
818 Fleming Street ✉ FL 33040 ☎ 294-7775
☎ (800) 278-4552 (toll free) 🖥 www.equatorresort.com
Very welcoming staff in a very attractive setting. Breakfasts are a treat. Watch out for the action in the hot tub in the early hours of the morning !

■ **Fleur de Key** (AC BF CC GLM H OS PI WH)
412 Frances Street ✉ FL 33040-6950 ☎ 296-4719
☎ (800) 932-9119 (toll free) 🖥 296-1994
🖥 www.fleurdekey.com
All rooms with fridge, private bath/WC, balcony. Rates US$ 150-280 (high-season) and US$ 70-160 (off-season), bf. incl. Formally known as Brass Key Guesthouse.

■ **Island House Key West** (AC B CC DR F G H NU OS PI SA VS WH WO) .
1129 Fleming Street ✉ FL 33040 *(Old town, near Duval St.)*
☎ 294-6284 ☎ (800) 890-6284 (toll free) 🖥 292-0051
🖥 ihkeywest@aol.com 🖥 www.islandhousekeywest.com
Located in Old Town. All rooms with AC, some with kitchenette, priv. bath/WC, fridge. Health Club with gym, steamroom,jacuzzi.

■ **Knowles House** (AC BF CC glm H PI)
1004 Eaton Street ✉ FL 33040-6925 ☎ 296-8132
☎ (800) 352-4414 (toll free) 🖥 296-2093
🖥 knowleshse@aol.com 🖥 www.members.aol.com/knowleshse
8 double rooms with bath or shower, SAT-TV, radio, own-key. Rates US$ 70-125 (off season), 109-165 (on season). Bf incl.

■ **Marrero's Guest Mansion** (AC BF CC GLM H OS PI WH) Office: 8-21 h
410 Fleming Street ✉ FL 33040 ☎ 294-6977 🖥 292-9030
🖥 Marreros@aol.com 🖥 www.gaytraveling.com/marreros/
Bicycle hire possible. Rates US$ 115-190 (high-season), US$ 85-140 (off-season), incl. Continental breakfast.

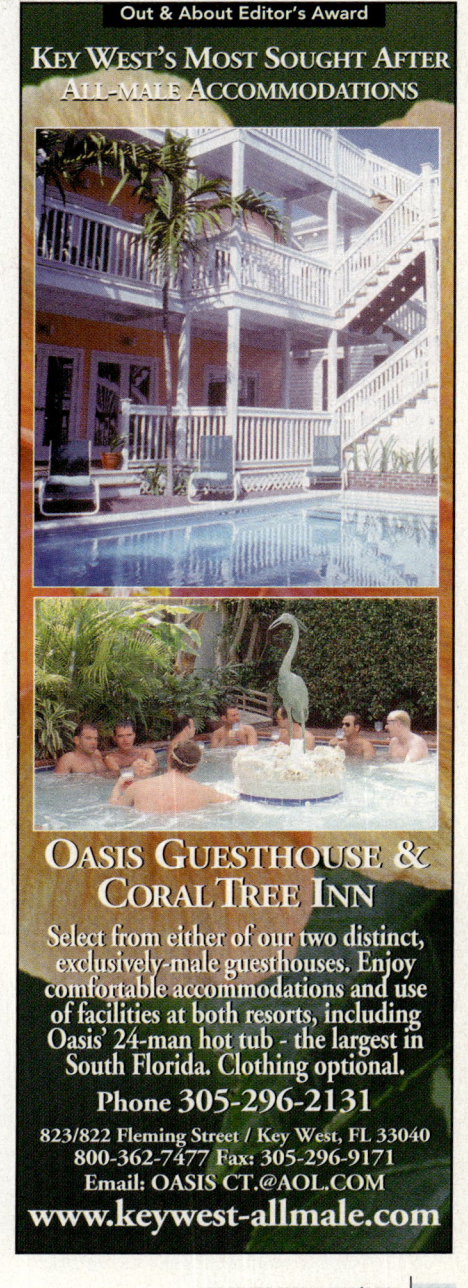

Out & About Editor's Award

KEY WEST'S MOST SOUGHT AFTER ALL-MALE ACCOMMODATIONS

OASIS GUESTHOUSE & CORAL TREE INN

Select from either of our two distinct, exclusively-male guesthouses. Enjoy comfortable accommodations and use of facilities at both resorts, including Oasis' 24-man hot tub - the largest in South Florida. Clothing optional.

Phone 305-296-2131
823/822 Fleming Street / Key West, FL 33040
800-362-7477 Fax: 305-296-9171
Email: OASIS CT.@AOL.COM

www.keywest-allmale.com

SPARTACUS 2001/2002 | 1223

USA/Florida Key West ▶ Miami

■ **Merlinn Guesthouse** (AC BF CC F glm H Pl s)
811 Simonton Street ✉ FL 33040 ☎ 296-3336 📠 296-3524
Centrally located. All rooms with priv. bath. Rates US$ 65-150.
■ **Nassau House B&B** (AC b BF CC glm H Pl) 9-21 h
1016 Fleming Street ✉ FL 33040 ☎ 296-8513 ☎ (800) 296-8513 (toll free) 📠 293-8423 ✉ nassau@conch.net
🌐 www.nassauhouse.com
■ **New Orleans House** (AC B BF CC G H NU PI WH)
724 Duval Street ✉ FL 33040 ☎ 293-9800 ☎ 293-9870
✉ NOHouseKW@aol.com 🌐 www.NewOrleansHouseKW.com
■ **Oasis Guest House** (AC B BF CC G H NU PI WH) Reservation 8-22 h.
823/822 Fleming Street ✉ FL 33040 ☎ 296-2131
☎ (800) 362-7177 (toll free) 📠 296-9171 ✉ oasisct@aol.com
🌐 www.keywest-allmale.com
All rooms with fridge, priv. bath, balcony, TV. Rates US$ 105-185 (high-season), US$ 80-125 (off-season). Out & About Editor's Award.
■ **Pilot House** (AC CC glm H NU PI WH) 9-18 h
414 Simonton Street ✉ FL 33040 (Old town) ☎ 293-6600
☎ (800) 648-3780 (toll-free) 📠 294-9298 ✉ pilotkw@aol.com
🌐 pilothousekeywest.com
Rates high season US$ 175-300, summer 100-200.
■ **Red Rooster Inn** (BF G H nu OS PI)
709 Truman Avenue ✉ FL 33040 ☎ 296-6558 📠 296-4822
✉ chelseahse@aol.com 🌐 www.chelseahse.com
■ **Terraza, La** (B BF CC F glm MA NU OS PI)
1125 Duval Street ✉ FL 33040 ☎ 296-6706 ☎ (800) 528-3320 (Toll-free) 📠 296-0438

APARTMENTS
■ **Southern Most Hospitality** (AC glm H msg NU PI WH)
524 Eaton Street, Suite 150 ✉ FL 33040 ☎ 294-3800
☎ (888) 294-3800 (Toll-free) 📠 294-9338
✉ KeyWestLodging@Sprynet 🌐 www.KeyWestLodging.com

HEALTH GROUPS
■ **AIDS Help, Inc.**
Truman Annex, PO Box 4374 ✉ FL 33040 ☎ 296-6196
☎ (800) 640-3867 (Toll-free)
Counselling, information and support for Monroe County's HIV+ population.
■ **Helpline, Inc.** 24 hours
PO Box 2186 ✉ FL 33045 ☎ 296-HELP ☎ 294-LINE
■ **Immuncare**
520 Southard Street ✉ FL 33040 ☎ 296-8593
Medical, nutritional, pharmaceutical, financial and social services to treat HIV.
■ **Old Town Medical Center** Mon-Fri 9-11.30 h
520 Southard Street ✉ FL 33040 ☎ 296-8593 ☎ 296-4990
📠 296-4868
General medical care, office and hospital.

CRUISING
-Duval Street
-Fleming Street
-Mallory Square (at sunset)
-Monroe Country Beach (Reynolds Street, Pier)

Lake Worth ☎ 407

BARS
■ **Palm Beaches Inn Exile** (B G MA S VS YG) Mon-Sat 15-2, Sun-24 h
6 South J Street ✉ FL 33460 (West Palm Area) ☎ 582-4144
Video nightclub.

VIDEO SHOPS
■ **Harold Video** (g VS)
4266 Lake Worth Road ☎ 964-2470

Lakeland ☎ 813

BARS
■ **Dockside** (B D F GLM S) 16-2 h
3770 Highway 92 ✉ FL 33804 ☎ 665-6021
■ **Green Parrot** (b D f G S SNU WE) Mon-Sat 16-2, Sun-24 h
1030 East Main Street ✉ FL 33801 ☎ 683-6021
German owners.

Madeira Beach ☎ 813

BARS
■ **CockTail Club** (B G MA)
14601 Gulf Boulevard ✉ FL 33108 ☎ 391-2680
Entrance in the rear of the building. Beach access.

Melbourne ☎ 407

BARS
■ **Saturdays Lounge** (B D GLM OS S) Tue-Sun 14-2 h
4060 West New Haven Avenue ✉ FL 32904 ☎ 724-1510

SWIMMING
-Beach at the end of the Eau Gallie Causeway
-Canova Beach (AYOR) (nights)
-Melbourne Harbor Marina (AYOR)

Miami ☎ 305

GAY INFO
■ **Switchboard of Miami Inc.** 0-24 h
444 Brickell Avenue, Suite 450 ✉ FL 33131 ☎ 358-1640
☎ 358-4357 (helpline) 📠 377-2269
🌐 www.switchboardmiami.org
Crisis counseling, referrals and information.

PUBLICATIONS
■ **Contax Guide** Tue-Fri 10-16 h
901 North East 79th Street ✉ FL 33138 ☎ 757-6333 📠 756-6488
✉ bwatson@contaxguide.com 🌐 www.contaxguide.com
Weekly magazine featuring national & regional news, community listings, maps and ads.
■ **TWN - The Weekly News** Tue-Fri 10-17 h
901 North East 79th Street ✉ FL 33138 ☎ 757-6333 📠 756-6488
✉ bwatson@theweeklynews.org 🌐 www.theweeklynews.org
South Florida's weekly gay newspaper featuring places of interest throughout the state, as well as reports and reviews. Free at gay venues.

TOURIST INFO
■ **Greater Miami Convention & Visitor Bureau**
701 Brickell Avenue, Suite 2700 ✉ FL 33131 ☎ 539-3000
📠 539-3113

BARS
■ **Cactus Bar + Grill** (AC B CC F G S SNU OS VS YG) Mon-Sat 15-3 h, Sun 12-3 h
2041 Biscayne Boulevard, Dade County ✉ FL 33137 ☎ 438-0662

GYM, SAUNA, STEAMROOM NOW OPEN!

KEY WEST'S LARGEST ALL MALE RESORT
GAY OWNED & OPERATED

- 34 Rooms
- Private Compound
- Clothing Optional
- Beautiful Heated Pool
- Gym (machines & free weights)
- Lockers Available
- Expansive 'Bun' Deck
- Indoor & Outdoor Jacuzzis
- Poolside Bar & Cafe
- Sauna
- Steamroom
- Complimentary Happy Hour
- Erotic Video Room
- 24 Hour Front Desk
- Friendly & Capable Staff

Daily, weekly, monthly & annual passes available.
Military men and college students (over 18) always half-price with ID.

ISLAND HOUSE KEY WEST
A TROPICAL RESORT FOR MEN

1129 Fleming St., Key West, FL 33040 • (305) 294-6284 • 800-890-6284
www.islandhousekeywest.com

USA/Florida — Miami ▶ Miami Beach

■ **Cactus Saloon** (B F G VS)
2041 Biscayne Boulevard ✉ FL 33137 ☎ 573-6025
■ **Eagle Miami** (B G P) 20-3 h
1252 Coral Way ☎ 860-0056
Cruise Bar.
■ **El Carol** (B g MA N) 11-3 h
930 South West Le Jeune Road/42nd Avenue ✉ FL 33134
☎ 448-9148
■ **Southpaw Saloon** (B G lj)
7005 Biscayne Boulevard/70th Street North East ✉ FL 33138
☎ 758-9362
■ **Splash** (AC B D GLM OS VS) 16-2 h, closed Mon
5922 South Dixie Highway ✉ FL 33143 ☎ 662-8779
■ **Stables** (B G LJ) 9-3 h
1641 South West 32nd Avenue ✉ FL 33145 *(Coral Gables)*
☎ 446-9137
■ **Waterfront. On the** (B D GLM S)
3615 N W South River Drive ✉ FL 33142 *(near airport)*
☎ 635-5500
The best Latin gay bar in town.

DANCECLUBS
■ **O'Zone** (! B D G MA) 21-5 h
6626 S Red Road/S W 57th Avenue ✉ FL 33143 ☎ 667-2888

RESTAURANTS
■ **Balans** (B BF F glm OS)
1022 Lincoln Road ✉ FL 33139
■ **Terrasse. La** (b F g)
429 Espanola Way, Coral Gables ✉ FL 33139 ☎ 538-2212

SEX SHOPS/BLUE MOVIES
■ **Bird Road Book & Video** (g VS) 0-24 h
6833 Bird Road ✉ FL 33155 ☎ 661-9103
■ **Biscayne Book & Video** 0-24 h
11711 Biscayne Boulevard ✉ FL 33181 ☎ 895-9009
■ **Cutler Ridge** 0-24 h
2316 South West 57th Avenue ✉ FL 33155 ☎ 266-5877
■ **Happy Adult Books** (g VS) 0-24 h
9514 South Dixie Highway ✉ FL 33156 ☎ 661-9349
■ **J+R Book And Video** 0-24 h
7455 South West 40th Street ✉ FL 33155 ☎ 262-6570
■ **Palace Videos** 0-24 h
190 North East 167th Street ✉ FL 33162 ☎ 949-8855
■ **Prime Time** (DR G VS) 0-24 h
14750 North East 16th Avenue ✉ FL 33161 ☎ 948-6745
Glory holes, very active.
■ **Red Road Books & Videos** (G VS) 0-24 h
2316 S Red Road ✉ FL 33155 ☎ 266-5877
■ **167 Street XXX** (g VS) 0-24 h
14 North East 167th Street ✉ FL 33162 ☎ 949-3828
Very active.

SAUNAS/BATHS
■ **Club Body Center** (b CC G MA P S SA SB VS WO) 0-24 h
2991 Coral Way ✉ FL 33145 ☎ 448-2214
Bath house with erotic shop. Tue and Fri at 22 h shows, Sun barbecue.

BOOK SHOPS
■ **Lambda Passages** (CC GLM) Sun 12-18, Mon-Sat 11-21 h
7545 Biscayne Boulevard ✉ FL 33138 ☎ 754-6900
Gay and lesbian video rental club and bookstore.

HOTELS
■ **Cactus Bed & Breakfast** (AC B CC F H MA PI S SNU WH)
2041 Biscayne Boulevard, Dade County ✉ FL 33137 ☎ 438-0662
🖷 438-9576.
■ **Miami River Inn** (BF CC GLM H OS PI WH)
118 South West South River Drive ✉ FL 33130 *(S.W. 2nd Street and S.W. 4th Avenue)* ☎ 325-0045 ☎ (800) HOTEL 89 (toll free)
🖷 325-9227 ✉ miami100@ix.netcom.com
Miami's only gay Bed & Breakfast. 40 rooms individually decorated. Historic buildings from 1906-1913. Centrally located across the Miami river. The only historic Inn in Miami.

GUEST HOUSES
■ **Brigham Garden's Guesthouse** (AC glm H)
1411 Collins Avenue ✉ FL 33139 *(centre of Art deco district, 1/2 block to the beach)* ☎ 531-1331 🖷 538-9898
✉ brighamg@bellsouth.net 🖳 www.brighamgardens.com
8 double rooms, 10 studios and 2 one bedroom-apartments with bath or shower, WC, cable TV, telephone, kitchenette. Rates double rooms US$ 60-95. Studios 75-125. Apartments 110-145. Additional bed US$ 5.

HELP WITH PROBLEMS
■ **Gay Lesbian Bisexual Hotline of Greater Miami**
7545 Biscayne Boulevard ☎ 759-3661

CRUISING
-Bayside Market (lots of Latin and Brasilian tourists)

Miami Beach ☎ 305

✱ Miami Beach (or *SoBe*, South Beach) is a very trendy place. It's interesting to take a look at the reasons for this: The most obvious reason is the *National Historic District*, consisting of 800 renovated Art-Deco-houses. A kitsch dream in pastel shades. Another reason is the clever way that the city government has used the media and dreamlike beach and palm scenery, to promote the city. The *Ocean Drive* is the boulevard next to the beach, where the beautiful and the wanna-be-beautiful saunter along. Parallel to it run Collins and Washington Avenue, which form one side of the gay right angle. The other side is the *Lincoln Road Mall*, a real pedestrian zone (!), in the US (!). Along one of these axes you'll find all gay establishments of the town in walkable distances. It is best to find accomodation in this area and save yourself renting a car. The best time to visit is between October and April, peak season around christmas right into January. Important event are the parties, which begin with *thanksgiving day* (last Thu in November). The climax of this party season is the Winter Party in February. SoBe is situated right next to a major city, Miami. And this city has many things to offer: Little Havanna (SW 8th Street/SW 11th Avenue), where the cuban immigrants have settled, Showtime in Seaquarium, or shopping and strolling around Bayside Marketplace, Coral Gables or Coconut Grove.

✱ Miami Beach (oder modisch *SoBe* für South Beach) ist trendy. Es lohnt sich, den Gründen dafür nachzuspüren. Der offensichtlichste Grund ist der *National Historic District*, 800 renovierte Art-Deco-Häuser. Ein Kitschtraum in Pastell. Ein weiterer Grund sind die Medien: die Stadtverwaltung hat -auch mit Hilfe der Strand-und-Palmen-Traumkulisse- in den letzten Jahren für verstärkte Medienpräsenz der Stadt gesorgt und sie damit noch bekannter gemacht. Und noch interessanter für die Medien. Der *Ocean Drive* ist die Flaniermeile der Schönen und Schön-Sein-Wollenden direkt am Strand, parallel dazu verlaufen Collins und Washington Avenue und bilden damit die eine Seite des schwulen rechten Winkels. Die andere Seite bildet die *Lincoln Road Mall*, eine richtige Fußgängerzone(!), und das in Amerika. Entlang dieser beiden Achsen finden sich alle schwulen Etablissements des Ortes innerhalb überschaubarer Distanzen. In

1226 *SPARTACUS* 2001/2002

Miami Beach — Florida/USA

Miami Beach

1. Abbey Hotel
2. ZMAX Travel & Transport
3. South Beach Vogue Fashion Shop
4. Nassau Suite Hotel
5. Villa Paradiso Guest House
6. Winterhaven Hotel
7. Beachcomber Hotel
8. Island House Guest House
9. Grillfish Restaurant
10. The Bayliss Guest House
11. Twist Bar
12. Lily Guesthouse
13. European Guest House
14. The Jefferson House Guest House
15. South Beach Villas Guest House
16. RGL Loading Zone Bar
17. Balans Restaurant
18. Salvation Danceclub

USA/Florida — Miami Beach

dieser Gegend sollte man auch übernachten, so daß man kein Auto benötigt. Die beste Zeit liegt zwischen Oktober und April, die Hochsaison um Weihnachten bis in den Januar. Wichtige Events sind die Parties, mit denen es nach *Thanksgiving* (letzter Do im Nov) los geht. Höhepunkt ist die Winter Party im Februar. SoBe liegt in direkter Nachbarschaft zu einer Großstadt, Miami nämlich. Und diese Stadt hat einiges zu bieten: Little Havanna (SW 8th Street/SW 11th Avenue), in dem sich die kubanischen Einwanderer niedergelassen haben, Showtime im Seaquarium und Shoppen und Bummeln im Bayside Marketplace, Coral Gables oder Coconut Grove.

Miami Beach (ou "SoBe" pour South Beach, comme disent les initiés) est l'endroit "in" de Floride. Voyons donc pourquoi! C'est d'abord grâce à ses 800 maisons art-déco soigneusement rénovées qui forment ce qu'on appelle le "National Historic District". Un vrai rêve dans les couleurs pastel! Les médias y sont également pour beaucoup. La municipalité a joué la carte de la presse et du cinéma et les investisseurs n'ont eu aucun mal à s'installer dans ce décor de rêve, sous les palmiers de Floride. SoBe y a gagné sur tous les plans: toujours plus célèbre, elle attiré encore plus d'investisseurs et d'entreprises. Ocean Drive, immédiatement au bord de la plage, est la promenade où l'on vient pour voir et être vu. Les dieux et les déesses du littoral s'y bousculent. Les simples mortels aussi. Les artères parallèles sont Collins et Washington Avenue. Elles délimitent le quartier gai avec, de l'autre côté, Lincoln Road Mall, une vraie zone piétonne, chose assez rare en Amérique. C'est le long de ces deux axes que l'on trouve tous les lieux gais de la ville. On peut tout faire à pied, donc pas besoin de voiture, si vous habitez dans le quartier. Le meilleur moment pour visiter Miami Beach, c'est entre octobre et avril. La fête bat son plein entre mi-décembre et mi-janvier. Les fêtes commencent après "Thanksgiving", le dernier jeudi de novembre. On atteint le summum en février avec la "Winter Party". Une des curiosités de SoBe, c'est sa proximité de Miami qui est, elle-même, n'est pas inintéressante: Little Havanna (SW 8th Street/SW 11th Avenue), son aquarium maritime (Seaquarium), ses boutiques et ses boulevards commerçants de Bayside Market, Coral Gables ou Coconut Grove.

Miami Beach (o como se suele decir hoy en día SoBe South Beach) está de moda. Una de las razones es el *National Historic District* que cuenta con 800 edificaciones recientemente reformados en el estilo Art-Deco, un cursi sueño en color pastel. Otra razón son los medios de comunicación que con ayuda de la municipalidad y la belleza de las playas y palmeras se han encargado de dar a conocer más la ciudad. El *Ocean Drive*, la pasarella de la gente guapa y de aquellos que desean serlo, se encuentra directamente junto a la playa, paralela a ella se localizan también las avenidas Collins y Washington. Estas forman uno de los centros gay de la ciudad. La *Lincoln Road Mall* es una zona peatonal (¡Y esto en Estados Unidas!) que también se distingue por su afluencia gay. A lo largo de estas calles y avenidas se encuentran los establecimientos gay del lugar. Es aconsejable pernoctar en esta zona, asi no se necesitará un automovil. Los mejores meses de visita son Octubre y Abril, el tiempo de mayor apogeo es la navidad. Los eventos más importantes son las fiestas que inician después del *Thanksgiving* (día de gracias) (último jueves de Noviembre). El punto culminante es la fiesta de invierno, que se celebra en Febrero. SoBe se localiza directamente en la vecindad de una gran ciudad: Miami, y esta ciudad tiene muchas cosas que ofrecer: Little Havanna (SW 8th. Street/SW 11th Avenue) en la que los emigrantes cubanos se han asentado. Recomendamos la visita al Seaquarium, asi como ir de compras en Bayside Marketplace, Coral Gables o Coconut Grove.

Miami Beach (o *SoBe*, South Beach) è molto alla moda per diversi motivi. Uno è il *National Historic District*, composto da 800 case ristrutturate, in stile art decò: un sogno kitsch dai colori pastello. Un altro motivo è dato dai mass media: l'amministrazione comunale, aiutata dagli scenari favolosi della spiaggia e delle palme, ha incentivato la presenza della città nei film e nelle riprese televisive rendendo Miami ancora più famosa e sempre più interessante come scenario cinetelevisivo. Direttamente sulla spiaggia, l'Ocean Drive è il passeggio dei belli e di coloro che desiderano esserlo; parallelamente cerrono la Collins e la Washington Avenue che insieme formano una parte della zona gay. L'altra parte è costituita dalla *Lincoln Road Mall*, una zona pedonale (molto rara in America). Lungo queste due vie, a piccola distanza, si trovano tutti i locali gay del luogo. Conviene alloggiare in questa zona per fare a meno dell'auto. Il periodo migliore per una visita è tra ottobre ed aprile mentre l'alta stagione va da Natale a gennaio. I *parties* sono eventi molto importanti: il primo è il *Thanksgiving* (l'ultimo giovedì di novembre) ed il culmine il *Winter Party* in febbraio. SoBe si trova in prossimità di Miami che offre a sua volta molti svaghi: Little Havanna (SW 8th Street/SW 11th Av.) dove giungevano gli immigrati cubani, Showtime nel Seaquarium o una passeggiata in Bayside Marketplace, Coral Gables e Coconut grove.

PUBLICATIONS

■ **Miamigo**
c/o Miamigo Publishing, Inc., 1234 Washington Avenue, Suite 200-202 ✉ FL 33139 ☎ 532-5051 🖷 532-5498
✉ miamigomag@aol.com 🌐 www.miamigo.com
Good quality monthly magazine featuring reports and listing on the gay scene in Florida.

BARS

■ **Boardwalk** (B G r SNU VS) 15-5 h
17008 Collins Avenue/Sunny Isles Causeway ✉ FL 33160 *(North Miami Beach)* ☎ 949-4119
Stripper Bar.

■ **Friends** (B G MA r S VS) 15-6 h
17032 Collins Avenue ☎ 949-4112

■ **Laundry**
721 North Lincoln Lane ✉ 33139 ☎ 531-7700

■ **Lucky`s** (B G)
1969 71st Street ✉ FL 33141 ☎ 868-0901

■ **RGR's Loading Zone** (B G LJ) 18-5 h
1426 A Alton Road ✉ FL 33139 ☎ 531-5623
Behind Dominos & Subway. Rear entrance in alley behind Starish of 14Ct. Check out the Leather Zone for the hottest Leather accessories.

■ **Twist** (! AC B CC D G lj MA N OS s SNU STV VS) 13-5 h
1057 Washington Avenue ✉ FL 33139 ☎ 538-9498

DANCECLUBS

■ **Amnesia**
136 Collins Avenue ☎ 531-5353

■ **Crobar**
1445 Washington Avenue ☎ 531-5027

■ **Level**
1235 Washington Avenue ☎ 532-1525

■ **Pump** (B D G YG) Fri, Sat 04-?
841 Washington Avenue ☎ 538 PUMP

■ **Salvation** (B D GLM) Sat 22-05:00h
1771 West Avenue ☎ 673-6508

■ **Score** (! B D G MA OS S VS YG) Thu, Fri & Sat 22-?, Sun 20-?
727 Lincoln Road ✉ FL 33139 *(South Beach, East of Meridian Ave.)* ☎ 535-1111
T-Dance on Sun. Busy every night. Popular.

■ **Shadow Lounge**
1532 Washington Avenue ☎ 531-9411

Miami Beach — Florida/USA

RESTAURANTS

■ **Balans** (AC B BF CC F GLM MA N OS WE SX) Sun-Thu 8-24 h, Fri-Sat 8-1 h
1022 Lincoln Road ✉ FL 33139 *(next to Colony Theatre and to new cinema complex)* ☎ 534-9191

■ **Caffe Torino** (B D F G S TV)
1437 Washington Avenue ✉ FL 33139 ☎ 351-5722
Good reasonably-priced Italian cuisine.

■ **Front Page Cafe** (BF CC F GLM OS) 8-2 h
607 Lincoln Road ✉ FL 33139 ☎ 538-3734

■ **Grillfish Restaurant** (F glm MA N) 18-? h
1444 Collins Avenue, ✉ FL 33139 *(Corner Esponola Way/Collins Avenue)* ☎ 538 99 08
Seafood restaurant. Price range US$ 7.95-14.95. Specializing in fresh grilled fish and diliciously sauced seafood pasta dishes.

■ **Norma's on the Beach** (F glm)
646 Lincoln Road ✉ FL 33139 ☎ 532-2809

■ **Palace Bar & Grill** (B F glm OS YG) 9-2 h
1200 Ocean Drive ✉ FL 33139 *(at 12th St.)* ☎ 531-9207
Popular on Sun after beach.

FITNESS STUDIOS

■ **Gold's**
17050 Collins Avenue ☎ 945-3218

PROPERTY SERVICES

■ **Bret Taylor-Real Estate**
420 Lincoln Road, Suite 260 ✉ FL 33139 ☎ 1-800-438-2783
📠 674-8980.

TRAVEL AND TRANSPORT

■ **ZMAX Travel and Tours, Inc.** (G) 10-18 h
420 Lincoln Road, Suite 239, PO Box 398179 ✉ FL 33139
☎ 532-0111 ☎ 800-864-6429 (toll-free) 📠 532-1222

HOTELS

■ **Abbey Hotel** (AC BF CC E F g H OS SOL NU)
300 21st Street ✉ FL 33139 ☎ 531-0031 ☎ (888) 61-ABBEY
📠 672-1663 📧 reservations@abbeyhotel.com
🖥 www.abbeyhotel.com
Art Deco elegant designed hotel-restaurant. Rooms with all facilities. Parking available.

■ **Beachcomber** (AC CC glm E H)
1340 Collins Avenue ✉ FL 33139 ☎ 531-3755 📠 673-8609
📧 southbcomber@worldnet.att.net

■ **Decowalk Hotel** (AC BF CC f g H) 9-18 h
928 Ocean Drive ✉ FL 33139 ☎ 531-5511

■ **Kenmore Hotel** (B f glm OS PI) 0-24 h
1050 Washington Avenue ✉ FL 33139 *(South Beach)* ☎ 674-1930
📠 534-6591

■ **Nassau Suite Hotel** (AC CC glm E H)
1414 Collins Avenue ✉ FL 33139 ☎ 534-0043 📠 534-3133
🖥 www.nassausuites.com

■ **Shelborne Beach Resort. The** (B F glm H OS PI WH WO) 24 h
1801 Collins Avenue ✉ FL 33139 *(directly at the South Beach ocean, Art Deco district)* ☎ 531-1271 ☎ 800-327-8757 (toll free)
📠 531-2206 📧 info@shelborne.com 🖥 www.shelborne.com

■ **Shore Club Resort** (B F glm H PI)
1901 Collins Avenue, ✉ FL 33139 ☎ 538-7811
☎ (800) 327-8330 (toll free)

■ **Surfcomber. The** (B BF glm H PI)
1717 Collins Avenue, ✉ FL 33139 ☎ 532-7715 ☎ 0130-815 526 (toll free from Europe) 📠 532-2780

■ **Winterhaven Hotel** (AC B CC f glm MA N OS)
1400 Ocean Drive ✉ FL 33139 *(South Beach)* ☎ 531-5571
☎ 800-395-2322 (toll free) 📠 538-3337

GUEST HOUSES

■ **Bayliss Guest House** (AC CC glm E H)
504 14th Street ✉ FL 33139 ☎ 531-3755

■ **European Guesthouse** (AC BF CC Glm H MA NU OS p WH) 8-24 h
721 Michigan Avenue ✉ FL 33139 *(in the center of the art deco district in South Beach)* ☎ 673-6665 📠 672-7442
📧 info@europeanguesthouse.com
🖥 www.europeanguesthouse.com
Walking distance to the beach and gay bars. 12 double rooms, 1 studio, all rooms with bath or shower and WC, balcony or terrace, telephone, Satellite TV, radio, air-conditioning.

ABBEY Hotel

- South Beach–Art Deco District
- New 50 Room Boutique Hotel
- Full Service Restaurant
- Room Service • Lobby Bar
- Fitness Room • 1 Block from Beach
- 2 Blocks fro Miami Beach Convention Center

For Information and to make Reservations:
Call **1-888-61-ABBEY** or
Visit us at
www.abbeyhotel.com

300 21st. Street,
Miami Beach, FL 33139
Tel: 305.531.0031
Fax: 305.672.1663

USA/Florida — Miami Beach

BEST CLOTHING OPTIONAL B&B in South Beach

from $149 — 3 night
$339 — 7 night

Valid May to Nov. 15
Single occupancy
Exceptions apply
All U can eat Buffet Breakfast
2 Nude Decks
Luxury Rooms

www.europeanguesthouse.com
E-mail: info@europeanguesthouse.com
721 Michigan avenue, Miami Beach, FL 33139
Reser. 305-673-6665   Fax. 305-672-7442

THE JEFFERSON HOUSE BED & BREAKFAST

Private Bath • Heated Pool
Tropical Garden • Sun Deck • Art Deco & Antiques
9 Luxury Rooms

SOBE'S ONLY B&B

Deluxe Gourmet Breakfast Included

*"Come Share Our Home
Just Blocks From the Beach"*

305-534-5247
Toll Free 877-599-5247 • FAX 305-534-5953
e-mail: sobejhouse@aol.com
www.thejeffersonhouse.com
1018 Jefferson Av., Miami Beach

THE GREAT VACATION ESCAPE IN THE HEART OF SOUTH BEACH

- Lush Tropical Surroundings
- Large Heated Pool & 8 Man Jacuzzi
- Spacious Luxury Villas
- Pampered Personal Attention
- Full Kitchens
- A/C / Color TV's / VCR King Size Beds
- Free Parking

SOUTH BEACH VILLAS
your south beach vacation guest house
(888) 429-SOBE

1201 WEST AVENUE • MIAMI BEACH FL. 33139 • PH 305.673.9600 • FAX 305.532.6200 • www.southbeachvillas.com

Miami Beach | Florida/USA

ISLAND HOUSE

South Beach's Largest All Gay Guesthouse

South Beach Miami Beach

1428 Collins Ave.
800-382-2422
305-864-2422
FAX 305-865-2220
www.islandhousesouthbeach.com
e-mail: ihsobe@bellsouth.net

IGLTA

USA/Florida — Miami Beach ▸ Orlando

■ **Island House** (AC BF CC G H) 9-23 h
1428 Collins Avenue ⊠ FL 33139 ☏ 864-2422
☏ (0800) 382-2422 (toll free) 📠 865-2220
📧 ihsobe@bellsouth.net 🖥 www.islandhousesouthbeach.com
Award-winning Island House, a fully restored historic Art Deco guesthouse, offers comfortably furnished accommodations for men, ranging from rooms to studios and suites. South Beach's biggest all-gay guesthouse.

■ **Island House Miami Beach** (AC CC Glm H msg NU OS) 9-18 h
715 82nd Street ⊠ FL 33141 ☏ 864-2422
📠 865-2220 📧 ihsobe@bellsouth.net
🖥 www.islandhousesouthbeach.com
Located in a quiet residential neighbourhood. Rooms & studios with fridge/kitchenette. Five minutes to gay nude beach. Check website for rates.

■ **Jefferson House B & B. The** (AC BF CC E GLM H MA OSA PI)
1018 Jefferson Avenue ⊠ FL 33139 *(South Beach)* ☏ 534-5247
☏ (877) 599-5247 (toll-free) 📠 534-5953
📧 sobejhouse@aol.com 🖥 www.thejeffersonhouse.com
Located near Flamingo park. All rooms with private entrance bath, color TV and telephone. Heated pool. Licensed.

■ **Key Guesthouse** (AC CC GLM H MA N OS) 0-24 h
835 Collins Avenue, ⊠ FL 33139 ☏ 535-9900 📠 535-0077

■ **Lily Guesthouse** (BF glm H)
835 Collins Avenue ⊠ FL 33139 ☏ 535-9900 ☏ 800-535-9959 (toll free) 📠 535-0077
In the heart of South beach, luxurious rooms with cable TV, answering machine, telephone and refrigerators.

■ **South Beach Villas** (AC BF CC G H MA PI WH) Office: 9-24 h
1201 West Avenue #4 ⊠ FL 33139 *(Between Alton and West Avenue)* ☏ 673-9600 ☏ (888) 429-7623 (toll free) 📠 532-6200
📧 gaysobe@aol.com 🖥 www.southbeachvillas.com
Renovated 16-unit Art Deco building with private courtyard, dazzling heated pool, jacuzzi and deluxe continental breakfasts. A lush and tropical oasis within walking distance of all the magic that makes South Beach the "American Riviera".

APARTMENTS
■ **Villa Paradiso** (AC CC glm H OS)
1415 Collins Avenue ⊠ FL 33139 ☏ 532-0616 📠 673-5874
📧 villap@gate.net

CRUISING
- Ocean Drive (particulary at 12th Street)
- Around the Flamingo Park (particulary at Meridian Avenue at 13th Street, the park closes from 24 to 5 h, also in the park from 5h)
- Bathhouses at Ocean Drive (10th and 14th Street)
- beach between 18th and 21 St. (from sunset)

Naples ☏ 941

BARS
■ **Galley. The** (AC B BF F GLM MA) 16-?, Sat Sun 11-? h
300 5th Avenue South #121 ⊠ FL 33940 ☏ 262-2509

CAFES
■ **Cafe Flamingo** (B g) 8-2, WE-1 h
947 3rd Avenue North ⊠ FL 33940 ☏ 262-8181

GENERAL GROUPS
■ **Gay People of Naples**
☏ 353-3126

HEALTH GROUPS
■ **AIDS-Hotline**
☏ 263-CARE

Ocala ☏ 904

BARS
■ **Connection** (B GLM N S) 15-2 h
3331 S. Pine Avenue (US 441) ☏ 620-2511

Orlando ☏ 407

GAY INFO
■ **Gay Lesbian & Bisexual Community Center of Central Florida (GLBCC)** (A AC CC d f GLM s) 11-21, Fri -18, Sat 12-19, Sun 13-18 h
934 North Mills Avenue ⊠ FL 32803 ☏ 425-4537 ☏ 843-4297
(24 h hotline) 📠 228-8230 📧 info@glbcc.org 🖥 www.glbcc.org
Social support community center.

PUBLICATIONS
■ **Watermark**
414 North Ferncreek Avenue ⊠ FL 32803 ☏ 481-2243
📠 481-2246 📧 tom@watermarkonline.com
🖥 www.watermarkonline.com
Florida biweekly "distinctive gay & lesbian publication" featuring news, travel, life style and community happenings.

BARS
■ **Cactus Club** (B F GLM OS) 14-2 h
1300 North Mills Avenue ⊠ FL 32803 ☏ 894-3041

■ **Club. The** (A B CC D GLM MA S STV) 21-? h
578 N. Orange Avenue ⊠ FL 32809 ☏ 872-0066
Especially busy Wed & Sat.

■ **Full Moon Saloon** (AC B d f G LJ MA OS VS) 12-2 h
500 North Orange Blossom Trail ⊠ FL 32805 ☏ 648-8725
Cruise bar. Monthly full moon parties.

CLUB ORLANDO ATHLETIC VENTURES
Healthy Life Choices

▸ OPEN 24 HOURS ▸
▸ WOLFF TANNING BEDS ▸
▸ ONE DAY MEMBERSHIPS ▸
▸ STEAM ROOM & SAUNA ▸
▸ CLEAN & MODERN FACILITIES ▸
▸ OUTDOOR POOL & PATIO ▸
▸ TROPICAL GARDEN & JACUZZI ▸
▸ PROPER ID REQUIRED ▸

VISIT OUR MEMBER CLUBS:
Dallas, Houston, St. Louis, New Orleans, Indianapolis, Cleveland, Columbus, and Ft. Lauderdale or visit us on the web at www.the-clubs.com

407.425.5005
450 E. COMPTON ST. · ORLANDO, FLORIDA

Orlando ▶ Port Richey | **Florida/USA**

■ **Hank's** (AC B d G lj) 12-2 h
5026 Edgewater Drive ✉ FL 32810 ☎ 291-2399
■ **Parliament House** (B G LJ S)
410 North Orange Blossom Trail ✉ FL 32805 ☎ 425-7571
■ **Southern Nights** (AC B D f GLM MA OS S tv) 16-2 h
375 South Bumby Avenue ✉ FL 32803 ☎ 898-0424

DANCECLUBS
■ **Power House Disco** (B D G S YG) 20-2 h
410 North Orange Blossom Trail ✉ FL 32805 (at Parliament House)
☎ 425-5771

RESTAURANTS
■ **Dog Out** (B F GLM) 0-24 h
410 North Orange Blossom Trail ✉ FL 32805 (at Parliament House Hotel) ☎ 305/425-7571
■ **Uncle Walt's Backstage** (! AC B CC d e F G MA S) 16-2 h
5454 International Drive ✉ FL 32819 (5 min from Disney, Universal, MGM) ☎ 351-4866
Cabaret shows Wed Fri Sat, 2 shows nightly, cover US$2-3. Piano Bar Thu Fri Happy hour. Appetizer menu, pizza, pasta.
■ **Union Deli** (BF CC F glm MA)
337 North Shine Avenue ☎ 894-5778

SEX SHOPS/BLUE MOVIES
■ **Leather Xplosion** (GLM LJ) 21-2 h
410 North Orange Blossom Trail ✉ FL 32805 ☎ 425-7571 ext139
Books, movies, videos, leather.

FITNESS STUDIOS
■ **Club Orlando Athletic Ventures** (AC CC f G MA P OS PI SA SB WH WO) 0-24 h
450 East Compton Street ✉ FL 32806 ☎ 425-5005
Sauna with complete gym equipment.

BOOK SHOPS
■ **Out & About Books** (AC CC GLM) Mon-Thu 10-20, Fri-Sat -21, Sun 12-19 h
930 North Mills Avenue ✉ FL 32803 ☎ 896-0204

GIFT & PRIDE SHOPS
■ **Rainbow City** (CC GLM)
934 North Mills Avenue ✉ FL 32803 ☎ 898-6096
Cards, T-shirts, magazines, bumper stickers, gifts.

LEATHER & FETISH SHOPS
■ **Eagle Shop** (LJ)
3400 S. Orange Blossom Trail ✉ FL 32839 ☎ 843-3374

HOTELS
■ **Parliament House** (B D F GLM H MA PI S WO)
410 North Orange Blossom Trail ✉ FL 32805 ☎ 425-7571
🗐 425-5881
■ **Veranda Bed & Breakfast. The** (AC CC BF glm msg OS PI WH WO) 7-19 (weekdays) 8-16 (weekends)
115 North Summerlin Avenue ✉ FL 32801 ☎ 849-0321
☎ (800) 420-6822 (toll free) 🗐 849-0321 💻 www.theverandabandb.com
Historic building. Rates US$89-159. Colour cable TV, telephone, kitchen, fridge, coffee/tea facilities.Complimentary bf.

GENERAL GROUPS
■ **Bears of Central Florida**
PO Box 647 ✉ FL 32802-0647

FETISH GROUPS
■ **Black Star MC**
c/o Loading Dock, 3400 South Orange Blossom Tr. ✉ FL 32839

HEALTH GROUPS
■ **AIDS-Hotline**
☎ (800) 342-2437 (toll free)
■ **VD Clinic**
832 West Central ✉ FL 32805 ☎ 420-3600

CRUISING
-Colonial Plaza Shopping Mall
-Eola Park & Drive (AYOR)
-Fashion Square Shopping Mall
-Rest Stop (AYOR) (on I-4 Buena Vista)

Panama City Beach ☎ 904

BARS
■ **Fiesta Room Lounge** (AC B D GLM lj MA r S STV) 20-3, Fri-Sat -4 h
110 Harrison Avenue ✉ FL 32401 ☎ 784-9311
■ **Royale Lounge. La** (AC B d GLM lj MA r) 15-3, Fri-Sat 16-4 h
100 Harrison Avenue ✉ FL 32401-2726 ☎ 784-9311

SWIMMING
-Seagrove Beach (NU) (west of Panama City Beach)
-Phillip's Inlet County Beach (½ mile West of Ramsgate Harbor)

Pensacola ☎ 850

BARS
■ **Emerald City** (AC B D GLM MA OS P s STV WE) Wed-Sun 15-3 h
406 East Wright Street ✉ FL 32501 ☎ 433-9491
■ **Red Carpet** (B D GLM QS S) 15-2.30 h
937 Warrington Road ✉ FL 32507 ☎ 453-9918
■ **Red Garter** (B D GLM S YG) 20-2h, closed Mon Tue
1 West Main Street ✉ FL 32501 ☎ 432-9188
■ **Roundup** (B G VS YG) Mon-Fri 15-2, Sat 13-2, Sun 13-1 h
706 East Gregory Street ✉ FL 32501 ☎ 438-8482

PRIVATE ACCOMMODATION
■ **Mill House Inn.B&B** (AC cc f GLM msg NU WH) all year
9603 Lillian Highway ✉ FL 32506 (West of town, on Perdido Bay)
☎ 455-3400 ☎ (888) 999-4575 (toll-free) 🗐 458-6397
💻 millhouseinn@aol.com 💻 millhouseinnbandb.com

SWIMMING
-Beach on Santa Rosa Island (Fort Picken's "BA" Beach)
-Gay Dunes Beach (Dunes and Trails 7 miles West of Navarre Beach)
-Penscola Beach

CRUISING
-Old Chimney (near bluff on scenic highway)

Port Richey ☎ 813

BARS
■ **BT's** (B CC G MA S) 18-2 h
7737 Grand Boulevard ☎ 841-7900

Saint Petersburg ☎ 813

PUBLICATIONS
■ **TLW - The Last Word Magazine**
PO Box 21512 ✉ FL 33742 ☎ (727) 579-4220 📠 (727) 579-4822
📧 tlastword@aol.com 💻 www.tlwmen.com
The Southeast's biweekly gay entertainment magazine for men.

BARS
■ **D.T.'s** (B G S) 14-2 h
2612 Central Avenue ✉ FL 33712 ☎ 327-8204
■ **Golden Arrow** (B G) 13-2 h
10604 Gandy Boulevard ✉ FL 33702 ☎ 577-7774
■ **Haymarket Pub** (B G MA) 16-2 h
8308 4th Street No. ☎ 577-9621
■ **New Connection** (B D GLM) 13-2 h
3100 3rd Avenue North ☎ 321-2112

RESTAURANTS
■ **Keystone Club Restaurant** (B F g) Mon-Fri 11.30-14.30 17-22 h
320 4th Street North ✉ FL 33701 ☎ 822-6600
Fresh seafood, French and domestic wines. Specialty: Prime Angus Beef Filets.

SEX SHOPS/BLUE MOVIES
■ **4th Street Books & Videos** (g VS)
1427 4th Street/14th Avenue ✉ FL 33706 ☎ 821-8824

HOTELS
■ **Suncoast Resort Hotel** (A AC B BF CC D F GLM H LJ MA OS PI SNU STV)
3000 34th Street, South ✉ FL 33711 *(only minutes from the Gulf of Mexico beaches)* ☎ 727/867-1111 📠 727/867-7068
💻 www.suncoastresort.com
120 hotel rooms & suites, 6 bars, 2 restaurants, 30,000 Sq. Ft. shopping mall, 15,000 Sq. Ft. convention area, 9 tennis courts, 2 volleyball courts, swimming pool.

FETISH GROUPS
■ **Adventurers-Suncoast MC**
PO BOX 8043 ✉ FL 33738

HEALTH GROUPS
■ **VD-Clinic**
500 7th Avenue ✉ FL 33706 ☎ 894-1184

SWIMMING
-Pass-a-Grille Beach (southern end)
-Treasure Island/Beach in front of Bedrox

CRUISING
-Bayshore Drive (from 2nd Street to Vinoy Park)
-Maximo Park
-Pass-a-Grille Beach (below 8th Street)
-Skyway Bridge Park

Sarasota ☎ 941

BARS
■ **Club Rowdy's** (AC B CC d DR G lj MA OS S VS) 12-2 h
1330 27th Street ✉ FL 34243 ☎ 953-5945
■ **H.G. Rooster's** (AC B d G MA OS s SNU VS) 15-2 h
1256 Old Stickney Point Road ✉ FL 34242 ☎ 346-3000

HOTELS
■ **Normandy Inn** (BF g H OS)
400 North Tamiami Trail ✉ FL 34236-4822 ☎ 366-8973
☎ (800) 282-8050 (Toll-free)
With own tropical outdoor cafe called "Billa Bowlegs Banana Patch".

GUEST HOUSES
■ **Vera's Place Bed & Breakfast** (AC BF G p Pl)
3913 Chapel Drive ✉ FL 34234 ☎ 351-3171
Private bath, heated pool, full breakfast.

CRUISING
-Gulfstream Avenue P (Ringling Boulevard and Gulfstream)
-North Lido Beach
-Palm Avenue (AYOR R)

Satellite Beach ☎ 407

SEX SHOPS/BLUE MOVIES
■ **Space Age Books & Temptations**
63 Ocean Boulevard ✉ FL 32937 ☎ 773-7660

South Beach

GAY INFO
☞ Miami Beach

Tallahassee ☎ 850

PUBLICATIONS
■ **Community News**
PO Box 14682 ✉ FL 32317-4682 ☎ 425.6397 📠 222.3783
📧 igranick@queerpress.com 💻 www.queerpress.com
Monthly magazine reporting on political and legislative issues affecting the G&L community.

BARS
■ **Brothers** (AC B CC D GLM OS S WE YG) 16-2 h
926 West Thorpe Street ✉ FL 32303 ☎ 386-2399
■ **Club Park Avenue** (B G S VS YG) 21-2 h
115 East Park Avenue ✉ FL 32301 ☎ 599-9143

CRUISING
-Rest Area US 319 North
-Florida State University (library)
-Last Lake (southwest on Route 373)
-Park by post office (opposite Club Park Avenue)

Tampa ☎ 813

GAY INFO
■ **Hotline** 19-23 h
1222 South Dale Mabry Street ✉ FL 33611 ☎ 229-8839
■ **Stonewall**
3225 S. MacDill Avd. S-220 ✉ FL 33629 ☎ 832-2878
📠 887-3544

PUBLICATIONS
■ **Gazette. The**
PO Box 2650, Brandon ✉ FL 33509-2650 ☎ 689-7566
☎ 654-6995 📧 gazette@tampabay.rr.com
Florida's gay and lesbian news magazine.

BARS
■ **Angel's** (B G MA SNU) Mon-Sun 11-?
4502 South Dale Mabry ✉ FL 33611 ☎ 831-9980
■ **Annex. The** (B G) 11-? h
2408 West Kennedy Boulevard ✉ FL 33609 ☎ 254-4188
■ **City Side** (B G OS S)
3810 Neptune Street ✉ FL 33629 ☎ 254-6466

Tampa ▶ Atlanta Florida - Georgia/USA

- **Club Matrix** (B D F GLM) 16-3, Thu-Sat -4.30, Sun 12-3 h
105 W. Martin Luther King Boulevard ☏ 237-8883
- **Howard Avenue Station** (B D G snu)
3003 North Howard Avenue ✉ FL 33607 ☏ 254-7194
- **Jungle** (AC B CC D GLM MA N OS VS) 15-3 h
3703 Henderson Boulevard ✉ FL 33609 ☏ 877-3290
- **Keith's Lounge** (B Glm N) 13-3 h
14905 North Nebraska Avenue ☏ 971-3576
- **Metropolis** (B G MA S)
3447 West Kennedy Boulevard ☏ 871-2410
- **Tampa Brigg. The** (AC B G LJ MA N OS SNU S) 15-03:00h
9002 North Florida Avenue ✉ FL 33604 (south of Busch Boulevard) ☏ 931-3396
Tampa's oldest gay owned and run bar. Male strippers Fri & Sat.
- **2606 Club** (AC B G lj MA) 20-3 h
2606 North Armenia Avenue ✉ FL 33607 ☏ 875-6993
Cruising western style bar.

DANCECLUBS

- **Pleasuredome** (! B D GLM STV)
1430 East 7th Avenue/15th Street ✉ FL 33605 (Ybor City) ☏ 247-2006

SEX SHOPS/BLUE MOVIES

- **Buddies Video** (G VS)
4322 W. Crest Avenue ✉ FL 33614 ☏ 876-8083
- **XTC** (glm VS)
4829 Lois Avenue ✉ FL 33614 ☏ 871-6900

SAUNAS/BATHS

- **Club Tampa Baths** (B f G NU P SA WH) 0-24 h
215 North 11th Street ✉ FL 33602 ☏ 223-5181

FITNESS STUDIOS

- **Metro Flex** (G WO)
2511 Swann Avenue ✉ FL 33609

FETISH GROUPS

- **FFA, Tampa Bay**
1230 East Mohawk Avenue ✉ FL 33610

CRUISING

- Picnic Island Park
- Ben T. Davis Beach (AYOR) (Campbell Causeway)

West Palm Beach ☏ 561

BARS

- **H.G. Rooster's** (AC B G MA OS s SNU VS) 15-3, Fri Sat -4 h
823 Belvedere Road ✉ FL 33405 ☏ 833-4045
- **Kozlow's** (B F glm OS) 12-2, Fri Sat-4 h
6205 Georgia Avenue ✉ FL 33405 ☏ 533-5355
- **5101 Bar** (B G N) Mon-Thu 7-3, Fri Sat-4, Sun 12-3 h
5101 South Dixie Highway ✉ FL 33405 ☏ 585-2379

HOTELS

- **Hibiscus House** (AC B BF CC glm MA OS PI) 24 h
501 30th Street ✉ FL 33407 (city centre) ☏ 863-5633
☏ (800) 203-4927 (Toll-free) 🖨 863-5633
📧 hibiscushouse@mymailstation.com 💻 www.hibiscushouse.com
Rates US$ 65-170 (low season), 95-250 (high season).

GUEST HOUSES

- **Casa Piña** (AC BF G H OS PI)
PO Box 17 602 ✉ FL 33416 ☏ 820-8872
📧 lambskul@ix.netcom.com

CRUISING

- Curry Park (AYOR)
- Dixie Highway (from Belvedere Boulevard to Forrest Hill)
- MacArthur Park Beach
- Seawall (summers)

Wilton Manors ☏ 954

PUBLICATIONS

- **Express. The**
1595 North East 26th Street ✉ FL 33305 ☏ 568-1880
🖨 568-5110 📧 publisher@expressgaynews.com
💻 www.expressgaynews.com
"County independent gay & lesbian newspaper" published twice a month.

CAFES

- **Chardees Courtyard Cafe** (BF F GLM MA) 7-15 h
2211 Wilton Drive ✉ FL 33305 ☏ 563-2499

RESTAURANTS

- **Chardees Dinner Club** (B CC d F GLM MA S) 16.30-1, Sun Brunch 11-15 h
2209 Wilton Drive ✉ FL 33305 ☏ 563-1800
Piano Bar. Traditional American cuisine.

USA-Georgia

Location: Southeast USA
Initials: GA
Time: GMT -5
Area: 153.952 km^2 / 62,966 sq mi.
Population: 7,486,000
Capital: Atlanta

Athens ☏ 706

DANCECLUBS

- **Boneshakers** (B D GLM MA OS) closed Sun
433 East Hancock Avenue ✉ GA 30601 ☏ 543-1555
A dance floor, a pool bar, a video bar, and a huge backyard.

Atlanta ☏ 404

GAY INFO

- **Atlanta Gay & Lesbian Center** 14-21 h EST
159 Ralph McGill Blvd., Suite 600 ✉ GA 30308 (Downtown, GLBT Community Center) ☏ 523-7500 📧 jpetty@agcl.org
💻 www.aglc.org

PUBLICATIONS

- **Etcetera Magazine**
151 Renaissance Parkway North East ✉ GA 30308 ☏ 888-0063
🖨 888-0910 📧 etc@mindspring.com 💻 www.etcmag.com
Queer full-color, glossy magazine distributed for free each week in six Southern states (Georgia, North Carolina, South Carolina, Tennessee, Alabama and North Florida).
- **Southern Voice**
1095 Zonolite Road #100 ✉ GA 30306 ☏ 876-1819
📧 ccrain@sovo.com 💻 www.sovo.com
Weekly G&L magazine covering all the Mid-South and the Gulf Coast.

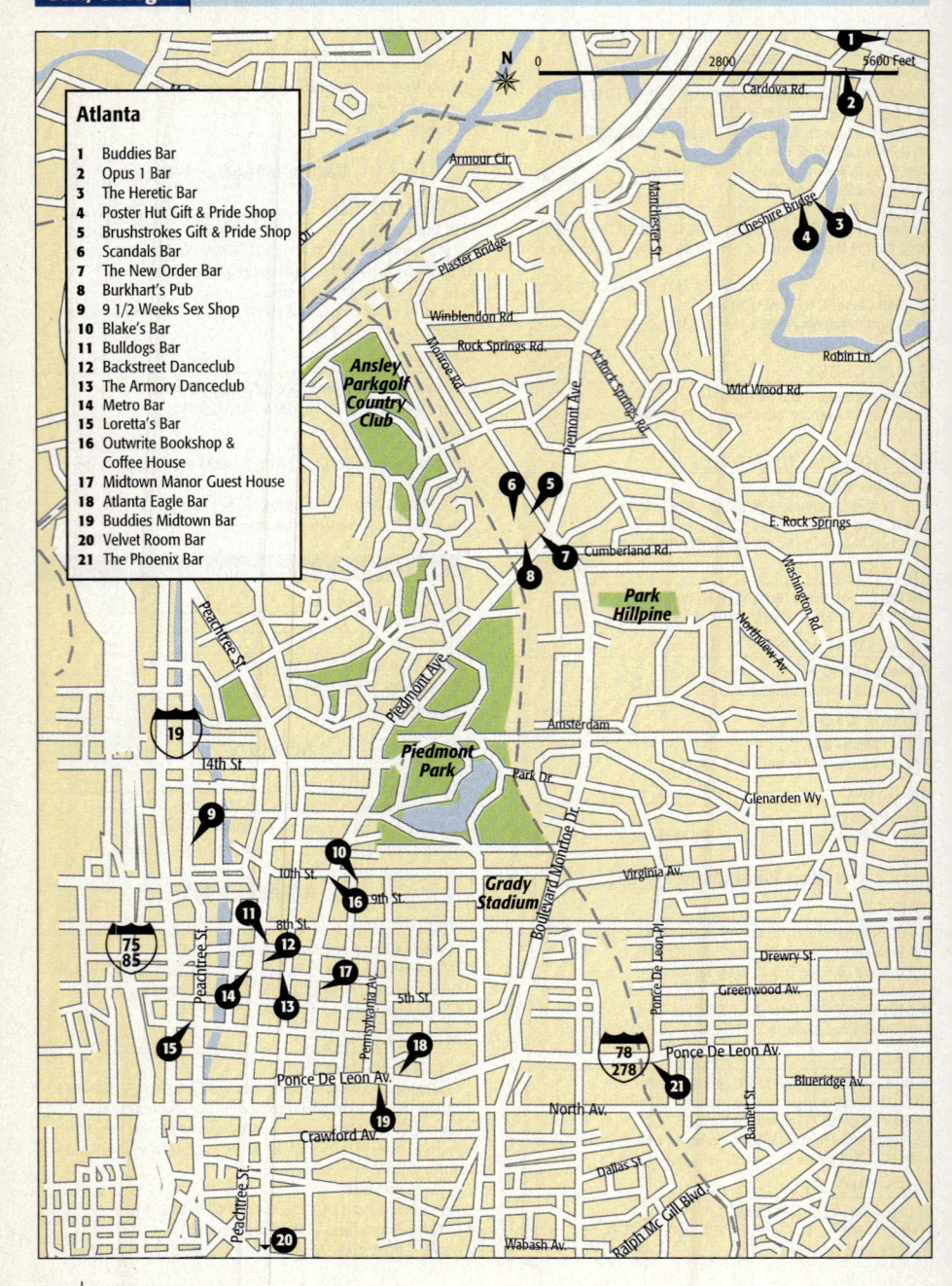

USA/Georgia — Atlanta

Atlanta

1. Buddies Bar
2. Opus 1 Bar
3. The Heretic Bar
4. Poster Hut Gift & Pride Shop
5. Brushstrokes Gift & Pride Shop
6. Scandals Bar
7. The New Order Bar
8. Burkhart's Pub
9. 9 1/2 Weeks Sex Shop
10. Blake's Bar
11. Bulldogs Bar
12. Backstreet Danceclub
13. The Armory Danceclub
14. Metro Bar
15. Loretta's Bar
16. Outwrite Bookshop & Coffee House
17. Midtown Manor Guest House
18. Atlanta Eagle Bar
19. Buddies Midtown Bar
20. Velvet Room Bar
21. The Phoenix Bar

Atlanta Georgia/USA

CULTURE
■ **Planet Claire**
753 Edgewood Avenue ✉ GA 30307 ☎ 522-5620
Gay community arts center.

TOURIST INFO
■ **Atlanta Convention & Visitor Bureau**
233 Peachtree Street NE, Ste. 2000 ✉ GA 30303 ☎ 521-6600

BARS
■ **Atlanta Eagle** (B D G LJ) 19-? h, Sun 17-? h
308 Ponce De Leon Avenue ✉ GA 30308 ☎ 873-2453
■ **Blake's** (B Glm MA N OS stv snu vs) 15-4, Sun Brunch 12-15 h
227 10th Street North East ✉ GA 30309 ☎ 892-5786
■ **Buddies Cheshire Square** (B G N MA)
2345 Cheshire Bridge Road, Cheshire Bridge ✉ GA 30324
☎ 634-5895
Four pool tables & 2 bars.
■ **Buddies Midtown** (B G) 16-4h
239 Ponce de Leon Avenue ✉ GA 30324 ☎ 872-2655
■ **Bulldogs** (B G LJ OS) Sun-Fri 14-4h, Sat -3h
893 Peachtree Street ✉ GA 30308 ☎ 872-3025
Cruisy. Popular Sun evening.
■ **Burkhart's Pub** (AC B CC G MA N OS s) 14-3 h
1492-F Piedmont Avenue ✉ GA 30309 *(Near Ansley Square)*
☎ 872-4403
The Original Gospel Girls with the Gospel Echos Sun 19.30 & 22.30h. Karaoke almost every night.
■ **Buzz. Le** (B D GLM MA OS)
585 Franklin Road *(Mariett)* ☎ (770) 424-1337
A liquor-Espresso Bar in the north suburbs.
■ **Club Colours** (B GLM MA stv)
1492 Piedmont Avenue North East *(Ansley Square)* ☎ 724-0611
Drag shows a couple nights a week.
■ **Heretic. The** (AC B D F G LJ MA s VS) 12-4 h
2069 Cheshire Bridge Road, Cheshire Bridge ✉ GA 30324
☎ 325-3061
Shows 1st/3rd Sun at 18 h. Wed & Sun parties with strict dress code for access to certain parts of the bar! Leather shop located inside the bar.
■ **Hoedowns** (B D GLM)
931 Monroe Drive ☎ 876-0001
Western-style bar with country music and dance courses.
■ **Loretta's** (B D glm S) 18-4h
908 Spring Street ☎ 874-8125
■ **Mary's** (B G MA) 20-2 h
1287 Glenwood Avenue *(East Atlanta)* ☎ 624-4311
■ **Metro** (B G MA SNU tv VS YG) 15-4 h
1080 Peachtree Street North East ✉ GA 30308 ☎ 874-9869
Video monitors show music videos. Go-go boys are at work seven nights a week. This is the bar that brings porn stars, dancers, and drag queens in from out of town for special appearances.
■ **Midtown Saloon & Grill** (B F GLM N) 14-2, Sat 12-2, Sun 13-2, restaurant Mon-Sat 17-21 h
736 Ponce de Leon Avenue ☎ 874-1655
■ **Miss Q's** (B G MA stv) 16-2, Sat-Sun 12-2, closed Mon, shows on Wed at 19.30 h
560-B Amsterdam Avenue North East ☎ 875-6255
A casual place with couches & music.
■ **Model T** (B G N stv)
699 Ponce De Leon Avenue ☎ 872-2209
■ **Moreland Tavern. The** (B F GLM N stv)
1196 Moreland Avenue South East ✉ GA 30316 ☎ 622-4650

■ **New Order Lounge** (AC B G MG N) 14-2 h, Fri & Sat -3h
1544 Piedmont Avenue ✉ GA 30324 *(on back side of Ansley Mall Shopping Centre)* ☎ 874-8247
■ **Opus 1** (B G N stv) Mon-Sat 21-?, Sun 12.30-? h
1086 Alco Street ✉ GA 30324 *(at Cheshire Bridge Road)*
☎ 634-6478
Show Sun. Known for cheap strong drinks.
■ **Phoenix. The** (B G MA N) Mon-Fri 9-4, Sat -3, Sun 12.30-4 h
567 Ponce de Leon Avenue ✉ GA 30308 ☎ 892-7871
■ **Scandals** (B f G N s) Mon-Fri 11.30-4, Sat -3, Sun 12.30-4 h
1510 G-Piedmont Road, Ansley ✉ GA 30324 ☎ 875-5957
One jukebox, one pool table, one bar.
■ **Sequel. The** (B D G STV)
708 Spring Street North West ✉ GA 30308 ☎ 874-8125
Jazz bar with smoked mirrors frequented mostly by a beautiful African-American male crowd.
■ **Velvet Room** (B GLM STV) Thu show at 22 h
1021 Peachtree Road ☎ 876-6275

CAFES
■ **Mary Mac's Tea Room** (! B F G N) Mon-Fri 11-21 h, Sat 17-21 h, Sun 11-15 h
224 Ponce de Leon Avenue, NE ✉ GA 30308 ☎ 876-1800
A good place to meet locals.

DANCECLUBS
■ **Armory** (B D F GLM) 16-3, Fri -4h
836 Juniper Street *(at 7th Street)* ☎ 881-9280
■ **Backstreet Atlanta** (AC B CC D f GLM MA stv WE) 0-24 h
845 Peachtree Street North East ✉ GA 30308 *(rear entrance)*
☎ 873-1986
Also featuring Charlie Brown's Cabaret. Very busy 3-6 h. Shows Thu-Sun.
■ **Deux Plex** (B D F G MA) Bistro: Tue-Sun 17-2.30, Club: Thu-Sun 23-3 h
1789 Cheshire Bridge Road ✉ GA 30324 ☎ 733-5900
Casual French-style bistro cuisine on the first floor, dance floor on the ground floor.
■ **Fusion** (B D GLM MA)
550-C Amsterdam Avenue ☎ 872-6411
Club with two water fountains with a hardwood dance populat with an African American crowd on Fri nights.
■ **Otherside** (B D f GLM S VS) 17-4 h
1924 Piedmont Avenue *(At Chesire Bridge)* ☎ 875-5238
Friendly black and white bar. Many special nights.
■ **Traxx** (B D G s OS) Sat 22-4 h
306 Luckie Street ✉ GA 30313 ☎ 681-5033

RESTAURANTS
■ **Babushka's** (F g)
469 North Highland Avenue ✉ GA 30307 ☎ 688-0836
Eastern European style cuisine.
■ **Cowtippers** (AC B CC F g OS)
1600 Piedmont Avenue ✉ GA 30316 ☎ 874-3751
■ **Einstein's** (AC B CC F g OS)
1077 Juniper ✉ GA 30309 ☎ 876-7925
■ **Mambo Restaurante Cubano** (F G)
1402 North Highland Avenue ✉ GA 30306 ☎ 876-2626
■ **Pleasant Pleasant** (E F g)
555 Peachtree Street ✉ GA 30303 ☎ 874-3223
■ **Prince George Inn** (AC F GLM MA N OS) Wed Thu 17-23, Fri Sat 17-24, Sun 12-15 (brunch), 17-22 h (dinner)
114 6th Street ✉ GA 30316 ☎ 724-4669

SPARTACUS 2001/2002 | 1237

USA/Georgia — Atlanta ▸ Augusta

■ **St. Agnes Tea Garden** (B F glm) Mon-Fri 8-14 h, 18-22 h, Sat Sun 8-23 h
222 E. Howard Avenue ☎ 370-1995
■ **Veni Vidi Vici** (E F g)
41 14th Street ✉ GA 30309 ☎ 875-8344

SEX SHOPS/BLUE MOVIES
■ **9 1/2 Weeks** (GLM)
2628 Piedmont Avenue ⊔ GA 30324
Lingerie, Cards, lotions, games, gifts, leather, adult toys, videos.

SAUNAS/BATHS
■ **Flex** (b f G MA PI SA SB VS) 0-24 h
76 4th Street North East ✉ GA 30308 ☎ 815-0456
Large heated pool and free condoms. Theme party 3rd Sat of the month 22-4 h, Patio Cookout 1st Sat of the month.

FITNESS STUDIOS
■ **Mid-City Fitness Center** (AC G SA SB WO) Mon-Thu 6-23 h, Fri -22 h, Sat 10-20 h, Sun 11-17 h
2201 Faulkner Road ✉ GA 30324 ☎ 321-6507

BOOK SHOPS
■ **Outwrite Bookstore & Coffeehouse** (! A AC CC F GLM MA OS) Sun-Thu 8-23 h, Fri Sat -24 h
991 Piedmont Avenue ✉ GA 30309 (at 10th St) ☎ 607-0082
Books, music, videos, cards, gifts, sandwiches, hot and iced drinks.

GIFT & PRIDE SHOPS
■ **Brushstrokes/Sensory Overload** (CC GLM) Sun-Thu 10-22, Fri Sat 10-23 h
1510 Piedmont Avenue N.E. ✉ GA 30324 ☎ 876-6557
Gifts, cards, videos and music. Also: "Capulets- A shop for Gift Givers", gay-owned and operated, at 1510 H Piedmont Ave. Same openig hours.www.capulets.com.
■ **Poster Hut** (GLM)
2175 Cheshire Bridge Road ✉ GA 30324 ☎ 633-7491
Gay Department Store. Clothing, leather, rubber, fetish, housewares, clocks, cards, stationery, posters, artwork.

LEATHER & FETISH SHOPS
■ **Gryphon Leathers**
2069 Cheshire Bridge Road ✉ GA 30324 ☎ 325-3061
■ **Mohawk Leather**
306 Ponce de Leon ✉ GA 30308 ☎ 873-2453

TRAVEL AND TRANSPORT
■ **Midtown Travel** 9-17 h, Sat 10-15 h
1830 Piedmont Road, #F ✉ GA 30324 ☎ 872-8308
Travel agency.

HOTELS
■ **Midtown Manor** (GLM H)
811 Piedmont Avenue, N.E., ✉ GA 30308 ☎ 872-5846
☎ (800) 724-4381 ✉ MidtownMoe@aol.com
🖥 www.trdigital.com/Midtown/Manor

GUEST HOUSES
■ **Abbett Inn** (AC BF CC GLM)
1746 Virginia Ave, College Park ✉ GA 30337 (Close to hartsfield Intern. Airport) ☎ 767-3708 📠 767-1626
✉ abbettinn@bellsouth.net 🖥 www.abbettinn.com

OUTWRITE BOOKSTORE & COFFEEHOUSE

YOUR ATLANTA WELCOME CENTER!

Thousands of Books, Magazines, Videos, the Best Collection of Music in Town, Colossal Baked Goods, Sandwiches, and Damn Good Coffee.

ATLANTA'S GAY & LESBIAN **OUTWRITE BOOKSTORE & COFFEEHOUSE**

Sun-Thur 8am-11pm
Fri & Sat 8am-midnight

991 PIEDMONT AVE. @ 10th ST.
MIDTOWN ATLANTA
TEL: (404) 607-0082
www.outwritebooks.com

The South's Source for Information on Our Lives.

GENERAL GROUPS
■ **Black & White Men Together**
☎ 794-2968

HEALTH GROUPS
■ **AIDS Information Line**
☎ 876-9944

HELP WITH PROBLEMS
■ **Gay Helpline** 18-23 h
☎ 892-0661

CRUISING
- Cabbage Town (AYOR) (Grant Park)
- Chattahoochee Park (AYOR) (nature trails)
- Cypress Street/"The Strip" (AYOR) (alley between Peachtree & West Peachtree from 6th to 8th Streets)
- Lenox Square Mall
- Peachtree Center Shopping Gallery (800 Peachtree N.E.)
- Piedmont Park (AYOR) (nature trails & botanical gardens)

Augusta ☎ 706

BARS
■ **Barracks, The** (B glm MA)
1923 Walton Way (entrance at the rear on Heckle Sreet)
☎ 481-8829
■ **Walton Way Station** (B D GLM MA S) 21-3 h, closed Sun
1632 Walton Way ☎ 733-2603

Augusta ▶ Hawaii | Georgia - Hawaii/USA

HOTELS

■ **Parliament Social Club** (B G H MA P)
1250 Gordon Highway ☎ 722-1155 ✉ info@p-house.com
🖥 www.p-house.com
Check website for more infos. Many special events.

Savannah ☎ 912

BARS

■ **Felicia's** (AC B CC D F GLM MA stv VS WE) Mon-Sat 16-3, Sun 16-2, shows Fri Sat 23 h
416 West Old Liberty Street ✉ GA 31401 (Next to Bank of America)
☎ 238-4788

GUEST HOUSES

■ **912 Barnard Bed & Breakfast** (AC BF f GLM H MA OS) all year round
912 Barnard Street ✉ GA 31401 (historic district) ☎ 234-9121
🖨 944-0996 ✉ 912barnard@msn.com 🖥 www.912barnard.com
2 single rooms with bath, shower, WC, balcony, TV, VCR, own key and room service. Casual, home-like atmosphere. Rates US$ 99 plus 12 % tax per room, per night, bf incl.

PRIVATE ACCOMMODATION

■ **Green Palm Inn** (AC BF cc glm H)
546 East President Street ✉ GA 31401 (historic district, near River-front) ☎ 447-8901 ☎ (888) 606-9510 🖨 233-9525
✉ greepalminn@aol.com 🖥 www.greenpalminn.com
Rooms with AC, bath, phone, radio, TV. Own key and car place. One studio with kitchen. Rates from US$ 99-169.

USA-Hawaii

Location: Pacific region USA
Initials: HI
Time: GMT -10
Area: 28.313 km² / 11,580 sq mi.
Population: 1,187.000
Capital: Honolulu
Important gay cities: Honolulu and Waikiki

Hawaii ☎ 808

PUBLICATIONS

■ **Honolulu Weekly** (GLM)
1200 Cottage Walk, Suite 214 ✉ HI 96817 ☎ 528-1475
🖨 528-3144 ✉ editorial@honoluluweekly.com
🖥 www.honoluluweekly.com
■ **Odyssey Magazine**
PMB 3247, 1750 Kalakaua Ave #103, Honolulu ✉ HI 96826
☎ 955-5959 ✉ odysseyhi@aol.com
🖥 www.hawaiiscene.com/odyssey
Monthly gay and lesbian magazine with infos and gossip.
■ **Outspoken**
PO Box 1746, Pahoa ✉ HI 96778 ☎ 935-2769
✉ outspokenhawaii@aol.com 🖥 www.outinhawaii.com
Queer resources and information for the island of Hawaii.

KAUAI
NIIHAU Kaloa
OAHU
Honolulu
MOLOKAI
LANAI
MAUI
KAHOOLAWE
Captain Cook
HAWAII

Pacific Ocean

USA/Hawaii — Hawaii-Captain Cook ▶ Hawaii-Pahoa

Hawaii-Captain Cook ☎ 808

GUEST HOUSES
■ **Hale Aloha Guest Ranch** (AC BF GLM MA msg NU OS WH) 8-20 h
84-4780 Mamalahoa Highway ✉ HI 96704 ☎ 328-3188
☎ (800) 897-3188 (toll free) 📠 328-8955
📧 vacation@halealoha.com 🖥 www.halealoha.com
Luxurious house located on the mountain side of Mauna Loa Volcano overlooking Kona coast of the Big Island of Hawaii. 3 guest rooms with shared bath and kitchen. Mastersuite with private jacuzzi tub. Rates: room US$ 70-80, suite $140. Bf incl.

Hawaii-Honaunau ☎ 808

TRAVEL AND TRANSPORT
■ **Matt's Rainbow Tours/Rainbow Handbook Hawaii** (GLM)
PO Box 100 ✉ HI 96726 ☎ 328-8654
Gay Tour Company & Gay Travel Guide book of Hawaii.

Hawaii-Kailua Kona ☎ 808

BARS
■ **Mask Bar & Grill** (B D F G STV) 18-2 h, disco Fri Sat 22.30-? h
75-5660 Kopiko Street ✉ HI 96740 (at Cathedral Plaza)
☎ 329-8558
■ **Other Side, The** (AC CC g MA N WE) Mon-Thu 12-24 h, Fri Sat -2 h
74-5484 A-120 Kaiwi Street ✉ HI 96740 (In old industrial area)
☎ 329-7226

HOTELS
■ **Big Island Guest House** (BF g H msg NU)
77-344 Nohealani Street ✉ HI 96740-9785 ☎ 324-6712
■ **Hale Kipa 'O Pele** (BF cc G H msg WH)
75-5852 Alii Drive ✉ HI 96745 ☎ 329-8676 ☎ (800) 528-2456
(toll-free) 📧 halekipa@gte.ne
■ **Plumeria House** (g H)
77-6546 Naniloa Drive ✉ HI 96740 ☎ 322-8164
Six miles south of Kailua, located between two beaches. Vacation rental with private bath, kitchenette, TV and phone.
■ **Royal Kona Resort** (BF CC g H msg PI S)
75-5852 Alii Drive ✉ HI 96740 ☎ 329-3111 ☎ (800) 774-5662
(toll-free) 📠 329-7230 📧 hhr@hawaiihotels.com
🖥 www.royalkona.com
Large, comfortable resort hotel.

SWIMMING
-**Honokohau Beach** (G NU) (On highway 19 between Kailua-Kona and Kona airport turn onto the road to Honokohau Boat Harbor. Take the first road to the right then follow the trail that leads north then to the left through the bushes. At the ocean the right end of the beach is the gayest.)

CRUISING
-**Kahaluu Beach Park** (near 5-mile-marker)

Hawaii-Kilauea ☎ 808

GUEST HOUSES
■ **Pali Kai Bed and Breakfast** (BF glm H PI WH)
PO Box 450 ✉ HI 96754 ☎ 828-6691 ☎ (800) 335-6968 (toll-free) 📠 828-1271 📧 Palikai@aloha.net 🖥 www.palikai.com
Hilltop with 360° views on ocean, mountains, waterfalls. Rates US$ 90 (+tax), cottage $125 (+tax).

APARTMENTS
■ **Kalihiwai Jungle Home** (AC G msg NU)
PO Box 717 ✉ HI 96754 ☎ 828-1626 📧 thomasw@aloha.net
🖥 www.hshawaii.com/kvp/jungle/
One luxury bedroom with full kitchen, Hawaiian art and furnishing, bath, fireplace and a large deck and hammock overlooking the waterfall, jungle and mountain landscape. Daily rates US$ 100-150.

CRUISING
-**Donkey Beach** (at Dirt Road, south of 12 mile marker, walk toward beach)

Hawaii-Pahoa ☎ 808

RESTAURANTS
■ **Godmother, The** (B BF CC d F glm MA OS) 8-15, 16-? h
PO Box 1163 ✉ HI 96778 (On the main street in historic Pahoa)
☎ 965-0055
Restaurant and bar. Italian cuisine.

HOTELS
■ **Kalani Resort** (A AC BF CC F glm H MA msg NU OS PI s SA WH WO)
RR2, Box 4500, Pahoa Beach Road ✉ HI 96778-9724 ☎ 965-7828
☎ (800) 800-6886 (toll-free) 📧 kalani@kalani.com
🖥 www.kalani.com
Oceanside getaway on a non-commercial coast. Also a healing & culture center offering various workshops and a yearly Pacific Men's gathering. Camping available.
■ **Volcano Ranch, The** (G H)
13-3775 Kalapana Highway ✉ HI 96778 ☎ 965-8800
🖥 haleakala.aloha-net/v-ranch

Cool HAWAII

KALANI Resort

1-800-800-6886 or **808-965-7828**

113 coastal acres in Hawaii's largest preserve. Comfortable cottages, lodges, Olympic pool/spa, delicious cuisine, dolphin/naturist beaches, thermal springs, waterfalls, gay events, Volcanos Nat'l Park *70°-80°F (21°-27°C) all year!

K A L A N I
RR2 Box 4500, Pahoa Beach Rd, HI 96778
e-mail: kalani@kalani.com • www.kalani.com

Hawaii-Pahoa ▸ Maui-Puunene | Hawaii/USA

GUEST HOUSES

■ **Huliaule'a Bed and Breakfast**
PO Box 10 30 ✉ HI 96778 ☎ 965-9175
Rates US$ 65-80 per night.
■ **Pamalu Guest House** (AC GLM MA msg NU PI SB)
RR2, Box 4023 ✉ HI 96778 *(8 km from Pahoa at Puna Coast)*
☎ 965-0830 🖷 965-6198
Private 5 acre guest ranch with bath/shower/WC, terrace, TV/Video room, 1 h to the Volcano Nationl Park. Work-out in nearby facilities. Different swimming possiblities: pool, ocean, fresh water lake, warm springs, snorkeling in underwater coral gardens.

Hawaii-Volcano Village ☎ 808

GUEST HOUSES

■ **Hale Ohia Cottages** (BF CC glm OS WH) 8-17 h
11-3968 Hale Ohia Boulevard, P.O. Box 758 ✉ HI 96785 *(1 mile from Hawaii Volcanoes National Park)* ☎ 967-7986
☎ (800) 455-3803 (toll free) 🖷 967-8610
✉ haleohia@bigisland.com 🖳 www.haleohia.com

Kauai-Anahola ☎ 808

GUEST HOUSES

■ **Mahina Kai Ocean Villa** (BF F glm H msg N OS PI WH)
4933 Aliomanu Road ✉ HI 96703 *(across from the beach)*
☎ 822-9451 🖳 joemoore@mahinakai.com 🖳 mahinakai@com

Kauai-Kapaa ☎ 808

BARS

■ **Sideout Bar and Grill** (B CC F GLM MA N s) Mon-Sun 12-2 h
4-1330 Kuhio Highway ✉ HI 96746 ☎ 822-7330

RESTAURANTS

■ **Buzz's Steak & Lobster** (B CC F g) lunch 11-15 h, happy hour 15-17 h, dinner 17-22.30 h
484 Kuhio Highway ✉ HI 96746 ☎ 822-7491
Located in the Coconut Plantation Market Place. Seafood, steaks, lobster. Tahitian interior design.

GUEST HOUSES

■ **Aloha Kauai B&B** (BF GLM H MA OS PI)
156 Lihau Street ✉ HI 96746 ☎ 822-6966 ☎ (800) 262-4852 (toll free)
Rooms with shared bath, TV, ceiling fan. Breakfast and sunset refreshments included.
■ **Hale Kahawai Bed & Breakfast** (G H)
185 Kahawai Place ✉ HI 96746 ☎ 822-1031 🖷 823-8220
■ **Royal Drive Cottages** (G H msg)
147 Royal Drive, Wailua ✉ HI 96746 ☎ 822-2321 🖷 822-7537
✉ sand@aloha.ne 🖳 www.planet-hawaii.com/~royal/

Maui ☎ 808

PUBLICATIONS

■ **Out in Maui**
c/o Both Sides Now, Inc., PO Box 5042, Kahului ✉ HI 96733-5042
☎ 248-4022 ☎ 244-4566 🖷 248-7501 ✉ gaymaui@maui.net
🖳 www.maui-tech.com/glom

SWIMMING

-**Little Beach** (g NU) (in Makena to the right of "Big Beach". Do not leave things in your car because of thiefs.)

Maui-Hana ☎ 808

APARTMENTS

■ **Hana Plantation Houses of Maui** (CC g H msg NU OS WH WO)
PO Box 489 ✉ HI 96713 ☎ 923-0772 ☎ (800)228-4262 (toll free) 🖷 922-6008 🖳 www.hana-maui.com

Maui-Kihei ☎ 808

APARTMENTS

■ **Makena Surf** (AC cc g H PI WH)
940 South Kihei Road ✉ HI 96753 *(30 min from airport, 2 min from the beach)* ☎ 879-1268 🖷 879-1455
🖳 luanakai@mauigateway.com 🖳 www.makenasurfrentals.com
All condominiums with AC, bath, phone, kitchen, TV, radio. Sport facilities.
■ **Wailana Inn** (AC G H)
14 Wailana Pl. ✉ HI 96753 ☎ 874-3131 ☎ (800) 399-3885 (toll free) 🖷 874-0454 🖳 www.wailanabeach.com
10 studios with kitchenette, air conditioning, phone and cable TV. Private sun deck with whirl pool. Barbecue grill.

Maui-Kula ☎ 808

GUEST HOUSES

■ **Camp Kula-Bed & Breakfast** (AC BF CC G H MA NU OS) all year
PO Box 111 ✉ HI 96790 ☎ 878-0000 ☎ 800-367-7546 (toll free) 🖷 878-2529
Centrally located on the lush slopes of the Haleakala Crater, near Haleakala National Park. No public transportation. Rental cars on Maui only.

Maui-Lahaina ☎ 808

HOTELS

■ **Royal Lahaina Resort** (AC B F BF CC g H msg PI WH)
2780 Kekaa Drive ✉ HI 96761 ☎ 661-3611 🖷 661-3538
✉ hhr@hawaiihotels.com 🖳 www.2maui.com
All rooms with shower/bath/WC, phone, TV, radio, safe.
■ **Wailuku Grand Hotel** (B F GLM H OS) Open all year.
2080 Vineyard Street ✉ HI 96793 ☎ 242-8191
In the center of Old Wailuku Town, 10 minutes from the beach. Shared bath, TV in room. Rates US$ 22.50-30.50.

Maui-Paia ☎ 808

HOTELS

■ **Huleo Point Flower Farm** (AC glm H PI WH)
PO Box 11 95 ✉ HI 96779 ☎ 572-1850 🖳 huelopt@maui.net
Half an hour to the airport on the road to Hana. Close to natural pools and waterfalls. Rates from US$ 135/night (2 people). Gay owned farm with beautiful views and luxurious apartments/flats.

Maui-Puunene ☎ 808

TRAVEL AND TRANSPORT

■ **Royal Hawaiian Weddings** (GLM) Mon-Fri 9-18 h
PO Box 424 ✉ HI 96784 ☎ 659-1866 ☎ (800) 659-1866 (toll free) 🖷 875-0623 ✉ jrenner@maui.net
🖳 www.hawaiigayweddings.com
Weddings for gays and lesbians from US$ 239,- up to 1.729,-.

USA/Hawaii — Maui Puunene ▶ Oahu-Honolulu

GUEST HOUSES

■ **Andrea`s Maui Condos** (GLM H msg Pl SA WH)
P.O.Box 1411 ✉ HI 96784 ☎ (800) 289-1522 🖷 879-6430
📧 andrea@maui.net 🖥 www.maui.net/~andrea
2 double rooms, 2 single rooms with bath/shower/WC, phone, TV, VCR, radio, own key.

Molokai-Kalua Koi ☎ 808

HOTELS

■ **Hana Plantation Houses** (g H)
PO Box 249 ✉ 96713 ☎ 248-7863 ☎ (800) 228-4262 (Toll free)

Oahu-Aiea ☎ 808

SEX SHOPS/BLUE MOVIES

■ **C'n'C**
Aiea Shopping Center ✉ HI 96701 ☎ 487-2944

Oahu-Honolulu ☎ 808

CULTURE

■ **Gallery Simonson** (a CC G)
758 Kapahulu, Box 328 ✉ HI 96816 ☎ 737-6275
☎ 737-6275 🖥 simonson@pixi.com
📧 www.douglassimonson.com
Paintings, drawings and prints of the mal nude. Mail order.

TOURIST INFO

■ **Hawaii National Tourist Office**
2270 Kalakaua Avenue, Suite 801 ✉ HI 96815 ☎ 923-1811
🖷 923-8991

BARS

■ **Hula's Bar & Lei Stand** (AC B D GLM S) 10-2 h
134 Kapahulu Avenue, Waikiki ✉ HI 96815 *(at Waikiki Grand Hotel, 2nd Floor)* ☎ 923-0669
Weekly events. Also Internet Café.

■ **In-Between** (B G N) 14-2 h
2155 Lau'ula Street, Waikiki *(behind Moose's)* ☎ 926-7060
Small & intimate bar for tourists and locals.

■ **Michelangelo** (B G MA s) 12-? h
444 Hobron Lane P-8, Waikiki ✉ HI *(Eaton Square)* ☎ 951-0008
Karaoke, Happy hour.

DANCECLUBS

■ **Angles Waikiki** (AC B D G S) 10-2 h
2256 Kuhio Avenue *(2nd floor)* ☎ 926-9766
Popular.

■ **Evolution Waikiki** (B D GLM MA S) 21-2 h
478 Ena Road *(2nd floor)* ☎ 946-6499
Brandnew club.

■ **Fusion** (AC B D G) 20-4 h
2260 Kuhio Avenue, Seaside ✉ HI 96815 *(2nd floor)* ☎ 924-2422
Popular, happy hour until 22 h.

■ **Venus** (B D glm S) 20-4 h
1349 Kapiolani Boulevard *(Below the China Hosue)* ☎ 955-2640
Live entertainment 6 nights a week, including male revues and femal impersonator shows. Gay Night every Sunday. Specials every night and many special surprise events.

RESTAURANTS

■ **Cafe Sistina** (B F glm)
1314 S. King Street ✉ HI 96814 *(Interstate Building)* ☎ 526-0071

MALE ART IN HAWAII

Paintings, drawings, prints of the male nude by Douglas Simonson. Send for free brochure or visit www.douglassimonson.com! MC, Visa, Amex, Discover. We ship everywhere! Simonson, 758 Kapahulu, Box 328, Honolulu HI 96816 USA. (Contact us for studio location.) Fax/ Phone: (808) 737-6275.
E-mail: simonson@pixi.com.

■ **JM Restaurant** (B F glm)
1040 Richards Street ✉ HI 96813 *(downtown)* ☎ 524-8789

■ **Pieces of Eight** (B F g) Dinner 17-23 h, Bar -2 h
250 Lewers Street, Waikiki ✉ HI 96815 ☎ 923-6646
Waikiki's original steak and seafood restaurant. Dinners served 17-23 daily; Piano-bar 19-24 h.

■ **Sunset Grill** (B F glm)
500 Ala Moana Boulevard ✉ HI 96813 ☎ 521-4409
Restaurant Row.

SAUNAS/BATHS

■ **Max's Gym** (AC b CC DR f G OS P SA SB VS WO YG) Mon-Sun 0-24 h
444 Hobron Lane, Eaton Square, PH1 ✉ HI 96815 *(in the shopping mall, 4th floor)* ☎ 951-8232
A private club for men, featuring a full bodybuilders gym with sports trainer equipment, free weights, steam room, sauna, showers, lockers, private video rooms and the outdoor Café Max.

TRAVEL AND TRANSPORT

■ **Pacific Ocean Holidays** (GLM) 9-17 h, closed Sat Sun
PO Box 882 45, ✉ HI 96830-6245 ☎ 923-2400
☎ (800) 735-6600 (toll free) 🖷 923-2499
📧 poh@gayhawaii.com
Gay Hawaii Vacation Packages.

VIDEO SHOPS

■ **Diamond Head Video** (AC CC g VS) 9-24 h
870 Kapahulu Avenue ✉ HI 96816 ☎ 735-6066

Oahu-Honolulu | Hawaii/USA

It's More Than a Video Store!

PHOTO: CADET • STUDIO 2000

ADULT VIDEOS

MAGAZINES

CALENDARS

ADULT NOVELTIES

GREETING CARDS

BOOKS • DVD'S

Want to buy X-rated videos?
Visit our adult department
online at www.adultdhv.com

870 Kapahulu Ave,
Just one mile from Waikiki!
Ph (808) 735-6066

Diamond Head Video

Open 9am-Midnight 365 days a year

USA/Hawaii - Illinois Oahu-Honolulu ▶ Chicago

HOTELS

■ **Coconut Plaza Hotel** (BF glm H PI)
450 Lewers Street, Waikiki ✉ HI 96815 ☎ 923-8828
☎ (800) 882-9696 📠 923-3473 💻 www.coconutplaza.com
Complementary daily breakfast buffet, in-room kitchenette and outdoor pool.

■ **Honolulu Hotel** (AC CC GLM H MA msg) 0-24 h
376 Kaiolu Street, Waikiki ✉ HI 96815 ☎ 926-2766
☎ (877) 922-3824 📠 922-5514 💻 hulagirl@hula.net
Parking available, 2 blocks from the beach. Theme rooms with complete kitchen, Rates from $49 per night to $105 per night.

■ **Waikiki Joy Hotel** (glm H PI SA SB WH)
320 Lewers Street, Waikiki ✉ HI 96815 ☎ 923-2300
☎ (800) 733-5569 (toll free) 📠 924-4010
All rooms and suites with private jacuzzi tubs, stereo system and air conditioning. Complimentary continental breakfast. Swimming pool, sauna, parking.

GUEST HOUSES

■ **Cabana at Waikiki** (AC BF G H OS WH WO) all year
2551 Cartwright Road, Waikiki ✉ HI 96815 *(5 mins to gay Queen's Surf Beach)* ☎ 926-5555 ☎ (877) 902-2121 (toll free)
📠 926-5566 ✉ reservations@cabana-waikiki.com
💻 www.cabana-waikiki.com
Close to the beach and shopping & entertainment. 15 charming single bedroom suites with kitchen. 8-man whirl pool.

HEALTH GROUPS

■ **Life Foundation. AIDS Service & Education** (GLM) Mon-Fri 9-17 h
233 Keawe St. Suite 126 ✉ HI 96813-5405 *(easily accesible by bus)*
☎ 521-2437 📠 521-1279 ✉ mail@.lifefoundation.org
💻 www.lifefoundation.org
Provides free confidential services with HIV/AIDS, and HIV prevention program for the community. Services include: case management, counseling and support groups, benefits and food assistance, weekly meals program, legal clinic, volunteer support, massage therapy, outreach programs, HIV testing.

SWIMMING

-**Ala Moana Beach Park** (Across from shopping center of the same name. The area where the beach start to curve at the Diamond Head end usually has a small gay crowd on weekdays.)
-**Diamond Head Beach** (Within walking distance of Waikiki. Gay area is just below the lighthouse.)
-**Queen's Surf** (G) (To get there, go towards Diamond Head on Kalakaua Avenue into Kapiolani Park and look for the pavilion on the right side. The grassy area between the pavilion and the snack bar: voilà! THE gay beach.)
-**Waikiki Beach** (Extremely long beach. The gay section is on the oceanside of the park, almost adjacent to Queen's Surf, approximately ½ of a mile east of the middle of the straight scene.)

Oahu-Kailua

CRUISING

-**Kailua Beach Park** (AYOR)
-**Kona Market Place**

Oahu-Kaneohe Bay ☎ 808

GUEST HOUSES

■ **Ali'i Bluffs Windward Bed & Breakfast** (BF glm H OS PI)
46-251 Ikiiki Street ✉ HI 96744 ☎ 235-1124 ☎ (800) 235-1151 (toll free) 📠 236-1877 ✉ donm@lava.net

Rates from $60-75 according to season. Luxurious home with pool and large breakfast.

USA-Idaho

Location: Northwest USA
Initials: ID
Time: GMT -7
Area: 216.456 km^2 / 88,530 sq mi.
Population: 1,210,000
Capital: Boise City

Boise ☎ 208

PUBLICATIONS

■ **Diversity News**
PO Box 323 ✉ ID 83701 ☎ 336-3870 mailbox 2 📠 323-0805
✉ editor@tcc-diversity.com
💻 www.tcc-diversity.com/diversityhome.htm
Idaho's LGBT monthly news magazine.

BARS

■ **Emerald City** (B D GLM) 10-2 h
415 S. 9th Street ✉ ID 83702 ☎ 342-5446
■ **Partners** (B gLM)
2210 Main Street ☎ 331-3551
■ **8th Street Balcony Pub** (B glm) 14-2 h
150 North 8th Street #224 ☎ 336-1313

GENERAL GROUPS

■ **TCC - The Community Center** Tue 18.30-21, Wed 18-21, Fri 19-21 (YG), Sat 10-14 h
919 North 27th Street ☎ 336-3870
✉ webmaster@tcc-diversity.com 💻 www.tcc-diversity.com
GLBT Community Center. Publishers of Diversity. Check website for more details.

CRUISING

-**Ann Morrison Park** (near archery range)
-**Front Street**

USA-Illinois

Location: Great Lakes region USA
Initials: IL
Time: GMT -6
Area: 150.007 km^2 / 61,352 sq mi.
Population: 11,896,000
Capital: Springfield

Chicago ☎ 312

✴ Winter can be quite hard in Chicago. The climate is severe, but it fits the tough, blue collar image of this city, which makes its money with steel, meatpacking and transportation. Could that be the reason why the competition for *International Mr. Leather* is held in Chicago each year on the Memorial Day weekend? The city has been known as the slaughter house of the nation, earning the nickname "Porkopolis". Of course, Chicago also has more sophisticated sides, eg. Shop 'til you drop in Water Tower Place. By taking a boat tour called the Architecture River Cruise, you can get a good look at the architectural designs of Sullivan, van der Rohe, Jahn or Wright. The great fire of 1871 destroyed much of downtown; the city has been rebuilt in a sleek, functional, modern style. The gay scene

Chicago | Illinois/USA

is concentrated around New Town, which is also known as Boys Town. A name that suits us just fine. Most of the gay bars and businesses are situated along North Halsted Street, between Barry Avenue and Grace Street. One highlight of the summer festival season is NortHalsted Market Days, a street festival held in late July or early August. The gay scene is quite diverse but not as glamorous as New York or LA. Although gay nightlife may not be very spectacular, there is also less attitude and snobbery than in some other cities. People in the Midwest tend to be friendly and outgoing. The easiest way to get around town is on the rapid transit trains, but you will need a car to visit the gay resorts of *Douglas* and *Saugatuck*, which are located on the eastern shore of Lake Michigan.

★ Nun gut: die Winter in Chicago können recht hart sein. Aber als odentlicher Chicagoer verläßt man seine Stadt dann selbstverständlich nicht. Das Wetter ist eben rauh, doch das paßt zum Arbeiter-Image dieser Stadt, die ihr Geld mit Stahl, Fleisch und Transporten verdient. Ist das vielleicht der Grund dafür, daß hier alljährlich am Memorial-Day-Wochenende die Wahlen zum *International Mr. Leather* stattfinden? Genausogut könnte es daran liegen, daß Chicago das Schlachthaus der Nation war und gerne "Porkopolis" (pork, engl. = Schweinefleisch) genannt wurde. Und aus den Häuten Tausender toter Tiere muß man doch was machen können, oder? Aber selbstverständlich hat Chicago auch milde Seiten: z.B. "Shop 'til you drop" im *Water Tower Place*. Vom Boot des *Architecture River Cruise* aus kann man die Werke von Sullivan, van der Rohe, Jahn oder Wright betrachten. Kein Wunder also, daß sich diese Stadt unschrill und schnörkellos präsentiert, verbrannte doch die Historie im großen Feuer von 1871. Die Chicagoer Szene konzentriert sich in *New Town* oder netter formuliert *Boystown*. Entlang der North Halsted Street findet sich hier zwischen Barry Avenue und Grace Street der größte Teil der schwulen Einrichtungen. Spektakuläre Auftritte sollte man von der Chicagoer Szene aber nicht erwarten. Der Outdoor-Höhepunkt ist z.B. das Straßenfest *NortHalsted Market Days* Ende Juli/Anfang August. So unspektakulär die Szene bei aller Reichhaltigkeit auch ist, so warmherzig sind doch die Menschen *in Middle-West*. Was auf den Aussenstehenden rauh wirken mag, entpuppt sich bei näherem Hinsehen als Empfang mit offenen Armen. In der Stadt kommt man mit der Hochbahn gut zu recht. Ein Auto benötigt man höchstens für einen Besuch der schwulen Badeorte *Douglas* und *Saugatuck*, die auf der anderen Seite des Lake Michigan liegen.

✱ D'accord, à Chicago, les hivers sont plutôt durs, mais tout habitant de Chicago qui se respecte ne met pas la clé sous le paillasson pour autant! Le climat est rude, ce qui correspond bien à l'image de cette ville industrielle qui a fait fortune dans les aciers, la viande et les transports. Rude et dure: voilà Chicago! Rien d'étonnant, donc, à ce qu'on organise ici tous les ans pour le week-end du Memorial Day les élections de M. Cuir International. Chicago, c'est aussi les abattoirs de la nation, ce qui lui vaut le nom de "Porkopolis". Et que fait-on des peaux des milliers de cochons égorgés chaque année? Des blousons et des pantalons de cuir! La boucle est bouclée. Mais Chicago a aussi de bons côtés, comme p. ex. le "Shop 'til you drop" dans le Water Tower Place. Depuis le bâteau de l'"Architecture River Cruise", on peut admirer les réalisations de Sullivan, van der Rohe, Jahn ou Wright. Le grand incendie de 1871 a entièrement détruit le centre-ville. Le nouveau Chicago est donc fonctionnel, lisse et sans fioriture. Les quartiers gais sont dans le district de Newton qu'on appelle aussi "Boystown", non sans un sourire entendu. C'est le long de Halsted Street (entre Grace Street et Barry Avenue) que l'on trouve la plupart des établissements gais. N'atten-

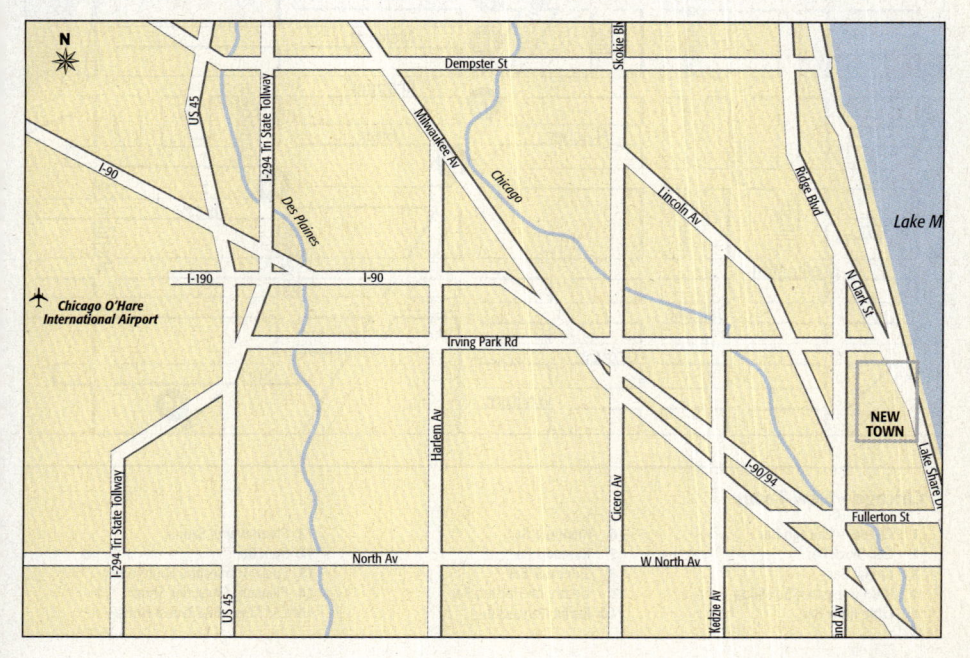

USA/Illinois Chicago

Chicago - New Town

1. Charlie's Chicago Bar
2. Cell Block Bar
3. Circuit Bar
4. RAM Bookstore Sex Shop
5. Little Jim's Bar
6. Manhole Bar
7. Roscoe's Bar
8. Sidetrack Bar
9. Gentry on Halsted Bar
10. Berlin Danceclub
11. Steamworks Sauna
12. Spin Bar
13. Lucky Horseshoe Lounge Bar
14. Pleasure Chest Sex Shop
15. Old Town B&B Guest House

Chicago | Illinois/USA

dez rien de spectaculaire de la vie gaie de Chicago! La plus belle fête en plein air a lieu fin juillet/début août: les "NortHalsted Market Days". Si le Chicago gai n'a rien d'extravagant, les gais, eux, sont en revanche très gentils et ouverts, à l'image des gens du Middle West. Même si, au premier abord, on peut avoir l'impression d'avoir affaire à des rustres. Le métro aérien est le meilleur moyen de se déplacer en ville. Une voiture n'est indispensable que pour aller voir Douglas et Saugatuck qui sont les stations balnéaires gaies sur l'autre rive du Michigan.

Hay que reconocer que los inviernos en Chicago pueden ser muy duros. Pero para sus habitantes no es ningúna razón de dejar su ciudad. El clima es duro, al igual que la imagen de la ciudad con sus obreros que ganan sus sueldos con acero, carne y transportes. La industria de carne de cerdo y el apodo "Porcopolis" (porc=en inglés carne de cerdo) no han sido una coincidencia. Quiza sea por ello que anualmente en el Memorial-Day-Weekend se lleva a cabo la elección del *International Mr. Gay Leather*. Pero Chicago tiene mucho más ofrecer, p. ej. "Shop'til you drop" en el *Water Tower Place*. Los trabajos artísticos de Sullivan, van der Rohe, Jahn o Wright, pueden ser observados desde el barco de *Architecture River Cruise*. El ambiente gay se concentra en el *New Town* que se conoce también como "Boystown". A largo de la North Halsted Street se encuentran la major parte de los establecimientos gay. El ambiente de la ciudad no es nada espectacular. Uno de los puntos festivos culminantes es la fiesta callejera *North Halsted Market Days* a finales de Julio e inicios de Agosto. La actitud agradable y amistosa de las personas en *Middle West* se refleja en la tranquilidad del ambiente gay. Dentro de la ciudad, el medio de transporte más utilizado lo es el metro. Un auto sería de gran ayuda si se desean visitar los balnearios *Douglas* y *Saugatuck* que se encuentran al otro lado del lago Michigan. En general la ciudad presenta hoy en día una imagen moderna y funcional, ya que en el gran fuego de 1871 se destruyó la gran parte de sus edificios históricos.

L'inverno a Chicago può essere veramente freddo, ma un verace abitante di Chicago naturalmente non lascia la città per questa ragione. Il tempo rigido è consono all'immagine operaia di questa città che guadagna i propri soldi con l'acciaio, la carne ed i trasporti; e forse questa la ragione per la quale proprio qui ha luogo durante il Memorial-Day-Weekend l'elezione dell'*International Mr Leather*? Chicago era in passato il macello del paese, e per questo veniva chiamata "Porkopolis". E con le pelli delle migliaia di animali uccisi bisognava pur far qualcosa, non è vero? Naturalmente Chicago ha anche lati più moderati: ad esempio "Shop 'til you drop" nella *Water Tower Place*. Dalla nave dell'*Architecture River Cruise* è possibile osservare le opere di Sullivan, van der Rohe, Jahn o Wright. Dal punto di vista architettonico Chicago si presenta monotona, senza fronzoli, perché nel 1871 fu vittima di un grave incendio. L'ambiente gay si concentra nella *New Town* o, meglio detto, nella *boystown*. La maggior parte dei locali gay si trova tra la Barry Avenue e la Grace street lungo la North Halsted street. Tuttavia non aspettatevi niente di spettacolare. Il culmine è la festa all'aperto di *North Halsted Market Days* alla fine di luglio, inizio di agosto. Se nel Middle West l'ambiente non è spettacolare le persone sono in compenso calde ed affettuose: all'inizio sono un po' riservate ma poi vi accoglieranno a braccia aperte. Per girare la città sono sufficienti i mezzi pubblici; vi servirà un'auto solo se visiterete le stazioni balneari di *Douglas* e *Saugatuck* situate sulla sponda opposta del lago Michigan.

GAY INFO

■ **Gay & Lesbian Visitors Center**
3713 North Broadway ✉ IL 60613 ☎ (773) 871-4190
🖷 (773) 871-1021 📧 info@GLChamber.org
💻 www.glchamber.org

PUBLICATIONS

■ **Chicago Free Press**
3714 North Broadway ✉ IL 60613 ☎ (773) 325-0005
🖷 (773) 325-0006 📧 neff@chicagofreepress.com
💻 www.chicagofreepress.com
Weekly GLBT newspaper free at gay venues.
■ **Gab Magazine**
3227 North Sheffield #4-R ✉ IL 60657 ☎ (773) 248-4542
🖷 (773) 248-7570 📧 gabmag@earthlink.net
■ **Gale**
c/o Propago Publishing Ink, 3227 N. Sheffield ✉ IL 60657
☎ (773) 248-7570 🖷 (773) 248-4542 📧 gabmag@earthlink.net
Weekly gay magazine avalaible for free at gay venues.
■ **Gay Chicago Magazine**
3115 North Broadway ✉ IL 60657-4522 ☎ (773) 327-7271
🖷 (773) 327-0112 📧 gaychimag@aol.com
Entertainment guide for the gay community, containing calendar of events, photos, columns and personal ads. Published weekly, 80-96 pages, US$ 2. Subscriptions available.
■ **Magayzine**
PO Box 408496 ✉ IL 60640 ☎ (773) 728-5278
☎ (877) 728-5200 🖷 (773) 728-6723 📧 magayzine2@aol.com
💻 www.magayzine.com
Regional gay entertainment publication distributed in Illinois and Middle West. Published every other week.
■ **Outlines, Nightlines, En La Vida, BLackline, Clout!**
c/o Lambda Publications Inc., 1115 West Belmont, Suite 2-D ✉ IL 60657 ☎ (773) 871-7610 🖷 871-7609 📧 outlines@suba.com
💻 www.outlineschicago.com
Gay and lesbian publications.

CULTURE

■ **Leather Archives and Museum** (GLM LZ) Sat 14-24 h (and by appointment)
6418 N Greenview Ave. ✉ IL 60625 *(2 blocks East of Ashland at Devon)* ☎ (773) 761-9200 🖷 545-6753
One of the largest collection in the world open to serious research by appointment only.

TOURIST INFO

■ **Chicago Convention & Visitor Bureau**
2301 South Lake Shore Drive ✉ IL 60616 ☎ 567-8500
🖷 567-8533

BARS

■ **Annex 3** (AC B CC G MA N s) 12-2 h
3160 North Clark Street ✉ IL 60657 ☎ (773) 327-5969
Very nice and comfortable.
■ **Baton Show Lounge** (! AC B GLM MA STV) 20-4, Sat -5 h, closed Mon
436 North Clark Street/Hubbard Street ✉ IL 60610 ☎ 644-5269
Great shows!
■ **Big Chicks** (B glm s tv) 12-2 h
5024 North Sheridan Road ✉ IL 60640 ☎ (773) 728-5811
■ **Buck's Saloon** (B CC GLM OS) 10-2, Sat 9-2, Sun 12-? h
3439 North Halsted Street ✉ IL 60657 ☎ 525-1125
■ **Buddies' Bar & Restaurant** (A AC B BF F GLM lj) 7-2 h, Sun 12-2 h, dining room closed Mon
3301 North Clark/Aldine ✉ IL 60657 ☎ 477-4066
■ **Cell Block** (B d DR G LJ MA VS) Mon-Fri 16-2, Sat 14-3, Sun -2 h
3702 North Halsted ✉ IL 60614 ☎ (773) 665-8064
■ **Charlies Chicago** (B d G) Sun Wed-Fri 15-4, Sat -5 h
3726 N. Broadway ✉ IL 60613 ☎ (773) 871-8887

USA/Illinois — Chicago

CHICAGO EAGLE
Where Leathermen Meet in the USA

Tuesday Leather Nights - Wednesday Free Pool Table
Sunday Night Movies @ 8:30 & 11:30pm

A Traditional Leather Bar
Home of International Mr. Leather, Inc.

Open Daily 8pm til 4am (5am on Sat.)
5015 N. CLARK ST - CHICAGO

■ **Charmer's** (AC B GLM MA N) Mon-Fri 16-2, Sat 16-3, Sun 12-2 h
1502 West Jarvis Avenue ✉ IL 60626 ☏ 465-3811
Neighbourhood bar with friendly atmosphere.

■ **Chicago Eagle** (AC B DR G LJ MA VS) 20-4, Sat -5 h
5015 North Clark Street ✉ IL 60640 *(next door to Man's Country Baths)* ☏ (773) 728-0050
Home of International Mr. Leather, Inc.

■ **Clark's on Clark** (B GLM MA) 16-4, Sat 16-5, Sun 20-4 h
5001 North Clark Street ✉ IL 60640 *(at Argyle)* ☏ (773) 728-2373

■ **Closet** (AC B D GLM VS) 14-4, Sat Sun 12-4 h
3325 North Broadway ✉ IL 60657 ☏ 477-8533

■ **Cocktail** (AC B GLM MA N VS) 16-2, WE 14-2 h
3359 North Halsted Street ✉ IL 60657 ☏ (773) 871-8123
Popular.

■ **Dandy's** (B GLM S) 12-? h
3729 N. Halsted Street ✉ IL 60613 ☏ 525-1200
Piano bar.

■ **Different Strokes** (AC B GLM MA N OS) Sun-Fri 12-2 h, Sat -3 h
4923 North Clark Street ✉ IL 60640 ☏ (773) 989-1958
Pleasant neighborhood bar. Comfortable setting with very friendly staff.

■ **Escapades** (B D GLM VS) 20-4, Sat -5, Sun 14-4 h
6301 South Harlem ✉ IL 60638 ☏ 229-0886

■ **Flash!** (B D GLM S) 19-2 h
1450 E. Algonquin, Schaumburg *(adjacent to 1450 East)*
☏ (708) 925-9696

■ **Gentry on Halsted** (AC B CC G MA S VS) Sun-Fri 16-2 h, Sat -3 h
3320 North Halsted Street ✉ IL 60657

■ **Gentry on State** (AC B CC G MA S VS) Sun-Fri 16-2 h, Sat -3 h
440 North State Street ✉ IL 60610 ☏ 664-1033

■ **Hideaway II** (B D G S VS WE YG) 16-2 h
7301 West Roosevelt Road, Forest Park ✉ IL 60130 *(near Harlem Avenue)* ☏ (708) 771-4459
Chicago's most popular bar on Mon night.

■ **Inn Exile** (A AC B d G MA N s VS) Sun-Fri 20-2, Sat -3 h
5758 West 65th Street ✉ IL 60638-5504 *(near Midway Airport)*
☏ (773) 582-3510

■ **Jeffery Pub** (AC B D GLM MA N VS) 11-4 h
7041 South Jeffrey Boulevard *(Jackson Park in Chicago's south shore neighborhood)* ☏ 363-8555
African American Bar.

■ **Legacy 21** (AC B D GLM MA N S VS WE) 20-4 h, Fri Sat piano player
3042 West Irving Park Road ✉ IL 60618 ☏ 588-9405

■ **Little Jim's** (AC B G LJ MA N r VS) 11-4 Sat- 5 h
3501 North Halsted Street ✉ IL 60657 *(at Cornelia Street)*
☏ (773) 871-6116
Very popular neighborhood bar. Large afternoon crowds daily.

■ **Lucky Horseshoe Lounge. The** (! AC B G MA OS SNU SOL) 14-2, Sat 12-3, Sun -2 h, nightly dancers
3169 North Halsted Street ✉ IL 60657 ☏ (773) 404-3169

■ **Manhandler** (AC B G MA OS) 12-4, Sat -5 h
1948 North Halsted Street ✉ IL 60614 *(at Armitage St.)*
☏ 871-3339
Friendly staff. Warm atmosphere.

■ **Manhole** (B D G LJ S VS) 21-4, Sat -5 h (best 1.30-4 h)
3458 North Halsted Street ✉ IL 60657 *(opposite Little Jim's)*
☏ (773) 975-9244
Front bar, at the back bar & disco Fri Sat dress code leather, rubber or shirtless.

RAM BOOKSTORE & VIDEO
IN CHICAGO
3511 N. Halsted St.
(773) 525-9528

FUN! FRIENDLY!
different strokes bar
4923 N. Clark St.
(773) 989-1958

■ **Marigold Bowling Arcade** (B G)
828 West Grace ✉ IL 60613 ☏ 935-8183
■ **Mr. B's** (AC B d G MA N) Wed-Sat 13-2 h, Sun-Thu 14-2 h
606 State Line Road, Calumet City (On Illinois/Indiana state line)
☏ (708) 862-1221
■ **North End, The** (AC B G MA N S VS WE) Mon-Fri 15-? h, Sat Sun 14-? h
3733 North Halsted Street ✉ IL 60613 (near Bradley Pl.)
☏ (773) 477-7999
Pool tables. Male dancers occasionally.
■ **Off The Line** (B gLM VS) Mon-Fri 17-2 h, Sat 12-2 h, Sun 12-2 h
1829 W. Montrose ✉ IL 60613 ☏ 528-1293
■ **Pour House** (AC B D GLM MA N WE) 20-4 h, closed Mon
103 155th Place, Calumet City ✉ IL 60409 ☏ (708) 891-3980
■ **Roscoe's Tavern & Café** (! A AC B D F GLM S OS VS YG) Mon-Fri 14-2 h, Sat-Sun 12-2 h
3356 North Halsted Street ✉ IL 60657 ☏ (773) 281-3355
One of the most popular bars and dance clubs in Chicago. A must.
■ **Second Story Bar** (B G)
157 East Ohio Street ✉ IL 60611 ☏ 923-9536
■ **Sidetrack** (! AC B GLM OS S VS WE YG) 15-2 h
3349 North Halsted Street ✉ IL 60657 (two doors south of Roscoe's)
☏ (773) 477-9189
This video-bar always attracts a very good and attractive crowd, especially after 21 h, and Sun late afternoons.
■ **Spin** (B Glm D VS) 16-2 h
800 West Belmont ✉ IL 60657 ☏ (773) 327-7711
■ **Temptations** (B D GLM S) 16-4 h
10235 W. Grand, Franklin Park ✉ IL 60131 ☏ (708) 455-0008
■ **Touché** (B G LJ) Mon-Fri 17-2 h, Sat Sun 15-? h
6412 North Clark Street ✉ IL 60626 ☏ 465-7400
■ **2nd Story Bar** (AC B G) Mon-Fri 12-2, Sat-Sun 15-2 h
157 East Ohio Street ✉ IL 60611 (1/2 block east of N Michigan Ave.)
☏ 923-9536

MEN'S CLUBS
■ **Circuit/ Rehab** (B D g MA S) Tue-Thu 21-2, Fri-4, Sat-5 h
3641 North Halsted Street ✉ IL 60613 (at Addison) ☏ 325-2233
Also karaoke nights. "Club Rehab" from 16h.

DANCECLUBS
■ **Berlin** (AC B D GLM SNU STV VS YG) Sun 18-4, Mon 20-4, Tue-Fri 17-4, Sat 20-5 h
954 West Belmont Avenue ✉ IL 60657 ☏ (773) 348-4975
Unique and worth stopping by. Always packed late in the evening. Best Thu after 22 h.
■ **Clubhouse** (B D G) Fri-Sat/Mon 23-? h
440 North Halsted Street ✉ IL 60622 ☏ 421-3588
■ **Crowbar Nightclub** (B D glm MA) 22-4 h, Mon Tue closed, G on Sun
1543 North Kingsbury ☏ 243-4800
■ **Generator** (B D GLM) 21-2 h
306 N. Halsted ✉ IL 60661 ☏ 243-8889
■ **Neo** (AC B D glm S VS WE YG) 21-4 h
2350 North Clark Street/Fullerton ✉ IL 60614 ☏ 528-2622
Progressive music.
■ **Numbers** (B D G OS vs) 16-4 h
6406 Clark Street ✉ IL 60626 ☏ 743-5772

RESTAURANTS
■ **Big Daddies** (F G) 11-? h
2914 North Broadway ✉ IL 60657 ☏ (773) 929-0922
■ **Chicago Diner** (B F g)
3411 North Halsted Street ✉ IL 60657 ☏ (773) 935-6696
Vegetarian cuisine.
■ **Cornelia** (B F GLM)
748 West Cornelia Avenue ✉ IL 60657 ☏ (773) 935-7793
■ **Fireplace Inn** (B F g)
1448 North Wells Street ✉ IL 60610 ☏ 664-5264
■ **Mama Mimi** (B F g)
111 West Hubbard Street ✉ IL 60610 ☏ 321-0776
■ **Sottosantos** (B F g)
5025 North Clark Street ✉ IL 60640 ☏ (773) 878-6360
■ **Voltaire** (B F Glm MA S)
3441 North Halsted Street ✉ IL 60657-6516 (between Rosco St. and Cornelia Ave.) ☏ (773) 281 9320
Contemporary American cuisine.

SHOWS
■ **Bailiwick's Pride Series** (AC CC GLM S) Performances Thu-Sun
1229 West Belmont ✉ IL 60657 ☏ (773) 883-1090
Greenhouse for gay and lesbian theater and performance.

USA/Illinois Chicago

MAN'S COUNTRY
Bath & Entertainment Complex
LOCKERS & ROOMS
Singles - Doubles - Fantasy S/M Suites
HUGE Whirlpool - Largest Steam Room - All Male Videos
NUDE StripperBOYZ on Stage
Friday & Saturday Nights
Regularly featuring your favorite XXX-Video Stars!
watch the shows on the net
www.SatyrSite.com

PRIVATE MEMBERSHIP CLUB
5017 N. Clark St., Chicago USA

■ **Zebra Crossing Theater** (GLM S)
4223 North Lincoln ✉ IL 60618 ☏ (773) 248-6401
Year-round gay-lesbian theater.

SEX SHOPS/BLUE MOVIES
■ **Banana Video**
4923 N. Clark ✉ IL 60640 *(2nd floor)* ☏ (773) 561-8322
■ **Bijou Theatre** (AC DR G OG SNU VS) 0-24 h
1349 North Wells Street/Schiller Street ✉ IL 60610 ☏ 337-3404
$ 13 admission, $ 1 membership.
■ **Cupid's Treasures** (CC glm MA TV WE) Mon-Thu 11-2 h, Fri Sat 11-1 h
3519 North Halstead Street ✉ IL 60657 ☏ (773) 348-3884
■ **Pleasure Chest** (g) 12-24 h
3143 North Broadway ✉ IL 60657 ☏ (773) 525-7151

■ **RAM Bookstore** (AC CC DR G MA VS)
3511 North Halsted Street ✉ IL 60657 ☏ (773) 525-9258

SAUNAS/BATHS
■ **Man's Country** (AC DR f G MA P S SB SNU VS WH) 0-24 h
5017 North Clark Street ✉ IL 60640 *(next to Chicago Eagle)*
☏ (773) 878-2070
Bath house and entertainment complex. Nude strip shows on Fri and Sat.
■ **Mans World** (AC G MA NU SB VS WH)
4862 North Clark Street *Mans World*
☏ (773) 728-0400
■ **Steamworks, The** (AC CC DR f G MA P SA SB VS WH WO) 0-24 h
3246 North Halsted Street ✉ IL 60657 *(north of Belmont St.)*
☏ (773) 929-6080
Many special events organised. Check website or call for special rates.

INTERNATIONAL MR. LEATHER
4 Days of Glory
5 Nights of Parties
50(+) Contestants
5,000 Spectators
Tickets & Information
I.M.L., Inc.
5015 N. Clark St.
Chicago, IL USA 60640
www.IMRL.com

Every May for 23 years

Chicago | Illinois/USA

STEAMWORKS

take the pressure off

BERKELEY CA CHICAGO IL SAN JUAN PR

24 HOUR MEN'S GYM / SAUNA

3246 North Halsted / Chicago / 773.929.6080 / www.SteamworksOnLine.com

OLD TOWN BED & BREAKFAST
CHICAGO

- Art Deco Mansion
- Four Guest Suites
- Full Kitchen
- Penthouse and Roof Gardens
- Gymnasium on Premises
- Conference Room
- Separate and Private Three Bedroom Guesthouse with Playroom and Private Sundecks
- Ideal Location and Parking

1442 N. North Park Avenue
Chicago, IL 60610

VOX: 312-440-9268

FAX: 312-440-2378

www.oldtownbandbchicago.com

USA/Illinois Chicago ▸ Springfield

BOOK SHOPS
■ **Unabridged Bookstore** (GLM) Mon-Fri 11-21 h, Sat 10-19 h, Sun 11-18 h
3251 North Broadway Street ✉ IL 60657 ☎ (773) 883-9119
Mixed bookstore with large gay/lesbian section.

LEATHER & FETISH SHOPS
■ **Male Hide Leathers, Inc** (GLM) Tue-Thu 12-20, Fri Sat 12-24 h
2816 North Lincoln Avenue ✉ IL 60657 ☎ (773) 929-0069

VIDEO SHOPS
■ **RJ's Videos**
3452 N. Halsted ✉ IL 60657 ☎ (773) 871-1810
■ **Specialty Video Films** (G VS)
3221 North Broadway ✉ IL 60657 ☎ (773) 248-3434
Also in 6307 North Clark St.Tel .878-3434.

HOTELS
■ **Abbott Hotel** (AC glm H)
721 West Belmont, ✉ IL 60657 ☎ (773) 248-2700
■ **Cass Hotel** (H)
640 North Wabash Avenue ✉ IL 60611 ☎ 787-4030
☎ (800) 2277-850 📠 787-8544
Central location. Rates from US$ 49.
■ **City Suites Hotel Chicago** (g H MA) 0-24 h
933 West Belmont Street ✉ IL 60657 ☎ (773) 404-3400
📠 (773) 404-3405
Close to gay bars.
■ **Diplomat Hotel** (AC glm H vs)
3208 North Sheffield ✉ IL 60657 ☎ (773) 549-6800
■ **Park Brompton Hotel** (g H MA) 7.30-23.30 h
528 West Brompton Place ✉ IL 60657 *(close to gay bars)*
☎ (773) 404-3499 📠 404-3495
Rates from US$ 79. Recommended.
■ **Surf Hotel** (g H MA)
555 West Surf Street ✉ IL 60657 ☎ (773) 528-8400
📠 (773) 528-8483

GUEST HOUSES
■ **Deeks Den** (AC CC G WH) Office: 9-23 h
1919 West Greenleaf Avenue ✉ IL 60626-2305 ☎ (773) 381-1118
📠 (773) 381-1116 📧 Deeksden@hotmail.com
■ **Old Town Bed & Breakfast** (AC BF CC F G H lj MA msg NU OS SOL WH WO)
1442 North North Park Avenue ✉ IL 60610-1327 ☎ 440-9268
📠 440-2378 💻 www.oldtownbandbchicago.com
Luxurious Art Deco mansion with only four guest suites. Large common rooms, restaurant kitchen, small gym, private roof decks, office and penthouse sitting room.
■ **Villa Toscana Guest House** (AC BF CC GLM H MA OS)
3447 North Halsted Street ✉ IL 60657-2414 ☎ (773) 404-2643
📠 (773) 404-3488 📧 rochus1@ibm.net
7 rooms with TV, telephone, some with shared bath. Continental bf. Garden.

PRIVATE ACCOMMODATION
■ **Carnitas Network. The**
75 East Wacker Drive, Suite 3600 ✉ IL 60601 ☎ 857-0801
📠 857-0805 📧 Gaycaritas@aol.com
💻 www.freedomweb.com/caritas/
Caritas offers bed & breakfast accommodations in private gay homes throughout America . Each host is carefully screened and inspected by Caritas, reasonable prices.

GENERAL GROUPS
■ **Chicago Area G&L Chamber of Commerce**
3713 North Halsted ✉ IL 60613-4198 ☎ (888) 452-4262
📠 (773) 871-1021 📧 visit@glchamber.org
💻 www.glchamber.org
Business owner association.
■ **Chicago Professional Networking Association** Meets at Ann Sather's Restaurant, 929 W. Belmont
990 W. Fullerton Avenue ✉ IL 60614 ☎ (773) 296-2762
Non-profit business and social networking. Call for more information.

FETISH GROUPS
■ **International Mr Leather, Inc.** (LJ)
5015 North Clark Street ✉ IL 60640 ☎ (773) 381-4650
☎ (800) 545-6753 📠 (773) 878-5184 📧 info@imrl.com
💻 www.imrl.com

HEALTH GROUPS
■ **AIDS Foundation of Chicago**
411 South Wells, Ste. 300 ✉ IL 60607 ☎ 922-2322 📠 922-2916
■ **AIDS Pastoral Care Network** 9-17 h or by appointment
☎ (773) 975-5180
■ **Test Positive Aware Network**
1258 West Belmont ✉ IL 60657 ☎ (773) 404-8815
HIV and fellowship & information network.

CRUISING
-Montrose Harbor (between Montrose Street and Foster Street. Cruisy from dusk-11 h.)
-Belmont Street "rocks" at the lakefront (WE afternoons during summer)
-Halsted and Broadway Streets (between Belmont and Addison. Many gay shops and restaurants)

Peoria ☎ 309

BARS
■ **Quench Room** (B GLM) 17-1 h
631 West Main Street ✉ IL 61606 ☎ 676-1079

SEX SHOPS/BLUE MOVIES
■ **Swingers World**
335 Adams Street ☎ 676-9275

CRUISING
-Bradley Park
-Detweiller Park (days)
-West Main Street (between 600 and 1600 blocks, by foot or car)

Springfield ☎ 217

BARS
■ **New Dimensions** (B D GLM VS) 21-? h
3036 Peoria Road ✉ IL 62702 ☎ 544-3861
■ **Smokey's Den** (B D GLM) Sun-Thu 16-1, Fri Sat 16-3 h
411 East Washington Street ✉ IL 62701 ☎ 522-0301

SEX SHOPS/BLUE MOVIES
■ **Expo One Books**
300 North 5th Street ✉ IL 62701 ☎ 544-5145

CRUISING
-Douglas Park (on I-94 North near Zion)
-Lake Springfield

USA-Indiana

Location: Central Northeast USA
Initials: IN
Time: GMT -5
Area: 94.328 km^2 / 38,580 sq mi.
Population: 5,864,000
Capital: Indianapolis

Bloomington ☏ 812

BARS

■ **Bullwinkle's** (B D GLM S) 17-3 h, closed Sun
201 South College ✉ IN 47404 ☏ 334-3232
■ **The Other Bar** (B GLM) 16-2 h, closed Sun
414 South Walnut Street ✉ IN 47401 ☏ 332-0033

SEX SHOPS/BLUE MOVIES

■ **College Avenue Adult Bookstore** (glm) 0-24 h
1013 North College Street ✉ IN 47401 ☏ 332-4160
Large gay section, very cruisy.

Fort Wayne ☏ 219

GAY INFO

■ **Gay/Lesbian Helpline** Mon-Thu 19-22, Fri Sat 19-24, Sun 18.30-21 h
☏ 744-1199

BARS

■ **After Dark** (B GLM MA N S VS) Mon-Sat 18-3.30 h, closed Sun
231 Pearl Street ✉ IN 46802 ☏ 424-6130
■ **Riff Raff's** (B F Glm N) Mon-Sat 16-3 h, closed Sun
2809 W Main Street ☏ 436-4166

Indianapolis ☏ 317

GAY INFO

■ **Out & About Indiana**
133 West Market Street #105 ✉ IN 46204-2801 ☏ 923-8550
📠 923-8505
Info service and social club for gays and lesbians.

PUBLICATIONS

■ **OUTlines**
133 West Market Street, #105 ✉ IN 46204-2801 ☏ 923-8550
📠 923-8505 📧 editor@indygaynews.com
🖥 www.indygaynews.com
The Indiana weekly Gay & Lesbian news magazine.
■ **Word. The**
501 Madison Avenue, Suite 307 ✉ IN 46225 ☏ 725-8840
📠 687-8840 📧 theword@dsl.telocity.com 🖥 www.indword.com
Monthly gay newspaper.

BARS

■ **Brothers Bar & Grill** (B F GLM)
822 North Illinois ✉ IN 46204 ☏ 636-1020
■ **Illusions** (B G MA N S)
1446 East Washington ☏ 266-0535
■ **Our Place** (B G MA OS) 16-3 h, closed Sun
231 East 16th Street ✉ IN 46202 ☏ 638-8138
■ **Ten. The** (B gLM N STV)
1218 North Pennsylvania ☏ 638-5802
Best drag shows in town

■ **Utopia** (B d F gLM WE) 17-2, Fri Sat -3 h
924 North Pennsylvania ✉ IN 46204 ☏ 638-0215
■ **The Varsity Lounge** (AC B BF CC F GLM MA WE) Mon-Sat 10-3, Sun 12-0.30 h
1517 North Pennsylvania Street ✉ IN 46202 ☏ 635-9998
Also restaurant.
■ **501 Tavern** (B G LJ MA) 17.30-3 h, closed Sun
501 North College ☏ 632-2100

CAFES

■ **Abbey. The** (b BF f glm)
771 North Massachusetts Avenue ☏ 269-8426

DANCECLUBS

■ **Metro & Colours** (B D F GLM OS) Mon-Sat 16-3 Sun 12-24 h
707 Massachusetts Avenue ✉ IN 46204 ☏ 639-6022
■ **The Unicorn Club** (B D G p SNU YG)
122 West 13th Street ✉ IN 46202 ☏ 262-9195
■ **The Vogue** (B D glm MA) Sun (G)
6259 North College Avenue ✉ IN 46220 ☏ 259-7029

RESTAURANTS

■ **Aesop's Tables** (B F glm)
600 North Massachusetts Avenue ☏ 631-0055
Good Mediterranean food
■ **Canary Café** (A AC CC b bf F glm MA N OS)
621 Ft. Wayne Avenue ✉ IN 46204 *(Downtown)* ☏ 635-6168

SEX SHOPS/BLUE MOVIES

■ **Bookland** (glm)
137 West Market ☏ 639-9864
Adult books
■ **115 New Jersey** (G)
115 New Jersey
Magazines and videos

SAUNAS/BATHS

■ **Club Indianapolis** (AC CC G MA P PI SA SB SOL WH WO) 0-24 h
620 North Capitol Avenue ✉ IN 46204 ☏ 635-5796
Sauna with complete gym equipment.
■ **Works. The** (b G H MA OS P SA SB VS WO)
4120 North Keystone Avenue ✉ IN 46205 ☏ 547-9210
Bath house with room to room telephone service and patio parties on Sun in summer.

BOOK SHOPS

■ **Borders Books** (glm)
5612 Castleton Corner Lane ✉ IN 46250 ☏ 849-8660
■ **Out Word Bound ... Books with Pride** (a CC GLM MA) 11.30-21, Fri 11.30-22, Sat 10-22, Sun 12-18 h
625 N. East Street *(Downtown)* ☏ 951-9100
Specialized in lesbian & gay books plus cards, magazines, pride items, gifts, mainstream books etc.

GENERAL GROUPS

■ **Fellowship**
PO Box 2331 ✉ IN 46206 ☏ 921-9713
Support group for lesbians and gay men
■ **PFLAG-Parents and Friends of Lesbians and Gays**
☏ 545-7034

FETISH GROUPS

■ **Circle City Leather**
PO Box 1632 ✉ IN 46206

USA/Indiana - Kansas | Indianapolis ▶ Topeka

HEALTH GROUPS
- **Circle City AIDS Coalition**
3951 North Meridian Street, Suite 200 ✉ IN 46208 ☎ 632-0123
- **Damien Center** 8.30-20.30 h
1350 North Pennsylvania Street ✉ IN 46202 ☎ 632-0123
📠 632-4362 🖥 www.damien.org
AIDS care center

HELP WITH PROBLEMS
- **Indianapolis Youth Group**
☎ 541-8726

RELIGIOUS GROUPS
- **Gay and Lesbian Jewish Group**
5413 Graceland Avenue ✉ IN 46208 ☎ 633-9285

SPORT GROUPS
- **Frontrunners** (GLM)
PO Box 88765 ✉ IN 46208-0765 ☎ 767-5034

CRUISING
- all AYOR
- Glendale Shopping Center (Sun only)
- Holiday Park
- American Legion Park

Lake Station ☎ 219

BARS
- **Axcis Nightclub & Lounge** (AC B D F GLM MA S SNU STV VS)
Mon-Sat 19-3 h, Sun 17-0.30 h
2415 Rush Street ✉ IN 46405 *(next to water tower)* ☎ 962-1017
Piano Lounge open Thu, Fri, Sat 22-1 h. Latin night on Mon. Popular on Fri.

New Albany ☎ 812

GUEST HOUSES
- **Beharrell House** (AC BF CC GLM H OS WO)
343 Beharrell Avenue ✉ IN 47150 *(near Louisville/Kentucky)*
☎ 944-0289
Small B&B in a restored 100 year old home with a big deck and yard. All rooms have ceiling fans, clock/radio and cable TV. Rates double/private bath US$ 95 and double/shared bath US$ 65 incl. continental bf.

South Bend ☎ 219

SHOWS
- **Seahorse II Cabaret** (AC B CC D GLM MA S STV VS) Wed-Sat 20-3.30 h, Sun -12.30 h
1902 Western ✉ IN 46619 ☎ 231-9139
Shows Wed-Sat at 22 and 1 h.

USA-Iowa

Location: Middlewest USA
Initials: IA
Time: GMT -6
Area: 145.754 km² / 59,613 sq mi.
Population: 2,852,000
Capital: Des Moines

Cedar Rapids ☎ 319

BARS
- **Warehouse Saloon** (B D G MA S) 17-2, Sun -24 h
525 H Street South West ✉ IA 52404 ☎ 365-9044

CRUISING
- Ellis Park (AYOR)
- Linndale Mall

Des Moines ☎ 515

GAY INFO
- **Gay Info Line** 24 hrs
☎ 279-2110

BARS
- **Blazing Saddles** (B G LJ) 11-2 h, Sun 16-24 h
416 East 5th Street ✉ IA 50309 ☎ 246-1299
- **Brass Garden** (B D GLM S YG) 18-2, Sun 18-24 h
112 East 4th Street ✉ IA 50309 ☎ 243-3965

SEX SHOPS/BLUE MOVIES
- **Gallery Book Store** 24 hrs.
1114 Walnut Street ✉ IA 50309 ☎ 244-2916

HOTELS
- **Kingman House** (BF glm H)
2920 Kingman Boulevard ✉ IA 50311 ☎ 279-7312

CRUISING
- Gay Loop (AYOR) (Keo Park between 4th and 5th Streets)
- Birdland Park (AYOR)
- Greenwood Park
- Margo Frankel Woods (AYOR)
- Valley West Mall (upper level)

Sioux City ☎ 712

DANCECLUBS
- **3 Cheers** (AC B D GLM MA N S TV) 21-2 h
414 20th Street ✉ IA 51104 ☎ 255-8005

USA-Kansas

Location: Middlewest USA
Initials: KS
Time: GMT -6
Area: 213.111 km² / 87,162 sq mi.
Population: 2,595,000
Capital: Topeka

Kansas City

GAY INFO
☞ Kansas City, Missouri

Topeka ☎ 785

CRUISING
- Gage Park (AYOR)
- Kansas Avenue (downtown by car)

Wichita ☏ 316

PUBLICATIONS
■ **Liberty Press**
PO Box 16315 ✉ KS 67216-0315 ☏ 652-7737 📠 685-1999
💻 editor@libertypress.net 💻 www.libertypress.net
Monthly GLBT publication.

BARS
■ **Our Fantasy** (B D GLM OS YG) 16-2 h closed Mon-Tue
3201 South Hillside ✉ KS 67216 ☏ 682-5494
■ **T-Room** (B GLM lj N) 12-2 h
1507 South Pawnee ✉ KS 67211 ☏ 262-9317

RESTAURANTS
■ **Harbour Restaurant. The** (F GLM)
3201 South Hillside ✉ KS 67216 ☏ 681-2746

USA-Kentucky

Location: Central East USA
Initials: KY
Time: GMT -5
Area: 104.665 km² / 42,807 sq mi.
Population: 3,908,000
Capital: Frankfort

Lexington ☏ 606

GAY INFO
■ **Lexington Gay and Lesbian Services** Wed-Fri 20-23 h
PO Box 114 71 ✉ KY 40575 ☏ 231-0335
Info and referrals; social events, newsletter.

BARS
■ **Bar, Inc. The** (A AC B CC D GLM lj MA N S STV) Mon-Fri 16-1 Sat-3.30 h
224 East Main Street ✉ KY 40507 *(On Main St. in front of Esplanade)* ☏ (859) 255-1551
■ **Crossings** (AC B G LJ OS S) 16-1 h, closed Sun
117 North Limestone Street ✉ KY 40507 ☏ 233-7266

SEX SHOPS/BLUE MOVIES
■ **Bookstore. The**
942 Winchester Road ✉ KY 40505 ☏ 252-2093

CRUISING
-Jacobson Park (AYOR)
-University of Kentucky (Fine Arts Building)
-Woodland Park

Louisville ☏ 502

GAY INFO
■ **Gay and Lesbian Hotline** 18-1 h
☏ 897-2475

PUBLICATIONS
■ **Letter. The** 9-15 h (EST)
PO Box 3882 ✉ KY 40201 ☏ 636-0295 💻 willnich@aol.com
💻 www.theletter.net
Monthly magazine.

BOOK SHOPS
■ **Carmichael's** (glm)
1295 Bardstown Road ✉ KY 40204 ☏ 456-6950

GENERAL GROUPS
■ **Bluegrass Bears Kentucky**
PO Box 370 01 ✉ KY 40233-7001

CRUISING
-The Falls (across Ohio River in Jeffersonville, Indiana)
-Central Park (4th and Magnolia)
-Fourth Street (between St. Catherine and Hill)
-Iroquois Park
-Cherokee Park (at the fountain)

Paducah ☏ 270

RESTAURANTS
■ **Tribeca Mexican Cuisine** (AC B CC F glm S) Mon-Sat 11-24 h, closed Mon
127 Market House Square ✉ KY 42001 ☏ 444-3960
Authentic Mexican food restaurant.

GUEST HOUSES
■ **1857 Bed & Breakfast** (AC BF CC GLM LJ WH)
127 Market House Square ✉ KY 42001 *(heart of downtown)*
☏ 444-3960 ☏ (800) 264-5607
Rooms with bath, phone, cable TV. Rates US$ 65-85. Completely renovated.

USA-Louisiana

Location: South USA
Initials: LA
Time: GMT -6
Area: 134.275 km² / 54,918 sq mi.
Population: 4,352,000
Capital: Baton Rouge

Baton Rouge ☏ 225

BARS
■ **Buddies** (B g)
450 Oklahoma ✉ LA 70802 ☏ 346-1191
■ **George's** (B G MA)
860 St. Louis Street ✉ LA 70802 ☏ 387-9798
■ **Hide-A-Way Club** (B G MA)
7367 Exchange Place ✉ LA 70806 ☏ 923-3632
■ **Mac's** (B G MA) 20-2 h
668 Main Street ✉ LA 70801 ☏ 387-9963

BOOK SHOPS
■ **Hibiscus Bookstore** (glm) Mon-Sat 11-18 h
635 Main Street ✉ LA 70801 *(downtown)* ☏ 387-4264

PRIVATE ACCOMMODATION
■ **Brentwood House** (AC BF F G NU VS WH wo)
PO Box 40872 ✉ LA 70835-0872 ☏ 924-4789 📠 924-1738
💻 tomsin@ix.hetcom.com
Home stays in residential area. Shared bath/wc. Weekly rates available.

CRUISING
-Capitol Lakes (AYOR) (and adjacent area)
-Cortana Mall
-Highland Road Park (AYOR)
-Louisiana State University (AYOR) (Allen Hall)

USA/Louisiana | Hammond ▶ New Orleans

Hammond ☎ 504

BARS

■ **Chances** (B D GLM MA) Fri Sat 21-2 h
42357 Veterans *(right off exit #40, I-12)* ☎ 542-9350

Lafayette ☎ 318

BARS

■ **Images** (B G MA)
524 West Jefferson ✉ LA 70501 ☎ 233-0070
■ **Ole Blue Note** (B g)
115 Spring Street ✉ LA 70501 ☎ 234-9232

CRUISING

-Garrard Park (AYOR)
-Northeast Louisiana University (library)
-U.S.L. Library and Wharton Hall (2nd and 3rd floor)

Lake Charles ☎ 318

BARS

■ **Billy B's** (B G MA)
704 Ryan ✉ LA 70601 ☎ 433-5457
■ **Crystal's** (B F glm YG) 20-3 h, closed Sun-Tue, Fri (G), Sat (L)
112 West Broad Street ✉ LA 70601 ☎ 433-5457

Metairie ☎ 504

BARS

■ **4-Seasons/The Out Back** (B G MA)
3229 North Causeway Boulevard ✉ LA 70002 ☎ 832-0659

New Orleans ☎ 504

✱ Feel like Scarlett O'Hara once in a lifetime? The more than decadent south state mansion *Nottoway* boasts enough rooms for living your romantic dreams and *Cajun country* in the west of New Orleans beautiful outing opportunities. But don't take your outing in summer; then the city is far too hot and humid. But while the heat recedes during the other seasons, the humidity stays, New Orleans being situated between *Lake Pontchartrain* and the gulf of Mexico. In between is rather little space, so that you can get along without a car in this not too big city. Be as it may, as a tourist you are likely to hang out in *Vieux Carré*, the enchanting old city center and tourist magnet. The more gay part of this quarter, which is also THE gay quarter of the city, is the area to the northeast of St. Ann Street. Newest events and locations can be drawn from the magazines *Ambush* or *Impact*. the most lively event in town is the *Mardi Gras*, THE (gay) festival in New Orleans. No other event shows more distinctly, what New Orleans is all about: a real multicultural feeling in this city, where Africans, Choctaw-Indians, French, Irish, Caribeans, Spanish and many more have left their marks. And, naturally, the gays, which are one of the many, colourful *communities* of the city. The Mardi Gras is in a very special way the "southern" art of celebrating, of music (jazz!), of good food and "laissez-faire", an art of living which can only prosper here. By the way: for the right morsel of romanticism take the river ferry from the aquarium to Audubon zoo, and ride the St. Charles Avenue Streetcar back into town.

★ Einmal im Leben fühlen wie Scarlett O'Hara? Das ultra-dekadente Südstaaten-Herrenhaus *Nottoway* hat genügend Zimmer für romantische Träume, und das *Cajun country* westlich von New Orleans bietet einige dieser Ausflugs-Perlen.

Ausflüge, für die man sich nicht den Sommer vormerken sollte. Die Stadt ist dann viel zu heiß und viel zu feucht. Obwohl die Hitze während des restlichen Jahres weicht, bleibt die Feuchtigkeit denn auf der einen Seite New Orleans' liegt der *Lake Pontchartrain*, auf der anderen der Golf von Mexiko.
Und dazwischen ist eher weniger Platz, so daß man in der nicht übermässig großen Stadt gut ohne Auto auskommt. Es ist so oder so sehr wahrscheinlich, daß man als Tourist meist im *Vieux Carré*, dem bezaubernden Altstadt-Touristenmagnet, unterwegs ist. Die schwulere Hälfte dieses Viertels, das auch DAS Homo-Viertel der Stadt ist, ist die Gegend nordöstlich der St. Ann Street. Was gerade genau angesagt ist, entnimmt man den Zeitungen *Ambush* oder *Impact*.
Die bunteste Seite der Stadt ist *Mardi Gras* (⇨ Events), DAS (schwule) Fest der Stadt. Keine andere Feier veranschaulicht besser, was New Orleans ausmacht: echtes Multi-Kulti-Feeling in einer Stadt, in der Afrikaner, Choctaw-Indianer, Franzosen, Iren, Kariben, Spanier und viele andere ihre Spuren hinterlassen haben. Und natürlich auch die Schwulen, die eben eine der vielen, bunten *communities* der Stadt sind. Mardi Gras, das ist in besonderem Maße die "südliche" Kunst des Feierns, der Musik (Jazz!), des guten Essens und des "Laissez-Faire", eine Kunst, die nur hier gedeihen kann.
Übrigens: für die richtige Prise Romantik zum Schluß nimmt man die Flußfähre vom Aquarium zum Audubon Zoo und fährt mit der St. Charles Avenue Streetcar zurück in die Stadt.

✱ Jouer Scarlett O'Hara au moins une fois dans sa vie? Oui, c'est possible! La demeure de Nottoway, symbole de la décadence du Sud, a suffisamment de chambres pour réaliser le plus romantique de vos rêves! Et le Pays Cajun, à l'ouest de la Nouvelle Orléans, regorge de curiosités touristiques. Tant d'excursions qu'on ferait mieux de faire en automne ou en hiver, car, l'été, la chaleur est tellement étouffante en Louisiane qu'on en reste collé au pavé. Si les températures deviennent supportables l'hiver, l'humidité, elle, reste pesante toute l'année, car sachez que la ville est coincée entre le Lac Pontchartrain et le Golfe du Mexique. La superficie de la ville est donc assez restreinte, ce qui offre l'avantage de pouvoir quasiment tout faire à pied: pas besoin de voiture! D'autant plus que quand on visite La Nouvelle Orléans, on a du mal de s'extraire du "Vieux Carré", le pôle d'attraction numéro 1 de la ville. Attention: c'est aussi le bastion gai de la Louisiane. 50% de sa superficie est entre les mains des gays, Commencez à St Ann Street et remontez vers le nord. Pour savoir quoi faire, quand et où aller, consultez les magasines gays locaux "Ambush" ou "Impact". La Nouvelle Orléans, c'est le carnaval, c'est "Mardi Gras". Aucune autre manifestation ne montre mieux le caractère multiculturel de la ville. Africains, Indiens Choctaw, Français, Irlandais, Espagnols et Antillais ont marqué la ville de leur empreinte. Les gais, eux aussi, forment une communauté qui, aujourd'hui, fait définitivement partie du décor et qui a aussi son mot à dire. Jazz, cuisine excellente, art de vivre et de faire la fête, ambiance laisser-faire décontractée: tout ça, c'est la Nouvelle Orléans! Au fait: Traversez le fleuve en bac pour aller de l'aquarium au zoo Audubon et revenez en ville avec le St Charles Avenue Street Car: un souvenir inoubliable!

● ¿Sentir como Escarlata O'Hara una vez en la vida? La ultra decadente mansión del estado sureño *Nottoway* tiene suficientes dormitorios para sueños románticos, y el *Cajun Country* al oeste de Nueva Orleans ofrece algunos sitios encantadores. Aunque so se deberían visitar precisamente en verano, ya que en estas fechas la ciudad es muy calurosa y humeda. Mientras que en el resto del año el calor cede, la humedad persiste, porque Nueva Orleans está situada entre el *Lake Pontchartrain* y el Golfo de México. La ciudad es pequeña, así que los trayectos se pueden hacer a pie. El centro turístico de la ciudad es el magnífico *Vieux Carré*. El sector gay de la ciu-

1256 | *SPARTACUS* 2001/2002

New Orleans | Louisiana/USA

New Orleans

1. Big Easy Guest House / Macarty Park Guest House / Copper Top Bar / La Dauphine Guest House
2. Faubourg Marigny Bookshop
3. Rober House Condos Apartments
4. Golden Lantern Bar
5. Ursulines Guest House
6. MRB Bar
7. Café Lafitte in Exile Bar
8. Bourbon Pub Bar
9. Good Friends Bar
10. Rawhide 2010 Bar
11. Wolfendale's Bar
12. Footloose Bar
13. Oz Danceclub
14. Corner Pocket Bar
15. The Roundup Bar
16. The Greenhouse Guest House
17. French Quarter B&B Guest House

SPARTACUS 2001/2002 | 1257

USA/Louisiana — New Orleans

dad esta en la región moroeste de la St. Ann Street. Las revistas *Ambush* o *Impact* informan sobre los sitios gay de moda. El acontecimiento gay anual de mayor relevancia es el *Mardi Gras*. Ninguna otra fiesta manifiesta de igual forma la especialidad de Nueva Orleans: un sentimiento multicultural en una ciudad en la que africanos, indios Chovtaw, franceses, irlandeses, caribeños, españoles y muchos otros, han dejado sus huellas. Y por supuesto los homosexuales que constituyen uno de los variopintos grupos de la ciudad. Mardi Gras es sobre todo la manifestación del arte sureño de celebrar fiestas, de la música (jazz), la buena comida y del dejar hacer "Laissez-Faire", un arte que solo aquí puede florecer. Consejo: Tome el barco del Aquarium en dirección Audubon Zoo y viaje con el St. Charles Avenue Streetcar de regreso a la ciudad.

E sentirsi per una volta come Scarlett O'Hara? L'ultra decadente casa padronale del sud *Nottoway* ha abbastanza stanze per sogni romantici e la *Cajun Country* ad ovest di New Orleans offre alcune di queste perle. Queste escursioni non sono consigliabili in estate, poichè la città è troppo calda ed umida. Mentre il caldo diminuisce durante il resto dell'anno l'umidità resta. New Orleans infatti è situata tra *Lake Pontchartrain* e il golfo del Messico. A causa di queste frontiere naturali la città non è molto grande pertanto non è necessaria un'auto per girarla. I turisti si muovono di solito nel *Vieux Carrè*, l'incantevole centro storico della città. Il quartiere gay occupa la metà del centro, nella zona a nord est dalla St. Ann Street. Otterrete ulteriori informazioni sui giornali *Ambush* o *Impact*. Il momento più colorato della città è il *Mardi Gras*, la festa gay per eccellenza. Nessun altro festeggiamento mostra meglio l'essenza di New Orleans: un vero spirito multiculturale in una città in cui africani, indiani Choctaw, francesi, irlandesi, centroamericani, spagnoli ed altri hanno lasciato le proprie tracce; naturalmente anche i gay formano una delle variopinte comunità della città. Mardi Gras rappresenta il modo di far festa tipico del sud, con musica (jazz), buona cucina ed il "laissez faire" che esiste solo qui. A proposito: se volete un po' di romanticismo prendete il battello da Aquarium a Audubon Zoo. Potrete poi rientrare in città con la St.Charles Avenue Streetcar.

GAY INFO

■ **Lesbian & Gay Community Center** (A GLM S) 12-19 h
2114 Decatur Street ✉ LA 70116 ☎ 522-1103
Refferals for lodging, meals, counseling, support group.

PUBLICATIONS

■ **Ambush Magazine**
828-A Bourbon Street ✉ LA 70116-3137 ☎ 522-8049
📠 522-0907 💻 webmaster@ambushmag.com
💻 www.ambushmag.com
Biweekly magazine.
■ **Impact News** Mon-Fri 10-18 h
PO Box 52079 ✉ LA 70152 ☎ 944-6722 ☎ (888) 944-6722
📠 944-6794 💻 mail@impactnews.com 💻 www.impactnews.com
Biweekly newspaper for Gulf South. Free at gay venues.

CULTURE

■ **Amistad Research Center. The**
Tulane University, 6823 St. Charles Avenue ✉ LA 70118
☎ 866-5535

TOURIST INFO

■ **New Orleans Metropolitan Convention & Visitors Bureau**
1520 Sugar Bowl Drive ✉ LA 70112 ☎ 566-5011 📠 566-5046
💻 www.nawlins.com

BARS

■ **Another Corner** (B G lj N snu)
2601 Royal Street ✉ LA 70117 ☎ 940-0666
A bar for bears and their friends.
■ **Big Daddy's** (B f GLM N) 0-24 h
2513 Royal Street ✉ LA 70117 ☎ 948-6288
■ **Cafe Lafitte & Balcony Bar** (AC B G lj MA VS) 0-24 h
901 Bourbon Street ✉ LA 70116 *(at Dumaine Street)* ☎ 522-8397
One of the oldest gay bar in the US. Very popular. 24 hours of D.J. music.
■ **Coppertop Bar** (AC B CC F G MA N) 0-24 h
706 Franklin Avenue ✉ LA 70117 ☎ 948-2300
■ **Corner Pocket. The** (B G LJ N SNU STV YG) 0-24 h
940 St. Louis Street ✉ LA 70112 *(at Burgundy Street)* ☎ 568-9829
SNU Thu-Sun 20-? h Popular on Fri.
■ **Country Club. The** (B GLM NU P PI WO) 10-6 h (closed in winter)
634 Louisa Street ✉ LA 70117 *(near Royal Street)* ☎ 945-0742
Two bars, hot tub. US$ 5 cover.
■ **Double Play** (B G N TV)
439 Dauphine Street ✉ LA 70116 ☎ 523-4517
Cruise bar formerly named "The Wild Side"; rather "wild" neighbourhood-bar.
■ **Footloose** (AC B G MA stv) Mon Tue Thu 14-2, Wed 16-2, Fri-Sun 0-24 h
700 North Rampart Street ✉ LA 70117 ☎ 524-7654
Drag show on WE.
■ **Friendly Bar. The** (B F GLM MA N)
2301 Chartres Street ✉ LA 70117 ☎ 943-8929
A pool table and a juke box.
■ **Golden Lantern** (B G MA N) 0-24 h
1239 Royal Street ✉ LA 70116 *(at Barracks)* ☎ 529-2860
Second-oldest gay bar in the French quarter. Friendly neighborhood bar.
■ **Good Friends Bar & Queen's Head Pub** (AC B GLM MA N VS) 0-24 h
740 Dauphine Street ✉ LA 70116 ☎ 566-7191
Especially popular in the early evening. Perfect meeting place.
■ **Mother Bob's** (B GLM MA TV)
542 North Rampart ☎ 566-1300
Weekly specials and other events.
■ **MRB / The Patio** (B F G snu) 0-24 h
515 Saint Phillip Street ✉ LA 70116 ☎ 524-2558
Cruise bar with strip-tease on WE.
■ **Phoenix & Men's Room** (B F G LJ) 0-24 h
941 Elysian Fields Avenue ✉ LA 70117 *(at Rampart Street)*
☎ 945-9264
Posters from gay bars around the world cover the walls downstairs. Upstairs, in The Men's Room, you'll find some dark corners, restraints hanging from the ceiling and a cage. Popular gathering for the town's leather crowd.
■ **Rawhide 2010** (AC B G LJ MA N) 0-24 h
740 Burgundy Street ✉ LA 70117 *(at Saint Ann Street)*
☎ 525-8106
■ **RK's Rainbow** (B GLM N s) 0-24 h
626 Saint Philip Street ☎ 566-7553
Open-to-the-street bar allowing you to enjoy all the sights and scenery in New Orleans.
■ **Roundup. The** (B G N OS stv tv) 0-24 h
819 Saint Louis Street ✉ LA 70112 ☎ 561-8340
Bar with an interestingly mixed crowed. Pocket pool, juke box, occasional shows, and a patio (open during the summer).

New Orleans — Louisiana/USA

■ **TT's** (B GLM N stv) 0-24 h
820 North Rampart Street ✉ LA 70116 ☎ 523-9521
Very mixed clientele.
■ **Voodo at Congo Square** (B GLM MA N)
718 North Rampart Street ✉ LA ☎ 527-0703
One of the wildest clubs in town, voted Neighborhood Bar of the Year 2000. Late night bar.
■ **Wolfendale's** (B D F G snu) 16-5, Thu-Sun (D) 22-? h
834 North Rampart Street ✉ LA 70116 ☎ 523-7764
African-American clientele.

DANCECLUBS

■ **Bourbon Pub & Parade Disco** (AC B D GLM VS YG s) 0-24 h
801 Bourbon Street ✉ LA 70116 ☎ 529-2107
One of the lagest gay dance club.
■ **Oz** (B D GLM SNU stv YG) 0-24 h
800 Bourbon Street ✉ LA 70116 ☎ 593-9491
Drag show on Wed.
■ **735 nightclub & bar** (B D glm MA S STV VS WE)
735 Bourbon Street ✉ LA ☎ 581-6740
Two dancefloors, live music, theme nights and nationally-known DJs. One of the best clubs in town.

RESTAURANTS

■ **Buffa's** (B F GLM) 22-2 h
1001 Esplanade Avenue ✉ LA 70116 ☎ 945-9373
Home cooking!
■ **Cafe Sbisa** (AC CC F glm OS) 17.30-22.30 h
1011 Decatur Street ✉ LA 70116na ☎ 522-5565
■ **Clover Grill** (AC BF CC F glm MA) 0-24 h
900 Bourbon Street ✉ LA 70116 (at Dumaine Street) ☎ 523-0904
■ **Lucky Cheng's** (AC B CC d F GLM MA N S TV WE) 18-23, Fri Sat - 24 h
720 Saint Louis Street ✉ LA 70130 (between Bourbon & Royal Street in the French quarter) ☎ 523-9560
Restaurant & bar. Asian Creole cuisine served by luscious drag queens. Nightly shows. Call for further infos.
■ **Mama Rosa's** (B CC F glm) Tue-Sun 10.30-23.30 h
616 North Rampart Street ✉ LA 70112 ☎ 523-5546
Italian food and sandwiches.
■ **Mona Lisa** (B CC F glm) Tue-Fri 17-23 h, Sat Sun 21-2 h
1212 Royal Street ✉ LA 70116 ☎ 522-6746
Pizza and salads.
■ **La Peniche** (B F g) 0-24 h
1940 Dauphine Street ✉ LA 70116 ☎ 943-1460
■ **Quarter Scene. The** (AC BF CC F glm) daily 8-24 h
900 Dumaine Street ✉ LA 70116 (French Quarter, Corner Dumaine/Dauphine St.) ☎ 522-6533
Good and inexpensive lunch meals. No alcoholic drinks.
■ **Vera Cruz** (B CC F glm)
1141 Decatur Street ✉ LA 70116 ☎ 561-8081
Mexican cuisine.

SAUNAS/BATHS

■ **Club. The** (b CC f G MA P SA SB SOL VS WH WO) 0-24 h
515 Toulouse Street ✉ LA 70130 ☎ 581-2402
Five levels of facilities with many special rooms.
■ **Flex** (G MA VS) 24 h
700 Baronne Street ✉ LA ☎ 598-3539

BOOK SHOPS

■ **Faubourg Marigny Books** (CC GLM) Mon-Fri 10-20, Sat-Sun 10-18 h
600 Frenchmen Street ✉ LA 70116 ☎ 943-9875

LEATHER & FETISH SHOPS

■ **Gargoyles Leather**
1205 Decatur Street ✉ LA 70116 ☎ 529-4387
Mail order available.
■ **Gay Mart**
808 North Rampart Street ✉ LA 70116 ☎ 523-5876
■ **Second Skin Leather Company** (GLM vs) 12-22, Sun 12-18 h
521 Rue Saint Philip ✉ LA 70116 (French Quarter, Downtown) ☎ 561-8167
Retail store, clothing&video. Mail order available.

HOTELS

■ **Frenchmen Hotel. The** (AC BF F glm H PI)
417 Frenchmen Street ✉ LA 70116 ☎ 948-2166 📠 943-2328
Rooms with bath, phone and TV.
■ **Garden District. The** (AC BF glm H OS)
2418 Magazine Street ✉ LA 70130 ☎ 895 43 02
Beautifully furnished Victorian town house built in 1890. All rooms with private bath, balconies, ceiling fans, open fire places and cable TV. Suites with full kitchens available. Call for detailed information and rates.
■ **Rathbone Inn** (AC BF g H WH) 8-19 h
1227 Esplanade Avenue ✉ LA 70116 ☎ 947-2100 ☎ (800) 947-2101 📠 947-7454
Rooms with priv. bath, kitchenette. Rates US$ 90-145.
■ **Rue Royal Inn** (AC CC g H) Office 8-19 h
1006 Royal Street ✉ LA 70116 ☎ 524-3900 ☎ (800) 776-3901 📠 558-0566
All rooms with priv. bath, fridge.

GUEST HOUSES

■ **Big Easy Guest House** (AC BF CC f GLM)
2633 Dauphine Street ✉ LA 70117 ☎ 943-3717 ☎ (800) 679-0640 (toll-free) 📧 BigEasyGH@aol.com
Located near the French Quarter. in a private home dated circa 1850. All rooms with private bath/WC, telephone, TV and private entrance. Lush, semi-tropical patio. Rooms furnished with lots of antiques. German spoken.
■ **Bon Maison Guest House** (AC CC glm H MA OS)
835 Bourbon Street ✉ LA 70116-3106 ☎ 561-8498 📠 561-8498
📧 bmgh@acadiacom.net 🌐 www.bonmaison.com
Small guest house in a restored townhouse (built in 1833). Hotel with garden and lovely planted patio with tables, chairs and outdoor grill. All rooms with private shower baths, kitchenette (refrigerator, microwave, toaster and coffee maker), air-condition, private phone and color cable TV. Rooms in the slave (!) quarter units US$ 75 and suites $125 (tax included).
■ **Bourgoyne Guest House** (AC cc glm H MA)
839 Bourbon Street ✉ LA 70116 (in French Quarter) ☎ 524-3621 ☎ 525-3983
Located on bustling Bourbon Street the Guesthouse is located in an 1830s Creole mansion with balconies, galleries, winding staircases and a lush, green courtyard. The two suites are furnished with antiques and have private bathrooms (one with solarium), TV and fully equipped kitchen. Rates US$ 70-160. Studio apartments available with double bed, dining area, private bath and kitchen. Rates US$ 80-170.
■ **Creole Inn** (AC CC G H MA OS)
2471 Dauphine Street ✉ LA 70117 (5 blocks to Freunch Quarter, 15 mins to Convention Center) ☎ 948-2217 (reservations) ☎ 948-2217 📠 948-3420 📧 creoleinn@aol.com 🌐 www.creoleinn.com

USA/Louisiana | New Orleans

1830'S PRIVATE HOME
BIG EASY GUEST HOUSE
2633 DAUPHINE ST., NEW ORLEANS, LA 70117
1-800-679-0640 • (504) 943-3717

E-mail: bigeasygh@aol.com

- Private Bath Entrance*
- TV - Phone - Central AC/Heat - Continental Breakfast*
- Microwave - Refrigerator - Ice Maker*
- Only 9 Blocks (4 to 5 minute walk) to French Quarter)*
- Minimum Night Stay may be Required Based on Double Occupancy*
- Regular $65 (2N) - Weekly $55 (7N)*
- Summer (June 15 to August 15) $50 (3N) Summer rate not Applicable to 4th July weekend*
- Special Events/Holidays*
- $130 TO $150 (Min. night p299)*
  All Rates Include Tax*
- MasterCard/Visa*

Please call between 8 am & 4 pm Central Standard Time
Color Brochure available upon request
GERMAN SPOKEN
*Rates subject to change

Royal Street Courtyard
2446 Royal Street
New Orleans, LA 70117

A 1844 historic all suite guesthouse with tropical courtyard and hot tub. Rates start at $55.00

**Toll Free
888-846-4004**

504-943-6818
Fax: 504-945-1212
E-mail: royalctyd@aol.com

La Dauphine & Creole Inn

*LaDauphine – 2316 Dauphine
www.ladauphine.com*

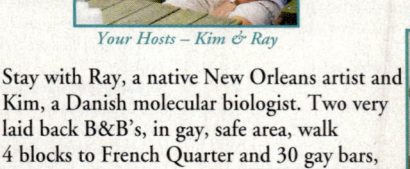

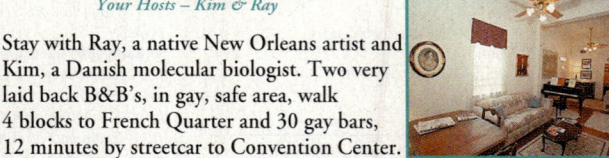

Your Hosts – Kim & Ray

*Creole Inn - 2471 Dauphine
www.creoleinn.com*

LaDauphine - Alec Baldwin Suite

Cyber Cafe in Creole Inn

Stay with Ray, a native New Orleans artist and Kim, a Danish molecular biologist. Two very laid back B&B's, in gay, safe area, walk 4 blocks to French Quarter and 30 gay bars, 12 minutes by streetcar to Convention Center. Roomy, private baths, cable TV/VCR, phone, cyber cafe, central air & heat, smoke-free inside. VISA, MC, AMEX, Diners, Discover. 3 night minimum. French, Danish, German, Spanish. Single - $65 - $85, Double $85 - $110. - Weekly Rates $450-$550.

Creole Inn - Living Room

Reservations - 504-948-2217   Fax 504-948-3720   IGLTA Member
email: ladauphine@aol.com   Visit our website: www.ladauphine.com

New Orleans | **Louisiana/USA**

Ursuline Guest House
708 Rue Des Ursulines
New Orleans, Louisiana 70116
504-525-8509
1-800-654-2351

■ **French Quarter B&B. The** (AC CC GLM H MA msg PI)
1132 Ursulines Street ✉ LA 70116 *(French Quarter)* ☎ 525-3390
🖷 593-9859
Full kitchen, 2 bedrooms, bath, living room, swimming pool. Rates Jun-Aug US$ 60-75, Sep-May 100-150.

■ **Greenhouse Inn. The** (BF E GLM H msg OS PI WH WO)
1212 Magazine Street ✉ LA 70130 ☎ 525-1333
☎ (800) 966-1303 🖷 525-1306 💻 GreenInn@aol.com
Comfortable guesthouse built in 1840. Swimmingpool and spa (open year round). All rooms with private bath/WC, color TV, video, minibar and telephone (with modem jacks).

■ **La Dauphine Résidence des Artistes** (AC CC G H MA OS)
2316 Rue Dauphine ✉ LA 70117 *(Downtown, 4 blocks walk to French Quarter; 12 mins trolley ride to Convention Centre)*
☎ 948-2217 🖷 948-3420 💻 LaDauphine@aol.com
💻 www.ladauphine.com
Renovated Victorian, 100-year-old house. Relaxed atmosphere. All rooms with private bath/WC, telephone, Sat-TV, video, hair-dryer, some with balcony. Rates single US$ 65-85 and double 85-110. Weekly discounts available. Non-smoking. Continental bf included. Dog on premises.

■ **Lafitte Guest House** (AC BF g H OS)
1003 Bourbon Street ✉ LA 70116 ☎ 581-2678 🖷 581-2678
Convenient location. All rooms with priv. bath, WC, telephone and some with balcony.

■ **Lion's Inn B&B** (AC BF CC G H MA PI WH)
2517 Chartres ✉ LA 70117 ☎ 945-2339 ☎ (800)485-6386
🖷 949-7321 💻 lions@gs.net 💻 www.lionsinn.com
Small B&B in renovated 140 year old Edwardian house. Beautiful garden with jacuzzi. All rooms with telephone, cable TV, radio and hair-dryer. Rates single/shared bath $45-70, double/shared bath $65-110, double/private bath $75-130, loft $100-150 depending on season. Continental bf incl.

■ **Macarty Park Guest House** (AC BF CC glm H PI WH) 8.30-22 h
3820 Burgundy Street ✉ LA 70117-5708 ☎ 943-4994
☎ (800) 521-2790 (toll-free) 🖷 943-4999
💻 goodtimes@macartypark.com 💻 www.macartypark.com
8 double rooms, 2 studios and 6 apartments in a cottage-style home all with bath/shower/WC, balcony, phone, fax, TV, radio, kitchenette (studios) and kitchen (apartments). Rates from $ 59-115 (double occupancy) continental bf included.

■ **Maison Dauphine** (AC BF glm H WH)
2460 Dauphine Street ✉ LA 70117 *(located in Foubourg Marigny, near the French Quarter (Vieux Carré))* ☎ 943-0861 🖷 943-0861
All suites feature living area, bedroom, private bath, direct-dial telephone, answering machine, refrigerator, microwave oven, TV, air condition and heating controls.

■ **Mazant Guesthouse** (AC BF glm H OS)
906 Mazant Street, LA 70117 ✉ LA 70117 ☎ 944-2662
30 min to the airport. Downtown neighborhood. Hotel with garden. All rooms with kitchenette.

■ **New Orleans Guest House** (AC b BF CC glm N) closed 20-25 Dec.
1118 Ursulines Street ✉ LA 70116 *(French Quarter)* ☎ 566-1177
☎ 566-1179
Built in 1848. The Slave Quarters have been renovated into guest units. All 14 rooms with private bath, TV, air-condition, radio and telephone. Rates US$ 79-99 incl. continental breakfast. All taxes extra.

■ **Olde Town Inn** (AC CC glm H)
1001 Marigny Street ✉ LA 70117 ☎ 949-5815
💻 www.fqaccommodations.com

■ **Pauger Guest Suites** (AC glm H MA OS PI) Office: 8-24 h
1750 North Rampart Street ✉ LA 70116 *(near French Quarter)*
☎ 944-2601
Rooms with private bath, telephone, cable-TV, refrigerator, microwave oven. Pool, car park, at walking distance to Gay venues. Rates single from US$ 50, double from $60. Weekly discount.

■ **Royal Barracks Guesthouse** (AC CC GLM MA N OS p VS WH) Reservations: 9-21 h
717 Barracks Street ✉ LA 70116 *(between Royal and Bourbon Street)* ☎ 529-7269 ☎ (888)-255-7269 🖷 529-7298
💻 rbgh@acadiacom.net 💻 www.rbgh.com
B&B in restored Victorian building in the historic French Quarter. Quiet location. All rooms with cable TV, radio, ceiling fan, private bath. Private patio with hot tub. Rates Sep-May US$ 85-145, Jun-Aug $65-110.

■ **Royal Street Courtyard** (G H OS)
2446 Royal Street ✉ LA 70177 ☎ 943-6818 🖷 945-1212
💻 royalctyd@aol.com

■ **Ursuline Guesthouse** (AC GLM H LJ MA OS WH) Office 9-21 h
708 Rue des Ursulines ✉ LA 70116 *(20 minutes to the airport, French Quarter)* ☎ 525-8509 ☎ (800) 654-2351 🖷 525-8408
Centrally located in the heart of local gay scene. All rooms with phone, bath/WC and balcony.

APARTMENTS

■ **Rober House Condos** (AC glm H OS PI)
822 Ursulines Street ✉ LA 70116 *(French Quarter)* ☎ 529-4663
🖷 527-6381

GENERAL GROUPS

■ **LAGPAC** (GLM)
PO Box 530 75 ✉ LA 70153 ☎ 527-0050

USA/Louisiana - Maine — New Orleans ▸ Ogunquit

■ **P-FLAG**
PO Box 15515 ✉ LA 70175 ☏ 895-3936

FETISH GROUPS
■ **Knights D'Orleans**
PO Box 508 12 ✉ LA 70150
■ **Lords of Leather**
PO Box 72105 ✉ LA 70172

HEALTH GROUPS
■ **Act up** Meeting Wed 20 h at 504 Frenchmen
☏ 944-4546
■ **Louisiana HIV/AIDS Hotline**
☏ (800) 992-4379
■ **New Orleans AIDS Task Force**
1407 Decatur Street ✉ LA 70116 ☏ 944-AIDS
■ **PWA Coalition**
☏ 944-3663
■ **RAIN Regional AIDS Interfaith Network**
☏ 523-3755

SPORT GROUPS
■ **Frontrunners Running Club**
☏ 523-3834
■ **New Orleans Gay and Lesbian Tennis Association**
☏ 482-2192

CRUISING
-Audubon Park (AYOR)
-Belle Promenade (West Bank)
-City Park (AYOR)
-Oakwood Shopping Center (AYOR)
-Riverwalk
-Tulane University (AYOR) (cafeteria, library & student union)
-U.N.O. (business administration building & library)
-Vieux Carre (especially Bourbon Street between Toulouse & Ursulines Streets)
-Woldenberg Park

St. Joseph ☏ 318

HOTELS
■ **Garrett Drake Guest House** (AC BF B G H PI)
PO Box 316, LA 71366 ✉ LA 71366 ☏ 766-4229
Priv. and shared baths.

USA-Maine

Location:	Northeast USA
Initials:	ME
Time:	GMT -5
Area:	91.653 km² / 37,486 sq mi.
Population:	1,242,000
Capital:	Augusta

Caribou ☏ 207

GAY INFO
■ **Northern Lambda** 19-21 h
PO Box 990 ✉ ME 04736 ☏ 498-2088
Operates in northeastern Maine and northwestern New Brunswick (Canada). It publishes a newsletter ten times yearly. Holds regular meetings and operates a library.

Naples ☏ 207

GUEST HOUSES
■ **Lamb's Mill Inn** (AC BF CC f GLM OS SB WH)
Lamb's Mill Road, ✉ ME 04055 *(Country Road 0.5 mile outside the town, Western Mountains, Lake Region of Maine).* ☏ 693-6253
✉ lambsmil@pivot.net 🖳 www.pivot.net/~lambsmil/
6 rooms with private baths, TV, refrigerator, AC. Rates US$ 90-120 in season (May-Nov) rest of the year US$ 70-100.

Ogunquit ☏ 207

✻ Located just 70 miles north of Boston, Ogunquit is the quieter and smaller alternative to Provincetown. The village itself is pretty and the beach is white and many miles long. Ogunquit is busy in the summer months and really peaceful for the rest of the year. There are a few gay bars but don't expect a party scene here. This is the perfect place to recover from the daily hassle, walk along the beach, visit the art galleries and have a romatic dinner in one of the good restaurants. There are several gay guest houses who offer good quality accomodation at very reasonable prices. To get to Ogunquit you need a car which is recommended anyway to explore the beautiful scenery. Many guest houses close after the Columbus Day Weekend in the middle of October.

✻ 120 Kilometer nördlich von Boston gelegen ist Ogunquit die kleinere und ruhigere Alternative zu Provincetown. Der hübsche Ort verfügt über lange, weiße Dünenstrände. Saison ist in Ogunquit im Sommer. Den Rest des Jahres geht es hier sehr beschaulich zu. Es gibt einige schwule Bars, doch sollte man an das Nachtleben keine zu große Erwartungen stellen. Dies ist der perfekte Ort um sich bei ausgiebigen Strandspaziergängen, einem Besuch in einer der zahlreichen Galerien oder bei einem gemütlichen Abendessen bei Kerzenschein, vom Streß des Alltags zu erholen. Die schwulen Pensionen bieten alle komfortable Unterkünfte zu sehr zivilen Preisen. Nach Ogunquit reist man am besten mit dem eigenen Auto, denn nur so läßt sich die schöne Umgebung bequem erkunden. Viele Pensionen schließen nach dem Columbus Day Wochenende Mitte Oktober.

✻ Située à 120 km au nord de Boston, Ogunquit offre une alternative plus calme et plus petite à la ville de province. Cette jolie ville possède de longues plages de dunes blanches. La saison la plus intéressante à Ogunquit, c'est l'été. Le reste de l'année, Ogunquit est assez calme. Il y a quelques bars gais, mais il ne faut pas s'attendre à trouver une vie nocturne particulièrement animée. Mais c'est l'endroit rêvé pour de longues promenades sur la plage, des visites dans quelques-unes des nombreuses galeries, ou pour un dîner comfortable aux chandelles pour se reposer du stress quotidien. Les pensions gaies offrent toutes un hébergement comfortable à des prix raisonnables. Il est préférable de se rendre à Ogunquit en voiture pour pouvoir visiter les alentours. Noter que de nombreuses pensions ferment leurs portes après le week-end de Colombus Day, fin Octobre.

✻ Situada a 120 km. al norte de Boston es una pequeña y tranquila alternativa a Provincetown. Ogunquit posee una linda y larga playa de arena blanca. La temporada alta es en verano, durante el resto del año la ciudad es bastante tranquila. Hay algunos bares gay, sin embargo no se debe esperar mucho de la marcha nocturna. Este es el lugar perfecto para hacer largo paseos por la playa, para visitar alguna de las numerosas galerías o para librarse del estrés cotidiano a la luz de las velas de una agradable cena en uno de sus restaurantes. Las pensiones gay ofrecen una confortable estancia a

Weitere Informationen erhältlich bei:

the uncommonplace
KEY WEST®

The Florida Keys & Key West
c/o Get It Across Tourism Marketing
Neumarkt 33
50677 Köln
Tel: (0221) 2336 451
Fax: (0221) 23336 450
flkeys@netcologne.de
www..fla-keys.com

Eine der besten gay-Unterkünfte der USA:
Alexander´s Guesthouse

ALEXANDER'S
GUESTHOUSE

1118 Fleming Street
Key West, Florida 33040
USA
Tel:(001) (305) 294-9919
Within North America:(800) 654-9919
Fax: (001) (305) 295-0257
e-mail: info@alexghouse.com
Internet: www.alexghouse.com

Für Reiseangebote (Flüge, Hotels, Mietwagen und vieles mehr) steht Euch das Reisebüro G-tours gerne zur Verfügung (Gay-Katalog kostenlos anfordern!):

G-tours
WELTWEIT REISEN

Reisebüro G-tours GmbH
Schwalbengasse 46
50667 Köln
Tel.: (0221) 925891-0
Fax: (0221) 925891-19
e-mail: G-tours@t-online.de
Internet: www.G-tours.de

Where there's freedom, there is expression.

KEY WEST
the gay destination

USA/Maine — Ogunquit ▶ Portland

precios relativamente comodos. Para llegar a Ogunquit se debe utilizar preferentemente un coche, solo así se puede apreciar lo hermoso de su paisaje. Muchas pensiones cierran sus puertas a mediados de octubre después del fin de semana de Columbus Day.

Situato a 120 km a nord di Boston, Ogunquit è la variante più piccola e tranquilla rispetto a Provincetown. Il posto carino è dotato di spiagge bianche. L'alta stagione è in estate. Ci sono varie bar gay, però è meglio di non aspettarsi troppo di una vita notturna. E il posto ideale per fare delle passeggiate, visitare una delle numerose gallerie d'arte o cenare in un dei piacevoli ristoranti al lume di candela. Le pensioni gay offrono alloggi a prezzi moderati. Conviene andare ad Ogunquit con la propria macchina, perché solo così si è in grado di conoscere i dintorni con facilità. Molte pensioni chiudono a metà ottobre dopo la fine settimana del Columbus Day.

TOURIST INFO
■ **Chamber of Commerce**
☎ 646-2939
Call for free information package

BARS
■ **Club. The** (AC B D G MA VS) 21-1, Sun 17-1 h
13 Main Street ✉ ME 03907 ☎ 646-6655
Dance and video bar.
■ **Front Porch** (AC B F GLM MA) May-15th Oct 16-1 h
PO Box 796 ✉ ME 03907 ☎ 646-3976
Small piano bar. Open on some WE in winter (special holidays).

RESTAURANTS
■ **Arrows** (b F glm) Tue-Sun 18-21 h
Berwick Road ✉ ME 03907 *(2.5 km north of center)* ☎ 361-1111
Open June-November
■ **Jonathan's** (A AC B CC F glm S) 17-21 h
2 Bourne Lane ✉ ME 03907 ☎ 646-4777
Continental food
■ **Lobster Shack. The** (b F glm)
Perkins Cove ☎ 646-2941

GUEST HOUSES
■ **Admiral's Inn** (AC BF CC glm H MA NU PI OS WH) all year
79 South Main Street ✉ ME 03907 ☎ 646-7093 📠 646-5241
📧 office@theadmiralsinn.com 💻 www.theadmiralsinn.com
Gay owned & operated, 18 units, restaurant & cocktail-lounge, hot tub.
■ **Beauport Inn** (AC BF CC f g MA OS WE)
102 Shore Road ✉ ME 03907 ☎ 646-8680
📧 lobster@cybertours.com 💻 ogun-online.com/beauport
4 rooms with private baths. No pets, no kids.
■ **Clipper Ship** (AC BF CC glm H) 1st May-15th Oct.
170 U.S. Route 1 ✉ ME 03907 ☎ 646-9735
B&B in two restored buidlings (dated 1820 & 1890) in central location. Short walk to the beach. All rooms with TV, some with private bath, own decks and kitchens. Rates US$ 40-85 (off season), US$ 55-130 (on season) incl. bf. Kids and pets welcome.
■ **Gazebo Inn** (AC BF glm H PI)
PO Box 668 ✉ ME 03907 ☎ 646-3733
Rates double/private bath US$ 65 (Oct-May) and $95 (June-Sep) incl. full gourmet bf. Close to the beach. On trolley line.
■ **Heritage of Ogunquit. The** (BF gLM H OS WH)
Marginal Avenue ✉ ME 03907 ☎ 646-7787
💻 wwwone-on-onepc.com/heritage
5 rooms with private and shared bath. Non-smoking rooms available. Kids welcome, no pets.

■ **Inn at Tall Chimneys. The** (AC BF CC GLM H WH) Apr-Nov
94 U.S. Route 1, ✉ ME 03907 ☎ 646-8974
Centrally located B&B. Rooms with Sat-TV, radio, hair-dryer. Some rooms with balcony. Two large decks.
■ **Inn at Two Village Square. The** (AC BF CC GLM MA PI SOL WH WO) Mid-May-Mid Oct, Office: 7-22 h
2 Village Square Lane, PO Box 864 ✉ ME 03907-0864 *(hillside overlooking the village square)* ☎ 646-5779 📠 646-6797
📧 Theinntvs@aol.com 💻 www.theinn.tv
Comfortable Victorian guesthouse with view over the village and ocean. Large decks, heated pool and hot tub. TV room, cozy fire-place. Secluded in-town setting. All rooms with AC and TV. Rates US$ 50-135.
■ **Leisure Inn** (AC BF G H OS) May 15-Oct 15
6 School Street ✉ ME 03907-2113 ☎ 646-2737
📧 ysaint@aol.com 💻 members.aol.com/reysaint
B&B in a restored building built in 1915. All rooms with TV, most with air-condition. On-site parking. Walking distance to bars and beach. No kids, no pets.
■ **Moon over Maine** (AC BF CC G H OS WH)
6 Berwick Road ✉ ME 03907 ☎ 646-6666 ☎ (800) 851-6837
📧 moonmaine@aol.com 💻 www.members.aol.com/moonmaine
All rooms with private bath, balcony, radio and SAT-TV. Rates USD 49-119 depending on season incl. cont. bf. Kids welcome, no pets.
■ **Ogunquit Beach Inn** (A AC B BF CC f GLM H MA) Check-in: 14-19 h
67 School Street ✉ ME 03907 *(Village center)* ☎ 646-1112
☎ 888-976-2463 📠 646-8858 📧 ogtbeachin@aol.com
💻 www.ogunquitbeachinn.com
Just 5 minutes from the beautiful beach. All rooms with Sat-TV, video, apartments with kitchenette, some with private baths. Rates US$ 75-125 depending on season. Apartment US$ 1200 per week (summer rates). Expanded continental bf served.
■ **Ogunquit House. The** (AC BF CC GLM H MA OS) 15 Mar-2 Jan, 8-22 h
3 Glen Avenue, ✉ ME 03907 ☎ 646-2967
📧 ogunquitHS@aol.com
In walking distance to the beach. All rooms with balcony.
■ **Rockmere Lodge B&B** (BF CC E glm H OS msg) all year round
40 Stearns Road ✉ ME 03907 ☎ 646-2985 📠 646-6947
📧 info@rockmere.com 💻 www.rockmere.com
Eight rooms oceanside B&B with private bath and TV. Rates double US$ 100-185 incl. cont. bf.
■ **White Rose Inn** (AC BF glm H)
64 South Main Street ✉ ME 03907 ☎ 646-3432
Rooms with private bath, TV, some with refrigerator and microwave. Rates US$ 85-109 (July-August), $39-60 (Sep-Apr) and $45-95 (May-June). Rooms with shared bath available (not from Sep-Apr) for $65-75 (July-Aug) and $45-65 (May-June). Breakfast buffet incl. in price. TV room.
■ **Yellow Monkey Guest House** (AC BF GLM H WH)
44 Main Street ✉ ME 03907 *(centre of town, short walk to beach, shops & restaurants)* ☎ 646-9056
Rooms with private and shared bath, TV in every room. Rates on request.

SWIMMING
Section G (go to the main beach, walk a few hundred meters to the left until you pass the dune opening)

Portland ☎ 207

BARS
■ **Blackstone's** (B GLM) 16-1, Sun 15-1 h
6 Pine Street ✉ ME 04102 ☎ 775-2885

Portland ▸ Baltimore | **Maine - Maryland/USA**

■ **Somewhere** (AC B CC f GLM MA N S VS) 16-1 h
117 Spring Street ✉ ME 04101 ☏ 871-9169
Piano Fri-Sun, Karaoke on Tue and Thu.

RESTAURANTS
■ **Katahdin** (b F glm) 17-22 h, closed Sun
106 Spring Street ☏ 774-1740

CRUISING
-Deering Oaks Park (AYOR) (off Park Avenue)
-Maine Mall (not very active)

Tenants Harbor ☏ 207
HOTELS
■ **East Wind Inn** (F glm H)
PO Box 149, ✉ ME 04860 ☏ 372-6366
Priv. and shared baths, telephone.

USA-Maryland
Location: East USA
Initials: MD
Time: GMT -5
Area: 32.134 km² / 13,142 sq mi.
Population: 5,094,000
Capital: Annapolis

Baltimore ☏ 410
GAY INFO
■ **Gay & Lesbian Switchboard** 19.30-22.30 h
☏ 837-8888

PUBLICATIONS
■ **Baltimore Alternative**
PO Box 23 51 ✉ MD 21203 ☏ 235-3401 🖷 889-5665
BaltAlt@aol.com 🖳 www.baltalt.com
Free monthly newspaper.
■ **Baltimore Gay Paper - BGP & Mid-Atlantic Gay Life**
241 West Chase Street ✉ MD 21201 ☏ 837-7748 🖷 837-8889
editor@bgp.org 🖳 www.bgp.org
Biweekly newspaper. Features local and international news, reviews, cultural events and classifed ads. 32 pages.

BARS
■ **Allégro** (B d GLM VS YG) 16-4 h, Tue men's night
1101 Cathedral Street ✉ MD 21201 ☏ 837-3906
■ **Baltimore Eagle** (B G LJ MA) 16-2 h
2022 North Charles Street ✉ MD 21218 *(Entrance on 21st Street)*
☏ 823-2453
■ **Club Atlantis** (AC B CC G SNU)
615 Fallsway ✉ MD 21202 ☏ 727-9099
■ **Club Bunns** (B G)
606 West Lexington Street ☏ 727-6064
■ **Club 1722** (B G)
1722 North Charles Street ☏ 727-7431
■ **Hippo** (B D G MA s TV)
1 West Eager Street ☏ 547-0069
■ **Leon's** (B F G MA) 11-2, lunch available 11-15 h
870 Park Avenue ✉ MD 21201 ☏ 301/539-4993
■ **Stagecoach** (B D GLM) 16-2 h
1003 N. Charles Street ☏ 547-0257

■ **Unicorn** (B D G MG N) Mon-Fri 19-2 h, Sat Sun 15-2 h
2218 Boston Street ✉ MD 21231 ☏ 342-8314

CAFES
■ **Coconuts Cafe** (B gLM)
331 West Madison Street ☏ 383-6064
Mainly women.

DANCECLUBS
■ **1722** (D glm YG)
1722 North Charles Street ☏ 727-7431
Very popular after-hour club. Bring your own bottle.

RESTAURANTS
■ **Central Station** (B F Glm MA N VS) 11.30-2 h
1001 N. Charles Street ☏ 752-7133
American cuisine. Also a popular gay bar.
■ **Gampy's** (b F glm) 11.30-2, Fri Sat 11.30-3 h
904 North Charles Street ✉ MD 21201 ☏ 837-9797
Typical American food from the different regions at reasonable prices. Recommended!
■ **Louie's Book Store Café** (b F g)
518 North Charles Street ☏ 962-1224
American cuisine. Also a bookstore.
■ **Mount Vernon Stable** (b F glm)
909 North Charles Street ☏ 685-7427

SEX SHOPS/BLUE MOVIES
■ **Big Top** (g) 0-24 h
429 East Baltimore Street ✉ MD 21202 ☏ 547-2495
■ **Center News**
205 West Lafayette Street ✉ MD 21201 *(near park)*
☏ 301/727-9544

BOOK SHOPS
■ **Lambda Rising** (AC CC GLM MA VS) 10-22 h
241 West Chase Street ✉ MD 21201 *(In Gay Community Center)*
☏ 234-0069
Gay, lesbian, bisexual and transgender books, videos, magazines and gifts. Free local guides.

TRAVEL AND TRANSPORT
■ **Adventures in Travel**
3900 North Charles Street ✉ MD 21218 ☏ 467-1161

HOTELS
■ **Mount Vernon Hotel** (AC B BF CC F glm H MA)
24 West Franklin St. ✉ MD 21201-5090 ☏ 727-2000
☏ (800) 537-8483 🖷 576-9300
Friendly hotel located in the Mount Vernon neighborhood, the area containing most of the gay bars. Rates from US$ 69 to US$ 109 per night.

GUEST HOUSES
■ **Chez Claire Bed & Breakfast** (AC BF CC GLM H MA p) 8-22 h
17 West Chase Street ✉ MD 21201-5404 *(in historic Mt. Vernan area)* ☏ 685-4666 ☏ 837-0996 🖳 allancolman@webtv.net
All rooms with telephone and TV. Rates single/double US$ 65-85 (bf incl.)
■ **Mr. Mole** (AC BF glm H)
1601 Bolton Street ✉ MD 21217 ☏ 728-1179
B&B in old town house. 5 suites with private and shared baths. Rates incl. bf US$ 80-145. Kids over 10 ok, no pets.

USA/Maryland - Massachusetts | Baltimore ▸ Boston

■ **William Page Inn** (AC BF CC e glm H MA WH)
8 Martin Street, Annapolis ✉ MD 21401-1716 *(in the historic district)* ☎ 626-1506 ☎ (800) 364-4160 🖨 263-4163
💻 williampageinn@aol.com 💻 williampageinn.com

GENERAL GROUPS
■ **Black and White Men/People of All Colors Together** 3rd Fri 19.30 h at 241 West Chase Street
PO Box 33186 ✉ MD 21218 ☎ 583-3938 🖨 235-3191
💻 bpbalt@aol.com

HEALTH GROUPS
■ **Chase Brexton Health Services**
1001 Cathedral Street ☎ 837-2050
Also provides mental health services.

Hagerstown ☎ 301

DANCECLUBS
■ **Headquarters** (B D F GLM S) 17-? h
41 North Potomac Street ✉ MD 21740 ☎ 797-1553

Silver Spring ☎ 301

HOTELS
■ **Northwood Inn** (g H)
10304 Eastwood Avenue ✉ MD 20901 ☎ 593-7027

USA-Massachusetts

Location: Northeast USA
Initials: MA
Time: GMT -5
Area: 27.337 km² / 11.180 sq mi.
Population: 6,118,000
Capital: Boston
Important gay cities: Boston and Provincetown

Amherst ☎ 413

GUEST HOUSES
■ **Ivy House B&B** (BF glm H)
1 Sunset Court ✉ MA 01002 ☎ 549-7554
💻 ivyhouse@shaysnet.com
Small B&B in restored colonial home. All rooms with private bath. Rates US$ 60-90 incl. bf. 100 miles west from Boston.

SWIMMING
-Cummington gay beach (Park car at Swift River Rest Stop on Route 9 and walk 1 mile through woods.)

Boston ☎ 617

PUBLICATIONS
■ **Bay Windows**
631 Tremont Street ✉ MA 02118-2034 ☎ 266-6670 🖨 266-5973
💻 jepperly@baywindows.com 💻 www.baywindows.com
Weekly publication, about 25 pages. US$ 0.50. Features news, arts & entertainment, interviews, media watch column.

TOURIST INFO
■ **Greater Boston Convention & Visitor Bureau**
Prudential Tower, Suite 400 ✉ MA 02199 ☎ 536-4100

BARS
■ **Boston Eagle** (B G LJ) 15-2 h
520 Tremont Street ✉ MA 02116 ☎ 542-4494
Cruise bar.
■ **Chaps** (B G LJ N)
100 Warrenton Street ☎ 695-9500
■ **Fritz** (B F GLM N) 12-2 h
26 Chandler Street ✉ MA 02116 *(at Berkeley)* ☎ 482-4428
Brunch Sat Sun 11-15.30 h.
■ **Jacques** (B D GLM stv)
79 Broadway Street ✉ MA 02116 *(at Piedmont Street, behind Howard Johnson's)* ☎ 426-8902
■ **Luxor** (AC B G VS YG) 16-1 h
69 Church Street ✉ MA 02116 *(at Stuart Street)* ☎ 423-6969
Comfortable video bar. Also: Mario's (restaurant) and Jox (sports bar).
■ **Machine** (B G MA)
1254/1256 Boylston Street ☎ 536-1950
■ **Paradise** (B D F G lj SNU) Thu 19-2 h
180 Massachusetts Avenue, Cambridge ✉ MA 02139
☎ 494-0700
Cruisy bar.
■ **Ramrod** (AC B DR G LJ) 12-2 h
1254 Boylston Street ✉ MA 02215 ☎ 266-2986
■ **119 Merrimac** (AC B G LJ N) 10.30-2, Sun 12-2 h
119 Merrimac Street/Stanford Street ✉ MA 02114 ☎ 367-0713

CAFES
■ **Everyday Cafe** (BF CC f g MA OS) Mon-Fri 7-21, Sat 9-21, Sun -17 h
517 Columbus Avenue ✉ MA 02118-3003 ☎ 536-2119
■ **Tremont Ice Cream** (b f G)
584 Tremont Street ✉ MA 02116 ☎ 247-8414

DANCECLUBS
■ **Avalon** (A AC B C D G MA STV)
15 Lansdowne Street ✉ MA 02215 *(in the Fenway)* ☎ 262-2424
Only Sun 9-2 h, straight all other days.
■ **Buzz** (B D GLM YG) Sat (G) 22-? h , Thu Fri (GLM)
67 Stuart Street ☎ 267-8969
Popular.
■ **Manray** (B D glm) Gay Thu "Campus" 21-1 h, Sat "Liquid" 19-? h
21A Brookline Street/Central Square, Cambridge ✉ MA 02139
☎ 864-0400

RESTAURANTS
■ **Club Café** (! AC B CC D e F GLM S VS) 11-2, dinner 18-22 h
209 Columbus Avenue ✉ MA 02116 *(at Berkeley)* ☎ 536-0966
Features some of Boston's best jazz musicians and exquisite American and continental cuisine. Highly reccommended.
■ **Mario's** (B F GLM MA) 17.30-22 h
69 Church Street ✉ MA 02116 ☎ 542-3776
Italian cuisine.
■ **On the Park** (A AC b BF CC F glm MA) Tue-Thu 7-30-22.30 h, Fri-Sat 17-30-23 h, Sat-Sun 9-15 h brunch.
1 Union Park ✉ MA 02118 ☎ 426-0862

SEX SHOPS/BLUE MOVIES
■ **Art Cinema I+II** (G)
204 Tremont Street ✉ MA 02116 ☎ 482-4661

BOOK SHOPS
■ **Downtown Books**
697 Washington Street ✉ MA 02111 ☎ 426-7844

Boston — Massachusetts/USA

overnight accomodation service — from § 50
· about 750 beds · more than 28 cities ·

enjoy bed & breakfast

complete offer see page Germany/Berlin

central booking office Berlin ☎ +49-30-23623610 4:30-9:00 pm local time
Fax +49-30-23623619 · info@ebab.com · www.ebab.com

■ **Glad Day Bookstore** (GLM) Mon-Thu 9.30-22 h, Fri Sat -23 h, Sun & holidays 12-21 h
673 Boylston Street ✉ MA 02116 ☎ 267-3010
■ **We think the World of you**
540 Tremont Street ✉ MA 02116 ☎ 423-1995

FASHION SHOPS
■ **Vernon's Specialties**
386 Moody Street ✉ MA 02154 *(Waltham)* ☎ 894-1744
All your needs for cross dressing, including on site beauty salon. Mailorder catalogue available.

VIDEO SHOPS
■ **The Movie Place** (CC G) 11-23 h
526 Tremont Street ✉ MA 02116 ☎ 482-9008
Video rentals, magazines & periodicals.

HOTELS
■ **Chandler Inn** (AC B BF GLM H lj MA)
26 Chandler Street ✉ MA 02116 *(at Berkeley)* ☎ (800) 842-4450
(toll-free) ☎ 482-3450 542-3228 inn3450@ix.netcom.com
 www.chandlerinn.com
Recently renovated B&B hotel located near Back Bay train station. Gay owned. Brunch Sat and Sun 11-15.30h. All rooms with priv. bath, WC and phone.
■ **463 Beacon Street Guest House** (glm H)
463 Beacon Street ✉ MA 02115 ☎ 536-1302
Single/double US$ 50-95, also special weekly rates available.

GUEST HOUSES
■ **Amsterdammertje** (AC bf GLM H MA OS)
PO Box 1731 ✉ MA 02205-1731 *(Near ocean)* ☎ 471-8454
 471-8454 www.bbonline.com/ma/am
Small B&B, 15 minutes by car from Downtown in a quiet neighborhood at the ocean. Rooms with shared bath, telephone, radio, TV, video and hair-dryer. Rates single US$ 69, double 99. Non-smoking.
■ **Oasis Guest House** (AC BF CC glm H OS) Office: 8-24 h
22 Edgerly Road ✉ MA 02115 *(Green Line-Convention Center)*
☎ 267-2262 267-1920 oasisgh@tiac.net
 www.oasisgh.com
15 minutes from the airport. Located in the heart of Boston, close to the gay scene. All rooms with phone, color TV, some with private bath and balcony. Rates from US$ 72-119.

PRIVATE ACCOMMODATION
■ **Enjoy Bed and Breakfast** (BF G H MA) 16.30-21 h (Central European Time)
Nollendorfplatz 5, 10777 Berlin - Germany ☎ +49 30 236 236 10
 +49 30 236 236 19 info@ebab.com ebab.com
Accommodation sharing agency. All with shower and BF. 20-25 Euro p.p.

GENERAL GROUPS
■ **Babson Gay & Lesbian Alliance**
PO Box 631, Babson Park ✉ MA 02157 *Wellesley*
■ **Greater Boston Gay Men's Association**
PO Box 10 09 ✉ MA 02205
Monthly meetings with guest speakers & informal social hour.
■ **LGBT Political Alliance of Masschussets**
PO Box 65, Back Bay Annex ✉ MA 02117 ☎ 338-4297
 alliance@masspride.net

FETISH GROUPS
■ **Leather Knights** 1st Thu
c/o Ramrod, 1254 Boylston Street ✉ MA 02215

BOSTON

Two Townhouses in The Heart Of Boston / Telephones / Color TV's / Central Air / Outdoor decks / Private Shared Baths / Continental Breakfast / Walk To All Major Sights & Nightlife / Reasonable Rates

O·A·S·I·S GUEST HOUSE B·O·S·T·O·N

OASIS GUEST HOUSE
22 Edgerly Road, Boston, MA 02115
617-267-2262 / Fax: 617 267-1920
E-mail: oasisgh@tiac.net   www.oasisgh.com

USA/Massachusetts | Boston ▸ Provincetown

HEALTH GROUPS

■ **AIDS Action Committee** Mon-Fri 12-20 h, Sat -18 h
131 Clarendon ✉ MA 02116 ☎ 437-6360
Direct services to people with AIDS; councelling for all concerned; education and advocacy.

■ **Fenway Community Health Center**
16 Haviland Street ✉ MA 02115 ☎ 267-0900 ☎ 267-9001 (Helpline).
Second location: 93 Mass Avenue. Sexually transmitted disease treatment; HIV education and testing program; general medicine; gay and lesbian victim recovery program.

SPECIAL INTEREST GROUPS

■ **Boston University Lesbian/Gay Law Association**
775 Commonwealth Avenue ✉ MA 02215 ☎ 353-9804
c/o Program, Resource Office, George Sherman Union

CRUISING

-Revere Beach (G NU) (2 miles north of Boston downtown, on the boulevard between Band Sand and Kelly's. Take the blue line to Revere Beach or Wonderland Station.)
-The Fens at Victoria Gardens (in the high reeds along the river, near Boylston Street)

Edgartown ☎ 508

HOTELS

■ **Captain Dexter House** (AC BF glm H MA OS)
35 Pease's Point Way, ✉ MA 02539 (PO Box 27 98) ☎ 627-7289

Ipswich

SWIMMING

-Crane's Beach (NU) (from sunrise to sunset. Off old Route 1. Fee varies from US$ 3 to 10 per car depending on season and day. Cape Cod style beach, the sand dunes at the southern end become very cruisy.)

Martha's Vineyard ☎ 508

HOTELS

■ **Captain Dexter House** (AC BF glm MA OS)
100 Main Street, Vineyard Haven ✉ MA 02568 ☎ 693-6564
Rates US $65-160.

GUEST HOUSES

■ **Martha's Place Inn** (AC BF CC GLM H MA OS) 9-21 h
114 Main Street, Vineyard Haven ✉ MA 02537 ☎ 693-0253
📧 info@marthasplace.com 🌐 www.marthasplace.com
Rates US$ 175-375 (in-season) and $125-275 (value season).

Northampton ☎ 413

GAY INFO

■ **Community Prideline**
☎ 584-4848

GENERAL GROUPS

■ **Venture Out** (glm)
☎ 584-3145
Outdoor adventure group. Weekly events.

CRUISING

-Route I-91 Springfield ⇌ Northampton, [P] behind Exit 17B
-Route I-91 Northampton ⇌ Springfield, [P] behind Exit 18 (near Easthampton and Holyoke)

Provincetown ☎ 508

✱ This is how *the gay resort par excellence* should be: Far from major cities (Boston being 150 km away) and situated at the end of a longstretched peninsula. It takes two and a half hours by car to reach Provincetown from Boston, taking Highway 6, which circulates *Cape Cod Bay*. Be prepared that crossing the bridge to the peninsula can take quite some time. Provincetown owes its development to artists, who moved and settled there at the beginning of the century. In the sixties the town became very popular for all those not conforming politically or sexually to the conservative norm. Best time to visit is between Memorial Day (May 30) and Labour Day (1st Monday in September). As there is no gay magazine in Provincetown it is best to obtain information at the *Provincetown Business Guild*, the gay "chamber of commerce", which also organizes the special event *Carnival Week* in mid August.

★ So gehört es sich für *den schwulen Badeort par excellence*: abseits einer Großstadt (Boston ist 150 km entfernt) und am Ende einer -in diesem Fall- Landzunge. Zweieinhalb Stunden benötigt man per Auto nach Provincetown von Boston aus, wenn man die *Cape Cod Bay* auf den Highway 6 umrundet. Es kann übrigens sehr lange dauern, bis man die Brücke auf die Landzunge überquert hat. Provincetown verdankt seine Entwicklung Künstlern, die seit Anfang des Jahrhunderts dorthin gezogen und sich niederliessen. Wirklich beliebt wurde der Ort dann in den 60er Jahren als Zuflucht für all jene, die politisch oder sexuell von der konservativen Norm abwichen. Die beste Zeit für einen Besuch liegt zwischen Memorial Day (30. Mai) und Labour Day (1. Montag im September). Es gibt keine schwule Zeitung in Provincetown, am besten besorgt man sich Infos bei der *Provincetown Business Guild*, der schwulen "Handelskammer", die übrigens auch Mitte August das special event *Carnival Week* veranstaltet.

✱ Provincetown est une station balnéaire idéale: loin de tout, au bout d'une presqu'île. Boston est à 150 km. Il faut deux heures et demie pour aller de Boston à Provincetown en voiture, par la "Highway 6" qui contourne Cape Code Bay. Provincetown doit sa renommée aux nombreux artistes qui, dès le début du siècle, y sont venus en villégiature, mais ce n'est que dans les années 60 qu'elle a définitivement acquis ses lettres de noblesse en offrant l'asile à tous ceux qui, victimes de persécutions politiques ou sexuelles, ont fui le conservatisme et l'étroitesse d'esprit de la société américaine. Le meilleur moment pour découvrir Provincetown, c'est fin mai (Memorial day, 30 mai) et début septembre (Labour Day, 1er lundi du mois). Il n'y a pas de magasines gais locaux à Provincetown. Pour savoir quoi faire, où sortir, comment et avec qui, adressez-vous à la "Provincetown Business Guild", une sorte de Chambre de Commerce gaie, qui organise chaque année mi-août la "Carnival Week".

◆ Provincetown se encuentra cerca de la gran ciudad Boston (a 150 km. de distancia) y al final de una pequeña península. Se puede decir que cuenta geograficamente con las condiciones ideales para ser denominada balneario gay. Con coche se tarda aproximadamente 2,5 horas desde Boston, si se va por la autopista 6 pasando por Cape Cod Boy. El traspaso del puente para llegar a la península suele tardar bastante. El desarrollo de Provincetown es de agradecer a los artistas que al inicio de este siglo se mudaron a vivir en este lugar. Este sitio tomó auge en la década de los '60 cuando muchos

Provincetown — Massachusetts/USA

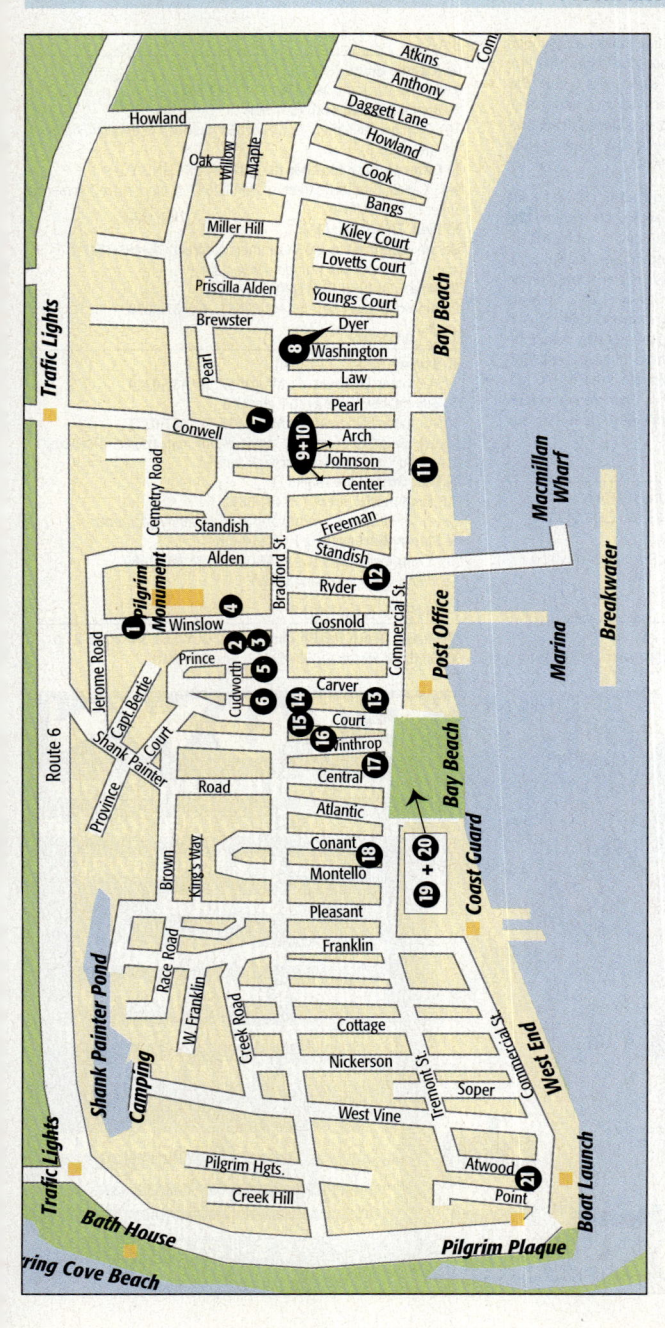

Provincetown

1. The Chicago Guest House
2. Six Webster Place Guest House
3. Fairbanks Inn Guest House
4. Howard's End Guest House
5. Crowne Pointe Historical Inn
6. Carl's Guest House
7. Admiral's Landing Guest House
8. Benchmark Inn
9. Elephant Walk Inn Guest House
10. Price Albert House Guest House
11. Captain and his Ship Guest House
12. Moffett Guest House
13. The Ranch Guest House
14. Brass Key Guest House
15. Revere Guest House
16. Watership Inn Guest House
17. White Wind Guest House
18. Grand View Inn Guest House
19. Pied Piper Bar
20. Boatslip Beach Club Hotel
21. The West End Inn Guest House

USA/Massachusetts — Provincetown

gays encontraron en él, el lugar de escape a la política sexual y las normas conservativas de la sociedad. La época ideal para visitar Provincetown es entre el Memorial Day (30 de Mayo) y el Labour Day (1er. lunes de Septiembre). No hay publicaciones gay. Informaciones sobre los acontecimientos del momento se obtienen del *Provincetown Business Guild*, la Camara de Comercio Gay. Que organiza también a mediados de agosto la *Carnival Week*.

Al margine di una grande città (Boston è a soli 150 km) e alla fine di una appendice di terra: ciò si addice alla stazione balneare gay per eccellenza. Provincetown dista due ore e mezza d'auto da Boston, percorrendo la Highway 6 lungo *Cape Cod Bay*. Provincetown deve il proprio sviluppo agli artisti che vi si trasferirono all'inizio del secolo. Anche se solo durante gli anni '60 è divenuta realmente ambita da tutti coloro che si distanziavano politicamente e sessualmente dalla norma. Il periodo migliore per una visita è tra Memorial day (30 maggio) e Labour day (primo lunedì di sett.). Provincetown non ha un proprio giornale gay. Potrete ottenere informazioni presso il *Provincetown Business Guild*, la "camera di commercio gay" che organizza a metà agosto la manifestazione *Carnival Week*.

GAY INFO

■ **Provincetown Business Guild** (GLM) Mon-Fri 9-14 h
115 Bradford Street ✉ MA 02657 ☎ 487-2313 487-1252
 pbguild@capecod.net www.ptown.org
Promotion of Gay & Lesbian tourism in Provincetown. Publisher of a free gay guide.

CULTURE

■ **Charles Batliuik Gallery** (A)
432 Commercial Street ✉ MA 02657 ☎ 487-3611 487-3611

BARS

■ **Atlantic House** (B D G LJ OS S) 11-1 h
8 Masonic Place ✉ MA 02657 ☎ 487-3821
■ **Boatslip Beach Club** (B G MA)
161 Commercial Street ✉ MA 02657 *(between Central and Atlantic)*
☎ 487-1669
■ **Gifford House Inn&Bar** (B CC G MA OS S SNU YG) 9-1 h
9-11 Carver/Bradford Street ✉ MA 02657 *(1 block from Commercial Street)* ☎ 487-0688
■ **Pied. The** (B glm MA)
On the waterfront at 193A Commercial Street ☎ 487-1527
After T-Dance popular with gays from 18 h.
■ **Steve's Alibi** (B GLM N STV) May-Sep
Commercial Street 291 ✉ MA 02657 ☎ 487-2890

RESTAURANTS

■ **Bayside Betsy's** (B F glm)
177 Commercial Street ✉ MA 02657 ☎ 487-0120
■ **Bubala's by the Bay** (b F glm OS)
183 Commercial Street ✉ MA 02657 ☎ 487-0773
Bayside dining-excellent food served all day from traditional seafood fare to fajita's, focaccio sandwiches & burgers.
■ **Post Office Cafe** (B glm F)
303 Commercial Street ☎ 487-3892
One of Provincetown's most popular year-round restaurants.
■ **Stormy Harbor** (BF g F OS S) 8-1 h
277 Commercial Street ✉ MA 02657 ☎ 487-1680
Cabaret and live vocals every night.

FITNESS STUDIOS

■ **Mussel Beach Health Club** (AC CC GLM SOL SA WO) 6-21 h
35 Bradford Street ✉ MA 02657 ☎ 487-0001

PROVINCETOWN

Come visit the gayest place on earth. Enjoy total freedom in your gay home away from home.

Experience our fabulous beaches and nightlife or plan a romantic escape in Spring, Fall or Winter.

Visit our website,
Call 508 487-2313 or Write for your Free Gay Guide to Provincetown.
PROVINCETOWN BUSINESS GUILD
P.O. Box 421-94 SP
Provincetown, MA 02657 USA

Visit your "Gay Home" Page!
WWW.PTOWN.ORG

Provincetown — Massachusetts/USA

■ **Provincetown Gym & Fitness Center Inc.** (AC CC GLM MA msg WO) 6-21 h (season) -20 h (off season)
81 Shank Painter Road ✉ MA 02657 *(across A&P Superstore)*
☎ 487-2776

BOOK SHOPS
■ **Now Voyager** (GLM) 10-23 h
357 Commercial Street ✉ MA 02657 ☎ 487-0848
Mysteries gay and lesbian books. Selected fiction and non-fiction.
■ **Provincetown Bookshop** (GLM) 10-23 h
246 Commercial Street ✉ MA 02657 ☎ 487-0964

TRAVEL AND TRANSPORT
■ **Provincetown Reservation System** 10-18 h
293 Commercial Street ✉ MA 02657 ☎ (800) 648-0364
🖷 487-6517 ✉ ptownres@ptownres.com 💻 www.ptownres.com
Room reservations, travel agency, tickets.
■ **Travel Network** (GLM) Summer: 8-20, Off-season: 9-17 h, closed Sun
4 Standish Street ✉ MA 02657 ☎ 487-6330
✉ intownres@aol.com 💻 www.intownreservations.com
A full service travel agency specializing in gay and lesbian travel.

HOTELS
■ **Boatslip Beach Club** (! B BF CC D F GLM H MA OS PI s) Apr-Oct
161 Commercial Street, PO Box 393 ✉ MA 02657 ☎ 487-1669
☎ (800) 451-7547 🖷 587-6021 ✉ boatslip@provincetown.com
💻 ww.provincetown.com/boatslip
Beach location, queen or double bed, private bath, TV and sea view. Rates US$ 65-160.
■ **Commons Guesthouse & Bistro. The** (B CC F GLM H MA N OS)
Jun-Sep: 8-24 h, Oct-May 16-24 h (closed Tue Wed)
386 Commercial Street ✉ MA 02657 ☎ 487-7800 🖷 487 6114
✉ commons@capecod.net
Hotel with restaurant & bar.
■ **Crowne Pointe Historic Inn** (AC BF B GLM H)
82 Bradford Street ✉ MA 02657 ☎ 487-6767 🖷 487-5554
💻 www.crownepointe.com
Winner of Out & About's "Editor's Choice Awards" for 2000.
■ **Gifford House Inn** (B BF CC D GLM H N OS STV) Office: 9-23 h
9-11 Carver Street ✉ MA 02657 ☎ 487-0688 ☎ (800) 434-0130
(Toll-free) 🖷 487-4918
Rooms with private bath. Rates USD 45-158. extra bed 20 incl. continental bf. More than 140 years old restored home situated on a hill overlooking the bay. Also danceclub and bar.

GUEST HOUSES
■ **Admiral's Landing** (AC BF CC G H MA OS VS) office: 8-22 h
158 Bradford Street ✉ MA 02657 ☎ 487-9665
☎ (800) 934-0925 (Toll-free) 🖷 487-4437
✉ admiral@capecod.net 💻 www.admiralslanding.com
Cottages with kitchenette. All rooms with bath, TV, VCR, phone, fridge and some with fireplaces. Non-smoking. Rates US$ 70-125.
■ **Aerie House and Beach Club** (AC BF CC G Ij MA NU OS WH WO) all year round
184 Bradford Street ✉ MA 02657 *(Atop Miller Hill, 5 mins walk to town centre)* ☎ 487-1197 ☎ (800) 487-1197 (toll-free)
✉ aerieptown@cs.com
Sweeping bay views, beach club on private bay beach. Rates US$ 50-200.
■ **Ampersand**
6 Cottage Street ✉ MA 02657 ☎ 487-0959
✉ ampersand@capecod.net
💻 www.capecod.net/ampersand

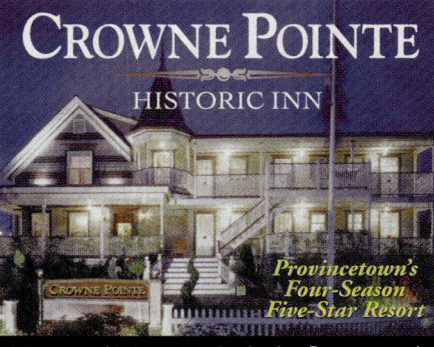

CROWNE POINTE
HISTORIC INN

Provincetown's Four-Season Five-Star Resort

Restored to its original splendor, Provincetown's most stately accommodations offer 40 graciously appointed rooms, suites and apartments, with the utmost in amenities. Enjoy the sweeping harbor views, lounge in the gardens, take a leisurely stroll to the many nearby points of interest or just curl up by one of the fireplaces. It's truly a four season resort.

Call us at (508) 487-6767
For reservations only call 877-CROWNE-1
www.crownepointe.com
82 Bradford Street, Provincetown, MA 02657

Lands End Inn

22 COMMERCIAL STREET
PROVINCETOWN
MA 02657
Telephone (508) 487-0706
800-276-7088

Unique rooms with spectacular views at the very tip of Cape Cod

SPARTACUS 2001/2002 1271

USA/Massachusetts — Provincetown

CARL'S GUEST HOUSE provincetown

"... Where strangers become friends"
CLEAN • COMFORTABLE • FRIENDLY
offering reasonable rates at all times!
Free Brochure and Rates MESSAGE
Write/Call: 1-800-348-CARL

OPEN YEAR ROUND
For RESERVATIONS and/or QUESTIONS
call: (508) 487-1650

E-Mail: info@carlsguesthouse.com
Web Page: www.carlsguesthouse.com

CARL, Your Host
68 Bradford St. (Corner of Court St.)
Provincetown, MA 02657

■ **Anchor Inn** (AC bf CC E Glm H WH) 9-21 h
175 Commercial Street ✉ MA 02657 ☎ 487-0432 487-6280
💻 ankrinn@capecod.net 🖥 www.anchorinnbeachhouse.com
All rooms with private bath, balcony.

■ **Archer Inn** (AC BF CC G H MA NU OS)
26 Bradford Street ✉ MA 02657 ☎ 487-2529 ☎ (800) 263-6574
(toll-free) 487-0079 💻 lamplite@lamplite.com
All rooms with TV, video, telephone, balcony, some with private bath. The B&B is located on top of a hill in a restored house built in the 1800s with a beautiful view.

■ **Bayshore** (CC GLM H OS) all year round
493 Commercial Street ✉ MA 02657-2413 ☎ 487-9133
487-0520 💻 BayShore@provincetown.com
🖥 www.provincetown.com/bayshore
See website and or call for details.

■ **Benchmark Inn** (AC BF CC E G H msg OS PI WH)
6-8 Dyer Street ✉ MA 02657 (central) ☎ 487-1542
☎ (800) 942-1542 (Toll-free) 487-3446
💻 parkhd@aol.com 🖥 www.CapeCodAccess.com/benchmark/
Rooms with telephone, TV, video, radio, minibar, safe, hair-dryer, some with balcony and kitchenette. Heated pool and spa room. Rates double/shared bath US$ 59-89, single room/shared bath 39-75 incl. bf. Additional bed US$ 30.

■ **Bradford-Carver House. The** (AC BF CC GLM H MA OS)
Office: 9-21 h
70 Bradford Street ✉ MA 02657-1363 *(Corner Bradford/Carver St.)*
☎ 487-4966 ☎ (0800) 826-9083 (toll-free) 487-7213
💻 bradcarver@capecod.net 🖥 www.capecod.net/bradfordcarver
Small Guesthouse in a historic home. All rooms have private bath, heating, AC, cable TV, video and refrigerator. Rates $ 49-129 (winter), 69-149 (spring/fall) and 109-199 (summer) incl. continental bf. Video library and TV room.

■ **Brass Key Guesthouse. The** (AC BF CC GLM H OS PI WH)
67 Commercial Street ✉ MA 02657 ☎ 487-9005 ☎ (800) 842-9858
(toll-free) 487-9020 💻 ptown@brasskey.com
🖥 www.brasskey.com
Historic sea captain's house built 1830's. All rooms with priv. bath, TV, VCR, phone, fridge. Rates US$ 220-400 (season) to 100-295 (off-season), bf incl.

■ **Captain and His Ship. The** (AC BF CC E glm H MA OS) 8-23 h
164 Commercial Street ✉ MA 02657 ☎ 487-1850
☎ (800) 400-2278 🖥 www.captainandhisship.com
Guesthouse in a restored captain's home built in the last century. All rooms with color TV, video, telephone and refrigerator, most with private bath, some with lovely water view. Rates room/private bath US$ 85-185 and with shared bath $ 65-105 depending on season. Continental bf incl. Smoke free establishment.

■ **Carl's Guest House** (AC CC G H MA NU OS SOL WH)
68 Bradford Street ✉ MA 02657 ☎ 487-1650 ☎ (800)-348-CARL
💻 info@CarlsGuestHouse.com 🖥 www.CarlsGuestHouse.com
Excellent location, clean, comfortable, friendly and affordable. Own pri-

vate sundeck. TV room. Rates single US$ 39-79, double 49-99, cottage 69-149. Men only.

■ **Carpe Diem Guesthouse** (AC BF CC GLM H OS WH)
12 Johnson Street ✉ MA 02657 *(Center of town; half a block from Harbor Beach)* ☎ 487-4242 ☎ (800) 487-0132 487-4242
💻 carpediem@capecod.net 🖥 www.carpediemguesthouse.com
13 double rooms with shower/WC, balcony or terrace, telephone, hair-dryer, air-conditioning, own key, room service, fax, video, heating and TV. Breakfast buffet incl. Car park. Rates double $70-250. German owned.

■ **Chicago House. The** (BF CC G H MA OS)
6 Winslow Street ✉ MA 02657 *(2 min from the centre)*
☎ 487-0537 ☎ (800) 733-7869 (toll-free)
💻 chicagohse@aol.com 🖥 www.chicagohse.com
6 private bath, 3 shared bath rooms, 2 apartments and a town house (up to 6 people). All rooms with TV, some with radio. Rates US $ 35-110.-

"This house on the quiet west end has undergone thorough renovation and emerged a winner. A large and comfortable common room, tasteful, yet understated guest rooms and friendly management make this a great choice"

Highly recommended

★★★★
OUT&ABOUT

W
WEST END INN

44 Commercial St.
Provincetown, MA 02657
508-487-9555
www.westendinn.com

1272 SPARTACUS 2001/2002

Provincetown | **Massachusetts/USA**

ANCHOR INN
Beach House

Provincetown's Finest Inn on the Waterfront

Our guestrooms offer private bath, individually-controlled heating and air conditioning, twin-line telephone with voicemail & dataport, TV/VCR, wet bar with sink and refrigerator and luxury bath amenities including robes and hairdryer. Many guestrooms feature deluxe showers, whirlpool baths and/or fireplaces. Sixteen rooms have balconies overlooking the harbor A complimentary continental breakfast buffet is served each morning.

175 Commercial St., Provincetown, MA 02657
1.800.858.2657   508.487.0432   Fax: 508.487.6280
Email: ankrinn@capecod.net
Web Site: www.anchorinnbeachhouse.com

USA/Massachusetts | Provincetown

www.provincetownfavorites.com

ADMIRAL'S LANDING
158 Bradford Street
508 487-9665
800 934-0925
Email: admiral@capecod.net
www.admiralslanding.com

Ampersand Guesthouse
6 Cottage Street
508 487-0959   800 574-9645
ampersand@capecod.net
www.capecod.net/ampersand

The Captain and his Ship
Guesthouse on Cape Cod
164 Commercial Street
508 487-1850
800 400-CAPT
www.captainandhisship.com

DEXTER'S INN
6 Conwell Street
508 487-1911
888 521-1999
dextersinn@aol.com
www.ptowndextersinn.com

ELEPHANT WALK INN
156 Bradford Street
508 487-2543
800 889-9255
elephant@capecod.net
www.elephantwalkinn.com

Provincetown | Massachusetts/USA

THE PRINCE ALBERT
GUEST HOUSE

166 Commercial Street — 508 487-0859   800 992-0859
princealbert@mediaone.net   www.princealbertguesthouse.net

ROMEO'S HOLIDAY

97 Bradford Street
508 487-6636
877 MY ROMEO
freenite@romeosholiday.com
www.romeosholiday.com

SUNSET INN

142 Bradford Street
508 487-9810
800 965-1801
Email: sunset1@capecod.net
www.sunsetinnptown.com

WATERSHIP INN

7 Winthrop Street
508 487-0094
800 330-9413
watership@capecod.net
www.capecod.net/watershipinn

WINDSOR COURT
Key West Style — Provincetown Charm

15 Cottage Street — 508 487-2620
windsorct@capecod.net
www.windsorcourtptown.com

PROVINCETOWN Favorites!

www.provincetownfavorites.com

Provincetown Favorites

USA/Massachusetts — Provincetown

■ **Dexter's Inn**
6 Conwell Street ✉ MA 36036 ☏ 487-1911
📧 dextersinn@aol.com 🖥 www.ptowndextersinn.com
■ **Dunes, The** (CC GLM H) 9-21 h
125 Bradford Street Ext. ✉ MA 02657 ☏ 487-1956
☏ (800)-475-1833 (toll free) 📠 487-2436
📧 jeff@thedunesprovincetown.com
🖥 www.thedunesprovincetown.com
Rates from $39 to $69, Apartments from $69 to $109.
■ **Elephant Walk Inn** (AC BF CC GLM H OS VS) Apr 1st-Nov 10th
156 Bradford Street ✉ MA 02657 ☏ 487-2543
☏ (800) 889-9255 (toll-free) 📧 elephant@capecod.net
🖥 www.elephantwalkinn.com
Rooms with shower/WC, phone, fridge, TV, video, ceiling fans, AC, heating and own key. Car park. Continental bf incl. Rates: double US$ 56-142, single 56-142, additional bed 30.
■ **Elm House** (AC BF G lj H)
9 Johnson Street ✉ MA 02657 ☏ 487-0793
FAX 487-7549 Close to the beach. Rates from US$ 50-85.
■ **Fairbanks Inn** (AC BF CC GLM H OS)
90 Bradford Street ✉ MA 02657 ☏ 487-0386
📧 info@fairbanksinn.com 🖥 www.fairbanksinn.com
Call for rates.
■ **Grand View Inn** (BF CC GLM MA OS)
4 Conant Street ✉ MA 02657 ☏ 487-9193
FAX 487-2894. Email: vanbelle@capecod.net. Located in picturesque West End of town with outside deck with a view on the bay. Rates US$ 45-100 (off season), 65-125 (on season) incl. continental bf.
■ **Howards End** (BF GLM H) all year round
5 Winslow Street ✉ MA 02657 (town centre) ☏ 487-0169
📧 howardsend@mediaone.net
Call for further information.
■ **John Randall House, The** (AC BF CC GLM H) 9-21 h
140 Bradford Street ✉ MA 02657-1435 ☏ 487-3533
☏ (800)573-6700 (toll free) 📠 487-3533
📧 jrhouse@capecod.net 🖥 www.capecod.net/johnrandall/
Free parking, priv. bath, cable TV, VCR
■ **Land's End Inn** (AC CC BF GLM H OS WH)
22 Commercial Street ✉ MA 02657 ☏ 487-0706
☏ (800) 276-7088 (toll-free)
Nicely furnished rooms and fully equipped apartments. Rates US$ 87-165 (off season) and 120-190 (high season). Suites with balcony and jacuzzi available (USD 185-285). Continental bf included. TV room.
■ **Moffett House** (CC G H LJ MA)
296 A Commercial Street ✉ MA 02657 ☏ 487-6615
☏ (800) 990 88 65 (toll-free)
■ **Pilgrim Colony Inn** (BF CC GLM H) May-Oct
670 Shore Road, North Truro ✉ MA 02652 ☏ 487-1100
🖥 www.pilgrimcolony.com
On the beach overlooking Cape Cod Bay and Provincetown harbour. All rooms with private bath. Rates US$ 69-99. Free continental bf. and newspaper each morning.
■ **Prince Albert Guest House, The** (AC G MA OS) 8-22 h
166 Commercial Street ✉ MA 02657 ☏ 487-0859
☏ (800) 992-0859 (toll-free) 📧 princealbert@mediaone.net
🖥 www.princealbertguesthouse.net
No smoking, 8 rooms with private baths, 2 with shared rooms. All rooms with color TV, video and small refrigerator + AC. Rates in season US$ 85-170.

■ **Ranch Guestlodge** (B BF G lj H MA OS VS)
198 Commercial Street, PO Box 26 ✉ MA 02657 (central)
☏ 487-1542 ☏ (800) 942-1542 (Toll-free) 📠 487-3446
📧 parknd@aol.com 🖥 www.CapeCodAccess.com/ranch
Sundeck and streetside patio. TV room and private bar. All rooms with shared bath. Sport activities nearby. Rates single US$ 39-75 and double US$ 59-39 coffee/tea included. Additional town $US 30.
■ **Revere Guest House** (AC bF CC GLM H) 9.30-21 h
14 Court Street ✉ MA 02657 ☏ 487-2292
📧 info@reverehouse.com 🖥 www.reverehouse.com
Small B&B in a restored Captain's home (dated 1830). All rooms with AC, TV, studio with kitchenette. Rates: $45-90 (off season): $70-155 (in season)
■ **Romeo's Holiday** (AC bf CC GLM LJ OS NU PI WH) 24 h
97 Bradford Street ✉ MA 02657 (in the city centre) ☏ 487-6636
📠 487-3082 📧 freenite@romeosholiday.com
🖥 www.romeosholiday.com
8 double rooms with shower/WC, TV radio owm key. Continental bf included. Hot tub. See webside or call for details.
■ **Seasons** (AC cc BF GLM H OS)
160 Bradford Street ✉ MA 02657 (central) ☏ 487-2283
☏ (800) 563-0113 (Toll-free) 📠 487-8748
📧 seasons@capecod.net 🖥 www.capecod.net/seasons
Bed and Breakfast with 5 double rooms with bath, cable TV, VCR, CD/radio. Car park and own key. Rates US$ 80-125.
■ **Six Webster Place** (AC BF CC Glm H OS SOL WH)
6 Webster Place ✉ MA 02657 ☏ 487-9242 📠 487-9242
📧 sixwebster@capecod.net 🖥 www.sixwebster.com
All rooms with shower/WC, TV, video, phone, fax, radio, own key.
■ **Sunset Inn** (AC BF CC GLM H NU OS) April 15-November 1
142 Bradford Street ✉ MA 02657 (one block to centre)
☏ 487-9810 ☏ (800) 965-1801 (toll-free) 📠 487-7820
📧 sunset1@capecod.net 🖥 www.sunsetinnptown.com
Rooms with shower/WC, telephone, TV, radio, own key. Non-smoking in the rooms. Homemade bf. Free parking. Rates US$ 49-135.
■ **Watership Inn** (bf CC GLM H MA OS)
7 Winthrop Street ✉ MA 02657 ☏ 487-0094
📧 watership@capecod.net 🖥 www.capecod.net/watershipinn
Built about 1820. Rooms mostly with private bath, color cable TV. Rates US$ 40-95 (winter) and $65-205 (summer) plus taxes, incl. continental bf. Big deck.
■ **West End Inn** (BF CC GLM H MA)
44 Commercial Street ✉ MA 02657 ☏ 487-9555
☏ (800) 559-1220 📠 487-8779 📧 warren@westendinn.com
🖥 www.westendinn.com
All rooms with private bath/WC, TV, video, fax, radio, minibar, kitchenette, hair-dryer, own key. Own car park. Rates US$ 89-219.
■ **Windsor Court**
15 Cottage Street ✉ 36406 ☏ 487-2620
📧 windsorct@capecod.net 🖥 www.windsorcourtptown.com
■ **White Wind Inn** (AC BF CC GLM H OS)
174 Commercial Street ✉ MA 02657 ☏ 487-1526
☏ (888) 449-WIND 📠 457-4792 📧 wwinn@capecod.net.
🖥 www.whidewindinn.com
Single rooms with bath/shower/WC, balcony, TV, video, radio, refrigerator. Rates US$ 75-225 (ind. bf) depenting on season.

HEALTH GROUPS

■ **Provincetown AIDS Support Group**
PO Box 15 22 ✉ MA 02667 ☏ 487-9445 📠 487-0565

SWIMMING

Herring Cove Beach (G MA)

Springfield ▶ Detroit Massachusetts - Michigan/USA

Springfield ☏ 413

BARS
■ **Jam's** (B GLM)
632 Page Boulevard ✉ MA 01104 ☏ 736-9734
■ **Just Friends** (B D G LJ) 11-2 h
23 Hampden Street ✉ MA 01103 *(three floors)* ☏ 781-5878
■ **The Quarry** (B G LJ) 21-2 h, closed Wed
382 Dwight Street ✉ MA 01103 ☏ 736-9384
■ **The Pub** (B D GLM S) Mon-Sat 21-2, Sun 16-2 h
382 Dwight Street ✉ MA 01103 ☏ 734-8123
Dance bar downstairs.

RESTAURANTS
■ **Rosie's Place** (b F glm) Wed-Sun 17-22 h
382 Dwight Street ✉ MA 01103 *(at the Pub Bar)* ☏ 734-8123

CRUISING
-Downtown Mall
-Forest Park (picnic area near Recreation Department)
-Liberty Street (AYOR)
-Springfield Bus Terminal (AYOR)

Ware ☏ 413

HOTELS
■ **Wildwood Inn. The** (AC BF cc glm H MA OS)
121 Church Street ✉ MA 01082 ☏ 967-7798 ☏ (800) 860-8098 (toll-free)
1.5 hours drive west from Boston. Rooms with shared and private bath. Rates US$ 50-95 incl. full bf.

Worcester ☏ 508

BARS
■ **Club 241** (B D F G YG) 14-2 h
241 Southbridge Street ✉ MA 01608 ☏ 755-9311
■ **Mailbox Lounge** (B G lj) 14-2 h
40 Grafton Street ✉ MA 01608 ☏ 799-4521
Leather night last Sat/month.

CRUISING
-Rest Stop (on 140, Upton)
-Block around Portland & Salem Streets

USA-Michigan

Location: Great Lakes region USA
Initials: MI
Time: GMT -5
Area: 250.465 km² / 102,440 sq mi.
Population: 9,774,000
Capital: Lansing
Important gay cities: Detroit and Saugatuck

Ann Arbor ☏ 734

GAY INFO
■ **Gay Hotline** Mon-Fri
☏ 662-1977

BARS
■ **\'aút\Bar** (AC B BF CC F GLM MA N OS) 16-2, kitchen hours: 16-23, Fri Sat -1, Sun -15 h
315 Braun Court ✉ MI 48104 ☏ 994-3677

DANCECLUBS
■ **Nectarine Ballroom** (B D GLM VS YG) Tue and Fri 21-2 h
510 East Liberty Street ✉ MI 48104 ☏ 994-5835

CRUISING
-Rest Stop (AYOR) (north on US 23 at 31 mile marker)
-Dexter Rest Stop (south side of I-94 West)

Detroit ☏ 313

PUBLICATIONS
■ **Between the Lines Newspaper**
20793 Farmington Road #25, Farmington ✉ MI 48336
☏ 248.615.7003 ☏ 248.615.7018 ✉ pridepblis@aol.com
🖳 www.betweenthelinesnews.com
Michigan's statewide weekly newspaper for the LGBT community.
■ **Cruise Magazine** Mon-Fri 11-17 h
660 Livernois, Ferndale ✉ MI 48220-2304 ☏ (248) 545-9040
🖨 (248) 545-1073 ✉ cruisedet@aol.com
Weekly news and entertainment publication serving Michigan, Ohio and Indiana gay/lesbian community.
■ **Metra Magazine**
PO Box 71844, Madison Heights ✉ MI 48071 ☏ 248.543.3500
🖨 248.548.1023 ✉ metramag@aol.com
🖳 hometown.aol.com/metramag/myhomepage/business.html
Biweekly gay & lesbian publication.

BARS
■ **Adam's Apple** (AC B f G MA N) 15-2 h
18931 West Warren Avenue ✉ MI 48228 *(local neighbourhood)* ☏ 240-8482
Clean, friendly atmosphere.
■ **Back Pocket** (B F G MA) 17-2 h
8832 Greenfield Road ✉ MI 48228 *(near Joy Road)* ☏ 272-8435
■ **Gigi's** (AC B CC D f GLM MA p r S SNU STV TV) Mon-Fri 12-2, Sat Sun 14-2 h
16920 West Warren Avenue ✉ MI 48228 *(near South Field freeway)* ☏ 584-6525
Two bars on different levels, dancing every night, shows on Mon, Thu, Fri and Sat.
■ **Gold Coast. Club** (B G SNU) Mon-Sat 19-?, Sun 15-? h.
2971 East Seven Mile Road/Mitchell Street ✉ MI 48234 ☏ 366-6135
Male dancers Mon-Sat 21 h, Sun 20 h. Draft beer $1.
■ **Hayloft Saloon** (B G MA) Mon-Sun
8070 Greenfield Avenue ✉ MI 48228 *(near Tireman)* ☏ 581-8913
■ **Karma** (B D glmM TV)
22901 Woodward Avenue, Ferndale ✉ MI 48203
☏ 248/541-1600
■ **Male Box. The** (B D G stv) Mon-Fri 14-2, Sat Sun 12-2 h
3537 East Seven Mile Road ✉ MI 48234 *(3 blocks East of the Gold Coast)* ☏ 892-5420
■ **Mirage** (B D GLM)
31 North Walnut, Mt. Clemens ✉ MI 48043 ☏ 810/913-1921
■ **Number's** (D F G VS) 20-4 h.
17518 Woodward ✉ MI 48203 ☏ 868-9145
After hours with grilled chicken, hamburgers, etc. Dancing downstairs and quieter lounge upstairs.
■ **Off Broadway** (B D GLM)
12215 Harper Avenue ✉ MI 48213 ☏ 521-0920
■ **Other Side. The** (B F G) after hours
16801 Plymouth Road ✉ MI 48227 *(near Southfield Freeway)* ☏ 836-2324

USA/Michigan — Detroit ▸ Grand Rapids

■ **Pronto Video Bar** (B f GLM)
608 Washington, Royal Oak ✉ MI 48307 ☏ 248/544-7900
■ **Rainbow Room** (B CC D GLM MA S STV VS) Wed-Sun 19-2, shows at 22.30 and 24 h
6640 East 8 Mile ✉ Mi 48234 ☏ 891-1020
■ **R&R Saloon** (B D DR G LJ)
7330 Michigan Avenue ✉ MI 48210 ☏ 849-2751
■ **Sam's Tiffany's on the Park** (B D G LJ OS)
17436 Woodward Avenue ✉ MI 48203 *(near Parkhurst)*
☏ 883-7162
Popular on Thu and Sun.
■ **Stiletto's** (B GLM S snu) Wed-Sun 10-2 h
1641 Middlebelt Road *(between Michigan and Cherry Hill)*
☏ 734/729-8980
■ **Stingers** (B D F GLM VS) Mon Fri 18-2, Sat Sun 20-2 h
19404 Sherwood Street ✉ MI 48234 *(side entrance)* ☏ 892-1765
■ **Woodward** (B d F G) DJ on WE
6426 Woodward Avenue ✉ MI 48202 *(near Milwaukee)*
☏ 872-0166

DANCECLUBS
■ **Backstreet** (B D G YG) Wed Sat 20-2 h
15606 Joy Road ✉ MI 48228 ☏ 272-8959
Popular.
■ **Menjo's** (B D G OS S) Mon-Wed 12-20, Thu Fri 12-2, Sat Sun 13-2 h
928 West McNichols Road/Hamilton Street ✉ MI 48203
☏ 863-3934
■ **Zippers** (B D G STV VS) Wed-Mon 21-? h
6221 East Davidson ✉ MI 48212 ☏ 892-8120

RESTAURANTS
■ **Como's Restaurant** (B F glm)
22812 Woodward Avenue, Ferndale ✉ MI 48220 *(at 9 Mile Roade)*
☏ 248/548-5005
■ **Dolce Vita. La** (A B d F GLM) Dancing Tue night. Dinner Wed-Sat
17546 Woodward ✉ MI 48220 *(Ferndale)* ☏ 856-0371
Very good Italian food, light jazz.
■ **Pronto** (B F glm)
608 South Washington, Royal Oak ✉ MI 48367 ☏ 248/544-7900
■ **Rhinoceros** (B F d GLM)
265 Riopelle ✉ MI 48207 ☏ 313/259-6937

SEX SHOPS/BLUE MOVIES
■ **Escape Book Store** 10-23 h, closed Sun
18728 West Warren Avenue ✉ MI 48228 ☏ 336-6558
■ **Fifth Wheel** (g) 10-24 h
9320 Michigan Avenue ✉ MI 48210 ☏ 846-8613

SAUNAS/BATHS
■ **TNT Complex** (G PI SA SB SOL VS WO) 0-24 h
13333 West Eight Road ✉ MI 48235 ☏ 341-5372

BOOK SHOPS
■ **Chosen Books** (GLM)
120 West 4th Street ✉ MI 48064 *(Royal Oak)* ☏ 543-7458
Literature, games, cards, posters, gifts.

GENERAL GROUPS
■ **Affirmations Community Center** (GLM)
195 West Mile, Ferndale ✉ MI 48220 ☏ 248/298-7105
■ **Triangle Foundation** (GLM)
19641 West Seven Mile Road ✉ MI 48219-2721 ☏ 537-3323
🖷 537-3379 🖳 www.tri.org
Michigan's statewide civil rights, advocacy and anti-violence organisation for gay, lesbian, bisexual and transgender people.

Douglas ☏ 616

HOTELS
■ **Lighthouse Motel** (AC BF glm H PI)
130th & Blue Star Highway ✉ MI 49406 ☏ 857-2271
Rooms with private and shared bath, all with kitchenette, fridge and TV.

GUEST HOUSES
■ **Douglas House B&B** (AC BF CC glm H OS) May-Oct
41 Spring Street ✉ MI 49406-140 ☏ 857-1119
Small B&B in private home. 4 rooms with private bath.
■ **Kirby House. The** (A AC BF CC glm MA NU OS PI WH)
294 West Center Bx 1124 ✉ MI 49406 ☏ 857-2904 🖷 857-2904
🖳 www.bbonline.com/mi/grandescape/
B&B in Victorian manorhouse.

Ellsworth ☏ 231

PRIVATE ACCOMMODATION
■ **Wunderschönes Bed & Breakfast** (BF F f GLM H lj MA msg OS WO)
12410 Antrim Drive ✉ MI 49729-9741 ☏ 599-2847
Rates US$ 80-90. Discounts for 3 days and longer stays. Private beach. Surrounded by golf course and nature preserve.

Flint ☏ 810

BARS
■ **State Bar** (B D GLM)
2512 South Dort ✉ MI 48507 ☏ 767-7050

DANCECLUBS
■ **Club Triangle** (B D GLM)
2101 South Dort ✉ MI 48507 ☏ 767-7552

Grand Rapids ☏ 616

GAY INFO
■ **Network (Gay/Lesbian Network of Western Michigan)** Mon-Fri 18-22 h
909 Cherry Street South East ✉ MI 49503 ☏ 458-3511
🖷 458-4294
Information and referral. Monthly publication.

BARS
■ **Cell. The** (B D G LJ VS)
76 South Division Avenue ☏ 454-5800
■ **City Limits** (B D GLM)
67 South Division Avenue ☏ 454-8003

DANCECLUBS
■ **Diversions** (B D F GLM MA VS)
10 Fountain Street NW ✉ MI 49503 ☏ 451-3800

SEX SHOPS/BLUE MOVIES
■ **Cini-Mini** (g) 11-2 h
415 Bridge Street NW ✉ MI 49501 ☏ 454-7531

SAUNAS/BATHS
■ **Diplomat Health Club** (G SA)
2324 South Division Avenue ✉ MI 4907-3051 ☏ 452-3754

BOOK SHOPS
■ **Sons & Daughters** (glm)
962 Cherry SE ✉ MI 49506 ☏ 459-8877

Grand Rapids ▶ Minneapolis/St. Paul — Michigan - Minnesota/USA

CRUISING
- Rest Stop (US 131 North)
- Rest Stop (I-96 West)
- Ann Street Park (AYOR)
- City Centre (downtown shopping mall)

Kalamazoo ☎ 616

BARS
■ **Brothers** (B D GLM)
209 Stockbridge ✉ MI 49001 ☎ 345-1960
■ **Missias** (B D glm)
562 Portage Street ✉ MI 49001 ☎ 381-4140

BOOK SHOPS
■ **Triangle World** (GLM)
551 Portage Street ✉ MI 49007 ☎ 373-4005

Lansing ☎ 517

BARS
■ **Club 505** (B D GLM)
505 East Shiawassee ✉ MI 48912 ☎ 374-6312
■ **Esquire** (B F Glm N OG) 12-2 h
1250 Turner ☎ 487-5338
■ **Spiral** (B D GLM)
1247 Center Street ✉ MI 48906 ☎ 371-3221

CRUISING
- Rest stop (AYOR) (on I-96, Okemos)
- Rest stop (AYOR) (on Highway 27, 1 mile north of 127)

Royal Oak ☎ 248

GAY INFO
☞ See Detroit

Saugatuck ☎ 616

HOTELS
■ **Dunes Resort, The** (AC B CC D F GLM H MA OS PI S) 9-2 h
PO Box 1132 ✉ MI 49453 ☎ 857-1401 🖷 857-4052
✉ mjones@duneresort.com 🖳 www.duneresort.com
Hotel & disco. One of the largest gay and lesbian resorts in the Midwest. Cabaret, game room & bistro. Call or see website for details.

GUEST HOUSES
■ **Grandma Arlene's House B&B** (BF CC GLM H OS WE WH) open Fri-Mon only
2135 Blue Star Highway, Fennville ✉ MI 49408 ☎ 543-4706
Small B&B with 4 single rooms with private baths, hair-dryer and color cable TV.
■ **Kirky House, The** (A AC BF CC glm H MA N NU OS PI WH) close for Christmas
294 West Center Street, PO Box 1734 ✉ MI 49453 ☎ 857-2904
☎ (800) 521-6473 (Toll-free) ✉ kirbyinn@aol.com
8 double rooms with shower/WC, heating, own key. Free bikes, good off street parking.
■ **Moore's Creek Inn** (BF CC glm H)
820 Holland Street ✉ MI 49453 ☎ 857-2411 ☎ (800) 838-5864 (Toll-free)
Small B&B in 1900s townhouse. All rooms with private bath. No kids, no pets.

CAMPING
■ **Camp It** (GLM)
Route 6635, 118th Avenue, Fennville ✉ MI 49408 ☎ 543-4335
Big campsight under gay management. TV lounge. Laundry facilities. Store and supermarket nearby. No kids.

SWIMMING
- Oval Beach

USA-Minnesota

Location: Great Lakes region USA
Initials: MN
Time: GMT -6
Area: 225.182 km^2 / 92,099 sq mi.
Population: 4,686,000
Capital: Saint Paul
Important gay cities: Minneapolis/Saint Paul

Minneapolis/St. Paul ☎ 612

GAY INFO
■ **Gay and Lesbian Community Action Council**
310 East 38th Street, Minneapolis ✉ MN 55409 ☎ 822-0127
☎ (800) 800-0350 (Toll-free)

PUBLICATIONS
■ **focusPoint**
PO Box 50188, Minneapolis ✉ MN 55405 ☎ 288-9008
🖷 288-9001 ✉ focuspointeditor@aol.com
Monthly GLBT newspaper.
■ **Lavender Magazine** (CC GLM) Mon-Fri 8.30-17 h
2344 Nicollet Avenue, Suite 300, Minneapolis ✉ MN 55404
☎ 871-2237 🖷 871-2650 ✉ info@lavendermagazine.com
🖳 www.lavendermagazine.com
Biweekly magazine. Online version available. One of the largest gay lesbi&transgender magazine in the Upper Midwest.

TOURIST INFO
■ **Greater Minneapolis Convention & Visitor Bureau** 8-17 h
33 S 6th Street, Minneapolis ✉ MN 55402 (4000 Multifoods Tower)
☎ 348-7000 🖷 335-5841 🖳 www.minneapolis.org

BARS
■ **Body Shop** (B G LJ)
1415 University Avenue West, St. Paul ✉ MN 55104 (in the back of the Town House) ☎ 646-7087
■ **Brass Rail** (B G N s) 10-1 h
422 Hennepin Avenue, Minneapolis ✉ MN 55401 ☎ 333-3016
■ **Club Metro** (AC B CC D F GLM MA OS S STV YG) Mon-Thu 16-1, Fri-Sat 15-1, Sun 14-1 h
733 Pierce Butler Rte, St. Paul ✉ MN 55104 ☎ 489-0002
■ **Gay 90's** (! B D F GLM lj MA S SNU STV VS) Mon-Sat 8-1, Sun 10-1 h
408 Hennepin Avenue, Minneapolis ✉ MN 55401 ☎ 333-7755
Upper Midwest's largest gay entertainment complex: 7 bars, 2 dance floors.
■ **Minneapolis Eagle** (B F G LJ MA)
515 Washington Avenue South ✉ MN 55403 ☎ 338-4214
■ **Over the Rainbow** (B GLM)
249 West 7th Street (St. Paul) ☎ 228-7180
■ **Saloon** (B D F G)
830 Hennepin Avenue, Minneapolis ✉ MN 55401 (at 9th Street)
☎ 332-0835
High energy dance music.

SPARTACUS 2001/2002 | 1279

USA/Minnesota - Mississippi | Minneapolis/St. Paul ▶ Jackson

■ **Town House** (AC B GLM MA) Mon-Fri 14-1, Sat Sun 12-1 h
1415 West University Avenue West, St. Paul ✉ MN 55104
☎ 646-7087
Western style bar.
■ **Trikkx** (B D F GLM MA s) Mon-Thu 16-1, Fri -3, Sat 18-3, Sun -1 h
490 North Robert Street ✉ MN 55101 ☎ 651/224-0703
German spoken.
■ **19 Bar** (AC B f GLM MA N OS) Mon-Fri 15-1, Sat-Sun 13-1 h
19 West 15th Street, Minneapolis ✉ MN 55403 ☎ 871-5553
Low prices, pool tables, voted best neighborhood bar 1999.

CAFES

■ **Cafe Wyrd** (b BF GLM) 7-1 h
1600 West Lake Street, Minneapolis ☎ 827-5710
■ **Cafe Zev** (b BF f glm) 7-1, Fri Sat -2 h
1362 LaSalle Avenue, Minneapolis ☎ 874-3377
Popular.

DANCECLUBS

■ **Ground Zero** (B D GLM MA) Thu (LJ)
15 Northeast 4th Street ☎ 378-5115

RESTAURANTS

■ **Black Forest Inn** (F glm)
1 East 26th Street, Minneapolis ✉ MN 55404 ☎ 872-0812
German food.

BOOK SHOPS

■ **A Brother's Touch** (AC CC GLM MA) Mon-Fri 10-21, Sat 11-20, Sun 12-17 h
2327 Hennepin Avenue South ✉ MN 55405 ☎ 377-6279
Books, cards, gifts, music, T-shirts, jewelry.

GIFT & PRIDE SHOPS

■ **Rainbow Road** (GLM) 10-22 h
109 West Grant Street, Minneapolis ✉ MN 55403 ☎ 872-8448
Bookstore/Variety Store.

HOTELS

■ **Hotel Amsterdam** (AC BF CC f G H p) 24 h
828 Hennepin Avenue, Minneapolis ✉ MN 55403 ☎ 288-0459
🖷 288-0461 ✉ hotel@scc.net 🖳 www.gaympls.com
European-style hotel. Gay bar and restaurant on-site. Rates for single rooms with shared bath USD 30-50.

GUEST HOUSES

■ **Como Villa B&B** (AC BF GLM H)
1371 West Nebraska Avenue, St. Paul ✉ MN 55108 ☎ 647-0471
Non-smoking establishment. No pets, no kids. Rooms with private and shared bath. Central location.

GENERAL GROUPS

■ **PFLAG**
PO Box 19290, Minneapolis ✉ MN 55419 ☎ 825-1660

FETISH GROUPS

■ **ATONS of Minneapolis**
PO Box 2311, Minneapolis ✉ MN 55402 ☎ 738-7343
Leather group for gay men.
■ **Girth & Mirth/Twin Cities**
PO Box 4288, Hopkins ✉ MN 55343 ☎ 934-4332
■ **Knights of Leather**
PO Box 582601, Minneapolis ✉ MN 55458-2601 ☎ 870-7473

HEALTH GROUPS

■ **AIDS Information** Mon-Fri 9-22, Sat 12-17 h
☎ 373-2437
■ **Aliveness Project**
730 East 38th Street, Minneapolis ✉ MN 55409 ☎ 822-7946
Support and services for people with AIDS, ARC and who are HIV positive.
■ **Minnesota AIDS Project** Mon-Fri 8.30-17.30 h
1400 Park Avenue ✉ MN 55404 ☎ 341-2060

HELP WITH PROBLEMS

■ **Gay & Lesbian Hotline** 12-24 h
☎ 822-8661 ☎ (0800) 800-0907 (toll-free)

SPECIAL INTEREST GROUPS

■ **Bisexual Connection**
PO Box 13158, Minneapolis ✉ MN 55414

SWIMMING

-**32nd Street Beach** (32nd Street & West Calhoun, gay beach)

CRUISING

-Hennepin Avenue (AYOR) (downtown)
-IDS Tower (indoor mall, "Crystal Court")
-Loring Park & Oak Grove (AYOR)
-Mississippi River Flats (AYOR) (East River Road, opposite Shriners Hospital)
-University of Minnesota (Minneapolis Campus, Gay Community Center, Coffman Memorial Union at 2nd floor, Northrop Auditorium at 3rd floor)

USA-Mississippi

Location: South USA
Initials: MS
Time: GMT -6
Area: 125.443 km² / 51,306 sq mi.
Population: 2,731,000
Capital: Jackson

Biloxi ☎ 601

BARS

■ **Joey's on the Beach**
878 Ravenwood Court ✉ MS 39532 ☎ 435-5639

CRUISING

-Beach Highway (between Biloxi and Gulfport)
-Edgewater Shopping Center (AYOR)
-Gulf Coast Beach (between Holiday Inn and Coliseum)

Hattiesburg ☎ 601

BARS

■ **Courtyard, The** (B D F GLM S)
107 E. Front Street ☎ 545-2714

Jackson ☎ 601

BARS

■ **Club City Lights** (b D GLM) Wed Fri-Sun 22-? h
200 North Mill Street ✉ MS 39201 (Mill & Amite) ☎ 353-0059
■ **Jack and Jill's** (AC B D f GLM lj MA s STV WE) Fri, Sat 21-? h
3911 Northview Drive ✉ MS 39206 ☎ 982-5225
Beer only bar.

Jackson ▶ Kansas City | Mississippi - Missouri/USA

■ **Jack's Construction Site** (AC B d f GLM lj MA N OS S) 17-? h
425 North Mart Plaza ✉ MS 39206 ☎ 362-3108
Beer only bar.
■ **Star. The** (AC B BF CC F GLM MA S) Mon-Sat 17-1, Sun 12-22 h
400 E. South Street, Hinds County ✉ MS 39201 *(across from main post office)* ☎ 352-5111
Piano bar. Also restaurant. Live music.

SEX SHOPS/BLUE MOVIES
■ **Heritage Video**
1515 Terry Road ✉ MS 39204 ☎ 354-5555
■ **Terry Road Bookstore**
1449 Terry Road ✉ MS 39204 ☎ 353-9196
Adult books and videos.

GENERAL GROUPS
■ **American Civil Liberties Union (ACLU) of Mississippi**
PO Box 2242 ✉ MS 39225 ☎ 355-6464
■ **Mississippi Gay & Lesbian Task Force**
PO Box 7737 ✉ MS 39284 ☎ 924-3333
Host of Lambda AA, Mississippi Phoenix Coalition, Mothers of AIDS Patients, Prime Timers and Overeaters Anonymous for Gays and Lesbians.

HEALTH GROUPS
■ **Adopt-A-Friend Project**
PO Box 2055 ✉ MS 39225 ☎ 924-3333
■ **HIV-PWA Project of Mississippi**
Drawer 8342 ✉ MS 39294 ☎ 371-3019
■ **Southern AIDS Commission - Jackson Office**
5565 Robinson Road, PO Box 8457 ✉ MS 39284-8457 ☎ 371-3019, 🖷 371-3156 📧 eddies2@prodigy.com
Also seat of MS Gay/Lesbian Alliance, Inc.
■ **Support Group for those Living with HIV/AIDS**
☎ 922-9687

HELP WITH PROBLEMS
■ **Gay & Lesbian Hotline**
☎ 435-2398
Action Line 24 hrs. for the Gulf Coast Area.

SPECIAL INTEREST GROUPS
■ **Aurora Transgender Support for Central Mississippi** (TV)
PO Box 1306, Florence ✉ MS 39073 ☎ 845-1328

CRUISING
-Jackson State Library
-Smith Park (AYOR)

USA-Missouri

Location: Middlewest USA
Initials: MO
Time: GMT -6
Area: 180.546 km² / 73,843 sq mi.
Population: 5,402,000
Capital: Jefferson City
Important gay cities: Kansas City and St. Louis

Kansas City ☎ 816

TOURIST INFO
■ **Greater Kansas City Convention & Visitor Bureau**
1100 Main Street ✉ MO 64105 ☎ 221-5242 🖷 691-3805

BARS
■ **Buddies Lounge** (B G MA N r) 6-3 h
3715 Main Street ✉ MO 64111 ☎ 561-2600
Popular
■ **Fox** (B G MA N)
7520 Shawnee Mission Parkway, Overland Park ☎ (913) 384-0369
■ **Mari's Saloon & Grill** (B F GLM N S)
1809 Grand Boulevard ✉ MO 64116 ☎ 283-0511
■ **Missy B's** (B G STV) Mon-Sat ?-3 h
805 West 39th Street ✉ MO 64111 ☎ 561-0625
Mon/Wed Drag shows, Fri/Sat live music & vocals
■ **Other Side** (B G VS) closed Sun
3611 Broadway ✉ MO 64111 ☎ 931-0501
Video bar.
■ **Sidekicks Saloon** (AC B CC d G MA r s VS) Mon-Sat 14-3 h, closed Sun
3707 Main Street ✉ MO 64111 ☎ 931-1430
■ **Tootsie's New Place** (B gLM MA N)
1822 Main Street ☎ 474-4638
■ **Vineyard** (B G MA S)
1108 Grand Avenue ☎ 421-1082

DANCECLUBS
■ **Cabaret Club** (B D G S SNU STV VS YG) ?-3 h
5025 Main Street ✉ MO 64112 *(near 50th St.)* ☎ 753-6504
Wed-Sun drag and strip shows.
■ **Dixie Belle Saloon** (B D F G LJ OS)
1922 Main Street ✉ MO 64108 ☎ 471-2424
Café, patio bar, cruise bar and leather shop.

RESTAURANTS
■ **Metropolis** (B F GLM)
303 Westport Road ☎ 753-1550

SEX SHOPS/BLUE MOVIES
■ **Erotic City** (glm) 0-24 h
8401 East Truman Road ☎ 252-3370
■ **Ray's Playpen** (glm) 0-24 h
3235 Main Street ☎ 753-7692

SAUNAS/BATHS
■ **1823 Club** (b G LJ MA OS P SA SOL VS) 0-24 h
1823 Wyandotte ✉ MO 64108

BOOK SHOPS
■ **Borders** (glm)
9108 Metcalf, Overland Park ☎ (913) 642-3642
■ **Larry's Gifts and Cards Inc.** (GLM) Mon-Fri 10-7, Sat 10-18.30, Sun 10-17 h
205 Westport Road ✉ MO 64111 ☎ 753-4757

LEATHER & FETISH SHOPS
■ **Spike's Leather**
1922 Main ✉ MO 64108 *(Downstairs at Dixie Belle)*

HOTELS
■ **Inn the Park** (BF glm H Pl)
3610 Gilham Road ✉ MO 64111 ☎ 931-0797
B&B in private home. All rooms with private bath, color cable TV and VCR.

SPARTACUS 2001/2002 | 1281

USA/Missouri — Kansas City ▶ St. Louis

GUEST HOUSES
■ **Doanleigh Inn, The** (AC BF CC E glm msg OS)
217 East 37th Street ✉ MO 64111 *(Hyde Park area)* ☎ 753-2667
🖨 531-5185 doanleigh@aol.com www.doanleigh.com
Luxury B&B in an old Georgian mansion with fireplaces and antique furnishings. All rooms with bath/WC, hair-dryer, balcony, telephone, Sat-TV, video and radio. Rates USD 85-150 incl. bf buffet. No pets, kids on request.

HEALTH GROUPS
■ **KC Free Health Clinic Midtown**
2 East 39th Street ✉ MO 64111 ☎ 753-5144
HIV-testing.

HELP WITH PROBLEMS
■ **Gay and Lesbian Alcoholics Anonymous**
☎ 531-9668
■ **Gay Talk Line** 18-24 h
☎ 931-4470

RELIGIOUS GROUPS
■ **Trinity United Methodist Church**
620 East Armour Boulevard ✉ MO 64109-2247 ☎ 931-1100
🖨 831-1101 TUMCkcmo@aol.com
 www.gbgm-umc.org/trinitymi01

CRUISING
-Rest Stop (on I-29 near airport)
-Country Club Plaza
-Liberty Memorial Mall (AYOR)
-Loose Park
-McGee (AYOR R) (between 10th and 11th Street)

Springfield ☎ 417

SEX SHOPS/BLUE MOVIES
■ **Sunshine News and Arcade**
3537 West Sunshine Street ✉ MO 65807 ☎ 831-2298

CRUISING
-Phelps Grove Park (AYOR)

St. Louis ☎ 314

GAY INFO
■ **Access Line**
☎ 533-6155
Infoline about gay life in St. Louis. Recorded message.
■ **Gay and Lesbian Community Center**
☎ 997-9897

PUBLICATIONS
■ **EXP Magazine**
4579 Laclede #110 ✉ MO 63108 ☎ 367-0397 ☎ 397-6244
🖨 727-1884 expmag@aol.com www.expmag.com
Biweekly newspaper covering the Missouri, Kansas & Montana.
■ **Vital Voice, The**
PO Box 170138 ✉ MO 63117 ☎ 865-3787 🖨 865-3073
 vitalvoicenews@aol.com
New (2000) biweekly GLBT newspaper.

TOURIST INFO
■ **St. Louis Convention & Visitors Commission**
One Metropolitan Square ✉ MO 63102 ☎ 421-1023
🖨 421-0394

BARS
■ **Alibi's** (B D F G S SNU STV)
3016 Arsenal ☎ 772-8989
■ **Clementine's** (AC B CC F G LJ MA N OS) Mon-Fri 10-1.30, Sat 8-1.30, Sun 11-24 h
2001 Menard Avenue ✉ MO 63104 *(at Allen Avenue)* ☎ 664-7869
Gay cruising bar & sidewalk restaurant for guys into leather, levis and western clothing.
■ **Drake Bar, The** (B G N OS) 16.45-1.30 h, closed Sun
3502 Fapin Street ✉ MO 63110 ☎ 685-1400
Piano nightly. Fri/Sat 21 h Jazz
■ **Grey Fox Pub** (B G MA N)
3503 South Spring ☎ 772-2150
■ **Loading Zone** (B GLM VS YG) closed Sun
16 South Euclid Avenue ✉ MO 63108 ☎ 361-4119
■ **Magnolia's** (B D F G lj S) 16-3, Sun 11-3 h
5-9 South Vandeventer ✉ MO 63108 ☎ 652-6500
Very popular restaurant, café, bar and disco.
■ **Mags** (B D F G LJ S VS) ß-
5 South Vandeventer ✉ MO 63108 ☎ 652-6500
■ **Nero Bianco** (B G MA N)
6 South Sarah ☎ 531-4123
The name "Black and White" in italian says it all.
■ **St. Louis Eagle, The** (B G LJ MA) Mon-Fri 15.30-1.30, Sat 12-1.30 h, closed Sun
17 South Vandeventer ✉ MO 63108 ☎ 535-4100

DANCECLUBS
■ **Complex Nightclub, The** (AC B CC D F G lj MA OS STV) 18-3 h. Food served Wed-Sun 18-22.30 h.
3515 Chouteau Avenue ✉ MO 63103 ☎ 772-2645
Dance club and restaurant.
■ **Faces** (B D DR G LJ S SNU STV VS)
130 4th Street

RESTAURANTS
■ **Angels** (B F GLM LJ) 11-3 h
3511 Chouteau Avenue ✉ MO 63103 ☎ 772-2645
American cuisine
■ **Duff's** (B F glm MA)
392 North Euclid Avenue ☎ 361-0522
American cuisine. Full bar.
■ **Niner Diner** (b F GLM)
9 South Vandeventer ☎ 652-0171
American cuisine.
■ **Ninth Street Abbey** (b F glm)
808 South 9th Street ☎ 621-9598
International cuisine.
■ **South City Diner** (b F glm) 0-24 h
3141 South Grand ☎ 772-6100
American cuisine.

SAUNAS/BATHS
■ **Club, The** (b CC f G MA P PI SA SB SOL VS WH WO) 0-24 h
2625 Samuel Shepard Drive ✉ MO 63103 *(near Jefferson)*
☎ 533-3666
Parties on Sat & Sun at 13 h on the outside heated pool-side.

BOOK SHOPS
■ **Left Bank Books** (A AC glm) 10-22, Sun 11-18 h
399 N. Euclid Avenue ✉ MO 63108 *(at McPherson)* ☎ 367-6731
General bookstore with large lesbi-gay section.
■ **Our World Too** (AC CC GLM MA) 10-21.30, Sun 12-20 h
11 South Vandeventer ✉ MO 63108-3221 ☎ 533-5322
Bookshop and mail order service.

St. Louis ▶ West Yellowstone | Missouri - Montana/USA

A St. Louis Guesthouse
INTIMATE GUESTHOUSE WITH FIVE SUITES
LOCATED IN HISTORIC SOULARD
CONVENIENT TO DOWNTOWN ST. LOUIS
ALL GAY, MOSTLY MALE CLIENTELE
GAY BAR AND RESTAURANT NEXT DOOR
CLOTHING-OPTIONAL COURTYARD WITH HOT TUB • NUDE SUNBATHING
MAKE US YOUR HOME AWAY FROM HOME WHEN YOU VISIT ST. LOUIS!
1032-38 ALLEN AVE., ST. LOUIS, MISSOURI 63104
PHONE: (314) 773-1016 • E-MAIL STLOUISGH@AOL.COM
HOMETOWN.AOL.COM/STLOUISGH/MYHOMEPAGE/BUSINESS.HTML

LEATHER & FETISH SHOPS
■ **Ngamson Leather & Lace**
2822 Cherokee ☎ 772-5218

GUEST HOUSES
■ **A St. Louis Guesthouse** (AC CC GLM msg OS WH)
1032-38 Allen Avenue ✉ MO 63104 *(in historic Soulard)*
☎ 773-1016 stlouisgh@aol.com
 hometown.aol.com/stlouisgh/myhomepage/business.html
Two suites with private bath, cable TV, VCR, fridge, small kitchen and phone. Rates US$ 75-110 per night.
■ **Brewer's House Bed & Breakfast** (AC BF CC GLM H Ij MA NU WH) reception 7-24 h
1829 Lami Street ✉ MO 63104 *(south of downtown near brewery)*
☎ 771-1542
Small B&B in historic home. Rooms with private bath, telephone, TV, video, radio, kitchen and hair-dryer. Rates USD 70-75 incl. continental bf.
■ **Napoleon's Retreat Bed & Breakfast** (AC BF CC f glm H MA) reception 7-22 h
1815 Lafayette Avenue ✉ MO 63104 *(1 mile from downtown in historical district)* ☎ 772-6979 (800) 700-9980 772-7675
 info@napoleonsretreat.com www.napoleonsretreat.com
4 rooms and 1 apartment in 1880s townhouse. Bath or shower, WC, telephone, TV, own key and room service. Rates single US$ 75-100, double 85-125. Full-board.

GENERAL GROUPS
■ **People of All Colors Together**
PO Box 8052 ✉ MO 63108 ☎ 231-6931

FETISH GROUPS
■ **Blue Max Cycle Club**
PO Box 233, Main Station ✉ MO 63166
■ **Gateway MC**
PO Box 140 55 ✉ MO 63178

HEALTH GROUPS
■ **VD Control**
634 North Grand Avenue ✉ MO 63103 ☎ 658-1025
Venereal diseases.

HELP WITH PROBLEMS
■ **St. Louis Gay & Lesbian Community Services** Gay/Lesbian Hotline 18-22 h daily
PO Box 232 27 ✉ MO 63156 ☎ 367-0084

SPECIAL INTEREST GROUPS
■ **GAMMA Support Group**
☎ 567-2076
Support group for gay men who are married, separated or divorced.

■ **St. Louis Gender Foundation** (TV)
☎ 997-9897
Support group for transgendered people.

USA-Montana
Location: North USA
Initials: MT
Time: GMT -7
Area: 380.850 km² / 155,767 sq mi.
Population: 879,000
Capital: Helena

Billings ☎ 406

BOOK SHOPS
■ **Barjon's** (g) Mon-Sat 9.30-17.30 h
2718 3rd Avenue North ✉ MT 59101 ☎ 252-4318
Alternative books with gay/lesbian titles.

Missoula ☎ 406

BARS
■ **AmVets** (B D f G MA S tv) ?-1.30 h
225 Ryman ✉ MT 59801 ☎ 728-3137
Popular after 22.30 h

CAFES
■ **Catalyst Espresso** (b glm MA)
111 N. Higgins Avenue ✉ MT 59801 ☎ 542-1337

Ronan ☎ 406

GUEST HOUSES
■ **North Crow Ranch** (BF GLM H MA msg NU OS WH) May-Oct
2360 North Crow Road ✉ MT 59864 *(5 miles north-east of Ronan)*
☎ 676-5169 gamine@ronan.net www.ronan.net/~gamine
The ranch features a tasteful balance of comfort and outdoor activity in a natural setting of forest, field and stream. Spend the night in a tent, ti-pi cabin or ranchhouse vacation on rental.

West Yellowstone ☎ 406

GUEST HOUSES
■ **Campobello Lodge at Bar N Ranch** (F GLM MA S WH)
3111 Targhee Pass Highway ✉ MT 89758 ☎ 646-9682
 barnranch@wyellowstone.com
 www.wyellowstone.com/bar-n-ranch
Rates on request.

USA/Nebraska - Nevada | Lincoln ▸ Las Vegas

USA-Nebraska
Location: Middlewest USA
Initials: NE
Time: GMT -6
Area: 200.358 km² / 81,946 sq mi.
Population: 1,657,000
Capital: Lincoln

Lincoln ☎ 402

BARS
■ **Panic. The** (B D GLM lj) Mon-Fri 16-1, Sat 13-1, Sun 13-23 h
200 South 18th Street ✉ NE 68508 ☎ 435-8764
■ **Q** (AC B D DR GLM lj MA SNU STV) Tue-Sun 20-1 h
226 South 9th Street ✉ NE 68508 ☎ 475-2269
Small cruise bar within the bar open on Fri Sat 22-1 h.

GIFT & PRIDE SHOPS
■ **Christie's Toy Box** Mon-Thu 9-23, Fri/Sat 9-24, Sun 12-21 h
2029 O Street ✉ NE 68510 ☎ 477-6566
Wide range of cards, movies toys and accessories.

LEATHER & FETISH SHOPS
■ **Boog's Rockand Roll Boutique** Mon-Fri 12-19 Sat 12-6 h
122 South 52nd Street/O Street ✉ NE 68501 ☎ 483-2263
Leather goods, costumes and undergarments.

GENERAL GROUPS
■ **Parents and Friends of Lesbians and Gays**
☎ 467-4599

HEALTH GROUPS
■ **Nebraska AIDS Project**
3818 Sheridan Boulevard ✉ NE 68506 ☎ 484-8100
☎ (800) 782-AIDS (Toll-free)

HELP WITH PROBLEMS
■ **Gay-Lesbian Youth Talkline**
☎ 473-7932

CRUISING
- Antelope, Pioneer, Wilderness and Van Dorn Parks (AYOR/police)
- I-80 Westbound (west of 56th Street exit AYOR)
- Gateway Mall
- University of Nebraska City Union (restrooms on 2nd floor)
- University of Nebraska Love Library (old building, 2nd floor)
- Route 77 (AYOR) (15 miles north, near Ceresco)
- 15th Street (between D & H, "Fruit Loop", very popular)

Omaha ☎ 402

BARS
■ **Diamond Bar** (B G lj N) Mon-Sat 21-1, Sun 12-1 h
712 South 16th Street ✉ NE 68102 ☎ 342-9595
■ **Max. The** (B D GLM S VS YG) 21-1 h
1417 Jackson Street ✉ NE 68102 ☎ 346-4110
Popular.
■ **Run. The** (B D G LJ) Sun-Thu 14-1, Sat 14-4 h
1715 Leavenworth Street ✉ NE 68102 *(near 18th)* ☎ 449-8703

CRUISING
- Milks Run (R) (Howard & Jackson Streets between 16th and 18th, nights)

- Benson Park
- Carter Lake
- Hanscom Park
- Towl Park (AYOR) (wooded area & jogging path)
- Westroads Shopping Center Mall

USA-Nevada
Location: West USA
Initials: NV
Time: GMT -8
Area: 286.367 km² / 117,124 sq mi.
Population: 1,677,000
Capital: Carson City
Important gay cities: Las Vegas and Reno

Lake Tahoe ☎ 702

GUEST HOUSES
■ **Lakeside Bed & Breakfast - Tahoe** (BF GLM H MA NU OS P SB VS WH)
PO Box 8, Crystal Bay ✉ NV 89402 ☎ 831-8281 📠 831-7329
📧 tahoeBnB@aol.com
2 double room and 1 suite with bath/shower/WC, telephone, fax, TV, video, radio, hair-dryer. Skiing in winter, swimming and boating in summer.

Las Vegas ☎ 702

GAY INFO
■ **Gay & Lesbian Community Center** 10-17 h
PO Box 70481 ✉ NV 89170 ☎ 733-9800 📧 tashahill@aol.com

PUBLICATIONS
■ **Las Vegas Bugle**
714 E Sahara Avenue #220 ✉ NV 89104 ☎ 369-6260
📠 369-9325 📧 editor@lvbugle.com 🌐 www.lvbugle.com
Biweekly magazine covering regional and national news, culture, ads. Good on-line version.

BARS
■ **Angles/Club Lace** (B GLM N VS YG) 0-24 h
4633 Paradise Road ✉ NV 89109 *(at Tropicana)* ☎ 733-9677
Angels is more popular with gay men while women prefer Club Lace.
■ **Back Door Lounge** (B G MA N) 0-24 h
1415 East Charleston ✉ NV 89104 *(downtown)* ☎ 385-2018
■ **Backstreet** (B d GLM N) 0-24 h
5012 South Arville Road ✉ NV 89118 *(off West Tropicana)*
☎ 876-1844
Western-style, country dancing on Fri and Sat.
■ **Bamboleos** (B G MA)
713 East Ogden Street ☎ 474-9060
Latino bar.
■ **Buffalo. The** (B G LJ MA VS) 0-24 h
4640 Paradise Road ✉ NV 89109 ☎ 733-8355
Popular. Home of the Satyricon Motorcycle Club.
■ **Choices** (B G N) 0-24 h
1729 East Charleston Boulevard ✉ NV 89104 ☎ 382-4791
■ **Eagle** (B d G lj MA STV)
5430 East Tropicana/Pecos ✉ NV 89121 *(at Pecos)* ☎ 458-8662
Poker machines.
■ **Flex** (B d GLM MA N snu) 0-24 h
4371 West Charleston Street ☎ 385-3539

Las Vegas — Nevada/USA

Gipsy (B D GLM S YG)
4605 Paradise Road ✉ NV 89119 ☎ 733-9677
Good Times (AC B D f GLM MA N s) 0-24 h
1775 East Tropicana Avenue #1 ✉ NV 89119 *(at Liberace Plaza)*
☎ 736-9494
Snick's Place (B G MG)
1402 South 4th Street ☎ 385-9298

CAFES
Mariposa Cafe (A AC F GLM MA OS s tv) 18-6 h
4643 Paradise Road ✉ NV 89119 ☎ 650-9009

DANCECLUBS
Freezone (b D F GLm S SNU TV) 24 h
610 East Naples ✉ NV 89109 *(across from the Buffalo)*
☎ 794-2300

SAUNAS/BATHS
Apollo Spa & Health Club (AC CC DR G MA N p SB SNU WH WO) 0-24 h
953 E. Sahara Avenue A-19 ✉ NV 80104 *(in Commercial Center)*
☎ 650-9191

BOOK SHOPS
Get Booked (GLM)
4643 Paradise Rd. ✉ NV 89109 *(opposite Angles/Club Lace)*
☎ 737-7780

GUEST HOUSES
Lucky You B&B (AC BF G H MA OS NU PI SA SB WH) all year
(2 blocks from Las Vegas Strip) ☎ 384-1129 384-1129
🖳 www.gayvegas.com/accomodation
Rooms with shower or shared bath, telephone, fax, TV, video, radio, hair-dryer, own key and room service. Hot tub. Full American bf incl. Call for more info on location.
Villas & Wedding Chapel (bf G H)
1205 Las Vegas Boulevard South ✉ NV 89104 *(North of the Stratosphere Tower on the East side of the Street; limousine service & bus stop at front door)* ☎ (800) 574-4450 (toll-free) ☎ 384-0771
 384-0190 🖳 www.vivalasvegasweddings.com
Ask for the super stretch limo & their different wedding and commitment ceremonies.

FETISH GROUPS
Desert Brotherhood MC
PO Box 71345 ✉ NV 89170

HEALTH GROUPS
AIDS Information
☎ 474-2437

SPECIAL INTEREST GROUPS
Las Vegas Bears
PO Box 34582 ✉ NV 89133 ☎ 658-7548
Neon Squares
PO Box 46161 ✉ NV 89114 ☎ 253-9485
GLB country and western dance group.

SWIMMING
Lake Mead (North on Las Vegas Blvd., past Hollywood Blvd. through the desert to the stop sign. Turn left and go on for exactly 4.8 miles, turn right on the gravel road at highway marker 8.0. Go left at every fork in the road. Park your car in the lot overlooking the lake.
Hike north for 5 min. into a little ravine and over a hill along a narrow trail.

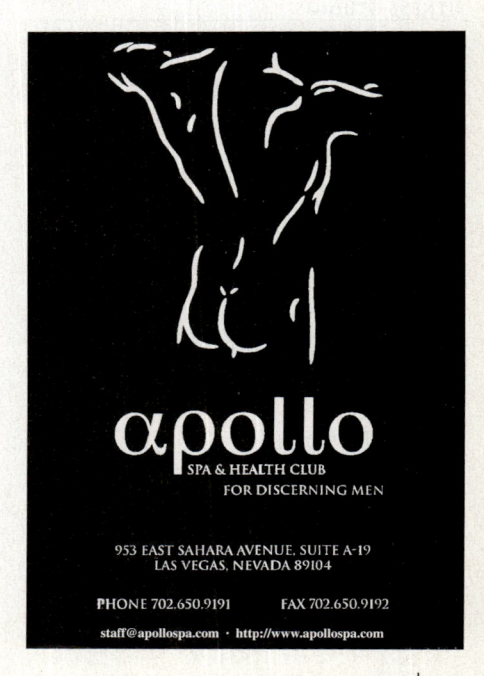

USA/Nevada - New Jersey | Reno ▶ Atlantic City

Reno ☎ 702

PUBLICATIONS
■ **Reno Informer Gay & Lesbian News**
PO Box 33337 ✉ NV 89533 ☎ 747-8833
💻 editor@reno-informer.com 🌐 www.reno-informer.com
Monthly magazine.

BARS
■ **Five Star Saloon** (B d f Glm s) 0-24 h
132 West Street ☎ 329-2878
■ **1099 Club** (B d f Glm lj MA S VS) 0-24 h
1099 South Virginia ✉ NV 89502 ☎ 329-1099
Popular western style bar.

MEN'S CLUBS
■ **Quest. The** (B D G) 12-5, WE 24 h
210 W. Commercial Row ✉ NV 84501 *(Downtown Reno)*
☎ (775) 333-2808
Late night hot spot.

DANCECLUBS
■ **Visions** (B D Glm YG) Mon-Thu 12-4, Fri 12-Mon 4 h
340 Kietzke Lane ✉ NV 89502 *(one block south of East Second Street)* ☎ 786-5455
Popular.

SEX SHOPS/BLUE MOVIES
■ **Suzie's Adult Video** (glm) 0-24 h
195 Kietzke Lane ✉ NV 89502 ☎ 786-8557
Wide selection of gay videos, magazines, cards etc.

FITNESS STUDIOS
■ **Steve's Gym** (G WO) 0-24 h
1030 West 2nd Street ☎ 323-7770

LEATHER & FETISH SHOPS
■ **Fantasy Fire**
1298 South Virginia ☎ 323-6969

GENERAL GROUPS
■ **Comstock Grizzlies**
PO Box 12102 ✉ NV 89510
Social group for gay men.

FETISH GROUPS
■ **Knights of Malta MC**
PO Box 7726 ✉ NV 89210

USA-New Hampshire

Location: Northeast USA
Initials: NH
Time: GMT -5
Area: 24.219 km^2 / 9,905 sq mi.
Population: 1,173,000
Capital: Concord

Centre Harbor ☎ 603

HOTELS
■ **Red Hill Inn** (AC B BF CC F glm OS PI WH) Office: 8-22 h
Route 25B/College Road, RFD 1, PO Box 99 M ✉ NH 03226
☎ 279-1001 💻 info@redhillinn.com 🌐 www.redhillinn.com
Countryside location. All rooms with priv. bath, WC and balcony.

Manchester ☎ 603

BARS
■ **Merrimac Club** (B D GLM P) Mon-Fri 11-1.30, Sat Sun 12-1.30 h
201 Merrimack Street ✉ NH 13103 ☎ 623-9362

Portsmouth ☎ 603

SEX SHOPS/BLUE MOVIES
■ **Peter's Palace** 9-23 h
Route 1 Bypass North ✉ NH 03801 *(near Myrtle and Rockingham)*
☎ 436-9622

CRUISING
-Hilton Part - Dover Point Road
-Pierce Island (dock area)

USA-New Jersey

Location: Northeast USA
Initials: NJ
Time: GMT -5
Area: 22.590 km^2 / 9,239 sq mi.
Population: 8,053,000
Capital: Trenton

Asbury Park ☎ 908

BARS
■ **Bond Street Bar** (B G)
208 Bond Street ✉ NJ 07712 ☎ 776-9766
■ **Down the Street** (B D F G S VS YG) 12-2 h
230 Cookman Avenue ✉ NJ 07712 ☎ 988-2163
Beergarden, beach crowd. Very popular.
■ **Phoenix. Club** (B D G S) 14.30-2.30 h
427 Cookman Avenue ☎ 775-9849

Atlantic City ☎ 609

BARS
■ **Brass Rail. The** (AC B f GLM MA N S SNU) 0-24 h
13 South Mt. Vernon Avenue ✉ NJ 08401-7003 ☎ 348-0192
Popular local bar, friendly atmosphere. Dinner and late snacks served.
■ **Rendezvous** (B d f G)
137 South New York Avenue ✉ NJ 08401 ☎ 347-8539
■ **Studio Six Video Dance Club** (AC B D G MA OS P SNU VS) 22-8 h
12 St. Mount Vernon Avenue ✉ NJ 08401 ☎ 348-3310
Hot dance club.

DANCECLUBS
■ **Reflections** (B D G)
South Carolina/Boardwalk ✉ NJ 08401

RESTAURANTS
■ **Mama Mott's** (f F G)
151 South New York Avenue ✉ NJ 08401 ☎ 345-8218

HOTELS
■ **Fraternity House. The** (AC G H)
18 South Mt. Vernon Avenue ✉ NJ 08401 ☎ 347-0808
All rooms with priv. baths.

1286 SPARTACUS 2001/2002

Atlantic City ▶ Albuquerque — New Jersey - New Mexico/USA

GUEST HOUSES
■ **Ocean House** (AC BF CC G MG NU VS) Office 10-22 h
127 South Ocean Avenue ✉ NJ 08401-7272 *(central, 100 yards form the beach)* ☎ 345-8203
Gay men only. Offers a comfortable place for men in a clothing optional and intimate atmosphere, where there is a possibility of meeting others with similar interests. Call for rates.

■ **Surfside Resort Hotel** (AC B CC D F GLM H MG OS P PI S SB WH) Bar 0-24, Disco 22-8 h
18 South Mt. Vernon Avenue ✉ 08401-7003 ☎ 347-7873
☎ (800) 888-277-SURF (Toll-free) 🖨 347-6668
🖳 www.studiosix.com
All rooms with private bath-rooms with hair-dryer, color-TV, refrigerator, suites available. Large private sundeck. The Brass Rail Tavern and Studio Six Video Dance Club are part of the hotel complex.

Boonton ☎ 201
DANCECLUBS
■ **Connexions** (B D G MA)
202 Myrtle Avenue ✉ NJ 07005 ☎ 263-4000

Cherry Hill ☎ 609
DANCECLUBS
■ **Gatsbys** (B D G YG)
760 Cuthbert Boulevard ✉ NJ 08002 ☎ 663-8744

CRUISING
-Cooper River Park

Hoboken ☎ 201
DANCECLUBS
■ **Excalibur 2001** (B D GLM S SNU STV)
1000 Jefferson Street ✉ NJ 07230 *(less than one hour drive from Manhattan)* ☎ 795-1023
Multi-level nightclub with 6 bars.

Jefferson Township ☎ 201
BARS
■ **Yacht Club. The** (B CC D f GLM MA s SNU) Mon-Sat 19-3, Sun 14-3 h
5190 Berkshire Valley Road ✉ NJ 07438 *(North Jersey)*
☎ 697-9780

Jersey City ☎ 201
BARS
■ **Uncle Joe's** (B G MA)
154 1st Street ✉ NJ 07302 *(North Jersey)* ☎ 653-9173

Morristown ☎ 973
HELP WITH PROBLEMS
■ **Helpline** 19.30-22.30 h
☎ 285-1595

SPECIAL INTEREST GROUPS
■ **Gay and Lesbian Youth in New Jersey (GALY-NJ)**
PO Box 137, Convent Sn. ✉ NJ 07961 ☎ 285-1595

Plainfield ☎ 908
PRIVATE ACCOMMODATION
■ **Pillars of Plainfield Bed & Breakfast. The** (AC BF CC glm H MA OS)
922 Central Avenue ✉ NJ 07060-2311 ☎ 753-0922
🖳 pillars2@Juno.com
B&B in a Victorian-Georgian mansion in the historic district. All suites have private bath, phone/voice mail, and cable-TV. Non-smoking. Dog on premises. Big garden.

River Edge ☎ 201
BARS
■ **Feathers** (B G) 21-2, Sat -3 h
77 Kinderkamack Road ✉ NJ 07661 *(North Jersey)* ☎ 342-6410

Somerset ☎ 908
BARS
■ **Den. The** (AC B CC DR f GLM lj MA N s VS) 20-2, Sun 17-2 h
700 Hamilton Street ✉ NJ 08873 ☎ 545-7354

Trenton ☎ 609
BARS
■ **Buddies Pub** (B GLM) 17-2, WE 18-2 h
677 South Broad Street ☎ 989-8566
■ **Center House Pub** (B glm) 16-2, WE 19-2 h
499 Center Street ☎ 599-9558

USA-New Mexico
Location: Southwest USA
Initials: NM
Time: GMT -7
Area: 314.939 km² / 128,810 sq mi.
Population: 1,730,000
Capital: Santa Fé

Albuquerque ☎ 505
GAY INFO
■ **Common Bond Community Center** 19-22 h
4013 Silver Avenue South East, PO Box 268 36 ✉ NM 87125
☎ 266-8041

PUBLICATIONS
■ **Out! magazine**
PO Box 27321 ✉ NM 87125, ☎ 253-2540 🖨 842-5144
🖳 mail@outmagazine.com 🖳 www.outmagazine.com
Monthly gay and lesbian magazine covering the New Mexico state.

BARS
■ **Albuquerque Social Club** (B GLM LJ MA P)
4021 Central Avenue North East ✉ NM 87198 ☎ 255-0887
■ **Foxes Lounge** (B G D MA) 10-2, Sun 12-24 h
8521 Central North East Avenue ☎ 255-3060
■ **Ranch. The** (B D G LJ) 11-2, Sun 12-24 h
8900 Central South East ✉ NM 87125 ☎ 275-1616

DANCECLUBS
■ **Albuquerque Mining** (B D G MA OS VS) 9-2 h
7209 Central Avenue North East ✉ NM 87108 ☎ 255-0925

USA/New Mexico — Albuquerque ▶ Santa Fe

■ **Pulse Nightclub** (AC B CC D GLM lj MA N OS SNU STV VS WE)
Wed-Sat 20-2 h, Sun-Tue special events
4100 Central Avenue South East ✉ NM 87108 *(in Nob Hill, on RT. 66)* ☎ 255-3334
Popular bar and nightclub.

SEX SHOPS/BLUE MOVIES
■ **Castle Superstore** (g VS) 0-24 h
5110 East Central Avenue S.E. ✉ NM 87108 ☎ 262-2266
Leather, lingerie, magazines, books, DVD's, toys and more.

FITNESS STUDIOS
■ **Pride Gym** (AC b CC f G MA msg OS P SB WH WO) Mon-Fri 7-22, Sat & Sun 10-18 h
1803 3rd Street N.W. ✉ NM 87102-1411 *(North of Downtown, 4 blocks south of Interstate 40 at Exit 158)* ☎ 242-7810

GIFT & PRIDE SHOPS
■ **In Crowd** (A AC CC) Mon-Sat 10-18, Sun 11-16 h
3106 Central South East ✉ NM 87106 ☎ 268-3750
Gift shop and gallery.

GUEST HOUSES
■ **Brittania & W.E. Mauger Estate** (AC BF CC f glm H MA)
701 Roma Avenue N.W. ✉ NM 87102 ☎ 242-8755
☎ (800) 719 9189 maugerbb@aol.com maugerbb.com
Each room has private bath, phone, TV, refrigerator. Rates US$ 79-179 incl bf. Evening wine and cheese.

HEALTH GROUPS
■ **New Mexico AIDS Services** Tue 17.30-19.39 h
4200 Silver South Eeast #D ✉ NM 87108 *(near Community Center)*
☎ 266-0911 266-5104
Information, HIV-testing, counselling, assistance.

Pecos ☎ 505

HOTELS
■ **Wilderness Inn** (G H)
PO Box 11 77 ✉ NM 87552 ☎ 757-6694
15 miles from Santa Fé.

Radium Springs ☎ 505

HOTELS
■ **Radium Hot Springs Resort** (B F GLM H Pl)
PO Box 40 ✉ NM 88054 ☎ 525-1983

Santa Fe ☎ 505

TOURIST INFO
■ **Convention & Visitor's Bureau**
☎ 984-6760 ☎ (800) 984-9984 (Toll-free)

CAFES
■ **Telecote Cafe** (BF f glm)
1203 Cerrillos Road ☎ 988-1362

DANCECLUBS
■ **Drama Club** (B D GLM STV)
126 North Guadelupe Street ☎ 988-4374
This is the only location im town that is really gay.

RESTAURANTS
■ **Blue Corn Cafe** (b F glm)
133 Water Street ☎ 984-1800
Good Mexican food.
■ **Geronimo** (AC B CC E F glm MA N OS) 11.30-14.30, 18-22 h
724 Canyon Road ✉ NM 87501 ☎ 982-1500
Very good Mediterranean cuisine.
■ **Santacafe** (b F glm OS) Mon- 11.30-14/18-22 h
231 Washington Avenue ✉ NM 87501 ☎ 984-1788
Very good Asian and Southwestern cuisine.
■ **Vanessie** (B F Glm)
434 West San Francisco Street ✉ NM 87501 ☎ 982-9966
Mixed restaurant, the bar is rather gay.

GUEST HOUSES
■ **Four Kachinas Inn** (BF glm H OS)
512 Webber Street ✉ NM 87501 ☎ 982-2550 989-1323
 4kachina@swcp.com
 www.southwesterninns.com/fourkach.htm
Small B&B with comfortable rooms all with private baths, color cable TV and private patios. Rates USD 75-130 incl. cont. bf. No pets.

Inn of the Turquoise Bear

SANTA FE
◆ ◆ ◆ ◆

a bed and breakfast for all seasons
headquarters for gay visitors to new mexico

◆ fireplaces, intimate courtyards, private baths & entrances
◆ walk to Plaza, museums, galleries
◆ superb breakfasts & sunset refreshments
◆ an acre of gardens, tall pines & flagstone paths
◆ featured in Our World *(International Gay & Lesbian Travel Magazine)*

For excellence, innovation and solid gay travel values

342 E. Buena Vista Street
Santa Fe, NM 87501-4423
800.396.4104
email: bluebear@newmexico.com

www.turquoisebear.net

IGLTA

Santa Fe ▶ Brentwood — New Mexico - New York/USA

■ **Hummingbird Ranch** (BF glm H)
Route 10, PO Box 111 ✉ NM 87501 ☎ 471-2921
Small guest house 7 miles from the city centre. Rooms with shared baths, kitchens, fridge, fireplace amd cable TV.

■ **Inn of the Turquoise Bear** (BF CC GLM H lj MA msg OS VS)
Office: 7-21 h
342 East Buena Vista Street ✉ NM 87501-4423 ☎ 983-0798
☎ (800) 396-4104 ⎙ 988-4225 ✉ bluebear@newmexico.com
✉ www.turquoisebear.com
Historical ambiance, walking distance to downtown attractions. All rooms with bath/shower/WC, balcony/patio, telephone, cable-TV, video and hair-dryer. Rates double US$ 95-195 incl. bf buffet. Afternoon wine & cheese hour. IGLTA member. Out & About Editor's Choice Award 1999, Preservation Award, City of Santa Fe 1999 & State of NM 2000.

■ **Open Sky B&B** (BF CC E GLM H msg OS WH)
134 Turqoise Trail ✉ NM 87505 ☎ (800) 244-2475
✉ SkyMiller@aol.com
✉ www.bestinns.net/USA/NM/opensky.html
Small B&B in ranch house. All rooms with private baths, fridge and color TV.

■ **Triangle Inn, The** (AC BF CC f GLM MA OS WH)
PO Box 32 35 ✉ NM 87501 ☎ 455-3375 ⎙ 455-3375
✉ triangleSF@aol.com ✉ www.roadrunner.com/~triangle/
Studios with shower/WC, balcony, TV/video, telephone, radio, kitchenette/kitchen and hair-dryer.

■ **Water Street Inn** (BF glm H)
427 West Water Street ☎ 984-1235
Comfortable rooms all with private bath.

CRUISING
-Rest Stop (on I-25 15 miles south of Santa Fe)
-DeVargas Mall

Thoreau ☎ 505

PRIVATE ACCOMMODATION
■ **Zuni Mountain Lodge & Tour** (AC BF F g lj MA os s)
PO Box 5114 ✉ NM 87323 ☎ 862-7769 ⎙ 862-7616
Private accommodation in remote location surrounded by pine forest overlooking high-mountain landscape.

USA-New York

Location: Northeast USA
Initials: NY
Time: GMT -5
Area: 141.080 km^2 / 57,701 sq mi.
Population: 18,137,000
Capital: Albany
Important gay cities: Fire Island and New York City

Albany ☎ 518

GAY INFO
■ **Capital District Lesbian/Gay Community Center** 19-23, Sat Sun 15-23 h
332 Hudson Avenue ✉ NY 12210 ☎ 462-6138

BARS
☞ See also Lake George, NY
■ **Club Phoenix** (B D G lj N S) 16-4 h
348 Central Avenue ✉ NY 12206 ☎ 462-4862

■ **JD's Playhouse** (B D G N)
519 Central Avenue ✉ NY 12206 ☎ 482-5816
■ **Oh-Bar** (AC B G MA N) 14-4 h
304 Lark Street ✉ NY 12210 ☎ 463-9004
■ **One Flight Up** (B D G WE) Wed-Sun 21-4 h
76 Central Avenue ✉ NY 12206 (above Waterworks) ☎ 465-6400

CRUISING
-Empire State Plaza (AYOR)
-Washington Park (AYOR)

Binghamton ☎ 607

BARS
■ **Numbers** (B D GLM lj S) Sun-Thu 21-1, Fri Sat 21-3 h
Upper Court Street ✉ NY 13904 (in Rocket Center) ☎ 775-3300
■ **Risky Business** (B D GLM MA VS) Sun-Thu 17-1, Fri Sat 20-3 h
201-203 State Street ✉ NY 13901 ☎ 723-1507
■ **Squiggy's** (B D GLM MA) Sun-Wed 20-1, Thu 17-1, Fri-Sat 17-3 h
34 Chenango Street ☎ 722-2299

CAFES
■ **Tom's Coffee Cards & Gifts**
176 1/2 Main Street ✉ NY 13905 ☎ 733-8500

CAMPING
■ **Hillside Campgrounds** (D G Pl)
PO Box 726 ✉ NY 13902 ☎ 756-2833

GENERAL GROUPS
■ **B/C Bears**
PO Box 1642 ✉ NY 13902
■ **Lesbian & Gay Studies Coalition**
#621, GSO, Box 514 SUNY-Binghamton ✉ NY 13902
☎ 617/729-7250
■ **PFLAG (Parents and Friends of Lesbians & Gays)**
PO Box 728, WVS ✉ NY 13905 ☎ 729-5616

HEALTH GROUPS
■ **AIDS Hotline**
☎ 723-6520
■ **Anonymous HIV Testing**
☎ 800-562-9423
■ **Broome County Health Department STD Clinic**
☎ 778-2839
■ **Southern Tier AIDS Program Office**
☎ 798-1706

SPECIAL INTEREST GROUPS
■ **LGBU University Union**
SUNY Binghamton ✉ NY 13902

CRUISING
-Oneida campground
-Rest Stop (on Route 81 North, lollipop heaven)
-Cole Park
-Greyhound Bus Depot (AYOR)

Brentwood ☎ 516

SEX SHOPS/BLUE MOVIES
■ **Heaven Sent Me** (DR g VS)
108 Cain Street ✉ NY 11717 ☎ 434-4777
Private video viewing booths.

USA/New York Buffalo ▸ Fire Island

Buffalo ☎ 716

PUBLICATIONS
■ **OUTCOME**
266 Elmwood Avenue PMB 226L ✉ NY 14222 ☎ 441-7476
📠 883-2756 ✉ outcomewny@aol.com
Monthly magazine deserving the Buffalo, Niagra Falls and Rochester communities.

BARS
■ **Buddies** (AC B CC D f G lj MA OS SNU STV) 13-4, Sat Sun 12-4 h
31 Johnson Park ✉ NY 14201-2348 ☎ 885-1313
Popular.
■ **Cathode Ray** (B G VS YG) 13-4 h
26 Allen Road ✉ NY 14202 ☎ 884-3615
■ **Club 153** (B GLM MA OS YG) Fri-Sat 22-4 h
153 Delaware Avenue ✉ NY 14213 ☎ 842-6825
■ **Compton's** (B G MA)
1239 Niagara Street ✉ NY 14213 ☎ 881-6769
■ **Stagedoor. The** (B G MG OS S) 17-4 h
20 Allen Street ✉ NY 14202
■ **Underground** (B D Glm MA) 16-4, Sat-Sun 12-4 h
274 Delaware Avenue ✉ NY 14202 ☎ 855-1040

CAFES
■ **Java Temple. The** (b BF f glm) WE -2 h
57 Allen Street

DANCECLUBS
■ **Club Marcella c/o Theater Place** (B D f glm SNU STV)
622 Main Street *(at Shea's)*
■ **Fuel** (B D G LJ MA)
884 Main Street

RESTAURANTS
■ **Mothers** (b F glm) WE -3 h
33 Virginia Place

SAUNAS/BATHS
■ **Sauna 655** (b f G P SA SB) 0-24 h
655 Main Street ✉ NY 14203 ☎ 852-2153

BOOK SHOPS
■ **Book & News** (glm)
3102 Delaware Avenue ✉ NY 14217 ☎ 877-5027
■ **Talking Leaves** (glm) Mon-Sat 10-18 h
3144 Main Street ✉ NY 14214 ☎ 837-8554

TRAVEL AND TRANSPORT
■ **Destinations Unlimited**
130 Theaterplace

HEALTH GROUPS
■ **AIDS Community Services**
☎ 847-2441
■ **AIDS Family Services**
320 Porter ✉ NY 14201 ☎ 881-7655
■ **Benedict House**
124 Plymouth Avenue ✉ NY 14201 ☎ 834-4940

SPECIAL INTEREST GROUPS
■ **Gay and Lesbian Youth Services (GLYS)** Mon, Tue, Thu, Fri 18-21 h
c/o YWCA, 190 Franklin Street ✉ NY 14322 *(lower level)*
☎ 855-0221 📠 855-0661 ✉ glyswny@juno.com

Catskill Mountains ☎ 518

GUEST HOUSES
■ **Palenville House B&B** (BF CC GLM H MA WH) all year
3292 Route 23 A; P.O.Box 465, Palenville ✉ NY 12463 *(2 hrs north of NYC)* ☎ 678-5649 ☎ (877) 689-5101 (Toll-free) 📠 678-9038
✉ Palenville@aol.com ✉ catskillsbb.com
Turn-of-the-century Victorian home. 5 double rooms with bath/shower/WC, TV, VCR, radio. Suites with fireplace and jacuzzi. 10 person hot tub. Rates US$ 75-145. Outdoor activities.
■ **Red Bear Inn** (A B BF CC F g H lj OS p WE)
HCI Box 40, Route 42, West Kill ✉ NY 12492 ☎ 989-6000
☎ 888-BEAR INN
Located 2 hours drive north of New York City close to the Hudson Valley. Private bath. Also bar and restaurant. Outdoor activities.

Fire Island ☎ 516

✳ Not that a misunderstanding emerges: Fire Island is no New York Provincetown and no Key West. It just doesn't have the size. New Yorkers own a house here, or know somebody who owns a house. Tourists must see where they find an accomodation. Both towns, which are of interest to gays, *Cherry Grove* and *Fire Island Pines* are, after all, more or less small villages. The tranquile and remote Fire Island can only be reached by ferry. The distance from New York to Sayville is approximately 70 km. This town is connected with The Pines by ferry (going regularly from May to October). The Pines is rather stylishly orientated, body conscious and very gay. Cherry Grove is prefered by middle-class gays and lesbians and occasionally by heterosexuals. Both lie quite near to one another. The one mile inbetween, also called the *Meat Rack*, is a highly frequented dune landscape. Nightlife does not exist in abundance; private parties prevail. A very well known and rewarding highlight of the year exists: The *Gay Men's Health Crisis Morning Party* in August.

✳ Nicht dass jetzt ein Mißverständnis entsteht: Fire Island ist kein New Yorker Provincetown oder Key West. Dafür reicht die Größe einfach nicht. Als New Yorker hat man hier ein Haus oder kennt jemanden mit Haus. Als Tourist muß man sehen, wo man unterkommt. Schließlich sind die beiden für Schwule interessanten Orte, *Cherry Grove* und *Fire Island Pines* eher kleine Dörfer.
Das ruhige und abgeschiedene Fire Island erreicht man nur per Fähre. Von New York City sind es etwa 70 km bis Sayville. Von dort gehen Fähren (Mai-Okt regelmässig) nach The Pines, das eher stylingorientiert, sehr körperbewußt und sehr schwul ist, und Cherry Grove, das von Lesben, Schwulen aus der Mittelschicht und gelegentlichen Heteros bevorzugt wird.
Beide Orte liegen nicht sonderlich weit auseinander: Auf der einen Meile dazwischen befindet sich eine hochfrequentierte Dünenlandschaft, auch *Meat Rack* genannt.
Das Nightlife ist nicht gerade üppig, denn vieles läuft eher auf privater Party-Ebene. Einen weithin bekannten und äußerst lohnenden Jahres-Höhepunkt gibt es trotzdem: Die *Gay Men's Health Crisis Morning Party* im August.

✳ Que les choses soient claires: Fire Island n'est pas le Provincetown ou le Key West des New Yorkais! Fire Island est bien trop petite! Les New Yorkais y ont soit une maison, soit un ami qui y possède une maison. Les touristes, eux, doivent se débrouiller eux-mêmes. Seuls Cherry Grove et Fire Island Pines sont intéressants pour les gais. Attention: ce ne sont que de petits villages! Pour jouir du calme de Fire Island, il faut d'abord prendre le bac. Il y a environ 70 km entre New York City et Sayville d'où on prend le bac (circule régulièrement de mai à octobre) jusqu'à The Pines et Cherry Grove.

Fire Island ▶ Lake George — New York/USA

Cherry Grove est plutôt fréquentée par les gais et les lesbiennes middle-class et quelques hétéros qui se sont égarés par là, alors que The Pines est presque exclusivement homo stylé, body-buildé. Entre les deux, il y a une dune assez fréquentée où l'on peut faire des rencontres. On l'appelle "Meat Rack". La vie nocturne est loin d'être trépidante. Les gens se retrouvent plutôt en privé. A Fire Island, l'évènement de l'année, c'est le "Gay Men's Health Crisis Morning Party" en août.

Hay que tener claro que Fire Island no es el Provincetown o el Key West de Nueva York, para ello es simple mente demasiado pequeña. Fire Island es una popular zona residencial para gente de Nueva York. De especial intéres para turistas gay son *Cherry Grove* y *Fire Island Pines* que en realidad no son más que pequeños pueblos. A la tranquila y retirada Fire Island se llega solo ferry. Desde Nueva York son aprox. 70 km. hasta Sayville. Desde este lugar parten los ferrys (entre mayo y octubre regularmente) hacia The Pines y Cherry Grove. The Pines es un sitio gay muy elegante, donde se da mucha importancia a la aparencia y los cuerpos entrenados; Cherry Grove es preferida y visitada por lesbianas y gays de la clase media incluso de vez en cuando por heterosexuales. Ambos sitios se encuentran tan solo separados por las muy frecuentadas dunas *Meat Roack*. La vida nocturna no es muy extensa, la mayor parte de ella se lleva a cabo en fiesta privadas. En agosto se vive el punto culminante anual gay, el *Gay Men's Health Crisis Mornig Party*.

Che non nascano malintesi: Fire Island non è nè una Provincetown nè una Key West di New York, non è abbastanza grande. Molti abitanti di New York hanno qui la seconda casa o conoscono qualcuno che ce l'ha. Per i turisti invece è più difficile trovare alloggio, poichè sia *Cherry Grove* che *Fire Island*, benchè siano luoghi interessanti per i gay, sono dei piccoli paesi; è possibile raggiungere la piccola ed isolata Fire Island per traghetto. Da New York City a Sayville vi sono solo 70 km. Da qui partono regolarmente dei traghetti per The Pines, località frequentata da gay dove regna il culto del corpo e della moda, e per Cherry Grove, frequentata da gay e lesbiche di classe media e da eterosessuali. Queste località non sono distanti tra loro: sono separate da un paesaggio di dune molto frequentato che viene chiamato *meat rack*. La vita notturna è piuttosto tranquilla poichè si svolge principalmente attraverso feste private. Tuttavia in agosto ha luogo l'avvenimento dell'anno che merita di essere conosciuto:il *Gay Men's Health Crisis Morning Party*.

BARS
■ **Blue Whale Bar** (B D g)
Picketty Ruff ✉ NY 11782 *(near Fire Island Boulevard)* ☎ 597-6131
■ **Ice Palace** (B D F G Pl S) Sun-Fri 12-4, Sat -8 h
Cherry Grove ✉ NY 11782 *(at Beach Hotel)* ☎ 597-6600
■ **Monster. The** (B D F GLM YG) 16-4, dinner 19-23.30 h
Ocean Walk, Cherry Grove ✉ NY 11782 *(near Dock Walk)* ☎ 597-6888
■ **Pines Pavillon** (B F D g) 16-18 h tea dance
Picketty Ruff at Fire Island Boulevard ✉ NY 11782 ☎ 597-6677

RESTAURANTS
■ **Cultured Elephant** (B F glm OS)
Picketty Ruff ✉ NY 11782 *(near Fire Island Boulevard)* ☎ 597-6060
■ **Top of the Bay** (B F G OG)
Dock Walk/Bay Walk, Cherry Grove ✉ NY 11782 ☎ 597-6699

HOTELS
■ **Cherry Grove Beach Hotel** (A AC B CC D GLM H lj MA msg NU OS PI STV TV WE) May 1-Oct 1
PO Box 537, Cherry Grove ✉ NY 11782 ☎ 597-6600
☎ 597-6651 🖳 grovehotel@aol.com 🖳 www.grovehotel.com

■ **Holly House** (BF G H) May 15th-Sep 30th
Holly Walk, Box 96, Cherry Grove ✉ NY 11782-4097 ☎ 597-6911
■ **Sea Crest** (b glm H)
Lewis Walk at Main Walk, Cherry Grove ✉ NY 11782 ☎ 597-6849

GUEST HOUSES
■ **Belvedere Guest House** (BF CC G H MA NU OS PI WH WO) May-Oct
33 Bay View Walk, Cherry Grove ✉ NY 11782 *(Sayville ferry service to Cherry Grove,on the bay)* ☎ 597-6448
🖳 belvederefireisland.com
Old mansion with garden, fountain and water views. Bf on WE only. 38 en suite rooms with balcony/terrace, TV, VCR, radio, own key.
■ **Carousel Guest House** (BF G H OS) May-Oct
PO Box 4001, Cherry Grove ✉ NY 11782-0998 ☎ 597-6612
Suburb location, 1 hour to the airport.
■ **Dune Point** (F GLM H) all year; 8-21 h
PO Box 78, Cherry Grove ✉ NY 11782 ☎ 597-6261 🛏 597-7048
Shared and private room facilities.
■ **Pines Place** (BF G H MA PI) May-Oct, closed in winter
PO Box 5309, Fire Island Pines ✉ NY 11782 *(Sayville Ferry Service to Fire Island Pines)* ☎ 597-6162 🛏 597-6162
🖳 PinesPlace@aol.com 🖳 www.pinesplace.com
All rooms with phone, TV, ocean-view with balcony, partly with own bath/WC. Rates on request.No credit cards.

CRUISING
-Anywhere and everywhere from the time you get on the ferry, but especially the west end of the boardwalk at The Pines and the "Meat Rack" and bushes between Cherry Grove & The Pines.

Ithaca ☎ 607

DANCECLUBS
■ **Common Ground** (B D F GLM MA OS S) Thu-Sun 16-1 h
1230 Danby Road (Route 96B) ✉ NY 14850 *(across American Legion)* ☎ 273-1505
Nightclub & restaurant.
■ **Tilt a Whirl** (B D G MA) Thu night
The Haunt, 114 West Green Street ✉ NY 14850 ☎ 273-1505

GENERAL GROUPS
■ **Cornell Lesbian Gay Bisexual Coalition**
207 Willard Strait Hall, Cornell University ✉ NY 14853
☎ 255-6482
■ **Ithaca Lesbian Gay & Bisexual Task Force**
PO Box 283 ✉ NY 14581

HEALTH GROUPS
■ **AIDS Hotline**
☎ 800-333-0892
■ **AIDS Work**
De Witt Office Complex, 215 North Cayuga Street ✉ NY 14850
☎ 272-4098

SPECIAL INTEREST GROUPS
■ **Ithaca College Gay & Lesbian Association**
Campus Union Building ✉ NY 14580 ☎ 274-3011

Lake George ☎ 518

HOTELS
■ **King Hendrick Motel** (AC F GLM H OS PI)
Route 9, Box 623 ✉ NY 12845 ☎ 792-0418
Centrally located, all units with kitchenette, priv. bath, balcony, color cable TV.

USA/New York — Long Island ▶ New York City

Long Island ☎ 516

HEALTH GROUPS
■ **Long Island AIDS Care** Mon-Fri 9-17, recorded messages -21 h, Sat-Sun 9-21 h
☎ 385-2437
Information, support services.

SWIMMING
-Jones Beach (G NU) (from South End Station left down the beach to the gay and nude area)

Long Island - Nassau County ☎ 516

BARS
■ **Blanche** (AC B GLM N OS S) 20-4 h
47-2 Boundary Avenue, South Farmingdale ✉ NY 11735
☎ 694-6906
■ **Pal Joey's** (B G) Mon-Thu 16-4, Fri-Sun 20-4 h
2457 Jerusalem Avenue, North Bellmore ✉ NY 11710
☎ 785-9301
■ **Porsche Club. The** (B D GLM)
1317 Broadway, Hewlett ✉ NY 11557   ☎ 374-3671

Long Island - Suffolk County ☎ 516

BARS
■ **Bunk House. The** (B D G LJ stv) 20-4 h
192 Montauk Highway, Sayville ✉ NY 11782   ☎ 567-2865
■ **Forever Green** (B d GLM) 20-? h
841 North Boom Avenue, Lindenhurst ✉ NY 11757   ☎ 226-9357
■ **Long Island Eagle** (AC B G LJ MA OS) Mon-Sat 21-4, Sun 16-4 h
94 N. Clinton Avenue, Bay Shore ✉ NY 11706   ☎ 968-2250
Home of L.I. Ravens M.C.
■ **Mr's** (B G)
608 Sunrise Highway, West Babylon ✉ NY 11702   ☎ 661-9580

SEX SHOPS/BLUE MOVIES
■ **Adult Shop** (g)
6083 Sunrise Highway, Holbrook ✉ NY 11741   ☎ 472-9519

HOTELS
■ **Cozy Cabins** (GLM H) 1st Apr-30th Nov
PO Box 848, Wainscott ✉ NY 11101   ☎ 537-1160
■ **132 North Main** (AC BF CC GLM H NU OS Pl) Memorial Day-Labor Day Weekend (Summer only)
132 North Main Street, East Hampton ✉ NY 11937 *(5 mins from town and beaches)* ☎ 324-2246 💻 tm132nmaine@aol.com
Centrally located, two hours from JFK-Airport. Hotel with garden and pool in private woods. All rooms with refrigerator, some with priv. bath.

Nassau

GAY INFO
☞ Long Island

New York ☎ 212

★ The centre of gay life is *Christopher Street*, where, on 28th June 1969, gays forcefully resisted the ongoing and arbitrary police raids. This historical site is an absolute must for every gay tourist.
It's best to visit New York in spring or autumn; Winter and summer in this extreme city can include extreme temperatures. The best way to get around town is the subway (and for going from the main airport JFK to city center). For going home after a night out in the gay scene we recommend taking a taxi. The *N.Y. Gay and Lesbian Community Center* is a help for orientating yourself. The biggest and most important gay-lesbian event in New York is the *Gay Pride Parade* in June.
But there are changes emerging. *The Village* (i.e. Greenwich Village), situated around *Sheridon Square*, is indeed still very colourful, but an equivalent and very trendy center of gay life has evolved in *Chelsea*, corner of 8th Avenue and West 17th Street, with a tendency of moving to the north above the 23rd Street.
Gay nightlife in New York has a decidedly long tradition. Areas like Times Square or The Village were already trendy places in the twenties. Nightclubbing in New York can sometimes be rather straining (starts late into the night; lively bustle often not before 1.00 a.m.), but it's also exceptionally easy going (no taboos concerning stimulants and dark rooms) and communicative (inquisitve tourists and lonely business men).
The gay public around Christopher Street may be a bit older, a bit rougher than elsewhere, but that doesn't diminish its popularity. But: *East Village* is slowly but surely overtaking its western neighbour as an artists center and quarter. *Chelsea* has evolved from a middle class residential area for whites and latinos to a new and modern gay Mecca of NY. This is for instance shown by the traditional gay bookshop *A Different Light* having moved to 7th Avenue. The redevelopment of the Chelsea Piers contributed to this. We'll have to wait and see, whether the plans to redevelop the area around *Times Square* will really displace the strip-shows and porn cinemas residing there.
A tip at the end: If time and travelplans allow, you should at least take a daytrip to *Fire Island*, the gay bathing mecca of the metropolis (look under *Fire Island*).
The listing is divided into 7 parts. We divided Manhattan into *Downtown*, *Village & Chelsea* (with city map), *Midtown* (with city map) and *Uptown*. There is an extra chapter for each of the 3 boroughs Bronx, Brooklyn, and Queens. Addresses on Long Island (look under *Long Island*) have been divided into *Nassau County* (west) and *Suffolk County* (east).

★ Der Mittelpunkt der schwulen Welt liegt in der *Christopher Street*, dort, wo sich am 28. Juni 1969 Schwule zum erstenmal massiv und handgreiflich gegen fortwährende willkürliche Polizeirazzien wehrten. Dieser historische Ort ist ein absolutes Muß für jeden homosexuellen Touristen.
Am besten sieht man sich New York im Frühjahr oder Herbst an, denn Winter und Sommer halten extreme Temperaturen für diese extreme Stadt bereit. Für die Wege in der Stadt (und vom Flughafen JFK in die Stadt) empfiehlt sich auf jeden Fall die *subway*. Taxis sind eher das optimale Verkehrsmittel für nächtliche Heimfahrten nach einer Szene-Tour. Das *N.Y. Gay and Lesbian Community Center* bietet sich als Orientierungshilfe an. Das wichtigste und größte schwullesbische Ereignis der Stadt ist die *Gay Pride Parade* im Juni.
In Manhattan konzentriert sich New Yorks schwules Leben. Und dies ist in Bewegung geraten: zwar ist *The Village* (i.e. Greenwich Village) um den *Sheridan Square* immer noch sehr bunt, aber ein gleichwertiger und angesagter Schwerpunkt schwulen Lebens hat sich in *Chelsea*, an der Ecke 8th Avenue und West 17th Street gebildet. Mit der Tendenz, sich Richtung Norden über die 23rd Street hinaus weiterzubewegen.
Schwules Nightlife hat in New York eine ausgesprochen lange Tradition und schon in den 20er Jahren waren Gegenden wie die Times Square oder das Village angesagt. Ausgehen in New York ist manch-

New York City — New York/USA

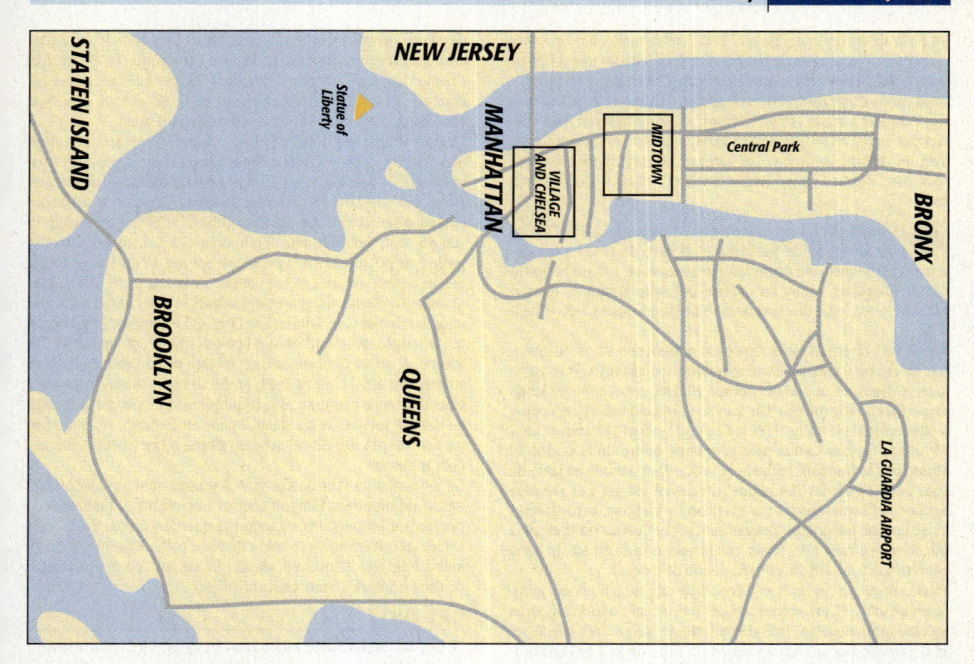

[Map: Staten Island, New Jersey, Manhattan (Statue of Liberty, Village and Chelsea, Midtown), Central Park, Bronx, Brooklyn, Queens, La Guardia Airport]

mal anstrengend, denn es geht spät los, Trubel kommt oft nicht vor 1 Uhr auf. Die Szene befindet sich zur Zeit im Umbruch, was auch an den Säuberungsaktionen des republikanischen Bürgermeisters Guiliani liegt. So wurden zahlreiche Darkrooms geschlossen. Geplant ist auch die Schließung von Sexshops, die sich näher als 1000 m an einer Kirche oder Schule befinden. Immer beliebter werden bei vielen Schwulen gepflegte Cocktail-Bars. Das *East Village* läuft seinem West-Pendant rund um die Christopher Street langsam den Rang als Künstlerviertel ab. *Chelsea* hat sich von einer Mittelklasse-Wohngegend für Weiße und Latinos zum neuen und modernen schwulen Mekka New Yorks entwickelt. Beitragen wird zu dieser Entwicklung sicherlich auch die Sanierung der Chelsea Piers. Die Sanierung der Gegend um den *Times Square* zeigt tatsächlich Wirkung: Disney-Millionen und Familienfreundlichkeit verdrängen den rauhen Charme der Schmuddel-Sex-Shops und Pornokinos. Ein Tip zum Schluß: Bei genügend Zeit im Reiseplan sollte ein zumindest eintägiger Besuch auf *Fire Island*, dem schwulen Bademekka der Metropole, eingeplant werden (siehe dort).

Das Listing ist in acht Teile untergliedert: Manhattan haben wir in *Downtown, Village & Chelsea* (mit Stadtplan), *Midtown* (mit Stadtplan) und *Uptown* gegliedert. Für jedes der Boroughs Bronx, Brooklyn und Queens gibt es ein kleines Extra-Kapitel. Adressen auf Long Island (siehe dort) haben wir nach *Nassau County* (westlicher Teil) und *Suffolk County* (östlicher Teil) sortiert.

✱ Si une rue sur terre peut se targuer d'être LA première rue gaie du monde, c'est bien la Christopher Street! Là où, pour la toute première fois, le 28 juin 1969, les gais se sont violemment rebellés contre les contrôles intempestifs et permanents de la police. La Christopher Street, c'est un lieu historique! Un must pour le touriste gai!

Le meilleur moment pour visiter New York, c'est au printemps ou en automne, car on y étouffe en été et on y gèle en hiver. Pour aller de Kennedy Airport en ville, comme pour les trajets quotidiens, il n'y a rien de mieux que le métro. Pour les trajets nocturnes d'une boîte à l'autre, le taxi est plus sûr et plus pratique. Pour commencer, allez donc faire un tour au "New York Gay and Lesbian Community Center". Vous y trouverez tous les renseignements et les tuyaux que vous cherchez. L'évènement numéro 1 au calendrier gai, c'est la "Gay Pride Parade" qui a lieu tous les ans en juin. Le bastion gay est -et a toujours été- Greenwich Village, surtout autour de Sheridan Square, même si, depuis quelque temps, c'est à Chelsea que ça bouge le plus, à la hauteur de la 8th Avenue et de West 17th Street en remontant jusqu'à la 23th Street.

La vie nocturne de New York, c'est quelque chose! Times Square et Greenwich Village sont les quartiers qui bougent la nuit et ce, depuis les années 20. Sortir à New York, ce n'est pas une sinécure: ça commence tard, les gens ne se montrent qu'après une heure du matin. Fatiguant, mais assez cool: les darkrooms, les stimulants et excitants de toute sorte ne choquent plus personne. Fatiguant, cool et aussi communicatif: les touristes et les gens de passage contribuent à rendre l'atmosphère conviviale et décontractée.

Dans la plupart des bars de Christopher Street, les gens ont passé la quarantaine et peuvent paraître un tantinet rudes. Ils n'en sont pas pour autant des brutes! Dans l'East Village (qui commence à faire concurrence au West Village), le public est plus jeune. Ce quartier plutôt middle-class est en train de devenir le quartier des artistes, la Mecque des jeunes gays blancs ou latinos. Un signe qui ne trompe pas: la librairie gay "A Different Light" a récemment déménagé pour s'installer dans la 7th Street. L'aménagement des quais de Chelsea va certainement accélérer cette métamorphose qu'est en train de connaître le quartier. Verra-t-on enfin disparaître les ciné porno et

SPARTACUS 2001/2002 | 1293

USA/New York — New York City

les peep shows de Times Square? Cela semble moins sûr! Un tuyau pour finir: s'il vous reste du temps, allez donc faire un tour à Fire Island, la station balnéaire gay de New York (Cf. rubrique Fire Island). Nous avons divisé New York en 7 parties: Manhattan avec Downtown, Village et Chelsea (plan), Midtown (plan) et Uptown. Pour chacun des autres arrondissements (Bronx, Brooklyn, et Queens), vous avez un chapitre particulier. Les adresses de Long Island sont classées sous "Nassau County" (partie ouest) et "Suffolk County" (partie est).

El punto central del mundo gay se encuentra en la *Christopher Street*, donde que el día 28 de junio de 1969 los homosexuales por primera vez protestaban masivamente, incluso haciendo uso de los puños, contra las redadas policiales arbitrarias al azar. Este sitio es un lugar de importante valor histórico para todo visitante gay.
Nueva York ofrece su mejor cara en la primavera o en otoño, mientras en verano y invierno las temperaturas son extremas. Para trasladarse dentro de la ciudad (y desde el aeropuerto) se recomienda el uso del *subway* (metro). Los taxis son el medio transporte óptimo a altas horas de la noche. El *N.Y. Gay and Lesbian Community Center* ofrece también ayuda para orientarse dentro de la ciudad. El evento gay-lesbiano más grande es la *Gay Pride Parade* en junio de cada año. Los barrios *The Village* (Greenwich Village) y el *Sheridan Square* son homosexuales por excelencia y tradición, pero también el igualmente importante y nuevo centro gay *Chelsea* en la esquina 8th. Avenue y West 17th. Street, con la tendencia de expansión hacia el norte sobre la 23rd Street se ha puesto de moda.
La vida nocturna gay en Nueva York tiene una larga tradición, incluso en los años '20 los alrededores del Time Square o las Village eran ya muy prometedoras. Vivir el ambiente de Nueva York puede ser muy cansado (las actividades inician no antes de la 1 de la madrugada), pero también muy agradable (estimulantes y cuartos oscuros no son tabú) y comunicativo (debido a los turistas curiosos y a los hombres de negocios solitarios). En los alrededores de la Christopher Street el público es un poco mayor y brusco. El *East Village* ha adquirido la fama de barrio artístico con el público correspondiente. *Chelsea* ha pasado de ser un barrio residencial de clase media para blancos y latinos, al nuevo centro moderno de la vida gay en Nuva York. Esto ha sido subrayado por la mudanza de la famosa librería *A Different Light* en la 7th. Avenue. La remodelación de Chelsea Piers contribuirá con seguridad a este desarrollo. Es de esperar que la nueva igagen que se está dando al sector cercano al *Times Square* no relege los muchos Strip-Shows y cines porno de los alrededores. Consejo: una vista a la Fire Island, esta es el balneario gay por excelencia de Nueva York.
El listado esta dividido en 7 partes: Manhattan la hemos dividido en *Downtown, Village & Chelsea* (con mapa), *Midtown* (con mapa) y *Uptown*. Para cada uno de los otros boroughs (Bronx, Brooklyn y Queens) hay un capítulo extra. Las direcciones de Long Island las hemos acomodado bajo los nombres *Nassau County* (parte este) y *Suffolk County* (parte oeste).

La *Christopher Street* è il centro del mondo gay, dove il 28 giugno 1969 per la prima volta i gay si sono difesi in massa, ed in modo aggressivo, contro le ripetute ed arbitrarie repressioni della polizia. Visitare questo luogo storico è un obbligo per ogni turista.
Le stagioni migliori per visitare New York sono la primavera e l'autunno considerato che in estate ed in inverno si registrano sempre temperature estreme. Per gli spostamenti urbani (anche dall'aereoporto JFK al centro) vi consigliamo di usare la *subway*. I taxi sono consigliabili per il rientro in albergo dopo una nottata nell'ambiente gay. Come punto di orientamento, esiste il *New York Gay and Lesbian Community Center*. L'evento gay più importante della città è la *Gay Pride Parade* in giugno. La vita gay di New York infatti si concentra soprattutto a Manhattan: le zone calde sono *The Village* (i.e. Greenwich Village), intorno a *Sheridan Square*, tuttora vivace e frizzante, e da poco *Chelsea*, all'angolo tra la 8th avenue e la West 17th street, che tende a svilupparsi verso la 23rd street.
La vita notturna gay di New York ha una lunga tradizione: già negli anni '20 zone come il Village o Times Square erano conosciute. Uscire di sera è spesso faticoso (il movimento inizia tardi, spesso non prima dell'una), ma l'ambiente è disinibito (vibratori e darkroom non sono un tabù) e comunicativo (i turisti e gli uomini d'affari in viaggio sono molto disponibili). Intorno alla Chirstopher street la gente è un po' ruvida e non più molto giovane. L'*East Village* sta cedendo il suo ruolo di quartiere artistico alla sua parte occidentale. Chelsea è divenuto, da quartiere residenziale della classe, media bianca e sudamericana, la mecca dei gay. Ciò è confermato anche dal trasferimento della tradizionale libreria *A different light* nella 7th avenue. A questo cambiamento contribuirà sicuramente anche la ristrutturazione del Chelsea Piers, anche se non è ancora sicuro se i piani di rinnovo di questa zona respingeranno i cinema a luce rossa e i locali di spogliarelli qui situati. In fine un consiglio: se avete tempo a sufficienza dedicate almeno un giorno a *Fire Island*, il lido gay della metropoli.
Gli indirizzi sono stati classificati in 8 gruppi: abbiamo diviso Manhattan in *Downtown, Village e Chelsea* (con piantina), *Midtown* (con piantina) e *Uptown*. Per ognuno dei quartieri Bronx, Brooklyn e Queens presentiamo un piccolo capitolo a parte. Abbiamo diviso gli indirizzi di Long Island (vedi elenco) in Nassau County (parte occidentale) e Suffolk County (parte orientale).

GAY INFO

■ **Gay & Lesbian Switchboard** Mon-Fri 16-24, Sat 11-17 (Eastern Standard time)
332 BleeckerStreet, Suite F-18 ✉ NY 10014 ☎ 989-0999
📠 (415) 552-5498 📧 glnh@glnh.org 💻 www.glnh.org

■ **Lesbian and Gay Community Services Center** (A AC CC d GLM MA S TV VS) 8-23 h
One Little West 12th Street ✉ NY 10014 *(West Village)*
☎ 620-7810 📠 924-2657 📧 info@gaycenter.org
💻 www.gaycenter.org
THE NYC Community center providing help and support in case of any problem, archival collection, library, museum, over 300 groups, social events, legal advice, and more. Bimonthly newsletter "Centervoice".

PUBLICATIONS

■ **Gayellow Pages** 12-17.30 h
PO Box 533, Village Station ✉ NY 10014 ☎ 674-0120
📠 (212) 420-1126 📧 gayellow_pages@juno.com
Annual regional guide, 96 pages. US$ 3.95.

■ **HX Magazine**
c/o Two Queens, 230 West 17th Street ✉ NY 10011 *(8th floor)*
☎ 352-3535 📠 352-3596 📧 advertising@hx.com
💻 www.hx.com
Good weekly gay nightlife and entertainment magazine available for free at gay venues. Lesbian version also available (HX for her).

■ **LGNY - Lesbian & Gay New York**
151 West 19th Street ✉ NY 10011 ☎ 691.1100 📠 691.6185
📧 editor@lgny.com 💻 www.lgny.com
Biweekly newspaper providing news, politics, commentary, health, features, arts and entertainment, and listings for New York City's large and diverse lesbian and gay community.

New York City — New York/USA

■ **Metrosource**
180 Varick Street ✉ NY 10014 (5th floor) ☎ 691-5127
📠 741-2978 📧 metrosourc@aol.com 💻 www.metrosource.com
Gay and lesbian guide to New York. Excellent articles about certain aspects of gay and lesbian lifestyle in the city, community and business directories. Published four times a year.
■ **New York Blade News** Mon-Fri 9-17 h
242 West 30th Street ✉ NY 10001 (4th floor) ☎ 268-2701
📠 268-2069 📧 news@nyblade.com 💻 www.nyblade.com
Newspaper covering national and local, arts and entertainment news, contains classifieds and some events listings.
■ **New York Gay and Lesbian Yellow Pages**
4200 Montrose Boulevard, Ste 480 ✉ TX 77006 ☎ 691-8960
💻 www.glyp.com
■ **Next**
121 Varick Street ✉ NY 10013 (6th floor) ☎ 627-0165
📠 627-0633
Weekly publication. Bar/Club guide. Info on New York's scene.
■ **Parlee Plus/Equal Time the News**
13 South Carl Avenue, Babylon ✉ NY 11704 ☎ (516) 587-8669
Monthly magazine with bar guide.
■ **Twist**
P.O. Box 7908 Rego Park ✉ NY 11374 ☎ (718) 381-8776
📠 (718) 366-8636
Small monthly magazine with info on the scene and bars listing available for free at gay venues.
■ **Vice Magazine**
c/o VICE Publishing Inc., PO Box 20281 ✉ NY 10011-0003
☎ 727-2787 📠 727-3190 📧 vice@mindspring.com
Gay monthly Magazine of Art, Entertainment and news. Subscription 12 issues $36/$46 foreign.

CULTURE

■ **National Museum of Lesbian and Gay History**
c/o Lesbian and Gay Gay Community Services Center, 208 West 13th Street ✉ NY 10011 (West Village)
New founded in 1989. Including library and archives.
■ **Pat Parker/Vito Russo Center Library** (GLM MA)
Mon-Thu 18-21, Sat 13-16 h
208 West 13th Street ✉ NY 10011 ☎ 620-7310 ext. 302
📧 library@gaycenter.org 💻 www.gaycenter.org
Over 10,000 books, 400 videos and 55 periodicals.

TOURIST INFO

■ **New York Convention & Visitor Bureau**
2 Columbus Circle ✉ NY 10019 ☎ 484-1200 📠 246-6310

ESCORTS & STUDIOS

■ **Campus Escorts** (CC G)
☎ (866) 2-22-6787
■ **Chelsea Guys**
☎ 533-5600
From college men to porn stars.

TRAVEL AND TRANSPORT

■ **Sailing Affairs** (F GLM MA OS)
404 East 11th Street ✉ NY 10009-4541 ☎ 228-5755 📠 228-8512
📧 sailingaff@aol.com
Captained sailboat charters for individuals or small groups. Day trips, sunset sails, weekends on 38 foot yacht. Gay owned and operated.

PRIVATE ACCOMMODATION

■ **Enjoy Bed and Breakfast** (BF G H MA) 16.30-21 h (Central European Time)
Nollendorfplatz 5, 10777 Berlin - Germany ☎ +49 30 236 236 10
📠 +49 30 236 236 19 📧 info@ebab.com 💻 ebab.com
Accommodation sharing agency. All with shower and BF. 20-25 Euro p.p.

Campus Escorts

NYCs Finest College–Age Escorts

(866)2-226787 CAMPUS

ONLINE: www.campusescorts.com

■ **New York Bed & Breakfast Reservation Center. The** (GLM)
☎ 977-3512
Wide range of Bed & Breakfast accomodations in private homes in New York City.
■ **Rainbow Roommates** (AC CC GLM MA) Mon-Fri 11-19, Sat 12-18 h
268 West 22nd Street ✉ NY 10011 (corner of 8th Street)
☎ 627-8612 📠 (800) 421-9733
📧 rainbowroommate@nycnet 💻 nycnet.com/rainbowroommates/
Gay roommate and real estate service.

GENERAL GROUPS

■ **ACLU Lesbian and Gay Rights Project**
132 West 43rd Street ✉ NY 10036 ☎ 944-9800
■ **ACT UP New York** Mon 19.30 h at LGCSC, 208 West 13th Street
☎ 642-5499 📠 966-4873 💻 www.actupny.org
■ **Asian and Friends New York**
☎ (718) 488-0630

USA/New York — New York City

Chelsea Guys

"we'll give you a hard time!"

for an hour...
for an evening...
for a weekend...

New York's Hottest Escorts
from college jocks to pornstars

(212) 533-5600
all major credit cards accepted   visit us online at: www.chelseaguys.com

---

■ **Center For Lesbian And Gay Studies. The (CLAGS)**
Graduate Center, City University of New York, 33 West 42nd Street
✉ NY 10036
■ **Coalition for Lesbian and Gay Rights**
☎ 627-1398
■ **Gay and Lesbian Anti-Violence Project** 0-24 h
☎ 807-0197
Counselling and referral.
■ **Heritage of Pride**
154 Christopher Street ✉ NY 10014 *(West Village)* ☎ 807-7433
Organises the annual Pride Week.
■ **Nineth Street Center** (GLM MA)
151 First Avenue, Suite 25 ✉ NY 10003 ☎ 228-5153
📧 nscenter@geocities.com 🖥 www.geocities.com/nscenter/
Small, non-profit organisation which offers supportive open discussion groups and peer coonceling on personal and social issues,based on the idea of Paul Rosenfels.Call for information.
■ **Twenty-Something**
c/o The Center, One Little West 12th Street ✉ NY 10014
☎ 439-8051
Youth group.

FETISH GROUPS

■ **Excelsior Motorcycle Club**
PO Box 1386, Bowling Green Station ✉ NY 10274-1130
■ **Gay Male S/M Activists (GMSMA)** (B f G p SA)
332 Bleecker Street, Suite D23 ✉ NY 10014 ☎ 727-9878
For safe and responsible S/M.
■ **Girth and Mirth Club of New York**
PO Box 10, Dept. G, Pelham ✉ NY 10803 ☎ 914/699-7735

■ **Golden Shower Association (GSA)**
332 Bleecker, # K-95 ✉ NY 10014
Its name says it all. Write for info on activities.
■ **Hot Ash**
PC Box 20147, London Terrace Station ✉ NY 10011
For cigar fetishists of every sexual orientation.
■ **Iron Guard NYC**
PO Box 291 Village Station ✉ NY 10014

HEALTH GROUPS

■ **Aids Hotline** 9-21 h
☎ 447-8200
NYC Department of Health.
■ **aidsinfonyc.org**
📧 webman@aidsinfonyc.org 🖥 www.aidsinfonyc.org
Extensive site with page providing information on Aids and related services in NYC.
■ **American Indian Community House HIV/AIDS Project (AICH)**
404 Lafayette Street ✉ NY 10003 *(2nd floor)* ☎ 598-0100
📧 thomasaich@aol.com
■ **Body Positive. The** Mon-Fri 9-18 h
19 Fulton Street, Suite 308 B ✉ NY 10038 ☎ 566-7333
📠 566-4539
Education, medical info and support groups. Publisher of a magazine about HIV and AIDS. Published monthly, about 48 pages. Free at gay venues. Also available in Spanish language edition.
■ **Central New York AIDS Hotline**
☎ (315) 475-AIDS
■ **Community Health Project** Tue Thu 18-21 h
208 West 13th Street ✉ NY 10011 *(West Village)(2nd floor)*
☎ 675-3559
Walk in clinic for VD, AIDS.

New York City | New York/USA

VistaVideo INTERNATIONAL

The World's Most Beautiful Men

www.vistamen.com

Producers of the Highest Quality Physique Fantasy Videos.
VistaVideo, P.O. Box 370706, Miami, FL 33137
We Ship Worldwide.

USA/New York — New York City

NEW YORK — from $ 50 —
overnight accomodation service
· about 750 beds · more than 28 cities ·

enjoy bed & breakfast

complete offer see page Germany/Berlin

central booking office Berlin ☎ +49-30-23623610 4:30-9:00 pm local time
Fax +49-30-23623619 · info@ebab.com · www.ebab.com

■ **Gay Men's Health Crisis**
Tisch Building, 129 West 20th Street ✉ NY 10011-1913
☎ 367-1000 367-1220
A not-for-profit, volunteer-based, and community-based organization committed to national leadership on the fight against Aids.

■ **H.E.L.P./Project Samaritan** Wed 20 h at the Center
Residential Health Care Facility, 1401 University Avenue ✉ NY 10452 ☎ 718/681-8700 718/681-8800 ✉ psiadm@aol.com
 www.aidsnyc.org/help-psi
66-bed nursing home for people with Aids/HIV who are recovering substance abusers.

HELP WITH PROBLEMS
■ **Alcoholics Anonymous**
☎ 683-3900
■ **Gay Men's Therapy Group**
420 West 24th Street, Suite 1B ☎ 243-8798

RELIGIOUS GROUPS
■ **Congregation Beth Simchat Torah** Service Fri 8.30 h
57 Bethune Street ✉ NY 10014 *(West Village)* ☎ 929-9498
New York's Gay and Lesbian Jewish Synagogue.

SPECIAL INTEREST GROUPS
■ **M.A.N.**
☎ 535-3914
Gay Male Social Nudists.
■ **MetroBears New York**
P.O. Box 1802 ✉ NY 10185-1802 ☎ 978-5080
Social organisation for bears and their admirers.
■ **Senior Action in a Gay Environment (SAGE)**
305 7th Avenue ✉ NY 10001 *(16th floor, Chelsea)* ☎ 741-2247
Organisation for senior lesbians and gays.

SPORT GROUPS
■ **Team New York**
P.O. Box 126 ✉ NY 10011 ☎ 439-8179
 members.aol.com/teamny1998
Umbrella organisation for athletes, sport teams and cultural festival participants who participates in the Gay Games.

New York - Bronx ☎ 718

BARS
■ **Up & Down Bar** (B GLM D S)
1306 Unionport Road ☎ 822-9585
Go-go girls and boys in the Bronx.

HEALTH GROUPS
■ **Gay Men's HIV+ Support Group** Mon 18-20 h
c/o Bronx AIDS Services, One Fordham Plaza No.903, ✉ NY 10458
☎ 295-5605

New York - Brooklyn ☎ 718

BARS
■ **Sanctuary Lounge** (B GLM)
444 7th Avenue ☎ 832-9800
Gay and lesbian mixed crowd.

DANCECLUBS
■ **Spectrum** (AC B D GLM MA OS SNU STV) Wed-Sat 21.30-4 h
802 54th Street ✉ NY 11220 ☎ 238-8213
The movie "Saturday Night Fever" was filmed here.

HEALTH GROUPS
■ **Brooklyn AIDS Task Force, Inc.**
☎ 212/783-0883
■ **Touch AIDS Community Dinners** Mon 17.30 h
Friends Meeting House, 110 Schermerhorn Street ☎ 518-2806
Free dinners for PWA's.

New York - Manhattan/Downtown ☎ 212

CULTURE
■ **Wessel and O'Connor Gallery** (G) Tue-Sun 11-18 h
242 West 26th Street ✉ NY 10001 *(Chelsea, between 7th and 8th Avenues)* ☎ 242-8811 242-8822 ✉ wesselocon@aol.com
 www.wesseloconnor.com

SEX SHOPS/BLUE MOVIES
■ **Ann Street Entertainment Center** (CC G VS) Mon-Fri 7-23, Sat 10-23, Sun 10-19 h
21 Ann Street ✉ NY 10038-2405 *(between Broadway and Nassau Streets)* ☎ 267-9760

SAUNAS/BATHS
■ **Wall Street Sauna** (B F G SA) Mon-Fri 11-20 h
1 Maiden Lane ✉ NY 10038 *(11th floor)* ☎ 233-890
Its name says it all.

New York - Manhattan/Midtown ☎ 212

BARS
■ **bs new york** (B G MA S VS) 14-4 h
405 3rd Avenue/29th Street ✉ NY 10016 ☎ 684-8376

New York City — New York/USA

New York City - Midtown

1. The Web Bar
2. The Townhouse Bar
3. Oscar Wilde Bar
4. Regents Bar
5. Spa 227 Fitness Club
6. Lion's Den Sex Shop
7. Stella's Bar
8. Don't Tell Mama Show
9. Cleo's 9th Avenue Saloon Bar
10. Mike's American Bar & Grill Restaurant
11. La Nueva Escuelita Danceclub

USA/New York — New York City

■ **Chase** (B G YG)
255 West 55th Street ✉ NY 10019 (between broadway and 8th avenue) ☏ 333-3400
70s-style coffee bar and cocktail lounge.
■ **Cleo's 9th Avenue Saloon** (B G MA N) 8-4 h
656 9th Avenue/46th Street ✉ NY 10036 (Lower West Side)
☏ 307-1503
■ **Comfort Zone. The** (B G VS)
405 3rd Avenue ✉ NY 10016 ☏ 684-8376
■ **Oscar Wilde** (AC B CC E f GLM MA N s) 16-4 h
221 East 58th Street ✉ NY 10022 (East Side. Between 2nd and 3rd Avenue) ☏ 486-7309
■ **Regents** (B G E F S) 12-4 h
317 East 53rd Street ✉ NY 10022 (between 1st & 2nd Avneues)
☏ 593-3091
■ **Stella's** (B Glm r S SNU) 12-4 h, shows WE
266 West 47 Street (east of Eight Avenue) ✉ NY 10036
☏ 575-1680
■ **Townhouse. The** (B E G MA) 16-3 h
236 East 58th Street ✉ NY 10022 (between 2nd and 3rd Avenue)
☏ 754-4649

DANCECLUBS

↪ You should always check the local gay magazines for up-to-date listings of parties and special events.
■ **New Escuelita. The** (B D glm) Mon, Thu-Sat 22-? h
301 West 39th Street ✉ NY 10018 ☏ 631-0588
Very latino.
■ **Web. The** (AC B CC D G LJ MA S SNU STV VS) 16-4 h
40 East 58th Street ✉ NY 10022 (between Park and Madison Streets)
☏ 308-1546
Mostly Asian crowd.

RESTAURANTS

■ **Mike's American Bar & Grill** (B F g)
650 10th Avenue ✉ NY 10036 (West Side) ☏ 246-4115
Popular.

SHOWS

■ **Don't Tell Mama** (B GLM S) 16-4 h
343 West 46th Street ✉ NY 10036 (between 8th and 9th Avenues)
☏ 757-0788
Two cabaret rooms.
■ **Gaiety** (f G R SNU) 12-?
201 West 46th Street ✉ NY 10036 (at Broadway) ☏ 221-8868
New York's oldest male burlesque.

SEX SHOPS/BLUE MOVIES

■ **International Film & Video** (g VS) Mon-Fri 9-17 h
453 West 47th Street ✉ NY 10036 ☏ 245-8039
Video rental.
■ **Lion's Den** (G VS) 9-1, Sat-Sun -2 h
230 East 53rd Street ✉ NY 10022 ☏ 753-7800
Videos, magazines, toys, and more.

SAUNAS/BATHS

■ **East Side Club** (f G MA P SA SB VS) 0-24 h
227 East 56th Street ✉ NY 10022 (near Bloomingdales and Citycorp Center, top floor) ☏ 753-2222
Safer sex sauna with free condoms and some seminars.
■ **Spa 227** (B f G msg p SA SOL) 0-24 h
227 East 54th Street ✉ NY 10022 (Near 3rd Avenue, 3rd floor)
☏ 754-0227

FITNESS STUDIOS

■ **Athletic Complex** (g)
3 Park Avenue ✉ NY 10016 (at southeast corner of 34th Street)
■ **Prescriptive Fitness** (g)
250 West 54th Street ✉ NY 10019 ☏ 307-7760

HOTELS

■ **Hotel Grand Union** (AC CC F g H MA)
34 East 32nd Street ✉ NY 10016 ☏ 683-5890 🖶 689-7397
Central location close to theatres and Greenwich Village. All rooms with priv. baths and TV.

New York - Manhattan/Uptown ☏ 212

BARS

■ **Brandy's Piano Bar** (B glm S)
235 East 84th Street/2nd Avenue ✉ NY 10028 (East Side)
☏ 650-1944
■ **Bridge. The** (B G MA) 16-4 h
309 East 60th Street ✉ NY 10028 (East-Side, between 2nd and 1st Avenue) ☏ 223-9104

New York City — New York/USA

■ **Candle Bar** (B G lj N MA) 14-4 h
309 Amsterdam Avenue/74th Street ✉ NY 10023 (*Upper West Side*)
☎ 874-9155
■ **Eight of Clubs** (B G MA N OS)
230 W. 75th Street/Broadway ✉ NY 10023 ☎ 580-7389
■ **Pegasus** (A AC B G MA N S SNU STV VS) 16-4 h
119 East 60th Street ✉ NY 10022 (*East Side*) ☎ 888-4702
Piano bar and club room with a cabaret stage. Asian crowd on WE.
■ **Toolbox. The** (B G S SNU VS) 12-2 h
1742 2nd Avenue ✉ NY 10022 (*East-Side, between 90th & 91st Streets*) ☎ 348-1288
Cruise Bar.
■ **Works. The** (AC B E GLM MG N S VS) 14-4 h
428 Columbus Avenue/81st Street ✉ NY 10024 (*Upper West Side*)
☎ 799-7365
Recently renovated and enlarged; special events nightly.

SHOWS

■ **Diva** (B F glm S)
306 East 81st Street/2nd Avenue ✉ NY 10028 (*Upper East Side*)
☎ 650-1928
Piano bar.

SEX SHOPS/BLUE MOVIES

■ **Les Hommes** (AC CC G MA VS) Sun-Thu 10-2, Fri, Sat 10-4 h
217-B West 80th Street ✉ NY 10024-7002 (*2nd floor*) ☎ 580-2445

HOTELS

■ **Sugar Hill • International House** (B f g H)
722 Saint Nicholas Avenue ✉ NY 10031 (*Harlem*) ☎ 926-7030
🖷 283-0108 💻 infohostel@aol.com 🌐 www.hostels.com/sugar/

CRUISING

—Central Park (enter from 72nd Street entrance. Near the lake on the west side you'll find "The Ramble")

New York - Manhattan/Village & Chelsea
☎ **212**

GAY INFO

⇒ This part includes Greenwich Village, the East Village and Chelsea.

CULTURE

■ **Ganymede Gallery** (A g)
220 West Houston Street ✉ NY 10014 (*Between 6th Avenue and Varrick Street*) ☎ 255-6755

BARS

■ **Androgyny** (B d TV YG) Tue-Thu 18-2, Fri 18-4, Sat 20-4 h
35 Crosby Street ✉ NY 10014 ☎ 613-0971
Lounge for transgenders and their admirers.
■ **B Bar** (! AC B D G YG) Tue 23-? h
40 East 4th Street ✉ NY 10003 ☎ 475-2220
The weekly party "Beige" on Tue attracts the trendiest gay fashion crowd of New York. Beautiful place, live DJs and handsome men. Not gay the rest of the week.
■ **Bar. The** (B G N) 13-4 h
68 2nd Avenue/4th Street ✉ NY 10003 (*East Village*) ☎ 674-9714
Very friendly atmosphere, good jukebox.
■ **Barracuda** (! AC B G MA S STV VS) 16-4 h
275 West 22nd Street ✉ NY 10011 (*Chelsea, between 7th and 8th Avenue*) ☎ 645-8613
DJs and drag shows nightly. Voted "Bar of the year 2000".

NEW YORK'S MOST POPULAR DANCE BAR

**DAILY HAPPY HOUR
2 FOR 1
4PM - 8PM**

SUNDAY TEA DANCE BEGINS AT 4PM

OPEN DAILY 'TIL 4AM

SPLASH 2000
splashbar.com

USA/New York — New York City

[Advertisement: g LOUNGE — 225 W. 19TH STREET NEW YORK CITY 10011 WWW.GLOUNGE.COM]

■ **Blu Bar** (B D G MA S SNU TV VS)
161 West 23rd Street ✉ NY 10011 *(Chelsea)* ☏ 633-6113
New dance bar with cyberstations.
■ **B.M.W. Bar** (A AC B BF CC F GLM lj MA N) Mon-Son 16-4 h
227 East 21 St. ✉ NY 10021 *(Gramercy 21 St. between 2nd&3rd Ave.)* ☏ 473-1959
Every day live music: Jazz, guitar. Cigar bar.
■ **Boiler Room. The** (B GLM YG) 16-4 h
86 East 4th Street ✉ NY 10003 *(East Village)* ☏ 254-7536
Large bar with an eclectic crowd of young men.
■ **Boots & Saddle** (B G lj) 8-4, Sun 12-4 h
76 Christopher Street ✉ NY 10014 *(West Village)* ☏ 929-9684
■ **Chi Chiz** (B f G) Mon-Sat 15-4; Sun 12-4 h
135 Christopher St. ✉ NY 10014 ☏ 462-0027
Popular, mainly among Afro-Americans. Sun 12-17h good brunch; Mon-Fri 17-20 2 for 1.
■ **Cock. The** (B GLM MA S STV) 21.30-4 h
188 Avenue A 12th St. ✉ NY 10009 ☏ 946-1871
Cabaret shows on Wed, Fri and Sat. Popular.
■ **Crazy Nannie's** (B D gLm MA)
21 South 7th Avenue ✉ NY 10011 ☏ 366-6312
Can be fun depending on the night. Check lovcal paper for events. "DQNY" parties on Mon.
■ **Dick's Bar** (B G N)
192 2nd Avenue/12th Street ✉ NY 10003 *(East Village)*
☏ 475-2071
■ **Dugout. The** (B d G MG N) 16-1 h
185 Christopher Street ✉ NY 10014 *(West Village)* ☏ 242-9113
■ **Dusk Lounge** (B Glm MA) Mon-Wed 18-2, Thu-Sat 18-4 h
147 west 24th Street ✉ NY 10011 ☏ 924-4490
New upscale lounge with a Florida atmosphere.

■ **G Lounge** (! AC B GLM MA N) 16-4 h
225 West 19th Street ✉ NY 10011 *(Chelsea between 7th & 8th Avenue)* ☏ 929-1085
Very popular modern bar. non-alcoholic Juice bar.
■ **Hangar. The** (! AC B G LJ MA N s SNU STV VS WO) Mon-Fri 15-4, Sat 14-4, Sun 13-4 h
115 Christopher Street ✉ NY 10014 *(West Village)* ☏ 627-2044
Popular hangout for locals and gay tourists.
■ **Hell** (AC B G MA) Sun-Thu 19-4, Fri Sat 17-4 h
59 Gansevoort Street/Washington Street ✉ NY 10014 *(West Village)*
☏ 727-1666
Bar and lounge with DJs in the meat-packing district.
■ **H2O** (AC B G MA S SNU)
443 East 6th Street ✉ NY 10009 *(East Village)(off Avenue A)*
☏ 979-9291
■ **I.C. Guyz** (B G S SNU) 20-4 h
443 East 6th Street ✉ NY 10003 *(East village)* ☏ 979-9291
Swimsuited bar hunks dance every hour.
■ **Julius** (B f GLM) Mon-Sat 11-4, Sun 12-4 h
159 West 10th Street ✉ NY 10014 *(West Village)* ☏ 929-9672
One of the oldest gay bars in NYC. Great hamburgers.
■ **Liquids** (B glm YG) 18-4 h
226 East 10th Street ✉ NY 10014 *(East Village)* ☏ 677-1717
Friendly mixed bar.
■ **Lure. The** (AC B G LJ MA VS) 20-4 h
409 West 13th Street/9th Avenue ✉ NY 10011 *(West Village)*
☏ 741-3919
For serious leather crowd. Mon foot night, Wed pork-fetish, Thu bears, WE leather.
■ **Marie's Crisis** (AC B G MA S) 16-4 h
59 Grove Street/7th Avenue ✉ NY 10014 *(West Village)*
☏ 243-9323
Piano bar from 17.30 at the weekend, Mon-Thu 21.30 h

USA/New York — New York City

■ **Meriken** (B F g)
189 7th Avenue/21st Street ✉ NY 10011 *(Chelsea)* ☎ 620-9684
Japanese cuisine.
■ **Paris Commune. The** (AC B CC F glm MA) 11-15, 18-24, Sat Sun 10-15.30 18-24 h
411 Bleecker Street ✉ NY 10014 *(West Village)* ☎ 929-0509
Reservation advisable. French cuisine.
■ **Restivo** (B F GLM MA N OS) 12-24 h
209 7th Avenue ✉ NY 10022 *(Chelsea, at 22nd Street)*
☎ 346-4133
Bar and restaurant. Italian cuisine.
■ **Salon de Sade** (B F glm LJ)
206 West 23rd Street ✉ NY 10010 ☎ 727-8642
Gastonomical house of pain where you can meet the local leather crowd and have your friend spanked for the desert. Funny.
■ **Stingy Lulu's** (B F glm)
129 Saint Mark's Place/Avenue A ✉ NY 10009 *(East Village)*
☎ 674-3545
American cuisine.
■ **Tiffany's Diner** (B F G)
222 West 4th Street ✉ NY 10014 *(West Village)* ☎ 242-1480

■ **Universal Grill** (B F GLM)
44 Bedford Street ✉ NY 10011 *(West Village)* ☎ 989-5621
Good brunch & American dinner.

SHOWS
■ **Bar d'O** (! B Glm MA S STV)
29 Bedford Street ✉ NY 10014 ☎ 627-1580
One of the world famous drag cabaret show of the world. Live singing by Joey Arias, Raven-O, Sherry Vine and the others. Gay only show nights.
■ **Duplex. The** (B d GLM MA S STV) 16-4 h
61 Christopher Street ✉ NY 10011 ☎ 255-5438
Cabaret/piano bar with singing staff and comics.2 dinks min. charge.Entrance $ 5-10.Groundfloor piano bar no charge.
■ **Lips** (B F GLM S STV) (see webside for details)
2 Bank Street ✉ NY 10014 *(at Greenwich Avenue)* ☎ 675-7710
Restaurant with drag show during dinner.
■ **Lucky Cheng's** (B F G S STV)
24 1st Avenue ✉ NY 10013 *(East Village)(at 2nd Street)*
☎ 473-0516
Original New York pan-Asian drag theme restaurant. Drag show in the basement.

1306 SPARTACUS 2001/2002

New York City | New York/USA

New York City - Manhattan / Village & Chelsea

1. Blu Bar
2. Barracuda Bar
3. Unicorn Sex Shop
4. Colonial House Inn Guest House
5. Rawhide Bar
6. B.M.W. Bar
7. A Different Light Bookshop
8. West Side Club Men's Club
9. Limelight Danceclub
10. Splash Bar
11. G Lounge Bar
12. Spike Bar
13. The Lure Bar
14. Hell Bar
15. J's Hangout Men's Club
16. Chelsea Pines Inn Guest House
17. Incentra Village House Guest House
18. Lesbian & Gay Community Center
19. Julius Bar
20. Pieces Bar
21. Oscar Wilde Bookshop
22. Stonewall Bar
23. The Monster Bar & Danceclub
24. Boots & Saddle Bar
25. Leather Man Leather Shop
26. Creative Visions Bookshop
27. Ty's Bar
28. The Hangar Bar
29. Two Potato Bar
30. Sneakers Bar
31. The Dugout Bar
32. Chi Chiz Bar
33. Christopher Street Bookshop
34. Factory Café
35. Marie's Crisis Bar
36. Vivid Video Sex Shop
37. Bar d'O
38. Dick's Bar
39. The Bar
40. Boiler Room Bar
41. Wonderbar

SPARTACUS 2001/2002 | 1305

USA/New York | New York City

CHELSEA

Madison Square Park

GREENWICH VILLAGE

New York City — New York/USA

■ **Meow Mix** (B D GLM S YG) Sat-Wed 17-4 h
269 East Houston Street ✉ NY 10029 ☎ 254-0688
Cute boys and girls.
■ **Mother** (AC B D glm TV YG) 22-6 h
432 West 14th Street ✉ NY 10014 ☎ 366-5680
Two floors bar with dance floor. Check in local papers for special events. Jackie 60 nights (cyber-fetish) last Tue of the month.
■ **Pieces** (B G MA S SNU VS) 14-4 h
8 Christopher Street ✉ NY 10014 *(West Village)* ☎ 929-9291
Tue karaoke and Thu go-go boys. Popular on Tue.
■ **Rawhide** (AC B G LJ MA N) Mon-Sat 8-4, Sun 12-4 h
212 8th Avenue ✉ NY 10016 *(Chelsea, at 21st Street)* ☎ 242-9332
Popular neighborhood bar for leather and western fans. GoGo-Boys at the weekend, 17-21 h happy hour.
■ **Sneakers** (B G MG N) 12-4 h
392 West Street ✉ NY 10014 *(West Village. Between Christopher & 10th Street)* ☎ 242-9830
Mon-Fri 17-21 h happy hour.
■ **Spike. The** (! B d F G lj) 21-4 h
120 11th Avenue/20th Street ✉ NY 10011 *(Chelsea)* ☎ 243-9688
Mixed during the week, LJ on weekends! Attracts leather fans from all the State.
■ **Splash** (! AC B D G lj S SNU VS YG) 16-4 h
50 West 17th Street/6th Avenue ✉ NY 10011 *(Chelsea)*
☎ 691-0073
Popular with a mixed crowd.
■ **Starlight Bar and Lounge** (AC B E GLM MA N) Wed, Thu, Sun 21-3, Fri, Sat -4 h
165 Avenue A ✉ NY 10009 *(between 10th and 11th Street)*
☎ 475-2172
The new lounge in the East Village. Same owners as Wonder Bar. Gay and Lesbian fashion and entertainment crowd.
■ **Stonewall** (B G s) 16-4 h
53 Christopher Street ✉ NY 10014 ☎ 463-0950
Where it all started. Now with a new look.
■ **Two Potato** (AC B F G MA S STV) 12-4 h
145 Christopher Street ✉ NY 10014 *(West Village)* ☎ 255-0286
African-American crowd. Great atmosphere. Thu-Sat shows at midnight.
■ **Ty's** (AC B G lj MG N) Mon-Fri 14-4, Sat Sun 13-4 h
114 Christopher Street ✉ NY 10014 *(West Village)* ☎ 741-9641
■ **View** (AC B G N VS YG) 14-4 h
232 8th Avenue/ 22nd Street ✉ NY 10011 *(Chelsea)* ☎ 929-2243
New Chelsea hot spot for heavy cruising.
■ **Wonder Bar** (AC B E GLM MA N) 18-4 h
505 East 6th Street/Avenue A ✉ NY 10003 *(East Village, between Avenues A & B)* ☎ 777-9105
Nice upscale gays and lesbians bar, entertainment crowd, live DJ nightly.

MEN'S CLUBS

■ **J's Hangout** (b DR G VS WE) 24-8 h
675 Hudson Street/14th Street ✉ NY 10014 ☎ 242-9292
After-hour sex club. Mon&Thu jerk-off-parties,Fri bondage $10 entrance.

CAFES

■ **Big Cup** (b f G MA) Mon-Thu 7-1, Fri-2, Sat 8-2 Sun 8-1 h
228 8th Ave ✉ NY 10011 *(between 21st and 22nd St.)* ☎ 206-0059
Tea & coffee house.
■ **Espresso Bar** (b f glm)
82 Christopher Street ✉ NY 10014 *(West Village)* ☎ 627-3870
One of the best sandwiches in town.

■ **Factory Café. The** (AB b f G MA) Mon-Thu 8-24, Fri -2, Sat 9-2 Sun-24 h
104 Christopher Street ✉ NY 10014
Friendly café with lots of tourists, popular in the afternoon and late evening. Also beer&wine.

DANCECLUBS

☞ *You should always check the local gay magazines for up-to-date listings of parties and special events.*
■ **Life** (AC B D glm YG) Sun (G) 23-4 h
158 Blecker Street ✉ NY 10014 *(at Thompson Street)* ☎ 420-1999
"Boy's Life" parties on Sundays. Mixed on Thu.
■ **Monster** (B D G) 16-4, Sat Sun 14-4 h
80 Grove Street/Sheridan Square ✉ NY 10014 *(West Village)*
☎ 924-3558
Popular West Village bar and disco. Lots of latin boys.

RESTAURANTS

■ **Brunetta's** (B F g OS)
190 1st Avenue ✉ NY 10009 *(East Village, between 11th & 12th Streets)* ☎ 228-4030
Very good Italian food, nice garden.
■ **Caffe Torino** (B F G) 17-24 h
139 West 10th Street ✉ NY 10014 *(West Village, between 6th and 7th Avenues)* ☎ 675-5554
Italian cuisine. Good, moderate prices.
■ **Candy Bar and Grill** (B F GLM) 16.30-4 h
131 8th Avenue ✉ NY 10014 *(At 16th Street, Chelsea)* ☎ 229-9702
■ **Chelsea Bistro and Bar** (AC B CC F glm MA) Mon-Thu 17.30-23, Fri 17.30-24, Sat 17-24, Sun 17-22.30 h
358 West 23rd Street ✉ NY 10011 *(Chelsea)* ☎ 727-2026
One of the best French restaurants in Manhattan.
■ **Chez Ma Tante** (b F g OS)
198 West 10th Street ✉ NY 10014 *(West Village)* ☎ 620-0223
■ **Circa** (B CC F glm lj OS YG) 11-16 h (lunch), Sun-Thu 18-0, Fri Sat -1 h
103 Second Avenue/6th Street ✉ NY 10003 *(East Village)*
☎ 777-4120
Restaurant-bar.
■ **Cola's** (B F glm)
148 8th Avenue ✉ NY 10011 *(Chelsea)* ☎ 633-8020
Popular
■ **Empire Diner** (B F g) 0-24 h
210 10th Avenue/22nd Street ✉ NY 10011 *(Chelsea)* ☎ 243-2736
Nice late night place.
■ **Flamingo East** (A AC B CC F glm YG) 18-4 h
219 2nd Avenue/13th Street ✉ NY 10003 *(East Village)*
☎ 533-2860
■ **Florent** (AC B BF F glm MA) Mon-Fri 9-5, Sat Sun 0-24 h
69 Gansevoort Street ✉ NY 10014 *(West Village)* ☎ 989-5779
Great French baguettes.
■ **Food Bar** (b e F Glm MA)
189 8th Avenue *(between 17th & 18th St.)* ☎ 243-2020
■ **Garage** (B F glm)
99 7th Avenue South ✉ NY 10014 ☎ 645-0600
American cuisine.
■ **Judy's Chelsea** (AC B CC F G MA S) Rest. 17-1 Fri&Sat- 2 Sun brunch 12-16; Cabaret daily from 20.30, Piano Bar daily 18-4 h
169 8th Ave ✉ NY 10019 ☎ 929-5410
Restaurant, Café and Piano bar.
■ **Mary Ann's** (B F g)
116 8th Avenue/16th Street ✉ NY 10011 *(Chelsea)* ☎ 633-0877
Mexican food.

New York City | New York/USA

SEX SHOPS/BLUE MOVIES
■ **Christopher Street Shop** (AC CC G MA VS) Sun, Thu 12-4, Fri, Sat 12-6 h
500 Hudson Street ✉ NY 10014-2818 *(at Christopher Street, West Village)* ☏ 463-0657
■ **Harmony Video** (G VS) 0-24 h
139 Christopher Street ✉ NY 10014 *(West Village)* ☏ 366-9059
Videos, magazines and cabins.
■ **Pleasure Chest. The** (AC CC glm)
156 7th Ave. South ✉ NY 10014 ☏ 242-2158
Dildos&toys.
■ **Unicorn** (AC CC G MA VS) Sun-Thu 12-4, Fri Sat 12-6 h
277c West 22nd Street ✉ NY 10011-2702 *(Chelsea, between 7th and 8th)* ☏ 924-2921
■ **Vivid Video** (CC G)
100 Christopher St. ✉ NY 10014 ☏ 352-8800
Videos,toys & sexy clothing.

CINEMAS
■ **All Male Jewel Theatre** (B DR VS) Sun-Thu 10-3, Fri Sat 10-5 h
100 3rd Avenue ✉ NY 10003 *(East Village)* ☏ 505-7320

SAUNAS/BATHS
■ **Steam** (f G MA msg SA SB WH WO) 0-24 h
585 8th Avenue ✉ NY 10018 *(near Time Square)* ☏ 947-4411
All male 24 h bathhouse.
■ **West Side Club** (B f G SA SB VS WO) 0-24 h
27 West 20th Street ✉ NY 10011 *(2nd floor)* ☏ 691-2700

FITNESS STUDIOS
■ **Chelsea Gym** (G)
267 West 17th Street/8th Avenue ✉ NY 10011 *(Chelsea)* ☏ 255-1150

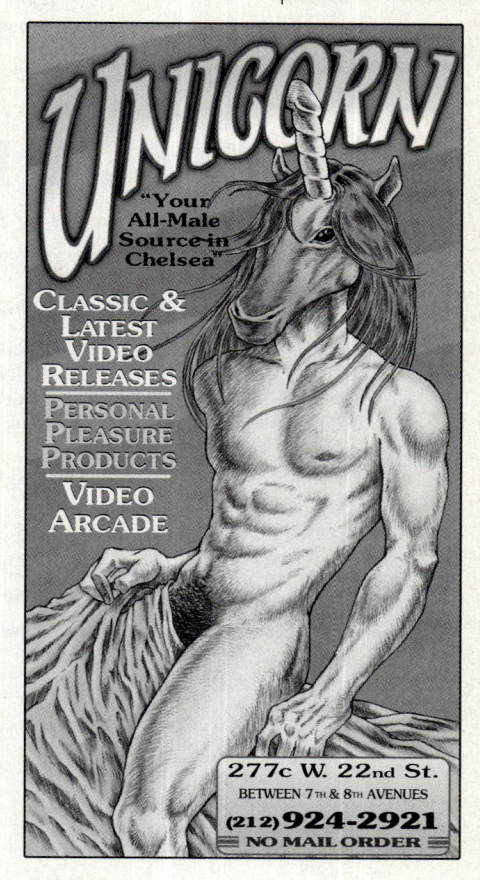

■ **David Barton Gym** (G)
552 6th Avenue/15th Street ✉ NY 10011 *(Chelsea)* ☏ 772-0004

BODY & BEAUTY SHOPS
■ **R.J. White Jewelry, Inc.** (AC CC GLM) Wed-Sat 13-19, Jul Aug: Tue-Fri 13-19 h
107 Christopher Street ✉ NY 10014 *(Between Hudson and Bleecker)* ☏ 242-0540

BOOK SHOPS
■ **Creative Visions** (AC CC GLM MA) 11-23 h
548 Hudson Street ✉ NY 10014 *(2 blocks north of Christopher Street, West Village)* ☏ 645-7573
Magazines, periodicals, travel guides, paperback framed art.
■ **Different Light. A** 11-22 h daily
151 West 19th Street ✉ NY 10011 *(Chelsea)* ☏ 989-4850
Over 7000 gay and lesbian books.
■ **Oscar Wilde Bookshop** (AC CC GLM) Sun-Fri 12-20, Sat -21 h
15 Christopher Street ✉ NY 10014 *(West Village)* ☏ 255-8097
World's oldest gay and lesbian bookshop. Large collection of rare & out of print books.

Creative Visions

New York's Gay Lesbian Bi Trans
Book Store & More
548 Hudson Street 212-645-7573
creativevisions.citysearch.com

UNICORN

"Your All-Male Source in Chelsea"

CLASSIC & LATEST VIDEO RELEASES
PERSONAL PLEASURE PRODUCTS
VIDEO ARCADE

277c W. 22nd St.
BETWEEN 7TH & 8TH AVENUES
(212) 924-2921
NO MAIL ORDER

USA/New York — New York City

Winner Out & About Editor's Choice Award
Outsanding Achievement in Gay Travel

CHELSEA PINES INN

The Cozy Bed and Breakfast in the Heart of Gay New York
Sheldon Post, Founder

Charming Rooms from $99

Features Include: Private or semi-private bath • Telephone/Cable TV with Free HBO
Refrigerator/Hair Dryer/Irons & ironing Boards in all rooms
Continental Breakfast featuring homemade bread, Krispy Kreme Donuts & Fresh Fruit
Air Conditioning/Central Heating • Walk to Christopher Street, bars, clubs, shops,

Advance Reservations Suggested • All Major Credit Cards Accepted

317 West 14th Street, New York City 10014
Tel: 212 929-1023   Fax: 212 620-5646   E-mail: cpiny@aol.com
Visit our website at www.chelseapinesinn.com

GIFT & PRIDE SHOPS
■ **Roger & Dave** Mon-Thu 12-21, Fri&Sat -23, Sun-18 h
123 7th Ave ✉ NY 10011 ☎ 645-4563
Crazy T-Shirts, postcards etc. Another branch in 224, 8th Ave,tel. 645-4563.

LEATHER & FETISH SHOPS
■ **DeMask N.Y.** (CC glm)
135 West 22nd Street ✉ NY 10011 *(Chelsea)(between 6th and 7th Avenue)* ☎ 352-2850
Ranging from street wear to heavy leather and rubber. NYC branch of the famous European fetish house.
■ **Leather Man** (CC G LJ) Mon-Sat 12-22 Sun 13-21 h
111 Christopher Street ✉ NY 10014 ☎ 243-5339
Sales and tailoring on own premises.
■ **Noose. The**
261 West 19th Street ✉ NY 10011 *(Chelsea)* ☎ 807-1789

TRAVEL AND TRANSPORT
■ **Acquarian Travel and Entertainment Service** 8-17 h
292 8th Avenue Suite 1 ✉ NY 10001 *(Chelsea)*
☎ 741-0708
Travel and accomodations agent.

VIDEO SHOPS
■ **Gay Pleasures** (AC CC GLM MA VS) 11-23 h
548 Hudson Street ✉ NY 10013 *(2 blocks north of Christopher Street, West Village)* ☎ 255-5256
8 mm film, slides, photos, gay videos.

Chelsea Mews Guesthouse
For Men
Friendly, Private & Affordable

Old-fashioned atmosphere
with Victorian Garden.
Furnished with Antiques.

convenient to all attractions,
transportation and shopping.

Advanced Reservations are advised.
344 W. 15th Street
New York, NY 10011
(212) 255-9174

New York City | New York/USA

Colonial House Inn

THE "INN" PLACE TO STAY

- Bed and Breakfast
- All rooms equipped with Phones, Cable TV, & A/C •
- Private/Shared Baths • Lounge • Roof Sundeck
- Some with Refrigerators and Fireplace
- Rooms from $80.00
- Conveniently located • Reservations suggested

Winner
Editor's Choice Award
Out & About 1994 - 2000

318 West 22nd Street • New York City, New York 10011
Telephone: 212-243-9669   Fax: 212-633-1612   Toll Free: 1-800-689-3779
email: houseinn@aol.com   •   www.colonialhouseinn.com

USA/New York — New York City ▸ Schenectady

HOTELS
■ **Hotel 17** (glm H) 24 h
225 East 17th Street ✉ NY 10003 (*Union Square Subway, Gramercy Park*) ☎ 475-2845 📠 677-8178 💻 hotel17@worldnet.att.net
💻 hotel17.citysearch.com
Beautiful hotel with kitsch/original decoration. Madonna was photographed here. Popular with drag queens. Rooftop where nude sunbathing is allowed; Guests not allowed in single room after 22 h at night.

GUEST HOUSES
■ **Chelsea Mews Guest House** (AC G H MA)
344 West 15 Street ✉ NY 10011 (*Chelsea*) ☎ 255-9174
3 doubles, 5 singles. All rooms with phone and own key. Rates US$ 85-165 with/without bath. Parking garage available.
■ **Chelsea Pines Inn** (AC BF CC GLM H OS)
317 West 14th Street ✉ NY 10014 (*Chelsea*) ☎ 929-1023
📠 620-5646 💻 cpiny@aol.com 💻 www.chelseapinesinn.com
In the Greenwich Village/Chelsea area, 30-45 minutes to airports. Rates US$ 89-139. Private and shared bath. All rooms with telephone, cable TV and refrigerator. Own key.
■ **Colonial House Inn** (A AC CC BF GLM H MA msg OS SOL WO) 24 h
318 West 22nd Street ✉ NY 10011 (*Chelsea. Between 8th and 9th Avenue*) ☎ 243-9669 📠 633-1612 💻 houseinn@aol.com
💻 www.colonialhouseinn.com
Located in Chelsea, 45 mins. to airport. 20 rooms, partly with private bath. Visa or MC accepted.
■ **Incentra Village House** (! AC CC GLM H) Tel only 9-21 h
32 8th Avenue ✉ NY 10014 (*West Village*) ☎ 206-0007
📠 604-0625
Historic Inn, downtown location, 12 km to the airport. All 12 rooms with TV, phone, kitchenette, priv. bath and WC. Nicely furnished, recommended! Rates: suites US$ 130-179, double 149-179, single 99-129 (+ tax).

New York - Queens ☎ 718

BARS
■ **Amnesia** (B d GLM MA) 12-4 h
32-03 Broadway, Astoria ☎ 204-7010
■ **Atlantis 2010** (B GLM D S STV SNU) 21-4 h
76-19 Roosevelt Avenue, Jackson Heights ✉ NY 11372
☎ 457-3939
■ **BS East/Breadstix** (AC B G MA SNU VS) Sun-Fri 17-?, Sat 19-? h
113-24 Queens Boulevard, Forest Hills ✉ NY 11375 (*Next to P.C. Richards*) ☎ 263-0300
Video bar with amateur strip show on Fri and live go-go boys on Sat.
■ **Friends Tavern** (B G) 16-4 h
78-11 Roosevelt Avenue, Jackson Heights ✉ NY 11372
☎ 397-7256
■ **Music Box** (B G N S)
40-08 74th Street, Jackson Heights ✉ NY 11372 ☎ 457-5306

DANCECLUBS
■ **Krash** (AC B CC D f GLM MA P r S SNU STV) Mon Thu-Sat & Holidays 22-5 h
34-48 Steinway Street, Astoria ✉ NY 11101 ☎ 937-2400
Very latino.

SAUNAS/BATHS
■ **Northern Men's Sauna** (G MA SA SB) 12-24 h
3365 Farrington Street ✉ NY 11372 (*Flushing, 1 block from Main St.& Northern Blvd*) ☎ 445-9775

HEALTH GROUPS
■ **AIDS Center of Queens County**
☎ 896-2500
or ☎ 275-2094. *Direct services for people with AIDS.*

CRUISING
-**Forest Park** (*the footpath parallel to Park Lane South beginning at Metropolitan Avenue, best at night*)
-**Roosevelt Avenue** (*woodside, between 69th and 79th Street*)

Niagara Falls ☎ 716

HOTELS
■ **Rainbow House** (BF F glm H)
423 Rainbow Boulevard ✉ NY 14303 ☎ 282-1135
25 minutes to the airport. Centrally located. All rooms with priv. bath and balcony.

Rochester ☎ 716

GAY INFO
■ **Empty Closet**
179 Atlantic Avenue ✉ NY 14607

BARS
■ **Anthony's** (B d GLM MA N) 12-2 h
522 East Main Street ✉ NY 14604 ☎ 325-2060
■ **Avenue Pub** (B GLM N)
522 Monroe Avenue ✉ NY 14607 ☎ 244-4960
■ **Bachelor Forum** (B D G LJ N)
670 University Avenue ✉ NY 14607 ☎ 325-6930
■ **Muthers** (B G N)
40 South Union Street
■ **Tara Cocktail Lounge** (B GLM MA) 12-2 h
153 Liberty Pole Way ✉ NY 14604 ☎ 232-4719
Popular piano bar.

SAUNAS/BATHS
■ **Rochester Spa and Body Club, The** (b G MA OS SA SB SOL VS WO) 0-24 h
153 Liberty Pole Way ✉ NY 14604 ☎ 454-1077
Newly renovated Spa in Downtown Rochester.

TRAVEL AND TRANSPORT
■ **Great Expectations Travel** 9-17 h
2349 Monroe Avenue ✉ NY 14618 ☎ 244-8430 📠 244-8749
💻 glenskalny@vanzile.com 💻 www.greatgaytravel.com

GENERAL GROUPS
■ **Gay Alliance of Genesee Valley** Mon-Thu 13-21.30, Fri 13-18 h
713 C Monroe Avenue ✉ NY 14607 ☎ 316/244-8640

Sayville ☎ 516

BARS
■ **Bunkhouse** (AC B D G MA N s VS) 19-4, Sun -3/4 h
192 North Main Street ✉ NY 11782 ☎ 567-2865

Schenectady ☎ 518

BARS
■ **Blythewood, The** (B F G) 21-4.30 h
50 North Jay Street ✉ NY 12305 ☎ 382-9755
■ **Clinton Street Pub** (B glm) 12-4 h
159 Clinton Street ✉ NY 12305 ☎ 382-9173

NEW YORK

A charming 1841 Guest House located in New York's Greenwich Village Historic District.

All rooms with private bath, air conditioner, television, and telephone.
Most with fireplace and kitchenette.
$99 single/$149 double
Suites $130/$179

INCENTRA VILLAGE HOUSE
32 Eighth Avenue, NYC 10014
(between West 12th St. and Jane St.)
Tel 212/206-0007
Fax 212/604-0625

Prices may increase during Holiday and Special Event periods and are subject to change.

USA/New York - North Carolina Seaford ▸ Charlotte

Seaford ☎ 516

BARS
- **Auntie M's** (AC B f GLM MA S SNU STV) 17-4 h
3547 Merrick Road ✉ NY 11783

Syracuse ☎ 315

GAY INFO
- **Gay Telephone Line** 19-23 h
☎ 423-3599

BARS
- **Armory Pub** (B G LJ r) 8-2 h
400 South Clinton Street ✉ NY 13202 ☎ 471-6318
- **Ryan's Someplace Else** (B D G VS YG) Thu-Sat 20-2, Sun 12-2 h
408-410 Pearl Street ✉ NY 13203 ☎ 471-9499
- **Trexx** (B D Glm S YG) Thu, Sun 20-2, Fri, Sat -4 h
319 N. Clinton Street ☎ 474-6288

SEX SHOPS/BLUE MOVIES
- **Boulevard Books** (g VS) 24 hrs
2576 Erie Boulevard ✉ NY 13214 ☎ 446-1595

CRUISING
- Thunder Park

Troy ☎ 518

SAUNAS/BATHS
- **River Street Club** (G MA P SA SB VS WH WO) 12-? h
540 River Strret ✉ NY 12180 (20 min from Albany, corner of Hoosick Street) ☎ 272-0340
New club with game (pool table) room, video lounge and cyber cafe.

Utica ☎ 315

BARS
- **Options** (B D GLM) 17-2 h, closed Mon-Tue
1724 Oriskany Boulevard, Yorkville ✉ NY 13502 ☎ 724-9231
- **That Place** (B D G LJ MA OS P s) 20-2, Fri 16-2 h
216 Bleecker Street ✉ NY 13501 ☎ 724-1446

BOOK SHOPS
- **Adult World**
319 Oriskany Boulevard, Yorkville ✉ NY 13495
- **Playtime Boutique**
626 Orinsky Boulevard, Yorkville ✉ NY 14395

GENERAL GROUPS
- **Lesbian and Gay Concerns Network**
c/o UU Church, 12 Ford Avenue, Oneonta, NY 13820

FETISH GROUPS
- **Utica Tri s, M.C., Gay Men's Leather & Levi Club** (G LJ)
PO Box 425 ✉ NY 13503-0425

White Plains ☎ 914

PUBLICATIONS
- **Gayzette**
156 South Broadway ✉ NY 10605 ☎ 328-6463 🖨 771-9663
📧 Gayzette1@aol.com
Monthly newspaper for New York, Bergen county, Westchester, Rockland, Fairfield (CT), Bergen (NJ), New York City and Long Island. Free at gay venues.

BARS
- **Stutz** (B D G S VS) Mon-Fri 17-4, Sat Sun 20-4 h
202 Westchester Avenue ✉ NY 10601 ☎ 761-3100

CRUISING
- Rest Stop (15 miles north on I-684)

USA-North Carolina

Location: East USA
Initials: NCA
Time: GMT -5
Area: 139.397 km^2 / 57.013 sq mi.
Population: 7,425,000
Capital: Raleigh

Asheville ☎ 828

BARS
- **Hairspray / Club Mix** (B G lj S) HC: 19-2.30, Barbershop: Tue-Sun 21-2.30, CM: Thu Fri 22-3, Sat 22-6 h
38 North French Broad Avenue ✉ NC 28801 ☎ 258-2027
- **O'Henry's** (AC B d GLM lj MA N P S SNU STV) 12-2 h
59 Haywood Street ✉ NC 28801 ☎ 254-1891

DANCECLUBS
- **Scandals** (B CC D f GLM MA P S STV VS WE) Fri, Sat 22-3 h
11 Grove Street ✉ NC 28801 ☎ 252-2838

HEALTH GROUPS
- **Western NC AIDS Project**
PO Box 2411 ✉ NC 28802 ☎ 252-7489

CRUISING
- "The Cage" (block around Federal Building)

Charlotte ☎ 704

PUBLICATIONS
- **Q-Notes**
PO Box 221841 ✉ NC 28222-1841 ☎ 531-9988 🖨 531-1361
📧 editor@q-notes.com 🌐 www.q-notes.com
Biweekly GLBT magazine.

BARS
- **Central Station** (B G MG)
2131 Central Avenue ☎ 377-0906
- **Chasers** (B d GLM P SNU VS) 17-2, Sun 16-2 h
3217 The Plaza ✉ NC ☎ 339-0500
- **Hartigan's Pub** (B GLM F N)
601 S. Cedar Street ☎ 347-1841
- **Liaisons** (AC B CC f Glm OS S VS) 16-1 h
316 Rensselaer Avenue ✉ NC 28203 ☎ 376-1617
Popular

CAFES
- **Tic Toc Coffee Shop** (A f g OS)
512 N. Tyron Street ☎ 375-5750

DANCECLUBS
- **Club Myxx** (B D glm P)
3110 N. Tyron Street ☎ 525-5001
- **Mythos** (AC B CC D g P STV YG) Wed-Thu 22-3 h, Fri 22-6 h, Sat 22-4 h, Sun var. special events.
300 North College Street ✉ NC 28202 (City center) ☎ 375-8765

Charlotte ▶ Raleigh — **North Carolina/USA**

■ **Scorpio's Lounge** (B D GLM S VS) 21-2 h
2301 Freedom Drive ✉ NC 28208 ☎ 373-9640
■ **300 East Stonewall** (B D GLM MA OS) WE -4 h
300 East Stonewall ☎ 347-4200
Very popular

RESTAURANTS
■ **Cosmos Café** (B F NG)
6th Street & N. College Street ☎ 372-3553
■ **Fat City** (B F NG)
3127 N. Davidson Street ☎ 343-0240
■ **300 East** (B F NG)
300 East Boulevard ☎ 332-6507

SEX SHOPS/BLUE MOVIES
■ **Independence News** (G MA VS)
3205 The Plaza ☎ 332-8430
■ **Queen City Video & News** (g MA VS)
2320 Wilkinson Boulevard ☎ 344-9459

BOOK SHOPS
■ **White Rabbit Books**
834 Central Avenue ☎ 377-4067
Good selection of magazines, videos and guides.

GIFT & PRIDE SHOPS
■ **Urban Evolution**
1329 East Boulevard ☎ 332-8644

HEALTH GROUPS
■ **AIDS Hotline** Mon-Fri 8.30-17 h
☎ 333-AIDS (2437)

CRUISING
-Freedom Park (AYOR)
-Plaza Road (AYOR R)
-South Park Shopping Mall

Durham ☎ 919

BARS
■ **Boxer's** (AC B D G S YG) Tue-Sat 20.30-3 h Sun 18-? h
5504 Chapel Hill Boulevard ✉ NC 27707 *(at Straw Valley, Route 15-501 at I-40)* ☎ 489-7678
■ **Boxer's Ringside** (B D G)
308 West Main St.

SEX SHOPS/BLUE MOVIES
■ **Atlantis Video News** (G VS) Mon-Thu 11-2, Fri Sat 11-17, Sun 13-2 h
522 East Main Street ✉ NC 27701 ☎ 682-7469
Gay magazines, video rentals, sex goods, peep shows.

Fayetteville ☎ 910

DANCECLUBS
■ **Spektrum** (B D G SNU STV) 17-3 h
107 Swain Street ☎ 868-4279
■ **Studio 315** (B D G MA SNU STV)
315 Hay Street

Greensboro ☎ 336

BARS
■ **The Palms** (B d GLM N S) 21-1.30 h
413 North Eugene Street ✉ NC 27401 ☎ 272-6307

DANCECLUBS
■ **Warehouse 29** (AC B D Glm OS P SNU VS WE) Fri-Sat 21.30-3.30, Sun 15-24 h, closed Mon-Thu
1011 Arnold Street ✉ NC 27405 ☎ 333-9333

GIFT & PRIDE SHOPS
■ **White Rabbit Books & Things** (GLM) Mon-Sat 10-21, Sun 12-20 h
1833 Spring Garden Street ✉ NC 27403 ☎ 272-7604

HEALTH GROUPS
■ **TRIAD Health Project**
PO Box 5716 ✉ NC 27435 ☎ 275-1654

Hickory ☎ 828

DANCECLUBS
■ **Club Cabaret** (B D GLM MA)
101 North Center Street ☎ 322-8103

Raleigh ☎ 919

PUBLICATIONS
■ **Front Page**
PO Box 27928 ✉ NC 27611 ☎ 829-0181 🖷 829-0830
✉ frntpage@aol.com 🖳 www.frontpagenews.com
Biweekly publication with local and international features, classifieds. Serving North and South Carolina.

BARS
■ **Flex** (B D G LJ) 17-?, Sun 14-? h
2 South West Street ☎ 832-8855
Special theme nights
■ **Legends** (AC B D Glm P S YG) Mon-Sat 20-1, Sun 17-1 h, Thu women only
330 West Hargett Street ✉ NC 27601 ☎ 831-8888
Very popular. Cruisy atmosphere.

DANCECLUBS
■ **Capital Corral** (AC B CC D G LJ MA P VS WE) 20-? h, Sun 16-? h
313 West Hargett ✉ NC 27601 ☎ 755-9599

SEX SHOPS/BLUE MOVIES
■ **Bachelor's Video** Mon-Thu 10-2, Fri-Sun 10-3 h
3411 South Wilmington Street ✉ NC 27603 *(next to Pizza Hut, no sign)* ☎ 779-0995
Gay books, magazines, video rental, peep shows.
■ **Our Place** (AC CC G MA VS) 24 h
327 West Hargett Street ✉ NC 27609 ☎ 833-8968
Video booths, video tapes, tape rentals.

BOOK SHOPS
■ **Adult Books** (g VS) 0-24 h
1433 South Wilmington Street ✉ NC 27603
Books, porno magazines, video rental, peep shows, sex goods.

GIFT & PRIDE SHOPS
■ **White Rabbit Books & Things** (GLM) Mon-Fri 11-21, Sat 11-19, Sun 13-18 h
309 West Martin Street ✉ NC 27601 ☎ 856-1429
Gay and lesbian articles from books to videos.

CRUISING
-West Hargett Street (around gay bars and bookstore)
-Unstead State Park (Glenwood Avenue, near Brownleigh Drive. In cars and around Lake Area. Take steps down to Lake-follow path to the left. Daytime only. Be discreet.)

USA/North Carolina - Ohio | Wilmington ▸ Cincinnati

Wilmington ☎ 910

BARS
■ **Mickey Ratz** (AC B D GLM MA OS P SNU STV) 17-2.30 h, closed Mon
115 South Front Street ✉ NC 28401 ☎ 251-1289

DANCECLUBS
■ **Nocturna** (AC D DR GLM OS S YG) 21-4 h
121 Grace Street ☎ 815-8583

GUEST HOUSES
■ **Inn on Orange. The** (CC glm H Pl)
410 Orange Street ✉ NC 28401 ☎ 815-0035 ☎ (800) 381-4666.

CRUISING
-Wrightsville Beach (north end)
-Hugh Macrae Park (Orange + 2nd Street, car cruising 20-0 h)

Wilson

CRUISING
-Parkwood Mall (mens restroom)
-Lake Wilson (parking lot near mens restroom)

USA-North Dakota

Location:	North USA
Initials:	ND
Time:	GMT -6
Area:	183.123 km² / 74,897 sq mi.
Population:	641,000
Capital:	Bismarck

Fargo ☎ 701

RESTAURANTS
■ **Fargo Fryn's Pan** (glm) 0-24 h
300 Main St ✉ ND 58103 ☎ 293-9952

BOOK SHOPS
■ **Adult Books and Cinema X**
417 NP Avenue, ✉ ND 58102 ☎ 232-9768

CRUISING
-Broadway (nights)
-Bus depot

USA-Ohio

Location:	Great Lakes region USA
Initials:	OH
Time:	GMT -5
Area:	116.103 km² / 47,486 sq mi.
Population:	11,186,000
Capital:	Columbus
Important gay cities:	Cincinnati, Cleveland and Columbus

Akron ☎ 330

BARS
■ **Adams Street Bar** (AC B D f G MA SNU STV) Mon-Fri 16.30-2.30, Sat 15-2.30, Sun 21-2.30 h
77 North Adams Street ✉ OH 44304 ☎ 434-9791
■ **Roseto Club** (B D F GLM) 18-1 h, closed Sun
627 South Arlington Street ✉ OH 44306 ☎ 724-4228
■ **Tear-ez** (B GLM MA) 11-2.30, Sun 23.30-2.30 h
360 South Main Street ☎ 376-0011
Popular

DANCECLUBS
■ **Interbelt Nite Club** (B D GLM VS WE YG) Mon, Wed, Fri-Sun 20-? h
70 North Howard Street ✉ OH 44308 ☎ 253-5700
The only all-gay disco in Akron. Patio bar in summer. Very popular.

SAUNAS/BATHS
■ **Akron Steam/Sauna** (G SB WH)
41 South Case Avenue ✉ OH 44305
■ **Club Akron Inc.** (G SA WH)
1339 East Market Street ✉ OH 44305 ☎ 784-0309

CRUISING
-Main Street near the Tear EZ and Club 358. (AYOR) (Also the side streets close by.)
-Main Street/Mill Street (in front of public library)
-Metropolitan Park in Goodyear Heights on Eastwood Avenue (in the parking lot by the baseball field)
-Railroad tracks under Talmadge Avenue/Glenwood Avenue

Canton ☎ 330

BARS
■ **La Casa's Golden Door** (B G MA N) 13-2.30 h
508 Cleveland Avenue N.W. ☎ 453-7432
■ **540 Club / Eagle** (AC B f G LJ N) Mon-Sat 21-2.30, Sun 18-2.30 h
540 Walnut Avenue North East ✉ OH 44702 (next to Y.M.C.A.)
☎ 456-8622

CAFES
■ **Sidestreet Cafe** (b BF f glm OS) 15-1 h
2360 Mahoning ☎ 453-8055

DANCECLUBS
■ **Boardwalk** (B D GLM MA S) 16-2.30 h, closed Sun
1227 West Tuscarawas Street ☎ 453-8000

Cincinnati ☎ 513

GAY INFO
■ **Gay and Lesbian Community Center** Mon-Fri 19-23 h
☎ 651-0070

BARS
■ **Colors** (B GLM MA N VS)
4042 Hamilton Avenue ✉ OH 45223 ☎ 681-6969
■ **Golden Lions** (B d GMG N S) 19-2.30 h
340 Ludlow Avenue ✉ OH 45202 ☎ 281-4179
■ **Milton's Tavern** (a B glm N)
301 Milton Street *(residential area, 1block north of Liberty at the Corner of Sycamore/Liberty St.)* ☎ 784-9938
New ownership.
■ **Plum Street Pipeline** (! AC B D f GLM lj MA S SNU STV OS YG) Sun-Thu 16-21.30, Fri Sat -3 h
241 West Court Street ✉ OH 45202 ☎ 241-5678
4 bars on 4 floors.
■ **Shirley's** (B D gLM) 20-2.30, Sun 16-2.30 h, closed Mon
2401 Vine Street ✉ OH 45219 ☎ 721-8483

Cincinnati ▶ Cleveland Ohio/USA

■ **Shooters** (B d G lj s) 16-2.30 h
927 Race Street ✉ OH 45219 ☏ 381-9900
■ **Simon Says** (B G N) 11-2.30, Sun 13-2.30 h
428 Walnut Street ✉ OH 45202 ☏ 381-8196
■ **Spurs** (B d G LJ s) 16-2.30 h
326 East 8th Street ☏ 621-2668
■ **Subway** (B D G N S) 17.30-2.30 h
609 Walnut Street ✉ OH 45202 ☏ 421-1294
■ **Vertigo** (B GLM MA N)
1 West Corry Street ☏ 684-9313

DANCECLUBS
■ **Dock** (B D GLM OS S VS) 20-2.30, Fri Sat 20-4 h
603 West Pete Rose Way ✉ OH 45202 ☏ 241-5623

RESTAURANTS
■ **Carol's On Main** (! B CC F GLM MA) Sun-Fri 11-2.30, Sat 16-2.30, meals -1 h
825 Main Street ✉ OH 45202 (downtown, between 8th&9th street) ☏ 651-2667
■ **Mullane's Parkside Cafe** (B F GLM MA)
723 Race Street ✉ OH 45202 ☏ 381-1331

LEATHER & FETISH SHOPS
■ **ACME Leather & Toy Co.** (G LJ) 16-2.30 h
326 East Eight Street ✉ OH 45202 (at Spurs) ☏ 241-6874

GUEST HOUSES
■ **Prospect Hill B&B** (AC BF CC e glm H WH)
408 Boal Street ✉ OH 45210 ☏ 421-4408 🖷 421-4408
🖳 www.bbonline.com/oh/prospect/
Old Victorian townhouse located on a hill overlooking the city. All rooms with Sat-TV, radio, fax, fireplaces and a sitting area. Rates double/shared bath USD-99-129 and double/private bath 109-129. A full bf buffet is incl. in the price. Non-smoking establishment.

SPORT GROUPS
■ **Frontrunners (and Walkers)**
☏ 651-0070

CRUISING
-Burnett Woods (AYOR)
-Mt. Airy Forest (AYOR)
-Mc Farland Street (between 3rd and 4th Street, after the bars close)

Cleveland ☏ 216
GAY INFO
■ **Lesbian & Gay Center** Mon-Fri 12-17 h
6600 Detroit Ave, PO Box 6177 ✉ OH 44101 ☏ 651-5428

PUBLICATIONS
■ **Gay People's Chronicle**
PO Box 5426 ✉ OH 44101 ☏ 631-8686 ☏ 426-5947
🖷 631-1052 🖳 editor@chronohio.com
🖳 www.gaypeopleschronicle.com
Weekly gay newspaper.

BARS
■ **Code Blue** (A AC B CC d GLM MA s SNU STV) closed Mon
1946 St. Clair Avenue ✉ OH 44114 ☏ 241-4663
■ **Five Cent Decision** (AC B D f GLM MA) 18-2.30 h
4365 State Road ✉ OH 44109 ☏ 661-1314

■ **Leather Stallion Saloon** (AC B G LJ MA OS s SNU) 15-2.30 h
2205 St. Clair Avenue ✉ OH 44114-4046 (downtown)
☏ 589-8588
Oldest gay bar in Cleveland, since 1970. Very popular Sun afternoon.
■ **MJ's Place** (B d G MA S) 16-2.30 h, closed Sun
11633 Lorain Ave. ✉ OH 44111 ☏ 476-1970
■ **Numbers** (B D G S VS YG) 22-3 h, closed Mon Thu
620 Frankfort Avenue ✉ OH 44113 ☏ 621-6900
Popular Wed/Sun
■ **Rockies** (AC B CC D G lj MA OS SNU VS) 16-2.3 h
9208 Detroit Avenue ✉ OH 44102 ☏ 961-3115
■ **Sexx** (B D G MA OS S) 10-2.30, Sun 12-2.30 h
11213 Detroit Avenue ✉ OH 44102 ☏ 221-8576
Cruise bar
■ **The Hawk** (B f G LJ s) 10-2.30 h, closed Sun
11217 Detroit Avenue ✉ OH 44102 (near 112th Street)
☏ 521-5443

DANCECLUBS
■ **Grid. The** (! AC B CC D G MA SNU VS YG) Mon-Thus 17-2.30 h, Fri-Sat 17-3 h, Sun 16-4.30 h
1281 West 9th Street ✉ OH 44113 (Warehouse district, downtown)
☏ 623-0113
Hight tech dance floor, tow levels, wideo, poo.l table, video games, pinball.
■ **U4ia Nite Club** (! B D Glm OS S tv WE) Fri-Sun 21.30-3 h
10630 Berea Road ✉ OH 44102 ☏ 631-7111
Cleveland's largest gay dance club.

RESTAURANTS
■ **My Friends** (B F glm MA)
11616 Detroit Avenue
Popular late-night restaurant

SEX SHOPS/BLUE MOVIES
■ **West Nine Street Video and News**
1273 West Ninth
Magazines, newspapers and wide selection of video titles

SAUNAS/BATHS
■ **Club. The** (b CC G MA OS SA SB SOL VS WH WO) 0-24 h
1448 West 32nd Street ✉ OH 44113 ☏ 961-2727
Bath house with sun deck and view on Lake Erie.
■ **Flex** (f G lj MA SA SB VS WH WO) 0-24 h
1293 West 9th Street ✉ OH 44113 (next to "The Grid" gay bar)
☏ 696-0595
One of the largest bathhouse in Ohio on 5 floors frequented by all types of men.

BOOK SHOPS
■ **Body Language** (CC GLM) 11-22, Sun 13 -18 h
11424 Lorain Avenue/West 115th Street ✉ OH 44111 (at Lorain)
☏ 251-3330
Books, cards, (leather)clothing, magazines and erotic videos & DVD's.
■ **Books & Magazines** Mon-Sat 9.30-17.15 h
5 Tation Road

GENERAL GROUPS
■ **Foot Fraternity** (G MA)
P.O.Box 24102 ✉ OH 44124 ☏ +1-440-449-4114
🖷 +1-440-449-0114
International group for friends of feed, etc.

HEALTH GROUPS
■ **Ohio Dept of Health AIDS Hotline** 13-23 h
PO Box 61 77 ✉ OH 44101 ☏ (800) 322-2437

USA/Ohio Cleveland ▶ Columbus

RELIGIOUS GROUPS
■ **Chevrei Tikva** 1st/3rd Fri
PO Box 181 20 ✉ OH 44118 ☎ 932-5551
Jewish gays & lesbians.

CRUISING
-Ambassador Bowling Lanes (Sun 13 h)
-Edgewater Park (AYOR)
-Metropolitan Park (AYOR) (Memphis & Tiedman Street)
-N. Chagrin Reservation Park (AYOR)

Columbus ☎ 614

GAY INFO
■ **Stonewall Columbus** (AC GLM MA) Mon-Thu 10-19, Fri -17 h
1160 North High Street ✉ OH 43201-2411 ☎ 299-7764
📠 299-4408 💻 stnwall@ix.netcom.com
Organization fighting for gay and lesbian rights in Ohio.

PUBLICATIONS
■ **Outlook Newspaper**
700 Ackerman Road #600 ✉ OH 43202 ☎ 268-8525
📠 261-8120 💻 editor@outlooknews.com
🖥 www.outlooknews.com
Biweekly GLB newspaper.
■ **Stonewall Journal**
PO Box 10814 ✉ OH 43101 ☎ 299.7764 📠 299.4408
💻 stnwall@ix.netcom.com 🖥 www.stonewall-columbus.org
Monthly GL publication.

BARS
■ **Club Diversity** (AC B CC GLM MA N s) Tue-Thu 16-1 h,
Fri 16-2.30, Sat 18-2.30 closed Sun, Mon
124 East Main Street ✉ OH 43215 *(Downtown Colombus)*
☎ 224 40 50
■ **Club 20** (B G N S) 13-2.30, Sat 11-2.30 h
20 East Duncan Street ✉ OH 43202 ☎ 261-9111
■ **Downtown Connection** (B G MA)
1156 North High Street ✉ OH 43201 ☎ 299-4880
Gay sports bar
■ **Eagle in Exile** (AC B G LJ MA WE) Wed-Sat 21-2.30 h
893 North 4th Street ✉ OH 43201 ☎ 294-0069
Strict dress code
■ **Grapevine Café** (AC B BF F GLM MA S) Tue-Sat 17-1,
Sun 12-23 h
73 East Gay Street ✉ OH 43215 *(Downtown)* ☎ 221-8463
Sun Brunch.
■ **Havana Video Lounge** (AC B CC G MA s VS) 17-2.30 h
862 North High Street ✉ OH 43215 *(in the heart of the Short North at First Avenue)* ☎ 421-9697
Bar with videos and cigar lounge.
■ **Remo's** (AC B CC d F G lj MA N SNU STV WE) Mon-Sat 9-2.30 h
1409 South High Street ✉ OH 43207 ☎ 443-4224
■ **Slammers** (B F GLM OS) 11-1, WE 15-1 h
202 East Long Street ✉ OH 43215 ☎ 224-8880
■ **Summit Station** (B gLM MA S)
2210 Summit Street ✉ OH 43201 ☎ 261-9634
■ **Tradewinds II** (B d G LJ) Tue-Sun 16-2.30, Disco Fri Sun 20-2.30 h, Sat 22-2.30 h
117 East Chestnut Street ✉ OH 43215 ☎ 461-4110
3rd Fri Club Centurion (GLM LJ)
■ **Tremont** (B G MG N S) 10-2.30, Sun 13-23 h
708 South High Street ✉ OH 43206 ☎ 445-9365

■ **Trends** (B G MA) 17-2.30 h
40 East Long Street ✉ OH 43215-2911 *(in front of Garage, near High Street)* ☎ 461-0076

CAFES
■ **Coffee Table** (A AC BF f GLM MA N OS WE) Mon-Thu 7-24, Fri -1,
Sat 8-1, Sun 9-22 h
731 North High Street ✉ OH 43215 ☎ 297-1177
■ **Hollywood & High** (AC BF CC f GLM OS) Mon-Thu 7-23, Fri -24,
Sat 8-24, Sun 9-22 h
850 North High Street ✉ OH 43215 ☎ 294-2233

DANCECLUBS
■ **Axis** (B D G MA) Thu-Sun 22-2.30 h
630 North High Street ✉ OH 43215 ☎ 291-4008
■ **Club Alive!** (b f D GLM MA)
203 King Avenue ✉ OH 43201 ☎ 297-8990
■ **Columbus Eagle** (D G MA SNU VS) 20-2.30 h
232 North 3rd Street ✉ OH 43215 *(at Hickory)* ☎ 228-2804
■ **Garage** (B D G STV OS) 17-2.30 h
40 East Long Street ✉ 43215-2911 *(behind Trends, near High Street)*
☎ 461-0076
Large dancefloor, especially popular with students on Sat
■ **Wall Street** (D GLM MA s STV VS) Wed-Sun 20-2.30 h, closed Mon&Tue
144 North Wall Street ✉ OH 43215 ☎ 464-2800

RESTAURANTS
■ **Antibes. L'** (AC B CC F glm) Tue-Thu 17-21, Fri Sat -22 h, closed Sun-Mon
772 North High Street, Suite 106 ✉ OH 43215-1456 *(Near the convention center, side entrance)* ☎ 291-1666
■ **King Avenue Coffeehouse** (A AC CC F glm MA) Mon 17-22, Tue-Thu 11-22, Fri-Sat -23 h, Sun brunch: 10-15, bistro 17-22 h
247 King Avenue ✉ OH 43201 *(near the corner of King and Neil Avenues)* ☎ 294-8287
Vegetarian cuisine. Lunch, dinner, juice bar, catering.
■ **Out on Main** (AC B CC F GLM MA s WE) 16-22, Fri,Sat -23, Sun Brunch 11-14.30, 17-21 h
122 East Main Street ✉ OH 43215 *(downtown)* ☎ 224-9510
Popular restaurant and bar. Delicious food.
■ **Union Station Video Café** (AC B CC F G MA VS) 11-2.30 h
630 North High Street ✉ OH 43201 *(one block north of the convention center in Short North)* ☎ 228-3546
Restaurant and video bar.

SAUNAS/BATHS
■ **Club Columbus** (AC CC G MA P PI SA SB WH WO) 0-24 h
795 West 5th Avenue ✉ OH 43212 ☎ 291-0049
Sauna with complete gym equipment.

BOOK SHOPS
■ **An Open Book** 10-22, Sun 10-20 h
761 North High Street ✉ OH 43215 ☎ 291-0080

VIDEO SHOPS
■ **Metro Video** (AC CC GLM) Mon-Sat 11-24, Sun 12-24 h
848 North High Street ✉ OH 43215 ☎ 291-7962

HOTELS
■ **Five Forty-Two** (AC BF GLM H OS)
542 Mohawk Street ☎ 621-1741
Small B&B. Room with private bath, color cable TV and VCR. Rates US$ 75-95. No kids or pets.

1316 *SPARTACUS* 2001/2002

Columbus ▶ Toledo Ohio/USA

GUEST HOUSES
■ **The Brewmaster's House** (AC BF G H) 24 h
1083 S. High Street ✉ OH 43206 *(Exit US Route 71-5 at Greenlawn to High, located lext to BP service station at corner of High and Greenlawn)* ☎ 449-8298 449-8663
 brewmastershouse@compuserve.com
 www.g-net.com/brewmastershouse

GENERAL GROUPS
■ **Capital LGB Association**
☎ 236-6269
Social group for LGB students at Capital University.
■ **Men of All Colors together**
1160 North High Street ✉ OH 43201-2411 ☎ 267-1610
■ **PFLAG-Parents, Families & Friends of Lesbians and Gays**
Meets 4th Sun 14-16 h at Unitarian Universalist Church, 93 West Weisheimer
PO Box 340101 ✉ OH 43234 ☎ 227-9355

FETISH GROUPS
■ **Dragon Leather Club**
PO Box 06417 ✉ OH 43206 ☎ 258-7100

HELP WITH PROBLEMS
■ **Coming Out Support Group for Men** 2nd/4th Mon 19 h
☎ 299-7764 299-4408

SPECIAL INTEREST GROUPS
■ **Columbus Asians and Friends** (GLM)
PO Box 10814 ✉ OH 43201 ☎ 488-4297
■ **The Columbus Gay Men's Chorus**
177 Naghten Street ✉ OH 43215-2613 ☎ 228-2462
■ **GLB Student Services**
OSU, Ohio Union, 1739 North High Street ✉ OH 43210
☎ 292-6100

CRUISING
-O.S.U. Botany and Zoology Building (Basement, Sep-Jun 9-21 h, Jul-Aug 9-17 h, closed Sat Sun)
-Larkins Hall (Gymnasium, 4th floor, 7-22 h)
-Ohio Union (AYOR) (Basement)
-The Beach (Whittier Street, west of High and Front Streets)
-Big Walnut Park (on Livingston Avenue east of Hamilton Street)
-Park of Roses (on North High, just north of Clintonville, next to public library)
-Bull Run Park (AYOR OG) (on Clime Road, west of Georgesville Road, before 23 h)
-Lou Berliner Park (AYOR) (on Greenlawn Avenue, between High Street and I-71, before 23 h, busy all year)

Dayton ☎ 937

GAY INFO
■ **Dayton GLB Hotline**
☎ 274-1776

BARS
■ **Asylum. The** (B G MA N)
605 East Patterson Boulevard
■ **City Cafe** (B BF f Glm MA r stv snu)
121 North Ludlow *(Talbot Towers Building)* ☎ 223-1377
Busy every night of the week. Various nightly entertainment, karaoke, strippers, drag shows, etc., mainly for gay men of all ages, very cruisy, pool table.

■ **D.J.'s Saloon** (AC B CC f G LJ MG OS SNU VS) Mon-Fri 12-2.30, Sat-Sun 15-2.30 h
237 North Main Street ✉ OH 45402 ☎ 223-7340
■ **Jessie's Celebrity Club** (AC B D E GLM lj MA SNU STV VS) Sun-Thu 20-2.30, Fri-Sat -4 h
850 North Main Street ✉ OH 45405 ☎ 461-2582
■ **Right Corner. The** (AC B CC GLM MA N) 12-2.30, Sun 13-2.30 h
105 East Third Street ✉ OH 45402 ☎ 228-1285
■ **Stage Door** (B G lj) 12-2.30 h
44 North Jefferson Street ✉ OH 45402 ☎ 223-7418
■ **1470 West** (B D G MA SNU STV)
34 North Jefferson ☎ 293-0066

FETISH GROUPS
■ **Great Lakes Leather Coalition**
PO Box 24426 ✉ OH 45424 ☎ 233-9162

CRUISING
-DeWeese Park
-Wright State University WSU (Library, Millet Hall on 2nd floor)

Lima ☎ 419

BARS
■ **Somewhere** (AC B D f GLM MA s SNU STV) Sun-Thu 19-?, Fri Sat 20-? h
804 West North Street ✉ OH 45801 ☎ 227-7288

Logan ☎ 740

HOTELS
■ **Summit Lodge Resort** (BF glm H PI SA WH)
PO Box 951-Code A ✉ OH 43138 ☎ 385-6822

GUEST HOUSES
■ **Spring Wood Hocking Hills Cabins** (b GLM H WH)
28560 Blackjack Road ✉ OH 43138 ☎ 385-2042
Cabins for 4 or 8 people with private baths, kitchenettes, refridgerators and fireplace. Kids ok. rates US$ 85-90.

Monroe ☎ 513

BARS
■ **Old Street Saloon** (B GLM MA N)
13 Old Street ✉ OH 45050 ☎ 539-9183

Newark ☎ 614

BARS
■ **Bulldog Lounge** (B G MA N)
35 North Third Street ✉ OH 43055 ☎ 345-9729

Springfield ☎ 937

BARS
■ **Chances** (B GLM MA OS P S) 20.30-2.30 h, Tue closed
1912-1914 Edwards Avenue ✉ OH 45503 ☎ 324-0383

Toledo ☎ 419

BARS
■ **Blue Jeans** (B F GLM)
3606 Sylvania Avenue ✉ OH 43623 ☎ 474-0690
■ **Bretz** (B D G VS) Mon-Thu 14-2.30, Fri Sat 14-4 h
2012 Adams Street ✉ OH 43624 ☎ 243-1900

USA/Ohio - Oregon — Toledo ▸ Medford

■ **Caesar's Show Bar** (B D glm) Wed-Sun 19-2.30 h
133 North Erie Street ✉ OH 43624 ☎ 241-5140
■ **Hooterville Station** (B D LJ) 17.30-2.30 h
119 North Erie Street ✉ OH 43624 ☎ 241-5140
■ **Rustler Saloon** (B G LJ) 14-2.30 h
4023 Monroe Street ✉ OH 43606 *(rear entrance)* ☎ 472-8278

CRUISING
-Franklin Park Mall
-Ontario Street (between Washington Street and Jefferson Street)
-Southwick Mall

Warren ☎ 330

BARS
■ **Queen of Hearts. The** (AC B d f GLM lj MA OS r snu) 14-2.30 h, Happy Hour 14-21 h
132-134 Pine Avenue South East ✉ OH 44481 ☎ 395-1100

DANCECLUBS
■ **Crazy Duck** (B D GLM MA S) 17-2.30, Sat 20-2.30 h
121 Pine Avenue ☎ 394-3825

Youngstown ☎ 330

BARS
■ **Sophie's Lounge** (B D f GLM lj MA r S SNU STV TV VS WE) Mon-Fri 17-2.30, Sat 21-2.30, Sun 22-2.30 h
2 East LaClede Avenue ✉ OH 44507 ☎ 782-8080

USA-Oklahoma

Location: Middlewest USA
Initials: OK
Time: GMT -6
Area: 181.048 km² / 74,048 sq mi.
Population: 3,317,000
Capital: Oklahoma City

Oklahoma City ☎ 405

GAY INFO
■ **Gay and Lesbian Community Services Center** 19-22, Fri Sat -24 h
☎ 525-2437

PUBLICATIONS
■ **Gayly Oklahoman** 9.30-17 h
PO Box 60930 ✉ OK 73146 ☎ 528-0800 🖨 528-0796
📧 gaylyok@aol.com 💻 www.gayly.com
Biweekly newspaper with events calendar, guide to Oklahoma, book review, classified ads.

BARS
■ **Copa. The** (B D GLM YG)
2200 North-West 39th Expressway ✉ OK 73112 *(at the Habana Inn)* ☎ 528-2221
■ **Finishline. The** (B D GLM lj) 12-? h
2200 North-West 39th Expressway ✉ OK 73112 *(at the Habana Inn)* ☎ 528-2221
■ **Park. The** (A B d G OS SNU VS) 17-2 h, Sun 15-2 h
2125 North West 39th Street ✉ OK 73112 ☎ 528-4690
■ **Tramps** (AC B d f G lj MA OS P r STV VS) 12-2 h
2201 North West 39th Street ✉ OK 73112 ☎ 521-9898

DANCECLUBS
■ **Angles** (B D GLM s VS YG) Wed-Sun 21-2 h, Tea dance Sun
2117 North West 39th Street ✉ OK 73112 ☎ 528-0050
Modern gay disco, video etc.
■ **Wreck Room. The** (D f YG) Fri Sat 21-? h
2127 North West 39th Street ☎ 525-7610
Non alcoholic drinks only.

HOTELS
■ **Habana Inn Gay Hotel Complex** (AC B BF CC D EF GLM H MA N PI STV)
2200 North West 39th Expressway ✉ OK 73112 ☎ 528-2221
☎ 800-988-22 21 (Reservation only) 🖨 528 04 96
💻 www.habanainn.com
30 double rooms, 145 single rooms. All rooms with shower/bath & WC, wash-basin, telephone, Satellite TV, Air-conditioning, heating. This huge gay complex has 2 swimming pols, 3 gay clubs, a restaurant, an adult gift shop and is located in the heart of the gay strip. Weekley rates available.

CRUISING
-Lake Heffner (AYOR)
-Shepperd Mall
-Trosper Park

Tulsa ☎ 918

BARS
■ **Lola's** (B G STV)
2630 East 15th Street ✉ OK 74104 ☎ 749-1563
■ **Silver Star Saloon** (B D G) Wed-Sun 19-2 h
1565 South Sheridan ✉ OK 74112 ☎ 834-4234
■ **Tool Box** (B D G LJ) 12-2 h
1338 East 3rd Street ✉ OK 74120 ☎ 584-1308

CRUISING
-Boulder and Boston (between 5th and 10th Streets)
-River Parks (at 21st Street)
-Turkey Mountain Park (61st and South Elwood Streets)
-Woodward Park

USA-Oregon

Location: Northwest USA
Initials: OR
Time: GMT -8
Area: 254.819 km² / 104,221 sq mi.
Population: 3,244,000
Capital: Salem

Eugene ☎ 541

BARS
■ **Club Arena** (AC B D GLM s VS) 21-2.30 h
959 Pearl Street ✉ OR 97401 ☎ 683-2360

GENERAL GROUPS
■ **MPowerment Project** Thu Fri 15-18, Sat 15-22 h
1414 Kincaid Street ✉ OR 97403 ☎ 683-4303

Medford ☎ 541

GIFT & PRIDE SHOPS
■ **Castle Superstore** (CC GLM TV) Sun-Thu 9-1, Fri&Sat - 2 h
1113 Progress Drive ✉ OR 97504 ☎ 608-9540
Vidoes, leather, lingerie, magazines, toys, novelties, books, DVD's.

Portland ▶ Salem Oregon/USA

Portland ☏ 503

PUBLICATIONS
■ **Just Out**
PO Box 14400 ✉ OR 97293-0400 ☏ 236-1252 📠 236-1257
💻 marty@justout.com
Oregon's biweekly GL publication.

BARS
■ **Boxx's** (B GLM VS YG) 12-2.30 h
1035 South West Stark Street ✉ OR 97205 ☏ 226-4171
Very popular gay night on Thu
■ **Brigg. The** (B D glm VS WE YG) 15-4 Sun-Thu, Thu (G), Fri-Sat (glm)
1035 South West Stark Street ✉ OR 97205 *(connected to Boxx's)*
☏ 226-4171
More straight.
■ **Eagle. The** (B DR G LJ MG VS)
1300 West Burnside Street ✉ OR 97209 ☏ 241-0105
Popular. Darkroom upstairs.
■ **Embers. The** (B D f GLM MA STV WE)
110 North West Broadway ✉ OR 97209 ☏ 222-3082
Very popular bar/disco, good nightly Drag shows.
■ **Scandals** (AC B F G MA) 11.30-2.30 h
1038 South West Stark Street ✉ OR 97205 ☏ 227 58 87
■ **Silverado** (B d F G MA SNU VS) 9-2.30 h
1217 South West Stark Street ✉ OR 97205 ☏ 224-4493
Wed-Sun 20-2h male strippers. Cruisy atmosphere. Very popular.
■ **Three Sisters Tavern** (B D F GLM) 12.30-2.30 h, Sat Sun 12.30-3 h
1125 South West Stark Street ☏ 228-0486
Latino crowd and latino dance music.

DANCECLUBS
■ **LaLuna** (B D GLM MA) Mon
215 South East 9th Street ☏ 241-5862
■ **Panorama** (b CC D g lj MA WE) Fri 21-4 h, Sat -4.30 h
341 SW 10th Street ✉ OR 97205 *(next to Boxx's and the Brigg)*
☏ 221-7262

RESTAURANTS
■ **Chameleon** (B F glm MA) 17-21.30 h
2000 North East 40th ☏ 460-0284
Good food. Popular with gays and lesbians.
■ **Hobo's** (b F glm S) 16-2 h
120 North West 3rd Avenue ✉ OR 97209 *(Old Town)* ☏ 224-3285
Popular for drinks and dinner after work.
■ **JOQ's** (B G MA)
2512 North East Broadway ☏ 287-4210
■ **Saucebox** (AC B CC D F f glm MA OS) Tue-Thu 11.30-24, Fri -2, Sat 17-2 h
214 South West Broadway ✉ OR 97205 ☏ 241-3393
Pan-Asian restaurant for dining and dancing.
■ **Starky's** (AC B CC F GLM MA OS) Mon-Sat 11-2 h, Sun 9.30-2 h
2913 SE Stark Street ✉ OR 97214 ☏ 230-7980

SHOWS
■ **Darcelle XV** (B CC F glm S STV) Wed-Sat 13-2 h
208 North West 3rd Avenue ✉ OR 97209 *(in Chinatown)*
☏ 222-5338

SAUNAS/BATHS
■ **Club Portland** (g SA)
303 South West 12th Avenue ✉ OR 97205 ☏ 227-9992

■ **Continental Club** (G SA)
303 SW 12th Ave. ✉ OR 97205 ☏ 227-9992

GUEST HOUSES
■ **Sullivan's Gulch B&B** (BF CC GLM H)
1744 North East Clackamas Street ✉ OR 97232 ☏ 331-1104
📠 331-1575 💻 thegulch@teleport.com
💻 www.sullivansgulch.com
Small B&B in a restored Portland home built in 1907; quiet neighbourhood. Smoke free establishment. All rooms with telephone, TV and radio, two with balcony. Rates room/private bath US$ 85 and with shared bath $ 70 and incl. an expanded continental bf.

GENERAL GROUPS
■ **Alliance. The** Tue-Fri 13-19 h. Meets Wed 11.30-12.30 h
12000 South West 48th Street ✉ OR 97219 ☏ 977-4131
📠 977-4740 💻 mfiorent@pcc.edu
■ **Gentle Giants of Oregon**
PO Box 1844 ✉ OR 97207 ☏ 241-4535
💻 chubstuf@teleport.com
■ **LGBA-Lesbian, Gay, Bisexual Alliance**
PO Box 751 ✉ OR 97201 ☏ 725-5681 💻 lgba@sg.ess.pdx.edu.
■ **Parents and Friends of Lesbians and Gays (PFLAG)**
PO Box 8944 ✉ OR 97207 ☏ 232-7676

HEALTH GROUPS
■ **Cascade AIDS Project - Speak to your Brother** 9-17 h
620 South West 5th Avenue, Suite 300 ✉ OR 97204 ☏ 223-5907
Service and information for HIV positive people and people living with Aids. Discussion groups, social activities, HIV-testing.
■ **HIV Center**
3835 South West Kelly Street ☏ 223-3444
■ **Names Project Portland Chapter**
PO Box 5423 ✉ OR 97228 ☏ 797-2881
💻 aidsquiltportland@aidsquilt.net

SPECIAL INTEREST GROUPS
■ **Cascade Bears**
625 South West 10th Avenue #125 ✉ OR 97205
■ **Portland Gay Men's Chorus**
PO Box 3223 ✉ OR 97208 ☏ 460-3689
■ **Sexual Minority Youth Recreation Center - SMYRC** (GLM S TV YG) Mon 16-22, Wed -23, Fri Sat -24 h
424 East Burnside ✉ OR 97214 ☏ 872-9664 📠 239.8107
💻 www.smyrc.org

SPORT GROUPS
■ **F.I.T.S. Gay and Lesbian Bowling League**
3031 South East Powell ✉ OR 97207 ☏ 581-1804 📠 581-1804

CRUISING
-Rest Stop (I-5, both sides)
-Columbia Park (AYOR)
-East Delta Park (showers)
-Rooster Rock State Park (East end of beach, 30 miles East of Portland)
-Sauvie's Island (West end of beach near parking lot)
-Washington Park (by Lewis and Clark Mounument, Burnside & 25th)

Salem ☏ 503

PUBLICATIONS
■ **Community News**
PO Box 663 ✉ OR 97308-0663 ☏ 363-0006
Oregon's oldest monthly gay & lesbian newspaper, 16 to 32 pages.

SPARTACUS 2001/2002 |1319

USA/Oregon - Pennsylvania — Tigard ▶ New Hope

Tigard ☎ 503

TRAVEL AND TRANSPORT
■ **Travel Shop. The** Mon-Fri 9-18, WE 10-14 h
10115 SW Nimbus Ave., Suite 600 ✉ OR 97223 ☎ 648-8533
☎ (888) 643- 8786 (toll-free) 🖷 624-1339
💻 thetravelshop@gay.com home.gay.com/thetravelshop

Tiller ☎ 514

CAMPING
■ **Kalles Family Ranch** (GLM MA)
233 Jackson Creek Road ✉ OR 97484 ☎ 825-3271 🖷 825-3299
✉ rkalles@pioneer-net.com www.coguide.com/out/kalles.htm
Large outdoor kitchen, wash house with bath and shower. Rates US$ 16 per night + US$ 2 for electric and water hookup. Only Gay and Lesbian campground in Oregon.

USA-Pennsylvania

Location: Northeast USA
Initials: PA
Time: GMT -5
Area: 119.291 km² / 48,790 sq mi.
Population: 12,020,000
Capital: Harrisburg
Important gay cities: Philadelphia, Pittsburgh

Altoona ☎ 814

BARS
■ **Escapade** (B GLM MA)
2523 Union Avenue ✉ PA 16602 ☎ 946-8155

HEALTH GROUPS
■ **AIDS Intervention Project**
PO Box 352 ✉ PA 16603 ☎ (1-800) 445-6262

HELP WITH PROBLEMS
■ **Gay, Lesbian, Bisexual Help line of Altoona**
☎ 942-8101

Erie ☎ 814

BARS
■ **Embers. The** (AC B D f GLM MA s)
1711 State Street ✉ PA 16501 ☎ 459-1711

RESTAURANTS
■ **Village Restaurant and Bar** (B F glm MA)
133 West 18th Street ☎ 452-0125

CRUISING
-Erie Mall (downtown)
-Preque Isle Park Beach

Harrisburg ☎ 717

GAY INFO
■ **Gay & Lesbian Switchboard** Mon-Fri 18-22 h
PO Box 872 ✉ PA 17108 ☎ 234-0328

BARS
■ **Mary's Brownstone** (B G lj MA)
412 Forster Street ☎ 234-7009
Country-western/neighborhood bar, some Levis/Leather scene, pool table.
■ **Neptune Lounge** (B d F G N s WE)
268 North Street ✉ PA 17101 ☎ 233-3078
■ **Strawberry Cafe** (B f G N) closed Sun
704 North 3rd Street ✉ PA 17113 ☎ 234-4228
Neighborhood bar with jukebox.

CAFES
■ **North Street Cafe** (A B glm s) Mond 6-21, Tue Wed -19, Thu-Sat -20, Sun -17 h
231 North Street ✉ PA 17101 ☎ 233-7194
Occasionally special shows, weekly poetry readings and other performance art events.

DANCECLUBS
■ **Stallions** (B D G s WE)
706 North Third Street ☎ 232-3060
Nightclub, games, dart board. DJ on weekends, shows.

RESTAURANTS
■ **Paper Moon. The**
268 North Street *(next to the Neptune Lounge)* ☎ 233-0581
Casual dining, good food, brunch on Sun.

GENERAL GROUPS
■ **Pennsylvania Council for Sexual Minorities**
238 Main Capital Building ✉ PA 17120

Lancaster ☎ 717

BARS
■ **Tally Ho** (B D GLM MA) 18-2 h, Sun 20-2 h
201 W. Orange Street *(Ground floor)* ☎ 299-0661

RESTAURANTS
■ **The Loft** (B F glm)
201 W. Orange Street ✉ PA17603 *(1st floor)* ☎ 299-0661
International cuisine.

GUEST HOUSES
■ **Maison Rouge B&B** (BF CC glm H OS)
2236 Marietta Avenue ✉ PA 17607 ☎ 399-3033
☎ (800) 309-3033
Small B&B in a beautifully restored Victorian home. All rooms with shower/WC. Rates US$ 85-125 incl. a full bf.

New Hope ☎ 215

BARS
■ **Cartwheel. The** (AC B CC D F GLM lj MA OS SNU STV VS) 11.30-2 h
437 Olde York Road ✉ PA 18938 *(at junction highway 202)*
☎ 862-0880
Popular bar and restaurant.

CAFES
■ **Cafe Galleria** (A BF f gLM)
93A Main Street ☎ 862-6860

RESTAURANTS
■ **Raven** (B F Glm H MA OS)
385 West Bridge Street ☎ 862-2081

New Hope ▶ Philadelphia | Pennsylvania/USA

Wildflowers Restaurant

Garden Café & Thai Corner
Gossip Bar
8 W. Mechanic St. New Hope, PA 18938
☎ +1 (215) 862 - 2241
Souvenir Guest House, Chiang Mai, Thailand

■ **Rosemont Cafe** (b BF F glm)
88 Kingwood-Stockton Road, Rosemont, NJ ☎ (609) 397-4097
20 minute drive from New Hope. Delicious food served all day. Reservation recommended. Try the desserts. No credit cards. Bring your own bottle.
■ **Wildflowers** (B F glm OS) Mon-Thu 12-22, Fri & Sat -23 h
8 West Mechanic Street ☎ 862-2241

BOOK SHOPS
■ **Book Gallery, The** (GLM)
19 West Mechanic Street ☎ 862-5110

GUEST HOUSES
■ **Fox & Hound Bed & Breakfast, The** (AC BF CC f GLM OS WH)
246 West Bridge Street ✉ PA 18938 ☎ 862-5082
☎ (800) 862-5082 📧 foxhound@bee.com
🌐 www.foxhoundinn.com
Romms with bath/WC, some with fireplaces, tub jacuzzis and first floor outside entrance. Rates from USD 75-170.
■ **Victorian Peacock B&B** (BF gLM H PI WH)
309 East Dark Hollow Road, Pipersville ☎ 766-1356
Comfortable B&B in a large Victorian estate. All rooms furnished with antiques. Rates US$ 65-165.

Philadelphia ☎ 215

✳ When talking about Philadelphia, you'll have to talk about Washington D.C. and New York City first. This may seem funny, but in the 18th century Philadelphia was on its way to become the most important city in the US. After all, here the 13 states of the union declared their independence from Great Britain on 4th July 1776 and here the US-constitution was developed in 1788. But soon New York took over the economical leadership of the country; Washington D.C. the political. Accordingly enormous gay scenes have evolved in both cities in the 20th century. Seen from hindsight: what a piece of luck for Philadelphia. No other Convention & Visitors Bureau in the US will provide you with such an allround gay information package (including gay-pertinent travelling news and a small gay guide in city-map format) about its city like the one in Philaphia. Being gay or lesbian is a very normal thing here in Philly, where the freedom of the US made its start. More gay infos about the city can be found in the *Philadelphia Gay News* or in its smaller rival, the *Au Courant*. The best time of the year for a visit here (and its greater neighbours) are spring and autumn. The biggest festivity of the local 'community' takes place in the middle of May: the *PrideFest*. So if you want to party, party, party, Philadelphia isn't quite the right place for you. But the mainstream-gay will find everything he needs, moreover on weekends, in the gay quarter between *Juniper* and *Quince Street* (east to west direction) and *Walnut* and *Pine Street* (north to south direction). Anyway: Most people come here to see the *Independence National Historic Park* with *Independence Hall* and *Liberty Bell*. They flock to *Walt Whitman House* in Camden, New Jersey, or take a cartrip to the country, to New Hope, Pennsylvania, which has become a popular gay outing destination.

✳ Will man etwas über Philadelphia erfahren, muß man zuerst über Washington, D.C. und New York City reden. Warum? Nun: Philadelphia war im 18. Jahrhundert auf dem Weg zur wichtigsten Stadt der USA. Schließlich erklärten sich hier am 4. Juli 1776 die 13 ersten Staaten der Union von Großbritannien unabhängig, und hier wurde 1788 die Verfassung der USA entwickelt. Bald aber übernahm New York die wirtschaftliche Führung des Landes, Washington D.C. die politische. Entsprechend haben sich dann im 20. Jahrhundert in beiden Städten überwältigende schwule Szenen entwickelt. Heute muß man sagen: was für ein Glücksfall für diese Stadt. Von keinem anderen Convention & Visitors Bureau der USA bekommt man auf Anfrage ein derart umfassendes schwules Info-Paket (inkl. einschlägiger Reise-News und einem kleinen Gay Guide im Stadtplanformat) wie von dem Philadelphias. Schwul oder lesbisch sein, das ist in Philly, wo die Freiheit der USA ihren Anfang nahm, eine recht normale Sache. Weitere schwule Infos über die Stadt findet man in den *Philadelphia Gay News* oder im *Au Courant*, dem kleineren Konkurrenten. Die besten Jahreszeiten für diese Stadt sind, wie für die großen Nachbarn, Herbst und Frühjahr. Mitte Mai findet auch das größte Fest der örtlichen "community" statt: *PrideFest*. Wer also Party, Party, Party will, ist nicht unbedingt richtig hier. Der Durchschnitts-Homosexuelle aber findet alles Notwendige, zumal am Wochenende und im schwulen Viertel zwischen (in Ost-West-Richtung) *Juniper* und *Quince Street* und (in Nord-Süd-Richtung) *Walnut* und *Pine Street*. Und sowieso: Man kommt doch hierher, um sich im *Independence National Historic Park* mit *Independence Hall* und *Liberty Bell* umzusehen. Man pilgert zum *Walt Whitman House* in Camden, New Jersey. Oder man macht per Auto einen Ausflug auf's Land, nach New Hope, Pennsylvania, das sich zu einem beliebten schwulen Ausflugsort gemausert hat.

✳ Pour parler de Philadelphie, il faut d'abord parler de Washington D.C. et de New York City. Cela vous étonne? Sachez qu'au 18ème siècle, Philadelphie était la ville la plus importante d'Amérique, car c'est ici que les 13 états de l'Union ont proclamé leur indépendance de la couronne britannique le 4 juillet 1776. C'est aussi ici que l'on a élaboré la Constitution américaine en 1788. Philadelphie a donc failli devenir capitale, mais c'était sans compter New York et Washington D.C. qui ont su se sont respectivement partagé le pouvoir économique et politique. Dans aucune autre ville des Etats-Unis, le

SPARTACUS 2001/2002 | 1321

USA/Pennsylvania — Philadelphia

Convention & Visitors Bureau ne met à votre disposition autant de brochures et d'informations purement homos. Cela va même jusqu'au petit plan gai de la ville! A "Philly", là où est née l'idée américaine de la Liberté, être gai ou lesbienne est la chose la plus naturelle du monde! Pour de plus amples informations, jetez un oeil dans les "Philadelphia Gay News" ou dans "Au courant". Comme pour New York et Washington, le printemps et l'automne sont les meilleurs saisons pour visiter la ville. Mi-mai a lieu la "Pride Fest", la manifestation gaie de la "communité". Si vous venez aux Etats-Unis pour faire la fête, encore la fête et toujours la fête, vous serez déçu par Philadelphie. Notez bien que l'homo de base trouve quand même tout ce dont il a besoin. Donc: pas de pénurie à Philadelphie! Les week-ends, ça bouge pas mal dans le quartier gai entre Juniper et Quince Street et Walnut et Pine Street. De toute façon, on vient à Philadelphie pour voir le "Independence National Historic Park", le "Independence Hall" et la "Liberty Bell". On fait son pélerinage à la "Withman House" à Camden, dans le New Jersey. On peut aussi aller à New Hope (Pensylvanie) en voiture ou en avion. C'est le lieu de villégiature des gais de la région.

Si se quiere saber algo sobre Filadelfia se debe hablar primeramente de Washington D.C. y de la ciudad de Nueva York. En el siglo XVIII Filadelfia se encontraba en el mejor camino para convertirse en la ciudad más importante de los Estados Unidos. El 4 de julio de 1776 se declararon independientes de la Gran Bretaña los primeros 13 estados norteamericanos y aqui se desarrolló también en 1778 la constitución de los E.E.U.U.. Muy pronto sería Nueva York la ciudad que tomaría el poder económico del país y Washington el político. En el siglo XX. se desarrollaron en ambas ciudades grandes centros gay. Hoy en día esto se puede considerar como una gran suerte para Filadelfia. En ninguna otra oficina para turistas ("Convention & Visitors Bureau") se obtienen informaciones tan detalladas para gays. Ser homosexual en Philly es una cosa bastante normal, que no es de extrañar, ya que esta ciudad es la cuna y el orgullo de la libertad estadounidense. Más informaciones gay se encuentran en el *Philadelphia Gay News* o en el *Au Courant*. La mejor época para visitar la ciudad son el otoño y la primavera. A mediados de mayo se lleva a cabo la *Pride Fest*, la celebración anual más importante. Aunque Filadelfia no es la ciudad adecuada para los que busquen solamente marcha y fiestas, homosexuales encuentran aquí todo lo que necesitan para satisfacer sus necesidades sobre todo los fines de semana. El sector gay de la ciudad se encuentra en dirección este-oeste en *Jupiter* y *Quince Street* y en dirección norte-sur *Walnut* y *Pine Street*. Puntos turísticos de atracción son el *Independence National Park* con *Independence Hall* y *Liberty Bell* o se puede vistar *Walt Whitman House* en Camden, Nueva Yersey. Recomendamos también una excursión en coche al New Hope, Pennsylvania que se ha convertido ultimamente en un destino turístico homosexual de moda.

E impossibile conoscere Philadelphia senza conoscere prima Washington D.C. e New York; è sorprendente, nel XVIII secolo Philadelphia stava per diventare la città più importante degli Stati Uniti: qui il 4 luglio 1776 tredici stati dell'Unione si dichiararono indipendenti dalla Gran Bretagna e sempre a Philadelphia, nel 1788, fu scritta la costituzione. Poco dopo però New York divenne il centro economico principale del paese e Washington D.C. quello politico. In entrambe le città si sono poi sviluppati degli ambienti gay di corrispondente importanza. Oggi bisogna dire che per Philadelphia è stata una fortuna. In nessun Convention e Visitors Bureau degli Stati Uniti si ricevono tante informazioni (incluse informazioni su viaggi gay ed una guida in forma di piantina) sulla vita gay come in quello di Philadelphia. In questa città, madre della libertà, essere omosessuale è veramente normale. Troverete ulteriori informazioni sulla vita gay sul *Philadelphia gay news* o sul meno importante *Au Courant*. Primavera ed autunno sono le stagioni migliori per visitare questa città. A metà maggio ha luogo la *Pride Fest*, la festa della "community" locale è l'unico evento importante per i gay. Per chi vuole solo fare festa, Philadelphia non è quindi il posto giusto. I gay più moderati invece saranno soddisfatti, specialmente durante il fine settimana, nel quartiere gay nella *Juniper* e *Quince Street* (in direzione est e ovest) e nella *Walnut* e *Pine street* (in direzione sud e nord). Visitate l'*Indipendence National Historic Park, Independence Hall* e il *Liberty Bell*. Fate un pellegrinaggio a *Walt Whitmann House* a Camden in New Jersey, o un'escursione in auto a New Hope, Pennsylvania, che è una località molto amata dai gay.

PUBLICATIONS

■ **Au Courant News Magazine**
PO Box 42741 ✉ PA 19101 ☎ 790-1179
Philadelphia's free, weekly publication. Available at gay venues.
■ **Philadelphia Gay News**
505 South 4th Street ✉ PA 19147 ☎ 625-8501 📠 925-6437
📧 tihey@epgn.com 🖥 www.epgn.com
Appears weekly and features reports and articles on Philadelphia's gay and Lesbian community, as well as on cultural events and lots of classified ads.

BARS

■ **Attic. The** (B G S STV)
16 South 2nd Street ☎ 928-0665
Tue drag shows and Thu "hard body dancers".
■ **Bike Stop** (AC B d f GLM LJ MA N VS) Mon-Fri 16-2, Sat Sun 14-2 h
204-206 South Quince Street ✉ PA 19107 *(near Locust Street)*
☎ 627-1662
■ **Post. The** (B CC f G lj SNU) 12-2
1705 Chancellor Street ✉ PA 19103 *(near 17th Street, next to Warwick Hotel)* ☎ 985 9720
■ **Shampoo** (AC B CC D DR GLM lj MA msg SNU STV TV WE) 21-2 h
417 North 8th Street ✉ PA 19123 ☎ 922-7500
■ **Sisters** (AC B D F f GLM MA S) 17-2, Sun 12-2 h
1320 Chancellor Street ✉ 19107 *(behind Woody's bar)*
☎ 735-0735
High-energy bar, restaurant, disco with shows, contest or events everyday.
■ **Venture Inn** (B F MG N) 12-2 h, dinner 17.30-23, Sun brunch 12-16 h
255 South Camac Street ✉ PA 19107 *(near Spruce Street)*
☎ 545-8731

DANCECLUBS

■ **Dennio Productions "Special Events"**
507 Pine Street, Suite 3 ✉ PA 19106 ☎ 931-0060
■ **Key West** (B D G SNU)
207 South Juniper Street ✉ PA 19107 ☎ 545-1578
■ **Woody's** (! B D Glm YG)
202 South 13th Street ✉ PA 19107 *(at Chancellor Street)*
☎ 545-1893
■ **12th Air Command** (B D f G MA SNU STV) 16-2 h
254 South 12th Street ✉ PA 19107 ☎ 545-8088

RESTAURANTS

■ **Astral Plane** (A AC B CC F f GLM LJ MA N OS) Lunch: Mon-Fri 11-14, Sun (brunch) 10.30-14.30, Dinner: Mon-Tue 17-24, Wed-Sun 15-2 h
1708 Lombard Street ✉ PA 19416 *(near 17th Street)* ☎ 546-6230
Romantic atmosphere restaurant with collectable pictures and objects and a Bohemian alcove.

Philadelphia — Pennsylvania/USA

Philadelphia

1. Adonis Sex Cinema
2. The Post Bar
3. Astral Plane Restaurant
4. Key West Danceclub
5. Chancellor Health & Spa Sauna
6. Woody's Danceclub
7. Club Body Center Sauna
8. Walnut Street Inn Guest House
9. Bike Stop Bar
10. 12th Air Command Danceclub
11. Venture Inn Bar
12. Giovanni's Room Bookshop
13. Backstage Restaurant
14. Judy's Cafe Restaurant

SPARTACUS 2001/2002

USA/Oregon - Pennsylvania — Philadelphia ▸ Pittsburgh

■ **Backstage** (AC B CC F glm) 16-2 h, dinner served from 18-23 h
614 South 4th Street ✉ PA 19147 *(near Kater)* ☎ 627-8907
Medium sized restaurant offering European specialties.
■ **Cheap Art Café** (A AC BF F f glm MA) 0-24 h
260 South 12th Street ✉ PA 19107 ☎ 735-6650
Diner-style food at reasonable prices. Vegetarian dishes available.
■ **Circa** (AC B CC d E F glm) Tue-Fri 11.30-14.30, Mon-Wed 17-22, Thu-Sat -23, Sun 16.30-21 h
1518 Walnut Street ✉ PA 19102 ☎ 545-6800
Mediterranean cuisine. Fri-Sat 22-? h (D GLM).
■ **Judy's Cafe** (AC B CC F glm N) Mon-Sat 17.30-?, Sun 10.30-15 h
3rd Street/Bainbridge Street ✉ PA 19147 ☎ 928-1968
Gay owned and operated restaurant.
■ **Waldorf Cafe** (b F glm)
20th Street/Lombard Street ☎ 985-1836
■ **Wildflowers** (AC B CC F glm MA) 12-22h, Fri, Sat - 23. Closed January-February.
8 W. Mechanic Street ✉ PA 18938 ☎ 862-2241
American and Thai food. Dinners from 7.50 $, Lunches from 5 $. Very romantic garden setting with fountains.

SEX SHOPS/BLUE MOVIES

■ **Adonis Cinema Complex** (G VS) 0-24 h
2026 Sansom Street ✉ PA 19103 *(near 20th Street)* ☎ 557-9511
■ **Danny's Adam & Eve** (AC CC g MA VS) 0-24 h
133 South 13th Street ✉ PA 19107 ☎ 925-5041
Magazines, videos and all male cinema upstair's.
■ **Tomcat** (G VS) 11-2 h
120 South 13th Street ✉ PA 19107 ☎ 985-9725

SAUNAS/BATHS

■ **Chancellor Health & Spa** (AC B F G SA SB WH WO) 0-24 h
1220 Chancellor Street ✉ PA 19107 ☎ 545-4098
■ **Club Body Center** (AC b CC G MA P SA SB VS WO) 0-24 h
120 South 13th Street ✉ PA 19107 *(2nd floor)* ☎ 735-9568

BOOK SHOPS

■ **Afterwords** (CC glm) Sun-Thu 11-22, Fri-Sat -24 h
218 South 12th Street ✉ PA 19107 ☎ 735-2393
Books, cards, gifts.
■ **Giovanni's Room** (AC CC GLM MA) Sun 13-19 h, Mon, Tue, Thu 11.30-21 h, Wed 11.30-19 h. Fri 11.30-22 h, Sa 10-22 h
345 South 12th Street ✉ PA 19107 ☎ 923-2960
Gay, lesbian & feminist bookstore. Americas world-class gay bookstore.

HOTELS

■ **Alexander Inn** (BF CC E GLM H WO)
304 South 12th Street ✉ PA 19107 *(central, adjacent to gay bars)*
☎ 923 3535   ☎ (877) ALEX-INN (toll-free) 📠 923 1004
📧 info@alexanderinn.com 💻 www.alexanderinn.com
Old Philadelphia hotel with designer rooms and art-deco furnishing. B&B atmosphere. Rooms with bath, phone, TV from US$ 89 incl. breakfast buffet. 24 hours fitness center.

GUEST HOUSES

■ **Glen Isle Farm** (CC g H)
130 S. LLoyd Avenue, Downington ✉ PA 19335 *(30 miles west of Philadelphia)* ☎ (610) 269-9100 📠 (610) 269-9191
Rates US$ 69-89.
■ **Uncles Inn** (AC B BF CC Glm H)
1220 Locust Street ✉ PA 19107 ☎ 546-6660 📠 546-1653
All rooms with color TV, ceiling fan, fridge and private baths. Pets ok. Rates USD 75-95 incl. cont. bf.

PHILADELPHIA

Alexander INN
THE INTIMATE LUXURY HOTEL

European Charm and amenities in a most convenient Center City location—very near to the Convention Center, Avenue of the Arts, Independence Hall, Antique Row, major museums, shopping, nightlife and the city's finest restaurants.

American Comfort in a historic building restored with 48 elegant guest rooms, each featuring luxurious bath with fluffy towels, DirecTV with 4 movie channels, phone with modem port. Continental Breakfast Buffet with fresh baked goods. 24-hour Fitness Center.   **Rooms from $99**

Spruce at Twelfth Street, Philadelphia, PA.
Call for rates, reservations or a color brochure:
Toll Free (USA only): **(877) ALEX-INN**   **(215) 923-3535**
Fax: (215) 923-1004   www.alexanderinn.com

IGLTA

■ **Walnut Street Inn** (AC BF CC GLM H)
1208 Walnut Street ✉ PA 19107 ☎ 546-7000 📠 546-7573
All rooms with private bath, radio, TV and hair-dryer. Rates USD 95 incl. cont. bf.

GENERAL GROUPS

■ **Pennsylvania Lesbian and Gay Task Force**
1616 Walnut Street, Suite 1005 ✉ PA 19103-5313 ☎ 772-2000
📠 772-2004 💻 www.op.net/plgtf

SPORT GROUPS

■ **GO! Philadelphia**
PO Box 15784 ✉ PA 19103 ☎ 969-8948
Outdoors club for gays and lesbians.

Pittsburgh ☎ 412

GAY INFO

■ **Gay and Lesbian Community Center** Mon-Fri 18.30-21.30, Sat 15-18 h
5808 Forward Avenue ✉ PA 15217 ☎ 422-0114

PUBLICATIONS

■ **Out**
1000 Ross Avenue ✉ PA 15221 ☎ 243-3350 📠 243-7989
📧 out@outpub.com 💻 www.outpub.com
Monthly publication serving Pennsylvania, Ohio, West Virginia. News, entertainment, calendar of events, classified ads.

CULTURE

■ **Pittsburgh International Lesbian & Gay Film Festival**
PO Box 81627 ✉ PA 15217 ☎ 232-3277

Pittsburgh ▶ State College | Pennsylvania/USA

BARS
■ **Bean Scene Cafe**
2104 Murray Avenue ✉ PA 15232 ☎ 422-7336
■ **Brewer's** (B G LJ MA N) 10-2 h
3315 Liberty Avenue ✉ PA 15201 ☎ 681-7991
Pool tables, juke box, colorful people.
■ **Club Havana** (B GLM MA)
5744 Ellsworth Avenue ✉ PA 15232 ☎ 661-2025
■ **Holiday Bar** (B G OS YG) Mon-Sat 14-2 h
4620 Forbes Avenue ✉ PA 15213 *(Oakland)* ☎ 682-8598
Cruisy atmosphere.
■ **Images** (B GLM VS) Mon-Sat 16-2 h
965 Liberty Avenue ✉ PA 15222 *(Downtown)* ☎ 391-9990
Karaoke.
■ **Real Luck Cafe** (AC B D F GLM MA N OS s SNU) 15-2, kitchen 17-24 h
1519 Penn Avenue ✉ PA 15222 *(Strip District)* ☎ 566-8988
2 floors.
■ **Tuscany** (B G MA)
1501 East Carson Street *(Southside)* ☎ 488-4545
Happy hours Sun-Fri 17-19 h

DANCECLUBS
■ **CJ Deighan's** (B D F GLM MA) 19-? h Wed (G)
2506 West Liberty Avenue ✉ PA 15226 *(South Hills)* ☎ 561-4044
■ **Donnie's Place** (B D GLM lj) 16-2, Sun 15-2 h
1226 Herron Avenue ✉ PA 15219 *(Polish Hill)* ☎ 682-9869
3 floors, lower level: Leather Central (LJ)
■ **House of Tilden** (B D GLM P) 20-3 h
941 Liberty Avenue ✉ PA 15222 *(Downtown)* ☎ 391-0804
After-hours club.
■ **Metropol** (B D glm S YG) 20-? h
1600 Smallman Street ✉ PA 15222 *(Strip District)* ☎ 261-2221
Popular Thu.
■ **Pegasus Lounge** (AC B D G lj MA s STV VS) Tue-Sat 21-2 h, closed Sun Mon
818 Liberty Avenue ✉ PA 15222 *(Downtown)* ☎ 281-2131
Most popular gay disco in town.
■ **Pittsburgh Eagle** (AC B f G LJ MA VS) Wed-Sat 21-2 h
1740 Eckert Street ✉ PA 15212 *(North Side)* ☎ 766-7222

RESTAURANTS
■ **Liberty Avenue Saloon** 11-14, 17-22, Sat Sun -23 h
941 Liberty Avenue *(Downtown)* ☎ 338-1533
Neighborhood bar and grill.
■ **New York, New York** (B F GLM S OS) Mon-Sat 16-2, Sun 14-2 h
5801 Ellsworth Avenue ✉ PA 15232 *(Shadyside)* ☎ 661-5600
American cuisine, brunch on Sun.
■ **Senator's Restaurant and Lounge** (B F GLM MA) Mon-Sat 16-? h
401 Hastings Street *(Point Breeze)* ☎ 362-1600
Seafood, steaks, daily specials.
■ **Sidekicks** (B F GLM MA) Mon-Fri 11-2, Sat,18- 2 h
931 Liberty Avenue ✉ PA 15222 *(Downtown)* ☎ 642-4435
Restaurant and cocktail bar.

SAUNAS/BATHS
■ **Arena Health Club** (B G SA) 0-24 h
2025 Forbes Avenue ✉ PA 15219 ☎ 471-8548

BOOK SHOPS
■ **Saint Elmo's** (glm) ?-21 h, Sun -16 h
2208 East Carson Street ✉ PA 15203 *(Southside)* ☎ 431-9100
Large selection of gay and lesbian books. Also music shop.

HOTELS
■ **Brewer's Hotel** (G H OS)
3315 Liberty Avenue ✉ PA 15201 *(above bar)* ☎ 681-7991
Inexpensive accomodation in boarding house. Rooms with shared baths.

GUEST HOUSES
■ **Inn on the Mexican War Street. The** (AC BF CC F GLM H)
604 West North Avenue ✉ PA 15212 ☎ 231 65 44
Located in the historic district. All rooms with bath/shower/WC, hair-dryer, baclony, telephone, TV, video, radio, apartments with kitchenette/kitchen.

GENERAL GROUPS
■ **Three Rivers Pride**
PO Box 81207 ✉ PA 15217-0207 ☎ 422-3060

HEALTH GROUPS
■ **AIDS Task Force**
905 West Street ✉ 15221-2833 *(4th floor)* ☎ 242-2500

HELP WITH PROBLEMS
■ **Persad Center Inc.**
5150 Penn Avenue ✉ PA 15224 ☎ 441-9786

SPECIAL INTEREST GROUPS
■ **Asians & Friends** (G MA)
PO Box 99191 ✉ PA 15233-4191 ☎ 521-1368 📠 521-1368
✉ afpgh@hotmail.com
🌐 www.qrd.org/QRD/www/orgs/afpgh/index.html
Meetings every 2nd Sat (Potluck Dinner) and last Sat (Business/Movie night) at 20 h. Publishers of the bi-monthly newsletter "Ring of Fire".
■ **Burgh Bears**
PO Box 1451 ✉ PA 15230-1451 ☎ 422-8850
■ **Renaissance City Choirs** Men´s rehearsal meets Mon 19.30-22 h at East Liberty Presbyterian Church
PO Box 10282 ✉ PA 15232 ☎ 362-9484
Gay and lesbian choir.

SPORT GROUPS
■ **Frontrunners**
☎ 243-1781
Gay & lesbian running group.
■ **Iron City Squares**
☎ 244-8196
GLB square dance group.

Reading ☎ 610

BARS
■ **Red Star** (B D G LJ OG) Winter Mon-Sat 17-2, summer Mon-Sat 20-2 h
11 South 10th Street ✉ PA 19602 ☎ 375-4116
■ **Scarab** (B D G YG) Tue-Sat 20-2 h, Sun Mon closed
724 Franklin Street ✉ PA 19611 ☎ 375-7878

CRUISING
-Mount Penn (above Reading, daytime along main drag starting at Pagoda. MA especially after 17 h.)

State College ☎ 814

GAY INFO
■ **Gay and Lesbian Switchboard** 18-21 h, closed Sun
PO Box 805 ✉ PA 16804 ☎ 237-1750

USA/Pennsylvania - Rhode Island — State College ▸ Providence

BARS
■ **Chumley's** (B glm) 18-2 Sun, 16-2 h
108 West College Avenue ✉ PA 16801 ☎ 238-4446

GENERAL GROUPS
■ **State College Gay Men's Alliance**
PO Box 545 ✉ PA 16804

CRUISING
-The Wall (100 block of College Avenue)
-Penn State (Hertzel Union Building, Recreation Hall and men's locker rooms)

Williamsport ☎ 717

BARS
■ **Court. The** (B CC GLM MA)
320 Court Street ☎ 326-3611

GENERAL GROUPS
■ **Gay, Lesbian Switchboard of North Central Pennsylvania**
c/o Susquehanna Lambda, PO Box 2510 ✉ PA 17703 ☎ 327-1411

Wycombe ☎ 215

HOTELS
■ **Wycombe Inn** (AC F GLM H OS)
1073 Mill Creek Road ✉ PA 05777 (Bucks Country) ☎ 598-7000
Suburb location, 70 min to the airport, 13km to gay scene of New Hope. All rooms with telephone, kitchenette, priv. bath and WC.

York ☎ 717

BARS
■ **Fourteen Karat** (B D F G VS) Mon-Sat 19-2 h, closed Sun
659 West Market Street ✉ PA 17406 ☎ 846-5029

CRUISING
-100 block of Duke and Queen Streets
-Saint George Street Square

USA-Rhode Island

Location: Northeast USA
Initials: RI
Time: GMT -5
Area: 4.002 km² / 1,636 sq mi.
Population: 987,000
Capital: Providence

Newport ☎ 401

GUEST HOUSES
■ **Hydrangea House. The** (A AC BF CC glm H msg) all year
16 Bellevue Avenue ✉ RI 02840 In the center of historic walking district) ☎ 846-4435 ☎ (800) 945-4667 📠 846-6602
✉ www.hydrangeahouse.com
9 elegant non-smoking rooms with bath, incl. bf. Rates US$ 125-300. Special winter rates.

■ **Prospect Hill Guest House** (AC b BF CC GLM H MA OS)
Bar: 13-1 h

32 Prospect Hill Street ✉ RI 02840 ☎ 847-7405
✉ prospectgh@aol.com ✉ www.impulz.net/buzzardsbay/newport
Small, nicely furnished, non-smoking guest house. All rooms with bath/WC, telephone, TV, radio, minibar and kitchenette (microwave, coffee maker, full sink and refrigerator). Extended continental bf (incl.) served in your room. Rates on request.

CRUISING
-First Beach(Eastons Beach)(in front of the concession stands)
-Purgatory Chasm-Tuckerman Avenue(Middletown)

Providence ☎ 401

PUBLICATIONS
■ **Options**
PO Box 6406 ✉ RI 02940-6406 ☎ 831-4519 📠 272-3247
✉ gayoptions@aol.com ✉ www.glbt.net/options

BARS
■ **Blinky`s** (AC B d GLM MA) Sun-Thu 12-1, Fri Sat 12-2 h
125 Washington Street ✉ RI 02903 ☎ 272-6950
■ **Changes** (B g)
525 Eddy Street ✉ RI 02903 ☎ 861-8025
■ **Club In-Town** (B G)
95 Eddy Street ✉ RI 02903 ☎ 621-8739
■ **Mirabar** (B D G S) 15-1 h
35 Richmond Street ✉ RI 02905 ☎ 331-6761
■ **Wheels** (AC B d f GLM lj MA N s YG)
125 Washington Street ✉ RI 02903
■ **Yukon Trading Co.** (AC B C D G LJ MA N) Sun-Thu 16-1 h, Fri Sat -2 h
124 Snow Street ✉ RI 02903 (near Weybossett Street) ☎ 274-6620

DANCECLUBS
■ **Galaxy** (B D G S) Sun Thu 12-1, Fri Sat 12-2 h
123 Empire Street ✉ RI 02903 ☎ 831-9206
Thu country & western night. Fri strip contest.
■ **Gerardo's** (B D F G S) Thu strip contest
1 Franklin Square ✉ RI 02903 ☎ 274-5560
■ **69 Union Street Station** (B D GLM s)
69 Union Street ✉ RI 02903 ☎ 331-2291

RESTAURANTS
■ **Gerardo's Supper Club** (B F GLM)
1 Franklin Square ✉ RI 02903 ☎ 274-5560

SEX SHOPS/BLUE MOVIES
■ **Upstairs Bookshop** (g)
255 Allans Avenue ✉ RI 02903 ☎ 785-1324

SAUNAS/BATHS
■ **Club Body Center** (b CC G MA P SB VS) 0-24 h
257 Weybosset Street ✉ RI 02903 ☎ 274-0298
Black-out party on Fri from 21 h.

HEALTH GROUPS
■ **Rhode Island Project AIDS Hotline** 9.30-20 h
☎ 277-6502

HELP WITH PROBLEMS
■ **GLBT Helpline of RI** Mon Wed Fri 19-22 h
PO Box 41297 ✉ RI 02940 ☎ 751-3322

USA-South Carolina

Location: Southeast USA
Initials: SC
Time: GMT -5
Area: 82.902 km² / 33.906 sq mi.
Population: 3,760,000
Capital: Columbia

Charleston ☎ 843

BARS
■ **Dudley's** (B D G N P) 16-?, Sun 14-? h
346 King Street ✉ SC 29401 ☎ 723-2784

RESTAURANTS
■ **Fannie's Diner** (B F glm) open all day
137 Market Street ✉ SC 29401 ☎ 723-7121
■ **Magnolias** (F g)
185 East Bay Street ✉ SC 29401 ☎ 577-7771
■ **Papillon** (F g)
41 Market Street ✉ SC 29401 ☎ 723-6510
Italian cuisine.
■ **82 Queen** (F g OS)
82 Queen Street ✉ SC 29401 ☎ 723-7591

HOTELS
■ **Charleston Beach B&B** (AC b BF GLM L nu OS PI WH)
118 West Arctic Avenue ✉ SC 29439 *(Folly Beach)* ☎ 588-9443
Close to Charleston, SC. Rate $75.
■ **Fifty Folly Place** (AC BF glm H OS)
50 Folly Road ✉ SC 29407 ☎ 571-4171
Hotel with garden, 25 min from downtown. All rooms with priv. bath and WC. US$ 50-90 (bf incl.).
■ **Mills House Hotel** (g H)
Meeting Street/Queen Street ✉ SC 29401 ☎ (800) 874-9600

GENERAL GROUPS
■ **Low Country Gay and Lesbian Alliance**
PO Box 98 ✉ SC 29401 ☎ 577-5139

Columbia ☎ 803

GAY INFO
■ **South Carolina Coalition of Lesbians and Gay Men** Tue-Fri 18-22 h, Sat 14-22 h, closed Sun Mon
1108 Woodrow Street ☎ 771-7713

PUBLICATIONS
■ **In Unison**
PO Box 8024 ✉ SC 29202 ☎ 771-0804 📧 NUnison@aol.com

BARS
■ **Art Bar** (a B d glm ng)
Lady Street *(one block north of Gervais)*
■ **Candy Shop** (B D GLM) Thu-Sun 23-? h
1903 Two Notch Road ✉ SC 29204
■ **Capital Club** (B GLM P)
1002 Gervais Street ✉ SC 29201 ☎ 256-6464
Private gentleman's club.
■ **Downtown** (B d G MA p r SNU)
1109 Assembly *(previously Ikon; across from State House)*
Gay strip bar.

CAFES
■ **Goatfeathers** (b F glm) 17-? h
2017 Divine

DANCECLUBS
■ **Metropolis** (! B D MA P S OS YG) 22-?, Fri-Sun 21-? h, closed Mon
1800 Blanding Street ✉ SC 29202 ☎ 799-8727
Large disco with three separate bars and terrace.

SEX SHOPS/BLUE MOVIES
■ **Big Ex-Citing Emporium**
4333 Fort Jackson Blvd. ☎ 738-3707
■ **Book Exchange**
2739 Broad River Road ☎ 772-6728
■ **Nicki's X-Citing Novelties**
3311 Broad River Road ☎ 798-1010

BOOK SHOPS
■ **Moxie**
631-C Hardon Street
Small gay section.

GENERAL GROUPS
■ **PFLAG Columbia**
PO Box 1838 ✉ SC 29202-1838
■ **SC Pride Center**
1108 Woodrow Street, PO Box 12648 ✉ SC 29211 ☎ 771-7713
■ **South Caralina Gay and Lesbian Business Guild**
PO Box 7913 ✉ SC 29202-7913
■ **Univ. of SC Bisexual, Gay and Lesbian Association**
PO Box 80098 ✉ SC 29225 ☎ 777-7716
■ **Youth Out Loud**
☎ 771-7713
Help hotline.

CRUISING
-Rest Stop (on I-26 South)
-Lake Murray Dam
-Univ of South Carolina (Russel House, Blatte PE Center lockers, pool and Thomas Cooper Library)
-Senate Street from Capitol to Gregg Street (ayor. Very busy at night)
-Main Street

Ehrhardt ☎ 803

HOTELS
■ **Ehrhardt Hall** (B H)
PO Box 246 ✉ SC 29801 ☎ 267-2020

Greenville ☎ 803

GAY INFO
■ **Gay Switchboard**
☎ 271-4207

BARS
■ **New Attitude** (B D GLM) Wed-Sun 21-2 h
706 West Washington Street ✉ SC 29601 ☎ 233-1387
■ **Stone Castle** (B D GLM S VS YG) 20-4, Sat Sun 20-2 h
8 Legrande Boulevard ☎ 235-9949

USA/South Carolina - Tennessee — Johns Island ▸ Memphis

Johns Island ☎ 843

RESTAURANTS
■ **St. Johns Island Cafe** (AC b BF CC F glm OS) Mon-Sat 7-21, Sun 9.30-14 h
3140 Maybank Highway ✉ SC 29455 (between downtown Charleston and Kiawah Island) ☎ 559-9090

Myrtle Beach ☎ 843

BARS
■ **Underground** (B G)
821 Main Street ☎ 448-5844

CRUISING
-Beach at 82nd Avenue
-Hurlock Park

USA-South Dakota

Location: North USA
Initials: SD
Time: GMT -6
Area: 199.744 km² / 81,695 sq mi.
Population: 738,000
Capital: Pierre

Rapid City ☎ 605

GUEST HOUSES
■ **Camp Michael Guesthouse** (AC BF F GLM MA WH)
13051 Bogus Jim Road ✉ SD 57702 ☎ 342-5590
✉ michael@campmike.com ● www.campmike.com
Secluded and quiet, located in the Black Hills, 12 miles from Rapid City. Rates single: US$ 59, couple US$ 69, discounts for 3 days or longer.

Sioux Falls ☎ 605

GAY INFO
■ **Gay Hotline and Lesbian Alliance Coalition** 24 hrs
☎ 332-4599
■ **Office, The**
2404 West Madison Street ✉ SD 57104 ☎ 335-9546
At the Metropolitan Community Church; coffeehouse and community center.

SEX SHOPS/BLUE MOVIES
■ **Studio One Book Store**
309 North Dakota Avenue ✉ SD 57102 ☎ 332-9316

CRUISING
-Faywick Park 2nd Avenue & 11th Street

USA-Tennessee

Location: Central East
Initials: TN
Time: GMT -6
Area: 109.158 km² / 44,645 sq mi.
Population: 5,368,000
Capital: Nashville
Important gay cities: Memphis, Nashville

Chatta ☎ 423

BARS
■ **Chuck's Bar** (AC B d DR f GLM LJ MA N OS S WE) Sun-Thu 18-1 h, Fri-Sat 18-3 h
27 W. Main Street ✉ TN 37408 (Downtown) ☎ 265-5405

GIFT & PRIDE SHOPS
■ **Condoms etc. Rainbow Merchandise** (AC CC) Sun-Thu 18-1 h, Fri-Sat 18-3 h
27 W. Main Street ✉ TN 37408 ☎ 266-3668

Greeneville ☎ 423

HOTELS
■ **Timberfell Lodge** (AC B BF F G LJ msg NU Pl SA WH)
Route 11 ✉ TN 37743 ☎ 234-0833 ☎ (800) 437-0118 (toll free).
Located in the Smokey Mountains. All rooms with TV and telephone. Rates US$ 84-144. Rooms with shared or private bath.

Knoxville ☎ 423

GAY INFO
■ **Gay/Lesbian Helpline** 19-23 h
☎ 521-6546

BARS
■ **Carousel II** (B D GLM S) 21-3 h
1501 White Avenue South ✉ TN 37920 ☎ 522-6966
■ **The Electric Ball Room** (AC B CC D f GLM lj MA SNU STV) Wed-Sun 20-3 h
1213 Western Avenue ✉ TN 37921 ☎ 525-6724

CRUISING
-Cumberland Avenue (around St. John's Church)
-Downtown between post office and Public Library
-Tyson Park (AYOR)

Memphis ☎ 901

BARS
■ **Another Bar** (B D G)
1351 Autumn ✉ TN 38104 ☎ 272-0903
■ **Fancy's** (B g)
887 South Highland ✉ TN 38111 ☎ 452-9286
■ **Jackie's** (B G)
1474 Madison Avenue ✉ TN 38104 ☎ 272-1104
■ **J-Wag's Lounge** (AC B CC d f GLM MA N OS r SNU STV) 0-24 h
1268 Madison Avenue ✉ TN 38104 ☎ 725-1909
■ **Pipeline** (B G LJ MA)
1382 Poplar Avenue ✉ TN 38104 ☎ 726-5263

SEX SHOPS/BLUE MOVIES
■ **Airport Bookmart**
2214 Brooks Road East ✉ TN 38132 ☎ 345-0657
■ **Paris Adult Theater** (g)
2432 Summer ✉ TN 38112 ☎ 323-2665

BOOK SHOPS
■ **Fantasy World** (g)
1814 Winchester Road ✉ TN 38116 ☎ 346-2086

LEATHER & FETISH SHOPS
■ **Men of Leather at J-Wag's** Mon-Thu 12-23, Fri Sat 13-1 h
1268 Madison Avenue ✉ TN 38104

Memphis ▸ Amarillo | **Tennessee - Texas/USA**

HEALTH GROUPS
■ **Memphis Center for Reproductive Health**
1462 Poplar Avenue ✉ TN 38104 ☎ 274-3550

Nashville ☎ 615

GAY INFO
■ **Nashville Gay and Lesbian Community Center** 18-21 h, Infoline daily 17-22 h.
703 Berry Road ✉ TN 37204 ☎ 297-0008
💻 www.nashcenter.org
The Center is the place to go for information regarding the Nashville gay community. The Center Library has more than 500 books.
■ **Nashville GayWeb**
💻 www.nashvillegayweb.com

PUBLICATIONS
■ **Query**
PO Box 24241 ✉ TN 37202-4241 ☎ 259-4135
✉ querynews@aol.com
Published weekly.
■ **Xenogeny News / Southern X-posure**
PO Box 110504 ✉ TN 37222 ☎ 831-1806 📠 831-1806
✉ xenogeny@home.com 💻 www.xenogeny.com

BARS
■ **Chute Complex. The** (B D F G MA)
2535 Franklin Road ✉ TN 37204 *(attached to The Nashville Eagle)*
☎ 297-4571
■ **Gas Lite Lounge. The** (AC B CC f GLM MA N s) 16.30-3 h
167 1/2 8th Avenue North ✉ TN 37203 ☎ 254-1278
Piano bar.
■ **Jungle. The** (AC B CC d F glm MA r SNU STV VS) 11-3 h
306 4th Avenue South ✉ TN 37201 ☎ 256-9411
Cruisy atmosphere
■ **Nashville Eagle. The** (B G LJ MA)
2535 Franklin Road *(attached to the Chute)* ☎ 297-4571
■ **Your Way Cafe and Bar** (B G N)
515 2nd Avenue South ✉ TN 37210 ☎ 256-9411

DANCECLUBS
■ **Connection. The** (! B D GLM MA)
901 Cowan Street ☎ 742-1166
Nashville's largest bar and danceclub.

RESTAURANTS
■ **Julian's Eatery** (B F GLM MA) Wed-Sun 20-24 h
901 Cowan Street *(at Connections)* ☎ 742-1166
Nouvelle American cuisine
■ **Town House Restaurant** (AC B BF CC F glm) Mon-Fri 8-14.30 h
165 8th Avenue North ✉ TN 37203 *(at Savage House Inn)*
☎ 254-1277
Southern-style cuisine
■ **World's End** (B F glm YG) 16-2 h
1713 Church Street ✉ TN 37203 *(near Vanderbilt University)*
☎ 329-3480
American cuisine

SEX SHOPS/BLUE MOVIES
■ **Metro News** 0-24 h
822 5th Avenue South ☎ 256-1310
Calls itself "the worlds largest adult bookstore".

GUEST HOUSES
■ **Savage House Inn. The** (AC BF CC glm H)
165 8th Avenue North ✉ TN 37203 ☎ 244-2229
Small B&B located in the oldest house in downtown Nashville. All rooms are furnished with antiques. Rooms have telephone, TV and some have private baths. Special rates for extended stays available. Conference facilities.

GENERAL GROUPS
■ **Girth and Mirth**
PO Box 121886 ✉ TN 37212
■ **Southeastern Gay Rodeo Association** Meets 2nd Sun 17 h at The Chute
☎ 226-7124
■ **Tennessee Vals** Meets 2nd Sat 19 h
PO Box 92335 ✉ TN 37209 ☎ 664-6883
💻 www.transgender.org
Group for crossdressers, transvestites and transgendered people.

FETISH GROUPS
■ **Conductors L/L** (G)
PO Box 40261 ✉ TN 37204-0261
onthly meetings at The Eagle, The Chute Complex, Nashville every 2nd Fri at 22.30 h.

HEALTH GROUPS
■ **Nashville CARES**
209 Tenth Avenue South, Suite 160 ☎ 845-4266
AIDS information and support.

HELP WITH PROBLEMS
■ **Gay and Lesbian AA** Wed 6.30-7.30 h
St. Ann's Episcopal, 5th and Woodland ☎ 298-1050

Rogersville ☎ 423

HOTELS
■ **Lee Valley Farm** (CC F GLM MA NU PI WH)
142 Drinnon Lane ✉ TN 37857 ☎ 272-4068
✉ eesfarm@usit.net
Cabins and campgrounds. Rates from US$ 50 (single) to 125 (couple). Sports activities incl. riding, hiking, fishing, etc.

USA-Texas

Location: South USA
Initials: TX
Time: GMT -6
Area: 695.676 km² / 284,531 sq mi.
Population: 19,439,000
Capital: Austin
Important gay cities: Austin, Dallas, Houston, San Antonio

Amarillo ☎ 806

BARS
■ **Sassy's** (B d GLM MA) 15-2 h
309 West 6th Street ✉ TX 79101 ☎ 374-3029
Live DJ on Wed, Fri and Sat, Tejano night (Margarita specials) on Thu.
■ **Whiskers** (B GLM) 12-2 h
1219 West 10th Street ✉ TX 79101 ☎ 371-8482

USA/Texas — Amarillo ▸ Austin

DANCECLUBS
■ **Bubba's** (B D G MA) Wed-Sat 18-2 h
519 East 10th Street ✉ TX 79101 ☏ 374-2435
Live DJ on Thu, Fri and Sat.
■ **212 Club** (B D G LJ MA) 14-2 h
212 West 6th Street, PO Box 2903 ✉ TX 79105 ☏ 372-7997
Fri and Sat live DJ from 22 h, Wed leather & uniform night.

RESTAURANTS
■ **OHMS Gallery Cafe & Catering** (A b F glm) Mon-Fri 11-30-1.30, Fri Sat 18.30-21 h
619 South Tyler Street ✉ TX 79101 ☏ 373-3233

Austin ☏ 512

GAY INFO
■ **Gay Hotline** 0-24 h
☏ 472-4357

BARS
■ **'Bout Time** (B CC GLM N) 14-2 h
9601 North I-35 ✉ TX 78753 *(at Rundberg)* ☏ 832-5339
Western-style bar with pool tables, video games, volleyball court.
■ **Chain Drive** (B CC G LJ MA) 14-2 h
504 Willow Street ✉ TX 78701 ☏ 480-9017
■ **Charlie's** (B CC D GLM snu) 14-2 h
1301 Lavaca Street ✉ TX 78701 *(at 13th Street)* ☏ 474-6481
■ **Forum. The** (AC B CC D G MA OS SNU STV VS WE) Sun-Thu 14-2, Fri-Sat -4 h
408 Congress Avenue ✉ TX 78701 *(corner of 4th Congress/Warehouse District)* ☏ 476-2900
■ **Splash** (B G lj OS SNU VS)
406 Brazos Street ☏ 477-6969

CAFES
■ **Carrusso's Cafe** (b BF f glm MA)
307 West 5th Street ☏ 457-0722

DANCECLUBS
■ **Boyz Cellar** (B D GLM snu) closed Mon-Tue
213 West 4th Street ☏ 479-8482
■ **Dick's Deja Disco** (B D GLM MA)
113 San Jacinto Boulevard ✉ TX 78705 *(at 2nd and San Jacinto)* ☏ 457-8010
A country dance club for Austin's gay and lesbian community.
■ **Oil Can Harrys** (AC B CC D GMA S OS SNU SJ) 14-2, Fri-Sat -4 h
211 West 4th Street ✉ TX 78701 *(near Guy Town)* ☏ 320-8823
Dance bar, patio, multiple bar areas, pool tables. Popular especially after 23 h.
■ **Rainbow Cattle Company** (B CC D GLM MA) 14-2 h
305 West 5th Street ✉ TX 78701 ☏ 472-5288
Western bar with large dance floor, pool tables and video games.
■ **1920's Club** (B F D GLM)
918 Congress Avenue ☏ 479-7979
Elegant gay club in Austin. They offer martinis, jazz and an all night kitchen.

RESTAURANTS
■ **Eastside Cafe** (B f glm) 11-22 h
2113 Manor Road ✉ TX 78722 ☏ 476-5858
■ **Manuel's** (A AC B CC F glm MA WE) 11-22.30, Sun brunch 12-15 h
310 Congress Avenue ✉ TX 78701 ☏ 472-7555
Mexican cuisine.

SHOWS
■ **Esther's Follies** (b D GLM S STV) Shows Thu 20, Fri-Sat 20 22 h
525 East 6th Street ☏ 320-0553

SEX SHOPS/BLUE MOVIES
■ **Pleasure Shop** (g VS) 0-24 h
603 West Oltorf/South 1st Street ✉ TX 78704 ☏ 447-1101
Adult videos
■ **Tapelenders** (GLM VS) 9-24, Sun 11-24 h
1114 West 5th Street #201 ✉ TX 78703

SAUNAS/BATHS
■ **Midtowne Spa** (b CC G MA OS SA SB VS WH WO) 0-24 h
5815 Airport Boulevard ✉ TX 78752 ☏ 302-9696
Bath house with an outdoor hot tub and many special rooms.

FITNESS STUDIOS
■ **World Gym** (G WO)
115 East 6th Street ☏ 479-0044
Cruisy atmosphere.

BOOK SHOPS
■ **BookPeople** (glm)
6th Street at Lamar Street ☏ 441-9757
Large selection of gay and lesbian books.

GUEST HOUSES
■ **Carrington's Bluff** (AC BF CC E glm H MA) 6.30-23 h
1900 David Street ✉ TX 78705 *(downtown)* ☏ (800) 649-3370
(toll-free) 🖷 476-4769 🖳 governorsinn@earthlink.net
🖳 www.governorsinnaustin.com
B&B in central location. All rooms with private bath, TV, radio and hair-dryer.
■ **Governor's Inn** (AC BF CC E glm H) 6.30-23 h
611 West 22nd Street ✉ TX 78705 *(downtown)* ☏ (800) 871-8908
(toll-free) 🖷 476-4769 🖳 governorsinn@earthlink.net
🖳 www.governorsinnaustin.com
B&B in nice old mansion. All rooms with private bath, TV, phone, radio and hair-dryer.
■ **Summit House B&B. The** (A AC B BF CC f G H LJ MA msg NU OS PI WH) Reception: 9.30-21.30
1204 Summit Street ✉ TX 78741-1158 ☏ 445-5304
🖳 summit@texas.net 🖳 www.summit.home.texas.net
Small B&B located on an old Indian campground just two blocks from the Colorado river. Rooms with private and shared baths, one studio with kitchenette.

HEALTH GROUPS
■ **AIDS Services of Austin**
☏ 451-2273

RELIGIOUS GROUPS
■ **Mishpachat Am Echad**
PO Box 9591 ✉ TX 78766 ☏ 451-7018
Jewish gays and lesbians.

SPECIAL INTEREST GROUPS
■ **Gay & Lesbian Student Association**
PO Box 275 ✉ TX 78713 ☏ 471-4387

SWIMMING
-**Hippie Hollow** (AYOR G NU) (Highway 2222 west to #620, turn left to the Mansfield Dam and follow the signs. You reach the gay area over the rocks east of the parking lot)

Austin ▶ Dallas **Texas/USA**

CRUISING
-Pease Park (along Lamar Boulevard near West 15th from 22 h)

Bryan ☎ 409

BARS
■ **Club. The** (B CC D GLM MA N STV) Tue-Sat 21-2 h
308 North Bryan Avenue ✉ TX 77803 *(in Bryan/College Station)*
☎ 823-6767

Corpus Christi ☎ 512

BARS
■ **Hidden Door** (B G lj) 11-2, Sun 12-2 h
802 South Staples Street ✉ TX 78404 ☎ 882-0183
■ **Numbers** (B GLM MA)
1214 Leopard Street ☎ 887-8445

DANCECLUBS
■ **Liquid 2000** (B D GLM)
208 North Water Street ☎ 888-8767

CRUISING
-Seawall (AYOR)

Dallas ☎ 214

GAY INFO
■ **Gay and Lesbian Community Center** Mon-Fri 9-21, Sat 10-18, Sun 12-17 h
2701 Reagan Street ✉ TX 75219 ☎ 528-9254 📠 522-4604
📧 glcc@resourcecenterdallas.org
🖥 www.resourcecenterdallas.org

PUBLICATIONS
■ **Dallas Voice**
3000 Carlisle Street #200 ✉ TX 75204 ☎ 754-8710 📠 969-7271
📧 editor@dallasvoice.com 🖥 www.dallasvoice.com
Weekly GL publication.
■ **Texas Triangle. The**
4001-C Cedar Springs Road ✉ TX 75219 ☎ 599-0155
📠 599-0156 📧 todd@txtriangle.com 🖥 www.txtriangle.com
Newspaper published weekly serving the GLBT Texan community.

TOURIST INFO
■ **Dallas Convention & Visitor Bureau**
1201 Elm Street, Suite 2000 ✉ TX 75270 ☎ 746-6677
📠 746-6688

BARS
■ **Brick. The** (AC B CC D LJ snu YG) 12-2, Fri-Sat -4 h
4117 Maple Street ✉ TX 75219 ☎ 521-3154
■ **Dallas Eagle** (B G LJ) 16-2 h, Sat after hours
2515 Inwood Street, #107 ✉ TX 75235 *(rear entrance)*
☎ 357-4375
■ **Fraternity House. The** (B D GLM MA S)
2525 Wycliff #120 ☎ 520-1415
Theme nights.
■ **Hidden Door** (B G LJ MA N)
5025 Bowser Street *(off Mahana and West of Lemmon Avenue and the Tollway)*
☎ 526-0103
Front and back bars, a patio, pool tables, video games in the home of Dallas leather's organizations.

■ **Hideaway Club** (B D GLM OS S) 8-2, Sun 12-2 h
4144 Buena Vista Street ☎ 559-4668
Nightly live cabaret entertainment, garden patio and quiet back bar.
■ **JR's Bar and Grill** (AC B F GLM MA s) 11-2, Sun 12-2 h
3923 Cedar Springs Road ✉ TX 75219 *(at Throckmorton)*
☎ 528-1004
■ **Moby Dick** (! B CC D G OS snu stv)
4011 Cedar Springs Road ☎ 520-6629
Three bar areas, pool tables. gorgeous men.
■ **Pub Pegasus** (B G N) Mon-Fri 10-2, Sat 8-2, Sun 12-2 h
3326 North Fitzhugh Road ✉ TX 75204 ☎ 559-4663
■ **Side 2 Bar** (B GLM N) 10-2 h
2615 Oaklawn Avenue ✉ TX 75219 ☎ 528-2026
■ **Studio** (B GLM MA N)
3851 Cedar Springs Road ☎ 521-7079
Formerly named Santa Fe.
■ **Throckmorton Mining Company** (AC B D G LJ) 15-4 h
3014 Throckmorton Street ✉ TX 75219 ☎ 559-0850
A dance/cruise club for men.
■ **Trestle** (B D GLM)
412 South Haskell Street ☎ 826-9988
Club drawing a late night and after hours clientele. Outdoor secluded patio, video games and pool tables available.
■ **Twisted Lemmon Club** (B G S SNU)
5006 Lemmon Avenue ☎ 219-5006
Live shoes, male dancers, aquariums,...
■ **Zippers** (B G lj N S SNU) 12-2 h
3333 North Fitzhugh Road ✉ TX 75204 ☎ 526-9519

DANCECLUBS
■ **Bamboleos** (B D GLM stv) Fri-Sun
5027 Lemmon Avenue ☎ 520-1124
Latin club with a large dancefloor and drag shows on Sun.
■ **Crews Inn** (B D G lj OS S YG) 12-2 h
3215 North Fitzhugh Avenue ✉ TX 75204 ☎ 524-9510
■ **Round-Up Saloon** (B D G LJ) 13-2 h
3912-14 Cedar Springs Road ✉ TX 75219 ☎ 522-9611
Western style bar and danceclub.
■ **Village Station** (B D G lj MA OS SNU VS) Wed-Sun 21-4 h
3911 Cedar Springs Road ✉ TX 75219 ☎ 559-0650

RESTAURANTS
■ **Hunky's** (B F glm)
4000 Cedar Springs Road ✉ TX 75219 ☎ 522-1812

SEX SHOPS/BLUE MOVIES
■ **Alternatives** (G VS)
1720 W. Mockingbird Lane ☎ 630-7071
■ **TapeLenders Video** (CC GLM VS) 9-24, Sun 11-24 h
3926 Cedar Springs Road ✉ TX 75219 ☎ 528-6344
One of the most complex gay and lesbian video libraries worldwide.

SAUNAS/BATHS
■ **Club. The** (cc f G MA PI SA SB WH WO) 0-24 h
2616 Swiss Avenue ✉ TX 75204 *(east side of downtown, near Deep Ellum Arts district)* ☎ 821-1990
Fitness and sauna with remodelled pool area. Membership required. Free Aids testing Tue 17-20 h. Barbecue on Sat Sun 13-16 h.
■ **Midtowne Spa** (AC CC DR F G MA OS P SA SB VS WH WO) 0-24 h
2509 Pacific Avenue ✉ TX 75226 ☎ 821-8989
Sauna located in a beautiful old warehouse built in 1910. Lots of fantasy rooms and beautiful rooftop with view of downtown.

USA/Texas — Dallas ▶ Galveston

BOOK SHOPS
■ **Crossroads Market Bookstore & Cafe** (AC CC GLM MA OS) 7-24 h
3930 Cedar Springs Road ✉ TX 75219 ☏ 521-8919

LEATHER & FETISH SHOPS
■ **Shades of Grey Leather** (CC) Mon-Thu 11-20, Fri Sat -22, Sun 12-18 h
3930-A Cedar Springs Road ✉ TX 75219-3518 ☏ 521-4739
Leather/Fetish/SM-shop. Men and women.

GUEST HOUSES
■ **Courtyard on the Trail** (AC BF glm H NU OS PI)
8045 Forest Trail ✉ TX 75238 ☏ 553-9700
Comfortable small B&B 6 miles from the city centre. Rooms with private baths, modem line, color cable TV and VCR. Private garden and sundeck. No kids and no pets.
■ **Inn on Fairmont** (BF CC GLM H OS WH)
3701 Fairmount ✉ TX 75219 ☏ 522-2800 📠 522-2898
Nicely furnished Bed & Breakfast in the heart of the Oak Lawn/Turtle Creek area close to clubs and bars. Seven bedrooms with private baths, and TV.
■ **Symphony House** (CC G H PI WH)
6327 Symphony Lane ✉ TX 75227 ☏ 388-9134
📧 SymphonyHouse@webtv.net
Room for up to ten people in four bedrooms; 2 bathrooms, 2 living areas, kitchen.

GENERAL GROUPS
■ **Men of All Colors Together**
PO Box 190611 ✉ TX 75219 ☏ 521-4765

HEALTH GROUPS
■ **AIDS Information Line** 9-21 h
☏ 559-2437

RELIGIOUS GROUPS
■ **Beth El Binah**
PO Box 191188 ✉ TX 75219 ☏ 497-1591
GLB Jews.

CRUISING
-Bachman Lake
-Cedar Springs Road (between Oaklawn & Dallas North Toll Road)
-Eastfield College (at night)
-Film World & Kit Kat Book Sore (Industrial Boulevard)
-Greyhound Bus Depot
-"Homo Heights" (Oakland and Lemmon Avenues)
-Kiest Park (best on Sun)
-Lee Park (AYOR)
-Mid Continent Truck Stop (on Big Town Boulevard off I-20, east of I-30)
-News Stand Adult Book Store on Cedar Springs Road
-Paris Book I & II (AYOR) (Harry Hines Boulevard)
-Red Letter News (AYOR) (Harry Hines Boulevard)
-Reverchon Park (AYOR) (trails and trees)
-S.M.U. Main Library (1st & 2nd floor)
-Tower Bay Park (Lake Lewisville)
-Town East Mall (Sears)
-White Rock Lake (AYOR)
-Cedar Springs Road (AYOR) (south of to Maple Street, between Regan and Knight Streets)

El Paso ☏ 915

BARS
■ **Apartment** (B G)
804 Myrtle Avenue ✉ TX 79901 *(near Virginia Avenue)*
■ **Whatever Lounge. The** (B G MA R) 14-2 h
701 E. Paisano Drive ✉ TX 79901 ☏ 533-0215

DANCECLUBS
■ **New Old Plantation** (B D GLM MA S VS) 21-2, Fri Sat 21-4 h, closed Mon Tue
301 South Ochoa Street ✉ TX 79901 ☏ 533-6055

HEALTH GROUPS
■ **Tillman Health Centre**
222 South Campell ✉ TX 79901 ☏ 543-3560

HELP WITH PROBLEMS
■ **AIDS Information Line**
☏ 543-3574 (English) ☏ 543-3575 (Spanish)

CRUISING
-Rest stop-20 miles on I-10 (AYOR) (tourists and truckers)
-Dyer Street (AYOR R) (after dark, weekends)
-McKelligon Canyon (off Alabama, near Beaumont Hospital)

Fort Worth ☏ 817

BARS
■ **Across the Street** (B D G) 20-2 h
659 South Jennings Avenue ✉ TX 76104 ☏ 332-0192
■ **Corral Club** (B G LJ MA N P)
621 Hemphill Street ☏ 335-0196
■ **Magnolia Station** (B G MA S) Wed-Sun 20-? h
600 West Magnolia Avenue ✉ TX 76104 ☏ 332-0415
■ **651** (B D G lj) 12-2 h
651 South Jennings Avenue ✉ TX 76104 ☏ 332-0745
Western style bar.

FETISH GROUPS
■ **Cowtown Leathermen** (G LJ)
PO Box 3494 ✉ TX 76113-3494
📧 cowtownleathermen@hotmail.com

CRUISING
-Rest Stop (on I-35 South)
-Benbrook Lake (AYOR) (off US 377, southwest of town)
-Forest Park (picnic area)
-Rockwood Park (days)
-T.C.U. (Burnett Library)

Galveston ☏ 409

BARS
■ **Cocktail Lounge** (AC B d f Glm lj MA N OS R S STV) 8-2, Sun 12-2 h
2501 Rosenburg ✉ TX 77550 ☏ 765-9092
Drag shows on week-ends.
■ **Evolution** (B D glm)
2214 Ships Mechanic Road ✉ TX 77550 ☏ 763-4212
■ **Kon Tiki** (B D glm SNU VS) 16-2 h
315 23rd Street ✉ TX 77550 ☏ 763-6264

Galveston ▶ Houston Texas/USA

■ **Robert's Lafitte** (AC B d f GLM lj MA N OS r s STV) 22-2, Sun 12-2 h
2501 Avenue Q ✉ TX 77550 *(1 block to the beach)* ☏ 765-9092
Oldest gay bar on the island, no cover charge, drag shows on WE. Patio.

SWIMMING
-Stewart Beach

Gun Barrel City ☏ 903
BARS
■ **Friends** (AC B CC d f GLM MA N OS P STV) Mon-Fri 16-24, Sat 15-1, Sun 15-24 h
602 South Gun Barrel Lane ✉ TX 75147 *(on highway 198, next to the Wagon Wheel Reastaurant)* ☏ 887-2061

Harker Heights ☏ 254
DANCECLUBS
■ **Krosover Club** (B D G MA N) 21-2, Sat -3, closed on Tue
1509 East Veterans Memorial Boulevard ✉ TX 76548 ☏ 680-5239

Houston ☏ 713
GAY INFO
■ **Gay & Lesbian Switchboard** 15-24 h
☏ 529-3211

PUBLICATIONS
■ **Houston Voice** Mon-Fri 9-18 h, closed Sat Sun
500 Lovett Boulevard #200 ✉ TX 77006 ☏ 529-8490
🖨 529-9531 📧 editor@houstonvoice.com
💻 www.houstonvoice.com
Weekly gay and lesbian newspaper.
■ **Houston's Gay and Lesbian Yellow Pages**
PO Box 660 45 ✉ TX 77266 ☏ 942-0084
■ **OutSmart Magazine**
3406 Audubon Place ✉ TX 77006 ☏ 520-7237 🖨 522-3275
📧 greg@outsmartmagazine.com 💻 www.outsmartmagazine.com
Monthly magazine published by Up&Out Communications covering community news both on a local and global scale.
■ **This Week in Texas-Twit**
811 Westheimer Road, #111 ✉ TX 77006 ☏ 527-9111
🖨 527-8948
Weekly free gay and lesbian news magazine. Available at most gay venues.

TOURIST INFO
■ **Greater Houston Convention & Visitor Bureau**
801 Congress ✉ TX 77002 ☏ 227-3100 🖨 227-1408

BARS
■ **Brazo's River Bottom** (B D Glm lj)
2400 Brazos Street ✉ TX 77706 ☏ 528-9192
Country western dance bar. Three bar areas, patio & pool tables. Dance lessons on certain nights.
■ **Briar Patch** (B G N) 14-2 h
2294 W. Holcomb ✉ TX 77030 ☏ 665-9678
■ **Chances** (B GLM MA N)
1100 Westheimer ☏ 523-7217
■ **Cousins** (B G S) Fri Sat shows
817 Fairview/Converse Street ✉ TX 77006 ☏ 528-9204

■ **E.J.'s** (AC B d f GLM lj MA N OS SNU STV) 7-2 h
2517 Ralph Street ✉ TX 77006 ☏ 527-9071
■ **JR's Bar & Grill** (A AC B CC GLM MA N S SNU VS WO) 12-2 h
804/808 Pacific Avenue ✉ TX 77006 *(near downtown)*
☏ 521-2519
Very popular and cruisy.
■ **Lazy J** (B G MA)
312 East Tuam Street ✉ TX 77006 ☏ 528-9343
■ **Lola's** (B glm N YG)
2327 Grant Street ✉ TX 77006 ☏ 528-8263
■ **Mary's** (B G LJ MA OS) Fri Sat -2 h
1022 Westheimer Road ✉ TX 77006 ☏ 527-9669
Cruisy atmosphere.
■ **Mela's Tejano Country** (B G LJ)
302 Taum Street ☏ 523-0747
Country/western bar.
■ **Montrose Mining Co.** (AC B CC G LJ MA N OS S SNU WO) Mon-Fri 16-2, Sat Sun 13-2 h
805 Pacific Avenue ✉ TX 77006 *(near downtown)* ☏ 529-7488
Very popular.
■ **Ripcord** (B G LJ MG OS r) Sun-Thu 13-2, Fri-Sat -4 h
715 Fairview ✉ TX 77006 ☏ 521-2792
■ **Sante Fe Bar and Patio** (A AC B CC GLM MA N S SNU VS WO) 12-2 h
804 Pacific Avenue ✉ TX 77006 *(near downtown)* ☏ 521-2519
Video and party bar.
■ **Venture-N** (AC B CC d DR G LJ MG N OS R SNU STV) 12-2 h
2923 South Main Street ✉ TX 77002 *(neat downtown)*
☏ 522-0000
■ **611 Hyde Park Pub** (AC B CC f G lj MA N OS r SNU) Mon-Sat 7-2, Sun 12-2 h
611 Hyde Park Boulevard/Stanford Street ✉ TX 77006 *(Montrose district)* ☏ 526-7070

CAFES
■ **Barnaby's Cafe** (B F glm) 11-22, Fri Sat -23 h
604 Fairview/Standford ☏ 522-0106
■ **Charlie's** (B F glm MA)
1102 Westheimer ✉ TX 77006 ☏ 522-3332

DANCECLUBS
■ **Club Inergy** (B D Glm MA)
5750 Chimney Rock ☏ 666-7310
Good sized dance club that attracts a Latino clientele.
■ **Numbers** (B D glm YG)
300 Westheimer *(between Montrose and downtown)* ☏ 526-6551
■ **Pacific Street** (AC B D G lj MA SNU VS) 20-2 h
710 Pacific Street ✉ TX 77006 ☏ 523-0213
Dance club with upstairs bar & balcony that overlooks the strip. Video screens, laser lights and male dancers in cages.
■ **Picasso** (B D GLM MA S SNU VS) closed Mon
2151 Richmond Avenue *(in Shepherd Plaza)* ☏ 520-8636
■ **Rich's** (A B CC D G OS VS YG)
2401 San Jacinto Street ✉ TX 77002 ☏ 759-9606
Two floors woth a large dance floor, an art lounge, avideo bar and a patio.
■ **South Beach** (AC B CC D E GLM MA S SNU STV VS WO YG) Wed-Sat 21-3, Sun 20-3 h
810 Pacific Avenue ✉ TX 77006 ☏ 521-9123
Most popular disco in town.

RESTAURANTS
■ **Baba Yega** (B CC F glm OS MA) 10-22 h
2607 Grant Street ✉ TX 77006 *(at Missouri Street)* ☏ 522-0042

USA/Texas — Houston ▶ San Antonio

■ **Chapultepec** (B F glm)
813 Richmond Avenue ✉ TX 77006 *(at Montrose)* ☏ 522-2365
Mexican food.
■ **La Strada** (B F glm MA)
5161 San Felipe *(at Sage)* ☏ 850-9999
Italian restaurant.

SEX SHOPS/BLUE MOVIES
■ **French Quarter** (G P VS)
3201 Louisiana Street ✉ TX 77006 ☏ 527-0782

SAUNAS/BATHS
■ **Club. The** (b CC G MA SA SB SOL P PI VS WH WO) 0-24 h
2205 Fannin Street ✉ TX 77002 ☏ 659-4998
Complete entertainment and physical fitness complex with outdoor pool parties on WE.
■ **Midtowne Spa** (b G MA OS PI SA SB SOL WH WO) 0-24 h
3100 Fannin Street ✉ TX 77004 ☏ 522-2379
Bath house with and outdoor garden patio for sun tanning and a steam room modelled after a dark cave with numerous caverns to explore. Many special rooms available.

BOOK SHOPS
■ **Crossroads Market Bookstore & Cafe** (AC CC f GLM MA) 7-24 h
1111 Westheimer Road ✉ TX 77006 ☏ 942-0147
■ **Inklings-an alternative bookshop** (AC CC GLM MA) Tue-Sat 10.30-18.30, Sun 12-17 h, closed Mon
1846 Richmond Avenue ✉ TX 77098 ☏ 521-3369
Books, music and information.

LEATHER & FETISH SHOPS
■ **Leather by Boots** (G LJ) 12-20 h
711 Fairview ✉ TX 77006 ☏ 526-6940
at the Ripcord Sat Sun 15-2 h ☏ 526-0444.

GUEST HOUSES
■ **Lovett Inn. The** (AC BF CC GLM H MA PI WH) Office: 10-20 h
501 Lovett Boulevard ✉ TX 77006 *(near downtown)* ☏ 522-5224
☏ 528-6708 ✉ lovettinn@aol.com 🖥 www.lovettinn.com
Rooms with private bath, TV, radio, balcony and coffee/tea, some rooms with bar, jacuzzi and VCR. Located in a 1920s Southern home. Prices range US$ 75-200.
■ **Montrose Inn** (AC BF CC G H) Office 9-22 h
408 Avondale ✉ TX 77006 *(close to gay bars)* ☏ 520-0206
☏ (800) 357-1228 (Toll-free)
Centrally located in the gay bar district. 7 double rooms, partly with shared bath.

GENERAL GROUPS
■ **Houston Gay and Lesbian Political Caucus** Meeting 1st Wed 19 h at Houston Lesbian and Gay Community Center
PO Box 666 64 ✉ TX 77266-6664 ☏ 521-1000 ☏ 861-8208
✉ hglpc@neosoft.com

HEALTH GROUPS
■ **Aid for AIDS**
PO Box 664 14 ✉ TX 77266 ☏ 526-6077
■ **AIDS Hotline** 9-21 h
☏ 524-2437

SPECIAL INTEREST GROUPS
■ **Lone Star Nudists** (G)
PO Box 66621 ✉ TX 77266 ☏ 866-8847 (24 h)
✉ Biearthguy@hotmail.com

SPORT GROUPS
■ **Houston Outdoor Group** (GLM)
PO Box 980893 ✉ TX 77098 ☏ 526-7688

CRUISING
-Bayland Park (on Bissonet)
-Corner of Michigan and Yupon "Club Luscene"
-Galleria Mall/Skating Rink (AYOR)
-Golden Star Theatre (r) (912 Prairie Street, 24 hours)
-Memorial Park and adjacent pathway (AYOR)
-Rest Stop (15 E. on I-10)
-Rest Stop (on I-10 / Columbia)
-Rice U (Memorial Center & Library)
-University of Houston (library, 2nd floor & all A.A. Hall)
-Vicinity of both bus depots
-Westheimer (Montrose)
-Y.M.C.A.

Lubbock ☏ 806

DANCECLUBS
■ **Club Luxor** (B D GLM) Thu-Sun 21-2 h
2211 4th Street ✉ TX 79415 ☏ 744-3744
Live DJs.

GENERAL GROUPS
■ **Lubbock Lesbian/Gay Alliance** 2nd Wed 19.30 h
PO Box 64746 ✉ TX 79464 ☏ 766-7184

San Antonio ☏ 210

BARS
■ **Annex** (B G LJ MA OS)
330 San Pedro Avenue ✉ TX 78212 ☏ 223-6957
■ **Eagle Mountain Saloon** (B GLM MA OS)
1902 McCullough Avenue ☏ 733-1516
■ **Mick's Hideaway** (B GLM MA N) 15-2 h
5307 Mc Cullough Avenue ✉ TX 78212 ☏ 828-4222
■ **Pegasus** (B D G MA OS SNU)
1402 North Main Avenue at Laurel ☏ 299-4222
Cruisy atmosphere.
■ **Rebar** (B G LJ MA)
826 San Pedro at Laurel *(upstairs at Woody's)* ☏ 271-9633
Cruising bar.
■ **Silver Dollar Saloon** (AC B G MA s OS VS) 14-2 h
1418 North Main Avenue ✉ TX 78212 ☏ 227-2623
■ **Sparks** (AC B D G MA SNU VS) 12-2 h
8011 Webbels ✉ TX 75218 ☏ 653-9941
■ **Woody's** (B G LJ MA)
826 San Pedro at Laurel ☏ 271-9633
■ **2015** (B D G N SNU)
2015 San Pedro Avenue ✉ TX 78212 ☏ 733-3365

DANCECLUBS
■ **Bonham Exchange** (AC B CC D GLM MA SNU) Mon-Tue closed, Wed-Fri 16-3 Sat 20-4 Sun 18-2 h
411 Bonham Street ✉ TX 78205 *(behind the Alamo)* ☏ 271-3811
Multi-level dance club in a 110 year old historical building hosting up to 2000 people.

San Antonio ▸ Salt Lake City — Texas - Utah/USA

■ **Saint** (B D GLM STV YG) Sun-Thu 22-2, Fri Sat -4 h
1430 North Main Avenue ✉ TX 78212 ☎ 225-7330

SEX SHOPS/BLUE MOVIES
■ **Apollo News** (glm)
2376 Austin Highway ☎ 653-3538
Adult bookshop.
■ **Encore-Video.com** (AC CC GLM MA) Mon-Thu 10-22, Fri Sat -24, Sun 12-19 h
1031 North East Loop 410 ✉ TX 78209-1205 *(next to airport)*
☎ 821-5345
Video rental and sales.

SAUNAS/BATHS
■ **Alternative Clubs, Inc.** (b G MA OS SA SOL PI WH WO) Mon-Fr 12-9, Sat Sun 0-24 h
827 East Elmira ✉ TX 78212 ☎ 223-2177
Bath house with outdoor patio and hairdresser. Also known as ACI.
■ **Executive Spa** (b G MA SA WO) 0-24 h
1121 Basse Road ✉ TX 78215 ☎ 732-4333

GIFT & PRIDE SHOPS
■ **Zebraz.com** (AC CC GLM MA) 11-21 h
1608 North Main Avenue ✉ TX 78212-8910 *(next to San Antonio College)* ☎ 472-2800
One of the largest gay and lesbian department store by mail: www.zebraz.com

GUEST HOUSES
■ **Adam House B&B** (BF glm H)
231 Adams Street ☎ 224-4791
Small B&B in 1900s home. All rooms with cable TV and private bath. No smoking.
■ **Painted Lady Inn on Broadway. The** (AC BF CC E GLM H MA msg OS WH) 7-22 h
620 Broadway ✉ TX 78215 *(downtown close to convention center Alamo)* ☎ 220-1092 🖷 299-4185 ✉ travel2sa@earthlink.net
💻 www.thepaintedladyinn.com
All rooms and suites with private bath, TV/VCR, radio, some with kitchenette. BF included, close to gayclubs.
■ **San Antonio Bed & Breakfast** (BF GLM H WH)
510 East Guenther ✉ TX 78210 ☎ 222-1828
Small B&B in a 1980s home. Rooms with private bath. Rates USD 89-100 incl. bf.

HELP WITH PROBLEMS
■ **Crisis Hotline** 0-24 h
☎ 227-4357

South Padre Island ☎ 956

HOTELS
■ **New Upper Deck. The** (AC B BF CC GLM H MA NU P PI VS WH WO)
120 East Atol Street, PO Box 2309 ✉ TX 78597 *(1/2 block to gay beach)* ☎ 761-5953 🖷 761-4288 ✉ spiup@aol.com
💻 www.NewUpperDeck.com
Hotel in resort area with nude beach, kitchen and laundry facilities, TV lounges. All rooms with priv. bath, TV, VCR and balcony. Nautical locker room. Clothing optional. Continental bf. Prices range US$ 55-120 (without tax).

USA-Utah

Location: West USA
Initials: UT
Time: GMT -7
Area: 219.902 km^2 / 89,940 sq mi.
Population: 2,059,000
Capital: Salt Lake City

Escalante ☎ 435

GUEST HOUSES
■ **Rainbow Country B&B and Tours** (AC BF CC glm H WH)
586 E. 300 Street, PO Box 333 ✉ UT 84726 ☎ 826-4567
☎ (800) 252-8824 *(toll-free).*
💻 rainbow@color-country.net. *Rates on request.*

Ogden ☎ 801

BARS
■ **Brass Rail** (B G MA) 15-1 h
103 27th Street ✉ UT 84401 ☎ 399-1374

Salt Lake City ☎ 801

GAY INFO
■ **Gay and Lesbian Community Center of Utah** (A AC GLM MA TV) 8-22 h
361 North 300 West ✉ UT 84101-2603 ☎ 539-8800
💻 thecenter@glccu.com 💻 www.glccu.com
Includes library with over 3,000 circulating items. Many different organizations meet here. Call for details. Also includes a coffee-shop.

PUBLICATIONS
■ **Pillar. The**
PO Box 57744 ✉ UT 84157-0744 ☎ 265-0066 🖷 261-2923
💻 PillarSLC@aol.com 💻 www.pillarmag.com
Magazine featuring news, events and information in the gay, lesbian, bisexual and transgendered community.

BARS
■ **Bricks** (AC B D g MA OS P S STV VS YG) Tue-Sat 21.30-2 h
579 West 200 South ✉ UT 84101 *(West side of downtown, 2 blocks west of Delta Center)* ☎ 328-0255
■ **Inbetween** (B D G OS)
579 West 200 South Street ✉ UT 84101 ☎ 328-3392
■ **Sun. The** (B D f glm P S OS YG) 12-? h
702 West 200 South Street ✉ UT 81104 ☎ 531-0833
Private members club.
■ **Trapp. The** (AC B CC D f GLM LJ MA OS P s VS)
102 South 600 West ✉ UT 84101 ☎ 531-8727
Country/Western music & dancing.

CAFES
■ **Coffee Garden. The** 7-22 h
898 East 900 Street ✉ UT 84104 *(northwest corner of 9th & 9th)*
☎ 355-3425

DANCECLUBS
■ **Club Vortex** (B D glm P)
#32 Exchange Place ✉ UT 84111 *(downtown)* ☎ 521-9292
Gay owned and operated. Salt Lake's hottest dance club. Private club.

USA/Utah - Virginia | Salt Lake City ▸ Cape Charles

SEX SHOPS/BLUE MOVIES
■ **Hyatt's Magazine Store** (AC CC glm MA VS) Mon-Sat 8-24, Sun 8-23 h
1350 South State ✉ UT 84115 ☎ 486-9925
Gay and lesbian magazines and videos.
■ **Video One** (GLM)
484 South 900 West ✉ UT 84101 ☎ 539-0300

HEALTH GROUPS
■ **People With AIDS Coalition of Utah** (CC GLM MA) Mon-Fri 10-16 h
1390 South 1100 East # 107 ✉ UT 84105 *(Sugerhouse area)*
☎ 484-2205 📠 466-6015 📧 pwacu@xmission.com
💻 www.pwacu.org
Also computers with internet access available.
■ **Utah AIDS Foundation**
1408 South 1100 East ✉ UT 84105 ☎ 487-2100 (Information hotline) ☎ 1-800-FON-AIDS

HELP WITH PROBLEMS
■ **Gay Helpline** 24 hrs
☎ 533-0927

SPECIAL INTEREST GROUPS
■ **Lesbian & Gay Chorus of Salt Lake City**
☎ 536-6040

CRUISING
- Liberty Park
- Memory Grove Park
- South Main (and surrounding area, evenings)
- Vicinity of Greyhound Bus Depot

USA-Vermont

Location: Northeast USA
Initials: VT
Time: GMT -5
Area: 24.903 km² / 10,185 sq mi.
Population: 589,000
Capital: Montpelier

Brattleboro ☎ 802

BARS
■ **Rainbow Cattle Co.** (AC B D GLM MA N) Wed-Sun 20-1 h
Route 5, East Dummerston ✉ VT 05301 ☎ 254-9830

Burlington ☎ 802

BARS
■ **135 Pearl** (AC B D GLM lj MA N s) 19.30-2, Fri Sun 17-2, Sat 17-1, dancing Thu-Sat 22-3 h
135 Pearl Street ✉ VT 05401 *(at the north end of Church Street)*
☎ 863-2343

HOTELS
■ **Black Bear Inn** (b BF CC F glm H OS)
4010 Bolton Access Road ✉ VT 05477 *(half an hour from Burlington)* ☎ 434-2126 📠 434-5161 📧 blkbear@wcvt.com
💻 www.blkbearinn.wcvt.com
Mountaintop country inn nestled in the heart of Vermont's Green Mountains. For nature and sport lovers. New England's Ski-in ski-out inn.

CRUISING
- Battery Park (North Public Beach)
- Main Square (opposite Bus Terminal)
- Univ of Vermont (Baily Howe Library, 3rd and 4rth floor)

Dorset ☎ 802

HOTELS
■ **Marble West Inn** (BF G H OS)
West Road ✉ VT 05251 ☎ 867-4155
Elegant country hospitality. priv. bath.

Richmond ☎ 802

PUBLICATIONS
■ **Out in the Mountains**
PO Box 1078 ✉ VT 05753 ☎ 434-6486 📠 434-7046
📧 editor@mountainpridemedia.org
💻 www.mountainpridemedia.org
The GLBT Vermont publication.

Shaftsbury ☎ 802

HOTELS
■ **Country Cousin B&B** (AC BF CC GLM H OS WH)
192 Old Depot Road ✉ VT 05262 ☎ 375-6985 📠 375-6985
A farmhouse with hot tub and swimming pond.

Stowe ☎ 802

HOTELS
■ **Buccaneer Country Lodge** (F glm H Pl)
1390 Mountain Road ✉ VT 05672 ☎ 253-4772
Priv. and shared baths, cable TV in room, hot tub.

Waterbury ☎ 802

GUEST HOUSES
■ **Grünberg Haus** (BF CC glm H MA OS SA WH)
Route 100 South, RR 2, Box 1595 SP ✉ VT 05676-9621 *(3 miles south of the village)* ☎ 244-7726 ☎ (800) 800-7760 (Toll-free)
📠 244-1283 📧 grunhaus@aol.com
💻 www.waterbury.org/grunberg
Handbuilt Austrian chalet.

USA-Virginia

Location: East USA
Initials: VA
Time: GMT -5
Area: 110.792 km² / 45,313 sq mi.
Population: 6,734,000
Capital: Richmond

Cape Charles ☎ 757

GUEST HOUSES
■ **Sea Gate Bed & Breakfast** (AC BF g H MA)
9 Tazewell Avenue ✉ VA 23310-3127 ☎ 331-2206 📠 331-2206
📧 seagate@pilot.infi.net
4 rooms with bath, balcony, phone, tv, radio. Rates US$ 80-90, add. bed $20.

Charlottesville ☎ 804

HEALTH GROUPS
■ **Men to Men C-ville AIDS/HIV Services Group**
☎ 979-7714

HELP WITH PROBLEMS
■ **Gay and Lesbian Helpline** Sun-Wed 20-23, Thu 19-21 h
☎ 971-4942

CRUISING
-Rest Stop (Route 64, west of Ivy)
-Lee Park (AYOR)

Norfolk ☎ 757

GAY INFO
■ **Gay Info Line** 19-22 h
☎ 423-0933

PUBLICATIONS
■ **Out & About of Virginia**
PO Box 1414 ✉ VA 23501 ☎ 583-7468 💻 vaoutabout@aol.com

BARS
■ **Charlotte's Web** (B D F GLM S)
6425 Tidewater Drive ☎ 853-5021
■ **Garage. The** (B F G lj) Mon-Fri 20-2, Sat 18-2, Sun 13-2 h
731 Granby Street ✉ VA 23510 ☎ 623-0303
■ **Nutty Buddys** (B g)
143 East Little Creek Road ✉ VA 23505 ☎ 588-6474

CAFES
■ **Charlies** (B F glm) 7-15 h
1800 Granby Street ☎ 625-0824

BOOK SHOPS
■ **Lambda Rising** (AC CC GLM MA VS) 10-22 h
9229 Granby Street ✉ VA 23503 ☎ 480-6969
Gay, lesbian, bisexual and transgender books, videos, magazines and gifts. Free local guides.
■ **Phoenix Rising** (GLM)
619 Colonial Avenue ✉ VA 23507 *(2nd floor)* ☎ 622-3701

CRUISING
-Ghent Gay Ghetto (around Colley and Princess Anne Road)
-Ocean View Public Park (AYOR)
-Watside Park (South Military Highway, days)

Richmond ☎ 804

GAY INFO
■ **Gay Information Line**
☎ 353-3626

BARS
■ **Babes** (B g)
Auburn Street/West Cary Street ✉ VA 23221 ☎ 355-9370
■ **Broadway Café** (B D F G) Mon-Fri 17-2 h
1624 West Broad Street ✉ VA 23220 ☎ 355-9931
■ **Fielden's** (B D G P YG) Wed-Sat 24-6 h
2033 West Broad Street ✉ VA 23220 ☎ 359-1963

BOOK SHOPS
■ **Biff's Carytown Bookstore** (glm) 10-18, Sun 10-15 h
2930 West Cary Street ✉ VA 23221 ☎ 359-4831

FETISH GROUPS
■ **Teddy Bear Leather Club**
PO Box 255 45 ✉ VA 23260-5545

CRUISING
-The Block (Grace and Franklin between Adams and 3rd)
-The Rocks (James River Park, North Bank near South end of Meadow St)
-Belle Isle (James River Park)
-Bryant Park (summer)
-Byrd Park (AYOR)
-Monroe Park
-Pumphouse Drive (summer)
-The Battle Abby (behind the VA museum)

Roanoke ☎ 540

PUBLICATIONS
■ **Shout!**
PO Box 21201 ✉ VA 24018 ☎ 989-1579 📠 989-1579
💻 shoutzine@aol.com 💻 www.shoutmag.com
Monthly magazine serving the Virginia GBLT community.

BARS
■ **Backstreet Café** (B F GLM MA)
356 Salem Avenue ☎ 345-1542

GIFT & PRIDE SHOPS
■ **Out Word Connection** (GLM)
114-A Kirk Avenue, SW ☎ 985-6886
E-mail outword@aol.com Gay pride shopping.

Virginia Beach ☎ 757

HOTELS
■ **Coral Sand Motel** (AC Glm H)
PO Box 1125, 2307 Pacific Avenue ✉ VA 23451-0125 ☎ 425-0872
☎ (800) 828-0872 (Toll-free)
One Block from ocean.

USA-Washington

Location: Northwest USA
Initials: WA
Time: GMT -8
Area: 184.672 km^2 / 75,530 sq mi.
Population: 5,610,000
Capital: Olympia

Kennewick ☎ 509

SEX SHOPS/BLUE MOVIES
■ **Castle Superstore Adult Retail** 24 hours
522 N. Columbia Center Boulevard ✉ WA 99336 ☎ 374-8276
Videos, leather, lingerie, magazines, toys, novelties, books, DVD's.

Kent ☎ 253

BARS
■ **Trax Bar & Grill** (B D F GLM)
226 1st Avenue South ✉ WA 98032 ☎ 854-8729
Gay bar and night club.

USA/Washington | **Lake Quinault ▶ Seattle**

Lake Quinault ☎ 206

HOTELS
■ **Rain Forest Resort Village** (B F GLM H s)
Route 1, PO Box 40 ✉ WA 98575 ☎ 288-2535
Suburb location. All rooms with kitchenette and priv. bath.

Port Angeles ☎ 360

GUEST HOUSES
■ **Maple Rose Inn** (BF CC g H WH WO)
112 Reservoir Road ✉ WA 98363 ☎ 457-3373
✉ maplerose@tenforward.com
🖥 www.northolympic.com/maplerose
Most rooms with kitchenette, cable-TV, VCR, telephone, private bath.

Seattle ☎ 206

PUBLICATIONS
■ **G.S.B.A. Guide & Directory**
2033 Sixth Avenue #804 ✉ WA 98121 ☎ 443-4722
Yearly directory to gay or gay friendly businesses.
■ **Seattle Gay News**
1605 12th Avenue #31 ✉ WA 98122 ☎ 324-4297 📠 322-7188
🖥 sgnl@sgn.org 🖥 www.gayseattle.com
Local weekly news & entertainment newspaper.

BARS
■ **C.C. Attle's** (B F G MA VS)
1501 E. Madison ✉ WA 98122 ☎ 726-0565
■ **Changes** (B G N)
2103 North 45th Street, Wallingford ✉ WA 98103 ☎ 545-8363
■ **Crescent. The** (b G OG)
1413 East Olive Way ☎ 720-8023
■ **Cuff Complex. The** (! AC B CC D F G lj MA VS) The Cuff: everyday 11-2, back bar, dance and patio: Thu, Fri Sat 21-2, Sun 18-2 h
1533 13th Avenue ✉ WA 98122 *(on Capitol Hill)* ☎ 323-1525
One of the most popular men's bar in Seattle.
■ **Double Header** (b d G LJ OG s)
407 2nd Avenue South *(near Washington)* ☎ 464-9918
Oldest gay bar on West Coast.
■ **Eagle** (B G LJ) 14-2 h
314 East Pike Street ✉ WA 98122 ☎ 621-7591
A man's rock-n-roll club.
■ **Elite II** (b G MA N)
1658 East Olive Way ☎ 322-7334
■ **Elite. The** (b G N)
622 Broadway East/Roy ☎ 324-4470
■ **Madison Pub** (AC B CC F GLM MA n) 12-2 h
1315 East Madison ✉ WA 98122 ☎ 325-6337
Bar primarily gay; all welcome.
■ **R Place** (b G MA VS) 14-2 h
619 East Pine Street ✉ WA 98122 ☎ 322-8828
Games.
■ **Re-bar** (B D glm S YG)
1114 Howell Street ✉ WA 98101 ☎ 233-9873
■ **Sea Wolf Saloon** (B d F G) 14-2 h
1413 14th Avenue ✉ WA 98122 ☎ 323-2158
■ **Timberline Tavern** (b GLM lj OS MA) 18-2 h
2015 Boren Avenue ✉ WA 98121 ☎ 622-6220
Largest country dance bar on West Coast with lessons Tue-Fri. 19.30-21 h

CAFES
■ **Glo's** (b BF glm) Wed-Fri 7-14, Sat-Sun 7.30-14.30 h
1621 E. Olive Way ✉ WA 98102 ☎ 324-2577

DANCECLUBS
■ **Neighbours** (B D F G YG)
1509 Broadway East/Pike Street ✉ WA 98122 *(entrance rear alley)*
☎ 324-5358
Also restaurant.
■ **Spintron** (B D GLM)
916 East Pike Street ✉ WA 98122 ☎ 568-6190

RESTAURANTS
■ **Broadway New American Grill. The** (F glm) Mon-Fri 10-2, Sat-Sun 9-2 h
314 Broadway East ✉ WA 98102 ☎ 328-7000
■ **Coastal Kitchen** (BF F glm)
429 15th Avenue East ✉ WA 98112 ☎ 322-1145
■ **Flora. Cafe** (F g)
2901 E. Madison ✉ WA 98112 ☎ 325-9100
■ **Hamburger Mary's** (B F g)
1526 East Olive Way ✉ WA 98122 *(upstairs)* ☎ 324-8112
■ **Hana's Lounge** (B F g)
1914 8th Avenue ✉ WA 98101 ☎ 340-1591
■ **Jack's Bistro** (B F G OS s)
405 15th Avenue East ✉ WA 98112 ☎ 324-9625
■ **Jade Pagoda** (B F g)
606 Broadway East ✉ WA 98102 ☎ 322-5900
■ **Mae's Cafe** (BF F glm) 7-15 h
6412 Phinney Avenue N. ✉ WA 98103 ☎ 782-1222
■ **Thumper's** (AC B CC F GLM MA OS S VS) 10-2 h
1500 East Madison ✉ WA 98122 ☎ 328-3800

SAUNAS/BATHS
■ **Club Seattle** (G SA P VS) 0-24 h
1520 Summit Avenue ✉ WA 98122 ☎ 329-2334
■ **Club Z** (DR f G LJ MA P SA VS) Mon-Thu 16-9, Fri 16-Mon 9 h
1117 Pike Street ✉ WA 98101 *(close to gay nightlife on Capitol Hill)*
☎ 622-9958
Three floors sauna, labyrinth, large SM rooms frequented by a leather crowd but not exclusively.

BOOK SHOPS
■ **Bailey-Coy Books** (CC glm) Mon-Thu, Sun 10-22, Fri, Sat 10-23 h
414 Broadway Avenue East ✉ WA 98102 *(Bus 7/43)* ☎ 322-8842
Large selection of gay/lesbian books.
■ **Beyond the Closet Bookstore** (CC GLM) Sun-Thu 10-23, Fri Sat - 24 h
518 East Pike Street ✉ WA 98122-3618 *(On Capitol Hill, corner of Belmont Ave/E. Pike St)* ☎ 324-4609
Exclusively gay & lesbian bookshop, carrying gay fiction, non-fiction, magazines and erotica.
■ **Fremont Place Book Co.** (gLM)
621 N. 35th ✉ WA 98103 ☎ 547-5970

LEATHER & FETISH SHOPS
■ **Pink Zone. The** (AC CC GLM MA) Mon-Sat 10-22, Sun 11-21 h
211 Broadway Avenue E ✉ WA 98112 *(on Capitol Hill)*
☎ 325-0050
Outrageous and fun fashion, tattoos and body piercing.

TRAVEL AND TRANSPORT
■ **Council Travel** (g)
219 Broadway Avenue East ✉ WA 98102 ☎ 329-4567
■ **It's Your World** (g)
1411 East Olive Way ✉ WA 98122 ☎ 328-0616

HOTELS
■ **Country Inn** (BF glm H)
685 Juniper, Issaquah ✉ WA 98027 ☎ 392-1010
Country living.

Seattle ▶ Huntington — Washington - West Virginia/USA

■ **Gaslight Inn** (bf CC GLM H MA OS PI)
1727 15th Avenue ✉ WA 98112 ☎ 325-3654
🖥 innkeepr@gaslight-inn.com 💻 www.gaslight-inn.com
■ **Landes House** (BF g H OS WH)
712 11th Avenue East ✉ WA 98102 ☎ 329-8781

GUEST HOUSES

■ **Bacon Mansion. The** (BF CC glm H) Office: 8-20 h
959 Broadway East ✉ WA 98102 ☎ 329-1864
☎ (800) 240-1864 (Toll-free) 📠 860-9025
🖥 info@baconmansion.com 💻 www.baconmansion.com
Rooms with phone, private voice-mail, TV, data. Rates US$ 79-159 incl. bf.
■ **Hill House B & B** (BF CC glm H)
1113 East John Street ✉ WA 98102 ☎ 720-7161
☎ (800) 720-7161 (Toll-free) 📠 323-0772
■ **Scandia House B & B** (BF GLM H MA)
2028 34th Avenue South ✉ WA 98144-4923 ☎ 725-7825
📠 721-3348 🖥 scandia@nwlink.com
Near Capitol Hill and downtown.
■ **Shafer Baillie Mansion B&B** (bf CC GLM H MA msg SOL) 8.30-21 h
907 14th Avenue East ✉ WA 98112 *(Capital Hill)* ☎ 322-4654
☎ (800) 922-4654 (toll-free) 📠 329-4654
🖥 smansion@sprynet.com
Suburban location, 5 blocks to gay bars. Most rooms with telephone, priv. bath, WC. Massage for $65 US p/h.

FETISH GROUPS

■ **Generic Leather Productions**
1122 East Pike Street #800 ✉ WA 98122
■ **Knights of Malta MC**
PO Box 210 52 ✉ WA 98111
■ **Seattle Men in Leather**
1122 East Pike Street ✉ WA 98122 ☎ 781-4461
🖥 info@seattlemeninleather.org 💻 www.seattlemeninleather.org
A gay men's social group promoting the Seattle men's leather community. Call or write for info on activities.

Silverdale ☎ 360

SEX SHOPS/BLUE MOVIES

■ **Castle Superstore Adult Retail** 24 hours
2789 NW Randall Way ✉ WA 98383 ☎ 308-0779
Videos, leather, lingerie, magazines, toys, novelties, books, DVD's.

Spokane ☎ 509

GAY INFO

■ **Gay and Lesbian Community Services** 24 hrs
☎ 489-2266

PUBLICATIONS

■ **Stonewall News Northwest**
PO Box 3994 ✉ WA 99220-3994 ☎ 456-8011 📠 455-7013
🖥 snnspokane@aol.com
Monthly GL publication.

BARS

■ **Hour Place** (B D F G S) 17-2 h
415 West Sprague ✉ WA 99204 ☎ 838-6947

SEX SHOPS/BLUE MOVIES

■ **Castle Superstore Adult Retail** 24 hours
11324 E. Sprague ✉ WA 99206
Videos, leather, lingerie, magazines, toys, novelties, books, DVD's.
■ **Spokane Arcade** 0-24 h
1125 West 1st Avenue ✉ WA 99204 ☎ 747-1621

CRUISING

-High Bridge (NU) (People's Park)
-Manito Park
-Mission Park

Tacoma ☎ 253

BARS

■ **Airport Tavern** (B G LJ)
5406 South Tacoma Way ✉ WA 98405 ☎ 475-9730
■ **Casey's Tavern** (B G LJ) 6-2 h
2810 6th Avenue ✉ WA 98406 ☎ 572-7961
■ **Twenty-fourth Street Tavern** (B D GLM S) 12-2 h
2405 Pacific Avenue ✉ WA 98402 ☎ 572-3748

RESTAURANTS

■ **Gold Ball Grill & Spirits** (B d F GLM MA OS) 14-2 h
2708 6th Avenue ✉ WA 98406 ☎ 627-0430

SEX SHOPS/BLUE MOVIES

■ **Castle Superstore Adult Retail** 24 hours
6015 Tacoma Mall Boulevard ✉ WA 98409 ☎ 471-0391
Videos, leather, lingerie, magazines, toys, novelties, books, DVD's.

CRUISING

-Nude beach (follow railroad track 1 mile north of Chambers Creek)
-Pacific Avenue (between 13th & 15th)

USA-West Virginia

Location: East USA
Initials: WV
Time: GMT -5
Area: 62.759 km^2 / 25,668 sq mi.
Population: 1,816,000
Capital: Charleston

Charleston ☎ 304

PUBLICATIONS

■ **abOUT West Virginia**
PO Box 2624 ✉ WV 25329-2624 ☎ 345-9938
🖥 aboutwv@hotmail.com 💻 www.pridewv.com
The West Virginia monthly GLBT publication.

BARS

■ **Grand Palace** (B D F GLM S VS) 17-3.30 h
617 Brooks Street ✉ WV 25301 *(near Smith Street)* ☎ 342-9532

SEX SHOPS/BLUE MOVIES

■ **Arcade News and Books**
230 Capitol Street ✉ WV 25301 ☎ 344-2281

CRUISING

-The Block (AYOR) (Summers, Donnally, Capitol & Christopher Street)

Huntington ☎ 304

BARS

■ **Driftwood Lounge** (AC B D f GLM LJ MA P p r S SNU STV VS)
Mon, Thu, Fri 17-3.30, Sat, Sun 14-? h
1121 7th Avenue ✉ WV 25701 *(near Marshall University Campus)*
☎ 696-9538

SPARTACUS 2001/2002 | 1339

USA/West Virginia - Wisconsin | Huntington ▸ Milwaukee

SEX SHOPS/BLUE MOVIES
■ **Fourth Avenue News**
1119 4th Avenue ✉ WV 25701 ☎ 525-6861

CRUISING
-5th and 7th Avenues (between 11th and 12th Streets)

USA-Wisconsin

Location: Great Lakes region USA
Initials: WI
Time: GMT -6
Area: 169.643 km² / 69,383 sq mi.
Population: 5,170,000
Capital: Madison

Appleton ☎ 920

BARS
■ **Rascals Bar & Grill** (B F GLM OS)
702 East Wisconsin ✉ WI 54911 ☎ 954-9262

Green Bay ☎ 920

BARS
■ **Brandy's II** (B G LJ)
1126 Main Street ✉ WI 54301 ☎ 437-3917
■ **Java's** (B GLM VS)
1106 Main Street ✉ WI 54301 ☎ 435-5476
■ **Napalese Lounge** (B D GLM) Sun-Thu 16-2, Fri Sat 16-2.30 h
515 South Broadway ✉ WI 54303 ☎ 432-9646
■ **Sass** (AC B d GLM MA N S) Tue-Thu 18-2, Fri-Sun 17-2.30 h
840 South Broadway ✉ WI 54304 ☎ 437-3377
■ **Za's** (AC BF CC D f G OS S YG)
1106 Main Street ✉ WI 54301 ☎ 435-5476

CRUISING
-Rest Stop (AYOR) (on US 41, South of DePere)
-Rest Stop (Wisconsin 141, eastside near city limits)

Lodi ☎ 608

GUEST HOUSES
■ **Prairie Garden Bed & Breakfast** (AC BF CC GLM MA msg NU OS VS WH)
West 13172 Highway 188 ✉ WI 53555 (half an hour north of Madison,WI, 3hrs north of Chicago) ☎ 592-5187
☎ 800-380-8427 (toll-free) ✉ prairiegarden@prairiegarden.com
🌐 www.prairiegarden.com
Near nude beach, rates start at $70 (bf. incl.).

Madison ☎ 608

GAY INFO
■ **Gay Center** Mon-Fri 9-17, 19-22 h
1127 University Avenue ✉ WI 53715 ☎ 255-4297

BARS
■ **Barracks. The - Club 5 - Foxhole. The - Planet Q** (AC B BF CC D GLM LJ MA OS S SNU STV TV VS) Restaurant: Tue-Sun 17-22, Sun brunch 10.30 14 h, Bars and club: Mon-Thu 16-2, Fri Sat -2.30, Sun 15-2 h
5 Applegate ✉ WI 53713 ☎ 277-9700
Gay and Lesbian restaurant, 3 bars, nightclub.

■ **Geraldine's** (B D GLM) 16-2 h
3052 East Washington Street ✉ WI 53704 ☎ 241-9335
■ **Greenbush** (B F glm) 16-2
914 Regent Street ✉ WI 53715 ☎ 257-2874
■ **Rod's** (AC B CC D DR f G H LJ MA S VS) 16-2.30 h
636 West Washington Avenue ✉ WI 53703 ☎ 255-0609
■ **Shamrock Tavern** (B D F glm) 11-2 h
117 West Main Street ✉ WI 53703 ☎ 255-5029

SWIMMING
-Mazomanie Beach (Nude beach-30 miles Northwest on Highway Y, 4 miles north to Laws Road, then turn onto gravel road, at the end. One of the best in the Midwest. Camping, swimming, campfires, fun, owls, fishing, trees, cameraderie, tolerance, beauty!)
-Lake Mendota

CRUISING
-Burrows Park
-Fairchild Street (opposite library near square)
-James Madison Park

Menomonee Falls ☎ 414

TRAVEL AND TRANSPORT
■ **Horizon Travel** Mon-Fri 9-17.30, Sat 11-14 h
N81 W15028 Appelton Avenue ✉ WI 53051 ☎ 255-0704
📠 255-0708

Milwaukee ☎ 414

GAY INFO
■ **Gay & Lesbian Community Center** (GLM)
PO Box 1686 ✉ WI 53201 ☎ 643-1652

PUBLICATIONS
■ **g-street magazine**
1212 First Avenue Suite 3, Eau Claire ☎ (877) 398-6918
📠 (715) 831-7985 ✉ publisher@g-street.com
🌐 www.g-street.com
Wisconsin & Minnesota monthly gay entertainment, news & travel magazine.
■ **In Step Magazine**
1661 North Water Street, Suite 411 ✉ WI 53202 ☎ 278-7480
📠 278-5868 ✉ instepnews@aol.com 🌐 www.instepnews.com
Wisconsin's LesBiGay community newspaper.

BARS
■ **B Bar** (B D GLM MA)
1579 South 2nd Street ☎ 672-5580
Dance bar
■ **Ballgame. The** (B F D G S VS) 12-2 h
196 South 2nd Street ✉ WI 53204 ☎ 273-7474
■ **Barbie's Playhouse** (B GLM)
700 East Meinecke ✉ WI 53212 ☎ 374-7441
■ **Boot Camp Saloon** (AC B G LJ OS) Sun-Thu 16-2, Fri Sat -2.30 h
209 East National Avenue ✉ WI 53204 ☎ 643-6900
Leather bar with parking and patio.
■ **C'est La Vie** (B D G N SNU YG) 12-2, Fri Sat 12-2.30 h, Fri Sat shows
231 South 2nd Street ✉ WI 53204 ☎ 291-9600
■ **Dish** (AC B D gLM) 17.30-22 h, closed Tue
235 South 2nd Street ✉ WI 53202 ☎ 273-3474
Popular lesbian bar, gays welcome.
■ **Fannies** (B D gLM)
200 East Washington ✉ WI 53204 ☎ 649-9003

1340 SPARTACUS 2001/2002

Milwaukee ▶ Thermopolis — Wisconsin - Wyoming/USA

■ **Fluid** (AC B CC G) 17-? h
819 South 2nd Street ✉ WI 53204 ☎ 645-8311
Cocktail lounge specializing in Martini's. Warm atmosphere with no attitude and friendly staff. Crowded on week-ends.
■ **Kathy's Nut Hut** (B F GLM S)
1500 West Scott ✉ WI 53201 ☎ 647-2673
■ **Milwaukee Eagle** (! B DR G LJ MA) 20-2 h
300 West Juneau Avenue *(at corner of North 3rd Street)*
☎ 273-6900
Dresscode for backroom only. Very popular.
■ **M&M Club** (AC B CC F GLM MA OS S) 11-2 (meals -23 h)
124 North Water Street ✉ WI 53202 ☎ 347-1962
Piano bar and restaurant.
■ **South Water Street Docks** (AC B G lj MA N s)
354 East National Avenue ✉ WI 53204 ☎ 225-9676
■ **Station 2** (B gLM N)
1534 West Grant Street ✉ WI 53215 ☎ 383-5755
■ **This is it** (AC B Glm MA N) 15-? h
418 East Wells Street ✉ WI 53202 ☎ 278-9192
Very diverse crowd. Friendly atmosphere.
■ **Triangle** (A B G MA N) Mon-Fri 17-?, Sat Sun 15-?
135 East National Avenue ✉ WI 53204 ☎ 383-9412
■ **Woody's** (B G MA N)
1579 South 2nd Street ✉ WI 53204 ☎ 672-0806
■ **1100 Club** (AC B BF d F Glm LJ MA S WE) Mon-Wed 7-2, Fri-Sat -2.30 h
1100 South 1st Street ✉ WI 53204 ☎ 647-9950
Western style Bar & Restaurant. Steaks and seafood.

CAFES

■ **Annex Cafe** (AC BF F GLM LJ MA YG) 10-4 h
1106 South 1st Street ✉ WI 53204 ☎ 672-1217
■ **Pier 221** (b BF f glm)
221 North Water Street ☎ 272-0555

DANCECLUBS

■ **Club 219** (B D GLM S VS) Mon-Thu 16-2, Fri Sat 15-2.30, Sun 15-2 h
219 South 2nd Street ✉ WI 53204 ☎ 276-2711
■ **Eagle** (B D G LJ)
300 West Juneau ✉ WI 53203 ☎ 273-6900
■ **La Cage** (! B F Glm S VS WE YG) 21-2, Sun 16-2 h
801 South 2nd Street ✉ WI 53204 ☎ 383-8330

RESTAURANTS

■ **Glass Menagerie at M&M Bar** (F GLM) Lunch, dinner & Sun brunch.
124 North Water Street ✉ WI 53202 ☎ 347-1962
■ **La Perla** (AC B CC F glm)
734 South 5th Street ✉ WI 53204 ☎ 645-9888
Mexican food.

SEX SHOPS/BLUE MOVIES

■ **J.R. News** (G) 0-24 h
831 North 27th Street ☎ 344-9686

BOOK SHOPS

■ **After Words Bookstore** Mon-Thu 11-22, Fri -23, Sat 10-23, Sun 12-18 h
2710 North Murray Avenue ✉ WI 53211 ☎ 963-9089

HOTELS

■ **Park East Hotel** (BF F glm H)
916 East State Street ✉ WI 53202 ☎ 276-8800
Gay friendly hotel overlooking the lake. Rooms with telephone, minibar, cable TV, video, and private bath, non smoking rooms available.

GENERAL GROUPS

■ **Milwaukee LGBT Community Center**
170 South 2nd Street ✉ WI 53204 ☎ 271 2656 🖷 271 2161
✉ execdirector@mkelgbt.org 🖳 www.mkelgbt.org
Social and educational programs provided

FETISH GROUPS

■ **Beer Town Badgers**
PO Box 840 ✉ WI 53201

HEALTH GROUPS

■ **AIDS Resource Center Of Wisconsin** Mon-Thu 8-21, Fri 8-17 h, closed Sat Sun
PO Box 510498 ✉ Wi 53203-0092 *(820 North Plankinton Avenue)*
☎ 273-1991 ☎ (800) 359-9272 (Toll-free) 🖷 273-2357
🖳 www.arcw.org
HIV counseling & testing, men's and women's support groups. Call for detailed information.

HELP WITH PROBLEMS

■ **Galano Club** (AA) 18-22 h
☎ 2796-6936
■ **Gay Hotline** 0-24 h
☎ 444-7331
■ **Gay People's Union Hotline** 19-21 h
☎ 562-7010

SPECIAL INTEREST GROUPS

■ **Girth & Mirth**
PO Box 862 ✉ WI 53201

CRUISING

-Astor Street (between Juneau and Kilbourn)
-Wisconsin Avenue (between 10th and 17th)

Superior ☎ 715

BARS

■ **JT's Bar & Grill** (AC B F GLM MA S SNU STV) Mon-Fri 15-?, Sat Sun 13-? h
1506 North 3rd ✉ WI 54880 ☎ 394-2580
■ **Trio Bar** (B gLM MA N) ?-2, Fri-Sun -2.30 h
802 Tower Avenue ✉ WI 54880 ☎ 392-5373

Wausau ☎ 715

BARS

■ **Oz** (B D GLM MA s) Mon-Sat 19-? h, Sun 17-? h, Wed and Sun Beer Bust
320 Washington Street ✉ WI 54403 *(next to the mall)* ☎ 842-3225

USA-Wyoming

Location: West USA
Initials: WY
Time: GMT -7
Area: 253.349 km² / 103,620 sq mi.
Population: 480,000
Capital: Cheyenne

Thermopolis ☎ 307

GUEST HOUSES

■ **Out West B+B** (CC glm H)
1344 Broadway ✉ WY 82443 ☎ 864-2700

United States of America

Sauna Guide & Gay Bathhouses International
252 Seiten/Pages, English / Deutsch / Français, ISBN 3-86187-155-6
US$ 17,95

Available from: Bookazine Company, Inc. · 75 Hook Road · Bayonne, NJ 07002
Toll-free (800) 584-3855 · www.bookazine.com

Uruguay

Location: South America
Initials: ROU
Time: GMT -3
International Country Code: ☎ 598 (leave first 0 after area codes
International Access Code: ☎ 00
Language: Spanish
Area: 175,016 km^2 / 68,500 sq mi.
Currency: 1 Uruguayan Peso (urug$) = 100 Centésimos
Population: 3,289,000
Capital: Montevideo
Religions: 78% Roman Catholic
Climate: Winters are cold and wet with frequent rainfalls. Summers are very hot with occasionally rainfalls. Best time for a visit is from October to April.

❋ Homosexuality is not illegal in Uruguay. We have no exact information on the legal situation at present. The gay scene is growing.

★ Homosexualität ist in Uruguay nicht illegal. Genauere juristische Informationen liegen uns nicht vor. Die Szene hat sich in den letzten Jahren beachtlich vergrößert.

❋ En Uruguay, l'homosexualité n'est pas un délit. C'est tout ce que nous pouvons dire à ce sujet. Ces derniers temps, on a ouvert de nombreux bars et boîtes de nuit.

⬢ La homosexualdad en Uruguay no es ilegal. Lastimosamente no poseemos informaciones legales más exactas. El ambiente gay ha crecido enormemente en los últimos años.

✖ L'omosessualità in Uruguay non è illegale. Non abbiamo a disposizione informazioni legali più precise. Negli ultimi anni l'ambiente gay si è esteso notevolmente.

Montevideo ☎ 02

GAY INFO
■ **Guía Triángulo Amatista**
Casilla de Correos 6346, C.P. 11000
Guide for gay travellers

BARS
■ **Avanti** (B D f GLM MA) 21-6 h
Avenida Fernández Crespo esq. Nicaragua
■ **Delmira** (f MG)
Bartolomé Mitre/Buenos Aires *(near Sarandi Pedestrian area)*

CAFES
■ **Ronda, La** (B glm MA)
Ciudadela 1182 esq. Canelones ☎ 903-1353
■ **Sorocabana** (B glm MA s) 8-24 h
Carlos Quijano 1377 ☎ 90-8861
Fri-Sun Show at 22 h.

DANCECLUBS
■ **Caín** (B D DR GLM Ma r snu) Thu-Sat 0-6 h
Cerro Largo 1833 esq. Arenal Grande
Every Thu strip show
■ **Casta** (AC B CC D E G MG s WE) Wed 22-2 h, Fri, Sat 24-5 h
Gonzalo Ramiriz 2121 ☎ 400 65 39
■ **Espejismo** (AC B D GLM MA r snu) Thu-Sun 0-6 h
Jackson 872/Lauro Müller ☎ 408 4736

■ **Ibiza** (b D g MA r snu stv) Thu-Sun 1-7 h
Ejido 1395 esq. Colonia ☎ 901 6728
Thu & Sun shows
■ **Insólito** (B D GLM MA r p stv) Thu-Sun 0-6 h
Cerro Largo 1281 esq. Yaguarón
■ **Milenio** (B D glm P S YG) Fri Sat 0-6
25 de Mayo 749 esq. Ciudadela *(two blocks from Plaza Hotel)*
■ **Piscotico** (B D DR GLM S SNU YG)
Galicia/Magallanes *(opp. Palacio Peñarol)*

RESTAURANTS
■ **Doña Flor Restaurant** (CC E F NG) Mon-Fri 12.30-15, 20.30-24, Sat 20.30-24 h
Boulevard Artigas 1034 ☎ 708 5751
French cuisine. Expensive.
■ **Posada del Puerto** (b F g) Mon-Sat 11.30-0.45, Sun -16 h
Peatonal Pérez Castellanos 2569 esq. Yacaré *(near the habour)*
☎ 915 4278
traditional local cuisine

SEX SHOPS/BLUE MOVIES
■ **Complement** (glm MA) Mon-Fri 10-20, Sat 10-14 h, Sun closed
Rio Nego 1320, 3rd floor, E 308 ☎ 908 1716
■ **Erotik Sex Shop** (glm MA) Mon-Fri 10-19, Sat -14 h
Avenida 18 de Julio 1953, apto. 204 ☎ 923 476

CINEMAS
■ **Cine Atlas** (G MA) 12.30-23 h
Uruguay 1167 ☎ 900-6477

Uruguay — Montevideo ▶ Punta del Este

■ **Cine Private** (G) 12.30-23 h
Convención 1290/San José ☏ 901 9779
■ **Cine Tres Cruces** (G) 12-23 h
Acevedo Díaz N° 1765 ☏ 402-5131
■ **Cinema Yi** (G MA) 14-23 h
Carlos Quijano 1275/Soriano ☏ 901-3368

ESCORTS & STUDIOS
■ **Agencia XTC**
☏ (094) 629 511

BOOK SHOPS
■ **Plazalibros** (G)
Av. 18 de Julio ☏ 902 6707

FASHION SHOPS
■ **Freaks** (GLM YG) Mon-Fri 10-19, Sat -13 h
Río Negro 940, Loc. 001, esq. 18 de Julio ☏ 901 7578
■ **Metal** (G YG) Mon-Sat 10-21 h
Wilson Ferreira Aldunate 1338 esq. 18 de Julio ☏ 902 5196

NEWS STANDS
■ **Librería Palace** (g) 9-24 h
Plaza Independencia 842 *(in the archs of Salvo-Palace)*
section with international gay magazines
■ **Magazine** (g) 9-24 h
Av. 18 de Julio esq. Paraguay ☏ 903-1950
section with international gay magazines

TRAVEL AND TRANSPORT
■ **Flypass-Wolesaler Tour operator**
Río Negro 1354, piso 4, Of. 19 ☏ 902 4050 ✉ 901 1092

HOTELS
■ **Continental** (AC BF H msg SA WO)
Paraguay 1373/Avenida 18 de Julio ☏ 902 2062 ✉ 900 2737
rates: single 65 US$, double 80 US$ incl bf
■ **Embajador** (AC BF H)
San José 1212 ☏ 902 0215 ✉ 902 0009
comfortable rooms with privat bath and color TV. Rates: single 66 US$, double 88 US$.

GENERAL GROUPS
■ **Comunidad Organizada GLTTB (Gay-Lésbica-Travest-Transexual y Bisexual) Uruguay**
Casilla de Correos 7415, C.P. 11.000 ☏ 575 3864
■ **E.E.L.M.S. (Encuentro Ecuménico para la Liberación de las minorías Sexuales)**
Casilla de Correos 1294, C.P. 11.000 📧 fefroq@adinet.com.uy
■ **Grupo DIVERSIDAD**
Casilla de Correos 7415, C.P. 11.000 ☏ 575-3864
📧 dmines@ucu.edu.uy

HEALTH GROUPS
■ **Asociación de Ayuda al Seropositivo (ASEPO)** 18.30-19.30
Bulevar Artigas 1515 ☏ 414 701
■ **Asociación de Meretrices Públicas de Uruguay** 15-19 h
Avenida Daniel Fernandez Crespo 1914 esq. La Paz ☏ 924 5275
information and counselling about AIDS

SWIMMING
-Playa Miramar (G MA) (Rambla Tomás Berreta, Bus 104/105 from downtown)
-Playa Turisferia (take bus from Avenida Italia direction Lagomar or Solymar till bus-stop Avenida Ing. Luis Giannattasio/Avenida de la Playa)
-Playa Chiuaua (NU) 120km east of Montevideo ▶ Punta del Este. at "Cabañas del Tío Tom" behind dunes AYOR.

CRUISING
-Avenida 18 de Julio (MA) (23-? h. Entre/between Plaza Independencia y/and Avenida Dr. Fernández Crespo)
-Rambla República del Perú (Entre/between la Plaza Daniel Muñoz y/and la Plaza W. Churchill)
-Avenida General Flores (YG) (21-? h. Entre/between Bulevar Jose Batlle and/y Ordoñez y Camino Corrales)
-Plaza de Ejército (YG) (21-? h)

Paysandú ☏ 0722

BARS
■ **Bahía Pub** (B g MA) 23-5 h
Proyectada Segunda esq. Enrique Chaplin
■ **Leyendas Pub** (B f glm MA) 20-5 h, closed Mon
Uruguay 699 esq. Dr. J. Silvan Fernández

CAFES
■ **Florencio** (B glm MA)
19 de Abril 932 ☏ 25 722

DANCECLUBS
■ **Brujas Internacional** (AYOR b D glm P S TV VS YG) 23-5 h
Luis Batlle Berres/25 de Mayo

RESTAURANTS
■ **Tres Pinos. Les** (B F glm MA) 11-15 & 19.30-2 h
Avenida España 1474 ☏ 26 252
international cuisine

CRUISING
-Avenida 18 de Julio (Entre/between Baltazar Brum y/and Cerrito)
-Plaza Artigas (actividad por la tarde/in the evening)
-Avenida España (Entre/between Bulevar Artigas y/and Cerrito)
-Zona de la Rambla (al final de/ at the end of Av. Brasil)

Piriapolis ☏ 0432

DANCECLUBS
■ **Vértigo** (B D glm YG) Fri Sat 0-5 h
Rambla de los Argentinos s/n° ✉ 20200 *(at the city limits)*

HOTELS
■ **Argentino** (AC BF B F H OS WO)
Rambla de los Argentinos & Armenia ☏ 30 54
■ **Miramar** (AC H)
Rambla de los Argentinos No. 1082 ☏ 25 44

Punta del Este ☏ 042

BARS
■ **Moby Dick Pub** (B g MA) daily open
Rambla General Artigas 650 *(at the habour)*

DANCECLUBS
■ **Morocha. La** (B D glm S YG) open only from december to february
La Barra de Maldonado
■ **Zona Franca** (B D G MA S) open only from december to february
Av. Gorlero esq. Calle 32

Port Villa | Vanuatu

Vanuatu

Location: Oceania
Initials: VU
Time: GMT +11
International Country Code: ☏ 678 (no area codes)
International Access Code: ☏ 00
Language: English and French; Bichelamar
Area: 12,190 km² / 4,706 sq mi.
Currency: 1 Vatu (VT)
Population: 183,000
Capital: Port-Vila (on Efate)
Religions: 80% Christian
Climate: Tropical climate that is effected by southeast trade winds.

※ Vanuatu, "the land that rises from the ocean", has seen the development of a modest gay scene. The capital, Port-Vila, is a small town of 34,000 inhabitants, mostly Melanesians, but also Polynesians, Europeans, Vietnamese, and Chinese. Melanesians traditionally have little difficulty dealing with the concept of homosexual desires. We have no exact information on the legal situation here, but it is supposedly more liberal on Vanuatu than on neighbouring islands. This is the perfect place for spending beautiful, quiet and relaxed holidays.

★ "Das Land, das sich aus dem Meer erhebt". Hier hat sich eine eher zurückhaltende schwule Szene entwickelt. Die Hauptstadt Port-Vila ist eine Kleinstadt mit knapp 34.000 Einwohnern, meist Melanesier, daneben Polynesier, Europäer, Vietnamesen und Chinesen. Den Melanesiern bereitet schwule Lust traditionell wenig Bauchschmerzen. Die zur Zeit gültigen Gesetze, sie liegen uns leider nicht im Einzelnen vor, sollen im Vergleich zu denen benachbarter Inseln im südlichen Pazifik eher liberal sein. Hier kann man einen schönen, ruhigen, entspannten Urlaub verbringen.

※ Le "Pays qui sort de la mer" (indépendant depuis le 30.7.1980) est un archipel de plus de 70 îles. Pas grand chose encore, au niveau gay. Port-Vila, la capitale de l'archipel, est une petite ville de 16.000 habitants, en majorité des Mélanésiens. Pour le reste, ce sont des Polynésiens, des Européens, des Vietnamiens et des Chinois. L'homosexualité ne semble pas être un sujet tabou. La législation actuelle (nous ne disposons, hélas, d'aucune information concrète) semble être plutôt tolérante, si on compare avec les autres pays du Pacifique Sud. Calme et détente assurés à Vanuatu!

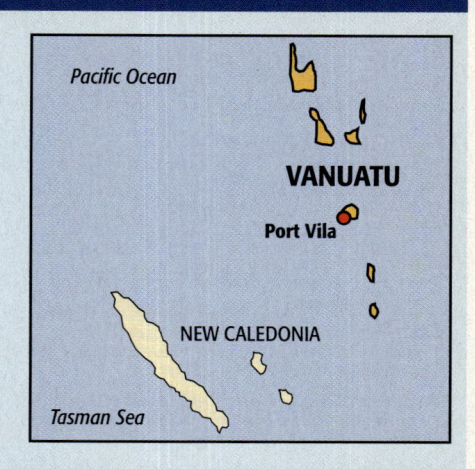

● "El país que sumerge del mar". Aqui se ha desarrollado un ambiente gay más bien discreto. La capital Port-Vila es una pequeña ciudad con apenas 16,000 habitantes, la mayoría melanesios, aparte de polinesios, europeos, vietnamitas y chinos. Tradicionalmente el deseo gay no ha sido cosa que les haya dado dolores de cabeza a los melanesios. Las leyes actualmente vigentes, desgraciadamente no las tenemos en detalle, parecen ser, en comparación con las de los demás vecinos de Pacífico Sur, más bien liberales. Aquí se pueden disfrutar unas vacaciones preciosas, tranquilas y relajadas.

✖ "La terra che sorge dall'oceano" è costituita da più di 70 isole. Si è sviluppata una vita gay di dimensioni alquanto modeste. La capitale, Port-Vila, è una piccola cittadina di 16,000 abitanti, in gran parte Melanesiani ma anche Polinesiani, Europei, Vietnamiti e Cinesi. Tradizionalmente, ai Melanesiani l'omosessualità non crea soverchi problemi. Non lo sappiamo con assoluta sicurezza, ma le notizie che ci sono giunte parlano di una situazione legale senz'altro più liberale che nelle isole vicine. Una vacanza bella, quieta e rilassante, quindi, che aspetta soltanto di essere assaporata fino in fondo.

Port Vila

BARS
■ **Bar Cascade** (B F g)
(south of town)
Late night cabaret.

■ **Houstalet. L'** (B D F g) 18-3 h
(south of town on road to Wharf)

■ **Prive** (B D P g YG) 21.30-3 h
(south of town on road to Wharf)

RESTAURANTS
■ **Pandanus Restaurant** (B F g) closed Mon
(on main road east of town)

CRUISING
-Around Cinema Hickson (south of town)

SPARTACUS 2001/2002 | 1345

Venezuela

Location: South America
Initials: YV
Time: GMT -4
International Country Code: ☎ 58 (leave the first 0 after area codes)
International Access Code: ☎ 00
Language: Spanish, in some areas Indian languages
Area: 912,050 km² / 352,143 sq mi.
Currency: 1 Bolivar (vB) = 100 Céntimos
Population: 23,242,000
Capital: Caracas
Religions: 93% Roman Catholic
Climate: Hot and humid tropical climate which is more moderate in the highlands.

There are no legal restrictions on homosexuality in this Latin American country, but a number of administrative barriers can make life difficult.

Es gibt in diesem lateinamerikanischen Land keine gesetzlichen Beschränkungen des Rechts auf Homosexualität, aber eine Reihe behördlicher Diskriminierungen.

Au Vénézuéla, l'homosexualité n'est pas un délit. Ce qui ne veut pas dire que les autorités fichent automatiquement la paix aux gays!

En este país sudamericano no existe ningún tipo de restricción legal del Derecho a la Homosexualidad, pero sí que existe una serie de discriminaciones por parte de las autoridades.

In questo paese latino-americano non esistono restrizioni contro l'omossessualità, ma la discriminazione operata dal governo è notevole.

Barquisimeto - Estado Lara ☎ 051

BARS
■ **Albert** (B glm MA)
Calle 38 (between Carreras 23 & 24)
■ **Bar Banana** (B glm MA)
Calle 14 (between Carreras 30 & 31)
■ **Dulce Pimienta** (B glm MA)
Calle 19 (between carreras 20 & 21)
■ **Johny's** (B glm MA)
Calle 18 (between carreras 29 & 30)
■ **El Tizón** (B f G MA r)
Carrera 16 (between Calle 29 and Calle 30)

DANCECLUBS
■ **Shonkry's** (! B D GLM)
Carrera 18/Calle 42

CRUISING
-Museo de Barquisimeto
-Ateneo de Barquisimeto
-Hotel Barquisimeto Hilton (Bar)

Caracas - Distrito Federal ☎ 02

TOURIST INFO
■ **Corpo Turismo**
Plaza Venezuela, Centro Capriles 7°

BARS
■ **Copa's Dancing Bar** (B D glm MA) 21-? h
Calle Guaicaipuro, Torre Taeca, El Rosal

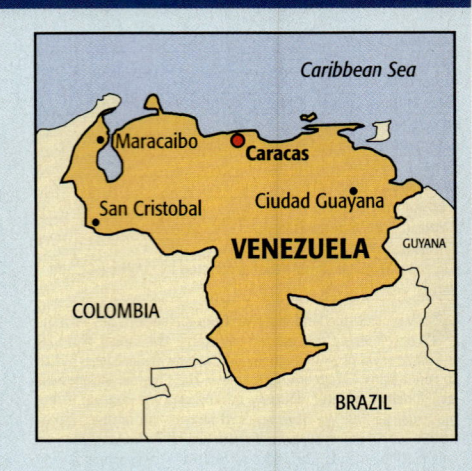

■ **La Cotorra** (B F G MA)
Centro Comercial, Paseo Las Mercedes (near Tamaro Hotel Inter-Continantal) ☎ 992 06 08
■ **Dos Barras** (! B F G MA)
Pasaje Ascunción (between Av. Abraham Lincoln/Casanova (near Plaza Venezuela/Sabana Grande Metro) ☎ 729 406
■ **El Rincón del Gabán** (! B G YG) 17-2 h, Fri Sat -5 h
Avenida San Antonio 38, Sabana Grande (beetween Av. Abraham Lincoln/Casanova, Pl. Venezuela Metro) ☎ 762 78 07
■ **Greenfields** (B D GLM MA)
Centro Commercial Las Mercedes
■ **Tasca Pullman** (B G MA) 18-5 h
Av. Francisco Solano Lopez (1st floor of Ovidio Building) ☎ 761 11 12
Popular
■ **Same Side. The** (B GLM MA SNU)
Av. Casanova/Calle El Colegio, Sabana Grande ☎ 76 60 54
Fri & Sat strip show,
■ **West Side. The** (B d G LJ SNU)
Calle Chacaíto, Chacaíto ☎ 952 75 15
■ **Tortilla** (B G MA) Mon-Sat 19-? h
Avenida San Antonio (between Av. Abraham Lincoln/Casanova, Pl. Venezuela Metro)

CAFES
■ **Cafe Con Leche** (B glm MA)
Av. Libertador, Edf. Libertador, Local 1-A, El BosQue ☎ 731 16 83

DANCECLUBS
■ **A Mi Manera** (glm)
C/ Madrid, Quinta Avileña ☎ 929-672

Caracas ▶ La Guaira | Venezuela

■ **Tiffany´s Club** (! B D e glm P VS YG) 23-5 h, Sun closed
(Av. San Juan Bosco) *(in the basement of the Cinte Altamira building)*
☏ 266 63 71
■ **Zig Zag** (B D G LJ YG) 15-7 h, Mon closed
Av. Libertador *(between Av. Las Acacias/Las Palmas, Metro Plaza Venezuela)*
Popular on Sun. Only recommended if you speak Spanish.

SAUNAS/BATHS

■ **Baños Turcos Suecos** (G MA msg SA SB) 7-21 h
Calle el Mango, Urb. San Antonio *(Metro Pl. Venezuela, near corner with Avenida Las Acacias)* ☏ 793 77 66
■ **Sauna Arcoiris** (G MA SA SB VS) 14 21 h
Av. Andrés Bello/Calle La Colina *(near Teatro Alberto Paz, Sateveca)*
☏ 793 71 81
Show on Sunday.

TRAVEL AND TRANSPORT

■ **Take A Break Tours** Mon-Fri 8.30-17.30 h, closed Sat Sun
Torre Britanica, Mezzanina 1, Sector A, Local 4, *(U-Altamira)*
☏ 263 49 42 🖷 263 39 30
Travelagency.

HOTELS

■ **Gran Melia Caracas Hotel** (B F H NG)
Av. Casanova & Recreo. Sabana Grande ☏ 762 81 11
New hotel with 432 rooms within walking distance to the gay nightlife. Rates from US$ 275.
■ **Tampa Hotel** (B BF CC F H NG OS)
Av. Fco.Solano Lopez No.9, Sabana Grande *(U-Sabana Grande)*
☏ 762 37 71 🖷 762 01 12
Recommended. Rates starting at US$ 51/Single.

HEALTH GROUPS

■ **ACCI - Acción Ciudadana Contra el SIDA**
☏ 232 79 38 🖷 235 92 15 ✉ accsi@ccs.internet.ve
🖳 internet.ve/accsi
■ **Hospital Universitario de Caracas** Mon-Fri 13-18 h
Piso 8 *(8th floor)* ☏ 662 88 05
Free diagnosis and treatment, contact tracing, health education activities on the subject of VD Prevention through conferences, interviews, television programmes, leaflets, etc..
■ **Unidad Sanitaria del Sur** Mon-Thu 12-15 h
Final de la Avenida Roosevelt ☏ 61 41 47

SWIMMING

-Playa Bahia de Cata (Maracay, about 3 hours from Caracas)
-Playa Camuri Chico (La Guayra & Pantaletu, very gay)
-Playa Camuri Grande (Naiguata)
-Playa Chuspa (La Sabana)
-Playa de los Angeles (AYOR)
-Playa Macuto Sheraton (next to the Hotel) (popular)
-Playa Marina Grande

CRUISING

-Centro Comercial Paseo Las Mercedes, Urb. Las Mercedes (AYOR)
-Centro Comercial Chacaito
-Centro Simon Bolivar, El Silencio
-Calle Real de Sabana Grande
-Centro Plaza (in front of United States Embassy, evenings)
-Plaza Candelaria (AYOR) (after 18 h)
-Avenida Francisco Solano (AYOR R)
-Avenida Casanova (r)
-Hotel Tamamaco (r)
-Cafés along Boulevard de Sabana Grande
-Centro Comercial Ciudad Tamanaco
-Avenida Abraham Lincoln (AYOR)
-Paseo Los Ilustres (AYOR)
-Plaza Caracas (AYOR)
-Plaza Diego de Lozada (AYOR)
-Ateneo de Caracas (WE) (Plaza Morelos)
-"El Circuito" (Car-cruising on Avenida Francisco Solano between Avenida Negrín and Avenida Los Jabillos)
-Parque Los Caobos (AYOR WE) (by Teresa Careños Theatre)
-Parque Central (AYOR WE) (by Hilton Hotel and including Contemporary Museum)

Cumana - Estado Sucre ☏ 094

SWIMMING

-Playa San Luis (Along the beach, near the "Vivero" and Hotel Los Bordones. Cruising activity. Let People ask for a cigarette. Sometimes R but not dangerous or expensive.)

Isla Margarita - Estado Nueva Esparta ☏ 095

BARS

■ **Hilton Hotel** (B H NG)
Calle los Uveros-Porlamar ☏ 62 33 33

DANCECLUBS

■ **Mosquito Coast** (AC B D F g MA OS R WE) 18-6 h
(behind Bella Vista Hotel) ☏ 61 35 24

RESTAURANTS

■ **Moise's Restaurant** (B F NG OS r)
Playa El Aqua
Gay owner, mostly straight crowd.

TRAVEL AND TRANSPORT

■ **New Life Tours** (g)
Avenida Joaquin Maneiro 53 - Pampatar ☏ 62 50 46
Travel Agency (IGTA-Member, accomodation, yacht charters)

CRUISING

-Avenida 4 de Mayo
-Avenida Santiago Mariño
-Playa Bella Vista (AYOR)(behind Mosquito Coast, best in the afternoon)
-Playa el Morro (AYOR)(in front of Sol y Mar, best in the afternoon)
-Beach between Playa Moreno and Playa Caracola (from the Hilton hotel 500m past the new harbour)

La Guaira - Distrito Federal ☏ 031

HOTELS

■ **Macuto Sheraton** (AC B D E F H NG PI SOL)
Urbanización Caraballeda, Avenida La Costanera ☏ 94 43 00
Separated from beach, where local beautiful, often bisexual young men do crowd. Bar extremely cruisy (20-1 h), some staff members are also gay. In the nearby village of Caraballeda, several bars and cafés open until 2 or 3 h (YG). All rooms are with telephone, priv. bath and balcony. Rates US$ 70-95.

SPARTACUS 2001/2002 | 1347

Venezuela | Maracaibo ▶ Valencia

Maracaibo - Estado Zulia ☏ 061

BARS
- **Bosque.El** (B G MA) Fri-Sun 21-4 h
Avenida 9 *(between Calles 76 and 77)*
- **Diamond White** (B D E G MA p YG)
Calle 77 *(Near Calle 3 D)*
- **Mara Bar** (B E g MA WE) 11-1 h
Avenida 2 *Hotel del Lago, Milagro*
- **Meson de Chimitas** (B D G MA YG) Thu-Sun 21-4 h
Avenida 13A/Calle 76
- **Stu Ricardo** (B G MA)
Avenida 3G/Calle 77
Bohemian atmosphere.
- **Union** (B G MA)
Avenida Bella Vista *(between Calle 83 & 84)*

CAFES
- **Kabuki** (B f G MA) 8-22 h
Boulevard 5 de Julio *(Calle 77 between Avenidas 12 and 13)*

HOTELS
- **Roma** (H NG MA)
Avenue Bella Vista/Calle 86 ☏ 22 08 68/33
You may rent a simple room by the hour or for the whole night. Single Bs 2.000/night.

CRUISING
- Centro Comercial Costa Verde (shopping mall)
- Avenue Bella Vista (off Avenue Cecilio Acosta)
- Boulevard 5 de Julio (Calle 77)
- Paseo Ciencias (ayor) (afternoons and nights)

Mérida - Cord de Mérida ☏ 074

CRUISING
- Plaza Bolivar
- Teleferico
- Parco Los Chorros de Milla

Puerto La Cruz - Estado Anzoátegui ☏ 081

BARS
- **Guatacarazo. El** (B NG r)
Paseo Colon Boulevard
- **Parranda** (B g)
Paseo Colon Boulevard
- **Studio** (B d e NG YG)
Avenue Americo Vepucio *(Morro resort area)*

DANCECLUBS
- **Con Sabor Latino** (AC B D GLM S) 20-4 h
Calle Bolivar *(Edificio Alsyru, 2nd floor)*
- **Hato. El** (B D G MA S) 24-5 h
Calle Democracia N° 6

HOTELS
- **Doral Beach** (B H NG PI)
Avenue Americo Vespucio, PO Box 42 75 ☏ 879 11
- **Melia Puerto La Cruz** (B BF F H NG OS PI)
(at the end of Paseo Colon) ☏ 69 13 11 🖷 69 12 41

SWIMMING
- Doral Beach
- Cangrjo Beach
- El Morro
- Silver Island
- Guanta Harbor
- Caracas Islands (within the Mochima National Park)
- Arapito Beach
- Colorada Beach

CRUISING
- Paseo Colon
- Plaza Bolivar
- Hotel Melia Beach
- Doral Beach
- Silver Island

San Cristóbal - Estado Táchira ☏ 076

HOTELS
- **Bella Vista** (B H NG)
Calle 9/Carrera 9
- **Tama** (B F H PI)
Avenida 19 de Abril *(Urb. Pirineos)* ☏ 55 44 77
Convenient location, 1 hour to the airport. All rooms with priv. bath, WC and telephone. Single Bs 375, double 430.

Valencia - Estado Carabobo ☏ 041

BARS
- **Cuevas de Louis Candela. Las** (B g)
Avenida Bolivar
- **Posada.La** (B G)
Los Sauces/Avenue Bolivar

CAFES
- **Cafeteria Atrium** (B F g)
Centro Prof. Avenue Bolivar

DANCECLUBS
- **Rose & Flower** (B D G VS YG)
Urb. Las Rosas, Lincoln Ave.
Very popular, two floors.

CRUISING
- Plaza Bolivar (in and around Hotel Intercontinental)

Vietnam

Name: Viet-nam
Location: South East Asia
Initials: VN
Time: GMT +7
International Country Code: ☎ 84
International Access Code: ☎ 00
Language: Vietnamese; partly French and English (in the south)
Area: 331,114 km² / 128,065 sq mi.
Currency: 1 Dong (D) = 100 Xu
Population: 76,520,000
Capital: Hanoi (Ha-noi)
Religions: 55% Buddhist, 5% Catholic
Climate: Tropical climate in the south, monsoon climate in the north with a hot, rainy season that lasts from mid-May to mid-September and warm, dry season between mid-October and mid-March.

❋ Vietnam has no laws prohibiting homosexuality, although there are strong penalties for prostitution. Homosexuality has strong roots in Vietnamese culture, although open public behaviour and Western gay lifestyles are not tolerated by Vietnamese society. Vietnam so far has no strictly-gay venues.
English is widely spoken everywhere in Vietnam. Very few people speak French, which is no longer politically correct.

❋ In Vietnam gibt es keine Gesetze, die sich gegen Homosexualität richten, jedoch ist Prostitution illegal und wird streng bestraft. Homosexualität ist in der vietnamesischen Kultur stark verwurzelt, auch wenn auffällige öffentliche Verhaltensweisen, wie der westliche schwule "lifestyle", von der vietnamesischen Gesellschaft nicht toleriert werden. Bisher hat sich in Vietnam keine organisierte homosexuelle Szene etablieren können.
Englisch ist weitverbreitet und wird von den meisten Menschen in Vietnam gesprochen. Wenige sprechen Französisch, jedoch gilt diese Sprache als politisch nicht korrekt.

❋ Le Vietnam n'a pas de lois condamnant l'homosexualité. De sévères peines sanctionnent par contre la prostitution. L'homosexualité a de profondes racines dans la culture vietnamienne mais un comportement ouvert similaire à celui des occidentaux ne serait pas toléré ici. Le Vietnam n'a pas encore une scène gaye bien établie.
L'anglais est courrament parlé dans tout le pays. Certaines personnes pratiquent encore le français bien que cette langue ne soit plus considérée comme politiquement correcte.

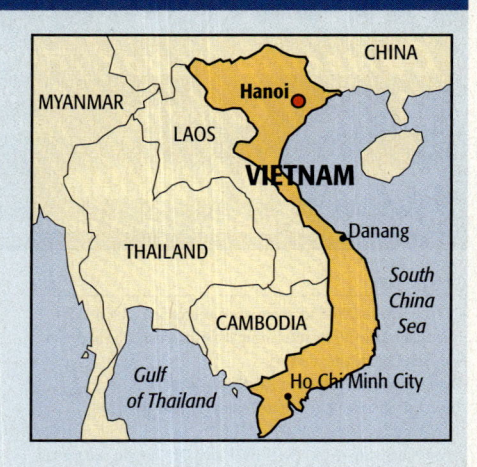

❋ En Vietnam no existen leyes en contra de la homosexualidad, pero la prostitución es ilegal y muy severamente castigada. La homosexualidad está muy arraigada en la sociedad vietnamita, si bien no se tolera un comportamiento llamativo en público, como lo es el estilo de vida gay occidental. Hasta el momento no se ha podido establecer un movimiento gay organizado.
La mayoría de los vietnamitas habla inglés. Pocos saben hablar francés, pero utilizar esta lengua no se considera políticamente correcto en Vietnam.

❋ In Vietnam non esistono leggi contro l'omosessualità, però la prostituzione è illegale e viene punita severamente. L'omosessualità ha forti radici nella cultura vietnamita pur non tolerando comportamenti poco discreti come anche lo stile di vita gay occidentale. Fin'ora non si trovano né locali per sesso né locali esclusivamente omosessuali.
La lingua inglese è molto diffusa e la maggior parte dei vietnamiti la parla. Pochi parlano anche il francese il che non è molto popolare per la storia coloniale del Vietnam.

NATIONAL GROUPS

■ **Nguyen Friendship Society**
🖥 www.GoVietnam.com/NFS
Underground AIDS prevention program for gay/bi men.

Ha Noi

BARS

■ **Café Lieu** (G N R)
20 Quang Trung Street/Ha Hoi Street
■ **GC** (AC B G R)
Bao Khanh Street
■ **Golden Cock**
5 Bao Khan Street ☎ 825 499
■ **Sparks Bar** (AC B g R)
88 Lo Duc Street

DANCECLUBS

■ **Apocalypse Now** (B g D)
338 Ba Trieu Street
■ **Metal Disco** (B g D)
Cua Nam Street

HOTELS

■ **Camellia Hotel** (H)
Thuoc Bac Street
■ **Trang An Hotel** (H)
51 Hang Gai Street

GUEST HOUSES

■ **Real Darling Café and Guesthouse** (H)
33 Hang Quat

Vietnam | Ha Noi ▶ Nha Trang

VIETNAM
Cambodia Laos Bali Thailand
local gay guides, private holidays, a world of new friends.

www.utopia-tours.com
Asia's gay & lesbian travel pioneers

Utopia Tours
info@utopia-tours.com

CRUISING
- Ba Dinh Square (AYOR R) (here you meet soldiers after dark)
- Hoan Kiem Lake (R) (particularly in the park around the bridge to Ngoc Son Pagoda after dark)
- Outdoor cafés at the bend in Bao Khanh Street
- Thien Quang Lake (R) (opposite Lenin Park after dark)
- Tran Hung Dao Street (AYOR)
- Quan Phong Lan (AYOR) (Near Hai Phong City Theatre and garden. Many sailors)

Hô Chi Minh City (Sai Gon)

BARS
■ **Quan 241** (B g F) Best after 19.30 h
Nguyen Thi Minh Khai (on the roundabout where Nguyen Thi Minh Khai, Ly Thai To and Nguyen Van Cu meet)

CAFES
■ **Bich Lien Coffee** (b BF g)
26 Dien Bien Phu Street, District 10
■ **Hao Thi Quán** (b BF g)
636 Le Hong Phong, District 10
Coffee house.
■ **Phong Cat Café** (b BF g) Sun mornings
Nguyen Van Troi Street (next to Saigon Lodge)
■ **343 Café** (b BF g)
343 Nguyen Trai Street, District 1
■ **373 Café** (b BF g)
373/44 Cach Mang Thang Tam, Tan Binh District

DANCECLUBS
■ **Apocalypse Now** (B D g OS R) 23-? h
29 Mac Thi Buoi Street, District 1 (at the end of Thi Sach Street)
■ **Long Van Cultural Entertainment Center** (B D g) On Mon
Dien Bien Phu Street, District 3
■ **Zouk** (B g D R)
191 Nguyen Hue, District 1 (Opposite Oscar Hotel)

RESTAURANTS
■ **Tu My 2** (! g F S)
53 Nguyen Thi Minh Khai, District 1

FITNESS STUDIOS
■ **Workers Club** (g SA SB PI WO)
55 Nguyen Thi Minh Khai Street
Cruisy especially in the showers and locker rooms below the pool in the late afternoon.

HOTELS
■ **Evergreen Hotel** (H)
261 Hai Ba Trung Street
■ **Hong Kong Mini Hotel** (H)
22 Bui Vien
■ **Thai Thien 1 Hotel** (g H)
31 Le Anh Xuan Street
■ **Thai Thien 2 Hotel** (g H)
142 Bui Thi Xuan Street
■ **181 Hotel** (NG)
181 Dinh Tien Hoang Street ☏ 829 7362

CRUISING
- Nguyen Binh Khiem Street, Nguyen Du Street and Nguyen Trung Ngan Street (AYOR) (after dark near the zoo)
- Sai Gon Superbowl (near the airport)
- Tu Xuong Street (AYOR) (Near the Cach Mang Thang Tam Roundabout and Café Cay Dua. After dark)
- Turtle Fountain (look for "Con Rùa" on street maps. After dark)
- Waterfront area at the end of Nguyen Hue Boulevard (AYOR) (After dark)

Hoi An

CRUISING
- Along the quay after sunset. Beware of hustlers.
- Main beach (especially at dawn and late afternoon)

Nha Trang

HOTELS
■ **Khatoco Hotel** (g H)
9 Biet Tru
■ **Vien Dong Hotel** (g H)
1 Tran Hung Dao

CRUISING
- Boulevard along the beach (At the sunset especially with motorbike)
- Palm groves along the beach (AYOR) Beware of huslers (after 23 h)

Yugoslavia

Name: Jugoslavija • Jugoslawien • Yougoslavie • Iugoslavia
Location: Southern central Europe
Initials: YU
Time: GMT +1
International Country Code: ☏ 381
International Access Code: ☏ 99
Language: Serbo-Croatian, Albanian
Area: 102.173 km² / 39,449 sq mi.
Currency: 1 Yugoslavian Dinar (Din) = 100 Para
Population: 10,616,000
Capital: Beograd (Belgrade)
Religions: 65% Orthodox, 19% Muslim, 4% Roman Catholic
Climate: Climate varies considerably with altitude and geographical location. The costal region is hot in summer.

✳ In all remaining parts of the former Yugoslavia, homosexuality is now legal. The only age of consent we have on record is that of Montenegro, set at 14 years.

✳ In allen Teilen Rest-Jugoslawiens ist Homosexualität heute legal. Wir kennen nur die montenegrinische Schutzaltersgrenze von 14 Jahren.

✳ L'homosexualité n'est plus en délit, dans ce qui reste de la Yougoslavie. Dans le Monténégro, la majorité sexuelle est fixée à 14 ans.

✳ La homosexualidad ya no es ilegal en todos los territorios del resto de Yugoslavia. La única edad de consentimiento de nuestro conocimiento es la de Montenegro: 14 años.

✖ In Serbia l'omosessualità è completamente proibita, mentre nel Montenegro si possono avere rapporti a partire dai 14 anni.

Beograd/Belgrado - Serbia ☏ 011

BARS
■ **Academia** (B D g S YG) 23-6 h
Raiceva/Knez Mihajlova ✉ 11000 *(Basement of Art & Design Academy)*
■ **Platoj Cafe Club** (B glm MA)
Vasina ulica ✉ 11000
■ **Prostor Club** differing days 23-4 h
Sarajevska 26 ✉ 11000 *(Near train station)*
■ **Saga Club** (B G MA) Sun 21-6 h
Marsala Tolbuhina/14 Decembra street ✉ 11000 *(Bus 19/21/22)*

CAFES
■ **Moskva Hotel** (B g OG)
Terazije Place ✉ 11000 *(At Sweet-Coffee-Shop)*

SAUNAS/BATHS
■ **Javno Kupatilo** (g)
Dusanova street ✉ 11000
Only on man's days.

GENERAL GROUPS
■ **Gay Yugoslav SM Initiative (GYSM)** (LJ P)
c/o Gogoljeva 98a/40 ✉ 11030 ☏ 545 585 ✉ rijzweep@freemail.nl
Contact group for gay SM.

HEALTH GROUPS
■ **Infektivna Klinika**
Klinicki center Srbije ✉ 11000 ☏ 68 33 66
HIV-screening. Ask for Dr. Jevtovic.

CRUISING
- Usce Park (ayor) (around Museum of Modern Art, at nights)
- Karadjordjev park (ayor) (JNA street, close to Slavija Place, opposite Sveti Sava Cathedral, at night)
- Ada Giganlija Lake
- Cvetni Trg to Srpskih Vladara street (opposite Yugoslovensko Dramsko Pozoriste)
- Zemunski gradski Park (in Zemun)
- Main Train/Main Bus station
- Zeleni Venac Bus Terminal
- Sremska street/Terazije place (underground passage)

Novi Sad - Serbia

BARS
■ **Queen** (B G P) Fri Sat 24-7 h
c/o Novi Sad Hotel ✉ 21000 *(Opposite Main train station)*

CAFES
■ **Atrium** (B glm) 24-? h
Pasiceva street ✉ 21000
■ **Royal** (g)
c/o Putnik Hotel, Ilije Ognjanovica street ✉ 21000 *(1st floor)*

Yugoslavia Novi Sad ▶ Ulcinj

DANCECLUBS
■ **Contrast** (B D G) Sun
Kisacka street ✉ 21000

CINEMAS
■ **Arena** (g) 10/17 h
Bul. Mihajla Pupina ✉ 21000 *(Behind Hotel Park)*
Only during porno-projection.

HEALTH GROUPS
■ **Higijenski Institut**
Bul. Revolucije ✉ 21000
Aids testing and information. Contact Dr. Borisa Vukovic.

CRUISING
-Garden in front of the rail way station (ayor) (at night)
-Futoski Park (Futoska street, behind Hotel Park, evenings)
-Becar Strand
-Kamenjar Beach
-Bus station (daytime)
-SPENS shopping center (ground floor)

Podgorica - Montenegro
CRUISING
-Park opposite Hotel Crna Gora (AYOR)
-Train and bus station

Subotica - Serbia ☎ 024
CRUISING
-Railway station
-Park opposite Main train station (only evenings)
-Park opposite City Sport center
-Palicko Jezero (NU) (very popular)

Ulcinj - Montenegro
SWIMMING
-Along the beach (12 km!)
-Camping area of "Ada" (NU)

Most HIV+ men try not to pass on HIV

+ve
I want to give him one - but I don't want to give him it

GMFA Gay Men Fighting AIDS

All GMFA's campaigns & actions are planned & executed by positive, negative and untested volunteers. To volunteer for GMFA write, phone

Kitwe ▸ Ndola City | Zambia

Zambia

Name: Sambia • Zambie
Location: Southern central Africa
Initials: Z
Time: GMT +2
International Country Code: ☎ 260 (leave the first 0 of the area codes)
International Access Code: ☎ 00
Language: English (official)
Area: 752,614 km^2 / 290,586 sq mi.
Currency: 1 Kwacha (K) = 100 Ngwee
Population: 9,666,000
Capital: Lusaka
Religions: 72% Christian
Climate: Tropical climate that is modified by altitude. The rainy season lasts from October to April.

❋ In Zambia homosexual relations between men of any age are illegal according to Articles 155-158 of the penal code. The maximum penalty is fourteen years imprisonment. In spite of this legislation, the administration occasionally insists that there are no homosexuals in Zambia, and that there is therefore nothing to punish. We have no information on the general attitude of society towards gays.

❋ Homosexuelle Beziehungen zwischen Männern jeden Alters sind gemäß den Artikeln 155-158 des Strafgesetzbuches illegal. Die Höchststrafe liegt bei 14 Jahren Gefängnis. Jedoch vertreten die Behörden des Landes gelegentlich die Meinung, in ihrem Staat gebe es gar keine Homosexuellen und somit sei auch nichts zu bestrafen. Über die Einstellung der Bevölkerung gegenüber Schwulen ist uns nichts bekannt.

❋ En Zambie, l'homosexualité masculine est un délit, même entre adultes consentants (articles 155 à 158 du code pénal). On risque un maximum de 14 ans de prison, même si, bizarrement, les autorités du pays affirment que l'homosexualité n'existe pas dans le pays. Nous ne sommes pas en mesure de dire si les gens, là-bas, sont plutôt homophobes ou homophiles.

❋ Las relaciones homosexuales entre hombres, sean de la edad que sean, constan como ilegales de acuerdo con los párrafos 155-158 del Código Penal. La pena máxima comprende 14 años de cárcel. Así y todo, las autoridades de este país sostienen a veces la opinión de que en Zambia no existen homosexuales-y asi tampoco hay nada que castigar. Sobre la actitud de la población hacia los gays sabemos casi nada.

❋ I paragrafi 155-158 del codice penale considerano illegali le relazioni omosessuali fra maschi di qualsiasi età. Quattordici anni di prigione rappresentano il massimo della pena comminabile. Nonostante tutto, però, il governo s'è dato gran pena per sottolineare che in Zambia il problema non esista. Non abbiamo informazioni sull'atteggiamento generale nei confronti dei gay.

Kitwe ☎ 02

BARS

■ **Cobalt Room Bar** (B d F H NG YG)
c/o Hotel Edingurgh, PO Box 218 00 *(city centre)* ☎ 21 68 63

CRUISING

-In front of the "Zamby"
-Squash Club (after business hours; also restaurant at Squash Club which is the only place where you may safely eat meat in Zambia; not far from city center)

Lusaka ☎ 01

BARS

■ **Lusaka Hotel** (ayor B D F g H WE)
Katondo Road, PO Box 300 44 ☎ 21 73 70
■ **Mukumbi Bar** (B H NG)
c/o Hotel Intercontinental, Haile Selassie Avenue *(top floor)*
☎ 21 23 66
Hotel rates upon request.

DANCECLUBS

■ **Moon City** (B D g) 22-5 h
(off Cairo Road, next to Bank of Zambia)
Although not gay, it is possible to meet gays in this huge disco.

Ndola City ☎ 02

BARS

■ **Copper Smith Arms Hotel** (B E F g H YG)
PO Box 710 63 *(opposite railway station)*
☎ 23 95
■ **Top Hat Bar** (B f g LJ YG)
(opposite Zambian Airways, St. Patrick's)

HOTELS

■ **Intercontinental Cuisine Hotel** (b d F H NG YG)
PO Box 715 38 *(in city center)*
☎ 47 75
■ **New Savoy Hotel** (b d F H NG YG)
2446 Buteko Avenue, PO Box 718 00 *(in city center)*
☎ 39 33

Zimbabwe

Name: Simbabwe
Location: Southern Africa
Initials: ZW
Time: GMT +1
International Country Code: ☏ 263 (leave the first 0 of area codes)
International Access Code: ☏ 00
Language: English
Area: 390 757 km² = 150,800 sq mi.
Currency: 1 Zimbabwe Dollar (Z$) = 100 Cents
Population: 11,689,000
Capital: Harare
Religions: 55% Christian
Climate: The summer rainy season from October to March is hot; winters are mild and dry. In the low lands the temperatures are more extreme with widespread Malaria during the summer months. The Eastern Highlands are wet and cool with evergreen forests.

✳ Under common law, in Zimbabwe sodomy is illegal between two men. In addition, there are clauses relating to public morality and "unnatural offences". No distinction is made between consensual and enforced sodomy. Technically speaking, any person who is homosexual or a prostitute or who earns money from such "practises" may not enter Zimbabwe. However, unless one is to declare oneself openly there is no problem in entering Zimbabwe. Cases of blackmail are on the increase and foreigners should be very wary of hustlers! AYOR!

The plight of homosexuals rose to international prominence in August 1995 when the Gays and Lesbians of Zimbabwe (GALZ) attempted to enter the Zimbabwe International Book Fair which had the theme "Human Rights and Justice". President Mugabe opened the fair with his now infamous "Pigs and Dogs" speech in which he referred to homosexuals as animals. Later he declared homosexuals had no rights at all and called on the police to "remove" them from the streets and throw them into prison.

Despite the homophobic campaigns from the government which are sanctioned by the church, there is a growing gay scene in Zimbabwe. There is even an annual Pride celebration in September/October each year!
(GALZ Organisation)

✳ Nach Gewohnheitsrecht ist Analverkehr zwischen Männern untersagt. Hinzu kommen Klauseln bezüglich der öffentlichen Moral und "widernatürlicher Handlungen". Zwischen freiwilligem und erzwungenem Analverkehr wird kein Unterschied gemacht. Also praktisch gesagt darf niemand, der homosexuell ist, sich prostituiert und Geld mit solchen "Praktiken" verdient, nach Zimbabwe einreisen. Dennoch gibt es für Personen, die sich zu ihrer Homosexualität bekennen keine Probleme bei der Einreise nach Zimbabwe. Fälle von Erpressung nehmen allerdings zu und Ausländer sollten sich vor Prostituierten in acht nehmen. Auf eigenes Risiko!

Die mißliche Lage der Homosexuellen wurde im August 1995 auf internationaler Ebene bekannt, als Schwule und Lesben Zimbabwes (GALZ) versuchten auf die internationale Buchmesse, die das Thema "Menschenrechte und Gerechtigkeit" hatte, zu gelangen. Zimbabwes Präsident Mugabe eröffnete die Messe mit seiner berüchtigten "Schweine und Hunde-Rede", in der er Homosexuelle mit Tieren auf eine Stufe stellte. Später gab er eine Erklärung ab, in der er sagte, daß Homosexuelle keine Rechte hätten und die Polizei dazu aufforderte sie von den Straßen zu entfernen und ins Gefängnis zu werfen. Trotz der homofeindlichen Kampagnen der Regierung, die von der Kirche sanktioniert werden, gibt es dennoch eine ständig wachsende Gay-Szene in Zimbabwe. Im September und Oktober jeden Jahres findet sogar eine Ehrenfeier unter den purpurfarbig blühenden Jacarandabäumen statt. (GALZ Organisation)

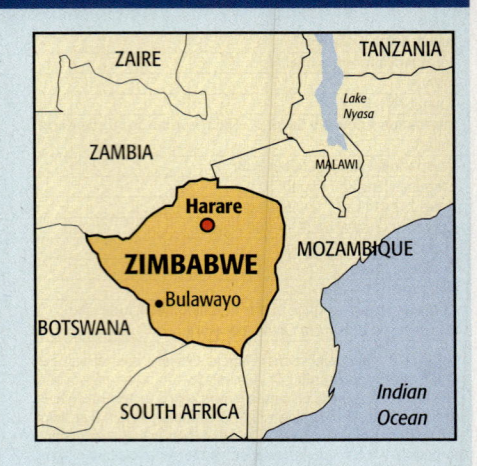

✳ Les lois du Zimbabwe interdisent la sodomie. Il existe en plus des clauses spéciales qui mentionnent la moralité publique et la "débauche contre nature". Aucune distinction n'est faite entre la sodomie consentie et celle contrainte. Théoriquement, toute personne qui est homosexuelle ou qui se prostitue ou qui gagne de l'argent avec l'une de ces pratiques n'est pas autorisée à séjourner dans le pays. Cependant, à moins que quelqu'un se décide à le déclarer à la douane, il n'y a aucun problème pour entrer dans le Zimbabwe.

Les cas de chantage sont de plus en plus courant dans le pays et on conseille les étrangers de se méfier des gigolos. A vos risques et périls !

La cause des gais au Zimbabwe a pris une dimension internationale en août 1995, lorsque l'association homosexuelle du pays "Gays and Lesbians of Zimbabwe (GALZ)" a tenté d'entrer dans le Salon International du Livre dont le thème était "droits de l'homme et justice". Le président Mugabe a inauguré le salon avec son désormais célèbre discours "cochons et chiens" dans lequel il comparait les gais à des animaux. Il déclara plus tard que les homosexuels n'avaient aucun droits et appela la police à les "ramasser" dans les rues pour les jeter en prison.

Malgré cette campagne homophobe du gouvernement soutenue d'ailleurs par l'église, une scène gaie se développe au Zimbabwe. Il y a même une Gay Pride qui se déroule chaque année au mois de septembre ou d'octobre.
(GALZ Organisation)

Harare Zimbabwe

De acuerdo con el derecho consuetudinario, la sodomía entre dos hombres es ilegal en Zimbabue. Además, hay párrafos relacionados con la moral pública y la "ofensa contra la naturaleza". No se distingue entre sodomía consensual y casos de sodomización contra voluntad. Es decir que cualquier persona homosexual o que se dedique a ganar dinero con estas "prácticas" no debería entrar en Zimbabue. De todas formas, siempre que uno no se declare abiertamente, no hay problema con un viaje a este país. Hay cada vez más casos de chantajes y extranjeros deberían tener cuidado con prostitutas. ¡¡Puede ser peligroso!!

La grave situación de los homosexuales fue centro de la atención internacional en agosto de 1995, cuando la organización de gays y lesbianas de Zimbabue, la GALZ, intentó acceder a la Feria Internacional del Libro, celebrada bajo el lema de "Derechos humanos y justicia". El presidente Mugabe inauguró la feria con su infame discurso "de cerdos y perros" en el que se refirió a los homosexuales como si fuesen animales. Más tarde declaró que los homosexuales no tenían ningún derecho y pidió a la policía que "limpiara" las calles de ellos y los metiera en la cárcel.

A pesar de las campañas homófobas del gobierno, sancionadas por la iglesia cristiana, el ambiente gay está cresciendo en Zimbabue, e incluso hay una celebración anual del orgullo gay (en septiembre u octubre), aunque se trate de celebraciones muy discretas.

(GALZ Organisation)

Secondo il diritto consuetudinario la sodomia tra uomini è illegale. Esistono inoltre delle clausole riguardanti la morale pubblica ed i "delitti contro natura". Non si fa distinzione tra sodomia consensuale e forzata. Questo significa praticamente che chiunque sia omosessuale, si prostituisca o guadagni soldi con queste "pratiche" non può entrare in Zimbabwe. Comunque, finché non si dichiara apertamente di essere omosessuali, si può entrare nel paese senza problemi. Tuttavia, i casi di ricatto sono in aumento e gli stranieri fanno bene a guardarsi dai rapporti sessuali a pagamento. Altrimenti: a proprio rischio e pericolo! La desolata situazione degli omosessuali divenne pubblica a livello internazionale nel agosto di 1995, quando i gay e le lesbiche dello Zimbabwe (GALZ) tentarono di entrare con la forza alla Fiera internazionale del libro, il cui motto era "Diritti umani e Giustizia". Il Presidente Mugabe aveva inaugurato la fiera con l'ormai tristemente famoso discorso dei "maiali e cani" in cui degradava gli omosessuali al livello di animali. In una dichiarazione rilasciata poi disse che gli omosessuali non hanno alcun diritto e incitò la polizia a "rimuoverli" dalle strade e a metterli in prigione.

Nonostante le campagne omofobiche del governo, che tra altro vengono sanzionate dalla chiesa, la scena gay in Zimbabwe sta crescendo. Ogni anno tra settembre e ottobre viene organizzato anche un gay-pride che ha luogo sotto le chiome color porpora degli alberi di jacaranda.

(GALZ Organisation)

NATIONAL GAY INFO

■ **GALZ - Gays and Lesbians of Zimbabwe** (GLM) Open Mon-Fri 9-17.30h, Sat 13-18h (social events)
35 Colenbrander Road, Milton Park Harare ☎ (04)741 736
📠 (04)741 736 ✉ galz@samara.co.zw
Contact GALZ for any information regarding visits to Zimbabwe.

Harare ☎ 04

GAY INFO

■ **Gay Tour Guides**
☎ 741 736
Gay tour guides and escort services.

BARS

■ **Bazarre Bar** (glm)
Kamfinsa Shopping Center
White scene.

■ **Beer Engine** (glm MA)
Best Western Jameson Hotel; Samora Machel Av.
Racially mixed.

■ **Time & Place** (AYOR B D glm)
Nelson Mandela Avenue /Rezende Street
AYOR. Younger black scene.

■ **Tipperary's Bar & Grill** (f glm)
Fife Avenue/ Leopold Takawira Street
Racially mixed.

CAFES

■ **Italian Bakery** (NG)
Avondale Shopping Center

Gays and Lesbians of Zimbabwe

– GALZ –

sexual rights are human rights

Safe haven for gays and lesbians
to meet and socialise in comfort

Membership open to all
-
The GALZ Centre
35 Colenbrander Road
Milton Park
Harare
Zimbabwe

Tel: +263 4 741736
Fax: +263 4 778165
e-mail: galz@samara.co.zw

Zimbabwe | Harare

Not gay but very cruisy.

DANCECLUBS

■ **Pensaoe** (NG OS)
Samora Machel Ave/ 8th Street
Racially very mixed.
■ **Stars** (B F MA)
Harare Sheraton Hotel
Upmarket. Live music. Mixed races and gays/straights.
■ **Wiggle** (B glm MA)
Park Street/Jason Moyo Avenue
Rave crowd. Very mixed.
■ **X-cape** (B gLm MA) (Fri)
Sam Levy's Village, Borrowdale
Upmarket, not exculsively gay but interesting especially for lesbians. White scene.

RESTAURANTS

■ **Blue Banana. The**
109 Fife Avenue *(between 2nd and 3rd Street)*
Thai cuisine. Gay-friendly atmosphere.
■ **Dolce Vita. La** (NG)
Avondale Shopping Center

PRIVATE ACCOMMODATION

■ **Jacaranda Pride**
PO Box A1915, Avondale ☎ 305 790
Please write for accommodation tips and rates.

CRUISING

Nibbles Coffee Shop - Eastgate Shopping Center.
Botanical Gardens - Belgravia area, AYOR - beware of the police.

International

INTERNATIONAL ORGANISATIONS

■ **Amnesty International Members for G&L Concerns**
77 Maitland Place, Suite 820 ✉ M4Y 2V6 Toronto, Canada
🖥 www.amnesty.org
Support human and gay rights worldwide by writing letters to governments urging them to respect international standards.

■ **European Gay and Lesbian Sports Federation (EGLSF)**
Breedstraat 28 ✉ 2513 TT Den Haag, The Netherlands ☏ +31 70 364 24 42

■ **European Pride Organizers Association**
c/o Hartmut Schönknecht, Elberfelder Straße 23 ✉ 10555 Berlin, Germany ☏ +49 30 392 53 11 📠 +49 30 392 43 19
Voluntarily working European network of Lesbian & Gay Pride Organizations and licenser of the Europride title.

■ **Federation of Gay Games**
584 Castro Street, Suite 343 ✉ CA 94114 San Francisco
☏ +1 415 6950-222

■ **International Gay and Lesbian Archives**
PO Box 69619, West Hollywood ✉ CA 90069 Los Angeles, USA
☏ +1 310 845-0271

■ **International Gay and Lesbian Travel Association (IGLTA)**
52 West Oakland Park Boulevard 237 ✉ FL 33311 Wilton Manors, USA ☏ +1 954 776-2626 ☏ +1 800 448-8550
📠 +1 954 776-3303 ✉ iglta@iglta.org 🖥 www.iglta.org
IGLTA is an international network of travel industry business and professionals dedicated to the support of its members who have joined together to encourage gay travel throughout the world. IGLTA is committed to the welfare of gay and lesbian travelers, and to "shrinking the gay globe". Spartacus is member of IGLTA.

■ **International Gay Penpals**
Ste. 320, PO Box 7304 ✉ CA 91603 Los Angeles, USA

■ **International Lesbian and Gay Association (ILGA)**
81 Rue du Marché au Charbon ✉ 1000 Bruxelles, Belgium
☏ +32 2 502 24 71 📠 +32 2 502 24 71
✉ ilga@ilga.org
🖥 www.ilga.org
ILGA's aim is to work for the equality of lesbians, gay men, bisexuals and transgendered people and their liberation from all forms of discrimination.

■ **Lesbian & Gay Hospitality Exchange International**
PO Box 612, Station C ✉ QC H2L 4K5 Montréal, Canada
☏ +1 514 593 03 00 📠 +1 514 593 03 00
✉ info@lghei.org 🖥 www.lghei.org
Non-profit home stay network, with 500 listings in 40 different countries.

■ **UNAIDS**
20 Avenue Appia ✉ 1211 Genève 27, Switzerland ☏ +41 22 791 36 66 ☏ +41 22 791 41 87
✉ unaids@unaids.org
🖥 www.unaids.org/contact/index.html
As the main advocate for global action on HIV/AIDS, UNAIDS leads, strengthens and supports an expanded response aimed at preventing the transmission of HIV, providing care and support, reducing the vulnerability of individuals and communities to HIV/AIDS, and alleviating the impact of the epidemic.

SPARTACUS Events Calendar 2001

February 9-25   Auckland, New Zealand: Hero 2001, Gay, Lesbian and Transgender Festival (Info: www.hero.org.nz)

February 27   New Orleans,LA, USA: Mardi Gras Day (Info: New Orleans Metropolitan Convention & Visitor Bureau, www.neworleanscvb.com)

March 3   Sydney, NSW, Australia: Gay and Lesbian Mardi Gras (Info: www.mardigras.com.au)

March 8-12   Miami Beach, Southbeach,FL, USA (Info: www.winterparty.com)

March 24-31   Lenzerheide, Switzerland: SWING (Skiing With International Gays, Info: Hotel Schweizer Hof, Tel.+41-81-384 0111)

March 18-25   Les Menuires, France: European Gay Ski Week (Info: www.alternative.holidays.com)

April 30-May 6   Philadelphia,PA,USA: Pride Fest America (Info: www.pridefest.org)

April 30   Amsterdam,Netherlands: Queensday

May 20-27   Berlin, Germany:10th European Gay/Lesbian Choir Festival 2001

May 24-28   Chicago, IL,USA: International Mr. Leather 2001 (Info: www.mrl.com/iml2001/)

June 1-30   Vienna, Austria: Europride 2001 (Info: +43-1-319 44 72 33, www.europride.at)

June 14-17   San Paulo, Brazil: Gay and Lesbian Parada do Orgulho

June 17-24   New York,NY,USA; NCY Pride Week 2001 (Info: www.nycpride.org)

SPARTACUS Events Calendar 2001

June 23-24 San Francisco,CA,USA: 2001 San Francisco Pride (Info: www.sf-pride.org)

June 23 Berlin,Germany:CSD Berlin (Info: www.csd-berlin.de)

June 30 London, Great Britain: London Mardi Gras 2001 (Info: www.londonmardigras.com)

July 6-8 Cologne,Germany: CSD Köln

July 8 Rome, Italy: International Gay and Lesbian Pride Roma 2001

August 2-5 Hanover,Germany: Eurogames 2001 (Info: www.eurogames.org)

August 18 Copenhagen, Denmark: Mermaid Pride Copenhagen (Info: www.mermaidpride.dk)

September 23 Munich,Germany: Oktoberfest, at the "Bräurosl" tent (Info: www.oktoberfest.de)

October 1-27 Perth,Australia: Lesbian & Gay Pride Western Australia (Info: www.pridewa.asn.au)

October 3-9 Montreal,Québec,Canada: XI. Black and Blue Festival. (Info: www.bbcm.org)

October 15-17 Atlanta, Georgia, USA: Inter Pride World Conference 2001 (Info: www.interpride.org)

November 2-3 Amsterdam, Netherlands: Leather Pride Amsterdam (Info: www.leatherpride.nl)

December 1 World Aids Day

-12h+
+11h
+10h
+9h
+8h
+7h
+6h
+5h
+4h
+3h
+2h
+1h
RUSSIA
Greenland (DK)
ICELA
CANADA
UNITED STATES OF AMERICA
E
Canary Islands (E)
AL
International Date Line
Hawaiian Islands (US)
MEXICO
CARRIBEAN
BRAZIL
FIJI
-13h
ARGENTINA
NEW ZEALAND
-12h
Midnight
1AM
2AM
3AM
4AM
5AM
6AM
7AM
8AM
9AM
10AM
11AM
N

-2h
-3h
-4h
-5h
-6h
-7h
-8h
-9h
-10h
-11h
-12h+
+11h
RUSSIA
PL
CHINA
JAPAN
INDIA
International Date Line
+10h
Hawaii
+11h
VANUATU
FIJI
MAURITIUS
Réunion (F)
AUSTRALIA
SOUTH AFRICA
NEW ZEALAND
M
2PM
3PM
4PM
5PM
6PM
7PM
8PM
9PM
10PM
11PM
Midnight
1AM

Index

This Index contains all countries, the states, territories and provinces of Australia, Canada and the US and all cities and islands that are listed in the Spartacus

A

A Coruña	936
Aabenraa	209
Aachen	361
Aalst	76
Aarau	989
Abano Terme	604
Aberdeen	1068
Aberystwyth	1068
Abidjan	692
Acapulco	722
Adana	1059
Adelaide	30
Adelong	11
Afrique du Sud	**863**
Agadir	733
Agaña	565
Agen	239
Agrigento	675
Aguada	162
Aguadulce	886
Aguascalientes	722
Ägypten	**223**
Ahaus	361
Ahlen	361
Aiea	1242
Aigues-Mortes	239
Aiguines	240
Airole	604
Aix-en-Provence	240
Aix-la-Chapelle (Aachen)	361
Aix-les-Bains	240
Ajaccio	256
Akaroa	796
Akron	1314
Alabama	1135
Alacant	886
Alajuela	185
Alanya	1059
Alaska	1136
Alassio	604
Alba	604
Albacete	886
Albania	**1**
Albanie	**1**
Albanien	**1**
Albany	1289
Alberta	118
Albertville	240
Albi	240
Ålborg	209
Albufeira	829
Albuquerque	1287
Albury	12
Aldershot	1068
Alemania	**347**
Alessandria	606
Ålesund	811
Alexandria	224
Alexandroúpolis	556
Algeciras	886
Alicante	886
Alice Springs	24
Alkmaar	742
Allauch	240
Allegany	1140
Allemagne	**347**
Almancil	829
Almaty	703
Almere	743
Almeria	887
Alost (Aalst)	76
Alphen aan de Rijn	743
Alta	811
Altenau	361
Altoona	1320
Al-Uqsur	224
al-Urdunn	**702**
Amarillo	1329
Amberes (Antwerpen)	77
Amberg	361
Ambilly	240
Amburgo (Hamburg)	448
Ameland	743
Amersfoort	743
Amherst	1266
Amiens	240
Amman	702
Amsterdam	743
Anaheim	1140
Anahola	1241
Anchorage	1136
Ancona	606
Åndalsnes	811
Angers	240
Anglet	241
Angoulême	241
Ankara	1059
Ann Arbor	1277
Annecy	241
Annemasse	241
Annonay	241
Annover (Hannover)	467
Anshan	173
Antalya	1059
Antibes	241
Antigonish	128
Antigua	566
Antillas Neerlandesas	**160**
Antilles Néerlandaises	**160**
Antofagasta	168
Antwerp (Antwerpen)	77
Antwerpen	77
Anvers (Antwerpen)	77
Anversa (Antwerpen)	77
Anzio	606
Aomori	695
Aosta	606
Apeldoorn	778
Appleton	1340
Aprica	606
Aquisgrana (Aachen)	361
Aracaju	99
Arbon	989
Arborea	674
Arcueil	243
Arequipa	819
Arezzo	606
Argelès-sur-Mer	243
Argentina	**2**
Argentine	**2**
Argentinien	**2**
Argenton-sur-Creuse	243
Århus	209
Arica	168
Arizona	1137
Arkansas	1139
Arkhangelsk	848
Arles	243
Arlon	81
Armação de Pêra	829
Armenia	181
Arnhem	778
Arpajon	243
Arras	243
Arrecife	930
Arriaga	723
Års	210
Aruba	**150**
Arzon	243
Asbury Park	1286
Ascha/Straubing	362
Aschaffenburg	362
Ascoli Piceno	606
Asheville	1312
Ashford	1068
Ashton-Under-Lyne	1069
Asilah	734
Asnelles	243
Asnières-sur-Seine	243
Aspen	1188
Assen	778
Assenede	81
Assuan	224
Asti	606
Astrakhan	848
Asunción	818

Index

Aswan ... 224	Baltimore, IRL ... 588	Belgrado ... 1351
Atacames ... 222	Baltimore, MD, USA ... 1265	**Belice ... 95**
Atenas (Athina) ... 556	Bamberg ... 362	Belize City ... 96
Atene (Athina) ... 556	Bandol ... 245	**Belize ... 95**
Athen (Athina) ... 556	Bandung ... 581	Bellinzona ... 991
Athènes (Athina) ... 556	Bangkok ... 1024	Belo Horizonte ... 99
Athens (Athina) ... 556	Bangor ... 1069	Bendigo ... 34
Athens ... 1235	Banjarmasin ... 581	Beni Mellal ... 734
Athina ... 556	Baños ... 222	Benidorm ... 916
Atlanta ... 1235	Bansin ... 363	Benoni ... 864
Atlantic City ... 1286	Baoding ... 173	Beograd ... 1351
Auburn ... 1142	**Barbade ... 151**	Berck ... 246
Auch ... 243	**Barbados ... 151**	Bergamo ... 607
Auckland ... 797	Barbate de Franco ... 903	Bergen (Mons), B ... 93
Augsburg ... 362	Barbentane ... 245	Bergen aan Zee ... 778
Augusta ... 1238	Barcelona ... 903	Bergen op Zoom ... 778
Aups ... 243	Bareggio ... 607	Bergen, N ... 811
Aurillac ... 243	Bari ... 607	Bergerac ... 246
Aurisina ... 606	Bar-le-Duc ... 245	Bergisch Gladbach ... 363
Austin ... 1330	Barnaul ... 850	Berkeley ... 1142
Australia ... 8	Barneville-Carteret ... 245	Berlin ... 363
Austrália ... 8	Barnsley ... 1069	Bern ... 991
Australian Capital Territory ... 10	Barnstaple ... 1069	Besançon ... 246
Australie ... 8	Barossa Valley ... 32	Best ... 778
Australien ... 8	Barquisimeto ... 1346	Béthune ... 246
Austria ... 44	Barranquilla ... 182	Bettendorf ... 715
Autriche ... 44	Barrydale ... 864	Béziers ... 246
Auxerre ... 243	Basel ... 989	**Bhárat ... 579**
Aveiro ... 829	Basilea (Basel) ... 989	Biarritz ... 247
Avellino ... 607	Bassano del Grappa ... 607	Biberach ... 411
Aviemore ... 1069	Basse-Terre, GUA ... 157	Bibione Pineta ... 610
Avignon ... 244	Basseterre, KN ... 166	Bidart ... 247
Avila ... 887	Bastia ... 256	Bideford ... 1070
Aviles ... 887	Batam ... 581	Biel ... 993
Aylesbury ... 1069	Bath ... 1069	Bielefeld ... 411
Ayr ... 1069	Bathurst ... 127	Biella ... 610
	Baton Rouge ... 1255	**Bielorusia ... 73**
B	Bay of Islands ... 800	**Biélorussie ... 73**
	Bayonne ... 245	Bielsko-Biala ... 824
Baarle Nassau ... 778	Bayrut ... 710	Bienne ... 993
Backnang ... 362	Beara ... 588	Bilbao ... 920
Bacolod ... 821	Beaulieu-sur-Mer ... 246	Billings ... 1283
Bad Honnef ... 362	Beaumont-Hague ... 246	Biloxi ... 1280
Bad Kreuznach ... 362	Beauvais ... 246	Bingen ... 412
Bad Tölz ... 362	Bedford ... 1070	Binghamton ... 1289
Badajoz ... 887	Bedzin ... 823	Birmingham, AL, USA ... 1135
Baden-Baden ... 362	Beek (Ubb) ... 778	Birmingham, GB ... 1070
Baguio ... 821	Beer Sheva ... 595	Biscarosse ... 247
Bahamas ... 150	Beijing ... 173	Bitterfeld ... 412
Bains-les-Bains ... 245	**Belarus ... 73**	Blackburn ... 1071
Bakersfield ... 1142	Belem ... 99	Blackpool ... 1071
Bâle (Basel) ... 989	Belfast ... 1070	Blagnac ... 248
Balearen (Balearic Islands) ... 887	Belfort ... 246	Blanes ... 921
Baléares, Iles (Balearic Islands) ... 887	**Bélgica ... 74**	Blankenberge ... 81
Baleares, Islas (Balearic Islands) ... 887	**België ... 74**	Bled ... 861
Baleari, Isole (Balearic Islands) ... 887	**Belgien ... 74**	Blenheim ... 800
Balearic Islands ... 887	**Belgio ... 74**	Bloemfontein ... 864
Bâlgarija ... 113	**Belgique ... 74**	Blois ... 248
Balikpapan ... 581	**Belgium ... 74**	Bloomington ... 1253
Ballarat ... 34	Belgrad (Beograd/Belgrado) ... 1351	Böblingen ... 412
Ballerup ... 210	Belgrade (Beograd/Belgrado) ... 1351	Bocholt ... 412

THE WORLD OF...
pjur
EROS
finest products · worldwide
360° Play-System
Spiel-Spender-System
pjur
EROS
COMFORT SYSTEM
super concentrated
BODYGLIDE
pjur
EROS
LIGHT LOVE
BODYGLIDE
pjur
EROS
WATER FORMULATION
LIQUID
Neu
New
pjur EROS Toys & Accessoires
Made in Germany
pjur group: www.pjurEROS.com
Luxembourg: Phone (++352) 748 989
Fax (++352) 748 990
USA (NYC): Phone (++1) 212-337-37
Fax (++1) 212-367-9389
pjur EROS "PLUG LINE"
pjur EROS "MILITARY LINE"
pjur EROS "REALISTIC LINE"
pjur EROS "FETISH LINE"

Index

Bochum 413	**Brazil 98**	**C**
Bodø 812	Breckenridge 1188	Cabourg 250
Bodrum 1059	Breda 779	Cadiz 921
Boekel 779	Bregenz 46	Caen 250
Bogor 582	Bréhal 249	Cagliari 674
Boise 1244	Bremen 415	Cagnes-sur-Mer 250
Boksburg 865	Bremerhaven 416	Cahors 250
Bolivia 96	Brentwood 1289	Caiolo 614
Bolivie 96	Brescia 614	Cairnryan 1079
Bolivien 96	**Brésil 98**	Cairns 27
Boll-Sinneringen 993	Breslau (Wroclaw) 827	Cairo 224
Bologna 610	Bressuire 249	Cala Millor 897
Bolton 1073	Brest 250	Calais 250
Bolzano 613	Briançon 250	Calama 168
Bombay 579	Bridgetown 152	Calgary 118
Bonaire 160	Bridgwater 1074	Calí 182
Bonifacio 256	Brig 993	California 1139
Bonn 413	Brighton 1074	Callantsoog 779
Bonnieux 248	Brindisi 614	Caloocan City 821
Boonton 1287	Brisbane 25	Calvi 256
Boonville 1142	Bristol 1078	Camaret-sur-Mer 251
Boracay Island 821	British-Columbia 120	**Cambodge 114**
Borås 972	Brive-la-Gaillarde 250	**Cambodia 114**
Bordeaux 248	Brno 195	**Cambogia 114**
Borken 414	Bruchsal 416	**Camboya 114**
Bormio 614	Bruges (Brugge) 82	Cambridge, GB 1079
Bosna i Hercegovina 97	Brügge (Brugge) 82	Cambridge, ON. CDN 129
Bosnia-Erzegovina 97	Brugge 82	Camerino 614
Bosnia-Herzegovina 97	Brujas (Brugge) 82	Campeche 723
Bosnie-Herzégovine 97	Brunnen 994	**Canada 116**
Bosnien & Herzegowina 97	Bruselas (Brussel/Bruxelles) 82	Canakkale 1059
Boston 1266	Brüssel (Brussel/Bruxelles) 82	Canarias, Islas (Canary Islands) 921
Bottrop 414	Brussel 82	Canarie, Isole (Canary Islands) 921
Bouc-Bel-Air 249	Brussels (Brussel/Bruxelles) . . . 82	Canaries, Iles (Canary Islands) 921
Boulder 1188	Bruxelles 82	Canary Islands 921
Boulogne Billancourt 249	Bryan 1331	Canberra 10
Boulogne-sur-Mer 249	Bucarest (Bucuresti) 845	Cancún 723
Bourg-en-Bresse 249	Bucuresti 845	Cangzhou 173
Bourges 249	Budapest 569	Canillas De Albaidas 933
Bournemouth 1073	Buena Park 1142	Cannes 251
Bourtange 779	Buenos Aires 3	Canosa di Puglia 615
Bowen Island 120	Buffalo 1290	Canterbury 1079
Bozen 613	Bugibba 718	Canton 1314
Bra 614	Bühl 416	Capalbio 615
Braamfontein 865	Bukarest (Bucuresti) 845	Cap-d'Agde 253
Bradenton 1198	**Bulgaria 113**	Cap-d'Ail 253
Bradford 1074	**Bulgarie 113**	Cape Charles 1336
Braffe 82	**Bulgarien 113**	Cape Schanck 34
Braga 829	Bulle 994	Cape Town 865
Bragança 830	Bundaberg 27	Capelle a.d. Ijssel 779
Brakpan 865	Burbank 1142	Cap-Ferret 253
Brandon 126	Burgas 113	Capo d'Orlando 676
Brasil 98	Burgos 921	Capri 615
Brasile 98	Burlington 1336	Captain Cook 1240
Brasilia 99	Burnham-on-Sea 1078	Caracas 1346
Brasilien 98	Burnley 1078	Caraïbes (Caribbean) 149
Brasov 845	Burra 32	Caraibi (Caribbean) 149
Bratislava 860	Bursa 1059	Carcassonne 253
Brattleboro 1336	Bury Saint Edmunds 1078	Carcès 254
Braunschweig 414	Bussum 779	Cardiff 1079
Bray-Dunes 249	Byron Bay 12	Caribbean 149

+++ register now +++ constantly updated +++ all current info

- Lifestyle
- Shopping
- Personals
- Adult Entertainment
- Gay Chat

www.SpartacusWorld.com

- Events
- Travel

Spartacus Gay Guide

- Free newsletter
- Entertainment

Launch date: 1st May 2001!

As purchaser of the jubilee edition of SPARTACUS International Gay Guide 2001/2002, after I have registered myself, I have the possibility to use and research in the SPARTACUS address data bank free of charge until the 31st December 2001.

The registration card should be completed in full, signed and sent off by post to:

SpartacusWorld.com GmbH
P.O. Box 17 01 23 • 10203 Berlin • Germany

Your personal password will be sent to you promptly.

+++ all current information +++ register now +++ constantly

Index

Caribou ... 1262	Chaumont ... 255	Cocoa Beach ... 1198
Carlisle ... 1079	Chauvry ... 255	Coffs Harbour ... 12
Carmel ... 1142	Cheb ... 196	Coimbra ... 830
Carnac ... 254	Chelmsford ... 1079	Colchester ... 1080
Cartagena, CO ... 182	Cheltenham Spa ... 1079	Colima ... 725
Cartagena, E ... 933	Chelyabinsk ... 850	Colmar ... 256
Carvoeiro ... 830	Chemnitz ... 417	Cologne (Köln) ... 480
Casablanca ... 734	Chengdu ... 173	Cologno Monzese ... 616
Casale Monferrato ... 615	Cherbourg ... 255	Colombes ... 256
Cascais ... 830	Cherkassy ... 1063	**Colombia ... 181**
Caserta ... 615	Cherry Hill ... 1287	**Colombie ... 181**
Cassano d'Adda ... 615	Chester ... 1080	Colombo ... 970
Cassis ... 254	Chesterfield ... 1080	Colonia (Köln) ... 480
Castelfranco Veneto ... 615	Chiang Mai ... 1040	Colorado Springs ... 1189
Castellamare di Stabia ... 616	Chiang Rai ... 1043	Colorado ... 1188
Castillon ... 254	Chicago ... 1244	Columbia ... 1327
Castlegar ... 120	Chichester ... 1080	Columbus ... 1316
Castres ... 254	Chico ... 1142	Como ... 616
Castro ... 168	Chicoutimi ... 138	Compiègne ... 256
Castroville ... 1142	Chieuti ... 616	Concarneau ... 256
Catania ... 676	Chihuahua ... 723	Concepción ... 168
Cathedral City ... 1142	**Chile ... 167**	Connecticut ... 1190
Catskill Mountains ... 1290	**Chili ... 167**	Constanta ... 846
Cauterets ... 254	Chillan ... 168	Conwy ... 1080
Cava dei Tirreni ... 616	**China ... 172**	Copenaghen (København) ... 211
Cavalaire-sur-Mer ... 254	**Chine ... 172**	Copenhagen (København) ... 211
Cebu ... 821	Chinon ... 255	Copenhague (København) ... 211
Cedar Rapids ... 1254	Chios ... 559	Corbara ... 256
Cefalù ... 677	**Chipre ... 192**	Córdoba, ARG ... 5
Celje ... 861	Cholet ... 255	Córdoba, E ... 933
Celle ... 417	Chongqing ... 173	Córdoba, MEX ... 725
Centre Harbor ... 1286	Chorzów Batory ... 824	**Corea del Sud ... 705**
Cerbère ... 254	Christ Church ... 152	**Corea del Sur ... 705**
Cerdeña (Sardegna) ... 674	Christchurch ... 800	**Corée du Sud ... 705**
Cerritos ... 1142	Chur ... 994	Corfou (Kérkyra) ... 559
Cervia Milano Marittima ... 616	**Chypre ... 192**	Corfu (Kérkyra) ... 559
Cesena ... 616	**Cile ... 167**	Corfù (Kérkyra) ... 559
Ceská Lipá ... 196	**Cina ... 172**	Cork ... 588
Ceská Republika ... 194	Cincinnati ... 1314	Corowa ... 12
Cha Am ... 1040	**Cipro ... 192**	Corpus Christi ... 1331
Châlons-sur-Marne ... 254	Città del Capo (Cape Town) ... 865	Corrençon-en-Vercors ... 256
Chalon-sur-Saône ... 254	Ciudad de Mexico ... 723	Corrientes ... 5
Chalupy ... 824	Ciudad del Cabo (Cape Town) ... 865	Corse ... 256
Chambéry ... 254	Ciudad del Carmen ... 725	Corsica (Corse) ... 256
Chamonix-Mont-Blanc ... 255	Ciudad Juarez ... 725	Cosenza ... 616
Charleroi ... 89	Civitanova Marche ... 616	**Costa d'Avorio ... 692**
Charleston, NZ ... 800	Civitavecchia ... 616	**Costa de Marfil ... 692**
Charleston, SC; USA ... 1327	Clamart ... 255	Costa Mesa ... 1142
Charleston, WV, USA ... 1339	Clare Valley ... 32	**Costa Rica ... 185**
Charlestown ... 166	Clear Lake ... 1142	**Côte d'Ivoire ... 692**
Charleville-Mézières ... 255	Clearwater ... 1198	Cotignac ... 257
Charlotte ... 1312	Clermont-Ferrand ... 255	Cottbus ... 418
Charlottesville ... 1337	Clermont-l'Hérault ... 256	Cournonsec ... 257
Charlottetown ... 138	Cleveland ... 1315	Courtrai (Kortrijk) ... 91
Chartres ... 255	Clichy ... 256	Coventry ... 1080
Châteaurenard ... 255	Cloverdale ... 1142	Cracovia (Kraków) ... 824
Château-Thierry ... 255	Cluj ... 846	Cracovie (Kraków) ... 824
Châtel-Censoir ... 255	Clunes ... 34	Creazzo ... 616
Châtellerault ... 255	Clusone ... 616	Creil ... 257
Châtillon-sur-Loire ... 255	Coburg ... 418	Crema ... 616
Chatta ... 1328	Cochabamba ... 96	Cremona ... 616

Index

Cres 190	Dendermonde. 90	Durham, NC, USA. 1313
Creta (Kriti) 559	Denia. 934	Durmersheim 422
Crete (Kriti) 559	**Denmark 207**	Düsseldorf. 422
Crète (Kriti) 559	Denpasar. 582	
Crewe 1080	Denver. 1189	**E**
Criel-sur-Mer. 257	Derby. 1082	
Croacia. 188	Derrygonnelly. 1082	East London 878
Croatia 188	Des Moines 1254	Eastbourne 1082
Croatie 188	Desenzano del Garda. 617	Eauze. 258
Croazia. 188	Detmold. 419	Echuca 34
Crotone 617	Detroit 1277	**Ecuador 221**
Croydon 1082	**Deutschland. 347**	Ede. 781
Cuba. 153	Deventer. 781	Edgartown. 1268
Cúcuta 182	Diamantina 100	Edinburgh 1083
Cuenca. 222	Dieppe. 257	Edmonton 119
Cuernavaca 725	Dijon 257	**Eesti 227**
Culiacan. 726	Dillenburg. 419	Eger 575
Cumana. 1347	**Dinamarca. 207**	**Egipto. 223**
Cuneo 617	Dinan 257	**Egitto 223**
Curepipe 720	Dinant 90	**Egypt 223**
Curitiba 100	Diou 257	**Egypte 223**
Cuxhaven. 418	District of Columbia 1192	Ehrhardt 1327
Cyprus 192	Divonne-les-Bains. 257	Eich 715
Czech Republic 194	Dnepropetrovsk 1063	Eilat 595
Czestochowa. 824	Doetinchem. 781	Eindhoven 782
	Dole 258	**Éire. 588**
D	Domburg. 781	Eisenach 427
	Dominican Republic 154	El Cairo (Cairo/El Qâhira) 224
Dade City. 1198	**Dominikanische Republik 154**	El Caribe (Caribbean) 149
Dalian 173	Donaueschingen. 419	El Iskandarya. 224
Dallas. 1331	Doncaster 1082	El Jadida 734
Damp 418	Donetsk 1063	El Paso 1332
Danemark 207	Doornik (Tournai). 94	El Qâhira 224
Dänemark 207	Dordrecht 781	**El Salvador. 225**
Danimarca 207	Dornbirn 46	Elba, Isola d' 618
Danmark 207	Dorset 1336	**Elfenbeinküste. 692**
Danzig (Gdansk) 824	Dortmund 419	Elgin 1086
Dargan. 12	Douai 258	Elizabeth 33
Darlaston. 1082	Douarnenez 258	**Ellás 555**
Darlington 1082	Douglas, GB 1082	Ellsworth 1278
Darmstadt 418	Douglas, MI, USA 1278	Embrun 258
Darwin 24	Draguignan 258	Emden 427
Davao 821	Drammen 812	Emmen 782
Dax. 257	Dresden. 420	Empoli 618
Daylesford. 34	Drummondville. 138	Engelberg 994
Dayton 1317	Dublin 589	Enna. 677
Daytona Beach 1198	Dubnica nad Váhom. 861	Enschede. 782
De Panne. 89	Dubrovnik 190	Ensenada. 726
Deakin 11	Ducey. 258	Epen. 784
Deauville 257	Duclair 258	Epernay 258
Debki 824	Duisburg 421	Epinal 258
Debrecen 574	Dumfries 1082	**Equateur 221**
Decin 196	Duncan 120	Eraclea Mare 618
Deißlingen. 419	Dundee 1082	Erfurt 427
Delaware. 1191	Dunedin 801	Erie. 1320
Delémont. 994	Dunkerque 258	Erlangen 427
Delft 779	Durango, CO, USA 1190	Esbjerg. 210
Delfzijl 779	Durango, MEX. 726	Escalante. 1335
Den Bosch 786	Durban 877	Eskilstuna 972
Den Haag 779	Durfort. 258	**Eslovaquia 860**
Den Helder 781	Durham, GB 1082	**Eslovenia 861**

Index

Espagne **883**	Flensburg. 429	**G**
España **883**	Fleury-d'Aude 259	
Espinho 830	Flint 1278	Gaeta. 623
Essaouira. 734	Florence (Firenze). 618	Gainesville. 1215
Essen 427	Florencia (Firenze) 618	Galashiels 1086
Esslingen 429	Florenz (Firenze). 618	Galéria 257
Estados Unidos **1129**	Florida 1197	Gallargues-le-Montueux. 259
Estambul 1060	Foggia 623	Gallipoli 623
Estepona 934	Foix 259	Galveston 1332
Estland. **227**	Folkestone. 1086	Galway. 592
Estocolmo (Stockholm) 976	Follo. 812	Gand (Gent) 90
Estonia. **227**	Fontainebleau 259	Gandia 934
Estonie. **227**	Førde 812	Gap 259
Estoril. 830	Forestville 1142	Garda. 623
Etampes. 258	Forlì 623	Gardanne 259
Etats-Unis. **1129**	Formentera 887	Garden Grove 1143
Etretat 258	Fort Erie. 129	Gateshead 1086
Eugene. 1318	Fort Lauderdale 1198	Gävle 972
Eureka Springs 1139	Fort Myers 1214	Gaziantep 1059
Eureka 1142	Fort Smith 1139	Gdansk 824
Evreux 258	Fort Walton Beach 1215	Gdynia 824
Exeter. 1086	Fort Wayne 1253	Geelong. 34
Eymoutiers 258	Fort Worth. 1332	Geislingen 446
Eze-sur-Mer. 258	Fortaleza 100	Gelsenkirchen 446
	Fort-de-France 159	Gemert 784
F	Fos-sur-Mer. 259	Gênes (Genova) 623
	Fouras 259	Geneva (Genève) 995
Fabriano 618	Foz do Iguaçu 101	Genève 995
Fairbanks. 1136	**France** **234**	Genf (Genève) 995
Falun 972	Francfort (Frankfurt/Main) 429	Genk 90
Famagusta. 193	**Francia** **234**	Genova 623
Fanø Sønderho 210	Francoforte (Frankfurt/Main). 429	Gent 90
Fano. 618	Frankenthal 429	Genua (Genova) 623
Fargo 1314	Frankfurt/Main 429	Georgia 1235
Farnham 1086	**Frankreich** **234**	**Germania**. **347**
Faro, Ilha de 830	Franschhoek 878	**Germany** **347**
Faxe Ladeplads 210	**Französisch-Polynesien**. **344**	Gerusalemme (Jerusalem) 595
Fayence 258	Frauenfeld 994	Gharb. 718
Fayetteville 1313	Fredericia 210	**Giamaica** **158**
Feldkirch 46	Fredericton 127	**Giappone** **693**
Fermo 618	Frederikshavn 210	**Gibilterra** **554**
Fernie. 120	Frederikstad 812	**Gibraltar** **554**
Ferrara 618	Fréhel 259	Gien 259
Fes 734	Freiberg 444	Gießen 446
Fidschi **228**	Freiburg, CH 994	Gigny-sur-Saône 259
Fielding 802	Freiburg, D 444	Gijón 934
Figeac 258	Fréjus 259	Ginebra (Genève) 995
Figueira da Foz 830	**French Polynesia** **344**	Ginevra (Genève) 995
Figueres. 934	Fresno 1143	**Giodania** **702**
Fiji **228**	Fribourg. 994	Girifalco 624
Filipinas **820**	Friedberg. 445	Girona 935
Filippine. **820**	Friedrichshafen 445	Gisborne 802
Finland. **229**	Fuengirola 934	Gjøvik. 812
Finlande. **229**	Fuerteventura 921	Gladbeck 446
Finlandia **229**	Fügen-Zillertal 46	Glasgow. 1086
Finnland. **229**	Fukuoka 695	Glendale 1137
Fire Island 1290	Fulda 445	Glenhaven 1143
Firenze. 618	Fullerton 1143	Gloucester 1087
Firostefani 564	Funchal 831	Gmunden 47
Fiyi **228**	Furnes (Veurne) 95	Gnandstein 446
Flagstaff. 1137		Godega di Sant'Urbano 625
		Goes. 784

Index

Sauna Guide & Gay Bathhouses International
252 Seiten/Pages, English / Deutsch / Français, ISBN 3-86187-155-6
US$ 17,95

Available from: Bookazine Company, Inc. · 75 Hook Road · Bayonne, NJ 07002
Toll-free (800) 584-3855 · www.bookazine.com

Goiânia 101	Gyöngyös 575	Helsinki 230
Golf-Juan 259		Herbignac 260
Gorgonzola 625	**H**	Herdecke 474
Görlitz 446		Hereford 1087
Göteborg 972	Ha Noi 1349	Herentals 91
Götene 973	Haapiti 344	Hergiswil am See 998
Göttingen 446	Haarlem 786	Hermanus 878
Gouda 784	Haderslev 210	Hermost Beach 1143
Gourin 259	Hagen 447	Herne Bay 1087
Gozo 718	Hagerstown 1266	Herne 474
Gran Bretagna 1066	Haicheng 174	Herning 210
Gran Canaria 921	Haifa 595	Herten 475
Granada 935	Hakodate 695	Hickory 1313
Granby 138	Halberstadt 447	Hildesheim 475
Grand Bay 720	Halifax 128	Hillerød 210
Grand Rapids 1278	Hallandale 1215	Hilversum 786
Grand Valley 129	Halle (Saale) 447	Hinwil 998
Grande Bretagne 1066	Halmstad 973	Hiroshima 695
Graz 47	Haltern 448	Hjørring 210
Great Britain 1066	Hamamatsu 695	Hô Chi Minh City (Sai Gon) 1350
Grèce 555	Hamar 812	Hobart 33
Grecia 555	Hambourg (Hamburg) 448	Hoboken 1287
Greece 555	Hamburg 448	Hoek van Holland 787
Green Bay 1340	Hamburgo (Hamburg) 448	Hof 475
Greeneville, TN, USA 1328	Hameln 467	Hoi An 1350
Greensboro 1313	Hamilton, NZ 802	Hokitika 803
Greenville, SC, USA 1327	Hamilton, ON, CDN 130	Holbæk 211
Greifswald 447	Hamm 467	Holiday 1215
Grenaa 210	Hammond 1256	Hollywood, CA, USA 1148
Grenada 156	Hana 1241	Hollywood, FL, USA 1215
Grenade 156	Hanau 467	Honaunau 1240
Grenoble 259	Hannover 467	**Honduras 567**
Grewesmühlen 447	Hannovre (Hannover) 467	Honfleur 260
Griechenland 555	Hanover, D (Hannover) 467	Hong Kong Island 175
Grignan 260	Hanover, RSA 878	**Hongrie 568**
Grimsby 1087	Harare 1355	Honolulu 1242
Grimstad 812	Harbin 174	Hoogeveen 787
Groningen 785	Harker Heights 1333	Hoorn 787
Großbritannien 1066	Harlow 1087	Horcon 168
Grosseto 625	Harrisburg 1320	Hossegor 260
Gruissan 260	Harrogate 1087	Hostka 196
Guadalajara 726	Harstad 812	Houplines 260
Guadalupe 156	Hartford 1190	Hourtin 260
Guadeloupe 156	Hasselt 91	Houston 1333
Guam 565	Hastings, GB 1087	Hove 1088
Guanajuato 727	Hastings, NZ 802	Hoyerswerda 475
Guangzhou 173	Hat Yai 1043	Hradec Králové 196
Guarujá 101	Hatfield 1124	**Hrvatska 188**
Guatemala 566	Hattiesburg 1280	Hua Hin 1043
Guatemala City 566	Haugesund 812	Huddersfield 1088
Guayaquil 222	Havana (La Habana) 153	Huesca 935
Guelph 129	Havanna (La Habana) 153	Hull 1088
Guérande 260	Hawaii 1239	Hulst 787
Guéret 260	Hebden Bridge 1087	**Hungary 568**
Guildford 1087	Heerlen 786	**Hungria 568**
Gulbarga 579	Heide 474	Hunter Valley Wine Country 12
Gulfport 1215	Heidelberg 474	Huntington Beach, CA; USA 1143
Gummersbach 447	Heilbronn 474	Huntington, WV, USA 1339
Gun Barrel City 1333	Helegeland 812	Huntsville 1135
Gunby 1087	Helsingborg 973	Hurstville 12
Gütersloh 447	Helsingør 210	Husum 475

Index

Huy . . . 91	Isle of Mull . . . 1088	Joue-les-Tours . . . 261
Hvar . . . 190	Isle of Wight . . . 1088	Juan-les-Pins . . . 261
Hyères . . . 260	Isleworth . . . 1088	**Jugoslavija . . . 1351**
	Isole Tremiti . . . 625	**Jugoslawien . . . 1351**
I	**Isole Vergini . . . 166**	Juneau . . . 1137
	Ispra . . . 625	**Jungferninseln . . . 166**
Ia . . . 564	**Israel . . . 594**	Jyväskylä . . . 231
Iasi . . . 846	**Israël . . . 594**	
Ibiza . . . 887	**Israele . . . 594**	**K**
Iceland . . . 576	Issy-les-Moulineaux . . . 261	
Idaho . . . 1244	Istanbul . . . 1060	Kaapstad (Cape Town) . . . 865
Idyllwild . . . 1143	**Italia . . . 598**	Kailua Kona . . . 1240
IJzendijke . . . 787	**Italie . . . 598**	Kailua . . . 1244
Il Cairo (Cairo/El Qâhira) . . . 224	**Italien . . . 598**	Kaina . . . 344
Ile-du-Levant . . . 260	**Italy . . . 598**	Kaiserslautern . . . 476
Iles Vierges . . . 166	Ithaca . . . 1291	Kaitaia . . . 803
Ile-sur-la-Sorgue . . . 261	**Iugoslavia . . . 1351**	Kalamata . . . 559
Ilhavo . . . 831	**Ivory Coast . . . 692**	Kalamazoo . . . 1279
Ilhéus . . . 101	Ivrea . . . 625	Kaliningrad . . . 850
Illinois . . . 1244	Ivry-sur-Seine . . . 261	Kalua Koi . . . 1242
Ilmenau . . . 475	Ixtapa Zihuatanejo . . . 727	Kaluga . . . 850
Inde . . . 579	Ixtapa . . . 731	**Kambodscha . . . 114**
Inden . . . 475	Izhevsk . . . 850	Kamloops . . . 121
India . . . 579	Izmir . . . 1061	**Kâmpuchéa . . . 114**
Indiana . . . 1253		**Kanada . . . 116**
Indianapolis . . . 1253	**J**	Kanaren (Canary Islands) . . . 921
Indien . . . 579		Kanazawa . . . 695
Indonesia . . . 580	Jackson . . . 1280	Kanegra . . . 190
Indonésie . . . 580	Jacksonville . . . 1216	Kaneohe Bay . . . 1244
Indonesien . . . 580	Jaén . . . 935	Kaniv . . . 1063
Indre Troms . . . 812	Jakarta . . . 582	Kansas City . . . 1281
Ingolstadt . . . 475	Jalapa . . . 727	Kansas . . . 1254
Innsbruck . . . 48	**Jamaica . . . 158**	Kaohsiung . . . 1021
Interlaken . . . 998	**Jamaïka . . . 158**	Kapaa . . . 1241
Invercargill . . . 803	**Jamaique . . . 158**	Kapstadt (Cape Town) . . . 865
Inverness . . . 1088	**Japan . . . 693**	Karibik (Caribbean) . . . 149
Iowa . . . 1254	**Japon . . . 693**	Karlovac . . . 190
Ipswich . . . 1088	Jasper . . . 1216	Karlovy Vary . . . 196
Ipswich . . . 1268	Javea . . . 936	Karlskrona . . . 974
Iquique . . . 169	Jayapura . . . 582	Karlsruhe . . . 476
Iraklion . . . 559	Jefferson Township . . . 1287	Karlstad . . . 974
Iran . . . 586	Jelenia Góra . . . 824	Karrebæksminde . . . 211
Irán . . . 586	Jember . . . 582	**Kasachstan . . . 703**
Îrân . . . 586	Jena . . . 476	Kassel . . . 478
Irapuato . . . 727	Jersey City . . . 1287	Kathmandu . . . 738
Ireland . . . 588	Jersey . . . 1089	Katowice . . . 824
Irkutsk . . . 850	Jerusalem . . . 595	Kauai . . . 1241
Irland . . . 588	Jerusalén (Jerusalem) . . . 595	Kaunas . . . 714
Irlanda . . . 588	Jesolo . . . 625	**Kazajstán . . . 703**
Irlande . . . 588	João Pessoa . . . 101	**Kazakhstan . . . 703**
Iruña . . . 953	Joensuu . . . 231	**Kazakistan . . . 703**
Ischia . . . 625	Johannesburg . . . 878	Kediri . . . 583
Iserlohn . . . 476	Johns Island . . . 1328	Kehl . . . 479
Isla de Chiloe . . . 168	Johore Bahru . . . 717	Kelowna . . . 121
Isla de Pascua . . . 169	Joliette . . . 138	Kempten . . . 479
Isla Margarita . . . 1347	Jönköping . . . 974	**Kenia . . . 704**
Island . . . 576	Jonquière . . . 138	Kennewick . . . 1337
Islanda . . . 576	**Jordan . . . 702**	Kent . . . 1337
Islande . . . 576	**Jordania . . . 702**	Kentucky . . . 1255
Islandia . . . 576	**Jordanie . . . 702**	**Kenya . . . 704**
Islas Virgenes . . . 166	**Jordanien . . . 702**	Kerak . . . 702

Index

Kérkyra 559
Key West 1216
Kharkov. 1063
Kibris **192**
Kidderminster 1089
Kiel. 479
Kielce. 824
Kiev (Kyiv) 1064
Kihei 1241
Kilauea 1240
Kilkenny. 592
Kimberley 879
King's Lynn 1089
Kingston, GB 1089
Kingston, JA. 158
Kingston, ON, CDN. 130
Kirchheim-Teck. 480
Kirkcaldy 1089
Kirov 850
Kisumu 704
Kitchener. 130
Kitwe 1353
Kitzingen. 480
Klagenfurt 49
Klaipëda 714
Kleve 480
Knokke-Heist. 91
Knoxville 1328
Knysna. 879
Kobe 695
København 211
Koblenz 480
Kochi 695
Koekelaere 91
Køge 219
Koh Samui. 1043
Kokura 695
Kolbnitz 49
Kolding 219
Köln 480
Koloubos. 564
Kolumbien **181**
Kongsvinger 813
Königstein. 499
Konstanz. 499
Kopenhagen (København). 211
Koprivnica 190
Korbach. 499
Korea-South **705**
Korfu (Kérkyra). 559
Korinthos. 559
Korolevu 228
Korsica (Corse) 256
Kortrijk. 91
Kos. 559
Kosice 861
Kostroma. 850
Koszalin. 824
Kotka 232
Koutsouras 559
Kowloon 180

Krakau (Kraków) 824
Kraków 824
Krefeld. 499
Krems 49
Kreta (Kriti) 559
Kristiansand 813
Kristianstad 974
Kristiansund 813
Kriti 559
Krk. 190
Kroatien. **188**
Kronach. 500
Krung Thep 1024
Kuala Lumpur. 717
Kuantan. 717
Kuba **153**
Kuching 717
Kula 1241
Kumamoto 695
Kuopio. 232
Kusadasi 1062
Kuta 583
Kuurne. 92
Kyiv 1064
Kyoto 695
Kypros **192**
Kyrenia 193

L

L'Aia (Den Haag) 779
La Barre-de-Monts 261
La Chaise-Dieu 261
La Ciotat 261
La Coruña 936
La Croix-Valmer 261
La Ferté-Gaucher 261
La Grande-Motte. 261
La Guaira. 1347
La Habana 153
La Havanne (La Habana) 153
La Haya (Den Haag) 779
La Haye (Den Haag) 779
La Laguna 932
La Louvière 92
La Maddalena 674
La Palma 930
La Panne (De Panne) 89
La Paz 727
La Paz 96
La Plaine-sur-Mer 261
La Plata 6
La Rochelle 261
La Roche-sur-Yon 262
La Saline 844
La Serena 169
La Seyne-sur-Mer 262
La Spezia 625
La Teste 262
La Tranche-sur-Mer 262
Lacanau 262

Lafayette 1256
Lagoa. 831
Lagos, P 831
Lagos, WAN. 809
Laguna Beach 1143
Lahaina 1241
Lahti. 232
Laibach (Ljubljana). 861
Lake Charles 1256
Lake George 1291
Lake Quinault 1338
Lake Station 1254
Lake Tahoe, CA, USA 1144
Lake Tahoe, NV, USA 1284
Lake Worth 1224
Lakeland 1224
L'Alpe-d'Huez 262
Lampeter. 1089
Lamure-sur-Azergues. 262
Lancaster, CA, USA. 1144
Lancaster, GB 1089
Lancaster, PA, USA 1320
Lanciano 625
Landau. 500
Landeronde. 262
Landshut 500
Lannion 262
Lansing 1279
Lantau Island. 180
Lanzarote 930
Laos **706**
L'Aquila 625
Larissa 559
Larnaca 193
Las Palmas 921
Las Terrenas 155
Las Vegas. 1284
Lashburn 147
Latina 625
Latvia **707**
Latvija **707**
Launceston 33
Lausana (Lausanne) 998
Lausanne 998
Lauzerte. 262
Laval 262
Lavaur 262
Le Caire (Cairo/El Qâhira) 224
Le Cannet 262
Le Cap (Cape Town) 865
Le Conquet 262
Le Croisic. 263
Le Grau-du-Roi 263
Le Havre 263
Le Lavandou 263
Le Mans 263
Le Palais 264
Le Pouliguen 264
Le Puy-en-Velay 264
Le Touquet 264
Lebanon. **710**

SPARTACUS 2001/2002 | 1373

Index

THE GAY MEDIA STORE

Bruno's
www.brunos.de

BÜCHER · MAGAZINE · DVD · VIDEOS · VIDEOVERLEIH

1374 *SPARTACUS* 2001/2002

Index

Lecce ... 625	Lincoln, NE, USA ... 1284	Lucca ... 626
Lecco ... 626	Lingen ... 502	Lucerne (Luzern) ... 1001
Leeds ... 1089	Linköping ... 974	Luchon ... 267
Leeuwarden ... 787	Linz ... 49	Lüdenscheid ... 503
Lefkosa ... 193	Lione (Lyon) ... 268	Ludwigsburg ... 504
Legnago - Verona ... 626	Lippstadt ... 503	Ludwigshafen ... 504
Legnano - Milano ... 626	Lisboa ... 832	Lugano ... 1000
Leicester ... 1090	Lisbon (Lisboa) ... 832	Luik (Liège) ... 92
Leiden ... 787	Lisbona (Lisboa) ... 832	Luleå ... 974
Leipzig ... 500	Lisbonne (Lisboa) ... 832	Lunay ... 268
Leiria ... 832	Lisieux ... 267	Lund ... 974
Lemgo ... 502	Lissabon (Lisboa) ... 832	Lüneburg ... 504
Lens ... 264	**Litauen ... 712**	Lunel ... 268
Leoben ... 49	**Lithuania ... 712**	Lusaka ... 1353
León, E. ... 936	Little Bromley ... 1090	**Lussemburgo ... 715**
Leon, MEX ... 727	Little Rock ... 1139	Luton ... 1115
León, NIC. ... 808	**Lituania ... 712**	Lutsk ... 1064
Leonberg ... 502	**Lituanie ... 712**	Lüttich (Liège) ... 92
Les Avirons ... 844	Liverpool ... 1090	Lützensommern ... 504
Les Rousses ... 264	Livigno ... 626	Luxembourg (City) ... 715
Les Saintes ... 157	Livorno ... 626	**Luxembourg ... 715**
Les Trois Islets ... 159	Ljubljana ... 861	**Luxemburg ... 715**
Lesbos ... 559	Llandrindod Wells ... 1091	**Luxemburgo ... 715**
Lethbridge ... 120	Llandudno ... 1091	Luxor ... 224
Letonia ... 707	Lleida ... 936	Luzern ... 1001
Lettland ... 707	Lloret de Mar ... 936	Lviv ... 1064
Lettonia ... 707	Llucmajor ... 897	Lynton ... 1115
Lettonie ... 707	Löbau ... 503	Lyon ... 268
Letzebuerg ... 715	Locarno ... 1000	
Leucate ... 264	Lodi ... 1340	**M**
Leura ... 12	Łódz ... 825	
Leuven ... 92	Logan ... 1317	Maastricht ... 787
Leuwen (Liège) ... 92	Loison-sous-Lens ... 267	Macapá ... 101
Levallois-Perret ... 264	Lommel ... 93	Maceió ... 101
Leverkusen ... 502	London, GB ... 1091	Macerata ... 626
Levin ... 803	London, ON, CDN ... 130	Mâcon ... 275
Lexington ... 1255	Londonderry ... 1114	Madeira Beach ... 1224
Liban ... 710	Londra (London) ... 1091	Madison ... 1340
Libano ... 710	Londres (London) ... 1091	Madrid ... 937
Libanon ... 710	Long Beach ... 1144	Magdeburg ... 504
Liberec ... 196	Long Island - Nassau County ... 1292	Magog ... 138
Lidköping ... 974	Long Island - Suffolk County ... 1292	**Magyar ... 568**
Liechtenstein ... 711	Long Island ... 1292	Mahé ... 857
Liège ... 92	Lons-le-Saunier ... 267	Mahina ... 344
Liegi (Liège) ... 92	Lopburi ... 1044	Maidenhead ... 1115
Lieja (Liège) ... 92	Lorient ... 267	Maidstone ... 1115
Lietuva ... 712	Los Angeles ... 1145	Mailand (Milano) ... 627
Lignières ... 93	Los Realejos ... 932	Maine ... 1262
L'Ile-Rousse ... 257	Losanna (Lausanne) ... 998	Mainz ... 505
Lille ... 264	Loughborough ... 1114	Makarska ... 190
Lillehammer ... 813	Louisiana ... 1255	Makasar ... 583
Lima, OH, USA ... 1317	Louisville ... 1255	Málaga ... 951
Lima, PE. ... 819	Louvain (Leuven) ... 92	Malang ... 584
Limassol ... 193	Louxor (Luxor/Al-Uqsur) ... 224	**Malasia ... 716**
Limburg ... 502	Lower Carlton ... 152	**Malaysia ... 716**
Limerick ... 592	Lowestoft ... 1115	**Malaysie ... 716**
Limoges ... 266	Luang Prabang ... 706	Malcesine ... 626
Limoges-Branchard ... 267	Lubbock ... 1334	Maleo ... 626
Limon ... 185	Lübeck ... 503	**Malesia ... 716**
Limoux ... 267	Lublin ... 825	Malines (Mechelen) ... 93
Lincoln, GB ... 1090	**Lubnan ... 710**	Mallorca ... 897

SPARTACUS 2001/2002 | 1375

Index

Malmö 975	Medellin 182	Mojokerto 584
Malta **718**	Medford 1318	Mol. 93
Malte **718**	Melbourne, FL, USA 1224	Molde 813
Manado 584	Melbourne, VIC, AUS 34	Molfetta 644
Managua 808	Memmingen 507	Molokai 1242
Manaus 102	Memphis 1328	Molyvos 559
Manchester, GB 1115	Mende 278	Mombasa 704
Manchester, NH, USA 1286	Menden 507	Monaco (München) 509
Manfredonia 627	Mendoza 6	Mönchengladbach 508
Manhattan 1298	Menen 93	Monchique 841
Manihi 344	Mennessis 278	Moncton 127
Manila 821	Menomonee Falls 1340	Mondorf-Les-Bains 716
Manitoba 126	Menton 278	**Monggol Ulus** **732**
Mannheim 505	Meran 627	**Mongolei** **732**
Mansfield 1118	Merano 627	**Mongolia** **732**
Mantova 627	Meransen 627	**Mongolie** **732**
Manuel Antonio 186	Merida, E. 952	Monroe 1317
Manzanillo 727	Mérida, MEX 727	Mons 93
Mar del Plata 6	Mérida, YV. 1318	Montabaur 508
Maracaibo 1348	**Messico** **721**	Montagu 879
Marbella 952	Messina 677	Montana 1283
Marburg 507	Mestre 627	Montargis 278
Marcelli di Numana 627	Metairie 1256	Montauban 278
Margate 1118	Metz 278	Montbéliard 279
Maribor 862	Metzingen 507	Montcombroux-les-Mines 279
Maricá 102	Meudon 278	Mont-de-Marsan 279
Mariehamn 232	Mexicali 727	Monte Isola 644
Marina di Bibbona 627	Mexico (Ciudad de Mexico) 723	Monte Rio 1158
Marina di Carrara 627	Mexico City (Ciudad de Mexico) 723	Montecatini Terme 644
Marina di Cecina 627	**Mexico** **721**	Montélimar 279
Marina di Pisa 627	**México** **721**	Monterey 1158
Marina di Ravenna 627	Mexiko (Ciudad de Mexico) 723	Monterrey 728
Marmande 275	**Mexique** **721**	Montesilvano 644
Maroc **733**	Miami Beach 1226	Montevideo 1343
Marocco **733**	Miami 1224	Montgomery 1136
Marokko **733**	Michigan 1277	Monthey 1002
Marrakech 734	Middelburg 788	Monticiano 644
Marruecos **733**	Middlesbrough 1118	Montpellier 279
Marsalforn 718	Milan (Milano) 627	Montréal 139
Marseille 275	Milano 627	Montreux 1003
Marsella (Marseille) 275	Millau 278	Mont-Tremblant 145
Marsiglia (Marseille) 275	Milton Keynes 1119	Monza 644
Martha's Vineyard 1268	Milwaukee 1340	Moorea 344
Martigues 278	Mimizan 278	Morelia 728
Martinica **159**	Minden 508	Morges 1003
Martinique **159**	Minneapolis 1279	Moritzburg 508
Maryland 1265	Minnesota 1279	Morlaix 281
Marysville 34	Minsk 73	Mornington 41
Massachusetts 1266	Mirandola 643	Morocco 733
Masterton 803	Mirtiotissa 559	Morristown 1287
Matosinhos 841	Miskolc 575	Mosca (Moskva) 850
Matsuyama 696	**Misr** **223**	Moscou (Moskva) 850
Maui 1241	Mississippi 1280	Moscú (Moskva) 850
Maurice **719**	Missoula 1283	Moskau (Moskva) 850
Mauricio **719**	Missouri 1281	Moskow (Moskva) 850
Mauritius **719**	Mitilini 559	Moskva 850
Maynooth 130	Mobile 1136	Most 196
Mazatlan 727	Modena 643	Moulins 281
Meaux 278	Modesto 1156	Mount Maunganui 803
Mechelen 93	Modica 644	Moustiers-Sainte-Marie 281
Medan 584	Moers 508	Mriehel 718

Index

Mühlhausen 528	Nerja 953	**Nippon** **693**
Mülheim a. d. Ruhr 508	Nerviano 646	Niterói 102
Mulhouse 281	**Netherlands** **739**	Nizhny Novgorod 853
München 509	**Netherlands Antilles** **160**	Nizza (Nice) 283
Munich (München) 509	Nettuno 646	Noirmoutier-en-l'Ile 291
Münster 528	Neubrandenburg 530	Nong Khai 1044
Murcia 952	Neuchâtel 1003	Noordwijk 789
Murmansk 853	Neufchâtel-en-Bray 282	Noosa 28
Myanma Pye **735**	Neuilly-en-Thelle 282	Norderney 530
Myanmar **735**	**Neukaledonien** **794**	Nordhorn 530
Mykonos 560	Neukirchen 530	Norfolk 1337
Myrtle Beach 1328	Neumünster 530	**Norge** **810**
	Neuseeland **795**	Norrköping 975
N	Neuss 530	North Carolina 1312
	Neustadt 530	North Dakota 1314
Naarden 788	Neu-Ulm 530	Northampton 1119
Nadi 228	Neuwied 530	Northampton 1268
Næstved 219	Nevada 1284	Northern Territory 24
Nafplion 563	Nevers 282	**Noruega** **810**
Nagasaki 696	**Nevis (Saint Kitts & Nevis)** **165**	**Norvège** **810**
Nagoya 696	New Albany 1254	**Norvegia** **810**
Naha 696	New Brunswick 127	**Norway** **810**
Nahariyya 596	**New Caledonia** **794**	**Norwegen** **810**
Nairobi 704	New Glasgow 129	Norwich 1120
Namen (Namur) 93	New Hampshire 1286	Nosara 185
Namibia **737**	New Haven 1191	Nottingham 1120
Namibie **737**	New Hope 1320	Nouméa 794
Namur 93	New Jersey 1286	**Nouvelle Calédonie** **794**
Nanaimo 121	New Mexico 1287	**Nouvelle Zélande** **795**
Nancy 281	New Orleans 1256	Nova Iguaçu 102
Nanjing 174	New Plymouth 804	Nova Scotia 128
Nantes 281	New South Wales 11	Novara 648
Naousa 563	New Westminster 121	Novi Sad 1351
Napier 803	New York City 1292	Novokuznetsk 853
Naples, FL, USA 1232	New York 1289	Novosibirsk 853
Naples, I (Napoli) 644	**New Zealand** **795**	**Nueva Caledonia** **794**
Naples, ME, USA 1262	Newark 1317	**Nueva Zelandia** **795**
Nápoles (Napoli) 644	Newcastle 12	Nuevo Laredo 728
Napoli 644	Newcastle-upon-Tyne 1119	Numana 648
Narbonne 282	Newfoundland 128	Numansdorp 789
Narita 696	Newport 1119	**Nuova Caledonia** **794**
Nashville 1329	Newport 1326	**Nuova Zelanda** **795**
Nassau 1292	Newton Abbot 1119	Nürnberg 531
Nassau 151	Nha Trang 1350	Nyiregyháza 575
Natal Midlands 879	Niagara Falls 1310	Nykøbing 219
Natal 102	**Nicaragua** **807**	Nyköping 976
Natanya 596	Nice 283	
Naucalpan de Juarez 728	Nicosia 193	**O**
Nazaré 841	Nicotera Marina 648	
Ndola City 1353	**Niederlande** **739**	Oahu 1242
Neapel (Napoli) 644	**Niederländische Antillen** **160**	Oakland 1158
Nebraska 1284	Niekerk 788	Oaxaca 728
Nederland **739**	Nieuwegein 788	Oberhausen 533
Nederlandse Antillen **160**	Nieuwpoort 93	Oberstdorf 534
Negril 159	**Nigeria** **808**	Oberursel 534
Neiva 183	Niigata 696	Ocala 1232
Nelson 121	Nijmegen 788	Oceanside 1158
Nelson 803	Nikolayev 1064	Odense 219
Nepal **738**	Nîmes 290	Odessa 1064
Nepál **738**	Nin 190	Offenbach 534
Népal **738**	Niort 291	Offenburg 534

SPARTACUS 2001/2002 | 1377

Die Nummer Eins unter Deutschlands schwulen Magazinen

männer aktuell

von mann zu mann

Einzelheft 14,80 DM

Probeabo: 3 Ausgaben für nur 29,60 DM

Hotline 030-6150030

Mail@maenneraktuell.de

männer aktuell, postfach 61 01 04, 10921 Berlin. Aktuelle Ausgabe: www.brunos.de

**Soap-Star
Laurent Daniels
Exklusiv entblättert**
im Heft 01/2001

Lifestyle, Unterhaltung, Service, Sex:

Jeden Monat die schärfsten Männer:
Jeff Palmer, Thom Barron, Ken Ryker

die neuesten Trends:
Mode, High-Tech, Musik und Bücher

die heissesten Reportagen:
Callboys, Schwule Knackis, Gay Manager

und die tollsten Promis im Interview:
Guido Westerwelle, Dolce & Gabbana, Stephen Gately

...und jeden Monat exklusiv einen Ralf-Könic-Comic!

Foto © by Andreas Bitesnich

Index

Ogden 1335	Paesi Bassi 739	Perrignier 327
Ogunquit 1262	Pahoa 1240	**Persekutan Tanah Malaysia** **716**
Ohio 1314	Paia 1241	Perth 41
Ohrigstad 880	**Paises Bajos** **739**	**Peru** **819**
Oia 564	Paisley 1121	**Perú** **819**
Oklahoma City 1318	Palembang 584	Perugia 651
Oklahoma 1318	Palermo 677	Perybere 720
Olbia 674	Palm Springs 1158	Pesaro 651
Oldenburg 534	Palma de Mallorca 897	Pescara 651
Oldham 1120	Palmerston North 804	Petange 716
Olinda, BR 103	Pals 953	Peterborough, GB 1121
Olinda, VIC, AUS 41	Pamiers 291	Peterborough, ON, CDN 131
Olomouc 196	Pamplona 953	Petite-Ile 844
Olonne-sur-Mer 291	Panajachel 566	Pforzheim 536
Olpe 535	**Panama** **817**	Philadelphia 1321
Olsztyn 825	Panama City Beach, FL, USA 1233	**Philippinen** **820**
Olten 1003	Panamá City, PA 817	**Philippines** **820**
Omaha 1284	Papéete 344	Phitsanuloke 1052
Ommen 789	Papenoo 345	Phnom Penh 115
Omsk 853	Papetoai 344	Phoenix 1137
Ontario 129	Paphos 193	Phuket 1052
Oostende 93	**Paraguay** **818**	Piacenza 651
Oostkapelle 789	Paray-le-Monial 291	**Pilipinas** **820**
Opole 825	Pardubice 196	Pinerolo 652
Orange 291	Parigi (Paris) 291	Pinet 327
Oranienburg 535	Parikia 563	Piotrków Trybunalski 825
Oranjestad 150	Paris 291	Pipaix 94
Orbetello 648	Parma 650	Piraeus 563
Orchamps 291	Pärnu 227	Piran 862
Örebro 976	Paros 563	Piriapolis 1344
Oregon 1318	Pasadena 1164	Pisa 652
Oristano 674	Passau 535	Pistoia 653
Orizaba 728	Pasto 183	Piteå 976
Orlando 1232	Pasuruan 584	Piton Saint Leu 844
Orléans 291	Pátrai 563	Pittem 94
Ormskirk 1120	Pattaya 1044	Pittsburgh 1324
Ortona 648	Patzcuaro 729	Plainfield 1287
Osaka 697	Pau 326	Platja d'Aro 954
Oshawa 131	Pavia 650	Plauen 536
Osijek 190	Paysandú 1344	Playa de las Americas 932
Oslo 813	**Pays-Bas** **739**	Playa de Palma 903
Osnabrück 535	Pechino (Beijing) 173	Playa del Carmen 729
Oss 789	Pecos 1288	Playa del Inglés 922
Österreich **44**	Pécs 575	Playa Jaco 185
Östersund 976	Pedreguer 954	Playa Tortuga 185
Ostrava 196	Pekanbaru 584	Plouarzel 327
Ottawa 131	Pékin (Beijing) 173	Plouescat 327
Oulu 232	Peking (Beijing) 173	Plouharnel 327
Ouro Preto 103	Penang 717	Plymouth 1121
Oviedo 953	Peniche 841	Plzen 196
Oxford 1120	Penmaenmawr 1121	Podgorica 1352
	Pennsylvania 1320	Poggibonsi 653
	Penrith 12	Pointe-à-Pitre 157
P	Pensacola 1233	Poissy 327
Pacy-sur-Eure 291	Penzance 1121	Poitiers 327
Padang 584	Peoria 1252	Pokolbin 13
Paderborn 535	Peregian Beach 28	**Poland** **823**
Paderno Fraciacorta 648	Périgueux 327	**Polen** **823**
Padova 648	Pernes-les-Fontaines 327	**Polinesia Francesa** **344**
Paducah 1255	**Pérou** **819**	**Polinesia Francese** **344**
Paea 345	Perpignan 327	**Pologne** **823**

1380 SPARTACUS 2001/2002

Index

Polonia 823
Polska 823
Poltava. 1064
Polynésie Française. 344
Pomona. 1164
Pompei 653
Ponorogo. 584
Ponsacco 653
Pont-Audemer. 327
Pontcarré. 328
Pont-d'Ain 328
Pont-de-Fillinges 328
Ponte San Pietro 653
Pontevedra 954
Pont-l'Abbé 328
Pordenone. 653
Porec 190
Pori 232
Port Angeles 1338
Port Elizabeth 880
Port Kembla 13
Port Louis 720
Port Richey 1233
Port Sydney. 132
Port Vila 1345
Portarlington 41
Portimão 841
Portland, ME, USA 1264
Portland, OR, USA. 1319
Porto Alegre 103
Porto Recanati. 653
Porto Rico 161
Porto Seguro 104
Porto Vehlo 104
Porto 841
Portogallo 828
Pörtschach am Wörther See 50
Portsmouth, GB 1121
Portsmouth, NH, USA. 1286
Portugal 828
Port-Vendres. 328
Positano. 654
Potenza 654
Potsdam 536
Poussan 328
Póvoa de Varzim. 841
Poznan 825
Prag (Praha) 197
Praga (Praha) 197
Prague (Praha) 197
Praha 197
Prathet Thai. 1023
Prato 654
Preßburg (Bratislava) 860
Preston 1122
Pretoria 880
Prievidza 861
Primosten 190
Prince George 121
Prince Rupert 121
Prince-Edward-Island 138

Prinsenbeek 789
Propriano 257
Prostejov 206
Providence 1326
Provincetown 1268
Ptuj. 862
Puebla de Zaragoza 729
Puerto Barrios. 567
Puerto de la Cruz 932
Puerto del Carmen 932
Puerto La Cruz 1348
Puerto Plata. 155
Puerto Princesa 822
Puerto Rico 161
Puerto San José. 567
Puerto Vallarta 729
Puerto Viejo. 186
Punaauia 345
Punta Arenas. 169
Punta del Este 1344
Puntagorda 930
Puntarenas 186
Purmerend 789
Pusan 705
Puunene 1241

Q

Quarteira 841
Québec (City) 145
Québec 138
Queensland. 24
Queenstown 804
Quepos 186
Queretaro 730
Quezon City 822
Quimper 328
Quito 222

R

Rab. 190
Rabat 735
Radium Springs. 1288
Radom 826
Ragusa 678
Raleigh. 1313
Ramatuelle 328
Rambouillet. 328
Ramsgate. 1118
Rangoon (Yangon) 736
Ranzanico 654
Rapid City 1328
Ravenna. 654
Ravensburg 536
Ravenscrag 147
Reading, GB 1122
Reading, PA, USA 1325
Recife. 104
Recklinghausen. 536
Red Bluff 1164

Red Deer 120
Redcar 1122
Redding 1164
Redhill 1122
Redwood City 1164
Regensburg 537
Reggio Calabria. 655
Reggio Emilia 655
Regina 147
Rehoboth Beach 1191
Reigate. 1122
Reims. 328
Rekkem 94
Remich. 716
Remoulins 328
Rendsburg. 537
Rennes 329
Reno 1286
Repubblica Ceca 194
Repubblica Dominicana 154
República Checa 194
República Dominicana 154
République Dominicaine 154
République Tchèque 194
Reseda. 1165
Reunion 843
Réunion 843
Reus. 954
Revelstoke 121
Reykjavik 577
Reynosa. 730
Rheine 537
Rhode Island. 1326
Riccione 655
Richmond, GB. 1122
Richmond, VA, USA 1337
Richmond, VT, USA. 1336
Riec-sur-Belon. 329
Rieti 655
Riga 708
Rijeka 190
Rillaar. 94
Rimini 655
Rimouski 146
Rio de Janeiro 104
Rio Verde. 107
Riva del Garda. 655
River Edge 1287
Riverside 1165
Roanoke 1337
Robertson, NSW, AUS. 13
Robertson, RSA. 881
Rocas de Santo Domingo. 169
Rochdale 1122
Rochefort. 329
Rochester, GB 1122
Rochester, NY, USA. 1310
Rockhampton 28
Rodez 329
Ródos. 563
Roermond 789

Index

Roeselare. 94	Saint Georges 147	Saint-Sébastien 333
Rogersville. 1329	Saint George's. 156	Saint-Thibéry 333
Rom (Roma) 655	Saint Helens 1124	Saint-Trojan-les-Bains. 333
Roma. 655	Saint Hyacinthe. 147	Saint-Tropez 333
Romania **844**	Saint Ives 1124	Saint-Vivien-de-Médoc 333
România **844**	Saint James 152	Salamanca. 954
Romans-sur-Isère 329	Saint Jérôme 147	Salatiga 584
Rome (Roma) 655	Saint John, NB, CDN. 127	Salem. 1319
Romorantin-Lanthenay 329	Saint John, VI, USA 166	Salerno 673
Ronan 1283	Saint John's, NF, CDN. 128	Salin-de-Giraud. 333
Roosendaal 789	Saint Joseph, BDS 152	Salisbury 1122
Roquebrune-Cap-Martin 329	Saint Joseph, LA, USA. 1262	Salon-de-Provence 333
Rosario. 6	Saint Julians 718	Salou 954
Rosenheim 537	**Saint Kitts & Nevis**. **165**	Salsomaggiore Terme. 673
Roskilde. 219	Saint Leonards on Sea 1124	Salt Lake City. 1335
Rosport 716	Saint Louis. 1282	Salt Spring Island 121
Rossiya. **846**	Saint Michael. 152	Salta 6
Rostock 537	Saint Paul 1279	Saltillo 730
Rostov-na-Donn 853	Saint Peter 152	Salvador 108
Rota 954	Saint Petersbourg (Saint Petersburg) . . 853	Salzburg. 50
Rotorua 804	Saint Petersburg, FL, USA. 1234	Samaná 155
Rottenbuch 538	Saint Petersburg, RUS. 853	Samara 187
Rotterdam 789	Saint Thomas 167	**Sambia**. **1353**
Rottweil 538	Saint-Brieuc. 330	Samedan 1003
Roubaix 329	Saint-Chamas 330	Samos 563
Rouen 329	Saint-Cirques-en-Montagne. 330	San Andrés 183
Roulers (Roeselare) 94	Saint-Clar. 330	San Antonio, RCA 169
Roumanie **844**	Saint-Denis 844	San Antonio, TX, USA 1334
Rouyn-Noranda 146	Saint-Denis-de-Jouhet 330	San Benedetto del Tronto 673
Rovaniemi 232	Saint-Dié 330	San Bernardino. 1166
Rovereto 673	Saint-Dizier 330	San Cristóbal. 1348
Rovinj. 191	Saint-Domingue (Santo Domingo) . . . 155	San Diego 1166
Royal Oak 1279	Sainte-Anne, GUA 158	San Francisco 1169
Royan 330	Sainte-Anne, MAR. 159	San Jose, CA, USA. 1186
Royaume-Uni (United Kingdom). . . **1066**	Saintes 331	San José, CR 187
Rue. 330	Saint-Etienne. 331	San Juan, ARG 6
Rumania **844**	Saint-Florent (Corse) 257	San Juan, PR 162
Rumänien **844**	Saint-Florent 331	San Luis Obispo 1187
Rumelange 716	Saint-François 157	San Luis Potosi 730
Runcorn/Halton 1122	Saint-Germain-en-Laye 331	San Miguel de Tucumán. 7
Rusia **846**	Saint-Gilles-Croix-de-Vie. 331	San Pedro de Atacama. 169
Russa Bianca **73**	Saint-Girons 331	San Pedro Sula 567
Rüsselsheim 538	Saint-Jean-de-Luz 331	San Pedro 1187
Russia **846**	Saint-Jean-de-Muzols. 331	San Petersburgo (Saint Petersburg) . . 853
Russian River. 1165	Saint-Julien-en-Born 331	San Pietroburgo (Saint Petersburg). . . 853
Russie **846**	Saint-Laurant-Nouant. 331	San Ramón 188
Rußland **846**	Saint-Lô 332	San Remo 673
Ryle 1088	Saint-Malo 332	San Salvador 226
Rylestone. 13	Saint-Martin 157	San Sebastian 954
Rzeszow. 826	Saint-Martin-d'Auxigny. 332	San Vincenzo. 674
	Saint-Martin-de-Jussac 332	Sandbach 1122
	Saint-Maur. 332	Sandefjord. 816
S	Saint-Meloir-des-Ondes 332	Sandförde 539
'S Hertogenbosch 786	Saint-Même-les-Carrières. 332	Sankt Gallen 1004
Saarbrücken 538	Saint-Michel 332	Sankt Ingbert. 540
Saarlouis 539	Saint-Nazaire. 332	Sankt Moritz 1004
Sabadell. 954	Saint-Paul-de-Vence 332	Sankt Petersburg (Saint Petersburg) . . 853
Sacramento. 1165	Saint-Pierre 844	Sankt Pölten 51
Saint Albans 1124	Saint-Quai-Portrieux 332	Sant Anthonis 791
Saint Croix 166	Saint-Raphaël 332	Sant Maarten 161
Saint François-Du-Lac. 147	Saint-Romain-en-Viennois 333	Santa Barbara 1187

Santa Cristina d'Aro 955	Scheveningen 791	Silverdale. . . . .
Santa Cruz de la Palma, E 930	Schiedam. 791	**Simbabwe** . . . .
Santa Cruz, BOL 97	Schöfflengrund 539	Simeiz . . . .
Santa Cruz, CA, USA. 1187	Schöllnach. 539	Simferopol' . . . . 1(
Santa Cruz, E. 933	Schwabach 539	**Singapore** **858**
Santa Fe, ARG 7	Schwäbisch Gmünd 539	**Singapore** **858**
Santa Fe, NM, USA 1288	**Schweden** **971**	**Singapour** **858**
Santa Margherita Ligure. 674	**Schweiz** **986**	**Singapur** **858**
Santa Maria. 109	Schwerin 539	Singen 540
Santa Marta. 183	Sciacca. 678	Sint-Niklaas 94
Santa Rosa. 1187	Scunthorpe 1122	Siófok. 575
Santafé de Bogotá 183	Seaford 1312	Sion 1003
Santander 955	Seattle 1338	Sioux City 1254
Santiago de Compostela 955	Sedan. 334	Sioux Falls 1328
Santiago, DOM 155	Sedona 1138	Siracusa. 678
Santiago, RCA 169	Segovia 955	Sitges 956
Sant'Ilario d'Enza 674	**Seicelle.** **857**	Sizilien (Sicilia) 675
Santo Domingo. 155	Seignosse 334	Skagen 219
Santo-Pietro-di-Tenda 257	Seinäjoki 233	Skiathos. 564
Santorini (Thira) 564	Semarang 584	Skibbereen 592
Santos 109	Sendai 699	Skien 816
São João Del Rei 109	**Senegal** **856**	Skövde. 976
São Luiz 109	**Sénégal** **856**	Slagelse 219
São Paulo 109	Senigallia 675	Slavonski Brod 191
São Vicente 112	Sennecey-le-Grand. 334	Slough 1123
Sapporo. 698	Sens 334	**Slovachia** **860**
Sarajevo. 98	Seoul 705	**Slovakia** **860**
Sarasota. 1234	Sept-Iles. 147	**Slovaquie** **860**
Saratov 853	Serignan 334	**Slovenia** **861**
Sardaigne (Sardegna). 674	**Sesel.** **857**	**Slovénie** **861**
Sardegna 674	Sesto Fiorentino 675	**Slovenija** **861**
Sardinia (Sardegna) 674	Sète 334	**Slovensko** **860**
Sardinien (Sardegna) 674	Setubal. 842	**Slowakei** **860**
Sartilly 333	Sevastopol' 1064	**Slowenien** **861**
Saskatchewan 147	Sevilla 955	Sneek. 791
Saskatoon 148	Sevran 334	Sochi 853
Sassari 674	**Seychellen** **857**	Soest 540
Sasso Marconi. 675	**Seychelles** **857**	Sofia (Sofija) 113
Satellite Beach. 1234	Shaftsbury 1336	Sofija 113
Sathlanalat Paxathipatai	Shanghai 174	Soissons. 334
Paxaxôn Lao **706**	Shanklin. 1088	Sölden 51
Saturnia 675	Sheffield, GB 1122	Solingen. 540
Saugatuck 1279	Shepton Mallet 1123	Solothurn 1003
Saumur 333	Sherbrooke 147	Somerset. 1287
Sausalito 1187	Sherman Oaks 1187	Sønderborg 220
Savanna la Mar 159	Shijiazhuang 175	Sondrio 679
Savannah 1239	**Shqipëria** **1**	Sonoma 1187
Savines-le-Lac 333	Shrewsbury 1123	Sonthofen 540
Savona. 675	Sibari 675	Sopot 826
Savonnières. 333	Sibenik. 191	Sopron. 575
Saxel 333	Sibiu. 846	Sorø 220
Sayville 1310	Sicile (Sicilia) 675	Sorrento 679
Sazaret. 334	Sicilia 675	Sotteville-les-Rouen 334
Scandicci 675	Sicily (Sicilia) 675	Soulac-sur-Mer 334
Scarborough, GB 1122	Sidmouth. 1123	Sousse 1056
Scarborough, WA, AUS. 43	Sidoarjo 585	**South Africa** **863**
Sceaux 334	Siegbur 539	South Australia 30
Schaan. 711	Siegen 539	South Beach 1234
Schaffhausen. 1003	Siena 679	South Bend 1254
Schagen 791	Sigmaringen 540	South Carolina 1327
Schenectady 1310	Silver Spring 1266	South Dakota 1328

***SPARTACUS* 2001/2002** | **1383**

Massage aus Strom –

Inklusive Video!

SLENDERTONE
LIVING LIFE AND LOVING IT

Perfekte Funktionen für ein Top-Ergebnis:

"Body Matched Impedance"
Eine eingebaute Sicherung gewährleistet, daß Slendertone-Geräte keine erhöhten Spannungswerte erzeugen können, selbst wenn Störungen an den Elektroden auftreten sollten. Diese Technologie bezeichnet Slendertone als "Body Matched Impedance" (Impedanz = Schein-Hautwiderstand).

"Multiplexing"
Eine Mehrfachschaltung bewirkt, daß der Strom immer zwischen dem Elektrodenpaar eines Muskels übertragen wird und nicht auf andere Elektroden, die andere Muskeln stimulieren.

"Safestart"
Vor Beginn einer jeden Anwendung müssen alle Regler auf Minimalstellung gebracht werden, damit nicht mit zu hoher Intensität begonnen wird. Alle Slendertone-Modelle sind mit einer Sicherheitsfunktion ausgestattet, die wir "Safestart" nennen. Das Gerät schaltet erst ein, wenn alle Regler auf Minimalstellung stehen.

Sicherheitspaket
"Safestart" (Sicherheitsstart), "Automatic Shutoff" (automatische Abschaltung), "Multiplexing" (Mehrfachschaltung), "Body Matched Impedance" (Impedanz = Schein-Hautwiderstand).

"Automatic Shutoff"
Nahezu alle Slendertone-Modelle sind mit einer automatischen Zeitschaltuhr ausgerüstet, die gewährleistet, daß Sie Ihre Muskulatur nicht überanstrengen.

DM 499,-/ Euro 255,13

Sofort-Lieferung frei Haus!
Bestellen ohne Risiko!
Mit 14 Tage Rückgaberecht

Index

für starke Körper mit Gefühl

Der "Body-Profile" von Slendertone ist das Ergebnis einer bis zur Perfektion gereiften Technologie: "Der Elektronischen-Muskel-Stimulation", kurz EMS. Muskelstimulation mittels Impulsströmen machte man sich früher nur in der Sport-Therapie nach Verletzungen zu Nutze. Inzwischen ist "EMS" weltweit ein Begriff, wenn es um passive Kontraktion der Muskeln geht. Für ein besseres Körpergefühl, Problemzonen-Fitness und Muskel-Kräftigung. Bequem im Sitzen, beim Lesen, Fernsehen, Arbeiten oder einfach nur zum Entspannen und Stimulieren. Für einen strammen, anziehenden Körper von der Brust bis zu den Waden.

Im mobilen Kompaktset mit:

- Slendertone Body Profile Muskelstimulationsgerät (inkl. Batterie)
- Dauerelektroden
- elastische Gurte
- Gürtel zum Anlegen des Body Profile
- Video (mehrsprachig) und eine bebilderte Bedienungsanleitung

Hair Remove -

für schnelles, gründliches Entfernen von Körperhaaren ohne Rasur! Einfach auftragen, wirken lassen, entfernen. Kein Ziepen und lange haarfrei mit **Hair Remove** 100 ml nur

DM 19,95/Euro 10,20

zzgl. Porto und Verpackungspauschale von DM 8,95 innerhalb Deutschlands.

! Hair Remove wird von vielen Bodybuilding-Profis wegen seiner unkomplizierten Anwendung vor Wettkämpfen empfohlen!

Info- und Bestell-Hotline:
0180 500 22 20

Koelbel-Trainingsforschung GmbH · Rendsburger Str. 14+16
30659 Hannover

Es gelten die Allgemeinen Geschäftsbedingungen (AGB) der Koelbel-Trainingsforschung, vertreten durch die GF W. Brandt und E. Schlüter

Index

South Padre Island 1335	Sundsvall 985	Tauranga 805
Southampton 1123	**Suomi 229**	Tavira 842
Southend-on-Sea 1123	Superior 1341	Tegucigalpa 567
Southport 1124	Surabaya 585	Tel-Aviv-Yafo 596
Spagna 883	Suresnes 335	Telford 1125
Spain 883	Surfer's Paradise 28	Tenants Harbor 1265
Spanien 883	Sutton in Ashfield 1125	Tenerife 932
Spárti 564	Suva 228	Tennessee 1328
Speightstown 152	Svendborg 220	Teresina 112
Spessa Po 680	**Sverige 971**	Tergnier 335
Speyer 540	**Svezia 971**	Termoli 680
Split 191	**Svizzera 986**	Termonde (Dendermonde) 90
Spokane 1339	Swansea 1125	Terneuzen 791
Spresiano 680	**Sweden 971**	Terni 680
Springfield, IL, USA 1252	Swindon 1125	Terschelling 792
Springfield, MA, USA 1277	Swinoujscie 826	Tetouan 735
Springfield, MO, USA 1282	**Switzerland 986**	Texas 1329
Springfield, OH, USA 1317	Sydney, NS, CDN 129	Texel 792
Sri Lanka 970	Sydney, NSW, USA 13	**Thailand 1023**
Stade 540	Sylt (Westerland - Sylt) 547	**Thailande 1023**
Stamford 1124	Syracuse 1312	The Hague (Den Haag) 779
Stanford 1187	Szczecin 826	Théoule-sur-Mer 335
Stanley 41	Szeged 575	Thermopolis 1341
State College 1325	Székesfehérvár 575	Thessaloníki 564
Stati Uniti 1129		Thiaroye 856
Stavanger 816	**T**	Thira 564
Stellenbosch 881		Thonon-les-Bains 335
Steyr 52	Tacoma 1339	Thoreau 1289
Stirling 1124	**Taehan Min'guk 705**	Thun 1004
Stoccarda (Stuttgart) 540	Tahiti 344	Thunder Bay 132
Stoccolma (Stockholm) 976	Tahoe Paradise 1188	Tianjin 175
Stockholm 976	Taichung 1021	Tielt 94
Stockport 1124	**Tailandia 1023**	Tienen 94
Stockton 1187	Tainan 1022	Tierlemont (Tienen) 94
Stoke-on-Trent 1124	Taipeh 1022	Tigard 1320
Stourbridge 1125	Taipei 1022	Tijuana 730
Stowe 1336	**Taiwan 1021**	Tilburg 792
Stralsund 540	**T'ai-wan 1021**	Tiller 1320
Strasbourg 334	Takaka 805	Timaru 805
Straßburg (Strasbourg) 334	Talca 171	Timisoara 846
Stratford 132	Talcahuano 171	Timmendorfer Strand 545
Stratford-Upon-Avon 1125	Talence 335	Tiradentes 113
Straubing 540	Tallahassee 1234	Tirana (Tiranë) 1
Stromboli 678	Tallinn 227	Tiranë 1
Stroud 1125	Talmont-Saint-Hilaire 335	Tisvilde 220
Stuttgart 540	Tampa 1234	Tiznit 735
Subotica 1352	Tampere 233	Tlaquepaque 731
Sucre 97	Tampico 730	Tofino 121
Sud Africa 863	Tamuning 565	Tokio (Tokyo) 699
Sudáfrica 863	Tanger 735	Tokyo 699
Südafrika 863	Tangier 735	Toledo 1317
Sudbury 132	Taormina 678	Toluca De Lerdo 731
Südkorea 705	Taranto 680	Tønsberg 816
Suecia 971	Tarare 335	Toowoomba 30
Suède 971	Tarbes 335	Topeka 1254
Suhl 545	Tarnos 335	Torino 680
Suid-Afrika 863	Tarquinia 680	Toronto 132
Suisse 986	Tarragona 964	Torquay 1125
Suiza 986	Tartu 228	Torre del Greco 683
Sukhothai 1056	Tasmania 33	Torre del Lago 683
Sunderland 1125	Taupo 805	Torrelavega 964

Index

Torremolinos....................964	**U**	Vendôme.......................342
Torres Novas...................842	Ubud..........................585	Venecia (Venezia)..............685
Torres Vedras..................842	**Ucrania.....................1062**	Venedig (Venezia)..............685
Torrevieja.....................966	Udine.........................683	Venezia.......................685
Torun.........................826	Udon Thani...................1056	**Venezuela..................1346**
Toulon........................336	**Ukraïna....................1062**	Venice (Venezia)...............685
Toulouse......................336	**Ukraine....................1062**	Venise (Venezia)...............685
Tournai........................94	Ulcinj.......................1352	Venlo.........................793
Tours.........................340	Ulm...........................546	Ventimiglia...................686
Townsville.....................30	Ulverstone.....................33	Ventura......................1188
Trang........................1056	Umag..........................191	Veracruz......................731
Trapani.......................679	Umeå..........................985	Vercelli......................686
Traunstein....................545	**Ungarn......................568**	Verdun........................342
Trento........................683	Ungheria......................568	**Vereinigte Staaten..........1129**
Trenton......................1287	**United Kingdom.............1066**	Vermont......................1336
Treviso.......................683	**United States of America..1129**	Vernon Bridge.................138
Trier.........................545	Unkel.........................546	Vernon........................126
Trieste.......................583	Unna..........................546	Verona........................686
Trogir........................191	Upland.......................1188	Verrières-le-Buisson..........342
Trois Rivières................147	Uppsala.......................985	Versailles....................342
Troisdorf.....................545	**Uruguay....................1343**	Verteuil-sur-Charente.........342
Trollhättan...................985	Uster........................1004	Vesterålen....................816
Tromsø........................816	Ustí nad Labem...............206	Veurne.........................95
Trondheim.....................816	Utah.........................1335	Vevey........................1004
Tropea........................683	Utica........................1312	Viana do Castelo..............842
Trou-aux-Biches...............720	Utrecht.......................792	Viangchan.....................706
Trouville-sur-Mer.............341	Uxbridge.....................1123	Viareggio.....................688
Troy.........................1312	Uzès..........................341	Viborg........................220
Troyes........................341		Vicenza.......................691
Truro........................1126	**V**	Vichy.........................342
Tschechische Republik......194	Vaasa.........................233	Victoria (State of), AUS......34
Tübingen......................545	Valence.......................341	Victoria, BC, CDN.............126
Tucson.......................1138	Valencia, E...................966	Victorville..................1188
Tulle.........................341	Valencia, YV.................1348	Viena (Wien)...................52
Tulsa........................1318	Valenciennes..................342	Vienna (Wien)..................52
Tumon.........................565	Vall de Ebo...................968	Vienne (Wien)..................52
Tunbridge Wells..............1126	Valladolid....................968	Vientiane.....................706
Tunesien...................1056	Vallejo......................1188	Viersen.......................546
Túnez......................1056	Valletta......................719	Vierzon.......................343
Tunis (City)................1056	Vallon-Pont-d'Arc............342	**Vietnam...................1349**
Tunis......................1056	Valparaiso....................171	**Viet-nam..................1349**
Tunisia....................1056	Vals-les-Bains...............342	Vieux-Boucau-les-Bains........343
Tunisie....................1056	Vancouver.....................122	Vigo..........................968
Turchia....................1057	Vanloese......................220	Vila Nova de Fâmilicão........842
Turin (Torino)................680	Vannes........................342	Vila Nova de Gaia.............842
Türkei.....................1057	**Vanuatu...................1345**	Vila Nova de Milfontes........843
Turkey.....................1057	Varazdin......................191	Vila Real de Santo Antonio....843
Türkiye....................1057	Varazze.......................683	Vilamoura.....................843
Turku.........................233	Varese........................683	Villach........................52
Turnhout.......................95	Varna.........................114	Villahermosa..................731
Turquia....................1057	Varsavia (Warszawa)...........826	Villard-de-Lans...............343
Turquie....................1057	Varsovia (Warszawa)...........826	Villeneuve-de-Marsan..........343
Tuttlingen....................546	Varsovie (Warszawa)...........826	Villeneuve-les-Avignon........343
Tuxpan........................731	Varzi.........................685	Villeneuve-les-Maguelonne.....343
Tuxtla Guiterrez..............731	Västerås......................985	Villeneuve-Loubet.............343
Tweed Heads....................23	Vechta........................546	Villers-sur-Mer...............343
Twjer.........................854	Veghel........................792	Villiers-les-Ormes............343
	Vejle.........................220	Villingen-Schwenningen........546
	Velden am Wörther See..........52	Vilnius.......................714
	Vendays-Montalivet............342	Viña del Mar..................171
		Vincennes.....................343

SPARTACUS 2001/2002 | **1387**

Index

Virgin Islands of the USA **166**	West Palm Beach 1235	**X**
Virginia Beach................... 1337	West Sacramento 1188	Xian 175
Virginia 1336	West Virginia.................... 1339	
Viseu 843	West Yellowstone 1283	**Y**
Visp 1004	Westerland 547	Yalta............................ 1065
Viterbo.......................... 691	Western Australia 41	Yangon 736
Viti............................. **228**	Wetzlar 549	**Yisra'él/Isra'il** **594**
Vitória, BR 113	Weymouth 1126	Yogyakarta 585
Vitoria, E 968	Whangarei....................... 807	Yokohama 701
Vitrolles 343	Whitby.......................... 1126	York, GB 1127
Vittorio Veneto 691	Whitby........................... 138	York, PA, USA 1326
Vlaardingen..................... 793	White Plains 1312	**Yougoslavie** **1351**
Vladivostok 854	Whitehorse 148	Youngstown 1318
Vlissingen 793	Wichelen 95	**Yugoslavia** **1351**
Volcano Village 1241	Wichita 1255	Yukon Territory................... 148
Volkenroda 547	Wien 52	Yuzhno 854
Völklingen 547	Wiener Neustadt.................. 72	Yverdon......................... 1004
Voronezh........................ 854	Wiesbaden 550	
Vrouwenpolder.................. 793	Wilderness 881	**Z**
	Wilhelmshaven 550	
W	Williamsport 1326	Zabrze 827
Waalre.......................... 793	Wilmington, DE, USA 1192	Zacatecas........................ 731
Waasmunster 95	Wilmington, NC, USA 1314	Zadar 191
Wageningen 793	Wilson 1314	Zagora 735
Waikanae 805	Wilton Manors 1235	Zagreb 191
Wakefield 1126	Winchester 1126	Zakopane........................ 827
Walbrzych 826	Windermere 1126	**Zambia**....................... **1353**
Wallasey 1126	Windhoek 737	**Zambie**....................... **1353**
Walnut Creek 1188	Windsor......................... 1126	Zamboanga del Sur 822
Walsall......................... 1126	Windsor......................... 138	Zandhuisen 793
Wanganui 805	Winnipeg........................ 126	Zandvoort 793
Warburton........................ 41	Winschoten 793	Zaporizhzhe 1065
Ware 1277	Winterthur...................... 1004	Zaragoza 969
Warren 1318	Wisconsin 1340	Zeist............................ 793
Warrington 1126	Wismar 550	Zhitomir........................ 1065
Warsaw (Warszawa)............. 826	Wissant 343	**Zhongguo**..................... **172**
Warschau (Warszawa)........... 826	Witten 551	Zihuatanejo 731
Warszawa 826	Woking 1126	Zilina 861
Washington D.C................ 1192	Wolfratshausen 551	**Zimbabwe** **1354**
Washington 1337	Wolfsburg 551	Ziqim 597
Waterbury..................... 1336	Wolfville......................... 129	Zoetermeer 793
Waterford 592	Wollongong...................... 23	Zug............................ 1019
Wausau 1341	Wolverhampton 1127	Zurich (Zürich) 1006
Weiden 547	Woodland Park 1190	Zürich 1006
Weimar 547	Worcester, GB 1127	Zurigo (Zürich) 1006
Weißrussland **73**	Worcester, MA, USA 1277	Zwickau 552
Wellington 805	Worthing 152	Zwolle 793
Wells-Next-The-Sea 1126	Wroclaw 827	**Zypern**........................ **192**
Wels 52	Wuhan 175	
Werribee 41	Wuppertal 551	
Wesel........................... 547	Würzburg 551	
West Coast 807	Wycombe 1326	
	Wyoming....................... 1341	

Index

Weitere Informationen erhältlich bei:

the uncommonplace
KEY WEST.

The Florida Keys & Key West
c/o Get It Across Tourism Marketing
Neumarkt 33
50677 Köln
Tel: (0221) 2336 451
Fax: (0221) 23336 450
flkeys@netcologne.de
www..fla-keys.com

Eine der besten gay-Unterkünfte der USA:
Alexander´s Guesthouse

ALEXANDER'S
GUESTHOUSE

1118 Fleming Street
Key West, Florida 33040
USA
Tel:(001) (305) 294-9919
Within North America:(800) 654-9919
Fax: (001) (305) 295-0357
e-mail: info@alexghouse.com
Internet: www.alexghouse.com

Für Reiseangebote (Flüge, Hotels, Mietwagen und vieles mehr) steht Euch das Reisebüro G-tours gerne zur Verfügung (Gay-Katalog kostenlos anfordern!):

G-tours
WELTWEIT REISEN

Reisebüro G-tours GmbH
Schwalbengasse 46
50667 Köln
Tel.: (0221) 925891-0
Fax: (0221) 925891-19
e-mail: G-tours@t-online.de
Internet: www.G-tours.de

Where there's freedom, there is expression.

KEY WEST
the gay destination

Notes

Notes

Notes

Notes

WORLD HITS MADE IN BERLIN

LOU BEGA

MARIANNE ROSENBERG

LA BOUCHE

EIFFEL 65

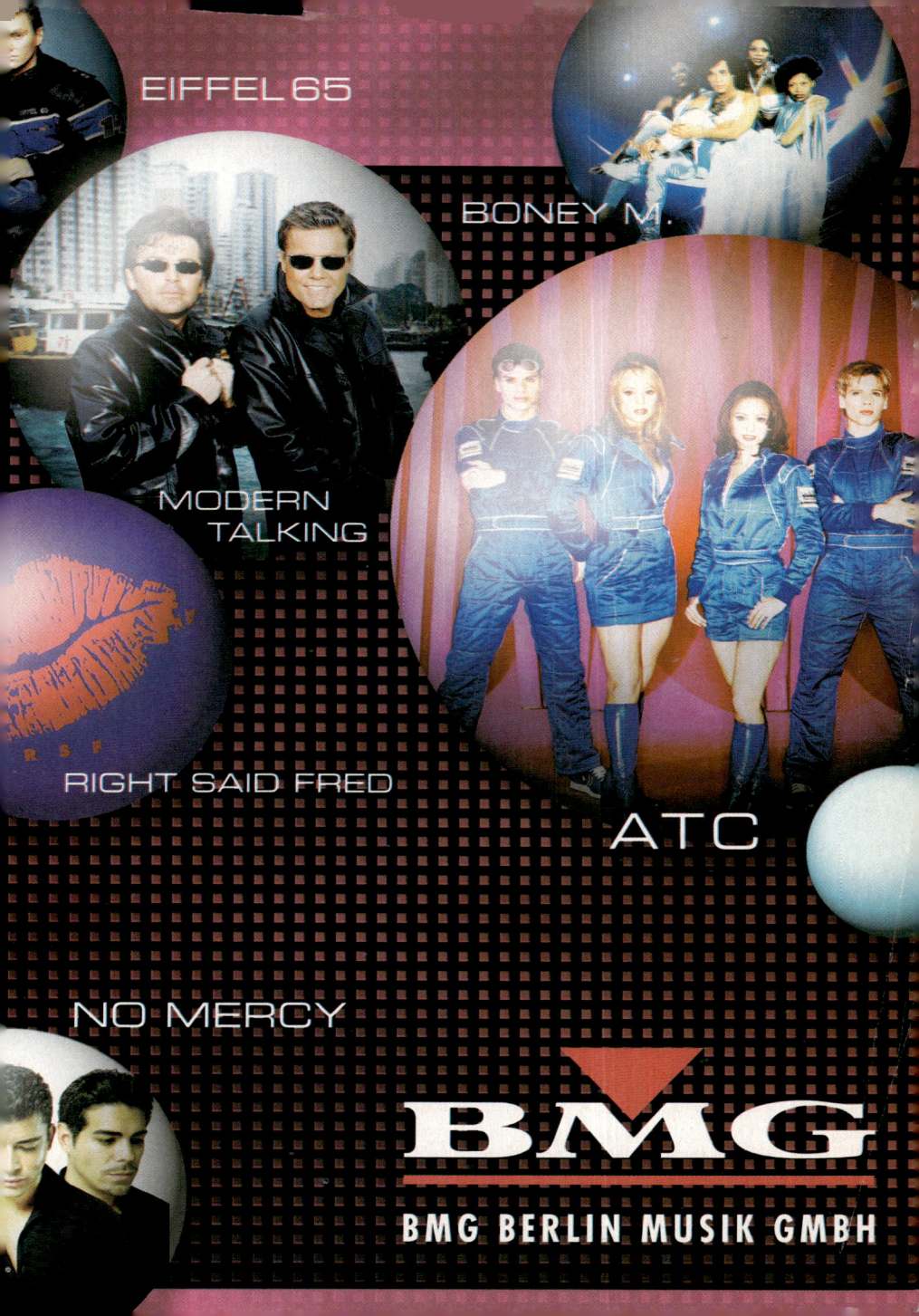

BONEY M.

MODERN TALKING

RIGHT SAID FRED

ATC

NO MERCY

BMG
BMG BERLIN MUSIK GMBH

君もやろう*

GIB AIDS KEINE CHANCE

***mach's mit.**

Telefonberatung: 0221-89 20 31 (www.aidsberatung.de). Kostenloses Informationsmaterial erhalten Sie bei: Bundeszentrale für gesundheitliche Aufklärung, 51101 Köln, oder im Internet: www.machsmit.de

SpartacusWorld.com
Registration Card

▶ As purchaser of the jubilee edition of
SPARTACUS INTERNATIONAL GAY GUIDE 2001/02,
after I have registered myself, I have the chance to use and research in the Spartacus address data bank free of charge until the 31.12.2001.

▶ The registration card should be completed in full, signed and sent off by post.

▶ Your personal password will be sent to you promptly.

☑ Yes, I would like to register with SpartacusWorld.com
As purchaser of the jubilee edition of **SPARTACUS INTERNATIONAL GAY GUIDE 2001/02**, after I have registered myself, I have the chance to use and research in the Spartacus address data bank free of charge until the 31.12.2001.

Name

First Name

Address

City / Post Code

Country

E-Mail

✗ Signature

I hereby confirm that all my details are correct as stated. I accept the general terms of business of SpartacusWorld.com ↳ www.SpartacusWorld.com

SpartacusWorld.com

▶ click and ▶ win!

www.spartacusworld.com

SpartacusWorld.com GmbH
Postfach 17 01 23

10203 Berlin
Germany